The Sporting News

BASEBALL GUIDE

1 9 9 4 E D I T I O N

Editors/Baseball Guide
CRAIG CARTER
DAVE SLOAN

PUBLISHING CO.

Francis P. Pandolfi, Chairman and Chief Executive Officer; **Nicholas H. Niles,** Publisher and President; **John D. Rawlings,** Editorial Director; **Kathy Kinkeade,** Vice President/Production; **Mike Nahrstedt,** Managing Editor; **Joe Hoppel,** Senior Editor; **Craig Carter, Tom Dienhart and Dave Sloan,** Associate Editors; **Mark Shimabukuro,** Assistant Editor; **George Puro,** Production Assistant; **Craig Mulcahy,** Editorial Assistant; **Bill Perry,** Director of Graphic Presentation; **Michael Bruner,** Art Director/Yearbooks and Books; **Steve Levin,** Photo Editor; **Gary Levy,** Editor of Special Projects; **Gary Brinker,** Director of Electronic Information Development; **Corby Ann Dolan,** Database Analyst; **Vern Kasal,** Composing Room Supervisor.

A Times Mirror
Company

EXPLANATION OF STATISTICAL ABBREVIATIONS

A: assists. **AB:** at-bats. **Avg.:** batting average (hits divided by at-bats). **BB:** bases on balls. **Bk.:** balks. **CG:** complete games. **CS:** caught stealing. **E:** errors. **ER:** earned runs. **ERA:** earned-run average (earned runs times nine divided by innings pitched). **G:** games. **GB:** games behind. **GF:** games finished. **GIDP:** grounding into double plays. **GS:** games started. **H:** hits. **HB:** hit batsmen. **HP:** hit by pitches. **HR:** home runs. **IBB:** intentional bases on balls. **IP:** innings pitched. **L:** losses. **OBP:** on-base percentage (hits plus bases on balls plus hit by pitches divided by at-bats plus bases on balls plus hit by pitches plus sacrifice flies). **Pct.:** winning percentage. **PO:** putouts. **Pos.:** position. **R:** runs. **RBI:** runs batted in. **SB:** stolen bases. **SF:** sacrifice flies (run-scoring flyouts). **SH:** sacrifice hits (bunts that advance one or more runners but result in the batter being retired at first base or reaching first on an error). **ShO:** shutouts. **Slg.:** slugging percentage (total bases divided by at-bats). **SO:** strikeouts. **Sv.:** saves. **TB:** total bases (hits plus doubles plus two times the number of triples plus three times the number of home runs). **TBF:** total batters faced. **TC:** total chances (putouts plus assists plus errors). **W:** wins. **WP:** wild pitches. **2B:** doubles. **3B:** triples.

World Series, A.L. Championship Series, N.L. Championship Series and All-Star Game highlights written by Joe Hoppel of The Sporting News.

Major league statistics compiled by MLB-IBM Baseball Information System.

Minor league statistics compiled by Howe Sportsdata International Inc., Boston.

Additional assistance provided by STATS, Inc., Lincolnwood, Ill., and Elias Sports Bureau, New York.

ISBN: 0-89204-485-3 (perfect-bound)
       0-89204-488-8 (comb-bound)

10 9 8 7 6 5 4 3 2 1

CONTENTS

1994 SEASON

Major League Baseball

Team information

MAJOR LEAGUE BASEBALL

COMMISSIONER'S OFFICE

Address
350 Park Avenue
New York, NY 10022
Telephone
212-339-7800
FAX
212-355-0007
Exec. director, broadcasting
David Alworth
Dir. of governmental relations
Eugene Callahan

Exec. dir., market development
Leonard Coleman
Director, special events
David Dziedzic
Exec. dir., security/facility management
Kevin Hallinan
Exec. dir., public relations
Richard Levin
Exec. dir., baseball operations
William Murray

General counsel
Thomas J. Ostertag
Director, minor league relations
Jimmie Lee Solomon
Director, broadcast administration
Leslie Sullivan
Chief financial officer
Jeffrey White
Exec. dir., licensing oper. and pres., MLBP
Rick White

AMERICAN LEAGUE

Address
350 Park Avenue
New York, NY 10022
Telephone
212-339-7600
President
Robert W. Brown, M.D.
Vice president
Gene Autry
Executive director of umpiring
Martin J. Springstead
Coordinator of umpire operations
Philip Janssen
Special assistant to the president
Richard Butler
V.p., admin. and media affairs
Phyllis Merhige
Director, waivers and player records
John G. Ricco
Assistant media affairs director
Joe Fitzgerald

Administrator of umpires/travel
Tess Basta-Marino
Administrative assistant
Carolyn Coen
Umpires
Larry Barnett
Joseph Brinkman
Alan Clark
Drew Coble
Derryl Cousins
Terry Craft
Donald Denkinger
James Evans
Dale Ford
Richard Garcia
Ted Hendry
John Hirschbeck
Mark Johnson
Jim Joyce
Kenneth Kaiser
Greg Kosc

Tim McClelland
Larry McCoy
James McKean
Chuck Meriwether
Durwood Merrill
Dan Morrison
Steve Palermo*
David Phillips
Rick Reed
Michael Reilly
John (Rocky) Roe
Dale Scott
John Shulock
Tim Tschida
Vic Voltaggio
Tim Welke
Larry Young
*Inactive status.

NATIONAL LEAGUE

Address
350 Park Avenue
New York, NY 10022
Telephone
212-339-7700
President and treasurer
William D. White
Senior vice president and secretary
Phyllis B. Collins
Vice president, media and public affairs
Katy Feeney
Director of umpire supervision
Ed Vargo
Asst. secretary and exec. dir., player records
Nancy Crofts
Executive secretary
Valerie Dietrich
Administrative assistant, umpires
Cathy Davis

Public relations assistant
Glenn Wilburn
Umpires
Wally Bell
Greg Bonin
Jerry Crawford
Gary Darling
Bob Davidson
Gerry Davis
Dana DeMuth
Bruce Froemming
Brian Gorman
Eric Gregg
Tom Hallion
Angel Hernandez
Mark Hirschbeck
Bill Hohn
Jeff Kellogg
Jerry Layne
Randy Marsh

John McSherry
Ed Montague
Larry Poncino
Frank Pulli
Jim Quick
Ed Rapuano Jr.
Charlie Reliford
Steve Rippley
Paul Runge
Terry Tata
Larry Vanover
Harry Wendelstedt
Joe West
Charlie Williams
Mike Winters

OTHER ORGANIZATIONS

**NATIONAL BASEBALL
HALL OF FAME AND MUSEUM**
Address
P.O. Box 590
Cooperstown, NY 13326

Telephone
607-547-7200
607-547-2044 (FAX)
President
Donald C. Marr Jr.

Vice president
William J. Guilfoile
Curator
William T. Spencer Jr.
Registrar
Peter P. Clark

Director of merchandising
Jeffrey D. Stevens
Controller
Frances L. Althiser
Librarian
Thomas R. Heitz

NATIONAL ASSOCIATION OF PROFESSIONAL BASEBALL LEAGUES

Address
P.O. Box A
St. Petersburg, FL 33731
Telephone
813-822-6937
813-821-5819 (FAX)
President
Mike Moore
Chief operating officer
Pat O'Conner
Special counsel
George E. Yund
General counsel
Ben Hayes
Exec. dir., special projects and events
Robert J. Sparks
Dir. of marketing and public relations
Ronald M. Myers
Director of information and trade show
Larry Wiederecht
Exec. dir., business administration
Ann Perkins

MAJOR LEAGUE BASEBALL PLAYERS ASSOCIATION

Address
12 E. 49th St., 24th Floor
New York, NY 10017
Telephone
212-826-0808
212-752-3649 (FAX)
Executive director and general counsel
Donald M. Fehr
Special assistant
Mark Belanger
Associate general counsel
Eugene D. Orza
Assistant general counsels
Lauren Rich
Michael Weiner
Doyle Pryor
Counsel
Arthur Schack
Director of licensing
Judy Heeter

PLAYER RELATIONS COMMITTEE

Address
350 Park Avenue
New York, NY 10022
Telephone
212-339-7400
212-371-2242 (FAX)
President and chief operating officer
Richard Ravitch
General counsel
Charles P. O'Connor
Associate counsels
Louis Melendez
John Westhoff
Contract administrator
Barbara Ernst
Director, public relations
Richard Levin

MAJOR LEAGUE BASEBALL UMPIRE DEVELOPMENT

Address
P.O. Box A
St. Petersburg, FL 33731
Telephone
813-823-1286
813-821-5819 (FAX)
Executive director
Edwin W. Lawrence
Director of field supervision
Mike Fitzpatrick

HOWE SPORTSDATA INTERNATIONAL INC.

Address
Boston Fish Pier
West Building No. 2, Suite 306
Boston, MA 02210
Telephone
617-951-0070
617-951-1379 (stats request)
617-737-9960 (FAX)
President
Jay Virshbo
Executive vice president
William Weiss

ELIAS SPORTS BUREAU

Address
500 Fifth Ave.
New York, NY 10110
Telephone
212-869-1530
212-354-0980 (FAX)
General manager
Seymour Siwoff

BASEBALL WRITERS' ASSOCIATION OF AMERICA

President
Rick Hummel,
St. Louis Post-Dispatch
Vice president
Paul Meyer,
Pittsburgh Post-Gazette
Secretary/treasurer
Jack O'Connell, Hartford Courant
Executive secretary
Jack Lang, SportsTicker
Board of directors
Neil Hohlfeld, Houston Chronicle
Dick Kaegel, Kansas City Star
Kevin Kernan,
San Diego Union-Tribune
Marty Noble, Newsday

MAJOR LEAGUE SCOUTING BUREAU

Address
23712 Birtcher Dr., Suite A
El Toro, CA 92630
Telephone
714-458-7600
714-458-9454 (FAX)
Director
Donald F. Pries
Board of directors
Sandy Alderson
Dan Duquette
Bob Gebhard
Lou Gorman
Roland Hemond
Joe Klein
Joe McIlvaine
Bill Murray
Donald F. Pries
Art Stewart

MAJOR LEAGUE UMPIRES ASSOCIATION

Address
1735 Market St., Suite 3420
Philadelphia, PA 19103
Telephone
215-979-3220
215-979-3201 (FAX)
General counsel
Richard G. Phillips

ASS'N OF PROFESSIONAL BASEBALL PLAYERS OF AMERICA

Address
12062 Valley View, Suite 211
Garden Grove, CA 92645
Telephone
714-892-9900
714-897-0233 (FAX)
President
John J. McHale
Secretary/treasurer
Chuck Stevens

BASEBALL ASSISTANCE TEAM INC.

Address
350 Park Avenue
New York, NY 10022
Telephone
212-339-7884
Chairman
Ralph Branca
President
Joe Garagiola
Vice presidents
Joe Black
Earl Wilson
Executive director
Frank Slocum
Secretary/treasurer
Tom Ostertag

MAJOR LEAGUE BASEBALL PLAYERS ALUMNI ASSOC.

Address
3637 4th St., North, Suite 480
St. Petersburg, FL 33704
Telephone
813-822-3399
813-822-6300 (FAX)
President
Brooks Robinson
Vice presidents
Bob Boone
Carl Erskine
Mike Hegan
Chuck Hinton
Al Kaline
Mike Schmidt
Rusty Staub
Billy Williams
Secretary/treasurer
Fred Valentine
Executive committee
Carl Warwick, Chairman
Jim Hannan, Vice chairman
Jim (Mudcat) Grant
Rich Hand
Jerry Moses
Board of directors
Hank Aguirre
Nellie Briles
Darrel Chaney
Denny Doyle
Jim (Mudcat) Grant
Rich Hand
Jim Hannan
Tug McGraw
Bob Miller
Jerry Moses
Dick Radatz
Brooks Robinson
Eddie Robinson
Ken Sanders
Tom Seaver
Fred Valentine
Carl Warwick
Bob Allison, Director emeritus

BALTIMORE ORIOLES
AMERICAN LEAGUE EAST DIVISION

1994 SCHEDULE

N Denotes night game (any game starting after 5 p.m.).
☐ Home games shaded.
* At Three Rivers Stadium in Pittsburgh.

APRIL

SUN	MON	TUE	WED	THU	FRI	SAT
					1	2
3	4 KC	5	6 N KC	7	8 N TEX	9 TEX
10 TEX	11 DET	12	13 DET	14 DET	15 N TEX	16 N TEX
17 N TEX	18	19 N CAL	20 N CAL	21 N CAL	22 N CAL	23 SEA
24 SEA	25 N OAK	26 OAK	27 N CAL	28 N CAL	29 N SEA	30 N SEA

MAY

SUN	MON	TUE	WED	THU	FRI	SAT
1 SEA	2	3 N OAK	4 N OAK	5	6 N CLE	7 CLE
8 CLE	9 N TOR	10 N TOR	11 N TOR	12	13 N MIN	14 N MIN
15 MIN	16	17 N BOS	18 N BOS	19 N BOS	20 N NY	21 NY
22 NY	23 N MIL	24 N MIL	25 MIL	26	27 N CHI	28 CHI
29 CHI	30 N DET	31 N DET				

JUNE

SUN	MON	TUE	WED	THU	FRI	SAT
			1 N DET	2 DET	3 N CHI	4 CHI
5 CHI	6 N KC	7 N KC	8 N KC	9	10 N BOS	11 BOS
12 BOS	13 N NY	14 N NY	15 N NY	16 N NY	17 N MIN	18 MIN
19 MIN	20 N MIL	21 N MIL	22 MIL	23	24 N TOR	25 TOR
26 N TOR	27 N CLE	28 N CLE	29 N CLE	30 N CLE		

JULY

SUN	MON	TUE	WED	THU	FRI	SAT
					1 N CAL	2 N CAL
3 CAL	4 N SEA	5 N GEA	6 N SEA	7 N OAK	8 N OAK	9 N OAK
10 N OAK	11 *	12 ALL-STAR GAME	13	14 N CAL	15 N CAL	16 N CAL
17 CAL	18 N SEA	19 N SEA	20 SEA	21 N OAK	22 N OAK	23 N OAK
24 OAK	25	26 N CLE	27 N CLE	28 N CLE	29 N TOR	30 N TOR
31 TOR						

AUGUST

SUN	MON	TUE	WED	THU	FRI	SAT
	1 N MIN	2 N MIN	3 MIN	4 N MIL	5 N MIL	6 N MIL
7 MIL	8 N NY	9 N NY	10 N NY	11 N BOS	12 N BOS	13 N BOS
14 BOS	15	16 N TEX	17 N TEX	18 N TEX	19 N KC	20 N KC
21 KC	22 N CHI	23 N CHI	24 CHI	25 N KC	26 N KC	27 N KC
28 KC	29	30 N CHI	31 N CHI			

SEPTEMBER

SUN	MON	TUE	WED	THU	FRI	SAT
				1 N CHI	2 N DET	3 N DET
4 DET	5 N TEX	6 N TEX	7 N TEX	8	9 N DET	10 DET
11 DET	12 N BOS	13 N BOS	14 N BOS	15	16 N NY	17 N NY
18 N NY	19 N MIN	20 N MIN	21 N MIN	22	23 N MIL	24 MIL
25 MIL	26 N TOR	27 N TOR	28 N TOR	29 N TOR	30 N CLE	

OCTOBER

SUN	MON	TUE	WED	THU	FRI	SAT
						1 CLE
2 CLE						

1994 SEASON

CLUB DIRECTORY

Managing general partner
Peter G. Angelos
Vice-chairman, bus. op. & finance
Joseph E. Foss
Chief administrative officer
Fred W. Arscott
Exec. vice president and general manager
Roland A. Hemond
Vice president, administrative personnel
Calvin Hill
Vice president, planning and development
Janet Marie Smith
Asst. g.m./dir. of player personnel
R. Douglas Melvin
Assistant to the general manager
Frank Robinson
Director of scouting
Gary Nickels
Special assistants to the vice president
Gordon Goldsberry
Fred Uhlman Sr.
Vice president, finance
Aric Holsinger
Director/ticket operations
Joseph R. Keough
Administrator/minor league operations
Andy Feffer
Assistant/player development and scouting
Leland MacPhail IV
Marketing coordinator
Michael Fiorelli
Traveling secretary
Philip E. Itzoe
Director of public relations
Richard L. Vaughn
Director of stadium services
Roy A. Sommerhof
Director of research and statistics
Eddie Epstein
Director of public affairs
Charles A. Steinberg, DDS
Director of sales operations
Vince Dunbar
Director, community services
Julia A. Wagner
Director, computer services
James L. Kline
Ticket office manager
Audrey Brown
Assistant director of public relations
Bob Miller
Director of marketing and advertising
David Cope

Assistant director of sales operations
Matt Dryer
Assistant director of scouting
Fred Uhlman Jr.
Assistant director of community services
Stacey Beckwith
Community services assistant
Kenneth R. Abrams
Coordinator of Orioles productions
Amy Nelson
Assistant director/stadium operations
Scott Indorf
Assistant ticket office managers
Joseph B. Codd
Denise C. Addicks
Publishing coordinator
Stephanie Kelly
Club physicians
Dr. Sheldon Goldgeier
Dr. Charles E. Silberstein
Trainers
Richie Bancells
Jamie Reed
Strength and conditioning
Tim Bishop
Scouts
Rick Arnold
Carlos Bernhardt
Jesus Carmona
John Cox
Ray Crone
Lane Decker
Manny Estrada
Paul Fryer
Jim Gilbert
John Green
Jesus Halabi
Jim Howard
Deacon Jones
Leo Labossiere
Mike Ledna
Ed Liberatore
Miguel Machado
Curt Motton
Lamar North
Camilo Nunez
Fred Petersen
Harry Shelton
Ed Sprague
John Stokoe
Mike Tullier
Earl Winn
Jerry Zimmerman

SPRING TRAINING ROSTER

Manager—Johnny Oates (28).

Coaches—Greg Biagini (24), Dick Bosman (17), Don Buford (73), Elrod Hendricks (44), Davey Lopes (15), Jerry Narron (34).

No.	PITCHERS	B/T	Ht./Wt.	Born	1993 clubs
	Benitez, Armando	R/R	6-4/180	11-3-72	Albany, Frederick
55	Cook, Mike	L/R	6-3/225	8-14-63	Rochester, Baltimore
	Eichhorn, Mark	R/R	6-3/210	11-21-60	Toronto
50	Fernandez, Sid	L/L	6-1/225	10-12-62	New York N.L., St. Lucie, Binghamton
	Forney, Rick	R/R	6-4/210	10-24-71	Frederick, Bowie
	Krivda, Rick	R/L	6-1/180	1-19-70	Bowie, Rochester
36	Manuel, Barry	R/R	5-11/185	8-12-65	Charlotte, Oklahoma City, Rochester
19	McDonald, Ben	R/R	6-7/214	11-24-67	Baltimore
48	McGehee, Kevin	R/R	6-0/190	1-18-69	Phoenix, Rochester, Baltimore
75	Mills, Alan	B/R	6-1/192	10-18-66	Baltimore
51	Moyer, Jamie	L/L	6-0/170	11-18-62	Rochester, Baltimore
35	Mussina, Mike	R/R	6-2/185	12-8-68	Baltimore, Bowie
46	O'Donoghue, John	L/L	6-6/198	5-26-69	Rochester, Baltimore
56	Oquist, Mike	R/R	6-2/170	5-30-68	Rochester, Baltimore
47	Pennington, Brad	L/L	6-5/205	4-14-69	Rochester, Baltimore
45	Poole, Jim	L/L	6-2/203	4-28-66	Baltimore
53	Rhodes, Arthur	L/L	6-2/206	10-24-69	Baltimore, Rochester
	Smith, Lee	R/R	6-6/269	12-4-57	St. Louis, New York A.L.

No.	CATCHERS	B/T	Ht./Wt.	Born	1993 clubs
23	Hoiles, Chris	R/R	6-0/213	3-20-65	Baltimore
41	Tackett, Jeff	R/R	6-2/205	12-1-65	Baltimore, Rochester
	Zaun, Greg	B/R	5-10/170	4-14-71	Bowie, Rochester

No.	INFIELDERS	B/T	Ht./Wt.	Born	1993 clubs
1	Alexander, Manny	R/R	5-10/165	3-20-71	Rochester, Baltimore
38	Carey, Paul	L/R	6-4/215	1-8-68	Rochester, Baltimore
10	Gomez, Leo	R/R	6-0/208	3-2-67	Baltimore, Rochester
36	Hulett, Tim	R/R	6-0/199	1-12-60	Baltimore
2	McLemore, Mark	B/R	5-11/207	10-4-64	Baltimore
	Palmeiro, Rafael	L/L	6-0/188	9-24-64	Texas
8	Ripken, Cal	R/R	6-4/220	8-24-60	Baltimore
21	Segui, David	B/L	6-1/202	7-19-66	Baltimore

No.	OUTFIELDERS	B/T	Ht./Wt.	Born	1993 clubs
9	Anderson, Brady	L/L	6-1/195	1-18-64	Baltimore
3	Baines, Harold	L/L	6-2/195	3-15-59	Baltimore, Bowie
18	Buford, Damon	R/R	5-10/170	6-12-70	Rochester, Baltimore
12	Devereaux, Mike	R/R	6-0/195	4-10-63	Baltimore, Bowie
	Hammonds, Jeffrey	R/R	6-0/195	3-5-71	Bowie, Rochester, Baltimore
42	Obando, Sherman	R/R	6-4/215	1-23-70	Baltimore, Bowie
	Ochoa, Alex	R/R	6-0/175	3-29-72	Frederick
	Smith, Mark	R/R	6-3/205	5-7-70	Rochester
28	Voigt, Jack	R/R	6-1/175	5-17-66	Rochester, Baltimore
	Wawruck, James	L/L	5-11/185	4-23-70	Bowie

BALLPARK INFORMATION

Ballpark (capacity, surface)
Oriole Park at Camden Yards
(48,079, grass)

Address
333 W. Camden St.
Baltimore, MD 21201

Business phone
410-685-9800

Ticket information
410-685-9800

Ticket prices
$15 (lower boxes)
$14 (terrace boxes)
$12 (upper boxes)
$12 (left field lower boxes)
$11 (left field upper boxes)
$8 (reserved seats)
$6 (left field upper reserved)
$4 (bleachers)

Field dimensions (from home plate)
To left field at foul line, 333 feet
To center field, 400 feet
To right field at foul line, 318

First game played
April 6, 1992 (Orioles 2, Indians 0)

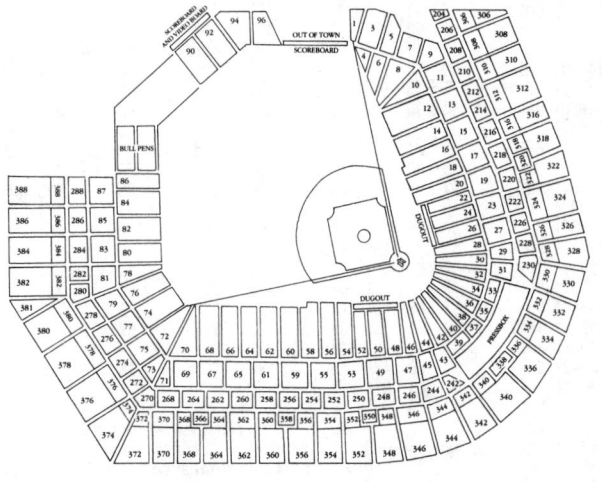

Class	Team	League	Manager
AAA	Rochester	International	Bob Miscik
AA	Bowie	Eastern	Pete Mackanin
A	Frederick	Carolina	Mike O'Berry
A	Albany	South Atlantic	Butch Wynegar
Rookie	Sarasota	Gulf Coast	Oneri Fleita
Rookie	Bluefield	Appalachian	Andy Etchebarren

▯ BROADCAST INFORMATION ▯

Radio: WBAL-AM (1090). Broadcasters: Fred Manfra, Jon Miller, Chuck Thompson.
TV: WMAR-TV (Channel 2). Broadcasters: Scott Garceau, Jon Miller, Brooks Robinson.
Cable TV: Home Team Sports. Broadcasters: Mel Procter, John Lowenstein, Jim Palmer.

SPRING TRAINING

Ballpark (city): Twin Lakes Park (Sarasota, Fla.) from February 17 through March 3; then home games will be played at Al Lang Stadium (St. Petersburg, Fla.).
Ticket information: 813-825-3334, 813-894-4773.

HISTORY

YEAR-BY-YEAR RECORDS

Year	Pos.	W	L	Pct.	GB	Year	Pos.	W	L	Pct.	GB
1901*	8th	48	89	.350	35½	1951†	8th	52	102	.338	46
1902†	2nd	78	58	.574	5	1952†	7th	64	90	.416	31
1903†	6th	65	74	.468	26½	1953†	8th	54	100	.351	46½
1904†	6th	65	87	.428	29	1954	7th	54	100	.351	57
1905†	8th	54	99	.354	40½	1955	7th	57	97	.370	39
1906†	5th	76	73	.510	16	1956	6th	69	85	.448	28
1907†	6th	69	83	.454	24	1957	5th	76	76	.500	21
1908†	4th	83	69	.546	6½	1958	6th	74	79	.484	17½
1909†	7th	61	89	.407	36	1959	6th	74	80	.481	20
1910†	8th	47	107	.305	57	1960	2nd	89	65	.578	8
1911†	8th	45	107	.296	56½	1961	3rd	95	67	.586	14
1912†	7th	53	101	.344	53	1962	7th	77	85	.475	19
1913†	8th	57	96	.373	39	1963	4th	86	76	.531	18½
1914†	5th	71	82	.464	28½	1964	3rd	97	65	.599	2
1915†	6th	63	91	.409	39½	1965	3rd	94	68	.580	8
1916†	5th	79	75	.513	12	1966	1st	97	63	.606	+ 9
1917†	7th	57	97	.370	43	1967	T6th	76	85	.472	15½
1918†	5th	58	64	.475	15	1968	2nd	91	71	.562	12
1919†	5th	67	72	.482	20½	1969	1st‡	109	53	.673	+19
1920†	4th	76	77	.497	21½	1970	1st‡	108	54	.667	+15
1921†	3rd	81	73	.526	17½	1971	1st‡	101	57	.639	+12
1922†	2nd	93	61	.604	1	1972	3rd	80	74	.519	5
1923†	5th	74	78	.487	24	1973	1st§	97	65	.599	+ 8
1924†	4th	74	78	.487	17	1974	1st§	91	71	.562	+ 2
1925†	3rd	82	71	.536	15	1975	2nd	90	69	.566	4½
1926†	7th	62	92	.403	29	1976	2nd	88	74	.543	10½
1927†	7th	59	94	.336	50½	1977	T2nd	97	64	.602	2½
1928†	3rd	82	72	.532	19	1978	4th	90	71	.559	9
1929†	4th	79	73	.520	26	1979	1st‡	102	57	.642	+ 8
1930†	6th	64	90	.416	38	1980	2nd	100	62	.617	3
1931†	5th	63	91	.409	45	1981	2nd/4th	59	46	.562	*
1932†	6th	63	91	.409	44	1982	2nd	94	68	.580	1
1933†	8th	55	96	.364	43½	1983	1st‡	98	64	.605	+ 6
1934†	6th	67	85	.441	33	1984	5th	85	77	.525	19
1935†	7th	65	87	.428	28½	1985	4th	83	78	.516	16
1936†	7th	57	95	.375	44½	1986	7th	73	89	.451	22½
1937†	8th	46	108	.299	56	1987	6th	67	95	.414	31
1938†	7th	55	97	.362	44	1988	7th	54	107	.335	34½
1939†	8th	43	111	.279	64½	1989	2nd	87	75	.537	2
1940†	6th	67	87	.435	23	1990	5th	76	85	.472	11½
1941†	T6th	70	84	.455	31	1991	6th	67	95	.414	24
1942†	3rd	82	69	.543	19½	1992	3rd	89	73	.549	7
1943†	6th	72	80	.474	25	1993	T3rd	85	77	.525	10
1944†	1st	89	65	.578	+ 1						
1945†	3rd	81	70	.536	6						
1946†	7th	66	88	.429	38						
1947†	8th	59	95	.383	38						
1948†	6th	59	94	.386	37						
1949†	7th	53	101	.344	44						
1950†	7th	58	96	.377	40						

*Franchise known as Milwaukee Brewers. †Franchise known as St. Louis Browns. ‡Won Championship Series. §Lost Championship Series. *First half 31-23; second 28-23.

MANAGERS

Name	Record	Years
Hugh Duffy	48-89	1901
Jimmy McAleer	551-632	'02-09
Jack O'Connor	47-107	1910
Bobby Wallace	57-134	'11-12
George Stovall	91-158	'12-13
Branch Rickey	139-179	'13-15
Fielder Jones	158-196	'16-18
Jimmy Austin	29-38	'18, '23
Jimmy Burke	172-180	'18-20
Lee Fohl	226-183	'21-23
George Sisler	218-241	'24-26
Dan Howley	220-239	'27-29
Bill Killefer	224-329	'30-33
Al Sothoron	2-6	1933
Rogers Hornsby	255-381	'33-37
		1952
Jim Bottomley	21-56	1937
Gabby Street	55-97	1938
Fred Haney	125-227	'39-41
Luke Sewell	432-410	41-46
Zack Taylor	235-410	1946
		'48-51
Marty Marion	96-161	'52-53
Jimmie Dykes	54-100	1954
Paul Richards	517-539	'55-61
Lum Harris	17-10	1961
Billy Hitchcock	163-161	'62-63
Hank Bauer	407-318	'64-68
Earl Weaver	1481-1060	'68-82
		'85-86
Cal Ripken Sr.	67-101	'87-88
Frank Robinson	230-285	88-91
Johnny Oates	228-221	'91-93

DAY BY DAY

Date	Opp.	Res.	Score	(Inn.*)	Hits	Opp. hits	Winning pitcher	Losing pitcher	Save	Record	Pos.	GB
4-5	Tex.	L	4-7		9	10	Lefferts	Sutcliffe	Henke	0-1	T5th	1
4-7	Tex.	L	1-3	(11)	9	6	Patterson	Frohwirth		0-2	T6th	2
4-9	At Sea.	L	0-6		9	6	Hanson	McDonald		0-3	7th	2½
4-10	At Sea.	W	5-3		9	5	Sutcliffe	Cummings	Olson	1-3	7th	2½
4-11	At Sea.	L	6-7	(12)	11	15	Swan	Williamson		1-4	7th	2½
4-12	At Tex.	L	3-6		10	8	Leibrandt	Mussina	Henke	1-5	7th	3
4-13	At Tex.	L	3-8		7	8	Rogers	Valenzuela		1-6	7th	4
4-14	At Tex.	W	6-5		9	11	McDonald	Ryan	Olson	2-6	7th	4
4-16	Cal.	W	4-1		7	9	Sutcliffe	Farrell	Olson	3-6	6th	3½
4-17	Cal.	L	5-7		8	9	Grahe	Pennington		3-7	7th	4½
4-18	Cal.	W	4-3		12	6	Mussina	Valera	Olson	4-7	7th	4½
4-20	Chi.	L	1-2	(14)	7	9	Pall	Mills		4-8	7th	6
4-22	Chi.	L	2-3		6	7	McDowell	Olson	Hernandez	4-9	7th	5½
4-23	At K.C.	L	6-7		7	8	Gardner	Rhodes	Montgomery	4-10	7th	5½
4-24	At K.C.	W	6-5		13	9	Mussina	Montgomery	Frohwirth	5-10	7th	5½
4-25	At K.C.	L	2-3		8	9	Appier	McDonald	Montgomery	5-11	7th	6½
4-26	At Chi.	L	0-7		7	9	Alvarez	Valenzuela		5-12	7th	7½
4-27	At Chi.	L	4-9		9	18	McDowell	Sutcliffe		5-13	7th	7½
4-28	Min.	W	8-4		10	7	Rhodes	Erickson		6-13	7th	6½
4-29	Min.	W	11-0		11	5	Mussina	Mahomes		7-13	6th	6½
4-30	K.C.	W	12-5		13	9	McDonald	Appier	Olson	8-13	6th	6½
5-1	K.C.	L	4-5		10	8	Sampen	Mills	Montgomery	8-14	6th	6½
5-2	K.C.	W	4-3		7	11	Frohwirth	Rasmussen		9-14	6th	5½
5-4	At Min.	L	3-4		4	12	Erickson	Rhodes	Aguilera	9-15	7th	6½
5-5	At Min.	W	3-0		8	2	Mussina	Banks		10-15	7th	5½
5-6	At Tor.	L	8-10		11	14	Cox	McDonald	Ward	10-16	7th	6
5-7	At Tor.	L	2-3		7	8	Eichhorn	Frohwirth		10-17	7th	7
5-8	At Tor.	W	6-3		9	5	Sutcliffe	Linton	Frohwirth	11-17	7th	6
5-9	At Tor.	W	4-3		8	8	Williamson	Ward	Olson	12-17	6th	5
5-10	Bos.	W	2-1		7	11	Frohwirth	Quantrill	Pennington	13-17	6th	5
5-11	Bos.	L	0-4		5	11	Clemens	McDonald		13-18	6th	6
5-12	Bos.	L	0-2		2	7	Darwin	Valenzuela	Russell	13-19	6th	7
5-14	At Det.	L	3-4		9	8	Henneman	Frohwirth		13-20	6th	7½
5-15	At Det.	L	3-5		8	7	Krueger	Mills		13-21	7th	8½
5-16	At Det.	W	3-2		10	6	Mussina	Haas	Olson	14-21	6th	7½
5-17	Cle.	L	0-2		4	6	Mesa	McDonald	Plunk	14-22	7th	8
5-18	Cle.	W	7-0		11	2	Valenzuela	M. Young		15-22	6th	8
5-19	Cle.	W	6-3		8	12	Sutcliffe	Scudder	Olson	16-22	6th	8
5-20	Cle.	L	1-3		3	13	Cook	Moyer	Lilliquist	16-23	6th	9
5-21	Mil.	L	3-9		7	10	Navarro	Mussina		16-24	7th	9
5-22	Mil.	W	5-4	(14)	14	10	Williamson	Maldonado		17-24	6th	9
5-23	Mil.	L	1-9		7	12	Eldred	Valenzuela		17-25	6th	10
5-24	At N.Y.	W	8-6		15	7	Sutcliffe	Cook	Olson	18-25	6th	9
5-25	At N.Y.	L	0-1		3	12	Wickman	Moyer	Farr	18-26	6th	10
5-26	At N.Y.	W	6-2		9	6	Mussina	Perez	Olson	19-26	6th	10
5-27	At N.Y.	W	4-3	(10)	6	9	Pennington	Farr		20-26	6th	9½
5-28	At Cal.	L	4-8		13	12	Valera	Valenzuela	Nelson	20-27	6th	9½
5-29	At Cal.	L	3-6		7	7	Langston	Frohwirth	Frey	20-28	6th	11
5-30	At Cal.	L	5-7		10	9	Finley	Moyer	Nelson	20-29	6th	10½
5-31	At Oak.	W	3-1		5	6	Mussina	Darling		21-29	6th	10
6-1	At Oak.	L	1-4		9	4	Hillegas	McDonald	Eckersley	21-30	6th	10
6-2	At Oak.	W	5-2		6	7	Valenzuela	Witt	Olson	22-30	6th	9
6-4	Sea.	W	6-5	(10)	8	11	Williamson	Swan		23-30	6th	8½
6-5	Sea.	W	5-3		8	10	Pennington	Hanson	Olson	24-30	6th	8½
6-6	Sea.	W	5-2		11	7	Mussina	Bosio	Olson	25-30	5th	8½
6-7	Oak.	W	3-2		7	5	Frohwirth	Gossage	Olson	26-30	5th	7½
6-8	Oak.	W	6-4		8	9	Mills	Davis	Olson	27-30	5th	7½
6-9	Oak.	W	7-4		15	10	Sutcliffe	Welch	Pennington	28-30	5th	7½
6-10	At Bos.	W	2-1		6	7	Moyer	Viola	Olson	29-30	4th	7½
6-11	At Bos.	W	16-4		16	8	Mussina	Dopson		30-30	4th	7½
6-12	At Bos.	W	5-1		9	6	Pennington	Harris		31-30	4th	7½
6-13	At Bos.	L	2-4		6	4	Clemens	Valenzuela	Russell	31-31	4th	7½
6-14	At Mil.	W	8-5		8	13	Sutcliffe	Wegman	Olson	32-31	4th	7½
6-15	At Mil.	W	4-2		8	5	Moyer	Bones	Pennington	33-31	4th	7½
6-16	At Mil.	L	2-7		5	12	Navarro	Mussina		33-32	4th	7½
6-18	At Cle.	W	4-1		8	8	McDonald	Mesa	Olson	34-32	4th	7
6-19	At Cle.	L	0-3		8	7	Clark	Valenzuela	Plunk	34-33	4th	8
6-20	At Cle.	W	6-3		11	8	Moyer	M. Young	Olson	35-33	4th	8
6-22	Det.	W	12-9		13	10	Poole	Krueger	Olson	36-33	4th	7
6-23	Det.	W	6-2		7	8	Sutcliffe	Moore		37-33	4th	6

— 11 —

Date	Opp.	Res.	Score (inn.*)	Hits	Opp. hits	Winning pitcher	Losing pitcher	Save	Record	Pos.	GB
6-24	Det.	W	6-2	11	9	McDonald	Leiter	Pennington	38-33	4th	5
6-25	N.Y.	W	7-6 (10)	13	8	Frohwirth	Howe		39-33	4th	4
6-26	N.Y.	W	12-10	16	15	Williamson	Wickman	Olson	40-33	4th	4
6-27	N.Y.	L	5-9	13	14	Perez	O'Donoghue	Howe	40-34	4th	5
6-28	Tor.	L	2-7	8	11	Stottlemyre	Sutcliffe	Leiter	40-35	4th	6
6-29	Tor.	L	1-2	9	5	Hentgen	McDonald	Ward	40-36	4th	7
6-30	Tor.	W	6-0	12	6	Valenzuela	Stewart		41-36	4th	6
7-1	At Chi.	W	1-0	3	5	Moyer	McDowell	Olson	42-36	4th	5½
7-2	At Chi.	L	1-12	6	13	Fernandez	Mussina		42-37	4th	5½
7-3	At Chi.	W	9-6	11	10	Williamson	Bere	Olson	43-37	4th	4½
7-4	At Chi.	L	1-3	3	4	Bolton	McDonald	Hernandez	43-38	4th	4½
7-5	At K.C.	L	1-7	9	9	Gubicza	Pennington		43-39	4th	4½
7-6	At K.C.	W	8-0	11	4	Moyer	Gardner		44-39	4th	4½
7-7	At K.C.	W	8-3	10	6	Mussina	Pichardo		45-39	4th	3½
7-8	Chi.	L	5-12	12	15	Bere	Sutcliffe		45-40	4th	3½
7-9	Chi.	W	15-6	14	10	McDonald	Bolton		46-40	4th	2½
7-10	Chi.	W	6-0	10	3	Valenzuela	Alvarez		47-40	4th	1½
7-11	Chi.	L	5-11	13	13	McDowell	Moyer		47-41	4th	1½
7-15	Min.	W	5-3	11	5	McDonald	Erickson	Olson	48-41	T2nd	1½
7-16	Min.	W	9-7	11	13	Mussina	Deshaies	Olson	49-41	2nd	½
7-17	Min.	L	2-4	9	7	Tapani	Sutcliffe	Aguilera	49-42	T3rd	½
7-18	Min.	W	7-2	9	6	Valenzuela	Guardado		50-42	T3rd	½
7-19	K.C.	W	6-5	11	10	Moyer	Rasmussen	Olson	51-42	3rd	½
7-20	K.C.	W	7-0	10	1	McDonald	Cone		52-42	1st	+½
7-21	K.C.	L	6-8	8	15	Brewer	Olson	Montgomery	52-43	2nd	½
7-22	At Min.	L	4-8	12	13	Banks	Sutcliffe	Trombley	52-44	4th	1½
7-23	At Min.	W	5-1	13	6	Valenzuela	Guardado		53-44	4th	½
7-24	At Min.	W	9-2	13	9	Moyer	Erickson	Poole	54-44	4th	½
7-25	At Min.	L	2-5	10	9	Deshaies	McDonald	Aguilera	54-45	4th	1½
7-27	At Tor.	L	5-6	9	11	Ward	Poole		54-46	4th	2½
7-28	At Tor.	L	4-5 (10)	9	8	Castillo	Williamson		54-47	4th	3½
7-30	Bos.	L	7-8	10	9	Quantrill	Moyer	Russell	54-48	4th	4
7-31	Bos.	W	4-0	10	3	McDonald	Clemens		55-48	4th	4
8-1	Bos.	L	1-2	5	10	Darwin	Sutcliffe	Russell	55-49	4th	5
8-2	Mil.	W	7-5	11	9	Williamson	Lloyd	Olson	56-49	4th	5
8-3	Mil.	W	13-8	15	10	Frohwirth	Bones		57-49	4th	5
8-4	Mil.	W	8-6	10	7	Rhodes	Eldred	Olson	58-49	4th	4
8-5	Mil.	W	3-1	7	8	McDonald	Novoa		59-49	4th	3
8-6	Cle.	W	8-1	11	8	Sutcliffe	Mutis		60-49	4th	3
8-7	Cle.	W	8-6	11	13	Mills	Tavarez	Olson	61-49	3rd	2
8-8	Cle.	W	7-6 (11)	13	12	Frohwirth	Plunk		62-49	T2nd	1
8-9	At Det.	W	4-1	6	4	Rhodes	Moore		63-49	2nd	½
8-10	At Det.	L	1-15	6	10	Doherty	McDonald		63-50	3rd	1½
8-11	At Det.	L	5-15	11	18	Gullickson	Sutcliffe		63-51	4th	2½
8-12	At Det.	L	11-17	16	20	Henneman	Frohwirth		63-52	4th	2½
8-13	At N.Y.	L	1-4	8	8	Abbott	Moyer		63-53	4th	2½
8-14	At N.Y.	L	2-4	5	8	Assenmacher	Williamson	Farr	63-54	4th	3½
8-15	At N.Y.	L	0-1	3	7	Kamieniecki	McDonald	Wickman	63-55	4th	4½
8-16	At Sea.	L	6-8	10	9	Fleming	Sutcliffe	Johnson	63-56	4th	5½
8-17	At Sea.	L	3-5	7	7	Bosio	Frohwirth	Power	63-57	4th	6½
8-18	At Sea.	W	8-1	12	8	Moyer	Hanson		64-57	4th	6½
8-20	Tex.	W	10-5	14	12	Mussina	Leibrandt	Frohwirth	65-57	4th	5½
8-21	Tex.	W	6-5 (12)	10	14	Mills	Henke		66-57	3rd	4½
8-22	Tex.	L	4-11	10	13	Brown	Rhodes		66-58	3rd	5½
8-23	Tex.	L	6-13	9	15	Rogers	Valenzuela		66-59	4th	5½
8-24	Cal.	W	1-0	2	4	Moyer	Finley	Mills	67-59	3rd	5½
8-25	Cal.	L	1-2	2	6	Langston	Mussina	Butcher	67-60	3rd	6½
8-26	Cal.	W	9-4	12	9	Williamson	Nelson		68-60	3rd	5½
8-27	At Tex.	L	4-5	4	7	Rogers	Frohwirth	Henke	68-61	5th	5½
8-28	At Tex.	L	1-11	5	12	Pavlik	Valenzuela		68-62	5th	5½
8-29	At Tex.	W	6-3	10	7	Moyer	Bohanon		69-62	5th	5½
8-31	At Cal.	W	8-2	13	6	Mussina	Leftwich		70-62	3rd	6
9-1	At Cal.	W	5-1	8	4	McDonald	Holzemer		71-62	3rd	6
9-2	At Cal.	W	4-3	13	7	Rhodes	Finley	Poole	72-62	3rd	5½
9-3	At Oak.	W	5-4 (13)	9	8	Mills	Eckersley		73-62	3rd	5
9-4	At Oak.	W	6-3	12	9	Moyer	Karsay		74-62	3rd	3½
9-5	At Oak.	W	9-2	16	8	Mussina	Welch		75-62	3rd	2½
9-6	Sea.	W	5-1	7	8	McDonald	Fleming	Mills	76-62	3rd	2
9-7	Sea.	L	2-3	6	4	Brad Holman	Rhodes	Power	76-63	3rd	2
9-8	Sea.	W	8-3	8	8	Poole	King		77-63	3rd	1
9-10	Oak.	L	9-12	11	13	Downs	Williamson	Eckersley	77-64	3rd	1½
9-11	Oak.	W	3-1	8	4	McDonald	Welch		78-64	3rd	1½
9-12	Oak.	W	14-5	14	9	Moyer	Darling		79-64	2nd	1½
9-13	At Bos.	L	4-6	8	12	Quantrill	Williamson	Harris	79-65	3rd	2

Date	Opp.	Res.	Score (inn.*)	Hits	Opp. hits	Winning pitcher	Losing pitcher	Save	Record	Pos.	GB
9-14	At Bos.	W	11-3	12	8	Valenzuela	Darwin		80-65	3rd	2
9-15	At Bos.	L	5-6	7	10	Clemens	Mussina	Harris	80-66	3rd	3
9-17	At Mil.	L	0-2	3	3	Eldred	McDonald		80-67	3rd	4
9-18	At Mil.	L	0-3	4	10	Miranda	Moyer	Orosco	80-68	3rd	5
9-19	At Mil.	W	8-4	15	8	Rhodes	Navarro	Mills	81-68	3rd	5
9-20	At Cle.	L	4-6	7	10	Milacki	Valenzuela	DiPoto	81-69	3rd	5½
9-21	At Cle.	W	7-6	14	13	Mills	DiPoto		82-69	3rd	5½
9-22	At Cle.	L	2-4	8	7	Hernandez	McDonald	DiPoto	82-70	3rd	5½
9-24	Det.	L	0-2	7	6	Doherty	Moyer		82-71	3rd	7
9-26 (1)	Det.	L	4-9	9	12	Gullickson	Rhodes		82-72	3rd	7½
9-26 (2)	Det.	L	5-6	13	14	Henneman	Mills	Boever	82-73	3rd	8
9-27	N.Y.	L	1-9	6	12	Kamieniecki	Sutcliffe		82-74	3rd	9
9-28	N.Y.	W	9-1	9	2	McDonald	Hitchcock		83-74	3rd	9
9-29	N.Y.	L	3-8	6	15	Key	Moyer		83-75	T3rd	10
9-30	Tor.	L	2-6	6	11	Leiter	Rhodes		83-76	4th	11
10-1	Tor.	W	7-2	12	8	Valenzuela	Stottlemyre		84-76	T3rd	10
10-2	Tor.	W	8-4	12	12	Sutcliffe	Hentgen	Mills	85-76	T3rd	9
10-3	Tor.	L	6-11	7	11	Brow	McDonald		85-77	T3rd	10

Monthly records: April (8-13), May (13-16), June (20-7), July (14-12), August (15-14), September (13-14), October (2-1).
*Innings, if other than nine.

HIGHLIGHTS

High point: From June 2-26, Baltimore won 19 of 22 games to climb from sixth place (10 games out) to fourth place (four games out).

Low point: Entering the season's final 19 games, Baltimore was just 1½ games out of first. But the Orioles proceeded to go 6-13, ending their title hopes.

Turning point: On September 13, the Orioles opened their final road trip of the season just 1½ games out of first. Baltimore went 3-6 to eliminate any serious hope of winning the division title.

Most valuable player: Catcher Chris Hoiles. He hit .310 with 29 homers and 82 RBIs to establish himself as one of the top-hitting catchers in baseball.

Most valuable pitcher: Righthander Mike Mussina. Even though shoulder and back problems sidelined him six weeks, he still led the Orioles with 14 victories.

Most improved player: Right fielder/second baseman Mark McLemore. A non-roster invitee to spring training, McLemore excelled in the first half and finished with a .284 average and a career-high 72 RBIs.

Most pleasant surprise: Lefthander Jamie Moyer. He was called up from Class AAA Rochester on May 20 and helped hold the rotation together with a 12-9 record and 3.43 ERA.

Biggest disappointment: First baseman Glenn Davis. The Orioles had reason to hope that they would get some return on the millions they had paid him the previous two seasons. But misfortune continued to dog Davis and he finally was released September 8.

Key injuries: Aside from Mussina's problems, top outfield prospect Jeffrey Hammonds was in and out of the lineup with a herniated disk in his neck. Righthander Gregg Olson missed most of the final two months of the season with a slightly torn ligament in his elbow. Righthander Rick Sutcliffe missed four weeks after left knee surgery. Designated hitter Harold Baines missed three weeks with a rib-cage injury. Third baseman Leo Gomez missed

much of the second half following left wrist surgery. Outfielders Brady Anderson and Mike Devereaux also spent time on the disabled list.

Notable: The Orioles were sold at a bankruptcy auction in August to Baltimore lawyer Peter Angelos. ... Baltimore posted consecutive winning seasons for the first time since 1984-85.

—PETER SCHMUCK

RECORDS

1993 regular-season record: 85-77 (T3rd in A.L. East); 48-33 at home; 37-44 on road; 38-40 vs. East; 47-37 vs. West; 24-23 vs. LHP; 61-54 vs. RHP; 75-63 on grass; 10-14 on turf; 22-24 in day-time; 63-53 at night; 21-21 in one-run games; 7-4 in extra-inning games; 0-1-0 in doubleheaders.

Team record last five years: 404-405 (.499), ranks 8th in league in that span).

TEAM LEADERS

Batting average: Mark McLemore (.284).
At-bats: Cal Ripken (641).
Runs: Brady Anderson, Cal Ripken (87).
Hits: Mark McLemore, Cal Ripken (165).
Total bases: Cal Ripken (269).
Doubles: Brady Anderson (36).
Triples: Brady Anderson (8).
Home runs: Chris Hoiles (29).
Runs batted in: Cal Ripken (90).
Stolen bases: Brady Anderson (24).
Slugging percentage: Chris Hoiles (.585).
On-base percentage: Chris Hoiles (.416).
Wins: Mike Mussina (14).
Earned-run average: Ben McDonald (3.39).
Complete games: Ben McDonald (7).
Shutouts: Mike Mussina, Fernando Valenzuela (2).
Saves: Gregg Olson (29).
Innings pitched: Ben McDonald (220⅓).
Strikeouts: Ben McDonald (171).

GAMES BY POSITION

Catcher: Chris Hoiles 124, Jeff Tackett 38, Mark Parent 21.
First base: David Segui 144, Glenn Davis 22, Paul Carey 9, Jack Voigt 5, Mike Pagliarulo 4.
Second base: Harold Reynolds 141, Mark McLemore 25, Tim Hulett 4.
Third base: Tim Hulett 75, Leo Gomez 70, Mike Pagliarulo 28, Mark McLemore 4, Jack Voigt 3.
Shortstop: Cal Ripken 162, Tim Hulett 8.
Outfield: Brady Anderson 140, Mike Devereaux 130, Mark McLemore 124, Jack Voigt 43, Damon Buford 30, Jeffrey Hammonds 23, Luis Mercedes 8, Sherman Obando 8, Chito Martinez 5, Mark Leonard 4, Lonnie Smith 4.
Designated hitter: Harold Baines 116, Sherman Obando 21, Damon Buford 17, Jack Voigt 9, Jeffrey Hammonds 8, Glenn Davis 7, Paul Carey 5, Lonnie Smith 5, Mark Leonard 3, Brady Anderson 3, Chris Hoiles 2, Tim Hulett 2, Chito Martinez 2, Luis Mercedes 2, Manny Alexander 1, Leo Gomez 1, Mark McLemore 1, Mark Parent 1, Harold Reynolds 1, David Segui 1.

TOP DRAFT CHOICES

1. **Jay Powell**, RHP, Mississippi State University.
2. **David Lamb**, SS, Newbury Park (Calif.) High School.
3. **Jimmy Walker**, RHP, University of Kansas.
4. **Jason Hackett**, LHP, Caravel Academy, Bear, Del.
5. **Mike Gargiulo**, C, Bishop McDevitt High School, Harrisburg, Pa.
6. **Brian Brewer**, LHP, Sacramento (Calif.) C.C.
7. **John Lombardi**, RHP/OF, Central Arizona J.C.
8. **Harry Berrios**, OF, Louisiana State University.
9. **Edwon Simmons**, SS, Leo High School, Chicago.
10. **Wes Hawkins**, OF, Louisiana Tech University.

BOSTON RED SOX
AMERICAN LEAGUE EAST DIVISION

1994 SCHEDULE

N Denotes night game (any game starting after 5 p.m.).
☐ Home games shaded.
* At Three Rivers Stadium in Pittsburgh.

APRIL

SUN	MON	TUE	WED	THU	FRI	SAT
					1	2
3	4 DET	5	6 DET	7 DET	8 CHI	9 CHI
10 CHI N	11 KC N	12 KC N	13 KC N	14	15 CHI N	16 CHI
17 CHI	18 CHI	19 OAK N	20 OAK N	21 OAK N	22 CAL N	23 CAL
24 CAL N	25 SEA N	26 SEA N	27 SEA N	28 OAK N	29 CAL N	30 CAL

MAY

SUN	MON	TUE	WED	THU	FRI	SAT
1 CAL N	2	3 SEA N	4 SEA N	5	6 NY N	7 NY
8 CAL N	9 MIL N	10 MIL N	11 MIL N	12 MIL N	13 TOR N	14 TOR
15 TOR N	16	17 BAL N	18 BAL N	19 BAL N	20 MIN N	21 MIN N
22 MIN	23 CLE N	24 CLE N	25 CLE N	26 TEX N	27 TEX N	28 TEX
29 TEX	30 KC N	31 KC N				

JUNE

SUN	MON	TUE	WED	THU	FRI	SAT
			1 KC N	2	3 TEX N	4 TEX
5 TEX N	6 DET N	7 DET N	8 DET	9	10 BAL N	11 BAL
12 BAL N	13 MIN N	14 MIN N	15 MIN N	16 CLE N	17 CLE N	18 CLE
19 CLE N	20 TOR N	21 TOR N	22 TOR	23	24 MIL N	25 MIL
26 MIL N	27 NY N	28 NY N	29 NY N	30 NY N		

JULY

SUN	MON	TUE	WED	THU	FRI	SAT
					1 OAK N	2 OAK
3 OAK	4 CAL N	5 CAL N	6 CAL N	7 SEA N	8 SEA N	9 SEA
10 SEA	11 *	12 ALL-STAR GAME	13	14 OAK N	15 OAK N	16 OAK
17 OAK N	18 CAL N	19 CAL N	20 CAL N	21 SEA N	22 SEA N	23 SEA
24 SEA	25	26 NY N	27 NY N	28 NY N	29 MIL N	30 MIL
31 MIL						

AUGUST

SUN	MON	TUE	WED	THU	FRI	SAT
	1 TOR N	2 TOR N	3 TOR	4 TOR N	5 CLE N	6 CLE
7 CLE N	8 MIN N	9 MIN N	10 MIN N	11 BAL N	12 BAL N	13 BAL
14 BAL	15	16 CHI N	17 CHI N	18 CHI N	19 DET N	20 DET
21 DET N	22 TEX N	23 TEX N	24 TEX N	25 DET N	26 DET N	27 DET
28 DET N	29 TEX N	30 TEX N	31 TEX N			

SEPTEMBER

SUN	MON	TUE	WED	THU	FRI	SAT
				1 KC N	2 KC N	3 KC
4 KC	5	6 CHI N	7 CHI N	8	9 KC N	10 KC
11 KC N	12 BAL N	13 BAL N	14 BAL N	15	16 MIN N	17 MIN
18 MIN	19	20 CLE N	21 CLE N	22 CLE N	23 TOR N	24 TOR
25 TOR N	26 MIL N	27 MIL N	28 MIL	29	30 NY N	

OCTOBER

SUN	MON	TUE	WED	THU	FRI	SAT
						1 NY N
2 NY						

1994 SEASON

CLUB DIRECTORY

Owner/majority general partner
JRY Corporation

President
John L. Harrington

Vice president and treasurer
William B. Gutfarb

Owner/general partner
Haywood C. Sullivan

Senior vice president and general manager
James (Lou) Gorman

Vice president and chief financial officer
Robert C. Furbush

Vice president baseball development
Edward M. Kasko

Assistant general manager
Elaine W. Steward

Director of scouting
Wayne Britton

Director of minor league operations
Edward P. Kenney

Assistant to player dev. and scouting
Erwin Bryant

Special assistant for player development
John M. Pesky

Traveling secretary
Steven W. August

Director of Florida Operations
William A. MacKay

Medical director
Arthur M. Pappas, M.D.

V.p., broadcasting and special projects
James P. Healey

Vice president, public relations
Richard L. Bresciani

Vice president, marketing
Lawrence C. Cancro

Vice president, stadium operations
Joseph F. McDermott

Director of baseball information
James A. Samia

Dir. of comm. relations & personnel admin.
Linda G. Ezell

Director of facilities management
Thomas L. Queenan Jr.

Director of food services
Patricia T. Flanagan

Dir. of parking and prop. maint.-buildings
Michael L. Silva

Director of ticket operations
Joseph P. Helyar

Superintendent of grounds and maintenance
Joseph F. Mooney

Controller
Stanley H. Tran

Staff accountant
Robin R. Yeingst

Manager of advertising/promotions
Lori T. McHugh

Manager of corporate sales
Robert G. Capilli

Manager of publications
Debra A. Matson

Manager of publicity
Kevin J. Shea

Major league special assignment scouts
Frank Malzone
Sabath A. Mele
Robert W. Schaefer

Scouts
Rafael Batista
Milton Bolling
Charles (Buzz) Bowers
Otho (Sonny) Bowers
Martin Crespo
Clark Crist
Ray Crone Jr.
Luis Delgado
Raymond Fagnant
Larry Flynn
Jack Lee
Frank Malzone
Steve McAllister
Howard McCullough
Sam Mele
Willie Paffen
Mike Rizzo
Phillip Rossi
Bob Schaefer
Alex Scott
Matt Sczesny
Joe Stephenson
Bob Sullivan
Larry Thomas
Fay Thompson
Luke Wrenn
Jeff Zona

Manager—Butch Hobson (17).

Coaches—Gary Allenson (32), Mike Easler (45), Mike Roarke (33), John Wathan (12), Frank White (20).

No.	PITCHERS	B/T	Ht./Wt.	Born	1993 clubs
43	Bailey, Cory	R/R	6-1/208	1-24-71	Pawtucket, Boston
29	Bankhead, Scott	R/R	5-10/185	7-31-63	Boston
59	Caruso, Joe	R/R	6-3/195	9-16-70	Pawtucket
54	Ciccarella, Joe	L/L	6-3/200	12-29-69	Pawtucket, New Britain
21	Clemens, Roger	R/R	6-4/220	8-4-62	Boston, Pawtucket
54	Conroy, Brian	B/R	6-2/185	8-29-68	Pawtucket
44	Darwin, Danny	R/R	6-3/195	10-25-55	Boston
60	Finnvold, Gar	R/R	6-5/195	3-11-68	Pawtucket
27	Harris, Greg A.	B/R	6-0/175	11-2-55	Boston
62	Henkel, Rob	R/R	6-3/190	11-23-70	Lynchburg
55	Hesketh, Joe	L/L	6-2/173	2-15-59	Boston
51	Melendez, Jose	R/R	6-2/175	9-2-65	Pawtucket, Boston
57	Minchey, Nate	R/R	6-7/210	8-31-69	Pawtucket, Boston
49	Quantrill, Paul	L/R	6-1/185	11-3-68	Boston
25	Russell, Jeff	R/R	6-3/205	9-2-61	Boston
50	Ryan, Ken	R/R	6-3/215	10-24-68	Boston, Pawtucket
	Sele, Aaron	R/R	6-5/205	6-25-70	Pawtucket, Boston
56	Taylor, Scott	L/L	6-1/190	8-2-67	Pawtucket, Boston
61	Vanegmond, Tim	R/R	6-2/180	5-31-69	New Britain
16	Viola, Frank	L/L	6-4/210	4-19-60	Boston

No.	CATCHERS	B/T	Ht./Wt.	Born	1993 clubs
15	Flaherty, John	R/R	6-1/195	10-21-67	Pawtucket, Boston
63	Hatteberg, Scott	L/R	6-1/185	12-14-69	New Britain, Pawtucket
3	Melvin, Bob	R/R	6-4/205	10-28-61	Boston
10	Valle, Dave	R/R	6-2/220	10-30-60	Seattle

No.	INFIELDERS	B/T	Ht./Wt.	Born	1993 clubs
45	Cooper, Scott	L/R	6-3/205	10-13-67	Boston
5	Fletcher, Scott	R/R	5-11/173	7-30-58	Boston
11	Naehring, Tim	R/R	6-2/205	2-1-67	Pawtucket, Boston
51	Ortiz, Luis	R/R	6-0/188	5-25-70	Pawtucket, Boston
13	Valentin, John	R/R	6-0/180	2-18-67	Pawtucket, Boston
42	Vaughn, Mo	L/R	6-1/225	12-15-67	Boston

No.	OUTFIELDERS	B/T	Ht./Wt.	Born	1993 clubs
38	Blosser, Greg	L/L	6-3/200	6-26-71	Pawtucket, Boston
10	Dawson, Andre	R/R	6-3/197	7-10-54	Boston
39	Greenwell, Mike	L/R	6-0/205	7-18-63	Boston
31	Hall, Billy	B/R	5-9/180	6-17-69	Wichita
22	Hatcher, Billy	R/R	5-10/190	10-4-60	Boston
65	Malave, Jose	R/R	6-2/194	5-31-71	Lynchburg
58	McNeely, Jeff	R/R	6-2/190	10-18-69	Pawtucket, Boston
1	Nixon, Otis	B/R	6-2/180	1-9-59	Atlanta
18	Quintana, Carlos	R/R	6-2/220	8-26-65	Boston
28	Zupcic, Bob	R/R	6-4/225	8-18-66	Boston

BALLPARK INFORMATION

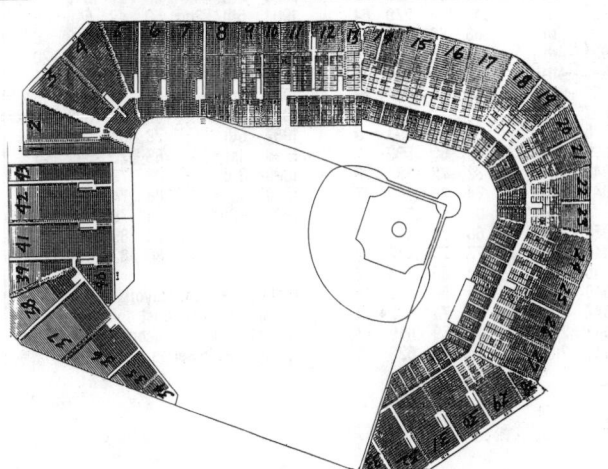

Ballpark (capacity, surface)
Fenway Park (33,871, grass)

Address
4 Yawkey Way
Boston, MA 02215

Business phone
617-267-9440

Ticket information
617-267-8661

Ticket prices
$16 (upper box)
$12 (grandstand)
$8 (bleachers)
$8 (standing room)

Field dimensions (from home plate)
To left field at foul line, 315 feet
To center field, 420 feet
To right field at foul line, 302 feet

First game played
April 20, 1912 (Red Sox 7, New York
Highlanders 6)

MINOR LEAGUE AFFILIATES

Class	Team	League	Manager
AAA	Pawtucket	International	Buddy Bailey
AA	New Britain	Eastern	Jim Pankovits
A	Lynchburg	Carolina	Mark Meleski
A	Sarasota	Florida State	DeMarlo Hale
A	Utica	New York-Pennsylvania	Dave Holt
Rookie	Gulf Coast Red Sox	Gulf Coast	Felix Maldonado

BROADCAST INFORMATION

Radio: WRKO-AM (680). Broadcasters: Joe Castiglione, Jerry Trupiano.
TV: WSBK-TV (Channel 38). Broadcasters: Sean McDonough, Bob Montgomery.
Cable TV: New England Sports Network. Broadcasters: Bob Kurtz, Jerry Remy.

SPRING TRAINING

Ballpark (city): City of Palms Park (Ft. Myers, Fla.).
Ticket information: 813-334-4700.

HISTORY

YEAR-BY-YEAR RECORDS

Year	Pos.	W	L	Pct.	GB	Year	Pos.	W	L	Pct.	GB
1901	2nd	79	57	.581	4	1950	3rd	94	60	.610	4
1902	3rd	77	60	.562	6½	1951	3rd	87	67	.565	11
1903	1st	91	47	.659	+14½	1952	6th	76	78	.494	19
1904	1st	95	59	.617	+1½	1953	4th	84	69	.549	16
1905	4th	78	74	.513	16	1954	4th	69	85	.448	42
1906	8th	49	105	.318	45½	1955	4th	84	70	.545	12
1907	7th	59	90	.396	32½	1956	4th	84	70	.545	13
1908	5th	75	79	.487	15½	1957	3rd	82	72	.532	16
1909	3rd	88	63	.583	9½	1958	3rd	79	75	.513	13
1910	4th	81	72	.529	22½	1959	5th	75	79	.487	19
1911	5th	78	75	.510	24	1960	7th	65	89	.422	32
1912	1st	105	47	.691	+14	1961	6th	76	86	.469	33
1913	4th	79	71	.527	15½	1962	8th	76	84	.475	19
1914	2nd	91	62	.595	8½	1963	7th	76	85	.472	28
1915	1st	101	50	.669	+2½	1964	8th	72	90	.444	27
1916	1st	91	63	.591	+2	1965	9th	62	100	.383	40
1917	2nd	90	62	.592	9	1966	9th	72	90	.444	26
1918	1st	75	51	.595	+2½	1967	1st	92	70	.568	+1
1919	6th	66	71	.482	20½	1968	4th	86	76	.531	17
1920	5th	72	81	.471	25½	1969	3rd	87	75	.537	22
1921	5th	75	79	.487	23½	1970	3rd	87	75	.537	21
1922	8th	61	93	.396	33	1971	3rd	85	77	.525	18
1923	8th	61	91	.401	37	1972	2nd	85	70	.548	½
1924	7th	67	87	.435	25	1973	2nd	89	73	.549	8
1925	8th	47	105	.309	49½	1974	3rd	84	78	.519	7
1926	8th	46	107	.301	44½	1975	1st†	95	65	.594	+4½
1927	8th	51	103	.331	59	1976	3rd	83	79	.512	15½
1928	8th	57	96	.373	43½	1977	T2nd	97	64	.602	2½
1929	8th	58	96	.377	48	1978	2nd‡	99	64	.607	1
1930	8th	52	102	.338	50	1979	3rd	91	69	.569	11½
1931	6th	62	90	.408	45	1980	4th	83	77	.519	19
1932	8th	43	111	.279	64	1981	5th/T2nd	59	49	.546	§
1933	7th	63	86	.423	34½	1982	3rd	89	73	.549	6
1934	4th	76	76	.500	24	1983	6th	78	84	.481	20
1935	4th	78	75	.510	16	1984	4th	86	76	.531	18
1936	6th	74	80	.481	28½	1985	5th	81	81	.500	18½
1937	5th	80	72	.526	21	1986	1st††	95	66	.590	+5½
1938	2nd	88	61	.591	9½	1987	5th	78	84	.481	20
1939	2nd	89	62	.589	17	1988	1st *	89	73	.549	+1
1940	T4th	82	72	.532	8	1989	3rd	83	79	.512	6
1941	2nd	84	70	.545	17	1990	1st *	88	74	.543	+2
1942	2nd	93	59	.612	9	1991	T2nd	84	78	.519	7
1943	7th	68	84	.447	29	1992	7th	73	89	.451	23
1944	4th	77	77	.500	12	1993	5th	80	82	.494	15
1945	7th	71	83	.461	17½						
1946	1st	104	50	.675	+12						
1947	3rd	83	71	.539	14						
1948	2nd*	96	59	.619	1						
1949	2nd	96	58	.623	1						

*Lost pennant playoff. †Won Championship Series. ‡Lost division playoff. §First half 30-26; second 29-23. ★ Lost Championship Series.

MANAGERS

Name	Record	Years
Jimmy Collins	455-376	'01-06
Chick Stahl	14-26	1906
George Huff	2-6	1907
Bob Unglaub	9-20	1907
Deacon McGuire	98-123	'07-08
Fred Lake	110-80	'08-09
Patsy Donovan	159-147	'10-11
Jake Stahl	144-88	'12-13
Bill Carrigan	489-500	'13-16
		'27-29
Jack Barry	90-62	1917
Ed Barrow	213-203	'18-20
Hugh Duffy	136-172	'21-22
Frank Chance	61-91	1923
Lee Fohl	160-299	'24-26
Heinie Wagner	52-102	1930
Shano Collins	73-134	'31-32
Marty McManus	95-153	'32-33
Bucky Harris	76-76	1934
Joe Cronin	1071-916	'35-47
Joe McCarthy	223-145	'48-50
Steve O'Neill	150-99	'50-51
Lou Boudreau	229-232	'52-54
Pinky Higgins	560-556	'55-59
		'60-62
Billy Jurges	59-63	'59-60
Johnny Pesky	147-179	'63-64
		1980
Billy Herman	128-182	'64-66
Pete Runnels	8-8	1966
Dick Williams	260-217	'67-69
Eddie Popowski	5-4	1969
Eddie Kasko	346-295	'70-73
Darrell Johnson	220-188	'74-76
Don Zimmer	411-304	'76-80
Ralph Houk	312-282	'81-84
John McNamara	297-273	'85-88
Joe Morgan	301-262	'88-91
Butch Hobson	153-171	'92-93

DAY BY DAY

Date	Opp.	Res.	Score	(inn.*)	Hits	Opp. hits	Winning pitcher	Losing pitcher	Save	Record	Pos.	GB
4-5	At K.C.	W	3-1		7	6	Clemens	Appier	Russell	1-0	T1st	...
4-7	At K.C.	W	3-2		10	5	Viola	Cone	Russell	2-0	1st	+2
4-8	At K.C.	W	9-4		15	4	Bankhead	Gubicza		3-0	1st	+1
4-9	At Tex.	L	1-3		5	5	Ryan	Dopson	Henke	3-1	1st	+½
4-10	At Tex.	W	10-2		14	9	Clemens	Lefferts		4-1	1st	+½
4-11	At Tex.	L	1-4		6	7	Brown	Darwin	Henke	4-2	1st	+½
4-13	Cle.	W	6-2		10	10	Viola	Mutis		5-2	1st	+½
4-14	Cle.	W	12-7		18	12	Hesketh	Bielecki		6-2	1st	+1
4-15	Cle.	W	4-3	(13)	10	13	Quantrill	Plunk		7-2	1st	+1½
4-16	Chi.	L	4-9		7	14	McDowell	Darwin		7-3	1st	+1
4-17	Chi.	W	5-1		11	5	Hesketh	McCaskill		8-3	1st	+1½
4-18	Chi.	W	4-0		10	9	Viola	Bolton		9-3	1st	+1½
4-19	Chi.	W	6-0		10	3	Dopson	Fernandez		10-3	1st	+2½
4-20	At Sea.	W	5-2		11	5	Clemens	Cummings	Russell	11-3	1st	+2½
4-21	At Sea.	L	0-5		4	10	Johnson	Darwin		11-4	1st	+½
4-22	At Sea.	L	0-7		0	11	Bosio	Hesketh		11-5	1st	+1
4-23	At Cal.	L	1-4		3	8	Langston	Viola		11-6	2nd	...
4-24	At Cal.	L	5-8		7	10	Crim	Bankhead	Valera	11-7	2nd	1
4-25	At Cal.	L	1-2		8	4	Sanderson	Clemens	Grahe	11-8	2nd	2
4-27	At Oak.	L	2-7		7	12	Witt	Darwin	Gossage	11-9	4th	2½
4-28	At Oak.	W	3-1		10	4	Viola	Welch	Russell	12-9	T2nd	1½
4-30	Cal.	W	6-1		7	3	Dopson	Farrell		13-9	2nd	2
5-1	Cal.	W	3-1		9	5	Clemens	Sanderson	Russell	14-9	2nd	1
5-2	Cal.	W	4-3		9	6	Darwin	Finley	Russell	15-9	T1st	...
5-3	Sea.	L	0-2		9	8	Hanson	Viola	Charlton	15-10	2nd	½
5-4	Sea.	L	6-7		10	13	Leary	Hesketh	Charlton	15-11	3rd	1½
5-5	Oak.	W	3-1		11	7	Quantrill	Nunez	Russell	16-11	2nd	½
5-6	Oak.	L	3-6		8	8	Witt	Clemens	Eckersley	16-12	2nd	1
5-7	At Mil.	W	1-0		4	3	Darwin	Wegman	Russell	17-12	2nd	1
5-8	At Mil.	L	3-6		10	5	Eldred	Quantrill	Henry	17-13	2nd	1
5-9	At Mil.	L	0-6		6	11	Boddicker	Hesketh		17-14	3rd	1
5-10	At Bal.	L	1-2		11	7	Frohwirth	Quantrill	Pennington	17-15	3rd	2
5-11	At Bal.	W	4-0		11	5	Clemens	McDonald		18-15	3rd	2
5-12	At Bal.	W	2-0		7	2	Darwin	Valenzuela	Russell	19-15	2nd	2
5-14	At Min.	L	3-4		5	8	Erickson	Viola	Aguilera	19-16	T2nd	2½
5-15	At Min.	L	4-7		8	11	Deshaies	Dopson	Aguilera	19-17	3rd	3½
5-16	At Min.	W	11-5		17	8	Hesketh	Hartley		20-17	T2nd	2½
5-17	Tor.	L	3-9		8	15	Hentgen	Clemens		20-18	T3rd	3
5-19	Tor.	W	10-5		11	11	Darwin	Stewart		21-18	3rd	3½
5-20	Tor.	L	3-4		8	8	Cox	Quantrill	Ward	21-19	T3rd	4½
5-21	N.Y.	W	7-2		10	11	Dopson	Perez		22-19	T3rd	4½
5-22	N.Y.	L	3-7		8	11	Witt	Clemens		22-20	4th	4½
5-23	N.Y.	W	5-2		8	6	Harris	Key	Russell	23-20	4th	4½
5-24	At Det.	W	6-5	(10)	17	9	Ryan	MacDonald	Russell	24-20	T3rd	3½
5-25	At Det.	L	1-4		4	4	Wells	Viola	Henneman	24-21	4th	4½
5-26	At Det.	L	2-4		6	6	Gullickson	Dopson	Knudsen	24-22	4th	5½
5-28	Tex.	W	4-1		8	2	Clemens	Pavlik	Russell	25-22	4th	4½
5-29	Tex.	W	15-1		14	6	Darwin	Burns		26-22	4th	4½
5-30	Tex.	W	6-5	(12)	14	16	Melendez	Bronkey		27-22	4th	3½
5-31	K.C.	L	3-5		8	10	Cone	Dopson	Montgomery	27-23	4th	4
6-1	K.C.	L	3-4		6	6	Haney	Quantrill	Montgomery	27-24	4th	4
6-2	K.C.	L	2-7		7	13	Appier	Clemens		27-25	4th	4
6-4	At Chi.	W	1-0		6	4	Harris	Hernandez	Russell	28-25	4th	3½
6-5	At Chi.	L	3-11		10	15	McDowell	Viola		28-26	4th	4½
6-6	At Chi.	L	3-4		7	6	Fernandez	Melendez	Hernandez	28-27	4th	5½
6-8	At Cle.	L	4-5		7	6	Lilliquist	Harris		28-28	4th	6
6-9	At Cle.	L	2-3		7	7	Young	Darwin	Plunk	28-29	4th	7
6-10	Bal.	L	1-2		7	6	Moyer	Viola	Olson	28-30	5th	8
6-11	Bal.	L	4-16		8	16	Mussina	Dopson		28-31	5th	9
6-12	Bal.	L	1-5		6	9	Pennington	Harris		28-32	5th	10
6-13	Bal.	W	4-2		4	6	Clemens	Valenzuela	Russell	29-32	5th	9
6-14	At N.Y.	L	0-4		3	5	Kamieniecki	Darwin		29-33	5th	10
6-15	At N.Y.	L	7-9		12	10	Heaton	Viola	Farr	29-34	5th	11
6-16	At N.Y.	W	7-1		11	3	Dopson	Perez		30-34	5th	10
6-17	At Tor.	L	0-7		2	14	Leiter	Quantrill		30-35	5th	11
6-18	At Tor.	L	2-11		7	14	Hentgen	Clemens		30-36	5th	11
6-19	At Tor.	L	4-9		8	13	Stewart	Darwin		30-37	5th	12
6-20	At Tor.	L	2-3	(12)	11	8	Timlin	Russell		30-38	5th	13
6-21	Min.	W	6-3		8	12	Dopson	Erickson	Russell	31-38	5th	12½
6-22	Min.	W	4-1		7	9	Quantrill	Deshaies	Russell	32-38	5th	11½

Date	Opp.	Res.	Score	(inn.*)	Hits	Opp. hits	Winning pitcher	Losing pitcher	Save	Record	Pos.	GB
6-23	Min.	W	3-1		10	5	Sele	Guardado	Harris	33-38	5th	10½
6-25	Det.	W	8-2		10	6	Darwin	Wells	Harris	34-38	5th	9
6-26	Det.	W	13-4		15	8	Melendez	Doherty		35-38	5th	9
6-27	Det.	W	8-2		14	8	Dopson	Gullickson		36-38	5th	9
6-28	Mil.	W	4-3		8	11	Harris	Henry		37-38	5th	9
6-29	Mil.	L	6-7		9	7	Fetters	Harris	Henry	37-39	5th	10
6-30	Mil.	W	12-2		15	6	Darwin	Miranda		38-39	5th	9
7-2	At Sea.	W	9-8		13	12	Viola	Hampton	Russell	39-39	5th	8
7-3	At Sea.	W	6-5		13	9	Harris	Charlton	Russell	40-39	5th	7
7-4	At Sea.	W	6-0		6	2	Quantrill	Bosio		41-39	5th	6
7-5	At Cal.	W	4-3	(11)	12	6	Ryan	Nelson		42-39	5th	5
7-6	At Cal.	L	2-3		6	6	Finley	Hesketh		42-40	5th	6
7-7	At Cal.	L	6-7		7	13	Linton	Russell		42-41	5th	6
7-8	At Oak.	W	11-9		11	13	Dopson	Van Poppel	Russell	43-41	5th	5
7-9	At Oak.	L	2-4		7	7	Darling	Quantrill	Eckersley	43-42	5th	5
7-10	At Oak.	W	5-0		11	6	Sele	Downs	Harris	44-42	5th	4
7-11	At Oak.	W	3-2		8	7	Darwin	Witt	Russell	45-42	5th	3
7-15	Sea.	L	2-3		6	9	Fleming	Viola	Hampton	45-43	5th	4
7-16	Sea.	W	5-3		10	9	Clemens	Hanson	Russell	46-43	5th	3
7-17	Sea.	W	4-3		8	8	Darwin	Bosio	Russell	47-43	5th	2
7-18	Sea.	W	7-6		8	8	Ryan	Charlton	Harris	48-43	5th	2
7-19	Cal.	W	8-6		16	10	Sele	Sanderson	Russell	49-43	5th	2
7-20	Cal.	W	2-1		11	11	Fossas	Nelson		50-43	4th	1½
7-21	Cal.	W	4-1		9	6	Clemens	Finley	Russell	51-43	3rd	1
7-22	Oak.	W	9-7		13	10	Ryan	Nunez	Russell	52-43	2nd	1
7-23	Oak.	W	6-5	(10)	13	6	Harris	Gossage		53-43	1st	...
7-24	Oak.	W	5-3		8	6	Sele	Downs	Russell	54-43	1st	...
7-25	Oak.	W	8-1		14	8	Viola	Welch	Quantrill	55-43	1st	...
7-26	At Mil.	L	2-3		5	7	Lloyd	Russell		55-44	2nd	½
7-27	At Mil.	L	2-3		5	9	Navarro	Darwin	Orosco	55-45	3rd	1½
7-28	At Mil.	W	8-4		11	6	Harris	Miranda		56-45	3rd	1½
7-29	At Mil.	W	7-3		9	11	Sele	Bones		57-45	3rd	1½
7-30	At Bal.	W	8-7		9	10	Quantrill	Moyer	Russell	58-45	3rd	½
7-31	At Bal.	L	0-4		3	10	McDonald	Clemens		58-46	3rd	1½
8-1	At Bal.	W	2-1		10	5	Darwin	Sutcliffe	Russell	59-46	3rd	1½
8-3	At Min.	L	1-6		8	11	Banks	Dopson		59-47	2nd	3
8-4	At Min.	W	5-4		11	12	Sele	Erickson	Russell	60-47	2nd	2
8-5	At Min.	W	2-1		6	5	Viola	Deshaies	Russell	61-47	2nd	1
8-6	At Det.	L	1-5		3	6	Gullickson	Clemens		61-48	2nd	2
8-7	At Det.	W	4-1		4	6	Darwin	Bergman	Russell	62-48	2nd	1
8-8	At Det.	L	1-5		7	9	Bolton	Dopson		62-49	T2nd	1
8-10	N.Y.	W	5-0		9	4	Viola	Kamieniecki	Hesketh	63-49	2nd	1
8-11	N.Y.	L	3-8		10	11	Key	Clemens	Wickman	63-50	2nd	2
8-12	N.Y.	L	1-4		2	9	Perez	Sele	Farr	63-51	3rd	2
8-13	Tor.	W	5-3		10	12	Darwin	Stottlemyre	Russell	64-51	3rd	1
8-14	Tor.	L	2-5		7	10	Hentgen	Dopson	Ward	64-52	3rd	2
8-15	Tor.	L	1-9		4	14	Stewart	Clemens		64-53	3rd	3
8-17	Chi.	L	2-3		10	9	McDowell	Sele	Hernandez	64-54	3rd	4½
8-18	Chi.	W	5-0		5	1	Darwin	Bere		65-54	3rd	4½
8-19	Cle.	L	1-5		8	11	Tavarez	Quantrill		65-55	3rd	5
8-20	Cle.	L	6-7		12	9	DiPoto	Russell		65-56	3rd	5
8-21	Cle.	L	5-10		13	12	Wertz	Harris		65-57	4th	5
8-22	Cle.	L	2-3	(11)	13	10	Kramer	Ryan	DiPoto	65-58	4th	6
8-24	At Tex.	L	3-4		12	7	Pavlik	Darwin	Henke	65-59	4th	6½
8-25	At Tex.	L	2-10		6	13	Dreyer	Quantrill		65-60	5th	7½
8-26	At Tex.	W	3-1		7	5	Viola	Brown	Russell	66-60	5th	6½
8-27	At K.C.	W	5-0		11	5	Clemens	Haney		67-60	4th	5½
8-28	At K.C.	W	2-1	(11)	9	5	Russell	Montgomery		68-60	4th	4½
8-29	At K.C.	L	4-5	(12)	12	13	Gubicza	Dopson		68-61	4th	5½
8-30	Tex.	W	7-3		10	6	Viola	Brown		69-61	4th	5½
8-31	Tex.	L	1-8		6	12	Rogers	Clemens		69-62	5th	6½
9-1	Tex.	L	7-9	(12)	14	13	Bronkey	Quantrill		69-63	5th	7½
9-3	K.C.	L	1-5		6	8	Appier	Darwin		69-64	5th	7½
9-4	K.C.	L	2-4		5	8	Cone	Ryan	Montgomery	69-65	5th	7½
9-5	K.C.	L	2-5		5	7	Gordon	Clemens		69-66	5th	7½
9-6	At Chi.	W	3-1		10	6	Bankhead	McDowell	Harris	70-66	4th	7
9-7	At Chi.	W	4-3		9	5	Darwin	Belcher	Ryan	71-66	4th	6
9-8	At Chi.	L	1-8		5	11	Bere	Dopson		71-67	5th	6
9-10 (1)	At Cle.	L	4-7		9	10	Ojeda	Clemens	DiPoto	71-68	5th	6½
9-10 (2)	At Cle.	W	5-4	(11)	12	9	Ryan	Wertz		72-68	5th	6
9-11	At Cle.	L	3-9		10	11	Lilliquist	Quantrill		72-69	5th	7
9-12	At Cle.	W	11-1		15	10	Minchey	Grimsley		73-69	5th	7
9-13	Bal.	W	6-4		12	8	Quantrill	Williamson	Harris	74-69	5th	6½
9-14	Bal.	L	3-11		8	12	Valenzuela	Darwin		74-70	5th	7½

— 18 —

Date	Opp.	Res.	Score	(inn.*)	Hits	Opp. hits	Winning pitcher	Losing pitcher	Save	Record	Pos.	GB
9-15	Bal.	W	6-5		10	7	Clemens	Mussina	Harris	75-70	4th	7½
9-16	At N.Y.	W	6-4		14	9	Viola	Kamienicki	Harris	76-70	4th	7
9-17	At N.Y.	L	4-5		7	10	Gibson	Dopson	Smith	76-71	4th	8
9-18	At N.Y.	L	3-4		11	10	Wickman	Harris		76-72	T4th	9
9-19	At N.Y.	W	8-3		13	5	Darwin	Tanana		77-72	4th	9
9-21	At Tor.	L	0-5		3	7	Stottlemyre	Clemens		77-73	3rd	10
9-22	At Tor.	L	7-5	(10)	11	12	Ryan	Timlin		78-73	4th	9
9-23	At Tor.	L	1-5		5	5	Stewart	Minchey		78-74	T4th	10
9-24	Min.	W	7-4		11	8	Ryan	Merriman		79-74	T4th	10
9-25	Min.	L	7-9	(10)	11	13	Aguilera	Harris	Willis	79-75	5th	11
9-26	Min.	L	2-5		11	11	Trombley	Quantrill	Aguilera	79-76	5th	11
9-28 (1)	Det.	W	11-6		15	10	Sele	Krueger		80-76	5th	11½
9-28 (2)	Det.	L	6-7	(11)	13	12	Henneman	Fossas	Knudsen	80-77	5th	12
9-29	Det.	L	7-8		13	16	Boever	Bailey	Henneman	80-78	5th	13
9-30	Det.	L	4-7		5	10	Knudsen	Taylor	Boever	80-79	5th	14
10-1	Mil.	L	4-8		8	14	Navarro	Harris		80-80	5th	14
10-2	Mil.	L	5-8		11	11	Bones	Minchey	Kiefer	80-81	5th	14
10-3	Mil.	L	3-6	(14)	5	9	Maldonado	Quantrill		80-82	5th	15

Monthly records: April (13-9), May (14-14), June (11-16), July (20-7), August (11-16), September (11-17), October (0-3).
*Innings, if other than nine.

HIGHLIGHTS

High point: From June 21-July 25, Boston won 25 of 30 games to move from fifth place (13 games behind) into a first-place tie.

Low point: After beating New York on August 10, the Red Sox were just one game out of first. But Boston closed the season by winning just 17 of its last 50 games, finishing in fifth place (15 games back).

Turning point: On August 10, the Red Sox had the best home record in the league (35-15) and began a 12-game homestand. Boston won just three of those 12 games, however, and never recovered.

Most valuable player: First baseman Mo Vaughn. With virtually no protection in the lineup, he hit .297 with 29 home runs and 101 RBIs.

Most valuable pitcher: Righthander Danny Darwin. Despite a 0-4 start, he led the staff with a career-high 15 wins.

Most improved player: Vaughn. Under hitting coach Mike Easler, Vaughn improved his batting average by 63 points, his home run total by 16 and his RBI count by 44 over his 1992 numbers. He also made strides defensively.

Most pleasant surprise: Righthander Aaron Sele. After just 14 starts at Class AAA, he was summoned June 22 and proceeded to win his first six decisions and finish 7-2 with a 2.74 ERA.

Biggest disappointment: Righthander Roger Clemens. He endured the first losing record (11-14) of his career and posted his worst-ever ERA (4.46).

Key injuries: Designated hitter Andre Dawson underwent arthroscopic surgery on his right knee May 6 and didn't begin to make a major contribution until the second half. Then he missed most of the final month with a fractured right wrist. Lefthander Frank Viola sprained his right ankle after getting off to a 4-1 start. He went 1-7 in his next 14 starts through July 20. With the team only 4½ games out of first, righthander Jeff Russell injured his left ankle August 29 and made just three appearances the rest of the season.

Notable: Left fielder Mike Greenwell made a great comeback from major right elbow surgery he underwent in 1992. He finished seventh in the league with a .315 batting average while hitting 13 home runs with 72 RBIs. . . . Righthander Greg Harris set a team record by appearing in 80 games. . . . Vaughn's 29 home runs were the most for a Red Sox lefthanded hitter since Fred Lynn hit 39 in 1979.

—JOE GIULIOTTI

RECORDS

1993 regular-season record: 80-82 (5th in A.L. East); 43-38 at home; 37-44 on road; 32-46 vs. East; 48-36 vs. West; 26-20 vs. LHP; 54-62 vs. RHP; 67-70 on grass; 13-12 on turf; 30-26 in daytime; 50-56 at night; 24-26 in one-run games; 8-7 in extra-inning games; 0-2 in doubleheaders.

Team record last five years: 408-402 (.504, ranks 6th in league in that span).

TEAM LEADERS

Batting average: Mike Greenwell (.315).
At-bats: Mike Greenwell (540).
Runs: Mo Vaughn (86).
Hits: Mike Greenwell (170).
Total bases: Mo Vaughn (283).
Doubles: John Valentin (40).
Triples: Mike Greenwell (6).
Home runs: Mo Vaughn (29).
Runs batted in: Mo Vaughn (101).
Stolen bases: Scott Fletcher (16).
Slugging percentage: Mo Vaughn (.525).
On-base percentage: Mo Vaughn (.390).
Wins: Danny Darwin (15).
Earned-run average: Frank Viola (3.14).
Complete games: Roger Clemens, Danny Darwin, Frank Viola (2).
Shutouts: Five tied (1).
Saves: Jeff Russell (33).
Innings pitched: Danny Darwin (229⅓).
Strikeouts: Roger Clemens (160).

GAMES BY POSITION

Catcher: Tony Pena 125, Bob Melvin 76, John Flaherty 13, Steve Lyons 1.
First base: Mo Vaughn 131, Carlos Quintana 53, Scott Cooper 2, Steve Lyons 1, Bob Melvin 1, Ernest Riles 1.
Second base: Scott Fletcher 116, Luis Rivera 27, Ernest Riles 20, Tim Naehring 15, Steve Lyons 9, Jeff Richardson 8, Billy Hatcher 2.
Third base: Scott Cooper 154, Ernest Riles 11, Tim Naehring 9, Luis Ortiz 5, Luis Rivera 2, Scott Fletcher 1, Steve Lyons 1, Jeff Richardson 1.
Shortstop: John Valentin 144, Luis Rivera 27, Jeff Richardson 5, Tim Naehring 4, Scott Fletcher 2, Scott Cooper 1.
Outfield: Mike Greenwell 134, Billy Hatcher 130, Bob Zupcic 122, Carlos Quintana 51, Ivan Calderon 47, Rob Deer 36, Andre Dawson 20, Jeff McNeely 13, Steve Lyons 10, Greg Blosser 9.
Designated hitter: Andre Dawson 97, Ivan Calderon 19, Mo Vaughn 19, Ernest Riles 15, Mike Greenwell 10, Tim Naehring 10, Luis Rivera 7, Bob Zupcic 5, Jeff Richardson 2, Greg Blosser 1, Jim Byrd 1, Scott Fletcher 1, Steve Lyons 1, Tony Pena 1.

TOP DRAFT CHOICES

1. **Trot Nixon**, OF, New Hanover High School, Wilmington, N.C.
2. **Jeff Suppan**, RHP, Crespi High School, Encino, Calif.
3. **Ryan McGuire**, 1B, UCLA.
4. **Shawn Senior**, LHP, North Carolina State University.
5. **Kevin Clark**, 3B, Cypress (Calif.) J.C.
6. **Peter Munro**, RHP, Cardoza High School, Bayside, N.Y.
7. **David Gibralter**, 3B, Duncanville (Tex.) High School.
8. **Sean DePaula**, RHP, Cushing Academy (Ashburnham, Mass.)
9. **Dean Peterson**, RHP, Allegheny (Pa.) J.C.
10. **Lou Merloni**, SS, Providence College.

CALIFORNIA ANGELS
AMERICAN LEAGUE WEST DIVISION

1994 SCHEDULE

N Denotes night game (any game starting after 5 p.m.).
▢ Home games shaded.
* At Three Rivers Stadium in Pittsburgh.

APRIL
SUN	MON	TUE	WED	THU	FRI	SAT
					1	2
3	4	5 N MIN	6 N MIN	7 N MIL	8 N MIL	9 MIL
10 MIL	11 N CLE	12 N CLE	13 N TOR	14 N TOR	15 N TOR	16 TOR
17 TOR	18	19 N BAL	20 N BAL	21 N BOS	22 N BOS	23 BOS
24 BOS	25 N NY	26 NY	27 N BAL	28 N BAL	29 N BOS	30 N BOS

MAY
SUN	MON	TUE	WED	THU	FRI	SAT
1 N BOS	2	3 N NY	4 N NY	5 N OAK	6 N OAK	7 N OAK
8 OAK	9 N TEX	10 N TEX	11 N TEX	12	13 N SEA	14 N SEA
15 SEA	16 N CHI	17 N CHI	18 N CHI	19 N KC	20 N KC	21 KC
22 KC	23 N DET	24 N DET	25 DET	26 N TOR	27 N TOR	28 TOR
29 TOR	30 N CLE	31 N CLE				

JUNE
SUN	MON	TUE	WED	THU	FRI	SAT
			1 N CLE	2	3 N MIL	4 N MIL
5 MIL	6 N MIN	7 N MIN	8 MIN	9 N DET	10 N DET	11 N DET
12 DET	13 N KC	14 N KC	15 N KC	16 N CHI	17 N CHI	18 CHI
19 CHI	20 N SEA	21 N SEA	22 N SEA	23	24 N TEX	25 N TEX
26 TEX	27 N OAK	28 N OAK	29 OAK	30		

JULY
SUN	MON	TUE	WED	THU	FRI	SAT
					1 N BAL	2 N BAL
3 BAL	4 N BOS	5 N BOS	6 N BOS	7 N NY	8 N NY	9 NY
10 NY	11 * 12 ALL-STAR GAME	13	14 N BAL	15 N BAL	16 N BAL
17 BAL	18 N BOS	19 N BOS	20 N BOS	21 N NY	22 N NY	23 N NY
24 NY	25 N OAK	26 OAK	27 N TEX	28 N TEX	29 N TEX	30 N TEX
31 N TEX						

AUGUST
SUN	MON	TUE	WED	THU	FRI	SAT
	1	2 N SEA	3 N SEA	4 N SEA	5 N CHI	6 N CHI
7 CHI	8 N KC	9 N KC	10 KC	11	12 N DET	13 N DET
14 DET	15	16 N MIL	17 N MIL	18 MIL	19 N MIN	20 N MIN
21 MIN	22	23 N MIL	24 N MIL	25 N MIL	26 N CLE	27 N CLE
28 CLE	29	30 N TOR	31 N TOR			

SEPTEMBER
SUN	MON	TUE	WED	THU	FRI	SAT
				1 N TOR	2 N CLE	3 CLE
4 CLE	5	6 N TOR	7 N TOR	8 N MIN	9 N MIN	10 N MIN
11 MIN	12	13 N DET	14 N DET	15	16 N KC	17 N KC
18 KC	19 N CHI	20 N CHI	21 N CHI	22 N SEA	23 N SEA	24 N SEA
25 SEA	26 N TEX	27 N TEX	28 N TEX	29 N OAK	30 N OAK	

OCTOBER
SUN	MON	TUE	WED	THU	FRI	SAT
						1 OAK
2 OAK						

1994 SEASON

CLUB DIRECTORY

Chairman of the board
Gene Autry
Board of directors
Gene Autry
Jackie Autry
Richard M. Brown
Stanley B. Schneider
John P. Singleton
Peter V. Ueberroth
President and chief executive officer
Richard M. Brown
Executive vice president
Jackie Autry
Senior vice president & general manager
Whitey Herzog
V.p., treasurer and chief financial officer
Ronald C. Shirley
V.p., civic affairs and broadcasting
Tom Seeberg
Asst. v.p. and director, facilities operations
Kevin Uhlich
Assistant vice president, media relations
Tim Mead
Asst. v.p., creative services & broadcasting
John Sevano
Assistant general manager
Bill Bavasi
Assistant to the general manager
Preston Gomez
Special assistant to the g.m.
Bob Harrison
Director, minor league operations
Ken Forsch
Traveling secretary
Frank Sims
Manager, baseball information
Larry Babcock
Director, sales and marketing
Craig Gerber
Manager, publications
Doug Ward
Controller
John Sullivan
Equipment manager
Ken Higdon
Visiting clubhouse
Brian Harkins
Director, community relations
Marie Moreno
Director, special projects
Corky Lippert
Director, ticket department
Sheila Brazelton
Supervisor, ticket services
Susan Weiss
Medical director
Dr. Robert K. Kerlan
Team physician, medicine
Dr. Jules Rasinski
Team physician, orthopedics
Dr. Lewis Yocum
Trainers
Ned Bergert
Rick Smith

Sports psychologist
Ken Ravizza
Director, scouting
Bob Fontaine Jr.
Coordinator of scouting operations
Tim Kelly
Director, international scouting
Ray Poitevint
Supervisor, international scouting
Lee Sigman
International cross-checker
Harry Smith
Scouts
Don Archer
Ted Brzenk
John Burden
Mike Cadahia
Joe Caro
Tom Davis
Orv Franchuk
Dave Garcia
Red Gaskill
Steve Gruwell
Fred Hatfield
Rick Ingalls
Bobby Johns
Nick Kamzic
Hal Keller
Tim Kelly
Matt Keough
Kris Kline
Tom Kotchman
Tony LaCava
Joe Lewis
Ron Marigny
Joe McDonald
Jim McLaughlin
Darrell Miller
Jon Neiderer
Tom Osowski
Dick Probola
Paul Robinson
Rich Schlenker
Terry Steeves
Jerry Streeter
Moose Stubing
Dale Sutherland
Rip Tutor
Jack Uhey
Ray Vince
International scouts
Pompeyo Davalillo
Eusebio Perez
Reuben Rodriguez
Duck Lee
Leo Figueroa
Wally Komatsubara
Marco Davalillo
Adrian Meagher
Jorge Ortiz

Manager—Buck Rodgers (7).

Coaches—Rod Carew (29), Chuck Hernandez (55), Bobby Knoop (2), Ken Macha (39), Max Olivares (72), Jimmie Reese (50).

No.	PITCHERS	B/T	Ht./Wt.	Born	1993 clubs
56	Anderson, Brian	B/L	6-1/190	4-26-72	Midland, Vancouver, California
23	Butcher, Mike	R/R	6-1/200	5-10-65	Vancouver, California
38	Farrell, John	R/R	6-4/210	8-4-62	California, Vancouver
31	Finley, Chuck	L/L	6-6/214	11-26-62	California
43	Gamez, Bob	L/L	6-5/185	11-18-68	Midland, Vancouver
19	Grahe, Joe	R/R	6-0/200	8-14-67	California, Vancouver
48	Hathaway, Hilly	L/L	6-4/195	9-12-69	Vancouver, California
42	Holzemer, Mark	L/L	6-0/165	8-20-69	Vancouver, California
37	Janicki, Pete	R/R	6-4/190	1-26-71	Palm Springs
12	Langston, Mark	R/L	6-2/184	8-20-60	California
	Lefferts, Craig	L/L	6-1/230	9-29-57	San Diego, Baltimore
45	Leftwich, Phil	R/R	6-5/205	5-19-69	Vancouver, California
18	Lewis, Scott	R/R	6-3/178	12-5-65	Midland, California, Vancouver
32	Magrane, Joe	R/L	6-6/230	7-2-64	St. Louis, California
27	Percival, Troy	R/R	6-3/200	8-9-69	Vancouver
25	Sebach, Kyle	R/R	6-4/195	9-6-71	Cedar Rapids
40	Springer, Russ	R/R	6-4/195	11-7-68	Vancouver, California
20	Swingle, Paul	R/R	6-0/185	12-21-66	Vancouver, California
34	Valera, Julio	R/R	6-2/215	10-13-68	California
28	Watson, Ron	L/R	6-5/240	9-12-68	Midland

No.	CATCHERS	B/T	Ht./Wt.	Born	1993 clubs
14	Dalesandro, Mark	R/R	6-0/185	5-14-68	Palm Springs, Midland, Vancouver
11	Myers, Greg	L/R	6-2/215	4-14-66	California
22	Turner, Chris	R/R	6-1/190	3-23-69	Vancouver, California

No.	INFIELDERS	B/T	Ht./Wt.	Born	1993 clubs
3	Brumley, Mike	B/R	5-10/155	4-9-63	Tucson, Houston
5	Correia, Rod	R/R	5-11/180	9-13-67	Vancouver, California
33	DiSarcina, Gary	R/R	6-1/178	11-19-67	California
1	Easley, Damion	R/R	5-11/185	11-11-69	California
10	Lovullo, Torey	B/R	6-0/185	7-25-65	California
17	Owen, Spike	B/R	5-10/170	4-19-61	New York A.L.
6	Snow, J.T.	B/L	6-2/202	2-26-68	California, Vancouver

No.	OUTFIELDERS	B/T	Ht./Wt.	Born	1993 clubs
16	Anderson, Garret	L/L	6-3/190	6-30-72	Vancouver
9	Curtis, Chad	R/R	5-10/175	11-6-68	California
44	Davis, Chili	B/R	6-3/217	1-17-60	California
21	Edmonds, Jim	L/L	6-1/190	6-27-70	Vancouver, California
6	Flora, Kevin	R/R	6-0/185	6-10-69	Vancouver
	Jackson, Bo	R/R	6-1/228	11-30-62	Chicago A.L.
24	Perez, Eduardo	R/R	6-4/215	9-11-69	Vancouver, California
15	Salmon, Tim	R/R	6-3/220	8-24-68	California
	Smith, Dwight	L/R	5-11/190	11-8-63	Chicago N.L., Daytona
36	Sweeney, Mark	L/L	6-1/195	10-26-69	Palm Springs, Midland

BALLPARK INFORMATION

Ballpark (capacity, surface)
Anaheim Stadium (64,593, grass)

Address
2000 Gene Autry Way
Anaheim, CA 92806

Business phones
714-937-7200
213-625-1123

Ticket Information
714-634-2000

Ticket prices
$13 (field & club level, MVP)
$11 (field & club level, box)
$10 (terrace level, MVP)
$9 (terrace level, box)
$8 (view level, lower box)
$7 (view level, upper box)
$5 (pavillion, reserved)

Field dimensions (from home plate)
To left field at foul line, 333 feet
To center field, 404 feet
To right field at foul line, 333 feet

First game played
April 19, 1966 (White Sox 3, Angels 1)

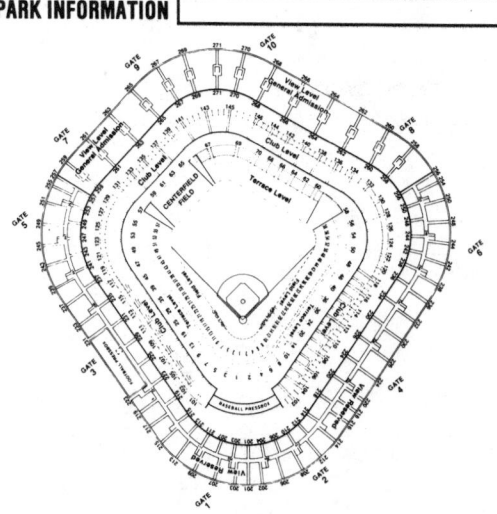

MINOR LEAGUE AFFILIATES

Class	Team	League	Manager
AAA	Vancouver	Pacific Coast	Max Oliveras
AA	Midland	Texas	Don Long
A	Lake Elsinore	California	Mario Mendoza
A	Quad City	Midwest	Mitch Seoane
A	Boise	Northwest	Tom Kotchman
Rookie	Mesa Angels	Arizona	Bill Lachemann

BROADCAST INFORMATION

Radio: KMPC-AM (710). Broadcasters: Bob Starr, Billy Sample. Spanish language station and broadcasters to be announced.
TV: KTLA-TV (Channel 5). Broadcasters: Ken Wilson, Ken Brett.
Cable TV: Prime Ticket. Broadcasters: To be announced.

SPRING TRAINING

Ballpark (city): Diablo Stadium (Tempe, Ariz.).
Ticket information: 602-678-2222 (Ticketron); 619-323-4143 (Angels Stadium).

HISTORY

YEAR-BY-YEAR RECORDS

Year	Pos.	W	L	Pct.	GB	Year	Pos.	W	L	Pct.	GB
1961*	8th	70	91	.435	38½	1980	6th	65	95	.406	31
1962*	3rd	86	76	.531	10	1981	4th/7th	51	59	.464	‡
1963*	9th	70	91	.435	34	1982	1st†	93	69	.574 +	3
1964*	5th	82	80	.506	17	1983	T5th	70	92	.432	29
1965*	7th	75	87	.463	27	1984	T2nd	81	81	.500	3
1966	6th	80	82	.494	18	1985	2nd	90	72	.556	1
1967	5th	84	77	.522	7½	1986	1st†	92	70	.568 +	5
1968	8th	67	95	.414	36	1987	T6th	75	87	.463	10
1969	3rd	71	91	.438	26	1988	4th	75	87	.463	29
1970	3rd	86	76	.531	12	1989	3rd	91	71	.562	8
1971	4th	76	86	.469	25½	1990	4th	80	82	.494	23
1972	5th	75	80	.484	18	1991	7th	81	81	.500	14
1973	4th	79	83	.488	15	1992	T5th	72	90	.444	24
1974	6th	68	94	.420	22	1993	T5th	71	91	.438	23
1975	6th	72	89	.447	25½						
1976	T4th	76	86	.469	14						
1977	5th	74	88	.457	28						
1978	T2nd	87	75	.537	5						
1979	1st†	88	74	.543 +	3						

*Franchise known as Los Angeles Angels through September 1, 1965.
†Lost Championship Series. ‡First half 31-29; second 20-30.

MANAGERS

Name	Record	Years
Bill Rigney	625-707	'61-69
Lefty Phillips	222-225	'69-71
Del Rice	75-80	1972
Bobby Winkles	109-127	'73-74
Dick Williams	147-194	'74-76
Norm Sherry	76-71	'76-77
Dave Garcia	60-66	'77-78
Jim Fregosi	237-249	'78-81
Gene Mauch	379-332	'81-82
		'85-87
John McNamara	151-173	'83-84
Cookie Rojas	75-87	1988
Doug Rader	232-216	'89-91
Buck Rodgers	163-199	'91-93

DAY BY DAY

Date	Opp.	Res.	Score (inn.*)	Hits	Opp. hits	Winning pitcher	Losing pitcher	Save	Record	Pos.	GB
4-6	Mil.	W	3-1	10	3	Langston	Wegman		1-0	T1st	...
4-7	Mil.	L	2-3	5	7	Eldred	Grahe	Henry	1-1	T3rd	1
4-9	Det.	W	7-5	12	4	Valera	Leiter		2-1	T2nd	1
4-10	Det.	L	2-5	5	8	Wells	Farrell	Henneman	2-2	T4th	1
4-11	Det.	W	7-6	13	11	Crim	Krueger	Grahe	3-2	3rd	1
4-12	At Mil.	W	12-5	12	12	Finley	Eldred	Valera	4-2	T2nd	1
4-14	At Mil.	W	12-2	16	5	Sanderson	Orosco		5-2	2nd	½
4-16	At Bal.	L	1-4	9	7	Sutcliffe	Farrell	Olson	5-3	2nd	½
4-17	At Bal.	W	7-5	9	8	Grahe	Pennington		6-3	2nd	½
4-18	At Bal.	L	3-4	6	12	Mussina	Valera	Olson	6-4	2nd	1½
4-20	Cle.	W	7-2	12	8	Sanderson	Mesa		7-4	2nd	½
4-21	Cle.	W	7-6	10	13	Farrell	Nagy	Frey	8-4	1st	+½
4-22	Cle.	W	8-0	12	2	Finley	Clark		9-4	1st	+1
4-23	Bos.	W	4-1	8	3	Langston	Viola		10-4	1st	+2
4-24	Bos.	W	8-5	10	7	Crim	Bankhead	Valera	11-4	1st	+2
4-25	Bos.	W	2-1	4	8	Sanderson	Clemens	Grahe	12-4	1st	+2
4-27	N.Y.	L	0-5	1	9	Key	Finley		12-5	1st	+2½
4-28	N.Y.	W	3-2	5	3	Langston	Abbott		13-5	1st	+2½
4-30	At Bos.	L	1-6	3	7	Dopson	Farrell		13-6	1st	+½
5-1	At Bos.	L	1-3	5	9	Clemens	Sanderson	Russell	13-7	1st	+½
5-2	At Bos.	L	3-4	6	9	Darwin	Finley	Russell	13-8	1st	+½
5-3	At Cle.	L	4-5	7	8	Lilliquist	Valera		13-9	1st	...
5-4	At Cle.	L	3-5	6	10	Cook	Lewis	Lilliquist	13-10	1st	...
5-5	At N.Y.	W	6-2	8	7	Farrell	Perez	Valera	14-10	1st	...
5-6	At N.Y.	W	3-1	8	5	Sanderson	Howe	Frey	15-10	1st	+½
5-7	Oak.	W	4-3	7	6	Finley	Downs	Valera	16-10	1st	+½
5-8	Oak.	L	2-6	8	11	Welch	Langston	Eckersley	16-11	2nd	½
5-9	Oak.	W	7-6	(10)	13	11	Grahe	Honeycutt		17-11	2nd	½
5-10	Min.	L	3-13	9	22	Banks	Farrell		17-12	T2nd	1½
5-11	Min.	W	5-3	8	10	Sanderson	Trombley	Grahe	18-12	2nd	½
5-12	Min.	L	2-5	9	10	Tapani	Finley	Aguilera	18-13	2nd	1½
5-14	K.C.	L	1-2	(10)	4	8	Cone	Valera	Montgomery	18-14	2nd	2½
5-15	K.C.	W	5-3	8	8	Lewis	Gubicza	Grahe	19-14	2nd	1½
5-16	K.C.	L	2-4	7	8	Appier	Farrell	Montgomery	19-15	2nd	2½
5-17	At Chi.	W	11-4	15	11	Sanderson	Stieb		20-15	2nd	1½
5-18	At Chi.	L	4-7	5	11	Alvarez	Finley	Hernandez	20-16	2nd	2½
5-19	At Chi.	W	2-0	8	5	Langston	McDowell	Grahe	21-16	2nd	1½
5-21	At Tex.	L	4-6	(10)	11	9	Henke	Crim		21-17	2nd	1½
5-22	At Tex.	L	2-4	7	7	Pavlik	Sanderson	Henke	21-18	3rd	1½
5-23	At Tex.	W	6-2	11	8	Valera	Burns	Grahe	22-18	2nd	1½
5-24	At Sea.	L	3-4	(14)	11	13	Henry	Crim		22-19	2nd	2
5-25	At Sea.	W	6-3	10	7	Finley	Leary	Frey	23-19	2nd	1
5-26	At Sea.	L	0-2	7	7	DeLucia	Lewis	Charlton	23-20	2nd	1
5-27	At Sea.	W	5-0	8	5	Sanderson	Converse		24-20	T1st	...
5-28	Bal.	W	8-4	12	13	Valera	Valenzuela	Nelson	25-20	1st	+1
5-29	Bal.	W	6-3	7	7	Langston	Frohwirth	Frey	26-20	1st	+2
5-30	Bal.	W	7-5	9	10	Finley	Moyer	Nelson	27-20	1st	+3
5-31	Tor.	L	5-10	11	9	Morris	Farrell		27-21	1st	+2
6-1	Tor.	L	0-8	2	12	Leiter	Sanderson		27-22	1st	+1
6-2	Tor.	L	6-7	10	13	Hentgen	Valera	Ward	27-23	T1st	...
6-4	At Det.	W	6-3	6	6	Langston	Henneman	Frey	28-23	2nd	½
6-5	At Det.	L	1-5	6	6	Doherty	Finley	MacDonald	28-24	2nd	½
6-6	At Det.	L	4-11	7	13	Gullickson	Farrell		28-25	T2nd	1½
6-7	At Tor.	L	2-4	11	10	Leiter	Sanderson	Ward	28-26	3rd	2½
6-8	At Tor.	L	6-14	13	13	Williams	Valera		28-27	3rd	2½
6-9	At Tor.	W	6-4	8	8	Langston	Stewart	Frey	29-27	T2nd	2½
6-11	Sea.	W	8-2	9	8	Finley	Hanson		30-27	T2nd	1½
6-12	Sea.	L	0-2	3	6	Fleming	Sanderson		30-28	3rd	1½
6-13	Sea.	L	7-12	12	18	Leary	Valera		30-29	3rd	2½
6-14	Tex.	W	8-2	10	5	Langston	Burns		31-29	T2nd	1½
6-15	Tex.	L	5-6	10	9	Leibrandt	Farrell	Henke	31-30	3rd	1½
6-16	Tex.	W	5-2	12	7	Finley	Brown	Nelson	32-30	3rd	1½
6-17	Tex.	L	2-18	7	18	Rogers	Sanderson		32-31	3rd	2
6-18	Chi.	W	9-8	12	11	Frey	Hernandez		33-31	T2nd	1
6-19	Chi.	W	5-4	5	7	Langston	Ruffcorn	Frey	34-31	2nd	1
6-20	Chi.	L	6-11	9	12	Alvarez	Springer		34-32	T2nd	1
6-21	At K.C.	W	4-3	3	13	Finley	Pichardo	Frey	35-32	T1st	...
6-22	At K.C.	L	3-5	9	14	Cone	Sanderson	Montgomery	35-33	3rd	1
6-23	At K.C.	W	8-7	11	13	Hathaway	Haney	Frey	36-33	T2nd	1
6-24	At K.C.	L	1-7	7	14	Appier	Langston	Montgomery	36-34	3rd	1½

Date	Opp.	Res.	Score	(inn.*)	Hits	Opp. hits	Winning pitcher	Losing pitcher	Save	Record	Pos.	GB
6-25	At Min.	L	5-8		14	12	Erickson	Springer	Aguilera	36-35	3rd	1½
6-26	At Min.	W	4-0		5	3	Finley	Banks		37-35	T2nd	1½
6-27	At Min.	L	0-2		4	6	Deshaies	Sanderson	Aguilera	37-36	T2nd	2½
6-29	At Oak.	L	7-8	(11)	10	18	Nunez	Patterson		37-37	3rd	2
6-30	At Oak.	L	4-5		8	9	Boever	Springer	Eckersley	37-38	3rd	2
7-1	At Oak.	L	3-6		9	11	Welch	Finley	Nunez	37-39	4th	2
7-2	Cle.	L	8-10		12	16	Slocumb	Nelson	Plunk	37-40	4th	3
7-3	Cle.	L	3-5		10	10	Mesa	Hathaway	Plunk	37-41	T4th	3
7-4	Cle.	W	7-6	(11)	12	12	Butcher	M. Young		38-41	T3rd	3
7-5	Bos.	L	3-4	(11)	6	12	Ryan	Nelson		38-42	4th	4
7-6	Bos.	W	3-2		6	6	Finley	Hesketh		39-42	4th	3
7-7	Bos.	W	7-6		13	7	Linton	Russell		40-42	T3rd	3
7-8	N.Y.	L	4-3		5	9	Frey	Perez		41-42	T3rd	3
7-9	N.Y.	L	2-3		5	12	Key	Langston		41-43	5th	3
7-10	N.Y.	W	4-2		12	9	Springer	Kamieniecki	Frey	42-43	5th	2
7-11	N.Y.	W	3-2	(14)	14	9	Linton	Monteleone		43-43	T4th	2
7-15	At Cle.	L	3-7		9	8	DiPoto	Sanderson		43-44	5th	3
7-16	At Cle.	W	2-1		8	7	Finley	Clark	Butcher	44-44	T4th	3
7-17	At Cle.	L	0-3		4	4	Mutis	Springer		44-45	5th	4
7-18	At Cle.	L	1-2		7	3	Lopez	Langston	DiPoto	44-46	5th	5
7-19	At Bos.	L	6-8		10	16	Sele	Sanderson	Russell	44-47	5th	5
7-20	At Bos.	L	1-2		11	11	Fossas	Nelson		44-48	5th	6
7-21	At Bos.	L	1-4		6	9	Clemens	Finley	Russell	44-49	5th	6
7-22	At N.Y.	L	1-12		5	10	Abbott	Springer		44-50	5th	7
7-23	At N.Y.	L	2-5		3	7	Hutton	Langston	Farr	44-51	5th	7
7-24	At N.Y.	L	3-5		8	11	Kamieniecki	Sanderson	Farr	44-52	5th	8
7-25	At N.Y.	L	8-9		12	14	Habyan	Frey		44-53	5th	8
7-26	Oak.	L	4-11		10	15	Darling	Finley		44-54	5th	9
7-27	Oak.	W	15-8		17	9	Grahe	Witt	Patterson	45-54	5th	9
7-28	Oak.	W	3-2		6	6	Langston	Van Poppel	Butcher	46-54	5th	9
7-29	Oak.	L	1-2		7	10	Welch	Leftwich	Eckersley	46-55	5th	9½
7-30	Min.	W	4-2		9	9	Hathaway	Deshaies	Butcher	47-55	5th	9½
7-31	Min.	W	4-3		7	8	Finley	Aguilera		48-55	5th	9½
8-1	Min.	L	2-9		9	16	Guardado	Springer		48-56	5th	10½
8-3	K.C.	W	3-2		6	7	Langston	Belinda	Butcher	49-56	5th	10
8-4	K.C.	L	2-3		8	10	Cone	Leftwich	Montgomery	49-57	5th	10
8-5	K.C.	W	5-4		8	9	Hathaway	Gordon	Frey	50-57	5th	9
8-6	At Chi.	W	7-3		16	8	Finley	Alvarez	Nelson	51-57	5th	8
8-7	At Chi.	L	4-6		10	10	McDowell	Farrell	Hernandez	51-58	5th	9
8-8	At Chi.	W	2-1		6	5	Langston	Bere	Butcher	52-58	5th	8
8-10	At Tex.	L	3-6		8	8	Ryan	Leftwich	Henke	52-59	5th	9½
8-11	At Tex.	W	4-1		13	6	Hathaway	Brown	Butcher	53-59	5th	8½
8-12	At Tex.	L	2-4		6	7	Rogers	Farrell	Henke	53-60	5th	8½
8-13	At Sea.	L	1-2		4	7	Hanson	Finley		53-61	5th	9½
8-14	At Sea.	L	2-7		8	8	Johnson	Langston		53-62	5th	10½
8-15	At Sea.	W	14-2		22	8	Leftwich	Leary		54-62	5th	9½
8-16	Det.	L	2-7		9	12	Gullickson	Hathaway		54-63	5th	10
8-17	Det.	L	3-9		7	10	Bolton	Farrell		54-64	5th	11
8-18	Det.	L	6-8		10	11	Knudsen	Frey	Henneman	54-65	5th	11
8-19	Mil.	W	5-4	(12)	10	12	Grahe	Lloyd		55-65	5th	10½
8-20	Mil.	L	2-7	(10)	6	8	Eldred	Frey		55-66	5th	11½
8-21	Mil.	W	7-6		9	12	Patterson	Maysey		56-66	5th	11½
8-22	Mil.	L	5-7		8	7	Henry	Magrane	Orosco	56-67	5th	12½
8-24	At Bal.	L	0-1		4	2	Moyer	Finley	Mills	56-68	5th	13
8-25	At Bal.	W	2-1		6	2	Langston	Mussina	Butcher	57-68	5th	12
8-26	At Bal.	L	4-9		9	12	Williamson	Nelson		57-69	5th	12½
8-27 (1)	At Mil.	L	6-7		9	8	Fetters	Holzemer		57-70	5th	13
8-27 (2)	At Mil.	L	3-4		11	9	Navarro	Nelson	Orosco	57-71	5th	13½
8-28	At Mil.	W	6-2		16	9	Finley	Bones	Butcher	58-71	5th	13½
8-29	At Mil.	W	6-1		10	7	Langston	Novoa		59-71	5th	13½
8-31	Bal.	L	2-8		6	13	Mussina	Leftwich		59-72	5th	15
9-1	Bal.	L	1-5		4	8	McDonald	Holzemer		59-73	5th	16
9-2	Bal.	L	3-4		7	13	Rhodes	Finley	Poole	59-74	5th	16
9-3	Tor.	W	4-1		9	6	Langston	Morris	Grahe	60-74	5th	16
9-4	Tor.	W	4-2		8	7	Magrane	Stottlemyre	Frey	61-74	5th	16
9-5	Tor.	W	5-1		11	6	Leftwich	Hentgen		62-74	5th	16
9-7	At Det.	L	6-10		8	15	Boever	Scott		62-75	5th	15½
9-8	At Det.	L	2-4		7	8	Doherty	Langston	Henneman	62-76	5th	16½
9-9	At Det.	W	6-0		12	6	Magrane	Gullickson		63-76	5th	16
9-10	At Tor.	L	4-10		10	14	Stottlemyre	Leftwich		63-77	5th	16
9-11	At Tor.	L	5-9		8	11	Hentgen	Hathaway		63-78	5th	17
9-12	At Tor.	L	1-4		6	7	Stewart	Finley	Ward	63-79	5th	17
9-13	Sea.	L	1-10		4	14	Bosio	Langston		63-80	5th	17
9-14	Sea.	W	9-2		13	8	Magrane	Hanson		64-80	5th	17

— 24 —

Date	Opp.	Res.	Score	(Inn.*)	Hits	Opp. hits	Winning pitcher	Losing pitcher	Save	Record	Pos.	GB
9-15	Sea.	W	15-1		19	3	Leftwich	Leary		65-80	5th	17
9-17	Tex.	W	2-1		6	6	Finley	Lefferts	Grahe	66-80	5th	17
9-18	Tex.	L	2-9		6	9	Brown	Langston		66-81	5th	17
9-19	Tex.	W	9-8		14	14	Scott	Henke	Grahe	67-81	5th	17
9-20	Chi.	L	2-10		7	15	Bere	Leftwich	McCaskill	67-82	5th	18
9-21	Chi.	W	8-0		15	7	Farrell	Fernandez	Frey	68-82	5th	17
9-22	Chi.	L	0-1		5	4	Alvarez	Finley	Hernandez	68-83	5th	18
9-23	Chi.	L	1-7		4	10	McDowell	Langston		68-84	5th	19
9-24	At K.C.	L	2-7	(5)	8	6	Pichardo	Magrane		68-85	5th	20
9-25	At K.C.	W	6-2		8	9	Leftwich	Cone	Grahe	69-85	5th	19½
9-26	At K.C.	L	8-9	(10)	17	10	Montgomery	Swingle		69-86	5th	20
9-27	At Min.	L	3-11		10	14	Banks	Finley		69-87	5th	21
9-28	At Min.	L	1-2		8	6	Tapani	Langston		69-88	5th	21
9-29	At Min.	L	2-3	(10)	6	9	Aguilera	Scott		69-89	T5th	22
9-30	At Min.	L	3-4		7	9	Brummett	Farrell	Aguilera	69-90	6th	22
10-1	At Oak.	L	2-7		4	11	Jimenez	Holzemer	Smithberg	69-91	6th	23
10-2	At Oak.	W	6-2		8	8	Finley	Welch		70-91	T5th	23
10-3	At Oak.	W	7-3		11	10	Langston	Witt	Grahe	71-91	T5th	23

Monthly records: April (13-6), May (14-15), June (10-17), July (11-17), August (11-17), September (10-18), October (2-1).
*Innings, if other than nine.

HIGHLIGHTS

High point: The Angels rushed out of the gate to a 13-5 start on April 28, good for a 2½-game lead.

Low point: On the heels of a 43-43 record at the All-Star break, California proceeded to lose 11 of its next 12 games. Before the skid, the Angels were just two games out of first. After the slide, they were nine games out.

Turning point: On May 27, righthander Scott Sanderson won his last game as an Angel. He was 7-2 at that point but went 0-9 until he finally was released July 28. Sanderson's No. 3 starter slot proved pivotal to the Angels because their two aces, lefthanders Mark Langston and Chuck Finley, won 16 games apiece, and the pitchers used in the Nos. 4 and 5 spots struggled.

Most valuable player: Designated hitter Chili Davis. His 27 home runs and career-high 112 RBIs provided sorely needed punch in the middle of the line-up.

Most valuable pitchers: Langston and Finley. No one else on the staff logged as many as 136 innings and seven wins. Yet Langston (3.20 ERA) and Finley (3.15) each worked more than 250 innings.

Most improved player: Center fielder Chad Curtis. He hit .285 and stole 48 bases in his second season in the big leagues.

Most pleasant surprise: Right fielder Tim Salmon. He hit .283 with 31 homers and 95 RBIs en route to winning A.L. Rookie of the Year honors.

Biggest disappointment: First baseman J.T. Snow. His .241 average, 16 homers and 57 RBIs were respectable, but when he hit .343 with six homers in April, expectations skyrocketed. So, his huge drop-off in May and June left the Angels wondering if he was still their first baseman of the future.

Key injuries: Righthander Julio Valera pitched with a torn ligament in his elbow before undergoing surgery in July. Shin splints ended second baseman Damion Easley's season in August. Third baseman Kelly Gruber (neck and left shoulder injuries) didn't play his first game until June 4 and played his last June 29.

Notable: Salmon became the first Angel ever to win Rookie of the Year honors. ... In a September restructuring of the front office, Senior Vice President Dan O'Brien was fired and Whitey Herzog's role was expanded as lone general manager. Then Herzog resigned in January and Bill Bavasi moved from assistant G.M. into Herzog's post.

—DAVE CUNNINGHAM

RECORDS

1993 regular-season record: 71-91 (T5th in A.L. West); 44-37 at home; 27-54 on road; 36-48 vs. East; 35-43 vs. West; 16-27 vs. LHP; 55-64 vs. RHP; 63-72 on grass; 8-19 on turf; 19-28 in day-time; 52-63 at night; 26-27 in one-run games; 4-8 in extra-inning games; 0-1-0 in doubleheaders.

Team record last five years: 395-415 (.488, ranks 10th in league in that span).

TEAM LEADERS

Batting average: Chad Curtis (.285).
At-bats: Chad Curtis (583).
Runs: Chad Curtis (94).
Hits: Chad Curtis (166).
Total bases: Tim Salmon (276).
Doubles: Tim Salmon (35).
Triples: Luis Polonia (6).
Home runs: Tim Salmon (31).
Runs batted in: Chili Davis (112).
Stolen bases: Luis Polonia (55).
Slugging percentage: Tim Salmon (.536).
On-base percentage: Tim Salmon (.382).
Wins: Chuck Finley, Mark Langston (16).
Earned-run average: Chuck Finley (3.15).
Complete games: Chuck Finley (13).
Shutouts: Chuck Finley (2).
Saves: Steve Frey (13).
Innings pitched: Mark Langston (256⅓).
Strikeouts: Mark Langston (196).

GAMES BY POSITION

Catcher: Greg Myers 97, Ron Tingley 58, John Orton 35, Chris Turner 25, Larry Gonzales 2.

First base: J.T. Snow 129, Rene Gonzales 31, Stan Javier 12, Ty Van Burkleo 12, Gary Gaetti 6, Torey Lovullo 1.

Second base: Torey Lovullo 76, Damion Easley 54, Kurt Stillwell 18, Rod Correia 11, Rene Gonzales 4, Chad Curtis 3, Stan Javier 2, Jim Walewander 2.

Third base: Rene Gonzales 79, Eduardo Perez 45, Kelly Gruber 17, Damion Easley 14, Torey Lovullo 14, Gary Gaetti 7, Rod Correia 3.

Shortstop: Gary DiSarcina 126, Rod Correia 40, Torey Lovullo 9, Kurt Stillwell 7, Jim Walewander 5, Rene Gonzales 5.

Outfield: Chad Curtis 151, Luis Polonia 141, Tim Salmon 140, Stan Javier 64, Jim Edmonds 17, Torey Lovullo 2, Kelly Gruber 1, John Orton 1, Jerome Walton 1.

Designated hitter: Chili Davis 150, Rod Correia 6, Gary Gaetti 5, Luis Polonia 4, Jerome Walton 4, Eduardo Perez 3, Jim Walewander 3, Greg Myers 2, Damion Easley 1, Kelly Gruber 1, Stan Javier 1, Torey Lovullo 1, Tim Salmon 1.

TOP DRAFT CHOICES

1. **Brian Anderson**, LHP, Wright State University.
2. **Ryan Hancock**, RHP, Brigham Young University.
3. **Matt Perisho**, LHP, McClintock High School, Tempe, Ariz.
4. **Andrew Lorraine**, LHP, Stanford University.
5. **Jose Cintron**, RHP, Yabucoa, Puerto Rico.
6. **Geoff Edsell**, RHP, Old Dominion University.
7. **George Arias**, 3B, University of Arizona.
8. **Tim Harkrider**, SS, University of Texas.
9. **Jamie Burke**, 3B, Oregon State University.
10. **Willard Brown**, RHP, Stetson University.

CHICAGO WHITE SOX
AMERICAN LEAGUE CENTRAL DIVISION

1994 SCHEDULE

N   Denotes night game (any game starting after 5 p.m.).
▢   Home games shaded.
*   At Three Rivers Stadium in Pittsburgh.

APRIL

SUN	MON	TUE	WED	THU	FRI	SAT
					1	2
3	4 TOR	N 5 TOR	N 6 TOR	7	N 8 BOS	N 9 BOS
10 BOS	11	N 12 NY	N 13 NY	14 NY	N 15 BOS	16 BOS
17 BOS	18 BOS	N 19 MIL	N 20 MIL	21 MIL	N 22 DET	N 23 DET
24 DET	N 25 MIL	N 26 MIL	N 27 CLE	N 28 CLE	N 29 DET	30 DET

MAY

SUN	MON	TUE	WED	THU	FRI	SAT
1 DET	2	N 3 CLE	N 4 CLE	5	N 6 KC	N 7 KC
8 KC	N 9 SEA	N 10 SEA	11	12	N 13 TEX	N 14 TEX
15 TEX	N 16 CAL	N 17 CAL	N 18 CAL	19	N 20 OAK	21 OAK
22 OAK	23	N 24 MIN	N 25 MIN	26	N 27 BAL	N 28 BAL
29 BAL	30 NY	31 NY				

JUNE

SUN	MON	TUE	WED	THU	FRI	SAT
		N 1 NY	2	N 3 BAL	N 4 BAL
5 BAL	6	N 7 TOR	N 8 TOR	N 9 MIN	N 10 MIN	11 MIN
12 MIN	N 13 OAK	N 14 OAK	N 15 OAK	N 16 CAL	N 17 CAL	N 18 CAL
19 CAL	N 20 TEX	N 21 TEX	N 22 SEA	N 23 SEA	24 SEA	N 25 SEA
26 SEA	27	N 28 KC	N 29 KC	N 30 KC		

JULY

SUN	MON	TUE	WED	THU	FRI	SAT
				N 1 MIL	N 2 MIL
3 MIL	N 4 MIL	N 5 DET	N 6 DET	7	N 8 MIL	N 9 MIL
10 MIL	11 ALL-STAR GAME	* 12	13	N 14 CLE	N 15 CLE	16 CLE
17 CLE	N 18 DET	N 19 DET	N 20 DET	21 CLE	N 22 CLE	23 CLE
24 CLE	N 25 KC	N 26 KC	N 27 KC	N 28 KC	N 29 SEA	N 30 SEA
31 SEA						

AUGUST

SUN	MON	TUE	WED	THU	FRI	SAT
	1	N 2 TEX	N 3 TEX	N 4 TEX	N 5 CAL	N 6 CAL
7 CAL	N 8 OAK	N 9 OAK	10 OAK	11	N 12 MIN	N 13 MIN
14 MIN	N 15 MIN	N 16 BOS	N 17 BOS	18 BOS	N 19 TOR	20 TOR
21 TOR	N 22 BAL	N 23 BAL	24 BAL	25 TOR	N 26 TOR	N 27 TOR
28 TOR	29	N 30 BAL	N 31 BAL			

SEPTEMBER

SUN	MON	TUE	WED	THU	FRI	SAT
				N 1 BAL	2 NY	3 NY
4 NY	5	N 6 BOS	N 7 BOS	8	N 9 NY	N 10 NY
11 NY	N 12 MIN	N 13 MIN	N 14 MIN	N 15 OAK	N 16 OAK	N 17 OAK
18 OAK	N 19 CAL	N 20 CAL	21 CAL	N 22 TEX	N 23 TEX	N 24 TEX
25 TEX	26	N 27 SEA	N 28 SEA	29 SEA	N 30 KC	

OCTOBER

SUN	MON	TUE	WED	THU	FRI	SAT
						1 N KC
2 KC						

1994 SEASON

CLUB DIRECTORY

Chairman
Jerry Reinsdorf
Vice chairman
Eddie Einhorn
Executive vice president
Howard Pizer
Senior v.p., major league operations
Ron Schueler
Senior v.p., marketing and broadcasting
Rob Gallas
Senior vice president, baseball
Jack Gould
Vice president, finance
Tim Buzard
Vice president, stadium operations
Terry Savarise
V.p., scouting and minor league operations
Larry Monroe
Director of baseball operations
Dan Evans
Special assistants to Ron Schueler
Ed Brinkman
Bart Johnson
Mike Pazik
Mike Squires
Dave Yoakum
Director of scouting
Duane Shaffer
Director of minor league operations
Steve Noworyta
Director of minor league instruction
Jim Snyder
Traveling secretary
Glen Rosenbaum
Assistant to the director of scouting
Grace Guerrero Zwit
Asst. to the director of baseball operations
Jeff Chaney
Major league computer scouting analyst
Mike Maziarka
Trainers
Herm Schneider
Mark Anderson
Director of conditioning
Steve Odgers
Team physicians
Dr. James Boscardin
Dr. Hugo Cuadros
Dr. Robert Daley
Dr. Bernard Feldman
Dr. David Orth
Dr. Scott Price
Dr. Lowell Scott Weil
Director of marketing and broadcasting
Mike Bucek
Director of advertising and promotions
Bob Grim

Director of public relations
Doug Abel
Director of community relations
Christine Makowski
Director of ticket sales
Bob Voight
Director of ticket operations
Bob Devoy
Controller
Bill Waters
Director of park operations
David Schaffer
Director of purchasing
Don Esposito
Assistant director of public relations
Scott Reifert
Scouting national cross-checker
George Bradley
Scouting supervisors
Mark Bernstein
Doug Laumann
Ed Pebley
Marti Wolever
Full-time scouts
Steve Arnieri
Juan Ramon Bernhardt
Kevin Burrell
Joseph Butler
Scott Cerny
Alex Cosmidis
Larry Grefer
Robert Harris
Warren Hughes
Miguel Ibarra
John Kazanas
Reginald Lewis
William Meyer
David Owen
Gary Pellant
Paul Provas
Michael Sgobba
Ken Stauffer
John Tumminia
Kenny Williams
Part-time scouts
Jose Bernhardt
Alonzo Ganther
Nino Giarratano
Joe Ingalls
Jack Jolly
George Kachigian
Dario Lodigiani
Jose Ortega
Al Otto
Victor Puig
Joe Thurman

Manager—Gene Lamont (33).
Coaches—Terry Bevington (18), Jackie Brown (41), Walt Hriniak (6),
Doug Mansolino (17), Joe Nossek (15), Dewey Robinson (55).

No.	PITCHERS	B/T	Ht./Wt.	Born	1993 clubs
40	Alvarez, Wilson	L/L	6-1/235	3-24-70	Chicago A.L., Nashville
	Andujar, Luis	R/R	6-1/160	11-22-72	Sarasota, Birmingham
	Baldwin, James	R/R	6-3/210	7-15-71	Birmingham, Nashville
51	Bere, Jason	R/R	6-3/185	5-26-71	Nashville, Chicago A.L.
	Boehringer, Brian	B/R	6-2/180	1-8-69	Sarasota, Birmingham
42	Bolton, Rodney	R/R	6-2/190	9-23-68	Chicago A.L., Nashville
48	DeLeon, Jose	R/R	6-3/226	12-20-60	Philadelphia, Chicago A.L.
48	Ellis, Robert	R/R	6-5/215	12-15-70	Sarasota, Birmingham
32	Fernandez, Alex	R/R	6-1/215	8-13-69	Chicago A.L.
39	Hernandez, Roberto	R/R	6-4/235	11-11-64	Chicago A.L.
25	McCaskill, Kirk	R/R	6-1/205	4-9-61	Chicago A.L., South Bend
29	McDowell, Jack	R/R	6-5/188	1-16-66	Chicago A.L.
31	Radinsky, Scott	L/L	6-3/204	3-3-68	Chicago A.L.
45	Ruffcorn, Scott	R/R	6-4/210	12-29-69	Birmingham, Chicago A.L., Nashville
	Schrenk, Steve	R/R	6-3/185	11-20-68	Birmingham, Nashville
49	Schwarz, Jeff	R/R	6-5/190	5-20-64	Nashville, Chicago A.L.
	Thomas, Larry	R/L	6-1/195	10-25-69	Nashville, Sarasota, Birmingham

No.	CATCHERS	B/T	Ht./Wt.	Born	1993 clubs
20	Karkovice, Ron	R/R	6-1/219	8-8-63	Chicago A.L.
10	LaValliere, Mike	L/R	5-9/205	8-18-60	Pittsburgh, Sarasota, Chicago A.L.
68	Lindsey, Doug	R/R	6-2/232	9-22-67	Scranton/Wilkes-Barre, Philadelphia, Chicago A.L.
5	Merullo, Matt	L/R	6-2/200	8-4-65	Nashville, Chicago A.L.

No.	INFIELDERS	B/T	Ht./Wt.	Born	1993 clubs
38	Beltre, Esteban	R/R	5-10/172	12-26-67	Nashville
28	Cora, Joey	B/R	5-8/155	5-14-65	Chicago A.L.
62	Denson, Drew	R/R	6-5/220	11-16-65	Nashville, Chicago A.L.
	DiSarcina, Glenn	L/R	6-0/175	4-29-70	Sarasota, Birmingham
	Durham, Ray	B/R	5-8/170	11-30-71	Birmingham
14	Franco, Julio	R/R	6-1/190	8-23-61	Texas
14	Grebeck, Craig	R/R	5-7/148	12-29-64	Chicago A.L.
13	Guillen, Ozzie	L/R	5-11/164	1-20-64	Chicago A.L.
53	Martin, Norberto	B/R	5-10/164	12-10-66	Nashville, Chicago A.L.
7	Sax, Steve	R/R	5-11/189	1-29-60	Chicago A.L.
35	Thomas, Frank	R/R	6-5/257	5-27-68	Chicago A.L.
23	Ventura, Robin	L/R	6-1/198	7-14-67	Chicago A.L.
57	Wilson, Brandon	R/R	6-1/170	2-26-69	Birmingham

No.	OUTFIELDERS	B/T	Ht./Wt.	Born	1993 clubs
	Battle, Allen	R/R	6-0/170	11-29-68	Arkansas
12	Huff, Mike	R/R	6-1/190	8-11-63	Nashville, Chicago A.L.
4	Jackson, Darrin	R/R	6-0/185	8-22-63	Toronto, New York N.L.
1	Johnson, Lance	L/L	5-11/160	7-6-63	Chicago A.L.
24	Newson, Warren	L/L	5-7/202	7-3-64	Nashville, Chicago A.L.
44	Pasqua, Dan	L/L	6-0/218	10-17-61	Chicago A.L.
30	Raines, Tim	B/R	5-8/186	9-16-59	Chicago A.L., Nashville

BALLPARK INFORMATION

Ballpark (capacity, surface)
Comiskey Park (44,321, grass)
Address
333 W. 35th St.
Chicago, IL 60616
Business phone
312-924-1000
Ticket information
312-924-1000
Ticket prices
$18 (club level)
$18 (lower deck box)
$13 (lower deck reserved)
$12 (upper deck box)
$10 (bleacher reserved)
$8 (upper deck reserved)
Field dimensions (from home plate)
To left field at foul line, 347 feet
To center field, 400 feet
To right field at foul line, 347 feet
First game played
April 18, 1991 (Tigers 16, White Sox 0)

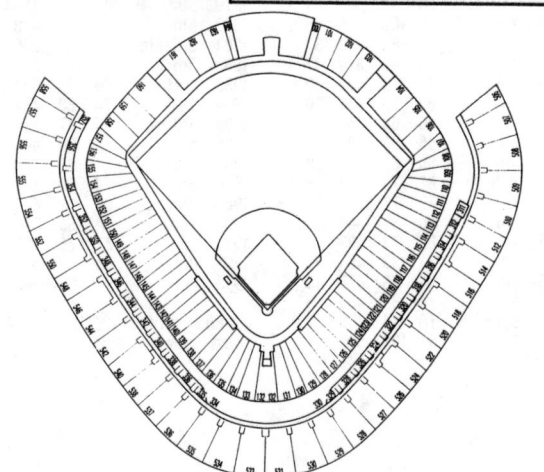

		MINOR LEAGUE AFFILIATES		

Class	Team	League	Manager
AAA	Nashville	American Association	Rick Renick
AA	Birmingham	Southern	Terry Francona
A	Prince William	Carolina	Dave Huppert
A	South Bend	Midwest	Mike Gellinger
A	Hickory	South Atlantic	Fred Kendall
Rookie	Sarasota	Gulf Coast	Mike Rojas

BROADCAST INFORMATION

Radio: WMAQ-AM (670). Broadcasters: John Rooney, Ed Farmer. WIND-AM (560, Spanish language). Broadcasters: Chico Carrasquel, Hector Molina.
TV: WGN-TV (Channel 9). Broadcasters: Ken Harrelson, Tom Paciorek.
Cable TV: SportsChannel. Broadcasters: Ken Harrelson, Tom Paciorek.

SPRING TRAINING

Ballpark (city): Ed Smith Stadium (Sarasota, Fla.).
Ticket information: 813-287-8844.

HISTORY

YEAR-BY-YEAR RECORDS

Year	Pos.	W	L	Pct.	GB		Year	Pos.	W	L	Pct.	GB
1901	1st	83	53	.610	+ 4		1949	6th	63	91	.409	34
1902	4th	74	60	.552	8		1950	6th	60	94	.390	38
1903	7th	60	77	.438	30½		1951	4th	81	73	.526	17
1904	3rd	89	65	.578	6		1952	3rd	81	73	.526	14
1905	2nd	92	60	.605	2		1953	3rd	89	65	.578	11½
1906	1st	93	58	.616	+ 3		1954	3rd	94	60	.610	17
1907	3rd	87	64	.576	5½		1955	3rd	91	63	.591	5
1908	3rd	88	64	.579	1½		1956	3rd	85	69	.552	12
1909	4th	78	74	.513	20		1957	2nd	90	64	.584	8
1910	6th	68	85	.444	35½		1958	2nd	82	72	.532	10
1911	4th	77	74	.510	24		1959	1st	94	60	.610	+ 5
1912	4th	78	76	.506	28		1960	3rd	87	67	.565	10
1913	5th	78	74	.513	17½		1961	4th	86	76	.531	23
1914	T6th	70	84	.455	30		1962	5th	85	77	.525	11
1915	3rd	93	61	.604	9½		1963	2nd	94	68	.580	10½
1916	2nd	89	65	.578	2		1964	2nd	98	64	.605	1
1917	1st	100	54	.649	+ 9		1965	2nd	95	67	.586	7
1918	6th	57	67	.460	17		1966	4th	83	79	.512	15
1919	1st	88	52	.629	+ 3½		1967	4th	89	73	.549	3
1920	2nd	96	58	.623	2		1968	T8th	67	95	.414	36
1921	7th	62	92	.403	36½		1969	5th	68	94	.420	29
1922	5th	77	77	.500	17		1970	6th	56	106	.346	42
1923	7th	69	85	.448	30		1971	3rd	79	83	.488	22½
1924	8th	66	87	.431	25½		1972	2nd	87	67	.565	5½
1925	5th	79	75	.513	18½		1973	5th	77	85	.475	17
1926	5th	81	72	.529	9½		1974	4th	80	80	.500	9
1927	5th	70	83	.458	29½		1975	5th	75	86	.466	22½
1928	5th	72	82	.468	29		1976	6th	64	97	.398	25½
1929	7th	59	93	.388	46		1977	3rd	90	72	.556	12
1930	7th	62	92	.403	40		1978	5th	71	90	.441	20½
1931	8th	56	97	.366	51		1979	5th	73	87	.456	14
1932	7th	49	102	.325	56½		1980	5th	70	90	.438	26
1933	6th	67	83	.447	31		1981	3rd/6th	54	52	.509	*
1934	8th	53	99	.349	47		1982	3rd	87	75	.537	6
1935	5th	74	78	.487	19½		1983	1st†	99	63	.611	+20
1936	3rd	81	70	.536	20		1984	T5th	74	88	.457	10
1937	3rd	86	68	.558	16		1985	3rd	85	77	.525	6
1938	6th	65	83	.439	32		1986	5th	72	90	.444	20
1939	4th	85	69	.552	22½		1987	5th	77	85	.475	8
1940	T4th	82	72	.532	8		1988	5th	71	90	.441	32½
1941	3rd	77	77	.500	24		1989	7th	69	92	.429	29½
1942	6th	66	82	.446	34		1990	2nd	94	68	.580	9
1943	4th	82	72	.532	16		1991	2nd	87	75	.537	8
1944	7th	71	83	.461	18		1992	3rd	86	76	.531	10
1945	6th	71	78	.477	15		1993	1st†	94	68	.580	+ 8
1946	5th	74	80	.481	30							
1947	6th	70	84	.455	27							
1948	8th	51	101	.336	44½							

*First half 31-22; second 23-30.
†Lost Championship Series.

MANAGERS

Name	Record	Years
Clark Griffith	157-113	'01-02
Nixey Callahan	309-329	'03-04
		'12-14
Fielder Jones	426-293	'04-08
Billy Sullivan	78-74	1909
Hugh Duffy	145-159	'10-11
Pants Rowland	339-247	'15-18
Kid Gleason	392-364	'19-23
Johnny Evers	66-87	1924
Eddie Collins	160-147	'25-26
Ray Schalk	102-125	'27-28
Lena Blackburne	99-133	'28-29
Donie Bush	118-189	'30-31
Lew Fonseca	120-196	'32-34
Jimmie Dykes	899-940	'34-46
Ted Lyons	185-245	'46-48
Jack Onslow	71-133	'49-50
Red Corriden	52-72	1950
Paul Richards	406-362	'51-54
		1976
Marty Marion	179-138	'54-56
Al Lopez	840-650	'57-65
		'68-69
Eddie Stanky	206-197	'66-68
Don Gutteridge	109-172	'69-70
Chuck Tanner	401-414	'70-75
Bob Lemon	124-112	'77-78
Larry Doby	37-50	1978
Don Kessinger	46-60	1979
Tony La Russa	522-510	'79-86
Jim Fregosi	193-226	'86-88
Jeff Torborg	250-235	'89-91
Gene Lamont	180-144	'92-93

DAY BY DAY

Date	Opp.	Res.	Score	(Inn.*)	Hits	Opp. hits	Winning pitcher	Losing pitcher	Save	Record	Pos.	GB
4-6	At Min.	W	10-5		13	9	McDowell	Tapani	Leach	1-0	T1st	...
4-7	At Min.	L	1-6		4	10	Deshaies	McCaskill	Aguilera	1-1	T3rd	1
4-8	At Min.	W	9-4		8	8	Fernandez	Mahomes		2-1	T2nd	½
4-9	N.Y.	L	6-11		10	15	Wickman	Pall		2-2	T4th	1½
4-10	N.Y.	L	0-12		7	16	Key	Bolton		2-3	6th	1½
4-11	N.Y.	W	6-4		9	12	McDowell	Monteleone	Hernandez	3-3	T4th	1½
4-12	Min.	L	2-3		5	6	Deshaies	McCaskill	Aguilera	3-4	6th	2½
4-13	Min.	W	4-0		9	3	Fernandez	Mahomes		4-4	T4th	2½
4-16	At Bos.	W	9-4		14	7	McDowell	Darwin		5-4	T3rd	1
4-17	At Bos.	L	1-5		5	11	Hesketh	McCaskill		5-5	4th	2
4-18	At Bos.	L	0-4		9	10	Viola	Bolton		5-6	4th	3
4-19	At Bos.	L	0-6		3	10	Dopson	Fernandez		5-7	T4th	3½
4-20	At Bal.	W	2-1	(14)	9	7	Pall	Mills		6-7	4th	2½
4-22	At Bal.	W	3-2		7	6	McDowell	Olson	Hernandez	7-7	4th	2½
4-23	At Tor.	W	5-4		5	11	McCaskill	Leiter	Hernandez	8-7	T3rd	2½
4-24	At Tor.	L	4-10		11	14	Guzman	Bolton		8-8	T3rd	3½
4-25	At Tor.	L	0-1		7	6	Stottlemyre	Fernandez	Ward	8-9	T3rd	4½
4-26	Bal.	W	7-0		9	7	Alvarez	Valenzuela		9-9	3rd	4
4-27	Bal.	W	9-4		18	9	McDowell	Sutcliffe		10-9	3rd	3
4-28	Mil.	W	11-2		12	9	McCaskill	Eldred		11-9	3rd	3
4-29	Mil.	W	7-4		13	7	Stieb	Boddicker	Radinsky	12-9	2nd	2½
4-30	Tor.	W	10-2		14	4	Fernandez	Stottlemyre		13-9	2nd	1½
5-1	Tor.	W	8-2		8	8	Alvarez	Morris		14-9	2nd	½
5-2	Tor.	L	1-6		5	10	Hentgen	McDowell	Cox	14-10	2nd	½
5-4	At Mil.	L	1-6		7	12	Boddicker	McCaskill		14-11	T2nd	...
5-5	At Mil.	W	3-1		10	5	Radinsky	Orosco	Hernandez	15-11	T2nd	...
5-7	Cle.	W	6-5		14	10	Alvarez	Nagy	Hernandez	16-11	2nd	½
5-8	Cle.	W	10-7		12	8	McDowell	C. Young	Hernandez	17-11	1st	+½
5-9	Cle.	W	6-5		12	10	Radinsky	Lilliquist		18-11	1st	+½
5-10	At Sea.	W	13-2		12	10	Fernandez	Hampton		19-11	1st	+½
5-11	At Sea.	L	3-4		4	9	Johnson	Stieb	Charlton	19-12	1st	+½
5-12	At Sea.	W	6-5		10	12	Alvarez	Cummings	Hernandez	20-12	1st	+½
5-14	At Tex.	W	4-0		4	4	McDowell	Brown		21-12	1st	+2½
5-15	At Tex.	L	4-6	(11)	11	12	Henke	Jones		21-13	1st	+½
5-16	At Tex.	W	15-8		17	12	Fernandez	Rogers	Thigpen	22-13	1st	+2½
5-17	Cal.	L	4-11		11	15	Sanderson	Stieb		22-14	1st	+½
5-18	Cal.	W	7-4		11	5	Alvarez	Finley	Hernandez	23-14	1st	+2½
5-19	Cal.	L	0-2		5	8	Langston	McDowell	Grahe	23-15	1st	+½
5-21	Oak.	L	11-12		12	12	Downs	Hernandez	Eckersley	23-16	1st	+½
5-22	Oak.	L	4-6		11	10	Witt	Stieb	Eckersley	23-17	1st	+½
5-23	Oak.	W	5-4	(10)	8	7	Hernandez	Gossage		24-17	1st	+½
5-25	K.C.	L	2-3		8	6	Gordon	McDowell	Montgomery	24-18	1st	+1
5-26	K.C.	L	3-4		3	10	Cone	Fernandez	Montgomery	24-19	1st	+1
5-27	K.C.	L	4-6		11	8	Haney	Bere	Montgomery	24-20	T1st	...
5-28	At N.Y.	L	0-4		3	9	Key	McCaskill		24-21	2nd	1
5-29	At N.Y.	L	2-8		2	11	Abbott	Alvarez		24-22	T2nd	2
5-30	At N.Y.	L	3-6		7	11	Wickman	McDowell	Farr	24-23	T2nd	3
6-1	At Det.	W	4-2		11	6	Fernandez	Gullickson	Hernandez	25-23	3rd	1½
6-2	At Det.	W	10-1		11	5	Bere	Moore		26-23	3rd	½
6-3	At Det.	L	3-5		5	9	Leiter	McCaskill		26-24	3rd	1½
6-4	Bos.	L	0-1		4	6	Harris	Hernandez	Russell	26-25	3rd	2½
6-5	Bos.	W	11-3		15	10	McDowell	Viola		27-25	3rd	1½
6-6	Bos.	W	4-3		6	7	Fernandez	Melendez	Hernandez	28-25	T2nd	1½
6-7	Det.	W	7-3		10	8	Bere	Moore	Pall	29-25	2nd	1½
6-8	Det.	L	4-6		10	8	Leiter	Schwarz	Henneman	29-26	2nd	1½
6-9	Det.	L	4-7		9	12	Wells	Alvarez	Henneman	29-27	T2nd	2½
6-11	At K.C.	W	6-1		10	10	McDowell	Cone		30-27	T2nd	1½
6-12	At K.C.	W	2-1	(15)	14	9	Schwarz	Meacham	Hernandez	31-27	2nd	½
6-13	At K.C.	L	4-5	(10)	9	9	Gordon	Pall		31-28	2nd	1½
6-14	At Oak.	L	3-7		5	11	Young	McCaskill		31-29	T2nd	1½
6-15	At Oak.	W	4-0		9	3	Alvarez	Welch		32-29	2nd	½
6-16	At Oak.	W	4-0		8	3	McDowell	Darling		33-29	2nd	½
6-17	At Oak.	L	2-5		9	7	Witt	Fernandez	Eckersley	33-30	2nd	1
6-18	At Cal.	L	8-9		11	12	Frey	Hernandez		33-31	2nd	1
6-19	At Cal.	L	4-5		7	5	Langston	Ruffcorn	Frey	33-32	3rd	2
6-20	At Cal.	W	11-6		12	9	Alvarez	Springer		34-32	T2nd	1
6-21	Tex.	W	7-6		10	10	McDowell	Brown	Hernandez	35-32	T1st	...
6-22	Tex.	W	3-2		9	8	Pall	Henke		36-32	T1st	...
6-23	Tex.	W	7-4		8	8	Bere	Pavlik		37-32	1st	+1
6-25	Sea.	L	2-3		8	7	Leary	Alvarez	Charlton	37-33	1st	+½

— 29 —

Date	Opp.	Res.	Score (inn.*)	Hits	Opp. hits	Winning pitcher	Losing pitcher	Save	Record	Pos.	GB
6-26	Sea.	W	7-4	12	11	McDowell	Hanson	Hernandez	38-33	1st	+½
6-27	Sea.	W	6-4	8	10	Fernandez	DeLucia	Hernandez	39-33	1st	+2½
6-28	At Cle.	L	0-2	9	7	Mesa	Bere	Plunk	39-34	1st	+½
6-29	At Cle.	L	2-8	7	14	Clark	Bolton		39-35	1st	+½
6-30	At Cle.	L	2-4	8	9	Cook	Alvarez	Hernandez	39-36	1st	+½
7-1	Bal.	L	0-1	5	3	Moyer	McDowell	Olson	39-37	1st	+1
7-2	Bal.	W	12-1	13	6	Fernandez	Mussina		40-37	1st	+1
7-3	Bal.	L	6-9	10	11	Williamson	Bere	Olson	40-38	T1st	...
7-4	Bal.	W	3-1	4	3	Bolton	McDonald	Hernandez	41-38	T1st	...
7-5	At Tor.	W	4-3	11	8	Alvarez	Hentgen	Hernandez	42-38	T1st	...
7-6	At Tor.	L	1-5	7	8	Stewart	McDowell		42-39	T1st	...
7-7	At Tor.	W	5-2	16	7	Fernandez	Guzman	Hernandez	43-39	1st	+1
7-8	At Bal.	W	12-5	15	12	Bere	Sutcliffe		44-39	1st	+1
7-9	At Bal.	L	6-15	10	14	McDonald	Bolton		44-40	1st	+1
7-10	At Bal.	L	0-6	3	10	Valenzuela	Alvarez		44-41	1st	+1
7-11	At Bal.	W	11-5	13	13	McDowell	Moyer		45-41	1st	+1
7-15	At Mil.	W	6-4	11	6	Fernandez	Fetters	Radinsky	46-41	1st	+1
7-16	At Mil.	W	4-3	8	5	Radinsky	Eldred	Hernandez	47-41	1st	+1
7-17	At Mil.	W	9-4	14	7	McDowell	Navarro		48-41	1st	+2
7-18	At Mil.	W	3-1	5	7	Radinsky	Henry	Hernandez	49-41	1st	+3
7-19	Tor.	L	7-15	9	21	Stewart	Bolton		49-42	1st	+2
7-20	Tor.	W	2-1	6	4	Fernandez	Guzman		50-42	1st	+2
7-21	Tor.	L	1-4	5	9	Leiter	Alvarez	Ward	50-43	1st	+½
7-22	Mil.	W	7-2	12	13	McDowell	Navarro		51-43	1st	+2½
7-23	Mil.	L	2-3	4	7	Orosco	Hernandez	Henry	51-44	1st	+½
7-24	Mil.	W	6-5	14	10	Radinsky	Fetters		52-44	1st	+2
7-25	Mil.	L	3-7	8	9	Eldred	Fernandez		52-45	1st	+2
7-26	Cle.	W	4-3	6	6	Schwarz	DiPoto	Hernandez	53-45	1st	+½
7-27	Cle.	W	7-4	11	11	McDowell	Mutis	Hernandez	54-45	1st	+2½
7-28	Cle.	W	9-4	6	10	Bere	Lopez		55-45	1st	+3½
7-30	At Sea.	W	6-4	(10)	15	7	Radinsky	DeLucia	Hernandez	56-45	1st	+3
7-31	At Sea.	W	13-10	15	13	Bolton	Hanson	Radinsky	57-45	1st	+4
8-1	At Sea.	W	4-0	6	2	McDowell	Bosio		58-45	1st	+5
8-2	At Tex.	L	8-9	13	7	Henke	Schwarz		58-46	1st	+5
8-3	At Tex.	W	11-6	18	9	McCaskill	Leibrandt		59-46	1st	+5½
8-4	At Tex.	L	2-5	4	11	Ryan	Fernandez	Henke	59-47	1st	+4½
8-5	At Tex.	L	1-7	9	12	Brown	Belcher	Carpenter	59-48	1st	+4½
8-6	Cal.	L	3-7	8	16	Finley	Alvarez	Nelson	59-49	1st	+3½
8-7	Cal.	W	6-4	10	10	McDowell	Farrell	Hernandez	60-49	1st	+4½
8-8	Cal.	L	1-2	5	6	Langston	Bere	Butcher	60-50	1st	+3½
8-9	Oak.	W	5-4	10	11	Fernandez	Witt	Hernandez	61-50	1st	+3½
8-10	Oak.	W	4-0	4	2	Belcher	Mohler		62-50	1st	+3½
8-11	Oak.	L	1-3	8	5	Van Poppel	Alvarez	Eckersley	62-51	1st	+3½
8-12	K.C.	L	2-4	7	10	Appier	McDowell		62-52	1st	+2½
8-13	K.C.	W	5-4	12	5	Cary	Montgomery	Hernandez	63-52	1st	+3½
8-14	K.C.	W	4-1	7	2	Fernandez	Cone	Radinsky	64-52	1st	+4½
8-15	K.C.	L	5-7	9	13	Gordon	Belcher	Montgomery	64-53	1st	+3½
8-17	At Bos.	W	3-2	9	10	McDowell	Sele	Hernandez	65-53	1st	+3½
8-18	At Bos.	L	0-5	1	5	Darwin	Bere		65-54	1st	+2½
8-20	At Min.	W	4-2	10	5	Fernandez	Erickson	Hernandez	66-54	1st	+3
8-21	At Min.	W	9-4	13	7	Belcher	Banks	Hernandez	67-54	1st	+4
8-22	At Min.	W	1-0	3	8	McDowell	Deshaies		68-54	1st	+4
8-23	N.Y.	L	5-6	(10)	10	11	Assenmacher	Radinsky	Farr	68-55	1st	+4
8-24	N.Y.	W	4-2	10	5	Alvarez	Abbott	Hernandez	69-55	1st	+4
8-25	N.Y.	L	5-7	10	12	Monteleone	Radinsky	Wickman	69-56	1st	+3½
8-27 (1)	Min.	W	7-3	11	9	Belcher	Deshaies		70-56	1st	+4
8-27 (2)	Min.	L	2-7	(10)	9	17	Casian	Pall		70-57	1st	+3½
8-28	Min.	W	4-1	7	6	Bere	Tapani		71-57	1st	+3½
8-29	Min.	W	13-5	18	12	McCaskill	Guardado		72-57	1st	+4½
8-30	Min.	W	4-1	7	3	Fernandez	Erickson	Hernandez	73-57	1st	+5½
8-31	At N.Y.	W	11-3	13	8	Alvarez	Hitchcock		74-57	1st	+5½
9-1	At N.Y.	W	5-3	11	9	McDowell	Assenmacher	Hernandez	75-57	1st	+5½
9-2	At N.Y.	L	1-7	4	10	Key	Belcher		75-58	1st	+5
9-3	At Det.	W	8-6	11	8	Bere	Doherty	Hernandez	76-58	1st	+6
9-4	At Det.	W	11-2	12	7	Fernandez	Gullickson		77-58	1st	+6
9-5	At Det.	W	5-3	11	8	Alvarez	Moore	Hernandez	78-58	1st	+6½
9-6	Bos.	L	1-3	6	10	Bankhead	McDowell	Harris	78-59	1st	+6
9-7	Bos.	L	3-4	5	9	Darwin	Belcher	Ryan	78-60	1st	+5
9-8	Bos.	W	8-1	11	5	Bere	Dopson		79-60	1st	+5
9-10	Det.	L	0-4	2	9	Moore	Fernandez		79-61	1st	+3½
9-11	Det.	W	3-1	9	5	Alvarez	Wells	Hernandez	80-61	1st	+3½
9-12	Det.	L	3-6	7	9	Doherty	McDowell	Davis	80-62	1st	+3½
9-13	At K.C.	L	0-9	4	12	Appier	Belcher		80-63	1st	+2½
9-14	At K.C.	W	8-3	14	7	Bere	Pichardo		81-63	1st	+3½

Date	Opp.	Res.	Score	(inn.*)	Hits	Opp. hits	Winning pitcher	Losing pitcher	Save	Record	Pos.	GB
9-15	At K.C.	W	10-6	(11)	14	15	Hernandez	Gubicza		82-63	1st	+3½
9-17	At Oak.	W	8-0		12	4	Alvarez	Welch		83-63	1st	+4½
9-18	At Oak.	L	2-3		5	8	Witt	McDowell	Eckersley	83-64	1st	+3½
9-19	At Oak.	W	3-1		8	6	Radinsky	Eckersley	Hernandez	84-64	1st	+4½
9-20	At Cal.	W	10-2		15	7	Bere	Leftwich	McCaskill	85-64	1st	+4½
9-21	At Cal.	L	0-8		7	15	Farrell	Fernandez	Frey	85-65	1st	+4½
9-22	At Cal.	W	1-0		4	5	Alvarez	Finley	Hernandez	86-65	1st	+5½
9-23	At Cal.	W	7-1		10	4	McDowell	Langston		87-65	1st	+6
9-24	Tex.	W	5-4		7	9	Hernandez	Patterson		88-65	1st	+7
9-26 (1)	Tex.	W	5-3		8	11	Bere	Rogers	Hernandez	89-65	1st	+7½
9-26 (2)	Tex.	L	2-3		7	9	Pavlik	Fernandez	Henke	89-66	1st	+7
9-27	Sea.	W	4-2		8	4	Alvarez	Fleming	McCaskill	90-66	1st	+7½
9-28	Sea.	L	2-5		8	6	Leary	Ruffcorn	Power	90-67	1st	+7
9-29	Sea.	W	3-2	(12)	11	10	Radinsky	Brad Holman		91-67	1st	+7
9-30	Sea.	L	1-2	(11)	8	10	Power	McCaskill		91-68	1st	+6
10-1	At Cle.	W	4-2		7	10	Fernandez	Clark	Hernandez	92-68	1st	+6
10-2	At Cle.	W	4-2	(10)	7	7	Howard	Hernandez	Drahman	93-68	1st	+7
10-3	At Cle.	W	4-0		11	6	Bere	Nagy		94-68	1st	+8

Monthly records: April (13-9), May (11-14), June (15-13), July (18-9), August (17-12), September (17-11), October (3-0).
*Innings, if other than nine.

HIGHLIGHTS

High point: On September 19 in Oakland, third baseman Robin Ventura hit a two-run homer in the ninth inning off Dennis Eckersley to give Chicago a 3-1 win and increase its lead over Texas to 4½ games. The Rangers didn't threaten again as the White Sox went on to win the A.L. West by eight games.

Low point: Chicago had its division lead trimmed to 2½ games on September 13 when it suffered a 9-0 pounding at Kansas City.

Turning point: Lefthander Wilson Alvarez returned from a one-game demotion to Class AAA to beat New York, 4-2, on August 24. From that point, Alvarez and rookie righthander Jason Bere, who won Minnesota on August 28, each won their last seven starts to help Chicago seal the division race.

Most valuable player: First baseman Frank Thomas. He became the first White Sox player to hit 40 homers (41) in a season. He ranked in the league's top 10 in nine offensive categories en route to winning A.L. MVP honors.

Most valuable pitcher: Righthander Jack McDowell. He won 22 games, the most by a White Sox hurler since 1983, and the A.L. Cy Young Award.

Most improved player: Righthander Alex Fernandez. He paced the staff with 169 strikeouts, and his 18 wins were one more than his combined totals from 1991 (nine) and '92 (eight).

Most pleasant surprise: Second baseman Joey Cora. He ranked second on the team in runs (95), led the league in sacrifice hits (19) and finished second in triples (13).

Biggest disappointment: Designated hitter George Bell. After hitting 25 home runs with 112 RBIs in 1992, Bell hit just 13 homers with 64 RBIs in '93.

Key injuries: Left fielder Tim Raines hurt his right thumb in April and missed six weeks. Bell underwent surgery on his right knee in July.

Notable: In winning their first division title since 1983, the White Sox led the league in ERA (3.70), outscored op-ponents 142-78 in the first inning and had the league's best road record (49-32). . . . Center fielder Lance Johnson led the league in triples (14) for the third straight year. . . . Chicago catchers paced the A.L. by throwing out 46.1 percent of opposing baserunners. . . . Gene Lamont won A.L. Manager of the Year honors. . . . On June 22, catcher Carlton Fisk set a major league record by catching his 2,226th career game. He was released June 28.

—JOE GODDARD

RECORDS

1993 regular-season record: 94-68 (1st in A.L. West); 45-36 at home; 49-32 on road; 48-36 vs. East; 46-32 vs. West; 27-22 vs. LHP; 67-46 vs. RHP; 77-61 on grass; 17-7 on turf; 27-22 in day-time; 67-46 at night; 23-20 in one-run games; 7-5 in extra-inning games; 0-2 in doubleheaders.

Team record last five years: 430-379 (.532, ranks 3rd in league in that span).

TEAM LEADERS

Batting average: Frank Thomas (.317).
At-bats: Joey Cora (579).
Runs: Frank Thomas (106).
Hits: Frank Thomas (174).
Total bases: Frank Thomas (333).
Doubles: Frank Thomas (36).
Triples: Lance Johnson (14).
Home runs: Frank Thomas (41).
Runs batted in: Frank Thomas (128).
Stolen bases: Lance Johnson (35).
Slugging percentage: Frank Thomas (.607).
On-base percentage: Frank Thomas (.426).
Wins: Jack McDowell (22).
Earned-run average: Wilson Alvarez (2.95).
Complete games: Jack McDowell (10).
Shutouts: Jack McDowell (4).
Saves: Roberto Hernandez (38).
Innings pitched: Jack McDowell (256⅔).
Strikeouts: Alex Fernandez (169).

GAMES BY POSITION

Catcher: Ron Karkovice 127, Mike La-Valliere 37, Carlton Fisk 25, Rick Wrona 4, Doug Lindsey 2.
First base: Frank Thomas 150, Dan Pasqua 32, Robin Ventura 4, Drew Denson 3.
Second base: Joey Cora 151, Craig Grebeck 16, Norberto Martin 5, Steve Sax 1.
Third base: Robin Ventura 155, Craig Grebeck 14, Joey Cora 3.
Shortstop: Ozzie Guillen 133, Craig Grebeck 46.
Outfield: Ellis Burks 146, Lance Johnson 146, Tim Raines 112, Bo Jackson 47, Mike Huff 43, Dan Pasqua 37, Steve Sax 32, Warren Newson 5.
Designated hitter: George Bell 102, Bo Jackson 36, Steve Sax 21, Warren Newson 10, Ivan Calderon 6, Matt Merullo 6, Dan Pasqua 6, Frank Thomas 4, Norberto Martin 1.

TOP DRAFT CHOICES

1. **Scott Christman**, LHP, Oregon State University.
2. **Greg Norton**, 3B, University of Oklahoma.
3. **Joe Bales**, RHP, Reed High School, Sparks, Nev.
4. **Dennis Twombley**, C, Patrick Henry High School, San Diego.
5. **David Lundquist**, RHP, Cochise County (Ariz.) C.C.
6. **Craig McClure**, OF, Columbine High School, Littleton, Colo.
7. **Ben Boulware**, 2B/OF, Cal Poly San Luis Obispo.
8. **Jason Goligoski**, SS, Western Montana College.
9. **Rich Pratt**, LHP, University of South Carolina.
10. **Zane Leiber**, RHP, Arizona Central J.C.

CLEVELAND INDIANS
AMERICAN LEAGUE CENTRAL DIVISION

N   Denotes night game (any game starting after 5 p.m.).
☐   Home games shaded.
*   At Three Rivers Stadium in Pittsburgh.

APRIL

SUN	MON	TUE	WED	THU	FRI	SAT
					1	2
3	4 SEA	5	6 N SEA	7 N SEA	8 KC	9 KC
10 KC	11 N CAL	12 N CAL	13 N CAL	14	15 N KC	16 N KC
17 KC	18	19 N MIN	20 N MIN	21 N MIN	22 N TEX	23 N TEX
24 TEX	25 N MIN	26 N MIN	27 N CHI	28 N CHI	29 N TEX	30 TEX

MAY

SUN	MON	TUE	WED	THU	FRI	SAT
1 TEX	2	3 N CHI	4 N CHI	5	6 N BAL	7 BAL
8 BAL	9 N NY	10 N NY	11 N NY	12 N DET	13 N DET
15 DET	16	17 N MIL	18 N MIL	19 N MIL	20 N TOR	21 TOR
22 TOR	23 TOR	24 N BOS	25 N BOS	26 N BOS	27 N OAK	28 OAK
29 OAK	30 N CAL	31 N CAL				

JUNE

SUN	MON	TUE	WED	THU	FRI	SAT
			1 N CAL	2	3 N OAK	4 OAK
5 N OAK	6 N SEA	7 N SEA	8 N SEA	9 N MIL	10 N MIL	11 N MIL
12 MIL	13 N TBR	14 N TOR	15 N TOR	16 N BOS	17 N BOS	18 BOS
19 BOS	20 N DET	21 N DET	22 N NY	23	24 N NY	25 N NY
26 N NY	27 N BAL	28 N BAL	29 N CAL	30 N BAL		

JULY

SUN	MON	TUE	WED	THU	FRI	SAT
					1 N MIN	2 N MIN
3 N MIN	4 N MIN	5 N TEX	6 N TEX	7 N TEX	8 N MIN	9 N MIN
10 MIN	11 N*	12 ALL-STAR GAME	13	14 N CHI	15 N CHI	16 N CHI
17 CHI	18 N TEX	19 N TEX	20 N TEX	21 N CHI	22 N CHI	23 N CHI
24 CHI	25	26 N BAL	27 N BAL	28 N BAL	29 N NY	30 N NY
31 NY						

AUGUST

SUN	MON	TUE	WED	THU	FRI	SAT
	1 N DET	2 N DET	3 N DET	4 N DET	5 N BOS	6 N BOS
7 BOS	8 N TOR	9 N TOR	10 N TOR	11	12 N MIL	13 N MIL
14 MIL	15	16 N OAK	17 N OAK	18 N OAK	19 N SEA	20 N SEA
21 SEA	22	23 N OAK	24 N OAK	25 N OAK	26 N CAL	27 N CAL
28 CAL	29	30 N KC	31 N KC			

SEPTEMBER

SUN	MON	TUE	WED	THU	FRI	SAT
				1 KC	2 N CAL	3 CAL
4 CAL	5 N KC	6 N KC	7 N KC	8	9 N SEA	10 N SEA
11 SEA	12 N MIL	13 N MIL	14 MIL	15 N TOR	16 N TOR	17 TOR
18 TOR	19 N BOS	20 N BOS	21 N BOS	22 N DET	23 N DET	24 DET
25 DET	26 N NY	27 N NY	28 N NY	29	30 N BAL	

OCTOBER

SUN	MON	TUE	WED	THU	FRI	SAT
						1 BAL
2 BAL						

CLUB DIRECTORY

Board of directors
Richard E. Jacobs
Martin J. Cleary
Gary L. Bryenton
Chairman of the board and CEO
Richard E. Jacobs
Executive vice president, general manager
John Hart
Executive vice president, business
Dennis Lehman
V.p., marketing and communications
Jeff Overton
Vice president
Martin J. Cleary
Vice president, public relations
Bob DiBiasio
Vice president, finance
Gregg Olson
Dir. of baseball operations/asst. g.m.
Dan O'Dowd
Director, scouting
Jay Robertson
Director, team travel
Mike Seghi
Director, minor league operations
Mark Shapiro
Administrator, player personnel
Wendy Hoppel
Administrator, scouting
Keith Boeck
Director, media relations
John Maroon
Assistant director, media relations
Susie Gharrity
Director, community relations
Glen Shumate
Manager, community relations
Eva Manning
Director, advertising
Valerie Arcuri
Director, promotions/sales
Jon Starrett
Director, broadcasting
Mike Lehr
Manager, advertising/publications
Kim Carpinello
Controller
Ken Stefanov
Director, ticket services
Connie Minadeo
Manager, box office
Tom McGrane
Director, ticket sales
Vic Gregovits
Coordinator, season/group sales
Diane Stack

Director, ballpark operations
Jim Folk
Director, merchandising/licensing
Jayne Churchmack
Home clubhouse manager
Stan Hunter
Equipment manager
Jeff Sipos
Visiting clubhouse manager
Cy Buynak
Medical director
William T. Wilder, M.D.
Head trainer
Jim Warfield
Assistant trainer
Paul Spicuzza
Strength and conditioning coach
Fernando Montes
Team physicians
Ronald Golovan, M.D.
Godofredo Domingo, M.D.
K.V. Gopal, M.D.
Zenos Vangelos, M.D.
Major league/spec. assignment scouts
Dan Carnevale
Dom Chiti
Tony DeMacio
Tom Giordano
Ted Simmons
Bill Werle
Mark Wiley
Full-time scouts
Luis Aponte
Steve Avila
Mark Baca
Brad Cameron
Ramon Conde
Tom Couston
Jeff Datz
Rene Gayo
Mark Germann
Don Jacoby
Gil Kubski
Allan Lewis
Winston Llenas
Guy Mader
Bob Mayer
Kasey McKeon
Jim Richardson
Max Semier
Jim Stevenson
Gary Tuck
Craig Wallenbrock

Manager—Mike Hargrove (21).

Coaches—Buddy Bell (26), Luis Isaac (13), Charlie Manual (42), Dave Nelson (14), Jeff Newman (55), Phil Regan (27).

No.	PITCHERS	B/T	Ht./Wt.	Born	1993 clubs
47	Barnes, Brian	L/L	5-9/170	3-25-67	Montreal
66	Bryant, Shawn	R/L	6-3/205	6-10-69	Canton/Akron
36	Carter, John	R/R	6-1/195	2-16-72	Columbus
54	Clark, Mark	R/R	6-5/225	5-12-68	Cleveland, Charlotte
63	Crawford, Carlos	R/R	6-1/185	10-4-71	Kinston
45	DiPoto, Jerry	R/R	6-2/200	5-24-68	Charlotte, Cleveland
56	Embree, Alan	L/L	6-2/185	1-23-70	Canton/Akron
48	Grimsley, Jason	R/R	6-3/180	8-7-67	Charlotte, Cleveland
53	Hernandez, Jeremy	R/R	6-6/195	7-6-66	San Diego, Cleveland
29	Kramer, Tom	B/R	6-0/205	1-9-68	Cleveland
28	Lilliquist, Derek	L/L	5-10/195	2-20-66	Cleveland
60	Logsdon, Kevin	B/L	5-11/215	12-23-70	Kinston
59	Lopez, Albie	R/R	6-2/205	8-18-71	Canton/Akron, Cleveland, Charlotte
32	Martinez, Dennis	R/R	6-1/180	5-14-55	Montreal
49	Mesa, Jose	R/R	6-3/225	5-22-66	Cleveland
23	Mlicki, Dave	R/R	6-4/190	6-8-68	Canton/Akron, Cleveland
41	Nagy, Charles	L/R	6-3/200	5-5-67	Cleveland, Canton/Akron
38	Plunk, Eric	R/R	6-6/220	9-3-63	Cleveland
50	Tavarez, Julian	R/R	6-2/165	5-22-73	Kinston, Canton/Akron, Cleveland
46	Wertz, Bill	R/R	6-6/220	1-15-67	Charlotte, Cleveland

No.	CATCHERS	B/T	Ht./Wt.	Born	1993 clubs
15	Alomar, Sandy	R/R	6-5/215	6-18-66	Cleveland, Charlotte
12	Levis, Jesse	L/R	5-9/180	4-14-68	Charlotte, Cleveland

No.	INFIELDERS	B/T	Ht./Wt.	Born	1993 clubs
9	Baerga, Carlos	B/R	5-11/200	11-4-68	Cleveland
57	Bell, David	R/R	5-10/170	9-14-72	Canton/Akron
10	Espinoza, Alvaro	R/R	6-0/190	2-19-62	Cleveland
20	Lewis, Mark	R/R	6-1/190	11-30-69	Charlotte, Cleveland
33	Murray, Eddie	B/R	6-2/220	2-24-56	New York N.L.
34	Perry, Herbert	R/R	6-2/210	9-15-69	Canton/Akron
11	Sorrento, Paul	L/R	6-2/220	11-17-65	Cleveland
25	Thome, Jim	L/R	6-4/220	8-27-70	Charlotte, Cleveland
13	Vizquel, Omar	B/R	5-9/165	4-24-67	Seattle

No.	OUTFIELDERS	B/T	Ht./Wt.	Born	1993 clubs
30	Amaro, Ruben	B/R	5-10/175	2-12-65	Scranton/Wilkes-Barre, Philadelphia
8	Belle, Albert	R/R	6-2/210	8-25-66	Cleveland
35	Kirby, Wayne	L/R	5-10/185	1-22-64	Charlotte, Cleveland
7	Lofton, Kenny	L/L	6-0/180	5-31-67	Cleveland
22	Maldonado, Candy	R/R	6-0/205	9-5-60	Chicago N.L., Cleveland
24	Ramirez, Manny	R/R	6-0/190	5-30-72	Canton/Akron, Charlotte, Cleveland
61	Ramirez, Omar	R/R	5-9/170	11-2-70	Canton/Akron
58	Ramos, Ken	L/L	6-0/185	6-8-67	Charlotte

BALLPARK INFORMATION

Ballpark (capacity, surface)
  Indians Park (42,400, grass)
Address
  2401 Ontario St.
  Cleveland, OH 44115
Business phone
  216-420-4200
Ticket information
  216-241-8888
Ticket prices
  $28 (club seating)
  $16 (field box)
  $14 (lower box & view box)
  $12 (lower reserved, upper box & mezzanine seating)
  $10 (upper reserved)
  $6 (reserved g.a.)
  $6 (bleachers)
Field dimensions (from home plate)
  To left field at foul line, 325 feet
  To center field, 405 feet
  To right field at foul line, 325 feet
First game played
  Scheduled for April 4, 1994

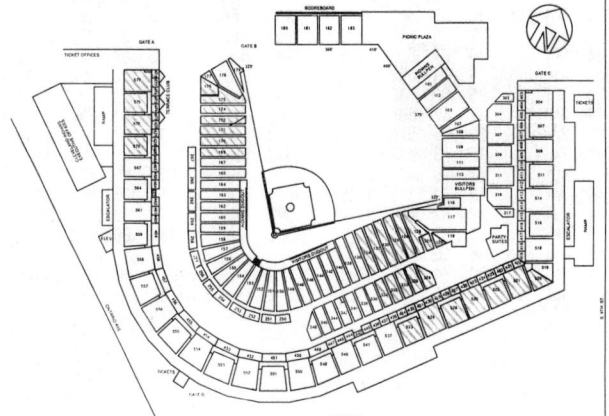

MINOR LEAGUE AFFILIATES

Class	Team	League	Manager
AAA	Charlotte	International	Brian Graham
AA	Canton/Akron	Eastern	Ted Kubiak
A	Kinston	Carolina	Dave Keller
A	Columbus, Ga.	South Atlantic	Mike Brown
A	Watertown	New York-Pennsylvania	Jeff Datz
Rookie	Burlington	Appalachian	Jim Gabella

BROADCAST INFORMATION

Radio: WKNR-AM (1220). Broadcasters: Tom Hamilton, Herb Score.
TV: WUAB-TV (Channel 43). Broadcasters: Mike Hegan, Jack Corrigan.
Cable TV: SportsChannel. Broadcasters: Rick Manning, John Sanders.

SPRING TRAINING

Ballpark (city): Chain O'Lakes (Winter Haven, Fla.).
Ticket information: 813-291-5803.

HISTORY

YEAR-BY-YEAR RECORDS

Year	Pos.	W	L	Pct.	GB	Year	Pos.	W	L	Pct.	GB
1901	7th	54	82	.397	29	1949	3rd	89	65	.578	8
1902	5th	69	67	.507	14	1950	4th	92	62	.597	6
1903	3rd	77	63	.550	15	1951	2nd	93	61	.604	5
1904	4th	86	65	.570	7½	1952	2nd	93	61	.604	2
1905	5th	76	78	.494	19	1953	2nd	92	62	.597	8½
1906	3rd	89	64	.582	5	1954	1st	111	43	.721	+ 8
1907	4th	85	67	.559	8	1955	2nd	93	61	.604	3
1908	2nd	90	64	.584	½	1956	2nd	88	66	.571	9
1909	6th	71	82	.464	27½	1957	6th	76	77	.497	21½
1910	5th	71	81	.467	32	1958	4th	77	76	.503	14½
1911	3rd	80	73	.523	22	1959	2nd	89	65	.578	5
1912	5th	75	78	.490	30½	1960	4th	76	78	.494	21
1913	3rd	86	66	.566	9½	1961	5th	78	83	.484	30½
1914	8th	51	102	.333	48½	1962	6th	80	82	.494	16
1915	7th	57	95	.375	44½	1963	T5th	79	83	.488	25½
1916	6th	77	77	.500	14	1964	T6th	79	83	.488	20
1917	3rd	88	66	.571	12	1965	5th	87	75	.537	15
1918	2nd	73	54	.575	2½	1966	5th	81	81	.500	17
1919	2nd	84	55	.604	3½	1967	8th	75	87	.463	17
1920	1st	98	56	.636	+ 2	1968	3rd	86	75	.534	16½
1921	2nd	94	60	.610	4½	1969	6th	62	99	.385	46½
1922	4th	78	76	.507	16	1970	5th	76	86	.469	32
1923	3rd	82	71	.536	16½	1971	6th	60	102	.370	43
1924	6th	67	86	.438	24½	1972	5th	72	84	.462	14
1925	6th	70	84	.455	27½	1973	6th	71	91	.438	26
1926	2nd	88	66	.571	3	1974	4th	77	85	.475	14
1927	6th	66	87	.431	43½	1975	4th	79	80	.497	15½
1928	7th	62	92	.403	39	1976	4th	81	78	.509	16
1929	3rd	81	71	.533	24	1977	5th	71	90	.441	28½
1930	4th	81	73	.536	21	1978	6th	69	90	.434	29
1931	4th	78	76	.506	30	1979	6th	81	80	.503	22
1932	4th	87	65	.572	19	1980	6th	79	81	.494	23
1933	4th	75	76	.497	23½	1981	6th/5th	52	51	.504	†
1934	3rd	85	69	.552	16	1982	T6th	78	84	.481	17
1935	3rd	82	71	.536	12	1983	7th	70	92	.432	28
1936	5th	80	74	.519	22½	1984	6th	75	87	.463	29
1937	4th	83	71	.539	19	1985	7th	60	102	.370	39½
1938	3rd	86	66	.566	13	1986	5th	84	78	.519	11½
1939	3rd	87	67	.565	20½	1987	7th	61	101	.377	37
1940	2nd	89	65	.578	1	1988	6th	78	84	.481	11
1941	T4th	75	79	.487	26	1989	6th	73	89	.451	16
1942	4th	75	79	.487	28	1990	4th	77	85	.475	11
1943	3rd	82	71	.536	15½	1991	7th	57	105	.352	34
1944	T5th	72	82	.468	17	1992	4th	76	86	.469	20
1945	5th	73	72	.503	11	1993	6th	76	86	.469	19
1946	6th	68	86	.442	36						
1947	4th	80	74	.519	17						
1948	1st*	97	58	.626	+ 1						

*Won pennant playoff. †First half 26-24; second 26-27.

MANAGERS

Name	Record	Years
Jimmy McAleer	54-82	1901
Bill Armour	232-195	'02-04
Nap Lajoie	377-309	'05-09
Deacon McGuire	91-117	'09-11
George Stovall	74-62	1911
Harry Davis	54-71	1912
Joe Birmingham	170-191	'12-15
Lee Fohl	327-310	'15-19
Tris Speaker	617-520	'19-26
Jack McCallister	66-87	1927
Rog. Peckinpaugh	490-481	'28-33
		1941
Walter Johnson	179-168	'33-35
Steve O'Neill	199-168	'35-37
Oscar Vitt	262-198	'38-40
Lou Boudreau	728-649	'42-50
Al Lopez	570-354	'51-56
Kerby Farrell	76-77	1957
Bobby Bragan	31-36	1958
Joe Gordon	184-19	'58-60
Jimmie Dykes	103-115	'60-61
Mel McGaha	80-82	1962
Birdie Tebbetts	269-298	'63-66
George Strickland	15-24	'66
Joe Adcock	75-87	1967
Alvin Dark	266-321	'68-71
Johnny Lipon	18-41	1971
Ken Aspromonte	220-260	'72-74
Frank Robinson	186-189	'75-77
Jeff Torborg	157-201	'77-79
Dave Garcia	247-244	'79-82
Mike Ferraro	40-60	1983
Pat Corrales	280-355	'83-87
Doc Edwards	173-207	'87-89
John Hart	8-11	1989
John McNamara	102-137	'90-91
Mike Hargrove	184-225	'91-93

DAY BY DAY

Date	Opp.	Res.	Score (Inn.*)	Hits	Opp. hits	Winning pitcher	Losing pitcher	Save	Record	Pos.	GB
4-5	N.Y.	L	1-9	3	16	Key	Nagy		0-1	T5th	1
4-7	N.Y.	W	4-2	12	6	Plunk	Abbott	Lilliquist	1-1	T2nd	1
4-8	N.Y.	W	15-5	17	12	Bielecki	Militello		2-1	2nd	1
4-9	At Tor.	L	10-13	16	14	Eichhorn	Power	Ward	2-2	T4th	1
4-10	At Tor.	L	4-5	9	7	Stottlemyre	Nagy	Ward	2-3	T5th	2
4-11	At Tor.	W	10-6	16	10	Clark	Morris	Lilliquist	3-3	T3rd	1
4-13	At Bos.	L	2-6	10	10	Viola	Mutis		3-4	T4th	2
4-14	At Bos.	L	7-12	12	18	Hesketh	Bielecki		3-5	5th	3
4-15	At Bos.	L	3-4 (13)	13	10	Quantrill	Plunk		3-6	5th	4
4-16	Tor.	W	13-1	19	7	Nagy	Morris		4-6	5th	3
4-17	Tor.	L	1-8	8	11	Hentgen	Clark		4-7	6th	4
4-18	Tor.	W	6-5	6	12	Mutis	Leiter	Lilliquist	5-7	6th	4
4-19	Tor.	L	1-7	6	12	Guzman	Bielecki		5-8	6th	5
4-20	At Cal.	L	2-7	8	12	Sanderson	Mesa		5-9	6th	6
4-21	At Cal.	L	6-7	13	10	Farrell	Nagy	Frey	5-10	7th	6
4-22	At Cal.	L	0-8	2	12	Finley	Clark		5-11	6th	6
4-24	At Oak.	W	10-3	15	7	Bielecki	Hillegas		6-11	6th	5½
4-25	At Oak.	W	6-0	13	3	Mesa	Davis		7-11	6th	5½
4-26	At Sea.	L	3-6	7	13	Johnson	Kramer		7-12	6th	6½
4-27	At Sea.	L	0-4	4	12	Bosio	Nagy		7-13	6th	6½
4-28	At Sea.	L	0-4	7	7	Hanson	Mutis	Charlton	7-14	6th	6½
4-30	Oak.	L	2-8 (10)	5	13	Gossage	Plunk		7-15	7th	8
5-1	Oak.	W	1-0	4	4	Mesa	Davis	Plunk	8-15	7th	7
5-2	Oak.	W	10-2	15	4	Nagy	Witt		9-15	7th	6
5-3	Cal.	W	5-4	8	7	Lilliquist	Valera		10-15	6th	5½
5-4	Cal.	W	5-3	10	6	Cook	Lewis	Lilliquist	11-15	6th	5½
5-5	Sea.	W	3-2	9	10	Bielecki	Cummings	Lilliquist	12-15	5th	4½
5-6	Sea.	L	5-9	6	16	Johnson	Mesa		12-16	6th	5
5-7	At Chi.	L	5-6	10	14	Alvarez	Nagy	Hernandez	12-17	6th	6
5-8	At Chi.	L	7-10	8	12	McDowell	C. Young	Hernandez	12-18	6th	6
5-9	At Chi.	L	5-6	10	12	Radinsky	Lilliquist		12-19	7th	6
5-11	K.C.	L	6-7	15	16	Appier	Cook	Montgomery	12-20	7th	7½
5-12	K.C.	W	6-2	7	10	Mesa	Gardner		13-20	7th	7½
5-13	K.C.	L	3-7	5	12	Pichardo	M. Young		13-21	7th	7½
5-14	At Mil.	L	2-5	10	10	Boddicker	C. Young	Henry	13-22	7th	8½
5-15	At Mil.	W	9-5	12	8	Cook	Bones		14-22	6th	8½
5-16	At Mil.	L	3-5	10	9	Navarro	Bielecki	Henry	14-23	7th	8½
5-17	At Bal.	W	2-0	6	4	Mesa	McDonald	Plunk	15-23	6th	8
5-18	At Bal.	L	0-7	2	11	Valenzuela	M. Young		15-24	7th	9
5-19	At Bal.	L	3-6	12	8	Sutcliffe	Scudder	Olson	15-25	7th	10
5-20	At Bal.	L	3-1	13	3	Cook	Moyer		16-25	7th	10
5-21	Det.	W	10-5	15	11	Bielecki	Gullickson	C. Young	17-25	6th	9
5-22	Det.	L	1-5	5	9	Moore	Mesa		17-26	7th	10
5-23	Det.	L	2-4	7	9	Leiter	M. Young	Henneman	17-27	7th	11
5-24	Tex.	W	4-1	8	1	Kramer	Brown		18-27	7th	10
5-25	Tex.	L	1-5	8	8	Leibrandt	Cook		18-28	7th	11
5-26	Tex.	W	7-6	10	10	Mesa	Rogers	Plunk	19-28	7th	11
5-28	At Min.	L	6-7	9	9	Aguilera	Power		19-29	7th	11
5-29	At Min.	L	3-9	6	15	Banks	Bielecki		19-30	7th	12
5-30	At Min.	L	2-8	6	15	Deshaies	Kramer	Trombley	19-31	7th	12
5-31	At N.Y.	L	2-8	8	14	Perez	Cook		19-32	7th	12½
6-1	At N.Y.	W	15-6	16	13	C. Young	Witt		20-32	7th	11½
6-2	At N.Y.	L	5-8	8	9	Key	M. Young	Farr	20-33	7th	11½
6-4	Min.	L	2-3	6	8	Deshaies	Hernandez	Aguilera	20-34	7th	12
6-5	Min.	W	7-6	13	12	Plunk	Trombley		21-34	7th	12
6-6	Min.	L	4-5	16	8	Erickson	Cook	Aguilera	21-35	7th	13
6-8	Bos.	W	5-4	6	7	Lilliquist	Harris		22-35	7th	12½
6-9	Bos.	W	3-2	7	7	Young	Darwin	Plunk	23-35	7th	12½
6-11	At Tex.	W	8-3	10	8	Slocumb	Brown		24-35	7th	13
6-12	At Tex.	W	10-9	15	14	M. Young	Rogers	Lilliquist	25-35	7th	13
6-13	At Tex.	L	1-5	6	6	Pavlik	Mesa		25-36	7th	13
6-14	At Det.	L	3-7	10	12	Wells	Bielecki		25-37	7th	14
6-15	At Det.	L	4-10	10	11	Krueger	Abbott		25-38	7th	15
6-16	At Det.	W	8-2	14	6	Kramer	Gullickson	Hernandez	26-38	7th	14
6-17	At Det.	L	5-9	4	11	Moore	Slocumb		26-39	7th	15
6-18	Bal.	L	1-4	8	8	McDonald	Mesa	Olson	26-40	7th	15
6-19	Bal.	W	3-0	7	8	Clark	Valenzuela	Plunk	27-40	7th	15
6-20	Bal.	L	3-6	8	11	Moyer	M. Young	Olson	27-41	7th	16
6-21	Mil.	W	3-0	8	4	Kramer	Navarro	Hernandez	28-41	7th	15½
6-22	Mil.	W	3-2	8	6	Slocumb	Eldred	Lilliquist	29-41	7th	14½

Date	Opp.	Res.	Score	(inn.*)	Hits	Opp. hits	Winning pitcher	Losing pitcher	Save	Record	Pos.	GB
6-23	Mil.	W	3-1		4	5	Mesa	Wegman	Hernandez	30-41	6th	13½
6-24	Mil.	L	3-5		3	10	Bones	Clark	Henry	30-42	7th	13½
6-25	K.C.	W	6-1		7	4	Cook	Gubicza		31-42	7th	12½
6-26	K.C.	W	7-4		7	8	Hernandez	DiPino	Plunk	32-42	6th	12½
6-27	K.C.	W	3-2		6	5	Plunk	Cone		33-42	6th	12½
6-28	Chi.	W	2-0		7	9	Mesa	Bere	Plunk	34-42	6th	12½
6-29	Chi.	W	8-2		14	7	Clark	Bolton		35-42	6th	12½
6-30	Chi.	W	4-2		9	8	Cook	Alvarez	Hernandez	36-42	6th	11½
7-2	At Cal.	W	10-8		16	12	Slocumb	Nelson	Plunk	37-42	6th	10½
7-3	At Cal.	W	5-3		10	10	Mesa	Hathaway	Plunk	38-42	6th	9½
7-4	At Cal.	L	6-7	(11)	12	12	Butcher	M. Young		38-43	6th	9½
7-5 (1)	At Oak.	L	5-6	(11)	12	9	Horsman	Cook	Eckersley	38-44	6th	9½
7-5 (2)	At Oak.	W	6-2		12	9	Clark	Young	Hernandez	39-44	6th	9
7-6	At Oak.	W	11-8		17	9	Plunk	Gossage	Hernandez	40-44	6th	9
7-7	At Oak.	L	0-3		4	9	Boever	Mesa	Eckersley	40-45	6th	9
7-9	At Sea.	L	4-6		10	8	Fleming	C. Young	Bosio	40-46	6th	8½
7-10	At Sea.	L	6-7		10	13	Bosio	Hernandez		40-47	6th	8½
7-11	At Sea.	L	4-5	(11)	9	16	Ayrault	Plunk		40-48	6th	8½
7-15	Cal.	W	7-3		8	9	DiPoto	Sanderson		41-48	6th	8½
7-16	Cal.	L	1-2		7	8	Finley	Clark	Butcher	41-49	6th	8½
7-17	Cal.	W	3-0		4	4	Mutis	Springer		42-49	6th	7½
7-18	Cal.	W	2-1		3	7	Lopez	Langston	DiPoto	43-49	6th	7½
7-19	Oak.	W	4-2		5	10	Young	Van Poppel	Hernandez	44-49	6th	7½
7-20	Oak.	W	9-5		11	11	Mesa	Mohler		45-49	6th	7
7-21	Oak.	L	2-7		6	13	Welch	Wertz		45-50	6th	7½
7-22	Sea.	L	2-3		9	6	Bosio	Mutis	Holman	45-51	6th	8½
7-23	Sea.	W	9-4		13	9	Lopez	Johnson		46-51	6th	7½
7-24	Sea.	L	5-6		8	13	Nelson	DiPoto	Holman	46-52	6th	8½
7-25	Sea.	W	11-9		11	12	Hernandez	Nelson	Lilliquist	47-52	6th	8½
7-26	At Chi.	L	3-4		6	6	Schwarz	DiPoto	Hernandez	47-53	6th	9
7-27	At Chi.	L	4-7		11	11	McDowell	Mutis	Hernandez	47-54	6th	10
7-28	At Chi.	L	4-9		10	6	Bere	Lopez		47-55	6th	11
7-30	At K.C.	L	0-3		5	8	Cone	Mesa		47-56	6th	11½
7-31	At K.C.	W	6-4		11	11	Kramer	Haney	Plunk	48-56	6th	11½
8-1	At K.C.	W	9-5		11	8	Wertz	Appier	Plunk	49-56	6th	11½
8-3	Det.	W	9-4	(7)	9	6	Lopez	Bergman	DiPoto	50-56	6th	12
8-4	Det.	L	3-8		9	10	Moore	Mesa		50-57	6th	12
8-5	Det.	W	8-4		8	12	Kramer	Doherty		51-57	6th	11
8-6	At Bal.	L	1-8		8	11	Sutcliffe	Mutis		51-58	6th	12
8-7	At Bal.	L	6-8		13	11	Mills	Tavarez	Olson	51-59	6th	12
8-8	At Bal.	L	6-7	(11)	12	13	Frohwirth	Plunk		51-60	6th	12
8-10	At Mil.	L	4-5	(10)	10	10	Henry	Plunk		51-61	6th	13
8-11	At Mil.	W	7-5		12	8	DiPoto	Orosco	Lilliquist	52-61	6th	13
8-12	At Mil.	W	8-6	(11)	14	8	DiPoto	Maldonado	Plunk	53-61	6th	12
8-13	Tex.	W	6-3		9	4	Hernandez	Lefferts		54-61	6th	11
8-14	Tex.	W	8-5		12	10	Tavarez	Dreyer	Plunk	55-61	6th	11
8-15	Tex.	L	1-4		4	6	Ryan	Mesa	Henke	55-62	6th	12
8-16	Tor.	L	1-4		6	11	Guzman	Ojeda	Ward	55-63	6th	13
8-17	Tor.	L	4-6		11	12	Morris	Kramer	Ward	55-64	6th	14
8-18	Tor.	L	6-7	(11)	10	12	Cox	Lilliquist	Ward	55-65	6th	15
8-19	At Bos.	W	5-1		11	8	Tavarez	Quantrill		56-65	6th	14½
8-20	At Bos.	W	7-6		9	12	DiPoto	Russell		57-65	6th	13½
8-21	At Bos.	W	10-5		12	13	Wertz	Harris		58-65	6th	12½
8-22	At Bos.	W	3-2	(11)	10	13	Kramer	Ryan	DiPoto	59-65	6th	12½
8-23	At Tor.	W	9-8		17	11	Hernandez	Eichhorn	DiPoto	60-65	6th	11½
8-24	At Tor.	L	6-8		11	11	Stottlemyre	Tavarez	Ward	60-66	6th	12½
8-25	At Tor.	L	7-10		11	17	Hentgen	Mesa	Ward	60-67	6th	13½
8-26	N.Y.	L	0-4		8	8	Hitchcock	Wertz	Wickman	60-68	6th	13½
8-27	N.Y.	W	9-2		14	8	Grimsley	Perez		61-68	6th	12½
8-28	N.Y.	W	8-4		16	10	Mutis	Key	Hernandez	62-68	6th	11½
8-29	N.Y.	L	8-14		13	16	Monteleone	Grimsley		62-69	6th	12½
8-31	At Min.	L	4-5	(22)	16	17	Merriman	Grimsley		62-70	6th	14
9-1	At Min.	W	12-7		22	10	Lilliquist	Trombley	Plunk	63-70	6th	14
9-2	At Min.	W	4-3		8	9	Kramer	Tapani	DiPoto	64-70	6th	13½
9-3	At N.Y.	W	7-3		12	9	Ojeda	Perez	DiPoto	65-70	6th	12½
9-4	At N.Y.	L	0-4		0	8	Abbott	Milacki		65-71	6th	12½
9-5	At N.Y.	L	2-7		5	16	Wickman	Mutis		65-72	6th	12½
9-7	Min.	L	0-6		4	10	Tapani	Grimsley		65-73	6th	12½
9-8	Min.	W	15-8		15	13	Mesa	Brummett		66-73	6th	11½
9-9	Min.	L	3-5	(12)	12	13	Aguilera	Lilliquist		66-74	6th	11½
9-10 (1)	Bos.	W	7-4		10	9	Ojeda	Clemens	DiPoto	67-74	6th	11½
9-10 (2)	Bos.	L	4-5	(11)	9	12	Ryan	Wertz		67-75	6th	12
9-11	Bos.	W	9-3		11	10	Lilliquist	Quantrill		68-75	6th	12
9-12	Bos.	L	1-11		10	15	Minchey	Grimsley		68-76	6th	13

Date	Opp.	Res.	Score	(inn.*)	Hits	Opp. hits	Winning pitcher	Losing pitcher	Save	Record	Pos.	GB
9-13	At Tex.	L	1-12		6	16	Brown	Mesa		68-77	6th	13½
9-14	At Tex.	W	2-0		8	5	Clark	Rogers	DiPoto	69-77	6th	13½
9-15	At Tex.	L	4-7		7	10	Carpenter	Hernandez	Henke	69-78	6th	14½
9-17	At Det.	W	3-1		8	7	Grimsley	Wells	DiPoto	70-78	6th	14½
9-18	At Det.	L	6-7		14	11	Bolton	Mesa	Davis	70-79	6th	15½
9-19	At Det.	W	12-2		16	7	Clark	Gullickson		71-79	6th	15½
9-20	Bal.	W	6-4		10	7	Milacki	Valenzuela	DiPoto	72-79	6th	15
9-21	Bal.	L	6-7		13	14	Mills	DiPoto		72-80	6th	16
9-22	Bal.	W	4-2		7	8	Hernandez	McDonald	DiPoto	73-80	6th	15
9-24	Mil.	L	8-11	(10)	12	19	Orosco	Lilliquist		73-81	6th	16½
9-25	Mil.	W	6-2		9	7	Clark	Navarro		74-81	6th	16½
9-26	Mil.	W	6-4		15	10	Hernandez	Ignasiak		75-81	6th	15½
9-27	At K.C.	L	5-6		8	10	Gubicza	DiPoto		75-82	6th	16½
9-28	At K.C.	W	3-2		10	9	Grimsley	Appier	Plunk	76-82	6th	16½
9-29	At K.C.	L	2-3		5	8	Montgomery	Hernandez		76-83	6th	17½
10-1	Chi.	L	2-4		10	7	Fernandez	Clark	Hernandez	76-84	6th	18
10-2	Chi.	L	2-4	(10)	7	7	Howard	Hernandez	Drahman	76-85	6th	18
10-3	Chi.	L	0-4		6	11	Bere	Nagy		76-86	6th	19

Monthly records: April (7-15), May (12-17), June (17-10), July (12-14), August (14-14), September (14-13), October (0-3).
*Innings, if other than nine.

HIGHLIGHTS

High point: In a 22-game span from June 25 to July 20, the Indians went 15-7 to improve their mark to 45-49, which gave them hope for a .500 finish.

Low point: The bottom dropped out of Cleveland's season before a game was even played. A March 22 boating accident took the lives of righthanders Steve Olin and Tim Crews and seriously injured lefthander Bob Ojeda. The Indians began a scramble for pitchers that lasted the entire year.

Turning point: On June 1, the Indians made deals for righthanders Heathcliff Slocumb and Jeremy Hernandez, both of whom helped stabilize the bullpen. Eventually, Slocumb was sent to Class AAA, but he and Hernandez bought Cleveland time until such prospects as righthanders Bill Wertz and Jerry DiPoto could make an impact.

Most valuable player: Left fielder Albert Belle. He batted .290 with 38 home runs and a big-league-best 129 RBIs.

Most valuable pitcher: Righthander Eric Plunk. He paced the team with 70 appearances and 15 saves while compiling a 2.79 ERA.

Most improved player: Center fielder Kenny Lofton. He improved his batting average 40 points (to .325) and led the league in steals (70). Lofton also scored 116 runs, an improvement of 20 over his 1992 total.

Most pleasant surprise: Right fielder Wayne Kirby. A career minor leaguer, Kirby seized his chance to win a regular job and became an ideal No. 2 hitter while also excelling defensively.

Biggest disappointment: In spring training, the battle for right field was a three-way fight among Mark Whiten, Glenallen Hill and Thomas Howard. It appeared to be a no-lose situation for the Indians, but none of the three took advantage of the opportunity and all eventually were traded.

Key injuries: Righthander Charles Nagy underwent shoulder surgery and was out from mid-May until the final day of the season. Ojeda did not return to action until August and then pitched only sporadically. Operations to pitching prospects Alan Embree (left elbow) and Dave Mlicki (right shoulder) cost each virtually the entire season. Catcher Sandy Alomar was limited to 64 games, mostly due to a back injury.

Notable: On April 8, second baseman Carlos Baerga became the first player ever to hit home runs from both sides of the plate in the same inning. . . . The Indians were swept by Chicago in their final series in Cleveland Stadium.

—SHELDON OCKER

RECORDS

1993 regular-season record: 76-86 (6th in A.L. East); 46-35 at home; 30-51 on road; 37-41 vs. East; 39-45 vs. West; 22-29 vs. LHP; 54-57 vs. RHP; 69-69 on grass; 7-17 on turf; 24-32 in daytime; 52-54 at night; 17-26 in one-run games; 2-12 in extra-inning games; 0-2 in doubleheaders.

Team record last five years: 359-451 (.443, ranks 14th in league in that span).

TEAM LEADERS

Batting average: Kenny Lofton (.325).
At-bats: Carlos Baerga (624).
Runs: Kenny Lofton (116).
Hits: Carlos Baerga (200).
Total bases: Albert Belle (328).
Doubles: Albert Belle (36).
Triples: Kenny Lofton (8).
Home runs: Albert Belle (38).
Runs batted in: Albert Belle (129).
Stolen bases: Kenny Lofton (70).
Slugging percentage: Albert Belle (.552).
On-base percentage: Kenny Lofton (.408).
Wins: Jose Mesa (10).
Earned-run average: Jose Mesa (4.92).
Complete games: Jose Mesa (3).
Shutouts: Jeff Mutis (1).
Saves: Eric Plunk (15).
Innings pitched: Jose Mesa (208⅔).
Strikeouts: Jose Mesa (118).

GAMES BY POSITION

Catcher: Junior Ortiz 95, Sandy Alomar 64, Jesse Levis 29, Lance Parrish 10.
First base: Paul Sorrento 144, Carlos Martinez 22, Randy Milligan 18, Reggie Jefferson 15.
Second base: Carlos Baerga 150, Jeff Treadway 19, Alvaro Espinoza 2.
Third base: Alvaro Espinoza 99, Jim Thome 47, Jeff Treadway 42, Carlos Martinez 35.
Shortstop: Felix Fermin 140, Alvaro Espinoza 35, Mark Lewis 13.
Outfield: Albert Belle 150, Kenny Lofton 146, Wayne Kirby 123, Thomas Howard 47, Glenallen Hill 39, Candy Maldonado 26, Paul Sorrento 3, Manny Ramirez 1.
Designated hitter: Reggie Jefferson 88, Manny Ramirez 21, Carlos Martinez 19, Glenallen Hill 18, Sam Horn 11, Albert Belle 9, Thomas Howard 7, Wayne Kirby 5, Carlos Baerga 4, Jeff Treadway 4, Candy Maldonado 2, Randy Milligan 1, Paul Sorrento 1.

TOP DRAFT CHOICES

1. **Daron Kirkreit,** RHP, UC Riverside.
2. **Casey Whitten,** LHP, Indiana State.
3. **J.J. Done,** RHP, Pace High School, Miami.
4. **Travis Driskill,** RHP, Texas Tech University.
5. **Kris Hanson,** RHP, University of Wisconsin-Whitewater.
6. **Matt Hobbie,** OF, Sarasota (Fla.) High School.
7. **Seth Greisinger,** RHP, McLean High School, Falls Church, Va.
8. **Steve Kline,** LHP, West Virginia University.
9. **Greg Thomas,** 1B, Vanderbilt University.
10. **Derrick Cook,** RHP, Robert E. Lee High School, Staunton, Va.

DETROIT TIGERS
AMERICAN LEAGUE EAST DIVISION

N Denotes night game (any game starting after 5 p.m.).
☐ Home games shaded.
* At Three Rivers Stadium in Pittsburgh.

APRIL

SUN	MON	TUE	WED	THU	FRI	SAT
					1	2
3	4 BOS	5	6 BOS	7 BOS N	8 N NY	9 N NY
10 NY	11 N BAL	12	13 BAL	14 BAL N	15 N NY	16 N NY
17 NY	18 N KC	19 KC	20 KC	21	22 N CHI	23 N CHI
24 CHI	25 N TEX	26 N TEX	27 N KC	28 N KC	29 N CHI	30 CHI

MAY

SUN	MON	TUE	WED	THU	FRI	SAT
1 CHI	2 N TEX	3 TEX	4 TEX	5	6 N SEA	7 SEA
8 SEA	9	10 N OAK	11 N OAK	12 OAK N	13 N CLE	14 CLE
15 CLE	16 N TOR	17 N TOR	18 N TOR	19	20 N MIL	21 MIL
22 MIL	23	24 N CAL	25 N CAL	26 CAL N	27 N MIN	28 N MIN
29 N MIN	30 N BAL	31 N BAL				

JUNE

SUN	MON	TUE	WED	THU	FRI	SAT
		1 N BAL	2 BAL N	3 N MIN	4 MIN	
5 MIN	6 N BOS	7 N BOS	8 N BOS	9 N CAL	10 N CAL	11 N CAL
12 CAL	13	14 N MIL	15 N MIL	16 MIL N	17 N TOR	18 TOR
19 TOR	20 N CLE	21 N CLE	22 CLE	23	24 N OAK	25 OAK
26 OAK	27 N SEA	28 N SEA	29 N SEA	30		

JULY

SUN	MON	TUE	WED	THU	FRI	SAT
					1 N TEX	2 N TEX
3 N TEX	4 N TEX	5 N CHI	6 N CHI	7 N CHI	8 N TEX	9 TEX
10 TEX	11 ALL-STAR GAME	12	13 N KC	14 N KC	15 N KC	16 N KC
17 N KC	18 N CHI	19 N CHI	20 CHI	21	22 N KC	23 N KC
24 KC	25	26 N SEA	27 N SEA	28 SEA N	29 N OAK	30 OAK
31 N OAK						

AUGUST

SUN	MON	TUE	WED	THU	FRI	SAT
	1 N CLE	2 N CLE	3 N CLE	4 N CLE	5 N TOR	6 TOR
7 TOR	8 N MIL	9 N MIL	10 N MIL	11 MIL N	12 N CAL	13 CAL
14 CAL	15	16 N MIN	17 N MIN	18 MIN N	19 N BOS	20 BOS
21 BOS	22 N MIN	23 N MIN	24 MIN	25 N BOS	26 N BOS	27 BOS
28 BOS	29 N NY	30 N NY	31 N NY			

SEPTEMBER

SUN	MON	TUE	WED	THU	FRI	SAT
				1 NY	2 N BAL	3 N BAL
4 BAL	5	6 N NY	7 N NY	8 NY N	9 N BAL	10 BAL
11 BAL	12	13 N CAL	14 N CAL	15	16 N MIL	17 MIL
18 MIL	19 N TOR	20 TOR N	21 N TOR	22 N CLE	23 N CLE	24 CLE
25 CLE	26 N OAK	27 N OAK	28 OAK	29	30 N SEA	

OCTOBER

SUN	MON	TUE	WED	THU	FRI	SAT
						1 N SEA
2 SEA						

CLUB DIRECTORY

Owners
Michael Ilitch
Marian Ilitch
Board of directors
Michael Ilitch, Chairman
Marian Ilitch
Charles P. Jones
Jay Bielfield
Denise Ilitch Lites
Ronald Ilitch
Michael Ilitch Jr.
Lisa Ilitch Murray
Atanas Ilitch
Christopher Ilitch
Carole Ilitch
Owner, chairman, president
Michael Ilitch
Owner, secretary treasurer
Marian Ilitch
Vice presidents
Atanas Ilitch
Christopher Ilitch
Senior director, general manager
Joe Klein
General counsel
Jay Bielfield
Chief financial officer
Gerald Pasternak
League affairs
John Ziegler
Urban development
Emmett Moten
Senior director, assistant general manager
Gary Vitto
Director minor league operations
Dave Miller
Director field operations
John Lipon
Assistant director equipment
Jim Schmakel
Asst. manager equipment and clubhouse
John Nelson
Traveling secretary
Bill Brown
Team physicians
Clarence S. Livingood, M.D.
David J. Collon, M.D.
Terry Lock, M.D.
Louis Saco, M.D. (Florida)
Head trainer
Russ Miller
Trainer
Pio DiSalvo
Strength and conditioning coach
Brad Andress

Scouting
Gary Blaylock
Gwen Keating
Minor league staff
Audrey Zielinski
Senior director public relations
Daniel Ewald
Director of marketing
Michael Dietz
Director of stadium operations
John Pettit
Controller
Scott Fisher
Director of community relations
Jim Price
Director ticket operations
Ken Marchetti
Director ticket sales
Gino D'Ambrosio
Marketing coordinator
James Brylewski
Season/group sales coordinator
Jodi Schroeder
Director of scouting
Jeff Scott
Scouts
Ruben Amaro
Arnie Beyeler
Wayne Blackburn
Gary Blaylock
Nathan Durst
Andy Hancock
Jack Hays
Harvey Koepf
Lou Laslo
Joe Lewis
Dennis Lieberthal
Juan Lopez
Jeff Malinoff
Stan Meek
John Mirabelli
Mark Monahan
Glenn Murdock
Ramon Pena
Dee Phillips
Dave Roberts
Joe Robinson
Don Rowland
Bill Schudlich
Steve Souchock
Clyde Weir
Dick Wiencek
Rob Wilfong

Manager—Sparky Anderson (11).
Coaches—Larry Herndon (31), Billy Muffett (56), Gene Roof (52), Dick Tracewski (53), Dan Whitmer (59).

No.	PITCHERS	B/T	Ht./Wt.	Born	1993 clubs
43	Bergman, Sean	R/R	6-4/205	4-11-70	Toledo, Detroit
26	Blomdahl, Ben	R/R	6-2/185	12-30-70	London, Toledo
37	Boever, Joe	R/R	6-1/200	10-4-60	Oakland, Detroit
49	Bolton, Tom	L/L	6-3/185	5-6-62	Detroit
48	Davis, Storm	R/R	6-4/225	12-26-61	Oakland, Detroit
44	Doherty, John	R/R	6-4/210	6-11-67	Detroit
48	Gardiner, Mike	B/R	6-0/200	10-19-65	Montreal, Ottawa, Toledo, Detroit
34	Gohr, Greg	R/R	6-3/205	10-29-67	Detroit, Toledo
42	Groom, Buddy	L/L	6-2/200	7-10-65	Toledo, Detroit
36	Gullickson, Bill	R/R	6-3/225	2-20-59	Lakeland, Toledo, Detroit
39	Henneman, Mike	R/R	6-4/205	12-11-61	Detroit
27	Knudsen, Kurt	R/R	6-3/200	2-20-67	Toledo, Detroit
30	Krueger, Bill	L/L	6-5/205	4-24-58	Detroit, Toledo
13	Leiter, Mark	R/R	6-3/210	4-13-63	Detroit
32	Lima, Jose	R/R	6-2/170	9-30-72	London
40	Lira, Felipe	R/R	6-0/170	4-26-72	London, Toledo
21	Moore, Mike	R/R	6-4/205	11-26-59	Detroit
16	Wells, David	L/L	6-4/225	5-20-63	Detroit
28	Withem, Shannon	R/R	6-3/185	9-21-72	Lakeland

No.	CATCHERS	B/T	Ht./Wt.	Born	1993 clubs
19	Kreuter, Chad	B/R	6-2/195	8-26-64	Detroit
12	Rowland, Rich	R/R	6-1/215	2-25-67	Toledo, Detroit
20	Tettleton, Mickey	B/R	6-2/212	9-16-60	Detroit

No.	INFIELDERS	B/T	Ht./Wt.	Born	1993 clubs
9	Barnes, Skeeter	R/R	5-10/180	3-7-57	Detroit
8	Brogna, Rico	L/L	6-2/200	4-18-70	Toledo
25	DuBose, Brian	L/R	6-3/208	5-17-71	Lakeland
45	Fielder, Cecil	R/R	6-3/250	9-21-63	Detroit
24	Fryman, Travis	R/R	6-1/194	3-25-69	Detroit
35	Gomez, Chris	R/R	6-1/183	6-16-71	Toledo, Detroit
7	Livingstone, Scott	L/R	6-0/198	7-15-65	Detroit
4	Phillips, Tony	B/R	5-10/175	4-25-59	Detroit
3	Trammell, Alan	R/R	6-0/185	2-21-58	Detroit
1	Whitaker, Lou	L/R	5-11/180	5-12-57	Detroit

No.	OUTFIELDERS	B/T	Ht./Wt.	Born	1993 clubs
29	Bautista, Danny	R/R	5-11/170	5-24-72	London, Detroit
17	Clark, Tony	B/R	6-8/205	6-15-72	Lakeland
22	Cuyler, Milt	B/R	5-10/185	10-7-68	Detroit
33	Davis, Eric	R/R	6-3/185	5-29-62	Los Angeles, Detroit
10	Hare, Shawn	L/L	6-1/200	3-26-67	Toledo
18	Pemberton, Rudy	R/R	6-1/185	12-17-69	London

BALLPARK INFORMATION

Ballpark (capacity, surface)
Tiger Stadium (52,416, grass)
Address
Tiger Stadium
Detroit, MI 48216
Business phone
313-962-4000
Ticket information
313-962-4000
Ticket prices
$15 (box seats)
$12 (reserved seats)
$8 (grandstand reserved seats)
$5 (bleacher seats)
Field dimensions (from home plate)
To left field at foul line, 340 feet
To center field, 440 feet
To right field at foul line, 325 feet
First game played
April 20, 1912 (Cleveland Naps 6, Tigers 5)

MINOR LEAGUE AFFILIATES

Class	Team	League	Manager
AAA	Toledo	International	Joe Sparks
AA	Trenton	Eastern	Tom Runnells
A	Fayetteville	South Atlantic	Mark Wagner
A	Lakeland	Florida State	Gerry Groninger
A	Jamestown	New York-Pennsylvania	Dave Anderson
Rookie	Bristol	Appalachian	Dwight Lowery

☐ BROADCAST INFORMATION ☐

Radio: WJR-AM (760). Broadcasters: Rick Rizzs, Bob Rathbun.
TV: WDIV-TV (Channel 4). Broadcasters: Al Kaline, George Kell.
Cable TV: Pro Am Sports Systems. Broadcasters: Jim Northrup, Jim Price.

SPRING TRAINING

Ballpark (city): Marchant Stadium (Lakeland, Fla.).
Ticket information: 813-499-8229.

HISTORY

YEAR-BY-YEAR RECORDS

Year	Pos.	W	L	Pct.	GB	Year	Pos.	W	L	Pct.	GB
1901	3rd	74	61	.548	8½	1950	2nd	95	59	.617	3
1902	7th	52	83	.385	30½	1951	5th	73	81	.474	25
1903	5th	65	71	.478	25	1952	8th	50	104	.325	45
1904	7th	62	90	.408	32	1953	6th	60	94	.390	40½
1905	3rd	79	74	.516	15½	1954	5th	68	86	.442	43
1906	6th	71	78	.477	21	1955	5th	79	75	.513	17
1907	1st	92	58	.613 +	1½	1956	5th	82	72	.532	15
1908	1st	90	63	.588 +	1	1957	4th	78	76	.506	20
1909	1st	98	54	.645 +	3½	1958	5th	77	77	.500	15
1910	3rd	86	68	.558	18	1959	4th	76	78	.494	18
1911	2nd	89	65	.578	13½	1960	6th	71	83	.461	26
1912	6th	69	84	.451	36½	1961	2nd	101	61	.623	8
1913	6th	66	87	.431	30	1962	4th	85	76	.528	10½
1914	4th	80	73	.523	19½	1963	T5th	79	83	.488	25½
1915	2nd	100	54	.649	2½	1964	4th	85	77	.525	14
1916	3rd	87	67	.565	4	1965	4th	89	73	.549	13
1917	4th	78	75	.510	21½	1966	3rd	88	74	.543	10
1918	7th	55	71	.437	20	1967	T2nd	91	71	.562	1
1919	4th	80	60	.571	8	1968	1st	103	59	.636 +12	
1920	7th	61	93	.396	37	1969	2nd	90	72	.556	19
1921	6th	71	82	.464	27	1970	4th	79	83	.488	29
1922	3rd	79	75	.513	15	1971	2nd	91	71	.562	12
1923	2nd	83	71	.539	16	1972	1st*	86	70	.551 +	½
1924	3rd	86	68	.558	6	1973	3rd	85	77	.525	12
1925	4th	81	73	.526	16½	1974	6th	72	90	.444	19
1926	6th	79	75	.513	12	1975	6th	57	102	.358	37½
1927	4th	82	71	.536	27½	1976	5th	74	87	.460	24
1928	6th	68	86	.442	33	1977	4th	74	88	.457	26
1929	6th	70	84	.455	36	1978	5th	86	76	.531	13½
1930	5th	75	79	.487	27	1979	5th	85	76	.528	18
1931	7th	61	93	.396	47	1980	5th	84	78	.519	19
1932	5th	76	75	.503	29½	1981	4th/T2nd	60	49	.550	†
1933	5th	75	79	.487	25	1982	4th	83	79	.512	12
1934	1st	101	53	.656 +	7	1983	2nd	92	70	.568	6
1935	1st	93	58	.616 +	3	1984	1st‡	104	58	.642	+15
1936	2nd	83	71	.539	19½	1985	3rd	84	77	.522	15
1937	2nd	89	65	.578	13	1986	3rd	87	75	.537	8½
1938	4th	84	70	.545	16	1987	1st*	98	64	.605 +	2
1939	5th	81	73	.526	26½	1988	2nd	88	74	.543	1
1940	1st	90	64	.584 +	1	1989	7th	59	103	.364	30
1941	T4th	75	79	.487	26	1990	3rd	79	83	.488	9
1942	5th	73	81	.474	30	1991	T2nd	84	78	.519	7
1943	5th	78	76	.506	20	1992	6th	75	87	.463	21
1944	2nd	88	66	.571	1	1993	T3rd	85	77	.525	10
1945	1st	88	65	.575 +	1½						
1946	2nd	92	62	.597	12						
1947	2nd	85	69	.552	12						
1948	5th	78	76	.506	18½						
1949	4th	87	67	.565	10						

*Lost Championship Series. †First half 31-26; second 29-23. ‡Won Championship Series.

MANAGERS

Name	Record	Years
George Stallings	74-61	1901
Frank Dwyer	52-83	1902
Ed Barrow	97-117	'03-04
Bobby Lowe	30-44	1904
Bill Armour	150-152	'05-06
Hugh Jennings	1131-972	'07-20
Ty Cobb	479-444	'21-26
George Moriarty	150-157	'27-28
Bucky Harris	516-557	'29-33
		'55-56
Del Baker	392-336	1933
		'38-42
Mickey Cochrane	379-278	'34-38
Steve O'Neill	509-414	'43-48
Red Rolfe	278-256	'49-52
Fred Hutchinson	155-235	'52-54
Jack Tighe	99-104	'57-58
Bill Norman	58-64	'58-59
Jimmie Dykes	118-115	'59-60
Joe Gordon	26-31	1960
Bob Scheffing	210-173	'61-63
Chuck Dressen	221-189	'63-65
		1966
Bob Swift	56-43	'65, '66
Frank Skaff	40-39	1966
Mayo Smith	363-285	'67-70
Billy Martin	248-204	'71-73
Joe Schultz	14-14	1973
Ralph Houk	366-443	'74-78
Les Moss	27-26	'1979
Sparky Anderson	1318-1102	'79-93

DAY BY DAY

Date	Opp.	Res.	Score (inn.*)	Hits	Opp. hits	Winning pitcher	Losing pitcher	Save	Record	Pos.	GB
4-5	At Oak.	L	4-9	9	10	Welch	Moore	Eckersley	0-1	T5th	1
4-7	At Oak.	L	7-12	13	10	Downs	Kiely		0-2	T6th	2
4-8	At Oak.	W	3-2	7	7	Doherty	Davis	Henneman	1-2	T5th	2
4-9	At Cal.	L	5-7	4	12	Valera	Leiter		1-3	6th	2
4-10	At Cal.	W	5-2	8	5	Wells	Farrell	Henneman	2-3	T5th	2
4-11	At Cal.	L	6-7	11	13	Crim	Krueger	Grahe	2-4	6th	2
4-13	Oak.	W	20-4	18	7	Moore	Davis		3-4	T4th	2
4-15	Oak.	W	3-2	7	9	Haas	Eckersley		4-4	4th	2½
4-16	Sea.	W	5-0	8	5	Wells	Johnson		5-4	T3rd	1½
4-17	Sea.	W	20-3	20	6	Krueger	Hampton		6-4	T2nd	1½
4-18	Sea.	W	8-7	12	13	MacDonald	Charlton		7-4	2nd	1½
4-19	Sea.	L	6-10	10	10	Hanson	Doherty	Henry	7-5	T2nd	2½
4-20	Tex.	W	3-1	5	4	Wells	Rogers	Henneman	8-5	2nd	2½
4-21	Tex.	W	5-4	7	14	Krueger	Lefferts	Henneman	9-5	2nd	1½
4-23	At Min.	W	12-4	14	7	Moore	Erickson		10-5	1st	...
4-24	At Min.	W	17-1	18	8	Doherty	Mahomes		11-5	1st	...
4-25	At Min.	W	16-5	14	8	Leiter	Guthrie		12-5	1st	+2
4-26	At K.C.	W	5-3	8	12	Bolton	Gubicza		13-5	1st	+2½
4-27	At K.C.	L	3-4 (10)	10	12	Meacham	Kiely		13-6	1st	+½
4-28	At Tex.	L	5-6 (11)	9	15	Henke	Munoz		13-7	1st	+½
4-29	At Tex.	W	3-1	7	5	Doherty	Leibrandt	Henneman	14-7	1st	+½
4-30	Min.	W	8-0	10	4	Wells	Banks		15-7	1st	+2
5-1	Min.	L	2-5	6	6	Tapani	Bolton	Aguilera	15-8	1st	+1
5-2	Min.	L	3-6	10	10	Trombley	Haas	Aguilera	15-9	T1st	...
5-4	K.C.	W	5-3	9	10	Johnson	Gordon	Henneman	16-9	1st	+1
5-5	K.C.	L	3-4	12	6	Montgomery	Wells		16-10	1st	+½
5-7	N.Y.	W	7-6 (12)	11	13	MacDonald	Kamieniecki		17-10	1st	+1
5-8	N.Y.	L	8-10 (11)	12	15	Farr	Johnson		17-11	1st	+1
5-9	N.Y.	L	2-11	12	14	Wickman	Doherty		17-12	1st	+½
5-10	N.Y.	W	2-1 (10)	5	5	MacDonald	Monteleone		18-12	1st	+½
5-11	At Tor.	W	12-7	14	13	Gullickson	Stottlemyre		19-12	1st	+½
5-12	At Tor.	W	13-8	16	11	Krueger	Hentgen	Henneman	20-12	1st	+2
5-13	At Tor.	L	5-6	10	10	Castillo	MacDonald		20-13	1st	+½
5-14	Bal.	W	4-3	8	9	Henneman	Frohwirth		21-13	1st	+2½
5-15	Bal.	W	5-3	7	8	Krueger	Mills		22-13	1st	+2½
5-16	Bal.	L	2-3	6	10	Mussina	Haas	Olson	22-14	1st	+2½
5-18	At Mil.	W	5-1	11	6	Leiter	Eldred		23-14	1st	+2
5-19	At Mil.	W	8-6	16	9	Doherty	Boddicker	Henneman	24-14	1st	+2
5-20	At Mil.	W	6-2	8	7	Wells	Wegman		25-14	1st	+2½
5-21	At Cle.	L	5-10	11	15	Bielecki	Gullickson	C. Young	25-15	1st	+2½
5-22	At Cle.	W	5-1	9	5	Moore	Mesa		26-15	1st	+2½
5-23	At Cle.	W	4-2	9	7	Leiter	M. Young	Henneman	27-15	1st	+3½
5-24	Bos.	L	5-6 (10)	9	17	Ryan	MacDonald	Russell	27-16	1st	+2½
5-25	Bos.	W	4-1	4	4	Wells	Viola	Henneman	28-16	1st	+2½
5-26	Bos.	W	4-2	6	6	Gullickson	Dopson	Knudsen	29-16	1st	+3½
5-28	At Sea.	L	3-4 (10)	9	8	Swan	Bolton		29-17	1st	+4
5-29	At Sea.	W	3-2	6	8	Leiter	Hanson	MacDonald	30-17	1st	+4
5-30	At Sea.	L	5-9	11	11	Charlton	Krueger		30-18	1st	+3
6-1	Chi.	L	2-4	6	11	Fernandez	Gullickson	Hernandez	30-19	1st	+½
6-2	Chi.	L	1-10	5	11	Bere	Moore		30-20	1st	+½
6-3	Chi.	W	5-3	9	5	Leiter	McCaskill		31-20	1st	+1
6-4	Cal.	L	3-6	6	6	Langston	Henneman	Frey	31-21	1st	...
6-5	Cal.	W	5-1	6	6	Doherty	Finley	MacDonald	32-21	1st	...
6-6	Cal.	W	11-4	13	7	Gullickson	Farrell		33-21	1st	+1
6-7	At Chi.	L	3-7	8	10	Bere	Moore	Pall	33-22	1st	...
6-8	At Chi.	W	6-4	8	10	Leiter	Schwarz	Henneman	34-22	1st	...
6-9	At Chi.	W	7-4	12	9	Wells	Alvarez	Henneman	35-22	1st	+1
6-10	Tor.	W	5-3	7	8	Doherty	Guzman	MacDonald	36-22	1st	+2
6-11	Tor.	W	6-1	8	6	Gullickson	Morris		37-22	1st	+3
6-12	Tor.	W	12-1	15	9	Moore	Leiter		38-22	1st	+4
6-13	Tor.	L	4-13	6	15	Hentgen	Leiter		38-23	1st	+3
6-14	Cle.	W	7-3	12	10	Wells	Bielecki		39-23	1st	+4
6-15	Cle.	W	10-4	11	10	Krueger	Abbott		40-23	1st	+4
6-16	Cle.	L	2-8	6	14	Kramer	Gullickson	Hernandez	40-24	1st	+3
6-17	Cle.	W	9-5	11	4	Moore	Slocumb		41-24	1st	+3
6-18	Mil.	L	3-6	8	11	Eldred	Leiter	Henry	41-25	1st	+2
6-19	Mil.	W	10-7	10	11	Wells	Wegman		42-25	1st	+2
6-20	Mil.	W	7-3	10	8	Doherty	Bones		43-25	1st	+2
6-22	At Bal.	L	9-12	10	13	Poole	Krueger	Olson	43-26	1st	+1
6-23	At Bal.	L	2-6	8	7	Sutcliffe	Moore		43-27	1st	+1

— 41 —

Date	Opp.	Res.	Score	(Inn.*)	Hits	Opp. hits	Winning pitcher	Losing pitcher	Save	Record	Pos.	GB
6-24	At Bal.	L	2-6		9	11	McDonald	Leiter	Pennington	43-28	1st	...
6-25	At Bos.	L	2-8		6	10	Darwin	Wells	Harris	43-29	1st	...
6-26	At Bos.	L	4-13		8	15	Melendez	Doherty		43-30	2nd	1
6-27	At Bos.	L	2-8		8	14	Dopson	Gullickson		43-31	2nd	2
6-28	At N.Y.	L	2-8		5	12	Key	Moore		43-32	2nd	3
6-29	At N.Y.	L	3-4	(10)	8	8	Munoz	Bolton		43-33	3rd	4
6-30	At N.Y.	L	0-7		3	10	Abbott	Wells		43-34	3rd	4
7-1	Tex.	L	5-8		10	14	Schooler	Doherty	Whiteside	43-35	3rd	4½
7-2	Tex.	W	6-4	(10)	7	5	Henneman	Patterson		44-35	3rd	3½
7-3	Tex.	L	5-11		13	15	Schooler	Knudsen		44-36	3rd	3½
7-4	Tex.	L	6-8		13	11	Pavlik	Leiter		44-37	3rd	3½
7-5	At Min.	L	3-13		11	17	Erickson	Wells		44-38	3rd	3½
7-6	At Min.	W	4-1		8	7	Doherty	Banks	Henneman	45-38	3rd	3½
7-7	At Min.	W	8-4		15	11	Gullickson	Deshaies		46-38	3rd	2½
7-8	At K.C.	L	5-6	(11)	11	18	Montgomery	Groom		46-39	3rd	2½
7-9	At K.C.	W	10-5		11	14	Bergman	Haney		47-39	3rd	1½
7-10	At K.C.	W	9-8		13	11	Knudsen	Sampen	Henneman	48-39	2nd	½
7-11	At K.C.	L	2-6		5	11	Appier	Doherty		48-40	2nd	½
7-15	At Tex.	L	7-12		8	17	Bohanon	Knudsen	Henke	48-41	T2nd	1½
7-16	At Tex.	L	6-9		10	12	Rogers	Wells	Henke	48-42	4th	1½
7-17	At Tex.	W	6-4		12	6	Gullickson	Pavlik	Henneman	49-42	T3rd	½
7-18	At Tex.	W	2-0		9	3	Doherty	Leibrandt		50-42	T3rd	½
7-19	Min.	L	2-4		6	10	Erickson	Bergman	Aguilera	50-43	4th	1½
7-20	Min.	L	3-4		4	11	Deshaies	Leiter	Aguilera	50-44	5th	2
7-21	Min.	L	2-7		7	14	Tapani	Wells	Willis	50-45	5th	2½
7-22	K.C.	L	6-12		7	16	Appier	Gullickson		50-46	5th	3½
7-23	K.C.	L	6-7		13	12	Pichardo	MacDonald	Montgomery	50-47	5th	3½
7-24	K.C.	L	3-6		7	7	Gordon	Bergman	Montgomery	50-48	5th	4½
7-25	K.C.	W	3-0		4	1	Moore	Cone		51-48	5th	4½
7-26	N.Y.	W	5-2		11	10	Wells	Key	Henneman	52-48	5th	4
7-27	N.Y.	L	2-5		7	12	Abbott	Gullickson	Farr	52-49	5th	5
7-28	N.Y.	L	7-12		11	18	Wickman	Doherty		52-50	5th	6
7-29	At Tor.	L	4-7		7	8	Castillo	Bolton	Ward	52-51	5th	7
7-30	At Tor.	W	8-5		19	11	Moore	Stewart	Henneman	53-51	5th	6
7-31	At Tor.	L	1-3		11	9	Timlin	Wells	Ward	53-52	5th	7
8-1	At Tor.	L	1-2		6	6	Morris	Henneman		53-53	5th	8
8-3	At Cle.	L	4-9	(7)	6	9	Lopez	Bergman	DiPoto	53-54	5th	9½
8-4	At Cle.	W	8-3		10	9	Moore	Mesa		54-54	5th	8½
8-5	At Cle.	L	4-8		12	8	Kramer	Doherty		54-55	5th	8½
8-6	Bos.	W	5-1		6	3	Gullickson	Clemens		55-55	5th	8½
8-7	Bos.	L	1-4		6	4	Darwin	Bergman	Russell	55-56	5th	8½
8-8	Bos.	W	5-1		9	7	Bolton	Dopson		56-56	5th	7½
8-9	Bal.	L	1-4		4	6	Rhodes	Moore		56-57	5th	8
8-10	Bal.	W	15-1		10	6	Doherty	McDonald		57-57	5th	8
8-11	Bal.	W	15-5		18	11	Gullickson	Sutcliffe		58-57	5th	8
8-12	Bal.	W	17-11		20	16	Henneman	Frohwirth		59-57	5th	7
8-13 (1)	At Mil.	L	1-6		6	8	Miranda	Groom		59-58	5th	7
8-13 (2)	At Mil.	L	1-7		6	10	Bones	Bolton		59-59	5th	7½
8-14	At Mil.	W	5-1		14	5	Moore	Higuera	Henneman	60-59	5th	7½
8-15	At Mil.	L	4-6		9	9	Eldred	Doherty	Maldonado	60-60	5th	8½
8-16	At Cal.	W	7-2		12	9	Gullickson	Hathaway		61-60	5th	8½
8-17	At Cal.	W	9-3		10	7	Bolton	Farrell		62-60	5th	8½
8-18	At Cal.	W	8-6		11	10	Knudsen	Frey	Henneman	63-60	5th	8½
8-20	Oak.	L	6-7		10	9	Witt	Doherty	Eckersley	63-61	5th	7½
8-21	Oak.	W	4-3		9	8	Gullickson	Downs	Davis	64-61	5th	7½
8-22	Oak.	W	5-3		8	7	Bolton	Van Poppel	Henneman	65-61	5th	7½
8-23	Oak.	W	9-0		13	1	Moore	Karsay		66-61	5th	6½
8-24	Sea.	W	4-1		7	3	Doherty	Hanson		67-61	5th	6½
8-25	Sea.	W	7-4		14	9	Gullickson	Leary	Davis	68-61	4th	6½
8-27	At Oak.	W	13-4		14	9	Bolton	Van Poppel		69-61	3rd	5
8-28	At Oak.	W	5-3		10	11	Moore	Karsay	Henneman	70-61	3rd	4
8-29	At Oak.	L	3-7		6	10	Welch	Doherty		70-62	3rd	5
8-30	At Sea.	W	13-2		16	5	Gullickson	Leary		71-62	3rd	5
8-31	At Sea.	L	4-5		6	11	Nelson	Henneman	Power	71-63	4th	6
9-1	At Sea.	L	3-9		9	13	Fleming	Moore		71-64	4th	7
9-3	Chi.	L	6-8		8	11	Bere	Doherty	Hernandez	71-65	4th	7
9-4	Chi.	L	2-11		7	12	Fernandez	Gullickson		71-66	4th	7
9-5	Chi.	L	3-5		8	11	Alvarez	Moore	Hernandez	71-67	4th	7
9-7	Cal.	W	10-6		15	9	Boever	Scott		72-67	5th	6
9-8	Cal.	W	4-2		8	7	Doherty	Langston	Henneman	73-67	4th	5
9-9	Cal.	L	0-6		6	12	Magrane	Gullickson		73-68	4th	5
9-10	At Chi.	W	4-0		9	2	Moore	Fernandez		74-68	4th	6
9-11	At Chi.	L	1-3		5	9	Alvarez	Wells	Hernandez	74-69	4th	6
9-12	At Chi.	W	6-3		9	7	Doherty	McDowell	Davis	75-69	4th	6

Date	Opp.	Res.	Score (Inn.*)	Hits	Opp. hits	Winning pitcher	Losing pitcher	Save	Record	Pos.	GB
9-14	Tor.	L	5-9	7	12	Guzman	Davis		75-70	4th	7
9-15	Tor.	L	8-14	13	19	Stottlemyre	Moore	Ward	75-71	5th	8
9-17	Cle.	L	1-3	7	8	Grimsley	Wells	DiPoto	75-72	5th	9
9-18	Cle.	W	7-6	11	14	Bolton	Mesa	Davis	76-72	T4th	9
9-19	Cle.	L	2-12	7	16	Clark	Gullickson		76-73	5th	10
9-20	Mil.	W	6-3	10	7	Moore	Bones	Boever	77-73	6th	9½
9-21	Mil.	L	4-7	13	10	Ignasiak	Davis	Orosco	77-74	5th	10½
9-22	Mil.	W	8-4	8	9	Wells	Eldred		78-74	5th	9½
9-24	At Bal.	W	2-0	6	7	Doherty	Moyer		79-74	T4th	10
9-26 (1)	At Bal.	W	9-4	12	9	Gullickson	Rhodes		80-74	4th	9½
9-26 (2)	At Bal.	W	6-5	14	13	Henneman	Mills	Boever	81-74	4th	9
9-28 (1)	At Bos.	L	6-11	10	15	Sele	Krueger		81-75	4th	10½
9-28 (2)	At Bos.	W	7-6 (11)	12	13	Henneman	Fossas	Knudsen	82-75	4th	10
9-29	At Bos.	W	8-7	16	13	Boever	Bailey	Henneman	83-75	T3rd	10
9-30	At Bos.	W	7-4	10	5	Knudsen	Taylor	Boever	84-75	3rd	10
10-1	At N.Y.	L	6-9	12	12	Wickman	Boever	Smith	84-76	T3rd	10
10-2	At N.Y.	W	4-1	12	8	Krueger	Abbott	Henneman	85-76	T3rd	9
10-3	At N.Y.	L	1-2	5	4	Munoz	Bolton		85-77	T3rd	10

Monthly records: April (15-7), May (15-11), June (13-16), July (10-18), August (18-11), September (13-12), October (1-2).
*Innings, if other than nine.

HIGHLIGHTS

High point: On June 20, the Tigers finished an 8-3 homestand and stood 43-25, good for a two-game lead in the A.L. East.

Low point: From June 22-August 3, Detroit lost 29 of 39 games to fall below .500 (53-54) and into fifth place, 9½ games out.

Turning point: The Tigers' season turned sour in one nightmarish half-inning. With a 43-25 mark and two-game lead, Detroit opened a nine-game road trip in Baltimore on June 22. Detroit knocked out Orioles ace Mike Mussina in the second inning and led, 7-3, after 5½ innings. But the Orioles proceeded to score eight runs in their half of the sixth en route to a 12-9 win. Detroit ended up going 0-9 on the trip on its way to its 10-29 skid.

Most valuable player: Infielder/outfielder Tony Phillips. Possibly the league's best leadoff hitter, Phillips hit a career-high .313 and became the first Tiger since Norm Cash in 1961 to reach base 300 times (313).

Most valuable pitcher: Righthander John Doherty. He led the team with 14 wins in his first full season in a big-league rotation. Doherty showed some inconsistency, but he maintained impeccable control (48 walks in 184⅔ innings).

Most improved player: Catcher Chad Kreuter. Always strong defensively, Kreuter had been an offensive liability since beginning his big-league career with Texas in 1988. But he hit .286 with 15 homers and 51 RBIs.

Most pleasant surprise: Center fielder Eric Davis. Lacking motivation at the time of his August 31 trade from Los Angeles, he hit six home runs in 23 games and played sparkling defense.

Biggest disappointment: Righthander Mike Moore. The club's primary free-agent signee after the '92 season, Moore posted a 5.22 ERA and allowed a league-leading 35 homers.

Key injuries: Center fielder Milt Cuyler went on the disabled list August 9 and never returned. First baseman Cecil Fielder played much of the second half on a sore right ankle.

Notable: The Tigers' 85-77 record was their best since 1988. ... Sparky Anderson passed Leo Durocher and Walter Alston to become the fifth-winningest manager of all time (2,081 wins). ... Righthander Mike Henneman passed John Hiller to become Detroit's all-time saves leader (128). ... On July 28, third baseman Travis Fryman became the first Tiger to hit for the cycle since Hoot Evers in 1950.

—REID CREAGER

RECORDS

1993 regular-season record: 85-77 (T3rd in A.L. East); 44-37 at home; 41-40 on road; 40-38 vs. East; 45-39 vs. West; 28-22 vs. LHP; 57-55 vs. RHP; 72-65 on grass; 13-12 on turf; 32-28 in daytime; 53-49 at night; 14-16 in one-run games; 4-7 in extra-inning games; 1-1 in doubleheaders.

Team record last five years: 382-428 (.472, ranks 11th in league in that span).

TEAM LEADERS

Batting average: Tony Phillips (.313).
At-bats: Travis Fryman (607).
Runs: Tony Phillips (113).
Hits: Travis Fryman (182).
Total bases: Travis Fryman (295).
Doubles: Travis Fryman (37).
Triples: Milt Cuyler (7).
Home runs: Mickey Tettleton (32).
Runs batted in: Cecil Fielder (117).
Stolen bases: Tony Phillips (16).
Slugging percentage: Mickey Tettleton (.492).
On-base percentage: Tony Phillips (.443).
Wins: John Doherty (14).
Earned-run average: David Wells (4.19).
Complete games: Mike Moore (4).
Shutouts: Mike Moore (3).
Saves: Mike Henneman (24).
Innings pitched: Mike Moore (213⅔).
Strikeouts: David Wells (139).

GAMES BY POSITION

Catcher: Chad Kreuter 112, Mickey Tettleton 56, Rich Rowland 17.
First base: Cecil Fielder 119, Mickey Tettleton 59, Skeeter Barnes 27, Chad Kreuter 1.
Second base: Lou Whitaker 110, Tony Phillips 51, Chris Gomez 17, Skeeter Barnes 10.
Third base: Travis Fryman 69, Scott Livingstone 35, Alan Trammell 35, Skeeter Barnes 13, Tony Phillips 1.
Shortstop: Travis Fryman 81, Alan Trammell 63, Chris Gomez 29, Skeeter Barnes 2.
Outfield: Tony Phillips 108, Rob Deer 86, Dan Gladden 86, Milt Cuyler 80, Mickey Tettleton 55, Gary Thurman 53, Kirk Gibson 32, Skeeter Barnes 18, Eric Davis 18, Danny Bautista 16, Alan Trammell 8.
Designated hitter: Kirk Gibson 76, Cecil Fielder 36, Scott Livingstone 32, Skeeter Barnes 13, Gary Thurman 8, Alan Trammell 6, Eric Davis 5, Dan Gladden 5, Rob Deer 4, Tony Phillips 4, Mickey Tettleton 4, Rich Rowland 3, Chad Kreuter 2, Danny Bautista 1, Travis Fryman 1, Chris Gomez 1.

TOP DRAFT CHOICES

1. **Matt Brunson**, SS, Cherry Creek High School, Englewood, Colo.
2. **Tony Fuduric**, RHP, Cardinal High School, Middlefield, Ohio.
3. **Cameron Smith**, RHP, Ithaca (N.Y.) College.
4. **Michael Wilson**, RHP, Blinn (Tex.) J.C.
5. **Jason Bass**, OF, O'Dea High School, Seattle.
6. **Brian Moehler**, RHP, University of North Carolina-Greensboro.
7. **Greg Granger**, RHP, Lake City (Fla.) C.C.
8. **Drew Christmon**, OF, University of Oklahoma.
9. **Lonny Landry**, OF, Flagler College (Fla.).
10. **R.A. Dickey**, RHP, Montgomery Bell Academy, Nashville.

KANSAS CITY ROYALS
AMERICAN LEAGUE CENTRAL DIVISION

1994 SCHEDULE

N   Denotes night game (any game starting after 5 p.m.).
▢   Home games shaded.
*   At Three Rivers Stadium in Pittsburgh.

APRIL

SUN	MON	TUE	WED	THU	FRI	SAT
					1	2
3	4 BAL	5	6 N BAL	7	8 N CLE	9 CLE
10 CLE	11 N BOS	12 N BOS	13 N BOS	14	15 N CLE	16 CLE
17 CLE	18 N DET	19 DET	20 N DET	21	22 N MIL	23 MIL
24 MIL	25 N TOR	26 N DET	27 N DET	28 DET	29 N MIL	30 N MIL

MAY

SUN	MON	TUE	WED	THU	FRI	SAT
1 MIL	2	3 N TOR	4 N TOR	5 TOR	6 N CHI	7 CHI
8 CHI	9 N MIN	10 N MIN	11 N MIN	12	13 N OAK	14 OAK
15 OAK	16 N SEA	17 N SEA	18 N SEA	19 N CAL	20 N CAL	21 N CAL
22 CAL	23	24 N TEX	25 N TEX	26 TEX	27 N NY	28 N NY
29 NY	30 N BOS	31 N BOS				

JUNE

SUN	MON	TUE	WED	THU	FRI	SAT
			1 N BOS	2	3 N NY	4 NY
5 NY	6 N BAL	7 N BAL	8 N BAL	9 N TEX	10 N TEX	11 N TEX
12 N TEX	13 N CAL	14 N CAL	15 N CAL	16 N SEA	17 N SEA	18 N SEA
19 SEA	20	21 N OAK	22 N OAK	23 OAK	24 N MIN	25 N MIN
26 MIN	27 N MIN	28 N CHI	29 N CHI	30 CHI		

JULY

SUN	MON	TUE	WED	THU	FRI	SAT
					1 N TOR	2 N TOR
3 TOR	4 N TOR	5 N MIL	6 N MIL	7 N MIL	8 N TOR	9 N TOR
10 TOR	11 *	12 ALL-STAR GAME	13	14 N DET	15 N DET	16 N DET
17 N DET	18 N MIL	19 N MIL	20 MIL	21	22 N DET	23 N DET
24 DET	25 N CHI	26 N CHI	27 N CHI	28 N CHI	29 N MIN	30 N MIN
31 MIN						

AUGUST

SUN	MON	TUE	WED	THU	FRI	SAT
	1 N OAK	2 N OAK	3 N OAK	4 OAK	5 N SEA	6 N SEA
7 N SEA	8 N CAL	9 N CAL	10 N CAL	11	12 N TEX	13 N TEX
14 TEX	15	16 N NY	17 N NY	18 N NY	19 N BAL	20 N BAL
21 BAL	22 N NY	23 N NY	24 N NY	25 N BAL	26 N BAL	27 N BAL
28 BAL	29	30 N CLE	31 N CLE			

SEPTEMBER

SUN	MON	TUE	WED	THU	FRI	SAT
				1 CLE	2 N BOS	3 N BOS
4 BOS	5 CLE	6 N CLE	7 N CLE	8	9 N BOS	10 BOS
11 BOS	12 N TEX	13 N TEX	14 N TEX	15	16 N CAL	17 N CAL
18 CAL	19 N SEA	20 N SEA	21 N SEA	22	23 N OAK	24 OAK
25 OAK	26 N MIN	27 N MIN	28 MIN	29	30 N CHI	

OCTOBER

SUN	MON	TUE	WED	THU	FRI	SAT
						1 N CHI
2 CHI						

1994 SEASON

CLUB DIRECTORY

Board of directors
  Gene A. Budig
  David D. Glass
  Mike Herman
  Charles Hughes
  Mrs. Ewing Kauffman
  Larry Kauffman
Chairman of the board & CEO
  David D. Glass
Exec. vice president and general manager
  Spencer (Herk) Robinson
Vice president, treasurer
  Charles Hughes
Vice president, finance
  Dale Rohr
Vice president, baseball operations
  George Brett
Vice president, govt. and consumer affairs
  Merle Wood
Vice president, public relations
  Dean Vogelaar
Vice president, administration
  Dennis Cryder
Director of scouting
  Art Stewart
Assistant general manager
  Jay Hinrichs
Director of minor league operations
  Bob Hegman
Director of marketing
  Mike Behymer
Director of stadium operations
  Tom Folk
Director of season ticket sales
  Joe Grigoli
Lancer coordinator
  Chris Muehlbach
Director of data processing
  Loretta Kratzberg
Director of benefits and compensation
  Tom Pfannenstiel
Director of accounting
  Pat Fleischmann
Traveling secretary
  Dave Witty
Assistant directors of public relations
  Steve Fink
  Barry Holmes

Assistant directors of marketing
  Mike Behymer
  Barry Holmes
Assistant director of stadium operations
  John Johnson
Stadium engineers
  Duane Robinson
  Chris Frank
Production manager
  Larry Magariel
Equipment manager
  Mike Burkhalter
Team physician
  Dr. Steve Joyce
Trainers
  Nick Swartz
  Steve Morrow
Scouts
  Frank Baez
  Allard Baird
  Carl Blando
  Bob Carter
  Balos Davis
  Doug Deutsch
  Larry Doughty
  Steve Flores
  Ken Gonzales
  Guy Hansen
  Dave Herrera
  Ray Jackson
  Gary Johnson
  Al Kubski
  Tony Levato
  Tom McDevitt
  Jeff McKay
  Chuck McMichael
  Brian Murphy
  Herb Raybourn
  Wil Rutenschroer
  Luis Silverio
  Jerry Stephens
  Jerry Terrell
  Terry Wetzel
  Stan Williams
  Dennis Woody

Manager—Hal McRae (11).

Coaches—Steve Boros (43), Glenn Ezell (44), Bruce Kison (42), Lee May (45), Jamie Quirk (9).

No.	PITCHERS	B/T	Ht./Wt.	Born	1993 clubs
55	Appier, Kevin	R/R	6-2/195	12-6-67	Kansas City
50	Belinda, Stan	R/R	6-3/215	8-6-66	Pittsburgh, Kansas City
29	Brewer, Billy	L/L	6-1/175	4-15-68	Kansas City
51	Burgos, Enrique	L/L	6-4/230	10-7-65	Omaha, Kansas City
17	Cone, David	L/R	6-1/190	1-2-63	Kansas City
36	Gordon, Tom	R/R	5-9/180	11-18-67	Kansas City
27	Granger, Jeff	R/L	6-4/200	12-16-71	Eugene, Kansas City
23	Gubicza, Mark	R/R	6-5/225	8-14-62	Kansas City
33	Haney, Chris	L/L	6-3/195	11-16-68	Omaha, Kansas City
58	Harris, Doug	R/R	6-4/205	9-27-69	Memphis
57	Magnante, Mike	L/L	6-1/190	6-17-65	Omaha, Kansas City
28	Meacham, Rusty	R/R	6-2/175	1-27-68	Kansas City, Omaha
21	Montgomery, Jeff	R/R	5-11/180	1-7-62	Kansas City
35	Pichardo, Hipolito	R/R	6-1/185	8-22-69	Kansas City

No.	CATCHERS	B/T	Ht./Wt.	Born	1993 clubs
	Jennings, Lance	R/R	6-0/195	10-3-71	Memphis
15	Macfarlane, Mike	R/R	6-1/195	4-12-64	Kansas City
24	Mayne, Brent	L/R	6-1/190	4-19-68	Kansas City
	Strickland, Chad	R/R	6-1/185	3-16-72	Wilmington

No.	INFIELDERS	B/T	Ht./Wt.	Born	1993 clubs
	Caraballo, Gary	R/R	5-11/205	7-11-71	Wilmington
3	Gaetti, Gary	R/R	6-0/200	8-19-58	California, Kansas City
7	Gagne, Greg	R/R	5-11/180	11-12-61	Kansas City
	Halter, Shane	R/R	5-10/160	11-8-69	Wilmington, Memphis
48	Hamelin, Bob	L/L	6-0/235	11-29-67	Omaha, Kansas City
25	Hiatt, Phil	R/R	6-3/200	5-1-69	Kansas City, Omaha
6	Howard, David	B/R	6-0/191	2-26-67	Kansas City, Omaha
12	Joyner, Wally	L/L	6-2/200	6-16-62	Kansas City
13	Lind, Jose	R/R	5-11/180	5-1-64	Kansas City
16	Miller, Keith	R/R	5-11/185	6-12-63	Kansas City, Omaha
	Randa, Joe	R/R	5-11/190	12-18-69	Memphis
3	Shumpert, Terry	R/R	5-11/185	8-16-66	Omaha, Kansas City
	Vitiello, Joe	R/R	6-2/215	4-11-70	Memphis

No.	OUTFIELDERS	B/T	Ht./Wt.	Born	1993 clubs
	Burton, Darren	B/R	6-1/185	9-16-72	Wilmington
	Coleman, Vince	B/R	6-1/185	9-22-61	New York N.L.
47	Goodwin, Tom	L/R	6-1/170	7-27-68	Los Angeles, Albuquerque
14	Gwynn, Chris	L/L	6-0/220	10-13-64	Kansas City
	Henderson, Dave	R/R	6-2/220	7-21-58	Oakland, Modesto, Tacoma
34	Jose, Felix	B/R	6-1/220	5-8-65	Kansas City
40	Koslofski, Kevin	L/R	5-8/175	9-24-66	Omaha, Kansas City
56	McRae, Brian	B/R	6-0/185	8-27-67	Kansas City
	Norman, Les	R/R	6-1/185	2-25-69	Memphis

BALLPARK INFORMATION

Ballpark (capacity, surface)
Kauffman Stadium (40,625, artificial)
Address
P.O. Box 419969
Kansas City, MO 64141-6969
Business phone
816-921-2200
Ticket information
816-921-8000
Ticket prices
$14 (club box)
$13 (field box)
$11 (plaza reserved)
$10 (view upper box)
$9 (view upper reserved)
$4.50 (Royal nights)
$6 (general admission)
Field dimensions (from home plate)
To left field at foul line, 330 feet
To center field, 410 feet
To right field at foul line, 330 feet
First game played
April 10, 1973 (Royals 12, Rangers 1)

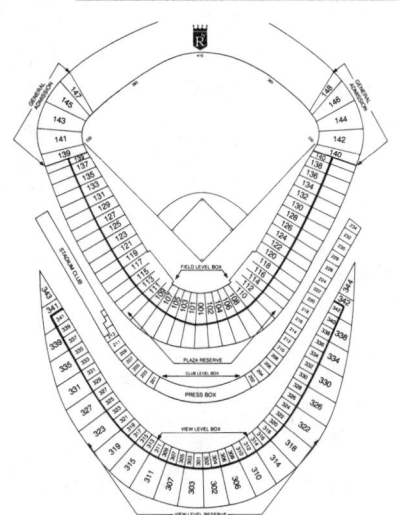

MINOR LEAGUE AFFILIATES

Class	Team	League	Manager
AAA	Omaha	American Association	Jeff Cox
AA	Memphis	Southern	Ron Johnson
A	Wilmington	Carolina	Mike Jirschele
A	Rockford	Midwest	John Mizerock
A	Eugene	Northwest	Brian Poldberg
Rookie	Gulf Coast Royals	Gulf Coast	Bob Herold

☐ BROADCAST INFORMATION ☐

Radio: WIBW-AM (580). Broadcasters: Denny Matthews, Fred White.
TV: KSMO-TV (Channel 62). Broadcasters: Dave Armstrong, Paul Splittorff.
Cable TV: None.

SPRING TRAINING

Ballpark (city): Baseball City Stadium (Baseball City, Fla.).
Ticket information: 813-424-2500.

HISTORY

YEAR-BY-YEAR RECORDS

Year	Pos.	W	L	Pct.	GB	Year	Pos.	W	L	Pct.	GB
1969	4th	69	93	.426	28	1984	1st*	84	78	.519	+ 3
1970	T4th	65	97	.401	33	1985	1st†	91	71	.562	+ 1
1971	2nd	85	76	.528	16	1986	T3rd	76	86	.469	16
1972	4th	76	78	.494	16½	1987	2nd	83	79	.512	2
1973	2nd	88	74	.543	6	1988	3rd	84	77	.522	19½
1974	5th	77	85	.475	13	1989	2nd	92	70	.568	7
1975	2nd	91	71	.562	7	1990	6th	75	86	.466	27½
1976	1st*	90	72	.556	+ 2½	1991	6th	82	80	.506	13
1977	1st*	102	60	.630	+ 8	1992	T5th	72	90	.444	24
1978	1st*	92	70	.568	+ 5	1993	3rd	84	78	.519	10
1979	2nd	85	77	.525	3						
1980	1st†	97	65	.599	+14						
1981	5th/1st	50	53	.485	‡§						
1982	2nd	90	72	.556	3						
1983	2nd	79	83	.488	20						

*Lost Championship Series. †Won Championship Series. ‡First half 20-30; second 30-23. §Lost division playoff.

MANAGERS

Name	Record	Years
Joe Gordon	69-93	1969
Charlie Metro	19-33	1970
Bob Lemon	207-218	'70-72
Jack McKeon	215-205	'73-75
Whitey Herzog	410-304	'74-79
Jim Frey	127-105	'80-81
Dick Howser	404-365	'81-86
Mike Ferraro	36-38	1986
Billy Gardner	62-64	1987
John Wathan	288-270	'87-91
Hal McRae	222-226	'91-93

DAY BY DAY

Date	Opp.	Res.	Score (inn.*)	Hits	Opp. hits	Winning pitcher	Losing pitcher	Save	Record	Pos.	GB
4-5	Bos.	L	1-3	6	7	Clemens	Appier	Russell	0-1	7th	1
4-7	Bos.	L	2-3	5	10	Viola	Cone	Russell	0-2	7th	2
4-8	Bos.	L	4-9	4	15	Bankhead	Gubicza		0-3	7th	2½
4-9	Min.	L	7-8	14	9	Trombley	Gardner	Aguilera	0-4	7th	3½
4-10	Min.	L	2-3	9	8	Banks	Appier	Aguilera	0-5	7th	3½
4-11	Min.	W	2-1	6	5	Gordon	Tapani	Montgomery	1-5	7th	3½
4-12	At N.Y.	L	1-4	8	8	Abbott	Cone		1-6	7th	4½
4-14	At N.Y.	L	5-6	6	12	Wickman	Gubicza	Farr	1-7	7th	5
4-15	At N.Y.	W	5-4	10	7	DiPino	Farr	Montgomery	2-7	7th	4½
4-16	At Min.	L	3-4 (10)	4	7	Guthrie	Meacham		2-8	7th	4½
4-17	At Min.	L	2-8	7	8	Deshaies	Cone	Hartley	2-9	7th	5½
4-18	At Min.	W	5-4	10	9	Pichardo	Erickson	Montgomery	3-9	7th	5½
4-20	Tor.	W	8-2	16	3	Appier	Stottlemyre		4-9	7th	4½
4-21	Tor.	W	6-5	12	8	Montgomery	Timlin		5-9	7th	4
4-22	Tor.	L	3-6	7	7	Hentgen	Cone		5-10	7th	5
4-23	Bal.	W	7-6	8	7	Gardner	Rhodes	Montgomery	6-10	7th	5
4-24	Bal.	L	5-6	9	13	Mussina	Montgomery	Frohwirth	6-11	7th	6
4-25	Bal.	W	3-2	9	8	Appier	McDonald	Montgomery	7-11	6th	6
4-26	Det.	L	3-5	12	8	Bolton	Gubicza		7-12	6th	6½
4-27	Det.	W	4-3 (10)	12	10	Meacham	Kiely		8-12	6th	5½
4-28	At Tor.	W	5-3	7	7	Gardner	Brow	Montgomery	9-12	5th	5½
4-29	At Tor.	L	0-8	5	15	Guzman	Pichardo		9-13	5th	6
4-30	At Bal.	L	5-12	9	13	McDonald	Appier	Olson	9-14	5th	6
5-1	At Bal.	W	5-4	8	10	Sampen	Mills	Montgomery	10-14	5th	5
5-2	At Bal.	L	3-4	11	7	Frohwirth	Rasmussen		10-15	6th	5
5-4	At Det.	L	3-5	10	9	Johnson	Gordon	Henneman	10-16	6th	4½
5-5	At Det.	W	4-3	6	12	Montgomery	Wells		11-16	6th	4½
5-7	Tex.	W	9-4	12	9	Pichardo	Ryan		12-16	6th	5
5-9	Tex.	L	1-2	6	2	Brown	Cone		12-17	T5th	6
5-11	At Cle.	W	7-6	16	15	Appier	Cook	Montgomery	13-17	5th	5½
5-12	At Cle.	L	2-6	10	7	Mesa	Gardner		13-18	6th	6½
5-13	At Cle.	W	7-3	12	5	Pichardo	M. Young		14-18	T5th	6
5-14	At Cal.	W	2-1 (10)	8	4	Cone	Valera	Montgomery	15-18	T5th	6
5-15	At Cal.	L	3-5	8	8	Lewis	Gubicza	Grahe	15-19	6th	6
5-16	At Cal.	W	4-2	8	7	Appier	Farrell	Montgomery	16-19	T5th	6
5-18	Oak.	W	6-1	10	4	Gardner	Welch		17-19	5th	5½
5-19	Oak.	W	13-8	14	14	Gordon	Hillegas	Montgomery	18-19	4th	4½
5-20	Oak.	L	1-4 (12)	9	9	Nunez	Gubicza	Eckersley	18-20	5th	5
5-21	Sea.	W	2-1	6	6	Haney	Johnson	Gordon	19-20	4th	4
5-22	Sea.	W	4-1	10	5	Appier	Converse		20-20	4th	3
5-23	Sea.	L	7-10	10	17	Swan	Montgomery	Charlton	20-21	4th	4
5-25	At Chi.	W	3-2	6	8	Gordon	McDowell	Montgomery	21-21	4th	3
5-26	At Chi.	W	4-3	10	3	Cone	Fernandez	Montgomery	22-21	4th	2
5-27	At Chi.	W	6-4	8	11	Haney	Bere	Montgomery	23-21	4th	1
5-28	At Mil.	L	1-5	4	10	Eldred	Appier		23-22	4th	2
5-29	At Mil.	W	6-5 (13)	15	8	Sampen	Austin	Montgomery	24-22	T2nd	2
5-30	At Mil.	L	2-8	10	10	Wegman	Pichardo		24-23	T2nd	3
5-31	At Bos.	W	5-3	10	8	Cone	Dopson	Montgomery	25-23	2nd	2
6-1	At Bos.	W	4-3	6	6	Haney	Quantrill	Montgomery	26-23	2nd	1
6-2	At Bos.	W	7-2	13	7	Appier	Clemens		27-23	T1st	...
6-3	Mil.	W	6-5	10	10	Gardner	Boddicker		28-23	1st	+½
6-4	Mil.	W	3-2	7	11	Brewer	Wegman	Montgomery	29-23	1st	+½
6-5	Mil.	L	2-8	5	9	Bones	Cone		29-24	1st	+½
6-6	Mil.	W	8-7	15	10	Meacham	Austin		30-24	1st	+½
6-7	N.Y.	W	8-3	15	9	Appier	Johnson		31-24	1st	+½
6-8	N.Y.	L	4-9	13	13	Howe	Brewer		31-25	1st	+½
6-9	N.Y.	W	10-3	11	10	Pichardo	Abbott		32-25	1st	+2½
6-11	Chi.	L	1-6	10	10	McDowell	Cone		32-26	1st	+½
6-12	Chi.	L	1-2 (15)	9	14	Schwarz	Meacham	Hernandez	32-27	1st	+½
6-13	Chi.	W	5-4 (10)	9	9	Gordon	Pall		33-27	1st	+½
6-14	At Sea.	L	3-6	6	8	Johnson	Gardner	Charlton	33-28	1st	+½
6-15	At Sea.	L	1-6	4	9	Converse	Pichardo		33-29	1st	+½
6-16	At Sea.	W	5-1	16	6	Cone	Hanson		34-29	1st	+½
6-18	At Oak.	L	9-10	15	10	Gossage	Gordon	Eckersley	34-30	1st	+1
6-19	At Oak.	W	3-0	9	4	Appier	Boever	Montgomery	35-30	1st	+1
6-20	At Oak.	L	1-4	9	5	Welch	Gardner	Eckersley	35-31	1st	+1
6-21	Cal.	L	3-4	13	3	Finley	Pichardo	Frey	35-32	T1st	...
6-22	Cal.	W	5-3	14	9	Cone	Sanderson	Montgomery	36-32	T1st	...
6-23	Cal.	L	7-8	13	11	Hathaway	Haney	Frey	36-33	T2nd	1
6-24	Cal.	W	7-1	14	7	Appier	Langston	Montgomery	37-33	2nd	½

Date	Opp.	Res.	Score	(inn.*)	Hits	Opp. hits	Winning pitcher	Losing pitcher	Save	Record	Pos.	GB
6-25	At Cle.	L	1-6		4	7	Cook	Gubicza		37-34	2nd	½
6-26	At Cle.	L	4-7		8	7	Hernandez	DiPino	Plunk	37-35	T2nd	1½
6-27	At Cle.	L	2-3		5	6	Plunk	Cone		37-36	T2nd	2½
6-28	At Tex.	W	4-2		8	8	Haney	Rogers	Montgomery	38-36	2nd	1½
6-29	At Tex.	L	3-4		6	6	Patterson	Sampen	Henke	38-37	2nd	1½
6-30	At Tex.	L	4-5		8	9	Bohanon	Gardner	Henke	38-38	2nd	1½
7-2	Tor.	W	3-2		10	8	Gubicza	Cox		39-38	2nd	1
7-3	Tor.	W	3-2		9	4	Cone	Morris	Montgomery	40-38	T1st	...
7-4	Tor.	W	3-1		7	7	Haney	Stottlemyre	Montgomery	41-38	T1st	...
7-5	Bal.	W	7-1		9	9	Gubicza	Pennington		42-38	T1st	...
7-6	Bal.	L	0-8		4	11	Moyer	Gardner		42-39	T1st	...
7-7	Bal.	L	3-8		6	10	Mussina	Pichardo		42-40	2nd	1
7-8	Det.	W	6-5	(11)	18	11	Montgomery	Groom		43-40	2nd	1
7-9	Det.	L	5-10		14	11	Bergman	Haney		43-41	2nd	1
7-10	Det.	L	8-9		11	13	Knudsen	Sampen	Henneman	43-42	T2nd	1
7-11	Det.	W	6-2		11	5	Appier	Doherty		44-42	T2nd	1
7-15	At Tor.	L	2-7		6	8	Leiter	Burgos		44-43	3rd	2
7-16	At Tor.	W	7-3		11	7	Haney	Morris	Montgomery	45-43	3rd	2
7-17	At Tor.	W	5-4		9	9	Gubicza	Cox	Montgomery	46-43	T2nd	2
7-18	At Tor.	L	3-4		5	10	Hentgen	Pichardo		46-44	T2nd	3
7-19	At Bal.	L	5-6		10	11	Moyer	Rasmussen	Olson	46-45	3rd	3
7-20	At Bal.	L	0-7		1	10	McDonald	Cone		46-46	3rd	4
7-21	At Bal.	W	8-6		15	8	Brewer	Olson	Montgomery	47-46	3rd	3
7-22	At Det.	W	12-6		16	7	Appier	Gullickson		48-46	3rd	3
7-23	At Det.	W	7-6		12	13	Pichardo	MacDonald	Montgomery	49-46	3rd	2
7-24	At Det.	W	6-3		7	7	Gordon	Bergman	Montgomery	50-46	2nd	2
7-25	At Det.	L	0-3		1	4	Moore	Cone		50-47	2nd	2
7-26 (1)	Tex.	W	12-3		21	9	Haney	Brown		51-47	2nd	2
7-26 (2)	Tex.	W	6-5		10	13	Rasmussen	Bohanon	Montgomery	52-47	2nd	1½
7-27	Tex.	L	0-1		9	1	Rogers	Appier	Henke	52-48	2nd	2½
7-28	Tex.	L	3-10		10	16	Pavlik	Pichardo		52-49	2nd	3½
7-29	Tex.	W	9-4		10	7	Gordon	Leibrandt	Gubicza	53-49	2nd	3
7-30	Cle.	W	3-0		8	5	Cone	Mesa		54-49	2nd	3
7-31	Cle.	L	4-6		11	11	Kramer	Haney	Plunk	54-50	2nd	4
8-1	Cle.	L	5-9		8	11	Wertz	Appier	Plunk	54-51	2nd	5
8-3	At Cal.	L	2-3		7	6	Langston	Belinda	Butcher	54-52	2nd	5½
8-4	At Cal.	W	3-2		10	8	Cone	Leftwich	Montgomery	55-52	2nd	4½
8-5	At Cal.	L	4-5		9	8	Hathaway	Gordon	Frey	55-53	T2nd	4½
8-6	Oak.	L	2-5		7	9	Van Poppel	Haney	Eckersley	55-54	3rd	4½
8-7	Oak.	W	5-2		8	4	Appier	Downs	Montgomery	56-54	T2nd	4½
8-8	Oak.	W	4-3		8	10	Pichardo	Darling	Montgomery	57-54	T2nd	3½
8-9	Sea.	W	7-6		11	11	Belinda	Power	Montgomery	58-54	2nd	3½
8-10	Sea.	W	4-1		10	8	Gordon	Fleming	Gubicza	59-54	2nd	3½
8-11	Sea.	L	3-4		8	8	Bosio	Haney	Power	59-55	2nd	3½
8-12	At Chi.	W	4-2		10	7	Appier	McDowell		60-55	2nd	2½
8-13	At Chi.	L	4-5		5	12	Cary	Montgomery	Hernandez	60-56	2nd	3½
8-14	At Chi.	L	1-4		2	7	Fernandez	Cone	Radinsky	60-57	2nd	4½
8-15	At Chi.	W	7-5		13	9	Gordon	Belcher	Montgomery	61-57	2nd	3½
8-17	At Min.	W	3-2		8	12	Haney	Deshaies	Montgomery	62-57	2nd	3½
8-18	At Min.	W	5-2		10	8	Appier	Tapani	Montgomery	63-57	2nd	2½
8-19	At Min.	W	4-2		11	7	Cone	Guardado		64-57	2nd	2
8-20	At N.Y.	L	2-7		5	11	Jean	Gordon		64-58	2nd	3
8-21	At N.Y.	L	2-3		5	9	Kamieniecki	Magnante	Farr	64-59	2nd	4
8-22	At N.Y.	W	7-0		12	4	Haney	Perez		65-59	2nd	4
8-23	Min.	L	2-3	(10)	11	9	Casian	Montgomery	Willis	65-60	2nd	4
8-24	Min.	W	5-3		10	8	Cone	Guardado	Montgomery	66-60	2nd	4
8-25	Min.	L	2-4		9	6	Erickson	Gordon	Willis	66-61	3rd	4
8-26	Min.	W	3-0		5	7	Magnante	Banks	Montgomery	67-61	2nd	3½
8-27	Bos.	L	0-5		5	11	Clemens	Haney		67-62	3rd	4
8-28	Bos.	L	1-2	(11)	5	9	Russell	Montgomery		67-63	3rd	5
8-29	Bos.	W	5-4	(12)	13	12	Gubicza	Dopson		68-63	3rd	5
8-30	At Mil.	L	1-2		4	7	Eldred	Gordon		68-64	3rd	6
8-31	At Mil.	W	6-5		11	7	Cadaret	Miranda	Montgomery	69-64	3rd	6
9-1	At Mil.	L	1-7		7	10	Navarro	Haney		69-65	3rd	7
9-3	At Bos.	W	5-1		8	6	Appier	Darwin		70-65	3rd	6½
9-4	At Bos.	W	4-2		8	5	Cone	Ryan	Montgomery	71-65	3rd	6½
9-5	At Bos.	W	5-2		7	5	Gordon	Clemens		72-65	2nd	6½
9-6	Mil.	L	2-3		7	5	Navarro	Cadaret	Orosco	72-66	3rd	6½
9-8	Mil.	L	1-2		2	7	Bones	Brewer		72-67	3rd	7
9-10	N.Y.	W	6-5		12	11	Montgomery	Howe		73-67	3rd	6
9-11	N.Y.	L	5-12		11	17	Wickman	Haney		73-68	3rd	7
9-12	N.Y.	W	10-2		9	8	Gordon	Hutton		74-68	3rd	6
9-13	Chi.	W	9-0		12	4	Appier	Belcher		75-68	3rd	5
9-14	Chi.	L	3-8		7	14	Bere	Pichardo		75-69	3rd	6

Date	Opp.	Res.	Score	(inn.*)	Hits	Opp. hits	Winning pitcher	Losing pitcher	Save	Record	Pos.	GB
9-15	Chi.	L	6-10	(11)	15	14	Hernandez	Gubicza		75-70	3rd	7
9-16	At Sea.	L	1-14		2	14	Johnson	Haney		75-71	T3rd	7½
9-17	At Sea.	W	6-3		10	8	Gordon	Fleming	Montgomery	76-71	3rd	7½
9-18	At Sea.	W	1-0		6	3	Appier	Bosio		77-71	3rd	6½
9-19	At Sea.	L	1-4		6	7	Hanson	Magnante	Power	77-72	3rd	7½
9-20	At Oak.	L	1-2		7	5	Van Poppel	Cone	Smithberg	77-73	3rd	8½
9-21	At Oak.	L	6-9		12	16	Downs	Gubicza		77-74	T3rd	8½
9-22	At Oak.	W	3-2	(10)	8	8	Montgomery	Smithberg		78-74	T3rd	8½
9-23	At Oak.	L	1-2		5	7	Witt	Appier	Eckersley	78-75	4th	9½
9-24	Cal.	W	7-2	(5)	6	8	Pichardo	Magrane		79-75	3rd	9½
9-25	Cal.	L	2-6		9	8	Leftwich	Cone	Grahe	79-76	3rd	10
9-26	Cal.	W	9-8	(10)	10	17	Montgomery	Swingle		80-76	3rd	9½
9-27	Cle.	W	6-5		10	8	Gubicza	DiPoto		81-76	3rd	9½
9-28	Cle.	L	2-3		9	10	Grimsley	Appier	Plunk	81-77	3rd	9½
9-29	Cle.	W	3-2		8	5	Montgomery	Hernandez		82-77	3rd	9½
10-1	At Tex.	L	0-2		4	4	Pavlik	Cone	Henke	82-78	3rd	10
10-2	At Tex.	W	7-4		12	10	Gordon	Brown	Montgomery	83-78	3rd	10
10-3	At Tex.	W	4-1		7	4	Appier	Dreyer	Montgomery	84-78	3rd	10

Monthly records: April (9-14), May (16-9), June (13-15), July (16-12), August (15-14), September (13-13), October (2-1).
*Innings, if other than nine.

HIGHLIGHTS

High point: From May 31-June 4, Kansas City won a season-high five games in a row and moved into first place (half-game lead). The Royals retained at least a share of the division lead through June 22.

Low point: Like 1992, the Royals staggered to a poor start, losing their first five games and nine of their first 11 to fall 5½ games behind.

Turning point: After splitting a four-game series in Chicago and sweeping three games from the Twins in Minnesota, Kansas City was within two games of the lead on August 19. But the Royals ran out of steam in New York, losing two of three games. Kansas City never recovered and, by September 1, was seven games out.

Most valuable player: Shortstop Greg Gagne. As expected, he played great defense. But his offense also was great. Gagne posted career highs in average (.280), hits (151) and RBIs (57).

Most valuable pitchers: Righthanders Kevin Appier and Jeff Montgomery. Appier won a career-high 18 games and paced the A.L. with a 2.56 ERA. Montgomery tied for the A.L. lead with 45 saves and had a 2.27 ERA.

Most improved player: Center fielder Brian McRae. After batting .223 in 1992, McRae registered a .282 average with a career-high 12 homers and 69 RBIs. Defensively, he was outstanding.

Most pleasant surprise: Third baseman Gary Gaetti. Released by California on June 3, Gaetti signed with the Royals and took over for struggling rookie Phil Hiatt. In 82 games with Kansas City, Gaetti delivered 14 homers, 46 RBIs and fine defense.

Biggest disappointment: Right fielder Felix Jose. Obtained from St. Louis to provide much-needed power, he injured his left shoulder in March and was unable to bat righthanded (his best side of the plate) for most of the season. Jose finished with just six homers and 43 RBIs.

Key injuries: Righthander Rusty Meacham missed most of the season with a sore elbow. Infielder Keith Miller played just 37 games because of an injury to his groin and left thumb. Infielder Curtis Wilkerson's season ended May 16 with a broken left ankle.

Notable: Designated hitter George Brett retired with 3,154 career hits. ... Owner Ewing M. Kauffman died August 1 of cancer. He was the founder of the expansion club, which began play in 1969. In his honor, Royals Stadium was renamed Kauffman Stadium.

—DICK KAEGEL

RECORDS

1993 regular-season record: 84-78 (3rd in A.L. West); 43-38 at home; 41-40 on road; 43-41 vs. East; 41-37 vs. West; 23-21 vs. LHP; 61-57 vs. RHP; 31-31 on grass; 53-47 on turf; 27-23 in daytime; 57-55 at night; 38-32 in one-run games; 8-6 in extra-inning games; 1-0-0 in doubleheaders.

Team record last five years: 405-404 (.501, ranks 7th in league in that span).

TEAM LEADERS

Batting average: Wally Joyner (.292).
At-bats: Brian McRae (627).
Runs: Wally Joyner (83).
Hits: Brian McRae (177).
Total bases: Brian McRae (259).
Doubles: Wally Joyner (36).
Triples: Brian McRae (9).
Home runs: Mike Macfarlane (20).
Runs batted in: George Brett (75).
Stolen bases: Felix Jose (31).
Slugging percentage: Wally Joyner (.467).
On-base percentage: Wally Joyner (.375).
Wins: Kevin Appier (18).
Earned-run average: Kevin Appier (2.56).
Complete games: David Cone (6).
Shutouts: Kevin Appier, David Cone, Chris Haney (1).
Saves: Jeff Montgomery (45).
Innings pitched: David Cone (254).
Strikeouts: David Cone (191).

GAMES BY POSITION

Catcher: Mike Macfarlane 114, Brent Mayne 68, Nelson Santovenia 4.

First base: Wally Joyner 140, Gary Gaetti 18, Bob Hamelin 15, Hubie Brooks 3, Chris Gwynn 1.

Second base: Jose Lind 136, Rico Rossy 24, Curtis Wilkerson 10, Terry Shumpert 6, David Howard 7, Keith Miller 3, Craig Wilson 1.

Third base: Gary Gaetti 72, Phil Hiatt 70, Keith Miller 21, Rico Rossy 16, Craig Wilson 15, David Howard 2.

Shortstop: Greg Gagne 159, Rico Rossy 11, Curtis Wilkerson 4, David Howard 3.

Outfield: Brian McRae 153, Felix Jose 144, Kevin McReynolds 104, Chris Gwynn 83, Hubie Brooks 40, Harvey Pulliam 26, Kevin Koslofski 13, Keith Miller 4, David Howard 1, Craig Wilson 1.

Designated hitter: George Brett 140, Hubie Brooks 9, Phil Hiatt 9, Keith Miller 6, Chris Gwynn 5, Gary Gaetti 1, Felix Jose 1, Kevin Koslofski 1, Brent Mayne 1, Kevin McReynolds 1.

TOP DRAFT CHOICES

1. **Jeff Granger,** LHP, Texas A&M University.
2. **None.**
3. **None.**
4. **Phil Grundy,** RHP, Western Carolina University.
5. **Phil Brassington,** RHP, Lamar University.
6. **Tyrone Frazier,** OF/SS, Woodlawn High School, Shreveport, La.
7. **Pat Flury,** RHP, J.C. of Southern Idaho.
8. **O.J. Rhone,** OF, Central Missouri State University.
9. **Chad Green,** OF, Mentor (Ohio) High School.
10. **Tom Buchman,** C, Shawnee Mission South High School, Lenexa, Kan.

MILWAUKEE BREWERS
AMERICAN LEAGUE CENTRAL DIVISION

N Denotes night game (any game starting after 5 p.m.).
☐ Home games shaded.
* At Three Rivers Stadium in Pittsburgh.

APRIL

SUN	MON	TUE	WED	THU	FRI	SAT
					1	2
3	4	5 OAK	6	N 7 OAK	N 8 CAL	9 CAL
10 CAL	11	12	N 13 TEX	N 14 TEX	N 15 SEA	16 SEA
17 SEA	18	N 19 CHI	N 20 CHI	N 21 CHI	N 22 KC	23 KC
24 KC	N 25 CHI	N 26 CHI	N 27 MIN	N 28 MIN	N 29 KC	30 KC

MAY

SUN	MON	TUE	WED	THU	FRI	SAT
1 KC	2	N 3 MIN	4 MIN	5	N 6 TOR	7 TOR
8 TOR	N 9 BOS	N 10 BOS	N 11 BOS	N 12 BOS	N 13 NY	14 NY
15 NY	16	N 17 CLE	N 18 CLE	N 19 CLE	N 20 DET	21 DET
22 DET	N 23 BAL	N 24 BAL	25 BAL	26	N 27 SEA	28 SEA
29 SEA	N 30 TEX	N 31 TEX				

JUNE

SUN	MON	TUE	WED	THU	FRI	SAT
			1 TEX	2	N 3 CAL	N 4 CAL
5 CAL	N 6 OAK	N 7 OAK	N 8 OAK	N 9 CLE	N 10 CLE	11 CLE
12 CLE	13	N 14 DET	N 15 DET	N 16 DET	N 17 NY	18 NY
19 NY	N 20 BAL	N 21 BAL	N 22 BAL	23	N 24 BOS	25 BOS
26 BOS	N 27 TOR	N 28 TOR	N 29 TOR	30 TOR		

JULY

SUN	MON	TUE	WED	THU	FRI	SAT
					N 1 CHI	2 CHI
3 CHI	N 4 CHI	N 5 KC	N 6 KC	N 7 KC	N 8 CHI	9 CHI
10 CHI	11 *	12 ALL-STAR GAME	13	N 14 MIN	N 15 MIN	16 MIN
17 MIN	N 18 KC	N 19 KC	N 20 KC	N 21 MIN	N 22 MIN	23 MIN
24 MIN	25	N 26 TOR	N 27 TOR	N 28 TOR	N 29 BOS	30 BOS
31 BOS						

AUGUST

SUN	MON	TUE	WED	THU	FRI	SAT
	1 NY	2 NY	N 3 BAL	4 BAL	N 5 BAL	6 BAL
7 BAL	N 8 DET	N 9 DET	N 10 DET	N 11 DET	N 12 CLE	13 CLE
14 CLE	15	N 16 CAL	N 17 CAL	N 18 CAL	N 19 OAK	20 OAK
21 OAK	N 22 OAK	N 23 CAL	N 24 CAL	N 25 CAL	N 26 OAK	27 OAK
28 OAK	29	N 30 SEA	31 SEA			

SEPTEMBER

SUN	MON	TUE	WED	THU	FRI	SAT
				1 SEA	N 2 TEX	3 TEX
4 TEX	5	N 6 SEA	7 SEA	N 8 SEA	N 9 TEX	10 TEX
11 TEX	12	N 13 CLE	14 CLE	N 15 CLE	N 16 DET	17 DET
18 DET	N 19 NY	N 20 NY	N 21 NY	N 22 NY	N 23 BAL	24 BAL
25 BAL	N 26 BOS	N 27 BOS	N 28 BOS	29	N 30 TOR	

OCTOBER

SUN	MON	TUE	WED	THU	FRI	SAT
						1 TOR
2 TOR						

CLUB DIRECTORY

President, chief executive officer
Allan H. (Bud) Selig
Senior vice president, baseball operations
Sal Bando
Senior vice president
Harry Dalton
Vice president, government affairs
Dick Hackett
Vice president, broadcast operations
Bill Haig
Vice president, finance
Dick Hoffmann
Vice president, stadium operations
Gabe Paul Jr.
Asst. vice president, baseball operations
Bruce Manno
Scouting director
Ken Califano
Senior consultant, baseball operations
Dee Fondy
Special assistants, baseball operations
Larry Haney
Chuck Tanner
Vice President & General counsel
Wendy Selig-Prieb
Assistant general counsel
Eugene (Pepi) Randolph
Director of baseball administration
Brian Small
Vice president of communications
Laurel Prieb
Director of community relations
Michael Downs
Vice president of marketing
John Cordova
Director of stadium administration
Terry Ann Peterson
Director of grounds
Gary Vandenberg
Director of media relations
Tom Skibosh
Director of player development
Fred Stanley
Dir. of administration & human resources
Tom Gausden
Director of publications
Mario Ziino
Director of ticket operations
John Barnes
Vice president of ticket sales
Jeff Eisenberg
Traveling secretary
Steve Ethier
Trainers
John Adam
Al Price
Strength and conditioning coach
John Rewolinski

Team physicians
Dr. Paul Jacobs
Dr. Dennis Sullivan
Dr. Drew Palin
Western crosschecker
Lou Snipp
Eastern crosschecker
Ed Durkin
Midwest supervisor
Fred Beene
Latin America supervisor
Felix Delgado
Northeast supervisor
Ron Rizzi
Northwest supervisor
Dick Foster
Southeast supervisor
Russ Bove
Southwest supervisor
Roland LeBlanc
Special assignment scout
Walter Youse
Scouts
Jeff Brookens
Tom Calvano
Kevin Christman
Dick Fanning
Miguel Flores
Bill Foley
Danny Garcia
Manola Hernandez
Ken Houp
Bob Hughes
Elvio Jiminez
Pete Jones
Harvey Kuenn Jr.
John Logan
Demie Mainieri
Frank Piet
Mike Powers
Lenny Randle
Jeff Ransom
Doug Reynolds
Pedro Rivera
Phil Rizzo
Alexis Salcedo
Richard Scarafia
Art Schuerman
Bob Sloan
Paul Tretiak
John Viney
Thomas Walsh
Red Whitsett
Ric Wilson
David Young

Manager—Phil Garner (3).

Coaches—Bill Castro (35), Gene Clines (12), Duffy Dyer (10), Tim Foli (14), Don Rowe (45).

No.	PITCHERS	B/T	Ht./Wt.	Born	1993 clubs
25	Bones, Ricky	R/R	6-0/190	4-7-69	Milwaukee
57	Boze, Marshall	R/R	6-1/212	5-23-71	Stockton, El Paso
	Bronkey, Jeff	R/R	6-3/210	9-18-65	Oklahoma City, Texas
59	Browne, Byron	R/R	6-7/190	8-8-70	Stockton
21	Eldred, Cal	R/R	6-4/235	11-24-67	Milwaukee
36	Fetters, Mike	R/R	6-4/215	12-19-64	Milwaukee
58	Gamez, Francisco	R/R	6-2/185	4-2-70	El Paso
28	Henry, Doug	R/R	6-4/205	12-10-63	Milwaukee
49	Higuera, Ted	B/L	5-10/180	11-9-58	New Orleans, Milwaukee
55	Hill, Tyrone	L/L	6-6/195	3-7-72	Stockton
40	Ignasiak, Michael	B/R	5-11/190	3-12-66	New Orleans, Milwaukee
43	Kiefer, Mark	R/R	6-4/184	11-13-68	El Paso, New Orleans, Milwaukee
37	Lloyd, Graeme	L/L	6-7/230	4-9-67	Milwaukee
38	Miranda, Angel	L/L	6-1/195	11-9-69	New Orleans, Milwaukee
31	Navarro, Jaime	R/R	6-4/225	3-27-68	Milwaukee
47	Orosco, Jesse	R/L	6-2/205	4-21-57	Milwaukee
60	Rogers, Charlie	R/R	6-0/180	8-21-68	El Paso
39	Scanlan, Bob	R/R	6-8/215	8-9-66	Chicago N.L.
54	Taylor, Scott	R/R	6-3/200	10-3-66	El Paso, New Orleans
46	Wegman, Bill	R/R	6-5/235	12-19-62	Milwaukee

No.	CATCHERS	B/T	Ht./Wt.	Born	1993 clubs
65	Matheny, Mike	R/R	6-3/205	9-22-70	El Paso
11	Nilsson, Dave	L/R	6-3/215	12-14-69	El Paso, Milwaukee, New Orleans
64	Stefanski, Mike	R/R	6-2/190	9-12-69	Stockton

No.	INFIELDERS	B/T	Ht./Wt.	Born	1993 clubs
26	Bell, Juan	B/R	5-11/175	3-29-68	Philadelphia, Milwaukee
13	Cirillo, Jeff	R/R	6-2/190	9-23-69	El Paso, New Orleans
32	Jaha, John	R/R	6-1/205	5-27-66	Milwaukee
16	Listach, Pat	B/R	5-9/170	9-12-67	Milwaukee, Beloit
9	Spiers, Bill	L/R	6-2/190	6-5-66	Milwaukee
5	Surhoff, B.J.	L/R	6-1/200	8-4-64	Milwaukee
2	Valentin, Jose	B/R	5-10/175	10-12-69	New Orleans, Milwaukee

No.	OUTFIELDERS	B/T	Ht./Wt.	Born	1993 clubs
1	Diaz, Alex	B/R	5-11/180	10-5-68	Milwaukee, New Orleans
24	Hamilton, Darryl	L/R	6-1/180	12-3-64	Milwaukee
30	Mieske, Matt	R/R	6-0/185	2-13-68	New Orleans, Milwaukee
33	O'Leary, Troy	L/L	6-0/190	8-4-69	New Orleans, Milwaukee
51	Singleton, Duane	L/R	6-1/170	8-6-72	El Paso
23	Vaughn, Greg	R/R	6-0/205	7-3-65	Milwaukee
52	Wachter, Derek	R/R	6-2/195	8-28-70	Stockton
27	Ward, Turner	B/R	6-2/182	4-11-65	Toronto, Knoxville

BALLPARK INFORMATION

Ballpark (capacity, surface)
County Stadium (53,192, grass)

Address
County Stadium
P.O. Box 3099 Milwaukee, WI
53201-3099

Business phone
414-933-4114

Ticket information
414-933-1818

Ticket prices
$18 (diamond box mezz.)
$17 (diamond box lower box)
$15 (mezzanine)
$14 (lower box)
$12 (upper box)
$11 (lower grandstand)
$8 (upper grandstand)
$7 (general admission)
$4 (bleachers)

Field dimensions (from home plate)
To left field at foul line, 315 feet
To center field, 402 feet
To right field at foul line, 315 feet

First game played
April 7, 1970 (Angels 12, Brewers 0)

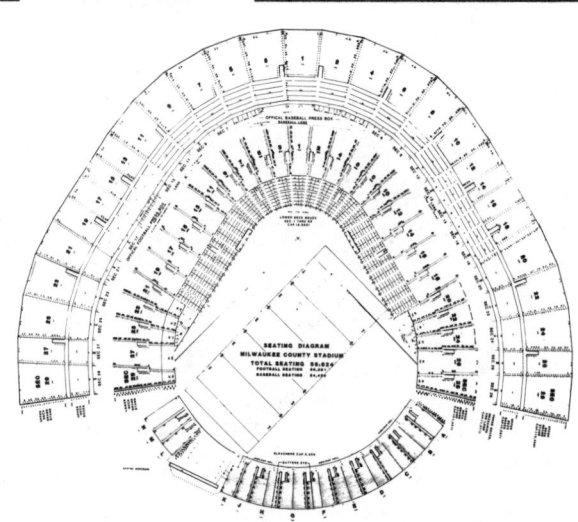

MINOR LEAGUE AFFILIATES

Class	Team	League	Manager
AAA	New Orleans	American Association	Chris Bando
AA	El Paso	Texas	Tim Ireland
A	Stockton	California	Lamar Johnson
A	Beloit	Midwest	Wayne Krenchicki
Rookie	Helena	Pioneer	To be announced
Rookie	Chandler Brewers	Arizona	Ralph Dickenson

BROADCAST INFORMATION

Radio: WTMJ-AM (620). Broadcasters: Bob Uecker, Pat Hughes.
TV: WVTV-TV (Channel 24). Broadcasters: Rory Markas, Del Crandall.
Cable TV: None.

SPRING TRAINING

Ballpark (city): Compadre Stadium (Chandler, Ariz.).
Ticket Information: 602-895-1200.

HISTORY

YEAR-BY-YEAR RECORDS

Year	Pos.	W	L	Pct.	GB
1969*	6th	64	98	.395	33
1970	T4th	65	97	.401	33
1971	6th	69	92	.429	32
1972	6th	65	91	.417	21
1973	5th	74	88	.457	23
1974	5th	76	86	.469	15
1975	5th	68	94	.420	28
1976	6th	66	95	.410	32
1977	6th	67	95	.414	33
1978	3rd	93	69	.574	6½
1979	2nd	95	66	.590	8
1980	3rd	86	76	.531	17
1981	3rd/1st	62	47	.569	†‡
1982	1st§	95	67	.586	+1
1983	5th	87	75	.537	11

Year	Pos.	W	L	Pct.	GB
1984	7th	67	94	.416	36½
1985	6th	71	90	.441	28
1986	6th	77	84	.478	18
1987	3rd	91	71	.562	7
1988	T3rd	87	75	.537	2
1989	4th	81	81	.500	8
1990	6th	74	88	.457	14
1991	4th	83	79	.512	8
1992	2nd	92	70	.568	4
1993	7th	69	93	.426	26

*Franchise known as Seattle Pilots. †First half 31-25; second 31-22. ‡Lost division playoff. §Won Championship Series.

MANAGERS

Name	Record	Years
Joe Schultz	64-98	1969
Dave Bristol	144-209	'70-72
Del Crandall	271-338	'72-75
Alex Grammas	133-190	'76-77
George Bamberger	377-351	'78-80
		'85-86
Buck Rodgers	124-102	'80-82
Harvey Kuenn	160-118	'82-83
Rene Lachemann	67-94	1984
Tom Trebelhorn	422-397	'86-91
Phil Garner	161-163	'92-93

DAY BY DAY

Date	Opp.	Res.	Score	(inn.*)	Hits	Opp. hits	Winning pitcher	Losing pitcher	Save	Record	Pos.	GB
4-6	At Cal.	L	1-3		3	10	Langston	Wegman		0-1	T3rd	1
4-7	At Cal.	W	3-2		7	5	Eldred	Grahe	Henry	1-1	T2nd	1
4-9	At Oak.	W	6-5		12	10	Manzanillo	Downs	Henry	2-1	T2nd	½
4-10	At Oak.	L	3-4		9	10	Welch	Bones	Eckersley	2-2	4th	1½
4-11	At Oak.	L	2-8		6	12	Hillegas	Wegman		2-3	5th	1½
4-12	Cal.	L	5-12		12	12	Finley	Eldred	Valera	2-4	T5th	2
4-14	Cal.	L	2-12		5	16	Sanderson	Orosco		2-5	6th	3½
4-17	Oak.	W	6-3		7	7	Wegman	Welch		3-5	5th	3½
4-18	Oak.	W	8-0		12	3	Eldred	Hillegas		4-5	5th	3½
4-20	At Min.	L	0-10		8	11	Banks	Navarro		4-6	5th	5
4-21	At Min.	W	10-8	(10)	12	12	Maldonado	Hartley	Henry	5-6	5th	4
4-22	At Min.	L	4-5		8	8	Deshaies	Wegman	Aguilera	5-7	5th	4
4-23	Tex.	W	3-0		8	1	Eldred	Brown	Orosco	6-7	5th	3
4-24	Tex.	L	4-15		11	12	Leibrandt	Manzanillo		6-8	5th	4
4-25	Tex.	L	1-6		3	10	Rogers	Navarro		6-9	5th	5
4-26	Min.	W	10-3		12	13	Bones	Tapani		7-9	5th	5
4-27	Min.	W	3-2		10	9	Wegman	Deshaies	Henry	8-9	5th	4
4-28	At Chi.	L	2-11		9	12	McCaskill	Eldred		8-10	5th	4
4-29	At Chi.	L	4-7		7	13	Stieb	Boddicker	Radinsky	8-11	5th	5
4-30	At Tex.	W	5-4		6	6	Lloyd	Patterson	Henry	9-11	5th	5
5-1	At Tex.	W	4-3	(12)	8	14	Lloyd	Patterson	Manzanillo	10-11	5th	4
5-2	At Tex.	L	2-13		4	15	Nen	Wegman	Bronkey	10-12	5th	4
5-3	At Tex.	L	2-9		6	14	Brown	Eldred		10-13	5th	4½
5-4	Chi.	W	6-1		12	7	Boddicker	McCaskill		11-13	5th	4½
5-5	Chi.	L	1-3		5	10	Radinsky	Orosco	Hernandez	11-14	6th	4½
5-7	Bos.	L	0-1		3	4	Darwin	Wegman	Russell	11-15	5th	5½
5-8	Bos.	W	6-3		5	10	Eldred	Quantrill	Henry	12-15	5th	4½
5-9	Bos.	W	6-0		11	6	Boddicker	Hesketh		13-15	5th	3½
5-11	At N.Y.	L	1-5		3	10	Witt	Navarro		13-16	5th	5
5-12	At N.Y.	W	4-1		9	5	Wegman	Key	Henry	14-16	5th	5
5-13	At N.Y.	L	2-4		5	8	Abbott	Eldred	Farr	14-17	5th	5
5-14	Cle.	W	5-2		10	10	Boddicker	C. Young	Henry	15-17	5th	5
5-15	Cle.	L	5-9		8	12	Cook	Bones		15-18	5th	6
5-16	Cle.	W	5-3		9	10	Navarro	Bielecki	Henry	16-18	5th	5
5-18	Det.	L	1-5		6	11	Leiter	Eldred		16-19	5th	6
5-19	Det.	L	6-8		9	16	Doherty	Boddicker	Henneman	16-20	5th	7
5-20	Det.	L	2-6		7	8	Wells	Wegman		16-21	5th	8
5-21	At Bal.	W	9-3		10	7	Navarro	Mussina		17-21	5th	7
5-22	At Bal.	L	4-5	(14)	10	14	Williamson	Maldonado		17-22	5th	8
5-23	At Bal.	W	9-1		12	7	Eldred	Valenzuela		18-22	5th	8
5-24	At Tor.	L	1-4		2	10	Stewart	Boddicker	Ward	18-23	5th	8
5-25	At Tor.	L	2-4		7	8	Guzman	Wegman	Ward	18-24	5th	9
5-26	At Tor.	W	8-1		14	10	Navarro	Morris		19-24	5th	9
5-27	At Tor.	W	9-3		15	6	Bones	Leiter		20-24	5th	8½
5-28	K.C.	W	5-1		10	4	Eldred	Appier		21-24	5th	7½
5-29	K.C.	L	5-6	(13)	8	15	Sampen	Austin	Montgomery	21-25	5th	8½
5-30	K.C.	W	8-2		10	10	Wegman	Pichardo		22-25	5th	7½
6-1	At Sea.	W	10-0		9	9	Navarro	Bosio		23-25	5th	6½
6-2	At Sea.	L	3-6		6	9	Nelson	Eldred	Charlton	23-26	5th	6½
6-3	At K.C.	L	5-6		10	10	Gardner	Boddicker		23-27	5th	7½
6-4	At K.C.	L	2-3		11	7	Brewer	Wegman	Montgomery	23-28	5th	7½
6-5	At K.C.	W	8-2		9	5	Bones	Cone		24-28	5th	7½
6-6	At K.C.	L	7-8		10	15	Meacham	Austin		24-29	6th	8½
6-7	Sea.	W	5-3		9	7	Eldred	Fleming	Henry	25-29	6th	7½
6-8	Sea.	W	2-1		8	5	Austin	Leary	Henry	26-29	6th	7½
6-9	Sea.	L	1-6		8	14	Johnson	Wegman		26-30	6th	8½
6-10	N.Y.	L	1-3		10	8	Wickman	Bones	Farr	26-31	6th	9½
6-11	N.Y.	L	4-5		9	9	Perez	Henry	Farr	26-32	6th	10½
6-12	N.Y.	W	9-1		11	6	Eldred	Johnson		27-32	6th	10½
6-13	N.Y.	L	5-9		10	11	Key	Boddicker	Howe	27-33	6th	10½
6-14	Bal.	L	5-8		13	8	Sutcliffe	Wegman	Olson	27-34	6th	11½
6-15	Bal.	L	2-4		5	8	Moyer	Bones	Pennington	27-35	6th	12½
6-16	Bal.	W	7-2		12	5	Navarro	Mussina		28-35	6th	11½
6-18	At Det.	W	6-3		11	8	Eldred	Leiter	Henry	29-35	6th	11
6-19	At Det.	L	7-10		11	10	Wells	Wegman		29-36	6th	12
6-20	At Det.	L	3-7		8	10	Doherty	Bones		29-37	6th	13
6-21	At Cle.	L	0-3		4	8	Kramer	Navarro	Hernandez	29-38	6th	13½
6-22	At Cle.	L	2-3		6	8	Slocumb	Eldred	Lilliquist	29-39	6th	13½
6-23	At Cle.	L	1-3		5	4	Mesa	Wegman	Hernandez	29-40	7th	13½
6-24	At Cle.	W	5-3		10	3	Bones	Clark	Henry	30-40	6th	12½

Date	Opp.	Res.	Score	(inn.*)	Hits	Opp. hits	Winning pitcher	Losing pitcher	Save	Record	Pos.	GB
6-25	Tor.	W	6-5		8	6	Fetters	Cox		31-40	6th	11½
6-26	Tor.	L	2-3		6	7	Guzman	Eldred	Ward	31-41	7th	12½
6-27	Tor.	L	4-5		6	11	Morris	Wegman	Ward	31-42	7th	13½
6-28	At Bos.	L	3-4		11	8	Harris	Henry		31-43	7th	14½
6-29	At Bos.	W	7-6		7	9	Fetters	Harris	Henry	32-43	7th	14½
6-30	At Bos.	L	2-12		6	15	Darwin	Miranda		32-44	7th	14½
7-2	At Min.	L	10-11		14	14	Casian	Fetters		32-45	7th	14½
7-3	At Min.	W	3-1		7	5	Bones	Tapani	Henry	33-45	7th	13½
7-4	At Min.	L	3-4		9	9	Guardado	Navarro	Aguilera	33-46	7th	13½
7-5	Tex.	L	4-5		9	8	Schooler	Lloyd	Patterson	33-47	7th	13½
7-6	Tex.	L	1-11		6	17	Leibrandt	Wegman		33-48	7th	14½
7-7	Tex.	W	7-6		12	10	Henry	Lefferts		34-48	7th	13½
7-8	Min.	W	15-3		23	8	Bones	Tapani		35-48	7th	12½
7-9	Min.	L	6-10		14	15	Willis	Navarro		35-49	7th	12½
7-10	Min.	W	5-4		13	10	Henry	Aguilera		36-49	7th	11½
7-11	Min.	W	5-4		7	9	Eldred	Banks	Henry	37-49	7th	10½
7-15	Chi.	L	4-6		6	11	Fernandez	Fetters	Radinsky	37-50	7th	11½
7-16	Chi.	L	3-4		5	8	Radinsky	Eldred	Hernandez	37-51	7th	11½
7-17	Chi.	L	4-9		7	14	McDowell	Navarro		37-52	7th	11½
7-18	Chi.	L	1-3		7	5	Radinsky	Henry	Hernandez	37-53	7th	12½
7-19	At Tex.	L	3-5		8	9	Ryan	Bones	Henke	37-54	7th	13½
7-20	At Tex.	L	1-5		5	7	Brown	Eldred		37-55	7th	14
7-22	At Chi.	L	2-7		13	12	McDowell	Navarro		37-56	7th	15
7-23	At Chi.	W	3-2		7	4	Orosco	Hernandez	Henry	38-56	7th	14
7-24	At Chi.	L	5-6		10	14	Radinsky	Fetters		38-57	7th	15
7-25	At Chi.	W	7-3		9	8	Eldred	Fernandez		39-57	7th	15
7-26	Bos.	W	3-2		7	5	Lloyd	Russell		40-57	7th	14½
7-27	Bos.	W	3-2		9	5	Navarro	Darwin	Orosco	41-57	7th	14½
7-28	Bos.	L	4-8		6	11	Harris	Miranda		41-58	7th	15½
7-29	Bos.	L	3-7		11	9	Sele	Bones		41-59	7th	16½
7-30	At N.Y.	L	4-8		10	12	Kamieniecki	Eldred	Howe	41-60	7th	16½
7-31	At N.Y.	L	4-5		8	7	Wickman	Lloyd		41-61	7th	17½
8-1	At N.Y.	W	9-2		13	9	Navarro	Perez		42-61	7th	17½
8-2	At Bal.	L	5-7		9	11	Williamson	Lloyd	Olson	42-62	7th	18½
8-3	At Bal.	L	8-13		10	15	Frohwirth	Bones		42-63	7th	19½
8-4	At Bal.	L	6-8		7	10	Rhodes	Eldred	Olson	42-64	7th	19½
8-5	At Bal.	L	1-3		8	7	McDonald	Novoa		42-65	7th	19½
8-6	At Tor.	L	10-11	(11)	17	19	Leiter	Henry		42-66	7th	20½
8-7	At Tor.	W	7-1		12	6	Miranda	Stottlemyre		43-66	7th	19½
8-8	At Tor.	W	5-2		8	7	Bones	Hentgen		44-66	7th	18½
8-10	Cle.	W	5-4	(10)	10	10	Henry	Plunk		45-66	7th	18½
8-11	Cle.	L	5-7		8	12	DiPoto	Orosco	Lilliquist	45-67	7th	19½
8-12	Cle.	L	6-8	(11)	8	14	DiPoto	Maldonado	Plunk	45-68	7th	19½
8-13 (1)	Det.	W	6-1		8	6	Miranda	Groom		46-68	7th	18½
8-13 (2)	Det.	W	7-1		10	6	Bones	Bolton		47-68	7th	18
8-14	Det.	L	1-5		5	14	Moore	Higuera	Henneman	47-69	7th	19
8-15	Det.	W	6-4		9	9	Eldred	Doherty	Maldonado	48-69	7th	19
8-16	At Oak.	L	1-4		4	6	Van Poppel	Novoa	Eckersley	48-70	7th	20
8-17	At Oak.	L	3-6		7	7	Karsay	Navarro	Eckersley	48-71	7th	21
8-18	At Oak.	L	1-2		5	5	Darling	Miranda	Eckersley	48-72	7th	22
8-19	At Cal.	L	4-5	(12)	12	10	Grahe	Lloyd		48-73	7th	22½
8-20	At Cal.	W	7-2	(10)	8	6	Eldred	Frey		49-73	7th	21½
8-21	At Cal.	L	6-7		12	9	Patterson	Maysey		49-74	7th	21½
8-22	At Cal.	W	7-5		7	8	Henry	Magrane	Orosco	50-74	7th	21½
8-24 (1)	Oak.	W	9-2		13	8	Bones	Honeycutt		51-74	7th	21½
8-24 (2)	Oak.	W	7-6	(13)	21	14	Maysey	Downs		52-74	7th	21
8-25	Oak.	W	12-2		14	9	Eldred	Witt		53-74	7th	20½
8-26	Oak.	W	5-3		4	6	Miranda	Mohler	Orosco	54-74	7th	19½
8-27 (1)	Cal.	W	7-6		8	9	Fetters	Holzemer		55-74	7th	18½
8-27 (2)	Cal.	W	4-3		9	11	Navarro	Nelson	Orosco	56-74	7th	18
8-28	Cal.	L	2-6		9	16	Finley	Bones	Butcher	56-75	7th	18
8-29	Cal.	L	1-6		7	10	Langston	Novoa		56-76	7th	19
8-30	K.C.	W	2-1		7	4	Eldred	Gordon		57-76	7th	19
8-31	K.C.	L	5-6		7	11	Cadaret	Miranda	Montgomery	57-77	7th	19½
9-1	K.C.	W	7-1		10	7	Navarro	Haney		58-77	7th	20
9-2	At Sea.	L	1-8		5	15	Bosio	Higuera		58-78	7th	20½
9-3	At Sea.	W	7-4	(12)	12	11	Orosco	Brad Holman	Maysey	59-78	6th	20
9-4	At Sea.	L	1-6		7	7	Leary	Eldred	Power	59-79	7th	19½
9-5	At Sea.	L	2-3		5	5	Johnson	Miranda		59-80	7th	19½
9-6	At K.C.	W	3-2		5	7	Navarro	Cadaret	Orosco	60-80	7th	19
9-8	At K.C.	W	2-1		7	2	Bones	Brewer		61-80	7th	17½
9-10	Sea.	L	3-10		8	13	Leary	Higuera		61-81	7th	18
9-11	Sea.	L	3-7		7	13	Johnson	Eldred	Brad Holman	61-82	7th	19
9-12	Sea.	L	4-5	(10)	13	9	Power	Orosco		61-83	7th	20

Date	Opp.	Res.	Score	(inn.*)	Hits	Opp. hits	Winning pitcher	Losing pitcher	Save	Record	Pos.	GB
9-13	N.Y.	L	1-3		7	11	Key	Navarro	Smith	61-84	7th	20½
9-14	N.Y.	L	5-12		12	14	Gibson	Bones		61-85	7th	21½
9-15	N.Y.	W	15-5		16	10	Higuera	Abbott		62-85	7th	21½
9-17	Bal.	W	2-0		3	3	Eldred	McDonald		63-85	7th	21½
9-18	Bal.	W	3-0		10	4	Miranda	Moyer	Orosco	64-85	7th	21½
9-19	Bal.	L	4-8		8	15	Rhodes	Navarro	Mills	64-86	7th	22½
9-20	At Det.	L	3-6		7	10	Moore	Bones	Boever	64-87	7th	23
9-21	At Det.	W	7-4		10	13	Ignasiak	Davis	Orosco	65-87	7th	23
9-22	At Det.	L	4-8		9	8	Wells	Eldred		65-88	7th	23
9-24	At Cle.	W	11-8	(10)	19	12	Orosco	Lilliquist		66-88	7th	23½
9-25	At Cle.	L	2-6		7	9	Clark	Navarro		66-89	7th	24½
9-26	At Cle.	L	4-6		10	15	Hernandez	Ignasiak		66-90	7th	24½
9-27	Tor.	L	0-2		7	7	Hentgen	Eldred	Ward	66-91	7th	25½
9-28	Tor.	L	4-6		8	10	Stewart	Maysey	Ward	66-92	7th	26½
9-29	Tor.	L	6-9		8	14	Eichhorn	Orosco	Ward	66-93	7th	27½
10-1	At Bos.	W	8-4		14	8	Navarro	Harris		67-93	7th	27
10-2	At Bos.	W	8-5		11	11	Bones	Minchey	Kiefer	68-93	7th	26
10-3	At Bos.	W	6-3	(14)	9	5	Maldonado	Quantrill		69-93	7th	26

Monthly records: April (9-11), May (13-14), June (10-19), July (9-17), August (16-16), September (9-16), October (3-0).
*Innings, if other than nine.

HIGHLIGHTS

High point: Following a 6-5 win at Oakland on April 9, Milwaukee was 2-1. It was the only time all season the Brewers were over .500. Following a loss to Toronto on June 27, Milwaukee settled into last place for good.

Low point: From June 2 to July 6, the Brewers compiled a 10-23 record to go from 23-25 (6½ games out) to 33-48 (14½), falling out of the A.L. East race before the All-Star break.

Turning point: June 1, when shortstop Pat Listach strained his right hamstring in a 10-0 victory at Seattle, which gave Milwaukee a 23-25 record. The Brewers' infield was never really in sync again, and the team fell into the aforementioned funk from which it never recovered.

Most valuable player: Left fielder Greg Vaughn. He made the All-Star team for the first time and collected 30 homers (a career high) and 97 RBIs.

Most valuable pitcher: Righthander Cal Eldred. He led the league in innings pitched (258) en route to pacing the team with 16 wins.

Most improved player: First baseman John Jaha. After a slow start, he hit .284 with 14 homers and 44 RBIs in the second half of the year to finish with 19 homers and 70 RBIs.

Most pleasant surprise: Lefthander Graeme Lloyd. The first Australian ever to pitch in the big leagues, Lloyd made a Brewers rookie-record 55 appearances and compiled a 3-4 record with a 2.83 ERA in 63⅔ innings.

Biggest disappointments: Righthanders Bill Wegman and Jaime Navarro. Both struggled from the start and never got going. Wegman missed most of the second half with physical problems, and Navarro was simply ineffective (5.33 ERA).

Key injuries: In early May, Milwaukee had three center fielders (Robin Yount, Darryl Hamilton and Alex Diaz) on the disabled list, which created some problems. Listach was limited to 98 games due to a variety of injuries. Wegman made just two appearances after the All-Star break.

Notable: The Brewers finished last for the first time since 1984 and the fifth time overall.... On September 15, lefthander Ted Higuera earned his first win since June 23, 1991. ... Eldred set a team record for strikeouts by a righthander (180).... On April 14, catcher Dave Nilsson combined with countryman Lloyd to form the first Australian battery in big-league annals.

— BOB BERGHAUS

RECORDS

1993 regular-season record: 69-93 (7th in A.L. East); 38-43 at home; 31-50 on road; 32-46 vs. East; 37-47 vs. West; 22-36 vs. LHP; 47-57 vs. RHP; 58-79 on grass; 11-14 on turf; 25-35 in daytime; 44-58 at night; 21-26 in one-run games; 8-6 in extra-inning games; 3-0-0 in doubleheaders.

Team record last five years: 399-411 (.493, ranks 9th in league in that span).

TEAM LEADERS

Batting average: Darryl Hamilton (.310).
At-bats: Greg Vaughn (569).
Runs: Greg Vaughn (97).
Hits: Darryl Hamilton (161).
Total bases: Greg Vaughn (274).
Doubles: B.J. Surhoff (38).
Triples: Bill Spiers (4).
Home runs: Greg Vaughn (30).
Runs batted in: Greg Vaughn (97).
Stolen bases: Darryl Hamilton (21).
Slugging percentage: Greg Vaughn (.482).
On-base percentage: Greg Vaughn (.369).
Wins: Cal Eldred (16).
Earned-run average: Cal Eldred (4.01).
Complete games: Cal Eldred (8).
Shutouts: Cal Eldred, Jaime Navarro (1).
Saves: Doug Henry (17).
Innings pitched: Cal Eldred (258).
Strikeouts: Cal Eldred (180).

GAMES BY POSITION

Catcher: Dave Nilsson 91, Tom Lampkin 60, Joe Kmak 50, B.J. Surhoff 3, Tim McIntosh 1.

First base: John Jaha 150, B.J. Surhoff 8, Kevin Seitzer 7, Robin Yount 7, Bill Doran 4, Dave Nilsson 4.

Second base: Bill Spiers 104, Juan Bell 47, Dickie Thon 22, Bill Doran 17, William Suero 8, John Jaha 1, Kevin Seitzer 1.

Third base: B.J. Surhoff 121, Kevin Seitzer 33, Dickie Thon 25, John Jaha 1, William Suero 1.

Shortstop: Pat Listach 95, Juan Bell 40, Dickie Thon 28, Jose Valentin 19, Bill Spiers 4, Kevin Seitzer 1.

Outfield: Darryl Hamilton 129, Robin Yount 114, Greg Vaughn 94, Tom Brunansky 71, Kevin Reimer 37, Alex Diaz 28, B.J. Surhoff 24, Matt Mieske 22, Troy O'Leary 15, Pat Listach 6, Juan Bell 3, Tom Lampkin 3, Ricky Bones 1, Kevin Seitzer 1.

Designated hitter: Kevin Reimer 83, Greg Vaughn 58, Dickie Thon 14, Tom Brunansky 6, Robin Yount 6, Dave Nilsson 4, Kevin Seitzer 3, Juan Bell 2, Alex Diaz 1, Darryl Hamilton 1, Tom Lampkin 1, Bill Spiers 1, B.J. Surhoff 1.

TOP DRAFT CHOICES

1a. **Jeff D'Amico**, RHP, Northeast High School, St. Petersburg, Fla.
1b. **Kelly Wunsch**, LHP, Texas A&M U.
1c. **Todd Dunn**, OF, U. of North Florida.
1d. **Joe Wagner**, RHP, U. of Central Florida.
2a. **Brian Banks**, C, Brigham Young U.
2b. **Danny Klassen**, SS, John Carrol High School, Port St. Lucie, Fla.
3. **George Preston**, RHP, Brenham (Tex.) HS
4. **Shane Sheldon**, RHP, Gordon (Ga.) J.C.
5. **Steve Duda**, RHP, Pepperdine U.
6. **Josh Zwisler**, C, St. Vincent HS, Akron, O.
7. **Mark Loretta**, SS, Northwestern U.
8. **Tano Tijerina**, RHP, Navarro (Tex.) J.C.
9. **Jon Hillis**, RHP, Rice University.
10. **Chris McInnes**, SS, Ricks (Idaho) J.C.

1994 SCHEDULE

N Denotes night game (any game starting after 5 p.m.).
▦ Home games shaded.
* At Three Rivers Stadium in Pittsburgh.

APRIL

SUN	MON	TUE	WED	THU	FRI	SAT
					1	2
3	4	5 N CAL	6 N CAL	7 N CAL	8 N OAK	9 N OAK
10 OAK	11 N SEA	12 N SEA	13 SEA	14 N OAK	15 N OAK	16 OAK
17 OAK	18	19 N CLE	20 N CLE	21 N CLE	22 N TOR	23 TOR
24 TOR	25 N CLE	26 N CLE	27 N MIL	28 N MIL	29 N TOR	30 TOR

MAY

SUN	MON	TUE	WED	THU	FRI	SAT
1 TOR	2	3 N MIL	4 MIL	5	6 N TEX	7 N TEX
8 TOR	9 N KC	10 N KC	11 N KC	12	13 N BAL	14 N BAL
15 BAL	16	17 N NY	18 N NY	19	20 N BOS	21 N BOS
22 BOS	23	24 N CHI	25 N CHI	26	27 N DET	28 N DET
29 N DET	30 N SEA	31 N SEA				

JUNE

SUN	MON	TUE	WED	THU	FRI	SAT
				2 SEA	3 N DET	4 DET
5 N DET	6 N CAL	7 N CAL	8 N CAL	9 N CHI	10 N CHI	11 N CHI
12 CHI	13 N BOS	14 N BOS	15 N BOS	16 N BAL	17 N BAL	18 N BAL
19 BAL	20 N NY	21 N NY	22 N NY	23	24 N KC	25 N KC
26 KC	27 N KC	28 N TEX	29 N TEX	30 TEX		

JULY

SUN	MON	TUE	WED	THU	FRI	SAT
					1 N CLE	2 CLE
3 N CLE	4 CLE	5 N TOR	6 N TOR	7 N TOR	8 N CLE	9 N CLE
10 CLE	11	* 12 ALL-STAR GAME	13	14 N MIL	15 N MIL	16 N MIL
17 MIL	18 N TOR	19 N TOR	20 N TOR	21 N MIL	22 N MIL	23 N MIL
24 MIL	25 N TEX	26 N TEX	27 TEX	28	29 N KC	30 N KC
31 KC						

AUGUST

SUN	MON	TUE	WED	THU	FRI	SAT
	1 N BAL	2 N BAL	3 BAL	4 N NY	5 N NY	6 N NY
7 NY	8 N BOS	9 N BOS	10 N BOS	11	12 N CHI	13 N CHI
14 CHI	15 N CHI	16 N DET	17 N DET	18 N DET	19 N CAL	20 N CAL
21 CAL	22 N DET	23 N DET	24 N DET	25 N SEA	26 N SEA	27 N SEA
28 SEA	29	30 N OAK	31 N OAK			

SEPTEMBER

SUN	MON	TUE	WED	THU	FRI	SAT
				1 OAK	2 N SEA	3 SEA
4 SEA	5 N OAK	6 N OAK	7 OAK	8 N CAL	9 N CAL	10 N CAL
11 CAL	12 N CHI	13 N CHI	14 N CHI	15	16 N BOS	17 BOS
18 BOS	19 N BAL	20 N BAL	21 BAL	22	23 N NY	24 NY
25 NY	26 N KC	27 N KC	28 N KC	29 N TEX	30 N TEX	

OCTOBER

SUN	MON	TUE	WED	THU	FRI	SAT
						1 N TEX
2 TEX						

1994 SEASON

CLUB DIRECTORY

Owner
Carl R. Pohlad
President
Jerry Bell
Chairman of executive committee
Howard Fox
Directors
Donald E. Benson
Paul R. Christen
James O. Pohlad
Robert C. Pohlad
William M. Pohlad
Robert E. Woolley
Executive v.p., baseball operations/g.m.
Andy MacPhail
Vice president, player personnel
Terry Ryan
Vice president, marketing/sales
Bill Mahre
Chief financial officer
Kevin Mather
Vice president, stadium operations
Matt Hoy
Director of minor leagues
Jim Rantz
Director of scouting
Mike Radcliff
Assistant general manager
Bill Smith
Director of media relations
Rob Antony
Traveling secretary
Remzi Kiratli

Club physicians
Dr. Leonard J. Michienzi
Dr. John Steubs
Scouts
Floyd Baker
Vernon Borning
Ellsworth Brown
Gene DeBoer
Dan Durst
Cal Ermer
Marty Esposito
Vern Followell
Earl Frishman
Scott Groot
Joel Lepel
Bill Lohr
Kevin Murphy
Al Newman
Clair Rierson
Eddie Robinson
Edwin Rodriguez
Mike Ruth
Herb Stein
Ricky Taylor
Brad Weitzel
Steve Williams
John Wilson
International scouts
Enrique Brito
Howard Norsetter
Johnny Sierra

SPRING TRAINING ROSTER

Manager—Tom Kelly (10).

Coaches—Terry Crowley (46), Ron Gardenhire (35), Rick Stelmaszek (43), Dick Such (42), Wayne Terwilliger (45).

No.	PITCHERS	B/T	Ht./Wt.	Born	1993 clubs
38	Aguilera, Rick	R/R	6-5/203	12-31-61	Minnesota
57	Brummett, Greg	R/R	6-0/186	4-20-67	Phoenix, San Francisco, Minnesota
49	Caridad, Ron	R/R	5-10/181	3-22-72	Fort Wayne
48	Casian, Larry	R/L	6-0/173	10-28-65	Minnesota, Portland
56	Correa, Jose	R/R	6-2/194	6-21-72	Fort Wayne
	Deshaies, Jim	L/L	6-5/222	6-23-60	Las Vegas, San Diego
19	Erickson, Scott	R/R	6-4/222	2-2-68	Minnesota
54	Garagozzo, Keith	L/L	6-0/170	10-25-69	Prince William, Albany/Colonie
18	Guardado, Eddie	R/L	6-0/193	10-2-70	Nashville, Minnesota
53	Guthrie, Mark	R/L	6-4/206	9-22-65	Minnesota
20	Mahomes, Pat	R/R	6-4/210	8-9-70	Minnesota, Portland
47	Merriman, Brett	R/R	6-2/216	7-15-66	Minnesota, Portland
55	Munoz, Oscar	R/R	6-3/210	9-25-69	Nashville, Portland
22	Pulido, Carlos	L/L	6-0/194	8-5-71	Portland
30	Ritchie, Todd	R/R	6-3/190	11-7-71	Nashville
44	Stevens, Dave	R/R	6-3/210	3-4-70	Iowa, Orlando
36	Tapani, Kevin	R/R	6-0/188	2-18-64	Minnesota
21	Trombley, Mike	R/R	6-2/208	4-14-67	Minnesota
51	Willis, Carl	L/R	6-4/213	12-28-60	Portland, Minnesota

No.	CATCHERS	B/T	Ht./Wt.	Born	1993 clubs
27	Durant, Mike	R/R	6-2/200	9-14-69	Nashville
16	Parks, Derek	R/R	6-0/217	9-29-68	Portland, Minnesota
9	Walbeck, Matt	B/R	5-11/190	10-2-69	Chicago N.L., Iowa
15	Webster, Lenny	R/R	5-9/195	2-10-65	Minnesota

No.	INFIELDERS	B/T	Ht./Wt.	Born	1993 clubs
39	Dunn, Steve	L/L	6-4/225	4-18-70	Nashville
4	Hale, Chip	L/R	5-11/191	12-2-64	Portland, Minnesota
7	Hocking, Denny	B/R	5-10/176	4-2-70	Nashville, Minnesota
14	Hrbek, Kent	L/R	6-4/260	5-21-60	Minnesota
11	Knoblauch, Chuck	R/R	5-9/181	7-7-68	Minnesota
31	Leius, Scott	R/R	6-3/208	9-24-65	Minnesota
2	Meares, Pat	R/R	6-0/184	9-6-68	Portland, Minnesota
17	Reboulet, Jeff	R/R	6-0/169	4-30-64	Minnesota
1	Scott, Gary	R/R	6-0/175	8-22-68	Indianapolis, Portland
37	Stahoviak, Scott	L/R	6-5/208	3-6-70	Nashville, Minnesota

No.	OUTFIELDERS	B/T	Ht./Wt.	Born	1993 clubs
25	Becker, Rich	B/L	5-10/180	2-1-72	Nashville, Minnesota
26	Bruett, J.T.	L/L	5-11/180	10-8-67	Minnesota, Portland
40	Cordova, Marty	R/R	6-0/200	7-10-69	Nashville
24	Mack, Shane	R/R	6-0/190	12-7-63	Minnesota
8	McCarty, David	R/L	6-5/207	11-23-69	Portland, Minnesota
5	Munoz, Pedro	R/R	5-10/203	9-19-68	Minnesota
34	Puckett, Kirby	R/R	5-9/215	3-14-61	Minnesota
32	Winfield, Dave	R/R	6-6/245	10-3-51	Minnesota

BALLPARK INFORMATION

Ballpark (capacity, surface)
Hubert H. Humphrey Metrodome
(56,783, artificial)

Address
501 Chicago Ave. South
Minneapolis, MN 55415

Business phone
612-375-1366

Ticket information
612-375-7444

Ticket prices
$17 (VIP level)
$15 (lower deck club level)
$12 (lower deck reserved)
$11 (upper deck club level)
$10 (upper deck reserved)
$7 (g.a., lower left field)
$4 (g.a., upper deck)

Field dimensions (from home plate)
To left field at foul line, 343 feet
To center field, 408 feet
To right field at foul line, 327 feet

First game played
April 6, 1982 (Mariners 11, Twins 7)

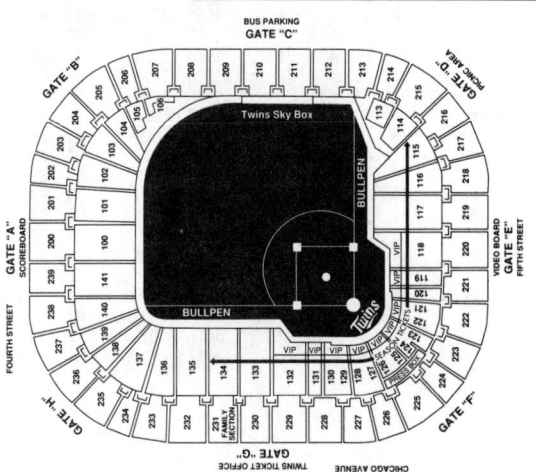

MINOR LEAGUE AFFILIATES

Class	Team	League	Manager
AAA	Salt Lake City	Pacific Coast	Scott Ullger
AA	Nashville	Southern	Phil Roof
A	Fort Myers	Florida State	Steve Liddle
A	Fort Wayne	Midwest	Jim Dwyer
Rookie	Elizabethton	Appalachian	Ray Smith
Rookie	Gulf Coast Twins	Gulf Coast	Jose Marzan

BROADCAST INFORMATION

Radio: WCCO-AM (830). Broadcasters: Herb Carneal, John Gordon.
TV: WCCO-TV (Channel 4). Broadcasters: George Frazier, Jim Kaat, Dick Bremer.
Cable TV: Midwest Sports Channel. Broadcasters: Jim Kaat, Dick Bremer, George Frazier.

SPRING TRAINING

Ballpark (city): Lee County Sports Complex (Fort Myers, Fla.).
Ticket information: 800-33-TWINS.

HISTORY

YEAR-BY-YEAR RECORDS

Year	Pos.	W	L	Pct.	GB	Year	Pos.	W	L	Pct.	GB
1901*	6th	61	72	.459	20½	1950*	5th	67	87	.435	31
1902*	6th	61	75	.449	22	1951*	7th	62	92	.403	36
1903*	8th	43	94	.314	47½	1952*	5th	78	76	.506	17
1904*	8th	38	113	.251	55½	1953*	5th	76	76	.500	23½
1905*	7th	64	87	.421	29½	1954*	6th	66	88	.429	45
1906*	7th	55	95	.367	37½	1955*	8th	53	101	.344	43
1907*	8th	49	102	.325	43½	1956*	7th	59	95	.383	38
1908*	7th	67	85	.441	22½	1957*	8th	55	99	.357	43
1909*	8th	42	110	.276	56	1958*	8th	61	93	.396	31
1910*	7th	66	85	.437	36½	1959*	8th	63	91	.409	31
1911*	7th	64	90	.416	38½	1960*	5th	73	81	.474	24
1912*	2nd	91	61	.599	14	1961	7th	70	90	.438	38
1913*	2nd	90	64	.584	6½	1962	2nd	91	71	.562	5
1914*	3rd	81	73	.526	19	1963	3rd	91	70	.565	13
1915*	4th	85	68	.556	17	1964	T6th	79	83	.488	20
1916*	7th	76	77	.497	14½	1965	1st	102	60	.630 +	7
1917*	5th	74	79	.484	25½	1966	2nd	89	73	.549	9
1918*	3rd	72	56	.563	4	1967	T2nd	91	71	.562	1
1919*	7th	56	84	.400	32	1968	7th	79	83	.488	24
1920*	6th	68	84	.447	29	1969	1st†	97	65	.599 +	9
1921*	4th	80	73	.523	18	1970	1st†	98	64	.605 +	9
1922*	6th	69	85	.448	25	1971	5th	74	86	.463	26½
1923*	4th	75	78	.490	23½	1972	3rd	77	77	.500	15½
1924*	1st	92	62	.597 +	2	1973	3rd	81	81	.500	13
1925*	1st	96	55	.636 +	8½	1974	3rd	82	80	.506	8
1926*	4th	81	69	.540	8	1975	4th	76	83	.478	20½
1927*	3rd	85	69	.552	25	1976	3rd	85	77	.525	5
1928*	4th	75	79	.487	26	1977	4th	84	77	.522	17½
1929*	5th	71	81	.467	34	1978	4th	73	89	.451	19
1930*	2nd	94	60	.610	8	1979	4th	82	80	.506	6
1931*	3rd	92	62	.597	16	1980	3rd	77	84	.478	19½
1932*	3rd	93	61	.604	14	1981	7th/4th	41	68	.376	‡
1933*	1st	99	53	.651 +	7	1982	7th	60	102	.370	33
1934*	7th	66	86	.434	34	1983	T5th	70	92	.432	29
1935*	6th	67	86	.438	27	1984	T2nd	81	81	.500	3
1936*	4th	82	71	.536	20	1985	T4th	77	85	.475	14
1937*	6th	73	80	.477	28½	1986	6th	71	91	.438	21
1938*	5th	75	76	.497	23½	1987	1st§	85	77	.525 +	2
1939*	6th	65	87	.428	41½	1988	2nd	91	71	.562	13
1940*	7th	64	90	.416	26	1989	5th	80	82	.494	19
1941*	T6th	70	84	.455	31	1990	7th	74	88	.457	29
1942*	7th	62	89	.411	39½	1991	1st§	95	67	.586 +	8
1943*	2nd	84	69	.549	13½	1992	2nd	90	72	.556	6
1944*	8th	64	90	.416	25	1993	T5th	71	91	.438	23
1945*	2nd	87	67	.565	1½						
1946*	4th	76	78	.494	28						
1947*	7th	64	90	.416	33						
1948*	7th	56	97	.366	40						
1949*	8th	50	104	.325	47						

*Franchise known as Washington Senators (original team). †Lost Championship Series. ‡First half 17-39; second 24-29. §Won Championship Series.

MANAGERS

Name	Record	Years
Jimmy Manning	61-72	1901
Tom Loftus	104-169	'02-03
Patsy Donovan	38-113	1904
Jake Stahl	119-182	'05-06
Joe Cantillon	158-297	'07-09
Jimmy McAleer	130-175	'10-11
Clark Griffith	693-646	'12-20
George McBride	80-73	1921
Clyde Milan	69-85	1922
Donie Bush	75-78	1923
Bucky Harris	1336-1416	'24-28
		'35-42
		'50-54
Walter Johnson	350-264	'29-32
Joe Cronin	165-139	'33-34
Ossie Bluege	375-394	'43-47
Joe Kuhel	106-201	'48-49
Chuck Dressen	116-212	'55-57
Cookie Lavagetto	271-384	'57-61
Sam Mele	524-436	'61-67
Cal Ermer	145-129	'67-68
Billy Martin	97-65	1969
Bill Rigney	208-184	'70-72
Frank Quilici	280-287	'72-75
Gene Mauch	378-394	'76-80
Johnny Goryl	34-38	'80-81
Billy Gardner	268-353	'81-85
Ray Miller	109-130	'85-86
Tom Kelly	598-559	'86-93

DAY BY DAY

Date	Opp.	Res.	Score (Inn.*)	Hits	Opp. hits	Winning pitcher	Losing pitcher	Save	Record	Pos.	GB
4-6	Chi.	L	5-10	9	13	McDowell	Tapani	Leach	0-1	T6th	1
4-7	Chi.	W	6-1	10	4	Deshaies	McCaskill	Aguilera	1-1	T3rd	1
4-8	Chi.	L	4-9	8	8	Fernandez	Mahomes		1-2	6th	1½
4-9	At K.C.	W	8-7	9	14	Trombley	Gardner	Aguilera	2-2	T4th	1½
4-10	At K.C.	W	3-2	8	9	Banks	Appier	Aguilera	3-2	T2nd	½
4-11	At K.C.	L	1-2	5	6	Gordon	Tapani	Montgomery	3-3	T4th	1½
4-12	At Chi.	W	3-2	6	5	Deshaies	McCaskill	Aguilera	4-3	5th	1½
4-13	At Chi.	L	0-4	3	9	Fernandez	Mahomes		4-4	T4th	2½
4-16	K.C.	W	4-3 (10)	7	4	Guthrie	Meacham		5-4	T3rd	1
4-17	K.C.	W	8-2	8	7	Deshaies	Cone	Hartley	6-4	3rd	1
4-18	K.C.	L	4-5	9	10	Pichardo	Erickson	Montgomery	6-5	3rd	2
4-20	Mil.	W	10-0	11	8	Banks	Navarro		7-5	3rd	1
4-21	Mil.	L	8-10 (10)	12	12	Maldonado	Hartley	Henry	7-6	3rd	1½
4-22	Mil.	W	5-4	8	8	Deshaies	Wegman	Aguilera	8-6	3rd	1½
4-23	Det.	L	4-12	7	14	Moore	Erickson		8-7	T3rd	2½
4-24	Det.	L	1-17	8	18	Doherty	Mahomes		8-8	T3rd	3½
4-25	Det.	L	5-16	8	14	Leiter	Guthrie		8-9	T3rd	4½
4-26	At Mil.	L	3-10	13	12	Bones	Tapani		8-10	5th	5
4-27	At Mil.	L	2-3	9	10	Wegman	Deshaies	Henry	8-11	5th	5
4-28	At Bal.	L	4-8	7	10	Rhodes	Erickson		8-12	6th	6
4-29	At Bal.	L	0-11	5	11	Mussina	Mahomes		8-13	6th	6½
4-30	At Det.	L	0-8	4	10	Wells	Banks		8-14	7th	6½
5-1	At Det.	W	5-2	6	6	Tapani	Bolton	Aguilera	9-14	6th	5½
5-2	At Det.	W	6-3	10	10	Trombley	Haas	Aguilera	10-14	5th	4½
5-4	Bal.	W	4-3	12	4	Erickson	Rhodes	Aguilera	11-14	5th	3
5-5	Bal.	L	0-3	2	8	Mussina	Banks		11-15	5th	4
5-7	At Sea.	W	5-4	8	11	Guthrie	Swan	Aguilera	12-15	5th	4½
5-8	At Sea.	L	2-7	6	9	Hanson	Deshaies		12-16	T5th	5
5-9	At Sea.	L	4-6	11	8	Leary	Erickson	Charlton	12-17	T5th	6
5-10	At Cal.	W	13-3	22	9	Banks	Farrell		13-17	5th	6
5-11	At Cal.	L	3-5	10	8	Sanderson	Trombley	Grahe	13-18	6th	6
5-12	At Cal.	W	5-2	10	9	Tapani	Finley	Aguilera	14-18	5th	6
5-14	Bos.	W	4-3	8	5	Erickson	Viola	Aguilera	15-18	T5th	6
5-15	Bos.	W	7-4	11	8	Deshaies	Dopson	Aguilera	16-18	5th	5
5-16	Bos.	L	5-11	8	17	Hesketh	Hartley		16-19	T5th	6
5-17	N.Y.	L	5-11	12	18	Key	Tapani		16-20	6th	6
5-18	N.Y.	L	3-5	9	8	Abbott	Trombley	Farr	16-21	6th	7
5-19	N.Y.	L	6-11	9	15	Monteleone	Erickson		16-22	6th	7
5-21	At Tor.	L	2-11	5	16	Morris	Deshaies		16-23	7th	7
5-22	At Tor.	L	0-7	6	13	Cox	Tapani		16-24	7th	7
5-23	At Tor.	L	1-2	7	7	Hentgen	Erickson	Ward	16-25	7th	8
5-25	At Oak.	L	1-3	7	6	Davis	Deshaies	Eckersley	16-26	7th	8
5-26	At Oak.	W	12-11	17	14	Tsamis	Boever		17-26	7th	7
5-28	Cle.	W	7-6	9	9	Aguilera	Power		18-26	7th	6½
5-29	Cle.	W	9-3	15	6	Banks	Bielecki		19-26	7th	6½
5-30	Cle.	W	8-2	15	6	Deshaies	Kramer	Trombley	20-26	6th	6½
5-31	Tex.	L	0-1	7	4	Leibrandt	Tapani	Henke	20-27	6th	6½
6-1	Tex.	W	7-5	10	7	Mahomes	Bohanon	Aguilera	21-27	6th	5½
6-2	Tex.	W	6-3	10	8	Banks	Pavlik	Aguilera	22-27	6th	4½
6-4	At Cle.	W	3-2	8	6	Deshaies	Hernandez	Aguilera	23-27	6th	5
6-5	At Cle.	L	6-7	12	13	Plunk	Trombley		23-28	6th	5
6-6	At Cle.	W	5-4	8	16	Erickson	Cook	Aguilera	24-28	6th	5
6-7	At Tex.	L	2-8	7	12	Pavlik	Mahomes		24-29	6th	6
6-8	At Tex.	W	3-2 (10)	9	9	Willis	Whiteside	Aguilera	25-29	5th	5
6-10	At Tex.	W	6-5	10	12	Tapani	Leibrandt	Aguilera	26-29	5th	5
6-11	Oak.	W	11-8	15	14	Trombley	Nunez	Aguilera	27-29	5th	4
6-12	Oak.	W	7-2	11	5	Deshaies	Witt		28-29	4th	3½
6-13	Oak.	L	6-7	12	15	Nunez	Tsamis	Eckersley	28-30	5th	4
6-14	Tor.	W	4-3	9	8	Casian	Cox	Willis	29-30	4th	3
6-15	Tor.	L	3-6	4	6	Guzman	Tapani	Ward	29-31	6th	3
6-16	Tor.	L	0-4	5	7	Morris	Erickson		29-32	6th	4
6-17	At NY	L	5-6	10	13	Munoz	Casian	Farr	29-33	6th	4½
6-18	At NY	L	0-5	9	5	Key	Guardado		29-34	6th	4½
6-19	At NY	L	4-8	7	9	Kamieniecki	Banks		29-35	6th	5½
6-20	At NY	L	0-8	6	13	Wickman	Tapani		29-36	6th	5½
6-21	At Bos.	L	3-6	12	8	Dopson	Erickson	Russell	29-37	6th	5½
6-22	At Bos.	L	1-4	9	7	Quantrill	Deshaies	Russell	29-38	6th	6½
6-23	At Bos.	L	1-3	5	10	Sele	Guardado	Harris	29-39	6th	7½
6-25	Cal.	W	8-5	12	14	Erickson	Springer	Aguilera	30-39	6th	6½
6-26	Cal.	L	0-4	3	5	Finley	Banks		30-40	6th	7½

— 59 —

Date	Opp.	Res.	Score	(inn.*)	Hits	Opp. hits	Winning pitcher	Losing pitcher	Save	Record	Pos.	GB
6-27	Cal.	W	2-0		6	4	Deshaies	Sanderson	Aguilera	31-40	6th	7½
6-28	Sea.	L	1-4		5	8	Fleming	Tapani	Charlton	31-41	6th	7½
6-29	Sea.	W	7-5		15	9	Trombley	Ayrault	Aguilera	32-41	6th	6½
6-30	Sea.	L	3-6		8	12	Johnson	Erickson	Charlton	32-42	6th	6½
7-1	Sea.	L	1-6		8	10	Hanson	Banks		32-43	7th	6½
7-2	Mil.	W	11-10		14	14	Casian	Fetters		33-43	7th	6½
7-3	Mil.	L	1-3		5	7	Bones	Tapani	Henry	33-44	7th	6½
7-4	Mil.	W	4-3		9	9	Guardado	Navarro	Aguilera	34-44	7th	6½
7-5	Det.	W	13-3		17	11	Erickson	Wells		35-44	7th	6½
7-6	Det.	L	1-4		7	8	Doherty	Banks	Henneman	35-45	7th	6½
7-7	Det.	L	4-8		11	15	Gullickson	Deshaies		35-46	7th	7½
7-8	At Mil.	L	3-15		8	23	Bones	Tapani		35-47	7th	8½
7-9	At Mil.	W	10-6		15	14	Willis	Navarro		36-47	7th	7½
7-10	At Mil.	L	4-5		10	13	Henry	Aguilera		36-48	7th	7½
7-11	At Mil.	L	4-5		9	7	Eldred	Banks	Henry	36-49	7th	8½
7-15	At Bal.	L	3-5		5	11	McDonald	Erickson	Olson	36-50	7th	9½
7-16	At Bal.	L	7-9		13	11	Mussina	Deshaies	Olson	36-51	7th	10½
7-17	At Bal.	W	4-2		7	9	Tapani	Sutcliffe	Aguilera	37-51	7th	10½
7-18	At Bal.	L	2-7		6	9	Valenzuela	Guardado		37-52	7th	11½
7-19	At Det.	W	4-2		10	6	Erickson	Bergman	Aguilera	38-52	7th	10½
7-20	At Det.	W	4-3		11	4	Deshaies	Leiter	Aguilera	39-52	7th	10½
7-21	At Det.	W	7-2		14	7	Tapani	Wells	Willis	40-52	7th	9½
7-22	Bal.	W	8-4		13	12	Banks	Sutcliffe	Trombley	41-52	6th	9½
7-23	Bal.	L	1-5		6	13	Valenzuela	Guardado		41-53	6th	9½
7-24	Bal.	L	2-9		9	13	Moyer	Erickson	Poole	41-54	6th	10½
7-25	Bal.	W	5-2		9	10	Deshaies	McDonald	Aguilera	42-54	6th	9½
7-27	At Sea.	L	8-10		13	12	DeLucia	Tsamis	Nelson	42-55	6th	11
7-28	At Sea.	W	5-1		9	5	Banks	Johnson	Casian	43-55	6th	11
7-29	At Sea.	L	3-4		7	10	Leary	Erickson	Power	43-56	6th	11½
7-30	At Cal.	L	2-4		9	9	Hathaway	Deshaies	Butcher	43-57	T6th	12½
7-31	At Cal.	L	3-4		8	7	Finley	Aguilera		43-58	T6th	13½
8-1	At Cal.	W	9-2		16	9	Guardado	Springer		44-58	6th	13½
8-3	Bos.	W	6-1		11	8	Banks	Dopson		45-58	6th	13
8-4	Bos.	L	4-5		12	11	Sele	Erickson	Russell	45-59	T6th	13
8-5	Bos.	L	1-2		5	6	Viola	Deshaies	Russell	45-60	T6th	13
8-6	N.Y.	W	4-3		12	4	Tapani	Wickman		46-60	T6th	12
8-7	N.Y.	W	6-5		13	11	Willis	Munoz		47-60	6th	12
8-8	N.Y.	L	6-8	(10)	9	9	Farr	Aguilera		47-61	6th	12
8-10	At Tor.	L	3-6		5	13	Stewart	Erickson	Ward	47-62	6th	13½
8-11	At Tor.	L	2-4		6	5	Guzman	Deshaies	Ward	47-63	6th	13½
8-12	At Tor.	W	9-2		13	6	Tapani	Morris		48-63	6th	12½
8-13	At Oak.	W	5-2		9	5	Guardado	Darling	Aguilera	49-63	6th	12½
8-14 (1)	At Oak.	W	5-1	(12)	9	7	Casian	Honeycutt		50-63	6th	13
8-14 (2)	At Oak.	W	6-2		8	10	Trombley	Downs	Tsamis	51-63	6th	12½
8-15	At Oak.	W	12-5		17	15	Erickson	Mohler		52-63	6th	11
8-17	K.C.	L	2-3		12	8	Haney	Deshaies	Montgomery	52-64	6th	12
8-18	K.C.	L	2-5		5	10	Appier	Tapani	Montgomery	52-65	6th	12
8-19	K.C.	L	2-4		7	11	Cone	Guardado		52-66	6th	12½
8-20	Chi.	L	2-4		5	10	Fernandez	Erickson	Hernandez	52-67	6th	13½
8-21	Chi.	L	4-9		7	13	Belcher	Banks	Hernandez	52-68	6th	14½
8-22	Chi.	L	0-1		8	3	McDowell	Deshaies		52-69	6th	15½
8-23	At K.C.	W	3-2	(10)	9	11	Casian	Montgomery	Willis	53-69	6th	14½
8-24	At K.C.	L	3-5		8	10	Cone	Guardado	Montgomery	53-70	6th	15½
8-25	At K.C.	W	4-2		6	9	Erickson	Gordon	Willis	54-70	6th	14½
8-26	At K.C.	L	0-3		7	5	Magnante	Banks	Montgomery	54-71	6th	15
8-27 (1)	At Chi.	L	3-7		9	11	Belcher	Deshaies		54-72	6th	15½
8-27 (2)	At Chi.	W	7-2	(10)	17	9	Casian	Pall		55-72	6th	15
8-28	At Chi.	L	1-4		6	7	Bere	Tapani		55-73	6th	16
8-29	At Chi.	L	5-13		12	18	McCaskill	Guardado		55-74	6th	17
8-30	At Chi.	L	1-4		3	7	Fernandez	Erickson	Hernandez	55-75	6th	18
8-31	Cle.	W	5-4	(22)	17	16	Merriman	Grimsley		56-75	6th	18
9-1	Cle.	L	7-12		10	22	Lilliquist	Trombley	Plunk	56-76	6th	19
9-2	Cle.	L	3-4		9	8	Kramer	Tapani	DiPoto	56-77	6th	19
9-3	Tex.	W	9-5		15	13	Brummett	Dreyer	Aguilera	57-77	6th	19
9-4	Tex.	L	4-6		9	13	Brown	Erickson	Henke	57-78	6th	20
9-5	Tex.	W	8-3		11	5	Banks	Rogers		58-78	6th	20
9-7	At Cle.	W	6-0		10	4	Tapani	Grimsley		59-78	6th	18½
9-8	At Cle.	L	8-15		13	15	Mesa	Brummett		59-79	6th	19½
9-9	At Cle.	W	5-3	(12)	13	12	Aguilera	Lilliquist		60-79	6th	19
9-10 (1)	At Tex.	L	3-4		8	13	Rogers	Banks	Henke	60-80	6th	19
9-10 (2)	At Tex.	L	2-3		7	8	Carpenter	Casian	Henke	60-81	6th	19½
9-11	At Tex.	L	4-7		5	12	Reed	Casian	Nelson	60-82	6th	20½
9-12	At Tex.	W	4-2		6	7	Tapani	Ryan	Aguilera	61-82	6th	19½
9-13	Oak.	L	2-7		6	17	Witt	Erickson		61-83	6th	19½

Date	Opp.	Res.	Score	(inn.*)	Hits	Opp. hits	Winning pitcher	Losing pitcher	Save	Record	Pos.	GB
9-14	Oak.	L	3-8		5	11	Karsay	Guardado	Smithberg	61-84	6th	2½
9-15	Oak.	L	2-15		8	18	Van Poppel	Banks		61-85	6th	21½
9-16	Oak.	W	5-4	(13)	13	9	Hartley	Smithberg		62-85	6th	21
9-17	Tor.	L	2-4		3	12	Hentgen	Tapani	Ward	62-86	6th	22
9-18	Tor.	L	1-5		7	8	Stewart	Erickson	Timlin	62-87	6th	22
9-19	Tor.	L	0-10		9	15	Guzman	Trombley		62-88	6th	23
9-21	At NY	W	5-4		11	8	Banks	Abbott	Aguilera	63-88	6th	22½
9-22	At NY	W	5-2		9	6	Tapani	Kamieniecki	Aguilera	64-88	6th	22½
9-24	At Bos.	L	4-7		8	11	Ryan	Merriman		64-89	T6th	24
9-25	At Bos.	W	9-7	(10)	13	11	Aguilera	Harris	Willis	65-89	T6th	23½
9-26	At Bos.	W	5-2		11	11	Trombley	Quantrill	Aguilera	66-89	T6th	23
9-27	Cal.	W	11-3		14	10	Banks	Finley		67-89	6th	23
9-28	Cal.	W	2-1		6	8	Tapani	Langston		68-89	6th	22
9-29	Cal.	W	3-2	(10)	9	6	Aguilera	Scott		69-89	T5th	22
9-30	Cal.	W	4-3		9	7	Brummett	Farrell	Aguilera	70-89	5th	21
10-1	Sea.	L	2-8		9	14	Johnson	Trombley		70-90	5th	22
10-2	Sea.	L	3-7		7	10	Fleming	Banks		70-91	T5th	23
10-3	Sea.	W	7-2		9	6	Tapani	Leary		71-91	T5th	23

Monthly records: April (8-14), May (12-13), June (12-15), July (11-16), August (13-17), September (14-14), October (1-2).
*Innings, if other than nine.

HIGHLIGHTS

High point: Following a win on April 22, the Twins owned an 8-6 record, prompting one local columnist to write that they were off to their best start in years. The next day, Minnesota began the first of three losing streaks that would last at least eight games.

Low point: The Twins set a team record by going winless on a road trip of seven or more games. From June 17-23, Minnesota lost four games in New York and then lost in Boston.

Turning point: Righthander Scott Erickson was placed on the disabled list April 3 with an injury to his left oblique muscles. Although he regained his stuff, he never seemed to regain his sharpness, and he finished with a major league-high 19 losses.

Most valuable player: Right fielder Kirby Puckett. Despite posting his lowest batting average (.296) since 1985, he still led the team in RBIs (89) and played excellent defense.

Most valuable pitcher: Righthander Rick Aguilera. He finished with 30 or more saves (34) for the fourth straight season and could have had bigger numbers had he pitched for a contender.

Most improved player: Second baseman Chip Hale. He had bounced around the organization since 1987 and hadn't hit over .300 at any level other than Class A. But in 1993 he hit .333 and was excellent in the clutch.

Most pleasant surprise: Shortstop Pat Meares. Thrust into the starting job when Scott Leius got hurt early in the season, Meares played well defensively and offensively before wearing out and slumping near the end.

Biggest disappointments: Erickson and righthander Kevin Tapani. Supposedly the leaders of the rotation, they combined to lose 34 games.

Key injuries: Lefthander Mark Guthrie was lost for the season on May 30 with an impinged vein in his shoulder. Leius was lost for the year on April 25 with right rotator cuff problems. Erickson began the season on the disabled list. First baseman Kent Hrbek and outfield-

ers Shane Mack and Pedro Munoz also spent time on the shelf.

Notable: Designated hitter Dave Winfield collected his 3,000th career hit September 16. . . . Puckett was named the MVP of the All-Star Game. . . . Tapani became the first Twins pitcher since 1961 to lead the team in wins with a losing record. . . . Brian Harper became just the fourth catcher in the last 40 years to hit .300 in three straight years.

—JIM SOUHAN

RECORDS

1993 regular-season record: 71-91 (T5th in A.L. West); 36-45 at home; 35-46 on road; 34-50 vs. East; 37-41 vs. West; 21-23 vs. LHP; 50-68 vs. RHP; 28-34 on grass; 43-57 on turf; 25-31 in daytime; 46-60 at night; 27-19 in one-run games; 10-2 in extra-inning games; 1-1-1 in doubleheaders.

Team record last five years: 410-400 (.506, ranks 5th in league in that span).

TEAM LEADERS

Batting average: Brian Harper (.304).
At-bats: Kirby Puckett (622).
Runs: Kirby Puckett (89).
Hits: Kirby Puckett (184).
Total bases: Kirby Puckett (295).
Doubles: Kirby Puckett (39).
Triples: Chuck Knoblauch, Shane Mack, Mike Pagliarulo (4).
Home runs: Kent Hrbek (25).
Runs batted in: Kirby Puckett (89).
Stolen bases: Chuck Knoblauch (29).
Slugging percentage: Kirby Puckett (.474).
On-base percentage: Chuck Knoblauch (.354).
Wins: Kevin Tapani (12).
Earned-run average: Willie Banks (4.04).
Complete games: Kevin Tapani (3).
Shutouts: Kevin Tapani (1).
Saves: Rick Aguilera (34).
Innings pitched: Kevin Tapani (225⅔).
Strikeouts: Kevin Tapani (150).

GAMES BY POSITION

Catcher: Brian Harper 134, Lenny Webster 45, Derek Parks 7.
First base: Kent Hrbek 115, Dave McCarty 36, Gene Larkin 18, Terry Jorgensen 9, Dave Winfield 5, Randy Bush 4, Mike Maksudian 4, Chip Hale 1.
Second base: Chuck Knoblauch 148, Chip Hale 21, Jeff Reboulet 11, Dennis Hocking 1.
Third base: Mike Pagliarulo 79, Terry Jorgensen 45, Jeff Reboulet 35, Chip Hale 19, Scott Stahoviak 19, Gene Larkin 2, Mike Maksudian 1.
Shortstop: Pat Meares 111, Jeff Reboulet 62, Dennis Hocking 12, Scott Leius 9, Terry Jorgensen 6, Chuck Knoblauch 6, Chip Hale 1.
Outfield: Kirby Puckett 139, Shane Mack 128, Pedro Munoz 102, Dave McCarty 67, Dave Winfield 31, Gene Larkin 28, J.T. Bruett 13, Derek Lee 13, Bernardo Brito 10, Rich Becker 3, Jeff Reboulet 3, Randy Bush 1, Chuck Knoblauch 1.
Designated hitter: Dave Winfield 105, Chip Hale 19, Kirby Puckett 17, Bernardo Brito 7, Brian Harper 7, Randy Bush 5, Gene Larkin 3, Kent Hrbek 2, Dave McCarty 2, Jeff Reboulet 1, Lenny Webster 1.

TOP DRAFT CHOICES

1a. **Torii Hunter**, OF, Pine Bluff (Ark.) H.S.
1b. **Jason Varitek**, C, Georgia Tech.
1c. **Marc Barcelo**, RHP, Arizona State U.
1d. **Kelsey Mucker**, OF, Lawrenceburg (Ind.) HS
2. **Dan Perkins**, RHP, Westminster Christian High School, Miami
3a. **Troy Carrasco**, LHP, Jesuit HS, Tampa.
3b. **Jose Valentin**, 3B, Manati, Puerto Rico.
4. **Toby Dollar**, RHP, Graham (Tex.) H.S.
5. **Jesse Ibarra**, 1B, Loyola Marymount U.
6. **Benj Sampson**, LHP, Ankeny (Iowa) H.S.
7. **Kelly Dransfeldt**, SS, Morris (Ill.) H.S.
8. **Ryan Lane**, SS, Bellefontaine (O.) H.S.
9. **Kevin Ohme**, LHP, U. of North Florida.
10. **Mark Merila**, 2B, U. of Minnesota.

NEW YORK YANKEES
AMERICAN LEAGUE EAST DIVISION

N   Denotes night game (any game starting after 5 p.m.).
☐   Home games shaded.
*   At Three Rivers Stadium in Pittsburgh.

APRIL

SUN	MON	TUE	WED	THU	FRI	SAT
					1	2
3	4 TEX	5	6 TEX	7	8 N DET	9 N DET
10 DET	11	12 N CHI	13 N CHI	14 N CHI	15 N DET	16 N DET
17 DET	18	19 N SEA	20 N SEA	21 N SEA	22 N OAK	23 OAK
24 OAK	25 N CAL	26 CAL	27 N SEA	28 N SEA	29 N OAK	30 OAK

MAY

SUN	MON	TUE	WED	THU	FRI	SAT
1 OAK	2	3 N CAL	4 N CAL	5	6 N BOS	7 BOS
8 BOS	9 N CLE	10 N CLE	11 N CLE	12 N CLE	13 N MIL	14 MIL
15 MIL	16 N MIN	17 N MIN	18 MIN	19	20 N BAL	21 BAL
22 BAL	23	24 N TOR	25 N TOR	26	27 N KC	28 N KC
29 KC	30 N CHI	31 N CHI				

JUNE

SUN	MON	TUE	WED	THU	FRI	SAT
			1 N CHI	2	3 N KC	4 KC
5 KC	6 N TEX	7 N TEX	8 N TEX	9 N TOR	10 N TOR	11 TOR
12 TOR	13 N BAL	14 N BAL	15 N BAL	16 N BAL	17 N MIL	18 MIL
19 MIL	20 N MIN	21 N MIN	22	23	24 N CLE	25 CLE
26 CLE	27 N BOS	28 N BOS	29 N BOS	30 N BOS		

JULY

SUN	MON	TUE	WED	THU	FRI	SAT
					1 N SEA	2 SEA
3 SEA	4 OAK	5 N OAK	6 N OAK	7	8 N CAL	9 N CAL
10 CAL	11 *	12 ALL-STAR GAME	13	14 N SEA	15 N SEA	16 N SEA
17 SEA	18 N OAK	19 N OAK	20 N OAK	21 N CAL	22 N CAL	23 CAL
24 CAL	25	26 N BOS	27 N BOS	28 BOS	29 N CLE	30 CLE
31 CLE						

AUGUST

SUN	MON	TUE	WED	THU	FRI	SAT
	1 N MIL	2 N MIL	3	4 MIL	5 N MIN	6 N MIN
7 MIN	8 N BAL	9 N BAL	10 N BAL	11 N TOR	12 N TOR	13 TOR
14 N TOR	15	16 N KC	17 N KC	18 N KC	19 N TEX	20 N TEX
21 TEX	22 N KC	23 N KC	24 N KC	25 N TEX	26 N TEX	27 TEX
28 TEX	29 N DET	30 N DET	31 N DET			

SEPTEMBER

SUN	MON	TUE	WED	THU	FRI	SAT
				1 DET	2 N CHI	3 CHI
4 N CHI	5	6 N DET	7 DET	8 N DET	9 N CHI	10 CHI
11 CHI	12	13 N TOR	14 N TOR	15 N TOR	16 N BAL	17 BAL
18 BAL	19 N MIL	20 N MIL	21 N MIL	22 MIL	23 N MIN	24 MIN
25 MIN	26 N CLE	27 N CLE	28 CLE	29	30 N BOS	

OCTOBER

SUN	MON	TUE	WED	THU	FRI	SAT
						1 BOS
2 BOS						

CLUB DIRECTORY

Principal owner
George M. Steinbrenner
General partner
Joseph A. Molloy
Executive vice president, general counsel
David W. Sussman
Senior vice president
Arthur Richman
Vice president and general manager
Gene Michael
Vice president, chief of operations
John C. Lawn
Vice president, marketing
John C. Fugazy
V.p., finance, chief financial officer
Barry Pincus
Vice president, community relations
Richard Kraft
Vice president
Ed Weaver
Director of office admin. and services
Harvey C. Winston
Vice president, ticket operations
Frank Swaine
V.p., player development and scouting
Bill Livesey
Senior advisor, baseball operations
Bill Bergesch
Asst. general manager, baseball operations
Tim McCleary
Asst. general manager, baseball admin.
Brian Cashman
Director of minor league operations
Mitch Lukevics
Coordinator of scouting
Kevin Elfering
Traveling secretary
David Szen
Director of stadium operations
Timothy D. Hassett
Director of customer services
Joel S. White
Director of video operations
John J. Franzone
Executive director of ticket operations
Jeff Kline
Ticket director
Ken Skrypek
Director of group and season sales
Debbie Tymon
Director of media relations and publicity
Rob Butcher
Asst. dir. of media relations and publicity
Marty Naughton

Director of special events
Bob Pelegrino
Director of publications
Tom Bannon
Team physician
Dr. Stuart Hershon
Head trainer
Gene J. Monahan
Assistant trainer
Steve Donohue
Major league scouts
Ted Uhlaender
Ron Hansen
Clyde King
Bob Lemon
Dick Tidrow
Scouting cross-checker
Jack Gills
Area supervisor scouts
Fernando Arango
Mark Batchko
Stephen Chandler
Joe DiCarlo
Lee Elder
Bill Geivett
Tim Kelly
Don Lindberg
Carl Moesche
Greg Orr
Joe Robison
Bill Schmidt
Jeff Taylor
Paul Turco
Leon Wurth
Foreign scouts
Joel Grampietro
Dick Groch
Rudy Santin
Luis Arroyo
Philip Elhage
Karl Heron
Pedro Ithier
Leo Lacle
Victor Mata
Raul Ortega
Arquimedes Rojas
Mike LaBossiere
Marc Pickard
Bruce Ross
Bill Saunders
Dennis Springenatic
Dale Tilleman

Manager—Buck Showalter (11).
Coaches—Clete Boyer (6), Brian Butterfield (55), Tony Cloninger (40), Billy Connors (36), Rick Down (48), Willie Randolph (30), Glenn Sherlock (53).

No.	PITCHERS	B/T	Ht./Wt.	Born	1993 clubs
25	Abbott, Jim	L/L	6-3/210	9-19-67	New York A.L.
43	Assenmacher, Paul	L/L	6-3/210	12-10-60	Chicago N.L., New York A.L.
	Pall, Donn	R/R	6-1/179	1-11-62	Chicago A.L.
35	Gibson, Paul	R/L	6-1/185	1-4-60	Norfolk, New York N.L., Columbus, New York A.L.
31	Hernandez, Xavier	L/R	6-2/185	8-16-65	Houston
42	Hitchcock, Sterling	L/L	6-1/192	4-29-71	Columbus, New York A.L.
57	Howe, Steve	L/L	5-11/198	3-10-58	New York A.L., Columbus
52	Hutton, Mark	R/R	6-6/225	2-6-70	Columbus, New York A.L.
28	Kamieniecki, Scott	R/R	6-0/195	4-19-64	New York A.L., Columbus
22	Key, Jimmy	R/L	6-1/185	4-22-61	New York A.L.
34	Militello, Sam	R/R	6-3/195	11-26-69	New York A.L., Columbus
54	Munoz, Bobby	R/R	6-7/237	3-3-68	Columbus, New York A.L.
64	Musset, Jose	R/R	6-3/186	9-18-68	Midland
33	Perez, Melido	R/R	6-4/210	2-15-66	New York A.L.
58	Rivera, Mariano	R/R	6-4/168	11-29-69	Greensboro, Gulf Coast Yankees
27	Wickman, Bob	R/R	6-1/212	2-6-69	New York A.L.

No.	CATCHERS	B/T	Ht./Wt.	Born	1993 clubs
13	Leyritz, Jim	R/R	6-0/195	12-27-63	New York A.L.
38	Nokes, Matt	L/R	6-1/210	10-31-63	New York A.L.
20	Stanley, Mike	R/R	6-0/192	6-25-63	New York A.L.

No.	INFIELDERS	B/T	Ht./Wt.	Born	1993 clubs
12	Boggs, Wade	L/R	6-2/197	6-15-58	New York A.L.
63	Davis, Russ	R/R	6-0/170	9-13-69	Columbus
46	Eenhoorn, Robert	R/R	6-3/170	2-9-68	Albany/Colonie
56	Fox, Andy	L/R	6-4/185	1-12-71	Albany/Colonie
2	Gallego, Mike	R/R	5-8/175	10-31-60	New York A.L.
59	Jordan, Kevin	R/R	6-1/185	10-9-69	Albany/Colonie
14	Kelly, Pat	R/R	6-0/182	10-14-67	New York A.L.
24	Maas, Kevin	L/L	6-3/204	1-20-65	New York A.L., Columbus
23	Mattingly, Don	L/L	6-0/200	4-20-61	New York A.L.
47	Silvestri, Dave	R/R	6-0/196	9-29-67	Columbus, New York A.L.
18	Velarde, Randy	R/R	6-0/192	11-24-62	New York A.L., Albany/Colonie

No.	OUTFIELDERS	B/T	Ht./Wt.	Born	1993 clubs
39	Humphreys, Mike	R/R	6-0/195	4-10-67	New York A.L., Columbus
61	Leach, Jay	L/L	6-2/200	3-14-69	Albany/Colonie
59	Masse, Billy	R/R	6-1/185	7-6-66	Columbus
21	O'Neill, Paul	L/L	6-4/215	2-25-63	New York A.L.
17	Polonia, Luis	L/L	5-8/150	10-12-64	California
62	Robertson, Jason	L/L	6-2/200	3-24-71	Albany/Colonie
60	Seefried, Tate	L/R	6-4/180	4-22-72	Prince William
45	Tartabull, Danny	R/R	6-1/204	10-30-62	New York A.L.
51	Williams, Bernie	B/R	6-2/200	9-13-68	New York A.L.
29	Williams, Gerald	R/R	6-2/190	8-10-66	Columbus, New York A.L.

BALLPARK INFORMATION

Ballpark (capacity, surface)
Yankee Stadium (57,545, grass)
Address
Yankee Stadium
E. 161 St. and River Ave.
Bronx, NY 10451
Business phone
212-293-4300
Ticket information
212-293-6000
Ticket prices
$17 (lower and loge box seats)
$15.50 (tier box seats)
$14.50 (lower reserves)
$11.50 (tier reserves)
$2 (senior citizens)
$6.50 (bleachers)
Field dimensions (from home plate)
To left field at foul line, 312 feet
To center field, 410 feet
To right field at foul line, 310 feet
First game played
April 18, 1923 (Yankees 4, Red Sox 1)

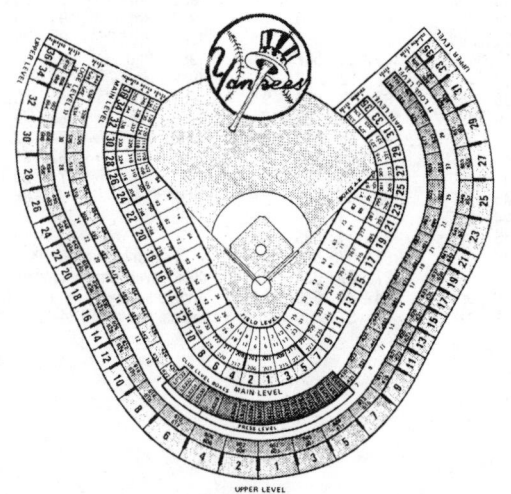

MINOR LEAGUE AFFILIATES

Class	Team	League	Manager
AAA	Columbus, O.	International	To be announced
AA	Albany/Colonie	Eastern	To be announced
A	Tampa	Florida State	To be announced
A	Greensboro	South Atlantic	Trey Hillman
A	Oneonta	New York-Pennsylvania	To be announced
Rookie	Tampa Yankees	Gulf Coast	Gary Denbo

BROADCAST INFORMATION

Radio: WABC-AM (770). Broadcasters: John Sterling, Michael Kay.
Cable TV: Madison Square Garden Network. Broadcasters: Dewayne Staats, Tony Kubek, Al Trautwig.

SPRING TRAINING

Ballpark (city): Fort Lauderdale Stadium (Fort Lauderdale, Fla.).
Ticket information: 305-776-1921.

HISTORY

YEAR-BY-YEAR RECORDS

Year	Pos.	W	L	Pct.	GB		Year	Pos.	W	L	Pct.	GB
1901*	5th	68	65	.511	13½		1950	1st	98	56	.636	+ 3
1902*	8th	50	88	.362	34		1951	1st	98	56	.636	+ 5
1903	4th	72	62	.537	17		1952	1st	95	59	.617	+ 2
1904	2nd	92	59	.609	1½		1953	1st	99	52	.656	+ 8½
1905	6th	71	78	.477	21½		1954	2nd	103	51	.669	8
1906	2nd	90	61	.596	3		1955	1st	96	58	.623	+ 3
1907	5th	70	78	.473	21		1956	1st	97	57	.630	+ 9
1908	8th	51	103	.331	39½		1957	1st	98	56	.636	+ 8
1909	5th	74	77	.490	23½		1958	1st	92	62	.597	+10
1910	2nd	88	63	.583	14½		1959	3rd	79	75	.513	15
1911	6th	76	76	.500	25½		1960	1st	97	57	.630	+ 8
1912	8th	50	102	.329	55		1961	1st	109	53	.673	+ 8
1913	7th	57	94	.377	38		1962	1st	96	66	.593	+ 5
1914	T6th	70	84	.455	30		1963	1st	104	57	.646	+10½
1915	5th	69	83	.454	32½		1964	1st	99	63	.611	+ 1
1916	4th	80	74	.519	11		1965	6th	77	85	.475	25
1917	6th	71	82	.464	28½		1966	10th	70	89	.440	26½
1918	4th	60	63	.488	13½		1967	9th	72	90	.444	20
1919	3rd	80	59	.576	7½		1968	5th	83	79	.512	20
1920	3rd	95	59	.617	3		1969	5th	80	81	.497	28½
1921	1st	98	55	.641	+ 4½		1970	2nd	93	69	.574	15
1922	1st	94	60	.610	+ 1		1971	4th	82	80	.506	21
1923	1st	98	54	.645	+16		1972	4th	79	76	.510	6½
1924	2nd	89	63	.586	2		1973	4th	80	82	.494	17
1925	7th	69	85	.448	30		1974	2nd	89	73	.549	2
1926	1st	91	63	.591	+ 3		1975	3rd	83	77	.519	12
1927	1st	110	44	.714	+19		1976	1st†	97	62	.610	+10½
1928	1st	101	53	.656	+ 2½		1977	1st†	100	62	.617	+ 2½
1929	2nd	88	66	.571	18		1978	1st†‡	100	63	.613	+ 1
1930	3rd	86	68	.558	16		1979	4th	89	71	.556	13½
1931	2nd	94	59	.614	13½		1980	1st§	103	59	.636	+ 3
1932	1st	107	47	.695	+13		1981	1st/6th	59	48	.551	†‡*
1933	2nd	91	59	.607	7		1982	5th	79	83	.488	16
1934	2nd	94	60	.610	7		1983	3rd	91	71	.562	7
1935	2nd	89	60	.597	3		1984	3rd	87	75	.537	17
1936	1st	102	51	.667	+19½		1985	2nd	97	64	.602	2
1937	1st	102	52	.662	+13		1986	2nd	90	72	.556	5½
1938	1st	99	53	.651	+ 9½		1987	4th	89	73	.549	9
1939	1st	106	45	.702	+17		1988	5th	85	76	.528	3½
1940	3rd	88	66	.571	2		1989	5th	74	87	.460	14½
1941	1st	101	53	.656	+17		1990	7th	67	95	.414	21
1942	1st	103	51	.669	+ 9		1991	5th	71	91	.438	20
1943	1st	98	56	.636	+13½		1992	T4th	76	86	.469	20
1944	3rd	83	71	.539	6		1993	2nd	88	74	.543	7
1945	4th	81	71	.533	6½							
1946	3rd	87	67	.565	17							
1947	1st	97	57	.630	+12							
1948	3rd	94	60	.610	2½							
1949	1st	97	57	.630	+ 1							

*Franchise known as Baltimore Orioles. †Won Championship Series. ‡Won division playoff. §Lost Championship Series. *First half 34-22; second 25-26.

MANAGERS

Name	Record	Years
John McGraw	94-96	'01-02
Wilbert Robinson	24-57	1902
Clark Griffith	419-370	'03-08
Kid Elberfeld	27-71	1908
George Stallings	152-136	'09-10
Hal Chase	86-80	'10-11
Harry Wolverton	50-102	1912
Frank Chance	117-168	'13-14
Rog. Peckinpaugh	10-10	1914
Bill Donovan	220-239	'15-17
Miller Huggins	1067-719	'18-29
Art Fletcher	6-5	1929
Bob Shawkey	86-68	1930
Joe McCarthy	1460-867	'31-46
Bill Dickey	57-48	1946
Johnny Neun	8-6	1946
Bucky Harris	191-117	'47-48
Casey Stengel	1149-696	'49-60
Ralph Houk	944-806	'61-63
		'66-73
Yogi Berra	192-148	1964
		'84-85
Johnny Keane	81-101	'65-66
Bill Virdon	142-124	'74-75
Billy Martin	501-345	'75-78
		'79, '83
		'85, '88
Bob Lemon	99-73	'78-79
		'81-82
Dick Howser	103-59	1980
Gene Michael	92-76	'81, '82
Clyde King	29-33	1982
Lou Piniella	224-193	'86-87
		1988
Dallas Green	56-65	1989
Bucky Dent	36-53	'89-90
Stump Merrill	120-155	'90-91
Buck Showalter	164-160	'92-93

DAY BY DAY

Date	Opp.	Res.	Score	(inn.*)	Hits	Opp. hits	Winning pitcher	Losing pitcher	Save	Record	Pos.	GB
4-5	At Cle.	W	9-1		16	3	Key	Nagy		1-0	T1st	...
4-7	At Cle.	L	2-4		6	12	Plunk	Abbott	Lilliquist	1-1	T2nd	1
4-8	At Cle.	L	5-15		12	17	Bielecki	Militello		1-2	T5th	2
4-9	At Chi.	W	11-6		15	10	Wickman	Pall		2-2	T4th	1
4-10	At Chi.	W	12-0		16	7	Key	Bolton		3-2	3rd	1
4-11	At Chi.	L	4-6		12	9	McDowell	Monteleone	Hernandez	3-3	T3rd	1
4-12	K.C.	W	4-1		8	8	Abbott	Cone		4-3	3rd	½
4-14	K.C.	W	6-5		12	6	Wickman	Gubicza	Farr	5-3	2nd	1
4-15	K.C.	L	4-5		7	10	DiPino	Farr	Montgomery	5-4	3rd	2
4-16	Tex.	W	5-3		11	8	Monteleone	Lefferts	Habyan	6-4	2nd	1
4-17	Tex.	L	0-9		6	11	Brown	Abbott		6-5	4th	2
4-18	Tex.	L	2-12		8	15	Leibrandt	Perez		6-6	4th	3
4-20	At Oak.	L	7-9	(10)	8	13	Gossage	Habyan		6-7	4th	4½
4-21	At Oak.	W	5-3		8	9	Monteleone	Honeycutt	Farr	7-7	T3rd	3½
4-22	At Oak.	W	5-1		7	7	Militello	Darling	Kamieniecki	8-7	T3rd	2½
4-23	At Sea.	L	3-6		10	10	Hampton	Abbott	Charlton	8-8	T3rd	2½
4-24	At Sea.	W	1-0	(11)	11	2	Howe	Swan	Farr	9-8	T3rd	2½
4-25	At Sea.	W	10-9		11	13	Monteleone	Henry	Farr	10-8	T3rd	2½
4-27	At Cal.	W	5-0		9	1	Key	Finley		11-8	3rd	2
4-28	At Cal.	L	2-3		3	5	Langston	Abbott		11-9	4th	2
4-30	Sea.	W	3-0		7	4	Perez	Cummings	Farr	12-9	4th	2½
5-1	Sea.	W	6-2		12	4	Witt	Johnson		13-9	3rd	1½
5-2	Sea.	W	3-2	(10)	8	7	Habyan	DeLucia		14-9	3rd	½
5-3	Oak.	L	2-4		4	8	Welch	Abbott	Eckersley	14-10	3rd	1
5-4	Oak.	W	4-2		7	4	Wickman	Hillegas	Farr	15-10	2nd	1
5-5	Cal.	L	2-6		7	8	Farrell	Perez	Valera	15-11	3rd	1
5-6	Cal.	L	1-3		5	8	Sanderson	Howe	Frey	15-12	3rd	1½
5-7	At Det.	L	6-7	(12)	13	11	MacDonald	Kamieniecki		15-13	4th	2½
5-8	At Det.	W	10-8	(11)	15	12	Farr	Johnson		16-13	3rd	1½
5-9	At Det.	W	11-2		14	12	Wickman	Doherty		17-13	2nd	½
5-10	At Det.	L	1-2	(10)	5	5	MacDonald	Monteleone		17-14	2nd	1½
5-11	Mil.	W	5-1		10	3	Witt	Navarro		18-14	2nd	1½
5-12	Mil.	L	1-4		5	9	Wegman	Key	Henry	18-15	3rd	2½
5-13	Mil.	W	4-2		8	5	Abbott	Eldred	Farr	19-15	T2nd	1½
5-14	Tor.	L	6-8		9	11	Ward	Monteleone		19-16	T2nd	2½
5-15	Tor.	W	4-3		7	10	Perez	Leiter	Farr	20-16	3rd	2½
5-16	Tor.	L	6-12		10	13	Stottlemyre	Witt		20-17	T2nd	2½
5-17	At Min.	W	11-5		18	12	Key	Tapani		21-17	2nd	2
5-18	At Min.	W	5-3		8	9	Abbott	Trombley	Farr	22-17	2nd	2
5-19	At Min.	W	11-6		15	9	Monteleone	Erickson		23-17	2nd	2
5-21	At Bos.	L	2-7		11	10	Dopson	Perez		23-18	2nd	2½
5-22	At Bos.	W	7-3		11	8	Witt	Clemens		24-18	2nd	2½
5-23	At Bos.	L	2-5		6	8	Harris	Key	Russell	24-19	T2nd	3½
5-24	Bal.	L	6-8		7	15	Sutcliffe	Cook	Olson	24-20	T3rd	3½
5-25	Bal.	W	1-0		12	3	Wickman	Moyer	Farr	25-20	3rd	3½
5-26	Bal.	L	2-6		6	9	Mussina	Perez	Olson	25-21	3rd	4½
5-27	Bal.	L	3-4	(10)	9	6	Pennington	Farr		25-22	3rd	5
5-28	Chi.	W	4-0		9	3	Key	McCaskill		26-22	T3rd	4
5-29	Chi.	W	8-2		11	2	Abbott	Alvarez		27-22	T2nd	4
5-30	Chi.	W	6-3		11	7	Wickman	McDowell	Farr	28-22	T2nd	3
5-31	Cle.	W	8-2		14	8	Perez	Cook		29-22	T2nd	2½
6-1	Cle.	L	6-15		13	16	C. Young	Witt		29-23	3rd	2½
6-2	Cle.	W	8-5		9	8	Key	M. Young	Farr	30-23	3rd	1½
6-4	At Tex.	L	3-5		8	7	Brown	Abbott	Henke	30-24	3rd	2
6-5	At Tex.	W	9-6		15	9	Monteleone	Lefferts	Farr	31-24	3rd	2
6-6	At Tex.	L	3-4		8	9	Rogers	Perez	Henke	31-25	3rd	3
6-7	At K.C.	L	3-8		9	15	Appier	Johnson		31-26	3rd	3
6-8	At K.C.	W	9-4		13	13	Howe	Brewer		32-26	3rd	3
6-9	At K.C.	L	3-10		10	11	Pichardo	Abbott		32-27	3rd	4
6-10	At Mil.	W	3-1		8	10	Wickman	Bones	Farr	33-27	3rd	4
6-11	At Mil.	W	5-4		9	9	Perez	Henry	Farr	34-27	3rd	4
6-12	At Mil.	L	1-9		6	11	Eldred	Johnson		34-28	3rd	5
6-13	At Mil.	W	9-5		11	10	Key	Boddicker	Howe	35-28	3rd	4
6-14	Bos.	W	4-0		5	3	Kamieniecki	Darwin		36-28	T2nd	4
6-15	Bos.	W	9-7		10	12	Heaton	Viola	Farr	37-28	T2nd	4
6-16	Bos.	L	1-7		3	11	Dopson	Perez		37-29	3rd	4
6-17	Min.	W	6-5		13	10	Munoz	Casian	Farr	38-29	3rd	4
6-18	Min.	W	5-0		5	9	Key	Guardado		39-29	3rd	3
6-19	Min.	W	8-4		9	7	Kamieniecki	Banks		40-29	3rd	3
6-20	Min.	W	8-0		13	6	Wickman	Tapani		41-29	3rd	3

Date	Opp.	Res.	Score	(Inn.*)	Hits	Opp. hits	Winning pitcher	Losing pitcher	Save	Record	Pos.	GB
6-22	At Tor.	L	4-5		8	12	Williams	Howe	Ward	41-30	3rd	3
6-23	At Tor.	W	4-3	15	7		Key	Stottlemyre	Farr	42-30	3rd	2
6-24	At Tor.	L	2-7		8	10	Hentgen	Kamienlecki		42-31	3rd	2
6-25	At Bal.	L	6-7	(10)	8	13	Frohwirth	Howe		42-32	3rd	2
6-26	At Bal.	L	10-12		15	16	Williamson	Wickman	Olson	42-33	3rd	3
6-27	At Bal.	W	9-5		14	13	Perez	O'Donoghue	Howe	43-33	3rd	3
6-28	Det.	W	8-2		12	5	Key	Moore		44-33	3rd	3
6-29	Det.	W	4-3	(10)	8	8	Munoz	Bolton		45-33	2nd	3
6-30	Det.	W	7-0		10	3	Abbott	Wells		46-33	2nd	2
7-2	At Oak.	L	3-4		6	8	Witt	Wickman		46-34	2nd	2
7-3	At Oak.	L	4-5		11	8	Boever	Perez	Eckersley	46-35	2nd	2
7-4	At Oak.	L	6-7		11	12	Hillegas	Munoz	Eckersley	46-36	2nd	2
7-5	At Sea.	W	6-3		6	7	Kanieniecki	Johnson	Howe	47-36	2nd	1
7-6	At Sea.	L	4-12		7	12	Hanson	Abbott		47-37	2nd	2
7-7	At Sea.	L	5-6		9	9	Leary	Wickman	Charlton	47-38	2nd	2
7-8	At Cal.	L	3-4		9	5	Frey	Perez		47-39	2nd	2
7-9	At Cal.	W	3-2		12	5	Key	Langston		48-39	2nd	1
7-10	At Cal.	L	2-4		9	12	Springer	Kamienlecki	Frey	48-40	3rd	1
7-11	At Cal.	L	2-3	(14)	9	14	Linton	Monteleone		48-41	3rd	1
7-15	Oak.	L	3-8		11	15	Mohler	Perez		48-42	4th	2
7-16	Oak.	W	10-3		17	7	Key	Downs		49-42	3rd	1
7-17	Oak.	W	9-5		14	6	Abbott	Witt		50-42	T1st	...
7-18	Oak.	W	13-6		18	14	Howe	Nunez		51-42	T1st	...
7-19	Sea.	W	8-2		12	8	Kamieniecki	Leary		52-42	1st	...
7-20	Sea.	L	5-9		10	12	Fleming	Howe		52-43	T2nd	½
7-21	Sea.	L	3-10		6	16	Hanson	Key		52-44	4th	1
7-22	Cal.	W	12-1		10	5	Abbott	Springer		53-44	3rd	1
7-23	Cal.	W	5-2		7	3	Hutton	Langston	Farr	54-44	T2nd	...
7-24	Cal.	W	5-3		11	8	Kamieniecki	Sanderson	Farr	55-44	T2nd	...
7-25	Cal.	W	9-8		14	12	Habyan	Frey		56-44	T2nd	...
7-26	At Det.	L	2-5		10	11	Wells	Key	Henneman	56-45	3rd	½
7-27	At Det.	W	5-2		12	7	Abbott	Gullickson	Farr	57-45	2nd	½
7-28	At Det.	W	12-7		18	11	Wickman	Doherty		58-45	2nd	½
7-30	Mil.	W	8-4		12	10	Kamieniecki	Eldred	Howe	59-45	T1st	...
7-31	Mil.	W	5-4		7	8	Wickman	Lloyd		60-45	T1st	...
8-1	Mil.	L	2-9		9	13	Navarro	Perez		60-46	2nd	1
8-2	Tor.	L	0-4		9	7	Stottlemyre	Abbott	Cox	60-47	3rd	2
8-3	Tor.	L	6-8		16	14	Hentgen	Munoz	Leiter	60-48	3rd	3
8-4	Tor.	W	6-2		9	8	Kamieniecki	Stewart		61-48	3rd	2
8-5	Tor.	W	5-4		7	6	Key	Leiter		62-48	3rd	1
8-6	At Min.	L	3-4		4	12	Tapani	Wickman		62-49	3rd	2
8-7	At Min.	L	5-6		11	13	Willis	Munoz		62-50	4th	2
8-8	At Min.	W	8-6	(10)	9	9	Farr	Aguilera		63-50	4th	1
8-10	At Bos.	L	0-5		4	9	Viola	Kamieniecki	Hesketh	63-51	4th	2
8-11	At Bos.	W	8-3		11	10	Key	Clemens	Wickman	64-51	3rd	2
8-12	At Bos.	W	4-1		9	2	Perez	Sele	Farr	65-51	2nd	1
8-13	Bal.	W	4-1		8	8	Abbott	Moyer		66-51	T1st	...
8-14	Bal.	W	4-2		8	5	Assenmacher	Williamson	Farr	67-51	T1st	...
8-15	Bal.	W	1-0		7	3	Kamieniecki	McDonald	Wickman	68-51	T1st	...
8-17 (1)	Tex.	W	11-4		16	10	Key	Brown		69-51	2nd	½
8-17 (2)	Tex.	L	2-3		6	5	Rogers	Perez	Henke	69-52	2nd	1
8-18	Tex.	L	2-4		10	9	Pavlik	Abbott	Henke	69-53	2nd	2
8-20	K.C.	W	7-2		11	5	Jean	Gordon		70-53	2nd	1
8-21	K.C.	W	3-2		9	5	Kamieniecki	Magnante	Farr	71-53	T1st	...
8-22	K.C.	L	0-7		4	12	Haney	Perez		71-54	2nd	1
8-23	At Chi.	W	6-5	(10)	11	10	Assenmacher	Radinsky	Farr	72-54	T1st	...
8-24	At Chi.	L	2-4		5	10	Alvarez	Abbott	Hernandez	72-55	2nd	1
8-25	At Chi.	W	7-5		12	10	Monteleone	Radinsky	Wickman	73-55	2nd	1
8-26	At Cle.	W	4-0		8	8	Hitchcock	Wertz	Wickman	74-55	T1st	...
8-27	At Cle.	L	2-9		8	14	Grimsley	Perez		74-56	T1st	...
8-28	At Cle.	L	4-8		10	16	Mutis	Key	Hernandez	74-57	T1st	...
8-29	At Cle.	W	14-8		16	13	Monteleone	Grimsley		75-57	T1st	...
8-31	Chi.	L	3-11		8	13	Alvarez	Hitchcock		75-58	2nd	1½
9-1	Chi.	L	3-5		9	11	McDowell	Assenmacher	Hernandez	75-59	2nd	2½
9-2	Chi.	W	7-1		10	4	Key	Belcher		76-59	2nd	2
9-3	Cle.	L	3-7		9	12	Ojeda	Perez	DiPoto	76-60	2nd	2
9-4	Cle.	W	4-0		8	0	Abbott	Milacki		77-60	2nd	1
9-5	Cle.	W	7-2		16	5	Wickman	Mutis		78-60	T1st	...
9-6	At Tex.	L	5-8		5	11	Pavlik	Kamieniecki		78-61	2nd	½
9-7	At Tex.	L	4-5		12	14	Carpenter	Assenmacher	Henke	78-62	2nd	½
9-8	At Tex.	L	1-4		7	8	Brown	Jean	Henke	78-63	2nd	½
9-10	At K.C.	L	5-6		11	12	Montgomery	Howe		78-64	2nd	1
9-11	At K.C.	W	12-5		17	11	Wickman	Haney		79-64	2nd	1
9-12	At K.C.	L	2-10		8	9	Gordon	Hutton		79-65	3rd	2

Date	Opp.	Res.	Score (Inn.*)	Hits	Opp. hits	Winning pitcher	Losing pitcher	Save	Record	Pos.	GB
9-13	At Mil.	W	3-1	11	7	Key	Navarro	Smith	80-65	2nd	1½
9-14	At Mil.	W	12-5	14	12	Gibson	Bones		81-65	2nd	1½
9-15	At Mil.	L	5-15	10	16	Higuera	Abbott		81-66	2nd	2½
9-16	Bos.	L	4-6	9	14	Viola	Kamieniecki	Harris	81-67	3rd	3
9-17	Bos.	W	5-4	10	7	Gibson	Dopson	Smith	82-67	2nd	3
9-18	Bos.	W	4-3	10	11	Wickman	Harris		83-67	2nd	3
9-19	Bos.	L	3-8	5	13	Darwin	Tanana		83-68	2nd	4
9-21	Min.	L	4-5	8	11	Banks	Abbott	Aguilera	83-69	2nd	5
9-22	Min.	L	2-5	6	9	Tapani	Kamieniecki	Aguilera	83-70	2nd	5
9-24	At Tor.	L	3-7	10	13	Guzman	Key		83-71	2nd	6½
9-25	At Tor.	L	1-3	4	4	Leiter	Tanana	Ward	83-72	3rd	7½
9-26	At Tor.	W	7-3	8	6	Abbott	Stottlemyre		84-72	2nd	6½
9-27	At Bal.	W	9-1	12	6	Kamieniecki	Sutcliffe		85-72	2nd	6½
9-28	At Bal.	L	1-9	2	9	McDonald	Hitchcock		85-73	2nd	7½
9-29	At Bal.	W	8-3	15	6	Key	Moyer		86-73	2nd	7½
10-1	Det.	W	9-6	12	12	Wickman	Boever	Smith	87-73	2nd	7
10-2	Det.	L	1-4	8	12	Krueger	Abbott	Henneman	87-74	2nd	7
10-3	Det.	W	2-1	4	5	Munoz	Bolton		88-74	2nd	7

Monthly records: April (12-9), May (17-13), June (17-11), July (14-12), August (15-13), September (11-15), October (2-1).
*Innings, if other than nine.

HIGHLIGHTS

High point: On September 4, lefthander Jim Abbott pitched a no-hitter against Cleveland, and the Yankees beat the Indians the next day to pull into a first-place tie with Toronto.

Low point: During a six-game homestand September 16-22, New York posted a 2-4 mark, dropping the Yankees five games behind Toronto and forcing them to sweep the Blue Jays in a three-game series at SkyDome on September 24-26 in order to stay in contention. Toronto won the first two games, and the Yankees were finished.

Turning point: In their last appearance at Arlington Stadium (September 6-8), the Yankees suffered a three-game sweep. It was the start of a three-city trip that saw New York go 3-6 and fail to capitalize on a six-game Toronto losing streak from September 3-9.

Most valuable player: Catcher Mike Stanley. He emerged from career backup status to have a career year (.305, 26 home runs, 84 RBIs).

Most valuable pitcher: Lefthander Jimmy Key. He set personal standards in victories (18) and strikeouts (173).

Most improved player: Righthander Scott Kamieniecki. He went from 6-14 in '92 to 10-7, filling a void in the rotation in the second half.

Most pleasant surprise: Infielder Mike Gallego. While rotating among second base, third base and shortstop, he hit .283 with 10 home runs and 54 RBIs.

Biggest disappointment: Righthander Melido Perez. After going 13-16 with a 2.87 ERA in '92, he endured an injury-plagued season in which he was 6-14 with a 5.19 ERA.

Key injuries: Nagging injuries to first baseman Don Mattingly (right wrist) and designated hitter Danny Tartabull (right shoulder) proved costly as both struggled in September, the Yankees' only losing month (11-15). Center fielder Bernie Williams played just 12 games in May because of a rib-cage injury. Infielder Randy Velarde suffered a fractured pelvis June 5 and didn't re-

turn until July 30. Righthander Sam Militello pitched only briefly for New York because of shoulder problems.

Notable: Abbott's no-hitter was the first nine-inning effort by a Yankee at home since Dave Righetti beat Boston in 1983. . . . New York (88-74) ended a stretch of four losing seasons. . . . George Steinbrenner resumed command of the Yankees on March 1. He had been banished from everyday control August 20, 1990, for his association with gambler Howard Spira.

—JACK O'CONNELL

RECORDS

1993 regular-season record: 88-74 (2nd in A.L. East); 50-31 at home; 38-43 on road; 44-34 vs. East; 44-40 vs. West; 32-26 vs. LHP; 56-48 vs. RHP; 77-61 on grass; 11-13 on turf; 35-18 in daytime; 53-56 at night; 20-20 in one-run games; 6-6 in extra-inning games; 0-0-1 in doubleheaders.

Team record last five years: 376-433 (.465, ranks 13th in league in that span).

TEAM LEADERS

Batting average: Paul O'Neill (.311).
At-bats: Bernie Williams (567).
Runs: Danny Tartabull (87).
Hits: Wade Boggs (169).
Total bases: Danny Tartabull (258).
Doubles: Paul O'Neill (34).
Triples: Bernie Williams (4).
Home runs: Danny Tartabull (31).
Runs batted in: Danny Tartabull (102).
Stolen bases: Pat Kelly (14).
Slugging percentage: Paul O'Neill (.504).
On-base percentage: Wade Boggs (.378).
Wins: Jimmy Key (18).
Earned-run average: Jimmy Key (3.00).
Complete games: Jim Abbott, Jimmy Key (4).
Shutouts: Jimmy Key (2).
Saves: Steve Farr (25).
Innings pitched: Jimmy Key (236⅔).
Strikeouts: Jimmy Key (173).

GAMES BY POSITION

Catcher: Mike Stanley 122, Matt Nokes 56, Jim Leyritz 12.
First base: Don Mattingly 130, Jim Leyritz 29, Kevin Maas 17, Hensley Meulens 3, Dion James 1.
Second base: Pat Kelly 125, Mike Gallego 52, Andy Stankiewicz 8.
Third base: Wade Boggs 134, Mike Gallego 27, Randy Velarde 16, Andy Stankiewicz 4, Dave Silvestri 3, Hensley Meulens 1.
Shortstop: Spike Owen 96, Mike Gallego 55, Randy Velarde 26, Dave Silvestri 4, Andy Stankiewicz 2.
Outfield: Bernie Williams 139, Paul O'Neill 138, Dion James 103, Danny Tartabull 50, Randy Velarde 50, Gerald Williams 37, Jim Leyritz 28, Hensley Meulens 24, Mike Humphreys 21.
Designated hitter: Danny Tartabull 88, Kevin Maas 31, Jim Leyritz 21, Matt Nokes 11, Wade Boggs 8, Don Mattingly 5, Mike Humphreys 3, Paul O'Neill 2, Spike Owen 2, Mike Stanley 2, Mike Gallego 1, Dion James 1, Andy Stankiewicz 1, Randy Velarde 1, Gerald Williams 1.

TOP DRAFT CHOICES

1. **Matt Drews**, RHP, Sarasota (Fla.) High School.
2. **None.**
3. **None.**
4. **Sloan Smith**, OF, Northwestern University.
5. **Mike Jerzembeck**, RHP, University of North Carolina.
6. **Kurt Bierek**, 1B, University of Southern California.
7. **Jim Musselwhite**, RHP, University of Georgia.
8. **Rob Trimble**, C/RHP, Texas A&M University.
9. **Clint Whitworth**, RHP, Oklahoma City University.
10. **Derek Shumpert**, OF, Aquinas-Mercy High School, St. Louis.

OAKLAND ATHLETICS
AMERICAN LEAGUE WEST DIVISION

1994 SCHEDULE

N Denotes night game (any game starting after 5 p.m.).
▨ Home games shaded.
* At Three Rivers Stadium in Pittsburgh.

APRIL

SUN	MON	TUE	WED	THU	FRI	SAT
					1	2
3	4	5 MIL	6	7 N MIL	8 N MIN	9 N MIN
10 MIN	11 N TOR	12 N TOR	13 N TOR	14 N MIN	15 N MIN	16 N MIN
17 MIN	18	19 N BOS	20 N BOS	21 BOS	22 N NY	23 NY
24 NY	25 N BAL	26 BAL	27 N BOS	28 BOS	29 N NY	30 NY

MAY

SUN	MON	TUE	WED	THU	FRI	SAT
1 NY	2	3 N BAL	4 N BAL	5 N CAL	6 N CAL	7 N CAL
8 CAL	9	10 N DET	11 N DET	12 N DET	13 N KC	14 N KC
15 KC	16 N TEX	17 N TEX	18 TEX	19	20 N CHI	21 N CHI
22 CHI	23 N SEA	24 N SEA	25 SEA	26	27 N CLE	28 CLE
29 CLE	30 N TOR	31 TOR				

JUNE

SUN	MON	TUE	WED	THU	FRI	SAT
			1 TOR	2	3 N CLE	4 CLE
5 CLE	6 N MIL	7 N MIL	8 N MIL	9	10 N SEA	11 N SEA
12 SEA	13 N CHI	14 N CHI	15 N CHI	16	17 N TEX	18 TEX
19 N TEX	20	21 N KC	22 N KC	23 KC	24 N DET	25 DET
26 DET	27 N CAL	28 CAL	29 CAL	30		

JULY

SUN	MON	TUE	WED	THU	FRI	SAT
					1 N BOS	2 BOS
3 BOS	4 N NY	5 N NY	6 N NY	7 N BAL	8 N BAL	9 BAL
10 BAL	11 ALL-STAR GAME	12	13	14 N BOS	15 N BOS	16 BOS
17 BOS	18 N NY	19 N NY	20 N NY	21 N BAL	22 N BAL	23 BAL
24 BAL	25	26 N CAL	27 CAL	28	29 N DET	30 DET
31 N DET						

AUGUST

SUN	MON	TUE	WED	THU	FRI	SAT
	1 N KC	2 N KC	3 N KC	4 N KC	5 N TEX	6 N TEX
7 TEX	8 N CHI	9 N CHI	10 N CHI	11 N SEA	12 N SEA	13 SEA
14 SEA	15	16 N CLE	17 CLE	18 N CLE	19 N MIL	20 MIL
21 MIL	22 N MIL	23 N CLE	24 N CLE	25 N CLE	26 N MIL	27 MIL
28 MIL	29	30 N MIN	31 MIN			

SEPTEMBER

SUN	MON	TUE	WED	THU	FRI	SAT
				1 MIN	2 N TOR	3 TOR
4 TOR	5 N MIN	6 N MIN	7 MIN	8	9 N TOR	10 TOR
11 TOR	12 N SEA	13 N SEA	14 N SEA	15 N CHI	16 N CHI	17 CHI
18 CHI	19 N TEX	20 N TEX	21 TEX	22	23 N KC	24 KC
25 KC	26 N DET	27 N DET	28 DET	29 N CAL	30 N CAL	

OCTOBER

SUN	MON	TUE	WED	THU	FRI	SAT
						1 CAL
2 CAL						

1994 SEASON

CLUB DIRECTORY

Owner/managing general partner
Walter A. Haas Jr.
Chairman and chief operating officer
Walter J. Haas
President and general manager
Sandy Alderson
Executive vice president
Andy Dolich
Vice president, finance
Kathleen McCracken
Vice president, admin. and personnel
Raymond B. Krise Jr.
Vice president & general counsel
George Schell
Asst. to the man. gen. partner, baseball
Bill Rigney
Asst. to the general manager
Billy Beane
Director of player development
Keith Lieppman
Special assistant for baseball operations
Karl Kuehl
Director of scouting
Dick Bogard
Assistant director of scouting
Eric Kubota
Director of baseball administration
Walt Jocketty
Director of Latin American scouting
Juan Marichal
Director of team travel
Mickey Morabito
Director of baseball information
Jay Alves
Assistant director, baseball administration
Pamela Pitts
Administrative asst., baseball operations
Jennella Roark
Administrative assistant, baseball relations
Doreen Alves
Admin. asst., stats and desktop publishing
Mike Selleck
Director of broadcasting
Tom Cordova
Director of media relations
Kathy Jacobson
Dir. of community affairs/speakers bureau
Dave Perron

Director of stadium operations
To be announced
Director of broadcast operations
Bill King
Director of business administration
Alan Ledford
Director of ticket sales
John Kamperschroer
Dir. of sponsor services & special events
Matt Strelo
Director of corporate sales
Doug Nelson
Director of purchasing & merchandising
David Alioto
Director of group sales and season tickets
Bettina Flores
Director of ticket operations
Shelley Landeros
Team physician
Dr. Allan Pont
Team orthopedist
Dr. Rick Bost
Trainers
Barry Weinberg
Larry Davis
Equipment manager
Steve Vucinich
Visiting clubhouse manager
Mike Thalblum
Scouts
Tony Arias
Mark Conkin
Tim Corcoran
Ed Crosby
Ron Elam
Grady Fuson
Bill Gayton
Tim Holt
Billy Merkel
Marty Miller
Steve Nichols
Chris Pittaro
J.P. Ricciardi
Rick Rodriguez
Will Schock
Ron Vaughn

Manager—Tony La Russa (10).
Coaches—Dave Duncan (18), Art Kusnyer (5), Jim Lefebvre (6), Dave McKay (8), Tommie Reynolds (47).

No.	PITCHERS	B/T	Ht./Wt.	Born	1993 clubs
55	Acre, Mark	R/R	6-8/235	9-16-68	Madison, Huntsville
62	Baker, Scott	L/L	6-2/175	5-18-70	Huntsville
53	Briscoe, John	R/R	6-3/185	9-22-67	Huntsville, Oakland, Tacoma
17	Darling, Ron	R/R	6-3/195	8-19-60	Oakland
31	Downs, Kelly	R/R	6-4/200	10-25-60	Oakland
43	Eckersley, Dennis	R/R	6-2/195	10-3-54	Oakland
26	Horsman, Vince	R/L	6-2/180	3-9-67	Tacoma, Oakland
47	Jimenez, Miguel	R/R	6-2/205	8-19-69	Huntsville, Tacoma, Oakland
20	Karsay, Steve	R/R	6-3/205	3-24-72	Knoxville, Huntsville, Oakland
52	Nunez, Edwin	R/R	6-5/240	5-27-63	Oakland
40	Reyes, Carlos	B/R	6-1/190	4-4-69	Greenville, Richmond
19	Righetti, Dave	L/L	6-4/219	11-28-58	San Francisco
61	Shaw, Curtis	L/L	6-1/190	8-16-69	Huntsville
51	Smithberg, Roger	R/R	6-3/210	3-21-66	Huntsville, Tacoma, Oakland
33	Sturtze, Tanyon	R/R	6-5/190	10-12-70	Huntsville
	Taylor, Bill	R/R	6-8/230	10-16-61	Richmond
59	Van Poppel, Todd	R/R	6-4/210	12-9-71	Tacoma, Oakland
35	Welch, Bob	R/R	6-3/198	11-3-56	Oakland
32	Witt, Bobby	R/R	6-2/205	5-11-64	Oakland

No.	CATCHERS	B/T	Ht./Wt.	Born	1993 clubs
48	Helfand, Eric	L/R	6-0/195	3-25-69	Huntsville, Oakland
2	Hemond, Scott	R/R	6-0/215	11-18-65	Oakland
45	Molina, Islay	R/R	6-1/200	6-3-71	Modesto
36	Steinbach, Terry	R/R	6-1/195	3-2-62	Oakland
56	Williams, George	B/R	5-10/190	4-22-69	Huntsville

No.	INFIELDERS	B/T	Ht./Wt.	Born	1993 clubs
23	Aldrete, Mike	L/L	5-11/185	1-29-61	Tacoma, Oakland
14	Bordick, Mike	R/R	5-11/175	7-21-65	Oakland
41	Cruz, Fausto	R/R	5-10/165	5-1-72	Modesto, Huntsville, Tacoma
13	Gates, Brent	B/R	6-1/180	3-14-70	Huntsville, Tacoma, Oakland
25	McGwire, Mark	R/R	6-5/225	10-1-63	Oakland
16	Neel, Troy	L/R	6-4/215	9-14-65	Oakland, Tacoma
3	Paquette, Craig	R/R	6-0/190	3-28-69	Tacoma, Oakland

No.	OUTFIELDERS	B/T	Ht./Wt.	Born	1993 clubs
12	Blankenship, Lance	R/R	6-0/185	12-6-63	Oakland
7	Brosius, Scott	R/R	6-1/185	8-15-66	Oakland, Tacoma
24	Henderson, Rickey	R/L	5-10/190	12-25-58	Oakland, Toronto
44	Herrera, Jose	L/L	6-0/165	8-30-72	Hagerstown, Madison
29	Javier, Stan	B/R	6-0/185	1-9-64	California
49	Lydy, Scott	R/R	6-5/190	10-26-68	Tacoma, Oakland
63	Moore, Kerwin	B/R	6-1/190	10-29-70	High Desert
21	Sierra, Ruben	B/R	6-1/200	10-6-65	Oakland
60	Young, Ernie	R/R	6-1/190	7-8-69	Modesto, Huntsville

Ballpark (capacity, surface)
  Oakland-Alameda County Coliseum
    (47,313, grass)
Address
  Oakland A's
  Oakland Coliseum
  7000 Coliseum Way
  Oakland, CA 94621-1918
Business phone
  510-638-4900
Ticket information
  510-568-5600
Ticket prices
  $14 (field level)
  $13 (plaza level)
  $7 (upper reserved)
  $4.50 (bleachers)
Field dimensions (from home plate)
  To left field at foul line, 330 feet
  To center field, 400 feet
  To right field at foul line, 330 feet
First game played
  April 17, 1968 (Orioles 4, Athletics 1)

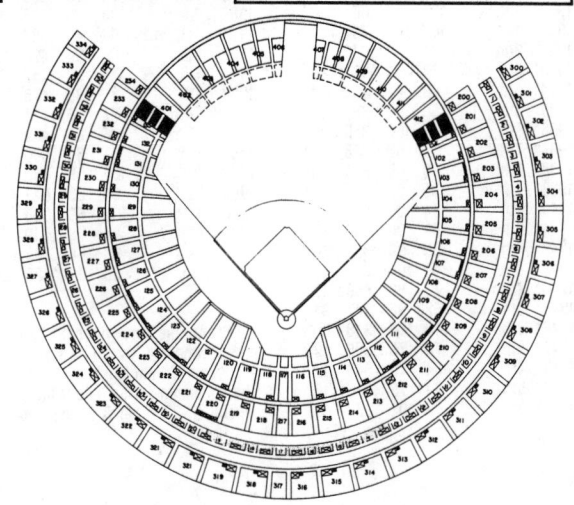

Class	Team	League	Manager
AAA	Tacoma	Pacific Coast	Casey Parsons
AA	Huntsville	Southern	Gary Jones
A	Modesto	California	Dick Scott
A	West Michigan	Midwest	Jim Colburn
A	Southern Oregon	Northwest	To be announced
Rookie	Scottsdale Athletics	Arizona	Tony DeFrancesco

BROADCAST INFORMATION

Radio: KNEW-AM (910). Broadcasters: Lon Simmons, Bill King, Ray Fosse. KNTA-AM (1430, Spanish language). Broadcasters: Amaury Pi-Gonzales, Erwin Higueros.
TV: KRON-TV (Channel 4). Broadcasters: Dick Stockton, Ray Fosse.
Cable TV: SportsChannel. Broadcasters: To be announced.

SPRING TRAINING

Ballpark (city): Phoenix Stadium (Phoenix, Ariz.).
Ticket information: 602-392-0074.

HISTORY

YEAR-BY-YEAR RECORDS

Year	Pos.	W	L	Pct.	GB	Year	Pos.	W	L	Pct.	GB
1901*	4th	74	62	.544	9	1951*	6th	70	84	.455	28
1902*	1st	83	53	.610	+ 5	1952*	4th	79	75	.513	16
1903*	2nd	75	60	.556	14½	1953*	7th	59	95	.383	41½
1904*	5th	81	70	.536	12½	1954*	8th	51	103	.331	60
1905*	1st	92	56	.622	+ 2	1955†	6th	63	91	.409	33
1906*	4th	78	67	.538	12	1956†	8th	52	102	.338	45
1907*	2nd	88	57	.607	1½	1957†	7th	59	94	.386	38½
1908*	6th	68	85	.444	22	1958†	7th	73	81	.474	19
1909*	2nd	95	58	.621	3½	1959†	7th	66	88	.429	28
1910*	1st	102	48	.680	+14½	1960†	8th	58	96	.377	39
1911*	1st	101	50	.669	+13½	1961†	T9th	61	100	.379	47½
1912*	3rd	90	62	.592	15	1962†	9th	72	90	.444	24
1913*	1st	96	57	.627	+ 6½	1963†	8th	73	89	.451	31½
1914*	1st	99	53	.651	+ 8½	1964†	10th	57	105	.352	42
1915*	8th	43	109	.283	58½	1965†	10th	59	103	.364	43
1916*	8th	36	117	.235	54½	1966†	7th	74	86	.463	23
1917*	8th	52	98	.359	44½	1967†	10th	62	99	.385	29½
1918*	8th	52	76	.406	24	1968	6th	82	80	.506	21
1919*	8th	36	104	.257	52	1969	2nd	88	74	.543	9
1920*	8th	48	106	.312	50	1970	2nd	89	73	.549	9
1921*	8th	53	100	.346	45	1971	1st‡	101	60	.627	+16
1922*	7th	65	89	.422	29	1972	1st§	93	62	.600	+ 5½
1923*	6th	69	83	.454	29	1973	1st§	94	68	.580	+ 6
1924*	5th	71	81	.467	20	1974	1st§	90	72	.556	+ 5
1925*	2nd	88	64	.579	8½	1975	1st‡	98	64	.605	+ 7
1926*	3rd	83	67	.553	6	1976	2nd	87	74	.540	2½
1927*	2nd	91	63	.591	19	1977	7th	63	98	.391	38½
1928*	2nd	98	55	.641	2½	1978	6th	69	93	.426	23
1929*	1st	104	46	.693	+18	1979	7th	54	108	.333	34
1930*	1st	102	52	.662	+ 8	1980	2nd	83	79	.512	14
1931*	1st	107	45	.704	+13½	1981	1st/2nd	64	45	.587	★†•
1932*	2nd	94	60	.610	13	1982	5th	68	94	.420	25
1933*	3rd	79	72	.523	19½	1983	4th	74	88	.457	25
1934*	5th	68	82	.453	31	1984	4th	77	85	.475	7
1935*	8th	58	91	.389	34	1985	T4th	77	85	.475	14
1936*	8th	53	100	.346	49	1986	T3rd	76	86	.469	16
1937*	7th	54	97	.358	46½	1987	3rd	81	81	.500	4
1938*	8th	53	99	.349	46	1988	1st§	104	58	.642	+13
1939*	7th	55	97	.362	51½	1989	1st§	99	63	.611	+ 7
1940*	8th	54	100	.351	36	1990	1st§	103	59	.636	+ 9
1941*	8th	64	90	.416	37	1991	4th	84	78	.519	11
1942*	8th	55	99	.357	48	1992	1st‡	96	66	.593	+ 6
1943*	8th	49	105	.318	49	1993	7th	68	94	.420	26
1944*	T5th	72	82	.468	17						
1945*	8th	52	98	.347	34½						
1946*	8th	49	105	.318	55						
1947*	5th	78	76	.506	19						
1948*	4th	84	70	.545	12½						
1949*	5th	81	73	.526	16						
1950*	8th	52	102	.338	46						

*Franchise known as Philadelphia A's. †Franchise known as Kansas City A's. ‡Lost Championship Series. §Won Championship Series. ★First half 37-23; second 27-22. •Won division playoff.

MANAGERS

Name	Record	Years
Connie Mack	3582-3814	'01-50
Jimmie Dykes	198-254	'51-53
Eddie Joost	51-103	1954
Lou Boudreau	151-260	'55-57
Harry Craft	162-196	'57-59
Bob Elliott	58-96	1960
Joe Gordon	26-33	1961
Hank Bauer	187-226	'61-62
		1969
Eddie Lopat	90-124	'63-64
Mel McGaha	45-91	'64-65
Haywood Sullivan	54-82	1965
Alvin Dark	314-291	'66-67
		'74-75
Luke Appling	10-30	1967
Bob Kennedy	82-80	1968
John McNamara	97-78	'69-70
Dick Williams	288-190	'71-73
Chuck Tanner	87-74	1976
Jack McKeon	71-105	'77, '78
Bobby Winkles	61-86	'77-78
Jim Marshall	54-108	1979
Billy Martin	215-218	'80-82
Steve Boros	94-112	'83-84
Jackie Moore	163-190	'84-86
Tony La Russa	577-474	'86-93

1993 REVIEW

DAY BY DAY

Date	Opp.	Res.	Score	(inn.*)	Hits	Opp. hits	Winning pitcher	Losing pitcher	Save	Record	Pos.	GB
4-5	Det.	W	9-4		10	9	Welch	Moore	Eckersley	1-0	T1st	...
4-7	Det.	W	12-7		10	13	Downs	Kiely		2-0	T1st	...
4-8	Det.	L	2-3		7	7	Doherty	Davis	Henneman	2-1	T2nd	½
4-9	Mil.	L	5-6		10	12	Manzanillo	Downs	Henry	2-2	T4th	1½
4-10	Mil.	W	4-3		10	9	Welch	Bones	Eckersley	3-2	T2nd	½
4-11	Mil.	W	8-2		12	6	Hillegas	Wegman		4-2	2nd	½
4-13	At Det.	L	4-20		7	18	Moore	Davis		4-3	3rd	2
4-15	At Det.	L	2-3		9	7	Haas	Eckersley		4-4	T3rd	2
4-17	At Mil.	L	3-6		7	7	Wegman	Welch		4-5	5th	2½
4-18	At Mil.	L	0-8		3	12	Eldred	Hillegas		4-6	5th	3½
4-20	N.Y.	W	9-7	(10)	13	8	Gossage	Habyan		5-6	5th	2½
4-21	N.Y.	L	3-5		9	8	Monteleone	Honeycutt	Farr	5-7	6th	3
4-22	N.Y.	L	1-5		7	7	Militello	Darling	Kamieniecki	5-8	6th	4
4-24	Cle.	L	3-10		7	15	Bielecki	Hillegas		5-9	6th	5½
4-25	Cle.	L	0-6		3	13	Mesa	Davis		5-10	7th	6½
4-27	Bos.	W	7-2		12	7	Witt	Darwin	Gossage	6-10	7th	5½
4-28	Bos.	L	1-3		4	10	Viola	Welch	Russell	6-11	7th	6½
4-30	At Cle.	W	8-2	(10)	13	5	Gossage	Plunk		7-11	6th	5½
5-1	At Cle.	L	0-1		4	4	Mesa	Davis	Plunk	7-12	7th	5½
5-2	At Cle.	L	2-10		4	15	Nagy	Witt		7-13	7th	5½
5-3	At NY	W	4-2		8	4	Welch	Abbott	Eckersley	8-13	7th	4½
5-4	At NY	L	2-4		4	7	Wickman	Hillegas	Farr	8-14	7th	4½
5-5	At Bos.	L	1-3		7	11	Quantrill	Nunez	Russell	8-15	7th	5½
5-6	At Bos.	W	6-3		8	8	Witt	Clemens	Eckersley	9-15	7th	5½
5-7	At Cal.	L	3-4		6	7	Finley	Downs	Valera	9-16	7th	6½
5-8	At Cal.	W	6-2		11	8	Welch	Langston	Eckersley	10-16	7th	6
5-9	At Cal.	L	6-7	(10)	11	13	Grahe	Honeycutt		10-17	7th	7
5-10	Tex.	L	4-7		9	11	Leibrandt	Darling	Henke	10-18	7th	8
5-11	Tex.	W	6-0		10	3	Witt	Rogers		11-18	7th	7
5-12	Tex.	W	8-7		12	8	Eckersley	Henke		12-18	7th	7
5-13	Tex.	L	5-9		12	18	Whiteside	Nunez		12-19	7th	7½
5-14	Sea.	W	2-1	(11)	10	10	Boever	DeLucia		13-19	7th	7½
5-15	Sea.	W	2-1		3	5	Gossage	Nelson		14-19	7th	6½
5-16	Sea.	L	0-7		1	11	Johnson	Witt		14-20	7th	7½
5-18	At K.C.	L	1-6		4	10	Gardner	Welch		14-21	7th	8
5-19	At K.C.	L	8-13		14	14	Gordon	Hillegas	Montgomery	14-22	7th	8
5-20	At K.C.	W	4-1	(12)	9	9	Nunez	Gubicza	Eckersley	15-22	7th	7½
5-21	At Chi.	W	12-11		12	12	Downs	Hernandez	Eckersley	16-22	6th	6½
5-22	At Chi.	W	6-4		10	11	Witt	Stieb	Eckersley	17-22	6th	5½
5-23	At Chi.	L	4-5	(10)	7	8	Hernandez	Gossage		17-23	6th	6½
5-25	Min.	W	3-1		6	7	Davis	Deshaies	Eckersley	18-23	6th	5½
5-26	Min.	L	11-12		14	17	Tsamis	Boever		18-24	6th	5½
5-28	Tor.	W	3-2		7	7	Witt	Cox	Honeycutt	19-24	6th	5
5-29	Tor.	L	3-5		7	12	Stewart	Welch	Ward	19-25	6th	6
5-30	Tor.	L	11-13		13	13	Cox	Mohler	Ward	19-26	7th	7
5-31	Bal.	L	1-3		6	5	Mussina	Darling		19-27	7th	7
6-1	Bal.	W	4-1		4	9	Hillegas	McDonald	Eckersley	20-27	7th	6
6-2	Bal.	L	2-5		7	6	Valenzuela	Witt	Olson	20-28	7th	6
6-4	At Tor.	L	3-4	(12)	12	10	Williams	Gossage		20-29	7th	7½
6-5	At Tor.	L	5-9		7	10	Guzman	Hillegas		20-30	7th	7½
6-6	At Tor.	W	10-3		12	10	Darling	Morris		21-30	7th	7½
6-7	At Bal.	L	2-3		5	7	Frohwirth	Gossage	Olson	21-31	7th	8½
6-8	At Bal.	L	4-6		9	8	Mills	Davis	Olson	21-32	7th	8½
6-9	At Bal.	L	4-7		10	15	Sutcliffe	Welch	Pennington	21-33	7th	9½
6-11	At Min.	L	8-11		14	15	Trombley	Nunez	Aguilera	21-34	7th	9½
6-12	At Min.	L	2-7		5	11	Deshaies	Witt		21-35	7th	10
6-13	At Min.	W	7-6		15	12	Nunez	Tsamis	Eckersley	22-35	7th	9½
6-14	Chi.	W	7-3		11	5	Young	McCaskill		23-35	7th	8½
6-15	Chi.	L	0-4		3	9	Alvarez	Welch		23-36	7th	8½
6-16	Chi.	L	0-4		3	8	McDowell	Darling		23-37	7th	9½
6-17	Chi.	W	5-2		7	9	Witt	Fernandez	Eckersley	24-37	7th	9
6-18	K.C.	W	10-9		10	15	Gossage	Gordon	Eckersley	25-37	7th	8
6-19	K.C.	L	0-3		4	9	Appier	Boever	Montgomery	25-38	7th	9
6-20	K.C.	W	4-1		5	9	Welch	Gardner	Eckersley	26-38	7th	8
6-21	At Sea.	W	5-3		14	8	Davis	DeLucia	Eckersley	27-38	7th	7
6-22	At Sea.	W	10-3		16	4	Witt	Converse		28-38	7th	7
6-23	At Sea.	L	7-8	(14)	16	14	Henry	Hillegas		28-39	7th	8
6-24	At Sea.	W	3-2		4	7	Eckersley	Johnson		29-39	7th	7½
6-26	At Tex.	L	7-10		14	15	Whiteside	Davis	Henke	29-40	7th	8
6-27	At Tex.	L	0-4		5	10	Brown	Witt		29-41	7th	9

Date	Opp.	Res.	Score	(Inn.*)	Hits	Opp. hits	Winning pitcher	Losing pitcher	Save	Record	Pos.	GB
6-29	Cal.	W	8-7	(11)	18	10	Nunez	Patterson		30-41	7th	7½
6-30	Cal.	W	5-4		9	8	Boever	Springer	Eckersley	31-41	7th	6½
7-1	Cal.	W	6-3		11	9	Welch	Finley	Nunez	32-41	6th	5½
7-2	N.Y.	W	4-3		8	6	Witt	Wickman		33-41	6th	5½
7-3	N.Y.	W	5-4		8	11	Boever	Perez	Eckersley	34-41	6th	4½
7-4	N.Y.	W	7-6		12	11	Hillegas	Munoz	Eckersley	35-41	6th	4½
7-5 (1)	Cle.	W	6-5		9	12	Horsman	Cook	Eckersley	36-41	6th	4½
7-5 (2)	Cle.	L	2-6		9	12	Clark	Young	Hernandez	36-42	6th	5
7-6	Cle.	L	8-11		9	17	Plunk	Gossage	Hernandez	36-43	6th	5
7-7	Cle.	W	3-0		9	4	Boever	Mesa	Eckersley	37-43	6th	5
7-8	Bos.	L	9-11		13	11	Dopson	Van Poppel	Russell	37-44	6th	6
7-9	Bos.	W	4-2		7	7	Darling	Quantrill	Eckersley	38-44	6th	5
7-10	Bos.	L	0-5		6	11	Sele	Downs	Harris	38-45	6th	5
7-11	Bos.	L	2-3		7	8	Darwin	Witt	Russell	38-46	6th	6
7-15	At NY	W	8-3		15	11	Mohler	Perez		39-46	6th	6
7-16	At NY	L	3-10		7	17	Key	Downs		39-47	6th	7
7-17	At NY	L	5-9		6	14	Abbott	Witt		39-48	6th	8
7-18	At NY	L	6-13		14	18	Howe	Nunez		39-49	6th	9
7-19	At Cle.	L	2-4		10	5	Young	Van Poppel	Hernandez	39-50	6th	9
7-20	At Cle.	L	5-9		11	11	Mesa	Mohler		39-51	6th	10
7-21	At Cle.	W	7-2		13	6	Welch	Wertz		40-51	6th	9
7-22	At Bos.	L	7-9		10	13	Ryan	Nunez	Russell	40-52	7th	10
7-23	At Bos.	L	5-6	(10)	6	13	Harris	Gossage		40-53	7th	10
7-24	At Bos.	L	3-5		6	8	Sele	Downs	Russell	40-54	7th	11
7-25	At Bos.	L	1-8		8	14	Viola	Welch	Quantrill	40-55	7th	11
7-26	At Cal.	W	11-4		15	10	Darling	Finley		41-55	7th	11
7-27	At Cal.	L	8-15		9	17	Grahe	Witt	Patterson	41-56	7th	12
7-28	At Cal.	L	2-3		6	6	Langston	Van Poppel	Butcher	41-57	7th	13
7-29	At Cal.	W	2-1		10	7	Welch	Leftwich	Eckersley	42-57	7th	12½
7-30	Tex.	W	4-1		7	8	Darling	Ryan	Eckersley	43-57	T6th	12½
7-31	Tex.	L	2-8		6	10	Brown	Witt		43-58	T6th	13½
8-1	Tex.	W	9-5		14	8	Van Poppel	Rogers		44-58	T6th	13½
8-3	Sea.	L	4-5		7	7	Johnson	Nunez	Power	44-59	7th	14
8-4	Sea.	W	5-4		7	9	Downs	Nelson		45-59	T6th	13
8-5	Sea.	L	2-3		6	7	Fleming	Witt	Charlton	45-60	T6th	13
8-6	At K.C.	W	5-2		9	7	Van Poppel	Haney	Eckersley	46-60	T6th	12
8-7	At K.C.	L	2-5		4	8	Appier	Downs	Montgomery	46-61	7th	13
8-8	At K.C.	L	3-4		10	8	Pichardo	Darling	Montgomery	46-62	7th	13
8-9	At Chi.	L	4-5		11	10	Fernandez	Witt	Hernandez	46-63	7th	14
8-10	At Chi.	L	0-4		2	4	Belcher	Mohler		46-64	7th	15
8-11	At Chi.	W	3-1		5	8	Van Poppel	Alvarez	Eckersley	47-64	7th	14
8-13	Min.	L	2-5		5	9	Guardado	Darling	Aguilera	47-65	7th	14½
8-14 (1)	Min.	L	1-5	(12)	7	9	Casian	Honeycutt		47-66	7th	15
8-14 (2)	Min.	L	2-6		10	8	Trombley	Downs	Tsamis	47-67	7th	15½
8-15	Min.	L	5-12		15	17	Erickson	Mohler		47-68	7th	16
8-16	Mil.	W	4-1		6	4	Van Poppel	Novoa	Eckersley	48-68	7th	15½
8-17	Mil.	W	6-3		7	7	Karsay	Navarro	Eckersley	49-68	7th	15½
8-18	Mil.	W	2-1		5	5	Darling	Miranda	Eckersley	50-68	7th	14½
8-20	At Det.	W	7-6		10	10	Witt	Doherty	Eckersley	51-68	7th	14½
8-21	At Det.	L	3-4		8	9	Gullickson	Downs	Davis	51-69	7th	15½
8-22	At Det.	L	3-5		7	8	Bolton	Van Poppel	Henneman	51-70	7th	16½
8-23	At Det.	L	0-9		1	13	Moore	Karsay		51-71	7th	16½
8-24 (1)	At Mil.	L	2-9		8	13	Bones	Honeycutt		51-72	7th	17
8-24 (2)	At Mil.	L	6-7	(13)	14	21	Maysey	Downs		51-73	7th	17½
8-25	At Mil.	L	2-12		9	14	Eldred	Witt		51-74	7th	18
8-26	At Mil.	L	3-5		5	4	Miranda	Mohler	Orosco	51-75	7th	18½
8-27	Det.	L	4-13		9	14	Bolton	Van Poppel		51-76	7th	19
8-28	Det.	L	3-5		11	10	Moore	Karsay	Henneman	51-77	7th	20
8-29	Det.	W	7-3		10	6	Welch	Doherty		52-77	7th	20
8-30	Tor.	L	2-4		7	9	Hentgen	Darling	Ward	52-78	7th	21
8-31	Tor.	L	2-3	(10)	9	11	Cox	Eckersley	Ward	52-79	7th	22
9-1	Tor.	L	3-8		5	9	Guzman	Mohler		52-80	7th	23
9-3	Bal.	L	4-5	(13)	8	9	Mills	Eckersley		52-81	7th	23
9-4	Bal.	L	3-6		9	12	Moyer	Karsay		52-82	7th	24½
9-5	Bal.	L	2-9		8	16	Mussina	Welch		52-83	7th	25½
9-7	At Tor.	W	11-7	(11)	12	10	Honeycutt	Castillo		53-83	7th	24
9-8	At Tor.	W	2-1		5	5	Witt	Ward	Eckersley	54-83	7th	24
9-9	At Tor.	W	7-4		10	8	Smithberg	Castillo	Eckersley	55-83	7th	23½
9-10	At Bal.	W	12-9		13	11	Downs	Williamson	Eckersley	56-83	7th	22½
9-11	At Bal.	L	1-3		4	8	McDonald	Welch		56-84	7th	23½
9-12	At Bal.	L	5-14		9	14	Moyer	Darling		56-85	7th	23½
9-13	At Min.	W	7-2		17	6	Witt	Erickson		57-85	7th	22½
9-14	At Min.	W	8-3		11	5	Karsay	Guardado	Smithberg	58-85	7th	22½
9-15	At Min.	W	15-2		18	8	Van Poppel	Banks		59-85	7th	22½

Date	Opp.	Res.	Score	(Inn.*)	Hits	Opp. hits	Winning pitcher	Losing pitcher	Save	Record	Pos.	GB
9-16	At Min.	L	4-5	(13)	9	13	Hartley	Smithberg		59-86	7th	23
9-17	Chi.	L	0-8		4	12	Alvarez	Welch		59-87	7th	23
9-18	Chi.	W	3-2		8	5	Witt	McDowell	Eckersley	60-87	7th	23
9-19	Chi.	L	1-3		6	8	Radinsky	Eckersley	Hernandez	60-88	7th	23
9-20	K.C.	W	2-1		5	7	Van Poppel	Cone	Smithberg	61-88	7th	23
9-21	K.C.	W	9-6		16	12	Downs	Gubicza		62-88	7th	23
9-22	K.C.	L	2-3	(10)	8	8	Montgomery	Smithberg		62-89	7th	23
9-23	K.C.	W	2-1		7	5	Witt	Appier	Eckersley	63-89	7th	23
9-24	At Sea.	W	5-3		9	8	Karsay	Bosio	Eckersley	64-89	T6th	24
9-25	At Sea.	W	7-2		10	7	Horsman	Power		65-89	T6th	23½
9-26	At Sea.	W	3-2	(12)	5	8	Briscoe	Ontiveros	Eckersley	66-89	T6th	23
9-28 (1)	At Tex.	L	0-2		4	7	Brown	Darling		66-90	7th	23
9-28 (2)	At Tex.	W	10-3		16	5	Witt	Bohanon		67-90	7th	23
9-29	At Tex.	L	6-11		12	13	Dreyer	Downs		67-91	7th	24
9-30	At Tex.	L	2-6		6	9	Rogers	Van Poppel		67-92	7th	24
10-1	Cal.	W	7-2		11	4	Jimenez	Holzemer	Smithberg	68-92	7th	23
10-2	Cal.	L	2-6		8	8	Finley	Welch		68-93	7th	25
10-3	Cal.	L	3-7		10	11	Langston	Witt	Grahe	68-94	7th	26

Monthly records: April (7-11), May (12-16), June (12-14), July (12-17), August (9-21), September (15-13), October (1-2).
*Innings, if other than nine.

HIGHLIGHTS

High point: The A's won a season-high seven consecutive games from June 29 through the first game of a double-header July 5. The streak pulled them to within 4½ games of first place.

Low point: Starting with a 4-3 loss at Detroit on August 21 and ending with a 9-2 loss to Baltimore on September 5, the A's dropped 15 of 16 games. At that point, Oakland was a season-worst 31 games below .500 (52-83).

Turning point: After reaching the All-Star break in fairly decent shape (38-46 record, six games out), Oakland embarked on its longest road trip of the season. The A's went 4-11, falling 12½ games back.

Most valuable player: Second baseman Brent Gates. Called up from the minors May 5, Gates became a regular and hit .290, collected 69 RBIs and seized the second base job for years to come.

Most valuable pitcher: Righthander Bobby Witt. He had some bumpy moments, but Witt's strong first half (8-6) and perfect September (5-0) carried him to a team-high 14 victories.

Most improved player: Designated hitter Troy Neel. Following a slow start, he was demoted on May 31 to Class AAA, where he found his swing. He was recalled June 17 and finished with a .290 average, 19 home runs and 63 RBIs.

Most pleasant surprise: First baseman Mike Aldrete. Signed as a minor league free agent in March, he stepped in when first baseman Mark McGwire got hurt and delivered a .267 average with a career-high 10 homers and a team-high seven pinch hits.

Biggest disappointments: Righthanders Ron Darling and Bob Welch. Darling did not collect the first of his five wins until June 6, and Welch finished with his fewest victories (nine) since 1986.

Key injuries: McGwire played in only 27 games due mostly to an injured left heel that required surgery in September. Among other key casualties were outfielder Lance Blankenship (right shoulder surgery in August), outfielder Jerry Browne (broke right hand in April) and catcher Terry Steinbach (broke right wrist in August).

Notable: Oakland finished below .500 (68-94) for the first time since 1986. ... The A's became the first team since the 1914-15 Philadelphia A's to fall from first place to sole possession of last place in consecutive seasons. ... Despite blowing a career-high 10 saves, righthander Dennis Eckersley became the first major league pitcher to earn 30 or more saves in six consecutive seasons.

—RON KROICHICK

RECORDS

1993 regular-season record: 68-94 (7th in A.L. West); 38-43 at home; 30-51 on road; 29-55 vs. East; 39-39 vs. West; 23-31 vs. LHP; 45-63 vs. RHP; 52-84 on grass; 16-10 on turf; 23-46 in day-time; 45-48 at night; 24-24 in one-run games; 7-11 in extra-inning games; 0-2 in doubleheaders.

Team record last five years: 450-360 (.556, ranks 2nd in league in that span).

TEAM LEADERS

Batting average: Brent Gates (.290).
At-bats: Ruben Sierra (630).
Runs: Rickey Henderson, Ruben Sierra (77).
Hits: Brent Gates (155).
Total bases: Ruben Sierra (246).
Doubles: Brent Gates (29).
Triples: Ruben Sierra (5).
Home runs: Ruben Sierra (22).
Runs batted in: Ruben Sierra (101).
Stolen bases: Rickey Henderson (31).
Slugging percentage: Brent Gates (.391).
On-base percentage: Brent Gates (.357).
Wins: Bobby Witt (14).
Earned-run average: Bobby Witt (4.21).
Complete games: Bobby Witt (5).
Shutouts: Bobby Witt (1).
Saves: Dennis Eckersley (36).
Innings pitched: Bobby Witt (220).
Strikeouts: Bobby Witt (131).

GAMES BY POSITION

Catcher: Terry Steinbach 86, Scott Hemond 75, Henry Mercedes 18, Eric Helfand 5.
First base: Mike Aldrete 59, Troy Neel 34, Mark McGwire 25, Kevin Seitzer 24, Terry Steinbach 15, Dale Sveum 14, Marcos Armas 12, Scott Brosius 11, Lance Blankenship 6, Jerry Browne 2, Scott Hemond 1.
Second base: Brent Gates 139, Lance Blankenship 19, Dale Sveum 4, Jerry Browne 3, Kurt Abbott 2, Kevin Seitzer 2, Mike Bordick 1, Scott Hemond 1.
Third base: Craig Paquette 104, Kevin Seitzer 46, Jerry Browne 13, Scott Brosius 10, Dale Sveum 7.
Shortstop: Mike Bordick 159, Kurt Abbott 6, Scott Brosius 6, Lance Blankenship 2, Dale Sveum 1.
Outfield: Ruben Sierra 133, Dave Henderson 76, Rickey Henderson 74, Lance Blankenship 66, Jerry Browne 56, Scott Brosius 46, Scott Lydy 38, Eric Fox 26, Mike Aldrete 20, Kurt Abbott 13, Scott Hemond 6, Kevin Seitzer 3, Marcos Armas 1, Craig Paquette 1, Dale Sveum 1.
Designated hitter: Troy Neel 85, Dave Henderson 28, Ruben Sierra 25, Rickey Henderson 18, Mike Aldrete 6, Terry Steinbach 6, Lance Blankenship 5, Scott Hemond 3, Kevin Seitzer 3, Marcos Armas 2, Scott Brosius 2, Eric Fox 2, Scott Lydy 2, Dale Sveum 2, Henry Mercedes 1, Craig Paquette 1.

TOP DRAFT CHOICES

1a. **John Wasdin**, RHP, Florida State U.
1b. **Willie Adams**, RHP, Stanford U.
2a. **Jeff D'Amico**, SS, Redmond (Wash.) HS
2b. **Mike Moschetti**, SS, La Mirada (Cal.) HS
3. **Tucker Barr**, C, Maclay HS, Tallahassee, Fla.
4. **Jason McDonald**, SS, U. of Houston.
5. **Andy Smith**, RHP, A.L. Brown High School, Kannapolis, N.C.
6. **Scott Spiezio**, 1B, U. of Illinois.
7. **Tim Kubinski**, LHP, UCLA.
8. **Leon Hamburg**, OF, Casa Roble High School, Orangevale, Calif.
9. **Damon Newman**, RHP, Fullerton (Cal.) JC
10. **John Phillips**, RHP, Bullard High School, Fresno, Calif.

SEATTLE MARINERS
AMERICAN LEAGUE WEST DIVISION

1994 SCHEDULE

N Denotes night game (any game starting after 5 p.m.).
☐ Home games shaded.
* At Three Rivers Stadium in Pittsburgh.

APRIL

SUN	MON	TUE	WED	THU	FRI	SAT
					1	2
3	4 CLE	5	6 N CLE	7 N CLE	8 N TOR	9 N TOR
10 TOR	11 N MIN	12 N MIN	13 N MIN	14	15 N MIL	16 N MIL
17 MIL	18	19 N NY	20 N NY	21 N NY	22 N BAL	23 N BAL
24 BAL	25 N BOS	26 N BOS	27 N NY	28 N NY	29 N BAL	30 N BAL

MAY

SUN	MON	TUE	WED	THU	FRI	SAT
1 BAL	2	3 N BOS	4 N BOS	5	6 N DET	7 N DET
8 DET	9 N CHI	10 N CHI	11 N CHI	12	13 N CAL	14 N CAL
15 CAL	16 N KC	17 N KC	18 N KC	19 N TEX	20 N TEX	21 N TEX
22 N TEX	23 N OAK	24 N OAK	25 OAK	26	27 N MIL	28 N MIL
29 MIL	30 N MIN	31 N MIN				

JUNE

SUN	MON	TUE	WED	THU	FRI	SAT
			1 MIN	2	3 N TOR	4 N TOR
5 TOR	6 N CLE	7 N CLE	8 N CLE	9	10 N OAK	11 N OAK
12 OAK	13 N TEX	14 N TEX	15 N TEX	16 N KC	17 N KC	18 N KC
19 KC	20 N CAL	21 N CAL	22 N CAL	23 N CHI	24 N CHI	25 N CHI
26 CHI	27 N DET	28 N DET	29 N DET	30		

JULY

SUN	MON	TUE	WED	THU	FRI	SAT
				N 1 NY	N 2 NY
3 NY	4 N BAL	5 N BAL	6 N BAL	7 N BOS	8 N BOS	9 N BOS
10 BOS	11	12 * ALL-STAR GAME	13	14 N NY	15 N NY	16 N NY
17 NY	18 N BAL	19 N BAL	20 N BAL	21 N BOS	22 N BOS	23 N BOS
24 BOS	25	26 N DET	27 N DET	28 N DET	29 N CHI	30 N CHI
31 CHI						

AUGUST

SUN	MON	TUE	WED	THU	FRI	SAT
	1	2 N CAL	3 N CAL	4 N CAL	5 N KC	6 N KC
7 N KC	8	9 N TEX	10 N TEX	11 N OAK	12 N OAK	13 N OAK
14 OAK	15	16 N TOR	17 N TOR	18 N TOR	19 N CLE	20 N CLE
21 CLE	22 N TOR	23 N TOR	24 N TOR	25 N MIN	26 N MIN	27 N MIN
28 MIN	29	30 N MIL	31 N MIL			

SEPTEMBER

SUN	MON	TUE	WED	THU	FRI	SAT
				1 MIL	2 N MIN	3 MIN
4 MIN	5	6 N MIL	7 N MIL	8 MIL	9 N CLE	10 N CLE
11 CLE	12 N OAK	13 N OAK	14 OAK	15	16 N TEX	17 N TEX
18 TEX	19 N KC	20 N KC	21 N KC	22 N CAL	23 N CAL	24 N CAL
25 CAL	26	27 N CHI	28 N CHI	29 CHI	30 N DET	

OCTOBER

SUN	MON	TUE	WED	THU	FRI	SAT
					N 1 DET
2 DET						

1994 SEASON

CLUB DIRECTORY

Chief executive officer
John Ellis
President and chief operating officer
Chuck Armstrong
Vice president, baseball operations
Woody Woodward
Vice president, communications
Randy Adamack
Vice president, finance and administration
Brian Beggs
Vice president, business development
Paul Isaki
Vice president, marketing and sales
Bob Gobrecht
V.p., scouting and player development
Roger Jongewaard
Director of baseball administration
Lee Pelekoudas
Assistant to v.p., baseball operations
George Zuraw
Minor league director
Jim Beattie
Coordinator of minor league instruction
George Zuraw
Director, team travel
Craig Detwiler
Director, community relations
Joe Chard
Director, corporate sponsorships
Beth Wojick
Director, marketing
Carl Weinstein
Director, promotions
Kevin Martinez
Director, public relations
Dave Aust
Director, stadium operations
Tony Pereira
Director of sales
Chris McCartney
Operations manager
Connie Zentner
Controller
Denise Podosek
Assistant director, public relations
Pete Vanderwarker
Exec. asst. to chairman and president
Shirley Ward
Payroll manager
Shirley Shreve
Player development and scouting assistant
Larry Beinfest
Public relations assistant
Molly Magan
Trainer
Rick Griffin
Home clubhouse and equipment manager
Henry Genzale

Club physicians
Dr. Larry Pedegana
Dr. Mitchel Storey
Club dentist
Dr. Richard Leshgold
Head groundskeeper
Wilbur Loo
Public address announcer
Tom Hutyler
Supervisor, international scouting
Gordon Blakely
Major league and special assignment scout
Bill Kearns
National supervisor and assignment scout
Benny Looper
Scouting supervisors
Ken Compton
Steve Pope
Chris Smith
Regular scouts
Maximo Alvarez
Fernando Arguelles
Brian Ballentine
Jeff Brisson
John Burden
Kendall Carter
Ramon de los Santos
Curtis Dishman
Miguel Escobar
Guy Gianni
Ron Hafner
Lewis Graham
Ron Hopkins
Gudalope Jabalera
Dan Jennings
Mark Jensen
Dave Karaff
John Leavitt
Gary McGraw
Jerry Marik
Omer Munoz
Glenn Murdock
Joe Nigro
Cotton Nye
Fran Oneto
Cliff Pastornicky
Mryon Pines
Don Poplin
Phil Pote
John Ramey
Louis Scheuermann
Douglas Scott
Roberto Valdez
Ray Vince
Jack Webber
Archie White
Bill Young

Manager—Lou Piniella (14).

Coaches—Lee Elia (4), Sammy Ellis (32), Ken Griffey Sr. (30), John McLaren (7), Sam Mejias (49), Sam Perlozzo (2).

No.	PITCHERS	B/T	Ht./Wt.	Born	1993 clubs
13	Ayala, Bobby	R/R	6-3/200	7-8-69	Indianapolis, Cincinnati
29	Bosio, Chris	R/R	6-3/225	4-3-63	Seattle
34	Buckley, Travis	R/R	6-4/210	6-15-70	Colorado Springs, Chattanooga, Jacksonville
40	Clayton, Craig	R/R	6-0/185	11-29-70	Riverside, Jacksonville
41	Converse, Jim	L/R	5-9/180	8-17-71	Calgary, Seattle
47	Cummings, John	L/L	6-3/200	5-10-69	Seattle, Jacksonville, Calgary
44	Darwin, Jeff	R/R	6-3/180	7-6-69	Jacksonville, Edmonton
55	DeLucia, Rich	R/R	6-0/185	10-7-64	Seattle, Calgary
35	Fleming, Dave	L/L	6-3/200	11-7-69	Jacksonville, Seattle
31	Harris, Reggie	R/R	6-1/190	8-12-68	Jacksonville, Calgary
	Hibbard, Greg	L/L	6-0/185	9-13-64	Chicago A.L.
38	Holman, Brad	R/R	6-5/200	2-9-68	Calgary, Seattle
51	Johnson, Randy	R/L	6-10/225	9-10-63	Seattle
50	King, Kevin	L/L	6-4/200	2-11-69	Riverside, Jacksonville, Seattle
43	Nelson, Jeff	R/R	6-8/235	11-17-66	Calgary, Seattle
12	Plantenberg, Erik	B/L	6-1/180	10-30-68	Jacksonville, Seattle
48	Power, Ted	R/R	6-4/215	1-31-55	Cleveland, Canton/Akron, Seattle
22	Salkeld, Roger	R/R	6-5/215	3-6-71	Jacksonville, Seattle
26	Wainhouse, Dave	L/R	6-2/185	11-7-67	Seattle, Calgary
39	Williams, Jeff	R/R	6-4/230	4-16-69	Rochester

No.	CATCHERS	B/T	Ht./Wt.	Born	1993 clubs
54	Christopherson, Eric	R/R	6-0/195	4-25-69	Arizona Giants, Shreveport
33	Haselman, Bill	R/R	6-3/220	5-25-66	Seattle
45	Howard, Chris	R/R	6-2/220	2-27-66	Calgary, Seattle
15	Sasser, Mackey	L/R	6-1/210	8-3-62	Seattle
6	Wilson, Dan	R/R	6-3/190	3-25-69	Cincinnati, Indianapolis

No.	INFIELDERS	B/T	Ht./Wt.	Born	1993 clubs
8	Amaral, Rich	R/R	6-0/175	4-1-62	Seattle
16	Blowers, Mike	R/R	6-2/210	4-24-65	Seattle
10	Fermin, Felix	R/R	5-11/170	10-9-63	Cleveland
18	Jefferson, Reggie	B/L	6-4/215	9-25-68	Cleveland
9	Manahan, Anthony	R/R	6-0/190	12-15-68	Calgary
11	Martinez, Edgar	R/R	5-11/190	1-2-63	Seattle, Jacksonville
23	Martinez, Tino	L/R	6-2/210	12-7-67	Seattle
28	Newfield, Marc	R/R	6-4/205	10-19-72	Jacksonville, Seattle
20	Pirkl, Greg	R/R	6-5/240	8-7-70	Calgary, Seattle
3	Rodriguez, Alex	R/R	6-3/190	7-27-75	DID NOT PLAY
17	Santana, Ruben	R/R	6-2/175	3-7-70	Jacksonville
1	Turang, Brian	R/R	5-10/170	6-14-67	Calgary, Seattle

No.	OUTFIELDERS	B/T	Ht./Wt.	Born	1993 clubs
5	Anthony, Eric	L/L	6-2/195	11-8-67	Houston
19	Buhner, Jay	R/R	6-3/210	8-13-64	Seattle
24	Griffey Jr., Ken	L/L	6-3/205	11-21-69	Seattle
27	Tinsley, Lee	B/R	5-10/185	3-4-69	Seattle, Calgary

BALLPARK INFORMATION

Ballpark (capacity, surface)
The Kingdome (59,702, artificial)

Address
P.O. Box 4100
411 First Ave. S.
Seattle, WA 98104

Business phone
206-628-3555

Ticket information
206-628-3555

Ticket prices
$15 (box)
$12 (club)
$8 (view)
$6 (general admission)
$6 (view, children 14 and under)
$4 (g.a., children 14 and under)

Field dimensions (from home plate)
To left field at foul line, 331 feet
To center field, 405 feet
To right field at foul line, 314 feet

First game played
April 6, 1977 (Angels 7, Mariners 0)

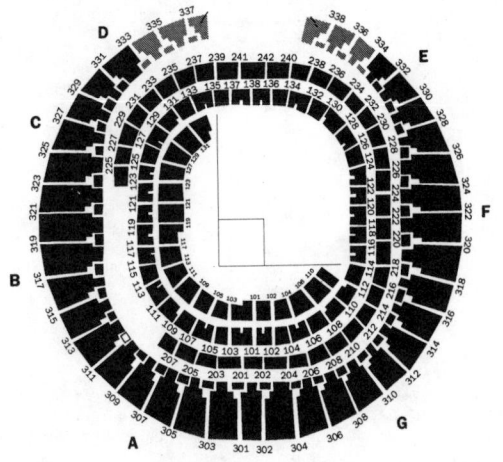

Class	Team	League	Manager
AAA	Calgary	Pacific Coast	Steve Smith
AA	Jacksonville	Southern	Marc Hill
A	Riverside	California	Dave Myers
A	Appleton	Midwest	Carlos Lezcano
A	Bellingham	Northwest	Mike Goff
Rookie	Peoria Mariners	Arizona	Marty Martinez

☐ BROADCAST INFORMATION ☐

Radio: KIRO-AM (710). Broadcasters: Dave Niehaus, Ron Fairly, Chip Carey, Ken Levine.
TV: KSTW-TV (Channel 11). Broadcasters: Dave Niehaus, Ron Fairly, Chip Carey, Ken Levine.
Cable TV: None.

☐ SPRING TRAINING ☐

Ballpark: Peoria Stadium (Peoria, Ariz.).
Ticket information: 602-784-4444.

HISTORY

☐ YEAR-BY-YEAR RECORDS ☐

Year	Pos.	W	L	Pct.	GB	Year	Pos.	W	L	Pct.	GB
1977	6th	64	98	.395	38	1987	4th	78	84	.481	7
1978	7th	56	104	.350	35	1988	7th	68	93	.422	35½
1979	6th	67	95	.414	21	1989	6th	73	89	.451	26
1980	7th	59	103	.364	38	1990	5th	77	85	.475	26
1981	6th/5th	44	65	.404	*	1991	5th	83	79	.512	12
1982	4th	76	86	.469	17	1992	7th	64	98	.395	32
1983	7th	60	102	.370	39	1993	4th	82	80	.506	12
1984	T5th	74	88	.457	10						
1985	6th	74	88	.457	17						
1986	7th	67	95	.414	25						

*First half 21-36; second 23-29.

☐ MANAGERS ☐

Name	Record	Years
Darrell Johnson	226-362	'77-80
Maury Wills	26-56	'80-81
Rene Lachemann	140-180	'81-83
Del Crandall	93-141	'83-84
Chuck Cottier	98-120	'84-86
Dick Williams	159-192	'86-88
Jimmy Snyder	45-60	1988
Jim Lefebvre	233-253	'89-91
Bill Plummer	64-98	1992
Lou Piniella	82-80	1993

DAY BY DAY

Date	Opp.	Res.	Score (inn.*)	Hits	Opp. hits	Winning pitcher	Losing pitcher	Save	Record	Pos.	GB
4-6	Tor.	W	8-1	11	7	Johnson	Morris		1-0	T1st	...
4-7	Tor.	L	0-2	3	5	Leiter	Bosio	Ward	1-1	T3rd	1
4-9	Bal.	W	6-0	6	9	Hanson	McDonald		2-1	T2nd	1
4-10	Bal.	L	3-5	5	9	Sutcliffe	Cummings	Olson	2-2	T4th	1
4-11	Bal.	W	7-6	(12)	15	11	Swan	Williamson		3-2	T4th	1½
4-13	At Tor.	L	5-6	7	11	Cox	Leary	Ward	3-3	T4th	2½
4-14	At Tor.	W	10-9	(10)	14	9	DeLucia	Hentgen	Charlton	4-3	T3rd	1½
4-15	At Tor.	L	1-3	5	10	Stottlemyre	Cummings	Ward	4-4	T3rd	2
4-16	At Det.	L	0-5	5	8	Wells	Johnson		4-5	6th	2
4-17	At Det.	L	3-20	6	20	Krueger	Hampton		4-6	6th	3
4-18	At Det.	L	7-8	13	12	MacDonald	Charlton		4-7	6th	4
4-19	At Det.	W	10-6	10	10	Hanson	Doherty	Henry	5-7	T4th	3½
4-20	Bos.	L	2-5	5	11	Clemens	Cummings	Russell	5-8	6th	3½
4-21	Bos.	W	5-0	10	4	Johnson	Darwin		6-8	5th	3
4-22	Bos.	W	7-0	11	0	Bosio	Hesketh		7-8	5th	3
4-23	N.Y.	W	6-3	10	10	Hampton	Abbott	Charlton	8-8	5th	3
4-24	N.Y.	L	0-1	(11)	2	11	Howe	Swan	Farr	8-9	5th	4
4-25	N.Y.	L	9-10	13	11	Monteleone	Henry	Farr	8-10	5th	5
4-26	Cle.	W	6-3	13	7	Johnson	Kramer		9-10	4th	4½
4-27	Cle.	W	4-0	12	4	Bosio	Nagy		10-10	4th	3½
4-28	Cle.	W	4-0	7	7	Hanson	Mutis	Charlton	11-10	4th	3½
4-30	At NY	L	0-3	4	7	Perez	Cummings	Farr	11-11	4th	3½
5-1	At NY	L	2-6	4	12	Witt	Johnson		11-12	4th	3½
5-2	At NY	L	2-3	(10)	7	8	Habyan	DeLucia		11-13	4th	3½
5-3	At Bos.	W	2-0	8	9	Hanson	Viola	Charlton	12-13	4th	2½
5-4	At Bos.	W	7-6	13	10	Leary	Hesketh	Charlton	13-13	4th	1½
5-5	At Cle.	L	2-3	10	9	Bielecki	Cummings	Lilliquist	13-14	4th	2½
5-6	At Cle.	W	9-5	16	6	Johnson	Mesa		14-14	4th	2½
5-7	Min.	L	4-5	11	8	Guthrie	Swan	Aguilera	14-15	4th	3½
5-8	Min.	W	7-2	9	6	Hanson	Deshaies		15-15	4th	3
5-9	Min.	W	6-4	8	11	Leary	Erickson	Charlton	16-15	4th	3
5-10	Chi.	L	2-13	10	12	Fernandez	Hampton		16-16	4th	4
5-11	Chi.	W	4-3	9	4	Johnson	Stieb	Charlton	17-16	4th	3
5-12	Chi.	L	5-6	12	10	Alvarez	Cummings	Hernandez	17-17	4th	4
5-14	At Oak.	L	1-2	(11)	10	10	Boever	DeLucia		17-18	4th	5
5-15	At Oak.	L	1-2	5	3	Gossage	Nelson		17-19	4th	5
5-16	At Oak.	W	7-0	11	1	Johnson	Witt		18-19	4th	5
5-17	At Tex.	W	16-9	23	14	Nelson	Lefferts		19-19	4th	4
5-18	At Tex.	L	2-3	10	8	Bohanon	DeLucia	Henke	19-20	4th	5
5-19	At Tex.	L	3-4	6	6	Henke	Hanson		19-21	5th	5
5-20	At Tex.	W	7-4	9	8	Leary	Leibrandt		20-21	4th	4½
5-21	At K.C.	L	1-2	6	6	Haney	Johnson	Gordon	20-22	5th	4½
5-22	At K.C.	L	1-4	5	10	Appier	Converse		20-23	5th	4½
5-23	At K.C.	W	10-7	17	10	Swan	Montgomery	Charlton	21-23	5th	4½
5-24	Cal.	W	4-3	(14)	13	11	Henry	Crim		22-23	4th	4
5-25	Cal.	L	3-6	7	10	Finley	Leary	Frey	22-24	5th	4
5-26	Cal.	W	2-0	7	7	DeLucia	Lewis	Charlton	23-24	5th	3
5-27	Cal.	L	0-5	5	8	Sanderson	Converse		23-25	5th	3
5-28	Det.	W	4-3	(10)	8	9	Swan	Bolton		24-25	5th	3
5-29	Det.	L	2-3	8	6	Leiter	Hanson	MacDonald	24-26	5th	3½
5-30	Det.	W	9-5	11	11	Charlton	Krueger		25-26	5th	3
6-1	Mil.	L	0-10	9	9	Navarro	Bosio		25-27	5th	3½
6-2	Mil.	W	6-3	9	6	Nelson	Eldred	Charlton	26-27	4th	2½
6-4	At Bal.	L	5-6	(10)	11	8	Williamson	Swan		26-28	5th	4
6-5	At Bal.	L	3-5	10	8	Pennington	Hanson	Olson	26-29	5th	4
6-6	At Bal.	L	2-5	7	11	Mussina	Bosio	Olson	26-30	5th	5
6-7	At Mil.	L	3-5	7	9	Eldred	Fleming	Henry	26-31	5th	6
6-8	At Mil.	L	1-2	5	8	Austin	Leary	Henry	26-32	6th	6
6-9	At Mil.	W	6-1	14	8	Johnson	Wegman		27-32	6th	6
6-11	At Cal.	L	2-8	8	9	Finley	Hanson		27-33	6th	6
6-12	At Cal.	W	2-0	6	3	Fleming	Sanderson		28-33	6th	5
6-13	At Cal.	W	12-7	18	12	Leary	Valera		29-33	6th	5
6-14	K.C.	W	6-3	8	6	Johnson	Gardner	Charlton	30-33	5th	4
6-15	K.C.	W	6-1	9	4	Converse	Pichardo		31-33	4th	3
6-16	K.C.	L	1-5	6	16	Cone	Hanson		31-34	4th	4
6-18	Tex.	W	3-2	9	7	Fleming	Pavlik	Charlton	32-34	4th	3
6-19	Tex.	W	6-5	8	7	Johnson	Burns	Charlton	33-34	4th	3
6-20	Tex.	W	13-2	12	5	Leary	Leibrandt		34-34	4th	2
6-21	Oak.	L	3-5	8	14	Davis	DeLucia	Eckersley	34-35	4th	2
6-22	Oak.	L	3-10	4	16	Witt	Converse		34-36	4th	3

Date	Opp.	Res.	Score	(Inn.*)	Hits	Opp. hits	Winning pitcher	Losing pitcher	Save	Record	Pos.	GB
6-23	Oak.	W	8-7	(14)	14	16	Henry	Hillegas		35-36	4th	3
6-24	Oak.	L	2-3		7	4	Eckersley	Johnson		35-37	4th	3½
6-25	At Chi.	W	3-2		7	8	Leary	Alvarez	Charlton	36-37	4th	2½
6-26	At Chi.	L	4-7		11	12	McDowell	Hanson	Hernandez	36-38	4th	3½
6-27	At Chi.	L	4-6		10	8	Fernandez	DeLucia	Hernandez	36-39	4th	4½
6-28	At Min.	W	4-1		8	5	Fleming	Tapani	Charlton	37-39	4th	3½
6-29	At Min.	L	5-7		9	15	Trombley	Ayrault	Aguilera	37-40	4th	3½
6-30	At Min.	W	6-3		12	8	Johnson	Erickson	Charlton	38-40	4th	2½
7-1	At Min.	W	6-1		10	8	Hanson	Banks		39-40	3rd	1½
7-2	Bos.	L	8-9		12	13	Viola	Hampton	Russell	39-41	3rd	2½
7-3	Bos.	L	5-6		9	13	Harris	Charlton	Russell	39-42	3rd	2½
7-4	Bos.	L	0-6		2	6	Quantrill	Bosio		39-43	5th	3½
7-5	N.Y.	L	3-6		7	4	Kanieniecki	Johnson	Howe	39-44	5th	4½
7-6	N.Y.	W	12-4		12	7	Hanson	Abbott		40-44	5th	3½
7-7	N.Y.	W	6-5		9	9	Leary	Wickman	Charlton	41-44	5th	3½
7-9	Cle.	W	6-4		8	10	Fleming	C. Young	Bosio	42-44	4th	3
7-10	Cle.	W	7-6		13	10	Bosio	Hernandez		43-44	4th	2
7-11	Cle.	W	5-4	(11)	16	9	Ayrault	Plunk		44-44	T4th	2
7-15	At Bos.	W	3-2		9	6	Fleming	Viola	Hampton	45-44	4th	2
7-16	At Bos.	L	3-5		9	10	Clemens	Hanson	Russell	45-45	4th	3
7-17	At Bos.	L	3-4		8	8	Darwin	Bosio	Russell	45-46	4th	4
7-18	At Bos.	L	6-7		9	8	Ryan	Charlton	Harris	45-47	4th	5
7-19	At NY	L	2-8		8	12	Kamieniecki	Leary		45-48	4th	5
7-20	At NY	W	9-5		12	10	Fleming	Howe		46-48	4th	5
7-21	At NY	W	10-3		16	6	Hanson	Key		47-48	4th	4
7-22	At Cle.	W	3-2		6	9	Bosio	Mutis	Holman	48-48	4th	4
7-23	At Cle.	L	4-9		9	13	Lopez	Johnson		48-49	4th	4
7-24	At Cle.	W	6-5		13	8	Nelson	DiPoto	Holman	49-49	4th	4
7-25	At Cle.	L	9-11		12	11	Hernandez	Nelson	Lilliquist	49-50	4th	4
7-27	Min.	W	10-8		12	13	DeLucia	Tsamis	Nelson	50-50	4th	4½
7-28	Min.	L	1-5		5	9	Banks	Johnson	Casian	50-51	4th	5½
7-29	Min.	W	4-3		10	7	Leary	Erickson	Power	51-51	4th	5
7-30	Chi.	L	4-6	(10)	7	15	Radinsky	DeLucia	Hernandez	51-52	4th	6
7-31	Chi.	L	10-13		13	15	Bolton	Hanson	Radinsky	51-53	4th	7
8-1	Chi.	L	0-4		2	6	McDowell	Bosio		51-54	4th	8
8-3	At Oak.	W	5-4		7	7	Johnson	Nunez	Power	52-54	4th	7½
8-4	At Oak.	L	4-5		9	7	Downs	Nelson		52-55	4th	7½
8-5	At Oak.	W	3-2		7	4	Fleming	Witt	Charlton	53-55	4th	6½
8-6	At Tex.	L	3-5		5	6	Rogers	Bosio	Henke	53-56	4th	6½
8-7	At Tex.	W	2-1		3	4	Hanson	Pavlik	Henry	54-56	4th	6½
8-8	At Tex.	L	1-7		7	7	Dreyer	Johnson		54-57	4th	6½
8-9	At K.C.	L	6-7		11	11	Belinda	Power	Montgomery	54-58	4th	7½
8-10	At K.C.	L	1-4		8	10	Gordon	Fleming	Gubicza	54-59	4th	8½
8-11	At K.C.	W	4-3		8	8	Bosio	Haney	Power	55-59	4th	7½
8-13	Cal.	W	2-1		7	4	Hanson	Finley		56-59	4th	7
8-14	Cal.	W	7-2		8	8	Johnson	Langston		57-59	4th	7
8-15	Cal.	L	2-14		8	22	Leftwich	Leary		57-60	4th	7
8-16	Bal.	W	8-6		9	10	Fleming	Sutcliffe	Johnson	58-60	4th	6½
8-17	Bal.	W	5-3		7	7	Bosio	Frohwirth	Power	59-60	4th	6½
8-18	Bal.	L	1-8		8	12	Moyer	Hanson		59-61	4th	6½
8-20	At Tor.	W	4-1		8	3	Johnson	Hentgen		60-61	4th	6½
8-21	At Tor.	W	5-2		7	10	Fleming	Stewart	Power	61-61	4th	6½
8-22	At Tor.	L	7-12		10	9	Guzman	Ontiveros		61-62	4th	7½
8-24	At Det.	L	1-4		3	7	Doherty	Hanson		61-63	4th	8
8-25	At Det.	L	4-7		9	14	Gullickson	Leary	Davis	61-64	4th	8
8-26	Tor.	W	6-3		7	10	Johnson	Stewart	Power	62-64	4th	7½
8-27	Tor.	W	7-6		8	11	Nelson	Williams	Plantenberg	63-64	4th	7
8-28	Tor.	W	2-1		4	7	Bosio	Cox	Power	64-64	4th	7
8-29	Tor.	L	2-6		7	11	Stottlemyre	Hanson		64-65	4th	8
8-30	Det.	L	2-13		5	16	Gullickson	Leary		64-66	4th	9
8-31	Det.	W	5-4		11	6	Nelson	Henneman	Power	65-66	4th	9
9-1	Det.	W	9-3		13	9	Fleming	Moore		66-66	4th	9
9-2	Mil.	W	8-1		15	5	Bosio	Higuera		67-66	4th	8
9-3	Mil.	L	4-7	(12)	11	12	Orosco	Brad Holman	Maysey	67-67	4th	8½
9-4	Mil.	W	6-1		7	7	Leary	Eldred	Power	68-67	4th	9
9-5	Mil.	W	3-2		5	5	Johnson	Miranda		69-67	4th	9
9-6	At Bal.	L	1-5		8	4	McDonald	Fleming	Mills	69-68	4th	9
9-7	At Bal.	W	3-2		4	6	Brad Holman	Rhodes	Power	70-68	4th	9
9-8	At Bal.	L	3-6		8	8	Poole	King		70-69	4th	9
9-10	At Mil.	W	10-3		13	8	Leary	Higuera		71-69	4th	8
9-11	At Mil.	W	7-3		13	7	Johnson	Eldred	Brad Holman	72-69	4th	8
9-12	At Mil.	W	5-4	(10)	9	13	Power	Orosco		73-69	4th	7
9-13	At Cal.	W	10-1		14	4	Bosio	Langston		74-69	4th	6
9-14	At Cal.	L	2-9		8	13	Magrane	Hanson		74-70	4th	7

Date	Opp.	Res.	Score	(inn.*)	Hits	Opp. hits	Winning pitcher	Losing pitcher	Save	Record	Pos.	GB
9-15	At Cal.	L	1-15		3	19	Leftwich	Leary		74-71	4th	8
9-16	K.C.	W	14-1		14	2	Johnson	Haney		75-71	T3rd	7½
9-17	K.C.	L	3-6		8	10	Gordon	Fleming	Montgomery	75-72	4th	8½
9-18	K.C.	L	0-1		3	6	Appier	Bosio		75-73	4th	8½
9-19	K.C.	W	4-1		7	6	Hanson	Magnante	Power	76-73	4th	8½
9-20	Tex.	L	1-2	(10)	6	10	Carpenter	Brad Holman	Henke	76-74	4th	9½
9-21	Tex.	W	8-0		9	3	Johnson	Leibrandt		77-74	T3rd	8½
9-22	Tex.	W	7-4		8	9	Fleming	Ryan	Power	78-74	T3rd	8½
9-24	Oak.	L	3-5		8	9	Karsay	Bosio	Eckersley	78-75	4th	10
9-25	Oak.	L	2-7		7	10	Horsman	Power		78-76	4th	10½
9-26	Oak.	L	2-3	(12)	8	5	Briscoe	Ontiveros	Eckersley	78-77	4th	11
9-27	At Chi.	L	2-4		4	8	Alvarez	Fleming	McCaskill	78-78	4th	12
9-28	At Chi.	W	5-2		6	8	Leary	Ruffcorn	Power	79-78	4th	11
9-29	At Chi.	L	2-3	(12)	10	11	Radinsky	Brad Holman		79-79	4th	12
9-30	At Chi.	W	2-1	(11)	10	8	Power	McCaskill		80-79	4th	11
10-1	At Min.	W	8-2		14	9	Johnson	Trombley		81-79	4th	11
10-2	At Min.	W	7-3		10	7	Fleming	Banks		82-79	4th	11
10-3	At Min.	L	2-7		6	9	Tapani	Leary		82-80	4th	12

Monthly records: April (11-11), May (14-15), June (13-14), July (13-13), August (14-13), September (15-13), October (2-1).
*Innings, if other than nine.

HIGHLIGHTS

High point: From July 6-15, Seattle won six games in a row to pull within two games of first place.

Low point: Following that high point, the Mariners lost 15 of their next 24 games to fall 8½ games off the pace. Seattle would get no closer than 4½ games behind the rest of the year.

Turning point: The Mariners began a three-game series against division-leading Chicago on July 30, only five games behind the White Sox. Seattle's bullpen blew a 4-2 lead in the ninth inning and Chicago scored twice in the 10th to win, 6-4, en route to a sweep.

Most valuable player: Center fielder Ken Griffey. He emerged as a premier slugger, posting career highs in home runs (45) and RBIs (109).

Most valuable pitcher: Lefthander Randy Johnson. He tied a club record with 19 victories and paced the major leagues with 308 strikeouts, becoming the first big leaguer to fan 300 batters since Nolan Ryan in 1989.

Most improved player: Second baseman Bret Boone. He began spring training as a regular but started the year in the minors. When he returned for good on July 30, he played solid defense and finished with 12 homers (a team record for second basemen).

Most pleasant surprise: Third baseman Mike Blowers. After making the team as a non-roster invitee, Blowers hit three grand slams and set career highs in virtually every offensive category.

Biggest disappointment: Left fielder Mike Felder. After signing as a free agent in the off-season, he boasted he would steal at least 60 bases. He ended up with 15 thefts and hit just .211.

Key injuries: Third baseman Edgar Martinez spent three stints on the disabled list, missing 112 games. Righthander Chris Bosio and lefthander Norm Charlton each went on the disabled list twice. First baseman Tino Martinez missed 50 games.

Notable: The Mariners' 82-80 mark was just the franchise's second winning record. ... Seattle paced the majors with a .985 fielding percentage. ... Johnson became the first lefthander to strike out 300 hitters since Steve Carlton did it for Philadelphia in 1972. ... Bosio hurled the second no-hitter in team history, beating Boston on April 22. ... On June 23 against Oakland, right fielder Jay Buhner became the first Mariner ever to hit for the cycle. ... Griffey tied a major league record by hitting home runs in eight straight games (July 20-28).

—JIM STREET

RECORDS

1993 regular-season record: 82-80 (4th in A.L. West); 46-35 at home; 36-45 on road; 44-40 vs. East; 38-40 vs. West; 35-18 vs. LHP; 47-62 vs. RHP; 26-36 on grass; 56-44 on turf; 21-24 in daytime; 61-56 at night; 29-27 in one-run games; 8-9 in extra-inning games; 0-0 in doubleheaders.

Team record last five years: 379-431 (.468, ranks 12th in league in that span).

TEAM LEADERS

Batting average: Ken Griffey (.309).
At-bats: Ken Griffey (582).
Runs: Ken Griffey (113).
Hits: Ken Griffey (180).
Total bases: Ken Griffey (359).
Doubles: Ken Griffey (38).
Triples: Mike Felder (5).
Home runs: Ken Griffey (45).
Runs batted in: Ken Griffey (109).
Stolen bases: Rich Amaral (19).
Slugging percentage: Ken Griffey (.617).
On-base percentage: Ken Griffey (.408).
Wins: Randy Johnson (19).
Earned-run average: Randy Johnson (3.24).
Complete games: Randy Johnson (10).
Shutouts: Randy Johnson (3).
Saves: Norm Charlton (18).
Innings pitched: Randy Johnson (255⅓).
Strikeouts: Randy Johnson (308).

GAMES BY POSITION

Catcher: Dave Valle 135, Bill Haselman 49, Chris Howard 4, Mackey Sasser 4, Mike Blowers 1.

First base: Tino Martinez 103, Dave Magadan 41, Greg Litton 13, Pete O'Brien 9, Greg Pirkl 5, Rich Amaral 3, Mike Blowers 1, Ken Griffey Jr. 1, Mackey Sasser 1.

Second base: Rich Amaral 77, Bret Boone 74, Greg Litton 17, Fernando Vina 16, Wally Backman 1, Brian Turang 1.

Third base: Mike Blowers 117, Dave Magadan 27, Rich Amaral 19, Edgar Martinez 16, Wally Backman 9, Greg Litton 7, Mike Felder 2, Brian Turang 2.

Shortstop: Omar Vizquel 155, Rich Amaral 14, Greg Litton 5, Fernando Vina 4.

Outfield: Jay Buhner 148, Ken Griffey Jr. 139, Mike Felder 95, Brian Turang 38, Mackey Sasser 37, Henry Cotto 34, Dann Howitt 29, Greg Litton 22, Lee Tinsley 6, Marc Newfield 5, Mike Blowers 2, Bill Haselman 2, Randy Johnson 1, Jeff Nelson 1, Pete O'Brien 1, Larry Sheets 1.

Designated hitter: Pete O'Brien 52, Edgar Martinez 24, Ken Griffey Jr. 19, Mackey Sasser 19, Henry Cotto 15, Marc Newfield 15, Greg Litton 12, Jay Buhner 10, Rich Amaral 9, Mike Felder 6, Tino Martinez 6, Larry Sheets 5, Bill Haselman 4, Mike Blowers 3, Dann Howitt 2, Dave Magadan 2, Greg Pirkl 2, Lee Tinsley 2, Fernando Vina 2, Omar Vizquel 2, Bret Boone 1, Erik Hanson 1, Brian Turang 1.

TOP DRAFT CHOICES

1. **Alex Rodriguez**, SS, Westminster Christian High School, Miami.
2. **None.**
3. **Ed Randolph**, 3B/OF, Roosevelt High School, Dallas.
4. **Mike Collett**, RHP, U. of Southern Cal.
5. **David Cooper**, RHP, Hesperia (Cal.) H.S.
6. **Kenny Cloude**, RHP, McDonough HS, Balt.
7. **Tim Schweitzer**, LHP, U. of Arizona.
8. **Greg Hillengas**, OF, Seminole (Fla.) H.S.
9. **Rob Krueger**, LHP, Western Michigan U.
10. **Dean Crow**, RHP, Baylor University.

TEXAS RANGERS
AMERICAN LEAGUE WEST DIVISION

N Denotes night game (any game starting after 5 p.m.).
▢ Home games shaded.
* At Three Rivers Stadium in Pittsburgh.

APRIL

SUN	MON	TUE	WED	THU	FRI	SAT
					1	2
3	4 N NY	5	6 N NY	7	8 N BAL	9 N BAL
10 BAL	11 MIL	12	13 N MIL	14 N MIL	15 N BAL	16 N BAL
17 BAL	18	19 N TOR	20 N TOR	21	22 N CLE	23 N CLE
24 CLE	25 N DET	26 N DET	27 N TOR	28 N TOR	29 N CLE	30 CLE

MAY

SUN	MON	TUE	WED	THU	FRI	SAT
1 CLE	2 N DET	3 N DET	4 DET	5	6 N MIN	7 N MIN
8 MIN	9 N CAL	10 N CAL	11 N CAL	12	13 N CHI	14 N CHI
15 CHI	16 N OAK	17 N OAK	18 OAK	19 N SEA	20 N SEA	21 N SEA
22 SEA	23 N KC	24 N KC	25 KC	26 N KC	27 N BOS	28 N BOS
29 BOS	30 N MIL	31 N MIL				

JUNE

SUN	MON	TUE	WED	THU	FRI	SAT
			1 MIL	2	3 N BOS	4 N BOS
5 BOS	6 N NY	7 N NY	8 N NY	9 N KC	10 N KC	11 N KC
12 KC	13 N SEA	14 N SEA	15 SEA	16 N OAK	17 N OAK	18 N OAK
19 OAK	20 N CHI	21 N CHI	22 CHI	23	24 N CAL	25 N CAL
26 CAL	27	28 N MIN	29 MIN	30 MIN		

JULY

SUN	MON	TUE	WED	THU	FRI	SAT
					1 N DET	2 N DET
3 N DET	4 N DET	5 N CLE	6 N CLE	7 N CLE	8 DET	9 DET
10 DET	11 * ALL-STAR GAME	12	13	14 N TOR	15 N TOR	16 N TOR
17 N TOR	18 N CLE	19 N CLE	20 N CLE	21 TOR	22 N TOR	23 TOR
24 TOR	25 N MIN	26 N MIN	27 N MIN	28 N CAL	29 N CAL	30 N CAL
31 N CAL						

AUGUST

SUN	MON	TUE	WED	THU	FRI	SAT
	1	2 N CHI	3 N CHI	4 N CHI	5 N OAK	6 N OAK
7 OAK	8 N SEA	9 N SEA	10 N SEA	11	12 N KC	13 N KC
14 KC	15	16 N BAL	17 N BAL	18 N BAL	19 N NY	20 N NY
21 NY	22 N BOS	23 N BOS	24 N BOS	25 N NY	26 N NY	27 NY
28 NY	29 N BOS	30 N BOS	31 N BOS			

SEPTEMBER

SUN	MON	TUE	WED	THU	FRI	SAT
				1 N MIL	2 N MIL	3
4 MIL	5 N BAL	6 N BAL	7 N BAL	8	9 N MIL	10 N MIL
11 MIL	12 N KC	13 N KC	14 KC	15	16 N SEA	17 N SEA
18 SEA	19 N OAK	20 N OAK	21 N OAK	22 N CHI	23 N CHI	24 CHI
25 CHI	26 N CAL	27 N CAL	28 N CAL	29 N MIN	30 N MIN	

OCTOBER

SUN	MON	TUE	WED	THU	FRI	SAT
						1 N MIN
2 MIN						

CLUB DIRECTORY

General partners
George W. Bush
Edward W. (Rusty) Rose
President
J. Thomas Schieffer
Vice president, general manager
Thomas A. Grieve
V.p., business operations/treasurer
John F. McMichael
Vice president, marketing
Martin B. Conway
Vice president, administration/secretary
Charles F. Wangner
Vice president, public relations
John C. Blake
Vice president, ballpark development
Jack W. Hill
Vice president, community development
Norman B. Lyons
General counsel
Gerald W. Haddock
Director of ballpark operations
Mat Stolley
Director of grounds
Jim Anglea
Asst. g.m., player personnel and scouting
Sandy Johnson
Assistant general manager
Wayne Krivsky
Director, player development
Marty Scott
Traveling secretary
Dan Schimek
Dir. of major league administration
Judy Johns
Admin. asst., baseball operations
Bob Garvey
Asst. to dir., player development
Monty Clegg
Admin. asst., scouting
Charlene Homuth
Major league scout/special assignments
Larry Hardy
Major league advance scout
Marc Sullivan
Director of medical services
Dr. Mike Mycoskie
Equipment and home clubhouse manager
Joe Macko
Visiting clubhouse manager
Zack Minasian
Video coordinator
Brian Harbert
Controller
Steve McNeill
Asst. to v.p., community development
Ray Burris
Director, corporate marketing
Dave Fendrick
Director, in-park entertainment
Chuck Morgan
Director, merchandising
Nancy McCusker

Corporate sales manager
Jodi Benefiel
Sales manager
Brad Zane
Promotions manager
Chuck Baugh
Director, sales
Ross Scott
Asst. to v.p., marketing
Jeannie Richards
Director, player relations
Taunee Paur
Dir., Span. broadcasting and Latin Am. liasion
Luis R. Mayoral
Director, publications
Eric Kolb
Assistant director, public relations
John Ralph
Assistant director, player relations
Sheila Bolduc
Assistant, special projects
Bobby Bragan
Admin. asst., public relations
Michelle Baugh
Scouting supervisors
Bill Earnhart
Bryan Lambe
Omar Minaya
Len Strelitz
Rudy Terrasas
Scouts
Hector Acevedo
Manuel Batista
Jim Benedict
Ray Blanco
Joe Branzell
Roney Calderon
Marco Cobos
Paddy Cottrell
Dick Coury
Mike Daughtry
Marc Delpiano
Jim Dreyer
Kip Fagg
Jim Fairey
Mario Gonzalez
Mike Grouse
Thomas Gushiken
Tim Hallgren
Larry Izzo
Robert Lavallee
Bob Meisner
Jose Offerman
Cornelio Pena
Mike Piatnik
Alan Regier
Antolin Reyes
Pat Rigby
Rodolfo Rosario
Don Shwery
Randy Taylor
Jim Terrell
Danilo Troncoso

Manager—Kevin Kennedy (44).

Coaches—Mickey Hatcher (43), Perry Hill (47), Jackie Moore (42), Dave Oliver (26), Claude Osteen (48), Willie Upshaw (46).

No.	PITCHERS	B/T	Ht./Wt.	Born	1993 clubs
	Armstrong, Jack	R/R	6-5/220	3-7-65	Florida
41	Brown, Kevin	R/R	6-4/195	3-14-65	Texas
56	Brumley, Duff	R/R	6-4/195	8-25-70	St. Petersburg, Arkansas, Tulsa
53	Burrows, Terry	L/L	6-1/185	11-28-68	Oklahoma City
31	Carpenter, Cris	R/R	6-1/185	4-5-65	Florida, Texas
24	Dreyer, Steve	R/R	6-3/180	11-19-69	Tulsa, Oklahoma City, Texas
30	Fajardo, Hector	R/R	6-4/200	11-6-70	Gulf Coast Rangers, Charlotte, Texas
50	Henke, Tom	R/R	6-5/225	12-21-57	Texas
40	Honeycutt, Rick	L/L	6-1/191	6-29-54	Oakland
	Howell, Jay	R/R	6-3/203	11-26-55	Atlanta
61	Hurst, James	L/L	6-0/160	6-1-67	Tulsa, Oklahoma City
28	Oliver, Darren	R/L	6-1/170	10-6-70	Tulsa, Texas
59	Pavlik, Roger	R/R	6-2/220	10-4-67	Oklahoma City, Texas
37	Rogers, Kenny	L/L	6-1/205	11-10-64	Texas
60	Santana, Julio	R/R	6-0/175	1-20-73	Gulf Coast Rangers
35	Smith, Dan	L/L	6-5/195	8-20-69	Charlotte, Oklahoma City
27	Whiteside, Matt	R/R	6-0/195	8-8-67	Texas, Oklahoma City

No.	CATCHERS	B/T	Ht./Wt.	Born	1993 clubs
7	Rodriguez, Ivan	R/R	5-9/205	11-30-71	Texas

No.	INFIELDERS	B/T	Ht./Wt.	Born	1993 clubs
22	Clark, Will	L/L	6-0/196	3-13-64	San Francisco
1	Frye, Jeff	R/R	5-9/165	8-31-66	Texas
23	Gil, Benji	R/R	6-2/182	10-6-72	Texas, Tulsa
58	Greer, Rusty	L/L	6-0/190	1-21-69	Tulsa, Oklahoma City
9	Huson, Jeff	L/R	6-3/180	8-15-64	Oklahoma City, Texas
2	Lee, Manuel	B/R	5-9/166	6-17-65	Texas
16	Palmer, Dean	R/R	6-2/195	12-27-68	Texas
5	Redus, Gary	R/R	6-1/195	11-1-56	Texas
10	Shave, Jon	R/R	6-0/180	11-4-67	Oklahoma City, Texas
20	Strange, Doug	B/R	6-2/170	4-13-64	Texas
36	Wilson, Desi	L/L	6-7/230	5-9-68	Charlotte

No.	OUTFIELDERS	B/T	Ht./Wt.	Born	1993 clubs
33	Canseco, Jose	R/R	6-4/240	7-2-64	Texas
12	Ducey, Rob	L/R	6-2/180	5-24-65	Oklahoma City, Texas
19	Gonzalez, Juan	R/R	6-3/215	10-16-69	Texas
18	Harris, Donald	R/R	6-1/185	11-12-67	Oklahoma City, Texas
15	Hulse, David	L/L	5-11/170	2-25-68	Texas
4	James, Chris	R/R	6-1/202	10-4-62	Houston, Texas
32	Lowery, Terrell	R/R	6-3/175	10-25-70	Charlotte, Tulsa
17	Peltier, Dan	L/L	6-1/200	6-30-68	Texas, Oklahoma City

BALLPARK INFORMATION

Ballpark (capacity, surface)
The Ballpark in Arlington
(48,100, grass)

Address
1000 Ballpark Way
Arlington, TX 76011

Business phone
817-273-5222

Ticket information
817-273-5222

Ticket prices
$16 (field box & club level box)
$14 (terr. box & club level reserved)
$10 (upper box)
$9 (upper reserved)
$8 (left field reserved)
$8 (upper & lower porch)
$6 (grandstand reserved, adults)
$3 (grandstand reserved, children 13 and under)
$4 (outfield bleachers, adults)
$2 (outfield bleachers, children 13 and under)

Field dimensions (from home plate)
To left field at foul line, 334 feet
To center field, 400 feet
To right field at foul line, 325 feet

First game played
Scheduled for April 11, 1994

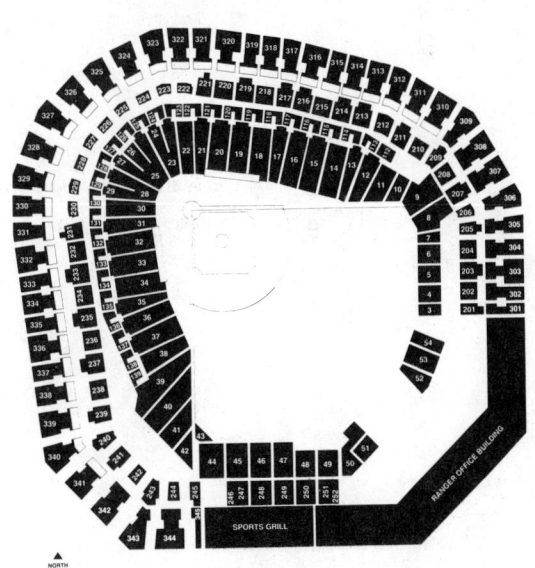

Class	Team	League	Manager
AAA	Oklahoma City	American Association	Bobby Jones
AA	Tulsa	Texas	Stan Cliburn
A	Charlotte	Florida State	Tommy Thompson
A	Charleston, S.C.	South Atlantic	Walt Williams
A	Hudson Valley	New York-Pennsylvania	Doug Sisson
Rookie	Gulf Coast Rangers	Gulf Coast	Chino Cadahia

☐ **BROADCAST INFORMATION** ☐

Radio: WBAP-AM (820). Broadcasters: Mark Holtz, Eric Nadel. KXEB-AM (910, Spanish language). Broadcasters: Mario Diaz, Luis Mayoral.
TV: KTVT-TV (Channel 11). Broadcasters: Steve Busby, Jim Sundberg.
Cable TV: Home Sports Entertainment. Broadcasters: Greg Lucas, Norm Hitzges.

┌──────────┐ **SPRING TRAINING** ┌──────────┐

Ballpark (city): Charlotte County Stadium (Port Charlotte, Fla.).
Ticket information: 813-625-9500, 813-624-2211.

HISTORY

┌──────────┐ **YEAR-BY-YEAR RECORDS** ┌──────────┐   ┌──────────┐ **MANAGERS** ┌──────────┐

Year	Pos.	W	L	Pct.	GB
1961*	T9th	61	100	.379	47½
1962*	10th	60	101	.373	35½
1963*	10th	56	106	.346	48½
1964*	9th	62	100	.383	37
1965*	8th	70	92	.432	32
1966*	8th	71	88	.447	25½
1967*	T6th	76	85	.472	15½
1968*	10th	65	96	.404	37½
1969*	4th	86	76	.531	23
1970*	6th	70	92	.432	38
1971*	5th	63	96	.396	38½
1972	6th	54	100	.351	38½
1973	6th	57	105	.352	37
1974	2nd	84	76	.525	5
1975	3rd	79	83	.488	19
1976	T4th	76	86	.469	14
1977	2nd	94	68	.580	8
1978	T2nd	87	75	.537	5
1979	3rd	83	79	.512	5

Year	Pos.	W	L	Pct.	GB
1980	4th	76	85	.472	20½
1981	2nd/3rd	57	48	.543	†
1982	6th	64	98	.395	29
1983	3rd	77	85	.475	22
1984	7th	69	92	.429	14½
1985	7th	62	99	.385	28½
1986	2nd	87	75	.537	5
1987	T6th	75	87	.463	10
1988	6th	70	91	.435	33½
1989	4th	83	79	.512	16
1990	3rd	83	79	.512	20
1991	3rd	85	77	.525	10
1992	4th	77	85	.475	19
1993	2nd	86	76	.531	8

*Franchise known as Washington Senators (second team). †First half 33-22; second 24-26.

Name	Record	Years
Mickey Vernon	135-227	'61-63
Gil Hodges	321-444	'63-67
Jim Lemon	65-96	1968
Ted Williams	273-364	'69-72
Whitey Herzog	47-91	1973
Del Wilber	1-0	1973
Billy Martin	137-141	'73-75
Frank Lucchesi	142-149	'75-77
Eddie Stanky	1-0	1977
Connie Ryan	2-4	1977
Billy Hunter	146-108	'77-78
Pat Corrales	160-164	'78-80
Don Zimmer	95-106	'81-82
Darrell Johnson	26-40	1982
Doug Rader	155-200	'83-85
Bobby Valentine	581-605	'85-92
Toby Harrah	32-44	1992
Kevin Kennedy	86-76	1993

DAY BY DAY

Date	Opp.	Res.	Score	(Inn.*)	Hits	Opp. hits	Winning pitcher	Losing pitcher	Save	Record	Pos.	GB
4-5	At Bal.	W	7-4		10	9	Lefferts	Sutcliffe	Henke	1-0	T1st	...
4-7	At Bal.	W	3-1	(11)	6	9	Patterson	Frohwirth		2-0	T1st	...
4-9	Bos.	W	3-1		5	5	Ryan	Dopson	Henke	3-0	1st	+1
4-10	Bos.	L	2-10		9	14	Clemens	Lefferts		3-1	1st	+½
4-11	Bos.	W	4-1		7	6	Brown	Darwin	Henke	4-1	1st	+½
4-12	Bal.	W	6-3		8	10	Leibrandt	Mussina	Henke	5-1	1st	+1
4-13	Bal.	W	8-3		8	7	Rogers	Valenzuela		6-1	1st	+1½
4-14	Bal.	L	5-6		11	9	McDonald	Ryan	Olson	6-2	1st	+½
4-16	At N.Y.	L	3-5		8	11	Monteleone	Lefferts	Habyan	6-3	1st	+½
4-17	At N.Y.	W	9-0		11	6	Brown	Abbott		7-3	1st	+½
4-18	At N.Y.	W	12-2		15	8	Leibrandt	Perez		8-3	1st	+1½
4-20	At Det.	L	1-3		4	5	Wells	Rogers	Henneman	8-4	1st	+½
4-21	At Det.	L	4-5		14	7	Krueger	Lefferts	Henneman	8-5	2nd	½
4-23	At Mil.	L	0-3		1	8	Eldred	Brown	Orosco	8-6	2nd	2
4-24	At Mil.	W	15-4		12	11	Leibrandt	Manzanillo		9-6	2nd	2
4-25	At Mil.	W	6-1		10	3	Rogers	Navarro		10-6	2nd	2
4-26	At Tor.	L	6-8		9	16	Morris	Lefferts	Ward	10-7	2nd	2½
4-27	At Tor.	L	3-4		4	8	Hentgen	Nen	Ward	10-8	2nd	2½
4-28	Det.	W	6-5	(11)	15	9	Henke	Munoz		11-8	2nd	2½
4-29	Det.	L	1-3		5	7	Doherty	Leibrandt	Henneman	11-9	3rd	3
4-30	Mil.	L	4-5		6	6	Lloyd	Patterson	Henry	11-10	3rd	3
5-1	Mil.	L	3-4	(12)	14	8	Lloyd	Patterson	Manzanillo	11-11	1st	+3
5-2	Mil.	W	13-2		15	4	Nen	Wegman	Bronkey	12-11	3rd	2
5-3	Mil.	W	9-2		14	6	Brown	Eldred		13-11	3rd	1
5-4	Tor.	W	3-2		9	7	Bohanon	Ward	Henke	14-11	T2nd	...
5-5	Tor.	W	7-1		12	5	Rogers	Stottlemyre		15-11	T2nd	...
5-7	At K.C.	L	4-9		9	12	Pichardo	Ryan		15-12	3rd	1½
5-9	At K.C.	W	2-1		2	6	Brown	Cone		16-12	3rd	1½
5-10	At Oak.	W	7-4		11	9	Leibrandt	Darling	Henke	17-12	T2nd	1½
5-11	At Oak.	L	0-6		3	10	Witt	Rogers		17-13	3rd	1½
5-12	At Oak.	L	7-8		8	12	Eckersley	Henke		17-14	3rd	2½
5-13	At Oak.	W	9-5		18	12	Whiteside	Nunez		18-14	3rd	2
5-14	Chi.	L	0-4		4	4	McDowell	Brown		18-15	3rd	2
5-15	Chi.	W	6-4	(11)	12	11	Henke	Jones		19-15	3rd	2
5-16	Chi.	L	8-15		12	17	Fernandez	Rogers	Thigpen	19-16	3rd	3
5-17	Sea.	L	9-16		14	23	Nelson	Lefferts		19-17	3rd	3
5-18	Sea.	W	3-2		8	10	Bohanon	DeLucia	Henke	20-17	3rd	3
5-19	Sea.	W	4-3		6	6	Henke	Hanson		21-17	3rd	2
5-20	Sea.	L	4-7		8	9	Leary	Leibrandt		21-18	3rd	2½
5-21	Cal.	W	6-4	(10)	9	11	Henke	Crim		22-18	3rd	1½
5-22	Cal.	W	4-2		7	7	Pavlik	Sanderson	Henke	23-18	2nd	½
5-23	Cal.	L	2-6		8	11	Valera	Burns	Grahe	23-19	3rd	1½
5-24	At Cle.	L	1-4		1	8	Kramer	Brown		23-20	3rd	2
5-25	At Cle.	W	5-1		8	8	Leibrandt	Cook		24-20	3rd	1
5-26	At Cle.	L	6-7		10	10	Mesa	Rogers	Plunk	24-21	3rd	1
5-28	At Bos.	L	1-4		2	8	Clemens	Pavlik	Russell	24-22	3rd	1½
5-29	At Bos.	L	1-15		6	14	Darwin	Burns		24-23	4th	2½
5-30	At Bos.	L	5-6	(12)	16	14	Melendez	Bronkey		24-24	4th	3½
5-31	At Min.	W	1-0		4	7	Leibrandt	Tapani	Henke	25-24	4th	2½
6-1	At Min.	L	5-7		7	10	Mahomes	Bohanon	Aguilera	25-25	4th	2½
6-2	At Min.	L	3-6		8	10	Banks	Pavlik	Aguilera	25-26	5th	2½
6-4	N.Y.	W	5-3		7	8	Brown	Abbott	Henke	26-26	4th	3
6-5	N.Y.	L	6-9		9	15	Monteleone	Lefferts	Farr	26-27	4th	3
6-6	N.Y.	W	4-3		9	8	Rogers	Perez	Henke	27-27	4th	3
6-7	Min.	W	8-2		12	7	Pavlik	Mahomes		28-27	4th	3
6-8	Min.	L	2-3	(10)	9	9	Willis	Whiteside	Aguilera	28-28	4th	3
6-10	Min.	L	5-6		12	10	Tapani	Leibrandt	Aguilera	28-29	4th	4
6-11	Cle.	L	3-8		8	10	Slocumb	Brown		28-30	4th	4
6-12	Cle.	L	9-10		14	15	M. Young	Rogers	Lilliquist	28-31	5th	4
6-13	Cle.	W	5-1		6	6	Pavlik	Mesa		29-31	4th	4
6-14	At Cal.	L	2-8		5	10	Langston	Burns		29-32	6th	4
6-15	At Cal.	W	6-5		9	10	Leibrandt	Farrell	Henke	30-32	5th	3
6-16	At Cal.	L	2-5		7	12	Finley	Brown	Nelson	30-33	5th	4
6-17	At Cal.	W	18-2		18	7	Rogers	Sanderson		31-33	4th	3½
6-18	At Sea.	L	2-3		7	9	Fleming	Pavlik	Charlton	31-34	5th	3½
6-19	At Sea.	L	5-6		7	8	Johnson	Burns	Charlton	31-35	5th	4½
6-20	At Sea.	L	2-13		5	12	Leary	Leibrandt		31-36	5th	4½
6-21	At Chi.	L	6-7		10	10	McDowell	Brown	Hernandez	31-37	5th	4½
6-22	At Chi.	L	2-3		9	9	Pall	Henke		31-38	5th	5½
6-23	At Chi.	L	4-7		8	8	Bere	Pavlik		31-39	5th	6½

— 83 —

Date	Opp.	Res.	Score	(inn.*)	Hits	Opp. hits	Winning pitcher	Losing pitcher	Save	Record	Pos.	GB
6-26	Oak.	W	10-7		15	14	Whiteside	Davis	Henke	32-39	5th	6
6-27	Oak.	W	4-0		10	5	Brown	Witt		33-39	5th	6
6-28	K.C.	L	2-4		8	8	Haney	Rogers	Montgomery	33-40	5th	6
6-29	K.C.	W	4-3		6	6	Patterson	Sampen	Henke	34-40	5th	5
6-30	K.C.	W	5-4		9	8	Bohanon	Gardner	Henke	35-40	5th	4
7-1	At Det.	W	8-5		14	10	Schooler	Doherty	Whiteside	36-40	5th	3
7-2	At Det.	L	4-6	(10)	5	7	Henneman	Patterson		36-41	5th	4
7-3	At Det.	W	11-5		15	13	Schooler	Knudsen		37-41	T4th	3
7-4	At Det.	W	8-6		11	13	Pavlik	Leiter		38-41	T3rd	3
7-5	At Mil.	W	5-4		8	9	Schooler	Lloyd	Patterson	39-41	3rd	3
7-6	At Mil.	W	11-1		17	6	Leibrandt	Wegman		40-41	3rd	2
7-7	At Mil.	L	6-7		10	12	Henry	Lefferts		40-42	T3rd	3
7-8	At Tor.	W	6-1		8	5	Rogers	Morris		41-42	4th	3
7-9	At Tor.	W	4-2		9	7	Pavlik	Stottlemyre	Henke	42-42	3rd	2
7-10	At Tor.	W	10-7		13	10	Lefferts	Hentgen	Henke	43-42	T2nd	1
7-11	At Tor.	W	11-6		13	11	Leibrandt	Stewart		44-42	T2nd	1
7-15	Det.	W	12-7		17	8	Bohanon	Knudsen	Henke	45-42	2nd	1
7-16	Det.	W	9-6		12	10	Rogers	Wells	Henke	46-42	2nd	1
7-17	Det.	L	4-6		6	12	Gullickson	Pavlik	Henneman	46-43	T2nd	2
7-18	Det.	L	0-2		3	9	Doherty	Leibrandt		46-44	T2nd	3
7-19	Mil.	W	5-3		9	9	Ryan	Bones	Henke	47-44	2nd	2
7-20	Mil.	W	5-1		7	5	Brown	Eldred		48-44	2nd	2
7-22	Tor.	L	7-8		13	15	Timlin	Carpenter	Ward	48-45	2nd	2½
7-23	Tor.	W	6-5		8	14	Lefferts	Hentgen	Henke	49-45	2nd	1½
7-24	Tor.	L	1-5		8	7	Stewart	Leibrandt	Ward	49-46	3rd	2½
7-25	Tor.	L	7-9		7	11	Timlin	Henke	Ward	49-47	3rd	2½
7-26 (1)	At K.C.	L	3-12		9	21	Haney	Brown		49-48	3rd	3½
7-26 (2)	At K.C.	L	5-6		13	10	Rasmussen	Bohanon	Montgomery	49-49	3rd	4
7-27	At K.C.	W	1-0		1	9	Rogers	Appier	Henke	50-49	3rd	4
7-28	At K.C.	W	10-3		16	10	Pavlik	Pichardo		51-49	3rd	4
7-29	At K.C.	L	4-9		7	10	Gordon	Leibrandt	Gubicza	51-50	3rd	4½
7-30	At Oak.	L	1-4		8	7	Darling	Ryan	Eckersley	51-51	3rd	5½
7-31	At Oak.	W	8-2		10	6	Brown	Witt		52-51	3rd	5½
8-1	At Oak.	L	5-9		8	14	Van Poppel	Rogers		52-52	3rd	6½
8-2	Chi.	W	9-8		7	13	Henke	Schwarz		53-52	3rd	6
8-3	Chi.	L	6-11		9	18	McCaskill	Leibrandt		53-53	3rd	6½
8-4	Chi.	W	5-2		11	4	Ryan	Fernandez	Henke	54-53	3rd	5½
8-5	Chi.	W	7-1		12	9	Brown	Belcher	Carpenter	55-53	T2nd	4½
8-6	Sea.	W	5-3		6	5	Rogers	Bosio	Henke	56-53	2nd	3½
8-7	Sea.	L	1-2		4	3	Hanson	Pavlik	Henry	56-54	T2nd	4½
8-8	Sea.	W	7-1		7	7	Dreyer	Johnson		57-54	T2nd	3½
8-10	Cal.	W	6-3		8	8	Ryan	Leftwich	Henke	58-54	3rd	4
8-11	Cal.	L	1-4		6	13	Hathaway	Brown	Butcher	58-55	3rd	4
8-12	Cal.	W	4-2		7	6	Rogers	Farrell	Henke	59-55	3rd	3
8-13	At Cle.	L	3-6		4	9	Hernandez	Lefferts		59-56	3rd	4
8-14	At Cle.	L	5-8		10	12	Tavarez	Dreyer	Plunk	59-57	3rd	5
8-15	At Cle.	W	4-1		6	4	Ryan	Mesa	Henke	60-57	3rd	4
8-17 (1)	At N.Y.	L	4-11		10	16	Key	Brown		60-58	3rd	5
8-17 (2)	At N.Y.	W	3-2		5	6	Rogers	Perez	Henke	61-58	3rd	4½
8-18	At N.Y.	W	4-2		9	10	Pavlik	Abbott	Henke	62-58	3rd	3½
8-20	At Bal.	L	5-10		12	14	Mussina	Leibrandt	Frohwirth	62-59	3rd	4½
8-21	At Bal.	L	5-6	(12)	14	10	Mills	Henke		62-60	3rd	5½
8-22	At Bal.	W	11-4		13	10	Brown	Rhodes		63-60	3rd	5½
8-23	At Bal.	W	13-6		15	9	Rogers	Valenzuela		64-60	3rd	4½
8-24	Bos.	W	4-3		7	12	Pavlik	Darwin	Henke	65-60	3rd	4½
8-25	Bos.	W	10-2		13	6	Dreyer	Quantrill		66-60	2nd	3½
8-26	Bos.	L	1-3		5	7	Viola	Brown	Russell	66-61	3rd	4
8-27	Bal.	W	5-4		7	4	Rogers	Frohwirth	Henke	67-61	2nd	3½
8-28	Bal.	W	11-1		12	5	Pavlik	Valenzuela		68-61	2nd	3½
8-29	Bal.	L	3-6		7	10	Moyer	Bohanon		68-62	2nd	4½
8-30	At Bos.	L	3-7		6	10	Viola	Brown		68-63	2nd	5½
8-31	At Bos.	W	8-1		12	6	Rogers	Clemens		69-63	2nd	5½
9-1	At Bos.	W	9-7	(12)	13	14	Bronkey	Quantrill		70-63	2nd	5½
9-3	At Min.	L	5-9		13	15	Brummett	Dreyer	Aguilera	70-64	2nd	6
9-4	At Min.	W	6-4		13	9	Brown	Erickson	Henke	71-64	2nd	6
9-5	At Min.	L	3-8		5	11	Banks	Rogers		71-65	3rd	7
9-6	N.Y.	W	8-5		11	5	Pavlik	Kamieniecki		72-65	2nd	6
9-7	N.Y.	W	5-4		14	12	Carpenter	Assenmacher	Henke	73-65	2nd	5
9-8	N.Y.	W	4-1		8	7	Brown	Jean	Henke	74-65	2nd	5
9-10 (1)	Min.	W	4-3		13	8	Rogers	Banks	Henke	75-65	2nd	4
9-10 (2)	Min.	W	3-2		8	7	Carpenter	Casian	Henke	76-65	2nd	3½
9-11	Min.	W	7-4		12	5	Reed	Casian	Nelson	77-65	2nd	3½
9-12	Min.	L	2-4		7	6	Tapani	Ryan	Aguilera	77-66	2nd	3½
9-13	Cle.	W	12-1		16	6	Brown	Mesa		78-66	2nd	2½

Date	Opp.	Res.	Score	(Inn.*)	Hits	Opp. hits	Winning pitcher	Losing pitcher	Save	Record	Pos.	GB
9-14	Cle.	L	0-2		5	8	Clark	Rogers	DiPoto	78-67	2nd	3½
9-15	Cle.	W	7-4		10	7	Carpenter	Hernandez	Henke	79-67	2nd	3½
9-17	At Cal.	L	1-2		6	6	Finley	Lefferts	Grahe	79-68	2nd	4½
9-18	At Cal.	W	9-2		9	6	Brown	Langston		80-68	2nd	3½
9-19	At Cal.	L	8-9		14	14	Scott	Henke	Grahe	80-69	2nd	4½
9-20	At Sea.	W	2-1	(10)	10	6	Carpenter	Brad Holman	Henke	81-69	2nd	4½
9-21	At Sea.	L	0-8		3	9	Johnson	Leibrandt		81-70	2nd	4½
9-22	At Sea.	L	4-7		9	8	Fleming	Ryan	Power	81-71	2nd	5½
9-24	At Chi.	L	4-5		9	7	Hernandez	Patterson		81-72	2nd	7
9-26 (1)	At Chi.	L	3-5		11	8	Bere	Rogers	Hernandez	81-73	2nd	7½
9-26 (2)	At Chi.	W	3-2		9	7	Pavlik	Fernandez	Henke	82-73	2nd	7
9-28 (1)	Oak.	W	2-0		7	4	Brown	Darling		83-73	2nd	7
9-28 (2)	Oak.	L	3-10		5	16	Witt	Bohanon		83-74	2nd	7
9-29	Oak.	W	11-6		13	12	Dreyer	Downs		84-74	2nd	7
9-30	Oak.	W	6-2		9	6	Rogers	Van Poppel		85-74	2nd	6
10-1	K.C.	W	2-0		4	4	Pavlik	Cone	Henke	86-74	2nd	6
10-2	K.C.	L	4-7		10	12	Gordon	Brown	Montgomery	86-75	2nd	7
10-3	K.C.	L	1-4		4	7	Appier	Dreyer	Montgomery	86-76	2nd	8

Monthly records: April (11-10), May (14-14), June (10-16), July (17-11), August (17-12), September (16-11), October (1-2).
*Innings, if other than nine.

HIGHLIGHTS

High point: The Rangers won 15 of 18 games from June 26-July 16, including a four-game sweep of Toronto in Sky-Dome. That improved their record to 46-42, one game out of first place. That was the closest Texas would come to the lead the rest of the season.

Low point: From June 14-23, the Rangers went 2-8 on a road trip. They dragged themselves home with a 31-39 record, 6½ games out of first place. Before they played another game, right fielder Jose Canseco was placed on the disabled list with a sore right elbow that eventually required season-ending surgery.

Turning point: Entering a game at California on September 19, Texas trailed first-place Chicago by 3½ games. The Rangers led California, 7-3, only to have the Angels rally and win, 9-8. Texas proceeded to lose four of its next five games and was eliminated.

Most valuable players: Left fielder Juan Gonzalez and first baseman Rafael Palmeiro. Gonzalez hit a league-leading 46 home runs, while Palmeiro hit 37.

Most valuable pitcher: Righthander Tom Henke. He saved a club-record 40 games with a 2.91 ERA.

Most improved player: Lefthander Kenny Rogers. Primarily a reliever his first four seasons, he became a front-line starter by winning a club-high 16 games.

Most pleasant surprise: Second baseman Doug Strange. After barely making the team in spring training, he stepped in when others got hurt and played solid defense while hitting .256 with 60 RBIs.

Biggest disappointments: Lefthanded pitchers Charlie Leibrandt, Craig Lefferts and Bob Patterson. They were a combined 14-23 with a 5.03 ERA.

Key injuries: Texas set team records for stints (27) and days (1,373) on the disabled list. Among the wounded: Canseco, Nolan Ryan, shortstop Manuel Lee, Leibrandt, outfielder Gary Redus, infielder Bill Ripken, Gonzalez and center fielder David Hulse.

Notable: Gonzalez, Palmeiro and third baseman Dean Palmer combined for 116 home runs, the most by three teammates since Davey Johnson (43), Darrell Evans (41) and Hank Aaron (40) hit 124 for Atlanta in 1973. . . . The Rangers played their last game in Arlington Stadium, which closed after 22 years. Texas will play in The Ballpark in Arlington in 1994. . . . In Ryan's final start, September 22 in Seattle, he failed to retire a batter.

—T.R. SULLIVAN

RECORDS

1993 regular-season record: 86-76 (2nd in A.L. West); 50-31 at home; 36-45 on road; 49-35 vs. East; 37-41 vs. West; 17-20 vs. LHP; 69-56 vs. RHP; 76-61 on grass; 10-15 on turf; 21-16 in day-time; 65-60 at night; 22-23 in one-run games; 6-5 in extra-inning games; 1-3 in doubleheaders.

Team record last five years: 414-396 (.511, ranks 4th in league in that span).

TEAM LEADERS

Batting average: Juan Gonzalez (.310).
At-bats: Rafael Palmeiro (597).
Runs: Rafael Palmeiro (124).
Hits: Rafael Palmeiro (176).
Total bases: Juan Gonzalez (339).
Doubles: Rafael Palmeiro (40).
Triples: David Hulse (10).
Home runs: Juan Gonzalez (46).
Runs batted in: Juan Gonzalez (118).
Stolen bases: David Hulse (29).
Slugging percentage: Juan Gonzalez (.632).
On-base percentage: Rafael Palmeiro (.371).
Wins: Kenny Rogers (16).
Earned-run average: Roger Pavlik (3.41).
Complete games: Kevin Brown (12).
Shutouts: Kevin Brown (3).
Saves: Tom Henke (40).
Innings pitched: Kevin Brown (233).
Strikeouts: Kevin Brown (142).

GAMES BY POSITION

Catcher: Ivan Rodriguez 134, Geno Petralli 39, John Russell 11.
First base: Rafael Palmeiro 160, Dan Peltier 5, Gary Redus 5, Mario Diaz 1, John Russell 1.
Second base: Doug Strange 135, Bill Ripken 34, Jon Shave 8, Jeff Huson 5, Geno Petralli 1, Gary Redus 1.
Third base: Dean Palmer 148, Mario Diaz 12, Doug Strange 9, Jeff Huson 2, Geno Petralli 1, Bill Ripken 1, John Russell 1.
Shortstop: Manuel Lee 72, Mario Diaz 57, Benji Gil 22, Bill Ripken 18, Jeff Huson 12, Jon Shave 9, Dean Palmer 1, Doug Strange 1.
Outfield: Juan Gonzalez 129, David Hulse 112, Doug Dascenzo 68, Gary Redus 61, Dan Peltier 55, Jose Canseco 49, Butch Davis 44, Donald Harris 38, Rob Ducey 26, Chris James 7, John Russell 1.
Designated hitter: Julio Franco 140, Butch Davis 11, Juan Gonzalez 10, Jose Canseco 9, Donald Harris 3, Steve Balboni 2, Doug Dascenzo 2, David Hulse 2, Jeff Huson 2, Geno Petralli 2, Manuel Lee 1, Gary Redus 1, Ivan Rodriguez 1.

TOP DRAFT CHOICES

1. **Mike Bell**, 3B, Moeller High School, Cincinnati.
2. **Edwin Diaz**, 2B, Vega Alta, Puerto Rico.
3. **Andrew Vessel**, OF, Kennedy High School, Richmond, Calif.
4. **Toure Knighton**, RHP, Tucson (Ariz.) High School.
5. **Rod Walker**, SS, Hyde Park High School, Chicago.
6. **Mark Ocasio**, RHP, Carolina, Puerto Rico.
7. **Dan Smith**, RHP, Girard (Kan.) High School.
8. **Jack Stanczak**, 3B, Villanova University.
9. **Pete Hartmann**, LHP, Oklahoma City University.
10. **Brian Thomas**, OF, Texas A&M University.

TORONTO BLUE JAYS
AMERICAN LEAGUE EAST DIVISION

1994 SCHEDULE

N Denotes night game (any game starting after 5 p.m.).
☐ Home games shaded.
* At Three Rivers Stadium in Pittsburgh.

APRIL

SUN	MON	TUE	WED	THU	FRI	SAT
					1	2
3	4 N CHI	5 N CHI	6 N CHI	7	8 N SEA	9 SEA
10 SEA	11 N OAK	12 N OAK	13 N OAK	14 N CAL	15 N CAL	16 N CAL
17 CAL	18	19 N TEX	20 N TEX	21	22 N MIN	23 MIN
24 MIN	25 N KC	26 N KC	27 N TEX	28 N TEX	29 N MIN	30 N MIN

MAY

SUN	MON	TUE	WED	THU	FRI	SAT
1 MIN	2	3 N KC	4 N KC	5 N KC	6 N MIL	7 MIL
8 MIL	9 N BAL	10 N BAL	11 N BAL	12	13 N BOS	14 BOS
15 N BOS	16 N DET	17 N DET	18 N DET	19	20 N CLE	21 CLE
22 CLE	23 N NY	24 N NY	25 NY	26	27 N CAL	28 CAL
29 CAL	30 N OAK	31 N OAK				

JUNE

SUN	MON	TUE	WED	THU	FRI	SAT
			1 OAK	2	3 N SEA	4 N SEA
5 SEA	6	7 N CHI	8 N CHI	9 N NY	10 N NY	11 NY
12 NY	13 N CLE	14 N CLE	15 N CLE	16	17 N DET	18 N DET
19 DET	20 N BOS	21 N BOS	22 N BOS	23	24 N BAL	25 BAL
26 N BAL	27 N MIL	28 N MIL	29 N MIL	30 MIL		

JULY

SUN	MON	TUE	WED	THU	FRI	SAT
					1 N KC	2 N KC
3 KC	4 N KC	5 N MIN	6 N MIN	7	8 N KC	9 N KC
10 KC	11 * ALL-STAR GAME	12	13	14 N TEX	15 N TEX	16 N TEX
17 N TEX	18 N MIN	19 N MIN	20 N MIN	21 N TEX	22 N TEX	23 TEX
24 TEX	25	26 N MIL	27 N MIL	28 N MIL	29 N BAL	30 N BAL
31 BAL						

AUGUST

SUN	MON	TUE	WED	THU	FRI	SAT
	1 N BOS	2 N BOS	3 BOS	4 N BOS	5 N DET	6 N DET
7 DET	8 N CLE	9 N CLE	10 CLE	11	12 N NY	13 N NY
14 N NY	15	16 N SEA	17 N SEA	18 N SEA	19 N OAK	20 N OAK
21 CHI	22 N SEA	23 N SEA	24 N SEA	25 N CHI	26 N CHI	27 N CHI
28 CHI	29	30 N CAL	31 N CAL			

SEPTEMBER

SUN	MON	TUE	WED	THU	FRI	SAT
				1 N CAL	2 N OAK	3 OAK
4 OAK	5 N CAL	6 N CAL	7	8 N OAK	9 N OAK	10 OAK
11 OAK	12	13 N NY	14 N NY	15 N NY	16 N CLE	17 CLE
18 CLE N	19 DET	20 N DET	21 N DET	22 N DET	23 N BOS	24 BOS
25 BOS N	26 BAL	27 N BAL	28 N BAL	29 N BAL	30 N MIL	

OCTOBER

SUN	MON	TUE	WED	THU	FRI	SAT
						1 MIL
2 MIL						

1994 SEASON
CLUB DIRECTORY

Chairman
P.N.T. Widdrington
President and chief executive officer
Paul Beeston
Executive vice president, baseball
Pat Gillick
Vice presidents, baseball
Bob Mattick
Al LaMacchia
Vice president, business
Bob Nicholson
Special asst. to the exec. v.p., baseball
Al Widmar
Assistant general manager
Gord Ash
Director, public relations
Howard Starkman
Director, stadium and ticket operations
George Holm
Director, marketing
Paul Markle
Director, finance
Susie Quigley
Director, scouting
Bob Engle
Director, international scouting
Wayne Morgan
Director, player development
Mel Queen
Director, Canadian scouting
Bill Byckowski
Director, minor league business
Ken Carson
Administrator, player personnel
Bob Nelson
Assistant director, public relations
Mark Leno
Asst. dir., tickets and box office manager
Randy Low
Assistant director, operations
Len Frejlich
Manager, group sales
Maureen Haffey
Manager, team travel
John Brioux
Manager, promotions and advertising
Rick Amos
Manager, com. relations and special events
Peter Cosentino
Manager, accounting
Cathy McNamara
Manager, employee compensations
Perry Nicoletta
Manager, information systems
Hans Frauenlob

Manager, ticket vault
Paul Goodyear
Manager, subscriber services
Mike Maunder
Manager, game operations
Mario Coutinho
Supervisor, grounds
Brad Bujold
Supervisor, office services
Mick Bazinet
Trainers
Tommy Craig
Brent Andrews
Strength and conditioning coordinator
Geoffrey Horne
Team physician
Dr. Ron Taylor
Coord., Latin Am. scouting & develop.
Epy Guerrero
Special assignment scouts
Moose Johnson
Gordon Lakey
Tim Wilken
Director, international scouting
Wayne Morgan
Advance scout
Don Welke
Scouts
David Blume
Chris Bourjos
Chris Buckley
Robert Campbell
John Cole
Ellis Dungan
Joe Ford
Tim Hewes
Tom Hinkle
Jim Hughes
Duane Larson
Ted Lekas
Ben McLure
Bill Moore
Andy Pienovi
Alvin Rittman
Jorge Rivera
Mike Russell
Joe Siers
Mark Snipp
Jerry Sobeck
Neil Summers
Ron Tostenson
Ramon Webster

SPRING TRAINING ROSTER

Manager—Cito Gaston (43).

Coaches—Bob Bailor (3), Galen Cisco (42), Larry Hisle (39), Dennis Holmberg, Nick Leyva (45), Gene Tenace (18).

No.	PITCHERS	B/T	Ht./Wt.	Born	1993 clubs
44	Brow, Scott	R/R	6-3/200	3-17-69	Knoxville, Toronto, Syracuse
49	Castillo, Tony	L/L	5-10/188	3-1-63	Syracuse, Toronto
50	Cox, Danny	R/R	6-4/250	9-21-59	Toronto
	Daniels, Lee	R/R	6-4/180	3-31-71	Dunedin, Hagerstown
32	Flener, Huck	B/L	5-11/185	2-25-69	Knoxville, Toronto
	Gray, Dennis	L/L	6-6/210	12-24-69	Dunedin
66	Guzman, Juan	R/R	5-11/195	10-28-66	Toronto
41	Hentgen, Pat	R/R	6-2/200	11-13-68	Toronto
28	Leiter, Al	L/L	6-3/215	10-23-65	Toronto
55	Menhart, Paul	R/R	6-2/190	3-25-69	Syracuse
38	Small, Aaron	R/R	6-5/200	11-23-71	Knoxville
	Spoljaric, Paul	R/L	6-3/205	9-24-70	Dunedin, Knoxville, Syracuse
34	Stewart, Dave	R/R	6-2/200	2-19-57	Toronto
30	Stottlemyre, Todd	L/R	6-3/200	5-20-65	Toronto
40	Timlin, Mike	R/R	6-4/210	3-10-66	Toronto, Dunedin
31	Ward, Duane	R/R	6-4/225	5-28-64	Toronto
54	Williams, Woody	R/R	6-0/190	8-19-66	Syracuse, Toronto, Dunedin

No.	CATCHERS	B/T	Ht./Wt.	Born	1993 clubs
10	Borders, Pat	R/R	6-2/200	5-14-63	Toronto
6	Delgado, Carlos	L/R	6-3/220	6-25-72	Knoxville, Toronto
27	Knorr, Randy	R/R	6-2/215	11-12-68	Toronto
53	Martinez, Angel	L/R	6-4/200	10-3-72	Hagerstown

No.	INFIELDERS	B/T	Ht./Wt.	Born	1993 clubs
12	Alomar, Roberto	B/R	6-0/185	2-5-68	Toronto
	Battle, Howard	R/R	6-0/208	3-25-72	Knoxville
	Brito, Tilson	R/R	6-0/170	5-28-72	Dunedin
70	Cedeno, Domingo	B/R	6-1/165	11-4-68	Syracuse, Toronto
11	Coles, Darnell	R/R	6-1/185	6-2-62	Toronto
19	Martinez, Domingo	R/R	6-2/215	8-4-67	Toronto, Syracuse
19	Molitor, Paul	R/R	6-0/180	8-22-56	Toronto
9	Olerud, John	L/L	6-5/218	8-5-68	Toronto
22	Schofield, Dick	R/R	5-10/179	11-21-62	Toronto, Dunedin
33	Sprague, Ed	R/R	6-2/210	7-25-67	Toronto
	Zosky, Eddie	R/R	6-0/180	2-10-68	Hagerstown, Syracuse

No.	OUTFIELDERS	B/T	Ht./Wt.	Born	1993 clubs
23	Bowers, Brent	L/R	6-3/190	5-2-71	Knoxville
2	Butler, Rob	L/L	5-11/185	4-10-70	Syracuse, Toronto
21	Canate, Willie	R/R	6-0/170	12-11-71	Indianapolis, Toronto, Knoxville, Syracuse
29	Carter, Joe	R/R	6-3/225	3-7-60	Toronto
	Green, Shawn	L/L	6-4/190	11-10-72	Knoxville, Toronto
	Holifield, Rick	L/L	6-2/180	3-25-70	Dunedin
17	Perez, Robert	R/R	6-3/205	6-4-69	Syracuse
25	White, Devon	B/R	6-2/190	12-29-62	Toronto

BALLPARK INFORMATION

Ballpark (capacity, surface)
SkyDome (50,516, artificial)
Address
One Blue Jay Way
Suite 3200
Toronto, Ontario M5V 1J1
Business phone
416-341-1000
Ticket information
416-341-1111
Ticket prices
$23 (esplanade IF, club level OF)
$18 (skydeck IF, esplanade OF)
$13 (skydeck)
$6 (skydeck outfield)
Field dimensions (from home plate)
To left field at foul line, 330 feet
To center field, 400 feet
To right field at foul line, 330 feet
First game played
June 5, 1989 (Brewers 5, Blue Jays 3)

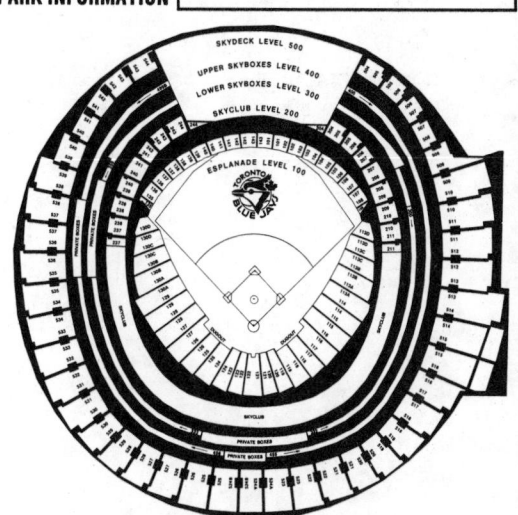

MINOR LEAGUE AFFILIATES

Class	Team	League	Manager
AAA	Syracuse	International	Bob Didier
AA	Knoxville	Southern	Garth Iorg
A	Hagerstown	South Atlantic	Omar Malave
A	Dunedin	Florida State	Jim Nettles
A	St. Catharines	New York-Pennsylvania	J.J. Cannon
Rookie	Medicine Hat	Pioneer	Darren Balsley
Rookie	Gulf Coast Blue Jays	Gulf Coast	Doug Ault

BROADCAST INFORMATION

Radio: THE-FAN (1430). Broadcasters: Tom Cheek, Jerry Howarth.
TV: CFTO-TV (Channel 9). Broadcasters: Don Chevrier, Tommy Hutton, Fergie Olver. CBC-TV (Channel 6). Broadcasters: Don Chevrier, Tommy Hutton, Fergie Olver.
Cable TV: The Sports Network. Broadcasters: Jim Hughson, Buck Martinez.

SPRING TRAINING

Ballpark (city): Dunedin Stadium at Grant Field (Dunedin, Fla.).
Ticket information: 813-733-0429.

HISTORY

YEAR-BY-YEAR RECORDS

Year	Pos.	W	L	Pct.	GB	Year	Pos.	W	L	Pct.	GB
1977	7th	54	107	.335	45½	1988	T3rd	87	75	.537	2
1978	7th	59	102	.366	40	1989	1st†	89	73	.549	+ 2
1979	7th	53	109	.327	50½	1990	2nd	86	76	.531	2
1980	7th	67	95	.414	36	1991	1st†	91	71	.562	+ 7
1981	7th/7th	37	69	.349	*	1992	1st‡	96	66	.593	+ 4
1982	T6th	78	84	.481	17	1993	1st‡	95	67	.586	+ 7
1983	4th	89	73	.549	9						
1984	2nd	89	73	.549	15						
1985	1st†	99	62	.615	+ 2						
1986	4th	86	76	.531	9½						
1987	2nd	96	66	.593	2						

*First half 16-42; second 21-27.
†Lost Championship Series. ‡Won Championship Series.

MANAGERS

Name	Record	Years
Roy Hartsfield	166-318	'77-79
Bobby Mattick	104-164	'80-81
Bobby Cox	355-292	'82-85
Jimy Williams	281-241	'86-89
Cito Gaston	445-329	'89-93

DAY BY DAY

Date	Opp.	Res.	Score (inn.*)	Hits	Opp. hits	Winning pitcher	Losing pitcher	Save	Record	Pos.	GB
4-6	At Sea.	L	1-8	7	11	Johnson	Morris		0-1	T3rd	1
4-7	At Sea.	W	2-0	5	3	Leiter	Bosio	Ward	1-1	T2nd	1
4-9	Cle.	W	13-10	14	16	Eichhorn	Power	Ward	2-1	T2nd	½
4-10	Cle.	W	5-4	7	9	Stottlemyre	Nagy	Ward	3-1	2nd	½
4-11	Cle.	L	6-10	10	16	Clark	Morris	Lilliquist	3-2	2nd	½
4-13	Sea.	W	6-5	11	7	Cox	Leary	Ward	4-2	2nd	½
4-14	Sea.	L	9-10	(10)	9	14	DeLucia	Hentgen	Charlton	4-3	3rd	1½
4-15	Sea.	W	3-1	10	5	Stottlemyre	Cummings	Ward	5-3	2nd	1½
4-16	At Cle.	L	1-13	7	19	Nagy	Morris		5-4	T3rd	1½
4-17	At Cle.	W	8-1	11	8	Hentgen	Clark		6-4	T2nd	1½
4-18	At Cle.	L	5-6	12	6	Mutis	Leiter	Lilliquist	6-5	3rd	2½
4-19	At Cle.	W	7-1	12	6	Guzman	Bielecki		7-5	T2nd	2½
4-20	At K.C.	L	2-8	3	16	Appier	Stottlemyre		7-6	3rd	3½
4-21	At K.C.	L	5-6	8	12	Montgomery	Timlin		7-7	T3rd	3½
4-22	At K.C.	W	6-3	7	7	Hentgen	Cone		8-7	T3rd	2½
4-23	Chi.	L	4-5	11	5	McCaskill	Leiter	Hernandez	8-8	T3rd	2½
4-24	Chi.	W	10-4	14	11	Guzman	Bolton		9-8	T3rd	2½
4-25	Chi.	W	1-0	6	7	Stottlemyre	Fernandez	Ward	10-8	T3rd	2½
4-26	Tex.	W	8-6	16	9	Morris	Lefferts	Ward	11-8	T2nd	2½
4-27	Tex.	W	4-3	8	4	Hentgen	Nen	Ward	12-8	2nd	1½
4-28	K.C.	L	3-5	7	7	Gardner	Brow	Montgomery	12-9	T2nd	1½
4-29	K.C.	W	8-0	15	5	Guzman	Pichardo		13-9	2nd	1½
4-30	At Chi.	L	2-10	4	14	Fernandez	Stottlemyre		13-10	3rd	2½
5-1	At Chi.	L	2-8	8	8	Alvarez	Morris		13-11	4th	2½
5-2	At Chi.	W	6-1	10	5	Hentgen	McDowell	Cox	14-11	4th	1½
5-4	At Tex.	L	2-3	7	9	Bohanon	Ward	Henke	14-12	4th	2½
5-5	At Tex.	L	1-7	5	12	Rogers	Stottlemyre		14-13	4th	2½
5-6	Bal.	W	10-8	14	11	Cox	McDonald	Ward	15-13	4th	2
5-7	Bal.	W	3-2	8	7	Eichhorn	Frohwirth		16-13	3rd	2
5-8	Bal.	L	3-6	5	9	Sutcliffe	Linton	Frohwirth	16-14	4th	2
5-9	Bal.	L	3-4	8	8	Williamson	Ward	Olson	16-15	4th	2
5-11	Det.	L	7-12	13	14	Gullickson	Stottlemyre		16-16	4th	3½
5-12	Det.	L	8-13	11	16	Krueger	Hentgen	Henneman	16-17	4th	4½
5-13	Det.	W	6-5	10	10	Castillo	MacDonald		17-17	4th	3½
5-14	At N.Y.	W	8-6	11	9	Ward	Monteleone		18-17	4th	3½
5-15	At N.Y.	L	3-4	10	7	Perez	Leiter	Farr	18-18	4th	4½
5-16	At N.Y.	W	12-6	13	10	Stottlemyre	Witt		19-18	4th	3½
5-17	At Bos.	W	9-3	15	8	Hentgen	Clemens		20-18	T3rd	3
5-19	At Bos.	L	5-10	11	11	Darwin	Stewart		20-19	4th	4½
5-20	At Bos.	W	4-3	8	8	Cox	Quantrill	Ward	21-19	T3rd	4½
5-21	Min.	W	11-2	16	5	Morris	Deshaies		22-19	T3rd	3½
5-22	Min.	W	7-0	13	6	Cox	Tapani		23-19	3rd	3½
5-23	Min.	W	2-1	7	7	Hentgen	Erickson	Ward	24-19	T2nd	3½
5-24	Mil.	W	4-1	10	2	Stewart	Boddicker	Ward	25-19	2nd	2½
5-25	Mil.	W	4-2	8	7	Guzman	Wegman	Ward	26-19	2nd	2½
5-26	Mil.	L	1-8	10	14	Navarro	Morris		26-20	2nd	3½
5-27	Mil.	L	3-9	6	15	Bones	Leiter		26-21	2nd	4
5-28	At Oak.	L	2-3	7	7	Witt	Cox	Honeycutt	26-22	T2nd	4
5-29	At Oak.	W	5-3	12	7	Stewart	Welch	Ward	27-22	T2nd	4
5-30	At Oak.	W	13-11	13	13	Cox	Mohler	Ward	28-22	T2nd	3
5-31	At Cal.	W	10-5	9	11	Morris	Farrell		29-22	T2nd	2½
6-1	At Cal.	W	8-0	12	2	Leiter	Sanderson		30-22	2nd	1½
6-2	At Cal.	W	7-6	13	10	Hentgen	Valera	Ward	31-22	2nd	½
6-4	Oak.	W	4-3	(12)	10	12	Williams	Gossage		32-22	2nd	...
6-5	Oak.	W	9-5	10	7	Guzman	Hillegas		33-22	2nd	...
6-6	Oak.	L	3-10	10	12	Darling	Morris		33-23	2nd	1
6-7	Cal.	W	4-2	10	11	Leiter	Sanderson	Ward	34-23	2nd	...
6-8	Cal.	W	14-6	13	13	Williams	Valera		35-23	2nd	...
6-9	Cal.	L	4-6	8	8	Langston	Stewart	Frey	35-24	2nd	1
6-10	At Det.	L	3-5	8	7	Doherty	Guzman	MacDonald	35-25	2nd	2
6-11	At Det.	L	1-6	6	8	Gullickson	Morris		35-26	2nd	3
6-12	At Det.	L	1-12	10	15	Moore	Leiter		35-27	2nd	4
6-13	At Det.	W	13-4	15	6	Hentgen	Leiter		36-27	2nd	3
6-14	At Min.	L	3-4	8	9	Casian	Cox	Willis	36-28	T2nd	4
6-15	At Min.	W	6-3	6	4	Guzman	Tapani	Ward	37-28	T2nd	4
6-16	At Min.	W	4-0	7	5	Morris	Erickson		38-28	2nd	3
6-17	Bos.	W	7-0	14	2	Leiter	Quantrill		39-28	2nd	3
6-18	Bos.	W	11-2	14	7	Hentgen	Clemens		40-28	2nd	2
6-19	Bos.	W	9-4	13	8	Stewart	Darwin		41-28	2nd	2
6-20	Bos.	W	3-2	(12)	8	11	Timlin	Russell		42-28	2nd	2

Date	Opp.	Res.	Score	(Inn.*)	Hits	Opp. hits	Winning pitcher	Losing pitcher	Save	Record	Pos.	GB
6-22	N.Y.	W	5-4		12	8	Williams	Howe	Ward	43-28	2nd	1
6-23	N.Y.	L	3-4		7	15	Key	Stottlemyre	Farr	43-29	2nd	1
6-24	N.Y.	W	7-2		10	8	Hentgen	Kamieniecki		44-29	2nd	...
6-25	At Mil.	L	5-6		6	8	Fetters	Cox		44-30	2nd	...
6-26	At Mil.	W	3-2		7	6	Guzman	Eldred	Ward	45-30	1st	+1
6-27	At Mil.	W	5-4		11	6	Morris	Wegman	Ward	46-30	1st	+2
6-28	At Bal.	W	7-2		11	8	Stottlemyre	Sutcliffe	Leiter	47-30	1st	+3
6-29	At Bal.	W	2-1		5	9	Hentgen	McDonald	Ward	48-30	1st	+3
6-30	At Bal.	L	0-6		6	12	Valenzuela	Stewart		48-31	1st	+2
7-2	At K.C.	L	2-3		8	10	Gubicza	Cox		48-32	1st	+2
7-3	At K.C.	L	2-3		4	9	Cone	Morris	Montgomery	48-33	1st	+2
7-4	At K.C.	L	1-3		7	7	Haney	Stottlemyre	Montgomery	48-34	1st	+2
7-5	Chi.	L	3-4		8	11	Alvarez	Hentgen	Hernandez	48-35	1st	+1
7-6	Chi.	W	5-1		8	7	Stewart	McDowell		49-35	1st	+2
7-7	Chi.	L	2-5		7	16	Fernandez	Guzman	Hernandez	49-36	1st	+2
7-8	Tex.	L	1-6		5	8	Rogers	Morris		49-37	1st	+2
7-9	Tex.	L	2-4		7	9	Pavlik	Stottlemyre	Henke	49-38	1st	+1
7-10	Tex.	L	7-10		10	13	Lefferts	Hentgen	Henke	49-39	1st	+ ½
7-11	Tex.	L	6-11		11	13	Leibrandt	Stewart		49-40	1st	+ ½
7-15	K.C.	W	7-2		8	6	Leiter	Burgos		50-40	1st	+ ½
7-16	K.C.	L	3-7		7	11	Haney	Morris	Montgomery	50-41	1st	+ ½
7-17	K.C.	L	4-5		9	9	Gubicza	Cox	Montgomery	50-42	1st	...
7-18	K.C.	W	4-3		10	5	Hentgen	Pichardo		51-42	T1st	...
7-19	At Chi.	W	15-7		21	9	Stewart	Bolton		52-42	T1st	...
7-20	At Chi.	L	1-2		4	6	Fernandez	Guzman		52-43	T2nd	½
7-21	At Chi.	W	4-1		9	5	Leiter	Alvarez	Ward	53-43	1st	+ ½
7-22	At Tex.	W	8-7		15	13	Timlin	Carpenter	Ward	54-43	1st	+1
7-23	At Tex.	L	5-6		14	8	Lefferts	Hentgen	Henke	54-44	T2nd	...
7-24	At Tex.	W	5-1		7	8	Stewart	Leibrandt	Ward	55-44	T2nd	...
7-25	At Tex.	W	9-7		11	7	Timlin	Henke	Ward	56-44	T2nd	...
7-27	Bal.	W	6-5		11	9	Ward	Poole		57-44	1st	+ ½
7-28	Bal.	W	5-4	(10)	8	9	Castillo	Williamson		58-44	1st	+ ½
7-29	Det.	W	7-4		8	7	Castillo	Bolton	Ward	59-44	1st	+1
7-30	Det.	L	5-8		11	19	Moore	Stewart	Henneman	59-45	T1st	...
7-31	Det.	W	3-1		9	11	Timlin	Wells	Ward	60-45	T1st	...
8-1	Det.	W	2-1		6	6	Morris	Henneman		61-45	1st	+1
8-2	At N.Y.	W	4-0		7	9	Stottlemyre	Abbott	Cox	62-45	1st	+2
8-3	At N.Y.	W	8-6		14	16	Hentgen	Munoz	Leiter	63-45	1st	+3
8-4	At N.Y.	L	2-6		8	9	Kamieniecki	Stewart		63-46	1st	+2
8-5	At N.Y.	L	4-5		6	7	Key	Leiter		63-47	1st	+1
8-6	Mil.	W	11-10	(11)	19	17	Leiter	Henry		64-47	1st	+2
8-7	Mil.	L	1-7		6	12	Miranda	Stottlemyre		64-48	1st	+1
8-8	Mil.	L	2-5		7	8	Bones	Hentgen		64-49	1st	+1
8-10	Min.	W	6-3		13	5	Stewart	Erickson	Ward	65-49	1st	+1
8-11	Min.	W	4-2		5	6	Guzman	Deshaies	Ward	66-49	1st	+2
8-12	Min.	L	2-9		6	13	Tapani	Morris		66-50	1st	+1
8-13	At Bos.	L	3-5		12	10	Darwin	Stottlemyre	Russell	66-51	T1st	...
8-14	At Bos.	W	5-2		10	7	Hentgen	Dopson	Ward	67-51	T1st	...
8-15	At Bos.	W	9-1		14	4	Stewart	Clemens		68-51	T1st	...
8-16	At Cle.	W	4-1		11	6	Guzman	Ojeda	Ward	69-51	1st	+ ½
8-17	At Cle.	W	6-4		12	11	Morris	Kramer	Ward	70-51	1st	+1
8-18	At Cle.	W	7-6	(11)	12	10	Cox	Lilliquist	Ward	71-51	1st	+2
8-20	Sea.	L	1-4		3	8	Johnson	Hentgen		71-52	1st	+1
8-21	Sea.	L	2-5		10	7	Fleming	Stewart	Power	71-53	T1st	...
8-22	Sea.	W	12-7		9	10	Guzman	Ontiveros		72-53	1st	+1
8-23	Cle.	L	8-9		11	17	Hernandez	Eichhorn	DiPoto	72-54	T1st	...
8-24	Cle.	W	8-6		11	11	Stottlemyre	Tavarez	Ward	73-54	1st	+1
8-25	Cle.	W	10-7		17	11	Hentgen	Mesa	Ward	74-54	1st	+1
8-26	At Sea.	L	3-6		10	7	Johnson	Stewart	Power	74-55	T1st	...
8-27	At Sea.	L	6-7		11	8	Nelson	Williams	Plantenberg	74-56	T1st	...
8-28	At Sea.	L	1-2		7	4	Bosio	Cox	Power	74-57	T1st	...
8-29	At Sea.	W	6-2		11	7	Stottlemyre	Hanson		75-57	T1st	...
8-30	At Oak.	W	4-2		9	7	Hentgen	Darling	Ward	76-57	1st	+ ½
8-31	At Oak.	W	3-2	(10)	11	9	Cox	Eckersley	Ward	77-57	1st	+ ½
9-1	At Oak.	W	8-3		9	5	Guzman	Mohler		78-57	2nd	5 ½
9-3	At Cal.	L	1-4		6	9	Langston	Morris	Grahe	78-58	1st	+2
9-4	At Cal.	L	2-4		7	8	Magrane	Stottlemyre	Frey	78-59	1st	+1
9-5	At Cal.	L	1-5		6	11	Leftwich	Hentgen		78-60	T1st	...
9-7	Oak.	L	7-11	(11)	10	12	Honeycutt	Castillo		78-61	1st	+ ½
9-8	Oak.	L	1-2		5	5	Witt	Ward	Eckersley	78-62	1st	+ ½
9-9	Oak.	L	4-7		8	10	Smithberg	Castillo	Eckersley	78-63	T1st	...
9-10	Cal.	W	10-4		14	10	Stottlemyre	Leftwich		79-63	1st	+1
9-11	Cal.	W	9-5		11	8	Hentgen	Hathaway		80-63	1st	+1
9-12	Cal.	W	4-1		7	6	Stewart	Finley	Ward	81-63	1st	+ ½

Date	Opp.	Res.	Score	(Inn.*)	Hits	Opp. hits	Winning pitcher	Losing pitcher	Save	Record	Pos.	GB
9-14	At Det.	W	9-5		12	7	Guzman	Davis		82-63	1st	+½
9-15	At Det.	W	14-8		19	13	Stottlemyre	Moore	Ward	83-63	1st	+2½
9-17	At Min.	W	4-2		12	3	Hentgen	Tapani	Ward	84-63	1st	+3
9-18	At Min.	W	5-1		8	7	Stewart	Erickson	Timlin	85-63	1st	+3
9-19	At Min.	W	10-0		15	9	Guzman	Trombley		86-63	1st	+4
9-21	Bos.	W	5-0		7	3	Stottlemyre	Clemens		87-63	1st	+5
9-22	Bos.	L	5-7	(10)	12	11	Ryan	Timlin		87-64	1st	+5
9-23	Bos.	W	5-1		5	5	Stewart	Minchey		88-64	1st	+5½
9-24	N.Y.	W	7-3		13	10	Guzman	Key		89-64	1st	+6½
9-25	N.Y.	W	3-1		4	4	Leiter	Tanana	Ward	90-64	1st	+7½
9-26	N.Y.	L	3-7		6	8	Abbott	Stottlemyre		90-65	1st	+6½
9-27	At Mil.	W	2-0		7	7	Hentgen	Eldred	Ward	91-65	1st	+6½
9-28	At Mil.	W	6-4		10	8	Stewart	Maysey	Ward	92-65	1st	+7½
9-29	At Mil.	W	9-6		14	8	Eichhorn	Orosco	Ward	93-65	1st	+7½
9-30	At Bal.	W	6-2		11	6	Leiter	Rhodes		94-65	1st	+7
10-1	At Bal.	L	2-7		8	12	Valenzuela	Stottlemyre		94-66	1st	+7
10-2	At Bal.	L	4-8		12	12	Sutcliffe	Hentgen	Mills	94-67	1st	+7
10-3	At Bal.	W	11-6		11	7	Brow	McDonald		95-67	1st	+7

Monthly records: April (13-10), May (16-12), June (19-9), July (12-14), August (17-12), September (17-8), October (1-2).
*Innings, if other than nine.

HIGHLIGHTS

High point: From September 10-21, Toronto won a season-high nine straight games. They began the streak tied with New York for first place and ended it with a five-game lead.

Low point: On May 12, the Blue Jays lost their fourth straight game, falling to 16-17 and 4½ games out of first.

Turning point: From September 3-9, the Blue Jays were swept in consecutive three-game series by California and Oakland and fell into a first-place tie. But they responded by winning 17 of their final 21 games to win the division.

Most valuable player: Second baseman Roberto Alomar. He set career highs in average (.326), homers (17), runs (109) and RBIs (93). Plus, he won his third Gold Glove.

Most valuable pitcher: Righthander Duane Ward. His 45 saves set a team record and tied for the A.L. lead. Ward led A.L. relievers with an average of 12.2 strikeouts per nine innings.

Most improved player: Righthander Pat Hentgen. He joined the rotation April 17 and finished with a 19-9 mark in his first full big-league season.

Most pleasant surprise: Third baseman Ed Sprague. Toronto wasn't sure the converted catcher could play third base, but he displayed good defense, hit 12 homers and drove in 73 runs.

Biggest disappointment: Righthander Jack Morris. He won just seven games and had a 6.19 ERA. Additionally, righthander Mike Timlin struggled to fill Ward's shoes as a setup man, and Darrin Jackson, obtained from San Diego for Derek Bell to play right field, was a total flop. He was traded to the New York Mets for shortstop Tony Fernandez in June.

Key injuries: Morris and righthander Todd Stottlemyre both went on the disabled list with shoulder injuries in May. Righthander Dave Stewart didn't pitch until May due to a forearm injury. Shortstop Dick Schofield broke his left forearm in May and missed 100 games.

Notable: First baseman John Olerud be-

came the first Blue Jay to win a batting title (.363) and carried a .400 average until August 2. ... Olerud, designated hitter Paul Molitor and Alomar finished 1-2-3 in the A.L. batting race, becoming the first teammates this century to accomplish the feat. ... With a win at Oakland on September 1, Toronto evened its all-time record at 1,334-1,334-2. It marked the first time the Blue Jays had been at .500 since they were 9-9 on April 27, 1977.

—STEVE MILTON

RECORDS

1993 regular-season record: 95-67 (1st in A.L. East); 48-33 at home; 47-34 on road; 50-28 vs. East; 45-39 vs. West; 22-25 vs. LHP; 73-42 vs. RHP; 39-24 on grass; 56-43 on turf; 38-16 in daytime; 57-51 at night; 23-22 in one-run games; 6-3 in extra-inning games; 0-0 in doubleheaders.

Team record last five years: 457-353 (.564, ranks 1st in league in that span).

TEAM LEADERS

Batting average: John Olerud (.363).
At-bats: Paul Molitor (636).
Runs: Paul Molitor (121).
Hits: Paul Molitor (211).
Total bases: John Olerud (330).
Doubles: John Olerud (54).
Triples: Tony Fernandez (9).
Home runs: Joe Carter (33).
Runs batted in: Joe Carter (121).
Stolen bases: Roberto Alomar (55).
Slugging percentage: John Olerud (.599).
On-base percentage: John Olerud (.473).
Wins: Pat Hentgen (19).
Earned-run average: Pat Hentgen (3.87).
Complete games: Jack Morris (4).
Shutouts: Juan Guzman, Al Leiter, Jack Morris, Todd Stottlemyre (1).
Saves: Duane Ward (45).
Innings pitched: Juan Guzman (221).
Strikeouts: Juan Guzman (194).

GAMES BY POSITION

Catcher: Pat Borders 138, Randy Knorr 39, Carlos Delgado 1.
First base: John Olerud 137, Paul Molitor 23, Domingo Martinez 7, Darnell Coles 1, Turner Ward 1.
Second base: Roberto Alomar 150, Alfredo Griffin 11, Luis Sojo 8, Domingo Cedeno 5.
Third base: Ed Sprague 150, Darnell Coles 16, Alfredo Griffin 6, Luis Sojo 3, Domingo Martinez 1.
Shortstop: Tony Fernandez 94, Dick Schofield 36, Alfredo Griffin 20, Domingo Cedeno 10, Luis Sojo 3.
Outfield: Joe Carter 151, Devon White 145, Turner Ward 65, Darrin Jackson 46, Darnell Coles 44, Rickey Henderson 44, Willie Canate 31, Rob Butler 16, Shawn Green 2.
Designated hitter: Paul Molitor 137, John Olerud 20, Joe Carter 3, Willie Canate 1, Darnell Coles 1, Carlos Delgado 1, Shawn Green 1.

TOP DRAFT CHOICES

1a. Chris Carpenter, RHP, Trinity High School, Manchester, N.H.
1b. Matt Farner, OF, East Pennsboro High School, Enola, Pa.
1c. Jeremy Lee, RHP, Galesburg (Ill.) H.S.
1d. Mark Lukasiewicz, LHP, Brevard (Fla.) CC
2a. Anthony Medrano, SS, Jordan High School, Long Beach, Calif.
2b. Ryan Jones, 1B, Irvine (Calif.) H.S.
3a. Mike Romano, RHP, Tulane U.
3b. Joe Young, RHP, Ainlay High School, Fort McMurray, Alberta.
4. Thad Busby, C/OF, Pace (Fla.) H.S.
5. Tim Bourne, SS, Muir H.S., Altadena, Cal.
6. Rob DeBoer, C, U. of South Carolina.
7. Donnie Barker, RHP, Leander (Tex.) H.S.
8. Matt Stone, LHP, Vista (Calif.) H.S.
9. Oreste Volkert, RHP, La Habra (Cal.) H.S.
10. Ruben Corral, RHP, Arroyo High School, El Monte, Calif.

ONTO BLUE

1994 SCHEDULE

N Denotes night game (any game starting after 5 p.m.).
▢ Home games shaded.
* At Three Rivers Stadium in Pittsburgh.

APRIL

SUN	MON	TUE	WED	THU	FRI	SAT
					1	2
3	4 SD N	5 SD N	6 SD	7 SD N	8 LA N	9 LA
10 LA	11 N	12 SF N	13 SF N	14 SF	15 CHI N	16 CHI
17 CHI N	18 STL N	19 STL N	20 STL	21	22 PIT N	23 PIT
24 PIT N	25 FLA N	26 FLA N	27 FLA	28 STL	29 PIT N	30 PIT

MAY

SUN	MON	TUE	WED	THU	FRI	SAT
1 PIT	2	3 FLA N	4 FLA N	5	6 MON N	7 MON
8 MON N	9 PHI N	10 PHI N	11 PHI	12	13 NY N	14 NY
15 NY	16	17 CIN N	18 CIN N	19 CIN N	20 COL N	21 COL
22 COL	23	24 HOU N	25 HOU N	26 HOU N	27 CHI N	28 CHI
29 CHI	30 SF	31 SF				

JUNE

SUN	MON	TUE	WED	THU	FRI	SAT
			1 SF	2	3 LA N	4 LA
5 LA N	6 SD N	7 SD N	8 SD N	9	10 HOU N	11 HOU
12 HOU	13 COL N	14 COL N	15 COL N	16 COL	17 CIN N	18 CIN
19 CIN N	20 NY N	21 NY N	22 NY N	23	24 PHI N	25 PHI
26 PHI N	27 MON N	28 MON N	29 MON N	30 FLA		

JULY

SUN	MON	TUE	WED	THU	FRI	SAT
					1 FLA N	2 FLA
3 FLA N	4 PIT N	5 PIT N	6 PIT	7	8 STL N	9 STL
10 STL	11 *	12 ALL-STAR GAME	13	14 FLA N	15 FLA N	16 FLA
17 FLA N	18 PIT N	19 PIT N	20 PIT N	21 STL N	22 STL	23 STL
24 STL N	25 MON N	26 MON N	27 MON	28	29 PHI N	30 PHI
31 PHI						

AUGUST

SUN	MON	TUE	WED	THU	FRI	SAT
	1 NY N	2 NY N	3 NY N	4	5 CIN N	6 CIN
7 CIN N	8 CIN N	9 COL N	10 COL N	11 COL	12 HOU N	13 HOU
14 HOU N	15 N	16 CHI N	17 CHI N	18 CHI	19 SD N	20 SD
21 SD	22	23 CHI N	24 CHI	25 CHI N	26 SD N	27 SD
28 N	29 LA N	30 LA N	31 LA			

SEPTEMBER

SUN	MON	TUE	WED	THU	FRI	SAT
				1 LA N	2 SF N	3 SF
4 SF	5 LA N	6 LA N	7 LA N	8 SF N	9 SF N	10 SF
11 SF N	12	13 HOU N	14 HOU N	15 HOU N	16 COL N	17 COL
18 COL	19	20 CIN N	21 CIN N	22 CIN N	23 NY N	24 NY
25 NY N	26 PHI N	27 PHI N	28 PHI	29	30 MON N	

OCTOBER

SUN	MON	TUE	WED	THU	FRI	SAT
						1 MON N
2 MON						

1994 SEASON

CLUB DIRECTORY

Owner
R.E. Turner III
Chairman of the board of directors
William C. Bartholomay
President
Stanley H. Kasten
Exec. vice president and general manager
John Schuerholz
Sr. vice president and asst. to the president
Henry L. Aaron
Senior v.p., administration
Bob Wolfe
V.p., dir. of marketing and broadcasting
Wayne Long
Vice president
Lee Douglas
Assistant general manager
Dean Taylor
Asst. general manager/player personnel
Chuck LaMar
Dir. of team travel and equipment manager
Bill Acree
Assistant director of player development
Rod Gilbreath
Assistant director of scouting
Don Mitchell
Scouting and player development asst.
Scott Proefrock
Special assistant/player personnel
Willie Stargell
Sr. dir. of promotions and civic affairs
Miles McRea
Controller
Chip Moore
Director of ticket sales
Paul Adams
Director of stadium operations and security
Larry Bowman
Director of community relations
Danny Goodwin
Director of merchandising
Robert A. Hope
Field director
Ed Mangan
Director of ticket operations
Ed Newman
Dir. of advertising and special events
Amy Richter
Dir. of community rel. and fan development
Dexter Santos
Director of public relations
Jim Schultz
Director of multicultural marketing
Peter Serrano
Media relations managers
Glen Serra
Phil Civins
Public relations assistant
Thurman Brooks
Community relations coordinator
Bob Prior
Licensing manager
Lynn Craven
Ad sales manager
Rodney Henderson
Special evens manager
Kathleen Hayes
Publications manager
Mike Ringering
Trainer
Dave Pursley
Assistant trainer
Jeff Porter

Club physician
Dr. David T. Watson
Associate physicians
Dr. John Cantwell
Dr. Robert Crow
Dr. Norman Elliott
Club orthopedists
Dr. Joe Chandler
Dr. Carl Fackler
Major league advance scout
John Van Ornum
Scouts
Eric Alexander
Mack Babitt
Butch Baccala
Doug Baker
Ray Belanger
Bart Braun
James Buchert
Jorge Calvo
Stu Cann
Joe Caputo
Bill Clark
Roy Clark
Ray Corbett
Hep Cronin
Phil Dale
Robert Dunning
Rob English
John Flannery
Rene Francisco
Jerry Gardner
Ralph Garr
Gil Garrido
Steve Givens
Pedro Gonzalez
John Hagemann
Bob Irwin
Bob Isabelle
Dean Jongewaard
Steve Jongewaard
Brian Kohlscheen
Deric Ladnier
Bill Lajoie
Scott Littlefield
Gerardo Lopez
Robert Lucas
Scott Nethery
Marco Paddy
Ernie Pedersen
Julian Perez
Rolando Petit
Jack Pierce
Jack Powell
Carlos Rios
Cristobal Santoya
Malcolm Seibert
Fred Shaffer
Alex Smith
Charlie Smith
Paul Snyder
John Stewart
Tony Stiel
Bob Turzilli
Giovanni Viceisza
Junior Vizcaino
Wes Westrum
Bill Wight
Dave Wilder
Don Williams
Richard Wilson

SPRING TRAINING ROSTER

Manager — Bobby Cox (6).

Coaches — Jim Beauchamp (37), Pat Corrales (39), Clarence Jones (28), Leo Mazzone (54), Jimy Williams (22).

No.	PITCHERS	B/T	Ht./Wt.	Born	1993 clubs
33	Avery, Steve	L/L	6-4/190	4-14-70	Atlanta
57	Bark, Brian	L/L	5-9/160	8-26-68	Richmond
36	Bedrosian, Steve	R/R	6-3/205	12-6-57	Atlanta
48	Birkbeck, Mike	R/R	6-2/190	3-10-61	Richmond
51	Borbon, Pedro	L/L	6-1/205	11-15-67	Richmond, Atlanta
47	Glavine, Tom	L/L	6-1/190	3-25-66	Atlanta
49	Hill, Milt	R/R	6-0/180	8-22-65	Indianapolis, Cincinnati
65	Koller, Jerry	R/R	6-3/190	6-30-72	Durham
31	Maddux, Greg	R/R	6-0/175	4-14-66	Atlanta
36	McMichael, Greg	R/R	6-3/215	12-1-66	Atlanta
50	Mercker, Kent	L/L	6-2/195	2-1-68	Atlanta
60	Murray, Matt	L/R	6-6/200	9-26-70	Macon
59	Potts, Michael	L/L	5-9/170	9-5-70	Greenville
29	Smoltz, John	R/R	6-3/185	5-15-67	Atlanta
30	Stanton, Mike	L/L	6-1/190	6-2-67	Atlanta
43	Wohlers, Mark	R/R	6-4/207	1-23-70	Richmond, Atlanta

No.	CATCHERS	B/T	Ht./Wt.	Born	1993 clubs
63	Ayrault, Joe	R/R	6-3/190	10-8-71	Durham
61	Houston, Tyler	L/R	6-2/210	1-17-71	Greenville, Richmond
8	Lopez, Javier	R/R	6-3/185	11-5-70	Richmond, Atlanta
7	O'Brien, Charlie	R/R	6-2/205	5-1-61	New York N.L.

No.	INFIELDERS	B/T	Ht./Wt.	Born	1993 clubs
2	Belliard, Rafael	R/R	5-6/160	10-24-61	Atlanta
4	Blauser, Jeff	R/R	6-0/170	11-8-65	Atlanta
15	Caraballo, Ramon	B/R	5-7/150	5-23-69	Richmond, Atlanta
64	Graffanino, Tony	R/R	6-1/175	6-6-72	Durham
16	Jones, Chipper	B/R	6-3/185	4-24-72	Richmond, Atlanta
18	Klesko, Ryan	L/L	6-3/220	6-12-71	Richmond, Atlanta
20	Lemke, Mark	B/R	5-9/167	8-13-65	Atlanta
27	McGriff, Fred	L/L	6-3/215	10-31-63	San Diego, Atlanta
45	Oliva, Jose	R/R	6-1/150	3-3-71	Richmond
32	Pecota, Bill	R/R	6-2/195	2-16-60	Atlanta
9	Pendleton, Terry	B/R	5-9/195	7-16-60	Atlanta

No.	OUTFIELDERS	B/T	Ht./Wt.	Born	1993 clubs
17	Brown, Jarvis	R/R	5-7/170	3-26-67	Las Vegas, San Diego
12	Gallagher, Dave	R/R	6-0/185	9-20-60	New York N.L.
5	Gant, Ron	R/R	6-0/172	3-2-65	Atlanta
66	Hughes, Troy	R/R	6-4/195	1-3-71	Greenville
23	Justice, David	L/L	6-3/200	4-14-66	Atlanta
25	Kelly, Mike	R/R	6-4/195	6-2-70	Richmond
24	Sanders, Deion	L/L	6-1/195	8-9-67	Atlanta
26	Tarasco, Tony	L/R	6-1/205	12-9-70	Richmond, Atlanta

BALLPARK INFORMATION

Ballpark (capacity, surface)
Atlanta-Fulton County Stadium
(52,710, grass)

Address
P.O. Box 4064
Atlanta, GA 30302

Business phone
404-522-7630

Ticket information
404-522-7630

Ticket prices
$18 (club level)
$15 (field level)
$12 (lower pavilion)
$10 (upper level)
$5 (upper pavilion)
$1 (g.a., children under 12)

Field dimensions (from home plate)
To left field at foul line, 330 feet
To center field, 402 feet
To right field at foul line, 330 feet

First game played
April 12, 1966 (Pirates 3, Braves 2)

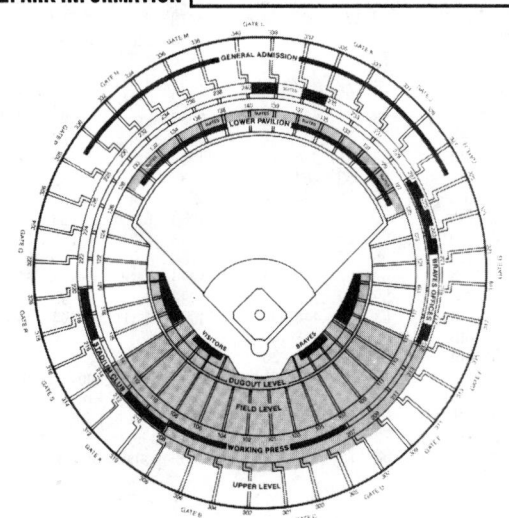

MINOR LEAGUE AFFILIATES

Class	Team	League	Manager
AAA	Richmond	International	Grady Little
AA	Greenville	Southern	Bruce Kimm
A	Durham	Carolina	Leon Roberts
A	Macon	South Atlantic	Randy Ingle
Rookie	Danville	Appalachian	Bruce Benedict
Rookie	Idaho Falls	Pioneer	Paul Runge
Rookie	Gulf Coast Braves	Gulf Coast	Jim Saul

BROADCAST INFORMATION

Radio: WGST-AM (640). Broadcasters: Skip Caray, Don Sutton, Pete Van Wieren, Joe Simpson. WPCH-FM (94.9). Broadcasters: Skip Caray, Don Sutton, Pete Van Wieren, Joe Simpson. **TV:** TBS-TV (Channel 17). Broadcasters: Skip Caray, Don Sutton, Pete Van Wieren, Joe Simpson. **Cable TV:** SportsSouth. Broadcasters: Chip Caray, Ernie Johnson.

SPRING TRAINING

Ballpark (city): Municipal Stadium (West Palm Beach, Fla.). **Ticket information:** 407-683-6100.

HISTORY

YEAR-BY-YEAR RECORDS

Year	Pos.	W	L	Pct.	GB	Year	Pos.	W	L	Pct.	GB
1901*	5th	69	69	.500	20½	1951*	4th	76	78	.494	20½
1902*	3rd	73	64	.533	29	1952*	7th	64	89	.418	32
1903*	6th	58	80	.420	32	1953†	2nd	92	62	.597	13
1904*	7th	55	98	.359	51	1954†	3rd	89	65	.578	8
1905*	7th	51	103	.331	54½	1955†	2nd	85	69	.552	13½
1906*	8th	49	102	.325	66½	1956†	2nd	92	62	.597	1
1907*	7th	58	90	.392	47	1957†	1st	95	59	.617 + 8	
1908*	6th	63	91	.409	36	1958†	1st	92	62	.597 + 8	
1909*	8th	45	108	.294	65½	1959†	T2nd	86	70	.551	2
1910*	8th	53	100	.346	50½	1960†	2nd	88	66	.571	7
1911*	8th	44	107	.291	54	1961†	4th	83	71	.539	10
1912*	8th	52	101	.340	52	1962*	5th	86	76	.531	15½
1913*	5th	69	82	.457	31½	1963†	6th	84	78	.519	15
1914*	1st	94	59	.614 +10½		1964†	5th	88	74	.543	5
1915*	2nd	83	69	.546	7	1965†	5th	86	76	.531	11
1916*	3rd	89	63	.586	4	1966	5th	85	77	.525	10
1917*	6th	72	81	.471	25½	1967	7th	77	85	.475	24½
1918*	7th	53	71	.427	28½	1968	5th	81	81	.500	16
1919*	6th	57	82	.410	38½	1969	1st‡	93	69	.574 + 3	
1920*	7th	62	90	.408	30	1970	5th	76	86	.469	26
1921*	4th	79	74	.516	15	1971	3rd	82	80	.506	8
1922*	8th	53	100	.346	39½	1972	4th	70	84	.455	25
1923*	7th	54	100	.351	41½	1973	5th	76	85	.472	22½
1924*	8th	53	100	.346	40	1974	3rd	88	74	.543	14
1925*	5th	70	83	.458	25	1975	5th	67	94	.416	40½
1926*	7th	66	86	.434	22	1976	6th	70	92	.432	32
1927*	7th	60	94	.390	34	1977	6th	61	101	.377	37
1928*	7th	50	103	.327	44½	1978	6th	69	93	.426	26
1929*	8th	56	98	.364	43	1979	6th	66	94	.413	23½
1930*	6th	70	84	.455	22	1980	4th	81	80	.503	11
1931*	7th	64	90	.416	37	1981	4th/5th	50	56	.472	§
1932*	5th	77	77	.500	13	1982	1st‡	89	73	.549 + 1	
1933*	4th	83	71	.539	9	1983	2nd	88	74	.543	3
1934*	4th	78	73	.517	16	1984	T2nd	80	82	.494	12
1935*	8th	38	115	.248	61½	1985	5th	66	96	.407	29
1936*	6th	71	83	.461	21	1986	6th	72	89	.447	23½
1937*	5th	79	73	.520	16	1987	5th	69	92	.429	20½
1938*	5th	77	75	.507	12	1988	6th	54	106	.338	39½
1939*	7th	63	88	.417	32½	1989	6th	63	97	.394	28
1940*	7th	65	87	.428	34½	1990	6th	65	97	.401	26
1941*	7th	62	92	.403	38	1991	1st*	94	68	.580 + 1	
1942*	7th	59	89	.399	44	1992	1st*	98	64	.605 + 8	
1943*	6th	68	85	.444	36½	1993	1st‡	104	58	.642 + 1	
1944*	6th	65	89	.422	40						
1945*	6th	67	85	.441	30						
1946*	4th	81	72	.529	15½						
1947*	3rd	86	68	.558	8						
1948*	1st	91	62	.595 + 6½							
1949*	4th	75	79	.487	22						
1950*	4th	83	71	.539	8						

*Franchise known as Boston Braves. †Franchise known as Milwaukee Braves. ‡Lost Championship Series. §First half 25-29; second 25-27. *Won Championship Series.

MANAGERS

Name	Record	Years
Frank Selee	69-69	1901
Al Buckenberger	186-242	'02-04
Fred Tenney	202-402	'05-07
		1911
Joe Kelley	63-91	1908
Frank Bowerman	23-55	1909
Harry Smith	22-53	1909
Fred Lake	53-100	1910
Johnny Kling	52-101	1912
George Stallings	579-597	'13-20
Fred Mitchell	186-274	'21-23
Dave Bancroft	249-363	'24-27
Jack Slattery	11-20	1928
Rogers Hornsby	39-83	1928
Emil Fuchs	56-98	1929
Bill McKechnie	560-666	'30-37
Casey Stengel	394-516	'38-43
Bob Coleman	107-140	'44-45
Del Bissonette	25-34	1945
Billy Southworth	424-358	'46-51
Tommy Holmes	61-69	'51-52
Charlie Grimm	341-285	'52-56
Fred Haney	341-231	'56-59
Chuck Dressen	159-124	'60-61
Birdie Tebbetts	98-89	'61-62
Bobby Bragan	310-287	'63-66
Billy Hitchcock	110-100	'66-67
Ken Silvestri	0-3	1967
Lum Harris	379-373	'68-72
Eddie Mathews	149-161	'72-74
Clyde King	96-101	'74-75
Connie Ryan	9-18	1975
Dave Bristol	131-192	'76-77
Ted Turner	0-1	1977
Bobby Cox	498-512	'78-81
		'90-92
Joe Torre	257-229	'82-84
Eddie Haas	50-71	1985
Bobby Wine	16-25	1985
Chuck Tanner	153-208	'86-88
Russ Nixon	234-274	'88-93

DAY BY DAY

Date	Opp.	Res.	Score	(Inn.*)	Hits	Opp. hits	Winning pitcher	Losing pitcher	Save	Record	Pos.	GB
4-5	At Chi.	W	1-0		5	5	Maddux	Morgan	Stanton	1-0	T1st	...
4-6	At Chi.	L	0-1		1	6	Guzman	Smoltz		1-1	T3rd	½
4-7	At Chi.	W	5-4	(10)	12	13	Howell	Scanlan		2-1	T1st	...
4-8	L.A.	W	6-1		8	5	Glavine	Candiotti		3-1	1st	+1
4-9	L.A.	W	2-0		5	3	Smith	Astacio	Stanton	4-1	1st	+2
4-10	L.A.	L	1-2	(10)	4	8	Hershiser	Howell	Gott	4-2	1st	+1
4-11	L.A.	W	3-0		4	4	Smoltz	R. Martinez	Stanton	5-2	1st	+1½
4-12	Chi.	L	1-5		7	14	Hibbard	Avery		5-3	1st	+½
4-13	Chi.	W	3-2		9	7	Glavine	Castillo	Stanton	6-3	1st	+½
4-14	Chi.	L	0-6		6	10	Harkey	Smith		6-4	2nd	...
4-15	At S.F.	L	1-6		6	10	Brantley	Maddux		6-5	3rd	½
4-16	At S.F.	L	0-1		6	4	Burkett	Smoltz	Beck	6-6	3rd	1½
4-17	At S.F.	W	2-0		8	3	Avery	Jackson	Stanton	7-6	3rd	½
4-18	At S.F.	L	12-13	(11)	9	16	Jackson	Bedrosian		7-7	3rd	1½
4-20	At Fla.	W	5-4		9	7	Maddux	Bowen	Stanton	8-7	3rd	1½
4-21	At Fla.	W	7-4		11	10	Smoltz	McClure	Stanton	9-7	3rd	½
4-22	At Fla.	L	3-4		8	9	Armstrong	Avery	Harvey	9-8	3rd	1½
4-23	At St.L.	W	3-1		8	4	Glavine	Murphy	Stanton	10-8	3rd	½
4-24	At St.L.	W	11-0		16	6	Smith	Tewksbury		11-8	2nd	½
4-25	At St.L.	L	3-7		8	14	Olivares	Maddux	Smith	11-9	3rd	½
4-26	Pit.	L	3-4	(11)	8	8	Minor	McMichael	Belinda	11-10	3rd	½
4-27	Pit.	L	2-6	(11)	6	11	Wakefield	Stanton	Wagner	11-11	3rd	1½
4-28	Fla.	L	1-3		10	7	McClure	Bedrosian	Harvey	11-12	3rd	2½
4-29	Fla.	L	5-6		10	10	Aquino	Smith	Hoffman	11-13	3rd	3½
4-30	St.L.	W	3-2	(11)	8	5	Stanton	Murphy		12-13	3rd	3½
5-1	St.L.	L	3-10		7	11	Magrane	Smoltz		12-14	4th	4½
5-2	St.L.	W	4-3		7	8	Mercker	Murphy	Stanton	13-14	3rd	4½
5-4	At Pit.	W	3-2		10	4	Glavine	Wakefield	Stanton	14-14	3rd	3½
5-5	At Pit.	L	1-4		7	8	Walk	Maddux	Belinda	14-15	3rd	4½
5-6	At Col.	W	13-3		15	3	Smoltz	Nied		15-15	3rd	4½
5-7	At Col.	W	13-5		16	11	Freeman	Parrett		16-15	3rd	4
5-8	At Col.	W	8-7		9	11	Mercker	Fredrickson	Stanton	17-15	3rd	3
5-9	At Col.	W	12-7		11	14	McMichael	Reed		18-15	3rd	2
5-10	At Hou.	L	2-5		11	5	Hernandez	Howell	D. Jones	18-16	3rd	2½
5-11	At Hou.	W	5-4		9	7	Smoltz	Drabek	Stanton	19-16	3rd	2
5-12	At Hou.	W	5-2		9	6	Avery	Swindell	Stanton	20-16	3rd	2
5-14	Phi.	W	10-7		12	10	Glavine	Mulholland	Stanton	21-16	3rd	1½
5-15	Phi.	W	5-3		6	7	Maddux	West	Stanton	22-16	3rd	1½
5-16	Phi.	L	4-5		8	10	Jackson	McMichael	Mit. Williams	22-17	3rd	2½
5-17	Mon.	W	5-2		11	6	Avery	Martinez	Stanton	23-17	3rd	2½
5-18	Mon.	L	0-1		5	7	Heredia	Smith	Wetteland	23-18	3rd	3½
5-19	Mon.	W	1-0		4	4	Glavine	Shaw		24-18	2nd	3½
5-21	At N.Y.	W	4-2		11	6	Maddux	Hillman		25-18	2nd	4
5-22	At N.Y.	L	1-6		8	10	Gooden	Smoltz		25-19	2nd	4
5-23	At N.Y.	W	2-1		7	4	Avery	Saberhagen	Stanton	26-19	2nd	4
5-25	At Cin.	W	5-0		12	7	Glavine	Ayala		27-19	2nd	4
5-26	At Cin.	L	0-4		1	7	Belcher	Maddux		27-20	2nd	4
5-27	At Cin.	L	4-5		7	12	Cadaret	McMichael		27-21	2nd	4
5-28	S.F.	W	7-4		9	16	Avery	Burkett	Stanton	28-21	2nd	3
5-29	S.F.	L	3-6		8	11	Brummett	Smith	Beck	28-22	2nd	4
5-30	S.F.	L	3-4		11	8	Burba	Glavine	Beck	28-23	2nd	5
5-31	S.D.	W	2-1		7	5	Maddux	Mason		29-23	2nd	4½
6-1	S.D.	L	1-2		7	4	Brocail	Smoltz	Ge. Harris	29-24	2nd	5½
6-2	S.D.	W	5-2		9	8	Avery	Benes	Stanton	30-24	2nd	5
6-3	S.D.	L	4-12		7	15	Gr. Harris	Smith		30-25	3rd	5
6-4	At L.A.	L	4-5		7	9	R. Martinez	Glavine	Gott	30-26	4th	5
6-5	At L.A.	L	1-5		5	12	Ke. Gross	Maddux		30-27	4th	6
6-6	At L.A.	W	2-0		6	5	Smoltz	Candiotti		31-27	4th	6
6-7	At S.D.	W	4-0		8	4	Avery	Benes		32-27	3rd	5½
6-8	At S.D.	L	4-5		10	8	Ge. Harris	Stanton		32-28	4th	5½
6-10	Cin.	L	1-3		6	8	Belcher	Glavine	Dibble	32-29	4th	6½
6-11	Cin.	W	6-5	(11)	14	12	Stanton	Pugh		33-29	3rd	6½
6-12	Cin.	W	7-2		9	5	Smoltz	Smiley		34-29	3rd	6½
6-13	Cin.	W	9-2		12	9	Avery	Roper		35-29	2nd	6½
6-14	N.Y.	L	4-7		12	13	Tanana	Smith		35-30	3rd	7
6-15	N.Y.	W	2-1		7	6	Glavine	Hillman		36-30	3rd	6
6-16	N.Y.	W	5-2		10	3	Maddux	Schourek		37-30	2nd	6
6-18	At Mon.	L	1-2		4	4	Martinez	Smoltz	Wetteland	37-31	2nd	7½
6-19	At Mon.	W	4-3		5	8	Wohlers	Rojas	Stanton	38-31	2nd	7½
6-20	At Mon.	W	5-1		11	8	Glavine	Shaw		39-31	2nd	7½

Date	Opp.	Res.	Score	(inn.*)	Hits	Opp. hits	Winning pitcher	Losing pitcher	Save	Record	Pos.	GB
6-21	At Phi.	W	8-1		13	7	Maddux	Schilling		40-31	2nd	7½
6-22	At Phi.	L	3-5		6	7	Jackson	Smith	Mit. Williams	40-32	2nd	7½
6-23	At Phi.	L	3-8		9	7	Rivera	Smoltz		40-33	2nd	8½
6-25	Hou.	W	8-2		10	6	Avery	Harnisch		41-33	2nd	9
6-26	Hou.	W	6-5		8	12	Stanton	D. Jones		42-33	2nd	8
6-27	Hou.	L	0-3		5	6	Kile	Maddux	Hernandez	42-34	2nd	9
6-29	Col.	W	6-4		10	7	Smoltz	Ruffin	Stanton	43-34	2nd	8½
6-30	Col.	W	3-2		7	6	Wohlers	Shepherd		44-34	2nd	7½
7-1	Col.	W	4-0		9	4	Glavine	Reynoso		45-34	2nd	7
7-2	Fla.	L	2-4		4	8	Hammond	Maddux	Harvey	45-35	2nd	8
7-3	Fla.	W	11-2		13	8	Smith	Aquino		46-35	2nd	7
7-4	Fla.	W	4-3		10	9	Stanton	Turner		47-35	2nd	7
7-5	Fla.	W	9-7		12	10	Wohlers	Corsi	Stanton	48-35	2nd	7
7-6	At St.L.	L	4-5		10	12	Guetterman	Stanton		48-36	2nd	8
7-7	At St.L.	L	1-3		5	10	Magrane	Maddux	Smith	48-37	2nd	8
7-8	At St.L.	L	1-7		5	13	Watson	Avery		48-38	2nd	9
7-9	At Fla.	W	5-1		7	5	Smoltz	Bowen		49-38	2nd	9
7-10	At Fla.	L	2-5		9	11	Armstrong	Glavine	Harvey	49-39	2nd	9
7-11	At Fla.	W	6-3		8	6	Maddux	Hough	Stanton	50-39	2nd	9
7-15	Pit.	W	4-0		6	6	Glavine	Tomlin		51-39	2nd	9
7-16	Pit.	W	3-2		4	9	Maddux	Cooke	Stanton	52-39	2nd	9
7-17	Pit.	L	3-4		5	11	Wagner	Smoltz	Belinda	52-40	2nd	9
7-18	Pit.	W	2-0		6	13	Avery	Smith	Stanton	53-40	2nd	8
7-19	St.L.	L	0-4		6	11	Osborne	Smith	Smith	53-41	2nd	9
7-20	St.L.	W	8-5		11	10	Wohlers	Cormier	Stanton	54-41	2nd	9
7-21	St.L.	W	14-2		18	5	Maddux	Magrane		55-41	2nd	9
7-22	At Pit.	L	7-8		14	11	Minor	Howell		55-42	2nd	10
7-23	At Pit.	W	6-2		14	4	Avery	Belinda		56-42	2nd	9
7-24	At Pit.	W	11-6		18	10	Bedrosian	Walk		57-42	2nd	9
7-25	At Pit.	W	13-1		21	4	Glavine	Tomlin		58-42	2nd	9
7-26	At Col.	W	12-7		14	11	Maddux	Leskanic		59-42	2nd	8
7-27	At Col.	W	10-5		14	4	Smoltz	Reynoso		60-42	2nd	8
7-28	At Col.	W	3-2		6	10	Wohlers	Reed	McMichael	61-42	2nd	7
7-29	At Hou.	L	0-2		4	3	Harnisch	Mercker		61-43	2nd	7½
7-30	At Hou.	W	4-1		7	7	Glavine	Drabek	McMichael	62-43	2nd	7½
7-31	At Hou.	W	4-3		8	9	Maddux	Kile	Stanton	63-43	2nd	7½
8-1	At Hou.	W	3-2		6	7	Smoltz	Swindell	McMichael	64-43	2nd	7½
8-3	Phi.	L	3-5		8	10	Mulholland	Avery	Mit. Williams	64-44	2nd	8½
8-4	Phi.	W	9-8		10	14	Howell	West	McMichael	65-44	2nd	7½
8-5	Phi.	L	4-10		8	10	Rivera	Maddux		65-45	2nd	8½
8-6	Mon.	L	2-8		5	13	Rueter	Smoltz		65-46	2nd	9½
8-7	Mon.	L	3-5	(10)	9	9	Scott	Stanton	Wetteland	65-47	2nd	9½
8-8	Mon.	W	3-2		5	7	Avery	Fassero	McMichael	66-47	2nd	8½
8-10	At N.Y.	W	3-2		8	9	Bedrosian	Hillman	McMichael	67-47	2nd	9
8-11	At N.Y.	W	4-2		6	6	Maddux	Fernandez		68-47	2nd	9
8-12	At N.Y.	W	8-4		10	4	Smoltz	Gooden		69-47	2nd	8½
8-13	At Cin.	W	14-0		14	1	Avery	Pugh		70-47	2nd	8½
8-14	At Cin.	W	4-2		6	3	Glavine	Roper	McMichael	71-47	2nd	7½
8-15	At Cin.	W	1-0		5	4	Maddux	Rijo		72-47	2nd	7½
8-17	L.A.	W	3-2		6	8	Smoltz	R. Martinez	McMichael	73-47	2nd	6½
8-18	L.A.	W	5-4	(12)	6	8	Bedrosian	McDowell		74-47	2nd	6½
8-19	L.A.	L	5-7		14	11	Ke. Gross	Glavine	Gott	74-48	2nd	7½
8-20	At Chi.	L	3-6		9	12	Morgan	Stanton	Myers	74-49	2nd	7½
8-21	At Chi.	W	6-3		14	10	Freeman	Plesac	McMichael	75-49	2nd	7½
8-22	At Chi.	W	4-3		11	7	Smoltz	Guzman	McMichael	76-49	2nd	7½
8-23	At S.F.	W	5-3		9	8	Avery	Wilson		77-49	2nd	6½
8-24	At S.F.	W	6-4		11	10	Glavine	Hickerson	McMichael	78-49	2nd	5½
8-25	At S.F.	W	9-1		16	6	Maddux	Swift		79-49	2nd	4½
8-27	Chi.	L	7-9		13	9	Boskie	Wohlers	Bautista	79-50	2nd	4½
8-28	Chi.	W	5-1		10	6	Avery	Guzman		80-50	2nd	4
8-29	Chi.	W	8-2		13	7	Glavine	Hibbard		81-50	2nd	4
8-31	S.F.	W	8-2		9	6	Maddux	Swift		82-50	2nd	3½
9-1	S.F.	L	2-3		4	7	Jackson	Wohlers	Beck	82-51	2nd	4½
9-2	S.F.	W	5-3		11	8	Wohlers	Brantley	McMichael	83-51	2nd	3½
9-3	S.D.	W	7-3		13	7	Glavine	Ashby		84-51	2nd	3½
9-4	S.D.	W	3-2		9	5	Mercker	Brocail	McMichael	85-51	2nd	3½
9-5	S.D.	W	3-2		9	6	Maddux	Martinez		86-51	2nd	3½
9-6	At L.A.	L	1-2		6	6	P. Martinez	Smoltz		86-52	2nd	3½
9-7	At L.A.	W	1-0		5	6	Avery	Astacio		87-52	2nd	2½
9-8	At L.A.	W	8-2		13	10	Glavine	R. Martinez		88-52	2nd	2
9-9	At S.D.	W	1-0	(10)	10	1	McMichael	Hoffman		89-52	2nd	1
9-10	At S.D.	W	3-2		5	6	Maddux	Worrell	McMichael	90-52	2nd	...
9-11	At S.D.	W	13-1		15	5	Smoltz	Benes		91-52	1st	+1
9-12	At S.D.	L	4-5		8	5	Sanders	Avery	Ge. Harris	91-53	1st	+1

Date	Opp.	Res.	Score	(inn.*)	Hits	Opp. hits	Winning pitcher	Losing pitcher	Save	Record	Pos.	GB
9-14	Cin.	W	10-3		14	11	Glavine	Ayala		92-53	1st	+2½
9-15	Cin.	W	7-6		13	13	Smith	Dibble		93-53	1st	+3½
9-16	Cin.	W	3-2	(12)	10	10	Bedrosian	Service		94-53	1st	+4
9-17	N.Y.	W	2-1	(10)	6	6	Howell	Maddux		95-53	1st	+4
9-18	N.Y.	L	2-3	(10)	6	15	Innis	Stanton	Gozzo	95-54	1st	+3
9-19	N.Y.	W	11-2		14	11	Glavine	Schourek		96-54	1st	+3
9-21	At Mon.	W	18-5		16	8	Smoltz	Hill		97-54	1st	+3½
9-22	At Mon.	L	1-6		4	9	Fassero	Avery		97-55	1st	+2½
9-23	At Mon.	W	6-3		9	7	Maddux	Martinez		98-55	1st	+2½
9-24	At Phi.	L	0-3		3	7	Greene	Glavine	Mit. Williams	98-56	1st	+1½
9-25	At Phi.	W	9-7		14	15	Bedrosian	Mason	McMichael	99-56	1st	+1½
9-26	At Phi.	W	7-2		9	5	Avery	Schilling		100-56	1st	+1½
9-28	Hou.	L	2-5		6	12	Harnisch	Maddux	D. Jones	100-57	T1st	...
9-29	Hou.	W	6-3		11	11	Glavine	Drabek	McMichael	101-57	1st	+1
9-30	Hou.	L	8-10		14	12	Hernandez	Smoltz		101-58	T1st	...
10-1	Col.	W	7-4		6	6	Avery	Harris	McMichael	102-58	T1st	...
10-2	Col.	W	10-1		14	5	Maddux	Reynoso		103-58	T1st	...
10-3	Col.	W	5-3		12	6	Glavine	Nied	McMichael	104-58	1st	+1

Monthly records: April (12-13), May (17-10), June (15-11), July (19-9), August (19-7), September (19-8), October (3-0).
*Innings, if other than nine.

HIGHLIGHTS

High point: After chasing San Francisco for much of the season, the Braves finally moved into sole possession of first place following a win at San Diego September 11. They didn't fall from first the rest of the way.

Low point: The Atlanta bullpen blew a ninth-inning lead at Pittsburgh on July 22, allowing four runs in an 8-7 loss. The defeat dropped the Braves 10 games behind the Giants, Atlanta's biggest deficit of the season.

Turning point: First baseman Fred McGriff was acquired in a trade from San Diego on July 18 and made his presence felt immediately. In his first game two days later, he hit a two-run homer as the Braves overcame a 5-0 deficit to defeat St. Louis, 8-5.

Most valuable player: Right fielder David Justice. He set career highs in homers (40) and RBIs (120), becoming only the fourth player in Atlanta annals to eclipse those levels in the same season.

Most valuable pitcher: Lefthander Tom Glavine. His 22 wins set a career high and tied for the league lead. It also was his third consecutive 20-win season, the best streak in the N.L. since Ferguson Jenkins won 20 from 1967-72.

Most improved player: Jeff Blauser. Aside from improved defense, he became the first Braves shortstop to hit over .300 since 1948, set a franchise record for runs scored by a shortstop (110) and drove in a career-high 73 runs.

Most pleasant surprise: Righthander Greg McMichael. He made the team as a middle reliever/setup man, was moved to closer in midseason and finished with 19 saves in 21 opportunities.

Biggest disappointment: Lefthander Mike Stanton. He had 27 saves by July 31, then hit a bad stretch and never recovered. He failed to collect another save and finished with a 4.67 ERA.

Key injuries: Catcher Greg Olson was on the disabled list from August 17 to September 1 with an inflamed tendon in his right forearm. Center fielder Deion Sanders was stricken with a respiratory infection and played sparingly over the final two months.

Notable: The Braves set a franchise record with 104 wins. ... Glavine and righthander Greg Maddux, who won his second straight Cy Young Award, gave the Braves a pair of 20-game winners for the first time since Warren Spahn and Lew Burdette in 1959. ... Before acquiring McGriff, Atlanta was 53-41 (.564). With McGriff, the Braves were 51-17 (.750).

—BILL ZACK

RECORDS

1993 regular-season record: 104-58 (1st in N.L. West); 51-30 at home; 53-28 on road; 49-35 vs. East; 55-23 vs. West; 29-15 vs. LHP; 75-43 vs. RHP; 82-43 on grass; 22-15 on turf; 26-15 in daytime; 77-43 at night; 37-22 in one-run games; 7-6 in extra-inning games; 0-0-0 in doubleheaders.

Team record last five years: 424-384 (.525), ranks 3rd in league in that span).

TEAM LEADERS

Batting average: Jeff Blauser (.305).
At-bats: Terry Pendleton (633).
Runs: Ron Gant (113).
Hits: Jeff Blauser (182).
Total bases: Ron Gant (309).
Doubles: Terry Pendleton (33).
Triples: Deion Sanders (6).
Home runs: David Justice (40).
Runs batted in: David Justice (120).
Stolen bases: Otis Nixon (47).
Slugging percentage: David Justice (.515).
On-base percentage: Jeff Blauser (.401).
Wins: Tom Glavine (22).
Earned-run average: Greg Maddux (2.36).
Complete games: Greg Maddux (8).
Shutouts: Tom Glavine (2).
Saves: Mike Stanton (27).
Innings pitched: Greg Maddux (267).
Strikeouts: John Smoltz (208).

GAMES BY POSITION

Catcher: Damon Berryhill 105, Greg Olson 81, Javier Lopez 7, Francisco Cabrera 2.

First base: Sid Bream 90, Fred McGriff 66, Brian Hunter 29, Francisco Cabrera 12, Ryan Klesko 3.

Second base: Mark Lemke 150, Rafael Belliard 24, Ramon Caraballo 5, Bill Pecota 4.

Third base: Terry Pendleton 161, Bill Pecota 23.

Shortstop: Jeff Blauser 161, Rafael Belliard 58, Chipper Jones 3.

Outfield: David Justice 157, Ron Gant 155, Otis Nixon 116, Deion Sanders 60, Tony Tarasco 12, Brian Hunter 2, Ryan Klesko 2, Bill Pecota 1.

TOP DRAFT CHOICES

1. None.
2. Andre King, OF, Stranahan High School, Fort Lauderdale, Fla.
3. Carl Schutz, LHP, Southeastern Louisiana University.
4. James Franklin, OF, Larue County High School, Hodgenville, Ky.
5. Del Mathews, 1B/LHP, Fernandina Beach (Fla.) High School.
6. Danny Magee, SS, Denham Springs (La.) High School.
7. Travis Cain, RHP, T.L. Hanna High School, Anderson, S.C.
8. Micah Bowie, LHP, Kingwood (Tex.) High School.
9. Jason Green, RHP, Contra Costa (Calif.) J.C.
10. Robert Sasser, OF, Oakland (Calif.) High School.

CHICAGO CUBS
NATIONAL LEAGUE CENTRAL DIVISION

1994 SCHEDULE

N   Denotes night game (any game starting after 5 p.m.).
☐   Home games shaded.
*   At Three Rivers Stadium in Pittsburgh.

APRIL

SUN	MON	TUE	WED	THU	FRI	SAT
					1	2
3	4 NY	5 NY	6 NY	7	8 MON	9 MON
10 MON	11 NY	12	13 NY	14 NY	15 ATL	16 ATL
17 ATL	18	19 N	20 HOU	21	22 N COL	23 COL
24 COL	25 N CIN	26 N CIN	27 N HOU	28 HOU	29 N COL	30 COL

MAY

SUN	MON	TUE	WED	THU	FRI	SAT
1 COL	2 N CIN	3 CIN	4 CIN	5	6 N PIT	7 N PIT
8 PIT	9 N STL	10 N STL	11 N STL	12 STL	13 N FLA	14 FLA
15 FLA	16 N SD	17 N SD	18 N SD	19	20 SF	21 SF
22 SF	23 N LA	24 N LA	25 N LA	26	27 N ATL	28 N ATL
29 ATL	30 N PHI	31 N PHI				

JUNE

SUN	MON	TUE	WED	THU	FRI	SAT
			1 PHI	2 N PHI	3 MON	4 MON
5 MON	6 N PHI	7 N PHI	8 PHI	9	10 N LA	11 LA
12 LA	13	14 N SD	15 N SD	16 N SD	17 SF	18 SF
19 SF	20	21 N FLA	22 N FLA	23 FLA	24 STL	25 STL
26 STL	27 N PIT	28 PIT	29 N PIT	30 N HOU		

JULY

SUN	MON	TUE	WED	THU	FRI	SAT
					1 N HOU	2 N HOU
3 HOU	4 COL	5 N COL	6 CBL	7 N HOU	8 HOU	9 HOU
10 N HOU	11	12 * ALL-STAR GAME	13	14 N CIN	15 N CIN	16 N CIN
17 CIN	18 N COL	19 N COL	20 COL	21	22 N CIN	23 CIN
24 CIN	25 N PIT	26 N PIT	27 N PIT	28 N PIT	29 N STL	30 N STL
31 STL						

AUGUST

SUN	MON	TUE	WED	THU	FRI	SAT
	1 N FLA	2 FLA	3 N FLA	4 FLA	5 N SD	6 SD
7 SD	8 N SF	9 SF	10 N SF	11	12 N LA	13 LA
14 LA	15	16 N ATL	17 N ATL	18 N ATL	19 N NY	20 NY
21 N NY	22 NY	23 N ATL	24 ATL	25 ATL	26 NY	27 NY
28 NY	29 N MON	30 N MON	31 N MON			

SEPTEMBER

SUN	MON	TUE	WED	THU	FRI	SAT
			1	2 N PHI	3 N PHI
4 PHI	5 N MON	6 N MON	7 MON	8 N PHI	9 PHI	10 PHI
11 PHI	12 N LA	13 N LA	14	15	16 N SD	17 SD
18 SD	19 SF	20 SF	21 SF	22	23 N FLA	24 FLA
25 FLA	26 N STL	27 N STL	28 STL	29	30 PIT	

OCTOBER

SUN	MON	TUE	WED	THU	FRI	SAT
						1 PIT
2 PIT						

1994 SEASON

CLUB DIRECTORY

Board of directors
Stanton R. Cook
Thomas G. Ayers
Charles T. Brumback
Frank W. Considine
Donald C. Grenesko
Andrew J. McKenna

Exec. vice president, baseball operations
Larry Himes

Assistant general manager
Syd Thrift

Vice president, baseball administration
Ned Colletti

Special player consultant
Hugh Alexander

Major League advance scout
Eddie Lyons

Traveling secretary
Jimmy Bank

V.p., baseball development and scouting
Al Goldis

Dir., player development administration
Scott Nelson

Executive v.p., business operations
Mark McGuire

Director, minor league business operations
Connie Kowal

Legal counsel
Donn Davis

Director, planning and control
Margaret Durkin

Manager, accounting
Jodi Norman

Manager, information systems
Carl Rice

V.p., marketing and broadcasting
John McDonough

Manager, sponsorship/advertising
Jay Blunk

Mgr., Cubs Care and community relations
Ellen Jensen

Mezz. box coordinator/broadcast services
Phil Bedella

Director, media relations
Sharon Pannozzo

Media information coordinator
Chuck Wasserstrom

Media relations assistant
Wanda Taylor

Manager, publications
Ernie Roth

Publications editor
Ed McGregor

Director, stadium operations
Tom Cooper

Asst. director, stadium operations
Paul Rathje

Event operations and security
To be announced

Director, ticket operations
Frank Maloney

Team physicians
John Marquardt, M.D.
Michael Schafer, M.D.

Head trainer
John Fierro

Assistant trainer
Brett Fischer

Physical development coordinator
Garrett Glemont

Equipment manager
Yosh Kawano

Assistant equipment manager
Dana Noeltner

Visiting clubhouse manager
Tom Hellmann

Dir., int'l scouting/national cross-checker
Southeast regional scouting supervisor
Danny Monzon

East national cross-checker
Rod Fridley

West national cross-checker
Larry Maxie

Midwest regional scouting supervisor
Doug Gassaway

East regional scouting supervisor
Bill Blitzer

West regional scouting supervisor
Jesse Flores

Scouting supervisor
Ed Ford

Scouting consultant
Vedie Himsl

Area scouts
Bill Capps
Frank DeMoss
Preston Douglas
Steve Fuller
John Gracio
Gene Handley
Elmore Hill
Joe Housey
Toney Howell
Spider Jorgensen
Buzzy Keller
Bobby Morgan
Bob Steinkamp
John Stockstill
Billy Swoope

SPRING TRAINING ROSTER

Manager—Tom Trebelhorn (41).

Coaches—Chuck Cottier (15), Moe Drabowsky, Marv Foley, Jose Martinez (3), Tony Muser (40), Billy Williams (26).

No.	PITCHERS	B/T	Ht./Wt.	Born	1993 clubs
23	Banks, Willie	R/R	6-1/202	2-27-69	Minnesota
38	Bautista, Jose	R/R	6-2/205	7-25-64	Chicago N.L.
47	Boskie, Shawn	R/R	6-3/200	3-28-67	Chicago N.L., Iowa
52	Bullinger, Jim	R/R	6-2/185	8-21-65	Iowa, Chicago N.L.
49	Castillo, Frank	R/R	6-1/190	4-1-69	Chicago N.L.
33	Dickson, Lance	R/L	6-1/190	10-19-69	Daytona, Orlando, Iowa
29	Guzman, Jose	R/R	6-3/195	4-9-63	Chicago N.L.
48	Hollins, Jessie	R/R	6-3/235	1-27-70	Chicago N.L.
	Ilsley, Blaise	L/L	6-1/195	4-9-64	Iowa
62	Luebbers, Larry	R/R	6-6/200	10-11-69	Indianapolis, Cincinnati
36	Morgan, Mike	R/R	6-2/220	10-8-59	Chicago N.L.
28	Myers, Randy	L/L	6-1/230	9-19-62	Chicago N.L.
55	Novoa, Rafael	L/L	6-1/190	10-26-67	New Orleans, Milwaukee
32	Plesac, Dan	L/L	6-5/215	2-4-62	Chicago N.L.
46	Trachsel, Steve	R/R	6-4/205	10-31-70	Iowa, Chicago N.L.
	Veres, Randy	R/R	6-3/210	11-25-65	Canton/Akron
43	Wendell, Turk	B/R	6-2/190	5-19-67	Iowa, Chicago N.L.

No.	CATCHERS	B/T	Ht./Wt.	Born	1993 clubs
	Cox, Darron	R/R	6-1/205	11-21-67	Chattanooga
2	Wilkins, Rick	L/R	6-2/210	6-4-67	Chicago N.L.

No.	INFIELDERS	B/T	Ht./Wt.	Born	1993 clubs
24	Buechele, Steve	R/R	6-2/200	9-26-61	Chicago N.L.
12	Dunston, Shawon	R/R	6-1/180	3-21-63	Chicago N.L.
	Franco, Matt	L/R	6-2/200	8-19-69	Orlando, Iowa
17	Grace, Mark	L/L	6-2/190	6-28-64	Chicago N.L.
2	Hernandez, Jose	R/R	6-1/180	7-14-69	Canton/Akron, Orlando, Iowa
11	Sanchez, Rey	R/R	5-9/170	10-5-67	Chicago N.L.
23	Sandberg, Ryne	R/R	6-2/190	9-18-59	Daytona, Orlando, Chicago N.L.
1	Shields, Tommy	R/R	6-0/185	8-14-64	Chicago N.L., Iowa
16	Vizcaino, Jose	B/R	6-1/180	3-26-68	Chicago N.L.

No.	OUTFIELDERS	B/T	Ht./Wt.	Born	1993 clubs
	Glanville, Doug	R/R	6-2/170	8-25-70	Daytona, Orlando
34	Hill, Glenallen	R/R	6-2/220	3-22-65	Cleveland, Chicago N.L.
27	May, Derrick	L/R	6-4/225	7-14-68	Chicago N.L.
25	Rhodes, Karl	L/L	6-0/195	8-21-68	Houston, Omaha, Iowa, Chicago N.L.
19	Roberson, Kevin	B/R	6-4/210	1-29-68	Iowa, Chicago N.L.
21	Sosa, Sammy	R/R	6-0/185	11-12-68	Chicago N.L.
	Timmons, Ozzie	R/R	6-2/205	9-18-70	Orlando
	Wilson, Willie	B/R	6-3/200	7-9-55	Chicago N.L.
39	Zambrano, Eddie	R/R	6-3/200	2-1-66	Iowa, Chicago N.L.

BALLPARK INFORMATION

Ballpark (capacity, surface)
Wrigley Field (38,765, grass)
Address
1060 W. Addison St.
Chicago, IL 60613-4397
Business phone
312-404-2827
Ticket information
312-404-2827
Ticket prices
$19 (club box)
$19 (field box)
$15 (terrace box)
$15 (upper deck box)
$15 (family section)
$12 (terrace reserved)
$9 (adult upper deck reserved)
$6 (under 14 upper deck reserved)
$10 (bleachers)
All weekday afternoon games in April,
May and September are less.
Field dimensions (from home plate)
To left field at foul line, 355 feet
To center field, 400 feet
To right field at foul line, 353 feet
First game played
April 20, 1916 (Cubs 7, Reds 6)

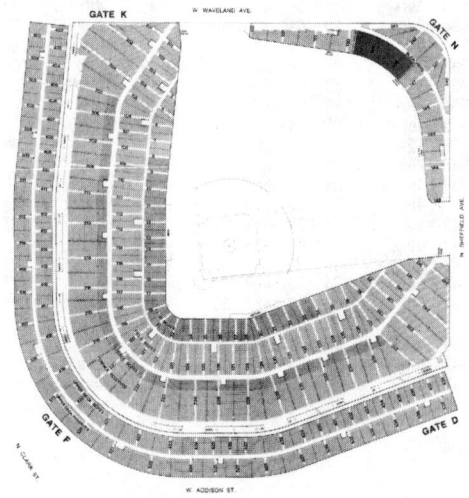

MINOR LEAGUE AFFILIATES

Class	Team	League	Manager
AAA	Iowa	American Association	Rick Patterson
AA	Orlando	Southern	Dave Trembley
A	Daytona	Florida State	Ken Bolek
A	Peoria	Midwest	Steve Roadcap
A	Williamsport	New York-Pennsylvania	Jerry Weinstein
Rookie	Huntington	Appalachian	Steve Kolinsky
Rookie	Osceola Cubs	Gulf Coast	John Noce

BROADCAST INFORMATION

Radio: WGN-AM (720). Broadcasters: Harry Caray, Thom Brennaman, Ron Santo.
TV: WGN-TV (Channel 9). Broadcasters: Harry Caray, Steve Stone, Thom Brennaman.
Cable TV: CLTV. Broadcasters: Harry Caray, Steve Stone.

SPRING TRAINING

Ballpark (city): HoHoKam Park (Mesa, Ariz.).
Ticket information: 800-638-4253.

HISTORY

YEAR-BY-YEAR RECORDS

Year	Pos.	W	L	Pct.	GB	Year	Pos.	W	L	Pct.	GB
1901	6th	53	86	.381	37	1949	8th	61	93	.396	36
1902	5th	68	69	.496	34	1950	7th	64	89	.418	26½
1903	3rd	82	56	.594	8	1951	8th	62	92	.403	34½
1904	2nd	93	60	.608	13	1952	5th	77	77	.500	19½
1905	3rd	92	61	.601	13	1953	7th	65	89	.422	40
1906	1st	116	36	.763	+20	1954	7th	64	90	.416	33
1907	1st	107	45	.704	+17	1955	6th	72	81	.471	26
1908	1st	99	55	.643	+1	1956	8th	60	94	.390	33
1909	2nd	104	49	.680	6½	1957	T7th	62	92	.403	33
1910	1st	104	50	.675	+13	1958	T5th	72	82	.468	20
1911	2nd	92	62	.597	7½	1959	T5th	74	80	.481	13
1912	3rd	91	59	.607	11½	1960	7th	60	94	.390	35
1913	3rd	88	65	.575	13½	1961	7th	64	90	.416	29
1914	4th	78	76	.506	16½	1962	9th	59	103	.364	42½
1915	4th	73	80	.477	17½	1963	7th	82	80	.506	17
1916	5th	67	86	.438	26½	1964	8th	76	86	.469	17
1917	5th	74	80	.481	24	1965	8th	72	90	.444	25
1918	1st	84	45	.651	+10½	1966	10th	59	103	.364	36
1919	3rd	75	65	.536	21	1967	3rd	87	74	.540	14
1920	T5th	75	79	.487	18	1968	3rd	84	78	.519	13
1921	7th	64	89	.418	30	1969	2nd	92	70	.568	8
1922	5th	80	74	.519	13	1970	2nd	84	78	.519	5
1923	4th	83	71	.539	12½	1971	T3rd	83	79	.512	14
1924	5th	81	72	.529	12	1972	2nd	85	70	.548	11
1925	8th	68	86	.442	27½	1973	5th	77	84	.478	5
1926	4th	82	72	.532	7	1974	6th	66	96	.407	22
1927	4th	85	68	.556	8½	1975	T5th	75	87	.463	17½
1928	3rd	91	63	.591	4	1976	4th	75	87	.463	26
1929	1st	98	54	.645	+10½	1977	4th	81	81	.500	20
1930	2nd	90	64	.584	2	1978	3rd	79	83	.488	11
1931	3rd	84	70	.545	17	1979	5th	80	82	.494	18
1932	1st	90	64	.584	+4	1980	6th	64	98	.395	27
1933	3rd	86	68	.558	6	1981	6th/5th	38	65	.369	*
1934	3rd	86	65	.570	8	1982	5th	73	89	.451	19
1935	1st	100	54	.649	+4	1983	5th	71	91	.438	19
1936	T2nd	87	67	.565	5	1984	1st†	96	65	.596	+6½
1937	2nd	93	61	.604	3	1985	4th	77	84	.478	23½
1938	1st	89	63	.586	+2	1986	5th	70	90	.438	37
1939	4th	84	70	.545	13	1987	6th	76	85	.472	18½
1940	5th	75	79	.487	25½	1988	4th	77	85	.475	24
1941	6th	70	84	.455	30	1989	1st†	93	69	.574	+6
1942	6th	68	86	.442	38	1990	T4th	77	85	.475	18
1943	5th	74	79	.484	30½	1991	4th	77	83	.481	20
1944	4th	75	79	.487	30	1992	4th	78	84	.481	18
1945	1st	98	56	.636	+3	1993	4th	84	78	.519	13
1946	3rd	82	71	.536	14½						
1947	6th	69	85	.448	25						
1948	8th	64	90	.416	27½						

*First half 15-37; second 23-28.
†Lost Championship Series.

MANAGERS

Name	Record	Years
Tom Loftus	53-86	'01
Frank Selee	295-223	'02-05
Frank Chance	753-379	'05-12
Johnny Evers	130-121	'13, '21
Hank O'Day	78-76	1914
Roger Bresnahan	73-80	1915
Joe Tinker	67-86	1916
Fred Mitchell	308-269	'17-20
Bill Killefer	299-292	'21-25
Rabbit Maranville	23-30	1925
George Gibson	12-14	1925
Joe McCarthy	442-321	'26-30
Rogers Hornsby	141-114	'30-32
Charlie Grimm	946-784	'32-38, '44-49, 1960
Gabby Hartnett	203-176	'38-40
Jimmy Wilson	213-258	'41-44
Roy Johnson	0-1	1944
Frank Frisch	141-196	'49-51
Phil Cavarretta	169-213	'51-53
Stan Hack	196-265	'54-56
Bob Scheffing	208-254	'57-59
Lou Boudreau	54-83	1960
Vedie Himsl*	10-21	1961
Harry Craft*	7-9	1961
Elvin Tappe*	46-69	'61-62
Lou Klein*	65-83	'61-62, 1965
Charlie Metro*	43-69	1962
Bob Kennedy	182-198	'63-65
Leo Durocher	535-526	'66-72
Whitey Lockman	157-162	'72-74
Jim Marshall	175-218	'74-76
Herman Franks	238-241	'77-79
Joe Amalfitano	66-116	1979, '80-81
Preston Gomez	38-52	1980
Lee Elia	127-158	'82-83
Charlie Fox	17-22	1983
Jim Frey	196-182	'84-86
John Vukovich	1-1	1986
Gene Michael	114-124	'86-87
Frank Lucchesi	8-17	1987
Don Zimmer	265-259	'88-91
Jim Essian	59-63	1991
Jim Lefebvre	162-162	'92-93

*College of Coaches.

DAY BY DAY

Date	Opp.	Res.	Score	(inn.*)	Hits	Opp. hits	Winning pitcher	Losing pitcher	Save	Record	Pos.	GB
4-5	Atl.	L	0-1		5	5	Maddux	Morgan	Stanton	0-1	T6th	1
4-6	Atl.	W	1-0		6	1	Guzman	Smoltz		1-1	T4th	1
4-7	Atl.	L	4-5	(10)	13	12	Howell	Scanlan		1-2	T6th	2
4-9	At Phi.	W	11-7		13	10	McElroy	Rivera	Myers	2-2	T5th	1½
4-10	At Phi.	L	4-5		3	7	Mulholland	Morgan	Mit. Williams	2-3	T5th	2
4-11	At Phi.	L	0-3		4	5	Schilling	Guzman		2-4	T6th	3
4-12	At Atl.	W	5-1		14	7	Hibbard	Avery		3-4	5th	3
4-13	At Atl.	L	2-3		7	9	Glavine	Castillo	Stanton	3-5	6th	4
4-14	At Atl.	W	6-0		10	6	Harkey	Smith		4-5	5th	4
4-16	Phi.	W	3-1		8	8	Morgan	Mulholland	Myers	5-5	T5th	3
4-17	Phi.	W	6-3		10	5	Guzman	Schilling	Myers	6-5	5th	2
4-18	Phi.	L	10-11	(11)	14	15	Mit. Williams	Scanlan	West	6-6	T5th	3
4-20	Hou.	W	2-1		6	3	Harkey	Portugal	Myers	7-6	T3rd	3
4-21	Hou.	L	0-2		6	10	Drabek	Morgan		7-7	T5th	3½
4-23	Cin.	W	7-4		11	11	Guzman	Pugh	Myers	8-7	T4th	3
4-24	Cin.	L	5-15		13	15	Browning	Hibbard		8-8	T4th	4
4-25	Cin.	W	2-1		8	3	Assenmacher	Belcher		9-8	4th	4
4-26	At Col.	W	6-3		10	16	Harkey	Nied	Myers	10-8	4th	4
4-27	At Col.	L	2-11		9	11	Henry	Morgan		10-9	5th	4
4-28	At Hou.	L	1-6		7	8	Swindell	Guzman		10-10	5th	5
4-29	At Hou.	L	4-5		8	11	Harnisch	Hibbard	D. Jones	10-11	5th	6
4-30	At Cin.	W	7-3		11	8	Slocumb	Belcher		11-11	T4th	6
5-1	At Cin.	L	4-9		9	16	Rijo	Harkey		11-12	T4th	6
5-2	At Cin.	W	4-3		10	5	Morgan	Smiley	Myers	12-12	T4th	6
5-4	Col.	L	13-14	(11)	21	17	Blair	McElroy		12-13	T4th	7
5-5	Col.	W	3-2		7	5	Hibbard	Reynoso	Myers	13-13	T4th	6
5-7	S.D.	L	1-2		6	6	Benes	Morgan	Ge. Harris	13-14	T4th	6½
5-8	S.D.	W	8-6		11	11	McElroy	Gomez	Myers	14-14	T4th	7
5-9	S.D.	L	4-5		13	10	Gr. Harris	Guzman	Ge. Harris	14-15	5th	8
5-10	L.A.	W	6-2		11	3	Hibbard	Astacio		15-15	T3rd	8
5-11	L.A.	W	2-1	(10)	13	8	Scanlan	Gott		16-15	T3rd	7
5-12	L.A.	L	3-9		8	16	McDowell	Morgan		16-16	T4th	8
5-14	Pit.	W	3-2		8	10	Harkey	Cooke	Myers	17-16	4th	7
5-15	Pit.	W	14-5		19	10	Guzman	Wakefield		18-16	3rd	6
5-16	Pit.	L	3-5		9	8	Walk	Hibbard	Belinda	18-17	4th	7
5-18	At St.L.	W	4-1		9	6	Castillo	Olivares	Myers	19-17	3rd	7½
5-19	At St.L.	W	5-3		8	8	Morgan	Murphy	Myers	20-17	3rd	6½
5-20	At St.L.	L	3-6		6	11	Tewksbury	Guzman	Smith	20-18	3rd	7½
5-21	At Fla.	L	3-5		9	9	Hoffman	Assenmacher	Harvey	20-19	4th	7½
5-22	At Fla.	W	2-1		8	7	Hibbard	Aquino	Myers	21-19	3rd	6½
5-23	At Fla.	L	2-4		6	6	Armstrong	Castillo	Harvey	21-20	4th	7½
5-25	S.F.	L	4-5		12	10	Burba	Myers	Beck	21-21	T4th	9
5-26	S.F.	W	4-2		6	8	Harkey	Swift	Myers	22-21	3rd	8
5-27	S.F.	W	5-4		9	13	Hibbard	Hickerson	Myers	23-21	3rd	7½
5-28	Mon.	T	2-2	(5)	4	7	....	....		23-21	3rd	8
5-29	Mon.	L	4-5		9	8	Martinez	Scanlan	Wetteland	23-22	3rd	9
5-30	Mon.	W	5-2		9	4	Bautista	Shaw		24-22	3rd	9
5-31	N.Y.	L	5-9		13	11	Gibson	Harkey		24-23	3rd	9
6-1	N.Y.	W	8-3		12	9	Hibbard	Draper	Myers	25-23	3rd	9
6-2	N.Y.	L	3-11		9	16	Gooden	Castillo		25-24	3rd	10
6-3	At Mon.	L	1-7		5	8	Martinez	Morgan		25-25	5th	10½
6-4	At Mon.	L	1-3		7	5	Shaw	Guzman	Wetteland	25-26	5th	10½
6-5	At Mon.	L	3-6		8	7	Fassero	Bautista	Wetteland	25-27	5th	11½
6-6	At Mon.	W	4-1		9	8	Hibbard	Hill	Myers	26-27	5th	11½
6-7	At N.Y.	L	2-7		7	12	Gooden	Castillo		26-28	5th	12½
6-8	At N.Y.	W	5-1		12	6	Morgan	Young	Myers	27-28	T4th	11½
6-9	At N.Y.	W	8-3		14	8	Guzman	Tanana		28-28	T4th	11½
6-11	At S.F.	L	2-7		8	13	Wilson	Hibbard		28-29	4th	13
6-12	At S.F.	L	4-5		7	14	Swift	McElroy	Beck	28-30	4th	14
6-13	At S.F.	L	3-5		9	11	Burkett	Morgan	Beck	28-31	5th	15
6-14	Fla.	W	6-3		12	7	Guzman	Armstrong	Myers	29-31	5th	14
6-15	Fla.	W	3-0		8	5	Castillo	Hough	Myers	30-31	4th	14
6-16	Fla.	W	6-4		9	8	Bullinger	Aquino	Myers	31-31	4th	13
6-17	St.L.	L	10-11		19	17	Cormier	Wendell	Smith	31-32	4th	13
6-18	St.L.	W	8-3		13	10	Boskie	Arocha	Myers	32-32	4th	13
6-19	St.L.	L	4-6		6	12	Osborne	Guzman	Smith	32-33	4th	14
6-20	St.L.	L	4-7		11	13	Tewksbury	Castillo	Smith	32-34	4th	15
6-21	At Pit.	W	5-1		7	4	Bautista	Smith		33-34	4th	14
6-22	At Pit.	L	2-7		3	10	Walk	Wendell		33-35	4th	15
6-23	At Pit.	L	4-9		15	12	Wagner	Boskie	Belinda	33-36	5th	16

Date	Opp.	Res.	Score	(inn.*)	Hits	Opp. hits	Winning pitcher	Losing pitcher	Save	Record	Pos.	GB
6-25	At L.A.	W	8-5	(10)	8	9	Myers	Gott		34-36	4th	16
6-26	At L.A.	L	4-5		10	11	McDowell	Scanlan	Gott	34-37	5th	16
6-27	At L.A.	L	1-3		6	12	Ke. Gross	Bautista		34-38	5th	16
6-28	At S.D.	W	4-3	(11)	10	9	Assenmacher	Mason	Myers	35-38	5th	15
6-29	At S.D.	W	10-5		15	11	Morgan	Worrell		36-38	5th	15
6-30	At S.D.	W	4-1		11	6	Guzman	Whitehurst	Myers	37-38	4th	14
7-2	At Col.	W	11-8		21	13	Bautista	Shepherd	Myers	38-38	4th	13
7-3	At Col.	L	4-5		8	13	Reed	Myers		38-39	4th	13
7-4	At Col.	L	1-3		5	10	Parrett	Morgan	Holmes	38-40	4th	14
7-5	At Col.	W	10-1		17	5	Harkey	Blair		39-40	4th	14
7-6	Cin.	W	3-2		10	12	Bautista	Rijo	Myers	40-40	4th	13
7-7	Cin.	L	3-4		9	13	Pugh	Hibbard	Dibble	40-41	4th	14
7-8	Cin.	L	3-7		9	10	Luebbers	Castillo	Reardon	40-42	4th	14
7-9	Hou.	W	5-2		9	5	Morgan	Drabek	Myers	41-42	4th	13
7-10 (1)	Hou.	L	0-4		1	7	Harnisch	Harkey		41-43	4th	14
7-10 (2)	Hou.	L	2-5		6	12	Williams	Guzman	Hernandez	41-44	4th	14½
7-11	Hou.	L	1-10		3	8	Portugal	Hibbard		41-45	5th	14½
7-15	Col.	W	1-0		5	5	Morgan	Blair		42-45	4th	13½
7-16	Col.	W	8-2		10	6	Guzman	Leskanic		43-45	4th	12½
7-17	Col.	W	5-1		7	5	Harkey	Reynoso		44-45	4th	11½
7-18	Col.	W	12-2	(7)	17	6	Hibbard	Parrett		45-45	4th	11½
7-19	At Cin.	W	6-4		9	9	Castillo	Luebbers	Myers	46-45	4th	11½
7-20	At Cin.	L	3-8		8	14	Belcher	Morgan	Spradlin	46-46	4th	12½
7-21	At Cin.	W	4-1		10	2	Guzman	Reardon	Myers	47-46	4th	12½
7-22	At Hou.	L	4-9		9	12	Williams	Harkey		47-47	4th	12½
7-23	At Hou.	L	1-5		7	8	Portugal	Hibbard	D. Jones	47-48	4th	13½
7-24	At Hou.	W	7-6		13	10	Castillo	Harnisch		48-48	4th	12½
7-25	At Hou.	W	3-1	(11)	10	8	Scanlan	D. Jones	Myers	49-48	4th	11½
7-26	S.D.	W	9-6	(11)	13	9	Boskie	Mauser		50-48	4th	11
7-27	S.D.	L	0-8		5	16	Benes	Harkey		50-49	4th	12
7-28	S.D.	W	8-6		9	10	Boskie	Brocail	Myers	51-49	4th	12
7-30	L.A.	W	2-1		4	6	Castillo	Astacio	Myers	52-49	4th	11½
7-31	L.A.	L	2-7	(13)	8	14	P. Martinez	Scanlan		52-50	4th	12½
8-1	L.A.	W	10-4		13	7	Guzman	Hershiser		53-50	4th	12½
8-2	Pit.	W	12-10		14	13	Scanlan	Minor	Myers	54-50	4th	12
8-3	Pit.	L	3-7		8	14	Smith	Hibbard		54-51	4th	13
8-4	Pit.	L	5-6		11	10	Ballard	Boskie	Neagle	54-52	4th	13
8-5	Pit.	L	2-5		5	11	Tomlin	Morgan	Dewey	54-53	4th	14
8-6	At St.L.	W	6-4		10	7	Bautista	Smith	Myers	55-53	4th	13
8-7	At St.L.	L	1-4		5	8	Tewksbury	Harkey	Smith	55-54	4th	14
8-8	At St.L.	W	2-1		9	8	Hibbard	Osborne	Myers	56-54	4th	13
8-9	At Fla.	L	2-3		9	8	Bowen	Castillo	Harvey	56-55	4th	13½
8-10	At Fla.	L	2-3	(15)	4	11	Aquino	Boskie		56-56	4th	14½
8-11	At Fla.	L	11-12		17	16	Lewis	Myers		56-57	4th	15½
8-12	At Fla.	W	5-1		9	7	Harkey	Armstrong		57-57	4th	15½
8-13	S.F.	L	1-4		4	6	Wilson	Hibbard	Beck	57-58	4th	16½
8-14	S.F.	W	3-2		14	7	Myers	Jackson		58-58	4th	15½
8-15	S.F.	L	7-9	(11)	15	16	Rogers	Myers		58-59	4th	16½
8-17 (1)	Mon.	W	7-2		11	5	Guzman	Martinez		59-59	4th	16½
8-17 (2)	Mon.	L	4-6		12	12	Rueter	Harkey	Wetteland	59-60	4th	17
8-18	Mon.	W	2-0		7	4	Hibbard	Hill	Bautista	60-60	4th	17
8-19	Mon.	L	2-10		6	8	Fassero	Castillo		60-61	4th	17
8-20	Atl.	W	6-3		12	9	Morgan	Stanton	Myers	61-61	4th	17
8-21	Atl.	L	3-6		10	14	Freeman	Plesac	McMichael	61-62	4th	17
8-22	Atl.	L	3-4		7	11	Smoltz	Guzman	McMichael	61-63	4th	17
8-23	At Mon.	L	0-1		5	5	Rueter	Hibbard	Wetteland	61-64	4th	17
8-24	At Mon.	W	6-5		10	12	Plesac	Hill	Myers	62-64	4th	17
8-25	At Mon.	L	3-7		7	13	Fassero	Morgan	Wetteland	62-65	4th	18
8-27	At Atl.	W	9-7		9	13	Boskie	Wohlers	Bautista	63-65	4th	17
8-28	At Atl.	L	1-5		6	10	Avery	Guzman		63-66	4th	17
8-29	At Atl.	L	2-8		7	13	Glavine	Hibbard		63-67	4th	18
8-30	Phi.	W	10-6	(11)	14	11	Plesac	Mason		64-67	4th	17
8-31	Phi.	L	0-7		4	12	Rivera	Morgan		64-68	4th	18
9-1	Phi.	L	1-4		6	8	Mulholland	Harkey		64-69	4th	19
9-2	N.Y.	L	3-8		8	11	Jones	Guzman		64-70	4th	19½
9-3	N.Y.	W	4-3		8	7	Hibbard	Tanana	Myers	65-70	4th	19½
9-4	N.Y.	W	9-8		17	12	Bautista	Franco	Myers	66-70	4th	18½
9-5	N.Y.	W	2-1		7	3	Bautista	Franco		67-70	4th	17½
9-6	At Phi.	W	7-6		9	12	Harkey	Mike Williams	Myers	68-70	4th	17½
9-7	At Phi.	W	5-4		9	12	Guzman	Rivera	Myers	69-70	4th	16½
9-8	At Phi.	W	8-5		11	10	Hibbard	West	Myers	70-70	4th	15½
9-9	At Phi.	L	8-10		15	14	Jackson	Bautista	West	70-71	4th	16½
9-10	At N.Y.	W	12-10		16	14	Scanlan	Maddux	Myers	71-71	4th	16½
9-11	At N.Y.	W	4-3		7	6	Harkey	Young	Myers	72-71	4th	15½

Date	Opp.	Res.	Score (inn.*)	Hits	Opp. hits	Winning pitcher	Losing pitcher	Save	Record	Pos.	GB
9-12	At N.Y.	L	0-5	4	14	Fernandez	Brennan		72-72	4th	15½
9-13	At S.F.	W	6-5	11	14	Hibbard	Sanderson	Myers	73-72	4th	15½
9-14	At S.F.	W	8-1	13	5	Bautista	Deshaies		74-72	4th	14½
9-15	At S.F.	W	3-1	7	4	Morgan	Torres	Myers	75-72	4th	14½
9-17	Fla.	L	0-2	3	5	Armstrong	Harkey	Harvey	75-73	4th	14½
9-18	Fla.	W	6-5	10	14	Brennan	Lewis	Myers	76-73	4th	14½
9-19	Fla.	L	1-2	4	4	Hammond	Trachsel	Harvey	76-74	4th	14½
9-20	St.L.	W	6-5	13	8	Morgan	Murphy	Myers	77-74	4th	14½
9-21	St.L.	W	13-3	16	10	Bautista	Tewksbury		78-74	4th	14½
9-22	St.L.	W	11-9	13	15	Boskie	Arocha	Myers	79-74	4th	14½
9-24	At Pit.	W	8-3	11	11	Hibbard	Walk	Bullinger	80-74	4th	14½
9-26 (1)	At Pit.	L	1-5	5	9	Wagner	Trachsel		80-75	4th	14
9-26 (2)	At Pit.	L	0-1	5	4	Wakefield	Morgan		80-76	4th	14½
9-27	At L.A.	W	7-3	10	8	Bautista	Hershiser	Myers	81-76	4th	14½
9-28	At L.A.	L	5-6	8	8	Ke. Gross	Harkey	Gott	81-77	4th	15½
9-29	At L.A.	W	6-1	12	10	Hibbard	Astacio	Myers	82-77	4th	14½
10-1	At S.D.	W	8-5	9	6	Brennan	Seminara		83-77	4th	14
10-2	At S.D.	L	3-7	10	10	Brocail	Morgan		83-78	4th	14
10-3	At S.D.	W	4-1	9	5	Wendell	Whitehurst	Myers	84-78	4th	13

Monthly records: April (11-11), May (13-12), June (13-15), July (15-12), August (12-18), September (18-9), October (2-1).
*Innings, if other than nine.

HIGHLIGHTS

High point: The Cubs won 20 of their last 28 games to finish with a winning record for only the third time in the last 20 years.
Low point: Right before their late-season success, the Cubs were six games under .500 (64-70 on September 2) and 19½ games out of first place. At that point, the expansion Florida Marlins were only 7½ games behind fourth-place Chicago.
Turning point: The Cubs went 8-2 on a 10-game road trip to Philadelphia, New York and San Francisco in early September, including a three-game sweep of the pennant-contending Giants.
Most valuable player: First baseman Mark Grace. He led the team in batting average, on-base percentage, hits, doubles and runs batted in and won his second straight Gold Glove.
Most valuable pitcher: Closer Randy Myers. The lefthanded reliever set a National League record for saves and took part in 65 percent of the Cubs' wins (53 saves, two victories).
Most improved player: Catcher Rick Wilkins. In his first full major league season, he became the only Cub catcher other than Gabby Hartnett to hit 30 home runs with a .300 batting average.
Most pleasant surprise: Shortstop Jose Vizcaino. Although he wore down toward the end of the season, Vizcaino proved he could be an everyday shortstop. He had more at-bats last season (551) than he had in his pre-1993 major league career (491).
Biggest disappointment: Righthander Mike Morgan. When the Cubs lost Greg Maddux to free agency in 1992, they figured Morgan would fill a big part of the void. Wrong. Morgan was the only Chicago starter among the top four to compile a losing record (10-15).
Key injuries: The Cubs' former All-Star double-play combination of second baseman Ryne Sandberg and shortstop Shawon Dunston never played together all year. Dunston missed virtually the entire season following back surgery, and Sandberg missed the first and last months with hand problems.
Notable: Outfielder Sammy Sosa became the first 30/30 player in club history. ...Greg Hibbard's 15 victories made him the first lefty to lead the Cubs in wins since Ken Holtzman won 11 games in 1966.

— DAVE van DYCK

RECORDS

1993 regular-season record: 84-78 (4th in N.L. East); 43-38 at home; 41-40 on road; 39-39 vs. East; 45-39 vs. West; 16-27 vs. LHP; 68-51 vs. RHP; 66-58 on grass; 18-20 on turf; 41-47 in day-time; 43-31 at night; 26-25 in one-run games; 6-6 in extra-inning games; 0-2-1 in doubleheaders.
Team record last five years: 409-399 (.506, ranks 5th in league in that span).

TEAM LEADERS

Batting average: Mark Grace (.325).
At-bats: Sammy Sosa (598).
Runs: Sammy Sosa (92).
Hits: Mark Grace (193).
Total bases: Sammy Sosa (290).
Doubles: Mark Grace (39).
Triples: Dwight Smith, Sammy Sosa (5).
Home runs: Sammy Sosa (33).
Runs batted in: Mark Grace (98).
Stolen bases: Sammy Sosa (36).
Slugging percentage: Sammy Sosa (.485).
On-base percentage: Mark Grace (.393).
Wins: Greg Hibbard (15).
Earned-run average: Greg Hibbard (3.96).
Complete games: Frank Castillo, Jose Guzman (2).
Shutouts: Jose Guzman, Mike Morgan (1).
Saves: Randy Myers (53).
Innings pitched: Mike Morgan (207⅔).
Strikeouts: Jose Guzman (163).

GAMES BY POSITION

Catcher: Rick Wilkins 133, Steve Lake 41, Matt Walbeck 11.
First base: Mark Grace 154, Doug Jennings 10, Steve Buechele 6, Eddie Zambrano 2, Tommy Shields 1.
Second base: Ryne Sandberg 115, Jose Vizcaino 34, Eric Yelding 32, Tommy Shields 7.
Third base: Steve Buechele 129, Jose Vizcaino 44, Tommy Shields 7, Eric Yelding 7.
Shortstop: Rey Sanchez 98, Jose Vizcaino 81, Shawon Dunston 2, Eric Yelding 1.
Outfield: Sammy Sosa 158, Derrick May 122, Dwight Smith 89, Willie Wilson 82, Kevin Roberson 51, Candy Maldonado 41, Glenallen Hill 21, Karl Rhodes 21, Eddie Zambrano 4, Tommy Shields 1, Eric Yelding 1.

TOP DRAFT CHOICES

1a. Brooks Kieschnick, OF/RHP, University of Texas.
1b. Jon Ratliff, RHP, LeMoyne College (N.Y.).
1c. Kevin Orie, SS, Indiana University.
2. None.
3. Vee Hightower, OF, Vanderbilt University.
4. Miguel Montilla, SS, North Bergen (N.J.) High School.
5. Matt Miller, LHP, Monterey High School, Lubbock, Tex.
6. Pat Cline, C, Manatee High School, Bradenton, Fla.
7. Scott Kendrick, RHP, Monroe-Woodbury High School, Central Valley, N.Y.
8. Chris Bryant, LHP, Brandon (Fla.) High School.
9. Bob Morris, 3B, University of Iowa.
10. Jamey Price, RHP, Texarkana (Tex.) C.C.

CINCINNATI REDS
NATIONAL LEAGUE CENTRAL DIVISION

1994 SCHEDULE

N Denotes night game (any game starting after 5 p.m.).
▢ Home games shaded.
* At Three Rivers Stadium in Pittsburgh.

APRIL
SUN	MON	TUE	WED	THU	FRI	SAT
					1	2
3 STL	4 N STL	5	6 N STL	7	8 N PHI	9 N PHI
10 PHI	11 N MON	12 N MON	13 N MON	14	15 N PHI	16 N PHI
17 PHI	18	19 N PIT	20 N PIT	21	22 N FLA	23 FLA
24 FLA	25 N CHI	26 N CHI	27 N PIT	28 N PIT	29 N FLA	30 N FLA

MAY
SUN	MON	TUE	WED	THU	FRI	SAT
1 FLA	2 N CHI	3 CHI	4 N CHI	5 N HOU	6 N HOU	7 N HOU
8 HOU	9 N SD	10 N SD	11 N SD	12	13 N SF	14 N SF
15 SF	16	17 N ATL	18 N ATL	19 N ATL	20 N LA	21 N LA
22 LA	23 N COL	24 N COL	25 N COL	26 COL	27 N NY	28 N NY
29 NY	30 N MON	31 N MON				

JUNE
SUN	MON	TUE	WED	THU	FRI	SAT
		1 N MON	2 N NY	3 N NY	4 N NY	
5 NY	6	7 N STL	8 STL	9 N COL	10 N COL	11 N COL
12 COL	13 N LA	14 N LA	15 N LA	16	17 N ATL	18 N ATL
19 ATL	20	21 N SF	22 N SF	23 N SF	24 N SD	25 N SD
26 SD	27 N HOU	28 N HOU	29 HOU	30 N PIT		

JULY
SUN	MON	TUE	WED	THU	FRI	SAT
					1 N PIT	2 N PIT
3 PIT	4 N FLA	5 N FLA	6 N FLA	7 N PIT	8 N PIT	9 N PIT
10 PIT	11	12 * ALL-STAR GAME	13	14 N CHI	15 N CHI	16 N CHI
17 CHI	18 N FLA	19 N FLA	20 N FLA	21	22 CHI	23 CHI
24 CHI	25 N HOU	26 N HOU	27 HOU	28 N SD	29 N SD	30 N SD
31 SD						

AUGUST
SUN	MON	TUE	WED	THU	FRI	SAT
	1 SF	2 SF	3 SF	4	5 N ATL	6 N ATL
7 ATL	8 N ATL	9 N LA	10 N LA	11 LA	12 N COL	13 N COL
14 COL	15 N PHI	16 N PHI	17 N PHI	18 PHI	19 N STL	20 N STL
21 STL	22 N PHI	23 N PHI	24 N PHI	25 STL	26 N STL	27 STL
28 STL	29 N NY	30 N NY	31 N NY			

SEPTEMBER
SUN	MON	TUE	WED	THU	FRI	SAT
				1 N MON	2 N MON	3 N MON
4 MON	5 N NY	6 N NY	7 N NY	8	9 N MON	10 N MON
11 MON	12	13 N COL	14 COL	15 N LA	16 N LA	17 N LA
18 LA	19 N ATL	20 N ATL	21 N ATL	22 N SF	23 N SF	24 N SF
25 SF	26 N SD	27 N SD	28 N SD	29 N HOU	30 N HOU	

OCTOBER
SUN	MON	TUE	WED	THU	FRI	SAT
						1 N HOU
2 HOU						

1994 SEASON

CLUB DIRECTORY

General partner
  Marge Schott
President and chief executive officer
  Marge Schott
General manager
  Jim Bowden
Director, player development
  Sheldon Bender
Director, scouting
  Julian Mock
Special assistant to the general manager
  Gene Bennett
Senior advisor/player personnel
  Tony Robello
Senior advisor/baseball operations
  Larry Barton Jr.
Major league scouts
  Jack McKeon
  John Stearns
Controller
  Ernie Brubaker
Director, stadium operations
  Tim O'Connell
Director, ticket department
  John O'Brien
Director, season ticket sales
  Pat McCaffrey
Director, group sales
  Susan Toomey
Director, marketing
  Chip Baker
Director, publicity
  Jon Braude
Director, speakers bureau
  Gordy Coleman
Traveling secretary
  Joel Pieper
Assistant publicity director
  Joe Kelley
Assistant ticket director
  Ken Ayer
Assistant/baseball operations
  Darrell Rodgers
Chief administrative assistant
  Joyce Pfarr
Administrative assistant, business
  Ginny Kamp
Administrative assistant, scouting
  Wilma Mann
Admin. assistant, player development
  Lois Schneider

Scouting secretary
  Lois Hudson
Trainers
  Greg Lynn
  Doug Spreen
Field superintendent
  Gary Wahoff
Equipment manager
  Bernie Stowe
Scouts
  Johnny Almaraz
  Jeff Barton
  Ray Bellino
  Fred Blair
  George Brill
  Jim Conner
  Robby Corsaro
  Clay Daniel
  Ed DeBenedetti
  Robert Filotei
  Craig Gambs
  Jim Grief
  Don Gust
  Fred Hayes
  Les Houser
  Vincent Javier
  David Jennings
  Gordan Kelly
  Eddie Kolo
  Fred Leon
  Anthony Lowe
  John Luedtke
  Mike Mangan
  Jose Moreno
  Miguel Nava
  Jorge Oquendo
  Jerry Raddatz
  Tom Severtson
  Douglas Stewart
  Bob Szymkowski
  Lee Toole
  Marion (Bo) Trumbo
  Jim Vennari
  Mike Wallace
  John Walsh
  Tom Wilson
  Jeff Zimmerman
  Murray Zuk
Scouting consultant
  Paul Campbell

Manager—Davey Johnson (15).

Coaches—Bob Boone (8), Don Gullett (35), Grant Jackson (3), Ray Knight (25), Joel Youngblood (2).

No.	PITCHERS	B/T	Ht./Wt.	Born	1993 clubs
49	Brantley, Jeff	R/R	5-10/189	9-5-63	San Francisco
32	Browning, Tom	L/L	6-1/190	4-28-60	Cincinnati
56	Carrasco, Hector	R/R	6-2/175	10-22-69	Kane County
62	Courtright, John	L/L	6-2/185	5-30-70	Chattanooga
49	Dibble, Rob	L/R	6-4/230	1-24-64	Cincinnati
56	Ferry, Mike	R/R	6-3/200	7-26-69	Chattanooga
54	Foster, Steve	R/R	6-0/180	8-16-66	Cincinnati
39	Hanson, Erik	R/R	6-6/215	5-18-65	Seattle
36	Holman, Brian	R/R	6-4/190	1-25-65	Seattle
67	Jarvis, Kevin	L/R	6-2/200	8-1-69	Winston-Salem, Chattanooga
31	McElroy, Chuck	L/L	6-0/195	10-1-67	Chicago N.L., Iowa
42	Patterson, Ken	L/L	6-4/230	7-8-64	California
65	Pierce, Jeff	R/R	6-1/200	6-7-69	Birmingham, Chattanooga
55	Powell, Ross	L/L	6-0/180	1-24-68	Indianapolis, Cincinnati
40	Pugh, Tim	R/R	6-6/230	1-26-67	Cincinnati
27	Rijo, Jose	R/R	6-2/215	5-13-65	Cincinnati
44	Roper, John	R/R	6-0/175	11-21-71	Indianapolis, Cincinnati
47	Ruffin, Johnny	R/R	6-3/170	7-29-71	Birmingham, Nashville, Indianapolis, Cincinnati
34	Service, Scott	R/R	6-6/226	2-26-67	Indianapolis, Colorado, Cincinnati
57	Smiley, John	L/L	6-4/212	3-17-65	Cincinnati
48	Spradlin, Jerry	B/R	6-7/231	6-14-67	Indianapolis, Cincinnati
53	Wickander, Kevin	L/L	6-3/205	1-4-65	Cleveland, Cincinnati, Indianapolis

No.	CATCHERS	B/T	Ht./Wt.	Born	1993 clubs
33	Dorsett, Brian	R/R	6-4/222	4-9-61	Indianapolis, Cincinnati
9	Oliver, Joe	R/R	6-3/220	7-24-65	Cincinnati

No.	INFIELDERS	B/T	Ht./Wt.	Born	1993 clubs
29	Boone, Bret	R/R	5-10/180	4-6-69	Calgary, Seattle
20	Branson, Jeff	L/R	6-0/175	1-26-67	Cincinnati
18	Costo, Tim	R/R	6-5/230	2-16-69	Cincinnati, Indianapolis
60	Dismuke, Jamie	L/R	6-1/210	10-17-69	Chattanooga
12	Greene, Willie	L/R	5-11/184	9-23-71	Indianapolis, Cincinnati
28	Harris, Lenny	L/R	5-10/220	10-28-64	Los Angeles
52	Koelling, Brian	R/R	6-1/185	6-11-69	Chattanooga, Cincinnati, Indianapolis
11	Larkin, Barry	R/R	6-0/196	4-28-64	Cincinnati
23	Morris, Hal	L/L	6-4/210	4-9-65	Indianapolis, Cincinnati

No.	OUTFIELDERS	B/T	Ht./Wt.	Born	1993 clubs
4	Brumfield, Jacob	R/R	6-0/185	5-27-65	Indianapolis, Cincinnati
61	Gibralter, Steve	R/R	6-0/185	10-9-72	Chattanooga
50	Gordon, Keith	R/R	6-1/205	1-22-69	Chattanooga, Cincinnati
22	Howard, Thomas	B/R	6-2/208	12-11-64	Cleveland, Cincinnati
26	Hyzdu, Adam	R/R	6-2/210	12-6-71	San Jose, Shreveport
30	Kelly, Bobby	R/R	6-2/202	10-1-64	Cincinnati
7	Mitchell, Kevin	R/R	5-11/248	1-13-62	Cincinnati
16	Sanders, Reggie	R/R	6-1/186	12-1-67	Cincinnati

Ballpark (capacity, surface)
Riverfront Stadium (52,952, artificial)
Address
100 Riverfront Stadium
Cincinnati, OH 45202
Business phone
513-421-4510
Ticket information
513-421-7337
Ticket prices
$11.50 (blue level box seats)
$10 (green level box seats)
$10 (yellow level box seats)
$9 (red level box seats)
$8 (green level reserved seats)
$6.50 (red level reserved seats)
$3.50 ("top six" reserved seats)
Field dimensions (from home plate)
To left field at foul line, 330 feet
To center field, 404 feet
To right field at foul line, 330 feet
First game played
June 30, 1970 (Braves 8, Reds 2)

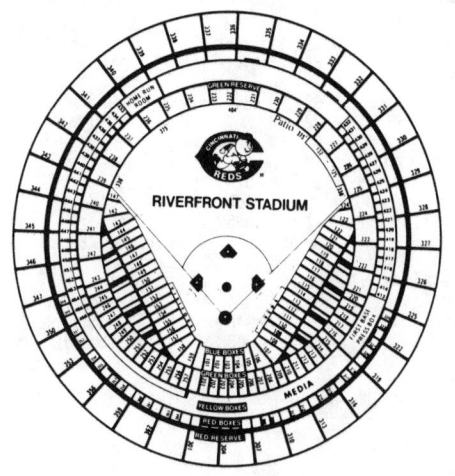

MINOR LEAGUE AFFILIATES

Class	Team	League	Manager
AAA	Indianapolis	American Association	Marc Bombard
AA	Chattanooga	Southern	Pat Kelly
A	Winston-Salem	Carolina	Mark Berry
A	Charleston, W.Va.	South Atlantic	Tom Nieto
Rookie	Billings	Pioneer	Donnie Scott
Rookie	Princeton	Appalachian	John Stearns

BROADCAST INFORMATION

Radio: WLW-AM (700). Broadcasters: Joe Nuxhall, Marty Brennaman.
TV: WLWT-TV (Channel 5). Broadcasters: Marty Brennaman, George Grande, Chris Welsh.
Cable TV: SportsChannel Cincinnati. Broadcasters: George Grande, Gordy Coleman.

SPRING TRAINING

Ballpark (city): Plant City Stadium (Plant City, Fla.).
Ticket information: 813-752-7337.

HISTORY

YEAR-BY-YEAR RECORDS

Year	Pos.	W	L	Pct.	GB	Year	Pos.	W	L	Pct.	GB
1901	8th	52	87	.374	38	1950	6th	66	87	.431	24½
1902	4th	70	70	.500	33½	1951	6th	68	86	.442	28½
1903	4th	74	65	.532	16½	1952	6th	69	85	.448	27½
1904	3rd	88	65	.575	18	1953	6th	68	86	.442	37
1905	5th	79	74	.516	26	1954	5th	74	80	.481	23
1906	6th	64	87	.424	51½	1955	5th	75	79	.487	23½
1907	6th	66	87	.431	41½	1956	3rd	91	63	.591	2
1908	5th	73	81	.474	26	1957	4th	80	74	.519	15
1909	4th	77	76	.503	33½	1958	4th	76	78	.494	16
1910	5th	75	79	.487	29	1959	T5th	74	80	.481	13
1911	6th	70	83	.458	29	1960	6th	67	87	.435	28
1912	4th	75	78	.490	29	1961	1st	93	61	.604 +	4
1913	7th	64	89	.418	37½	1962	3rd	98	64	.605	3½
1914	8th	60	94	.390	34½	1963	5th	86	76	.531	13
1915	7th	71	83	.461	20	1964	T2nd	92	70	.568	1
1916	T7th	60	93	.392	33½	1965	4th	89	73	.549	8
1917	4th	78	76	.506	20	1966	7th	76	84	.475	18
1918	3rd	68	60	.531	15½	1967	4th	87	75	.537	14½
1919	1st	96	44	.686 +	9	1968	4th	83	79	.512	14
1920	3rd	82	71	.536	10½	1969	3rd	89	73	.549	4
1921	6th	70	83	.458	24	1970	1st*	102	60	.630 +14½
1922	2nd	86	68	.558	7	1971	T4th	79	83	.488	11
1923	2nd	91	63	.591	4½	1972	1st*	95	59	.617 +10½
1924	4th	83	70	.542	10	1973	1st†	99	63	.611 +	3½
1925	3rd	80	73	.523	15	1974	2nd	98	64	.605	4
1926	2nd	87	67	.565	2	1975	1st*	108	54	.667 +20
1927	5th	75	78	.490	18½	1976	1st*	102	60	.630 +10
1928	5th	78	74	.513	16	1977	2nd	88	74	.543	10
1929	7th	66	88	.429	33	1978	2nd	92	69	.571	2½
1930	7th	59	95	.383	33	1979	1st†	90	71	.559 +	1½
1931	8th	58	96	.377	43	1980	3rd	89	73	.549	3½
1932	8th	60	94	.390	30	1981	2nd/2nd	66	42	.611	‡
1933	8th	58	94	.382	33	1982	6th	61	101	.377	28
1934	8th	52	99	.344	42	1983	6th	74	88	.457	17
1935	6th	68	85	.444	31½	1984	5th	70	92	.432	22
1936	5th	74	80	.481	18	1985	2nd	89	72	.553	5½
1937	8th	56	98	.364	40	1986	2nd	86	76	.531	10
1938	4th	82	68	.547	6	1987	2nd	84	78	.519	6
1939	1st	97	57	.630 + 4½		1988	2nd	87	74	.540	7
1940	1st	100	53	.654 +12		1989	5th	75	87	.463	17
1941	3rd	88	66	.571	12	1990	1st*	91	71	.562 +	5
1942	4th	76	76	.500	29	1991	5th	74	88	.457	20
1943	2nd	87	67	.565	18	1992	2nd	90	72	.556	8
1944	3rd	89	65	.578	16	1993	5th	73	89	.451	31
1945	7th	61	93	.396	37						
1946	6th	67	87	.435	30						
1947	5th	73	81	.474	21						
1948	7th	64	89	.418	27						
1949	7th	62	92	.403	35						

*Won Championship Series. †Lost Championship Series. ‡First half 35-21; second 31-21.

MANAGERS

Name	Record	Years
Biddy McPhee	79-124	'01-02
Frank Bancroft	9-7	1902
Joe Kelley	275-230	'02-05
Ned Hanlon	130-174	'06-07
John Ganzel	73-81	1908
Clark Griffith	222-238	'09-11
Hank O'Day	75-78	1912
Joe Tinker	64-89	1913
Buck Herzog	165-226	'14-16
Chris. Mathewson	164-176	'16-18
Heinie Groh	7-3	1918
Pat Moran	425-329	'19-23
Jack Hendricks	469-450	'24-29
Dan Howley	177-285	'30-32
Donie Bush	58-94	1933
Bob O'Farrell	30-60	1934
Chuck Dressen	214-282	'34-37
Bobby Wallace	5-20	1937
Bill McKechnie	747-632	'38-46
Johnny Neun	117-137	'47-48
Bucky Walters	81-123	'48-49
Luke Sewell	176-234	'50-52
Rogers Hornsby	91-106	'52-53
Buster Mills	4-4	'1953
Birdie Tebbetts	372-357	'54-58
Jimmie Dykes	24-17	1958
Mayo Smith	35-45	1959
Fred Hutchinson	443-372	'59-64
Dick Sisler	121-94	'64-65
Don Heffner	37-46	1966
Dave Bristol	298-265	'66-69
Sparky Anderson	863-586	'70-78
John McNamara	279-244	'79-82
Russ Nixon	101-131	'82-83
Vern Rapp	51-70	1984
Pete Rose	426-388	'84-89
Tommy Helms	14-21	1989
Lou Piniella	255-231	'90-92
Tony Perez	20-24	1993
Dave Johnson	53-65	1993

DAY BY DAY

Date	Opp.	Res.	Score	(Inn.°)	Hits	Opp. hits	Winning pitcher	Losing pitcher	Save	Record	Pos.	GB
4-5	Mon.	W	2-1		8	6	Rijo	Martinez	Dibble	1-0	T1st	...
4-7	Mon.	L	1-5		3	7	Hill	Smiley	Rojas	1-1	T3rd	½
4-8	Mon.	L	11-14		14	16	Barnes	Henry	Rojas	1-2	T3rd	1½
4-9	At St.L.	L	2-8		5	11	Arocha	Browning		1-3	T5th	2½
4-10	At St.L.	L	1-2	(10)	11	9	Perez	Foster		1-4	7th	2½
4-11	At St.L.	W	4-3		17	6	Pugh	Tewksbury	Dibble	2-4	7th	2½
4-12	At Phi.	L	4-5		6	6	DeLeon	Foster	Mit. Williams	2-5	7th	2½
4-13	At Phi.	L	1-4		4	9	Greene	Belcher	Mit. Williams	2-6	7th	3½
4-14	At Phi.	L	2-9		6	16	Rivera	Browning		2-7	7th	3½
4-16	N.Y.	L	1-3		8	5	Schourek	Rijo	Franco	2-8	7th	4½
4-17	N.Y.	L	1-4		6	7	Tanana	Smiley	Maddux	2-9	7th	4½
4-18	N.Y.	W	3-2		9	5	Foster	Saberhagen	Dibble	3-9	7th	4½
4-20	At Pit.	W	5-0		10	3	Belcher	Tomlin		4-9	7th	4½
4-21	At Pit.	W	8-7	(12)	16	14	Foster	Candelaria		5-9	7th	3½
4-22	At Pit.	L	4-5		4	9	Wakefield	Smiley		5-10	7th	4½
4-23	At Chi.	L	4-7		11	11	Guzman	Pugh	Myers	5-11	7th	4½
4-24	At Chi.	W	15-5		15	13	Browning	Hibbard		6-11	6th	4½
4-25	At Chi.	L	1-2		3	8	Assenmacher	Belcher		6-12	6th	4½
4-26	Fla.	W	3-0		5	3	Rijo	Hough		7-12	5th	3½
4-27	Fla.	L	3-4		12	4	Hoffman	Ayala	Harvey	7-13	T6th	4½
4-28	Pit.	W	4-2		5	11	Pugh	Otto	Reardon	8-13	T5th	4½
4-30	Chi.	L	3-7		8	11	Slocumb	Belcher		8-14	T5th	6
5-1	Chi.	W	9-4		16	9	Rijo	Harkey		9-14	5th	6
5-2	Chi.	L	3-4		5	10	Morgan	Smiley	Myers	9-15	T5th	7
5-4	At Fla.	L	6-9		8	12	Hammond	Pugh	Harvey	9-16	7th	7
5-5	At Fla.	W	6-2		6	9	Browning	Bowen		10-16	T6th	7
5-6	At Hou.	W	5-4		11	6	Hill	D. Jones		11-16	T5th	6½
5-7	At Hou.	W	7-5		12	9	Rijo	Swindell	Reardon	12-16	5th	6½
5-8	At Hou.	L	1-12		7	15	Kile	Smiley		12-17	T5th	6½
5-9	At Hou.	L	3-6		7	10	Harnisch	Pugh	D. Jones	12-18	6th	6½
5-10	S.D.	W	6-5		11	15	Browning	Taylor	Reardon	13-18	T5th	6
5-11	S.D.	W	4-2		9	7	Hill	Whitehurst	Cadaret	14-18	4th	5½
5-12	S.D.	W	3-2	(5)	7	5	Rijo	Benes		15-18	4th	5½
5-13	S.D.	W	7-1		10	5	Smiley	Eiland		16-18	4th	5½
5-14	Col.	W	13-5		15	10	Pugh	Ashby		17-18	4th	4½
5-15	Col.	W	5-3		10	11	Hill	Reynoso	Reardon	18-18	4th	4½
5-16	Col.	W	14-2		15	10	Roper	Nied		19-18	4th	4½
5-17	At L.A.	L	4-5	(10)	16	10	Gott	Landrum		19-19	4th	5½
5-18	At L.A.	L	1-9		6	8	Ke. Gross	Smiley		19-20	4th	6½
5-19	At L.A.	L	2-5		5	11	Candiotti	Pugh	Gott	19-21	4th	7½
5-20	At S.F.	L	1-6		5	11	Wilson	Browning		19-22	4th	8½
5-21	At S.F.	L	0-3		3	9	Swift	Belcher	Beck	19-23	4th	9½
5-22	At S.F.	W	6-2		11	9	Rijo	Black		20-23	4th	8½
5-23	At S.F.	L	2-3		5	5	Jackson	Landrum		20-24	5th	9½
5-25	Atl.	L	0-5		7	12	Glavine	Ayala		20-25	5th	10½
5-26	Atl.	W	4-0		7	1	Belcher	Maddux		21-25	5th	9½
5-27	Atl.	W	5-4		12	7	Cadaret	McMichael		22-25	5th	8½
5-28	At N.Y.	W	5-2	(10)	11	6	Smiley	Young	Ayala	23-25	5th	7½
5-29	At N.Y.	L	3-4		11	6	Tanana	Pugh	Franco	23-26	5th	8½
5-30	At N.Y.	W	8-4		14	6	Ayala	Schourek		24-26	5th	8½
5-31	Phi.	W	6-4		11	7	Reardon	Anderson	Dibble	25-26	5th	8
6-1	Phi.	L	3-6		9	11	Andersen	Cadaret	Mit. Williams	25-27	5th	8½
6-2	Phi.	L	2-5		8	10	Rivera	Smiley	Mit. Williams	25-28	5th	9½
6-3	St.L.	L	2-9		12	17	Kilgus	Pugh		25-29	5th	9½
6-5	St.L.	W	6-2		10	8	Belcher	Tewksbury		26-29	5th	9
6-6	St.L.	L	1-5		5	7	Magrane	Rijo		26-30	5th	14
6-7	At Mon.	W	12-3		18	8	Smiley	Heredia		27-30	5th	9½
6-8	At Mon.	L	2-4		8	8	Martinez	Pugh	Wetteland	27-31	5th	9½
6-9	At Mon.	W	3-2	(12)	11	11	Cadaret	Gardiner	Ayala	28-31	5th	9½
6-10	At Atl.	W	3-1		8	6	Belcher	Glavine	Dibble	29-31	5th	9
6-11	At Atl.	L	5-6	(11)	12	14	Stanton	Pugh		29-32	5th	10
6-12	At Atl.	L	2-7		5	9	Smoltz	Smiley		29-33	5th	11
6-13	At Atl.	L	2-9		9	12	Avery	Roper		29-34	5th	12
6-15	S.F.	W	10-5		17	12	Belcher	Brantley		30-34	5th	11
6-16	S.F.	L	5-6	(10)	9	10	Jackson	Ayala	Beck	30-35	5th	12
6-17	S.F.	L	1-5		1	9	Swift	Smiley		30-36	5th	13
6-18	L.A.	W	4-3	(10)	8	6	Ayala	Gott		31-36	5th	13
6-19	L.A.	W	8-4		19	10	Browning	Hershiser	Ayala	32-36	5th	13
6-20	L.A.	L	3-6		5	10	Astacio	Belcher	Gott	32-37	5th	14
6-21	At Col.	L	4-5	(10)	6	9	Reed	Reardon		32-38	5th	15

Date		Opp.	Res.	Score	(inn.*)	Hits	Opp. hits	Winning pitcher	Losing pitcher	Save	Record	Pos.	GB
6-22		At Col.	W	16-13		18	17	Wickander	Grant	Dibble	33-38	5th	14
6-23		At Col.	L	5-15		13	16	Parrett	Pugh		33-39	5th	15
6-24		At S.D.	W	6-4		13	10	Ayala	Mason	Dibble	34-39	5th	15
6-25		At S.D.	W	6-2		11	4	Belcher	Whitehurst		35-39	5th	15
6-26		At S.D.	L	0-2		5	6	Brocail	Rijo	Ge. Harris	35-40	5th	15
6-27		At S.D.	W	7-1	(11)	11	11	Dibble	Ge. Harris		36-40	5th	15
6-29		Hou.	W	3-0		7	6	Browning	Drabek	Dibble	37-40	5th	14½
6-30		Hou.	W	5-4		10	11	Reardon	Osuna		38-40	5th	13½
7-1		Hou.	L	1-8		8	10	Harnisch	Rijo		38-41	5th	14
7-2	(1)	Pit.	L	9-10		10	14	Otto	Ayala	Belinda	38-42	5th	15
7-2	(2)	Pit.	W	9-1		10	7	Pugh	Wakefield		39-42	5th	14½
7-3		Pit.	W	5-3		12	7	Luebbers	Walk	Dibble	40-42	5th	13½
7-4		Pit.	W	7-2		10	11	Browning	Wagner	Spradlin	41-42	5th	13½
7-5		Pit.	W	6-4		13	8	Belcher	Neagle	Dibble	42-42	5th	13½
7-6		At Chi.	L	2-3		12	10	Bautista	Rijo	Myers	42-43	5th	14½
7-7		At Chi.	W	4-3		13	9	Pugh	Hibbard	Dibble	43-43	5th	13½
7-8		At Chi.	W	7-3		10	9	Luebbers	Castillo	Reardon	44-43	5th	13½
7-9		At Pit.	L	1-4		8	9	Walk	Browning	Belinda	44-44	5th	14½
7-10		At Pit.	W	10-7		19	8	Service	Wagner	Dibble	45-44	5th	13½
7-11		At Pit.	L	2-3		7	9	Minor	Reardon		45-45	5th	14½
7-15		Fla.	W	7-4		10	7	Belcher	Hammond	Reardon	46-45	5th	14½
7-16		Fla.	W	4-0		10	8	Rijo	Rapp		47-45	5th	14½
7-17		Fla.	L	3-6		7	9	Armstrong	Browning		47-46	5th	14½
7-18		Fla.	W	5-3		8	6	Pugh	Hough	Dibble	48-46	5th	13½
7-19		Chi.	L	4-6		9	9	Castillo	Luebbers	Myers	48-47	5th	14½
7-20		Chi.	W	8-3		14	8	Belcher	Morgan	Spradlin	49-47	5th	14½
7-21		Chi.	L	1-4		2	10	Guzman	Reardon	Myers	49-48	5th	15½
7-22		At Fla.	W	7-3		10	10	Browning	Armstrong		50-48	5th	15½
7-23		At Fla.	W	3-2		5	9	Ayala	Lewis	Dibble	51-48	5th	14½
7-24		At Fla.	L	0-2		5	6	Bowen	Luebbers	Harvey	51-49	5th	15½
7-25		At Fla.	L	3-7		4	13	Nen	Belcher	Harvey	51-50	5th	16½
7-26		At Hou.	W	6-1		10	5	Rijo	Kile		52-50	5th	15½
7-27		At Hou.	L	5-6		9	10	Williams	Browning	D. Jones	52-51	5th	16½
7-28		At Hou.	L	2-4		12	10	Portugal	Pugh	Hernandez	52-52	5th	16½
7-30		S.D.	L	9-11		10	14	Hoffman	Reardon	Davis	52-53	5th	17½
7-31		S.D.	W	6-3		9	4	Rijo	Ashby	Dibble	53-53	5th	17½
8-1		S.D.	L	1-3		5	9	Benes	Browning	Ge. Harris	53-54	5th	18½
8-2		Col.	W	6-2		11	10	Pugh	Blair		54-54	5th	18
8-3		Col.	W	5-4	(10)	7	5	Spradlin	Leskanic		55-54	5th	18
8-4		Col.	W	9-3		13	9	Roper	Harris		56-54	5th	17
8-5		Col.	W	11-4		12	9	Rijo	Bottenfield		57-54	4th	17
8-6		At L.A.	L	2-3		8	11	P. Martinez	Dibble		57-55	4th	18
8-7		At L.A.	W	9-6		13	12	Spradlin	Hershiser	Dibble	58-55	4th	17
8-8		At L.A.	W	8-5		9	6	Ruffin	McDowell	Dibble	59-55	4th	16
8-9		At S.F.	L	7-10		12	14	Burba	Ruffin	Beck	59-56	5th	17
8-10		At S.F.	L	1-2		2	6	Swift	Rijo	Beck	59-57	5th	18
8-11		At S.F.	L	0-6		4	10	Burkett	Ayala		59-58	5th	19
8-13		Atl.	L	0-14		1	14	Avery	Pugh		59-59	4th	20
8-14		Atl.	L	2-4		3	6	Glavine	Roper	McMichael	59-60	5th	20
8-15		Atl.	L	0-1		4	5	Maddux	Rijo		59-61	5th	21
8-16		N.Y.	L	2-6		7	10	Fernandez	Luebbers	Maddux	59-62	5th	21½
8-17		N.Y.	W	6-0		9	7	Ayala	Gooden		60-62	5th	20½
8-18		N.Y.	L	2-12		5	12	Tanana	Pugh		60-63	5th	21½
8-20		Mon.	W	4-2		11	9	Reardon	Rojas	Dibble	61-63	5th	21
8-21		Mon.	L	3-6		4	9	Henry	Roper	Wetteland	61-64	5th	22
8-22		Mon.	L	2-7		6	15	Martinez	Ayala		61-65	5th	23
8-23		At N.Y.	W	6-2		6	6	Pugh	Gooden		62-65	5th	22
8-24		At N.Y.	L	4-5		4	8	Maddux	Spradlin		62-66	5th	22
8-25		At N.Y.	W	4-1		9	4	Rijo	Hillman		63-66	5th	21
8-27		At Phi.	W	8-5		10	8	Ruffin	Mit. Williams	Dibble	64-66	5th	20
8-28		At Phi.	W	9-5		15	12	Service	Thigpen		65-66	5th	19½
8-29		At Phi.	L	0-12		5	17	Jackson	Pugh		65-67	5th	20½
8-30		At St.L.	W	10-3		17	11	Rijo	Arocha	Ruffin	66-67	5th	20½
8-31		At St.L.	L	6-7		11	11	Murphy	Dibble		66-68	5th	20½
9-1		At St.L.	L	4-7		8	11	Tewksbury	Reardon	Perez	66-69	5th	21½
9-3		Phi.	L	2-14		3	13	Greene	Ayala		66-70	5th	22
9-4		Phi.	W	6-5		12	10	Rijo	Jackson	Service	67-70	5th	22
9-5		Phi.	L	3-5		8	15	Schilling	Pugh	Mit. Williams	67-71	5th	22
9-7	(1)	St.L.	W	14-13		19	17	Reardon	Murphy		68-71	5th	21½
9-7	(1)	St.L.	L	2-15		7	11	Tewksbury	Luebbers		68-72	5th	22
9-8		St.L.	W	6-2		10	12	Ayala	Watson	Ruffin	69-72	5th	21½
9-10		At Mon.	L	3-4	(10)	10	6	Rojas	Dibble		69-73	5th	21
9-11		At Mon.	L	2-4		7	9	Boucher	Powell	Wetteland	69-74	5th	22
9-12		At Mon.	L	2-3		7	10	Wetteland	Service		69-75	5th	22

— 108 —

Date	Opp.	Res.	Score	(inn.*)	Hits	Opp. hits	Winning pitcher	Losing pitcher	Save	Record	Pos.	GB
9-14	At Atl.	L	3-10		11	14	Glavine	Ayala		69-76	5th	23
9-15	At Atl.	L	6-7		13	13	Smith	Dibble		69-77	5th	24
9-16	At Atl.	L	2-3	(12)	10	10	Bedrosian	Service		69-78	5th	25
9-17	S.F.	L	0-13		7	17	Swift	Roper		69-79	5th	26
9-18	S.F.	L	1-6		6	9	Burkett	Pugh		69-80	5th	26
9-19	S.F.	L	3-7		8	6	Sanderson	Ayala		69-81	5th	27
9-20	L.A.	L	2-5		4	12	R. Martinez	Rijo	Worrell	69-82	5th	27½
9-21	L.A.	L	3-5	(11)	8	9	McDowell	Reardon	Trlicek	69-83	5th	28½
9-22	L.A.	L	1-3		6	8	Ke. Gross	Roper	Worrell	69-84	5th	28½
9-23	L.A.	W	11-2		11	7	Pugh	Candiotti		70-84	5th	28½
9-24	At Col.	L	2-9		4	10	Reed	Ayala		70-85	5th	28½
9-25	At Col.	W	6-0		11	1	Rijo	Harris		71-85	5th	28½
9-26	At Col.	L	7-12		12	12	Reynoso	Luebbers		71-86	5th	29½
9-28	At S.D.	L	4-11		6	15	Worrell	Powell		71-87	5th	29½
9-29	At S.D.	W	8-0		8	1	Pugh	Sanders		72-87	5th	29½
10-1	Hou.	L	0-2		8	10	Swindell	Rijo		72-88	5th	30
10-2	Hou.	L	1-3		5	10	Portugal	Powell	Hernandez	72-89	5th	31
10-3	Hou.	W	7-4		10	9	Ayala	Juden	Service	73-89	5th	31

Monthly records: April (8-14), May (17-12), June (13-14), July (15-13), August (13-15), September (6-19), October (1-2).
*Innings, if other than nine.

HIGHLIGHTS

High point: The Reds won a season-high seven straight games from May 10-16 to climb to within 4½ games of the first-place San Francisco Giants in the National League West.

Low point: Just one week after the winning streak ended, General Manager Jim Bowden fired rookie manager Tony Perez (over the phone). The team was demoralized by the departure of its popular leader and never recovered under new Manager Davey Johnson.

Turning point: On May 17 at Dodger Stadium, outfielder Cesar Hernandez, a defensive replacement, misplayed Cory Snyder's fly ball to left field in the ninth inning, a miscue that allowed Los Angeles to rally from a 4-1 deficit to a 5-4 victory. The defeat snapped the Reds' seven-game winning streak and set the tone for a 1-6 West Coast trip that ended with Perez's dismissal.

Most valuable player: Third baseman Chris Sabo. He led the team in home runs, doubles, games and hits and finished second in runs batted in.

Most valuable pitcher: Righthander Jose Rijo. He would have won 20 games with just a little support from the offense and the bullpen. The Reds scored only eight runs in Rijo's nine defeats, and the relief corps blew six Rijo leads in the eighth and ninth innings.

Most improved player: Catcher Joe Oliver, who established career highs in home runs (14) and RBIs (75).

Most pleasant surprise: Rookie right-hander Johnny Ruffin. Acquired from the Chicago White Sox for Tim Belcher on July 31, Ruffin went 1-0 with two saves and a 2.56 ERA in his final 18 appearances with the Reds.

Biggest disappointment: Lefthander John Smiley. The free-agent signee was 3-9 with a 5.62 ERA in 18 starts before being placed on the disabled list July 3 with a bone spur in his left elbow.

Key injuries: Who didn't get hurt? The projected starting eight (Oliver, Hal Morris, Bip Roberts, Barry Larkin, Sabo, Kevin Mitchell, Bobby Kelly and Reggie Sanders) played only four games together all year. All told, the Reds lost 798 man-games via the disabled list.

Notable: The Reds finished more than 30 games out of first place (31) for the first time since 1953. . . . Their record was 3-75 when trailing after eight innings. . . . The Reds' 12-game losing streak from September 10-22 was the club's longest since 1945. . . . The Reds used a team-record 51 players.

—JEFF HORRIGAN

RECORDS

1993 regular-season record: 73-89 (5th in N.L. West); 41-40 at home; 32-49 on road; 39-45 vs. East; 34-44 vs. West; 19-28 vs. LHP; 54-61 vs. RHP; 20-30 on grass; 53-59 on turf; 21-26 in daytime; 52-63 at night; 16-25 in one-run games; 6-8 in extra-inning games; 0-0-2 in doubleheaders.

Team record last five years: 403-407 (.498, ranks 7th in league in that span).

TEAM LEADERS

Batting average: Reggie Sanders (.274).
At-bats: Chris Sabo (552).
Runs: Reggie Sanders (90).
Hits: Chris Sabo (143).
Total bases: Chris Sabo (243).
Doubles: Chris Sabo (33).
Triples: Juan Samuel, Reggie Sanders (4).
Home runs: Chris Sabo (21).
Runs batted in: Reggie Sanders (83).
Stolen bases: Reggie Sanders (27).
Slugging percentage: Reggie Sanders (.444).
On-base percentage: Reggie Sanders (.343).
Wins: Jose Rijo (14).
Earned-run average: Jose Rijo (2.48).
Complete games: Tim Belcher (4).
Shutouts: Tim Belcher (2).
Saves: Rob Dibble (19).
Innings pitched: Jose Rijo (257⅓).
Strikeouts: Jose Rijo (227).

GAMES BY POSITION

Catcher: Joe Oliver 133, Dan Wilson 35, Brian Dorsett 18.
First base: Hal Morris 98, Randy Milligan 61, Joe Oliver 12, Juan Samuel 6, Brian Dorsett 3, Tim Costo 2, Jack Daugherty 2, Jeff Branson 1.
Second base: Juan Samuel 70, Bip Roberts 64, Jeff Branson 45, Jacob Brumfield 4, Brian Koelling 3.
Third base: Chris Sabo 148, Jeff Branson 14, Willie Greene 5, Juan Samuel 4, Bip Roberts 3, Tim Costo 2.
Shortstop: Barry Larkin 99, Jeff Branson 59, Keith Kessinger 11, Willie Greene 10, Brian Koelling 2, Bip Roberts 1.
Outfield: Reggie Sanders 137, Jacob Brumfield 96, Kevin Mitchell 87, Bobby Kelly 77, Thomas Howard 37, Tim Costo 26, Cesar Hernandez 23, Gary Varsho 21, Greg Tubbs 21, Cecil Espy 18, Jack Daugherty 16, Bip Roberts 11, Randy Milligan 9, Tommy Gregg 4, Juan Samuel 3, Keith Gordon 2, Keith Hughes 2, Joe Oliver 1.

TOP DRAFT CHOICES

1. **Pat Watkins**, OF, East Carolina University.
2. **Scott Sullivan**, RHP, Auburn University.
3a. **Steve Wilkerson**, RHP, Grand Canyon (Ariz.) University.
3b. **Brad Tweedlie**, RHP, Western Carolina University.
4. **Samuel Osorio**, OF, Loiza, Puerto Rico.
5. **Paul Bako**, C, University of Southwestern Louisiana.
6. **David Caldwell**, LHP, Northeast Texas C.C.
7. **Darren Hall**, OF, Lincoln High School, San Diego.
8. **Pete Harvell**, LHP, University of Tennessee.
9. **John Ambrose**, RHP, Memorial High School, Evansville, Ind.
10. **Chris Sexton**, OF/2B, Miami (Ohio) University.

COLORADO ROCKIES
NATIONAL LEAGUE WEST DIVISION

1994 SCHEDULE

N Denotes night game (any game starting after 5 p.m.).
▨ Home games shaded.
* At Three Rivers Stadium in Pittsburgh.
DH Doubleheader.

APRIL

SUN	MON	TUE	WED	THU	FRI	SAT
				N 1		2
3	4 PHI	5	6 N PHI	7 PHI	8 N PIT	9 PIT
10 PIT	11 PHI	12	13 N PHI	14 N PHI	15 N MON	16 MON
17 MON	18 N FLA	19 N FLA	20 FLA	21	22 N CHI	23 CHI
24 CHI	25 N STL	26 N STL	27 N FLA	28 FLA	29 CHI	30 CHI

MAY

SUN	MON	TUE	WED	THU	FRI	SAT
1 CHI	2	3 N STL	4 N STL	5	6 N SD	7 N SD
8 SD	9 N SF	10 N SF	11 SF	12	13 N HOU	14 N HOU
15 HOU	16 N LA	17 N LA	18 N LA	19 N LA	20 N ATL	21 N ATL
22 ATL	23 N CIN	24 N CIN	25 N CIN	26 CIN	27 N MON	28 MON
29 MON	30 N NY	31 N NY				

JUNE

SUN	MON	TUE	WED	THU	FRI	SAT
			1 N NY	2	3 N PIT	4 N PIT
5 PIT	6 N NY	7 N NY	8 N NY	9 N CIN	10 N CIN	11 N CIN
12 CIN	13 N ATL	14 N ATL	15 N ATL	16 N ATL	17 N LA	18 N LA
19 LA	20 N HOU	21 N HOU	22 HOU	23	24 N SF	25 N SF
26 N SF	27 DH SD	28 SD	29 SD N	30 N STL		

JULY

SUN	MON	TUE	WED	THU	FRI	SAT
					N 1 STL	N 2 STL
3 STL	4 N CHI	5 N CHI	6 CHI	7 N FLA	8 N FLA	9 N FLA
10 N FLA	11 *	12 ALL-STAR GAME	13	14 N STL	15 N STL	16 N STL
17 STL	18 N CHI	19 N CHI	20 CHI	21	22 N FLA	23 N FLA
24 FLA	25 N SD	26 N SD	27 SD	28 N SF	29 N SF	30 N SF
31 SF						

AUGUST

SUN	MON	TUE	WED	THU	FRI	SAT
	1 N HOU	2 N HOU	3 N HOU	4 N HOU	5 N LA	6
7 LA	8 N LA	9 N ATL	10 N ATL	11 N ATL	12 N CIN	13 N CIN
14 CIN	15 N MON	16 N MON	17 N MON	18	19 N PHI	20 PHI
21 PHI	22 N MON	23 N MON	24 MON	25	26 N PHI	27 PHI
28 PHI	29 N PIT	30 N PIT	31 PIT			

SEPTEMBER

SUN	MON	TUE	WED	THU	FRI	SAT
				1 N NY	2 N NY	3 NY
4 NY	5 N PIT	6 N PIT	7 PIT	8 N NY	9 N NY	10 NY
11 NY	12 N CIN	13 CIN	14	15 N ATL	16 N ATL	17 ATL
18 ATL	19 N LA	20 N LA	21 LA	22	23 N HOU	24 HOU
25 HOU	26	27 N SF	28 SF	29 N SD	30 SD	

OCTOBER

SUN	MON	TUE	WED	THU	FRI	SAT
						1 SD
2 SG						

1994 SEASON

CLUB DIRECTORY

Chairman, president and CEO
Jerry McMorris
Executive vice president, operations
John McHale
Senior vice president/general manager
Bob Gebhard
Sr. v.p./secretary and corporate counsel
Clark Weaver
Senior vice president, chief financial officer
Hal Roth
Vice president, sales and marketing
Dave Glazier
Vice president, finance
Michael Kent
General counsel
Paul Jacobs
Assistant general manager
Walt Jocketty
Senior director of ticket sales
Sue Ann McClaren
Senior director of corporate sales
Tom Manoogian
Senior director of operations
Keli McGregor
Director of player development
Dick Balderson
Director of scouting
Pat Daugherty
Director of team travel
Peter Durso
Director of publications
Jimmy Oldham
Director of public relations
Mike Swanson
Director of stadium services
Kevin Kahn
Director of ticket operations
Chuck Javernick
Assistant director of player development
Paul Egins
Assistant director of scouting
Jay Darnell
Manager of community relations
Jackie Sarmiento
Manager of marketing services
Wendy Jobe
Manager of promotions and special events
Alan Bossart

Secretary, scouting department
Penny Biever
Special assignment scout
Jeff Scott
National cross-checker scouts
Herb Hippauf
Jeff Schugel
Regional cross-checker scouts
Bruce Andrew
Dave Holliday
Robyn Lynch
Major league advance scout
Pat Dobson
Major league scouts
Jim Fanning
Bill Harford
Mel Nelson
Scouts
Mark Corey
Ty Coslow
Dar Cox
Abe Flores
Mike Garlatti
Al Hargesheimer
Larry High
Bert Holt
Greg Hopkins
Pat Jones
Jimmy Lester
Bill Mackenzie
Frank Mattox
Brian McRobie
Danny Montgomery
Steve Murray
Lance Nichols
Art Pontarelli
Ed Santa
Reed Spencer
Ron Steele
Tom Wheeler
International scouts
Cristobal A. Giron
Julian Gonzalez
Angel Hermoso
Jim Hovorka
Atanacio Mendez
Jorge Posada

Manager—Don Baylor (25).

Coaches—Larry Bearnarth (36), Dwight Evans (24), Gene Glynn (2), Ron Hassey (29), Bill Plummer (41), Don Zimmer (23).

No.	PITCHERS	B/T	Ht./Wt.	Born	1993 clubs
54	Arteaga, Ivan	L/R	6-2/220	7-20-72	Burlington, West Palm Beach
19	Blair, Willie	R/R	6-1/185	12-18-65	Colorado
46	Bottenfield, Kent	B/R	6-3/225	11-14-68	Montreal, Colorado
49	Fredrickson, Scott	R/R	6-3/215	8-19-67	Colorado Springs, Colorado
44	Freeman, Marvin	R/R	6-7/222	4-10-63	Atlanta, Richmond
22	Harkey, Mike	R/R	6-5/235	10-25-66	Orlando, Chicago N.L.
31	Harris, Greg W.	R/R	6-2/195	12-1-63	San Diego, Colorado
48	Hawblitzel, Ryan	R/R	6-2/170	4-30-71	Colorado Springs
40	Holmes, Darren	R/R	6-0/200	4-25-66	Colorado, Colorado Springs
45	Leskanic, Curt	R/R	6-0/180	4-2-68	Wichita, Colorado Springs, Colorado
54	Moore, Marcus	B/R	6-5/195	11-2-70	Central Valley, Colorado Springs, Colorado
43	Munoz, Mike	L/L	6-2/200	7-12-65	Detroit, Colorado Springs, Colorado
17	Nied, David	R/R	6-2/185	12-22-68	Colorado, Central Valley, Colorado Springs
28	Painter, Lance	L/L	6-1/195	7-21-67	Colorado Springs, Colorado
35	Pisciotta, Marc	R/R	6-5/240	8-7-70	Augusta, Salem
39	Reed, Steve	R/R	6-2/205	3-11-66	Colorado, Colorado Springs
42	Reynoso, Armando	R/R	6-0/196	5-1-66	Colorado Springs, Colorado
18	Ruffin, Bruce	B/L	6-2/213	10-4-63	Colorado
30	Shepherd, Keith	R/R	6-2/197	1-21-68	Colorado Springs, Colorado

No.	CATCHERS	B/T	Ht./Wt.	Born	1993 clubs
7	Girardi, Joe	R/R	5-11/195	10-14-64	Colorado, Colorado Springs
32	Owens, Jayhawk	R/R	6-1/200	2-10-69	Colorado Springs, Colorado
16	Sheaffer, Danny	R/R	6-0/190	8-21-61	Colorado
22	Wedge, Eric	R/R	6-3/220	1-27-68	Central Valley, Colorado Springs, Colorado

No.	INFIELDERS	B/T	Ht./Wt.	Born	1993 clubs
15	Castellano, Pedro	R/R	6-1/180	3-11-70	Colorado Springs, Colorado
9	Castilla, Vinny	R/R	6-1/180	7-4-67	Colorado
37	Gainer, Jay	L/L	6-0/190	10-8-66	Colorado Springs, Colorado
14	Galarraga, Andres	R/R	6-3/235	6-18-61	Colorado
13	Hayes, Charlie	R/R	6-0/215	5-29-65	Colorado
4	Liriano, Nelson	B/R	5-10/165	6-3-64	Central Valley, Colorado Springs, Colorado
8	Mejia, Roberto	R/R	5-11/165	4-14-72	Colorado Springs, Colorado
20	Van Burkleo, Ty	L/L	6-5/225	10-7-63	Vancouver, California
22	Weiss, Walt	B/R	6-0/175	11-28-63	Florida

No.	OUTFIELDERS	B/T	Ht./Wt.	Born	1993 clubs
10	Bichette, Dante	R/R	6-3/225	11-18-63	Colorado
26	Burks, Ellis	R/R	6-2/205	9-11-64	Chicago A.L.
20	Johnson, Howard	B/R	5-10/195	11-29-60	New York N.L.
11	Sherman, Darrell	L/L	5-9/160	12-4-67	San Diego, Las Vegas
21	Young, Eric	R/R	5-9/180	5-18-67	Colorado

Ballpark (capacity, surface)
  Mile High Stadium (76,100, grass)
Address
  2850 W. 20th Ave.
  Denver, CO 80211
Business phone
  303-292-0200
Ticket information
  303-762-5437
Ticket prices
  $16 (VIP field)
  $14 (infield plaza)
  $12 (VIP field, OF plaza, IF mezz.)
  $10 (OF plaza, OF mezz. and IF terr.)
  $8 (OF terr. and IF view)
  $5 (OF view and reserved pavilion)
  $4 (reserved general admission)
  $1 (rockpile—reserved)
Field dimensions (from home plate)
  To left field at foul line, 333 feet
  To center field, 423 feet
  To right field at foul line, 370
First game played
  April 5, 1993 (Mets 3, Rockies 0)

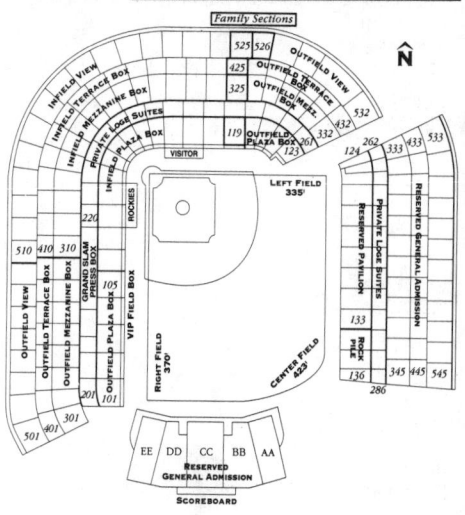

MINOR LEAGUE AFFILIATES

Class	Team	League	Manager
AAA	Colorado Springs	Pacific Coast	Brad Mills
AA	New Haven	Eastern	Paul Zuvella
A	Central Valley	California	Bill Hayes
A	Asheville	South Atlantic	Tony Torchia
A	Bend	Northwest	Rudy Jaramillo
Rookie	Chandler	Arizona	P.J. Carey

BROADCAST INFORMATION

Radio: KOA-AM (850). Broadcasters: Wayne Hagin, Jeff Kingery.
TV: KWGN-TV (Channel 2). Broadcasters: Charlie Jones, To be announced.
Cable TV: None.

SPRING TRAINING

Ballpark (city): Hi Corbett Field (Tucson, Ariz.).
Ticket information: 602-327-9467.

HISTORY

YEAR-BY-YEAR RECORDS

Year	Pos.	W	L	Pct.	GB
1993	6th	67	95	.414	37

MANAGERS

Name	Record	Years
Don Baylor	67-95	1993

DAY BY DAY

Date	Opp.	Res.	Score	(Inn.*)	Hits	Opp. hits	Winning pitcher	Losing pitcher	Save	Record	Pos.	GB
4-5	At N.Y.	L	0-3		4	8	Gooden	Nied		0-1	T5th	1
4-7	At N.Y.	L	1-6		2	10	Saberhagen	Ruffin		0-2	6th	2
4-9	Mon.	W	11-4		18	10	Smith	Bottenfield		1-2	T3rd	2
4-10	Mon.	W	9-5		7	12	Nied	Martinez		2-2	T2nd	1
4-11	Mon.	L	9-19		16	22	Jones	Henry		2-3	T5th	2
4-13	N.Y.	L	4-8		11	12	Saberhagen	Holmes		2-4	4th	2½
4-14	N.Y.	L	3-6		7	12	Fernandez	Smith	Maddux	2-5	5th	2½
4-15	N.Y.	W	5-3		4	6	Nied	Gooden		3-5	4th	2
4-16	At Mon.	L	2-3		6	5	Bottenfield	Henry	Rojas	3-6	5th	3
4-17	At Mon.	W	9-1		14	10	Ruffin	Martinez		4-6	5th	2
4-18	At Mon.	L	2-4		4	9	Hill	Wayne		4-7	6th	3
4-20	At St.L.	L	0-5		5	9	Arocha	Smith	Olivares	4-8	6th	4
4-21	At St.L.	W	11-2		14	6	Nied	Magrane		5-8	T5th	3
4-22	At St.L.	L	2-5		7	9	Perez	Wayne	Smith	5-9	6th	4
4-23	Fla.	W	5-4		7	12	Reed	Hammond	Holmes	6-9	T4th	3
4-24	Fla.	L	1-2		10	6	Aquino	Ashby	Harvey	6-10	5th	4
4-25	Fla.	L	1-11		6	14	Bowen	Smith		6-11	5th	4
4-26	Chi.	L	3-6		16	10	Harkey	Nied	Myers	6-12	6th	4
4-27	Chi.	W	11-2		11	9	Henry	Morgan		7-12	5th	4
4-28	St.L.	L	6-7		11	8	Murphy	Holmes	Smith	7-13	7th	5
4-29	St.L.	L	2-5		9	14	Tewksbury	Ashby	Smith	7-14	7th	6
4-30	At Fla.	W	6-2		12	6	Reynoso	Bowen		8-14	6th	6
5-1	At Fla.	L	6-7	(12)	11	11	Harvey	Reed		8-15	7th	7
5-2	At Fla.	W	2-1		6	7	Henry	Armstrong	Holmes	9-15	T5th	7
5-4	At Chi.	W	14-13	(11)	17	21	Blair	McElroy		10-15	5th	6
5-5	At Chi.	L	2-3		5	7	Hibbard	Reynoso	Myers	10-16	T6th	7
5-6	Atl.	L	3-13		3	15	Smoltz	Nied		10-17	7th	7½
5-7	Atl.	L	5-13		11	16	Freeman	Parrett		10-18	7th	8½
5-8	Atl.	L	7-8		11	9	Mercker	Fredrickson	Stanton	10-19	7th	8½
5-9	Atl.	L	7-12		14	11	McMichael	Reed		10-20	7th	8½
5-10	S.F.	W	7-4		7	13	Reynoso	Wilson		11-20	7th	8
5-11	S.F.	L	3-5		7	13	Swift	Nied	Beck	11-21	7th	8½
5-12	S.F.	L	2-8		3	16	Black	Henry		11-22	7th	9½
5-13	S.F.	L	8-13		14	13	Burkett	Ruffin		11-23	7th	10½
5-14	At Cin.	L	5-13		10	15	Pugh	Ashby		11-24	7th	10½
5-15	At Cin.	L	3-5		11	10	Hill	Reynoso	Reardon	11-25	7th	11½
5-16	At Cin.	L	2-14		10	15	Roper	Nied		11-26	7th	12½
5-17	At S.D.	L	0-4		3	6	Benes	Henry		11-27	7th	13½
5-18	At S.D.	W	2-1	(11)	11	9	Wayne	Rodriguez	Holmes	12-27	7th	13½
5-19	At S.D.	L	3-7		3	7	Gr. Harris	Painter		12-28	7th	14½
5-20	At S.D.	L	4-5	(11)	5	10	Ge. Harris	Holmes		12-29	7th	15½
5-21	At L.A.	L	0-8		5	12	Hershiser	Nied		12-30	7th	17
5-22	At L.A.	L	3-4		7	8	McDowell	Henry	Gott	12-31	7th	16½
5-23	At L.A.	L	0-4		3	4	R. Martinez	Blair		12-32	7th	17½
5-25	At Hou.	W	7-5		11	11	Wayne	Hernandez	Ashby	13-32	7th	17½
5-26	At Hou.	W	3-2		12	8	Smith	D. Jones	Parrett	14-32	7th	16½
5-27	At Hou.	L	0-8		7	12	Drabek	Nied		14-33	7th	16½
5-28	Phi.	L	9-15		15	20	Rivera	Henry		14-34	7th	16½
5-29	Phi.	L	0-6		6	8	Mulholland	Blair		14-35	7th	17½
5-30	Phi.	L	1-18		6	19	Greene	Painter		14-36	7th	18½
5-31	Pit.	W	6-2		12	9	Reynoso	Wakefield		15-36	7th	18
6-1	Pit.	L	6-8		12	12	Walk	Smith		15-37	7th	18½
6-2	Pit.	L	3-5		4	12	Petkovsek	Parrett	Belinda	15-38	7th	19½
6-4	At Phi.	W	2-1		7	10	Blair	Mulholland	Wayne	16-38	7th	18
6-5	At Phi.	L	2-6		7	9	Greene	Reynoso		16-39	7th	19
6-6	At Phi.	L	7-11		12	18	Schilling	Ashby		16-40	7th	20
6-8	At Pit.	W	4-1		9	4	Ruffin	Wagner	Shepherd	17-40	7th	19
6-9	At Pit.	L	1-4		7	9	Neagle	Blair	Belinda	17-41	7th	20
6-11	Hou.	W	5-4		8	12	Parrett	Hernandez	Holmes	18-41	7th	20
6-12	Hou.	W	14-11		20	13	Shepherd	D. Jones		19-41	7th	20
6-13	Hou.	W	9-1		14	6	Ruffin	Swindell		20-41	7th	20
6-14	L.A.	L	4-9		9	12	Astacio	Blair		20-42	7th	20½
6-15	L.A.	L	4-12		12	16	McDowell	Shepherd		20-43	7th	20½
6-16	L.A.	W	7-6		12	9	Reynoso	Ke. Gross	Grant	21-43	7th	20½
6-18	S.D.	L	1-11		8	12	Gr. Harris	Ruffin		21-44	7th	22
6-19	S.D.	W	17-3		18	9	Blair	Taylor		22-44	7th	22
6-20	S.D.	W	3-1		8	8	Reed	Mason	Holmes	23-44	7th	22
6-21	Cin.	W	5-4	(10)	9	6	Reed	Reardon		24-44	7th	22
6-22	Cin.	L	13-16		17	18	Wickander	Grant	Dibble	24-45	7th	22
6-23	Cin.	W	15-5		16	13	Parrett	Pugh		25-45	7th	22

— 113 —

Date	Opp.	Res.	Score (inn.*)	Hits	Opp. hits	Winning pitcher	Losing pitcher	Save	Record	Pos.	GB
6-24	At S.F.	L	2-17	7	20	Burkett	Blair		25-46	7th	23
6-25	At S.F.	L	2-7	8	12	Hickerson	Henry		25-47	7th	24
6-26	At S.F.	W	5-1	15	7	Reynoso	Wilson		26-47	7th	23
6-27	At S.F.	L	0-5	2	7	Swift	Leskanic		26-48	7th	24
6-29	At Atl.	L	4-6	7	10	Smoltz	Ruffin	Stanton	26-49	7th	24½
6-30	At Atl.	L	2-3	6	7	Wohlers	Shepherd		26-50	7th	24½
7-1	At Atl.	L	0-4	4	9	Glavine	Reynoso		26-51	7th	25
7-2	Chi.	L	8-11	13	21	Bautista	Shepherd	Myers	26-52	7th	26
7-3	Chi.	W	5-4	13	8	Reed	Myers		27-52	7th	25
7-4	Chi.	W	3-1	10	5	Parrett	Morgan	Holmes	28-52	7th	25
7-5	Chi.	L	1-10	5	17	Harkey	Blair		28-53	7th	26
7-6	Fla.	W	8-3	12	7	Reynoso	Hough		29-53	7th	26
7-7	Fla.	W	6-5	12	9	Reed	Harvey		30-53	7th	25
7-8	Fla.	W	3-2	5	3	Leskanic	Rapp	Holmes	31-53	7th	25
7-9	At St.L.	W	5-4	10	11	Moore	Smith	Holmes	32-53	7th	25
7-10	At St.L.	L	3-9	5	12	Osborne	Henry		32-54	7th	25
7-11	At St.L.	W	4-1	9	6	Reynoso	Tewksbury	Reed	33-54	6th	25
7-15	At Chi.	L	0-1	5	5	Morgan	Blair		33-55	7th	26
7-16	At Chi.	L	2-8	6	10	Guzman	Leskanic		33-56	7th	27
7-17	At Chi.	L	1-5	5	7	Harkey	Reynoso		33-57	7th	27
7-18	At Chi.	L	2-12	(7)	8	17	Hibbard	Parrett		33-58	7th	27
7-19	At Fla.	L	1-3	8	5	Bowen	Bottenfield	Harvey	33-59	7th	28
7-20	At Fla.	W	6-3	13	8	Blair	Hammond	Holmes	34-59	7th	28
7-21	At Fla.	L	4-6	10	11	Rapp	Leskanic	Harvey	34-60	7th	29
7-22	St.L.	W	7-6	14	10	Holmes	Burns		35-60	7th	29
7-23	St.L.	L	11-13	17	16	Watson	Reed	Smith	35-61	7th	29
7-24	St.L.	W	9-8	13	13	Bottenfield	Osborne	Holmes	36-61	7th	29
7-25	St.L.	L	4-5	(11)	10	15	Olivares	Wayne	Guetterman	36-62	7th	30
7-26	Atl.	L	7-12	11	14	Maddux	Leskanic		36-63	7th	30
7-27	Atl.	L	5-10	4	14	Smoltz	Reynoso		36-64	7th	31
7-28	Atl.	L	2-3	10	6	Wohlers	Reed	McMichael	36-65	7th	31
7-30	S.F.	L	4-10	9	16	Brummett	Harris		36-66	7th	32
7-31	S.F.	L	3-4	7	11	Swift	Bottenfield	Beck	36-67	7th	33
8-1	S.F.	L	5-6	9	6	Burkett	Reynoso	Beck	36-68	7th	34
8-2	At Cin.	L	2-6	10	11	Pugh	Blair		36-69	7th	34½
8-3	At Cin.	L	4-5	(10)	5	7	Spradlin	Leskanic		36-70	7th	35½
8-4	At Cin.	L	3-9	9	13	Roper	Harris		36-71	7th	35½
8-5	At Cin.	L	4-11	9	12	Rijo	Bottenfield		36-72	7th	36½
8-6 (1)	At S.D.	L	3-6	10	14	Benes	Reynoso	Hoffman	36-73	7th	37½
8-6 (2)	At S.D.	L	2-6	6	16	Sanders	Blair		36-74	7th	38
8-8	At S.D.	W	5-2	9	6	Sanford	Brocail	Holmes	37-74	7th	36½
8-9	At L.A.	W	3-2	(11)	9	9	Reed	Gott	Holmes	38-74	7th	36½
8-10	At L.A.	W	4-2	11	7	Bottenfield	Astacio		39-74	7th	36½
8-11	At L.A.	W	3-2	15	7	Reynoso	R. Martinez	Reed	40-74	7th	36½
8-12	At L.A.	W	4-1	6	7	Blair	Hershiser		41-74	7th	36
8-13	At Hou.	W	5-3	11	6	Wayne	D. Jones	Holmes	42-74	7th	36
8-14	At Hou.	L	0-9	3	12	Harnisch	Harris		42-75	7th	37
8-15	At Hou.	W	4-3	8	6	Ruffin	Hernandez	Holmes	43-75	7th	36
8-17	Phi.	L	7-10	12	15	Rivera	Reynoso	Mit. Williams	43-76	7th	36
8-18	Phi.	L	6-7	8	11	Thigpen	Ruffin	Mit. Williams	43-77	7th	37
8-19	Phi.	W	6-5	11	12	Moore	Mason	Holmes	44-77	7th	37
8-21 (1)	N.Y.	W	4-3	7	5	Harris	Innis	Holmes	45-77	7th	36½
8-21 (2)	N.Y.	W	8-6	10	6	Reed	Jones	Holmes	46-77	T6th	36
8-22	N.Y.	W	4-3	5	7	Munoz	Fernandez	Reed	47-77	6th	36
8-23	At Phi.	W	3-2	(13)	12	8	Wayne	Mason	Holmes	48-77	6th	35
8-24	At Phi.	L	2-4	6	8	Jackson	Blair	Mit. Williams	48-78	T6th	35
8-25	At Phi.	L	5-8	10	11	Schilling	Sanford		48-79	7th	35
8-26	At N.Y.	L	1-7	4	10	Gooden	Harris		48-80	7th	35½
8-27	At N.Y.	L	2-3	6	8	Fernandez	Bottenfield	Innis	48-81	7th	35½
8-28	At N.Y.	W	7-5	7	8	Reynoso	Jones	Holmes	49-81	7th	35
8-29	At N.Y.	W	6-1	9	5	Painter	Tanana		50-81	7th	35
8-30	Mon.	L	1-6	5	8	Fassero	Sanford	Rojas	50-82	7th	36
8-31	Mon.	L	3-14	13	15	Heredia	Harris		50-83	7th	36
9-1	Mon.	L	3-11	5	15	Martinez	Bottenfield		50-84	7th	37
9-3	Pit.	W	7-6	11	10	Holmes	Dewey		51-84	7th	36½
9-4	Pit.	W	10-4	14	13	Painter	Wakefield		52-84	7th	36½
9-5	Pit.	W	4-1	8	6	Ruffin	Walk	Holmes	53-84	T6th	36½
9-6	At Mon.	L	3-4	9	4	Scott	Reed	Wetteland	53-85	7th	36½
9-7	At Mon.	L	3-4	8	7	Martinez	Moore	Wetteland	53-86	7th	36½
9-8	At Mon.	L	1-6	6	9	Rueter	Reynoso	Scott	53-87	7th	37
9-9	At Pit.	W	10-7	(12)	16	11	Wayne	Johnston		54-87	7th	36
9-10	At Pit.	W	9-8	(11)	14	13	Moore	Minor	Holmes	55-87	T6th	35
9-11	At Pit.	W	3-2	11	5	Bottenfield	Wakefield	Ruffin	56-87	6th	35
9-12	At Pit.	L	3-4	9	6	Menendez	Munoz		56-88	T6th	35

Date	Opp.	Res.	Score	(inn.*)	Hits	Opp. hits	Winning pitcher	Losing pitcher	Save	Record	Pos.	GB
9-14 (1)	Hou.	W	9-4		16	14	Reynoso	Drabek	Ruffin	57-88	6th	35
9-14 (2)	Hou.	W	6-5	(10)	11	10	Holmes	Hernandez		58-88	6th	34½
9-15	Hou.	W	6-4		14	12	Munoz	Williams	Holmes	59-88	6th	34½
9-16	Hou.	W	6-3		13	10	Ruffin	T. Jones	Holmes	60-88	6th	34½
9-17	L.A.	W	12-3		17	10	Nied	Candiotti		61-88	6th	34½
9-18	L.A.	L	0-9		7	11	Astacio	Hurst		61-89	6th	34½
9-19	L.A.	W	8-5		12	7	Reynoso	P. Martinez	Holmes	62-89	6th	34½
9-20	S.D.	L	7-11		9	9	Seminara	Harris	Hoffman	62-90	6th	35
9-21	S.D.	W	15-4		17	7	Blair	Worrell		63-90	6th	35
9-22	S.D.	W	11-4		12	9	Nied	Benes		64-90	6th	34
9-24	Cin.	W	9-2		10	4	Reed	Ayala		65-90	6th	33½
9-25	Cin.	L	0-6		1	11	Rijo	Harris		65-91	6th	34½
9-26	Cin.	W	12-7		12	12	Reynoso	Luebbers		66-91	6th	34½
9-28	At S.F.	L	4-6		14	4	Hickerson	Nied	Beck	66-92	6th	34½
9-29	At S.F.	W	5-3		9	7	Reed	Torres	Holmes	67-92	6th	34½
10-1	At Atl.	L	4-7		6	6	Avery	Harris	McMichael	67-93	6th	35
10-2	At Atl.	L	1-10		5	14	Maddux	Reynoso		67-94	6th	36
10-3	At Atl.	L	3-5		6	12	Glavine	Nied	McMichael	67-95	6th	37

Monthly records: April (8-14), May (7-22), June (11-14), July (10-17), August (14-16), September (17-9), October (0-3).
*Innings, if other than nine.

HIGHLIGHTS

High point: From August 8 to the end of the season, Colorado went 31-21. The run included a four-game sweep of the Dodgers in Los Angeles, the first time an expansion team had ever taken a four-game series in the park of an established team. The streak allowed the Rockies to set an N.L. expansion record for victories (67) and avoid last place.

Low point: As if a 2-17 slide in May wasn't bad enough, Colorado endured a 13-game losing streak from July 25 through August 6.

Turning point: The Rockies reworked their rotation in July, which led to stability in the bullpen and success the final two months. The bullpen, which had a 7.18 ERA at the All-Star break, posted a 4.36 ERA in the second half. From August 1 to the end of the season, the relievers had a 3.79 ERA.

Most valuable player: First baseman Andres Galarraga. He became the first expansion player to win a batting title, hitting a big-league-best .370.

Most valuable pitcher: Righthander Darren Holmes. After struggling early, he was sent to Class AAA on May 5 with a 17.19 ERA. Upon returning May 17, he had 23 saves and a 2.43 ERA.

Most improved player: Lefthander Bruce Ruffin. His season and career turned around after July 1, when Colorado decided to make him a full-time setup man for Holmes. In that role, he went 3-1 with a 2.40 ERA.

Most pleasant surprise: Righthander Armando Reynoso. He wound up being the No. 1 starter, even though he didn't debut with Colorado until April 30. Reynoso finished at 12-11 with a 4.00 ERA.

Biggest disappointments: Righthanders Bryn Smith and Greg Harris. Both veterans failed to stabilize the rotation. Smith went 2-4 with an 8.49 ERA before being released June 2. Harris, acquired July 26 from San Diego, was 1-8 with a 6.50 ERA with Colorado.

Key injuries: Galarraga was disabled twice (right hamstring and right knee), missing 41 games. Righthander David Nied hurt his elbow June 3 and didn't pitch again until September 12.

Notable: The Rockies set a major league attendance mark, drawing 4,483,350 fans. . . . Galarraga and third baseman Charlie Hayes each drove in 98 runs, an expansion record, and Hayes set an expansion mark with 175 hits and 45 doubles. Right fielder Dante Bichette set an expansion record with 93 runs.

—TRACY RINGOLSBY

RECORDS

1993 regular-season record: 67-95 (6th in N.L. West); 39-42 at home; 28-53 on road; 36-48 vs. East; 31-47 vs. West; 14-27 vs. LHP; 53-68 vs. RHP; 53-72 on grass; 14-23 on turf; 26-32 in daytime; 41-63 at night; 26-20 in one-run games; 8-4 in extra-inning games; 2-1-0 in doubleheaders.

Team record last five years: 67-95 (.414, ranks 13th in league in that span).

TEAM LEADERS

Batting average: Andres Galarraga (.370).
At-bats: Charlie Hayes (573).
Runs: Dante Bichette (93).
Hits: Charlie Hayes (175).
Total bases: Charlie Hayes (299).
Doubles: Charlie Hayes (45).
Triples: Eric Young (8).
Home runs: Charlie Hayes (25).
Runs batted in: Andres Galarraga, Charlie Hayes (98).
Stolen bases: Eric Young (42).
Slugging percentage: Andres Galarraga (.602).
On-base percentage: Andres Galarraga (.403).
Wins: Armando Reynoso (12).
Earned-run average: Armando Reynoso (4.00).
Complete games: Armando Reynoso (4).
Shutouts: None.
Saves: Darren Holmes (25).
Innings pitched: Armando Reynoso (189).
Strikeouts: Bruce Ruffin (126).

GAMES BY POSITION

Catcher: Joe Girardi 84, Danny Sheaffer 65, Jayhawk Owens 32, Eric Wedge 1.
First base: Andres Galarraga 119, Jerald Clark 37, Jim Tatum 12, Pedro Castellano 10, Jay Gainer 7, Danny Sheaffer 7, Freddie Benavides 1.
Second base: Eric Young 79, Roberto Mejia 65, Freddie Benavides 19, Nelson Liriano 16, Pedro Castellano 4.
Third base: Charlie Hayes 154, Pedro Castellano 13, Jim Tatum 6, Freddie Benavides 5, Nelson Liriano 1, Danny Sheaffer 1.
Shortstop: Vinny Castilla 104, Freddie Benavides 48, Nelson Liriano 35, Pedro Castellano 5, Charlie Hayes 1.
Outfield: Dante Bichette 137, Jerald Clark 96, Alex Cole 93, Daryl Boston 79, Chris Jones 70, Eric Young 52, Dale Murphy 13, Gerald Young 11, Jim Tatum 3, Danny Sheaffer 2.

TOP DRAFT CHOICES

1. **Jamey Wright,** RHP, Westmoore High School, Oklahoma City, Okla.
2. **Bryan Rekar,** RHP, Bradley University.
3. **Joel Moore,** RHP, Bradley University.
4. **Doug Walls,** RHP, Muscatine (Iowa) C.C.
5. **Mike Zolecki,** RHP, St. Mary's (Tex.) University.
6. **Chad Gambill,** OF, Clearwater (Fla.) High School.
7. **John Thomson,** RHP, Blinn (Tex.) J.C.
8. **Kyle Houser,** SS, Duncanville (Tex.) High School.
9. **John Myrow,** OF, UCLA.
10. **Edgard Velazquez,** OF, Colegio Hostos High School, Puerto Rico.

FLORIDA MARLINS
NATIONAL LEAGUE EAST DIVISION

1994 SCHEDULE

N Denotes night game (any game starting after 5 p.m.).
▢ Home games shaded.
* At Three Rivers Stadium in Pittsburgh.

APRIL
SUN	MON	TUE	WED	THU	FRI	SAT
					1	2
3	4	5 N LA	6 N LA	7 N LA	8 N SD	9 N SD
10 N SD	11	12 N HOU	13 N HOU	14 N HOU	15 N SF	16 N SF
17 SF	18 N COL	19 N COL	20 COL	21	22 N CIN	23 N CIN
24 CIN	25 N ATL	26 N ATL	27 N COL	28 COL	29 N CIN	30 N CIN

MAY
SUN	MON	TUE	WED	THU	FRI	SAT
1 CIN	2	3 N ATL	4 N ATL	5 N PHI	6 N PHI	7 N PHI
8 PHI	9 N PIT	10 N PIT	11 N PIT	12	13 N CHI	14 N CHI
15 CHI	16 N NY	17 N NY	18 N NY	19	20 N STL	21 N STL
22 STL	23 N MON	24 N MON	25 N MON	26	27 N SF	28 N SF
29 SF	30 N HOU	31 N HOU				

JUNE
SUN	MON	TUE	WED	THU	FRI	SAT
			1 N HOU	2	3 N SD	4 N SD
5 N SD	6 N LA	7 N LA	8 N LA	9 N PIT	10 N PIT	11 N PIT
12 PIT	13 N STL	14 N STL	15 N STL	16 N NY	17 N NY	18 N NY
19 NY	20	21 N CHI	22 N CHI	23 N CHI	24 N MON	25 N MON
26 MON	27 N PHI	28 N PHI	29 PHI	30 N ATL		

JULY
SUN	MON	TUE	WED	THU	FRI	SAT
					1 N ATL	2 N ATL
3 N ATL	4 CIN	5 N CIN	6 N CIN	7 N COL	8 N COL	9 N COL
10 N COL	11	12 * ALL-STAR GAME	13	14 N ATL	15 N ATL	16 N ATL
17 ATL	18 N CIN	19 N CIN	20 N CIN	21	22 N COL	23 N COL
24 COL	25 N PHI	26 N PHI	27 PHI	28	29 N MON	30 N MON
31 N MON						

AUGUST
SUN	MON	TUE	WED	THU	FRI	SAT
	1 N CHI	2 CHI	3 CHI	4 N CHI	5 N NY	6 N NY
7 NY	8 N STL	9 N STL	10 N STL	11 N STL	12 N PIT	13 N PIT
14 PIT	15	16 N SF	17 SF	18 N SF	19 N LA	20 N LA
21 LA	22	23 N SD	24 N SD	25 N SD	26 N LA	27 N LA
28 LA	29 N SD	30 N SD	31 N SD			

SEPTEMBER
SUN	MON	TUE	WED	THU	FRI	SAT
				1	2 N HOU	3 N HOU
4 HOU	5 N SF	6 N SF	7 SF	8	9 N HOU	10 N HOU
11 N HOU	12	13 N PIT	14 N PIT	15 N PIT	16 N STL	17 N STL
18 STL	19 N NY	20 N NY	21 N NY	22	23 N CHI	24 N CHI
25 CHI	26 N MON	27 N MON	28 N MON	29 N MON	30 PHI	

OCTOBER
SUN	MON	TUE	WED	THU	FRI	SAT
					1 N PHI	
2 PHI						

1994 SEASON

CLUB DIRECTORY

Chairman
H. Wayne Huizenga
Exec. vice president and general manager
David Dombrowski
Vice president of business operations
Richard Andersen
Vice president of broadcasting
Dean Jordan
Vice president of finance & administration
Jonathan Mariner
Vice president of sales and marketing
Donald Smiley
Special counsel
James J. Blosser
Special consultant
Richard C. Rochon
Assistant general manager
Frank Wren
Director of scouting & special asst. to g.m.
Gary Hughes
Director of Latin American operations and special consultant to the general manager
Angel Vasquez
Director of player development & special asst. to g.m.
John Boles
Senior adviser, player personnel
Whitey Lockman
Director of minor league administration
Dan Lunetta
Associate director of scouting and director of international operations
Orrin Freeman
Director of team travel
John Panagakis
Asst. dir. of Latin American operations
Al Avila
Dir. of facility management
M. Bruce Schulze
Director of merchandising
Steve Stock
Director of ticket operations
Bill Galante
Director of international relations
Tony Perez
Director of group sales and advertising
Bob Kramm
Dir. of corporate sales and sponsorships
Neal Bendesky
Director of community relations
Jorge Arrizurieta
Director of player services
Bonnie Fisher Lundquist
Director of media relations
Chuck Pool
Assistant directors of media relations
Mark Geddis
Adolfo Salgueiro

Director of Brevard County operations
Ken Lehner
Equipment manager
Mike Wallace
Team physician
Dr. Dan Kanell
Head trainer
Larry Starr
Major league scouts
Ken Kravec
Scott Reid
John Young
National crosschecker
Jax Robertson
Regional crosscheckers
Dick Egan
Murray Cook
Greg Zunino
Scouts
Kelvin Bowles
Ty Brown
John Castleberry
Brad Del Barba
Lou Fitzgerald
William George
Jim Hendry
Stan Saleski
Stan Zielinski
Ed Bockman
Richard Bordi
Al Geddes
Bill Serena
Charlie Silvera
Keith Snider
Matthew King
Robert Laurie
Grady Mack
Steve Minor
Francis Oneto
James Pentland
Bill Scherrer
Tim Schmidt
Bill Singer
Wally Walker
DeJon Watson
Jeff Wren
Director Dominican Republic operations
Jesus Alou
Dominican Republic scouts
Edmundo Borrome
Julian Camilo
Pablo Lantigua
Puerto Rico scout
Cucho Rodriguez
Venezuela scout
Levy Ochoa

SPRING TRAINING ROSTER

Manager—Rene Lachemann (15).

Coaches—Marcel Lachemann (53), Vada Pinson (28), Doug Rader (12), Frank Reberger (33), Cookie Rojas (1).

No.	PITCHERS	B/T	Ht./Wt.	Born	1993 clubs
46	Bowen, Ryan	R/R	6-0/185	2-10-68	Florida
56	De La Hoya, Javier	R/R	6-0/162	2-21-70	San Antonio
50	Drahman, Brian	R/R	6-3/231	11-7-66	Nashville, Chicago A.L.
11	Hammond, Chris	L/L	6-1/195	1-21-66	Florida
34	Harvey, Bryan	R/R	6-2/212	6-2-63	Florida
49	Hough, Charlie	R/R	6-2/190	1-5-48	Florida
58	Klink, Joe	L/L	5-11/175	2-3-62	Florida
24	Lewis, Richie	R/R	5-10/175	1-25-66	Florida
59	Long, Steve	R/R	6-4/210	7-17-69	Binghamton
44	Miller, Kurt	R/R	6-5/205	8-24-72	Tulsa, Edmonton
47	Mutis, Jeff	L/L	6-2/185	12-20-66	Cleveland, Charlotte
32	Myers, Mike	L/L	6-3/197	6-26-69	Edmonton
31	Nen, Robb	R/R	6-4/200	11-28-69	Texas, Oklahoma City, Florida
48	Rapp, Pat	R/R	6-3/205	7-13-67	Edmonton, Florida
42	Rodriguez, Rich	L/L	6-0/200	3-1-63	San Diego, Florida
54	Turner, Matt	R/R	6-5/215	2-18-67	Edmonton, Florida
35	Weathers, Dave	R/R	6-3/205	9-25-69	Edmonton, Florida
38	Whisenant, Matt	B/L	6-3/200	6-8-71	Kane County
45	Yaughn, Kip	R/R	6-0/180	7-20-69	High Desert, Edmonton

No.	CATCHERS	B/T	Ht./Wt.	Born	1993 clubs
13	Natal, Bob	R/R	5-11/190	11-13-65	Edmonton, Florida
16	O'Halloran, Greg	L/R	6-2/205	5-21-68	Syracuse
09	Santiago, Benito	R/R	6-1/185	3-9-65	Florida

No.	INFIELDERS	B/T	Ht./Wt.	Born	1993 clubs
7	Abbott, Kurt	R/R	6-0/170	6-2-69	Tacoma, Oakland
26	Arias, Alex	R/R	6-3/185	11-20-67	Florida
8	Barberie, Bret	B/R	5-11/180	8-16-67	Florida, Edmonton, Gulf Coast Marlins
30	Browne, Jerry	B/R	5-10/170	2-3-66	Oakland, Tacoma
14	Clark, Tim	L/R	6-3/210	2-10-69	High Desert
4	Colbrunn, Greg	R/R	6-0/200	7-26-69	West Palm Beach, Montreal, Ottawa
39	Destrade, Orestes	B/R	6-4/230	5-8-62	Florida
18	Magadan, Dave	L/R	6-3/205	9-30-62	Florida, Seattle
37	Martinez, Ramon D.	B/R	6-0/165	9-8-69	High Desert
6	Renteria, Rick	R/R	5-9/175	12-25-61	Florida

No.	OUTFIELDERS	B/T	Ht./Wt.	Born	1993 clubs
21	Carr, Chuck	B/R	5-10/165	8-10-68	Florida, Gulf Coast Marlins
25	Carrillo, Matias	L/L	5-11/190	2-24-63	Mexico City Tigers, Florida
19	Conine, Jeff	R/R	6-1/220	6-27-66	Florida
3	Everett, Carl	B/R	6-0/181	6-3-70	High Desert, Florida, Edmonton
10	Sheffield, Gary	R/R	5-11/190	11-18-68	San Diego, Florida
20	Tavarez, Jesus	B/R	6-0/170	3-26-71	High Desert
17	Whitmore, Darrell	L/R	6-1/210	11-18-68	Edmonton, Florida
30	Wilson, Nigel	L/L	6-1/185	1-12-70	Edmonton, Florida

BALLPARK INFORMATION

Ballpark (capacity, surface)
Joe Robbie Stadium (47,662, grass)

Address
2269 N.W. 199th St.
Miami, Fla. 33056

Business phone
305-626-7400

Ticket information
305-779-7070

Ticket prices
$20 (club level section B)
$13 (club level section C)
$13 (terrace box)
$9 (mezzanine reserved)
$8 (outfield reserved, adult)
$3.50 (outfield res., 12 and under)
$4 (general admission, adult)
$1.50 (g.a., 12 and under)
* does not include $5 license fee

Field dimensions (from home plate)
To left field at foul line, 335 feet
To center field, 410 feet
To right field at foul line, 345

First game played
April 5, 1993 (Marlins 6, Dodgers 3)

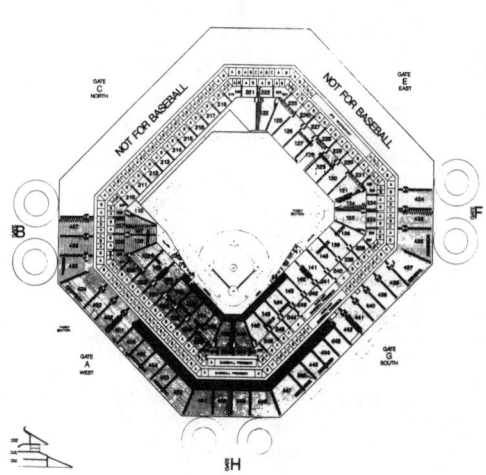

MINOR LEAGUE AFFILIATES

Class	Team	League	Manager
AAA	Edmonton	Pacific Coast	Sal Rende
AA	Portland	Eastern	Carlos Tosca
A	Brevard County	Florida State	Fredi Gonzalez
A	Kane County	Midwest	Lynn Jones
A	Elmira	New York-Pennsylvania	Jim Hendry
Rookie	Gulf Coast Marlins	Gulf Coast	Juan Bustabad

☐ BROADCAST INFORMATION ☐

Radio: WQAM-AM (560). Broadcasters: Joe Angel, Dave O'Brien. WCMQ-AM (1210, Spanish language). Broadcasters: Felo Ramirez, Manolo Alvarez. **TV:** WBFS-TV (Channel 33). Broadcasters: Jay Randolph, Gary Carter. **Cable TV:** The Sunshine Network. Broadcasters: Jay Randolph, Gary Carter.

SPRING TRAINING

Ballpark (city): Spacecoast Stadium (Melbourne, Fla.). **Ticket information:** 407-633-9200.

HISTORY

YEAR-BY-YEAR RECORDS

Year	Pos.	W	L	Pct.	GB
1993	6th	64	98	.395	33

MANAGERS

Name	Record	Years
Rene Lachemann	64-98	1993

DAY BY DAY

Date		Opp.	Res.	Score	(inn.*)	Hits	Opp. hits	Winning pitcher	Losing pitcher	Save	Record	Pos.	GB
4-5		L.A.	W	6-3		14	8	Hough	Hershiser	Harvey	1-0	T1st	...
4-6		L.A.	L	2-4		8	8	R. Martinez	Armstrong	Worrell	1-1	T4th	1
4-7		L.A.	L	2-4		9	9	Ke. Gross	Hammond	McDowell	1-2	T6th	2
4-9		S.D.	L	1-2		5	8	Gr. Harris	Harvey		1-3	7th	2½
4-10		S.D.	W	2-1		4	5	Hough	Eiland	Harvey	2-3	T5th	2
4-11		S.D.	L	2-6		8	13	Benes	Armstrong	Ge. Harris	2-4	T6th	3
4-12		At S.F.	L	3-4	(11)	4	9	Beck	Klink		2-5	7th	4
4-13		At S.F.	L	1-3		6	6	Burba	Aquino	Beck	2-6	7th	5
4-14		At S.F.	W	6-4		13	9	Bowen	Swift	Harvey	3-6	7th	5
4-16		At Hou.	L	3-9		12	15	Swindell	Hough		3-7	7th	5
4-17		At Hou.	W	9-4		11	5	Armstrong	Williams		4-7	7th	4
4-18		At Hou.	L	0-3		4	4	Harnisch	Hammond	D. Jones	4-8	7th	5
4-20		Atl.	L	4-5		7	9	Maddux	Bowen	Stanton	4-9	7th	6
4-21		Atl.	L	4-7		10	11	Smoltz	McClure	Stanton	4-10	7th	6½
4-22		Atl.	W	4-3		9	8	Armstrong	Avery	Harvey	5-10	7th	5½
4-23		At Col.	L	4-5		12	7	Reed	Hammond	Holmes	5-11	7th	6½
4-24		At Col.	W	2-1		6	10	Aquino	Ashby	Harvey	6-11	7th	6½
4-25		At Col.	W	11-1		14	6	Bowen	Smith		7-11	7th	6½
4-26		At Cin.	L	0-3		3	5	Rijo	Hough	Reardon	7-12	7th	7½
4-27		At Cin.	W	4-3		4	12	Hoffman	Ayala	Harvey	8-12	7th	6½
4-28		At Atl.	W	3-1		7	10	McClure	Bedrosian	Harvey	9-12	6th	6½
4-29		At Atl.	W	6-5		10	10	Aquino	Smith	Hoffman	10-12	6th	6½
4-30		Col.	L	2-6		6	12	Reynoso	Bowen		10-13	6th	7½
5-1		Col.	W	7-6	(12)	9	11	Harvey	Reed		11-13	6th	6½
5-2		Col.	L	1-2		7	6	Henry	Armstrong	Holmes	11-14	6th	7½
5-4		Cin.	W	9-6		12	8	Hammond	Pugh	Harvey	12-14	6th	7½
5-5		Cin.	L	2-6		9	6	Browning	Bowen		12-15	6th	7½
5-7		At N.Y.	L	0-4		4	7	Gooden	Hough		12-16	6th	8½
5-8		At N.Y.	W	4-2		11	4	Armstrong	Schourek	Harvey	13-16	6th	8½
5-9		At N.Y.	W	6-4		10	10	Hammond	Tanana	Harvey	14-16	6th	8½
5-10		At N.Y.	L	0-1		3	3	Saberhagen	Bowen		14-17	6th	9½
5-11		At Mon.	L	4-6		9	10	Rojas	Carpenter	Wetteland	14-18	6th	9½
5-12		At Mon.	W	10-7		16	10	Lewis	Nabholz	Harvey	15-18	6th	9½
5-13		At Mon.	L	4-5		10	9	Wetteland	Corsi		15-19	6th	10
5-14		At St.L.	L	2-7		9	13	Tewksbury	Hammond		15-20	6th	10
5-15		At St.L.	W	8-0		11	6	Bowen	Magrane		16-20	6th	9
5-16		At St.L.	L	0-1		5	5	Smith	Hoffman		16-21	6th	10
5-17		Phi.	L	3-10		9	17	Rivera	Hough		16-22	6th	11
5-18		Phi.	L	0-6		6	8	Greene	Armstrong		16-23	6th	12
5-19		Phi.	W	5-3		7	3	Lewis	Davis	Harvey	17-23	6th	11
5-21		Chi.	W	5-3		9	9	Hoffman	Assenmacher	Harvey	18-23	6th	10½
5-22		Chi.	L	1-2		7	8	Hibbard	Aquino	Myers	18-24	6th	10½
5-23		Chi.	W	4-2		6	6	Armstrong	Castillo	Harvey	19-24	6th	10½
5-25		At Pit.	L	0-2		4	8	Cooke	Hough		19-25	6th	12
5-26		At Pit.	W	5-4		9	3	Hammond	Wagner	Harvey	20-25	6th	11
5-27		At Pit.	L	8-13		16	13	Walk	Bowen		20-26	6th	11½
5-28		Hou.	W	5-4	(12)	12	14	Lewis	Edens		21-26	6th	11½
5-29		Hou.	L	2-4		4	9	Kile	Hough	D. Jones	21-27	6th	12½
5-30		Hou.	L	1-2		5	8	Harnisch	Aquino	D. Jones	21-28	6th	13½
6-1	(1)	S.F.	W	7-3		12	12	Hammond	Swift		22-28	6th	13
6-1	(2)	S.F.	L	3-4		9	8	Black	Bowen	Beck	22-29	6th	13½
6-2		S.F.	L	2-3		12	7	Burkett	Armstrong	Beck	22-30	6th	14½
6-4		At S.D.	W	6-2		10	6	Hough	Hurst		23-30	6th	13½
6-5		At S.D.	W	3-1		7	6	Aquino	Mason	Harvey	24-30	6th	13½
6-6		At S.D.	W	9-2		9	9	Hammond	Brocail		25-30	6th	13½
6-7		At L.A.	W	5-3		7	5	Lewis	Worrell	Harvey	26-30	6th	13½
6-8		At L.A.	L	1-2		8	4	Astacio	Armstrong	Gott	26-31	6th	13½
6-10		Pit.	W	4-3		8	7	Turner	Otto	Harvey	27-31	6th	14
6-11		Pit.	W	11-3		21	7	Aquino	Wakefield		28-31	6th	14
6-12		Pit.	W	5-2		5	11	Hammond	Walk	Harvey	29-31	5th	14
6-13		Pit.	W	5-2		8	10	Bowen	Minor	Harvey	30-31	4th	14
6-14		At Chi.	L	3-6		7	12	Guzman	Armstrong	Myers	30-32	4th	15
6-15		At Chi.	L	0-3		5	8	Castillo	Hough	Myers	30-33	5th	15
6-16		At Chi.	L	4-6		8	9	Bullinger	Aquino	Myers	30-34	5th	15
6-17		At Phi.	W	4-1		9	4	Hammond	Jackson	Harvey	31-34	5th	14
6-18		At Phi.	L	3-7		9	8	Rivera	Bowen		31-35	5th	15
6-19		At Phi.	L	2-5		9	12	Mulholland	Armstrong	Mit. Williams	31-36	6th	16
6-20		At Phi.	L	3-4		8	6	Greene	Hoffman	Mit. Williams	31-37	6th	17
6-21		St.L.	L	3-4		7	11	Magrane	Aquino	Smith	31-38	6th	17
6-22		St.L.	W	7-5		12	9	Hammond	Cormier	Harvey	32-38	6th	17

Date	Opp.	Res.	Score (inn.*)	Hits	Opp. hits	Winning pitcher	Losing pitcher	Save	Record	Pos.	GB
6-23	St.L.	L	3-4	9	8	Arocha	Bowen	Smith	32-39	6th	18
6-25	Mon.	W	3-1	5	3	Armstrong	Hill	Harvey	33-39	6th	18
6-26	Mon.	L	2-4	10	7	Bottenfield	Hough	Wetteland	33-40	6th	18
6-27	Mon.	W	9-2	10	6	Hammond	Barnes		34-40	6th	17
6-29	N.Y.	L	9-10 (12)	15	16	Telgheder	Turner		34-41	6th	17½
6-30	N.Y.	L	1-7	8	14	Saberhagen	Armstrong		34-42	6th	17½
7-1	N.Y.	W	7-5	11	8	Hough	Gooden	Harvey	35-42	6th	16½
7-2	At Atl.	W	4-2	8	4	Hammond	Maddux	Harvey	36-42	6th	16
7-3	At Atl.	L	2-11	8	13	Smith	Aquino		36-43	6th	16
7-4	At Atl.	L	3-4	9	10	Stanton	Turner		36-44	6th	17
7-5	At Atl.	L	7-9	10	12	Wohlers	Corsi	Stanton	36-45	6th	18
7-6	At Col.	L	3-8	7	12	Reynoso	Hough		36-46	6th	18
7-7	At Col.	L	5-6	9	12	Reed	Harvey		36-47	6th	19
7-8	At Col.	L	2-3	3	5	Leskanic	Rapp	Holmes	36-48	6th	19
7-9	Atl.	L	1-5	5	7	Smoltz	Bowen		36-49	6th	19
7-10	Atl.	W	5-2	11	9	Armstrong	Glavine	Harvey	37-49	6th	19
7-11	Atl.	L	3-6	6	8	Maddux	Hough	Stanton	37-50	6th	19
7-15	At Cin.	L	4-7	7	10	Belcher	Hammond	Reardon	37-51	6th	19
7-16	At Cin.	L	0-4	8	10	Rijo	Rapp		37-52	6th	19
7-17	At Cin.	W	6-3	9	7	Armstrong	Browning		38-52	6th	18
7-18	At Cin.	L	3-5	6	8	Pugh	Hough	Dibble	38-53	6th	19
7-19	Col.	W	3-1	5	8	Bowen	Bottenfield	Harvey	39-53	6th	19
7-20	Col.	L	3-6	8	13	Blair	Hammond	Holmes	39-54	6th	20
7-21	Col.	W	6-4	11	10	Rapp	Leskanic	Harvey	40-54	6th	20
7-22	Cin.	L	3-7	10	10	Browning	Armstrong		40-55	6th	20
7-23	Cin.	L	2-3	9	5	Ayala	Lewis	Dibble	40-56	6th	21
7-24	Cin.	W	2-0	6	5	Bowen	Luebbers	Harvey	41-56	6th	20
7-25	Cin.	W	7-3	13	4	Nen	Belcher	Harvey	42-56	6th	19
7-27	At N.Y.	L	3-4	6	6	Gooden	Rapp	Franco	42-57	6th	20
7-28	At N.Y.	L	4-5	10	12	Young	Harvey		42-58	6th	21
7-29	At N.Y.	W	2-1	4	7	Hough	Tanana	Harvey	43-58	6th	21
7-30	At Mon.	L	1-11	6	18	Nabholz	Bowen		43-59	6th	21
7-31	At Mon.	L	5-6	11	10	Wetteland	Turner		43-60	6th	22
8-1	At Mon.	W	5-4	12	5	Turner	Barnes	Harvey	44-60	6th	22
8-2	At St.L.	L	3-5	15	10	Tewksbury	Armstrong	Smith	44-61	6th	22½
8-3	At St.L.	W	1-0	10	6	Hough	Osborne	Harvey	45-61	6th	22½
8-4	At St.L.	L	2-10	9	11	Watson	Bowen		45-62	6th	22½
8-5	At St.L.	L	6-16	11	19	Arocha	Hammond		45-63	6th	23½
8-6	Phi.	W	4-3	5	8	Aquino	Mason	Harvey	46-63	6th	22½
8-7	Phi.	L	7-8 (10)	12	9	Mit. Williams	Turner		46-64	6th	23½
8-8	Phi.	W	6-5	8	9	Hough	Mulholland	Harvey	47-64	6th	22½
8-9	Chi.	W	3-2	8	9	Bowen	Castillo	Harvey	48-64	6th	22
8-10	Chi.	W	3-2 (15)	11	4	Aquino	Boskie		49-64	6th	22
8-11	Chi.	W	12-11	16	17	Lewis	Myers		50-64	6th	22
8-12	Chi.	L	1-5	7	9	Harkey	Armstrong		50-65	6th	23
8-13	At Pit.	L	3-8	10	9	Smith	Hough		50-66	6th	24
8-14	At Pit.	W	8-3	12	9	Bowen	Walk	Harvey	51-66	6th	23
8-15	At Pit.	L	3-4 (11)	12	10	Minor	Aquino		51-67	6th	24
8-17	At Hou.	L	0-4	3	8	Kile	Rapp		51-68	6th	25
8-18	At Hou.	L	1-2	7	9	Swindell	Klink	T. Jones	51-69	6th	26
8-19	At Hou.	L	3-8	9	12	Portugal	Hough		51-70	6th	26
8-20	At S.F.	W	5-4	8	7	Turner	Jackson	Harvey	52-70	6th	26
8-21	At S.F.	L	4-7	10	9	Sanderson	Hammond	Beck	52-71	6th	26
8-22	At S.F.	L	6-7	12	10	Rogers	Harvey		52-72	6th	26
8-24	Hou.	L	0-4	6	9	Swindell	Armstrong		52-73	6th	26½
8-25	Hou.	L	2-3	3	10	Portugal	Hough	Hernandez	52-74	6th	27½
8-26	Hou.	W	5-4 (13)	12	13	Lewis	D. Jones		53-74	6th	27
8-27	S.F.	W	7-4	13	9	Rapp	Burkett		54-74	6th	26
8-29	S.F.	L	3-9	6	15	Torres	Hammond		54-75	6th	26½
8-30	S.F.	L	1-5	8	9	Sanderson	Armstrong		54-76	6th	26½
8-31	S.D.	W	2-1	4	8	Hough	Worrell	Harvey	55-76	6th	26½
9-1	S.D.	L	5-13	6	17	Benes	Bowen		55-77	6th	27½
9-2	S.D.	W	8-2	16	7	Rapp	Sanders		56-77	6th	27
9-3	L.A.	L	4-5 (13)	14	13	Daal	Johnstone		56-78	6th	28
9-4	L.A.	L	4-9	8	13	Hershiser	Armstrong		56-79	6th	28
9-5	L.A.	W	4-3	11	5	Turner	McDowell	Harvey	57-79	6th	28
9-6	At S.D.	W	2-0	7	3	Weathers	Benes	Harvey	58-79	6th	27
9-7	At S.D.	L	4-6	9	11	Hoffman	Aquino	Ge. Harris	58-80	6th	27
9-8	At S.D.	L	2-3	6	6	Seminara	Hammond	Ge. Harris	58-81	6th	27
9-9	At L.A.	L	5-6 (10)	9	13	Trlicek	Turner		58-82	6th	28
9-10	At L.A.	W	2-1	3	6	Hough	Ke. Gross	Harvey	59-82	6th	28½
9-11	At L.A.	W	3-2	6	10	Weathers	Candiotti	Harvey	60-82	6th	27
9-12	At L.A.	L	0-1	5	6	Astacio	Rapp		60-83	6th	27
9-14	Pit.	L	0-1 (6)	4	3	Wagner	Hammond		60-84	6th	27½

Date	Opp.	Res.	Score (Inn.*)	Hits	Opp. hits	Winning pitcher	Losing pitcher	Save	Record	Pos.	GB
9-15	Pit.	L	1-8	5	8	Cooke	Hough		60-85	6th	28½
9-16	Pit.	L	0-10	3	19	Ballard	Weathers		60-86	6th	29
9-17	At Chi.	W	2-0	5	3	Armstrong	Harkey	Harvey	61-86	6th	28
9-18	At Chi.	L	5-6	14	10	Brennan	Lewis	Myers	61-87	6th	29
9-19	At Chi.	W	2-1	4	4	Hammond	Trachsel	Harvey	62-87	6th	28
9-20	At Phi.	L	1-7	7	12	Schilling	Hough		62-88	6th	29
9-21	At Phi.	L	3-5	7	7	Pall	Rodriguez		62-89	6th	30
9-22	At Phi.	L	1-2	(12)	11	10	Mason	Harvey	Mit. Williams	62-90	6th	31
9-24	St.L.	L	5-9	6	15	Lancaster	Johnstone		62-91	6th	32
9-25	St.L.	W	2-1	5	3	Armstrong	Watson		63-91	6th	31
9-26	St.L.	L	7-10	12	15	Olivares	Weathers		63-92	6th	31
9-27	Mon.	W	3-1	9	4	Rapp	Fassero	Rodriguez	64-92	6th	31
9-28	Mon.	L	2-3	4	8	Martinez	Armstrong	Wetteland	64-93	6th	32
9-29	Mon.	L	2-5	6	12	Nabholz	Hammond		64-94	6th	32
9-30	Mon.	L	3-5	8	8	Shaw	Lewis	Wetteland	64-95	6th	32
10-1	N.Y.	L	1-4	6	9	Telgheder	Weathers		64-96	6th	33
10-2	N.Y.	L	1-7	4	12	Fernandez	Rapp		64-97	6th	33
10-3	N.Y.	L	2-9	(8½)	6	12	Schourek	Armstrong		64-98	6th	33

Monthly records: April (10-13), May (11-15), June (13-14), July (9-18), August (12-16), September (9-19), October (0-3).
*Innings, if other than nine.

HIGHLIGHTS

High point: On June 13, Florida completed a four-game sweep of Pittsburgh to pull within a game of .500 (30-31) and into sole possession of fourth place.

Low point: From September 12 to the end of the season, the Marlins won just four of 20 games.

Turning point: On June 24, Florida traded righthander Trevor Hoffman and two minor league pitchers to San Diego for lefthander Rich Rodriguez and third baseman Gary Sheffield, who less than a month later became the first expansion player to start in an All-Star Game. Sheffield signed a four-year deal in September and will be the centerpiece of the Marlins' offense.

Most valuable player: Shortstop Walt Weiss. He answered all questions about his durability by appearing in 158 games en route to enjoying his best season offensively, batting .266 with 50 runs, 39 RBIs and 79 walks.

Most valuable pitcher: Righthander Bryan Harvey. Nabbed from California in the expansion draft, he had 45 saves, a 1.70 ERA and 73 strikeouts in 69 innings.

Most improved player: Center fielder Chuck Carr. A .208 career hitter entering 1993, Carr hit .267, led the N.L. in stolen bases with 58 and made many spectacular catches.

Most pleasant surprise: Infielder Rick Renteria. After winning a roster spot the last week of spring training, he became the team's best player off the bench and paced Florida with a .347 average with men in scoring position.

Biggest disappointment: Catcher Benito Santiago. He endured the worst season of his career, batting a career-low .230 and playing subpar defense.

Key injuries: Righthander Pat Rapp underwent knee surgery in the spring and began the year in Class AAA before being recalled July 5. Second baseman Bret Barberie went on the disabled list twice (left elbow and left knee). Righthander Luis Aquino spent time on the

D.L. with a shoulder problem.

Notable: Montreal turned the first triple play in Joe Robbie Stadium on September 29. . . . Left fielder Jeff Conine became the first expansion player to appear in 162 games. . . . Florida drew 3,064,847 fans, becoming only the 10th team in major league history to reach the 3 million mark. . . . The Marlins suffered just one rainout (May 31) after it was feared that Miami's tropical weather would wash out many games.

—GORDON EDES

RECORDS

1993 regular-season record: 64-98 (6th in N.L. East); 35-46 at home; 29-52 on road; 30-48 vs. East; 34-50 vs. West; 21-27 vs. LHP; 43-71 vs. RHP; 54-70 on grass; 10-28 on turf; 15-20 in daytime; 49-78 at night; 25-37 in one-run games; 4-7 in extra-inning games; 0-0-1 in doubleheaders.

Team record last five years: 64-98 (.395), ranks 14th in league in that span).

TEAM LEADERS

Batting average: Jeff Conine (.292).
At-bats: Jeff Conine (595).
Runs: Chuck Carr, Jeff Conine (75).
Hits: Jeff Conine (174).
Total bases: Jeff Conine (240).
Doubles: Jeff Conine (24).
Triples: Benito Santiago (6).
Home runs: Orestes Destrade (20).
Runs batted in: Orestes Destrade (87).
Stolen bases: Chuck Carr (58).
Slugging percentage: Orestes Destrade (.406).
On-base percentage: Walt Weiss (.367).
Wins: Chris Hammond (11).
Earned-run average: Charlie Hough (4.27).
Complete games: Ryan Bowen (2).
Shutouts: Ryan Bowen (1).
Saves: Bryan Harvey (45).
Innings pitched: Charlie Hough (204⅓).
Strikeouts: Charlie Hough (126).

GAMES BY POSITION

Catcher: Benito Santiago 136, Bob Natal 38, Steve Decker 5, Terry McGriff 3, Mitch Lyden 2.
First base: Orestes Destrade 152, Jeff Conine 43, Dave Magadan 2.
Second base: Bret Barberie 97, Rick Renteria 45, Alex Arias 30, Gus Polidor 1.
Third base: Gary Sheffield 66, Dave Magadan 63, Rick Renteria 25, Alex Arias 22, Gus Polidor 1.
Shortstop: Walt Weiss 153, Alex Arias 18.
Outfield: Jeff Conine 147, Chuck Carr 139, Darrell Whitmore 69, Greg Briley 67, Junior Felix 52, Henry Cotto 46, Matias Carrillo 16, Scott Pose 10, Geronimo Berroa 9, Carl Everett 8, Monty Fariss 8, Nigel Wilson 3, Rick Renteria 1, Benito Santiago 1.

TOP DRAFT CHOICES

1. **Marc Valdes**, RHP, University of Florida.
2. **John Roskos**, C, Cibola High School, Rio Rancho, N.M.
3. **Dan Ehler**, RHP, South Hills High School, Covina, Calif.
4. **Thomas Howard**, LHP, Titusville (Fla.) High School.
5. **Ernie Delgado**, RHP, Sunnyside High School, Tucson, Ariz.
6. **Paul Thornton**, RHP, Georgia Southern University.
7. **Todd Dunwoody**, OF, Harrison High School, West Lafayette, Ind.
8. **Billy McMillon**, OF, Clemson University.
9. **Brady Babin**, SS, St. Amant High School, Gonzales, La.
10. **Ryan Filbeck**, RHP, Rancho Santiago (Calif.) J.C.

HOUSTON ASTROS
NATIONAL LEAGUE CENTRAL DIVISION

N Denotes night game (any game starting after 5 p.m.).
▨ Home games shaded.
* At Three Rivers Stadium in Pittsburgh.

APRIL

SUN	MON	TUE	WED	THU	FRI	SAT
					1	2
3	4 MON	5 N MON	6 N MON	7	8 N NY	9 N NY
10 NY	11	12 N FLA	13 N FLA	14 N FLA	15 N NY	16 N NY
17 NY	18	19 N CHI	20 CHI	21	22 N STL	23 N STL
24 STL	25 N PIT	26 N PIT	27 N CHI	28 CHI	29 N STL	30 N STL

MAY

SUN	MON	TUE	WED	THU	FRI	SAT
1 STL	2	3 N PIT	4 N PIT	5 N CIN	6 N CIN	7 N CIN
8 CIN	9 N LA	10 N LA	11 N LA	12	13 N COL	14 N COL
15 COL	16 N SF	17 N SF	18 N SF	19 N SD	20 N SD	21 N SD
22 SD	23	24 N ATL	25 N ATL	26 N ATL	27 N PHI	28 N PHI
29 PHI	30 N FLA	31 N FLA				

JUNE

SUN	MON	TUE	WED	THU	FRI	SAT
			1 N FLA	2 N	3 N PHI	4 N PHI
5 PHI	6 N MON	7 N MON	8 N MON	9	10 N ATL	11 N ATL
12 ATL	13 SF	14 SF	15 SF	16 SF	17 N SD	18 N SD
19 SD	20 N COL	21 N COL	22 COL	23	24 N LA	25 N LA
26 LA	27 N CIN	28 N CIN	29 CIN	30 N CHI		

JULY

SUN	MON	TUE	WED	THU	FRI	SAT
					1 N CHI	2 N CHI
3 CHI	4 N STL	5 N STL	6 N STL	7 N CHI	8 CHI	9 CHI
10 N CHI	11 N	12 * ALL-STAR GAME	13	14 N PIT	15 N PIT	16 PIT
17 PIT	18 N STL	19 N STL	20 STL	21 N PIT	22 N PIT	23 N PIT
24 PIT	25 N CIN	26 N CIN	27 CIN	28	29 N LA	30 N LA
31 LA						

AUGUST

SUN	MON	TUE	WED	THU	FRI	SAT
	1 N COL	2 N COL	3 N COL	4 N COL	5 N SF	6 N SF
7 SF	8	9 N SD	10 N SD	11 N SD	12 N ATL	13 N ATL
14 ATL	15 N ATL	16 N NY	17 N NY	18 N NY	19 N MON	20 N MON
21 MON	22	23 N NY	24 N NY	25 N NY	26 N MON	27 N MON
28 MON	29 N PHI	30 N PHI	31 N PHI			

SEPTEMBER

SUN	MON	TUE	WED	THU	FRI	SAT
				1 N	2 N FLA	3 N FLA
4 FLA	5 N PHI	6 N PHI	7 N PHI	8	9 N FLA	10 N FLA
11 FLA	12	13 N ATL	14 N ATL	15 N ATL	16 N SF	17 SF
18 SF	19 N SD	20 N SD	21 N SD	22	23 N COL	24 COL
25 COL	26 N LA	27 N LA	28 N LA	29 N CIN		

OCTOBER

SUN	MON	TUE	WED	THU	FRI	SAT
						1 N CIN
2 CIN						

Owner and chairman of the board
  Drayton McLane Jr.
Senior vice president
  G.W. Sanford Jr.
Vice president
  Bob McClaren
General manager
  Bob Watson
Director of player administration
  Tim Hellmuth
Director of baseball administration
  Barry Waters
Director of minor league operations
  Fred Nelson
Director of scouting
  Dan O'Brien
Director of public relations
  Rob Matwick
Assistant director of public relations
  Tyler Barnes
Asst. to dir. of minor leagues and scouting
  Tim Purapura
Asst. dir. of scouting and dir. of int'l. dev.
  David Rawnsley
Coordinator of publications
  Warren Miller
Dir. of data base, marketing & ticket services
  Randy Crimmins
Vice president, marketing
  Ted Haracz
Director of sales
  John Sorrentino
Director of broadcasting
  Jamie Hildreth
Director of communications
  Pam Gardner
Director of group sales
  Debra Fulmer
Marketing operations manager
  Derrick Grubbs
Director of community services
  Amy Kress

Scouts
  Bob Blair
  Stan Boroski
  Ralph Bratton
  Gerry Craft
  Jug DeFord
  Chuck Edmondson
  Orlando Estevez
  James Farrar
  Ben Galante
  Brian Granger
  Sterling Housley
  Dan Huston
  Marc Johnson
  Brian Keegan
  Bill Kelso
  Bob King
  David Lakey
  Julio Linares
  Bobby Macias
  Mike Maggert
  Walt Matthews
  Tom Mooney
  Joe Pittman
  Jim Pransky
  Deron Rombach
  Nelson Rood
  Rich Schroeder
  Mark Servais
  Tad Slowik
  Lynwood Stallings
  Kevin Stein
  Frankie Thon
  Paul Weaver
  Gene Wellman
  Greg Whitworth
Advance scouts
  George Brophy
  Dick Hager
  Bob Skinner

SPRING TRAINING ROSTER

Manager—Terry Collins (2).
Coaches—Matt Galante (48), Steve Henderson (55), Ben Hines (56), Julio Linares (1), Mel Stottlemyre (30).

No.	PITCHERS	B/T	Ht./Wt.	Born	1993 clubs
49	Dougherty, Jim	R/R	6-0/210	3-8-68	Jackson
15	Drabek, Doug	R/R	6-1/185	7-25-62	Houston
46	Edens, Tom	L/R	6-2/188	6-9-61	Osceola, Tucson, Houston
44	Gallaher, Kevin	R/R	6-3/190	8-1-68	Osceola, Jackson
38	Hampton, Mike	R/L	5-10/190	9-9-72	Seattle, Jacksonville
27	Harnisch, Pete	R/R	6-0/207	9-23-66	Houston
35	Hudek, John	B/R	6-1/190	8-8-66	Toledo, Tucson
42	Jean, Domingo	R/R	6-2/175	1-9-69	Albany/Colonie, Columbus, New York A.L., Prince William
59	Jones, Todd	L/R	6-3/200	4-24-68	Tucson, Houston
57	Kile, Darryl	R/R	6-5/185	12-2-68	Houston
51	Morman, Alvin	L/L	6-3/210	1-6-69	Jackson
29	Osuna, Al	R/L	6-3/200	8-10-65	Tucson, Houston
37	Reynolds, Shane	R/R	6-3/210	3-26-68	Tucson, Houston
21	Swindell, Greg	R/L	6-3/225	1-2-65	Houston
53	Williams, Brian	R/R	6-2/195	2-15-69	Houston, Tucson
99	Williams, Mitch	L/L	6-4/205	11-17-64	Philadelphia

No.	CATCHERS	B/T	Ht./Wt.	Born	1993 clubs
20	Eusebio, Tony	R/R	6-2/180	4-27-67	Tucson
9	Servais, Scott	R/R	6-2/195	6-4-67	Houston
6	Taubensee, Eddie	L/R	6-4/205	10-31-68	Houston
36	Tucker, Scooter	R/R	6-2/205	11-18-66	Tucson, Houston

No.	INFIELDERS	B/T	Ht./Wt.	Born	1993 clubs
5	Bagwell, Jeff	R/R	6-0/195	5-27-68	Houston
7	Biggio, Craig	R/R	5-11/180	12-14-65	Houston
11	Caminiti, Ken	B/R	6-0/200	4-21-63	Houston
10	Cedeno, Andujar	R/R	6-1/168	8-21-69	Houston
3	Donnels, Chris	L/R	6-0/185	4-21-66	Houston
2	Miller, Orlando	R/R	6-1/180	1-13-69	Tucson
18	Mouton, James	R/R	5-9/175	12-29-68	Tucson
65	Petagine, Roberto	L/L	6-1/172	6-7-71	Jackson
4	Stankiewicz, Andy	R/R	5-9/165	8-10-64	Columbus, New York A.L.

No.	OUTFIELDERS	B/T	Ht./Wt.	Born	1993 clubs
64	Ansley, Willie	R/R	6-2/200	12-15-69	Tucson
	Bass, Kevin	B/R	6-0/190	5-12-59	Houston
16	Castillo, Braulio	R/R	6-0/160	5-13-68	Colorado Springs, Tucson
25	Felder, Mike	B/R	5-9/175	11-18-62	Seattle
12	Finley, Steve	L/L	6-2/180	3-12-65	Houston
26	Gonzalez, Luis	L/R	6-2/180	9-3-67	Houston
60	Hatcher, Chris	R/R	6-3/220	1-7-69	Jackson
19	Hunter, Brian L.	R/R	6-4/180	3-5-71	Jackson
63	Mota, Gary	R/R	6-0/195	10-6-70	Jackson
62	White, Jimmy	L/R	6-1/170	12-1-72	Osceola

BALLPARK INFORMATION

Ballpark (capacity, surface)
The Astrodome (53,821, artificial)
Address
P.O. Box 288
Houston, TX 77001-0288
Business phone
713-799-9500
Ticket information
713-799-9555
Ticket prices
$17 (star deck)
$14 (field level)
$12 (mezzanine)
$10 (skybox)
$9 (loge level)
$6 (upper box)
$5 (upper reserved)
$5 (skybox club)
$4 (adult pavilion)
$1 (youth pavilion)
Field dimensions (from home plate)
To left field at foul line, 330 feet
To center field, 400 feet
To right field at foul line, 330 feet
First game played
April 12, 1965 (Phillies 2, Astros 0)

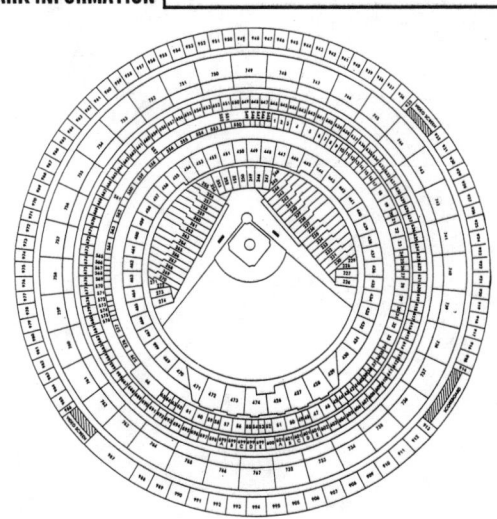

Class	Team	League	Manager
AAA	Tucson	Pacific Coast	Rick Sweet
AA	Jackson	Texas	Sal Butera
A	Osceola	Florida State	Tim Tolman
A	Quad City	Midwest	To be announced
A	Auburn	New York-Pennsylvania	To be announced
Rookie	Gulf Coast Astros	Gulf Coast	To be announced

BROADCAST INFORMATION

Radio: KPRC-AM (940). Broadcasters: Milo Hamilton, Larry Dierker, Bill Brown, Vince Cotroneo. KXYZ-AM (1320, Spanish language). Broadcasters: Francisco Ernesto Ruiz.
TV: KTXH-TV (Channel 20). Broadcasters: Milo Hamilton, Larry Dierker, Bill Brown.
Cable TV: Home Sports Entertainment. Broadcasters: Milo Hamilton, Enos Cabell, Bill Worrell, Bill Brown.

SPRING TRAINING

Ballpark (city): Osceola County Stadium (Kissimmee, Fla.).
Ticket information: 407-933-2520.

HISTORY

YEAR-BY-YEAR RECORDS

Year	Pos.	W	L	Pct.	GB	Year	Pos.	W	L	Pct.	GB
1962*	8th	64	96	.400	36½	1981	3rd/1st	61	49	.555	§★
1963*	9th	66	96	.407	33	1982	5th	77	85	.475	12
1964*	9th	66	96	.407	27	1983	3rd	85	77	.525	6
1965	9th	65	97	.401	32	1984	T2nd	80	82	.494	12
1966	8th	72	90	.444	23	1985	T3rd	83	79	.512	12
1967	9th	69	93	.426	32½	1986	1st‡	96	66	.593	+10
1968	10th	72	90	.444	25	1987	3rd	76	86	.469	14
1969	5th	81	81	.500	12	1988	5th	82	80	.506	12½
1970	4th	79	83	.488	23	1989	3rd	86	76	.531	6
1971	T4th	79	83	.488	11	1990	T4th	75	87	.463	16
1972	2nd	84	69	.549	10½	1991	6th	65	97	.401	29
1973	4th	82	80	.506	17	1992	4th	81	81	.500	17
1974	4th	81	81	.500	21	1993	3rd	85	77	.525	19
1975	6th	64	97	.398	43½						
1976	3rd	80	82	.494	22						
1977	3rd	81	81	.500	17						
1978	5th	74	88	.457	21						
1979	2nd	89	73	.549	1½						
1980	1st†‡	93	70	.571	+1						

*Franchise known as Houston Colt .45s. †Won division playoff. ‡Lost Championship Series. §Lost division playoff. ★First half 28-29; second 33-20.

MANAGERS

Name	Record	Years
Harry Craft	191-280	'62-64
Lum Harris	70-105	'64-65
Grady Hatton	164-221	'66-68
Harry Walker	355-353	'68-72
Leo Durocher	98-95	'72-73
Preston Gomez	128-161	'73-75
Bill Virdon	544-522	'75-82
Bob Lillis	276-261	'82-85
Hal Lanier	254-232	'86-88
Art Howe	392-418	'89-93

DAY BY DAY

Date	Opp.	Res.	Score	(Inn.*)	Hits	Opp. hits	Winning pitcher	Losing pitcher	Save	Record	Pos.	GB
4-5	Phi.	L	1-3		4	6	Mulholland	Drabek		0-1	T5th	1
4-6	Phi.	L	3-5		7	9	Schilling	Swindell	Mit. Williams	0-2	7th	1½
4-7	Phi.	L	3-6	(10)	9	10	DeLeon	Bell	Mit. Williams	0-3	7th	2
4-9	At N.Y.	W	7-3	(10)	10	8	D. Jones	Young		1-3	T5th	2½
4-10	At N.Y.	W	6-3		13	8	Drabek	Gooden		2-3	T4th	1½
4-11	At N.Y.	W	5-4		11	7	Swindell	Schourek	D. Jones	3-3	T2nd	1½
4-13	At Mon.	W	9-6		10	9	Williams	Rojas		4-3	3rd	1
4-14	At Mon.	W	9-5		14	6	Portugal	Gardiner		5-3	1st	...
4-15	At Mon.	L	1-2		6	4	Jones	Drabek	Rojas	5-4	2nd	½
4-16	Fla.	W	9-3		15	12	Swindell	Hough		6-4	2nd	½
4-17	Fla.	L	4-9		5	11	Armstrong	Williams		6-5	2nd	½
4-18	Fla.	W	3-0		4	4	Harnisch	Hammond	D. Jones	7-5	2nd	½
4-20	At Chi.	L	1-2		3	6	Harkey	Portugal	Myers	7-6	2nd	1½
4-21	At Chi.	W	2-0		10	6	Drabek	Morgan		8-6	2nd	½
4-23	At Pit.	W	4-2		7	4	Swindell	Neagle	D. Jones	9-6	1st	...
4-24	At Pit.	W	8-4		14	10	Hernandez	Candelaria		10-6	1st	+½
4-25	At Pit.	L	2-7		5	11	Tomlin	Portugal		10-7	1st	...
4-26	St.L.	L	2-3		6	6	Magrane	Drabek	Smith	10-8	1st	...
4-27	St.L.	W	9-2		12	4	Kile	Cormier	Williams	11-8	1st	...
4-28	Chi.	W	6-1		8	7	Swindell	Guzman		12-8	1st	...
4-29	Chi.	W	5-4		11	8	Harnisch	Hibbard	D. Jones	13-8	1st	...
4-30	Pit.	W	11-2		13	6	Portugal	Walk	Hernandez	14-8	1st	...
5-1	Pit.	W	7-3		11	7	Drabek	Tomlin		15-8	1st	...
5-2	Pit.	L	2-6		9	12	Cooke	Swindell		15-9	2nd	1
5-4	At St.L.	L	1-6		6	12	Tewksbury	Harnisch		15-10	2nd	1
5-5	At St.L.	W	6-3		12	6	Portugal	Osborne	D. Jones	16-10	2nd	1
5-6	Cin.	L	4-5		6	11	Hill	D. Jones		16-11	2nd	1½
5-7	Cin.	L	5-7		9	12	Rijo	Swindell	Reardon	16-12	2nd	2½
5-8	Cin.	W	12-1		15	7	Kile	Smiley		17-12	2nd	1½
5-9	Cin.	W	6-3		10	7	Harnisch	Pugh	D. Jones	18-12	2nd	½
5-10	Atl.	W	5-2		5	11	Hernandez	Howell	D. Jones	19-12	1st	+½
5-11	Atl.	L	4-5		7	9	Smoltz	Drabek	Stanton	19-13	2nd	½
5-12	Atl.	L	2-5		6	9	Avery	Swindell	Stanton	19-14	2nd	1½
5-14	L.A.	W	9-1		13	5	Harnisch	Candiotti		20-14	2nd	1
5-15	L.A.	W	7-1		10	6	Portugal	Hershiser		21-14	2nd	1
5-16	L.A.	W	3-2		9	8	Drabek	P. Martinez	D. Jones	22-14	2nd	1
5-17	At S.F.	L	7-8	(10)	10	15	Burba	D. Jones		22-15	2nd	2
5-18	At S.F.	L	2-7		7	10	Burkett	Kile		22-16	2nd	3
5-19	At S.F.	L	3-6		8	6	Brantley	Harnisch		22-17	3rd	4
5-21	At S.D.	L	2-3	(10)	9	7	Rodriguez	D. Jones		22-18	3rd	4½
5-22	At S.D.	L	4-9		5	14	Benes	Drabek		22-19	3rd	5½
5-23	At S.D.	W	9-7		16	9	Swindell	Eiland	D. Jones	23-19	3rd	5½
5-25	Col.	L	5-7		11	11	Wayne	Hernandez	Ashby	23-20	3rd	6½
5-26	Col.	L	2-3		8	12	Smith	D. Jones	Parrett	23-21	3rd	5½
5-27	Col.	W	8-0		12	7	Drabek	Nied		24-21	3rd	5½
5-28	At Fla.	L	4-5	(12)	14	12	Lewis	Edens		24-22	T3rd	5½
5-29	At Fla.	W	4-2		9	4	Kile	Hough	D. Jones	25-22	T3rd	5½
5-30	At Fla.	W	2-1		8	5	Harnisch	Aquino	D. Jones	26-22	3rd	5½
5-31	Mon.	W	2-1		4	5	D. Jones	Rojas		27-22	3rd	5
6-1	Mon.	L	1-2		8	5	Wetteland	Drabek		27-23	T3rd	5½
6-2	Mon.	W	5-4		9	9	D. Jones	Rojas		28-23	3rd	5½
6-4	N.Y.	W	7-2		10	6	Harnisch	Tanana		29-23	2nd	4
6-5	N.Y.	W	7-5		13	9	Kile	Maddux	Hernandez	30-23	2nd	4
6-6	N.Y.	W	5-4		11	11	Osuna	Schourek	D. Jones	31-23	2nd	4
6-7	At Phi.	L	5-7		9	13	Jackson	Swindell	Mit. Williams	31-24	2nd	4½
6-8	At Phi.	W	6-3		7	7	Kile	Rivera	D. Jones	32-24	2nd	3½
6-9	At Phi.	L	0-8		6	12	Mulholland	Harnisch		32-25	2nd	4½
6-11	At Col.	L	4-5		12	8	Parrett	Hernandez	Holmes	32-26	2nd	5½
6-12	At Col.	L	11-14		13	20	Shepherd	D. Jones		32-27	2nd	6½
6-13	At Col.	L	1-9		6	14	Ruffin	Swindell		32-28	T3rd	7½
6-15	S.D.	L	0-3		6	7	Whitehurst	Harnisch	Ge. Harris	32-29	4th	7½
6-16	S.D.	W	5-4		10	10	Portugal	Brocail	Osuna	33-29	4th	7½
6-17	S.D.	W	4-1		6	7	Kile	Benes	Williams	34-29	T3rd	7½
6-18	S.F.	L	0-5		6	12	Black	Drabek		34-30	T3rd	8½
6-19	S.F.	L	3-10		7	13	Burkett	Swindell		34-31	T3rd	9½
6-20	S.F.	L	5-8		9	10	Brantley	Williams	Beck	34-32	4th	10½
6-21	At L.A.	L	0-7		2	13	R. Martinez	Portugal		34-33	4th	11½
6-22	At L.A.	W	5-1		9	9	Kile	Ke. Gross		35-33	4th	10½
6-23	At L.A.	W	5-3		7	6	Drabek	Gott	Williams	36-33	T3rd	10½
6-24	At L.A.	W	1-0		8	8	Swindell	Hershiser	Osuna	37-33	3rd	10½

Date	Opp.	Res.	Score	(inn.°)	Hits	Opp. hits	Winning pitcher	Losing pitcher	Save	Record	Pos.	GB
6-25	At Atl.	L	2-8		6	10	Avery	Harnisch		37-34	3rd	11½
6-26	At Atl.	L	5-6		12	8	Stanton	D. Jones		37-35	T3rd	11½
6-27	At Atl.	W	3-0		6	5	Kile	Maddux	Hernandez	38-35	T3rd	11½
6-29	At Cin.	L	0-3		6	7	Browning	Drabek	Dibble	38-36	4th	12
6-30	At Cin.	L	4-5		11	10	Reardon	Osuna		38-37	4th	12
7-1	At Cin.	W	8-1		10	8	Harnisch	Rijo		39-37	4th	11½
7-2	St.L.	W	7-1		5	9	Portugal	Magrane		40-37	4th	11½
7-3	St.L.	W	6-0		14	6	Kile	Cormier		41-37	T3rd	10½
7-4	St.L.	W	9-4		14	8	Drabek	Arocha		42-37	T3rd	10½
7-5	St.L.	L	4-10		10	14	Osborne	Swindell		42-38	T3rd	11½
7-6	Pit.	L	3-10		10	12	Ballard	Harnisch		42-39	4th	12½
7-7	Pit.	L	2-5		7	14	Wagner	Portugal	Belinda	42-40	4th	12½
7-8	Pit.	W	10-4		12	10	Kile	Smith		43-40	4th	12½
7-9	At Chi.	L	2-5		5	9	Morgan	Drabek	Myers	43-41	4th	13½
7-10 (1)	At Chi.	W	4-0		7	1	Harnisch	Harkey		44-41	4th	12½
7-10 (2)	At Chi.	W	5-2		12	6	Williams	Guzman	Hernandez	45-41	T3rd	12
7-11	At Chi.	W	10-1		8	3	Portugal	Hibbard		46-41	T3rd	12
7-15	At St.L.	L	2-4		11	8	Arocha	Drabek	Smith	46-42	4th	13
7-16	At St.L.	W	7-6		17	12	Edens	Guetterman	D. Jones	47-42	4th	13
7-17	At St.L.	L	3-5		9	6	Tewksbury	Williams	Smith	47-43	4th	13
7-18	At St.L.	L	6-7	(11)	12	13	Guetterman	D. Jones		47-44	4th	13
7-19	At Pit.	W	4-2		12	6	Harnisch	Walk	D. Jones	48-44	4th	13
7-20	At Pit.	L	1-2		4	5	Tomlin	Drabek		48-45	4th	14
7-21	At Pit.	W	5-3		5	8	Kile	Cooke	D. Jones	49-45	T3rd	14
7-22	Chi.	W	9-4		12	9	Williams	Harkey		50-45	3rd	14
7-23	Chi.	W	5-1		8	7	Portugal	Hibbard	D. Jones	51-45	3rd	13
7-24	Chi.	L	6-7		10	13	Castillo	Harnisch		51-46	T3rd	14
7-25	Chi.	L	1-3	(11)	8	10	Scanlan	D. Jones	Myers	51-47	T3rd	15
7-26	Cin.	L	1-6		5	10	Rijo	Kile		51-48	4th	15
7-27	Cin.	W	6-5		10	9	Williams	Browning	D. Jones	52-48	T3rd	15
7-28	Cin.	W	4-2		10	12	Portugal	Pugh	Hernandez	53-48	T3rd	14
7-29	Atl.	W	2-0		3	4	Harnisch	Mercker		54-48	3rd	13½
7-30	Atl.	L	1-4		7	7	Glavine	Drabek	McMichael	54-49	3rd	14½
7-31	Atl.	L	3-4		9	8	Maddux	Kile	Stanton	54-50	4th	15½
8-1	Atl.	L	2-3		7	6	Smoltz	Swindell	McMichael	54-51	4th	16½
8-3	L.A.	W	6-1		10	5	Portugal	Ke. Gross	Hernandez	55-51	3rd	16½
8-4	L.A.	L	2-4		10	7	Candiotti	Harnisch	Gott	55-52	4th	16½
8-5	L.A.	L	2-5		5	11	Astacio	Drabek	Gott	55-53	5th	17½
8-6	At S.F.	L	3-4		10	9	Burkett	Kile	Beck	55-54	5th	18½
8-7	At S.F.	W	6-5		8	7	Swindell	Sanderson	D. Jones	56-54	5th	17½
8-8	At S.F.	W	4-1		9	9	Portugal	Hickerson	D. Jones	57-54	5th	16½
8-9	At S.D.	W	5-4	(10)	11	9	Hernandez	Hoffman	D. Jones	58-54	3rd	16½
8-10	At S.D.	L	2-7		8	10	Ashby	Drabek		58-55	3rd	17½
8-11	At S.D.	W	9-6		11	6	Kile	Benes	D. Jones	59-55	3rd	17½
8-12	At S.D.	W	5-3		8	13	Swindell	Hoffman	D. Jones	60-55	3rd	17
8-13	Col.	L	3-5		6	11	Wayne	D. Jones	Holmes	60-56	3rd	18
8-14	Col.	W	9-0		12	3	Harnisch	Harris		61-56	3rd	17
8-15	Col.	L	3-4		6	8	Ruffin	Hernandez	Holmes	61-57	3rd	18
8-17	Fla.	W	4-0		8	3	Kile	Rapp		62-57	3rd	17
8-18	Fla.	W	2-1		9	7	Swindell	Klink	T. Jones	63-57	3rd	17
8-19	Fla.	W	8-3		12	9	Portugal	Hough		64-57	3rd	17
8-20	Phi.	L	4-6		9	4	West	T. Jones	Mit. Williams	64-58	3rd	17
8-21	Phi.	W	3-2	(10)	10	8	D. Jones	Andersen		65-58	3rd	17
8-22	Phi.	W	7-3		11	8	Kile	Rivera		66-58	3rd	17
8-24	At Fla.	W	4-0		9	6	Swindell	Armstrong		67-58	3rd	15½
8-25	At Fla.	W	3-2		10	3	Portugal	Hough	Hernandez	68-58	3rd	14½
8-26	At Fla.	L	4-5	(13)	13	12	Lewis	D. Jones		68-59	3rd	15
8-27	At Mon.	L	1-3		8	4	Martinez	Drabek	Wetteland	68-60	3rd	15
8-28	At Mon.	L	3-7		7	10	Rueter	Kile	Rojas	68-61	3rd	15½
8-29	At Mon.	L	2-3		8	6	Hill	Swindell	Wetteland	68-62	3rd	16½
8-30	At N.Y.	L	4-5		8	9	Maddux	Hernandez	Franco	68-63	3rd	17½
8-31	At N.Y.	W	10-2		18	5	Harnisch	Gooden		69-63	3rd	16½
9-1	At N.Y.	W	3-2		5	8	Drabek	Fernandez	D. Jones	70-63	3rd	16½
9-3	Mon.	L	0-3		5	7	Rueter	Kile	Wetteland	70-64	3rd	17
9-4	Mon.	L	5-7		9	11	Hill	Swindell	Wetteland	70-65	3rd	18
9-5	Mon.	W	7-1		10	5	Portugal	Fassero		71-65	4th	19
9-6	N.Y.	W	7-2		7	4	Harnisch	Fernandez	Hernandez	72-65	3rd	17
9-7	N.Y.	W	4-3	(10)	7	11	T. Jones	Franco		73-65	3rd	16
9-8	N.Y.	W	7-1		9	0	Kile	Tanana		74-65	3rd	15½
9-10	At Phi.	L	2-6		9	12	Schilling	Swindell		74-66	3rd	15
9-11	At Phi.	W	4-1		8	3	Portugal	Mike Williams	T. Jones	75-66	3rd	15
9-12	At Phi.	W	9-2		11	7	Harnisch	Rivera		76-66	3rd	14
9-14 (1)	At Col.	L	4-9		14	16	Reynoso	Drabek	Ruffin	76-67	3rd	15
9-14 (2)	At Col.	L	5-6	(10)	10	11	Holmes	Hernandez		76-68	3rd	15½

Date	Opp.	Res.	Score	(inn.*)	Hits	Opp. hits	Winning pitcher	Losing pitcher	Save	Record	Pos.	GB
9-15	At Col.	L	4-6		12	14	Munoz	Williams	Holmes	76-69	3rd	16½
9-16	At Col.	L	3-6		10	13	Ruffin	T. Jones	Holmes	76-70	3rd	17½
9-17	S.D.	W	3-0		7	1	Harnisch	Benes		77-70	3rd	17½
9-18	S.D.	W	4-2		6	6	Drabek	Sanders		78-70	3rd	16½
9-19	S.D.	L	3-6		10	9	Ashby	Kile	Davis	78-71	3rd	17½
9-20	S.F.	L	2-7		9	10	Deshaies	Swindell		78-72	3rd	18
9-21	S.F.	W	6-0		10	3	Portugal	Torres		79-72	3rd	18
9-22	S.F.	L	0-1		5	7	Swift	Harnisch	Beck	79-73	3rd	18
9-23	S.F.	L	0-7		3	12	Burkett	Drabek		79-74	3rd	19
9-24	At L.A.	L	3-6		5	12	Astacio	Kile		79-75	4th	19
9-25	At L.A.	W	12-4		18	9	Swindell	P. Martinez		80-75	3rd	19
9-26	At L.A.	W	5-4		8	8	Portugal	R. Martinez	D. Jones	81-75	3rd	19
9-28	At Atl.	W	5-2		12	6	Harnisch	Maddux	D. Jones	82-75	3rd	18
9-29	At Atl.	L	3-6		11	11	Glavine	Drabek	McMichael	82-76	3rd	19
9-30	At Atl.	W	10-8		12	14	Hernandez	Smoltz		83-76	3rd	18
10-1	At Cin.	W	2-0		10	8	Swindell	Rijo		84-76	3rd	18
10-2	At Cin.	W	3-1		10	5	Portugal	Powell	Hernandez	85-76	3rd	18
10-3	At Cin.	L	4-7		9	10	Ayala	Juden	Service	85-77	3rd	19

Monthly records: April (14-8), May (13-14), June (11-15), July (16-13), August (15-13), September (14-13), October (2-1).
*Innings, if other than nine.

HIGHLIGHTS

High point: After being swept by Philadelphia in a three-game, season-opening series, Houston won 15 of 20 games to earn a share of the division lead through May 1.

Low point: The Astros never got the hang of playing in Colorado, losing all seven games at Mile High Stadium. Overall, the Astros were 2-11 against the Rockies, the worst record for an established team against an expansion team in baseball history.

Turning point: Following a June 8 win at Philadelphia, the Astros were 3½ games out of first place. They went 6-13 the rest of the month, fell 12½ games behind San Francisco and were never closer than 10½ games from first place the rest of the season.

Most valuable player: First baseman Jeff Bagwell. He hit .320 with 20 homers and 88 RBIs. His season and 304 consecutive-games-played streak ended with a broken left hand September 12.

Most valuable pitcher: Righthander Mark Portugal. He won his final 12 decisions en route to an 18-4 mark and 2.77 ERA.

Most improved player: Shortstop Andujar Cedeno. He hit .283 (an increase of 110 points from '92) with 11 homers and 56 RBIs and improved greatly afield.

Most pleasant surprise: Catcher Scott Servais. He had 10 home runs as a professional (all in the minors) entering the season, but Servais hit 11 in 258 at-bats in '93.

Biggest disappointments: Righthander Doug Drabek and lefthander Greg Swindell. The free agents were a combined 21-31. Drabek paced the N.L. with 18 losses, while Swindell went 2-7 from May to July.

Key injuries: Bagwell's injury was key. Center fielder Steve Finley was slowed by Bell's palsy during spring training and suffered a broken right wrist in April. Swindell spent three weeks on the disabled list with a shoulder strain.

Notable: On September 8, righthander Darryl Kile no-hit New York. ... The Astros established club records for home runs (138), batting average (.267), doubles (288), extra-base hits (460), total bases (2,235) and slugging percentage (.409). ... Despite leading Houston to an 85-77 record and its first upper-division finish since 1989, General Manager Bill Wood and Manager Art Howe were fired. Bob Watson was promoted from assistant G.M. to general manager, and Pittsburgh bullpen coach Terry Collins was named manager.

—NEIL HOHLFELD

RECORDS

1993 regular-season record: 85-77 (3rd in N.L. West); 44-37 at home; 41-40 on road; 51-33 vs. East; 34-44 vs. West; 28-26 vs. LHP; 57-51 vs. RHP; 27-24 on grass; 58-53 on turf; 29-24 in daytime; 56-53 at night; 19-25 in one-run games; 4-8 in extra-inning games; 1-1-0 in doubleheaders.

Team record last five years: 392-418 (.484, ranks 9th in league in that span).

TEAM LEADERS

Batting average: Jeff Bagwell (.320).
At-bats: Craig Biggio (610).
Runs: Craig Biggio (98).
Hits: Craig Biggio (175).
Total bases: Craig Biggio (289).
Doubles: Craig Biggio (41).
Triples: Steve Finley (5).
Home runs: Craig Biggio (21).
Runs batted in: Jeff Bagwell (88).
Stolen bases: Luis Gonzalez (20).
Slugging percentage: Jeff Bagwell (.516).
On-base percentage: Jeff Bagwell (.388).
Wins: Mark Portugal (18).
Earned-run average: Mark Portugal (2.77).
Complete games: Doug Drabek (7).
Shutouts: Pete Harnisch (4).
Saves: Doug Jones (26).
Innings pitched: Doug Drabek (237⅔).
Strikeouts: Pete Harnisch (185).

GAMES BY POSITION

Catcher: Eddie Taubensee 90, Scott Servais 82, Eddie Tucker 8.
First base: Jeff Bagwell 140, Chris Donnels 23, Jim Lindeman 9, Jack Daugherty 1.
Second base: Craig Biggio 155, Casey Candaele 19, Chris Donnels 1, Rick Parker 1.
Third base: Ken Caminiti 143, Chris Donnels 31, Casey Candaele 4, Mike Brumley 1, Andujar Cedeno 1.
Shortstop: Andujar Cedeno 149, Jose Uribe 41, Casey Candaele 14, Mike Brumley 1, Rick Parker 1.
Outfield: Luis Gonzalez 149, Steve Finley 140, Eric Anthony 131, Kevin Bass 64, Chris James 34, Casey Candaele 17, Rick Parker 16, Karl Rhodes 4, Mike Brumley 1, Jack Daugherty 1.

TOP DRAFT CHOICES

1. **Billy Wagner**, LHP, Ferrum (Va.) College.
2. **None.**
3. **None.**
4. **Steve Verduzco**, SS, San Jose, Calif.
5. **Derek Root**, 1B, St. Edward High School, Lakewood, Ohio.
6. **Jamie Saylor**, SS, North Garland High School, Garland, Tex.
7. **Jaime Bluma**, RHP, Wichita State University.
8. **Mike Diorio**, RHP, Seward County (Kan.) C.C.
9. **Brett Callan**, C, San Diego Mesa J.C.
10. **Kary Bridges**, 3B, University of Mississippi.

LOS ANGELES DODGERS
NATIONAL LEAGUE WEST DIVISION

1994 SCHEDULE

N Denotes night game (any game starting after 5 p.m.).
▨ Home games shaded.
* At Three Rivers Stadium in Pittsburgh.

APRIL

SUN	MON	TUE	WED	THU	FRI	SAT
					1 N FLA	2 N ATL
3	4	5 FLA	6 N FLA	7 N FLA	8 N ATL	9 N ATL
10 ATL	11 N STL	12	13 N STL	14 N STL	15 N PIT	16 N PIT
17 PIT	18 N PHI	19 N PHI	20 N NY	21 N NY	22 N MON	23 N MON
24 N MON	25	26 N PHI	27 N PHI	28 N PHI	29 N NY	30 NY

MAY

SUN	MON	TUE	WED	THU	FRI	SAT
1 NY	2 N MON	3 N MON	4 MON	5 N SF	6 N SF	7 SF
8 N SF	9 N HOU	10 N HOU	11 N HOU	12	13 N SD	14 N SD
15 SD	16 N COL	17 N COL	18 N COL	19 N COL	20 N CIN	21 N CIN
22 CIN	23 N CHI	24 N CHI	25 N CHI	26	27 N PIT	28 N PIT
29 PIT	30 N STL	31 N STL				

JUNE

SUN	MON	TUE	WED	THU	FRI	SAT
			1 N STL	2	3 N ATL	4 N ATL
5 ATL	6 N FLA	7 N FLA	8 N FLA	9	10 N CHI	11 CHI
12 CHI	13 N CIN	14 N CIN	15 N CIN	16	17 N COL	18 N COL
19 COL	20 N SD	21 N SD	22 SD	23	24 N HOU	25 N HOU
26 HOU	27 N SF	28 N SF	29 N SF	30 N PHI		

JULY

SUN	MON	TUE	WED	THU	FRI	SAT
					1 N PHI	2 N PHI
3 PHI	4 N MON	5 MON	6 N MON	7 N NY	8 N NY	9 N NY
10 NY	11 ALL-STAR GAME	12	13	14 N PHI	15 N PHI	16 N PHI
17 PHI	18 N NY	19 N NY	20 N NY	21	22 N MON	23 N MON
24 MON	25 N SF	26 N SF	27 SF	28	29 N HOU	30 N HOU
31 HOU						

AUGUST

SUN	MON	TUE	WED	THU	FRI	SAT
	1 N SD	2 N SD	3 N SD	4 N SD	5 N COL	6 COL
7 COL	8 N COL	9 N CIN	10 N CIN	11 N CIN	12 N CHI	13 N CHI
14 CHI	15	16 N PIT	17 N PIT	18 N PIT	19 N FLA	20 N FLA
21 FLA	22	23 N PIT	24 N PIT	25 N PIT	26 N FLA	27 N FLA
28 FLA	29 N ATL	30 N ATL	31 N ATL			

SEPTEMBER

SUN	MON	TUE	WED	THU	FRI	SAT
				1 N ATL	2 N STL	3 STL
4 STL	5 N ATL	6 N ATL	7 N ATL	8	9 N STL	10 N STL
11 STL	12 N CHI	13 N CHI	14 CHI	15 N CIN	16 N CIN	17 N CIN
18 CIN	19 N COL	20 N COL	21 COL	22	23 N SD	24 N SD
25 SD	26 N HOU	27 N HOU	28 N HOU	29 HOU	30 N SF	

OCTOBER

SUN	MON	TUE	WED	THU	FRI	SAT
						1 N SF
2 SF						

1994 SEASON

CLUB DIRECTORY

Board of directors
Peter O'Malley
Harry M. Bardt
Roland Seidler
Mrs. Roland (Terry) Seidler
President
Peter O'Malley
Executive vice president
Fred Claire
Vice president, communications
Tom Hawkins
Vice president, finance
Bob Graziano
Vice president, marketing
Barry Stockhamer
Vice president, stadium operations
Bob Smith
Vice president, ticketing
Walter Nash
Vice president, treasurer
Roland Seidler
Vice president, Campo Las Palmas
Ralph Avila
Assistant secretary and general counsel
Santiago Fernandez
Director, accounting and finance
Bill Foltz
Director, advertising and special events
Paul Kalil
Director, broadcasting and publications
Brent Shyer
Director, community relations
Don Newcombe
Director, community services
Monique Brandon
Dir., human resources and administration
Irene Tanji
Director, management information services
Mike Mularky
Director, minor league operations
Charlie Blaney
Director, scouting
Terry Reynolds
Director, publicity
Jay Lucas
Assistant director, publicity
Chuck Harris
Traveling secretary
Bill DeLury
Director, ticket operations
Debra Duncan
Director, ticket marketing
Allan Erselius
Club physicians
Dr. Frank W. Jobe
Dr. Michael F. Mellman
Dr. Herndon Harding

Scouts
Eleodoro Arias
Eddie Bane
Bill Barkley
Gil Bassetti
Rick Birmingham
Bob Bishop
Gib Bodet
Flores Bolivar
Mike Brito
Joe Campbell
Jim Chapman
Bob Darwin
Eddie Fajardo Rodriguez
Lin Garrett
Ossie Alvarez Gonzalez
Rafael Gonzalez
Michael Hankins
Dick Hanlon
Dennis Haren
Gail Henley
Hank Jones
Lon Joyce
John Keenan
Gary LaRocque
Juan Latigua
Don LeJohn
Carl Lowenstine
Manuel Lunar
Teodoro Mata
Dale McReynolds
Bob Miske
Tommy Mixon
Victor Nazario
Alberto Osorio
Deni Pacini
Camilo Pasqual
Pablo Peguero
Cornelio Pena
Jose Pena
Claude Pelletier
Bill Pleis
Silvano Quesada
Mark Sheehy
Jim Stoeckel
Dick Teed
Tom Thomas
Glen Van Proyen
Special assignment scouts
Mel Didier
Art Howe
Jerry Stephenson
Gary Sutherland

SPRING TRAINING ROSTER

Manager—Tom Lasorda (2).

Coaches—Joe Amalfitano (8), Mark Cresse (58), Manny Mota (11), Ron Perranoski (16), Bill Russell (18), Reggie Smith.

No.	PITCHERS	B/T	Ht./Wt.	Born	1993 clubs
56	Astacio, Pedro	R/R	6-2/190	11-28-69	Los Angeles
49	Candiotti, Tom	R/R	6-2/215	8-31-57	Los Angeles
64	Castro, Nelson	R/R	6-1/165	12-10-71	Bakersfield, San Antonio
54	Daal, Omar	L/L	6-3/175	3-1-72	Albuquerque, Los Angeles
52	DeSilva, John	R/R	6-0/190	9-30-67	Toledo, Detroit, Los Angeles
35	Gott, Jim	R/R	6-4/229	8-3-59	Los Angeles
46	Gross, Kevin	R/R	6-5/227	6-8-61	Los Angeles
57	Gross, Kip	R/R	6-2/194	8-24-64	Albuquerque, Los Angeles
63	Hansell, Greg	R/R	6-5/213	3-12-71	Albuquerque
55	Hershiser, Orel	R/R	6-3/198	9-16-58	Los Angeles
48	Martinez, Ramon J.	L/R	6-4/176	3-22-68	Los Angeles
17	McDowell, Roger	R/R	6-1/197	12-21-60	Los Angeles
65	Parra, Jose	R/R	5-11/160	11-28-72	San Antonio
68	Rodriguez, Felix	R/R	6-1/170	12-5-72	Vero Beach
36	Trlicek, Rick	R/R	6-2/200	4-26-69	Los Angeles
62	VanRyn, Ben	L/L	6-5/185	8-19-71	San Antonio, Albuquerque
61	Williams, Todd	R/R	6-3/185	2-13-71	Albuquerque
50	Wilson, Steve	L/L	6-4/224	12-13-64	Los Angeles, Albuquerque
38	Worrell, Todd	R/R	6-5/222	9-28-59	Los Angeles, Bakersfield, Albuquerque

No.	CATCHERS	B/T	Ht./Wt.	Born	1993 clubs
27	Brooks, Jerry	R/R	6-0/195	3-23-67	Albuquerque, Los Angeles
26	Hernandez, Carlos	R/R	5-11/218	5-24-67	Los Angeles
31	Piazza, Mike	R/R	6-3/197	9-4-68	Los Angeles

No.	INFIELDERS	B/T	Ht./Wt.	Born	1993 clubs
	Blanco, Henry	R/R	5-11/168	8-29-71	San Antonio
21	Bournigal, Rafael	R/R	5-11/165	5-12-66	Albuquerque, Los Angeles
25	Busch, Mike	R/R	6-5/241	7-7-68	Albuquerque
70	Coomer, Ron	R/R	5-11/195	11-18-66	Birmingham, Nashville
14	DeShields, Delino	L/R	6-1/175	1-15-69	Montreal
5	Hansen, Dave	L/R	6-0/195	11-24-68	Los Angeles
71	Ingram, Garey	R/R	5-11/180	7-25-70	San Antonio
23	Karros, Eric	R/R	6-4/216	11-4-67	Los Angeles
30	Offerman, Jose	B/R	6-0/165	11-8-68	Los Angeles
60	Pye, Eddie	R/R	5-10/175	2-13-67	Albuquerque
29	Wallach, Tim	R/R	6-3/202	9-14-57	Los Angeles

No.	OUTFIELDERS	B/T	Ht./Wt.	Born	1993 clubs
7	Ashley, Billy	R/R	6-7/227	7-11-70	Albuquerque, Los Angeles
22	Butler, Brett	L/L	5-10/161	6-15-57	Los Angeles
43	Mondesi, Raul	R/R	5-11/202	3-12-71	Albuquerque, Los Angeles
26	Rodriguez, Henry	L/L	6-1/200	11-8-67	Albuquerque, Los Angeles
28	Snyder, Cory	R/R	6-3/206	11-11-62	Los Angeles
44	Strawberry, Darryl	L/L	6-6/215	3-12-62	Los Angeles, Albuquerque
20	Webster, Mitch	B/L	6-1/191	5-16-59	Los Angeles

BALLPARK INFORMATION

Ballpark (capacity, surface)
Dodger Stadium (56,000, grass)
Address
1000 Elysian Park Ave.
Los Angeles, CA 90012
Business phone
213-224-1500
Ticket information
213-224-1400
Ticket prices
$11 & $13 (box seats)
$8 & $9 (reserved seats)
$6 (top deck and pavilion)
$3 (g.a., youth 12 and under)
Field dimensions (from home plate)
To left field at foul line, 330 feet
To center field, 395 feet
To right field at foul line, 330 feet
First game played
April 10, 1962 (Reds 6, Dodgers 3)

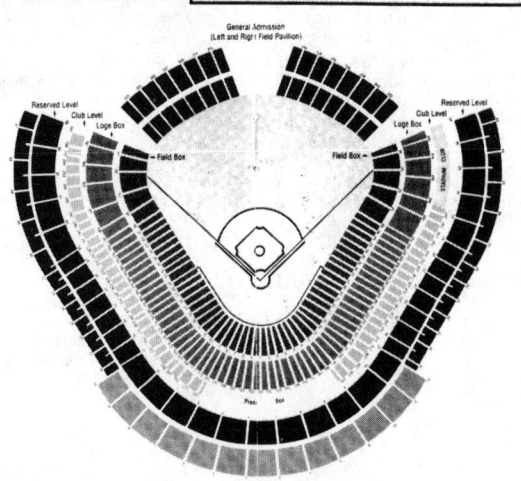

MINOR LEAGUE AFFILIATES

Class	Team	League	Manager
AAA	Albuquerque	Pacific Coast	Rick Dempsey
AA	San Antonio	Texas	Tom Beyers
A	Bakersfield	California	John Shelby
A	Vero Beach	Florida State	John Debus
A	Yakima	Northwest	Joe Vavra
Rookie	Great Falls	Pioneer	Ron Roenicke

BROADCAST INFORMATION

Radio: KABC-AM (790). Broadcasters: Vin Scully, Rick Monday, Ross Porter. KWKW-AM (1330, Spanish language). Broadcasters: Jaime Jarrin, Rene Cardenas.

TV: KTLA-TV (Channel 5). Broadcasters: Vin Scully, Ross Porter.

SPRING TRAINING

Ballpark (city): Holman Stadium (Vero Beach, Fla.).
Ticket information: 407-569-4900.

HISTORY

YEAR-BY-YEAR RECORDS

Year	Pos.	W	L	Pct.	GB	Year	Pos.	W	L	Pct.	GB
1901*	3rd	79	57	.581	9½	1951*	2nd†	97	60	.618	1
1902*	2nd	75	63	.543	27½	1952*	1st	96	57	.627 +	4½
1903*	5th	70	66	.515	19	1953*	1st	105	49	.682	+13
1904*	6th	56	97	.366	50	1954*	2nd	92	62	.597	5
1905*	8th	48	104	.316	56½	1955*	1st	98	55	.641	+13½
1906*	5th	66	86	.434	50	1956*	1st	93	61	.604 +	1
1907*	5th	65	83	.439	40	1957*	3rd	84	70	.545	11
1908*	7th	53	101	.344	46	1958	7th	71	83	.461	21
1909*	6th	55	98	.359	55½	1959	1st‡	88	68	.564 +	2
1910*	6th	64	90	.416	40	1960	4th	82	72	.532	13
1911*	7th	64	86	.427	33½	1961	2nd	89	65	.578	4
1912*	7th	58	95	.379	46	1962	2nd†	102	63	.618	1
1913*	6th	65	84	.436	34½	1963	1st	99	63	.611 +	6
1914*	5th	75	79	.487	19½	1964	T6th	80	82	.494	13
1915*	3rd	80	72	.526	10	1965	1st	97	65	.599 +	2
1916*	1st	94	60	.610 +	2½	1966	1st	95	67	.586 +	1½
1917*	7th	70	81	.464	26½	1967	8th	73	89	.451	28½
1918*	5th	57	69	.452	25½	1968	7th	76	86	.469	21
1919*	5th	69	71	.493	27	1969	4th	85	77	.525	8
1920*	1st	93	61	.604 +	7	1970	2nd	87	74	.540	14½
1921*	5th	77	75	.507	16½	1971	2nd	89	73	.549	1
1922*	6th	76	78	.494	17	1972	3rd	85	70	.548	10½
1923*	6th	76	78	.494	19½	1973	2nd	95	66	.590	3½
1924*	2nd	92	62	.597	1½	1974	1st§	102	60	.630 +	4
1925*	T6th	68	85	.444	27	1975	2nd	88	74	.543	20
1926*	6th	71	82	.464	17½	1976	2nd	92	70	.568	10
1927*	6th	65	88	.425	28½	1977	1st§	98	64	.605	+10
1928*	6th	77	76	.503	17½	1978	1st§	95	67	.586 +	2½
1929*	6th	70	83	.458	28½	1979	3rd	79	83	.488	11½
1930*	4th	86	68	.558	6	1980	2nd★	92	71	.564	1
1931*	4th	79	73	.520	21	1981	1st/4th	63	47	.573	•§◆
1932*	3rd	81	73	.526	9	1982	2nd	88	74	.543	1
1933*	6th	65	88	.425	26½	1983	1st■	91	71	.652 +	3
1934*	6th	71	81	.467	23½	1984	4th	79	83	.488	13
1935*	5th	70	83	.458	29½	1985	1st■	95	67	.586 +	5½
1936*	7th	67	87	.435	25	1986	5th	73	89	.451	23
1937*	6th	62	91	.405	33½	1987	4th	73	89	.451	17
1938*	7th	69	80	.463	18½	1988	1st§	94	67	.584 +	7
1939*	3rd	84	69	.549	12½	1989	4th	77	83	.481	14
1940*	2nd	88	65	.575	12	1990	2nd	86	76	.531	5
1941*	1st	100	54	.649 +	2½	1991	2nd	93	69	.574	1
1942*	2nd	104	50	.675	2	1992	6th	63	99	.389	35
1943*	3rd	81	72	.529	23½	1993	4th	81	81	.500	23
1944*	7th	63	91	.409	42						
1945*	3rd	87	67	.565	11						
1946*	2nd†	96	60	.615	2						
1947*	1st	94	60	.610 +	5						
1948*	3rd	84	70	.545	7½						
1949*	1st	97	57	.630 +	1						
1950*	2nd	89	65	.578	2						

*Franchise known as Brooklyn Dodgers. †Lost pennant playoff. ‡Won pennant playoff. §Won Championship Series. ★Lost division playoff. • Won division playoff. ◆First half 36-21; second 27-26. ■Lost Championship Series.

MANAGERS

Name	Record	Years
Ned Hanlon	328-387	'01-05
Patsy Donovan	184-270	'06-08
Harry Lumley	55-98	1909
Bill Dahlen	251-355	'10-13
Wilbert Robinson	1375-1341	'14-31
Max Carey	146-161	'32-33
Casey Stengel	208-251	'34-36
Burleigh Grimes	131-171	'37-38
Leo Durocher	738-565	'39-46
		1948
Clyde Sukeforth	2-0	1947
Burt Shotton	326-215	1947
		'48-50
Chuck Dressen	298-166	'51-53
Walter Alston	2040-1613	'54-76
Tommy Lasorda	1422-1282	'76-93

DAY BY DAY

Date	Opp.	Res.	Score	(inn.*)	Hits	Opp. hits	Winning pitcher	Losing pitcher	Save	Record	Pos.	GB
4-5	At Fla.	L	3-6		8	14	Hough	Hershiser	Harvey	0-1	T5th	1
4-6	At Fla.	W	4-2		8	8	R. Martinez	Armstrong	Worrell	1-1	T3rd	1
4-7	At Fla.	W	4-2		9	9	Ke. Gross	Hammond	McDowell	2-1	T1st	...
4-8	At Atl.	L	1-6		5	8	Glavine	Candiotti		2-2	2nd	1
4-9	At Atl.	L	0-2		3	5	Smith	Astacio	Stanton	2-3	2nd	2
4-10	At Atl.	W	2-1	(10)	8	4	Hershiser	Howell	Gott	3-3	T2nd	1
4-11	At Atl.	L	0-3		4	4	Smoltz	R. Martinez	Stanton	3-4	4th	2
4-13	St.L.	L	7-9		14	13	Lancaster	P. Martinez	Smith	3-5	5th	2½
4-14	St.L.	L	1-2	(15)	4	12	Lancaster	Trlicek	Smith	3-6	4th	2½
4-15	St.L.	L	2-4		7	7	Arocha	Ke. Gross	Smith	3-7	5th	3
4-16	Pit.	W	7-4		15	10	Hershiser	Wakefield	Gott	4-7	4th	3
4-17	Pit.	W	6-3		11	5	R. Martinez	Otto		5-7	4th	2
4-18	Pit.	W	6-4		11	9	Ke. Gross	Walk	Wilson	6-7	4th	2
4-20	At Mon.	L	3-7		5	9	Nabholz	Candiotti		6-8	4th	3
4-21	At Mon.	L	4-6		3	7	Jones	Astacio	Barnes	6-9	4th	3
4-22	At Mon.	L	1-3		4	7	Fassero	Hershiser	Rojas	6-10	5th	4
4-23	At Phi.	L	0-2		5	5	Schilling	R. Martinez		6-11	6th	4
4-24	At Phi.	L	3-7		10	10	Jackson	Ke. Gross	Mit. Williams	6-12	7th	5
4-25	At Phi.	L	2-5		5	6	Greene	Candiotti	Mit. Williams	6-13	7th	5
4-27	At N.Y.	W	4-1		2	3	Hershiser	Gooden		7-13	T6th	4½
4-28	Mon.	W	6-1		8	9	Astacio	Martinez		8-13	T5th	4½
4-29	Mon.	L	3-7		9	14	Hill	R. Martinez		8-14	6th	5½
4-30	Phi.	L	6-7		15	7	Ayrault	Daal	Mit. Williams	8-15	7th	6½
5-1	Phi.	W	5-1		11	6	Candiotti	Rivera		9-15	6th	6½
5-2	Phi.	L	1-9		6	13	Mulholland	Hershiser		9-16	7th	7½
5-4	N.Y.	W	8-4		14	10	Astacio	Tanana		10-16	6th	6½
5-5	N.Y.	W	6-5		14	9	P. Martinez	Maddux	Gott	11-16	5th	6½
5-7	At S.F.	L	5-8		10	14	Black	Ke. Gross		11-17	6th	7½
5-8	At S.F.	W	5-2	(12)	10	12	Gott	Burba		12-17	T5th	6½
5-9	At S.F.	W	6-4		8	3	Hershiser	Brantley	Gott	13-17	5th	5½
5-10	At Chi.	L	2-6		3	11	Hibbard	Astacio		13-18	T5th	6
5-11	At Chi.	L	1-2	(10)	8	13	Scanlan	Gott		13-19	6th	6½
5-12	At Chi.	W	9-3		16	8	McDowell	Morgan		14-19	5th	6½
5-14	At Hou.	L	1-9		5	13	Harnisch	Candiotti		14-20	T5th	7
5-15	At Hou.	L	1-7		6	10	Portugal	Hershiser		14-21	T5th	8
5-16	At Hou.	L	2-3		8	9	Drabek	P. Martinez	D. Jones	14-22	T5th	9
5-17	Cin.	W	5-4	(10)	10	16	Gott	Landrum		15-22	T5th	9
5-18	Cin.	W	9-1		8	6	Ke. Gross	Smiley		16-22	5th	9
5-19	Cin.	W	5-2		11	5	Candiotti	Pugh	Gott	17-22	5th	9
5-21	Col.	W	8-0		12	5	Hershiser	Nied		18-22	5th	9½
5-22	Col.	W	4-3		8	7	McDowell	Henry	Gott	19-22	5th	8½
5-23	Col.	W	4-0		8	3	R. Martinez	Blair		20-22	4th	8½
5-24	S.D.	W	5-4		9	8	Ke. Gross	Gr. Harris	P. Martinez	21-22	4th	8
5-25	S.D.	W	10-9	(10)	17	15	P. Martinez	Mason		22-22	4th	8
5-26	S.D.	W	8-3		11	8	Wilson	Whitehurst		23-22	4th	7
5-28	At Pit.	W	7-2		12	8	Astacio	Tomlin		24-22	T3rd	5½
5-29	At Pit.	W	6-1		12	4	R. Martinez	Otto		25-22	T3rd	5½
5-30	At Pit.	L	3-5		9	8	Cooke	Ke. Gross	Belinda	25-23	4th	6½
5-31	At St.L.	W	5-1		13	4	Candiotti	Tewksbury		26-23	4th	6
6-1	At St.L.	W	11-6		14	9	P. Martinez	Magrane		27-23	T3rd	5½
6-2	At St.L.	L	4-5		9	9	Osborne	Astacio	Smith	27-24	4th	6½
6-4	Atl.	W	5-4		9	7	R. Martinez	Glavine	Gott	28-24	3rd	5
6-5	Atl.	W	5-1		12	5	Ke. Gross	Maddux		29-24	3rd	5
6-6	Atl.	L	0-2		5	6	Smoltz	Candiotti		29-25	3rd	6
6-7	Fla.	L	3-5		5	7	Lewis	Worrell	Hoffman	29-26	4th	6½
6-8	Fla.	W	2-1		4	8	Astacio	Armstrong	Gott	30-26	3rd	5½
6-10	At S.D.	L	2-14		8	14	Whitehurst	R. Martinez		30-27	3rd	6½
6-11	At S.D.	L	4-5		8	8	Gomez	Gott		30-28	4th	7½
6-12	At S.D.	W	6-4		10	11	Daal	Mason	Gott	31-28	4th	7½
6-13	At S.D.	W	2-1		9	8	Hershiser	Gr. Harris	Gott	32-28	T3rd	7½
6-14	At Col.	W	9-4		12	9	Astacio	Blair		33-28	2nd	7
6-15	At Col.	W	12-4		16	12	McDowell	Shepherd		34-28	2nd	6
6-16	At Col.	L	6-7		9	12	Reynoso	Ke. Gross	Grant	34-29	3rd	7
6-18	At Cin.	L	3-4	(10)	6	8	Ayala	Gott		34-30	T3rd	8½
6-19	At Cin.	L	4-8		10	19	Browning	Hershiser	Ayala	34-31	T3rd	9½
6-20	At Cin.	W	6-3		10	5	Astacio	Belcher	Gott	35-31	3rd	9½
6-21	Hou.	W	7-0		13	2	R. Martinez	Portugal		36-31	3rd	9½
6-22	Hou.	L	1-5		9	9	Kile	Ke. Gross		36-32	3rd	9½
6-23	Hou.	L	3-5		6	7	Drabek	Gott	Williams	36-33	T3rd	10½
6-24	Hou.	L	0-1		8	8	Swindell	Hershiser	Osuna	36-34	4th	11½

Date		Opp.	Res.	Score	(inn.*)	Hits	Opp. hits	Winning pitcher	Losing pitcher	Save	Record	Pos.	GB
6-25		Chi.	L	5-8	(10)	9	8	Myers	Gott		36-35	4th	12½
6-26		Chi.	W	5-4		11	10	McDowell	Scanlan	Gott	37-35	T3rd	11½
6-27		Chi.	W	3-1		12	6	Ke. Gross	Bautista		38-35	T3rd	11½
6-28		S.F.	L	4-0		5	7	P. Martinez	Jackson		39-35	3rd	10½
6-29		S.F.	L	1-3		4	7	Burkett	Hershiser	Beck	39-36	2nd	8½
6-30		S.F.	W	5-3		10	6	P. Martinez	Rogers	Gott	40-36	3rd	10½
7-2		At Mon.	W	4-3		9	7	R. Martinez	Barnes	Gott	41-36	3rd	10½
7-3		At Mon.	L	4-6		8	12	Martinez	Ke. Gross	Wetteland	41-37	T3rd	10½
7-4		At Mon.	W	1-0	(11)	7	7	Gott	Shaw	McDowell	42-37	T3rd	10½
7-5		At Phi.	L	5-9		9	11	Greene	Hershiser		42-38	T3rd	11½
7-6		At Phi.	W	7-5		13	8	Astacio	Schilling	Gott	43-38	3rd	11½
7-7		At Phi.	L	6-7	(20)	17	12	Mike Williams	Trlicek		43-39	3rd	11½
7-8	(1)	At N.Y.	W	11-8		17	17	Ke. Gross	Telgheder		44-39	3rd	11½
7-8	(2)	At N.Y.	L	3-6	(10)	8	8	Innis	Nichols		44-40	3rd	12
7-9		At N.Y.	W	6-2		11	9	Hershiser	Tanana		45-40	3rd	12
7-10		At N.Y.	L	6-7		11	7	Saberhagen	Astacio	Franco	45-41	T3rd	12
7-11		At N.Y.	W	2-1		10	7	P. Martinez	Gooden	Gott	46-41	T3rd	12
7-15		Mon.	W	3-2		4	9	R. Martinez	D. Martinez	Gott	47-41	3rd	12
7-16		Mon.	W	2-1		10	6	P. Martinez	Wetteland		48-41	3rd	12
7-17		Mon.	L	6-9	(10)	8	13	Gardiner	Daal	Wetteland	48-42	2nd	9
7-18		Mon.	W	2-1		8	6	Candiotti	Shaw	P. Martinez	49-42	3rd	11
7-19		Phi.	L	5-7		8	11	Mason	Daal	Mit. Williams	49-43	3rd	12
7-20		Phi.	L	2-8		6	15	Jackson	R. Martinez		49-44	3rd	13
7-21		Phi.	L	0-7		6	11	Greene	Hershiser		49-45	T3rd	14
7-22		N.Y.	L	5-10		12	10	Saberhagen	Ke. Gross	Young	49-46	4th	15
7-23		N.Y.	W	5-2		8	5	Candiotti	Tanana		50-46	4th	14
7-24		N.Y.	W	5-4	(10)	8	11	Gott	Young		51-46	T3rd	14
7-25		N.Y.	L	0-4		5	8	Hillman	R. Martinez		51-47	T3rd	15
7-26		At S.F.	W	15-1		17	5	Hershiser	Hickerson		52-47	3rd	14
7-27		At S.F.	L	2-3		3	9	Burkett	Ke. Gross	Beck	52-48	T3rd	15
7-28		At S.F.	W	2-1		8	5	Candiotti	Black	Gott	53-48	T3rd	14
7-30		At Chi.	L	1-2		6	4	Castillo	Astacio	Myers	53-49	4th	15
7-31		At Chi.	W	7-2	(13)	14	8	P. Martinez	Scanlan		54-49	3rd	15
8-1		At Chi.	L	4-10		7	13	Guzman	Hershiser		54-50	3rd	16
8-3		At Hou.	L	1-6		5	10	Portugal	Ke. Gross	Hernandez	54-51	4th	17
8-4		At Hou.	W	4-2		7	10	Candiotti	Harnisch	Gott	55-51	3rd	16
8-5		At Hou.	W	5-2		11	5	Astacio	Drabek	Gott	56-51	3rd	16
8-6		Cin.	W	3-2		11	8	P. Martinez	Dibble		57-51	3rd	16
8-7		Cin.	L	6-9		12	13	Spradlin	Hershiser	Dibble	57-52	3rd	16
8-8		Cin.	L	5-8		6	9	Ruffin	McDowell	Dibble	57-53	3rd	16
8-9		Col.	L	2-3	(11)	9	9	Reed	Gott	Holmes	57-54	4th	17
8-10		Col.	L	2-4		7	11	Bottenfield	Astacio		57-55	4th	18
8-11		Col.	L	2-3		7	15	Reynoso	R. Martinez	Reed	57-56	4th	19
8-12		Col.	L	1-4		7	6	Blair	Hershiser		57-57	5th	19½
8-13		S.D.	L	1-4		8	11	Whitehurst	Ke. Gross	Ge. Harris	57-58	5th	20½
8-14		S.D.	W	4-3		8	13	Candiotti	Brocail	Gott	58-58	4th	19½
8-15		S.D.	W	4-2		10	8	Astacio	Ashby	Gott	59-58	4th	19½
8-17		At Atl.	L	2-3		8	6	Smoltz	R. Martinez	McMichael	59-59	4th	19½
8-18		At Atl.	L	4-5	(12)	8	6	Bedrosian	McDowell		59-60	4th	20½
8-19		At Atl.	W	7-5		11	14	Ke. Gross	Glavine	Gott	60-60	4th	20½
8-20		At St.L.	W	3-2		6	9	Worrell	Smith	Gott	61-60	4th	19½
8-21		At St.L.	W	8-4		11	5	Astacio	Urbani		62-60	4th	19½
8-22		At St.L.	W	3-0		8	4	R. Martinez	Tewksbury		63-60	4th	19½
8-23		Pit.	W	6-1		14	8	Hershiser	Smith		64-60	4th	18½
8-24		Pit.	W	13-4		15	8	Ke. Gross	Walk		65-60	4th	17½
8-25		Pit.	L	1-2	(12)	10	8	Neagle	Gott		65-61	4th	17½
8-27		St.L.	L	2-3	(10)	5	9	Murphy	P. Martinez	Smith	65-62	4th	17½
8-28		St.L.	L	3-4		11	9	Tewksbury	R. Martinez	Smith	65-63	4th	18
8-29		St.L.	W	8-3		16	6	Hershiser	Watson		66-63	4th	18
8-31		At Pit.	L	2-6		4	12	Johnston	Ke. Gross		66-64	4th	18½
9-1		At Pit.	L	1-5		8	9	Cooke	Candiotti		66-65	4th	19½
9-2		At Pit.	W	4-0		11	4	Astacio	Ballard		67-65	4th	18½
9-3		At Fla.	W	5-4	(13)	13	14	Daal	Johnstone		68-65	4th	18½
9-4		At Fla.	W	9-4		13	8	Hershiser	Armstrong		69-65	4th	18½
9-5		At Fla.	L	3-4		5	11	Turner	McDowell	Harvey	69-66	3rd	18½
9-6		Atl.	W	2-1		6	6	P. Martinez	Smoltz		70-66	4th	18½
9-7		Atl.	L	0-1		5	5	Avery	Astacio	McMichael	70-67	4th	18½
9-8		Atl.	L	2-8		10	13	Glavine	R. Martinez		70-68	4th	19
9-9		Fla.	W	6-5	(10)	13	9	Trlicek	Turner		71-68	4th	18
9-10		Fla.	L	1-2		6	3	Hough	Ke. Gross	Harvey	71-69	4th	18
9-11		Fla.	L	2-3		10	9	Weathers	Candiotti	Harvey	71-70	4th	19
9-12		Fla.	W	1-0		6	5	Astacio	Rapp		72-70	4th	18
9-13		At S.D.	L	3-4	(11)	9	4	Ge. Harris	Gott		72-71	4th	18½
9-14		At S.D.	W	5-3		6	6	Hershiser	Brocail	Worrell	73-71	4th	18½

Date	Opp.	Res.	Score	(inn.*)	Hits	Opp. hits	Winning pitcher	Losing pitcher	Save	Record	Pos.	GB
9-15	At S.D.	W	5-4		8	12	Ke. Gross	Tim Worrell	Todd Worrell	74-71	4th	18½
9-17	At Col.	L	3-12		10	17	Nied	Candiotti		74-72	4th	20
9-18	At Col.	W	9-0		11	7	Astacio	Hurst		75-72	4th	19
9-19	At Col.	L	5-8		7	12	Reynoso	P. Martinez	Holmes	75-73	4th	20
9-20	At Cin.	W	5-2		12	4	R. Martinez	Rijo	Worrell	76-73	4th	19½
9-21	At Cin.	W	5-3	(11)	9	8	McDowell	Reardon	Trlicek	77-73	4th	19½
9-22	At Cin.	W	3-1		8	6	Ke. Gross	Roper	Worrell	78-73	4th	18½
9-23	At Cin.	L	2-11		7	11	Pugh	Candiotti		78-74	4th	18½
9-24	Hou.	W	6-3		12	5	Astacio	Kile		79-74	3rd	18½
9-25	Hou.	L	4-12		9	18	Swindell	P. Martinez		79-75	4th	19½
9-26	Hou.	L	4-5		8	8	Portugal	R. Martinez	D. Jones	79-76	4th	20½
9-27	Chi.	L	3-7		8	10	Bautista	Hershiser	Myers	79-77	4th	21
9-28	Chi.	W	6-5		8	8	Ke. Gross	Harkey	Gott	80-77	4th	20
9-29	Chi.	L	1-6		10	12	Hibbard	Astacio	Myers	80-78	4th	21
9-30	S.F.	L	1-3		4	10	Swift	Candiotti	Beck	80-79	4th	21
10-1	S.F.	L	7-8		12	11	Burkett	R. Martinez	Beck	80-80	4th	22
10-2	S.F.	L	3-5		10	9	Brantley	Hershiser	Beck	80-81	4th	23
10-3	S.F.	W	12-1		14	6	Ke. Gross	Torres		81-81	4th	23

Monthly records: April (8-15), May (18-8), June (14-13), July (14-13), August (12-15), September (14-15), October (1-2).
*Innings, if other than nine.

HIGHLIGHTS

High point: From May 17 to June 15, Los Angeles won 20 of 26 games, including a major league-high 11 wins in a row, to move from a tie for fifth place to a tie for second, six games out of first. It was the closest Los Angeles would get to first the rest of the season.

Low point: After that run, the Dodgers lost seven of their next nine games to fall 12½ games off the pace.

Turning point: On June 15, the Dodgers won at Colorado, 12-4. But there were two bench-clearing brawls as well as a play at second base in which the Rockies' Andres Galarraga slid into Jody Reed, who injured his left elbow and was sidelined for a month. Los Angeles was 12-13 minus Reed.

Most valuable player: Catcher Mike Piazza. He surprised everyone by hitting .318 with 35 homers and 112 RBIs en route to capturing N.L. Rookie of the Year honors.

Most valuable pitchers: Righthanders Tom Candiotti and Pedro Astacio. Candiotti was 8-10, but his 3.12 ERA ranked seventh in the league. Astacio led the staff with 14 wins.

Most improved player: Shortstop Jose Offerman. He displayed more confidence and athletic ability defensively and became a force on offense, driving in 62 runs, the most by a Dodger shortstop since 1976.

Most pleasant surprise: Righthander Pedro Martinez. He was summoned from Class AAA on April 9 and proceeded to strike out 119 batters in 107 innings while finishing at 10-5 with a 2.61 ERA.

Biggest disappointments: Righthander Todd Worrell and right fielder Darryl Strawberry. Worrell got hurt in April and finished with five saves and a 6.05 ERA. Strawberry played in just 32 games and had almost as many errors (four) as homers (five).

Key injuries: Strawberry (back) and Worrell (forearm and elbow) both spent two stints on the disabled list. Reed's injury also was costly.

Notable: Piazza's homer total was the most ever by a rookie big-league catcher. ... The Dodgers had three players—center fielder Brett Butler (39), Offerman (30) and left fielder Eric Davis (33)—steal 30 or more bases for the first time since 1903. ... Infielder Dave Hansen collected a team-record 18 pinch hits. ... First baseman Eric Karros became the first Dodger to hit at least 20 homers in his first two seasons.

—GORDON VERRELL

RECORDS

1993 regular-season record: 81-81 (4th in N.L. West); 41-40 at home; 40-41 on road; 42-42 vs. East; 39-39 vs. West; 30-24 vs. LHP; 51-57 vs. RHP; 64-61 on grass; 17-20 on turf; 21-24 in day-time; 60-57 at night; 27-27 in one-run games; 10-12 in extra-inning games; 0-0-1 in doubleheaders.

Team record last five years: 400-408 (.495, ranks 8th in league in that span).

TEAM LEADERS

Batting average: Mike Piazza (.318).
At-bats: Eric Karros (619).
Runs: Mike Piazza (81).
Hits: Brett Butler (181).
Total bases: Mike Piazza (307).
Doubles: Cory Snyder (33).
Triples: Brett Butler (10).
Home runs: Mike Piazza (35).
Runs batted in: Mike Piazza (112).
Stolen bases: Brett Butler (39).
Slugging percentage: Mike Piazza (.561).
On-base percentage: Brett Butler (.387).
Wins: Pedro Astacio (14).
Earned-run average: Tom Candiotti (3.12).
Complete games: Orel Hershiser (5).
Shutouts: Ramon Martinez (3).
Saves: Jim Gott (25).
Innings pitched: Orel Hershiser (215⅔).
Strikeouts: Tom Candiotti (155).

GAMES BY POSITION

Catcher: Mike Piazza 146, Carlos Hernandez 43.
First base: Eric Karros 157, Henry Rodriguez 13, Cory Snyder 12, Mike Piazza 1, Mike Sharperson 1, Tim Wallach 1.
Second base: Jody Reed 132, Lenny Harris 35, Mike Sharperson 17, Rafael Bournigal 4.
Third base: Tim Wallach 130, Cory Snyder 23, Dave Hansen 18, Lenny Harris 17, Mike Sharperson 6.
Shortstop: Jose Offerman 158, Rafael Bournigal 4, Lenny Harris 3, Mike Sharperson 3, Cory Snyder 2.
Outfield: Brett Butler 155, Cory Snyder 115, Eric Davis 103, Mitch Webster 56, Henry Rodriguez 48, Raul Mondesi 40, Darryl Strawberry 29, Tom Goodwin 12, Billy Ashley 11, Jerry Brooks 2, Lenny Harris 2, Mike Sharperson 1.

TOP DRAFT CHOICES

1. **Darren Dreifort**, RHP, Wichita State University.
2. **None.**
3. **Dax Winslett**, RHP, Arizona State University.
4. **Nathan Bland**, LHP, Mountain Brook (Ala.) High School.
5. **Scott Hunter**, C, Northeast High School, Philadelphia.
6. **Nate Yeskie**, RHP, Carson High School, Carson City, Nev.
7. **Doug Newstrom**, 1B, Arizona State University.
8. **Jose Prado**, RHP, University of Miami (Fla.).
9. **Matt Schwenke**, C, UCLA.
10. **John Vukson**, RHP/3B, Sanger High School, Fresno, Calif.

MONTREAL EXPOS
NATIONAL LEAGUE EAST DIVISION

1994 SCHEDULE

- **N** Denotes night game (any game starting after 5 p.m.).
- ▨ Home games shaded.
- * At Three Rivers Stadium in Pittsburgh.

APRIL

SUN	MON	TUE	WED	THU	FRI	SAT
					1	2
3	4 N HOU	5 N HOU	6 N HOU	7	8 CHI	9 CHI
10 CHI	11 N CIN	12 N CIN	13 N CIN	14	15 N COL	16 COL
17 COL	18 N SF	19 SF	20 N SD	21 SD	22 N LA	23 LA
24 N LA	25	26 N SF	27 SF	28	29 N SD	30 SD

MAY

SUN	MON	TUE	WED	THU	FRI	SAT
1 SD	2 N LA	3 N LA	4 LA	5	6 N ATL	7 ATL
8 ATL	9 N NY	10 N NY	11 NY	12	13 N STL	14 STL
15 STL	16 N PHI	17 N PHI	18 PHI	19	20 N PIT	21 PIT
22 PIT	23 N FLA	24 N FLA	25 FLA	26	27 N COL	28 COL
29 COL	30 N CIN	31 N CIN				

JUNE

SUN	MON	TUE	WED	THU	FRI	SAT
			1 N CIN	2	3 CHI	4 CHI
5 CHI	6 N HOU	7 N HOU	8 N NY	9 N NY	10 N NY	11 NY
12 NY	13 N PIT	14 N PIT	15 PIT	16	17 N PHI	18 N PHI
19 N PHI	20 N STL	21 N STL	22 STL	23	24 N FLA	25 N FLA
26 FLA	27 N ATL	28 N ATL	29 ATL	30 N SF		

JULY

SUN	MON	TUE	WED	THU	FRI	SAT
					1 N SF	2 SF
3 SF	4 N LA	5 LA	6 N LA	7 N SD	8 N SD	9 SD
10 SD	11 N	12 ALL-STAR GAME	13	14 N SF	15 N SF	16 SF
17 SF	18 N SB	19 N SB	20 N SD	21	22 N LA	23 N LA
24 LA	25 N ATL	26 N ATL	27 ATL	28	29 N FLA	30 N FLA
31 N FLA						

AUGUST

SUN	MON	TUE	WED	THU	FRI	SAT
	1 N STL	2 N STL	3 N STL	4 N PHI	5 N PHI	6 PHI
7 PHI	8 N PIT	9 N PIT	10 N PIT	11	12 N NY	13 NY
14 NY	15 N COL	16 N COL	17 COL	18	19 N HOU	20 N HOU
21 HOU	22 N COL	23 N COL	24 COL	25	26 N HOU	27 N HOU
28 HOU	29 N CHI	30 N CHI	31 CHI			

SEPTEMBER

SUN	MON	TUE	WED	THU	FRI	SAT
				1	2 N CIN	3 N CIN
4 CIN	5 N CHI	6 N CHI	7 CHI	8	9 N CIN	10 N CIN
11 CIN	12 N NY	13 N NY	14 NY	15	16 N PIT	17 N PIT
18 PIT	19 N PHI	20 N PHI	21 PHI	22	23 N STL	24 N STL
25 STL	26 N FLA	27 N FLA	28 FLA	29 N ATL	30	

OCTOBER

SUN	MON	TUE	WED	THU	FRI	SAT
						1 N ATL
2 ATL						

1994 SEASON

CLUB DIRECTORY

President and general partner
Claude R. Brochu

Chairman of the board
Jacques Menard

Vice chairmen of the board
Jacques Berube
Claude Blanchet
Jocelyn Proteau

V.p., player personnel and general manager
Dan Duquette

Vice president, baseball operations
Bill Stoneman

Vice president, finance
Laurier M. Carpentier

Director, financial planning & admin.
Michel Buissiere

Manager, accounting services
Constance Jodoin

Vice president, sales
Mag Kassis

Director, scouting
Kevin Malone

Director, minor league field operations
Herm Starrette

Director, team travel
Erik Ostling

Director, minor league operations
Kent Qualls

International scouting supervisor
Fred Ferreira

Executive advisor, baseball operations
Eddie Haas

General mgr., West Palm Beach operations
Rob Rabenecker

Administrative assistant, scouting
Gregg Leonard

Admin. asst., minor league operations
Neal Huntington

V.p., marketing and communications
Richard Morency

Vice president, business operations
Claude Delorme

Director, corporate sponsorships, media
Carole Boivin

Director, events
Claudine Cook

Director, promotions
Luigi Carolo

Director, ticket office
Chantal Dalpe

Director, media services
Monique Giroux

Director, media relations
Richard Griffin

Director, advertising
Johanne Heroux

Director, stadium operations
Pierre Touzin

Director, merchandising
Susan LeBlanc

Director, group sales
Ronald Martineau

Director, season ticket sales
Claude Chabot

Public relations representative
Ron Piche

Club physician
Dr. Robert Brodrick

Club orthopedist
Dr. Larry Coughlin

Scouts
Dennis Cardoza
Doug Carpenter
Emilio Carrasquel
Carl Cassell
Ed Creech
Arturo DeFreitas
Richard DeHart
Phil Favia
Fred Ferreira
Joe Ferrone
Jim Fleming
Joe Frisina
Eddie Haas
Jim Holden
John Hughes
Dave Jauss
Bob Johnson
Jeff Kahn
Gregg Leonard
Dave Littlefield
Juan Loyola
Bill MacKenzie
Kevin Malone
Dave Malpass
Rene Marchand
Roberto Mazur
Roy McMillan
Tomas Morales
Carlos Moreno
Mike Murphy
Bob Oldis
Rene Picota
Hank Sargent
Scott Stanley
Pat Sullivan
Fred Wright

Manager—Felipe Alou (17).

Coaches—Pierre Arsenault (67), Tommy Harper (21), Tim Johnson (1), Joe Kerrigan (45), Jerry Manual (6), Luis Pujols (31).

No.	PITCHERS	B/T	Ht./Wt.	Born	1993 clubs
	Alvarez, Tavo	R/R	6-3/225	11-25-71	Ottawa
41	Batista, Miguel	R/R	6-1/170	2-19-71	Harrisburg
38	Boucher, Denis	R/L	6-1/195	3-7-68	Las Vegas, Ottawa, Montreal
49	Cornelius, Reid	R/R	6-0/185	6-2-70	Harrisburg
58	Eischen, Joey	L/L	6-1/190	5-25-70	Harrisburg, Ottawa
13	Fassero, Jeff	L/L	6-1/195	1-5-63	Montreal
34	Heredia, Gil	R/R	6-1/205	10-26-65	Ottawa, Montreal
44	Hill, Ken	R/R	6-2/200	12-14-65	Montreal, Ottawa
53	Looney, Brian	L/L	5-10/185	9-26-69	West Palm Beach, Harrisburg, Montreal
45	Martinez, Pedro J.	R/R	5-11/170	7-25-71	Albuquerque, Los Angeles
43	Nabholz, Chris	L/L	6-5/210	1-5-67	Montreal, Ottawa
50	Risley, Bill	R/R	6-2/215	5-29-67	Ottawa, Montreal
27	Rojas, Mel	R/R	5-11/195	12-10-66	Montreal
42	Rueter, Kirk	L/L	6-3/195	12-1-70	Harrisburg, Ottawa, Montreal
54	Scott, Tim	R/R	6-2/205	11-16-66	San Diego, Montreal
31	Shaw, Jeff	R/R	6-2/200	7-7-66	Ottawa, Montreal
57	Wetteland, John	R/R	6-2/215	8-21-66	West Palm Beach, Montreal
	White, Gabe	L/L	6-2/200	11-20-71	Harrisburg, Ottawa
20	Young, Pete	R/R	6-0/225	3-19-68	Ottawa, Montreal

No.	CATCHERS	B/T	Ht./Wt.	Born	1993 clubs
24	Fletcher, Darrin	L/R	6-1/198	10-3-66	Montreal
19	Laker, Tim	R/R	6-2/190	11-27-69	Montreal, Ottawa
2	Spehr, Tim	R/R	6-2/200	7-2-66	Montreal, Ottawa

No.	INFIELDERS	B/T	Ht./Wt.	Born	1993 clubs
	Andrews, Shane	R/R	6-1/215	8-28-71	Harrisburg
12	Benavides, Freddie	R/R	6-2/185	4-7-66	Colorado, Colorado Springs
5	Berry, Sean	R/R	5-11/200	3-22-66	Montreal
12	Cordero, Wilfredo	R/R	6-2/190	10-3-71	Montreal
	Hardge, Mike	R/R	5-11/190	1-27-72	West Palm Beach, Harrisburg
3	Lansing, Mike	R/R	6-0/180	4-3-68	Montreal
	Martin, Chris	R/R	6-1/170	1-25-68	Harrisburg
	Milligan, Randy	R/R	6-1/225	11-27-61	Cincinnati, Cleveland

No.	OUTFIELDERS	B/T	Ht./Wt.	Born	1993 clubs
18	Alou, Moises	R/R	6-3/190	7-3-66	Montreal
	Benitez, Yamil	R/R	6-2/190	10-5-72	Burlington
30	Floyd, Cliff	L/R	6-4/220	12-5-72	Harrisburg, Ottawa, Montreal
7	Frazier, Lou	B/R	6-2/175	1-26-65	Montreal
9	Grissom, Marquis	R/R	5-11/190	4-17-67	Montreal
	Murray, Glenn	R/R	6-2/200	11-23-70	Harrisburg
16	Pride, Curtis	L/R	5-11/200	12-17-68	Harrisburg, Ottawa, Montreal
23	Vander Wal, John	L/L	6-2/190	4-29-66	Montreal
33	Walker, Larry	L/R	6-3/215	12-1-66	Montreal
37	White, Rondell	R/R	6-1/205	2-23-72	Harrisburg, Ottawa, Montreal
	Woods, Tyrone	R/R	6-1/220	8-19-69	Harrisburg

BALLPARK INFORMATION

Ballpark (capacity, surface)
Olympic Stadium (46,500, artificial)
Address
4549 Pierre-de-Coubertin Ave.
Montreal, QC H1V 3N7
Business phone
514-253-3434
Ticket information
800-GO-EXPOS
Ticket prices
$22 (VIP box seats)
$17 (box seats)
$9 (terrace)
$5 (general admission)
$5 (bleachers)
Field dimensions (from home plate)
To left field at foul line, 325 feet
To center field, 404 feet
To right field at foul line, 325 feet
First game played
April 15, 1977 (Phillies 7, Expos 2)

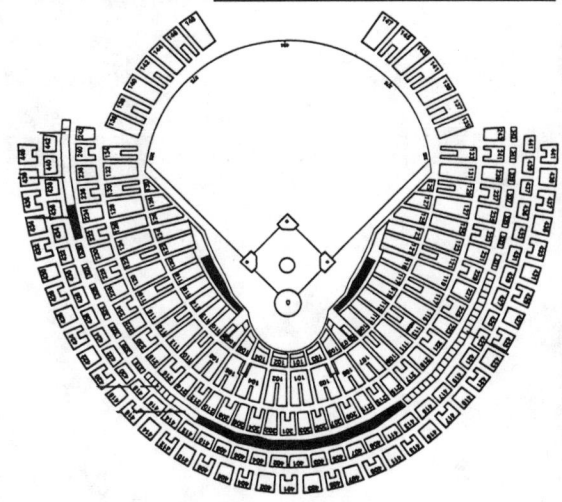

MINOR LEAGUE AFFILIATES

Class	Team	League	Manager
AAA	Ottawa	International	Jim Tracy
AA	Harrisburg	Eastern	David Jauss
A	West Palm Beach	Florida State	Rob Leary
A	Burlington	Midwest	Lorenzo Bundy
A	Vermont	New York-Pennsylvania	Terry Kennedy
Rookie	Gulf Coast Expos	Gulf Coast	Nelson Norman
Rookie	Mendoza Expos	Dominican Summer	Carlos Gil

BROADCAST INFORMATION

Radio: CICQ-AM (600). Broadcasters: Dave VanHorne, Ken Singleton, Bobby Winkles, Elliott Price. CKAC-AM (73, French language). Broadcasters: Rodger Brulotte, Jacques Doucet, Alain Chantelois.
TV: CFCF-TV CBFT (2, French language). Broadcasters: Claude Raymond, Camille Dube.
Cable TV: The Sports Network. Broadcasters: Ken Singleton, Dave Van-Horne. RDS (French language). Broadcasters: Rodger Brulotte, Denis Casavant.

SPRING TRAINING

Ballpark (city): Municipal Stadium (West Palm Beach, Fla.).
Ticket information: 407-684-6801.

HISTORY

YEAR-BY-YEAR RECORDS

Year	Pos.	W	L	Pct.	GB	Year	Pos.	W	L	Pct.	GB
1969	6th	52	110	.321	48	1984	5th	78	83	.484	18
1970	6th	73	89	.451	16	1985	3rd	84	77	.522	16½
1971	5th	71	90	.441	25½	1986	4th	78	83	.484	29½
1972	5th	70	86	.449	26½	1987	3rd	91	71	.562	4
1973	4th	79	83	.488	3½	1988	3rd	81	81	.500	20
1974	4th	79	82	.491	8½	1989	4th	81	81	.500	12
1975	T5th	75	87	.463	17½	1990	3rd	85	77	.525	10
1976	6th	55	107	.340	46	1991	6th	71	90	.441	26½
1977	5th	75	87	.463	26	1992	2nd	87	75	.537	9
1978	4th	76	86	.469	14	1993	2nd	94	68	.580	3
1979	2nd	95	65	.594	2						
1980	2nd	90	72	.556	1						
1981	3rd/1st	60	48	.556	*†‡						
1982	3rd	86	76	.531	6						
1983	3rd	82	80	.506	8						

*Won division playoff. †Lost Championship Series. ‡First half 30-25; second 30-23.

MANAGERS

Name	Record	Years
Gene Mauch	499-627	'69-75
Karl Kuehl	43-85	1976
Charlie Fox	12-22	1976
Dick Williams	350-322	'77-81
Jim Fanning	116-103	'81-82
		1984
Bill Virdon	146-147	'83-84
Buck Rodgers	520-499	'85-91
Tom Runnells	68-81	'91-92
Felipe Alou	164-123	'92-93

DAY BY DAY

Date	Opp.	Res.	Score	(inn.*)	Hits	Opp. hits	Winning pitcher	Losing pitcher	Save	Record	Pos.	GB
4-5	At Cin.	L	1-2		6	8	Rijo	Martinez	Dibble	0-1	T6th	1
4-7	At Cin.	W	5-1		7	3	Hill	Smiley	Rojas	1-1	T4th	1½
4-8	At Cin.	W	14-11		16	14	Barnes	Henry	Rojas	2-1	T4th	1
4-9	At Col.	L	4-11		10	18	Smith	Bottenfield		2-2	T5th	1½
4-10	At Col.	L	5-9		12	7	Nied	Martinez		2-3	T5th	2
4-11	At Col.	W	19-9		22	16	Jones	Henry		3-3	4th	2
4-13	Hou.	L	6-9		9	10	Williams	Rojas		3-4	5th	3½
4-14	Hou.	L	5-9		6	14	Portugal	Gardiner		3-5	6th	4½
4-15	Hou.	W	2-1		4	6	Jones	Drabek	Rojas	4-5	T5th	4
4-16	Col.	W	3-2		5	6	Bottenfield	Henry	Rojas	5-5	T5th	3
4-17	Col.	L	1-9		10	14	Ruffin	Martinez		5-6	6th	3
4-18	Col.	W	4-2		9	4	Hill	Wayne		6-6	T5th	3
4-20	L.A.	W	7-3		9	5	Nabholz	Candiotti		7-6	T3rd	3
4-21	L.A.	W	6-4		7	3	Jones	Astacio	Barnes	8-6	T2nd	2½
4-22	L.A.	W	3-1		7	4	Fassero	Hershiser	Rojas	9-6	T2nd	1½
4-23	S.F.	W	7-2		14	6	Martinez	Wilson	Barnes	10-6	2nd	1½
4-24	S.F.	W	6-1		13	4	Hill	Burba		11-6	2nd	1½
4-25	S.F.	L	1-4		4	10	Swift	Nabholz	Beck	11-7	2nd	2½
4-26	At S.D.	W	6-4		10	9	Jones	Taylor	Wetteland	12-7	2nd	2½
4-27	At S.D.	L	1-4		4	7	Benes	Bottenfield		12-8	2nd	2½
4-28	At L.A.	L	1-6		9	8	Astacio	Martinez		12-9	T2nd	3½
4-29	At L.A.	W	7-3		14	9	Hill	R. Martinez		13-9	T2nd	3½
4-30	At S.F.	L	2-5		8	14	Swift	Nabholz		13-10	T2nd	4½
5-1	At S.F.	L	3-7		10	12	Brantley	Jones		13-11	3rd	4½
5-2	At S.F.	L	3-4	(11)	14	7	Jackson	Fassero		13-12	3rd	5½
5-4	S.D.	W	6-1		10	5	Martinez	Gr. Harris		14-12	3rd	5½
5-5	S.D.	W	6-5		10	8	Wetteland	Rodriguez		15-12	T2nd	4½
5-7	At Pit.	W	1-0		6	8	Nabholz	Tomlin	Wetteland	16-12	2nd	4½
5-8	At Pit.	L	9-10	(10)	14	10	Belinda	Bottenfield		16-13	2nd	5½
5-9	At Pit.	L	5-6	(11)	12	11	Minor	Barnes		16-14	2nd	6½
5-11	Fla.	W	6-4		10	9	Rojas	Carpenter	Wetteland	17-14	2nd	6
5-12	Fla.	L	7-10		10	16	Lewis	Nabholz	Harvey	17-15	T2nd	7
5-13	Fla.	W	5-4		9	10	Wetteland	Corsi		18-15	2nd	6½
5-14	N.Y.	W	8-7		8	13	Aldred	Innis	Wetteland	19-15	2nd	5½
5-15	N.Y.	W	2-1		6	6	Nabholz	Saberhagen	Barnes	20-15	2nd	4½
5-16	N.Y.	W	4-3	(12)	11	7	Fassero	Young		21-15	2nd	4½
5-17	At Atl.	L	2-5		6	11	Avery	Martinez	Stanton	21-16	2nd	5½
5-18	At Atl.	W	1-0		7	5	Heredia	Smith	Wetteland	22-16	2nd	5½
5-19	At Atl.	L	0-1		4	4	Glavine	Shaw		22-17	2nd	5½
5-20	At Phi.	L	3-9		7	8	Schilling	Nabholz		22-18	2nd	6½
5-21	At Phi.	W	6-2		9	4	Hill	Jackson	Rojas	23-18	2nd	5½
5-22	At Phi.	W	6-5		13	7	Fassero	Mit. Williams	Wetteland	24-18	2nd	4½
5-23	At Phi.	L	7-14		5	15	Mulholland	Heredia	West	24-19	2nd	5½
5-24	St.L.	L	1-4	(11)	8	7	Cormier	Rojas	Smith	24-20	2nd	6½
5-25	St.L.	W	4-2		7	7	Fassero	Tewksbury	Wetteland	25-20	2nd	6½
5-26	St.L.	W	6-0		12	4	Hill	Magrane		26-20	2nd	5½
5-28	At Chi.	T	2-2	(5)	7	4	....	....		26-20	2nd	6
5-29	At Chi.	W	5-4		8	9	Martinez	Scanlan	Wetteland	27-20	2nd	6
5-30	At Chi.	L	2-5		4	9	Bautista	Shaw		27-21	2nd	7
5-31	At Hou.	L	1-2		5	4	D. Jones	Rojas		27-22	2nd	7
6-1	At Hou.	W	2-1		5	8	Wetteland	Drabek		28-22	2nd	7
6-2	At Hou.	L	4-5		9	9	D. Jones	Rojas		28-23	2nd	8
6-3	Chi.	W	7-1		8	5	Martinez	Morgan		29-23	2nd	7½
6-4	Chi.	W	3-1		5	7	Shaw	Guzman	Wetteland	30-23	2nd	6½
6-5	Chi.	W	6-3		7	8	Fassero	Bautista	Wetteland	31-23	2nd	6½
6-6	Chi.	L	1-4		8	9	Hibbard	Hill	Myers	31-24	2nd	7½
6-7	Cin.	L	3-12		8	18	Smiley	Heredia		31-25	2nd	8½
6-8	Cin.	W	4-2		8	8	Martinez	Pugh	Wetteland	32-25	2nd	7½
6-9	Cin.	L	2-3	(12)	11	11	Cadaret	Gardiner	Ayala	32-26	2nd	8½
6-10	At St.L.	L	4-7		9	11	Tewksbury	Rojas	Smith	32-27	2nd	9½
6-11	At St.L.	L	0-1		3	7	Magrane	Bottenfield	Smith	32-28	3rd	10½
6-12	At St.L.	L	3-13		8	13	Cormier	Nabholz		32-29	3rd	11½
6-13	At St.L.	W	3-1		8	6	Martinez	Arocha	Wetteland	33-29	3rd	11½
6-14	Phi.	L	3-10		8	8	Mulholland	Shaw		33-30	3rd	12½
6-15	Phi.	W	8-4		9	11	Barnes	Greene		34-30	3rd	11½
6-16	Phi.	W	4-3	(10)	5	9	Rojas	West		35-30	3rd	10½
6-18	Atl.	W	2-1		4	4	Martinez	Smoltz	Wetteland	36-30	3rd	10
6-19	Atl.	L	3-4		8	5	Wohlers	Rojas	Stanton	36-31	3rd	11
6-20	Atl.	L	1-5		8	11	Glavine	Shaw		36-32	3rd	12
6-21	At N.Y.	L	3-8		9	9	Telgheder	Barnes	Maddux	36-33	3rd	12

Date	Opp.	Res.	Score	(inn.*)	Hits	Opp. hits	Winning pitcher	Losing pitcher	Save	Record	Pos.	GB
6-22	At N.Y.	W	6-3		6	10	Rojas	Young	Wetteland	37-33	3rd	12
6-23	At N.Y.	W	4-3		7	6	Martinez	Tanana	Wetteland	38-33	3rd	12
6-25	At Fla.	L	1-3		3	5	Armstrong	Hill	Harvey	38-34	3rd	13
6-26	At Fla.	W	4-2		7	10	Bottenfield	Hough	Wetteland	39-34	3rd	12
6-27	At Fla.	L	2-9		6	10	Hammond	Barnes		39-35	3rd	11
6-28	Pit.	L	5-9	(10)	9	12	Wakefield	Scott		39-36	3rd	12
6-29	Pit.	W	9-2		12	4	Nabholz	Wagner		40-36	3rd	12
6-30	Pit.	W	9-1		7	3	Gardiner	Neagle	Fassero	41-36	3rd	11
7-1	Pit.	W	7-5		10	10	Rojas	Cooke	Wetteland	42-36	3rd	10
7-2	L.A.	L	3-4		7	9	R. Martinez	Barnes	Gott	42-37	3rd	10 ½
7-3	L.A.	W	6-4		12	8	Martinez	Ke. Gross	Wetteland	43-37	3rd	9 ½
7-4	L.A.	L	0-1	(11)	7	7	Gott	Shaw	McDowell	43-38	3rd	10 ½
7-5	S.F.	L	4-10		12	14	Burkett	Gardiner		43-39	3rd	11 ½
7-6	S.F.	L	5-13		10	13	Hickerson	Bottenfield		43-40	3rd	11 ½
7-7	S.F.	W	3-0		5	2	Rueter	Brummett	Wetteland	44-40	3rd	11 ½
7-8	S.D.	W	5-4		6	9	Martinez	Gr. Harris	Wetteland	45-40	3rd	10 ½
7-9	S.D.	W	6-1		11	3	Nabholz	Worrell		46-40	3rd	9 ½
7-10	S.D.	W	3-2		7	6	Young	Ge. Harris		47-40	3rd	9 ½
7-11	S.D.	W	5-4		13	11	Wetteland	Ge. Harris	Martinez	48-40	3rd	8 ½
7-15	At L.A.	L	2-3		9	4	R. Martinez	D. Martinez	Gott	48-41	3rd	8 ½
7-16	At L.A.	L	1-2		6	10	P. Martinez	Wetteland		48-42	3rd	8 ½
7-17	At L.A.	W	9-6	(10)	13	8	Gardiner	Daal	Wetteland	49-42	3rd	7 ½
7-18	At L.A.	L	1-2		6	8	Candiotti	Shaw	P. Martinez	49-43	3rd	8 ½
7-19	At S.F.	L	2-6		11	11	Burba	Nabholz		49-44	3rd	9 ½
7-20	At S.F.	L	3-8		7	11	Swift	Martinez		49-45	3rd	10 ½
7-21	At S.F.	L	3-4		6	7	Hickerson	Rojas	Beck	49-46	3rd	11 ½
7-22	At S.D.	W	10-5		11	9	Hill	Benes		50-46	3rd	10 ½
7-23	At S.D.	W	5-0		10	6	Fassero	Brocail	Rojas	51-46	3rd	10 ½
7-24	At S.D.	L	4-11		4	12	Worrell	Nabholz		51-47	3rd	10 ½
7-25	At S.D.	W	5-4	(10)	9	8	Wetteland	Ge. Harris	Rojas	52-47	3rd	9 ½
7-27	At Pit.	W	8-6		11	12	Scott	Johnston	Wetteland	53-47	3rd	9 ½
7-28	At Pit.	L	2-3		11	11	Petkovsek	Shaw		53-48	3rd	10 ½
7-29	At Pit.	W	3-2	(11)	10	7	Wetteland	Minor	Heredia	54-48	3rd	10 ½
7-30	Fla.	W	11-1		18	6	Nabholz	Bowen		55-48	3rd	9 ½
7-31	Fla.	W	6-5		10	11	Wetteland	Turner		56-48	3rd	9 ½
8-1	Fla.	L	4-5		5	12	Turner	Barnes	Harvey	56-49	3rd	10 ½
8-2	N.Y.	L	3-4		7	11	Saberhagen	Hill	Franco	56-50	3rd	11
8-3	N.Y.	W	3-1		9	7	Fassero	Tanana	Wetteland	57-50	3rd	11
8-4	N.Y.	W	3-1		5	4	Nabholz	Fernandez	Wetteland	58-50	3rd	10
8-5	N.Y.	L	9-12	(13)	15	14	Draper	Wetteland	Young	58-51	3rd	11
8-6	At Atl.	W	8-2		13	5	Rueter	Smoltz		59-51	3rd	10
8-7	At Atl.	W	5-3	(10)	9	9	Scott	Stanton	Wetteland	60-51	3rd	10
8-8	At Atl.	L	2-3		7	5	Avery	Fassero	McMichael	60-52	3rd	10
8-10	At Phi.	L	2-5		5	7	Schilling	Nabholz		60-53	3rd	11
8-11	At Phi.	L	5-6		9	9	West	Wetteland		60-54	3rd	12
8-12	At Phi.	L	4-7		8	12	Mason	Scott	Mit. Williams	60-55	3rd	13
8-13	St.L.	W	4-3	(11)	8	9	Wetteland	Magrane		61-55	3rd	13
8-14	St.L.	L	0-2		5	6	Watson	Fassero	Smith	61-56	3rd	13
8-15	St.L.	W	7-1		9	10	Heredia	Arocha		62-56	3rd	13
8-17 (1)	At Chi.	L	2-7		5	11	Guzman	Martinez		62-57	3rd	14
8-17 (2)	At Chi.	W	6-4		12	12	Rueter	Harkey	Wetteland	63-57	3rd	13 ½
8-18	At Chi.	L	0-2		4	7	Hibbard	Hill	Bautista	63-58	3rd	14 ½
8-19	At Chi.	W	10-2		8	6	Fassero	Castillo		64-58	3rd	13 ½
8-20	At Cin.	L	2-4		9	11	Reardon	Rojas	Dibble	64-59	3rd	14 ½
8-21	At Cin.	W	6-3		9	4	Henry	Roper	Wetteland	65-59	3rd	13 ½
8-22	At Cin.	W	7-2		15	6	Martinez	Ayala		66-59	3rd	12 ½
8-23	Chi.	W	1-0		5	5	Rueter	Hibbard	Wetteland	67-59	3rd	11 ½
8-24	Chi.	L	5-6		12	10	Plesac	Hill	Myers	67-60	3rd	12 ½
8-25	Chi.	W	7-3		13	7	Fassero	Morgan	Wetteland	68-60	3rd	12 ½
8-27	Hou.	W	3-1		4	8	Martinez	Drabek	Wetteland	69-60	3rd	11 ½
8-28	Hou.	W	7-3		10	7	Rueter	Kile	Rojas	70-60	3rd	10 ½
8-29	Hou.	W	3-2		6	8	Hill	Swindell	Wetteland	71-60	3rd	10 ½
8-30	At Col.	W	6-1		8	5	Fassero	Sanford	Rojas	72-60	2nd	9 ½
8-31	At Col.	W	14-3		15	13	Heredia	Harris		73-60	2nd	9 ½
9-1	At Col.	W	11-3		15	5	Martinez	Bottenfield		74-60	2nd	9 ½
9-3	At Hou.	W	3-0		7	5	Rueter	Kile	Wetteland	75-60	2nd	9 ½
9-4	At Hou.	W	7-5		11	9	Hill	Swindell	Wetteland	76-60	2nd	8 ½
9-5	At Hou.	L	1-7		5	10	Portugal	Fassero		76-61	2nd	7 ½
9-6	Col.	W	4-3		5	5	Scott	Reed	Wetteland	77-61	2nd	8 ½
9-7	Col.	W	4-3		7	8	Martinez	Moore	Wetteland	78-61	2nd	7 ½
9-8	Col.	W	6-1		9	6	Rueter	Reynoso	Scott	79-61	2nd	6 ½
9-10	Cin.	W	4-3	(10)	6	10	Rojas	Dibble		80-61	2nd	7
9-11	Cin.	W	4-2		9	7	Boucher	Powell	Wetteland	81-61	2nd	6
9-12	Cin.	W	3-2		10	7	Wetteland	Service		82-61	2nd	5

Date	Opp.	Res.	Score	(Inn.*)	Hits	Opp. hits	Winning pitcher	Losing pitcher	Save	Record	Pos.	GB
9-14	At St.L.	W	12-9		16	13	Rueter	Watson	Wetteland	83-61	2nd	4½
9-15	At St.L.	L	4-5		10	8	Perez	Barnes		83-62	2nd	5½
9-16	At St.L.	W	4-3		9	12	Fassero	Tewksbury	Wetteland	84-62	2nd	5
9-17	Phi.	W	8-7	(12)	12	9	Scott	Mit. Williams		85-62	2nd	4
9-18	Phi.	L	4-5		5	10	Greene	Boucher	Mit. Williams	85-63	2nd	5
9-19	Phi.	W	6-5		7	10	Scott	Mit. Williams		86-63	2nd	4
9-21	Atl.	L	5-18		8	16	Smoltz	Hill		86-64	2nd	5½
9-22	Atl.	W	6-1		9	4	Fassero	Avery		87-64	2nd	5½
9-23	Atl.	L	3-6		7	9	Maddux	Martinez		87-65	2nd	6
9-24	At N.Y.	W	6-3		12	4	Nabholz	Jones	Wetteland	88-65	2nd	6
9-25	At N.Y.	W	4-1		10	7	Boucher	Hillman	Heredia	89-65	2nd	5
9-26	At N.Y.	L	3-9		5	16	Telgheder	Hill		89-66	2nd	6
9-27	At Fla.	L	1-3		4	9	Rapp	Fassero	Rodriguez	89-67	2nd	6
9-28	At Fla.	W	3-2		8	4	Martinez	Armstrong	Wetteland	90-67	2nd	5
9-29	At Fla.	W	7-1		12	6	Nabholz	Hammond		91-67	2nd	5
9-30	At Fla.	W	5-3		8	8	Shaw	Lewis	Wetteland	92-67	2nd	4
10-1	Pit.	W	6-3		10	8	Heredia	Wagner	Wetteland	93-67	2nd	4
10-2	Pit.	L	2-4		6	7	Ballard	Henry	Dewey	93-68	2nd	4
10-3	Pit.	W	3-1		14	5	Boucher	Hope	Wetteland	94-68	2nd	3

Monthly records: April (13-10), May (14-12), June (14-14), July (15-12), August (17-12), September (19-7), October (2-1).
*Innings, if other than nine.

HIGHLIGHTS

High point: After the Expos beat Philadelphia, 6-5, on September 19, they were within four games of the first-place Phils in the National League East.
Low point: Team morale was at rock-bottom following a 4-3 loss at San Francisco on July 21. It was Montreal's fourth straight defeat, and lefthander Kirk Rueter was removed from the game after suffering what appeared to be a serious knee injury while taking a toss at first base from fellow rookie Frank Bolick. It was a routine play but Bolick, whose defensive deficiencies were glaring, botched the play. After the game, dejected Expo players spoke openly about how the season seemed pointless.
Turning point: The Expos won nine consecutive games from August 25 through September 4 to pull within 8½ games of the Phillies, setting the stage for their late-season run.
Most valuable player: Outfielder Marquis Grissom. He keyed Montreal's run into pennant contention with nine three-hit games after August 3.
Most valuable pitcher: Righthander John Wetteland. He saved a club-record 43 games, a total that would have been greater had he not started the season on the disabled list after breaking the big toe on his right foot in a fit of anger during spring training.
Most improved player: Catcher Darrin Fletcher. His 60 runs batted in were the most by an Expo catcher since Gary Carter's 106 in 1984.
Most pleasant surprise: Infielder Mike Lansing. Just two years removed from Class A, he won a utility job in spring training and finished the year with a .287 average and 23 stolen bases.
Biggest disappointment: Righthander Ken Hill. Although he started the season 6-0, he suffered a hamstring injury May 21 and won just three more games.
Key injuries: In addition to pitchers Hill and Wetteland, outfielder Moises Alou suffered a frightening, season-ending injury when he dislocated his left ankle and fractured the fibula in his left leg in a baserunning incident September 16. Second baseman Delino DeShields finished strong after spraining a ligament in his left thumb August 11.
Notable: The Expos' 94 victories and 55 home wins rank as the second-best totals in franchise history, behind the 95 victories/56 home wins of 1979.

— JEFF BLAIR

RECORDS

1993 regular-season record: 94-68 (2nd in N.L. East); 55-26 at home; 39-42 on road; 46-32 vs. East; 48-36 vs. West; 28-23 vs. LHP; 66-45 vs. RHP; 24-25 on grass; 70-43 on turf; 22-28 in daytime; 72-40 at night; 32-24 in one-run games; 9-8 in extra-inning games; 0-0-1 in doubleheaders.
Team record last five years: 418-391 (.517, ranks 4th in league in that span).

TEAM LEADERS

Batting average: Marquis Grissom (.298).
At-bats: Marquis Grissom (630).
Runs: Marquis Grissom (104).
Hits: Marquis Grissom (188).
Total bases: Marquis Grissom (276).
Doubles: Wil Cordero (32).
Triples: Delino DeShields (7).
Home runs: Larry Walker (22).
Runs batted in: Marquis Grissom (95).
Stolen bases: Marquis Grissom (53).
Slugging percentage: Moises Alou (.483).
On-base percentage: Delino DeShields (.389).
Wins: Dennis Martinez (15).
Earned-run average: Ken Hill (3.23).
Complete games: Ken Hill, Dennis Martinez (2).
Shutouts: None.
Saves: John Wetteland (43).
Innings pitched: Dennis Martinez (224⅔).
Strikeouts: Jeff Fassero (140).

GAMES BY POSITION

Catcher: Darrin Fletcher 127, Tim Spehr 49, Tim Laker 43, Joe Siddall 15, Tim McIntosh 5.
First base: Greg Colbrunn 61, Frank Bolick 51, John Vander Wal 42, Oreste Marrero 32, Derrick White 17, Randy Ready 13, Archi Cianfrocco 11, Cliff Floyd 10, Lou Frazier 8, Larry Walker 4, Joe Siddall 1.
Second base: Delino DeShields 123, Randy Ready 28, Mike Lansing 25, Charlie Montoyo 3, Lou Frazier 1.
Third base: Sean Berry 96, Mike Lansing 81, Frank Bolick 24, Randy Ready 3, Wilfredo Cordero 2.
Shortstop: Wilfredo Cordero 134, Mike Lansing 51.
Outfield: Marquis Grissom 157, Moises Alou 136, Larry Walker 132, Lou Frazier 60, John Vander Wal 38, Rondell White 21, Ted Wood 8, Tim McIntosh 7, Curtis Pride 2, Joe Siddall 1, Matt Stairs 1.

TOP DRAFT CHOICES

1a. Chris Schwab, OF, Cretin High School, Eagan, Minn.
1b. Josue Estrada, OF, Rio Piedras, Puerto Rico.
2a. Martin Mainville, RHP, Marquette High School, Montreal.
2b. Brad Fullmer, 3B, Montclair Prep High School, Chatsworth, Calif.
3. Jason Baker, RHP, Robert E. Lee High School, Midland, Tex.
4. Ronnie Hall, OF, Tustin (Calif.) High School.
5. Nate Brown, LHP, University of California.
6. Jeff Foster, 3B, University of Tennessee.
7. Donnie Fowler, RHP, Spring (Tex.) High School.
8. Neal Weber, LHP, Cuesta (Calif.) C.C.
9. Jayson Durocher, RHP, Horizon High School, Scottsdale, Ariz.
10. Trace Coquillette, OF, Sacramento (Calif.) C.C.

NEW YORK METS
NATIONAL LEAGUE EAST DIVISION

1994 SCHEDULE

N Denotes night game (any game starting after 5 p.m.).
▢ Home games shaded.
* At Three Rivers Stadium in Pittsburgh.

APRIL
SUN	MON	TUE	WED	THU	FRI	SAT
					1	2
3	4 CHI	5 CHI	6 CHI	7	8 N HOU	9 N HOU
10 HOU	11 CHI	12	13 CHI	14 N CHI	15 N HOU	16 HOU
17 HOU	18 N SD	19 N SD	20 N LA	21 N LA	22 N SF	23 SF
24 SF	25	26 N SD	27 N SD	28	29 N LA	30 LA

MAY
SUN	MON	TUE	WED	THU	FRI	SAT
1 LA	2 N SF	3 N SF	4 N SF	5 N STL	6 N STL	7 N STL
8 STL	9 N MON	10 N MON	11 N MON	12	13 N ATL	14 ATL
15 ATL	16 N FLA	17 N FLA	18 N FLA	19	20 N PHI	21 N PHI
22 PHI	23	24 N PIT	25 N PIT	26 N PIT	27 N CIN	28 CIN
29 CIN	30 N COL	31 N COL				

JUNE
SUN	MON	TUE	WED	THU	FRI	SAT
		1	2 N COL	3 N CIN	4 N CIN
5 CIN	6 N COL	7 N COL	8 COL	9 N MON	10 N MON	11 MON
12 MON	13 N PHI	14 N PHI	15 N PHI	16 N FLA	17 N FLA	18 FLA
19 N FLA	20 N ATL	21 N ATL	22 N ATL	23	24 N PIT	25 N PIT
26 PIT	27 N STL	28 N STL	29 STL	30 N SD		

JULY
SUN	MON	TUE	WED	THU	FRI	SAT
					1 N SD	2 N SD
3 SD	4 SF	5 N SF	6 N SF	7 N LA	8 N LA	9 LA
10 LA	11	12 ALL-STAR GAME	13	14 N SD	15 N SD	16 SD
17 SD	18 N LA	19 N LA	20 N LA	21	22 N SF	23 SF
24 SF	25 N STL	26 N STL	27 N STL	28	29 N PIT	30 N PIT
31 PIT						

AUGUST
SUN	MON	TUE	WED	THU	FRI	SAT
	1 N ATL	2 N ATL	3 N ATL	4	5 N FLA	6 N FLA
7 FLA	8 N PHI	9 N PHI	10 N PHI	11 N PHI	12 N MON	13 N MON
14 MON	15	16 N HOU	17 N HOU	18 HOU	19 N CHI	20 N CHI
21 CHI	22 N CHI	23 N HOU	24 N HOU	25 HOU	26 N CHI	27 CHI
28 CHI	29 N CIN	30 N CIN	31 N CIN			

SEPTEMBER
SUN	MON	TUE	WED	THU	FRI	SAT
				1	2 N COL	3 COL
4 COL	5 N CIN	6 N CIN	7 N CIN	8	9 N COL	10 COL
11 COL	12 N MON	13 N MON	14 MON	15	16 N PHI	17 PHI
18 PHI	19 N FLA	20 N FLA	21 N FLA	22	23 N ATL	24 N ATL
25 ATL	26 N PIT	27 N PIT	28 N PIT	29 PIT	30 N STL	

OCTOBER
SUN	MON	TUE	WED	THU	FRI	SAT
						1 STL
2 STL						

1994 SEASON

CLUB DIRECTORY

Chairman of the board
Nelson Doubleday
President and chief executive officer
Fred Wilpon
Directors
Nelson Doubleday
Fred Wilpon
John C. Diller
Saul B. Katz
Joe McIlvaine
Marvin B. Tepper
Fay T. Vincent
Special advisor to the board of directors
Richard Cummins
Executive v.p., baseball operations
Joe McIlvaine
Executive v.p., business operations
John C. Diller
Asst. vice president, baseball operations
Gerald H. Hunsicker
Special asst. to the exec. v.p., baseball op.
Ed Lynch
Director of scouting
John Barr
Director of minor league operations
Steve Phillips
Admin. assistant, scouting
Scott Brown
Admin. assistant, minor league operations
Jim Duquette
Baseball administrator
Maureen Cooke
Travel director
Bob O'Hara
Senior v.p. and consultant
J. Frank Cashen
Senior v.p. and treasurer
Harold W. O'Shaughnessy
Vice president, broadcasting
Mike Ryan
Vice president, marketing
Mark Bingham
Vice president, stadium operations
Bob Mandt
Vice president, ticket sales and services
Bill Ianniciello
Secretary and general counsel
David Howard
Controller
Rick Iandoli
Dir., administration and data processing
Russ Richardson
Director of amateur baseball relations
Tommy Holmes
Director, community outreach
Jill Knee
Community outreach representatives
Bud Harrelson
Mookie Wilson
Dir., Diamond View suites and marketing rep.
Philip Bernstein

Director of promotions
James Plummer
Director of public relations
Jay Horwitz
Director, ticket operations
Dan DeMato
Director, ticket sales
Randye Ringler
Assistant director, public relations
Craig Sanders
Manager, data processing
Tom Doyle
Manager, customer relations
Joann Galardy
Stadium manager
John McCarthy
Admin. asst. to exec. v.p., business op.
Pat Owens
Marketing representative
Jill Grabill
Club physicians
Dr. David Altchek
Dr. David Dines
Club psychologist/E.A.P.
Dr. Allan Lans
Team trainers
Steve Garland
Sam McCrary
Scouts
Paul Baretta
Larry Chase
Carmen Fusco
Dick Gernert
Mark Giegler
Rob Guzik
R.J. Harrison
Marty Harvat
Darrell Johnson
Roland Johnson
Buddy Kerr
Craig Kornfeld
Dave Lottsfeldt
Joe Mason
Jim Miller
Bob Minor
Harry Minor
Joe Nigro
Carlos Pascual
Mark Ralston
Jim Reeves
Paul Ricciarini
Junior Roman
Bob Rossi
Eddy Toledo
Terry Tripp
Bob Wellman
Jim Woodward
Jack Zduriencik

SPRING TRAINING ROSTER

Manager—Dallas Green (46).

Coaches—Mike Cubbage (4), Frank Howard (55), Tom McCraw (27), Greg Pavlick (52), Steve Swisher (8), Bobby Wine (7).

No.	PITCHERS	B/T	Ht./Wt.	Born	1993 clubs
63	Castillo, Juan	R/R	6-5/205	6-23-70	Binghamton
31	Franco, John	L/L	5-10/185	9-17-60	New York N.L.
16	Gooden, Dwight	R/R	6-3/210	11-16-64	New York N.L.
45	Gozzo, Mauro	R/R	6-3/212	3-7-66	Norfolk, New York N.L.
35	Greer, Kenny	R/R	6-2/215	5-12-67	Columbus, New York N.L.
53	Hillman, Eric	L/L	6-10/225	4-27-66	Norfolk, New York N.L.
67	Jacome, Jason	L/L	6-1/155	11-24-70	St. Lucie, Binghamton
28	Jones, Bobby	R/R	6-4/210	2-10-70	Norfolk, New York N.L.
51	Maddux, Mike	L/R	6-2/188	8-27-61	New York N.L.
39	Manzanillo, Josias	R/R	6-0/190	10-16-67	Milwaukee, New Orleans, Norfolk, New York N.L.
17	Saberhagen, Bret	R/R	6-1/200	4-11-64	New York N.L.
48	Schourek, Pete	L/L	6-5/205	5-10-69	New York N.L.
34	Seminara, Frank	R/R	6-2/205	5-16-67	San Diego, Las Vegas
32	Smith, Pete	R/R	6-2/200	2-27-66	Atlanta
38	Telgheder, David	R/R	6-3/212	11-11-66	Norfolk, New York N.L.
49	Vitko, Joe	R/R	6-8/210	2-1-70	Gulf Coast Mets, St. Lucie
26	Walker, Pete	R/R	6-2/195	4-8-69	Binghamton
47	Wegmann, Tom	R/R	6-0/185	8-29-68	Norfolk
19	Young, Anthony	R/R	6-2/200	1-19-66	New York N.L., Norfolk

No.	CATCHERS	B/T	Ht./Wt.	Born	1993 clubs
64	Fordyce, Brook	R/R	6-1/185	5-7-70	Norfolk
9	Hundley, Todd	B/R	5-11/185	5-27-69	New York N.L.
21	Kmak, Joe	R/R	6-0/185	5-3-63	Milwaukee, New Orleans
10	Olson, Greg	R/R	6-0/200	9-6-60	Atlanta
33	Stinnett, Kelly	R/R	5-11/195	2-14-70	Charlotte

No.	INFIELDERS	B/T	Ht./Wt.	Born	1993 clubs
23	Bogar, Timothy	R/R	6-2/198	10-28-66	New York N.L.
3	Huskey, Butch	R/R	6-3/244	11-10-71	Binghamton, New York N.L.
12	Kent, Jeff	R/R	6-1/185	3-7-68	New York N.L.
61	Ledesma, Aaron	R/R	6-2/200	6-3-71	Binghamton
18	McKnight, Jeff	B/R	6-0/180	2-18-63	New York N.L.
36	Navarro, Tito	B/R	5-10/165	9-12-70	Norfolk, Gulf Coast Mets, New York N.L.
	Rivera, Luis	R/R	5-9/175	1-3-64	Boston
62	Veras, Quilvio	B/R	5-9/166	4-3-71	Binghamton
15	Zinter, Alan	B/R	6-2/185	5-19-68	Binghamton

No.	OUTFIELDERS	B/T	Ht./Wt.	Born	1993 clubs
25	Bonilla, Bobby	B/R	6-3/240	2-23-63	New York N.L.
5	Burnitz, Jeromy	L/R	6-0/190	4-15-69	Norfolk, New York N.L.
22	McReynolds, Kevin	R/R	6-1/225	10-16-59	Kansas City
6	Orsulak, Joe	L/L	6-1/205	5-31-62	New York N.L.
60	Sanders, Tracy	L/R	6-2/200	7-26-69	Canton/Akron, Wichita
44	Thompson, Ryan	R/R	6-3/200	11-4-67	New York N.L., Norfolk

BALLPARK INFORMATION

Ballpark (capacity, surface)
Shea Stadium (55,601, grass)
Address
Roosevelt Ave. and 126th St.
Flushing, NY 11368
Business phone
718-507-6387
Ticket information
718-507-8499
Ticket prices
$15 (box)
$12 (upper level box)
$12 (loge and mezzanine reserved)
$6.50 (bk. rows, loge & mezz. res.)
$6.50 (upper level reserved)
$1 (senior citizens)
Field dimensions (from home plate)
To left field at foul line, 338 feet
To center field, 410 feet
To right field at foul line, 338 feet
First game played
April 17, 1964 (Pirates 4, Mets 3)

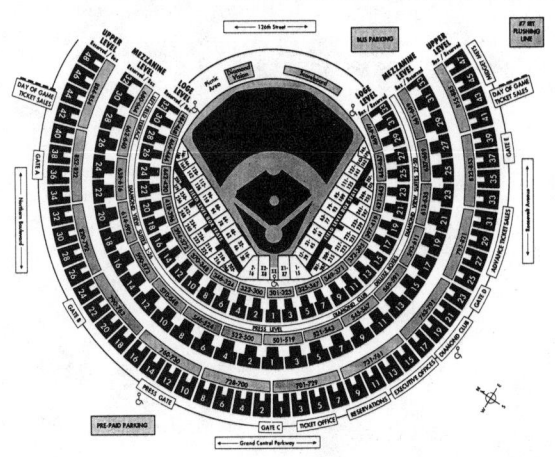

MINOR LEAGUE AFFILIATES

Class	Team	League	Manager
AAA	Norfolk	International	Bobby Valentine
AA	Binghamton	Eastern	John Tamargo
A	St. Lucie	Florida State	Rafael Landestoy
A	Columbia	South Atlantic	Ron Washington
A	Pittsfield	New York-Pennsylvania	Howie Freiling
Rookie	Kingsport	Appalachian	Ron Gideon
Rookie	Gulf Coast Mets	Gulf Coast	Junior Roman

BROADCAST INFORMATION

Radio: WFAN-AM (660). Broadcasters: Gary Cohen, Bob Murphy.
TV: WWOR-TV (Channel 9). Broadcasters: Ralph Kiner, Tim McCarver, Gary Thorne.
Cable TV: SportsChannel. Broadcasters: Ralph Kiner, Fran Healy, Rusty Staub.

SPRING TRAINING

Ballpark (city): St. Lucie County Stadium (Port St. Lucie, Fla.).
Ticket information: 407-871-2115.

HISTORY

YEAR-BY-YEAR RECORDS

Year	Pos.	W	L	Pct.	GB	Year	Pos.	W	L	Pct.	GB
1962	10th	40	120	.250	60½	1980	5th	67	95	.414	24
1963	10th	51	111	.315	48	1981	5th/4th	41	62	.398	†
1964	10th	53	109	.327	40	1982	6th	65	97	.401	27
1965	10th	50	112	.309	47	1983	6th	68	94	.420	22
1966	9th	66	95	.410	28½	1984	2nd	90	72	.556	6½
1967	10th	61	101	.377	40½	1985	2nd	98	64	.605	3
1968	9th	73	89	.451	24	1986	1st*	108	54	.667	+21½
1969	1st*	100	62	.617	+ 8	1987	2nd	92	70	.568	3
1970	3rd	83	79	.512	6	1988	1st‡	100	60	.625	+15
1971	T3rd	83	79	.512	14	1989	2nd	87	75	.537	6
1972	3rd	83	73	.532	13½	1990	2nd	91	71	.562	4
1973	1st*	82	79	.509	+ 1½	1991	5th	77	84	.478	20½
1974	5th	71	91	.438	17	1992	5th	72	90	.444	24
1975	T3rd	82	80	.506	10½	1993	7th	59	103	.364	38
1976	3rd	86	76	.531	15						
1977	6th	64	98	.395	37						
1978	6th	66	96	.407	24						
1979	6th	63	99	.389	35						

*Won Championship Series. †First half 17-34; second 24-28. ‡Lost Championship Series.

MANAGERS

Name	Record	Years
Casey Stengel	175-404	'62-65
Wes Westrum	142-237	'65-67
Salty Parker	4-7	1967
Gil Hodges	339-309	'68-71
Yogi Berra	292-296	'72-75
Roy McMillan	26-27	1975
Joe Frazier	101-106	'76-77
Joe Torre	286-240	'77-81
George Bamberger	81-127	'82-83
Frank Howard	52-64	1983
Davey Johnson	595-417	'84-90
Bud Harrelson	145-129	'90-91
Mike Cubbage	3-4	1991
Jeff Torborg	85-115	'92-93
Dallas Green	46-78	1993

DAY BY DAY

Date	Opp.	Res.	Score (inn.*)	Hits	Opp. hits	Winning pitcher	Losing pitcher	Save	Record	Pos.	GB
4-5	Col.	W	3-0	8	4	Gooden	Nied		1-0	T1st	...
4-7	Col.	W	6-1	10	2	Saberhagen	Ruffin		2-0	2nd	½
4-9	Hou.	L	3-7 (10)	8	10	D. Jones	Young		2-1	4th	1
4-10	Hou.	L	3-6	8	13	Drabek	Gooden		2-2	T4th	1½
4-11	Hou.	L	4-5	7	11	Swindell	Schourek	D. Jones	2-3	5th	2½
4-13	At Col.	W	8-4	12	11	Saberhagen	Holmes		3-3	4th	3
4-14	At Col.	W	6-3	12	7	Fernandez	Smith	Maddux	4-3	4th	3
4-15	At Col.	L	3-5	6	4	Nied	Gooden		4-4	4th	3½
4-16	At Cin.	W	3-1	5	8	Schourek	Rijo	Franco	5-4	4th	2½
4-17	At Cin.	W	4-1	7	6	Tanana	Smiley	Maddux	6-4	4th	1½
4-18	At Cin.	L	2-3	5	9	Foster	Saberhagen	Dibble	6-5	4th	2½
4-20	S.F.	L	1-4 (11)	3	8	Righetti	Maddux	Beck	6-6	6th	3½
4-21	S.F.	W	10-0	12	8	Gooden	Brantley		7-6	4th	3
4-22	S.F.	L	4-13	5	19	Burkett	Schourek		7-7	T5th	3
4-23	S.D.	W	6-1	6	8	Tanana	Gr. Harris		8-7	T4th	3
4-24	S.D.	L	3-5	6	11	Seminara	Saberhagen	Ge. Harris	8-8	T4th	4
4-25	S.D.	L	8-9	9	10	Scott	Young	Ge. Harris	8-9	6th	5
4-27	L.A.	L	1-4	3	2	Hershiser	Gooden		8-10	6th	5½
4-28	At S.F.	L	3-4	7	12	Beck	Innis		8-11	7th	6½
4-29	At S.F.	L	5-10	9	12	Black	Saberhagen	Jackson	8-12	7th	7½
4-30	At S.D.	L	6-7	10	14	Rodriguez	Young	Ge. Harris	8-13	7th	8½
5-1	At S.D.	L	3-5	6	16	Ge. Harris	Maddux		8-14	7th	8½
5-2	At S.D.	W	3-2	9	7	Gooden	Benes		9-14	7th	8½
5-4	At L.A.	L	4-8	10	14	Astacio	Tanana		9-15	7th	9½
5-5	At L.A.	L	5-6	9	14	P. Martinez	Maddux	Gott	9-16	7th	9½
5-7	Fla.	W	4-0	7	4	Gooden	Hough		10-16	7th	9½
5-8	Fla.	L	2-4	4	11	Armstrong	Schourek	Harvey	10-17	7th	10½
5-9	Fla.	L	4-6	10	10	Hammond	Tanana	Harvey	10-18	7th	11½
5-10	Fla.	W	1-0	3	3	Saberhagen	Bowen		11-18	7th	11½
5-11	At St.L.	L	4-7	12	13	Osborne	Hillman	Smith	11-19	7th	11½
5-12	At St.L.	L	5-6	9	9	Perez	Maddux		11-20	7th	12½
5-13	At St.L.	W	4-0	6	6	Schourek	Cormier		12-20	7th	12
5-14	At Mon.	L	7-8	13	8	Aldred	Innis	Wetteland	12-21	7th	12
5-15	At Mon.	L	1-2	6	6	Nabholz	Saberhagen	Barnes	12-22	7th	12
5-16	At Mon.	L	3-4 (12)	7	11	Fassero	Young		12-23	7th	13
5-17	Pit.	L	4-9	7	14	Tomlin	Gooden		12-24	7th	14
5-18	Pit.	L	8-10	17	16	Otto	Schourek	Belinda	12-25	7th	15
5-19	Pit.	W	6-4 (10)	10	10	Franco	Minor		13-25	7th	14
5-21	Atl.	L	2-4	6	11	Maddux	Hillman		13-26	7th	14½
5-22	Atl.	W	6-1	10	8	Gooden	Smoltz		14-26	7th	13½
5-23	Atl.	L	1-2	4	7	Avery	Saberhagen	Stanton	14-27	7th	14½
5-24	At Phi.	L	3-6	5	10	Greene	Tanana		14-28	7th	15½
5-25	At Phi.	L	2-4	7	8	Schilling	Schourek		14-29	7th	16½
5-26	At Phi.	W	5-4	8	7	Franco	Mit. Williams	Innis	15-29	7th	15½
5-28	Cin.	L	2-5 (10)	6	11	Smiley	Young	Ayala	15-30	7th	16½
5-29	Cin.	W	4-3	6	11	Tanana	Pugh	Franco	16-30	7th	16½
5-30	Cin.	L	4-8	6	14	Ayala	Schourek		16-31	7th	17½
5-31	At Chi.	W	9-5	11	13	Gibson	Harkey		17-31	7th	16½
6-1	At Chi.	L	3-8	9	12	Hibbard	Draper	Myers	17-32	7th	17½
6-2	At Chi.	W	11-3	16	9	Gooden	Castillo		18-32	7th	17½
6-4	At Hou.	L	2-7	6	10	Harnisch	Tanana		18-33	7th	17½
6-5	At Hou.	L	5-7	9	13	Kile	Maddux	Hernandez	18-34	7th	18½
6-6	At Hou.	L	4-5	11	11	Osuna	Schourek	D. Jones	18-35	7th	19½
6-7	Chi.	W	7-2	12	7	Gooden	Castillo		19-35	7th	19½
6-8	Chi.	L	1-5	6	12	Morgan	Young	Myers	19-36	7th	19½
6-9	Chi.	L	3-8	8	14	Guzman	Tanana		19-37	7th	20½
6-10	Phi.	L	6-7	11	14	West	Gibson	Mit. Williams	19-38	7th	21½
6-11	Phi.	L	2-5	5	5	Schilling	Schourek		19-39	7th	22½
6-12	Phi.	L	0-3	6	7	Jackson	Gooden		19-40	7th	23½
6-13	Phi.	L	3-5	7	11	Rivera	Young	Mit. Williams	19-41	7th	24½
6-14	At Atl.	W	7-4	13	12	Tanana	Smith		20-41	7th	24½
6-15	At Atl.	L	1-2	6	7	Glavine	Hillman		20-42	7th	24½
6-16	At Atl.	L	2-5	3	10	Maddux	Schourek		20-43	7th	24½
6-17	At Pit.	L	2-6	6	10	Walk	Gooden		20-44	7th	24½
6-18	At Pit.	L	2-5	6	8	Wagner	Young		20-45	7th	25½
6-19	At Pit.	L	3-8	10	13	Toliver	Tanana	Minor	20-46	7th	26½
6-20	At Pit.	L	2-3	5	7	Belinda	Saberhagen		20-47	7th	26½
6-21	Mon.	W	8-3	9	9	Telgheder	Barnes	Maddux	21-47	7th	26½
6-22	Mon.	L	3-6	10	6	Rojas	Young	Wetteland	21-48	7th	27½
6-23	Mon.	L	3-4	6	7	Martinez	Tanana	Wetteland	21-49	7th	28½

Date	Opp.	Res.	Score	(inn.*)	Hits	Opp. hits	Winning pitcher	Losing pitcher	Save	Record	Pos.	GB
6-25	St.L.	L	5-8		12	12	Olivares	Saberhagen	Smith	21-50	7th	29½
6-26	St.L.	L	2-4		6	7	Tewksbury	Gooden	Smith	21-51	7th	29½
6-27	St.L.	L	3-5		11	8	Magrane	Young	Smith	21-52	7th	29½
6-29	At Fla.	W	10-9	(12)	16	15	Telgheder	Turner		22-52	7th	29
6-30	At Fla.	W	7-1		14	8	Saberhagen	Armstrong		23-52	7th	28
7-1	At Fla.	L	5-7		8	11	Hough	Gooden	Harvey	23-53	7th	28
7-2	S.F.	L	1-3	(5)	3	7	Burba	Young		23-54	7th	28½
7-3	S.F.	W	6-3		12	10	Telgheder	SWift	Franco	24-54	7th	27½
7-4	S.F.	L	8-10		12	17	Jackson	Maddux	Beck	24-55	7th	28½
7-5	S.D.	L	7-12		12	19	Whitehurst	Schourek		24-56	7th	29½
7-6	S.D.	W	9-7		16	10	Gooden	Brocail		25-56	7th	28½
7-7	S.D.	L	0-2		1	5	Benes	Young	Ge. Harris	25-57	7th	29½
7-8 (1)	L.A.	L	8-11		17	17	Ke. Gross	Telgheder		25-58	7th	29½
7-8 (2)	L.A.	W	6-3	(10)	8	8	Innis	Nichols		26-58	7th	29
7-9	L.A.	L	2-6		9	11	Hershiser	Tanana		26-59	7th	29
7-10	L.A.	W	7-6		7	11	Saberhagen	Astacio	Franco	27-59	7th	29
7-11	L.A.	L	1-2		7	10	P. Martinez	Gooden	Gott	27-60	7th	29
7-15	At S.F.	L	1-8		6	13	Swift	Hillman		27-61	7th	29
7-16	At S.F.	L	2-4		6	7	Hickerson	Gooden	Beck	27-62	7th	29
7-17	At S.F.	W	3-1		12	3	Tanana	Burkett	Franco	28-62	7th	28
7-18	At S.F.	W	12-6		11	9	Schourek	Brummett		29-62	7th	28
7-19	At S.D.	W	2-1	(10)	8	6	Franco	Ge. Harris		30-62	7th	29
7-20	At S.D.	L	1-4		4	11	Gr. Harris	Telgheder		30-63	7th	29
7-21	At S.D.	W	5-2		6	7	Gooden	Whitehurst	Franco	31-63	7th	29
7-22	At L.A.	W	10-5		10	12	Saberhagen	Ke. Gross	Young	32-63	7th	28
7-23	At L.A.	L	2-5		5	8	Candiotti	Tanana		32-64	7th	29
7-24	At L.A.	L	4-5	(10)	11	8	Gott	Young		32-65	7th	29
7-25	At L.A.	W	4-0		8	5	Hillman	R. Martinez		33-65	7th	29
7-27	Fla.	W	4-3		6	6	Gooden	Rapp	Franco	34-65	7th	28
7-28	Fla.	W	5-4		12	10	Young	Harvey		35-65	7th	28
7-29	Fla.	L	1-2		7	4	Hough	Tanana	Harvey	35-66	7th	29
7-30	At St.L.	L	2-3		6	7	Watson	Fernandez	Smith	35-67	7th	29
7-31	At St.L.	L	3-4		9	12	Arocha	Hillman	Smith	35-68	7th	29½
8-1	At St.L.	W	10-3		16	7	Gooden	Burns		36-68	7th	30
8-2	At Mon.	W	4-3		11	7	Saberhagen	Hill	Franco	37-68	7th	29½
8-3	At Mon.	L	1-3		7	9	Fassero	Tanana	Wetteland	37-69	7th	30½
8-4	At Mon.	L	1-3		4	5	Nabholz	Fernandez	Wetteland	37-70	7th	30½
8-5	At Mon.	W	12-9	(13)	14	15	Draper	Wetteland	Young	38-70	7th	30½
8-7 (1)	Pit.	L	1-2		9	7	Cooke	Gooden	Dewey	38-71	7th	31
8-7 (2)	Pit.	W	10-8		17	13	Maddux	Neagle	Young	39-71	7th	30½
8-8	Pit.	L	2-3		5	10	Smith	Tanana		39-72	7th	30½
8-10	Atl.	L	2-3		9	8	Bedrosian	Hillman	McMichael	39-73	7th	31½
8-11	Atl.	L	2-4		6	6	Maddux	Fernandez		39-74	7th	32½
8-12	Atl.	L	4-8		4	10	Smoltz	Gooden		39-75	7th	33½
8-13	At Phi.	L	5-9		8	7	Thigpen	Young		39-76	7th	34½
8-14	At Phi.	W	9-5		10	10	Jones	Jackson	Innis	40-76	7th	33½
8-15	At Phi.	L	4-5		6	9	West	Young	Mit. Williams	40-77	7th	34½
8-16	At Cin.	W	6-2		10	7	Fernandez	Luebbers	Maddux	41-77	7th	34
8-17	At Cin.	L	0-6		7	9	Ayala	Gooden		41-78	7th	35
8-18	At Cin.	W	12-2		12	5	Tanana	Pugh		42-78	7th	35
8-21 (1)	At Col.	L	3-4		5	7	Harris	Innis	Holmes	42-79	7th	35
8-21 (2)	At Col.	L	6-8		6	10	Reed	Jones	Holmes	42-80	7th	35½
8-22	At Col.	L	3-4		7	5	Munoz	Fernandez	Reed	42-81	7th	35½
8-23	Cin.	L	2-6		6	6	Pugh	Gooden		42-82	7th	35½
8-24	Cin.	W	5-4		8	4	Maddux	Spradlin		43-82	7th	35½
8-25	Cin.	L	1-4		4	9	Rijo	Hillman		43-83	7th	36½
8-26	Col.	W	7-1		10	4	Gooden	Harris		44-83	7th	36
8-27	Col.	W	3-2		8	6	Fernandez	Bottenfield	Innis	45-83	7th	35
8-28	Col.	L	5-7		8	7	Reynoso	Jones	Holmes	45-84	7th	35
8-29	Col.	L	1-6		5	9	Painter	Tanana		45-85	7th	36
8-30	Hou.	W	5-4		9	8	Maddux	Hernandez	Franco	46-85	7th	35
8-31	Hou.	L	2-10		5	18	Harnisch	Gooden		46-86	7th	36
9-1	Hou.	L	2-3		8	5	Drabek	Fernandez	D. Jones	46-87	7th	37
9-2	At Chi.	W	8-3		11	8	Jones	Guzman		47-87	7th	36½
9-3	At Chi.	L	3-4		7	8	Hibbard	Tanana	Myers	47-88	7th	37½
9-4	At Chi.	L	8-9		12	17	Bautista	Franco	Myers	47-89	7th	37½
9-5	At Chi.	L	1-2		3	7	Bautista	Franco		47-90	7th	37½
9-6	At Hou.	L	2-7		4	7	Harnisch	Fernandez	Hernandez	47-91	7th	38½
9-7	At Hou.	L	3-4	(10)	11	7	T. Jones	Franco		47-92	7th	38½
9-8	At Hou.	L	1-7		0	9	Kile	Tanana		47-93	7th	38½
9-10	Chi.	L	10-12		14	16	Scanlan	Maddux	Myers	47-94	7th	40
9-11	Chi.	L	3-4		6	7	Harkey	Young	Myers	47-95	7th	40
9-12	Chi.	W	5-0		14	4	Fernandez	Brennan		48-95	7th	39
9-13	Phi.	L	0-5		6	9	Greene	Jones		48-96	7th	40

Date	Opp.	Res.	Score	(inn.*)	Hits	Opp. hits	Winning pitcher	Losing pitcher	Save	Record	Pos.	GB
9-14	Phi.	W	5-4		7	9	Tanana	Jackson	Franco	49-96	7th	39
9-15	Phi.	L	3-6		10	12	Schilling	Schourek	Mit. Williams	49-97	7th	40
9-17	At Atl.	L	1-2	(10)	6	6	Howell	Maddux		49-98	7th	40
9-18	At Atl.	W	3-2	(10)	15	6	Innis	Stanton	Gozzo	50-98	7th	40
9-19	At Atl.	L	2-11		11	14	Glavine	Schourek		50-99	7th	40
9-20	At Pit.	L	2-6		9	13	Wagner	Hillman	Johnston	50-100	7th	41
9-21	At Pit.	W	4-3		9	8	Telgheder	Cooke	Maddux	51-100	7th	41
9-22	At Pit.	W	6-5	(10)	12	10	Franco	Johnston		52-100	7th	41
9-24	Mon.	L	3-6		4	12	Nabholz	Jones	Wetteland	52-101	7th	42
9-25	Mon.	L	1-4		7	10	Boucher	Hillman	Heredia	52-102	7th	42
9-26	Mon.	W	9-3		16	5	Telgheder	Hill		53-102	7th	41
9-27	St.L.	L	3-4		7	7	Murphy	Gozzo	Perez	53-103	7th	42
9-28	St.L.	W	6-1		9	9	Schourek	Arocha		54-103	7th	42
9-29	St.L.	W	1-0	(17)	3	3	Greer	Lancaster		55-103	7th	41
9-30	St.L.	W	3-2		7	10	Hillman	Watson		56-103	7th	40
10-1	At Fla.	W	4-1		9	6	Telgheder	Weathers		57-103	7th	40
10-2	At Fla.	W	7-1		12	4	Fernandez	Rapp		58-103	7th	39
10-3	At Fla.	W	9-2	(8½)	12	6	Schourek	Armstrong		59-103	7th	38

Monthly records: April (8-13), May (9-18), June (6-21), July (12-16), August (11-18), September (10-17), October (3-0).
*Innings, if other than nine.

HIGHLIGHTS

High point: The Mets won six of their first 10 games to trail Philadelphia by only 1½ games in the N.L. East.

Low point: From April 18, when right-hander Bret Saberhagen squandered a two-run, eighth-inning lead in a 3-2 loss at Cincinnati, until June 30, when they finally won a second consecutive game, the Mets went 17-48 and their deficit in the standings increased from 2½ to 28 games.

Turning point: After showing some signs of life after the All-Star break, the Mets collapsed after outfielder Vince Coleman threw a powerful firecracker into a group of people outside Dodger Stadium on July 24, injuring three people. The incident diffused the team's focus, which was never particularly sharp anyway.

Most valuable player: First baseman Eddie Murray. He had defensive flaws, but no one contributed more than Murray, whose 100 runs batted in and 27 home runs compared favorably to outfielder Bobby Bonilla's 87 and 34.

Most valuable pitcher: Righthander Dwight Gooden. The Doctor worked 208⅔ innings and, with any luck, could have reversed his 12-15 record.

Most improved player: Second baseman Jeff Kent. In his first full year in the majors, he emerged as a fine offensive player (.270 average, 21 homers, 80 RBIs). His defense improved as well.

Most pleasant surprise: Outfielder Ryan Thompson. After being recalled to replace an injured Howard Johnson on July 24, Thompson, who had hit .125 in 40 at-bats in April before being demoted, rebounded to bat .270 with 18 doubles, one triple, 11 home runs and 25 RBIs after the recall.

Biggest disappointments: Johnson and Saberhagen. HoJo struggled until a broken wrist ended his season July 22, and Saberhagen didn't pitch well before undergoing operations on his right elbow and left knee.

Key injuries: Closer John Franco was unable to pitch in April because of residual pain in his surgically repaired left elbow. Kidney stones diminished shortstop Tony Fernandez's skills, at least until a June 11 trade to the Blue Jays apparently cured him.

Notable: Dallas Green succeeded Jeff Torborg as manager May 19. . . . The Mets' 59-103 record equaled the worst record ever by an established team in an expansion season.

—MARTY NOBLE

RECORDS

1993 regular-season record: 59-103 (7th in N.L. East); 28-53 at home; 31-50 on road; 30-48 vs. East; 29-55 vs. West; 13-37 vs. LHP; 46-66 vs. RHP; 47-77 on grass; 12-26 on turf; 21-38 in daytime; 38-65 at night; 19-35 in one-run games; 8-7 in extra-inning games; 0-1-2 in doubleheaders. **Team record last five years:** 386-423 (.477, ranks 12th in league in that span).

TEAM LEADERS

Batting average: Eddie Murray (.285).
At-bats: Eddie Murray (610).
Runs: Bobby Bonilla (81).
Hits: Eddie Murray (174).
Total bases: Eddie Murray (285).
Doubles: Eddie Murray (28).
Triples: Vince Coleman (8).
Home runs: Bobby Bonilla (34).
Runs batted in: Eddie Murray (100).
Stolen bases: Vince Coleman (38).
Slugging percentage: Bobby Bonilla (.522).
On-base percentage: Bobby Bonilla (.352).
Wins: Dwight Gooden (12).
Earned-run average: Dwight Gooden (3.45).
Complete games: Dwight Gooden (7).
Shutouts: Dwight Gooden (2).
Saves: John Franco (10).
Innings pitched: Dwight Gooden (208⅔).
Strikeouts: Dwight Gooden (149).

GAMES BY POSITION

Catcher: Todd Hundley 123, Charlie O'Brien 65, Jeff McKnight 1.
First base: Eddie Murray 154, Jeff McKnight 10, Dave Gallagher 9, Bobby Bonilla 6, Joe Orsulak 4.
Second base: Jeff Kent 127, Chico Walker 24, Doug Saunders 22, Jeff McKnight 15, Timothy Bogar 6.
Third base: Howard Johnson 67, Bobby Bonilla 52, Chico Walker 23, Butch Huskey 13, Jeff Kent 12, Jeff McKnight 9, Timothy Bogar 7, Doug Saunders 4.
Shortstop: Timothy Bogar 66, Kevin Baez 52, Tony Fernandez 48, Jeff McKnight 29, Jeff Kent 2, Tito Navarro 2, Doug Saunders 1.
Outfield: Joe Orsulak 114, Vince Coleman 90, Bobby Bonilla 85, Jeromy Burnitz 79, Ryan Thompson 76, Dave Gallagher 72, Darrin Jackson 26, Chico Walker 15, Ced Landrum 3, Wayne Housie 2.

TOP DRAFT CHOICES

1. **Kirk Presley,** RHP, Tupelo (Miss.) High School.
2. **Eric Ludwick,** RHP, UNLV.
3. **Mike Welch,** RHP, University of Southern Maine.
4. **Bill Koch,** RHP, West Babylon (N.Y.) High School.
5. **Fletcher Bates,** OF, New Hanover High School, Wilmington, N.C.
6. **Matt Terrell,** OF, Western Michigan University.
7. **Scott Adair,** RHP, Norte Vista High School, Riverside, Calif.
8. **Paul Petrulis,** SS, Mississippi State University.
9. **Joe Atwater,** LHP, South Alamance High School, Graham, N.C.
10. **Derek Sutton,** LHP, Indian Hills (Iowa) C.C.

PHILADELPHIA PHILLIES
NATIONAL LEAGUE EAST DIVISION

N   Denotes night game (any game starting after 5 p.m.).
☐   Home games shaded.
*   At Three Rivers Stadium in Pittsburgh.

APRIL

SUN	MON	TUE	WED	THU	FRI	SAT
					1	2
3	4 COL	5	6 N COL	7 COL	8 N CIN	9 N CIN
10 CIN	11 COL	12	13 N COL	14 N COL	15 N CIN	16 N CIN
17 CIN	18 N LA	19 LA	20	21 SF	22 N SD	23 N SD
24 SD	25	26 N LA	27 N LA	28	29 N SF	30 N SF

MAY

SUN	MON	TUE	WED	THU	FRI	SAT
1 SF	2 N SD	3 N SB	4 N SD	5 N FLA	6 N FLA	7 N FLA
8 FLA	9 N ATL	10 N ATL	11 N ATL	12 N PIT	13 N PIT	14 N PIT
15 PIT	16 N MON	17 N MON	18 MON	19	20 N NY	21 N NY
22 NY	23 N STL	24 N STL	25 N STL	26	27 N HOU	28 N HOU
29 HOU	30 N CHI	31 N CHI				

JUNE

SUN	MON	TUE	WED	THU	FRI	SAT
			1 CHI	2 N CHI	3 N HOU	4 N HOU
5 HOU	6 N CHI	7 N CHI	8 N CHI	9 N STL	10 N STL	11 N STL
12 STL	13 N NY	14 N NY	15 N NY	16	17 N MON	18 N MON
19 MON	20 N PIT	21 N PIT	22 PIT	23	24 N ATL	25 N ATL
26 ATL	27 N FLA	28 N FLA	29 FLA	30 N LA		

JULY

SUN	MON	TUE	WED	THU	FRI	SAT
					1 N LA	2 N LA
3 LA	4 N SD	5 N SD	6 SD	7 SF	8 N SF	9 N SF
10 SF	11	12* ALL-STAR GAME	13	14 N LA	15 N LA	16 N LA
17 LA	18 N SF	19 N SF	20 SF	21	22 N SD	23 N SD
24 SD	25 N FLA	26 N FLA	27 N FLA	28	29 N ATL	30 N ATL
31 ATL						

AUGUST

SUN	MON	TUE	WED	THU	FRI	SAT
	1	2 N PIT	3 N PIT	4 PIT	5 N MON	6 N MON
7 MON	8 N NY	9 N NY	10 N NY	11 N NY	12 N STL	13 N STL
14 STL	15	16 N CIN	17 N CIN	18 CIN	19 N COL	20 N COL
21 COL	22 N CIN	23 N CIN	24 CIN	25	26 N COL	27 N COL
28 COL	29 N HOU	30 N HOU	31 N HOU			

SEPTEMBER

SUN	MON	TUE	WED	THU	FRI	SAT
				1	2 N CHI	3 N CHI
4 CHI	5 N HOU	6 N HOU	7 N HOU	8	9 N CHI	10 CHI
11 CHI	12	13 N STL	14 N STL	15 N STL	16 N NY	17 NY
18 NY	19 N MON	20 N MON	21 N MON	22 N MON	23 N PIT	24 N PIT
25 PIT	26 N ATL	27 N ATL	28 N ATL	29	30 N FLA	

OCTOBER

SUN	MON	TUE	WED	THU	FRI	SAT
						1 N FLA
2 FLA						

CLUB DIRECTORY

President/CEO/general partner
Bill Giles
Partners
Claire S. Betz
Estate of John Drew Betz
Tri-Play Associates (Alexander K. Buck, J. Mahlon Buck Jr., William C. Buck)
Fitz Eugene Dixon Jr.
Mrs. Rochelle Levy
Executive v.p. and chief operating officer
David Montgomery
Executive secretary
Nancy Nolan
Secretary and general counsel
William Y. Webb
Dir., planning/develop. and super boxes
Tom Hudson
Senior vice president, general manager
Lee Thomas
Player personnel administrator
Ed Wade
Director, player development
Del Unser
Director, scouting
Mike Arbuckle
Assistant to the president
Paul Owens
Business manager, minor leagues
Bill Gargano
Traveling secretary
Eddie Ferenz
Senior vice president, finance and planning
Jerry Clothier
Vice president, public relations
Larry Shenk
Broadcaster/director speakers' bureau
Chris Wheeler
Director, community relations
Regina Castellani
Administrator, public relations
Karen Nocella
Manager, media relations
Gene Dias
Manager, publicity
Leigh Tobin
Vice president, marketing
Dennis Mannion
Director, promotions
Frank Sullivan
Manager, advertising and broadcasting
Jo-Anne Levy-Lamoreaux
Manager, entertainment
Chris Legault
Manager, marketing services
Kurt Funk
Manager, corporate marketing
Dave Buck

Vice president, ticket sales and operations
Richard Deats
Director, sales
Rory McNeil
Director, sales operations
John Weber
Director, ticket department
Dan Goroff
Manager, group sales
Kathy Killian
Director, information systems
Brian Lamoreaux
Director, stadium operations
Mike DiMuzio
Club physician
Dr. Phillip Marone
Club trainers
Jeff Cooper
Mark Andersen
National supervisor
Mark Wolever
Regional supervisor, scouts
Dick Lawlor
Tony Roig
Bob Reasonover
Special assignment, major league scouts
Ray Shore
Jimmy Stewart
Advance scout, major leagues
Hank King
Special assignment scouts
Bing Devine
Jay Hankins
Larry Rojas
Regular scouts
Sal Agostinelli
Emil Belich
Tom Ferguson
Jim Fregosi Jr.
Jose Gomez
Eli Grba
Bill Harper
Ken Hultzapple
John Kennedy
Jerry Lafferty
George Lauzerique
Jose Leiva
Terry Logan
Fred Mazuca
Lloyd Merritt
Willie Montanez
Arthur Parrack
Bob Poole
David Sirak
Mitch Sokel
Roy Tanner
Scott Trcka

SPRING TRAINING ROSTER

Manager—Jim Fregosi (11).

Coaches—Larry Bowa (2), Denis Menke (14), Johnny Podres (46), Mel Roberts (26), Mike Ryan (9), John Vukovich (18).

No.	PITCHERS	B/T	Ht./Wt.	Born	1993 clubs
42	Borland, Toby	R/R	6-6/186	5-29-69	Reading, Scranton/Wilkes-Barre
52	Bottalico, Ricky	L/R	6-1/200	8-26-69	Clearwater, Reading
31	Brink, Brad	R/R	6-2/208	1-20-65	Scranton/Wilkes-Barre, Philadelphia
57	Foster, Kevin	R/R	6-1/160	1-13-69	Jacksonville, Scranton/Wilkes-Barre, Philadelphia
28	Green, Tyler	R/R	6-5/192	2-18-70	Philadelphia, Scranton/Wilkes-Barre
49	Greene, Tommy	R/R	6-5/222	4-6-67	Philadelphia
27	Jackson, Danny	R/L	6-0/220	1-5-62	Philadelphia
23	Jones, Doug	R/R	6-2/195	6-24-57	Houston
37	Juden, Jeff	R/R	6-7/245	1-19-71	Tucson, Houston
48	Mason, Roger	R/R	6-6/226	9-18-58	San Diego, Philadelphia
45	Mulholland, Terry	R/L	6-3/212	3-9-63	Philadelphia
53	Patterson, Jeff	R/R	6-2/200	10-1-68	Scranton/Wilkes-Barre
34	Rivera, Ben	R/R	6-6/250	1-11-68	Philadelphia
38	Schilling, Curt	R/R	6-4/225	11-14-66	Philadelphia
51	Slocumb, Heathcliff	R/R	6-3/220	6-7-66	Iowa, Chicago N.L., Cleveland, Charlotte
56	Wells, Bob	R/R	6-0/180	11-1-66	Clearwater, Scranton/Wilkes-Barre
40	West, David	L/L	6-6/255	9-1-64	Philadelphia
41	Williams, Mike	R/R	6-2/199	7-29-68	Scranton/Wilkes-Barre, Philadelphia

No.	CATCHERS	B/T	Ht./Wt.	Born	1993 clubs
10	Daulton, Darren	L/R	6-2/202	1-3-62	Philadelphia
24	Lieberthal, Mike	R/R	6-0/170	1-18-72	Scranton/Wilkes-Barre
3	Pratt, Todd	R/R	6-3/225	2-9-67	Philadelphia, Scranton/Wilkes-Barre

No.	INFIELDERS	B/T	Ht./Wt.	Born	1993 clubs
5	Batiste, Kim	R/R	6-0/200	3-15-68	Philadelphia
7	Duncan, Mariano	R/R	6-0/200	3-13-63	Philadelphia
15	Hollins, Dave	B/R	6-1/215	5-25-66	Philadelphia
17	Jordan, Ricky	R/R	6-3/210	5-26-65	Philadelphia
29	Kruk, John	L/L	5-10/220	2-9-61	Philadelphia
12	Morandini, Mickey	L/R	5-11/180	4-22-66	Philadelphia
55	Schall, Gene	R/R	6-3/190	6-5-70	Reading, Scranton/Wilkes-Barre
19	Stocker, Kevin	B/R	6-1/175	2-13-70	Scranton/Wilkes-Barre, Philadelphia

No.	OUTFIELDERS	B/T	Ht./Wt.	Born	1993 clubs
44	Chamberlain, Wes	R/R	6-2/216	4-13-66	Philadelphia
4	Dykstra, Lenny	L/L	5-10/195	2-10-63	Philadelphia
8	Eisenreich, Jim	L/L	5-11/200	4-18-59	Philadelphia
	Geisler, Phil	L/L	6-3/195	10-23-69	Clearwater, Reading
22	Incaviglia, Pete	R/R	6-1/235	4-2-64	Philadelphia
59	Jackson, Jeff	R/R	6-2/212	1-2-72	Reading
16	Longmire, Tony	L/R	6-1/199	8-12-68	Scranton/Wilkes-Barre, Philadelphia
58	Marsh, Tom	R/R	6-2/180	12-27-65	Scranton/Wilkes-Barre
25	Thompson, Milt	L/R	5-11/203	1-5-59	Philadelphia

BALLPARK INFORMATION

Ballpark (capacity, surface)
Veterans Stadium (62,382, artificial)

Address
P.O. Box 7575
Philadelphia, PA 19101

Business phone
215-463-6000

Ticket information
215-463-1000

Ticket prices
$14 (field box)
$12 (sections 258-274)
$12 (terrace box)
$12 (loge box)
$9 (reserved, 600 level)
$5 (reserved, 700 level)

Field dimensions (from home plate)
To left field at foul line, 330 feet
To center field, 408 feet
To right field at foul line, 330 feet

First game played
April 10, 1971 (Phillies 4, Expos 1)

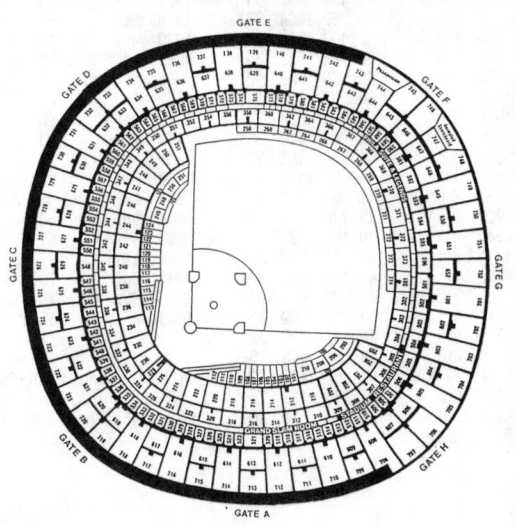

MINOR LEAGUE AFFILIATES

Class	Team	League	Manager
AAA	Scranton/Wilkes-Barre	International	Mike Quade
AA	Reading	Eastern	Bill Dancy
A	Clearwater	Florida State	Don McCormack
A	Spartanburg	South Atlantic	Roy Majtyka
A	Batavia	New York-Pennsylvania	Al LeBoeuf
Rookie	Martinsville	Appalachian	Ramon Henderson

BROADCAST INFORMATION

Radio: WOGL-AM (1210). Broadcasters: Harry Kalas, Richie Ashburn, Chris Wheeler, Andy Musser.
TV: WPHL-TV (Channel 17). Broadcasters: Andy Musser, Richie Ashburn, Harry Kalas, Chris Wheeler.
Cable TV: PRISM, SportsChannel. Broadcasters: Garry Maddox, Chris Wheeler, Kent Tekulve, Andy Musser.

SPRING TRAINING

Ballpark (city): Jack Russell Stadium (Clearwater, Fla.).
Ticket information: 215-463-1000.

YEAR-BY-YEAR RECORDS

Year	Pos.	W	L	Pct.	GB	Year	Pos.	W	L	Pct.	GB
1901	2nd	83	57	.593	7½	1950	1st	91	63	.591	+2
1902	7th	56	81	.409	46	1951	5th	73	81	.474	23½
1903	7th	49	86	.363	39½	1952	4th	87	67	.565	9½
1904	8th	52	100	.342	53½	1953	T3rd	83	71	.539	22
1905	4th	83	69	.546	21½	1954	4th	75	79	.487	22
1906	4th	71	82	.464	45½	1955	4th	77	77	.500	21½
1907	3rd	83	64	.565	21½	1956	5th	71	83	.461	22
1908	4th	83	71	.539	16	1957	5th	77	77	.500	19
1909	5th	74	79	.484	36½	1958	8th	69	85	.448	23
1910	4th	78	75	.510	25½	1959	8th	64	90	.416	23
1911	4th	79	73	.520	19½	1960	8th	59	95	.383	36
1912	5th	73	79	.480	30½	1961	8th	47	107	.305	46
1913	2nd	88	63	.583	12½	1962	7th	81	80	.503	20
1914	6th	74	80	.481	20½	1963	4th	87	75	.537	12
1915	1st	90	62	.592	+7	1964	T2nd	92	70	.568	1
1916	2nd	91	62	.595	2½	1965	6th	85	76	.528	11½
1917	2nd	87	65	.572	10	1966	4th	87	75	.537	8
1918	6th	55	68	.447	26	1967	5th	82	80	.506	19½
1919	8th	47	90	.343	47½	1968	T7th	76	86	.469	21
1920	8th	62	91	.405	30½	1969	5th	63	99	.389	37
1921	8th	51	103	.331	43½	1970	5th	73	88	.453	15½
1922	7th	57	96	.373	35½	1971	6th	67	95	.414	30
1923	8th	50	104	.325	45½	1972	6th	59	97	.378	37½
1924	7th	55	96	.364	37	1973	6th	71	91	.438	11½
1925	T6th	68	85	.444	27	1974	3rd	80	82	.494	8
1926	8th	58	93	.384	29½	1975	2nd	86	76	.531	6½
1927	8th	51	103	.331	43	1976	1st*	101	61	.623	+9
1928	8th	43	109	.283	51	1977	1st*	101	61	.623	+5
1929	5th	71	82	.464	27½	1978	1st*	90	72	.556	+1½
1930	8th	52	102	.338	40	1979	4th	84	78	.519	14
1931	6th	66	88	.429	35	1980	1st†	91	71	.562	+1
1932	4th	78	76	.506	12	1981	1st/3rd	59	48	.551	‡§
1933	7th	60	92	.395	31	1982	2nd	89	73	.549	3
1934	7th	56	93	.376	37	1983	1st†	90	72	.556	+6
1935	7th	64	89	.418	35½	1984	4th	81	81	.500	15½
1936	8th	54	100	.351	38	1985	5th	75	87	.463	26
1937	7th	61	92	.399	34½	1986	2nd	86	75	.534	21½
1938	8th	45	105	.300	43	1987	T4th	80	82	.494	15
1939	8th	45	106	.298	50½	1988	6th	65	96	.404	35½
1940	8th	50	103	.327	50	1989	6th	67	95	.414	26
1941	8th	43	111	.279	57	1990	T4th	77	85	.475	18
1942	8th	42	109	.278	62½	1991	3rd	78	84	.481	20
1943	7th	64	90	.416	41	1992	6th	70	92	.432	26
1944	8th	61	92	.399	43½	1993		97	65	.599	+3
1945	8th	46	108	.299	52						
1946	5th	69	85	.448	28						
1947	T7th	62	92	.403	32						
1948	6th	66	88	.429	25½						
1949	3rd	81	73	.526	16						

*Lost Championship Series. †Won Championship Series. ‡Lost division playoff. §First half 34-21; second 25-27.

MANAGERS

Name	Record	Years
Bill Shettsline	139-138	'01-02
Chief Zimmer	49-86	1903
Hugh Duffy	206-251	'04-06
Bill Murray	240-214	'07-09
Red Dooin	392-370	'10-14
Pat Moran	323-257	'15-18
Jack Coombs	18-44	1919
Gavvy Cravath	91-137	'19-20
Bill Donovan	31-71	1921
Kaiser Wilhelm	77-128	'21-22
Art Fletcher	231-378	'23-26
Stuffy McInnis	51-103	1927
Burt Shotton	370-439	'28-33
Jimmy Wilson	280-477	'34-38
Hans Lobert	42-111	'38, '42
Doc Prothro	138-320	'39-41
Bucky Harris	40-53	1943
Fred Fitzsimmons	102-179	'43-45
Ben Chapman	197-277	'45-48
Dusty Cooke	6-6	1948
Eddie Sawyer	390-424	'48-52, '58-60
Steve O'Neill	182-140	'52-54
Terry Moore	35-42	1954
Mayo Smith	264-281	'55-58
Eddie Sawyer	94-132	'58-60
Andy Cohen	1-0	1960
Gene Mauch	645-684	'60-68
George Myatt	21-35	'68, '69
Bob Skinner	92-123	'68-69
Frank Lucchesi	166-233	'70-72
Paul Owens	161-158	1972, '83-84
Danny Ozark	594-510	'73-79
Dallas Green	169-130	'79-81
Pat Corrales	132-115	'82-83
John Felske	190-194	'85-87
Lee Elia	111-142	'87-88
John Vukovich	5-4	1988
Nick Leyva	148-189	'89-91
Jim Fregosi	241-232	'91-93

DAY BY DAY

Date	Opp.	Res.	Score	(inn.*)	Hits	Opp. hits	Winning pitcher	Losing pitcher	Save	Record	Pos.	GB
4-5	At Hou.	W	3-1		6	4	Mulholland	Drabek		1-0	T1st	...
4-6	At Hou.	W	5-3		9	7	Schilling	Swindell	Mit. Williams	2-0	1st	+½
4-7	At Hou.	W	6-3	(10)	10	9	DeLeon	Bell	Mit. Williams	3-0	T1st	+½
4-9	Chi.	L	7-11		10	13	McElroy	Rivera	Myers	3-1	T2nd	½
4-10	Chi.	W	5-4		7	3	Mulholland	Morgan	Mit. Williams	4-1	T1st	...
4-11	Chi.	W	3-0		5	4	Schilling	Guzman		5-1	1st	+1
4-12	Cin.	W	5-4		6	6	DeLeon	Foster	Mit. Williams	6-1	1st	+1½
4-13	Cin.	W	4-1		9	4	Greene	Belcher	Mit. Williams	7-1	1st	+1½
4-14	Cin.	W	9-2		16	6	Rivera	Browning		8-1	1st	+1½
4-16	At Chi.	L	1-3		8	8	Morgan	Mulholland	Myers	8-2	1st	+1
4-17	At Chi.	L	3-6		5	10	Guzman	Schilling	Myers	8-3	1st	+1
4-18	At Chi.	W	11-10	(11)	15	14	Mit. Williams	Scanlan	West	9-3	1st	+2
4-20	S.D.	W	4-3	(14)	10	7	Ayrault	Hernandez		10-3	1st	+2
4-22	S.D.	L	1-2		5	8	Benes	Mulholland	Rodriguez	10-4	1st	+1½
4-23	L.A.	W	2-0		5	5	Schilling	R. Martinez		11-4	1st	+1½
4-24	L.A.	W	7-3		10	10	Jackson	Ke. Gross	Mit. Williams	12-4	1st	+1½
4-25	L.A.	W	5-2		6	5	Greene	Candiotti	Mit. Williams	13-4	1st	+2½
4-26	S.F.	W	9-8	(10)	11	9	Andersen	Minutelli		14-4	1st	+2½
4-27	S.F.	L	3-6		7	9	Burkett	Mulholland	Beck	14-5	1st	+2½
4-28	At S.D.	W	5-3		11	9	Schilling	Gr. Harris	Mit. Williams	15-5	1st	+3½
4-29	At S.D.	W	5-3		9	8	Jackson	Seminara	Mit. Williams	16-5	1st	+3½
4-30	At L.A.	W	7-6		7	15	Ayrault	Daal	Mit. Williams	17-5	1st	+4½
5-1	At L.A.	L	1-5		6	11	Candiotti	Rivera		17-6	1st	+3½
5-2	At L.A.	W	9-1		13	6	Mulholland	Hershiser		18-6	1st	+4½
5-4	At S.F.	W	4-3	(12)	10	7	Andersen	Righetti	Mit. Williams	19-6	1st	+4½
5-5	At S.F.	L	2-11		8	15	Swift	Jackson		19-7	1st	+4½
5-7	St.L.	W	4-3		8	5	Greene	Magrane	Mit. Williams	20-7	1st	+4½
5-8	St.L.	W	2-1	(10)	6	10	Mulholland	Perez		21-7	1st	+5½
5-9	St.L.	W	6-5		10	8	Davis	Smith	Mit. Williams	22-7	1st	+6½
5-10	Pit.	W	5-1		8	4	Jackson	Walk		23-7	1st	+7
5-11	Pit.	L	4-8		11	13	Wagner	Davis		23-8	1st	+6
5-12	Pit.	W	4-1		6	5	Greene	Tomlin		24-8	1st	+7
5-14	At Atl.	L	7-10		10	12	Glavine	Mulholland	Stanton	24-9	1st	+5½
5-15	At Atl.	L	3-5		7	6	Maddux	West	Stanton	24-10	1st	+4½
5-16	At Atl.	W	5-4		10	8	Jackson	McMichael	Mit. Williams	25-10	1st	+4½
5-17	At Fla.	W	10-3		17	9	Rivera	Hough		26-10	1st	+5½
5-18	At Fla.	W	6-0		8	6	Greene	Armstrong		27-10	1st	+5½
5-19	At Fla.	L	3-5		3	7	Lewis	Davis	Harvey	27-11	1st	+5½
5-20	Mon.	W	9-3		8	7	Schilling	Nabholz		28-11	1st	+6½
5-21	Mon.	L	2-6		4	9	Hill	Jackson	Rojas	28-12	1st	+5½
5-22	Mon.	L	5-6		7	13	Fassero	Mit. Williams	Wetteland	28-13	1st	+4½
5-23	Mon.	W	14-7		15	5	Mulholland	Heredia	West	29-13	1st	+5½
5-24	N.Y.	W	6-3		10	5	Greene	Tanana		30-13	1st	+6½
5-25	N.Y.	W	4-2		8	7	Schilling	Schourek		31-13	1st	+6½
5-26	N.Y.	L	4-5		7	8	Franco	Mit. Williams	Innis	31-14	1st	+5½
5-28	At Col.	W	15-9		20	15	Rivera	Henry		32-14	1st	+6
5-29	At Col.	W	6-0		8	6	Mulholland	Blair		33-14	1st	+6
5-30	At Col.	W	18-1		19	6	Greene	Painter		34-14	1st	+7
5-31	At Cin.	L	4-6		7	11	Reardon	Anderson	Dibble	34-15	1st	+7
6-1	At Cin.	W	6-3		11	9	Andersen	Cadaret	Mit. Williams	35-15	1st	+7
6-2	At Cin.	W	5-2		10	8	Rivera	Smiley	Mit. Williams	36-15	1st	+8
6-4	Col.	L	1-2		10	7	Blair	Mulholland	Wayne	36-16	1st	+6½
6-5	Col.	W	6-2		9	7	Greene	Reynoso		37-16	1st	+6½
6-6	Col.	W	11-7		18	12	Schilling	Ashby		38-16	1st	+7½
6-7	Hou.	W	7-5		13	9	Jackson	Swindell	Mit. Williams	39-16	1st	+8½
6-8	Hou.	L	3-6		7	7	Kile	Rivera	D. Jones	39-17	1st	+7½
6-9	Hou.	W	8-0		12	6	Mulholland	Harnisch		40-17	1st	+8½
6-10	At N.Y.	W	7-6		14	11	West	Gibson	Mit. Williams	41-17	1st	+9½
6-11	At N.Y.	W	5-2		5	5	Schilling	Schourek		42-17	1st	+10½
6-12	At N.Y.	W	3-0		7	6	Jackson	Gooden		43-17	T1st	+10½
6-13	At N.Y.	W	5-3		11	7	Rivera	Young	Mit. Williams	44-17	1st	+11½
6-14	At Mon.	W	10-3		8	8	Mulholland	Shaw		45-17	1st	+11½
6-15	At Mon.	L	4-8		11	9	Barnes	Greene		45-18	1st	+10½
6-16	At Mon.	L	3-4	(10)	9	5	Rojas	West		45-19	1st	+9½
6-17	Fla.	L	1-4		4	9	Hammond	Jackson	Harvey	45-20	1st	+8½
6-18	Fla.	W	7-3		8	9	Rivera	Bowen		46-20	1st	+9½
6-19	Fla.	W	5-2		12	9	Mulholland	Armstrong	Mit. Williams	47-20	1st	+9½
6-20	Fla.	W	4-3		6	8	Greene	Hoffman	Mit. Williams	48-20	1st	+9½
6-21	Atl.	L	1-8		7	13	Maddux	Schilling		48-21	1st	+8½
6-22	Atl.	W	5-3		7	6	Jackson	Smith	Mit. Williams	49-21	1st	+9½

Date		Opp.	Res.	Score	(inn.*)	Hits	Opp. hits	Winning pitcher	Losing pitcher	Save	Record	Pos.	GB
6-23		Atl.	W	8-3		7	9	Rivera	Smoltz		50-21	1st	+9½
6-25		At Pit.	W	8-6		10	9	DeLeon	Candelaria	Mit. Williams	51-21	1st	+9½
6-26		At Pit.	L	2-4		6	9	Cooke	Schilling		51-22	1st	+8½
6-27		At Pit.	L	3-4	(10)	9	11	Belinda	Mit. Williams		51-23	1st	+7½
6-28		At St.L.	L	1-3		8	7	Cormier	Jackson	Smith	51-24	1st	+6½
6-29		At St.L.	W	13-10		17	13	Rivera	Urbani		52-24	1st	+7½
6-30		At St.L.	L	3-9		9	14	Osborne	Greene		52-25	1st	+6½
7-1		At St.L.	L	5-14		12	15	Tewksbury	Schilling		52-26	1st	+5½
7-2	(1)	S.D.	L	2-5		6	8	Ettles	Mulholland	Ge. Harris	52-27	1st	+5½
7-2	(2)	S.D.	W	6-5	(10)	10	6	Mit. Williams	Hoffman		53-27	1st	+6
7-3		S.D.	L	4-6		10	12	Gr. Harris	Jackson	Ge. Harris	53-28	1st	+6
7-4		S.D.	W	8-4		16	9	Rivera	Worrell		54-28	1st	+7
7-5		L.A.	W	9-5		11	9	Greene	Hershiser		55-28	1st	+7
7-6		L.A.	L	5-7		8	13	Astacio	Schilling	Gott	55-29	1st	+6
7-7		L.A.	W	7-6	(20)	12	17	Mike Williams	Trlicek		56-29	1st	+6
7-8		S.F.	L	2-13		9	20	Swift	Jackson		56-30	1st	+5
7-9		S.F.	L	8-15		13	23	Black	Rivera		56-31	1st	+5
7-10		S.F.	W	8-3		12	7	Greene	Burkett		57-31	1st	+5
7-11		S.F.	L	2-10		10	18	Hickerson	Schilling		57-32	1st	+5
7-15		At S.D.	L	2-5		8	5	Gr. Harris	Jackson	Davis	57-33	1st	+4
7-16		At S.D.	L	3-5		8	9	Martinez	Greene	Davis	57-34	1st	+4
7-17		At S.D.	L	2-4		5	8	Benes	Mulholland	Ge. Harris	57-35	1st	+3
7-18		At S.D.	W	6-3		9	8	Schilling	Brocail	Mit. Williams	58-35	1st	+3
7-19		At L.A.	W	7-5		11	8	Mason	Daal	Mit. Williams	59-35	1st	+3
7-20		At L.A.	W	8-2		15	6	Jackson	R. Martinez		60-35	1st	+4
7-21		At L.A.	W	7-0		11	6	Greene	Hershiser		61-35	1st	+5
7-22		At S.F.	L	1-4		5	6	Burkett	Mulholland	Beck	61-36	1st	+5
7-23		At S.F.	W	2-1	(14)	8	8	West	Jackson	Mit. Williams	62-36	1st	+5
7-24		At S.F.	L	4-5		11	6	Burba	Rivera	Beck	62-37	1st	+5
7-25		At S.F.	L	2-5		4	9	Swift	Jackson	Righetti	62-38	1st	+4
7-27		St.L.	W	10-7		18	9	Mason	Magrane	Mit. Williams	63-38	1st	+5
7-28		St.L.	W	14-6		17	9	Mulholland	Guetterman		64-38	1st	+6
7-29		St.L.	W	6-4		7	8	West	Murphy	Mit. Williams	65-38	1st	+7
7-30		Pit.	L	2-4		6	9	Walk	Rivera	Belinda	65-39	1st	+6
7-31		Pit.	W	10-2		15	9	Jackson	Tomlin		66-39	1st	+6½
8-1		Pit.	W	5-4		12	14	Mason	Cooke	Mit. Williams	67-39	1st	+7
8-3		At Atl.	W	5-3		10	8	Mulholland	Avery	Mit. Williams	68-39	1st	+7½
8-4		At Atl.	L	8-9		14	10	Howell	West	McMichael	68-40	1st	+6½
8-5		At Atl.	W	10-4		10	8	Rivera	Maddux		69-40	1st	+6½
8-6		At Fla.	L	3-4		8	5	Aquino	Mason	Harvey	69-41	1st	+6½
8-7		At Fla.	W	8-7	(10)	9	12	Mit. Williams	Turner		70-41	1st	+6½
8-8		At Fla.	L	5-6		9	8	Hough	Mulholland	Harvey	70-42	1st	+6½
8-10		Mon.	W	5-2		7	5	Schilling	Nabholz		71-42	1st	+6
8-11		Mon.	W	6-5		9	9	West	Wetteland		72-42	1st	+7
8-12		Mon.	W	7-4		12	8	Mason	Scott	Mit. Williams	73-42	1st	+8
8-13		N.Y.	W	9-5		7	8	Thigpen	Young		74-42	1st	+9
8-14		N.Y.	L	5-9		10	10	Jones	Jackson	Innis	74-43	1st	+8
8-15		N.Y.	W	5-4		9	6	West	Young	Mit. Williams	75-43	1st	+9
8-17		At Col.	W	10-7		15	12	Rivera	Reynoso	Mit. Williams	76-43	1st	+9
8-18		At Col.	W	7-6		11	8	Thigpen	Ruffin	Mit. Williams	77-43	1st	+9
8-19		At Col.	L	5-6		12	11	Moore	Mason	Holmes	77-44	1st	+8
8-20		At Hou.	W	6-4		9	9	West	T. Jones	Mit. Williams	78-44	1st	+9
8-21		At Hou.	L	2-3	(10)	8	10	D. Jones	Andersen		78-45	1st	+9
8-22		At Hou.	L	3-7		8	11	Kile	Rivera		78-46	1st	+9
8-23		Col.	L	2-3	(13)	8	12	Wayne	Mason	Holmes	78-47	1st	+9
8-24		Col.	W	4-2		8	6	Jackson	Blair	Mit. Williams	79-47	1st	+10
8-25		Col.	W	8-5		11	10	Schilling	Sanford		80-47	1st	+11
8-27		Cin.	L	5-8		8	10	Ruffin	Mit. Williams	Dibble	80-48	1st	+10
8-28		Cin.	L	5-9		12	15	Service	Thigpen		80-49	1st	+9
8-29		Cin.	W	12-0		17	5	Jackson	Pugh		81-49	1st	+10
8-30		At Chi.	L	6-10	(11)	11	14	Plesac	Mason		81-50	1st	+9½
8-31		At Chi.	W	7-0		12	4	Rivera	Morgan		82-50	1st	+9½
9-1		At Chi.	W	4-1		8	6	Mulholland	Harkey		83-50	1st	+9½
9-3		At Cin.	W	14-2		13	3	Greene	Ayala		84-50	1st	+9½
9-4		At Cin.	L	5-6		10	12	Rijo	Jackson	Service	84-51	1st	+8½
9-5		At Cin.	W	5-3		15	8	Schilling	Pugh	Mit. Williams	85-51	1st	+7½
9-6		Chi.	L	6-7		12	9	Harkey	Mike Williams	Myers	85-52	1st	+8½
9-7		Chi.	L	4-5		12	9	Guzman	Rivera	Myers	85-53	1st	+7½
9-8		Chi.	L	5-8		10	11	Hibbard	West	Myers	85-54	1st	+6½
9-9		Chi.	W	10-8		14	15	Jackson	Bautista	West	86-54	1st	+7
9-10		Hou.	W	6-2		12	9	Schilling	Swindell		87-54	1st	+7
9-11		Hou.	L	1-4		3	8	Portugal	Mike Williams	T. Jones	87-55	1st	+6
9-12		Hou.	L	2-9		7	11	Harnisch	Rivera		87-56	1st	+5
9-13		At N.Y.	W	5-0		9	6	Greene	Jones		88-56	1st	+5½

Date	Opp.	Res.	Score	(inn.*)	Hits	Opp. hits	Winning pitcher	Losing pitcher	Save	Record	Pos.	GB
9-14	At N.Y.	L	4-5		9	7	Tanana	Jackson	Franco	88-57	1st	+4½
9-15	At N.Y.	W	6-3		12	10	Schilling	Schourek	Mit. Williams	89-57	1st	+5½
9-17	At Mon.	L	7-8	(12)	9	12	Scott	Mit. Williams		89-58	1st	+4
9-18	At Mon.	W	5-4		10	5	Greene	Boucher	Mit. Williams	90-58	1st	+5
9-19	At Mon.	L	5-6		10	7	Scott	Mit. Williams		90-59	1st	+4½
9-20	Fla.	W	7-1		12	7	Schilling	Hough		91-59	1st	+4½
9-21	Fla.	W	5-3		7	7	Pall	Rodriguez	Mit. Williams	92-59	1st	+5½
9-22	Fla.	W	2-1	(12)	10	11	Mason	Harvey		93-59	1st	+5½
9-24	Atl.	W	3-0		7	3	Greene	Glavine	Mit. Williams	94-59	1st	+6
9-25	Atl.	L	7-9		15	14	Bedrosian	Mason	McMichael	94-60	1st	+5
9-26	Atl.	L	2-7		5	9	Avery	Schilling		94-61	1st	+5
9-27	At Pit.	W	6-4		8	10	Rivera	Cooke	Mit. Williams	95-61	1st	+6
9-28	At Pit.	W	10-7		18	10	Thigpen	Robertson		96-61	1st	+6
9-29	At Pit.	L	1-9		5	10	Walk	Foster	Johnston	96-62	1st	+5
9-30	At Pit.	L	0-5		4	9	Wakefield	Greene		96-63	1st	+4
10-1	At St.L.	W	4-2		6	6	Schilling	Olivares	Mit. Williams	97-63	1st	+4
10-2	At St.L.	L	4-5	(10)	9	7	Murphy	Mike Williams		97-64	1st	+4
10-3	At St.L.	L	0-2		7	2	Guetterman	Mit. Williams	Perez	97-65	1st	+3

Monthly records: April (17-5), May (17-10), June (18-10), July (14-14), August (16-11), September (14-13), October (1-2).
*Innings, if other than nine.

HIGHLIGHTS

High point: Philadelphia opened the season with a three-game sweep of the Astros in Houston, setting the Phillies' worst-to-first campaign in motion. A four-game sweep of the Mets in New York from June 10-13 hiked Philadelphia's lead to a season-high 11½ games and helped the Phillies pull away.

Low point: After losing three of four games at home to San Francisco prior to the All-Star break, the Phillies opened the second half by losing three straight games in San Diego. That dropped Philadelphia's lead to three games, the lowest it dipped for the rest of the year.

Turning point: On July 27, St. Louis came to Philadelphia trailing the Phillies by four games. But Philadelphia swept the three-game series, dropping the Cardinals seven games back and breaking their spirit.

Most valuable player: Center fielder Lenny Dykstra. Among other things, he led the majors with 143 runs scored, the most in the N.L. since 1932, and became just the third N.L. player since 1958 to reach base 300 times.

Most valuable pitcher: Righthander Curt Schilling. The MVP of the N.L. playoffs, he went 16-7 and led the staff in innings (235⅓) and strikeouts (186).

Most improved player: Left fielder Pete Incaviglia. In 1991 and '92, he combined to hit 22 homers with 82 RBIs in 686 at-bats. Last year, he clubbed 24 home runs with a career-high 89 RBIs in 368 at-bats.

Most pleasant surprise: Shortstop Kevin Stocker. He made his big-league debut July 7 and cemented his grasp on the position by playing well in the field and batting .324 in 70 games.

Biggest disappointment: Righthander Ben Rivera. After going 7-3 with a 2.82 ERA with the Phillies in 1992, he went 13-9 with an ugly 5.02 ERA.

Key injuries: Third baseman Dave Hollins was on the disabled list June 11-28 with a broken right wrist. Lefthander

Terry Mulholland missed over three weeks in September with a strained hip. **Notable:** The Phillies drew over 3 million fans (3,137,674) for the first time ever. ... Philadelphia became just the third team since 1900 to go from last to first place in consecutive seasons.

—BILL BROWN

RECORDS

1993 regular-season record: 97-65 (1st in N.L. East); 52-29 at home; 45-36 on road; 47-31 vs. East; 50-34 vs. West; 31-18 vs. LHP; 66-47 vs. RHP; 30-19 on grass; 67-46 on turf; 25-20 in daytime; 72-45 at night; 23-20 in one-run games; 11-7 in extra-inning games; 0-0-1 in doubleheaders.

Team record last five years: 389-421 (.480, ranks 11th in league in that span).

TEAM LEADERS

Batting average: John Kruk (.316).
At-bats: Lenny Dykstra (637).
Runs: Lenny Dykstra (143).
Hits: Lenny Dykstra (194).
Total bases: Lenny Dykstra (307).
Doubles: Lenny Dykstra (44).
Triples: Mickey Morandini (9).
Home runs: Darren Daulton, Pete Incaviglia (24).
Runs batted in: Darren Daulton (105).
Stolen bases: Lenny Dykstra (37).
Slugging percentage: Darren Daulton, Lenny Dykstra (.482).
On-base percentage: John Kruk (.430).
Wins: Curt Schilling, Tommy Greene (16).
Earned-run average: Terry Mulholland (3.25).
Complete games: Tommy Greene, Terry Mulholland, Curt Schilling (7).
Shutouts: Tommy Greene, Terry Mulholland, Curt Schilling (2).
Saves: Mitch Williams (43).
Innings pitched: Curt Schilling (235⅓).
Strikeouts: Curt Schilling (186).

GAMES BY POSITION

Catcher: Darren Daulton 146, Todd Pratt 26, Doug Lindsey 2.
First base: John Kruk 144, Ricky Jordan 33, Jim Eisenreich 1.
Second base: Mickey Morandini 111, Mariano Duncan 65.
Third base: Dave Hollins 143, Kim Batiste 58, Jeff Manto 6, Joe Millette 3.
Shortstop: Kevin Stocker 70, Mariano Duncan 24, Kim Batiste 24, Juan Bell 22, Joe Millette 7, Jeff Manto 1.
Outfield: Lenny Dykstra 160, Jim Eisenreich 137, Milt Thompson 106, Pete Incaviglia 97, Wes Chamberlain 76, Ruben Amaro 16, Tony Longmire 2.

TOP DRAFT CHOICES

1. **Wayne Gomes**, RHP, Old Dominion University.
2. **Scott Rolen**, 3B, Jasper (Ind.) High School.
3. **Josh Watts**, OF, Ironwood High School, Glendale, Ariz.
4. **Jeffrey Key**, OF, Newton County High School, Covington, Ga.
5. **Thomas Franek**, RHP, Mesa State College (Colo.).
6. **Blair Fowler**, RHP, Everett (Wash.) High School.
7. **Scott Sladovnik**, OF, Westside High School, Omaha, Neb.
8. **Bo Hamilton**, RHP, Cleveland (Tex.) High School.
9. **Nelson Metheney**, RHP, Clinch Valley College (Va.).
10. **Silvio Censale**, LHP, University of Miami (Fla.).

PHILADELPHIA PHILLIES

1994 SEASON

PITTSBURGH PIRATES
NATIONAL LEAGUE CENTRAL DIVISION

1994 SEASON

N Denotes night game (any game starting after 5 p.m.).
▦ Home games shaded.
* At Three Rivers Stadium in Pittsburgh.

APRIL

SUN	MON	TUE	WED	THU	FRI	SAT
					1	2
3	4 SF	5 SF	6 SF	7	8 N COL	9 N COL
10 COL	11	12 N SD	13 N SD	14 N SD	15 N LA	16 N LA
17 LA	18	19 N CIN	20 N CIN	21	22 N ATL	23 N ATL
24 ATL	25 N HOU	26 N HOU	27 N CIN	28 N CIN	29 N ATL	30 N ATL

MAY

SUN	MON	TUE	WED	THU	FRI	SAT
1 ATL	2	3 N HOU	4 N HOU	5	6 N CHI	7 N CHI
8 CHI	9 N FLA	10 N FLA	11 N FLA	12 N PHI	13 N PHI	14 N PHI
15 PHI	16 N STL	17 N STL	18 N STL	19	20 N MON	21 N MON
22 MON	23	24 N NY	25 N NY	26 N NY	27 N LA	28 N LA
29 LA	30 N SD	31 N SD				

JUNE

SUN	MON	TUE	WED	THU	FRI	SAT
			1 SD	2	3 N COL	4 N COL
5 COL	6 N SF	7 N SF	8 N SF	9 N FLA	10 N FLA	11 N FLA
12 FLA	13 N MON	14 N MON	15 N MON	16	17 N STL	18 N STL
19 STL	20 N PHI	21 N PHI	22 PHI	23	24 N NY	25 N NY
26 NY	27 N CHI	28 CHI	29 N CHI	30 N CIN		

JULY

SUN	MON	TUE	WED	THU	FRI	SAT
					1 N CIN	2 N CIN
3 CIN	4 N ATL	5 N ATL	6 N ATL	7 N CIN	8 N CIN	9 N CIN
10 CIN	11 *	12 ALL-STAR GAME	13	14 N HOU	15 N HOU	16 N HOU
17 HOU	18 N ATL	19 N ATL	20 N ATL	21 N HOU	22 N HOU	23 N HOU
24 HOU	25 N CHI	26 N CHI	27 N CHI	28 N CHI	29 N NY	30 N NY
31 NY						

AUGUST

SUN	MON	TUE	WED	THU	FRI	SAT
	1	2 N PHI	3 N PHI	4	5 N STL	6 N STL
7 STL	8 N MON	9 N MON	10 N MON	11 N MON	12 N FLA	13 N FLA
14 N FLA	15	16 N LA	17 N LA	18 N LA	19 N SF	20 N SF
21 SF	22	23 N LA	24 N LA	25 N LA	26 N SF	27 N SF
28 SF	29 N COL	30 N COL	31 COL			

SEPTEMBER

SUN	MON	TUE	WED	THU	FRI	SAT
				1 N SD	2 N SD	3
4 SD	5 N COL	6 N COL	7 COL	8	9 N SD	10 N SD
11 SD	12	13 N FLA	14 N FLA	15 N FLA	16 N MON	17 N MON
18 MON	19 N STL	20 N STL	21 N STL	22	23 N PHI	24 N PHI
25 PHI	26 N NY	27 N NY	28 N NY	29 N NY	30 CHI	

OCTOBER

SUN	MON	TUE	WED	THU	FRI	SAT
						1 CHI
2 CHI						

CLUB DIRECTORY

Board of directors
Joe L. Brown
Frank V. Cahouet
Richard M. Cyert
Douglas D. Danforth
Eugene Litman
John Marous
John H. McConnell
Tom Murphy
Thomas H. O'Brien
Paul H. O'Neill
David M. Roderick
Vincent A. Sarni
Mark Sauer
Harvey M. Walken
Chairman of the exec. comm. of the board
Vincent Sarni
President and chief executive officer
Mark Sauer
Sr. v.p. and general manager
Cam Bonifay
Special assistants to the general manager
Leland Maddox
Ken Parker
Pete Vuckovich
Lenny Yochim
Vice president, finance and administration
Kenneth C. Curcio
Vice President, broadcasting & adv. sales
Mark Driscoll
Vice president, marketing and operations
Steven N. Greenberg
Assistant vice president, finance
Patti Mistick
Traveling secretary
Greg Johnson
Director of ticket operations
Gary Remlinger
Senior director of sales and marketing
Bob Derda
Sales manager, broadcasting & promotions
Mark Ferraco
Director of major league baseball admin.
John Sirignano
Director of Bradenton baseball operations
Jeff Podobnik
Director of community relations
Patty Paytas
Director of community services and sales
Al Gordon
Director of corporate relations
Nellie Briles

Director of finance
Jim Plake
Director of information systems
Sanjay Chakrabarty
Director of in-game entertainment
Mike Gordon
Director of media relations
Jim Trdinich
Director of merchandising
Joe Billetdeaux
Director of minor league operations
Chet Montgomery
Director of promotions
Kathy Guy
Director of publicity
Jim Lachimia
Director of operations
Dennis DaPra
Director of scouting
Paul Tinnell
Assistant director of public relations
Sally O'Leary
Club physician
Dr. Joseph Coroso
Team orthopedist
Dr. Jack Failla
Trainers
Kent Biggerstaff
Dave Tumbas
Equipment manager
Roger Wilson
Scouting coordinators
Ron King
Fred Wright
Scouting supervisors
Tom Barnard
Dana Brown
Bill Bryk
Pablo Cruz
Larry D'Amato
Steve Demeter
Angel Figueroa
Steve Fleming
Dave Klipstein
Carlos Loreto
Scott Lovekamp
Jose Luna
Boyd Odom
Ed Roebuck
George Swain
Mike Williams

Manager—Jim Leyland (10).

Coaches—Rich Donnelly (45), Milt May (39), Ray Miller (31), Tommy Sandt (37), Bill Virdon (19), Spin Williams (54).

No.	PITCHERS	B/T	Ht./Wt.	Born	1993 clubs
26	Cooke, Steve	R/L	6-6/229	1-14-70	Pittsburgh
52	De Los Santos, Mariano	R/R	5-10/200	7-13-70	Salem, Carolina
50	Dewey, Mark	R/R	6-0/216	1-3-65	Buffalo, Pittsburgh
56	Hope, John	R/R	6-3/206	12-21-70	Carolina, Buffalo, Pittsburgh
64	Johnston, Joel	R/R	6-4/234	3-8-67	Buffalo, Pittsburgh
53	McCurry, Jeff	R/R	6-7/210	1-21-70	Salem, Carolina
32	Miceli, Dan	R/R	6-0/207	9-9-70	Memphis, Carolina, Pittsburgh
55	Minor, Blas	R/R	6-3/203	3-20-66	Pittsburgh
15	Neagle, Denny	L/L	6-2/217	9-13-68	Pittsburgh, Buffalo
34	Pena, Alejandro	R/R	6-1/228	6-25-59	Pittsburgh
48	Powell, Dennis	R/L	6-3/227	8-13-63	Calgary, Seattle
30	Ramirez, Roberto	R/L	5-11/170	8-17-72	Mexico City Red Devils
41	Smith, Zane	L/L	6-1/207	12-28-60	Carolina, Pittsburgh
29	Tomlin, Randy	L/L	5-10/182	6-14-66	Pittsburgh, Carolina
43	Wagner, Paul	R/R	6-1/202	11-14-67	Pittsburgh
49	Wakefield, Tim	R/R	6-2/204	8-2-66	Pittsburgh, Carolina
44	White, Rick	R/R	6-4/215	12-23-68	Carolina, Buffalo
46	Zimmerman, Mike	R/R	6-0/180	2-6-69	Buffalo, Carolina

No.	CATCHERS	B/T	Ht./Wt.	Born	1993 clubs
2	Encarnacion, Angelo	R/R	5-8/180	4-18-73	Salem, Buffalo
57	Goff, Jerry	L/R	6-3/207	4-12-64	Buffalo, Pittsburgh
42	Osik, Keith	R/R	6-0/195	10-22-68	Carolina
11	Slaught, Don	R/R	6-1/185	9-11-58	Pittsburgh

No.	INFIELDERS	B/T	Ht./Wt.	Born	1993 clubs
48	Aude, Rich	R/R	6-5/209	7-13-71	Carolina, Buffalo, Pittsburgh
3	Bell, Jay	R/R	6-0/185	12-11-65	Pittsburgh
27	Brown, Michael	L/L	6-7/235	11-4-71	Salem
16	Foley, Tom	L/R	6-1/185	9-9-59	Pittsburgh
13	Garcia, Carlos	R/R	6-1/193	10-15-67	Pittsburgh
14	Hunter, Brian R.	R/L	6-0/195	3-4-68	Atlanta, Richmond
7	King, Jeff	R/R	6-1/183	12-26-64	Pittsburgh
6	Merced, Orlando	L/R	5-11/185	11-2-66	Pittsburgh
5	Sandoval, Jose	R/R	5-11/170	8-25-69	Buffalo, Mexico City Red Devils
51	Womack, Tony	L/R	5-9/153	9-25-69	Salem, Carolina, Pittsburgh
36	Young, Kevin	R/R	6-2/219	6-16-69	Pittsburgh

No.	OUTFIELDERS	B/T	Ht./Wt.	Born	1993 clubs
47	Bullett, Scott	L/L	6-2/190	12-25-68	Buffalo, Pittsburgh
24	Cameron, Stanton	R/R	6-5/195	7-5-69	Bowie
35	Clark, Dave	L/R	6-2/209	9-3-62	Pittsburgh
30	Cummings, Midre	L/R	6-0/196	10-14-71	Carolina, Buffalo, Pittsburgh
28	Martin, Al	L/L	6-2/210	11-24-67	Pittsburgh
23	McClendon, Lloyd	R/R	6-0/208	1-11-59	Pittsburgh
25	Pennyfeather, William	R/R	6-2/215	5-25-68	Buffalo, Pittsburgh
18	Van Slyke, Andy	L/R	6-2/198	12-21-60	Pittsburgh, Carolina

BALLPARK INFORMATION

Ballpark (capacity, surface)
  Three Rivers Stadium
  (47,972, artificial)

Address
  600 Stadium Circle
  Pittsburgh, PA 15212

Business phone
  412-323-5000

Ticket information
  412-321-2827

Ticket prices
  $14 (club boxes)
  $10 (terrace boxes)
  $8 (reserved seats)
  $5 (general admission)
  $2.50 (g.a., children 12 and under)

Field dimensions (from home plate)
  To left field at foul line, 335 feet
  To center field, 400 feet
  To right field at foul line, 335 feet

First game played
  July 16, 1970 (Reds 3, Pirates 2)

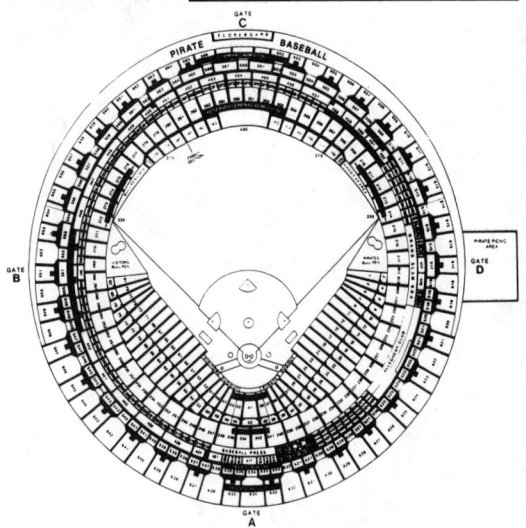

Class	Team	League	Manager
AAA	Buffalo	American Association	Doc Edwards
AA	Carolina	Southern	Bobby Meacham
A	Salem	Carolina	Trent Jewett
A	Augusta	South Atlantic	Scott Little
A	Welland, Ont.	New York-Pennsylvania	Jeff Banister
Rookie	Bradenton Pirates	Gulf Coast	Woody Huyke

BROADCAST INFORMATION

Radio: KDKA-AM (1020). Broadcasters: Lanny Frattare, Steve Blass.
TV: KDKA-TV (Channel 2). Broadcasters: Lanny Frattare, Steve Blass.
Cable TV: KBL Sports Network. Broadcasters: Lanny Frattare, Steve Blass.

SPRING TRAINING

Ballpark (city): McKechnie Field (Bradenton, Fla.).
Ticket Information: 813-748-4610.

HISTORY

YEAR-BY-YEAR RECORDS

Year	Pos.	W	L	Pct.	GB	Year	Pos.	W	L	Pct.	GB
1901	1st	90	49	.647	+ 7½	1950	8th	57	96	.373	33½
1902	1st	103	36	.741	+27½	1951	7th	64	90	.416	32½
1903	1st	91	49	.650	+ 6½	1952	8th	42	112	.273	54½
1904	4th	87	66	.569	19	1953	8th	50	104	.325	55
1905	2nd	96	57	.627	9	1954	8th	53	101	.344	44
1906	3rd	93	60	.608	23½	1955	8th	60	94	.390	38½
1907	2nd	91	63	.591	17	1956	7th	66	88	.429	27
1908	T2nd	98	56	.636	1	1957	T7th	62	92	.403	33
1909	1st	110	42	.724	+ 6½	1958	2nd	84	70	.545	8
1910	3rd	86	67	.562	17½	1959	4th	78	76	.506	9
1911	3rd	85	69	.552	14½	1960	1st	95	59	.617	+ 7
1912	2nd	93	58	.616	10	1961	6th	75	79	.487	18
1913	4th	78	71	.523	21½	1962	4th	93	68	.578	8
1914	7th	69	85	.448	25½	1963	8th	74	88	.457	25
1915	5th	73	81	.474	18	1964	T6th	80	82	.494	13
1916	6th	65	89	.422	29	1965	3rd	90	72	.556	7
1917	8th	51	103	.331	47	1966	3rd	92	70	.568	3
1918	4th	65	60	.520	17	1967	6th	81	81	.500	20½
1919	4th	71	68	.511	24½	1968	6th	80	82	.494	17
1920	4th	79	75	.513	14	1969	3rd	88	74	.543	12
1921	2nd	90	63	.588	4	1970	1st*	89	73	.549	+ 5
1922	T3rd	85	69	.552	8	1971	1st†	97	65	.599	+ 7
1923	3rd	87	67	.565	8½	1972	1st*	96	59	.619	+11
1924	3rd	90	63	.588	3	1973	3rd	80	82	.494	2½
1925	1st	95	58	.621	+ 8½	1974	1st*	88	74	.543	+ 1½
1926	3rd	84	69	.549	4½	1975	1st*	92	69	.571	+ 6½
1927	1st	94	60	.610	+ 1½	1976	2nd	92	70	.568	9
1928	4th	85	67	.559	9	1977	2nd	96	66	.593	5
1929	2nd	88	65	.575	10½	1978	2nd	88	73	.547	1½
1930	5th	80	74	.519	12	1979	1st†	98	64	.605	+ 2
1931	5th	75	79	.487	26	1980	3rd	83	79	.512	8
1932	2nd	86	68	.558	4	1981	4th/6th	46	56	.451	‡
1933	2nd	87	67	.565	5	1982	4th	84	78	.519	8
1934	5th	74	76	.493	19½	1983	2nd	84	78	.519	6
1935	4th	86	67	.562	13½	1984	6th	75	87	.463	21½
1936	4th	84	70	.545	8	1985	6th	57	104	.354	43½
1937	3rd	86	68	.558	10	1986	6th	64	98	.395	44
1938	2nd	86	64	.573	2	1987	T4th	80	82	.494	15
1939	6th	68	85	.444	28½	1988	2nd	85	75	.531	15
1940	4th	78	76	.506	22½	1989	5th	74	88	.457	19
1941	4th	81	73	.526	19	1990	1st*	95	67	.586	+ 4
1942	5th	66	81	.449	36½	1991	1st*	98	64	.605	+14
1943	4th	80	74	.519	25	1992	1st*	96	66	.593	+ 9
1944	2nd	90	63	.588	14½	1993	5th	75	87	.463	22
1945	4th	82	72	.532	16						
1946	7th	63	91	.409	34						
1947	T7th	62	92	.403	32						
1948	4th	83	71	.539	8½						
1949	6th	71	83	.461	26						

*Lost Championship Series. †Won Championship Series. ‡First half 25-23; second 21-33.

MANAGERS

Name	Record	Years
Fred Clarke	1343-909	'01-15
Jimmy Callahan	85-129	'16-17
Honus Wagner	1-4	1917
Hugo Bezdek	166-187	'17-19
George Gibson	401-330	'20-22
		'32-34
Bill McKechnie	409-293	'22-26
Donie Bush	246-178	'27-29
Jewel Ens	176-167	'29-31
Pie Traynor	457-406	'34-39
Frank Frisch	539-528	'40-46
Spud Davis	1-2	1946
Billy Herman	61-92	1947
Bill Burwell	1-0	1947
Billy Meyer	317-452	'48-52
Fred Haney	163-299	'53-55
Bobby Bragan	102-155	'56-57
Danny Murtaugh	1115-950	'57-64
		1967
		'70-71
		'73-76
Harry Walker	224-184	'65-67
Larry Shepard	164-155	'68-69
Alex Grammas	4-1	1969
Bill Virdon	163-128	'72-73
Chuck Tanner	711-685	'77-85
Jim Leyland	667-627	'86-93

DAY BY DAY

Date	Opp.	Res.	Score	(Inn.*)	Hits	Opp. hits	Winning pitcher	Losing pitcher	Save	Record	Pos.	GB
4-6	S.D.	W	9-4		15	4	Wakefield	Benes	Candelaria	1-0	T2nd	½
4-8	S.D.	W	5-4		9	5	Walk	Gr. Harris	Belinda	2-0	T1st	½
4-9	S.F.	W	6-5		10	10	Minor	Beck	Belinda	3-0	1st	+½
4-10	S.F.	L	5-12		7	14	Burba	Cooke		3-1	3rd	½
4-11	S.F.	L	3-4		6	7	Burkett	Wakefield	Beck	3-2	3rd	1½
4-12	At S.D.	W	4-2		10	5	Otto	Gr. Harris	Belinda	4-2	T2nd	1½
4-13	At S.D.	W	6-4		14	9	Walk	Gomez	Wagner	5-2	T2nd	1½
4-14	At S.D.	W	11-7		17	13	Minor	Seminara		6-2	T2nd	1½
4-15	At S.D.	W	5-4	(13)	12	12	Moeller	Hernandez	Belinda	7-2	T2nd	1
4-16	At L.A.	L	4-7		10	15	Hershiser	Wakefield	Gott	7-3	T2nd	1
4-17	At L.A.	L	3-6		5	11	R. Martinez	Otto		7-4	T2nd	1
4-18	At L.A.	L	4-6		9	11	Ke. Gross	Walk	Wilson	7-5	T2nd	2
4-20	Cin.	L	0-5		3	10	Belcher	Tomlin		7-6	T3rd	3
4-21	Cin.	L	7-8	(12)	14	16	Foster	Candelaria		7-7	T5th	3½
4-22	Cin.	W	5-4		9	4	Wakefield	Smiley		8-7	4th	2½
4-23	Hou.	L	2-4		4	7	Swindell	Neagle	D. Jones	8-8	6th	3½
4-24	Hou.	L	4-8		10	14	Hernandez	Candelaria		8-9	6th	4½
4-25	Hou.	W	7-2		11	5	Tomlin	Portugal		9-9	5th	4½
4-26	At Atl.	W	4-3	(11)	8	8	Minor	McMichael	Belinda	10-9	5th	4½
4-27	At Atl.	W	6-2	(11)	11	6	Wakefield	Stanton	Wagner	11-9	T3rd	3½
4-28	At Cin.	L	2-4		11	5	Pugh	Otto	Reardon	11-10	4th	4½
4-30	At Hou.	L	2-11		6	13	Portugal	Walk	Hernandez	11-11	T4th	6
5-1	At Hou.	L	3-7		7	11	Drabek	Tomlin		11-12	T4th	6
5-2	At Hou.	W	6-2		12	9	Cooke	Swindell		12-12	T4th	6
5-4	Atl.	L	2-3		4	10	Glavine	Wakefield	Stanton	12-13	T4th	7
5-5	Atl.	W	4-1		8	7	Walk	Maddux	Belinda	13-13	T4th	6
5-7	Mon.	L	0-1		8	6	Nabholz	Tomlin	Wetteland	13-14	T4th	6½
5-8	Mon.	W	10-9	(10)	10	14	Belinda	Bottenfield		14-14	T4th	7
5-9	Mon.	W	6-5	(11)	11	12	Minor	Barnes		15-14	3rd	7
5-10	At Phi.	L	1-5		4	8	Jackson	Walk		15-15	T3rd	8
5-11	At Phi.	W	8-4		13	11	Wagner	Davis		16-15	T3rd	7
5-12	At Phi.	L	1-4		5	6	Greene	Tomlin		16-16	T4th	8
5-14	At Chi.	L	2-3		10	8	Harkey	Cooke	Myers	16-17	5th	8
5-15	At Chi.	L	5-14		10	19	Guzman	Wakefield		16-18	5th	8
5-16	At Chi.	W	5-3		8	9	Walk	Hibbard	Belinda	17-18	5th	8
5-17	At N.Y.	W	9-4		14	7	Tomlin	Gooden		18-18	5th	8
5-18	At N.Y.	W	10-8		16	17	Otto	Schourek	Belinda	19-18	T4th	8
5-19	At N.Y.	L	4-6	(10)	10	10	Franco	Minor		19-19	T4th	8
5-21	St.L.	L	8-10	(11)	14	14	Lancaster	Wagner	Perez	19-20	5th	8½
5-22	St.L.	W	4-2		8	6	Walk	Osborne	Belinda	20-20	5th	7½
5-23	St.L.	L	3-4	(10)	7	10	Smith	Minor	Perez	20-21	5th	8½
5-25	Fla.	W	2-0		8	4	Cooke	Hough		21-21	T4th	9
5-26	Fla.	L	4-5		3	9	Hammond	Wagner	Harvey	21-22	5th	9
5-27	Fla.	W	13-8		13	16	Walk	Bowen		22-22	5th	8½
5-28	L.A.	L	2-7		8	12	Astacio	Tomlin		22-23	5th	9½
5-29	L.A.	L	1-6		4	12	R. Martinez	Otto		22-24	5th	10½
5-30	L.A.	W	5-3		8	9	Cooke	Ke. Gross	Belinda	23-24	5th	10½
5-31	At Col.	L	2-6		9	12	Reynoso	Wakefield		23-25	5th	10½
6-1	At Col.	W	8-6		12	12	Walk	Smith		24-25	5th	10½
6-2	At Col.	W	5-3		12	4	Petkovsek	Parrett	Belinda	25-25	5th	10½
6-3	At S.F.	W	2-1		10	2	Neagle	Brummett	Minor	26-25	4th	10
6-4	At S.F.	W	3-2		8	7	Cooke	Brantley	Belinda	27-25	T3rd	9
6-5	At S.F.	L	2-3		6	5	Wilson	Wakefield	Beck	27-26	T3rd	10
6-6	At S.F.	L	1-7		7	11	Swift	Walk		27-27	4th	11
6-8	Col.	L	1-4		4	9	Ruffin	Wagner	Shepherd	27-28	T4th	11½
6-9	Col.	W	4-1		9	7	Neagle	Blair	Belinda	28-28	T4th	11½
6-10	At Fla.	L	3-4		7	8	Turner	Otto	Harvey	28-29	5th	12½
6-11	At Fla.	L	3-11		7	21	Aquino	Wakefield		28-30	5th	13½
6-12	At Fla.	L	2-5		11	5	Hammond	Walk	Harvey	28-31	6th	14½
6-13	At Fla.	L	2-5		10	8	Bowen	Minor	Harvey	28-32	6th	15½
6-14	At St.L.	L	3-8		8	11	Osborne	Neagle	Perez	28-33	6th	16½
6-15	At St.L.	L	3-6		8	10	Tewksbury	Cooke	Smith	28-34	6th	16½
6-16	At St.L.	L	2-3		6	9	Magrane	Smith	Smith	28-35	6th	16½
6-17	N.Y.	W	6-2		10	6	Walk	Gooden		29-35	6th	15½
6-18	N.Y.	W	5-2		8	6	Wagner	Young		30-35	6th	15½
6-19	N.Y.	W	8-3		13	10	Toliver	Tanana	Minor	31-35	5th	15½
6-20	N.Y.	W	3-2		7	5	Belinda	Saberhagen		32-35	5th	15½
6-21	Chi.	L	1-5		4	7	Bautista	Smith		32-36	5th	15½
6-22	Chi.	W	7-2		10	3	Walk	Wendell		33-36	5th	15½
6-23	Chi.	W	9-4		12	15	Wagner	Boskie	Belinda	34-36	4th	15½

Date		Opp.	Res.	Score	(inn.*)	Hits	Opp. hits	Winning pitcher	Losing pitcher	Save	Record	Pos.	GB
6-25		Phi.	L	6-8		9	10	DeLeon	Candelaria	Mit. Williams	34-37	5th	16½
6-26		Phi.	W	4-2		9	6	Cooke	Schilling		35-37	4th	15½
6-27		Phi.	W	4-3	(10)	11	9	Belinda	Mit. Williams		36-37	4th	14½
6-28		At Mon.	W	9-5	(10)	12	9	Wakefield	Scott		37-37	4th	13½
6-29		At Mon.	L	2-9		4	12	Nabholz	Wagner		37-38	4th	14½
6-30		At Mon.	L	1-9		3	7	Gardiner	Neagle	Fassero	37-39	5th	14½
7-1		At Mon.	L	5-7		10	10	Rojas	Cooke	Wetteland	37-40	5th	14½
7-2	(1)	At Cin.	W	10-9		14	10	Otto	Ayala	Belinda	38-40	5th	14
7-2	(2)	At Cin.	L	1-9		7	10	Pugh	Wakefield		38-41	5th	14½
7-3		At Cin.	L	3-5		7	12	Luebbers	Walk	Dibble	38-42	5th	14½
7-4		At Cin.	L	2-7		11	10	Browning	Wagner	Spradlin	38-43	5th	15½
7-5		At Cin.	L	4-6		8	13	Belcher	Neagle	Dibble	38-44	5th	16½
7-6		At Hou.	W	10-3		12	10	Ballard	Harnisch		39-44	5th	15½
7-7		At Hou.	W	5-2		14	7	Wagner	Portugal	Belinda	40-44	5th	15½
7-8		At Hou.	L	4-10		10	12	Kile	Smith		40-45	5th	15½
7-9		Cin.	W	4-1		9	8	Walk	Browning	Belinda	41-45	5th	14½
7-10		Cin.	L	7-10		8	19	Service	Wagner	Dibble	41-46	5th	15½
7-11		Cin.	W	3-2		9	7	Minor	Reardon		42-46	4th	14½
7-15		At Atl.	L	0-4		6	6	Glavine	Tomlin		42-47	5th	14½
7-16		At Atl.	L	2-3		9	4	Maddux	Cooke	Stanton	42-48	5th	14½
7-17		At Atl.	W	4-3		11	5	Wagner	Smoltz	Belinda	43-48	5th	13½
7-18		At Atl.	L	0-2		13	6	Avery	Smith	Stanton	43-49	5th	14½
7-19		Hou.	L	2-4		6	12	Harnisch	Walk	D. Jones	43-50	5th	15½
7-20		Hou.	W	2-1		5	4	Tomlin	Drabek		44-50	5th	15½
7-21		Hou.	L	3-5		8	5	Kile	Cooke	D. Jones	44-51	5th	16½
7-22		Atl.	L	8-7		11	14	Minor	Howell		45-51	5th	15½
7-23		Atl.	L	2-6		4	14	Avery	Belinda		45-52	5th	16½
7-24		Atl.	L	6-11		10	18	Bedrosian	Walk		45-53	5th	16½
7-25		Atl.	L	1-13		4	21	Glavine	Tomlin		45-54	5th	16½
7-27		Mon.	L	6-8		12	11	Scott	Johnston	Wetteland	45-55	5th	17½
7-28		Mon.	W	3-2		11	11	Petkovsek	Shaw		46-55	5th	17½
7-29		Mon.	L	2-3	(11)	7	10	Wetteland	Minor	Heredia	46-56	5th	18½
7-30		At Phi.	W	4-2		9	6	Walk	Rivera	Belinda	47-56	5th	17½
7-31		At Phi.	L	2-10		9	15	Jackson	Tomlin		47-57	5th	18½
8-1		At Phi.	L	4-5		14	12	Mason	Cooke	Mit. Williams	47-58	5th	19½
8-2		At Chi.	L	10-12		13	14	Scanlan	Minor	Myers	47-59	5th	20
8-3		At Chi.	W	7-3		14	8	Smith	Hibbard		48-59	5th	20
8-4		At Chi.	W	6-5		10	11	Ballard	Boskie	Neagle	49-59	5th	19
8-5		At Chi.	W	5-2		11	5	Tomlin	Morgan	Dewey	50-59	5th	19
8-7	(1)	At N.Y.	W	2-1		7	9	Cooke	Gooden	Dewey	51-59	5th	18½
8-7	(2)	At N.Y.	L	8-10		13	17	Maddux	Neagle	Young	51-60	5th	19
8-8		At N.Y.	W	3-2		10	5	Smith	Tanana		52-60	5th	18
8-9		St.L.	L	3-7		5	10	Watson	Walk		52-61	5th	18½
8-10		St.L.	L	2-4		11	9	Arocha	Johnston	Smith	52-62	5th	19½
8-11		St.L.	W	8-6		12	10	Dewey	Burns		53-62	5th	19½
8-12		St.L.	W	5-4	(11)	14	9	Johnston	Burns		54-62	5th	19½
8-13		Fla.	W	8-3		9	10	Smith	Hough		55-62	5th	19½
8-14		Fla.	L	3-8		9	12	Bowen	Walk	Harvey	55-63	5th	19½
8-15		Fla.	W	4-3	(11)	10	12	Minor	Aquino		56-63	5th	19½
8-17		S.F.	W	10-3		13	10	Cooke	Burkett		57-63	5th	19½
8-18		S.F.	L	6-9		11	15	Wilson	Smith		57-64	5th	20½
8-19		S.F.	L	3-6		6	7	Hickerson	Walk	Beck	57-65	5th	20½
8-20		At S.D.	W	7-6		14	11	Petkovsek	Davis	Dewey	58-65	5th	20½
8-22		At S.D.	W	10-5		14	10	Cooke	Benes		59-65	5th	19
8-23		At L.A.	L	1-6		8	14	Hershiser	Smith		59-66	5th	19
8-24		At L.A.	L	4-13		8	15	Ke. Gross	Walk		59-67	5th	20
8-25		At L.A.	W	2-1	(12)	8	10	Neagle	Gott		60-67	5th	20
8-27		S.D.	L	6-10		8	12	Benes	Cooke	Hoffman	60-68	5th	20
8-28		S.D.	L	3-5		6	9	Sanders	Smith	Ge. Harris	60-69	5th	20
8-29	(1)	S.D.	W	7-4		12	9	Walk	Ashby	Dewey	61-69	5th	20
8-29	(2)	S.D.	L	0-11		6	14	Brocail	Hope		61-70	5th	20½
8-31		L.A.	W	6-2		12	4	Johnston	Ke. Gross		62-70	5th	20
9-1		L.A.	W	5-1		9	8	Cooke	Candiotti		63-70	5th	20
9-2		L.A.	L	0-4		4	11	Astacio	Ballard		63-71	5th	20½
9-3		At Col.	L	6-7		10	11	Holmes	Dewey		63-72	5th	21½
9-4		At Col.	L	4-10		13	14	Painter	Wakefield		63-73	5th	21½
9-5		At Col.	L	1-4		6	8	Ruffin	Walk	Holmes	63-74	5th	21½
9-6		At S.F.	L	1-4		4	8	Sanderson	Wagner	Beck	63-75	5th	22½
9-7		At S.F.	W	4-3		7	4	Menendez	Jackson	Dewey	64-75	5th	21½
9-9		Col.	L	7-10	(12)	11	16	Wayne	Johnston		64-76	5th	22
9-10		Col.	L	8-9	(11)	13	14	Moore	Minor	Holmes	64-77	5th	23
9-11		Col.	L	2-3		5	11	Bottenfield	Wakefield	Ruffin	64-78	5th	23
9-12		Col.	W	4-3		6	9	Menendez	Munoz		65-78	5th	22
9-14		At Fla.	W	1-0	(6)	3	4	Wagner	Hammond		66-78	5th	21½

Date	Opp.	Res.	Score	(Inn.*)	Hits	Opp. hits	Winning pitcher	Losing pitcher	Save	Record	Pos.	GB
9-15	At Fla.	W	8-1		8	5	Cooke	Hough		67-78	5th	21½
9-16	At Fla.	W	10-0		19	3	Ballard	Weathers		68-78	5th	21
9-17	At St.L.	W	2-1		11	6	Minor	Urbani	Dewey	69-78	5th	20
9-18	At St.L.	L	1-8		6	11	Cormier	Wakefield		69-79	5th	21
9-19	At St.L.	L	6-7		11	9	Perez	Dewey		69-80	5th	21
9-20	N.Y.	W	6-2		13	9	Wagner	Hillman	Johnston	70-80	5th	21
9-21	N.Y.	L	3-4		8	9	Telgheder	Cooke	Maddux	70-81	5th	22
9-22	N.Y.	L	5-6	(10)	10	12	Franco	Johnston		70-82	5th	23
9-24	Chi.	L	3-8		11	11	Hibbard	Walk	Bullinger	70-83	5th	24
9-26 (1)	Chi.	W	5-1		9	5	Wagner	Trachsel		71-83	5th	22½
9-26 (2)	Chi.	W	1-0		4	5	Wakefield	Morgan		72-83	5th	22
9-27	Phi.	L	4-6		10	8	Rivera	Cooke	Mit. Williams	72-84	5th	23
9-28	Phi.	L	7-10		10	18	Thigpen	Robertson		72-85	5th	24
9-29	Phi.	W	5-3		10	5	Walk	Foster	Johnston	73-85	5th	23
9-30	Phi.	W	5-0		9	4	Wakefield	Greene		74-85	5th	22
10-1	At Mon.	L	3-6		8	10	Heredia	Wagner	Wetteland	74-86	5th	23
10-2	At Mon.	W	4-2		7	6	Ballard	Henry	Dewey	75-86	5th	22
10-3	At Mon.	L	1-3		5	14	Boucher	Hope	Wetteland	75-87	5th	22

Monthly records: April (11-11), May (12-14), June (14-14), July (10-18), August (15-13), September (12-15), October (1-2).
*Innings, if other than nine.

HIGHLIGHTS

High point: A 7-2 start resembled the kind of April superiority that sparked the Pirates to N.L. East titles in 1990, '91 and '92. During that streak, Pittsburgh occupied first place for one day.

Low point: A 0-7 trip through Florida and St. Louis from June 10-16 dropped the Pirates below .500 for good. On June 14, center fielder Andy Van Slyke broke his right collarbone after he crashed into the wall at Busch Stadium. He wasn't taken off the disabled list until August 27.

Turning point: Van Slyke's injury guaranteed the Pirates weren't going to contend. He missed 66 games and had just 81 at-bats the rest of the season. His injury robbed the lineup of a key offensive and defensive performer.

Most valuable player: Shortstop Jay Bell. He enjoyed a breakthrough season defensively, ending Ozzie Smith's 13-year Gold Glove reign. He also had career highs in runs, hits, triples, walks, stolen bases and average.

Most valuable pitcher: None. This staff was too inexperienced, injured and inept for anyone to consistently rise above mediocrity. The staff ERA of 4.77 was Pittsburgh's worst in 40 years.

Most improved player: Third baseman Jeff King. He batted .295 with 98 RBIs despite hitting only nine home runs. He also became a solid fielder.

Most pleasant surprise: Left fielder Al Martin. The Pirates weren't sure how the rookie would handle major league pitching, but he hit .281 with 64 RBIs and a team-leading 18 homers.

Biggest disappointment: Righthander Tim Wakefield. The rookie sensation of 1992 flopped in '93. He finished at 6-11 with a 5.61 ERA and was optioned to Class AA on July 9 before being recalled September 1.

Key injuries: Van Slyke's was the biggest, but the pitching staff was crushed by injuries to lefthanders Zane Smith (shoulder) and Randy Tomlin (elbow). Neither was able to pitch 100 innings or provide needed leadership.

Notable: General Manager Ted Simmons resigned for health reasons June 19 and assistant G.M. Cam Bonifay was promoted to Simmons' post. . . . Pittsburgh turned a triple play against St. Louis on August 10. . . . Three rookies were in the opening-day lineup (second baseman Carlos Garcia, Martin and first baseman Kevin Young) for the first time since 1952.

—JOHN MEHNO

RECORDS

1993 regular-season record: 75-87 (5th in N.L. East); 40-41 at home; 35-46 on road; 39-39 vs. East; 36-48 vs. West; 21-31 vs. LHP; 54-56 vs. RHP; 26-24 on grass; 49-63 on turf; 21-22 in daytime; 54-65 at night; 29-19 in one-run games; 10-8 in extra-inning games; 1-0-3 in doubleheaders.

Team record last five years: 438-372 (.541, ranks 1st in league in that span).

TEAM LEADERS

Batting average: Orlando Merced (.313).
At-bats: Jeff King (611).
Runs: Jay Bell (102).
Hits: Jay Bell (187).
Total bases: Jay Bell (264).
Doubles: Jeff King (35).
Triples: Jay Bell (9).
Home runs: Al Martin (18).
Runs batted in: Jeff King (98).
Stolen bases: Carlos Garcia (18).
Slugging percentage: Al Martin (.481).
On-base percentage: Orlando Merced (.414).
Wins: Bob Walk (13).
Earned-run average: Steve Cooke (3.89).
Complete games: Steve Cooke, Tim Wakefield, Bob Walk (3).
Shutouts: Tim Wakefield (2).
Saves: Stan Belinda (19).
Innings pitched: Steve Cooke (210⅔).
Strikeouts: Steve Cooke (132).

GAMES BY POSITION

Catcher: Don Slaught 105, Tom Prince 59, Jerry Goff 14, Mike LaValliere 1.
First base: Kevin Young 135, Orlando Merced 42, Tom Foley 12, Rich Aude 7, Lloyd McClendon 6, Ben Shelton 2.
Second base: Carlos Garcia 140, Tom Foley 35, John Wehner 3, Jeff King 2.
Third base: Jeff King 156, Tom Foley 7, Kevin Young 6, John Wehner 3.
Shortstop: Jay Bell 154, Tom Foley 6, Tony Womack 6, Carlos Garcia 3, Jeff King 2.
Outfield: Albert Martin 136, Orlando Merced 109, Dave Clark 91, Andy Van Slyke 78, Lloyd McClendon 61, Lonnie Smith 60, Scott Bullett 19, William Pennyfeather 17, John Wehner 13, Midre Cummings 11, Andy Tomberlin 7, Ben Shelton 6, Glenn Wilson 5, Rich Aude 1.

TOP DRAFT CHOICES

1a. Charles Peterson, OF, Laurens (S.C.) High School.
1b. Jermaine Allensworth, OF, Purdue University.
1c. Charles Rice, 1B, Parker High School, Birmingham, Ala.
2a. Kevin Pickford, LHP, West High School, Clovis, Calif.
2b. Jose Delgado, SS, Carolina, Puerto Rico.
3. Derek Swafford, OF/2B, Ventura (Calif.) High School.
4. Kerry Ward, RHP, Edison (Fla.) C.C.
5. Jason Temple, RHP, Woodhaven (Mich.) High School.
6. Shane McGill, RHP, Campbell High School, Smyrna, Ga.
7. Akili Smith, OF, Lincoln High School, San Diego.
8. Sean Hagen, SS, Brighton High School, Sandy, Utah.
9. Rayon Reid, RHP, Miami-Dade (Fla.) C.C. North.
10. Terrence Staton, 1B/LHP, West High School, Elyria, Ohio.

ST. LOUIS CARDINALS
NATIONAL LEAGUE CENTRAL DIVISION

1994 SCHEDULE

N Denotes night game (any game starting after 5 p.m.).
⬜ Home games shaded.
* At Three Rivers Stadium in Pittsburgh.

APRIL

SUN	MON	TUE	WED	THU	FRI	SAT
					1	2
3 N CIN	4 N CIN	5	6 N CIN	7	8 N SF	9 SF
10 SF	11 N LA	12	13 N LA	14 LA N	15 N SD	16 SD
17 SD N	18 N ATL	19 N ATL	20 N ATL	21	22 N HOU	23 HOU
24 HOU N	25 N COL	26 N COL	27 N ATL	28 ATL N	29 N HOU	30 N HOU

MAY

SUN	MON	TUE	WED	THU	FRI	SAT
1 HOU	2	3 N COL	4 N COL	5 N NY	6 N NY	7 N NY
8 NY N	9 N CHI	10 N CHI	11 N CHI	12 CHI N	13 N MON	14 MON
15 MON	16 N PIT	17 N PIT	18 N PIT	19	20 N FLA	21 N FLA
22 FLA N	23 N PHI	24 N PHI	25 N PHI	26	27 N SD	28 N SD
29 SD N	30 N LA	31 N LA				

JUNE

SUN	MON	TUE	WED	THU	FRI	SAT
			1 N LA	2	3 N SF	4 N SF
5 SF	6	7 N CIN	8 N CIN	9 N PHI	10 N PHI	11 N PHI
12 N PHI	13 N FLA	14 N FLA	15 FLA N	16 N PIT	17 N PIT	18 N PIT
19 N PIT	20 N MON	21 N MON	22 MON	23	24 CHI	25 CHI
26 CHI N	27 N NY	28 N NY	29 N NY	30 N COL		

JULY

SUN	MON	TUE	WED	THU	FRI	SAT
				N COL	1 N COL	2 COL
3 COL	4 N HOU	5 N HOU	6 N HOU	7	8 N ATL	9 N ATL
10 ATL	11 *	12 ALL-STAR GAME	13	14 N COL	15 N COL	16 N COL
17 COL N	18 N HOU	19 N HOU	20 HOU N	21 N ATL	22 N ATL	23 N ATL
24 N ATL	25 N NY	26 N NY	27 N NY	28	29 N CHI	30 N CHI
31 CHI						

AUGUST

SUN	MON	TUE	WED	THU	FRI	SAT
	1 N MON	2 N MON	3 N MON	4 N MON	5 N PIT	6 N PIT
7 PIT	8 N FLA	9 N FLA	10 N FLA	11 N FLA	12 N PHI	13 N PHI
14 PHI	15 N SD	16 N SD	17 N SD	18	19 N CIN	20 N CIN
21 CIN	22 N SF	23 N SF	24 N SF	25 N CIN	26 N CIN	27 N CIN
28 CIN	29	30 SF	31 SF			

SEPTEMBER

SUN	MON	TUE	WED	THU	FRI	SAT
				1 SF	2 N LA	3 N LA
4 LA	5 N SD	6 N SD	7 N SD	8	9 N LA	10 N LA
11 LA	12 N PHI	13 N PHI	14 N PHI	15 N FLA	16 N FLA	17 N FLA
18 FLA N	19 N PIT	20 N PIT	21	22	23 N MON	24 N MON
25 MON N	26 N CHI	27 N CHI	28 CHI	29	30 N NY	

OCTOBER

SUN	MON	TUE	WED	THU	FRI	SAT
						1 NY
2 NY						

1994 SEASON

CLUB DIRECTORY

Chairman of the board
August A. Busch III
Vice chairman
Fred L. Kuhlmann
President and chief executive officer
Stuart F. Meyer
Vice president, business operations
Mark Gorris
Controller
Brad Wood
Vice president, general manager
Dal Maxvill
Admin. asst. to the president and CEO
Elaine Milo
Admin. asst. to the v.p., general manager
Judy Carpenter Barada
Admin. asst., business operations
Renee Garrett
Vice president, marketing
Marty Hendin
Admin. asst. to the v.p., marketing
Mary Ellen Edmiston
Director of promotions
Nancy Trammell
Director of player development
Mike Jorgensen
Director of scouting
Marty Maier
Asst. to player development and scouting
Scott Smulczenski
Public relations manager
Brian Bartow
Dir. of broadcasting and market develop.
Dan Farrell
Promotions supervisor
Thane Van Breusegen
Director of group sales
Joe Strohm
Director, target marketing
Ted Savage
Director, ticket systems
Josephine Arnold

Director, human resources
Marian Rhodes
Director, ticket services
Kevin Wade
Director, tickets and office administration
Colin Allsop
Manager, office services
Patti McCormick
Traveling secretary
C.J. Cherre
Club physician
Dr. Stan London
Scouting supervisors
Jorge Aranzamendi
Jim Bayens
Jim Belz
Randy Benson
John DiPuglia
Manuel Guerra
Marty Keough
Tom McCormack
Joe Morlan
Scott Nichols
Jay North
Joe Rigoli
Mike Roberts
Hal Smith
Roger Smith
Special assignment scouts
Jack Hubbard
Fred McAlister
Regular scouts
James Brown
Roy Cromer
Roberto Diaz
Manuel Espinosa
Cecil Espy
Charles Menzhuber
Ramon Ortiz
Joe Popek
Kenneth Thomas

SPRING TRAINING ROSTER

Manager—Joe Torre (9).

Coaches—Jose Cardenal (7), Chris Chambliss (10), Joe Coleman (40), Bucky Dent (30), Gaylen Pitts (4), Red Schoendienst (2).

No.	PITCHERS	B/T	Ht./Wt.	Born	1993 clubs
43	Arocha, Rene	R/R	6-0/180	2-24-66	St. Louis
48	Batchelor, Richard	R/R	6-1/195	4-8-67	Albany/Colonie, Columbus, St. Louis
58	Cimorelli, Frank	R/R	6-0/175	8-2-68	Arkansas, Louisville
61	Coleman, Paul	R/R	5-11/200	12-9-70	Arkansas
52	Cormier, Rheal	L/L	5-10/185	4-23-67	St. Louis
72	Creek, Doug	L/L	5-10/205	3-1-69	Louisville, Arkansas
66	Davis, Clint	R/R	6-3/205	9-26-69	St. Petersburg, Arkansas
35	Dixon, Steve	L/L	6-0/190	8-3-69	Louisville, St. Louis
62	Eversgerd, Bryan	R/L	6-1/190	2-11-69	Arkansas
60	Frascatore, John	R/R	6-1/200	2-4-70	Springfield
36	Kilgus, Paul	L/L	6-1/185	2-2-62	Louisville, St. Louis
46	Murphy, Rob	L/L	6-2/215	5-26-60	St. Louis
00	Olivares, Omar	R/R	6-1/193	7-6-67	St. Louis
42	Perez, Mike	R/R	6-0/187	10-19-64	St. Louis, Arkansas
39	Tewksbury, Bob	R/R	6-4/208	11-30-60	St. Louis
34	Urbani, Tom	L/L	6-1/190	1-21-68	Louisville, St. Louis
38	Watson, Allen	L/L	6-3/190	11-18-70	Louisville, St. Louis

No.	CATCHERS	B/T	Ht./Wt.	Born	1993 clubs
19	Pagnozzi, Tom	R/R	6-1/190	7-30-62	St. Louis, Louisville
12	Pappas, Erik	R/R	6-0/190	4-25-66	Louisville, St. Louis

No.	INFIELDERS	B/T	Ht./Wt.	Born	1993 clubs
18	Alicea, Luis	B/R	5-9/177	7-29-65	St. Louis
33	Brewer, Rod	L/L	6-3/218	2-24-66	St. Louis
57	Cholowsky, Dan	R/R	6-0/195	10-30-70	St. Petersburg, Arkansas
44	Cromer, Tripp	R/R	6-2/165	11-21-67	Louisville, St. Louis
71	Deak, Darrell	B/R	6-0/180	7-5-69	Arkansas
68	Holbert, Aaron	R/R	6-0/160	1-9-73	St. Petersburg
25	Jefferies, Gregg	B/R	5-10/185	8-1-67	St. Louis
11	Oquendo, Jose	B/R	5-10/171	7-4-63	St. Louis
21	Pena, Geronimo	B/R	6-1/195	3-29-67	St. Louis, Louisville
28	Perry, Gerald	L/R	6-0/201	10-30-60	St. Louis
5	Royer, Stan	R/R	6-3/221	8-31-67	Louisville, St. Louis
1	Smith, Ozzie	B/R	5-10/168	12-26-54	St. Louis
27	Zeile, Todd	R/R	6-1/190	9-9-65	St. Louis

No.	OUTFIELDERS	B/T	Ht./Wt.	Born	1993 clubs
55	Bradshaw, Terry	L/R	6-0/180	2-3-69	St. Petersburg
23	Gilkey, Bernard	R/R	6-0/190	9-24-66	St. Louis
3	Jordan, Brian	R/R	6-1/205	3-29-67	St. Louis, Louisville
16	Lankford, Ray	L/L	5-11/198	6-5-67	St. Louis
47	Mabry, John	L/L	6-4/195	10-17-70	Arkansas, Louisville
64	Shabazz, Basil	R/R	6-0/190	1-31-72	Springfield
23	Whiten, Mark	B/R	6-3/215	11-25-66	St. Louis

BALLPARK INFORMATION

Ballpark (capacity, surface)
Busch Stadium (57,000, artificial)
Address
250 Stadium Plaza
St. Louis, MO 63102
Business phone
314-421-3060
Ticket information
314-421-3060
Ticket prices
$14 (box)
$10.50 (reserved)
$5.50 (general admission)
$5 (bleachers)
Field dimensions (from home plate)
To left field at foul line, 330 feet
To center field, 402 feet
To right field at foul line, 330 feet
First game played
May 12, 1966 (Cardinals 4, Braves 3)

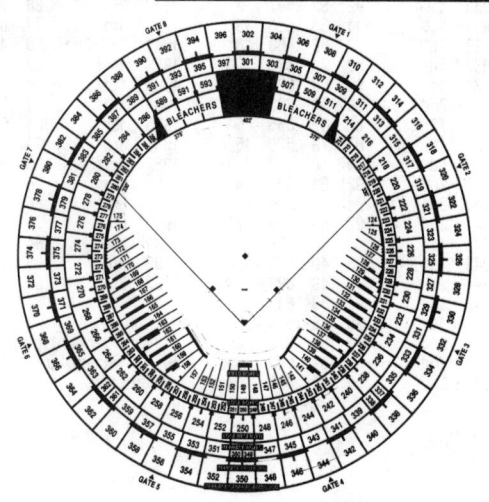

MINOR LEAGUE AFFILIATES

Class	Team	League	Manager
AAA	Louisville	American Association	Joe Pettini
AA	Arkansas	Texas	Chris Maloney
A	St. Petersburg	Florida State	Mike Ramsey
A	Madison	Midwest	To be announced
A	Savannah	South Atlantic	To be announced
A	New Jersey	New York-Pennsylvania	To be announced
Rookie	Johnson City	Appalachian	To be announced
Rookie	Chandler Cardinals	Arizona	To be announced

□ BROADCAST INFORMATION □

Radio: KMOX-AM (1120). Broadcasters: Jack Buck, Mike Shannon, Joe Buck.
TV: KPLR-TV (Channel 11). Broadcasters: Joe Buck, Al Hrabosky.
Cable TV: Prime Network. Broadcasters: Joe Buck, Al Hrabosky.

SPRING TRAINING

Ballpark (city): Al Lang Stadium (St. Petersburg, Fla.).
Ticket information: 813-896-4641.

HISTORY

YEAR-BY-YEAR RECORDS

Year	Pos.	W	L	Pct.	GB	Year	Pos.	W	L	Pct.	GB
1901	4th	76	64	.543	14½	1950	5th	78	75	.510	12½
1902	6th	56	78	.418	44½	1951	3rd	81	73	.526	15½
1903	8th	43	94	.314	46½	1952	3rd	88	66	.571	8½
1904	5th	75	79	.487	31½	1953	T3rd	83	71	.539	22
1905	6th	58	96	.377	47½	1954	6th	72	82	.468	25
1906	7th	52	98	.347	63	1955	7th	68	86	.442	30½
1907	8th	52	101	.340	55½	1956	4th	76	78	.494	17
1908	8th	49	105	.318	50	1957	2nd	87	67	.565	8
1909	7th	54	98	.355	56	1958	T5th	72	82	.468	20
1910	7th	63	90	.412	40½	1959	7th	71	83	.461	16
1911	5th	75	74	.503	22	1960	3rd	86	68	.558	9
1912	6th	63	90	.412	41	1961	5th	80	74	.519	13
1913	8th	51	99	.340	49	1962	6th	84	78	.519	17½
1914	3rd	81	72	.529	13	1963	2nd	93	69	.574	6
1915	6th	72	81	.471	18½	1964	1st	93	69	.574 +	1
1916	T7th	60	93	.392	33½	1965	7th	80	81	.497	16½
1917	3rd	82	70	.539	15	1966	6th	83	79	.512	12
1918	8th	51	78	.395	33	1967	1st	101	60	.627 +	10½
1919	7th	54	83	.394	40½	1968	1st	97	65	.599 +	9
1920	T5th	75	79	.487	18	1969	4th	87	75	.537	13
1921	3rd	87	66	.569	7	1970	4th	76	86	.469	13
1922	T3rd	85	69	.552	8	1971	2nd	90	72	.556	7
1923	5th	79	74	.516	16	1972	4th	75	81	.481	21½
1924	6th	65	89	.422	28½	1973	2nd	81	81	.500	1½
1925	4th	77	76	.503	18	1974	2nd	86	75	.534	1½
1926	1st	89	65	.578 +	2	1975	T3rd	82	80	.506	10½
1927	2nd	92	61	.601	1½	1976	5th	72	90	.444	29
1928	1st	95	59	.617 +	2	1977	3rd	83	79	.512	18
1929	4th	78	74	.513	20	1978	5th	69	93	.426	21
1930	1st	92	62	.597 +	2	1979	3rd	86	76	.531	12
1931	1st	101	53	.656 +13		1980	4th	74	88	.457	17
1932	T6th	72	82	.468	18	1981	2nd/2nd	59	43	.578	†
1933	5th	82	71	.536	9½	1982	1st‡	92	70	.568 +	3
1934	1st	95	58	.621 +	2	1983	4th	79	83	.488	11
1935	2nd	96	58	.623	4	1984	3rd	84	78	.519	12½
1936	T2nd	87	67	.565	5	1985	1st‡	101	61	.623 +	3
1937	4th	81	73	.526	15	1986	3rd	79	82	.491	28½
1938	6th	71	80	.470	17½	1987	1st‡	95	67	.586 +	3
1939	2nd	92	61	.601	4½	1988	5th	76	86	.469	25
1940	3rd	84	69	.549	16	1989	3rd	86	76	.531	7
1941	2nd	97	56	.634	2½	1990	6th	70	92	.432	25
1942	1st	106	48	.688 +	2	1991	2nd	84	78	.519	14
1943	1st	105	49	.682 +18		1992	3rd	83	79	.512	13
1944	1st	105	49	.682 +14½		1993	3rd	87	75	.537	10
1945	2nd	95	59	.617	3						
1946	1st*	98	58	.628 +	2						
1947	2nd	89	65	.578	5						
1948	2nd	85	69	.552	6½						
1949	2nd	96	58	.623	1						

*Won pennant playoff. †First half 30-20; second 29-23. ‡Won Championship Series.

MANAGERS

Name	Record	Years
Patsy Donovan	175-236	'01-03
Kid Nichols	94-108	'04-05
Jimmy Burke	17-32	1905
Stanley Robison	22-35	1905
John McCloskey	153-304	'06-08
Roger Bresnahan	255-352	'09-12
Miller Huggins	346-415	'13-17
Jack Hendricks	51-78	1918
Branch Rickey	458-485	'19-25
Rogers Hornsby	153-116	'25-26
Bob O'Farrell	92-61	1927
Bill McKechnie	129-88	'28-29
Billy Southworth	620-346	1929 '40-45
Gabby Street	312-242	'30-33
Frank Frisch	458-354	'33-38
Mike Gonzalez	9-13	'38, '40
Ray Blades	106-85	'39-40
Eddie Dyer	446-325	'46-50
Marty Marion	81-73	1951
Eddie Stanky	260-238	'52-55
Harry Walker	51-67	1955
Fred Hutchinson	232-220	'56-58
Stan Hack	3-7	1958
Solly Hemus	190-192	'59-61
Johnny Keane	317-249	'61-64
Red Schoendienst	1028-944	'65-76 1980
Vern Rapp	89-90	'77-78
Ken Boyer	166-190	'78-80
Whitey Herzog	835-739	1980 '81-90
Joe Torre	278-266	'90-93

DAY BY DAY

Date	Opp.	Res.	Score	(inn.*)	Hits	Opp. hits	Winning pitcher	Losing pitcher	Save	Record	Pos.	GB
4-6	S.F.	L	1-2		7	8	Burkett	Tewksbury	Beck	0-1	T6th	1
4-7	S.F.	W	6-2		13	8	Cormier	Wilson	Smith	1-1	T4th	1½
4-8	S.F.	W	2-1		4	5	Osborne	Rogers	Smith	2-1	T4th	1
4-9	Cin.	W	8-2		11	5	Arocha	Browning		3-1	T2nd	½
4-10	Cin.	W	2-1	(10)	9	11	Perez	Foster		4-1	T1st	...
4-11	Cin.	L	3-4		6	17	Pugh	Tewksbury	Dibble	4-2	2nd	1
4-13	At L.A.	W	9-7		13	14	Lancaster	P. Martinez	Smith	5-2	T2nd	1½
4-14	At L.A.	W	2-1	(15)	12	4	Lancaster	Trlicek	Smith	6-2	T2nd	1½
4-15	At L.A.	W	4-2		7	7	Arocha	Ke. Gross	Smith	7-2	T2nd	1
4-16	At S.D.	L	1-5		4	6	Benes	Magrane		7-3	T2nd	1
4-17	At S.D.	L	1-2		6	7	Gr. Harris	Cormier	Ge. Harris	7-4	2nd	1
4-18	At S.D.	L	6-10		12	13	Scott	Perez	Rodriguez	7-5	T2nd	2
4-20	Col.	W	5-0		9	5	Arocha	Smith	Olivares	8-5	2nd	2
4-21	Col.	L	2-11		6	14	Nied	Magrane		8-6	T2nd	2½
4-22	Col.	W	5-2		9	7	Perez	Wayne	Smith	9-6	T2nd	1½
4-23	Atl.	L	1-3		4	8	Glavine	Murphy	Stanton	9-7	3rd	2½
4-24	Atl.	L	0-11		6	16	Smith	Tewksbury		9-8	3rd	3½
4-25	Atl.	W	7-3		14	8	Olivares	Maddux	Smith	10-8	3rd	3½
4-26	At Hou.	W	3-2		6	6	Magrane	Drabek	Smith	11-8	3rd	3½
4-27	At Hou.	L	2-9		4	12	Kile	Cormier	Williams	11-9	T3rd	3½
4-28	At Col.	W	7-6		8	11	Murphy	Holmes	Smith	12-9	T2nd	3½
4-29	At Col.	W	5-2		14	9	Tewksbury	Ashby	Smith	13-9	T2nd	3½
4-30	At Atl.	L	2-3	(11)	5	8	Stanton	Murphy		13-10	T2nd	4½
5-1	At Atl.	W	10-3		11	7	Magrane	Smoltz		14-10	2nd	3½
5-2	At Atl.	L	3-4		8	7	Mercker	Murphy	Stanton	14-11	2nd	4½
5-4	Hou.	W	6-1		12	6	Tewksbury	Harnisch		15-11	2nd	4½
5-5	Hou.	L	3-6		6	12	Portugal	Osborne	D. Jones	15-12	T2nd	4½
5-7	At Phi.	L	3-4		5	8	Greene	Magrane	Mit. Williams	15-13	3rd	5½
5-8	At Phi.	L	1-2	(10)	10	6	Mulholland	Perez		15-14	3rd	6½
5-9	At Phi.	L	5-6		8	10	Davis	Smith	Mit. Williams	15-15	4th	7½
5-11	N.Y.	W	7-4		13	12	Osborne	Hillman	Smith	16-15	T3rd	7
5-12	N.Y.	W	6-5		9	9	Perez	Maddux		17-15	T2nd	7
5-13	N.Y.	L	0-4		6	6	Schourek	Cormier		17-16	3rd	7½
5-14	Fla.	W	7-2		13	9	Tewksbury	Hammond		18-16	3rd	6½
5-15	Fla.	L	0-8		6	11	Bowen	Magrane		18-17	4th	6½
5-16	Fla.	W	1-0		5	5	Smith	Hoffman		19-17	3rd	6½
5-18	Chi.	L	1-4		6	9	Castillo	Olivares	Myers	19-18	T4th	8
5-19	Chi.	L	3-5		8	8	Morgan	Murphy	Myers	19-19	T4th	8
5-20	Chi.	W	6-3		11	6	Tewksbury	Guzman	Smith	20-19	4th	8
5-21	At Pit.	W	10-8	(11)	14	14	Lancaster	Wagner	Perez	21-19	3rd	5
5-22	At Pit.	L	2-4		6	8	Walk	Osborne	Belinda	21-20	4th	7
5-23	At Pit.	W	4-3	(10)	10	7	Smith	Minor	Perez	22-20	3rd	7
5-24	At Mon.	W	4-1	(11)	7	8	Cormier	Rojas	Smith	23-20	3rd	7
5-25	At Mon.	L	2-4		7	7	Fassero	Tewksbury	Wetteland	23-21	3rd	8
5-26	At Mon.	L	0-6		4	12	Hill	Magrane		23-22	4th	8
5-28	S.D.	W	3-2		10	10	Perez	Rodriguez	Smith	24-22	4th	8
5-29	S.D.	L	4-7		11	11	Gr. Harris	Olivares	Ge. Harris	24-23	4th	9
5-30	S.D.	W	10-4		13	9	Arocha	Taylor		25-23	4th	9
5-31	L.A.	L	1-5		4	13	Candiotti	Tewksbury		25-24	4th	9
6-1	L.A.	L	6-11		9	14	P. Martinez	Magrane		25-25	4th	10
6-2	L.A.	W	5-4		9	9	Osborne	Astacio	Smith	26-25	4th	10
6-3	At Cin.	W	9-2		17	9	Kilgus	Pugh		27-25	3rd	9½
6-5	At Cin.	L	2-6		8	10	Belcher	Tewksbury		27-26	T3rd	10
6-6	At Cin.	W	5-1		7	5	Magrane	Rijo		28-26	3rd	10
6-8	At S.F.	W	4-3		7	9	Arocha	Burkett	Smith	29-26	3rd	9½
6-9	At S.F.	L	1-3		11	5	Black	Osborne	Beck	29-27	3rd	10½
6-10	Mon.	W	7-4		11	9	Tewksbury	Rojas	Smith	30-27	3rd	10½
6-11	Mon.	W	1-0		7	3	Magrane	Bottenfield	Smith	31-27	2nd	10½
6-12	Mon.	W	13-3		13	8	Cormier	Nabholz		32-27	2nd	10½
6-13	Mon.	L	1-3		6	8	Martinez	Arocha	Wetteland	32-28	2nd	11½
6-14	Pit.	W	8-3		11	8	Osborne	Neagle	Perez	33-28	2nd	11½
6-15	Pit.	W	6-3		10	8	Tewksbury	Cooke	Smith	34-28	2nd	10½
6-16	Pit.	W	3-2		9	6	Magrane	Smith	Smith	35-28	2nd	9½
6-17	At Chi.	W	11-10		17	19	Cormier	Wendell	Smith	36-28	2nd	8½
6-18	At Chi.	L	3-8		10	13	Boskie	Arocha	Myers	36-29	2nd	9½
6-19	At Chi.	W	6-4		12	6	Osborne	Guzman	Smith	37-29	2nd	9½
6-20	At Chi.	W	7-4		13	11	Tewksbury	Castillo	Smith	38-29	2nd	9½
6-21	At Fla.	W	4-3		11	7	Magrane	Aquino	Smith	39-29	2nd	8½
6-22	At Fla.	L	5-7		9	12	Hammond	Cormier	Harvey	39-30	2nd	9½
6-23	At Fla.	W	4-3		8	9	Arocha	Bowen	Smith	40-30	2nd	9½

— 161 —

Date		Opp.	Res.	Score	(Inn.*)	Hits	Opp. hits	Winning pitcher	Losing pitcher	Save	Record	Pos.	GB
6-25		At N.Y.	W	8-5		12	12	Olivares	Saberhagen	Smith	41-30	2nd	9½
6-26		At N.Y.	W	4-2		7	6	Tewksbury	Gooden	Smith	42-30	2nd	8½
6-27		At N.Y.	W	5-3		8	11	Magrane	Young	Smith	43-30	2nd	7½
6-28		Phi.	W	3-1		7	8	Cormier	Jackson	Smith	44-30	2nd	6½
6-29		Phi.	L	10-13		13	17	Rivera	Urbani		44-31	2nd	7½
6-30		Phi.	W	9-3		14	9	Osborne	Greene		45-31	2nd	6½
7-1		Phi.	W	14-5		15	12	Tewksbury	Schilling		46-31	2nd	5½
7-2		At Hou.	L	1-7		9	5	Portugal	Magrane		46-32	2nd	6
7-3		At Hou.	L	0-6		6	14	Kile	Cormier		46-33	2nd	6
7-4		At Hou.	L	4-9		8	14	Drabek	Arocha		46-34	2nd	7
7-5		At Hou.	W	10-4		14	10	Osborne	Swindell		47-34	2nd	7
7-6		Atl.	W	5-4		12	10	Guetterman	Stanton		48-34	2nd	6
7-7		Atl.	W	3-1		10	5	Magrane	Maddux	Smith	49-34	2nd	6
7-8		Atl.	W	7-1		13	5	Watson	Avery		50-34	2nd	5
7-9		Col.	L	4-5		11	10	Moore	Smith	Holmes	50-35	2nd	5
7-10		Col.	W	9-3		12	5	Osborne	Henry		51-35	2nd	5
7-11		Col.	L	1-4		6	9	Reynoso	Tewksbury	Reed	51-36	2nd	5
7-15		Hou.	W	4-2		8	11	Arocha	Drabek	Smith	52-36	2nd	4
7-16		Hou.	L	6-7		12	17	Edens	Guetterman	D. Jones	52-37	2nd	4
7-17		Hou.	W	5-3		6	9	Tewksbury	Williams	Smith	53-37	2nd	3
7-18		Hou.	W	7-6	(11)	13	12	Guetterman	D. Jones		54-37	2nd	3
7-19		At Atl.	W	4-0		11	6	Osborne	Smith		55-37	2nd	3
7-20		At Atl.	L	5-8		10	11	Wohlers	Cormier	Stanton	55-38	2nd	4
7-21		At Atl.	L	2-14		5	18	Maddux	Magrane		55-39	2nd	5
7-22		At Col.	L	6-7		10	14	Holmes	Burns		55-40	2nd	5
7-23		At Col.	W	13-11		16	17	Watson	Reed	Smith	56-40	2nd	5
7-24		At Col.	L	8-9		13	13	Bottenfield	Osborne	Holmes	56-41	2nd	5
7-25		At Col.	W	5-4	(11)	15	10	Olivares	Wayne	Guetterman	57-41	2nd	4
7-27		At Phi.	L	7-10		9	18	Mason	Magrane	Mit. Williams	57-42	2nd	5
7-28		At Phi.	L	6-14		9	17	Mulholland	Guetterman		57-43	2nd	6
7-29		At Phi.	L	4-6		8	7	West	Murphy	Mit. Williams	57-44	2nd	7
7-30		N.Y.	W	3-2		7	6	Watson	Fernandez	Smith	58-44	2nd	6
7-31		N.Y.	W	4-3		12	9	Arocha	Hillman	Smith	59-44	2nd	6½
8-1		N.Y.	L	3-10		7	16	Gooden	Burns		59-45	2nd	7
8-2		Fla.	W	5-3		10	15	Tewksbury	Armstrong	Smith	60-45	2nd	6½
8-3		Fla.	L	0-1		6	10	Hough	Osborne	Harvey	60-46	2nd	7½
8-4		Fla.	W	10-2		11	9	Watson	Bowen		61-46	2nd	6½
8-5		Fla.	W	16-6		19	11	Arocha	Hammond		62-46	2nd	6½
8-6		Chi.	L	4-6		7	10	Bautista	Smith	Myers	62-47	2nd	6½
8-7		Chi.	W	4-1		8	5	Tewksbury	Harkey	Smith	63-47	2nd	6½
8-8		Chi.	L	1-2		8	9	Hibbard	Osborne	Myers	63-48	2nd	6½
8-9		At Pit.	W	7-3		10	5	Watson	Walk		64-48	2nd	6
8-10		At Pit.	W	4-2		9	11	Arocha	Johnston	Smith	65-48	2nd	6
8-11		At Pit.	L	6-8		10	12	Dewey	Burns		65-49	2nd	7
8-12		At Pit.	L	4-5	(11)	9	14	Johnston	Burns		65-50	2nd	8
8-13		At Mon.	L	3-4	(11)	9	8	Wetteland	Magrane		65-51	2nd	9
8-14		At Mon.	W	2-0		6	5	Watson	Fassero	Smith	66-51	2nd	8
8-15		At Mon.	L	1-7		10	9	Heredia	Arocha		66-52	2nd	9
8-17		S.D.	W	8-4		9	10	Tewksbury	Benes		67-52	2nd	9
8-18		S.D.	W	4-0		8	4	Osborne	Brocail	Murphy	68-52	2nd	9
8-19		S.D.	W	3-2		7	3	Perez	Davis	Smith	69-52	2nd	8
8-20		L.A.	L	2-3		9	6	Worrell	Smith	Gott	69-53	2nd	9
8-21		L.A.	L	4-8		5	11	Astacio	Urbani		69-54	2nd	9
8-22		L.A.	L	0-3		4	8	R. Martinez	Tewksbury		69-55	2nd	9
8-23		At S.D.	L	5-7		7	10	Martinez	Osborne	Ge. Harris	69-56	2nd	9
8-24		At S.D.	L	4-17		8	14	Ashby	Watson		69-57	2nd	10
8-25		At S.D.	L	1-2	(10)	8	9	Ge. Harris	Guetterman		69-58	2nd	11
8-27		At L.A.	W	3-2	(10)	9	5	Murphy	P. Martinez	Smith	70-58	2nd	10
8-28		At L.A.	W	4-3		9	11	Tewksbury	R. Martinez	Smith	71-58	2nd	9
8-29		At L.A.	L	3-8		6	16	Hershiser	Watson		71-59	2nd	9
8-30		Cin.	L	3-10		11	17	Rijo	Arocha	Ruffin	71-60	3rd	10
8-31		Cin.	W	7-6		11	11	Murphy	Dibble		72-60	3rd	10
9-1		Cin.	W	7-4		11	8	Tewksbury	Reardon	Perez	73-60	3rd	10
9-3		S.F.	L	1-6		7	9	Deshaies	Watson		73-61	3rd	11
9-4		S.F.	L	1-3		8	8	Torres	Arocha	Beck	73-62	3rd	11
9-5		S.F.	W	7-6		14	11	Olivares	Burba		74-62	3rd	11
9-7	(1)	At Cin.	L	13-14		17	19	Reardon	Murphy		74-63	3rd	10½
9-7	(1)	At Cin.	W	15-2		11	7	Tewksbury	Luebbers		75-63	3rd	10
9-8		At Cin.	L	2-6		12	10	Ayala	Watson	Ruffin	75-64	3rd	10
9-9		At S.F.	W	9-4		14	5	Arocha	Deshaies		76-64	3rd	10
9-10		At S.F.	W	6-2		9	6	Urbani	Torres		77-64	3rd	10
9-11		At S.F.	W	3-1		6	12	Tewksbury	Swift	Perez	78-64	3rd	9
9-12		At S.F.	W	4-2		9	7	Cormier	Burkett	Kilgus	79-64	3rd	8
9-14		Mon.	L	9-12		13	16	Rueter	Watson	Wetteland	79-65	3rd	8½

Date	Opp.	Res.	Score	(Inn.*)	Hits	Opp. hits	Winning pitcher	Losing pitcher	Save	Record	Pos.	GB
9-15	Mon.	W	5-4		8	10	Perez	Barnes		80-65	3rd	8½
9-16	Mon.	L	3-4		12	9	Fassero	Tewksbury	Wetteland	80-66	3rd	9
9-17	Pit.	L	1-2		6	11	Minor	Urbani	Dewey	80-67	3rd	9
9-18	Pit.	W	8-1		11	6	Cormier	Wakefield		81-67	3rd	9
9-19	Pit.	W	7-6		9	11	Perez	Dewey		82-67	3rd	8
9-20	At Chi.	L	5-6		8	13	Morgan	Murphy	Myers	82-68	3rd	9
9-21	At Chi.	L	3-13		10	16	Bautista	Tewksbury		82-69	3rd	10
9-22	At Chi.	L	9-11		15	13	Boskie	Arocha	Myers	82-70	3rd	11
9-24	At Fla.	W	9-5		15	6	Lancaster	Johnstone		83-70	3rd	11
9-25	At Fla.	L	1-2		3	5	Armstrong	Watson		83-71	3rd	11
9-26	At Fla.	W	10-7		15	12	Olivares	Weathers		84-71	3rd	10
9-27	At N.Y.	W	4-3		7	7	Murphy	Gozzo	Perez	85-71	3rd	10
9-28	At N.Y.	L	1-6		9	9	Schourek	Arocha		85-72	3rd	11
9-29	At N.Y.	L	0-1	(17)	3	3	Greer	Lancaster		85-73	3rd	11
9-30	At N.Y.	L	2-3		10	7	Hillman	Watson		85-74	3rd	11
10-1	Phi.	L	2-4		6	6	Schilling	Olivares	Mit. Williams	85-75	3rd	12
10-2	Phi.	W	5-4	(10)	7	9	Murphy	Mike Williams		86-75	3rd	11
10-3	Phi.	W	2-0		2	7	Guetterman	Mit. Williams	Perez	87-75	3rd	10

Monthly records: April (13-10), May (12-14), June (20-7), July (14-13), August (13-16), September (13-14), October (2-1).
*Innings, if other than nine.

HIGHLIGHTS

High point: The Cardinals whipped first-place Philadelphia, three games to one, in a four-game series from June 28 through July 1 to pull within 5½ games of the Phillies in the N.L. East.

Low point: After sweeping a three-game series at home against San Diego on August 17-19, the Cardinals proceeded to lose three at home to Los Angeles and three more at San Diego to fall 11 games off the pace.

Turning point: After shutting out the Braves the night before, the Cardinals lost, 8-5, at Atlanta on July 20 in a game they led, 5-0, after six innings. They went on to lose seven of their next nine games on the 10-game trip.

Most valuable player: First baseman Gregg Jefferies. Jefferies led the team in average and stolen bases, and his down-and-dirty style of play also gave the Cards a certain spunk.

Most valuable pitcher: Righthander Bob Tewksbury. After a slow start, he turned his season around and won 17 games.

Most improved player: Outfielder Mark Whiten. Acquired from Cleveland during spring training, he nearly tripled his home run total and more than doubled his RBI output from the previous year.

Most pleasant surprises: Outfielder Bernard Gilkey and third baseman Todd Zeile. Gilkey not only hit .305 as a full-time player, but also developed into a power source as well (16 home runs and 70 runs batted in while batting mostly leadoff). After knocking in just 48 runs in '92, Zeile totaled 103 RBIs and hit a career-high 17 homers.

Biggest disappointment: Outfielder Ray Lankford. In 1992, he probably ranked as one of the top 10 players in the league. After suffering a wrist injury and later a shoulder separation, he had only seven homers and 14 stolen bases in '93.

Key injuries: The Cards lost setup men Mike Perez, Les Lancaster and Paul Kilgus in July. Second baseman Geronimo Pena was sidelined for more than a month with a broken foot. Outfielder Brian Jordan missed the final month with a bad shoulder.

Notable: On September 7, Whiten did something that no player in big-league history had ever done—hit four home runs and drive in 12 runs in the same game. . . . The Cardinals hit 118 homers, their highest total in 30 years. . . . The Cards committed 159 errors, 65 more than they did in 1992.

—RICK HUMMEL

RECORDS

1993 regular-season record: 87-75 (3rd in N.L. East); 49-32 at home; 38-43 on road; 42-36 vs. East; 45-39 vs. West; 28-17 vs. LHP; 59-58 vs. RHP; 27-23 on grass; 60-52 on turf; 31-19 in daytime; 56-56 at night; 30-25 in one-run games; 9-6 in extra-inning games; 0-0-1 in doubleheaders.

Team record last five years: 410-400 (.506, ranks 6th in league in that span).

TEAM LEADERS

Batting average: Gregg Jefferies (.342).
At-bats: Todd Zeile (571).
Runs: Bernard Gilkey (99).
Hits: Gregg Jefferies (186).
Total bases: Bernard Gilkey (268).
Doubles: Bernard Gilkey (40).
Triples: Brian Jordan, Ozzie Smith (6).
Home runs: Mark Whiten (25).
Runs batted in: Todd Zeile (103).
Stolen bases: Gregg Jefferies (46).
Slugging percentage: Gregg Jefferies (.485).
On-base percentage: Gregg Jefferies (.408).
Wins: Bob Tewksbury (17).
Earned-run average: Rene Arocha (3.78).
Complete games: Bob Tewksbury (2).
Shutouts: None.
Saves: Lee Smith (43).
Innings pitched: Bob Tewksbury (213⅔).
Strikeouts: Bob Tewksbury (97).

GAMES BY POSITION

Catcher: Tom Pagnozzi 92, Erik Pappas 63, Hector Villanueva 17, Marc Ronan 6.

First base: Gregg Jefferies 140, Rod Brewer 32, Gerald Perry 15, Tracy Woodson 11, Bernard Gilkey 3, Erik Pappas 2, Stan Royer 2.

Second base: Luis Alicea 96, Geronimo Pena 64, Jose Oquendo 16, Tim Jones 7, Gregg Jefferies 1.

Third base: Todd Zeile 153, Tracy Woodson 28, Stan Royer 10, Luis Alicea 1.

Shortstop: Ozzie Smith 134, Jose Oquendo 22, Tim Jones 21, Tripp Cromer 9.

Outfield: Mark Whiten 148, Bernard Gilkey 134, Ray Lankford 121, Brian Jordan 65, Rod Brewer 33, Erik Pappas 16, Ozzie Canseco 5, Lonnie Maclin 5, Luis Alicea 4, Gerald Perry 1.

TOP DRAFT CHOICES

1. **Alan Benes**, RHP, Creighton University.

2a. **Nate Dishington**, 1B, Hoover (Calif.) High School.

2b. **Gerald Witasick**, RHP, University of Maryland-Baltimore County.

3. **Eliezer Marrero**, C, Coral Gables (Fla.) High School.

4. **Darrell Nicholas**, OF, University of New Orleans.

5. **Marc Ottmers**, RHP, Texas-Pan American.

6. **David Carroll**, LHP, Manatee (Fla.) J.C.

7. **Jeff Berblinger**, 2B, University of Kansas.

8. **Rantie Harper**, OF, Point Loma (Calif.) High School.

9. **Mike Windham**, RHP, University of North Florida.

10. **Mike Martin**, RHP, Walters (Tenn.) State C.C.

SAN DIEGO PADRES
NATIONAL LEAGUE WEST DIVISION

1994 SCHEDULE

N Denotes night game (any game starting after 5 p.m.).
▢ Home games shaded.
* At Three Rivers Stadium in Pittsburgh.
DH Doubleheader.

APRIL
SUN	MON	TUE	WED	THU	FRI	SAT
					1	2
3	4 N ATL	5 N ATL	6 N ATL	7 ATL	8 N FLA	9 N FLA
10 N FLA	11 N	12 N PIT	13 N PIT	14 N PIT	15 N STL	16 N STL
17 N STL	18 N NY	19 N NY	20 N MON	21 MON	22 N PHI	23 N PHI
24 PHI	25 N	26 N NY	27 N NY	28	29 N MON	30 MON

MAY
SUN	MON	TUE	WED	THU	FRI	SAT
1 MON	2 N PHI	3 N	4 N PHI	5 N PHI		6 N COL
8 COL	9 N CIN	10 N CIN	11 N CIN	12	13 N LA	14 N LA
15 LA	16 N CHI	17 N CHI	18 N	19 N HOU	20 N HOU	21 N HOU
22 HOU	23 N SF	24 N SF	25 N SF	26 N SF	27 N STL	28 N STL
29 STL	30 N PIT	31 N PIT				

JUNE
SUN	MON	TUE	WED	THU	FRI	SAT
			1 PIT	2 N FLA	3 N FLA	4 N FLA
5 N FLA	6 N ATL	7 N ATL	8 ATL	9	10 N SF	11 N SF
12 SF	13	14 N CHI	15 N CHI	16 CHI	17 N HOU	18 N HOU
19 HOU	20 N LA	21 N LA	22 N LA	23	24 N CIN	25 N CIN
26 CIN	27 N COL	28 DH COL	29 N COL	30 N NY		

JULY
SUN	MON	TUE	WED	THU	FRI	SAT
					1 N NY	2 N NY
3 NY	4 N PHI	5 N PHI	6 PHI	7 N MON	8 N MON	9 N MON
10 MON	11 N ALL-STAR GAME	12 *	13 N	14 N NY	15 N NY	16 N NY
17 NY	18 N MON	19 N MON	20 N MON	21 N	22 N PHI	23 N PHI
24 PHI	25 N COL	26 N COL	27 N COL	28 N CIN	29 N CIN	30 N CIN
31 CIN						

AUGUST
SUN	MON	TUE	WED	THU	FRI	SAT
	1 N LA	2 N LA	3 N LA	4 LA	5 N CHI	6 N CHI
7 CHI	8 N	9 N HOU	10 N HOU	11 HOU	12 N SF	13 N SF
14 SF	15 N STL	16 N STL	17 N STL	18 N	19 N ATL	20 N ATL
21 ATL	22	23 N FLA	24 N FLA	25 FLA	26 N ATL	27 N ATL
28 N ATL	29 N FLA	30 N FLA	31 N FLA			

SEPTEMBER
SUN	MON	TUE	WED	THU	FRI	SAT
				1 N PIT	2 N PIT	3
4 PIT	5 STL	6 N STL	7 N STL	8	9 N PIT	10 N PIT
11 PIT	12 N SF	13 N SF	14 N SF	15	16 N CHI	17 N CHI
18 CHI	19 N HOU	20 N HOU	21 N HOU	22	23 N LA	24 LA
25 LA	26	27 N CIN	28 N CIN	29 N CIN	30 N COL	

OCTOBER
SUN	MON	TUE	WED	THU	FRI	SAT
						1 COL
2 COL						

1994 SEASON

CLUB DIRECTORY

Chairman
Tom Werner

Vice chairmen
Art Engel
Russell Goldsmith
Art Rivkin

Partners
Malin Burnham
Bruce Corwin
John Earhart
Jack Goodall
Keith Matson
Michael Monk
Leon Parma
Robert Payne
Peter Peckham
Ernest Rady
Scott Wolfe

President
Dick Freeman

Executive Vice President
Bill Adams

V.p./baseball operations and g.m.
Randy Smith

Vice President/stadium operations
Doug Duennes

Vice President/marketing
Don Johnson

V.p./game operations & special events
Andy Strasberg

Vice president/finance
Bob Wells

Assistant general manager
Reggie Waller

Special assistant to the general manager
Brad Sloan

Major league scouts
Ken Bracey
Randy Johnson

Advance scout
Steve Lubratich

Director/administrative services
Lucy Freeman

Director/media relations
Jim Ferguson

Director/minor league administration
Priscilla Oppenheimer

Director/promotions sales
Tom Ryba

Director/scouting
Kevin Towers

Director/ticket operations
Dave Gilmore

Director/ticket sales
Jack Autry

Director/video and special projects
Mark Guglielmo

Director/merchandising
Michael Babida

Controller
Bob Croasdale

Traveling secretary
John Mattei

Club physician
Scripps Clinic

National supervisor
Ross Sapp

East Coast supervisor
Bob Cummings

Midwestern supervisor
Logan White

Area scouts
Howard Bowens
Dave Finley
Denny Galehouse
Ronquito Garcia
Donnie Lyle
Mark McKnight
Tim McWilliams
Juan Melo
Rene Mons
Patrick Murtaugh
Gary Roenicke
Bruce Seid
Greg Smith
Van Smith
Scipio Spinks
Jeff Wetherby

Part-time scouts
Pedro Avila
Mike Becker
Billy Castell
Julio Coronado
Timothy Harkness
Cesar Jarquin
William Killian
Darryl Milne
Earl Smith

Manager—Jim Riggleman (8).

Coaches—Dave Bialas (32), Bruce Bochy (15), Rob Picciolo (5), Dan Radison (22), Merv Rettenmund (16), Sonny Siebert (34).

No.	PITCHERS	B/T	Ht./Wt.	Born	1993 clubs
43	Ashby, Andy	R/R	6-5/190	7-11-67	Colorado, Colorado Springs, San Diego
35	Beckett, Robbie	R/L	6-5/235	7-16-72	Rancho Cucamonga
40	Benes, Andy	R/R	6-6/240	8-20-67	San Diego
55	Berumen, Andres	R/R	6-1/205	4-5-71	High Desert, Wichita
45	Bochtler, Doug	R/R	6-3/185	7-5-70	Colorado Springs, Central Valley, Las Vegas
49	Brocail, Doug	L/R	6-5/235	5-16-67	Las Vegas, San Diego
48	Davis, Mark	L/L	6-4/215	10-19-60	Philadelphia, San Diego
38	Elliott, Donnie	R/R	6-4/190	9-20-68	Richmond, Las Vegas
39	Florie, Bryce	R/R	6-0/185	5-21-70	Wichita
33	Harris, Gene	R/R	5-11/195	12-5-64	San Diego
51	Hoffman, Trevor	R/R	6-0/205	10-13-67	Florida, San Diego
47	Martinez, Jose	R/R	6-2/155	4-1-71	Edmonton, Las Vegas
42	Martinez, Pedro A.	L/L	6-2/185	11-29-68	Las Vegas, San Diego
52	Mauser, Tim	R/R	6-0/195	10-4-66	Scranton/Wilkes-Barre, Philadelphia, San Diego
27	Sanders, Scott	R/R	6-4/215	3-25-69	Las Vegas, San Diego
37	Taylor, Kerry	R/R	6-3/200	1-25-71	San Diego
41	Whitehurst, Wally	R/R	6-3/200	4-11-64	Wichita, San Diego
58	Worrell, Tim	R/R	6-4/220	7-5-67	Las Vegas, San Diego

No.	CATCHERS	B/T	Ht./Wt.	Born	1993 clubs
11	Ausmus, Brad	R/R	5-11/190	4-14-69	Colorado Springs, San Diego
28	Johnson, Brian	R/R	6-2/210	1-8-68	Las Vegas

No.	INFIELDERS	B/T	Ht./Wt.	Born	1993 clubs
25	Bruno, Julio	R/R	5-10/170	10-15-72	Rancho Cucamonga, Wichita
26	Cianfrocco, Archi	R/R	6-5/215	10-6-66	Montreal, Ottawa, San Diego
12	Gardner, Jeff	L/R	5-11/175	2-4-64	San Diego
7	Gutierrez, Ricky	R/R	6-1/175	5-23-70	Las Vegas, San Diego
53	Holbert, Ray	R/R	6-0/170	9-25-70	Wichita
17	Hyers, Tim	L/L	6-1/185	10-3-71	Knoxville
1	Lopez, Luis	B/R	5-11/175	9-4-70	Las Vegas, San Diego
18	Shipley, Craig	R/R	6-1/190	1-7-63	San Diego
31	Staton, Dave	R/R	6-5/225	4-12-68	Wichita, Rancho Cucamonga, Las Vegas, San Diego
23	Velasquez, Guillermo	L/R	6-3/225	4-23-68	San Diego, Las Vegas

No.	OUTFIELDERS	B/T	Ht./Wt.	Born	1993 clubs
21	Bean, Billy	L/L	6-0/190	5-11-64	Las Vegas, San Diego
4	Bell, Derek	R/R	6-2/215	12-11-68	San Diego
30	Clark, Phil	R/R	6-0/200	5-6-68	San Diego
67	Curtis, Randy	L/L	5-11/185	1-16-71	St. Lucie
19	Gwynn, Tony	L/L	5-11/215	5-9-60	San Diego
20	McDavid, Ray	L/R	6-3/190	7-20-71	Wichita
56	Moore, Vince	L/L	6-1/175	9-22-71	Durham, Rancho Cucamonga
10	Nieves, Melvin	B/R	6-2/210	12-28-71	Richmond, Las Vegas, San Diego
9	Pegues, Steve	R/R	6-2/190	5-21-68	Las Vegas
24	Plantier, Phil	L/R	5-11/195	1-27-69	San Diego

BALLPARK INFORMATION

Ballpark (capacity, surface)
San Diego/Jack Murphy Stadium
(46,510, grass)

Address
P.O. Box 2000
San Diego, CA 92112-2000

Business phone
619-283-4494

Ticket information
619-283-4494

Ticket prices
$11 (field, plaza and press reserved)
$9.50 (loge reserved)
$7 (grandstand reserved)
$5 (pavilion admission, plaza sections 48-60 & 45a-58a)

Field dimensions (from home plate)
To left field at foul line, 327 feet
To center field, 405 feet
To right field at foul line, 327 feet

First game played
April 8, 1969 (Padres 2, Astros 1)

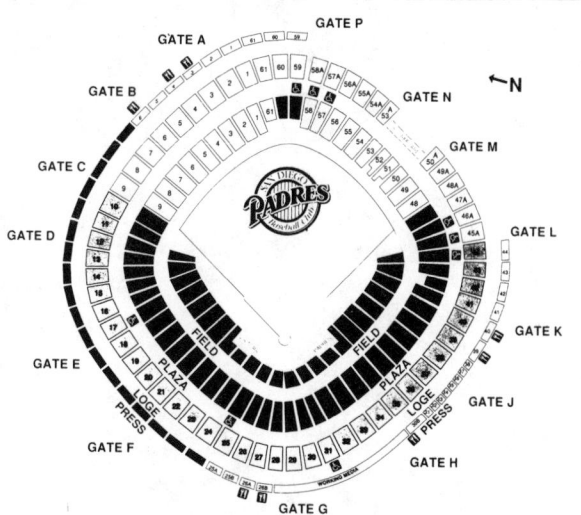

MINOR LEAGUE AFFILIATES

Class	Team	League	Manager
AAA	Las Vegas	Pacific Coast	Russ Nixon
AA	Wichita	Texas	Keith Champion
A	Rancho Cucamonga	California	Tim Flannery
A	Waterloo	Midwest	Ed Romero
A	Spokane	Northwest	Tye Waller
Rookie	Peoria Padres	Arizona	Barry Moss

BROADCAST INFORMATION

Radio: KFMB-AM (760). Broadcasters: Jerry Coleman, Bob Chandler, Ted Leitner. XEXX-AM (1420, Spanish language). Broadcasters: Mario Thomas, Eduardo Ortega.
TV: KUSI-TV (Channel 51). Broadcasters: Jerry Coleman, Bob Chandler, Ted Leitner.
Cable TV: Prime Ticket Network. Broadcasters: Jerry Coleman, Bob Chandler, Ted Leitner.

SPRING TRAINING

Ballpark (city): Peoria Stadium (Peoria, Ariz.).
Ticket information: 602-878-4337.

HISTORY

YEAR-BY-YEAR RECORDS

Year	Pos.	W	L	Pct.	GB	Year	Pos.	W	L	Pct.	GB
1969	6th	52	110	.321	41	1983	4th	81	81	.500	10
1970	6th	63	99	.389	39	1984	1st†	92	70	.568	+12
1971	6th	61	100	.379	28½	1985	T3rd	83	79	.512	12
1972	6th	58	95	.379	36½	1986	4th	74	88	.457	22
1973	6th	60	102	.370	39	1987	6th	65	97	.401	25
1974	6th	60	102	.370	42	1988	3rd	83	78	.516	11
1975	4th	71	91	.438	37	1989	2nd	89	73	.549	3
1976	5th	73	89	.451	29	1990	T4th	75	87	.463	16
1977	5th	69	93	.426	29	1991	3rd	84	78	.519	10
1978	4th	84	78	.519	11	1992	3rd	82	80	.506	16
1979	5th	68	93	.422	22	1993	7th	61	101	.377	43
1980	6th	73	89	.451	19½						
1981	6th/6th	41	69	.373	*						
1982	4th	81	81	.500	8						

*First half 23-33; second 18-36.
†Won Championship Series.

MANAGERS

Name	Record	Years
Preston Gomez	180-306	'69-72
Don Zimmer	114-186	'72-73
John McNamara	224-310	'74-77
Alvin Dark	49-65	1977
Roger Craig	152-171	'78-79
Jerry Coleman	73-89	1980
Frank Howard	41-69	1981
Dick Williams	337-311	'82-85
Steve Boros	74-88	1986
Larry Bowa	81-127	'87-88
Jack McKeon	193-164	'88-90
Greg Riddoch	200-194	'90-92
Jim Riggleman	65-109	'92-93

DAY BY DAY

Date	Opp.	Res.	Score	(Inn.*)	Hits	Opp. hits	Winning pitcher	Losing pitcher	Save	Record	Pos.	GB
4-6	At Pit.	L	4-9		4	15	Wakefield	Benes	Candelaria	0-1	T5th	1
4-8	At Pit.	L	4-5		5	9	Walk	Gr. Harris	Belinda	0-2	T5th	2
4-9	At Fla.	W	2-1		8	5	Gr. Harris	Harvey		1-2	T3rd	2
4-10	At Fla.	L	1-2		5	4	Hough	Eiland	Harvey	1-3	6th	2
4-11	At Fla.	W	6-2		13	8	Benes	Armstrong	Ge. Harris	2-3	T5th	2
4-12	Pit.	L	2-4		5	10	Otto	Gr. Harris	Belinda	2-4	6th	3
4-13	Pit.	L	4-6		9	14	Walk	Gomez	Wagner	2-5	6th	3
4-14	Pit.	L	7-11		13	17	Minor	Seminara		2-6	6th	3
4-15	Pit.	L	4-5	(13)	12	12	Moeller	Hernandez	Belinda	2-7	T6th	3½
4-16	St.L.	W	5-1		6	4	Benes	Magrane		3-7	6th	3½
4-17	St.L.	W	2-1		7	6	Gr. Harris	Cormier	Ge. Harris	4-7	6th	2½
4-18	St.L.	W	10-6		13	12	Scott	Perez	Rodriguez	5-7	6th	2½
4-20	At Phi.	L	3-4	(14)	7	10	Ayrault	Hernandez		5-8	5th	3½
4-22	At Phi.	W	2-1		8	5	Benes	Mulholland	Rodriguez	6-8	4th	3
4-23	At N.Y.	L	1-6		8	6	Tanana	Gr. Harris		6-9	T4th	3
4-24	At N.Y.	W	5-3		11	6	Seminara	Saberhagen	Ge. Harris	7-9	4th	4
4-25	At N.Y.	W	9-8		10	9	Scott	Young	Ge. Harris	8-9	4th	2
4-26	Mon.	L	4-6		9	10	Jones	Taylor	Wetteland	8-10	4th	2
4-27	Mon.	W	4-1		7	4	Benes	Bottenfield		9-10	4th	2
4-28	Phi.	L	3-5		9	11	Schilling	Gr. Harris	Mit. Williams	9-11	4th	3
4-29	Phi.	L	3-5		8	9	Jackson	Seminara	Mit. Williams	9-12	4th	4
4-30	N.Y.	W	7-6		14	10	Rodriguez	Young	Ge. Harris	10-12	4th	4
5-1	N.Y.	W	5-3		16	6	Ge. Harris	Maddux		11-12	3rd	4
5-2	N.Y.	L	2-3		7	9	Gooden	Benes		11-13	4th	5
5-4	At Mon.	L	1-6		5	10	Martinez	Gr. Harris		11-14	4th	5
5-5	At Mon.	L	5-6		8	10	Wetteland	Rodriguez		11-15	4th	6
5-7	At Chi.	W	2-1		6	6	Benes	Morgan	Ge. Harris	12-15	4th	6
5-8	At Chi.	L	6-8		11	11	McElroy	Gomez	Myers	12-16	4th	6
5-9	At Chi.	W	5-4		10	13	Gr. Harris	Guzman	Ge. Harris	13-16	4th	5
5-10	At Cin.	L	5-6		15	11	Browning	Taylor	Reardon	13-17	4th	5½
5-11	At Cin.	L	2-4		7	9	Hill	Whitehurst	Cadaret	13-18	5th	6
5-12	At Cin.	L	2-3	(5)	5	7	Rijo	Benes		13-19	6th	7
5-13	At Cin.	L	1-7		5	10	Smiley	Eiland		13-20	6th	8
5-14	S.F.	W	3-1		6	6	Gr. Harris	Brantley		14-20	T5th	7
5-15	S.F.	L	0-3		4	4	Wilson	Taylor	Beck	14-21	T5th	8
5-16	S.F.	L	4-9		9	13	Swift	Whitehurst		14-22	T5th	9
5-17	Col.	W	4-0		6	3	Benes	Henry		15-22	T6th	9
5-18	Col.	L	1-2	(11)	9	11	Wayne	Rodriguez	Holmes	15-23	6th	10
5-19	Col.	W	7-3		7	3	Gr. Harris	Painter		16-23	6th	10
5-20	Col.	W	5-4	(11)	10	5	Ge. Harris	Holmes		17-23	6th	10
5-21	Hou.	W	3-2	(10)	7	9	Rodriguez	D. Jones		18-23	6th	10
5-22	Hou.	W	9-4		14	5	Benes	Drabek		19-23	6th	9
5-23	Hou.	L	7-9		9	16	Swindell	Eiland	D. Jones	19-24	6th	10
5-24	At L.A.	L	4-5		8	9	Ke. Gross	Gr. Harris	P. Martinez	19-25	6th	10½
5-25	At L.A.	L	9-10	(10)	15	17	P. Martinez	Mason		19-26	6th	11½
5-26	At L.A.	L	3-8		8	11	Wilson	Whitehurst		19-27	6th	11½
5-28	At St.L.	L	2-3		10	10	Perez	Rodriguez	Smith	19-28	6th	11
5-29	At St.L.	W	7-4		11	11	Gr. Harris	Olivares	Ge. Harris	20-28	6th	11
5-30	At St.L.	L	4-10		9	13	Arocha	Taylor		20-29	6th	12
5-31	At Atl.	L	1-2		5	7	Maddux	Mason		20-30	6th	12½
6-1	At Atl.	W	2-1		4	7	Brocail	Smoltz	Ge. Harris	21-30	6th	12
6-2	At Atl.	L	2-5		8	9	Avery	Benes	Stanton	21-31	6th	12½
6-3	At Atl.	W	12-4		15	7	Gr. Harris	Smith		22-31	6th	12
6-4	Fla.	L	2-6		6	10	Hough	Hurst		22-32	6th	12
6-5	Fla.	L	1-3		6	7	Aquino	Mason	Harvey	22-33	6th	13
6-6	Fla.	L	2-9		9	9	Hammond	Brocail		22-34	6th	14
6-7	Atl.	L	0-4		4	8	Avery	Benes		22-35	6th	14½
6-8	Atl.	W	5-4		8	10	Ge. Harris	Stanton		23-35	6th	13½
6-10	L.A.	W	14-2		14	8	Whitehurst	R. Martinez		24-35	6th	13½
6-11	L.A.	W	5-4		8	8	Gomez	Gott		25-35	6th	13½
6-12	L.A.	L	4-6		11	10	Daal	Mason	Gott	25-36	6th	14½
6-13	L.A.	L	1-2		8	9	Hershiser	Gr. Harris	Gott	25-37	6th	15½
6-15	At Hou.	W	3-0		7	6	Whitehurst	Harnisch	Ge. Harris	26-37	6th	14½
6-16	At Hou.	L	4-5		10	10	Portugal	Brocail	Osuna	26-38	6th	15½
6-17	At Hou.	L	1-4		7	6	Kile	Benes	Williams	26-39	6th	16½
6-18	At Col.	W	11-1		12	8	Gr. Harris	Ruffin		27-39	6th	16½
6-19	At Col.	L	3-17		9	18	Blair	Taylor		27-40	6th	17½
6-20	At Col.	L	1-3		8	8	Reed	Mason	Holmes	27-41	6th	18½
6-21	At S.F.	L	1-2		8	8	Wilson	Brocail	Beck	27-42	6th	19½
6-22	At S.F.	W	2-1		8	6	Benes	Swift	Ge. Harris	28-42	6th	18½

Date		Opp.	Res.	Score	(inn.*)	Hits	Opp. hits	Winning pitcher	Losing pitcher	Save	Record	Pos.	GB
6-23		At S.F.	L	2-6		6	10	Black	Gr. Harris		28-43	6th	19½
6-24		Cin.	L	4-6		10	13	Ayala	Mason	Dibble	28-44	6th	20½
6-25		Cin.	L	2-6		4	11	Belcher	Whitehurst		28-45	6th	21½
6-26		Cin.	W	2-0		6	5	Brocail	Rijo	Ge. Harris	29-45	6th	20½
6-27		Cin.	L	1-7	(11)	11	11	Dibble	Ge. Harris		29-46	6th	21½
6-28		Chi.	L	3-4	(11)	9	10	Assenmacher	Mason	Myers	29-47	6th	21½
6-29		Chi.	L	5-10		11	15	Morgan	Worrell		29-48	6th	22½
6-30		Chi.	L	1-4		6	11	Guzman	Whitehurst	Myers	29-49	6th	22½
7-2	(1)	At Phi.	W	5-2		8	6	Ettles	Mulholland	Ge. Harris	30-49	6th	22½
7-2	(2)	At Phi.	L	5-6	(10)	6	10	Mit. Williams	Hoffman		30-50	6th	23
7-3		At Phi.	W	6-4		12	10	Gr. Harris	Jackson	Ge. Harris	31-50	6th	22
7-4		At Phi.	L	4-8		7	16	Rivera	Worrell		31-51	6th	23
7-5		At N.Y.	W	12-7		19	12	Whitehurst	Schourek		32-51	6th	23
7-6		At N.Y.	L	7-9		10	16	Gooden	Brocail		32-52	6th	24
7-7		At N.Y.	W	2-0		5	1	Benes	Young	Ge. Harris	33-52	6th	23
7-8		At Mon.	L	4-5		9	6	Martinez	Gr. Harris	Wetteland	33-53	6th	24
7-9		At Mon.	L	1-6		3	11	Nabholz	Worrell		33-54	6th	25
7-10		At Mon.	L	2-3		6	7	Young	Ge. Harris		33-55	6th	25
7-11		At Mon.	L	4-5		11	13	Wetteland	Ge. Harris	Martinez	33-56	6th	26
7-15		Phi.	W	5-2		5	8	Gr. Harris	Jackson	Davis	34-56	6th	26
7-16		Phi.	W	5-3		9	8	Martinez	Greene	Davis	35-56	6th	26
7-17		Phi.	W	4-2		8	5	Benes	Mulholland	Ge. Harris	36-56	6th	25
7-18		Phi.	L	3-6		8	9	Schilling	Brocail	Mit. Williams	36-57	5th	25
7-19		N.Y.	L	1-2	(10)	6	8	Franco	Ge. Harris		36-58	6th	28
7-20		N.Y.	W	4-1		11	4	Gr. Harris	Telgheder		37-58	6th	26
7-21		N.Y.	L	2-5		7	6	Gooden	Whitehurst	Franco	37-59	6th	27
7-22		Mon.	L	5-10		9	11	Hill	Benes		37-60	6th	28
7-23		Mon.	L	0-5		6	10	Fassero	Brocail	Rojas	37-61	6th	28
7-24		Mon.	W	11-4		12	4	Worrell	Nabholz		38-61	6th	28
7-25		Mon.	L	4-5	(10)	8	9	Wetteland	Ge. Harris	Rojas	38-62	6th	29
7-26		At Chi.	L	6-9	(11)	9	13	Boskie	Mauser		38-63	6th	29
7-27		At Chi.	W	8-0		16	5	Benes	Harkey		39-63	6th	29
7-28		At Chi.	L	6-8		10	9	Boskie	Brocail	Myers	39-64	6th	29
7-30		At Cin.	W	11-9		14	10	Hoffman	Reardon	Davis	40-64	6th	29
7-31		At Cin.	L	3-6		4	9	Rijo	Ashby	Dibble	40-65	6th	30
8-1		At Cin.	W	3-1		9	5	Benes	Browning	Ge. Harris	41-65	6th	30
8-3		S.F.	L	7-12		9	12	Burba	Davis		41-66	6th	31
8-4		S.F.	W	11-10	(12)	19	19	Martinez	Hickerson		42-66	6th	30
8-5		S.F.	L	3-5		7	6	Swift	Ashby	Beck	42-67	6th	31
8-6	(1)	Col.	W	6-3		14	10	Benes	Reynoso	Hoffman	43-67	6th	31
8-6	(2)	Col.	W	6-2		16	6	Sanders	Blair		44-67	6th	30½
8-8		Col.	L	2-5		6	9	Sanford	Brocail	Holmes	44-68	6th	30
8-9		Hou.	L	4-5	(10)	9	11	Hernandez	Hoffman	D. Jones	44-69	6th	31
8-10		Hou.	W	7-2		10	8	Ashby	Drabek		45-69	6th	31
8-11		Hou.	L	6-9		6	11	Kile	Benes	D. Jones	45-70	6th	32
8-12		Hou.	L	3-5		13	8	Swindell	Hoffman	D. Jones	45-71	6th	32½
8-13		At L.A.	W	4-1		11	8	Whitehurst	Ke. Gross	Ge. Harris	46-71	6th	32½
8-14		At L.A.	L	3-4		13	8	Candiotti	Brocail	Gott	46-72	6th	32½
8-15		At L.A.	L	2-4		8	10	Astacio	Ashby	Gott	46-73	6th	33½
8-17		At St.L.	L	4-8		10	9	Tewksbury	Benes		46-74	6th	33½
8-18		At St.L.	L	0-4		4	8	Osborne	Brocail	Murphy	46-75	6th	34½
8-19		At St.L.	L	2-3		3	7	Perez	Davis	Smith	46-76	6th	35½
8-20		Pit.	L	6-7		11	14	Petkovsek	Davis	Dewey	46-77	6th	35½
8-22		Pit.	L	5-10		10	14	Cooke	Benes		46-78	7th	37
8-23		St.L.	W	7-5		10	7	Martinez	Osborne	Ge. Harris	47-78	6th	36
8-24		St.L.	W	17-4		14	8	Ashby	Watson		48-78	T6th	35
8-25		St.L.	W	2-1	(10)	9	8	Ge. Harris	Guetterman		49-78	6th	34
8-27		At Pit.	W	10-6		12	8	Benes	Cooke	Hoffman	50-78	6th	33
8-28		At Pit.	W	5-3		9	6	Sanders	Smith	Ge. Harris	51-78	6th	32½
8-29	(1)	At Pit.	L	4-7		9	12	Walk	Ashby	Dewey	51-79	6th	33½
8-29	(2)	At Pit.	W	11-0		14	6	Brocail	Hope		52-79	6th	33
8-31		At Fla.	L	1-2		8	4	Hough	Worrell	Harvey	52-80	6th	33½
9-1		At Fla.	W	13-5		17	6	Benes	Bowen		53-80	6th	33½
9-2		At Fla.	L	2-8		7	16	Rapp	Sanders		53-81	6th	33½
9-3		At Atl.	L	3-7		7	13	Glavine	Ashby		53-82	6th	34½
9-4		At Atl.	L	2-3		5	9	Mercker	Brocail	McMichael	53-83	6th	35½
9-5		At Atl.	L	2-3		6	9	Maddux	Martinez		53-84	T6th	36½
9-6		Fla.	L	0-2		3	7	Weathers	Benes	Harvey	53-85	T6th	36½
9-7		Fla.	W	6-4		11	9	Hoffman	Aquino	Ge. Harris	54-85	6th	35½
9-8		Fla.	W	3-2		6	6	Seminara	Hammond	Ge. Harris	55-85	6th	35
9-9		Atl.	L	0-1	(10)	1	10	McMichael	Hoffman		55-86	6th	35
9-10		Atl.	L	2-3		6	5	Maddux	Worrell	McMichael	55-87	T6th	35
9-11		Atl.	L	1-13		5	15	Smoltz	Benes		55-88	7th	36
9-12		Atl.	W	5-4		5	8	Sanders	Avery	Ge. Harris	56-88	T6th	35

Date	Opp.	Res.	Score	(inn.*)	Hits	Opp. hits	Winning pitcher	Losing pitcher	Save	Record	Pos.	GB
9-13	L.A.	W	4-3	(11)	4	9	Ge. Harris	Gott		57-88	6th	34½
9-14	L.A.	L	3-5		6	6	Hershiser	Brocail	Worrell	57-89	7th	35½
9-15	L.A.	L	4-5		12	8	Ke. Gross	Tim Worrell	Todd Worrell	57-90	7th	36½
9-17	At Hou.	L	0-3		1	7	Harnisch	Benes		57-91	7th	38
9-18	At Hou.	L	2-4		6	6	Drabek	Sanders		57-92	7th	38
9-19	At Hou.	W	6-3		9	10	Ashby	Kile	Davis	58-92	7th	38
9-20	At Col.	W	11-7		9	9	Seminara	Harris	Hoffman	59-92	7th	37½
9-21	At Col.	L	4-15		7	17	Blair	Worrell		59-93	7th	38½
9-22	At Col.	L	4-11		9	12	Nied	Benes		59-94	7th	38½
9-24	At S.F.	L	3-4	(10)	8	6	Beck	Ge. Harris		59-95	7th	39
9-25	At S.F.	L	1-3		5	9	Torres	Ashby	Beck	59-96	7th	40
9-26	At S.F.	L	2-5		5	12	Swift	Brocail		59-97	7th	41
9-27	At S.F.	L	4-8		6	14	Burkett	Benes	Beck	59-98	7th	41½
9-28	Cin.	W	11-4		15	6	Worrell	Powell		60-98	7th	40½
9-29	Cin.	L	0-8		1	8	Pugh	Sanders		60-99	7th	41½
10-1	Chi.	L	5-8		6	9	Brennan	Seminara		60-100	7th	42
10-2	Chi.	W	7-3		10	10	Brocail	Morgan		61-100	7th	42
10-3	Chi.	L	1-4		5	9	Wendell	Whitehurst	Myers	61-101	7th	43

Monthly records: April (10-12), May (10-18), June (9-19), July (11-16), August (12-15), September (8-19), October (1-2).
*Innings, if other than nine.

HIGHLIGHTS

High point: There probably was none. San Diego never had a .500 record, but the Padres did muster a season-high five-game winning streak from August 23-28.

Low point: The trades of third baseman Gary Sheffield, the defending N.L. batting champion, to Florida on June 24 and of first baseman Fred McGriff, the league's defending home run champ, to Atlanta on July 18 outraged the fans and made the players realize just how deep the owners were ready to slash the payroll.

Turning point: A season-high seven-game losing streak from August 14-22 pushed the Padres into last place, where they eventually would finish with 101 losses. It marked San Diego's first 100-loss season since 1974.

Most valuable player: Right fielder Tony Gwynn. He provided stability amid a fire sale of talent, batting .358 (second in the N.L.) and committing just five errors.

Most valuable pitcher: Righthander Andy Benes. Despite going 2-8 in his final 10 starts, the first-time All-Star finished at 15-15 with a 3.78 ERA and provided experience to a young staff.

Most improved player: Shortstop Ricky Gutierrez. After opening the season in Class AAA, the rookie established himself as the everyday shortstop by hitting .251 and ranking fourth among N.L. shortstops in fielding (.971).

Most pleasant surprise: Left fielder Phil Plantier. The Padres expected him to hit for power, but even they were amazed by his 34 homers and 100 RBIs.

Biggest disappointment: Catcher Dan Walters. The heir apparent to departed Benito Santiago, Walters struggled early and was sent to Class AAA on May 25. He was recalled September 7 and finished with a .202 average.

Key injuries: For the third consecutive year, Gwynn's season was cut short because of injury. His left knee required surgery September 12. Righthander Wally Whitehurst was limited to 19 starts because of elbow and shoulder problems.

Notable: General Manager Joe McIlvaine, fed up with the payroll cuts and embarrassing trades dictated by ownership, resigned in June. Randy Smith was hired to replace McIlvaine. At 30, Smith became the youngest G.M. in baseball. . . . The cost-cutting continued under Smith. By season's end, the Padres had trimmed their payroll to $10.3 million, the lowest in the majors.

—CHRIS DE LUCA

RECORDS

1993 regular-season record: 61-101 (7th in N.L. West); 34-47 at home; 27-54 on road; 34-50 vs. East; 27-51 vs. West; 23-32 vs. LHP; 38-69 vs. RHP; 50-75 on grass; 11-26 on turf; 19-32 in daytime; 42-69 at night; 18-34 in one-run games; 5-13 in extra-inning games; 1-0-2 in doubleheaders.

Team record last five years: 391-419 (.483, ranks 10th in league in that span).

TEAM LEADERS

Batting average: Tony Gwynn (.358).
At-bats: Derek Bell (542).
Runs: Ricky Gutierrez (76).
Hits: Tony Gwynn (175).
Total bases: Tony Gwynn (243).
Doubles: Tony Gwynn (41).
Triples: Jeff Gardner (7).
Home runs: Phil Plantier (34).
Runs batted in: Phil Plantier (100).
Stolen bases: Derek Bell (26).
Slugging percentage: Phil Plantier (.509).
On-base percentage: Tony Gwynn (.398).
Wins: Andy Benes (15).
Earned-run average: Andy Benes (3.78).
Complete games: Andy Benes, Greg Harris (4).
Shutouts: Andy Benes (2).
Saves: Gene Harris (23).
Innings pitched: Andy Benes (230⅔).
Strikeouts: Andy Benes (179).

GAMES BY POSITION

Catcher: Kevin Higgins 59, Brad Ausmus 49, Bob Geren 49, Dan Walters 26, Phil Clark 11.

First base: Fred McGriff 83, Guillermo Velasquez 38, Archi Cianfrocco 31, Phil Clark 24, Billy Bean 12, Dave Staton 12, Tim Teufel 8, Kevin Higgins 3, Bob Geren 1.

Second base: Jeff Gardner 133, Tim Teufel 52, Luis Lopez 15, Craig Shipley 12, Ricky Gutierrez 6, Kevin Higgins 1.

Third base: Gary Sheffield 67, Archi Cianfrocco 64, Craig Shipley 37, Derek Bell 19, Tim Teufel 9, Phil Clark 5, Ricky Gutierrez 4, Kevin Higgins 4, Kurt Stillwell 3, Jeff Gardner 1, Bob Geren 1.

Shortstop: Ricky Gutierrez 117, Craig Shipley 38, Kurt Stillwell 30, Jeff Gardner 1.

Outfield: Phil Plantier 134, Derek Bell 125, Tony Gwynn 121, Billy Bean 54, Jarvis Brown 43, Phil Clark 36, Darrell Sherman 26, Melvin Nieves 15, Guillermo Velasquez 6, Ricky Gutierrez 5, Craig Shipley 5, Kevin Higgins 3.

TOP DRAFT CHOICES

1. **Derrek Lee,** 1B, El Camino High School, Sacramento, Calif.
2. **Matt LaChappa,** LHP, El Capitan High School, Lakeside, Calif.
3. **Matt Clement,** RHP, Butler (Pa.) Area High School.
4. **Tim Miller,** RHP, Williamsport (Pa.) High School.
5. **Harold Garrett,** RHP, Brentwood (Tenn.) Academy.
6. **Greg Keagle,** RHP, Florida International University.
7. **Jason Schlutt,** LHP, University of Central Florida.
8. **Derek Mix,** RHP, San Bernardino Valley (Calif.) J.C.
9. **Jason Thompson,** 1B, University of Arizona.
10. **Stacy Kleiner,** C/3B, Taft High School, Tarzana, Calif.

SAN FRANCISCO GIANTS
NATIONAL LEAGUE WEST DIVISION

1994 SCHEDULE

N Denotes night game (any game starting after 5 p.m.).
☐ Home games shaded.
* At Three Rivers Stadium in Pittsburgh.

APRIL

SUN	MON	TUE	WED	THU	FRI	SAT
					1	2
3	4 PIT	5 PIT	6 PIT	7 N	8 N STL	9 STL
10 STL	11	12 N ATL	13 N ATL	14 N ATL	15 N FLA	16 FLA
17 FLA	18	19 N MON	20 N MON	21 N PHI	22 N NY	23 NY
24 NY	25	26 N MON	27 N MON	28 N	29 N PHI	30 PHI

MAY

SUN	MON	TUE	WED	THU	FRI	SAT
1 PHI	2 N NY	3 N NY	4 N NY	5 N LA	6 N LA	7 LA
8 N LA	9 N COL	10 N COL	11 COL	12	13 N CIN	14 CIN
15 CIN	16 N HOU	17 N HOU	18 N HOU	19	20 N CHI	21 CHI
22 CHI	23 N SD	24 N SD	25 N SD	26	27 N FLA	28 FLA
29 FLA	30 ATL	31 ATL				

JUNE

SUN	MON	TUE	WED	THU	FRI	SAT
			N 1 ATL	2	3 N STL	4 N STL
5 STL	6 N PIT	7 N PIT	8 N PIT	9	10 N SD	11 N SD
12 SD	13 N HOU	14 N HOU	15 N HOU	16 N HOU	17 N CHI	18 CHI
19 CHI	20	21 N CIN	22 N CIN	23 N CIN	24 N COL	25 COL
26 COL	27 N LA	28 N LA	29 N LA	30 N MON		

JULY

SUN	MON	TUE	WED	THU	FRI	SAT
					N 1 MON	2 MON
3 MON	4 N NY	5 N NY	6 N NY	7 N PHI	8 N PHI	9 PHI
10 PHI	11 *	12 ALL-STAR GAME	13	14 N MON	15 N MON	16 MON
17 MON	18 N PHI	19 N PHI	20 PHI	21	22 N NY	23 NY
24 NY	25 N LA	26 N LA	27 N LA	28 N COL	29 N COL	30 COL
31 COL						

AUGUST

SUN	MON	TUE	WED	THU	FRI	SAT
	1 CIN	2 CIN	3 CIN	4	5 N HOU	6 N HOU
7 N HOU	8 N CHI	9 N CHI	10 CHI	11	12 N SD	13 N SD
14 SD	15	16 FLA	17 FLA	18 FLA	19 N PIT	20 N PIT
21 PIT	22 N STL	23 N STL	24 N STL	25	26 N PIT	27 N PIT
28 PIT	29	30 STL	31 STL			

SEPTEMBER

SUN	MON	TUE	WED	THU	FRI	SAT
				1 STL	2 N ATL	3 ATL
4 ATL	5 N FLA	6 N FLA	7 N FLA	8 N ATL	9 N ATL	10 ATL
11 ATL	12 N SD	13 N SD	14 SD	15	16 N HOU	17 HOU
18 HOU	19 N CHI	20 N CHI	21 CHI	22	23 N CIN	24 CIN
25 CIN	26 N COL	27 N COL	28 COL	29 N LA	30 LA	

OCTOBER

SUN	MON	TUE	WED	THU	FRI	SAT
					N 1 LA	1 LA
2 LA						

1994 SEASON

CLUB DIRECTORY

President and managing general partner
Peter A. Magowan
Executive vice president
Larry Baer
Senior vice president and general manager
Bob Quinn
Senior vice president, business operations
Pat Gallagher
Asst. to the general manager and v.p. of scouting and player personnel
Brian Sabean
V.p./baseball admin. and operations
Tony Siegle
Vice president, finance
John Yee
Vice president, stadium operations
Jorge Costa
Director of public relations
Bob Rose
Director of community development
Jan Hutchins
Director of marketing
Mario Alioto
Director of retail operations
Robert Tolifson
Director of stadium operations
Gene Telucci
Director of travel
Dirk Smith
Director of legal and governmental affairs
Jack Bair
Publicity coordinator
Robin Carr Locke
Media relations manager
Jim Moorehead
Coordinator of scouting
Bob Hartsfield
National cross-checker
Randy Waddill
Western cross-checker
Doug Mapson

Southern cross-checker
Larry Osborne
Coordinator of Latin American operations
Luis Rosa
Scouts
Claudio Brito
Jose Cassino
Art Chapman
Richard Cole
Pablo Delgado
Nino Escalera
Bob Gardner
George Genovese
Herman Hannah
Chuck Hensley
Carlos Hernandez
Diego Herrera
Andres James
Elvio Jimenez
Mike Keenan
Tom Korenek
Jose Marcano
Jerry Marik
Alan Marr
Abraham Martinez
Doug McMillan
Tony Michalak
Bob Myrick
Rick Ragazzo
Hector Rivera
Gary Robinson
Milton Rosario
John Shafer
Joe Strain
Todd Thomas
Gene Thompson
Mike Toomey
Elanis Westbrooks
Tom Zimmer

Manager—Dusty Baker (12).

Coaches—Bobby Bonds (16), Bob Brenly (15), Wendell Kim (20), Bob Lillis (5), Dick Pole (48), Denny Sommers (58).

No.	PITCHERS	B/T	Ht./Wt.	Born	1993 clubs
47	Beck, Rod	R/R	6-1/236	8-3-68	San Francisco
34	Burba, Dave	R/R	6-4/240	7-7-66	San Francisco
33	Burkett, John	R/R	6-2/211	11-28-64	San Francisco
53	Carlson, Dan	R/R	6-1/185	1-26-70	Phoenix, Shreveport
39	Hancock, Chris	L/L	6-3/175	9-12-69	Shreveport
41	Hickerson, Bryan	L/L	6-2/203	10-13-63	San Francisco
42	Jackson, Mike	R/R	6-2/223	12-22-64	San Francisco
36	Menendez, Tony	R/R	6-2/190	2-20-65	Buffalo, Pittsburgh
55	Monteleone, Rich	R/R	6-2/214	3-22-63	New York A.L.
19	Portugal, Mark	R/R	6-0/190	10-30-62	Houston
28	Rogers, Kevin	B/L	6-1/198	8-20-68	San Francisco
46	Rosselli, Joe	R/L	6-1/170	5-28-72	Shreveport
26	Swift, Bill	R/R	6-0/191	10-27-61	San Francisco
35	Torres, Salomon	R/R	5-11/165	3-11-72	Shreveport, Phoenix, San Francisco
50	VanLandingham, Bill	R/R	6-2/210	7-16-70	San Jose, Phoenix
32	Wilson, Trevor	L/L	6-0/204	6-7-66	San Francisco, San Jose

No.	CATCHERS	B/T	Ht./Wt.	Born	1993 clubs
54	Jensen, Marcus	B/R	6-4/195	12-14-72	Clinton
8	Manwaring, Kirt	R/R	5-11/203	7-15-65	San Francisco
52	Reed, Jeff	L/R	6-2/190	11-12-62	San Francisco, San Jose

No.	INFIELDERS	B/T	Ht./Wt.	Born	1993 clubs
18	Benjamin, Mike	R/R	6-0/169	11-22-65	San Francisco, San Jose
14	Benzinger, Todd	B/R	6-1/195	2-11-63	San Francisco
10	Clayton, Royce	R/R	6-0/183	1-2-70	San Francisco
21	Faries, Paul	R/R	5-10/170	2-20-65	Phoenix, San Francisco
7	Patterson, John	B/R	5-9/168	2-11-67	San Jose, San Francisco
31	Phillips, J.R.	L/L	6-1/185	4-29-70	Phoenix, San Francisco
23	Scarsone, Steve	R/R	6-2/195	4-11-66	Phoenix, San Francisco
6	Thompson, Robby	R/R	5-11/173	5-10-62	San Francisco
9	Williams, Matt	R/R	6-2/216	11-28-65	San Francisco

No.	OUTFIELDERS	B/T	Ht./Wt.	Born	1993 clubs
25	Bonds, Barry	L/L	6-1/185	7-24-64	San Francisco
45	Carreon, Mark	R/L	6-0/195	7-9-63	San Francisco
38	Faneyte, Rikkert	R/R	6-1/170	5-31-69	Phoenix, San Francisco
29	Hosey, Steve	R/R	6-3/225	4-2-69	Phoenix, San Francisco
56	Jones, Dax	R/R	5-9/180	8-4-70	Shreveport
2	Lewis, Darren	R/R	6-0/189	8-28-67	San Francisco
1	Martinez, Dave	L/L	5-10/175	9-26-64	San Francisco, Phoenix
51	McGee, Willie	B/R	6-1/185	11-2-58	San Francisco
17	Mercedes, Luis	R/R	6-3/195	2-20-68	Baltimore, San Francisco, Phoenix

BALLPARK INFORMATION

Ballpark (capacity, surface)
Candlestick Park (60,000, grass)
Address
Candlestick Park
San Francisco, CA 94124
Business phone
415-468-3700
Ticket information
415-467-8000
Ticket prices
$15 (lower box)
$12 (upper box)
$12 (lower reserved)
$7 (upper reserved)
$6 (pavilion)
$5 (bleachers)
Field dimensions (from home plate)
To left field at foul line, 335 feet
To center field, 400 feet
To right field at foul line, 328 feet
First game played
April 12, 1960 (Giants 3, Cardinals 1)

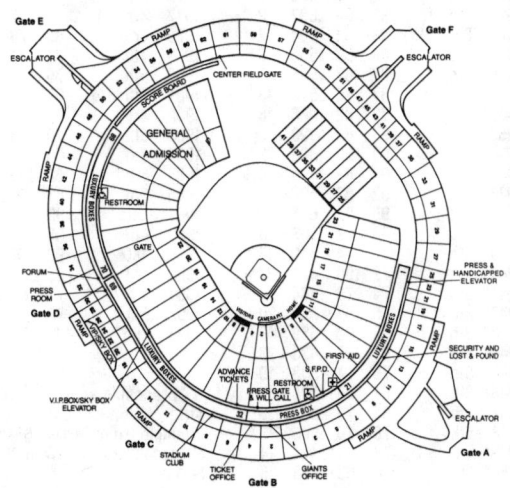

MINOR LEAGUE AFFILIATES

Class	Team	League	Manager
AAA	Phoenix	Pacific Coast	Carlos Alfonso
AA	Shreveport	Texas	Ron Wotus
A	San Jose	California	Dick Dietz
A	Clinton	Midwest	Jack Mull
A	Everett	Northwest	To be announced
Rookie	Scottsdale	Arizona	Alan Bannister

BROADCAST INFORMATION

Radio: KNBR-AM (680). Broadcasters: Hank Greenwald, Ted Robinson. KIQI-AM (1010, Spanish language). Broadcasters: Julio Gonzales, Edgard Martinez.
TV: KTVU-TV (Channel 2). Broadcasters: Ted Robinson, Mike Krukow, Joe Morgan.
Cable TV: SportsChannel Pacific. Broadcasters: Duane Kuiper, Mike Krukow, Joe Morgan.

SPRING TRAINING

Ballpark (city): Scottsdale Stadium (Scottsdale, Ariz.).
Ticket information: 602-990-7972.

HISTORY

YEAR-BY-YEAR RECORDS

Year	Pos.	W	L	Pct.	GB	Year	Pos.	W	L	Pct.	GB
1901*	7th	52	85	.380	37	1951*	1st†	98	59	.624	+ 1
1902*	8th	48	88	.353	53½	1952*	2nd	92	62	.597	4½
1903*	2nd	84	55	.604	6½	1953*	5th	70	84	.455	35
1904*	1st	106	47	.693	+13	1954*	1st	97	57	.630	+ 5
1905*	1st	105	48	.686	+ 9	1955*	3rd	80	74	.519	18½
1906*	2nd	96	56	.632	20	1956*	6th	67	87	.435	26
1907*	4th	82	71	.536	25½	1957*	6th	69	85	.448	26
1908*	T2nd	98	56	.636	1	1958	3rd	80	74	.519	12
1909*	3rd	92	61	.601	18½	1959	3rd	83	71	.539	4
1910*	2nd	91	63	.591	13	1960	5th	79	75	.513	16
1911*	1st	99	54	.647	+ 7½	1961	3rd	85	69	.552	8
1912*	1st	103	48	.682	+10	1962	1st†	103	62	.624	+ 1
1913*	1st	101	51	.664	+12½	1963	3rd	88	74	.543	11
1914*	2nd	84	70	.545	10½	1964	4th	90	72	.556	3
1915*	8th	69	83	.454	21	1965	2nd	95	67	.586	2
1916*	4th	86	66	.566	7	1966	2nd	93	68	.578	1½
1917*	1st	98	56	.636	+10	1967	2nd	91	71	.562	10½
1918*	2nd	71	53	.573	10½	1968	2nd	88	74	.543	9
1919*	2nd	87	53	.621	9	1969	2nd	90	72	.556	3
1920*	2nd	86	68	.558	7	1970	3rd	86	76	.531	16
1921*	1st	94	59	.614	+ 4	1971	1st‡	90	72	.556	+ 1
1922*	1st	93	61	.604	+ 7	1972	5th	69	86	.445	26½
1923*	1st	95	58	.621	+ 4½	1973	3rd	88	74	.543	11
1924*	1st	93	60	.608	+ 1½	1974	5th	72	90	.444	30
1925*	2nd	86	66	.566	8½	1975	3rd	80	81	.497	27½
1926*	5th	74	77	.490	13½	1976	4th	74	88	.457	28
1927*	3rd	92	62	.597	2	1977	4th	75	87	.463	23
1928*	2nd	93	61	.604	2	1978	3rd	89	73	.549	6
1929*	3rd	84	67	.556	13½	1979	4th	71	91	.438	19½
1930*	3rd	87	67	.565	5	1980	5th	75	86	.466	17
1931*	2nd	87	65	.572	13	1981	5th/3rd	56	55	.505	§
1932*	T6th	72	82	.468	18	1982	3rd	87	75	.537	2
1933*	1st	91	61	.599	+ 5	1983	5th	79	83	.488	12
1934*	2nd	93	60	.608	2	1984	6th	66	96	.407	26
1935*	3rd	91	62	.595	8½	1985	6th	62	100	.383	33
1936*	1st	92	62	.597	+ 5	1986	3rd	83	79	.512	13
1937*	1st	95	57	.625	+ 3	1987	1st‡	90	72	.556	+ 6
1938*	3rd	83	67	.553	5	1988	4th	83	79	.512	11½
1939*	5th	77	74	.510	18½	1989	1st*	92	70	.568	+ 3
1940*	6th	72	80	.474	27½	1990	3rd	85	77	.525	6
1941*	5th	74	79	.484	25½	1991	4th	75	87	.463	19
1942*	3rd	85	67	.559	20	1992	5th	72	90	.444	26
1943*	8th	55	98	.359	49½	1993	2nd	103	59	.636	1
1944*	5th	67	87	.435	38						
1945*	5th	78	74	.513	19						
1946*	8th	61	93	.396	36						
1947*	4th	81	73	.526	13						
1948*	5th	78	76	.506	13½						
1949*	5th	73	81	.474	24						
1950*	3rd	86	68	.558	5						

*Franchise known as New York Giants. †Won pennant playoff. ‡Lost Championship Series. §First half 27-32; second 29-23. *Won Championship Series.

MANAGERS

Name	Record	Years
George Davis	52-85	1901
Horace Fogel	18-23	1902
Heinie Smith	5-27	1902
John McGraw	2604-1801	'02-32
Bill Terry	823-661	'32-41
Mel Ott	464-530	'42-48
Leo Durocher	637-523	'48-55
Bill Rigney	406-430	'56-60
		1976
Tom Sheehan	46-50	1960
Alvin Dark	366-370	'61-64
Herman Franks	367-280	'65-68
Clyde King	109-95	'69-70
Charlie Fox	348-327	'70-74
Wes Westrum	118-129	'74-75
Joe Altobelli	225-239	'77-79
Dave Bristol	85-98	'79-80
Frank Robinson	264-277	'81-84
Danny Ozark	24-32	1984
Jim Davenport	56-88	1985
Roger Craig	586-566	'85-92
Dusty Baker	103-59	1993

DAY BY DAY

Date		Opp.	Res.	Score	(inn.*)	Hits	Opp. hits	Winning pitcher	Losing pitcher	Save	Record	Pos.	GB
4-6		At St.L.	W	2-1		8	7	Burkett	Tewksbury	Beck	1-0	T1st	...
4-7		At St.L.	L	2-6		8	13	Cormier	Wilson	Smith	1-1	T3rd	1
4-8		At St.L.	L	1-2		5	4	Osborne	Rogers	Smith	1-2	T3rd	1½
4-9		At Pit.	L	5-6		10	10	Minor	Beck	Belinda	1-3	T5th	2½
4-10		At Pit.	W	12-5		14	7	Burba	Cooke		2-3	T4th	1½
4-11		At Pit.	W	4-3		7	6	Burkett	Wakefield	Beck	3-3	T2nd	1½
4-12		Fla.	W	4-3	(11)	9	4	Beck	Klink		4-3	2nd	½
4-13		Fla.	W	3-1		6	6	Burba	Aquino	Beck	5-3	2nd	½
4-14		Fla.	L	4-6		9	13	Bowen	Swift	Harvey	5-4	3rd	½
4-15		Atl.	W	6-1		10	6	Brantley	Maddux		6-4	1st	+½
4-16		Atl.	W	1-0		4	6	Burkett	Smoltz	Beck	7-4	1st	+½
4-17		Atl.	L	0-2		3	8	Avery	Jackson	Stanton	7-5	1st	+½
4-18		Atl.	W	13-12	(11)	16	9	Jackson	Bedrosian		8-5	1st	+½
4-20		At N.Y.	W	4-1	(11)	8	3	Righetti	Maddux	Beck	9-5	1st	+1½
4-21		At N.Y.	L	0-10		8	12	Gooden	Brantley		9-6	1st	+½
4-22		At N.Y.	W	13-4		19	5	Burkett	Schourek		10-6	1st	+1
4-23		At Mon.	L	2-7		6	14	Martinez	Wilson	Barnes	10-7	2nd	...
4-24		At Mon.	L	1-6		4	13	Hill	Burba		10-8	3rd	1
4-25		At Mon.	W	4-1		10	4	Swift	Nabholz	Beck	11-8	2nd	...
4-26		At Phi.	L	8-9	(10)	9	11	Andersen	Minutelli		11-9	2nd	...
4-27		At Phi.	W	6-3		9	7	Burkett	Mulholland	Beck	12-9	2nd	...
4-28		N.Y.	W	4-3		12	7	Beck	Innis		13-9	2nd	...
4-29		N.Y.	W	10-5		12	9	Black	Saberhagen	Jackson	14-9	2nd	...
4-30		Mon.	W	5-2		14	8	Swift	Nabholz		15-9	2nd	...
5-1		Mon.	W	7-3		12	10	Brantley	Jones		16-9	2nd	...
5-2		Mon.	W	4-3	(11)	7	14	Jackson	Fassero		17-9	1st	+1
5-4		Phi.	L	3-4	(12)	7	10	Andersen	Righetti	Mit. Williams	17-10	1st	+1
5-5		Phi.	W	11-2		15	8	Swift	Jackson		18-10	1st	+1
5-7		L.A.	W	8-5		14	10	Black	Ke. Gross		19-10	1st	+2½
5-8		L.A.	L	2-5	(12)	12	10	Gott	Burba		19-11	1st	+1½
5-9		L.A.	L	4-6		3	8	Hershiser	Brantley	Gott	19-12	1st	+½
5-10		At Col.	L	4-7		13	7	Reynoso	Wilson		19-13	2nd	½
5-11		At Col.	W	5-3		13	7	Swift	Nied	Beck	20-13	1st	+½
5-12		At Col.	W	8-2		16	3	Black	Henry		21-13	1st	+1½
5-13		At Col.	W	13-8		13	14	Burkett	Ruffin		22-13	1st	+2
5-14		At S.D.	L	1-3		6	6	Gr. Harris	Brantley		22-14	1st	+1
5-15		At S.D.	W	3-0		4	4	Wilson	Taylor	Beck	23-14	1st	+1
5-16		At S.D.	W	9-4		13	9	Swift	Whitehurst		24-14	1st	+1
5-17		Hou.	W	8-7	(10)	15	10	Burba	D. Jones		25-14	1st	+2
5-18		Hou.	W	7-2		10	7	Burkett	Kile		26-14	1st	+3
5-19		Hou.	W	6-3		6	8	Brantley	Harnisch		27-14	1st	+3½
5-20		Cin.	W	6-1		11	5	Wilson	Browning		28-14	1st	+4
5-21		Cin.	W	3-0		9	3	Swift	Belcher	Beck	29-14	1st	+4
5-22		Cin.	L	2-6		9	11	Rijo	Black		29-15	1st	+4
5-23		Cin.	W	3-2		5	5	Jackson	Landrum		30-15	1st	+4
5-25		At Chi.	W	5-4		10	12	Burba	Myers	Beck	31-15	1st	+4
5-26		At Chi.	L	2-4		8	6	Harkey	Swift	Myers	31-16	1st	+4
5-27		At Chi.	L	4-5		13	9	Hibbard	Hickerson	Myers	31-17	1st	+4
5-28		At Atl.	L	4-7		16	9	Avery	Burkett	Stanton	31-18	1st	+3
5-29		At Atl.	W	6-3		11	8	Brummett	Smith	Beck	32-18	1st	+4
5-30		At Atl.	W	4-3		8	11	Burba	Glavine	Beck	33-18	1st	+5
6-1	(1)	At Fla.	L	3-7		12	12	Hammond	Swift		33-19	1st	+4½
6-1	(2)	At Fla.	W	4-3		8	9	Black	Bowen	Beck	34-19	1st	+5
6-2		At Fla.	W	3-2		7	12	Burkett	Armstrong	Beck	35-19	1st	+5
6-3		Pit.	L	1-2		2	10	Neagle	Brummett	Minor	35-20	1st	+5
6-4		Pit.	L	2-3		7	8	Cooke	Brantley	Belinda	35-21	1st	+4
6-5		Pit.	W	3-2		5	6	Wilson	Wakefield	Beck	36-21	1st	+4
6-6		Pit.	W	7-1		11	7	Swift	Walk		37-21	1st	+4
6-8		St.L.	L	3-4		9	7	Arocha	Burkett	Smith	37-22	1st	+3½
6-9		St.L.	W	3-1		5	11	Black	Osborne	Beck	38-22	1st	+4½
6-11		Chi.	W	7-2		13	8	Wilson	Hibbard		39-22	1st	+5½
6-12		Chi.	W	5-4		14	7	Swift	McElroy	Beck	40-22	1st	+6½
6-13		Chi.	W	5-3		11	9	Burkett	Morgan	Beck	41-22	1st	+6½
6-15		At Cin.	L	5-10		12	17	Belcher	Brantley		41-23	1st	+6
6-16		At Cin.	W	6-5	(10)	10	9	Jackson	Ayala	Beck	42-23	1st	+6
6-17		At Cin.	W	5-1		9	1	Swift	Smiley		43-23	1st	+6½
6-18		At Hou.	W	5-0		12	6	Black	Drabek		44-23	1st	+7½
6-19		At Hou.	W	10-3		13	7	Burkett	Swindell		45-23	1st	+7½
6-20		At Hou.	W	8-5		10	9	Brantley	Williams	Beck	46-23	1st	+7½
6-21		S.D.	W	2-1		8	8	Wilson	Brocail	Beck	47-23	1st	+7½

Date	Opp.	Res.	Score	(inn.*)	Hits	Opp. hits	Winning pitcher	Losing pitcher	Save	Record	Pos.	GB
6-22	S.D.	L	1-2		6	8	Benes	Swift	Ge. Harris	47-24	1st	+7½
6-23	S.D.	W	6-2		10	6	Black	Gr. Harris		48-24	1st	+8½
6-24	Col.	W	17-2		20	7	Burkett	Blair		49-24	1st	+9
6-25	Col.	W	7-2		12	8	Hickerson	Henry		50-24	1st	+9
6-26	Col.	L	1-5		7	15	Reynoso	Wilson		50-25	1st	+8
6-27	Col.	W	5-0		7	2	Swift	Leskanic		51-25	1st	+9
6-28	At L.A.	L	0-4		7	5	P. Martinez	Jackson		51-26	1st	+8½
6-29	At L.A.	W	3-1		7	4	Burkett	Hershiser	Beck	52-26	1st	+8½
6-30	At L.A.	L	3-5		6	10	P. Martinez	Rogers	Gott	52-27	1st	+7½
7-2	At N.Y.	W	3-1	(5)	7	3	Burba	Young		53-27	1st	+8
7-3	At N.Y.	L	3-6		10	12	Telgheder	Swift	Franco	53-28	1st	+7
7-4	At N.Y.	W	10-8		17	12	Jackson	Maddux	Beck	54-28	1st	+7
7-5	At Mon.	W	10-4		14	12	Burkett	Gardiner		55-28	1st	+7
7-6	At Mon.	W	13-5		13	10	Hickerson	Bottenfield		56-28	1st	+8
7-7	At Mon.	L	0-3		2	5	Rueter	Brummett	Wetteland	56-29	1st	+8
7-8	At Phi.	W	13-2		20	9	Swift	Jackson		57-29	1st	+9
7-9	At Phi.	W	15-8		23	13	Black	Rivera		58-29	1st	+9
7-10	At Phi.	L	3-8		7	12	Greene	Burkett		58-30	1st	+9
7-11	At Phi.	W	10-2		18	10	Hickerson	Schilling		59-30	1st	+9
7-15	N.Y.	W	8-1		13	6	Swift	Hillman		60-30	1st	+9
7-16	N.Y.	W	4-2		7	6	Hickerson	Gooden	Beck	61-30	1st	+9
7-17	N.Y.	L	1-3		3	12	Tanana	Burkett	Franco	61-31	1st	+9
7-18	N.Y.	L	6-12		9	11	Schourek	Brummett		61-32	1st	+8
7-19	Mon.	W	6-2		11	11	Burba	Nabholz		62-32	1st	+9
7-20	Mon.	W	8-3		11	7	Swift	Martinez		63-32	1st	+9
7-21	Mon.	W	4-3		7	6	Hickerson	Rojas	Beck	64-32	1st	+9
7-22	Phi.	W	4-1		6	5	Burkett	Mulholland	Beck	65-32	1st	+10
7-23	Phi.	L	1-2	(14)	8	6	West	Jackson	Mit. Williams	65-33	1st	+9
7-24	Phi.	W	5-4		6	11	Burba	Rivera	Beck	66-33	1st	+9
7-25	Phi.	W	5-2		9	4	Swift	Jackson	Righetti	67-33	1st	+9
7-26	L.A.	L	1-15		5	17	Hershiser	Hickerson		67-34	1st	+8
7-27	L.A.	W	3-2		9	3	Burkett	Ke. Gross	Beck	68-34	1st	+8
7-28	L.A.	L	1-2		5	8	Candiotti	Black	Gott	68-35	1st	+7
7-30	At Col.	W	10-4		16	9	Brummett	Harris		69-35	1st	+7½
7-31	At Col.	W	4-3		11	7	Swift	Bottenfield	Beck	70-35	1st	+7½
8-1	At Col.	W	6-5		6	9	Burkett	Reynoso	Beck	71-35	1st	+7½
8-3	At S.D.	W	12-7		12	9	Burba	Davis		72-35	1st	+8½
8-4	At S.D.	L	10-11	(12)	19	19	Martinez	Hickerson		72-36	1st	+7½
8-5	At S.D.	W	5-3		6	7	Swift	Ashby	Beck	73-36	1st	+8½
8-6	Hou.	W	4-3		9	10	Burkett	Kile	Beck	74-36	1st	+9½
8-7	Hou.	L	5-6		7	8	Swindell	Sanderson	D. Jones	74-37	1st	+9½
8-8	Hou.	L	1-4		9	9	Portugal	Hickerson	D. Jones	74-38	1st	+8½
8-9	Cin.	W	10-7		14	12	Burba	Ruffin	Beck	75-38	1st	+9
8-10	Cin.	W	2-1		6	2	Swift	Rijo	Beck	76-38	1st	+9
8-11	Cin.	W	6-0		10	4	Burkett	Ayala		77-38	1st	+9
8-13	At Chi.	W	4-1		6	4	Wilson	Hibbard	Beck	78-38	1st	+8½
8-14	At Chi.	L	2-3		7	14	Myers	Jackson		78-39	1st	+7½
8-15	At Chi.	W	9-7	(11)	16	15	Rogers	Myers		79-39	1st	+7½
8-17	At Pit.	L	3-10		10	13	Cooke	Burkett		79-40	1st	+6½
8-18	At Pit.	W	9-6		15	11	Wilson	Smith		80-40	1st	+6½
8-19	At Pit.	W	6-3		7	6	Hickerson	Walk	Beck	81-40	1st	+7½
8-20	Fla.	L	4-5		7	8	Turner	Jackson	Harvey	81-41	1st	+7½
8-21	Fla.	W	7-4		9	10	Sanderson	Hammond	Beck	82-41	1st	+7½
8-22	Fla.	W	7-6		10	12	Rogers	Harvey		83-41	1st	+7½
8-23	Atl.	L	3-5		8	9	Avery	Wilson		83-42	1st	+6½
8-24	Atl.	L	4-6		10	11	Glavine	Hickerson	McMichael	83-43	1st	+5½
8-25	Atl.	L	1-9		6	16	Maddux	Swift		83-44	1st	+4½
8-27	At Fla.	L	4-7		9	13	Rapp	Burkett		83-45	1st	+4½
8-29	At Fla.	W	9-3		15	6	Torres	Hammond		84-45	1st	+4
8-30	At Fla.	W	5-1		9	8	Sanderson	Armstrong		85-45	1st	+4½
8-31	At Atl.	L	2-8		6	9	Maddux	Swift		85-46	1st	+3½
9-1	At Atl.	W	3-2		7	4	Jackson	Wohlers	Beck	86-46	1st	+4½
9-2	At Atl.	L	3-5		8	11	Wohlers	Brantley	McMichael	86-47	1st	+3½
9-3	At St.L.	W	6-1		9	7	Deshaies	Watson		87-47	1st	+3½
9-4	At St.L.	W	3-1		8	8	Torres	Arocha	Beck	88-47	1st	+3½
9-5	At St.L.	L	6-7		11	14	Olivares	Burba		88-48	1st	+3½
9-6	Pit.	W	4-1		8	4	Sanderson	Wagner	Beck	89-48	1st	+3½
9-7	Pit.	L	3-4		4	7	Menendez	Jackson	Dewey	89-49	1st	+2½
9-9	St.L.	L	4-9		5	14	Arocha	Deshaies		89-50	1st	+1
9-10	St.L.	L	2-6		6	9	Urbani	Torres		89-51	1st	...
9-11	St.L.	L	1-3		12	6	Tewksbury	Swift	Perez	89-52	2nd	1
9-12	St.L.	L	2-4		7	9	Cormier	Burkett	Kilgus	89-53	2nd	1
9-13	Chi.	L	5-6		14	11	Hibbard	Sanderson	Myers	89-54	2nd	1½
9-14	Chi.	L	1-8		5	13	Bautista	Deshaies		89-55	2nd	2½

Date	Opp.	Res.	Score	(Inn.*)	Hits	Opp. hits	Winning pitcher	Losing pitcher	Save	Record	Pos.	GB
9-15	Chi.	L	1-3		4	7	Morgan	Torres	Myers	89-56	2nd	3½
9-17	At Cin.	W	13-0		17	7	Swift	Roper		90-56	2nd	4
9-18	At Cin.	W	6-1		9	6	Burkett	Pugh		91-56	2nd	3
9-19	At Cin.	W	7-3		6	8	Sanderson	Ayala		92-56	2nd	3
9-20	At Hou.	W	7-2		10	9	Deshaies	Swindell		93-56	2nd	2½
9-21	At Hou.	L	0-6		3	10	Portugal	Torres		93-57	2nd	3½
9-22	At Hou.	W	1-0		7	5	Swift	Harnisch	Beck	94-57	2nd	2½
9-23	At Hou.	W	7-0		12	3	Burkett	Drabek		95-57	2nd	2½
9-24	S.D.	W	4-3	(10)	6	8	Beck	Ge. Harris		96-57	2nd	1½
9-25	S.D.	W	3-1		9	5	Torres	Ashby	Beck	97-57	2nd	1½
9-26	S.D.	W	5-2		12	5	Swift	Brocail		98-57	2nd	1½
9-27	S.D.	W	8-4		14	6	Burkett	Benes	Beck	99-57	2nd	1
9-28	Col.	W	6-4		4	14	Hickerson	Nied	Beck	100-57	T1st	...
9-29	Col.	L	3-5		7	9	Reed	Torres	Holmes	100-58	2nd	1
9-30	At L.A.	W	3-1		10	4	Swift	Candiotti	Beck	101-58	T1st	...
10-1	At L.A.	W	8-7		11	12	Burkett	R. Martinez	Beck	102-58	T1st	...
10-2	At L.A.	W	5-3		9	10	Brantley	Hershiser	Beck	103-58	T1st	...
10-3	At L.A.	L	1-12		6	14	Ke. Gross	Torres		103-59	2nd	1

Monthly records: April (15-9), May (18-9), June (19-9), July (18-8), August (15-11), September (16-12), October (2-1).
*Innings, if other than nine.

HIGHLIGHTS

High point: On July 22, San Francisco won its fourth straight game to open a 10-game lead over Atlanta, the Giants' largest of the season.

Low point: The Giants suffered an eight-game losing streak from September 7-15. San Francisco began the skid with a 3½-game lead and ended it trailing the Braves by 3½ games.

Turning point: On September 2 in Atlanta, the Giants blew a 3-0 lead to the Braves and lost, 5-3. It was the final meeting between the two teams and kept San Francisco from building a 5½-game lead over Atlanta.

Most valuable player: Left fielder Barry Bonds. He set career highs in average (.336), homers (46) and RBIs (123) en route to winning his third N.L. MVP award in four years. He also stole 29 bases and won his fourth straight Gold Glove.

Most valuable pitcher: Righthander Rod Beck. The Giants wound up with aces in righthanders John Burkett (22-7) and Bill Swift (21-8). But the key to the staff was Beck, who saved 48 games.

Most improved player: Shortstop Royce Clayton. Following a disappointing rookie season, he hit .282 with 70 RBIs, which tied a team record for RBIs by a shortstop.

Most pleasant surprise: Burkett. He had never won more than 14 games, but Burkett got off to a 7-0 start, made the All-Star team and wound up tying for the league lead in wins.

Biggest disappointment: First baseman Will Clark. He hit just .218 through May 26 and finished with only 14 homers (his lowest total since his rookie year, 1986) and 73 RBIs.

Key injuries: Lefthanders Trevor Wilson (shoulder) and Bud Black (elbow) were on the disabled list three times each. Clark, second baseman Robby Thompson, third baseman Matt Williams, right fielder Willie McGee and center fielder Darren Lewis also spent time on the D.L.

Notable: The last team to win 100 games and finish in second place was the 1980 Baltimore Orioles. . . . Dusty Baker won more games (103) than any rookie manager in N.L. history. . . . Burkett and Swift became the Giants' first 20-win tandem since Juan Marichal and Gaylord Perry in 1966. . . . Lewis set a major league record for consecutive errorless games (267) July 16. He finished the season with no errors, extending his streak to 316 games (770 chances). . . . Bonds, Thompson, Williams and catcher Kirt Manwaring all won Gold Gloves.

—LARRY STONE

RECORDS

1993 regular-season record: 103-59 (2nd in N.L. West); 50-31 at home; 53-28 on road; 50-34 vs. East; 53-25 vs. West; 34-22 vs. LHP; 69-37 vs. RHP; 78-47 on grass; 25-12 on turf; 54-26 in daytime; 49-33 at night; 29-18 in one-run games; 8-5 in extra-inning games; 0-0-1 in doubleheaders.

Team record last five years: 427-383 (.527, ranks 2nd in league in that span).

TEAM LEADERS

Batting average: Barry Bonds (.336).
At-bats: Matt Williams (579).
Runs: Barry Bonds (129).
Hits: Barry Bonds (181).
Total bases: Barry Bonds (365).
Doubles: Barry Bonds (38).
Triples: Darren Lewis (7).
Home runs: Barry Bonds (46).
Runs batted in: Barry Bonds (123).
Stolen bases: Darren Lewis (46).
Slugging percentage: Barry Bonds (.677).
On-base percentage: Barry Bonds (.458).
Wins: John Burkett (22).
Earned-run average: Bill Swift (2.82).
Complete games: John Burkett (2).
Shutouts: John Burkett, Bill Swift (1).
Saves: Rod Beck (48).
Innings pitched: Bill Swift (232⅔).
Strikeouts: Bill Swift (157).

GAMES BY POSITION

Catcher: Kirt Manwaring 130, Jeff Reed 37, Craig Colbert 10, Andy Allanson 8, Jim McNamara 4.

First base: Will Clark 129, Todd Benzinger 40, Steve Scarsone 6, J.R. Phillips 5, Mark Carreon 3, Andy Allanson 2.

Second base: Robby Thompson 128, Mike Benjamin 23, Steve Scarsone 20, Paul Faries 7, Craig Colbert 2, Erik Johnson 2.

Third base: Matt Williams 144, Mike Benjamin 16, Steve Scarsone 8, Todd Benzinger 1, Craig Colbert 1, Paul Faries 1, Erik Johnson 1.

Shortstop: Royce Clayton 153, Mike Benjamin 23, Paul Faries 4, Erik Johnson 1.

Outfield: Barry Bonds 157, Darren Lewis 131, Willie McGee 126, Dave Martinez 73, Mark Carreon 41, Todd Benzinger 7, Rikkert Faneyte 6, Luis Mercedes 5, Steve Hosey 1.

TOP DRAFT CHOICES

1. Steve Soderstrom, RHP, Fresno State University.

2a. Chris Singleton, OF, University of Nevada.

2b. Macey Brooks, OF, Kecoughtan High School, Hampton, Va.

2c. Brett King, SS, University of South Florida.

3. Don Denbow, OF, Blinn (Tex.) J.C.

4. Jay Canizaro, SS, Blinn (Tex.) J.C.

5. Heath Altman, RHP, University of North Carolina-Wilmington.

6. Pat Ryan, RHP, Apopka (Fla.) High School.

7. Keith Williams, OF, Clemson University.

8. Brett Smith, RHP, Arizona State University.

9. Ivan Alvarez, LHP, Canoga Park, Calif.

10. Jason Myers, LHP, Chaffey (Calif.) J.C.

1993 REVIEW

Year in review

A.L. Championship Series

N.L. Championship Series

World Series

All-Star Game

Notable performances

Transactions

Award winners

Miscellaneous

Necrology

YEAR IN REVIEW

By STEVE GIETSCHIER

For a few precious weeks toward the middle of 1993, baseball seemed to put aside its problems. Roughly from the All-Star break in July until the last sparks from SkyDome's celebratory World Series fireworks burned out, fans enjoyed an unusual interval during which baseball's on-the-field activities tended to eclipse its troubles.

Perhaps this hiatus had its roots in the stubborn and naive perception that baseball will always be with us, no matter what. More likely, though, this cockeyed optimism was nurtured by an exciting regular season, including one particularly special pennant race, and more than two weeks of post-season play full of improbability.

It was a year in which baseball saw the retirement of three legends and quests to hit .400 by batters in both leagues. It survived a concerted effort to speed up play that chopped a minute off the length of the average game. And it tolerated the lack of a commissioner for the entire year, the expiration of the Basic Agreement in December and the apparent end of the divisional alignment that had served the sport well since 1969.

The National League inaugurated its 118th season with ceremonies marking the debut of two expansion teams that brought its membership to 14. Both the Florida Marlins and the Colorado Rockies began their histories by winning their first spring-training games and their home openers. Both, too, avoided the ignominy of a last-place finish. The Marlins wound up sixth in the N.L. East, ahead of the New York Mets, and the Rockies were sixth in the N.L. West, ahead of the San Diego Padres.

The Rockies proved to be incredibly popular with their fans. They reached the 1 million mark in attendance in their 17th home date, faster than any other team in major league history. In addition, they became the first N.L. team to go over the 4 million mark in attendance. Their total of 4,483,350 set a big-league record as well and included marks for average attendance (56,751), opening-day and single-game attendance (80,227), night game (72,208), three-game series (212,475) and four-game series (251,521).

Stunning climax to season

The season came to a stunning climax on Saturday night, October 23, when Joe Carter of the Toronto Blue Jays lashed Mitch Williams' 2-2 pitch over the left-field fence to end the World Series as it had never been ended before. Carter's ninth-inning, three-run homer pulled out an 8-6 victory for the Jays over the Philadelphia Phillies and gave them their second straight Series crown, four games to two.

Carter's sudden blow was immediately compared to other glorious moments in postseason home run history: to 1951, when Bobby Thomson of the New York Giants hit a three-run homer off Ralph Branca in the bottom of the ninth to snatch the N.L. pennant from the Brooklyn Dodgers; to the seventh game of the 1960 Series, when Bill Mazeroski broke a 9-9 tie with a ninth-inning homer off Ralph Terry of the New York Yankees to win the Series for the Pittsburgh Pirates; and to 1988, when Kirk Gibson of the Los Angeles Dodgers became the first player to win a Series game with a come-from-behind home run in the last inning.

Carter's line drive stands alone in Series play. Unlike Mazeroski's, it erased a one-run deficit; and unlike Gibson's, it came in the Series' last game, not the first.

The Blue Jays thus became the first team to win consecutive World Series championships since the New York Yankees of 1977-78. Despite turning over more than one-third of its roster in the off-season, Toronto added this impressive triumph to a record of postseason appearances that now includes three straight American League East titles and five in the last nine years. For this achievement, THE SPORTING NEWS named Executive Vice President Pat Gillick and Manager Cito Gaston as its Sportsmen of the Year.

Toronto started the season sluggishly and was actually a game below .500 and 4½ games behind the surprising Detroit Tigers on May 12. Newly acquired pitcher Dave Stewart spent the season's first month on the disabled list and managed to win only four games before the All-Star break. Nevertheless, the Blue Jays reached first place June 26, fell back a bit and then were either tied for the lead or in first place outright from July 20 on. The Yankees proved to be dogged pursuers and last tied for first place September 9. But the Jays won 17 of their last 21 games to finish seven games ahead.

Toronto's offense was fueled by three players with more than 100 runs batted in—Carter (121), Paul Molitor (111) and John Olerud (107), who also hit .400 into August before winning the batting title at .363. Molitor (211) and Olerud (200) finished first and second in the league in hits, and Olerud, Molitor (.332) and Roberto Alomar (.326) became the first teammates in A.L. history to finish 1-2-3 in the batting race. Pat Hentgen led the team in victories with 19, and Duane Ward became the first Blue Jay to win or share the A.L. save title with 45.

Chicago wins A.L. West

The Chicago White Sox won the A.L. West crown for the first time since 1983, winning the division by eight games over the Texas Rangers. Chicago moved into sole possession of first place to stay July 7 and clinched the flag September 27 by beating the Seattle Mariners, 4-2, on a three-run homer by Bo Jackson. The Oakland Athletics, division champions in 1988, 1989, 1990 and 1992, fell all the way to last place.

Chicago was paced by first baseman Frank Thomas and by the youngest starting pitching rotation—average age, 24—ever to win a division title. Thomas ranked in the league's top 10 in nine offensive categories. He hit .317, drove in 128 runs and set a franchise record with 41 homers, 15 of which (along with 35 RBIs) came in the first inning. He had three four-hit games and an 18-game hitting streak, and he reached base safely in 138 of the 153 games in which he played. Thomas won the A.L. Most Valuable Player award, and THE SPORTING NEWS named him Major League Player of the Year.

White Sox pitching was just as impressive. The staff topped the league with a 3.70 earned-run average, and the starters led the league with 76 victories, seven shutouts, a 3.72 ERA and 1,067½ innings pitched. Cy Young Award winner and A.L. Pitcher of the Year Jack McDowell won a league-leading 22 games, including 10 of his last 15 starts. Alex Fernandez, Wilson Alvarez and rookie Jason Bere contributed 18, 15 and 12 victories, respectively. Reliever Roberto Hernandez chalked up 38 saves, second highest in club history, in 44 opportunities.

Phillies complete reversal

By winning their first N.L. East title since 1983, the Phillies became the third team since 1900 to go from last place to first in one season. Manager Jim Fregosi's unkempt upstarts put the race away early. They won 28 of their first 40 games and built a seven-game lead over the Montreal Expos by the end of May. St. Louis closed the gap to three games in mid-July, but Philadelphia pulled away to clinch the pennant September 28.

The Phillies featured a balanced lineup that led the league in hits, walks, runs and RBIs. Lenny Dykstra became the first N.L. player ever to lead the league in at-bats (637) and walks (129) in the same season. He also took league honors in hits (194) and runs (143, the most in the N.L. since 1932). Darren Daulton and Pete Incaviglia hit 24 home runs each, and four players (Daulton, Dave Hollins, Incaviglia and John Kruk) drove in at least 85 runs apiece.

The gutsy Philadelphia pitching staff led the league in strikeouts and complete games. Curt Schilling and Tommy Greene each won 16 games, and Williams earned a club-record 43 saves.

Braves rule on last day

The Atlanta Braves won their third straight N.L. West championship, but not until the season's final day. The Braves trailed the San Francisco Giants by 9½ games as late as August 7 before gaining ground inexorably on the team that occupied first place from May 10 to September 10. San Francisco went 19-13 in September/October, but Atlanta lost only 15 games after July 31 to nip the Giants at the wire.

On July 18, Braves General Manager John Schuerholz traded three minor leaguers to the Padres to acquire first baseman Fred McGriff. He made his Atlanta debut two days later in a game delayed two hours by a fire in a hospitality suite on the press level of Atlanta-Fulton County Stadium. The fire damaged 2,000 seats and put some electronic systems out of operation. But when the game against the Cardinals began, McGriff hit a home run in an 8-5 Braves triumph. He went on to hit .310 for his new team with 19 home runs and 55 RBIs in just 68 games, 51 of which Atlanta won. David Justice contributed 40 homers and 120 RBIs, and Ron Gant added 36 homers and 117 RBIs to an offense that outscored the opposition, 165-94, in September/October.

Pitcher Greg Maddux, acquired as a free agent on December 9, 1992, won 20 games and led the league in complete games, ERA and innings pitched. He won the N.L. Cy Young Award for the second straight year and was named THE SPORTING NEWS' N.L. Pitcher of the Year. Tom Glavine recorded his third consecutive season with 20 victories or more, and Steve Avery and John Smoltz added 18 and 15 wins, respectively. Mike Stanton earned 27 saves, and rookie Greg McMichael came on to notch 19.

Blue Jays opportunistic

The White Sox's pitching staff, so sterling throughout the regular season, failed to perform up to standards in the A.L. Championship Series, won by Toronto, four games to two. The opportunistic Blue Jays collected 65 hits, a six-game A.L. playoff record, and were aided by seven White Sox errors.

Toronto won the first two games on the road, 7-3 (despite walks to 10 White Sox batters) and 3-1. In Game 1, Molitor had four hits, including a home run and three RBIs, in a contest that was more than slightly upstaged by the rumored announcement of Michael Jordan's retirement from the Chicago Bulls. Stewart used his customary savvy postseason pitching to win Game 2.

Chicago tied the series at SkyDome on a seven-hitter by Alvarez and a 7-4 victory in Game 4 keyed by home runs by Thomas and Lance Johnson.

Jose Guzman bested McDowell in Game 5, as he had in Game 1. This time, Guzman walked only one batter, and Ed Sprague and Alomar provided the hitting heroics. Stewart, voted the series MVP, held the White Sox at bay again in Game 6. Pat Borders drove in two runs in the second inning, but Chicago countered with two in the third. Toronto tallied again in the fourth on two errors and a Borders groundout and then tucked the game and the pennant away with three more runs in the ninth.

Underdog role for Phils

After winning 104 games to overtake the Giants, the Braves appeared to be a good bet to barge past the Phillies into the World Series. Even a 4-3, 10-inning victory by Philadelphia in Game 1 seemed to matter little as Atlanta came back to win the next two games.

In Game 4, however, the Braves' superb offensive machine was shut down by veteran left-hander Danny Jackson. The Phillies, despite striking out 15 times and leaving 15 men on base, escaped with a 2-1 triumph made secure by a dazzling catch by left fielder Milt Thompson with two on and two out in the eighth inning.

The next afternoon, Philadelphia eked out another 4-3 victory in extra innings behind Schilling, who was named series MVP despite winning neither game he started. The Phils saw a three-run lead wiped out in the bottom of the ninth, but Dykstra hit a homer in the 10th to give his team a 3-2 lead in games.

Game 6 was almost anticlimactic. Maddux pitched ineffectively after being hit on the leg by a Mickey Morandini line drive and gave up two runs in the third, fifth and sixth innings. Williams closed out Atlanta in the ninth as the Phillies won the fifth N.L. pennant in their long history.

The Blue Jays and the Phillies split the first two games of the World Series in Toronto. The Jays won Game 1 on homers by Devon White and Olerud, but Philadelphia bounced back to defeat Stewart in Game 2.

As the Series shifted to Veterans Stadium, Manager Gaston had to decide what to do with Molitor, who was unable to be a designated hitter in the N.L. park. Gaston benched Olerud for Game 3 and replaced him with Molitor, who responded with a single, a triple and a homer as Toronto won, 10-3. The Jays also won Game 4, a record-setting fandango marked by 14 walks, 32 hits, eight doubles, two triples, three home runs and a six-run Toronto comeback in the eighth from a 14-9 deficit.

Carter vs. Williams

Schilling shut out the Blue Jays on five hits in Game 5 to cut Toronto's lead to three games to two. Back in Toronto, the Phillies scored five runs in the seventh to take a 6-5 lead in Game 6. In the ninth inning, Rickey Henderson walked, White flied out and Molitor singled to center before Carter came to the plate and settled the issue against Williams.

Each member of the Blue Jays voted a full share of Series winnings received $127,920.77. Philadel-

phia's full shares came to $91,222.27.

Superstars call it quits

The 1993 season marked the last go-round in the major leagues for pitcher Nolan Ryan of the Rangers. After having announced February 11 that his record 27th season would be his last, Ryan hoped that '93 would prove to be a suitable finale to his outstanding career. But he incurred four major injuries and spent three stints on the disabled list, making only 13 starts and finishing the year at 5-5 with 46 strikeouts and a 4.88 ERA. His last appearance was a September 22 start against the Mariners. He pitched to six batters, got none of them out and left the game after tearing the ulnar collateral ligament in his right elbow.

Still, Ryan ended his career holding or sharing 53 league and major league records. He finished with 324 victories (tied for 11th best of all time), 5,714 strikeouts and seven no-hitters.

George Brett of the Kansas City Royals also retired at the conclusion of the season, his 21st year in the majors. He singled in his final at-bat to close his career with 3,154 hits and a .305 batting average. Brett hit his 300th career home run May 13 and stole his 200th career base July 29, thus joining Willie Mays and Henry Aaron as the only players in major league history to have 3,000 hits, 300 homers and 200 stolen bases.

Dave Winfield added his name to the 3,000-hit list September 16 vs. Oakland. Playing for the Minnesota Twins, his fifth team in a 20-year career, Winfield, in the throes of an 18-for-110 slump, collected his 2,999th hit off Kelly Downs and his 3,000th against Dennis Eckersley.

Veteran Carlton Fisk was released by the Chicago White Sox on June 28, just four days after he set a major league record by catching his 2,226th game, surpassing Bob Boone.

Three no-hit games

Three pitchers recorded no-hitters in 1993, one more than in the previous season. Chris Bosio of the Mariners no-hit the Boston Red Sox, 7-0, on April 22. He walked two, struck out four and was backed by a superb fielding play by second baseman Bret Boone in the fifth inning.

Jim Abbott, acquired by the Yankees in a trade with the California Angels in December 1992, no-hit the Cleveland Indians, 4-0, on September 4. Abbott walked five but didn't let a baserunner advance past first.

Four days later, Darryl Kile of the Houston Astros pitched the National League's only no-hitter and the ninth in Astros history. He beat the Mets, 7-1, striking out nine.

Offenses muscle up

Overall offense soared remarkably in 1993 and prompted new charges that the composition of the baseball had been enhanced. Home runs jumped 16.8 percent in the A.L. and 55 percent in the N.L., some of this no doubt attributable to expansion. The National League's batting average rose 12 points to .264, highest in 39 years, and the American League's increased eight points to .267, highest since 1980. Correspondingly, ERAs also rose, from 3.50 to 4.04 in the N.L. and from 3.94 to 4.32 in the A.L.

McDowell was the American League's only 20-game winner. He also led the league with four shutouts. Kansas City's Kevin Appier topped all pitchers with a 2.56 ERA, and the Mariners' Randy Johnson led the league with 308 strikeouts.

Glavine shared the N.L. lead in victories (22) with John Burkett of the Giants. Bill Swift of San Francisco won 21 games, and Pete Harnisch of the Astros topped the league in shutouts with four. Jose Rijo of the Cincinnati Reds finished first in strikeouts with 227.

Thomas did not sweep all A.L. offensive honors. League leaders included Juan Gonzalez of the Rangers with 46 home runs, Albert Belle of the Indians with 129 RBIs and Cleveland's Kenny Lofton with 70 stolen bases.

The Giants' Barry Bonds led the N.L. in homers (46) and RBIs (123) to win his third Most Valuable Player award in four seasons. Chuck Carr of the Marlins stole a league-leading 58 bases, and Andres Galarraga of the Rockies hit .370 to win the batting crown.

Baerga and Whiten excel

Carlos Baerga of the Indians became the first player in major league history to hit home runs from both sides of the plate in the same inning. On April 8, in a 15-5 victory over the Yankees, Baerga hit a two-run homer off lefthander Steve Howe with none out in the seventh inning. When Cleveland batted around, he hit a two-out, bases-empty homer off righthander Steve Farr.

Mark Whiten of the Cardinals put together one of the greatest single-game offensive performances in major league history September 7, when he hit four homers and drove in 12 runs in a 15-2 St. Louis victory over Cincinnati in the second game of a doubleheader. Whiten hit a grand slam in the first inning, fouled out in the fourth, hit three-run homers in the sixth and seventh and smashed a two-run shot in the ninth. He is the 12th player to hit four home runs in one game and only the second, besides Jim Bottomley, to drive in 12 runs in one game.

Andre Dawson of the Red Sox became the 25th player in big-league history to reach the 400-homer plateau April 15 against Cleveland. Dale Murphy ended his career two homers short of 400 when he retired from Colorado on May 27.

Ken Griffey of Seattle tied a major league record by hitting home runs in eight consecutive games. And Sparky Anderson got credit for his 2,000th victory as a manager when the Tigers defeated the A's, 3-2, on April 15.

Pitcher Anthony Young of the Mets set a major league record by losing 27 games in a row. He tied the previous mark, 23, on June 22 and lost his 27th on July 24. Four days later, he earned a victory in the Mets' 5-3 win over the Marlins.

Lee Smith set a major league record when he recorded his 358th career save April 13. The next day, he set the N.L. record for career saves with 301.

Ripken extends streak

Cal Ripken of the Baltimore Orioles played in all 162 of his team's games, thereby extending his streak of consecutive games played to 1,897. He is 233 games shy of Lou Gehrig's major league record of 2,130.

Major league attendance rose to 70,256,459, an all-time high, thanks in part to the presence of the two new N.L. clubs. The Marlins drew 3,064,847, and the Dodgers and Phillies also exceeded the 3 million mark. Five other N.L. teams topped 2 million.

N.L. attendance jumped more than 53 percent, but this figure was misleading because the league amended how it defines paid attendance. Like the A.L., the N.L. now counts total tickets sold instead of tickets used.

A.L. attendance increased nearly 5 percent to 33,332,603, with Toronto and Baltimore setting club records and 11 teams exceeding 2 million.

Tragedy in Florida

Cleveland's Steve Olin and Tim Crews were killed and teammate Bob Ojeda was seriously injured in a boating accident on a lake near Orlando, Fla., on March 22. The families of the three pitchers were picnicking at a house Crews owned on an off-day in the Indians' spring-training schedule. Just after dark, the players, riding in a fishing boat piloted by Crews, slammed into the side of a long dock at high speed. An investigation later showed that Crews' blood-alcohol level was 0.14 percent, over the state's legal limit of 0.10 percent.

Olin was killed instantly, and Crews died the next morning of a brain injury. Ojeda underwent surgery for severe damage to his scalp and was released from the hospital three days later. He underwent therapy and did not pitch again for the Indians until August 6.

Mets' circus atmosphere

The Mets became the first team to fire a manager in 1993 when they dismissed Jeff Torborg on May 19 and replaced him with Dallas Green, a Mets scout since 1991. Under Torborg, in the second year of a four-year contract, the Mets had gotten off to a 13-25 start despite being favored by many to win the N.L. East.

New York did little better for Green (46-78). The Mets' decline was marked by injuries, subpar performances, abysmal morale and several destructive incidents that embarrassed the team's owners and forced the resignation of Al Harazin as general manager.

On July 7, pitcher Bret Saberhagen tossed a firecracker at reporters in the Mets' clubhouse. On July 24, outfielder Vince Coleman threw a much larger firecracker out a car window as he and other players were leaving Dodger Stadium. The explosion injured three people, including a two-year-old girl, and Coleman was placed on administrative leave. Three days later, Saberhagen squirted liquid bleach at reporters.

Coleman was charged with a felony and sued by the family he injured. In November, his attorney arranged for Coleman to plead guilty to a misdemeanor. He was given a one-year suspended sentence, put on probation for three years, fined $1,000 and required to perform 200 hours of community service. Coleman also agreed to make restitution to the family. In the interim, however, Mets co-Owner Fred Wilpon had announced that Coleman would never again wear a Mets uniform despite the year remaining on his contract.

Five days after Torborg got the ax, the Reds engineered the fifth-quickest firing of a first-year manager in baseball history when they discharged Tony Perez and hired Davey Johnson after only 44 games. The Reds were 20-24 under Perez, and they compiled a 53-65 record under his successor.

After the season, two other managers lost their jobs. The Chicago Cubs fired their 10th manager in 10 years when they dismissed Jim Lefebvre despite only their third winning season since 1972. On October 13, the Cubs hired Tom Trebelhorn, a Chicago coach for two years, who had previously managed the Milwaukee Brewers.

Houston hired Terry Collins, who had managed 11 years in the minor leagues, as its new manager November 17. He replaced Art Howe, who had directed the Astros to a third-place finish in the N.L. West.

Owners struggle with issues

Baseball's owners continued to struggle with the various components of what they insist is the game's precarious financial structure. They met throughout the year in an attempt to settle several outstanding problems: to hire a new commissioner, to resolve their differences over increased revenue sharing, to approve a new television package, to expand the playoffs to eight teams and to reach a new collective bargaining agreement that perhaps would incorporate a salary cap with the Major League Baseball Players Association. At year's end, only the television package was in place.

Baseball has been without a commissioner since the forced resignation of Francis T. (Fay) Vincent on September 7, 1992. The Executive Council appointed a search committee January 12 headed by Chairman William C. Bartholomay of Atlanta. The committee, whose other members were Jackie Autry of the Angels, Paul Beeston of the Blue Jays, Douglas Danforth of the Pirates, Fred Kuhlmann of the Cardinals, Carl Pohlad of the Twins, Haywood Sullivan of the Red Sox and the Mets' Wilpon, reported progress periodically. Often the names of prominent individuals in and out of sports were advanced in the press as front-runners. At the end of the year, however, the committee had not yet brought its work to a conclusion.

The need to share revenue from local TV and radio contracts has been advanced for a few years by teams located in so-called small markets. Owners of these teams argue that if teams in large media markets do not consent to share this revenue, baseball's competitive balance will be upset irrevocably and the continued existence of small-market teams will be jeopardized.

Richard Ravitch, president of the Player Relations Committee, urged the owners to link any agreement on revenue sharing to their quest for a salary cap or some other adjustment to the player-compensation system. The owners accepted this viewpoint in February, agreeing with Ravitch, who serves as baseball's chief labor negotiator, that creating more of a common economic interest will help the owners deal more effectively with the players association.

Ravitch formally presented a revenue-sharing proposal to the owners August 10, but the exact details were kept confidential. Endorsement of any revenue-sharing plan would require affirmative votes from 21 of the 28 clubs, and at year's end, no such approval had been given.

Postseason changes proposed

In January, Red Sox President John Harrington, chairman of the schedule-format committee, reported to the owners on surveys that showed fans favorably disposed to expanding the number of teams in postseason play from four to eight. Two months later, the owners took a non-binding vote that approved splitting each league into three divisions, adding a preliminary round of playoffs and perhaps incorporating interleague play into the schedule.

Responding to criticism that expanded playoffs would dilute the importance of the regular season, Bud Selig, chairman of the Executive Council, said, "It's not an excessive number of teams. Anyone who thinks eight teams is excessive is arithmetically incorrect."

Still, it was uncertain whether the owners would opt to support a three-division system that would bring one wild-card team from each league into the first round of the playoffs or retain the two-division system and add second-place finishers to the playoffs. The schedule-format committee studied this question and made a preliminary decision in favor of a two-division plan that would match the first-place team from one division against the second-place team from the other division in each league. After further consideration, the committee recommended instead a proposal to retain the two divisions but omit the crisscross.

On June 17, the owners approved the preliminary playoff round by a 26-2 vote, but left the specific format undecided because of questions about how home games would be assigned. "It would be a disadvantage for the first-place team to play the first two games away," said George Steinbrenner, commenting on an idea putting each division champion at home for the final three games of a preliminary best-of-five series.

Donald Fehr, executive director of the players association, repeatedly warned that no alteration in the playoff system could occur without the union's sanction. On August 23, Fehr announced the union would be inclined to approve a new round of playoff games, but that the players favored realignment of each league into three divisions, with one wild-card team included in the playoff mix.

Perhaps surprisingly, the owners agreed with this idea. On September 9, they voted, 27-1, to split each league into three divisions—East, Central and West—and to match the three division champs and the second-place team with the best won-lost record in a best-of-five first round.

Amid heated discussion about how this arrangement would affect the various pennant races, the owners also agreed to retain a balanced schedule as a means to effect a scheme for realignment that all teams would approve. When the Pittsburgh Pirates consented September 14 to be placed in the N.L. Central and allow the Atlanta Braves to join the N.L. East, the following makeup took shape:

N.L. East: Atlanta, Florida, Montreal, New York, Philadelphia.

N.L. Central: Chicago, Cincinnati, Houston, Pittsburgh, St. Louis.

N.L. West: Colorado, Los Angeles, San Diego, San Francisco.

A.L. East: Baltimore, Boston, Detroit, New York, Toronto.

A.L. Central: Chicago, Cleveland, Kansas City, Milwaukee, Minnesota.

A.L. West: California, Oakland, Seattle, Texas.

Still, at year's end, the owners had not yet obtained approval of the players association, the two sides disagreeing about how revenue from the new round of playoffs should be divided. Basically, the owners wanted to restrict the players to a certain percentage of revenue from the first three games and the union argued for a share of revenue from all games.

Joint television venture

On May 8, Major League Baseball announced a joint venture with NBC and ABC to televise baseball for the next six seasons. Under the agreement, no rights fees will be paid by the networks. Instead, the three parties decided to form a partnership, later named the Baseball Network, to produce and market the telecasts. Baseball will get 87.5 percent of net revenues up to $160 million, with the two networks splitting the rest.

The agreement, approved by an owners conference call May 28, covers the All-Star Game, the 12 weeks of the regular season following the All-Star Game and all postseason play. A June coin flip determined that in 1994 NBC will show the All-Star Game and the League Championship Series and ABC will show the proposed preliminary playoff round and the World Series.

Regular-season telecasts, all of which will be regionalized, will be divided between the networks. ABC will televise a game on the Saturday night following the All-Star Game, followed by two Monday nights and three Saturday nights. NBC will then televise games on six Friday nights.

Under the agreement, born as baseball faced the prospect of declining revenue as a four-year contract with CBS expired, playoff games can be played simultaneously, but may have staggered starting times. World Series weekend games will start no later than 7:20, Eastern time.

In September, baseball reached a separate agreement with ESPN on a six-year, $255 million contract to televise three games per week. ESPN's package will include Wednesday-night doubleheaders and Sunday-night games, the latter including a special season-opening telecast April 3.

Basic Agreement expires

Adding to baseball's turmoil came the expiration of baseball's collective bargaining contract, the Basic Agreement, on December 31. The Player Relations Committee had announced its intention to reopen the agreement in December 1992, one year short of its expiration. Yet, throughout 1993, precious little bargaining took place. Concerned that the owners might implement unilateral changes in the player-compensation system after the expiration of the agreement, Fehr held out the possibility of a player strike sometime during 1993.

When Ravitch confirmed in writing on August 16 that the owners would neither lock the players out during spring training of 1994 nor change the rules governing free agency or salary arbitration, Fehr withdrew the threat of a strike. As the contract expired, meaningful bargaining was not occurring.

Reds owner suspended

On February 3, the Executive Council suspended Marge Schott, principal owner and general partner of the Reds, for making racial and ethnic slurs "indicating an insensitivity that cannot be accepted or tolerated by anyone in baseball." The council unanimously imposed four sanctions on Schott: suspended her for one year, commencing

March 1, 1993; fined her $25,000; directed her to attend and complete a multicultural training program; and reprimanded and censured her in the strongest terms. The council's decision was widely criticized in the media as too lenient.

Schott was ordered not to participate in the day-to-day activities of the club and to refrain from using the owner's box when she attended Reds games until May 1, but she was allowed to keep control of the club and to remain general partner. The council offered her reinstatement effective November 1, 1993, if she complied with the terms of the suspension.

Charges that Schott made racial and anti-Semitic remarks as a matter of course had first been lodged in November 1992, when depositions taken in a lawsuit filed by a former Reds employee were made public. Further allegations came shortly thereafter from Sharon Jones, a former Oakland employee.

On December 1, 1992, the Executive Council appointed a committee composed of N.L. President Bill White, A.L. President Bobby Brown, Jackie Autry and Douglas Danforth to examine the charges. While the investigation was pending, the Rev. Jesse Jackson met with the council to discuss baseball's racial problems. Schott apologized for making "insensitive remarks which I now realize have hurt others." The Reds also adopted an equal employment opportunity program and promoted Darrell Rodgers, an African American, to assistant for baseball operations.

The investigative committee gave its report to Robert Bennett, Schott's attorney, on December 23, and he submitted a response January 20. Both Schott and Bennett appeared before the Executive Council on January 22. Schott served her suspension without serious incident and was reinstated November 1.

The Schott case sparked renewed criticism that baseball was not making sufficient progress in increasing minority participation.

Steinbrenner returns

George Steinbrenner returned to active control of the Yankees on March 1. He originally had been banned for life by Commissioner Francis T. (Fay) Vincent on August 20, 1990, for his involvement with gambler Howard Spira. Following some protracted legal proceedings involving several minority owners of the Yankees, Vincent reduced the ban on July 24, 1992, to a 30-month suspension.

Major league owners voted unanimously by telephone conference call October 3 to approve the sale of the Orioles from Eli Jacobs to a group headed by attorney Peter Angelos. Jacobs was forced to put the team up for sale after he entered personal backruptcy with debts exceeding assets by more than $170 million. The Angelos group—which includes author Tom Clancy, Cincinnati businessman William O. DeWitt Jr., movie

director Barry Levinson, broadcaster Jim McKay and tennis player Pam Shriver—made a successful bid of $173 million, the most ever for a professional sports franchise, at a U.S. Bankrupty Court auction August 2.

On January 12, the owners approved the sale of the Giants from Bob Lurie to a group headed by Peter Magowan for $100 million.

In April, Ewing Kauffman, chairman of the board of the Royals, unveiled a plan to have operating control of the club pass to a board of directors composed of business leaders, civic leaders and philanthropists in order that the Royals stay in Kansas City. Kauffman died August 1, and on August 23, David D. Glass, president and chief executive officer of Wal-Mart Stores Inc., was elected chairman of the board, and Mike Herman, past president and chief operating officer of the Kauffman Foundation, was elected president.

In November, the JRY Corporation, holders of two of the three general-partnership shares of the Red Sox, announced the purchase of the third share from Haywood Sullivan.

The Padres accepted the resignation of their general manager, Joe McIlvaine, on June 9, when it became clear that McIlvaine was not comfortable implementing the plans of Owner Tom Werner to pare the team's payroll drastically. Under McIlvaine, San Diego traded high-salaried players Tony Fernandez, Darrin Jackson and Craig Lefferts. Benito Santiago and Randy Myers were lost through free agency.

Randy Smith, the 30-year-old assistant general manager of the Rockies, replaced McIlvaine and soon traded third baseman Gary Sheffield to the Marlins, McGriff to the Braves and pitchers Bruce Hurst and Greg Harris to the Rockies. McIlvaine returned to the Mets, for whom he had worked previously, as their executive vice president of baseball operations.

A bundle for Fielder

The largest free-agent contract finalized before the season began was signed by Cecil Fielder. He agreed with the Tigers on a five-year deal worth $36 million.

A salary study done by the Associated Press after the season revealed that 273 players made $1 million or more in 1993. The number of players making $3 million or more jumped from 71 in 1992 to 103, and those making at least $5 million rose from five to 13.

Ryne Sandberg of the Cubs topped the salary chart at $6,379,213, followed by two Mets, Bobby Bonilla at $6.2 million and Dwight Gooden at $6,166,667, according to the AP.

The Major League Baseball Players Association calculated the average salary of all players at $1,076,089, up 4.6 percent, the lowest annual percentage increase since 1987.

A total of 118 players filed for salary arbitration

in January. According to the Associated Press, these players increased their average salary from $756,911 in 1992 to $1,586,332 in 1993, a jump of 110 percent. In dollar terms, the average raise of $829,421 was the largest in the 19-year history of arbitration.

Eighteen cases proceeded all the way through the hearing and award stages, with the clubs winning 12 times. The six players who won their cases received an average raise of 174 percent. The 12 who lost got an average increase of 55 percent. The 100 who signed before a hearing settled for an average hike of 113 percent.

Jack McDowell won a salary of $4 million (up from $1.6 million in 1992), and Greg Hibbard got the biggest percentage increase, a 555 percent gain from $210,000 to $1.375 million.

Free-agent signings again made news. First baseman Will Clark signed a five-year, $30 million contract with Texas. Pitcher Sid Fernandez (three years, $9 million) and first baseman Rafael Palmeiro (five years, $30.5 million) both agreed to

terms with the Orioles. Outfielder Otis Nixon became a member of the Red Sox (two years, $7 million), and outfielder Rickey Henderson rejoined Oakland (two years, $8.6 million).

Andres Galarraga re-signed with the Rockies (four years, $12 million), and third baseman Matt Williams remained with the Giants (five years, $30.75 million).

Fans in Cleveland and Texas bade farewell to Cleveland Stadium and Arlington Stadium and looked forward to 1994, when Indians Park and the Ballpark in Arlington are scheduled to open. Donald Fehr, on the other hand, expressed a different view in February: "For the first time," he said, surveying the problems confronting the game, "players have fundamental doubts that the industry as a whole is going to be run very well for the foreseeable future."

Doubts or not, major league baseball endured in 1993 as it has for more than a century. Here's how that season wound up on the field:

FINAL STANDINGS

AMERICAN LEAGUE

EAST DIVISION

Team	Tor.	N.Y.	Det.	Bal.	Bos.	Cle.	Mil.	Chi.	Tex.	K.C.	Sea.	Min.	Cal.	Oak.	W	L	Pct.	GB
Toronto	...	8	7	8	10	9	8	6	5	4	5	10	8	7	95	67	.586	.....
New York	5	...	9	7	7	7	9	8	3	6	7	8	6	6	88	74	.543	7
Detroit	6	4	...	8	7	7	8	5	6	5	7	6	8	8	85	77	.525	10
Baltimore	5	6	5	...	6	8	8	4	4	7	7	8	7	10	85	77	.525	10
Boston	3	6	6	7	...	5	5	7	6	5	7	7	7	9	80	82	.494	15
Cleveland	4	6	6	5	8	...	8	3	7	7	3	4	7	8	76	86	.469	19
Milwaukee	5	4	5	5	8	5	...	3	4	7	4	7	5	7	69	93	.426	26

WEST DIVISION

Team	Chi.	Tex.	K.C.	Sea.	Min.	Cal.	Oak.	Tor.	N.Y.	Det.	Bal.	Bos.	Cle.	Mil.	W	L	Pct.	GB
Chicago	...	8	6	9	10	6	7	6	4	7	8	5	9	9	94	68	.580	.....
Texas	5	...	6	5	6	7	8	7	9	6	8	6	5	8	86	76	.531	8
Kansas City	7	7	...	7	7	7	6	8	6	7	5	7	5	5	84	78	.519	10
Seattle	4	8	6	...	9	7	4	7	5	5	5	5	9	8	82	80	.506	12
Minnesota	3	7	6	4	...	9	8	2	4	6	4	5	8	5	71	91	.438	23
California	7	6	6	6	4	...	6	4	6	4	5	5	5	7	71	91	.438	23
Oakland	6	5	7	9	5	7	...	5	6	4	2	3	4	5	68	94	.420	26

NATIONAL LEAGUE

EAST DIVISION

Team	Phi.	Mon.	St.L.	Chi.	Pit.	Fla.	N.Y.	Atl.	S.F.	Hou.	L.A.	Cin.	Col.	S.D.	W	L	Pct.	GB
Philadelphia	...	7	8	6	7	9	10	6	4	7	10	8	9	6	97	65	.599	.....
Montreal	6	...	7	8	8	9	5	3	7	6	8	9	10		94	68	.580	3
St. Louis	5	6	...	5	9	9	8	6	8	6	6	7	7	5	87	75	.537	10
Chicago	7	5	8	...	5	6	8	5	6	4	7	7	8	8	84	78	.519	13
Pittsburgh	6	5	4	8	...	7	9	5	5	5	4	4	9		75	87	.463	22
Florida	4	5	4	7	6	...	4	5	4	3	5	5	5	7	64	98	.395	33
New York	3	4	5	5	4	9	...	3	4	1	4	6	6	5	59	103	.364	38

WEST DIVISION

Team	Atl.	S.F.	Hou.	L.A.	Cin.	Col.	S.D.	Phi.	Mon.	St.L.	Chi.	Pit.	Fla.	N.Y.	W	L	Pct.	GB
Atlanta	...	7	8	8	10	13	9	6	7	6	7	7	7	9	104	58	.642	.....
San Francisco	6	...	10	6	11	10	10	8	9	4	6	7	8	8	103	59	.636	1
Houston	5	3	...	9	7	2	8	5	5	6	8	7	9	11	85	77	.525	19
Los Angeles	5	7	4	...	8	6	9	2	6	6	5	8	7	8	81	81	.500	23
Cincinnati	3	2	6	5	...	9	9	4	4	5	5	8	7	6	73	89	.451	31
Colorado	0	3	11	7	4	...	6	3	3	5	4	8	7	6	67	95	.414	37
San Diego	4	3	5	4	4	7	...	6	2	7	4	3	5	7	61	101	.377	43

NOTE: Read across for wins, down for losses.

A.L. CHAMPIONSHIP SERIES

GAME 1

HIGHLIGHTS
TORONTO 7, CHICAGO 3

Why the Blue Jays won: Paul Molitor and Ed Sprague picked up where they left off the last time they were in postseason play. Molitor, who hadn't seen postseason action since batting .355 for Milwaukee in the 1982 World Series (in which he had a record five-hit game), stroked a run-scoring single and a two-run home run and collected four hits overall. Sprague, a hero in the 1992 Series when he clubbed a game-winning homer in Game 2 for Toronto, also contributed four hits, including a two-run triple in the fourth inning.

Why the White Sox lost: Jack McDowell, who pitched like Grover Cleveland Alexander while winning 22 games in the regular season, pitched more like Grover Cleveland in the League Championship Series opener. He was hammered for 13 hits and seven runs in 6⅔ innings.

The turning points:

1. John Olerud's double in Toronto's three-run fifth. With the White Sox ahead, 3-2, Olerud, the A.L. batting champion, came up with runners on the corners and two out. He slashed a drive into the gap in right-center, sending Roberto Alomar and Joe Carter across the plate and giving the Blue Jays the lead for good. Molitor followed with a single that scored Olerud.

2. Chicago's inability to take advantage of Toronto starter Juan Guzman's wildness. Guzman walked eight batters and uncorked three wild pitches in his six innings of work, but the Blue Jays' righthander worked out of trouble time and again. He induced the White Sox to leave eight men on base in the first four innings, his Houdini act capped by Ellis Burks' fly-ball out with the bases loaded in Chicago's fourth.

Notable: His troubles aside, Guzman improved his career league-playoff record to 4-0. . . . Deciding that the better part of valor is indeed discretion, Guzman walked Chicago slugger Frank Thomas three times. Then, in the ninth, reliever Duane Ward doled out Thomas' fourth base on balls of the night. Thomas had drilled 41 homers and knocked in 128 runs in the regular season. . . . Chicago Bulls superstar Michael Jordan threw out the ceremonial first ball at Comiskey Park, then stunned the sports world the next day by throwing in the towel as a pro basketball player. Rumors of Jordan's retirement had spread among the media—and into the Comiskey throng—as Game 1 unfolded.

Quotable: "It's nice to be on his side for a change," said Toronto Manager Cito Gaston, alluding to Molitor, who spent 15 seasons with Milwaukee be-

fore signing a free-agent contract with the Blue Jays over the winter. "I've seen those kinds of games from him all year."

BOX SCORE
TUESDAY, OCTOBER 5, AT CHICAGO

Toronto	AB	R	H	RBI	PO	A
Henderson, lf	6	0	0	0	3	0
White, cf	5	0	2	0	2	0
Alomar, 2b	4	1	0	0	4	4
Carter, rf	5	1	2	0	2	0
Olerud, 1b	4	3	3	2	7	0
Molitor, dh	5	2	4	3	0	0
T. Fernandez, ss	5	0	1	0	2	2
Sprague, 3b	5	0	4	2	0	0
Borders, c	5	0	1	0	7	1
Guzman, p	0	0	0	0	0	4
Cox, p	0	0	0	0	0	0
D. Ward, p	0	0	0	0	0	0
Totals	44	7	17	7	27	11

Chicago	AB	R	H	RBI	PO	A
Raines, lf	5	0	2	1	1	0
Cora, 2b	3	0	0	0	4	0
Thomas, dh	1	0	1	0	0	0
Ventura, 3b	3	0	0	0	0	3
Burks, rf	5	0	1	0	3	0
Pasqua, 1b	3	1	0	0	6	1
Johnson, cf	4	1	0	0	3	0
Karkovice, c	3	0	0	0	8	1
Guillen, ss	4	1	2	2	2	4
McDowell, p	0	0	0	0	0	0
DeLeon, p	0	0	0	0	0	0
Radinsky, p	0	0	0	0	0	0
McCaskill, p	0	0	0	0	0	0
Totals	31	3	6	3	27	9

Toronto .... 0 0 0   2 3 0   2 0 0—7
Chicago .... 0 0 0   3 0 0   0 0 0—3

Toronto	IP	H	R	ER	BB	SO
Guzman (W)	6	5	3	2	8	3
Cox	2	1	0	0	0	2
D. Ward	1	0	0	0	2	2

Chicago	IP	H	R	ER	BB	SO
McDowell (L)	6⅔	13	7	7	2	4
DeLeon	1	2	0	0	0	1
Radinsky	⅓	0	0	0	0	1
McCaskill	1	2	0	0	0	2

E—Olerud, Cora. DP—Toronto 1. LOB—Toronto 12, Chicago 13. 2B—Burks, Olerud. 3B—Sprague. HR—Molitor. SB—Guillen, Raines. CS—Raines. SH—Karkovice. HBP—By Guzman (Pasqua). WP—Guzman 3. U—Evans, plate; Kosc, first; Shulock, second; Hendry, third; Tschida, left field; Kaiser, right field. T—3:38. A—46,246.

GAME 2

HIGHLIGHTS
TORONTO 3, CHICAGO 1

Why the Blue Jays won: Veteran righthander Dave Stewart delivered his usual big-game performance, allowing only one run and four hits over six innings. Stewart ran his career League Championship Series record to 7-0, with a 1.99 earned-run average.

Why the White Sox lost: They continued to muff scoring opportunities. Having left 13 men on base in Game 1, the Sox stranded 10 more runners in this contest.

The turning points:

1. Nursing a 3-1 lead, Stewart yielded two singles and a walk in the sixth and faced a bases-loaded, no-out situation. But he proceeded to retire Dan Pasqua on a fly ball, Lance Johnson on a popup and pinch-hitter Warren Newson on a grounder back to the mound. The two-run lead remained intact.

2. After filling the bases with two out in the first inning, Chicago had to settle for one run. The White Sox got that run on a wild pitch before Pasqua struck out with runners on second and third base.

Notable: Toronto's Paul Molitor established a League Championship Series record (for one series) with hits in six consecutive at-bats. After his four-hit spree in Game 1, he rapped a second-inning single and a fourth-inning double off Chicago's Alex Fernandez in Game 2. . . . For the second straight game, Frank Thomas, Chicago's regular first baseman, was used as the designated hitter as Manager Gene Lamont tried to protect the slugger's ailing left arm. While Pasqua subbed for Thomas at first, DH specialists Bo Jackson and George Bell rode the bench. . . . A fourth-inning single extended Toronto catcher Pat Borders' postseason hitting streak to 16 games, one shy of the record set by the Yankees' Hank Bauer in World Series competition in the 1950s.

Quotable: Commenting on his decision to keep Stewart in the game when the 36-year-old pitcher loaded the bases with none out in the sixth, Blue Jays Manager Cito Gaston said: "I can't think of anyone in the bullpen who I would want out there in that situation over him." . . . "Aggressiveness overcomes any fear you have," Stewart said of his response to working in tight spots. . . . Jackson, addressing his and other players' reaction to the White Sox's lineup maneuvering at first base and DH: "We've reached the conclusion that we are one man short (offensively). And it shows." . . . "Personally, I did my job," said the White Sox's Fernandez, who in eight innings allowed only one earned run. Fernandez, just 24 years old, was coming off an 18-9 season in which he fashioned a 3.13 ERA.

BOX SCORE

WEDNESDAY, OCTOBER 6, AT CHICAGO

Toronto	AB	R	H	RBI	PO	A
Henderson, lf	3	1	0	0	3	0
White, cf	4	0	2	0	3	0
Alomar, 2b	4	0	0	1	2	1
Carter, rf	4	0	1	0	1	0
Olerud, 1b	4	0	1	0	4	3
Molitor, dh	4	1	2	0	0	0
T. Fernandez, ss	3	1	1	1	3	1
Sprague, 3b	3	0	0	0	2	1

	AB	R	H	RBI	PO	A
Borders, c	4	0	1	0	7	0
Stewart, p	0	0	0	0	2	0
Leiter, p	0	0	0	0	0	0
D. Ward, p	0	0	0	0	0	0
Totals	33	3	8	2	27	6

Chicago	AB	R	H	RBI	PO	A
Raines, lf	4	1	1	0	0	1
Cora, 2b	5	0	0	0	2	9
Thomas, dh	3	0	2	0	0	0
Ventura, 3b-1b	3	0	1	0	4	0
Burks, rf	2	0	0	0	1	0
Pasqua, 1b	3	0	0	0	7	1
Grebeck, ph-3b	1	0	1	0	0	0
Johnson, cf	4	0	1	0	3	0
Karkovice, c	1	0	0	0	3	0
Newson, ph	1	0	0	0	0	0
LaValliere, c	1	0	1	0	2	0
Guillen, ss	4	0	0	0	4	5
A. Fernandez, p	0	0	0	0	1	0
Hernandez, p	0	0	0	0	0	0
Totals	32	1	7	0	27	16

Toronto	1 0 0	2 0 0	0 0 0	— 3
Chicago	1 0 0	0 0 0	0 0 0	— 1

Toronto	IP	H	R	ER	BB	SO
Stewart (W)	6	4	1	1	4	5
Leiter	2	2	0	0	1	2
D. Ward (S)	1	1	0	0	0	0

Chicago	IP	H	R	ER	BB	SO
A. Fernandez (L)	8	8	3	1	3	5
Hernandez	1	0	0	0	0	0

E—Pasqua, Cora. DP—Chicago 2, Toronto 1. LOB—Toronto 6, Chicago 10. 2B—Johnson, Molitor. SH—Karkovice. WP—Stewart. U—Kosc, plate; Shulock, first; Hendry, second; Tschida, third; Kaiser, left field; Evans, right field. T—3:00. A—46,101.

GAME 3

HIGHLIGHTS

CHICAGO 6, TORONTO 1

Why the White Sox won: They sent lefthander Wilson Alvarez to the mound against a Toronto team that had compiled a losing record against lefthanded pitching (23-27) in 1993—and Alvarez gave the Sox the lift they needed. Alvarez, who put together a 15-8 regular-season mark and had a glittering earned-run average of 2.95, tossed a complete-game seven-hitter. Six of the hits he allowed were singles.

Why the Blue Jays lost: Toronto staff ace Pat Hentgen, a 19-game winner in '93, proved no mystery to the White Sox. He was rocked for nine hits and six runs in three-plus innings. Getting roughed up at SkyDome was nothing new for Hentgen, who had posted a 7-6 record and 4.77 ERA at the Blue Jays' home park in '93 compared with 12-3 and 2.91 figures away from the dome.

The turning points:

1. Moaning over the lack of two-out hits in this series, Chicago got five such hits and two walks in the third inning. The result was a five-run salvo that featured two-run singles by Ellis Burks and Lance Johnson.

2. The White Sox's ability to get to starter Hent-

gen. Against Toronto relievers Danny Cox, Mark Eichhorn and Tony Castillo, Chicago collected three hits and no runs in six innings.

Notable: Chicago won Game 3 despite another sizable left-on-base total (10). . . . The White Sox's Bo Jackson, who had expressed considerable displeasure over his bench-warming role in Games 1 and 2, got an opportunity to show what he could do. Serving as Chicago's designated hitter (as Frank Thomas returned to first base), Jackson went 0-for-4 and struck out three times. . . . Toronto's Pat Borders saw his postseason hitting streak stopped at 16 games. . . . The best road team in the American League at 49-32 in '93, the White Sox showed that SkyDome was just the tonic they needed to cure—or at least alleviate—their playoff ills. . . . Chicago's outfield accounted for eight of the team's 12 hits, with Tim Raines leading the way with two doubles and two singles.

Quotable: The victory was a big one for the White Sox, and no one enjoyed it more than right fielder Burks. As a member of the Boston Red Sox in 1988 and 1990 championship-series play, Burks played on teams that compiled a record of 0-8. After the first two games of the '93 A.L. playoffs, Burks' teams had a 0-10 postseason mark. "Yeah, it's great to get the monkey off my back," Burks said. "It was a long time. Thought it would never happen."

| | | BOX SCORE | | |

FRIDAY, OCTOBER 8, AT TORONTO

Chicago	AB	R	H	RBI	PO	A
Raines, lf	5	1	4	0	4	0
Cora, 2b	3	1	2	0	3	3
Thomas, 1b	3	1	1	1	7	1
Ventura, 3b	2	1	0	1	0	1
Burks, rf	5	1	2	2	4	0
Jackson, dh	4	0	0	0	0	0
Johnson, cf	5	0	2	2	1	0
Karkovice, c	4	0	0	0	6	0
Guillen, ss	4	1	1	0	2	1
Alvarez, p	0	0	0	0	0	2
Totals	35	6	12	6	27	7

Toronto	AB	R	H	RBI	PO	A
Henderson, lf	3	1	1	0	0	0
White, cf	4	0	1	1	3	0
Molitor, dh	4	0	1	0	0	0
Carter, rf	4	0	0	0	1	0
Olerud, 1b	4	0	2	0	14	1
Alomar, 2b	3	0	1	0	0	4
T. Fernandez, ss	3	0	1	0	2	1
Sprague, 3b	3	0	0	0	0	4
Borders, c	3	0	0	0	6	3
Hentgen, p	0	0	0	0	1	0
Cox, p	0	0	0	0	0	1
Eichhorn, p	0	0	0	0	0	0
Castillo, p	0	0	0	0	0	1
Totals	31	1	7	1	27	15

Chicago			0 0 5	1 0 0	0 0 0—6
Toronto			0 0 1	0 0 0	0 0 0—1

Chicago	IP	H	R	ER	BB	SO
Alvarez (W)	9	7	1	1	2	6

Toronto	IP	H	R	ER	BB	SO
Hentgen (L)	*3	9	6	6	2	3
Cox	3	2	0	0	2	3
Eichhorn	2	1	0	0	1	1
Castillo	1	0	0	0	0	1

*Pitched to two batters in fourth.

E—Henderson. DP—Chicago 2, Toronto 1. LOB—Chicago 10, Toronto 5. 2B—Raines 2, Henderson. SB—Johnson, Henderson. CS—Burks, White. SH—Cora. SF—Ventura. U—Shulock, plate; Hendry, first; Tschida, second; Kaiser, third; Evans, left field; Kosc, right field. T—2:56. A—51,783.

	GAME 4	

| | HIGHLIGHTS | |

CHICAGO 7, TORONTO 4

Why the White Sox won: Fleet center fielder Lance Johnson did what comes naturally—and what doesn't—as Chicago deadlocked the playoffs at two victories apiece. With two on, two out and the score tied 3-3 in the sixth inning, Johnson, the A.L. leader in triples in 1991, 1992 and 1993, tripled to right-center to give Chicago a lead it never relinquished. In the second inning—to the surprise of almost everyone—he had cracked a home run, a two-run shot, off Todd Stottlemyre. Johnson had not homered in 540 regular-season at-bats.

Why the Blue Jays lost: Stottlemyre, not one of Toronto's front-line starters (he went 11-12 in '93 with a 4.84 ERA and allowed 204 hits in 176⅔ innings), simply wasn't up to the task. Besides allowing Johnson's triple and homer that netted four runs, he also yielded a homer to Frank Thomas in his six innings of work.

The turning points:

1. Tim Belcher's strong performance while working in relief of Jason Bere, Chicago's 22-year-old starter who had been a regular-season phenom with a 12-5 record. Belcher came on with one out in the Toronto third—the Blue Jays had cuffed Bere for three runs in that inning—and snuffed out the fire. Over 3⅔ innings, Belcher allowed one run and three hits. He was credited with the victory.

2. After Stottlemyre allowed Chicago to seize a 5-3 lead, Blue Jay relievers Al Leiter and Mike Timlin couldn't keep Toronto in the game. They permitted a total of two runs and five hits in three innings.

Notable: White Sox leadoff hitter Tim Raines rapped three singles and stretched his series hit total to 10 over four games. Johnson boosted his RBI total to six.

Quotable: "I try to hit triples," Johnson said. "If I was going to go out and try to hit home runs, I'd hit seven or eight a year and be out of the game in two years. So, I hit my home runs in batting practice and catch one every now and then in a game." Johnson's career homer total in 2,599 at-bats: four. . . . White Sox Manager Gene Lamont, commenting on the early hook for Bere: "During the (regular) season, I probably wouldn't have gone

— 188 —

to a reliever, but in the playoffs—trying to get even—I thought it was the thing to do." ... While disappointed in the consecutive losses to Chicago at SkyDome, Toronto Manager Cito Gaston was keeping his cool. "Nobody said this was going to be easy," Gaston said. "I said before the series I thought these teams were pretty well matched. So, it's even. It's not like it's the end of the world."

Chicago	AB	R	H	RBI	PO	A
Raines, lf	5	1	3	0	3	1
Cora, 2b	5	0	1	1	2	3
Thomas, 1b	3	1	1	1	7	0
Ventura, 3b	5	0	2	1	2	2
Burks, rf	4	2	1	0	3	0
Jackson, dh	2	1	0	0	0	0
Johnson, cf	4	1	2	4	3	0
Karkovice, c	4	0	0	0	6	0
Guillen, ss	4	1	1	0	0	1
Bere, p	0	0	0	0	0	0
Belcher, p	0	0	0	0	1	1
McCaskill, p	0	0	0	0	0	0
Radinsky, p	0	0	0	0	0	0
Hernandez, p	0	0	0	0	0	0
Totals	36	7	11	7	27	8
Toronto	**AB**	**R**	**H**	**RBI**	**PO**	**A**
Henderson, lf	3	1	0	0	1	0
White, cf	4	1	2	0	3	0
Alomar, 2b	5	1	2	2	4	2
Carter, rf	4	0	2	2	2	1
Olerud, 1b	4	0	0	0	7	0
Molitor, dh	4	0	0	0	0	0
T. Fernandez, ss	3	0	2	0	1	3
Sprague, 3b	4	0	0	0	0	2
Borders, c	4	1	1	0	6	0
Stottlemyre, p	0	0	0	0	2	0
Leiter, p	0	0	0	0	0	0
Timlin, p	0	0	0	0	1	1
Totals	35	4	9	4	27	11

Chicago .... 0 2 0   0 0 3   1 0 1—7
Toronto .... 0 0 3   0 0 1   0 0 0—4

Chicago	IP	H	R	ER	BB	SO
Bere	2⅓	5	3	3	2	3
Belcher (W)	3⅔	3	1	1	3	1
McCaskill	1⅓	1	0	0	1	1
Radinsky	⅔	0	0	0	0	0
Hernandez (S)	1	0	0	0	0	0
Toronto	**IP**	**H**	**R**	**ER**	**BB**	**SO**
Stottlemyre (L)	6	6	5	5	4	4
Leiter	⅔	2	1	1	1	0
Timlin	2⅓	3	1	1	0	2

DP—Toronto 1. LOB—Chicago 7, Toronto 11. 2B—Alomar. 3B—Johnson, White. HR—Thomas, Johnson. HBP—By Bere (Olerud). WP—Belcher. Balk—Stottlemyre. U—Hendry, plate; Tschida, first; Kaiser, second; Evans, third; Kosc, left field; Shulock, right field. T—3:30. A—51,889.

TORONTO 5, CHICAGO 3

Why the Blue Jays won: Righthander Juan Guzman was as effective in Game 5 as he was ineffective in Game 1—and he came out a winner in both in-

stances. After an eight-walk performance in the opener, Guzman settled down in this game and allowed only one base on balls and three hits over seven innings.

Why the White Sox lost: Jack McDowell pitched about like he did in Game 1—in other words, terribly. This time, he gave up five hits, three walks and three runs in only 2⅓ innings—meaning that in nine innings of work in the 1993 A.L. playoffs he had been rocked for 18 hits and 10 runs. Also, Chicago's offense pretty much shot blanks until the ninth, when the White Sox made a too-little, too-late run.

The turning points:

1. Toronto's offense, while hardly potent, was pesky. The Blue Jays notched single runs in each of the first four innings and collected their final run in the seventh on a base hit by Ed Sprague, who earlier in the game had contributed a sacrifice fly. Roberto Alomar went 3-for-3 with one RBI and one run scored, while Paul Molitor scored twice.

2. Toronto reliever Duane Ward's ability to extricate himself from a jam in the ninth. Entering the inning with a 5-1 lead to protect, Ward yielded a two-run homer to Robin Ventura and hit Ellis Burks with a two-out pitch. With the potential tying run at the plate in the person of Bo Jackson, Ward proceeded to strike out Chicago's DH, who was now 0-for-10 in the series with six strikeouts.

Notable: Guzman retired the first 13 batters he faced, then allowed a home run by Burks. ... White Sox catcher Ron Karkovice was 0-for-14 with six strikeouts after five games. ... Toronto stole five bases in Game 5, three of them by Alomar, who had 55 steals during the regular season. ... Besides his game-ending strikeout against Ward with a man on base, Jackson also fanned with two men on and two out in the seventh when Chicago trailed by a 4-1 score. Guzman got Jackson that time.

Quotable: Jackson, who had voiced unhappiness over being benched for Games 1 and 2, said he was "frustrated at the last at-bat, that's all. I don't have any excuses. I fouled off a few pitches I should have hit on the button." Jackson also insisted that the "one man short" remark attributed to him earlier in the series was merely a case of "repeating what someone else said." ... McDowell said his money pitch, the split-fingered fastball, simply wasn't doing what it did in the regular season. "It's not really mechanics," he said. "It's one of those things that comes and goes."

Chicago	AB	R	H	RBI	PO	A
Raines, lf	4	1	1	0	3	0
Cora, 2b	3	0	0	0	2	2
Thomas, 1b	4	0	0	0	5	1
Ventura, 3b	4	1	1	2	1	1
Burks, rf	3	1	2	1	2	0

	AB	R	H	RBI	PO	A
Jackson, dh	4	0	0	0	0	0
Johnson, cf	3	0	0	0	0	0
Karkovice, c	2	0	0	0	7	1
Guillen, ss	3	0	1	0	4	1
McDowell, p	0	0	0	0	0	1
DeLeon, p	0	0	0	0	0	0
Radinsky, p	0	0	0	0	0	0
Hernandez, p	0	0	0	0	0	0
Totals	30	3	5	3	24	7

Toronto	AB	R	H	RBI	PO	A
Henderson, lf	5	1	2	0	0	0
White, cf	5	1	2	0	3	0
Alomar, 2b	3	1	3	1	2	4
Carter, rf	5	0	1	0	2	0
Olerud, 1b	3	0	1	1	8	2
Molitor, dh	3	2	1	0	0	0
T. Fernandez, ss	4	0	2	0	2	1
Sprague, 3b	3	0	1	2	1	0
Borders, c	4	0	1	0	9	0
Guzman, p	0	0	0	0	0	0
Castillo, p	0	0	0	0	0	0
D. Ward, p	0	0	0	0	0	0
Totals	35	5	14	4	27	7

Chicago	0 0 0	0 1 0	0 0 2—3
Toronto	1 1 1	1 0 0	1 0 x—5

Chicago	IP	H	R	ER	BB	SO
McDowell (L)	2⅓	5	3	3	3	1
DeLeon	3⅔	5	1	1	1	5
Radinsky	⅓	1	1	1	1	0
Hernandez	1⅔	3	0	0	0	1

Toronto	IP	H	R	ER	BB	SO
Guzman (W)	7	3	1	1	1	6
Castillo	1	0	0	0	1	0
D. Ward	1	2	2	2	0	3

E—McDowell. DP—Chicago 1, Toronto 2. LOB—Chicago 3, Toronto 12. 2B—Henderson, White, Molitor. HR—Burks, Ventura. SB—Henderson, Alomar 3, Borders. CS—Henderson. SF—Sprague. HBP—By D. Ward (Burks). WP—McDowell. U—Tschida, plate; Kaiser, first; Evans, second; Kosc, third; Shulock, left field; Hendry, right field. T—3:09. A—51,375.

GAME 6

HIGHLIGHTS

TORONTO 6, CHICAGO 3

Why the Blue Jays won: Big-game pitcher Dave Stewart delivered the goods. Again. Allowing only four hits and two runs over 7⅓ innings, he improved his career League Championship Series record to 8-0 in 10 starts (his team also won his two no-decision games). Catcher Pat Borders, a .355 hitter in 18 postseason games entering this series, went 2-for-4 and drove home three of the Blue Jays' runs. He rapped a bases-loaded single in the second inning, putting Toronto ahead 2-0, and then collected an RBI in the fourth on a force-out grounder.

Why the White Sox lost: They unraveled defensively, committing three errors that led to three unearned runs, and couldn't exploit a bases-full situation in the third into a big inning—even with heavy hitters Frank Thomas and Robin Ventura coming up.

The turning points:

1. With the outcome still in doubt going into the

ninth inning—Toronto was clinging to a 3-2 lead—Devon White provided the Jays with an insurance run when he homered off Scott Radinsky. It was the 12th hit of the series for White. Paul Molitor put the game virtually out of reach later in the ninth when he stroked a two-run triple.

2. After filling the bases with one out in the third, Chicago got only two runs—courtesy of a walk to Thomas and a grounder by Ventura. While the White Sox tied the game at 2-2, the inning seemed more like a lost opportunity.

Notable: The triumph was Stewart's fourth pennant-clinching victory in six seasons. . . . Chicago starter Alex Fernandez, a tough-luck loser in Game 2, pitched well once again. He allowed only two earned runs and seven hits over seven innings. In his two playoff appearances, Fernandez posted a record of 0-2 but had an ERA of 1.80. . . . The White Sox's World Series drought continued. The Sox haven't played in the fall classic since 1959—and they haven't won the Series since 1917. Toronto, meanwhile, would be making its second straight Series appearance.

Quotable: Thomas, responding to the bases-loaded walk he received from Stewart: "Walking me there, I thought it was pretty smart. I wasn't going to let those men stay on base. Instead of getting two runs that inning (the third), we should have had three or four." . . . "I'm living a childhood dream as an adult playing a child's game," said Stewart, alluding to his gaudy record in the A.L. playoffs over the years. . . . Chicago's Tim Raines, on the fact his team lost all three games played at Comiskey Park: "When you have a team of 25 guys and nothing works at home, it's just frustrating to take. If it was one or two or three guys, you could understand. But it was the whole ball club."

BOX SCORE

TUESDAY, OCTOBER 12, AT CHICAGO

Toronto	AB	R	H	RBI	PO	A
Henderson, lf	5	0	0	0	2	0
White, cf	5	1	3	1	1	0
Alomar, 2b	5	0	1	0	2	4
Carter, rf	5	1	1	0	4	0
Olerud, 1b	4	2	1	0	8	1
Molitor, dh	3	2	1	2	0	0
T. Fernandez, ss	4	0	1	0	2	0
Sprague, 3b	3	0	1	0	2	2
Borders, c	4	0	2	3	6	0
Stewart, p	0	0	0	0	0	0
D. Ward, p	0	0	0	0	0	0
Totals	38	6	10	6	27	7

Chicago	AB	R	H	RBI	PO	A
Raines, lf	4	1	1	0	1	0
Cora, 2b	3	0	0	0	5	3
Thomas, 1b	3	0	1	1	5	1
Ventura, 3b	3	0	0	1	2	0
Burks, rf	4	0	1	0	2	0
Newson, dh	4	1	1	1	0	0
Johnson, cf	3	0	0	0	5	0
LaValliere, c	2	0	0	0	6	0
Karkovice, pr-c	1	0	0	0	0	0
Guillen, ss	3	1	1	0	0	2
A. Fernandez, p	0	0	0	0	1	1

	AB	R	H	RBI	PO	A
McCaskill, p	0	0	0	0	0	2
Radinsky, p	0	0	0	0	0	0
Hernandez, p	0	0	0	0	0	0
Totals	30	3	5	3	27	9

Chicago	IP	H	R	ER	BB	SO
A. Fernandez (L)	7	7	3	2	3	5
McCaskill	1⅓	0	0	0	0	0
Radinsky	⅓	2	3	1	0	0
Hernandez	⅓	1	0	0	0	0

Toronto .... 0 2 0 1 0 0 0 0 3—6
Chicago .... 0 0 2 0 0 0 0 0 1—3

Toronto	IP	H	R	ER	BB	SO
Stewart (W)	7⅓	4	2	2	4	3
D. Ward (S)	1⅔	1	1	1	1	3

E—Cora, Ventura, Radinsky. DP—Toronto 1. LOB—Toronto 10, Chicago 7. 2B—Borders, Guillen. 3B—Molitor. HR—White, Newson. SB—Alomar. SH—T. Fernandez, Guillen. HBP—By Stewart (Cora), by A. Fernandez (Molitor). WP—Stewart. U—Kaiser, plate; Evans, first; Kosc, second; Shulock, third; Hendry, left field; Tschida, right field. T—3:31. A—45,527.

STATISTICS

TORONTO BLUE JAYS' BATTING AND FIELDING AVERAGES

Player, position	G	AB	R	H	TB	2B	3B	HR	RBI	BB	IBB	SO	Avg.	PO	A	E	Avg.
White, cf	6	27	3	12	18	1	1	1	2	1	0	5	.444	15	0	0	1.000
Molitor, dh	6	23	7	9	16	2	1	1	5	3	1	3	.391	0	0	0	.000
Olerud, 1b	6	23	5	8	9	1	0	0	3	4	0	1	.348	48	9	1	.983
T. Fernandez, ss	6	22	1	7	7	0	0	0	1	2	2	4	.318	12	8	0	1.000
Alomar, 2b	6	24	3	7	8	1	0	0	4	4	0	3	.292	14	19	0	1.000
Sprague, 3b	6	21	0	6	8	0	1	0	4	2	1	4	.286	5	9	0	1.000
Carter, rf	6	27	2	7	7	0	0	0	2	1	0	5	.259	12	1	0	1.000
Borders, c	6	24	1	6	7	1	0	0	3	0	0	6	.250	41	4	0	1.000
Henderson, lf	6	25	4	3	5	2	0	0	0	4	0	5	.120	9	0	1	.900
Castillo, p	2	0	0	0	0	0	0	0	0	0	0	0	.000	0	1	0	1.000
Cox, p	2	0	0	0	0	0	0	0	0	0	0	0	.000	0	1	0	1.000
Eichhorn, p	1	0	0	0	0	0	0	0	0	0	0	0	.000	0	0	0	.000
Guzman, p	2	0	0	0	0	0	0	0	0	0	0	0	.000	0	4	0	1.000
Hentgen, p	1	0	0	0	0	0	0	0	0	0	0	0	.000	1	0	0	1.000
Leiter, p	2	0	0	0	0	0	0	0	0	0	0	0	.000	0	0	0	.000
Stewart, p	2	0	0	0	0	0	0	0	0	0	0	0	.000	2	0	0	1.000
Stottlemyre, p	1	0	0	0	0	0	0	0	0	0	0	0	.000	2	0	0	1.000
Timlin, p	1	0	0	0	0	0	0	0	0	0	0	0	.000	1	1	0	1.000
D. Ward, p	4	0	0	0	0	0	0	0	0	0	0	0	.000	0	0	0	.000
Totals	6	216	26	65	85	8	3	2	24	21	4	36	.301	162	57	2	.991

CHICAGO WHITE SOX' BATTING AND FIELDING AVERAGES

Player, position	G	AB	R	H	TB	2B	3B	HR	RBI	BB	IBB	SO	Avg.	PO	A	E	Avg.
Grebeck, ph-3b	1	1	0	1	1	0	0	0	0	0	0	0	1.000	0	0	0	.000
Raines, lf	6	27	5	12	14	2	0	0	1	2	0	2	.444	12	2	0	1.000
Thomas, dh - 1b	6	17	2	6	9	0	0	1	3	10	2	5	.353	24	3	0	1.000
LaValliere, c	2	3	0	1	1	0	0	0	0	1	0	0	.333	8	0	0	1.000
Burks, rf	6	23	4	7	11	1	0	1	3	3	0	5	.304	15	0	0	1.000
Guillen, ss	6	22	4	6	7	1	0	0	2	0	0	2	.273	12	14	0	1.000
Johnson, cf	6	23	2	5	11	1	1	1	6	2	0	1	.217	15	0	0	1.000
Ventura, 3b - 1b	6	20	2	4	7	0	0	1	5	6	2	6	.200	9	6	1	.938
Newson, ph-dh	2	5	1	1	4	0	0	1	1	0	0	1	.200	0	0	0	.000
Cora, 2b	6	22	1	3	3	0	0	0	1	3	0	6	.136	18	20	3	.927
Alvarez, p	1	0	0	0	0	0	0	0	0	0	0	0	.000	0	2	0	1.000
Belcher, p	1	0	0	0	0	0	0	0	0	0	0	0	.000	1	1	0	1.000
Bere, p	1	0	0	0	0	0	0	0	0	0	0	0	.000	0	0	0	.000
DeLeon, p	2	0	0	0	0	0	0	0	0	0	0	0	.000	0	0	0	.000
A. Fernandez, p	2	0	0	0	0	0	0	0	0	0	0	0	.000	2	1	0	1.000
Hernandez, p	4	0	0	0	0	0	0	0	0	0	0	0	.000	0	0	0	.000
McCaskill, p	3	0	0	0	0	0	0	0	0	0	0	0	.000	0	2	0	1.000
McDowell, p	2	0	0	0	0	0	0	0	0	0	0	0	.000	0	1	1	.500
Radinsky, p	4	0	0	0	0	0	0	0	0	0	0	0	.000	0	0	1	.000
Pasqua, 1b	2	6	1	0	0	0	0	0	0	1	0	2	.000	13	2	1	.938
Jackson, dh	3	10	1	0	0	0	0	0	0	3	0	6	.000	0	0	0	.000
Karkovice, c-pr	6	15	0	0	0	0	0	0	0	1	0	7	.000	30	2	0	1.000
Totals	6	194	23	46	68	5	1	5	22	32	4	43	.237	159	56	7	.968

TORONTO BLUE JAYS' PITCHING RECORDS

Pitcher	G	GS	CG	IP	H	R	ER	HR	BB	IBB	SO	HB	WP	W	L	Pct.	ERA
Cox	2	0	0	5	3	0	0	0	2	2	5	0	0	0	0	.000	0.00
Castillo	2	0	0	2	0	0	0	1	0	1	0	0	0	0	0	.000	0.00
Eichhorn	1	0	0	2	1	0	0	0	1	0	1	0	0	0	0	.000	0.00
Stewart	2	2	0	13⅓	8	3	3	0	8	0	8	1	2	2	0	1.000	2.03
Guzman	2	2	0	13	8	4	3	1	9	1	9	1	3	2	0	1.000	2.08

Pitcher	G	GS	CG	IP	H	R	ER	HR	BB	IBB	SO	HB	WP	W	L	Pct.	ERA
Leiter	2	0	0	2⅔	4	1	1	0	2	1	2	0	0	0	0	.000	3.38
Timlin	1	0	0	2⅓	3	1	1	0	0	0	2	0	0	0	0	.000	3.86
D. Ward	4	0	0	4⅔	4	3	3	2	3	0	8	1	0	0	0	.000	5.79
Stottlemyre	1	1	0	6	6	5	5	2	4	0	4	0	0	0	1	.000	7.50
Hentgen	1	1	0	3	9	6	6	0	2	0	3	0	0	0	1	.000	18.00
Totals	6	6	0	54	46	23	22	5	32	4	43	3	5	4	2	.667	3.67

No shutouts. Saves—Ward 2.

CHICAGO WHITE SOX' PITCHING RECORDS

Pitcher	G	GS	CG	IP	H	R	ER	HR	BB	IBB	SO	HB	WP	W	L	Pct.	ERA
Hernandez	4	0	0	4	4	0	0	0	0	0	1	0	0	0	0	.000	0.00
McCaskill	3	0	0	3⅔	3	0	0	0	1	0	3	0	0	0	0	.000	0.00
Alvarez	1	1	1	9	7	1	1	0	2	0	6	0	0	1	0	1.000	1.00
A. Fernandez	2	2	0	15	15	6	3	0	6	3	10	1	0	0	2	.000	1.80
DeLeon	2	0	0	4⅔	7	1	1	0	1	0	6	0	0	0	0	.000	1.93
Belcher	1	0	0	3⅔	3	1	1	0	3	1	1	0	1	1	0	1.000	2.45
McDowell	2	2	0	9	18	10	10	1	5	0	5	0	1	0	2	.000	10.00
Radinsky	4	0	0	1⅔	3	4	2	1	1	0	1	0	0	0	0	.000	10.80
Bere	1	1	0	2⅓	5	3	3	0	2	0	3	1	0	0	0	.000	11.57
Totals	6	6	1	53	65	26	21	2	21	4	36	2	2	2	4	.333	3.57

No shutouts. Save—Hernandez.

COMPOSITE SCORE BY INNINGS

Toronto	2	3	5	6	3	1	3	0	3—26
Chicago	1	2	7	4	1	3	1	0	4—23

MISCELLANEOUS STATISTICS

Sacrifice hits—Cora 2, Karkovice 2, T. Fernandez, Guillen.
Sacrifice flies—Sprague, Ventura.
Stolen bases—Alomar 4, Henderson 2, Borders, Guillen, Johnson, Raines.
Caught stealing—Burks, Henderson, Raines, White.
Double plays—Guillen and Thomas 2; T. Fernandez, Alomar and Olerud; Alomar, T. Fernandez and Olerud; Pasqua, Guillen and A. Fernandez; Cora, Guillen and Pasqua; Borders and T. Fernandez; Alvarez, Cora and Thomas; Sprague, Alomar and Olerud; Alomar and Olerud; Olerud and T. Fernandez; Alomar and T. Fernandez.
Left on bases—Toronto 12, 6, 5, 11, 12, 10—56; Chicago 13, 10, 10, 7, 3, 7—50.
Hit by pitcher—By Guzman (Pasqua), by Bere (Olerud), by D. Ward (Burks), by Stewart (Cora), by A. Fernandez (Molitor).
Passed balls—None.
Balks—Stottlemyre.
Time of games—First game, 3:38; second game, 3:00; third game, 2:56; fourth game, 3:30; fifth game, 3:09; sixth game, 3:31.
Attendance—First game, 46,246; second game, 46,101; third game, 51,783; fourth game, 51,889; fifth game, 51,375; sixth game, 45,527.
Umpires—Evans, Kosc, Shulock, Hendry, Tschida and Kaiser.
Official scorers—Neil MacCarl, Toronto official scorer; Bob Rosenberg, Chicago White Sox official scorer.

N.L. CHAMPIONSHIP SERIES

HIGHLIGHTS

PHILADELPHIA 4, ATLANTA 3

Why the Phillies won: Reserve infielder Kim Batiste proved he could take as well as give away. Inserted into the game at third base for defensive purposes, the Phils' Batiste threw away a potential double-play ball in the ninth inning, an error that helped the Braves tie the score at 3-3 on Otis Nixon's groundout. But in the bottom of the 10th, Batiste followed John Kruk's one-out double with a game-winning single down the third-base line.

Why the Braves lost: Their big offensive guns—Ron Gant, Fred McGriff, David Justice and Terry Pendleton—were held in check by righthander Curt Schilling, who was coming off a 16-7 season. Schilling struck out the first five batters he faced, a League Championship Series record, and fanned 10 batters in his eight innings of work.

The turning points:

1. Mitch Williams, pitching his second inning in relief of Schilling, struck out Tony Tarasco with two men in scoring position in the top of the 10th to keep the game deadlocked at 3-3. Williams had allowed two-out hits to Pendleton (a single) and Greg Olson (a double).

2. Batiste's ability to keep his cool after his defensive lapse. Even veteran players have been known to let their fielding affect their hitting, but the 25-year-old Batiste proved unflinching in a pressure-packed situation.

Notable: The Phils, who finished last in the National League East in 1992, took step one in their quest to become the first East champions to win the N.L. playoffs since St. Louis defeated San Francisco in 1987. ... Before Game 1, the last time Williams had appeared in postseason play was in 1989 when, as a member of the Cubs, he yielded a pennant-deciding hit to the Giants' Will Clark in the eighth inning of Game 5 of the N.L. playoffs.

Quotable: "I was just hoping I would get a chance to redeem myself," said Batiste, who had been a tough out in the regular season (he batted .282 in part-time duty). "I was really thinking about it before I went to the plate. There was so much encouragement from the bench. I couldn't have felt better." ... Kruk, on Schilling's stellar effort: "We're expected to score runs. We're not known for defense or pitching. It would have been demoralizing (to lose) because we don't expect to get games pitched like that." ... "Schilling never really throws you a nice fat one," said McGriff, the slugging first baseman whom the Braves obtained from San Diego in mid-July. "He's always inside, outside, up and down. It's tough to really zone in." ... Schilling, on his response to Manager Jim

Fregosi's decision to go to the bullpen in the ninth: "I couldn't have argued any harder to get out of the electric chair than I argued to stay in that game."

BOX SCORE

WEDNESDAY, OCTOBER 6, AT PHILADELPHIA

Atlanta	AB	R	H	RBI	PO	A
Nixon, cf	4	0	2	2	2	0
Blauser, ss	4	0	0	0	1	1
Gant, lf	4	1	1	0	0	1
McMichael, p	0	0	0	0	0	1
McGriff, 1b	5	0	1	0	10	0
Justice, rf	4	0	0	1	3	0
Pendleton, 3b	5	0	1	0	3	2
Berryhill, c	3	0	0	0	8	0
Pecota, ph	0	1	0	0	0	0
Olson, c	1	0	1	0	0	0
Lemke, 2b	4	0	1	0	1	6
Tarasco, pr-lf	1	0	0	0	0	0
Avery, p	2	1	2	0	0	0
Sanders, ph	1	0	0	0	0	0
Mercker, p	0	0	0	0	0	0
Belliard, ph-2b	0	0	0	0	0	0
Totals	38	3	9	3	28	11

Philadelphia	AB	R	H	RBI	PO	A
Dykstra, cf	4	1	1	0	3	0
Duncan, 2b	5	0	1	0	3	0
Kruk, 1b	4	2	1	1	4	1
Hollins, 3b	4	0	1	0	2	1
Batiste, 3b	1	0	1	1	0	0
Daulton, c	3	0	0	0	12	0
Incaviglia, lf	4	1	2	1	3	0
Thompson, pr-lf	0	0	0	0	1	0
Chamberlain, rf	3	0	2	0	0	0
Mit. Williams, p	0	0	0	0	0	0
Stocker, ss	3	0	0	0	2	3
Schilling, p	3	0	0	0	0	0
Eisenreich, rf	1	0	0	0	0	0
Totals	35	4	9	3	30	5

```
Atlanta ........................... 0 0 1   1 0 0   0 0 1   0—3
Philadelphia ..................... 1 0 0   1 0 1   0 0 0   1—4
```

One out when winning run scored.

Atlanta	IP	H	R	ER	BB	SO
Avery	6	5	3	3	4	5
Mercker	2	2	0	0	1	2
McMichael (L)	1⅓	2	1	1	0	0

Philadelphia	IP	H	R	ER	BB	SO
Schilling	8	7	2	2	2	10
Mit. Williams (W)	2	2	1	0	2	2

E—Batiste. DP—Atlanta 1. LOB—Atlanta 11, Philadelphia 8. 2B—Nixon, Olson, Avery, Dykstra, Kruk, Hollins, Chamberlain 2. HR—Incaviglia. SH—Belliard. SF—Justice. WP—Avery. U—Froemming, plate; Pulli, first; Tata, second; Quick, third; Crawford, left field; West, right field. T—3:33. A—62,012.

HIGHLIGHTS

ATLANTA 14, PHILADELPHIA 3

Why the Braves won: They proved from the get-go that their high-powered offense wouldn't go quietly this time around. First baseman Fred McGriff, who hit 37 homers and drove in 101 runs in the regular season, tore into a Tommy Greene pitch and hammered it into the upper reaches of the stadium, the mammoth first-inning homer staking Atlanta to a 2-0 lead.

Why the Phillies lost: Greene wasn't invincible at Philadelphia's Veterans Stadium, after all. Having posted a 10-0 record at home in 1993, Greene proved he was human—and then some—by allowing the Braves seven hits and seven runs in only 2⅓ innings.

The turning points:

1. If McGriff's homer came a bit too early to be considered the decisive blow of the game (some argued nonetheless that it was), the Braves' offensive fireworks in the third inning surely did the job. With one out in the third, Jeff Blauser belted a bases-empty homer, Terry Pendleton hit a two-run single and Damon Berryhill slammed a three-run homer. Good night, Phillies.

2. The Phillies couldn't break through against Braves righthander Greg Maddux in the first inning. Down 2-0 at the time, Philadelphia had a two-on, one-out situation and its No. 4 and 5 hitters coming to bat. But Maddux, a 20-game winner during the regular season, induced Dave Hollins to fly to center and struck out Darren Daulton. Instead of getting right back into the game, the Phillies had been turned away. And after the Phils were retired 1-2-3 in the second, blowout time came in the next inning.

Notable: McGriff's blast was only the seventh in the 23-season history of Veterans Stadium to reach the upper deck in right field. . . . Atlanta reeled off six consecutive hits in the third inning, tying the N.L. playoff mark set by St. Louis against the Braves in Game 1 of the 1982 championship series. Four hits into the record-tying hit spree, Atlanta's David Justice drew a walk (a non-factor in determining a streak). . . . Pendleton also homered for the Braves, the fifth-inning smash being his first homer in 28 league playoff games.

Quotable: "It was important to get on top and set a tone," said McGriff, who set some kind of a tone with his 438-foot home run in the first inning. . . . "He (McGriff) got us going big time," Braves Manager Bobby Cox said. "I think that was the key hit of the game." . . . Maddux, assessing his first-inning jam: "You don't want to get two runs and then turn around and give it right back to them." He didn't. . . . "If anything deflated (the Phillies)," Pendleton said, "it was Maddux getting out of the first inning."

	AB	R	H	RBI	PO	A
Belliard, pr-ss	1	1	0	0	0	0
Gant, lf	5	1	2	3	1	0
McGriff, 1b	5	2	3	2	5	2
Stanton, p	0	0	0	0	0	0
Tarasco, rf	0	0	0	0	0	0
Justice, rf	3	1	0	0	1	0
Sanders, cf	0	0	0	0	0	0
Pendleton, 3b	5	2	3	3	1	0
Berryhill, c	5	1	1	3	11	0
Lemke, 2b	5	1	0	0	0	2
Maddux, p	4	1	1	0	3	2
Bream, 1b	1	1	1	0	1	0
Totals	43	14	16	14	27	6

Philadelphia	AB	R	H	RBI	PO	A
Dykstra, cf	4	1	1	1	1	0
Morandini, 2b	5	0	1	0	1	5
Kruk, 1b	3	1	2	0	10	0
Hollins, 3b	3	1	1	2	0	0
Daulton, c	4	0	1	0	8	1
Andersen, p	0	0	0	0	0	0
Eisenreich, rf	4	0	0	0	3	0
Thompson, lf	4	0	0	0	2	0
Stocker, ss	4	0	1	0	1	1
Greene, p	0	0	0	0	0	0
Thigpen, p	0	0	0	0	0	0
Longmire, ph	1	0	0	0	0	0
Rivera, p	0	0	0	0	0	0
Chamberlain, ph	1	0	0	0	0	0
Mason, p	0	0	0	0	0	0
Jordan, ph	0	0	0	0	0	0
West, p	0	0	0	0	0	0
Pratt, c	1	0	0	0	1	0
Totals	34	3	7	3	27	7

Atlanta	2 0 6	0 1 0	0 4 1—14
Philadelphia	0 0 0	2 0 0	0 0 1— 3

Atlanta	IP	H	R	ER	BB	SO
Maddux (W)	7	5	2	2	3	8
Stanton	1	1	0	0	0	0
Wohlers	1	1	1	1	0	3

Philadelphia	IP	H	R	ER	BB	SO
Greene (L)	2⅓	7	7	7	2	2
Thigpen	⅔	1	1	1	0	1
Rivera	2	1	1	1	1	2
Mason	2	1	0	0	0	1
West	1	4	4	3	1	2
Andersen	1	2	1	1	0	1

E—Stocker, Morandini. LOB—Atlanta 6, Philadelphia 8. 2B—Nixon, Gant 2. HR—McGriff, Blauser, Berryhill, Hollins, Pendleton, Dykstra. SB—Morandini. CS—Nixon. PB—Daulton. U—Pulli, plate; Tata, first; Quick, second; Crawford, third; West, left field; Froemming, right field. T—3:14. A—62,436.

BOX SCORE

THURSDAY, OCTOBER 7, AT PHILADELPHIA

Atlanta	AB	R	H	RBI	PO	A
Nixon, cf	4	2	3	2	3	0
Wohlers, p	0	0	0	0	0	0
Blauser, ss	5	1	2	1	1	0

GAME 3

HIGHLIGHTS

ATLANTA 9, PHILADELPHIA 4

Why the Braves won: Coming off their 14-run, 16-hit outburst in Game 2, they resumed batting practice against the Phillies' pitching—although it took a little time for them to find their groove. Trailing 2-0 entering the bottom of the sixth at Atlanta-Fulton County Stadium, the Braves hit Philadelphia with a five-spot—David Justice's two-run double was the key blow—and took control behind lefthander Tom Glavine, a 22-game winner during the regular season. In the seventh, Mark Lemke's three-run double highlighted a four-run inning that vaulted Atlanta into a 9-2 lead.

Why the Phillies lost: Philadelphia lefthander Terry Mulholland went from the sublime to the ridiculous. He shut out the Braves' vaunted attack through five innings but then couldn't get anyone out in the sixth, an inning in which he faced five batters and gave up three singles, a walk and a double.

The turning points:

1. Atlanta's ability to get into the Phillies' shaky bullpen five-plus innings into the game. While Mulholland was charged with five runs (four of them earned), the Phils still were within striking distance (5-2) when the sixth inning ended. However, Philadelphia relievers Larry Andersen and David West were tagged for four runs in the seventh, and the N.L. East champions were left staring at a seven-run deficit.

2. Glavine's ability to keep his team close until the Braves finally hauled out the heavy artillery.

Notable: John Kruk, the grubbiest-looking player among the Phils' scruffy-but-talented cast, drove in three of Philadelphia's runs with a triple, a homer and a groundout. ... Glavine was 0-4 in championship-series play entering the 1993 N.L. playoffs. ... In Games 2 and 3 of this series, the Phils' bullpen was torched for 12 hits and 10 earned runs in 9 ⅔ innings.

Quotable: "I didn't go out there to get the monkey off my back as much as I did to help get this team a win," Glavine said. "I'm not trying to make up for what's happened the last two years (0-2 records in both the 1991 and 1992 N.L. playoffs). Regardless of what I do here, I'm not going to be able to erase the last two years." ... Justice's big double in the sixth was his lone hit thus far (in 11 at-bats) in the '93 playoffs. "The bottom line is not my batting average," Justice said. "If I hit .300 and we're down two games to one, I feel terrible. I'd rather be hitting .091 and be where we are." ... Mulholland, bothered by hip problems in '93, said he "expected to go out there and pitch till I was no longer needed, whether it was five innings, six innings or nine innings. You don't take these things lightly. I know the guys were looking for good things from me, and I just couldn't come through for them. I thought I was ready."

BOX SCORE

SATURDAY, OCTOBER 9, AT ATLANTA

Philadelphia	AB	R	H	RBI	PO	A
Dykstra, cf	5	0	1	0	1	0
Duncan, 2b	5	2	2	0	1	4
Kruk, 1b	4	1	2	3	10	0
Hollins, 3b	3	0	0	0	1	0
Daulton, c	4	0	0	0	7	1
Incaviglia, lf	4	0	0	0	2	0
Chamberlain, rf	4	1	1	0	1	0
Stocker, ss	4	0	3	0	1	1
Mulholland, p	2	0	0	0	0	2
Mason, p	0	0	0	0	0	0

	AB	R	H	RBI	PO	A
Thompson, ph	1	0	0	0	0	0
Andersen, p	0	0	0	0	0	1
West, p	0	0	0	0	0	0
Thigpen, p	0	0	0	0	0	0
Eisenreich, ph	1	0	1	1	0	0
Totals	37	4	10	4	24	9
Atlanta	AB	R	H	RBI	PO	A
Nixon, cf	5	0	1	0	2	0
Blauser, ss	4	2	2	0	0	4
Gant, lf	4	1	0	0	2	0
McGriff, 1b	4	2	2	1	14	0
Pendleton, 3b	4	2	2	2	1	2
Justice, rf	4	1	1	2	2	0
Berryhill, c	3	1	1	0	6	0
Lemke, 2b	4	0	2	3	0	4
Glavine, p	3	0	0	0	0	3
Cabrera, ph	1	0	0	0	0	0
Mercker, p	0	0	0	0	0	0
McMichael, p	0	0	0	0	0	0
Totals	36	9	12	8	27	13

Philadelphia .... 0 0 0   1 0 1   0 1 1—4
Atlanta .... 0 0 0   0 0 5   4 0 x—9

Philadelphia	IP	H	R	ER	BB	SO
Mulholland (L)	*5	9	5	4	1	2
Mason	1	0	0	0	0	1
Andersen	⅓	2	3	3	1	0
West	⅔	1	1	1	1	2
Thigpen	1	0	0	0	1	2
Atlanta	IP	H	R	ER	BB	SO
Glavine (W)	7	6	2	2	0	5
Mercker	1	1	1	1	1	0
McMichael	1	3	1	1	0	1

*Pitched to five batters in sixth.

E—Duncan. LOB—Philadelphia 7, Atlanta 7. 2B—Chamberlain, Stocker, Eisenreich, Blauser, Gant, McGriff, Justice, Lemke. 3B—Duncan 2, Kruk. HR—Kruk. SB—Hollins. CS—Nixon. U—Tata, plate; Quick, first; Crawford, second; West, third; Froemming, left field; Pulli, right field. T—2:44. A—52,032.

GAME 4

HIGHLIGHTS

PHILADELPHIA 2, ATLANTA 1

Why the Phillies won: They got sound pitching and timely hitting from veteran lefthander Danny Jackson, who hurled one-run ball over 7 ⅔ innings and broke a 1-1 tie in the fourth with a run-scoring single off John Smoltz.

Why the Braves lost: Despite thwarting the Phillies' offense time and again, Atlanta couldn't generate any real offense of its own and left 11 men on base.

The turning points:

1. With two Braves on base and two out in the eighth inning, Phils left fielder Milt Thompson made a leaping catch of a drive off the bat of Mark Lemke. If the ball had gotten past Thompson, Atlanta would have seized the lead and moved within three outs of taking a 3-1 edge in games.

2. With two Braves on base and no one out in the ninth inning, Philadelphia reliever Mitch Williams squirmed out of trouble by inducing a force-out grounder by Jeff Blauser and getting Ron Gant

to hit into a double play. Williams had contributed to the threat, misplaying Otis Nixon's bunt attempt after pinch-hitter Bill Pecota had led off the inning with a single.

Notable: Incredibly, the Phillies stranded 15 runners and struck out 15 times but still managed to win. John Kruk left five men on base and fanned four times, while Kevin Stocker went down on strikes only once but left six men stranded.

Quotable: Braves Manager Bobby Cox, on Jackson's performance: "That was one of the best games I've seen him pitch since he pitched for Kansas City years ago." ... "When somebody talks bad about you and tells you you're not going to be that good, it ticks you off," said Jackson, whose poor performances in the 1990 World Series (with the Reds) and the 1992 N.L. playoffs (with the Pirates) were brought up repeatedly. "I knew I was going to have a good game tonight. I believe in myself, and my teammates believe in me. I know what I can do. I've been there before." Entering 1993 postseason play, Jackson's playoff/World Series ERA over eight games stood at 2.81—much to the surprise of his critics. ... Thompson, on his crucial catch of Lemke's eighth-inning smash: "It was a situation where I first took a couple of steps in to try to have a chance at home in case there was a base hit. I knew the ball was hit real well, but I got a good read on the ball and I knew I had a chance at it. I knew when I hit the warning track that I still had two steps and was able to jump and catch it. The main thing on a play like that is holding onto the ball when you hit the wall. ... This is the most important catch I've made, from an emotional standpoint."

| | BOX SCORE | |

SUNDAY, OCTOBER 10, AT ATLANTA

Philadelphia	AB	R	H	RBI	PO	A
Dykstra, cf	3	0	2	0	2	0
Morandini, 2b	5	0	2	0	5	1
Kruk, 1b	5	0	0	0	6	1
Hollins, 3b	4	0	1	0	1	1
Batiste, 3b	0	0	0	0	1	0
Daulton, c	1	1	0	0	6	1
Eisenreich, rf	5	0	1	0	2	0
Thompson, lf	4	1	1	0	3	0
Stocker, ss	4	0	0	1	1	4
Jackson, p	4	0	1	1	0	0
Mit. Williams, p	0	0	0	0	0	1
Totals	35	2	8	2	27	9

Atlanta	AB	R	H	RBI	PO	A
Nixon, cf	3	0	1	0	1	0
Blauser, ss	4	0	0	0	2	1
Gant, lf	5	0	0	0	4	0
McGriff, 1b	4	1	2	0	3	1
Pendleton, 3b	4	0	1	0	0	0
Justice, rf	4	0	2	0	1	0
Olson, c	2	0	0	0	10	0
Berryhill, ph-c	1	0	1	0	5	0
Lemke, 2b	4	0	1	1	1	2
Smoltz, p	1	0	0	0	0	0
Mercker, p	0	0	0	0	0	0
Cabrera, ph	1	0	1	0	0	0
Sanders, pr	0	0	0	0	0	0

	AB	R	H	RBI	PO	A
Wohlers, p	0	0	0	0	0	0
Pecota, ph	1	0	1	0	0	0
Totals	34	1	10	1	27	4

Philadelphia	0 0 0	2 0 0	0 0 0—2
Atlanta	0 1 0	0 0 0	0 0 0—1

Philadelphia	IP	H	R	ER	BB	SO
Jackson (W)	7⅔	9	1	1	2	6
Mit. Williams (S)	1⅓	1	0	0	0	0

Atlanta	IP	H	R	ER	BB	SO
Smoltz (L)	6⅓	8	2	0	5	10
Mercker	⅔	0	0	0	0	0
Wohlers	2	0	0	0	3	5

E—Mit. Williams, Lemke. DP—Philadelphia 1. LOB—Philadelphia 15, Atlanta 11. 2B—Thompson, McGriff, Pendleton, Lemke. CS—Gant. SH—Nixon 2. SF—Stocker. HBP—By Jackson (Olson). WP—Wohlers. U—Quick, plate; Crawford, first; West, second; Froemming, third; Pulli, left field; Tata, right field. T—3:33. A—52,032.

| | GAME 5 | |

| | HIGHLIGHTS | |

PHILADELPHIA 4, ATLANTA 3

Why the Phillies won: Starter Curt Schilling pitched splendidly, as he had in Game 1—and with the same result, a no-decision. Plus, Lenny Dykstra, a team leader par excellence, came through in the clutch, blasting a game-winning home run in the 10th inning.

Why the Braves lost: They couldn't turn a stirring ninth-inning rally into a full-fledged "miracle" comeback. Down 3-0 entering the ninth, the Braves struck for three runs in a spine-tingling inning—but couldn't cash in the fourth one despite having the potential game-winning run just 90 feet from home plate with one out.

The turning points:

1. Mitch Williams' strikeout of Mark Lemke with one out in the ninth and the game tied, 3-3. Schilling, who had gotten the Phillies in position to win with eight shutout innings, gave way to Williams in the ninth after a leadoff walk to Jeff Blauser and an error by third baseman Kim Batiste (a defensive replacement) on a grounder hit by Ron Gant. Fred McGriff singled home Blauser, and David Justice delivered a sacrifice fly. Terry Pendleton and pinch-hitter Francisco Cabrera, Atlanta's 1992 playoff hero, followed with singles, Cabrera's hit deadlocking the score. But Williams struck out Lemke when a medium-range fly ball would have won it for the Braves, and the Phils' Wild Thing then got pinch-hitter Bill Pecota on a fly ball to end the inning.

2. Under the theory that you never have enough runs at the "launching pad," Atlanta-Fulton County Stadium, the Phillies entered the ninth trying to build on a 2-0 lead. Probably hoping for at least two runs, the Phils gladly settled for one—Darren Daulton's leadoff homer off reliever Greg McMichael, who had just entered the game.

Notable: After two playoff starts, the Phils' Schilling had a 1.69 ERA and 19 strikeouts in 16 innings. His record: 0-0. . . . Now down three games to two with the series shifting back to Philadelphia, the Braves remained remarkably upbeat. And why not. They had Greg Maddux ready for Game 6 and, if needed, Tom Glavine for Game 7. Combined, they won 42 regular-season games in 1993. . . . Seven years to the day earlier, Dykstra, playing for the Mets, hit a game-winning homer in the ninth against Houston in Game 3 of the N.L. playoffs.

Quotable: "I am leaned on by my teammates, my coaches and my manager," said the 30-year-old Dykstra, comparing his leadership role with the Phillies with his free-and-easy days with the Mets. "If I don't have success, I've let them down. We were in command the whole way (in Game 5). We felt it still was our game when Mitch got out of it in the ninth. But I knew we had to do something that next inning."

BOX SCORE

MONDAY, OCTOBER 11, AT ATLANTA

Philadelphia	AB	R	H	RBI	PO	A
Dykstra, cf	5	1	1	1	2	0
Duncan, 2b	5	1	1	0	1	2
Andersen, p	0	0	0	0	0	0
Kruk, 1b	4	0	1	0	6	0
Hollins, 3b	4	0	0	0	0	1
Batiste, 3b	0	0	0	0	1	0
Daulton, c	3	1	2	1	13	0
Incaviglia, lf	4	1	0	0	3	0
Thompson, lf	0	0	0	0	1	0
Chamberlain, rf	3	0	1	1	1	2
Eisenreich, rf	0	0	0	0	1	0
Stocker, ss	4	0	0	0	1	3
Schilling, p	2	0	0	0	0	0
Mit. Williams, p	0	0	0	0	0	0
Morandini, ph-2b	1	0	0	0	0	0
Totals	35	4	6	4	30	8

Atlanta	AB	R	H	RBI	PO	A
Nixon, cf	4	0	0	0	4	0
Blauser, ss	4	1	1	0	0	3
Gant, lf	5	1	1	0	1	0
McGriff, 1b	4	1	2	1	8	0
Justice, rf	2	0	0	1	6	0
Pendleton, 3b	4	0	1	0	1	1
Berryhill, c	3	0	1	0	7	0
Cabrera, ph-c	1	0	1	1	1	0
Lemke, 2b	4	0	0	0	2	2
Avery, p	2	0	0	0	0	2
Mercker, p	0	0	0	0	0	0
Sanders, ph	1	0	0	0	0	0
McMichael, p	0	0	0	0	0	0
Pecota, ph	1	0	0	0	0	0
Wohlers, p	0	0	0	0	0	0
Totals	35	3	7	3	30	8

Philadelphia	1 0 0	1 0 0	0 0 1	1—4
Atlanta	0 0 0	0 0 0	0 0 3	0—3

Philadelphia	IP	H	R	ER	BB	SO
Schilling	*8	4	2	1	3	9
Mit. Williams (W)	1	3	1	1	0	1
Andersen (S)	1	0	0	0	0	2

Atlanta	IP	H	R	ER	BB	SO
Avery	7	4	2	1	2	5
Mercker	1	0	0	0	0	2

	AB	R	H	RBI	PO	A
McMichael	1	1	1	1	0	0
Wohlers (L)	1	1	1	1	0	1

*Pitched to two batters in ninth.

E—Batiste, Gant. LOB—Philadelphia 5, Atlanta 6. 2B—Kruk. HR—Daulton, Dykstra. SH—Schilling. SF—Chamberlain, Justice. WP—Avery. U—Crawford, plate; West, first; Froemming, second; Pulli, third; Tata, left field; Quick, right field. T—3:21. A—52,032.

GAME 6

HIGHLIGHTS

PHILADELPHIA 6, ATLANTA 3

Why the Phillies won: Tommy Greene returned to the Veterans Stadium form he had exhibited during the regular season—or at least approximated it. He yielded five hits and three runs over seven innings. Also, the Phils got key hits—extra-base hits—from Darren Daulton in the third inning, Dave Hollins in the fifth and Mickey Morandini in the sixth. Daulton lashed a two-run double, Hollins a two-run homer and Morandini a two-run triple.

Why the Braves lost: Greg Maddux wasn't his Cy Young Award-winning self (he won the honor in 1992 and would repeat in 1993). He gave up six hits and six runs (five earned) in 5⅔ innings. Ron Gant and David Justice, two of Atlanta's big boppers, continued to struggle offensively, both going 0-for-4. Combined, they went 8-for-48 (.167) in the series.

The turning points:

1. Morandini's hard smash off Maddux's leg in the first inning. While the Braves' righthander stayed in the game and later offered no excuses for his subpar performance, he seemed to labor with his pitches.

2. A rock-solid two innings from Philadelphia's much-maligned bullpen.

Notable: The N.L. pennant was only the fifth in Phillies history. Other flags came in 1915, 1950, 1980 and 1983. . . . Despite his 0-0 record in this League Championship Series, Phillies righthander Curt Schilling had something to show for his efforts—the Most Valuable Player honor. Schilling pitched masterfully in Games 1 and 5, extra-inning triumphs by the Phils in which reliever Mitch Williams received credit for the victories after blowing save opportunities. . . . Williams, Mr. Excitement because of his propensity toward wildness, pitched the ninth inning in Game 6 and, to the surprise of most, retired the Braves in order. David West also had a 1-2-3 inning in the eighth.

Quotable: . "They had their ace (Maddux) out there," Lenny Dykstra said. "He's the best right-handed pitcher in baseball. But sometimes you can't control what's meant to be. This was meant to be since spring training." . . . "Everyone says this is a team with a lot of characters, but we have character," Phillies Manager Jim Fregosi said. "And 10 years from now, they can all look in the mirror and say we were champions." . . . Maddux, on the effects of the wicked grounder that struck him in the first inning and caused a deep calf bruise: "Would I have pitched better if I didn't get hit? I can't tell you.""This is a team you dream about," Greene said. "We're not flamboyant. We'll fight you in the mud and the rain, we'll get down and get dirty and it doesn't matter." . . . Justice, on the Braves' failure to win a third straight N.L. pennant: "The magic went out."

BOX SCORE

WEDNESDAY, OCTOBER 13, AT PHILADELPHIA

Atlanta	AB	R	H	RBI	PO	A
Nixon, cf	3	1	1	0	1	0
Blauser, ss	4	1	2	3	2	5
Gant, lf	4	0	0	0	2	0
McGriff, 1b	1	0	0	0	9	1
Justice, rf	4	0	0	0	1	0
Pendleton, 3b	4	0	1	0	1	0
Berryhill, c	4	0	0	0	5	0
Lemke, 2b	3	1	1	0	2	3
Maddux, p	0	0	0	0	1	3
Mercker, p	0	0	0	0	0	0
Sanders, ph	1	0	0	0	0	0
McMichael, p	0	0	0	0	0	0
Wohlers, p	0	0	0	0	0	0
Pecota, ph	1	0	0	0	0	0
Totals	29	3	5	3	24	12

Philadelphia	AB	R	H	RBI	PO	A
Dykstra, cf	4	2	1	0	4	0
Morandini, 2b	5	1	1	2	2	3
Kruk, 1b	4	0	0	0	7	0
Hollins, 3b	2	1	1	2	1	1
Batiste, 3b	0	0	0	0	0	0
Daulton, c	4	0	2	2	8	0
Eisenreich, rf	4	0	0	0	1	0
Thompson, lf	4	1	2	0	1	0
Stocker, ss	3	0	0	0	4	1
Greene, p	0	1	0	0	0	3
Jordan, ph	1	0	0	0	0	0
West, p	0	0	0	0	0	1
Mit. Williams, p	0	0	0	0	0	0
Totals	31	6	7	6	27	9

Atlanta	0 0 0	0 1 0	2 0 0—3
Philadelphia	0 0 2	0 2 2	0 0 x—6

Atlanta	IP	H	R	ER	BB	SO
Maddux (L)	5⅔	6	6	5	4	3
Mercker	⅓	0	0	0	0	0
McMichael	⅔	1	0	0	2	0
Wohlers	1⅓	0	0	0	0	1

Philadelphia	IP	H	R	ER	BB	SO
Greene (W)	7	5	3	3	5	5
West	1	0	0	0	0	1
Mit. Williams (S)	1	0	0	0	0	2

E—Justice, Lemke, Maddux, Thompson. DP—Philadelphia 1. LOB—Atlanta 6, Philadelphia 9. 2B—Daulton. 3B—Morandini. HR—Hollins, Blauser. SH—Maddux 2, Greene 2. PB—Daulton. U—West, plate; Froemming, first; Pulli, second; Tata, third; Quick, left field; Crawford, right field. T—3:04. A—62,502.

STATISTICS

PHILADELPHIA PHILLIES' BATTING AND FIELDING AVERAGES

Player, position	G	AB	R	H	TB	2B	3B	HR	RBI	BB	IBB	SO	Avg.	PO	A	E	Avg.
Batiste, 3b	4	1	0	1	1	0	0	0	1	0	0	0	1.000	2	0	2	.500
Chamberlain, rf-ph	4	11	1	4	7	3	0	0	1	1	1	3	.364	2	2	0	1.000
Dykstra, cf	6	25	5	7	14	1	0	2	2	5	1	8	.280	13	0	0	1.000
Duncan, 2b	3	15	3	4	8	0	2	0	0	0	0	5	.267	5	6	1	.917
Daulton, c	6	19	2	5	9	1	0	1	3	6	1	3	.263	54	3	0	1.000
Kruk, 1b	6	24	4	6	13	2	1	1	5	4	0	5	.250	43	2	0	1.000
Morandini, 2b-ph	4	16	1	4	6	0	1	0	2	0	0	3	.250	8	9	1	.944
Jackson, p	1	4	0	1	1	0	0	0	1	0	0	3	.250	0	0	0	.000
Thompson, pr-lf-ph	6	13	2	3	4	1	0	0	1	1	1	2	.231	8	0	1	.889
Hollins, 3b	6	20	2	4	11	1	0	2	4	5	0	4	.200	5	4	0	1.000
Stocker, ss	6	22	0	4	5	1	0	0	1	2	2	5	.182	10	13	1	.958
Incaviglia, lf	3	12	2	2	5	0	0	1	1	0	0	3	.167	8	0	0	1.000
Eisenreich, rf-ph	6	15	0	2	3	1	0	0	1	0	0	2	.133	6	0	0	1.000
Andersen, p	3	0	0	0	0	0	0	0	0	0	0	0	.000	0	1	0	1.000
Greene, p	2	0	1	0	0	0	0	0	0	1	0	0	.000	0	3	0	1.000
Mason, p	2	0	0	0	0	0	0	0	0	0	0	0	.000	0	0	0	.000
Rivera, p	1	0	0	0	0	0	0	0	0	0	0	0	.000	0	0	0	.000
Thigpen, p	2	0	0	0	0	0	0	0	0	0	0	0	.000	0	0	0	.000
West, p	3	0	0	0	0	0	0	0	0	0	0	0	.000	0	1	0	1.000
Mit. Williams, p	4	0	0	0	0	0	0	0	0	0	0	0	.000	0	1	1	.500
Jordan, ph	2	1	0	0	0	0	0	0	0	0	1	0	.000	0	0	0	.000
Longmire, ph	1	1	0	0	0	0	0	0	0	0	0	1	.000	0	0	0	.000
Pratt, c	1	1	0	0	0	0	0	0	0	0	0	1	.000	1	0	0	1.000
Mulholland, p	2	2	0	0	0	0	0	0	0	0	0	0	.000	0	2	0	1.000
Schilling, p	2	5	0	0	0	0	0	0	0	0	0	2	.000	0	0	0	.000
Totals	6	207	23	47	87	11	4	7	22	26	6	51	.227	165	47	7	.968

ATLANTA BRAVES' BATTING AND FIELDING AVERAGES

Player, position	G	AB	R	H	TB	2B	3B	HR	RBI	BB	IBB	SO	Avg.	PO	A	E	Avg.
Bream, 1b	1	1	1	1	1	0	0	0	0	0	0	0	1.000	1	0	0	1.000
Cabrera, ph-c	3	3	0	2	2	0	0	0	1	0	0	1	.667	1	0	0	1.000
Avery, p	2	4	1	2	3	1	0	0	0	0	0	1	.500	0	2	0	1.000

Player, position	G	AB	R	H	TB	2B	3B	HR	RBI	BB	IBB	SO	Avg.	PO	A	E	Avg.
McGriff, 1b	6	23	6	10	15	2	0	1	4	4	1	7	.435	49	4	0	1.000
Nixon, cf	6	23	3	8	10	2	0	0	4	5	0	6	.348	13	0	0	1.000
Pendleton, 3b	6	26	4	9	13	1	0	1	5	0	0	2	.346	7	5	0	1.000
Olson, c	2	3	0	1	2	1	0	0	0	0	0	1	.333	10	0	0	1.000
Pecota, ph	4	3	1	1	1	0	0	0	0	1	0	1	.333	0	0	0	.000
Blauser, ss	6	25	5	7	14	1	0	2	4	4	0	7	.280	6	14	0	1.000
Maddux, p	2	4	1	1	1	0	0	0	0	0	0	1	.250	4	5	1	.900
Berryhill, c	6	19	2	4	7	0	0	1	3	1	0	5	.211	42	0	0	1.000
Lemke, 2b	6	24	2	5	7	2	0	0	4	1	0	6	.208	6	19	2	.926
Gant, lf	6	27	4	5	8	3	0	0	3	2	0	9	.185	10	1	1	.917
Justice, rf	6	21	2	3	4	1	0	0	4	3	0	3	.143	14	0	1	.933
McMichael, p	4	0	0	0	0	0	0	0	0	0	0	0	.000	0	1	0	1.000
Mercker, p	5	0	0	0	0	0	0	0	0	0	0	0	.000	0	0	0	.000
Stanton, p	1	0	0	0	0	0	0	0	0	0	0	0	.000	0	0	0	.000
Wohlers, p	4	0	0	0	0	0	0	0	0	0	0	0	.000	0	0	0	.000
Belliard, ph-2b-ss	2	1	1	0	0	0	0	0	0	0	0	1	.000	0	0	0	.000
Smoltz, p	1	1	0	0	0	0	0	0	0	0	1	0	.000	0	0	0	.000
Tarasco, pr-lf-rf	2	1	0	0	0	0	0	0	0	0	0	1	.000	0	0	0	.000
Glavine, p	1	3	0	0	0	0	0	0	0	0	0	0	.000	0	3	0	1.000
Sanders, ph-cf-pr	5	3	0	0	0	0	0	0	0	0	0	1	.000	0	0	0	.000
Totals	6	215	33	59	88	14	0	5	32	22	1	54	.274	163	54	5	.977

PHILADELPHIA PHILLIES' PITCHING RECORDS

Pitcher	G	GS	CG	IP	H	R	ER	HR	BB	IBB	SO	HB	WP	W	L	Pct.	ERA
Mason	2	0	0	3	1	0	0	0	0	0	2	0	0	0	0	.000	0.00
Jackson	1	1	0	7⅔	9	1	1	0	2	0	6	1	0	1	0	1.000	1.17
Schilling	2	2	0	16	11	4	3	0	5	0	19	0	0	0	0	.000	1.69
Mit. Williams	4	0	0	5⅓	6	2	1	0	2	0	5	0	0	2	0	1.000	1.69
Rivera	1	0	0	2	1	1	1	1	1	0	2	0	0	0	0	.000	4.50
Thigpen	2	0	0	1⅔	1	1	1	0	1	0	3	0	0	0	0	.000	5.40
Mulholland	1	1	0	5	9	5	4	0	1	0	2	0	0	0	1	.000	7.20
Greene	2	2	0	9⅓	12	10	10	3	7	0	7	0	0	1	1	.500	9.64
West	3	0	0	2⅔	5	5	4	0	2	0	5	0	0	0	0	.000	13.50
Andersen	3	0	0	2⅓	4	4	4	0	1	1	3	0	0	0	0	.000	15.43
Totals	6	6	0	55	59	33	29	5	22	1	54	1	0	4	2	.667	4.75

No shutouts. Saves—Mit. Williams 2, Andersen.

ATLANTA BRAVES' PITCHING RECORDS

Pitcher	G	GS	CG	IP	H	R	ER	HR	BB	IBB	SO	HB	WP	W	L	Pct.	ERA
Smoltz	1	1	0	6⅓	8	2	0	0	5	0	10	0	0	0	1	.000	0.00
Stanton	1	0	0	1	1	0	0	0	1	0	0	0	0	0	0	.000	0.00
Mercker	5	0	0	5	3	1	1	0	2	0	4	0	0	0	0	.000	1.80
Glavine	1	1	0	7	6	2	2	0	0	0	5	0	0	1	0	1.000	2.57
Avery	2	2	0	13	9	5	4	1	6	3	10	0	2	0	0	.000	2.77
Wohlers	4	0	0	5⅓	2	2	2	2	3	1	10	0	1	0	1	.000	3.38
Maddux	2	2	0	12⅔	11	8	7	2	7	1	11	0	0	1	1	.500	4.97
McMichael	4	0	0	4	7	3	3	1	2	1	1	0	0	0	1	.000	6.75
Totals	6	6	0	54⅓	47	23	19	7	26	6	51	0	3	2	4	.333	3.15

No shutouts or saves.

SCORE BY INNINGS

Philadelphia	2	0	2	7	2	4	0	1	3	2—23
Atlanta	2	1	7	1	2	5	6	4	5	0—33

MISCELLANEOUS STATISTICS

Sacrifice hits—Greene 2, Maddux 2, Nixon 2, Belliard, Schilling.
Sacrifice flies—Justice 2, Chamberlain, Stocker.
Stolen bases—Hollins, Morandini.
Caught stealing—Nixon 2, Gant.
Double plays—Pendleton, Lemke and McGriff; Morandini and Kruk; Morandini, Stocker and Kruk.
Left on bases—Philadelphia 8, 8, 7, 15, 5, 9—52; Atlanta 11, 6, 7, 11, 6, 6—47.
Hit by pitcher—By Jackson (Olson).
Passed balls—Daulton 2.
Balks—None.
Time of games—First game, 3:33; second game, 3:14; third game, 2:44; fourth game, 3:33; fifth game, 3:21; sixth game, 3:04.
Attendance—First game, 62,012; second game, 62,436; third game, 52,032; fourth game, 52,032; fifth game, 52,032; sixth game, 62,502.
Umpires—Froemming, Pulli, Tata, Quick, Crawford and West.
Official scorers—Bob Kenney, Camden (N.J.) Courier-Post; Paul Newberry, Atlanta official scorer; Nick Peters, Sacramento Bee.

WORLD SERIES

| HIGHLIGHTS |

TORONTO 8, PHILADELPHIA 5

Why the Blue Jays won: Their solid top-to-bottom batting order was just too much for the Phillies. Eight Toronto players collected at least one hit, and six Blue Jays managed at least one RBI. The result was that the Phillies were unable to hold leads of 2-0, 3-2 and 4-3. The Jays' big blows were a fifth-inning home run by Devon White, which tied the score at 4-4, and a sixth-inning homer by John Olerud, which thrust Toronto into a 5-4 lead.

Why Phillies lost: Righthander Curt Schilling, the Most Valuable Player in the National League playoffs, didn't turn in an MVP-caliber performance. He was scored upon in five of seven innings and yielded six earned runs and eight hits.

The turning points:

1. Al Leiter's strikeout of the Phillies' John Kruk with the bases loaded and two out in the sixth inning. The game was tied, 4-4, at the time. Reliever Leiter not only put out the fire, but also started it. He allowed three hits and one walk in the inning but escaped unscathed—thanks to a double-play grounder off the bat of Milt Thompson and the Kruk strikeout.

2. Roberto Alomar's two-run double in the seventh. It gave the Blue Jays some breathing room, boosting their lead—which had been only 5-4 at the start of the inning—to 8-4. The Blue Jays had scored earlier in the seventh on two singles and White's double.

Notable: While Kruk struck out in a key situation, he also cracked three singles and drove in two runs for the Phillies. . . . Blue Jays starter Juan Guzman and relievers Leiter and Duane Ward struck out 11 Phillies, with Mariano Duncan, Darren Daulton, Jim Eisenreich and Ricky Jordan each going down on strikes twice. . . . White, who batted .444 in the American League playoffs, went 2-for-4 and scored three of Toronto's runs. . . . Olerud, the A.L. batting champion and a .348 hitter in the playoffs, showed no signs of letting up. He went 2-for-3, scored two runs and had one RBI.

Quotable: "It was a little nerve-racking," winning pitcher Leiter said of his first World Series appearance. "I played little mind games, thinking I was in Clearwater (Fla.) in spring training." . . . "I didn't do the job they pay me to do," Schilling said. "I failed and when I fail, the whole team has to pay for it. We got the lead three times and I gave it back." . . . Phils left fielder Thompson, on his three-base error of White's leadoff fly ball in the third inning that helped Toronto tie the score at 3-3: "We both (center fielder Lenny Dykstra and Thompson) called for it, and I just missed it. That's all there was to it. With 50,000 (fans) screaming, it's tough to hear anything out there."

| BOX SCORE |

SATURDAY, OCTOBER 16, AT TORONTO

Philadelphia	AB	R	H	RBI	PO	A
Dykstra, cf	4	1	1	0	1	0
Duncan, 2b	5	2	3	0	2	5
Kruk, 1b	4	2	3	2	9	0
Hollins, 3b	4	0	0	0	2	1
Daulton, c	4	0	1	1	5	1
Eisenreich, rf	5	0	1	1	3	0
Jordan, dh	5	0	1	0	0	0
Thompson, lf	3	0	0	0	1	0
aIncaviglia, ph-lf	1	0	0	0	0	0
Stocker, ss	3	0	1	0	1	2
Schilling, p	0	0	0	0	0	2
West, p	0	0	0	0	0	0
Andersen, p	0	0	0	0	0	0
Mason, p	0	0	0	0	0	0
Totals	38	5	11	4	24	11

Toronto	AB	R	H	RBI	PO	A
Henderson, lf	3	1	1	0	0	0
White, cf	4	3	2	2	2	0
Alomar, 2b	4	0	1	2	2	2
Carter, rf	3	1	1	1	1	0
Olerud, 1b	3	2	2	1	9	0
Molitor, dh	4	0	1	1	0	0
Fernandez, ss	3	0	0	1	1	2
Sprague, 3b	4	0	1	0	0	3
Borders, c	4	1	1	0	12	0
Guzman, p	0	0	0	0	0	1
Leiter, p	0	0	0	0	0	0
D. Ward, p	0	0	0	0	0	0
Totals	32	8	10	8	27	8

Philadelphia	2 0 1	0 1 0	0 0 1—5
Toronto	0 2 1	0 1 1	3 0 x—8

Philadelphia	IP	H	R	ER	BB	SO
Schilling (L)	6⅓	8	7	6	2	3
West	*0	2	1	1	0	0
Andersen	⅔	0	0	0	1	1
Mason	1	0	0	0	0	1

Toronto	IP	H	R	ER	BB	SO
Guzman	5	5	4	4	4	6
Leiter (W)	2⅔	4	0	0	1	2
D. Ward (S)	1⅓	2	1	0	0	3

*Pitched to two batters in seventh.

Bases on balls—Off Schilling 2 (Henderson, Fernandez), off Andersen 1 (Olerud), off Guzman 4 (Dykstra, Hollins, Kruk, Daulton), off Leiter 1 (Stocker).

Strikeouts—By Schilling 3 (Alomar, Borders, Sprague), by Andersen 1 (Carter), by Mason 1 (Sprague), by Guzman 6 (Duncan, Eisenreich, Jordan 2, Daulton, Thompson), by Leiter 2 (Kruk, Eisenreich), by D. Ward 3 (Duncan, Hollins, Daulton).

aFouled out for Thompson in eighth. E—Thompson, Alomar, Carter, Sprague. DP—Philadelphia 1, Toronto 1. LOB—Philadelphia 11, Toronto 4. 2B—White, Alomar. 3B—Duncan. HR—White, Olerud. SB—Dykstra, Duncan, Alomar, CS—Fernandez. SF—Carter. WP—Guzman. PB—Daulton. U—Phillips, plate; Runge, first; Johnson, second; Williams, third; McClelland, left field; DeMuth, right field. T—3:27. A—52,011.

PLAY BY PLAY

FIRST INNING

Philadelphia—Dykstra walked and stole second. Duncan struck out. Kruk singled to left, scoring Dykstra. Hollins walked. Daulton singled to right, scoring Kruk as Hollins went to third on an error by the right fielder. Eisenreich and Jordan struck out.

Toronto—Henderson walked. White grounded into a double play, shortstop to second to first baseman. Alomar struck out.

SECOND INNING

Philadelphia—Thompson grounded to the pitcher. Stocker grounded to first. Dykstra grounded to second.

Toronto—Carter singled to center. Olerud singled to left, Carter went to second. Carter went to third and Olerud to second on a passed ball. Molitor singled to second, scoring Carter as Olerud went to third. Fernandez reached on a fielder's choice as Olerud scored and Molitor was forced, second baseman to shortstop. Sprague singled to center, Fernandez went to second. Borders lined to first. Henderson flied to Eisenreich.

THIRD INNING

Philadelphia—Duncan singled to left and stole second. Kruk singled to right, scoring Duncan. Hollins flied to center. Daulton struck out. Eisenreich reached on a fielder's choice as Kruk was forced, shortstop to second baseman.

Toronto—White reached third on an error by the left fielder. Alomar popped to third. Carter hit a sacrifice fly to Eisenreich, scoring White. Olerud grounded to the pitcher.

FOURTH INNING

Philadelphia—Jordan and Thompson struck out. Stocker flied to center.

Toronto—Molitor flied to right. Fernandez walked. Fernandez was caught trying to steal second, catcher to second baseman. Sprague grounded to short.

FIFTH INNING

Philadelphia—Dykstra lined to second. Duncan tripled to left. Duncan scored on a wild pitch. Kruk walked. Hollins grounded to first as Kruk went to second. Daulton was walked intentionally. Eisenreich grounded to third.

Toronto—Borders struck out. Henderson grounded to second. White homered to right. Alomar popped to third.

SIXTH INNING

Philadelphia—Leiter now pitching. Jordan singled to right. Thompson grounded into a double play, shortstop to first baseman. Stocker walked. Dykstra singled to center, Stocker went to second. Duncan singled to center, Stocker went to third and Dykstra to second. Kruk struck out.

Toronto—Carter grounded out to the pitcher. Olerud homered to right. Molitor and Fernandez grounded to second.

SEVENTH INNING

Philadelphia—Hollins grounded to third. Daulton grounded to second. Eisenreich struck out.

Toronto—Sprague struck out. Borders singled to center. Henderson singled to left, Borders went to third. West now pitching. White doubled to left, scoring Borders as Henderson went to third. Alomar doubled to left, scoring Henderson and White. Andersen now pitching. Carter struck out. Alomar stole third. Olerud was walked intentionally. Molitor flied to left.

EIGHTH INNING

Philadelphia—Jordan grounded to third. Incaviglia, pinch-hitting for Thompson, fouled to the catcher. Stocker singled to center. Dykstra reached on an error by the second baseman as Stocker went to second. D. Ward now pitching. Duncan struck out.

Toronto—Incaviglia now in left field and Mason pitching. Fernandez lined to center. Sprague struck out. Borders

grounded to third.

NINTH INNING

Philadelphia—Kruk singled to third and went to second on a wild throw error by the first baseman. Hollins and Daulton struck out. Eisenreich singled to left, scoring Kruk. Jordan flied to right.

HIGHLIGHTS

PHILADELPHIA 6, TORONTO 4

Why the Phillies won: Jim Eisenreich, not known for his power, capped a five-run third with a three-run homer off Dave Stewart, who was coming off Most Valuable Player honors in the A.L. playoffs.

Why the Blue Jays lost: They couldn't contain Lenny Dykstra. The Phillies' catalyst coaxed a rally-starting walk from Stewart in the third, homered off Blue Jays reliever Tony Castillo in the seventh and twice crashed into SkyDome's center-field wall to make outstanding catches (of balls hit by Devon White in the third inning and Roberto Alomar in the fourth).

The turning points:

1. Stewart's wildness in the third. Walking the leadoff hitter in an inning often comes back to haunt a pitcher, and walking the first two batters can be downright dangerous. Sure enough, after Dykstra and Mariano Duncan started the inning by drawing bases on balls, both came around to score—Dykstra on a single by John Kruk and Duncan on a single by Dave Hollins.

2. Toronto's mini-uprising in the eighth was held to just that. Paul Molitor, the Blue Jays' lusty-hitting designated hitter, doubled to start the inning and, after stealing third base with one out, scored on John Olerud's sacrifice fly to cut Philadelphia's lead—once a 5-0 cushion—to 6-4. Alomar then walked, bringing the potential tying run to the plate in Tony Fernandez. But before Fernandez could complete his at-bat, Alomar, after stealing second base, broke for third and was nailed on a spin move by Phillies reliever Mitch Williams.

Notable: Phils lefthander Terry Mulholland, while hardly at the top of his game, pitched well enough (seven hits and three runs in 5⅔ innings) to win. ... Kruk, a .316 hitter in the regular season, collected two singles to extend his two-game hit total to five in this fall classic. ... Joe Carter's fourth-inning home run with a man aboard was the Toronto outfielder's third homer in eight World Series games. ... Molitor, who pummeled Chicago pitching for a .391 average in the A.L. playoffs, was off to a 3-for-7 start in the World Series.

Quotable: Eisenreich, who suffers from Tourette syndrome (a neurological disorder that at times causes uncontrollable muscular movements), was out of baseball in 1985 in 1986 but, with the help of medication, has battled back to have a fine career. "Sure, (Tourette) has been something I don't like to think about," said Eisenreich, who signed with the Phils as a free agent in January 1993. "But it's part of life, and I deal with it." ... Dykstra, on Eisenreich: "No one really thinks about Jim's problem or anything. All we know is that dude can hit." ... Dykstra, on his own standout two-way performance: "I think I can play with anyone."

BOX SCORE

SUNDAY, OCTOBER 17, AT TORONTO

Philadelphia	AB	R	H	RBI	PO	A
Dykstra, cf	4	2	2	1	4	0
Duncan, 2b	4	1	1	0	3	2
Kruk, 1b	5	1	2	1	5	1
Hollins, 3b	4	1	2	1	2	1
Batiste, 3b	0	0	0	0	0	1
Daulton, c	5	0	1	0	7	1
Eisenreich, rf	4	1	1	3	4	0
Incaviglia, lf	4	0	1	0	1	0
aThompson, pr-lf	0	0	0	0	0	0
Jordan, dh	4	0	1	0	0	0
Stocker, ss	3	0	1	0	0	2
Mulholland, p	0	0	0	0	1	0
Mason, p	0	0	0	0	0	0
Mit. Williams, p	0	0	0	0	0	1
Totals	37	6	12	6	27	9

Toronto	AB	R	H	RBI	PO	A
Henderson, lf	3	0	0	0	2	0
White, cf	4	0	1	0	1	0
Molitor, dh	3	2	2	0	0	0
Carter, rf	4	1	1	2	2	0
Olerud, 1b	3	0	0	1	8	0
Alomar, 2b	3	1	1	0	3	5
Fernandez, ss	3	0	2	1	1	0
Sprague, 3b	4	0	0	0	1	4
bGriffin, pr	0	0	0	0	0	0
Borders, c	4	0	1	0	8	1
Stewart, p	0	0	0	0	1	0
Castillo, p	0	0	0	0	0	0
Eichhorn, p	0	0	0	0	0	0
Timlin, p	0	0	0	0	0	0
Totals	31	4	8	4	27	10

Philadelphia	0 0 5	0 0 0	1 0 0—6
Toronto	0 0 0	2 0 1	0 1 0—4

Philadelphia	IP	H	R	ER	BB	SO
Mulholland (W)	5⅔	7	3	3	2	4
Mason	1⅔	1	1	1	0	2
Mit. Williams (S)	1⅔	0	0	0	2	0

Toronto	IP	H	R	ER	BB	SO
Stewart (L)	6	6	5	5	4	6
Castillo	1	3	1	1	0	0
Eichhorn	⅓	1	0	0	1	0
Timlin	1⅔	2	0	0	0	2

Bases on balls—Off Mulholland 2 (Henderson, Molitor), off Mit. Williams 2 (Alomar, Fernandez), off Stewart 4 (Eisenreich, Dykstra, Duncan, Hollins), off Eichhorn 1 (Stocker).
Strikeouts—By Mulholland 4 (White, Alomar, Henderson, Sprague), by Mason 2 (White, Carter), by Stewart 6 (Hollins, Incaviglia 2, Duncan, Kruk, Eisenreich), by Timlin 2 (Duncan, Hollins).
aRan for Incaviglia in eighth. bRan for Sprague in ninth. DP—Philadelphia 1, Toronto 1. LOB—Philadelphia 9, Toronto 5. 2B—White, Molitor, Fernandez. HR—Carter, Dykstra, Eisenreich, Alomar. SB—Molitor, Alomar. CS—Stocker, Henderson, Alomar. SF—Olerud. U—Runge, plate; Johnson, first; Williams, second; McClelland, third; DeMuth, left field; Phillips, right field. T—3:35. A—52,062.

PLAY BY PLAY

FIRST INNING

Philadelphia—Dykstra flied to left. Duncan singled to short and went to second on a balk. Kruk grounded out to the pitcher, unassisted, as Duncan went to third. Hollins struck out.

Toronto—Henderson walked. White struck out. Henderson was caught trying to steal second, catcher to second baseman. Molitor walked. Carter flied to right.

SECOND INNING

Philadelphia—Daulton flied to short. Eisenreich walked. Incaviglia flied to left. Jordan singled to left, Eisenreich went to third. Stocker grounded to second.

Toronto—Olerud grounded to the pitcher, unassisted. Alomar struck out. Fernandez flied to right.

THIRD INNING

Philadelphia—Dykstra walked and advanced on a wild pitch. Duncan walked. Kruk singled to left, scoring Dykstra as Duncan went to third. Hollins singled to center, scoring Duncan as Kruk went to second. Daulton grounded to first as Kruk went to third and Hollins to second. Eisenreich homered to right, scoring Kruk and Hollins. Incaviglia struck out. Jordan grounded to third.

Toronto—Sprague fouled to the catcher. Borders singled to right. Henderson struck out. White flied to right.

FOURTH INNING

Philadelphia—Stocker singled to left. Dykstra flied to right. Stocker was caught trying to steal second, catcher to second baseman. Duncan struck out.

Toronto—Molitor singled to center. Carter homered to left, scoring Molitor. Olerud fouled to third. Alomar flied to center. Fernandez singled to left. Sprague struck out.

FIFTH INNING

Philadelphia—Kruk struck out. Hollins walked. Daulton reached on a fielder's choice as Hollins was forced at second, third baseman to second baseman. Eisenreich struck out.

Toronto—Borders grounded to short. Henderson flied to right. White doubled to left. Molitor grounded to second.

SIXTH INNING

Philadelphia—Incaviglia struck out. Jordan grounded to second. Stocker fouled to third.

Toronto—Carter lined to left. Olerud grounded to the first baseman, who tossed to the pitcher covering first. Alomar singled to left. Fernandez doubled to left, scoring Alomar. Mason now pitching. Sprague flied to center.

SEVENTH INNING

Philadelphia—Castillo now pitching. Dykstra homered to right. Duncan flied to right. Kruk singled to right. Hollins singled to right as Kruk went to second. Daulton grounded to second as Kruk went to third and Hollins to second. Eisenreich flied to center.

Toronto—Borders grounded to third. Henderson flied to left. White struck out.

EIGHTH INNING

Philadelphia—Eichhorn now pitching. Incaviglia singled to third. Thompson now pinch-running for Incaviglia. Jordan grounded to third as Thompson went to second. Stocker walked. Timlin now pitching. Dykstra singled to right as Thompson went to third and Stocker to second. Duncan struck out. Kruk grounded to second.

Toronto—Thompson now in left field. Molitor doubled to left. Carter struck out. Mit. Williams now pitching. Molitor stole third. Olerud hit a sacrifice fly to right, scoring Molitor. Alomar walked. Alomar stole second. Alomar caught trying to steal third, pitcher to third baseman.

NINTH INNING

Philadelphia—Hollins struck out. Daulton singled to first.

Eisenreich grounded into a double play, third baseman to second baseman to first baseman.

Toronto—Batiste now at third. Fernandez walked. Sprague reached first as Fernandez was forced at second, third baseman to second baseman. Griffin now pinch-running for Sprague. Borders grounded into a double play, shortstop to second baseman to first baseman.

GAME 3

HIGHLIGHTS

TORONTO 10, PHILADELPHIA 3

Why the Blue Jays won: Toronto Manager Cito Gaston shook up his lineup—he sent A.L. batting champion John Olerud to the bench so he could keep red-hot Paul Molitor in the batting order—and came out a big winner. With the DH rule not in effect in the National League champions' ballpark, Gaston benched Olerud, a lefthanded-hitting first baseman, against Phillies lefthander Danny Jackson and replaced him with his regular DH, Molitor. The Jays proceeded to go on a 13-hit spree, with Molitor tripling home two runs in the first inning and ripping a bases-empty home run in the third. Roberto Alomar hit three singles and a triple, scored two runs and batted in two.

Why the Phillies lost: They could do little against Toronto starter Pat Hentgen, a 19-game winner who had been hammered in his lone appearance in the A.L. playoffs. Hentgen permitted only five hits and one run over six innings and struck out five batters in the first three innings.

The turning points:

1. After falling behind by a 3-0 score in the top of the first at Veterans Stadium, the Phillies made some noise of their own in the bottom half of the inning—but to no avail. After leadoff hitter Lenny Dykstra struck out, Mariano Duncan and John Kruk followed with singles and moved to third and second base, respectively, when Toronto right fielder Joe Carter overran Kruk's hit. But Hentgen then struck out cleanup man Dave Hollins and No. 5 hitter Darren Daulton. Crisis averted.

2. The failure of Philadelphia's bullpen to keep the Phillies in the game. While starter Jackson was shaky at best, relievers Ben Rivera and Larry Andersen let the game get away. They pitched a total of 2⅓ innings and were roughed up for seven hits and six runs.

Notable: The start of the game was delayed one hour, 12 minutes by rain. Still, the game was completed with no problem, keeping alive the remarkable record of every World Series game ever played having gone at least 8½ innings. . . . The Blue Jays rapped three triples in Game 3. . . . Alomar stole two bases, increasing his total to four in this Series.

Quotable: "I was relaxed at first base," Molitor said of his rare use defensively, "though I wasn't coordinated on a couple of plays. Whatever Cito decides, his players are going to make it work." . . . "I really felt I had to redeem myself," said Hent-

gen, alluding to his subpar effort in Game 3 of the A.L. playoffs. "I felt I let my teammates down in the LCS. We were ahead 2-0 (in games) over the White Sox and I let them back in. I was determined not to let that happen again." . . . Hentgen, on his first-inning jam: "I told myself that I had to strike Hollins out, don't let him put the ball in play and get the run in. The first inning was a big lift for me."

BOX SCORE

TUESDAY, OCTOBER 19, AT PHILADELPHIA

Toronto	AB	R	H	RBI	PO	A
Henderson, lf	4	2	2	0	1	0
White, cf	4	2	1	1	3	0
Molitor, 1b	4	3	3	3	7	1
Carter, rf	4	1	1	1	1	0
Alomar, 2b	5	2	4	2	1	4
Fernandez, ss	3	0	2	2	3	3
Sprague, 3b	4	0	0	1	0	0
Borders, c	4	0	0	0	10	0
Hentgen, p	3	0	0	0	0	0
Cox, p	1	0	0	0	1	0
D. Ward, p	0	0	0	0	0	0
Totals	36	10	13	10	27	8

Philadelphia	AB	R	H	RBI	PO	A
Dykstra, cf	5	0	1	0	2	0
Duncan, 2b	5	0	2	1	2	3
Kruk, 1b	3	1	2	0	7	0
Hollins, 3b	3	0	0	0	1	2
Daulton, c	3	0	0	0	4	0
Eisenreich, rf	4	0	1	1	4	0
Incaviglia, lf	3	0	0	0	3	0
Thigpen, p	0	0	0	0	0	1
bMorandini, ph	0	0	0	0	0	0
Andersen, p	0	0	0	0	0	0
Stocker, ss	4	0	1	0	3	3
Jackson, p	1	0	0	0	0	0
aChamberlain, ph	1	0	0	0	0	0
Rivera, p	0	0	0	0	0	0
Thompson, lf	2	2	2	1	1	0
Totals	34	3	9	3	27	9

Toronto	3 0 1	0 0 1	3 0 2—10			
Philadelphia	0 0 0	0 0 1	1 0 1— 3			

Toronto	IP	H	R	ER	BB	SO
Hentgen (W)	6	5	1	1	3	6
Cox	2	3	1	1	2	2
D. Ward	1	1	1	1	0	2

Philadelphia	IP	H	R	ER	BB	SO
Jackson (L)	5	6	4	4	1	1
Rivera	1⅓	4	4	4	2	3
Thigpen	1⅔	0	0	0	1	0
Andersen	1	3	2	2	0	0

Bases on Balls—Off Hentgen 3 (Hollins, Kruk, Daulton), off Cox 2 (Kruk, Morandini), off Jackson 1 (White), off Rivera 2 (Borders, Molitor), off Thigpen 1 (Fernandez).

Strikeouts—By Hentgen 6 (Dykstra, Hollins, Daulton, Incaviglia 2, Jackson), by Cox 2 (Stocker 2), by D. Ward 2 (Duncan, Kruk), by Jackson 1 (Sprague), by Rivera 3 (Sprague, Hentgen, Carter).

aGrounded into double play for Jackson in fifth. bWalked for Thigpen in eighth. E—Carter. DP—Toronto 2, Philadelphia 9. LOB—Toronto 7, Philadelphia 9. 2B—Henderson, White, Molitor, Alomar. HR—Thompson, Molitor. SB—Alomar 2. SF—Carter, Fernandez, Sprague. HBP—By Thigpen (Henderson). U—Johnson, plate; Williams, first; McClelland, second; DeMuth, third; Phillips, left field; Runge, right field. T—3:16. A—62,689.

FIRST INNING

Toronto—Henderson singled to center. White walked. Molitor tripled to right-center, scoring Henderson and White. Carter hit a sacrifice fly to right, scoring Molitor. Alomar lined to third. Fernandez lined to right.

Philadelphia—Dykstra struck out. Duncan singled to left. Kruk singled to center and went to second as the right fielder bobbled the ball for an error. Duncan advanced to third on the play. Hollins and Daulton struck out.

SECOND INNING

Toronto—Sprague grounded to short. Borders grounded to second. Hentgen popped to second.

Philadelphia—Eisenreich grounded to short. Incaviglia struck out. Stocker grounded to second.

THIRD INNING

Toronto—Henderson flied to right. White popped to second. Molitor homered to left. Carter singled to center. Alomar singled to short as Carter went to second. Fernandez singled to first as Carter went to third and Alomar to second. Sprague struck out.

Philadelphia—Jackson struck out. Dykstra grounded to first. Duncan flied to center.

FOURTH INNING

Toronto—Borders flied to left. Hentgen grounded to short. Henderson fouled to left.

Philadelphia—Kruk doubled to right. Hollins walked. Daulton popped to second. Eisenreich lined to left. Incaviglia flied to center.

FIFTH INNING

Toronto—White and Molitor grounded to third. Carter lined to left.

Philadelphia—Stocker singled to right. Chamberlain, pinch-hitting for Jackson, grounded into a double play, second baseman to shortstop to first baseman. Dykstra flied to center.

SIXTH INNING

Toronto—Rivera now pitching. Alomar singled to left, then stole second and third. Fernandez hit a sacrifice fly to Eisenreich, scoring Alomar. Sprague struck out. Borders walked. Hentgen struck out.

Philadelphia—Duncan fouled to first. Kruk walked. Hollins lined to right. Daulton walked. Eisenreich singled to center, scoring Kruk as Daulton went to second. Incaviglia struck out.

SEVENTH INNING

Toronto—Henderson doubled to right-center. White tripled to right, scoring Henderson. Molitor lined to left. Carter struck out. Alomar singled to right, scoring White as Molitor went to third. Thigpen now pitching and Thompson in left field. Fernandez walked. Sprague hit a sacrifice fly to left, scoring Molitor. Borders lined to center.

Philadelphia—Cox now pitching. Stocker struck out. Thompson singled to second. Dykstra singled to right, Thompson went to third. Duncan singled to center, scoring Thompson as Dykstra went to second. Kruk walked. Hollins grounded into a double play, first baseman to shortstop to pitcher covering first.

EIGHTH INNING

Toronto—Cox grounded to short. Henderson was hit by a pitch. Henderson picked off first, pitcher to first baseman. White popped to short.

Philadelphia—Daulton popped to short. Eisenreich grounded to second. Morandini, pinch-hitting for Thigpen, walked. Stocker struck out.

NINTH INNING

Toronto—Andersen now pitching. Molitor singled to short.

Carter reached first on a fielder's choice as Molitor was out at second, second baseman to shortstop. Alomar tripled to right-center, scoring Carter. Fernandez singled to short, scoring Alomar. Sprague reached first on a fielder's choice as Fernandez was out at second, second baseman to shortstop. Borders lined to center.

Philadelphia—D. Ward now pitching. Thompson homered to right. Dykstra grounded to second. Duncan and Kruk struck out.

GAME 4

| HIGHLIGHTS |

TORONTO 15, PHILADELPHIA 14

Why the Blue Jays won: No deficit was too large to overcome—the Phillies had leads of 6-3, 12-7 and 14-9—as the Jays continued to maul a Philadelphia pitching staff that by the end of the Series would have an earned-run average of 7.57.

Why the Phillies lost: Lenny Dykstra wasn't allowed to pitch. The Phils' make-it-happen center fielder did virtually everything else. He walloped a double and two homers, scored four runs, drove in four runs, stole a base and had an assist.

The turning points:

1. When Toronto first showed its resiliency in the third inning. Trailing 6-3, the Blue Jays battled back to seize the lead. After John Olerud drew a one-out walk off Phillies starter Tommy Greene, Paul Molitor, Tony Fernandez and Pat Borders followed with singles, inching the Jays within one run and sending Greene to the showers. A forceout grounder and a base on balls brought Devon White to the plate with the bases loaded, and White singled home the tying and go-ahead runs off Roger Mason.

2. When Toronto showed its resiliency again, this time in the eighth inning. Down by a 14-9 score, the Blue Jays struck for six runs in a stunning rally capped by a two-run single by Rickey Henderson and a two-run triple by White. Both key hits, which came with two out, were off Phils reliever Mitch Williams, who allowed two inherited runners and three other Blue Jays to score in his brief stint (two-thirds of an inning).

Notable: Dykstra, coming off a 19-homer season (by far his best power year in the majors), ran his postseason homer total to nine over 30 games. Projected over a full season, that would compute to 48 home runs. . . . Molitor remained in the lineup for the Jays, taking over this time for Ed Sprague at third base. First baseman Olerud returned to the lineup. . . . Fernandez and Phils left fielder Milt Thompson, not exactly big boppers on their robust-hitting clubs, each drove in five runs in the highest-scoring game in postseason history. . . . The contest also was the longest in World Series history, running 4 hours, 14 minutes.

Quotable: "There are not many words to describe it," Dykstra said of the goings-on in Game 4. "I could care less about what I did personally. We were in control of it the whole way. And they just kept pounding and pounding. It was an unbelievable game." ... "Yeah, I guess it was a hitters night," Williams said. "But still, I have no excuse. I just stunk. This is tough. Real tough." ... "Everyone's seeing the ball well," White said. "It seems like the pitchers are just throwing it in there, but this time of year everybody's 'zoned in.' " ... "It's been a weird year for me," said Fernandez, who began the season with the New York Mets but returned to his old club, the Blue Jays, in a June trade. "God works in mysterious ways."

BOX SCORE

WEDNESDAY, OCTOBER 20, AT PHILADELPHIA

Toronto	AB	R	H	RBI	PO	A
Henderson, lf	5	2	2	2	1	0
White, cf	5	2	3	4	3	0
Alomar, 2b	6	1	2	1	0	5
Carter, rf	6	2	3	0	2	0
Olerud, 1b	4	2	1	0	8	0
Molitor, 3b	4	2	2	2	0	1
Griffin, 3b	0	0	0	0	0	0
Fernandez, ss	6	2	3	5	4	2
Borders, c	4	1	1	1	9	0
Stottlemyre, p	0	0	0	0	0	0
Butler, ph	1	1	0	0	0	0
Leiter, p	1	0	1	0	0	0
Castillo, p	1	0	0	0	0	0
Sprague, ph	1	0	0	0	0	0
Timlin, p	0	0	0	0	0	0
D. Ward, p	0	0	0	0	0	0
Totals	44	15	18	15	27	8

Philadelphia	AB	R	H	RBI	PO	A
Dykstra, cf	5	4	3	4	0	1
Duncan, 2b	6	1	3	1	4	4
Kruk, 1b	5	0	0	0	10	1
Hollins, 3b	4	3	2	0	3	3
Daulton, c	3	2	1	3	6	0
Eisenreich, rf	4	2	1	1	3	0
Thompson, lf	5	1	3	5	2	0
Stocker, ss	4	0	0	0	2	2
Greene, p	1	1	1	0	0	0
Mason, p	1	0	0	0	0	0
Jordan, ph	1	0	0	0	0	0
West, p	0	0	0	0	0	0
Chamberlain, ph	1	0	0	0	0	0
Andersen, p	0	0	0	0	0	0
Mit. Williams, p	0	0	0	0	0	0
Morandini, ph	1	0	0	0	0	0
Thigpen, p	0	0	0	0	0	0
Totals	41	14	14	14	27	11

Toronto			3 0 4	0 0 2	0 6 0—15
Philadelphia			4 2 0	1 5 1	1 0 0—14

Toronto	IP	H	R	ER	BB	SO
Stottlemyre	2	3	6	6	4	1
Leiter	2⅔	8	6	6	0	1
Castillo (W)	2⅓	3	2	2	3	1
Timlin	⅔	0	0	0	0	2
D. Ward (S)	1⅓	0	0	0	0	2

Philadelphia	IP	H	R	ER	BB	SO
Greene	2⅓	7	7	7	4	1
Mason	2⅔	2	0	0	1	2
West	1	3	2	2	0	0
Andersen	1⅓	2	3	3	1	2
Mit. Williams (L)	⅔	3	3	3	1	1
Thigpen	1	1	0	0	0	0

Bases on balls—Off Stottlemyre 4 (Dykstra, Hollins, Daulton, Eisenreich), off Castillo 3 (Stocker, Kruk, Hollins), off Greene 4 (White, Molitor, Stottlemyre, Olerud), off Mason 1 (Henderson), off Andersen 1 (Olerud), off Mit. Williams 1 (Borders).

Strikeouts—By Stottlemyre 1 (Kruk), by Leiter 1 (Daulton), by Castillo 1 (Chamberlain), by Timlin 2 (Stocker, Morandini), by D. Ward 2 (Dykstra, Kruk), by Greene 1 (White), by Mason 2 (Alomar, Fernandez), by Andersen 2 (Castillo, Henderson), by Mit. Williams 1 (Sprague).

aHit into force play for Stottlemyre in third. bGrounded out for Mason in fifth. cStruck out for West in sixth. dStruck out for Castillo in eighth. eStruck out for Mit. Williams in eighth. LOB—Toronto 10, Philadelphia 8. 2B—Henderson, White, Carter, Leiter, Dykstra, Hollins, Thompson, Molitor. 3B—White, Thompson. HR—Dykstra 2, Daulton. SB—Henderson, White, Dykstra, Duncan. HBP—By Castillo (Daulton), by West (Molitor). U—Williams, plate; McClelland, first; DeMuth, second; Phillips, third; Runge, left field; Johnson, right field. T—4:14. A—62,731.

PLAY BY PLAY

FIRST INNING

Toronto—Henderson doubled to center. White walked. Alomar fouled to left. Carter singled to third, Henderson went to third and Alomar to second. Olerud popped to first. Molitor walked, scoring Henderson as Alomar went to third and Carter to second. Fernandez singled to right, scoring White and Carter as Molitor went to third. Borders lined to left.

Philadelphia—Dykstra walked. Duncan flied to right. Dykstra stole second. Kruk struck out. Hollins and Daulton walked. Eisenreich walked, scoring Dykstra. Thompson tripled to center, scoring Hollins, Daulton and Eisenreich. Stocker grounded to first.

SECOND INNING

Toronto—Stottlemyre walked. Henderson fouled to first. White struck out. Alomar singled to center, Stottlemyre went to second but was out trying for third, center fielder to shortstop to third baseman.

Philadelphia—Greene singled to center. Dykstra homered to right, scoring Greene. Duncan flied to center. Kruk grounded to second. Hollins popped to the catcher.

THIRD INNING

Toronto—Carter popped to second. Olerud walked. Molitor singled to right, Olerud went to third. Fernandez singled to right, scoring Olerud as Molitor went to third. Borders singled to left, scoring Molitor as Fernandez went to second. Butler, pinch-hitting for Stottlemyre against Mason, reached on a fielder's choice as Borders was retired at second, first baseman to second baseman. Fernandez went to third on the play. Henderson walked. White singled to right, scoring Fernandez and Butler as Henderson went to second. Henderson stole third and White stole second. Alomar struck out.

Philadelphia—Leiter now pitching. Daulton struck out. Eisenreich grounded to short. Thompson grounded to second.

FOURTH INNING

Toronto—Carter popped to short. Olerud popped to third. Molitor fouled to right.

Philadelphia—Stocker popped to Fernandez. Mason lined to center. Dykstra doubled to right. Duncan singled to center, scoring Dykstra. Kruk lined to right.

FIFTH INNING

Toronto—Fernandez struck out. Borders grounded to third. Leiter doubled to left. Henderson grounded to second.

Philadelphia—Hollins singled to third. Daulton homered to right, scoring Hollins. Eisenreich singled to second. Thompson doubled to left, scoring Eisenreich. Stocker grounded to third. Jordan, pinch-hitting for Mason, grounded to short. Dykstra homered to right, scoring Thompson. Duncan singled to center. Castillo now pitching. Duncan stole second. Kruk grounded to second.

SIXTH INNING

Toronto—West now pitching. White doubled to left. Alomar singled to center, scoring White. Carter flied to right. Olerud singled to left, Alomar went to third. Molitor was hit by a pitch. Fernandez grounded to Duncan as Alomar scored, Olerud went to third and Molitor went to second. Borders flied to right.

Philadelphia—Hollins doubled to left-center. Daulton flied to left. Eisenreich popped to the catcher. Thompson singled to second, scoring Hollins. Stocker walked. Chamberlain, pinch-hitting for West, struck out.

SEVENTH INNING

Toronto—Andersen now pitching. Castillo and Henderson struck out. White fouled to third.

Philadelphia—Dykstra grounded to second. Duncan singled to short. Kruk and Hollins walked. Daulton was hit by a pitch, scoring Duncan as Kruk went to third and Hollins to second. Eisenreich popped to short. Thompson reached on a fielder's choice as Daulton was forced at second, second baseman to shortstop.

EIGHTH INNING

Toronto—Alomar grounded to third. Carter singled to right. Olerud walked. Molitor reached second on an error by the third baseman. Carter scored and Olerud went to third on the play. Mit. Williams now pitching. Fernandez singled to left, scoring Olerud as Molitor went to third. Borders walked. Sprague, pinch-hitting for Castillo, struck out. Henderson singled to center, scoring Molitor and Fernandez as Borders went to second. White tripled to right-center, scoring Borders and Henderson. Alomar grounded to third.

Philadelphia—Timlin now pitching. Stocker struck out. Morandini pinch-hitting for Mit. Williams, struck out. D. Ward now pitching. Dykstra struck out.

NINTH INNING

Toronto—Thigpen now pitching. Carter doubled to left. Olerud grounded to second, Carter went to third. Molitor grounded to short. Fernandez grounded to second.

Philadelphia—Griffin now at third. Duncan popped to short. Kruk struck out. Hollins flied to center.

GAME 5

PHILADELPHIA 2, TORONTO 0

Why the Phillies won: The night after the Phillies' pitching staff had been brutalized for 15 runs and 18 hits, righthander Curt Schilling came through with a godsend performance for the N.L. champions. In a remarkable effort on the heels of a record-setting slugfest, Schilling spun a five-hit shutout and breathed new life into the Phils.

Why the Blue Jays lost: They fell behind early and couldn't take advantage of the few opportunities they did have.

The turning points:

1. The top of the eighth inning. Pat Borders and pinch-hitter Rob Butler led off with singles for the Blue Jays, who were trying to cut into the 2-0 deficit they had faced since the second inning. Rickey Henderson then rapped a grounder that deflected off the glove of Schilling, who scrambled after the ball and caught Willie Canate, running for Borders, between third base and home. After Canate was retired in a rundown, Devon White struck out and Roberto Alomar grounded to second.

2. The top of the sixth inning. After Blue Jays starting pitcher Juan Guzman struck out against

Schilling, Henderson and White walked and Alomar, hitting .474 at this juncture of the Series, strolled to the plate. Alomar, the American League's No. 3 batsman in 1993 at .326, couldn't get the job done against Schilling, bouncing into a second-to-short-to-first double play.

Notable: The Phils, on the brink of elimination with a three-games-to-one deficit entering Game 5, struck quickly in their attempt to stay alive. Lenny Dykstra was his usual catalytic self. After drawing a leadoff walk in the first inning, Dykstra stole second, advanced to third on catcher Borders' throwing error and scored on John Kruk's ground-out.... With pitcher Schilling on deck and two out in the second inning, rookie shortstop Kevin Stocker came to bat with Darren Daulton on third base. The Jays elected to pitch to Stocker, who rammed a run-scoring double down the right-field line.

Quotable: "Honest to God, I don't think we had any choice but for him (Schilling) to pitch nine," Kruk said. "Our bullpen was depleted. And if it wasn't depleted, it was shellshocked." ... "I've always gone out with the attitude that if I don't go nine, I'm not doing my job," said Schilling, whose seven complete games in the regular season tied for second place among N.L. pitchers. ... Catcher Daulton, trying to ease the pregame pressure on his pitcher, told Schilling: "Just keep them under 14." ... "I was thinking two runs is not enough to beat me, not with this (the Blue Jays') offense," Toronto's Guzman said.

BOX SCORE

THURSDAY, OCTOBER 21, AT PHILADELPHIA

Toronto	AB	R	H	RBI	PO	A
Henderson, lf	3	0	0	0	2	0
White, cf	3	0	0	0	1	0
Alomar, 2b	3	0	1	0	2	2
Carter, rf	4	0	0	0	4	0
Olerud, 1b	4	0	0	0	5	0
Molitor, 3b	4	0	1	0	0	1
Fernandez, ss	3	0	0	0	1	1
Borders, c	3	0	2	0	6	1
aCanate, pr	0	0	0	0	0	0
Knorr, c	0	0	0	0	3	0
Guzman, p	2	0	0	0	0	0
bButler, ph	1	0	1	0	0	0
Cox, p	0	0	0	0	0	0
Totals	30	0	5	0	24	5

Philadelphia	AB	R	H	RBI	PO	A
Dykstra, cf	2	1	0	0	6	0
Duncan, 2b	4	0	0	0	3	3
Kruk, 1b	3	0	1	1	5	1
Hollins, 3b	3	0	1	0	1	1
Batiste, 3b	0	0	0	0	0	0
Daulton, c	4	1	1	0	6	2
Eisenreich, rf	4	0	0	0	2	0
Thompson, lf	3	0	0	0	2	0
Stocker, ss	2	0	1	1	2	3
Schilling, p	2	0	1	0	0	1
Totals	27	2	5	2	27	11

Toronto	0 0 0	0 0 0	0 0 0—0			
Philadelphia	1 1 0	0 0 0	0 0 x—2			

Toronto	IP	H	R	ER	BB	SO
Guzman (L)	7	5	2	1	4	6
Cox	1	0	0	0	2	3

Philadelphia	IP	H	R	ER	BB	SO
Schilling (W)	9	5	0	0	3	6

Bases on balls—Off Guzman 4 (Dykstra 2, Thompson, Stocker), off Cox 2 (Kruk, Hollins), off Schilling 3 (Alomar, Henderson, White).

Strikeouts—By Guzman 6 (Hollins, Schilling, Duncan, Kruk, Stocker, Dykstra), by Cox 3 (Daulton, Eisenreich, Thompson), by Schilling 6 (Fernandez, White 2, Carter, Guzman, Olerud).

aRan for Borders in eighth. bSingled for Guzman in eighth. E—Borders, Duncan. DP—Toronto 1, Philadelphia 3. LOB—Toronto 6, Philadelphia 8. 2B—Daulton, Stocker. SB—Dykstra. CS—Alomar. SH—Schilling. U—McClelland, plate; DeMuth, first; Phillips, second; Runge, third; Johnson, left field; Williams, right field. T—2:53. A—62,706.

PLAY BY PLAY

FIRST INNING
Toronto—Henderson grounded to second. White flied to center. Alomar walked. Carter flied to center.

Philadelphia—Dykstra walked. Dykstra stole second and reached third on a throwing error by the catcher. Duncan flied to right.

SECOND INNING
Toronto—Olerud lined to left. Molitor flied to right. Fernandez struck out.

Philadelphia—Daulton doubled to left-center. Eisenreich grounded to first, Daulton went to third. Thompson flied to left. Stocker doubled to right, scoring Daulton. Schilling struck out.

THIRD INNING
Toronto—Borders singled to right. Guzman grounded into a double play, first baseman to shortstop to second baseman. Henderson flied to center.

Philadelphia—Dykstra flied to center. Duncan grounded to third. Kruk singled to center. Hollins singled to right, Kruk went to second. Daulton popped to second.

FOURTH INNING
Toronto—White struck out. Alomar singled to right. Carter struck out as Alomar was caught trying to steal second, catcher to second baseman.

Philadelphia—Eisenreich grounded to second. Thompson and Stocker walked. Thompson went to third and Stocker to second as Schilling sacrificed, catcher to second baseman covering first. Dykstra was walked intentionally. Duncan struck out.

FIFTH INNING
Toronto—Olerud flied to right. Molitor reached first on an error by the second baseman. Fernandez lined to left. Borders flied to center.

Philadelphia—Kruk struck out. Hollins and Daulton flied to right.

SIXTH INNING
Toronto—Guzman struck out. Henderson and White walked. Alomar grounded into a double play, second baseman to shortstop to first baseman.

Philadelphia—Eisenreich lined to left. Thompson lined to right. Stocker struck out.

SEVENTH INNING
Toronto—Carter grounded to third. Olerud struck out. Molitor singled to short. Fernandez flied to center.

Philadelphia—Schilling singled to right. Dykstra struck out. Duncan grounded into a double play, shortstop to first baseman.

EIGHTH INNING
Toronto—Borders singled to left. Canate now pinch-running for Borders. Butler, pinch-hitting for Guzman, singled to right, Canate went to third. Henderson reached on a fielder's choice as Canate was tagged out, pitcher to catcher to third baseman. Butler went to second on the play. White struck out. Alomar grounded to second.

Philadelphia—Cox now pitching and Knorr catching. Kruk and Hollins walked. Daulton, Eisenreich and Thompson struck out.

NINTH INNING
Toronto—Batiste now at third. Carter popped to second. Olerud grounded to short. Molitor lined to center.

GAME 6

HIGHLIGHTS

TORONTO 8, PHILADELPHIA 6

Why the Blue Jays won: Veteran outfielder Joe Carter hit one of the most dramatic home runs in baseball history. With Toronto leading the 1993 World Series three games to two but trailing, 6-5, in the ninth inning of Game 6, the Blue Jays went to work against reliever Mitch Williams. Rickey Henderson walked on four pitches and, after Devon White flied out, Paul Molitor singled to center field. That brought up Carter, who in the last eight seasons had driven in more than 100 runs seven times (and had 98 RBIs in his "off" year). Williams and Carter battled to a 2-2 count as the Toronto crowd cheered wildly for a game-tying hit and maybe more. Carter supplied the latter, ripping Williams' next pitch over the left-field wall. The Jays were 8-6 victors and Series champions.

Why the Phillies lost: They simply had no one to entrust with the one-run lead they had built with a five-run seventh (which featured a three-run homer by Lenny Dykstra). When Williams took the mound in the bottom of the ninth, he was one of five Philadelphia pitchers with a Series ERA in double figures.

The turning points:

1. When Williams was called upon to pitch the ninth. While that assessment might seem unfair to a man who registered 43 saves for the Phillies in the regular season (and boasted a career total of 186), there was a genuine sense of foreboding as the 28-year-old lefthander made his way from the bullpen to the mound. For one thing, Williams usually was true to his "Wild Thing" nickname—and reliance on a wild pitcher in a one-run game was cause for major concern (or, in some observers' view, simply asking for trouble). Second, and perhaps most prominent in everyone's mind, was the specter of Williams' most recent outing—a horrific, losing effort three nights earlier in Game 4.

2. When the Blue Jays rocked Phils starter Terry Mulholland for three first-inning runs, an indication that Toronto's mashers might well get a crack at the Phillies' relief corps.

Notable: In the 89 Series played before the '93 classic, none had ended with a come-from-behind homer. In fact, only one game in 531 Series contests had ever concluded in such a fashion, with the Dodgers' Kirk Gibson providing that outcome in the opener of the 1988 Series. . . . Dykstra finished with four home runs against the Jays, which tied him for second for most homers in one Series. . . . The Jays were the first team since the Yankees of 1977-78 to repeat as Series winners.

Quotable: "As I told him after the game, he's the one who got us here," Phils Manager Jim Fregosi said of Williams. . . . "With Mitch out there, we knew something good was going to happen (for Toronto)," Carter said. "And it did." . . . Williams' reaction to his "goat" role: "I didn't do the job for two games in the World Series. It's happened before, when I didn't do the job in a couple of games. I have to look at it like maybe we wouldn't have been here if I hadn't done the job I did during the year. Well, we got here and I let us down. I'm not going to sit here and make excuses. I threw the pitch that cost us the World Series. That's tough to deal with, but I'm going to deal with it."

BOX SCORE

SATURDAY, OCTOBER 23, AT TORONTO

Philadelphia	AB	R	H	RBI	PO	A
Dykstra, cf	3	1	1	3	5	0
Duncan, dh	5	1	1	0	0	0
Kruk, 1b	3	0	0	0	6	0
Hollins, 3b	5	1	1	1	0	1
Batiste, 3b	0	0	0	0	0	0
Daulton, c	4	1	1	0	3	0
Eisenreich, rf	5	0	2	1	2	0
Thompson, lf	3	0	0	0	4	0
Incaviglia, ph-lf	0	0	0	1	3	0
Stocker, ss	3	1	0	0	0	1
Morandini, 2b	4	1	1	0	2	0
Mulholland, p	0	0	0	0	0	1
Mason, p	0	0	0	0	0	0
West, p	0	0	0	0	0	0
Andersen, p	0	0	0	0	0	0
Mit. Williams, p	0	0	0	0	0	0
Totals	35	6	7	6	25	3

Toronto	AB	R	H	RBI	PO	A
Henderson, lf	4	1	0	0	2	0
White, cf	4	1	0	0	6	0
Molitor, dh	5	3	3	2	0	0
Carter, rf	4	1	1	4	3	0
Olerud, 1b	3	1	1	0	6	0
Griffin, pr-3b	0	0	0	0	0	0
Alomar, 2b	4	1	3	1	1	3
Fernandez, ss	3	0	0	0	1	0
Sprague, 3b-1b	2	0	0	1	3	2
Borders, c	4	0	2	0	5	0
Stewart, p	0	0	0	0	0	1
Cox, p	0	0	0	0	0	0
Leiter, p	0	0	0	0	0	0
D. Ward, p	0	0	0	0	0	0
Totals	33	8	10	8	27	6

Philadelphia						
Philadelphia	0 0 0	1 0 0	5 0 0—6			
Toronto	3 0 0	1 1 0	0 0 3—8			

One out when winning run scored.

Philadelphia	IP	H	R	ER	BB	SO
Mulholland	5	7	5	5	1	1
Mason	2 1/3	1	0	0	0	2
West	†0	0	0	0	1	0
Andersen	2/3	0	0	0	1	0
Mit. Williams (L)	1/3	2	3	3	1	0

Toronto	IP	H	R	ER	BB	SO
Stewart	*6	4	4	4	4	2
Cox	1/3	3	2	2	1	1
Leiter	1 2/3	0	0	0	1	2
D. Ward (W)	1	0	0	0	0	0

*Pitched to three batters in seventh.
†Pitched to one batter in eighth.

Bases on balls—Off Mulholland 1 (White), off West 1 (Olerud), off Andersen 1 (Sprague), off Mit. Williams 1 (Henderson), off Stewart 4 (Kruk 2, Dykstra, Stocker), off Cox 1 (Daulton), off Leiter 1 (Dykstra).

Strikeouts—By Mulholland 1 (White), by Mason 2 (Fernandez, White), by Stewart 2 (Dykstra, Duncan), by Cox 1 (Kruk), by Leiter 2 (Stocker, Morandini).

aHit sacrifice fly for Thompson in seventh. bRan for Olerud in eighth. E—Alomar, Sprague. LOB—Philadelphia 9, Toronto 7. 2B—Daulton, Olerud, Alomar. 3B—Molitor. HR—Molitor, Dykstra, Carter. SB—Dykstra, Duncan. SF—Incaviglia, Carter, Sprague. HBP—By Andersen (Fernandez). U—DeMuth, plate; Phillips, first; Runge, second; Johnson, third; Williams, left field; McClelland, right field. T—3:27. A—52,195.

PLAY BY PLAY

FIRST INNING

Philadelphia—Dykstra struck out. Duncan flied to right. Kruk walked. Hollins flied to right.

Toronto—Henderson lined to center. White walked. Molitor tripled to right, scoring White. Carter hit a sacrifice fly to left, scoring Molitor. Olerud doubled to left-center. Alomar singled to left-center, scoring Olerud. Fernandez flied to center.

SECOND INNING

Philadelphia—Daulton flied to left. Eisenreich lined to left. Thompson grounded to third.

Toronto—Sprague flied to center. Borders singled to center. Henderson popped to second. White struck out.

THIRD INNING

Philadelphia—Stocker and Morandini flied to center. Dykstra walked. Duncan struck out.

Toronto—Molitor lined to left. Carter grounded to first. Olerud flied to left.

FOURTH INNING

Philadelphia—Kruk grounded to the pitcher. Hollins fouled to third. Daulton doubled to left. Eisenreich singled to center, scoring Daulton. Thompson grounded to second.

Toronto—Alomar doubled to left. Fernandez grounded to Stocker, Alomar went to third. Sprague hit a sacrifice fly to Eisenreich, scoring Alomar. Borders singled to center. Henderson grounded to the pitcher.

FIFTH INNING

Philadelphia—Stocker lined to short. Morandini reached first on an error by the second baseman. Dykstra flied to right. Duncan reached first on an error by the third baseman, Morandini went to second. Kruk walked. Hollins grounded to first.

Toronto—White lined to right. Molitor homered to left. Carter grounded to third. Olerud lined to center.

SIXTH INNING

Philadelphia—Daulton flied to center. Eisenreich grounded to second. Thompson fouled to third.

Toronto—Mason now pitching. Alomar singled to right-center. Fernandez struck out. Sprague flied to left. Borders popped to first.

SEVENTH INNING

Philadelphia—Stocker walked. Morandini singled to left, Stocker went to third. Dykstra homered to right, scoring Stocker and Morandini. Cox now pitching. Duncan singled to center. Kruk struck out. Duncan stole second. Hollins singled to center, scoring Duncan. Daulton walked. Eisenreich singled to the pitcher, Hollins went to third and Daulton to second. Leiter now pitching. Incaviglia, pinch-hitting for Thompson, hit a sacrifice fly to center, scoring Hollins as Daulton went to third. Stocker struck out.

Toronto—Incaviglia now in left field. Henderson flied to left. White struck out. Molitor lined to center.

EIGHTH INNING

Philadelphia—Morandini struck out. Dykstra walked. Duncan popped to second. Dykstra stole second. Kruk grounded to third.

Toronto—Carter flied to left. West now pitching. Olerud

walked. Griffin now pinch-running for Olerud. Andersen now pitching. Alomar grounded to first, Griffin went to second. Fernandez was hit by a pitch. Sprague walked. Borders popped to second.

NINTH INNING

Philadelphia—D. Ward now pitching, Griffin at third and Sprague at first. Hollins flied to center. Daulton grounded to second. Eisenreich flied to center.

Toronto—Mit. Williams now pitching and Batiste at third. Henderson walked. White flied to left. Molitor singled to center, Henderson went to second. Carter homered to left, scoring Henderson and Molitor.

STATISTICS

TORONTO BLUE JAYS' BATTING AND FIELDING AVERAGES

Player, position	G	AB	R	H	TB	2B	3B	HR	RBI	BB	IBB	SO	Avg.	PO	A	E	Avg.
Leiter, p	3	1	0	1	2	1	0	0	0	0	0	0	1.000	0	0	0	.000
Molitor, dh-1b-3b	6	24	10	12	24	2	2	2	8	3	0	0	.500	7	3	0	1.000
Butler, ph	2	2	1	1	1	0	0	0	0	0	0	0	.500	0	0	0	.000
Alomar, 2b	6	25	5	12	16	2	1	0	6	2	0	3	.480	9	21	2	.938
Fernandez, ss	6	21	2	7	8	1	0	0	9	3	0	3	.333	11	8	0	1.000
Borders, c	6	23	2	7	7	0	0	0	1	2	0	1	.304	50	2	1	.981
White, cf	6	24	8	7	17	3	2	1	7	4	0	7	.292	16	0	0	1.000
Carter, rf	6	25	6	7	14	1	0	2	8	0	0	4	.280	13	0	2	.867
Olerud, 1b	5	17	5	4	8	1	0	1	2	4	1	1	.235	36	0	0	1.000
Henderson, lf	6	22	6	5	7	2	0	0	2	5	0	2	.227	8	0	0	1.000
Sprague, 3b-ph-1b	5	15	0	1	1	0	0	0	2	1	0	6	.067	4	9	2	.867
Cox, p	3	1	0	0	0	0	0	0	0	0	0	0	.000	1	0	0	1.000
Canate, pr	1	0	0	0	0	0	0	0	0	0	0	0	.000	0	0	0	.000
Eichhorn, p	1	0	0	0	0	0	0	0	0	0	0	0	.000	0	0	0	.000
Griffin, pr-3b	3	0	0	0	0	0	0	0	0	0	0	0	.000	3	0	0	1.000
Knorr, c	1	0	0	0	0	0	0	0	0	0	0	0	.000	0	0	0	.000
Stewart, p	2	0	0	0	0	0	0	0	0	0	0	0	.000	1	1	0	1.000
Stottlemyre, p	1	0	0	0	0	0	0	0	0	1	0	0	.000	0	0	0	.000
Timlin, p	2	0	0	0	0	0	0	0	0	0	0	0	.000	0	0	0	.000
D. Ward, p	4	0	0	0	0	0	0	0	0	0	0	0	.000	0	0	0	.000
Castillo, p	2	1	0	0	0	0	0	0	0	0	0	1	.000	0	0	0	.000
Guzman, p	2	2	0	0	0	0	0	0	0	0	0	1	.000	0	1	0	1.000
Hentgen, p	1	3	0	0	0	0	0	0	0	0	0	1	.000	0	0	0	.000
Totals	6	206	45	64	105	13	5	6	45	25	1	30	.311	159	45	7	.967

Butler—Grounded into force out for Stottlemyre in third inning of fourth game; singled for Guzman in eighth inning of fifth game.

Canate—Ran for Borders in eighth inning of fifth game.

Griffin—Ran for Sprague in ninth inning of second game; ran for Olerud in eighth inning of sixth game.

Sprague—Struck out for Castillo in eighth inning of fourth game.

PHILADELPHIA PHILLIES' BATTING AND FIELDING AVERAGES

Player, position	G	AB	R	H	TB	2B	3B	HR	RBI	BB	IBB	SO	Avg.	PO	A	E	Avg.
Greene, p	1	1	1	1	1	0	0	0	0	0	0	0	1.000	0	0	0	.000
Schilling, p	2	2	0	1	1	0	0	0	0	0	0	1	.500	0	3	0	1.000
Dykstra, cf	6	23	9	8	21	1	0	4	8	7	1	4	.348	18	1	0	1.000
Kruk, 1b	6	23	4	8	9	1	0	0	4	7	0	7	.348	42	3	0	1.000
Duncan, 2b-dh	6	29	5	10	12	0	1	0	2	1	0	7	.345	11	17	1	.966
Thompson, lf-pr	5	16	3	5	11	1	1	1	6	1	0	2	.313	10	0	1	.909
Hollins, 3b	6	23	5	6	7	1	0	0	2	6	0	5	.261	9	9	0	1.000
Eisenreich, rf	6	26	3	6	9	0	0	1	7	2	0	4	.231	18	0	0	1.000
Daulton, c	6	23	4	5	10	2	0	1	4	4	1	5	.217	31	4	0	1.000
Stocker, ss	6	19	1	4	5	1	0	0	1	5	0	5	.211	8	13	0	1.000
Jordan, dh-ph	3	10	0	2	2	0	0	0	0	0	0	2	.200	0	0	0	.000
Morandini, ph-2b	3	5	1	1	1	0	0	0	0	1	0	2	.200	2	0	0	1.000
Incaviglia, ph-lf	4	8	0	1	1	0	0	0	1	0	0	4	.125	7	0	0	1.000
Andersen, p	4	0	0	0	0	0	0	0	0	0	0	0	.000	0	0	0	.000
Batiste, 3b	2	0	0	0	0	0	0	0	0	0	0	0	.000	0	1	0	1.000
Mulholland, p	2	0	0	0	0	0	0	0	0	0	0	0	.000	1	1	0	1.000
Rivera, p	1	0	0	0	0	0	0	0	0	0	0	0	.000	0	0	0	.000
Thigpen, p	2	0	0	0	0	0	0	0	0	0	0	0	.000	0	1	0	1.000
West, p	3	0	0	0	0	0	0	0	0	0	0	0	.000	0	0	0	.000
Mit. Williams, p	3	0	0	0	0	0	0	0	0	0	0	0	.000	0	1	0	1.000
Jackson, p	1	1	0	0	0	0	0	0	0	0	0	1	.000	0	0	0	.000

Player, position	G	AB	R	H	TB	2B	3B	HR	RBI	BB	IBB	SO	Avg.	PO	A	E	Avg.
								BATTING							FIELDING		
Mason, p	4	1	0	0	0	0	0	0	0	0	0	0	.000	0	0	0	.000
Chamberlain, ph	2	2	0	0	0	0	0	0	0	0	0	1	.000	0	0	0	.000
Totals	6	212	36	58	90	7	2	7	35	34	2	50	.274	157	54	2	.991

Chamberlain—Grounded into double play for Jackson in fifth inning of third game; struck out for West in sixth inning of fourth game.

Incaviglia—Fouled out for Thompson in eighth inning of first game; hit sacrifice fly for Thompson in seventh inning of sixth game.

Jordan—Grounded out for Mason in fifth inning of fourth game.

Morandini—Walked for Thigpen in eighth inning of third game; struck out for Mit. Williams in eighth inning of fourth game.

Thompson—Ran for Incaviglia in eighth inning of second game.

TORONTO BLUE JAYS' PITCHING RECORDS

Pitcher	G	GS	CG	IP	H	R	ER	HR	BB	IBB	SO	HB	WP	W	L	Pct.	ERA
Timlin	2	0	0	2⅓	2	0	0	0	0	0	4	0	0	0	0	.000	0.00
Eichhorn	1	0	0	⅓	1	0	0	0	1	0	0	0	0	0	0	.000	0.00
Hentgen	1	1	0	6	5	1	1	0	3	0	6	0	0	1	0	1.000	1.50
D. Ward	4	0	0	4⅔	3	2	1	1	0	0	7	0	0	1	0	1.000	1.93
Guzman	2	2	0	12	10	6	5	0	8	2	12	0	1	0	1	.000	3.75
Stewart	2	2	0	12	10	9	9	2	8	0	8	0	1	0	1	.000	6.75
Leiter	3	0	0	7	12	6	6	2	2	0	5	0	0	1	0	1.000	7.71
Castillo	2	0	0	3⅓	6	3	3	1	3	0	1	1	0	1	0	1.000	8.10
Cox	3	0	0	3⅓	6	3	3	0	5	0	6	0	0	0	0	.000	8.10
Stottlemyre	1	1	0	2	3	6	6	1	4	0	1	0	0	0	0	.000	27.00
Totals	6	6	0	53	58	36	34	7	34	2	50	1	2	4	2	.667	5.77

No shutouts. Saves—D. Ward 2.

PHILADELPHIA PHILLIES' PITCHING RECORDS

Pitcher	G	GS	CG	IP	H	R	ER	HR	BB	IBB	SO	HB	WP	W	L	Pct.	ERA
Thigpen	2	0	0	2⅔	1	0	0	0	1	0	0	1	0	0	0	.000	0.00
Mason	4	0	0	7⅔	4	1	1	0	1	0	7	0	0	0	0	.000	1.17
Schilling	2	2	1	15⅓	13	7	6	2	5	0	9	0	0	1	1	.500	3.52
Mulholland	2	2	0	10⅔	14	8	8	2	3	0	5	0	0	1	0	1.000	6.75
Jackson	1	1	0	5	6	4	4	1	1	0	1	0	0	0	1	.000	7.20
Andersen	4	0	0	3⅔	5	5	5	0	3	1	3	1	0	0	0	.000	12.27
Mit. Williams	3	0	0	2⅔	5	6	6	1	4	0	1	0	0	0	2	.000	20.25
Greene	1	1	0	2⅓	7	7	7	0	4	0	1	0	0	0	0	.000	27.00
Rivera	1	0	0	1⅓	4	4	4	0	2	0	3	0	0	0	0	.000	27.00
West	3	0	0	1	5	3	3	0	1	0	0	1	0	0	0	.000	27.00
Totals	6	6	1	52⅓	64	45	44	6	25	1	30	3	0	2	4	.333	7.57

Shutout—Schilling. Save—Mit. Williams.

COMPOSITE SCORE BY INNINGS

Toronto	9	2	6	3	2	5	6	7	5—45	
Philadelphia	7	3	6	2	6	2	8	0	2—36	

MISCELLANEOUS STATISTICS

Sacrifice hits—Schilling.

Sacrifice flies—Carter 3, Sprague 2, Fernandez, Incaviglia, Olerud.

Stolen bases—Alomar 4, Dykstra 4, Duncan 3, Henderson, Molitor, White.

Caught stealing—Alomar 2, Fernandez, Henderson, Stocker.

Double plays—Stocker, Duncan and Kruk 2; Fernandez and Olerud; Sprague, Alomar and Olerud; Alomar, Fernandez and Molitor; Molitor, Fernandez and Cox; Fernandez and Olerud; Kruk, Stocker and Duncan; Daulton and Duncan; Duncan, Stocker and Kruk.

Left on bases—Toronto 4, 5, 7, 10, 6, 7—39; Philadelphia 11, 9, 9, 8, 8, 9—54.

Hit by pitcher—By Thigpen (Henderson), by Castillo (Daulton), by West (Molitor), by Andersen (Fernandez).

Passed balls—Daulton.

Balks—None.

Time of games—First game, 3:27; second game, 3:35; third game, 3:16; fourth game, 4:14; fifth game, 2:53; sixth game, 3:27.

Attendance—First game, 52,011; second game, 52,062; third game, 62,689; fourth game, 62,731; fifth game, 62,706; sixth game, 52,195.

Umpires—Phillips (A.L.), Runge (N.L.), Johnson (A.L.), Williams (N.L.), McClelland (A.L.) and DeMuth (N.L.).

Official scorers—Neil Hohlfeld, BBWAA; Bob Kenney, Camden (N.J.) Courier-Post; Dave Nightingale; Joe Sawchuck, Toronto official scorer.

ALL-STAR GAME

HIGHLIGHTS

AMERICAN LEAGUE 9, NATIONAL LEAGUE 3

Why the American League won: Kirby Puckett shook off his All-Star Game blues and, after a shaky first inning, the A.L. pitching staff got down to business. Puckett, who had failed to collect an extra-base hit in seven previous All-Star contests, walloped a bases-empty home run in the second inning and then contributed a run-scoring double in the junior circuit's three-run outburst in the fifth inning, a flurry that broke a 2-2 tie and sent the A.L. winging toward its sixth straight victory in a series that had begun six decades earlier. After A.L. starter Mark Langston was rocked for a two-run homer by Gary Sheffield in the first inning and permitted a hit and a walk in the second inning, his six successors allowed only one run and four hits and didn't walk a batter.

Why the National League lost: In the big picture, it seemed to lack the stable of bright young stars that the A.L. possessed. In the smaller scheme of things, the National League pitching staff just couldn't handle A.L. hitters, failing to hold the Americans scoreless for more than one inning at a time.

The turning points:

1. The Americans' three-run sixth, which turned the game into a runaway. The A.L. had led by a not-so-comfortable 5-3 score entering the bottom half of that frame, when two runs were scored on wild pitches by John Smoltz.

2. Roberto Alomar's game-tying homer in the third inning, a blow that appeared to put the swagger back into the A.L.

Notable: The Atlanta factor took its toll. Braves Manager Bobby Cox, who directed the N.L. squad, saw his record dip to 0-4 against the A.L. His Braves lost World Series to A.L. teams in 1991 and 1992 and his N.L. All-Stars fell in '92 before losing again in this game. Also, Atlanta right fielder David Justice and Braves shortstop Jeff Blauser committed the only errors of the game, Braves righthander Smoltz uncorked those two errant pitches and Atlanta lefthander Steve Avery was charged with three sixth-inning runs (none of which were earned, however). Things got so bad that Baltimore fans began to mock Braves fans' war chant. . . . While the game didn't qualify as dull, the highlight nonetheless was Randy Johnson's third-inning strikeout of John Kruk. Johnson, the 6-foot-10, hard-throwing lefthander for the Seattle Mariners, sailed a pitch far over Kruk's head and the Phillies' first baseman proceeded to bail out on the next three pitches. In a moment of comic relief, Kruk swung feebly on strike three and

headed for the relative safety of his first base station. . . . Free-agent acquisition Barry Bonds, on his way to a monster season with the Giants, stroked two doubles for the N.L. . . . Toronto Manager Cito Gaston caused a stir—a crescendo of boos, actually—in the ninth inning when he didn't call upon Orioles standout pitcher Mike Mussina, who was warming up in the bullpen. As it turned out, Mussina was working out on his own and was never projected for use in the game.

Quotable: "It's tough to hit when you're laughing," said Kruk, alluding to his at-bat against Johnson. "It's also tough to hit when you're dead. If he was going to hit me, he was going to have to hit a moving target."

BOX SCORE

National League	AB	R	H	RBI	PO	A
Grissom, cf (Expos)	3	0	0	0	1	0
Kelly, cf (Reds)	1	0	0	0	0	1
Bonds, lf (Giants)	3	2	2	0	1	0
Bonilla, lf (Mets)	1	0	1	0	2	0
Sheffield, 3b (Marlins)	3	1	2	2	0	2
Hollins, 3b (Phillies)	1	0	1	0	1	0
Kruk, 1b (Phillies)	3	0	0	0	7	0
Galarraga, 1b (Rockies)....	1	0	0	0	0	0
Larkin, ss (Reds)	2	0	0	1	2	1
Blauser, ss (Braves)	1	0	0	0	1	2
Grace, dh (Cubs)	3	0	0	0	0	0
cJefferies, ph-dh (Cards) .	1	0	0	0	0	0
Justice, rf (Braves)	3	0	1	0	1	0
Gwynn, rf (Padres)	1	0	0	0	0	0
Daulton, c (Phillies)	3	0	0	0	4	0
Piazza, c (Dodgers)	1	0	0	0	3	0
Sandberg, 2b (Cubs)	1	0	0	0	0	2
Bell, 2b (Pirates)	1	0	0	0	1	1
Mulholland, p (Phillies)	0	0	0	0	0	0
Benes, p (Padres)	0	0	0	0	0	0
Burkett, p (Giants)	0	0	0	0	0	0
Avery, p (Braves)	0	0	0	0	0	0
Smoltz, p (Braves)	0	0	0	0	0	0
Beck, p (Giants)	0	0	0	0	0	0
Harvey, p (Marlins)	0	0	0	0	0	0
Totals............................	33	3	7	3	24	9

American League	AB	R	H	RBI	PO	A
Alomar, 2b (Blue Jays)	3	1	1	1	0	0
Baerga, 2b (Indians)	2	1	0	0	0	1
Molitor, dh (Blue Jays)	1	0	0	0	0	0
aBelle, ph-dh (Indians).....	1	2	1	1	0	0
bThomas, ph-dh (W. Sox)	1	0	1	0	0	0
Griffey, cf (Mariners)	3	1	1	1	2	0
White, cf (Blue Jays)	2	1	1	1	1	0
Carter, rf (Blue Jays)	3	0	1	0	1	0
Gonzalez, rf (Rangers)	1	0	0	0	1	0
Olerud, 1b (Blue Jays)	2	0	0	0	4	0
Fielder, 1b (Tigers)	1	0	0	0	4	0
Puckett, lf (Twins)	3	1	2	2	1	0
Vaughn, lf (Brewers)	1	1	1	0	0	0
Ripken, ss (Orioles)	3	0	0	0	1	2
Fryman, ss (Tigers)	1	0	0	0	1	1
Boggs, 3b (Yankees)	1	0	0	0	1	0
Cooper, 3b (Red Sox)	2	0	0	0	1	0
Rodriguez, c (Rangers)	2	1	1	0	3	0
Steinbach, c (A's)	2	0	1	1	6	0

	AB	R	H	RBI	PO	A
Langston, p (Angels)	0	0	0	0	0	1
Johnson, p (Mariners)	0	0	0	0	0	1
McDowell, p (White Sox) ..	0	0	0	0	0	0
Key, p (Yankees)	0	0	0	0	0	0
Montgomery, p (Royals) ...	0	0	0	0	0	0
Aguilera, p (Twins)	0	0	0	0	0	0
Ward, p (Blue Jays)	0	0	0	0	0	0
Totals	35	9	11	7	27	6

National League 2 0 0		0 0 1		0 0 0—3		
American League 0 1 1		0 3 3		1 0 x—9		

National League	IP	H	R	ER	BB	SO
Mulholland (Phillies)..	2	1	1	1	2	0
Benes (Padres)	2	2	1	1	0	2
Burkett (Giants)	2/3	4	3	3	0	1
Avery (Braves)	1	1	3	3	0	1
Smoltz (Braves).........	1/3	0	0	0	1	0
Beck (Giants)	1	2	1	1	0	1
Harvey (Marlins)	1	1	0	0	0	2

American League	IP	H	R	ER	BB	SO
Langston (Angels)	2	3	2	2	1	2
Johnson (Mariners) ...	2	0	0	0	0	1
McDowell (W. Sox).....	1	0	0	0	0	0
Key (Yankees)	1	2	1	1	0	1
Montgomery (Royals)	1	0	0	0	0	1
Aguilera (Twins)	1	2	0	0	0	2
Ward (Blue Jays)	1	0	0	0	0	2

Winning pitcher—McDowell. Losing pitcher—Burkett. aSingled for Molitor in fifth. bSingled for Belle in eighth. cStruck out for Grace in ninth. E—Justice, Blauser. LOB—N.L. 5, A.L. 7. 2B—Bonds 2, Rodriguez, Puckett, White, Steinbach, Hollins. HR—Sheffield, Puckett, Alomar. SB—White. SF—Larkin. HBP—By Burkett (Fielder). WP—Smoltz 2. BB—Off Mulholland 2 (Molitor, Boggs), off Avery 1 (Belle), off Smoltz 1 (Gonzalez), off Langston 1 (Sandberg). SO—By Benes 2 (Griffey, Ripken), by Burkett 1 (Carter), by Avery 1 (Steinbach), by Beck 1 (Cooper), by Harvey 2 (Baerga, Gonzalez), by Langston 2 (Larkin, Grissom), by Johnson 1 (Kruk), by Key 1 (Kruk), by Montgomery 1 (Daulton), by Aguilera 2 (Kelly, Blauser), by Ward 2 (Jefferies, Piazza). U—McKean (A.L.), plate; Davidson (N.L.), first; Reilly (A.L.), second; Darling (N.L.), third; Scott (A.L.), left field; M. Hirschbeck (N.L.), right field. Official scorers—Bob Brown (Orioles Gazette), Neil Hohlfeld (BBWAA) , Bill Stetka (Orioles official scorer). T—2:49. A—48,147.

Players listed on rosters but not used: N.L.—Glavine, Kile, L. Smith; A.L.—Hentgen, Mussina.

PLAY BY PLAY

FIRST INNING

N.L.—Grissom fouled to third. Bonds doubled to right. Sheffield homered to left, scoring Bonds. Kruk flied to left. Larkin struck out.

A.L.—Alomar grounded to third. Molitor walked. Griffey grounded to first, Molitor went to second. Carter popped to short.

SECOND INNING

N.L.—Grace grounded to second. Justice singled to center. Daulton grounded to the pitcher, Justice went to second. Sandberg walked. Grissom struck out.

A.L.—Olerud grounded to second. Puckett homered to center. Ripken grounded to short. Boggs walked. Rodriguez flied to right.

THIRD INNING

N.L.—Johnson now pitching. Bonds grounded to short. Sheffield popped to short. Kruk struck out.

A.L.—Benes now pitching. Alomar homered to right. Molitor flied to left. Griffey struck out. Carter singled to left. Olerud forced Carter at second base, shortstop unassisted.

FOURTH INNING

N.L.—Larkin flied to right. Grace grounded to the pitcher. Justice flied to center.

A.L.—Puckett grounded to second. Ripken struck out. Boggs lined to left.

FIFTH INNING

N.L.—McDowell now pitching and Fielder at first. Daulton grounded to first. Sandberg grounded to short. Grissom flied to center.

A.L.—Burkett now pitching, Kelly in center and Bell at second. Rodriguez doubled to left. Alomar grounded to second, Rodriguez went to third. Belle, pinch-hitting for Molitor, singled to right, scoring Rodriguez. During the play Belle went to second on an error by the right fielder. Griffey singled to right, scoring Belle, and Griffey went to second on the right fielder's throw to the plate. Carter struck out. Fielder was hit by a pitch. Puckett doubled to left, scoring Griffey, and Fielder went to third. Avery now pitching. Ripken grounded to third.

SIXTH INNING

N.L.—Key now pitching, Vaughn in left, White in center, Gonzalez in right, Baerga at second, Cooper at third and Steinbach catching. Bonds doubled to right. Sheffield singled to left, Bonds went to third. Kruk struck out. Larkin hit a sacrifice fly to center, scoring Bonds. Grace grounded to first.

A.L.—Bonilla now in left, Galarraga at first, Hollins at third and Blauser at short. Cooper flied to left. Steinbach struck out. Baerga reached first on an error by the shortstop. Belle walked, Baerga went to second. White doubled to right, scoring Baerga, and Belle went to third. Smoltz now pitching. Smoltz threw a wild pitch, scoring Belle and moving White to third. Gonzalez walked. Smoltz threw a wild pitch, scoring White and moving Gonzalez to second. Fielder flied to left.

SEVENTH INNING

N.L.—Montgomery now pitching and Fryman at short. Justice flied to right. Daulton struck out. Bell popped to third.

A.L.—Beck now pitching, Piazza catching and Gwynn in right. Vaughn singled to left. Fryman popped to short. Cooper struck out. Steinbach doubled to right, scoring Vaughn. Steinbach was out trying for third, center fielder to shortstop to third baseman.

EIGHTH INNING

N.L.—Aguilera now pitching. Kelly struck out. Bonilla singled to right. Hollins doubled to right, Bonilla went to third. Galarraga popped to short. Blauser struck out.

A.L.—Harvey now pitching. Baerga struck out. Thomas, pinch-hitting for Belle, singled to center. White forced Thomas at second base, shortstop to second baseman. White stole second. Gonzalez struck out.

NINTH INNING

N.L.—Ward now pitching. Jefferies, pinch-hitting for Grace, struck out. Gwynn grounded to short. Piazza struck out.

NOTABLE PERFORMANCES

CHRIS BOSIO

APRIL 22
Seattle 7, Boston 0 (N)

BOSTON	ab	r	h	bi	SEATTLE	ab	r	h	bi
Riles, 2b	3	0	0	0	Felder, lf	4	0	1	1
Quintana, rf	2	0	0	0	Cotto, dh	3	0	0	0
Greenwell, lf	3	0	0	0	Sasser, dh	1	0	0	0
Dawson, dh	3	0	0	0	Griffey, cf	4	0	0	0
Vaughn, 1b	3	0	0	0	Buhner, rf	3	1	0	0
Calderon, cf	3	0	0	0	Boone, 2b	4	2	3	2
Cooper, 3b	3	0	0	0	T. Martinez, 1b	3	1	1	0
Valentin, ss	3	0	0	0	Blowers, 3b	4	1	2	1
Pena, c	3	0	0	0	Valle, c	4	1	2	2
					Vizquel, ss	4	1	2	0
TOTALS	26	0	0	0	TOTALS	34	7	11	6

Boston .... 0 0 0   0 0 0   0 0 0—0
Seattle .... 0 2 2   1 0 2   0 0 x—7

E—Greenwell (1). DP—Boston 1, Seattle 1. LOB—Boston 1, Seattle 6. HR—Boone (1). SB—Felder (4), Blowers (1).

BOSTON	IP	H	R	ER	BB	K
Hesketh (L 2-1)	3	6	5	5	2	1
Quantrill	2⅔	4	2	1	0	2
Fossas	⅓	0	0	0	0	0
Harris	1	0	0	0	1	2
Ryan	1	1	0	0	0	0

SEATTLE	IP	H	R	ER	BB	K
Bosio (W 1-1)	9	0	0	0	2	4

Hesketh pitched to two batters in the 4th.
T—2:12. A—13,604. Umpires—HP, Voltaggio. 1B, Kaiser. 2B, Johnson. 3B, McKean.

JIM ABBOTT

SEPTEMBER 4
New York 4, Cleveland 0 (D)

CLEVELAND	ab	r	h	bi	NEW YORK	ab	r	h	bi
Lofton, cf	3	0	0	0	Boggs, 3b	4	1	1	0
Fermin, ss	4	0	0	0	James, lf	4	1	2	1
Baerga, 2b	4	0	0	0	G. Williams, lf	0	0	0	0
Belle, lf	3	0	0	0	Mattingly, 1b	3	0	1	0
Milligan, 1b	1	0	0	0	Tartabull, dh	4	0	1	0
Ramirez, dh	3	0	0	0	O'Neill, rf	4	0	0	0
Maldonado, rf	3	0	0	0	B. Williams, cf	3	0	1	0
Thome, 3b	2	0	0	0	Nokes, c	4	0	1	0
Ortiz, c	1	0	0	0	Gallego, 2b	3	1	0	0
Alomar, c	1	0	0	0	Velarde, ss	3	1	1	1
TOTALS	25	0	0	0	TOTALS	32	4	8	2

Cleveland .... 0 0 0   0 0 0   0 0 0—0
New York .... 0 0 3   0 1 0   0 0 x—4

E—Lofton (7), Thome (3). DP—New York 2. LOB—Cleveland 3, New York 7. 2B—James (17). HR—Velarde (6). SB—B. Williams (7).

CLEVELAND	IP	H	R	ER	BB	K
Milacki (L 0-1)	5⅓	6	4	2	3	2
Wertz	2⅔	2	0	0	0	2

NEW YORK	IP	H	R	ER	BB	K
Abbott (W 10-11)	9	0	0	0	5	3

T—2:33. A—27,225. Umpires—HP, Hendry. 1B, Evans. 2B, Craft. 3B, Hickox.

DARRYL KILE

SEPTEMBER 8
Houston 7, New York 1 (N)

NEW YORK	ab	r	h	bi	HOUSTON	ab	r	h	bi
Thompson, cf	3	0	0	0	Biggio, 2b	4	0	1	0
Walker, ph	1	0	0	0	Candaele, cf	4	1	1	1
McKnight, ss	2	1	0	0	Finley, cf	0	1	0	0
Murray, 1b	3	0	0	0	Bagwell, 1b	4	1	2	1
Orsulak, lf	3	0	0	0	Anthony, rf	4	0	0	0
Gallagher, lf	0	0	0	0	Caminiti, 3b	3	2	1	1
Burnitz, rf	3	0	0	0	Gonzalez, lf	4	0	2	2
Kent, 2b	3	0	0	0	Servais, c	4	0	0	0
Huskey, 3b	3	0	0	0	Cedeno, ss	4	2	2	1
Hundley, c	3	0	0	0	Kile, p	2	0	0	0
Tanana, p	1	0	0	0					
Landrum, ph	1	0	0	0					
Manzanillo, p	0	0	0	0					
Telgheder, p	0	0	0	0					
Navarro, ph	1	0	0	0					
TOTALS	27	1	0	0	TOTALS	33	7	9	6

New York .... 0 0 0   1 0 0   0 0 0—1
Houston .... 0 1 2   0 1 0   0 3 x—7

E—Murray (15), Huskey (1), Tanana (1), Bagwell (9). DP—New York 1. LOB—Houston 4. 2B—Biggio (39), Bagwell (37), Cedeno (20). HR—Caminiti (12), Cedeno (7). SH—Kile.

NEW YORK	IP	H	R	ER	BB	K
Tanana (L 6-15)	5	7	4	4	0	0
Manzanillo	2⅔	2	3	0	1	4
Telgheder	⅓	0	0	0	0	0

HOUSTON	IP	H	R	ER	BB	K
Kile (W 15-6)	9	0	1	0	1	9

WP—Kile. T—2:11. A—15,684. Umpires—HP, Montague. 1B, Hirschbeck. 2B, Froemming. 3B, Winters.

LOW-HIT GAMES

AMERICAN LEAGUE

ONE-HIT GAMES

Date   **Pitcher(s), Team, Opponent, Result—Player with hit**

4-23   Cal Eldred (8 innings) and Jesse Orosco (1 inning), Milwaukee vs. Texas, W 3-0—Rafael Palmeiro (double in first)
4-27   Jimmy Key, New York at California, W 5-0—Gary DiSarcina (single in sixth)
5-16   Randy Johnson, Seattle at Oakland, W 7-0—Lance Blankenship (single in ninth)
5-24   Tom Kramer, Cleveland vs. Texas, W 4-1—Julio Franco (home run in fourth)
7-20   Ben McDonald, Baltimore vs. Kansas City, W 7-0—Gary Gaetti (single in fourth)
7-25   Mike Moore, Detroit vs. Kansas City, W 3-0—Wally Joyner (single in second)
7-27   Kevin Appier, Kansas City vs. Texas, L 1-0—Rafael Palmeiro (home run in seventh)
8-18   Danny Darwin, Boston vs. Chicago, W 5-0—Dan Pasqua (triple in eighth)
8-23   Mike Moore, Detroit vs. Oakland, W 9-0—Scott Lydy (single in sixth)

TWO-HIT GAMES

Date   **Pitcher(s), Team, Opponent, Result—Player(s) with hits**

4-22   Chuck Finley, California vs. Cleveland, W 8-0—Alvaro Espinoza (single in third), Kenny Lofton (single in third)

4-24   Melido Perez (9 innings), Steve Howe (1 inning) and Steve Farr (1 inning), New York at Seattle, W 1-0—Ken Griffey (single in first), Rich Amaral (single in third)

5-5   Mike Mussina, Baltimore at Minnesota, W 3-0—Mike Pagliarulo (double in third), Chuck Knoblauch (single in sixth)

5-9   David Cone, Kansas City vs. Texas, L 2-1—Julio Franco (single in fourth), Juan Gonzalez (home run in fourth)

5-12   Danny Darwin (7⅔ innings), Greg Harris (⅓ inning) and Jeff Russell (1 inning), Boston at Baltimore, W 2-0—David Segui (single in third and double in eighth)

5-18   Fernando Valenzuela, Baltimore vs. Cleveland, W 7-0—Felix Fermin (single in third), Glenallen Hill (double in eighth)

5-24   Dave Stewart (7 innings), Mike Timlin (1 inning) and Duane Ward (1 inning), Toronto vs. Milwaukee, W 4-1—Robin Yount (home run in fifth), John Jaha (single in fifth)

5-28   Roger Clemens (8 innings) and Jeff Russell (1 inning), Boston vs. Texas, W 4-1—Rafael Palmeiro (single in second), Ivan Rodriguez (triple in seventh)

5-29   Jim Abbott (8 innings) and Bobby Munoz (1 inning), New York vs. Chicago, W 8-2—Bo Jackson (single in eighth), Ron Karkovice (home run in eighth)

6-1   Al Leiter (5⅓ innings), Mark Eichhorn (1⅔ innings), Tony Castillo (1 inning) and Duane Ward (1 inning), Toronto at California, W 8-0—Luis Polonia (single in fourth), Tim Salmon (single in ninth)

6-17   Al Leiter, Toronto vs. Boston, W 7-0—Mike Greenwell (single in fourth), Billy Hatcher (single in sixth)

7-4   Paul Quantrill, Boston at Seattle, W 6-0—Jay Buhner (single in second), Mackey Sasser (double in second)

8-1   Jack McDowell, Chicago at Seattle, W 4-0—Bret Boone (triple in second), Ken Griffey (single in third)

8-10   Tim Belcher, Chicago vs. Oakland, W 4-0—Brent Gates (singles in fourth and ninth)

8-12   Melido Perez (7⅔ innings), Paul Assenmacher (⅓ inning) and Steve Farr (1 inning), New York at Boston, W 4-1—Billy Hatcher (double in sixth), John Valentin (double in eighth)

8-14   Alex Fernandez (8⅔ innings) and Scott Radinsky (⅓ inning), Chicago vs. Kansas City, W 4-1—Brian McRae (single in first), Brent Mayne (home run in second)

8-24   Chuck Finley, California at Baltimore, L 1-0—Cal Ripken (single in first), Brady Anderson (single in fifth)

8-25   Mark Langston (8 innings) and Mike Butcher (1 inning), California at Baltimore, W 2-1—Cal Ripken (single in seventh), Chris Hoiles (single in ninth)

9-8   Ricky Bones, Milwaukee at Kansas City, W 2-1—Kevin McReynolds (home run in second), Greg Gagne (single in third)

9-10   Mike Moore, Detroit at Chicago, W 4-0—Ron Karkovice (single in fifth), Lance Johnson (single in seventh)

9-16   Randy Johnson (7⅓ innings), Jeff Nelson (⅔ innings) and Steve Ontiveros (1 inning), Seattle vs. Kansas City, W 14-1—Brian McRae (double in eighth), Craig Wilson (double in ninth)

9-28   Ben McDonald, Baltimore vs. New York, W 9-1—Dion James (single in fourth), Don Mattingly (single in sixth)

NATIONAL LEAGUE

ONE-HIT GAMES

Date   **Pitcher(s), Team, Opponent, Result—Player with hit**

4-6   Jose Guzman, Chicago vs. Atlanta, W 1-0—Otis Nixon (single in ninth)

5-26   Tim Belcher, Cincinnati vs. Atlanta, W 4-0—Deion Sanders (double in first)

6-17   Bill Swift (8 innings) and Kevin Rogers (1 inning), San Francisco at Cincinnati, W 5-1—Kevin Mitchell (single in eighth)

7-7   Andy Benes (8 innings) and Gene Harris (1 inning), San Diego at New York, W 2-0—Jeff Kent (single in second)

7-10   Pete Harnisch, Houston at Chicago, W 4-0—Mark Grace (single in seventh)

8-13   Steve Avery (6 innings), Marvin Freeman (1 inning), Kent Mercker (1 inning) and Jay Howell (1 inning), Atlanta vs. Cincinnati, W 14-0—Chris Sabo (single in fifth)

9-9   Kent Mercker (6 innings), Mark Wohlers (2 innings) and Greg McMichael (2 innings), Atlanta at San Diego, W 1-0—Luis Lopez (single in eighth)

9-17   Pete Harnisch, Houston vs. San Diego, W 3-0—Jarvis Brown (single in sixth)

9-25   Jose Rijo, Cincinnati at Colorado, W 6-0—Charlie Hayes (single in second)

9-29   Tim Pugh, Cincinnati at San Diego, W 8-0—Billy Bean (single in ninth)

TWO-HIT GAMES

Date   **Pitcher(s), Team, Opponent, Result—Player(s) with hits**

4-7   Bret Saberhagen (8 innings) and Mike Maddux (1 inning), New York vs. Colorado, W 6-1—Jim Tatum (single in sixth), Dante Bichette (home run in seventh)

4-27   Dwight Gooden (8 innings) and Jeff Innis (1 inning), New York vs. Los Angeles, L 4-1—Mike Piazza (home run in second), Orel Hershiser (single in eighth)

6-3   Denny Neagle (5⅓ innings), Dave Otto (1⅔ innings) and Blas Minor (2 innings), Pittsburgh at San Francisco, W 2-1—Willie McGee (single in second), Darren Lewis (double in sixth)

6-21   Ramon Martinez, Los Angeles vs. Houston, W 7-0—Craig Biggio (single in first), Luis Gonzalez (double in second)

6-27   Bill Swift (8 innings) and Mike Jackson (1 inning), San Francisco vs. Colorado, W 5-0—Alex Cole (single in first), Freddie Benavides (double in seventh)

7-7   Kirk Rueter (8⅓ innings) and John Wetteland (⅔ innings), Montreal vs. San Francisco, W 3-0—Steve Scarsone (single in first), Mike Benjamin (single in eighth)

7-21   Jose Guzman (7 innings), Bob Scanlan (1 inning) and Randy Myers (1 inning), Chicago at Cincinnati, W 4-1—Hal Morris (single in fifth), Joe Oliver (single in fifth)

8-10   Bill Swift (8 innings) and Rod Beck (1 inning), San Francisco vs. Cincinnati, W 2-1—, Reggie Sanders (single in fifth), Kevin Mitchell (home run in seventh)

10-3   Terry Mulholland (4 innings), Ben Rivera (2 innings), Mitch Williams (1 inning) and Larry Andersen (1 inning), Philadelphia at St. Louis, L 2-0—Mark Whiten (singles in fourth and seventh)

10-STRIKEOUT GAMES

AMERICAN LEAGUE

Team	No.	Pitchers
Seattle	16	Randy Johnson 14, Chris Bosio 1, Erik Hanson 1.
Boston	7	Roger Clemens 3, Aaron Sele 3, Danny Darwin 1.
Kansas City	6	Kevin Appier 3, Tom Gordon 2, David Cone 1.
Chicago	5	Wilson Alvarez 2, Jason Bere 2, Jack McDowell 1.
Texas	5	Kevin Brown 2, Roger Pavlik 2, Kenny Rogers 1.
California	4	Chuck Finley 2, Mark Langston 1, Julio Valera 1.
Toronto	4	Juan Guzman 3, Todd Stottlemyre 1.
New York	3	Melido Perez 2, Jimmy Key 1.
Baltimore	2	Ben McDonald 1, Mike Mussina 1.
Detroit	2	David Wells 2.
Milwaukee	2	Cal Eldred 1, Angel Miranda 1.
Oakland	2	Bobby Witt 2.
Minnesota	1	Willie Banks 1.
Cleveland	0	None.

NATIONAL LEAGUE

Team	No.	Pitchers
Houston	9	Pete Harnisch 4, Doug Drabek 2, Greg Swindell 2, Darryl Kile 1.
Cincinnati	5	Jose Rijo 4, Tim Belcher 1.
Philadelphia	4	Tommy Greene 2, Terry Mulholland 1, Curt Schilling 1.
Atlanta	3	John Smoltz 2, Greg Maddux 1.
Chicago	2	Jose Guzman 2.
Montreal	2	Jeff Fassero 2.
Florida	1	Jack Armstrong 1.
New York	1	Sid Fernandez 1.
Pittsburgh	1	Steve Cooke 1.
San Diego	1	Andy Benes 1.
San Francisco	1	Bill Swift 1.
Colorado	0	None.
Los Angeles	0	None.
St. Louis	0	None.

15-STRIKEOUT GAMES

Date	Pitcher, Team, Opponent	IP	H	R	ER	BB	SO	Result
6-14	Randy Johnson, Seattle vs. Kansas City	8	6	3	3	0	15	W 6-3
9-16	Randy Johnson, Seattle vs. Kansas City	7⅓	1	1	1	6	15	W 14-1

1-0 GAMES

AMERICAN LEAGUE

Date	Winner	Loser	Inn.*	Site
4-24	†Steve Howe, New York	†Russ Swan, Seattle	11	Seattle
4-25	†Todd Stottlemyre, Toronto	Alex Fernandez, Chicago	8	Toronto
5-1	†Jose Mesa, Cleveland	†Storm Davis, Oakland	1	Cleveland
5-7	†Danny Darwin, Boston	Bill Wegman, Milwaukee	2	Milwaukee
5-25	†Bob Wickman, New York	†Jamie Moyer, Baltimore	5	New York
5-31	†Charlie Leibrandt, Texas	†Kevin Tapani, Minnesota	2	Minnesota
6-4	†Greg Harris, Boston	†Roberto Hernandez, Chicago	9	Chicago
7-1	†Jamie Moyer, Baltimore	Jack McDowell, Chicago	3	Chicago
7-27	†Kenny Rogers, Texas	Kevin Appier, Kansas City	7	Kansas City
8-15	†Scott Kamieniecki, New York	Ben McDonald, Baltimore	8	New York
8-22	Jack McDowell, Chicago	†Jim Deshaies, Minnesota	1	Minnesota
8-24	†Jamie Moyer, Baltimore	Chuck Finley, California	1	Baltimore
9-18	Kevin Appier, Kansas City	Chris Bosio, Seattle	3	Seattle
9-22	†Wilson Alvarez, Chicago	Chuck Finley, California	4	California

PLAYERS HITTING HOME RUNS IN 1-0 GAMES: 4-25—Darrin Jackson, Toronto; 5-25—Pat Kelly, New York; 7-27—Rafael Palmeiro, Texas; 8-15—Don Mattingly, New York; 8-22—Frank Thomas, Chicago; 9-18—Felix Jose, Kansas City.

*Inning in which run was scored.   †Did not pitch complete game.

NATIONAL LEAGUE

Date	Winner	Loser	Inn.*	Site
4-5	†Greg Maddux, Atlanta	†Mike Morgan, Chicago	1	Chicago
4-6	Jose Guzman, Chicago	†John Smoltz, Atlanta	1	Chicago
4-16	†John Burkett, San Francisco	John Smoltz, Atlanta	5	San Francisco
5-7	†Chris Nabholz, Montreal	†Randy Tomlin, Pittsburgh	4	Pittsburgh
5-10	Bret Saberhagen, New York	Ryan Bowen, Florida	1	New York
5-16	†Lee Smith, St. Louis	†Trevor Hoffman, Florida	9	St. Louis
5-18	†Gil Heredia, Montreal	†Pete Smith, Atlanta	6	Atlanta
5-19	Tom Glavine, Atlanta	†Jeff Shaw, Montreal	2	Atlanta
6-11	†Joe Magrane, St. Louis	†Kent Bottenfield, Montreal	5	St. Louis
6-24	†Greg Swindell, Houston	Orel Hershiser, Los Angeles	4	Los Angeles
7-4	†Jim Gott, Los Angeles	†Jeff Shaw, Montreal	11	Montreal
7-15	Mike Morgan, Chicago	†Willie Blair, Colorado	4	Chicago
8-3	†Charlie Hough, Florida	†Donovan Osborne, St. Louis	2	St. Louis
8-15	Greg Maddux, Atlanta	†Jose Rijo, Cincinnati	3	Cincinnati
8-23	†Kirk Rueter, Montreal	Greg Hibbard, Chicago	2	Montreal

Date	Winner	Loser	Inn.*	Site
9-7	†Steve Avery, Atlanta	†Pedro Astacio, Los Angeles	8	Los Angeles
9-9	†Greg McMichael, Atlanta	†Trevor Hoffman, San Diego	10	San Diego
9-12	Pedro Astacio, Los Angeles	†Pat Rapp, Florida	6	Los Angeles
9-14	Paul Wagner, Pittsburgh	Chris Hammond, Florida	1	Florida
9-22	†Bill Swift, San Francisco	†Pete Harnisch, Houston	7	Houston
9-26‡	Tim Wakefield, Pittsburgh	†Mike Morgan, Chicago	1	Pittsburgh
9-29	†Kenny Greer, New York	†Les Lancaster, St. Louis	17	New York

PLAYERS HITTING HOME RUNS IN 1-0 GAMES: 5-19—Ron Gant, Atlanta; 6-11—Bernard Gilkey, St. Louis; 8-3—Benito Santiago, Florida; 9-9—Ron Gant, Atlanta; 9-14—Carlos Garcia, Pittsburgh.

*Inning in which run was scored.   †Did not pitch complete game.   ‡Second game of doubleheader.

FOUR OR MORE HITS IN ONE GAME

AMERICAN LEAGUE

Team	No.	Hitters
Detroit	19	Travis Fryman 6, Cecil Fielder 2, Dan Gladden 2, Tony Phillips 2, Milt Cuyler 1, Chris Gomez 1, Chad Kreuter 1, Scott Livingstone 1, Mickey Tettleton 1, Alan Trammell 1, Lou Whitaker 1.
Cleveland	17	Carlos Baerga 5, Kenny Lofton 4, Albert Belle 2, Sandy Alomar 1, Alvaro Espinoza 1, Felix Fermin 1, Thomas Howard 1, Reggie Jefferson 1, Wayne Kirby 1.
Toronto	17	Paul Molitor 5, Roberto Alomar 4, John Olerud 3, Devon White 2, Joe Carter 1, Tony Fernandez 1, Ed Sprague 1.
Oakland	16	Mike Bordick 2, Jerry Browne 2, Rickey Henderson 2, Ruben Sierra 2, Kurt Abbott 1, Brent Gates 1, Scott Hemond 1, Mark McGwire 1, Troy Neel 1, Craig Paquette 1, Kevin Seitzer 1, Terry Steinbach 1.
Minnesota	15	Shane Mack 3, Kirby Puckett 3, Chuck Knoblauch 2, Pedro Munoz 2, Dave Winfield 2, Brian Harper 1, Terry Jorgensen 1, Dave McCarty 1.
Milwaukee	14	Darryl Hamilton 3, Pat Listach 3, B.J. Surhoff 3, Greg Vaughn 2, Juan Bell 1, Kevin Reimer 1, Robin Yount 1.
New York	12	Wade Boggs 3, Bernie Williams 3, Don Mattingly 2, Pat Kelly 1, Paul O'Neill 1, Mike Stanley 1, Randy Velarde 1.
Seattle	12	Jay Buhner 4, Bret Boone 2, Ken Griffey 2, Rich Amaral 1, Mike Blowers 1, Tino Martinez 1, Omar Vizquel 1.
Texas	12	Juan Gonzalez 3, Julio Franco 2, Rafael Palmeiro 2, Ivan Rodriguez 2, Dave Hulse 1, Dean Palmer 1, Doug Strange 1.
Chicago	11	Tim Raines 3, Frank Thomas 3, Steve Sax 2, Ozzie Guillen 1, Bo Jackson 1, Lance Johnson 1.
Kansas City	11	George Brett 3, Greg Gagne 3, Brian McRae 3, Felix Jose 2.
Boston	10	Mo Vaughn 5, Billy Hatcher 2, Scott Fletcher 1, Mike Greenwell 1, Bob Zupcic 1.
Baltimore	7	Mark McLemore 4, Mike Devereaux 1, Mike Pagliarulo 1, Cal Ripken 1.
California	7	Chad Curtis 2, Luis Polonia 1, J.T. Snow 2, Stan Javier 1.

NATIONAL LEAGUE

Team	No.	Hitters
San Francisco	22	Barry Bonds 4, Kirt Manwaring 4, Robby Thompson 3, Will Clark 2, Willie McGee 2, Steve Scarsone 2, Matt Williams 2, Royce Clayton 1, Darren Lewis 1, Dave Martinez 1.
Colorado	18	Andres Galarraga 4, Dante Bichette 3, Jerald Clark 2, Eric Young 2, Freddie Benavides 1, Daryl Boston 1, Vinny Castilla 1, Joe Girardi 1, Charlie Hayes 1, Nelson Liriano 1, Roberto Mejia 1.
Chicago	14	Ryne Sandberg 3, Mark Grace 2, Rey Sanchez 2, Sammy Sosa 2, Jose Vizcaino 2, Steve Buechele 1, Derrick May 1, Willie Wilson 1.
St. Louis	14	Gregg Jefferies 4, Bernard Gilkey 3, Ozzie Smith 3, Brian Jordan 2, Mark Whiten 1, Todd Zeile 1.
Cincinnati	13	Kevin Mitchell 3, Hal Morris 2, Bip Roberts 2, Juan Samuel 2, Bobby Kelly 1, Barry Larkin 1, Chris Sabo 1, John Smiley 1.
Philadelphia	13	John Kruk 3, Lenny Dykstra 2, Ruben Amaro 1, Kim Batiste 1, Darren Daulton 1, Mariano Duncan 1, Jim Eisenreich 1, Dave Hollins 1, Pete Incaviglia 1, Ricky Jordan 1.
Los Angeles	12	Brett Butler 3, Mike Piazza 3, Eric Davis 1, Dave Hansen 1, Eric Karros 1, Jose Offerman 1, Jody Reed 1, Cory Snyder 1.
San Diego	12	Tony Gwynn 6, Archi Cianfrocco 1, Phil Clark 1, Ricky Gutierrez 1, Fred McGriff 1, Gary Sheffield 1, Tim Teufel 1.
Atlanta	11	David Justice 2, Terry Pendleton 2, Deion Sanders 2, Damon Berryhill 1, Jeff Blauser 1, Sid Bream 1, Ron Gant 1, Mark Lemke 1.
Florida	11	Chuck Carr 2, Jeff Conine 2, Dave Magadan 2, Rich Renteria 2, Alex Arias 1, Orestes Destrade 1, Walt Weiss 1.
Pittsburgh	11	Carlos Garcia 3, Jeff King 2, Dave Clark 1, Al Martin 1, Orlando Merced 1, Don Slaught 1, Andy Van Slyke 1, Kevin Young 1.
New York	9	Todd Hundley 2, Joe Orsulak 2, Tim Bogar 1, Jeromy Burnitz 1, Vince Coleman 1, Eddie Murray 1, Ryan Thompson 1.
Houston	8	Luis Gonzalez 3, Craig Biggio 2, Jeff Bagwell 1, Andujar Cedeno 1, Eddie Taubensee 1.
Montreal	8	Marquis Grissom 2, Mike Lansing 2, Moises Alou 1, Greg Colbrunn 1, Larry Walker 1, Rondell White 1.

FIVE- AND SIX-HIT GAMES

Date	Player, Team, Opponent	AB	R	H	2B	3B	HR	RBI	Result
4-11	Mike Lansing, Montreal at Colorado	7	3	5	0	0	1	2	W 19-9
4-14	Tim Teufel, San Diego vs. Pittsburgh	5	0	5	1	0	0	3	L 11-7
4-18	Tony Gwynn, San Diego vs. St. Louis	5	3	5	0	0	1	2	W 10-6

Date	Player, Team, Opponent	AB	R	H	2B	3B	HR	RBI	Result
4-29	John Olerud, Toronto vs. Kansas City	5	2	5	2	0	0	1	W 8-0
4-30	Tony Gwynn, San Diego vs. New York	5	1	5	1	0	0	3	W 7-6
5-3	Julio Franco, Texas vs. Milwaukee	5	2	5	0	0	1	3	W 9-2
5-4	Sammy Sosa, Chicago vs. Colorado (11 inn.)	6	3	5	1	0	2	5	L 14-13
5-17	Rich Amaral, Seattle at Texas	5	1	5	1	0	0	1	W 16-9
5-17	John Kruk, Philadelphia at Florida	6	3	5	1	0	0	2	W 10-3
6-9	Mark McLemore, Baltimore vs. Oakland	5	3	5	0	0	0	3	W 7-4
6-12	Robby Thompson, San Francisco vs. Chicago	5	0	5	1	0	0	3	W 5-4
6-17	Ozzie Smith, St. Louis at Chicago	5	1	5	3	0	0	6	W 11-10
6-24	Robby Thompson, San Francisco vs. Colorado	5	4	5	0	0	2	3	W 17-2
7-2	Sammy Sosa, Chicago at Colorado	6	2	6	1	0	0	2	W 11-8
7-21	Jay Buhner, Seattle at New York	5	2	5	1	0	1	3	W 10-3
7-27	Tony Gwynn, San Diego at Chicago	5	0	5	2	0	0	3	W 8-0
7-27	John Kruk, Philadelphia vs. St. Louis	5	3	5	1	0	0	3	W 10-7
7-28	Travis Fryman, Detroit vs. New York	5	2	5	2	1	1	4	L 12-7
8-4	Tony Gwynn, San Diego vs. San Francisco (12 inn.)	7	2	6	2	0	0	0	W 11-10
8-15	Kirby Puckett, Minnesota at Oakland	5	2	5	0	0	2	4	W 12-5
8-24*	Kevin Reimer, Milwaukee vs. Oakland	6	4	6	2	0	0	0	W 7-6

*Second game of doubleheader.

HITTING STREAKS OF 15 OR MORE GAMES

AMERICAN LEAGUE

G	Player, Team	Span of streak
26	John Olerud, Toronto	May 26-June 22
21	Bernie Williams, New York	Aug. 1-Aug. 23
19	Brian Harper, Minnesota	July 20-Aug. 12
18	Chad Curtis, California	Aug. 18-Sept. 5
	Reggie Jefferson, Cleveland	July 27-Aug. 22
	Frank Thomas, Chicago	June 9-June 28
17	Carlos Baerga, Cleveland	May 24-June 14
	Chuck Knoblauch, Minnesota	July 29-Aug. 18
16	Mike Greenwell, Boston	June 19-July 6
	Rafael Palmeiro, Texas	June 29-July 17
	Alan Trammell, Detroit	Aug. 9-Aug. 28
	Mo Vaughn, Boston	Aug. 19-Sept. 5
15	Chad Curtis, California	July 26-Aug. 11
	Mike Gallego, New York	May 22-June 28
	Don Mattingly, New York	July 3-July 20
	Paul Molitor, Toronto	July 17-Aug. 1
	John Olerud, Toronto	July 10-July 28
	Harold Reynolds, Baltimore	June 24-July 8
	B.J. Surhoff, Milwaukee	May 26-June 10

NATIONAL LEAGUE

G	Player, Team	Span of streak
21	Delino DeShields, Montreal	June 28-July 21
	Robby Thompson, San Francisco	May 8-June 1
20	Kevin Mitchell, Cincinnati	June 1-June 30
18	Mariano Duncan, Philadelphia	Aug. 28-Sept. 19
17	Gregg Jefferies, St. Louis	July 22-Aug. 20
	Ryne Sandberg, Chicago	Aug. 19-Sept. 5
16	Gregg Jefferies, St. Louis	June 17-July 3
	Erik Pappas, St. Louis	May 14-June 5
	Jose Vizcaino, Chicago	Apr. 27-May 15
	Todd Zeile, St. Louis	June 29-July 18
15	Bret Barberie, Florida	Aug. 7-Aug. 22
	Jay Bell, Pittsburgh	July 24-Aug. 8
	Chuck Carr, Florida	July 30-Aug. 14
	Andres Galarraga, Colorado	Sept. 3-Sept. 17
	Jeff Gardner, San Diego	Apr. 26-May 14
	Jeff King, Pittsburgh	Aug. 4-Aug. 19
	Derrick May, Chicago	June 23-July 9
	Matt Williams, San Francisco	Apr. 27-May 13

MULTI-HOMER GAMES

AMERICAN LEAGUE

Team	No.	Hitters
Texas	14	Juan Gonzalez 5, Rafael Palmeiro 5, Dean Palmer 2, Chris James 1, Gary Redus 1.
Detroit	13	Cecil Fielder 5, Travis Fryman 2, Eric Davis 1, Rob Deer 1, Dan Gladden 1, Kirk Gibson 1, Chad Kreuter 1, Mickey Tettleton 1.
Cleveland	12	Albert Belle 6, Carlos Baerga 2, Glenallen Hill 1, Sam Horn 1, Manny Ramirez 1, Paul Sorrento 1.
Minnesota	10	Pedro Munoz 3, Kent Hrbek 2, Kirby Puckett 2, Bernardo Brito 1, Shane Mack 1, Dave Winfield 1.
Chicago	9	Frank Thomas 3, Ron Karkovice 2, George Bell 1, Ellis Burks 1, Tim Raines 1, Robin Ventura 1.
Oakland	8	Mark McGwire 4, Troy Neel 2, Dave Henderson 1, Rickey Henderson 1, Kevin Seitzer 1.
Seattle	8	Ken Griffey 5, Jay Buhner 2, Mike Blowers 1.
California	6	Chili Davis 3, Tim Salmon 2, J.T. Snow 1.
Toronto	6	Joe Carter 2, Roberto Alomar 1, Paul Molitor 1, John Olerud 1, Devon White 1.

Team	No.	Hitters
Baltimore	5	Chris Hoiles 3, Brady Anderson 1, Cal Ripken 1.
Milwaukee	5	Greg Vaughn 4, John Jaha 1.
New York	5	Matt Nokes 2, Mike Gallego 1, Kevin Maas 1, Danny Tartabull 1.
Boston	3	Rob Deer 1, John Valentin 1, Mo Vaughn 1.
Kansas City	3	George Brett 2, Wally Joyner 1.

NATIONAL LEAGUE

Team	No.	Hitters
San Francisco	18	Barry Bonds 7, Matt Williams 4, Robby Thompson 3, Todd Benzinger 2, Will Clark 1, Dave Martinez 1.
Philadelphia	12	Darren Daulton 4, Pete Incaviglia 3, John Kruk 2, Wes Chamberlain 1, Lenny Dykstra 1, Todd Pratt 1.
Atlanta	11	Ron Gant 3, Fred McGriff 3, David Justice 2, Jeff Blauser 1, Mark Lemke 1, Terry Pendleton 1.
New York	10	Bobby Bonilla 5, Jeff Kent 2, Tim Bogar 1, Eddie Murray 1, Ryan Thompson 1.
Chicago	9	Sammy Sosa 5, Rick Wilkins 2, Dwight Smith 1, Derrick May 1.

Team	No.	Hitters
Colorado	8	Daryl Boston 2, Chris Jones 2, Vinny Castilla 1, Charlie Hayes 1, J. Owens 1, Eric Young 1.
Los Angeles	8	Mike Piazza 5, Eric Karros 2, Cory Snyder 1.
San Diego	5	Phil Plantier 3, Derek Bell 1, Gary Shef-field 1.
St. Louis	5	Ricky Jordan 2, Mark Whiten 2, Gregg Jefferies 1.

Team	No.	Hitters
Cincinnati	5	Kevin Mitchell 2, Randy Milligan 1, Hal Morris 1, Joe Oliver 1.
Florida	4	Orestes Destrade 2, Greg Briley 1, Gary Sheffield 1.
Houston	4	Craig Biggio 1, Ken Caminiti 1, Luis Gonzalez 1, Eddie Taubensee 1.
Montreal	4	Moises Alou 2, Sean Berry 2.
Pittsburgh	4	Carlos Garcia 1, Jeff King 1, Don Slaught 1, Lonnie Smith 1.

THREE-HOMER AND FOUR-HOMER GAMES

Date	Player, Team, Opponent	AB	R	H	2B	3B	HR	RBI	Result
6-17	Carlos Baerga, Cleveland at Detroit	4	3	3	0	0	3	5	L 9-5
8-23	Joe Carter, Toronto vs. Cleveland	4	3	3	0	0	3	4	L 9-8
8-28	Juan Gonzalez, Texas vs. Baltimore	4	3	3	0	0	3	5	W 11-1
9-7*	Mark Whiten, St. Louis at Cincinnati	5	4	4	0	0	4	12	W 15-2

*Second game of doubleheader.

GRAND SLAMS

AMERICAN LEAGUE

Date	Batter	Pitcher	Inn.*	Site
4-5	Eric Fox, Oakland	Tom Bolton, Detroit	8	Oakland
4-7	Cecil Fielder, Detroit	Kelly Downs, Oakland	5	Oakland
4-9	Kirk Gibson, Detroit	Scott Sanderson, California	1	California
4-9	Jim Leyritz, New York	Bobby Thigpen, Chicago	8	Chicago
4-13	Omar Vizquel, Seattle	Danny Cox, Toronto	6	Toronto
4-21	Kent Hrbek, Minnesota	Graeme Lloyd, Milwaukee	5	Minnesota
4-23	Dave Winfield, Minnesota	Mike Moore, Detroit	3	Minnesota
4-24	Mickey Tettleton, Detroit	Mike Trombley, Minnesota	7	Minnesota
4-25	Pete O'Brien, Seattle	Mike Witt, New York	3	Seattle
4-30	Frank Thomas, Chicago	Todd Stottlemyre, Toronto	3	Chicago
5-16	Mike Blowers, Seattle	Bobby Witt, Oakland	6	Oakland
5-16	Ellis Burks, Chicago	Kenny Rogers, Texas	2	Texas
5-16	Dean Palmer, Texas	Alex Fernandez, Chicago	4	Texas
5-17	Mike Blowers, Seattle	Craig Lefferts, Texas	4	Texas
5-21	Kevin Reimer, Milwaukee	Mike Mussina, Baltimore	3	Baltimore
6-2	Ron Karkovice, Chicago	Mike Moore, Detroit	1	Detroit
6-8	Joe Carter, Toronto	Darryl Scott, California	5	Toronto
6-12	Kirby Puckett, Minnesota	Bobby Witt, Oakland	3	Minnesota
6-14	Bernie Williams, New York	Danny Darwin, Boston	5	New York
6-17	Juan Gonzalez, Texas	Ken Patterson, California	5	California
6-20	George Bell, Chicago	Russ Springer, California	1	California
6-20	Mickey Tettleton, Detroit	Ricky Bones, Milwaukee	1	Detroit
6-22	Chris Hoiles, Baltimore	Kurt Knudsen, Detroit	6	Baltimore
6-23	Jay Buhner, Seattle	Kelly Downs, Oakland	1	Seattle
6-25	Paul Sorrento, Cleveland	Tom Gordon, Kansas City	8	Cleveland
6-26	Ellis Burks, Chicago	Erik Hanson, Seattle	3	Chicago
6-26	Chili Davis, California	Willie Banks, Minnesota	6	Minnesota
6-29	Kenny Lofton, Cleveland	Rodney Bolton, Chicago	4	Cleveland
6-30	Mike Stanley, New York	David Wells, Detroit	3	New York
7-2	Robin Ventura, Chicago	Mike Mussina, Baltimore	4	Chicago
7-3	Julio Franco, Texas	Bob MacDonald, Detroit	7	Detroit
7-8	Mo Vaughn, Boston	Todd Van Poppel, Oakland	1	Oakland
7-10	Dan Gladden, Detroit	Dennis Rasmussen, Kansas City	4	Kansas City
7-18	Mike Stanley, New York	Rich Gossage, Oakland	7	New York
7-20	Carlos Baerga, Cleveland	Joe Boever, Oakland	2	Cleveland
7-20	Mike Stanley, New York	Dave Fleming, Seattle	3	New York
7-23	Wally Joyner, Kansas City	Bob MacDonald, Detroit	7	Detroit
7-25	Mo Vaughn, Boston	Rick Honeycutt, Oakland	5	Boston
7-27	Ken Griffey, Seattle	Kevin Tapani, Minnesota	3	Seattle
7-28	Robin Ventura, Chicago	Albie Lopez, Cleveland	1	Chicago
7-29	Greg Gagne, Kansas City	Bob Patterson, Texas	7	Kansas City
7-30	Harold Baines, Baltimore	Frank Viola, Boston	4	Baltimore
8-4	Kevin Seitzer, Milwaukee	Brad Pennington, Baltimore	9	Baltimore
8-10	Julio Franco, Texas	Phil Leftwich, California	1	Texas
8-10	Dan Gladden, Detroit	Ben McDonald, Baltimore	4	Detroit
8-11	Mike Blowers, Seattle	Chris Haney, Kansas City	6	Kansas City
8-11	Dan Gladden, Detroit	Anthony Telford, Baltimore	3	Detroit
8-12	Chad Kreuter, Detroit	Jim Poole, Baltimore	6	Detroit
8-20	Mike Aldrete, Oakland	John Doherty, Detroit	4	Detroit

Date	Batter	Pitcher	Inn.*	Site
8-21	Mike Pagliarulo, Baltimore	Nolan Ryan, Texas	1	Baltimore
8-29	Roberto Alomar, Toronto	Erik Hanson, Seattle	3	Seattle
9-5	Gary Gaetti, Kansas City	Roger Clemens, Boston	6	Boston
9-11	Kirby Puckett, Minnesota	Roger Pavlik, Texas	5	Texas
9-15	Tim Salmon, California	Tim Leary, Seattle	4	California
9-22	Dann Howitt, Seattle	Nolan Ryan, Texas	1	Seattle
9-25	Ruben Sierra, Oakland	Ted Power, Seattle	8	Seattle
10-1	Dave Henderson, Oakland	Mark Holzemer, California	3	Oakland

*Inning in which grand slam was hit.

NATIONAL LEAGUE

Date	Batter	Pitcher	Inn.*	Site
4-8	Bobby Kelly, Cincinnati	Chris Nabholz, Montreal	2	Cincinnati
4-24	Joe Oliver, Cincinnati	Dan Plesac, Chicago	7	Chicago
4-24	Chris Sabo, Cincinnati	Greg Hibbard, Chicago	1	Chicago
4-25	Junior Felix, Florida	Scott Aldred, Colorado	4	Colorado
5-1	Jeff Conine, Florida	David Nied, Colorado	5	Florida
5-4	Chris Sabo, Cincinnati	Chris Hammond, Florida	4	Florida
5-4	Jim Tatum, Colorado	Dan Plesac, Chicago	8	Chicago
5-8	Sid Bream, Atlanta	Willie Blair, Colorado	8	Colorado
5-9	Mariano Duncan, Philadelphia	Lee Smith, St. Louis	8	Philadelphia
5-10	Darren Daulton, Philadelphia	Bob Walk, Pittsburgh	7	Philadelphia
5-12	Chuck Carr, Florida	Chris Nabholz, Montreal	2	Montreal
5-18	Eric Davis, Los Angeles	John Smiley, Cincinnati	5	Los Angeles
5-20	Pete Incaviglia, Philadelphia	Chris Nabholz, Montreal	1	Philadelphia
6-14	Jim Eisenreich, Philadelphia	Mel Rojas, Montreal	9	Montreal
6-24	Barry Bonds, San Francisco	Willie Blair, Colorado	2	San Francisco
6-28	Dave Hansen, Los Angeles	Mike Jackson, San Francisco	9	Los Angeles
7-1	Brian Jordan, St. Louis	Mark Davis, Philadelphia	3	St. Louis
7-10	Mickey Morandini, Philadelphia	Dave Righetti, San Francisco	8	Philadelphia
7-18	Dave Gallagher, New York	Mike Jackson, San Francisco	9	San Francisco
7-21	Francisco Cabrera, Atlanta	Rod Brewer, St. Louis	8	Atlanta
7-26	Charlie Hayes, Colorado	Jay Howell, Atlanta	8	Colorado
7-28	Darren Daulton, Philadelphia	Omar Olivares, St. Louis	8	Philadelphia
7-28	Todd Zeile, St. Louis	Terry Mulholland, Philadelphia	1	Philadelphia
8-4	Luis Alicea, St. Louis	Richie Lewis, Florida	3	St. Louis
8-4	Chris Sabo, Cincinnati	Greg Harris, Colorado	5	Cincinnati
8-5	Jeromy Burnitz, New York	Dennis Martinez, Montreal	5	Montreal
8-11	Billy Bean, San Diego	Darryl Kile, Houston	3	San Diego
8-13	Kim Batiste, Philadelphia	Anthony Young, New York	9	Philadelphia
8-20	Jeff Conine, Florida	Jeff Brantley, San Francisco	8	San Francisco
8-21	Larry Walker, Montreal	John Roper, Cincinnati	1	Cincinnati
8-23	Phil Plantier, San Diego	Donovan Osborne, St. Louis	1	San Diego
8-27	Derrick May, Chicago	Mike Stanton, Atlanta	7	Atlanta
8-30	Rick Wilkins, Chicago	Roger Mason, Philadelphia	11	Chicago
9-2	Todd Hundley, New York	Jose Guzman, Chicago	3	Chicago
9-7	Mark Whiten, St. Louis	Larry Luebbers, Cincinnati	1	Cincinnati
9-9	Todd Zeile, St. Louis	Terry Bross, San Francisco	6	San Francisco
9-14	Ron Gant, Atlanta	Bobby Ayala, Cincinnati	2	Atlanta
9-20	Jay Gainer, Colorado	Doug Brocail, San Diego	4	Colorado
9-21	Fred McGriff, Atlanta	Gil Heredia, Montreal	5	Montreal
9-26	Jeff Kent, New York	Ken Hill, Montreal	5	New York
9-28	Mariano Duncan, Philadelphia	Denny Neagle, Pittsburgh	7	Pittsburgh

*Inning in which grand slam was hit.

TRANSACTIONS

JANUARY 2
White Sox organization signed P Barry Jones, a free agent.

JANUARY 4
Braves signed IF Bill Pecota, a free agent formerly with Mets.

Mets organization signed P Mickey Weston, a free agent.

Pirates signed OF Lonnie Smith, a free agent formerly with Braves.

White Sox signed OF Ellis Burks, a free agent formerly with Red Sox.

JANUARY 5
Astros organization signed SS Jose Uribe, a free agent formerly with Giants, and OF Jack Daugherty, a free agent.

Athletics re-signed 1B Mark McGwire, a free agent.

Cardinals organization signed C Erik Pappas, a free agent.

Indians organization signed P Cliff Young, a free agent.

JANUARY 6
Blue Jays re-signed P Mark Eichhorn, a free agent.

Orioles organization signed 2B Mark McLemore, a free agent.

JANUARY 7
Astros signed OF Kevin Bass, a free agent formerly with Mets.

Cardinals signed P Rob Murphy, a free agent formerly with Astros.

Cubs signed P Jeff D. Robinson, a free agent formerly with Angels.

JANUARY 8
Astros signed OF Chris James, a free agent formerly with Giants.

Blue Jays re-signed SS Alfredo Griffin, a free agent.

Brewers re-signed OF Robin Yount, a free agent.

Dodgers organization signed C Lance Parrish, a free agent formerly with Mariners.

Mariners released P Yorkis Perez.

White Sox organization signed P Chuck Cary, a free agent.

JANUARY 11
Blue Jays organization signed P Tony Castillo, a free agent.

Padres organization signed P Juan Agosto, a free agent.

Rangers organization signed IF Doug Strange, a free agent.

JANUARY 12
Astros organization signed P Eric Bell, a free agent.

Orioles re-signed P Mark Williamson, a free agent.

JANUARY 13
Cardinals signed P Les Lancaster, a free agent formerly with Tigers.

Dodgers organization signed P Lee Guetterman, a free agent.

Giants organization signed OF Mark Carreon, a free agent formerly with Tigers.

Rangers signed P Craig Lefferts, a free agent formerly with Orioles, 1B/OF Gary Redus, a free agent formerly with Pirates, and Rangers organization signed IF Mario Diaz, a free agent.

Reds sold contract of 2B Bill Doran to Brewers.

JANUARY 14
Athletics traded DH Harold Baines to Orioles for P Bobby Chouinard and P Allen Plaster.

Giants signed 1B/OF Todd Benzinger, a free agent formerly with Dodgers, and Giants organization signed C Andy Allanson, a free agent.

Pirates organization signed OF Glenn Wilson, a free agent.

Reds signed 2B Juan Samuel, a free agent formerly with Royals.

JANUARY 15
Angels traded 1B Lee Stevens to Expos for P Jeff Tuss; Tuss announced his retirement and Expos sent P Keith Morrison to Angels to complete deal (January 21). Angels organization signed OF Stan Javier, a free agent.

Blue Jays organization signed SS Dick Schofield, a free agent formerly with Mets.

Dodgers organization signed P Rod Nichols, a free agent.

Giants signed IF Dave Anderson, a free agent formerly with Dodgers and Giants organization signed C Jeff Reed, a free agent.

Twins organization re-signed OF Bernardo Brito, a free agent.

JANUARY 18
Red Sox organization re-signed P Tony Fossas, a free agent.

JANUARY 19
Astros organization signed P Mark Grant, a free agent.

Reds organization signed P Jeff Reardon, a free agent formerly with Braves.

JANUARY 20
Angels organization signed IF Jim Walewander, a free agent.

Brewers granted 1B/OF Franklin Stubbs free agency and Brewers organization traded 1B Oreste Marrero and IF Charlie Montoyo to Expos organization for OF Todd Samples and P Ron Gerstein.

Phillies signed OF Jim Eisenreich, a free agent formerly with Royals.

Pirates organization signed C Jerry Goff, a free agent.

JANUARY 21
Astros released P Rich Scheid.

Athletics organization re-signed P Kevin Campbell, a free agent, and signed P Joe Boever, a free agent formerly with Astros, and IF Dale Sveum, a free agent.

Mets re-signed OF Dave Gallagher, a free agent.

Rockies signed P Jeff Parrett, a free agent formerly with Athletics.

JANUARY 22
Braves organization signed P Jay Howell, a free agent.

Mets organization re-signed P Paul Gibson, a free agent.

JANUARY 23
Orioles organization signed P Mike Cook, a free agent.

JANUARY 26
Athletics organization signed P Jeff Ballard, a free agent.

JANUARY 27
Marlins organization signed P Joe Klink, a free agent.

Royals organization signed DH/OF Hubie Brooks and P Frank DiPino, both free agents.

JANUARY 28
Brewers signed OF Tom Brunansky, a free agent formerly with Red Sox.

JANUARY 29
Angels organization signed OF Jerome Walton, a free agent.

Athletics organization signed P Bob Milacki, a free agent.

FEBRUARY 1
Astros organization signed OF Jim Lindeman, a free agent.

Athletics signed 3B Kevin Seitzer, a free agent formerly with Brewers.

Rangers organization signed 2B Bill Ripken, a free agent.

FEBRUARY 2
Brewers organization signed SS Dickie Thon, a free agent.

Yankees organization signed P Neal Heaton, a free agent.

FEBRUARY 5

Brewers sold contract of P Archie Corbin to Expos.

Giants organization signed P Tim Layana, a free agent.

White Sox organization re-signed C Carlton Fisk, a free agent.

FEBRUARY 8

Rangers organization signed OF Steve Balboni, a free agent.

FEBRUARY 10

Tigers signed OF Kirk Gibson, a free agent.

FEBRUARY 11

Angels signed P Scott Sanderson, a free agent formerly with Yankees.

Padres signed C Mike Scioscia, a free agent formerly with Dodgers.

FEBRUARY 16

Athletics organization signed P Edwin Nunez, a free agent.

FEBRUARY 17

Tigers organization re-signed P Dave Johnson, a free agent.

FEBRUARY 20

Marlins organization signed IF Rick Renteria, a free agent.

FEBRUARY 22

Astros organization signed OF Mike Brumley, a free agent.

Royals traded IF Greg Jefferies and OF Ed Gerald to Cardinals for OF Felix Jose and IF/OF Craig Wilson.

FEBRUARY 24

Cubs organization signed OF/IF Steve Lyons, a free agent.

Twins organization signed OF Ced Landrum, a free agent.

FEBRUARY 26

Red Sox released DH/1B Jack Clark.

FEBRUARY 27

Orioles organization signed P Fernando Valenzuela, a free agent.

FEBRUARY 28

Padres organization re-signed P Dave Eiland, a free agent.

MARCH 1

Red Sox signed P Jeff Russell, a free agent formerly with Athletics.

MARCH 2

Royals organization signed IF/OF Randy Ready, a free agent.

Twins released P Paul Abbott.

MARCH 9

Brewers released P Ron Robinson.

MARCH 12

Athletics organization released P Jeff Ballard.

MARCH 16

Angels released P Tim Fortugno.

Brewers released P Larry Stanford.

Dodgers claimed P Rick Trlicek on waivers from Blue Jays.

Mariners released P Mike Schooler.

MARCH 18

Giants released IF Dave Anderson.

MARCH 20

Orioles traded IF Steve Scarsone to Giants for OF Mark Leonard.

Rangers released P Terry Bross.

MARCH 21

Marlins granted P Jeff Tabaka free agency.

Padres traded 1B Jay Gainer to Rockies for P Denis Boucher.

MARCH 23

Expos claimed OF Ted Wood on waivers from Giants and Expos organization signed 1B Jack Clark.

Reds organization released IF Eric Yelding.

MARCH 24

Indians organization released OF/1B Mike Aldrete.

Red Sox released C John Marzano.

MARCH 25

Mariners released OF Greg Briley.

Padres traded C Tom Lampkin to Brewers for future considerations; deal later settled in cash.

MARCH 26

Giants organization signed P Terry Bross, a free agent.

Reds organization released OF Tommy Gregg.

Rockies released P Calvin Jones.

Tigers claimed OF Gary Thurman on waivers from Royals.

Twins traded P Gary Wayne and P Bob Wassenaar to Rockies for P Brett Merriman.

MARCH 27

Athletics organization signed OF/1B Mike Aldrete, a free agent.

Indians organization signed P Paul Abbott, a free agent. Reds traded P Chris Hammond to Marlins for 3B Gary Scott and a player to be named later; Marlins sent P Hector Carrasco to Reds to complete deal (September 10). Reds organization re-signed OF Tommy Gregg, a free agent.

Royals sold contract of P Luis Aquino to Marlins.

MARCH 28

Cubs organization released OF/IF Steve Lyons.

MARCH 29

Athletics organization claimed C/IF Scott Hemond on waivers from White Sox and released P Bob Milacki.

MARCH 30

Astros released P Jason Grimsley and granted OF Mike Simms free agency.

Blue Jays released P David Wells and sold contract of P Bob MacDonald to Tigers.

Cubs released P Jeff D. Robinson and Cubs organization signed IF Eric Yelding.

Dodgers organization released P Lee Guetterman.

Expos released 1B Lee Stevens.

Orioles released OF/1B Doug Jennings.

Padres traded OF Darrin Jackson to Blue Jays for OF Derek Bell and OF Stoney Briggs.

Red Sox released P Matt Young.

White Sox released OF Shawn Abner.

MARCH 31

Indians traded OF Mark Whiten to Cardinals for P Mark Clark and SS Juan Andujar.

Marlins traded P Brian Griffiths to Giants for IF Andres Santana; Marlins assigned Santana to Edmonton of the Pacific Coast League; Marlins signed OF Greg Briley, a free agent.

APRIL 1

Orioles claimed P Erik Schullstrom on waivers from Padres.

APRIL 2

Marlins traded P Jamie McAndrew to Brewers for P Tom McGraw.

Padres claimed OF Phil Clark on waivers from Tigers.

Pirates traded IF Jeff Richardson to Red Sox for P Daryl Irvine.

APRIL 3

Braves organization reacquired P Bill Taylor from Blue Jays, who had selected him from Richmond in 1992 Rule 5 major league draft.

Brewers granted P Otis Green free agency.

Cubs organization signed OF/1B Doug Jennings, a free agent.

Red Sox organization signed IF Ernest Riles, a free agent.

Rockies signed OF Dale Murphy, a free agent.

Royals organization reacquired P Dera Clark from Dodgers, who had selected him from Omaha in 1992 Rule 5 major league draft.

Tigers signed P David Wells, a free agent.

Twins re-signed 3B Mike Pagliarulo, a free agent.

APRIL 4
Angels signed P Ken Patterson, a free agent.

Mets organization released P Paul Gibson.

APRIL 5
Mariners signed IF Wally Backman, a free agent.

Twins organization signed P Steve Ontiveros, a free agent.

APRIL 6
Indians organization signed P Bob Milacki and P Matt Young, both free agents.

APRIL 7
Indians organization signed P Jason Grimsley, a free agent.

APRIL 8
Royals organization released IF/OF Randy Ready.

APRIL 11
Pirates released C Mike LaValliere.

APRIL 13
Braves traded P Mark Davis to Phillies for P Brad Hassinger; Braves assigned Hassinger to Durham of the Carolina League.

Reds sold contract of OF Willie Canate to Blue Jays and sold contract of P Dwayne Henry to Mariners.

APRIL 14
Expos claimed C/OF Tim McIntosh on waivers from Brewers.

Mets organization re-signed P Paul Gibson, a free agent.

APRIL 15
Braves released P Ken Dayley.

APRIL 17
Twins organization released OF Ced Landrum.

APRIL 19
Dodgers claimed P Steve Parris on waivers from Phillies and assigned him to San Antonio of the Texas League.

APRIL 20
Dodgers organization signed P Ken Dayley, a free agent.

APRIL 23
Astros granted OF Karl Rhodes free agency.

Mets claimed P Jeff Kaiser on waivers from Reds.

White Sox organization signed C Mike LaValliere, a free agent.

APRIL 26
Mariners claimed P Zak Shinall on waivers from Indians and claimed P Steve Parris on waivers from Dodgers.

Royals traded P Mike Boddicker to Brewers for a player to be named later; deal later settled in cash.

APRIL 27
Pirates organization signed P Jeff Ballard, a free agent.

Royals organization signed OF Karl Rhodes, a free agent.

APRIL 29
Expos claimed P Scott Aldred on waivers from Rockies.

Orioles traded OF Luis Mercedes to Giants for P Kevin McGehee; Orioles assigned McGehee to Rochester of the International League.

Reds claimed P Travis Buckley on waivers from Rockies.

MAY 1
Cardinals organization signed P Lee Guetterman, a free agent.

MAY 7
Dodgers organization released C Lance Parrish.

Indians traded P Kevin Wickander to Reds for a player to be named later; Reds sent P Todd Ruyak to Indians to complete deal (June 4). Indians signed C Lance Parrish, a free agent.

Mariners claimed P Len Picota on waivers from Expos.

Orioles organization signed IF/OF Randy Ready, a free agent.

Red Sox organization signed OF/IF Steve Lyons, a free agent.

MAY 11
Pirates claimed P Mark Dewey on waivers from Mets.

MAY 12
Tigers granted P Mike Munoz free agency.

MAY 14
Mets signed OF Ced Landrum, a free agent.

Rockies organization signed P Mike Munoz, a free agent.

MAY 17
Mariners released IF Wally Backman.

MAY 18
Marlins released P Bob McClure.

MAY 19
Rockies released OF Gerald Young and granted P Mark Knudson free agency.

MAY 20
Astros traded P Mark Grant to Rockies for OF Braulio Castillo; Astros assigned Castillo to Tucson of the Pacific Coast League.

Padres organization released P Juan Agosto.

Rangers granted C John Russell free agency.

MAY 23
White Sox released P Dave Stieb.

MAY 24
Astros organization signed P Juan Agosto, a free agent.

Mariners released P Andy Nezelek.

Reds traded P Travis Buckley to Mariners for 1B Charles "Bubba" Smith; Mariners assigned Buckley to Jacksonville of the Southern League.

MAY 27
Expos claimed P Cliff Brantley on waivers from Phillies.

Padres granted P Dave Eiland free agency.

Rockies placed OF Dale Murphy on the voluntarily retired list.

MAY 29
Indians organization signed P Dave Eiland, a free agent.

MAY 30
Indians released C Lance Parrish.

MAY 31
Angels released P Chuck Crim.

JUNE 1
Brewers claimed SS Juan Bell on waivers from Phillies.

Cubs traded P Heathcliff Slocumb to Indians for SS Jose Hernandez; Cubs assigned Hernandez to Orlando of the Southern League.

Padres traded P Jeremy Hernandez to Indians for OF Tracy Sanders and P Fernando Hernandez.

Rangers released P Danny Leon.

JUNE 2
Dodgers claimed P Jonathan Hurst on waivers from Expos.

Rockies released P Bryn Smith.

JUNE 3
Angels released 3B Gary Gaetti.

Reds organization signed OF Gerald Young, a free agent.

JUNE 4
White Sox released P Barry Jones.

JUNE 8
Expos released OF Matt Stairs.

JUNE 11
Mets released P Paul Gibson and traded SS Tony Fernandez to Blue Jays for OF Darrin Jackson.

JUNE 12
Brewers traded P Josias Manzanillo to Mets for OF Wayne Housie; Brewers assigned Housie to New Orleans of the American Association.

Phillies traded P Bob Ayrault to Mariners for P Kevin Foster.

JUNE 14
Royals organization signed P Dave Stieb, a free agent.

JUNE 15
Mets organization reacquired 2B Fernando Vina from Mariners, who had selected him from Tidewater in 1992 Rule 5 major league draft.

JUNE 17
Angels claimed P Doug Linton on waivers from Blue Jays.

Athletics released SS Dale Sveum.

Pirates released IF/OF Glenn Wilson and Pirates organization re-signed Wilson.

JUNE 18
Yankees organization signed P Paul Gibson, a free agent.

JUNE 19
Indians released P Mike Bielecki.

Royals signed 3B Gary Gaetti, a free agent.

JUNE 20
Expos organization released 1B Jack Clark.

JUNE 22
Dodgers organization released P Ken Dayley.

JUNE 23
Expos traded IF/OF Archi Cianfrocco to Padres for P Tim Scott.

JUNE 24
Padres traded 3B Gary Sheffield and P Rich Rodriguez to Marlins for P Trevor Hoffman, P Jose Martinez and P Andres Beruman; Padres assigned Martinez to Las Vegas of the Pacific Coast League and Beruman to Wichita of the Texas League.

JUNE 27
Mariners organization signed IF Dale Sveum, a free agent.

Marlins traded 3B Dave Magadan to Mariners for OF Henry Cotto and P Jeff Darwin.

Twins released OF/1B Randy Bush.

Yankees released P Neal Heaton.

JUNE 28
Rockies claimed P Scott Service on waivers from Reds.

White Sox released C Carlton Fisk.

JUNE 30
Reds traded 3B Gary Scott to Twins for P Alan Newman and IF Tom Houk; Twins assigned Scott to Portland of the Pacific Coast League and Reds assigned Newman to Indianapolis of the American Association and Houk to Chattanooga of the Southern League.

JULY 2
Phillies released P Mark Davis.

JULY 3
Padres traded P Roger Mason to for P Tim Mauser.

JULY 7
Reds claimed P Scott Service on waivers from Rockies.

JULY 9
Athletics released P Storm Davis.

Pirates released P John Candelaria.

JULY 10
Padres traded P Denis Boucher to Expos for IF Austin Manahan and future considerations; deal later settled in cash. Expos assigned Boucher to Ottawa of the International League. Padres signed P Mark Davis, a free agent.

JULY 12
Astros traded OF Jack Daugherty to Reds for OF Steve Carter; Astros assigned Carter to Tucson of the Pacific Coast League.

JULY 14
Expos granted P Jimmy Jones free agency.

JULY 16
Rockies traded P Butch Henry to Expos for P Kent Bottenfield.

Rockies granted P Rudy Seanez free agency.

JULY 17
Marlins traded P Cris Carpenter to Rangers for P Robb Nen and P Kurt Miller.

JULY 18
Padres traded 1B Fred McGriff to Braves for OF Mel Nieves, P Donnie Elliott and OF Vince Moore.

JULY 20
Reds organization released OF Gerald Young.

JULY 21
Mariners released DH/1B Pete O'Brien.

JULY 22
Padres organization signed P Rudy Seanez, a free agent.

Rangers traded P Todd Burns to Cardinals for a player to be named later; Cardinals sent P Duff Brumley to Rangers to complete deal (July 30).

JULY 23
Indians released P Ted Power.

JULY 24
Mariners organization signed P Mark Grater, a free agent.

Tigers signed P Storm Davis, a free agent.

JULY 25
Royals released P Frank DiPino.

JULY 26
Athletics released 3B Kevin Seitzer.

Brewers placed P Mike Boddicker on the voluntarily retired list.

Reds released P Greg Cadaret.

Padres traded P Bruce Hurst and P Greg W. Harris to Rockies for C Brad Ausmus, P Doug Bochtler and a player to be named later; Rockies sent P Andy Ashby to Padres to complete deal (July 27). Padres released IF Kurt Stillwell.

JULY 28
Mariners signed P Ted Power, a free agent.

Rockies released P Mark Grant.

JULY 29
Astros claimed P John Hudek on waivers from Tigers.

Brewers signed 3B Kevin Seitzer, a free agent.

JULY 30
Cubs traded P Paul Assenmacher to Yankees as part of a three-way deal in which Yankees sent P John Habyan to Royals and Royals sent OF Karl Rhodes to Cubs; Cubs assigned Rhodes to Iowa of the American Association.

Rangers signed C John Russell, a free agent.

Royals signed P Greg Cadaret, a free agent.

JULY 31
Athletics traded OF Rickey Henderson to Blue Jays for P Steve Karsay and a player to be named later; Blue Jays sent OF Jose Herrera to A's to complete deal (August 6).

Mariners released P Steve Parris.

Pirates traded P Stan Belinda to Royals for P Jon Lieber and P Dan Miceli.

Reds traded P Tim Belcher to White Sox for P Johnny Ruffin and P Jeff Pierce; Reds assigned Ruffin to Indianapolis of the American Association and Pierce to Chattanooga of the Southern League.

Royals organization released P Dave Stieb.

AUGUST 1
Angels signed IF Kurt Stillwell, a free agent.

AUGUST 3
Giants claimed P Scott Sanderson on waivers from Giants.

AUGUST 4
Indians organization traded P Dave Eiland to Rangers organization for P Gerald Alexander and P Allan Anderson. Indians assigned Alexander to Canton/Akron of the Eastern League and Anderson to Charlotte of the International League.

AUGUST 5
Royals granted P Rick Reed free agency.

AUGUST 7
Mariners organization signed OF Gerald Young, a free agent.
AUGUST 8
Brewers granted 2B William Suero free agency.

Cardinals released P Joe Magrane and C Hector Villanueva.
AUGUST 9
Dodgers claimed P Bob Ayrault on waivers from Mariners.

Indians released P Matt Young.

Orioles claimed P Barry Manuel on waivers from Rangers and Orioles organization released IF/OF Randy Ready.
AUGUST 10
Expos signed IF/OF Randy Ready, a free agent.

Twins organization traded P Steve Ontiveros to Mariners organization for OF Greg Shockey.

White Sox traded P Bobby Thigpen to Phillies for P Jose DeLeon.
AUGUST 11
Rangers organization signed P Rick Reed, a free agent.
AUGUST 12
Blue Jays organization signed P Matt Young, a free agent.
AUGUST 15
Athletics released P Joe Boever.

Twins traded 3B Mike Pagliarulo to Orioles for a player to be named later; Orioles sent P Erik Schullstrom to Twins to complete deal and Twins assigned Schullstrom to Nashville of the Southern League (August 16).
AUGUST 16
Expos released P Cliff Brantley.
AUGUST 17
Red Sox released OF Ivan Calderon.

Reds traded 1B Randy Milligan to Indians for a player to be named later; Indians sent OF Thomas Howard to Reds to complete deal (August 20).
AUGUST 18
Rangers granted C John Russell free agency.
AUGUST 19
Cubs traded OF Candy Maldonado to Indians for OF Glenallen Hill.

Pirates released P Dave Otto.
AUGUST 20
Angels organization released OF Jerome Walton, and signed P Joe Magrane and P Mark Grant, both free agents.
AUGUST 21
Tigers signed P Joe Boever, a free agent, and traded OF Rob Deer to Red Sox for a player to be named later.
AUGUST 22
Expos released P Mike Gardiner.
AUGUST 26
Brewers released P Chris George.

Reds claimed OF Phil Dauphin on waivers from Cubs.
AUGUST 27
Astros claimed P Rick Huisman on waivers from Giants.
AUGUST 28
Twins traded P Jim Deshaies to Giants for P Aaron Fultz, SS Andres Duncan and a player to be named later; Twins assigned Fultz to Ft. Wayne of the Midwest League and Duncan to Ft. Myers of the Florida State League. Giants sent P Greg Brummett to Twins to complete deal (September 1).
AUGUST 30
Reds granted OF Tommy Gregg free agency.
AUGUST 31
Cardinals traded P Lee Smith to Yankees for P Richard Batchelor.

Dodgers traded OF Eric Davis to Tigers for a player to be named later; Tigers sent P John DeSilva to Dodgers to complete deal (September 7).

White Sox signed OF Ivan Calderon, a free agent.

Yankees released P Andy Cook.
SEPTEMBER 1
Rangers re-signed C John Russell, a free agent.

White Sox traded P Donn Pall to Phillies for a player to be named later; Phillies sent C Doug Lindsey to White Sox to complete deal (September 8).
SEPTEMBER 2
Brewers traded OF/1B Larry Sheets to Mariners for a player to be named later; deal later settled in cash.
SEPTEMBER 3
Angels released P Gene Nelson.
SEPTEMBER 7
Angels released 3B Kelly Gruber.
SEPTEMBER 8
Blue Jays organization released P Matt Young.

Pirates traded OF Lonnie Smith to Orioles for two players to be named later; Orioles sent OF Stanton Cameron and P Terry Farrar to complete deal (September 14). Pirates released 1B Mike Bell.

Orioles released 1B Glenn Davis.
SEPTEMBER 9
Mets released OF Darren Reed.
SEPTEMBER 11
Expos released P Scott Aldred.

Rangers released P Mike Schooler and signed P Gene Nelson, a free agent.
SEPTEMBER 14
Angels released P Doug Linton.
SEPTEMBER 15
White Sox released P Ramon Garcia.
SEPTEMBER 17
Astros traded OF Chris James to Rangers for P Dave Gandolph.

Mets traded P Frank Tanana to Yankees for P Kenny Greer.

Yankees released P Jeff Johnson.
SEPTEMBER 20
Cardinals released P Todd Burns.
SEPTEMBER 22
Marlins claimed P Javier De La Hoya on waivers from Dodgers.
SEPTEMBER 27
Marlins released OF Greg Briley.
SEPTEMBER 29
Mets released P Mike Draper.
OCTOBER 4
Angels claimed OF Mike Brumley on waivers from Astros.

Mariners released P Dwayne Henry, OF/1B Larry Sheets and OF Dann Howitt.

Marlins released P Scott Chiamparino.

Mets released IF/OF Chico Walker and OF Ced Landrum.

Royals placed DH George Brett on the voluntarily retired list.
OCTOBER 5
Braves claimed P Milt Hill on waivers from Reds.

Brewers released P Matt Maysey and P James Austin.
OCTOBER 6
Giants released P Larry Carter.
OCTOBER 7
Marlins claimed 1B Greg Colbrunn on waivers from Expos.
OCTOBER 8
Astros released P Rob Mallicoat.

Athletics released P Curt Young.

Tigers released P Dave Johnson.
OCTOBER 12
Cubs released C Steve Lake.

Rockies released P Kevin Ritz.

OCTOBER 13
White Sox released DH George Bell.
OCTOBER 14
Rangers placed P Nolan Ryan on voluntarily retired list.
Reds claimed P Brian Holman on waivers from Mariners.
OCTOBER 15
Brewers placed 2B Bill Doran on the voluntarily retired list.
Dodgers claimed P Mike Milchin on waivers from Cardinals.
Padres released C Mike Scioscia.
OCTOBER 22
Brewers released P Rob Wishnevski.
OCTOBER 24
Twins organization re-signed OF Bernardo Brito, a free agent.
OCTOBER 25
Angels organization released IF Kurt Stillwell and signed P Jimmy Jones, a free agent.
Braves released P Marvin Freeman.
OCTOBER 27
Cardinals organization signed C Terry McGriff, a free agent.
OCTOBER 29
Rockies signed P Marvin Freeman, a free agent formerly with Braves.
NOVEMBER 1
Giants organization re-signed IF Erik Johnson, a free agent.
NOVEMBER 2
Padres organization signed OF Lonnie Maclin, a free agent.
Phillies traded OF Ruben Amaro to Indians for P Heathcliff Slocumb.
Mariners traded P Erik Hanson and 2B Bret Boone to Reds for C Dan Wilson and P Bobby Ayala.
NOVEMBER 3
Marlins organization signed C Ron Tingley, a free agent.
NOVEMBER 4
Reds organization signed OF Jerome Walton, a free agent.
NOVEMBER 5
Blue Jays released P Jack Morris.
NOVEMBER 6
Angels organization released P Jimmy Jones.
NOVEMBER 7
Tigers re-signed P Joe Boever, a free agent.
NOVEMBER 8
Blue Jays organization re-signed P Danny Cox, a free agent.
NOVEMBER 9
Giants released P Dave Righetti and signed P Rich Monteleone, a free agent.
Mariners traded 3B Dave Magadan to Marlins for P Jeff Darwin and cash.
Tigers re-signed P Storm Davis, a free agent.
NOVEMBER 10
Rockies released P Jeff Parrett.
White Sox sold contract of P Brian Drahman to Marlins.
NOVEMBER 11
Mariners re-signed P Reggie Harris, a free agent.
NOVEMBER 12
Blue Jays sold contract of P Greg O'Halloran to Marlins.
Dodgers organization signed C Tom Prince, a free agent.
Mariners released P Russ Swan.
Marlins organization signed IF Jim Walewander, a free agent.
Rangers organization signed C Jim McNamara, a free agent.
NOVEMBER 13
Giants re-signed 2B Robby Thompson, a free agent.
NOVEMBER 15
Brewers released P Carlos Maldonado.

Pirates released 1B Ben Shelton.
NOVEMBER 16
Angels released P Darryl Scott.
Athletics re-signed OF/1B Mike Aldrete, a free agent.
Mariners re-signed P Ted Power, a free agent.
Royals organization re-signed C Nelson Santovenia, a free agent.
NOVEMBER 17
Braves traded 1B Brian Hunter to Pirates for a player to be named later.
Mets organization signed OF Doug Dascenzo, a free agent.
NOVEMBER 18
Braves claimed OF Jarvis Brown on waivers from Padres.
Giants released C/IF Craig Colbert.
Mariners released C Brian Deak.
Mets claimed C Joe Kmak on waivers from Brewers.
Padres released P Rudy Seanez.
Rockies claimed OF Darrell Sherman on waivers from Padres.
NOVEMBER 19
Expos traded 2B Delino DeShields to Dodgers for P Pedro Martinez.
Rangers organization re-signed OF Butch Davis, a free agent.
Rockies signed OF/3B Howard Johnson, a free agent formerly with Mets.
NOVEMBER 21
Giants signed P Mark Portugal, a free agent formerly with Astros.
Royals organization signed P Paul Abbott, a free agent.
NOVEMBER 22
Angels organization signed P Mike Hartley, a free agent.
Orioles signed P Sid Fernandez, a free agent formerly with Mets, and released OF Chito Martinez.
Pirates organization signed IF Tracy Woodson, a free agent.
Rangers signed 1B Will Clark, a free agent formerly with Giants.
Reds released P Chris Bushing.
White Sox organization signed OF Greg Tubbs, a free agent.
NOVEMBER 23
Reds organization signed C Steve Lake, a free agent.
NOVEMBER 24
Braves traded P Pete Smith to Mets for OF Dave Gallagher and released C/IF Francisco Cabrera.
Brewers claimed OF Turner Ward on waivers from Blue Jays.
Cubs re-signed OF Glenallen Hill, a free agent.
Phillies re-signed OF Jim Eisenreich, a free agent, and released P Kyle Abbott.
Rangers signed P Rick Honeycutt, a free agent formerly with Athletics.
Reds organization signed IF Casey Candaele and IF Kurt Stillwell, both free agents.
Twins traded P Willie Banks to Cubs for P Dave Stevens and C Matt Walbeck.
Kintetsu Buffaloes of Japan Pacific League signed P Kyle Abbott, a free agent formerly with Phillies.
Orix Blue Wave of Japan Pacific League signed IF/C Francisco Cabrera, a free agent formerly with Braves.
NOVEMBER 26
Braves signed C Charlie O'Brien, a free agent.
Yankees released OF Hensley Meulens.
Chiba Lotte Orions of Japan Pacific League signed OF Hensley Meulens, a free agent formerly with Yankees.
NOVEMBER 27
Astros traded P Xavier Hernandez to Yankees for P Domingo Jean and IF Andy Stankiewicz.
Pirates organization signed 1B Frank Bolick, a free agent.
NOVEMBER 28
Blue Jays released P Juan de la Rosa.

Royals organization signed P Dennis Moeller, a free agent.

NOVEMBER 29

Dodgers released P Jonathan Hurst.

Giants organization signed C Allan Anderson, a free agent.

Indians released P Mike Christopher.

Marlins claimed P Jeff Mutis on waivers from Indians.

NOVEMBER 30

Rockies signed OF Ellis Burks, a free agent formerly with White Sox.

DECEMBER 1

Phillies signed 3B Tom Quinlan, a free agent.

Reds re-signed IF Lenny Harris, a free agent formerly with Dodgers.

White Sox organization signed OF Dann Howitt, a free agent.

Seibu Lions of Japan Pacific League signed 3B Mike Pagliarulo, a free agent formerly with Orioles.

DECEMBER 2

Indians signed P Dennis Martinez, a free agent formerly with Expos, and 1B Eddie Murray, a free agent formerly with Mets.

Orioles re-signed DH Harold Baines and IF Tim Hulett, both free agents, and released C Mark Parent.

Phillies traded P Mitch Williams to Astros for P Doug Jones and P Jeff Juden.

Rockies organization signed OF Ty Van Burkleo, a free agent.

DECEMBER 3

Cubs signed P Randy Veres, a free agent.

DECEMBER 4

Rockies organization signed P Bruce Walton, a free agent.

DECEMBER 6

Braves released C Greg Olson.

Rockies re-signed 1B Andres Galarraga, a free agent.

Twins organization signed P Kevin Campbell, a free agent.

Chunichi Dragons of Japan Central League signed OF Dion James and P Dwayne Henry, both free agents.

DECEMBER 7

Astros re-signed OF Kevin Bass, a free agent.

Athletics re-signed P Edwin Nunez, a free agent, and signed OF Stan Javier, a free agent formerly with Angels.

Red Sox signed OF Otis Nixon, a free agent formerly with Braves.

Royals re-signed P Mark Gubicza, a free agent.

Twins organization signed C Tim McIntosh, a free agent.

White Sox re-signed P Jose Deleon, a free agent.

DECEMBER 8

Cardinals re-signed P Paul Kilgus, a free agent.

Reds signed P Ken Patterson, a free agent formerly with Angels.

Royals released P Mark Gardner.

DECEMBER 9

Royals organization signed P Bob Milacki, a free agent.

Yankees traded SS Spike Owen and cash to Angels for P Jose Musset.

DECEMBER 10

Astros traded OF Eric Anthony to Mariners for OF Mike Felder and P Mike Hampton.

Cubs released P Bill Brennan and traded P Chuck McElroy to Reds for P Larry Luebbers, P Mike Anderson and C Darron Cox.

Padres traded P Frank Seminara, OF Tracy Sanders and a player to be named later to Mets for OF Randy Curtis and a player to be named later; Mets sent P Marc Kroon to Padres and Padres sent SS Pablo Martinez to Mets to complete deal (December 13).

DECEMBER 12

Orioles signed 1B Rafael Palmeiro, a free agent formerly with Rangers, and released OF Mark Leonard.

DECEMBER 13

Indians released 1B/DH Sam Horn and traded 1B Randy Mil-

ligan to Expos for a player to be named later; Expos sent P Brian Barnes to Indians to complete deal (December 17).

Tigers re-signed P David Wells, a free agent.

Twins organization signed OF Chito Martinez, a free agent.

DECEMBER 14

Cardinals organization traded OF Ozzie Canseco to Brewers organization for OF Tony Diggs.

Cubs organization signed C Mark Parent, C/IF Mike Maksudian and 2B Todd Haney, all free agents.

Dodgers organization signed IF Jeff Treadway, a free agent.

Expos organization re-signed IF Randy Ready, a free agent.

Orioles organization signed P Mark Eichhorn, a free agent formerly with Blue Jays, and C Rich Gedman, a free agent.

Rangers organization signed C Mike Scioscia, a free agent.

Royals organization re-signed P Scott Ruskin, a free agent.

DECEMBER 15

Expos organization signed OF Matt Stairs, a free agent.

Giants signed P Tony Menendez, a free agent.

Indians signed P Calvin Jones, a free agent.

Pirates signed P Archie Corbin, a free agent.

White Sox signed DH Julio Franco, a free agent formerly with Rangers.

DECEMBER 16

Expos organization signed 1B Ben Shelton, a free agent.

Mets organization signed IF Jeff Manto, OF Jim Lindeman and OF Rick Parker, all free agents.

Royals organization re-signed 3B Gary Gaetti, a free agent.

Hanshin Tigers of Japan Central League signed OF Rob Deer, a free agent formerly with Red Sox.

Yomiuri Giants of Japan Central League signed OF Dan Gladden, a free agent formerly with Tigers.

DECEMBER 17

Athletics signed OF Rickey Henderson, a free agent formerly with Blue Jays.

Mets organization signed P Doug Linton, a free agent.

Pirates organization signed P Dennis Powell and P Scott Scudder, both free agents.

DECEMBER 18

Rangers organization re-signed IF Bill Ripken, a free agent.

DECEMBER 19

Cubs traded P Bob Scanlan to Brewers for P Rafael Novoa and OF Mike Carter.

DECEMBER 20

Athletics traded IF Kurt Abbott to Marlins for OF Kerwin Moore.

Giants organization signed IF/OF Rex Hudler, a free agent who played in Japan in 1993.

Indians organization re-signed C Junior Ortiz, a free agent.

Marlins re-signed P Charlie Hough, a free agent.

Mariners traded SS Omar Vizquel to Indians for SS Felix Fermin, 1B Reggie Jefferson and cash.

Mets signed C Greg Olson, a free agent.

Rangers organization signed P Bruce Hurst, a free agent formerly with Rockies.

Yankees signed OF Luis Polonia, a free agent formerly with Angels.

DECEMBER 21

Blue Jays orgranization signed P Greg Cadaret, a free agent.

Brewers re-signed IF Bill Spiers and OF Alex Diaz, both free agents.

Cardinals re-signed 1B Gerald Perry, a free agent.

Yankees organization signed P James Austin, a free agent.

DECEMBER 22

Cubs re-signed P Shawn Boskie, a free agent.

Indians organization signed IF Tim Jones, a free agent.

Mariners claimed P Jeff Williams on waivers from Orioles.

Rockies re-signed OF Chris Jones, a free agent.

Royals re-signed IF Keith Miller, a free agent.

White Sox re-signed OF Tim Raines, a free agent.

Yankees organization signed 1B/DH Sam Horn, a free agent.

DECEMBER 23

Athletics signed P Dave Righetti, a free agent formerly with Giants.

Rockies organization re-signed OF Jim Tatum, a free agent.

DECEMBER 27

White Sox traded IF Ron Coomer to Dodgers for P Isidro Martinez.

DECEMBER 28

Astros organization signed OF Jesse Barfield, a free agent.

White Sox signed OF Darrin Jackson, a free agent formerly with Mets.

DECEMBER 30

Red Sox signed C Dave Valle, a free agent formerly with Mariners.

AWARD WINNERS

THE SPORTING NEWS

AMERICAN LEAGUE

Pitcher of the Year: Jack McDowell, Chicago
Rookie Player of the Year: Tim Salmon, California, OF
Rookie Pitcher of the Year: Aaron Sele, Boston
Fireman of the Year: Jeff Montgomery, Kansas City
Manager of the Year: Gene Lamont, Chicago

NATIONAL LEAGUE

Pitcher of the Year: Greg Maddux, Atlanta
Rookie Player of the Year: Mike Piazza, Los Angeles, C
Rookie Pitcher of the Year: Kirk Rueter, Montreal
Fireman of the Year: Randy Myers, Chicago
Manager of the Year: Bobby Cox, Atlanta

MAJOR LEAGUE

Player of the Year: Frank Thomas, Chicago (A.L.)
Executive of the Year: Lee Thomas, Philadelphia

MINOR LEAGUE

Player of the Year: Cliff Floyd, Harrisburg, Eastern
Manager of the Year: Jim Tracy, Harrisburg, Eastern
Executive of the Year: Todd Vander Woude, Harrisburg, Eastern

BASEBALL WRITERS' ASSOCIATION OF AMERICA

AMERICAN LEAGUE

MOST VALUABLE PLAYER

Player, Team	1	2	3	4	5	6	7	8	9	10	Pts.
Frank Thomas, Chicago	28	-	-	-	-	-	-	-	-	-	392
Paul Molitor, Toronto	-	13	5	3	1	4	-	1	1	-	209
John Olerud, Toronto	-	4	11	4	4	3	1	1	-	-	198
Juan Gonzalez, Texas	-	4	4	10	4	3	1	1	-	1	185
Ken Griffey Jr., Seattle	-	4	5	7	7	2	1	-	-	1	182
Roberto Alomar, Toronto	-	3	2	1	1	2	5	3	2	3	102
Albert Belle, Cleveland	-	-	-	1	4	3	3	4	5	1	81
Rafael Palmeiro, Texas	-	-	-	-	1	3	4	3	2	2	52
Jack McDowell, Chicago	-	-	-	1	2	3	1	3	1	2	51
Carlos Baerga, Cleveland	-	-	1	-	1	2	2	2	5	2	50
Jimmy Key, New York	-	-	-	1	2	-	1	2	-	-	29
Joe Carter, Toronto	-	-	-	-	1	1	3	-	-	2	25
Mike Stanley, New York	-	-	-	-	-	-	1	1	3	2	15
Jeff Montgomery, Kansas City	-	-	-	-	-	-	1	3	1	-	15
Kenny Lofton, Cleveland	-	-	-	-	-	-	1	-	2	3	11
Tony Phillips, Detroit	-	-	-	-	-	-	-	1	2	3	10
Chris Hoiles, Baltimore	-	-	-	-	-	-	1	-	2	2	10
Mo Vaughn, Boston	-	-	-	-	-	-	1	1	-	1	8
Don Mattingly, New York	-	-	-	-	-	1	-	1	-	-	7
Cal Ripken, Baltimore	-	-	-	-	-	1	-	1	-	-	7
Alex Fernandez, Chicago	-	-	-	-	-	1	-	-	-	-	4
Duane Ward, Toronto	-	-	-	-	-	-	-	1	-	-	3
Greg Gagne, Kansas City	-	-	-	-	-	-	-	1	-	-	3
Kevin Appier, Kansas City	-	-	-	-	-	-	-	-	1	1	1
Cecil Fielder, Detroit	-	-	-	-	-	-	-	-	-	1	1
Randy Johnson, Seattle	-	-	-	-	-	-	-	-	-	1	1

Fourteen points awarded for a first-place vote, nine for second and on down to one for 10th.

MANAGER OF THE YEAR

Manager, Team	1	2	3	Pts.
Gene Lamont, Chicago	8	9	5	72
Buck Showalter, New York	7	8	4	63
Cito Gaston, Toronto	6	5	4	49
Kevin Kennedy, Texas	3	3	4	28
Lou Piniella, Seattle	3	2	3	24
Mike Hargrove, Cleveland	1	-	5	10
Johnny Oates, Baltimore	-	1	2	5
Butch Hobson, Boston	-	-	1	1

Five points awarded for a first-place vote, three for second and one for third.

CY YOUNG AWARD

Pitcher, Team	1	2	3	Pts.
Jack McDowell, Chicago	21	6	1	124
Randy Johnson, Seattle	6	14	3	75
Kevin Appier, Kansas City	1	4	13	30
Jimmy Key, New York	-	2	8	14
Duane Ward, Toronto	-	1	2	5
Pat Hentgen, Toronto	-	1	-	3
Juan Guzman, Toronto	-	-	1	1

Five points awarded for a first-place vote, three for second and one for third.

ROOKIE OF THE YEAR

Player, Team	1	2	3	Pts.	Player, Team	1	2	3	Pts.
Tim Salmon, California	28	-	-	140	Brent Gates, Oakland	-	1	4	7
Jason Bere, Chicago	-	18	5	59	Troy Neel, Oakland	-	1	2	5
Aaron Sele, Boston	-	3	10	19	Gerry DiPoto, Cleveland	-	-	1	1
Wayne Kirby, Cleveland	-	3	3	12	David Hulse, Texas	-	-	1	1
Rich Amaral, Seattle	-	2	2	8					

Five points awarded for a first-place vote, three for second and one for third.

MOST VALUABLE PLAYER

Player, Team	1	2	3	4	5	6	7	8	9	10	Pts.
Barry Bonds, San Francisco	24	4	-	-	-	-	-	-	-	-	372
Lenny Dykstra, Philadelphia	4	20	3	1	-	-	-	-	-	-	267
David Justice, Atlanta	-	3	5	8	7	3	-	1	-	-	183
Fred McGriff, San Diego/Atlanta	-	1	12	4	3	3	1	1	2	-	177
Ron Gant, Atlanta	-	-	8	9	3	5	-	-	3	-	176
Matt Williams, San Francisco	-	-	-	2	7	3	5	2	3	-	103
Darren Daulton, Philadelphia	-	-	-	-	4	5	3	5	1	1	79
Marquis Grissom, Montreal	-	-	-	2	-	2	6	4	3	-	66
Mike Piazza, Los Angeles	-	-	-	-	3	-	3	3	3	4	49
Andres Galarraga, Colorado	-	-	-	1	-	1	3	4	3	3	45
Gregg Jefferies, St. Louis	-	-	-	-	-	3	1	2	-	3	28
Rod Beck, San Francisco	-	-	-	-	1	2	-	-	3	1	23
Greg Maddux, Atlanta	-	-	-	1	-	-	-	2	-	4	17
Bryan Harvey, Florida	-	-	-	-	-	-	2	1	-	3	14
Robby Thompson, San Francisco	-	-	-	-	-	-	1	-	2	3	11
Jeff Blauser, Atlanta	-	-	-	-	-	-	-	1	1	2	9
John Kruk, Philadelphia	-	-	-	-	-	-	1	-	2	-	9
Mark Grace, Chicago	-	-	-	-	-	-	1	1	-	1	8
Jay Bell, Pittsburgh	-	-	-	-	-	-	1	-	-	-	4
Jeff Bagwell, Houston	-	-	-	-	-	-	-	1	-	-	3
Tony Gwynn, San Diego	-	-	-	-	-	-	-	-	1	-	2
Randy Myers, Chicago	-	-	-	-	-	-	-	-	1	-	2
Jose Rijo, Cincinnati	-	-	-	-	-	-	-	-	1	-	2
John Burkett, San Francisco	-	-	-	-	-	-	-	-	-	1	1
Tom Glavine, Atlanta	-	-	-	-	-	-	-	-	-	1	1
John Wetteland, Montreal	-	-	-	-	-	-	-	-	-	1	1

Fourteen points awarded for a first-place vote, nine for second and on down to one for 10th.

CY YOUNG AWARD

Pitcher, Team	1	2	3	Pts.
Greg Maddux, Atlanta	22	2	3	119
Bill Swift, San Francisco	2	15	6	61
Tom Glavine, Atlanta	4	7	8	49
John Burkett, San Francisco	-	3	-	9
Jose Rijo, Cincinnati	-	1	5	8
Tommy Greene, Philadelphia	-	-	2	2
Mark Portugal, Houston	-	-	2	2
Bryan Harvey, Florida	-	-	1	1
Randy Myers, Chicago	-	-	1	1

Five points awarded for a first-place vote, three for second and one for third.

MANAGER OF THE YEAR

Manager, Team	1	2	3	Pts.
Dusty Baker, San Francisco	15	9	3	105
Jim Fregosi, Philadelphia	11	11	4	92
Felipe Alou, Montreal	2	2	11	27
Bobby Cox, Atlanta	-	6	9	27
Don Baylor, Colorado	-	-	1	1

Five points awarded for a first-place vote, three for second and one for third.

ROOKIE OF THE YEAR

Player, Team	1	2	3	Pts.
Mike Piazza, Los Angeles	28	-	-	140
Greg McMichael, Atlanta	-	12	4	40
Jeff Conine, Florida	-	7	10	31
Chuck Carr, Florida	-	4	6	18
Al Martin, Pittsburgh	-	2	-	6
Kevin Stocker, Philadelphia	-	1	1	4
Wil Cordero, Montreal	-	1	-	3
Kirk Rueter, Montreal	-	1	-	3
Carlos Garcia, Pittsburgh	-	-	2	2
Pedro Martinez, Los Angeles	-	-	2	2
Steve Cooke, Pittsburgh	-	-	1	1
Ricky Gutierrez, San Diego	-	-	1	1
Armando Reynoso, Colorado	-	-	1	1

Five points awarded for a first-place vote, three for second and one for third.

MISCELLANEOUS

ATTENDANCE

AMERICAN LEAGUE

	Home	Road
Baltimore	3,644,965	2,190,759
Boston	2,422,021	2,542,249
California	2,057,460	2,286,647
Chicago	2,581,091	2,571,969
Cleveland	2,177,908	2,216,318
Detroit	1,971,421	2,387,312
Kansas City	1,934,578	2,378,624
Milwaukee	1,688,080	2,269,151
Minnesota	2,048,673	2,300,021
New York	2,416,965	2,603,338
Oakland	2,035,025	2,326,919
Seattle	2,051,853	2,307,636
Texas	2,244,616	2,401,762
Toronto	4,057,947	2,549,898
Totals	**33,332,603**	**33,332,603**

NATIONAL LEAGUE

	Home	Road
Atlanta	3,884,725	2,944,157
Chicago	2,653,763	2,592,790
Cincinnati	2,453,232	2,532,257
Colorado	4,483,350	2,695,071
Florida	3,064,847	2,701,068
Houston	2,084,546	2,421,566
Los Angeles	3,170,392	2,663,828
Montreal	1,641,437	2,620,064
New York	1,873,183	2,660,426
Philadelphia	3,137,674	2,666,219
Pittsburgh	1,650,593	2,507,346
St. Louis	2,844,328	2,612,017
San Diego	1,375,432	2,534,072
San Francisco	2,606,354	2,772,975
Totals	**36,923,856**	**36,923,856**

DEBUTS

Player	Pos.	Team	Birth date	Birthplace	Debut
Abbott, Kurt Thomas	PR	Oakland	6- 2-69	Zanesville, O.	9-7
Anderson, Brian James	P	California	4-26-72	Virginia Beach, Va.	9-10
Anderson, Michael James	P	Cincinnati	7-30-66	Austin, Tex.	9-7
Armas, Marcos Rafael	1B	Oakland	8- 5-69	Puerto Pirtu, Venezuela	5-25
Arocha, Rene	P	St. Louis	2-24-66	Havana, Cuba	4-9
Aude, Richard Thomas	PH	Pittsburgh	7-13-71	Van Nuys, Calif.	9-9
Ausmus, Bradley David	C	San Diego	4-14-69	New Haven, Conn.	7-28
Bailey, Phillip Cory	P	Boston	1-24-71	Herrin, Ill.	9-1
Batchelor, Richard Anthony	P	St. Louis	4- 8-67	Florence, S.C.	9-3
Bautista, Daniel	DH	Detroit	5-24-72	Santo Domingo, D.R.	9-15
Becker, Richard Goodhard	OF	Minnesota	2- 1-72	Aurora, Ill.	9-10
Bere, Jason Phillip	P	Chicago A.L.	5-26-71	Cambridge, Mass.	5-27
Bergman, Sean F.	P	Detroit	4-11-70	Joliet, Ill.	7-7
Blosser, Gregory Brent	PH	Boston	6-26-71	Bradenton, Fla.	9-5
Bogar, Timothy Paul	SS	New York N.L.	10-28-66	Indianapolis	5-28
Bolick, Frank Charles	3B	Montreal	6-28-66	Ashland, Pa.	4-5
Bolton, Rodney Earl	P	Chicago A.L.	9-23-68	Chattanooga, Tenn.	4-10
Brewer, William Robert	P	Kansas City	4-15-68	Fort Worth, Tex.	4-8
Bronkey, Jacob Jeffery	P	Texas	9-18-65	Kabul, Afghanistan	6-14
Brooks, Jerome Edward	PR	Los Angeles	3-23-67	Syracuse, N.Y.	9-6
Brow, Scott John	P	Toronto	3-17-69	Butte, Mont.	4-28
Brummett, Gregory Scott	P	San Francisco	4-20-67	Wichita, Kan.	5-29
Buford, Damon Jackson	OF	Baltimore	6-12-70	Baltimore	5-4
Bullett, Scott Douglas	OF	Pittsburgh	12-25-68	Martinsburg, W.Va.	7-16
Burgos, Enrique	P	Kansas City	10- 7-65	Chorrera, Panama	7-15
Burnitz, Jeromy Neal	OF	New York N.L.	4-15-69	Westminster, Calif.	6-21
Bushing, Christopher Shaun	P	Cincinnati	11- 4-67	Rockville Center, N.Y.	9-3
Butler, Robert Frank	OF	Toronto	4-10-70	East York, Ont.	6-12
Byrd, James Edward	DH	Boston	10- 3-68	WeWahitchca, Fla.	5-31
Canate, Emisael William	OF	Toronto	12-11-71	Maracaibo, Venezuela	7-5
Caraballo, Ramon	2B	Atlanta	5-23-69	Rio San Juan, D.R.	9-9
Carey, Paul Stephen	PH	Baltimore	1- 8-68	Boston	7-4
Castellano, Pedro Orlando	1B	Colorado	3-11-70	Lara, Venezuela	5-30
Cedeno, Domingo	SS	Toronto	11- 4-68	La Romana, D.R.	5-19
Converse, James Daniel	P	Seattle	8-17-71	San Francisco	5-22
Cook, Andrew Bernard	P	New York A.L.	8-30-67	Memphis, Tenn.	5-9
Correia, Ronald Douglas	SS	California	9-13-67	Providence, R.I.	6-20
Cromer, Roy Bunyan III	PR	St. Louis	11-27-67	Lake City, S.C.	9-7
Cummings, John Russell	P	Seattle	5-10-69	Torrance, Calif.	4-10
Cummings, Midre Almeric	OF	Pittsburgh	10-14-71	St. Croix, Virgin Islands	9-10
Daal, Omar Jose Cordaro	P	Los Angeles	3- 1-72	Maracaibo, Venezuela	4-23
Delgado, Carlos Juan	C	Toronto	6-25-72	Aguadilla, P.R.	10-1
DeSilva, John Reed	P	Detroit	9-30-67	Fort Bragg, Calif.	8-15
DiPoto, Gerard Peter III	P	Cleveland	5-24-68	Jersey City, N.J.	5-11
Dixon, Steven Ross	P	St. Louis	8- 3-69	Cincinnati	9-7

Player	Pos.	Team	Birth date	Birthplace	Debut
Draper, Michael Anthony	P	New York N.L.	9-14-66	Hagerstown, Md.	4-10
Dreyer, Steven William	P	Texas	11-19-69	Ames, Ia.	8-8
Edmonds, James Patrick	OF	California	6-27-70	Fullerton, Calif.	9-9
Ettles, Mark Edward	P	San Diego	10-30-66	Perth, Australia	6-5
Everett, Carl Edward	OF	Florida	6- 3-70	Tampa, Fla.	7-1
Faneyte, Rikkert	OF	San Francisco	5-31-69	Amsterdam, Netherlands	8-29
Flener, Gregory Alan	P	Toronto	2-25-69	Austin, Tex.	9-14
Fletcher, Edward Paul	P	Philadelphia	1-14-67	Gallipolis, O.	7-11
Floyd, Cornelius Clifford	1B	Montreal	12- 5-72	Chicago	9-18
Foster, Kevin Christopher	P	Philadelphia	1-13-69	Evanston, Ill.	9-12
Frazier, Arthur Louis	PH	Montreal	1-26-65	St. Louis	4-8
Fredrickson, Scott Eric	P	Colorado	8-19-67	Manchester, N.H.	4-29
Gainer, Jonathan Keith	1B	Colorado	10- 8-66	Panama City, Fla.	5-14
Gates, Brent Robert	2B	Oakland	3-14-70	Grand Rapids, Mich.	5-5
Gil, Romar Benjamin	SS	Texas	10- 6-72	Tijuana, Mexico	4-5
Gohr, Gregory James	P	Detroit	10-29-67	Santa Clara, Calif.	4-7
Gomez, Chris Cory	SS	Detroit	6-16-71	Los Angeles	7-19
Gomez, Patrick Alexander	P	San Diego	3-17-68	Roseville, Calif.	4-6
Gonzales, Lawrence Christopher	1B	California	3-28-67	Covina, Calif.	6-12
Gordon, Keith Bradley	OF	Cincinnati	1-22-69	Bethesda, Md.	7-9
Granger, Jeffrey Adam	P	Kansas City	12-16-71	San Pedro, Calif.	9-16
Green, Shawn David	DH	Toronto	11-10-72	Des Plaines, Ill.	9-28
Green, Tyler Scott	P	Philadelphia	2-18-70	Inglewood, Colo.	4-9
Greer, Kenneth William	P	New York N.L.	5-12-67	Boston	9-29
Guardado, Edward Adrian	P	Minnesota	10- 2-70	Stockton, Calif.	6-13
Gutierrez, Ricardo	OF	San Diego	5-23-70	Miami	4-13
Hamelin, Robert James III	PH	Kansas City	11-29-67	Elizabeth, N.J.	9-12
Hammonds, Jeffrey Bryan	DH	Baltimore	3- 5-71	Plainfield, N.J.	6-25
Hampton, Michael William	P	Seattle	9- 9-72	Brooksville, Fla.	6-29
Helfand, Eric James	C	Oakland	3-25-69	Erie, Pa.	9-4
Hiatt, Philip Farrell	3B	Kansas City	5- 1-69	Pensacola, Fla.	4-7
Higgins, Kevin W.	C	San Diego	1-22-67	San Gabriel, Calif.	5-29
Hocking, Dennis Lee	SS	Minnesota	4- 2-70	Torrance, Calif.	9-10
Hoffman, Trevor William	P	Florida	10-13-67	Bellflower, Calif.	4-6
Holman, Bradley Thomas	P	Seattle	2- 9-68	Kansas City, Kan.	7-4
Holzemer, Mark Harold	P	California	8-20-69	Littleton, Colo.	8-21
Hope, John Alan	P	Pittsburgh	12-21-70	Fort Lauderdale, Fla.	8-29
Howard, Christian	P	Chicago A.L.	11-18-65	Lynn, Mass.	9-21
Huskey, Robert Leon	3B	New York N.L.	11-10-71	Anadarko, Okla.	9-8
Hutton, Mark Steven	P	New York A.L.	2- 6-70	South Adelaide, Aust.	7-23
Jean, Domingo	P	New York A.L.	1- 9-69	San Pedro de Macoris, D.R.	8-8
Jimenez, Miguel Anthony	P	Oakland	8-19-69	New York, N.Y.	9-12
Johnson, Erik Anthony	SS	San Francisco	10-11-65	Oakland, Calif.	7-8
Johnstone, John William	P	Florida	11-25-68	Liverpool, N.Y.	9-3
Jones, Larry Wayne	SS	Atlanta	4-24-72	Deland, Fla.	9-11
Jones, Robert Joseph	P	New York N.L.	2-10-70	Fresno, Calif.	8-14
Jones, Todd Barton	P	Houston	4-24-68	Marietta, Ga.	7-7
Karsay, Stefan Andrew	P	Oakland	3-24-72	Flushing, N.Y.	8-17
Kessinger, Robert Keith	SS	Cincinnati	2-19-67	Forrest City, Ark.	9-15
Kiefer, Mark Andrew	P	Milwaukee	11-13-68	Orange, Calif.	9-20
King, Kevin Ray	P	Seattle	2-11-69	Atwater, Calif.	9-2
Kmak, Joseph Robert	C	Milwaukee	5- 3-63	Napa, Calif.	4-6
Koelling, Brian Wayne	2B	Cincinnati	6-11-69	Cincinnati	8-21
Lansing, Michael Thomas	2B	Montreal	4- 3-68	Rawlins, Wyo.	4-7
Lee, Derek Gerald	OF	Minnesota	7-28-66	Chicago	6-27
Leftwich, Phillip Dale	P	California	5-19-69	Lynchburg, Va.	7-29
Leskanic, Curtis John	P	Colorado	4- 2-68	Homestead, Pa.	6-27
Lloyd, Graeme John	P	Milwaukee	4- 9-67	Victoria, Aust.	4-11
Longmire, Anthony Eugene	OF	Philadelphia	8-12-68	Vallejo, Calif.	9-3
Looney, Brian James	P	Montreal	9-26-69	New Haven, Conn.	9-26
Lopez, Albert Anthony	P	Cleveland	8-18-71	Mesa, Ariz.	7-6
Lopez, Luis Santos	2B	San Diego	9- 4-70	Cidra, P.R.	9-7
Luebbers, Larry Christopher	P	Cincinnati	10-11-69	Cincinnati	7-3
Lyden, Mitchell Scott	C	Florida	12-14-64	Portland, Ore.	6-16
Lydy, Donald Scott	OF	Oakland	10-26-68	Mesa, Ariz.	5-18
Maclin, Lonnie Lee Jr.	OF	St. Louis	2-17-67	Clayton, Mo.	9-7
Marrero, Oreste Vilato	1B	Montreal	10-31-69	Bayamon, Puerto Rico	8-12
Martin, Norberto Edonal	PR	Chicago A.L.	12-10-66	Santo Domingo, D.R.	9-20
Martinez, Pedro Aquino	P	San Diego	11-29-68	Villa Mella, D.R.	6-29
Mauser, Timothy Edward	P	Philadelphia	10- 4-66	Fort Worth, Tex.	5-28
McCarty, David Andrew	OF	Minnesota	11-23-69	Houston	5-17
McGehee, George Kevin	P	Baltimore	1-18-69	Alexandria, La.	8-23
McMichael, Gregory Winston	P	Atlanta	12- 1-66	Knoxville, Tenn.	4-12
McNeely, Jeffrey Laverne	PR	Boston	10-18-69	Monroe, N.C.	9-5
Meares, Patrick James	SS	Minnesota	9- 6-68	Salina, Kan.	5-5
Mejia, Roberto Antonio Diaz	2B	Colorado	4-14-72	Hato Mayor, D.R.	7-15

Player	Pos.	Team	Birth date	Birthplace	Debut
Merriman, Brett Alan	P	Minnesota	7-15-66	Jacksonville, Fla.	4-8
Miceli, Daniel	P	Pittsburgh	9- 9-70	Newark, N.J.	9-9
Mieske, Matthew Todd	OF	Milwaukee	2-13-68	Midland, Mich.	5-3
Minchey, Nathan Derek	P	Boston	8-31-69	Austin, Tex.	9-12
Miranda, Angel	P	Milwaukee	11- 9-69	Arecibo, P.R.	6-5
Mohler, Michael Ross	P	Oakland	7-26-68	Dayton, O.	4-7
Mondesi, Raul	OF	Los Angeles	3-12-71	San Cristobal, D.R.	7-19
Montoyo, Jose Carlos	2B	Montreal	10-17-65	Manati, Puerto Rico	9-7
Moore, Marcus Braymont	P	Colorado	11- 2-70	Oakland, Calif.	7-9
Munoz, Roberto	P	New York A.L.	3- 3-68	Rio Piedras, P.R.	9-6
Navarro, Norberto Rodriguez	SS	New York N.L.	9-12-70	Rio Pedras, P.R.	9-6
Nen, Robert Allen	P	Texas	11-28-69	San Pedro, Calif.	4-10
Newfield, Marc Alexander	DH	Seattle	10-19-72	Sacramento, Calif.	7-6
Obando, Sherman Omar	OF	Baltimore	1-23-70	Changuinola, Panama	4-10
O'Donoghue, John Preston	P	Baltimore	5-26-69	Wilmington, Del.	6-27
O'Leary, Troy Franklin	OF	Milwaukee	8- 4-69	Compton, Calif.	5-9
Oliver, Darren Christopher	P	Texas	10- 6-70	Kansas City, Mo.	9-1
Oquist, Michael Lee	P	Baltimore	5-30-68	La Junta, Colo.	8-14
Ortiz, Luis Alberto	3B	Boston	5-25-70	Santo Domingo, D.R.	8-31
Owens, Claude J.	C	Colorado	2-10-69	Cincinnati	6-6
Painter, Lance T.	P	Colorado	7-21-67	Bedford, England	5-19
Paquette, Craig Howard	3B	Oakland	3-28-69	Long Beach, Calif.	6-1
Pennington, Brad Lee	P	Baltimore	4-14-69	Salem, Ind.	4-17
Perez, Eduardo Antancio	3B	California	9-11-69	Cincinnati	7-27
Phillips, Charles Gene	1B	San Francisco	4-29-70	West Covina, Calif.	9-3
Pirkl, Gregory Daniel	1B	Seattle	8- 7-70	Long Beach, Calif.	8-13
Plantenberg, Erik John	P	Seattle	10-30-68	Renton, Wash.	7-31
Pose, Scott Vernon	OF	Florida	2-11-67	Davenport, Ia.	4-5
Powell, Ross John	P	Cincinnati	1-24-68	Grand Rapids, Mich.	9-5
Pride, Curtis John	OF	Montreal	12-17-68	Washington, D.C.	9-14
Ramirez, Manuel Aristides	DH	Cleveland	5-30-72	Santo Domingo, D.R.	9-2
Roberson, Kevin Lynn	OF	Chicago N.L.	1-29-68	Decatur, Ill.	7-15
Robertson, Richard Wayne	P	Pittsburgh	9-15-68	Nacogdoches, Tex.	4-30
Ronan, Edward Marcus	C	St. Louis	9-19-69	Ozark, Ala.	9-21
Roper, John Christopher	P	Cincinnati	11-21-71	Southern Pines, N.C.	5-16
Rueter, Kirk Wesley	P	Montreal	12- 1-70	Nashville, Tenn.	7-7
Ruffcorn, Scott Patrick	P	Chicago A.L.	12-29-69	New Braunfels, Tex.	6-19
Ruffin, Johnny Renando	P	Cincinnati	7-29-71	Butler, Ala.	8-8
Salkeld, Roger W.	P	Seattle	3- 6-71	Burbank, Calif.	9-8
Sanders, Scott Gerald	P	San Diego	3-25-69	Hannibal, Mo.	8-6
Saunders, Douglas Long	2B	New York N.L.	12-13-69	Lakewood, Calif.	6-13
Schwarz, Jeffrey William	P	Chicago A.L.	5-20-64	Fort Pierce, Fla.	4-24
Scott, Darryl Nelson	P	California	8- 6-68	Fresno, Calif.	6-2
Sele, Aaron Helmer	P	Boston	6-25-70	Golden Valley, Minn.	6-23
Shave, Jonathan Taylor	SS	Texas	11- 4-67	Waycross, Ga.	5-15
Shelton, Benjamin Davis	PH	Pittsburgh	9-21-69	Chicago	6-16
Sherman, Darrell Edward	PH	San Diego	12- 4-67	Los Angeles	4-8
Shinall, Zakary Sebastien	P	Seattle	10-14-68	St. Louis	5-12
Shouse, Brian Douglas	P	Pittsburgh	9-26-68	Effingham, Ill.	7-31
Siddall, Joseph Todd	C	Montreal	10-25-67	Windsor, Ont.	7-28
Smithberg, Roger Craig	P	Oakland	3-21-66	Elgin, Ill.	9-1
Spradlin, Jerry Carl	P	Cincinnati	6-14-67	Fullerton, Calif.	7-2
Stahoviak, Scott Edmund	3B	Minnesota	3- 6-70	Waukegan, Ill.	9-10
Staton, David Allen	1B	San Diego	4-12-68	Seattle	9-8
Stocker, Kevin Douglas	SS	Philadelphia	2-13-70	Spokane, Wash.	7-7
Swingle, Paul Christopher	P	California	12-21-66	Inglewood, Calif.	9-7
Tarasco, Anthony Giacinto	OF	Atlanta	12- 9-70	New York, N.Y.	4-30
Tavarez, Julian	P	Cleveland	5-22-73	Santiago, D.R.	8-7
Taylor, Kerry Thomas	P	San Diego	1-25-71	Bemidji, Minn.	4-13
Telgheder, David William	P	New York N.L.	11-11-66	Middletown, N.Y.	6-12
Tinsley, Lee Owen	OF	Seattle	3- 4-69	Shelbyville, Ky.	4-6
Tomberlin, Andy Lee	PH	Pittsburgh	11- 7-66	Monroe, N.C.	8-12
Torres, Salomon Ramirez	P	San Francisco	3-11-72	San Pedro de Macoris, D.R.	8-29
Trachsel, Stephen Christopher	P	Chicago N.L.	10-31-70	Oxnard, Calif.	9-19
Tsamis, George Alex	P	Minnesota	6-14-67	Campbell, Calif.	4-26
Tubbs, Gregory Alan	OF	Cincinnati	8-31-62	Smithville, Tenn.	8-1
Turang, Brian Craig	OF	Seattle	6-14-67	Long Beach, Calif.	8-13
Turner, Christopher Wan	C	California	3-23-69	Bowling Green, Ky.	8-27
Turner, William Mathew	P	Florida	2-18-67	Lexington, Ky.	4-23
Urbani, Thomas James	P	St. Louis	1-21-68	Santa Cruz, Calif.	4-21
Van Burkleo, Tyler Lee	1B	California	10- 7-63	Oakland, Calif.	7-28
Vina, Fernando	2B	Seattle	4-16-69	Sacramento, Calif.	4-11
Walbeck, Matthew Lovick	C	Chicago N.L.	10- 2-69	Sacramento, Calif.	4-7
Watson, Allen K.	P	St. Louis	11-18-70	Jamaica, N.Y.	7-8
Wendell, Steven John	P	Chicago N.L.	5-19-67	Pittsfield, Mass.	6-17
Wertz, William Charles	P	Cleveland	1-15-67	Cleveland	5-22

Player	Pos.	Team	Birth date	Birthplace	Debut
White, Derrick Ramon	1B	Montreal	10-12-69	San Rafael, Calif.	7-22
White, Rondell Bernard	OF	Montreal	2-23-72	Milledgeville, Ga.	9-1
Whitmore, Darrell Lamont	OF	Florida	11-18-68	Front Royal, Va.	6-25
Williams, Gregory Scott	P	Toronto	8-19-66	Houston	5-13
Wilson, Nigel Edward	OF	Florida	1-12-70	Oshawa, Ont.	9-8
Womack, Anthony Darrell	PR	Pittsburgh	9-25-69	Danville, Va.	9-10
Worrell, Timothy Howard	P	San Diego	7- 5-67	Pasadena, Calif.	6-25
Zambrano, Eduardo Jose	OF	Chicago N.L.	2- 1-66	Maracaibo, Venezuela	9-19

SALARY ARBITRATION RESULTS

WINNERS

Player, Team	Salary awarded	Team's offer
Jack McDowell, Chicago White Sox	$4,000,000	$3,150,000
Bip Roberts, Cincinnati	$3,900,000	$2,700,000
Darrin Jackson, San Diego	$2,100,000	$1,500,000
Andy Benes, San Diego	$2,050,000	$1,550,000
Randy Velarde, New York Yankees	$1,050,000	$600,000
John Dopson, Boston	$750,000	$485,000

LOSERS

Player, Team	Salary awarded	Player's request
Mark Grace, Chicago	$3,100,000	$4,100,000
Kevin Brown, Texas	$2,800,000	$3,400,000
Jim Abbott, New York Yankees	$2,350,000	$3,500,000
Jeff Brantley, San Francisco	$1,500,000	$2,600,000
Marquis Grissom, Montreal	$1,500,000	$1,950,000
Erik Hanson, Seattle	$1,250,000	$2,300,000
Kenny Rogers, Texas	$1,000,000	$1,500,000
Jeff King, Pittsburgh	$675,000	$1,075,000
Jerry Browne, Oakland	$625,000	$1,950,000
John Habyan, New York Yankees	$600,000	$830,000
Mark Lemke, Atlanta	$550,000	$925,000
Carlos Quintana, Boston	$340,000	$850,000

1993 FREE-AGENT FILINGS

AMERICAN LEAGUE

Baltimore: Harold Baines, Tim Hulett, Mike Pagliarulo, Harold Reynolds, Lonnie Smith, Rick Sutcliffe, Fernando Valenzuela.
Boston: Rob Deer, John Dopson, Steve Lyons, Tony Pena, Ernest Riles, Luis Rivera.
California: Rene Gonzales, Stan Javier, Luis Polonia.
Chicago: Tim Belcher, Ellis Burks, Ivan Calderon, Jose DeLeon, Bo Jackson, Tim Raines.
Cleveland: Bob Ojeda, Junior Ortiz, Jeff Treadway.
Detroit: Storm Davis, Dan Gladden, Kirk Gibson, David Wells.
Kansas City: Hubie Brooks, Greg Cadaret, Gary Gaetti, Mark Gubicza, Dennis Rasmussen.
Milwaukee: Kevin Seitzer, Dickie Thon, Robin Yount.
Minnesota: Brian Harper.
New York: Steve Farr, Dion James, Lee Smith, Frank Tanana, Mike Witt.
Oakland: Mike Aldrete, Jerry Browne, Rich Gossage, Dave Henderson, Rick Honeycutt, Edwin Nunez.
Seattle: Tim Leary, Ted Power, Dave Valle.
Texas: Julio Franco, Craig Lefferts, Charlie Leibrandt, Rafael Palmeiro, Geno Petralli.
Toronto: Danny Cox, Mark Eichhorn, Tony Fernandez, Alfredo Griffin, Rickey Henderson.

NATIONAL LEAGUE

Atlanta: Sid Bream, Jay Howell, Otis Nixon.
Chicago: None.
Cincinnati: Jeff Reardon, Bip Roberts, Chris Sabo, Juan Samuel.
Colorado: Daryl Boston, Andres Galarraga, Bruce Hurst.
Florida: Henry Cotto, Charlie Hough, Walt Weiss.
Houston: Kevin Bass, Mark Portugal, Jose Uribe.
Los Angeles: Jody Reed.
Montreal: Dennis Martinez, Randy Ready.
New York: Sid Fernandez, Howard Johnson, Eddie Murray, Charlie O'Brien.
Philadelphia: Larry Andersen, Jim Eisenreich, Bobby Thigpen.
Pittsburgh: Bob Walk.
St. Louis: Lee Guetterman, Les Lancaster, Gerald Perry.
San Diego: Tim Teufel.
San Francisco: Will Clark, Jim Deshaies, Scott Sanderson, Robby Thompson.

MAJOR LEAGUE DRAFT

(Listed in order of selection)

Player	Pos.	Drafted by	Drafted from (major league organization)
Carlos Reyes	P	Oakland	Richmond, International League (Braves)
Kelly Stinnett	C	New York N.L.	Charlotte, International League (Indians)
Jose Mercedes	P	Milwaukee	Rochester, International League (Orioles)
Tim Hyers	1B	San Diego	Syracuse, International League (Blue Jays)
Steve Long	P	Florida	Norfolk, International League (Mets)
Keith Garagozzo	P	Minnesota	Columbus, International League (Yankees)
Marc Pisciotta	P	Colorado	Buffalo, American Association (Pirates)
Adam Hyzdu	OF	Cincinnati	Phoenix, Pacific Coast League (Giants)
William Hall	2B	Boston	Las Vegas, Pacific Coast League (Padres)
Eric Christopherson	C	Seattle	Phoenix, Pacific Coast League (Giants)
Allen Battle	OF	Chicago A.L.	Louisville, American Association (Cardinals)

NECROLOGY

Al Aber, 65, at Garfield Heights, O., on May 20. Lefthander Aber, pitching for three teams, compiled a 24-25 record in six big-league seasons. His best year was 1955, when he went 6-3 for the Tigers with a 3.38 earned-run average. Overall, he pitched in 168 games—138 of them in relief.

Joe Abreu, 76, at Hayward, Calif., on March 17. Infielder Abreu appeared in nine games for the 1942 Reds.

Bob Alexander, 70, at Oceanside, Calif., on April 7. Alexander pitched in four games for the 1955 Orioles and in five games for the 1957 Indians.

Ethan Allen, 89, at Brookings, Ore., on September 15. Outfielder Allen batted .300 over 13 major league seasons. He hit a career-high .330 for the Phillies in 1934, a season in which he tied for the National League lead in doubles with 42. A former baseball coach at Yale—one of his players was a first baseman named George Bush—Allen also created a popular board game, All-Star Baseball.

Tom Alston, 62, at Winston-Salem, N.C., on December 30. First baseman Alston was the first black player for the Cardinals, breaking into the majors with the St. Louis club on April 13, 1954. Alston, who hit home runs in his second and third games with the Cards, batted .244 in a big-league career that consisted of 91 games spread over four seasons.

Merlyn Anthony, 66, at Yuba City, Calif., on February 2. Anthony was an American League umpire from 1969 through 1975.

Bill Antonello, 65, at Fridley, Minn., on March 4. Outfielder Antonello saw action in 40 games for the 1953 Dodgers, one of the best teams in Brooklyn's storied history.

Bill Atwood, 81, in an automobile accident at Snyder, Tex., on September 14. Atwood, a catcher, played in 342 games for the Phillies from 1936-40.

George Armstrong, 69, at Orange, N.J., on July 24. Catcher Armstrong appeared in eight games for the 1946 Athletics.

Wayne Belardi, 63, at Santa Cruz, Calif., on October 21. Pinch-hitter/first baseman Belardi appeared in 69 games for the 1953 Dodgers and hit 11 homers in 163 at-bats.

Charlie Bishop, 69, at Lawrenceville, Ga., on July 5. Bishop pitched for the Athletics in their last three seasons in Philadelphia, 1952-54, and in their first season in Kansas City, 1955. He had a 10-22 career record.

Marv Blaylock, 64, at Conway, Ark., on October 23. Blaylock was the Phillies' No. 1 first baseman in 1956, a year in which he batted .254 with 10 homers and 50 RBIs. Overall, he hit .235 in 287 big-league games.

Ed Boland, 84, at Clearwater, Fla., on February 5. Outfielder Boland saw limited duty for the Phillies in 1934 and 1935 and for the Senators in 1944.

Cecil Bolton, 89, at Jackson, Miss., on August 25. First baseman Bolton played in four games for the 1928 Indians.

Earl Browne, 81, at Whittier, Calif., on January 12. Outfielder/first baseman Browne played 105 of his 143 big-league games for the 1937 Phillies, batting .292 in 332 at-bats.

Roy Campanella, 71, at Woodland Hills, Calif., on June 26. A three-time Most Valuable Player in the N.L., Campanella was one of the great players on Brooklyn teams that won five pennants and one World Series title during his 10 years in the big leagues. He had a monster season in 1953, walloping 41 homers and knocking in 142 runs. As Campanella and the Dodgers prepared for their move to Los Angeles in 1958, the veteran catcher and future Hall of Famer suffered injuries in a car crash that left him a quadriplegic.

Ben Chapman, 84, at Hoover, Ala., on July 7. Chapman was a .302 hitter over 15 big-league seasons. The outfielder added speed to a thunderous Yankees lineup, stealing 61 bases for a 1931 New York team that boasted four 100-RBI men (one of whom was Chapman himself). Chapman, the first A.L. batter in All-Star Game history, wound up playing for seven major league clubs.

Gus Cherry, 75, at Chicago on April 10. A former minor league pitcher, Cherry owned the Class AAA Omaha franchise from 1985-91.

Eddie Chiles, 83, at Fort Worth, Tex., on August 22. Chiles, who made millions in the petroleum industry, owned the Texas Rangers in the 1980s.

Pat Cooper, 75, at Charlotte, N.C., on March 15. Cooper pitched in one game for the Athletics in 1946 and was a pinch-hitter/first baseman in 13 games for the Philadelphia club in 1947.

Joe Coscarart, 83, at Sequim, Wash., on April 5. Infielder Coscarart played 190 big-league games—all for Boston's N.L. club—in 1935 and 1936.

Tim Crews, 31, of injuries suffered in a March 22 boating accident, at Orlando, Fla., on March 23. Crews made 277 relief appearances for the Dodgers from 1987-92. His best season was 1990, when he pitched in 66 games and posted an ERA of 2.77. Crews was a member of the Indians at the time of his death, having signed as a free agent in January 1993.

Jimmie Crutchfield, 83, at Chicago on March 31. Crutchfield was a longtime Negro leagues outfielder whose most prominent years were spent with the Pittsburgh Crawfords.

Francis Dale, 72, at Victoria Falls, Zimbabwe, on November 28. Dale was president of the Cincinnati Reds from 1967-73.

John Dantonio, 73, at New Orleans on May 28. Catcher Dantonio appeared in 50 games for the 1944-45 Dodgers.

Jimmy DeShong, 83, at Lower Paxton, Pa., on October 16. A righthander who compiled a 47-44 record in seven seasons in the majors, DeShong was an 18-game winner for the 1936 Senators.

Bill Dickey, 86, at Little Rock, Ark., on November 12. A Hall of Fame catcher for the Yankees, he began his big-league career in the glory days of Babe Ruth and Lou Gehrig and finished it in the heyday of Joe DiMaggio. Dickey batted .313 in 17 seasons with the Yankees. His best years were 1936, when he hit .362, and 1937, when he drove in 133 runs. Dickey also was a manager and coach for the Yanks.

Don Drysdale, 56, at Montreal on July 3. A tall, side-wheeling righthander who wasn't afraid to brush back hitters, Drysdale won 209 games for the Brooklyn and Los Angeles Dodgers in a big-league career that lasted from 1956 through 1969. Drysdale's most memorable seasons were 1962, when he won 25 games and copped the Cy Young Award, and 1968, when he pitched 58 consecutive scoreless innings. The Hall of Famer was a member of the Dodgers' broadcast team at the time of his death.

Paul Easterling, 87, at Reidsville, Ga., on March 15. Outfielder Easterling saw action with the Tigers in 1928 and 1930 and had a brief stint with the Athletics in 1938. In '28, he batted .325 in 114 at-bats.

Augie Galan, 81, at Fairfield, Calif., on December 28. Galan, the first player in N.L. history to hit homers from both sides of the plate in the same game, batted .287 in 16 big-league seasons and played in three World Series. In 1935, outfielder Galan played in every game for the Cubs, who won 21 consecutive games in September and captured the N.L. pennant.

Charlie Gehringer, 89, at Bloomfield Hills, Mich., on January 21. Hall of Famer Gehringer, who spent all of his 19 major league seasons with the Tigers, was a .320 career hitter who led the A.L. in batting in 1937 en route to league MVP honors. He scored more than 100 runs in a season 12 times and topped the 100-RBI mark on seven occasions.

Izzy Goldstein, 85, at Delray Beach, Fla., on September 24. Goldstein pitched in 16 big-league games, all for the 1932 Tigers, and posted a 3-2 record.

Oscar Grimes, 77, at Westlake, O., on May 19. Grimes saw duty at all four infield positions while playing for the Indians, Yankees and Athletics from 1938-46. He batted .256 in 602 games.

Granny Hamner, 66, at Philadelphia on September 12. Shortstop for the Phillies' "Whiz Kids" pennant-winners of 1950 and a .429 hitter in the '50 World Series, Hamner batted .262 over 17 major league seasons.

Roy Henshaw, 81, at La Grange, Ill., on June 8. Lefthander Henshaw compiled a 33-40 record over eight big-league seasons. His best year was 1935, when he went 13-5 and hurled three shutouts for the Cubs. Henshaw appeared in the World Series that season.

Jesse Hill, 86, at Pasadena, Calif., on August 31. An outfielder for the Yankees, Senators and Athletics from 1935-37, Hill hit .289 in 295 games. He later was football coach and athletic director at the University of Southern California.

Tex Hughson, 77, at Austin, Tex., on August 6. Hughson, a cog in the Red Sox's rotation in the 1940s, compiled a 96-54 record in the majors. Twice a 20-game winner, he led the A.L. in winning percentage in 1944 with a figure of .783 (18 victories, five losses) and finished his career with a mark of .640.

Alex Hooks, 86, at Edgewood, Tex., on June 19. First baseman Hooks appeared in 15 games for the 1935 Athletics.

Joe Hutcheson, 88, at Tyler, Tex., on February 23. Hutcheson, an outfielder, played in the majors in 1933. Appearing in 55 games with the Dodgers, he batted .234 and hit six home runs.

Buck Jordan, 86, at Salisbury, N.C., on March 18. First baseman Jordan, who played for the Giants, Senators, Braves, Reds and Phillies in a 10-year major league career, was one of the N.L.'s top hitters in 1936, when he batted .323.

Milt Jordan, 65, at Ithaca, N.Y., on May 13. Jordan pitched in eight games for the 1953 Tigers.

Ewing Kauffman, 76, at Kansas City, Mo., on August 1. Kauffman was owner of the Royals from the expansion club's founding in 1969 to the time of his death. Founder of a prominent pharmaceuticals firm, he was instrumental in returning major league baseball to Kansas City, which had lost the Athletics to Oakland after the 1967 season.

Vern Kennedy, 85, at Mendon, Mo., on January 28. Kennedy, who fashioned a 104-132 record in the majors from 1934-45, achieved his greatest fame with the White Sox, for whom he pitched a no-hitter in 1935 and won 21 games in 1936. Even as an octogenarian, Kennedy was an active athlete, competing in Senior Olympics competition.

John Kerr, 94, at Long Beach, Calif., on October 19. Kerr, an infielder, played for the Tigers, White Sox and Senators while seeing eight seasons of major league duty in the 1920s and 1930s. He made a pinch-running appearance for Washington in the 1933 World Series.

Fred Koenig, 61, at Chouteau, Okla., on January 12. Koenig was a coach in the 1970s and 1980s for the Angels, Cardinals, Rangers, Cubs and Indians.

Mark Koenig, 90, at Willows, Calif., on April 22. Koenig was the shortstop for the 1927 Yankees, considered by many the greatest team in baseball history. Koenig hit .285 in the '27 regular season and .500 in that year's World Series. He played in two other Series for the Yankees and in one each for the Cubs and Giants.

Cal Koonce, 52, at Hope Mills, N.C., on October 28. Koonce, who made 40 relief appearances for the World Series-winning Mets in 1969, pitched for 10 seasons in the majors and compiled a 47-49 record. Primarily a starter early in his big-league career, he posted a 10-10 mark for the Cubs in 1962.

Sam Langford, 93, at Plainview, Tex., on July 31. Outfielder Langford played in 131 big-league games—110 of them for Cleveland in 1928. He batted .276 that season.

Hank Leiber, 82, at Tucson, Ariz., on November 8. In 1935, his first season of full-time duty in the majors, outfielder Leiber batted .331 for the Giants with 22 home runs and 107 RBIs. Overall, Leiber played 10 seasons in the big leagues and hit .288 with 101 homers and 518 RBIs.

Lenny Levy, 79, at Palm Desert, Calif., on February 2. Levy was an on-again, off-again coach for the Pirates from the late 1930s to the early 1960s.

Bob Maier, 77, at South Plainfield, N.J., on August 4. Maier played only one season in the majors, but that was as the No. 1 third baseman for the pennant-winning Tigers of 1945. Maier appeared in 132 regular-season games and batted .263, but he made only one appearance—as a pinch-hitter—in the '45 Series, also won by Detroit.

R.L. (Bob) Miller, 54, in an automobile accident at Rancho Bernardo, Calif., on August 6. Miller, whose 74 appearances for the Dodgers in 1964 led the N.L., pitched for 10 big-league teams in a 17-year career (he made two tours with two clubs, the Mets and Padres). He saw relief duty in three World Series. Miller was an advance scout for the Giants at the time of his death.

Johnny Mize, 80, at Demorest, Ga., on June 2. Mize won or shared four N.L. home run crowns while playing for the Cardinals (1936-41) and Giants (1942-49) and late in his career was a valuable contributor to the Yankees as a part-time player and pinch-hitting specialist. Known for his slugging exploits, Hall of Famer Mize also was a gifted all-around hitter—as attested by his 1939 N.L. batting championship and his .364 batting mark two years earlier.

Joe Muich, 89, at St. Louis on July 2. Muich made three relief appearances for the 1924 Braves.

Larry Napp, 77, at Plantation, Fla., on July 7. Napp was an A.L. umpire from 1951-74. He was the third base umpire in Game 5 of the 1956 World Series, when the Yankees' Don Larsen pitched a perfect game against Brooklyn.

Steve Olin, 27, in a boating accident on Little Lake Nellie, Fla., on March 22. Olin had recorded 29 saves for the Indians in 1992, compiling an 8-5 record in 72 appearances. In four big-league seasons, he was 16-19 with 48 saves in 195 games.

Emmett O'Neill, 75, at Sparks, Nev., on October 11. O'Neill went 6-11 and 8-11 as a member of the Red Sox's rotation in 1944 and 1945 and pitched four seasons in the majors overall.

Joe Orrell, 75, at Chula Vista, Calif., on January 12. Righthander Orrell fashioned a 4-4 record and a 3.01 ERA for the Tigers from 1943-45.

Bubba Phillips, 63, at Hattiesburg, Miss., on June 22. A platoon third baseman for the pennant-winning 1959 White Sox, Phillips enjoyed his best of 10 big-league seasons in 1961, when he hit 18 home runs and drove in 72 runs for the Indians.

Nick Polly, 75, at Chicago on January 17. Infielder Polly appeared in 10 games for the 1937 Dodgers and in four games for the 1945 Red Sox.

Harlan Pyle, 87, at Beatrice, Neb., on January 13. Pyle pitched in two games for the 1928 Reds.

Frank Quinn, 65, at Boynton Beach, Fla., on January 11. A baseball teammate of George Bush's at Yale, Quinn went on to pitch in a total of nine games for the Red Sox in 1949 and 1950.

Bobby Reeves, 88, at Chattanooga, Tenn., on June 4. An infielder with the Senators and the Red Sox from 1926-31, Reeves batted .252 in 502 major league games.

Rip Repulski, 65, at Waite Park, Minn., on February 10. Outfielder Repulski broke into the majors in 1953 with the Cardinals, playing between Hall of Famers-to-be Stan Musial and Enos Slaughter and hitting .275 with 15 homers. A nine-year major leaguer, he appeared in the 1959 World Series with the Dodgers.

Al (Skippy) Roberge, 76, at Lowell, Mass., on June 7. Roberge, an infielder, played 177 games for the Braves in the 1940s.

Ted Sadowski, 57, at Shaler Township, Pa., on July 18. Righthander Sadowski pitched in 43 big-league games, 41 of them in relief, for the original Senators (1960) and the transplanted version of the team, the Minnesota Twins (1961-62).

Hal Schumacher, 82, at Cooperstown, N.Y., on April 21. Spending his entire 13-year major league career with the Giants, he won a total of 61 games over three seasons (1933-35) before settling into a seven-year groove in which he won 13 games four times, 12 games twice and 11 games once.

Bob Seeds, 86, at Erick, Okla., on October 28. Seeds, a nine-season major leaguer, hit home runs in four consecutive innings for Newark in a 1938 International League game, a contest in which he drove in 12 runs. In Newark's next game, Seeds blasted three more homers.

Al Sima, 71, at Suffern, N.Y., on August 17. Lefthander Sima put together an 11-21 record over four major league seasons. After pitching for the Senators in 1950, 1951 and 1953, he toiled for the White Sox and Athletics in 1954.

Walter Stephenson, 82, at Shreveport, La., on July 4. Catcher Stephenson was used sparingly (32 games) in three big-league seasons but appeared in one game of the 1935 World Series for the Cubs.

George Stumpf, 82, at Metairie, La., on March 6. Outfielder Stumpf, who played for the Red Sox from 1931-33 and for the White Sox in 1936, batted .235 in 118 major league games.

Quincy Trouppe, 80, at Creve Coeur, Mo., on August 10. Veteran Negro leagues player Trouppe, long foiled by the majors' color barrier, didn't crash the big leagues until he was 39 years old. He caught in six games for the Indians in 1952.

Thurman Tucker, 75, at Oklahoma City, Okla., on May 7. Tucker, the starting center fielder for the champion Indians in the final game of the 1948 World Series, batted .255 in a nine-season major league career.

Lee Walls, 60, at Los Angeles on October 11. Outfielder Walls played 10 seasons in the majors, enjoying his best year in 1958, when he hit 24 homers for the Cubs and batted .304. He was the first player to take dead aim on the left-field screen at the Los Angeles Coliseum (which became home of the Dodgers in '58 upon their move from Brooklyn to Los Angeles). In the ninth big-league game played at the Coliseum, Walls hammered three homers over the screen, which stood 40 feet high and was 251 feet from home plate.

Burgess Whitehead, 83, at Windsor, N.C., on November 25. Whitehead was a reserve infielder for the 1934 World Series champion Cardinals—but saw plenty of action (100 games) for that year's Gas House Gang. The regular second baseman for the Giants in 1936 and 1937, Whitehead played in three World Series overall.

Bob Wright, 101, at Carmichael, Calif., on July 30. Wright pitched briefly for the Cubs in 1915—a year before they became tenants of Wrigley Field.

Cliff Young, 29, in a truck accident at Willis, Tex., on November 4. Lefthander Young, who had made a total of 28 appearances for California in 1990 and 1991, pitched in 21 games for Cleveland in 1993 and went 3-3 with a 4.62 ERA.

1993 A.L. STATISTICS

Batting

Designated hitting

Pinch-hitting

Pitching

Fielding

Miscellaneous

BATTING

TEAM

Team	Avg.	G	AB	R	H	TB	2B	3B	HR	RBI	SH	SF	HP	BB	Int. BB	SO	SB	CS	GI DP	LOB	ShO	Slg.	OBP
New York	.279	162	5615	821	1568	2444	294	24	178	793	22	50	43	629	47	910	39	35	149	1247		.435	.353
Toronto	.279	162	5579	847	1556	2434	317	42	159	796	46	54	52	588	57	861	170	49	138	1187	1	.436	.350
Cleveland	.275	162	5619	790	1547	2296	264	31	141	747	39	72	49	488	57	843	159	55	131	1128		.409	.335
Detroit	.275	162	5620	899	1546	2438	282	38	178	853	33	52	35	765	50	1122	104	63	101	1312	2	.434	.362
Texas	.267	162	5510	835	1472	2377	284	39	181	780	69	56	48	483	56	984	113	67	111	1034	6	.431	.329
Baltimore	.267	162	5508	786	1470	2276	287	24	157	744	49	56	41	655	52	930	73	54	131	1202	11	.413	.346
Chicago	.265	162	5483	776	1454	2256	228	44	162	731	72	61	33	604	52	834	106	57	126	1150	14	.411	.338
Minnesota	.264	162	5601	693	1480	2158	261	27	121	642	27	37	51	493	35	850	83	59	150	1145	13	.385	.327
Boston	.264	162	5496	686	1451	2170	319	29	114	644	80	49	62	508	69	871	73	38	146	1154	8	.395	.330
Kansas City	.263	162	5522	675	1455	2194	294	35	125	641	48	51	52	428	50	936	100	75	107	1090	7	.397	.320
Seattle	.260	162	5494	734	1429	2232	272	24	161	681	63	51	56	624	73	901	91	68	132	1200	9	.406	.339
California	.260	162	5391	684	1399	2048	259	24	114	644	50	46	38	564	39	930	169	100	129	*1089	8	.380	.331
Milwaukee	.258	162	5525	733	1426	2091	240	25	125	688	57	45	40	555	52	932	138	93	117	1112	4	.378	.328
Oakland	.254	162	5543	715	1408	2184	260	21	158	679	46	49	33	622	45	1048	141	59	125	1188	3	.394	.330
Totals	.267	1134	77506	10674	20661	31598	3861	427	2074	10063	701	729	633	8006	734	12952	1549	872	1793	16238	110	.408	.337

INDIVIDUAL

TOP 15 QUALIFIERS FOR BATTING CHAMPIONSHIP

Minimum 502 plate appearances.   *Lefthanded batter.   †Switch-hitter.

Player, Team	Avg.	G	AB	R	H	TB	2B	3B	HR	RBI	SH	SF	HP	BB	Int. BB	SO	SB	CS	GI DP	Slg.	OBP
Olerud, John, Toronto*	.363	158	551	109	200	330	54	2	24	107	0	7	7	114	33	65	0	2	12	.599	.473
Molitor, Paul, Toronto	.332	160	636	121	211	324	37	5	22	111	1	8	3	77	3	71	22	4	13	.509	.402
Alomar, Roberto, Toronto†	.326	153	589	109	192	290	35	6	17	93	4	5	5	80	5	67	55	15	13	.492	.408
Lofton, Kenny, Cleveland*	.325	148	569	116	185	232	28	8	1	42	2	4	1	81	6	83	70	14	8	.408	.408
Baerga, Carlos, Cleveland†	.321	154	624	105	200	303	28	6	21	114	3	13	6	34	7	68	15	4	17	.486	.355
Thomas, Frank, Chicago	.317	153	549	106	174	333	36	0	41	128	0	13	2	112	23	54	4	2	10	.607	.426
Greenwell, Mike, Boston*	.315	146	540	77	170	259	38	6	13	72	2	3	4	54	12	46	5	4	17	.480	.379
Phillips, Tony, Detroit†	.313	151	566	113	177	225	27	0	7	57	1	4	4	132	5	102	16	11	11	.398	.443
O'Neill, Paul, New York*	.311	141	498	71	155	251	34	1	20	75	0	3	2	44	5	69	2	4	13	.504	.367
Johnson, Lance, Chicago*	.311	147	540	75	168	214	18	14	0	47	3	0	0	36	1	33	35	7	10	.396	.354
Hoiles, Chris, Baltimore	.310	126	419	80	130	245	28	0	29	82	3	3	9	69	4	94	1	1	10	.585	.416
Gonzalez, Juan, Texas	.310	140	536	105	166	339	33	1	46	118	0	1	13	37	7	99	4	1	12	.632	.368
Hamilton, Darryl, Milwaukee*	.310	135	520	74	161	211	21	1	9	48	4	1	3	45	5	62	21	13	9	.406	.367
Griffey, Ken, Seattle*	.309	156	582	113	180	359	38	3	45	109	0	7	6	96	25	91	17	9	14	.617	.408
Harper, Brian, Minnesota	.304	147	530	52	161	225	26	1	12	73	0	5	9	29	9	29	1	3	15	.425	.347

DEPARTMENTAL LEADERS: G—Ripken, Bal., 162; AB—Ripken, Bal., 641; R—Palmeiro, Tex., 124; H—Molitor, Tor., 211; TB—Griffey, Sea., 359; 1B—Lofton, Cle., 148; 2B—Olerud, Tor., 54; 3B—Johnson, Chi., 14; HR—Gonzalez, Tex., 46; RBI—Belle, Cle., 129; SH—Cora, Chi., 19; SF—Belle, Cle., 14; HP—Valle, Sea., 17; BB—Phillips, Det., 132; IBB—Olerud, Tor., 33; SO—Deer, Det.-Bos., 169; SB—Lofton, Cle., 70; CS—Curtis, Cal., Polonia, Cal., 24; GIDP—Sprague, Tor., 23; Slg. Pct.—Gonzalez, Tex., .632; OB. Pct.—Olerud, Tor., .473.

ALL PLAYERS

*Lefthanded batter.   †Switch-hitter.

Player, Team	Avg.	G	AB	R	H	TB	2B	3B	HR	RBI	SH	SF	HP	BB	Int. BB	SO	SB	CS	GI DP	Slg.	OBP
Abbott, Kurt, Oakland	.246	20	61	11	15	25	1	0	3	9	3	0	0	3	0	20	2	0	3	.410	.281
Aldrete, Mike, Oakland*	.267	95	255	40	68	113	13	1	10	33	3	0	0	34	2	45	1	1	7	.443	.353
Alexander, Manny, Baltimore	.000	3	0	1	0	0	0	0	0	0	0	0	0	0	0	0	0	0	0	.000	.000
Alomar, Roberto, Toronto†	.326	153	589	109	192	290	35	6	17	93	4	5	5	80	5	67	55	15	13	.492	.408
Alomar, Sandy, Cleveland	.270	64	215	24	58	85	7	1	6	32	1	4	6	11	0	28	3	1	3	.395	.318
Amaral, Rich, Seattle	.290	110	373	53	108	137	24	1	1	44	7	5	3	33	0	54	19	11	5	.367	.348
Anderson, Brady, Baltimore*	.263	142	560	87	147	238	36	8	13	66	6	6	10	82	4	99	24	12	4	.425	.363
Armas, Marcos, Oakland	.194	15	31	4	7	6	1	0	1	0	0	1	0	1	0	12	1	0	0	.355	.242
Backman, Wally, Seattle*	.138	10	29	2	4	11	2	0	1	0	0	0	1	1	0	8	0	0	0	.138	.167
Baerga, Carlos, Cleveland†	.321	154	624	105	200	303	28	6	21	114	3	13	6	34	7	68	15	4	17	.486	.355
Baines, Harold, Baltimore*	.313	118	416	64	130	212	22	0	20	78	1	6	0	57	9	52	0	1	14	.510	.390
Balboni, Steve, Texas	.600	2	5	0	3	3	0	0	0	0	0	0	0	0	0	2	0	0	0	.600	.600
Barnes, Skeeter, Detroit	.281	84	160	24	45	61	8	1	2	27	4	5	0	11	0	19	5	5	2	.381	.318
Bautista, Danny, Detroit	.311	17	61	6	19	25	3	0	1	9	0	1	0	1	0	10	3	1	1	.410	.317
Becker, Rich, Minnesota†	.286	3	7	3	2	4	2	0	0	0	0	0	0	5	0	4	1	1	0	.571	.583
Bell, George, Chicago	.217	102	410	36	89	149	17	2	13	64	0	9	4	13	2	49	1	1	14	.363	.243
Bell, Juan, Milwaukee†	.234	91	286	42	67	92	6	2	5	29	3	1	1	36	0	64	6	6	4	.322	.321
Belle, Albert, Cleveland	.290	159	594	93	172	328	36	3	38	129	1	14	8	76	13	96	23	12	18	.552	.370
Blankenship, Lance, Oakland	.190	94	252	43	48	64	8	1	2	23	6	1	2	67	0	64	13	5	9	.254	.363
Blosser, Greg, Boston*	.071	17	28	1	2	3	1	0	0	1	0	0	0	2	0	7	1	0	0	.107	.133
Blowers, Mike, Seattle	.280	127	379	55	106	180	23	3	15	57	3	1	2	44	3	98	1	5	12	.475	.357
Boggs, Wade, New York*	.302	143	560	83	169	203	26	1	2	59	1	0	0	74	4	49	0	1	10	.363	.378
Boone, Bret, Seattle	.251	76	271	31	68	120	12	2	12	38	6	4	4	17	1	52	2	3	6	.443	.301
Borders, Pat, Toronto	.254	138	488	38	124	181	30	0	9	55	7	3	2	20	2	66	2	2	18	.371	.325
Bordick, Mike, Oakland	.249	159	546	60	136	170	21	2	3	48	10	6	11	60	2	58	10	10	9	.311	.332
Brett, George, Kansas City*	.266	145	560	69	149	243	31	3	19	75	0	10	3	39	9	67	7	5	20	.434	.312
Brito, Bernardo, Minnesota	.241	27	54	8	13	27	2	0	4	8	0	0	0	1	0	20	0	1	1	.500	.255
Bronkey, Jeff, Texas	.000	21	1	0	0	0	0	0	0	0	0	0	0	0	0	0	0	0	0	.000	.000

Player, Team	Avg.	G	AB	R	H	TB	2B	3B	HR	RBI	SH	SF	HP	BB	Int. BB	SO	SB	CS	GI DP	Slg.	OBP
Brooks, Hubie, Kansas City	.286	75	168	14	48	63	12	0	1	24	0	1	1	11	1	27	0	1	5	.375	.331
Brosius, Scott, Oakland	.249	70	213	26	53	83	10	1	6	25	3	2	1	14	0	37	6	0	6	.390	.296
Browne, Jerry, Oakland†	.250	76	260	27	65	84	13	0	2	19	2	2	0	22	0	17	4	0	9	.323	.306
Bruett, J.T., Minnesota*	.250	17	20	2	5	7	2	0	0	1	0	0	1	1	0	4	0	0	1	.350	.318
Brunansky, Tom, Milwaukee	.183	80	224	20	41	72	7	3	6	29	2	0	0	25	0	59	3	4	5	.321	.265
Buford, Damon, Baltimore	.228	53	79	18	18	29	5	0	2	9	1	0	1	9	0	19	2	2	1	.367	.315
Buhner, Jay, Seattle	.272	158	563	91	153	268	28	3	27	98	2	8	2	100	11	144	2	5	12	.476	.379
Burks, Ellis, Chicago	.275	146	499	75	137	220	24	4	17	74	3	8	4	60	2	97	6	9	11	.441	.352
Bush, Randy, Minnesota*	.156	35	45	1	7	9	2	0	0	3	0	0	0	7	1	13	0	0	3	.200	.269
Butler, Rob, Toronto*	.271	17	48	8	13	17	4	0	0	2	0	0	1	7	0	12	2	2	0	.354	.375
Calderon, Ivan, Bos.-Chi.	.209	82	239	26	50	67	10	2	1	22	2	2	1	21	1	33	4	2	12	.280	.274
Canate, Willie, Toronto	.213	38	47	12	10	13	0	0	1	3	2	1	1	6	0	15	1	1	2	.277	.309
Canseco, Jose, Texas	.255	60	231	30	59	105	14	1	10	46	0	3	3	16	2	62	6	6	6	.455	.308
Carey, Paul, Baltimore*	.213	18	47	1	10	11	1	0	0	3	0	0	0	5	0	14	0	0	4	.234	.288
Carter, Joe, Toronto	.254	155	603	92	153	295	33	5	33	121	0	10	9	47	5	113	8	3	10	.489	.312
Cedeno, Domingo, Toronto†	.174	15	46	5	8	8	0	0	0	7	2	1	0	1	0	10	1	0	2	.174	.188
Coles, Darnell, Toronto	.253	64	194	26	49	72	9	1	4	26	1	2	4	16	1	29	1	1	3	.371	.319
Cooper, Scott, Boston*	.279	156	526	67	147	209	29	3	9	63	4	3	5	58	15	81	5	2	8	.397	.355
Cora, Joey, Chicago†	.268	153	579	95	155	202	15	13	2	51	19	4	9	67	0	63	20	8	14	.349	.351
Correia, Rod, California	.266	64	128	12	34	39	5	0	0	9	5	0	4	6	0	20	2	4	1	.305	.319
Cotto, Henry, Seattle	.190	54	105	10	20	27	1	0	2	7	1	0	1	2	0	22	5	4	0	.257	.213
Curtis, Chad, California	.285	152	583	94	166	215	25	3	6	59	7	7	4	70	2	89	48	24	16	.369	.361
Cuyler, Milt, Detroit†	.213	82	249	46	53	78	11	7	0	19	4	1	3	19	0	53	13	2	2	.313	.276
Dascenzo, Doug, Texas†	.199	76	146	20	29	42	5	1	2	10	3	1	0	8	0	22	2	0	1	.288	.239
Davis, Butch, Texas	.245	62	159	24	39	66	10	4	3	20	5	0	1	5	1	28	3	1	0	.415	.273
Davis, Chili, California†	.243	153	573	74	139	252	32	0	27	112	0	0	1	71	12	135	4	1	18	.440	.327
Davis, Eric, Detroit	.253	23	75	14	19	40	1	1	6	15	0	0	0	14	1	18	2	2	4	.533	.371
Davis, Glenn, Baltimore	.177	30	113	8	20	26	3	0	1	9	1	1	1	7	0	29	0	1	2	.230	.232
Dawson, Andre, Boston	.273	121	461	44	126	196	29	1	13	67	0	7	13	17	4	49	2	1	18	.425	.313
Deer, Rob, Det.-Bos.	.210	128	466	66	98	180	17	1	21	55	0	3	5	58	1	169	5	2	6	.386	.303
Delgado, Carlos, Toronto*	.000	2	1	0	0	0	0	0	0	0	0	0	0	1	0	0	0	0	0	.000	.500
Denson, Drew, Chicago†	.200	4	5	0	1	1	0	0	0	0	0	0	0	0	0	2	0	0	0	.200	.200
Devereaux, Mike, Baltimore	.250	131	527	72	132	211	31	3	14	75	2	4	1	43	0	99	3	3	13	.400	.306
Diaz, Alex, Milwaukee†	.319	32	69	9	22	24	2	0	0	1	3	0	0	0	0	12	5	3	3	.348	.319
Diaz, Mario, Texas	.273	71	205	24	56	74	10	1	2	24	7	5	1	8	0	13	1	0	6	.361	.297
DiSarcina, Gary, California	.238	126	416	44	99	130	20	1	3	45	5	3	6	15	0	38	5	7	13	.313	.273
Doran, Bill, Milwaukee†	.217	28	60	7	13	17	4	0	0	6	0	1	0	6	1	3	1	0	3	.283	.284
Ducey, Rob, Texas*	.282	27	85	15	24	42	6	3	2	9	2	2	0	10	2	17	2	3	1	.494	.351
Easley, Damion, California	.313	73	230	33	72	95	13	2	2	22	1	2	3	28	2	35	6	5	5	.413	.392
Edmonds, Jim, California*	.246	18	61	5	15	21	4	1	0	4	0	0	0	2	1	16	0	2	1	.344	.270
Espinoza, Alvaro, Cleveland	.278	129	263	34	73	100	15	0	4	27	8	3	1	8	0	36	2	2	7	.380	.298
Felder, Mike, Seattle†	.211	109	342	31	72	92	7	5	1	20	7	1	2	22	2	34	15	9	2	.269	.262
Fermin, Felix, Cleveland	.263	140	480	48	126	152	16	2	2	45	5	1	4	24	1	14	4	5	12	.317	.303
Fernandez, Tony, Toronto†	.306	94	353	45	108	156	18	9	4	50	5	1	0	31	3	26	15	8	13	.442	.361
Fielder, Cecil, Detroit	.267	154	573	80	153	266	23	0	30	117	0	5	4	90	15	125	0	1	22	.464	.368
Fisk, Carlton, Chicago	.189	25	53	2	10	13	0	0	1	4	1	1	1	2	0	11	0	1	0	.245	.228
Flaherty, John, Boston	.120	13	25	3	3	5	2	0	0	2	1	0	1	2	0	6	0	0	0	.200	.214
Fletcher, Scott, Boston	.285	121	480	81	137	193	31	5	5	45	6	3	5	37	1	35	16	3	12	.402	.341
Fox, Eric, Oakland†	.143	29	56	5	8	12	1	0	1	5	3	0	0	2	0	7	0	2	0	.214	.172
Franco, Julio, Texas	.289	144	532	85	154	233	31	3	14	84	5	7	1	62	4	95	9	3	16	.438	.360
Fryman, Travis, Detroit	.300	151	607	98	182	295	37	5	22	97	1	6	4	77	1	128	9	4	8	.486	.379
Gaetti, Gary, Cal.-K.C.	.245	102	331	40	81	145	20	1	14	50	2	7	8	21	0	87	1	3	5	.438	.300
Gagne, Greg, Kansas City	.280	159	540	66	151	219	32	3	10	57	4	4	0	33	1	93	10	12	7	.406	.319
Gallego, Mike, New York	.283	119	403	63	114	166	20	1	10	54	3	5	4	50	0	65	3	2	16	.412	.364
Gates, Brent, Oakland†	.290	139	535	64	155	209	29	2	7	69	6	8	4	56	4	75	7	3	17	.391	.357
Gibson, Kirk, Detroit*	.261	116	403	62	105	174	18	6	13	62	0	3	4	44	4	87	15	6	2	.432	.337
Gil, Benji, Texas	.123	22	57	3	7	7	0	0	0	2	4	0	0	5	0	22	1	2	0	.123	.194
Gladden, Dan, Detroit	.267	91	356	52	95	154	16	2	13	56	4	2	3	21	0	50	8	5	14	.433	.312
Gomez, Chris, Detroit	.250	46	128	11	32	41	7	1	0	11	3	0	1	9	0	17	2	2	2	.320	.304
Gomez, Leo, Baltimore	.197	71	244	30	48	85	7	0	10	25	3	2	3	32	1	60	0	1	2	.348	.295
Gonzales, Larry, California	.500	2	2	0	1	1	0	0	0	1	0	0	0	1	0	0	0	0	0	.500	.667
Gonzales, Rene, California	.251	118	335	34	84	107	17	0	2	31	2	2	1	49	2	45	5	5	12	.319	.346
Gonzalez, Juan, Texas	.310	140	536	105	166	339	33	1	46	118	0	1	13	37	7	99	4	1	12	.632	.368
Grebeck, Craig, Chicago	.226	72	190	25	43	51	5	0	1	12	7	0	0	26	0	26	1	2	9	.268	.319
Green, Shawn, Toronto*	.000	3	6	0	0	0	0	0	0	0	0	0	0	0	0	1	0	0	0	.000	.000
Greenwell, Mike, Boston*	.315	146	540	77	170	259	38	6	13	72	2	3	4	54	12	46	5	4	17	.480	.379
Griffey, Ken, Seattle*	.309	156	582	113	180	359	38	3	45	109	0	7	6	96	25	91	17	9	14	.617	.408
Griffin, Alfredo, Toronto†	.211	46	95	15	20	23	3	0	0	3	4	0	0	3	0	13	0	3	3	.242	.235
Gruber, Kelly, California	.277	18	65	10	18	30	3	0	3	9	2	0	1	2	0	11	0	0	2	.462	.309
Guillen, Ozzie, Chicago*	.280	134	457	44	128	171	23	4	4	50	13	6	0	10	4	41	5	4	6	.374	.292
Gwynn, Chris, Kansas City*	.300	103	287	36	86	111	14	4	1	25	2	2	1	24	5	34	0	1	7	.387	.354
Hale, Chip, Minnesota*	.333	69	186	25	62	79	6	1	3	27	2	1	6	18	0	17	2	1	3	.425	.408
Hamelin, Bob, Kansas City*	.224	16	49	2	11	20	3	0	2	5	0	0	0	6	0	15	0	0	2	.408	.309
Hamilton, Darryl, Milwaukee*	.310	135	520	74	161	211	21	1	9	48	4	1	3	45	5	62	21	13	9	.406	.367
Hammonds, Jeffrey, Baltimore	.305	33	105	10	32	49	8	0	3	19	1	2	2	2	1	16	4	0	3	.467	.312
Hanson, Erik, Seattle	.000	33	0	2	0	0	0	0	0	0	0	0	0	0	0	0	0	0	0	.000	.000
Harper, Brian, Minnesota	.304	147	530	52	161	225	26	1	12	73	0	5	9	29	9	29	1	3	15	.425	.347
Harris, Donald, Texas	.197	40	76	10	15	20	2	0	1	8	3	1	1	5	0	18	0	1	0	.263	.253
Haselman, Bill, Seattle	.255	58	137	21	35	58	8	0	5	16	2	2	1	12	0	19	2	1	5	.423	.316
Hatcher, Billy, Boston	.287	136	508	71	146	203	24	3	9	57	11	4	11	28	4	46	14	7	14	.400	.336
Helfand, Eric, Oakland*	.231	8	13	1	3	3	0	0	0	1	0	0	0	1	0	4	0	0	0	.231	.231
Hemond, Scott, Oakland	.256	91	215	31	55	89	16	0	6	26	6	1	7	32	0	55	14	5	2	.414	.353
Henderson, Dave, Oakland	.220	107	382	37	84	163	19	0	20	53	0	8	4	32	0	113	0	1	9	.427	.275
Henderson, Rickey, Oak.-Tor.	.289	134	481	114	139	228	22	2	21	59	1	4	4	120	7	65	53	8	9	.474	.432
Hiatt, Phil, Kansas City	.218	81	238	30	52	87	12	1	7	36	0	2	7	16	0	82	6	3	8	.366	.285
Hill, Glenallen, Cleveland	.224	66	174	19	39	65	7	2	5	25	1	4	1	11	1	50	7	3	3	.374	.268
Hocking, Denny, Minnesota†	.139	15	36	7	5	6	1	0	0	0	0	0	0	6	0	8	1	0	1	.167	.262

Player, Team	Avg.	G	AB	R	H	TB	2B	3B	HR	RBI	SH	SF	HP	BB	Int. BB	SO	SB	CS	GI DP	Slg.	OBP
Hoiles, Chris, Baltimore	.310	126	419	80	130	245	28	0	29	82	3	3	9	69	4	94	1	1	10	.585	.416
Horn, Sam, Cleveland*	.455	12	33	8	15	28	1	0	4	8	0	1	1	1	0	5	0	0	1	.848	.472
Howard, Chris, Seattle	.000	4	1	0	0	0	0	0	0	0	0	0	0	0	0	0	0	0	0	.000	.000
Howard, David, Kansas City†	.333	15	24	5	8	10	0	1	0	2	2	1	0	2	0	5	1	0	0	.417	.370
Howard, Thomas, Cleveland†	.236	74	178	26	42	58	7	0	3	23	0	4	0	12	0	42	5	1	5	.326	.278
Howitt, Dann, Seattle*	.211	32	76	6	16	27	3	1	2	8	0	0	0	4	0	18	0	0	0	.355	.250
Hrbek, Kent, Minnesota*	.242	123	392	60	95	183	11	1	25	83	3	4	1	71	6	57	4	2	12	.467	.357
Huff, Mike, Chicago	.182	43	44	4	8	13	2	0	1	6	1	2	1	9	0	15	1	0	0	.295	.321
Hulett, Tim, Baltimore	.300	85	260	40	78	99	15	0	2	23	1	2	3	23	1	56	1	2	5	.381	.361
Hulse, Dave, Texas*	.290	114	407	71	118	150	9	10	1	29	5	2	1	26	1	57	29	9	9	.369	.333
Humphreys, Mike, New York	.171	25	35	6	6	13	2	1	1	6	0	1	0	4	0	11	2	1	0	.371	.250
Huson, Jeff, Texas*	.133	23	45	3	6	9	1	1	0	2	1	0	0	0	0	10	0	0	0	.200	.133
Jackson, Bo, Chicago	.232	85	284	32	66	123	9	0	16	45	0	1	0	23	1	106	0	2	5	.433	.289
Jackson, Darrin, Toronto	.216	46	176	15	38	61	8	0	5	19	5	0	0	8	0	53	0	2	9	.347	.250
Jaha, John, Milwaukee	.264	153	515	78	136	214	21	0	19	70	4	4	8	51	4	109	13	9	6	.416	.337
James, Chris, Texas	.355	8	31	5	11	21	1	0	3	7	0	0	0	3	0	6	0	0	0	.677	.412
James, Dion, New York*	.332	115	343	62	114	160	21	2	7	36	1	1	2	31	1	31	0	0	5	.466	.390
Javier, Stan, California*	.291	92	237	33	69	96	10	4	3	28	1	3	1	27	1	33	12	2	7	.405	.362
Jefferson, Reggie, Cleveland†	.249	113	366	35	91	136	11	2	10	34	3	1	5	28	7	78	1	3	7	.372	.310
Johnson, Lance, Chicago*	.311	147	540	75	168	214	18	14	0	47	3	0	0	36	1	33	35	7	10	.396	.354
Jorgensen, Terry, Minnesota	.224	59	152	15	34	44	7	0	1	12	0	1	0	9	0	21	1	0	7	.289	.270
Jose, Felix, Kansas City†	.253	149	499	64	126	174	24	3	6	43	1	2	1	36	5	95	31	13	5	.349	.303
Joyner, Wally, Kansas City*	.292	141	497	83	145	232	36	3	15	65	2	5	3	66	13	67	5	9	6	.467	.375
Karkovice, Ron, Chicago	.228	128	403	60	92	171	17	1	20	54	11	4	6	29	1	126	2	2	12	.424	.287
Kelly, Pat, New York	.273	127	406	49	111	158	24	1	7	51	10	6	5	24	0	68	14	11	9	.389	.317
Kirby, Wayne, Cleveland*	.269	131	458	71	123	170	19	5	6	60	7	6	3	37	2	58	17	5	8	.371	.323
Kmak, Joe, Milwaukee	.218	51	110	9	24	29	5	0	0	7	1	0	2	14	0	13	6	2	2	.264	.317
Knoblauch, Chuck, Minnesota	.277	153	602	82	167	208	27	4	2	41	4	5	9	65	1	44	29	11	11	.346	.354
Knorr, Randy, Toronto	.248	39	101	11	25	44	3	2	4	20	2	0	0	9	0	29	0	0	2	.436	.309
Koslofski, Kevin, Kansas City*	.269	15	26	4	7	10	0	0	1	2	1	0	1	4	0	5	0	1	1	.385	.387
Kreuter, Chad, Detroit†	.286	119	374	59	107	181	23	3	15	51	2	3	3	49	4	92	2	1	5	.484	.371
LaValliere, Mike, Chicago*	.258	37	97	6	25	27	2	0	0	8	7	2	0	4	0	14	0	1	1	.278	.282
Lampkin, Tom, Milwaukee*	.198	73	162	22	32	52	8	0	4	25	2	4	0	20	3	26	7	3	2	.321	.280
Larkin, Gene, Minnesota†	.264	56	144	17	38	50	7	1	1	19	2	4	2	21	3	16	0	1	5	.347	.357
Lee, Derek, Minnesota*	.152	15	33	3	5	6	1	0	0	4	0	0	0	1	0	4	0	0	0	.182	.176
Lee, Manny, Texas†	.220	73	205	31	45	53	3	1	1	12	9	1	2	22	3	39	2	4	2	.259	.300
Leius, Scott, Minnesota	.167	10	18	4	3	3	0	0	0	2	0	2	0	2	0	4	0	1	1	.167	.227
Leonard, Mark, Baltimore*	.067	10	15	1	1	2	1	0	0	3	0	0	0	3	0	7	0	0	0	.133	.190
Levis, Jesse, Cleveland*	.175	31	63	7	11	13	2	0	0	4	1	1	0	2	0	10	0	0	0	.206	.197
Lewis, Mark, Cleveland	.250	14	52	6	13	18	2	0	1	5	1	0	0	0	0	7	3	0	1	.346	.250
Leyritz, Jim, New York	.309	95	259	43	80	136	14	0	14	53	0	1	8	37	3	59	0	0	12	.525	.410
Lind, Jose, Kansas City	.248	136	431	33	107	124	13	2	0	37	13	5	2	13	0	36	3	2	7	.288	.271
Lindsey, Doug, Chicago	.000	2	1	0	0	0	0	0	0	0	0	0	0	0	0	0	0	0	0	.000	.000
Listach, Pat, Milwaukee†	.244	98	356	50	87	113	15	1	3	30	5	2	3	37	0	70	18	9	7	.317	.319
Litton, Greg, Seattle	.299	72	174	25	52	78	17	0	3	25	5	1	1	18	2	30	0	1	6	.448	.366
Livingstone, Scott, Detroit*	.293	98	304	39	89	109	10	2	2	39	1	6	0	19	1	32	1	3	4	.359	.328
Lofton, Kenny, Cleveland*	.325	148	569	116	185	232	28	8	1	42	2	4	1	81	6	83	70	14	8	.408	.408
Lovullo, Torey, California†	.251	116	367	42	92	130	20	0	6	30	3	2	1	36	1	49	7	6	8	.354	.318
Lydy, Scott, Oakland	.225	41	102	11	23	34	5	0	2	7	0	0	1	8	0	39	2	0	1	.333	.288
Lyons, Steve, Boston*	.130	28	23	4	3	4	1	0	0	0	0	0	0	2	0	5	1	0	0	.174	.200
Maas, Kevin, New York*	.205	59	151	20	31	62	4	0	9	25	0	1	1	24	2	32	1	1	2	.411	.316
Macfarlane, Mike, Kansas City	.273	117	388	55	106	193	27	0	20	67	1	6	16	40	2	83	2	5	8	.497	.360
Mack, Shane, Minnesota	.276	128	503	66	139	207	30	4	10	61	3	2	4	41	1	76	15	5	13	.412	.335
Magadan, Dave, Seattle*	.259	71	228	27	59	73	11	0	1	21	2	3	0	36	3	33	2	0	9	.320	.356
Maksudian, Mike, Minnesota*	.167	5	12	2	2	3	1	0	0	2	0	1	0	4	0	2	0	0	2	.250	.353
Maldonado, Candy, Cleveland	.247	28	81	11	20	37	2	0	5	20	1	1	0	11	2	18	0	1	2	.457	.333
Martin, Norberto, Chicago*	.357	8	14	3	5	5	0	0	0	2	0	0	0	1	0	1	0	0	0	.357	.400
Martinez, Chito, Baltimore*	.000	8	15	0	0	0	0	0	0	0	0	0	0	4	2	4	0	0	0	.000	.211
Martinez, Carlos, Cleveland	.244	80	262	26	64	89	10	0	5	31	0	3	0	20	3	29	1	1	5	.340	.295
Martinez, Domingo, Toronto	.286	8	14	2	4	7	0	0	1	3	0	0	0	0	0	7	0	0	0	.500	.333
Martinez, Edgar, Seattle	.237	42	135	20	32	51	7	0	4	13	1	1	0	28	1	19	0	0	4	.378	.366
Martinez, Tino, Seattle*	.265	109	408	48	108	186	25	1	17	60	3	3	5	45	9	56	0	3	7	.456	.343
Mattingly, Don, New York*	.291	134	530	78	154	236	27	2	17	86	0	3	2	61	9	42	0	0	20	.445	.364
Mayne, Brent, Kansas City*	.254	71	205	22	52	69	9	1	2	22	3	1	1	7	1	31	3	2	6	.337	.317
Maysey, Matt, Milwaukee	1.000	23	1	0	1	1	0	0	0	0	0	0	0	0	0	0	0	0	0	1.000	1.000
McCarty, Dave, Minnesota	.214	98	350	36	75	100	15	2	2	21	1	1	0	19	0	80	2	6	13	.286	.257
McGwire, Mark, Oakland	.333	27	84	16	28	61	6	0	9	24	0	1	1	21	5	19	0	1	0	.726	.467
McLemore, Mark, Baltimore†	.284	148	581	81	165	214	27	5	4	72	11	6	1	64	4	92	21	15	21	.368	.353
McNeely, Jeff, Boston	.297	21	37	10	11	14	1	1	0	1	0	0	0	7	0	9	6	0	0	.378	.409
McRae, Brian, Kansas City†	.282	153	627	78	177	259	28	9	12	69	14	3	4	37	1	105	23	14	8	.413	.325
McReynolds, Kevin, Kansas City	.245	110	351	44	86	149	22	4	11	42	1	3	1	37	6	56	2	2	8	.425	.316
Meares, Pat, Minnesota	.251	111	346	33	87	107	14	3	0	33	4	3	1	7	0	52	4	5	11	.309	.266
Melvin, Bob, Boston	.222	77	176	13	39	55	7	0	3	23	3	3	1	7	0	44	0	0	2	.313	.251
Mercedes, Henry, Oakland	.213	20	47	5	10	12	2	0	0	3	0	0	1	2	0	15	1	1	0	.255	.260
Mercedes, Luis, Baltimore	.292	10	24	1	7	9	2	0	0	0	1	0	0	5	0	4	1	1	1	.375	.414
Merullo, Matt, Chicago*	.050	8	20	1	1	1	0	0	0	1	0	0	0	0	0	1	0	0	1	.050	.050
Meulens, Hensley, New York	.170	30	53	8	9	18	1	1	2	5	0	0	0	8	0	19	0	1	2	.340	.279
Mieske, Matt, Milwaukee	.241	23	58	9	14	23	0	0	3	7	1	0	0	4	0	15	0	0	2	.397	.290
Miller, Kevin, Kansas City	.167	37	108	9	18	21	3	0	0	3	0	1	0	8	0	19	3	1	3	.194	.229
Milligan, Randy, Cleveland	.426	19	47	7	20	27	7	0	0	7	0	0	0	14	0	4	0	0	0	.574	.557
Molitor, Paul, Toronto	.332	160	636	121	211	324	37	5	22	111	0	8	3	77	3	71	22	4	13	.509	.402
Munoz, Pedro, Minnesota	.233	104	326	34	76	128	11	1	13	38	0	0	3	25	2	97	1	2	7	.393	.294
Myers, Greg, California*	.255	108	290	27	74	105	10	0	7	40	3	3	2	17	2	47	3	3	8	.362	.298
Naehring, Tim, Boston	.331	39	127	14	42	55	10	0	1	17	3	1	0	10	0	26	1	0	3	.433	.377
Neel, Troy, Oakland*	.290	123	427	59	124	202	21	0	19	63	0	2	4	49	5	101	3	5	7	.473	.367
Newfield, Marc, Seattle	.227	22	66	5	15	21	3	0	1	7	0	1	1	2	0	18	0	1	2	.318	.257
Newson, Warren, Chicago*	.300	26	40	9	12	18	0	0	2	6	0	0	0	9	1	12	0	0	2	.450	.429

Player, Team	Avg.	G	AB	R	H	TB	2B	3B	HR	RBI	SH	SF	HP	BB	Int. BB	SO	SB	CS	GI DP	Slg.	OBP
Nilsson, Dave, Milwaukee*	.257	100	296	35	76	111	10	2	7	40	4	3	0	37	5	36	3	6	10	.375	.336
Nokes, Matt, New York*	.249	76	217	25	54	92	8	0	10	35	0	3	2	16	2	31	0	0	4	.424	.303
Obando, Sherman, Baltimore	.272	31	92	8	25	36	2	0	3	15	0	1	0	4	0	26	0	0	1	.391	.309
O'Brien, Pete, Seattle*	.257	72	210	30	54	82	7	0	7	27	0	3	0	26	4	21	0	0	8	.390	.335
O'Leary, Troy, Milwaukee*	.293	19	41	3	12	15	3	0	0	3	3	0	0	5	0	9	0	0	1	.366	.370
Olerud, John, Toronto*	.363	158	551	109	200	330	54	2	24	107	0	7	7	114	33	65	0	2	12	.599	.473
Olson, Gregg, Baltimore	.000	50	1	0	0	0	0	0	0	0	0	0	0	0	0	1	0	0	0	.000	.000
O'Neill, Paul, New York*	.311	141	498	71	155	251	34	1	20	75	0	3	2	44	5	69	2	4	13	.504	.367
Orosco, Jesse, Milwaukee	.000	57	1	0	0	0	0	0	0	0	0	0	0	0	0	1	0	0	0	.000	.000
Ortiz, Junior, Cleveland	.221	95	249	19	55	68	13	0	0	20	4	1	5	11	1	26	1	0	10	.273	.267
Ortiz, Luis, Boston	.250	9	12	0	3	3	0	0	0	1	0	0	0	0	0	2	0	0	0	.250	.250
Orton, John, California	.189	37	95	5	18	26	5	0	1	4	2	0	1	7	0	24	1	2	1	.274	.252
Owen, Spike, New York†	.234	103	334	41	78	104	16	2	2	20	3	1	0	29	2	30	3	2	6	.311	.294
Pagliarulo, Mike, Min.-Bal.*	.303	116	370	55	112	172	25	4	9	44	2	1	6	26	2	49	6	7	7	.465	.357
Palmeiro, Rafael, Texas*	.295	160	597	124	176	331	40	2	37	105	2	9	5	73	22	85	22	3	8	.554	.371
Palmer, Dean, Texas	.245	148	519	88	127	261	31	2	33	96	0	5	8	53	4	154	11	10	5	.503	.321
Paquette, Craig, Oakland	.219	105	393	35	86	150	20	4	12	46	1	1	0	14	2	108	4	2	7	.382	.245
Parent, Mark, Baltimore	.259	22	54	7	14	28	2	0	4	12	3	1	0	3	0	14	0	0	1	.519	.293
Parks, Derek, Minnesota	.200	7	20	3	4	4	0	0	0	1	0	0	0	1	0	2	0	0	0	.200	.238
Parrish, Lance, Cleveland	.200	10	20	2	4	8	1	0	1	2	0	0	0	4	0	5	1	0	2	.400	.333
Pasqua, Dan, Chicago*	.205	78	176	22	36	63	10	1	5	20	1	3	0	26	1	51	2	2	3	.358	.302
Peltier, Dan, Texas*	.269	65	160	23	43	55	7	1	1	17	1	1	1	20	0	27	0	4	3	.344	.352
Pena, Tony, Boston	.181	126	304	20	55	78	11	0	4	19	13	3	2	25	0	46	1	3	12	.257	.246
Perez, Eduardo, California	.250	52	180	16	45	67	6	2	4	30	0	1	2	9	0	39	5	4	4	.372	.292
Petralli, Geno, Texas†	.241	59	133	16	32	40	5	0	1	13	1	0	0	22	3	17	2	0	5	.301	.348
Phillips, Tony, Detroit†	.313	151	566	113	177	225	27	0	7	57	1	4	4	132	5	102	16	11	11	.398	.443
Pirkl, Greg, Seattle	.174	7	23	1	4	7	0	0	1	4	0	0	0	0	0	4	0	0	2	.304	.174
Polonia, Luis, California*	.271	152	576	75	156	188	17	6	1	32	8	3	2	48	7	53	55	24	7	.326	.328
Puckett, Kirby, Minnesota	.296	156	622	89	184	295	39	3	22	89	1	5	7	47	7	93	8	6	15	.474	.349
Pulliam, Harvey, Kansas City	.258	27	62	7	16	24	5	0	1	6	0	0	1	2	0	14	0	0	3	.387	.292
Quintana, Carlos, Boston	.244	101	303	31	74	82	5	0	1	19	5	2	2	31	2	52	1	0	13	.271	.317
Raines, Tim, Chicago†	.306	115	415	75	127	199	16	4	16	54	2	2	3	64	4	35	21	7	7	.480	.401
Ramirez, Manny, Cleveland	.170	22	53	5	9	16	1	0	2	5	0	0	0	2	0	8	0	0	3	.302	.200
Reboulet, Jeff, Minnesota	.258	109	240	33	62	73	8	0	1	15	5	1	2	35	0	37	5	5	6	.304	.356
Redus, Gary, Texas	.288	77	222	28	64	102	12	4	6	31	0	3	0	23	1	35	4	4	3	.459	.351
Reimer, Kevin, Milwaukee*	.249	125	437	53	109	172	22	1	13	60	1	4	5	30	4	72	5	4	12	.394	.303
Reynolds, Harold, Baltimore†	.252	145	485	64	122	162	20	4	4	47	10	5	4	66	3	47	12	11	4	.334	.343
Richardson, Jeff, Boston	.208	15	24	3	5	7	2	0	0	2	2	0	0	1	0	3	0	0	0	.292	.240
Riles, Ernest, Boston*	.189	94	143	15	27	50	8	0	5	20	2	3	2	20	3	40	1	3	5	.350	.292
Ripken, Cal, Baltimore	.257	162	641	87	165	269	26	3	24	90	0	6	6	65	19	58	1	4	17	.420	.329
Ripken, Bill, Texas	.189	50	132	12	25	29	4	0	0	11	5	1	4	11	0	19	0	2	6	.220	.270
Rivera, Luis, Boston	.208	62	130	13	27	40	8	1	1	7	2	1	1	11	0	36	1	2	2	.308	.273
Rodriguez, Ivan, Texas	.273	137	473	56	129	195	28	4	10	66	5	8	4	29	3	70	8	7	16	.412	.315
Rossy, Rico, Kansas City	.221	46	86	10	19	29	4	0	2	12	1	0	1	9	0	11	0	0	6	.337	.302
Rowland, Rich, Detroit	.217	21	46	2	10	13	3	0	0	4	1	0	0	5	0	16	0	0	1	.283	.294
Russell, John, Texas	.227	18	22	1	5	9	1	0	1	3	0	0	2	2	0	10	0	0	0	.409	.292
Salmon, Tim, California	.283	142	515	93	146	276	35	1	31	95	0	8	5	82	5	135	5	6	6	.536	.382
Santovenia, Nelson, Kansas City	.125	4	8	0	1	1	0	0	0	0	0	0	0	1	0	2	0	0	0	.125	.222
Sasser, Mackey, Seattle*	.218	83	188	18	41	58	10	2	1	21	0	4	1	15	6	30	1	0	7	.309	.274
Sax, Steve, Chicago	.235	57	119	20	28	36	5	0	1	8	2	0	0	8	0	6	7	3	1	.303	.283
Schofield, Dick, Toronto	.191	36	110	11	21	26	1	2	0	5	2	0	0	16	0	25	3	0	1	.236	.294
Segui, David, Baltimore†	.273	146	450	54	123	180	27	0	10	60	3	8	0	58	4	53	2	1	18	.400	.351
Seitzer, Kevin, Oak.-Mil.	.269	120	417	45	112	165	16	2	11	57	3	5	2	44	1	48	7	7	14	.396	.338
Shave, Jon, Texas	.319	14	47	3	15	17	2	0	0	7	3	2	0	0	0	8	1	3	0	.362	.306
Sheets, Larry, Seattle*	.118	11	17	0	2	3	1	0	0	1	0	0	1	2	0	1	0	0	2	.176	.250
Shumpert, Terry, Kansas City	.100	8	10	0	1	1	0	0	0	0	1	0	0	2	0	2	1	0	0	.100	.250
Sierra, Ruben, Oakland†	.233	158	630	77	147	246	23	5	22	101	0	10	0	52	16	97	25	5	17	.390	.288
Silvestri, Dave, New York	.286	7	21	4	6	10	1	0	1	4	0	0	0	5	0	3	0	0	1	.476	.423
Smith, Lonnie, Baltimore	.208	9	24	8	5	12	1	0	2	3	0	0	0	8	0	10	0	0	0	.500	.406
Snow, J.T., California†	.241	129	419	60	101	171	18	2	16	57	7	6	2	55	4	88	3	0	10	.408	.328
Sojo, Luis, Toronto	.170	19	47	5	8	10	2	0	0	6	2	1	0	4	0	2	0	3	3	.213	.231
Sorrento, Paul, Cleveland*	.257	148	463	75	119	201	26	1	18	65	0	4	2	58	11	121	3	1	10	.434	.340
Spiers, Bill, Milwaukee*	.238	113	340	43	81	103	8	4	2	36	9	4	4	29	2	51	9	8	11	.303	.302
Sprague, Ed, Toronto	.260	150	546	50	142	211	31	1	12	73	2	6	10	32	1	85	1	0	23	.386	.310
Stahoviak, Scott, Minnesota*	.193	20	57	7	11	15	4	0	0	1	0	0	0	3	0	22	0	2	2	.263	.233
Stankiewicz, Andy, New York	.000	16	9	5	0	0	0	0	0	0	0	0	0	1	0	1	0	0	0	.000	.100
Stanley, Mike, New York	.305	138	423	70	129	226	17	1	26	84	0	6	5	57	4	85	1	1	10	.534	.389
Steinbach, Terry, Oakland	.285	104	389	47	111	162	19	1	10	43	0	1	3	25	1	65	3	3	13	.416	.333
Stillwell, Kurt, California†	.262	22	61	2	16	22	2	2	0	3	1	2	0	4	0	11	2	0	2	.361	.299
Strange, Doug, Texas†	.256	145	484	58	124	174	29	0	7	60	8	4	3	43	3	69	6	4	12	.360	.318
Suero, William, Milwaukee	.286	15	14	0	4	4	0	0	0	0	0	0	0	5	0	3	0	1	1	.286	.333
Surhoff, B.J., Milwaukee*	.274	148	552	66	151	216	38	3	7	79	4	5	2	36	5	47	12	9	9	.391	.318
Sveum, Dale, Oakland†	.177	30	79	12	14	24	2	1	2	6	1	0	0	16	1	21	0	0	2	.304	.316
Tackett, Jeff, Baltimore	.172	39	87	8	15	18	3	0	0	9	2	1	0	13	0	28	0	0	5	.207	.277
Tartabull, Danny, New York	.250	138	513	87	128	258	33	2	31	102	0	4	2	92	9	156	0	0	8	.503	.363
Tettleton, Mickey, Detroit†	.245	152	522	79	128	257	25	4	32	110	0	6	0	109	12	139	3	7	5	.492	.372
Thomas, Frank, Chicago	.317	153	549	106	174	333	36	0	41	128	0	13	2	112	23	54	4	2	10	.607	.426
Thome, Jim, Cleveland*	.266	47	154	28	41	73	11	0	7	22	0	5	4	29	1	36	2	1	3	.474	.385
Thon, Dickie, Milwaukee	.269	85	245	23	66	81	10	1	1	33	3	5	0	22	3	39	6	5	4	.331	.324
Thurman, Gary, Detroit	.213	75	89	22	19	25	2	2	0	13	1	1	0	11	0	30	7	0	2	.281	.297
Tingley, Ron, California	.200	58	90	7	18	25	7	0	0	12	3	1	1	9	0	22	1	2	4	.278	.277
Tinsley, Lee, Seattle†	.158	11	19	2	3	7	1	0	1	2	0	0	2	0	0	9	0	0	1	.368	.238
Trammell, Alan, Detroit	.329	112	401	72	132	199	25	3	12	60	4	2	2	38	2	38	12	8	7	.496	.388
Treadway, Jeff, Cleveland*	.303	97	221	25	67	89	14	1	2	27	1	2	2	14	2	21	1	1	6	.403	.347
Turang, Brian, Seattle	.250	40	140	22	35	48	11	1	0	7	1	0	2	17	0	20	6	2	3	.343	.340
Turner, Chris, California	.280	25	75	9	21	29	5	0	1	13	0	1	1	9	0	16	1	1	1	.387	.360
Valentin, John, Boston	.278	144	468	50	130	209	40	3	11	66	16	4	2	49	2	77	3	4	9	.447	.346

Player, Team	Avg.	G	AB	R	H	TB	2B	3B	HR	RBI	SH	SF	HP	BB	Int. BB	SO	SB	CS	GI DP	Slg.	OBP
Valentin, Jose, Milwaukee†	.245	19	53	10	13	21	1	2	1	7	2	0	1	7	1	16	1	0	1	.396	.344
Valle, Dave, Seattle	.258	135	423	48	109	167	19	0	13	63	8	4	17	48	4	56	1	0	18	.395	.354
Van Burkleo, Ty, California*	.152	12	33	2	5	11	3	0	1	1	0	0	0	6	0	9	1	0	0	.333	.282
Vaughn, Greg, Milwaukee	.267	154	569	97	152	274	28	2	30	97	0	4	5	89	14	118	10	7	6	.482	.369
Vaughn, Mo, Boston*	.297	152	539	86	160	283	34	1	29	101	0	7	8	79	23	130	4	3	14	.525	.390
Velarde, Randy, New York	.301	85	226	28	68	106	13	2	7	24	3	2	4	18	2	39	2	2	12	.469	.360
Ventura, Robin, Chicago*	.262	157	554	85	145	240	27	1	22	94	1	6	3	105	16	82	1	6	18	.433	.379
Vina, Fernando, Seattle*	.222	24	45	5	10	12	2	0	0	2	1	0	3	4	0	3	6	0	0	.267	.327
Vizquel, Omar, Seattle†	.255	158	560	68	143	167	14	2	2	31	13	3	4	50	2	71	12	14	7	.298	.319
Voigt, Jack, Baltimore	.296	64	152	32	45	76	11	1	6	23	0	0	0	25	0	33	1	0	3	.500	.395
Walewander, Jim, California†	.125	12	8	2	1	1	0	0	0	3	0	1	0	5	0	1	1	1	0	.125	.429
Walton, Jerome, California	.000	5	2	2	0	0	0	0	0	0	0	0	0	1	0	2	1	0	0	.000	.333
Ward, Turner, Toronto†	.192	72	167	20	32	52	4	2	4	28	3	4	1	23	2	26	3	3	7	.311	.287
Webster, Lenny, Minnesota	.198	49	106	14	21	26	2	0	1	8	0	0	1	11	1	8	1	0	1	.245	.274
Whitaker, Lou, Detroit*	.290	119	383	72	111	172	32	1	9	67	7	4	4	78	4	46	3	3	5	.449	.412
White, Devon, Toronto†	.273	146	598	116	163	262	42	6	15	52	3	3	7	57	1	127	34	4	3	.438	.341
Wilkerson, Curtis, Kansas City†	.143	12	28	1	4	4	0	0	0	0	0	0	0	1	0	6	2	0	1	.143	.172
Williams, Bernie, New York†	.268	139	567	67	152	227	31	4	12	68	1	3	4	53	4	106	9	9	17	.400	.333
Williams, Gerald, New York	.149	42	67	11	10	18	2	3	0	6	0	1	2	1	0	14	2	0	2	.269	.183
Wilson, Craig, Kansas City	.265	21	49	6	13	17	1	0	1	3	1	0	0	7	0	6	1	1	0	.347	.357
Winfield, Dave, Minnesota	.271	143	547	72	148	242	27	2	21	76	0	2	0	45	2	106	2*	3	15	.442	.325
Wrona, Rick, Chicago	.125	4	8	0	1	1	0	0	0	1	0	0	0	0	0	4	0	0	0	.125	.125
Yount, Robin, Milwaukee	.258	127	454	62	117	172	25	3	8	51	5	6	5	44	5	93	9	2	12	.379	.326
Zupcic, Bob, Boston	.241	141	286	40	69	103	24	2	2	26	8	3	2	27	2	54	5	2	7	.360	.308

AWARDED FIRST BASE ON OBSTRUCTION OR CATCHER'S INTERFERENCE—Steinbach, Oakland 2 (Ortiz, Petralli); Cooper, Boston (Parks); Gomez, Baltimore (Macfarlane).

PLAYERS WITH TWO OR MORE TEAMS

Player, Team	Avg.	G	AB	R	H	TB	2B	3B	HR	RBI	SH	SF	HP	BB	Int. BB	SO	SB	CS	GI DP	Slg.	OBP
Boever, Joe, Detroit	.000	19	0	0	0	0	0	0	0	0	0	0	0	0	0	0	0	0	0	.000	.000
Boever, Joe, Oakland	.000	42	0	0	0	0	0	0	0	0	0	0	0	0	0	0	0	0	0	.000	.000
Calderon, Ivan, Boston	.221	73	213	25	47	62	8	2	1	19	2	2	1	21	1	28	4	2	10	.291	.291
Calderon, Ivan, Chicago	.115	9	26	1	3	5	2	0	0	3	0	0	0	0	0	5	0	0	2	.192	.115
Davis, Storm, Detroit	.000	24	0	0	0	0	0	0	0	0	0	0	0	0	0	0	0	0	0	.000	.000
Davis, Storm, Oakland	.000	19	0	0	0	0	0	0	0	0	0	0	0	0	0	0	0	0	0	.000	.000
Deer, Rob, Boston	.196	38	143	18	28	57	6	1	7	16	0	0	2	20	0	49	2	0	2	.399	.303
Deer, Rob, Detroit	.217	90	323	48	70	123	11	0	14	39	0	3	3	38	1	120	3	2	4	.381	.302
Gaetti, Gary, California	.180	20	50	3	9	11	2	0	0	4	1	0	5	0	0	12	1	0	3	.220	.250
Gaetti, Gary, Kansas City	.256	82	281	37	72	134	18	1	14	46	2	6	8	16	0	75	0	3	2	.477	.309
Habyan, John, Kansas City	.000	12	0	0	0	0	0	0	0	0	0	0	0	0	0	0	0	0	0	.000	.000
Habyan, John, New York	.000	36	0	0	0	0	0	0	0	0	0	0	0	0	0	0	0	0	0	.000	.000
Henderson, Rickey, Oakland	.327	90	318	77	104	176	19	1	17	47	0	2	2	85	6	46	31	6	8	.553	.469
Henderson, Rickey, Toronto	.215	44	163	37	35	52	3	1	4	12	1	2	2	35	1	19	22	2	1	.319	.356
Linton, Doug, California	.000	19	0	0	0	0	0	0	0	0	0	0	0	0	0	0	0	0	0	.000	.000
Linton, Doug, Toronto	.000	4	0	0	0	0	0	0	0	0	0	0	0	0	0	0	0	0	0	.000	.000
Nelson, Gene, California	.000	46	0	0	0	0	0	0	0	0	0	0	0	0	0	0	0	0	0	.000	.000
Nelson, Gene, Texas	.000	6	0	0	0	0	0	0	0	0	0	0	0	0	0	0	0	0	0	.000	.000
Pagliarulo, Mike, Baltimore*	.325	33	117	24	38	65	9	0	6	21	0	0	1	8	0	15	0	0	2	.556	.373
Pagliarulo, Mike, Minnesota*	.292	83	253	31	74	107	16	4	3	23	2	1	5	18	2	34	6	5	5	.423	.350
Power, Ted, Cleveland	.000	20	0	0	0	0	0	0	0	0	0	0	0	0	0	0	0	0	0	.000	.000
Power, Ted, Seattle	.000	25	0	0	0	0	0	0	0	0	0	0	0	0	0	0	0	0	0	.000	.000
Reed, Rick, Kansas City	.000	1	0	0	0	0	0	0	0	0	0	0	0	0	0	0	0	0	0	.000	.000
Reed, Rick, Texas	.000	2	0	0	0	0	0	0	0	0	0	0	0	0	0	0	0	0	0	.000	.000
Seitzer, Kevin, Milwaukee	.290	47	162	21	47	74	6	0	7	30	1	1	1	17	0	15	3	0	7	.457	.359
Seitzer, Kevin, Oakland	.255	73	255	24	65	91	10	2	4	27	2	4	1	27	1	33	4	7	7	.357	.324

DESIGNATED HITTING

TEAM

Team	Avg.	AB	R	H	TB	2B	3B	HR	RBI	SH	SF	HP	BB	Int. BB	SO	SB	CS	GI DP	Slg.	OBP
Toronto	.308	639	116	197	301	36	4	20	101	1	10	4	80	6	77	20	4	13	.471	.383
Detroit	.284	616	97	175	268	27	6	18	103	1	9	2	89	11	119	17	10	7	.435	.372
Baltimore	.280	617	93	173	281	27	0	27	104	2	8	1	75	11	107	1	1	19	.455	.355
Texas	.277	631	104	175	269	34	3	18	97	5	8	2	65	5	118	9	3	20	.426	.343
Minnesota	.273	641	82	175	265	35	2	17	78	1	1	1	53	1	106	2	4	17	.413	.329
Boston	.265	635	77	168	272	35	3	21	94	2	11	13	41	7	100	6	3	23	.428	.317
Oakland	.257	630	87	162	269	27	1	26	86	2	7	3	73	5	161	13	6	13	.427	.334
Kansas City	.255	647	79	165	265	34	3	20	80	0	10	4	46	10	83	7	6	22	.410	.304
New York	.253	612	96	155	298	33	1	36	124	0	7	6	89	10	157	0	1	10	.487	.350
Seattle	.253	597	86	151	235	25	1	19	77	4	9	3	85	13	92	7	4	20	.394	.344
Milwaukee	.252	623	87	157	255	29	3	21	90	2	3	6	67	9	124	13	9	14	.409	.329
Cleveland	.251	618	70	155	253	17	3	25	72	3	9	5	48	12	118	8	4	12	.409	.306
California	.245	624	83	153	269	35	0	27	119	0	1	1	74	12	146	5	5	19	.431	.326
Chicago	.214	654	69	140	239	27	3	22	103	2	10	4	33	3	127	4	3	19	.365	.252
Totals	.262	8784	1226	2301	3739	421	33	317	1328	25	103	55	918	115	1635	112	63	228	.426	.332

INDIVIDUAL

TOP 15 DESIGNATED HITTERS

Minimum 100 at-bats. *Lefthanded batter. †Switch-hitter.

Player, Team	Avg.	G	AB	R	H	TB	2B	3B	HR	RBI	SH	SF	HP	BB	Int. BB	SO	SB	CS	GI DP	Slg.	OBP
Baines, Harold, Baltimore*	.313	116	415	64	130	212	22	0	20	78	1	6	0	57	9	52	0	0	14	.511	.391
Molitor, Paul, Toronto	.311	137	543	107	169	260	32	4	17	90	1	8	3	68	3	60	20	2	13	.479	.386
Franco, Julio, Texas	.289	140	529	85	153	232	31	3	14	83	5	7	1	61	4	94	9	3	16	.439	.360
Fielder, Cecil, Detroit	.277	36	130	21	36	61	7	0	6	28	0	2	1	29	6	24	0	0	4	.469	.407
Neel, Troy, Oakland*	.274	85	318	43	87	147	15	0	15	44	0	2	2	34	4	79	3	2	6	.462	.346
Dawson, Andre, Boston	.266	97	380	38	101	164	22	1	13	56	0	6	12	14	3	38	1	0	15	.432	.308
Brett, George, Kansas City*	.265	140	555	68	147	239	29	3	19	74	0	10	3	39	9	66	7	5	20	.431	.311
Reimer, Kevin, Milwaukee*	.261	83	307	40	80	128	19	1	9	36	0	2	5	19	1	48	3	4	9	.417	.312
Tartabull, Danny, New York*	.260	88	327	57	85	166	21	0	20	70	0	1	2	58	6	94	0	0	5	.508	.374
Winfield, Dave, Minnesota	.258	105	414	54	107	168	23	1	12	49	0	1	0	33	1	79	2	2	13	.406	.313
Jefferson, Reggie, Cleveland†	.256	88	316	33	81	125	10	2	10	31	3	1	3	21	6	69	1	3	6	.396	.308
O'Brien, Pete, Seattle*	.253	52	170	27	43	65	4	0	6	21	0	3	0	21	2	18	0	0	7	.382	.330
Vaughn, Greg, Milwaukee	.251	58	219	37	55	97	9	0	11	38	0	1	1	39	8	57	4	1	1	.443	.365
Gibson, Kirk, Detroit*	.248	76	278	39	69	111	13	4	7	40	0	3	1	36	3	62	14	5	2	.399	.333
Davis, Chili, California†	.243	150	572	74	139	252	32	0	27	112	0	0	1	70	12	135	4	1	17	.441	.327

ALL DESIGNATED HITTERS

*Lefthanded batter. †Switch-hitter.

Player, Team	Avg.	G	AB	R	H	TB	2B	3B	HR	RBI	SH	SF	HP	BB	Int. BB	SO	SB	CS	GI DP	Slg.	OBP
Aldrete, Mike, Oakland*	.421	6	19	3	8	10	2	0	0	2	1	0	0	2	0	3	0	0	1	.526	.476
Amaral, Rich, Seattle	.370	9	27	3	10	16	4	1	0	8	2	1	0	1	0	2	1	0	1	.593	.379
Anderson, Brady, Baltimore*	.000	2	1	2	0	0	0	0	0	0	0	0	0	0	0	0	0	0	0	.000	.000
Armas, Marcos, Oakland	.000	2	2	0	0	0	0	0	0	0	0	0	0	0	0	0	0	0	0	.000	.000
Baerga, Carlos, Cleveland†	.412	4	17	1	7	10	1	1	0	4	0	2	0	2	1	2	0	0	0	.588	.429
Baines, Harold, Baltimore*	.313	116	415	64	130	212	22	0	20	78	1	6	0	57	9	52	0	0	14	.511	.391
Balboni, Steve, Texas	.600	2	5	0	3	3	0	0	0	0	0	0	0	0	0	2	0	0	0	.600	.600
Barnes, Skeeter, Detroit	.323	13	31	6	10	17	2	1	1	5	0	0	0	2	0	2	1	0	1	.548	.364
Bell, George, Chicago	.217	102	410	36	89	149	17	2	13	64	0	9	4	13	2	49	1	1	14	.363	.243
Bell, Juan, Milwaukee†	.000	2	0	1	0	0	0	0	0	0	0	0	0	0	0	0	0	0	0	.000	.000
Belle, Albert, Cleveland	.400	9	30	7	12	27	0	0	5	11	0	3	1	5	1	2	2	0	1	.900	.462
Blankenship, Lance, Oakland	.333	5	3	0	1	1	0	0	0	1	1	0	0	0	0	0	0	0	0	.333	.333
Blosser, Greg, Boston*	.000	1	4	0	0	0	0	0	0	0	0	0	0	0	0	2	0	0	0	.000	.000
Blowers, Mike, Seattle	.000	3	1	0	0	0	0	0	0	1	0	0	0	1	0	0	0	0	0	.000	.000
Boggs, Wade, New York*	.375	8	32	6	12	17	3	1	0	7	0	2	0	4	1	2	0	0	1	.531	.421
Boone, Bret, Seattle	.500	1	2	0	1	1	0	0	0	0	0	0	0	1	0	1	0	0	0	.500	.667
Brett, George, Kansas City*	.265	140	555	68	147	239	29	3	19	74	0	10	3	39	9	66	7	5	20	.431	.311
Brito, Bernardo, Minnesota	.304	7	23	4	7	14	1	0	2	5	0	0	0	0	0	9	0	0	1	.609	.304
Brooks, Hubie, Kansas City	.267	9	30	4	8	12	4	0	0	2	0	0	0	1	0	5	0	0	1	.400	.290
Brosius, Scott, Oakland	.600	2	5	1	3	4	1	0	0	0	0	0	0	0	0	1	0	0	0	.800	.600
Brunansky, Tom, Milwaukee	.000	6	10	0	0	0	0	0	0	0	1	0	0	1	0	4	0	1	1	.000	.091
Buford, Damon, Baltimore	.500	17	4	8	2	3	1	0	0	1	0	0	0	0	0	1	1	0	0	.750	.500
Buhner, Jay, Seattle	.171	10	35	3	6	14	2	0	2	5	0	1	0	4	1	7	0	0	1	.400	.250
Bush, Randy, Minnesota*	.167	5	18	1	3	4	1	0	0	1	0	0	0	1	0	5	0	0	0	.222	.211
Calderon, Ivan, Bos.-Chi.	.213	25	80	6	17	22	3	1	0	7	1	1	0	3	0	15	0	1	4	.275	.238
Canate, Willie, Toronto	.000	1	1	0	0	0	0	0	0	0	0	0	0	0	0	0	0	0	0	.000	.000
Canseco, Jose, Texas	.167	9	36	4	6	9	0	0	1	5	0	1	0	2	0	12	0	0	2	.250	.225
Carey, Paul, Baltimore	.067	5	15	0	1	1	0	0	0	0	0	0	0	0	0	4	0	0	2	.067	.176
Carter, Joe, Toronto	.385	3	13	4	5	11	0	0	2	2	0	0	0	0	0	4	0	0	0	.846	.385
Coles, Darnell, Toronto	.000	1	4	0	0	0	0	0	0	0	0	0	0	0	0	0	0	0	0	.000	.000
Correia, Rod, California	.000	6	0	1	0	0	0	0	0	0	0	0	0	0	0	0	0	0	0	.000	.000
Cotto, Henry, Seattle	.250	15	20	1	5	5	0	0	0	2	0	0	0	0	0	5	0	1	0	.250	.250

Player, Team	Avg.	G	AB	R	H	TB	2B	3B	HR	RBI	SH	SF	HP	BB	Int. BB	SO	SB	CS	GI DP	Slg.	OBP
Dascenzo, Doug, Texas†	.000	2	1	1	0	0	0	0	0	0	0	0	0	0	0	0	0	0	0	.000	.000
Davis, Butch, Texas	.250	11	8	4	2	6	1	0	1	1	0	0	0	0	0	0	0	0	0	.750	.250
Davis, Chili, California†	.243	150	572	74	139	252	32	0	27	112	0	0	1	70	12	135	4	1	17	.441	.327
Davis, Eric, Detroit	.182	5	11	2	2	2	0	0	0	0	0	0	0	5	1	2	0	0	1	.182	.438
Davis, Glenn, Baltimore	.107	7	28	1	3	3	0	0	0	0	0	0	0	2	0	8	0	1	0	.107	.167
Dawson, Andre, Boston	.266	97	380	38	101	164	22	1	13	56	0	6	12	14	3	38	1	0	15	.432	.308
Deer, Rob, Det.-Bos.	.222	6	18	2	4	7	0	0	1	3	0	1	0	2	0	7	0	1	0	.389	.286
Delgado, Carlos, Toronto*	.000	1	1	0	0	0	0	0	0	0	0	0	0	0	0	0	0	0	0	.000	.000
Diaz, Alex, Milwaukee†	.000	1	0	1	0	0	0	0	0	0	0	0	0	0	0	0	1	0	0	.000	.000
Easley, Damion, California	1.000	1	1	0	1	2	1	0	0	0	0	0	0	0	0	0	0	0	0	2.000	1.000
Felder, Mike, Seattle†	.222	6	9	1	2	2	0	0	0	0	0	0	1	1	1	2	1	1	0	.222	.364
Fielder, Cecil, Detroit	.277	36	130	21	36	61	7	0	6	28	0	2	1	29	6	24	0	0	4	.469	.407
Fletcher, Scott, Boston	.333	1	3	1	1	1	0	0	0	0	0	0	0	0	0	0	0	0	0	.333	.333
Fox, Eric, Oakland†	.000	2	1	0	0	0	0	0	0	0	0	0	0	0	0	0	0	0	0	.000	.000
Franco, Julio, Texas	.289	140	529	85	153	232	31	3	14	83	5	7	1	61	4	94	9	3	16	.439	.360
Fryman, Travis, Detroit	.250	1	4	1	1	1	0	0	0	0	0	0	0	0	0	0	0	0	0	.250	.250
Gaetti, Gary, Cal.-K.C.	.222	6	18	2	4	4	0	0	0	4	0	1	0	4	0	1	0	0	1	.222	.348
Gibson, Kirk, Detroit*	.248	76	278	39	69	111	13	4	7	40	0	3	1	36	3	62	14	5	2	.399	.333
Gladden, Dan, Detroit	.333	5	12	1	4	4	0	0	0	0	0	0	0	0	0	1	0	0	0	.333	.333
Gomez, Chris, Detroit	.000	1	0	1	0	0	0	0	0	0	0	0	0	0	0	0	0	0	0	.000	.000
Gomez, Luis, Baltimore	.000	1	4	0	0	0	0	0	0	0	0	0	0	0	0	0	0	0	0	.000	.000
Gonzalez, Juan, Texas	.220	10	41	5	9	17	2	0	2	5	0	0	0	2	1	9	0	0	1	.415	.256
Green, Shawn, Toronto*	.000	1	4	0	0	0	0	0	0	0	0	0	0	0	0	1	0	0	0	.000	.000
Greenwell, Mike, Boston*	.324	10	34	3	11	21	2	1	2	6	0	1	1	2	0	5	1	0	1	.618	.368
Griffey, Ken, Seattle*	.309	19	68	15	21	41	5	0	5	13	0	1	1	13	4	18	3	0	1	.603	.422
Gruber, Kelly, California	.000	1	4	0	0	0	0	0	0	0	0	0	0	0	0	2	0	1	0	.000	.000
Gwynn, Chris, Kansas City*	.250	5	16	0	4	4	0	0	0	1	0	0	0	1	0	1	0	0	0	.250	.294
Hale, Chip, Minnesota*	.380	19	71	12	27	31	1	0	1	10	1	0	1	8	0	3	0	1	1	.437	.450
Hamilton, Darryl, Milwaukee*	.000	1	0	1	0	0	0	0	0	0	0	0	0	0	0	0	0	0	0	.000	.000
Hammonds, Jeffrey, Baltimore	.190	8	21	2	4	7	0	0	1	2	1	0	0	1	1	3	0	0	0	.333	.227
Hanson, Erik, Seattle	.000	1	0	1	0	0	0	0	0	0	0	0	0	0	0	0	0	0	0	.000	.000
Harper, Brian, Minnesota	.276	7	29	1	8	10	2	0	0	4	0	0	1	0	0	4	0	0	0	.345	.300
Harris, Donald, Texas	.000	3	0	2	0	0	0	0	0	0	0	0	0	0	0	0	0	0	0	.000	.000
Haselman, Bill, Seattle	.417	4	12	3	5	8	0	0	1	3	0	1	0	3	0	2	1	0	0	.667	.500
Hemond, Scott, Oakland	.000	3	1	1	0	0	0	0	0	0	0	0	0	0	0	1	0	0	0	.000	.000
Henderson, Dave, Oakland	.160	28	100	9	16	31	3	0	4	14	0	3	0	11	0	35	0	0	1	.310	.237
Henderson, Rickey, Oakland	.292	16	48	10	14	23	3	0	2	3	0	0	1	17	1	15	3	2	1	.479	.477
Hiatt, Phil, Kansas City	.176	9	17	3	3	7	1	0	1	2	0	0	0	0	0	6	0	0	0	.412	.176
Hill, Glenallen, Cleveland	.127	18	55	4	7	14	1	0	2	6	0	0	0	4	1	18	2	1	1	.255	.183
Hoiles, Chris, Baltimore	.200	2	5	1	1	2	1	0	0	0	0	0	0	3	1	3	0	0	0	.400	.500
Horn, Sam, Cleveland*	.469	11	32	8	15	28	1	0	4	8	0	1	1	0	4	0	0	1	.875	.486
Howard, Thomas, Cleveland†	.227	7	22	3	5	6	1	0	0	1	0	1	0	1	0	3	0	0	0	.273	.217
Howitt, Dann, Seattle*	.200	2	5	0	1	1	0	0	0	0	0	0	0	0	0	1	0	0	0	.200	.200
Hrbek, Kent, Minnesota*	.333	2	6	1	2	5	0	0	1	2	0	0	0	0	0	0	0	0	0	.833	.333
Hulett, Tim, Baltimore	.000	2	2	0	0	0	0	0	0	0	0	0	0	0	0	0	0	0	0	.000	.000
Hulse, Dave, Texas*	.500	2	2	1	1	1	0	0	0	2	0	0	0	0	0	0	0	0	1	.500	.500
Humphreys, Mike, New York	.333	3	3	0	1	2	1	0	0	0	0	0	0	0	0	1	0	0	0	.667	.333
Jackson, Bo, Chicago	.213	36	127	16	27	51	3	0	7	25	0	1	0	8	0	54	0	1	2	.402	.257
James, Dion, New York*	1.000	1	1	0	1	1	0	0	0	0	0	0	0	0	0	0	0	0	0	1.000	1.000
Javier, Stan, California†	.500	1	2	0	1	1	0	0	0	0	0	0	0	0	0	1	0	0	0	.500	.500
Jefferson, Reggie, Cleveland†	.256	88	316	33	81	125	10	2	10	31	3	1	3	21	6	69	1	3	6	.396	.308
Jose, Felix, Kansas City†	.250	1	4	0	1	1	0	0	0	0	0	0	0	0	0	1	0	0	0	.250	.250
Kirby, Wayne, Cleveland*	.000	5	3	0	0	0	0	0	0	0	0	0	0	1	0	0	0	0	0	.000	.250
Kreuter, Chad, Detroit†	.500	2	2	1	1	1	0	0	0	0	0	0	0	0	0	0	0	0	0	.500	.500
Lampkin, Tom, Milwaukee*	.000	1	1	0	0	0	0	0	0	0	0	0	0	0	0	0	0	0	0	.000	.000
Larkin, Gene, Minnesota†	.300	3	10	0	3	6	1	0	0	3	0	0	0	4	0	0	0	0	1	.600	.500
Lee, Manny, Texas†	.000	1	0	1	0	0	0	0	0	0	0	0	0	0	0	0	0	0	0	.000	.000
Leonard, Mark, Baltimore*	.000	3	9	0	0	0	0	0	0	2	0	2	0	1	0	4	0	0	0	.000	.083
Leyritz, Jim, New York	.290	21	69	9	20	35	3	0	4	13	0	0	2	7	1	20	0	0	3	.507	.372
Litton, Greg, Seattle	.421	12	19	3	8	9	1	0	0	3	1	0	0	2	0	4	0	0	0	.474	.476
Livingstone, Scott, Detroit*	.341	32	85	14	29	36	2	1	1	17	1	3	0	7	0	11	0	1	0	.424	.379
Lydy, Scott, Oakland	.000	2	1	0	0	0	0	0	0	0	0	0	0	0	0	0	0	0	0	.000	.000
Lyons, Steve, Boston*	.000	1	0	1	0	0	0	0	0	0	0	0	0	0	0	0	0	0	0	.000	.000
Maas, Kevin, New York*	.196	31	107	14	21	41	2	0	6	17	0	1	1	17	2	24	0	1	0	.383	.310
Magadan, Dave, Seattle*	.333	2	9	2	3	3	0	0	0	1	0	0	1	0	0	0	0	2	.333	.400
Maldonado, Candy, Cleveland	.000	2	3	0	0	0	0	0	0	0	0	0	0	2	0	0	0	0	0	.000	.400
Martin, Norberto, Chicago	.500	1	2	0	1	1	0	0	0	1	0	0	0	0	0	0	0	0	0	.500	.500
Martinez, Chito, Baltimore*	.000	2	6	0	0	0	0	0	0	0	0	0	0	0	0	2	0	0	0	.000	.000
Martinez, Carlos, Cleveland	.151	19	73	4	11	15	1	0	1	2	0	0	0	3	1	11	1	0	0	.205	.184
Martinez, Edgar, Seattle	.232	24	82	16	19	32	4	0	3	8	1	0	0	18	1	10	0	4	.390	.370
Martinez, Tino, Seattle*	.222	6	18	2	4	7	0	0	1	3	0	0	0	9	2	4	0	0	0	.389	.481
Mattingly, Don, New York*	.227	5	22	2	5	12	1	0	2	3	0	0	0	3	0	3	0	0	1	.545	.227
Mayne, Brent, Kansas City*	.000	1	4	0	0	0	0	0	0	0	0	0	0	1	1	0	0	0	0	.000	.200
McCarty, Dave, Minnesota	.500	2	2	1	1	1	0	0	0	0	0	0	0	1	0	0	0	0	0	.500	.667
McLemore, Mark, Baltimore†	.250	1	4	0	1	1	0	0	0	0	0	0	0	0	0	0	0	0	1	.250	.250
McNeely, Jeff, Boston	.000	3	0	1	0	0	0	0	0	0	0	0	0	0	0	0	0	0	0	.000	.000
McReynolds, Kevin, Kansas City	.000	1	4	0	0	0	0	0	0	0	0	0	0	0	0	1	0	0	1	.000	.000
Mercedes, Henry, Oakland	.000	1	1	0	0	0	0	0	0	0	0	0	0	0	0	1	0	0	0	.000	.000
Mercedes, Luis, Baltimore	.000	2	1	1	0	0	0	0	0	0	0	0	0	0	0	0	0	0	0	.000	.000
Merullo, Matt, Chicago*	.056	6	18	1	1	1	0	0	0	0	0	0	0	0	0	1	0	0	0	.056	.056
Miller, Kevin, Kansas City	.063	6	16	4	1	1	0	0	0	0	0	0	0	2	0	3	0	0	0	.063	.211
Milligan, Randy, Cleveland	.000	1	1	0	0	0	0	0	0	0	0	0	0	4	0	0	0	0	0	.000	.800
Molitor, Paul, Toronto	.311	137	543	107	169	260	32	4	17	90	1	8	3	68	3	60	20	2	13	.479	.386
Myers, Greg, California*	.429	2	7	0	3	3	0	0	0	2	0	0	0	0	0	0	0	0	0	.429	.429
Naehring, Tim, Boston	.302	10	43	4	13	18	5	0	0	10	1	0	0	2	0	10	1	0	1	.419	.333
Neel, Troy, Oakland*	.274	85	318	43	87	147	15	0	15	44	0	2	2	34	4	79	3	2	6	.462	.346
Newfield, Marc, Seattle	.259	15	54	4	14	20	3	0	1	7	0	1	1	2	0	6	0	1	1	.370	.293

Player, Team	Avg.	G	AB	R	H	TB	2B	3B	HR	RBI	SH	SF	HP	BB	Int. BB	SO	SB	CS	GI DP	Slg.	OBP
Newson, Warren, Chicago*	.182	10	22	5	4	7	0	0	1	1	0	0	0	6	1	8	0	0	1	.318	.357
Nilsson, Dave, Milwaukee*	.200	4	15	2	3	3	0	0	0	1	0	0	0	1	0	3	0	1	1	.200	.250
Nokes, Matt, New York*	.220	11	41	7	9	22	1	0	4	12	0	1	1	3	0	9	0	0	1	.537	.283
Obando, Sherman, Baltimore	.278	21	72	7	20	28	2	0	2	11	0	0	1	4	0	20	0	0	1	.389	.325
O'Brien, Pete, Seattle*	.253	52	170	27	43	65	4	0	6	21	0	3	0	21	2	18	0	0	7	.382	.330
Olerud, John, Toronto*	.315	20	73	5	23	30	4	0	1	9	0	2	1	12	3	12	0	2	0	.411	.409
O'Neill, Paul, New York*	.200	2	5	0	1	2	1	0	0	0	0	0	0	0	0	2	0	0	1	.400	.200
Ortiz, Luis, Boston	.000	3	3	0	0	0	0	0	0	0	0	0	0	0	0	1	0	0	0	.000	.000
Owen, Spike, New York†	.000	2	1	0	0	0	0	0	0	0	0	0	0	0	0	1	0	0	0	.000	.000
Paquette, Craig, Oakland	.000	1	1	0	0	0	0	0	0	0	0	0	0	0	0	0	0	0	0	.000	.000
Parent, Mark, Baltimore	1.000	1	1	0	1	1	0	0	0	0	0	0	0	0	0	0	0	0	0	1.000	1.000
Pasqua, Dan, Chicago*	.222	6	18	2	4	7	1	1	0	0	0	0	0	1	0	4	0	0	0	.389	.263
Pena, Tony, Boston	.000	1	0	1	0	0	0	0	0	0	0	0	0	0	0	0	0	0	0	.000	.000
Perez, Eduardo, California	.000	3	1	1	0	0	0	0	0	0	0	0	0	0	0	0	0	0	0	.000	.000
Petralli, Geno, Texas†	.250	2	4	1	1	1	0	0	0	1	0	0	0	0	0	0	0	0	0	.250	.250
Phillips, Tony, Detroit†	.438	4	16	4	7	11	1	0	1	4	0	0	0	3	1	3	0	1	0	.688	.526
Pirkl, Greg, Seattle	.000	2	4	0	0	0	0	0	0	0	0	0	0	0	0	2	0	0	0	.000	.000
Polonia, Luis, California*	.188	4	16	2	3	3	0	0	0	0	0	0	0	1	0	3	1	3	0	.188	.235
Puckett, Kirby, Minnesota	.254	17	63	7	16	25	6	0	1	4	0	0	0	5	0	5	0	1	1	.397	.309
Ramirez, Manny, Cleveland	.184	21	49	5	9	16	1	0	2	5	0	0	0	2	0	8	0	0	2	.327	.216
Reboulet, Jeff, Minnesota	.000	1	1	0	0	0	0	0	0	0	0	0	0	0	0	0	0	0	0	.000	.000
Redus, Gary, Texas	.000	1	1	0	0	0	0	0	0	0	0	0	0	0	0	0	0	0	0	.000	.000
Reimer, Kevin, Milwaukee*	.261	83	307	40	80	128	19	1	9	36	0	2	5	19	1	48	3	4	9	.417	.312
Riles, Ernest, Boston*	.323	15	31	8	10	20	1	0	3	7	0	1	0	5	0	9	1	1	1	.645	.405
Rivera, Luis, Boston	.250	7	4	2	1	1	0	0	0	0	0	0	0	1	0	2	0	1	0	.250	.400
Rodriguez, Ivan, Texas	.000	1	4	0	0	0	0	0	0	0	0	0	0	0	0	0	0	0	0	.000	.000
Rowland, Rich, Detroit	.200	3	5	1	1	1	0	0	0	0	0	0	0	0	0	2	0	0	0	.200	.200
Salmon, Tim, California	.750	1	4	2	3	5	2	0	0	1	0	0	0	1	0	1	0	0	1	1.250	.800
Sasser, Mackey, Seattle*	.149	19	47	2	7	8	1	0	0	1	0	1	0	6	2	8	1	0	1	.170	.241
Sax, Steve, Chicago	.235	21	17	5	4	5	1	0	0	2	1	0	0	2	0	2	3	1	0	.294	.316
Segui, David, Baltimore†	.000	1	1	0	0	0	0	0	0	0	0	0	0	0	0	0	0	0	0	.000	.000
Seitzer, Kevin, Oak.-Mil.	.385	6	13	2	5	8	0	0	1	5	0	0	1	1	0	1	1	1	2	.615	.467
Sheets, Larry, Seattle*	.167	5	12	0	2	3	1	0	0	1	0	0	0	2	0	0	0	1	0	.250	.286
Sierra, Ruben, Oakland†	.216	25	102	15	22	39	3	1	4	17	0	2	0	6	0	20	6	1	3	.382	.255
Smith, Lonnie, Baltimore	.308	5	13	3	4	10	0	0	2	3	0	0	0	3	0	6	0	0	0	.769	.438
Sorrento, Paul, Cleveland*	.000	1	1	0	0	0	0	0	0	0	0	0	0	0	0	1	0	0	0	.000	.000
Stankiewicz, Andy, New York	.000	1	0	1	0	0	0	0	0	0	0	0	0	0	0	0	0	0	0	.000	.000
Stanley, Mike, New York	.000	2	3	0	0	0	0	0	0	2	0	2	0	0	0	1	0	0	0	.000	.000
Steinbach, Terry, Oakland	.474	6	19	2	9	12	0	0	1	4	0	0	0	1	0	3	1	0	1	.632	.500
Surhoff, B.J., Milwaukee*	.000	1	4	0	0	0	0	0	0	0	0	0	0	1	0	1	0	0	0	.000	.200
Sveum, Dale, Oakland†	.143	2	7	0	1	1	0	0	0	1	0	0	0	2	0	2	0	0	0	.143	.333
Tartabull, Danny, New York	.260	88	327	57	85	166	21	0	20	70	0	1	2	58	6	94	0	0	5	.508	.374
Tettleton, Mickey, Detroit†	.300	4	10	2	3	6	0	0	1	2	0	0	0	4	0	2	0	0	0	.600	.500
Thomas, Frank, Chicago	.412	4	17	3	7	13	3	0	1	7	0	0	0	3	0	4	0	0	1	.765	.500
Thon, Dickie, Milwaukee	.211	14	38	1	8	8	0	0	0	4	1	0	0	4	0	7	2	2	1	.211	.286
Thurman, Gary, Detroit	.500	8	2	1	1	1	0	0	0	0	0	0	0	0	0	1	1	0	0	.500	.500
Tinsley, Lee, Seattle†	.000	2	3	0	0	0	0	0	0	0	0	0	0	0	0	1	0	0	1	.000	.000
Trammell, Alan, Detroit	.400	6	20	2	8	10	2	0	0	3	0	0	0	3	0	4	1	1	0	.500	.478
Treadway, Jeff, Cleveland*	.500	4	16	4	8	12	1	0	1	4	0	0	0	3	2	0	1	0	0	.750	.579
Turang, Brian, Seattle	.000	1	0	1	0	0	0	0	0	0	0	0	0	0	0	0	0	0	0	.000	.000
Vaughn, Greg, Milwaukee	.251	58	219	37	55	97	9	0	11	38	0	1	1	39	8	57	4	1	1	.443	.365
Vaughn, Mo, Boston*	.239	19	67	10	16	29	4	0	3	11	0	2	0	12	4	19	0	0	2	.433	.346
Velarde, Randy, New York	.000	1	1	0	0	0	0	0	0	0	0	0	0	0	0	0	0	0	0	.000	.000
Vina, Fernando, Seattle*	.000	2	0	1	0	0	0	0	0	0	0	0	0	0	0	0	0	0	0	.000	.000
Vizquel, Omar, Seattle†	.000	2	0	1	0	0	0	0	0	0	0	0	0	0	0	0	0	0	0	.000	.000
Voigt, Jack, Baltimore	.400	9	15	4	6	13	1	0	2	7	0	0	0	2	0	1	0	0	1	.867	.471
Walewander, Jim, California†	.000	3	0	0	0	0	0	0	0	0	0	0	0	0	0	0	1	0	0	.000	.000
Walton, Jerome, California	.000	4	0	1	0	0	0	0	0	0	0	0	0	0	0	0	0	0	0	.000	.000
Webster, Lenny, Minnesota	.250	1	4	1	1	1	0	0	0	0	0	0	0	0	0	1	0	0	0	.250	.250
Winfield, Dave, Minnesota	.258	105	414	54	107	168	23	1	12	49	0	1	0	33	1	79	2	2	13	.406	.313
Yount, Robin, Milwaukee	.350	6	20	2	7	12	1	2	0	6	0	0	0	1	0	4	1	0	0	.600	.381
Zupcic, Bob, Boston	.000	5	1	2	0	0	0	0	0	0	0	0	0	0	0	1	0	0	0	.000	.000

DESIGNATED HITTERS WITH TWO OR MORE TEAMS

Player, Team	Avg.	G	AB	R	H	TB	2B	3B	HR	RBI	SH	SF	HP	BB	Int. BB	SO	SB	CS	GI DP	Slg.	OBP
Calderon, Ivan, Boston	.246	19	57	5	14	17	1	1	0	4	1	1	0	3	0	10	0	1	3	.298	.279
Calderon, Ivan, Chicago	.130	6	23	1	3	5	2	0	0	3	0	0	0	0	0	5	0	0	1	.217	.130
Deer, Rob, Detroit	.300	4	10	1	3	6	0	0	1	3	0	1	0	0	0	3	0	1	0	.600	.273
Deer, Rob, Boston	.125	2	8	1	1	1	0	0	0	0	0	0	0	2	0	4	0	0	0	.125	.300
Gaetti, Gary, California	.176	5	17	2	3	3	0	0	0	3	0	1	0	2	0	4	0	0	1	.176	.250
Gaetti, Gary, Kansas City	1.000	1	1	0	1	1	0	0	0	1	0	0	0	2	0	0	0	0	0	1.000	1.000
Seitzer, Kevin, Oakland	.250	3	4	0	1	1	0	0	0	0	0	0	0	0	0	1	0	1	1	.250	.400
Seitzer, Kevin, Milwaukee	.444	3	9	2	4	7	0	0	1	5	0	0	1	1	0	0	1	0	1	.778	.500

The following designated hitters, each of whom appeared in at least one game, had no plate appearances: Huson, Jeff, Texas (2); Richardson, Jeff, Boston (2); Alexander, Manny, Baltimore; Bautista, Danny, Detroit; Bosio, Chris, Seattle; Byrd, Jim, Boston; Gallego, Mike, New York; Koslofski, Kevin, Kansas City; Lovullo, Torey, California; Reynolds, Harold, Baltimore; Spiers, Bill, Milwaukee; Williams, Gerald, New York.

PINCH-HITTING

TEAM

Team	Avg.	AB	R	H	TB	2B	3B	HR	RBI	SH	SF	HP	BB	Int. BB	SO	SB	CS	GI DP	Slg.	OBP
Detroit	.316	98	15	31	44	7	0	2	26	0	1	1	12	1	18	0	1	0	.449	.393
Texas	.315	108	13	34	49	7	1	2	21	4	0	0	11	1	28	2	1	2	.454	.378
New York	.272	125	18	34	55	7	1	4	21	2	0	1	15	3	37	1	1	1	.440	.355
California	.272	103	11	28	43	2	2	3	15	2	1	1	15	2	24	0	0	4	.417	.367
Seattle	.267	131	11	35	50	6	0	3	26	3	4	0	13	6	24	3	0	5	.382	.324
Kansas City	.260	127	15	33	44	11	0	0	23	0	2	0	18	0	33	0	0	1	.346	.347
Oakland	.250	100	13	25	41	5	1	3	17	1	2	0	13	2	21	1	1	1	.410	.330
Minnesota	.222	135	11	30	42	6	0	2	20	0	3	0	21	2	29	1	0	3	.311	.340
Cleveland	.205	161	13	33	52	7	0	4	19	0	1	1	15	1	37	0	1	3	.323	.275
Milwaukee	.193	109	9	21	26	3	1	0	12	1	0	0	11	3	20	0	0	6	.239	.267
Chicago	.187	75	10	14	17	0	0	1	7	0	0	0	12	1	19	0	0	2	.227	.299
Toronto	.185	27	1	5	8	0	0	1	5	0	0	1	2	0	7	0	0	0	.296	.267
Baltimore	.185	54	9	10	11	1	0	0	10	0	1	1	11	3	18	0	0	0	.204	.328
Boston	.179	134	5	24	37	10	0	1	18	0	1	0	17	4	33	0	2	6	.276	.270
Totals	.240	1487	154	357	519	72	6	26	240	13	13	9	186	29	348	8	7	34	.349	.326

INDIVIDUAL

TOP 10 PINCH-HITTERS

Minimum 20 at-bats.   *Lefthanded batter.   †Switch-hitter.

Player, Team	Avg.	G	AB	R	H	TB	2B	3B	HR	RBI	SH	SF	HP	BB	Int. BB	SO	SB	CS	GI DP	Slg.	OBP
James, Dion, New York*	.409	27	22	5	9	9	0	0	0	3	1	0	0	3	0	5	0	0	0	.409	.480
Myers, Greg, California*	.320	28	25	3	8	15	1	0	2	8	0	1	0	0	0	3	0	0	1	.600	.308
Brooks, Hubie, Kansas City*	.303	36	33	2	10	11	1	0	0	8	0	1	0	2	0	10	0	0	0	.333	.333
Sasser, Mackey, Seattle*	.261	35	23	3	6	9	3	0	0	6	0	1	0	5	4	6	0	0	1	.391	.379
Javier, Stan, California†	.259	32	27	2	7	11	0	2	0	4	0	0	0	5	1	6	0	0	1	.407	.375
Treadway, Jeff, Cleveland*	.250	39	36	2	9	13	1	0	1	2	0	0	0	2	0	6	0	0	0	.361	.289
Redus, Gary, Texas	.238	24	21	2	5	8	0	0	1	5	0	0	0	2	0	5	1	1	0	.381	.304
Howard, Thomas, Cleveland†	.200	28	25	2	5	8	3	0	0	3	0	0	0	3	0	7	0	0	0	.320	.286
Riles, Ernest, Boston*	.170	56	47	2	8	15	4	0	1	9	0	1	0	7	3	14	0	2	2	.319	.273
Felder, Mike, Seattle†	.130	26	23	0	3	3	0	0	0	3	1	0	0	2	0	2	2	0	1	.130	.200

NOTE: Only 10 batters (rather than the usual 15) are listed above since they are the only players to have the minimum 20 pinch-hit at-bats during the 1993 American League season.

ALL PINCH-HITTERS

*Lefthanded batter.   †Switch-hitter.

Player, Team	Avg.	G	AB	R	H	TB	2B	3B	HR	RBI	SH	SF	HP	BB	Int. BB	SO	SB	CS	GI DP	Slg.	OBP
Abbott, Kurt, Oakland	.500	2	2	1	1	4	0	0	1	1	0	0	0	0	0	0	0	0	0	2.000	.500
Aldrete, Mike, Oakland*	.412	19	17	4	7	13	1	1	1	4	0	0	0	2	1	4	1	0	0	.765	.474
Alomar, Roberto, Toronto†	.500	2	2	0	1	1	0	0	0	0	0	0	0	0	0	0	0	0	0	.500	.500
Alomar, Sandy, Cleveland	.500	2	2	0	1	1	0	0	0	0	0	0	0	0	0	0	0	0	0	.500	.500
Amaral, Rich, Seattle	.600	7	5	1	3	4	1	0	0	2	1	1	0	0	0	1	0	0	0	.800	.500
Anderson, Brady, Baltimore*	.000	1	1	0	0	0	0	0	0	0	0	0	0	0	0	0	0	0	0	.000	.000
Armas, Marcos, Oakland	.000	2	2	0	0	0	0	0	0	0	0	0	0	0	0	0	0	0	0	.000	.000
Backman, Wally, Seattle*	.000	1	1	0	0	0	0	0	0	0	0	0	0	0	0	0	0	0	0	.000	.000
Baerga, Carlos, Cleveland†	.000	1	1	0	0	0	0	0	0	0	0	0	0	0	0	0	0	0	0	.000	.000
Baines, Harold, Baltimore*	.333	8	6	1	2	2	0	0	0	2	0	0	0	1	0	1	0	0	0	.333	.429
Balboni, Steve, Texas	.000	1	1	0	0	0	0	0	0	0	0	0	0	0	0	1	0	0	0	.000	.000
Barnes, Skeeter, Detroit	.353	19	17	1	6	7	1	0	0	6	0	1	0	1	0	5	0	0	0	.412	.368
Bell, Juan, Milwaukee†	.000	2	1	0	0	0	0	0	0	0	0	0	0	1	0	1	0	0	0	.000	.500
Belle, Albert, Cleveland	.000	1	1	0	0	0	0	0	0	0	0	0	0	0	0	0	0	0	0	.000	.000
Blankenship, Lance, Oakland	.400	8	5	2	2	2	0	0	0	1	1	0	0	2	0	0	0	0	0	.400	.571
Blosser, Greg, Boston*	.000	9	7	0	0	0	0	0	0	0	0	0	0	2	0	1	0	0	0	.000	.222
Blowers, Mike, Seattle	.333	8	6	0	2	2	0	0	0	3	0	0	0	1	0	0	0	0	0	.333	.429
Boggs, Wade, New York*	.167	6	6	0	1	1	0	0	0	0	0	0	0	0	0	2	0	0	0	.167	.167
Bordick, Mike, Oakland	.000	2	2	0	0	0	0	0	0	0	0	0	0	0	0	1	0	0	0	.000	.000
Brett, George, Kansas City*	.333	6	6	1	2	4	2	0	0	0	0	0	0	0	0	1	0	0	0	.667	.333
Brito, Bernardo, Minnesota	.083	13	12	0	1	2	1	0	0	1	0	0	0	1	0	5	0	0	0	.167	.154
Brooks, Hubie, Kansas City	.303	36	33	2	10	11	1	0	0	8	0	1	0	2	0	10	0	0	0	.333	.333
Brosius, Scott, Oakland	.333	7	6	0	2	3	1	0	0	0	0	0	0	1	0	1	0	0	0	.500	.429
Browne, Jerry, Oakland†	.100	13	10	2	1	2	1	0	0	3	0	1	0	2	0	2	0	0	0	.200	.231
Bruett, J.T., Minnesota*	.250	5	4	1	1	2	1	0	0	1	0	0	0	0	0	0	0	0	0	.500	.250
Brunansky, Tom, Milwaukee	.000	9	8	0	0	0	0	0	0	0	0	0	0	1	0	2	0	0	1	.000	.111
Buford, Damon, Baltimore	.333	3	3	0	1	1	0	0	0	0	0	0	0	0	0	2	0	0	0	.333	.333
Buhner, Jay, Seattle	.500	3	2	1	1	4	0	0	1	0	0	0	0	0	0	1	0	0	0	2.000	.333
Burks, Ellis, Chicago	.400	5	5	0	2	2	0	0	0	0	0	0	0	0	0	1	0	0	0	.400	.400
Bush, Randy, Minnesota*	.211	27	19	0	4	5	1	0	0	2	0	0	0	6	1	5	0	0	1	.263	.400
Butler, Rob, Toronto*	.000	1	1	0	0	0	0	0	0	0	0	0	0	0	0	0	0	0	0	.000	.000
Calderon, Ivan, Bos.-Chi.	.071	16	14	0	1	1	0	0	0	0	0	0	0	2	0	3	0	0	2	.071	.188
Canate, Willie, Toronto	.000	3	3	0	0	0	0	0	0	0	0	0	0	0	0	0	0	0	0	.000	.000
Canseco, Jose, Texas	.000	3	3	0	0	0	0	0	0	0	0	0	0	0	0	1	0	0	0	.000	.000
Carey, Paul, Baltimore*	.000	6	6	0	0	0	0	0	0	0	0	0	0	0	0	2	0	0	0	.000	.000

Player, Team	Avg.	G	AB	R	H	TB	2B	3B	HR	RBI	SH	SF	HP	BB	Int. BB	SO	SB	CS	GI DP	Slg.	OBP
Carter, Joe, Toronto	.000	1	1	0	0	0	0	0	0	0	0	0	0	0	0	0	0	0	0	.000	.000
Cedeno, Domingo, Toronto†	.000	1	1	0	0	0	0	0	0	0	0	0	0	0	0	1	0	0	0	.000	.000
Coles, Darnell, Toronto	.250	5	4	1	1	4	0	0	1	3	0	0	0	1	0	0	0	0	0	1.000	.400
Cooper, Scott, Boston*	.500	5	4	1	2	3	1	0	0	0	0	0	0	1	0	1	0	0	0	.750	.600
Cora, Joey, Chicago†	.000	3	3	0	0	0	0	0	0	0	0	0	0	0	0	2	0	0	0	.000	.000
Cotto, Henry, Seattle	.300	13	10	0	3	3	0	0	0	0	0	0	0	0	0	3	0	0	0	.300	.300
Curtis, Chad, California	.500	2	2	1	1	1	0	0	0	0	0	0	0	0	0	0	0	0	0	.500	.500
Cuyler, Milt, Detroit†	.000	2	2	0	0	0	0	0	0	0	0	0	0	0	0	1	0	0	0	.000	.000
Dascenzo, Doug, Texas†	.545	14	11	3	6	8	2	0	0	0	1	0	0	1	0	2	0	0	0	.727	.583
Davis, Butch, Texas	.333	10	9	1	3	5	2	0	0	0	1	0	0	0	0	2	0	0	0	.556	.333
Davis, Chili, California†	.000	2	1	0	0	0	0	0	0	0	0	0	0	1	0	0	0	0	1	.000	.500
Davis, Eric, Detroit	.000	3	2	0	0	0	0	0	0	0	0	0	0	1	0	0	0	0	0	.000	.333
Davis, Glenn, Baltimore	.000	1	1	0	0	0	0	0	0	0	0	0	0	0	0	1	0	0	0	.000	.000
Dawson, Andre, Boston	.500	4	4	0	2	3	1	0	0	3	0	0	0	0	0	1	0	0	1	.750	.500
Deer, Rob, Det.-Bos.	.250	8	8	1	2	5	0	0	1	1	0	0	0	0	0	2	0	0	1	.625	.250
Delgado, Carlos, Toronto*	.000	1	1	0	0	0	0	0	0	0	0	0	0	0	0	0	0	0	0	.000	.000
Denson, Drew, Chicago†	.250	4	4	0	1	1	0	0	0	0	0	0	0	0	0	2	0	0	0	.250	.250
Diaz, Alex, Milwaukee†	.250	4	4	1	1	2	1	0	0	0	0	0	0	0	0	1	0	0	0	.500	.250
Diaz, Mario, Texas	.333	3	3	0	1	1	0	0	0	0	0	0	0	0	0	2	0	0	0	.333	.333
DiSarcina, Gary, California	.000	1	1	0	0	0	0	0	0	0	0	0	0	0	0	0	0	0	0	.000	.000
Doran, Bill, Milwaukee†	.200	11	10	1	2	2	0	0	0	1	0	0	0	1	1	0	0	0	1	.200	.273
Ducey, Rob, Texas*	1.000	1	1	0	1	2	1	0	0	0	0	0	0	0	0	0	0	0	0	2.000	1.000
Easley, Damion, California	.333	4	3	2	1	1	0	0	0	0	0	0	0	1	0	0	0	0	0	.333	.500
Edmonds, Jim, California*	1.000	1	1	1	1	2	1	0	0	0	0	0	0	0	0	0	0	0	0	2.000	1.000
Espinoza, Alvaro, Cleveland	.250	8	8	1	2	3	1	0	0	0	0	0	0	0	0	0	0	0	3	.375	.250
Felder, Mike, Seattle†	.130	26	23	0	3	3	0	0	0	3	1	0	0	2	0	2	2	0	1	.130	.200
Fielder, Cecil, Detroit	.000	1	1	0	0	0	0	0	0	0	0	0	0	0	0	0	0	0	0	.000	.000
Fisk, Carlton, Chicago	.000	3	3	0	0	0	0	0	0	0	0	0	0	0	0	2	0	0	0	.000	.000
Fletcher, Scott, Boston	.000	4	4	0	0	0	0	0	0	1	0	0	0	0	0	0	0	0	0	.000	.000
Fox, Eric, Oakland†	.000	3	3	0	0	0	0	0	0	0	0	0	0	0	0	0	0	0	0	.000	.000
Franco, Julio, Texas	.333	4	3	0	1	1	0	0	0	1	0	0	0	1	0	1	0	0	0	.333	.500
Fryman, Travis, Detroit	.000	1	0	0	0	0	0	0	0	0	0	0	0	1	0	0	0	0	0	.000	1.000
Gaetti, Gary, Cal.-K.C.	.125	8	8	0	1	1	0	0	0	1	0	0	0	0	0	2	0	0	0	.125	.125
Gagne, Greg, Kansas City	.000	1	1	0	0	0	0	0	0	0	0	0	0	0	0	0	0	0	0	.000	.000
Gallego, Mike, New York	.000	2	1	0	0	0	0	0	0	0	0	0	0	0	0	0	0	0	0	.000	.000
Gates, Brent, Oakland†	.333	4	3	1	1	1	0	0	0	1	0	0	0	1	1	1	0	0	0	.333	.500
Gibson, Kirk, Detroit*	.182	13	11	0	2	3	1	0	0	3	0	0	1	1	0	3	0	0	0	.273	.308
Gladden, Dan, Detroit	.250	5	4	0	1	1	0	0	0	0	0	0	0	1	0	1	0	0	0	.250	.400
Gonzales, Rene, California	.400	9	5	0	2	2	0	0	0	0	0	0	0	4	1	3	0	0	0	.400	.667
Gonzalez, Juan, Texas	1.000	1	1	0	1	1	0	0	0	1	0	0	0	0	0	0	0	0	0	1.000	1.000
Grebeck, Craig, Chicago	.000	3	3	0	0	0	0	0	0	0	0	0	0	0	0	1	0	0	0	.000	.000
Greenwell, Mike, Boston*	.000	5	3	1	0	0	0	0	0	0	0	0	0	2	0	0	0	0	0	.000	.400
Griffin, Alfredo, Toronto†	.000	2	2	0	0	0	0	0	0	0	0	0	0	0	0	1	0	0	0	.000	.000
Guillen, Ozzie, Chicago*	.333	3	3	0	1	1	0	0	0	1	0	0	0	0	0	1	0	0	0	.333	.333
Gwynn, Chris, Kansas City*	.375	21	16	3	6	7	1	0	0	4	0	0	0	3	0	4	0	0	0	.438	.474
Hale, Chip, Minnesota*	.412	21	17	2	7	8	1	0	0	6	0	0	2	2	0	3	0	0	0	.471	.524
Hamelin, Bob, Kansas City*	.000	1	1	0	0	0	0	0	0	0	0	0	0	0	0	1	0	0	0	.000	.000
Hamilton, Darryl, Milwaukee*	.000	7	5	0	0	0	0	0	0	0	0	0	0	1	1	0	0	0	0	.000	.167
Hammonds, Jeffrey, Baltimore	1.000	2	2	0	2	2	0	0	0	0	0	0	0	0	0	0	0	0	0	1.000	1.000
Harper, Brian, Minnesota	.625	10	8	1	5	9	1	0	1	5	0	0	0	2	1	1	0	0	0	1.125	.700
Harris, Donald, Texas	.333	3	3	0	1	1	0	0	0	2	0	0	0	0	0	1	0	0	0	.333	.333
Haselman, Bill, Seattle	.167	6	6	1	1	4	0	0	1	1	0	0	0	0	0	2	0	0	1	.667	.167
Hatcher, Billy, Boston	.250	4	4	0	1	1	0	0	0	1	0	0	0	0	0	0	0	0	0	.250	.250
Helfand, Eric, Oakland*	.333	3	3	1	1	1	0	0	0	0	0	0	0	0	0	0	0	0	0	.333	.333
Hemond, Scott, Oakland	.333	4	3	0	1	2	1	0	0	0	0	0	0	1	0	1	0	0	0	.667	.500
Henderson, Dave, Oakland	.125	9	8	0	1	1	0	0	0	2	0	1	0	0	0	2	0	0	0	.125	.111
Henderson, Rickey, Oakland	.000	3	2	0	0	0	0	0	0	0	0	0	0	1	0	1	0	0	0	.000	.333
Hiatt, Phil, Kansas City	.000	4	2	1	0	0	0	0	0	0	0	0	0	2	0	0	0	0	0	.000	.500
Hill, Glenallen, Cleveland	.200	14	10	1	2	5	0	0	1	1	0	0	0	0	0	3	0	0	0	.500	.200
Hocking, Denny, Minnesota†	.000	5	5	0	0	0	0	0	0	0	0	0	0	0	0	1	0	0	0	.000	.000
Hoiles, Chris, Baltimore	.000	3	3	0	0	0	0	0	0	0	0	0	0	0	0	2	0	0	0	.000	.000
Horn, Sam, Cleveland*	.000	2	1	0	0	0	0	0	0	0	0	0	0	1	0	1	0	0	0	.000	.500
Howard, David, Kansas City†	.000	1	0	0	0	0	0	0	0	0	0	0	0	1	0	0	0	0	0	.000	1.000
Howard, Thomas, Cleveland†	.200	28	25	2	5	8	3	0	0	3	0	0	0	3	0	7	0	0	0	.320	.286
Howitt, Dann, Seattle*	.000	4	4	0	0	0	0	0	0	0	0	0	0	0	0	1	0	0	0	.000	.000
Hrbek, Kent, Minnesota*	.125	11	8	1	1	1	0	0	0	0	0	0	0	3	0	2	0	0	0	.125	.364
Huff, Mike, Chicago	.000	3	2	0	0	0	0	0	0	0	0	0	0	1	0	1	0	0	0	.000	.333
Hulett, Tim, Baltimore	.167	7	6	2	1	2	1	0	0	2	0	0	0	1	0	2	0	0	0	.333	.286
Hulse, Dave, Texas*	1.000	5	5	3	5	7	0	1	0	3	0	0	0	0	0	0	1	0	0	1.400	1.000
Humphreys, Mike, New York	.143	7	7	0	1	2	1	0	0	0	0	0	0	0	0	2	0	0	0	.286	.143
Huson, Jeff, Texas*	.000	3	3	0	0	0	0	0	0	0	0	0	0	0	0	1	0	0	0	.000	.000
Jackson, Bo, Chicago	.375	8	8	2	3	6	0	0	1	2	0	0	0	0	0	3	0	0	0	.750	.375
Jaha, John, Milwaukee	.000	4	4	0	0	0	0	0	0	0	0	0	0	0	0	1	0	0	0	.000	.000
James, Chris, Texas	.000	1	1	0	0	0	0	0	0	0	0	0	0	0	0	1	0	0	0	.000	.000
James, Dion, New York*	.409	27	22	5	9	9	0	0	0	3	1	0	0	3	1	3	0	0	0	.409	.480
Javier, Stan, California†	.259	32	27	2	7	11	0	2	0	4	0	0	0	5	1	6	0	0	1	.407	.375
Jefferson, Reggie, Cleveland†	.176	21	17	1	3	6	0	0	1	4	0	0	1	3	0	4	0	1	0	.353	.333
Johnson, Lance, Chicago*	.000	2	2	1	0	0	0	0	0	0	0	0	0	0	0	0	0	0	0	.000	.000
Jorgensen, Terry, Minnesota	.000	6	3	0	0	0	0	0	0	0	0	0	0	3	0	0	0	0	0	.000	.500
Jose, Felix, Kansas City†	.222	11	9	1	2	3	1	0	0	0	0	0	0	2	0	3	0	0	0	.333	.364
Joyner, Wally, Kansas City*	.000	2	1	0	0	0	0	0	0	1	0	0	0	1	0	0	0	0	0	.000	.500
Karkovice, Ron, Chicago	.000	3	2	1	0	0	0	0	0	0	0	0	0	1	0	1	0	0	0	.000	.333
Kelly, Pat, New York	.000	2	2	0	0	0	0	0	0	0	0	0	0	0	0	1	0	0	0	.000	.000
Kirby, Wayne, Cleveland*	.000	12	10	1	0	0	0	0	0	0	0	0	0	1	0	2	0	0	0	.000	.091
Kmak, Joe, Milwaukee	.000	1	1	0	0	0	0	0	0	0	0	0	0	0	0	0	0	0	0	.000	.000
Knoblauch, Chuck, Minnesota	.000	4	4	0	0	0	0	0	0	0	0	0	0	0	0	0	0	0	0	.000	.000
Knorr, Randy, Toronto	.000	1	1	0	0	0	0	0	0	0	0	0	0	0	0	1	0	0	0	.000	.000

Player, Team	Avg.	G	AB	R	H	TB	2B	3B	HR	RBI	SH	SF	HP	BB	Int. BB	SO	SB	CS	GI DP	Slg.	OBP
Koslofski, Kevin, Kansas City*	.000	1	1	0	0	0	0	0	0	0	0	0	0	0	0	0	0	0	0	.000	.000
Kreuter, Chad, Detroit†	.500	11	8	3	4	9	2	0	1	7	0	0	0	3	0	2	0	0	1	1.125	.636
Lampkin, Tom, Milwaukee*	.154	18	13	2	2	2	0	0	0	2	0	0	0	2	0	3	0	0	0	.154	.267
Larkin, Gene, Minnesota†	.286	16	14	3	4	4	0	0	0	1	0	0	0	2	0	0	0	0	1	.286	.375
Lee, Derek, Minnesota*	.200	5	5	0	1	2	1	0	0	2	0	0	0	0	0	1	0	0	0	.400	.200
Leonard, Mark, Baltimore*	.000	5	2	0	0	0	0	0	0	1	0	1	0	1	0	1	0	0	0	.000	.250
Levis, Jesse, Cleveland*	.125	8	8	0	1	1	0	0	0	0	0	0	0	0	0	3	0	0	0	.125	.125
Leyritz, Jim, New York	.308	17	13	3	4	5	1	0	0	5	0	0	1	3	2	4	0	0	0	.385	.471
Lind, Jose, Kansas City	1.000	1	1	0	1	1	0	0	0	2	0	0	0	0	0	0	0	0	0	1.000	1.000
Listach, Pat, Milwaukee†	.500	2	2	0	1	1	0	0	0	0	0	0	0	0	0	0	0	0	0	.500	.500
Litton, Greg, Seattle	.400	18	15	1	6	7	1	0	0	2	1	0	0	0	0	1	0	0	0	.467	.400
Livingstone, Scott, Detroit*	.333	11	9	1	3	3	0	0	0	1	0	0	0	0	0	0	0	0	0	.333	.333
Lofton, Kenny, Cleveland*	.000	2	2	0	0	0	0	0	0	0	0	0	0	0	0	0	0	0	0	.000	.000
Lovullo, Torey, California†	.417	15	12	2	5	8	0	0	1	3	0	0	0	3	0	4	0	0	0	.667	.533
Lydy, Scott, Oakland	.000	2	1	0	0	0	0	0	0	0	0	0	0	0	0	0	0	0	0	.000	.000
Lyons, Steve, Boston*	.200	6	5	0	1	2	1	0	0	0	0	0	0	1	0	1	0	0	0	.400	.333
Maas, Kevin, New York*	.250	14	12	2	3	7	1	0	1	4	0	0	0	1	0	4	1	0	0	.583	.308
Macfarlane, Mike, Kansas City	.417	15	12	0	5	7	2	0	0	3	0	1	0	2	0	4	0	0	0	.583	.467
Mack, Shane, Minnesota	.000	1	1	0	0	0	0	0	0	0	0	0	0	0	0	0	0	0	0	.000	.000
Magadan, Dave, Seattle*	.375	9	8	2	3	3	0	0	0	1	0	0	1	1	1	2	0	0	0	.375	.444
Maksudian, Mike, Minnesota*	.000	1	1	0	0	0	0	0	0	0	0	0	0	1	0	0	0	0	0	.000	.000
Maldonado, Candy, Cleveland	.500	6	6	0	3	4	1	0	0	4	0	0	0	0	0	0	0	0	0	.667	.500
Martin, Norberto, Chicago†	.000	1	1	0	0	0	0	0	0	0	0	0	0	0	0	0	0	0	0	.000	.000
Martinez, Carlos, Cleveland	.125	9	8	1	1	4	0	0	1	4	0	1	0	0	0	0	0	0	0	.500	.111
Martinez, Chito, Baltimore*	.000	5	3	0	0	0	0	0	0	0	0	0	0	2	2	1	0	0	0	.000	.400
Martinez, Domingo, Toronto	.500	2	2	1	1	1	0	0	0	2	0	0	0	0	0	0	0	0	0	.500	.500
Martinez, Edgar, Seattle	1.000	2	1	1	1	4	0	0	1	2	0	0	0	1	0	0	0	0	0	4.000	1.000
Mattingly, Don, New York*	.500	2	2	0	1	1	0	0	0	1	0	0	0	0	0	0	0	0	0	.500	.500
Mayne, Brent, Kansas City*	.250	4	4	1	1	2	1	0	0	0	0	0	0	0	0	0	0	0	0	.500	.250
McCarty, Dave, Minnesota	.200	6	5	1	1	1	0	0	0	0	0	0	0	1	0	2	0	0	0	.200	.333
McGwire, Mark, Oakland	.000	2	1	0	0	0	0	0	0	0	0	0	0	1	0	0	0	0	0	.000	.500
McNeely, Jeff, Boston	.000	1	1	0	0	0	0	0	0	0	0	0	0	0	0	0	0	0	0	.000	.000
McRae, Brian, Kansas City†	.000	3	3	0	0	0	0	0	0	0	0	0	0	0	0	1	0	0	0	.000	.000
McReynolds, Kevin, Kansas City	.125	19	16	3	2	3	1	0	0	2	0	0	0	3	0	7	0	0	0	.188	.263
Meares, Pat, Minnesota	.000	1	1	0	0	0	0	0	0	0	0	0	0	0	0	0	0	0	0	.000	.000
Melvin, Bob, Boston	.333	3	3	0	1	1	0	0	0	2	0	0	0	0	0	1	0	0	0	.333	.333
Mercedes, Henry, Oakland	.000	2	2	0	0	0	0	0	0	0	0	0	0	0	0	0	0	0	0	.000	.000
Merullo, Matt, Chicago*	.000	3	3	0	0	0	0	0	0	0	0	0	0	0	0	0	0	0	0	.000	.000
Meulens, Hensley, New York	.143	9	7	1	1	2	1	0	0	0	0	0	0	2	0	2	0	1	0	.286	.333
Miller, Kevin, Kansas City	.000	6	5	0	0	0	0	0	0	0	0	0	0	0	0	1	0	0	0	.000	.000
Milligan, Randy, Cleveland	.500	7	4	1	2	2	0	0	0	1	0	0	0	3	0	0	0	0	0	.500	.714
Munoz, Pedro, Minnesota	.000	3	3	0	0	0	0	0	0	0	0	0	0	0	0	0	0	0	0	.000	.000
Myers, Greg, California*	.320	28	25	3	8	15	1	0	2	8	0	1	0	0	0	3	0	0	1	.600	.308
Naehring, Tim, Boston	.333	6	6	0	2	3	1	0	0	0	0	0	0	0	0	2	0	0	0	.500	.333
Neel, Troy, Oakland*	.143	8	7	1	1	1	0	0	0	3	0	0	0	1	0	1	0	0	0	.143	.250
Newfield, Marc, Seattle	.000	3	3	0	0	0	0	0	0	0	0	0	0	0	0	1	0	0	0	.000	.000
Newson, Warren, Chicago*	.455	14	11	3	5	5	0	0	0	3	0	0	0	3	0	4	0	0	0	.455	.571
Nilsson, Dave, Milwaukee*	.250	4	4	0	1	1	0	0	0	3	0	0	0	0	0	1	0	0	0	.250	.250
Nokes, Matt, New York*	.556	11	9	2	5	12	1	0	2	4	0	0	0	1	0	3	0	0	1	1.333	.600
Obando, Sherman, Baltimore	.000	3	2	1	0	0	0	0	0	0	0	0	1	0	0	1	0	0	0	.000	.333
O'Brien, Pete, Seattle*	.200	14	10	0	2	2	0	0	0	3	0	1	0	1	1	1	0	0	1	.200	.250
O'Leary, Troy, Milwaukee*	.500	2	2	0	1	2	1	0	0	2	0	0	0	0	0	0	0	0	0	1.000	.500
Olerud, John, Toronto*	.000	1	1	0	0	0	0	0	0	0	0	0	0	0	0	0	0	0	0	.000	.000
O'Neill, Paul, New York*	.083	13	12	0	1	1	0	0	0	1	0	0	0	1	0	3	0	0	0	.083	.154
Ortiz, Junior, Cleveland	.000	2	2	0	0	0	0	0	0	0	0	0	0	0	0	0	0	0	0	.000	.000
Ortiz, Luis, Boston	.200	5	5	0	1	1	0	0	0	0	0	0	0	0	0	2	0	0	0	.200	.200
Orton, John, California	.000	3	2	0	0	0	0	0	0	0	0	0	1	0	0	0	0	0	0	.000	.000
Owen, Spike, New York†	.000	5	4	0	0	0	0	0	0	0	0	0	0	1	0	2	0	0	0	.000	.200
Pagliarulo, Mike, Min.-Bal.*	.222	11	9	1	2	5	0	0	1	3	0	0	1	1	0	4	0	0	0	.556	.364
Palmeiro, Rafael, Texas*	.000	2	1	1	0	0	0	0	0	0	0	0	0	1	1	0	0	0	0	.000	.500
Paquette, Craig, Oakland	.250	4	4	0	1	2	1	0	0	0	0	0	0	0	0	0	0	0	0	.500	.250
Parent, Mark, Baltimore	.500	2	2	0	1	1	0	0	0	0	0	0	0	0	0	0	0	0	0	.500	.500
Parrish, Lance, Cleveland	.000	1	1	0	0	0	0	0	0	0	0	0	0	0	0	0	0	0	0	.000	.000
Pasqua, Dan, Chicago*	.143	10	7	0	1	1	0	0	0	0	0	0	0	3	0	1	0	0	1	.143	.400
Peltier, Dan, Texas*	.000	10	8	1	0	0	0	0	0	0	0	0	0	2	0	3	0	0	0	.000	.200
Perez, Eduardo, California	.000	5	4	0	0	0	0	0	0	0	0	0	1	0	0	2	0	0	0	.000	.200
Petralli, Geno, Texas†	.077	19	13	1	1	1	0	0	0	2	1	0	0	2	0	2	0	0	2	.077	.200
Phillips, Tony, Detroit†	.667	4	3	2	2	2	0	0	0	0	0	0	0	1	1	0	0	0	0	.667	.750
Polonia, Luis, California*	.250	9	8	0	2	2	0	0	0	0	0	0	0	0	0	2	0	1	0	.250	.250
Pulliam, Harvey, Kansas City	.167	7	6	1	1	2	1	0	0	0	0	0	0	1	0	1	0	0	1	.333	.286
Quintana, Carlos, Boston	.182	11	11	0	2	2	0	0	0	0	0	0	0	0	0	2	0	0	0	.182	.182
Raines, Tim, Chicago†	.250	8	4	2	1	1	0	0	0	0	0	0	0	4	1	0	0	0	0	.250	.625
Ramirez, Manny, Cleveland	.250	4	4	1	1	1	0	0	0	0	0	0	0	0	0	1	0	0	0	.250	.250
Reboulet, Jeff, Minnesota	.200	6	5	1	1	1	0	0	0	0	0	0	0	1	0	1	0	0	0	.200	.333
Redus, Gary, Texas	.238	24	21	2	5	8	0	0	1	5	0	0	0	2	0	5	1	1	0	.381	.304
Reimer, Kevin, Milwaukee*	.182	13	11	1	2	2	0	0	0	0	0	0	0	2	0	4	0	0	1	.182	.308
Reynolds, Harold, Baltimore†	.333	3	3	0	1	2	1	0	0	0	0	0	0	0	0	1	0	0	0	.333	.333
Richardson, Jeff, Boston	.000	2	2	0	0	0	0	0	0	0	0	0	0	0	0	0	0	0	0	.000	.000
Riles, Ernest, Boston*	.170	56	47	2	8	15	4	0	1	9	0	1	0	7	3	14	0	2	2	.319	.273
Ripken, Bill, Texas	.000	1	0	0	0	0	0	0	0	0	0	1	0	0	0	0	0	0	0	.000	.000
Rivera, Luis, Boston	.250	4	4	0	1	2	1	0	0	0	0	0	0	0	0	0	0	0	0	.500	.250
Rodriguez, Ivan, Texas	.750	4	4	0	3	3	0	0	0	2	0	0	0	0	0	1	0	0	0	.750	.750
Rossy, Rico, Kansas City	.500	2	2	1	1	2	1	0	0	0	0	0	0	0	0	0	0	0	0	1.000	.500
Rowland, Rich, Detroit	.667	3	3	1	2	2	0	0	0	0	0	0	0	0	0	0	0	0	0	.667	.667
Russell, John, Texas	.400	7	5	0	2	3	1	0	0	2	0	0	0	2	0	2	0	0	0	.600	.571
Santovenia, Nelson, Kansas City	.000	1	1	0	0	0	0	0	0	0	0	0	0	0	0	0	0	0	0	.000	.000
Sasser, Mackey, Seattle*	.261	35	23	3	6	9	3	0	0	6	0	1	0	5	4	6	0	0	1	.391	.379

Player, Team	Avg.	G	AB	R	H	TB	2B	3B	HR	RBI	SH	SF	HP	BB	Int. BB	SO	SB	CS	GI DP	Slg.	OBP
Sax, Steve, Chicago	.000	8	8	1	0	0	0	0	0	1	0	0	0	0	0	0	0	0	0	.000	.000
Segui, David, Baltimore†	.000	3	2	0	0	0	0	0	0	0	0	0	0	1	1	1	0	0	0	.000	.333
Seitzer, Kevin, Oak.-Mil.	.154	14	13	0	2	2	0	0	0	1	0	0	0	1	0	4	0	1	1	.154	.214
Sheets, Larry, Seattle*	.200	7	5	0	1	2	1	0	0	1	0	0	0	0	0	1	0	0	1	.400	.200
Sierra, Ruben, Oakland†	.000	2	2	0	0	0	0	0	0	0	0	0	0	0	0	1	0	0	0	.000	.000
Smith, Lonnie, Baltimore	.000	1	0	1	0	0	0	0	0	0	0	0	0	1	0	0	0	0	0	.000	1.000
Snow, J.T., California†	.000	2	2	0	0	0	0	0	0	0	0	0	0	0	0	0	0	0	0	.000	.000
Sojo, Luis, Toronto	.000	1	1	0	0	0	0	0	0	0	0	0	0	0	0	0	0	0	0	.000	.000
Sorrento, Paul, Cleveland*	.231	15	13	2	3	4	1	0	0	0	0	0	0	2	1	6	0	0	0	.308	.333
Spiers, Bill, Milwaukee*	.333	4	3	2	1	3	0	1	0	2	0	0	0	1	0	0	0	0	0	1.000	.500
Stahoviak, Scott, Minnesota*	.000	5	5	0	0	0	0	0	0	0	0	0	0	0	0	4	0	0	0	.000	.000
Stanley, Mike, New York	.273	15	11	3	3	4	1	0	0	0	0	0	0	2	0	5	0	0	0	.364	.385
Steinbach, Terry, Oakland	.250	4	4	0	1	1	0	0	0	1	0	0	0	0	0	0	0	0	1	.250	.250
Stillwell, Kurt, California†	.500	3	2	0	1	1	0	0	0	0	0	0	0	1	0	0	0	0	0	.500	.667
Strange, Doug, Texas†	.333	13	12	1	4	8	1	0	1	3	0	0	0	0	0	4	0	0	0	.667	.333
Suero, William, Milwaukee	.500	6	6	0	3	3	0	0	0	0	0	0	0	0	0	0	0	0	1	.500	.500
Surhoff, B.J., Milwaukee*	.400	5	5	1	2	2	0	0	0	0	0	0	0	0	0	0	0	0	0	.400	.400
Sveum, Dale, Oakland†	.429	7	7	1	3	6	0	0	1	1	0	0	0	0	0	2	0	0	0	.857	.429
Tartabull, Danny, New York	.000	1	0	0	0	0	0	0	0	0	0	0	0	1	1	0	0	0	0	.000	1.000
Tettleton, Mickey, Detroit†	.250	6	4	0	1	1	0	0	0	1	0	0	0	2	0	1	0	1	0	.250	.500
Thome, Jim, Cleveland*	.000	2	2	0	0	0	0	0	0	0	0	0	0	0	0	1	0	0	0	.000	.000
Thon, Dickie, Milwaukee	.250	19	16	1	4	5	1	0	0	1	1	0	0	2	1	1	0	0	1	.313	.333
Thurman, Gary, Detroit	1.000	1	1	0	1	1	0	0	0	0	0	0	0	0	0	0	0	0	0	1.000	1.000
Tingley, Ron, California	.000	1	0	0	0	0	0	0	0	0	0	1	0	0	0	0	0	0	0	.000	.000
Tinsley, Lee, Seattle†	.200	6	5	1	1	1	0	0	0	0	0	0	0	1	0	3	0	0	0	.200	.333
Trammell, Alan, Detroit	.182	12	11	2	2	3	1	0	0	2	0	0	0	1	0	2	0	0	0	.273	.250
Treadway, Jeff, Cleveland*	.250	39	36	2	9	13	1	0	1	2	0	0	0	2	0	6	0	0	0	.361	.289
Turang, Brian, Seattle	.500	3	2	0	1	1	0	0	0	0	0	0	0	1	0	0	0	0	0	.500	.667
Valentin, John, Boston	.000	2	1	0	0	0	0	0	0	0	0	0	0	1	0	0	0	0	0	.000	.500
Van Burkleo, Ty, California*	.000	1	1	0	0	0	0	0	0	0	0	0	0	0	0	1	0	0	0	.000	.000
Vaughn, Greg, Milwaukee	.000	2	2	0	0	0	0	0	0	0	0	0	0	0	0	1	0	0	0	.000	.000
Vaughn, Mo, Boston*	.000	3	2	0	0	0	0	0	0	1	0	0	0	1	1	1	0	0	0	.000	.333
Velarde, Randy, New York	.308	15	13	2	4	10	1	1	1	2	1	0	0	0	0	2	0	0	0	.769	.308
Ventura, Robin, Chicago*	.000	2	2	0	0	0	0	0	0	0	0	0	0	0	0	0	0	0	0	.000	.000
Vina, Fernando, Seattle*	.000	1	1	0	0	0	0	0	0	0	0	0	0	0	0	0	0	0	0	.000	.000
Vizquel, Omar, Seattle†	1.000	1	1	0	1	1	0	0	0	0	0	0	0	0	0	0	0	0	0	1.000	1.000
Voigt, Jack, Baltimore	.200	13	10	4	2	2	0	0	0	1	0	0	0	3	0	4	0	0	0	.200	.385
Ward, Turner, Toronto†	.286	8	7	0	2	2	0	0	0	0	0	0	1	0	0	2	0	0	0	.286	.375
Webster, Lenny, Minnesota	.000	3	3	0	0	0	0	0	0	0	0	0	0	0	0	0	0	0	0	.000	.000
Whitaker, Lou, Detroit*	.313	18	16	4	5	7	2	0	0	5	0	0	0	0	0	2	0	0	0	.438	.313
White, Devon, Toronto†	.000	1	0	0	0	0	0	0	0	0	0	0	0	1	0	0	0	0	0	.000	1.000
Williams, Gerald, New York	.250	4	4	0	1	1	0	0	0	1	0	0	0	0	0	2	0	0	1	.250	.250
Wilson, Craig, Kansas City	.167	7	6	1	1	1	0	0	0	1	0	0	0	1	0	0	0	0	0	.167	.286
Winfield, Dave, Minnesota	.400	5	5	0	2	2	0	0	0	1	0	0	0	0	0	0	0	0	1	.400	.400
Yount, Robin, Milwaukee	.200	5	5	0	1	1	0	0	0	1	0	0	0	0	0	2	0	0	0	.200	.200
Zupcic, Bob, Boston	.222	9	9	1	2	3	1	0	0	0	0	0	0	0	0	1	0	0	1	.333	.222

PINCH-HITTERS WITH TWO OR MORE TEAMS

Player, Team	Avg.	G	AB	R	H	TB	2B	3B	HR	RBI	SH	SF	HP	BB	Int. BB	SO	SB	CS	GI DP	Slg.	OBP
Calderon, Ivan, Boston	.100	12	10	0	1	1	0	0	0	0	0	0	0	2	0	3	0	0	1	.100	.250
Calderon, Ivan, Chicago	.000	4	4	0	0	0	0	0	0	0	0	0	0	0	0	1	0	0	0	.000	.000
Deer, Rob, Detroit	.333	6	6	1	2	5	0	0	1	1	0	0	0	0	0	1	0	0	0	.833	.333
Deer, Rob, Boston	.000	2	2	0	0	0	0	0	0	0	0	0	0	0	0	1	0	0	1	.000	.000
Gaetti, Gary, California	.000	7	7	0	0	0	0	0	0	0	0	0	0	0	0	2	0	0	0	.000	.000
Gaetti, Gary, Kansas City	1.000	1	1	0	1	1	0	0	0	1	0	0	0	0	0	0	0	0	0	1.000	1.000
Pagliarulo, Mike, Minnesota*	.286	8	7	1	2	5	0	0	1	2	0	0	1	0	0	3	0	0	0	.714	.375
Pagliarulo, Mike, Baltimore*	.000	3	2	0	0	0	0	0	0	1	0	0	0	1	0	1	0	0	0	.000	.333
Seitzer, Kevin, Oakland	.333	7	6	0	2	2	0	0	0	1	0	0	0	1	0	2	0	1	0	.333	.429
Seitzer, Kevin, Milwaukee	.000	7	7	0	0	0	0	0	0	0	0	0	0	0	0	2	0	0	1	.000	.000

PITCHING

TEAM

Team	W	L	ERA	G	CG	ShO	Sv.	IP	H	TBF	R	ER	HR	SH	SF	HB	BB	Int. BB	SO	WP	Bk.
Chicago	94	68	3.70	162	16	11	48	1454.0	1398	6173	664	598	125	54	41	40	566	36	974	51	7
Boston	80	82	3.77	162	9	11	44	1452.1	1379	6201	698	609	127	58	60	48	552	87	997	42	11
Kansas City	84	78	4.04	162	16	6	48	1445.1	1379	6145	694	649	105	41	52	44	571	36	985	76	7
Seattle	82	80	4.20	162	22	10	41	1453.2	1421	6254	731	678	135	55	45	66	605	56	1083	57	6
Toronto	95	67	4.21	162	11	11	50	1441.1	1441	6269	742	674	134	38	52	32	620	38	1023	83	8
Texas	86	76	4.28	162	20	6	45	1438.1	1476	6232	751	684	144	48	42	44	562	42	957	52	14
Baltimore	85	77	4.31	162	21	10	42	1442.2	1427	6183	745	691	153	51	42	38	579	50	900	41	2
California	71	91	4.34	162	26	6	41	1430.1	1482	6203	770	690	153	53	61	51	550	35	843	55	7
New York	88	74	4.35	162	11	13	38	1431.1	1467	6200	761	695	170	50	47	29	552	58	899	33	5
Milwaukee	69	93	4.45	162	26	6	29	1447.0	1511	6285	792	716	153	50	76	60	522	58	810	45	7
Cleveland	76	86	4.58	162	7	8	45	1445.2	1591	6384	813	735	182	48	41	39	591	53*	888	41	5
Detroit	85	77	4.65	162	11	7	36	1436.2	1547	6308	837	742	188	56	57	48	542	92	828	68	5
Minnesota	71	91	4.71	162	5	3	44	1444.1	1591	6286	830	756	148	42	66	45	514	34	901	43	13
Oakland	68	94	4.90	162	8	2	42	1452.1	1551	6456	846	791	157	57	47	49	680	59	864	39	6
Totals	1134	1134	4.32	1134	209	110	593	20222.1	20661	87579	10674	9708	2074	701	729	633	8006	734	12952	726	103

NOTE—Totals for earned runs for several clubs do not agree with the composite total for all pitchers of each respective club due to instances in which provisions of Section 10.18(i) of the Scoring Rules were applied. The following differences are to be noted: Baltimore pitchers add to 693; Boston pitchers add to 614; California pitchers add to 693; Chicago pitchers add to 601; Detroit pitchers add to 751; Milwaukee pitchers add to 718; Minnesota pitchers add to 759; New York pitchers add to 698; Seattle pitchers add to 679; Toronto pitchers add to 676.

INDIVIDUAL

TOP 15 QUALIFIERS FOR EARNED-RUN AVERAGE TITLE

Minimum 162 innings.   *Lefthanded pitcher.

Pitcher, Team	W	L	ERA	G	GS	CG	ShO	GF	Sv.	IP	H	TBF	R	ER	HR	SH	SF	HB	BB	Int. BB	SO	WP	Bk.
Appier, Kevin, Kansas City	18	8	2.56	34	34	5	1	0	0	238.2	183	953	74	68	8	3	5	1	81	3	186	5	0
Alvarez, Wilson, Chicago*	15	8	2.95	31	31	1	1	0	0	207.2	168	877	78	68	14	13	6	7	122	8	155	2	1
Key, Jimmy, New York*	18	6	3.00	34	34	4	2	0	0	236.2	219	948	84	79	26	6	9	1	43	1	173	3	0
Fernandez, Alex, Chicago	18	9	3.13	34	34	3	1	0	0	247.1	221	1004	95	86	27	9	3	6	67	5	169	8	0
Viola, Frank, Boston*	11	8	3.14	29	29	2	1	0	0	183.2	180	787	76	64	12	8	7	6	72	5	91	5	0
Finley, Chuck, California*	16	14	3.15	35	35	13	2	0	0	251.1	243	1065	108	88	22	11	7	6	82	1	187	8	1
Langston, Mark, California*	16	11	3.20	35	35	7	0	0	0	256.1	220	1039	100	91	22	3	8	1	85	2	196	10	2
Johnson, Randy, Seattle*	19	8	3.24	35	34	10	3	1	1	255.1	185	1043	97	92	22	8	7	16	99	1	308	8	2
Darwin, Danny, Boston	15	11	3.26	34	34	2	1	0	0	229.1	196	919	93	83	31	6	9	3	49	8	130	5	1
Cone, David, Kansas City	11	14	3.33	34	34	6	1	0	0	254.0	205	1060	102	94	20	7	9	10	114	2	191	14	2
McDowell, Jack, Chicago	22	10	3.37	34	34	10	4	0	0	256.2	261	1067	104	96	20	8	6	3	69	6	158	8	1
McDonald, Ben, Baltimore	13	14	3.39	34	34	7	1	0	0	220.1	185	914	92	83	17	7	4	5	86	4	171	7	1
Pavlik, Roger, Texas	12	6	3.41	26	26	2	0	0	0	166.1	151	712	67	63	16	6	4	5	80	3	131	6	0
Bosio, Chris, Seattle	9	9	3.45	29	24	3	1	2	1	164.1	138	678	75	63	14	7	4	6	59	3	119	5	0
Hanson, Erik, Seattle	11	12	3.47	31	30	7	0	0	0	215.0	215	898	91	83	17	10	4	6	60	6	163	8	0

DEPARTMENTAL LEADERS: W—McDowell, Chi., 22; L—Erickson, Min., 19; G—Harris, Bos., 80; GS—Eldred, Mil., Moore, Det., 36; CG—Finley, Cal., 13; ShO—McDowell, Chi., 4; GF—Ward, Tor., 70; Sv.—Montgomery, K.C., Ward, Tor., 45; IP—Eldred, Mil., 258; H—Erickson, Min., 266; TBF—Eldred, Mil., 1087; R—Erickson, Min., 138; ER—Navarro, Mil., 127; HR—Moore, Det., 35; SH—Alvarez, Chi., 13; SF—Navarro, Mil., 17; HB—Johnson, Sea., 16; TBB—Alvarez, Chi., 122; IBB—Harris, Bos., Quantrill, Bos., 14; SO—Johnson, Sea., 308; WP—Guzman, Tor., 26; Bk.—Banks, Min., Rogers, Tex., 5.

ALL PITCHERS

*Lefthanded pitcher.

Pitcher, Team	W	L	ERA	G	GS	CG	ShO	GF	Sv.	IP	H	TBF	R	ER	HR	SH	SF	HB	BB	Int. BB	SO	WP	Bk.
Abbott, Jim, New York*	11	14	4.37	32	32	4	1	0	0	214.0	221	906	115	104	22	12	4	3	73	4	95	9	0
Abbott, Paul, Cleveland	0	1	6.38	5	5	0	0	0	0	18.1	19	84	15	13	5	0	0	0	11	1	7	1	0
Aguilera, Rick, Minnesota	4	3	3.11	65	0	0	0	61	34	72.1	60	287	25	25	9	2	1	1	14	3	59	1	0
Alvarez, Wilson, Chicago*	15	8	2.95	31	31	1	1	0	0	207.2	168	877	78	68	14	13	6	7	122	8	155	2	1
Anderson, Brian, California*	0	0	3.97	4	1	0	0	3	0	11.1	11	45	5	5	1	0	0	0	2	0	4	0	0
Appier, Kevin, Kansas City	18	8	2.56	34	34	5	1	0	0	238.2	183	953	74	68	8	3	5	1	81	3	186	5	0
Assenmacher, Paul, N.Y.*	2	2	3.12	26	0	0	0	6	0	17.1	10	71	6	6	0	4	0	1	9	3	11	0	0
Austin, Jim, Milwaukee	1	2	3.82	31	0	0	0	8	0	33.0	28	137	15	14	3	1	0	1	13	1	15	4	0
Ayrault, Bob, Seattle	1	1	3.45	14	0	0	0	6	0	19.2	18	80	8	7	1	2	0	6	1	7	0	0
Bailey, Phil, Boston	0	1	3.45	11	0	0	0	5	0	15.2	12	66	7	6	0	1	0	0	12	3	11	2	1
Bankhead, Scott, Boston	2	1	3.50	40	0	0	0	4	0	64.1	59	272	28	25	7	3	4	0	29	3	47	1	0
Banks, Willie, Minnesota	11	12	4.04	31	30	0	0	1	0	171.1	186	754	91	77	17	4	4	3	78	2	138	9	5
Belcher, Tim, Chicago	3	5	4.40	12	11	1	1	0	0	71.2	64	296	36	35	8	2	1	1	27	0	34	0	0
Belinda, Stan, Kansas City	1	1	4.28	23	0	0	0	7	0	27.1	30	116	13	13	2	2	0	1	6	0	25	2	0
Bere, Jason, Chicago	12	5	3.47	24	24	1	0	0	0	142.2	109	610	60	55	12	4	2	5	81	0	129	6	0
Bergman, Sean, Detroit	1	4	5.67	9	6	1	0	1	0	39.2	47	189	29	25	6	3	2	1	23	3	19	3	1
Bielecki, Mike, Cleveland	4	5	5.90	13	13	0	0	0	0	68.2	90	317	47	45	8	0	2	2	23	3	38	1	0
Boddicker, Mike, Milwaukee	3	5	5.67	10	10	1	0	0	0	54.0	77	249	35	34	6	1	1	4	15	1	24	0	0
Boever, Joe, Det.-Det.	6	3	3.61	61	0	0	0	22	3	102.1	101	449	50	41	9	5	7	4	44	7	63	1	0
Bohanon, Brian, Texas*	4	4	4.76	36	8	0	0	0	0	92.2	107	418	54	49	8	2	5	4	46	3	45	10	0
Bolton, Rodney, Chicago	2	6	7.44	9	8	0	0	0	0	42.1	55	197	40	35	4	1	4	1	16	0	17	4	0
Bolton, Tom, Detroit*	6	6	4.47	43	8	0	0	9	0	102.2	113	462	57	51	5	7	2	7	45	10	66	5	1
Bones, Ricky, Milwaukee	11	11	4.86	32	31	3	0	1	0	203.2	222	883	122	110	28	5	7	8	63	3	63	6	1

— 250 —

Pitcher, Team	W	L	ERA	G	GS	CG	ShO	GF	Sv.	IP	H	TBF	R	ER	HR	SH	SF	HB	BB	Int. BB	SO	WP	Bk.
Bosio, Chris, Seattle	9	9	3.45	29	24	3	1	2	1	164.1	138	678	75	63	14	7	4	6	59	3	119	5	0
Brewer, Billy, Kansas City*	2	2	3.46	46	0	0	0	14	0	39.0	31	157	16	15	6	1	1	0	20	4	28	2	1
Briscoe, John, Oakland	1	0	8.03	17	0	0	0	6	0	24.2	26	122	25	22	2	0	2	0	26	3	24	5	0
Bronkey, Jeff, Texas	1	1	4.00	21	0	0	0	6	1	36.0	39	152	20	16	4	1	2	1	11	4	18	2	0
Brow, Scott, Toronto	1	1	6.00	6	3	0	0	1	0	18.0	19	83	15	12	2	1	2	1	10	1	7	0	0
Brown, Kevin, Texas	15	12	3.59	34	34	12	3	0	0	233.0	228	1001	105	93	14	5	3	15	74	5	142	8	1
Brummett, Greg, Minnesota*	2	1	5.74	5	5	0	0	0	0	26.2	29	115	17	17	3	0	3	0	15	1	10	0	0
Burgos, Enrique, K.C.*	0	1	9.00	5	0	0	0	3	0	5.0	5	28	5	5	0	0	0	1	6	1	6	3	0
Burns, Todd, Texas	0	4	4.57	25	5	0	0	8	0	65.0	63	288	36	33	6	2	3	2	32	3	35	3	2
Butcher, Mike, California	1	0	2.86	23	0	0	0	11	8	28.1	21	124	12	9	2	1	3	2	15	1	24	0	0
Cadaret, Greg, Kansas City*	1	1	2.93	13	0	0	0	3	0	15.1	14	62	5	5	0	1	0	1	7	0	2	0	0
Campbell, Kevin, Oakland	0	0	7.31	11	0	0	0	4	0	16.0	20	77	13	13	1	0	1	1	11	1	9	0	0
Canseco, Jose, Texas	0	0	27.00	1	0	0	0	1	0	1.0	2	8	3	3	0	0	1	0	3	0	0	0	0
Carpenter, Cris, Texas	4	1	4.22	27	0	0	0	8	1	32.0	35	139	15	15	4	1	3	2	12	1	27	2	0
Cary, Chuck, Chicago*	1	0	5.23	16	0	0	0	4	0	20.2	22	96	12	12	1	1	4	3	11	0	10	4	0
Casian, Larry, Minnesota*	5	3	3.02	54	0	0	0	8	1	56.2	59	241	23	19	1	3	3	1	14	2	31	2	0
Castillo, Tony, Toronto*	3	2	3.38	51	0	0	0	10	0	50.2	44	211	19	19	4	5	2	0	22	5	28	1	0
Charlton, Norm, Seattle*	1	3	2.34	34	0	0	0	29	18	34.2	22	141	12	9	4	0	1	0	17	0	48	6	0
Christopher, Mike, Cleveland	0	0	3.86	9	0	0	0	3	0	11.2	14	51	6	5	3	0	0	2	1	0	8	0	0
Clark, Mark, Cleveland	7	5	4.28	26	15	1	0	1	0	109.1	119	454	55	52	18	1	1	1	25	1	57	1	0
Clemens, Roger, Boston	11	14	4.46	29	29	2	1	0	0	191.2	175	808	99	95	17	5	7	11	67	4	160	3	1
Cone, David, Kansas City	11	14	3.33	34	34	6	1	0	0	254.0	205	1060	102	94	20	7	9	10	114	2	191	14	2
Converse, Jim, Seattle	1	3	5.31	4	4	0	0	0	0	20.1	23	93	12	12	0	0	1	0	14	2	10	0	0
Cook, Andy, New York	0	1	5.06	4	0	0	0	3	0	5.1	4	28	3	3	1	0	0	0	7	0	4	2	0
Cook, Dennis, Cleveland*	5	5	5.67	25	0	0	0	2	0	54.0	62	233	36	34	9	3	2	2	16	1	34	0	1
Cook, Mike, Baltimore	0	0	0.00	2	0	0	0	0	0	3.0	1	13	0	0	0	0	0	0	2	1	3	1	0
Cox, Danny, Toronto	7	6	3.12	44	0	0	0	13	2	83.2	73	348	31	29	8	0	1	0	29	5	84	5	0
Crim, Chuck, California	2	2	5.87	11	0	0	0	3	0	15.1	17	67	11	10	2	2	1	2	5	1	10	0	0
Cummings, John, Seattle*	0	6	6.02	10	8	1	0	0	0	46.1	59	207	34	31	6	0	2	2	16	2	19	1	1
Darling, Ron, Oakland	5	9	5.16	31	29	3	0	1	0	178.0	198	793	107	102	22	5	6	5	72	5	95	3	1
Darwin, Danny, Boston	15	11	3.26	34	34	2	1	0	0	229.1	196	919	93	83	31	6	9	3	49	8	130	5	1
Davis, Chili, California	0	0	0.00	1	0	0	0	1	0	2.0	0	7	0	0	0	0	0	1	0	0	0	0	0
Davis, Storm, Oak.-Det.	2	8	5.05	43	8	0	0	12	4	98.0	93	428	57	55	9	2	3	3	48	6	73	0	0
Dayley, Ken, Toronto*	0	0	0.00	2	0	0	0	0	0	0.2	1	7	2	0	0	0	0	0	4	0	2	0	0
DeLeon, Jose, Chicago	0	0	1.74	11	0	0	0	1	0	10.1	5	37	2	2	2	0	0	1	3	0	6	0	0
DeLucia, Rich, Seattle	3	6	4.64	30	1	0	0	11	0	42.2	46	195	24	22	5	1	1	1	23	3	48	4	0
Deshaies, Jim, Minnesota*	11	13	4.41	27	27	1	0	0	0	167.1	159	693	85	82	24	4	7	6	51	1	80	0	4
DeSilva, John, Detroit	0	0	9.00	1	0	0	0	1	0	1.0	2	4	1	1	0	0	0	0	0	0	0	0	0
DiPino, Frank, Kansas City*	1	1	6.89	11	0	0	0	5	0	15.2	21	74	12	12	2	0	2	2	6	0	5	0	0
DiPoto, Jerry, Cleveland	4	4	2.40	46	0	0	0	26	11	56.1	57	247	21	15	0	3	2	1	30	7	41	0	0
Doherty, John, Detroit	14	11	4.44	32	31	3	2	1	0	184.2	205	780	104	91	19	5	4	5	48	7	63	4	1
Dopson, John, Boston	7	11	4.97	34	28	1	1	3	0	155.2	170	681	93	86	16	8	8	2	59	12	89	1	3
Downs, Kelly, Oakland	5	10	5.64	42	12	0	0	12	0	119.2	135	539	80	75	14	3	4	2	60	8	66	4	1
Drahman, Brian, Chicago	0	0	0.00	4	0	0	0	4	1	5.1	7	23	0	0	0	0	0	0	2	0	3	0	0
Dreyer, Steve, Texas	3	3	5.71	10	6	0	0	1	0	41.0	48	186	26	26	7	0	1	0	20	1	23	0	0
Eckersley, Dennis, Oakland	2	4	4.16	64	0	0	0	52	36	67.0	67	276	32	31	7	2	2	2	13	4	80	0	0
Eichhorn, Mark, Toronto	3	1	2.72	54	0	0	0	16	0	72.2	76	309	26	22	3	3	2	2	22	7	47	2	0
Eldred, Cal, Milwaukee	16	16	4.01	36	36	8	1	0	0	258.0	232	1087	120	115	32	5	12	10	91	5	180	2	0
Erickson, Scott, Minnesota	8	19	5.19	34	34	1	0	0	0	218.2	266	976	138	126	17	10	13	10	71	1	116	5	0
Fajardo, Hector, Texas	0	0	0.00	1	0	0	0	1	0	0.2	0	2	0	0	0	0	0	0	0	0	1	0	0
Farr, Steve, New York	2	2	4.21	49	0	0	0	37	25	47.0	44	211	22	22	8	3	4	2	28	4	39	2	0
Farrell, John, California	3	12	7.35	21	17	0	0	1	0	90.2	110	420	74	74	22	2	2	7	44	3	45	3	0
Fernandez, Alex, Chicago	18	9	3.13	34	34	3	1	0	0	247.1	221	1004	95	86	27	9	3	6	67	5	169	8	0
Fetters, Mike, Milwaukee	3	3	3.34	45	0	0	0	14	0	59.1	59	246	29	22	4	5	5	2	22	4	23	0	0
Finley, Chuck, California*	16	14	3.15	35	35	13	2	0	0	251.1	243	1065	108	88	22	11	7	6	82	1	187	8	1
Fleming, Dave, Seattle*	12	5	4.36	26	26	1	1	0	0	167.1	189	737	84	81	15	4	8	6	67	6	75	2	0
Flener, Huck, Toronto*	0	0	4.05	6	0	0	0	1	0	6.2	7	30	3	3	0	0	0	0	4	1	2	1	0
Fossas, Tony, Boston*	1	1	5.18	71	0	0	0	19	0	40.0	38	175	28	23	4	0	1	2	15	4	39	1	1
Frey, Steve, California*	2	3	2.98	55	0	0	0	28	13	48.1	41	212	20	16	1	4	1	3	26	1	22	3	0
Frohwirth, Todd, Baltimore*	6	7	3.83	70	0	0	0	30	3	96.1	91	411	47	41	7	7	2	3	44	8	50	1	0
Garces, Rich, Minnesota	0	0	0.00	3	0	0	0	1	0	4.0	4	18	2	0	0	0	0	0	2	0	3	0	0
Gardiner, Mike, Detroit	0	0	3.97	10	0	0	0	1	0	11.1	12	51	5	5	0	1	0	0	7	1	4	2	0
Gardner, Mark, Kansas City	4	6	6.19	17	16	0	0	0	0	91.2	92	387	65	63	17	1	7	4	36	0	54	2	0
Gibson, Paul, New York*	2	0	3.06	20	0	0	0	9	0	35.1	31	142	15	12	4	0	3	0	9	0	25	0	0
Gohr, Greg, Detroit	0	0	5.96	16	0	0	0	0	0	22.2	26	108	15	15	1	1	1	2	14	2	23	1	0
Gonzales, Rene, California	0	0	0.00	1	0	0	0	1	0	1.0	0	3	0	0	0	0	0	0	0	0	0	0	0
Gordon, Tom, Kansas City	12	6	3.58	48	14	2	0	18	1	155.2	125	651	65	62	11	6	6	1	77	5	143	17	0
Gossage, Rich, Oakland	4	5	4.53	39	0	0	0	12	1	47.2	49	213	24	24	6	0	2	1	26	2	40	4	0
Grahe, Joe, California	4	1	2.86	45	0	0	0	32	11	56.2	54	247	22	18	5	2	3	2	25	4	31	3	0
Granger, Jeff, Kansas City*	0	0	27.00	1	0	0	0	0	0	1.0	3	8	3	3	0	0	0	0	2	0	1	0	0
Grater, Mark, Detroit	0	0	5.40	6	0	0	0	1	0	5.0	6	25	3	3	0	0	0	0	4	1	1	0	0
Grimsley, Jason, Cleveland	3	4	5.31	10	6	0	0	0	0	42.1	52	194	26	25	3	1	0	1	20	1	27	2	0
Groom, Buddy, Detroit*	0	2	6.14	19	3	0	0	8	0	36.2	48	170	25	25	4	2	4	2	13	5	15	2	1
Guardado, Eddie, Min.*	3	8	6.18	19	16	0	0	2	0	94.2	123	426	68	65	13	1	3	1	36	2	46	0	0
Gubicza, Mark, Kansas City	5	8	4.66	49	6	0	0	12	2	104.1	128	474	61	54	2	6	2	4	43	8	80	12	0
Gullickson, Bill, Detroit	13	9	5.37	28	28	2	0	0	0	159.1	186	699	106	95	28	6	7	3	44	3	70	2	0
Guthrie, Mark, Minnesota*	2	1	4.71	22	0	0	0	0	0	21.0	20	94	11	11	2	1	2	0	16	2	15	1	3
Guzman, Juan, Toronto	14	3	3.99	33	33	2	1	0	0	221.0	211	963	107	98	17	5	9	3	110	2	194	26	1
Haas, Dave, Detroit	1	2	6.11	20	0	0	0	5	0	28.0	45	131	20	19	9	2	1	0	8	5	17	0	0
Habyan, John, N.Y.-K.C.	2	1	4.15	48	0	0	0	23	1	56.1	59	239	27	26	6	0	2	0	20	4	39	0	2
Hampton, Mike, Seattle*	1	3	9.53	13	3	0	0	0	0	17.0	28	95	20	18	3	1	1	0	17	3	8	1	1
Haney, Chris, Kansas City*	9	9	6.02	23	23	1	1	0	0	124.0	141	556	87	83	13	3	4	5	53	2	65	6	1
Hanson, Erik, Seattle	11	12	3.47	31	30	7	0	0	0	215.0	215	898	91	83	17	10	4	5	60	6	163	8	0
Harris, Greg, Boston	6	7	3.77	80	0	0	0	24	8	112.1	95	494	55	47	7	0	4	10	60	14	103	8	1
Hartley, Mike, Minnesota	1	2	4.00	53	0	0	0	21	1	81.0	86	359	38	36	4	4	6	7	36	3	57	0	0
Hathaway, Hilly, California*	4	3	5.02	11	11	0	0	0	0	57.1	71	253	35	32	6	1	3	5	26	1	11	5	1
Heaton, Neal, New York*	1	0	6.00	18	0	0	0	9	0	27.0	34	128	19	18	6	0	1	3	11	1	15	2	0

Pitcher, Team	W	L	ERA	G	GS	CG	ShO	GF	Sv.	IP	H	TBF	R	ER	HR	SH	SF	HB	BB	Int. BB	SO	WP	Bk.
Henke, Tom, Texas	5	5	2.91	66	0	0	0	60	40	74.1	55	302	25	24	7	3	3	1	27	3	79	3	0
Henneman, Mike, Detroit	5	3	2.64	63	0	0	0	50	24	71.2	69	316	28	21	4	5	2	2	32	8	58	4	0
Henry, Doug, Milwaukee	4	4	5.56	54	0	0	0	41	17	55.0	67	260	37	34	7	5	4	3	25	8	38	4	0
Henry, Dwayne, Seattle	2	1	6.67	31	1	0	0	15	2	54.0	56	249	40	40	6	3	4	2	35	4	35	7	0
Hentgen, Pat, Toronto	19	9	3.87	34	32	3	0	0	0	216.1	215	926	103	93	27	6	5	7	74	0	122	11	1
Hernandez, Jeremy, Cle.	6	5	3.14	49	0	0	0	22	8	77.1	75	321	33	27	12	2	5	0	27	6	44	2	0
Hernandez, Roberto, Chicago.	3	4	2.29	70	0	0	0	67	38	78.2	66	314	21	20	6	2	2	0	20	1	71	2	0
Hesketh, Joe, Boston*	3	4	5.06	28	5	0	0	8	1	53.1	62	246	35	30	4	4	2	0	29	4	34	4	2
Higuera, Ted, Milwaukee*	1	3	7.20	8	8	0	0	0	0	30.0	43	148	24	24	4	1	1	1	16	2	27	0	3
Hillegas, Shawn, Oakland	3	6	6.97	18	11	0	0	4	0	60.2	78	288	48	47	8	3	2	4	33	1	29	1	0
Hitchcock, Sterling, N.Y.*	1	2	4.65	6	6	0	0	0	0	31.0	32	135	18	16	4	0	2	1	14	1	26	3	2
Holman, Brad, Seattle	1	3	3.72	19	0	0	0	9	3	36.1	27	152	17	15	1	1	0	5	16	2	17	2	0
Holzemer, Mark, California*	0	3	8.87	5	4	0	0	1	0	23.1	34	117	24	23	2	1	0	3	13	0	10	1	0
Honeycutt, Rick, Oakland*	1	4	2.81	52	0	0	0	7	1	41.2	30	174	18	13	2	7	4	1	20	6	21	0	0
Horsman, Vince, Oakland*	2	0	5.40	40	0	0	0	5	0	25.0	25	116	15	15	2	0	3	0	15	1	17	1	0
Howard, Chris, Chicago*	1	0	0.00	3	0	0	0	0	0	2.1	2	10	0	0	0	0	0	0	3	1	1	0	0
Howe, Steve, New York*	3	5	4.97	51	0	0	0	19	4	50.2	58	215	31	28	7	5	2	3	10	4	19	0	0
Hutton, Mark, New York	1	1	5.73	7	4	0	0	2	0	22.0	24	104	17	14	2	2	2	1	17	0	12	0	0
Ignasiak, Mike, Milwaukee	1	1	3.65	27	0	0	0	4	0	37.0	32	158	17	15	2	1	1	2	21	4	28	0	0
Jean, Domingo, New York	1	1	4.46	10	6	0	0	1	0	40.1	37	176	20	20	7	0	1	0	19	1	20	1	0
Jimenez, Miguel, Oakland	1	4	4.00	5	4	0	0	0	0	27.0	27	120	12	12	5	0	0	1	16	0	13	0	0
Johnson, Dave, Detroit	1	1	12.96	6	0	0	0	2	0	8.1	13	46	13	12	3	0	1	2	5	1	7	1	0
Johnson, Jeff, New York*	0	2	30.38	2	2	0	0	0	0	2.2	12	22	10	9	1	0	0	0	2	0	0	0	0
Johnson, Randy, Seattle*	19	8	3.24	35	34	10	3	1	0	255.1	185	1043	97	92	22	8	7	16	99	1	308	8	2
Jones, Barry, Chicago	1	1	8.59	4	0	0	0	1	0	7.1	14	38	8	7	2	1	0	0	3	0	7	0	0
Kamieniecki, Scott, N.Y.	10	7	4.08	30	20	2	0	4	1	154.1	163	659	73	70	17	3	5	3	59	7	72	2	0
Karsay, Steve, Oakland	3	3	4.04	8	8	0	0	0	0	49.0	49	210	23	22	4	0	2	2	16	1	33	1	0
Key, Jimmy, New York*	18	6	3.00	34	34	4	2	0	0	236.2	219	948	84	79	26	6	9	1	43	1	173	3	0
Kiefer, Mark, Milwaukee	0	0	0.00	6	0	0	0	4	1	9.1	3	37	0	0	0	0	1	0	5	0	7	0	0
Kiely, John, Detroit	0	2	7.71	8	0	0	0	5	0	11.2	13	59	11	10	2	1	0	1	13	5	5	2	0
King, Kevin, Seattle*	0	1	6.17	13	0	0	0	3	0	11.2	9	49	8	8	3	2	1	4	1	8	0	0
Knudsen, Kurt, Detroit	3	2	4.78	30	0	0	0	7	2	37.2	41	171	22	20	9	2	3	4	16	2	29	2	0
Kramer, Tom, Cleveland	7	3	4.02	39	16	1	0	6	0	121.0	126	535	60	54	19	3	2	2	59	7	71	1	0
Krueger, Bill, Detroit*	6	4	3.40	32	7	0	0	7	0	82.0	90	356	43	31	6	3	4	30	5	60	8	0
Langston, Mark, California*	16	11	3.20	35	35	7	0	0	0	256.1	220	1039	100	91	22	3	8	1	85	2	196	10	2
Leach, Terry, Chicago	0	0	2.81	14	0	0	0	8	1	16.0	15	64	5	5	0	0	1	1	2	1	3	0	0
Leary, Tim, Seattle	11	9	5.05	33	27	0	0	6	0	169.1	202	746	104	95	21	5	1	8	58	5	68	6	2
Lefferts, Craig, Texas*	3	9	6.05	52	8	0	0	9	0	83.1	102	373	57	56	17	6	3	1	28	3	58	0	1
Leftwich, Phil, California	4	6	3.79	12	12	1	0	0	0	80.2	81	343	35	34	5	3	1	3	27	1	31	1	0
Leibrandt, Charlie, Texas*	9	10	4.55	26	26	1	0	0	0	150.1	169	656	84	76	15	8	4	4	45	5	89	5	2
Leiter, Al, Toronto*	9	6	4.11	34	12	1	1	4	2	105.0	93	454	52	48	8	3	4	56	2	66	2	2
Leiter, Mark, Detroit	6	6	4.73	27	13	1	0	4	0	106.2	111	471	61	56	17	3	5	3	44	5	70	5	0
Lewis, Scott, California	1	2	4.22	15	4	0	0	2	0	32.0	37	142	16	15	3	2	7	2	12	1	10	1	0
Lilliquist, Derek, Cleveland*	4	4	2.25	56	2	0	0	28	10	64.0	64	271	20	16	5	6	2	1	19	5	40	1	0
Linton, Doug, Tor.-Cal.	2	1	7.36	23	1	0	0	6	0	36.2	46	178	30	30	8	0	3	1	23	1	23	2	0
Lloyd, Graeme, Milwaukee*	3	4	2.83	55	0	0	0	12	0	63.2	64	269	24	20	5	1	2	3	13	3	31	4	0
Lopez, Albie, Cleveland	3	1	5.98	9	9	0	0	0	0	49.2	49	222	34	33	7	1	1	1	32	1	25	0	0
MacDonald, Bob, Detroit*	3	3	5.35	68	0	0	0	24	0	65.2	67	293	42	39	8	4	5	1	33	5	39	3	1
Magnante, Mike, K.C.*	1	2	4.08	7	6	0	0	0	0	35.1	37	145	16	16	3	1	1	1	11	1	16	1	0
Magrane, Joe, California*	2	3	3.94	8	8	0	0	0	0	48.0	48	209	27	21	4	4	3	0	21	0	24	4	0
Mahomes, Pat, Minnesota	1	5	7.71	12	5	0	0	4	0	37.1	47	173	34	32	8	1	1	16	0	23	3	0
Maldonado, Carlos, Mil.	2	2	4.58	29	0	0	0	9	1	37.1	40	167	20	19	2	4	4	0	17	5	18	1	0
Manzanillo, Josias, Mil.	1	1	9.53	10	1	0	0	4	1	17.0	22	86	20	18	1	2	2	2	10	3	10	1	0
Maysey, Matt, Milwaukee	1	2	5.73	23	0	0	0	12	1	22.0	28	105	14	14	4	2	2	1	13	1	10	4	0
McCaskill, Kirk, Chicago	4	8	5.23	30	14	0	0	6	2	113.2	144	502	71	66	12	2	3	1	36	6	65	6	0
McDonald, Ben, Baltimore	13	14	3.39	34	34	7	1	0	0	220.1	185	914	92	83	17	7	4	5	86	4	171	7	1
McDowell, Jack, Chicago	22	10	3.37	34	34	10	4	0	0	256.2	261	1067	104	96	20	8	6	3	69	6	158	8	1
McGehee, Kevin, Baltimore	0	0	5.94	5	0	0	0	1	0	16.2	18	75	11	11	5	1	1	2	7	2	7	1	0
Meacham, Rusty, K.C.	2	2	5.57	15	0	0	0	11	0	21.0	31	104	15	13	2	0	1	3	5	1	13	0	0
Melendez, Jose, Boston	2	1	2.25	9	0	0	0	5	0	16.0	10	63	4	4	2	0	2	0	5	3	14	0	0
Merriman, Brett, Minnesota	1	1	9.67	19	0	0	0	10	0	27.0	36	135	29	29	3	2	3	23	2	14	1	0
Mesa, Jose, Cleveland	10	12	4.92	34	33	3	0	0	0	208.2	232	897	122	114	21	9	9	7	62	2	118	8	2
Milacki, Bob, Cleveland	1	1	3.38	5	2	0	0	0	0	16.0	19	74	8	6	3	0	0	0	11	0	7	0	0
Militello, Sam, New York	1	1	6.75	3	2	0	0	0	0	9.1	10	46	8	7	1	0	0	2	7	1	5	0	0
Mills, Alan, Baltimore	5	4	3.23	45	0	0	0	18	4	100.1	80	421	39	36	14	4	4	51	5	68	3	0
Minchey, Nate, Boston	1	2	3.55	5	5	1	0	0	0	33.0	35	141	16	13	5	1	0	2	8	0	18	2	0
Miranda, Angel, Milwaukee*	4	5	3.30	22	17	2	0	0	0	120.0	100	502	53	44	12	3	2	52	4	88	4	2
Mlicki, Dave, Cleveland	0	0	3.38	3	3	0	0	0	0	13.1	11	58	6	5	2	0	0	2	6	0	7	2	0
Mohler, Mike, Oakland*	1	6	5.60	42	9	0	0	4	0	64.1	57	290	45	40	10	5	2	2	44	4	42	0	1
Monteleone, Rich, New York	7	4	4.94	42	0	0	0	11	0	85.2	85	369	52	47	14	4	5	0	35	10	50	1	0
Montgomery, Jeff, K.C.	7	5	2.27	69	0	0	0	63	45	87.1	65	347	22	22	3	5	1	2	23	4	66	3	0
Moore, Mike, Detroit	13	9	5.22	36	36	4	0	0	0	213.2	227	942	135	124	35	4	8	3	89	10	89	9	0
Morris, Jack, Toronto	7	12	6.19	27	27	4	1	0	0	152.2	189	702	116	105	18	4	3	5	65	2	103	14	1
Moyer, Jamie, Baltimore*	12	9	3.43	25	25	3	1	0	0	152.0	154	630	63	58	11	3	1	6	38	2	90	1	1
Munoz, Bobby, New York	3	3	5.32	38	0	0	0	12	0	45.2	48	208	27	27	1	1	3	0	26	5	33	2	0
Munoz, Mike, Detroit*	0	1	6.00	8	0	0	0	3	0	3.0	4	19	2	2	1	0	0	1	0	0	1	0	0
Mussina, Mike, Baltimore	14	6	4.46	25	25	3	2	0	0	167.2	163	693	84	83	20	6	4	3	44	2	117	5	0
Mutis, Jeff, Cleveland*	3	6	5.78	17	13	1	1	1	0	81.0	93	364	56	52	14	0	2	7	33	2	29	1	0
Nagy, Charles, Cleveland	2	6	6.29	9	9	1	0	0	0	48.2	66	223	38	34	6	2	1	2	13	1	30	2	0
Navarro, Jamie, Milwaukee	11	12	5.33	35	34	5	1	0	0	214.1	254	955	135	127	21	6	17	11	73	4	114	11	0
Nelson, Gene, Cal.-Tex.	0	5	3.12	52	0	0	0	22	5	60.2	60	265	28	21	3	4	2	4	25	4	35	2	0
Nelson, Jeff, Seattle	5	3	4.35	71	0	0	0	13	1	60.0	57	269	30	29	5	2	4	8	34	10	61	2	0
Nen, Robb, Texas	1	1	6.35	9	3	0	0	3	0	22.2	28	113	17	16	1	0	1	0	26	0	12	2	1
Nielsen, Jerry, California*	0	0	8.03	10	0	0	0	3	0	12.1	18	62	13	11	1	1	3	1	4	0	8	0	1
Novoa, Rafael, Milwaukee*	0	3	4.50	15	7	2	0	0	0	56.0	58	249	32	28	7	4	4	22	2	17	1	0
Nunez, Edwin, Oakland	3	6	3.81	56	0	0	0	16	1	75.2	89	341	36	32	2	5	4	0	29	2	58	4	2
O'Donoghue, John, Bal.*	0	1	4.58	11	1	0	0	3	0	19.2	22	90	12	10	4	0	0	1	10	1	16	0	0

— 252 —

																				Int.			
Pitcher, Team	W	L	ERA	G	GS	CG	ShO	GF	Sv.	IP	H	TBF	R	ER	HR	SH	SF	HB	BB	BB	SO	WP	Bk.
Ojeda, Bob, Cleveland*	2	1	4.40	9	7	0	0	0	0	43.0	48	194	22	21	5	4	3	0	21	0	27	3	0
Oliver, Darren, Texas*	0	0	2.70	2	0	0	0	0	0	3.1	2	14	1	1	1	0	0	0	1	1	4	0	0
Olson, Gregg, Baltimore	0	2	1.60	50	0	0	0	45	29	45.0	37	188	9	8	1	2	2	0	18	3	44	5	0
Ontiveros, Steve, Seattle	0	2	1.00	14	0	0	0	8	0	18.0	18	72	3	2	0	1	0	0	6	2	13	1	0
Oquist, Mike, Baltimore	0	0	3.86	5	0	0	0	2	0	11.2	12	50	5	5	0	0	0	0	4	1	8	0	0
Orosco, Jesse, Milwaukee*	3	5	3.18	57	0	0	0	27	8	56.2	47	233	25	20	2	1	2	3	17	3	67	3	1
Pall, Dann, Chicago	2	3	3.22	39	0	0	0	9	1	58.2	62	251	25	21	5	6	1	2	11	3	29	3	0
Patterson, Bob, Texas*	2	4	4.78	52	0	0	0	29	1	52.2	59	224	28	28	8	1	2	1	11	0	46	0	0
Patterson, Ken, California*	1	1	4.58	46	0	0	0	9	1	59.0	54	255	30	30	7	2	1	0	35	5	36	2	0
Pavlik, Roger, Texas	12	6	3.41	26	26	2	0	0	0	166.1	151	712	67	63	18	6	4	5	80	3	131	6	0
Pennington, Bill, Baltimore*	3	2	6.55	34	0	0	0	16	4	33.0	34	158	25	24	7	2	1	2	25	0	39	3	0
Perez, Melido, New York	6	14	5.19	25	25	0	0	0	0	163.0	173	718	103	94	22	4	2	1	64	5	148	3	1
Pichardo, Hector, K.C.	7	8	4.04	30	25	2	0	2	0	165.0	183	720	85	74	10	3	8	6	53	2	70	5	3
Plantenberg, Erik, Seattle*	0	0	6.52	20	0	0	0	4	1	9.2	11	53	7	7	0	1	0	1	12	1	3	1	0
Plunk, Eric, Cleveland	4	5	2.79	70	0	0	0	40	15	71.0	61	306	29	22	5	4	2	0	30	4	77	6	0
Poole, Jim, Baltimore*	2	1	2.15	55	0	0	0	11	2	50.1	30	197	18	12	2	3	2	0	21	5	29	0	0
Powell, Dennis, Seattle*	0	0	4.15	33	0	0	0	7	0	47.2	42	197	22	22	7	5	2	1	24	2	32	2	0
Power, Ted, Cle.-Sea.	2	4	5.46	34	0	0	0	24	13	45.1	57	206	28	27	3	3	2	0	17	4	27	2	0
Quantrill, Paul, Boston	6	12	3.91	49	14	1	1	8	1	138.0	151	594	73	60	13	4	2	4	44	14	66	0	1
Radinsky, Scott, Chicago*	8	2	4.28	73	0	0	0	24	4	54.2	61	250	33	26	3	2	0	1	19	3	44	0	4
Rasmussen, Dennis, K.C.*	1	2	7.45	9	4	0	0	3	0	29.0	40	138	25	24	4	0	1	1	14	1	12	2	0
Reed, Rick, K.C.-Tex.	1	0	5.87	3	0	0	0	0	0	7.2	12	36	5	5	1	0	0	2	2	0	5	0	0
Rhodes, Arthur, Baltimore*	5	6	6.51	17	17	0	0	0	0	85.2	91	387	62	62	16	2	3	1	49	1	49	2	0
Rogers, Kenny, Texas*	16	10	4.10	35	33	5	0	0	0	208.1	210	885	108	95	18	7	5	4	71	2	140	6	5
Ruffcorn, Scott, Chicago	0	2	8.10	3	2	0	0	1	0	10.0	9	46	11	9	2	1	1	0	10	0	2	1	0
Russell, Jeff, Boston	1	4	2.70	51	0	0	0	48	33	46.2	39	189	16	14	1	1	4	1	14	1	45	2	0
Ryan, Ken, Boston	7	2	3.60	47	0	0	0	26	1	50.0	43	223	23	20	2	4	4	3	29	5	49	3	0
Ryan, Nolan, Texas	5	5	4.88	13	13	0	0	0	0	66.1	54	291	47	36	5	2	2	1	40	0	46	3	0
Salkeld, Roger, Seattle	0	0	2.51	3	2	0	0	0	0	14.1	13	61	4	4	0	0	0	1	4	0	13	0	0
Sampen, Bill, Kansas City	2	2	5.89	18	0	0	0	3	0	18.1	25	89	12	12	1	2	0	4	9	0	9	2	0
Sanderson, Scott, California	7	11	4.46	21	21	4	1	0	0	135.1	153	576	77	67	15	6	8	5	27	5	66	1	2
Schooler, Mike, Texas	3	0	5.55	17	0	0	0	7	0	24.1	30	111	17	15	3	2	0	0	10	1	16	1	0
Schwarz, Jeff, Chicago	2	2	3.71	41	0	0	0	10	0	51.0	35	218	21	21	1	0	3	3	38	2	41	5	1
Scott, Darryl, California	1	2	5.85	16	0	0	0	2	0	20.0	19	90	13	13	1	0	2	1	11	1	13	2	0
Scudder, Scott, Cleveland	0	1	9.00	2	1	0	0	1	0	4.0	5	20	4	4	0	0	0	1	4	0	1	0	0
Seitzer, Kevin, Milwaukee	0	0	0.00	1	0	0	0	1	0	0.1	0	1	0	0	0	0	0	0	0	0	1	0	0
Sele, Aaron, Boston	7	2	2.74	18	18	0	0	0	0	111.2	100	484	42	34	5	2	5	7	48	2	93	5	0
Shinall, Zak, Seattle	0	0	3.38	1	0	0	0	0	0	2.2	4	14	1	1	1	0	0	0	2	0	0	0	0
Slocumb, Heathcliff, Cle.	3	1	4.28	10	0	0	0	5	0	27.1	28	122	14	13	3	1	2	0	12	2	18	0	0
Slusarski, Joe, Oakland	0	0	5.19	2	1	0	0	0	0	8.2	9	43	5	5	1	2	0	0	11	3	1	0	0
Smith, Lee, New York	0	0	0.00	8	0	0	0	8	3	8.0	4	33	0	0	0	1	0	1	5	1	11	0	0
Smithberg, Roger, Oakland	1	2	2.75	13	0	0	0	9	3	19.2	13	76	7	6	2	2	0	1	7	2	4	1	0
Springer, Russ, California	1	6	7.20	14	9	1	0	3	0	60.0	73	278	48	48	11	1	1	3	32	1	31	6	0
Stewart, Dave, Toronto	12	8	4.44	26	26	0	0	0	0	162.0	146	687	86	80	23	3	4	4	72	0	96	4	1
Stieb, Dave, Chicago	1	3	6.04	4	4	0	0	0	0	22.1	27	107	17	15	1	2	1	0	14	0	11	0	0
Stottlemyre, Todd, Toronto	11	12	4.84	30	28	1	1	0	0	176.2	204	786	107	95	11	5	11	3	69	5	98	7	1
Sutcliffe, Rick, Baltimore	10	10	5.75	29	28	3	0	0	0	166.0	212	763	112	106	23	4	3	6	74	5	80	1	0
Swan, Russ, Seattle*	3	3	9.15	23	0	0	0	6	0	19.2	25	100	20	20	2	1	0	2	18	1	10	0	0
Swingle, Paul, California	0	1	8.38	9	0	0	0	2	0	9.2	15	49	9	9	2	0	1	0	6	0	6	0	0
Tackett, Jeff, Baltimore	0	0	0.00	1	0	0	0	1	0	1.0	1	5	0	0	0	0	0	0	1	0	0	0	0
Tanana, Frank, New York*	0	2	3.20	3	3	0	0	0	0	19.2	18	88	10	7	2	0	0	0	7	1	12	0	0
Tapani, Kevin, Minnesota	12	15	4.43	36	35	3	1	0	0	225.2	243	964	123	111	21	3	5	6	57	1	150	4	0
Tavarez, Julian, Cleveland	2	2	6.57	8	7	0	0	0	0	37.0	53	172	29	27	7	0	1	2	13	2	19	3	1
Taylor, Scott, Boston*	0	1	8.18	16	0	0	0	3	0	11.0	14	59	10	10	1	1	0	1	12	3	8	0	0
Telford, Anthony, Baltimore	0	0	9.82	3	0	0	0	2	0	7.1	11	34	8	8	3	0	0	1	6	1	6	1	0
Thigpen, Bobby, Chicago	0	0	5.71	25	0	0	0	11	1	34.2	51	166	25	22	5	0	3	5	12	0	19	0	0
Timlin, Mike, Toronto	4	2	4.69	54	0	0	0	27	1	55.2	63	254	32	29	7	1	3	1	27	3	49	1	0
Trombley, Mike, Minnesota	6	6	4.88	44	10	0	0	8	2	114.1	131	506	72	62	15	3	7	3	41	4	85	5	0
Tsamis, George, Minnesota*	1	2	6.19	41	0	0	0	18	1	68.1	86	309	51	47	9	2	6	3	27	5	30	1	1
Valenzuela, Fernando, Bal.*	8	10	4.94	32	31	5	2	0	0	178.2	179	768	104	98	18	4	7	4	79	2	78	8	0
Valera, Julio, California	3	6	6.62	19	5	0	0	8	4	53.0	77	246	44	39	8	4	1	2	15	2	28	2	0
Van Poppel, Todd, Oakland	6	6	5.04	16	16	0	0	0	0	84.0	76	380	50	47	10	1	2	2	62	0	47	3	0
Viola, Frank, Boston*	11	8	3.14	29	29	2	1	0	0	183.2	180	787	76	64	12	8	7	6	72	5	91	5	0
Wainhouse, Dave, Seattle	0	0	27.00	3	0	0	0	0	0	2.1	7	20	7	7	1	0	0	1	5	0	2	0	0
Ward, Duane, Toronto	2	3	2.13	71	0	0	0	70	45	71.2	49	282	17	17	4	0	2	1	25	2	97	7	0
Wegman, Bill, Milwaukee	4	14	4.48	20	18	5	0	0	0	120.2	135	514	70	60	13	3	11	2	34	5	50	0	0
Welch, Bob, Oakland	9	11	5.29	30	28	0	0	0	0	166.2	208	746	102	98	25	10	3	7	56	5	63	1	0
Wells, Dave, Detroit*	11	9	4.19	32	30	0	0	0	0	187.0	183	776	93	87	26	3	3	7	42	6	139	13	0
Wertz, Bill, Cleveland	2	3	3.62	34	0	0	0	7	0	59.2	54	262	28	24	5	1	1	1	32	2	53	0	0
Whiteside, Matt, Texas	2	1	4.32	60	0	0	0	10	1	73.0	78	305	37	35	7	2	1	1	23	6	39	0	2
Wickander, Kevin, Cle.*	0	0	4.15	11	0	0	0	1	0	8.2	15	44	7	4	3	0	0	0	3	0	3	1	0
Wickman, Bob, New York	14	4	4.63	41	19	1	1	9	4	140.0	156	629	82	72	13	4	1	5	69	7	70	2	0
Williams, Woody, Toronto	3	1	4.38	30	0	0	0	9	0	37.0	40	172	18	18	2	2	1	1	22	3	24	2	1
Williamson, Mark, Baltimore	7	5	4.91	48	1	0	0	12	0	88.0	106	386	54	48	5	6	6	0	25	8	45	2	0
Willis, Carl, Minnesota	3	0	3.10	53	0	0	0	21	5	58.0	56	236	23	20	2	2	1	0	17	5	44	3	0
Witt, Bobby, Oakland	14	13	4.21	35	33	5	1	0	0	220.0	226	950	112	103	16	9	8	3	91	5	131	8	1
Witt, Mike, New York	3	2	5.27	9	9	0	0	0	0	41.0	39	183	26	24	7	1	0	3	22	0	30	1	0
Young, Cliff, Cleveland*	3	3	4.62	21	7	0	0	3	1	60.1	74	271	35	31	9	1	1	3	18	1	31	0	0
Young, Curt, Oakland*	1	1	4.30	3	3	0	0	0	0	14.2	14	64	7	7	5	0	0	0	6	0	4	0	0
Young, Matt, Cleveland*	1	6	5.21	22	6	0	0	2	0	74.1	75	347	45	43	8	4	1	3	57	0	65	5	1

PITCHERS WITH TWO OR MORE TEAMS

																				Int.			
Pitcher, Team	W	L	ERA	G	GS	CG	ShO	GF	Sv.	IP	H	TBF	R	ER	HR	SH	SF	HB	BB	BB	SO	WP	Bk.
Boever, Joe, Oakland	4	2	3.86	42	0	0	0	19	0	79.1	87	353	40	34	8	2	3	4	33	4	49	1	0
Boever, Joe, Detroit	2	1	2.74	19	0	0	0	3	3	23.0	14	96	10	7	1	3	4	0	11	3	14	0	0

Pitcher, Team	W	L	ERA	G	GS	CG	ShO	GF	Sv.	IP	H	TBF	R	ER	HR	SH	SF	HB	BB	Int. BB	SO	WP	Bk.
Davis, Storm, Oakland	2	6	6.18	19	8	0	0	2	0	62.2	68	284	45	43	5	1	2	2	33	2	37	2	0
Davis, Storm, Detroit	0	2	3.06	24	0	0	0	10	4	35.1	25	144	12	12	4	1	1	1	15	4	36	1	0
Habyan, John, New York	2	1	4.04	36	0	0	0	21	1	42.1	45	181	20	19	5	0	2	0	16	2	29	0	2
Habyan, John, Kansas City	0	0	4.50	12	0	0	0	2	0	14.0	14	58	7	7	1	0	0	0	4	2	10	0	0
Linton, Doug, Toronto	0	1	6.55	4	1	0	0	0	0	11.0	11	55	8	8	0	0	2	1	9	0	4	0	0
Linton, Doug, California	2	0	7.71	19	0	0	0	6	0	25.2	35	123	22	22	8	0	1	0	14	1	19	2	0
Nelson, Gene, California	0	5	3.08	46	0	0	0	20	4	52.2	50	231	25	18	3	3	4	2	23	4	31	1	0
Nelson, Gene, Texas	0	0	3.38	6	0	0	0	2	1	8.0	10	34	3	3	0	0	0	1	1	4	1	0	
Power, Ted, Cleveland	0	2	7.20	20	0	0	0	6	0	20.0	30	101	17	16	2	2	1	0	8	3	11	1	0
Power, Ted, Seattle	2	2	3.91	25	0	0	0	18	13	25.1	27	105	11	11	1	1	1	0	9	1	16	1	0
Reed, Rick, Kansas City	0	0	9.82	1	0	0	0	0	0	3.2	6	18	4	4	0	0	0	1	1	0	3	0	0
Reed, Rick, Texas	1	0	2.25	2	0	0	0	0	0	4.0	6	18	1	1	1	0	0	1	1	0	2	0	0

NOTE—The following pitchers combined to pitch shutout games: Baltimore (4)—Moyer and Olson; Valenzuela and Williamson; McDonald, Williamson and Olson; Moyer and Mills; Boston (6)—Darwin and Russell; Darwin, Harris and Russell; Darwin, Fossas, Harris and Russell; Sele and Harris; Viola and Hesketh; Clemens, Harris and Bankhead; California (3)—Langston and Grahe; Magrane, Lewis and Frey; Farrell and Frey; Chicago (4)—Alvarez and Radinsky; Alvarez and Schwarz; Alvarez and Hernandez; Bere, Belcher and DeLeon; Cleveland (7)—Mesa, Lilliquist and Plunk 2; Mesa and Lilliquist; Clark, Hernandez and Plunk; Kramer and Hernandez; Mesa, Hernandez, Lilliquist and Plunk; Clark and DiPoto; Detroit (2)—Wells, Kiely and Henneman; Wells and Gohr; Kansas City (3)—Appier and Montgomery; Magnante, Belinda and Montgomery; Appier and Gubicza; Milwaukee (4)—Eldred and Henry; Eldred and Orosco; Boddicker, Lloyd and Fetters; Miranda and Orosco; Minnesota (2)—Banks, Mahomes and Merriman; Deshaies and Aguilera; New York (9)—Perez, Howe and Farr 2; Key and Habyan; Wickman and Farr; Kamieniecki and Munoz; Key, Munoz and Howe; Abbott and Gibson; Kamieniecki, Assenmacher and Wickman; Hitchcock and Wickman; Oakland (1)—Mohler, Campbell, Boever and Eckersley; Seattle (5)—Hanson, DeLucia and Charlton; Bosio, DeLucia and Charlton; Hanson, Nelson, Swan and Charlton; Hanson, Swan, Nelson and Charlton; Johnson, DeLucia and Charlton; Texas (3)—Leibrandt, Whiteside and Henke; Rogers and Henke; Pavlik and Henke; Toronto (7)—Leiter, Timlin and Ward; Stottlemyre and Ward; Stottlemyre, Cox, Eichhorn and Timlin; Leiter, Eichhorn, Castillo and Ward; Stottlemyre and Cox; Guzman and Ward; Hentgen, Castillo, Timlin and Ward.

FIELDING

TEAM

Team	Pct.	G	PO	A	E	TC	DP	TP	PB
Seattle	.985	162	4361	1726	90	6177	173	0	13
Kansas City	.984	162	4336	1709	97	6142	150	0	15
Baltimore	.984	162	4328	1789	100	6217	171	0	6
Minnesota	.984	162	4333	1755	100	6188	160	0	21
New York	.983	162	4315	1889	105	6309	166	0	7
Toronto	.982	162	4324	1582	107	6013	144	0	6
Oakland	.982	162	4357	1625	111	6093	161	0	15
Chicago	.982	162	4362	1665	112	6139	153	0	15
California	.980	162	4291	1694	120	6105	161	0	10
Boston	.980	162	4357	1692	122	6171	155	0	11
Texas	.979	162	4315	1780	132	6227	145	0	18
Detroit	.979	162	4310	1777	132	6219	148	0	8
Milwaukee	.979	162	4341	1632	131	6104	148	0	12
Cleveland	.976	162	4337	1661	148	6146	174	0	9
Totals	.981	1134	60667	23976	1607	86250	2209	0	166

INDIVIDUAL

FIRST BASEMEN

*Throws lefthanded.

Leader, Team	Pct.	G	PO	A	E	TC	DP
MATTINGLY, N.Y.*	.998	130	1258	84	3	1345	123

Player, Team	Pct.	G	PO	A	E	TC	DP
Aldrete, Oakland*	.995	59	370	28	2	400	39
Amaral, Seattle	1.000	3	4	0	0	4	2
Armas, Oakland	1.000	12	74	4	0	78	4
Barnes, Detroit	.984	27	113	9	2	124	6
Blankenship, Oakland	1.000	6	12	0	0	12	1
Blowers, Seattle	1.000	1	1	0	0	1	0
Brooks, Kansas City	1.000	3	19	3	0	22	1
Brosius, Oakland	1.000	11	68	2	0	70	7
Browne, Oakland	.909	2	8	2	1	11	3
Bush, Minnesota*	1.000	4	13	0	0	13	2
Carey, Baltimore*	.970	9	64	1	2	67	7
Coles, Toronto	1.000	1	1	0	0	1	0
Cooper, Boston	1.000	2	1	0	0	1	1
Davis, Baltimore	.990	22	190	12	2	204	19
Denson, Chicago	.800	3	4	0	1	5	1
Diaz, Texas	1.000	1	1	0	0	1	0
Doran, Milwaukee	1.000	4	16	2	0	18	2
Fielder, Detroit	.991	119	971	78	10	1059	84
Gaetti, Cal.-K.C.	.993	24	134	12	1	147	13
R. Gonzales, California	.989	31	163	10	2	175	24
Griffey, Seattle*	1.000	1	1	0	0	1	0
Gwynn, Kansas City*	1.000	1	12	1	0	13	1
Hale, Minnesota	1.000	1	5	1	0	6	1
Hamelin, Kansas City*	.986	15	129	9	2	140	10
Hemond, Oakland	1.000	1	5	0	0	5	0
Hrbek, Minnesota	.995	115	940	81	5	1026	98
Jaha, Milwaukee	.992	150	1186	128	10	1324	116
James, New York*	1.000	1	1	0	0	1	0
Javier, California	.971	12	64	2	2	68	2
Jefferson, Cleveland*	.976	15	112	10	3	125	10
Jorgensen, Minnesota	.977	9	36	6	1	43	5
Joyner, Kansas City*	.994	140	1116	145	7	1268	116
Kreuter, Detroit	1.000	1	5	1	0	6	0
Larkin, Minnesota	.985	18	123	6	2	131	10
Leyritz, New York	.993	29	260	13	2	275	22
Litton, Seattle	1.000	13	86	8	0	94	15
Lovullo, California	.000	1	0	0	0	0	0
Lyons, Boston	.000	1	0	0	0	0	0
Maas, New York*	.984	17	115	5	2	122	13
Magadan, Seattle	.991	41	308	19	3	330	33
Maksudian, Minnesota	1.000	4	28	6	0	34	3
Martinez, Cleveland	.973	22	135	7	4	146	12
Martinez, Toronto	1.000	7	25	4	0	29	2
T. Martinez, Seattle	.997	103	932	60	3	995	89

Player, Team	Pct.	G	PO	A	E	TC	DP
Mattingly, New York*	.998	130	1258	84	3	1345	123
McCarty, Minnesota*	.994	36	278	30	2	310	24
McGwire, Oakland	1.000	25	197	14	0	211	20
Melvin, Boston	1.000	1	5	1	0	6	1
Meulens, New York	1.000	3	5	0	0	5	0
Milligan, Cleveland	1.000	18	101	7	0	108	16
Molitor, Toronto	.985	23	178	14	3	195	16
Neel, Oakland	.981	34	236	22	5	263	25
Nilsson, Milwaukee	1.000	4	27	3	0	30	3
O'Brien, Seattle*	.988	9	76	8	1	85	10
Olerud, Toronto*	.992	137	1160	97	10	1267	107
Pagliarulo, Baltimore	1.000	4	26	2	0	28	3
Palmeiro, Texas*	.997	160	1388	147	5	1540	133
Pasqua, Chicago*	.987	32	147	9	2	158	14
Peltier, Texas*	1.000	5	8	0	0	8	0
Pirkl, Seattle	1.000	5	42	5	0	47	8
Quintana, Boston	.991	53	320	21	3	344	30
Redus, Texas	.957	5	21	1	1	23	5
Riles, Boston	1.000	1	1	0	0	1	0
Russell, Texas	1.000	1	9	0	0	9	0
Sasser, Seattle	1.000	1	2	0	0	2	0
Segui, Baltimore*	.996	144	1152	98	5	1255	122
Seitzer, Oak.-Mil.	1.000	31	211	18	0	229	28
Snow, California*	.995	129	1010	81	6	1097	103
Sorrento, Cleveland	.995	144	1012	86	6	1104	107
Steinbach, Oakland	.982	15	102	9	2	113	9
Surhoff, Milwaukee	1.000	8	28	2	0	30	2
Sveum, Oakland	.976	14	116	5	3	124	11
Tettleton, Detroit	.992	59	364	24	3	391	41
Thomas, Chicago	.989	150	1222	83	15	1320	128
Van Burkleo, Cal.*	1.000	12	99	3	0	102	8
Vaughn, Boston	.987	131	1110	70	16	1196	104
Ventura, Chicago	1.000	4	7	0	0	7	1
Voigt, Baltimore	1.000	5	26	2	0	28	3
T. Ward, Toronto	1.000	1	3	0	0	3	0
Winfield, Minnesota	1.000	5	29	1	0	30	3
Yount, Milwaukee	1.000	7	43	1	0	44	7

FIRST BASEMEN WITH TWO OR MORE TEAMS

Player, Team	Pct.	G	PO	A	E	TC	DP
Gaetti, California	1.000	6	37	2	0	39	2
Gaetti, Kansas City	.991	18	97	10	1	108	11
Seitzer, Oakland	1.000	24	168	17	0	185	24
Seitzer, Milwaukee	1.000	7	43	1	0	44	4

SECOND BASEMEN

Leader, Team	Pct.	G	PO	A	E	TC	DP
LIND, Kansas City	.994	136	269	362	4	635	75

Player, Team	Pct.	G	PO	A	E	TC	DP
Abbott, Oakland	.000	2	0	0	0	0	0
Alomar, Toronto	.980	150	254	439	14	707	92
Amaral, Seattle	.975	77	151	206	9	366	48
Backman, Seattle	1.000	1	0	1	0	1	0
Baerga, Cleveland	.979	150	347	445	17	809	108
Barnes, Detroit	1.000	10	7	10	0	17	1
Bell, Milwaukee	.983	47	115	114	4	233	33
Blankenship, Oakland	.957	19	32	56	4	92	13
Boone, Seattle	.991	74	140	177	3	320	55
Bordick, Oakland	1.000	1	5	2	0	7	2
Browne, Oakland	1.000	3	5	9	0	14	1
Cedeno, Toronto	1.000	5	2	11	0	13	1
Cora, Chicago	.974	151	295	410	19	724	85
Correia, California	1.000	11	30	19	0	49	6
Curtis, California	1.000	3	2	1	0	3	0
Doran, Milwaukee	.964	17	28	26	2	56	5
Easley, California	.978	54	101	125	5	231	26
Espinoza, Cleveland	.900	2	6	3	1	10	2
Fletcher, Boston	.982	116	217	371	11	599	68
Gallego, New York	.978	52	83	143	5	231	36
Gates, Oakland	.981	139	281	431	14	726	88
Gomez, Detroit	.988	17	37	45	1	83	7
R. Gonzales, California	1.000	4	4	3	0	7	1
Grebeck, Chicago	1.000	16	29	53	0	82	13
Griffin, Toronto	.978	11	22	23	1	46	6
Hale, Minnesota	.952	21	23	36	3	62	8
Hatcher, Boston	.000	2	0	0	0	0	0
Hemond, Oakland	1.000	1	2	1	0	3	1
Hocking, Minnesota	1.000	1	4	4	0	8	2
Howard, Kansas City	.927	7	15	23	3	41	2
Hulett, Baltimore	1.000	4	10	8	0	18	3
Huson, Texas	1.000	5	8	6	0	14	2
Jaha, Milwaukee	1.000	1	1	0	0	1	0
Javier, California	1.000	2	2	0	0	2	0
Kelly, New York	.978	125	245	369	14	628	84
Knoblauch, Minnesota	.988	148	298	425	9	732	98
Lind, Kansas City	.994	136	269	362	4	635	75
Litton, Seattle	1.000	17	21	27	0	48	9
Lovullo, California	.981	91	184	220	8	412	67
Lyons, Boston	1.000	9	6	15	0	21	2
Martin, Chicago	.957	5	13	9	1	23	4
McLemore, Baltimore	1.000	25	53	59	0	112	19
Miller, Kansas City	.900	3	3	6	1	10	1
Naehring, Boston	.973	15	36	35	2	73	10
Petralli, Texas	1.000	1	1	0	0	1	0
Phillips, Detroit	.985	51	106	159	4	269	33
Reboulet, Minnesota	1.000	11	14	16	0	30	6
Redus, Texas	.000	1	0	0	0	0	0
Reynolds, Baltimore	.986	141	306	396	10	712	110
Richardson, Boston	1.000	8	9	24	0	33	3
Riles, Boston	1.000	20	22	45	0	67	8
Ripken, Texas	.992	34	52	73	1	126	16
Rivera, Boston	.969	27	36	57	3	96	13
Rossy, Kansas City	.987	24	29	48	1	78	11
Sax, Chicago	1.000	1	0	3	0	3	0
Seitzer, Oak.-Mil.	1.000	3	3	7	0	10	2
Shave, Texas	1.000	8	9	17	0	26	3
Shumpert, K.C.	1.000	8	11	11	0	22	3
Sojo, Toronto	1.000	8	9	11	0	20	2
Spiers, Milwaukee	.971	104	209	226	13	448	53
Stankiewicz, New York	1.000	6	7	10	0	17	4
Stillwell, California	.952	18	39	41	4	84	6
Strange, Texas	.980	135	272	362	13	647	81
Suero, Milwaukee	.944	8	5	12	1	18	1
Sveum, Oakland	1.000	4	4	7	0	11	1
Thon, Milwaukee	.960	22	40	32	3	75	9
Treadway, Cleveland	.949	19	29	45	4	78	8
Turang, Seattle	1.000	1	1	0	0	1	0
Vina, Seattle	1.000	16	25	38	0	63	12
Walewander, Cal.	1.000	2	2	3	0	5	1
Whitaker, Detroit	.981	110	236	322	11	569	75
Wilkerson, K.C.	1.000	10	5	16	0	21	3
Wilson, Kansas City	.800	1	1	3	1	5	0

SECOND BASEMEN WITH TWO OR MORE TEAMS

Player, Team	Pct.	G	PO	A	E	TC	DP
Seitzer, Oakland	1.000	2	2	6	0	8	1
Seitzer, Milwaukee	1.000	1	1	1	0	2	1

THIRD BASEMEN

Leader, Team	Pct.	G	PO	A	E	TC	DP
BOGGS, New York	.970	134	75	311	12	398	29

Player, Team	Pct.	G	PO	A	E	TC	DP
Amaral, Seattle	.972	19	5	30	1	36	7
Backman, Seattle	.857	9	4	14	3	21	0
Barnes, Detroit	.963	13	9	17	1	27	0
Blowers, Seattle	.951	117	66	225	15	306	14
Boggs, New York	.970	134	75	311	12	398	29
Brosius, Oakland	1.000	10	2	19	0	21	2
Browne, Oakland	.880	13	6	16	3	25	2
Coles, Toronto	.882	16	11	19	4	34	0
Cooper, Boston	.937	154	111	244	24	379	22
Cora, Chicago	1.000	3	1	3	0	4	0
Correia, California	1.000	3	1	0	0	1	0
Diaz, Texas	1.000	12	8	19	0	27	2
Easley, California	.977	14	10	32	1	43	3
Espinoza, Cleveland	.937	99	42	107	10	159	9
Felder, Oakland	1.000	2	0	3	0	3	1
Fletcher, Boston	.000	1	0	0	0	0	0
Fryman, Detroit	.976	69	44	120	4	168	10
Gaetti, Cal.-K.C.	.970	79	51	141	6	198	16
Gallego, New York	.973	27	18	53	2	73	5
Gomez, Baltimore	.951	70	48	145	10	203	16
R. Gonzales, California	.956	79	63	156	10	229	20
Grebeck, Chicago	.923	14	6	18	2	26	2
Griffin, Toronto	1.000	6	3	5	0	8	0
Gruber, California	.938	17	18	42	4	64	3
Hale, Minnesota	.974	19	11	26	1	38	2
Hiatt, Kansas City	.909	70	45	114	16	175	6
Howard, Kansas City...	1.000	2	1	0	0	1	0
Hulett, Baltimore	.963	75	48	161	8	217	23
Huson, Texas	.750	2	1	2	1	4	0
Jaha, Milwaukee	.000	1	0	0	0	0	0
Jorgensen, Minnesota	.982	45	27	85	2	114	8
Larkin, Minnesota	.000	2	0	0	0	0	0
Litton, Seattle	1.000	7	1	6	0	7	1
Livingstone, Detroit	.955	62	33	94	6	133	6
Lovullo, California	.929	14	14	25	3	42	2
Lyons, Boston	.000	1	0	0	0	0	0
Magadan, Seattle	.972	27	17	53	2	72	5
Maksudian, Minnesota	.000	1	0	0	0	0	0
Martinez, Cleveland	.934	35	27	44	5	76	5
Martinez, Toronto	.000	1	0	0	0	0	0
E. Martinez, Seattle	.889	16	5	11	2	18	1
McLemore, Baltimore..	.800	4	0	8	2	10	0
Meulens, New York	.000	1	0	0	0	0	0
Miller, Kansas City	.889	21	11	29	5	45	2
Naehring, Boston	1.000	9	6	6	0	12	2
Ortiz, Boston	1.000	5	2	2	0	4	1
Pagliarulo, Min.-Bal.	.969	107	69	184	8	261	17
Palmer, Texas	.922	148	85	258	29	372	21
Paquette, Oakland	.950	104	81	165	13	259	17
Perez, California	.962	45	24	101	5	130	7
Petralli, Texas	.000	1	0	0	0	0	0
Phillips, Detroit	.333	1	0	1	2	3	0
Reboulet, Minnesota	.978	35	22	65	2	89	7
Richardson, Boston	1.000	1	0	1	0	1	0
Riles, Boston	1.000	11	3	8	0	11	0
Ripken, Texas	.667	1	1	1	1	3	0
Rivera, Boston	1.000	2	1	3	0	4	1
Rossy, Kansas City	1.000	16	2	7	0	9	0
Russell, Texas	.000	1	0	0	0	0	0
Seitzer, Oak.-Mil.	.937	79	53	125	12	190	13
Silvestri, New York	.800	3	0	8	2	10	0
Sojo, Toronto	.667	3	1	1	1	3	0
Sprague, Toronto	.955	150	127	232	17	376	21
Stahoviak, Minnesota.	.922	19	9	38	4	51	1
Stankiewicz, New York	1.000	4	0	5	0	5	0
Strange, Texas	1.000	9	4	12	0	16	2

Player, Team	Pct.	G	PO	A	E	TC	DP
Suero, Milwaukee	1.000	1	1	1	0	2	1
Surhoff, Milwaukee	.949	121	101	216	17	334	19
Sveum, Oakland	1.000	7	5	4	0	9	1
Thome, Cleveland	.950	47	29	86	6	121	10
Thon, Milwaukee	.977	25	12	30	1	43	2
Trammell, Detroit	.938	35	19	56	5	80	7
Treadway, Cleveland	.933	42	17	66	6	89	5
Turang, Seattle	.000	2	0	0	0	0	0
Velarde, New York	.955	16	5	16	1	22	2
Ventura, Chicago	.965	155	112	278	14	404	26
Voigt, Baltimore	1.000	3	0	1	0	1	0
Wilson, Kansas City	1.000	15	7	19	0	26	4

THIRD BASEMEN WITH TWO OR MORE TEAMS

Player, Team	Pct.	G	PO	A	E	TC	DP
Gaetti, California	.857	7	1	5	1	7	1
Gaetti, Kansas City	.974	72	50	136	5	191	15
Pagliarulo, Minnesota	.984	79	42	137	3	182	11
Pagliarulo, Baltimore	.937	28	27	47	5	79	6
Seitzer, Oakland	.933	46	31	66	7	104	6
Seitzer, Milwaukee	.942	33	22	59	5	86	7

SHORTSTOPS

Leader, Team	Pct.	G	PO	A	E	TC	DP
GAGNE, Kansas City	.986	159	266	451	10	727	93

Player, Team	Pct.	G	PO	A	E	TC	DP
Abbott, Oakland	.938	6	3	12	1	16	2
Amaral, Seattle	1.000	14	20	34	0	54	14
Barnes, Detroit	.500	2	0	1	1	2	0
Bell, Milwaukee	.962	40	67	110	7	184	20
Blankenship, Oakland	1.000	2	1	8	0	9	1
Bordick, Oakland	.982	159	280	418	13	711	108
Brosius, Oakland	.857	6	0	6	1	7	2
Cedeno, Toronto	.973	10	8	28	1	37	4
Cooper, Boston	.000	1	0	0	0	0	0
Correia, California	.981	40	56	102	3	161	16
Diaz, Texas	.986	57	81	134	3	218	27
DiSarcina, California	.975	126	193	362	14	569	77
Espinoza, Cleveland	.985	35	18	47	1	66	13
Fermin, Cleveland	.960	140	211	346	23	580	87
Fernandez, Toronto	.985	94	196	260	7	463	62
Fletcher, Boston	.000	2	0	0	0	0	0
Fryman, Detroit	.953	81	125	262	19	406	60
Gagne, Kansas City	.986	159	266	451	10	727	93
Gallego, New York	.976	55	68	172	6	246	35
Gil, Texas	.954	22	27	76	5	108	10
Gomez, Detroit	.963	29	32	73	4	109	16
R. Gonzales, California	1.000	5	3	1	0	4	1
Grebeck, Chicago	.983	46	56	114	3	173	25
Griffin, Toronto	.960	20	34	38	3	75	9
Guillen, Chicago	.972	133	189	361	16	566	82
Hale, Minnesota	.000	1	0	0	0	0	0
Hocking, Minnesota	.971	12	15	19	1	35	9
Howard, Kansas City	1.000	3	1	5	0	6	0
Hulett, Baltimore	1.000	8	0	7	0	7	0
Huson, Texas	.909	12	16	34	5	55	8
Jorgensen, Minnesota	1.000	6	2	4	0	6	0
Knoblauch, Minnesota	1.000	6	2	6	0	8	1
Lee, Texas	.968	72	96	205	10	311	35
Leius, Minnesota	.947	9	10	26	2	38	7
Lewis, Cleveland	.964	13	22	31	2	55	10
Listach, Milwaukee	.975	95	127	267	10	404	53
Litton, Seattle	1.000	5	2	8	0	10	2
Lovullo, California	1.000	9	4	4	0	8	1
Meares, Minnesota	.961	111	165	304	19	488	70
Naehring, Boston	1.000	4	3	3	0	6	3
Owen, New York	.968	96	116	312	14	442	44
Palmer, Texas	1.000	1	1	0	0	1	0
Reboulet, Minnesota	.982	62	85	134	4	223	27
Richardson, Boston	1.000	5	2	6	0	8	2
Ripken, Baltimore	.977	162	226	495	17	738	101
Ripken, Texas	1.000	18	27	49	0	76	12
Rivera, Boston	.963	27	28	51	3	82	14
Rossy, Kansas City	1.000	11	11	21	0	32	7
Schofield, Toronto	.977	36	61	106	4	171	23
Seitzer, Milwaukee	1.000	1	1	1	0	2	0
Shave, Texas	.917	9	13	20	3	36	6
Silvestri, New York	.955	4	9	12	1	22	4
Sojo, Toronto	.974	8	14	23	1	38	6
Spiers, Milwaukee	1.000	4	1	4	0	5	2
Stankiewicz, New York	.000	1	0	0	0	0	0
Stillwell, California	.944	7	7	10	1	18	3
Strange, Texas	.000	1	0	0	0	0	0
Sveum, Oakland	1.000	1	3	1	0	4	0
Thon, Milwaukee	.966	28	28	57	3	88	8
Trammell, Detroit	.989	63	79	181	3	263	24
Valentin, Boston	.971	144	238	432	20	690	96
Valentin, Milwaukee	.922	19	20	51	6	77	9
Velarde, New York	.972	26	31	74	3	108	18
Vina, Seattle	1.000	4	3	2	0	5	0
Vizquel, Seattle	.980	155	245	475	15	735	108
Walewander, Cal.	1.000	6	7	10	0	17	3
Wilkerson, K.C.	1.000	4	3	9	0	12	0

OUTFIELDERS

Leader, Team	Pct.	G	PO	A	E	TC	DP
RAINES, Chicago	1.000	112	200	5	0	205	2

Player, Team	Pct.	G	PO	A	E	TC	DP
Abbott, Oakland	.971	13	33	1	1	35	0
Aldrete, Oakland*	1.000	20	37	0	0	37	0
Anderson, Baltimore*	.993	140	296	7	2	305	0
Armas, Oakland	1.000	1	3	0	0	3	0
Barnes, Detroit	1.000	18	29	0	0	29	0
Bautista, Detroit	1.000	16	38	2	0	40	0
Becker, Minnesota*	.875	3	7	0	1	8	0
Bell, Milwaukee	.750	3	3	0	1	4	0
Belle, Cleveland	.986	150	338	16	5	359	7
Blankenship, Oakland	.994	66	162	1	1	164	0
Blosser, Boston*	1.000	9	11	1	0	12	0
Blowers, Seattle	1.000	2	2	0	0	2	0
Bones, Milwaukee	.000	1	0	0	0	0	0
Brito, Minnesota	1.000	10	12	1	0	13	0
Brooks, Kansas City	.966	40	53	3	2	58	1
Brosius, Oakland	.991	46	103	2	1	106	0
Browne, Oakland	.985	56	130	1	2	133	0
Bruett, Minnesota*	.857	13	12	0	2	14	0
Brunansky, Mil.	.987	71	146	4	2	152	0
Buford, Baltimore	.984	30	61	2	1	64	1
Buhner, Seattle	.978	148	263	8	6	277	2
Burks, Chicago	.982	146	313	6	6	325	1
Bush, Minnesota*	.000	1	0	0	0	0	0
Butler, Toronto*	.970	16	32	0	1	33	0
Calderon, Chicago	1.000	47	94	2	0	96	0
Canate, Toronto	1.000	31	38	2	0	40	1
Canseco, Texas	.970	49	94	4	3	101	2
Carter, Toronto	.974	151	289	7	8	304	0
Coles, Toronto	.957	44	65	1	3	69	0
Cotto, Seattle	.983	34	59	0	1	60	0
Curtis, California	.980	151	426	13	9	448	6
Cuyler, Detroit	.968	80	211	2	7	220	1
Dascenzo, Texas*	.990	68	91	5	1	97	2
Davis, Texas	.960	44	94	2	4	100	1
E. Davis, Detroit	.981	18	52	0	1	53	0
Dawson, Boston	1.000	20	42	0	0	42	0
Deer, Det.-Bos.	.973	122	286	7	8	301	3
Devereaux, Baltimore	.988	130	311	8	4	323	3
Diaz, Milwaukee	.979	28	46	1	1	48	0
Ducey, Texas	1.000	26	51	1	0	52	0
Edmonds, California*	.981	17	47	4	1	52	2
Felder, Seattle	.987	95	143	9	2	154	0
Fox, Oakland*	1.000	26	47	0	0	47	1
Gibson, Detroit*	.987	32	76	0	1	77	0
Gladden, Detroit	.986	86	196	9	3	208	1
Gonzalez, Texas	.985	129	265	5	4	274	0
Green, Toronto*	1.000	2	1	0	0	1	0
Greenwell, Boston	.993	134	261	6	2	269	1

Player, Team	Pct.	G	PO	A	E	TC	DP
Griffey, Seattle*	.991	139	316	8	3	327	3
Gruber, California	1.000	1	2	0	0	2	0
Gwynn, Kansas City*	.994	83	149	6	1	156	0
Hamilton, Milwaukee	.992	129	340	10	3	353	1
Hammonds, Baltimore	.961	23	47	2	2	51	0
Harris, Texas	.943	38	47	3	3	53	0
Haselman, Seattle	.000	2	0	0	0	0	0
Hatcher, Boston	.993	130	284	6	2	292	2
Hemond, Oakland	1.000	6	2	0	0	2	0
D. Henderson, Oakland	.991	76	205	7	2	214	4
R. Henderson, Oak.-Tor.*	.974	118	258	6	7	271	1
Hill, Cleveland	.940	39	62	1	4	67	0
Howard, Kansas City	.000	1	0	0	0	0	0
Howard, Cleveland	.977	47	81	3	2	86	1
Howitt, Seattle	1.000	29	42	1	0	43	0
Huff, Chicago	1.000	43	40	0	0	40	0
Hulse, Texas*	.988	112	244	3	3	250	0
Humphreys, New York	1.000	21	14	0	0	14	0
Jackson, Chicago	.989	47	89	5	1	95	2
Jackson, Toronto	.989	46	86	2	1	89	0
James, Texas	1.000	7	14	0	0	14	0
James, New York*	.966	103	140	4	5	149	1
Javier, California	.981	64	101	2	2	105	0
Johnson, Chicago*	.980	146	427	7	9	443	1
Johnson, Seattle*	.000	1	0	0	0	0	0
Jose, Kansas City	.972	144	237	6	7	250	3
Kirby, Cleveland	.983	123	273	19	5	297	5
Knoblauch, Minnesota	1.000	1	2	0	0	2	0
Koslofski, Kansas City	1.000	13	20	2	0	22	2
Lampkin, Milwaukee	.000	3	0	0	0	0	0
Larkin, Minnesota	1.000	28	33	1	0	34	1
Lee, Minnesota	1.000	13	15	0	0	15	0
Leonard, Baltimore	.833	4	5	0	1	6	0
Leyritz, New York	1.000	28	42	1	0	43	0
Listach, Milwaukee	1.000	6	8	0	0	8	0
Litton, Seattle	1.000	22	25	3	0	28	1
Lofton, Cleveland*	.979	146	402	11	9	422	3
Lovullo, California	1.000	2	6	0	0	6	0
Lydy, Oakland	.958	38	67	2	3	72	0
Lyons, Boston	1.000	10	5	0	0	5	0
Mack, Minnesota	.986	128	347	8	5	360	1
Maldonado, Cleveland	.976	26	39	1	1	41	0
Martinez, Baltimore*	1.000	5	2	0	0	2	0
McCarty, Minnesota*	.959	67	134	8	6	148	1
McLemore, Baltimore	.987	124	282	13	4	299	4
McNeely, Boston	.917	13	22	0	2	24	0
McRae, Kansas City	.983	153	394	4	7	405	3
McReynolds, K.C.	.990	104	191	5	2	198	0
Mercedes, Baltimore	1.000	8	11	1	0	12	1
Meulens, New York	1.000	24	27	0	0	27	0
Mieske, Milwaukee	.936	22	43	1	3	47	0
Miller, Kansas City	1.000	4	4	0	0	4	0
Munoz, Minnesota	.983	102	172	5	3	180	2
Nelson, Seattle	.000	1	0	0	0	0	0
Newfield, Seattle	.000	5	0	0	0	0	0
Newson, Chicago*	1.000	5	5	0	0	5	0
Obando, Baltimore	.929	8	13	0	1	14	0
O'Brien, Seattle*	1.000	1	1	0	0	1	0
O'Leary, Milwaukee*	1.000	19	32	1	0	33	0
O'Neill, New York*	.992	138	230	7	2	239	0
Orton, California	1.000	1	1	0	0	1	0
Paquette, Oakland	1.000	1	1	0	0	1	0
Pasqua, Chicago*	.984	37	57	3	1	61	1
Peltier, Texas*	.950	55	72	4	4	80	2
Phillips, Detroit	.969	108	215	5	7	227	1
Polonia, California*	.983	141	286	12	5	303	3
Puckett, Minnesota	.994	139	312	13	2	327	2
Pulliam, Kansas City	.971	26	33	0	1	34	0
Quintana, Boston	1.000	51	92	4	0	96	1
Raines, Chicago	1.000	112	200	5	0	205	2
Ramirez, Cleveland	1.000	1	3	0	0	3	0
Reboulet, Minnesota	1.000	3	1	0	0	1	0
Redus, Texas	.981	61	103	3	2	108	0
Reimer, Milwaukee	.962	37	75	1	3	79	0
Russell, Texas	.000	1	0	0	0	0	0
Salmon, California	.980	140	335	12	7	354	2
Sasser, Seattle	.946	37	50	3	3	56	0
Sax, Chicago	1.000	32	39	0	0	39	0
Seitzer, Oak.-Mil.	1.000	4	8	0	0	8	0
Sheets, Seattle	1.000	1	1	0	0	1	0
Sierra, Oakland	.977	133	291	9	7	307	3
Smith, Baltimore	1.000	4	5	1	0	6	0
Sorrento, Cleveland	1.000	3	3	0	0	3	0
Spiers, Milwaukee	1.000	7	3	1	0	4	0
Surhoff, Milwaukee	.975	24	37	2	1	40	0
Sveum, Oakland	.000	1	0	0	0	0	0
Tartabull, New York	.978	50	88	3	2	93	2
Tettleton, Detroit	.980	55	92	4	2	98	1
Thurman, Detroit	.950	53	54	3	3	60	1
Tinsley, Seattle	.900	6	9	0	1	10	0
Trammell, Detroit	.941	8	15	1	1	17	0
Turang, Seattle	.986	38	71	2	1	74	0
Vaughn, Milwaukee	.986	94	214	1	3	218	1
Velarde, New York	.932	50	66	2	5	73	0
Voigt, Baltimore	.987	43	75	3	1	79	0
Walton, California	1.000	1	2	0	0	2	0
T. Ward, Toronto	.990	65	94	2	1	97	0
White, Toronto	.993	145	399	6	3	408	2
B. Williams, New York	.989	139	366	5	4	375	0
G. Williams, New York	.956	37	41	2	2	45	0
Wilson, Kansas City	.000	1	0	0	0	0	0
Winfield, Minnesota	1.000	31	62	2	0	64	0
Yount, Milwaukee	.997	114	299	6	1	306	1
Zupcic, Boston	.979	122	179	7	4	190	2

OUTFIELDERS WITH TWO OR MORE TEAMS

Player, Team	Pct.	G	PO	A	E	TC	DP
Deer, Detroit	.975	86	192	5	5	202	3
Deer, Boston	.970	36	94	2	3	99	0
R. Henderson, Oak.*	.974	74	182	5	5	192	1
R. Henderson, Tor.*	.975	44	76	1	2	79	0
Seitzer, Oakland	1.000	3	4	0	0	4	0
Seitzer, Milwaukee	1.000	1	4	0	0	4	0

CATCHERS

Leader, Team	Pct.	G	PO	A	E	TC	DP	PB
STANLEY, N.Y.	.996	122	652	46	3	701	5	6

Player, Team	Pct.	G	PO	A	E	TC	DP	PB
Alomar, Cleveland	.984	64	342	25	6	373	4	3
Blowers, Seattle	1.000	1	1	0	0	1	0	0
Borders, Toronto	.986	138	869	80	13	962	12	6
Delgado, Toronto	1.000	1	2	0	0	2	0	0
Fisk, Chicago	1.000	25	75	5	0	80	0	2
Flaherty, Boston	1.000	13	35	9	0	44	1	1
L. Gonzales, Cal.	1.000	2	4	0	0	4	0	0
Harper, Minnesota	.988	134	736	64	10	810	6	18
Haselman, Seattle	.992	49	236	17	2	255	2	5
Helfand, Oakland	1.000	5	25	5	0	30	1	0
Hemond, Oakland	.991	75	395	38	4	437	5	10
Hoiles, Baltimore	.993	124	696	64	5	765	11	2
Howard, Seattle	1.000	4	5	0	0	5	0	0
Karkovice, Chi.	.994	127	769	63	5	837	4	9
Kmak, Milwaukee	1.000	50	172	23	0	195	4	4
Knorr, Toronto	1.000	39	168	20	0	188	4	0
Kreuter, Detroit	.988	112	517	69	7	593	10	4
LaValliere, Chi.	1.000	37	164	28	0	192	2	4
Lampkin, Mil.	.978	60	242	24	6	272	2	1
Levis, Cleveland	.991	29	109	7	1	117	4	1
Leyritz, New York	1.000	12	31	1	0	32	0	1
Lindsey, Chicago	1.000	2	3	0	0	3	0	0
Lyons, Boston	.000	1	0	0	0	0	0	0
Macfarlane, K.C.	.985	114	647	68	11	726	11	8
Mayne, K.C.	.995	68	356	27	2	385	1	5
McIntosh, Mil.	.000	1	0	0	0	0	0	0
Melvin, Boston	.994	76	304	18	2	324	4	5
Mercedes, Oak.	.987	18	66	10	1	77	1	1
Myers, California	.986	97	369	44	6	419	5	5

Leader, Team	Pct.	G	PO	A	E	TC	DP	PB
Nilsson, Mil.	.981	91	430	30	9	469	3	7
Nokes, New York ..	.992	56	245	19	2	266	0	1
Ortiz, Cleveland	.990	95	441	58	5	504	13	2
Orton, California ...	.980	35	184	17	4	205	4	1
Parent, Baltimore .	.989	21	83	5	1	89	0	1
Parks, Minnesota .	.970	7	28	4	1	33	1	2
Parrish, Cleveland	.950	10	47	10	3	60	1	3
Pena, Boston........	.995	125	698	53	4	755	8	5
Petralli, Texas	.990	39	178	11	2	191	4	2
Rodriguez, Texas..	.991	134	801	76	8	885	6	14
Rowland, Detroit...	.988	17	75	7	1	83	1	0
Russell, Texas	1.000	11	21	0	0	21	0	2
Santovenia, K.C. ...	1.000	4	14	1	0	15	0	2
Sasser, Seattle......	1.000	4	8	1	0	9	0	0
Stanley, New York	.996	122	652	46	3	701	5	6
Steinbach, Oak.	.989	86	422	38	5	465	9	4
Surhoff, Mil.	1.000	3	9	0	0	9	0	0
Tackett, Baltimore	.989	38	167	16	2	185	1	3
Tettleton, Detroit..	.997	56	268	19	1	288	1	4
Tingley, California	.995	58	200	20	1	221	3	3
Turner, California .	.992	25	116	14	1	131	0	1
Valle, Seattle.........	.995	135	881	71	5	957	13	8
Webster, Min.	1.000	45	177	13	0	190	1	1
Wrona, Chicago....	1.000	4	12	0	0	12	0	0

PITCHERS

Leader, Team	Pct.	G	PO	A	E	TC	DP
FERNANDEZ, Chicago	1.000	34	18	38	0	56	2

Player, Team	Pct.	G	PO	A	E	TC	DP
Abbott, New York*	.979	32	4	42	1	47	3
Abbott, Cleveland	.833	5	2	3	1	6	0
Aguilera, Minnesota	1.000	65	12	8	0	20	0
Alvarez, Chicago*	.971	31	5	28	1	34	2
Anderson, California* .	1.000	0	0	1	0	1	0
Appier, Kansas City.....	.976	34	26	14	1	41	4
Assenmacher, N.Y.*	.500	26	0	1	1	2	1
Austin, Milwaukee	1.000	31	1	4	0	5	0
Ayrault, Seattle	1.000	14	0	2	0	2	0
Bailey, Boston	1.000	11	0	5	0	5	0
Bankhead, Boston	.833	40	1	4	1	6	0
Banks, Minnesota	.824	31	13	15	6	34	1
Belcher, Chicago	1.000	12	6	6	0	12	2
Belinda, Kansas City ...	1.000	23	0	1	0	1	1
Bere, Chicago	.926	24	11	14	2	27	1
Bergman, Detroit	1.000	9	3	6	0	9	1
Bielecki, Cleveland	1.000	13	5	11	0	16	1
Boddicker, Milwaukee.	.875	10	5	9	2	16	1
Boever, Oak.-Det.	.955	61	9	12	1	22	1
Bohanon, Texas*	1.000	36	5	18	0	23	3
Bolton, Chicago	1.000	9	4	9	0	13	0
Bolton, Detroit*	.913	43	6	15	2	23	2
Bones, Milwaukee	.980	32	26	22	1	49	2
Bosio, Seattle...............	.971	29	13	21	1	35	2
Brewer, Kansas City*..	.714	46	1	4	2	7	0
Briscoe, Oakland	1.000	17	1	4	0	5	0
Bronkey, Texas	1.000	21	3	10	0	13	1
Brow, Toronto..............	1.000	6	3	8	0	11	1
Brown, Texas	.959	34	29	42	3	74	2
Brummett, Minnesota..	1.000	5	1	2	0	3	0
Burgos, Kansas City*..	1.000	5	0	1	0	1	0
Burns, Texas	.818	25	6	3	2	11	1
Butcher, California	1.000	23	1	1	0	2	0
Cadaret, Kansas City*	1.000	13	2	2	0	4	0
Campbell, Oakland	1.000	11	0	1	0	1	0
Canseco, Texas............	.000	1	0	0	0	0	0
Carpenter, Texas.........	1.000	27	1	4	0	5	0
Cary, Chicago*	1.000	16	1	4	0	5	0
Casian, Minnesota*	1.000	54	4	4	0	8	0
Castillo, Toronto*........	.923	51	3	9	1	13	1
Charlton, Seattle*	1.000	34	0	2	0	2	1
Christopher, Cleveland	1.000	9	0	1	0	1	0
Clark, Cleveland	.875	26	4	10	2	16	0
Clemens, Boston	.969	29	11	20	1	32	1

Player, Team	Pct.	G	PO	A	E	TC	DP
Cone, Kansas City	.980	34	24	24	1	49	3
Converse, Seattle	1.000	4	2	6	0	8	0
Cook, New York	1.000	4	0	1	0	1	0
Cook, Cleveland*	.800	25	2	6	2	10	1
Cook, Baltimore	.000	2	0	0	0	0	0
Cox, Toronto	.889	44	4	4	1	9	0
Crim, California	1.000	11	0	5	0	5	0
Cummings, Seattle*	.818	10	3	6	2	11	0
Darling, Oakland..........	.967	31	12	17	1	30	0
Darwin, Boston	.957	34	14	31	2	47	2
Davis, California	.000	1	0	0	0	0	0
S. Davis, Oak.-Det.	.950	43	5	14	1	20	1
Dayley, Toronto*	.000	2	0	0	0	0	0
DeLeon, Chicago	.000	11	0	0	0	0	0
DeLucia, Seattle	1.000	30	2	7	0	9	0
Deshaies, Minnesota*.	1.000	27	4	22	0	26	0
DeSilva, Detroit............	.000	1	0	0	0	0	0
DiPino, Kansas City*...	1.000	11	0	3	0	3	0
DiPoto, Cleveland	.875	46	4	10	2	16	1
Doherty, Detroit	.872	32	14	20	5	39	1
Dopson, Boston	1.000	34	17	22	0	39	0
Downs, Oakland	1.000	42	3	10	0	13	2
Drahman, Chicago	1.000	5	0	1	0	1	0
Dreyer, Texas	1.000	10	2	4	0	6	0
Eckersley, Oakland	1.000	64	0	5	0	5	0
Eichhorn, Toronto	1.000	54	7	18	0	25	1
Eldred, Milwaukee.......	.964	36	26	27	2	55	4
Erickson, Minnesota ...	.945	34	18	34	3	55	3
Fajardo, Texas.............	.000	1	0	0	0	0	0
Farr, New York	1.000	49	6	10	0	16	0
Farrell, California	1.000	21	5	11	0	16	0
Fernandez, Chicago	1.000	34	18	38	0	56	2
Fetters, Milwaukee.......	.923	45	5	7	1	13	4
Finley, California*	.878	35	10	26	5	41	0
Fleming, Seattle*	1.000	26	9	28	0	37	1
Flener, Toronto*	1.000	6	2	2	0	4	0
Fossas, Boston*	.875	71	1	6	1	8	0
Frey, California*	1.000	55	2	6	0	8	0
Frohwirth, Baltimore ...	.967	70	8	21	1	30	3
Garces, Minnesota	.000	3	0	0	0	0	0
Gardiner, Detroit..........	1.000	10	0	2	0	2	0
Gardner, Kansas City ..	.917	17	6	5	1	12	1
Gibson, New York*	1.000	20	3	4	0	7	1
Gohr, Detroit	1.000	16	1	1	0	2	1
R. Gonzales, California	1.000	1	0	1	0	1	0
Gordon, Kansas City ...	.951	48	18	21	2	41	0
Gossage, Oakland	.889	39	5	3	1	9	0
Grahe, California	1.000	45	3	13	0	16	1
Granger, Kansas City*	.000	1	0	0	0	0	0
Grater, Detroit..............	.000	6	0	0	0	0	0
Grimsley, Cleveland.....	1.000	10	4	4	0	8	0
Groom, Detroit*	.889	19	1	7	1	9	0
Guardado, Minnesota*	1.000	19	6	9	0	15	1
Gubicza, Kansas City ..	.947	49	11	7	1	19	0
Gullickson, Detroit.......	1.000	28	11	24	0	35	1
Guthrie, Minnesota*	1.000	22	0	5	0	5	0
Guzman, Toronto..........	.964	33	11	16	1	28	0
Haas, Detroit................	1.000	20	2	5	0	7	1
Habyan, N.Y.-K.C.	1.000	48	5	7	0	12	0
Hampton, Seattle*........	.667	13	0	2	1	3	0
Haney, Kansas City*...	1.000	23	7	19	0	26	0
Hanson, Seattle	.943	31	25	25	3	53	3
Harris, Boston	.875	80	8	13	3	24	1
Hartley, Minnesota.......	.900	53	7	2	1	10	0
Hathaway, California* ..	1.000	11	4	10	0	14	4
Heaton, New York*......	1.000	18	1	6	0	7	0
Henke, Texas	1.000	66	6	10	0	16	0
Henneman, Detroit	.917	63	6	5	1	12	0
Henry, Milwaukee	1.000	54	5	7	0	12	0
Henry, Seattle	1.000	31	1	1	0	2	0
Hentgen, Toronto..........	.971	34	12	22	1	35	1
Hernandez, Cleveland .	.933	49	3	11	1	15	1
Hernandez, Chicago	.929	70	2	11	1	14	1
Hesketh, Boston*	.900	28	2	7	1	10	1
Higuera, Milwaukee* ..	1.000	8	3	0	0	3	0

Player, Team	Pct.	G	PO	A	E	TC	DP
Hillegas, Oakland	.889	18	1	7	1	9	0
Hitchcock, New York*	1.000	6	1	3	0	4	0
Holman, Seattle	1.000	19	1	3	0	4	0
Holzemer, California*	1.000	5	0	5	0	5	0
Honeycutt, Oakland*	.875	52	2	5	1	8	1
Horsman, Oakland*	1.000	40	0	2	0	2	0
Howard, Chicago*	.000	3	0	0	0	0	0
Howe, New York*	.938	51	2	13	1	16	0
Hutton, New York	.750	7	1	2	1	4	0
Ignasiak, Milwaukee	1.000	27	0	3	0	3	0
Jean, New York	1.000	10	1	6	0	7	0
Jimenez, Oakland	.000	5	0	0	0	0	0
Johnson, Detroit	.500	6	1	0	1	2	0
Johnson, New York*	.500	2	1	0	1	2	0
Johnson, Seattle*	1.000	35	10	29	0	39	2
Jones, Chicago	1.000	6	1	0	0	1	0
Kamieniecki, N.Y.	1.000	30	17	23	0	40	1
Karsay, Oakland	1.000	8	2	3	0	5	0
Key, New York*	.922	34	14	33	4	51	1
Kiefer, Milwaukee	1.000	6	1	1	0	2	0
Kiely, Detroit	1.000	8	0	5	0	5	2
King, Seattle*	.500	13	0	1	1	2	0
Knudsen, Detroit	1.000	30	4	3	0	7	0
Kramer, Cleveland	.957	39	9	13	1	23	0
Krueger, Detroit*	1.000	32	2	10	0	12	1
Langston, California*	.966	35	10	47	2	59	4
Leach, Chicago	1.000	14	1	0	0	1	0
Leary, Seattle	1.000	33	14	28	0	42	3
Lefferts, Texas*	.947	52	6	12	1	19	0
Leftwich, California	.941	12	5	11	1	17	2
Leibrandt, Texas*	.964	26	9	45	2	56	5
Leiter, Toronto*	.941	34	4	12	1	17	0
Leiter, Detroit	.889	27	5	11	2	18	1
Lewis, California	.750	15	5	1	2	8	0
Lilliquist, Cleveland*	.909	56	1	9	1	11	0
Linton, Tor.-Cal.	1.000	23	2	3	0	5	0
Lloyd, Milwaukee*	.941	55	4	12	1	17	1
Lopez, Cleveland	.846	9	5	6	2	13	0
MacDonald, Detroit*	.941	68	3	13	1	17	0
Magnante, K.C.*	1.000	7	4	6	0	10	0
Magrane, California*	.955	8	4	17	1	22	2
Mahomes, Minnesota	1.000	12	4	4	0	8	1
Maldonado, Mil.	.889	29	3	5	1	9	1
Manzanillo, Mil.	1.000	10	2	5	0	7	1
Maysey, Milwaukee	.600	23	1	2	2	5	0
McCaskill, Chicago	.938	30	7	23	2	32	4
McDonald, Baltimore	.966	34	15	42	2	59	2
McDowell, Chicago	.957	34	23	43	3	69	2
McGehee, Baltimore	1.000	5	2	2	0	4	0
Meacham, K.C.	1.000	15	2	4	0	6	1
Melendez, Boston	1.000	9	1	3	0	4	0
Merriman, Minnesota	1.000	19	1	4	0	5	0
Mesa, Cleveland	.936	34	15	29	3	47	0
Milacki, Cleveland	1.000	5	0	3	0	3	0
Militello, New York	1.000	3	2	1	0	3	0
Mills, Baltimore	.857	45	7	11	3	21	2
Minchey, Boston	.800	5	1	3	1	5	0
Miranda, Milwaukee*	.895	22	4	13	2	19	1
Mlicki, Cleveland	1.000	3	1	1	0	2	0
Mohler, Oakland*	.917	42	2	9	1	12	2
Monteleone, New York	.952	42	9	11	1	21	0
Montgomery, K.C.	1.000	69	6	13	0	19	0
Moore, Detroit	.972	36	27	43	2	72	3
Morris, Toronto	.913	27	11	10	2	23	1
Moyer, Baltimore*	.975	25	14	25	1	40	1
Munoz, New York	1.000	38	1	6	0	7	1
Munoz, Detroit*	1.000	8	0	1	0	1	0
Mussina, Baltimore	1.000	25	12	19	0	31	1
Mutis, Cleveland*	1.000	17	3	17	0	20	1
Nagy, Cleveland	.957	9	8	14	1	23	2
Navarro, Milwaukee	.946	35	14	21	2	37	2
Nelson, Cal.-Tex.	1.000	52	4	8	0	12	1
Nelson, Seattle	1.000	71	3	12	0	15	2
Nen, Texas	1.000	9	5	2	0	7	1
Nielsen, California*	1.000	10	1	1	0	2	0
Novoa, Milwaukee*	1.000	15	4	6	0	10	0
Nunez, Oakland	.938	56	7	8	1	16	1
O'Donoghue, Bal.*	.667	11	1	1	1	3	0
Ojeda, Cleveland*	1.000	9	3	9	0	12	1
Oliver, Texas*	.500	2	0	1	1	2	0
Olson, Baltimore	1.000	50	2	7	0	9	0
Ontiveros, Seattle	.667	14	0	2	1	3	2
Oquist, Baltimore	1.000	5	1	0	0	1	0
Orosco, Milwaukee*	1.000	57	1	19	0	20	0
Pall, Chicago	.938	39	4	11	1	16	0
Patterson, Texas*	1.000	52	3	7	0	10	0
Patterson, California*	.900	46	1	8	1	10	0
Pavlik, Texas	.925	26	10	27	3	40	2
Pennington, Bal.*	1.000	34	1	2	0	3	0
Perez, New York	1.000	25	5	17	0	22	0
Pichardo, K.C.	1.000	30	20	27	0	47	1
Plantenberg, Seattle*	1.000	20	3	1	0	4	1
Plunk, Cleveland	.875	70	5	2	1	8	0
Poole, Baltimore*	.917	55	4	7	1	12	0
Powell, Seattle*	1.000	33	3	5	0	8	0
Power, Cle.-Sea.	1.000	45	0	5	0	5	0
Quantrill, Boston	.957	49	4	18	1	23	3
Radinsky, Chicago*	.833	73	1	9	2	12	0
Rasmussen, K.C.*	1.000	9	0	5	0	5	0
Reed, K.C.-Tex.	1.000	3	3	1	0	4	0
Rhodes, Baltimore*	.917	17	2	9	1	12	0
Rogers, Texas*	.941	35	18	46	4	68	4
Ruffcorn, Chicago	.000	3	0	0	3	3	0
Russell, Boston	1.000	51	2	10	0	12	0
Ryan, Boston	.909	47	3	7	1	11	0
Ryan, Texas	.625	13	1	4	3	8	0
Salkeld, Seattle	1.000	3	0	2	0	2	0
Sampen, Kansas City	1.000	18	2	2	0	4	0
Sanderson, Cal.	.929	21	11	15	2	28	1
Schooler, Texas	1.000	17	1	3	0	4	0
Schwarz, Chicago	.800	41	3	1	1	5	0
Scott, California	.000	16	0	0	0	0	0
Scudder, Cleveland	.000	2	0	0	0	0	0
Seitzer, Milwaukee	.000	1	0	0	0	0	0
Sele, Boston	.706	18	3	9	5	17	1
Shinall, Seattle	1.000	1	1	0	0	1	0
Slocumb, Cleveland	1.000	20	1	2	0	3	1
Slusarski, Oakland	1.000	2	1	2	0	3	1
Smith, New York	1.000	8	0	1	0	1	0
Smithberg, Oakland	1.000	13	2	6	0	8	0
Springer, California	1.000	14	3	2	0	5	0
Stewart, Toronto	1.000	26	13	9	0	22	1
Stieb, Chicago	.667	4	0	2	1	3	1
Stottlemyre, Toronto	.968	30	11	19	1	31	2
Sutcliffe, Baltimore	.975	29	9	30	1	40	2
Swan, Seattle*	1.000	23	0	6	0	6	0
Swingle, California	1.000	9	0	1	0	1	0
Tackett, Baltimore	.000	1	0	0	0	0	0
Tanana, New York*	.500	3	0	1	1	2	0
Tapani, Minnesota	1.000	36	17	32	0	49	2
Tavarez, Cleveland	1.000	8	2	3	0	5	2
Taylor, Boston*	1.000	16	0	1	0	1	0
Telford, Baltimore	1.000	3	1	2	0	3	0
Thigpen, Chicago	1.000	25	1	2	0	3	1
Timlin, Toronto	.944	54	7	10	1	18	1
Trombley, Minnesota	1.000	44	6	19	0	25	2
Tsamis, Minnesota*	1.000	41	7	14	0	21	2
Valenzuela, Bal.*	.923	32	11	37	4	52	1
Valera, California	.900	19	4	5	1	10	1
Van Poppel, Oakland	1.000	16	6	4	0	10	1
Viola, Boston*	.911	29	10	31	4	45	1
Wainhouse, Seattle	.000	3	0	0	0	0	0
D. Ward, Toronto	1.000	71	1	5	0	6	0
Wegman, Milwaukee	.943	20	12	21	2	35	4
Welch, Oakland	1.000	30	16	26	0	42	2
Wells, Detroit*	.970	32	10	22	1	33	0
Wertz, Cleveland	.800	34	4	0	1	5	0
Whiteside, Texas	.857	60	5	7	2	14	3
Wickander, Cle.*	.000	11	0	0	0	0	0
Wickman, New York	.929	41	7	19	2	28	1

Player, Team	Pct.	G	PO	A	E	TC	DP
Williams, Toronto	1.000	30	5	6	0	11	1
Williamson, Baltimore	1.000	48	8	10	0	18	0
Willis, Minnesota	1.000	53	2	6	0	8	0
Witt, Oakland	.944	35	12	39	3	54	5
Witt, New York	1.000	9	1	6	0	7	0
C. Young, Cleveland*	1.000	21	4	5	0	9	1
Young, Oakland*	1.000	3	0	3	0	3	0
M. Young, Cleveland*	.933	22	4	10	1	15	0

PITCHERS WITH TWO OR MORE TEAMS

Player, Team	Pct.	G	PO	A	E	TC	DP
Boever, Oakland	1.000	42	7	10	0	17	1

Player, Team	Pct.	G	PO	A	E	TC	DP
Boever, Detroit	.800	19	2	2	1	5	0
S. Davis, Oakland	.933	19	3	11	1	15	1
S. Davis, Detroit	1.000	24	2	3	0	5	0
Habyan, New York	1.000	36	1	6	0	7	0
Habyan, Kansas City	1.000	12	4	1	0	5	0
Linton, Toronto	1.000	4	2	0	0	2	0
Linton, California	1.000	19	0	3	0	3	0
Nelson, California	1.000	46	4	7	0	11	1
Nelson, Texas	1.000	6	0	1	0	1	0
Power, Cleveland	1.000	20	0	1	0	1	0
Power, Seattle	1.000	25	0	4	0	4	0
Reed, Kansas City	1.000	1	2	0	0	2	0
Reed, Texas	1.000	2	1	1	0	2	0

MISCELLANEOUS

SHUTOUT GAMES

Read across for wins, down for losses.

Team	Tor.	Det.	N.Y.	Mil.	Bos.	Sea.	Tex.	Bal.	K.C.	Cle.	Chi.	Cal.	Min.	Oak.	W	L	Pct.
Toronto	..	0	1	1	2	1	0	0	1	0	1	1	3	0	11	1	.917
Detroit	0	..	0	0	0	1	1	1	1	0	1	0	1	1	7	2	.778
New York	0	1	..	0	1	2	0	2	0	2	2	1	2	0	13	4	.765
Milwaukee	0	0	0	..	1	1	1	2	0	0	0	0	1	1	6	4	.600
Boston	0	0	1	1	..	1	0	2	1	0	4	0	0	1	11	8	.579
Seattle	0	0	0	0	3	..	1	1	0	2	0	2	0	1	10	9	.526
Texas	0	0	1	0	0	0	..	0	2	0	0	0	1	2	6	6	.500
Baltimore	1	0	0	0	1	0	0	..	2	1	2	1	2	0	10	11	.476
Kansas City	0	0	1	0	0	1	0	0	..	1	1	0	1	1	6	7	.462
Cleveland	0	0	0	1	0	0	1	2	0	..	1	1	0	2	8	10	.444
Chicago	0	0	0	0	0	1	1	1	0	1	..	1	2	4	11	14	.440
California	0	1	0	0	0	1	0	0	0	1	2	..	1	0	6	8	.429
Minnesota	0	0	0	1	0	0	0	0	0	1	0	1	..	0	3	13	.188
Oakland	0	0	0	0	0	0	1	0	0	1	0	0	0	..	2	13	.133
Lost	1	2	4	4	8	9	6	11	7	10	14	8	13	13	110	110	.500

HOME RECORD

Read across for home wins, down for road losses.

Team	Tex.	N.Y.	Tor.	Bal.	Sea.	Cle.	Chi.	Det.	Cal.	K.C.	Bos.	Oak.	Mil.	Min.	W	L	Pct.
Texas	..	5	3	4	4	3	4	3	4	3	4	5	4	4	50	31	.617
New York	2	..	3	4	4	4	4	5	4	4	4	4	4	4	50	31	.617
Toronto	2	4	..	4	3	4	3	4	5	3	6	2	3	5	48	33	.593
Baltimore	2	3	3	..	5	5	2	3	4	2	5	5	5	5	48	33	.593
Seattle	5	3	4	4	..	6	1	4	4	4	2	1	4	4	46	35	.568
Cleveland	4	4	2	3	3	..	3	3	5	4	4	4	5	2	46	35	.568
Chicago	5	2	3	4	4	6	..	2	2	2	3	3	4	5	45	36	.556
Detroit	3	3	3	5	5	4	1	..	4	2	4	5	4	1	44	37	.543
California	4	4	3	3	3	4	3	2	..	3	5	4	3	3	44	37	.543
Kansas City	4	4	5	3	4	3	2	3	4	..	1	4	3	3	43	38	.531
Boston	4	3	2	3	3	3	4	4	6	0	..	5	2	4	43	38	.531
Oakland	4	4	1	1	3	2	3	3	4	5	2	..	5	1	38	43	.469
Milwaukee	2	2	1	3	2	3	1	3	2	4	4	6	..	5	38	43	.469
Minnesota	4	2	1	3	2	4	1	1	6	2	3	3	4	..	36	45	.444
Lost on road	45	43	34	44	45	51	32	40	54	40	44	51	50	46	619	515	.546

ROAD RECORD

Read across for road wins, down for home losses.

Team	Chi.	Tor.	K.C.	Det.	N.Y.	Bos.	Bal.	Tex.	Sea.	Min.	Mil.	Oak.	Cle.	Cal.	W	L	Pct.
Chicago	..	3	4	5	2	2	4	3	5	5	5	4	3	4	49	32	.605
Toronto	3	..	1	3	4	4	3	2	5	5	5	5	3	4	47	34	.580
Kansas City	5	3	..	4	2	6	2	3	3	4	2	2	2	3	41	40	.506
Detroit	4	3	3	..	1	3	3	3	2	5	4	3	3	4	41	40	.506
New York	4	2	2	4	..	3	3	1	3	4	5	2	3	2	38	43	.469
Boston	3	1	5	2	3	..	4	2	4	3	3	4	2	1	37	44	.457
Baltimore	2	2	3	2	3	4	..	2	2	3	3	5	3	3	37	44	.457
Texas	1	4	3	3	4	2	4	..	1	2	4	3	2	3	36	45	.444
Seattle	3	3	2	1	2	3	1	3	..	5	4	3	3	3	36	45	.444
Minnesota	2	1	4	5	2	2	1	3	2	..	1	5	4	3	35	46	.432
Milwaukee	2	4	3	2	2	4	2	2	2	2	..	1	2	3	31	50	.383
Oakland	3	4	2	1	2	1	1	1	6	4	0	..	2	3	30	51	.370
Cleveland	0	2	3	3	2	4	2	3	0	2	3	4	..	2	30	51	.370
California	4	1	3	2	2	0	2	2	3	1	4	2	1	..	27	54	.333
Lost at home	36	33	38	37	31	38	33	31	35	45	43	43	35	37	515	619	.454

PITCHING AGAINST EACH CLUB

BALTIMORE—85-77

Pitcher	Bos. W-L	Cal. W-L	Chi. W-L	Cle. W-L	Det. W-L	K.C. W-L	Mil. W-L	Min. W-L	N.Y. W-L	Oak. W-L	Sea. W-L	Tex. W-L	Tor. W-L	Totals W-L
Frohwirth	1-0	0-1	0-0	1-0	0-2	1-0	1-0	0-0	1-0	1-0	0-1	0-2	0-1	6-7
McDonald	1-1	1-0	1-1	1-2	1-1	2-1	1-1	1-1	1-1	1-1	1-1	1-0	0-3	13-14
Mills	0-0	0-0	0-1	2-0	0-2	0-1	0-0	0-0	0-0	2-0	0-0	1-0	0-0	5-4

| | Bos. | Cal. | Chi. | Cle. | Det. | K.C. | Mil. | Min. | N.Y. | Oak. | Sea. | Tex. | Tor. | Totals |
Pitcher	W-L	W-L	W-L	W-L	W-L	W-L	W-L	W-L	W-L	W-L	W-L	W-L	W-L	W-L
Moyer	1-1	1-1	1-1	1-1	0-1	2-0	1-1	1-0	0-3	2-0	1-0	1-0	0-0	12-9
Mussina	1-1	2-1	0-1	0-0	1-0	2-0	0-2	3-0	1-0	2-0	1-0	1-1	0-0	14-6
O'Donoghue	0-0	0-0	0-0	0-0	0-0	0-0	0-0	0-0	0-1	0-0	0-0	0-0	0-0	0-1
Olson	0-0	0-0	0-1	0-0	0-0	0-1	0-0	0-0	0-0	0-0	0-0	0-0	0-0	0-2
Pennington	1-0	0-1	0-0	0-0	0-0	0-1	0-0	0-0	1-0	0-0	1-0	0-0	0-0	3-2
Poole	0-0	0-0	0-0	0-0	1-0	0-0	0-0	0-0	0-0	0-0	1-0	0-0	0-1	2-1
Rhodes	0-0	1-0	0-0	0-0	1-1	0-1	2-0	1-1	0-0	0-0	0-1	0-1	0-1	5-6
Sutcliffe	0-1	1-0	0-2	2-0	1-1	0-0	1-0	0-2	1-1	1-0	1-1	0-1	2-1	10-10
Valenzuela	1-2	0-1	1-1	1-2	0-0	0-0	0-1	2-0	0-0	1-0	0-0	0-3	2-0	8-10
Williamson	0-1	1-0	1-0	0-0	0-0	0-0	2-0	0-0	1-1	0-1	1-1	0-0	1-1	7-5
Totals	6-7	7-5	4-8	8-5	5-8	7-5	8-5	8-4	6-7	10-2	7-5	4-8	5-8	85-77

No-decisions—Cook, McGehee, Oquist, Tackett, Telford.

BOSTON—80-82

| | Bal. | Cal. | Chi. | Cle. | Det. | K.C. | Mil. | Min. | N.Y. | Oak. | Sea. | Tex. | Tor. | Totals |
Pitcher	W-L	W-L	W-L	W-L	W-L	W-L	W-L	W-L	W-L	W-L	W-L	W-L	W-L	W-L
Bailey	0-0	0-0	0-0	0-0	0-1	0-0	0-0	0-0	0-0	0-0	0-0	0-0	0-0	0-1
Bankhead	0-0	0-1	1-0	0-0	0-0	1-0	0-0	0-0	0-0	0-0	0-0	0-0	0-0	2-1
Clemens	3-1	2-1	0-0	0-1	0-1	2-2	0-0	0-0	0-2	0-1	2-0	2-1	0-4	11-14
Darwin	2-1	1-0	2-1	0-1	2-0	0-1	2-1	0-0	1-1	1-1	1-1	1-2	2-1	15-11
Dopson	0-1	1-0	1-1	0-0	1-2	0-2	0-0	1-2	2-1	1-0	0-0	0-1	0-1	7-11
Fossas	0-0	1-0	0-0	0-0	0-1	0-0	0-0	0-0	0-0	0-0	0-0	0-0	0-0	1-1
Harris	0-1	0-0	1-0	0-2	0-0	0-0	2-2	0-1	1-1	1-0	1-0	0-0	0-0	6-7
Hesketh	0-0	0-1	1-0	1-0	0-0	0-0	0-1	1-0	0-0	0-2	0-0	0-0	0-0	3-4
Melendez	0-0	0-0	0-1	0-0	1-0	0-0	0-0	0-0	0-0	0-0	0-0	1-0	0-0	2-1
Minchey	0-0	0-0	0-0	1-0	0-0	0-0	0-1	0-0	0-0	0-0	0-0	0-0	0-1	1-2
Quantrill	2-1	0-0	0-0	1-2	0-0	0-0	0-2	1-1	0-0	1-1	1-0	0-2	0-2	6-12
Russell	0-0	0-1	0-0	0-1	0-0	1-0	0-1	0-0	0-0	0-0	0-0	0-0	0-1	1-4
Ryan	0-0	1-0	0-0	1-1	1-0	0-1	0-0	1-0	0-0	1-0	1-0	0-0	1-0	7-2
Sele	0-0	1-0	0-1	0-0	1-0	0-0	1-0	2-0	0-1	2-0	0-0	0-0	0-0	7-2
Taylor	0-0	0-0	0-0	0-0	0-1	0-0	0-0	0-0	0-0	0-0	0-0	0-0	0-0	0-1
Viola	0-1	0-1	1-1	1-0	0-1	1-0	0-0	1-1	2-1	2-0	1-2	2-0	0-0	11-8
Totals	7-6	7-5	7-5	5-8	6-7	5-7	5-8	7-5	6-7	9-3	7-5	6-6	3-10	80-82

CALIFORNIA—71-91

| | Bal. | Bos. | Chi. | Cle. | Det. | K.C. | Mil. | Min. | N.Y. | Oak. | Sea. | Tex. | Tor. | Totals |
Pitcher	W-L	W-L	W-L	W-L	W-L	W-L	W-L	W-L	W-L	W-L	W-L	W-L	W-L	W-L
Butcher	0-0	0-0	0-0	1-0	0-0	0-0	0-0	0-0	0-0	0-0	0-0	0-0	0-0	1-0
Crim	0-0	1-0	0-0	0-0	1-0	0-0	0-0	0-0	0-0	0-0	0-1	0-1	0-0	2-2
Farrell	0-1	0-1	1-1	1-0	0-3	0-1	0-0	0-2	1-0	0-0	0-0	0-2	0-1	3-12
Finley	1-2	1-2	1-2	2-0	0-1	1-0	2-0	2-2	0-1	2-2	2-1	2-0	0-1	16-14
Frey	0-0	0-0	1-0	0-0	0-1	0-0	0-1	0-0	1-1	0-0	0-0	0-0	0-0	2-3
Grahe	1-0	0-0	0-0	0-0	0-0	0-0	1-1	0-0	0-0	2-0	0-0	0-0	0-0	4-1
Hathaway	0-0	0-0	0-0	0-1	0-1	2-0	0-0	1-0	0-0	0-0	0-0	1-0	0-1	4-3
Holzemer	0-1	0-0	0-0	0-0	0-0	0-0	0-1	0-0	0-0	0-1	0-0	0-0	0-0	0-3
Langston	2-0	1-0	3-1	0-1	1-1	1-1	2-0	0-1	1-2	2-1	0-2	1-1	2-0	16-11
Leftwich	0-1	0-0	0-1	0-0	0-0	1-1	0-0	0-0	0-1	2-0	0-1	1-1	0-0	4-6
Lewis	0-0	0-0	0-0	0-1	0-0	1-0	0-0	0-0	0-0	0-0	0-1	0-0	0-0	1-2
Linton	0-0	1-0	0-0	0-0	0-0	0-0	0-0	0-0	1-0	0-0	0-0	0-0	0-0	2-0
Magrane	0-0	0-0	0-0	0-0	1-0	0-1	0-1	0-0	0-0	1-0	0-0	0-0	1-0	3-2
Nelson	0-1	0-2	0-0	0-1	0-0	0-0	0-1	0-0	0-0	0-0	0-0	0-0	0-0	0-5
Patterson	0-0	0-0	0-0	0-0	0-0	0-0	1-0	0-0	0-0	0-1	0-0	0-0	0-0	1-1
Sanderson	0-0	1-2	1-0	1-1	0-0	0-1	0-0	1-0	1-1	0-0	1-1	0-2	0-2	7-11
Scott	0-0	0-0	0-0	0-0	0-1	1-0	0-0	0-1	0-0	0-0	1-0	0-0	0-0	1-2
Springer	0-0	0-0	0-1	0-1	0-0	0-0	0-0	0-2	1-1	0-1	0-0	0-0	0-0	1-6
Swingle	0-0	0-0	0-0	0-0	0-0	0-0	0-0	0-0	0-0	0-0	0-0	0-0	0-1	0-1
Valera	1-1	0-0	0-0	0-1	1-0	0-1	0-0	0-0	0-0	0-0	0-1	1-0	0-2	3-6
Totals	5-7	5-7	7-6	5-7	4-8	6-7	7-5	4-9	6-6	6-7	6-7	6-7	4-8	71-91

No-decisions—Anderson, Davis, R. Gonzales, Nielsen.

CHICAGO—94-68

| | Bal. | Bos. | Cal. | Cle. | Det. | K.C. | Mil. | Min. | N.Y. | Oak. | Sea. | Tex. | Tor. | Totals |
Pitcher	W-L	W-L	W-L	W-L	W-L	W-L	W-L	W-L	W-L	W-L	W-L	W-L	W-L	W-L
Alvarez	1-1	0-0	3-1	1-1	2-1	0-0	0-0	0-0	2-1	2-1	2-1	0-0	2-1	15-8
Belcher	0-0	0-1	0-0	0-0	0-0	0-2	0-0	2-0	0-1	1-0	0-0	0-1	0-0	3-5
Bere	1-1	1-1	1-1	2-1	3-0	1-1	0-0	1-0	0-0	0-0	0-0	2-0	0-0	12-5
Bolton	1-1	0-1	0-0	0-1	0-0	0-0	0-0	0-0	0-1	0-0	1-0	0-0	0-2	2-6
Cary	0-0	0-0	0-0	0-0	0-0	0-0	0-0	0-0	0-0	0-0	0-0	0-0	0-0	1-0
Fernandez	1-0	1-1	0-1	1-0	2-1	1-1	1-1	4-0	0-0	1-1	2-0	1-2	3-1	18-9
Hernandez	0-0	0-1	0-1	0-0	0-0	1-0	0-1	0-0	0-0	1-1	0-0	1-0	0-0	3-4
Howard	0-0	0-0	0-0	1-0	0-0	0-0	0-0	0-0	0-0	0-0	0-0	0-0	0-0	1-0
Jones	0-0	0-0	0-0	0-0	0-0	0-0	0-0	0-0	0-0	0-0	0-0	0-1	0-0	0-1
McCaskill	0-0	0-1	0-0	0-0	0-1	0-0	1-1	1-2	0-0	0-1	0-1	1-0	1-0	4-8

Pitcher	Bal. W-L	Bos. W-L	Cal. W-L	Cle. W-L	Det. W-L	K.C. W-L	Mil. W-L	Min. W-L	N.Y. W-L	Oak. W-L	Sea. W-L	Tex. W-L	Tor. W-L	Totals W-L
McDowell	3-1	3-1	2-1	2-0	0-1	1-2	2-0	2-0	2-1	1-1	2-0	2-0	0-2	22-10
Pall	1-0	0-0	0-0	0-0	0-0	0-1	0-0	0-1	0-1	0-0	0-0	1-0	0-0	2-3
Radinsky	0-0	0-0	0-0	1-0	0-0	0-0	4-0	0-0	0-2	1-0	2-0	0-0	0-0	8-2
Ruffcorn	0-0	0-0	0-1	0-0	0-0	0-0	0-0	0-0	0-0	0-0	0-1	0-0	0-0	0-2
Schwarz	0-0	0-0	0-0	1-0	0-1	1-0	0-0	0-0	0-0	0-0	0-0	0-1	0-0	2-2
Stieb	0-0	0-0	0-1	0-0	0-0	0-0	1-0	0-0	0-0	0-1	0-1	0-0	0-0	1-3
Totals	8-4	5-7	6-7	9-3	7-5	6-7	9-3	10-3	4-8	7-6	9-4	8-5	6-6	94-68

No-decisions—DeLeon, Drahman, Leach, Thigpen.

CLEVELAND—76-86

Pitcher	Bal. W-L	Bos. W-L	Cal. W-L	Chi. W-L	Det. W-L	K.C. W-L	Mil. W-L	Min. W-L	N.Y. W-L	Oak. W-L	Sea. W-L	Tex. W-L	Tor. W-L	Totals W-L
Abbott	0-0	0-0	0-0	0-0	0-1	0-0	0-0	0-0	0-0	0-0	0-0	0-0	0-0	0-1
Bielecki	0-0	0-1	0-0	0-0	0-1	0-0	0-1	0-1	1-0	1-0	1-0	0-0	0-1	4-5
Clark............	1-0	0-0	0-2	1-1	1-0	0-0	1-1	0-0	0-0	1-0	0-0	1-0	1-1	7-5
Cook	1-0	0-0	1-0	1-0	0-0	1-1	1-0	0-1	0-1	0-1	0-0	0-1	0-0	5-5
DiPoto	0-1	1-0	1-0	0-1	0-0	0-1	2-0	0-0	0-0	0-0	0-1	0-0	0-0	4-4
Grimsley	0-0	0-1	0-0	0-0	1-0	1-0	0-0	0-2	1-1	0-0	0-0	0-0	0-0	3-4
Hernandez....	1-0	0-0	0-0	0-1	0-0	1-1	1-0	0-1	0-0	0-0	1-1	1-1	1-0	6-5
Kramer	0-0	1-0	0-0	0-0	2-0	1-0	1-0	1-1	0-0	0-0	0-1	1-0	0-1	7-3
Lilliquist.......	0-0	2-0	1-0	0-1	0-0	0-0	0-1	1-1	0-0	0-0	0-0	0-0	0-1	4-4
Lopez	0-0	0-0	1-0	0-1	1-0	0-0	0-0	0-0	0-0	0-0	1-0	0-0	0-0	3-1
Mesa............	1-1	0-0	1-1	1-0	0-3	1-1	1-0	1-0	0-0	3-1	0-1	1-3	0-1	10-12
Milacki	1-0	0-0	0-0	0-0	0-0	0-0	0-0	0-0	0-1	0-0	0-0	0-0	0-0	1-1
Mutis	0-1	0-1	1-0	0-1	0-0	0-0	0-0	0-0	1-1	0-0	0-2	0-0	1-0	3-6
Nagy............	0-0	0-0	0-1	0-2	0-0	0-0	0-0	0-0	0-1	1-0	0-1	0-0	1-1	2-6
Ojeda	0-0	1-0	0-0	0-0	0-0	0-0	0-0	1-0	0-0	0-0	0-0	0-0	0-1	2-1
Plunk..........	0-1	0-1	0-0	0-0	0-0	1-0	0-1	1-0	1-0	1-1	0-0	0-1	0-0	4-5
Power	0-0	0-0	0-0	0-0	0-0	0-0	0-0	0-1	0-0	0-0	0-0	0-0	0-1	0-2
Scudder........	0-1	0-0	0-0	0-0	0-0	0-0	0-0	0-0	0-0	0-0	0-0	0-0	0-0	0-1
Slocumb	0-0	0-0	1-0	0-0	0-1	0-0	1-0	0-0	0-0	0-0	0-0	1-0	0-0	3-1
Tavarez	0-1	1-0	0-0	0-0	0-0	0-0	0-0	0-0	0-0	0-0	0-0	1-0	0-1	2-2
Wertz...........	0-0	1-1	0-0	0-0	0-0	1-0	0-0	0-0	0-1	0-1	0-0	0-0	0-0	2-3
C. Young......	0-0	1-0	0-0	0-1	0-0	0-0	0-0	0-1	1-0	1-0	0-1	0-0	0-0	3-3
M. Young......	0-2	0-0	0-1	0-0	0-1	0-1	0-0	0-0	0-1	0-0	0-0	1-0	0-0	1-6
Totals	5-8	8-5	7-5	3-9	6-7	7-5	8-5	4-8	6-7	8-4	3-9	7-5	4-9	76-86

No-decisions—Christopher, Mlicki, Wickander.

DETROIT—85-77

Pitcher	Bal. W-L	Bos. W-L	Cal. W-L	Chi. W-L	Cle. W-L	K.C. W-L	Mil. W-L	Min. W-L	N.Y. W-L	Oak. W-L	Sea. W-L	Tex. W-L	Tor. W-L	Totals W-L
Bergman	0-0	0-1	0-0	0-0	0-1	1-1	0-0	0-1	0-0	0-0	0-0	0-0	0-0	1-4
Boever	0-0	1-0	1-0	0-0	0-0	0-0	0-0	0-0	0-1	0-0	0-0	0-0	0-0	2-1
Bolton	0-0	1-0	1-0	0-0	1-0	1-0	0-1	0-1	0-2	2-0	0-1	0-0	0-1	6-6
S. Davis........	0-0	0-0	0-0	0-0	0-0	0-0	0-1	0-0	0-0	0-0	0-0	0-0	0-1	0-2
Doherty	2-0	0-1	2-0	1-1	0-1	0-1	2-1	2-0	0-2	1-2	1-1	2-1	1-0	14-11
Groom..........	0-0	0-0	0-0	0-0	0-0	0-1	0-0	0-0	0-0	0-0	0-0	0-0	0-0	0-2
Gullickson....	2-0	2-1	2-1	0-2	0-3	0-1	0-0	1-0	0-1	1-0	2-0	1-0	2-0	13-9
Haas............	0-1	0-0	0-0	0-0	0-0	0-0	0-0	0-1	0-0	1-0	0-0	0-0	0-0	1-2
Henneman....	3-0	1-0	0-1	0-0	0-0	0-0	0-0	0-0	0-0	0-0	0-1	1-0	0-1	5-3
Johnson	0-0	0-0	0-0	0-0	0-0	1-0	0-0	0-0	0-1	0-0	0-0	0-0	0-0	1-1
Kiely	0-0	0-0	0-0	0-0	0-0	0-1	0-0	0-0	0-0	0-1	0-0	0-0	0-0	0-2
Knudsen.......	0-0	1-0	1-0	0-0	0-0	1-0	0-0	0-0	0-0	0-0	0-2	0-0	0-0	3-2
Krueger	1-1	0-1	0-1	0-0	1-0	0-0	0-0	0-0	1-0	0-0	1-1	1-0	1-0	6-4
Leiter...........	0-1	0-0	0-1	2-0	1-0	0-0	1-1	1-1	0-0	0-0	1-0	0-1	0-1	6-6
MacDonald...	0-0	0-1	0-0	0-0	0-0	0-1	0-0	0-0	2-0	0-0	1-0	0-0	0-1	3-3
Moore	0-2	0-0	0-0	1-3	3-0	1-0	2-0	1-0	0-1	3-1	0-1	0-0	2-1	13-9
Munoz	0-0	0-0	0-0	0-0	0-0	0-0	0-0	0-0	0-0	0-0	0-0	0-1	0-0	0-1
Wells	0-0	1-1	1-0	1-1	1-1	0-1	3-0	1-2	1-1	0-0	1-0	1-1	0-1	11-9
Totals	8-5	7-6	8-4	5-7	7-6	5-7	8-5	6-6	4-9	8-4	7-5	6-6	6-7	85-77

No-decisions—DeSilva, Gardiner, Gohr, Grater.

KANSAS CITY—84-78

Pitcher	Bal. W-L	Bos. W-L	Cal. W-L	Chi. W-L	Cle. W-L	Det. W-L	Mil. W-L	Min. W-L	N.Y. W-L	Oak. W-L	Sea. W-L	Tex. W-L	Tor. W-L	Totals W-L
Appier..........	1-1	2-1	2-0	2-0	1-2	2-0	0-1	1-1	1-0	2-1	2-0	1-1	1-0	18-8
Belinda	0-0	0-0	0-1	0-0	0-0	0-0	0-0	0-0	0-0	0-0	1-0	0-0	0-0	1-1
Brewer..........	1-0	0-0	0-0	0-0	0-0	0-0	1-1	0-0	0-1	0-0	0-0	0-0	0-0	2-2
Burgos..........	0-0	0-0	0-0	0-0	0-0	0-0	0-0	0-0	0-0	0-0	0-0	0-0	0-1	0-1
Cadaret	0-0	0-0	0-0	0-0	0-0	0-0	1-1	0-0	0-0	0-0	0-0	0-0	0-0	1-1
Cone	0-1	2-1	3-1	1-2	1-1	0-1	0-1	2-1	0-1	0-1	1-0	0-2	1-1	11-14
DiPino..........	0-0	0-0	0-0	0-0	0-1	0-0	0-0	0-0	1-0	0-0	0-0	0-0	0-0	1-1
Gardner........	1-1	0-0	0-0	0-0	0-1	0-0	0-0	1-0	0-1	0-0	1-0	0-1	1-0	4-6

Pitcher	Bal. W-L	Bos. W-L	Cal. W-L	Chi. W-L	Cle. W-L	Det. W-L	Mil. W-L	Min. W-L	N.Y. W-L	Oak. W-L	Sea. W-L	Tex. W-L	Tor. W-L	Totals W-L
Gordon	0-0	1-0	0-1	3-0	0-0	1-1	0-1	1-1	1-1	1-1	2-0	2-0	0-0	12-6
Gubicza	1-0	1-1	0-1	0-1	1-1	0-1	0-0	0-0	0-1	0-2	0-0	0-0	2-0	5-8
Haney	0-0	1-1	0-1	1-0	0-1	0-1	0-1	1-0	1-1	0-1	1-2	2-0	2-0	9-9
Magnante	0-0	0-0	0-0	0-0	0-0	0-0	0-0	0-0	0-1	0-0	0-1	0-0	0-0	1-2
Meacham	0-0	0-0	0-0	0-1	0-0	1-0	1-0	0-1	0-0	0-0	0-0	0-0	0-0	2-2
Montgomery	0-1	0-1	1-0	0-1	1-0	2-0	0-0	0-1	1-0	1-0	0-1	0-0	1-0	7-5
Pichardo	0-1	0-0	1-1	0-1	1-0	0-1	0-1	1-0	1-0	1-0	0-1	1-1	0-2	7-8
Rasmussen	0-2	0-0	0-0	0-0	0-0	0-0	0-0	0-0	0-0	0-0	0-0	1-0	0-0	1-2
Sampen	1-0	0-0	0-0	0-0	0-0	0-1	1-0	0-0	0-0	0-0	0-0	0-1	0-0	2-2
Totals	5-7	7-5	7-6	7-6	5-7	7-5	5-7	7-6	6-6	6-7	7-6	7-6	8-4	84-78

No-decisions—Granger, Habyan, Reed.

MILWAUKEE—69-93

Pitcher	Bal. W-L	Bos. W-L	Cal. W-L	Chi. W-L	Cle. W-L	Det. W-L	K.C. W-L	Min. W-L	N.Y. W-L	Oak. W-L	Sea. W-L	Tex. W-L	Tor. W-L	Totals W-L
Austin	0-0	0-0	0-0	0-0	0-0	0-0	0-2	0-0	0-0	0-0	1-0	0-0	0-0	1-2
Boddicker	0-0	1-0	0-0	1-1	1-0	0-1	0-1	0-0	0-1	0-0	0-0	0-0	0-1	3-5
Bones	0-2	1-1	0-1	0-0	1-1	1-2	2-0	3-0	0-2	1-1	0-0	0-1	2-0	11-11
Eldred	2-1	1-0	2-1	1-2	0-1	2-2	2-0	1-0	1-2	2-0	1-3	1-2	0-2	16-16
Fetters	0-0	1-0	1-0	0-2	0-0	0-0	0-0	0-1	0-0	0-0	0-0	0-0	1-0	3-3
Henry	0-0	0-1	1-0	0-1	1-0	0-0	0-0	1-0	0-1	0-0	0-0	1-0	0-1	4-4
Higuera	0-0	0-0	0-0	0-0	0-0	0-0	0-1	0-0	1-0	0-0	0-2	0-0	0-0	1-3
Ignasiak	0-0	0-0	0-0	0-0	0-1	1-0	0-0	0-0	0-0	0-0	0-0	0-0	0-0	1-1
Lloyd	0-1	1-0	0-1	0-0	0-0	0-0	0-0	0-0	0-1	0-0	0-0	2-1	0-0	3-4
Maldonado	0-1	1-0	0-0	0-0	0-1	0-0	0-0	1-0	0-0	0-0	0-0	0-0	0-0	2-2
Manzanillo	0-0	0-0	0-0	0-0	0-0	0-0	0-0	0-0	0-0	1-0	0-0	0-1	0-0	1-1
Maysey	0-0	0-0	0-1	0-0	0-0	0-0	0-0	0-0	0-0	1-0	0-0	0-0	0-1	1-2
Miranda	1-0	0-2	0-0	0-0	0-0	1-0	0-1	0-0	0-0	1-1	0-1	0-0	1-0	4-5
Navarro	2-1	2-0	1-0	0-2	1-2	0-0	2-0	0-3	1-2	0-1	1-0	0-1	1-0	11-12
Novoa	0-1	0-0	0-1	0-0	0-0	0-0	0-0	0-0	0-0	0-1	0-0	0-0	0-0	0-3
Orosco	0-0	0-0	0-1	1-1	1-1	0-0	0-0	0-0	0-0	0-0	1-1	0-0	0-1	3-5
Wegman	0-1	0-1	0-1	0-0	0-1	0-2	1-1	1-1	1-0	1-1	0-1	0-2	0-2	4-14
Totals	5-8	8-5	5-7	3-9	5-8	5-8	7-5	7-5	4-9	7-5	4-8	4-8	5-8	69-93

No-decisions—Kiefer.

MINNESOTA—71-91

Pitcher	Bal. W-L	Bos. W-L	Cal. W-L	Chi. W-L	Cle. W-L	Det. W-L	K.C. W-L	Mil. W-L	N.Y. W-L	Oak. W-L	Sea. W-L	Tex. W-L	Tor. W-L	Totals W-L
Aguilera	0-0	1-0	1-1	0-0	2-0	0-0	0-0	0-1	0-1	0-0	0-0	0-0	0-0	4-3
Banks	1-1	1-0	2-1	0-1	1-0	0-2	1-1	1-1	1-1	0-1	1-2	2-1	0-0	11-12
Brummett	0-0	0-0	1-0	0-0	0-1	0-0	0-0	0-0	0-0	0-0	0-0	1-0	0-0	2-1
Casian	0-0	0-0	0-0	1-0	0-0	0-0	1-0	1-0	0-1	1-0	0-0	0-2	1-0	5-3
Deshaies	1-1	1-2	1-1	2-2	2-0	1-1	1-1	1-1	0-0	1-1	0-1	0-0	0-2	11-13
Erickson	1-3	1-2	1-0	0-2	1-0	2-1	1-1	0-0	0-1	0-3	0-1	0-4		8-19
Guardado	0-2	0-1	1-0	0-1	0-0	0-0	0-2	1-0	0-1	1-1	0-0	0-0	0-0	3-8
Guthrie	0-0	0-0	0-0	0-0	0-0	0-0	0-1	1-0	0-0	0-0	1-0	0-0	0-0	2-1
Hartley	0-0	0-1	0-0	0-0	0-0	0-0	0-0	0-1	0-0	1-0	0-0	0-0	0-0	1-2
Mahomes	0-1	0-0	0-0	0-2	0-0	0-0	0-0	0-0	0-0	0-0	0-0	1-1	0-0	1-5
Merriman	0-0	0-1	0-0	0-0	0-0	0-0	0-0	0-0	0-0	0-0	0-0	0-0	0-0	1-1
Tapani	1-0	0-0	2-0	0-2	1-1	2-0	0-2	0-3	2-2	0-0	1-1	2-1	1-3	12-15
Trombley	0-0	1-0	0-1	0-0	0-2	1-0	1-0	0-0	0-1	2-0	1-1	0-0	0-1	6-6
Tsamis	0-0	0-0	0-0	0-0	0-0	0-0	0-0	0-0	0-0	1-1	0-0	0-0	0-0	1-2
Willis	0-0	0-0	0-0	0-0	0-0	0-0	0-0	1-0	1-0	0-0	0-0	1-0	0-0	3-0
Totals	4-8	5-7	9-4	3-10	8-4	6-6	6-7	5-7	4-8	8-5	4-9	7-6	2-10	71-91

No-decisions—Garces.

NEW YORK—88-74

Pitcher	Bal. W-L	Bos. W-L	Cal. W-L	Chi. W-L	Cle. W-L	Det. W-L	K.C. W-L	Mil. W-L	Min. W-L	Oak. W-L	Sea. W-L	Tex. W-L	Tor. W-L	Totals W-L
Abbott	1-0	0-0	1-1	1-1	1-1	2-1	1-1	1-1	1-1	1-1	0-2	0-3	1-1	11-14
Assenmacher	1-0	0-0	0-0	1-1	0-0	0-0	0-0	0-0	0-0	0-0	0-0	0-1	0-0	2-2
Cook	0-1	0-0	0-0	0-0	0-0	0-0	0-0	0-0	0-0	0-0	0-0	0-0	0-0	0-1
Farr	0-1	0-0	0-0	0-0	0-0	1-0	0-1	0-0	1-0	0-0	0-0	0-0	0-0	2-2
Gibson	0-0	1-0	0-0	0-0	0-0	0-0	0-0	1-0	0-0	0-0	0-0	0-0	0-0	2-0
Habyan	0-0	0-0	1-0	0-0	0-0	0-0	0-0	0-0	0-0	0-1	1-0	0-0	0-0	2-1
Heaton	0-0	1-0	0-0	0-0	0-0	0-0	0-0	0-0	0-0	0-0	0-0	0-0	0-0	1-0
Hitchcock	0-1	0-0	0-0	0-1	1-0	0-0	0-0	0-0	0-0	0-0	0-0	0-0	0-0	1-2
Howe	0-1	0-0	0-1	0-0	0-0	0-0	1-1	0-0	0-0	1-0	1-1	0-0	0-1	3-5
Hutton	0-0	0-0	1-0	0-0	0-0	0-0	0-1	0-0	0-0	0-0	0-0	0-0	0-0	1-1
Jean	0-0	0-0	0-0	0-0	0-0	0-0	1-0	0-0	0-0	0-0	0-1	0-0	0-0	1-1
Johnson	0-0	0-0	0-0	0-0	0-0	0-0	0-1	0-1	0-0	0-0	0-0	0-0	0-0	0-2
Kamieniecki	2-0	1-2	1-1	0-0	0-0	0-1	1-0	1-0	1-1	0-0	2-0	0-1	1-1	10-7
Key	1-0	1-1	2-0	3-0	2-1	1-1	0-0	2-1	2-0	1-0	0-1	1-0	2-1	18-6

Pitcher	Bal. W-L	Bos. W-L	Cal. W-L	Chi. W-L	Cle. W-L	Det. W-L	K.C. W-L	Mil. W-L	Min. W-L	Oak. W-L	Sea. W-L	Tex. W-L	Tor. W-L	Totals W-L
Militello	0-0	0-0	0-0	0-0	0-1	0-0	0-0	0-0	0-0	1-0	0-0	0-0	0-0	1-1
Monteleone	0-0	0-0	0-1	1-1	1-0	0-1	0-0	0-0	1-0	1-0	1-0	2-0	0-1	7-4
Munoz	0-0	0-0	0-0	0-0	0-0	2-0	0-0	0-0	1-1	0-1	0-0	0-0	0-1	3-3
Perez	1-1	1-2	0-2	0-0	1-2	0-0	0-1	1-1	0-0	0-2	1-0	0-3	1-0	6-14
Tanana	0-0	0-1	0-0	0-0	0-0	0-0	0-0	0-0	0-0	0-0	0-0	0-0	0-1	0-2
Wickman	1-1	1-0	0-0	2-0	1-0	3-0	2-0	2-0	1-1	1-1	0-1	0-0	0-0	14-4
Witt	0-0	1-0	0-0	0-0	0-1	0-0	0-0	1-0	0-0	0-0	1-0	0-0	0-1	3-2
Totals	7-6	7-6	6-6	8-4	7-6	9-4	6-6	9-4	8-4	6-6	7-5	3-9	5-8	88-74

No-decisions—Smith.

OAKLAND—68-94

Pitcher	Bal. W-L	Bos. W-L	Cal. W-L	Chi. W-L	Cle. W-L	Det. W-L	K.C. W-L	Mil. W-L	Min. W-L	N.Y. W-L	Sea. W-L	Tex. W-L	Tor. W-L	Totals W-L
Boever	0-0	0-0	1-0	0-0	1-0	0-0	0-1	0-0	0-1	1-0	1-0	0-0	0-0	4-2
Briscoe	0-0	0-0	0-0	0-0	0-0	0-0	0-0	0-0	0-0	0-0	1-0	0-0	0-0	1-0
Darling	0-2	1-0	1-0	0-1	0-0	0-0	0-1	1-0	0-1	0-1	0-0	1-2	1-1	5-9
Davis	0-1	0-0	0-0	0-0	0-2	0-2	0-0	0-0	1-0	0-0	1-0	0-1	0-0	2-6
Downs	1-0	0-2	0-1	1-0	0-0	1-1	1-1	0-2	0-1	0-1	1-0	0-1	0-0	5-10
Eckersley	0-1	0-0	0-0	0-1	0-0	0-1	0-0	0-0	0-0	0-0	1-0	1-0	0-1	2-4
Gossage	0-1	0-1	0-0	0-0	1-1	0-0	1-0	0-0	0-0	1-0	1-0	0-0	0-1	4-5
Hillegas	1-0	0-0	0-0	0-0	0-1	0-0	0-0	1-1	0-0	1-1	0-1	0-0	0-1	3-6
Honeycutt	0-0	0-0	0-1	0-0	0-0	0-0	0-0	0-1	0-1	0-1	0-0	0-0	1-0	1-4
Horsman	0-0	0-0	0-0	0-0	1-0	0-0	0-0	0-0	0-0	0-0	1-0	0-0	0-0	2-0
Jimenez	0-0	0-0	1-0	0-0	0-0	0-0	0-0	0-0	0-0	0-0	0-0	0-0	0-0	1-0
Karsay	0-1	0-0	0-0	0-0	0-0	0-2	0-0	1-0	1-0	0-0	1-0	0-0	0-0	3-3
Mohler	0-0	0-0	0-0	0-1	0-1	0-0	0-1	0-1	1-0	0-0	0-0	0-0	0-2	1-6
Nunez	0-0	0-2	1-0	0-0	0-0	0-0	1-0	0-0	1-1	0-1	0-1	0-1	0-0	3-6
Smithberg	0-0	0-0	0-0	0-0	0-0	0-0	0-1	0-0	0-1	0-0	0-0	0-0	1-0	1-2
Van Poppel	0-0	0-1	0-1	1-0	0-1	0-2	2-0	1-0	1-0	0-0	0-0	1-1	0-0	6-6
Welch	0-3	0-2	3-1	0-2	1-0	2-0	1-1	1-1	0-0	1-0	0-0	0-0	0-1	9-11
Witt	0-1	2-1	0-2	3-1	0-1	1-0	1-0	0-1	1-1	1-1	1-2	2-2	2-0	14-13
Young	0-0	0-0	0-0	1-0	0-1	0-0	0-0	0-0	0-0	0-0	0-0	0-0	0-0	1-1
Totals	2-10	3-9	7-6	6-7	4-8	4-8	7-6	5-7	5-8	6-6	9-4	5-8	5-7	68-94

No-decisions—Campbell, Seitzer, Slusarski.

SEATTLE—82-80

Pitcher	Bal. W-L	Bos. W-L	Cal. W-L	Chi. W-L	Cle. W-L	Det. W-L	K.C. W-L	Mil. W-L	Min. W-L	N.Y. W-L	Oak. W-L	Tex. W-L	Tor. W-L	Totals W-L
Ayrault	0-0	0-0	0-0	0-0	1-0	0-0	0-0	0-0	0-1	0-0	0-0	0-0	0-0	1-1
Bosio	1-1	1-2	1-0	0-1	3-0	0-0	1-1	1-1	0-0	0-0	0-1	0-1	1-1	9-9
Charlton	0-0	0-2	0-0	0-0	0-0	1-1	0-0	0-0	0-0	0-0	0-0	0-0	0-0	1-3
Converse	0-0	0-0	0-1	0-0	0-0	0-0	0-1	0-0	0-0	0-0	0-1	0-0	0-0	1-3
Cummings	0-1	0-1	0-0	0-1	0-1	0-0	0-0	0-0	0-0	0-1	0-0	0-0	0-1	0-6
DeLucia	0-0	0-0	1-0	0-2	0-0	0-0	0-0	0-0	1-0	0-1	0-2	0-1	0-0	3-6
Fleming	1-1	1-0	1-0	0-1	1-0	1-0	0-2	0-1	2-0	1-0	1-0	2-0	1-0	12-5
Hampton	0-0	0-1	0-0	0-1	0-0	0-1	0-0	0-0	0-0	1-0	0-0	0-0	0-0	1-3
Hanson	1-2	1-1	1-2	0-2	1-0	1-2	1-1	0-0	2-0	2-0	0-0	1-1	0-1	11-12
Henry	0-0	0-0	1-0	0-0	0-0	0-0	0-0	0-0	0-0	0-1	1-0	0-0	0-0	2-1
Brad Holman	1-0	0-0	0-0	0-1	0-0	0-0	0-0	0-1	0-0	0-0	0-0	0-1	0-0	1-3
Johnson	0-0	1-0	1-0	1-0	2-1	0-1	2-1	3-0	2-1	0-2	2-1	2-1	3-0	19-8
King	0-1	0-0	0-0	0-0	0-0	0-0	0-0	0-0	0-0	0-0	0-0	0-0	0-0	0-1
Leary	0-0	1-0	1-3	2-0	0-0	0-2	0-0	2-1	2-1	1-1	0-0	2-0	0-1	11-9
Nelson	0-0	0-0	0-0	0-0	1-1	1-0	0-0	1-0	0-0	0-0	0-2	1-0	1-0	5-3
Ontiveros	0-0	0-0	0-0	0-0	0-0	0-0	0-0	0-0	0-0	0-0	0-1	0-0	0-1	0-2
Power	0-0	0-0	0-0	1-0	0-0	0-0	0-1	1-0	0-0	0-0	0-1	0-0	0-0	2-2
Swan	1-1	0-0	0-0	0-0	0-0	1-0	1-0	0-0	0-1	0-1	0-0	0-0	0-0	3-3
Totals	5-7	5-7	7-6	4-9	9-3	5-7	6-7	8-4	9-4	5-7	4-9	8-5	7-5	82-80

No-decisions—Plantenberg, Powell, Salkeld, Shinall, Wainhouse.

TEXAS—86-76

Pitcher	Bal. W-L	Bos. W-L	Cal. W-L	Chi. W-L	Cle. W-L	Det. W-L	K.C. W-L	Mil. W-L	Min. W-L	N.Y. W-L	Oak. W-L	Sea. W-L	Tor. W-L	Totals W-L
Bohanon	0-1	0-0	0-0	0-0	0-0	1-0	1-1	0-0	0-1	0-0	0-1	1-0	1-0	4-4
Bronkey	0-0	1-1	0-0	0-0	0-0	0-0	0-0	0-0	0-0	0-0	0-0	0-0	0-0	1-1
Brown	1-0	1-2	1-2	1-2	1-2	0-0	1-2	2-1	1-0	3-1	3-0	0-0	0-0	15-12
Burns	0-0	0-1	0-2	0-0	0-0	0-0	0-0	0-0	0-0	0-0	0-0	0-1	0-0	0-4
Carpenter	0-0	0-0	0-0	0-0	1-0	0-0	0-0	0-0	1-0	1-0	0-0	1-0	0-1	4-1
Dreyer	0-0	1-0	0-0	0-0	0-1	0-0	0-1	0-0	0-1	0-0	1-0	1-0	0-0	3-3
Henke	0-1	0-0	1-1	2-1	0-0	1-0	0-0	0-0	0-0	0-0	0-1	1-0	0-1	5-5
Lefferts	1-0	0-1	0-1	0-0	0-1	0-1	0-0	0-1	0-0	0-2	0-0	0-1	2-1	3-9
Leibrandt	1-1	0-0	1-0	0-1	1-0	0-2	0-1	2-0	1-1	1-0	1-0	0-3	1-1	9-10
Nen	0-0	0-0	0-0	0-0	0-0	0-0	0-0	1-0	0-0	0-0	0-0	0-0	0-1	1-1
Patterson	1-0	0-0	0-0	0-1	0-0	0-1	1-0	0-2	0-0	0-0	0-0	0-0	0-0	2-4

Pitcher	Bal. W-L	Bos. W-L	Cal. W-L	Chi. W-L	Cle. W-L	Det. W-L	K.C. W-L	Mil. W-L	Min. W-L	N.Y. W-L	Oak. W-L	Sea. W-L	Tor. W-L	Totals W-L
Pavlik	1-0	1-1	1-0	1-1	1-0	1-1	2-0	0-0	1-1	2-0	0-0	0-2	1-0	12-6
Reed	0-0	0-0	0-0	0-0	0-0	0-0	0-0	0-0	1-0	0-0	0-0	0-0	0-0	1-0
Rogers	3-0	1-0	2-0	0-2	0-3	1-1	1-1	1-0	1-1	2-0	1-2	1-0	2-0	16-10
Ryan	0-1	1-0	1-0	1-0	1-0	0-0	0-1	1-0	0-1	0-0	0-1	0-1	0-0	5-5
Schooler	0-0	0-0	0-0	0-0	0-0	2-0	0-0	1-0	0-0	0-0	0-0	0-0	0-0	3-0
Whiteside	0-0	0-0	0-0	0-0	0-0	0-0	0-0	0-0	0-1	0-0	2-0	0-0	0-0	2-1
Totals	8-4	6-6	7-6	5-8	5-7	6-6	6-7	8-4	6-7	9-3	8-5	5-8	7-5	86-76

No-decisions—Canseco, Fajardo, Nelson, Oliver.

TORONTO—95-67

Pitcher	Bal. W-L	Bos. W-L	Cal. W-L	Chi. W-L	Cle. W-L	Det. W-L	K.C. W-L	Mil. W-L	Min. W-L	N.Y. W-L	Oak. W-L	Sea. W-L	Tex. W-L	Totals W-L
Brow	1-0	0-0	0-0	0-0	0-0	0-0	0-0	0-1	0-0	0-0	0-0	0-0	0-0	1-1
Castillo	1-0	0-0	0-0	0-0	0-0	2-0	0-0	0-0	0-0	0-0	0-2	0-0	0-0	3-2
Cox	1-0	1-0	0-0	0-0	1-0	0-0	0-2	0-1	1-1	0-0	2-1	1-1	0-0	7-6
Eichhorn	1-0	0-0	0-0	0-0	1-1	0-0	0-0	1-0	0-0	0-0	0-0	0-0	0-0	3-1
Guzman	0-0	0-0	0-0	1-2	2-0	1-1	1-0	2-0	3-0	1-0	2-0	1-0	0-0	14-3
Hentgen	1-1	3-0	2-1	1-1	2-0	1-1	2-0	1-1	2-0	1-0	0-2	1-2	2-0	19-9
Leiter	1-0	1-0	2-0	1-1	0-1	0-1	1-0	1-1	0-0	1-2	0-0	1-0	0-0	9-6
Linton	0-1	0-0	0-0	0-0	0-0	0-0	0-0	0-0	0-0	0-0	0-0	0-0	0-0	0-1
Morris	0-0	0-0	1-1	0-1	1-2	1-1	0-2	1-1	2-1	0-0	0-1	0-1	1-1	7-12
Stewart	0-1	3-1	1-1	2-0	0-0	1-0	0-0	2-0	2-0	0-1	1-0	0-2	1-1	12-8
Stottlemyre	1-1	1-1	1-1	1-1	2-0	1-1	0-2	0-1	0-0	2-2	0-0	0-2	2-0	11-12
Timlin	0-0	1-1	0-0	0-0	0-0	1-0	0-1	0-0	0-0	0-0	0-0	0-0	2-0	4-2
D. Ward	1-1	0-0	0-0	0-0	0-0	0-0	0-0	0-0	0-0	1-0	0-1	0-0	0-1	2-3
Williams	0-0	0-0	1-0	0-0	0-0	0-0	0-0	0-0	0-0	1-0	1-0	0-1	0-0	3-1
Totals	8-5	10-3	8-4	6-6	9-4	7-6	4-8	8-5	10-2	8-5	7-5	5-7	5-7	95-67

No-decisions—Dayley, Flener.

HOME RUNS BY PARKS

	At Bal.	At Bos.	At Cal.	At Chi.	At Cle.	At Det.	At K.C.	At Mil.	At Min.	At N.Y.	At Oak.	At Sea.	At Tex.	At Tor.	Totals 1993	Totals 1992
Baltimore	87	6	5	3	4	11	4	5	3	4	6	7	6	6	157	148
Boston	6	54	6	4	8	4	1	6	1	4	3	8	3	6	114	84
California	3	2	64	3	3	3	3	6	3	6	7	3	1	7	114	88
Chicago	6	4	5	82	2	13	4	4	7	8	5	12	9	1	162	110
Cleveland	3	5	5	6	69	10	1	8	2	7	7	4	4	10	141	127
Detroit	8	6	6	5	6	103	5	0	15	3	4	2	4	11	178	182
Kansas City	3	7	5	10	6	8	50	5	5	6	5	2	7	6	125	75
Milwaukee	6	5	6	5	4	11	3	53	5	8	2	3	4	10	125	116
Minnesota	6	1	8	4	5	3	3	3	56	5	11	7	6	3	121	104
New York	9	2	6	6	9	9	11	7	12	88	5	6	6	2	178	163
Oakland	7	5	8	7	4	3	2	6	7	9	78	8	8	6	158	142
Seattle	7	2	6	7	15	12	3	3	2	9	8	74	9	4	161	149
Texas	15	1	9	5	8	7	8	5	7	6	8	3	90	9	181	159
Toronto	2	7	9	5	9	5	1	7	1	10	7	1	5	90	159	163
1993 total	168	107	148	152	152	202	99	118	126	173	156	140	162	171	2074	....
1992 total	144	91	104	116	156	181	65	86	112	158	149	141	134	139	....	1776

AT BALTIMORE (168):

Baltimore (87)—Hoiles 16, Ripken 14, Baines 12, Devereaux 8, Gomez 7, Segui 6, Voigt 5, Pagliarulo 3, Anderson 2, Hammonds 2, Hulett 2, McLemore 2, Obando 2, Reynolds 2, Smith 2, Davis 1, Parent 1. **Boston (6)**—Dawson 2, Calderon 1, Fletcher 1, Pena 1, Vaughn 1. **California (3)**—Easley 1, Perez 1, Snow 1. **Chicago (6)**—Thomas 2, Burks 1, Guillen 1, Jackson 1, Karkovice 1. **Cleveland (3)**—Alomar 2, Belle 1. **Detroit (8)**—Fielder 2, Fryman 2, E. Davis 1, Phillips 1, Tettleton 1. **Kansas City (3)**—Brett 1, Macfarlane 1, Mayne 1. **Milwaukee (6)**—Vaughn 2, Jaha 1, Reimer 1, Seitzer 1, Surhoff 1. **Minnesota (6)**—Hrbek 2, Munoz 2, Harper 1, Winfield 1. **New York (9)**—Leyritz 2, Mattingly 2, O'Neill 1, Silvestri 1, Stanley 1, Tartabull 1, B. Williams 1. **Oakland (7)**—Abbott 1, Aldrete 1, Brosius 1, Hemond 1, Neel 1, Sierra 1, Sveum 1. **Seattle (7)**—Griffey 2, Blowers 1, Buhner 1, Cotto 1, Haselman 1, Valle 1. **Texas (15)**—Palmer 6, Gonzalez 2, Redus 2, Davis 1, Diaz 1, Franco 1, Palmeiro 1, Strange 1. **Toronto (2)**—Carter 2.

AT BOSTON (107):

Baltimore (6)—Baines 2, Hoiles 2, Anderson 1, Ripken 1. **Boston (54)**—Vaughn 13, Dawson 8, Valentin 7, Greenwell 6, Hatcher 5, Cooper 3, Deer 3, Fletcher 2, Pena 2, Riles 2, Melvin 1, Rivera 1, Zupcic 1. **California (2)**—Myers 1, Salmon 1. **Chicago (4)**—Burks 1, Karkovice 1, Thomas 1, Ventura 1. **Cleveland (5)**—Belle 2, Jefferson 2, Baerga 1. **Detroit (6)**—Deer 2, Tettleton 2, Fryman 1, Kreuter 1. **Kansas City (7)**—McRae 3, Brett 2, Gaetti 1, Joyner 1. **Milwaukee (5)**—Mieske 1, Nilsson 1, Reimer 1, Vaughn 1, Yount 1. **Minnesota (1)**—Hrbek 1. **New York (2)**—O'Neill 1, Tartabull 1. **Oakland (5)**—R. Henderson 2, McGwire 2, Gates 1. **Seattle (2)**—T. Martinez 1, Valle 1. **Texas (1)**—Gonzalez 1. **Toronto (7)**—Carter 2, Coles 1, Molitor 1, Olerud 1, Sprague 1, White 1.

AT CALIFORNIA (148):

Baltimore (5)—Baines 1, Devereaux 1, Pagliarulo 1, Ripken 1, Segui 1. **Boston (6)**—Greenwell 2, Cooper 1, Dawson 1, Hatcher 1, Vaughn 1. **California (64)**—Salmon 23, Davis 13, Snow 10, Lovullo 4, Myers 4, Curtis 3, DiSarcina 2, Perez 2, R. Gonzales 1, Gruber 1, Van Burkleo 1. **Chicago (5)**—Bell 2, Karkovice 2, Jackson 1. **Cleveland (5)**—Baerga 2, Hill 2, Kirby 1. **Detroit (6)**—Fielder 1, Gibson 1, Livingstone 1, Tettleton 1, Trammell 1, Whitaker 1. **Kansas City (5)**—Brett 1, Gagne 1, Joyner 1, Macfarlane 1, McRae 1. **Milwaukee (6)**—Vaughn 2, Jaha 1, Nilsson 1, Seitzer 1, Yount 1. **Minnesota (8)**—Hrbek 2, Mack 2, Winfield 2, Brito 1, Pagliarulo 1. **New York (6)**—Tartabull 3, Gallego 2, B. Williams 1. **Oakland (8)**—D. Henderson 3, Sierra 3, R. Henderson 1, Steinbach 1. **Seattle (6)**—Valle 2, Blowers 1, Boone 1, Griffey 1, T. Martinez 1. **Texas (9)**—Gonzalez 2, James 2, Palmeiro 2, Palmer 2, Canseco 1. **Toronto (9)**—Alomar 3, Olerud 3, Sprague 2, Borders 1.

AT CHICAGO (152):

Baltimore (3)—Devereaux 1, Hammonds 1, Ripken 1. **Boston (4)**—Deer 2, Melvin 1, Vaughn 1. **California (3)**—Davis 1, R. Gonzales 1, Snow 1. **Chicago (82)**—Thomas 26, Ventura 12, Jackson 9, Bell 7, Burks 7, Raines 7, Karkovice 6, Guillen 3, Newson 2, Pasqua 2, Sax 1. **Cleveland (6)**—Sorrento 2, Belle 1, Hill 1, Martinez 1, Treadway 1. **Detroit (5)**—E. Davis 2, Tettleton 2, Whitaker 1. **Kansas City (10)**—Gagne 2, Joyner 2, Macfarlane 2, Brett 1, Jose 1, Mayne 1, McReynolds 1. **Milwaukee (5)**—Brunansky 1, Hamilton 1, Lampkin 1, Reimer 1, Vaughn 1. **Minnesota (4)**—Brito 1, Hrbek 1, Jorgensen 1, Winfield 1. **New York (6)**—Tartabull 3, Velarde 2, Leyritz 1. **Oakland (7)**—D. Henderson 3, Steinbach 2, R. Henderson 1, Paquette 1. **Seattle (7)**—Griffey 3, Blowers 1, Buhner 1, Haselman 1, Magadan 1. **Texas (5)**—Hulse 1, James 1, Palmeiro 1, Palmer 1, Redus 1. **Toronto (5)**—Olerud 2, Carter 1, Knorr 1, Molitor 1.

AT CLEVELAND (152):

Baltimore (4)—Baines 1, Hoiles 1, Pagliarulo 1, Ripken 1. **Boston (8)**—Cooper 1, Deer 1, Greenwell 1, Melvin 1, Naehring 1, Pena 1, Valentin 1, Vaughn 1. **California (3)**—Salmon 2, Curtis 1. **Chicago (2)**—Jackson 1, Ventura 1. **Cleveland (69)**—Belle 20, Baerga 8, Sorrento 8, Thome 5, Jefferson 4, Kirby 4, Maldonado 4, Alomar 3, Espinoza 3, Howard 3, Horn 2, Martinez 2, Lewis 1, Lofton 1, Parrish 1. **Detroit (6)**—Fielder 2, Fryman 2, Kreuter 1, Tettleton 1. **Kansas City (6)**—Brett 2, Gwynn 2, Jose 1, Joyner 1, Macfarlane 1. **Milwaukee (4)**—Jaha 2, Vaughn 1, Yount 1. **Minnesota (5)**—Harper 1, Hrbek 1, Mack 1, Munoz 1, Puckett 1. **New York (9)**—Tartabull 3, Nokes 2, Kelly 1, O'Neill 1, Stanley 1, B. Williams 1. **Oakland (4)**—Browne 1, Hemond 1, Sierra 1, Steinbach 1. **Seattle (15)**—Griffey 5, Buhner 2, T. Martinez 2, E. Martinez 2, Valle 2, Amaral 1, O'Brien 1. **Texas (5)**—Franco 2, Gonzalez 2, Canseco 1, Davis 1, Palmeiro 1, Strange 1. **Toronto (9)**—Alomar 3, Olerud 3, Carter 1, Molitor 1, T. Ward 1.

AT DETROIT (202):

Baltimore (11)—Devereaux 2, Gomez 2, Anderson 1, Hoiles 1, Obando 1, Parent 1, Reynolds 1, Ripken 1, Segui 1. **Boston (4)**—Cooper 1, Fletcher 1, Hatcher 1, Riles 1. **California (3)**—Javier 1, Lovullo 1, Salmon 1. **Chicago (13)**—Bell 3, Karkovice 2, Raines 2, Thomas 2, Ventura 2, Cora 1, Pasqua 1. **Cleveland (10)**—Baerga 3, Horn 2, Hill 1, Jefferson 1, Maldonado 1, Sorrento 1, Thome 1. **Detroit (103)**—Fielder 20, Tettleton 16, Fryman 13, Gladden 11, Deer 9, Kreuter 9, Trammell 6, Gibson 5, Whitaker 5, E. Davis 3, Phillips 3, Barnes 2, Livingstone 1. **Kansas City (8)**—Brett 2, Joyner 2, Gagne 1, Macfarlane 1, McReynolds 1, Pulliam 1. **Milwaukee (11)**—Jaha 2, Reimer 2, Bell 1, Brunansky 1, Lampkin 1, Seitzer 1, Surhoff 1, Vaughn 1, Yount 1. **Minnesota (3)**—Harper 1, Mack 1, Puckett 1. **New York (9)**—Mattingly 3, Tartabull 2, Kelly 1, Nokes 1, O'Neill 1, Owen 1. **Oakland (3)**—Aldrete 1, Neel 1, Sierra 1. **Seattle (12)**—Griffey 5, O'Brien 2, Valle 2, Buhner 1, Felder 1, T. Martinez 1. **Texas (7)**—Palmer 3, Franco 2, Palmeiro 2. **Toronto (5)**—Fernandez 2, Molitor 2, Olerud 1.

AT KANSAS CITY (99):

Baltimore (4)—Hoiles 2, Anderson 1, McLemore 1. **Boston (1)**—Vaughn 1. **California (3)**—Gruber 1, Javier 1, Myers 1. **Chicago (4)**—Karkovice 1, Raines 1, Thomas 1, Ventura 1. **Cleveland (1)**—Belle 1. **Detroit (5)**—Fryman 1, Gibson 1, Gladden 1, Kreuter 1, Tettleton 1. **Kansas City (50)**—McReynolds 8, Brett 7, Macfarlane 7, Gaetti 6, McRae 5, Hiatt 4, Joyner 4, Gagne 3, Jose 2, Rossy 2, Hamelin 1, Wilson 1. **Milwaukee (3)**—Jaha 1, Listach 1, Vaughn 1. **Minnesota (3)**—Hale 1, Puckett 1, Winfield 1. **New York (11)**—O'Neill 3, Leyritz 2, Gallego 1, Kelly 1, Mattingly 1, Nokes 1, Stanley 1, B. Williams 1. **Oakland (2)**—Gates 1, Neel 1. **Seattle (3)**—Blowers 1, Griffey 1, Howitt 1. **Texas (8)**—Gonzalez 5, Palmeiro 3. **Toronto (1)**—Olerud 1.

AT MILWAUKEE (118):

Baltimore (5)—Anderson 2, Baines 1, McLemore 1, Segui 1. **Boston (6)**—Vaughn 3, Riles 2, Hatcher 1. **California (6)**—Davis 2, Easley 1, Orton 1, Salmon 1, Snow 1. **Chicago (4)**—Burks 2, Raines 1, Ventura 1. **Cleveland (8)**—Belle 4, Baerga 2, Kirby 1, Martinez 1. **Kansas City (5)**—Joyner 2, Brooks 1, Gaetti 1, Macfarlane 1. **Milwaukee (53)**—Vaughn 12, Reimer 8, Hamilton 5, Jaha 5, Nilsson 5, Seitzer 4, Surhoff 4, Bell 2, Brunansky 2, Spiers 2, Lampkin 1, Mieske 1, Valentin 1, Yount 1. **Minnesota (3)**—Winfield 2, Hrbek 1. **New York (7)**—James 1, Leyritz 1, Maas 1, Mattingly 1, O'Neill 1, Stanley 1, Tartabull 1. **Oakland (6)**—Seitzer 2, Aldrete 1, Bordick 1, D. Henderson 1, Neel 1. **Seattle (3)**—Blowers 1, Boone 1, O'Brien 1. **Texas (5)**—Gonzalez 2, Canseco 1, Palmer 1, Redus 1. **Toronto (7)**—Carter 2, Fernandez 2, Martinez 1, Molitor 1, T. Ward 1, White 1.

AT MINNESOTA (126):

Baltimore (3)—Anderson 2, Hoiles 1. **Boston (1)**—Zupcic 1. **California (3)**—Davis 1, Lovullo 1, Snow 1. **Chicago (7)**—Raines 3, Fisk 1, Karkovice 1, Pasqua 1, Thomas 1. **Cleveland (2)**—Baerga 1, Fermin 1. **Detroit (15)**—Tettleton 4, Kreuter 2, Phillips 2, Trammell 2, Deer 1, Fielder 1, Fryman 1, Gibson 1, Whitaker 1. **Kansas City (5)**—Gaetti 2, Brett 1, Hiatt 1, McRae 1. **Milwaukee (5)**—Vaughn 3, Bell 1, Thon 1. **Minnesota (56)**—Hrbek 12, Puckett 12, Winfield 12, Harper 6, Mack 3, Knoblauch 2, McCarty 2, Munoz 2, Pagliarulo 2, Hale 1, Larkin 1, Webster 1. **New York (12)**—O'Neill 2, Stanley 2, Tartabull 2, Gallego 1, James 1, Leyritz 1, Maas 1, Mattingly 1, Nokes 1. **Oakland (7)**—Abbott 1, Brosius 1, Hemond 1, R. Henderson 1, Neel 1, Paquette 1, Steinbach 1. **Seattle (2)**—Buhner 1, Griffey 1. **Texas (7)**—Dascenzo 1, Franco 1, Gonzalez 1, Lee 1, Palmer 1, Rodriguez 1, Strange 1. **Toronto (1)**—White 1.

AT NEW YORK (173):

Baltimore (4)—Hoiles 2, Devereaux 1, Ripken 1. **Boston (4)**—Cooper 1, Greenwell 1, Valentin 1, Vaughn 1. **California (6)**—Davis 3, DiSarcina 1, Myers 1, Salmon 1. **Chicago (8)**—Karkovice 2, Raines 2, Thomas 2, Burks 1, Cora 1. **Cleveland (7)**—Belle 3, Ramirez 2, Baerga 1, Jefferson 1. **Detroit (3)**—Bautista 1, Tettleton 1, Trammell 1. **Kansas City (6)**—Macfarlane 2, Gaetti 1, Gagne 1, Hiatt 1, Jose 1. **Milwaukee (8)**—Hamilton 2, Bell 1, Brunansky 1, Jaha 1, Lampkin 1, Listach 1, Mieske 1. **Minnesota (5)**—Munoz 3, Hale 1, Hrbek 1. **New York (88)**—Stanley 17, Tartabull 11, Mattingly 8, O'Neill 8, Maas 7, Leyritz 6, Gallego 5, James 5, B. Williams 5, Kelly 4, Nokes 4, Velarde 4, Boggs 1, Humphreys 1, Meulens 1, Owen 1. **Oakland (9)**—R. Henderson 2, McGwire 2, Sierra 2, Aldrete 1, D. Henderson 1, Neel 1. **Seattle (9)**—T. Martinez 3, Buhner 2, Griffey 2, Sasser 1, Tinsley 1. **Texas (6)**—Palmer 2, Canseco 1, Dascenzo 1, Gonzalez 1, Rodriguez 1. **Toronto (10)**—Carter 2, Molitor 2, Olerud 2, White 2, Alomar 1, Borders 1.

— 268 —

AT OAKLAND (156):

Baltimore (6) —Anderson 2, Hoiles 2, Pagliarulo 1, Segui 1. **Boston (3)** —Vaughn 2, Hatcher 1. **California (7)** —Davis 3, Snow 2, Javier 1, Salmon 1. **Chicago (5)** —Bell 1, Burks 1, Karkovice 1, Thomas 1, Ventura 1. **Cleveland (7)** —Belle 2, Alomar 1, Fermin 1, Jefferson 1, Martinez 1, Sorrento 1. **Detroit (4)** —Tettleton 2, Fielder 1, Trammell 1. **Kansas City (5)** —Brett 2, Gaetti 1, Hamelin 1, Koslofski 1. **Milwaukee (2)** —Jaha 1, Vaughn 1. **Minnesota (11)** —Hrbek 3, Brito 2, Puckett 2, Harper 1, Mack 1, Munoz 1, Reboulet 1. **New York (5)** —Tartabull 2, Boggs 1, Velarde 1, B. Williams 1. **Oakland (78)** —Neel 11, Sierra 9, R. Henderson 8, Paquette 8, D. Henderson 7, Aldrete 5, McGwire 5, Steinbach 5, Gates 4, Brosius 3, Hemond 3, Blankenship 2, Bordick 2, Seitzer 2, Armas 1, Browne 1, Fox 1, Lydy 1. **Seattle (8)** —Boone 2, Buhner 2, Blowers 1, Griffey 1, O'Brien 1, Valle 1. **Texas (8)** —Gonzalez 3, Palmeiro 3, Davis 1, Palmer 1. **Toronto (7)** —Henderson 2, Carter 1, Jackson 1, Knorr 1, Olerud 1, Sprague 1.

AT SEATTLE (140):

Baltimore (7) —Anderson 2, Baines 1, Devereaux 1, Hoiles 1, Parent 1, Reynolds 1. **Boston (8)** —Cooper 2, Dawson 2, Vaughn 2, Greenwell 1, Valentin 1. **California (3)** —Curtis 1, Perez 1, Polonia 1. **Chicago (12)** —Thomas 3, Burks 2, Jackson 2, Ventura 2, Grebeck 1, Huff 1, Pasqua 1. **Cleveland (4)** —Belle 2, Jefferson 1, Sorrento 1. **Detroit (2)** —Gibson 1, Gladden 1. **Kansas City (2)** —Jose 1, Macfarlane 1. **Milwaukee (3)** —Jaha 2, Hamilton 1. **Minnesota (7)** —Winfield 2, Harper 1, Hrbek 1, Mack 1, Munoz 1, Puckett 1. **New York (6)** —Stanley 2, Mattingly 1, Meulens 1, Nokes 1, B. Williams 1. **Oakland (8)** —D. Henderson 3, Paquette 2, R. Henderson 1, Neel 1, Sierra 1. **Seattle (74)** —Griffey 21, Buhner 13, T. Martinez 9, Blowers 8, Boone 7, Valle 4, Haselman 3, Litton 3, Howitt 1, E. Martinez 1, Newfield 1, O'Brien 1, Pirkl 1, Vizquel 1. **Texas (3)** —Gonzalez 1, Palmeiro 1, Palmer 1. **Toronto (1)** —Alomar 1.

AT TEXAS (162):

Baltimore (6) —Ripken 3, Hoiles 1, Parent 1, Voigt 1. **Boston (3)** —Vaughn 2, Valentin 1. **California (1)** —Salmon 1. **Chicago (9)** —Karkovice 3, Burks 2, Jackson 2, Thomas 1, Ventura 1. **Cleveland (4)** —Baerga 1, Hill 1, Sorrento 1, Thome 1. **Detroit (4)** —Fielder 1, Gibson 1, Kreuter 1, Tettleton 1. **Kansas City (7)** —Gaetti 2, Gagne 2, Hiatt 1, Macfarlane 1, McReynolds 1. **Milwaukee (4)** —Vaughn 2, Brunansky 1, Yount 1. **Minnesota (6)** —Munoz 3, Puckett 2, Mack 1. **New York (6)** —O'Neill 2, Gallego 1, Stanley 1, Tartabull 1, B. Williams 1. **Oakland (8)** —Sierra 2, Aldrete 1, Brosius 1, Gates 1, D. Henderson 1, R. Henderson 1, Lydy 1. **Seattle (9)** —Buhner 3, Blowers 1, Boone 1, Cotto 1, Griffey 1, E. Martinez 1, O'Brien 1. **Texas (90)** —Gonzalez 24, Palmeiro 22, Palmer 12, Rodriguez 7, Canseco 6, Franco 6, Strange 4, Ducey 2, Redus 2, Diaz 1, Harris 1, Peltier 1, Petralli 1, Russell 1. **Toronto (5)** —Alomar 1, Borders 1, Carter 1, Molitor 1, Olerud 1.

AT TORONTO (171):

Baltimore (6) —Baines 2, Buford 2, Gomez 1, Ripken 1. **Boston (6)** —Greenwell 2, Deer 1, Fletcher 1, Quintana 1, Vaughn 1. **California (7)** —Davis 4, Curtis 1, Gruber 1, Turner 1. **Chicago (1)** —Thomas 1. **Cleveland (10)** —Sorrento 4, Baerga 2, Belle 2, Espinoza 1, Treadway 1. **Detroit (11)** —Gibson 3, Deer 2, Fielder 2, Fryman 2, Phillips 1, Whitaker 1. **Kansas City (6)** —Joyner 2, Macfarlane 2, McRae 2. **Milwaukee (10)** —Jaha 3, Vaughn 3, Yount 2, Listach 1, Surhoff 1. **Minnesota (3)** —Puckett 2, Harper 1. **New York (2)** —Leyritz 1, Tartabull 1. **Oakland (6)** —Sierra 2, Abbott 1, D. Henderson 1, Neel 1, Sveum 1. **Seattle (4)** —Griffey 2, Buhner 1, Vizquel 1. **Texas (9)** —Palmer 3, Franco 2, Gonzalez 2, Palmeiro 1, Rodriguez 1. **Toronto (90)** —Carter 21, Molitor 13, White 10, Olerud 9, Alomar 8, Sprague 8, Borders 6, Jackson 4, Coles 3, Henderson 2, Knorr 2, T. Ward 2, Canate 1, Fernandez 1.

1993 N.L. STATISTICS

Batting

Pinch-hitting

Pitching

Fielding

Miscellaneous

BATTING

TEAM

Team	Avg.	G	AB	R	H	TB	2B	3B	HR	RBI	SH	SF	HP	BB	Int. BB	SO	SB	CS	GI DP	LOB	ShO	Slg.	OBP
San Francisco .	.276	162	5557	808	1534	2373	269	33	168	759	102	50	46	516	88	930	120	65	121	1155	5	.427	.340
Philadelphia	.274	162	5685	877	1555	2422	297	51	156	811	84	51	42	665	70	1049	91	32	107	1281	2	.426	.351
Colorado..........	.273	162	5517	758	1507	2329	278	59	142	704	70	52	46	388	40	944	146	90	125	978	13	.422	.323
St. Louis	.272	162	5551	758	1508	2192	262	34	118	724	59	54	27	588	50	882	153	72	128	1177	8	.395	.341
Chicago	.270	163	5627	738	1521	2327	259	32	161	706	67	42	34	446	61	923	100	43	131	1133	10	.414	.325
Pittsburgh	.267	162	5549	707	1482	2179	267	50	110	664	76	52	55	536	50	972	92	55	129	1199	6	.393	.335
Houston	.267	162	5464	716	1459	2235	288	37	138	656	82	47	40	497	58	911	103	60	125	1116	8	.409	.330
Cincinnati	.264	162	5517	722	1457	2185	261	28	137	669	63	66	32	485	42	1025	142	59	104	1125	10	.396	.324
Atlanta	.262	162	5515	767	1444	2248	239	29	169	712	73	50	36	560	46	946	125	48	127	1165	9	.408	.331
Los Angeles	.261	162	5588	675	1458	2138	234	28	130	639	107	47	27	492	48	937	126	61	105	1162	8	.383	.321
Montreal	.257	163	5493	732	1411	2118	270	36	122	682	100	54	48	542	65	860	228	56	95	1166	5	.386	.326
San Diego	.252	162	5503	679	1386	2140	239	28	153	633	80	50	59	443	43	1046	92	41	111	1090	8	.389	.312
New York	.248	162	5448	672	1350	2126	228	37	158	632	89	47	24	448	43	879	79	50	108	1011	4	.390	.305
Florida	.248	162	5475	581	1356	1897	197	31	94	542	58	43	51	498	39	1054	117	56	122	1183	14	.346	.314
Totals	.264	1135	77489	10190	20427	30909	3588	513	1956	9533	110	701	567	7104	743	13358	1714	788	1638	15941	110	.399	.327

INDIVIDUAL

TOP 15 QUALIFIERS FOR BATTING CHAMPIONSHIP

Minimum 502 plate appearances.   *Lefthanded batter.   †Switch-hitter.

Player, Team	Avg.	G	AB	R	H	TB	2B	3B	HR	RBI	SH	SF	HP	BB	Int. BB	SO	SB	CS	GI DP	Slg.	OBP
Galarraga, Andres, Colorado	.370	120	470	71	174	283	35	4	22	98	0	6	6	24	12	73	2	4	9	.602	.403
Gwynn, Tony, San Diego*	.358	122	489	70	175	243	41	3	7	59	1	7	1	36	11	19	14	1	18	.497	.398
Jefferies, Gregg, St. Louis†	.342	142	544	89	186	264	24	3	16	83	0	4	2	62	7	32	46	9	15	.485	.408
Bonds, Barry, San Francisco* ...	.336	159	539	129	181	365	38	4	46	123	0	7	2	126	43	79	29	12	11	.677	.458
Grace, Mark, Chicago*	.325	155	594	86	193	282	39	4	14	98	1	9	1	71	14	32	8	4	25	.475	.393
Bagwell, Jeff, Houston	.320	142	535	76	171	276	37	4	20	88	0	9	3	62	6	73	13	4	20	.516	.388
Piazza, Mike, Los Angeles	.318	149	547	81	174	307	24	2	35	112	0	6	3	46	6	86	3	4	10	.561	.370
Kruk, John, Philadelphia*	.316	150	535	100	169	254	33	5	14	85	0	5	0	111	10	87	6	2	11	.475	.430
Merced, Orlando, Pittsburgh*	.313	137	447	68	140	198	26	4	8	70	0	2	1	77	10	64	3	3	9	.443	.414
Thompson, Robby, San Francisco .	.312	128	494	85	154	245	30	2	19	65	9	4	7	45	0	97	10	4	7	.496	.375
Bichette, Dante, Colorado	.310	141	538	93	167	283	43	5	21	89	0	8	7	28	2	99	14	8	7	.526	.348
Bell, Jay, Pittsburgh	.310	154	604	102	187	264	32	9	9	51	13	1	6	77	6	122	16	10	16	.437	.392
Sandberg, Ryne, Chicago	.309	117	456	67	141	188	20	0	9	45	2	6	2	37	1	62	9	2	12	.412	.359
Hayes, Charlie, Colorado	.305	157	573	89	175	299	45	2	25	98	1	8	5	43	6	82	11	6	25	.522	.355
Gilkey, Bernard, St. Louis...........	.305	137	557	99	170	268	40	5	16	70	0	5	4	56	2	66	15	10	16	.481	.370

DEPARTMENTAL LEADERS: G—Conine, Fla., 162; AB—Dykstra, Phi., 637; R—Dykstra, Phi., 143; H—Dykstra, Phi., 194; TB—Bonds, S.F., 365; 1B—Butler, L.A., 149; 2B—Hayes, Col., 45; 3B—Finley, Hou., 13; HR—Bonds, S.F., 46; RBI—Bonds, S.F., 123; SH—Offerman, L.A., 25; SF—Gonzalez, Hou., 10; HP—Blauser, Atl., 16; BB—Dykstra, Phi., 129; IBB—Bonds, S.F., 43; SO—Snyder, L.A., 147; SB—Carr, Fla., 58; CS—Carr, Fla., 22; GIDP—Grace, Chi., Hayes, Col., 25; Slg. Pct.—Bonds, S.F., .677; OB. Pct.—Bonds, S.F., .458.

ALL PLAYERS

*Lefthanded batter.   †Switch-hitter.

Player, Team	Avg.	G	AB	R	H	TB	2B	3B	HR	RBI	SH	SF	HP	BB	Int. BB	SO	SB	CS	GI DP	Slg.	OBP
Alicea, Luis, St. Louis†	.279	115	362	50	101	135	19	3	3	46	1	7	4	47	2	54	11	1	9	.373	.362
Allanson, Andy, San Francisco...	.167	13	24	3	4	5	1	0	0	2	1	0	0	1	0	2	0	0	1	.208	.200
Alou, Moises, Montreal	.286	136	482	70	138	233	29	6	18	85	3	7	5	38	9	53	17	6	9	.483	.340
Amaro, Ruben, Philadelphia†	.333	25	48	7	16	25	2	2	1	6	3	1	0	6	0	5	0	0	1	.521	.400
Andersen, Larry, Philadelphia	1.000	64	1	0	1	1	0	0	0	0	0	0	0	0	0	0	0	0	0	1.000	1.000
Anderson, Mike, Cincinnati.........	.000	3	1	0	0	0	0	0	0	0	0	0	0	0	0	0	0	0	0	.000	.000
Anthony, Eric, Houston*	.249	145	486	70	121	193	19	4	15	66	0	2	2	49	2	88	3	5	9	.397	.319
Aquino, Luis, Florida	.080	38	25	1	2	2	0	0	0	4	0	0	0	0	0	7	0	0	0	.080	.080
Arias, Alex, Florida	.269	96	249	27	67	80	5	1	2	20	1	3	3	27	0	18	1	1	5	.321	.344
Armstrong, Jack, Florida	.152	36	66	3	10	11	1	0	0	3	4	0	0	0	0	29	0	0	2	.167	.152
Arocha, Rene, St. Louis	.103	32	58	3	6	7	1	0	0	3	7	0	0	2	0	24	0	0	0	.121	.133
Ashby, Andy, Col.-S.D.	.139	32	36	3	5	6	1	0	0	1	2	0	0	2	0	9	0	0	0	.167	.184
Ashley, Billy, Los Angeles	.243	14	37	0	9	9	0	0	0	0	0	0	0	2	0	11	0	0	0	.243	.282
Assenmacher, Paul, Chicago*	.500	46	2	0	1	1	0	0	0	0	0	0	0	0	0	0	0	0	0	.500	.500
Astacio, Pedro, Los Angeles	.161	31	62	4	10	10	0	0	0	2	7	0	0	0	0	26	0	1	0	.161	.161
Aude, Rich, Pittsburgh	.115	13	26	1	3	4	1	0	0	4	0	0	0	1	0	7	0	0	0	.154	.148
Ausmus, Brad, San Diego	.256	49	160	18	41	66	8	1	5	12	0	0	0	6	0	28	2	0	2	.413	.283
Avery, Steve, Atlanta*	.160	35	75	4	12	16	4	0	0	5	8	0	0	2	0	19	0	1	1	.213	.182
Ayala, Bobby, Cincinnati	.095	43	21	1	2	3	1	0	0	1	2	0	0	0	0	7	0	1	0	.143	.095
Ayrault, Bob, Philadelphia	.000	10	2	0	0	0	0	0	0	0	0	0	0	2	0	0	0	0	0	.000	.000
Baez, Kevin, New York	.183	52	126	10	23	32	9	0	0	7	4	0	0	13	1	17	0	0	1	.254	.259
Bagwell, Jeff, Houston	.320	142	535	76	171	276	37	4	20	88	0	9	3	62	6	73	13	4	20	.516	.388
Ballard, Jeff, Pittsburgh*	.364	25	11	0	4	5	1	0	0	0	1	0	0	0	0	4	0	0	0	.455	.364
Barberie, Bret, Florida†	.277	99	375	45	104	139	16	2	5	33	5	3	7	33	2	58	2	4	7	.371	.344
Barnes, Brian, Montreal*	.150	52	20	1	3	3	0	0	0	2	2	0	0	1	0	9	0	0	0	.150	.190
Bass, Kevin, Houston†	.284	111	229	31	65	92	18	0	3	37	2	0	1	26	3	31	7	1	4	.402	.359
Batchelor, Rich, St. Louis...........	.000	9	1	0	0	0	0	0	0	0	0	0	0	0	0	0	0	0	0	.000	.000
Batiste, Kim, Philadelphia	.282	79	156	14	44	68	7	1	5	29	0	1	1	3	2	29	0	1	3	.436	.298

Player, Team	Avg.	G	AB	R	H	TB	2B	3B	HR	RBI	SH	SF	HP	BB	Int. BB	SO	SB	CS	GI DP	Slg.	OBP
Bautista, Jose, Chicago	.190	61	21	1	4	4	0	0	0	1	2	0	0	4	0	0	0	0	0	.190	.190
Bean, Billy, San Diego*	.260	88	177	19	46	70	9	0	5	32	2	5	2	6	1	29	2	4	4	.395	.284
Beck, Rod, San Francisco	.000	76	4	0	0	0	0	0	0	0	1	0	0	0	0	3	0	0	0	.000	.000
Bedrosian, Steve, Atlanta	.000	49	2	0	0	0	0	0	0	0	0	0	0	0	0	2	0	0	0	.000	.000
Belcher, Tim, Cincinnati	.200	22	50	2	10	11	1	0	0	7	3	0	1	0	0	15	0	1	0	.220	.216
Belinda, Stan, Pittsburgh	.000	40	1	0	0	0	0	0	0	0	0	0	0	0	0	1	0	0	0	.000	.000
Bell, Derek, San Diego	.262	150	542	73	142	226	19	1	21	72	0	8	12	23	5	122	26	5	7	.417	.303
Bell, Jay, Pittsburgh	.310	154	604	102	187	264	32	9	9	51	13	1	6	77	6	122	16	10	16	.437	.392
Bell, Juan, Philadelphia†	.200	24	65	5	13	21	6	1	0	7	2	0	1	5	0	12	0	1	0	.323	.268
Belliard, Rafael, Atlanta	.228	91	79	6	18	23	5	0	0	6	3	0	3	4	0	13	0	0	1	.291	.291
Benavides, Freddie, Colorado	.286	74	213	20	61	86	10	3	3	26	3	1	0	6	1	27	3	2	4	.404	.305
Benes, Andy, San Diego	.125	34	72	5	9	15	3	0	1	4	14	0	1	1	0	33	0	0	0	.208	.149
Benjamin, Mike, San Francisco...	.199	63	146	22	29	48	7	0	4	16	6	0	4	9	2	23	0	3	3	.329	.264
Benzinger, Todd, San Francisco†..	.288	86	177	25	51	80	7	2	6	26	1	3	0	13	1	35	0	2	3	.452	.332
Berroa, Geronimo, Florida	.118	14	34	3	4	5	1	0	0	0	0	0	0	2	0	7	0	0	2	.147	.167
Berry, Sean, Montreal	.261	122	299	50	78	139	15	2	14	49	3	6	2	41	6	70	12	2	4	.465	.348
Berryhill, Damon, Atlanta†	.245	115	335	24	82	128	18	2	8	43	2	3	2	21	1	64	0	0	7	.382	.291
Bichette, Dante, Colorado	.310	141	538	93	167	283	43	5	21	89	0	8	7	28	2	99	14	8	7	.526	.348
Biggio, Craig, Houston	.287	155	610	98	175	289	41	5	21	64	4	5	10	77	7	93	15	17	10	.474	.373
Black, Bud, San Francisco*	.243	16	37	2	9	9	0	0	0	3	3	0	0	2	0	8	0	0	1	.243	.282
Blair, Willie, Colorado	.111	46	36	1	4	5	1	0	0	4	3	0	0	1	0	19	0	0	0	.139	.135
Blauser, Jeff, Atlanta	.305	161	597	110	182	260	29	2	15	73	5	7	16	85	0	109	16	6	13	.436	.401
Bogar, Tim, New York	.244	78	205	19	50	72	13	0	3	25	1	1	3	14	2	29	0	1	2	.351	.300
Bolick, Frank, Montreal†	.211	95	213	25	45	70	13	0	4	24	0	2	4	23	2	37	1	0	4	.329	.298
Bonds, Barry, San Francisco*	.336	159	539	129	181	365	38	4	46	123	0	7	2	126	43	79	29	12	11	.677	.458
Bonilla, Bobby, New York†	.265	139	502	81	133	262	21	3	34	87	0	8	0	72	11	96	3	3	12	.522	.352
Boskie, Shawn, Chicago	.273	39	11	2	3	3	0	0	0	0	0	0	0	0	0	3	0	0	0	.273	.273
Boston, Daryl, Colorado*	.261	124	291	46	76	135	15	1	14	40	0	1	2	26	1	57	1	6	5	.464	.325
Bottenfield, Kent, Mon.-Col.†	.220	37	50	2	11	11	0	0	0	3	3	0	1	1	0	15	1	0	0	.220	.250
Boucher, Denis, Montreal	.167	5	6	0	1	2	1	0	0	0	2	0	0	0	0	3	0	0	0	.333	.167
Bournigal, Rafael, Los Angeles...	.500	8	18	0	9	10	1	0	0	3	0	0	0	0	0	2	0	0	0	.556	.500
Bowen, Ryan, Florida	.118	27	51	3	6	9	1	1	0	3	3	0	0	1	0	15	0	0	0	.176	.135
Branson, Jeff, Cincinnati*	.241	125	381	40	92	118	15	1	3	22	8	4	0	19	2	73	4	1	4	.310	.275
Brantley, Jeff, San Francisco	.107	53	28	1	3	3	0	0	0	3	1	0	0	0	0	9	0	0	1	.107	.107
Bream, Sid, Atlanta*	.260	117	277	33	72	115	14	1	9	35	1	2	0	31	3	43	4	2	6	.415	.332
Brennan, Bill, Chicago	.000	8	1	0	0	0	0	0	0	0	1	0	0	1	0	1	0	0	0	.000	.500
Brewer, Rod, St. Louis*	.286	110	147	15	42	56	8	0	2	20	2	2	1	17	5	26	1	0	5	.381	.359
Briley, Greg, Florida*	.194	120	170	17	33	48	6	0	3	12	1	1	1	12	0	42	6	2	5	.282	.250
Brink, Brad, Philadelphia	.000	2	1	0	0	0	0	0	0	0	0	0	0	0	0	0	0	0	0	.000	.000
Brocail, Doug, San Diego*	.182	30	33	4	6	6	0	0	0	0	11	0	0	0	0	8	2	0	0	.182	.182
Brooks, Jerome, Los Angeles	.222	9	9	2	2	6	1	0	1	1	0	0	0	0	0	2	0	0	0	.667	.222
Brown, Jarvis, San Diego	.233	47	133	21	31	44	9	2	0	8	2	1	6	15	0	26	3	3	4	.331	.335
Browning, Tom, Cincinnati*	.216	21	37	4	8	12	1	0	1	4	4	1	0	2	0	6	0	0	0	.324	.250
Brumfield, Jacob, Cincinnati	.268	103	272	40	73	114	17	3	6	23	3	2	1	21	4	47	20	8	1	.419	.321
Brumley, Mike, Houston*	.300	8	10	1	3	3	0	0	0	2	0	0	0	1	0	3	0	1	0	.300	.364
Brummett, Greg, San Francisco..	.000	8	15	0	0	0	0	0	0	0	2	0	0	1	0	5	0	0	0	.000	.063
Buechele, Steve, Chicago	.272	133	460	53	125	201	27	2	15	65	4	3	5	48	5	87	1	1	12	.437	.345
Bullett, Scott, Pittsburgh*	.200	23	55	2	11	15	0	2	0	4	0	1	0	3	0	15	3	2	1	.273	.237
Bullinger, Jim, Chicago	.000	15	1	0	0	0	0	0	0	0	0	0	0	0	0	0	0	0	0	.000	.000
Burba, Dave, San Francisco	.294	54	17	1	5	6	1	0	0	2	3	0	0	1	0	7	0	0	1	.353	.333
Burkett, John, San Francisco	.118	34	76	7	9	9	0	0	0	4	12	0	0	5	0	31	0	0	4	.118	.173
Burnitz, Jeromy, New York*	.243	86	263	49	64	125	10	6	13	38	2	2	1	38	4	66	3	6	2	.475	.339
Burns, Todd, St. Louis	.000	24	3	0	0	0	0	0	0	0	0	0	0	0	0	1	0	0	0	.000	.000
Butler, Brett, Los Angeles*	.298	156	607	80	181	225	21	10	1	42	14	4	5	86	1	69	39	19	6	.371	.387
Cabrera, Francisco, Atlanta	.241	70	83	8	20	35	3	0	4	11	0	0	8	1	21	0	0	2	.422	.308
Cadaret, Greg, Cincinnati*	.000	34	2	0	0	0	0	0	0	0	1	0	0	0	0	0	0	0	0	.000	.000
Caminiti, Ken, Houston†	.262	143	543	75	142	212	31	0	13	75	1	3	0	49	10	88	8	5	15	.390	.321
Candaele, Casey, Houston†	.240	75	121	18	29	40	8	0	1	7	0	0	0	10	0	14	2	3	0	.331	.298
Candiotti, Tom, Los Angeles	.133	33	60	1	8	10	2	0	0	2	9	0	0	1	0	13	0	0	2	.167	.148
Canseco, Ozzie, St. Louis	.176	6	17	0	3	3	0	0	0	0	0	0	0	1	0	3	0	0	0	.176	.222
Carpenter, Cris, Florida	.000	29	0	0	0	0	0	0	0	0	1	0	0	0	0	0	0	0	0	.000	.000
Carr, Chuck, Florida†	.267	142	551	75	147	182	19	2	4	41	7	4	2	49	0	74	58	22	6	.330	.327
Carreon, Mark, San Francisco	.327	78	150	22	49	81	9	1	7	33	0	5	1	13	2	16	1	0	8	.540	.373
Carrillo, Matias, Florida*	.255	24	55	4	14	20	6	0	0	3	1	0	1	1	0	7	0	5	1	.364	.281
Castellano, Pedro, Colorado	.183	34	71	12	13	24	2	0	3	7	0	0	0	8	0	16	1	1	1	.338	.266
Castilla, Vinny, Colorado	.255	105	337	36	86	136	9	7	9	30	0	5	2	13	4	45	2	5	10	.404	.283
Castillo, Frank, Chicago	.163	29	43	1	7	7	0	0	0	3	8	0	0	1	0	3	0	0	2	.163	.182
Cedeno, Andujar, Houston	.283	149	505	69	143	208	24	4	11	56	4	5	3	48	9	97	9	7	17	.412	.346
Chamberlain, Wes, Philadelphia	.282	96	284	34	80	140	20	2	12	45	0	4	1	17	3	51	2	1	8	.493	.320
Cianfrocco, Archi, Mon.-S.D.	.243	96	296	30	72	123	11	2	12	48	2	5	3	17	1	69	2	0	9	.416	.287
Clark, Dave, Pittsburgh*	.271	110	277	43	75	123	11	2	11	46	0	2	1	38	5	58	1	0	10	.444	.358
Clark, Jerald, Colorado	.282	140	478	65	135	212	26	6	13	67	3	1	10	20	2	60	9	6	12	.444	.324
Clark, Phil, San Diego	.313	102	240	33	75	119	17	0	9	33	1	2	5	8	2	31	2	0	2	.496	.345
Clark, Will, San Francisco*	.283	132	491	82	139	212	27	2	14	73	1	6	6	63	6	68	2	2	10	.432	.367
Clayton, Royce, San Francisco ...	.282	153	549	54	155	204	21	5	6	70	8	7	5	38	2	91	11	10	16	.372	.331
Colbert, Craig, San Francisco	.162	23	37	2	6	11	2	0	1	5	0	0	3	1	0	13	0	0	0	.297	.225
Colbrunn, Greg, Montreal	.255	70	153	15	39	60	9	0	4	23	1	3	1	6	1	33	4	2	1	.392	.282
Cole, Alex, Colorado*	.256	126	348	50	89	106	9	4	0	24	4	2	2	43	3	58	30	13	6	.305	.339
Coleman, Vince, New York†	.279	92	373	64	104	140	14	8	2	25	3	2	0	21	1	58	38	13	2	.375	.316
Conine, Jeff, Florida	.292	162	595	75	174	240	24	3	12	79	0	6	5	52	2	135	2	2	14	.403	.351
Cooke, Steve, Pittsburgh	.155	32	71	4	11	13	2	0	0	5	6	1	1	0	0	17	0	0	4	.183	.164
Cordero, Wil, Montreal	.248	138	475	56	118	184	32	2	10	58	4	1	7	34	8	60	12	3	12	.387	.308
Cormier, Rheal, St. Louis*	.234	38	47	5	11	13	2	0	0	4	6	0	0	0	0	11	0	0	1	.277	.234
Costo, Tim, Cincinnati	.224	31	98	13	22	36	5	0	3	12	0	0	4	4	0	17	0	0	1	.367	.250
Cotto, Henry, Florida	.296	54	135	16	40	56	7	0	3	14	1	2	1	3	0	18	11	1	3	.415	.312
Cromer, Tripp, St. Louis	.087	10	23	1	2	2	0	0	0	0	0	0	1	0	0	6	0	0	0	.087	.125
Cummings, Midre, Pittsburgh*	.111	13	36	5	4	5	1	0	0	3	0	1	0	4	0	9	0	0	1	.139	.195

Player, Team	Avg.	G	AB	R	H	TB	2B	3B	HR	RBI	SH	SF	HP	BB	Int. BB	SO	SB	CS	GI DP	Slg.	OBP
Daal, Omar, Los Angeles*	.000	47	0	0	0	0	0	0	0	0	0	0	0	1	0	0	0	0	0	.000	1.000
Daugherty, Jack, Hou.-Cin.†	.226	50	62	7	14	22	2	0	2	9	0	1	0	11	0	15	0	0	0	.355	.338
Daulton, Darren, Philadelphia*	.257	147	510	90	131	246	35	4	24	105	0	8	2	117	12	111	5	0	2	.482	.392
Davis, Eric, Los Angeles	.234	108	376	57	88	147	17	0	14	53	0	4	1	41	6	88	33	5	8	.391	.308
Davis, Mark, Phi.-S.D.*	.250	60	4	1	1	1	0	0	0	0	1	0	0	0	0	1	0	0	0	.250	.250
DeLeon, Jose, Philadelphia	.000	24	6	0	0	0	0	0	0	0	0	0	0	0	0	5	0	0	1	.000	.000
Decker, Steve, Florida	.000	8	15	0	0	0	0	0	0	1	0	1	0	3	0	3	0	0	2	.000	.158
Deshaies, Jim, San Francisco*	.000	5	5	0	0	0	0	0	0	0	0	0	0	0	0	3	0	0	0	.000	.000
DeShields, Delino, Montreal*	.295	123	481	75	142	179	17	7	2	29	4	2	3	72	3	64	43	10	6	.372	.389
Destrade, Orestes, Florida†	.255	153	569	61	145	231	20	3	20	87	1	6	3	58	8	130	0	2	17	.406	.324
Dewey, Mark, Pittsburgh	.000	21	0	0	0	0	0	0	0	0	0	0	0	1	0	0	0	0	0	.000	1.000
Dibble, Rob, Cincinnati*	1.000	45	1	0	1	1	0	0	0	1	0	0	0	0	0	0	0	0	0	1.000	1.000
Donnels, Chris, Houston*	.257	88	179	18	46	70	14	2	2	24	0	1	0	19	0	33	2	0	6	.391	.327
Dorsett, Brian, Cincinnati	.254	25	63	7	16	26	4	0	2	12	0	0	3	0	0	14	0	0	1	.413	.288
Drabek, Doug, Houston	.085	34	71	2	6	11	2	0	1	3	9	0	0	2	0	22	0	0	3	.155	.110
Draper, Mike, New York	.667	29	3	1	2	2	0	0	0	0	0	0	0	0	0	1	0	0	0	.667	.667
Duncan, Mariano, Philadelphia...	.282	124	496	68	140	207	26	4	11	73	4	2	4	12	0	88	6	5	13	.417	.304
Dunston, Shawon, Chicago	.400	7	10	3	4	6	2	0	0	2	0	0	0	0	0	1	0	0	0	.600	.400
Dykstra, Lenny, Philadelphia*	.305	161	637	143	194	307	44	6	19	66	0	5	2	129	9	64	37	12	8	.482	.420
Edens, Tom, Houston	.000	38	1	0	0	0	0	0	0	0	0	0	0	0	0	1	0	0	0	.000	.000
Eiland, Dave, San Diego	.083	10	12	1	1	1	0	0	0	0	3	0	0	0	0	4	0	0	0	.083	.083
Eisenreich, Jim, Philadelphia*	.318	153	362	51	115	161	17	4	7	54	3	2	1	26	5	36	5	0	6	.445	.363
Espy, Cecil, Cincinnati†	.233	40	60	6	14	16	2	0	0	5	0	2	0	14	0	13	2	2	2	.267	.368
Ettles, Mark, San Diego	.000	14	2	0	0	0	0	0	0	0	0	0	0	0	0	0	0	0	0	.000	.000
Everett, Carl, Florida†	.105	11	19	0	2	2	0	0	0	0	0	0	0	1	0	9	1	0	0	.105	.150
Faneyte, Rikkert, San Francisco.	.133	7	15	2	2	2	0	0	0	0	0	0	0	2	0	4	0	0	0	.133	.235
Faries, Paul, San Francisco	.222	15	36	6	8	12	2	1	0	4	1	1	0	1	0	4	2	0	1	.333	.237
Fariss, Monty, Florida	.172	18	29	3	5	9	2	1	0	2	0	0	0	5	0	13	0	0	2	.310	.294
Fassero, Jeff, Montreal*	.063	56	32	3	2	3	1	0	0	5	5	0	0	1	0	23	0	0	0	.094	.091
Felix, Junior, Florida†	.238	57	214	25	51	85	11	1	7	22	0	0	1	10	1	50	2	1	6	.397	.276
Fernandez, Sid, New York*	.094	18	32	2	3	3	0	0	0	2	8	0	0	2	0	13	0	0	2	.094	.147
Fernandez, Tony, New York†	.225	48	173	20	39	51	5	2	1	14	3	2	1	25	0	19	6	2	3	.295	.323
Finley, Steve, Houston*	.266	142	545	69	145	210	15	13	8	44	6	3	3	28	1	65	19	6	8	.385	.304
Fletcher, Darrin, Montreal*	.255	133	396	33	101	150	20	1	9	60	5	4	6	34	2	40	0	0	7	.379	.320
Floyd, Cliff, Montreal*	.226	10	31	3	7	10	0	0	1	2	0	0	0	0	0	9	0	0	1	.323	.226
Foley, Tom, Pittsburgh*	.253	86	194	18	49	71	11	1	3	22	2	4	0	11	1	26	0	0	4	.366	.287
Foster, Kevin, Philadelphia	.000	2	0	0	0	0	0	0	0	0	0	0	0	0	0	0	0	0	0	.000	.000
Foster, Steve, Cincinnati	.000	17	0	0	0	0	0	0	0	0	1	0	0	0	0	0	0	0	0	.000	.000
Franco, John, New York*	.000	35	1	0	0	0	0	0	0	0	0	0	0	0	0	0	0	0	0	.000	.000
Frazier, Lou, Montreal†	.286	112	189	27	54	66	7	1	1	16	5	1	0	16	0	24	17	2	3	.349	.340
Fredrickson, Scott, Colorado	.000	25	3	0	0	0	0	0	0	0	0	0	0	0	0	3	0	0	0	.000	.000
Freeman, Marvin, Atlanta	.000	21	0	0	0	0	0	0	0	0	2	0	0	0	0	0	0	0	0	.000	.000
Gainer, Jay, Colorado*	.171	23	41	4	7	16	0	0	3	6	0	0	0	4	0	12	1	1	0	.390	.244
Galarraga, Andres, Colorado	.370	120	470	71	174	283	35	4	22	98	0	6	6	24	12	73	2	4	9	.602	.403
Gallagher, Dave, New York	.274	99	201	34	55	89	12	2	6	28	7	1	0	20	1	18	1	1	7	.443	.338
Gant, Ron, Atlanta	.274	157	606	113	166	309	27	4	36	117	0	7	2	67	2	117	26	9	14	.510	.345
Garcia, Carlos, Pittsburgh	.269	141	546	77	147	218	25	5	12	47	6	5	9	31	2	67	18	11	9	.399	.316
Gardiner, Mike, Montreal†	.000	24	4	0	0	0	0	0	0	0	0	0	0	1	0	3	0	0	0	.000	.200
Gardner, Jeff, San Diego*	.262	140	404	53	106	144	21	7	1	24	1	1	1	45	0	69	2	6	3	.356	.337
Geren, Bob, San Diego	.214	58	145	8	31	46	6	3	1	6	4	0	0	13	4	28	0	0	4	.317	.278
Gilkey, Bernard, St. Louis	.305	137	557	99	170	268	40	5	16	70	0	5	4	56	2	66	15	10	16	.481	.370
Girardi, Joe, Colorado	.290	86	310	35	90	123	14	5	3	31	12	1	3	24	0	41	6	6	6	.397	.346
Glavine, Tom, Atlanta*	.173	36	81	3	14	15	1	0	0	3	11	0	0	4	0	27	0	0	1	.185	.212
Goff, Jerry, Pittsburgh*	.297	14	37	5	11	19	2	0	2	6	1	0	0	8	1	9	0	0	0	.514	.422
Gomez, Pat, San Diego*	.000	28	5	0	0	0	0	0	0	0	1	0	0	1	0	0	0	0	0	.000	.000
Gonzalez, Luis, Houston*	.300	154	540	82	162	247	34	3	15	72	3	10	10	47	7	83	20	9	9	.457	.361
Gooden, Dwight, New York	.200	30	70	5	14	26	2	2	2	9	6	0	0	11	0	11	0	1	0	.371	.200
Goodwin, Tom, Los Angeles*	.294	30	17	6	5	6	1	0	0	1	0	0	0	1	0	4	1	2	1	.353	.333
Gordon, Keith, Cincinnati	.167	3	6	0	1	1	0	0	0	0	0	0	0	0	0	2	0	0	0	.167	.167
Gott, Jim, Los Angeles	.000	62	1	0	0	0	0	0	0	0	0	0	0	0	0	1	0	0	0	.000	.000
Grace, Mark, Chicago*	.325	155	594	86	193	282	39	4	14	98	1	9	1	71	14	32	8	4	25	.475	.393
Green, Tyler, Philadelphia	.000	3	2	0	0	0	0	0	0	0	0	0	0	0	0	2	0	0	0	.000	.000
Greene, Tommy, Philadelphia	.222	32	72	9	16	24	2	0	2	10	6	1	0	5	0	20	0	0	1	.333	.269
Greene, Willie, Cincinnati*	.160	15	50	7	8	17	1	1	2	5	0	1	0	2	0	19	0	1	1	.340	.189
Gregg, Tommy, Cincinnati*	.167	10	12	1	2	2	0	0	0	1	0	0	0	1	0	2	0	0	0	.167	.154
Grissom, Marquis, Montreal	.298	157	630	104	188	276	27	2	19	95	0	8	3	52	6	76	53	10	9	.438	.351
Gross, Kevin, Los Angeles	.203	33	64	6	13	18	2	0	1	7	8	0	1	5	0	32	0	0	1	.281	.271
Guetterman, Lee, St. Louis*	.500	40	2	0	1	2	1	0	0	0	0	0	0	0	0	0	0	0	1	1.000	.500
Gutierrez, Ricky, San Diego	.251	133	438	76	110	145	10	5	5	26	1	1	5	50	2	97	4	3	7	.331	.334
Guzman, Jose, Chicago	.111	30	63	1	7	7	0	0	0	2	9	0	0	1	0	15	0	0	1	.111	.125
Gwynn, Tony, San Diego*	.358	122	489	70	175	243	41	3	7	59	1	7	1	36	11	19	14	1	18	.497	.398
Hammond, Chris, Florida*	.190	33	63	10	12	20	0	1	2	4	5	0	0	9	0	26	0	0	1	.317	.292
Hansen, Dave, Los Angeles*	.362	84	105	13	38	53	3	0	4	30	0	1	0	21	3	13	0	1	0	.505	.465
Harkey, Mike, Chicago	.093	28	54	0	5	6	1	0	0	5	0	0	0	1	0	18	0	0	1	.111	.109
Harnisch, Pete, Houston	.104	33	67	6	7	9	2	0	0	2	10	0	1	2	0	19	0	0	3	.134	.143
Harris, Gene, San Diego	.000	59	1	0	0	0	0	0	0	0	0	0	0	0	0	0	0	0	0	.000	.000
Harris, Greg, S.D.-Col.	.137	35	73	2	10	13	3	0	0	4	5	0	0	5	0	25	0	0	0	.178	.188
Harris, Lenny, Los Angeles*	.238	107	160	20	38	52	6	1	2	11	1	0	0	15	4	15	3	1	4	.325	.303
Hayes, Charlie, Colorado	.305	157	573	89	175	299	45	2	25	98	1	8	5	43	6	82	11	6	25	.522	.355
Henry, Butch, Col.-Mon.*	.083	30	24	1	2	2	0	0	0	2	3	1	0	1	0	3	0	0	0	.083	.115
Henry, Dwayne, Cincinnati	.000	3	1	0	0	0	0	0	0	0	0	0	0	0	0	0	0	0	0	.000	.000
Heredia, Gil, Montreal	.154	20	13	1	2	3	1	0	0	0	4	0	0	0	0	3	0	0	0	.231	.154
Hernandez, Carlos, Los Angeles .	.253	50	99	6	25	36	5	0	2	7	1	0	0	2	0	11	0	0	0	.364	.267
Hernandez, Cesar, Cincinnati	.083	27	24	3	2	2	0	0	0	1	1	0	0	1	0	1	1	0	0	.083	.120
Hernandez, Jeremy, San Diego ...	.000	21	1	0	0	0	0	0	0	0	0	0	0	0	0	0	0	0	0	.000	.000
Hernandez, Xavier, Houston*	.000	72	5	0	0	0	0	0	0	0	0	0	0	0	0	2	0	0	0	.000	.000
Hershiser, Orel, Los Angeles	.356	34	73	11	26	30	4	0	0	6	8	0	0	2	0	5	0	1	1	.411	.373

Player, Team	Avg.	G	AB	R	H	TB	2B	3B	HR	RBI	SH	SF	HP	BB	Int. BB	SO	SB	CS	GI DP	Slg.	OBP
Hibbard, Greg, Chicago*	.092	32	65	4	6	7	1	0	0	3	3	0	0	2	0	17	0	0	1	.108	.119
Hickerson, Bryan, San Francisco*	.143	47	28	1	4	4	0	0	0	4	4	0	0	1	0	13	0	0	0	.143	.172
Higgins, Kevin, San Diego*	.221	71	181	17	40	46	4	1	0	13	1	1	3	16	0	17	0	1	7	.254	.294
Hill, Glenallen, Chicago	.345	31	87	14	30	67	7	0	10	22	0	0	0	6	0	21	1	0	1	.770	.387
Hill, Ken, Montreal	.115	29	52	4	6	8	2	0	0	3	14	0	0	4	0	15	0	0	0	.154	.179
Hill, Milton, Cincinnati	.000	19	2	0	0	0	0	0	0	0	0	0	0	0	0	2	0	0	0	.000	.000
Hillman, Eric, New York*	.159	27	44	2	7	8	1	0	0	0	6	0	1	0	0	14	0	0	0	.182	.178
Hoffman, Trevor, Fla.-S.D.	.143	67	7	0	1	1	0	0	0	0	0	0	0	0	0	1	0	0	0	.143	.143
Hollins, Dave, Philadelphia†	.273	143	543	104	148	240	30	4	18	93	0	7	5	85	5	109	2	3	15	.442	.372
Hope, John, Pittsburgh	.077	7	13	0	1	1	0	0	0	0	0	0	0	0	0	7	0	0	0	.077	.077
Hosey, Steve, San Francisco	.500	3	2	0	1	2	1	0	0	1	0	0	0	1	0	1	0	0	0	1.000	.667
Hough, Charlie, Florida	.032	34	63	1	2	2	0	0	0	1	4	0	1	2	0	20	0	0	4	.032	.076
Housie, Wayne, New York†	.188	18	16	2	3	4	1	0	0	1	0	0	0	1	0	1	0	0	0	.250	.235
Howard, Thomas, Cincinnati†	.277	38	141	22	39	65	8	3	4	13	0	1	0	12	0	21	5	6	4	.461	.331
Hughes, Keith, Cincinnati*	.000	3	4	0	0	0	0	0	0	0	0	0	0	0	0	0	0	0	0	.000	.000
Hundley, Todd, New York†	.228	130	417	40	95	149	17	2	11	53	2	4	2	23	7	62	1	1	10	.357	.269
Hunter, Brian, Atlanta	.138	37	80	4	11	16	3	1	0	8	0	3	0	2	1	15	0	0	1	.200	.153
Hurst, Bruce, S.D.-Col.*	.000	5	1	0	0	0	0	0	0	0	1	0	0	0	0	1	0	0	0	.000	.000
Huskey, Butch, New York	.146	13	41	2	6	7	1	0	0	3	0	2	0	1	1	13	0	0	0	.171	.159
Incaviglia, Pete, Philadelphia	.274	116	368	60	101	195	16	3	24	89	0	7	6	21	1	82	1	1	9	.530	.318
Innis, Jeff, New York	.000	67	0	0	0	0	0	0	0	0	2	0	0	0	0	0	0	0	0	.000	.000
Jackson, Danny, Philadelphia	.077	32	65	3	5	7	2	0	0	2	12	0	1	3	0	37	0	0	0	.108	.130
Jackson, Darrin, New York	.195	31	87	4	17	21	1	0	1	7	1	1	0	2	0	22	0	0	1	.241	.211
Jackson, Mike, San Francisco	.667	81	3	1	2	4	2	0	0	1	0	0	0	0	0	1	0	0	0	1.333	.667
James, Chris, Houston	.256	65	129	19	33	63	10	1	6	19	1	2	1	15	2	34	2	0	2	.488	.333
Jefferies, Gregg, St. Louis†	.342	142	544	89	186	264	24	3	16	83	0	4	2	62	7	32	46	9	15	.485	.408
Jennings, Doug, Chicago*	.250	42	52	8	13	24	3	1	2	8	0	0	2	3	0	10	0	0	3	.462	.316
Johnson, Erik, San Francisco	.400	4	5	1	2	4	2	0	0	0	0	0	0	0	0	1	0	0	0	.800	.400
Johnson, Howard, New York†	.238	72	235	32	56	89	8	2	7	26	0	2	0	43	3	43	6	4	3	.379	.354
Johnston, Joel, Pittsburgh	.333	33	6	1	2	3	1	0	0	0	1	0	0	0	0	2	0	0	0	.500	.333
Jones, Bobby, New York	.050	9	20	0	1	1	0	0	0	0	2	0	0	0	0	7	0	0	0	.050	.050
Jones, Chipper, Atlanta†	.667	8	3	2	2	3	1	0	0	0	0	0	0	1	0	1	0	0	0	1.000	.750
Jones, Chris, Colorado	.273	86	209	29	57	94	11	4	6	31	5	1	0	10	1	48	9	4	6	.450	.305
Jones, Jimmy, Montreal	.111	12	9	0	1	1	0	0	0	0	3	0	0	2	0	3	0	0	1	.111	.273
Jones, Tim, St. Louis*	.262	29	61	13	16	22	6	0	0	1	2	0	1	9	0	8	2	2	0	.361	.366
Jordan, Brian, St. Louis	.309	67	223	33	69	121	10	6	10	44	0	3	4	12	0	35	6	6	6	.543	.351
Jordan, Ricky, Philadelphia	.289	90	159	21	46	67	4	1	5	18	0	2	1	8	1	32	0	0	2	.421	.324
Justice, David, Atlanta*	.270	157	585	90	158	301	15	4	40	120	0	4	3	78	12	90	3	5	9	.515	.357
Karros, Eric, Los Angeles	.247	158	619	74	153	253	27	2	23	80	0	3	2	34	1	82	0	1	17	.409	.287
Kelly, Bobby, Cincinnati	.319	78	320	44	102	152	17	3	9	35	0	3	2	17	0	43	21	5	10	.475	.354
Kent, Jeff, New York	.270	140	496	65	134	221	24	0	21	80	6	4	8	30	2	88	4	4	11	.446	.320
Kessinger, Keith, Cincinnati†	.259	11	27	4	7	11	1	0	1	3	0	1	0	4	0	4	0	0	1	.407	.344
Kile, Darryl, Houston	.094	32	53	5	5	9	1	0	1	8	0	0	0	3	0	20	0	0	0	.170	.143
Kilgus, Paul, St. Louis*	.200	22	5	0	1	1	0	0	0	0	0	0	0	0	0	2	0	0	0	.200	.200
King, Jeff, Pittsburgh	.295	158	611	82	180	248	35	3	9	98	1	8	4	59	4	54	8	6	17	.406	.356
Klesko, Ryan, Atlanta*	.353	22	17	3	6	13	1	0	2	5	0	0	0	3	1	4	0	0	0	.765	.450
Klink, Joe, Florida*	.000	59	2	0	0	0	0	0	0	0	1	0	0	0	0	0	0	0	0	.000	.000
Knudson, Mark, Colorado	.000	4	1	0	0	0	0	0	0	0	0	0	0	0	0	1	0	0	0	.000	.000
Koelling, Brian, Cincinnati	.067	7	15	2	1	1	0	0	0	0	0	0	1	0	0	2	0	0	0	.067	.125
Kruk, John, Philadelphia*	.316	150	535	100	169	254	33	5	14	85	0	5	0	111	10	87	6	2	11	.475	.430
Lake, Steve, Chicago	.225	44	120	11	27	48	6	0	5	13	2	0	0	4	3	19	0	0	8	.400	.250
Laker, Tim, Montreal	.198	43	86	3	17	21	2	1	0	7	3	1	1	2	0	16	2	0	2	.244	.222
Lancaster, Les, St. Louis	.000	50	4	0	0	0	0	0	0	0	1	0	0	1	0	2	0	0	0	.000	.200
Landrum, Bill, Cincinnati	.000	18	0	0	0	0	0	0	0	0	0	0	0	1	0	0	0	0	0	.000	1.000
Landrum, Ced, New York*	.263	22	19	2	5	6	1	0	0	1	1	0	0	0	0	5	0	0	1	.316	.263
Lankford, Ray, St. Louis*	.238	127	407	64	97	141	17	3	7	45	1	3	3	81	7	111	14	14	5	.346	.366
Lansing, Mike, Montreal	.287	141	491	64	141	181	29	1	3	45	10	3	5	46	2	56	23	5	16	.369	.352
Larkin, Barry, Cincinnati	.315	100	384	57	121	171	20	3	8	51	1	3	1	51	6	33	14	1	13	.445	.394
LaValliere, Mike, Pittsburgh*	.200	1	5	0	1	1	0	0	0	0	0	0	0	0	0	0	0	0	0	.200	.200
Layana, Tim, San Francisco	.000	1	0	0	0	0	0	0	0	0	0	0	0	0	0	0	0	0	0	.000	.000
Lemke, Mark, Atlanta†	.252	151	493	52	124	168	19	2	7	49	5	6	0	65	13	50	1	2	21	.341	.335
Leskanic, Curt, Colorado	.154	18	13	0	2	3	1	0	0	1	1	0	0	1	0	6	0	0	3	.231	.214
Lewis, Darren, San Francisco	.253	136	522	84	132	169	17	7	2	48	12	1	1	30	0	40	46	15	4	.324	.302
Lewis, Richie, Florida	.500	57	2	0	1	1	0	0	0	1	1	0	0	0	0	1	0	0	0	.500	.500
Lindeman, Jim, Houston	.348	9	23	2	8	11	3	0	0	0	0	0	0	0	0	7	0	0	1	.478	.348
Lindsey, Doug, Philadelphia	.500	2	2	0	1	1	0	0	0	1	0	0	0	0	0	0	0	0	0	.500	.500
Liriano, Nelson, Colorado†	.305	48	151	28	46	64	6	3	2	15	5	1	0	18	2	22	6	4	6	.424	.376
Longmire, Tony, Philadelphia*	.231	11	13	1	3	3	0	0	0	1	0	0	0	0	0	1	0	0	0	.231	.231
Looney, Brian, Montreal*	.000	3	1	0	0	0	0	0	0	0	0	0	0	0	0	1	0	0	0	.000	.000
Lopez, Javy, Atlanta	.375	8	16	1	6	12	1	1	1	2	0	0	1	0	0	2	0	0	0	.750	.412
Lopez, Luis, San Diego†	.116	17	43	1	5	6	1	0	0	1	0	1	0	0	0	8	0	0	0	.140	.114
Luebbers, Larry, Cincinnati	.250	14	24	1	6	7	1	0	0	0	1	0	1	0	0	8	0	0	0	.292	.280
Lyden, Mitch, Florida	.300	6	10	2	3	6	0	0	1	1	0	0	0	0	0	4	0	0	0	.600	.300
Maclin, Lonnie, St. Louis*	.077	12	13	2	1	1	0	0	0	1	0	0	0	0	0	5	1	0	0	.077	.071
Maddux, Greg, Atlanta	.165	36	91	5	15	16	1	0	0	4	10	0	0	1	0	32	0	0	1	.176	.174
Maddux, Mike, New York*	.000	58	3	0	0	0	0	0	0	0	0	0	0	0	0	3	0	0	0	.000	.000
Magadan, Dave, Florida*	.286	66	227	22	65	89	12	0	4	29	0	3	1	44	4	30	0	1	3	.392	.400
Magrane, Joe, St. Louis	.114	22	35	2	4	5	1	0	0	1	4	0	0	1	0	20	0	0	3	.143	.139
Maldonado, Candy, Chicago	.186	70	140	8	26	40	5	0	3	15	0	0	1	13	0	40	0	3	3	.286	.260
Manto, Jeff, Philadelphia	.056	8	18	0	1	1	0	0	0	1	0	0	0	1	0	3	0	0	0	.056	.105
Manwaring, Kirt, San Francisco	.275	130	432	48	119	151	15	1	5	49	5	2	6	41	13	76	1	3	14	.350	.345
Manzanillo, Josias, New York	.000	6	1	0	0	0	0	0	0	0	0	0	0	0	0	1	0	0	0	.000	.000
Marrero, Oreste, Montreal*	.210	32	81	10	17	27	5	1	1	4	0	0	0	14	0	16	1	3	0	.333	.326
Martin, Al, Pittsburgh*	.281	143	480	85	135	231	26	8	18	64	2	3	1	42	5	122	16	9	5	.481	.338
Martinez, Dave, San Francisco*.	.241	91	241	28	58	87	12	1	5	27	0	0	0	27	3	39	6	3	5	.361	.317
Martinez, Dennis, Montreal	.159	36	69	1	11	13	2	0	0	4	9	2	0	2	0	17	0	0	1	.188	.178
Martinez, Pedro A., San Diego*	.000	32	4	0	0	0	0	0	0	1	2	0	0	0	0	2	0	0	0	.000	.000

— 275 —

Player, Team	Avg.	G	AB	R	H	TB	2B	3B	HR	RBI	SH	SF	HP	BB	Int. BB	SO	SB	CS	GI DP	Slg.	OBP
Martinez, Pedro J., Los Angeles..	.000	66	4	0	0	0	0	0	0	0	2	0	0	0	0	3	0	0	0	.000	.000
Martinez, Ramon, Los Angeles*..	.129	32	70	2	9	10	1	0	0	2	7	1	0	0	0	23	0	0	1	.143	.127
Mason, Roger, S.D.-Phi.	.167	68	6	0	1	1	0	0	0	0	0	0	0	0	0	2	0	0	0	.167	.167
Mauser, Tim, Phi.-S.D.	.000	36	6	1	0	0	0	0	0	0	0	0	0	1	0	3	0	0	0	.000	.143
May, Derrick, Chicago*	.295	128	465	62	137	196	25	2	10	77	0	6	1	31	6	41	10	3	15	.422	.336
McClendon, Lloyd, Pittsburgh..	.221	88	181	21	40	59	11	1	2	19	1	2	0	23	1	17	0	3	4	.326	.306
McDowell, Roger, Los Angeles..	.500	54	2	0	1	1	0	0	0	0	0	0	0	0	0	1	0	0	0	.500	.500
McElroy, Chuck, Chicago*	.000	49	6	0	0	0	0	0	0	0	0	0	0	0	0	3	0	0	0	.000	.000
McGee, Willie, San Francisco†	.301	130	475	53	143	185	28	1	4	46	3	2	1	38	7	67	10	9	12	.389	.353
McGriff, Fred, S.D.-Atl.*	.291	151	557	111	162	306	29	2	37	101	0	5	2	76	6	106	5	3	14	.549	.375
McGriff, Terry, Florida	.000	3	7	0	0	0	0	0	0	0	0	0	0	1	0	2	0	0	0	.000	.125
McIntosh, Tim, Montreal	.095	20	21	2	2	3	1	0	0	2	0	0	0	0	0	7	0	0	0	.143	.095
McKnight, Jeff, New York†	.256	105	164	19	42	53	3	1	2	13	3	2	1	13	0	31	0	0	3	.323	.311
McMichael, Greg, Atlanta	.000	74	4	0	0	0	0	0	0	0	0	0	0	0	0	2	0	0	1	.000	.000
McNamara, Jim, San Francisco*	.143	4	7	0	1	1	0	0	0	1	0	0	0	0	0	1	0	0	0	.143	.143
Mejia, Roberto, Colorado	.231	65	229	31	53	92	14	5	5	20	4	1	1	13	1	63	4	1	2	.402	.275
Menendez, Tony, Pittsburgh	.000	14	1	0	0	0	0	0	0	0	0	0	0	0	0	1	0	0	0	.000	.000
Merced, Orlando, Pittsburgh*	.313	137	447	68	140	198	26	4	8	70	0	2	1	77	10	64	3	3	9	.443	.414
Mercedes, Luis, San Francisco	.160	18	25	1	4	6	0	1	0	3	1	0	2	1	0	3	0	1	0	.240	.250
Mercker, Kent, Atlanta*	.000	43	13	0	0	0	0	0	0	0	0	0	0	0	0	6	0	0	0	.000	.000
Miller, Paul, Pittsburgh	.000	3	2	0	0	0	0	0	0	0	0	0	0	0	0	0	0	0	0	.000	.000
Millette, Joe, Philadelphia	.200	10	10	3	2	2	0	0	0	2	3	0	0	1	0	2	0	0	1	.200	.273
Milligan, Randy, Cincinnati	.274	83	234	30	64	95	11	1	6	29	0	1	1	46	0	49	0	2	3	.406	.394
Minor, Blas, Pittsburgh	.200	65	10	1	2	3	1	0	0	0	0	0	1	0	0	7	0	0	0	.300	.273
Minutelli, Gino, San Francisco* ..	.000	9	4	0	0	0	0	0	0	0	0	0	0	0	0	2	0	0	0	.000	.000
Mitchell, Kevin, Cincinnati	.341	93	323	56	110	194	21	3	19	64	0	4	1	25	4	48	1	0	14	.601	.385
Mondesi, Raul, Los Angeles	.291	42	86	13	25	42	3	1	4	10	1	0	0	4	0	16	4	1	1	.488	.322
Montoyo, Charlie, Montreal	.400	4	5	1	2	3	1	0	0	3	0	0	0	0	0	0	0	0	0	.600	.400
Moore, Marcus, Colorado†	.000	27	1	0	0	0	0	0	0	0	0	0	0	0	0	1	0	0	0	.000	.000
Morandini, Mickey, Philadelphia* .	.247	120	425	57	105	151	19	9	3	33	4	2	5	34	2	73	13	2	7	.355	.309
Morgan, Mike, Chicago	.061	32	66	1	4	6	2	0	0	1	5	0	0	2	0	22	0	0	1	.091	.088
Morris, Hal, Cincinnati*	.317	101	379	48	120	159	18	0	7	49	0	6	2	34	4	51	2	2	5	.420	.371
Mulholland, Terry, Philadelphia..	.065	29	62	3	4	4	0	0	0	0	8	0	0	1	0	27	0	0	0	.065	.079
Murphy, Dale, Colorado	.143	26	42	1	6	7	1	0	0	7	0	2	0	5	1	15	0	0	5	.167	.224
Murphy, Rob, St. Louis*	.500	73	2	0	1	1	0	0	0	0	1	0	0	0	0	1	0	0	0	.500	.500
Murray, Eddie, New York†	.285	154	610	77	174	285	28	1	27	100	0	9	0	40	4	61	2	2	24	.467	.325
Myers, Randy, Chicago*	.500	74	2	0	1	2	1	0	0	2	1	0	0	1	0	0	0	0	1	1.000	.667
Nabholz, Chris, Montreal*	.128	26	39	1	5	5	0	0	0	1	3	0	0	1	0	9	0	0	0	.128	.150
Natal, Rob, Florida	.214	41	117	3	25	34	4	1	1	6	3	1	4	6	0	22	1	0	6	.291	.273
Navarro, Tito, New York*	.059	12	17	1	1	1	0	0	0	1	1	0	0	0	0	4	0	1	0	.059	.059
Neagle, Denny, Pittsburgh*	.000	50	14	0	0	0	0	0	0	0	2	0	0	0	0	4	0	0	1	.000	.000
Nen, Robb, Florida	.000	15	4	0	0	0	0	0	0	0	0	0	0	0	0	0	0	0	0	.000	.000
Nied, David, Colorado	.174	16	23	3	4	4	0	0	0	2	3	0	0	3	0	8	0	0	0	.174	.269
Nieves, Melvin, San Diego†	.191	19	47	4	9	15	0	0	2	3	0	0	1	3	0	21	0	0	0	.319	.255
Nixon, Otis, Atlanta†	.269	134	461	77	124	145	12	3	1	24	5	5	0	61	2	63	47	13	10	.315	.351
O'Brien, Charlie, New York	.255	67	188	15	48	71	11	0	4	23	3	1	2	14	1	14	1	1	4	.378	.312
Offerman, Jose, Los Angeles†	.269	158	590	77	159	195	21	6	1	62	25	8	2	71	7	75	30	13	12	.331	.346
Olivares, Omar, St. Louis	.269	59	26	1	7	8	1	0	0	2	3	0	0	0	0	7	0	0	1	.308	.269
Oliver, Joe, Cincinnati	.239	139	482	40	115	185	28	0	14	75	2	9	1	27	2	91	0	0	13	.384	.276
Olson, Greg, Atlanta	.225	83	262	23	59	81	10	0	4	24	2	1	1	29	0	27	1	0	11	.309	.304
Oquendo, Jose, St. Louis†	.205	46	73	7	15	15	0	0	0	4	3	1	0	12	1	8	0	0	5	.205	.314
Orsulak, Joe, New York*	.284	134	409	59	116	163	15	4	8	35	0	2	2	28	1	25	5	4	6	.399	.331
Osborne, Donovan, St. Louis*	.204	29	49	4	10	11	1	0	0	3	7	0	0	3	0	13	0	0	2	.224	.250
Otto, Dave, Pittsburgh*	.222	28	18	0	4	7	1	1	0	4	1	0	0	0	0	6	0	0	0	.389	.222
Owens, J., Colorado	.209	33	86	12	18	32	5	0	3	6	0	0	2	6	1	30	1	0	1	.372	.277
Pagnozzi, Tom, St. Louis	.258	92	330	31	85	123	15	1	7	41	0	5	1	19	6	30	1	0	7	.373	.296
Painter, Lance, Colorado*	.300	10	10	2	3	5	0	1	0	1	3	0	0	1	0	5	0	0	0	.500	.364
Pappas, Erik, St. Louis	.276	82	228	25	63	78	12	0	1	28	0	3	0	35	2	35	1	3	7	.342	.368
Parker, Rick, Houston	.333	45	45	11	15	18	3	0	0	4	1	0	0	3	0	8	1	2	2	.400	.375
Parrett, Jeff, Colorado	.091	40	11	0	1	1	0	0	0	0	0	0	0	0	0	5	0	0	0	.091	.091
Patterson, John, San Francisco†	.188	16	16	1	3	6	0	0	1	2	0	0	0	0	0	5	0	1	0	.375	.188
Pecota, Bill, Atlanta	.323	72	62	17	20	24	2	1	0	5	1	0	0	2	0	5	1	1	3	.387	.344
Pena, Geronimo, St. Louis†	.256	74	254	34	65	103	19	2	5	30	4	2	4	25	0	71	13	5	3	.406	.330
Pendleton, Terry, Atlanta†	.272	161	633	81	172	258	33	1	17	84	3	7	3	36	5	97	5	1	18	.408	.311
Pennyfeather, William, Pittsburgh	.206	21	34	4	7	8	1	0	0	2	0	0	0	1	0	6	0	1	1	.235	.206
Perez, Mike, St. Louis	.000	65	1	0	0	0	0	0	0	0	0	0	0	1	0	0	0	0	0	.000	.500
Perry, Gerald, St. Louis*	.337	96	98	21	33	50	5	0	4	16	0	0	0	18	2	23	1	1	4	.510	.440
Phillips, J.T., San Francisco*	.313	11	16	1	5	11	1	1	1	4	0	0	0	0	0	5	0	0	0	.688	.313
Piazza, Mike, Los Angeles	.318	149	547	81	174	307	24	2	35	112	0	6	3	46	6	86	3	4	10	.561	.370
Plantier, Phil, San Diego*	.240	138	462	67	111	235	20	1	34	100	1	5	7	61	7	124	4	5	4	.509	.335
Plesac, Dan, Chicago*	.000	57	1	0	0	0	0	0	0	0	0	0	0	0	0	0	0	0	0	.000	.000
Polidor, Gus, Florida	.167	7	6	0	1	2	1	0	0	0	0	0	0	0	0	2	0	0	0	.333	.167
Portugal, Mark, Houston	.231	33	65	4	15	18	0	0	1	8	10	2	0	3	0	13	0	0	2	.277	.257
Pose, Scott, Florida*	.195	15	41	0	8	10	2	0	0	3	0	0	0	2	0	4	0	2	0	.244	.233
Powell, Ross, Cincinnati*	.000	9	1	0	0	0	0	0	0	0	0	0	0	0	0	0	0	0	0	.000	.000
Pratt, Todd, Philadelphia	.287	33	87	8	25	46	6	0	5	13	1	1	1	5	0	19	0	0	2	.529	.330
Pride, Curtis, Montreal*	.444	10	9	3	4	10	1	1	1	5	0	0	0	0	0	3	1	0	0	1.111	.444
Prince, Tom, Pittsburgh	.196	66	179	14	35	55	14	0	2	24	2	3	7	13	2	38	1	1	5	.307	.272
Pugh, Tim, Cincinnati	.222	31	54	2	12	13	1	0	0	1	7	0	1	0	0	20	0	0	0	.241	.236
Rapp, Pat, Florida	.194	16	31	3	6	7	1	0	0	2	2	0	0	1	0	11	0	0	0	.226	.219
Ready, Randy, Montreal*	.254	40	134	22	34	47	8	1	1	10	1	0	1	23	0	8	2	1	4	.351	.367
Reardon, Jeff, Cincinnati	.000	58	2	0	0	0	0	0	0	0	0	0	0	0	0	2	0	0	0	.000	.000
Reed, Jeff, San Francisco*	.261	66	119	10	31	52	3	0	6	12	0	1	0	16	4	22	0	1	2	.437	.346
Reed, Jody, Los Angeles	.276	132	445	48	123	154	21	2	2	31	17	3	1	38	10	40	1	3	16	.346	.333
Reed, Steve, Colorado	.000	64	9	0	0	0	0	0	0	0	2	0	0	0	0	3	0	0	0	.000	.000
Renteria, Rich, Florida	.255	103	263	27	67	86	9	2	2	30	3	1	2	21	1	31	0	2	8	.327	.314
Reynolds, Shane, Houston	.500	5	2	0	1	1	0	0	0	0	0	0	0	0	0	0	0	0	0	.500	.500

Player, Team	Avg.	G	AB	R	H	TB	2B	3B	HR	RBI	SH	SF	HP	BB	Int. BB	SO	SB	CS	GI DP	Slg.	OBP
Reynoso, Armando, Colorado	.127	31	63	4	8	14	0	0	2	4	6	0	0	3	0	20	0	0	0	.222	.167
Rhodes, Karl, Hou.-Chi.*	.278	20	54	12	15	28	2	1	3	7	0	0	0	11	0	9	2	0	0	.519	.400
Righetti, Dave, San Francisco*	1.000	51	1	0	1	1	0	0	0	1	0	0	0	0	0	0	0	0	0	1.000	1.000
Rijo, Jose, Cincinnati	.268	36	82	5	22	29	4	0	1	8	12	0	0	3	0	18	0	0	2	.354	.294
Rivera, Ben, Philadelphia	.098	30	51	3	5	5	0	0	0	0	13	0	0	3	0	24	0	0	0	.098	.148
Roberson, Kevin, Chicago†	.189	62	180	23	34	67	4	1	9	27	0	0	3	12	0	48	0	1	2	.372	.251
Roberts, Bip, Cincinnati†	.240	83	292	46	70	86	13	0	1	18	0	3	3	38	1	46	26	6	2	.295	.330
Rodriguez, Henry, Los Angeles*	.222	76	176	20	39	73	10	0	8	23	0	1	0	11	2	39	1	0	1	.415	.266
Rodriguez, Rich, S.D.-Fla.*	.000	70	2	0	0	0	0	0	0	0	0	0	0	0	0	0	0	0	1	.000	.000
Rogers, Kevin, San Francisco*	.000	64	3	0	0	0	0	0	0	0	0	0	0	0	0	2	0	0	0	.000	.000
Rojas, Mel, Montreal	.083	66	12	0	1	1	0	0	0	0	0	0	0	0	0	7	0	0	0	.083	.083
Ronan, Marc, St. Louis*	.083	6	12	0	1	1	0	0	0	0	0	0	0	0	0	5	0	0	0	.083	.083
Roper, John, Cincinnati	.179	16	28	1	5	5	0	0	0	2	1	0	0	0	0	11	0	0	1	.179	.179
Royer, Stan, St. Louis	.304	24	46	4	14	19	2	0	1	8	0	0	0	2	0	14	0	1	2	.413	.333
Rueter, Kirk, Montreal*	.077	14	26	0	2	2	0	0	0	3	8	0	0	3	0	10	0	0	0	.077	.172
Ruffin, Bruce, Colorado†	.080	59	25	1	2	3	1	0	0	0	3	0	0	3	0	10	0	0	0	.120	.179
Ruffin, Johnny, Cincinnati	.333	21	3	0	1	1	0	0	0	0	0	0	0	0	0	1	0	0	1	.333	.333
Saberhagen, Bret, New York	.111	19	45	2	5	6	1	0	0	0	8	0	0	5	0	10	0	0	1	.133	.200
Sabo, Chris, Cincinnati	.259	148	552	86	143	243	33	2	21	82	2	8	6	43	5	105	6	4	10	.440	.315
Samuel, Juan, Cincinnati	.230	103	261	31	60	90	10	4	4	26	0	2	3	23	3	53	9	7	2	.345	.298
Sanchez, Rey, Chicago	.282	105	344	35	97	112	11	2	0	28	9	2	3	15	7	22	1	1	8	.326	.316
Sandberg, Ryne, Chicago	.309	117	456	67	141	188	20	0	9	45	2	6	2	37	1	62	9	2	12	.412	.359
Sanders, Deion, Atlanta*	.276	95	272	42	75	123	18	6	6	28	1	2	3	16	3	42	19	7	3	.452	.321
Sanders, Reggie, Cincinnati	.274	138	496	90	136	220	16	4	20	83	3	8	5	51	7	118	27	10	10	.444	.343
Sanders, Scott, San Diego	.063	9	16	0	1	1	0	0	0	1	4	0	0	0	0	6	0	0	0	.063	.063
Sanderson, Scott, San Francisco	.000	11	14	1	0	0	0	0	0	0	1	0	0	1	0	11	0	0	0	.000	.067
Sanford, Mo, Colorado	.000	11	8	0	0	0	0	0	0	0	1	0	0	1	0	4	0	0	0	.000	.111
Santiago, Benito, Florida	.230	139	469	49	108	178	19	6	13	50	0	4	5	37	2	88	10	7	9	.380	.291
Saunders, Doug, New York	.209	28	67	8	14	16	2	0	0	0	3	0	0	3	0	4	0	0	2	.239	.243
Scanlan, Bob, Chicago	.500	70	2	0	1	1	0	0	0	2	1	1	0	0	0	1	0	0	0	.500	.333
Scarsone, Steve, San Francisco	.252	44	103	16	26	41	9	0	2	15	4	1	0	4	0	32	0	1	0	.398	.278
Schilling, Curt, Philadelphia	.147	34	75	3	11	12	1	0	0	2	13	0	0	2	0	19	0	0	0	.160	.169
Schourek, Pete, New York*	.219	41	32	2	7	7	0	0	0	4	3	1	0	3	0	11	0	0	2	.219	.278
Scott, Tim, S.D.-Mon.	.000	56	4	0	0	0	0	0	0	0	1	0	0	0	0	4	0	0	0	.000	.000
Seminara, Frank, San Diego	.200	18	10	1	2	2	0	0	0	0	1	0	0	0	0	1	0	0	0	.200	.200
Servais, Scott, Houston	.244	85	258	24	63	107	11	0	11	32	3	3	5	22	2	45	0	0	6	.415	.313
Service, Scott, Col.-Cin.	.143	30	7	0	1	1	0	0	0	1	0	0	0	0	0	3	0	0	0	.143	.143
Sharperson, Mike, Los Angeles	.256	73	90	13	23	33	4	0	2	10	0	1	1	5	0	17	2	0	2	.367	.299
Shaw, Jeff, Montreal	.067	55	15	1	1	1	0	0	0	0	0	0	0	0	0	6	0	0	0	.067	.067
Sheaffer, Danny, Colorado	.278	82	216	26	60	83	9	1	4	32	2	6	1	8	0	15	2	3	9	.384	.299
Sheffield, Gary, S.D.-Fla.	.294	140	494	67	145	235	20	5	20	73	0	7	9	47	6	64	17	5	11	.476	.361
Shelton, Ben, Pittsburgh	.250	15	24	3	6	13	1	0	2	7	0	0	0	3	0	3	0	0	2	.542	.333
Shepherd, Keith, Colorado	.000	14	2	0	0	0	0	0	0	0	0	0	0	0	0	0	0	0	0	.000	.000
Sherman, Darrell, San Diego*	.222	37	63	8	14	15	1	0	0	2	1	1	3	6	0	8	2	1	0	.238	.315
Shields, Tommy, Chicago	.176	20	34	4	6	7	1	0	0	1	0	0	0	2	0	10	0	0	1	.206	.222
Shipley, Craig, San Diego	.235	105	230	25	54	75	9	0	4	22	1	1	3	10	0	31	12	3	3	.326	.275
Siddall, Joe, Montreal*	.100	19	20	0	2	3	1	0	0	1	0	0	0	1	1	5	0	0	0	.150	.143
Slaught, Don, Pittsburgh	.300	116	377	34	113	166	19	2	10	55	4	4	6	29	2	56	2	1	13	.440	.356
Slocumb, Heathcliff, Chicago	.000	10	1	0	0	0	0	0	0	0	0	0	0	0	0	1	0	0	0	.000	.000
Smiley, John, Cincinnati*	.250	18	32	2	8	9	1	0	0	5	5	1	0	1	0	10	0	0	0	.281	.265
Smith, Bryn, Colorado	.000	11	6	0	0	0	0	0	0	0	0	0	0	1	0	1	1	0	0	.000	.143
Smith, Dwight, Chicago*	.300	111	310	51	93	153	17	5	11	35	1	3	3	25	1	51	8	6	3	.494	.355
Smith, Lee, St. Louis	.000	55	2	0	0	0	0	0	0	0	0	0	0	0	0	1	0	0	0	.000	.000
Smith, Lonnie, Pittsburgh	.286	94	199	35	57	88	5	4	6	24	3	2	5	43	2	42	9	4	3	.442	.422
Smith, Ozzie, St. Louis†	.288	141	545	75	157	194	22	6	1	53	7	7	1	43	1	18	21	8	11	.356	.337
Smith, Pete, Atlanta	.222	20	27	2	6	7	1	0	0	5	3	1	0	1	0	11	0	0	0	.259	.241
Smith, Zane, Pittsburgh*	.080	14	25	0	2	2	0	0	0	0	4	0	0	0	0	6	0	0	0	.080	.080
Smoltz, John, Atlanta	.183	35	71	2	13	14	1	0	0	4	11	0	0	9	0	24	1	1	2	.197	.275
Snyder, Cory, Los Angeles	.266	143	516	61	137	205	33	1	11	56	2	1	4	47	3	147	4	1	8	.397	.331
Sosa, Sammy, Chicago	.261	159	598	92	156	290	25	5	33	93	0	1	4	38	6	135	36	11	14	.485	.309
Spehr, Tim, Montreal	.230	53	87	14	20	32	6	0	2	10	3	2	1	6	1	20	2	0	0	.368	.281
Spradlin, Jerry, Cincinnati†	.000	37	2	0	0	0	0	0	0	0	0	0	0	0	0	1	0	0	0	.000	.000
Stairs, Matt, Montreal*	.375	6	8	1	3	4	1	0	0	2	0	0	0	0	0	1	0	0	1	.500	.375
Staton, Dave, San Diego	.262	17	42	7	11	29	3	0	5	9	0	0	1	3	0	12	0	0	2	.690	.326
Stillwell, Kurt, San Diego†	.215	57	121	9	26	33	4	0	1	11	2	0	1	11	2	22	4	3	2	.273	.286
Stocker, Kevin, Philadelphia†	.324	70	259	46	84	108	12	3	2	31	4	1	8	30	11	43	5	0	8	.417	.409
Strawberry, Darryl, Los Angeles*	.140	32	100	12	14	31	2	0	5	12	0	2	2	16	1	19	1	0	1	.310	.267
Swift, Bill, San Francisco	.263	34	80	12	21	22	1	0	0	4	10	1	0	5	0	19	0	0	3	.275	.302
Swindell, Greg, Houston	.183	31	60	3	11	12	1	0	0	4	10	0	0	0	0	16	0	0	0	.200	.183
Tanana, Frank, New York*	.155	29	58	3	9	12	1	1	0	5	3	0	0	2	0	11	0	1	0	.207	.183
Tarasco, Tony, Atlanta*	.229	24	35	6	8	10	2	0	0	2	0	1	1	0	0	5	0	1	1	.286	.243
Tatum, Jim, Colorado	.204	92	98	7	20	28	5	0	1	12	0	2	1	5	0	27	0	0	0	.286	.245
Taubensee, Eddie, Houston*	.250	94	288	26	72	112	11	1	9	42	1	2	0	21	5	44	1	0	8	.389	.299
Taylor, Kerry, San Diego	.000	36	12	0	0	0	0	0	0	0	1	0	0	0	0	8	0	0	0	.000	.000
Telgheder, Dave, New York	.067	24	15	0	1	2	1	0	0	0	4	0	0	1	0	8	0	0	0	.133	.125
Teufel, Tim, San Diego	.250	96	200	26	50	86	11	2	7	31	3	1	0	27	0	39	2	2	9	.430	.338
Tewksbury, Bob, St. Louis	.203	33	69	4	14	15	1	0	0	5	7	0	0	4	0	27	0	0	1	.217	.247
Thigpen, Bobby, Philadelphia	.000	17	1	0	0	0	0	0	0	0	0	0	0	0	0	0	0	0	0	.000	.000
Thompson, Milt, Philadelphia*	.262	129	340	42	89	119	14	2	4	44	3	2	2	40	9	57	9	4	8	.350	.341
Thompson, Robby, San Francisco	.312	128	494	85	154	245	30	2	19	65	9	4	7	45	0	97	10	4	7	.496	.375
Thompson, Ryan, New York	.250	80	288	34	72	128	19	2	11	26	5	1	3	19	4	81	2	7	5	.444	.302
Toliver, Freddie, Pittsburgh	.000	12	2	0	0	0	0	0	0	0	0	0	0	0	0	1	0	0	0	.000	.000
Tomberlin, Andy, Pittsburgh*	.286	27	42	4	12	17	0	1	1	5	0	0	1	2	0	14	0	0	0	.405	.333
Tomlin, Randy, Pittsburgh*	.182	18	33	3	6	6	0	0	0	1	2	0	0	1	0	4	0	0	1	.182	.206
Torres, Salomon, San Francisco	.231	8	13	0	3	3	0	0	0	0	3	0	0	0	0	4	0	0	1	.231	.231
Trachsel, Steve, Chicago	.167	3	6	1	1	1	0	0	0	0	0	0	0	1	0	2	0	0	0	.167	.286
Trlicek, Ricky, Los Angeles	.250	41	4	0	1	1	0	0	0	0	0	0	0	0	0	3	0	0	0	.250	.250

Player, Team	Avg.	G	AB	R	H	TB	2B	3B	HR	RBI	SH	SF	HP	BB	Int. BB	SO	SB	CS	GI DP	Slg.	OBP
Tubbs, Greg, Cincinnati	.186	35	59	10	11	14	0	0	1	2	0	0	1	14	0	10	3	1	0	.237	.351
Tucker, Eddie, Houston	.192	9	26	1	5	6	1	0	0	3	0	0	0	2	0	3	0	0	0	.231	.250
Turner, Matt, Florida	.000	55	0	0	0	0	0	0	0	0	0	0	0	0	0	2	0	0	0	.000	.000
Urbani, Tom, St. Louis*	.188	18	16	2	3	3	0	0	0	0	2	0	0	2	0	6	0	0	1	.188	.278
Uribe, Jose, Houston†	.245	45	53	4	13	14	1	0	0	3	4	0	1	8	4	5	1	0	1	.264	.355
Vander Wal, John, Montreal*	.233	106	215	34	50	80	7	4	5	30	0	1	1	27	2	30	6	3	4	.372	.320
Van Slyke, Andy, Pittsburgh* ...	.310	83	323	42	100	145	13	4	8	50	0	4	2	24	5	40	11	2	13	.449	.357
Varsho, Gary, Cincinnati*	.232	77	95	8	22	34	6	0	2	11	3	1	1	9	0	19	1	0	1	.358	.302
Velasquez, Guillermo, San Diego* .	.210	79	143	7	30	41	2	0	3	20	0	1	0	13	2	35	0	0	3	.287	.274
Villanueva, Hector, St. Louis.......	.145	17	55	7	8	18	1	0	3	9	0	0	0	4	1	17	0	0	3	.327	.203
Vizcaino, Jose, Chicago†	.287	151	551	74	158	197	19	4	4	54	8	9	3	46	2	71	12	9	9	.358	.340
Wagner, Paul, Pittsburgh............	.190	44	42	2	8	8	0	0	0	1	4	0	0	1	0	14	0	0	0	.190	.209
Wakefield, Tim, Pittsburgh	.163	24	43	3	7	12	2	0	1	3	4	0	0	0	0	11	0	0	0	.279	.163
Walbeck, Matt, Chicago†	.200	11	30	2	6	11	2	0	1	6	0	0	0	1	0	6	0	0	0	.367	.226
Walk, Bob, Pittsburgh	.121	32	58	2	7	8	1	0	0	2	7	0	1	0	0	15	0	0	0	.138	.136
Walker, Chico, New York†	.225	115	213	18	48	72	7	1	5	19	0	2	0	14	0	29	7	0	3	.338	.271
Walker, Larry, Montreal*	.265	138	490	85	130	230	24	5	22	86	0	6	6	80	20	76	29	7	8	.469	.371
Wallach, Tim, Los Angeles.........	.222	133	477	42	106	163	19	1	12	62	1	9	3	32	2	70	0	2	10	.342	.271
Walters, Dan, San Diego	.202	27	94	6	19	25	3	0	1	10	0	1	0	7	2	13	0	0	2	.266	.255
Walton, Bruce, Montreal	.000	4	1	0	0	0	0	0	0	0	0	0	0	0	0	0	0	0	0	.000	.000
Watson, Allen, St. Louis*	.231	16	26	0	6	9	3	0	0	2	1	0	0	1	0	2	0	0	1	.346	.259
Wayne, Gary, Colorado*	1.000	65	1	0	1	1	0	0	0	2	0	0	0	0	0	0	0	0	0	1.000	1.000
Weathers, Dave, Florida.............	.100	14	10	0	1	1	0	0	0	0	3	0	0	0	0	7	0	0	0	.100	.100
Webster, Mitch, Los Angeles†	.244	88	172	26	42	58	6	2	2	14	4	3	2	11	2	24	4	6	3	.337	.293
Wedge, Eric, Colorado...............	.182	9	11	2	2	2	0	0	0	1	0	0	0	0	0	4	0	0	0	.182	.182
Wehner, John, Pittsburgh	.143	29	35	3	5	5	0	0	0	0	2	0	0	6	1	10	0	0	0	.143	.268
Weiss, Walt, Florida†	.266	158	500	50	133	154	14	2	1	39	5	4	3	79	13	73	7	3	5	.308	.367
Wendell, Turk, Chicago†	.143	7	7	0	1	1	0	0	0	0	0	0	0	0	0	3	0	0	0	.143	.143
West, David, Philadelphia*	.400	76	5	0	2	3	1	0	0	2	0	0	0	0	0	2	0	0	0	.600	.400
Wetteland, John, Montreal	.000	70	4	0	0	0	0	0	0	0	1	0	0	0	0	3	0	0	0	.000	.000
White, Derrick, Montreal.............	.224	17	49	6	11	20	3	0	2	4	0	0	1	2	1	12	2	0	1	.408	.269
White, Rondell, Montreal	.260	23	73	9	19	30	3	1	2	15	2	1	0	7	0	16	1	2	2	.411	.321
Whitehurst, Wally, San Diego	.083	21	24	1	2	2	0	0	0	0	10	0	0	0	0	11	0	0	1	.083	.083
Whiten, Mark, St. Louis†	.253	152	562	81	142	238	13	4	25	99	0	4	2	58	9	110	15	8	11	.423	.323
Whitmore, Darrell, Florida*	.204	76	250	24	51	75	8	2	4	19	2	0	5	10	0	72	4	2	8	.300	.249
Wickander, Kevin, Cincinnati* ...	.000	33	2	0	0	0	0	0	0	0	0	0	0	0	0	1	0	0	0	.000	.000
Wilkins, Rick, Chicago*	.303	136	446	78	135	250	23	1	30	73	0	1	3	50	13	99	2	1	6	.561	.376
Williams, Brian, Houston	.200	42	10	2	2	3	1	0	0	0	3	0	0	0	0	4	0	0	0	.300	.200
Williams, Mitch, Philadelphia* ...	1.000	65	1	0	1	1	0	0	0	1	0	0	0	0	0	0	0	0	0	1.000	1.000
Williams, Matt, San Francisco	.294	145	579	105	170	325	33	4	38	110	0	9	4	27	4	80	1	3	12	.561	.325
Williams, Mike, Philadelphia	.083	17	12	1	1	1	0	0	0	0	3	0	0	0	0	3	0	0	1	.083	.083
Wilson, Dan, Cincinnati..............	.224	36	76	6	17	20	3	0	0	8	2	1	0	9	4	16	0	0	2	.263	.302
Wilson, Glenn, Pittsburgh	.143	10	14	0	2	2	0	0	0	0	1	0	0	0	0	5	0	0	0	.143	.143
Wilson, Nigel, Florida*	.000	7	16	0	0	0	0	0	0	0	0	0	0	0	0	11	0	0	0	.000	.000
Wilson, Steve, Los Angeles*	.000	25	2	0	0	0	0	0	0	0	0	0	0	0	0	0	0	0	0	.000	.000
Wilson, Trevor, San Francisco*..	.138	22	29	2	4	7	0	0	1	2	8	0	1	1	0	10	1	0	2	.241	.194
Wilson, Willie, Chicago†	.258	105	221	29	57	77	11	3	1	11	1	1	3	11	1	40	7	2	2	.348	.301
Womack, Tony, Pittsburgh*	.083	15	24	5	2	2	0	0	0	0	1	0	0	3	0	3	2	0	0	.083	.185
Wood, Ted, Montreal*	.192	13	26	4	5	6	1	0	0	3	3	0	0	3	1	3	0	0	0	.231	.276
Woodson, Tracy, St. Louis	.208	62	77	4	16	18	2	0	0	2	0	1	0	1	0	14	0	0	1	.234	.215
Worrell, Tim, San Diego	.032	21	31	1	1	2	1	0	0	1	2	0	0	0	0	15	0	0	0	.065	.032
Yelding, Eric, Chicago	.204	69	108	14	22	32	5	1	1	10	4	0	0	11	2	22	3	2	3	.296	.277
Young, Anthony, New York	.143	39	14	0	2	2	0	0	0	0	2	0	0	1	0	3	0	0	1	.143	.200
Young, Eric, Colorado................	.269	144	490	82	132	173	16	8	3	42	4	4	4	63	3	41	42	19	9	.353	.355
Young, Gerald, Colorado†	.053	19	19	5	1	1	0	0	0	1	0	0	0	4	0	1	0	1	2	.053	.217
Young, Kevin, Pittsburgh	.236	141	449	38	106	154	24	3	6	47	5	9	9	36	3	82	2	2	10	.343	.300
Young, Pete, Montreal................	.000	4	1	0	0	0	0	0	0	0	0	0	0	0	0	0	0	0	0	.000	.000
Zambrano, Eddie, Chicago	.294	8	17	1	5	5	0	0	0	2	0	0	1	0	3	0	1	0	0	1	.294	.333
Zeile, Todd, St. Louis.................	.277	157	571	82	158	247	36	1	17	103	0	6	0	70	5	76	5	4	15	.433	.352

AWARDED FIRST BASE ON CATCHER'S INTERFERENCE—Cedeno, Houston 4 (Berryhill, Higgins, Owens, Walters); Anthony, Houston (Piazza); Ausmus, San Diego (Lopez); Barberie, Florida (Hernandez); Biggio, Houston (Pagnozzi); Cianfrocco, San Diego (Berryhill); Kelly, Cincinnati (Daulton); Santiago, Florida (Higgins); Smith, Chicago (Prince); Van Slyke, Pittsburgh (Colbert); Walker, New York (Walters).

PLAYERS WITH TWO OR MORE TEAMS

Player, Team	Avg.	G	AB	R	H	TB	2B	3B	HR	RBI	SH	SF	HP	BB	Int. BB	SO	SB	CS	GI DP	Slg.	OBP
Aldred, Scott, Colorado*	.000	5	0	0	0	0	0	0	0	0	0	0	0	0	0	0	0	0	0	.000	.000
Aldred, Scott, Montreal*	.000	3	0	0	0	0	0	0	0	0	0	0	0	0	0	0	0	0	0	.000	.000
Ashby, Andy, Colorado	.267	20	15	1	4	4	0	0	0	1	0	0	0	0	3	0	0	0	.267	.267
Ashby, Andy, San Diego.............	.048	12	21	2	1	2	1	0	0	0	2	0	0	2	0	6	0	0	0	.095	.130
Bottenfield, Kent, Colorado†	.269	14	26	1	7	7	0	0	0	3	2	0	0	1	0	10	1	0	0	.269	.296
Bottenfield, Kent, Montreal†	.167	23	24	1	4	4	0	0	0	0	1	0	1	0	0	5	0	0	0	.167	.200
Cianfrocco, Archi, Montreal	.235	12	17	3	4	8	1	0	1	1	0	0	0	0	0	5	0	0	1	.471	.235
Cianfrocco, Archi, San Diego	.244	84	279	27	68	115	10	2	11	47	2	5	3	17	1	64	2	0	9	.412	.289
Daugherty, Jack, Cincinnati†	.220	46	59	7	13	21	2	0	2	9	0	1	0	11	0	15	0	0	3	.356	.338
Daugherty, Jack, Houston†	.333	4	3	0	1	1	0	0	0	0	0	0	0	0	0	0	0	0	0	.333	.333
Davis, Mark, Philadelphia*	.333	25	3	1	1	1	0	0	0	0	0	0	0	0	0	0	0	0	0	.333	.333
Davis, Mark, San Diego*	.000	35	1	0	0	0	0	0	0	0	1	0	0	0	0	0	0	0	0	.000	.000
Grant, Mark, Colorado...............	.000	14	0	0	0	0	0	0	0	0	0	0	0	0	0	0	0	0	0	.000	.000
Grant, Mark, Houston.................	.000	6	0	0	0	0	0	0	0	0	0	0	0	0	0	0	0	0	0	.000	.000
Harris, Greg, Colorado...............	.050	13	20	0	1	1	0	0	0	1	1	1	0	1	0	9	0	0	0	.050	.091
Harris, Greg, San Diego.............	.170	22	53	2	9	12	3	0	0	3	4	1	0	4	0	16	0	0	0	.226	.224
Henry, Butch, Colorado†	.091	20	22	1	2	2	0	0	0	2	2	1	0	1	0	3	0	0	0	.091	.125
Henry, Butch, Montreal*	.000	10	2	0	0	0	0	0	0	0	1	0	0	0	0	0	0	0	0	.000	.000

Player, Team	Avg.	G	AB	R	H	TB	2B	3B	HR	RBI	SH	SF	HP	BB	Int. BB	SO	SB	CS	GI DP	Slg.	OBP
Hoffman, Trevor, Florida	.000	28	2	0	0	0	0	0	0	0	0	0	0	0	0	0	0	0	0	.000	.000
Hoffman, Trevor, San Diego	.200	39	5	0	1	1	0	0	0	0	0	0	0	0	0	1	0	0	0	.200	.200
Hurst, Bruce, Colorado*	.000	3	1	0	0	0	0	0	0	0	0	0	0	0	0	1	0	0	0	.000	.000
Hurst, Bruce, San Diego*	.000	2	0	0	0	0	0	0	0	0	1	0	0	0	0	0	0	0	0	.000	.000
Kaiser, Jeff, Cincinnati	.000	3	0	0	0	0	0	0	0	0	0	0	0	0	0	0	0	0	0	.000	.000
Kaiser, Jeff, New York	.000	6	0	0	0	0	0	0	0	0	0	0	0	0	0	0	0	0	0	.000	.000
Mason, Roger, Philadelphia	.333	34	3	0	1	1	0	0	0	0	0	0	0	0	0	1	0	0	0	.333	.333
Mason, Roger, San Diego	.000	34	3	0	0	0	0	0	0	0	0	0	0	0	0	1	0	0	0	.000	.000
Mauser, Tim, Philadelphia	.000	8	4	0	0	0	0	0	0	0	0	0	0	1	0	2	0	0	0	.000	.200
Mauser, Tim, San Diego	.000	28	2	1	0	0	0	0	0	0	0	0	0	0	0	1	0	0	0	.000	.000
McGriff, Fred, Atlanta*	.310	68	255	59	79	156	18	1	19	55	0	1	1	34	2	51	1	0	5	.612	.392
McGriff, Fred, San Diego*	.275	83	302	52	83	150	11	1	18	46	0	4	1	42	4	55	4	3	9	.497	.361
Rhodes, Karl, Chicago*	.288	15	52	12	15	28	2	1	3	7	0	0	0	11	0	9	2	0	0	.538	.413
Rhodes, Karl, Houston*	.000	5	2	0	0	0	0	0	0	0	0	0	0	0	0	0	0	0	0	.000	.000
Rodriguez, Rich, Florida*	.000	36	2	0	0	0	0	0	0	0	0	0	0	0	0	0	0	0	1	.000	.000
Rodriguez, Rich, San Diego*	.000	34	0	0	0	0	0	0	0	0	0	0	0	0	0	0	0	0	0	.000	.000
Scott, Tim, Montreal	.000	32	2	0	0	0	0	0	0	0	0	0	0	0	0	2	0	0	0	.000	.000
Scott, Tim, San Diego	.000	24	2	0	0	0	0	0	0	0	1	0	0	0	0	2	0	0	0	.000	.000
Service, Scott, Cincinnati	.143	27	7	0	1	1	0	0	0	1	0	0	0	0	0	3	0	0	0	.143	.143
Service, Scott, Colorado	.000	3	0	0	0	0	0	0	0	0	0	0	0	0	0	0	0	0	0	.000	.000
Sheffield, Gary, Florida	.292	72	236	33	69	113	8	3	10	37	0	4	6	29	6	34	12	4	2	.479	.378
Sheffield, Gary, San Diego	.295	68	258	34	76	122	12	2	10	36	0	3	3	18	0	30	5	1	9	.473	.344

PINCH-HITTING

TEAM

Team	Avg.	AB	R	H	TB	2B	3B	HR	RBI	SH	SF	HP	BB	Int. BB	SO	SB	CS	GI DP	Slg.	OBP
St. Louis	.278	216	29	60	81	9	0	4	34	1	4	0	35	4	52	1	1	3	.375	.373
New York	.277	271	26	75	97	8	4	2	26	6	1	0	21	1	47	3	1	4	.358	.328
Atlanta	.264	220	24	58	86	13	0	5	34	2	1	1	21	3	48	1	0	7	.391	.329
Philadelphia	.253	198	23	50	65	7	1	2	26	3	5	1	19	1	46	0	0	5	.328	.314
Pittsburgh	.252	242	32	61	95	11	1	7	28	3	5	1	43	7	59	5	0	6	.393	.361
Montreal	.249	229	22	57	82	11	1	4	38	2	2	1	17	3	52	9	1	3	.358	.301
Houston	.246	224	24	55	74	13	0	2	25	3	0	1	22	1	47	0	1	9	.330	.316
Chicago	.243	235	35	57	98	11	3	8	30	3	1	1	21	3	60	4	0	5	.417	.306
Colorado	.234	261	29	61	84	7	2	4	32	0	3	1	20	1	72	7	1	7	.322	.288
Los Angeles	.233	257	23	60	81	9	0	4	29	1	1	1	24	2	60	0	3	7	.315	.300
San Diego	.220	277	28	61	83	10	0	4	41	4	5	2	24	1	75	3	0	9	.300	.282
Cincinnati	.187	198	18	37	54	8	0	3	26	3	4	1	26	3	52	2	2	4	.273	.279
San Francisco	.179	218	19	39	61	8	1	4	21	1	5	1	20	2	53	3	1	4	.280	.246
Florida	.133	210	17	28	32	2	1	0	11	2	2	3	22	0	66	1	1	12	.152	.224
Totals	.233	3256	349	759	1073	127	14	53	401	34	39	15	335	32	789	39	12	85	.330	.304

INDIVIDUAL

TOP 15 PINCH-HITTERS

Minimum 20 at-bats.   *Lefthanded batter.   †Switch-hitter.

Player, Team	Avg.	G	AB	R	H	TB	2B	3B	HR	RBI	SH	SF	HP	BB	Int. BB	SO	SB	CS	GI DP	Slg.	OBP
Sanders, Deion, Atlanta*	.429	34	28	6	12	19	4	0	1	5	0	0	0	3	0	1	0	0	0	.679	.484
Smith, Dwight, Chicago*	.375	28	24	5	9	14	3	1	0	5	0	0	0	4	1	0	0	0	.583	.444
Gallagher, Dave, New York	.370	32	27	4	10	14	2	1	0	4	1	0	0	4	0	4	0	1	1	.519	.452
Jones, Chris, Colorado	.364	25	22	3	8	12	0	2	0	3	0	0	0	3	0	4	2	0	0	.545	.440
Clark, Phil, San Diego	.351	40	37	3	13	18	2	0	1	7	1	1	0	1	1	5	0	0	1	.486	.359
Bream, Sid, Atlanta*	.345	34	29	2	10	14	1	0	1	6	0	0	0	5	1	5	0	0	3	.483	.441
Perry, Gerald, St. Louis*	.343	88	70	13	24	37	4	0	3	14	0	0	0	15	1	16	1	1	2	.529	.459
Orsulak, Joe, New York*	.333	33	30	4	10	11	1	0	0	4	0	0	0	2	0	1	0	0	0	.367	.375
Hansen, Dave, Los Angeles*	.327	69	55	5	18	25	1	0	2	18	0	0	0	11	1	9	0	0	0	.455	.439
McKnight, Jeff, New York†	.322	64	59	7	19	24	0	1	1	7	2	1	0	2	0	12	0	0	0	.407	.339
Thompson, Milt, Philadelphia*	.320	30	25	5	8	12	2	1	0	3	1	1	0	3	0	5	0	0	1	.480	.379
Jordan, Ricky, Philadelphia	.302	61	53	7	16	18	2	0	0	5	0	2	0	5	1	13	0	0	1	.340	.350
Woodson, Tracy, St. Louis	.292	26	24	3	7	8	1	0	0	0	0	0	0	1	0	5	0	0	0	.333	.320
Brewer, Rod, St. Louis*	.286	51	42	6	12	17	2	0	1	6	0	1	0	6	1	7	0	0	0	.405	.367
Carreon, Mark, San Francisco	.286	39	35	3	10	15	2	0	1	8	0	2	0	2	1	4	1	0	0	.429	.308

ALL PINCH-HITTERS

*Lefthanded batter.   †Switch-hitter.

Player, Team	Avg.	G	AB	R	H	TB	2B	3B	HR	RBI	SH	SF	HP	BB	Int. BB	SO	SB	CS	GI DP	Slg.	OBP
Alicea, Luis, St. Louis†	.353	22	17	4	6	7	1	0	0	4	0	1	0	4	0	3	0	0	0	.412	.455
Allanson, Andy, San Francisco	.250	4	4	1	1	1	0	0	0	0	0	0	0	0	0	0	0	0	0	.250	.250
Alou, Moises, Montreal	.333	3	3	0	1	1	0	0	0	0	0	0	0	0	0	0	0	0	0	.333	.333
Amaro, Ruben, Philadelphia†	.000	9	8	1	0	0	0	0	0	0	0	0	1	0	0	1	0	0	0	.000	.000
Anthony, Eric, Houston*	.125	16	16	0	2	2	0	0	0	0	0	0	0	0	0	3	0	0	1	.125	.125
Arias, Alex, Florida	.160	30	25	2	4	4	0	0	0	0	0	0	0	4	0	3	0	0	4	.160	.276
Ashley, Billy, Los Angeles	.333	4	3	0	1	1	0	0	0	0	0	0	0	1	0	0	0	0	0	.333	.500
Aude, Rich, Pittsburgh	.167	6	6	0	1	1	0	0	0	1	0	0	0	0	0	3	0	0	0	.167	.167
Baez, Kevin, New York	.000	1	1	0	0	0	0	0	0	0	0	0	0	0	0	0	0	0	0	.000	.000
Bagwell, Jeff, Houston	.500	3	2	1	1	1	0	0	0	2	0	0	0	1	0	0	0	0	0	.500	.667
Barberie, Bret, Florida†	.000	2	2	0	0	0	0	0	0	0	0	0	0	0	0	2	0	0	0	.000	.000
Barnes, Brian, Montreal*	.000	1	1	0	0	0	0	0	0	0	0	0	0	0	0	1	0	0	0	.000	.000
Bass, Kevin, Houston†	.269	57	52	5	14	18	4	0	0	7	0	0	0	4	0	9	0	0	2	.346	.321
Batiste, Kim, Philadelphia	.000	2	0	0	0	0	0	0	0	0	0	0	1	0	0	0	0	0	0	.000	1.000
Bean, Billy, San Diego*	.222	32	27	3	6	9	0	0	1	9	0	2	0	2	0	4	0	0	1	.333	.258
Bell, Derek, San Diego	.000	8	8	0	0	0	0	0	0	0	0	0	0	0	0	3	0	0	0	.000	.000
Bell, Juan, Philadelphia†	.000	2	1	0	0	0	0	0	0	0	0	0	1	0	0	1	0	0	0	.000	.000
Belliard, Rafael, Atlanta	.500	6	4	0	2	2	0	0	0	0	1	0	1	0	0	1	0	0	0	.500	.600
Benavides, Freddie, Colorado	.200	5	5	0	1	1	0	0	0	0	0	0	0	0	0	0	0	0	0	.200	.200
Benjamin, Mike, San Francisco	.000	1	0	0	0	0	0	0	0	0	0	0	1	0	0	0	0	0	0	.000	.000
Benzinger, Todd, San Francisco†	.195	47	41	5	8	13	3	1	0	4	0	2	0	4	0	7	0	1	1	.317	.255
Berroa, Geronimo, Florida	.000	5	5	0	0	0	0	0	0	0	0	0	0	0	0	0	0	0	2	.000	.000
Berry, Sean, Montreal	.233	33	30	4	7	11	1	0	1	7	0	0	1	2	1	10	3	0	0	.367	.303
Berryhill, Damon, Atlanta†	.167	13	12	0	2	3	1	0	0	2	0	0	0	1	0	2	0	0	0	.250	.231
Bichette, Dante, Colorado	.000	4	4	0	0	0	0	0	0	0	0	0	0	0	0	1	0	0	0	.000	.000
Blauser, Jeff, Atlanta	.000	2	2	1	0	0	0	0	0	0	0	0	0	0	0	0	0	0	1	.000	.000
Bogar, Tim, New York	.000	4	4	0	0	0	0	0	0	0	0	0	0	0	0	2	0	0	0	.000	.000
Bolick, Frank, Montreal†	.212	33	33	1	7	8	1	0	0	3	0	0	0	0	0	7	1	0	1	.242	.212
Bonds, Barry, San Francisco*	.000	3	3	0	0	0	0	0	0	0	0	0	0	0	0	2	0	0	0	.000	.000
Bonilla, Bobby, New York†	.000	2	0	0	0	0	0	0	0	0	0	0	0	2	1	0	0	0	0	.000	1.000
Boston, Daryl, Colorado*	.243	52	37	5	9	12	0	0	1	4	0	0	0	3	1	11	0	0	1	.324	.300
Bournigal, Rafael, Los Angeles	.500	2	2	0	1	1	0	0	0	0	0	0	0	0	0	0	0	0	0	.500	.500

Player, Team	Avg.	G	AB	R	H	TB	2B	3B	HR	RBI	SH	SF	HP	BB	Int. BB	SO	SB	CS	GI DP	Slg.	OBP
Branson, Jeff, Cincinnati*	.353	20	17	0	6	6	0	0	0	1	0	0	0	1	0	4	0	0	1	.353	.389
Bream, Sid, Atlanta*	.345	34	29	2	10	14	1	0	1	8	0	0	0	5	1	5	0	0	3	.483	.441
Brewer, Rod, St. Louis*	.286	51	42	6	12	17	2	0	1	6	0	1	0	6	1	7	0	0	0	.405	.367
Briley, Greg, Florida*	.196	66	56	8	11	12	1	0	0	2	0	0	1	7	0	15	1	0	2	.214	.297
Brooks, Jerome, Los Angeles	.125	8	8	1	1	2	1	0	0	0	0	0	0	0	0	2	0	0	0	.250	.125
Brown, Jarvis, San Diego	.200	5	5	1	1	1	0	0	0	0	0	0	0	0	0	2	0	0	1	.200	.200
Brumfield, Jacob, Cincinnati	.000	6	5	0	0	0	0	0	0	0	0	0	0	1	0	1	0	1	0	.000	.167
Brumley, Mike, Houston†	.286	7	7	0	2	2	0	0	0	2	0	0	0	0	0	2	0	1	0	.286	.286
Buechele, Steve, Chicago	.000	3	3	0	0	0	0	0	0	0	0	0	0	0	0	1	0	0	0	.000	.000
Bullett, Scott, Pittsburgh*	.500	5	4	1	2	2	0	0	0	0	0	0	0	1	0	1	1	0	0	.500	.600
Burnitz, Jeromy, New York*	.300	10	10	1	3	3	0	0	0	0	0	0	0	0	0	2	0	0	0	.300	.300
Butler, Brett, Los Angeles*	.000	1	1	0	0	0	0	0	0	0	0	0	0	0	0	1	0	0	0	.000	.000
Cabrera, Francisco, Atlanta	.176	57	51	3	9	13	1	0	1	6	0	0	0	5	1	16	0	0	2	.255	.250
Caminiti, Ken, Houston†	.000	1	1	0	0	0	0	0	0	0	0	0	0	0	0	0	0	0	0	.000	.000
Candaele, Casey, Houston†	.194	40	36	7	7	8	1	0	0	0	0	0	0	4	0	5	0	0	0	.222	.275
Canseco, Ozzie, St. Louis	.000	1	0	0	0	0	0	0	0	0	0	0	0	1	0	0	0	0	0	.000	1.000
Carr, Chuck, Florida†	.000	1	1	0	0	0	0	0	0	0	0	0	0	0	0	1	0	0	0	.000	.000
Carreon, Mark, San Francisco	.286	39	35	3	10	15	2	0	1	8	0	2	0	2	1	4	1	0	0	.429	.308
Carrillo, Matias, Florida*	.000	9	9	0	0	0	0	0	0	0	0	0	0	0	0	5	0	0	1	.000	.000
Castellano, Pedro, Colorado	.167	6	6	1	1	1	0	0	0	1	0	0	0	0	0	2	0	0	0	.167	.167
Castilla, Vinny, Colorado	.000	2	2	0	0	0	0	0	0	0	0	0	0	0	0	0	0	0	0	.000	.000
Cedeno, Andujar, Houston	1.000	1	1	0	1	1	0	0	0	0	0	0	0	0	0	0	0	0	0	1.000	1.000
Chamberlain, Wes, Philadelphia	.200	22	20	3	4	5	1	0	0	1	0	0	0	2	0	6	0	0	2	.250	.273
Cianfrocco, Archi, Mon.-S.D.	1.000	3	2	1	2	3	1	0	0	0	0	0	0	1	0	0	0	0	0	1.500	1.000
Clark, Dave, Pittsburgh*	.136	29	22	5	3	9	0	0	2	4	0	0	0	7	3	8	1	0	0	.409	.345
Clark, Jerald, Colorado	.250	16	16	2	4	5	1	0	0	1	0	0	0	0	0	4	0	0	0	.313	.250
Clark, Phil, San Diego	.351	40	37	3	13	18	2	0	1	7	1	1	0	1	1	5	0	0	1	.486	.359
Clark, Will, San Francisco*	.000	3	2	0	0	0	0	0	0	0	0	0	0	1	0	0	0	0	0	.000	.333
Clayton, Royce, San Francisco	.000	1	1	0	0	0	0	0	0	0	0	0	0	0	0	1	0	0	0	.000	.000
Colbert, Craig, San Francisco	.000	13	11	1	0	0	0	0	0	0	0	0	0	1	0	4	0	0	0	.000	.083
Colbrunn, Greg, Montreal	.400	13	10	2	4	8	1	0	1	3	0	1	0	2	1	2	0	0	0	.800	.462
Cole, Alex, Colorado*	.214	31	28	1	6	7	1	0	0	1	0	0	0	2	0	8	2	1	1	.250	.267
Coleman, Vince, New York†	.333	3	3	1	1	1	0	0	0	0	0	0	0	0	0	0	0	0	0	.333	.333
Conine, Jeff, Florida	.250	4	4	0	1	1	0	0	0	1	0	0	0	1	0	0	0	0	0	.250	.250
Cordero, Wil, Montreal	.250	4	4	1	1	1	0	0	0	0	0	0	0	0	0	3	0	0	0	.250	.250
Costo, Tim, Cincinnati	.333	3	3	1	1	1	0	0	0	0	0	0	0	0	0	0	0	0	0	.333	.333
Cotto, Henry, Florida	.083	13	12	0	1	1	0	0	0	2	0	1	0	0	0	3	0	0	2	.083	.077
Cromer, Tripp, St. Louis	.000	1	1	0	0	0	0	0	0	0	0	0	0	0	0	1	0	0	0	.000	.000
Cummings, Midre, Pittsburgh*	.000	2	2	0	0	0	0	0	0	0	0	0	0	0	0	0	0	0	0	.000	.000
Daugherty, Jack, Hou.-Cin.†*	.185	34	27	3	5	6	1	0	0	2	0	1	0	6	0	8	0	0	0	.222	.324
Daulton, Darren, Philadelphia*	.500	4	2	0	1	1	0	0	0	2	0	0	0	2	0	1	0	0	0	.500	.750
Davis, Eric, Los Angeles	.000	2	2	0	0	0	0	0	0	0	0	0	0	0	0	2	0	0	0	.000	.000
Decker, Steve, Florida	.000	3	2	0	0	0	0	0	0	0	0	0	0	1	0	0	0	0	0	.000	.333
Destrade, Orestes, Florida†	.000	2	1	0	0	0	0	0	0	0	0	0	0	1	0	1	0	0	0	.000	.500
Donnels, Chris, Houston*	.206	38	34	1	7	10	3	0	0	6	0	0	0	4	0	9	0	0	3	.294	.289
Dorsett, Brian, Cincinnati	.250	8	8	1	2	2	0	0	0	2	0	0	0	0	0	2	0	0	0	.250	.250
Duncan, Mariano, Philadelphia	.400	10	10	2	4	7	0	0	1	5	0	0	0	0	0	3	0	0	0	.700	.400
Dunston, Shawon, Chicago	.400	5	5	1	2	3	1	0	0	1	0	0	0	0	0	1	0	0	0	.600	.400
Dykstra, Lenny, Philadelphia*	.000	1	1	0	0	0	0	0	0	0	0	0	0	0	0	0	0	0	0	.000	.000
Eisenreich, Jim, Philadelphia*	.143	25	21	2	3	3	0	0	0	1	0	0	0	1	0	3	0	0	0	.143	.182
Espy, Cecil, Cincinnati†	.182	25	22	0	4	4	0	0	0	2	1	0	0	2	0	3	0	1	2	.182	.240
Everett, Carl, Florida†	.000	3	3	0	0	0	0	0	0	0	0	0	0	0	0	3	0	0	0	.000	.000
Faneyte, Rikkert, San Francisco	.000	1	1	0	0	0	0	0	0	0	0	0	0	0	0	1	0	0	0	.000	.000
Faries, Paul, San Francisco	.000	1	1	0	0	0	0	0	0	0	0	0	0	0	0	0	0	0	0	.000	.000
Fariss, Monty, Florida	.100	11	10	1	1	1	0	0	0	0	0	0	0	1	0	6	0	0	1	.100	.182
Felix, Junior, Florida†	.200	5	5	1	1	1	0	0	0	0	0	0	0	0	0	2	0	0	0	.200	.200
Finley, Steve, Houston*	.667	3	3	1	2	3	1	0	0	0	0	0	0	0	0	0	0	0	0	1.000	.667
Fletcher, Darrin, Montreal*	.438	20	16	1	7	11	1	0	1	6	1	0	0	3	0	2	0	0	0	.688	.526
Floyd, Cliff, Montreal*	.000	2	2	0	0	0	0	0	0	0	0	0	0	0	0	2	0	0	0	.000	.000
Foley, Tom, Pittsburgh*	.281	36	32	3	9	15	1	1	1	5	0	2	0	1	0	6	0	0	0	.469	.286
Frazier, Lou, Montreal†	.250	50	48	6	12	13	1	0	0	4	0	0	0	2	0	10	2	0	1	.271	.280
Gainer, Jay, Colorado*	.188	16	16	2	3	9	0	0	2	5	0	0	0	0	0	9	0	0	0	.563	.188
Galarraga, Andres, Colorado	.000	1	1	0	0	0	0	0	0	0	0	0	0	0	0	0	0	0	0	.000	.000
Gallagher, Dave, New York	.370	32	27	4	10	14	2	1	0	4	1	0	0	4	0	4	0	1	1	.519	.452
Gant, Ron, Atlanta	.000	2	1	1	0	0	0	0	0	0	0	0	0	1	0	0	0	0	0	.000	.500
Garcia, Carlos, Pittsburgh	.500	4	2	0	1	1	0	0	0	1	0	0	0	1	0	0	0	0	0	.500	.500
Gardner, Jeff, San Diego*	.118	22	17	1	2	2	0	0	0	1	0	1	0	2	0	4	0	0	0	.118	.200
Geren, Bob, San Diego	.250	9	8	0	2	3	1	0	0	0	0	0	0	1	0	3	0	0	0	.375	.250
Gilkey, Bernard, St. Louis	1.000	1	1	0	1	1	0	0	0	0	0	0	0	0	0	0	0	0	0	1.000	1.000
Girardi, Joe, Colorado	.000	3	1	2	0	0	0	0	0	0	0	0	0	2	0	0	0	0	0	.000	.667
Goff, Jerry, Pittsburgh*	.500	2	2	0	1	1	0	0	0	1	0	0	0	0	0	0	0	0	0	.500	.500
Gomez, Pat, San Diego*	.000	1	1	0	0	0	0	0	0	0	0	0	0	0	0	1	0	0	0	.000	.000
Gonzalez, Luis, Houston*	.500	9	6	0	3	3	0	0	0	1	1	0	0	2	1	0	0	0	0	.500	.625
Gooden, Dwight, New York	1.000	1	1	0	1	3	0	1	0	0	0	0	0	0	0	0	0	0	0	3.000	1.000
Goodwin, Tom, Los Angeles*	.200	6	5	0	1	1	0	0	0	0	0	0	0	1	0	2	0	1	0	.200	.333
Gordon, Keith, Cincinnati	.000	1	1	0	0	0	0	0	0	0	0	0	0	0	0	1	0	0	0	.000	.000
Grace, Mark, Chicago*	.000	1	1	0	0	0	0	0	0	0	0	0	0	0	0	0	0	0	0	.000	.000
Greene, Willie, Cincinnati*	.000	1	1	0	0	0	0	0	0	0	0	0	0	0	0	1	0	0	0	.000	.000
Gregg, Tommy, Cincinnati*	.000	7	5	0	0	0	0	0	0	0	0	0	0	1	0	0	0	0	0	.000	.167
Grissom, Marquis, Montreal	.000	1	1	0	0	0	0	0	0	1	0	0	0	0	0	0	0	0	0	.000	.000
Gutierrez, Ricky, San Diego	.250	11	8	1	2	2	0	0	0	4	0	0	0	2	0	3	0	0	0	.250	.400
Gwynn, Tony, San Diego*	.000	2	2	0	0	0	0	0	0	0	0	0	0	0	0	0	0	0	1	.000	.000
Hammond, Chris, Florida*	.000	1	1	0	0	0	0	0	0	0	0	0	0	0	0	0	0	0	0	.000	.000
Hansen, Dave, Los Angeles*	.327	69	55	5	18	25	1	0	2	18	0	0	0	11	1	9	0	0	0	.455	.439
Harris, Lenny, Los Angeles*	.178	56	45	2	8	10	2	0	0	1	1	0	0	3	0	9	0	1	2	.222	.229
Hayes, Charlie, Colorado	.167	6	6	1	1	1	0	0	0	1	0	0	0	0	0	1	0	0	1	.167	.167
Hernandez, Carlos, Los Angeles	.182	11	11	1	2	2	0	0	0	0	0	0	0	0	0	3	0	0	0	.182	.182

Player, Team	Avg.	G	AB	R	H	TB	2B	3B	HR	RBI	SH	SF	HP	BB	Int. BB	SO	SB	CS	GI DP	Slg.	OBP
Hernandez, Cesar, Cincinnati	.000	2	2	0	0	0	0	0	0	0	0	0	0	0	0	1	0	0	0	.000	.000
Higgins, Kevin, San Diego*	.154	16	13	1	2	2	0	0	0	0	1	0	0	2	0	2	0	0	0	.154	.267
Hill, Glenallen, Chicago	.444	13	9	4	4	10	0	0	2	4	0	0	0	4	0	2	1	0	0	1.111	.615
Hill, Ken, Montreal	.000	1	1	0	0	0	0	0	0	0	0	0	0	0	0	0	0	0	0	.000	.000
Hosey, Steve, San Francisco	.000	2	1	0	0	0	0	0	0	0	0	0	0	1	0	1	0	0	0	.000	.500
Housie, Wayne, New York†	.214	15	14	2	3	4	1	0	0	1	0	0	0	1	0	1	0	0	0	.286	.267
Howard, Thomas, Cincinnati†	.250	4	4	2	1	2	1	0	0	0	0	0	0	0	0	1	1	0	0	.500	.250
Hughes, Keith, Cincinnati*	.000	2	2	0	0	0	0	0	0	0	0	0	0	0	0	0	0	0	0	.000	.000
Hundley, Todd, New York†	.200	19	15	1	3	4	1	0	0	2	0	0	0	3	0	2	0	0	1	.267	.333
Hunter, Brian, Atlanta	.091	12	11	0	1	1	0	0	0	2	0	1	0	0	0	4	0	0	0	.091	.083
Incaviglia, Pete, Philadelphia	.250	27	24	0	6	7	1	0	0	5	0	1	0	2	0	9	0	0	0	.292	.296
Jackson, Darrin, New York	.250	8	8	2	2	2	0	0	0	0	0	0	0	0	0	3	0	0	0	.250	.250
James, Chris, Houston	.259	33	27	3	7	15	2	0	2	6	0	0	1	3	0	8	0	0	1	.556	.355
Jefferies, Gregg, St. Louis†	1.000	3	1	0	1	1	0	0	0	2	0	1	0	1	0	0	0	0	0	1.000	.667
Jennings, Doug, Chicago*	.167	34	30	5	5	15	2	1	2	7	0	0	1	1	0	7	0	0	0	.500	.219
Johnson, Erik, San Francisco	.000	1	1	0	0	0	0	0	0	0	0	0	0	0	0	1	0	0	0	.000	.000
Johnson, Howard, New York†	.000	4	3	0	0	0	0	0	0	0	0	0	0	1	0	2	0	0	0	.000	.250
Jones, Chipper, Atlanta†	.500	3	2	1	1	1	0	0	0	0	0	0	0	1	0	1	0	0	0	.500	.667
Jones, Chris, Colorado	.364	25	22	3	8	12	0	2	0	3	0	0	0	3	0	4	2	0	0	.545	.440
Jones, Tim, St. Louis*	.000	1	0	0	0	0	0	0	0	0	0	0	0	1	0	0	0	0	0	.000	1.000
Jordan, Brian, St. Louis	.000	3	2	0	0	0	0	0	0	0	0	0	0	0	0	0	0	0	0	.000	.000
Jordan, Ricky, Philadelphia	.302	61	53	7	16	18	2	0	0	5	0	2	0	5	1	13	0	0	1	.340	.350
Karros, Eric, Los Angeles	.000	1	1	0	0	0	0	0	0	0	0	0	0	0	0	0	0	0	0	.000	.000
Kent, Jeff, New York	.000	1	1	0	0	0	0	0	0	0	0	0	0	0	0	1	0	0	0	.000	.000
King, Jeff, Pittsburgh	.000	1	1	0	0	0	0	0	0	0	0	0	0	0	0	0	0	0	0	.000	.000
Klesko, Ryan, Atlanta*	.400	19	15	3	6	13	1	0	2	5	0	0	0	3	1	4	0	0	0	.867	.500
Koelling, Brian, Cincinnati	.000	1	1	0	0	0	0	0	0	0	0	0	0	0	0	0	0	0	0	.000	.000
Kruk, John, Philadelphia*	.143	9	7	0	1	1	0	0	0	1	0	1	0	1	0	2	0	0	1	.143	.222
Lake, Steve, Chicago	.333	3	3	1	1	1	0	0	0	1	0	0	0	0	0	1	0	0	0	.333	.333
Laker, Tim, Montreal	.333	3	3	0	1	1	0	0	0	0	0	0	0	0	0	0	0	0	0	.333	.333
Landrum, Ced, New York*	.278	19	18	1	5	6	1	0	0	1	1	0	0	0	0	4	0	0	0	.333	.278
Lankford, Ray, St. Louis*	.125	8	8	1	1	2	1	0	0	0	0	0	0	0	0	2	0	0	0	.250	.125
Lansing, Mike, Montreal	.250	5	4	0	1	1	0	0	0	0	0	0	0	1	0	1	0	0	0	.250	.400
Lemke, Mark, Atlanta†	.000	1	1	0	0	0	0	0	0	0	0	0	0	0	0	0	0	0	0	.000	.000
Lewis, Darren, San Francisco	.222	10	9	1	2	2	0	0	0	0	0	0	0	1	0	1	1	0	0	.222	.300
Lindeman, Jim, Houston	.000	4	4	0	0	0	0	0	0	0	0	0	0	0	0	1	0	0	0	.000	.000
Liriano, Nelson, Colorado†	.667	4	3	0	2	2	0	0	0	0	0	0	0	1	0	0	0	0	0	.667	.750
Longmire, Tony, Philadelphia*	.375	8	8	0	3	3	0	0	0	1	0	0	0	0	0	0	0	0	0	.375	.375
Lopez, Javy, Atlanta	.000	2	2	0	0	0	0	0	0	0	0	0	0	0	0	0	0	0	0	.000	.000
Lopez, Luis, San Diego†	1.000	1	1	1	1	2	1	0	0	0	0	0	0	0	0	0	0	0	0	1.000	1.000
Lyden, Mitch, Florida	.250	4	4	1	1	1	0	0	0	0	0	0	0	0	0	3	0	0	0	.250	.250
Maclin, Lonnie, St. Louis*	.000	5	5	0	0	0	0	0	0	0	0	0	0	0	0	0	0	0	0	.000	.000
Magadan, Dave, Florida*	.000	2	2	0	0	0	0	0	0	0	0	0	0	0	0	1	0	0	0	.000	.000
Maldonado, Candy, Chicago	.167	33	30	1	5	10	2	0	1	2	0	0	0	3	0	9	0	0	0	.333	.242
Manto, Jeff, Philadelphia	.000	1	1	0	0	0	0	0	0	0	0	0	0	0	0	0	0	0	0	.000	.000
Martin, Al, Pittsburgh*	.357	14	14	4	5	8	0	0	1	1	0	0	0	0	0	6	2	0	0	.571	.357
Martinez, Dennis, Montreal	.000	1	0	0	0	0	0	0	0	1	0	1	0	0	0	0	0	0	0	.000	.000
Martinez, Dave, San Francisco*	.150	25	20	2	3	4	1	0	0	0	0	0	0	5	1	4	1	0	1	.200	.320
May, Derrick, Chicago*	.100	12	10	1	1	1	0	0	0	0	0	0	0	2	2	2	0	0	1	.100	.250
McClendon, Lloyd, Pittsburgh	.188	40	32	5	6	9	3	0	0	4	0	1	0	7	1	2	0	0	2	.281	.325
McGee, Willie, San Francisco†	.143	8	7	0	1	2	1	0	0	0	0	0	0	1	0	2	0	0	0	.286	.250
McGriff, Fred, Atlanta*	.500	2	2	0	1	2	1	0	0	0	0	0	0	0	0	0	0	0	0	1.000	.500
McGriff, Terry, Florida	.000	1	1	0	0	0	0	0	0	0	0	0	0	0	0	0	0	0	0	.000	.000
McIntosh, Tim, Montreal	.091	11	11	0	1	2	1	0	0	2	0	0	0	0	0	3	0	0	0	.182	.091
McKnight, Jeff, New York†	.322	64	59	7	19	24	0	1	1	7	2	1	0	2	0	12	0	0	0	.407	.339
McNamara, Jim, San Francisco*	.000	1	1	0	0	0	0	0	0	0	0	0	0	0	0	1	0	0	0	.000	.000
Merced, Orlando, Pittsburgh*	.600	19	15	2	9	14	2	0	1	5	0	0	0	4	1	3	0	0	0	.933	.684
Mercedes, Luis, San Francisco	.000	13	12	0	0	0	0	0	0	0	0	0	1	0	0	4	0	0	0	.000	.077
Milligan, Randy, Cincinnati	.357	15	14	0	5	7	2	0	0	4	0	0	0	1	0	6	0	0	0	.500	.400
Mitchell, Kevin, Cincinnati	.000	6	3	1	0	0	0	0	0	0	0	0	0	3	1	2	0	0	0	.000	.500
Mondesi, Raul, Los Angeles	.429	7	7	1	3	4	1	0	0	0	0	0	0	0	0	2	0	0	0	.571	.429
Montoyo, Charlie, Montreal	.333	3	3	0	1	1	0	0	0	1	0	0	0	0	0	0	0	0	0	.333	.333
Morandini, Mickey, Philadelphia*	.273	14	11	3	3	6	0	0	1	2	0	0	0	3	0	1	0	0	0	.545	.429
Morris, Hal, Cincinnati*	.000	6	4	0	0	0	0	0	0	0	0	0	0	2	2	0	0	0	0	.000	.333
Murphy, Dale, Colorado	.000	14	11	0	0	0	0	0	0	1	0	1	0	2	0	7	0	0	3	.000	.143
Myers, Randy, Chicago*	.000	1	1	0	0	0	0	0	0	0	0	0	0	0	0	0	0	0	1	.000	.000
Natal, Rob, Florida	.000	3	2	0	0	0	0	0	0	0	0	0	0	1	0	0	0	0	0	.000	.333
Navarro, Tito, New York†	.125	9	8	0	1	1	0	0	0	1	1	0	0	0	0	2	0	0	1	.125	.125
Nieves, Melvin, San Diego†	.000	7	6	0	0	0	0	0	0	0	0	0	0	1	0	4	0	0	0	.000	.143
Nixon, Otis, Atlanta†	.154	13	13	0	2	3	1	0	0	0	2	0	0	0	0	6	0	0	0	.231	.154
O'Brien, Charlie, New York	.333	3	3	0	1	1	0	0	0	0	0	0	0	0	0	0	0	0	0	.333	.333
Offerman, Jose, Los Angeles†	.000	1	1	0	0	0	0	0	0	0	0	0	0	0	0	0	0	0	0	.000	.000
Olivares, Omar, St. Louis	.000	1	1	0	0	0	0	0	0	0	0	0	0	0	0	0	0	0	0	.000	.000
Oliver, Joe, Cincinnati	.333	3	3	0	1	2	1	0	0	1	0	0	0	0	0	0	0	0	1	.667	.333
Olson, Greg, Atlanta	.000	3	3	0	0	0	0	0	0	0	0	0	0	0	0	1	0	0	1	.000	.000
Oquendo, Jose, St. Louis†	.167	8	6	0	1	1	0	0	0	0	0	0	1	0	0	3	0	0	0	.167	.286
Orsulak, Joe, New York*	.333	33	30	4	10	11	1	0	0	4	0	0	0	2	0	0	1	0	0	.367	.375
Owens, J., Colorado	.000	2	2	0	0	0	0	0	0	0	0	0	0	0	0	1	0	0	0	.000	.000
Pagnozzi, Tom, St. Louis	.000	1	1	0	0	0	0	0	0	0	0	0	0	0	0	0	0	0	0	.000	.000
Pappas, Erik, St. Louis	.000	6	3	0	0	0	0	0	0	1	0	0	0	2	0	2	0	0	0	.000	.400
Parker, Rick, Houston	.294	21	17	6	5	6	1	0	0	1	0	0	0	3	0	4	0	0	1	.353	.400
Patterson, John, San Francisco†	.188	16	16	1	3	6	0	0	1	2	0	0	0	0	0	5	0	0	0	.375	.188
Pecota, Bill, Atlanta	.267	33	30	4	8	9	1	0	0	3	1	0	0	2	0	2	1	0	0	.300	.313
Pena, Geronimo, St. Louis†	.000	8	6	0	0	0	0	0	0	0	0	0	0	0	0	5	0	0	0	.000	.000
Pendleton, Terry, Atlanta†	.000	1	1	0	0	0	0	0	0	0	0	0	0	0	0	0	0	0	0	.000	.000
Pennyfeather, William, Pittsburgh	.000	5	5	0	0	0	0	0	0	0	0	0	0	0	0	1	0	0	0	.000	.000
Perry, Gerald, St. Louis*	.343	88	70	13	24	37	4	0	3	14	0	0	0	15	1	16	1	1	2	.529	.459

Player, Team	Avg.	G	AB	R	H	TB	2B	3B	HR	RBI	SH	SF	HP	BB	Int. BB	SO	SB	CS	GI DP	Slg.	OBP
Phillips, J.T., San Francisco*	.167	6	6	0	1	1	0	0	0	1	0	0	0	0	0	3	0	0	0	.167	.167
Piazza, Mike, Los Angeles	.000	5	5	0	0	0	0	0	0	0	0	0	0	0	0	2	0	0	2	.000	.000
Plantier, Phil, San Diego*	.000	6	5	0	0	0	0	0	0	0	0	0	0	1	0	2	0	0	0	.000	.167
Polidor, Gus, Florida	.200	5	5	0	1	2	1	0	0	0	0	0	0	0	0	1	0	0	0	.400	.200
Pose, Scott, Florida*	.000	5	5	0	0	0	0	0	0	0	0	0	0	0	0	1	0	0	0	.000	.000
Pratt, Todd, Philadelphia	.167	7	6	0	1	2	1	0	0	0	0	0	0	0	0	1	0	0	0	.333	.167
Pride, Curtis, Montreal*	.500	8	8	3	4	10	1	1	1	5	0	0	0	0	0	3	1	0	0	1.250	.500
Prince, Tom, Pittsburgh	.375	9	8	1	3	6	3	0	0	0	0	0	0	1	0	0	0	0	1	.750	.444
Ready, Randy, Montreal	.000	1	1	0	0	0	0	0	0	0	0	0	0	0	0	0	0	0	0	.000	.000
Reed, Jeff, San Francisco*	.182	37	33	3	6	12	0	0	2	3	0	0	0	3	0	10	0	0	2	.364	.250
Reed, Jody, Los Angeles	1.000	1	1	0	1	1	0	0	0	0	0	0	0	0	0	0	0	0	0	1.000	1.000
Renteria, Rich, Florida	.161	37	31	2	5	7	0	1	0	4	2	0	1	3	0	5	0	1	3	.226	.257
Rhodes, Karl, Hou.-Cin.*	.000	3	3	0	0	0	0	0	0	0	0	0	0	0	0	1	0	0	0	.000	.000
Roberson, Kevin, Chicago*	.077	15	13	1	1	4	0	0	1	2	0	0	0	2	0	6	0	0	0	.308	.200
Roberts, Bip, Cincinnati†	.000	5	3	1	0	0	0	0	0	0	0	0	0	2	0	2	0	0	0	.000	.400
Rodriguez, Henry, Los Angeles*	.267	18	15	3	4	8	1	0	1	3	0	0	0	1	0	6	0	0	1	.533	.313
Royer, Stan, St. Louis	.333	12	12	0	4	4	0	0	0	2	0	0	0	0	0	4	0	0	0	.333	.333
Samuel, Juan, Cincinnati	.167	20	18	1	3	6	0	0	1	3	0	0	0	2	0	6	0	0	0	.333	.250
Sanchez, Rey, Chicago	.400	10	10	2	4	4	0	0	0	1	0	0	0	0	0	3	0	0	1	.400	.400
Sandberg, Ryne, Chicago	.333	3	3	0	1	1	0	0	0	0	0	0	0	0	0	1	0	0	0	.333	.333
Sanders, Deion, Atlanta*	.429	34	28	6	12	19	4	0	1	5	0	0	0	3	0	1	0	0	0	.679	.484
Sanders, Reggie, Cincinnati	.000	1	1	0	0	0	0	0	0	0	0	0	0	0	0	0	0	0	0	.000	.000
Santiago, Benito, Florida	.200	7	5	0	1	1	0	0	0	1	0	1	0	1	0	2	0	0	0	.200	.286
Saunders, Doug, New York	.000	1	0	0	0	0	0	0	0	0	1	0	0	0	0	0	0	0	0	.000	.000
Scarsone, Steve, San Francisco	.300	12	10	1	3	3	0	0	0	1	0	1	0	1	0	4	0	0	0	.300	.333
Servais, Scott, Houston	.000	5	5	0	0	0	0	0	0	0	0	0	0	0	0	3	0	0	0	.000	.000
Service, Scott, Cincinnati	.000	1	1	0	0	0	0	0	0	0	0	0	0	0	0	0	0	0	0	.000	.000
Sharperson, Mike, Los Angeles	.255	53	47	5	12	17	2	0	1	4	0	1	1	3	0	11	0	0	1	.362	.308
Sheaffer, Danny, Colorado	.286	9	7	0	2	2	0	0	0	3	0	1	0	0	0	0	0	0	1	.286	.250
Sheffield, Gary, S.D.-Fla.	.250	6	4	1	1	1	0	0	0	0	0	0	0	2	0	1	0	0	0	.250	.500
Shelton, Ben, Pittsburgh	.143	8	7	1	1	4	0	0	1	1	0	0	0	1	0	2	0	0	1	.571	.250
Sherman, Darrell, San Diego*	.417	14	12	3	5	6	1	0	0	0	0	0	2	0	0	1	0	0	0	.500	.500
Shields, Tommy, Chicago	.143	7	7	1	1	1	0	0	0	0	0	0	0	0	0	3	0	0	0	.143	.143
Shipley, Craig, San Diego	.214	31	28	2	6	7	1	0	0	5	0	0	0	3	0	3	2	0	0	.250	.290
Siddall, Joe, Montreal*	.000	3	3	0	0	0	0	0	0	0	0	0	0	0	0	1	0	0	0	.000	.000
Slaught, Don, Pittsburgh	.462	15	13	1	6	9	0	0	1	3	0	0	0	2	0	0	0	0	1	.692	.533
Smith, Dwight, Chicago*	.375	28	24	5	9	14	3	1	0	5	0	0	0	3	0	4	1	0	0	.583	.444
Smith, Lonnie, Pittsburgh	.258	44	31	7	8	10	2	0	0	0	0	1	0	12	1	10	1	0	1	.323	.465
Smith, Ozzie, St. Louis†	.000	7	5	1	0	0	0	0	0	1	0	1	0	1	0	0	0	0	0	.000	.143
Snyder, Cory, Los Angeles	.200	7	5	0	1	2	1	0	0	0	0	0	0	1	0	1	0	0	0	.400	.333
Sosa, Sammy, Chicago	.500	3	2	0	1	1	0	0	0	0	0	0	0	1	1	0	0	0	0	.500	.667
Spehr, Tim, Montreal	.000	4	3	0	0	0	0	0	0	0	1	0	0	0	0	0	0	0	0	.000	.000
Stairs, Matt, Montreal*	.400	5	5	1	2	3	1	0	0	1	0	0	0	0	0	1	0	0	0	.600	.400
Staton, Dave, San Diego	.500	6	6	1	3	7	1	0	1	1	0	0	0	0	0	2	0	0	0	1.167	.500
Stillwell, Kurt, San Diego†	.231	27	26	3	6	6	0	0	0	2	0	0	0	1	0	9	1	0	1	.231	.259
Strawberry, Darryl, Los Angeles*	.333	3	3	1	1	1	0	0	0	0	0	0	0	0	0	0	0	0	0	.333	.333
Tarasco, Tony, Atlanta*	.308	13	13	3	4	6	2	0	0	1	0	0	0	0	0	3	0	0	0	.462	.308
Tatum, Jim, Colorado	.254	74	67	5	17	25	5	0	1	11	0	1	1	3	0	19	0	0	1	.373	.292
Taubensee, Eddie, Houston*	.286	8	7	0	2	3	1	0	0	0	0	0	0	1	0	2	0	0	1	.429	.375
Teufel, Tim, San Diego	.094	36	32	5	3	7	1	0	1	5	0	0	0	3	0	15	0	0	2	.219	.171
Thompson, Milt, Philadelphia*	.320	30	25	5	8	12	2	1	0	3	1	1	0	3	0	5	0	0	1	.480	.379
Thompson, Ryan, New York	1.000	3	1	0	1	1	0	0	0	0	0	0	0	0	0	0	0	0	0	1.000	1.000
Thompson, Robby, San Francisco	.500	2	2	1	1	2	1	0	0	2	0	0	0	0	0	0	0	0	0	1.000	.500
Tomberlin, Andy, Pittsburgh*	.222	20	18	1	4	4	0	0	0	0	0	0	1	1	0	7	0	0	0	.222	.300
Tubbs, Greg, Cincinnati	.000	10	9	1	0	0	0	0	0	0	0	0	0	1	0	3	0	0	0	.000	.100
Tucker, Eddie, Houston	.000	1	1	0	0	0	0	0	0	0	0	0	0	0	0	0	0	0	0	.000	.000
Uribe, Jose, Houston†	1.000	3	1	0	1	1	0	0	0	0	2	0	0	0	0	0	0	0	0	1.000	1.000
Vander Wal, John, Montreal*	.233	37	30	2	7	9	2	0	0	3	0	0	0	5	1	4	2	1	1	.300	.343
Van Slyke, Andy, Pittsburgh*	.000	6	6	0	0	0	0	0	0	0	0	0	0	0	0	1	0	0	0	.000	.000
Varsho, Gary, Cincinnati*	.205	58	44	6	9	17	2	0	2	8	3	1	1	5	0	11	1	0	0	.386	.294
Velasquez, Guillermo, San Diego*	.250	39	32	2	8	11	0	0	1	11	0	1	0	5	0	11	0	0	1	.344	.342
Vizcaino, Jose, Chicago†	.250	11	8	1	2	2	0	0	0	0	1	0	0	2	0	2	0	0	0	.250	.400
Walbeck, Matt, Chicago	.333	3	3	0	1	1	0	0	0	0	0	0	0	0	0	0	0	0	0	.333	.333
Walker, Chico, New York†	.231	72	65	3	15	22	2	1	1	5	0	0	0	6	0	12	2	0	1	.338	.296
Walker, Larry, Montreal*	.000	2	2	0	0	0	0	0	0	0	0	0	0	0	0	1	0	0	0	.000	.000
Wallach, Tim, Los Angeles	.000	5	5	0	0	0	0	0	0	0	0	0	0	0	0	0	0	0	0	.000	.000
Walters, Dan, San Diego	.000	1	1	0	0	0	0	0	0	0	0	0	0	0	0	0	0	0	0	.000	.000
Webster, Mitch, Los Angeles†	.171	38	35	4	6	6	0	0	0	2	0	0	0	3	0	10	1	0	2	.171	.237
Wedge, Eric, Colorado	.250	8	8	2	2	2	0	0	0	1	0	0	0	0	0	2	0	0	0	.250	.250
Wehner, John, Pittsburgh	.000	15	9	0	0	0	0	0	0	0	1	0	0	4	1	3	0	0	0	.000	.308
Weiss, Walt, Florida†	.000	7	6	1	0	0	0	0	0	0	0	0	0	1	0	1	0	0	0	.000	.143
White, Rondell, Montreal	.000	3	1	0	0	0	0	0	0	1	0	0	0	1	0	0	0	0	0	.000	.500
Whiten, Mark, St. Louis†	.333	6	6	1	2	2	0	0	0	3	0	0	0	0	0	1	0	0	0	.333	.333
Whitmore, Darrell, Florida*	.000	7	6	0	0	0	0	0	0	0	0	0	1	0	0	4	0	0	0	.000	.143
Wilkins, Rick, Chicago*	.444	10	9	2	4	10	0	0	2	2	0	0	0	0	0	3	0	0	0	1.111	.444
Williams, Matt, San Francisco	.000	1	1	0	0	0	0	0	0	0	0	0	0	0	0	0	0	0	0	.000	.000
Wilson, Dan, Cincinnati	.333	3	3	1	1	2	1	0	0	2	0	0	0	0	0	1	0	0	0	.667	.333
Wilson, Glenn, Pittsburgh	.000	5	4	0	0	0	0	0	0	0	1	0	0	0	0	4	0	0	0	.000	.000
Wilson, Nigel, Florida*	.000	4	4	0	0	0	0	0	0	0	0	0	0	0	0	4	0	0	0	.000	.000
Wilson, Willie, Chicago†	.243	42	37	7	9	13	2	1	0	4	1	1	0	3	0	8	1	0	1	.351	.293
Womack, Tony, Pittsburgh*	.000	3	3	0	0	0	0	0	0	0	0	0	0	0	0	0	0	0	0	.000	.000
Wood, Ted, Montreal*	.000	6	5	1	0	0	0	0	0	0	0	0	0	1	0	1	0	0	0	.000	.167
Woodson, Tracy, St. Louis	.292	26	24	3	7	8	1	0	0	0	0	0	0	1	0	5	0	0	0	.333	.320
Yelding, Eric, Chicago	.182	23	22	2	4	5	1	0	0	1	0	1	0	0	0	4	1	0	1	.227	.182
Young, Eric, Colorado	.357	16	14	4	5	5	0	0	0	0	0	0	0	2	0	3	3	0	0	.357	.438
Young, Gerald, Colorado†	.000	7	5	1	0	0	0	0	0	0	0	0	0	2	0	0	0	0	0	.000	.286
Young, Kevin, Pittsburgh	.333	8	6	1	2	2	0	0	0	2	0	1	0	1	0	2	0	0	0	.333	.375

Player, Team	Avg.	G	AB	R	H	TB	2B	3B	HR	RBI	SH	SF	HP	BB	Int. BB	SO	SB	CS	GI DP	Slg.	OBP
Zambrano, Eddie, Chicago	.667	3	3	1	2	2	0	0	0	1	0	0	0	0	0	1	0	0	0	.667	.667
Zeile, Todd, St. Louis	.333	5	3	0	1	1	0	0	0	1	0	0	0	2	2	0	0	0	1	.333	.600

PINCH-HITTERS WITH TWO OR MORE TEAMS

Player, Team	Avg.	G	AB	R	H	TB	2B	3B	HR	RBI	SH	SF	HP	BB	Int. BB	SO	SB	CS	GI DP	Slg.	OBP
Cianfrocco, Archi, Montreal	1.000	1	1	0	1	2	1	0	0	0	0	0	0	0	0	0	0	0	0	2.000	1.000
Cianfrocco, Archi, San Diego	1.000	2	1	1	1	1	0	0	0	0	0	0	0	1	0	0	0	0	0	1.000	1.000
Daugherty, Jack, Houston†	.333	3	3	0	1	1	0	0	0	0	0	0	0	0	0	0	0	0	0	.333	.333
Daugherty, Jack, Cincinnati†	.167	31	24	3	4	5	1	0	0	2	0	1	0	6	0	8	0	0	0	.208	.323
Rhodes, Karl, Houston*	.000	1	1	0	0	0	0	0	0	0	0	0	0	0	0	0	0	0	0	.000	.000
Rhodes, Karl, Chicago*	.000	2	2	0	0	0	0	0	0	0	0	0	0	0	0	1	0	0	0	.000	.000
Sheffield, Gary, San Diego	.000	1	1	0	0	0	0	0	0	0	0	0	0	0	0	0	0	0	1	.000	.000
Sheffield, Gary, Florida	.333	5	3	1	1	1	0	0	0	0	0	0	0	2	0	1	0	0	0	.333	.600

PITCHING

TEAM

Team	W	L	ERA	G	CG	ShO	Sv.	IP	H	TBF	R	ER	HR	SH	SF	HB	BB	Int. BB	SO	WP	Bk.
Atlanta	104	58	3.14	162	18	16	46	1455.0	1297	6015	559	507	101	77	39	22	480	59	1036	46	9
Houston	85	77	3.49	162	18	14	42	1441.1	1363	6079	630	559	117	79	43	41	476	52	1056	60	12
Los Angeles	81	81	3.50	162	17	9	36	1472.2	1406	6274	662	573	103	76	48	37	567	68	1043	47	20
Montreal	94	68	3.55	163	8	7	61	1456.2	1369	6191	682	574	119	82	40	47	521	38	934	46	12
San Francisco	103	59	3.61	162	4	9	50	1456.2	1385	6077	636	585	168	74	38	50	442	46	982	33	18
Philadelphia	97	65	3.95	162	24	11	46	1472.2	1419	6360	740	647	129	65	42	37	573	33	1117	74	7
New York	59	103	4.05	162	16	8	22	1438.0	1483	6151	744	647	139	87	58	50	434	61	867	32	14
St. Louis	87	75	4.09	162	5	7	54	1453.0	1553	6196	744	660	152	80	57	43	383	50	775	40	7
Florida	64	98	4.13	162	4	5	48	1440.1	1437	6261	724	661	135	80	50	32	598	58	945	85	20
Chicago	84	78	4.18	163	8	5	56	1449.2	1514	6178	739	673	153	69	51	43	470	61	905	43	21
San Diego	61	101	4.23	162	8	6	32	1437.2	1470	6267	772	675	148	89	62	34	558	72	957	57	14
Cincinnati	73	89	4.51	162	11	8	37	1434.0	1510	6218	785	718	158	77	40	44	508	36	996	47	8
Pittsburgh	75	87	4.77	162	12	5	34	1445.2	1557	6247	806	766	153	93	55	46	485	43	832	55	11
Colorado	67	95	5.41	162	9	0	35	1431.1	1664	6471	967	860	181	82	78	41	609	66	913	82	22
Totals	1134	1134	4.04	1135	162	110	599	20284.2	20427	86985	10190	9105	1956	1110	701	567	7104	743	13358	747	195

NOTE—Totals for earned runs for several clubs do not agree with the composite total for all pitchers of each respective club due to instances in which provisions of Section 10.18(i) of the Scoring Rules were applied. The following differences are to be noted: Cincinnati pitchers add up to 719; Colorado pitchers add up to 865; Florida pitchers add up to 664; Philadelphia pitchers add to 649; St. Louis pitchers add to 662; San Francisco pitchers add to 587.

INDIVIDUAL

TOP 15 QUALIFIERS FOR EARNED-RUN AVERAGE TITLE

Minimum 162 innings.   *Lefthanded pitcher.

Pitcher, Team	W	L	ERA	G	GS	CG	ShO	GF	Sv.	IP	H	TBF	R	ER	HR	SH	SF	HB	BB	Int. BB	SO	WP	Bk.
Maddux, Greg, Atlanta	20	10	2.36	36	36	8	1	0	0	267.0	228	1064	85	70	14	15	7	6	52	7	197	5	1
Rijo, Jose, Cincinnati	14	9	2.48	36	36	2	1	0	0	257.1	218	1029	76	71	19	13	3	2	62	2	227	0	1
Portugal, Mark, Houston	18	4	2.77	33	33	1	1	0	0	208.0	194	876	75	64	10	11	3	4	77	3	131	9	2
Swift, Bill, San Francisco	21	8	2.82	34	34	1	1	0	0	232.2	195	928	82	73	18	4	2	6	55	5	157	4	0
Avery, Steve, Atlanta*	18	6	2.94	35	35	3	1	0	0	223.1	216	891	81	73	14	12	8	0	43	5	125	3	1
Harnisch, Pete, Houston	16	9	2.98	33	33	5	4	0	0	217.2	171	896	84	72	20	9	4	6	79	5	185	3	1
Candiotti, Tom, Los Angeles	8	10	3.12	33	32	2	0	0	0	213.2	192	898	86	74	12	15	9	6	71	1	155	6	0
Glavine, Tom, Atlanta*	22	6	3.20	36	36	4	2	0	0	239.1	236	1014	91	85	16	10	2	2	90	7	120	4	0
Hill, Ken, Montreal	9	7	3.23	28	28	2	0	0	0	183.2	163	780	84	66	7	9	7	6	74	7	90	6	2
Mulholland, Terry, Phi.*	12	9	3.25	29	28	7	2	0	0	191.0	177	786	80	69	20	5	4	3	40	2	116	5	0
Greene, Tommy, Phi.	16	4	3.42	31	30	7	2	0	0	200.0	175	834	84	76	12	9	3	9	62	3	167	15	0
Martinez, Ramon, L.A.	10	12	3.44	32	32	4	3	0	0	211.2	202	918	88	81	15	12	5	4	104	9	127	2	2
Gooden, Dwight, New York	12	15	3.45	29	29	7	2	0	0	208.2	188	866	89	80	16	11	7	9	61	1	149	5	2
Kile, Darryl, Houston	15	8	3.51	32	26	4	2	0	0	171.2	152	733	73	67	12	5	7	15	69	1	141	9	3
Astacio, Pedro, Los Angeles	14	9	3.57	31	31	3	2	0	0	186.1	165	777	80	74	14	7	8	5	68	5	122	8	9

DEPARTMENTAL LEADERS: W—Burkett, S.F., Glavine, Atl., 22; L—Drabek, Hou., 18; G—Jackson, S.F., 81; GS—Glavine, Atl., Maddux, Atl., Rijo, Cin., 36; CG—Maddux, Atl., 8; ShO—Harnisch, Hou., 4; GF—Beck, S.F., 71; Sv.—Myers, Chi., 53; IP—Maddux, Atl., 267; H—Tewksbury, St.L., 258; TBF—Maddux, Atl., 1064; R—Gr. Harris, S.D.-Col., 127; ER—Walk, Pit., 118; HR—Gr. Harris, S.D.-Col., 33; SH—Bottenfield, Mon.-Col., 21; SF—Armstrong, Fla., Hibbard, Chi., Hillman, N.Y., 10; HB—Kile, Hou., 15; TBB—R. Martinez, L.A., 104; IBB—Hershiser, L.A., Hoffman, Fla.-S.D., 13; SO—Rijo, Cin., 227; WP—Greene, Phi., 15; Bk.—Astacio, L.A., 9.

ALL PITCHERS

*Lefthanded pitcher.

Pitcher, Team	W	L	ERA	G	GS	CG	ShO	GF	Sv.	IP	H	TBF	R	ER	HR	SH	SF	HB	BB	Int. BB	SO	WP	Bk.
Agosto, Juan, Houston*	0	0	6.00	6	0	0	0	3	0	6.0	8	26	4	4	1	0	0	0	6	0	3	0	1
Aldred, Scott, Col.-Mon.*	1	0	9.00	8	0	0	0	2	0	12.0	19	65	14	12	2	2	0	1	10	1	9	2	0
Andersen, Larry, Phi.	3	2	2.92	64	0	0	0	13	0	61.2	54	256	22	20	4	2	0	1	21	2	67	2	1
Anderson, Mike, Cincinnati	0	0	18.56	3	0	0	0	0	0	5.1	10	30	11	11	3	0	0	0	3	0	4	0	0
Aquino, Luis, Florida	6	8	3.42	38	13	0	0	5	0	110.2	115	471	43	42	6	7	2	5	40	1	67	4	0
Armstrong, Jack, Florida	9	17	4.49	36	33	0	0	2	0	196.1	210	879	105	98	29	8	10	7	78	6	118	7	2
Arocha, Rene, St. Louis	11	8	3.78	32	29	1	0	0	0	188.0	197	774	89	79	20	8	5	3	31	2	96	3	1
Ashby, Andy, Col.-S.D.	3	10	6.80	32	21	0	0	3	1	123.0	168	577	100	93	19	6	7	4	56	5	77	6	3
Assenmacher, Paul, Chi.*	2	1	3.49	46	0	0	0	15	0	38.2	44	166	15	15	5	0	0	0	13	3	34	0	0
Astacio, Pedro, Los Angeles	14	9	3.57	31	31	3	2	0	0	186.1	165	777	80	74	14	7	8	5	68	5	122	8	9
Avery, Steve, Atlanta*	18	6	2.94	35	35	3	1	0	0	223.1	216	891	81	73	14	12	8	0	43	5	125	3	1
Ayala, Bobby, Cincinnati	7	10	5.60	43	9	0	0	8	3	98.0	106	450	72	61	16	9	2	7	45	4	65	5	0
Ayrault, Bob, Philadelphia	2	0	9.58	10	0	0	0	3	0	10.1	18	59	11	11	1	0	0	1	10	1	8	1	0
Ballard, Jeff, Pittsburgh*	4	1	4.86	25	5	0	0	4	0	53.2	70	234	31	29	3	5	1	2	15	3	16	2	0
Barnes, Brian, Montreal*	2	6	4.41	52	8	0	0	8	3	100.0	105	442	53	49	9	8	3	0	48	2	60	5	1
Batcheler, Rich, St. Louis	0	0	8.10	9	0	0	0	2	0	10.0	14	45	12	9	1	1	2	0	3	1	4	0	0
Bautista, Jose, Chicago	10	3	2.82	58	7	1	0	14	2	111.2	105	459	38	35	11	4	3	5	27	3	63	4	1
Beck, Rod, San Francisco	3	1	2.16	76	0	0	0	71	48	79.1	57	309	20	19	11	6	3	3	13	4	86	4	0
Bedrosian, Steve, Atlanta	5	2	1.63	49	0	0	0	12	0	49.2	34	198	11	9	4	3	4	2	14	2	33	5	1
Belcher, Tim, Cincinnati	9	6	4.47	22	22	4	2	0	0	137.0	134	590	72	68	11	6	3	7	47	4	101	6	0
Belinda, Stan, Pittsburgh	3	1	3.61	40	0	0	0	37	19	42.1	35	171	18	17	4	1	2	1	11	4	30	0	0
Bell, Eric, Houston*	0	1	6.14	10	0	0	0	2	0	7.1	10	34	5	5	0	0	0	0	2	0	2	0	0

Pitcher, Team	W	L	ERA	G	GS	CG	ShO	GF	Sv.	IP	H	TBF	R	ER	HR	SH	SF	HB	BB	Int. BB	SO	WP	Bk.
Benes, Andy, San Diego	15	15	3.78	34	34	4	2	0	0	230.2	200	968	111	97	23	10	6	4	86	7	179	14	2
Black, Bud, San Francisco*	8	2	3.56	16	16	0	0	0	0	93.2	89	394	44	37	13	8	4	2	33	2	45	0	4
Blair, Willie, Colorado	6	10	4.75	46	18	1	0	5	0	146.0	184	664	90	77	20	10	8	3	42	4	84	6	1
Borbon, Pedro, Atlanta*	0	0	21.60	3	0	0	0	0	0	1.2	3	11	4	4	0	1	0	0	3	0	2	0	0
Boskie, Shawn, Chicago	5	3	3.43	39	2	0	0	10	0	65.2	63	277	30	25	7	4	1	7	21	2	39	5	0
Bottenfield, Kent, Mon.-Col.	5	10	5.07	37	25	1	0	2	0	159.2	179	710	102	90	24	21	4	6	71	3	63	4	1
Boucher, Denis, Montreal*	3	1	1.91	5	5	0	0	0	0	28.1	24	111	7	6	1	0	3	0	3	1	14	0	2
Bowen, Ryan, Florida	8	12	4.42	27	27	2	1	0	0	156.2	156	693	83	77	11	5	4	3	87	7	98	10	4
Brantley, Jeff, San Francisco.	5	6	4.28	53	12	0	0	9	0	113.2	112	496	60	54	19	5	5	7	46	2	76	3	4
Brennan, Bill, Chicago	2	1	4.20	8	1	0	0	0	0	15.0	16	65	8	7	2	0	1	1	8	1	11	0	0
Brewer, Rod, St. Louis*	0	0	45.00	1	0	0	0	1	0	1.0	3	8	5	5	1	0	0	0	2	0	1	0	0
Brink, Brad, Philadelphia	0	0	3.00	2	0	0	0	1	0	6.0	3	24	2	2	1	0	0	0	3	0	8	1	0
Brocail, Doug, San Diego	4	13	4.56	24	24	0	0	0	0	128.1	143	571	75	65	16	10	8	4	42	4	70	4	1
Bross, Terry, San Francisco	0	0	9.00	2	0	0	0	1	0	2.0	3	10	2	2	1	0	0	0	1	0	1	0	0
Browning, Tom, Cincinnati*	7	7	4.74	21	20	0	0	0	0	114.0	159	505	61	60	15	4	2	1	20	2	53	1	1
Brummett, Greg, S.F.	2	3	4.70	8	8	0	0	0	0	46.0	53	196	25	24	9	1	2	0	13	1	20	2	2
Bullinger, Jim, Chicago	1	0	4.32	15	0	0	0	6	1	16.2	18	75	9	8	1	0	1	0	9	0	10	0	0
Burba, Dave, San Francisco	10	3	4.25	54	5	0	0	9	0	95.1	95	408	49	45	14	6	3	3	37	5	88	4	0
Burkett, John, S.F.	22	7	3.65	34	34	2	1	0	0	231.2	224	942	100	94	18	8	4	11	40	4	145	1	2
Burns, Todd, St. Louis	0	4	6.16	24	0	0	0	5	0	30.2	32	131	21	21	8	3	2	0	9	6	10	0	1
Bushing, Chris, Cincinnati	0	0	12.46	6	0	0	0	2	0	4.1	9	25	7	6	1	0	1	0	4	0	3	2	0
Cadaret, Greg, Cincinnati*	2	1	4.96	34	0	0	0	15	1	32.2	40	158	19	18	3	3	0	1	23	5	23	2	0
Candelaria, John, Pit.*	0	3	8.24	24	0	0	0	6	1	19.2	25	92	19	18	2	1	1	1	9	1	17	1	0
Candiotti, Tom, Los Angeles	8	10	3.12	33	32	2	0	0	0	213.2	192	898	86	74	12	15	9	6	71	1	155	6	0
Carpenter, Cris, Florida	0	1	2.89	29	0	0	0	9	0	37.1	29	154	15	12	1	1	1	2	13	2	26	5	0
Castillo, Frank, Chicago	5	8	4.84	29	25	2	0	0	0	141.1	162	614	83	76	20	10	3	9	39	4	84	5	3
Cooke, Steve, Pittsburgh*	10	10	3.89	32	32	3	1	0	0	210.2	207	882	101	91	22	13	6	3	59	4	132	3	3
Cormier, Rheal, St. Louis*	7	6	4.33	38	21	1	0	4	0	145.1	163	619	80	70	18	10	4	4	27	3	75	6	0
Corsi, Jim, Florida	0	2	6.64	15	0	0	0	6	0	20.1	28	97	15	15	1	3	1	0	10	3	7	0	0
Daal, Omar, Los Angeles*	2	3	5.09	47	0	0	0	12	0	35.1	36	155	20	20	5	2	2	0	21	3	19	1	2
Davis, Mark, Phi.-S.D.*	1	5	4.26	60	0	0	0	13	4	69.2	79	327	37	33	10	4	1	1	44	7	70	2	1
DeLeon, Jose, Philadelphia	3	0	3.26	24	3	0	0	6	0	47.0	39	207	25	17	5	3	2	5	27	3	34	5	0
Deshaies, Jim, S.F.*	2	2	4.24	5	4	0	0	1	0	17.0	24	77	9	8	2	1	0	1	6	0	5	1	0
DeSilva, John, Los Angeles	0	0	6.75	3	0	0	0	2	0	5.1	6	23	4	4	0	0	0	0	1	0	6	0	0
Dewey, Mark, Pittsburgh	1	2	2.36	21	0	0	0	17	7	26.2	14	108	8	7	0	3	3	3	10	1	14	0	0
Dibble, Rob, Cincinnati	1	4	6.48	45	0	0	0	37	19	41.2	34	196	33	30	8	1	0	2	42	0	49	4	0
Dixon, Steve, St. Louis*	0	0	33.75	4	0	0	0	0	0	2.2	7	20	10	10	1	2	0	0	5	0	2	0	0
Drabek, Doug, Houston	9	18	3.79	34	34	7	2	0	0	237.2	242	991	108	100	18	14	8	3	60	12	157	12	0
Draper, Mike, New York	1	1	4.25	29	1	0	0	11	0	42.1	53	184	22	20	2	3	5	0	14	3	16	0	1
Edens, Tom, Houston	1	1	3.12	38	0	0	0	20	0	49.0	47	203	17	17	4	4	1	0	19	7	21	3	0
Eiland, Dave, San Diego	0	3	5.21	10	9	0	0	0	0	48.1	58	217	33	28	5	2	2	1	17	1	14	1	0
Ettles, Mark, San Diego	1	0	6.50	14	0	0	0	5	0	18.0	23	81	16	13	4	0	2	0	4	1	9	3	0
Fassero, Jeff, Montreal*	12	5	2.29	56	15	1	0	10	1	149.2	119	616	50	38	7	7	4	0	54	0	140	5	0
Fernandez, Sid, New York*	5	6	2.93	18	18	1	1	0	0	119.2	82	469	42	39	17	3	1	3	36	0	81	2	0
Fletcher, Ed, Philadelphia	0	0	0.00	1	0	0	0	0	0	0.1	0	1	0	0	0	0	0	0	0	0	0	1	0
Foster, Kevin, Philadelphia	0	1	14.85	2	1	0	0	0	0	6.2	13	40	11	11	3	0	0	0	7	0	6	2	0
Foster, Steve, Cincinnati	2	2	1.75	17	0	0	0	7	0	25.2	23	105	8	5	1	1	0	1	5	2	16	0	0
Franco, John, New York*	4	3	5.20	35	0	0	0	30	10	36.1	46	172	24	21	6	4	1	1	19	3	29	5	0
Fredrickson, Scott, Colorado	0	1	6.21	25	0	0	0	4	0	29.0	33	137	25	20	3	2	2	1	17	2	20	4	1
Freeman, Marvin, Atlanta	2	0	6.08	21	0	0	0	5	0	23.2	24	103	16	16	1	0	0	1	10	2	25	3	0
Gardiner, Mike, Montreal	2	3	5.21	24	2	0	0	3	0	38.0	40	173	28	22	3	1	3	1	19	2	21	0	0
Gibson, Paul, New York*	1	1	5.19	8	0	0	0	1	0	8.2	14	42	6	5	1	0	0	0	2	0	12	1	0
Glavine, Tom, Atlanta*	22	6	3.20	36	36	4	2	0	0	239.1	236	1014	91	85	16	10	2	2	90	7	120	4	0
Gomez, Pat, San Diego*	1	2	5.12	27	1	0	0	6	0	31.2	35	144	19	18	2	1	4	0	19	4	26	2	0
Gooden, Dwight, New York	12	15	3.45	29	29	7	2	0	0	208.2	188	866	89	80	16	11	7	9	61	1	149	5	2
Gott, Jim, Los Angeles	4	8	2.32	62	0	0	0	45	25	77.2	71	313	23	20	6	7	2	1	17	5	67	5	0
Gozzo, Mauro, New York	0	1	2.57	10	0	0	0	5	1	14.0	11	57	5	4	1	0	0	0	5	1	6	0	0
Grant, Mark, Hou.-Col.	0	1	7.46	20	0	0	0	9	1	25.1	34	114	24	21	4	0	2	0	11	3	14	2	0
Green, Tyler, Philadelphia	0	0	7.36	3	2	0	0	1	0	7.1	16	41	9	6	1	0	0	0	5	0	7	2	0
Greene, Tommy, Phi.	16	4	3.42	31	30	7	2	0	0	200.0	175	834	84	76	12	9	9	3	62	3	167	15	0
Greer, Kenny, New York	1	0	0.00	1	0	0	0	1	0	1.0	0	3	0	0	0	0	0	0	0	0	2	0	0
Gross, Kevin, Los Angeles	13	13	4.14	33	32	3	0	1	0	202.1	224	892	110	93	15	11	6	5	74	7	150	2	5
Gross, Kip, Los Angeles	0	0	0.60	10	0	0	0	0	0	15.0	13	59	1	1	0	0	0	0	4	0	12	0	0
Guetterman, Lee, St. Louis*	3	3	2.93	40	0	0	0	14	1	46.0	41	192	18	15	1	1	2	2	16	5	19	1	0
Guzman, Jose, Chicago	12	10	4.34	30	30	2	1	0	0	191.0	188	819	98	92	25	8	5	3	74	6	163	6	5
Hammond, Chris, Florida*	11	12	4.66	32	32	1	0	0	0	191.0	207	826	106	99	18	10	2	1	66	2	108	10	5
Harkey, Mike, Chicago	10	10	5.26	28	28	1	0	0	0	157.1	187	676	100	92	17	8	8	3	43	4	67	1	3
Harnisch, Pete, Houston	16	9	2.98	33	33	5	4	0	0	217.2	171	896	84	72	20	9	4	6	79	5	185	3	1
Harris, Gene, San Diego	6	6	3.03	59	0	0	0	48	23	59.1	57	269	27	20	3	5	2	1	37	8	39	7	0
Harris, Greg, S.D.-Col.	11	17	4.59	35	35	4	0	0	0	225.1	239	975	127	115	33	14	4	7	69	9	123	6	6
Harvey, Bryan, Florida	1	5	1.70	59	0	0	0	54	45	69.0	45	264	14	13	4	3	6	0	13	2	73	0	1
Henry, Butch, Col.-Mon.*	3	9	6.12	30	16	1	0	4	0	103.0	135	467	76	70	15	6	6	1	28	2	47	1	0
Henry, Dwayne, Cincinnati	0	1	3.86	3	0	0	0	1	0	4.2	6	26	8	2	0	0	0	0	4	1	2	1	0
Heredia, Gil, Montreal	4	2	3.92	20	9	1	0	2	2	57.1	66	246	28	25	4	4	1	2	14	2	40	0	0
Hernandez, Jeremy, S.D.	0	2	4.72	21	0	0	0	9	0	34.1	41	146	19	18	2	2	1	0	7	1	26	0	2
Hernandez, Xavier, Houston	4	5	2.61	72	0	0	0	29	9	96.2	75	389	37	28	6	3	3	1	28	3	101	6	0
Hershiser, Orel, Los Angeles	12	14	3.59	33	33	5	1	0	0	215.2	201	913	106	86	17	12	4	7	72	13	141	7	0
Hibbard, Greg, Chicago*	15	11	3.96	31	31	1	0	0	0	191.0	209	800	96	84	19	9	10	3	47	9	82	1	2
Hickerson, Bryan, S.F.*	7	5	4.26	47	15	0	0	5	0	120.1	137	525	58	57	14	11	4	1	39	3	69	4	0
Hill, Ken, Montreal	9	7	3.23	28	28	2	0	0	0	183.2	163	780	84	66	7	9	7	6	74	7	90	6	2
Hill, Milt, Cincinnati	3	0	5.65	19	0	0	0	2	0	28.2	34	125	18	18	5	0	3	0	9	1	23	1	0
Hillman, Eric, New York*	2	9	3.97	27	22	3	1	1	0	145.0	173	627	83	64	12	10	10	4	24	2	60	0	1
Hoffman, Trevor, Fla.-S.D.	4	6	3.90	67	0	0	0	26	5	90.0	80	391	43	39	10	4	5	1	39	13	79	5	0
Holmes, Darren, Colorado	3	3	4.05	62	0	0	0	51	25	66.2	56	274	31	30	6	0	0	2	20	1	60	2	1
Hope, John, Pittsburgh	0	2	4.03	7	7	0	0	0	0	38.0	47	166	19	17	2	5	1	2	8	3	8	1	0
Hough, Charlie, Florida	9	16	4.27	34	34	0	0	0	0	204.1	202	876	109	97	20	11	7	8	71	2	126	11	4
Howell, Jay, Atlanta	3	3	2.31	54	0	0	0	22	0	58.1	48	233	16	15	3	3	4	0	16	4	37	0	2

Pitcher, Team	W	L	ERA	G	GS	CG	ShO	GF	Sv.	IP	H	TBF	R	ER	HR	SH	SF	HB	Int. BB	BB	SO	WP	Bk.
Hurst, Bruce, S.D.-Col.*	0	2	7.62	5	5	0	0	0	0	13.0	15	60	12	11	1	1	0	0	6	0	9	1	1
Innis, Jeff, New York	2	3	4.11	67	0	0	0	30	3	76.2	81	345	39	35	5	9	1	6	38	12	36	3	1
Jackson, Danny, Phi.*	12	11	3.77	32	32	2	1	0	0	210.1	214	919	105	88	12	14	8	4	80	2	120	4	0
Jackson, Mike, S.F.	6	6	3.03	81	0	0	0	17	1	77.1	58	317	28	26	7	4	2	3	24	6	70	2	2
Johnston, Joel, Pittsburgh	2	4	3.38	33	0	0	0	16	2	53.1	38	210	20	20	7	4	0	0	19	5	31	1	0
Johnstone, John, Florida	0	2	5.91	7	0	0	0	3	0	10.2	16	54	8	7	1	0	0	0	7	0	5	1	0
Jones, Bobby, New York	2	4	3.65	9	9	0	0	0	0	61.2	61	265	35	25	6	5	3	2	22	3	35	1	0
Jones, Doug, Houston	4	10	4.54	71	0	0	0	60	26	85.1	102	381	46	43	7	9	4	5	21	6	66	3	0
Jones, Jimmy, Montreal	4	1	6.35	12	6	0	0	3	0	39.2	47	175	34	28	6	1	0	0	9	0	21	1	1
Jones, Todd, Houston	1	2	3.13	27	0	0	0	8	2	37.1	28	150	14	13	4	2	1	1	15	2	25	1	1
Juden, Jeff, Houston	0	1	5.40	2	0	0	0	1	0	5.0	4	23	3	3	1	0	1	0	4	1	7	0	0
Kaiser, Jeff, Cin.-N.Y.*	0	0	7.88	9	0	0	0	3	0	8.0	10	37	7	7	1	0	1	0	5	1	9	0	0
Kile, Darryl, Houston	15	8	3.51	32	26	4	2	0	0	171.2	152	733	73	67	12	5	7	15	69	1	141	9	3
Kilgus, Paul, St. Louis*	1	0	0.63	22	1	0	0	7	1	28.2	18	109	2	2	1	0	0	1	8	1	21	0	0
Klink, Joe, Florida*	0	2	5.02	59	0	0	0	10	0	37.2	37	168	22	21	0	2	3	0	24	4	22	1	2
Knudson, Mark, Colorado	0	0	22.24	4	0	0	0	2	0	5.2	16	39	14	14	4	0	0	0	5	0	3	2	0
Lancaster, Les, St. Louis	4	1	2.93	50	0	0	0	12	0	61.1	56	259	24	20	5	5	1	1	21	5	36	5	0
Landrum, Bill, Cincinnati	0	2	3.74	18	0	0	0	6	0	21.2	18	86	9	9	1	2	0	0	6	1	14	0	0
Layana, Tim, San Francisco..	0	0	22.50	1	0	0	0	0	0	2.0	7	15	5	5	1	1	0	0	1	1	1	0	0
Leskanic, Curt, Colorado	1	5	5.37	18	8	0	0	1	0	57.0	59	260	40	34	7	5	4	2	27	1	30	8	2
Lewis, Richie, Florida	6	3	3.26	57	0	0	0	14	0	77.1	68	341	37	28	7	8	4	1	43	6	65	9	1
Looney, Brian, Montreal*	0	0	3.00	3	1	0	0	1	0	6.0	8	28	2	2	0	0	0	2	0	7	0	1
Luebbers, Larry, Cincinnati	2	5	4.54	14	14	0	0	0	0	77.1	74	332	49	39	7	4	5	1	38	3	38	4	0
Maddux, Greg, Atlanta	20	10	2.36	36	36	8	1	0	0	267.0	228	1064	85	70	14	15	7	6	52	7	197	5	1
Maddux, Mike, New York	3	8	3.60	58	0	0	0	31	5	75.0	67	320	34	30	3	7	6	4	27	7	57	4	1
Magrane, Joe, St. Louis*	8	10	4.97	22	20	0	0	2	0	116.0	127	499	68	64	15	6	7	5	37	3	38	4	0
Manzanillo, Josias, N.Y.	0	0	3.00	6	0	0	0	2	0	12.0	8	54	7	4	1	1	1	0	9	0	11	0	0
Martinez, Dennis, Montreal	15	9	3.85	35	34	2	0	1	0	224.2	211	945	110	96	27	10	4	11	64	7	138	2	4
Martinez, Pedro A., S.D.*	3	1	2.43	32	0	0	0	9	0	37.0	23	148	11	10	4	0	0	1	13	1	32	0	0
Martinez, Pedro J., L.A.	10	5	2.61	65	2	0	0	20	2	107.0	76	444	34	31	5	0	5	4	57	4	119	3	1
Martinez, Ramon, L.A.	10	12	3.44	32	32	4	3	0	0	211.2	202	918	88	81	15	12	5	4	104	9	127	2	2
Mason, Roger, S.D.-Phi.	5	12	4.06	68	0	0	0	29	0	99.2	90	417	48	45	10	7	5	2	34	5	71	2	3
Mauser, Tim, Phi.-S.D.	0	1	4.00	36	0	0	0	16	0	54.0	51	235	28	24	6	1	1	1	24	5	46	2	0
McClure, Bob, Florida*	1	1	7.11	14	0	0	0	1	0	6.1	13	36	5	5	2	0	0	0	5	0	6	0	0
McDowell, Roger, L.A.	5	3	2.25	54	0	0	0	19	2	68.0	76	300	32	17	2	3	1	2	30	10	27	5	0
McElroy, Chuck, Chicago*	2	2	4.56	49	0	0	0	11	0	47.1	51	214	30	24	4	5	1	1	25	5	31	3	0
McMichael, Greg, Atlanta	2	3	2.06	74	0	0	0	40	19	91.2	68	365	22	21	3	4	2	0	29	4	89	6	1
Menendez, Tony, Pittsburgh	2	0	3.00	14	0	0	0	3	0	21.0	20	85	8	7	4	1	1	0	4	0	13	0	0
Mercker, Kent, Atlanta*	3	1	2.86	43	6	0	0	9	0	66.0	52	283	24	21	2	0	0	2	36	3	59	5	1
Miceli, Dan, Pittsburgh	0	0	5.06	9	0	0	0	1	0	5.1	4	25	3	3	0	0	0	0	4	0	4	0	1
Miller, Paul, Pittsburgh	0	0	5.40	3	2	0	0	1	0	10.0	15	47	6	6	2	2	0	0	2	0	2	1	0
Minor, Blas, Pittsburgh	8	6	4.10	65	0	0	0	18	2	94.1	94	398	43	43	8	6	4	4	26	3	84	5	0
Minutelli, Gino, S.F.*	0	1	3.77	9	0	0	0	4	0	14.1	7	64	9	6	2	1	2	0	15	0	10	1	0
Moeller, Dennis, Pittsburgh*..	1	0	9.92	10	0	0	0	3	0	16.1	26	82	20	18	2	1	0	1	7	1	13	1	2
Moore, Marcus, Colorado	3	1	6.84	27	0	0	0	8	0	26.1	30	128	25	20	4	0	4	1	20	0	13	4	0
Morgan, Mike, Chicago	10	15	4.03	32	32	1	1	0	0	207.2	206	883	100	93	15	11	5	7	74	8	111	8	2
Mulholland, Terry, Phi.*	12	9	3.25	29	28	7	2	0	0	191.0	177	786	80	69	20	5	4	3	40	2	116	5	0
Munoz, Mike, Colorado*	2	1	4.50	21	0	0	0	7	0	18.0	21	82	12	9	1	3	2	0	9	3	16	2	0
Murphy, Rob, St. Louis*	5	7	4.87	73	0	0	0	23	1	64.2	73	279	37	35	8	4	2	1	20	6	41	5	0
Myers, Randy, Chicago*	2	4	3.11	73	0	0	0	69	53	75.1	65	313	26	26	7	1	2	1	26	2	86	3	0
Nabholz, Chris, Montreal*	9	8	4.09	26	21	1	0	2	0	116.2	100	505	57	53	9	7	4	8	63	4	74	7	0
Neagle, Denny, Pittsburgh*	3	5	5.31	50	7	0	0	13	1	81.1	82	360	49	48	10	1	1	3	37	3	73	5	0
Nen, Robb, Florida	1	0	7.02	15	1	0	0	2	0	33.1	35	159	28	26	5	1	1	0	20	0	27	4	0
Nichols, Rod, Los Angeles	0	1	5.68	4	0	0	0	2	0	6.1	9	28	5	4	1	0	0	2	2	3	0	0
Nied, David, Colorado	5	9	5.17	16	16	1	0	0	0	87.0	99	394	53	50	8	9	7	1	42	4	46	1	1
Olivares, Omar, St. Louis	5	3	4.17	58	9	0	0	11	1	118.2	134	537	60	55	10	4	9	4	54	7	63	4	3
Osborne, Donovan, St.L.*	10	7	3.76	26	26	1	0	0	0	155.2	153	657	73	65	18	6	2	7	47	4	83	4	0
Osuna, Al, Houston*	1	1	3.20	44	0	0	0	6	2	25.1	17	107	10	9	3	4	1	1	13	2	21	3	0
Otto, Dave, Pittsburgh*	3	4	5.03	28	8	0	0	7	0	68.0	85	306	40	38	9	6	1	3	28	1	30	4	0
Painter, Lance, Colorado*	2	2	6.00	10	6	1	0	2	0	39.0	52	166	26	26	5	1	0	0	9	0	16	2	0
Pall, Donn, Philadelphia	1	0	2.55	8	0	0	0	2	0	17.2	15	69	7	5	1	1	0	0	3	0	11	0	1
Parrett, Jeff, Colorado	3	3	5.38	40	6	0	0	13	1	73.2	78	341	47	44	6	4	5	2	45	9	66	11	1
Perez, Mike, St. Louis	7	2	2.48	65	0	0	0	25	7	72.2	65	299	24	20	4	5	1	1	20	1	58	2	0
Petkovsek, Mark, Pittsburgh	3	0	6.96	26	0	0	0	8	0	32.1	43	145	25	25	7	4	1	0	9	2	14	4	0
Plesac, Dan, Chicago*	2	1	4.74	57	0	0	0	12	0	62.2	74	276	37	33	10	4	3	0	21	6	47	5	2
Portugal, Mark, Houston	18	4	2.77	33	33	1	1	0	0	208.0	194	876	75	64	10	11	3	4	77	3	131	9	2
Powell, Ross, Cincinnati*	0	3	4.41	9	1	0	0	1	0	16.1	13	66	8	8	1	2	0	0	6	0	17	0	0
Pugh, Tim, Cincinnati	10	15	5.26	31	27	3	1	3	0	164.1	200	738	102	96	19	6	5	7	59	1	94	3	2
Rapp, Pat, Florida	4	6	4.02	16	16	1	0	0	0	94.0	101	412	49	42	7	8	4	2	39	1	57	6	0
Reardon, Jeff, Cincinnati	4	6	4.09	58	0	0	0	32	8	61.2	66	267	34	28	4	4	5	0	10	0	35	2	0
Reed, Steve, Colorado	9	5	4.48	64	0	0	0	14	3	84.1	80	347	47	42	13	2	3	3	30	5	51	1	0
Reynolds, Shane, Houston	0	0	0.82	5	1	0	0	0	0	11.0	11	49	4	1	0	0	0	0	6	1	10	0	0
Reynoso, Armando, Colorado	12	11	4.00	30	30	4	0	0	0	189.0	206	830	101	84	22	5	8	9	63	7	117	7	6
Righetti, Dave, S.F.*	1	1	5.70	51	0	0	0	15	1	47.1	58	210	31	30	11	2	0	1	17	0	31	1	0
Rijo, Jose, Cincinnati	14	9	2.48	36	36	2	1	0	0	257.1	218	1029	76	71	19	13	3	2	62	2	227	0	1
Risley, Bill, Montreal	0	0	6.00	2	0	0	0	1	0	3.0	2	14	3	2	1	1	0	1	2	0	2	0	0
Rivera, Ben, Philadelphia	13	9	5.02	30	28	1	1	0	0	163.0	175	742	99	91	16	5	5	6	85	4	123	13	0
Robertson, Rich, Pittsburgh*.	0	1	6.00	9	0	0	0	2	0	9.0	15	44	6	6	1	0	0	4	0	5	0	0
Rodriguez, Rich, S.D.-Fla.*	2	4	3.79	70	0	0	0	21	3	76.0	73	331	38	32	10	5	0	2	38	3	43	3	0
Rogers, Kevin, S.F.*	2	2	2.68	64	0	0	0	24	0	80.2	71	334	28	24	3	0	1	4	28	5	62	3	0
Rojas, Mel, Montreal	5	8	2.95	66	0	0	0	25	10	88.1	80	378	39	29	6	8	6	4	30	3	48	5	0
Roper, John, Cincinnati	2	5	5.63	16	15	0	0	0	0	80.0	92	360	51	50	10	5	4	3	36	3	54	5	1
Rueter, Kirk, Montreal*	8	0	2.73	14	14	1	0	0	0	85.2	85	341	33	26	5	1	0	0	18	1	31	0	0
Ruffin, Bruce, Colorado*	6	5	3.87	59	12	0	0	8	2	139.2	145	619	71	60	10	4	5	1	69	9	126	8	0
Ruffin, Johnny, Cincinnati	2	1	3.58	21	0	0	0	5	2	37.2	36	159	16	15	4	1	0	1	11	1	30	2	0
Ruskin, Scott, Cincinnati*	0	0	18.00	4	0	0	0	1	0	1.0	3	8	2	2	1	0	0	0	2	0	0	0	0
Saberhagen, Bret, New York	7	7	3.29	19	19	4	1	0	0	139.1	131	556	55	51	11	6	6	3	17	4	93	2	2

Pitcher, Team	W	L	ERA	G	GS	CG	ShO	GF	Sv.	IP	H	TBF	R	ER	HR	SH	SF	HB	BB	Int. BB	SO	WP	Bk.
Sanders, Scott, San Diego	3	3	4.13	9	9	0	0	0	0	52.1	54	231	32	24	4	1	2	1	23	1	37	0	1
Sanderson, Scott, S.F.	4	2	3.51	11	8	0	0	1	0	48.2	48	201	20	19	12	3	2	1	7	2	36	0	3
Sanford, Mo, Colorado	1	2	5.30	11	6	0	0	1	0	35.2	37	166	25	21	4	4	2	0	27	0	36	2	1
Scanlan, Bob, Chicago	4	5	4.54	70	0	0	0	13	0	75.1	79	323	41	38	6	2	6	3	28	7	44	0	2
Schilling, Curt, Phi.	16	7	4.02	34	34	7	2	0	0	235.1	234	982	114	105	23	9	7	4	57	6	186	9	3
Schourek, Pete, New York*	5	12	5.96	41	18	0	0	6	0	128.1	168	586	90	85	13	3	8	3	45	7	72	1	2
Scott, Tim, S.D.-Mon.	7	2	3.01	56	0	0	0	18	1	71.2	69	317	28	24	4	3	2	4	34	2	65	2	1
Seanez, Rudy, San Diego	0	0	13.50	3	0	0	0	3	0	3.1	8	20	6	5	1	1	0	0	2	0	1	0	0
Seminara, Frank, San Diego	3	3	4.47	18	7	0	0	0	0	46.1	53	212	30	23	5	6	2	3	21	3	22	1	0
Service, Scott, Col.-Cin.	2	2	4.30	29	0	0	0	7	2	46.0	44	197	24	22	6	2	4	2	16	4	43	0	0
Shaw, Jeff, Montreal	2	7	4.14	55	8	0	0	13	0	95.2	91	404	47	44	12	5	2	7	32	2	50	2	0
Shepherd, Keith, Colorado	1	3	6.98	14	1	0	0	3	1	19.1	26	85	16	15	4	1	1	1	4	0	7	1	0
Shouse, Brian, Pittsburgh*	0	0	9.00	6	0	0	0	1	0	4.0	7	22	4	4	1	0	1	0	2	0	3	1	0
Slocumb, Heathcliff, Chicago	1	0	3.38	10	0	0	0	4	0	10.2	7	42	5	4	0	1	0	4	0	4	0	0
Smiley, John, Cincinnati*	3	9	5.62	18	18	2	0	0	0	105.2	117	455	69	66	15	10	3	2	31	0	60	2	1
Smith, Bryn, Colorado	2	4	8.49	11	5	0	0	2	0	29.2	47	150	29	28	2	2	4	3	11	1	9	1	0
Smith, Lee, St. Louis	2	4	4.50	55	0	0	0	48	43	50.0	49	206	25	25	11	0	2	0	9	1	49	1	0
Smith, Pete, Atlanta	4	8	4.37	20	14	0	0	2	0	90.2	92	390	45	44	15	6	5	2	36	3	53	1	1
Smith, Zane, Pittsburgh*	3	7	4.55	14	14	1	0	0	0	83.0	97	353	43	42	5	6	0	0	22	3	32	2	0
Smoltz, John, Atlanta	15	11	3.62	35	35	3	1	0	0	243.2	208	1028	104	98	23	13	4	6	100	12	208	13	1
Spradlin, Jerry, Cincinnati	2	1	3.49	37	0	0	0	16	2	49.0	44	193	20	19	4	3	4	0	9	0	24	3	1
Stanton, Mike, Atlanta*	4	6	4.67	63	0	0	0	41	27	52.0	51	236	35	27	4	5	2	0	29	7	43	1	0
Swift, Bill, San Francisco	21	8	2.82	34	34	1	1	0	0	232.2	195	928	82	73	18	4	2	6	55	5	157	4	0
Swindell, Greg, Houston*	12	13	4.16	31	30	1	1	0	0	190.1	215	818	98	88	24	13	3	1	40	3	124	2	2
Tanana, Frank, New York*	7	15	4.48	29	29	0	0	0	0	183.0	198	784	100	91	26	12	4	9	48	7	104	7	2
Taylor, Kerry, San Diego	0	5	6.45	36	7	0	0	9	0	68.1	72	326	53	49	5	10	3	4	49	0	45	4	0
Telgheder, Dave, New York*	6	2	4.76	24	7	0	0	7	0	75.2	82	325	40	40	10	2	1	4	21	2	35	1	0
Tewksbury, Bob, St.L.	17	10	3.83	32	32	2	0	0	0	213.2	258	907	99	91	15	15	9	6	20	1	97	2	0
Thigpen, Bobby, Phi.	3	1	6.05	17	0	0	0	5	0	19.1	23	88	13	13	2	2	1	1	9	1	10	0	1
Toliver, Freddie, Pittsburgh*	1	0	3.74	12	0	0	0	3	0	21.2	20	90	10	9	2	2	3	2	8	0	14	0	0
Tomlin, Randy, Pittsburgh*	4	8	4.85	18	18	1	0	0	0	98.1	109	411	57	53	11	8	8	5	15	0	44	4	2
Torres, Salomon, S.F.	3	5	4.03	8	8	0	0	0	0	44.2	37	196	21	20	5	7	1	1	27	3	23	3	1
Trachsel, Steve, Chicago	0	2	4.58	3	3	0	0	0	0	19.2	16	78	10	10	4	1	1	0	3	0	14	1	0
Trlicek, Ricky, Los Angeles	1	2	4.08	41	0	0	0	18	1	64.0	59	267	32	29	3	2	0	2	21	4	41	4	1
Turner, Matt, Florida	4	5	2.91	55	0	0	0	26	0	68.0	55	279	23	22	7	6	4	1	26	9	59	6	1
Urbani, Tom, St. Louis*	1	3	4.65	18	9	0	0	2	0	62.0	73	283	44	32	4	4	6	0	26	2	33	1	1
Valdez, Sergio, Montreal	0	0	9.00	4	0	0	0	1	0	3.0	4	14	4	3	1	0	0	0	1	0	2	0	0
Wagner, Paul, Pittsburgh	8	8	4.27	44	17	1	1	9	2	141.1	143	599	72	67	15	6	7	1	42	4	114	12	0
Wakefield, Tim, Pittsburgh	6	11	5.61	24	20	3	2	1	0	128.1	145	595	83	80	14	7	9	5	75	2	59	6	0
Walk, Bob, Pittsburgh	13	14	5.68	32	32	3	0	0	0	187.0	214	822	121	118	23	10	9	5	70	5	80	2	3
Walton, Bruce, Montreal	0	0	9.53	4	0	0	0	3	0	5.2	11	32	6	6	1	0	0	0	3	0	0	1	0
Watson, Allen, St. Louis*	6	7	4.60	16	15	0	0	0	1	86.0	90	373	53	44	11	6	4	3	28	2	49	2	1
Wayne, Gary, Colorado*	5	3	5.05	65	0	0	0	21	1	62.1	68	283	40	35	3	8	3	7	26	8	49	9	1
Weathers, Dave, Florida	2	3	5.12	14	6	0	0	2	0	45.2	57	202	26	26	3	2	0	1	13	1	34	6	0
Wendell, Turk, Chicago	1	2	4.37	7	4	0	0	1	0	22.2	24	98	13	11	0	2	0	0	8	1	15	1	1
West, David, Philadelphia*	6	4	2.92	76	0	0	0	27	3	86.1	60	375	37	28	6	8	2	5	51	4	87	3	0
Weston, Mickey, New York	0	0	7.94	4	0	0	0	1	0	5.2	11	30	5	5	0	0	0	1	1	0	2	0	0
Wetteland, John, Montreal	9	3	1.37	70	0	0	0	58	43	85.1	58	344	17	13	3	5	1	2	28	3	113	7	0
Whitehurst, Wally, S.D.	4	7	3.83	21	19	0	0	1	0	105.2	109	441	47	45	11	5	8	3	30	5	57	5	1
Wickander, Kevin, Cin.*	1	0	6.75	33	0	0	0	8	0	25.1	32	126	20	19	5	1	0	2	19	1	20	4	1
Williams, Brian, Houston	4	4	4.83	42	5	0	0	12	3	82.0	76	357	48	44	7	5	3	4	38	4	56	9	2
Williams, Mike, Philadelphia	1	3	5.29	17	4	0	0	2	0	51.0	50	221	32	30	5	1	0	0	22	2	33	2	0
Williams, Mitch, Phi.*	3	7	3.34	65	0	0	0	57	43	62.0	56	281	30	23	3	4	2	2	44	1	60	6	0
Wilson, Steve, Los Angeles*	1	0	4.56	25	0	0	0	4	1	25.2	30	120	13	13	2	1	1	0	14	4	23	0	0
Wilson, Trevor, S.F.*	7	5	3.60	22	18	1	0	1	0	110.0	110	455	45	44	8	6	3	6	40	3	57	0	0
Wohlers, Mark, Atlanta	6	2	4.50	46	0	0	0	13	0	48.0	37	199	25	24	2	5	1	1	22	3	45	0	0
Worrell, Tim, San Diego	2	7	4.92	21	16	0	0	1	0	100.2	104	443	63	55	11	8	5	0	43	5	52	3	0
Worrell, Todd, Los Angeles	1	1	6.05	35	0	0	0	22	5	38.2	46	167	28	26	6	3	6	0	11	1	31	1	0
Young, Anthony, New York	1	16	3.77	39	10	1	0	19	3	100.1	103	445	62	42	8	11	3	1	42	9	62	0	2
Young, Pete, Montreal	1	0	3.38	4	0	0	0	2	0	5.1	4	20	2	2	1	0	0	0	0	0	3	0	0

PITCHERS WITH TWO OR MORE TEAMS

Pitcher, Team	W	L	ERA	G	GS	CG	ShO	GF	Sv.	IP	H	TBF	R	ER	HR	SH	SF	HB	BB	Int. BB	SO	WP	Bk.
Aldred, Scott, Colorado*	0	0	10.80	5	0	0	0	1	0	6.2	10	40	10	8	1	2	0	1	9	1	5	1	0
Aldred, Scott, Montreal*	1	0	6.75	3	0	0	0	1	0	5.1	9	25	4	4	1	0	0	1	3	0	4	1	0
Ashby, Andy, Colorado	0	4	8.50	20	9	0	0	3	1	54.0	89	277	54	51	5	3	3	3	32	4	33	2	3
Ashby, Andy, San Diego	3	6	5.48	12	12	0	0	0	0	69.0	79	300	46	42	14	3	4	1	24	1	44	4	0
Bottenfield, Kent, Montreal	2	5	4.12	23	11	0	0	2	0	83.0	93	373	49	38	11	11	1	5	33	2	33	4	1
Bottenfield, Kent, Colorado	3	5	6.10	14	14	1	0	0	0	76.2	86	337	53	52	13	10	3	1	38	1	30	0	0
Davis, Mark, Philadelphia*	1	2	5.17	25	0	0	0	4	0	31.1	35	154	22	18	4	1	0	1	24	1	28	1	0
Davis, Mark, San Diego*	0	3	3.52	35	0	0	0	9	4	38.1	44	173	15	15	6	3	1	0	20	6	42	1	1
Grant, Mark, Houston	0	0	0.82	6	0	0	0	3	0	11.0	11	44	4	1	0	0	1	0	5	2	8	0	0
Grant, Mark, Colorado	0	1	12.56	14	0	0	0	6	0	14.1	23	68	20	20	4	0	1	0	6	1	8	2	0
Harris, Greg, San Diego	10	9	3.67	22	22	4	0	0	0	152.0	151	639	65	62	18	8	2	3	39	6	83	2	3
Harris, Greg, Colorado	1	8	6.50	13	13	0	0	0	0	73.1	88	336	62	53	15	6	2	4	30	3	40	4	3
Henry, Butch, Colorado	2	8	6.59	20	15	1	0	1	0	84.2	117	390	66	62	14	6	5	1	24	2	39	1	0
Henry, Butch, Montreal*	1	1	3.93	10	1	0	0	3	0	18.1	18	77	10	8	1	0	0	0	4	0	8	0	0
Hoffman, Trevor, Florida	2	2	3.28	28	0	0	0	13	2	35.2	24	152	13	13	5	2	1	0	19	7	26	3	0
Hoffman, Trevor, San Diego	2	4	4.31	39	0	0	0	13	3	54.1	56	239	30	26	5	2	4	1	20	6	53	2	0
Hurst, Bruce, San Diego*	0	1	12.46	2	2	0	0	0	0	4.1	9	26	7	6	0	1	0	0	3	0	6	1	1
Hurst, Bruce, Colorado*	1	1	5.19	3	3	0	0	0	0	8.2	8	34	5	5	1	0	0	0	3	0	6	1	1
Kaiser, Jeff, Cincinnati*	0	0	2.70	3	0	0	0	1	0	3.1	4	16	1	1	0	0	0	0	1	0	2	0	0
Kaiser, Jeff, New York*	0	0	11.57	6	0	0	0	2	0	4.2	6	21	6	6	1	0	1	0	3	0	5	0	0
Mason, Roger, San Diego	0	7	3.24	34	0	0	0	14	0	50.0	43	207	20	18	1	6	3	2	18	4	39	1	2
Mason, Roger, Philadelphia	5	5	4.89	34	0	0	0	15	0	49.2	47	210	28	27	9	1	2	0	16	1	32	1	1

Pitcher, Team	W	L	ERA	G	GS	CG	ShO	GF	Sv.	IP	H	TBF	R	ER	HR	SH	SF	HB	BB	Int. BB	SO	WP	Bk.
Mauser, Tim, Philadelphia	0	0	4.96	8	0	0	0	1	0	16.1	15	71	9	9	1	0	0	1	7	0	14	1	0
Mauser, Tim, San Diego	0	1	3.58	28	0	0	0	15	0	37.2	36	164	19	15	5	1	1	0	17	5	32	1	0
Rodriguez, Rich, San Diego* ..	2	3	3.30	34	0	0	0	10	2	30.0	34	133	15	11	2	2	0	1	9	3	22	1	0
Rodriguez, Rich, Florida*	0	1	4.11	36	0	0	0	11	1	46.0	39	198	23	21	8	3	0	1	24	5	21	2	0
Scott, Tim, San Diego.............	2	0	2.39	24	0	0	0	2	0	37.2	38	169	13	10	1	2	2	4	15	0	30	1	1
Scott, Tim, Montreal...............	5	2	3.71	32	0	0	0	16	1	34.0	31	148	15	14	3	1	0	0	19	2	35	1	0
Service, Scott, Colorado........	0	0	9.64	3	0	0	0	0	0	4.2	8	24	5	5	1	0	2	1	1	0	3	0	0
Service, Scott, Cincinnati.......	2	2	3.70	26	0	0	0	7	2	41.1	36	173	19	17	5	2	2	1	15	4	40	0	0

NOTE—The following pitchers combined to pitch shutout games: Atlanta (11)—Maddux and Stanton; Smith and Stanton; Smoltz and Stanton; Avery and Stanton; Smith and Freeman; Glavine and McMichael; Glavine, McMichael and Stanton; Avery, McMichael and Stanton; Avery, Freeman, Mercker and Howell; Avery and McMichael; Mercker, Wohlers and McMichael; Chicago (3)—Harkey, Scanlan and Myers; Castillo, Assenmacher, Scanlan and Myers; Hibbard, Myers and Bautista; Cincinnati (4)—Rijo, Foster and Reardon; Browning, Reardon and Dibble; Rijo and Dibble; Ayala and Service; Florida (4)—Bowen and Harvey; Hough and Harvey; Weathers and Harvey; Armstrong and Harvey; Houston (4)—Harnisch and Jones; Swindell, Williams and Osuna; Kile and Hernandez; Swindell, Hernandez and Jones; Los Angeles (3)—Candiotti and P. Martinez; Candiotti, P. Martinez, Daal, Gott and McDowell; Astacio and Gott; Montreal (7)—Rueter and Wetteland 2; Nabholz, Rojas and Wetteland; Heredia, Rojas and Wetteland; Hill and Rojas; Fassero and Rojas; Rueter, Rojas and Wetteland; New York (3)—Gooden and Draper; Schourek and Franco; Jones, Innis, Gozzo and Greer; Philadelphia (3)—Greene and Mason; Jackson and Mason; Greene and Mit. Williams; Pittsburgh (1)—Hope, Ballard, Menendez and Neagle; St. Louis (7)—Arocha and Olivares; Osborne and Smith; Magrane, Kilgus and Smith; Osborne, Murphy, Olivares and Smith; Watson, Burns and Smith; Osborne and Murphy; Arocha, Guetterman, Kilgus, Lancaster and Perez; San Diego (4)—Whitehurst, Rodriguez and Ge. Harris; Brocail and Ge. Harris; Benes and Ge. Harris; Brocail, Hoffman and Davis; San Francisco (7)—Swift and Beck 2; Burkett and Beck; Wilson, Righetti and Beck; Black and Jackson; Swift and Jackson; Burkett and Rogers.

FIELDING

TEAM

Team	Pct.	G	PO	A	E	TC	DP	TP	PB
San Francisco	.984	162	4370	1733	101	6204	169	0	15
Pittsburgh	.983	162	4337	1816	105	6258	161	1	19
Atlanta	.983	162	4365	1769	108	6242	146	0	13
Chicago	.982	163	4349	1889	115	6353	162	0	14
Cincinnati	.980	162	4302	1633	121	6056	133	0	12
Florida	.980	162	4321	1703	125	6149	130	0	29
Houston	.979	162	4324	1651	126	6101	141	0	7
Los Angeles	.979	162	4418	1838	133	6389	141	0	15
Philadelphia	.977	162	4418	1536	141	6095	123	0	12
St. Louis	.975	162	4359	1890	159	6408	157	1	14
New York	.975	162	4314	1781	156	6251	143	0	4
Montreal	.975	163	4370	1827	159	6356	144	2	14
San Diego	.974	162	4313	1616	160	6089	129	0	20
Colorado	.973	162	4294	1760	167	6221	149	0	11
Totals	.978	1135	60854	24442	1876	87172	2028	4	199

INDIVIDUAL

FIRST BASEMEN

*Throws lefthanded.

Leader, Team	Pct.	G	PO	A	E	TC	DP
YOUNG, Pittsburgh	.998	135	1116	101	3	1220	108

Player, Team	Pct.	G	PO	A	E	TC	DP
Allanson, S.F.	1.000	2	8	0	0	8	0
Aude, Pittsburgh	1.000	7	47	3	0	50	6
Bagwell, Houston	.993	140	1200	113	9	1322	106
Bean, San Diego*	1.000	12	51	3	0	54	5
Benavides, Colorado	1.000	1	2	0	0	2	1
Benzinger, S.F.	1.000	40	289	15	0	304	27
Bolick, Montreal	.992	51	333	33	3	369	28
Bonilla, New York	.981	6	50	1	1	52	4
Branson, Cincinnati	1.000	1	10	1	0	11	0
Bream, Atlanta*	.996	90	627	62	3	692	62
Brewer, St. Louis*	.991	32	101	5	1	107	13
Buechele, Chicago	1.000	6	18	0	0	18	3
Cabrera, Atlanta	1.000	12	61	10	0	71	4
Carreon, S.F.*	1.000	3	6	2	0	8	1
Castellano, Colorado	.955	10	37	5	2	44	6
Cianfrocco, Mon.-S.D.	.995	42	195	21	1	217	21
Clark, Colorado	.984	37	284	16	5	305	29
Clark, San Diego	.976	24	144	20	4	168	12
Clark, San Francisco*	.988	129	1078	88	14	1180	113
Colbrunn, Montreal	.995	61	372	27	2	401	31
Conine, Florida	1.000	43	151	14	0	165	11
Costo, Cincinnati	1.000	2	2	1	0	3	0
Daugherty, Hou.-Cin.*	1.000	3	20	2	0	22	1
Destrade, Florida	.987	152	1313	90	19	1422	109
Donnels, Houston	.988	23	157	9	2	168	14
Dorsett, Cincinnati	1.000	3	8	0	0	8	0
Eisenreich, Phi.*	1.000	1	5	0	0	5	0
Floyd, Montreal	1.000	10	79	4	0	83	5
Foley, Pittsburgh	.972	12	31	4	1	36	3
Frazier, Montreal	.970	8	27	5	1	33	1
Gainer, Colorado*	.982	7	52	2	1	55	3
Galarraga, Colorado	.990	119	1018	103	11	1132	88
Gallagher, New York	1.000	9	22	1	0	23	0
Geren, San Diego	1.000	1	1	0	0	1	0
Gilkey, St. Louis	1.000	3	24	1	0	25	2
Grace, Chicago*	.997	154	1456	112	5	1573	134
Higgins, San Diego	1.000	3	5	0	0	5	1
Hunter, Atlanta*	.994	29	164	13	1	178	19
Jefferies, St. Louis	.993	140	1279	76	9	1364	114
Jennings, Colorado*	1.000	10	80	2	0	82	8
Jordan, Philadelphia	.990	33	201	4	2	207	20
Karros, Los Angeles	.992	157	1335	147	12	1494	118
Klesko, Atlanta*	1.000	3	8	0	0	8	0
Kruk, Philadelphia*	.993	144	1149	69	8	1226	79

Player, Team	Pct.	G	PO	A	E	TC	DP
Lindeman, Houston	1.000	9	40	5	0	45	6
Magadan, Florida	1.000	2	5	1	0	6	0
Marrero, Montreal*	.991	32	194	15	2	211	21
McClendon, Pit.	1.000	6	14	2	0	16	1
McGriff, S.D.-Atl.*	.987	149	1203	92	17	1312	102
McKnight, New York	1.000	10	35	5	0	40	5
Merced, Pittsburgh	.993	42	276	20	2	298	23
Milligan, Cincinnati	.994	61	468	56	3	527	47
Morris, Cincinnati*	.994	98	746	75	5	826	61
Murray, New York	.988	154	1319	111	18	1448	118
Oliver, Cincinnati	1.000	12	34	2	0	36	5
Orsulak, New York*	1.000	4	16	1	0	17	0
Pappas, St. Louis	1.000	2	6	0	0	6	1
Perry, St. Louis	.976	15	77	3	2	82	5
Phillips, S.F.*	.971	5	32	2	1	35	1
Piazza, Los Angeles	1.000	1	2	0	0	2	1
Ready, Montreal	.960	13	87	8	4	99	5
Rodriguez, L.A.*	1.000	13	70	6	0	76	2
Royer, St. Louis	1.000	2	19	1	0	20	0
Samuel, Cincinnati	1.000	6	11	3	0	14	0
Scarsone, S.F.	1.000	6	9	0	0	9	0
Sharperson, L.A.	.000	1	0	0	0	0	0
Sheaffer, Colorado	1.000	7	6	4	0	10	1
Shelton, Pittsburgh*	1.000	2	10	1	0	11	1
Shields, Chicago	1.000	1	0	1	0	1	0
Siddall, Montreal	.000	1	0	0	0	0	0
Snyder, Los Angeles	1.000	12	22	3	0	25	1
Staton, San Diego	1.000	12	66	14	0	80	10
Tatum, Colorado	.978	12	41	4	1	46	6
Teufel, San Diego	.958	8	21	2	1	24	0
Vander Wal, Mon.*	.988	42	237	13	3	253	17
Velasquez, San Diego	.984	38	221	21	4	246	20
Walker, Montreal	1.000	4	43	3	0	46	2
Wallach, Los Angeles	1.000	1	9	1	0	10	1
D. White, Montreal	.993	17	129	8	1	138	16
Woodson, St. Louis	.981	11	49	2	1	52	7
Young, Pittsburgh	.998	135	1116	101	3	1220	108
Zambrano, Chicago	.929	2	13	0	1	14	1

TRIPLE PLAYS: Jefferies, St. Louis; Ready, Montreal; Young, Pittsburgh.

FIRST BASEMEN WITH TWO OR MORE TEAMS

Player, Team	Pct.	G	PO	A	E	TC	DP
Cianfrocco, Montreal	1.000	11	45	2	0	47	6
Cianfrocco, San Diego	.994	31	150	19	1	170	15
Daugherty, Houston*	.000	1	0	0	0	0	0
Daugherty, Cin.*	1.000	2	20	2	0	22	1
McGriff, San Diego*	.983	83	640	47	12	699	50
McGriff, Atlanta*	.992	66	563	45	5	613	52

SECOND BASEMEN

Leader, Team	Pct.	G	PO	A	E	TC	DP
REED, Los Angeles	.993	132	280	413	5	698	76

Player, Team	Pct.	G	PO	A	E	TC	DP
Alicea, St. Louis	.978	96	202	280	11	493	61
Arias, Florida	.987	30	59	88	2	149	15
Barberie, Florida	.982	97	201	303	9	513	62
Belliard, Atlanta	.987	24	26	50	1	77	7
Benavides, Colorado	.986	19	30	39	1	70	7
Benjamin, S.F.	.991	23	54	54	1	109	23
Biggio, Houston	.982	155	306	447	14	767	90
Bogar, New York	.963	6	13	13	1	27	6
Bournigal, L.A.	1.000	4	0	1	0	1	0
Branson, Cincinnati	.974	45	80	105	5	190	28
Brumfield, Cincinnati	.842	4	6	10	3	19	3
Candaele, Houston	1.000	19	15	19	0	34	3
Caraballo, Atlanta	1.000	5	4	3	0	7	0
Castellano, Colorado	1.000	4	10	7	0	17	2
Colbert, San Francisco	1.000	2	0	1	0	1	0
DeShields, Montreal	.983	123	243	381	11	635	74
Donnels, Houston	1.000	1	1	3	0	4	2
Duncan, Philadelphia	.969	65	109	168	9	286	29
Faries, San Francisco	1.000	7	12	18	0	30	3
Foley, Pittsburgh	.993	35	70	64	1	135	19
Frazier, Montreal	1.000	1	1	1	0	2	0
Garcia, Pittsburgh	.983	140	296	343	11	650	84
Gardner, San Diego	.983	133	213	294	9	516	48
Gutierrez, San Diego	1.000	6	1	14	0	15	0
Harris, Los Angeles	.987	35	56	92	2	150	11
Higgins, San Diego	.000	1	0	0	0	0	0
Jefferies, St. Louis	1.000	1	2	1	0	3	1
Johnson, S.F.	1.000	2	1	0	0	1	0
Jones, St. Louis	1.000	7	8	9	0	17	1
Kent, New York	.969	127	250	311	18	579	68
King, Pittsburgh	.900	2	3	6	1	10	2
Koelling, Cincinnati	.941	3	4	12	1	17	1
Lansing, Montreal	.956	25	35	52	4	91	11
Lemke, Atlanta	.982	150	329	442	14	785	100
Liriano, Colorado	.944	16	19	32	3	54	7
Lopez, San Diego	.983	15	23	34	1	58	5
McKnight, New York	.930	15	17	23	3	43	3
Mejia, Colorado	.963	65	126	184	12	322	38
Montoyo, Montreal	.000	3	0	0	0	0	0
Morandini, Phi.	.990	111	208	288	5	501	48
Oquendo, St. Louis	1.000	16	25	24	0	49	6
Parker, Houston	1.000	1	1	0	0	1	0
Pecota, Atlanta	1.000	4	5	1	0	6	1
Pena, St. Louis	.966	64	140	200	12	352	47
Polidor, Florida	.000	1	0	0	0	0	0
Ready, Montreal	.968	28	46	75	4	125	17
Reed, Los Angeles	.993	132	280	413	5	698	76
Renteria, Florida	.989	45	70	116	2	188	16
Roberts, Cincinnati	.984	64	136	172	5	313	31
Samuel, Cincinnati	.971	70	135	164	9	308	33
Sandberg, Chicago	.988	115	209	347	7	563	76
Saunders, New York	.956	22	36	50	4	90	18
Scarsone, S.F.	1.000	20	40	35	0	75	10
Sharperson, L.A.	.945	17	24	28	3	55	8
Shields, Chicago	1.000	7	6	12	0	18	3
Shipley, San Diego	.968	12	11	19	1	31	1
Teufel, San Diego	.990	52	85	117	2	204	22
Thompson, S.F.	.988	128	273	384	8	665	95
Vizcaino, Chicago	.986	34	66	76	2	144	23
Walker, New York	.976	24	40	43	2	85	8
Wehner, Pittsburgh	1.000	3	1	4	0	5	2
Yelding, Chicago	.984	32	48	76	2	126	14
Young, Colorado	.962	79	153	228	15	396	43

TRIPLE PLAYS: Garcia, Pittsburgh; Lansing, Montreal; Pena, St. Louis.

THIRD BASEMEN

Leader, Team	Pct.	G	PO	A	E	TC	DP
BUECHELE, Chicago	.975	129	79	232	8	319	24

Player, Team	Pct.	G	PO	A	E	TC	DP
Alicea, St. Louis	.000	1	0	0	0	0	0
Arias, Florida	.975	22	13	26	1	40	2
Batiste, Philadelphia	.956	58	24	41	3	68	2
Bell, San Diego	.820	19	12	29	9	50	3
Benavides, Colorado	1.000	5	0	6	0	6	0
Benjamin, S.F.	.936	16	10	34	3	47	3
Benzinger, S.F.	.000	1	0	0	0	0	0
Berry, Montreal	.936	96	66	153	15	234	13
Bogar, New York	1.000	7	4	11	0	15	2
Bolick, Montreal	.875	24	5	30	5	40	3
Bonilla, New York	.929	52	40	103	11	154	6
Branson, Cincinnati	.958	14	7	16	1	24	0
Brumley, Houston	.000	1	0	0	0	0	0
Buechele, Chicago	.975	129	79	232	8	319	24
Caminiti, Houston	.942	143	123	264	24	411	23
Candaele, Houston	1.000	4	0	1	0	1	0
Castellano, Colorado	.909	13	4	16	2	22	1
Cedeno, Houston	1.000	1	2	1	0	3	0
Cianfrocco, San Diego	.932	64	48	76	9	133	8
Clark, San Diego	1.000	5	2	6	0	8	1
Colbert, San Francisco	1.000	1	1	1	0	2	1
Cordero, Montreal	.625	2	2	3	3	8	0
Costo, Cincinnati	1.000	2	0	1	0	1	0
Donnels, Houston	.898	31	11	42	6	59	5
Faries, San Francisco	.000	1	0	0	1	1	0
Foley, Pittsburgh	.958	7	4	19	1	24	1
Gardner, San Diego	.000	1	0	0	1	1	0
Geren, San Diego	1.000	1	0	3	0	3	0
Greene, Cincinnati	1.000	5	2	9	0	11	0
Gutierrez, San Diego	1.000	4	2	5	0	7	0
Hansen, Los Angeles	.927	18	11	27	3	41	1
Harris, Los Angeles	.889	17	2	6	1	9	0
Hayes, Colorado	.954	154	123	292	20	435	22
Higgins, San Diego	1.000	4	1	1	0	2	0
Hollins, Philadelphia	.914	143	73	215	27	315	9
Huskey, New York	.923	13	9	27	3	39	2
Johnson, S.F.	1.000	1	0	1	0	1	0
Johnson, New York	.944	67	52	135	11	198	11
Kent, New York	.925	12	9	28	3	40	5
King, Pittsburgh	.964	156	105	353	17	475	28
Lansing, Montreal	.942	81	50	162	13	225	19
Liriano, Colorado	1.000	1	1	0	0	1	0
Magadan, Florida	.961	63	50	121	7	178	12
Manto, Philadelphia	1.000	6	2	7	0	9	0
McKnight, New York	.846	9	3	8	2	13	0
Millette, Philadelphia	1.000	3	0	4	0	4	0
Pecota, Atlanta	1.000	23	3	12	0	15	0
Pendleton, Atlanta	.959	161	128	319	19	466	32
Polidor, Florida	1.000	1	1	0	0	1	0
Ready, Montreal	1.000	3	2	9	0	11	0
Renteria, Florida	1.000	25	14	35	0	49	4
Roberts, Cincinnati	1.000	3	1	4	0	5	0
Royer, St. Louis	.857	10	3	15	3	21	1
Sabo, Cincinnati	.967	148	79	242	11	332	16
Samuel, Cincinnati	1.000	4	2	4	0	6	0
Saunders, New York	1.000	4	1	2	0	3	1
Scarsone, S.F.	.929	8	4	9	1	14	1
Sharperson, L.A.	.833	6	3	2	1	6	0
Sheaffer, Colorado	.000	1	0	0	0	0	0
Sheffield, S.D.-Fla.	.899	133	79	225	34	338	15
Shields, Chicago	1.000	7	2	9	0	11	1
Shipley, San Diego	.974	37	17	20	1	38	4
Snyder, Los Angeles	.884	23	12	26	5	43	3
Stillwell, San Diego	1.000	3	2	3	0	5	0
Tatum, Colorado	.800	6	3	1	1	5	1
Teufel, San Diego	1.000	9	3	5	0	8	0
Vizcaino, Chicago	.979	44	25	70	2	97	6
Walker, New York	.907	23	12	37	5	54	3
Wallach, Los Angeles	.958	130	112	228	15	355	14
Wehner, Pittsburgh	1.000	3	0	3	0	3	1

Player, Team	Pct.	G	PO	A	E	TC	DP
Williams, S.F.	.970	144	117	266	12	395	34
Woodson, St. Louis	.909	28	7	23	3	33	3
Yelding, Chicago	.923	7	3	9	1	13	1
Young, Pittsburgh	1.000	6	6	11	0	17	0
Zeile, St. Louis	.923	153	83	310	33	426	26

TRIPLE PLAY: Berry, Montreal.

THIRD BASEMEN WITH TWO OR MORE TEAMS

Player, Team	Pct.	G	PO	A	E	TC	DP
Sheffield, San Diego	.905	67	41	102	15	158	11
Sheffield, Florida	.894	66	38	123	19	180	4

SHORTSTOPS

Leader, Team	Pct.	G	PO	A	E	TC	DP
BELL, Pittsburgh	.986	154	256	527	11	794	100

Player, Team	Pct.	G	PO	A	E	TC	DP
Arias, Florida	.945	18	22	30	3	55	8
Baez, New York	.967	52	57	117	6	180	24
Batiste, Philadelphia	.943	24	48	67	7	122	13
Bell, Philadelphia	.909	22	33	57	9	99	11
Bell, Pittsburgh	.986	154	256	527	11	794	100
Belliard, Atlanta	1.000	58	27	49	0	76	11
Benavides, Colorado	.937	48	66	113	12	191	19
Benjamin, S.F.	.982	23	10	45	1	56	7
Blauser, Atlanta	.970	161	189	426	19	634	86
Bogar, New York	.972	66	88	193	8	289	34
Bournigal, L.A.	1.000	4	5	13	0	18	3
Branson, Cincinnati	.978	59	88	138	5	231	28
Brumley, Houston	1.000	1	0	1	0	1	0
Candaele, Houston	.933	14	9	19	2	30	1
Castellano, Colorado	1.000	5	4	5	0	9	1
Castilla, Colorado	.975	104	141	282	11	434	67
Cedeno, Houston	.955	149	153	375	25	553	78
Clayton, S.F.	.963	153	251	449	27	727	103
Cordero, Montreal	.941	134	161	370	33	564	61
Cromer, St. Louis	.912	9	13	18	3	34	3
Duncan, Philadelphia	.945	59	71	136	12	219	21
Dunston, Chicago	1.000	2	5	0	0	5	0
Faries, San Francisco	1.000	4	3	5	0	8	0
Fernandez, New York	.975	48	83	150	6	239	28
Foley, Pittsburgh	.935	6	11	18	2	31	6
Garcia, Pittsburgh	1.000	3	3	4	0	7	3
Gardner, San Diego	1.000	1	1	0	0	1	0
Greene, Cincinnati	.978	10	17	28	1	46	8
Gutierrez, San Diego	.971	117	190	286	14	490	55
Harris, Los Angeles	1.000	3	2	1	0	3	0
Hayes, Colorado	.000	1	0	0	0	0	0
Johnson, S.F.	.000	1	0	0	0	0	0
Jones, Atlanta	1.000	3	1	1	0	2	0
Jones, St. Louis	.976	21	26	54	2	82	8
Kent, New York	.800	2	2	2	1	5	0
Kessinger, Cincinnati	.935	11	7	22	2	31	5
King, Pittsburgh	1.000	2	0	3	0	3	0
Koelling, Cincinnati	1.000	2	2	0	0	2	0
Lansing, Montreal	.961	51	51	122	7	180	23
Larkin, Cincinnati	.965	99	159	281	16	456	56
Liriano, Colorado	.975	35	45	71	3	119	13
Manto, Philadelphia	1.000	1	0	1	0	1	0
McKnight, New York	.943	29	31	52	5	88	11
Millette, Phi.	1.000	7	3	14	0	17	1
Navarro, New York	1.000	2	8	7	0	15	0
Offerman, L.A.	.950	158	250	454	37	741	95
Oquendo, St. Louis	.988	22	27	58	1	86	9
Parker, Houston	.000	1	0	0	0	0	0
Roberts, Cincinnati	.000	1	0	0	0	0	0
Sanchez, Chicago	.969	98	158	316	15	489	60
Saunders, New York	.000	1	0	0	0	0	0
Sharperson, L.A.	.909	3	2	8	1	11	1
Shipley, San Diego	.964	38	50	82	5	137	10
O. Smith, St. Louis	.974	134	251	451	19	721	98

Player, Team	Pct.	G	PO	A	E	TC	DP
Snyder, Los Angeles	1.000	2	4	3	0	7	3
Stillwell, San Diego	.921	30	45	60	9	114	12
Stocker, Philadelphia	.958	70	118	202	14	334	44
Uribe, Houston	.944	41	34	51	5	90	20
Vizcaino, Chicago	.968	81	126	264	13	403	43
Weiss, Florida	.977	153	229	406	15	650	80
Womack, Pittsburgh	.971	6	11	22	1	34	6
Yelding, Chicago	.500	1	0	1	1	2	0

TRIPLE PLAYS: Bell, Pittsburgh; Cordero, Montreal; O. Smith, St. Louis.

OUTFIELDERS

Leader, Team	Pct.	G	PO	A	E	TC	DP
BUTLER, L.A.*	1.000	155	369	6	0	375	0

Player, Team	Pct.	G	PO	A	E	TC	DP
Alicea, St. Louis	1.000	4	8	1	0	9	0
Alou, Montreal	.985	136	254	11	4	269	2
Amaro, Philadelphia	.963	16	25	1	1	27	1
Anthony, Houston*	.988	131	233	6	3	242	0
Ashley, Los Angeles	1.000	11	11	3	0	14	0
Aude, Pittsburgh	.000	1	0	0	1	1	0
Bass, Houston	.989	64	83	3	1	87	0
Bean, San Diego*	.987	54	71	6	1	78	0
Bell, San Diego	.976	125	322	8	8	338	4
Benzinger, S.F.	1.000	7	10	0	0	10	0
Berroa, Florida	.833	9	9	1	2	12	0
Bichette, Colorado	.973	137	308	14	9	331	3
Bonds, S.F.*	.984	157	310	7	5	322	0
Bonilla, New York	.969	85	148	8	5	161	1
Boston, Colorado*	.985	79	124	5	2	131	1
Brewer, St. Louis*	.960	33	47	1	2	50	0
Briley, Florida	.986	67	71	2	1	74	0
Brooks, Los Angeles	.000	2	0	0	0	0	0
Brown, San Diego	.982	43	109	2	2	113	0
Brumfield, Cincinnati	.978	96	172	6	4	182	1
Brumley, Houston	1.000	1	1	0	0	1	0
Bullett, Pittsburgh*	1.000	19	35	1	0	36	0
Burnitz, New York	.977	79	165	6	4	175	2
Butler, Los Angeles*	1.000	155	369	6	0	375	0
Candaele, Houston	.958	17	22	1	1	24	0
Canseco, St. Louis	.500	5	1	0	1	2	0
Carr, Florida	.985	139	393	7	6	406	2
Carreon, S.F.*	.943	41	48	2	3	53	0
Carrillo, Florida*	1.000	16	21	0	0	21	0
Chamberlain, Phi.	.993	76	131	10	1	142	3
Clark, Pittsburgh	.957	91	132	3	6	141	1
Clark, Colorado	.966	96	192	7	7	206	1
Clark, San Diego	.963	36	74	5	3	82	0
Cole, Colorado*	.982	93	219	5	4	228	1
Coleman, New York	.982	90	162	5	3	170	1
Conine, Florida	.992	147	252	11	2	265	0
Costo, Cincinnati	.980	26	49	1	1	51	0
Cotto, Florida	.977	46	85	1	2	88	0
Cummings, Pittsburgh	1.000	11	21	0	0	21	0
Daugherty, Hou.-Cin.*	.923	17	12	0	1	13	0
Davis, Los Angeles	.991	103	221	7	2	230	2
Dykstra, Phi.*	.979	160	469	2	10	481	0
Eisenreich, Phi.*	.996	137	218	6	1	225	0
Espy, Cincinnati	.931	18	25	2	2	29	0
Everett, Florida	.857	8	6	0	1	7	0
Faneyte, S.F.	1.000	6	10	0	0	10	0
Fariss, Florida	1.000	8	13	0	0	13	0
Felix, Florida	.940	52	91	3	6	100	0
Finley, Houston*	.988	140	329	12	4	345	4
Frazier, Montreal	.986	60	70	3	1	74	0
Gallagher, New York	1.000	72	117	6	0	123	0
Gant, Atlanta	.962	155	271	5	11	287	1
Gilkey, St. Louis	.969	134	227	19	8	254	2
Gonzalez, Houston	.978	149	347	10	8	365	2
Goodwin, Los Angeles	1.000	12	8	0	0	8	0
Gordon, Cincinnati	1.000	2	2	0	0	2	0

Player, Team	Pct.	G	PO	A	E	TC	DP
Gregg, Cincinnati*	1.000	4	2	0	0	2	0
Grissom, Montreal	.984	157	416	8	7	431	3
Gutierrez, San Diego....	1.000	5	1	0	0	1	0
Gwynn, San Diego*	.981	121	244	8	5	257	2
Harris, Los Angeles	1.000	2	1	0	0	1	0
Hernandez, Cincinnati.	.970	23	30	2	1	33	0
Higgins, San Diego	.000	3	0	0	0	0	0
Hill, Chicago	.957	21	42	2	2	46	1
Hosey, San Francisco .	.000	1	0	0	0	0	0
Housie, New York	.000	2	0	0	0	0	0
Howard, Cincinnati.....	.987	37	73	4	1	78	1
Hughes, Cincinnati*	.000	2	0	0	0	0	0
Hunter, Atlanta*	1.000	2	4	0	0	4	0
Incaviglia, Phi	.971	97	164	4	5	173	1
Jackson, New York	1.000	26	51	4	0	55	2
James, Houston	.958	34	65	4	3	72	1
Jones, Colorado	.983	70	114	2	2	118	0
Jordan, St. Louis	.973	65	140	4	4	148	0
Justice, Atlanta*	.985	157	323	9	5	337	2
Kelly, Cincinnati	.995	77	198	3	1	202	1
Klesko, Atlanta*	.000	2	0	0	0	0	0
Landrum, New York	.000	3	0	0	0	0	0
Lankford, St. Louis*	.978	121	312	6	7	325	0
Lewis, San Francisco..	1.000	131	344	4	0	348	3
Longmire, Phi.	1.000	2	4	0	0	4	0
Maclin, St. Louis*	1.000	5	3	0	0	3	0
Maldonado, Chicago ...	.914	41	50	3	5	58	2
Martin, Pittsburgh*	.975	136	268	6	7	281	0
Martinez, S.F.*	.993	73	131	6	1	138	2
May, Chicago	.970	122	220	8	7	235	1
McClendon, Pit.	.967	61	84	3	3	90	1
McGee, San Francisco	.979	126	224	9	5	238	1
McIntosh, Montreal	1.000	7	3	0	0	3	0
Merced, Pittsburgh	.965	109	209	11	8	228	5
Mercedes, S.F.	1.000	5	5	0	0	5	0
Milligan, Cincinnati	.833	9	9	1	2	12	0
Mitchell, Cincinnati	.957	87	149	7	7	163	2
Mondesi, Los Angeles .	.951	40	55	3	3	61	1
Murphy, Colorado	1.000	13	16	1	0	17	0
Nieves, San Diego	.931	15	27	0	2	29	0
Nixon, Atlanta	.990	116	308	4	3	315	1
Oliver, Cincinnati	.000	1	0	0	0	0	0
Orsulak, New York*	.978	114	215	9	5	229	1
Pappas, St. Louis	1.000	16	37	0	0	37	0
Parker, Houston	1.000	16	17	0	0	17	0
Pecota, Atlanta	1.000	1	1	0	0	1	0
Pennyfeather, Pit	1.000	17	21	0	0	21	0
Perry, St. Louis	1.000	1	2	0	0	2	0
Plantier, S.D.	.990	134	272	14	3	289	3
Pose, Florida	1.000	10	14	0	0	14	0
Pride, Montreal	1.000	2	2	0	0	2	0
Renteria, Florida	.000	1	0	0	0	0	0
Rhodes, Hou.-Chi.*	.971	18	33	1	1	35	0
Roberson, Chicago	.963	51	77	2	3	82	0
Roberts, Cincinnati	.938	11	15	0	1	16	0
Rodriguez, L.A.*	.984	48	57	3	1	61	0
Samuel, Cincinnati	.800	3	3	1	1	5	0
Sanders, Atlanta*	.986	60	137	1	2	140	1
Sanders, Cincinnati	.975	137	312	3	8	323	0
Santiago, Florida	.000	1	0	0	0	0	0
Sharperson, L.A.	.000	1	0	0	0	0	0
Sheaffer, Colorado	.000	2	0	0	0	0	0
Shelton, Pittsburgh*	.889	6	7	1	1	9	0
Sherman, San Diego*	1.000	26	47	0	0	47	0
Shields, Chicago	.000	1	0	0	0	0	0
Shipley, San Diego	1.000	5	6	0	0	6	0
Siddall, Montreal	.000	1	0	0	0	0	0
Smith, Chicago	.955	89	163	5	8	176	2
L. Smith, Pit.	.981	60	104	1	2	107	0
Snyder, L.A.	.979	115	172	14	4	190	1
Sosa, Chicago	.976	158	344	17	9	370	4
Stairs, Montreal	1.000	1	1	0	0	1	0
Strawberry, L.A.*	.905	29	37	1	4	42	0
Tarasco, Atlanta	1.000	12	11	0	0	11	0
Tatum, Colorado	1.000	3	1	0	0	1	0

Player, Team	Pct.	G	PO	A	E	TC	DP
Thompson, Phi	.994	106	162	6	1	169	1
Thompson, New York..	.987	76	228	4	3	235	0
Tomberlin, Pit.*	1.000	7	9	1	0	10	0
Tubbs, Cincinnati	.975	21	38	1	1	40	0
Van Slyke, Pit.	.995	78	205	2	1	208	1
Vander Wal, Mon.*	.972	38	34	1	1	36	0
Varsho, Cincinnati	1.000	22	27	1	0	28	1
Velasquez, San Diego..	1.000	6	4	0	0	4	0
Walker, New York	.947	15	16	2	1	19	0
Walker, Montreal	.979	132	273	13	6	292	2
Webster, L.A.*	.950	56	75	1	4	80	0
Wehner, Pittsburgh	1.000	13	16	1	0	17	0
R. White, Montreal	1.000	21	33	0	0	33	0
Whiten, St. Louis	.971	148	329	9	10	348	1
Whitmore, Florida	.979	69	140	3	3	146	1
Wilson, Pittsburgh	.875	5	5	2	1	8	0
Wilson, Florida*	1.000	3	4	0	0	4	0
Wilson, Chicago	.991	82	109	1	1	111	0
Wood, Montreal*	1.000	8	16	0	0	16	0
Yelding, Chicago	1.000	1	1	0	0	1	0
E. Young, Colorado	.972	52	101	2	3	106	1
G. Young, Colorado	.882	11	15	0	2	17	0
Zambrano, Chicago	1.000	4	1	0	0	1	0

OUTFIELDERS WITH TWO OR MORE TEAMS

Player, Team	Pct.	G	PO	A	E	TC	DP
Daugherty, Houston* ..	1.000	1	1	0	0	1	0
Daugherty, Cin.*	.917	16	11	0	1	12	0
Rhodes, Houston*	1.000	4	2	0	0	2	0
Rhodes, Chicago*	.970	14	31	1	1	33	0

CATCHERS

Leader, Team	Pct.	G	PO	A	E	TC	DP	PB
MANWARING, S.F..	.998	130	739	70	2	811	12	11

Player, Team	Pct.	G	PO	A	E	TC	DP	PB
Allanson, S.F.	1.000	8	30	0	0	30	0	0
Ausmus, S.D.	.975	49	272	34	8	314	5	2
Berryhill, Atlanta..	.990	105	570	52	6	628	2	6
Cabrera, Atlanta...	1.000	2	4	0	0	4	0	0
Clark, San Diego ..	.964	11	23	4	1	28	1	0
Colbert, S.F.	.982	10	51	3	1	55	0	0
Daulton, Phi.	.991	146	981	67	9	1057	19	12
Decker, Florida	.968	5	28	2	1	31	0	0
Dorsett, Cin.	1.000	18	111	5	0	116	0	0
Fletcher, Montreal	.988	127	620	41	8	669	3	4
Geren, San Diego ..	.993	49	251	26	2	279	6	4
Girardi, Colorado...	.989	84	478	46	6	530	7	2
Goff, Pittsburgh ...	.984	14	54	7	1	62	1	2
Hernandez, L.A....	.966	43	181	15	7	203	1	1
Higgins, S.D.	.983	59	308	31	6	345	1	10
Hundley, N.Y.	.988	123	592	63	8	663	6	4
LaValliere, Pit.	1.000	1	12	0	0	12	0	1
Lake, Chicago	.985	41	168	27	3	198	1	2
Laker, Montreal	.987	43	136	18	2	156	2	9
Lindsey, Phi.	1.000	2	3	0	0	3	0	1
Lopez, Atlanta	.975	7	37	2	1	40	0	1
Lyden, Florida	1.000	2	4	0	0	4	0	0
Manwaring, S.F.	.998	130	739	70	2	811	12	11
McGriff, Florida	1.000	3	12	0	0	12	0	0
McIntosh, Mon.....	1.000	5	5	1	0	6	0	0
McKnight, N.Y.....	.000	1	0	0	0	0	0	0
McNamara, S.F.....	1.000	4	12	0	0	12	0	0
Natal, Florida	1.000	38	196	18	0	214	2	6
O'Brien, N.Y.	.986	65	325	39	5	369	5	0
Oliver, Cin.	.992	133	791	68	7	866	8	11
Olson, Atlanta	.988	81	445	35	6	486	6	6
Owens, Colorado...	.957	32	138	19	7	164	3	3
Pagnozzi, St.L.	.991	92	421	44	4	469	4	9
Pappas, St.L.	.982	63	294	32	6	332	5	3
Piazza, L.A.	.989	146	899	98	11	1008	10	14
Pratt, Phi.	.989	26	169	7	2	178	3	0
Prince, Pit.	.984	59	271	31	5	307	6	6
Reed, S.F.	1.000	37	180	14	0	194	4	4

Leader, Team	Pct.	G	PO	A	E	TC	DP	PB
Ronan, St. Louis ...	1.000	6	29	0	0	29	0	1
Santiago, Florida..	.987	136	740	64	11	815	4	23
Servais, Houston ..	.996	82	493	40	2	535	9	4
Sheaffer, Col.	.994	65	331	28	2	361	5	6
Siddall, Montreal ..	1.000	15	33	5	0	38	0	1
Slaught, Pit.	.993	105	539	51	4	594	10	10
Spehr, Montreal	.954	49	166	22	9	197	3	0
Taubensee, Hou....	.992	90	551	41	5	597	5	3
Tucker, Houston ...	1.000	8	56	3	0	59	0	0
Villanueva, St.L....	1.000	17	86	3	0	89	0	1
Walbeck, Chicago..	1.000	11	49	2	0	51	0	1
Walters, S.D.........	.970	26	138	21	5	164	1	4
Wedge, Colorado ..	1.000	1	6	1	0	7	0	0
Wilkins, Chicago ...	.996	133	717	89	3	809	9	11
Wilson, Cincinnati	.994	35	146	9	1	156	2	1

PITCHERS

Leader, Team	Pct.	G	PO	A	E	TC	DP
TEWKSBURY, St.L.	1.000	32	19	46	0	65	2

Player, Team	Pct.	G	PO	A	E	TC	DP
Agosto, Houston *......	.000	6	0	0	0	0	0
Aldred, Col.-Mon.* ...	1.000	8	0	2	0	2	0
Andersen, Phi.	.875	64	3	4	1	8	1
Anderson, Cincinnati ...	1.000	3	0	1	0	1	0
Aquino, Florida	.976	38	10	30	1	41	5
Armstrong, Florida	.953	36	13	28	2	43	1
Arocha, St. Louis	.902	32	9	28	4	41	3
Ashby, Col.-S.D.	1.000	32	15	19	0	34	1
Assenmacher, Chi.*	1.000	46	1	3	0	4	1
Astacio, Los Angeles...	.952	31	23	17	2	42	1
Avery, Atlanta *	1.000	35	4	47	0	51	2
Ayala, Cincinnati	.786	43	12	10	6	28	1
Ayrault, Philadelphia ..	1.000	10	0	1	0	1	0
Ballard, Pittsburgh*...	.941	25	4	12	1	17	3
Barnes, Montreal*......	1.000	52	3	15	0	18	1
Batchelor, St. Louis...	1.000	9	1	1	0	2	0
Bautista, Chicago.......	.941	58	14	18	2	34	2
Beck, San Francisco ...	.889	76	0	8	1	9	1
Bedrosian, Atlanta	1.000	49	3	5	0	8	0
Belcher, Cincinnati......	.923	22	13	11	2	26	0
Belinda, Pittsburgh	1.000	40	4	4	0	8	0
Bell, Houston*	.000	10	0	0	0	0	0
Benes, San Diego........	.969	34	17	14	1	32	2
Black, San Francisco*	.926	16	3	22	2	27	2
Blair, Colorado..........	1.000	46	9	16	0	25	0
Borbon, Atlanta*	.000	3	0	0	0	0	0
Boskie, Chicago..........	.889	39	3	5	1	9	0
Bottenfield, Mon.-Col..	.953	37	9	32	2	43	5
Boucher, Montreal*......	1.000	5	1	4	0	5	0
Bowen, Florida..........	.939	27	7	24	2	33	0
Brantley, S.F.............	.882	53	6	9	2	17	0
Brennan, Chicago.......	1.000	8	2	2	0	4	0
Brewer, St. Louis*	.000	1	0	0	0	0	0
Brink, Philadelphia	.000	2	0	0	1	1	0
Brocail, San Diego	.933	24	8	20	2	30	1
Bross, San Francisco..	.000	2	0	0	0	0	0
Browning, Cincinnati*	1.000	21	10	21	0	31	2
Brummett, S.F.............	1.000	8	4	6	0	10	0
Bullinger, Chicago.......	1.000	15	1	1	0	2	0
Burba, San Francisco .	.950	54	7	12	1	20	0
Burkett, S.F................	1.000	34	21	36	0	57	2
Burns, St. Louis	1.000	24	1	2	0	3	0
Bushing, Cincinnati......	.000	6	0	0	0	0	0
Cadaret, Cincinnati* ...	1.000	34	2	4	0	6	0
Candelaria, Pit.*........	.000	24	0	0	0	0	0
Candiotti, Los Angeles	.930	33	10	30	3	43	3
Carpenter, Florida	1.000	29	2	8	0	10	1
Castillo, Chicago	.976	29	7	34	1	42	1
Cooke, Pittsburgh*......	.909	32	7	23	3	33	0
Cormier, St. Louis*......	.921	38	8	27	3	38	2
Corsi, Florida	1.000	15	1	4	0	5	0
Daal, Los Angeles*......	1.000	47	5	6	0	11	0
Davis, Phi.-S.D.*	.846	60	3	8	2	13	1

Player, Team	Pct.	G	PO	A	E	TC	DP
DeLeon, Philadelphia ..	1.000	24	2	3	0	5	0
Deshaies, S.F.*	1.000	5	0	3	0	3	0
DeSilva, Los Angeles...	.000	3	0	0	0	0	0
Dewey, Pittsburgh.......	1.000	21	2	6	0	8	0
Dibble, Cincinnati	1.000	45	5	4	0	9	2
Dixon, St. Louis*	1.000	4	0	1	0	1	0
Drabek, Houston.........	1.000	34	19	32	0	51	2
Draper, New York	.909	29	2	8	1	11	0
Edens, Houston	.929	38	3	10	1	14	0
Eiland, San Diego	.923	10	4	8	1	13	2
Ettles, San Diego	1.000	14	0	4	0	4	0
Fassero, Montreal*	.900	56	5	22	3	30	0
Fernandez, New York*	1.000	18	2	10	0	12	1
Fletcher, Philadelphia .	1.000	1	0	0	0	0	0
Foster, Philadelphia .	1.000	2	1	0	0	1	0
Foster, Cincinnati.......	1.000	17	0	2	0	2	0
Franco, New York*......	1.000	35	3	9	0	12	0
Fredrickson, Colorado.	1.000	25	4	1	0	5	0
Freeman, Atlanta	1.000	21	1	0	0	1	0
Gardiner, Montreal	1.000	24	1	5	0	6	0
Gibson, New York*	1.000	8	0	1	0	1	0
Glavine, Atlanta*.........	.964	36	17	36	2	55	4
Gomez, San Diego*......	.750	27	0	3	1	4	0
Gooden, New York	.956	29	19	24	2	45	1
Gott, Los Angeles	1.000	62	8	8	0	16	1
Gozzo, New York.........	.000	10	0	0	0	0	0
Grant, Hou.-Col...........	1.000	20	1	6	0	7	1
Green, Philadelphia	.000	3	0	0	1	1	0
Greene, Philadelphia ...	.966	31	5	23	1	29	3
Greer, New York........	.000	1	0	0	0	0	0
Ke. Gross, L.A............	1.000	33	11	40	0	51	1
Kip Gross, L.A............	1.000	10	0	3	0	3	0
Guetterman, St.L.*	.714	40	1	4	2	7	0
Guzman, Chicago	.889	30	12	28	5	45	1
Hammond, Florida*......	.909	32	8	32	4	44	1
Harkey, Chicago	.853	28	9	20	5	34	2
Harnisch, Houston	.900	33	3	15	2	20	0
Harris, San Diego	1.000	59	5	10	0	15	0
Harris, S.D.-Col.	.947	35	17	37	3	57	3
Harvey, Florida............	1.000	59	3	5	0	8	0
Henry, Col.-Mon.*	.944	30	5	12	1	18	1
Henry, Cincinnati.........	1.000	3	1	0	0	1	0
Heredia, Montreal	1.000	20	4	11	0	15	1
Hernandez, San Diego .	1.000	21	0	6	0	6	0
Hernandez, Houston.....	1.000	72	1	8	0	9	0
Hershiser, L.A.............	.955	33	20	43	3	66	1
Hibbard, Chicago*.......	1.000	31	6	26	0	32	2
Hickerson, S.F.*	.941	47	4	12	1	17	0
Hill, Montreal	.984	28	24	38	1	63	2
Hill, Atlanta	.800	19	4	0	1	5	0
Hillman, New York*......	.889	27	11	21	4	36	1
Hoffman, Fla.-S.D........	1.000	67	6	11	0	17	0
Holmes, Colorado........	.929	62	7	6	1	14	1
Hope, Pittsburgh	.917	7	1	10	1	12	0
Hough, Florida	.979	34	6	41	1	48	1
Howell, Atlanta	1.000	54	4	7	0	11	0
Hurst, S.D.-Col.*	1.000	5	0	4	0	4	0
Innis, New York	1.000	67	7	13	0	20	1
Jackson, Phi.*	.892	32	7	26	4	37	3
Jackson, S.F.	.941	81	3	13	1	17	0
Johnston, Pit.	1.000	33	4	5	0	9	0
Johnstone, Florida	1.000	7	1	1	0	2	0
Jones, New York	1.000	9	5	8	0	13	0
D. Jones, Houston.......	.933	71	2	12	1	15	0
Jones, Montreal	1.000	12	4	4	0	8	1
T. Jones, Houston........	1.000	27	4	2	0	6	0
Juden, Houston...........	.000	2	0	0	0	0	0
Kaiser, Cin.-N.Y.*	1.000	9	0	1	0	1	0
Kile, Houston	.889	32	9	15	3	27	0
Kilgus, St. Louis*	1.000	22	4	3	0	7	0
Klink, Florida*	1.000	59	3	2	0	5	0
Knudson, Colorado......	.500	4	0	1	1	2	0
Lancaster, St. Louis.....	1.000	50	3	6	0	9	0
Landrum, Cincinnati ...	1.000	18	1	6	0	7	1
Layana, S.F.................	1.000	1	0	1	0	1	0
Leskanic, Colorado......	.909	18	5	5	1	11	2

Player, Team	Pct.	G	PO	A	E	TC	DP
Lewis, Florida	.941	57	3	13	1	17	1
Looney, Montreal*	1.000	3	0	1	0	1	0
Luebbers, Cincinnati	.857	14	4	8	2	14	1
Maddux, Atlanta	.933	36	39	59	7	105	5
Maddux, New York	.957	58	6	16	1	23	1
Magrane, St. Louis*	.964	22	8	19	1	28	1
Manzanillo, New York	.000	6	0	0	0	0	0
Martinez, Montreal	.984	35	17	46	1	64	1
P. Martinez, L.A.	1.000	65	4	4	0	8	1
Martinez, San Diego*	.857	32	2	4	1	7	0
R. Martinez, L.A.	1.000	32	28	31	0	59	4
Mason, S.D.-Phi.	1.000	68	2	8	0	10	0
Mauser, Phi.-S.D.	.944	36	6	11	1	18	2
McClure, Florida*	1.000	14	0	1	0	1	0
McDowell, L.A.	.921	54	11	24	3	38	3
McElroy, Chicago*	1.000	49	3	5	0	8	1
McMichael, Atlanta	.962	74	7	18	1	26	2
Menendez, Pittsburgh	.750	14	1	2	1	4	0
Mercker, Atlanta*	.833	43	1	4	1	6	0
Miceli, Pittsburgh	.000	9	0	0	0	0	0
Miller, Pittsburgh	.500	3	0	1	1	2	0
Minor, Pittsburgh	1.000	65	8	15	0	23	0
Minutelli, S.F.*	1.000	9	0	1	0	1	0
Moeller, Pittsburgh*	1.000	10	2	2	0	4	0
Moore, Colorado	.333	27	0	1	2	3	0
Morgan, Chicago	.978	32	11	33	1	45	3
Mulholland, Phi.*	.941	29	5	27	2	34	1
Munoz, Colorado*	1.000	21	1	4	0	5	0
Murphy, St. Louis*	.917	73	3	8	1	12	1
Myers, St. Louis*	1.000	73	1	7	0	8	0
Nabholz, Montreal*	1.000	26	6	17	0	23	1
Neagle, Pittsburgh*	1.000	50	1	5	0	6	0
Nen, Florida	1.000	15	1	4	0	5	1
Nichols, L.A.	1.000	4	1	2	0	3	1
Nied, Colorado	1.000	16	4	16	0	20	0
Olivares, St. Louis	.918	58	9	36	4	49	3
Osborne, St. Louis*	1.000	26	8	24	0	32	1
Osuna, Houston*	.667	44	0	2	1	3	0
Otto, Pittsburgh*	1.000	28	4	13	0	17	1
Painter, Colorado*	1.000	10	1	9	0	10	0
Pall, Philadelphia	1.000	8	1	2	0	3	0
Parrett, Colorado	.923	40	3	9	1	13	0
Perez, St. Louis	1.000	65	2	12	0	14	2
Petkovsek, Pit.	1.000	26	0	10	0	10	0
Plesac, Chicago*	.900	57	0	9	1	10	2
Portugal, Houston	.961	33	21	28	2	51	2
Powell, Cincinnati*	.667	9	0	2	1	3	0
Pugh, Cincinnati	.970	31	9	23	1	33	1
Rapp, Florida	.952	16	5	15	1	21	0
Reardon, Cincinnati	.833	58	4	6	2	12	0
Reed, Colorado	.944	64	3	14	1	18	1
Reynolds, Houston	1.000	5	0	1	0	1	0
Reynoso, Colorado	.895	30	16	35	6	57	5
Righetti, S.F.*	1.000	51	2	5	0	7	0
Rijo, Cincinnati	1.000	36	27	35	0	62	8
Risley, Montreal	1.000	2	1	0	0	1	0
Rivera, Philadelphia	.957	30	8	14	1	23	1
Robertson, Pit.*	.000	9	0	0	0	0	0
Rodriguez, S.D.-Fla.*	.941	70	6	10	1	17	2
Rogers, S.F.*	.900	64	2	7	1	10	1
Rojas, Montreal	1.000	66	7	9	0	16	1
Roper, Cincinnati	1.000	16	7	8	0	15	0
Rueter, Montreal*	.963	14	7	19	1	27	4
Ruffin, Colorado*	.958	59	7	16	1	24	3
Ruffin, Cincinnati	1.000	21	4	5	0	9	0
Ruskin, Cincinnati*	.000	4	0	0	0	0	0
Saberhagen, New York	.957	19	14	30	2	46	0
Sanders, San Diego	1.000	9	3	2	0	5	0
Sanderson, S.F.	1.000	11	2	8	0	10	0
Sanford, Colorado	.625	11	3	2	3	8	0
Scanlan, Chicago	1.000	70	3	6	0	9	0
Schilling, Phi.	1.000	34	6	36	0	42	1
Schourek, New York*	1.000	41	5	17	0	22	2
Scott, S.D.-Mon.	.917	56	3	8	1	12	1
Seanez, San Diego	1.000	3	0	1	0	1	0
Seminara, San Diego	.875	18	8	6	2	16	0

Player, Team	Pct.	G	PO	A	E	TC	DP
Service, Col.-Cin.	1.000	29	6	5	0	11	0
Shaw, Montreal	1.000	55	8	16	0	24	1
Shepherd, Colorado	.714	14	3	2	2	7	0
Shouse, Pittsburgh*	1.000	6	0	1	0	1	0
Slocumb, Chicago	1.000	10	2	2	0	4	1
Smiley, Cincinnati*	1.000	18	7	16	0	23	0
Smith, Colorado	1.000	11	2	8	0	10	1
L. Smith, St. Louis	1.000	55	0	1	0	1	0
Smith, Atlanta	1.000	20	7	14	0	21	0
Z. Smith, Pit.*	1.000	14	8	8	0	16	2
Smoltz, Atlanta	1.000	35	29	23	0	52	1
Spradlin, Cincinnati	1.000	37	2	2	0	4	0
Stanton, Atlanta*	.909	63	1	9	1	11	1
Swift, San Francisco	.910	34	17	44	6	67	3
Swindell, Houston*	.971	31	2	32	1	35	0
Tanana, New York*	.971	29	11	22	1	34	1
Taylor, San Diego	1.000	36	4	7	0	11	0
Telgheder, New York	1.000	24	4	9	0	13	0
Tewksbury, St. Louis	1.000	32	19	46	0	65	2
Thigpen, Phi.	1.000	17	0	3	0	3	1
Toliver, Pittsburgh	1.000	12	1	1	0	2	0
Tomlin, Pittsburgh*	.964	18	9	18	1	28	2
Torres, San Francisco	1.000	8	4	9	0	13	0
Trachsel, Chicago	1.000	3	1	5	0	6	0
Trlicek, Los Angeles	1.000	41	7	12	0	19	2
Turner, Florida	1.000	55	3	11	0	14	0
Urbani, St. Louis*	.933	18	2	12	1	15	1
Valdez, Montreal	.000	4	0	0	0	0	0
Wagner, Pittsburgh	1.000	44	9	13	0	22	3
Wakefield, Pit.	.852	24	8	15	4	27	2
Walk, Pittsburgh	.946	32	12	23	2	37	4
Walton, Montreal	1.000	4	1	1	0	2	0
Watson, St. Louis*	.929	16	3	10	1	14	1
Wayne, Colorado*	1.000	65	0	9	0	9	1
Weathers, Florida	1.000	14	5	3	0	8	0
Wendell, Chicago	1.000	7	7	1	0	8	0
West, Philadelphia*	.750	76	2	4	2	8	1
Weston, New York	1.000	4	0	1	0	1	0
Wetteland, Montreal	.667	70	1	5	3	9	0
Whitehurst, San Diego	.913	21	3	18	2	23	2
Wickander, Cin.*	1.000	33	0	3	0	3	0
Williams, Houston	.964	42	7	20	1	28	0
Mit. Williams, Phi.*	.714	65	2	3	2	7	0
Mike Williams, Phi.	1.000	17	2	6	0	8	1
Wilson, Los Angeles*	.857	25	2	4	1	7	0
Wilson, S.F.*	1.000	22	3	13	0	16	2
Wohlers, Atlanta	1.000	46	6	6	0	12	1
Worrell, Los Angeles	1.000	35	1	4	0	5	0
Worrell, San Diego	.944	21	6	11	1	18	0
Young, New York	.885	39	9	14	3	26	1
Young, Montreal	1.000	4	0	1	0	1	0

PITCHERS WITH TWO OR MORE TEAMS

Player, Team	Pct.	G	PO	A	E	TC	DP
Aldred, Colorado*	1.000	5	0	1	0	1	0
Aldred, Montreal*	1.000	3	0	1	0	1	0
Ashby, Colorado	1.000	20	5	12	0	17	0
Ashby, San Diego	1.000	12	10	7	0	17	1
Bottenfield, Montreal	.947	23	8	10	1	19	4
Bottenfield, Colorado	.958	14	1	22	1	24	1
Davis, Philadelphia*	1.000	25	0	3	0	3	0
Davis, San Diego*	.800	35	3	5	2	10	1
Grant, Houston	1.000	6	1	4	0	5	0
Grant, Colorado	1.000	14	0	2	0	2	1
Harris, San Diego	.973	22	13	23	1	37	3
Harris, Colorado	.900	13	4	14	2	20	0
Henry, Colorado*	.941	20	5	11	1	17	1
Henry, Montreal*	1.000	10	0	1	0	1	0
Hoffman, Florida	1.000	28	2	7	0	9	0
Hoffman, San Diego	1.000	39	4	4	0	8	0
Hurst, San Diego*	1.000	2	0	1	0	1	0
Hurst, Colorado*	1.000	3	0	3	0	3	0
Kaiser, Cincinnati*	.000	3	0	0	0	0	0
Kaiser, New York*	1.000	6	0	1	0	1	0
Mason, San Diego	1.000	34	2	6	0	8	0

Player, Team	Pct.	G	PO	A	E	TC	DP	Player, Team	Pct.	G	PO	A	E	TC	DP
Mason, Philadelphia....	1.000	34	0	2	0	2	0	Scott, San Diego..........	.875	24	1	6	1	8	0
Mauser, Phi.................	1.000	8	4	3	0	7	1	Scott, Montreal............	1.000	32	2	2	0	4	1
Mauser, San Diego	.909	28	2	8	1	11	1	Service, Colorado	1.000	3	3	1	0	4	0
Rodriguez, San Diego*	1.000	34	3	1	0	4	0	Service, Cincinnati	1.000	26	3	4	0	7	0
Rodriguez, Florida*	.923	36	3	9	1	13	2								

MISCELLANEOUS

Read across for wins, down for losses.

Team	Phi.	N.Y.	S.F.	Atl.	Hou.	Mon.	L.A.	St.L.	Pit.	Cin.	S.D.	Chi.	Fla.	Col.	W	L	Pct.
Philadelphia	..	2	0	1	1	0	2	0	0	1	0	2	1	1	11	2	.846
New York	0	..	1	0	0	0	1	2	0	0	0	1	2	1	8	4	.667
San Francisco	0	0	..	1	3	0	0	0	0	3	1	0	0	1	9	5	.643
Atlanta	0	0	1	..	0	1	4	1	2	3	2	1	0	1	16	9	.640
Houston	0	0	1	2	..	0	1	1	0	1	1	2	3	2	14	8	.636
Montreal	0	0	1	1	1	..	0	1	1	0	1	1	0	0	7	5	.583
Los Angeles	0	0	1	0	1	1	..	1	1	0	0	0	1	3	9	8	.529
St. Louis	1	0	0	1	0	2	0	..	0	0	1	0	1	1	7	8	.467
Pittsburgh	1	0	0	0	0	0	0	0	..	0	0	1	3	0	5	6	.455
Cincinnati	0	1	0	1	1	0	0	0	1	..	1	0	2	1	8	10	.444
San Diego	0	1	0	0	0	0	0	0	1	1	..	1	0	1	6	8	.429
Chicago	0	0	0	2	0	1	0	0	0	0	0	..	1	1	5	10	.333
Florida	0	0	0	0	0	0	0	2	0	1	1	1	..	0	5	14	.263
Colorado	0	0	0	0	0	0	0	0	0	0	0	0	0	..	0	13	.000
Lost	2	4	5	9	8	5	8	8	6	10	8	10	14	13	110	110	.500

Read across for home wins, down for road losses.

Team	Mon.	Phi.	Atl.	S.F.	St.L.	Hou.	Chi.	L.A.	Cin.	Pit.	Col.	Fla.	S.D.	N.Y.	W	L	Pct.
Montreal	..	4	2	3	4	4	5	4	4	5	5	4	6	5	55	26	.679
Philadelphia	5	..	3	2	6	3	3	5	4	4	4	6	3	4	52	29	.642
Atlanta	3	3	..	3	4	3	3	5	6	3	6	3	5	4	51	30	.630
San Francisco	6	4	3	..	1	4	3	2	6	3	4	4	6	4	50	31	.617
St. Louis	4	5	4	3	..	4	2	1	4	5	3	5	5	4	49	32	.605
Houston	3	2	2	1	4	..	4	4	4	3	2	5	4	6	44	37	.543
Chicago	3	3	2	3	4	2	..	4	3	3	5	4	3	4	43	38	.531
Los Angeles	4	1	3	3	1	2	3	..	4	5	3	3	5	4	41	40	.506
Cincinnati	2	2	2	1	3	3	3	3	..	5	7	4	5	2	41	40	.506
Pittsburgh	3	4	2	2	3	2	4	3	3	..	2	4	3	5	40	41	.494
Colorado	2	1	0	1	2	7	3	3	4	4	..	4	4	4	39	42	.481
Florida	3	3	2	2	2	2	5	2	3	4	3	..	3	1	35	46	.432
San Diego	2	3	2	2	6	3	1	3	2	0	5	2	..	3	34	47	.420
New York	2	1	1	2	3	1	2	2	2	2	4	4	2	..	28	53	.346
Lost on road	42	36	28	28	43	40	40	41	49	46	53	52	54	50	602	532	.531

Read across for road wins, down for home losses.

Team	S.F.	Atl.	Phi.	Hou.	Chi.	L.A.	Mon.	St.L.	Pit.	Cin.	N.Y.	Fla.	Col.	S.D.	W	L	Pct.
San Francisco	..	3	4	6	3	4	3	3	4	5	4	4	6	4	53	28	.654
Atlanta	4	..	3	5	4	3	4	2	4	4	5	4	7	4	53	28	.654
Philadelphia	2	3	..	4	3	5	2	2	3	4	6	3	5	3	45	36	.556
Houston	2	3	3	..	4	5	2	2	4	3	5	4	0	4	41	40	.506
Chicago	3	3	4	2	..	3	2	4	2	4	4	2	3	5	41	40	.506
Los Angeles	4	2	1	2	2	..	2	5	3	4	4	3	4	4	40	41	.494
Montreal	0	3	3	2	3	3	..	3	3	4	4	4	4	4	39	42	.481
St. Louis	5	2	0	2	3	5	2	..	4	3	4	4	0	4	38	43	.469
Pittsburgh	3	3	2	3	4	1	2	1	..	1	4	3	2	6	35	46	.432
Cincinnati	1	1	2	3	3	2	2	3	3	..	4	3	2	4	32	49	.395
New York	2	2	2	0	3	2	2	2	4	4	..	5	2	3	31	50	.383
Florida	2	3	1	1	2	3	2	2	2	2	3	..	2	4	29	52	.358
Colorado	2	0	2	4	1	4	1	3	4	0	2	3	..	2	28	53	.346
San Diego	1	2	3	2	3	1	0	1	3	2	4	2	3	..	27	54	.333
Lost at home	31	30	29	37	38	40	26	32	41	40	53	46	42	47	532	602	.469

ATLANTA—104-58

Pitcher	Chi. W-L	Cin. W-L	Col. W-L	Fla. W-L	Hou. W-L	L.A. W-L	Mon. W-L	N.Y. W-L	Phi. W-L	Pit. W-L	St.L. W-L	S.D. W-L	S.F. W-L	Totals W-L
Avery	1-1	2-0	1-0	0-1	2-0	1-0	2-1	1-0	1-1	2-0	0-1	2-1	3-0	18-6
Bedrosian	0-0	1-0	0-0	0-1	0-0	1-0	0-0	1-0	1-0	0-0	0-0	0-0	0-1	5-2
Freeman	1-0	0-0	1-0	0-0	0-0	0-0	0-0	0-0	0-0	0-0	0-0	0-0	0-0	2-0

Pitcher	Chi. W-L	Cin. W-L	Col. W-L	Fla. W-L	Hou. W-L	L.A. W-L	Mon. W-L	N.Y. W-L	Phi. W-L	Pit. W-L	St.L. W-L	S.D. W-L	S.F. W-L	Totals W-L
Glavine	2-0	3-1	2-0	0-1	2-0	2-2	2-0	2-0	1-1	3-0	1-0	1-0	1-1	22-6
Howell	1-0	0-0	0-0	0-0	0-1	0-1	0-0	1-0	1-0	0-1	0-0	0-0	0-0	3-3
Maddux	1-0	1-1	2-0	2-1	1-2	0-1	1-0	3-0	2-1	1-1	1-2	3-0	2-1	20-10
McMichael	0-0	0-1	1-0	0-0	0-0	0-0	0-0	0-0	0-1	0-1	0-0	1-0	0-0	2-3
Mercker	0-0	0-0	1-0	0-0	0-1	0-0	0-0	0-0	0-0	0-0	1-0	1-0	0-0	3-1
Smith	0-1	1-0	0-0	1-1	0-0	1-0	0-1	0-1	0-1	0-0	1-1	0-1	0-1	4-8
Smoltz	1-1	1-0	3-0	2-0	2-1	3-1	1-2	1-1	0-1	0-1	0-1	1-1	0-1	15-11
Stanton	0-1	1-0	0-0	1-0	1-0	0-0	0-1	0-1	0-0	0-1	1-1	0-1	0-0	4-6
Wohlers	0-1	0-0	2-0	1-0	0-0	0-0	1-0	0-0	0-0	0-0	1-0	0-0	1-1	6-2
Totals	7-5	10-3	13-0	7-5	8-5	8-5	7-5	9-3	6-6	7-5	6-6	9-4	7-6	104-58

No-decisions—Borbon.

CHICAGO—84-78

Pitcher	Atl. W-L	Cin. W-L	Col. W-L	Fla. W-L	Hou. W-L	L.A. W-L	Mon. W-L	N.Y. W-L	Phi. W-L	Pit. W-L	St.L. W-L	S.D. W-L	S.F. W-L	Totals W-L
Assenmacher	0-0	1-0	0-0	0-1	0-0	0-0	0-0	0-0	0-0	0-0	0-0	1-0	0-0	2-1
Bautista	0-0	1-0	1-0	0-0	0-0	1-1	1-1	2-0	0-1	1-0	2-0	0-0	1-0	10-3
Boskie	1-0	0-0	0-0	0-1	0-0	0-0	0-0	0-0	0-0	0-2	2-0	2-0	0-0	5-3
Brennan	0-0	0-0	0-0	1-0	0-0	0-0	0-0	0-1	0-0	0-0	0-0	1-0	0-0	2-1
Bullinger	0-0	0-0	0-0	1-0	0-0	0-0	0-0	0-0	0-0	0-0	0-0	0-0	0-0	1-0
Castillo	0-1	1-1	0-0	1-2	1-0	1-0	0-1	0-2	0-0	0-0	1-1	0-0	0-0	5-8
Guzman	1-2	2-0	1-0	1-0	0-2	1-0	1-1	1-1	2-1	1-0	0-2	1-1	0-0	12-10
Harkey	1-0	0-1	3-0	1-1	1-2	0-1	0-1	1-1	1-1	1-0	0-1	0-1	1-0	10-10
Hibbard	1-1	0-2	2-0	1-0	0-3	2-0	2-1	2-0	1-0	1-2	0-0	0-0	2-2	15-11
McElroy	0-0	0-0	0-0	0-0	0-0	0-0	0-0	0-0	1-0	0-0	0-0	1-0	0-1	2-2
Morgan	1-1	1-1	1-2	0-0	1-1	0-1	0-2	1-0	1-2	0-0	2-0	1-2	1-1	10-15
Myers	0-0	0-0	0-1	0-1	0-0	1-0	0-0	0-0	0-0	0-0	0-0	0-0	1-2	2-4
Plesac	0-1	0-0	0-0	0-0	0-0	0-0	1-0	0-0	0-0	0-0	0-0	0-0	0-0	2-1
Scanlan	0-1	0-0	0-0	0-0	1-0	1-2	0-1	1-0	0-1	1-0	0-0	0-0	0-0	4-5
Slocumb	0-0	1-0	0-0	0-0	0-0	0-0	0-0	0-0	0-0	0-0	0-0	0-0	0-0	1-0
Trachsel	0-0	0-0	0-0	0-1	0-0	0-0	0-0	0-0	0-0	0-1	0-0	0-0	0-0	0-2
Wendell	0-0	0-0	0-0	0-0	0-0	0-0	0-0	0-0	0-0	0-1	0-1	1-0	0-0	1-2
Totals	5-7	7-5	8-4	6-7	4-8	7-5	5-8	8-5	7-6	5-8	8-5	8-4	6-6	84-78

CINCINNATI—73-89

Pitcher	Atl. W-L	Chi. W-L	Col. W-L	Fla. W-L	Hou. W-L	L.A. W-L	Mon. W-L	N.Y. W-L	Phi. W-L	Pit. W-L	St.L. W-L	S.D. W-L	S.F. W-L	Totals W-L
Ayala	0-2	0-0	0-1	1-1	1-0	1-0	0-1	2-0	0-1	0-1	1-0	1-0	0-3	7-10
Belcher	2-0	1-2	0-0	1-1	0-0	0-1	0-0	0-0	0-1	2-0	1-0	1-0	1-1	9-6
Browning	0-0	1-0	0-0	2-1	1-1	1-0	0-0	0-1	1-1	0-0	0-1	1-1	0-1	7-7
Cadaret	1-0	0-0	0-0	0-0	0-0	0-0	1-0	0-0	0-1	0-0	0-0	0-0	0-0	2-1
Dibble	0-1	0-0	0-0	0-0	0-0	0-1	0-1	0-0	0-0	0-0	0-1	1-0	0-0	1-4
Foster	0-0	0-0	0-0	0-0	0-0	0-0	0-0	1-0	0-1	1-0	0-1	0-0	0-0	2-2
Henry	0-0	0-0	0-0	0-0	0-0	0-0	0-1	0-0	0-0	0-0	0-0	0-0	0-0	0-1
Hill	0-0	0-0	1-0	0-0	1-0	0-0	0-0	0-0	0-0	0-0	0-0	1-0	0-0	3-0
Landrum	0-0	0-0	0-0	0-0	0-0	0-1	0-0	0-0	0-0	0-0	0-0	0-0	0-1	0-2
Luebbers	0-0	1-1	0-1	0-1	0-0	0-0	0-0	0-1	0-0	1-0	0-1	0-0	0-0	2-5
Powell	0-0	0-0	0-0	0-0	0-1	0-0	0-1	0-0	0-0	0-0	0-0	0-1	0-0	0-3
Pugh	0-2	1-1	2-1	1-1	0-2	1-1	0-1	1-2	0-2	2-0	1-1	1-0	0-1	10-15
Reardon	0-0	0-0	1-0	0-0	1-0	1-0	1-0	0-0	1-0	0-1	1-1	0-1	0-0	4-6
Rijo	0-1	1-1	2-0	2-0	2-2	0-1	1-0	1-1	1-0	0-1	1-1	2-1	1-1	14-9
Roper	0-2	0-0	2-0	0-0	0-0	0-1	0-1	0-0	0-0	0-0	0-0	0-0	0-0	2-5
Ruffin	0-0	0-0	0-0	0-0	0-0	1-0	0-0	0-0	1-0	0-0	0-0	0-0	0-1	2-1
Service	0-1	0-0	0-0	0-0	0-0	0-0	0-0	0-1	1-0	1-0	0-0	0-0	0-0	2-2
Smiley	0-1	0-1	0-0	0-0	0-1	0-1	1-1	1-1	0-1	0-1	0-0	1-0	0-0	3-9
Spradlin	0-0	0-0	1-0	0-0	0-0	0-0	0-0	0-1	0-0	0-0	0-0	0-0	0-0	2-1
Wickander	0-0	0-0	1-0	0-0	0-0	0-0	0-0	0-0	0-0	0-0	0-0	0-0	0-0	1-0
Totals	3-10	5-7	9-4	7-5	6-7	5-8	4-8	6-6	4-8	8-4	5-7	9-4	2-11	73-89

No-decisions—Anderson, Bushing, Kaiser, Ruskin.

COLORADO—67-95

Pitcher	Atl. W-L	Chi. W-L	Cin. W-L	Fla. W-L	Hou. W-L	L.A. W-L	Mon. W-L	N.Y. W-L	Phi. W-L	Pit. W-L	St.L. W-L	S.D. W-L	S.F. W-L	Totals W-L
Ashby	0-0	0-0	0-1	0-1	0-0	0-0	0-0	0-0	0-1	0-0	0-1	0-0	0-0	0-4
Blair	0-0	1-2	0-1	1-0	0-0	1-2	0-0	0-0	1-2	0-1	0-0	2-1	0-1	6-10
Bottenfield	0-0	0-0	0-1	0-1	0-0	1-0	0-1	0-1	0-0	1-0	1-0	0-0	0-1	3-5
Fredrickson	0-1	0-0	0-0	0-0	0-0	0-0	0-0	0-0	0-0	0-0	0-0	0-0	0-0	0-1
Grant	0-0	0-0	0-1	0-0	0-0	0-0	0-0	0-0	0-0	0-0	0-0	0-0	0-0	0-1
Harris	0-1	0-0	0-2	0-0	0-1	0-0	0-1	1-1	0-0	0-0	0-0	0-1	0-1	1-8
Henry	0-0	1-0	0-0	1-0	0-0	0-1	0-2	0-0	0-1	0-0	0-1	0-1	0-2	2-8
Holmes	0-0	0-0	0-0	0-0	1-0	0-0	0-0	0-1	0-0	1-0	1-1	0-1	0-0	3-3
Hurst	0-0	0-0	0-0	0-0	0-0	0-0	0-1	0-0	0-0	0-0	0-0	0-0	0-0	0-1
Leskanic	0-1	0-1	0-1	1-1	0-0	0-0	0-0	0-0	0-0	0-0	0-0	0-0	0-1	1-5

Pitcher	Atl. W-L	Chi. W-L	Cin. W-L	Fla. W-L	Hou. W-L	L.A. W-L	Mon. W-L	N.Y. W-L	Phi. W-L	Pit. W-L	St.L. W-L	S.D. W-L	S.F. W-L	Totals W-L
Moore	0-0	0-0	0-0	0-0	0-0	0-0	0-1	0-0	1-0	1-0	1-0	0-0	0-0	3-1
Munoz	0-0	0-0	0-0	0-0	1-0	0-0	0-0	1-0	0-0	0-1	0-0	0-0	0-0	2-1
Nied	0-2	0-1	0-1	0-0	0-1	1-1	1-0	1-1	0-0	0-0	1-0	1-0	0-2	5-9
Painter	0-0	0-0	0-0	0-0	0-0	0-0	0-0	1-0	0-1	1-0	0-0	0-1	0-0	2-2
Parrett	0-1	1-1	1-0	0-0	1-0	0-0	0-0	0-0	0-0	0-1	0-0	0-0	0-0	3-3
Reed	0-2	1-0	2-0	2-1	0-0	1-0	0-1	1-0	0-0	0-0	0-1	1-0	1-0	9-5
Reynoso	0-3	0-2	1-1	2-0	1-0	3-0	0-1	1-0	0-2	1-0	1-0	0-1	2-1	12-11
Ruffin	0-1	0-0	0-0	0-0	3-0	0-0	1-0	0-1	0-1	2-0	0-0	1-0	0-1	6-5
Sanford	0-0	0-0	0-0	0-0	0-0	0-0	0-0	0-0	0-1	0-0	0-0	1-0	0-0	1-2
Shepherd	0-1	0-1	0-0	0-0	1-0	0-1	0-0	0-0	0-0	0-0	0-0	0-0	0-0	1-3
Smith	0-0	0-0	0-0	0-1	1-0	0-0	1-0	0-1	0-0	0-1	0-1	0-0	0-0	2-4
Wayne	0-0	0-0	0-0	0-0	2-0	0-0	0-1	0-0	1-0	1-0	0-2	1-0	0-0	5-3
Totals	0-13	4-8	4-9	7-5	11-2	7-6	3-9	6-6	3-9	8-4	5-7	6-7	3-10	67-95

No-decisions—Aldred, Knudson, Service.

FLORIDA—64-98

Pitcher	Atl. W-L	Chi. W-L	Cin. W-L	Col. W-L	Hou. W-L	L.A. W-L	Mon. W-L	N.Y. W-L	Phi. W-L	Pit. W-L	St.L. W-L	S.D. W-L	S.F. W-L	Totals W-L
Aquino	1-1	1-2	0-0	1-0	0-1	0-0	0-0	0-0	1-0	1-1	0-1	1-1	0-1	6-8
Armstrong	2-0	2-2	1-1	0-1	1-1	0-3	1-1	1-2	0-2	0-0	1-1	0-1	0-2	9-17
Bowen	0-2	1-0	1-1	2-1	0-0	0-0	0-1	0-1	0-1	2-1	1-2	0-1	1-1	8-12
Carpenter	0-0	0-0	0-0	0-0	0-0	0-0	0-1	0-0	0-0	0-0	0-0	0-0	0-0	0-1
Corsi	0-1	0-0	0-0	0-0	0-0	0-0	0-1	0-0	0-0	0-0	0-0	0-0	0-0	0-2
Hammond	1-0	1-0	1-1	0-2	0-1	0-1	1-1	1-0	1-0	2-1	1-2	1-1	1-2	11-12
Harvey	0-0	0-0	0-0	1-1	0-0	0-0	0-0	0-1	0-1	0-0	0-0	0-1	0-1	1-5
Hoffman	0-0	1-0	1-0	0-0	0-0	0-0	0-0	0-1	0-0	0-1	0-0	0-0	0-0	2-2
Hough	0-1	0-1	0-2	0-1	0-4	2-0	0-1	2-1	1-2	0-3	1-0	3-0	0-0	9-16
Johnstone	0-0	0-0	0-0	0-0	0-0	0-1	0-0	0-0	0-0	0-0	0-1	0-0	0-0	0-2
Klink	0-0	0-0	0-0	0-0	0-0	0-0	0-0	0-0	0-0	0-0	0-0	0-1	0-0	0-2
Lewis	0-0	1-1	0-1	0-0	2-0	1-0	1-1	0-0	1-0	0-0	0-0	0-0	0-0	6-3
McClure	1-1	0-0	0-0	0-0	0-0	0-0	0-0	0-0	0-0	0-0	0-0	0-0	0-0	1-1
Nen	0-0	0-0	1-0	0-0	0-0	0-0	0-0	0-0	0-0	0-0	0-0	0-0	0-0	1-0
Rapp	0-0	0-0	0-1	1-1	0-1	0-1	1-0	0-2	0-0	0-0	1-0	1-0	0-0	4-6
Rodriguez	0-0	0-0	0-0	0-0	0-0	0-0	0-0	0-0	0-1	0-0	0-0	0-0	0-0	0-1
Turner	0-1	0-0	0-0	0-0	0-0	1-1	1-1	0-1	0-1	1-0	0-0	0-0	1-0	4-5
Weathers	0-0	0-0	0-0	0-0	0-0	1-0	0-0	0-1	0-0	0-1	0-1	1-0	0-0	2-3
Totals	5-7	7-6	5-7	5-7	3-9	5-7	5-8	4-9	4-9	6-7	4-9	7-5	4-8	64-98

HOUSTON—85-77

Pitcher	Atl. W-L	Chi. W-L	Cin. W-L	Col. W-L	Fla. W-L	L.A. W-L	Mon. W-L	N.Y. W-L	Phi. W-L	Pit. W-L	St.L. W-L	S.D. W-L	S.F. W-L	Totals W-L
Bell	0-0	0-0	0-0	0-0	0-0	0-0	0-0	0-0	0-1	0-0	0-0	0-0	0-0	0-1
Drabek	0-3	1-1	0-1	1-1	0-0	2-1	0-3	2-0	0-1	1-1	1-2	1-2	0-2	9-18
Edens	0-0	0-0	0-0	0-0	0-1	0-0	0-0	0-0	0-0	0-0	1-0	0-0	0-0	1-1
Harnisch	2-1	2-1	2-0	1-0	2-0	1-1	0-0	3-0	1-1	1-1	0-1	1-1	0-2	16-9
Hernandez	2-0	0-0	0-0	0-4	0-0	0-0	0-0	0-1	0-0	1-0	1-0	0-0	0-0	4-5
D. Jones	0-1	0-1	0-1	0-3	0-1	0-0	2-0	1-0	1-0	0-0	0-1	0-1	0-1	4-10
T. Jones	0-0	0-0	0-0	0-1	0-0	0-0	0-0	1-0	0-1	0-0	0-0	0-0	0-0	1-2
Juden	0-0	0-0	0-1	0-0	0-0	0-0	0-0	0-0	0-0	0-0	0-0	0-0	0-0	0-1
Kile	1-1	0-0	1-1	0-0	2-0	1-1	0-2	2-0	2-0	2-0	2-0	2-1	0-2	15-8
Osuna	0-0	0-0	0-1	0-0	0-0	0-0	0-0	1-0	0-0	0-0	0-0	0-0	0-0	1-1
Portugal	0-0	2-1	2-0	0-0	2-0	3-1	2-0	0-0	1-0	1-2	2-0	1-0	2-0	18-4
Swindell	0-2	1-0	1-1	0-1	3-0	2-0	0-2	1-0	0-3	1-1	0-1	2-0	1-2	12-13
Williams	0-0	2-0	1-0	0-1	0-1	0-0	1-0	0-0	0-0	0-0	0-1	0-0	0-1	4-4
Totals	5-8	8-4	7-6	2-11	9-3	9-4	5-7	11-1	5-7	7-5	6-6	8-5	3-10	85-77

No-decisions—Agosto, Grant, Reynolds.

LOS ANGELES—81-81

Pitcher	Atl. W-L	Chi. W-L	Cin. W-L	Col. W-L	Fla. W-L	Hou. W-L	Mon. W-L	N.Y. W-L	Phi. W-L	Pit. W-L	St.L. W-L	S.D. W-L	S.F. W-L	Totals W-L
Astacio	0-2	0-3	1-0	2-1	2-0	2-0	1-1	1-1	1-0	2-0	1-1	1-0	0-0	14-9
Candiotti	0-2	0-0	1-1	0-1	0-1	1-1	1-1	1-0	1-1	0-1	1-0	1-0	1-1	8-10
Daal	0-0	0-0	0-0	0-0	1-0	0-0	0-1	0-0	0-2	0-0	0-0	1-0	0-0	2-3
Gott	0-0	0-2	1-1	0-1	0-0	0-1	1-0	1-0	0-1	0-0	0-2	1-0	0-0	4-8
Ke. Gross	2-0	2-0	2-0	0-1	1-1	0-2	0-1	1-1	0-1	2-2	0-1	2-1	1-2	13-13
Hershiser	1-0	0-2	0-2	1-1	1-1	0-2	0-1	2-0	0-3	2-0	1-0	2-0	2-2	12-14
P. Martinez	1-0	1-0	1-0	0-1	0-0	0-2	1-0	2-0	0-0	0-0	1-2	1-0	2-0	10-5
R. Martinez	1-3	0-0	1-0	1-1	1-0	1-1	2-1	0-1	0-2	2-0	1-1	0-1	0-1	10-12
McDowell	0-1	2-0	1-1	2-0	0-1	0-0	0-0	0-0	0-0	0-0	0-0	0-0	0-0	5-3
Nichols	0-0	0-0	0-0	0-0	0-0	0-0	0-0	0-1	0-1	0-0	0-0	0-0	0-0	0-1
Trlicek	0-0	0-0	0-0	0-0	1-0	0-0	0-0	0-0	0-1	0-0	0-1	0-0	0-0	1-2

Pitcher	Atl. W-L	Chi. W-L	Cin. W-L	Col. W-L	Fla. W-L	Hou. W-L	Mon. W-L	N.Y. W-L	Phi. W-L	Pit. W-L	St.L. W-L	S.D. W-L	S.F. W-L	Totals W-L
Wilson	0-0	0-0	0-0	0-0	0-0	0-0	0-0	0-0	0-0	0-0	0-0	1-0	0-0	1-0
Worrell	0-0	0-0	0-0	0-0	0-1	0-0	0-0	0-0	0-0	0-0	1-0	0-0	0-0	1-1
Totals	5-8	5-7	8-5	6-7	7-5	4-9	6-6	8-4	2-10	8-4	6-6	9-4	7-6	81-81

No-decisions—DeSilva, Kip Gross.

MONTREAL—94-68

Pitcher	Atl. W-L	Chi. W-L	Cin. W-L	Col. W-L	Fla. W-L	Hou. W-L	L.A. W-L	N.Y. W-L	Phi. W-L	Pit. W-L	St.L. W-L	S.D. W-L	S.F. W-L	Totals W-L
Aldred	0-0	0-0	0-0	0-0	0-0	0-0	0-0	1-0	0-0	0-0	0-0	0-0	0-0	1-0
Barnes	0-0	0-0	1-0	0-0	0-2	0-0	0-1	0-1	1-0	0-1	0-1	0-0	0-0	2-6
Bottenfield	0-0	0-0	0-0	1-1	1-0	0-0	0-0	0-0	0-0	0-1	0-1	0-1	0-1	2-5
Boucher	0-0	0-0	0-1	0-0	0-0	0-0	0-0	1-0	0-1	1-0	0-0	0-0	0-0	3-1
Fassero	1-1	3-0	0-0	1-0	0-1	0-1	1-0	2-0	1-0	0-0	2-1	1-0	0-1	12-5
Gardiner	0-0	0-0	0-1	0-0	0-0	0-1	1-0	0-0	0-0	1-0	0-0	0-0	0-1	2-3
Henry	0-0	0-0	1-0	0-0	0-0	0-0	0-0	0-0	0-1	0-0	0-0	0-0	0-0	1-1
Heredia	1-0	0-0	0-1	1-0	0-0	0-0	0-0	0-0	0-1	1-0	1-0	0-0	0-0	4-2
Hill	0-1	0-3	1-0	1-0	0-1	2-0	1-0	0-2	1-0	0-0	1-0	1-0	1-0	9-7
Jones	0-0	0-0	0-0	1-0	0-0	1-0	1-0	0-0	0-0	0-0	0-0	1-0	0-1	4-1
Martinez	1-2	2-1	2-1	2-2	1-0	1-0	1-2	1-0	0-0	0-0	1-0	2-0	1-1	15-9
Nabholz	0-0	0-0	0-0	0-0	2-1	0-0	1-0	3-0	0-2	2-0	0-1	1-1	0-3	9-8
Rojas	0-1	0-0	1-1	0-0	1-0	0-3	0-0	1-0	1-0	1-0	0-2	0-0	0-1	5-8
Rueter	1-0	2-0	0-0	1-0	0-0	2-0	0-0	0-0	0-0	0-0	1-0	0-0	1-0	8-0
Scott	1-0	0-0	0-0	1-0	0-0	0-0	0-0	0-0	2-1	1-1	0-0	0-0	0-0	5-2
Shaw	0-2	1-1	0-0	0-0	1-0	0-0	0-2	0-0	0-1	0-1	0-0	0-0	0-0	2-7
Wetteland	0-0	0-0	1-0	0-0	2-0	1-0	0-1	0-1	0-1	1-0	1-0	3-0	0-0	9-3
Young	0-0	0-0	0-0	0-0	0-0	0-0	0-0	0-0	0-0	0-0	0-0	1-0	0-0	1-0
Totals	5-7	8-5	8-4	9-3	8-5	7-5	6-6	9-4	6-7	8-5	7-6	10-2	3-9	94-68

No-decisions—Looney, Risley, Valdez, Walton.

NEW YORK—59-103

Pitcher	Atl. W-L	Chi. W-L	Cin. W-L	Col. W-L	Fla. W-L	Hou. W-L	L.A. W-L	Mon. W-L	Phi. W-L	Pit. W-L	St.L. W-L	S.D. W-L	S.F. W-L	Totals W-L
Draper	0-0	0-1	0-0	0-0	0-0	0-0	0-0	1-0	0-0	0-0	0-0	0-0	0-0	1-1
S. Fernandez	0-1	1-0	1-0	2-1	1-0	0-2	0-0	0-1	0-0	0-0	0-1	0-0	0-0	5-6
Franco	0-0	0-2	0-0	0-0	0-0	0-1	0-0	0-0	1-0	2-0	0-0	1-0	0-0	4-3
Gibson	0-0	1-0	0-0	0-0	0-0	0-0	0-0	0-0	0-1	0-0	0-0	0-0	0-0	1-1
Gooden	1-1	2-0	0-2	2-1	2-1	0-2	0-2	0-0	0-1	0-3	1-1	3-0	1-1	12-15
Gozzo	0-0	0-0	0-0	0-0	0-0	0-0	0-0	0-0	0-0	0-0	0-1	0-0	0-0	0-1
Greer	0-0	0-0	0-0	0-0	0-0	0-0	0-0	0-0	0-0	0-0	1-0	0-0	0-0	1-0
Hillman	0-3	0-0	0-1	0-0	0-0	0-0	1-0	0-1	0-0	0-1	1-2	0-0	0-1	2-9
Innis	1-0	0-0	0-0	0-1	0-0	0-0	1-0	0-1	0-0	0-0	0-0	0-0	0-1	2-3
Jones	0-0	1-0	0-0	0-2	0-0	0-0	0-0	0-1	1-1	0-0	0-0	0-0	0-0	2-4
Maddux	0-1	0-1	1-0	0-0	0-0	1-1	0-1	0-0	0-0	1-0	0-1	0-1	0-2	3-8
Saberhagen	0-1	0-0	0-1	2-0	2-0	0-0	2-0	1-1	0-0	0-1	0-1	0-1	0-1	7-7
Schourek	0-2	0-0	1-1	0-0	1-1	0-2	0-0	0-0	0-3	0-1	2-0	0-1	1-1	5-12
Tanana	1-0	0-2	3-0	0-1	0-2	0-2	0-3	0-2	1-1	0-2	0-0	1-0	1-0	7-15
Telgheder	0-0	0-0	0-0	0-0	2-0	0-0	0-1	2-0	0-0	1-0	0-0	0-1	1-0	6-2
Young	0-0	0-2	0-1	0-0	1-0	0-1	0-1	0-2	0-3	0-1	0-1	0-3	0-1	1-16
Totals	3-9	5-8	6-6	6-6	9-4	1-11	4-8	4-9	3-10	4-9	5-8	5-7	4-8	59-103

No-decisions—Kaiser, Manzanillo, Weston.

PHILADELPHIA—97-65

Pitcher	Atl. W-L	Chi. W-L	Cin. W-L	Col. W-L	Fla. W-L	Hou. W-L	L.A. W-L	Mon. W-L	N.Y. W-L	Pit. W-L	St.L. W-L	S.D. W-L	S.F. W-L	Totals W-L
Andersen	0-0	0-0	1-1	0-0	0-0	0-1	0-0	0-0	0-0	0-0	0-0	0-0	2-0	3-2
Ayrault	0-0	0-0	0-0	0-0	0-0	1-0	0-0	0-0	0-0	0-0	1-0	0-0	0-0	2-0
Davis	0-0	0-0	0-0	0-0	0-1	0-0	0-0	0-0	0-0	0-1	1-0	0-0	0-0	1-2
DeLeon	0-0	0-0	0-0	1-0	0-0	1-0	0-0	0-0	0-0	1-0	0-0	0-0	0-0	3-0
Foster	0-0	0-0	0-0	0-0	0-0	0-0	0-0	0-0	0-0	0-1	0-0	0-0	0-0	0-1
Greene	1-0	0-0	2-0	2-0	2-0	0-0	3-0	1-1	2-0	1-1	1-1	0-1	1-0	16-4
Jackson	2-0	1-0	1-1	1-0	0-1	1-0	2-0	0-1	1-2	0-0	0-1	1-2	0-3	12-11
Mason	0-1	0-1	0-0	0-2	1-1	0-0	1-0	1-0	0-0	1-0	1-0	0-0	0-0	5-5
Mulholland	1-1	2-1	0-0	1-1	1-1	2-0	1-0	2-0	0-0	0-0	2-0	0-3	0-2	12-9
Pall	0-0	0-0	0-0	0-0	1-0	0-0	0-0	0-0	0-0	0-0	0-0	0-0	0-0	1-0
Rivera	2-0	1-2	2-0	2-0	2-0	0-3	0-1	0-0	1-0	1-1	1-0	1-0	0-2	13-9
Schilling	0-2	1-1	1-0	2-0	1-0	2-0	1-1	2-0	3-0	0-1	1-1	2-0	0-1	16-7
Thigpen	0-0	0-0	0-1	1-0	0-0	0-0	0-0	0-0	1-0	1-0	0-0	0-0	0-0	3-1
West	0-2	0-1	0-0	0-0	0-0	1-0	0-0	1-1	2-0	0-0	1-0	0-0	1-0	6-4
Mike Williams	0-0	0-1	0-0	0-0	0-0	0-1	1-0	0-0	0-0	0-0	0-1	0-0	0-0	1-3
Mit. Williams	0-0	1-0	0-1	0-0	1-0	0-0	0-0	0-3	0-1	0-1	0-1	1-0	0-0	3-7
Totals	6-6	6-7	8-4	9-3	9-4	7-5	10-2	7-6	10-3	7-6	8-5	6-6	4-8	97-65

No-decisions—Brink, Fletcher, Green, Mauser.

PITTSBURGH—75-87

Pitcher	Atl. W-L	Chi. W-L	Cin. W-L	Col. W-L	Fla. W-L	Hou. W-L	L.A. W-L	Mon. W-L	N.Y. W-L	Phi. W-L	St.L. W-L	S.D. W-L	S.F. W-L	Totals W-L
Ballard	0-0	1-0	0-0	0-0	1-0	1-0	0-1	1-0	0-0	0-0	0-0	0-0	0-0	4-1
Belinda	0-1	0-0	0-0	0-0	0-0	0-0	0-0	1-0	1-0	1-0	0-0	0-0	0-0	3-1
Candelaria	0-0	0-0	0-1	0-0	0-0	0-1	0-0	0-0	0-0	0-1	0-0	0-0	0-0	0-3
Cooke	0-1	0-1	0-0	0-0	2-0	1-1	2-0	0-1	1-1	1-2	0-1	1-1	2-1	10-10
Dewey	0-0	0-0	0-0	0-1	0-0	0-0	0-0	0-0	0-0	0-0	1-1	0-0	0-0	1-2
Hope	0-0	0-0	0-0	0-0	0-0	0-0	0-0	0-1	0-0	0-0	0-0	0-1	0-0	0-2
Johnston	0-0	0-0	0-0	0-1	0-0	0-0	1-0	0-1	0-1	0-0	1-1	0-0	0-0	2-4
Menendez	0-0	0-0	0-0	1-0	0-0	0-0	0-0	0-0	0-0	0-0	0-0	0-0	1-0	2-0
Minor	2-0	0-1	1-0	0-1	1-1	0-0	0-0	1-1	0-1	0-0	1-1	1-0	1-0	8-6
Moeller	0-0	0-0	0-0	0-0	0-0	0-0	0-0	0-0	0-0	0-0	0-0	1-0	0-0	1-0
Neagle	0-0	0-0	0-1	1-0	0-0	0-1	1-0	0-1	0-1	0-1	0-0	0-1	1-0	3-5
Otto	0-0	0-0	1-1	0-0	0-1	0-0	0-2	0-0	1-0	0-0	0-0	1-0	0-0	3-4
Petkovsek	0-0	0-0	0-0	1-0	0-0	0-0	0-0	1-0	0-0	0-0	0-0	1-0	0-0	3-0
Robertson	0-0	0-0	0-0	0-0	0-0	0-0	0-0	0-0	0-0	0-1	0-0	0-0	0-0	0-1
Z. Smith	0-1	1-1	0-0	0-0	1-0	0-0	0-1	0-0	1-0	0-0	0-1	0-1	0-1	3-7
Toliver	0-0	0-0	0-0	0-0	0-0	0-0	0-0	0-0	1-0	0-0	0-0	0-0	0-0	1-0
Tomlin	0-2	1-0	0-1	0-0	0-0	2-1	0-1	0-1	1-0	0-2	0-0	0-0	0-0	4-8
Wagner	1-0	2-0	0-2	0-1	1-0	1-0	0-0	0-2	2-0	1-0	0-1	0-0	0-1	8-8
Wakefield	1-1	1-1	1-1	0-3	0-1	0-0	0-1	0-0	1-0	1-0	0-1	1-0	0-2	6-11
Walk	1-1	2-1	1-1	1-1	1-2	0-2	0-2	0-0	1-0	2-1	1-1	3-0	0-2	13-14
Totals	5-7	8-5	4-8	4-8	7-6	5-7	4-8	5-8	9-4	6-7	4-9	9-3	5-7	75-87

No-decisions—Miceli, Miller, Shouse.

ST. LOUIS—87-75

Pitcher	Atl. W-L	Chi. W-L	Cin. W-L	Col. W-L	Fla. W-L	Hou. W-L	L.A. W-L	Mon. W-L	N.Y. W-L	Phi. W-L	Pit. W-L	S.D. W-L	S.F. W-L	Totals W-L
Arocha	0-0	0-2	1-1	1-0	2-0	1-1	1-0	0-2	1-1	0-0	1-0	1-0	2-1	11-8
Burns	0-0	0-0	0-0	0-1	0-0	0-0	0-0	0-0	0-1	0-0	0-2	0-0	0-0	0-4
Cormier	0-1	1-0	0-0	0-0	0-1	0-2	0-0	2-0	0-1	1-0	0-0	0-1	2-0	7-6
Guetterman	1-0	0-0	0-0	0-0	0-0	1-1	0-0	0-0	0-0	1-1	0-0	0-1	0-0	3-3
Kilgus	0-0	0-0	1-0	0-0	0-0	0-0	0-0	0-0	0-0	0-0	0-0	0-0	0-0	1-0
Lancaster	0-0	0-0	0-0	0-0	1-0	0-0	2-0	0-0	0-1	0-0	1-0	0-0	0-0	4-1
Magrane	2-1	0-0	1-0	0-1	1-1	1-1	0-1	1-2	1-0	0-2	1-0	0-1	0-0	8-10
Murphy	0-3	0-2	1-1	1-0	0-0	0-0	1-0	0-0	1-0	1-1	0-0	0-0	0-0	5-7
Olivares	1-0	0-1	0-0	1-0	1-0	0-0	0-0	0-0	1-0	0-0	0-1	1-0	0-0	5-3
Osborne	1-0	1-1	0-0	1-1	0-1	1-1	1-0	0-0	1-0	1-0	1-1	1-1	1-1	10-7
Perez	0-0	0-0	1-0	1-0	0-0	0-0	0-0	0-0	1-0	0-1	1-0	2-1	0-0	7-2
L. Smith	0-0	0-1	0-0	0-1	1-0	0-0	0-1	0-0	0-0	0-1	1-0	0-0	0-0	2-4
Tewksbury	0-1	3-1	2-2	1-1	2-0	2-0	1-2	1-2	1-0	1-0	1-0	1-0	1-1	17-10
Urbani	0-0	0-0	0-0	0-0	0-0	0-0	0-1	0-0	0-0	0-1	0-1	0-0	1-0	1-3
Watson	1-0	0-0	0-1	1-0	1-1	0-0	0-1	1-1	1-1	0-0	1-0	0-1	0-1	6-7
Totals	6-6	5-8	7-5	7-5	9-4	6-6	6-6	6-7	8-5	5-8	9-4	5-7	8-4	87-75

No-decisions—Batchelor, Brewer, Dixon.

SAN DIEGO—61-101

Pitcher	Atl. W-L	Chi. W-L	Cin. W-L	Col. W-L	Fla. W-L	Hou. W-L	L.A. W-L	Mon. W-L	N.Y. W-L	Phi. W-L	Pit. W-L	St.L. W-L	S.F. W-L	Totals W-L
Ashby	0-1	0-0	0-1	0-0	0-0	2-0	0-1	0-0	0-0	0-0	0-1	1-0	0-2	3-6
Benes	0-3	2-0	1-1	2-1	2-1	1-3	0-0	1-1	1-1	2-0	1-2	1-1	1-1	15-15
Brocail	1-1	1-1	1-0	0-1	0-1	0-1	0-2	0-1	0-1	0-1	1-0	0-1	0-2	4-13
Davis	0-0	0-0	0-0	0-0	0-0	0-0	0-0	0-0	0-0	0-0	0-1	0-1	0-1	0-3
Eiland	0-0	0-0	0-1	0-0	0-1	0-1	0-0	0-0	0-0	0-0	0-0	0-0	0-0	0-3
Ettles	0-0	0-0	0-0	0-0	0-0	0-0	0-0	0-0	0-0	1-0	0-0	0-0	0-0	1-0
Gomez	0-0	0-1	0-0	0-0	0-0	0-0	1-0	0-0	0-0	0-0	0-1	0-0	0-0	1-2
Gr. Harris	1-0	1-0	0-0	2-0	0-0	0-0	0-2	0-2	1-1	2-1	0-2	2-0	1-1	10-9
Ge. Harris	1-0	0-0	0-1	1-0	1-0	0-0	1-0	0-3	1-1	0-0	1-0	0-1	0-1	6-6
Hernandez	0-0	0-0	0-0	0-0	0-0	0-0	0-0	0-0	0-0	0-1	0-1	0-0	0-0	0-2
Hoffman	0-1	0-0	1-0	0-0	1-0	0-2	0-0	0-0	0-0	0-1	0-0	0-0	0-0	2-4
Hurst	0-0	0-0	0-0	0-0	0-1	0-0	0-0	0-0	0-0	0-0	0-0	0-0	0-0	0-1
Martinez	0-1	0-0	0-0	0-0	0-0	0-0	0-0	0-0	0-0	1-0	0-0	1-0	1-0	3-1
Mason	0-1	0-1	0-1	0-1	0-1	0-0	0-2	0-0	0-0	0-0	0-0	0-0	0-0	0-7
Mauser	0-0	0-1	0-0	0-0	0-0	0-0	0-0	0-0	0-0	0-0	0-0	0-0	0-0	0-1
Rodriguez	0-0	0-0	0-0	0-1	0-0	1-0	0-0	0-1	1-0	0-0	0-0	0-1	0-0	2-3
Sanders	1-0	0-0	0-1	1-0	0-1	0-1	0-1	0-0	0-0	0-0	1-0	0-0	0-0	3-3
Scott	0-0	0-0	0-0	0-0	0-0	0-0	0-0	0-0	1-0	0-0	0-1	1-0	0-0	2-0
Seminara	0-0	0-1	0-0	1-0	1-0	0-0	0-0	0-0	1-0	0-1	0-1	0-0	0-0	3-3
Taylor	0-0	0-0	0-1	0-1	0-0	0-0	0-0	0-1	0-0	0-0	0-0	0-1	0-1	0-5
Whitehurst	0-0	0-2	0-2	0-0	0-0	1-0	2-1	0-0	1-1	0-0	0-0	0-0	0-1	4-7
Worrell	0-1	0-1	1-0	0-1	0-1	0-0	0-0	1-1	0-0	0-1	0-0	0-0	0-0	2-7
Totals	4-9	4-8	4-9	7-6	5-7	5-8	4-9	2-10	7-5	6-6	3-9	7-5	3-10	61-101

No-decisions—Seanez.

SAN FRANCISCO—103-59

Pitcher	Atl. W-L	Chi. W-L	Cin. W-L	Col. W-L	Fla. W-L	Hou. W-L	L.A. W-L	Mon. W-L	N.Y. W-L	Phi. W-L	Pit. W-L	St.L. W-L	S.D. W-L	Totals W-L
Beck	0-0	0-0	0-0	0-0	1-0	0-0	0-0	0-0	1-0	0-0	0-1	0-0	1-0	3-1
Black	0-0	0-0	0-1	1-0	1-0	1-0	1-1	0-0	1-0	1-0	0-0	1-0	1-0	8-2
Brantley	1-1	0-0	0-1	0-0	0-0	2-0	1-1	1-0	0-1	0-0	0-1	0-0	0-1	5-6
Brummett	1-0	0-0	0-0	1-0	0-0	0-0	0-0	0-1	0-1	0-0	0-1	0-0	0-0	2-3
Burba	1-0	1-0	1-0	0-0	1-0	1-0	0-1	1-1	0-1	1-0	1-0	0-1	1-0	10-3
Burkett	1-1	1-0	2-0	3-0	1-1	4-0	3-0	1-0	1-1	2-1	1-1	1-2	1-0	22-7
Deshaies	0-0	0-1	0-0	0-0	0-0	1-0	0-0	0-0	0-0	0-0	0-0	1-1	0-0	2-2
Hickerson	0-1	0-1	0-0	2-0	0-0	0-1	0-1	2-0	1-0	1-0	1-0	0-0	0-1	7-5
Jackson	2-1	0-1	2-0	0-0	0-1	0-0	0-1	1-0	0-0	0-1	0-1	0-0	0-0	6-6
Minutelli	0-0	0-0	0-0	0-0	0-0	0-0	0-0	0-0	0-0	0-1	0-0	0-0	0-0	0-1
Righetti	0-0	0-0	0-0	0-0	0-0	0-0	0-0	0-0	1-0	0-1	0-0	0-0	0-0	1-1
Rogers	0-0	1-0	0-0	0-0	1-0	0-0	0-0	0-0	0-0	0-0	0-1	0-0	0-0	1-2
Sanderson	0-0	0-1	1-0	0-0	2-0	0-1	0-1	0-0	0-0	0-0	1-0	0-0	0-0	4-2
Swift	0-2	1-1	4-0	3-0	0-2	1-0	1-0	3-0	1-1	3-0	0-0	0-1	3-1	21-8
Torres	0-0	0-1	0-0	0-1	1-0	0-1	0-1	0-0	0-0	0-0	0-0	1-1	1-0	3-5
Wilson	0-1	2-0	1-0	0-2	0-0	0-0	0-0	0-1	0-0	0-0	2-0	0-1	2-0	7-5
Totals	6-7	6-6	11-2	10-3	8-4	10-3	6-7	9-3	8-4	8-4	7-5	4-8	10-3	103-59

No-decisions—Bross, Layana.

HOME RUNS BY PARKS

	At Atl.	At Chi.	At Cin.	At Col.	At Fla.	At Hou.	At L.A.	At Mon.	At N.Y.	At Phi.	At Pit.	At St.L.	At S.D.	At S.F.	Totals 1993	1992
Atlanta	78	6	10	18	7	5	1	5	5	3	8	4	6	13	169	138
Chicago	7	76	3	6	7	5	6	6	7	12	2	8	10	6	161	104
Cincinnati	4	9	69	7	7	7	3	3	5	2	5	4	5	7	137	99
Colorado	3	4	6	77	4	3	6	6	6	4	6	7	7	3	142	....
Florida	4	7	2	6	44	3	2	4	3	2	5	3	3	6	94	....
Houston	5	5	3	6	6	62	6	2	8	6	3	6	10	10	138	96
Los Angeles	2	2	7	9	4	3	66	2	7	5	4	6	8	5	130	72
Montreal	1	3	8	12	4	3	3	62	8	3	4	2	5	4	122	102
New York	2	14	6	5	11	6	6	7	75	5	4	6	6	5	158	93
Philadelphia	5	8	5	15	8	5	3	5	7	80	4	2	4	5	156	118
Pittsburgh	2	11	5	5	5	6	2	2	1	0	64	2	4	1	110	106
St. Louis	6	7	8	7	3	2	4	0	3	5	8	59	4	2	118	94
San Diego	3	8	7	4	1	4	4	3	7	4	8	6	87	7	153	135
San Francisco	8	10	11	7	5	4	3	5	5	6	7	6	9	82	168	105
1993 total	130	170	150	184	116	118	114	112	147	137	131	118	166	163	1956	....
1992 total	117	108	120	....	....	90	59	98	91	116	88	107	151	117	....	1262

AT ATLANTA (130):

Atlanta (78)—Justice 18, Gant 17, Pendleton 9, McGriff 8, Berryhill 6, Bream 5, Blauser 4, Lemke 3, Olson 3, Klesko 2, Cabrera 1, Nixon 1, Sanders 1. **Chicago (7)**—Grace 2, Hill 1, May 1, Sandberg 1, Sosa 1, Wilkins 1. **Cincinnati (4)**—Brumfield 2, Branson 1, Mitchell 1. **Colorado (4)**—Bichette 1, Jones 1, Mejia 1. **Florida (4)**—Sheffield 2, Magadan 1, Natal 1. **Houston (5)**—Cedeno 2, Bagwell 1, Biggio 1, Finley 1. **Los Angeles (2)**—Davis 1, Piazza 1. **Montreal (1)**—Walker 1. **New York (2)**—Jackson 1, Murray 1. **Philadelphia (5)**—Incaviglia 2, Chamberlain 1, Daulton 1, Hollins 1. **Pittsburgh (2)**—Foley 1, L. Smith 1. **St. Louis (6)**—Jefferies 2, Jordan 2, Pagnozzi 1, Whiten 1. **San Diego (3)**—Bell 1, McGriff 1, Plantier 1. **San Francisco (8)**—Bonds 4, Clark 1, Patterson 1, Reed 1, Thompson 1.

AT CHICAGO (170):

Atlanta (6)—Blauser 2, Gant 1, Justice 1, Lopez 1, McGriff 1. **Chicago (76)**—Sosa 23, Wilkins 10, Buechele 8, Smith 6, Grace 5, Hill 5, Sandberg 5, Roberson 4, May 3, Jennings 2, Lake 1, Maldonado 1, Vizcaino 1, Walbeck 1, Yelding 1. **Cincinnati (9)**—Brumfield 2, Mitchell 2, Sabo 2, Oliver 1, Roberts 1, Sanders 1. **Colorado (4)**—Clark 1, Girardi 1, Hayes 1, Tatum 1. **Florida (7)**—Destrade 3, Arias 1, Conine 1, Lyden 1, Weiss 1. **Houston (5)**—Gonzalez 2, Anthony 1, Bagwell 1, Finley 1. **Los Angeles (2)**—Harris 1, Mondesi 1. **Montreal (3)**—Colbrunn 1, Fletcher 1, Ready 1. **New York (14)**—Bonilla 5, Hundley 3, Thompson 3, Walker 2, Murray 1. **Philadelphia (8)**—Kruk 3, Chamberlain 2, Hollins 2, Dykstra 1. **Pittsburgh (11)**—Garcia 3, Merced 2, Slaught 2, Bell 1, Martin 1, McClendon 1, L. Smith 1. **St. Louis (7)**—Gilkey 2, Pagnozzi 1, Pena 1, Royer 1, Whiten 1, Zeile 1. **San Diego (8)**—Clark 2, Geren 1, Gwynn 1, McGriff 1, Plantier 1, Sheffield 1, Velasquez 1. **San Francisco (10)**—Bonds 3, Williams 3, McGee 2, Manwaring 1, Thompson 1.

AT CINCINNATI (150):

Atlanta (10)—Gant 4, Justice 2, Sanders 2, Bream 1, McGriff 1. **Chicago (3)**—Buechele 1, Roberson 1, Sosa 1. **Cincinnati (69)**—Sabo 12, Mitchell 10, Sanders 8, Oliver 7, Milligan 5, Kelly 4, Larkin 4, Branson 2, Daugherty 2, Dorsett 2, Greene 2, Howard 2, Morris 2, Browning 1, Brumfield 1, Kessinger 1, Rijo 1, Samuel 1, Tubbs 1, Varsho 1. **Colorado (6)**—Bichette 2, Boston 1, Castellano 1, Castilla 1, Gainer 1. **Florida (2)**—Santiago 1, Whitmore 1. **Houston (3)**—Donnels 1, Gonzalez 1, Servais 1. **Los Angeles (7)**—Karros 2, Piazza 2, Davis 1, Harris 1, Snyder 1. **Montreal (8)**—Walker 3, Alou 2, Berry 2, Grissom 1. **New York (6)**—Johnson 2, Murray 2, Burnitz 1, Hundley 1. **Philadelphia (5)**—Batiste 1, Daulton 1, Greene 1, Hollins 1, Pratt 1. **Pittsburgh (5)**—Slaught 2, Bell 1, Foley 1, Merced 1. **St. Louis (8)**—Whiten 4, Brewer 1, Pena 1, Villanueva 1, Zeile 1. **San Diego (7)**—Plantier 2, Benes 1, Cianfrocco 1, Gwynn 1, McGriff 1, Teufel 1. **San Francisco (11)**—Williams 5, Benzinger 2, Bonds 2, Martinez 2.

AT COLORADO (184):

Atlanta (18)—Blauser 4, Justice 4, Gant 3, Bream 2, Lemke 2, McGriff 2, Sanders 1. **Chicago (6)**—Wilkins 2, Buechele 1, Lake 1, Maldonado 1, Smith 1. **Cincinnati (7)**—Sanders 3, Kelly 1, Mitchell 1, Morris 1, Samuel 1. **Colorado (77)**—Hayes 17, Galarraga 13, Bichette 11, Clark 8, Castilla 5, Benavides 3, Boston 3, Mejia 3, E. Young 3, Girardi 2, Jones 2, Owens 2, Sheaffer 2, Castellano 1, Gainer 1, Reynoso 1. **Florida (6)**—Conine 2, Cotto 2, Felix 2. **Houston (6)**—Biggio 3, Finley 1, Gonzalez 1, Servais 1. **Los Angeles (9)**—Karros 2, Piazza 2, Brooks 1, Mondesi 1, Reed 1, Rodriguez 1, Snyder 1. **Montreal (12)**—Berry 3, Grissom 3, Lansing 2, Cianfrocco 1, Cordero 1, Spehr 1, Walker 1. **New York (5)**—Kent 2, Bonilla 1, Burnitz 1, Thompson 1. **Philadelphia (15)**—Daulton 3, Dykstra 2, Kruk 2, Batiste 1, Chamberlain 1, Duncan 1, Eisenreich 1, Greene 1, Hollins 1, Incaviglia 1, Stocker 1. **Pittsburgh (5)**—Clark 1, King 1, Merced 1, Slaught 1, Van Slyke 1. **St. Louis (7)**—Zeile 3, Whiten 2, Brewer 1, Gilkey 1. **San Diego (4)**—Bell 2, Bean 1, Sheffield 1. **San Francisco (7)**—Williams 3, Bonds 2, Carreon 1, Manwaring 1.

AT FLORIDA (116):

Atlanta (7)—Justice 4, Blauser 1, Gant 1, Lemke 1. **Chicago (7)**—Smith 2, Wilkins 2, Buechele 1, Lake 1, Sosa 1. **Cincinnati (7)**—Sabo 2, Sanders 2, Kelly 1, Oliver 1, Samuel 1. **Colorado (4)**—Galarraga 2, Bichette 1, Boston 1. **Florida (44)**—Destrade 9, Santiago 6, Conine 5, Sheffield 4, Carr 3, Felix 3, Magadan 3, Whitmore 3, Barberie 2, Briley 2, Renteria 2, Arias 1, Cotto 1. **Houston (6)**—Taubensee 2, Anthony 1, Biggio 1, Caminiti 1, Gonzalez 1. **Los Angeles (6)**—Butler 1, Hansen 1, Karros 1, Rodriguez 1, Snyder 1, Wallach 1. **Montreal (2)**—Berry 1, Pride 1. **New York (11)**—Burnitz 2, Kent 2, Murray 2, Walker 2, Gooden 1, Hundley 1, Thompson 1. **Philadelphia (8)**—Daulton 3, Incaviglia 2, Chamberlain 1, Duncan 1, Eisenreich 1. **Pittsburgh (5)**—Bell 2, Garcia 1, Martin 1, Van Slyke 1. **St. Louis (3)**—Gilkey 1, Jefferies 1, Pagnozzi 1. **San Diego (1)**—Sheffield 1. **San Francisco (5)**—Benzinger 3, Clark 1, Thompson 1.

AT HOUSTON (118):

Atlanta (5)—Gant 2, Cabrera 1, Justice 1, McGriff 1. **Chicago (5)**—Roberson 2, Lake 1, Sandberg 1, Wilkins 1. **Cincinnati (7)**—Sanders 2, Kelly 1, Milligan 1, Mitchell 1, Oliver 1, Sabo 1. **Colorado (3)**—Boston 1, Hayes 1, Liriano 1. **Florida (3)**—Barberie 1, Felix 1, Santiago 1. **Houston (62)**—Bagwell 9, Biggio 8, Gonzalez 8, Cedeno 6, James 6, Anthony 5, Caminiti 5, Servais 5, Taubensee 4, Bass 2, Drabek 1, Finley 1, Kile 1, Portugal 1. **Los Angeles (3)**—Hansen 1, Karros 1, Piazza 1. **Montreal (3)**—Grissom 2, R. White 1. **New York (6)**—Kent 2, Burnitz 1, Johnson 1, Murray 1, Orsulak 1. **Philadelphia (5)**—Chamberlain 1, Daulton 1, Hollins 1, Incaviglia 1, Morandini 1. **Pittsburgh (6)**—King 4, Slaught 1, Wakefield 1. **St. Louis (2)**—Jefferies 1, Jordan 1. **San Diego (4)**—McGriff 2, Plantier 2. **San Francisco (4)**—Bonds 1, Clark 1, Martinez 1, Williams 1.

AT LOS ANGELES (114):

Atlanta (1)—Berryhill 1. **Chicago (6)**—Sosa 2, Wilkins 2, Hill 1, Vizcaino 1. **Cincinnati (3)**—Oliver 1, Sabo 1, Sanders 1. **Colorado (3)**—Boston 1, Castellano 1, Castilla 1. **Florida (2)**—Destrade 1, Santiago 1. **Houston (6)**—Anthony 1, Bagwell 1, Caminiti 1, Cedeno 1, Finley 1, Gonzalez 1. **Los Angeles (66)**—Piazza 21, Karros 13, Davis 7, Rodriguez 5, Snyder 5, Wallach 4, Strawberry 3, Hansen 2, Mondesi 2, Hernandez 1, Offerman 1, Sharperson 1, Webster 1. **Montreal (5)**—Vander Wal 2, Alou 1, Bolick 1, Grissom 1. **New York (6)**—Murray 2, Bonilla 1, Gallagher 1, Kent 1, Orsulak 1. **Philadelphia (3)**—Daulton 1, Dykstra 1, Hollins 1. **Pittsburgh (2)**—Garcia 1, Tomberlin 1. **St. Louis (4)**—Jefferies 1, Lankford 1, Pagnozzi 1, Perry 1. **San Diego (4)**—Bell 2, Cianfrocco 1, McGriff 1. **San Francisco (3)**—Bonds 2, Thompson 1.

AT MONTREAL (112):

Atlanta (5)—Gant 2, Pendleton 2, McGriff 1. **Chicago (6)**—May 2, Hill 1, Sandberg 1, Smith 1, Wilkins 1. **Cincinnati (3)**—Brumfield 1, Oliver 1, Sanders 1. **Colorado (6)**—Bichette 2, Galarraga 2, Clark 1, Hayes 1. **Florida (4)**—Briley 1, Carr 1, Santiago 1, Sheffield 1. **Houston (2)**—Finley 1, Taubensee 1. **Los Angeles (2)**—Strawberry 1, Wallach 1. **Montreal (62)**—Walker 13, Alou 10, Grissom 9, Cordero 8, Berry 5, Fletcher 5, Bolick 2, Colbrunn 2, DeShields 2, Frazier 1, Lansing 1, Marrero 1, Vander Wal 1, D. White 1, R. White 1. **New York (7)**—Bonilla 3, Kent 2, Burnitz 1, Hundley 1. **Philadelphia (5)**—Daulton 1, Dykstra 1, Eisenreich 1, Hollins 1, Kruk 1. **Pittsburgh (2)**—Martin 1, Slaught 1. **San Diego (3)**—Gwynn 1, McGriff 1, Plantier 1. **San Francisco (5)**—Bonds 2, Carreon 1, Clark 1, Williams 1.

AT NEW YORK (147):

Atlanta (5)—Justice 3, Blauser 1, Gant 1. **Chicago (7)**—Wilkins 4, Buechele 1, Grace 1, Roberson 1. **Cincinnati (5)**—Sanders 2, Costo 1, Larkin 1, Oliver 1. **Colorado (6)**—Castilla 2, Bichette 1, Clark 1, Galarraga 1, Reynoso 1. **Florida (3)**—Barberie 1, Destrade 1, Felix 1. **Houston (8)**—Biggio 2, Anthony 1, Bagwell 1, Caminiti 1, Candaele 1, Gonzalez 1, Taubensee 1. **Los Angeles (7)**—Piazza 3, Davis 1, Karros 1, Sharperson 1, Wallach 1. **Montreal (8)**—Berry 2, Alou 1, Fletcher 1, Floyd 1, Grissom 1, Spehr 1, Walker 1. **New York (75)**—Bonilla 18, Murray 15, Kent 9, Burnitz 6, Hundley 5, Orsulak 5, Thompson 5, Johnson 3, Coleman 2, McKnight 2, Bogar 1, Gallagher 1, Gooden 1, O'Brien 1, Walker 1. **Philadelphia (7)**—Incaviglia 2, Jordan 2, Batiste 1, Chamberlain 1, Duncan 1. **Pittsburgh (1)**—Bell 1. **St. Louis (3)**—Gilkey 1, Pena 1, Zeile 1. **San Diego (7)**—Bell 2, Cianfrocco 2, Plantier 2, Teufel 1. **San Francisco (5)**—Carreon 2, Benjamin 1, Bonds 1, Clayton 1.

AT PHILADELPHIA (137):

Atlanta (3)—Cabrera 1, Gant 1, Justice 1. **Chicago (12)**—Grace 3, May 3, Buechele 1, Hill 1, Lake 1, Vizcaino 1, Wilkins 1, Wilson 1. **Cincinnati (2)**—Howard 1, Sabo 1. **Colorado (6)**—Jones 2, Bichette 1, Boston 1, Hayes 1, Mejia 1. **Florida (2)**—Destrade 2. **Houston (6)**—Biggio 2, Bass 1, Donnels 1, Finley 1, Servais 1. **Los Angeles (3)**—Davis 1, Piazza 1, Wallach 1. **Montreal (3)**—Alou 1, Berry 1, Bolick 1. **New York (5)**—Bogar 2, Bonilla 2, Gallagher 1. **Philadelphia (80)**—Incaviglia 15, Dykstra 12, Daulton 10, Hollins 9, Kruk 8, Chamberlain 5, Duncan 5, Pratt 4, Eisenreich 3, Jordan 3, Morandini 2, Thompson 2, Batiste 1, Stocker 1. **St. Louis (5)**—Gilkey 2, Jefferies 1, Whiten 1, Zeile 1. **San Diego (4)**—McGriff 2, Geren 1, Shipley 1. **San Francisco (6)**—Bonds 2, Clark 1, McGee 1, Scarsone 1, Williams 1.

AT PITTSBURGH (131):

Atlanta (8)—Blauser 2, Justice 2, Gant 1, McGriff 1, Pendleton 1, Sanders 1. **Chicago (2)**—Maldonado 1, Rhodes 1. **Cincinnati (5)**—Larkin 1, Mitchell 1, Oliver 1, Samuel 1, Varsho 1. **Colorado (4)**—Galarraga 3, Hayes 1. **Florida (5)**—Destrade 2, Sheffield 1, Conine 1. **Houston (3)**—Anthony 1, Bagwell 1, Servais 1. **Los Angeles (5)**—Davis 1, Hernandez 1, Piazza 1, Snyder 1, Wallach 1. **Montreal (4)**—Colbrunn 1, Fletcher 1, Grissom 1, Walker 1. **New York (4)**—Bonilla 1, Burnitz 1, Gallagher 1, O'Brien 1. **Philadelphia (4)**—Duncan 1, Amaro 1, Batiste 1. **Pittsburgh (64)**—Martin 15, Clark 8, Garcia 7, Young 6, Van Slyke 5, King 4, L. Smith 4, Bell 3, Merced 3, Goff 2, Prince 2, Shelton 2, Foley 1, McClendon 1, Slaught 1. **St. Louis (8)**—Jordan 3, Pagnozzi 2, Whiten 2, Gilkey 1. **San Diego (8)**—Plantier 4, Bell 1, McGriff 1, Sheffield 1, Velasquez 1. **San Francisco (7)**—Bonds 2, Benzinger 1, Clark 1, McGee 1, Thompson 1, Williams 1.

AT ST. LOUIS (118):

Atlanta (4)—Bream 1, Cabrera 1, Lemke 1, Pendleton 1. **Chicago (8)**—Sosa 2, Wilkins 2, Buechele 1, Roberson 1, Sandberg 1, Smith 1. **Cincinnati (4)**—Costo 2, Howard 1, Morris 1. **Colorado (6)**—Bichette 1, Clark 1, Galarraga 1, Hayes 1, Jones 1, Sheaffer 1. **Florida (3)**—Conine 1, Destrade 1, Santiago 1. **Houston (6)**—Biggio 2, Anthony 1, Bagwell 1, Caminiti 1, Taubensee 1. **Los Angeles (4)**—Snyder 2, Davis 1, Karros 1. **Montreal (2)**—Alou 1, Walker 1. **New York (6)**—Bonilla 2, Gallagher 1, Murray 1, Orsulak 1, Thompson 1. **Philadelphia (2)**—Incaviglia 1, Thompson 1. **Pittsburgh (2)**—Clark 1, Slaught 1. **St. Louis (59)**—Whiten 12, Jefferies 10, Zeile 8, Gilkey 7, Lankford 6, Jordan 4, Perry 3, Alicea 2, Pena 2, Villanueva 2, Pagnozzi 1, Pappas 1, O. Smith 1. **San Diego (6)**—Plantier 3, Bell 1, Clark 1, McGriff 1. **San Francisco (6)**—Williams 3, Bonds 1, Carreon 1, Phillips 1.

AT SAN DIEGO (166):

Atlanta (6)—Gant 2, McGriff 2, Justice 1, Pendleton 1. **Chicago (10)**—Grace 3, Sosa 3, Rhodes 2, Hill 1, Wilkins 1. **Cincinnati (5)**—Kelly 1, Larkin 1, Mitchell 1, Morris 1, Sabo 1. **Colorado (7)**—Boston 4, Bichette 1, Clark 1, Sheaffer 1. **Florida (3)**—Barberie 1, Santiago 1, Hammond 1. **Houston (10)**—Anthony 2, Bagwell 2, Biggio 2, Caminiti 2, Cedeno 1, Servais 1. **Los Angeles (6)**—Piazza 2, Wallach 2, Karros 1, Ke. Gross 1. **Montreal (5)**—Alou 1, Cordero 1, Fletcher 1, Walker 1, D. White 1. **New York (6)**—O'Brien 2, Bonilla 1, T. Fernandez 1, Johnson 1, Murray 1. **Philadelphia (4)**—Daulton 2, Dykstra 2. **Pittsburgh (4)**—Bell 1, Clark 1, Merced 1, Van Slyke 1. **St. Louis (4)**—Whiten 2, Alicea 1, Zeile 1. **San Diego (87)**—Plantier 16, Bell 12, McGriff 7, Cianfrocco 6, Clark 6, Sheffield 6, Gutierrez 5, Teufel 5, Ausmus 4, Bean 4, Gwynn 4, Staton 3, Nieves 2, Shipley 2, Gardner 1, Geren 1, Stillwell 1, Velasquez 1, Walters 1. **San Francisco (9)**—Bonds 3, Clark 3, Martinez 1, Thompson 1, Williams 1.

AT SAN FRANCISCO (163):

Atlanta (13)—Justice 3, Pendleton 3, McGriff 2, Berryhill 1, Blauser 1, Gant 1, Olson 1, Sanders 1. **Chicago (6)**—Wilkins 3, Buechele 1, May 1, Vizcaino 1. **Cincinnati (7)**—Mitchell 2, Morris 2, Kelly 1, Larkin 1, Sabo 1. **Colorado (7)**—Boston 2, Hayes 2, Gainer 1, Liriano 1, Owens 1. **Florida (6)**—Conine 2, Destrade 1, Santiago 1, Sheffield 1, Hammond 1. **Houston (10)**—Bagwell 3, Anthony 2, Caminiti 2, Cedeno 1, Finley 1, Servais 1. **Los Angeles (8)**—Davis 1, Karros 1, Piazza 1, Reed 1, Rodriguez 1, Strawberry 1, Wallach 1, Webster 1. **Montreal (4)**—Vander Wal 2, Alou 1, Grissom 1. **New York (5)**—Kent 3, Gallagher 1, Murray 1. **Philadelphia (5)**—Daulton 1, Duncan 1, Eisenreich 1, Hollins 1, Thompson 1. **Pittsburgh (1)**—Slaught 1. **St. Louis (2)**—Gilkey 1, Zeile 1. **San Diego (7)**—Plantier 2, Staton 2, Ausmus 1, Cianfrocco 1, Shipley 1. **San Francisco (82)**—Bonds 21, Williams 19, Thompson 13, Clark 5, Clayton 5, Reed 5, Benjamin 3, Manwaring 3, Carreon 2, Lewis 2, Colbert 1, Martinez 1, Scarsone 1, Wilson 1.

HISTORY

All-time results

Award winners

Hall of Fame

ALL-TIME RESULTS

AMERICAN LEAGUE CHAMPIONS

Year	Team	Manager	Year	Team	Manager
1901	Chicago	Clark Griffith	1950	New York	Casey Stengel
1902	Philadelphia	Connie Mack	1951	New York	Casey Stengel
1903	Boston	Jimmy Collins	1952	New York	Casey Stengel
1904	Boston	Jimmy Collins	1953	New York	Casey Stengel
1905	Philadelphia	Connie Mack	1954	Cleveland	Al Lopez
1906	Chicago	Fielder Jones	1955	New York	Casey Stengel
1907	Detroit	Hugh Jennings	1956	New York	Casey Stengel
1908	Detroit	Hugh Jennings	1957	New York	Casey Stengel
1909	Detroit	Hugh Jennings	1958	New York	Casey Stengel
1910	Philadelphia	Connie Mack	1959	Chicago	Al Lopez
1911	Philadelphia	Connie Mack	1960	New York	Casey Stengel
1912	Boston	Jake Stahl	1961	New York	Ralph Houk
1913	Philadelphia	Connie Mack	1962	New York	Ralph Houk
1914	Philadelphia	Connie Mack	1963	New York	Ralph Houk
1915	Boston	Bill Carrigan	1964	New York	Yogi Berra
1916	Boston	Bill Carrigan	1965	Minnesota	Sam Mele
1917	Chicago	Pants Rowland	1966	Baltimore	Hank Bauer
1918	Boston	Ed Barrow	1967	Boston	Dick Williams
1919	Chicago	Kid Gleason	1968	Detroit	Mayo Smith
1920	Cleveland	Tris Speaker	1969	Baltimore (E)	Earl Weaver
1921	New York	Miller Huggins	1970	Baltimore (E)	Earl Weaver
1922	New York	Miller Huggins	1971	Baltimore (E)	Earl Weaver
1923	New York	Miller Huggins	1972	Oakland (W)	Dick Williams
1924	Washington	Bucky Harris	1973	Oakland (W)	Dick Williams
1925	Washington	Bucky Harris	1974	Oakland (W)	Al Dark
1926	New York	Miller Huggins	1975	Boston (E)	Darrell Johnson
1927	New York	Miller Huggins	1976	New York (E)	Billy Martin
1928	New York	Miller Huggins	1977	New York (E)	Billy Martin
1929	Philadelphia	Connie Mack	1978	New York (E)	Billy Martin, Bob Lemon
1930	Philadelphia	Connie Mack	1979	Baltimore (E)	Earl Weaver
1931	Philadelphia	Connie Mack	1980	Kansas City (W)	Jim Frey
1932	New York	Joe McCarthy	1981	New York (E)	Gene Michael, Bob Lemon
1933	Washington	Joe Cronin	1982	Milwaukee (E)	Buck Rodgers, Harvey Kuenn
1934	Detroit	Mickey Cochrane	1983	Baltimore (E)	Joe Altobelli
1935	Detroit	Mickey Cochrane	1984	Detroit (E)	Sparky Anderson
1936	New York	Joe McCarthy	1985	Kansas City (W)	Dick Howser
1937	New York	Joe McCarthy	1986	Boston (E)	John McNamara
1938	New York	Joe McCarthy	1987	Minnesota (W)	Tom Kelly
1939	New York	Joe McCarthy	1988	Oakland (W)	Tony La Russa
1940	Detroit	Del Baker	1989	Oakland (W)	Tony La Russa
1941	New York	Joe McCarthy	1990	Oakland (W)	Tony La Russa
1942	New York	Joe McCarthy	1991	Minnesota (W)	Tom Kelly
1943	New York	Joe McCarthy	1992	Toronto (E)	Cito Gaston
1944	St. Louis	Luke Sewell	1993	Toronto (E)	Cito Gaston
1945	Detroit	Steve O'Neill			
1946	Boston	Joe Cronin			
1947	New York	Bucky Harris			
1948	Cleveland*	Lou Boudreau			
1949	New York	Casey Stengel			

*Defeated Boston in one-game playoff.

NATIONAL LEAGUE CHAMPIONS

Year	Team	Manager	Year	Team	Manager
1876	Chicago	Albert Spalding	1891	Boston	Frank Selee
1877	Boston	Harry Wright	1892	Boston	Frank Selee
1878	Boston	Harry Wright	1893	Boston	Frank Selee
1879	Providence	George Wright	1894	Baltimore	Edward Hanlon
1880	Chicago	Adrian Anson	1895	Baltimore	Edward Hanlon
1881	Chicago	Adrian Anson	1896	Baltimore	Edward Hanlon
1882	Chicago	Adrian Anson	1897	Boston	Frank Selee
1883	Boston	John Morrill	1898	Boston	Frank Selee
1884	Providence	Frank Bancroft	1899	Brooklyn	Edward Hanlon
1885	Chicago	Adrian Anson	1900	Brooklyn	Edward Hanlon
1886	Chicago	Adrian Anson	1901	Pittsburgh	Fred Clarke
1887	Detroit	William Watkins	1902	Pittsburgh	Fred Clarke
1888	New York	James Mutrie	1903	Pittsburgh	Fred Clarke
1889	New York	James Mutrie	1904	New York	John McGraw
1890	Brooklyn	William McGunnigle	1905	New York	John McGraw

Year	Team	Manager	Year	Team	Manager
1906	Chicago	Frank Chance	1953	Brooklyn	Charlie Dressen
1907	Chicago	Frank Chance	1954	New York	Leo Durocher
1908	Chicago	Frank Chance	1955	Brooklyn	Walter Alston
1909	Pittsburgh	Fred Clarke	1956	Brooklyn	Walter Alston
1910	Chicago	Frank Chance	1957	Milwaukee	Fred Haney
1911	New York	John McGraw	1958	Milwaukee	Fred Haney
1912	New York	John McGraw	1959	Los Angeles‡	Walter Alston
1913	New York	John McGraw	1960	Pittsburgh	Danny Murtaugh
1914	Boston	George Stallings	1961	Cincinnati	Fred Hutchinson
1915	Philadelphia	Pat Moran	1962	San Francisco§	Al Dark
1916	Brooklyn	Wilbert Robinson	1963	Los Angeles	Walter Alston
1917	New York	John McGraw	1964	St. Louis	Johnny Keane
1918	Chicago	Fred Mitchell	1965	Los Angeles	Walter Alston
1919	Cincinnati	Pat Moran	1966	Los Angeles	Walter Alston
1920	Brooklyn	Wilbert Robinson	1967	St. Louis	Red Schoendienst
1921	New York	John McGraw	1968	St. Louis	Red Schoendienst
1922	New York	John McGraw	1969	New York (E)	Gil Hodges
1923	New York	John McGraw	1970	Cincinnati (W)	Sparky Anderson
1924	New York	John McGraw	1971	Pittsburgh (E)	Danny Murtaugh
1925	Pittsburgh	Bill McKechnie	1972	Cincinnati (W)	Sparky Anderson
1926	St. Louis	Rogers Hornsby	1973	New York (E)	Yogi Berra
1927	Pittsburgh	Donie Bush	1974	Los Angeles (W)	Walter Alston
1928	St. Louis	Bill McKechnie	1975	Cincinnati (W)	Sparky Anderson
1929	Chicago	Joe McCarthy	1976	Cincinnati (W)	Sparky Anderson
1930	St. Louis	Gabby Street	1977	Los Angeles (W)	Tommy Lasorda
1931	St. Louis	Gabby Street	1978	Los Angeles (W)	Tommy Lasorda
1932	Chicago	Charlie Grimm	1979	Pittsburgh (E)	Chuck Tanner
1933	New York	Bill Terry	1980	Philadelphia (E)	Dallas Green
1934	St. Louis	Frank Frisch	1981	Los Angeles (W)	Tommy Lasorda
1935	Chicago	Charlie Grimm	1982	St. Louis (E)	Whitey Herzog
1936	New York	Bill Terry	1983	Philadelphia (E)	Pat Corrales, Paul Owens
1937	New York	Bill Terry			
1938	Chicago	Gabby Hartnett	1984	San Diego (W)	Dick Williams
1939	Cincinnati	Bill McKechnie	1985	St. Loius (E)	Whitey Herzog
1940	Cincinnati	Bill McKechnie	1986	New York (E)	Dave Johnson
1941	Brooklyn	Leo Durocher	1987	St. Louis (E)	Whitey Herzog
1942	St. Louis	Billy Southworth	1988	Los Angeles (W)	Tommy Lasorda
1943	St. Louis	Billy Southworth	1989	San Francisco (W)	Roger Craig
1944	St. Louis	Billy Southworth	1990	Cincinnati (W)	Lou Piniella
1945	Chicago	Charlie Grimm	1991	Atlanta (W)	Bobby Cox
1946	St. Louis*	Eddie Dyer	1992	Atlanta (W)	Bobby Cox
1947	Brooklyn	Burt Shotton	1993	Philadelphia (E)	Jim Fregosi
1948	Boston	Billy Southworth			
1949	Brooklyn	Burt Shotton			
1950	Philadelphia	Eddie Sawyer			
1951	New York†	Leo Durocher			
1952	Brooklyn	Charlie Dressen			

*Defeated Brooklyn, two games to none, in playoff for pennant. †Defeated Brooklyn, two games to one, in playoff for pennant. ‡Defeated Milwaukee, two games to none, in playoff for pennant. §Defeated Los Angeles, two games to one, in playoff for pennant.

WORLD SERIES

Year	Winner over Loser
1903	Boston A.L. over Pittsburgh N.L., 5 games to 3.
1904	No Series.
1905	New York N.L. over Philadelphia A.L., 4-1.
1906	Chicago A.L. over Chicago N.L., 4-2.
1907	Chicago N.L. over Detroit A.L., 4-0 with 1 tie.
1908	Chicago N.L. over Detroit A.L., 4-1.
1909	Pittsburgh N.L. over Detroit A.L., 4-3.
1910	Philadelphia A.L. over Chicago N.L., 4-1.
1911	Philadelphia A.L. over New York N.L., 4-2.
1912	Boston A.L. over New York N.L., 4-3 with 1 tie.
1913	Philadelphia A.L. over New York N.L., 4-1.
1914	Boston N.L. over Philadelphia A.L., 4-0.
1915	Boston A.L. over Philadelphia N.L., 4-1.
1916	Boston A.L. over Brooklyn N.L., 4-1.
1917	Chicago A.L. over New York N.L., 4-2.
1918	Boston A.L. over Chicago N.L., 4-2.
1919	Cincinnati N.L. over Chicago A.L., 5-3.
1920	Cleveland A.L. over Brooklyn N.L., 5-2.
1921	New York N.L. over New York A.L., 5-3.
1922	New York N.L. over New York A.L., 4-0 with 1 tie.
1923	New York A.L. over New York N.L., 4-2.
1924	Washington A.L. over New York N.L., 4-3.
1925	Pittsburgh N.L. over Washington A.L., 4-3.
1926	St. Louis N.L. over New York A.L., 4-3.
1927	New York A.L. over Pittsburgh, N.L., 4-0.
1928	New York A.L. over St. Louis N.L., 4-0.
1929	Philadelphia A.L. over Chicago N.L., 4-1.
1930	Philadelphia A.L. over St. Louis N.L., 4-2.
1931	St. Louis N.L. over Philadelphia A.L., 4-3.
1932	New York A.L. over Chicago N.L., 4-0.
1933	New York N.L. over Washington A.L., 4-1.
1934	St. Louis N.L. over Detroit A.L., 4-3.
1935	Detroit A.L. over Chicago N.L., 4-2.
1936	New York A.L. over New York N.L., 4-2.
1937	New York A.L. over New York N.L., 4-1.
1938	New York A.L. over Chicago N.L., 4-0.
1939	New York A.L. over Cincinnati N.L., 4-0.
1940	Cincinnati N.L. over Detroit A.L., 4-3.
1941	New York A.L. over Brooklyn N.L., 4-1.
1942	St. Louis N.L. over New York A.L., 4-1.
1943	New York A.L. over St. Louis, N.L., 4-1.
1944	St. Louis N.L. over St. Louis A.L., 4-2.
1945	Detroit A.L. over Chicago N.L., 4-3.
1946	St. Louis N.L. over Boston A.L., 4-3.
1947	New York A.L. over Brooklyn, N.L., 4-3.
1948	Cleveland A.L. over Boston N.L., 4-2.
1949	New York A.L. over Brooklyn N.L., 4-1.
1950	New York A.L. over Philadelphia N.L., 4-0.

Year	Winner	Loser
1951	New York A.L. over New York N.L., 4-2.
1952	New York A.L. over Brooklyn N.L., 4-3.
1953	New York A.L. over Brooklyn N.L., 4-2.
1954	New York N.L. over Cleveland A.L., 4-0.
1955	Brooklyn N.L. over New York A.L., 4-3.
1956	New York A.L. over Brooklyn N.L., 4-3.
1957	Milwaukee N.L. over New York A.L., 4-3.
1958	New York A.L. over Milwaukee N.L., 4-3.
1959	Los Angeles N.L. over Chicago A.L., 4-2.
1960	Pittsburgh N.L. over New York A.L., 4-3.
1961	New York A.L. over Cincinnati N.L., 4-1.
1962	New York A.L. over San Francisco N.L., 4-3.
1963	Los Angeles N.L. over New York A.L., 4-0.
1964	St. Louis N.L. over New York A.L., 4-3.
1965	Los Angeles N.L. over Minnesota A.L., 4-3.
1966	Baltimore A.L. over Los Angeles N.L., 4-0.
1967	St. Louis N.L. over Boston A.L., 4-3.
1968	Detroit A.L. over St. Louis N.L., 4-3.
1969	New York N.L. over Baltimore A.L., 4-1.
1970	Baltimore A.L. over Cincinnati N.L., 4-1.
1971	Pittsburgh N.L. over Baltimore A.L., 4-3.
1972	Oakland A.L. over Cincinnati N.L., 4-3.

Year	Winner	Loser
1973	Oakland A.L. over New York N.L., 4-3.
1974	Oakland A.L. over Los Angeles N.L., 4-1.
1975	Cincinnati N.L. over Boston A.L., 4-3.
1976	Cincinnati N.L. over New York A.L., 4-0.
1977	New York A.L. over Los Angeles N.L., 4-2.
1978	New York A.L. over Los Angeles N.L., 4-2.
1979	Pittsburgh N.L. over Baltimore A.L., 4-3.
1980	Philadelphia N.L. over Kansas City A.L., 4-2.
1981	Los Angeles N.L. over New York A.L., 4-2.
1982	St. Louis N.L. over Milwaukee A.L., 4-3.
1983	Baltimore A.L. over Philadelphia N.L., 4-1.
1984	Detroit A.L. over San Diego N.L., 4-1.
1985	Kansas City A.L. over St. Louis N.L., 4-3.
1986	New York N.L. over Boston A.L., 4-3.
1987	Minnesota A.L. over St. Louis N.L., 4-3.
1988	Los Angeles N.L. over Oakland A.L., 4-1.
1989	Oakland A.L. over San Francisco N.L., 4-0.
1990	Cincinnati N.L. over Oakland A.L., 4-0.
1991	Minnesota A.L. over Atlanta N.L., 4-3.
1992	Toronto A.L. over Atlanta N.L., 4-2.
1993	Toronto A.L. over Philadelphia N.L., 4-2.

CHAMPIONSHIP SERIES

AMERICAN LEAGUE

Year	Winner	Loser
1969	Baltimore (East) over Minnesota (West), 3 games to 0.
1970	Baltimore (East) over Minnesota (West), 3-0.
1971	Baltimore (East) over Oakland (West), 3-0.
1972	Oakland (West) over Detroit (East), 3-2.
1973	Oakland (West) over Baltimore (East), 3-2.
1974	Oakland (West) over Baltimore (East), 3-1.
1975	Boston (East) over Oakland (West), 3-0.
1976	New York (East) over Kansas City (West), 3-2.
1977	New York (East) over Kansas City (West), 3-2.
1978	New York (East) over Kansas City (West), 3-1.
1979	Baltimore (East) over California (West), 3-1.
1980	Kansas City (West) over New York (East), 3-0.
1981	New York (East) over Oakland (West), 3-0.
1982	Milwaukee (East) over California (West), 3-2.
1983	Baltimore (East) over Chicago (West), 3-1.
1984	Detroit (East) over Kansas City (West), 3-0.
1985	Kansas City (West) over Toronto (East), 4-3.
1986	Boston (East) over California (West), 4-3.
1987	Minnesota (West) over Detroit (East), 4-1.
1988	Oakland (West) over Boston (East), 4-0.
1989	Oakland (West) over Toronto (East), 4-1.
1990	Oakland (West) over Boston (East), 4-0.
1991	Minnesota (West) over Toronto (East), 4-1.
1992	Toronto (East) over Oakland (West), 4-2.
1993	Toronto (East) over Chicago (West), 4-2.

NATIONAL LEAGUE

Year	Winner	Loser
1969	New York (East) over Atlanta (West), 3 games to 0.
1970	Cincinnati (West) over Pittsburgh (East), 3-0.
1971	Pittsburgh (East) over San Francisco (West), 3-1.
1972	Cincinnati (West) over Pittsburgh (East), 3-2.
1973	New York (East) over Cincinnati (West), 3-2.
1974	Los Angeles (West) over Pittsburgh (East), 3-1.
1975	Cincinnati (West) over Pittsburgh (East), 3-0.
1976	Cincinnati (West) over Philadelphia (East), 3-0.
1977	Los Angeles (West) over Philadelphia (East), 3-1.
1978	Los Angeles (West) over Philadelphia (East), 3-1.
1979	Pittsburgh (East) over Cincinnati (West), 3-0.
1980	Philadelphia (East) over Houston (West), 3-2.
1981	Los Angeles (West) over Montreal (East), 3-2.
1982	St. Louis (East) over Atlanta (West), 3-0.
1983	Philadelphia (East) over Los Angeles (West), 3-1.
1984	San Diego (West) over Chicago (East), 3-2.
1985	St. Louis (East) over Los Angeles (West), 4-2.
1986	New York (East) over Houston (West), 4-2.
1987	St. Louis (East) over San Francisco (West), 4-3.
1988	Los Angeles (West) over New York (East), 4-3.
1989	San Francisco (West) over Chicago (East), 4-1.
1990	Cincinnati (West) over Pittsburgh (East), 4-2.
1991	Atlanta (West) over Pittsburgh (East), 4-3.
1992	Atlanta (West) over Pittsburgh (East), 4-3.
1993	Philadelphia (East) over Atlanta (West), 4-2.

ALL-STAR GAME

Date	Site	Score (Winner)	Winning pitcher (Losing pitcher)	Winning manager (Losing manager)	Att.
7-6-33	Comiskey Park Chicago	4-2 (A.L.)	Lefty Gomez, Yankees (Bill Hallahan, Cardinals)	Connie Mack, Athletics (John McGraw, Giants)	47,595
7-10-34	Polo Grounds New York	9-7 (A.L.)	Mel Harder, Indians (Van Mungo, Dodgers)	Joe Cronin, Senators (Bill Terry, Giants)	48,363
7-8-35	Municipal Stadium Cleveland	4-1 (A.L.)	Lefty Gomez, Yankees (Bill Walker, Cardinals)	Mickey Cochrane, Tigers (Frankie Frisch, Cardinals)	69,831
7-7-36	Braves Field Boston	4-3 (N.L.)	Dizzy Dean, Cardinals (Lefty Grove, Red Sox)	Charlie Grimm, Cubs (Joe McCarthy, Yankees)	25,556
7-7-37	Griffith Stadium Washington	8-3 (A.L.)	Lefty Gomez, Yankees (Dizzy Dean, Cardinals)	Joe McCarthy, Yankees (Bill Terry, Giants)	31,391
7-6-38	Crosley Field Cincinnati	4-1 (N.L.)	Johnny Vander Meer, Reds (Lefty Gomez, Yankees)	Bill Terry, Giants (Joe McCarthy, Yankees)	27,067
7-11-39	Yankee Stadium New York	3-1 (A.L.)	Tommy Bridges, Tigers (Bill Lee, Cubs)	Joe McCarthy, Yankees (Gabby Hartnett, Cubs)	62,892
7-9-40	Sportsman's Park St. Louis	4-0 (N.L.)	Paul Derringer, Reds (Red Ruffing, Yankees)	Bill McKechnie, Reds (Joe Cronin, Red Sox)	32,373

Date	Site	Score (Winner)	Winning pitcher (Losing pitcher)	Winning manager (Losing manager)	Att.
7-8-41	Briggs Stadium Detroit	7-5 (A.L.)	Ed Smith, White Sox (Claude Passeau, Cubs)	Del Baker, Tigers (Bill McKechnie, Reds)	54,674
7-6-42	Polo Grounds New York	3-1 (A.L.)	Spud Chandler, Yankees (Mort Cooper, Cardinals)	Joe McCarthy, Yankees (Leo Durocher, Dodgers)	34,178
7-13-43	Shibe Park Philadelphia	5-3 (A.L.)	Dutch Leonard, Senators (Mort Cooper, Cardinals)	Joe McCarthy, Yankees (Billy Southworth, Cardinals)	31,938
7-11-44	Forbes Field Pittsburgh	7-1 (N.L.)	Ken Raffensberger, Phillies (Tex Hughson, Red Sox)	Billy Southworth, Cardinals (Joe McCarthy, Yankees)	29,589
1945	No game played.				
7-9-46	Fenway Park Boston	12-0 (A.L.)	Bob Feller, Indians (Claude Passeau, Cubs)	Steve O'Neill, Tigers (Charlie Grimm, Cubs)	34,906
7-8-47	Wrigley Field Chicago	2-1 (A.L.)	Frank Shea, Yankees (Johnny Sain, Braves)	Joe Cronin, Red Sox (Eddie Dyer, Cardinals)	41,123
7-13-48	Sportsman's Park St. Louis	5-2 (A.L.)	Vic Raschi, Yankees (Johnny Schmitz, Cubs)	Bucky Harris, Yankees (Leo Durocher, Dodgers)	34,009
7-12-49	Ebbets Field Brooklyn	11-7 (A.L.)	Virgil Trucks, Tigers (Don Newcombe, Dodgers)	Lou Boudreau, Indians (Billy Southworth, Braves)	32,577
7-11-50	Comiskey Park Chicago	4-3* (N.L.)	Ewell Blackwell, Reds (Ted Gray, Tigers)	Burt Shotton, Dodgers (Casey Stengel, Yankees)	46,127
7-10-51	Briggs Stadium Detroit	8-3 (N.L.)	Sal Maglie, Giants (Ed Lopat, Yankees)	Eddie Sawyer, Phillies (Casey Stengel, Yankees)	52,075
7-8-52	Shibe Park Philadelphia	3-2† (N.L.)	Bob Rush, Cubs (Bob Lemon, Indians)	Leo Durocher, Giants (Casey Stengel, Yankees)	32,785
7-14-53	Crosley Field Cincinnati	5-1 (N.L.)	Warren Spahn, Braves (Allie Reynolds, Yankees)	Chuck Dressen, Dodgers (Casey Stengel, Yankees)	30,846
7-13-54	Municipal Stadium Cleveland	11-9 (A.L.)	Dean Stone, Senators (Gene Conley, Braves)	Casey Stengel, Yankees (Walter Alston, Dodgers)	68,751
7-12-55	Milwaukee Co. Stadium Milwaukee	6-5‡ (N.L.)	Gene Conley, Braves (Frank Sullivan, Red Sox)	Leo Durocher, Giants (Al Lopez, Indians)	45,643
7-10-56	Griffith Stadium Washington	7-3 (N.L.)	Bob Friend, Pirates (Billy Pierce, White Sox)	Walter Alston, Dodgers (Casey Stengel, Yankees)	28,843
7-9-57	Busch Stadium St. Louis	6-5 (A.L.)	Jim Bunning, Tigers (Curt Simmons, Phillies)	Casey Stengel, Yankees (Walter Alston, Dodgers)	30,693
7-8-58	Memorial Stadium Baltimore	4-3 (A.L.)	Early Wynn, White Sox (Bob Friend, Pirates)	Casey Stengel, Yankees (Fred Haney, Braves)	48,829
7-7-59	Forbes Field Pittsburgh	5-4 (N.L.)	Johnny Antonelli, Giants (Whitey Ford, Yankees)	Fred Haney, Braves (Casey Stengel, Yankees)	35,277
8-3-59	Memorial Coliseum Los Angeles	5-3 (A.L.)	Jerry Walker, Orioles (Don Drysdale, Dodgers)	Casey Stengel, Yankees (Fred Haney, Braves)	55,105
7-11-60	Municipal Stadium Kansas City	5-3 (N.L.)	Bob Friend, Pirates (Bill Monbouquette, Red Sox)	Walter Alston, Dodgers (Al Lopez, White Sox)	30,619
7-13-60	Yankee Stadium New York	6-0 (N.L.)	Vernon Law, Pirates (Whitey Ford, Yankees)	Walter Alston, Dodgers (Al Lopez, White Sox)	38,362
7-11-61	Candlestick Park San Francisco	5-4§ (N.L.)	Stu Miller, Giants (Hoyt Wilhelm, Orioles)	Danny Murtaugh, Pirates (Paul Richards, Orioles)	44,115
7-31-61	Fenway Park Boston	1-1 (tie)		Paul Richards, Orioles (A.L.) Danny Murtaugh, Pirates (N.L.)	31,851
7-10-62	District of Col. Stad. Washington	3-1 (N.L.)	Juan Marichal, Giants (Camilo Pascual, Twins)	Fred Hutchinson, Reds (Ralph Houk, Yankees)	45,480
7-30-62	Wrigley Field Chicago	9-4 (A.L.)	Ray Herbert, White Sox (Art Mahaffey, Phillies)	Ralph Houk, Yankees (Fred Hutchinson, Reds)	38,359
7-9-63	Municipal Stadium Cleveland	5-3 (N.L.)	Larry Jackson, Cubs (Jim Bunning, Tigers)	Alvin Dark, Giants (Ralph Houk, Yankees)	44,160
7-7-64	Shea Stadium New York	7-4 (N.L.)	Juan Marichal, Giants (Dick Radatz, Red Sox)	Walter Alston, Dodgers (Al Lopez, White Sox)	50,850
7-13-65	Metropolitan Stadium Bloomington, Minn.	6-5 (N.L.)	Sandy Koufax, Dodgers (Sam McDowell, Indians)	Gene Mauch, Phillies (Al Lopez, White Sox)	46,706
7-12-66	Busch Stadium St. Louis	2-1§ (N.L.)	Gaylord Perry, Giants (Pete Richert, Senators)	Walter Alston, Dodgers (Sam Mele, Twins)	49,936
7-11-67	Anaheim Stadium Anaheim, Calif.	2-1★ (N.L.)	Don Drysdale, Dodgers (Jim Hunter, Athletics)	Walter Alston, Dodgers (Hank Bauer, Orioles)	46,309
7-9-68	Astrodome Houston	1-0 (N.L.)	Don Drysdale, Dodgers (Luis Tiant, Indians)	Red Schoendienst, Cardinals (Dick Williams, Red Sox)	48,321
7-23-69	R.F.K. Stadium Washington	9-3 (N.L.)	Steve Carlton, Cardinals (Mel Stottlemyre, Yankees)	Red Schoendienst, Cardinals (Mayo Smith, Tigers)	45,259
7-14-70	Riverfront Stadium Cincinnati	5-4‡ (N.L.)	Claude Osteen, Dodgers (Clyde Wright, Angels)	Gil Hodges, Mets (Earl Weaver, Orioles)	51,838
7-13-71	Tiger Stadium Detroit	6-4 (A.L.)	Vida Blue, Athletics (Dock Ellis, Pirates)	Earl Weaver, Orioles (Sparky Anderson, Reds)	53,559
7-25-72	Atlanta Stadium Atlanta	4-3§ (N.L.)	Tug McGraw, Mets (Dave McNally, Orioles)	Danny Murtaugh, Pirates (Earl Weaver, Orioles)	53,107
7-24-73	Royals Stadium Kansas City	7-1 (N.L.)	Rick Wise, Cardinals (Bert Blyleven, Twins)	Sparky Anderson, Reds (Dick Williams, Athletics)	40,849
7-23-74	Three Rivers Stadium Pittsburgh	7-2 (N.L.)	Ken Brett, Pirates (Luis Tiant, Red Sox)	Yogi Berra, Mets (Dick Williams, Athletics)	50,706

Date	Site	Score (Winner)	Winning pitcher (Losing pitcher)	Winning manager (Losing manager)	Att.
7-15-75	Milwaukee Co. Stadium Milwaukee	6-3 (N.L.)	Jon Matlack, Mets (Jim Hunter, Yankees)	Walter Alston, Dodgers (Alvin Dark, Athletics)	51,480
7-13-76	Veterans Stadium Philadelphia	7-1 (N.L)	Randy Jones, Padres (Mark Fidrych, Tigers)	Sparky Anderson, Reds (Darrell Johnson, Red Sox)	63,974
7-19-77	Yankee Stadium New York	7-5 (N.L.)	Don Sutton, Dodgers (Jim Palmer, Orioles)	Sparky Anderson, Reds (Billy Martin, Yankees)	56,683
7-11-78	San Diego Stadium San Diego	7-3 (N.L.)	Bruce Sutter, Cubs (Rich Gossage, Yankees)	Tommy Lasorda, Dodgers (Billy Martin, Yankees)	51,549
7-17-79	Kingdome Seattle	7-6 (N.L.)	Bruce Sutter, Cubs (Jim Kern, Rangers)	Tommy Lasorda, Dodgers (Bob Lemon, Yankees)	58,905
7-8-80	Dodger Stadium Los Angeles	4-2 (N.L.)	Jerry Reuss, Dodgers (Tommy John, Yankees)	Chuck Tanner, Pirates (Earl Weaver, Orioles)	56,088
8-9-81	Municipal Stadium Cleveland	5-4 (N.L.)	Vida Blue, Giants (Rollie Fingers, Brewers)	Dallas Green, Phillies (Jim Frey, Royals)	72,086
7-13-82	Olympic Stadium Montreal	4-1 (N.L.)	Steve Rogers, Expos (Dennis Eckersley, Red Sox)	Tommy Lasorda, Dodgers (Billy Martin, Athletics)	59,057
7-6-83	Comiskey Park Chicago	13-3 (A.L.)	Dave Stieb, Blue Jays (Mario Soto, Reds)	Harvey Kuenn, Brewers (Whitey Herzog, Cardinals)	43,801
7-10-84	Candlestick Park San Francisco	3-1 (N.L.)	Charlie Lea, Expos (Dave Stieb, Blue Jays)	Paul Owens, Phillies (Joe Altobelli, Orioles)	57,756
7-16-85	Metrodome Minneapolis	6-1 (N.L.)	LaMarr Hoyt, Padres (Jack Morris, Tigers)	Dick Williams, Padres (Sparky Anderson, Tigers)	54,960
7-15-86	Astrodome Houston	3-2 (A.L.)	Roger Clemens, Red Sox (Dwight Gooden, Mets)	Dick Howser, Royals (Whitey Herzog, Cardinals)	45,774
7-14-87	Oak.-Alameda Co. Col. Oakland	2-0 • (N.L.)	Lee Smith, Cubs (Jay Howell, Athletics)	Dave Johnson, Mets (John McNamara, Red Sox)	49,671
7-12-88	Riverfront Stadium Cincinnati	2-1 (A.L.)	Frank Viola, Twins (Dwight Gooden, Mets)	Tom Kelly, Twins (Whitey Herzog, Cardinals)	55,837
7-11-89	Anaheim Stadium Anaheim, Calif.	5-3 (A.L.)	Nolan Ryan, Rangers (John Smoltz, Braves)	Tony La Russa, Athletics (Tommy Lasorda, Dodgers)	64,036
7-10-90	Wrigley Field Chicago	2-0 (A.L.)	Bret Saberhagen, Royals (Jeff Brantley, Giants)	Tony La Russa, Athletics (Roger Craig, Giants)	39,071
7-9-91	SkyDome Toronto	4-2 (A.L.)	Jimmy Key, Blue Jays (Dennis Martinez, Expos)	Tony La Russa, Athletics (Lou Piniella, Reds)	52,383
7-14-92	Jack Murphy Stadium San Diego	13-6 (A.L.)	Kevin Brown, Rangers (Tom Glavine, Braves)	Tom Kelly, Twins (Bobby Cox, Braves)	59,372
7-13-93	Oriole Park at Camden Yards, Baltimore	9-3 (A.L.)	Jack McDowell, White Sox (John Burkett, Giants)	Cito Gaston, Blue Jays (Bobby Cox, Braves)	48,147

*14 innings.   †5 innings (rain).   ‡12 innings.   §10 innings.   ★15 innings.   •13 innings.

AWARD WINNERS

MOST VALUABLE PLAYER

AMERICAN LEAGUE

Year	Player, Team, Pos.	Points
1929—	Al Simmons, Philadelphia, OF	40
1930—	Joe Cronin, Washington, SS	52
1931—	Lou Gehrig, New York, 1B	40
1932—	Jimmie Foxx, Philadelphia, 1B	46
1933—	Jimmie Foxx, Philadelphia, 1B	49
1934—	Lou Gehrig, New York, 1B	51
1935—	Hank Greenberg, Detroit, 1B	64
1936—	Lou Gehrig, New York, 1B	55
1937—	Charley Gehringer, Detroit, 2B	78
1938—	Jimmie Foxx, Boston, 1B	304
1939—	Joe DiMaggio, New York, OF	280
1940—	Hank Greenberg, Detroit, OF	292
1941—	Joe DiMaggio, New York, OF	291
1942—	Joe Gordon, New York, 2B	270
1943—	Spud Chandler, New York, P	246
1944—	Bobby Doerr, Boston, 2B	
1945—	Eddie Mayo, Detroit, 2B	

NATIONAL LEAGUE

Year	Player, Team, Pos.	Points
1929—	No selection	
1930—	Bill Terry, New York, 1B	47
1931—	Chuck Klein, Philadelphia, OF	40
1932—	Chuck Klein, Philadelphia, OF	46
1933—	Carl Hubbell, New York, P	64
1934—	Dizzy Dean, St. Louis, P	57
1935—	Arky Vaughan, Pittsburgh, SS	42
1936—	Carl Hubbell, New York, P	61
1937—	Joe Medwick, St. Louis, OF	70
1938—	Ernie Lombardi, Cincinnati, C	229
1939—	Bucky Walters, Cincinnati, P	303
1940—	Frank McCormick, Cincinnati, 1B	274
1941—	Dolf Camilli, Brooklyn, 1B	300
1942—	Mort Cooper, St. Loius, P	263
1943—	Stan Musial, St. Louis, OF	267
1944—	Marty Marion, St. Louis, SS	
1945—	Tommy Holmes, Boston, OF	

PLAYER AND PITCHER OF THE YEAR

AMERICAN LEAGUE

Year	Player, Team, Pos.
1948—	Lou Boudreau, Cleveland, SS
	Bob Lemon, Cleveland, P
1949—	Ted Williams, Boston, OF
	Ellis Kinder, Boston, P
1950—	Phil Rizzuto, New York, SS
	Bob Lemon, Cleveland, P
1951—	Ferris Fain, Philadelphia, 1B
	Bob Feller, Cleveland, P
1952—	Luke Easter, Cleveland, 1B
	Bobby Shantz, Philadelphia, P
1953—	Al Rosen, Cleveland, 3B
	Bob Porterfield, Washington, P
1954—	Bobby Avila, Cleveland, 2B
	Bob Lemon, Cleveland, P
1955—	Al Kaline, Detroit, OF
	Whitey Ford, New York, P
1956—	Mickey Mantle, New York, OF
	Billy Pierce, Chicago, P
1957—	Ted Williams, Boston, OF
	Billy Pierce, Chicago, P
1958—	Jackie Jensen, Boston, OF
	Bob Turley, New York, P
1959—	Nellie Fox, Chicago, 2B
	Early Wynn, Chicago, P
1960—	Roger Maris, New York, OF
	Chuck Estrada, Baltimore, P
1961—	Roger Maris, New York, OF
	Whitey Ford, New York, P
1962—	Mickey Mantle, New York, OF
	Dick Donovan, Cleveland, P
1963—	Al Kaline, Detroit, OF
	Whitey Ford, New York, P
1964—	Brooks Robinson, Baltimore, 3B
	Dean Chance, Los Angeles, P
1965—	Tony Oliva, Minnesota, OF
	Jim Grant, Minnesota, P
1966—	Frank Robinson, Baltimore, OF
	Jim Kaat, Minnesota, P
1967—	Carl Yastrzemski, Boston, OF
	Jim Lonborg, Boston, P
1968—	Ken Harrelson, Boston, OF
	Denny McLain, Detroit, P
1969—	Harmon Killebrew, Minnesota, 1B-3B
	Denny McLain, Detroit, P

NATIONAL LEAGUE

Year	Player, Team, Pos.
1948—	Stan Musial, St. Louis, OF - 1B
	Johnny Sain, Boston, P
1949—	Enos Slaughter, St. Louis, OF
	Howard Pollet, St. Louis, P
1950—	Ralph Kiner, Pittsburgh, OF
	Jim Konstanty, Philadelphia, P
1951—	Stan Musial, St. Louis, OF
	Preacher Roe, Brooklyn, P
1952—	Hank Sauer, Chicago, OF
	Robin Roberts, Philadelphia, P
1953—	Roy Campanella, Brooklyn, C
	Warren Spahn, Milwaukee, P
1954—	Willie Mays, New York, OF
	Johnny Antonelli, New York, P
1955—	Duke Snider, Brooklyn, OF
	Robin Roberts, Philadelphia, P
1956—	Hank Aaron, Milwaukee, OF
	Don Newcombe, Brooklyn, P
1957—	Stan Musial, St. Louis, 1B
	Warren Spahn, Milwaukee, P
1958—	Ernie Banks, Chicago, SS
	Warren Spahn, Milwaukee, P
1959—	Ernie Banks, Chicago, SS
	Sam Jones, San Francisco, P
1960—	Dick Groat, Pittsburgh, SS
	Vern Law, Pittsburgh, P
1961—	Frank Robinson, Cincinnati, OF
	Warren Spahn, Milwaukee, P
1962—	Maury Wills, Los Angeles, SS
	Don Drysdale, Los Angeles, P
1963—	Hank Aaron, Milwaukee, OF
	Sandy Koufax, Los Angeles, P
1964—	Ken Boyer, St. Louis, 3B
	Sandy Koufax, Los Angeles, P
1965—	Willie Mays, San Francisco, OF
	Sandy Koufax, Los Angeles, P
1966—	Roberto Clemente, Pittsburgh, OF
	Sandy Koufax, Los Angeles, P
1967—	Orlando Cepeda, St. Louis, 1B
	Mike McCormick, San Francisco, P
1968—	Pete Rose, Cincinnati, OF
	Bob Gibson, St. Louis, P
1969—	Willie McCovey, San Francisco, 1B
	Tom Seaver, New York, P

Year	Player, Team, Pos.	Year	Player, Team, Pos.
1970—	Harmon Killebrew, Minnesota, 3B Sam McDowell, Cleveland, P	1970—	Johnny Bench, Cincinnati, C Bob Gibson, St. Louis, P
1971—	Tony Oliva, Minnesota, OF Vida Blue, Oakland, P	1971—	Joe Torre, St. Louis, 3B Ferguson Jenkins, Chicago, P
1972—	Dick Allen, Chicago, 1B Wilbur Wood, Chicago, P	1972—	Billy Williams, Chicago, OF Steve Carlton, Philadelphia, P
1973—	Reggie Jackson, Oakland, OF Jim Palmer, Baltimore, P	1973—	Bobby Bonds, San Francisco, OF Ron Bryant, San Francisco, P
1974—	Jeff Burroughs, Texas, OF Jim Hunter, Oakland, P	1974—	Lou Brock, St. Louis, OF Mike Marshall, Los Angeles, P
1975—	Fred Lynn, Boston, OF Jim Palmer, Baltimore, P	1975—	Joe Morgan, Cincinnati, 2B Tom Seaver, New York, P
1976—	Thurman Munson, New York, C Jim Palmer, Baltimore, P	1976—	George Foster, Cincinnati, OF Randy Jones, San Diego, P
1977—	Rod Carew, Minnesota, 1B Nolan Ryan, California, P	1977—	George Foster, Cincinnati, OF Steve Carlton, Philadelphia, P
1978—	Jim Rice, Boston, OF Ron Guidry, New York, P	1978—	Dave Parker, Pittsburgh, OF Vida Blue, San Francisco, P
1979—	Don Baylor, California, OF Mike Flanagan, Baltimore, P	1979—	Keith Hernandez, St. Louis, 1B Joe Niekro, Houston, P
1980—	George Brett, Kansas City, 3B Steve Stone, Baltimore, P	1980—	Mike Schmidt, Philadelphia, 3B Steve Carlton, Philadelphia, P
1981—	Tony Armas, Oakland, OF Jack Morris, Detroit, P	1981—	Andre Dawson, Montreal, OF Fernando Valenzuela, Los Angeles, P
1982—	Robin Yount, Milwaukee, SS Dave Stieb, Toronto, P	1982—	Dale Murphy, Atlanta, OF Steve Carlton, Philadelphia, P
1983—	Cal Ripken Jr., Baltimore, SS LaMarr Hoyt, Chicago, P	1983—	Dale Murphy, Atlanta, OF John Denny, Philadelphia, P
1984—	Don Mattingly, New York, 1B Willie Hernandez, Detroit, P	1984—	Ryne Sandberg, Chicago, 2B Rick Sutcliffe, Chicago, P
1985—	Don Mattingly, New York, 1B Bret Saberhagen, Kansas City, P	1985—	Willie McGee, St. Louis, OF Dwight Gooden, New York, P
1986—	Don Mattingly, New York, 1B Roger Clemens, Boston, P	1986—	Mike Schmidt, Philadelphia, 3B Mike Scott, Houston, P
1987—	George Bell, Toronto, OF Jimmy Key, Toronto, P	1987—	Andre Dawson, Chicago, OF Rick Sutcliffe, Chicago, P
1988—	Jose Canseco, Oakland, OF Frank Viola, Minnesota, P	1988—	Andy Van Slyke, Pittsburgh, OF Orel Hershiser, Los Angeles, P
1989—	Ruben Sierra, Texas, OF Bret Saberhagen, Kansas City, P	1989—	Kevin Mitchell, San Francisco, OF Mark Davis, San Diego, P
1990—	Cecil Fielder, Detroit, 1B Bob Welch, Oakland, P	1990—	Barry Bonds, Pittsburgh, OF Doug Drabek, Pittsburgh, P
1991—	Cal Ripken Jr., Baltimore, SS Roger Clemens, Boston, P	1991—	Barry Bonds, Pittsburgh, OF Tom Glavine, Atlanta, P

PITCHER OF THE YEAR

AMERICAN LEAGUE

Year	Player, Team, Pos.
1992—	Dennis Eckersley, Oakland
1993—	Jack McDowell, Chicago

NATIONAL LEAGUE

Year	Player, Team, Pos.
1992—	Greg Maddux, Chicago
1993—	Greg Maddux, Atlanta

ROOKIE OF THE YEAR

1946—Combined selection—Del Ennis, Philadelphia NL, OF
1947—Combined selection—Jackie Robinson, Brooklyn NL, 1B
1948—Combined selection—Richie Ashburn, Philadelphia NL, OF

AMERICAN LEAGUE

Year	Player, Team, Pos.
1949—	Roy Sievers, St. Louis, OF
1950—	Combined selection—Whitey Ford, New York, A.L., P
1951—	Minnie Minoso, Chicago, OF
1952—	Clint Courtney, St. Louis, C
1953—	Harvey Kuenn, Detroit, SS
1954—	Bob Grim, New York, P
1955—	Herb Score, Cleveland, P
1956—	Luis Aparicio, Chicago, SS
1957—	Tony Kubek, New York, IF-OF (No pitcher named)
1958—	Albie Pearson, Washington, OF Ryne Duren, New York, P

NATIONAL LEAGUE

Year	Player, Team, Pos.
1949—	Don Newcombe, Brooklyn, P
1951—	Willie Mays, New York, OF
1952—	Joe Black, Brooklyn, P
1953—	Jim Gilliam, Brooklyn, 2B
1954—	Wally Moon, St. Louis, OF
1955—	Bill Virdon, St. Louis, OF
1956—	Frank Robinson, Cincinnati, OF
1957—	Ed Bouchee, Philadelphia, 1B Jack Sanford, Philadelphia, P
1958—	Orlando Cepeda, San Francisco, 1B Carlton Willey, Milwaukee, P

Year	Player, Team, Pos.	Year	Player, Team, Pos.
1959—	Bob Allison, Washington, OF	1959—	Willie McCovey, San Francisco, 1B
1960—	Ron Hansen, Baltimore, SS	1960—	Frank Howard, Los Angeles, OF
1961—	Dick Howser, Kansas City, SS	1961—	Billy Williams, Chicago, OF
	Don Schwall, Boston, P		Ken Hunt, Cincinnati, P
1962—	Tom Tresh, New York, OF-SS	1962—	Ken Hubbs, Chicago, 2B
1963—	Pete Ward, Chicago, 3B	1963—	Pete Rose, Cincinnati, 2B
	Gary Peters, Chicago, P		Ray Culp, Philadelphia, P
1964—	Tony Oliva, Minnesota, OF	1964—	Dick Allen, Philadelphia, 3B
	Wally Bunker, Baltimore, P		Billy McCool, Cincinnati, P
1965—	Curt Blefary, Baltimore, OF	1965—	Joe Morgan, Houston, 2B
	Marcelino Lopez, California, P		Frank Linzy, San Francisco, P
1966—	Tommie Agee, Chicago, OF	1966—	Tommy Helms, Cincinnati, 3B
	Jim Nash, Kansas City, P		Don Sutton, Los Angeles, P
1967—	Rod Carew, Minnesota, 2B	1967—	Lee May, Cincinnati, 1B
	Tom Phoebus, Baltimore, P		Dick Hughes, St. Louis, P
1968—	Del Unser, Washington, OF	1968—	Johnny Bench, Cincinnati, C
	Stan Bahnsen, New York, P		Jerry Koosman, New York, P
1969—	Carlos May, Chicago, OF	1969—	Coco Laboy, Montreal, 3B
	Mike Nagy, Boston, P		Tom Griffin, Houston, P
1970—	Roy Foster, Cleveland, OF	1970—	Bernie Carbo, Cincinnati, OF
	Bert Blyleven, Minnesota, P		Carl Morton, Montreal, P
1971—	Chris Chambliss, Cleveland, 1B	1971—	Earl Williams, Atlanta, C
	Bill Parsons, Milwaukee, P		Reggie Cleveland, St. Louis, P
1972—	Carlton Fisk, Boston, C	1972—	Dave Rader, San Francisco, C
	Dick Tidrow, Cleveland, P		Jon Matlack, New York, P
1973—	Al Bumbry, Baltimore, OF	1973—	Gary Matthews, San Francisco, OF
	Steve Busby, Kansas City, P		Steve Rogers, Montreal, P
1974—	Mike Hargrove, Texas, 1B	1974—	Greg Gross, Houston, OF
	Frank Tanana, California, P		John D'Acquisto, San Francisco, P
1975—	Fred Lynn, Boston, OF	1975—	Gary Carter, Montreal, OF-C
	Dennis Eckersley, Cleveland, P		John Montefusco, San Francisco, P
1976—	Butch Wynegar, Minnesota, C	1976—	Larry Herndon, San Francisco, OF
	Mark Fidrych, Detroit, P		Butch Metzger, San Diego, P
1977—	Mitchell Page, Oakland, OF	1977—	Andre Dawson, Montreal, OF
	Dave Rozema, Detroit, P		Bob Owchinko, San Diego, P
1978—	Paul Molitor, Milwaukee, 2B	1978—	Bob Horner, Atlanta, 3B
	Rich Gale, Kansas City, P		Don Robinson, Pittsburgh, P
1979—	Pat Putnam, Texas 1B	1979—	Jeff Leonard, Houston, OF
	Mark Clear, California, P		Rick Sutcliffe, Los Angeles, P
1980—	Joe Charboneau, Cleveland, OF	1980—	Lonnie Smith, Philadelphia, OF
	Britt Burns, Chicago, P		Bill Gullickson, Montreal, P
1981—	Rich Gedman, Boston, C	1981—	Tim Raines, Montreal, OF
	Dave Righetti, New York, P		Fernando Valenzuela, Los Angeles, P
1982—	Cal Ripken Jr., Baltimore, SS-3B	1982—	Johnny Ray, Pittsburgh, 2B
	Ed Vande Berg, Seattle, P		Steve Bedrosian, Atlanta, P
1983—	Ron Kittle, Chicago, OF	1983—	Darryl Strawberry, New York, OF
	Mike Boddicker, Baltimore, P		Craig McMurtry, Atlanta, P
1984—	Alvin Davis, Seattle, 1B	1984—	Juan Samuel, Philadelphia, 2B
	Mark Langston, Seattle, P		Dwight Gooden, New York, P
1985	Ozzie Guillen, Chicago, SS	1985—	Vince Coleman, St. Louis, OF
	Teddy Higuera, Milwaukee, P		Tom Browning, Cincinnati, P
1986—	Jose Canseco, Oakland, OF	1986—	Robby Thompson, San Francisco, 2B
	Mark Eichhorn, Toronto, P		Todd Worrell, St. Louis, P
1987—	Mark McGwire, Oakland, 1B	1987—	Benito Santiago, San Diego, C
	Mike Henneman, Detroit, P		Mike Dunne, Pittsburgh, P
1988—	Walt Weiss, Oakland, SS	1988—	Mark Grace, Chicago, 1B
	Bryan Harvey, California, P		Tim Belcher, Los Angeles, P
1989—	Craig Worthington, Baltimore, 3B	1989—	Jerome Walton, Chicago, OF
	Tom Gordon, Kansas City, P		Andy Benes, San Diego, P
1990—	Sandy Alomar Jr., Cleveland, C	1990—	David Justice, Atlanta, OF
	Kevin Appier, Kansas City, P		Mike Harkey, Chicago, P
1991—	Chuck Knoblauch, Minnesota, 2B	1991—	Jeff Bagwell, Houston, 1B
	Juan Guzman, Toronto, P		Al Osuna, Houston, P
1992—	Pat Listach, Milwaukee, SS	1992—	Eric Karros, Los Angeles, 1B
	Cal Eldred, Milwaukee, P		Tim Wakefield, Pittsburgh, P
1993—	Tim Salmon, California, OF	1993—	Mike Piazza, Los Angeles, C
	Aaron Sele, Boston, P		Kirk Rueter, Montreal, P

FIREMAN OF THE YEAR

AMERICAN LEAGUE

Year	Player, Team
1960—	Mike Fornieles, Boston
1961—	Luis Arroyo, New York
1962—	Dick Radatz, Boston

NATIONAL LEAGUE

Year	Player, Team
1960—	Lindy McDaniel, St. Louis
1961—	Stu Miller, San Francisco
1962—	Roy Face, Pittsburgh

Year	Player, Team	Year	Player, Team
1963—	Stu Miller, Baltimore	1963—	Lindy McDaniel, Chicago
1964—	Dick Radatz, Boston	1964—	Al McBean, Pittsburgh
1965—	Eddie Fisher, Chicago	1965—	Ted Abernathy, Chicago
1966—	Jack Aker, Kansas City	1966—	Phil Regan, Los Angeles
1967—	Minnie Rojas, California	1967—	Ted Abernathy, Cincinnati
1968—	Wilbur Wood, Chicago	1968—	Phil Regan, L.A.-Chicago
1969—	Ron Perranoski, Minnesota	1969—	Wayne Granger, Cincinnati
1970—	Ron Perranoski, Minnesota	1970—	Wayne Granger, Cincinnati
1971—	Ken Sanders, Milwaukee	1971—	Dave Giusti, Pittsburgh
1972—	Sparky Lyle, New York	1972—	Clay Carroll, Cincinnati
1973—	John Hiller, Detroit	1973—	Mike Marshall, Montreal
1974—	Terry Forster, Chicago	1974—	Mike Marshall, Los Angeles
1975—	Rich Gossage, Chicago	1975—	Al Hrabosky, St. Louis
1976—	Bill Campbell, Minnesota	1976—	Rawly Eastwick, Cincinnati
1977—	Bill Campbell, Boston	1977—	Rollie Fingers, San Diego
1978—	Rich Gossage, New York	1978—	Rollie Fingers, San Diego
1979—	Mike Marshall, Minnesota	1979—	Bruce Sutter, Chicago
	Jim Kern, Texas		
1980—	Dan Quisenberry, Kansas City	1980—	Rollie Fingers, San Diego
			Tom Hume, Cincinnati
1981—	Rollie Fingers, Milwaukee	1981—	Bruce Sutter, St. Louis
1982—	Dan Quisenberry, Kansas City	1982—	Bruce Sutter, St. Louis
1983—	Dan Quisenberry, Kansas City	1983—	Al Holland, Philadelphia
			Lee Smith, Chicago
1984—	Dan Quisenberry, Kansas City	1984—	Bruce Sutter, St. Louis
1985—	Dan Quisenberry, Kansas City	1985—	Jeff Reardon, Montreal
1986—	Dave Righetti, New York	1986—	Todd Worrell, St. Louis
1987—	Dave Righetti, New York	1987—	Steve Bedrosian, Philadelphia
	Jeff Reardon, Minnesota		
1988—	Dennis Eckersley, Oakland	1988—	John Franco, Cincinnati
1989—	Jeff Russell, Texas	1989—	Mark Davis, San Diego
1990—	Bobby Thigpen, Chicago	1990—	John Franco, New York
1991—	Dennis Eckersley, Oakland	1991—	Lee Smith, St. Louis
	Bryan Harvey, California		
1992—	Dennis Eckersley, Oakland	1992—	Doug Jones, Houston
			Lee Smith, St. Louis
1993—	Jeff Montgomery, Kansas City	1993—	Randy Myers, Chicago

MAJOR LEAGUE PLAYER OF THE YEAR

Year	Player, Team	Year	Player, Team	Year	Player, Team
1936—	Carl Hubbell, New York NL	1956—	Mickey Mantle, New York AL	1975—	Joe Morgan, Cincinnati NL
1937—	Johnny Allen, Cleveland AL	1957—	Ted Williams, Boston AL	1976—	Joe Morgan, Cincinnati NL
1938—	Johnny Vander Meer, Cin. NL	1958—	Bob Turley, New York AL	1977—	Rod Carew, Minnesota AL
1939—	Joe DiMaggio, New York AL	1959—	Early Wynn, Chicago AL	1978—	Ron Guidry, New York AL
1940—	Bob Feller, Cleveland AL	1960—	Bill Mazeroski, Pittsburgh NL	1979—	Willie Stargell, Pittsburgh NL
1941—	Ted Williams, Boston AL	1961—	Roger Maris, New York AL	1980—	George Brett, Kansas City AL
1942—	Ted Williams, Boston AL	1962—	Maury Wills, Los Angeles NL	1981—	Fernando Valenzuela, L.A. NL
1943—	Spud Chandler, New York AL		Don Drysdale, Los Angeles NL	1982—	Robin Yount, Milwaukee AL
1944—	Marty Marion, St. Louis NL	1963—	Sandy Koufax, Los Angeles NL	1983—	Cal Ripken Jr., Baltimore AL
1945—	Hal Newhouser, Detroit AL	1964—	Ken Boyer, St. Louis NL	1984—	Ryne Sandberg, Chicago NL
1946—	Stan Musial, St. Louis NL	1965—	Sandy Koufax, Los Angeles NL	1985—	Don Mattingly, New York AL
1947—	Ted Williams, Boston AL	1966—	Frank Robinson, Baltimore AL	1986—	Roger Clemens, Boston AL
1948—	Lou Boudreau, Cleveland AL	1967—	Carl Yastrzemski, Boston AL	1987—	George Bell, Toronto AL
1949—	Ted Williams, Boston AL	1968—	Denny McLain, Detroit AL	1988—	Orel Hershiser, Los Angeles NL
1950—	Phil Rizzuto, New York AL	1969—	Willie McCovey, San Fran. NL	1989—	Kevin Mitchell, San Fran. NL
1951—	Stan Musial, St. Louis NL	1970—	Johnny Bench, Cincinnati NL	1990—	Barry Bonds, Pittsburgh NL
1952—	Robin Roberts, Philadelphia NL	1971—	Joe Torre, St. Louis NL	1991—	Cal Ripken Jr., Baltimore AL
1953—	Al Rosen, Cleveland AL	1972—	Billy Williams, Chicago NL	1992—	Gary Sheffield, San Diego NL
1954—	Willie Mays, New York NL	1973—	Reggie Jackson, Oakland AL	1993—	Frank Thomas, Chicago AL
1955—	Duke Snider, Brooklyn NL	1974—	Lou Brock, St. Louis NL		

MAJOR LEAGUE MANAGER OF THE YEAR

Year	Manager, Team	Year	Manager, Team	Year	Manager, Team
1936—	Joe McCarthy, New York AL	1944—	Luke Sewell, St. Louis AL	1952—	Eddie Stanky, St. Louis NL
1937—	Bill McKechnie, Boston NL	1945—	Ossie Bluege, Washington AL	1953—	Casey Stengel, New York AL
1938—	Joe McCarthy, New York AL	1946—	Eddie Dyer, St. Louis NL	1954—	Leo Durocher, New York AL
1939—	Leo Durocher, Brooklyn NL	1947—	Bucky Harris, New York AL	1955—	Walter Alston, Brooklyn NL
1940—	Bill McKechnie, Cincinnati NL	1948—	Bill Meyer, Pittsburgh NL	1956—	Birdie Tebbetts, Cincinnati NL
1941—	Billy Southworth, St. Louis NL	1949—	Casey Stengel, New York AL	1957—	Fred Hutchinson, St. Louis NL
1942—	Billy Southworth, St. Louis NL	1950—	Red Rolfe, Detroit AL	1958—	Casey Stengel, New York AL
1943—	Joe McCarthy, New York AL	1951—	Leo Durocher, New York NL	1959—	Walter Alston, Los Angeles NL

Year	Manager, Team	Year	Manager, Team	Year	Manager, Team
1960—	Danny Murtaugh, Pit. NL	1975—	Darrell Johnson, Boston AL	1988—	Tony La Russa, Oakland AL
1961—	Ralph Houk, New York AL	1976—	Danny Ozark, Philadelphia NL		Tom Lasorda, L.A. NL (tie)
1962—	Bill Rigney, Los Angeles AL	1977—	Earl Weaver, Baltimore AL		Jim Leyland, Pit. NL (tie)
1963—	Walter Alston, Los Angeles NL	1978—	George Bamberger, Mil. AL	1989—	Frank Robinson, Baltimore AL
1964—	Johnny Keane, St. Louis NL	1979—	Earl Weaver, Baltimore AL		Don Zimmer, Chicago NL
1965—	Sam Mele, Minnesota AL	1980—	Bill Virdon, Houston NL	1990—	Jeff Torborg, Chicago AL
1966—	Hank Bauer, Baltimore AL	1981—	Billy Martin, Oakland AL		Jim Leyland, Pittsburgh NL
1967—	Dick Williams, Boston AL	1982—	Whitey Herzog, St. Louis NL	1991—	Tom Kelly, Minnesota AL
1968—	Mayo Smith, Detroit AL	1983—	Tony La Russa, Chicago AL		Bobby Cox, Atlanta NL
1969—	Gil Hodges, New York NL	1984—	Jim Frey, Chicago NL	1992—	Tony La Russa, Oakland AL
1970—	Danny Murtaugh, Pit. NL	1985—	Bobby Cox, Toronto AL		Jim Leyland, Pittsburgh NL
1971—	Charlie Fox, San Francisco NL	1986—	John McNamara, Boston AL	1993—	Johnny Oates, Baltimore AL
1972—	Chuck Tanner, Chicago AL		Hal Lanier, Houston NL		Bobby Cox, Atlanta NL
1973—	Gene Mauch, Montreal NL	1987—	Sparky Anderson, Detroit AL		
1974—	Bill Virdon, New York AL		Buck Rodgers, Montreal NL		

MAJOR LEAGUE EXECUTIVE OF THE YEAR

Year	Executive, Team	Year	Executive, Team	Year	Executive, Team
1936—	Branch Rickey, St. Louis NL	1956—	Gabe Paul, Cincinnati NL	1976—	Joe Burke, Kansas City AL
1937—	Ed Barrow, New York AL	1957—	Frank Lane, St. Louis NL	1977—	Bill Veeck, Chicago AL
1938—	Warren Giles, Cincinnati NL	1958—	Joe Brown, Pittsburgh NL	1978—	Spec Richardson, San Fran. NL
1939—	Larry MacPhail, Brooklyn NL	1959—	Buzzie Bavasi, L.A. NL	1979—	Hank Peters, Baltimore AL
1940—	Walter Briggs Sr., Detroit AL	1960—	George Weiss, New York AL	1980—	Tal Smith, Houston NL
1941—	Ed Barrow, New York AL	1961—	Dan Topping, New York AL	1981—	John McHale, Montreal NL
1942—	Branch Rickey, St. Louis NL	1962—	Fred Haney, Los Angeles AL	1982—	Harry Dalton, Milwaukee AL
1943—	Clark Griffith, Washington AL	1963—	Bing Devine, St. Louis NL	1983—	Hank Peters, Baltimore AL
1944—	Billy DeWitt, St. Louis AL	1964—	Bing Devine, St. Louis NL	1984—	Dallas Green, Chicago NL
1945—	Phil Wrigley, Chicago NL	1965—	Cal Griffith, Minnesota AL	1985—	John Schuerholz, K.C. AL
1946—	Tom Yawkey, Boston AL	1966—	Lee MacPhail, Comm. Office	1986—	Frank Cashen, New York NL
1947—	Branch Rickey, Brooklyn NL	1967—	Dick O'Connell, Boston AL	1987—	Al Rosen, San Francisco AL
1948—	Bill Veeck, Cleveland AL	1968—	Jim Campbell, Detroit AL	1988—	Fred Claire, Los Angeles NL
1949—	Bob Carpenter, Philadelphia NL	1969—	John Murphy, New York NL	1989—	Roland Hemond, Baltimore AL
1950—	George Weiss, New York AL	1970—	Harry Dalton, Baltimore AL	1990—	Bob Quinn, Cincinnati NL
1951—	George Weiss, New York AL	1971—	Cedric Tallis, Kansas City AL	1991—	Andy MacPhail, Minnesota AL
1952—	George Weiss, New York AL	1972—	Roland Hemond, Chicago AL	1992—	Dan Duquette, Montreal NL
1953—	Lou Perini, Milwaukee NL	1973—	Bob Howsam, Cincinnati NL	1993—	Lee Thomas, Philadelphia NL
1954—	Horace Stoneham, New York NL	1974—	Gabe Paul, New York AL		
1955—	Walter O'Malley, Brooklyn NL	1975—	Dick O'Connell, Boston AL		

GOLD GLOVE TEAMS

1957
MAJORS
P—Bobby Shantz, N.Y. AL
C—Sherm Lollar, Chicago AL
1B—Gil Hodges, Brooklyn NL
2B—Nellie Fox, Chicago AL
3B—Frank Malzone, Boston AL
SS—Roy McMillan, Cin. NL
OF—Minnie Minoso, Chicago AL
OF—Willie Mays, N.Y. NL
OF—Al Kaline, Detroit AL

1958
AMERICAN LEAGUE
P—Bobby Shantz, New York
C—Sherm Lollar, Chicago
1B—Vic Power, Cleveland
2B—Frank Bolling, Detroit
3B—Frank Malzone, Boston
SS—Luis Aparicio, Chicago
OF—Norm Siebern, New York
OF—Jimmy Piersall, Boston
OF—Al Kaline, Detroit

NATIONAL LEAGUE
P—Harvey Haddix, Cincinnati
C—Del Crandall, Milwaukee
1B—Gil Hodges, Los Angeles
2B—Bill Mazeroski, Pitt.
3B—Ken Boyer, St. Louis
SS—Roy McMillan, Cin.
OF—Frank Robinson, Cin.
OF—Willie Mays, San Fran.
OF—Hank Aaron, Milwaukee

1959
AMERICAN LEAGUE
P—Bobby Shantz, New York
C—Sherm Lollar, Chicago
1B—Vic Power, Cleveland
2B—Nellie Fox, Chicago
3B—Frank Malzone, Boston
SS—Luis Aparicio, Chicago
OF—Minnie Minoso, Cleveland
OF—Al Kaline, Detroit
OF—Jackie Jensen, Boston

NATIONAL LEAGUE
P—Harvey Haddix, Pittsburgh
C—Del Crandall, Milwaukee
1B—Gil Hodges, Los Angeles
2B—Charley Neal, Los Angeles
3B—Ken Boyer, St. Louis
SS—Roy McMillan, Cincinnati
OF—Jackie Brandt, San Fran.
OF—Willie Mays, San Francisco
OF—Hank Aaron, Milwaukee

1960
AMERICAN LEAGUE
P—Bobby Shantz, New York
C—Earl Battey, Washington
1B—Vic Power, Cleveland
2B—Nellie Fox, Chicago
3B—Brooks Robinson, Baltimore
SS—Luis Aparicio, Chicago
OF—Minnie Minoso, Chicago
OF—Jim Landis, Chicago
OF—Roger Maris, New York

NATIONAL LEAGUE
P—Harvey Haddix, Pittsburgh
C—Del Crandall, Milwaukee
1B—Bill White, St. Louis
2B—Bill Mazeroski, Pittsburgh
3B—Ken Boyer, St. Louis
SS—Ernie Banks, Chicago
OF—Wally Moon, Los Angeles
OF—Willie Mays, San Francisco
OF—Hank Aaron, Milwaukee

1961
AMERICAN LEAGUE
P—Frank Lary, Detroit
C—Earl Battey, Chicago
1B—Vic Power, Cleveland
2B—Bobby Richardson, N.Y.
3B—Brooks Robinson, Baltimore
SS—Luis Aparicio, Chicago
OF—Al Kaline, Detroit
OF—Jimmy Piersall, Cleveland
OF—Jim Landis, Chicago

NATIONAL LEAGUE
P—Bobby Shantz, Pittsburgh
C—John Roseboro, Los Angeles
1B—Bill White, St. Louis
2B—Bill Mazeroski, Pittsburgh
3B—Ken Boyer, St. Louis
SS—Maury Wills, Los Angeles
OF—Willie Mays, San Francisco
OF—Roberto Clemente, Pittsburgh
OF—Vada Pinson, Cincinnati

1962
AMERICAN LEAGUE
P—Jim Kaat, Minnesota
C—Earl Battey, Minnesota
1B—Vic Power, Minnesota
2B—Bobby Richardson, N.Y.
3B—Brooks Robinson, Baltimore
SS—Luis Aparicio, Chicago
OF—Jim Landis, Chicago
OF—Mickey Mantle, New York
OF—Al Kaline, Detroit

NATIONAL LEAGUE
P—Bobby Shantz, St. Louis
C—Del Crandall, Milwaukee
1B—Bill White, St. Louis
2B—Ken Hubbs, Chicago
3B—Jim Davenport, S.F.
SS—Maury Wills, Los Angeles
OF—Willie Mays, San Francisco
OF—Roberto Clemente, Pittsburgh
OF—Bill Virdon, Pittsburgh

1963
AMERICAN LEAGUE
P—Jim Kaat, Minnesota
C—Elston Howard, New York
1B—Vic Power, Minnesota
2B—Bobby Richardson, N.Y.
3B—Brooks Robinson, Baltimore
SS—Zoilo Versalles, Minnesota
OF—Al Kaline, Detroit
OF—Carl Yastrzemski, Boston
OF—Jim Landis, Chicago

NATIONAL LEAGUE
P—Bobby Shantz, St. Louis
C—Johnny Edwards, Cincinnati
1B—Bill White, St. Louis
2B—Bill Mazeroski, Pittsburgh
3B—Ken Boyer, St. Louis
SS—Bobby Wine, Philadelphia
OF—Willie Mays, San Francisco
OF—Roberto Clemente, Pittsburgh
OF—Curt Flood, St. Louis

1964
AMERICAN LEAGUE
P—Jim Kaat, Minnesota
C—Elston Howard, New York
1B—Vic Power, Los Angeles
2B—Bobby Richardson, N.Y.
3B—Brooks Robinson, Baltimore
SS—Luis Aparicio, Baltimore
OF—Al Kaline, Detroit
OF—Jim Landis, Chicago
OF—Vic Davalillo, Cleveland

NATIONAL LEAGUE
P—Bobby Shantz, Philadelphia
C—Johnny Edwards, Cincinnati
1B—Bill White, St. Louis
2B—Bill Mazeroski, Pittsburgh
3B—Ron Santo, Chicago
SS—Ruben Amaro, Philadelphia
OF—Willie Mays, San Francisco
OF—Roberto Clemente, Pittsburgh
OF—Curt Flood, St. Louis

1965
AMERICAN LEAGUE
P—Jim Kaat, Minnesota
C—Bill Freehan, Detroit
1B—Joe Pepitone, New York
2B—Bobby Richardson, N.Y.
3B—Brooks Robinson, Baltimore
SS—Zoilo Versalles, Minnesota
OF—Al Kaline, Detroit
OF—Tom Tresh, New York
OF—Carl Yastrzemski, Boston

NATIONAL LEAGUE
P—Bob Gibson, St. Louis
C—Joe Torre, Atlanta
1B—Bill White, St. Louis
2B—Bill Mazeroski, Pittsburgh
3B—Ron Santo, Chicago
SS—Leo Cardenas, Cincinnati
OF—Willie Mays, San Francisco
OF—Roberto Clemente, Pittsburgh
OF—Curt Flood, St. Louis

1966
AMERICAN LEAGUE
P—Jim Kaat, Minnesota
C—Bill Freehan, Detroit
1B—Joe Pepitone, New York
2B—Bobby Knoop, California
3B—Brooks Robinson, Balt.
SS—Luis Aparicio, Baltimore
OF—Al Kaline, Detroit
OF—Tommie Agee, Chicago
OF—Tony Oliva, Minnesota

NATIONAL LEAGUE
P—Bob Gibson, St. Louis
C—John Roseboro, Los Angeles
1B—Bill White, Philadelphia
2B—Bill Mazeroski, Pittsburgh
3B—Ron Santo, Chicago
SS—Gene Alley, Pittsburgh
OF—Willie Mays, San Francisco
OF—Curt Flood, St. Louis
OF—Roberto Clemente, Pittsburgh

1967
AMERICAN LEAGUE
P—Jim Kaat, Minnesota
C—Bill Freehan, Detroit
1B—George Scott, Boston
2B—Bobby Knoop, California
3B—Brooks Robinson, Balt.
SS—Jim Fregosi, California
OF—Carl Yastrzemski, Boston
OF—Paul Blair, Baltimore
OF—Al Kaline, Detroit

NATIONAL LEAGUE
P—Bob Gibson, St. Louis
C—Randy Hundley, Chicago
1B—Wes Parker, Los Angeles
2B—Bill Mazeroski, Pittsburgh
3B—Ron Santo, Chicago
SS—Gene Alley, Pittsburgh
OF—Roberto Clemente, Pittsburgh
OF—Curt Flood, St. Louis
OF—Willie Mays, San Francisco

1968
AMERICAN LEAGUE
P—Jim Kaat, Minnesota
C—Bill Freehan, Detroit
1B—George Scott, Boston
2B—Bobby Knoop, California
3B—Brooks Robinson, Balt.
SS—Luis Aparicio, Chicago
OF—Mickey Stanley, Detroit
OF—Carl Yastrzemski, Boston
OF—Reggie Smith, Boston

NATIONAL LEAGUE
P—Bob Gibson, St. Louis
C—Johnny Bench, Cincinnati
1B—Wes Parker, Los Angeles
2B—Glenn Beckert, Chicago
3B—Ron Santo, Chicago
SS—Dal Maxvill, St. Louis
OF—Willie Mays, San Francisco
OF—Roberto Clemente, Pittsburgh
OF—Curt Flood, St. Louis

1969
AMERICAN LEAGUE
P—Jim Kaat, Minnesota
C—Bill Freehan, Detroit
1B—Joe Pepitone, New York
2B—Dave Johnson, Baltimore
3B—Brooks Robinson, Balt.
SS—Mark Belanger, Baltimore
OF—Paul Blair, Baltimore
OF—Mickey Stanley, Detroit
OF—Carl Yastrzemski, Boston

NATIONAL LEAGUE
P—Bob Gibson, St. Louis
C—Johnny Bench, Cincinnati
1B—Wes Parker, Los Angeles
2B—Felix Millan, Atlanta
3B—Clete Boyer, Atlanta
SS—Don Kessinger, Chicago
OF—Roberto Clemente, Pittsburgh
OF—Curt Flood, St. Louis
OF—Pete Rose, Cincinnati

1970
AMERICAN LEAGUE
P—Jim Kaat, Minnesota
C—Ray Fosse, Cleveland
1B—Jim Spencer, California
2B—Dave Johnson, Baltimore
3B—Brooks Robinson, Balt.
SS—Luis Aparicio, Chicago
OF—Mickey Stanley, Detroit
OF—Paul Blair, Baltimore
OF—Ken Berry, Chicago

NATIONAL LEAGUE
P—Bob Gibson, St. Louis
C—Johnny Bench, Cincinnati
1B—Wes Parker, Los Angeles
2B—Tommy Helms, Cincinnati
3B—Doug Rader, Houston
SS—Don Kessinger, Chicago
OF—Roberto Clemente, Pittsburgh
OF—Tommie Agee, New York
OF—Pete Rose, Cincinnati

1971

AMERICAN LEAGUE
P—Jim Kaat, Minnesota
C—Ray Fosse, Cleveland
1B—George Scott, Boston
2B—Dave Johnson, Baltimore
3B—Brooks Robinson, Balt.
SS—Mark Belanger, Baltimore
OF—Paul Blair, Baltimore
OF—Amos Otis, Kansas City
OF—Carl Yastrzemski, Boston

NATIONAL LEAGUE
P—Bob Gibson, St. Louis
C—Johnny Bench, Cincinnati
1B—Wes Parker, Los Angeles
2B—Tommy Helms, Cincinnati
3B—Doug Rader, Houston
SS—Bud Harrelson, New York
OF—Roberto Clemente, Pittsburgh
OF—Bobby Bonds, San Francisco
OF—Willie Davis, Los Angeles

1972

AMERICAN LEAGUE
P—Jim Kaat, Minnesota
C—Carlton Fisk, Boston
1B—George Scott, Milwaukee
2B—Doug Griffin, Boston
3B—Brooks Robinson, Baltimore
SS—Ed Brinkman, Detroit
OF—Paul Blair, Baltimore
OF—Bobby Murcer, New York
OF—Ken Berry, California

NATIONAL LEAGUE
P—Bob Gibson, St. Louis
C—Johnny Bench, Cincinnati
1B—Wes Parker, Los Angeles
2B—Felix Millan, Atlanta
3B—Doug Rader, Houston
SS—Larry Bowa, Philadelphia
OF—Roberto Clemente, Pittsburgh
OF—Cesar Cedeno, Houston
OF—Willie Davis, Los Angeles

1973

AMERICAN LEAGUE
P—Jim Kaat, Chicago
C—Thurman Munson, New York
1B—George Scott, Milwaukee
2B—Bobby Grich, Baltimore
3B—Brooks Robinson, Baltimore
SS—Mark Belanger, Baltimore
OF—Paul Blair, Baltimore
OF—Amos Otis, Kansas City
OF—Mickey Stanley, Detroit

NATIONAL LEAGUE
P—Bob Gibson, St. Louis
C—Johnny Bench, Cincinnati
1B—Mike Jorgensen, Montreal
2B—Joe Morgan, Cincinnati
3B—Doug Rader, Houston
SS—Roger Metzger, Houston
OF—Bobby Bonds, San Francisco
OF—Cesar Cedeno, Houston
OF—Willie Davis, Los Angeles

1974

AMERICAN LEAGUE
P—Jim Kaat, Chicago
C—Thurman Munson, New York
1B—George Scott, Milwaukee
2B—Bobby Grich, Baltimore
3B—Brooks Robinson, Baltimore
SS—Mark Belanger, Baltimore
OF—Paul Blair, Baltimore
OF—Amos Otis, Kansas City
OF—Joe Rudi, Oakland

NATIONAL LEAGUE
P—Andy Messersmith, Los Angeles
C—Johnny Bench, Cincinnati
1B—Steve Garvey, Los Angeles
2B—Joe Morgan, Cincinnati
3B—Doug Rader, Houston
SS—Dave Concepcion, Cincinnati
OF—Cesar Cedeno, Houston
OF—Cesar Geronimo, Cincinnati
OF—Bobby Bonds, San Francisco

1975

AMERICAN LEAGUE
P—Jim Kaat, Chicago
C—Thurman Munson, New York
1B—George Scott, Milwaukee
2B—Bobby Grich, Baltimore
3B—Brooks Robinson, Baltimore
SS—Mark Belanger, Baltimore
OF—Paul Blair, Baltimore
OF—Joe Rudi, Oakland
OF—Fred Lynn, Boston

NATIONAL LEAGUE
P—Andy Messersmith, Los Angeles
C—Johnny Bench, Cincinnati
1B—Steve Garvey, Los Angeles
2B—Joe Morgan, Cincinnati
3B—Ken Reitz, St. Louis
SS—Dave Concepcion, Cincinnati
OF—Cesar Cedeno, Houston
OF—Cesar Geronimo, Cincinnati
OF—Garry Maddox, Philadelphia

1976

AMERICAN LEAGUE
P—Jim Palmer, Baltimore
C—Jim Sundberg, Texas
1B—George Scott, Milwaukee
2B—Bobby Grich, Baltimore
3B—Aurelio Rodriguez, Detroit
SS—Mark Belanger, Baltimore
OF—Joe Rudi, Oakland
OF—Dwight Evans, Boston
OF—Rick Manning, Cleveland

NATIONAL LEAGUE
P—Jim Kaat, Philadelphia
C—Johnny Bench, Cincinnati
1B—Steve Garvey, Los Angeles
2B—Joe Morgan, Cincinnati
3B—Mike Schmidt, Philadelphia
SS—Dave Concepcion, Cincinnati
OF—Cesar Cedeno, Houston
OF—Cesar Geronimo, Cincinnati
OF—Garry Maddox, Philadelphia

1977

AMERICAN LEAGUE
P—Jim Palmer, Baltimore
C—Jim Sundberg, Texas
1B—Jim Spencer, Chicago
2B—Frank White, Kansas City
3B—Graig Nettles, New York
SS—Mark Belanger, Baltimore
OF—Juan Beniquez, Texas
OF—Carl Yastrzemski, Boston
OF—Al Cowens, Kansas City

NATIONAL LEAGUE
P—Jim Kaat, Philadelphia
C—Johnny Bench, Cincinnati
1B—Steve Garvey, Los Angeles
2B—Joe Morgan, Cincinnati
3B—Mike Schmidt, Philadelphia
SS—Dave Concepcion, Cincinnati
OF—Cesar Geronimo, Cincinnati
OF—Garry Maddox, Philadelphia
OF—Dave Parker, Pittsburgh

1978

AMERICAN LEAGUE
P—Jim Palmer, Baltimore
C—Jim Sundberg, Texas
1B—Chris Chambliss, New York
2B—Frank White, Kansas City
3B—Graig Nettles, New York
SS—Mark Belanger, Baltimore
OF—Fred Lynn, Boston
OF—Dwight Evans, Boston
OF—Rick Miller, California

NATIONAL LEAGUE
P—Phil Niekro, Atlanta
C—Bob Boone, Philadelphia
1B—Keith Hernandez, St. Louis
2B—Dave Lopes, Los Angeles
3B—Mike Schmidt, Philadelphia
SS—Larry Bowa, Philadelphia
OF—Garry Maddox, Philadelphia
OF—Dave Parker, Pittsburgh
OF—Ellis Valentine, Montreal

1979

AMERICAN LEAGUE
P—Jim Palmer, Baltimore
C—Jim Sundberg, Texas
1B—Cecil Cooper, Milwaukee
2B—Frank White, Kansas City
3B—Buddy Bell, Texas
SS—Rick Burleson, Boston
OF—Dwight Evans, Boston
OF—Sixto Lezcano, Milwaukee
OF—Fred Lynn, Boston

NATIONAL LEAGUE
P—Phil Niekro, Atlanta
C—Bob Boone, Philadelphia
1B—Keith Hernandez, St. Louis
2B—Manny Trillo, Philadelphia
3B—Mike Schmidt, Philadelphia
SS—Dave Concepcion, Cincinnati
OF—Garry Maddox, Philadelphia
OF—Dave Parker, Pittsburgh
OF—Dave Winfield, San Diego

1980

AMERICAN LEAGUE
P—Mike Norris, Oakland
C—Jim Sundberg, Texas
1B—Cecil Cooper, Milwaukee
2B—Frank White, Kansas City
3B—Buddy Bell, Texas
SS—Alan Trammell, Detroit
OF—Fred Lynn, Boston
OF—Dwayne Murphy, Oakland
OF—Willie Wilson, Kansas City

NATIONAL LEAGUE
P—Phil Niekro, Atlanta
C—Gary Carter, Montreal
1B—Keith Hernandez, St. Louis
2B—Doug Flynn, New York
3B—Mike Schmidt, Philadelphia
SS—Ozzie Smith, San Diego
OF—Andre Dawson, Montreal
OF—Garry Maddox, Philadelphia
OF—Dave Winfield, San Diego

1981

AMERICAN LEAGUE
P—Mike Norris, Oakland
C—Jim Sundberg, Texas
1B—Mike Squires, Chicago
2B—Frank White, Kansas City
3B—Buddy Bell, Texas
SS—Alan Trammell, Detroit
OF—Dwayne Murphy, Oakland
OF—Dwight Evans, Boston
OF—Rickey Henderson, Oakland

NATIONAL LEAGUE
P—Steve Carlton, Philadelphia
C—Gary Carter, Montreal
1B—Keith Hernandez, St. Louis
2B—Manny Trillo, Philadelphia
3B—Mike Schmidt, Philadelphia
SS—Ozzie Smith, San Diego
OF—Andre Dawson, Montreal
OF—Garry Maddox, Philadelphia
OF—Dusty Baker, Los Angeles

1982

AMERICAN LEAGUE
P—Ron Guidry, New York
C—Bob Boone, California
1B—Eddie Murray, Baltimore
2B—Frank White, Kansas City
3B—Buddy Bell, Texas
SS—Robin Yount, Milwaukee
OF—Dwight Evans, Boston
OF—Dave Winfield, New York
OF—Dwayne Murphy, Oakland

NATIONAL LEAGUE
P—Phil Niekro, Atlanta
C—Gary Carter, Montreal
1B—Keith Hernandez, St. Louis
2B—Manny Trillo, Philadelphia
3B—Mike Schmidt, Philadelphia
SS—Ozzie Smith, St. Louis
OF—Andre Dawson, Montreal
OF—Dale Murphy, Atlanta
OF—Garry Maddox, Philadelphia

1983

AMERICAN LEAGUE
P—Ron Guidry, New York
C—Lance Parrish, Detroit
1B—Eddie Murray, Baltimore
2B—Lou Whitaker, Detroit
3B—Buddy Bell, Texas
SS—Alan Trammell, Detroit
OF—Dwight Evans, Boston
OF—Dave Winfield, New York
OF—Dwayne Murphy, Oakland

NATIONAL LEAGUE
P—Phil Niekro, Atlanta
C—Tony Pena, Pittsburgh
1B—Keith Hernandez, St.L.-N.Y.
2B—Ryne Sandberg, Chicago
3B—Mike Schmidt, Philadelphia
SS—Ozzie Smith, St. Louis
OF—Andre Dawson, Montreal
OF—Dale Murphy, Atlanta
OF—Willie McGee, St. Louis

1984

AMERICAN LEAGUE
P—Ron Guidry, New York
C—Lance Parrish, Detroit
1B—Eddie Murray, Baltimore
2B—Lou Whitaker, Detroit
3B—Buddy Bell, Texas
SS—Alan Trammell, Detroit
OF—Dwight Evans, Boston
OF—Dave Winfield, New York
OF—Dwayne Murphy, Oakland

NATIONAL LEAGUE
P—Joaquin Andujar, St. Louis
C—Tony Pena, Pittsburgh
1B—Keith Hernandez, New York
2B—Ryne Sandberg, Chicago
3B—Mike Schmidt, Philadelphia
SS—Ozzie Smith, St. Louis
OF—Dale Murphy, Atlanta
OF—Bob Dernier, Chicago
OF—Andre Dawson, Montreal

1985

AMERICAN LEAGUE
P—Ron Guidry, New York
C—Lance Parrish, Detroit
1B—Don Mattingly, New York
2B—Lou Whitaker, Detroit
3B—George Brett, Kansas City
SS—Alfredo Griffin, Oakland
OF—Gary Pettis, California
OF—Dave Winfield, New York
OF—Dwight Evans, Boston (tie)
     Dwayne Murphy, Oakland (tie)

NATIONAL LEAGUE
P—Rick Reuschel, Pittsburgh
C—Tony Pena, Pittsburgh
1B—Keith Hernandez, New York
2B—Ryne Sandberg, Chicago
3B—Tim Wallach, Montreal
SS—Ozzie Smith, St. Louis
OF—Willie McGee, St. Louis
OF—Dale Murphy, Atlanta
OF—Andre Dawson, Montreal

1986

AMERICAN LEAGUE
P—Ron Guidry, New York
C—Bob Boone, California
1B—Don Mattingly, New York
2B—Frank White, Kansas City
3B—Gary Gaetti, Minnesota
SS—Tony Fernandez, Toronto
OF—Gary Pettis, California
OF—Jesse Barfield, Toronto
OF—Kirby Puckett, Minnesota

NATIONAL LEAGUE
P—Fernando Valenzuela, L.A.
C—Jody Davis, Chicago
1B—Keith Hernandez, New York
2B—Ryne Sandberg, Chicago
3B—Mike Schmidt, Philadelphia
SS—Ozzie Smith, St. Louis
OF—Tony Gwynn, San Diego
OF—Dale Murphy, Atlanta
OF—Willie McGee, St. Louis

1987

AMERICAN LEAGUE
P—Mark Langston, Seattle
C—Bob Boone, California
1B—Don Mattingly, New York
2B—Frank White, Kansas City
3B—Gary Gaetti, Minnesota
SS—Tony Fernandez, Toronto
OF—Jesse Barfield, Toronto
OF—Kirby Puckett, Minnesota
OF—Dave Winfield, New York

NATIONAL LEAGUE
P—Rick Reuschel, Pitt.-S.F.
C—Mike LaValliere, Pittsburgh
1B—Keith Hernandez, New York
2B—Ryne Sandberg, Chicago
3B—Terry Pendleton, St. Louis
SS—Ozzie Smith, St. Louis
OF—Eric Davis, Cincinnati
OF—Tony Gwynn, San Diego
OF—Andre Dawson, Chicago

1988

AMERICAN LEAGUE
P—Mark Langston, Seattle
C—Bob Boone, California
1B—Don Mattingly, New York
2B—Harold Reynolds, Seattle
3B—Gary Gaetti, Minnesota
SS—Tony Fernandez, Toronto
OF—Kirby Puckett, Minnesota
OF—Devon White, California
OF—Gary Pettis, Detroit

NATIONAL LEAGUE
P—Orel Hershiser, Los Angeles
C—Benito Santiago, San Diego
1B—Keith Hernandez, New York
2B—Ryne Sandberg, Chicago
3B—Tim Wallach, Montreal
SS—Ozzie Smith, St. Louis
OF—Andy Van Slyke, Pittsburgh
OF—Eric Davis, Cincinnati
OF—Andre Dawson, Chicago

1989
AMERICAN LEAGUE
P—Bret Saberhagen, Kansas City
C—Bob Boone, Kansas City
1B—Don Mattingly, New York
2B—Harold Reynolds, Seattle
3B—Gary Gaetti, Minnesota
SS—Tony Fernandez, Toronto
OF—Kirby Puckett, Minnesota
OF—Devon White, California
OF—Gary Pettis, Detroit

NATIONAL LEAGUE
P—Ron Darling, New York
C—Benito Santiago, San Diego
1B—Andres Galarraga, Montreal
2B—Ryne Sandberg, Chicago
3B—Terry Pendleton, St. Louis
SS—Ozzie Smith, St. Louis
OF—Andy Van Slyke, Pittsburgh
OF—Tony Gwynn, San Diego
OF—Eric Davis, Cincinnati

1990
AMERICAN LEAGUE
P—Mike Boddicker, Boston
C—Sandy Alomar Jr., Cleveland
1B—Mark McGwire, Oakland
2B—Harold Reynolds, Seattle
3B—Kelly Gruber, Toronto
SS—Ozzie Guillen, Chicago
OF—Ken Griffey Jr., Seattle
OF—Ellis Burks, Boston
OF—Gary Pettis, Texas

NATIONAL LEAGUE
P—Greg Maddux, Chicago
C—Benito Santiago, San Diego
1B—Andres Galarraga, Montreal
2B—Ryne Sandberg, Chicago
3B—Tim Wallach, Montreal
SS—Ozzie Smith, St. Louis
OF—Barry Bonds, Pittsburgh
OF—Andy Van Slyke, Pittsburgh
OF—Tony Gwynn, San Diego

1991
AMERICAN LEAGUE
P—Mark Langston, California
C—Tony Pena, Boston
1B—Don Mattingly, New York
2B—Roberto Alomar, Toronto
3B—Robin Ventura, Chicago
SS—Cal Ripken, Baltimore
OF—Ken Griffey Jr., Seattle
OF—Kirby Puckett, Minnesota
OF—Devon White, Toronto

NATIONAL LEAGUE
P—Greg Maddux, Chicago
C—Tom Pagnozzi, St. Louis
1B—Will Clark, San Francisco
2B—Ryne Sandberg, Chicago
3B—Matt Williams, San Francisco
SS—Ozzie Smith, St. Louis
OF—Barry Bonds, Pittsburgh
OF—Andy Van Slyke, Pittsburgh
OF—Tony Gwynn, San Diego

1992
AMERICAN LEAGUE
P—Mark Langston, California
C—Ivan Rodriguez, Texas
1B—Don Mattingly, New York
2B—Roberto Alomar, Toronto
3B—Robin Ventura, Chicago
SS—Cal Ripken, Baltimore
OF—Ken Griffey Jr., Seattle
OF—Kirby Puckett, Minnesota
OF—Devon White, Toronto

NATIONAL LEAGUE
P—Greg Maddux, Chicago
C—Tom Pagnozzi, St. Louis
1B—Mark Grace, Chicago
2B—Jose Lind, Pittsburgh
3B—Terry Pendleton, Atlanta
SS—Ozzie Smith, St. Louis
OF—Barry Bonds, Pittsburgh
OF—Andy Van Slyke, Pittsburgh
OF—Larry Walker, Montreal

1993
AMERICAN LEAGUE
P—Mark Langston, California
C—Ivan Rodriguez, Texas
1B—Don Mattingly, New York
2B—Roberto Alomar, Toronto
3B—Robin Ventura, Chicago
SS—Omar Vizquel, Seattle
OF—Ken Griffey Jr., Seattle
OF—Kenny Lofton, Cleveland
OF—Devon White, Toronto

NATIONAL LEAGUE
P—Greg Maddux, Atlanta
C—Kirt Manwaring, San Francisco
1B—Mark Grace, Chicago
2B—Robby Thompson, San Fran.
3B—Matt Williams, San Francisco
SS—Jay Bell, Pittsburgh
OF—Barry Bonds, San Francisco
OF—Marquis Grissom, Montreal
OF—Larry Walker, Montreal

SILVER SLUGGER TEAMS

1980
AMERICAN LEAGUE
1B—Cecil Cooper, Milwaukee
2B—Willie Randolph, New York
3B—George Brett, Kansas City
SS—Robin Yount, Milwaukee
OF—Ben Oglivie, Milwaukee
OF—Al Oliver, Texas
OF—Willie Wilson, Kansas City
C—Lance Parrish, Detroit
DH—Reggie Jackson, New York

NATIONAL LEAGUE
1B—Keith Hernandez, St. Louis
2B—Manny Trillo, Philadelphia
3B—Mike Schmidt, Philadelphia
SS—Garry Templeton, St. Louis
OF—Dusty Baker, Los Angeles
OF—Andre Dawson, Montreal
OF—George Hendrick, St. Louis
C—Ted Simmons, St. Louis
P—Bob Forsch, St. Louis

1981
AMERICAN LEAGUE
1B—Cecil Cooper, Milwaukee
2B—Bobby Grich, California
3B—Carney Lansford, Boston
SS—Rick Burleson, California
OF—Rickey Henderson, Oakland
OF—Dwight Evans, Boston
OF—Dave Winfield, New York
C—Carlton Fisk, Chicago
DH—Al Oliver, Texas

NATIONAL LEAGUE
1B—Pete Rose, Philadelphia
2B—Manny Trillo, Philadelphia
3B—Mike Schmidt, Philadelphia
SS—Dave Concepcion, Cincinnati
OF—Andre Dawson, Montreal
OF—George Foster, Cincinnati
OF—Dusty Baker, Los Angeles
C—Gary Carter, Montreal
P—Fernando Valenzuela, L.A.

1982
AMERICAN LEAGUE
1B—Cecil Cooper, Milwaukee
2B—Damaso Garcia, Toronto
3B—Doug DeCinces, California
SS—Robin Yount, Milwaukee
OF—Dave Winfield, New York
OF—Willie Wilson, Kansas City
OF—Reggie Jackson, California
C—Lance Parrish, Detroit
DH—Hal McRae, Kansas City

NATIONAL LEAGUE
1B—Al Oliver, Montreal
2B—Joe Morgan, San Francisco
3B—Mike Schmidt, Philadelphia
SS—Dave Concepcion, Cincinnati
OF—Dale Murphy, Atlanta
OF—Pedro Guerrero, Los Angeles
OF—Leon Durham, Chicago
C—Gary Carter, Montreal
P—Don Robinson, Pittsburgh

1983

AMERICAN LEAGUE
1B—Eddie Murray, Baltimore
2B—Lou Whitaker, Detroit
3B—Wade Boggs, Boston
SS—Cal Ripken Jr., Baltimore
OF—Jim Rice, Boston
OF—Dave Winfield, New York
OF—Lloyd Moseby, Toronto
C—Lance Parrish, Detroit
DH—Don Baylor, New York

NATIONAL LEAGUE
1B—George Hendrick, St. Louis
2B—Johnny Ray, Pittsburgh
3B—Mike Schmidt, Philadelphia
SS—Dickie Thon, Houston
OF—Andre Dawson, Montreal
OF—Dale Murphy, Atlanta
OF—Jose Cruz, Houston
C—Terry Kennedy, San Diego
P—Fernando Valenzuela, L.A.

1984

AMERICAN LEAGUE
1B—Eddie Murray, Baltimore
2B—Lou Whitaker, Detroit
3B—Buddy Bell, Texas
SS—Cal Ripken Jr., Baltimore
OF—Tony Armas, Boston
OF—Jim Rice, Boston
OF—Dave Winfield, New York
C—Lance Parrish, Detroit
DH—Andre Thornton, Cleveland

NATIONAL LEAGUE
1B—Keith Hernandez, New York
2B—Ryne Sandberg, Chicago
3B—Mike Schmidt, Philadelphia
SS—Garry Templeton, San Diego
OF—Dale Murphy, Atlanta
OF—Jose Cruz, Houston
OF—Tony Gwynn, San Diego
C—Gary Carter, Montreal
P—Rick Rhoden, Pittsburgh

1985

AMERICAN LEAGUE
1B—Don Mattingly, New York
2B—Lou Whitaker, Detroit
3B—George Brett, Kansas City
SS—Cal Ripken Jr., Baltimore
OF—Rickey Henderson, New York
OF—Dave Winfield, New York
OF—George Bell, Toronto
C—Carlton Fisk, Chicago
DH—Don Baylor, New York

NATIONAL LEAGUE
1B—Jack Clark, St. Louis
2B—Ryne Sandberg, Chicago
3B—Tim Wallach, Montreal
SS—Hubie Brooks, Montreal
OF—Willie McGee, St. Louis
OF—Dale Murphy, Atlanta
OF—Dave Parker, Cincinnati
C—Gary Carter, New York
P—Rick Rhoden, Pittsburgh

1986

AMERICAN LEAGUE
1B—Don Mattingly, New York
2B—Frank White, Kansas City
3B—Wade Boggs, Boston
SS—Cal Ripken Jr., Baltimore
OF—George Bell, Toronto
OF—Kirby Puckett, Minnesota
OF—Jesse Barfield, Toronto
C—Lance Parrish, Detroit
DH—Don Baylor, Boston

NATIONAL LEAGUE
1B—Glenn Davis, Houston
2B—Steve Sax, Los Angeles
3B—Mike Schmidt, Philadelphia
SS—Hubie Brooks, Montreal
OF—Tony Gwynn, San Diego
OF—Tim Raines, Montreal
OF—Dave Parker, Cincinnati
C—Gary Carter, New York
P—Rick Rhoden, Pittsburgh

1987

AMERICAN LEAGUE
1B—Don Mattingly, New York
2B—Lou Whitaker, Detroit
3B—Wade Boggs, Boston
SS—Alan Trammell, Detroit
OF—George Bell, Toronto
OF—Dwight Evans, Boston
OF—Kirby Puckett, Minnesota
C—Matt Nokes, Detroit
DH—Paul Molitor, Milwaukee

NATIONAL LEAGUE
1B—Jack Clark, St. Louis
2B—Juan Samuel, Philadelphia
3B—Tim Wallach, Montreal
SS—Ozzie Smith, St. Louis
OF—Andre Dawson, Chicago
OF—Eric Davis, Cincinnati
OF—Tony Gwynn, San Diego
C—Benito Santiago, San Diego
P—Bob Forsch, St. Louis

1988

AMERICAN LEAGUE
1B—George Brett, Kansas City
2B—Julio Franco, Cleveland
3B—Wade Boggs, Boston
SS—Alan Trammell, Detroit
OF—Kirby Puckett, Minnesota
OF—Jose Canseco, Oakland
OF—Mike Greenwell, Boston
C—Carlton Fisk, Chicago
DH—Paul Molitor, Milwaukee

NATIONAL LEAGUE
1B—Andres Galarraga, Montreal
2B—Ryne Sandberg, Chicago
3B—Bobby Bonilla, Pittsburgh
SS—Barry Larkin, Cincinnati
OF—Darryl Strawberry, New York
OF—Andy Van Slyke, Pittsburgh
OF—Kirk Gibson, Los Angeles
C—Benito Santiago, San Diego
P—Tim Leary, Los Angeles

1989

AMERICAN LEAGUE
1B—Fred McGriff, Toronto
2B—Julio Franco, Texas
3B—Wade Boggs, Boston
SS—Cal Ripken Jr., Baltimore
OF—Kirby Puckett, Minnesota
OF—Ruben Sierra, Texas
OF—Robin Yount, Milwaukee
C—Mickey Tettleton, Baltimore
DH—H. Baines, Chicago-Texas

NATIONAL LEAGUE
1B—Will Clark, San Francisco
2B—Ryne Sandberg, Chicago
3B—Howard Johnson, New York
SS—Barry Larkin, Cincinnati
OF—Kevin Mitchell, San Francisco
OF—Tony Gwynn, San Diego
OF—Eric Davis, Cincinnati
C—Craig Biggio, Houston
P—Don Robinson, San Francisco

1990

AMERICAN LEAGUE
1B—Cecil Fielder, Detroit
2B—Julio Franco, Texas
3B—Kelly Gruber, Toronto
SS—Alan Trammell, Detroit
OF—Rickey Henderson, Oakland
OF—Jose Canseco, Oakland
OF—Ellis Burks, Boston
C—Lance Parrish, California
DH—Dave Parker, Milwaukee

NATIONAL LEAGUE
1B—Eddie Murray, Los Angeles
2B—Ryne Sandberg, Chicago
3B—Matt Williams, San Francisco
SS—Barry Larkin, Cincinnati
OF—Barry Bonds, Pittsburgh
OF—Bobby Bonilla, Pittsburgh
OF—Darryl Strawberry, New York
C—Benito Santiago, San Diego
P—Don Robinson, San Francisco

1991

AMERICAN LEAGUE
1B—Cecil Fielder, Detroit
2B—Julio Franco, Texas
3B—Wade Boggs, Boston
SS—Cal Ripken Jr., Baltimore
OF—Jose Canseco, Oakland
OF—Joe Carter, Toronto
OF—Ken Griffey Jr., Seattle
C—Mickey Tettleton, Detroit
DH—Frank Thomas, Chicago

NATIONAL LEAGUE
1B—Will Clark, San Francisco
2B—Ryne Sandberg, Chicago
3B—Howard Johnson, New York
SS—Barry Larkin, Cincinnati
OF—Barry Bonds, Pittsburgh
OF—Bobby Bonilla, Pittsburgh
OF—Ron Gant, Atlanta
C—Benito Santiago, San Diego
P—Tom Glavine, Atlanta

1992

AMERICAN LEAGUE

1B—Mark McGwire, Oakland
2B—Roberto Alomar, Toronto
3B—Edgar Martinez, Seattle
SS—Travis Fryman, Detroit
OF—Joe Carter, Toronto
OF—Juan Gonzalez, Texas
OF—Kirby Puckett, Minnesota
C—Mickey Tettleton, Detroit
DH—Dave Winfield, Toronto

NATIONAL LEAGUE

1B—Fred McGriff, San Diego
2B—Ryne Sandberg, Chicago
3B—Gary Sheffield, San Diego
SS—Barry Larkin, Cincinnati
OF—Barry Bonds, Pittsburgh
OF—Andy Van Slyke, Pittsburgh
OF—Larry Walker, Montreal
C—Darren Daulton, Philadelphia
P—Dwight Gooden, New York

1993

AMERICAN LEAGUE

1B—Frank Thomas, Chicago
2B—Carlos Baerga, Cleveland
3B—Wade Boggs, New York
SS—Cal Ripken Jr., Baltimore
OF—Albert Belle, Cleveland
OF—Juan Gonzalez, Texas
OF—Ken Griffey Jr., Seattle
C—Mike Stanley, New York
DH—Paul Molitor, Toronto

NATIONAL LEAGUE

1B—Fred McGriff, S.D.-Atl.
2B—Robby Thompson, San Fran.
3B—Matt Williams, San Francisco
SS—Jay Bell, Pittsburgh
OF—Barry Bonds, San Francisco
OF—Lenny Dykstra, Philadelphia
OF—David Justice, Atlanta
C—Mike Piazza, Los Angeles
P—Orel Hershiser, Los Angeles

MAJOR LEAGUE ALL-STAR TEAMS

1925

1B—Jim Bottomley, St. Louis NL
2B—Rogers Hornsby, St. Louis NL
SS—Glenn Wright, Pittsburgh NL
3B—Pie Traynor, Pittsburgh NL
OF—Kiki Cuyler, Pittsburgh NL
OF—Max Carey, Pittsburgh NL
OF—Goose Goslin, Washington AL
C—Mickey Cochrane, Phil. AL
P—Walter Johnson, Washington AL
P—Ed Rommel, Philadelphia AL
P—Dazzy Vance, Brooklyn NL

1926

1B—George Burns, Cleveland AL
2B—Rogers Hornsby, St. Louis NL
SS—Joe Sewell, Cleveland AL
3B—Pie Traynor, Pittsburgh NL
OF—Goose Goslin, Washington AL
OF—John Mostil, Chicago AL
OF—Babe Ruth, New York AL
C—Bob O'Farrell, St. Louis NL
P—Herb Pennock, New York AL
P—George Uhle, Cleveland AL
P—Grover Alexander, St. Louis NL

1927

1B—Lou Gehrig, New York AL
2B—Rogers Hornsby, New York NL
SS—Travis Jackson, New York NL
3B—Pie Traynor, Pittsburgh NL
OF—Babe Ruth, New York AL
OF—Al Simmons, Philadelphia AL
OF—Paul Waner, Pittsburgh NL
C—Gabby Hartnett, Chicago NL
P—Charley Root, Chicago NL
P—Ted Lyons, Chicago AL

1928

1B—Lou Gehrig, New York AL
2B—Rogers Hornsby, Boston NL
SS—Travis Jackson, New York NL
3B—Fred Lindstrom, New York NL
OF—Babe Ruth, New York AL
OF—Heinie Manush, St. Louis AL
OF—Paul Waner, Pittsburgh NL
C—Mickey Cochrane, Phil. AL
P—Lefty Grove, Philadelphia AL
P—Waite Hoyt, New York AL

1929

1B—Jimmie Foxx, Philadelphia AL
2B—Rogers Hornsby, Chicago NL
SS—Travis Jackson, New York NL
3B—Pie Traynor, Pittsburgh, NL
OF—Al Simmons, Philadelphia AL
OF—Hack Wilson, Chicago NL
OF—Babe Ruth, New York AL
C—Mickey Cochrane, Phil. AL
P—Lefty Grove, Philadelphia AL
P—Burleigh Grimes, Pittsburgh NL

1930

1B—Bill Terry, New York NL
2B—Frank Frisch, St. Louis NL
SS—Joe Cronin, Washington AL
3B—Fred Lindstrom, New York NL
OF—Al Simmons, Philadelphia AL
OF—Hack Wilson, Chicago NL
OF—Babe Ruth, New York AL
C—Mickey Cochrane, Phil. AL
P—Lefty Grove, Philadelphia AL
P—Wes Ferrell, Cleveland AL

1931

1B—Lou Gehrig, New York AL
2B—Frank Frisch, St. Louis NL
SS—Joe Cronin, Washington AL
3B—Pie Traynor, Pittsburgh AL
OF—Al Simmons, Philadelphia AL
OF—Earl Averill, Cleveland AL
OF—Babe Ruth, New York AL
C—Mickey Cochrane, Phil. AL
P—Lefty Grove, Philadelphia AL
P—George Earnshaw, Phil. AL

1932

1B—Jimmie Foxx, Philadelphia AL
2B—Tony Lazzeri, New York AL
SS—Joe Cronin, Washington AL
3B—Pie Traynor, Pittsburgh NL
OF—Lefty O'Doul, Brooklyn NL
OF—Earl Averill, Cleveland AL
OF—Chuck Klein, Philadelphia NL
C—Bill Dickey, New York AL
P—Lefty Grove, Philadelphia AL
P—Lon Warneke, Chicago NL

1933

1B—Jimmie Foxx, Philadelphia AL
2B—Charley Gehringer, Detroit AL
SS—Joe Cronin, Washington AL
3B—Pie Traynor, Pittsburgh NL
OF—Al Simmons, Chicago AL
OF—Wally Berger, Boston NL
OF—Chuck Klein, Philadelphia NL
C—Bill Dickey, New York AL
P—Alvin Crowder, Washington AL
P—Carl Hubbell, New York NL

1934

1B—Lou Gehrig, New York AL
2B—Charley Gehringer, Detroit AL
SS—Joe Cronin, Washington AL
3B—Mike Higgins, Philadelphia AL
OF—Al Simmons, Chicago AL
OF—Earl Averill, Cleveland AL
OF—Mel Ott, New York NL
C—Mickey Cochrane, Detroit AL
P—Lefty Gomez, New York AL
P—Schoolboy Rowe, Detroit AL
P—Dizzy Dean, St. Louis NL

1935

1B—Hank Greenberg, Detroit AL
2B—Charley Gehringer, Detroit AL
SS—Arky Vaughan, Pittsburgh NL
3B—Pepper Martin, St. Louis NL
OF—Joe Medwick, St. Louis NL
OF—Doc Cramer, Philadelphia AL
OF—Mel Ott, New York NL
C—Mickey Cochrane, Detroit AL
P—Carl Hubbell, New York NL
P—Dizzy Dean, St. Louis NL

1936

1B—Lou Gehrig, New York AL
2B—Charley Gehringer, Detroit AL
SS—Luke Appling, Chicago AL
3B—Mike Higgins, Philadelphia AL
OF—Joe Medwick, St. Louis NL
OF—Earl Averill, Cleveland AL
OF—Mel Ott, New York NL
C—Bill Dickey, New York AL
P—Carl Hubbell, New York NL
P—Dizzy Dean, St. Louis NL

1937

1B—Lou Gehrig, New York AL
2B—Charley Gehringer, Detroit AL
SS—Dick Bartell, New York NL
3B—Red Rolfe, New York AL
OF—Joe Medwick, St. Louis NL
OF—Joe DiMaggio, New York AL
OF—Paul Waner, Pittsburgh NL
C—Gabby Hartnett, Chicago NL
P—Carl Hubbell, New York NL
P—Red Ruffing, New York AL

1938

1B—Jimmie Foxx, Boston AL
2B—Charley Gehringer, Detroit AL
SS—Joe Cronin, Boston AL
3B—Red Rolfe, New York AL
OF—Joe Medwick, St. Louis NL
OF—Joe DiMaggio, New York AL
OF—Mel Ott, New York NL
C—Bill Dickey, New York AL
P—Red Ruffing, New York AL
P—Lefty Gomez, New York AL
P—Johnny Vander Meer, Cin. NL

1939

1B—Jimmie Foxx, Boston AL
2B—Joe Gordon, New York AL
SS—Joe Cronin, Boston AL
3B—Red Rolfe, New York AL
OF—Joe Medwick, St. Louis NL
OF—Joe DiMaggio, New York AL
OF—Ted Williams, Boston AL
C—Bill Dickey, New York AL
P—Red Ruffing, New York AL
P—Bob Feller, Cleveland AL
P—Bucky Walters, Cincinnati NL

1940

1B—Frank McCormick, Cin. NL
2B—Joe Gordon, New York AL
SS—Luke Appling, Chicago AL
3B—Stan Hack, Chicago NL
OF—Hank Greenberg, Detroit AL
OF—Joe DiMaggio, New York AL
OF—Ted Williams, Boston AL
C—Harry Danning, New York NL
P—Bob Feller, Cleveland AL
P—Bucky Walters, Cincinnati NL
P—Paul Derringer, Cincinnati NL

1941

1B—Dolf Camilli, Brooklyn NL
2B—Joe Gordon, New York AL
SS—Cecil Travis, Washington AL
3B—Stan Hack, Chicago NL
OF—Ted Williams, Boston AL
OF—Joe DiMaggio, New York AL
OF—Pete Reiser, Brooklyn NL
C—Bill Dickey, New York AL
P—Bob Feller, Cleveland AL
P—Whitlow Wyatt, Brooklyn NL
P—Thornton Lee, Chicago AL

1942

1B—Johnny Mize, New York NL
2B—Joe Gordon, New York AL
SS—Johnny Pesky, Boston AL
3B—Stan Hack, Chicago NL
OF—Ted Williams, Boston AL
OF—Joe DiMaggio, New York AL
OF—Enos Slaughter, St. Louis NL
C—Mickey Owen, Brooklyn NL
P—Mort Cooper, St. Louis NL
P—Tiny Bonham, New York AL
P—Tex Hughson, Boston AL

1943

1B—Rudy York, Detroit AL
2B—Billy Herman, Brooklyn NL
SS—Luke Appling, Chicago AL
3B—Billy Johnson, New York AL
OF—Dick Wakefield, Detroit AL
OF—Stan Musial, St. Louis NL
OF—Bill Nicholson, Chicago NL
C—Walker Cooper, St. Louis NL
P—Spud Chandler, New York AL
P—Mort Cooper, St. Louis NL
P—Rip Sewell, Pittsburgh NL

1944

1B—Ray Sanders, St. Louis NL
2B—Bobby Doerr, Boston AL
SS—Marty Marion, St. Louis NL
3B—Bob Elliott, Pittsburgh NL
OF—Stan Musial, St. Louis NL
OF—Dick Wakefield, Detroit AL
OF—Dixie Walker, Brooklyn, NL
C—Walker Cooper, St. Louis NL
P—Hal Newhouser, Detroit AL
P—Mort Cooper, St. Louis NL
P—Dizzy Trout, Detroit AL

1945

1B—Phil Cavarretta, Chicago NL
2B—George Stirnweiss, New York AL
SS—Marty Marion, St. Louis NL
3B—Whitey Kurowski, St. Louis NL
OF—Tommy Holmes, Boston NL
OF—Andy Pafko, Chicago NL
OF—Goody Rosen, Brooklyn NL
C—Paul Richards, Detroit AL
P—Hal Newhouser, Detroit AL
P—Boo Ferriss, Boston AL
P—Hank Borowy, Chicago NL

1946

1B—Stan Musial, St. Louis NL
2B—Bobby Doerr, Boston AL
SS—Johnny Pesky, Boston AL
3B—George Kell, Detroit AL
OF—Ted Williams, Boston AL
OF—Dom DiMaggio, Boston AL
OF—Enos Slaughter, St. Louis NL
C—Aaron Robinson, New York AL
P—Hal Newhouser, Detroit AL
P—Bob Feller, Cleveland AL
P—Boo Ferriss, Boston AL

1947

1B—Johnny Mize, New York NL
2B—Joe Gordon, Cleveland AL
SS—Lou Boudreau, Cleveland AL
3B—George Kell, Detroit AL
OF—Ted Williams, Boston AL
OF—Joe DiMaggio, New York AL
OF—Ralph Kiner, Pittsburgh NL
C—Walker Cooper, New York NL
P—Ewell Blackwell, Cincinnati NL
P—Bob Feller, Cleveland AL
P—Ralph Branca, Brooklyn NL

1948

1B—Johnny Mize, New York NL
2B—Joe Gordon, Cleveland AL
SS—Lou Boudreau, Cleveland AL
3B—Bob Elliott, Boston NL
OF—Ted Williams, Boston AL
OF—Joe DiMaggio, New York AL
OF—Stan Musial, St. Louis NL
C—Birdie Tebbetts, Boston AL
P—Johnny Sain, Boston NL
P—Bob Lemon, Cleveland AL
P—Harry Brecheen, St. Louis NL

1949

1B—Tommy Henrich, New York AL
2B—Jackie Robinson, Brooklyn NL
SS—Phil Rizzuto, New York AL
3B—George Kell, Detroit AL
OF—Ted Williams, Boston AL
OF—Stan Musial, St. Louis NL
OF—Ralph Kiner, Pittsburgh NL
C—Roy Campanella, Brooklyn NL
P—Mel Parnell, Boston AL
P—Ellis Kinder, Boston AL
P—Joe Page, New York AL

1950

1B—Walt Dropo, Boston AL
2B—Jackie Robinson, Brooklyn NL
SS—Phil Rizzuto, New York AL
3B—George Kell, Detroit AL
OF—Stan Musial, St. Louis NL
OF—Ralph Kiner, Pittsburgh NL
OF—Larry Doby, Cleveland AL
C—Yogi Berra, New York AL
P—Vic Raschi, New York AL
P—Bob Lemon, Cleveland AL
P—Jim Konstanty, Philadelphia NL

1951

1B—Ferris Fain, Philadelphia AL
2B—Jackie Robinson, Brooklyn NL
SS—Phil Rizzuto, New York AL
3B—George Kell, Detroit AL
OF—Stan Musial, St. Louis NL
OF—Ted Williams, Boston AL
OF—Ralph Kiner, Pittsburgh NL
C—Roy Campanella, Brooklyn NL
P—Sal Maglie, New York NL
P—Preacher Roe, Brooklyn NL
P—Allie Reynolds, New York AL

1952

1B—Ferris Fain, Philadelphia AL
2B—Jackie Robinson, Brooklyn NL
SS—Phil Rizzuto, New York AL
3B—George Kell, Boston AL
OF—Stan Musial, St. Louis NL
OF—Hank Sauer, Chicago NL
OF—Mickey Mantle, New York AL
C—Yogi Berra, New York AL
P—Robin Roberts, Philadelphia NL
P—Bobby Shantz, Philadelphia AL
P—Allie Reynolds, New York AL

1953

1B—Mickey Vernon, Washington AL
2B—Red Schoendienst, St. Louis NL
SS—Pee Wee Reese, Brooklyn NL
3B—Al Rosen, Cleveland AL
OF—Stan Musial, St. Louis NL
OF—Duke Snider, Brooklyn NL
OF—Carl Furillo, Brooklyn NL
C—Roy Campanella, Brooklyn NL
P—Robin Roberts, Philadelphia NL
P—Warren Spahn, Milwaukee NL
P—Bob Porterfield, Washington AL

1954

1B—Ted Kluszewski, Cincinnati NL
2B—Bobby Avila, Cleveland AL
SS—Alvin Dark, New York NL
3B—Al Rosen, Cleveland AL
OF—Willie Mays, New York NL
OF—Stan Musial, St. Louis NL
OF—Duke Snider, Brooklyn NL
C—Yogi Berra, New York AL
P—Bob Lemon, Cleveland AL
P—Johnny Antonelli, New York NL
P—Robin Roberts, Philadelphia NL

1955

1B—Ted Kluszewski, Cincinnati NL
2B—Nellie Fox, Chicago AL
SS—Ernie Banks, Chicago NL
3B—Ed Mathews, Milwaukee NL
OF—Duke Snider, Brooklyn NL
OF—Ted Williams, Boston AL
OF—Al Kaline, Detroit AL
C—Roy Campanella, Brooklyn NL
P—Robin Roberts, Philadelphia NL
P—Don Newcombe, Brooklyn NL
P—Whitey Ford, New York AL

1956

1B—Ted Kluszewski, Cincinnati NL
2B—Nellie Fox, Chicago AL
SS—Harvey Kuenn, Detroit AL
3B—Ken Boyer, St. Louis NL
OF—Mickey Mantle, New York AL
OF—Hank Aaron, Milwaukee NL
OF—Ted Williams, Boston AL
C—Yogi Berra, New York AL
P—Don Newcombe, Brooklyn NL
P—Whitey Ford, New York AL
P—Billy Pierce, Chicago AL

1957

1B—Stan Musial, St. Louis NL
2B—Red Schoendienst, N.Y.-Mil. NL
SS—Gil McDougald, New York AL
3B—Ed Mathews, Milwaukee NL
OF—Mickey Mantle, New York AL
OF—Ted Williams, Boston AL
OF—Willie Mays, New York NL
C—Yogi Berra, New York AL
P—Warren Spahn, Milwaukee NL
P—Billy Pierce, Chicago NL
P—Jim Bunning, Detroit AL

1958

1B—Stan Musial, St. Louis NL
2B—Nellie Fox, Chicago AL
SS—Ernie Banks, Chicago NL
3B—Frank Thomas, Pittsburgh NL
OF—Ted Williams, Boston AL
OF—Willie Mays, San Francisco NL
OF—Hank Aaron, Milwaukee NL
C—Del Crandall, Milwaukee NL
P—Bob Turley, New York AL
P—Warren Spahn, Milwaukee NL
P—Bob Friend, Pittsburgh NL

1959

1B—Orlando Cepeda, S.F. NL
2B—Nellie Fox, Chicago AL
SS—Ernie Banks, Chicago NL
3B—Ed Mathews, Milwaukee NL
OF—Minnie Minoso, Cleveland AL
OF—Willie Mays, San Francisco NL
OF—Hank Aaron, Milwaukee NL
C—Sherm Lollar, Chicago AL
P—Early Wynn, Chicago AL
P—Sam Jones, San Francisco NL
P—Johnny Antonelli, S.F. NL

1960

1B—Bill Skowron, New York AL
2B—Bill Mazeroski, Pittsburgh NL
SS—Ernie Banks, Chicago NL
3B—Ed Mathews, Milwaukee NL
OF—Minnie Minoso, Chicago AL
OF—Willie Mays, San Francisco NL
OF—Roger Maris, New York AL
C—Del Crandall, Milwaukee NL
P—Vernon Law, Pittsburgh NL
P—Warren Spahn, Milwaukee NL
P—Ernie Broglio, St. Louis NL

1961

AMERICAN LEAGUE

1B—Norm Cash, Detroit
2B—Bobby Richardson, New York
SS—Tony Kubek, New York
3B—Brooks Robinson, Baltimore
OF—Mickey Mantle, New York
OF—Roger Maris, New York
OF—Rocky Colavito, Detroit
C—Elston Howard, New York
P—Whitey Ford, New York
P—Frank Lary, Detroit

NATIONAL LEAGUE

1B—Orlando Cepeda, San Francisco
2B—Frank Bolling, Milwaukee
SS—Maury Wills, Los Angeles
3B—Ken Boyer, St. Louis
OF—Willie Mays, San Francisco
OF—Frank Robinson, Cincinnati
OF—Roberto Clemente, Pittsburgh
C—Smoky Burgess, Pittsburgh
P—Joey Jay, Cincinnati
P—Warren Spahn, Milwaukee

1962

AMERICAN LEAGUE

1B—Norm Siebern, Kansas City
2B—Bobby Richardson, New York
SS—Tom Tresh, New York
3B—Brooks Robinson, Baltimore
OF—Leon Wagner, Los Angeles
OF—Mickey Mantle, New York
OF—Al Kaline, Detroit
C—Earl Battey, Minnesota
P—Ralph Terry, New York
P—Dick Donovan, Cleveland

NATIONAL LEAGUE

1B—Orlando Cepeda, San Francisco
2B—Bill Mazeroski, Pittsburgh
SS—Maury Wills, Los Angeles
3B—Ken Boyer, St. Louis
OF—Tommy Davis, Los Angeles
OF—Willie Mays, San Francisco
OF—Frank Robinson, Cincinnati
C—Del Crandall, Milwaukee
P—Don Drysdale, Los Angeles
P—Bob Purkey, Cincinnati

1963

AMERICAN LEAGUE

1B—Joe Pepitone, New York
2B—Bobby Richardson, New York
SS—Luis Aparicio, Baltimore
3B—Frank Malzone, Boston
OF—Carl Yastrzemski, Boston
OF—Albie Pearson, Los Angeles
OF—Al Kaline, Detroit
C—Elston Howard, New York
P—Whitey Ford, New York
P—Gary Peters, Chicago

NATIONAL LEAGUE

1B—Bill White, St. Louis
2B—Jim Gilliam, Los Angeles
SS—Dick Groat, St. Louis
3B—Ken Boyer, St. Louis
OF—Tommy Davis, Los Angeles
OF—Willie Mays, San Francisco
OF—Hank Aaron, Milwaukee
C—John Edwards, Cincinnati
P—Sandy Koufax, Los Angeles
P—Juan Marichal, San Francisco

1964

AMERICAN LEAGUE

1B—Dick Stuart, Boston
2B—Bobby Richardson, New York
SS—Jim Fregosi, Los Angeles
3B—Brooks Robinson, Baltimore
OF—Harmon Killebrew, Minnesota
OF—Mickey Mantle, New York
OF—Tony Oliva, Minnesota
C—Elston Howard, New York
P—Dean Chance, Los Angeles
P—Gary Peters, Chicago

NATIONAL LEAGUE

1B—Bill White, St. Louis
2B—Ron Hunt, New York
SS—Dick Groat, St. Louis
3B—Ken Boyer, St. Louis
OF—Billy Williams, Chicago
OF—Willie Mays, San Francisco
OF—Roberto Clemente, Pittsburgh
C—Joe Torre, Milwaukee
P—Sandy Koufax, Los Angeles
P—Jim Bunning, Philadelphia

1965

AMERICAN LEAGUE

1B—Fred Whitfield, Cleveland
2B—Bobby Richardson, New York
SS—Zoilo Versalles, Minnesota
3B—Brooks Robinson, Baltimore
OF—Carl Yastrzemski, Boston
OF—Jimmie Hall, Minnesota
OF—Tony Oliva, Minnesota
C—Earl Battey, Minnesota
P—Jim Grant, Minnesota
P—Mel Stottlemyre, New York

NATIONAL LEAGUE

1B—Willie McCovey, San Francisco
2B—Pete Rose, Cincinnati
SS—Maury Wills, Los Angeles
3B—Deron Johnson, Cincinnati
OF—Willie Stargell, Pittsburgh
OF—Willie Mays, San Francisco
OF—Hank Aaron, Milwaukee
C—Joe Torre, Milwaukee
P—Sandy Koufax, Los Angeles
P—Juan Marichal, San Francisco

1966

AMERICAN LEAGUE

1B—Boog Powell, Baltimore
2B—Bobby Richardson, New York
SS—Luis Aparicio, Baltimore
3B—Brooks Robinson, Baltimore
OF—Frank Robinson, Baltimore
OF—Al Kaline, Detroit
OF—Tony Oliva, Minnesota
C—Paul Casanova, Washington
P—Jim Kaat, Minnesota
P—Earl Wilson, Detroit

NATIONAL LEAGUE

1B—Felipe Alou, Atlanta
2B—Pete Rose, Cincinnati
SS—Gene Alley, Pittsburgh
3B—Ron Santo, Chicago
OF—Willie Stargell, Pittsburgh
OF—Willie Mays, San Francisco
OF—Roberto Clemente, Pittsburgh
C—Joe Torre, Atlanta
P—Sandy Koufax, Los Angeles
P—Juan Marichal, San Francisco

1967

AMERICAN LEAGUE

1B—Harmon Killebrew, Minnesota
2B—Rod Carew, Minnesota
SS—Jim Fregosi, California
3B—Brooks Robinson, Baltimore
OF—Carl Yastrzemski, Boston
OF—Al Kaline, Detroit
OF—Frank Robinson, Baltimore
C—Bill Freehan, Detroit
P—Jim Lonborg, Boston
P—Earl Wilson, Detroit

NATIONAL LEAGUE

1B—Orlando Cepeda, St. Louis
2B—Bill Mazeroski, Pittsburgh
SS—Gene Alley, Pittsburgh
3B—Ron Santo, Chicago
OF—Hank Aaron, Atlanta
OF—Jim Wynn, Houston
OF—Roberto Clemente, Pittsburgh
C—Tim McCarver, St. Louis
P—Mike McCormick, San Francisco
P—Ferguson Jenkins, Chicago

1968

AMERICAN LEAGUE

1B—Boog Powell, Baltimore
2B—Rod Carew, Minnesota
SS—Luis Aparicio, Chicago
3B—Brooks Robinson, Baltimore
OF—Ken Harrelson, Boston
OF—Willie Horton, Detroit
OF—Frank Howard, Washington
C—Bill Freehan, Detroit
P—Dave McNally, Baltimore
P—Denny McLain, Detroit

NATIONAL LEAGUE

1B—Willie McCovey, San Francisco
2B—Tommy Helms, Cincinnati
SS—Don Kessinger, Chicago
3B—Ron Santo, Chicago
OF—Billy Williams, Chicago
OF—Curt Flood, St. Louis
OF—Pete Rose, Cincinnati
C—Johnny Bench, Cincinnati
P—Bob Gibson, St. Louis
P—Juan Marichal, San Francisco

1969

AMERICAN LEAGUE

1B—Boog Powell, Baltimore
2B—Rod Carew, Minnesota
SS—Rico Petrocelli, Boston
3B—Harmon Killebrew, Minnesota
OF—Frank Howard, Washington
OF—Paul Blair, Baltimore
OF—Reggie Jackson, Oakland
C—Bill Freehan, Detroit
RHP—Denny McLain, Detroit
LHP—Mike Cuellar, Baltimore

NATIONAL LEAGUE

1B—Willie McCovey, San Francisco
2B—Glenn Beckert, Chicago
SS—Don Kessinger, Chicago
3B—Ron Santo, Chicago
OF—Cleon Jones, New York
OF—Matty Alou, Pittsburgh
OF—Hank Aaron, Atlanta
C—Johnny Bench, Cincinnati
RHP—Tom Seaver, New York
LHP—Steve Carlton, St. Louis

1970

AMERICAN LEAGUE

1B—Boog Powell, Baltimore
2B—Dave Johnson, Baltimore
SS—Luis Aparicio, Chicago
3B—Harmon Killebrew, Minnesota
OF—Frank Howard, Washington
OF—Reggie Smith, Boston
OF—Tony Oliva, Minnesota
C—Ray Fosse, Cleveland
RHP—Jim Perry, Minnesota
LHP—Sam McDowell, Cleveland

NATIONAL LEAGUE

1B—Willie McCovey, San Francisco
2B—Glenn Beckert, Chicago
SS—Don Kessinger, Chicago
3B—Tony Perez, Cincinnati
OF—Billy Williams, Chicago
OF—Bobby Tolan, Cincinnati
OF—Hank Aaron, Atlanta
C—Johnny Bench, Cincinnati
RHP—Bob Gibson, St. Louis
LHP—Jim Merritt, Cincinnati

1971

AMERICAN LEAGUE

1B—Norm Cash, Detroit
2B—Cookie Rojas, Kansas City
SS—Leo Cardenas, Minnesota
3B—Brooks Robinson, Baltimore
OF—Merv Rettenmund, Baltimore
OF—Bobby Murcer, New York
OF—Tony Oliva, Minnesota
C—Bill Freehan, Detroit
RHP—Jim Palmer, Baltimore
LHP—Vida Blue, Oakland

NATIONAL LEAGUE

1B—Lee May, Cincinnati
2B—Glenn Beckett, Chicago
SS—Bud Harrelson, New York
3B—Joe Torre, St. Louis
OF—Willie Stargell, Pittsburgh
OF—Willie Davis, Los Angeles
OF—Hank Aaron, Atlanta
C—Manny Sanguillen, Pittsburgh
RHP—Ferguson Jenkins, Chicago
LHP—Steve Carlton, St. Louis

1972

AMERICAN LEAGUE

1B—Dick Allen, Chicago
2B—Rod Carew, Minnesota
SS—Luis Aparicio, Boston
3B—Brooks Robinson, Baltimore
OF—Joe Rudi, Oakland
OF—Bobby Murcer, New York
OF—Richie Scheinblum, Kansas City
C—Carlton Fisk, Boston
RHP—Gaylord Perry, Cleveland
LHP—Wilbur Wood, Chicago

NATIONAL LEAGUE

1B—Willie Stargell, Pittsburgh
2B—Joe Morgan, Cincinnati
SS—Chris Speier, San Francisco
3B—Ron Santo, Chicago
OF—Billy Williams, Chicago
OF—Cesar Cedeno, Houston
OF—Roberto Clemente, Pittsburgh
C—Johnny Bench, Cincinnati
RHP—Ferguson Jenkins, Chicago
LHP—Steve Carlton, Philadelphia

1973

AMERICAN LEAGUE

1B—John Mayberry, Kansas City
2B—Rod Carew, Minnesota
SS—Bert Campaneris, Oakland
3B—Sal Bando, Oakland
OF—Reggie Jackson, Oakland
OF—Amos Otis, Kansas City
OF—Bobby Murcer, New York
C—Thurman Munson, New York
RHP—Jim Palmer, Baltimore
LHP—Ken Holtzman, Oakland

NATIONAL LEAGUE

1B—Tony Perez, Cincinnati
2B—Dave Johnson, Atlanta
SS—Bill Russell, Los Angeles
3B—Darrell Evans, Atlanta
OF—Bobby Bonds, San Francisco
OF—Cesar Cedeno, Houston
OF—Pete Rose, Cincinnati
C—Johnny Bench, Cincinnati
RHP—Tom Seaver, New York
LHP—Ron Bryant, San Francisco

1974

AMERICAN LEAGUE

1B—Dick Allen, Chicago
2B—Rod Carew, Minnesota
SS—Bert Campaneris, Oakland
3B—Sal Bando, Oakland
OF—Joe Rudi, Oakland
OF—Paul Blair, Baltimore
OF—Jeff Burroughs, Texas
C—Thurman Munson, New York
DH—Tommy Davis, Baltimore
RHP—Jim Hunter, Oakland
LHP—Mike Cuellar, Baltimore

NATIONAL LEAGUE

1B—Steve Garvey, Los Angeles
2B—Joe Morgan, Cincinnati
SS—Dave Concepcion, Cincinnati
3B—Mike Schmidt, Philadelphia
OF—Lou Brock, St. Louis
OF—Jim Wynn, Los Angeles
OF—Richie Zisk, Pittsburgh
C—Johnny Bench, Cincinnati
RHP—Andy Messersmith, Los Angeles
LHP—Don Gullett, Cincinnati

1975

AMERICAN LEAGUE

1B—John Mayberry, Kansas City
2B—Rod Carew, Minnesota
SS—Toby Harrah, Texas
3B—Graig Nettles, New York
OF—Jim Rice, Boston
OF—Fred Lynn, Boston
OF—Reggie Jackson, Oakland
C—Thurman Munson, New York
DH—Willie Horton, Detroit
RHP—Jim Palmer, Baltimore
LHP—Jim Kaat, Chicago

NATIONAL LEAGUE

1B—Steve Garvey, Los Angeles
2B—Joe Morgan, Cincinnati
SS—Larry Bowa, Philadelphia
3B—Bill Madlock, Chicago
OF—Greg Luzinski, Philadelphia
OF—Al Oliver, Pittsburgh
OF—Dave Parker, Pittsburgh
C—Johnny Bench, Cincinnati
RHP—Tom Seaver, New York
LHP—Randy Jones, San Diego

1976

AMERICAN LEAGUE

1B—Chris Chambliss, New York
2B—Bobby Grich, Baltimore
3B—George Brett, Kansas City
SS—Mark Belanger, Baltimore
OF—Joe Rudi, Oakland
OF—Mickey Rivers, New York
OF—Reggie Jackson, Baltimore
C—Thurman Munson, New York
DH—Hal McRae, Kansas City
RHP—Jim Palmer, Baltimore
LHP—Frank Tanana, California

NATIONAL LEAGUE

1B—Willie Montanez, San Fran.-Atl.
2B—Joe Morgan, Cincinnati
3B—Mike Schmidt, Philadelphia
SS—Dave Concepcion, Cincinnati
OF—George Foster, Cincinnati
OF—Cesar Cedeno, Houston
OF—Ken Griffey, Cincinnati
C—Bob Boone, Philadelphia
RHP—Don Sutton, Los Angeles
LHP—Randy Jones, San Diego

1977

AMERICAN LEAGUE

1B—Rod Carew, Minnesota
2B—Willie Randolph, New York
3B—Graig Nettles, New York
SS—Rick Burleson, Boston
OF—Jim Rice, Boston
OF—Larry Hisle, Minnesota
OF—Bobby Bonds, California
C—Carlton Fisk, Boston
DH—Hal McRae, Kansas City
RHP—Nolan Ryan, California
LHP—Frank Tanana, California

NATIONAL LEAGUE

1B—Steve Garvey, Los Angeles
2B—Joe Morgan, Cincinnati
3B—Mike Schmidt, Philadelphia
SS—Garry Templeton, St. Louis
OF—George Foster, Cincinnati
OF—Dave Parker, Pittsburgh
OF—Greg Luzinski, Philadelphia
C—Ted Simmons, St. Louis
RHP—Rick Reuschel, Chicago
LHP—Steve Carlton, Philadelphia

1978

AMERICAN LEAGUE

1B—Rod Carew, Minnesota
2B—Frank White, Kansas City
3B—Graig Nettles, New York
SS—Robin Yount, Milwaukee
OF—Jim Rice, Boston
OF—Larry Hisle, Milwaukee
OF—Fred Lynn, Boston
C—Jim Sundberg, Texas
DH—Rusty Staub, Detroit
RHP—Jim Palmer, Baltimore
LHP—Ron Guidry, New York

NATIONAL LEAGUE

1B—Steve Garvey, Los Angeles
2B—Dave Lopes, Los Angeles
3B—Pete Rose, Cincinnati
SS—Larry Bowa, Philadelphia
OF—George Foster, Cincinnati
OF—Dave Parker, Pittsburgh
OF—Jack Clark, San Francisco
C—Ted Simmons, St. Louis
RHP—Gaylord Perry, San Diego
LHP—Vida Blue, San Francisco

1979

AMERICAN LEAGUE

1B—Cecil Cooper, Milwaukee
2B—Bobby Grich, California
3B—George Brett, Kansas City
SS—Roy Smalley, Minnesota
OF—Jim Rice, Boston
OF—Fred Lynn, Boston
OF—Ken Singleton, Baltimore
C—Darrell Porter, Kansas City
DH—Don Baylor, California
RHP—Jim Kern, Texas
LHP—Mike Flanagan, Baltimore

NATIONAL LEAGUE

1B—Keith Hernandez, St. Louis
2B—Dave Lopes, Los Angeles
3B—Mike Schmidt, Philadelphia
SS—Garry Templeton, St. Louis
OF—Dave Kingman, Chicago
OF—Omar Moreno, Pittsburgh
OF—Dave Winfield, San Diego
C—Ted Simmons, St. Louis
RHP—Joe Niekro, Houston
LHP—Steve Carlton, Philadelphia

1980

AMERICAN LEAGUE

1B—Cecil Cooper, Milwaukee
2B—Willie Randolph, New York
3B—George Brett, Kansas City
SS—Robin Yount, Milwaukee
OF—Ben Oglivie, Milwaukee
OF—Al Bumbry, Baltimore
OF—Reggie Jackson, New York
DH—Reggie Jackson, New York
C—Rick Cerone, New York
RHP—Steve Stone, Baltimore
LHP—Tommy John, New York

NATIONAL LEAGUE

1B—Keith Hernandez, St. Louis
2B—Manny Trillo, Philadelphia
3B—Mike Schmidt, Philadelphia
SS—Garry Templeton, St. Louis
OF—Dusty Baker, Los Angeles
OF—Cesar Cedeno, Houston
OF—George Hendrick, St. Louis
C—Gary Carter, Montreal
RHP—Jim Bibby, Pittsburgh
LHP—Steve Carlton, Philadelphia

1981

AMERICAN LEAGUE

1B—Cecil Cooper, Milwaukee
2B—Bobby Grich, California
3B—Buddy Bell, Texas
SS—Rick Burleson, California
OF—Rickey Henderson, Oakland
OF—Dwayne Murphy, Oakland
OF—Tony Armas, Oakland
C—Jim Sundberg, Texas
DH—Richie Zisk, Seattle
RHP—Jack Morris, Detroit
LHP—Ron Guidry, New York

NATIONAL LEAGUE

1B—Pete Rose, Philadelphia
2B—Manny Trillo, Philadelphia
3B—Mike Schmidt, Philadelphia
SS—Dave Concepcion, Cincinnati
OF—George Foster, Cincinnati
OF—Andre Dawson, Montreal
OF—Pedro Guerrero, Los Angeles
C—Gary Carter, Montreal
RHP—Tom Seaver, Cincinnati
LHP—Fernando Valenzuela, Los Ang.

1982

AMERICAN LEAGUE

1B—Cecil Cooper, Milwaukee
2B—Damaso Garcia, Toronto
3B—Doug DeCinces, California
SS—Robin Yount, Milwaukee
OF—Dave Winfield, New York
OF—Gorman Thomas, Milwaukee
OF—Dwight Evans, Boston
C—Lance Parrish, Detroit
DH—Hal McRae, Kansas City
RHP—Dave Stieb, Toronto
LHP—Geoff Zahn, California

NATIONAL LEAGUE

1B—Al Oliver, Montreal
2B—Manny Trillo, Philadelphia
3B—Mike Schmidt, Philadelphia
SS—Ozzie Smith, St. Louis
OF—Lonnie Smith, St. Louis
OF—Dale Murphy, Atlanta
OF—Pedro Guerrero, Los Angeles
C—Gary Carter, Montreal
RHP—Steve Rogers, Montreal
LHP—Steve Carlton, Philadelphia

1983

AMERICAN LEAGUE

1B—Eddie Murray, Baltimore
2B—Lou Whitaker, Detroit
3B—Wade Boggs, Boston
SS—Cal Ripken, Baltimore
OF—Jim Rice, Boston
OF—Dave Winfield, New York
OF—Lloyd Moseby, Toronto
C—Carlton Fisk, Chicago
DH—Greg Luzinski, Chicago
RHP—LaMarr Hoyt, Chicago
LHP—Ron Guidry, New York

NATIONAL LEAGUE

1B—George Hendrick, St. Louis
2B—Glenn Hubbard, Atlanta
3B—Mike Schmidt, Philadelphia
SS—Dickie Thon, Houston
OF—Dale Murphy, Atlanta
OF—Andre Dawson, Montreal
OF—Tim Raines, Montreal
C—Tony Pena, Pittsburgh
RHP—John Denny, Philadelphia
LHP—Larry McWilliams, Pittsburgh

1984

AMERICAN LEAGUE

1B—Don Mattingly, New York
2B—Lou Whitaker, Detroit
3B—Buddy Bell, Texas
SS—Cal Ripken, Baltimore
OF—Tony Armas, Boston
OF—Dwight Evans, Boston
OF—Dave Winfield, New York
C—Lance Parrish, Detroit
DH—Dave Kingman, Oakland
RHP—Mike Boddicker, Baltimore
LHP—Willie Hernandez, Detroit

NATIONAL LEAGUE

1B—Keith Hernandez, New York
2B—Ryne Sandberg, Chicago
3B—Mike Schmidt, Philadelphia
SS—Ozzie Smith, St. Louis
OF—Dale Murphy, Atlanta
OF—Jose Cruz, Houston
OF—Tony Gwynn, San Diego
C—Gary Carter, Montreal
RHP—Rick Sutcliffe, Chicago
LHP—Mark Thurmond, San Diego

1985

AMERICAN LEAGUE
1B—Don Mattingly, New York
2B—Damaso Garcia, Toronto
3B—Wade Boggs, Boston
SS—Cal Ripken, Baltimore
OF—Rickey Henderson, New York
OF—Harold Baines, Chicago
OF—Phil Bradley, Seattle
C—Carlton Fisk, Chicago
DH—Don Baylor, New York
RHP—Bret Saberhagen, Kansas City
LHP—Ron Guidry, New York

NATIONAL LEAGUE
1B—Keith Hernandez, New York
2B—Tom Herr, St. Louis
3B—Tim Wallach, Montreal
SS—Ozzie Smith, St. Louis
OF—Dave Parker, Cincinnati
OF—Willie McGee, St. Louis
OF—Dale Murphy, Atlanta
C—Gary Carter, New York
RHP—Dwight Gooden, New York
LHP—John Tudor, St. Louis

1986

AMERICAN LEAGUE
1B—Don Mattingly, New York
2B—Tony Bernazard, Cleveland
3B—Wade Boggs, Boston
SS—Tony Fernandez, Toronto
OF—Jim Rice, Boston
OF—George Bell, Toronto
OF—Kirby Puckett, Minnesota
C—Rich Gedman, Boston
DH—Don Baylor, Boston
RHP—Roger Clemens, Boston
LHP—Teddy Higuera, Milwaukee

NATIONAL LEAGUE
1B—Keith Hernandez, New York
2B—Steve Sax, Los Angeles
3B—Mike Schmidt, Philadelphia
SS—Ozzie Smith, St. Louis
OF—Tim Raines, Montreal
OF—Tony Gwynn, San Diego
OF—Dave Parker, Cincinnati
C—Gary Carter, New York
RHP—Mike Scott, Houston
LHP—Fernando Valenzuela, Los Ang.

1987

AMERICAN LEAGUE
1B—Don Mattingly, New York
2B—Willie Randolph, New York
3B—Wade Boggs, Boston
SS—Alan Trammell, Detroit
OF—George Bell, Toronto
OF—Kirby Puckett, Minnesota
OF—Dwight Evans, Boston
C—Matt Nokes, Detroit
DH—Paul Molitor, Milwaukee
RHP—Roger Clemens, Boston
LHP—Jimmy Key, Toronto

NATIONAL LEAGUE
1B—Jack Clark, St. Louis
2B—Juan Samuel, Philadelphia
3B—Tim Wallach, Montreal
SS—Ozzie Smith, St. Louis
OF—Andre Dawson, Chicago
OF—Tony Gwynn, San Diego
OF—Eric Davis, Cincinnati
C—Benito Santiago, San Diego
RHP—Rick Sutcliffe, Chicago
LHP—Zane Smith, Atlanta

1988

AMERICAN LEAGUE
1B—George Brett, Kansas City
2B—Johnny Ray, California
3B—Wade Boggs, Boston
SS—Alan Trammell, Detroit
OF—Kirby Puckett, Minnesota
OF—Mike Greenwell, Boston
OF—Jose Canseco, Oakland
C—Ernie Whitt, Toronto
DH—Harold Baines, Chicago
RHP—Dave Stewart, Oakland
LHP—Frank Viola, Minnesota

NATIONAL LEAGUE
1B—Will Clark, San Francisco
2B—Ryne Sandberg, Chicago
3B—Bobby Bonilla, Pittsburgh
SS—Barry Larkin, Cincinnati
OF—Darryl Strawberry, New York
OF—Andy Van Slyke, Pittsburgh
OF—Kevin McReynolds, New York
C—Mike LaValliere, Pittsburgh
RHP—Orel Hershiser, Los Angeles
LHP—Danny Jackson, Cincinnati

1989

AMERICAN LEAGUE
1B—Fred McGriff, Toronto
2B—Julio Franco, Texas
3B—Carney Lansford, Oakland
SS—Cal Ripken, Baltimore
OF—Ruben Sierra, Texas
OF—Kirby Puckett, Minnesota
OF—Robin Yount, Milwaukee
C—Mickey Tettleton, Baltimore
DH—Harold Baines, Chicago-Texas
RHP—Bret Saberhagen, Kansas City
LHP—Chuck Finley, California

NATIONAL LEAGUE
1B—Will Clark, San Francisco
2B—Ryne Sandberg, Chicago
3B—Howard Johnson, New York
SS—Shawon Dunston, Chicago
OF—Tony Gwynn, San Diego
OF—Kevin Mitchell, San Francisco
OF—Eric Davis, Cincinnati
C—Benito Santiago, San Diego
RHP—Mike Scott, Houston
LHP—Mark Davis, San Diego

1990

AMERICAN LEAGUE
1B—Cecil Fielder, Detroit
2B—Julio Franco, Texas
3B—Kelly Gruber, Toronto
SS—Alan Trammell, Detroit
OF—Rickey Henderson, Oakland
OF—Jose Canseco, Oakland
OF—Ellis Burks, Boston
C—Carlton Fisk, Chicago
DH—Dave Parker, Milwaukee
RHP—Bob Welch, Oakland
LHP—Chuck Finley, California

NATIONAL LEAGUE
1B—Eddie Murray, Los Angeles
2B—Ryne Sandberg, Chicago
3B—Matt Williams, San Francisco
SS—Barry Larkin, Cincinnati
OF—Barry Bonds, Pittsburgh
OF—Bobby Bonilla, Pittsburgh
OF—Darryl Strawberry, New York
C—Mike Scioscia, Los Angeles
RHP—Doug Drabek, Pittsburgh
LHP—Frank Viola, New York

1991

AMERICAN LEAGUE
1B—Cecil Fielder, Detroit
2B—Julio Franco, Texas
3B—Wade Boggs, Boston
SS—Cal Ripken, Baltimore
OF—Jose Canseco, Oakland
OF—Joe Carter, Toronto
OF—Ken Griffey Jr., Seattle
C—Mickey Tettleton, Detroit
RHP—Roger Clemens, Boston
LHP—Jim Abbott, California

NATIONAL LEAGUE
1B—Will Clark, San Francisco
2B—Ryne Sandberg, Chicago
3B—Terry Pendleton, Atlanta
SS—Barry Larkin, Cincinnati
OF—Barry Bonds, Pittsburgh
OF—Bobby Bonilla, Pittsburgh
OF—Ron Gant, Atlanta
C—Benito Santiago, San Diego
RHP—Jose Rijo, Cincinnati
LHP—Tom Glavine, Atlanta

1992

AMERICAN LEAGUE
1B—Mark McGwire, Oakland
2B—Roberto Alomar, Toronto
3B—Edgar Martinez, Seattle
SS—Travis Fryman, Detroit
OF—Joe Carter, Toronto
OF—Mike Devereaux, Baltimore
OF—Kirby Puckett, Minnesota
C—Mickey Tettleton, Detroit
RHP—Jack McDowell, Chicago
LHP—Dave Fleming, Seattle

NATIONAL LEAGUE
1B—Fred McGriff, San Diego
2B—Ryne Sandberg, Chicago
3B—Gary Sheffield, San Diego
SS—Barry Larkin, Cincinnati
OF—Barry Bonds, Pittsburgh
OF—Andy Van Slyke, Pittsburgh
OF—Larry Walker, Montreal
C—Darren Daulton, Philadelphia
RHP—Greg Maddux, Chicago
LHP—Tom Glavine, Atlanta

1993

AMERICAN LEAGUE
1B—Frank Thomas, Chicago
2B—Carlos Baerga, Cleveland
3B—Travis Fryman, Detroit
SS—Cal Ripken Jr., Baltimore
OF—Albert Belle, Cleveland
OF—Juan Gonzalez, Texas
OF—Ken Griffey Jr., Seattle
C—Mike Stanley, New York
DH—Paul Molitor, Toronto
RHP—Jack McDowell, Chicago
LHP—Jimmy Key, New York

NATIONAL LEAGUE
1B—Fred McGriff, S.D.-Atl.
2B—Robby Thompson, San Fran.
3B—Matt Williams, San Francisco
SS—Jay Bell, Pittsburgh
OF—Barry Bonds, San Francisco
OF—Lenny Dykstra, Philadelphia
OF—David Justice, Atlanta
C—Mike Piazza, Los Angeles
RHP—Greg Maddux, Atlanta
LHP—Steve Avery, Atlanta

MINOR LEAGUE PLAYER OF THE YEAR

Year	Player, Team, League
1936	John Vander Meer, Durham, Piedmont
1937	Charlie Keller, Newark, International
1938	Fred Hutchinson, Seattle, Pacific Coast
1939	Lou Novikoff, Tulsa-Los Angeles
1940	Phil Rizzuto, Kansas City, American Association
1941	John Lindell, Newark, International
1942	Dick Barrett, Seattle, Pacific Coast
1943	Chet Covington, Scranton, Eastern
1944	Rip Collins, Albany, Eastern
1945	Gil Coan, Chattanooga, Southern
1946	Sibby Sisti, Indianapolis, American Association
1947	Hank Sauer, Syracuse, International
1948	Gene Woodling, San Francisco, Pacific Coast
1949	Orie Arntzen, Albany, Eastern
1950	Frank Saucier, San Antonio, Texas
1951	Gene Conley, Hartford, Eastern
1952	Bill Skowron, Kansas City, American Association
1953	Gene Conley, Toledo, American Association
1954	Herb Score, Indianapolis, American Association
1955	John Murff, Dallas, Texas
1956	Steve Bilko, Los Angeles, Pacific Coast
1957	Norm Siebern, Denver, American Association
1958	Jim O'Toole, Nashville, Southern
1959	Frank Howard, Victoria-Spokane
1960	Willie Davis, Spokane, Pacific Coast
1961	Howie Koplitz, Birmingham, Southern
1962	Bob Bailey, Columbus, International
1963	Don Buford, Indianapolis, International
1964	Mel Stottlemyre, Richmond, International
1965	Joe Foy, Toronto, International
1966	Mike Epstein, Rochester, International
1967	Johnny Bench, Buffalo, International
1968	Merv Rettenmund, Rochester, International
1969	Danny Walton, Oklahoma City, American Association
1970	Don Baylor, Rochester, International
1971	Bobby Grich, Rochester, International
1972	Tom Paciorek, Albuquerque, Pacific Coast
1973	Steve Ontiveros, Phoenix, Pacific Coast
1974	Jim Rice, Pawtucket, International
1975	Hector Cruz, Tulsa, American Association
1976	Pat Putnam, Asheville, Western Carolina
1977	Ken Landreaux, S.L.C., Pacific Coast-El Paso, Texas
1978	Champ Summers, Indianapolis, American Association
1979	Mark Bomback, Vancouver, Pacific Coast
1980	Tim Raines, Denver, American Association
1981	Mike Marshall, Albuquerque, Pacific Coast
1982	Ron Kittle, Edmonton, Pacific Coast
1983	Kevin McReynolds, Las Vegas, Pacific Coast
1984	Alan Knicely, Wichita, American Association
1985	Jose Canseco, Hunt., Southern-Tac., Pacific Coast
1986	Tim Pyznarski, Las Vegas, Pacific Coast
1987	Randy Milligan, Tidewater, International
1988	Sandy Alomar Jr., Las Vegas, Pacific Coast
	Gary Sheffield, Denver, American Association (tie)
1989	Sandy Alomar Jr., Las Vegas, Pacific Coast
1990	Jose Offerman, Albuquerque, Pacific Coast
1991	Pedro Martinez, Albuquerque, Pacific Coast
1992	Tim Salmon, Edmonton, Pacific Coast
1993	Cliff Floyd, Harrisburg, Eastern

MINOR LEAGUE MANAGER OF THE YEAR

Year	Manager, Team, League
1936	Al Sothoron, Milwaukee, American Association
1937	Jake Flowers, Salisbury, Eastern Shore
1938	Paul Richards, Atlanta, Southern
1939	Bill Meyer, Kansas City, American Association
1940	Larry Gilbert, Nashville, Southern
1941	Burt Shotton, Columbus, American Association
1942	Eddie Dyer, Columbus, American Association
1943	Nick Cullop, Columbus, American Association
1944	Al Thomas, Baltimore, International
1945	Lefty O'Doul, San Francisco, Pacific Coast
1946	Clay Hopper, Montreal, International
1947	Nick Cullop, Milwaukee, American Association
1948	Casey Stengel, Oakland, Pacific Coast
1949	Fred Haney, Hollywood, Pacific Coast
1950	Rollie Hemsley, Columbus, American Association
1951	Charlie Grimm, Milwaukee, American Association
1952	Luke Appling, Memphis, Southern
1953	Bobby Bragan, Hollywood, Pacific Coast
1954	Kerby Farrell, Indianapolis, American Association
1955	Bill Rigney, Minneapolis, American Association
1956	Kerby Farrell, Indianapolis, American Association
1957	Ben Geraghty, Wichita, American Association
1958	Cal Ermer, Birmingham, Southern
1959	Pete Reiser, Victoria, Texas
1960	Mel McGaha, Toronto, International
1961	Kerby Farrell, Buffalo, International
1962	Ben Geraghty, Jacksonville, International
1963	Rollie Hemsley, Indianapolis, International
1964	Harry Walker, Jacksonville, International

Year	Player, Team, League
1965	Grady Hatton, Oklahoma City, Pacific Coast
1966	Bob Lemon, Seattle, Pacific Coast
1967	Bob Skinner, San Diego, Pacific Coast
1968	Jack Tighe, Toledo, International
1969	Clyde McCullough, Tidewater, International
1970	Tom Lasorda, Spokane, Pacific Coast
1971	Del Rice, Salt Lake City, Pacific Coast
1972	Hank Bauer, Tidewater, International
1973	Joe Morgan, Charleston, International
1974	Joe Altobelli, Rochester, International
1975	Joe Frazier, Tidewater, International
1976	Vern Rapp, Denver, American Association
1977	Tommy Thompson, Arkan., Texas
1978	Les Moss, Evansville, American Association
1979	Vern Benson, Syracuse, International
1980	Hal Lanier, Springfield, American Association
1981	Del Crandall, Albuquerque, Pacific Coast
1982	George Scherger, Indianapolis, American Association
1983	Bill Dancy, Reading, Eastern
1984	Bob Rodgers, Indianapolis, American Association
1985	Jim Fregosi, Louisville, American Association
1986	Joe Sparks, Indianapolis, American Association
1987	Terry Collins, Albuquerque, Pacific Coast
1988	Joe Sparks, Indianapolis, American Association
1989	Bob Bailor, Syracuse, International
1990	Sal Rende, Omaha, American Association
1991	Chris Chambliss, Greenville, Southern
1992	Grady Little, Greenville, Southern
1993	Jim Tracy, Harrisburg, Eastern

MINOR LEAGUE EXECUTIVE OF THE YEAR (HIGHER CLASSIFICATIONS, 1936-1992)

(Restricted to Class AAA starting in 1963)

Year	Executive, Team, League
1936	Earl Mann, Atlanta, Southern
1937	Robert LaMotte, Savannah, Sally
1938	Louis McKenna, St. Paul, American Association
1939	Bruce Dudley, Louisville, American Association

Year	Player, Team, League
1940	Roy Hamey, Kansas City, American Association
1941	Emil Sick, Seattle, Pacific Coast
1942	Bill Veeck, Milwaukee, American Association
1943	Clarence Rowland, Los Angeles, Pacific Coast

Year	Executive, Team, League		Year	Executive, Team, League
1944—	William Mulligan, Seattle, Pacific Coast		1969—	Bill Gardner, Louisville, International
1945—	Bruce Dudley, Louisville, American Association		1970—	Dick King, Wichita, American Association
1946—	Earl Mann, Atlanta, Southern		1971—	Carl Steinfeldt Jr., Rochester, International
1947—	William Purnhage, Waterloo, I.I.I.		1972—	Don Labbruzzo, Evansville, American Association
1948—	Edward Glennon, Birmingham, Southern		1973—	Merle Miller, Tucson, Pacific Coast
1949—	Ted Sullivan, Indianapolis, American Association		1974—	John Carbray, Sacramento, Pacific Coast
1950—	Clearnce (Brick) Laws, Oakland, Pacific Coast		1975—	Stan Naccarato, Tacoma, Pacific Coast
1951—	Robert Howsam, Denver, West		1976—	Art Teece, Salt Lake City, Pacific Coast
1952—	Jack Cooke, Toronto, International		1977—	George Sisler Jr., Columbus, International
1953—	Richard Burnett, Dallas, Texas		1978—	Willie Sanchez, Albuquerque, Pacific Coast
1954—	Edward Stumpf, Indianapolis, American Association		1979—	George Sisler Jr., Columbus, International
1955—	Dewey Soriano, Seattle, Pacific Coast		1980—	Jim Burris, Denver, American Association
1956—	Robert Howsam, Denver American Association		1981—	Pat McKernan, Albuquerque, Pacific Coast
1957—	John Stiglmeier, Buffalo, International		1982—	A. Ray Smith, Louisville, American Association
1958—	Edward Glennon, Birmingham, Southern		1983—	A. Ray Smith, Louisville, American Association
1959—	Edward Leishman, Salt Lake City, Pacific Coast		1984—	Mike Tamburro, Pawtucket, International
1960—	Ray Winder, Little Rock, Southern		1985—	Patty Cox Hampton, Oklahoma City, Amer. Assoc.
1961—	Elten Schiller, Omaha, American Association		1986—	Bob Goughan, Rochester, International
1962—	George Sisler Jr., Rochester, International		1987—	Stu Kehoe, Vancouver, Pacific Coast
1963—	Lewis Matlin, Hawaii, Pacific Coast		1988—	Bob Rich, Buffalo, American Association
1964—	Edward Leishman, San Diego, Pacific Coast		1989—	Larry Schmittou, Nashville, American Association
1965—	Harold Cooper, Columbus, International		1990—	Greg Corns, Phoenix, Pacific Coast
1966—	John Quinn Jr., Hawaii, Pacific Coast		1991—	Tom Maloney, Denver, American Association
1967—	Hillman Lyons, Richmond, International		1992—	Lou Schwechheimer, Pawtucket, International
1968—	Gabe Paul Jr., Tulsa, Pacific Coast			

MINOR LEAGUE EXECUTIVE OF THE YEAR (LOWER CLASSIFICATIONS, 1950-1990)

(Separate awards for Class AA and Class A started in 1963; for Short Class A in 1988)

Year	Executive, Team, League		Year	Executive, Team, League
1950—	H. Cooper, Hutch'son, West. A.		1975—	Jim Paul, El Paso, Texas
1951—	O. W. (Bill) Hayes, Triple, B.S.			Cordy Jensen, Eugene, Northwest
1952—	Hillman Lyons, Danville, MOV		1976—	Woodrow Reid, Chattanooga, Southern
1953—	Carl Roth, Peoria, I.I.I.			Don Buchheister, Cedar Rapids, Midwest
1954—	James Meagham, Cedar Rapids, I.I.I.		1977—	Jim Paul, El Paso, Texas
1955—	John Petrakis, Dubuque, MOV			Harry Pells, Quad Cities, Midwest
1956—	Marvin Milkes, Fresno, California		1978—	Larry Schmittou, Nashville, Southern
1957—	Richard Wagner, Lincoln, West.			Dave Hersh, Appleton, Midwest
1958—	Gerald Waring, Macon, Sally		1979—	Bill Rigney Jr., Midland, Texas
1959—	Clay Dennis, Des Moines, I.I.I.			Tom Romenesko, Greensboro, W.C.
1960—	Hubert Kittle, Yakima, Northwest		1980—	Frances Crockett, Charlotte, Southern
1961—	David Steele, Fresno, California			Tom Romenesko, Greensboro, W.C.
1962—	John Quinn Jr., San Jose, California		1981—	Allie Prescott, Memphis, Southern
1963—	Hugh Finnerty, Tulsa, Texas			Dan Overstreet, Hagerstown, Caro.
	Ben Jewell, M. Valley, Pioneer		1982—	Art Clarkson, Birmingham, Southern
1964—	Glynn West, Birmingham, Southern			Bob Carruesco, Stockton, California
	Jas. Bayens, Rock Hill, W. Car.		1983—	Edward Kenney, New Britain, Eastern
1965—	Dick Butler, Dallas-Ft. Worth, Texas			Terry Reynolds, Vero Beach, Florida State
	Ken. Blackman, Quad Cities, Midwest		1984—	Bruce Baldwin, Greenville, Southern
1966—	Tom Fleming, Evansville, Southern			Dave Tarrolly, Beloit, Midwest
	Cappy Harada, Lodi, California		1985—	Ben Bernard, Albany-Colonie, Eastern
1967—	Robert Quinn, Reading, Eastern			Pete Vonachen, Peoria, Midwest
	Pat Williams, Spar'burg, W.C.		1986—	Bill Davidson, Midland, Texas
1968—	Phil Howser, Charlotte, Southern			Rob Dlugozima, Durham, Carolina
	Merle Miller, Burlington, Midwest		1987—	Joe Preseren, Tulsa, Texas
1969—	Charlie Blaney, Albuquerque, Texas			Skip Weisman, Greensboro, South Atlantic
	Bill Gorman, Visalia, California		1988—	Bill Valentine, Arkansas, Texas
1970—	Carl Sawatski, Arkansas, Texas			Dennis Bastien, Charleston (W.Va.), South Atlantic
	Bob Williams, Bakersfield, California			Bob Beban, Eugene, Northwest
1971—	Miles Wolff, Savannah, Dixie A.		1989—	Chuck Domino, Reading, Eastern
	Ed Holtz, Appleton, Midwest			John Baxter, South Bend, Midwest
1972—	John Begzos, S. Antonio, Texas			Bill Pereira, Boise, Northwest
	Bob Piccinini, Modesto, California		1990—	Joe Preseren, Tulsa, Texas
1973—	Dick Kravitz, Jacksonville, Southern			Dan Chapman, Stockton, California
	Fritz Colschen, Clinton, Midwest			Dave Baggott, Salt Lake City, Pioneer
1974—	Jim Paul, El Paso, Texas			
	Bing Russell, Portland, Northwest			

MINOR LEAGUE EXECUTIVE OF THE YEAR

Year	Executive, Team, League
1993—	Todd Vander Woude, Harrisburg, Eastern (AA)

MOST VALUABLE PLAYER

AMERICAN LEAGUE

Year	Player, Team, Pos.	Points
1931—	Lefty Grove, Philadelphia, P	78
1932—	Jimmie Foxx, Philadelphia, 1B	75
1933—	Jimmie Foxx, Philadelphia, 1B	74
1934—	Mickey Cochrane, Detroit, C	67
1935—	Hank Greenberg, Detroit, 1B	*80
1936—	Lou Gehrig, New York, 1B	73
1937—	Charley Gehringer, Detroit, 2B	78
1938—	Jimmie Foxx, Boston, 1B	305
1939—	Joe DiMaggio, New York, OF	280
1940—	Hank Greenberg, Detroit, OF	292
1941—	Joe DiMaggio, New York, OF	291
1942—	Joe Gordon, New York, 2B	270
1943—	Spud Chandler, New York, P	246
1944—	Hal Newhouser, Detroit, P	236
1945—	Hal Newhouser, Detroit, P	236
1946—	Ted Williams, Boston, OF	224
1947—	Joe DiMaggio, New York, OF	202
1948—	Lou Boudreau, Cleveland, SS	324
1949—	Ted Williams, Boston, OF	272
1950—	Phil Rizzuto, New York SS	284
1951—	Yogi Berra, New York, C	184
1952—	Bobby Shantz, Philadelphia, P	280
1953—	Al Rosen, Cleveland, 3B	*336
1954—	Yogi Berra, New York, C	230
1955—	Yogi Berra, New York, C	218
1956—	Mickey Mantle, New York, OF	*336
1957—	Mickey Mantle, New York, OF	233
1958—	Jackie Jensen, Boston, OF	233
1959—	Nellie Fox, Chicago, 2B	295
1960—	Roger Maris, New York, OF	225
1961—	Roger Maris, New York, OF	202
1962—	Mickey Mantle, New York, OF	234
1963—	Elston Howard, New York, C	248
1964—	Brooks Robinson, Baltimore, 3B	269
1965—	Zoilo Versalles, Minnesota, SS	275
1966—	Frank Robinson, Baltimore, OF	*280
1967—	Carl Yastrzemski, Boston, OF	275
1968—	Denny McLain, Detroit, P	*280
1969—	Harmon Killebrew, Minnesota, 1B-3B	294
1970—	Boog Powell, Baltimore, 1B	234
1971—	Vida Blue, Oakland, P	268
1972—	Dick Allen, Chicago, 1B	321
1973—	Reggie Jackson, Oakland, OF	*336
1974—	Jeff Burroughs, Texas, OF	248
1975—	Fred Lynn, Boston, OF	326
1976—	Thurman Munson, New York, C	304
1977—	Rod Carew, Minnesota, 1B	273
1978—	Jim Rice, Boston, OF	352
1979—	Don Baylor, California, OF	347
1980—	George Brett, Kansas City, 3B	335
1981—	Rollie Fingers, Milwaukee, P	319
1982—	Robin Yount, Milwaukee, SS	385
1983—	Cal Ripken Jr., Baltimore, SS	322
1984—	Willie Hernandez, Detroit, P	306
1985—	Don Mattingly, New York, 1B	367
1986—	Roger Clemens, Boston, P	339
1987—	George Bell, Toronto, OF	332
1988—	Jose Canseco, Oakland, OF	*392
1989—	Robin Yount, Milwaukee, OF	256
1990—	Rickey Henderson, Oakland, OF	317
1991—	Cal Ripken Jr., Baltimore, SS	318
1992—	Dennis Eckersley, Oakland, P	306
1993—	Frank Thomas, Chicago, 1B	*392

*Unanimous selection.

NATIONAL LEAGUE

Year	Player, Team, Pos.	Points
1931—	Frank Frisch, St. Louis, 2B	65
1932—	Chuck Klein, Philadelphia, OF	78
1933—	Carl Hubbell, New York, P	77
1934—	Dizzy Dean, St. Louis, P	78
1935—	Gabby Hartnett, Chicago, C	75
1936—	Carl Hubbell, New York, P	60
1937—	Joe Medwick, St. Louis, OF	70
1938—	Ernie Lombardi, Cincinnati, C	229
1939—	Bucky Walters, Cincinnati, P	303
1940—	Frank McCormick, Cincinnati, 1B	274
1941—	Dolf Camilli, Brooklyn, 1B	300
1942—	Mort Cooper, St. Louis, P	263
1943—	Stan Musial, St. Louis, OF	267
1944—	Marty Marion, St. Louis, SS	190
1945—	Phil Cavarretta, Chicago, 1B	279
1946—	Stan Musial, St. Louis, 1B	319
1947—	Bob Elliott, Boston, 3B	205
1948—	Stan Musial, St. Louis, OF	303
1949—	Jackie Robinson, Brooklyn, 2B	264
1950—	Jim Konstanty, Philadelphia, P	286
1951—	Roy Campanella, Brooklyn, C	243
1952—	Hank Sauer, Chicago, OF	226
1953—	Roy Campanella, Brooklyn, C	297
1954—	Willie Mays, New York, OF	283
1955—	Roy Campanella, Brooklyn, C	226
1956—	Don Newcombe, Brooklyn, P	223
1957—	Hank Aaron, Milwaukee, OF	239
1958—	Ernie Banks, Chicago, SS	283
1959—	Ernie Banks, Chicago, SS	232½
1960—	Dick Groat, Pittsburgh, SS	276
1961—	Frank Robinson, Cincinnati, OF	219
1962—	Maury Wills, Los Angeles, SS	209
1963—	Sandy Koufax, Los Angeles, P	237
1964—	Ken Boyer, St. Louis, 3B	243
1965—	Willie Mays, San Francisco, OF	224
1966—	Roberto Clemente, Pittsburgh, OF	218
1967—	Orlando Cepeda, St. Louis, 1B	*280
1968—	Bob Gibson, St. Louis, P	242
1969—	Willie McCovey, San Francisco, 1B	265
1970—	Johnny Bench, Cincinnati, C	326
1971—	Joe Torre, St. Louis, 3B	318
1972—	Johnny Bench, Cincinnati, C	263
1973—	Pete Rose, Cincinnati, OF	274
1974—	Steve Garvey, Los Angeles, 1B	270
1975—	Joe Morgan, Cincinnati, 2B	321½
1976—	Joe Morgan, Cincinnati, 2B	311
1977—	George Foster, Cincinnati, OF	291
1978—	Dave Parker, Pittsburgh, OF	320
1979—	Willie Stargell, Pittsburgh, 1B	216
	Keith Hernandez, St. Louis, 1B	216
1980—	Mike Schmidt, Philadelphia, 3B	*336
1981—	Mike Schmidt, Philadelphia, 3B	321
1982—	Dale Murphy, Atlanta, OF	283
1983—	Dale Murphy, Atlanta, OF	318
1984—	Ryne Sandberg, Chicago, 2B	326
1985—	Willie McGee, St. Louis, OF	280
1986—	Mike Schmidt, Philadelphia, 3B	287
1987—	Andre Dawson, Chicago, OF	269
1988—	Kirk Gibson, Los Angeles, OF	272
1989—	Kevin Mitchell, San Francisco, OF	314
1990—	Barry Bonds, Pittsburgh, OF	331
1991—	Terry Pendleton, Atlanta, 3B	274
1992—	Barry Bonds, Pittsburgh, OF	304
1993—	Barry Bonds, San Francisco, OF	372

CY YOUNG MEMORIAL AWARD

Year	Pitcher, Team	Votes
1956	Don Newcombe, Brooklyn	10
1957	Warren Spahn, Milwaukee	15
1958	Bob Turley, New York AL	5
1959	Early Wynn, Chicago AL	13
1960	Vernon Law, Pittsburgh	8
1961	Whitey Ford, New York AL	9
1962	Don Drysdale, Los Angeles NL	14
1963	Sandy Koufax, Los Angeles NL	*20
1964	Dean Chance, Los Angeles AL	17
1965	Sandy Koufax, Los Angeles NL	*20
1966	Sandy Koufax, Los Angeles NL	*20
1967	A.L.—Jim Lonborg, Boston	18
	N.L.—Mike McCormick, San Francisco	18
1968	A.L.—Denny McLain, Detroit	*20
	N.L.—Bob Gibson, St. Louis	*20
1969	A.L.—Denny McLain, Detroit	10
	Mike Cuellar, Baltimore	10
	N.L.—Tom Seaver, New York	23
1970	A.L.—Jim Perry, Minnesota	55
	N.L.—Bob Gibson, St. Louis	118
1971	A.L.—Vida Blue, Oakland	98
	N.L.—Fergie Jenkins, Chicago	97
1972	A.L.—Gaylord Perry, Cleveland	64
	N.L.—Steve Carlton, Philadelphia	*120
1973	A.L.—Jim Palmer, Baltimore	88
	N.L.—Tom Seaver, New York	71
1974	A.L.—Jim Hunter, Oakland	90
	N.L.—Mike Marshall, Los Angeles	96
1975	A.L.—Jim Palmer, Baltimore	98
	N.L.—Tom Seaver, New York	98
1976	A.L.—Jim Palmer, Baltimore	108
	N.L.—Randy Jones, San Diego	96
1977	A.L.—Sparky Lyle, New York	56½
	N.L.—Steve Carlton, Philadelphia	*104
1978	A.L.—Ron Guidry, New York	*140
	N.L.—Gaylord Perry, San Diego	116
1979	A.L.—Mike Flanagan, Baltimore	136
	N.L.—Bruce Sutter, Chicago	72
1980	A.L.—Steve Stone, Baltimore	100
	N.L.—Steve Carlton, Philadelphia	118
1981	A.L.—Rollie Fingers, Milwaukee	126
	N.L.—Fernando Valenzuela, Los Angeles	70
1982	A.L.—Pete Vuckovich, Milwaukee	87
	N.L.—Steve Carlton, Philadelphia	112
1983	A.L.—LaMarr Hoyt, Chicago	116
	N.L.—John Denny, Philadelphia	103
1984	A.L.—Willie Hernandez, Detroit	88
	N.L.—Rick Sutcliffe, Chicago	*120
1985	A.L.—Bret Saberhagen, Kansas City	127
	N.L.—Dwight Gooden, New York	*120
1986	A.L.—Roger Clemens, Boston	*140
	N.L.—Mike Scott, Houston	98
1987	A.L.—Roger Clemens, Boston	124
	N.L.—Steve Bedrosian, Philadelphia	57
1988	A.L.—Frank Viola, Minnesota	138
	N.L.—Orel Hershiser, Los Angeles	*120
1989	A.L.—Bret Saberhagen, Kansas City	138
	N.L.—Mark Davis, San Diego	107
1990	A.L.—Bob Welch, Oakland	107
	N.L.—Doug Drabek, Pittsburgh	118
1991	A.L.—Roger Clemens, Boston	119
	N.L.—Tom Glavine, Atlanta	110
1992	A.L.—Dennis Eckersley, Oakland	107
	N.L.—Greg Maddux, Chicago	112
1993	A.L.—Jack McDowell, Chicago	124
	N.L.—Greg Maddux, Atlanta	119

*Unanimous selection.

ROOKIE OF THE YEAR

1947—Combined selection—Jackie Robinson, Brooklyn NL, 1B.
1948—Combined selection—Alvin Dark, Boston NL, SS.

AMERICAN LEAGUE

Year	Player, Team, Pos.	Votes
1949	Roy Sievers, St. Louis, OF	10
1950	Walt Dropo, Boston, 1B	15
1951	Gil McDougald, New York, 3B	13
1952	Harry Byrd, Philadelphia, P	9
1953	Harvey Kuenn, Detroit, SS	23
1954	Bob Grim, New York, P	15
1955	Herb Score, Cleveland, P	18
1956	Luis Aparicio, Chicago, SS	22
1957	Tony Kubek, New York, IF-OF	23
1958	Albie Pearson, Washington, OF	14
1959	Bob Allison, Washington, OF	18
1960	Ron Hansen, Baltimore, SS	22
1961	Don Schwall, Boston, P	7
1962	Tom Tresh, New York, OF-SS	13
1963	Gary Peters, Chicago, P	10
1964	Tony Oliva, Minnesota, OF	19
1965	Curt Blefary, Baltimore, OF	12
1966	Tommie Agee, Chicago, OF	16
1967	Rod Carew, Minnesota, 2B	19
1968	Stan Bahnsen, New York, P	17
1969	Lou Piniella, Kansas City, OF	9
1970	Thurman Munson, New York, C	23
1971	Chris Chambliss, Cleveland, 1B	11
1972	Carlton Fisk, Boston, C	*24
1973	Al Bumbry, Baltimore, OF	13½
1974	Mike Hargrove, Texas, 1B	16½
1975	Fred Lynn, Boston, OF	23
1976	Mark Fidrych, Detroit, P	22
1977	Eddie Murray, Baltimore, DH-1B	12½

NATIONAL LEAGUE

Year	Player, Team, Pos.	Votes
1949	Don Newcombe, Brooklyn, P	21
1950	Sam Jethroe, Boston, OF	11
1951	Willie Mays, New York, OF	18
1952	Joe Black, Brooklyn, P	19
1953	Jim Gilliam, Brooklyn, 2B	11
1954	Wally Moon, St. Louis, OF	17
1955	Bill Virdon, St. Louis, OF	15
1956	Frank Robinson, Cincinnati, OF	*24
1957	Jack Sanford, Philadelphia, P	16
1958	Orlando Cepeda, San Francisco, 1B	*†21
1959	Willie McCovey, San Francisco, 1B	*24
1960	Frank Howard, Los Angeles, OF	12
1961	Billy Williams, Chicago, OF	10
1962	Ken Hubbs, Chicago, 2B	19
1963	Pete Rose, Cincinnati, 2B	17
1964	Dick Allen, Philadelphia, 3B	18
1965	Jim Lefebvre, Los Angeles, 2B	13
1966	Tommy Helms, Cincinnati, 3B	12
1967	Tom Seaver, New York, P	11
1968	Johnny Bench, Cincinnati, C	10½
1969	Ted Sizemore, Los Angeles, 2B	14
1970	Carl Morton, Montreal, P	11
1971	Earl Williams, Atlanta, C	18
1972	Jon Matlack, New York, P	11
1973	Gary Matthews, San Francisco, OF	11
1974	Bake McBride, St. Louis, OF	16
1975	John Montefusco, San Francisco, P	12
1976	Butch Metzger, San Diego, P	11
	Pat Zachry, Cincinnati, P	11
1977	Andre Dawson, Montreal, OF	10

Year	Player, Team, Pos.	Votes	Year	Player, Team, Pos.	Votes
1978—	Lou Whitaker, Detroit, 2B	21	1978—	Bob Horner, Atlanta, 3B	12½
1979—	John Castino, Minnesota, 3B	7	1979—	Rick Sutcliffe, Los Angeles, P	20
	Alfredo Griffin, Toronto, SS	7			
1980—	Joe Charboneau, Cleveland, OF	103	1980—	Steve Howe, Los Angeles, P	80
1981—	Dave Righetti, New York, P	127	1981—	Fernando Valenzuela, Los Angeles, P	107
1982—	Cal Ripken, Baltimore, SS-3B	132	1982—	Steve Sax, Los Angeles, 2B	63
1983—	Ron Kittle, Chicago, OF	104	1983—	Darryl Strawberry, New York, OF	109
1984—	Alvin Davis, Seattle, 1B	134	1984—	Dwight Gooden, New York, P	118
1985—	Ozzie Guillen, Chicago, SS	101	1985—	Vince Coleman, St. Louis, OF	*120
1986—	Jose Canseco, Oakland, OF	110	1986—	Todd Worrell, St. Louis, P	118
1987—	Mark McGwire, Oakland, 1B	*140	1987—	Benito Santiago, San Diego, C	*120
1988—	Walt Weiss, Oakland, SS	103	1988—	Chris Sabo, Cincinnati, 3B	79
1989—	Gregg Olson, Baltimore, P	136	1989—	Jerome Walton, Chicago, OF	116
1990—	Sandy Alomar Jr., Cleveland, C	*140	1990—	Dave Justice, Atlanta, OF	118
1991—	Chuck Knoblauch, Minnesota, 2B	136	1991—	Jeff Bagwell, Houston, 1B	118
1992—	Pat Listach, Milwaukee, SS	122	1992—	Eric Karros, Los Angeles, 1B	116
1993—	Tim Salmon, California, OF	*140	1993—	Mike Piazza, Los Angeles, C	*140

*Unanimous selection. †Three writers did not vote.

MANAGER OF THE YEAR

AMERICAN LEAGUE

Year	Manager, Team	Points
1983—	Tony La Russa, Chicago	17
1984—	Sparky Anderson, Detroit	96
1985—	Bobby Cox, Toronto	104
1986—	John McNamara, Boston	95
1987—	Sparky Anderson, Detroit	90
1988—	Tony La Russa, Oakland	103
1989—	Frank Robinson, Baltimore	125
1990—	Jeff Torborg, Chicago	128
1991—	Tom Kelly, Minnesota	138
1992—	Tony La Russa, Oakland	132
1993—	Gene Lamont, Chicago	72

NATIONAL LEAGUE

Year	Manager, Team	Points
1983—	Tommy Lasorda, Los Angeles	10
1984—	Jim Frey, Chicago	101
1985—	Whitey Herzog, St. Louis	86
1986—	Hal Lanier, Houston	108
1987—	Buck Rodgers, Montreal	92
1988—	Tommy Lasorda, Los Angeles	101
1989—	Don Zimmer, Chicago	118
1990—	Jim Leyland, Pittsburgh	99
1991—	Bobby Cox, Atlanta	96
1992—	Jim Leyland, Pittsburgh	109
1993—	Dusty Baker, San Francisco	105

EARLY MOST VALUABLE PLAYER AWARDS

CHALMERS AWARD

AMERICAN LEAGUE

Year	Player, Team, Pos.	Points
1911—	Ty Cobb, Detroit, OF	64
1912—	Tris Speaker, Boston, OF	59
1913—	Walter Johnson, Washington, P	54
1914—	Eddie Collins, Philadelphia, 2B	63

NATIONAL LEAGUE

Year	Player, Team, Pos.	Points
1911—	Frank Schulte, Chicago, OF	29
1912—	Larry Doyle, New York, 2B	48
1913—	Jake Daubert, Brooklyn, 1B	50
1914—	Johnny Evers, Boston, 2B	50

LEAGUE AWARDS

AMERICAN LEAGUE

Year	Player, Team, Pos.	Points
1922—	George Sisler, St. Louis, 1B	59
1923—	Babe Ruth, New York, OF	64
1924—	Walter Johnson, Washington, P	55
1925—	Roger Peckinpaugh, Washington, SS	45
1926—	George Burns, Cleveland, 1B	63
1927—	Lou Gehrig, New York, 1B	56
1928—	Mickey Cochrane, Philadelphia, C	53
1929—	No selection	

NATIONAL LEAGUE

Year	Player, Team, Pos.	Points
1922—	No selection	
1923—	No selection	
1924—	Dazzy Vance, Brooklyn, P	74
1925—	Rogers Hornsby, St. Louis, 2B	73
1926—	Bob O'Farrell, St. Louis, C	79
1927—	Paul Waner, Pittsburgh, OF	72
1928—	Jim Bottomley, St. Louis, 1B	76
1929—	Rogers Hornsby, Chicago, 2B	60

HALL OF FAME

Name	Des.*	Elec. year	Votes rec.†	Votes cast‡	% of vote	Teams as player
Aaron, Hank	P	1982	406	415	97.8	Milwaukee NL, Atlanta NL, Milwaukee AL
Alexander, Grover C.	P	1938	212	262	80.9	Philadelphia NL, Chicago NL, St. Louis NL
Alston, Walter	M	1983	CV	—	—	St. Louis NL
Anson, Cap	P	1939	C1	—	—	Chicago NL
Aparicio, Luis	P	1984	341	403	84.6	Chicago AL, Baltimore AL, Boston AL
Appling, Luke	P	1964	189	225	84	Chicago AL
Averill, Earl	P	1975	CV	—	—	Cleveland AL, Detroit AL, Boston AL
Baker, Home Run	P	1955	CV	—	—	Philadelphia AL, New York AL
Bancroft, Dave	P	1971	CV	—	—	Philadelphia NL, New York NL, Boston NL, Brooklyn NL
Banks, Ernie	P	1977	321	383	83.8	Chicago NL
Barlick, Al	U	1989	CV	—	—	
Barrow, Ed	E	1953	CV	—	—	
Beckley, Jake	P	1971	CV	—	—	Pittsburgh NL, Pittsburgh PL, New York NL, Cincinnati NL, St. Louis NL
Bell, Cool Papa	P	1974	SCNL	—	—	Negro Leagues
Bench, Johnny	P	1989	431	447	96.4	Cincinnati NL
Bender, Chief	P	1953	CV	—	—	Philadelphia AL, Philadelphia NL, Chicago AL
Berra, Yogi	P	1972	339	396	85.6	New York AL, New York NL
Bottomley, Jim	P	1974	CV	—	—	St. Louis NL, Cincinnati NL, St. Louis AL
Boudreau, Lou	P	1970	232	300	77.3	Cleveland AL, Boston AL
Bresnahan, Roger	P	1945	C2	—	—	Washington NL, Chicago NL, Baltimore AL, New York NL, St. Louis NL
Brock, Lou	P	1985	315	395	79.7	Chicago NL, St. Louis NL
Brouthers, Dan	P	1945	C2	—	—	Troy NL, Buffalo NL, Detroit NL, Boston NL, Boston PL, Boston AA, Brooklyn NL, Baltimore NL, Louisville NL, Philadelphia NL, New York NL
Brown, Three Finger	P	1949	C2	—	—	St. Louis NL, Chicago NL, Cincinnati NL
Bulkeley, Morgan	E	1937	CC	—	—	
Burkett, Jesse	P	1946	C2	—	—	New York NL, Cleveland NL, St. Louis NL, St. Louis AL, Boston AL
Campanella, Roy	P	1969	270	340	79.4	Brooklyn NL
Carew, Rod	P	1991	401	447	89.7	Minnesota AL, California AL
Carey, Max	P	1961	CV	—	—	Pittsburgh NL, Brooklyn NL
Carlton, Steve	P	1993	436	455	95.8	St. Louis NL, Philadelphia NL, San Francisco NL, Chicago AL, Cleveland AL, Minnesota AL
Cartwright, Alexander	O	1938	CC	—	—	
Chadwick, Henry	O	1938	CC	—	—	
Chance, Frank	P	1946	C2	—	—	Chicago NL, New York AL
Chandler, Happy	E	1982	CV	—	—	
Charleston, Oscar	P	1976	SCNL	—	—	Negro Leagues
Chesbro, Jack	P	1946	C2	—	—	Pittsburgh NL, New York AL, Boston AL
Clarke, Fred	P	1945	C2	—	—	Louisville NL, Pittsburgh NL
Clarkson, John	P	1963	CV	—	—	Worcester NL, Chicago NL, Boston NL, Cleveland NL
Clemente, Roberto	P	1973	393	424	92.7	Pittsburgh NL
Cobb, Ty	P	1936	222	226	98.2	Detroit AL, Philadelphia AL
Cochrane, Mickey	P	1947	128	161	79.5	Philadelphia AL, Detroit AL
Collins, Eddie	P	1939	213	274	77.7	Philadelphia AL, Chicago AL
Collins, Jimmy	P	1945	C2	—	—	Boston NL, Louisville NL, Boston AL, Philadelphia AL
Combs, Earle	P	1970	CV	—	—	New York AL
Comiskey, Charley	F/P	1939	C1	—	—	St. Louis AA, Chicago PL, Cincinnati NL
Conlan, Jocko	U	1974	CV	—	—	Chicago AL
Connolly, Tommy	U	1953	CV	—	—	
Connor, Roger	P	1976	CV	—	—	Troy NL, New York NL, New York PL, Philadelphia NL, St. Louis NL
Coveleski, Stan	P	1969	CV	—	—	Philadelphia AL, Cleveland AL, Washington AL, New York AL
Crawford, Sam	P	1957	CV	—	—	Cincinnati NL, Detroit AL
Cronin, Joe	P	1956	152	193	78.8	Pittsburgh NL, Washington AL, Boston AL
Cummings, Candy	P	1939	C1	—	—	Hartford NL, Cincinnati NL
Cuyler, Kiki	P	1968	CV	—	—	Pittsburgh NL, Chicago NL, Cincinnati NL, Brooklyn NL
Dandridge, Ray	P	1987	CV	—	—	Negro Leagues
Dean, Dizzy	P	1953	209	264	79.2	St. Louis NL, Chicago NL, St. Louis AL
Delahanty, Ed	P	1945	C2	—	—	Philadelphia NL, Cleveland PL, Washington AL
Dickey, Bill	P	1954	202	252	80.2	New York AL
Dihigo, Martin	P	1977	SCNL	—	—	Negro Leagues
DiMaggio, Joe	P	1955	223	251	88.8	New York AL
Doerr, Bobby	P	1986	CV	—	—	Boston AL
Drysdale, Don	P	1984	316	403	78.4	Brooklyn NL, Los Angeles NL
Duffy, Hugh	P	1945	C2	—	—	Chicago NL, Chicago PL, Boston AA, Boston NL, Milwaukee AL, Philadelphia NL
Evans, Billy	U	1973	CV	—	—	
Evers, Johnny	P	1946	C2	—	—	Chicago NL, Boston NL, Philadelphia NL, Chicago AL
Ewing, Buck	P	1939	C1	—	—	Troy NL, New York NL, New York PL, Cleveland NL, Cincinnati NL

Name	Des.*	Elec. year	Votes rec.†	Votes cast‡	% of vote	Teams as player
Faber, Red	P	1964	CV	—	—	Chicago AL
Feller, Bob	P	1962	150	160	93.8	Cleveland AL
Ferrell, Rick	P	1984	CV	—	—	St. Louis AL, Boston AL, Washington AL
Fingers, Rollie	P	1992	349	430	81.2	Oakland AL, San Diego NL, Milwaukee AL
Flick, Elmer	P	1963	CV	—	—	Philadelphia NL, Philadelphia AL, Cleveland AL
Ford, Whitey	P	1974	284	365	77.8	New York AL
Foster, Rube	P	1981	CV	—	—	Negro Leagues
Foxx, Jimmie	P	1951	179	226	79.2	Philadelphia AL, Boston AL, Chicago NL, Philadelphia NL
Frick, Ford	E	1970	CV	—	—	
Frisch, Frank	P	1947	136	161	84.5	New York NL, St. Louis NL
Galvin, Pud	P	1965	CV	—	—	Buffalo NL, Pittsburgh AA, Pittsburgh NL, Pittsburgh PL, St. Louis NL
Gehrig, Lou	P	1939	SE	—	—	New York AL
Gehringer, Charley	P	1949	159	187	85.0	Detroit AL
Gibson, Bob	P	1981	337	401	84.0	St. Louis NL
Gibson, Josh	P	1972	SCNL	—	—	Negro Leagues
Giles, Warren	E	1979	CV	—	—	
Gomez, Lefty	P	1972	CV	—	—	New York AL, Washington AL
Goslin, Goose	P	1968	CV	—	—	Washington AL, St. Louis AL, Detroit AL
Greenberg, Hank	P	1956	164	193	85.0	Detroit AL, Pittsburgh NL
Griffith, Clark	M	1946	C2	—	—	St. Louis AA, Boston AA, Chicago NL, Chicago AL, New York AL, Cincinnati NL, Washington AL
Grimes, Burleigh	P	1964	CV	—	—	Pittsburgh NL, Brooklyn NL, New York NL, Boston NL, St. Louis NL, Chicago NL, New York AL
Grove, Lefty	P	1947	123	161	76.4	Philadelphia AL, Boston AL
Hafey, Chick	P	1971	CV	—	—	St. Louis NL, Cincinnati NL
Haines, Jesse	P	1970	CV	—	—	Cincinnati NL, St. Louis NL
Hamilton, Billy	P	1961	CV	—	—	Kansas City AA, Philadelphia NL, Boston NL
Harridge, Will	E	1972	CV	—	—	
Harris, Bucky	M	1975	CV	—	—	Washington AL, Detroit AL
Hartnett, Gabby	P	1955	195	251	77.7	Chicago NL, New York NL
Heilmann, Harry	P	1952	203	234	86.8	Detroit AL, Cincinnati NL
Herman, Billy	P	1975	CV	—	—	Chicago NL, Brooklyn NL, Boston NL, Pittsburgh NL
Hooper, Harry	P	1971	CV	—	—	Boston AL, Chicago AL
Hornsby, Rogers	P	1942	182	233	78.1	St. Louis NL, New York NL, Boston NL, Chicago NL, St. Louis AL
Hoyt, Waite	P	1969	CV	—	—	New York NL, Boston AL, New York AL, Detroit AL, Philadelphia AL, Brooklyn NL, Pittsburgh NL
Hubbard, Cal	U	1976	CV	—	—	
Hubbell, Carl	P	1947	140	161	87.0	New York NL
Huggins, Miller	M	1964	CV	—	—	Cincinnati NL, St. Louis NL
Hunter, Catfish	P	1987	315	413	76.3	Kansas City AL, Oakland AL, New York AL
Irvin, Monte	P	1973	SCNL	—	—	New York NL, Chicago NL, Negro Leagues
Jackson, Reggie	P	1993	396	423	93.6	Kansas City AL, Oakland AL, Baltimore AL, New York AL, California AL
Jackson, Travis	P	1982	CV	—	—	New York NL
Jenkins, Ferguson	P	1991	334	447	74.7	Philadelphia NL, Chicago NL, Texas AL, Boston AL
Jennings, Hugh	P	1945	C2	—	—	Louisville AA, Louisville NL, Baltimore NL, Brooklyn NL, Philadelphia NL, Detroit AL
Johnson, Ban	E	1937	CC	—	—	
Johnson, Judy	P	1975	SCNL	—	—	Negro Leagues
Johnson, Walter	P	1936	189	226	83.6	Washington AL
Joss, Addie	P	1978	CV	—	—	Cleveland AL
Kaline, Al	P	1980	340	385	88.3	Detroit AL
Keefe, Tim	P	1964	CV	—	—	Troy NL, New York AA, New York NL, New York PL, Philadelphia NL
Keeler, Willie	P	1939	207	274	75.5	New York NL, Brooklyn, NL, Baltimore NL, New York AL
Kell, George	P	1983	CV	—	—	Philadelphia AL, Detroit AL, Boston AL, Chicago AL, Baltimore AL
Kelley, Joe	P	1971	CV	—	—	Boston NL, Pittsburgh NL, Baltimore NL, Brooklyn NL, Baltimore AL, Cincinnati NL
Kelly, George	P	1973	CV	—	—	New York NL, Pittsburgh NL, Cincinnati NL, Chicago NL, Brooklyn NL
Kelly, Mike	P	1945	C2	—	—	Cincinnati NL, Chicago NL, Boston NL, Boston PL, Cincinnati AA, Boston AA, New York NL
Killebrew, Harmon	P	1984	335	403	83.1	Washington AL, Minnesota AL, Kansas City AL
Kiner, Ralph	P	1975	273	362	75.4	Pittsburgh NL, Chicago NL, Cleveland AL
Klein, Chuck	P	1980	CV	—	—	Philadelphia NL, Chicago NL, Pittsburgh NL
Klem, Bill	U	1953	CV	—	—	
Koufax, Sandy	P	1972	344	396	86.9	Brooklyn NL, Los Angeles NL
Lajoie, Nap	P	1937	168	201	83.6	Philadelphia NL, Philadelphia AL, Cleveland AL
Landis, Kenesaw M.	E	1944	C2	—	—	
Lazzeri, Tony	P	1991	CV	—	—	New York AL, Chicago NL, Brooklyn NL, New York NL
Lemon, Bob	P	1976	305	388	78.6	Cleveland AL
Lindstrom, Fred	P	1976	CV	—	—	New York NL, Pittsburgh NL, Chicago NL, Brooklyn NL
Lloyd, John Henry	P	1977	SCNL	—	—	Negro Leagues
Lombardi, Ernie	P	1986	CV	—	—	Brooklyn NL, Cincinnati NL, Boston NL, New York NL
Lopez, Al	M	1977	CV	—	—	Brooklyn NL, Boston NL, Pittsburgh NL, Cleveland AL
Lyons, Ted	P	1955	217	251	86.5	Chicago AL
Mack, Connie	M	1937	CC	—	—	Washington NL, Buffalo PL, Pittsburgh NL

Name	Des.*	Elec. year	Votes rec.†	Votes cast‡	% of vote	Teams as player
MacPhail, Larry	E	1978	CV	—	—	
Mantle, Mickey	P	1974	322	365	88.2	New York AL
Manush, Heinie	P	1964	CV	—	—	Detroit AL, St. Louis AL, Washington AL, Boston AL, Brooklyn NL, Pittsburgh NL
Maranville, Rabbit	P	1954	209	252	82.9	Boston NL, Pittsburgh NL, Chicago NL, Brooklyn NL, St. Louis NL
Marichal, Juan	P	1983	313	374	83.7	San Francisco NL, Boston AL, Los Angeles NL
Marquard, Rube	P	1971	CV	—	—	New York NL, Brooklyn NL, Cincinnati NL, Boston NL
Mathews, Eddie	P	1978	301	379	79.4	Boston NL, Milwaukee NL, Atlanta NL, Houston NL, Detroit AL
Mathewson, Christy	P	1936	205	226	90.7	New York NL, Cincinnati NL
Mays, Willie	P	1979	409	432	94.7	New York (Giants)NL, San Francisco NL, New York (Mets)NL
McCarthy, Joe	M	1957	CV	—	—	
McCarthy, Tommy	P	1946	C2	—	—	Boston UA, Boston NL, Philadelphia NL, St. Louis AA, Brooklyn NL
McCovey, Willie	P	1986	346	425	81.4	San Francisco NL, San Diego NL, Oakland AL
McGinnity, Joe	P	1946	C2	—	—	Baltimore NL, Brooklyn NL, Baltimore AL, New York NL
McGowan, Bill	U	1992	CV	—	—	
McGraw, John	M	1937	CC	—	—	Baltimore AA, Baltimore NL, St. Louis NL, Baltimore AL, New York NL
McKechnie, Bill	M	1962	CV	—	—	Pittsburgh NL, Boston NL, New York AL, New York NL, Cincinnati
Medwick, Joe	P	1968	240	283	84.8	St. Louis NL, Brooklyn NL, New York NL, Boston NL
Mize, Johnny	P	1981	CV	—	—	St. Louis NL, New York NL, New York AL
Morgan, Joe	P	1990	363	444	81.8	Houston NL, Cincinnati NL, San Francisco NL, Philadelphia NL, Oakland AL
Musial, Stan	P	1969	317	340	93.2	St. Louis NL
Newhouser, Hal	P	1992	CV	—	—	Detroit AL, Cleveland AL
Nichols, Kid	P	1949	C2	—	—	Boston NL, St. Louis NL, Philadelphia NL
O'Rourke, Jim	P	1945	C2	—	—	Boston NL, Providence NL, Buffalo NL, New York NL, Washington NL, New York PL
Ott, Mel	P	1951	197	226	87.2	New York NL
Paige, Satchel	P	1971	SCNL	—	—	Cleveland AL, St. Louis AL, Kansas City AL, Negro Leagues
Palmer, Jim	P	1990	411	444	92.6	Baltimore AL
Pennock, Herb	P	1948	94	121	77.7	Philadelphia AL, Boston AL, New York AL
Perry, Gaylord	P	1991	342	447	76.5	San Francisco NL, Cleveland AL, Texas AL, San Diego NL, New York AL, Atlanta NL, Seattle AL, Kansas City AL
Plank, Eddie	P	1946	C2	—	—	Philadelphia AL, St. Louis AL
Radbourn, Hoss	P	1939	C1	—	—	Buffalo NL, Providence NL, Boston NL, Boston PL, Cincinnati NL
Reese, Pee Wee	P	1984	CV	—	—	Brooklyn NL, Los Angeles NL
Rice, Sam	P	1963	CV	—	—	Washington AL, Cleveland AL
Rickey, Branch	E	1967	CV	—	—	St. Louis AL, New York AL
Rixey, Eppa	P	1963	CV	—	—	Philadelphia NL, Cincinnati NL
Roberts, Robin	P	1976	337	388	86.9	Philadelphia NL, Baltimore AL, Houston NL, Chicago NL
Robinson, Brooks	P	1983	344	374	92.0	Baltimore AL
Robinson, Frank	P	1982	370	415	89.2	Cincinnati NL, Baltimore AL, Los Angeles NL, California AL, Cleveland AL
Robinson, Jackie	P	1962	124	160	77.5	Brooklyn NL
Robinson, Wilbert	M	1945	C2	—	—	Philadelphia AA, Baltimore AA, Baltimore NL, St. Louis NL, Baltimore AL
Roush, Edd	P	1962	CV	—	—	Chicago AL, New York NL, Cincinnati NL
Ruffing, Red	P	1967	266	306	86.9	Boston AL, New York AL, Chicago AL
Rusie, Amos	P	1977	CV	—	—	Indianapolis NL, New York NL, Cincinnati NL
Ruth, Babe	P	1936	215	226	95.1	Boston AL, New York AL, Boston NL
Schalk, Ray	P	1955	CV	—	—	Chicago AL, New York NL
Schoendienst, Red	P	1989	CV	—	—	St. Louis NL, New York (Giants)NL, Milwaukee NL
Seaver, Tom	P	1992	425	430	98.8	New York NL, Cincinnati NL, Chicago AL, Boston AL
Sewell, Joe	P	1977	CV	—	—	Cleveland AL, New York AL
Simmons, Al	P	1953	199	264	75.4	Philadelphia AL, Chicago AL, Detroit AL, Washington AL, Boston NL, Cincinnati NL, Boston AL
Sisler, George	P	1939	235	274	85.8	St. Louis AL, Washington AL, Boston NL
Slaughter, Enos	P	1985	CV	—	—	St. Louis NL, New York AL, Kansas City AL, Milwaukee NL
Snider, Duke	P	1980	333	385	86.5	Brooklyn NL, Los Angeles NL, New York NL, San Francisco NL
Spahn, Warren	P	1973	316	380	83.2	Boston NL, Milwaukee NL, New York NL, San Francisco NL
Spalding, Al	P	1939	C1	—	—	Chicago NL
Speaker, Tris	P	1937	165	201	82.1	Boston AL, Cleveland AL, Washington AL, Philadelphia AL
Stargell, Willie	P	1988	352	427	82.4	Pittsburgh NL
Stengel, Casey	M	1966	CV	—	—	Brooklyn NL, Pittsburgh NL, Philadelphia NL, New York NL, Boston NL
Terry, Bill	P	1954	195	252	77.4	New York NL
Thompson, Sam	P	1974	CV	—	—	Detroit NL, Philadelphia NL, Detroit AL
Tinker, Joe	P	1946	C2	—	—	Chicago NL, Cincinnati NL
Traynor, Pie	P	1948	93	121	76.9	Pittsburgh NL
Vance, Dazzy	P	1955	205	251	81.7	Pittsburgh NL, New York AL, Brooklyn NL, St. Louis NL, Cincinnati NL
Vaughan, Arky	P	1985	CV	—	—	Pittsburgh NL, Brooklyn NL
Veeck, Bill	E	1991	CV	—	—	
Waddell, Rube	P	1946	C2	—	—	Louisville NL, Pittsburgh NL, Chicago NL, Philadelphia AL, St. Louis AL
Wagner, Honus	P	1936	215	226	95.1	Louisville NL, Pittsburgh NL
Wallace, Bobby	P	1953	CV	—	—	Cleveland NL, St. Louis NL, St. Louis AL
Walsh, Ed	P	1946	C2	—	—	Chicago AL, Boston NL

Name	Des.*	Elec. year	Votes rec.†	Votes cast‡	% of vote	Teams as player
Waner, Lloyd	P	1967	CV	—	—	Pittsburgh NL, Boston NL, Cincinnati NL, Philadelphia NL, Brooklyn NL
Waner, Paul	P	1952	195	234	83.3	Pittsburgh NL, Brooklyn NL, Boston NL, New York AL
Ward, John Montgomery	P	1964	CV	—	—	Providence NL, New York NL, Brooklyn PL, Brooklyn NL
Weiss, George	E	1971	CV	—	—	
Welch, Mickey	P	1973	CV	—	—	Troy NL, New York NL
Wheat, Zack	P	1959	CV	—	—	Brooklyn NL, Philadelphia AL
Wilhelm, Hoyt	P	1985	331	395	83.8	New York NL, St. Louis NL, Cleveland AL, Baltimore AL, Chicago AL, California AL, Atlanta NL, Chicago NL, Los Angeles NL
Williams, Billy	P	1987	354	413	85.7	Chicago NL, Oakland AL
Williams, Ted	P	1966	282	302	93.4	Boston AL
Wilson, Hack	P	1979	CV	—	—	New York NL, Chicago NL, Brooklyn NL, Philadelphia NL
Wright, George	M	1937	CC	—	—	Boston NL, Providence NL
Wright, Harry	M	1953	CV	—	—	Boston NL
Wynn, Early	P	1972	301	396	76.0	Washington AL, Cleveland AL, Chicago AL
Yastrzemski, Carl	P	1989	423	447	94.6	Boston AL
Yawkey, Tom	E	1980	CV	—	—	
Young, Cy	P	1937	153	201	76.1	Cleveland NL, St. Louis NL, Boston AL, Cleveland AL, Boston NL
Youngs, Ross	P	1972	CV	—	—	New York NL

*Designation for which he was honored. Abbreviations: E—executive; F—founder; M—manager; O—organizer; P—player; U—umpire.

†Where an abbreviation is listed rather than a vote total, the enshrinee was selected by one of the following groups: Centennial Commission (CC), committee of old-time players and writers (C1), committee on old-timers (C2), Committee on Veterans (CV), special election by Baseball Writers' Association of America (SE) or Special Committee on Negro Leagues (SCNL).

‡Votes cast by eligible members of the Baseball Writers' Association of America.

League abbreviations: AA—American Association; AL—American League; NL—National League; PL—Players League; UA—Union Association.

MINOR LEAGUES

Farm systems

American Association

International League

Mexican League

Pacific Coast League

Eastern League

Southern League

Texas League

California League

Carolina League

Florida State League

Midwest League

New York-Pennsylvania League

Northwest League

South Atlantic League

Appalachian League

Arizona League

Dominican Summer League

Gulf Coast League

Pioneer League

Minor League Index

FARM SYSTEMS

BALTIMORE (6): AAA—Rochester. AA—Bowie. A—Frederick, Albany. Rookie—Sarasota, Bluefield.

BOSTON (6): AAA—Pawtucket. AA—New Britain. A—Lynchburg, Sarasota, Utica. Rookie—Gulf Coast Red Sox.

CALIFORNIA (6): AAA—Vancouver. AA—Midland. A—Boise, Lake Elsinore, Quad City. Rookie—Mesa Angels.

CHICAGO (6): AAA—Nashville. AA—Birmingham. A—Hickory, Prince William, South Bend. Rookie—Sarasota.

CLEVELAND (6): AAA—Charlotte. AA—Canton/Akron. A—Columbus (Ga.), Kinston, Watertown. Rookie—Burlington.

DETROIT (6): AAA—Toledo. AA—Trenton. A—Fayetteville, Jamestown, Lakeland. Rookie—Bristol.

KANSAS CITY (6): AAA—Omaha. AA—Memphis. A—Eugene, Rockford, Wilmington. Rookie—Gulf Coast Royals.

MILWAUKEE (6): AAA—New Orleans. AA—El Paso. A—Beloit, Stockton. Rookie—Chandler Brewers, Helena.

MINNESOTA (6): AAA—Salt Lake City. AA—Nashville. A—Fort Myers, Fort Wayne. Rookie—Elizabethton, Gulf Coast Twins.

NEW YORK (6): AAA—Columbus (O.). AA—Albany/Colonie. A—Greensboro, Oneonta, Tampa. Rookie—Tampa Yankees.

OAKLAND (6): AAA—Tacoma. AA—Huntsville. A—Modesto, Southern Oregon, West Michigan. Rookie—Scottsdale Athletics.

SEATTLE (6): AAA—Calgary. AA—Jacksonville. A—Appleton, Bellingham, Riverside. Rookie—Peoria Mariners.

TEXAS (6): AAA—Oklahoma City. AA—Tulsa. A—Charlotte, Charleston (S.C.), Hudson Valley. Rookie—Gulf Coast Rangers.

TORONTO (7): AAA—Syracuse. AA—Knoxville. A—Dunedin, Hagerstown, St. Catharines. Rookie—Gulf Coast Blue Jays, Medicine Hat.

ATLANTA (7): AAA—Richmond. AA—Greenville. A—Durham, Macon. Rookie—Danville, Gulf Coast Braves, Idaho Falls.

CHICAGO (7): AAA—Iowa. AA—Orlando. A—Daytona, Peoria, Williamsport. Rookie—Huntington, Gulf Coast Cubs.

CINCINNATI (6): AAA—Indianapolis. AA—Chattanooga. A—Winston-Salem, Charleston (W.Va.). Rookie—Billings, Princeton.

COLORADO (6): AAA—Colorado Springs. AA—New Haven. A—Asheville, Bend, Central Valley. Rookie—Chandler.

FLORIDA (6): AAA—Edmonton. AA—Portland (Me.). A—Brevard County, Elmira, Kane County. Rookie—Gulf Coast Marlins.

HOUSTON (6): AAA—Tucson. AA—Jackson. A—Auburn, Osceola, Quad City. Rookie—Gulf Coast Astros.

LOS ANGELES (6): AAA—Albuquerque. AA—San Antonio. A—Bakersfield, Vero Beach, Yakima. Rookie—Great Falls.

MONTREAL (7): AAA—Ottawa. AA—Harrisburg. A—Burlington, Vermont, West Palm Beach. Rookie—Gulf Coast Expos, Mendoza Expos.

NEW YORK (7): AAA—Norfolk. AA—Binghamton. A—Columbia, Pittsfield, St. Lucie. Rookie—Gulf Coast Mets, Kingsport.

PHILADELPHIA (6): AAA—Scranton/Wilkes-Barre. AA—Reading. A—Batavia, Clearwater, Spartanburg. Rookie—Martinsville.

PITTSBURGH (6): AAA—Buffalo. AA—Carolina. A—Augusta, Salem, Welland (Ont.). Rookie—Bradenton Pirates.

ST. LOUIS (8): AAA—Louisville. AA—Arkansas. A—Madison, New Jersey, St. Petersburg, Savannah. Rookie—Chandler Cardinals, Johnson City.

SAN DIEGO (6): AAA—Las Vegas. AA—Wichita. A—Rancho Cucamonga, Spokane, Waterloo. Rookie—Peoria Padres.

SAN FRANCISCO (6): AAA—Phoenix. AA—Shreveport. A—Clinton, Everett, San Jose. Rookie—Scottsdale.

AMERICAN ASSOCIATION

FINAL STANDINGS

EASTERN DIVISION

Team	W	L	T	Pct.	GB
Nashville (White Sox)	81	62	0	.566	....
Buffalo (Pirates)	71	73	0	.493	10½
Louisville (Cardinals)	68	76	0	.472	13½
Indianapolis (Reds)	66	77	0	.462	15

WESTERN DIVISION

Team	W	L	T	Pct.	GB
Iowa (Cubs)	85	59	0	.590	....
New Orleans (Brewers)	80	64	0	.556	5
Omaha (Royals)	70	74	0	.486	15
Oklahoma City (Rangers)	54	90	0	.375	31

COMPOSITE

Team	Iowa	Nash.	N.O	Buf.	Oma.	Lou.	Ind.	O.C.	W	L	T	Pct.	GB
Iowa (Cubs)	....	10	11	15	15	10	10	14	85	59	0	.590	....
Nashville (White Sox)	8	....	10	15	8	13	17	10	81	62	0	.566	3½
New Orleans (Brewers)	13	8	....	11	11	10	10	17	80	64	0	.556	5
Buffalo (Pirates)	3	9	7	....	11	11	15	16	71	73	0	.493	14
Omaha (Royals)	9	10	13	7	....	6	10	15	70	74	0	.486	15
Louisville (Cardinals)	8	11	8	9	12	....	9	11	68	76	0	.472	17
Indianapolis (Reds)	8	6	8	8	8	15	....	13	66	77	0	.462	18½
Oklahoma City (Rangers)	10	8	7	8	9	7	5	....	54	90	0	.375	31

Major league affiliations in parentheses.

Iowa club represented Des Moines, Ia.

Playoffs—Iowa defeated Nashville, four games to three, to win league championship.

Regular-season attendance—Buffalo, 1,058,620; Indianapolis, 300,397; Iowa, 446,860; Louisville, 643,833; Nashville, 438,745; New Orleans, 161,846; Oklahoma City, 364,673; Omaha, 384,972. Total, 3,799,946. Playoffs (7 games), 29,245. Class AAA All-Star Game at Albuquerque, 10,541.

Managers—Buffalo, Doc Edwards; Indianapolis, Marc Bombard; Iowa, Marv Foley; Louisville, Jack Krol; Nashville, Rick Renick; New Orleans, Chris Bando; Oklahoma City, Bobby Jones; Omaha, Jeff Cox.

All-Star team: 1B—Bob Hamelin, Omaha; 2B—Norberto Martin, Nashville; 3B—Keith Lockhart, Louisville; SS—Esteban Beltre, Nashville; OF—Eddie Zambrano, Iowa; Karl Rhodes, Omaha-Iowa; Rob Ducey, Oklahoma City; C—Matt Walbeck, Iowa; DH—Steve Balboni, Oklahoma City; RHP—Roy Smith, Buffalo; LHP—Blaise Ilsley, Iowa; Reliever—Tony Menendez, Buffalo; Rookie of the Year—Willie Greene, Indianapolis; Most Valuable Player—Eddie Zambrano, Iowa; Manager of the Year—Rick Renick, Nashville.

BATTING

TEAM

Team	Avg.	G	AB	R	OR	H	TB	2B	3B	HR	RBI	SH	SF	HP	BB	Int. BB	SO	SB	CS	LOB
Nashville	.281	143	4841	731	631	1362	2117	270	31	141	683	31	54	475	31	863	108	52	992
New Orleans	.276	144	4712	685	638	1300	1925	274	33	95	623	74	50	50	500	39	694	118	74	973
Omaha	.274	144	4787	710	679	1311	2097	258	33	154	662	46	58	43	477	21	715	100	52	974
Iowa	.270	144	4864	706	656	1312	2091	291	22	148	657	56	40	38	445	40	895	100	65	932
Louisville	.268	144	4884	639	671	1308	2045	256	32	139	600	34	38	32	412	30	878	40	38	974
Indianapolis	.267	143	4761	644	686	1270	2008	295	31	127	594	48	26	33	440	30	845	77	46	954
Buffalo	.261	144	4781	684	667	1246	2013	263	39	142	631	51	50	35	450	33	869	75	49	936
Oklahoma City	.257	144	4797	656	827	1235	1890	235	45	110	608	37	45	44	483	20	891	51	47	955

INDIVIDUAL

(Leading qualifiers for batting championship—389 or more plate appearances)

*Bats lefthanded.   †Switch-hitter.

Player, Team	Avg.	G	AB	R	H	TB	2B	3B	HR	RBI	SH	SF	HP	BB	Int. BB	SO	SB	CS
Merullo, Matt, Nashville*	.332	103	352	50	117	185	30	1	12	65	1	2	3	28	6	47	0	2
Costo, Tim, Indianapolis	.326	106	362	49	118	185	30	2	11	57	1	1	5	22	1	60	3	2
Morman, Russ, Buffalo	.320	119	409	79	131	235	34	2	22	77	0	5	2	48	4	59	0	3
Rhodes, Karl, 88 Oma.-35 Iowa*	.318	123	490	112	156	295	43	3	30	89	4	5	2	58	8	82	16	8
Caceres, Edgar, New Orleans†	.317	114	420	73	133	172	20	2	5	45	3	3	1	35	5	39	7	4
Martin, Norberto, Nashville†	.309	137	580	87	179	239	21	6	9	74	12	6	2	26	0	59	31	5
Ducey, Rob, Oklahoma City*	.303	105	389	68	118	206	17	10	17	56	0	4	1	46	2	97	17	9
Zambrano, Eddie, Iowa	.303	133	469	95	142	271	29	2	32	115	2	7	6	54	11	93	10	7
Shumpert, Terry, Omaha	.300	111	413	70	124	197	29	1	14	59	21	6	6	41	0	62	36	8
Lockhart, Keith, Louisville*	.300	132	467	66	140	209	24	3	13	68	2	6	7	60	4	43	3	3

Departmental leaders: G—Hamelin, Martin, 137; AB—Martin, 580; R—Rhodes, 112; H—Martin, 179; TB—Rhodes, 295; 2B—Rhodes, 43; 3B—Ducey, Jones, 10; HR—Balboni, 36; RBI—Zambrano, 115; SH—Shumpert, 21; SF—Sheets, 10; HP—Denson, 23; BB—Hamelin, 82; IBB—Zambrano, 11; SO—Cron, 114; SB—Shumpert, 36; CS—Bullett, 17.

(All players—listed alphabetically)

Player, Team	Avg.	G	AB	R	H	TB	2B	3B	HR	RBI	SH	SF	HP	BB	Int. BB	SO	SB	CS
Abner, Shawn, Omaha	.246	37	134	14	33	49	6	2	2	16	0	0	1	8	0	20	2	2
Afenir, Troy, Indianapolis	.240	84	254	29	61	103	14	2	8	35	2	0	11	0	53	2	1
Alvarez, Clemente, Nashville	.207	11	29	1	6	6	0	0	0	2	2	0	0	1	0	4	0	0
Anderson, Kent, 69 Iowa-24 Ind.	.238	93	273	34	65	87	13	0	3	22	1	2	1	25	2	35	3	2
Anderson, Mike, Indianapolis	.000	23	32	0	0	0	0	0	0	0	1	0	1	0	0	12	0	0
Anderson, Paul, Louisville	.100	16	10	0	1	2	1	0	0	0	0	0	0	0	3	0	0
Aude, Rich, Buffalo	.375	21	64	17	24	45	9	0	4	16	0	1	1	10	0	15	0	0
Ayala, Bobby, Indianapolis	.000	5	4	0	0	0	0	0	0	0	0	0	0	0	0	3	0	0
Backlund, Brett, Buffalo	.167	5	6	0	1	1	0	0	0	0	0	0	0	0	0	2	0	0
Balboni, Steve, Oklahoma City	.244	126	471	67	115	245	22	0	36	108	0	7	6	51	4	98	0	1

Player, Team	Avg.	G	AB	R	H	TB	2B	3B	HR	RBI	SH	SF	HP	BB	Int. BB	SO	SB	CS
Ballard, Jeff, Buffalo*	.176	12	17	1	3	4	1	0	0	1	0	0	0	2	0	5	0	0
Barbara, Don, New Orleans*	.294	84	255	34	75	99	10	1	4	38	1	6	1	42	2	38	1	3
Beasley, Tony, Buffalo	.189	30	95	9	18	21	3	0	0	8	4	1	2	4	0	17	1	0
Beatty, Blaine, Buffalo*	.333	20	3	1	1	1	0	0	0	0	0	0	0	0	0	1	0	0
Bell, Mike, Buffalo*	.155	32	97	12	15	33	4	1	4	13	2	5	2	9	0	28	0	0
Beltre, Esteban, Nashville	.292	134	489	67	143	199	24	4	8	52	5	0	3	33	1	102	18	6
Bennett, Chris, Indianapolis	.000	3	2	0	0	0	0	0	0	0	0	0	0	0	0	2	0	0
Berger, Mike, Oklahoma City	.286	6	14	2	4	4	0	0	0	1	0	0	0	1	0	3	0	0
Boskie, Shawn, Iowa	.250	11	4	0	1	2	1	0	0	1	1	0	0	0	0	1	0	0
Brady, Doug, Nashville†	.000	2	3	0	0	0	0	0	0	0	0	0	0	0	0	0	0	0
Brennan, Bill, Iowa	.200	28	20	1	4	4	0	0	0	5	4	0	2	0	0	7	0	0
Brumfield, Jacob, Indianapolis	.325	33	126	23	41	69	14	1	4	19	2	1	1	6	0	14	11	0
Buckels, Gary, Louisville	.400	40	5	0	2	2	0	0	0	1	2	1	0	1	0	2	0	0
Bullett, Scott, Buffalo*	.287	110	408	62	117	145	13	6	1	30	0	0	1	39	0	67	28	17
Bullinger, Jim, Iowa	.000	49	2	1	0	0	0	0	0	0	0	0	0	1	0	0	0	0
Byington, John, New Orleans	.280	123	436	58	122	192	33	2	11	63	2	5	6	35	4	32	3	2
Caceres, Edgar, New Orleans†	.317	114	420	73	133	172	20	2	5	45	3	3	1	35	5	39	7	4
Canate, William, Indianapolis	.000	3	5	0	0	0	0	0	0	0	0	0	0	0	0	1	0	0
Canseco, Ozzie, Louisville	.240	44	154	20	37	84	6	1	13	33	0	1	0	15	4	59	1	2
Carter, Mike, New Orleans	.276	104	369	49	102	139	18	5	3	31	11	4	4	17	0	52	20	11
Carter, Steve, Indianapolis*	.269	68	212	21	57	79	13	0	3	22	1	0	3	10	4	27	6	0
Cecena, Jose, Buffalo	.000	6	1	0	0	0	0	0	0	0	0	0	0	0	0	0	0	0
Cepicky, Scott, Nashville*	.212	45	137	22	29	70	3	1	12	27	0	1	1	19	0	51	0	1
Chance, Tony, Iowa	.282	101	294	50	83	154	23	0	16	46	2	4	1	38	2	73	5	5
Cimorelli, Frank, Louisville	.000	27	0	0	0	0	0	0	0	0	0	0	0	1	0	0	0	1
Cirillo, Jeff, New Orleans	.293	58	215	31	63	89	13	2	3	32	4	0	3	29	0	33	2	1
Cole, Victor, 6 Buf.-6 N.O.†	.000	12	1	0	0	0	0	0	0	0	0	0	0	0	0	1	0	0
Coomer, Ron, Nashville	.313	59	211	34	66	124	19	0	13	51	0	3	1	10	1	29	1	2
Cooper, Gary, Buffalo	.269	102	349	66	94	173	27	2	16	63	4	3	4	52	2	88	2	3
Costo, Tim, Indianapolis	.326	106	362	49	118	185	30	2	11	57	1	1	5	22	1	60	3	2
Coughlin, Kevin, Nashville*	.571	2	7	0	4	5	1	0	0	3	0	0	0	0	0	1	0	0
Creek, Doug, Louisville*	.400	2	5	1	2	2	0	0	0	0	0	0	0	0	0	0	0	0
Cromer, Tripp, Louisville	.275	85	309	39	85	134	8	4	11	33	2	0	2	15	3	60	1	3
Cron, Chris, Nashville	.257	126	460	69	118	211	27	0	22	68	3	4	8	61	5	114	2	1
Culberson, Calvain, Indianapolis	.000	2	2	0	0	0	0	0	0	0	0	0	0	0	0	0	0	0
Cummings, Midre, Buffalo*	.276	60	232	36	64	105	12	1	9	21	0	2	0	22	4	45	5	1
Czajkowski, Jim, Iowa†	.000	42	1	0	0	0	0	0	0	0	0	0	0	0	0	0	0	0
Dalton, Mike, Buffalo	.000	25	2	1	0	0	0	0	0	0	0	0	0	1	0	1	0	0
Dascenzo, Doug, Oklahoma City†	.248	38	157	21	39	54	8	2	1	13	2	1	0	16	0	16	6	5
Dauphin, Phil, 20 Iowa-8 Ind.*	.240	28	75	5	18	27	4	1	1	4	0	0	0	12	2	13	2	0
Davis, Doug, Oklahoma City	.207	83	241	34	50	76	10	2	4	21	2	2	6	43	0	48	2	1
Davis, Mark, New Orleans	.174	10	23	4	4	10	1	1	1	2	0	1	2	3	0	11	0	1
Denson, Drew, Nashville	.281	136	513	82	144	252	36	0	24	103	0	8	23	46	7	98	0	0
Dewey, Mark, Buffalo	.000	22	1	0	0	0	0	0	0	0	0	0	0	0	0	1	0	0
Diaz, Alex, New Orleans†	.291	16	55	8	16	18	2	0	0	5	1	0	0	3	1	6	7	0
Diaz, Kiki, Omaha	.273	57	154	21	42	51	5	2	0	14	4	2	1	7	0	15	0	0
Diaz, Mario, Oklahoma City	.328	48	177	24	58	83	12	2	3	20	1	2	1	7	0	15	3	1
Diggs, Tony, New Orleans†	.259	11	27	4	7	10	3	0	0	1	1	0	0	3	0	6	4	2
Distefano, Benny, Oklahoma City*	.222	116	414	51	92	137	17	5	6	34	2	3	6	31	1	64	2	1
Dixon, Steve, Louisville*	.500	52	2	0	1	1	0	0	0	0	0	0	0	0	0	0	0	0
Dorsett, Brian, Indianapolis	.299	77	278	38	83	164	27	0	18	57	0	5	3	28	2	53	2	0
Dozier, D.J., Louisville	.230	45	139	24	32	62	10	1	6	15	1	1	0	18	0	43	0	4
Ducey, Rob, Oklahoma City*	.303	105	389	68	118	206	17	10	17	56	0	4	1	46	2	97	17	9
Edge, Tim, Buffalo	.000	1	2	0	0	0	0	0	0	0	0	0	0	0	0	0	0	0
Ellis, Paul, Louisville*	.200	50	125	12	25	31	6	0	0	8	0	1	1	13	2	16	0	0
Encarnacion, Angelo, Buffalo	.333	3	9	1	3	3	0	0	0	2	0	0	0	0	0	0	0	0
Espy, Cecil, Indianapolis†	.229	25	83	10	19	22	3	0	0	7	0	0	0	6	0	16	2	0
Farrell, Mike, New Orleans*	1.000	27	1	1	1	1	0	0	0	0	0	0	0	1	0	0	0	0
Figueroa, Bien, Louisville	.239	93	272	44	65	84	17	1	0	15	1	1	3	16	1	27	1	1
Finn, John, New Orleans	.281	117	335	47	94	114	13	2	1	37	9	0	6	33	1	36	27	9
Fireovid, Steve, Oklahoma City†	.000	8	1	0	0	0	0	0	0	0	0	0	0	0	0	0	0	0
Fitzgerald, Mike, New Orleans	.259	102	297	35	77	119	21	0	7	35	5	3	2	35	1	45	3	2
Franco, Matt, Iowa*	.291	62	199	24	58	98	17	4	5	29	0	3	1	16	3	30	4	1
Fulton, Ed, Louisville*	.211	61	147	13	31	45	5	0	3	18	1	3	1	11	0	27	0	2
Gilbert, Shawn, Nashville	.227	104	278	28	63	84	17	2	0	17	2	1	2	12	0	41	6	2
Goff, Jerry, Buffalo*	.251	104	362	52	91	166	27	3	14	69	0	7	1	55	4	82	1	1
Gomez, Rudy, Iowa	.150	9	20	0	3	3	0	0	0	0	0	0	0	1	0	8	0	0
Grayum, Richie, Iowa*	.143	4	7	0	1	1	0	0	0	0	0	0	0	0	0	2	0	0
Green, Gary, Indianapolis	.188	72	218	15	41	54	7	0	2	14	7	0	0	11	0	30	1	1
Green, Tom, Buffalo	.346	8	26	3	9	11	2	0	0	9	0	2	0	2	0	7	0	0
Greene, Willie, Indianapolis*	.267	98	341	62	91	176	19	0	22	58	2	2	1	51	2	83	2	4
Greer, Rusty, Oklahoma City*	.222	8	27	6	6	11	2	0	1	4	0	0	0	5	0	7	0	0
Gregg, Tommy, Indianapolis*	.318	71	198	34	63	106	12	5	7	30	1	1	1	26	0	28	3	5
Grott, Matt, Indianapolis*	.125	33	8	1	1	1	0	0	0	0	0	0	0	1	0	3	0	0
Guetterman, Lee, Louisville*	1.000	25	1	1	1	1	0	0	0	0	0	0	0	1	0	0	0	0
Hall, Joe, Nashville	.290	116	424	66	123	196	33	5	10	58	1	2	4	52	3	56	10	9
Hamelin, Bob, Omaha*	.259	137	479	77	124	236	19	3	29	84	0	9	5	82	9	94	8	3
Hancock, Lee, Buffalo*	.167	11	12	0	2	3	1	0	0	1	0	0	2	0	0	4	0	0
Hanlon, Larry, Oklahoma City	.223	121	376	45	84	112	16	0	4	37	5	4	7	41	0	71	5	6
Harris, Donald, Oklahoma City	.253	96	367	48	93	142	13	9	6	40	4	5	4	23	0	89	4	4
Hartsock, Jeff, Iowa	.250	9	4	0	1	1	0	0	0	0	0	0	0	0	0	2	0	0
Hernandez, Cesar, Indianapolis	.257	84	272	30	70	105	12	4	5	22	1	2	3	9	0	63	5	7
Hernandez, Jose, Iowa	.250	6	24	3	6	7	1	0	0	3	0	0	1	0	0	2	0	0
Hiatt, Phil, Omaha	.235	12	51	8	12	23	2	0	3	10	0	0	1	4	0	20	0	0
Hill, Milt, Indianapolis	.286	20	7	1	2	2	0	0	0	0	1	0	0	0	0	3	0	0
Hope, John, Buffalo	.000	4	5	0	0	0	0	0	0	0	0	0	0	0	0	1	0	0
Housie, Wayne, New Orleans†	.274	64	113	22	31	39	6	1	0	7	4	0	1	18	0	21	6	2
Howard, Dave, Omaha†	.255	47	157	15	40	52	8	2	0	18	4	3	1	7	0	20	3	1
Huff, Mike, Nashville	.294	92	344	65	101	149	12	6	8	32	1	2	6	64	0	43	18	7
Hughes, Keith, Indianapolis*	.286	82	283	55	81	156	28	4	13	42	1	1	2	41	2	61	5	0
Hunter, Bobby, Buffalo†	.000	11	1	0	0	0	0	0	0	0	0	0	0	0	0	0	0	0
Hurst, James, Oklahoma City*	.000	19	1	2	0	0	0	0	0	0	0	0	0	0	0	0	0	0
Huson, Jeff, Oklahoma City*	.289	24	76	11	22	30	5	0	1	10	0	0	0	13	0	10	1	3
Ilsley, Blaise, Iowa*	.286	48	14	2	4	5	1	0	0	0	1	0	0	0	0	2	0	0

— 340 —

Player, Team	Avg.	G	AB	R	H	TB	2B	3B	HR	RBI	SH	SF	HP	BB	Int. BB	SO	SB	CS
Irvine, Daryl, Buffalo	.000	37	0	0	0	0	0	0	0	0	0	0	0	1	0	0	0	0
Jackson, Chuck, Oklahoma City	.316	85	316	51	100	150	24	4	6	43	1	2	0	34	1	53	0	2
Jennings, Doug, Iowa*	.294	65	228	38	67	110	20	1	7	37	0	2	4	29	2	64	3	4
Jensen, John, Iowa*	.177	25	62	5	11	20	3	0	2	8	0	0	0	7	0	18	2	1
Jeter, Shawn, Nashville*	.208	43	149	14	31	43	2	2	2	22	1	0	0	6	1	38	6	3
Johnson, Earnie, Iowa*	.000	9	1	0	0	0	0	0	0	0	0	0	0	0	0	1	0	0
Johnston, Joel, Buffalo	.000	26	0	0	0	0	0	0	0	0	0	0	1	0	0	0	0	0
Jones, Tim, Louisville*	.289	101	408	72	118	175	22	10	5	46	2	4	2	44	1	67	13	8
Jordan, Brian, Louisville	.375	38	144	24	54	86	13	2	5	35	0	2	3	16	0	17	9	4
Kappesser, Bob, New Orleans	.091	4	11	0	1	2	1	0	0	2	0	0	0	1	0	4	0	0
Kennedy, Bo, Indianapolis	.143	39	14	2	2	3	1	0	0	1	2	0	0	3	0	10	0	0
Kennedy, Darryl, Oklahoma City	.063	6	16	2	1	1	0	0	0	0	1	0	0	3	0	4	0	0
Kessinger, Keith, Indianapolis†	.283	35	120	17	34	49	9	0	2	15	1	0	1	14	4	14	0	1
Kilgus, Paul, Louisville*	.222	10	9	2	2	2	0	0	0	0	0	0	0	0	0	3	0	0
Kingery, Mike, Omaha*	.263	116	399	61	105	164	19	5	10	41	3	2	2	36	1	24	9	3
Kiser, Garland, New Orleans*	.000	52	2	0	0	0	0	0	0	0	0	0	0	0	0	2	0	0
Kmak, Joe, New Orleans	.303	24	76	9	23	33	3	2	1	13	0	0	0	8	0	14	1	0
Knapp, Mike, Omaha	.290	70	200	22	58	71	7	0	2	19	3	1	3	34	0	32	2	4
Knox, Kerry, Louisville*	.000	7	5	0	0	0	0	0	0	0	0	0	0	0	0	2	0	0
Koelling, Brian, Indianapolis	.222	2	9	1	2	2	0	0	0	0	0	0	1	0	0	1	0	1
Komminsk, Brad, Nashville	.266	118	383	55	102	157	18	2	11	49	2	3	1	52	3	92	7	8
Koslofski, Kevin, Omaha*	.276	111	395	58	109	162	22	5	7	45	3	2	2	43	3	73	15	7
Kremblas, Frank, Indianapolis	.243	108	341	38	83	130	15	4	8	46	3	0	0	42	2	78	7	4
Kremers, Jimmy, New Orleans	.265	51	155	29	41	78	10	0	9	26	2	3	0	21	1	44	0	0
Lampkin, Tom, New Orleans*	.325	25	80	18	26	37	5	0	2	10	1	0	3	18	2	4	5	4
Leiper, Tim, Buffalo*	.327	75	208	21	68	99	15	5	2	33	0	6	2	11	2	18	1	3
Lewis, Dan, Iowa*	.197	42	122	10	24	40	7	3	1	13	1	1	1	7	1	23	0	0
Lockhart, Keith, Louisville*	.300	132	467	66	140	209	24	3	13	68	2	6	7	60	4	43	3	3
Lofton, Rod, Indianapolis	.667	2	3	0	2	2	0	0	0	2	0	1	0	0	0	1	0	0
Long, Kevin, Omaha*	.255	17	51	7	13	15	2	0	0	4	1	1	0	2	0	13	3	0
Lonigro, Greg, Iowa	.254	43	114	14	29	43	5	0	3	10	6	1	0	10	0	16	2	2
Luebbers, Larry, Indianapolis	.000	15	12	0	0	0	0	0	0	0	2	0	0	0	0	5	0	0
Lukachyk, Rob, New Orleans*	.167	8	24	5	4	11	1	0	2	6	2	0	0	3	0	6	0	0
Lynch, Dave, Indianapolis*	.250	59	4	2	1	1	0	0	0	0	0	0	0	1	0	1	0	0
Lyons, Barry, Louisville	.269	107	401	36	108	181	19	0	18	65	1	4	2	15	1	64	0	1
Mabry, John, Louisville*	.143	4	7	0	1	1	0	0	0	1	0	0	0	0	0	1	0	0
Maclin, Lonnie, Louisville*	.277	62	220	29	61	89	10	3	4	18	0	0	2	16	2	48	4	4
Magallanes, Ever, Oklahoma City*	.310	33	116	16	36	44	6	1	0	18	2	0	1	10	2	17	0	3
Martin, Norberto, Nashville†	.309	137	580	87	179	239	21	6	9	74	12	6	2	26	0	59	31	5
Marx, Tim, Buffalo	.143	4	14	0	2	3	1	0	0	0	0	0	0	2	0	4	0	0
McAndrew, Jamie, New Orleans	.000	28	1	0	0	0	0	0	0	0	0	0	0	0	0	1	0	0
McCoy, Trey, Oklahoma City	.250	8	28	6	7	19	1	1	3	11	0	0	1	5	0	5	0	0
McElroy, Chuck, Iowa*	.333	9	3	0	1	1	0	0	0	0	1	0	0	0	0	1	0	0
McGinnis, Russ, Omaha	.291	78	275	53	80	152	20	2	16	54	0	5	7	42	1	44	1	0
McMurtry, Craig, Buffalo	.111	31	9	1	1	2	1	0	0	0	3	0	1	0	0	2	1	0
Meier, Kevin, Indianapolis	.100	27	20	1	2	2	0	0	0	1	3	0	0	1	0	4	0	0
Menendez, Tony, Buffalo	.000	54	1	0	0	0	0	0	0	0	0	0	0	0	0	0	0	0
Mercado, Orlando, Iowa	.357	8	28	4	10	15	2	0	1	5	0	0	1	0	0	6	0	0
Merchant, Mark, Indianapolis†	.167	3	6	2	1	2	1	0	0	1	0	0	1	0	0	3	0	0
Merullo, Matt, Nashville*	.332	103	352	50	117	185	30	1	12	65	1	2	3	28	4	47	0	2
Mieske, Matt, New Orleans	.260	60	219	36	57	99	14	2	8	22	2	0	3	27	3	46	6	4
Milchin, Mike, Louisville*	.091	35	22	1	2	5	1	0	1	3	0	1	0	2	0	8	0	0
Miller, Keith A., Omaha	.292	6	24	2	7	10	1	1	0	2	0	0	0	0	0	2	1	0
Miller, N. Keith, Oklahoma City†	.285	95	316	37	90	124	19	0	5	45	1	4	2	50	4	65	2	1
Miller, Paul, Buffalo	.143	10	7	0	1	1	0	0	0	1	1	0	0	0	0	3	0	0
Miranda, Angel, New Orleans*	.000	10	1	0	0	0	0	0	0	0	0	0	0	0	0	1	0	0
Moeller, Dennis, Buffalo	.182	24	11	0	2	2	0	0	0	0	2	0	0	1	0	3	0	0
Moore, Brad, Indianapolis	.000	22	3	0	0	0	0	0	0	0	1	0	0	0	0	1	0	0
Morman, Russ, Buffalo	.320	119	409	79	131	235	34	2	22	77	0	5	2	48	4	59	0	3
Morris, Hal, Indianapolis*	.462	3	13	4	6	11	0	1	1	5	0	0	1	1	0	2	0	1
Morris, John, Louisville*	.239	20	71	13	17	28	5	0	2	9	0	1	1	7	0	14	1	2
Morris, Rod, Oklahoma City*	.212	12	33	4	7	9	2	0	0	1	2	0	0	0	0	7	0	0
Morrow, Timmie, Oklahoma City	.259	7	27	2	7	9	2	0	0	5	0	1	0	1	0	6	0	0
Mota, Jose, Omaha†	.282	105	330	46	93	117	11	2	3	35	3	5	2	34	0	34	27	10
Munoz, Omer, Buffalo	.217	40	129	7	28	40	4	1	2	16	2	1	1	3	2	11	0	0
Newman, Alan, Indianapolis*	.000	9	3	0	0	0	0	0	0	0	0	0	0	0	0	3	0	0
Newson, Warren, Nashville*	.341	61	176	40	60	84	8	2	4	21	0	3	1	38	4	38	5	2
Nilsson, Dave, New Orleans*	.344	17	61	9	21	30	6	0	1	9	1	1	0	5	0	6	0	1
Noboa, Junior, Indianapolis	.283	45	180	27	51	64	11	1	0	14	0	1	1	14	2	8	4	2
O'Leary, Troy, New Orleans*	.273	111	388	65	106	161	32	1	7	59	6	5	2	43	7	61	6	3
Ortiz, Javier, Omaha	.286	3	7	0	2	2	0	0	0	2	0	0	0	1	0	3	0	1
Pagnozzi, Tom, Louisville	.279	12	43	5	12	18	3	0	1	1	0	0	0	0	0	3	0	0
Pappas, Erik, Louisville	.338	21	71	19	24	44	6	1	4	13	0	0	0	11	0	12	0	2
Patterson, Dave, Louisville	.278	80	180	26	50	71	6	0	5	16	2	0	1	27	2	27	0	0
Pedre, George, Iowa	.211	68	232	27	49	84	12	1	7	21	5	1	2	13	0	47	2	1
Peltier, Dan, Oklahoma City*	.321	48	187	28	60	98	15	4	5	33	0	2	0	19	4	27	2	2
Pena, Geronimo, Louisville†	.174	7	23	4	4	5	1	0	0	0	1	0	1	1	0	4	1	0
Pennyfeather, William, Buffalo	.249	112	457	54	114	180	18	3	14	41	8	1	1	18	2	92	10	12
Petkovsek, Mark, Buffalo	.167	17	12	1	2	2	0	0	0	1	2	0	0	1	0	1	0	0
Petralli, Geno, Oklahoma City†	.200	6	20	2	4	8	1	0	1	1	0	0	0	3	0	3	0	0
Powell, Ross, Louisville*	.182	30	22	1	4	4	0	0	0	0	2	0	0	2	0	3	0	1
Prager, Howard, Louisville	.263	63	209	27	55	84	17	0	4	28	0	1	2	24	1	37	0	0
Pulliam, Harvey, Omaha	.264	54	208	28	55	80	10	0	5	26	0	0	1	17	1	36	1	0
Raines, Tim, Nashville†	.455	3	11	3	5	6	1	0	0	2	0	0	0	2	0	0	2	1
Ramsey, Fernando, Iowa	.270	134	545	76	147	206	30	7	5	42	9	0	2	25	2	72	13	13
Rhodes, Karl, 88 Oma.-35 Iowa*	.318	123	490	112	156	295	43	3	30	89	4	5	2	58	8	82	16	8
Riesgo, Nikco, New Orleans	.291	27	79	9	23	37	5	3	1	12	0	1	0	3	0	16	0	1
Roberson, Kevin, Iowa*	.304	67	263	48	80	150	20	1	16	50	0	3	4	19	3	66	3	2
Robertson, Rich, Buffalo*	.125	23	16	1	2	2	0	0	0	0	2	0	0	0	0	5	0	0
Robinson, Scott, Indianapolis	.364	9	11	0	4	5	1	0	0	2	0	0	0	0	0	5	0	0
Rohde, Dave, Buffalo†	.244	131	464	64	113	172	22	2	11	48	5	6	3	50	3	46	4	5
Rohrmeier, Dan, Omaha†	.248	118	432	51	107	187	23	3	17	70	1	7	3	23	0	59	2	1
Romero, Mandy, Buffalo†	.228	42	136	11	31	45	6	1	2	14	1	1	0	6	1	21	1	0
Roper, John, Indianapolis	.000	12	3	0	0	0	0	0	0	0	0	0	0	0	0	1	0	0

Player, Team	Avg.	G	AB	R	H	TB	2B	3B	HR	RBI	SH	SF	HP	BB	Int. BB	SO	SB	CS
Rossy, Rico, Omaha	.298	37	131	25	39	66	10	1	5	21	0	1	3	20	1	19	3	2
Royer, Stan, Louisville	.280	98	368	46	103	170	19	0	16	54	3	5	0	33	2	74	2	0
Ruffin, Johnny, 29 Nash. -3 Ind.	.000	32	1	0	0	0	0	0	0	0	0	0	0	0	0	0	0	0
Ruskin, Scott, Indianapolis	.000	50	3	0	0	0	0	0	0	0	0	0	0	0	0	0	0	0
Sable, Luke, Oklahoma City	.207	94	295	42	61	72	11	0	0	17	3	0	4	28	0	47	3	3
Sandoval, Jose, Buffalo	.230	65	209	23	48	74	7	2	5	21	1	1	1	13	2	37	1	0
Santovenia, Nelson, Omaha	.237	81	274	33	65	111	13	0	11	42	0	7	3	12	1	50	0	1
Sauveur, Rich, Indianapolis*	.143	5	7	1	1	1	0	0	0	0	0	0	0	1	0	3	0	0
Savinon, Odalis, Louisville	.203	35	59	10	12	15	1	1	0	2	1	0	0	4	0	13	0	2
Schreiber, Bruce, Buffalo	.200	15	40	0	8	9	1	0	0	2	1	0	0	2	0	11	0	0
Scott, Gary, Indianapolis	.211	77	284	39	60	83	12	1	3	18	2	2	4	21	0	33	2	1
Sebra, Bob, Louisville	.111	28	27	3	3	3	0	0	0	2	0	2	0	1	0	3	0	0
Service, Scott, Indianapolis	.000	21	1	0	0	0	0	0	0	0	0	0	0	0	0	0	0	0
Shave, Jon, Oklahoma City	.263	100	399	58	105	140	17	3	4	41	9	1	2	20	0	60	4	3
Sheets, Larry, New Orleans*	.280	127	457	60	128	212	28	1	18	98	1	10	7	31	9	52	3	6
Shelton, Ben, Buffalo	.277	65	173	25	48	73	8	1	5	22	0	3	24	0	44	0	0	
Shields, Tommy, Iowa	.287	84	314	48	90	135	16	1	9	48	2	2	6	26	1	46	10	6
Shines, Razor, Indianapolis†	.276	65	192	24	53	81	13	0	5	35	1	3	0	18	2	27	1	0
Shouse, Brian, Buffalo*	.000	48	3	0	0	0	0	0	0	0	0	0	0	0	0	3	0	0
Shumpert, Terry, Omaha	.300	111	413	70	124	197	29	1	14	59	21	6	6	41	0	62	36	8
Smith, Greg, Iowa†	.282	131	500	82	141	197	27	1	9	54	9	8	3	53	1	61	25	11
Smith, Roy, Buffalo	.077	28	26	2	2	2	0	0	0	0	3	0	0	0	0	6	0	0
Snider, Van, Louisville*	.265	118	423	54	112	191	29	4	14	56	4	4	0	24	2	98	3	1
Sparks, Steve, New Orleans	.000	31	1	0	0	0	0	0	0	0	0	0	0	0	0	1	0	0
Spradlin, Jerry, Indianapolis†	.000	34	5	0	0	0	0	0	0	0	1	0	0	0	0	4	0	0
Stephens, Ray, Oklahoma City	.228	97	333	29	76	116	15	2	7	49	2	7	2	32	2	78	0	2
Stephenson, Phil, Omaha*	.306	20	72	12	22	43	7	1	4	8	0	0	0	5	0	12	0	0
Stevens, Dave, Iowa	.000	24	1	0	0	0	0	0	0	0	0	0	0	0	0	1	0	0
Suero, William, New Orleans	.226	46	124	14	28	37	4	1	1	13	2	3	1	21	0	17	8	7
Swartzbaugh, Dave, Iowa	.000	26	4	0	0	0	0	0	0	0	0	0	0	0	0	3	0	0
Tabaka, Jeff, New Orleans	.000	54	2	0	0	0	0	0	0	0	0	0	0	0	0	2	0	0
Tedder, Scott, Nashville*	.288	47	111	24	32	46	5	0	3	15	1	0	0	14	0	15	2	2
Thomas, Skeets, Louisville*	.276	108	377	30	104	148	15	1	9	40	0	1	3	15	4	75	1	0
Tomberlin, Andy, Buffalo*	.285	68	221	41	63	122	11	6	12	45	1	2	4	18	3	48	3	0
Trachsel, Steve, Iowa	.280	27	25	5	7	8	1	0	0	1	2	0	0	2	0	5	0	0
Tracy, Jim, 17 Buf. - 12 Ind.	.182	29	11	1	2	3	1	0	0	1	1	0	0	0	0	7	0	0
Tubbs, Greg, Indianapolis	.305	97	334	59	102	161	21	4	10	45	1	3	2	42	3	65	15	11
Urbani, Tom, Louisville*	.143	19	7	1	1	2	1	0	0	0	1	0	0	1	0	4	0	0
Valentin, Jose, New Orleans†	.247	122	389	56	96	155	22	5	9	53	14	4	8	47	2	87	9	10
Varsho, Gary, Indianapolis*	.289	32	121	19	35	54	8	1	3	18	3	0	2	15	1	13	1	2
Villanueva, Hector, Louisville	.242	40	124	13	30	54	9	0	5	20	0	1	1	16	1	18	0	0
Vindivich, Paul, Omaha	.000	2	2	0	0	0	0	0	0	0	0	0	0	0	0	1	0	0
Vosberg, Ed, Iowa*	.000	52	1	0	0	0	0	0	0	0	0	0	0	0	0	0	0	0
Wade, Scott, Iowa	.170	47	147	14	25	42	8	0	3	15	1	2	2	12	0	42	9	3
Walbeck, Matt, Iowa†	.281	87	331	31	93	133	18	2	6	43	2	2	2	18	4	47	1	2
Walker, Mike, Iowa	.000	12	0	0	0	0	0	0	0	0	1	0	0	0	0	0	0	0
Watson, Allen, Louisville*	.364	17	22	0	8	10	2	0	0	1	2	0	0	0	0	1	0	0
Wehner, John, Buffalo	.252	89	330	61	83	130	22	2	7	34	2	2	1	40	2	53	17	3
Wendell, Turk, Iowa†	.071	25	14	1	1	1	0	0	0	0	3	0	0	0	0	3	0	1
White, Rick, Buffalo	.000	7	5	0	0	0	0	0	0	0	0	0	0	0	0	2	0	0
Williams, Eddie, New Orleans	.259	8	27	2	7	12	0	1	1	4	0	1	0	7	0	4	0	0
Williams, Jimmy, Iowa*	.091	17	11	0	1	1	0	0	0	0	0	2	0	0	0	5	0	0
Wilson, Craig, Omaha	.278	65	234	26	65	89	13	1	3	28	1	1	1	20	0	24	7	4
Wilson, Dan, Indianapolis	.262	51	191	18	50	66	11	1	1	17	3	1	1	19	1	31	1	0
Wilson, Glenn, Buffalo	.279	61	201	32	56	108	14	1	12	43	0	4	3	16	2	38	0	1
Wiseman, Dennis, Louisville	.375	33	8	3	3	4	1	0	0	0	2	0	0	0	0	3	0	0
Worthington, Craig, Iowa	.273	132	469	63	128	190	23	0	13	66	1	2	1	59	3	91	1	1
Wrona, Rick, Nashville	.212	73	184	24	39	61	13	0	3	22	4	3	2	11	0	35	0	1
Yacopino, Ed, New Orleans†	.203	23	69	7	14	19	3	1	0	2	0	0	0	11	1	9	0	1
Young, Gerald, Indianapolis†	.301	32	103	15	31	44	10	0	1	6	2	1	1	18	3	7	7	2
Zambrano, Eddie, Iowa	.303	133	469	95	142	271	29	2	32	115	2	7	6	54	11	93	10	7
Zimmerman, Mike, Buffalo	.500	33	2	0	1	1	0	0	0	0	0	0	0	0	0	0	0	0

The following pitchers, listed alphabetically by club, with games in parentheses, had no plate appearances, primarily through use of designated hitters:

BUFFALO—Neagle, Denny (3); Piatt, Doug (2); Toliver, Fred (13).

INDIANAPOLIS—Arnsberg, Brad (6); Kaiser, Jeff (1); Wickander, Kevin (1).

IOWA—Corbett, Sherman (8); Dickson, Lance (2); Dyer, Mike (14); Slocumb, Heathcliff (10); Steenstra, Ken (1); Wallace, Derek (1).

LOUISVILLE—Arnsberg, Brad (23); Barber, Brian (1); Compres, Fidel (21); Ozuna, Gabe (35).

NASHVILLE—Alvarez, Wilson (1); Baldwin, Jim (10); Barfield, John (14); Bere, Jason (8); Bolton, Rodney (18); Campos, Frank (20); Carter, Jeff (12); Cary, Chuck (1); Dabney, Fred (51); Drahman, Brian (54); Garcia, Ramon (7); Howard, Chris (43); Jones, Barry (7); Keyser, Brian (30); Leach, Terry (5); Merigliano, Frank (7); Mongiello, Mike (39); Ruffcorn, Scott (7); Ruffin, Johnny (29); Schrenk, Steve (21); Schwarz, Jeff (7); Stieb, Dave (1); Thomas, Larry (18).

NEW ORLEANS—Austin, Jim (8); Cole, Victor (6); Farmer, Howard (20); Higuera, Ted (3); Hunter, Jim (39); Ignasiak, Mike (35); Johnson, Dane (13); Kiefer, Mark (5); Maldonado, Carlos (12); Manzanillo, Josias (1); Maysey, Matt (29); Nolte, Eric (7); Novoa, Rafael (20); Rightnowar, Ron (4); Taylor, Scott (12); Wishnevski, Bob (52).

OKLAHOMA CITY—Acker, Jim (6); Alberro, Jose (12); Alexander, Jerry (10); Anderson, Allan (19); Bohanon, Brian (2); Bronkey, Jeff (29); Brown, Bob (30); Burrows, Terry (27); Dreyer, Steve (16); Eiland, Dave (7); Helling, Ricky (2); Lee, Mark (52); Lefferts, Craig (1); Leon, Danilo (13); Manuel, Barry (21); Nen, Robb (6); Oliveras, Francisco (44); Pavlik, Roger (6); Perez, David (2); Reed, Rick (5); Sadecki, Steve (12); Schooler, Mike (28); Shaw, Cedric (28); Smith, Dan (3); Whiteside, Matt (8).

OMAHA—Ahern, Brian (6); Boddicker, Mike (3); Brown, Keith (26); Burgos, Enrique (48); Campbell, Jim (27); Clark, Dera (51); Curry, Steve (33); DiPino, Frank (15); Gardner, Mark (8); Haney, Chris (8); Magnante, Mike (33); Meacham, Russ (7); Pierce, Ed (12); Rasmussen, Dennis (17); Reed, Rick (19); Roesler, Mike (4); Sampen, Bill (33); Sanchez, Alex (16); Shifflett, Steve (43); Stieb, Dave (9).

GRAND SLAMS—Roberson, 2; Afenir, Barbara, Chance, Coomer, Cron, Ducey, Fitzgerald, Hughes, Kremblas, Kremers, Morman, Newson, Rhodes, Shave, Stephens, Tomberlin, Valentin, Walbeck, Zambrano, 1 each.

AWARDED FIRST BASE ON CATCHER'S INTERFERENCE—Brumfield (Romero); Jensen (Romero); Knapp (D. Davis); Kremers (Romero).

PITCHING

TEAM

Team	ERA	G	CG	ShO	Sv.	IP	H	R	ER	HR	HB	BB	Int. BB	SO	WP	Bk.
Nashville	3.88	143	10	4	40	1250.1	1182	631	539	117	36	448	37	910	90	11
New Orleans	4.05	144	19	6	37	1250.0	1226	638	562	147	46	433	24	857	51	17
Louisville	4.25	144	13	5	31	1256.1	1311	671	593	137	43	432	38	815	66	15
Iowa	4.27	144	7	10	42	1278.1	1285	656	607	114	60	482	19	930	87	9
Buffalo	4.32	144	9	7	39	1248.1	1322	667	599	114	39	443	27	677	57	9
Indianapolis	4.34	144	8	5	37	1230.2	1248	686	594	142	33	534	49	880	63	11
Omaha	4.47	144	13	11	30	1244.0	1289	679	618	160	27	392	14	817	51	9
Oklahoma City	5.33	144	8	1	30	1249.1	1481	827	740	125	45	518	36	764	81	20

INDIVIDUAL

(Leading qualifiers for earned-run average leadership—115 or more innings)

*Throws lefthanded.

Pitcher, Team	W	L	Pct.	ERA	G	GS	CG	GF	ShO	Sv.	IP	H	R	ER	HR	HB	BB	Int. BB	SO	WP
Bolton, Nashville	10	1	.909	2.88	18	16	1	1	0	1	115.2	108	40	37	10	3	37	2	75	11
Watson, Louisville*	5	4	.556	2.91	17	17	2	0	0	0	120.2	101	46	39	13	4	31	0	86	2
Reed, 19 Oma.-5 O.C.	12	7	.632	3.32	24	24	4	0	2	0	162.2	159	68	60	21	3	16	1	79	3
Campos, Nashville	7	5	.583	3.55	19	19	2	0	0	0	116.2	104	60	46	13	7	58	0	86	14
Anderson, Indianapolis	10	6	.625	3.75	23	23	2	0	1	0	151.0	150	73	63	10	4	56	5	111	8
Sparks, New Orleans	9	13	.409	3.84	29	28	7	0	1	0	180.1	174	89	77	17	5	80	1	104	7
Schrenk, Nashville	6	8	.429	3.90	21	20	0	0	0	0	122.1	117	61	53	11	3	47	3	78	6
McAndrew, New Orleans	11	6	.647	3.94	27	25	5	0	1	0	166.2	172	78	73	19	2	45	3	97	5
Ilsley, Iowa*	12	7	.632	3.94	48	16	0	13	0	4	134.2	147	61	59	10	4	32	2	78	7
Trachsel, Iowa	13	6	.684	3.96	27	26	1	1	1	0	170.2	170	78	75	20	6	45	0	135	4

Departmental leaders: G—Lynch, 59; W—L. Smith, 15; L—Burrows, 15; Pct.—Bolton, .909; GS—Brennan, L. Smith, Sparks, 28; CG—Sparks, 7; GF—Drahman, 50; ShO—Reed, 2; Sv.—Ruskin, 28; IP—Sparks, 180.1; H—Brennan, 180; R—Burrows, 107; ER—Burrows, 98; HR—Powell, 27; HB—Brennan, 15; BB—Sparks, 80; IBB—Drahman, Lynch, 8; SO—Brennan, 143; WP—Brennan, 23.

(All pitchers—listed alphabetically)

Pitcher, Team	W	L	Pct.	ERA	G	GS	CG	GF	ShO	Sv.	IP	H	R	ER	HR	HB	BB	Int. BB	SO	WP
Acker, Oklahoma City	0	1	.000	8.31	6	0	0	3	0	0	4.1	7	4	4	0	0	4	1	2	1
Ahern, Omaha	1	2	.333	5.68	6	5	0	0	0	0	19.0	18	17	12	3	0	13	0	16	1
Alberro, Oklahoma City	0	0	.000	6.88	12	0	0	7	0	0	17.0	25	15	13	2	0	11	0	14	4
Alexander, Oklahoma City	1	2	.333	9.25	10	3	0	4	0	0	24.1	40	27	25	9	4	9	1	13	4
Alvarez, Nashville*	0	1	.000	2.84	1	1	0	0	0	0	6.1	7	2	2	0	0	2	0	8	0
Anderson, Oklahoma City*	2	8	.200	5.32	19	18	0	1	0	1	115.0	137	72	68	13	5	37	0	52	6
Anderson, Indianapolis	10	6	.625	3.75	23	23	2	0	1	0	151.0	150	73	63	10	4	56	5	111	8
Anderson, Louisville	3	5	.375	4.89	11	11	2	0	0	0	70.0	74	41	38	7	2	14	0	32	7
Arnsberg, 6 Ind.-23 Lou.	0	2	.000	5.31	29	0	0	14	0	0	40.2	47	24	24	6	0	27	3	19	7
Austin, New Orleans	1	2	.333	5.06	8	3	0	0	0	0	16.0	17	11	9	3	0	7	0	7	4
Ayala, Indianapolis	0	2	.000	5.67	5	5	0	0	0	0	27.0	36	19	17	1	1	12	1	19	1
Backlund, Buffalo	0	4	.000	10.55	5	5	0	0	0	0	21.1	30	25	25	5	2	14	0	10	0
Baldwin, Nashville	5	4	.556	2.61	10	10	1	0	0	0	69.0	43	21	20	5	0	36	0	61	3
Ballard, Buffalo*	6	1	.857	2.29	12	12	1	0	0	0	74.2	79	22	19	4	2	17	0	40	0
Barber, Louisville*	0	1	.000	4.76	1	1	0	0	0	0	5.2	4	3	3	0	0	4	0	5	0
Barfield, Nashville*	3	1	.750	4.11	14	4	0	4	0	1	35.0	36	19	16	3	1	11	2	15	3
Beatty, Buffalo*	2	3	.400	5.50	20	4	0	5	0	1	36.0	51	25	22	2	2	8	0	14	3
Bennett, Indianapolis	0	0	.000	4.85	3	2	0	0	0	0	13.0	21	8	7	1	0	1	0	10	0
Bere, Nashville	5	1	.833	2.37	8	8	0	0	0	0	49.1	36	19	13	1	1	25	1	52	2
Boddicker, Omaha	0	2	.000	4.60	3	3	0	0	0	0	15.2	18	9	8	3	0	4	0	12	0
Bohanon, Oklahoma City*	0	1	.000	6.43	2	2	0	0	0	0	7.0	7	6	5	1	1	3	0	7	1
Bolton, Nashville	10	1	.909	2.88	18	16	1	1	0	1	115.2	108	40	37	10	3	37	2	75	11
Boskie, Iowa	6	1	.857	4.27	11	11	1	0	0	0	71.2	70	35	34	4	7	21	0	35	1
Brennan, Iowa	10	7	.588	4.42	28	28	2	0	1	0	179.0	180	96	88	13	15	64	0	143	23
Bronkey, Oklahoma City	2	2	.500	2.65	29	0	0	26	0	14	37.1	29	11	11	2	0	7	2	19	2
Brown, Omaha	13	8	.619	4.84	26	25	1	1	0	0	148.2	166	85	80	25	3	36	0	98	3
Brown, Oklahoma City	5	8	.385	6.09	30	16	0	4	0	1	99.0	134	83	67	7	2	41	3	60	6
Buckels, Louisville	4	2	.667	5.42	40	4	0	7	0	1	88.0	116	58	53	12	1	25	6	64	9
Bullinger, Iowa	4	6	.400	3.42	49	3	0	37	0	20	73.2	64	29	28	3	4	43	5	74	13
Burgos, Omaha*	2	4	.333	3.16	48	0	0	26	0	9	62.2	36	26	22	4	1	37	0	91	9
Burrows, Oklahoma City*	7	15	.318	6.39	27	25	1	0	0	0	138.0	171	107	98	19	2	76	0	74	8
Campbell, Omaha*	3	5	.375	5.04	27	4	0	6	0	0	55.1	72	33	31	6	2	17	0	33	3
Campos, Nashville	7	5	.583	3.55	19	19	2	0	0	0	116.2	104	60	46	13	7	58	0	86	14
Carter, Nashville	2	4	.333	6.99	11	6	0	2	0	0	37.1	43	30	29	4	0	17	0	21	1
Cary, Nashville*	0	1	.000	9.00	1	0	0	0	0	0	2.0	4	2	2	0	0	2	0	1	0
Cecena, Buffalo	0	1	.000	4.91	6	0	0	0	0	0	7.1	12	10	4	1	0	8	0	7	0
Chance, Iowa	0	0	.000	18.00	1	0	0	0	0	0	1.0	2	2	2	1	0	0	0	3	0
Cimorelli, Louisville	2	1	.667	2.72	27	0	0	13	0	2	43.0	34	15	13	1	3	25	5	24	7
Clark, Omaha	4	4	.500	4.37	51	0	0	19	0	5	82.1	86	43	40	16	0	30	2	53	4
Cole, 6 Buf.-6 N.O.	1	5	.167	8.91	12	7	0	0	0	0	32.1	44	32	32	5	1	31	0	19	1
Compres, Louisville	3	5	.375	6.91	21	0	0	11	0	0	27.1	41	26	21	5	2	19	5	18	2
Corbett, Iowa*	0	1	.000	3.77	8	0	0	1	0	0	14.1	11	6	6	1	3	4	1	9	0
Creek, Louisville*	0	0	.000	3.21	2	2	0	0	0	0	14.0	10	5	5	0	1	9	0	9	2
Culberson, Indianapolis	1	0	1.000	0.69	2	2	0	0	0	0	13.0	9	2	1	1	0	7	0	9	0
Curry, Omaha	6	7	.462	4.88	33	21	1	2	0	0	145.2	141	86	79	14	5	56	0	91	5
Czaikowski, Iowa	7	5	.583	3.84	42	0	0	18	0	0	70.1	64	31	30	3	3	32	2	43	4
Dabney, Nashville*	2	5	.286	4.86	51	0	0	15	0	3	63.0	65	43	34	7	9	21	0	44	3
Dalton, Buffalo*	3	1	.750	4.11	25	0	0	8	0	2	35.0	37	16	16	2	2	12	2	16	1
Dewey, Buffalo	2	0	1.000	1.23	22	0	0	11	0	6	29.1	21	9	4	2	3	5	0	17	0
Dickson, Iowa*	0	1	.000	10.38	2	2	0	0	0	0	4.1	6	5	5	0	0	1	0	3	1
DiPino, Omaha*	1	2	.333	2.78	15	0	0	8	0	1	22.2	21	9	7	3	2	4	1	9	0
Dixon, Louisville*	5	7	.417	5.05	57	0	0	41	0	20	67.2	57	39	38	4	4	33	7	61	2
Drahman, Nashville	9	4	.692	2.91	54	0	0	50	0	20	55.2	59	29	18	3	2	19	8	49	6
Dreyer, Oklahoma City	4	6	.400	3.03	16	16	1	0	0	0	107.0	108	39	36	5	2	31	1	59	4
Dyer, Iowa	1	0	1.000	4.81	14	0	0	3	0	0	24.1	18	14	13	4	0	20	0	18	2
Eiland, Oklahoma City	3	1	.750	4.29	7	7	1	0	0	0	35.2	39	18	17	1	1	9	0	15	0
Farmer, New Orleans	4	3	.571	5.73	20	13	1	1	0	0	75.1	93	52	48	8	1	24	1	55	2

— 343 —

Pitcher, Team	W	L	Pct.	ERA	G	GS	CG	GF	ShO	Sv.	IP	H	R	ER	HR	HB	BB	Int. BB	SO	WP
Farrell, New Orleans*	9	9	.500	4.86	26	26	3	0	1	0	152.0	164	92	82	22	6	32	1	63	2
Figueroa, Louisville	0	0	.000	0.00	1	0	0	0	0	0	1.1	0	0	0	0	0	1	0	0	0
Fireovid, Oklahoma City	1	1	.500	7.59	7	4	0	1	0	0	21.1	35	24	18	3	1	4	0	14	4
Franco, Iowa	0	0	.000	36.00	1	0	0	1	0	0	1.0	5	4	4	2	0	1	0	1	1
Fulton, Louisville	0	0	.000	0.00	2	0	0	2	0	0	3.0	1	0	0	0	0	1	0	3	0
Garcia, Nashville	4	1	.800	4.01	7	7	1	0	1	0	42.2	45	22	19	5	3	11	0	25	1
Gardner, Omaha	4	2	.667	2.79	8	8	1	0	0	0	48.1	34	17	15	7	1	19	2	41	1
Grott, Indianapolis*	7	5	.583	3.59	33	0	0	10	0	1	100.1	88	45	40	8	1	40	2	73	7
Guetterman, Louisville*	2	1	.667	2.94	25	0	0	7	0	2	33.2	35	11	11	0	2	12	3	20	3
Hall, Nashville	0	0	.000	0.00	1	0	0	1	0	0	1.0	1	0	0	0	0	0	0	1	0
Hancock, Buffalo*	2	6	.250	4.91	11	11	0	0	0	0	66.0	73	38	36	4	0	14	0	30	2
Haney, Omaha*	6	1	.857	2.27	8	7	2	0	0	0	47.2	43	13	12	2	1	14	0	32	2
Hartsock, Iowa	0	4	.000	6.32	9	9	0	0	0	0	47.0	68	35	33	6	1	20	1	17	1
Helling, Oklahoma City	1	1	.500	1.64	2	2	1	0	0	0	11.0	5	3	2	0	0	3	0	17	0
Higuera, New Orleans*	0	1	.000	9.00	3	3	0	0	0	0	8.0	11	11	8	1	0	7	0	7	1
Hill, Indianapolis	3	5	.375	4.08	20	5	0	9	0	2	53.0	53	27	24	1	3	17	4	45	2
Hope, Buffalo	2	1	.667	6.33	4	4	0	0	0	0	21.1	30	16	15	4	1	2	0	6	2
Howard, Nashville*	4	3	.571	3.38	43	0	0	17	0	3	66.2	55	32	25	9	0	16	4	53	7
Hunter, Buffalo	0	1	.000	9.64	11	0	0	0	0	0	14.0	18	15	15	2	2	10	1	8	2
Hunter, New Orleans	5	2	.714	4.19	39	0	0	8	0	1	68.2	82	40	32	8	6	25	2	35	1
Hurst, Oklahoma City*	4	6	.400	4.53	16	14	2	0	0	0	91.1	106	50	46	13	3	29	1	60	1
Ignasiak, New Orleans	6	0	1.000	1.09	35	0	0	18	0	9	57.2	26	10	7	4	1	20	2	61	3
Ilsley, Iowa*	12	7	.632	3.94	48	16	0	13	0	4	134.2	147	61	59	10	4	32	2	78	7
Irvine, Buffalo	1	3	.250	4.30	37	0	0	11	0	0	46.0	41	24	22	4	1	26	1	19	2
Johnson, New Orleans	0	0	.000	2.40	13	0	0	8	0	6	15.0	11	4	4	2	0	4	1	10	1
Johnson, Iowa*	1	1	.500	3.21	9	0	0	5	0	1	14.0	12	5	5	3	0	4	0	11	0
Johnston, Buffalo	1	3	.250	7.76	26	0	0	14	0	1	31.1	30	28	27	5	3	25	2	26	5
Jones, Nashville	0	0	.000	2.60	7	0	0	2	0	2	17.1	16	5	5	3	0	2	0	19	2
Kaiser, Indianapolis*	0	0	.000	0.00	1	0	0	0	0	0	1.0	0	0	0	0	0	0	0	2	0
Kennedy, Indianapolis	3	7	.300	4.96	39	14	0	10	0	1	118.0	135	76	65	16	0	47	5	79	1
Keyser, Nashville	9	5	.643	4.66	30	18	2	4	0	1	121.2	142	70	63	8	1	27	4	44	4
Kiefer, New Orleans	3	2	.600	5.08	5	5	0	0	0	0	28.1	28	20	16	4	0	17	0	23	4
Kilgus, Louisville*	7	1	.875	2.65	9	9	4	0	1	0	68.0	59	21	20	10	1	19	0	54	3
Kiser, New Orleans*	5	4	.556	5.40	50	0	0	12	0	1	66.2	69	43	40	10	3	24	3	42	2
Knapp, Omaha	0	0	.000	13.50	1	0	0	1	0	0	2.0	6	3	3	0	0	0	0	0	0
Knox, Louisville*	1	4	.200	4.50	7	7	1	0	1	0	44.0	48	25	22	6	3	10	0	24	2
Kremblas, Indianapolis	0	0	.000	21.60	1	0	0	0	0	0	1.2	6	4	4	2	0	0	0	2	0
Leach, Nashville	0	0	.000	3.18	5	0	0	1	0	1	5.2	4	2	2	0	0	0	0	4	0
Lee, Oklahoma City*	5	3	.625	4.34	52	1	0	21	0	4	101.2	112	61	49	4	0	43	5	65	4
Lefferts, Oklahoma City*	0	1	.000	7.50	1	1	0	0	0	0	6.0	9	5	5	1	0	2	0	1	0
Leon, Oklahoma City	2	2	.500	5.52	13	1	0	5	0	0	31.0	28	21	19	3	8	26	4	33	6
Luebbers, Indianapolis	4	7	.364	4.16	15	15	0	0	0	0	84.1	81	45	39	7	6	47	5	51	1
Lynch, Indianapolis	9	4	.692	3.21	59	0	0	27	0	1	84.0	73	41	30	3	2	48	8	76	3
Magnante, Omaha*	2	6	.250	3.67	33	13	0	5	0	2	105.1	97	46	43	7	4	29	2	74	6
Maldonado, New Orleans	1	0	1.000	0.47	12	0	0	9	0	7	19.1	13	1	1	0	0	7	1	14	0
Manuel, Oklahoma City	2	2	.500	7.99	21	0	0	10	0	2	23.2	29	21	21	1	0	16	1	19	3
Manzanillo, New Orleans	0	1	.000	9.00	1	0	0	1	0	0	1.1	1	1	1	0	0	0	0	3	0
Maysey, New Orleans	0	3	.000	4.13	29	5	0	6	0	2	52.1	48	25	24	8	0	14	1	40	2
McAndrew, New Orleans	11	6	.647	3.94	27	25	5	0	1	0	166.2	172	78	73	19	2	45	3	97	5
McElroy, Iowa*	0	1	.000	4.60	9	0	0	4	0	2	15.2	19	10	8	1	0	9	0	13	1
McMurtry, Buffalo	6	4	.600	3.44	30	13	1	6	1	1	96.2	102	44	37	6	3	38	4	63	3
Meacham, Omaha	0	0	.000	4.82	7	0	0	2	0	0	9.1	10	5	5	1	0	1	0	10	0
Meier, Louisville	8	6	.571	5.80	27	24	1	0	0	0	135.0	156	95	87	21	7	44	0	98	5
Menendez, Buffalo	4	5	.444	2.42	54	0	0	39	0	24	63.1	50	20	17	5	3	21	2	48	5
Merigliano, Nashville	0	1	.000	6.48	4	0	0	4	0	0	8.1	7	6	6	0	0	6	0	10	2
Milchin, Louisville*	3	7	.300	3.95	32	17	1	6	0	0	111.2	108	56	49	18	1	43	0	72	5
Miller, Buffalo	3	1	.750	4.47	10	10	0	0	0	0	52.1	57	28	26	2	1	14	1	25	0
Miranda, New Orleans*	0	1	.000	3.44	9	2	0	1	0	0	18.1	11	8	7	3	0	10	0	24	2
Moeller, Buffalo*	3	4	.429	4.34	24	11	0	4	0	0	76.2	85	43	37	13	1	21	3	38	4
Mongiello, Nashville	6	4	.600	4.25	39	9	1	19	0	7	91.0	88	44	43	10	4	41	3	73	7
Moore, Indianapolis	0	1	.000	5.86	21	1	0	6	0	0	43.0	46	28	28	4	2	22	1	22	9
Neagle, Buffalo*	0	0	.000	0.00	3	0	0	1	0	0	3.1	3	0	0	0	0	2	0	6	0
Nen, Oklahoma City	0	2	.000	6.67	6	5	0	0	0	0	28.1	45	22	21	3	2	18	0	12	2
Newman, Indianapolis*	1	3	.250	8.55	8	3	0	3	0	0	20.0	24	23	19	3	1	27	0	15	5
Nolte, New Orleans*	0	0	.000	6.35	7	0	0	2	0	0	5.2	7	4	4	1	1	2	0	3	0
Novoa, New Orleans*	10	5	.667	3.42	20	18	2	0	1	0	113.0	105	55	43	20	5	38	3	74	4
Oliveras, Oklahoma City	4	8	.333	5.68	44	7	0	12	0	2	123.2	146	81	78	16	5	52	6	77	7
Ozuna, Louisville	4	4	.000	2.93	35	0	0	20	0	4	40.0	32	16	13	7	3	18	2	41	1
Patterson, Louisville	0	0	.000	9.00	1	0	0	1	0	0	1.0	2	1	1	0	0	1	0	1	0
Pavlik, Oklahoma City	3	2	.600	1.70	6	6	0	0	0	0	37.0	26	12	7	1	2	14	0	32	1
Perez, Oklahoma City	1	0	1.000	12.27	2	0	0	1	0	0	7.1	8	10	10	1	0	4	0	3	2
Petkovsek, Buffalo	3	4	.429	4.33	14	11	1	0	0	0	70.2	74	38	34	8	2	16	0	27	3
Piatt, Buffalo	1	0	1.000	27.00	2	0	0	0	0	0	1.0	3	3	3	0	0	1	0	0	0
Pierce, Omaha*	0	2	.000	5.45	12	2	0	3	0	0	34.2	40	24	21	6	1	13	1	20	0
Powell, Indianapolis*	10	10	.500	4.11	28	27	4	1	0	0	179.2	159	89	82	27	5	71	1	133	13
Rasmussen, Omaha*	7	8	.467	5.03	17	17	3	0	1	0	105.2	124	68	59	16	1	27	0	59	4
Reed, 19 Oma.-5 O.C.	12	7	.632	3.32	24	24	4	0	2	0	162.2	159	68	60	21	3	16	1	79	3
Rightnowar, New Orleans	0	0	.000	10.38	4	0	0	1	0	0	8.2	19	10	10	1	1	2	0	8	0
Robertson, Buffalo*	9	8	.529	4.28	23	23	2	0	0	0	132.1	141	67	63	9	2	52	2	71	10
Robinson, Indianapolis	2	5	.286	6.42	9	9	0	0	0	0	47.2	55	43	34	14	1	24	2	29	1
Roesler, Omaha	1	1	.500	6.16	4	3	0	0	0	0	19.0	21	14	13	3	0	10	0	6	1
Roper, Indianapolis	3	5	.375	4.45	12	12	0	0	0	0	54.2	56	33	27	12	3	30	1	42	2
Ruffcorn, Nashville	2	2	.500	2.80	7	6	1	0	0	0	45.0	30	16	14	5	0	8	1	44	3
Ruffin, 29 Nash.-3 Ind.	4	5	.444	3.11	32	0	0	14	0	2	66.2	51	25	23	5	1	18	5	75	10
Ruskin, Indianapolis*	1	5	.167	5.14	49	2	0	42	0	28	56.0	60	34	32	8	0	22	3	41	1
Sable, Oklahoma City	0	0	.000	0.00	2	0	0	2	0	0	3.0	0	0	0	0	0	0	1	0	0
Sadecki, Oklahoma City	0	3	.000	7.08	12	2	1	3	0	0	20.1	22	17	16	4	3	15	1	13	1
Sampen, Omaha	1	2	.333	3.41	33	0	0	28	0	8	37.0	37	16	14	1	2	13	1	34	1
Sanchez, Omaha	2	8	.200	8.12	16	9	1	3	0	0	51.0	62	46	46	7	0	28	1	31	6
Sauveur, Indianapolis*	2	0	1.000	1.82	5	5	0	0	0	0	34.2	41	10	7	2	2	7	2	21	0
Schooler, Oklahoma City*	1	3	.250	5.91	28	0	0	20	0	5	45.2	59	33	30	3	0	11	3	31	5
Schrenk, Nashville	6	8	.429	3.90	21	20	0	0	0	0	122.1	117	61	53	11	3	47	3	78	6
Schwarz, Nashville	0	0	.000	2.45	7	0	0	2	0	0	11.0	1	3	3	0	0	12	1	8	0
Sebra, Louisville	9	12	.429	4.90	27	26	1	0	0	0	145.0	173	91	79	13	4	52	2	83	7

Pitcher, Team	W	L	Pct.	ERA	G	GS	CG	GF	ShO	Sv.	IP	H	R	ER	HR	HB	BB	Int. BB	SO	WP
Service, Indianapolis	4	2	.667	4.45	21	1	0	13	0	2	30.1	25	16	15	5	0	17	3	28	1
Shaw, Oklahoma City*	2	6	.250	7.91	28	5	0	11	0	0	52.1	78	47	46	8	2	36	3	28	6
Shifflett, Omaha	3	3	.500	4.98	43	0	0	27	0	5	56.0	78	34	31	7	0	15	3	31	2
Shouse, Buffalo*	1	0	1.000	3.83	48	0	0	14	0	2	51.2	54	24	22	7	2	17	2	25	1
Slocumb, Iowa	1	0	1.000	1.50	10	0	0	10	0	7	12.0	7	2	2	0	0	8	0	10	0
Smith, Oklahoma City*	1	2	.333	4.70	3	3	0	0	0	0	15.1	16	11	8	2	1	5	0	12	0
Smith, Buffalo	15	11	.577	4.13	28	28	4	0	1	0	167.2	178	87	77	15	5	38	0	87	7
Sparks, New Orleans	9	13	.409	3.84	29	28	7	0	1	0	180.1	174	89	77	17	5	80	1	104	7
Spradlin, Indianapolis	3	2	.600	3.49	34	0	0	8	0	1	56.2	58	24	22	4	0	12	2	46	2
Steenstra, Iowa	1	0	1.000	6.75	1	1	0	0	0	0	6.2	9	5	5	2	0	4	0	6	0
Stevens, Iowa	4	0	1.000	4.19	24	0	0	15	0	4	34.1	24	16	16	3	1	14	2	29	1
Stieb, 1 Nash.-9 Oma.	3	4	.429	6.09	10	9	1	0	1	0	54.2	72	40	37	10	2	14	0	21	3
Swartzbaugh, Iowa	4	6	.400	5.30	26	9	0	5	0	1	86.2	92	57	51	16	5	44	1	69	6
Tabaka, New Orleans*	6	6	.500	3.24	53	0	0	22	0	1	58.1	50	26	21	3	3	30	2	63	7
Taylor, New Orleans	5	1	.833	2.31	12	8	1	3	0	0	62.1	48	17	16	3	2	21	1	47	1
Thomas, Nashville*	4	6	.400	5.99	18	18	1	0	0	0	100.2	114	73	67	15	1	32	4	67	4
Toliver, Buffalo	1	3	.250	3.65	13	0	0	10	0	1	12.1	13	5	5	0	0	9	4	11	0
Tomberlin, Buffalo*	0	0	.000	0.00	2	0	0	2	0	0	2.0	0	0	0	0	0	3	0	1	1
Trachsel, Iowa	13	6	.684	3.96	27	26	1	1	1	0	170.2	170	78	75	20	6	46	0	135	4
Tracy, 15 Buf.-12 Ind.	4	9	.308	5.24	27	10	2	3	0	0	77.1	85	54	45	11	3	32	3	36	5
Urbani, Louisville*	9	5	.643	2.47	18	13	0	2	0	1	94.2	86	29	26	4	2	23	1	65	2
Vosberg, Iowa*	5	1	.833	3.57	52	0	0	20	0	3	63.0	67	32	25	7	2	22	5	64	7
Walker, Iowa	1	1	.500	2.70	12	0	0	3	0	0	23.1	22	8	7	1	2	9	0	11	3
Wallace, Iowa	0	0	.000	11.25	1	1	0	0	0	0	4.0	8	5	5	0	0	1	0	2	0
Watson, Louisville*	5	4	.556	2.91	17	17	2	0	0	0	120.2	101	46	39	13	4	31	0	86	2
Wendell, Iowa	10	8	.556	4.60	25	25	3	0	0	0	148.2	148	88	76	9	6	47	0	110	9
White, Buffalo	0	3	.000	3.54	7	3	0	1	0	0	28.0	25	13	11	1	0	8	0	16	1
Whiteside, Oklahoma City	2	1	.667	5.56	8	0	0	6	0	1	11.1	17	7	7	1	0	8	4	10	1
Wickander, Indianapolis*	0	0	.000	0.00	1	1	0	0	0	0	3.0	2	0	0	0	0	1	0	2	1
Williams, Iowa*	5	3	.625	3.46	17	13	0	1	0	0	78.0	74	32	30	5	1	37	0	49	3
Wiseman, Louisville	7	9	.438	5.06	33	13	1	7	0	1	112.0	144	79	63	10	3	23	4	39	1
Wishnevski, New Orleans	5	3	.625	4.09	52	0	0	33	0	10	70.1	68	34	32	9	9	17	2	72	3
Zimmerman, Buffalo	3	1	.750	4.08	33	0	0	8	0	1	46.1	45	23	21	5	0	28	3	32	2

BALKS—Burrows, Moeller, 5 each; A. Anderson, Curry, 4 each; R. Brown, Robinson, Schrenk, Sebra, Watson, Wendell, 3 each; P. Anderson, Dyer, Farrell, Howard, Kiser, Knox, Leon, McAndrew, Oliveras, Powell, Rasmussen, Roper, Schooler, Sparks, Williams, 2 each; Austin, Baldwin, Barber, Bennett, K. Brown, Campbell, Carter, Clark, Compres, Dabney, Farmer, Grott, Guetterman, Higuera, Ignasiak, Irvine, Keyser, Lee, Lynch, Maysey, Meier, Newman, Novoa, Robertson, Schwarz, L. Smith, Tabaka, Taylor, Thomas, Trachsel, Tracy, Vosberg, Whiteside, Wiseman, Wishnevski, 1 each.

COMBINATION SHUTOUTS—Ballard-Menendez, Beatty-Neagle-Zimmerman, McMurtry-Toliver, Smith-Menendez, Tracy-Dalton, Buffalo; Hill-Grott, Kennedy-Ruskin, Luebbers-Kennedy-Lynch-Spradlin-Ruskin, Luebbers-Service, Indianapolis; Boskie-Ilsley-Slocumb, Brennan-Ilsley, Ilsley-Stevens, Ilsley-Stevens-Bullinger, Ilsley-Swartzbaugh, Ilsley-Swartzbaugh-Vosberg-Czajkowski-Johnson, Wendell-Ilsley-Bullinger, Wendell-Stevens, Iowa; Urbani-Guetterman, Urbani-Guetterman-Ozuna, Wiseman-Dixon, Louisville; Baldwin-Drahman, Baldwin-Schrenk-Mongiello, Thomas-Bolton, Nashville; McAndrew-Tabaka, Taylor-Tabaka, New Orleans; Leon-Lee, Oklahoma City; Boddicker-Haney-Burgos, Curry-Clark-Burgos, Gardner-Shifflett-Sampen, Magnante-Clark, Magnante-Shifflett, Roesler-Burgos-Sampen, Sanchez-Clark-Curry-Burgos, Omaha.

NO-HIT GAMES—None.

FIELDING

TEAM

Team	Pct.	G	PO	A	E	DP	PB
Iowa	.980	144	3835	1648	114	166	20
Louisville	.979	144	3769	1603	115	141	12
New Orleans	.978	144	3750	1538	121	143	20
Omaha	.977	144	3732	1572	127	159	19
Buffalo	.976	144	3745	1668	134	186	15
Oklahoma City	.975	144	3748	1568	135	145	14
Nashville	.973	143	3751	1621	148	126	15
Indianapolis	.971	143	3692	1432	152	117	16

Triple play—Louisville.

INDIVIDUAL

FIRST BASEMEN

*Throws lefthanded.

Player, Team	Pct.	G	PO	A	E	DP
Afenir, Indianapolis	.989	10	86	7	1	8
Aude, Buffalo	.995	18	174	13	1	17
Balboni, Oklahoma City	1.000	7	59	10	0	2
Barbara, New Orleans*	.994	81	676	44	4	61
Bell, Buffalo*	.995	21	174	16	1	23
Berger, Oklahoma City	1.000	1	2	0	0	0
Byington, New Orleans	1.000	19	129	11	0	15
Caceres, New Orleans	.993	26	134	13	1	18
Canseco, Louisville	.979	14	85	8	2	4
Cepicky, Nashville	.929	2	13	0	1	2
Costo, Indianapolis	.992	67	468	30	4	41
Cron, Nashville	.993	91	766	63	6	67
Davis, Oklahoma City	1.000	2	11	1	0	3
Denson, Nashville	.981	56	534	48	11	38
Distefano, Oklahoma City*	.987	42	364	23	5	43
Dorsett, Indianapolis	.932	7	50	5	4	2
Fitzgerald, New Orleans	.941	5	26	6	2	3
Franco, Iowa	.996	52	445	39	2	47
Fulton, Louisville	1.000	1	11	0	0	2
Gregg, Indianapolis*	.980	43	312	29	7	32
HAMELIN, Omaha*	.991	127	1104	90	11	116
Hughes, Indianapolis*	1.000	5	24	2	0	1
Jennings, Iowa*	.996	48	433	36	2	50
Kiser, New Orleans*	1.000	1	1	0	0	0
Knapp, Omaha	1.000	1	3	0	0	0
Kremers, New Orleans	.983	5	52	5	1	12
Leiper, Buffalo	1.000	5	55	1	0	7
Lewis, Iowa*	1.000	8	62	8	0	9
Lockhart, Louisville	1.000	1	0	1	0	0
Lonigro, Iowa	1.000	1	3	0	0	1
Lyons, Louisville	.986	51	449	32	7	44
McGinnis, Omaha	.979	14	87	8	2	11
Merullo, Nashville	.889	1	8	0	1	0
Miller, Oklahoma City	.995	48	400	25	2	44
Morman, Buffalo	.991	89	814	60	8	97
Morris, Indianapolis*	1.000	3	26	3	0	1
O'Leary, New Orleans*	1.000	1	2	0	0	0
Patterson, Louisville	.992	46	339	23	3	36
Peltier, Oklahoma City*	.986	37	328	21	5	30
Prager, Louisville*	.984	43	344	22	6	33
Riesgo, New Orleans	1.000	3	22	1	0	3
Rohrmeier, Omaha	1.000	2	1	0	0	0
Royer, Louisville	1.000	6	48	1	0	6
Sable, Oklahoma City	1.000	1	1	0	0	0
Sheets, New Orleans	.994	24	155	9	1	14
Shelton, Buffalo*	.979	24	170	13	4	27
Shines, Indianapolis	.967	23	199	9	7	17
Stephens, Oklahoma City	.991	16	107	8	1	11
Stephenson, Omaha*	.983	7	49	10	1	5
Suero, New Orleans*	1.000	2	10	0	0	0
Tedder, Nashville*	1.000	1	1	0	0	0
Valentin, New Orleans	1.000	1	1	0	0	0
Varsho, Indianapolis	1.000	3	21	0	0	3
Villanueva, Louisville	.987	9	71	3	1	8
Williams, New Orleans	1.000	1	6	1	0	0
Wilson, Omaha	.909	1	10	0	1	1
Worthington, Iowa	1.000	2	6	1	0	0
Zambrano, Iowa	.988	48	391	32	5	44

SECOND BASEMEN

Player, Team	Pct.	G	PO	A	E	DP
K. Anderson, 9 Iowa-1 Ind.	.976	10	13	27	1	5
Beasley, Buffalo	.959	28	68	74	6	23
Brady, Nashville	.800	2	1	3	1	0
Byington, New Orleans	.914	7	13	19	3	6
Caceres, New Orleans	.983	63	115	175	5	42
Carter, New Orleans	1.000	1	1	1	0	0
Cirillo, New Orleans	1.000	4	4	13	0	5
Diaz, Omaha	.931	10	11	16	2	5
Diaz, Oklahoma City	.984	15	21	41	1	4
Figueroa, Louisville	.988	16	40	44	1	9
Finn, New Orleans	.968	56	97	116	7	29
Gilbert, Nashville	1.000	7	12	22	0	4
Gomez, Iowa	1.000	1	2	2	0	0
Huff, Nashville	1.000	1	1	2	0	0
Huson, Oklahoma City	.962	6	11	14	1	5
Jackson, Oklahoma City	1.000	1	1	4	0	1
Jones, Louisville	.988	86	176	250	5	58
Kessinger, Indianapolis	1.000	6	9	10	0	1
Koelling, Indianapolis	1.000	2	5	8	0	1
Kremblas, Indianapolis	.982	21	47	64	2	13
Lockhart, Louisville	.980	45	74	127	4	31
Lonigro, Iowa	.984	12	27	34	1	0
Magallanes, Oklahoma City	.986	24	56	82	2	27
Martin, Nashville	.976	137	291	438	18	86
Mota, Omaha	.971	32	52	83	4	23
Munoz, Buffalo	.962	23	37	64	4	21
Noboa, Indianapolis	.989	42	73	112	2	28
Patterson, Louisville	.667	2	0	2	1	0
Pena, Louisville	1.000	6	10	18	0	2
Rohde, Buffalo	.974	53	104	160	7	49
Sable, Oklahoma City	.975	22	55	64	3	18
Schreiber, Buffalo	1.000	1	3	3	0	2
Scott, Indianapolis	.964	77	161	187	13	40
Shave, Oklahoma City	.973	86	164	232	11	55
Shumpert, Omaha	.972	108	190	303	14	73
SMITH, Iowa	.983	126	241	396	11	98
Suero, New Orleans	.953	36	70	72	7	19
Wehner, Buffalo	.968	44	106	139	8	37

Triple play—Lockhart.

SHORTSTOPS

Player, Team	Pct.	G	PO	A	E	DP
K. Anderson, 58 Iowa-11 Ind.	.969	69	106	171	9	44
Beltre, Nashville	.952	134	190	404	30	77
Caceres, New Orleans	.976	27	25	55	2	11
Carter, New Orleans	1.000	1	0	1	0	1
Cirillo, New Orleans	1.000	1	0	3	0	0
Cooper, Buffalo	1.000	1	2	1	0	2
Costo, Indianapolis	.500	1	0	1	1	0
Cromer, Louisville	.969	85	123	253	12	59
Diaz, Omaha	.947	29	41	66	6	14
Diaz, Oklahoma City	.943	7	15	18	2	4
Figueroa, Louisville	.971	51	77	156	7	38
Finn, New Orleans	.958	9	10	13	1	3
Gilbert, Nashville	.873	13	17	31	7	7
Gomez, Iowa	1.000	2	2	8	0	3
Green, Indianapolis	.951	71	76	176	13	28
Greene, Indianapolis	1.000	6	8	21	0	4
HANLON, Oklahoma City	.961	117	198	337	22	71
Hernandez, Iowa	.976	6	14	26	1	7
Howard, Buffalo	.964	46	76	137	8	34
Huson, Oklahoma City	.955	6	6	15	1	4
Jackson, Oklahoma City	1.000	1	1	4	0	1
Jones, Louisville	.962	15	11	39	2	5
Kessinger, Indianapolis	.985	28	41	91	2	22
Kremblas, Indianapolis	.916	41	47	84	12	14
Leiper, Buffalo	1.000	1	0	1	0	0
Lonigro, Iowa	.957	20	28	60	4	13
Martin, Nashville	1.000	1	1	4	0	0
Mota, Omaha	.966	56	75	125	7	29
Munoz, Buffalo	.954	15	20	42	3	6
Riesgo, New Orleans	.714	2	0	5	2	0
Rohde, Buffalo	.972	64	101	211	9	51
Rossy, Omaha	.958	27	44	93	6	25
Sable, Oklahoma City	.909	5	9	11	2	4
Sandoval, Buffalo	.966	60	86	200	10	50
Schreiber, Buffalo	.976	7	16	24	1	2
Shave, Oklahoma City	.973	15	26	45	2	12
Shields, Iowa	.950	66	121	186	16	55
Valentin, New Orleans	.951	119	211	351	29	80

THIRD BASEMEN

Player, Team	Pct.	G	PO	A	E	DP
K. Anderson, Indianapolis	.923	9	6	18	2	2
Byington, New Orleans	.971	82	67	165	7	16
Caceres, New Orleans	1.000	9	7	15	0	2
Cirillo, New Orleans	.972	53	42	129	5	18
Coomer, Nashville	.895	58	30	107	16	6
Cooper, Buffalo	.932	73	38	153	14	23
Costo, Indianapolis	.897	13	6	29	4	7
Cron, Nashville	.924	32	24	61	7	6
Davis, Oklahoma City	.944	20	7	27	2	1
Diaz, Omaha	.931	16	12	15	2	1
Diaz, Oklahoma City	1.000	26	17	46	0	6
Figueroa, Louisville	.966	14	13	15	1	2
Finn, New Orleans	1.000	4	2	3	0	1
Gilbert, Nashville	.909	41	12	68	8	7
Goff, Buffalo	1.000	2	1	5	0	1
Gomez, Iowa	.833	3	0	10	2	2
Greene, Indianapolis	.905	92	69	150	23	6
Hall, Nashville	.926	28	7	56	5	4
Hiatt, Omaha	.946	12	11	24	2	3
Huson, Oklahoma City	.976	14	17	23	1	2
Jackson, Oklahoma City	.966	41	16	99	4	11
Kremblas, Indianapolis	.951	35	29	87	6	9
Leiper, Buffalo	.938	22	16	44	4	7
Lockhart, Louisville	.950	48	27	107	7	5
Lofton, Indianapolis	.833	2	2	3	1	0
Lonigro, Iowa	1.000	4	2	8	0	0
Magallanes, Oklahoma City	.960	9	8	16	1	2
McGinnis, Omaha	.959	45	28	88	5	7
Miller, Omaha	.909	6	2	8	1	0
Miller, Oklahoma City	.941	5	1	15	1	0
Mota, Omaha	.600	4	0	3	2	1
Noboa, Indianapolis	1.000	1	0	2	0	0
Patterson, Louisville	1.000	7	4	11	0	0
Pedre, Iowa	1.000	1	0	1	0	0
Rohde, Buffalo	.833	7	1	14	3	1
Rossy, Omaha	.976	16	10	31	1	5
Royer, Louisville	.960	85	61	201	11	18
Sable, Oklahoma City	.941	41	25	71	6	12
Schreiber, Buffalo	.833	7	4	11	3	4
Shields, Iowa	.980	17	10	40	1	3
Shines, Indianapolis	.900	5	2	7	1	1
Wehner, Buffalo	.941	47	27	107	9	17
Williams, New Orleans	.952	6	8	12	1	1
Wilson, Omaha	.951	60	40	115	8	14
WORTHINGTON, Iowa	.940	124	71	240	20	22

Triple play—Royer.

OUTFIELDERS

Player, Team	Pct.	G	PO	A	E	DP
Abner, Omaha	.988	34	75	4	1	2
Bell, Buffalo*	1.000	10	12	0	0	0
Brumfield, Indianapolis	.951	33	74	4	4	0
Bullett, Buffalo*	.970	102	222	6	7	1
Caceres, New Orleans	1.000	1	1	1	0	1
Canseco, Louisville	.967	25	28	1	1	0
Carter, New Orleans	.977	100	243	9	6	1
Carter, Indianapolis	.971	53	95	4	3	0
Cepicky, Nashville	.960	24	20	4	1	0
Chance, Iowa	.985	75	130	5	2	1
Cooper, Buffalo	1.000	30	49	1	0	0
Costo, Indianapolis	1.000	29	42	1	0	0
Coughlin, Nashville*	1.000	2	3	0	0	0
Cummings, Buffalo	.978	58	90	1	2	1
Dascenzo, Oklahoma City*	.984	38	118	4	2	3
Dauphin, 16 Iowa-7 Ind.*	.953	23	40	1	2	1
Davis, Oklahoma City	1.000	2	6	0	0	0
Davis, New Orleans	1.000	6	15	1	0	0
Diaz, New Orleans	1.000	13	38	1	0	0
Diggs, New Orleans	1.000	10	25	1	0	0
Distefano, Oklahoma City*	.954	72	119	5	6	1
Dozier, Louisville	.940	40	60	3	4	1
Ducey, Oklahoma City	.973	100	244	8	7	1
Espy, Indianapolis	1.000	19	33	2	0	0
Finn, New Orleans	.960	52	66	6	3	0
Fitzgerald, New Orleans	1.000	3	1	0	0	0
Franco, Iowa	1.000	3	5	0	0	0
Gilbert, Nashville	.955	33	40	2	2	0
Grayum, Iowa	1.000	1	2	0	0	0
Green, Indianapolis	1.000	7	18	0	0	0
Greer, Oklahoma City*	1.000	8	16	0	0	0
Gregg, Indianapolis*	1.000	12	18	0	0	0
Hall, Nashville	.989	85	169	7	2	1
Harris, New Orleans	.976	94	241	5	6	2
Hernandez, Indianapolis	.985	75	183	9	3	1
Housie, New Orleans	1.000	59	86	3	0	1
Huff, Nashville	.986	88	206	3	3	5
Hughes, Indianapolis*	.965	72	136	3	5	1
Huson, Oklahoma City	1.000	3	5	0	0	0
Jackson, Oklahoma City	.973	41	66	5	2	0
Jennings, Iowa*	1.000	6	9	0	0	0
Jensen, Iowa	.923	20	23	1	2	0
Jeter, Nashville	.955	41	80	4	4	1
Jordan, Louisville	1.000	37	75	2	0	0
KINGERY, Omaha*	.996	105	212	15	1	5
Komminsk, Nashville	.983	108	160	9	3	2
Koslofski, Omaha	.983	109	285	13	6	3
Kremblas, Indianapolis	.909	20	29	1	3	0
Lampkin, New Orleans	1.000	2	2	0	0	0

Player, Team	Pct.	G	PO	A	E	DP
Leiper, Buffalo	1.000	33	57	3	0	1
Lockhart, Louisville	.984	31	56	5	1	0
Long, Omaha*	1.000	15	33	4	0	1
Lukachyk, New Orleans	1.000	8	14	0	0	0
Mabry, Louisville	1.000	1	3	0	0	0
Maclin, Louisville*	1.000	59	100	2	0	0
McAndrew, New Orleans	1.000	1	1	0	0	0
Merchant, Indianapolis	1.000	1	1	0	0	0
Mieske, New Orleans	.983	57	114	4	2	0
Miller, Oklahoma City	.966	39	55	2	2	0
Morris, Louisville	.980	20	46	2	1	0
Morris, Oklahoma City*	1.000	12	18	1	0	0
Morrow, Oklahoma City	1.000	7	17	0	0	0
Newson, Nashville*	.988	49	74	7	1	1
O'Leary, New Orleans*	.970	110	187	8	6	1
Ortiz, Omaha	1.000	3	5	0	0	0
Patterson, Louisville	1.000	7	4	0	0	0
Peltier, Oklahoma City*	1.000	11	18	1	0	0
Pennyfeather, Buffalo	.987	111	293	21	4	4
Prager, Louisville*	.969	23	29	2	1	0
Pulliam, Omaha	.948	43	102	7	6	2
Raines, Nashville	1.000	2	3	0	0	0
Ramsey, Iowa	.977	127	292	7	7	5
Rhodes, 84 Oma.-35 Iowa*	.963	119	192	17	8	2
Riesgo, New Orleans	1.000	15	26	0	0	0
Roberson, Iowa	.966	64	110	4	4	0
Rohde, Buffalo	1.000	7	11	0	0	0
Rohrmeier, Omaha	1.000	39	70	2	0	0
Sable, Oklahoma City	.980	23	48	0	1	0
Savinon, Louisville	1.000	31	51	3	0	0
Sheets, New Orleans	1.000	32	38	4	0	1
Shelton, Buffalo*	.964	17	25	2	1	2
Snider, Louisville	.969	103	212	8	7	2
Sparks, New Orleans	1.000	1	1	0	0	0
Stephenson, Omaha*	1.000	8	24	0	0	0
Suero, New Orleans	1.000	1	3	0	0	0
Tedder, Nashville*	1.000	41	65	3	0	0
Thomas, Louisville	.957	97	191	7	9	1
Tomberlin, Buffalo*	.957	60	104	7	5	1
Tubbs, Indianapolis	.971	91	195	7	6	2
Varsho, Indianapolis	.923	26	48	0	4	0
Wade, Iowa	1.000	34	67	3	0	1
Wilson, Buffalo	.984	25	59	4	1	0
Yacopino, New Orleans*	.978	23	44	1	1	0
Young, Indianapolis	1.000	28	53	0	0	0
Zambrano, Iowa	.984	70	112	8	2	0

Triple play—Prager.

CATCHERS

Player, Team	Pct.	G	PO	A	E	DP	PB
Afenir, Indianapolis	.979	37	219	13	5	0	6
C. Alvarez, Nashville	1.000	11	75	0	0	0	1
Davis, Oklahoma City	.994	57	326	23	2	5	4
Distefano, Oklahoma City*	.923	2	12	0	1	0	1
Dorsett, Indianapolis	.993	61	389	45	3	4	5
Edge, Buffalo	1.000	1	2	1	0	1	0
Ellis, Louisville	1.000	45	192	14	0	0	1
Encarnacion, Buffalo	1.000	3	14	1	0	0	1
Fitzgerald, New Orleans	.990	65	362	26	4	8	6
Fulton, Louisville	.990	43	182	18	2	1	5
Goff, Buffalo	.987	100	499	48	7	2	12
Hall, Nashville	1.000	5	15	2	0	0	1
Kappesser, New Orleans	.964	4	22	5	1	0	2
Kennedy, Oklahoma City	.973	6	35	1	1	0	1
Kmak, New Orleans	.984	20	106	18	2	1	2
Knapp, Omaha	.988	67	357	43	5	9	6
Kremers, New Orleans	.978	38	202	19	5	2	5
Lampkin, New Orleans	.982	20	150	12	3	1	3
Lyons, Louisville	.995	39	192	21	1	5	1
Marx, Buffalo	1.000	4	21	1	0	0	0
McGinnis, Omaha	1.000	8	59	6	0	0	0
Mercado, Iowa	1.000	8	73	5	0	0	1
Merullo, Nashville	.985	83	427	40	7	3	10
Nilsson, New Orleans	.984	11	55	7	1	1	2
Pagnozzi, Louisville	.966	12	51	6	2	1	2
Pappas, Louisville	.978	21	131	5	3	0	0
Pedre, Iowa	.998	60	383	40	1	3	9
Petralli, Oklahoma City	.857	1	5	1	1	0	1
Romero, Buffalo	.973	36	168	13	5	2	2
Santovenia, Omaha	.990	77	446	44	5	7	13
Stephens, Oklahoma City	.977	81	419	50	11	6	7
Villanueva, Louisville	.992	18	117	11	1	1	3
WALBECK, Iowa	.998	79	496	64	1	9	10
Wilson, Indianapolis	.994	50	314	24	2	5	5
Wrona, Nashville	.989	72	400	52	5	7	3

Triple play—Villanueva.

PITCHERS

Player, Team	Pct.	G	PO	A	E	DP
Acker, Oklahoma City	.667	6	0	2	1	0
Ahern, Omaha	1.000	6	0	3	0	0
Alberro, Oklahoma City	1.000	12	1	1	0	0

Player, Team	Pct.	G	PO	A	E	DP
Alexander, Oklahoma City	.333	10	0	1	2	0
Anderson, Oklahoma City*	.969	19	5	26	1	1
M. Anderson, Indianapolis	.962	23	9	16	1	2
Anderson, Louisville	1.000	11	9	13	0	1
Arnsberg, 6 Ind.-23 Lou.	1.000	29	3	9	0	2
Austin, New Orleans	1.000	8	0	1	0	0
Ayala, Indianapolis	.889	5	2	6	1	1
Backlund, Buffalo	1.000	5	3	4	0	0
Baldwin, Nashville	1.000	10	6	7	0	0
Ballard, Buffalo*	1.000	12	6	18	0	4
Barber, Louisville	1.000	1	1	0	0	0
Barfield, Nashville*	1.000	14	5	12	0	1
Beatty, Buffalo*	.875	20	3	4	1	0
Bere, Nashville	1.000	8	4	8	0	0
Boddicker, Omaha	1.000	3	2	1	0	0
Bolton, Nashville	1.000	18	9	18	0	1
Boskie, Iowa	.947	11	6	12	1	1
Brennan, Omaha	.906	28	14	34	5	5
Bronkey, Oklahoma City	1.000	29	2	4	0	0
Brown, Omaha	.963	26	2	24	1	1
Brown, Oklahoma City	.950	30	4	15	1	0
Buckels, Louisville	.867	40	3	10	2	0
Bullinger, Iowa	1.000	49	5	10	0	0
Burgos, Omaha*	1.000	48	4	14	0	1
Burrows, Oklahoma City*	.968	27	5	25	1	2
Campbell, Omaha*	.917	27	2	9	1	2
Campos, Indianapolis	.944	19	9	8	1	1
Carter, Nashville	1.000	11	1	9	0	1
Cecena, Buffalo	1.000	6	0	1	0	0
Cimorelli, Louisville	.909	27	4	6	1	1
Clark, Omaha	1.000	51	6	9	0	2
Cole, 6 Buf.-6 N.O.	1.000	12	1	3	0	0
Compres, Louisville	1.000	21	3	1	0	0
Corbett, Iowa*	1.000	8	1	2	0	0
Creek, Louisville*	1.000	2	0	2	0	0
Culberson, Indianapolis	1.000	2	0	1	0	0
Curry, Omaha	.902	33	8	29	4	4
Czajkowski, Iowa	1.000	42	4	11	0	0
Dabney, Nashville*	.957	51	11	11	1	1
Dalton, Buffalo*	1.000	25	2	7	0	0
Dewey, Buffalo	1.000	22	1	7	0	0
DiPino, Omaha*	1.000	15	3	3	0	2
Dixon, Louisville*	.857	57	1	11	2	1
Drahman, Nashville	.857	54	3	3	1	0
Dreyer, Oklahoma City	.963	16	6	20	1	0
Dyer, Iowa	1.000	14	2	1	0	1
Eiland, Oklahoma City	1.000	7	1	8	0	0
Farmer, New Orleans	1.000	20	2	10	0	0
Farrell, New Orleans*	.939	26	8	23	2	4
Figueroa, Louisville	1.000	1	0	1	0	0
Fireovid, Oklahoma City	1.000	7	2	6	0	0
Garcia, Nashville	1.000	7	3	8	0	1
Gardner, Omaha	1.000	8	5	5	0	0
Grott, Indianapolis*	1.000	33	3	7	0	0
Guetterman, Louisville*	.917	25	5	6	1	0
Hall, Nashville	1.000	1	0	1	0	0
Hancock, Buffalo*	.905	11	8	11	2	1
Haney, Omaha*	.923	8	2	10	1	2
Hartsock, Iowa	.900	9	2	7	1	0
Helling, Oklahoma City	.500	2	1	0	1	0
Higuera, New Orleans*	1.000	3	0	2	0	0
Hill, Indianapolis	1.000	20	2	5	0	1
Hope, Buffalo	1.000	4	2	2	0	0
Howard, Nashville*	.778	43	2	5	2	0
Hunter, New Orleans	1.000	39	3	19	0	3
Hunter, Buffalo	1.000	11	2	1	0	0
Hurst, Oklahoma City*	.917	16	1	10	1	0
Ignasiak, New Orleans	.923	35	3	9	1	0
Ilsley, Iowa*	.979	48	11	35	1	5
Irvine, Buffalo	1.000	37	7	11	0	1
Johnson, New Orleans	1.000	13	1	2	0	0
Johnson, Iowa*	1.000	9	1	2	0	0
Johnston, Buffalo	1.000	26	1	3	0	0
Jones, Nashville	1.000	7	3	2	0	0
Kaiser, Indianapolis*	1.000	1	1	0	0	0
Kennedy, Indianapolis	1.000	39	5	18	0	0
Keyser, Nashville	1.000	30	19	25	0	2
Kiefer, New Orleans	.889	5	1	7	1	0
Kilgus, Louisville*	.909	9	2	18	2	1
Kiser, New Orleans*	1.000	50	2	5	0	1
Knox, Louisville*	1.000	7	2	11	0	0
Leach, Nashville	1.000	5	3	1	0	0
Lee, Oklahoma City	.889	52	4	12	2	1
Lefferts, Oklahoma City*	1.000	1	0	1	0	0
Leon, Oklahoma City	.857	13	2	4	1	0
Luebbers, Indianapolis	1.000	15	4	14	0	2
Lynch, Indianapolis*	.963	59	5	21	1	1
Magnante, Omaha*	.967	33	10	19	1	4
Maldonado, New Orleans	1.000	12	0	1	0	0
Manuel, Indianapolis	.889	21	2	6	1	0
Maysey, New Orleans	1.000	29	3	2	0	0
McAndrew, New Orleans	.969	27	15	16	1	2
McElroy, Iowa*	1.000	9	1	5	0	1
McMurtry, Buffalo	.929	30	6	20	2	0
Meacham, Omaha	1.000	7	2	3	0	1

Player, Team	Pct.	G	PO	A	E	DP	Player, Team	Pct.	G	PO	A	E	DP
Meier, Louisville	.957	27	8	14	1	0	Schooler, Oklahoma City	1.000	28	4	10	0	1
Menendez, Buffalo	1.000	54	6	7	0	4	Schrenk, Nashville	.963	21	9	17	1	1
Merigliano, Nashville	1.000	7	1	0	0	0	Schwarz, Nashville	1.000	7	0	3	0	0
Milchin, Louisville*	1.000	32	4	9	0	0	Sebra, Louisville	.955	27	16	26	2	2
Miller, Buffalo	1.000	10	0	7	0	0	Service, Indianapolis	1.000	21	0	3	0	1
Miranda, New Orleans*	1.000	9	0	4	0	0	Shaw, Oklahoma City*	.917	28	2	9	1	0
Moeller, Buffalo*	1.000	24	7	9	0	0	Shifflett, Omaha	1.000	43	4	11	0	0
Mongiello, Nashville	1.000	39	4	5	0	1	Shouse, Buffalo*	1.000	48	3	9	0	1
Moore, Indianapolis	.800	21	0	4	1	0	Slocumb, Iowa	1.000	10	2	3	0	0
Nen, Oklahoma City	1.000	6	0	4	0	0	Smith, Oklahoma City*	.800	3	0	4	1	0
Newman, Indianapolis*	.750	8	0	3	1	2	Smith, Buffalo	.969	28	12	19	1	2
Nolte, New Orleans*	1.000	7	0	2	0	0	SPARKS, New Orleans	1.000	29	9	41	0	2
Novoa, New Orleans*	.824	20	3	11	3	1	Spradlin, Indianapolis	1.000	34	3	7	0	0
Oliveras, Oklahoma City	.944	44	8	26	2	3	Stevens, Iowa	1.000	24	2	2	0	1
Ozuna, Louisville	1.000	35	2	5	0	0	Stieb, 1 Nash.-9 Oma.	1.000	10	6	13	0	0
Pavlik, Oklahoma City	.889	6	2	6	1	0	Swartzbaugh, Iowa	.875	26	9	12	3	3
Perez, Oklahoma City	1.000	2	0	2	0	0	Tabaka, New Orleans*	.900	53	2	7	1	1
Petkovsek, Buffalo	1.000	14	5	17	0	3	Taylor, New Orleans	1.000	12	4	9	0	2
Piatt, Buffalo	1.000	2	0	1	0	0	Thomas, Nashville*	.950	18	5	14	1	0
Pierce, Omaha*	1.000	12	0	6	0	1	Toliver, Buffalo	1.000	13	0	1	0	0
Powell, Indianapolis*	1.000	28	4	14	0	1	Trachsel, Iowa	.970	27	11	21	1	0
Rasmussen, Omaha*	.909	17	7	23	3	2	Tracy, 15 Buf.-12 Ind.	.955	27	12	9	1	2
Reed, 19 Oma.-5 O.C.	.931	24	13	14	2	4	Urbani, Louisville*	1.000	18	1	14	0	2
Robertson, Buffalo*	.962	23	6	19	1	1	Vosberg, Iowa*	.920	52	6	17	2	1
Robinson, Indianapolis	1.000	9	4	5	0	0	Walker, Iowa	1.000	12	0	3	0	0
Roesler, Omaha	1.000	4	1	1	0	0	Watson, Louisville*	1.000	17	12	17	0	2
Roper, Indianapolis	.933	12	5	9	1	0	Wendell, Iowa	.933	25	10	18	2	2
Ruffcorn, Nashville	.923	7	3	9	1	1	White, Iowa	1.000	7	0	2	0	0
Ruffin, 29 Nash.-3 Ind.	.867	32	6	7	2	1	Whiteside, Oklahoma City	1.000	8	0	1	0	0
Ruskin, Indianapolis*	1.000	49	2	6	0	1	Williams, Iowa*	.955	17	7	14	1	0
Sadecki, Oklahoma City	1.000	12	0	3	0	0	Wiseman, Louisville	.957	33	11	11	1	1
Sampen, Omaha	1.000	33	2	9	0	1	Wishnevski, New Orleans	1.000	52	5	3	0	0
Sanchez, Omaha	.857	16	6	6	2	0	Zimmerman, Buffalo	1.000	33	1	8	0	0
Sauveur, Indianapolis*	1.000	5	2	5	0	0							

The following players did not have any fielding statistics at the positions indicated or appeared only as a designated hitter, pinch-hitter or pinch-runner: Afenir, of; W. Alvarez, p; Bennett, p; Berger, of; Bohanon, p; Canate, of; S. Carter, ss; Cary, p; Chance, 1b, p; Dickson, p; Farrell, of; Figueroa, of; Fitzgerald, 3b; Franco, 2b, p; Fulton, p; Hanlon, 3b; Jackson, 1b; Knapp, p; Kremblas, p; Kremers, of; Manzanillo, p; McCoy, dh; Keith Miller (Oklahoma City), 2b; Moore, of; Mota, of; Neagle, p; Noboa, of; Patterson, p; Pedre, 1b; Riesgo, 3b; Rightnowar, p; Sable, p; Steenstra, p; Tomberlin, p; Valentin, of; Vindivich, ph; Wallace, p; Wehner, of; Wickander, p.

LEAGUE CHAMPIONS

Year	Team	Pct.	Year	Team	Pct.	Year	Team	Pct.
1902—	Indianapolis	.683	1942—	Kansas City	.549	1972—	Wichita	.621
1903—	St. Paul	.657		Columbus (3rd)‡	.532		Evansville*	.593
1904—	St. Paul	.646	1943—	Milwaukee	.596	1973—	Iowa	.610
1905—	Columbus	.658		Columbus (3rd)‡	.532		Tulsa*	.504
1906—	Columbus	.615	1944—	Milwaukee	.667	1974—	Indianapolis	.578
1907—	Columbus	.584		Louisville (3rd)‡	.574		Tulsa*	.567
1908—	Indianapolis	.601	1945—	Milwaukee	.604	1975—	Evansville*	.566
1909—	Louisville	.554		Louisville (3rd)‡	.545		Denver	.596
1910—	Minneapolis	.637	1946—	Louisville†	.601	1976—	Denver*	.632
1911—	Minneapolis	.600	1947—	Kansas City	.608		Omaha	.574
1912—	Minneapolis	.636		Milwaukee (3rd)†	.513	1977—	Omaha	.563
1913—	Milwaukee	.599	1948—	Indianapolis	.649		Denver*	.522
1914—	Milwaukee	.590		St. Paul (3rd)‡	.558	1978—	Indianapolis	.578
1915—	Louisville	.597	1949—	St. Paul	.608		Omaha*	.489
1916—	Louisville	.605		Indianapolis (2nd)‡	.604	1979—	Evansville*	.574
1917—	Indianapolis	.588	1950—	Minneapolis	.584		Oklahoma City	.533
1918—	Kansas City	.589		Columbus (3rd)‡	.549	1980—	Denver	.676
1919—	St. Paul	.610	1951—	Milwaukee†	.623		Springfield*	.551
1920—	St. Paul	.701	1952—	Milwaukee	.656	1981—	Omaha	.581
1921—	Louisville	.583		Kansas City (2nd)‡	.578		Denver*	.559
1922—	St. Paul	.641	1953—	Toledo	.584	1982—	Indianapolis*	.551
1923—	Kansas City	.675		Kansas City (2nd)‡	.571		Omaha	.518
1924—	St. Paul	.578	1954—	Indianapolis	.625	1983—	Louisville	.578
1925—	Louisville	.635		Louisville (2nd)‡	.556		Denver‡	.545
1926—	Louisville	.629	1955—	Minneapolis†	.597	1984—	Denver	.513
1927—	Toledo	.601	1956—	Indianapolis†	.597		Louisville‡	.510
1928—	Indianapolis	.593	1957—	Wichita	.604	1985—	Oklahoma City	.556
1929—	Kansas City	.665		Denver (2nd)†	.584		Louisville*	.521
1930—	Louisville	.608	1958—	Charleston	.589	1986—	Indianapolis*	.563
1931—	St. Paul	.623		Minneapolis (3rd)‡	.536		Denver	.535
1932—	Minneapolis	.595	1959—	Louisville§	.599	1987—	Denver	.564
1933—	Columbus*	.604		Omaha§	.516		Indianapolis‡	.536
	Minneapolis	.562		Minneapolis (2nd)‡	.586	1988—	Indianapolis*	.627
1934—	Minneapolis	.570	1960—	Denver	.571		Omaha	.570
	Columbus*	.556		Louisville (2nd)‡	.556	1989—	Indianapolis*	.596
1935—	Minneapolis	.591	1961—	Indianapolis	.573		Omaha	.507
1936—	Milwaukee†	.584		Louisville (2nd)‡	.533	1990—	Omaha*	.589
1937—	Columbus†	.584	1962—	Indianapolis	.605		Nashville	.585
1938—	St. Paul	.596		Louisville (4th)‡	.486	1991—	Buffalo	.566
	Kansas City (2nd)‡	.556	1963-1968—Did not operate.				Denver*	.549
1939—	Kansas City	.695	1969—	Omaha	.607	1992—	Buffalo	.604
	Louisville (4th)‡	.490	1970—	Omaha*	.529		Oklahoma City*	.514
1940—	Kansas City	.625		Denver	.504	1993—	Iowa*	.590
	Louisville (4th)‡	.500	1971—	Indianapolis	.604		Nashville	.566
1941—	Columbus†	.621		Denver*	.521			

*Won playoff (East vs. West). †Won championship and four-team playoff. ‡Won four-team playoff. §Respective Eastern and Western division winners.

INTERNATIONAL LEAGUE

FINAL STANDINGS

EAST DIVISION

Team	W	L	T	Pct.	GB
Rochester (Orioles)	74	67	0	.525	....
Ottawa (Expos)	73	69	0	.514	1½
Scranton-Wilkes Barre (Phillies)	62	80	0	.437	12½
Pawtucket (Red Sox)	60	82	0	.423	14½
Syracuse (Blue Jays)	59	82	1	.418	15

WEST DIVISION

Team	W	L	T	Pct.	GB
Charlotte (Indians)	86	55	0	.610	....
Richmond (Braves)	80	62	0	.563	6½
Columbus (Yankees)	78	62	1	.557	7½
Norfolk (Mets)	70	71	0	.496	16
Toledo (Tigers)	65	77	0	.458	21½

COMPOSITE

Team	Char.	Rich.	Col.	Roc.	Ott.	Nor.	Tol.	SWB	Paw.	Syr.	W	L	T	Pct.	GB
Charlotte (Indians)	....	10	8	8	9	12	11	8	9	11	86	55	0	.610	....
Richmond (Braves)	8	....	8	10	6	9	9	9	10	11	80	62	0	.563	6½
Columbus (Yankees)	10	10	....	7	6	11	10	10	7	7	78	62	1	.557	7½
Rochester (Orioles)	5	4	7	....	12	9	7	11	7	12	74	67	0	.525	12
Ottawa (Expos)	5	8	8	6	....	3	8	11	13	11	73	69	0	.514	13½
Norfolk (Mets)	6	9	6	5	11	....	8	8	9	8	70	71	0	.496	16
Toledo (Tigers)	7	9	8	7	6	10	....	7	6	5	65	77	0	.458	21½
Scranton-Wilkes Barre (Phillies)	6	5	4	7	7	6	7	....	10	10	62	80	0	.437	24½
Pawtucket (Red Sox)	5	4	7	11	5	5	8	8	....	7	60	82	0	.423	26½
Syracuse (Blue Jays)	3	3	6	6	7	6	6	9	8	11	59	82	1	.418	27

Major league affiliations in parentheses.

Playoffs—Charlotte defeated Richmond, three games to one; Rochester defeated Ottawa, three games to two; Charlotte defeated Rochester, three games to two, to win league championship.

Regular-season attendance—Charlotte, 403,029; Columbus, 580,570; Norfolk, 529,708; Ottawa, 663,926; Pawtucket, 466,428; Richmond, 553,076; Rochester, 361,676; Scranton-Wilkes Barre, 531,620; Syracuse, 262,760; Toledo, 274,047. Total—4,606,840. Playoffs (14 games)—60,030. Class AAA All-Star Game at Albuquerque—10,541.

Managers—Charlotte, Charlie Manuel; Columbus, Stump Merrill; Norfolk, Clint Hurdle; Ottawa, Mike Quade; Pawtucket, Buddy Bailey; Richmond, Grady Little; Rochester, Bob Miscik; Scranton-Wilkes Barre, George Culver; Syracuse, Nick Leyva (through July 16), and Bob Didier (from July 17); Toledo, Joe Sparks. Managerial record of team with more than one manager: Syracuse, Leyva, 36-56-1, Didier, 23-26.

All-Star team: 1B—Ryan Klesko, Richmond; 2B—Tommy Hinzo, Rochester; 3B—Jim Thome, Charlotte; SS—Chipper Jones, Richmond; OF—Tony Longmire, Scranton-Wilkes Barre; Billy Masse, Columbus; Tony Tarasco, Richmond; C—Javier Lopez, Richmond; DH—Sam Horn, Charlotte; Starting Pitcher—Aaron Sele, Pawtucket; Relief Pitcher—Billy Taylor, Richmond; Most Valuable Player—Jim Thome, Charlotte; Most Valuable Pitcher—Aaron Sele, Pawtucket; Rookie of the Year—Chipper Jones, Richmond; Manager of the Year—Mike Quade, Ottawa.

BATTING

TEAM

Team	Avg.	G	AB	R	OR	H	TB	2B	3B	HR	RBI	SH	SF	HP	BB	Int. BB	SO	SB	CS	LOB
Charlotte	.283	141	4852	769	635	1371	2251	245	40	185	713	39	40	44	456	40	886	58	43	997
Richmond	.277	142	4827	746	606	1335	2152	236	49	161	697	29	31	51	467	35	966	112	68	975
Rochester	.265	141	4844	718	633	1283	2013	258	41	130	671	26	37	56	500	28	994	92	43	1016
Columbus	.264	141	4651	693	668	1228	1988	267	38	139	648	21	44	41	536	22	962	105	78	948
Ottawa	.264	142	4679	649	586	1233	1778	229	32	84	587	55	44	80	531	44	925	120	70	1055
Toledo	.258	142	4677	611	650	1205	1837	225	37	111	555	41	37	34	410	27	816	158	76	917
Syracuse	.256	142	4660	564	684	1194	1803	213	48	100	515	57	38	49	342	20	970	67	66	883
Scranton-WB	.256	142	4758	603	649	1218	1819	260	37	89	545	48	36	58	417	28	727	97	42	969
Norfolk	.253	141	4680	537	610	1182	1710	190	49	80	483	59	33	32	426	37	772	154	78	940
Pawtucket	.249	142	4766	566	699	1188	1754	200	21	108	535	37	28	37	404	19	952	81	55	947

INDIVIDUAL

(Leading qualifiers for batting championship—383 or more plate appearances)

*Bats lefthanded.   †Switch-hitter.

Player, Team	Avg.	G	AB	R	H	TB	2B	3B	HR	RBI	SH	SF	HP	BB	Int. BB	SO	SB	CS
Thome, Jim, Charlotte*	.332	115	410	85	136	240	21	4	25	102	0	4	7	76	8	94	1	3
Tarasco, Tony, Richmond*	.330	93	370	73	122	196	15	7	15	53	4	3	1	36	3	54	19	11
Jones, Chipper, Richmond†	.325	139	536	97	174	268	31	12	13	89	3	6	1	57	5	70	23	8
Masse, Billy, Columbus	.316	117	402	81	127	225	35	3	19	91	1	4	8	82	0	68	17	7
Carey, Paul, Rochester	.311	96	325	63	101	165	20	4	12	50	1	2	5	65	11	92	0	0
Rodriguez, Victor, Scranton-WB	.305	118	442	59	135	201	24	3	12	64	6	3	3	17	0	40	2	4
Lopez, Javy, Richmond	.305	100	380	56	116	194	23	2	17	74	0	3	6	12	1	53	1	6
Longmire, Tony, Scranton-WB*	.304	120	447	63	136	198	36	4	6	67	4	4	3	41	6	71	12	4
Perez, Robert, Syracuse	.294	138	524	72	154	236	26	10	12	64	5	1	4	24	1	65	13	15
Ortiz, Luis, Pawtucket	.294	102	402	45	118	202	28	1	18	81	0	4	2	13	3	74	1	1

Departmental leaders: G—Quinlan, 141; AB—Hinzo, 560; R—C. Jones, 97; H—C. Jones, 174; TB—C. Jones, 268; 2B—Longmire, 36; 3B—C. Jones, 12; HR—Horn, 38; RBI—Thome, 102; SH—Paredes, 11; SF—Allred, 8; HP—Hansen, 27; BB—Masse, 82; IBB—Carey, 11; SO—Quinlan, 156; SB—Bullock, 45; CS—Cangelosi, 18.

(All players—listed alphabetically)

Player, Team	Avg.	G	AB	R	H	TB	2B	3B	HR	RBI	SH	SF	HP	BB	Int. BB	SO	SB	CS
Abbott, Kyle, Scranton-WB*	.120	27	25	4	3	3	0	0	0	0	1	0	0	2	0	11	0	0
Alexander, Manny, Rochester	.244	120	471	55	115	172	23	8	6	51	2	1	4	22	0	60	19	7
Allen, Ronnie, Scranton-WB	.000	5	5	0	0	0	0	0	0	0	1	0	0	0	0	1	0	0

Player, Team	Avg.	G	AB	R	H	TB	2B	3B	HR	RBI	SH	SF	HP	BB	Int. BB	SO	SB	CS
Allison, Tom, Norfolk†	.235	13	34	9	8	8	0	0	0	3	0	1	0	8	0	7	0	0
Allred, Beau, Charlotte*	.245	120	347	59	85	164	13	3	20	61	2	8	7	45	3	57	4	3
Alomar, Sandy, Charlotte	.364	12	44	8	16	24	5	0	1	8	0	0	1	5	1	8	0	0
Alstead, Jason, Rochester*	.178	23	45	8	8	9	1	0	0	4	2	0	0	5	0	8	2	1
Alvarez, Tavo, Ottawa	.059	25	17	1	1	1	0	0	0	0	3	0	0	0	0	4	0	0
Amaro, Ruben, Scranton-WB†	.291	101	412	76	120	187	30	5	9	37	3	3	5	31	2	44	25	4
Baez, Kevin, Norfolk	.258	63	209	23	54	73	11	1	2	21	2	1	1	20	1	29	0	2
Bark, Brian, Richmond*	.313	29	16	2	5	5	0	0	0	0	0	0	1	0	2	0	0	
Barker, Tim, Ottawa	.228	51	167	25	38	51	5	1	2	14	7	1	3	26	0	42	5	3
Bieser, Steve, Scranton-WB†	.253	26	83	3	21	25	4	0	0	4	1	0	1	2	0	14	3	0
Bilardello, Dann, Norfolk	.241	48	145	13	35	52	6	1	3	15	2	0	4	9	0	22	1	0
Birkbeck, Mike, Richmond	.125	27	16	1	2	2	0	0	0	0	2	0	0	0	0	7	0	0
Blosser, Greg, Pawtucket*	.228	130	478	66	109	204	22	2	23	66	1	4	2	58	5	139	3	3
Bolick, Frank, Ottawa†	.125	2	8	0	1	1	0	0	0	0	0	0	0	0	0	0	0	0
Borland, Toby, Scranton-WB	.000	26	1	0	0	0	0	0	0	0	0	0	0	0	0	1	0	0
Boucher, Denis, Ottawa	.000	11	3	0	0	0	0	0	0	0	0	0	0	0	0	1	0	0
Brady, Pat, Scranton-WB*	.228	63	189	28	43	85	10	4	8	26	0	3	1	49	0	40	1	4
Brantley, Cliff, 7 SWB-6 Ott.	.000	13	3	1	0	0	0	0	0	0	2	0	0	0	0	1	0	0
Brink, Brad, Scranton-WB	.000	18	12	0	0	0	0	0	0	0	0	0	0	0	0	4	0	0
Brito, Mario, Norfolk	.000	23	1	0	0	0	0	0	0	0	0	0	0	0	0	1	0	0
Brogna, Rico, Toledo*	.273	129	483	55	132	201	30	3	11	59	4	4	2	31	2	94	7	5
Bryant, Scott, Ottawa	.283	112	364	48	103	160	19	1	12	65	0	6	2	53	3	90	1	2
Buford, Damon, Rochester	.284	27	116	24	33	44	6	1	1	4	1	0	0	16	0	16	10	2
Bullock, Eric, Norfolk*	.254	117	437	55	111	165	26	8	4	48	1	4	1	52	5	56	45	15
Burlingame, Dennis, Richmond	.000	6	2	0	0	0	0	0	0	0	0	0	0	0	0	1	0	0
Burnitz, Jeromy, Norfolk*	.227	65	255	33	58	103	15	3	8	44	0	3	2	25	2	53	10	7
Butler, Rob, Syracuse*	.284	55	208	30	59	77	11	2	1	14	3	2	3	15	2	29	7	5
Byrd, Jim, Pawtucket	.177	117	378	33	67	96	12	4	3	26	5	0	9	18	1	111	10	9
Campbell, Darrin, Richmond	.183	54	115	21	21	35	9	1	1	11	0	1	1	11	0	30	0	0
Canale, George, Charlotte*	.216	73	208	32	45	71	8	0	6	27	0	1	0	26	3	47	2	1
Canate, William, Syracuse	.250	7	24	3	6	12	0	0	2	5	0	0	0	5	0	3	0	2
Cangelosi, John, Toledo†	.292	113	439	73	128	177	23	4	6	42	5	2	5	56	3	59	39	18
Caraballo, Ramon, Richmond†	.272	126	470	73	128	180	25	9	3	41	7	5	7	30	3	81	20	14
Carey, Paul, Rochester	.311	96	325	63	101	165	20	4	12	50	1	2	5	65	11	92	0	0
Carpenter, Bubba, Columbus*	.266	70	199	29	53	77	9	0	5	17	0	1	3	29	3	35	2	2
Carter, Andy, Scranton-WB*	.000	30	7	0	0	0	0	0	0	0	0	0	0	0	0	6	0	0
Castaldo, Vince, Ottawa*	.241	77	241	22	58	75	9	1	2	45	0	7	3	29	2	49	0	4
Cedeno, Domingo, Syracuse†	.272	103	382	58	104	146	16	10	2	28	8	2	1	33	2	67	15	10
Chick, Bruce, Pawtucket	.305	29	82	8	25	37	6	0	2	12	2	1	0	6	0	24	0	3
Cianfrocco, Archi, Ottawa	.298	50	188	21	56	86	14	2	4	27	0	4	2	7	0	33	4	2
Clayton, Royal, Columbus	.000	48	1	0	0	0	0	0	0	0	0	0	0	0	0	1	0	0
Cockrell, Alan, Charlotte	.276	96	275	31	76	116	12	2	8	39	2	3	2	23	0	59	0	0
Colbrunn, Greg, Ottawa	.273	6	22	4	6	7	1	0	0	8	0	1	0	1	0	2	1	0
Combs, Pat, Scranton-WB*	.000	15	3	1	0	0	0	0	0	0	1	0	0	2	0	1	0	0
Coolbaugh, Scott, Rochester	.245	118	421	52	103	191	26	4	18	67	1	2	2	27	2	110	0	0
Cross, Jesse, Syracuse	1.000	29	1	0	1	1	0	0	0	0	0	0	0	0	0	0	0	0
Crowley, Jim, Pawtucket	.171	12	35	2	6	6	0	0	0	2	0	0	0	2	0	10	0	0
Cruz, Ivan, Toledo*	.226	115	402	44	91	156	18	4	13	50	0	2	3	30	2	85	1	1
Davidson, Mark, Charlotte	.281	101	263	39	74	117	12	2	9	36	5	1	4	27	3	52	1	1
Davis, Glenn, Rochester	.250	7	24	2	6	9	1	0	0	3	0	0	2	0	0	8	0	0
Davis, Russ, Columbus	.255	113	424	63	108	212	24	1	26	83	2	6	3	40	2	118	1	1
Dejardin, Bobby, Columbus†	.275	103	360	45	99	145	17	7	5	37	4	3	1	34	0	44	10	8
de la Rosa, Juan, Syracuse	.227	60	198	17	45	71	10	2	4	15	4	1	1	7	0	41	4	4
Dellicarri, Joe, Norfolk	.077	7	13	0	1	1	0	0	0	1	0	0	0	2	0	5	1	0
Dickerson, Bobby, Rochester	.250	40	88	12	22	36	3	1	3	18	4	0	2	4	0	18	0	1
Dostal, Bruce, 6 SWB-88 Roch.*	.294	94	310	46	91	122	12	5	3	30	4	3	2	41	4	78	14	6
Duey, Kyle, Syracuse	.000	11	2	0	0	0	0	0	0	0	0	0	0	0	0	0	0	0
Eischen, Joey, Ottawa*	.000	6	2	0	0	0	0	0	0	0	1	0	0	0	0	1	0	0
Elliott, Donnie, Richmond	.000	18	9	0	0	0	0	0	0	0	1	0	0	0	0	5	0	0
Fernandez, Jose, Scranton-WB*	.188	16	32	2	6	7	1	0	0	1	1	0	0	4	0	11	0	0
Filer, Tom, Norfolk	.077	22	13	0	1	1	0	0	0	0	1	0	0	1	0	5	0	0
Flaherty, John, Pawtucket*	.271	105	365	29	99	139	22	0	6	35	2	2	5	26	1	41	0	2
Fletcher, Paul, Scranton-WB	.167	34	18	2	3	4	1	0	0	2	0	0	1	0	0	8	0	0
Floyd, Cliff, Ottawa*	.240	32	125	12	30	42	3	0	2	18	0	1	1	16	3	34	2	2
Fordyce, Brook, Norfolk	.259	116	409	33	106	137	21	2	2	41	3	6	5	26	3	62	2	2
Fortugno, Tim, Ottawa*	.000	28	2	0	0	0	0	0	0	0	0	0	0	0	0	2	0	0
Foster, Kevin, Scranton-WB	.250	17	4	0	1	1	0	0	0	0	0	0	0	0	0	2	0	0
Gaddy, Bob, Scranton-WB.	.500	23	2	0	1	1	0	0	0	0	0	0	0	0	0	0	0	0
Garcia, Cheo, Pawtucket	.260	96	373	48	97	131	16	3	4	32	1	3	2	24	0	45	3	8
Gardiner, Mike, 5 Ott.-4 Tol.	.000	9	1	0	0	0	0	0	0	0	1	0	0	0	0	1	0	0
Garner, Kevin, Ottawa*	.273	36	99	15	27	57	9	0	7	28	0	1	0	15	6	31	0	0
Gedman, Rich, Columbus*	.262	89	275	30	72	123	15	0	12	35	0	0	0	35	5	63	0	4
Giannelli, Ray, Syracuse*	.253	127	411	51	104	163	18	4	11	42	2	5	3	38	1	79	1	6
Givens, Jim, Toledo†	.257	44	148	18	38	46	4	2	0	13	2	1	1	10	0	19	6	3
Gladden, Dan, Toledo	.393	7	28	6	11	15	1	0	1	7	1	0	0	2	0	4	0	0
Gomez, Chris, Toledo	.245	87	277	29	68	84	12	2	0	20	6	2	3	23	0	37	6	2
Gomez, Leo, Rochester	.200	4	15	3	3	4	1	0	0	1	0	0	0	3	0	4	0	0
Gozzo, Mauro, Norfolk	.077	28	13	0	1	1	0	0	0	0	4	0	0	0	0	4	0	0
Green, Tyler, Scranton-WB	.200	28	5	1	1	1	0	0	0	0	0	0	0	0	0	3	0	0
Groom, Buddy, Toledo*	.000	16	1	0	0	0	0	0	0	0	0	0	0	0	0	1	0	0
Hall, Drew, Scranton-WB*	.000	61	2	0	0	0	0	0	0	0	0	0	0	0	0	1	0	0
Hammonds, Jeffrey, Rochester	.311	36	151	25	47	73	9	1	5	23	1	2	2	5	0	27	6	3
Haney, Todd, Ottawa	.291	136	506	69	147	194	30	4	3	46	5	2	3	36	1	56	11	6
Hansen, Terrel, Ottawa	.230	108	352	45	81	130	19	0	10	39	2	4	27	18	0	103	1	1
Hare, Shawn, Toledo*	.264	130	470	81	124	219	29	3	20	76	0	5	2	34	5	90	8	4
Hatteberg, Scott, Pawtucket*	.189	18	53	6	10	13	0	0	1	2	0	1	0	6	0	12	0	0
Henderson, Derek, Syracuse	.370	14	27	2	10	11	1	0	0	3	0	0	3	0	7	0	2	
Henry, Butch, Ottawa*	.250	5	4	1	1	1	0	0	0	1	0	0	0	1	0	0	0	0
Heredia, Gil, Ottawa	.182	16	11	0	2	3	1	0	0	1	0	0	0	0	0	4	0	0
Hernandez, Kiki, Columbus	.241	22	54	8	13	20	4	0	1	8	1	2	1	6	1	12	0	0
Hill, Ken, Ottawa	.000	1	1	0	0	0	0	0	0	0	0	0	0	0	0	0	0	0
Hillman, Eric, Norfolk*	.417	10	12	2	5	10	1	2	0	2	0	0	0	0	0	4	0	0
Hinzo, Tommy, Rochester†	.271	136	560	83	152	205	25	5	6	69	8	6	11	37	0	78	29	12
Hirtensteiner, Rick, Ottawa*	.214	10	14	1	3	3	0	0	0	0	0	0	0	2	1	3	1	0

Player, Team	Avg.	G	AB	R	H	TB	2B	3B	HR	RBI	SH	SF	HP	BB	Int. BB	SO	SB	CS
Holland, Tim, Rochester	.107	9	28	4	3	5	2	0	0	0	0	0	1	0	9	0	0
Holman, Shawn, Richmond	.182	37	11	1	2	2	0	0	0	0	0	0	0	0	4	0	0
Horn, Sam, Charlotte*	.269	122	402	62	108	241	17	1	38	96	0	7	2	60	8	131	1	0
Hostetler, Mike, Richmond	.333	9	3	0	1	1	0	0	0	0	3	0	0	0	0	1	0	0
Housie, Wayne, Norfolk†	.209	16	67	5	14	17	0	0	1	5	1	1	0	3	0	13	7	0
Houston, Tyler, Richmond*	.139	13	36	4	5	11	1	1	1	3	0	0	0	1	0	8	0	0
Howard, Tim, Norfolk*	.264	64	197	18	52	72	7	2	3	16	0	1	1	10	2	13	2	1
Humphreys, Mike, Columbus	.288	92	330	59	95	133	16	2	6	42	2	2	3	52	2	57	18	15
Hunter, Bert, Norfolk	.170	23	53	7	9	11	2	0	0	1	0	0	0	10	0	14	2	1
Hunter, Brian, Richmond	.242	30	99	16	24	49	7	0	6	26	0	3	0	10	0	21	4	2
Hurst, Jody, Toledo	.250	61	200	26	50	78	6	2	6	27	0	4	1	17	1	35	15	1
Hurst, Jonathan, Ottawa	.000	8	1	0	0	0	0	0	0	0	1	0	0	0	0	1	0	0
Hyde, Mickey, Scranton-WB	.167	2	6	1	1	1	0	0	0	0	0	0	0	0	0	1	0	0
Hymel, Gary, Ottawa	.000	3	3	0	0	0	0	0	0	0	0	0	0	0	0	2	0	0
Ingram, Riccardo, Toledo	.270	123	415	41	112	179	20	4	13	62	0	5	5	32	5	66	9	7
Johnson, Judd, Richmond	.000	49	2	0	0	0	0	0	0	0	0	0	0	0	0	1	0	0
Jones, Barry, Richmond*	.167	11	30	1	5	5	0	0	0	4	1	0	1	2	0	6	0	0
Jones, Bobby, Norfolk	.125	24	24	2	3	5	0	1	0	1	2	0	0	2	0	8	0	0
Jones, Chipper, Richmond†	.325	139	536	97	174	268	31	12	13	89	3	6	1	57	5	70	23	8
Jones, Jimmy, Ottawa	.000	3	2	0	0	0	0	0	0	0	0	0	0	1	0	1	0	0
Jones, Ron, Richmond*	.291	79	203	25	59	98	9	0	10	41	2	1	1	25	3	29	0	1
Kelly, Mike, Richmond	.243	123	424	63	103	175	13	1	19	58	0	1	14	36	1	109	11	7
Kirby, Wayne, Charlotte*	.289	17	76	10	22	41	6	2	3	7	0	0	0	3	0	10	4	2
Klesko, Ryan, Richmond*	.274	98	343	59	94	178	14	2	22	74	0	4	2	47	4	69	4	3
Knoblauh, Jay, Columbus	.187	56	171	23	32	57	13	0	4	21	0	0	2	9	0	46	1	0
Kowitz, Brian, Richmond*	.267	12	45	10	12	19	1	3	0	8	2	1	1	5	0	8	1	0
Kremers, Jimmy, Ottawa*	.200	4	15	1	3	6	0	0	1	2	0	0	0	1	1	2	0	0
Kunkel, Jeff, Charlotte	.281	115	430	65	121	194	34	3	11	46	5	0	9	13	0	104	12	8
Laker, Tim, Ottawa	.230	56	204	26	47	69	10	0	4	23	0	1	1	21	0	41	3	2
Landrum, Ced, Norfolk*	.291	69	275	39	80	118	13	5	5	29	3	0	1	19	2	30	16	6
Langbehn, Greg, Norfolk	.000	49	0	0	0	0	0	0	0	0	1	0	0	0	0	0	0	0
Legg, Greg, Scranton-WB*	.280	73	225	27	63	82	13	3	0	25	3	0	1	19	1	23	2	2
Leonard, Mark, Rochester	.276	97	330	57	91	167	23	1	17	58	0	6	10	60	4	81	0	1
Levis, Jesse, Charlotte*	.248	47	129	10	32	46	6	1	2	20	1	2	1	15	1	12	0	2
Lewis, Mark, Charlotte	.284	126	507	93	144	233	30	4	17	67	8	3	2	34	4	76	9	5
Lieberthal, Mike, Scranton-WB	.262	112	382	35	100	138	17	0	7	40	1	4	6	24	3	32	0	1
Lindsey, Doug, Scranton-WB	.174	38	121	9	21	33	4	1	2	7	0	0	5	0	24	0	0
Livesey, Jeff, Columbus	.247	34	89	9	22	33	5	0	2	8	2	0	0	2	0	18	0	0
Longmire, Tony, Scranton-WB*	.304	120	447	63	136	198	36	4	6	67	4	4	3	41	6	71	12	4
Lopez, Javy, Richmond	.305	100	380	56	116	194	23	2	17	74	0	3	6	12	1	53	1	6
Lopez, Luis, Charlotte	.314	67	242	36	76	127	15	0	12	37	0	2	1	6	2	17	0	0
Loynd, Mike, Richmond	.071	18	14	0	1	2	1	0	0	0	0	0	0	0	0	10	0	0
Lyons, Steve, Pawtucket*	.213	67	197	24	42	60	6	0	4	18	2	1	0	26	3	50	3	4
Maas, Kevin, Columbus*	.279	28	104	14	29	47	6	0	4	18	0	1	1	19	2	22	0	1
Mack, Quinn, Ottawa*	.095	8	21	1	2	2	0	0	0	0	0	0	1	0	3	0	0
Malzone, John, Pawtucket*	.237	75	207	14	49	62	7	0	2	15	0	0	1	12	0	24	2	1
Manto, Jeff, Scranton-WB	.289	106	388	62	112	195	30	1	17	88	0	6	5	55	3	58	4	1
Manzanillo, Josias, Norfolk	.000	14	10	0	0	0	0	0	0	0	0	0	0	0	0	4	0	0
Marsh, Tom, Scranton-WB	.286	78	315	45	90	158	16	8	12	57	1	3	4	14	2	47	10	4
Martin, Jeff, Pawtucket	.211	9	19	5	4	8	1	1	0	1	2	1	0	4	0	9	1	0
Martinez, Carlos, Charlotte	.367	20	79	17	29	47	7	1	3	12	0	1	0	4	0	15	2	0
Martinez, Chito, Rochester*	.262	43	145	14	38	64	11	0	5	23	2	0	0	11	0	34	0	0
Martinez, Domingo, Syracuse	.273	127	465	50	127	227	24	2	24	79	0	4	10	31	6	115	4	5
Martinez, Luis, Norfolk	.248	66	202	18	50	67	3	1	4	22	6	2	1	10	2	28	0	0
Marzano, John, Charlotte	.111	3	9	0	1	1	0	0	0	0	0	0	0	1	0	1	0	0
Masse, Billy, Columbus	.316	117	402	81	127	225	35	3	19	91	1	4	8	82	0	68	17	7
Mathile, Mike, Ottawa	.091	31	11	1	1	3	0	1	0	3	0	3	0	0	0	5	0	0
McIntosh, Tim, Ottawa	.292	27	106	15	31	58	7	1	6	21	0	2	0	10	2	22	1	0
McNeely, Jeff, Pawtucket	.261	129	498	65	130	156	14	3	2	35	10	2	3	43	1	102	40	7
Melendez, Jose, Pawtucket	.000	19	1	0	0	0	0	0	0	0	0	0	0	0	0	0	0	0
Mercado, Orlando, Charlotte	.143	10	21	0	3	3	0	0	0	0	1	0	1	2	1	5	0	0
Meulens, Hensley, Columbus	.204	75	279	39	57	113	14	0	14	45	0	3	3	32	0	92	6	2
Millette, Joe, Scranton-WB	.224	107	343	27	77	99	15	2	1	24	7	1	5	19	2	56	5	4
Milstien, Dave, Pawtucket	.252	88	258	28	65	82	8	3	1	18	2	1	2	10	0	31	1	3
Mitchell, Keith, Richmond	.232	110	353	59	82	119	23	1	4	44	3	3	2	44	0	48	9	5
Montalvo, Rob, Syracuse	.214	85	234	25	50	58	6	1	0	16	10	3	0	21	0	47	1	1
Montoyo, Charlie, Ottawa	.279	99	319	43	89	114	18	2	1	43	6	5	4	71	0	37	0	9
Monzon, Jose, Syracuse	.239	71	197	14	47	63	7	0	3	21	4	0	0	11	0	37	0	1
Moore, Bobby, Richmond	.667	1	3	2	2	2	0	0	0	0	0	0	0	1	0	0	1	0
Mordecai, Mike, Richmond	.268	72	205	29	55	71	8	1	2	14	1	0	1	14	0	33	10	2
Mota, Carlos, Charlotte	.200	14	25	4	5	6	1	0	0	4	1	0	0	2	0	6	1	0
Nabholz, Chris, Ottawa*	.200	5	5	0	1	1	0	0	0	1	0	0	0	0	0	1	0	0
Naehring, Tim, Pawtucket	.307	55	202	38	62	94	9	1	7	36	3	1	0	35	3	27	0	2
Navarro, Tito, Norfolk†	.282	96	273	35	77	90	11	1	0	16	7	2	0	33	1	39	19	3
Nieves, Melvin, Richmond†	.278	78	273	38	76	122	10	3	10	36	1	1	2	25	4	84	4	5
Nixon, Donell, Charlotte	.333	20	24	8	8	8	0	0	0	0	0	0	0	2	0	3	3	1
O'Halloran, Greg, Syracuse*	.267	109	322	32	86	115	14	3	3	35	0	4	2	13	3	54	2	1
Oliva, Jose, Richmond	.235	125	412	63	97	192	20	6	21	65	0	1	4	35	2	134	1	5
Ortiz, Luis, Pawtucket	.294	102	402	45	118	202	28	1	18	81	0	4	2	13	3	74	1	1
Palacios, Rey, Rochester	.000	1	1	0	0	0	0	0	0	0	0	0	0	0	0	0	0	0
Paredes, Johnny, Toledo	.257	133	471	70	121	154	19	4	2	41	11	3	4	47	1	45	21	13
Parent, Mark, Rochester	.247	92	332	47	82	139	15	0	14	56	0	1	0	40	0	71	0	1
Patterson, Jeff, Scranton-WB	.000	62	1	0	0	0	0	0	0	0	0	0	0	0	0	0	0	0
Perez, Robert, Syracuse	.294	138	524	72	154	236	26	10	12	64	5	1	4	24	1	65	13	15
Pevey, Marty, Toledo*	.274	62	175	11	48	64	8	1	2	18	1	1	0	16	2	36	3	3
Pratt, Todd, Scranton-WB	.222	3	9	1	2	3	1	0	0	1	0	0	0	1	0	1	0	0
Pride, Curtis, Ottawa*	.302	69	262	55	79	116	11	4	6	22	2	0	3	34	1	61	29	12
Quinlan, Tom, Syracuse	.236	141	461	63	109	187	20	5	16	53	2	6	19	56	2	156	6	1
Ramirez, Manny, Charlotte	.317	40	145	38	46	100	12	0	14	36	0	3	2	27	1	35	1	1
Ramos, John, Columbus	.259	49	158	17	41	51	7	0	1	18	0	2	0	19	1	32	1	2
Ramos, Ken, Charlotte*	.292	132	480	77	140	187	16	11	3	41	7	3	0	47	4	41	12	8
Ready, Randy, Rochester	.289	84	305	48	88	138	17	3	9	46	1	3	1	50	2	37	4	0
Reimink, Bob, Toledo†	.197	66	193	18	38	48	7	0	1	10	1	0	0	23	2	41	4	0
Richardson, Jeff, Pawtucket	.321	9	28	2	9	10	1	0	0	1	1	0	1	0	0	6	0	0

Player, Team	Avg.	G	AB	R	H	TB	2B	3B	HR	RBI	SH	SF	HP	BB	Int. BB	SO	SB	CS
Rightnowar, Ron, Toledo	.000	22	1	0	0	0	0	0	0	0	0	0	0	0	0	1	0	0
Riles, Ernie, Pawtucket*	.278	6	18	4	5	11	0	0	2	6	0	2	0	3	0	0	0	0
Robertson, Rod, Toledo†	.235	121	409	54	96	149	13	2	12	48	5	4	3	27	1	76	15	7
Robinson, Dwight, Norfolk*	.143	3	7	0	1	1	0	0	0	0	0	0	0	0	0	0	0	0
Robinson, Nap, 19 Rich.-1 Char	.000	20	6	0	0	0	0	0	0	0	0	0	0	0	0	6	0	0
Rodriguez, Boi, Richmond*	.267	88	236	34	63	108	13	1	10	22	0	0	1	26	3	55	4	1
Rodriguez, Carlos, Columbus†	.253	57	154	25	39	53	9	1	1	11	2	1	3	20	0	10	2	1
Rodriguez, Ruben, Pawtucket	.320	32	97	12	31	39	5	0	1	10	0	0	2	1	0	14	1	1
Rodriguez, Victor, Scranton-WB	.305	118	442	59	135	201	24	3	12	64	6	3	3	17	0	40	2	4
Ross, Sean, Pawtucket*	.225	26	80	14	18	26	2	0	2	5	0	1	2	2	0	12	4	2
Rowland, Rich, Toledo	.268	96	325	58	87	178	24	2	21	59	0	3	3	51	3	72	1	6
Rueter, Kirk, Ottawa*	.333	7	3	0	1	1	0	0	0	0	2	0	0	0	0	1	0	0
Ryan, Sean, Scranton-WB†	.221	66	208	14	46	58	9	0	1	16	1	2	2	26	1	39	0	0
Sanchez, Gordon, Columbus*	.173	25	75	12	13	19	2	2	0	6	1	0	1	8	1	21	0	2
Sandy, Tim, Norfolk*	.250	6	16	1	4	5	1	0	0	1	0	0	0	0	0	3	0	1
Santangelo, Frank, Ottawa†	.274	131	453	86	124	161	21	2	4	45	8	4	14	59	4	52	18	8
Saunders, Doug, Norfolk	.247	105	356	37	88	118	12	6	2	24	7	1	3	44	1	63	6	5
Schaefer, Jeff, Charlotte	.279	133	448	53	125	172	20	3	7	43	8	2	2	21	0	61	5	8
Schall, Gene, Scranton-WB	.237	40	139	16	33	53	6	1	4	16	1	1	7	19	1	38	4	2
Scott, Shawn, Syracuse†	.210	103	290	30	61	72	9	1	0	18	10	0	1	23	0	60	7	5
Sellers, Rick, Toledo	.283	18	46	6	13	25	4	1	2	7	0	0	1	3	0	8	0	1
Shaw, Jeff, Ottawa	.500	2	2	0	1	1	0	0	0	0	0	0	0	0	0	1	0	0
Siddall, Joe, Ottawa*	.213	48	136	14	29	38	6	0	1	16	3	2	0	19	5	33	2	2
Silvestri, Dave, Columbus	.269	120	428	76	115	209	26	4	20	65	0	4	3	68	4	127	6	9
Simons, Doug, Ottawa*	.250	34	8	1	2	2	0	0	0	0	3	0	0	1	0	1	0	0
Smith, Mark, Rochester	.280	129	485	69	136	201	27	1	12	68	0	2	9	37	3	90	4	6
Smith, Ottis, Norfolk	.333	5	3	1	1	1	0	0	0	2	0	0	0	0	0	0	0	0
Sojo, Luis, Syracuse	.218	43	142	17	31	45	7	2	1	12	4	0	0	8	0	12	2	1
Sparks, Don, Columbus	.284	128	475	63	135	215	33	7	11	72	1	6	4	29	0	83	0	3
Sparks, Greg, Pawtucket*	.172	58	198	7	34	52	6	0	4	21	1	2	2	14	0	54	0	3
Spehr, Tim, Ottawa	.199	46	141	15	28	48	6	1	4	13	0	1	6	14	1	35	2	1
Springer, Steve, Norfolk	.267	131	484	52	129	198	22	4	13	69	2	3	3	31	8	85	5	6
Stairs, Matt, Ottawa	.280	34	125	18	35	52	4	2	3	20	1	0	2	11	1	15	4	1
Stankiewicz, Andy, Columbus	.242	90	331	45	80	102	12	5	0	32	4	3	3	29	0	46	12	8
Stevens, Lee, Syracuse*	.264	116	401	61	106	180	30	1	14	66	0	4	1	39	3	85	2	4
Stinnett, Kelly, Charlotte	.274	98	288	42	79	113	10	3	6	33	0	1	2	17	1	52	0	0
Stocker, Kevin, Scranton-WB†	.233	83	313	54	73	98	14	1	3	17	8	0	7	29	2	56	17	6
Strange, Don, Richmond	.000	34	1	0	0	0	0	0	0	0	0	0	0	0	0	0	0	0
Stubbs, Franklin, Pawtucket*	.237	94	334	47	79	144	18	1	15	58	1	1	0	51	1	82	3	3
Tackett, Jeff, Rochester	.320	8	25	1	8	10	2	0	0	2	0	1	2	3	0	8	0	0
Tarasco, Tony, Richmond*	.330	93	370	73	122	196	15	7	15	53	4	3	1	36	3	54	19	11
Tatum, Willie, Pawtucket†	.083	7	24	5	2	5	1	1	0	2	0	1	0	3	0	4	0	0
Taylor, Sam, Scranton-WB*	.241	67	191	24	46	73	7	1	6	25	0	2	3	20	3	36	4	2
Telgheder, Dave, Norfolk	.000	13	9	0	0	0	0	0	0	0	2	0	0	0	0	7	0	0
Thome, Jim, Charlotte*	.332	115	410	85	136	240	21	4	25	102	0	4	7	76	8	94	1	3
Thompson, Ryan, Norfolk	.259	60	224	39	58	109	11	2	12	34	0	2	5	24	2	81	6	3
Thoutsis, Paul, Pawtucket*	.319	60	216	30	69	93	10	1	4	27	1	0	2	24	1	28	1	0
Twardoski, Mike, Norfolk*	.281	131	427	66	120	166	15	2	9	38	2	4	1	69	6	65	9	11
Valdez, Sergio, Ottawa	.333	30	3	0	1	1	0	0	0	0	0	0	0	0	0	0	0	0
Valentin, John, Pawtucket	.333	2	9	3	3	4	1	0	0	1	0	0	0	0	0	1	0	0
Vargas, Hector, Ottawa	.183	36	93	10	17	22	3	1	0	6	2	0	1	15	1	25	3	3
Viera, John, Columbus*	.500	2	6	2	3	4	1	0	0	1	0	0	0	3	0	0	0	0
Vina, Fernando, Norfolk*	.230	73	287	24	66	92	6	4	4	27	4	1	4	7	2	17	16	11
Voigt, Jack, Rochester	.361	18	61	16	22	39	6	1	3	11	0	0	0	14	0	14	0	1
Wade, Scott, Norfolk	.190	23	79	10	15	38	3	1	6	13	0	0	1	5	0	32	0	0
Waller, Casey, Scranton-WB†	.176	58	170	19	30	42	7	1	1	13	0	1	1	10	1	20	2	0
Walton, Bruce, Ottawa	.000	40	1	0	0	0	0	0	0	0	0	0	0	0	0	0	0	0
Wearing, Melvin, Rochester	.235	112	379	52	89	149	14	2	14	61	0	6	5	55	3	109	5	1
Wegmann, Tom, Norfolk	.300	46	10	0	3	3	0	0	0	0	1	0	0	0	0	3	0	0
Wells, Bob, Scranton-WB	.000	11	1	0	0	0	0	0	0	0	0	0	0	0	0	1	0	0
Weston, Mickey, Norfolk	.077	21	13	0	1	1	0	0	0	0	1	0	0	0	0	6	0	0
White, Derrick, Ottawa	.281	67	249	32	70	99	15	1	4	29	0	3	3	20	2	52	10	7
White, Gabe, Ottawa*	.000	6	2	0	0	0	0	0	0	0	0	0	0	0	0	0	0	0
White, Rondell, Ottawa	.380	37	150	28	57	90	8	2	7	32	0	3	2	12	1	20	10	1
Willard, Jerry, Richmond*	.319	107	317	37	101	146	21	0	8	44	0	2	3	60	6	63	0	0
Williams, Cary, Scranton-WB	.216	78	232	27	50	69	15	2	0	14	3	2	3	23	0	27	3	4
Williams, Gerald, Columbus	.283	87	336	53	95	150	19	6	8	38	1	6	2	20	1	66	29	12
Williams, Mike, Scranton-WB	.091	14	11	2	1	1	0	0	0	0	0	0	0	1	0	6	0	0
Williams, Ted, Toledo†	.247	68	194	21	48	64	7	3	1	16	5	1	1	10	0	45	22	5
Winningham, Herm, 59 Paw.-36 Nor.*	.254	95	338	46	86	125	10	4	7	33	3	2	1	37	0	73	15	6
Wood, Ted, Ottawa*	.255	83	231	39	59	81	11	4	1	21	2	1	2	38	3	54	12	2
Woodall, Brad, Richmond†	.500	12	12	3	6	7	1	0	0	1	0	0	0	0	0	6	0	0
Yacopino, Ed, Rochester†	.149	17	47	6	7	8	1	0	0	5	0	0	1	0	0	6	0	0
Yan, Julian, Syracuse	.266	91	278	30	74	114	9	5	7	36	1	3	1	14	0	91	3	2
Young, Pete, Ottawa	.667	48	3	0	2	2	0	0	0	1	0	0	0	0	0	0	0	0
Zaun, Gregg, Rochester†	.256	21	78	10	20	31	4	2	1	11	0	2	0	11	0	11	0	0
Zosky, Eddie, Syracuse	.215	28	93	9	20	25	5	0	0	8	2	3	4	1	0	20	0	1

The following pitchers, listed alphabetically by club, with games in parentheses, had no plate appearances, primarily through use of designated hitters:

CHARLOTTE—Abbott, Paul (4); Anderson, Allan (7); August, Don (14); Byrd, Paul (14); Charland, Colin (6); Christopher, Mike (50); Clark, Mark (2); Curtis, Mike (7); DiPoto, Jerry (34); Eiland, Dave (8); Grimsley, Jason (28); Lopez, Albie (3); McCarthy, Tom (45); Milacki, Bob (21); Mutis, Jeff (12); Ogea, Chad (29); Robinson, Napoleon (1); Scudder, Scott (24); Shinall, Zak (1); Slocumb, Heathcliff (24); Solano, Julio (3); Wells, Terry (6); Wertz, Bill (28); Young, Cliff (5); Young, Matt (3).

COLUMBUS—Batchelor, Rich (15); Cook, Andy (21); DeLaRosa, Francisco (31); Gibson, Paul (3); Gogolewski, Doug (28); Greer, Kenny (46); Hines, Rich (43); Hitchcock, Sterling (16); Howe, Steve (2); Hutton, Mark (21); Jean, Domingo (7); Johnson, Jeff (19); Kamieniecki, Scott (1); Militello, Sam (7); Munoz, Roberto (22); Ojala, Kirt (31); Popplewell, Tom (1); Quirico, Rafael (5); Seiler, Keith (1); Stanford, Don (36); Taylor, Wade (7); Witt, Mike (4).

NORFOLK—Gibson, Paul (14); Gunderson, Eric (6); Kaiser, Jeff (21); Lazorko, Jack (2); Marshall, Randy (4); Plummer, Dale (47); Vann, Brandy (53); Young, Anthony (3).

OTTAWA—Farmer, Howard (2); Perez, Yorkis (20); Picota, Len (8); Risley, Bill (41); Rosario, Dave (22).

PAWTUCKET—Bailey, Cory (52); Caruso, Joe (36); Ciccarella, Joe (12); Clemens, Roger (1); Conroy, Brian (19); Finnvold, Gar (24); Florence, Don (57); Gakeler, Dan (6); Livernois, Derek (27); Minchey, Nate (29); Plympton, Jeff (30); Riley, Ed (14); Ryan, Ken (18); Sele, Aaron (14); Shea, John (12); Taylor, Scott (47).

RICHMOND—Borbon, Pedro (52); Freeman, Marvin (2); Lovelace, Vance (5); Polley, Dale (10); Reyes, Carlos (18); St. Claire, Randy (6); Taylor, Bill (59); Wohlers, Mark (25).

ROCHESTER—Bielecki, Mike (9); Clements, Pat (8); Cook, Mike (57); Dedrick, Jim (1); DuBois, Brian (3); Krivda, Rick (5); Manuel, Barry (9); McGehee, Kevin (20); Moyer, Jamie (8); O'Donoghue, John (22); Oquist, Mike (28); Pennington, Brad (17); Rhodes, Arthur (6); Ricci, Chuck (4); Satre, Jason (15); Schulze, Don (39); Searcy, Steve (16); Stephan, Todd (29); Telford, Anthony (38); Valenzuela, Fernando (1); Williams, Jeff (33); Wood, Brian (30).

SCRANTON-WILKES BARRE—Ayrault, Bob (5); Mauser, Tim (19); Parris, Steve (3).

SYRACUSE—Adkins, Steve (5); Akerfelds, Darrel (41); Bailes, Scott (19); Blohm, Pete (30); Brow, Scott (20); Brown, Tim (28); Castillo, Tony (1); Hall, Darren (60); Linton, Doug (13); Menhart, Paul (25); Ohlms, Mark (47); St. Claire, Randy (14); Spoljaric, Paul (18); Terrell, Walt (8); Ward, Tony (35); Williams, Woody (12); Young, Matt (7).

TOLEDO—Bergman, Sean (19); Blomdahl, Ben (11); Carlyle, Ken (15); Corbett, Sherman (5); DeSilva, John (25); Fraser, Bill (53); Gardiner, Mike (4); Gohr, Greg (18); Gomez, Henrique (6); Gonzales, Francisco (29); Grater, Mark (28); Gullickson, Bill (1); Haas, Dave (2); Hudek, John (16); Johnson, Dave (9); Kiely, John (37); Knudsen, Kurt (23); Krueger, Bill (3); Lira, Felipe (5); Lumley, Mike (6); Ritchie, Wally (62); Warren, Brian (24).

GRAND SLAMS—Masse, 3; Stubbs, 2; Alexander, Allred, Castaldo, Cianfrocco, Cockrell, Coolbaugh, Cruz, Dickerson, C. Jones, Kelly, Klesko, Lewis, L. Lopez, C. Martinez, D. Martinez, Oliva, Ortiz, V. Rodriguez, Spehr, Thome, Wearing, R. White, Yan, 1 each.

AWARDED FIRST BASE ON CATCHER'S INTERFERENCE—Blosser 4 (Spehr 2, Parent, Rowland); Schaefer 4 (Gedman 2, Bilardello, O'Halloran); Houston 2 (Lieberthal, Tackett); Bullock (Sanchez); DeJardin (J. Lopez); Dostal (Hatteberg); Fordyce (O'Halloran); Klesko (Tackett); Knoblauh (Spehr); McIntosh (J. Lopez); Siddall (Lieberthal).

PITCHING

TEAM

Team	ERA	G	CG	ShO	Sv.	IP	H	R	ER	HR	HB	BB	Int. BB	SO	WP	Bk.
Ottawa	3.65	142	8	10	33	1232.0	1211	586	499	92	41	402	33	844	60	1
Richmond	3.74	142	4	8	33	1235.1	1209	606	513	94	53	456	40	1024	62	4
Norfolk	3.77	141	17	9	36	1247.1	1276	610	522	89	48	357	37	845	48	2
Charlotte	3.94	141	13	5	41	1239.1	1228	635	543	140	35	368	26	861	65	8
Rochester	4.04	141	9	8	37	1248.2	1249	633	560	128	45	496	28	965	71	6
Scranton-WB	4.14	142	13	7	27	1240.1	1198	649	571	113	56	465	34	912	85	5
Columbus	4.37	141	4	9	39	1226.2	1263	668	595	114	51	527	32	819	63	9
Syracuse	4.39	142	10	6	27	1221.0	1238	684	595	127	56	485	34	882	75	8
Pawtucket	4.43	142	13	9	34	1244.1	1285	699	612	156	62	479	15	911	67	6
Toledo	4.53	142	10	2	28	1218.2	1280	686	613	134	44	454	21	907	51	6

INDIVIDUAL

(Leading qualifiers for earned-run average leadership—114 or more innings)

*Throws lefthanded.

Pitcher, Team	W	L	Pct.	ERA	G	GS	CG	GF	ShO	Sv.	IP	H	R	ER	HR	HB	BB	Int. BB	SO	WP
McGehee, Rochester	7	6	.538	2.96	20	20	2	0	0	0	133.2	124	53	44	14	7	37	1	92	3
Birkbeck, Richmond	13	8	.619	3.11	27	26	1	0	0	0	159.1	143	67	55	10	9	41	0	136	11
Cross, Syracuse	8	6	.571	3.16	29	25	0	0	0	0	151.0	137	68	53	13	5	53	1	127	9
Hutton, Columbus	10	4	.714	3.18	21	21	0	0	0	0	133.0	98	52	47	14	10	53	0	112	2
Grimsley, Charlotte	6	6	.500	3.39	28	19	3	5	1	0	135.1	138	64	51	10	1	49	1	102	18
Gozzo, Norfolk	8	11	.421	3.45	28	28	2	0	0	0	190.1	208	88	73	0	9	49	7	97	6
Johnson, Columbus*	7	6	.538	3.45	19	17	3	0	1	0	114.2	125	55	44	7	5	47	2	59	4
Oquist, Rochester	9	8	.529	3.50	28	21	2	1	1	0	149.1	144	62	58	20	2	41	1	128	5
Clayton, Columbus	7	6	.538	3.54	47	11	0	21	0	8	117.0	119	56	46	12	2	31	3	66	3
Jones, Norfolk	12	10	.545	3.63	24	24	6	0	3	0	166.0	149	72	67	9	11	32	2	126	11

Departmental leaders: G—Patterson, Ritchie, 62; W—Birkbeck, Ogea, 13; L—Minchey, 14; Pct.—M. Williams, .818; GS—Minchey, Ogea, 29; CG—Minchey, 7; GF—B. Taylor, 26; ShO—B. Jones, 3; Sv.—B. Taylor, 26; IP—Minchey, 194.2; H—Gozzo, 208; R—Minchey, 108; ER—Fletcher, 88; HR—Ogea, 26; HB—B. Jones, 11; BB—Bark, 72; IBB—Patterson, 11; SO—Birkbeck, DeSilva, 136; WP—Fletcher, 21.

(All pitchers—listed alphabetically)

Pitcher, Team	W	L	Pct.	ERA	G	GS	CG	GF	ShO	Sv.	IP	H	R	ER	HR	HB	BB	Int. BB	SO	WP
Abbott, Scranton-WB*	12	10	.545	3.95	27	27	2	0	0	0	173.0	163	85	76	21	4	62	0	109	11
Abbott, Charlotte	0	1	.000	6.63	4	4	0	0	0	0	19.0	25	16	14	4	0	7	0	12	3
Adkins, Syracuse*	0	0	.000	4.91	5	0	0	0	0	0	3.2	4	2	2	0	0	3	0	1	1
Akerfelds, Syracuse	3	4	.429	4.36	40	1	0	15	0	4	64.0	68	36	31	5	5	30	2	34	8
Allen, Scranton-WB	0	2	.000	5.18	5	5	0	0	0	0	24.1	30	15	14	3	1	8	1	12	1
Alvarez, Ottawa	7	10	.412	4.22	25	25	1	0	0	0	140.2	163	80	66	10	4	55	2	77	6
Anderson, Charlotte*	0	0	.000	9.64	7	0	0	2	0	0	14.0	30	15	15	4	0	4	0	5	1
August, Charlotte	3	1	.750	5.48	14	5	0	5	0	0	44.1	57	29	27	9	1	10	0	24	1
Ayrault, Scranton-WB	0	1	.000	1.23	5	1	0	3	0	0	7.1	8	2	1	0	0	3	1	9	0
Bailes, Syracuse*	0	1	.000	2.21	19	0	0	10	0	2	20.1	19	10	5	1	2	3	2	22	0
Bailey, Pawtucket	4	5	.444	2.88	52	0	0	40	0	20	65.2	48	21	21	1	1	31	3	59	5
Bark, Richmond*	12	9	.571	3.67	29	28	1	0	1	0	162.0	153	81	66	13	9	72	4	110	9
Batchelor, Columbus	1	1	.500	2.76	15	0	0	14	0	6	16.1	14	5	5	0	1	8	1	17	3
Bergman, Toledo	8	9	.471	4.38	19	19	3	0	0	0	117.0	124	62	57	9	8	53	0	91	6
Bielecki, Rochester	5	3	.625	5.03	9	9	0	0	0	0	48.1	56	33	27	4	1	16	1	31	6
Bilardello, Norfolk	0	0	.000	0.00	2	0	0	2	0	0	2.0	0	0	0	0	0	0	0	0	0
Birkbeck, Richmond	13	8	.619	3.11	27	26	1	0	0	0	159.1	143	67	55	10	9	41	0	136	11
Blohm, Syracuse*	2	6	.250	5.44	30	9	0	3	0	0	102.2	122	67	62	9	3	52	2	57	11
Blomdahl, Toledo*	3	4	.429	4.88	11	10	0	0	0	0	62.2	67	34	34	8	2	19	0	27	4
Borbon, Richmond*	5	5	.500	4.23	52	0	0	15	0	1	76.2	71	40	36	7	2	42	9	95	3
Borland, Scranton-WB	2	4	.333	5.76	26	0	0	15	0	1	29.2	31	20	19	4	1	20	3	26	2
Boucher, Ottawa*	6	0	1.000	2.72	11	6	0	1	0	0	43.0	36	13	13	0	1	11	0	22	3
Brantley, 7 SWB-6 Ott.	2	8	.200	6.50	13	11	0	1	0	0	54.0	81	44	39	7	3	37	1	37	6
Brink, Scranton-WB	7	7	.500	4.22	18	18	2	0	0	0	106.2	104	53	50	10	5	27	1	89	6
Brito, Ottawa	2	0	1.000	1.32	23	0	0	9	0	2	34.0	25	6	5	0	1	17	0	29	3
Brow, Syracuse	6	8	.429	4.38	20	19	2	0	0	0	121.1	119	63	59	8	6	37	1	64	4

— 353 —

Pitcher, Team	W	L	Pct.	ERA	G	GS	CG	GF	ShO	Sv.	IP	H	R	ER	HR	HB	BB	Int. BB	SO	WP
Brown, Syracuse	5	13	.278	4.47	28	25	3	2	1	0	151.0	159	85	75	16	7	35	4	87	4
Burlingame, Richmond	2	0	1.000	4.91	6	1	0	0	0	0	14.2	12	9	8	0	2	14	1	5	2
Byrd, Charlotte	7	4	.636	3.89	14	14	1	0	1	0	81.0	80	43	35	9	6	30	0	54	4
Cangelosi, Toledo*	0	0	.000	81.00	1	0	0	0	0	0	0.2	7	6	6	0	0	1	0	0	2
Carlyle, Toledo	2	10	.167	6.42	15	14	1	0	0	0	75.2	88	59	54	13	1	36	1	43	4
Carter, Scranton-WB*	7	7	.500	4.54	30	13	0	6	0	0	109.0	104	59	55	7	8	35	0	68	10
Caruso, Pawtucket	5	10	.333	5.44	36	17	2	6	0	0	122.1	138	82	74	15	7	68	0	65	5
Castillo, Syracuse*	0	0	.000	0.00	1	0	0	0	0	0	6.0	4	2	0	0	0	2	0	2	0
Charland, Charlotte*	1	0	1.000	6.75	6	1	0	0	0	0	14.2	20	12	11	1	0	5	0	16	3
Christopher, Charlotte	3	6	.333	3.22	50	0	0	46	0	22	50.1	51	21	18	2	0	6	4	36	2
Ciccarella, Pawtucket*	0	1	.000	5.60	12	0	0	2	0	0	17.2	27	13	11	2	2	12	0	8	0
Clark, Charlotte	1	0	1.000	2.08	2	2	0	0	0	0	13.0	9	5	3	0	0	2	0	12	0
Clayton, Columbus	7	6	.538	3.54	47	11	0	21	0	8	117.0	119	56	46	12	2	31	3	66	3
Clemens, Pawtucket	0	0	.000	0.00	1	1	0	0	0	0	3.2	1	0	0	0	1	4	0	8	0
Clements, Rochester*	0	0	.000	5.91	8	0	0	2	0	1	10.2	14	7	7	0	0	8	0	8	2
Combs, Scranton-WB*	0	0	.000	4.84	15	15	1	0	0	0	83.2	97	57	45	8	4	27	1	60	7
Conroy, Pawtucket	5	7	.417	5.86	19	19	0	0	0	0	106.0	126	74	69	24	2	40	0	64	6
Cook, Columbus	6	7	.462	6.54	21	20	0	0	0	0	118.1	149	91	86	14	7	49	3	47	4
Cook, Charlotte*	3	2	.600	5.06	12	6	0	3	0	0	42.2	46	26	24	6	2	6	1	40	1
Cook, Rochester	6	7	.462	3.10	57	6	0	38	0	13	81.1	77	39	28	3	5	48	9	74	11
Corbett, Toledo*	0	0	.000	4.76	5	0	0	1	0	0	5.2	6	3	3	0	1	2	0	6	0
Cross, Syracuse	8	6	.571	3.16	29	25	0	0	0	0	151.0	137	68	53	13	5	53	1	127	9
Curtis, Charlotte*	2	1	.667	5.23	7	0	0	2	0	0	10.1	10	6	6	2	0	3	2	10	1
Dedrick, Rochester	1	0	1.000	2.57	1	1	1	0	0	0	7.0	6	2	2	0	0	3	0	3	0
Dejardin, Columbus	0	0	.000	0.00	3	0	0	0	0	0	5.0	3	0	0	0	0	1	0	1	0
DeLaRosa, Columbus	1	1	.500	6.45	31	0	0	12	0	1	44.2	45	34	32	4	2	31	3	31	4
DeSilva, Toledo	7	10	.412	3.69	25	24	1	0	0	0	161.0	145	73	66	13	0	60	2	136	6
DiPoto, Charlotte	6	3	.667	1.93	34	0	0	27	0	12	46.2	34	10	10	2	1	13	2	44	4
DuBois, Rochester*	0	2	.000	9.00	3	3	0	0	0	0	13.0	20	13	13	3	1	4	0	10	0
Duey, Syracuse	2	1	.667	4.05	11	0	0	4	0	1	20.0	19	10	9	1	0	7	1	13	3
Eiland, Charlotte	1	3	.250	5.30	8	8	0	0	0	0	35.2	42	22	21	8	1	12	0	13	0
Eischen, Ottawa*	2	2	.500	3.54	6	6	0	0	0	0	40.2	34	18	16	3	0	15	0	29	1
Elliott, Richmond	8	5	.615	4.72	18	18	1	0	0	0	103.0	108	65	54	16	0	39	0	99	5
Farmer, Toledo	0	1	.000	11.25	2	0	0	1	0	0	4.0	7	5	5	1	1	0	1	1	0
Filer, Norfolk	2	10	.167	3.79	22	20	0	0	0	0	123.1	132	64	52	10	5	34	4	65	3
Finnvold, Pawtucket	5	9	.357	3.77	24	24	0	0	0	0	136.0	128	68	57	21	4	51	0	123	3
Fletcher, Scranton-WB	4	12	.250	5.66	34	19	2	5	1	0	140.0	146	99	88	21	9	60	3	116	21
Florence, Pawtucket*	7	8	.467	3.36	57	0	0	18	0	2	59.0	56	24	22	6	0	18	5	46	8
Fortugno, Ottawa*	2	1	.667	3.60	28	4	0	7	0	1	40.0	28	17	16	4	4	31	4	42	7
Foster, Scranton-WB	1	1	.500	3.93	17	9	1	0	0	0	71.0	63	32	31	7	3	29	0	59	5
Fraser, Toledo	10	7	.588	4.69	53	1	0	35	0	8	71.0	79	44	37	10	2	24	6	63	2
Freeman, Richmond	0	0	.000	2.25	2	2	0	0	0	0	4.0	4	1	1	0	1	1	0	5	0
Gaddy, Scranton-WB*	1	4	.200	5.59	23	2	0	10	0	0	48.1	54	35	30	4	3	29	5	40	2
Gakeler, Pawtucket	0	1	.000	7.50	6	0	0	3	0	0	12.0	21	11	10	1	0	9	0	8	2
Gardiner, 5 Ott.-4 Tol.	1	2	.333	2.70	9	5	0	2	0	1	30.0	23	11	9	2	0	11	0	35	3
Gibson, 14 Nor.-3 Col.*	2	1	.667	0.64	17	1	0	12	0	8	28.0	14	2	2	0	0	6	0	36	0
Gogolewski, Columbus	5	3	.625	4.38	28	0	0	8	0	3	51.1	63	32	25	4	1	14	0	32	3
Gohr, Toledo	3	10	.231	5.80	18	17	2	1	0	0	107.0	127	74	69	16	5	38	2	77	5
Gomez, Toledo	1	1	.500	6.61	6	2	1	3	0	0	16.1	21	12	12	5	1	4	0	15	0
Gonzales, Toledo*	6	3	.667	3.95	29	15	2	3	0	0	109.1	116	56	48	12	3	37	1	71	4
Gozzo, Norfolk	8	11	.421	3.45	28	28	2	0	0	0	190.1	208	88	73	10	9	49	7	97	6
Grater, Toledo	1	2	.333	8.13	28	0	0	20	0	4	31.0	42	31	28	8	1	12	0	31	2
Green, Scranton-WB	6	10	.375	3.95	28	14	4	6	0	0	118.1	102	62	52	8	5	43	2	87	8
Greer, Columbus	9	4	.692	4.42	46	0	0	21	0	6	79.1	78	41	39	5	2	36	6	50	2
Grimsley, Charlotte	6	6	.500	3.39	28	19	3	5	1	0	135.1	138	64	51	10	1	49	1	102	18
Groom, Toledo*	9	3	.750	2.74	16	15	0	0	0	0	102.0	98	34	31	5	2	30	1	78	2
Gullickson, Toledo	1	0	1.000	9.00	1	1	0	0	0	0	6.0	8	6	6	4	0	0	0	4	0
Gunderson, Norfolk*	3	2	.600	3.71	6	5	1	0	0	0	34.0	41	16	14	5	2	9	1	26	1
Haas, Toledo	0	0	.000	18.69	2	2	0	0	0	0	4.1	8	9	9	0	1	6	0	2	1
Hall, Syracuse	6	7	.462	5.33	60	0	0	41	0	13	79.1	75	51	47	10	4	31	4	68	5
Hall, Scranton-WB*	2	2	.500	2.76	61	0	0	29	0	7	65.1	55	25	20	3	5	23	5	62	3
Hare, Toledo*	0	0	.000	0.00	1	0	0	1	0	0	1.0	2	0	0	0	0	0	0	1	0
Henry, Ottawa	3	1	.750	3.73	5	5	1	0	0	0	31.1	34	15	13	2	0	1	0	25	0
Heredia, Ottawa	8	4	.667	2.98	16	16	1	0	0	0	102.2	97	46	34	7	3	26	2	66	6
Hill, Ottawa	0	0	.000	0.00	1	1	0	0	0	0	4.0	1	0	0	0	0	1	0	0	0
Hillman, Norfolk*	6	2	.750	2.21	10	9	3	1	1	0	61.0	52	18	15	2	2	12	1	27	2
Hines, Columbus*	2	5	.286	4.02	43	0	0	17	0	4	56.0	50	28	25	3	1	34	6	40	2
Hitchcock, Columbus*	3	5	.375	4.81	16	16	0	0	0	0	76.2	80	43	41	8	6	28	0	85	1
Holman, Richmond	12	7	.632	4.18	37	22	0	3	0	0	155.0	174	88	72	12	5	46	3	101	8
Hostetler, Richmond	1	3	.250	5.06	9	9	0	0	0	0	48.0	50	29	27	5	4	18	2	36	0
Howe, Columbus*	0	1	.000	10.13	2	2	0	0	0	0	2.2	6	3	3	0	0	1	0	1	0
Hudek, Toledo	1	3	.250	5.82	16	5	0	2	0	0	38.2	44	26	25	2	1	22	0	32	2
Hurst, Ottawa	1	5	.167	6.63	8	8	0	0	0	0	36.2	44	31	27	6	2	17	0	28	0
Hutton, Columbus	10	4	.714	3.18	21	21	0	0	0	0	133.0	98	52	47	14	10	53	0	112	2
Jean, Columbus	2	2	.500	2.82	7	7	1	0	0	0	44.2	40	15	14	2	2	13	1	39	3
Johnson, Toledo	1	0	1.000	0.00	9	0	0	0	0	1	17.1	6	0	0	0	0	5	1	8	0
Johnson, Columbus*	7	6	.538	3.45	19	17	3	0	1	0	114.2	125	55	44	7	5	47	2	59	4
Johnson, Richmond*	4	2	.667	2.65	49	2	0	8	0	0	85.0	85	28	25	3	3	22	2	55	3
Jones, Norfolk	12	10	.545	3.63	24	24	6	0	3	0	166.0	149	72	67	9	11	32	2	126	11
Jones, Ottawa	1	0	1.000	1.20	3	3	0	0	0	0	15.0	10	2	2	0	0	5	0	12	0
Kaiser, Norfolk*	1	1	.500	5.64	21	0	0	15	0	9	22.1	23	15	14	2	0	6	0	23	3
Kamieniecki, Columbus	1	0	1.000	1.50	1	1	0	0	0	0	6.0	5	1	1	0	0	0	0	4	0
Kiely, Toledo	3	4	.429	3.88	37	0	0	16	0	4	58.0	65	34	25	8	1	25	1	48	2
Knudsen, Toledo	2	2	.500	3.78	23	0	0	15	0	6	33.1	24	15	14	3	1	11	1	39	2
Krivda, Rochester*	3	0	1.000	1.89	5	5	0	0	0	0	33.1	20	7	7	2	1	16	0	23	1
Krueger, Toledo*	1	0	1.000	1.59	3	3	0	0	0	0	11.1	11	2	2	0	3	6	0	8	0
Langbehn, Norfolk*	2	2	.500	5.43	49	0	0	16	0	2	69.2	76	46	42	5	3	34	3	58	5
Lazorko, Norfolk	0	0	.000	3.38	2	0	0	1	0	0	2.2	4	1	1	0	1	0	2	0	0
Linton, Syracuse	2	6	.250	5.32	13	7	0	4	0	2	47.1	48	29	28	11	3	14	3	42	2
Lira, Toledo	1	2	.333	4.60	5	5	0	0	0	0	31.1	32	18	16	5	1	11	1	23	0
Livernois, Pawtucket	2	6	.250	5.72	27	14	0	4	0	0	85.0	89	55	54	13	6	37	2	69	11
Lopez, Charlotte	1	0	1.000	2.25	3	2	0	0	0	0	12.0	8	3	3	1	0	2	0	7	0
Lovelace, Richmond*	0	0	.000	5.00	5	0	0	1	0	0	9.0	10	5	5	0	0	6	0	7	1
Loynd, Richmond	8	5	.615	3.85	18	18	1	0	1	0	107.2	98	53	46	9	7	34	1	85	7

Pitcher, Team	W	L	Pct.	ERA	G	GS	CG	GF	ShO	Sv.	IP	H	R	ER	HR	HB	BB	Int. BB	SO	WP
Lumley, Toledo	0	2	.000	6.57	6	2	0	2	0	0	12.1	13	10	9	1	5	8	0	7	1
Lyons, Pawtucket	0	0	.000	9.00	2	0	0	2	0	0	2.0	3	5	2	1	0	2	0	4	1
Manuel, Rochester	1	1	.500	3.66	9	0	0	2	0	0	19.2	14	8	8	2	1	7	0	11	0
Manzanillo, Norfolk	1	5	.167	3.11	14	12	2	1	1	0	84.0	82	40	29	3	2	25	1	79	0
Marshall, Norfolk*	0	2	.000	19.64	4	1	0	1	0	0	7.1	19	18	16	2	0	4	1	3	1
Mathile, Ottawa	9	9	.500	4.17	31	21	2	6	2	1	140.1	147	74	65	9	6	41	1	56	7
Mauser, Scranton-WB	2	0	1.000	0.87	19	0	0	19	0	10	20.2	10	2	2	1	0	5	0	25	4
McCarthy, Charlotte	6	5	.545	4.11	45	2	0	11	0	2	105.0	104	55	48	15	5	26	4	61	5
McGehee, Rochester	7	6	.538	2.96	20	20	2	0	0	0	133.2	124	53	44	14	7	37	1	92	3
Melendez, Pawtucket	2	3	.400	5.40	19	0	0	10	0	2	35.0	37	24	21	7	2	7	0	31	2
Menhart, Syracuse	9	10	.474	3.64	25	25	4	0	0	0	151.0	143	74	61	16	7	67	4	108	8
Milacki, Charlotte	4	3	.571	3.39	21	7	0	8	0	4	71.2	59	31	27	6	0	19	1	46	4
Militello, Columbus	1	3	.250	5.73	7	7	0	0	0	0	33.0	36	22	21	7	1	20	0	39	4
Milstien, Pawtucket	0	0	.000	15.19	5	0	0	5	0	0	5.1	9	9	9	1	2	4	0	4	0
Minchey, Pawtucket	7	14	.333	4.02	29	29	7	0	2	0	194.2	182	103	87	22	10	50	1	113	8
Moyer, Rochester*	6	0	1.000	1.67	8	8	1	0	1	0	54.0	42	13	10	2	3	13	0	41	0
Munoz, Columbus	3	1	.750	1.44	22	1	0	18	0	10	31.1	24	6	5	0	0	8	0	16	1
Mutis, Charlotte*	6	0	1.000	2.62	12	11	3	0	0	0	75.2	64	27	22	1	3	25	3	59	1
Nabholz, Ottawa*	1	1	.500	4.39	5	5	0	0	0	0	26.2	24	15	13	1	0	7	0	20	0
O'Donoghue, Rochester*	7	4	.636	3.88	22	20	2	1	1	0	127.2	122	60	55	11	3	41	0	111	3
Ogea, Charlotte	13	8	.619	3.81	29	29	2	0	0	0	181.2	169	91	77	26	2	54	0	135	6
Ohlms, Syracuse	3	6	.333	7.05	47	0	0	24	0	5	60.0	85	50	47	7	3	42	4	37	8
Ojala, Columbus*	8	9	.471	5.50	31	20	0	3	0	0	126.0	145	85	77	13	3	71	2	83	13
Oquist, Rochester	9	8	.529	3.50	28	21	2	1	1	0	149.1	144	62	58	20	2	41	1	128	5
Parris, Scranton-WB	0	0	.000	12.71	3	0	0	0	0	0	5.2	9	9	8	3	1	3	0	4	1
Patterson, Scranton-WB	7	5	.583	2.69	62	0	0	31	0	8	93.2	79	32	28	3	2	42	11	68	8
Pennington, Rochester*	1	2	.333	3.45	17	0	0	14	0	8	15.2	12	11	6	0	0	13	0	19	1
Perez, Ottawa*	0	1	.000	3.60	20	0	0	12	0	5	20.0	14	12	8	0	0	7	0	17	3
Picota, Ottawa	0	1	.000	7.36	8	0	0	3	0	0	7.1	12	6	6	1	0	5	1	3	0
Plummer, Norfolk	7	3	.700	5.16	47	2	0	25	0	4	75.0	93	47	43	6	6	26	2	47	0
Plympton, Pawtucket	2	1	.667	4.44	30	0	0	12	0	1	50.2	54	33	25	7	2	15	0	48	4
Polley, Richmond*	1	0	1.000	3.93	10	0	0	3	0	0	18.1	21	9	8	1	1	11	1	14	0
Popplewell, Columbus	0	0	.000	4.50	1	0	0	0	0	0	2.0	2	1	1	0	0	1	0	2	0
Quirico, Columbus*	2	0	1.000	7.36	5	2	0	0	0	0	11.0	12	10	9	3	0	7	0	16	1
Reyes, Richmond	1	0	1.000	3.77	18	1	0	11	0	1	28.2	30	12	12	2	3	11	3	30	2
Rhodes, Rochester*	1	1	.500	4.05	6	6	0	0	0	0	26.2	26	12	12	5	0	15	0	33	5
Ricci, Rochester	0	0	.000	5.63	4	0	0	3	0	0	8.0	11	5	5	1	0	3	0	6	0
Rightnowar, Toledo	2	2	.500	3.55	22	6	0	4	0	1	58.1	57	32	23	3	7	19	0	32	2
Riley, Pawtucket*	4	4	.500	5.01	14	13	2	0	0	0	70.0	90	45	39	8	1	23	0	44	6
Risley, Ottawa	2	4	.333	2.69	41	0	0	12	0	1	63.2	51	26	19	7	3	34	3	74	5
Ritchie, Toledo*	1	0	1.000	4.76	62	0	0	14	0	4	45.1	44	26	24	5	0	15	2	29	2
Robertson, Toledo	0	0	.000	0.00	1	0	0	1	0	0	0.1	0	0	0	0	0	0	0	0	0
Robinson, 19 Rich. - 1 Char.	4	6	.400	5.81	20	6	0	3	0	0	52.2	62	37	34	7	3	26	1	43	4
Rodriguez, Columbus	0	0	.000	0.00	1	0	0	0	0	0	1.0	2	0	0	0	0	0	0	0	0
Rosario, Ottawa*	1	1	.500	3.58	22	0	0	12	0	0	27.2	22	12	11	1	0	21	4	28	0
Rueter, Ottawa*	4	2	.667	2.70	7	7	1	0	0	0	43.1	46	20	13	7	0	3	0	27	0
Ryan, Pawtucket	0	2	.000	2.49	18	0	0	15	0	8	25.1	19	9	7	1	2	17	4	22	2
St. Claire, 6 Rich. - 14 Syra.	1	2	.333	2.93	20	0	0	2	0	0	30.2	34	14	10	0	0	6	0	16	2
Satre, Rochester	4	5	.444	5.85	15	15	0	0	0	0	80.0	87	57	52	12	6	45	0	42	9
Schulze, Rochester	8	5	.615	4.10	39	9	1	20	0	7	96.2	111	49	44	10	7	24	2	65	5
Scudder, Charlotte	7	7	.500	5.03	23	22	2	0	0	0	136.0	148	92	76	21	7	52	1	64	5
Searcy, Rochester*	2	1	.667	6.00	16	0	0	5	0	1	15.0	19	10	10	2	0	15	0	12	0
Seiler, Columbus*	0	0	.000	13.50	1	0	0	0	0	0	2.0	2	3	3	1	0	2	1	1	0
Sele, Pawtucket	8	2	.800	2.19	14	14	2	0	1	0	94.1	74	30	23	8	5	23	0	87	1
Shaw, Ottawa	0	0	.000	0.00	2	1	0	0	0	0	4.0	5	0	0	0	0	2	0	1	0
Shea, Pawtucket*	2	2	.500	7.00	12	3	0	1	0	0	36.0	51	31	28	6	0	19	0	20	1
Shinall, Charlotte	0	0	.000	54.00	1	0	0	0	0	0	0.2	3	4	4	0	0	1	0	0	0
Simons, Ottawa*	7	7	.500	4.75	34	13	1	6	0	0	115.2	134	67	61	13	2	16	2	75	3
Slocumb, Charlotte	3	2	.600	3.56	23	0	0	9	0	1	30.1	25	14	12	2	0	11	1	25	2
Smith, Norfolk*	0	2	.000	6.38	5	3	0	1	0	0	18.1	22	14	13	3	0	10	0	11	1
Solano, Charlotte	0	0	.000	7.50	3	0	0	0	0	0	6.0	7	5	5	1	0	3	1	5	1
Sparks, Pawtucket*	0	0	.000	0.00	1	0	0	1	0	0	1.0	1	1	0	0	0	1	0	0	0
Spoljaric, Syracuse*	8	7	.533	5.29	18	18	1	0	1	0	95.1	97	63	56	14	2	52	0	88	8
Stanford, Columbus	5	3	.625	5.04	36	7	0	19	0	0	103.2	119	65	58	13	6	56	3	44	11
Stephan, Rochester	3	7	.300	5.10	29	10	0	8	0	1	95.1	98	58	54	11	1	35	4	71	2
Strange, Richmond	1	2	.333	3.88	34	0	0	19	0	1	46.1	45	24	20	1	0	19	6	34	4
Taylor, Richmond	2	4	.333	1.98	59	0	0	55	0	26	68.1	56	19	15	3	2	26	7	81	1
Taylor, Pawtucket*	7	7	.500	4.04	47	8	0	10	0	1	122.2	132	61	55	12	3	48	0	88	2
Taylor, Columbus	3	1	.750	4.45	7	5	0	0	0	0	30.1	31	17	15	3	2	11	1	16	2
Telford, Rochester	7	7	.500	4.27	38	6	0	12	0	2	90.2	98	51	43	10	3	33	3	66	6
Telgheder, Norfolk	7	3	.700	2.95	13	12	0	1	0	0	76.1	81	29	25	6	3	19	1	52	1
Terrell, Syracuse	0	1	.000	5.30	8	6	0	1	0	0	35.2	41	25	21	5	2	11	0	20	1
Valdez, Ottawa	5	3	.625	3.12	30	4	0	6	0	1	83.2	77	31	29	3	6	22	2	53	7
Valenzuela, Rochester*	0	1	.000	10.80	1	1	0	0	0	0	3.1	6	4	4	0	0	3	0	1	0
Vann, Norfolk	4	4	.500	3.22	53	0	0	34	0	11	64.1	53	28	23	7	2	33	4	52	6
Walton, Ottawa	4	4	.500	1.05	40	0	0	38	0	16	42.2	32	12	5	2	0	8	2	40	0
Ward, Syracuse*	1	2	.333	3.70	35	1	0	12	0	1	41.1	37	22	17	7	4	25	3	45	1
Warren, Toledo	2	2	.500	3.44	24	1	0	11	0	0	36.2	40	17	14	3	2	11	2	26	3
Wegmann, Norfolk	5	3	.625	3.23	44	2	0	14	0	2	86.1	68	33	31	8	1	34	8	99	4
Wells, Scranton-WB	1	1	.500	2.79	11	0	0	3	0	0	19.1	19	7	6	1	1	5	0	8	2
Wells, Charlotte*	0	0	.000	4.26	6	0	0	0	0	0	6.1	9	5	3	0	0	6	1	5	2
Wertz, Charlotte	7	2	.778	1.95	28	1	0	9	0	0	50.2	42	18	11	4	1	14	4	47	1
Weston, Norfolk	10	9	.526	4.24	21	20	3	1	0	0	127.1	149	77	60	10	2	18	2	41	4
White, Ottawa*	2	1	.667	3.12	6	6	1	0	1	0	40.1	38	15	14	3	1	6	0	28	2
Willard, Richmond	0	0	.000	0.00	1	0	0	1	0	0	1.0	0	0	0	0	0	0	0	2	0
Williams, Rochester	2	5	.286	5.76	33	5	0	11	0	1	86.0	95	59	55	10	4	47	3	59	8
Williams, Scranton-WB	9	2	.818	2.87	14	13	1	1	1	0	97.1	93	34	31	7	2	16	0	53	0
Williams, Syracuse	1	1	.500	2.20	12	0	0	11	0	3	16.1	15	5	4	2	0	5	3	16	0
Witt, Columbus	1	0	1.000	1.98	3	3	0	0	0	0	13.2	13	3	3	1	0	5	0	11	0
Wohlers, Richmond	1	3	.250	1.84	25	0	0	20	0	4	29.1	21	7	6	0	1	11	0	39	2
Wood, Rochester	1	2	.333	2.70	30	2	0	15	0	3	53.1	47	20	16	4	0	32	4	59	4
Woodall, Richmond*	5	3	.625	4.21	10	9	0	0	0	0	57.2	59	32	27	6	1	16	0	45	1
Yan, Syracuse	0	0	.000	18.00	2	0	0	2	0	0	2.0	4	4	4	1	0	0	1	1	0
Young, Norfolk	1	1	.500	1.13	3	3	0	0	0	0	16.0	14	2	2	1	0	5	0	8	0

Pitcher, Team	W	L	Pct.	ERA	G	GS	CG	GF	ShO	Sv.	IP	H	R	ER	HR	HB	BB	Int. BB	SO	WP
Young, Charlotte*	3	1	.750	2.15	5	5	1	0	1	0	37.2	30	10	9	4	0	2	0	21	0
Young, 3 Char. -7 Syra.*	5	1	.833	2.37	10	8	1	1	0	0	49.1	33	15	13	2	5	19	0	55	0
Young, Ottawa	4	5	.444	3.72	48	0	0	16	0	1	72.2	63	32	30	5	6	33	10	46	2

BALKS—Ogea, 4; A. Cook, Stanford, 3 each; Bergman, Blohm, Brow, Carlyle, D. Cook, Green, 2 each; Bailey, Birkbeck, Borbon, Borland, Burlingame, Byrd, Carter, Caruso, Clements, Cross, DeSilva, Fortugno, D. Hall, Hines, Hutton, Langbehn, Lira, Menhart, Mutis, Ojala, Oquist, Patterson, Pennington, Plympton, Reyes, Rhodes, Riley, Ryan, Schulze, Spoljaric, S. Taylor, Wegmann, J. Williams, 1 each.

COMBINATION SHUTOUTS—Mutis-McCarthy-Christopher, Young-Grimsley-DiPoto, Charlotte; Clayton-Greer, Clayton-Munoz, Hitchcock-Greer, Hitchcock-Quirico-Batchelor, Hutton-DeLaRosa, Hutton-Hines-Clayton, Jean-Clayton, Witt-Stanford-Greer-Batchelor, Columbus; Gozzo-Langbehn-Kaiser, Jones-Gibson, Jones-Langbehn, Manzanillo-Vann-Plummer, Norfolk; Boucher-Young-Perez, Fortugno-Valdez, Heredia-Perez, Heredia-Shaw-Picota, Jones-Valdez, Nabholz-Mathile-Young-Simons, Nabholz-Walton, Ottawa; Clemens-Riley-Plympton, Conroy-Taylor-Ryan, Finnvold-Florence-Ryan, Finnvold-Melendez, Finnvold-Taylor, Livernois-Bailey, Pawtucket; Bark-Johnson-Taylor-Wohlers, Bark-Taylor, Bark-Wohlers, Birkbeck-Borbon-Wohlers, Birkbeck-Johnson-Wohlers-Taylor, Birkbeck-Robinson-Strange-Johnson, Richmond; McGehee-Schulze-Cook, McGehee-Williams, O'Donoghue-Cook, Stephan-O'Donoghue, Telford-Wood-Cook, Rochester; Allen-Carter, Green-Hall, Williams-Hall, Scranton-Wilkes Barre; Cross-Akerfelds, Menhart-Bailes-Linton, Spoljaric-Ohlms, Young-Hall, Syracuse; Groom-Johnson-Ritchie-Fraser-Grater, Toledo.

PERFECT GAME—Brown, Syracuse, defeated Toledo, 2-0 (second game), June 1.

NO-HIT GAMES—Nabholz-Walton, Ottawa, defeated Richmond, 4-0, May 24; Green, Scranton-Wilkes Barre, defeated Ottawa, 3-1 (first game), July 4.

FIELDING

TEAM

Team	Pct.	G	PO	A	E	DP	PB	Team	Pct.	G	PO	A	E	DP	PB
Columbus	.975	141	3680	1556	134	158	16	Ottawa	.973	142	3696	1575	147	120	11
Charlotte	.975	141	3718	1558	136	130	10	Scranton W.B.	.972	142	3721	1393	147	107	10
Rochester	.974	141	3746	1440	137	124	14	Syracuse	.971	142	3663	1503	153	130	18
Toledo	.974	142	3656	1484	137	136	5	Richmond	.970	142	3706	1515	164	133	26
Norfolk	.974	141	3742	1605	144	167	16	Pawtucket	.968	142	3733	1453	174	145	7

Triple plays—Columbus, Norfolk, Syracuse.

INDIVIDUAL

FIRST BASEMEN

*Throws lefthanded.

Player, Team	Pct.	G	PO	A	E	DP
Allred, Charlotte*	1.000	1	2	0	0	0
Bieser, Scranton W.B.	1.000	1	5	0	0	0
Bilardello, Norfolk	1.000	11	89	6	0	11
Brady, Scranton W.B.	.969	18	118	6	4	10
BROGNA, Toledo*	.992	116	937	97	8	102
Canale, Charlotte	.986	63	532	23	8	45
Carey, Rochester*	.993	91	752	53	6	70
Cianfrocco, Ottawa	.994	18	147	12	1	15
Cockrell, Charlotte	1.000	8	33	4	0	5
Colbrunn, Ottawa	1.000	6	50	1	0	3
Coolbaugh, Rochester	1.000	7	65	3	0	4
Cruz, Toledo*	.993	28	268	27	2	23
Davis, Rochester	1.000	5	28	7	0	2
Dickerson, Rochester	.900	7	6	3	1	1
Fernandez, Scranton W.B.	1.000	2	12	0	0	1
Floyd, Ottawa*	.983	31	272	23	5	23
Garner, Ottawa	.923	1	11	1	1	0
Gedman, Columbus	.750	1	3	0	1	0
Giannelli, Syracuse	1.000	3	19	1	0	1
Hansen, Ottawa	.978	20	171	11	4	7
Hare, Toledo*	1.000	2	1	0	0	0
Horn, Charlotte*	.983	7	58	0	1	5
Hunter, Richmond*	1.000	22	165	15	0	14
Klesko, Richmond	.985	66	569	42	9	60
Kunkel, Charlotte	.992	39	234	21	2	26
Laker, Ottawa	1.000	1	9	0	0	2
Lindsey, Scranton W.B.	1.000	2	12	1	0	0
L. Lopez, Charlotte	.990	52	396	20	4	32
Lyons, Pawtucket	.978	14	129	2	3	14
Maas, Columbus*	.976	27	270	20	7	27
Manto, Scranton W.B.	.995	53	347	35	2	27
Martinez, Charlotte	.988	17	78	6	1	8
Martinez, Syracuse	.986	121	991	104	16	94
McIntosh, Ottawa	1.000	1	6	1	0	1
Mercado, Charlotte	1.000	1	11	0	0	0
Meulens, Columbus	.958	18	164	17	8	24
Milstein, Pawtucket	.992	36	242	20	2	21
Montoyo, Ottawa	1.000	1	8	2	0	1
Mordecai, Richmond	1.000	1	8	1	0	1
O'Halloran, Syracuse	1.000	1	8	0	0	0
Ramos, Columbus	1.000	6	48	2	0	7
Ready, Rochester	1.000	12	94	9	0	6
Rodriguez, Columbus	1.000	4	6	0	0	1
Rodriguez, Richmond	.984	35	281	20	5	25
Rodriguez, Pawtucket	1.000	3	7	0	0	0
Rodriguez, Scranton W.B.	1.000	2	5	0	0	0
Ryan, Scranton W.B.	.992	45	335	24	3	32
Schall, Scranton W.B.	.991	39	287	28	3	22
Siddall, Ottawa	.929	3	12	1	1	3

Player, Team	Pct.	G	PO	A	E	DP
Sojo, Syracuse	1.000	1	2	0	0	0
Sparks, Columbus	.993	91	795	61	6	91
Sparks, Pawtucket*	.982	46	354	30	7	36
Springer, Norfolk	.993	14	125	11	1	14
Stevens, Syracuse*	1.000	8	56	4	0	7
Stubbs, Pawtucket*	.983	49	389	28	7	52
Tatum, Pawtucket	1.000	7	60	0	0	10
Thoutsis, Columbus	1.000	1	1	0	0	0
Twardoski, Norfolk*	.992	124	1087	80	9	126
Voigt, Rochester	1.000	2	18	1	0	1
Wearing, Rochester	.988	32	240	11	3	17
D. White, Ottawa	.988	67	632	49	8	57
Willard, Richmond	.982	34	248	23	5	17
Yan, Syracuse	.987	21	143	12	2	13

Triple plays—D. Martinez, D. Sparks, Twardoski.

SECOND BASEMEN

Player, Team	Pct.	G	PO	A	E	DP
Allison, Norfolk	.964	6	12	15	1	2
Caraballo, Richmond	.960	121	211	345	23	64
Cedeno, Syracuse	.957	28	42	68	5	13
Crowley, Pawtucket	.969	9	13	18	1	1
Dejardin, Columbus	.980	63	118	182	6	41
Dickerson, Rochester	1.000	2	4	5	0	1
Garcia, Rochester	.957	90	205	220	19	70
Giannelli, Syracuse	.970	82	113	207	10	39
Haney, Ottawa	.976	125	235	388	15	76
Henderson, Syracuse	1.000	2	1	5	0	1
Hinzo, Rochester	.966	136	267	415	24	75
Howard, Norfolk	1.000	2	4	5	0	1
Kunkel, Charlotte	.982	31	34	75	2	13
Legg, Scranton W.B.	.976	55	83	124	5	20
L. Lopez, Charlotte	1.000	3	3	2	0	0
Lyons, Pawtucket	.929	2	4	9	1	1
Malzone, Pawtucket	.935	18	21	22	3	4
Martinez, Norfolk	.900	2	5	4	1	1
Millette, Scranton W.B.	.967	49	92	114	7	26
Milstien, Pawtucket	.974	22	53	58	3	16
Montalvo, Syracuse	.982	40	46	66	2	20
Montoyo, Ottawa	.984	12	21	39	1	6
Mordecai, Richmond	.973	27	62	83	4	25
Naehring, Pawtucket	.988	15	36	48	1	10
PAREDES, Toledo	.980	132	270	369	13	91
Ready, Rochester	1.000	3	7	11	0	3
Richardson, Pawtucket	.900	3	3	6	1	3
Riles, Pawtucket	1.000	1	1	2	0	0
Robertson, Syracuse	.886	14	21	41	8	11
Rodriguez, Columbus	1.000	11	20	40	0	13
Rodriguez, Scranton W.B.	.989	39	80	96	2	22
Santangelo, Ottawa	.967	5	16	13	1	3

Player, Team	Pct.	G	PO	A	E	DP
Saunders, Norfolk	.973	101	209	322	15	78
Schaefer, Charlotte	.970	129	250	386	20	91
Sojo, Syracuse	.953	19	27	55	4	13
Sparks, Columbus	1.000	1	0	1	0	0
Springer, Norfolk	1.000	1	2	2	0	1
Stankiewicz, Columbus	.989	72	129	236	4	51
Vargas, Ottawa	1.000	5	7	12	0	2
Vina, Norfolk	.974	33	83	101	5	28
Waller, Scranton W.B.	.983	15	26	31	1	13

Triple play—Cedeno.

THIRD BASEMEN

Player, Team	Pct.	G	PO	A	E	DP
Allison, Norfolk	.889	3	2	6	1	1
Bolick, Ottawa	1.000	2	0	4	0	0
Brady, Scranton W.B.	1.000	4	0	12	0	1
Castaldo, Ottawa	.922	56	23	96	10	5
Cianfrocco, Ottawa	.895	10	5	12	2	2
Coolbaugh, Rochester	.912	110	82	156	23	18
Crowley, Pawtucket	.857	3	1	5	1	0
Davis, Columbus	.922	109	71	225	25	24
Dejardin, Columbus	.750	2	0	6	2	2
Dellicarri, Norfolk	1.000	1	0	2	0	0
Dickerson, Rochester	.909	9	1	9	1	2
Giannelli, Syracuse	1.000	4	0	3	0	0
Gomez, Rochester	1.000	3	1	5	0	0
Hansen, Ottawa	.714	3	0	5	2	1
Howard, Norfolk	.818	16	6	12	4	3
Humphreys, Columbus	.786	6	2	9	3	1
Kunkel, Charlotte	.943	26	8	25	2	0
Legg, Scranton W.B.	.750	4	3	6	3	0
L. Lopez, Charlotte	.800	7	4	4	2	0
Lyons, Pawtucket	.929	6	3	10	1	1
Malzone, Pawtucket	.876	50	30	69	14	10
Manto, Scranton W.B.	.961	54	50	98	6	14
Martinez, Norfolk	.955	19	8	34	2	1
Martinez, Charlotte	.960	12	7	17	1	0
Martinez, Syracuse	.714	3	1	4	2	0
Meulens, Columbus	.000	1	0	0	3	0
Millette, Scranton W.B.	1.000	1	1	3	0	0
Milstien, Pawtucket	.914	14	7	25	3	3
Montoyo, Ottawa	.930	51	29	90	9	14
Mordecai, Richmond	.900	15	3	24	3	0
Naehring, Pawtucket	.967	20	18	40	2	5
Oliva, Richmond	.929	121	44	205	19	13
Ortiz, Pawtucket	.928	63	41	114	12	11
Pevey, Toledo	1.000	1	1	1	0	1
QUINLAN, Syracuse	.957	140	128	273	18	25
Ready, Rochester	.930	27	18	48	5	4
Reimink, Toledo	.924	58	30	92	10	6
Richardson, Pawtucket	1.000	2	1	4	0	0
Riles, Pawtucket	1.000	1	2	4	0	0
Robertson, Toledo	.930	90	59	154	16	21
Robinson, Norfolk	1.000	2	4	2	0	1
Rodriguez, Columbus	.881	24	3	34	5	3
Rodriguez, Richmond	1.000	1	1	2	0	0
Rodriguez, Scranton W.B.	.963	64	44	86	5	8
Santangelo, Ottawa	.848	15	7	21	5	2
Silvestri, Columbus	1.000	8	9	16	0	0
Sojo, Syracuse	1.000	2	2	3	0	1
Sparks, Columbus	.875	6	3	11	2	3
Springer, Norfolk	.945	113	70	241	18	37
Stankiewicz, Columbus	.971	15	7	27	1	2
Thome, Charlotte	.951	114	67	226	15	18
Twardoski, Norfolk*	1.000	1	0	4	0	0
Vargas, Ottawa	.929	21	13	39	4	1
Voigt, Rochester	1.000	3	2	3	0	1
Waller, Scranton W.B.	.840	32	16	47	12	3

SHORTSTOPS

Player, Team	Pct.	G	PO	A	E	DP
ALEXANDER, Rochester	.966	119	184	335	18	71
Allison, Norfolk	1.000	1	0	1	0	0
Baez, Norfolk	.950	63	94	193	15	40
Barker, Ottawa	.955	51	85	148	11	27
Byrd, Pawtucket	.940	116	202	314	33	64
Cedeno, Syracuse	.946	78	108	174	16	43
Davis, Columbus	.971	5	14	20	1	7
Dejardin, Columbus	1.000	9	11	21	0	5
Dellicarri, Norfolk	.824	4	7	7	3	3
Dickerson, Rochester	.957	18	19	47	3	10
Givens, Toledo	.957	43	57	119	8	23
C. Gomez, Toledo	.961	87	133	261	16	57
Haney, Ottawa	1.000	7	10	13	0	2
Henderson, Syracuse	.914	11	10	22	3	5
Holland, Rochester	.939	8	10	21	2	5
C. Jones, Richmond	.931	129	195	381	43	74
Kunkel, Charlotte	.983	14	14	45	1	6
Legg, Scranton W.B.	1.000	1	0	2	0	0
Lewis, Charlotte	.961	125	168	403	23	81
Martinez, Norfolk	.952	37	61	97	8	29

Player, Team	Pct.	G	PO	A	E	DP
Millette, Scranton W.B.	.939	58	75	140	14	18
Milstien, Pawtucket	.933	12	21	35	4	7
Montalvo, Syracuse	.940	39	45	97	9	13
Montoyo, Ottawa	.966	37	43	99	5	19
Mordecai, Richmond	.966	17	19	37	2	11
Naehring, Pawtucket	.986	16	25	45	1	13
Navarro, Norfolk	.861	8	14	17	5	6
Oliva, Richmond	1.000	1	0	1	0	0
Quinlan, Syracuse	1.000	1	2	2	0	2
Richardson, Pawtucket	.889	4	4	12	2	1
Riles, Pawtucket	.900	2	2	7	1	2
Robertson, Toledo	.984	15	18	42	1	7
Rodriguez, Columbus	.992	36	51	72	1	17
Rodriguez, Scranton W.B.	.939	12	11	20	2	3
Santangelo, Ottawa	.979	54	84	149	5	32
Schaefer, Charlotte	1.000	5	3	7	0	3
Silvestri, Columbus	.966	105	171	283	16	73
Sojo, Syracuse	1.000	1	1	2	0	1
Stankiewicz, Columbus	.800	1	2	2	1	1
Stocker, Scranton W.B.	.961	81	122	248	15	47
Valentin, Pawtucket	1.000	2	8	9	0	4
Vargas, Ottawa	.833	1	2	3	1	0
Vina, Norfolk	.955	37	60	131	9	26
Zosky, Syracuse	.960	27	48	71	5	18

Triple plays—Baez, Montalvo, Silvestri.

OUTFIELDERS

Player, Team	Pct.	G	PO	A	E	DP
Allred, Charlotte*	.978	115	212	9	5	4
Alstead, Rochester	1.000	21	29	2	0	0
Amaro, Scranton W.B.	.982	99	272	8	5	2
Bieser, Scranton W.B.	.978	18	44	0	1	0
Blosser, Pawtucket*	.968	115	199	13	7	1
Brady, Scranton W.B.	1.000	30	63	1	0	0
Bryant, Ottawa	.978	73	126	5	3	1
Buford, Rochester	.962	27	73	3	3	1
Bullock, Norfolk*	.980	115	195	6	4	1
Burnitz, Norfolk	.993	65	133	9	1	2
Butler, Syracuse*	.989	55	93	1	1	0
Canate, Syracuse	1.000	6	9	2	0	1
Cangelosi, Toledo*	.973	112	251	5	7	0
Carpenter, Columbus*	.969	56	91	3	3	1
Castaldo, Ottawa	.800	2	3	1	1	0
Chick, Pawtucket	.981	29	51	0	1	0
Cianfrocco, Ottawa	1.000	25	36	2	0	0
Cockrell, Charlotte	.955	68	100	6	5	0
Davidson, Charlotte	.987	88	147	8	2	2
Dejardin, Columbus	.971	18	33	1	1	0
de la Rosa, Syracuse	.984	54	122	1	2	0
Dostal, 4 SWB-83 Roch.*	.985	87	188	6	3	1
Garcia, Pawtucket	1.000	1	1	0	0	0
Gladden, Toledo	.846	7	11	0	2	0
Hammonds, Rochester	1.000	30	72	1	0	0
Hansen, Ottawa	.976	72	120	2	3	0
Hare, Toledo*	.975	106	189	5	5	1
Hernandez, Columbus	1.000	1	1	0	0	0
Hirtensteiner, Ottawa*	1.000	8	6	1	0	0
Housie, Norfolk	.977	16	40	2	1	0
Howard, Norfolk	.953	27	35	6	2	3
Humphreys, Columbus	.983	80	170	7	3	1
Hunter, Norfolk	.931	19	27	0	2	0
Hunter, Richmond*	1.000	5	9	0	0	0
Hurst, Toledo*	.933	55	93	5	7	1
Hyde, Scranton W.B.	1.000	2	2	0	0	0
Ingram, Toledo	.988	104	167	2	2	0
L. Jones, Richmond	.933	9	14	0	1	0
R. Jones, Richmond	1.000	23	25	1	0	0
KELLY, Richmond	.993	117	270	6	2	1
Kirby, Charlotte	1.000	17	38	1	0	1
Klesko, Richmond*	.875	18	18	3	3	0
Knoblauh, Columbus	.992	52	123	3	1	0
Kowitz, Richmond*	.955	12	20	1	1	0
Kunkel, Charlotte	.982	30	54	2	1	0
Landrum, Norfolk	.972	64	134	3	4	1
Leonard, Rochester	.985	69	127	2	2	1
Longmire, Scranton W.B.	.976	107	195	5	5	1
L. Lopez, Charlotte	1.000	8	17	0	0	0
Lyons, Pawtucket	.970	42	57	7	2	3
Mack, Ottawa*	1.000	4	11	1	0	0
Marsh, Scranton W.B.	.957	64	145	10	7	5
Martinez, Norfolk	1.000	7	6	2	0	0
Martinez, Syracuse	1.000	2	4	0	0	0
Martinez, Rochester*	.911	29	36	5	4	2
Masse, Columbus	.976	99	154	10	4	3
McIntosh, Columbus	.964	14	26	1	1	0
McNeely, Pawtucket	.963	127	284	6	11	1
Meulens, Columbus	.928	56	100	3	8	1
Mitchell, Richmond	.960	102	138	7	6	1
Montalvo, Syracuse	1.000	9	18	1	0	1
Moore, Richmond	1.000	1	1	0	0	0
Mordecai, Richmond	1.000	7	4	0	0	0
Nieves, Richmond	.949	68	124	5	7	1
Ortiz, Pawtucket	1.000	6	4	0	0	0

— 357 —

Player, Team	Pct.	G	PO	A	E	DP
Perez, Syracuse	.960	137	278	13	12	3
Pevey, Toledo	.714	4	5	0	2	0
Pride, Ottawa	.986	68	136	3	2	1
Ramirez, Charlotte	.961	39	70	3	3	0
Ramos, Charlotte*	.991	124	205	11	2	0
Ready, Rochester	.975	25	37	2	1	0
Robertson, Toledo	.875	5	7	0	1	0
Ross, Pawtucket*	1.000	19	32	0	0	0
Sandy, Norfolk	1.000	6	5	0	0	0
Santangelo, Ottawa	.979	59	139	3	3	1
Scott, Syracuse	.985	91	193	4	3	3
Siddall, Ottawa	1.000	3	3	0	0	0
Silvestri, Columbus	1.000	1	3	0	0	0
Smith, Rochester	.975	127	261	9	7	1
Sojo, Syracuse	1.000	13	14	0	0	0
Sparks, Pawtucket*	1.000	2	2	1	0	0
Stairs, Ottawa	1.000	29	49	4	0	1
Stevens, Syracuse*	.981	85	145	8	3	0
Tarasco, Richmond	.987	92	143	8	2	3
Taylor, Scranton W.B.*	.979	53	92	3	2	1
Thompson, Norfolk	.973	59	138	4	4	0
Thoutsis, Pawtucket	.968	54	90	0	3	0
Twardoski, Norfolk*	1.000	5	9	1	0	0
Viera, Columbus*	.750	3	2	1	1	0
Vina, Norfolk	1.000	1	3	0	0	0
Voigt, Rochester	.950	14	18	1	1	0
Wade, Norfolk	.882	21	30	0	4	0
Wearing, Rochester	1.000	16	26	1	0	0
Wegmann, Norfolk	1.000	2	1	0	0	0
R. White, Ottawa	.988	35	79	0	1	0
C. Williams, Scranton W.B.	.983	72	168	4	3	2
Williams, Columbus	.985	79	191	6	3	1
Williams, Toledo	.941	60	94	2	6	0
Winningham, 55 Paw.-34 Nor.	.975	89	187	5	5	1
Wood, Ottawa*	1.000	70	108	6	0	0
Yacopino, Rochester*	1.000	14	24	1	0	0

Triple play—G. Williams.

CATCHERS

Player, Team	Pct.	G	PO	A	E	DP	PB
Alomar, Charlotte	1.000	5	20	1	0	0	0
Bieser, Scranton W.B.	1.000	6	41	3	0	1	0
Bilardello, Norfolk	.967	30	150	25	6	3	4
Campbell, Rochester	.992	51	243	13	2	1	2
Fernandez, Scranton W.B.	1.000	4	12	2	0	0	0
Flaherty, Pawtucket	.986	101	626	78	10	7	5
Fordyce, Norfolk	.990	114	735	67	8	11	12
Gedman, Columbus	.991	84	495	47	5	3	8
Hatteberg, Pawtucket	.964	18	131	4	5	0	0
Hernandez, Columbus	.976	22	76	7	2	0	2
Houston, Richmond	.959	12	69	2	3	1	2
Hymel, Ottawa	1.000	3	5	0	0	0	0
Kremers, Ottawa	1.000	2	6	1	0	0	0
Laker, Ottawa	.971	53	332	37	11	4	4
Levis, Charlotte	.986	45	266	22	4	1	5
Lieberthal, Scranton W.B.	.985	106	659	75	11	5	6
Lindsey, Scranton W.B.	.983	31	202	30	4	2	3
Livesey, Columbus	.986	33	132	13	2	1	3
Lopez, Richmond	.987	96	718	70	10	8	15
Lyons, Pawtucket	1.000	1	1	0	0	0	0
Manto, Scranton W.B.	1.000	2	4	1	0	0	0
Martin, Pawtucket	1.000	7	31	2	0	0	0
Marzano, Charlotte	.929	3	12	1	1	0	0
McIntosh, Ottawa	.988	11	71	10	1	1	0
Mercado, Charlotte	1.000	10	51	3	0	0	0
Montalvo, Syracuse	1.000	1	2	0	0	0	0
Monzon, Syracuse	.983	70	359	56	7	5	8
Mordecai, Richmond	1.000	3	2	0	0	0	0
Mota, Charlotte	.959	13	44	3	2	0	2
O'Halloran, Syracuse	.983	95	535	49	10	6	10
Palacios, Rochester	1.000	1	4	1	0	0	0
PARENT, Rochester	.995	86	549	63	3	11	11
Pevey, Toledo	.985	53	298	25	5	4	0
Pratt, Scranton W.B.	1.000	2	11	0	0	0	0
Rodriguez, Pawtucket	.983	27	157	15	3	1	2
Rowland, Toledo	.988	88	569	64	8	6	3
Sanchez, Columbus	.982	25	145	16	3	5	3
Sellers, Toledo	1.000	14	74	7	0	2	2
Siddall, Ottawa	.983	41	206	32	4	3	6
Spehr, Ottawa	.978	43	248	24	6	0	1
Stinnett, Charlotte	.985	95	495	48	8	4	3
Tackett, Rochester	.967	8	56	3	2	0	0
Willard, Richmond	.993	47	254	25	2	3	9
Zaun, Rochester	.975	21	141	18	4	4	0

PITCHERS

Player, Team	Pct.	G	PO	A	E	DP
Abbott, Scranton W.B.*	1.000	27	10	15	0	1
Abbott, Charlotte	1.000	4	1	2	0	0
Adkins, Syracuse*	1.000	5	0	2	0	0
Akerfelds, Syracuse	1.000	40	3	4	0	0

Player, Team	Pct.	G	PO	A	E	DP
Allen, Scranton W.B.	1.000	5	3	5	0	0
Alvarez, Ottawa	.846	25	10	34	8	3
Anderson, Charlotte*	1.000	7	1	0	0	0
August, Charlotte	.875	14	4	3	1	0
Ayrault, Scranton W.B.	1.000	5	0	1	0	0
Bailes, Syracuse*	.800	19	1	3	1	0
Bailey, Pawtucket	1.000	52	7	8	0	1
Bark, Richmond*	.967	29	7	22	1	1
Batchelor, Columbus	1.000	15	0	1	0	0
Bergman, Toledo	1.000	19	12	23	0	2
Bielecki, Rochester	.941	9	6	10	1	0
Birkbeck, Richmond	1.000	27	17	34	0	4
Blohm, Syracuse	.871	30	8	19	4	2
Blomdahl, Toledo	1.000	11	3	5	0	0
Borbon, Richmond*	.813	52	2	11	3	0
Borland, Scranton W.B.	1.000	26	1	6	0	0
Boucher, Ottawa*	.900	11	2	7	1	1
Brantley, 7 SWB-6 Ott.	1.000	13	6	8	0	2
Brink, Scranton W.B.	.810	18	9	8	4	0
Brito, Ottawa	1.000	23	3	4	0	0
Brow, Syracuse	.943	20	9	24	2	1
Brown, Syracuse	.929	28	12	14	2	1
Burlingame, Richmond	1.000	8	1	9	0	0
Byrd, Charlotte	.909	14	2	8	1	0
Cangelosi, Syracuse	1.000	1	1	0	0	0
Carlyle, Toledo	.938	15	6	9	1	1
Carter, Scranton W.B.*	.929	30	4	9	1	2
Caruso, Pawtucket	1.000	36	7	11	0	1
Castillo, Syracuse*	1.000	1	1	1	0	0
Charland, Charlotte*	.500	1	0	1	0	0
Christopher, Charlotte	1.000	50	5	7	0	1
Ciccarella, Pawtucket*	1.000	12	1	4	0	0
Clark, Charlotte	1.000	2	0	2	0	0
Clayton, Columbus	.976	47	12	28	1	3
Clemens, Pawtucket	1.000	1	0	1	0	0
Clements, Rochester*	1.000	8	1	9	0	0
Combs, Scranton W.B.*	.813	15	3	10	3	0
Conroy, Pawtucket	.929	19	6	7	1	0
Cook, Columbus	1.000	21	10	27	0	2
Cook, Charlotte*	1.000	12	1	9	0	0
Cook, Rochester	.706	57	5	7	5	2
Corbett, Toledo*	1.000	5	0	1	0	0
Cross, Syracuse	1.000	29	9	25	0	1
Curtis, Charlotte*	1.000	7	0	3	0	0
Dedrick, Rochester	1.000	1	2	3	0	0
DeLaRosa, Columbus	.889	31	2	6	1	0
DeSilva, Toledo	.925	25	17	20	3	0
DiPoto, Charlotte	1.000	34	1	4	0	0
DuBois, Rochester*	1.000	3	0	4	0	0
Duey, Syracuse	.500	11	1	0	1	1
Eiland, Charlotte	1.000	8	4	8	0	1
Eischen, Ottawa*	1.000	6	0	7	0	0
Elliott, Richmond	.955	18	8	13	1	1
Farmer, Ottawa	.500	2	0	1	1	0
Filer, Norfolk	.962	22	5	20	1	3
Finnvold, Pawtucket	.944	24	9	8	1	1
Fletcher, Scranton W.B.	.875	34	12	9	3	0
Florence, Pawtucket*	.944	57	3	14	1	0
Fortugno, Ottawa*	.833	28	1	9	2	0
Foster, Scranton W.B.	1.000	17	7	8	0	1
Fraser, Toledo	.769	53	5	5	3	0
Freeman, Richmond	1.000	2	2	0	0	0
Gaddy, Scranton W.B.*	.692	23	3	6	4	0
Gakeler, Pawtucket	1.000	6	0	2	0	0
Gardiner, 5 Ott.-4 Tol.	1.000	9	0	6	0	0
Gibson, 14 Nor.-3 Col.*	1.000	17	0	1	0	0
Gogolewski, Columbus	1.000	28	1	3	0	0
Gohr, Toledo	.947	18	8	10	1	0
Gonzales, Toledo*	1.000	29	9	25	0	1
GOZZO, Norfolk	1.000	28	17	36	0	3
Grater, Toledo	1.000	28	7	2	0	0
Green, Scranton W.B.	.833	28	7	18	5	1
Greer, Columbus	1.000	46	4	12	0	1
Grimsley, Charlotte	.808	28	10	11	5	0
Groom, Toledo*	1.000	16	4	19	0	0
Gullickson, Toledo	1.000	1	2	0	0	0
Gunderson, Norfolk*	.800	6	0	4	1	0
Hall, Scranton W.B.*	1.000	61	4	4	0	1
Hall, Syracuse	.963	60	11	15	1	1
Henry, Ottawa*	1.000	5	4	4	0	0
Heredia, Ottawa	.973	16	16	20	1	1
Hill, Ottawa	1.000	1	0	1	0	0
Hillman, Norfolk*	.917	10	2	9	1	1
Hines, Columbus*	.667	43	2	4	3	0
Hitchcock, Columbus*	.900	16	3	6	1	0
Holman, Richmond	.947	37	16	20	2	3
Hostetler, Richmond	1.000	9	4	7	0	0
Hudek, Toledo	1.000	16	1	6	0	0
Hurst, Ottawa	.875	8	2	5	1	0
Hutton, Columbus	1.000	21	7	21	0	2
Jean, Columbus	1.000	7	4	7	0	1
Johnson, Toledo	1.000	9	2	7	0	0
Johnson, Richmond*	1.000	49	2	10	0	1
Johnson, Columbus*	1.000	19	4	26	0	2
Jones, Ottawa	1.000	3	0	4	0	1

Player, Team	Pct.	G	PO	A	E	DP	Player, Team	Pct.	G	PO	A	E	DP
Jones, Norfolk	1.000	24	10	23	0	4	Robinson, 19 Rich.-1 Char.	1.000	20	6	4	0	1
Kaiser, Norfolk*	1.000	21	3	2	0	1	Rosario, Ottawa*	.889	22	0	8	1	1
KamienIecki, Columbus	1.000	1	0	2	0	0	Rueter, Ottawa*	1.000	7	3	10	0	0
Kiely, Toledo	.833	37	4	1	1	0	Ryan, Pawtucket	1.000	18	1	3	0	0
Knudsen, Toledo	1.000	23	0	4	0	0	St. Claire, 6 Rich.-14 Syra.	1.000	20	1	8	0	0
Krivda, Rochester*	1.000	5	0	2	0	0	Satre, Rochester	1.000	15	4	5	0	0
Krueger, Toledo*	1.000	3	1	1	0	0	Schulze, Rochester	.931	39	9	18	2	2
Langbehn, Norfolk*	1.000	49	5	7	0	0	Scudder, Charlotte	.955	23	7	14	1	3
Linton, Syracuse	1.000	13	3	9	0	0	Searcy, Rochester*	1.000	16	1	1	0	0
Lira, Toledo	1.000	5	6	1	0	1	Seiler, Columbus*	.000	1	0	0	1	0
Livernois, Pawtucket	.955	27	7	14	1	0	Sele, Pawtucket	1.000	14	3	11	0	2
A. Lopez, Charlotte	1.000	3	2	0	0	0	Shaw, Ottawa	1.000	2	1	1	0	1
Lovelace, Richmond*	1.000	5	0	1	0	0	Shea, Pawtucket*	1.000	12	3	7	0	1
Loynd, Richmond	.966	18	10	18	1	3	Shinall, Charlotte	1.000	1	0	1	0	0
Lumley, Toledo	1.000	6	0	5	0	0	Simons, Ottawa*	1.000	34	5	14	0	1
Manuel, Rochester	.667	9	0	2	1	0	Slocumb, Charlotte	.875	23	4	3	1	0
Manzanillo, Norfolk	1.000	14	5	8	0	3	Smith, Norfolk*	1.000	5	1	5	0	0
Marshall, Norfolk*	1.000	4	0	2	0	0	Solano, Charlotte	1.000	3	0	1	0	0
Mathile, Ottawa	1.000	31	13	26	0	2	Spoljaric, Syracuse*	.864	18	4	15	3	1
Mauser, Scranton W.B.	1.000	19	0	4	0	0	Stanford, Columbus	.909	36	3	7	1	1
McCarthy, Charlotte	.960	45	10	14	1	1	Stephan, Rochester	.929	29	2	11	1	2
McGehee, Rochester	1.000	20	6	12	0	1	Strange, Richmond	1.000	34	5	4	0	0
Melendez, Pawtucket	.800	19	3	1	1	0	Taylor, Pawtucket*	.941	47	7	25	2	3
Menhart, Syracuse	.867	25	20	19	6	2	Taylor, Columbus	1.000	7	2	3	0	1
Milacki, Charlotte	.952	21	6	14	1	0	Taylor, Richmond	.929	59	3	10	1	2
Militello, Columbus	.750	7	1	5	2	1	Telford, Rochester	.885	38	7	16	3	1
Milstien, Pawtucket	1.000	5	1	1	0	0	Telgheder, Norfolk	.941	13	4	12	1	1
Minchey, Pawtucket	1.000	29	17	22	0	1	Terrell, Syracuse	.889	8	3	5	1	0
Moyer, Rochester*	1.000	8	4	13	0	2	Valdez, Ottawa	.958	30	7	16	1	0
Munoz, Columbus	1.000	22	3	3	0	1	Vann, Rochester	1.000	53	0	11	0	0
Mutis, Charlotte*	.931	12	5	22	2	0	Walton, Ottawa	1.000	40	3	4	0	0
Nabholz, Ottawa*	.889	5	3	5	1	0	Ward, Syracuse*	.833	35	0	10	2	1
O'Donoghue, Rochester*	.929	22	5	21	2	0	Warren, Toledo	1.000	24	5	10	0	0
Ogea, Charlotte	.911	29	14	27	4	1	Wegmann, Norfolk	1.000	44	8	10	0	2
Ohlms, Syracuse	1.000	47	8	12	0	2	Wells, Scranton W.B.	1.000	11	2	1	0	1
Ojala, Columbus*	.963	31	7	19	1	3	Wells, Charlotte*	1.000	6	0	3	0	0
Oquist, Rochester	.962	28	7	18	1	1	Wertz, Charlotte	.889	28	1	15	2	0
Parris, Scranton W.B.	1.000	3	0	3	0	0	Weston, Norfolk	.929	21	8	18	2	2
Patterson, Scranton W.B.	.867	62	6	7	2	0	G. White, Ottawa*	.800	5	2	2	1	0
Pennington, Rochester*	.000	17	0	0	1	0	Willard, Richmond	1.000	1	0	1	0	0
Perez, Ottawa*	.500	20	0	1	1	0	Williams, Syracuse	1.000	12	2	7	0	1
Picota, Ottawa	1.000	8	0	1	0	0	Williams, Rochester	.786	33	4	7	3	1
Plummer, Norfolk	.905	47	4	15	2	1	M. Williams, Scranton W.B.	.923	14	12	12	2	1
Plympton, Pawtucket	.941	30	6	10	1	1	Witt, Columbus	1.000	3	3	3	0	0
Polley, Richmond*	1.000	10	0	2	0	0	Wohlers, Richmond	1.000	25	3	3	0	0
Quirico, Columbus*	1.000	5	1	3	0	0	Wood, Rochester	1.000	30	2	4	0	0
Reyes, Richmond	1.000	18	2	5	0	0	Woodall, Richmond*	1.000	10	1	5	0	0
Rhodes, Rochester*	1.000	6	1	4	0	0	Yan, Charlotte	1.000	2	0	1	0	0
Ricci, Rochester	1.000	4	1	0	0	0	Young, Norfolk	1.000	3	2	2	0	1
Rightnowar, Toledo	.941	22	8	8	1	0	Young, Norfolk	1.000	48	6	12	0	1
Riley, Pawtucket*	1.000	14	1	9	0	0	C. Young, Charlotte*	1.000	5	3	4	0	0
Risley, Ottawa	.875	41	2	5	1	0	M. Young, 3 Char.-7 Syra.*	.917	10	4	7	1	1
Ritchie, Toledo	1.000	62											

The following players did not have any fielding statistics at the positions indicated or appeared only as a designated hitter, pinch-hitter or pinch-runner: Amaro, 2b; Bilardello, p; Caraballo, of; Clayton, of; Dejardin, 1b, p; Dellicarri, 2b; Garcia, ss; H. Gomez, p; Haas, p; D. Hall, of; Hare, p; Howe, p; Ingram, 3b; Lazorko, p; Lyons, p; Montalvo, 3b; Nixon, pr, dh, ph; Popplewell, p; Robertson, p; C. Rodriguez, p; Siddall, 3b; G. Sparks, p; Valenzuela, p.

LEAGUE CHAMPIONS

Year	Team	Pct.	Year	Team	Pct.	Year	Team	Pct.
1884—	Trenton	.520	1914—	Providence	.617	1941—	Newark	.649
1885—	Syracuse	.584	1915—	Buffalo	.632		Montreal (2nd)†	.584
1886—	Utica	.646	1916—	Buffalo	.586	1942—	Newark	.601
1887—	Toronto	.644	1917—	Toronto	.604		Syracuse (3rd)†	.513
1888—	Syracuse	.723	1918—	Toronto	.693	1943—	Toronto	.625
1889—	Detroit	.649	1919—	Baltimore	.671		Syracuse (3rd)†	.536
1890—	Detroit	.617	1920—	Baltimore	.719	1944—	Baltimore‡	.553
1891—	Buffalo (reg. season)	.727	1921—	Baltimore	.717	1945—	Montreal	.621
	Buffalo (supplem'l)	.680	1922—	Baltimore	.689		Newark (2nd)†	.582
1892—	Providence	.615	1923—	Baltimore	.677	1946—	Montreal‡	.649
	Binghamton*	.667	1924—	Baltimore	.709	1947—	Jersey City	.610
1893—	Erie	.606	1925—	Baltimore	.633		Syracuse (3rd)†	.575
1894—	Providence	.696	1926—	Toronto	.657	1948—	Montreal‡	.614
1895—	Springfield	.687	1927—	Buffalo	.667	1949—	Buffalo	.584
1896—	Providence	.602	1928—	Rochester	.549		Montreal (3rd)†	.545
1897—	Syracuse	.632	1929—	Rochester	.613	1950—	Rochester	.609
1898—	Montreal	.586	1930—	Rochester	.629		Baltimore (3rd)†	.556
1899—	Rochester	.624	1931—	Rochester	.601	1951—	Montreal‡	.617
1900—	Providence	.616	1932—	Newark	.649	1952—	Montreal	.629
1901—	Rochester	.642	1933—	Newark	.622		Rochester (3rd)†	.619
1902—	Toronto	.669		Buffalo (4th)†	.494	1953—	Rochester	.630
1903—	Jersey City	.742	1934—	Newark	.608		Montreal (2nd)†	.586
1904—	Buffalo	.657		Toronto (3rd)†	.559	1954—	Toronto	.630
1905—	Providence	.638	1935—	Montreal	.597		Syracuse (4th)§	.510
1906—	Buffalo	.607		Syracuse (2nd)†	.565	1955—	Montreal	.617
1907—	Toronto	.619	1936—	Buffalo‡	.610		Rochester (4th)†	.497
1908—	Baltimore	.593	1937—	Newark‡	.717	1956—	Toronto	.566
1909—	Rochester	.596	1938—	Newark‡	.684		Rochester (2nd)†	.553
1910—	Rochester	.601	1939—	Jersey City	.582	1957—	Toronto	.575
1911—	Rochester	.645		Rochester (2nd)†	.556		Buffalo (2nd)†	.571
1912—	Toronto	.595	1940—	Rochester	.611	1958—	Montreal‡	.588
1913—	Newark	.625		Newark (2nd)†	.594	1959—	Buffalo	.582

INTERNATIONAL LEAGUE

CLASS AAA

INTERNATIONAL LEAGUE

Year	Team	Pct.
	Havana (3rd)†	.523
1960—	Toronto‡	.649
1961—	Columbus	.597
	Buffalo (3rd)†	.559
1962—	Jacksonville	.610
	Atlanta (3rd)†	.539
1963—	Syracuse x	.533
	Indianapolis‡	.562
1964—	Jacksonville	.589
	Rochester (4th)†	.532
1965—	Columbus	.582
	Toronto (3rd)†	.556
1966—	Rochester	.565
	Toronto (2nd-tied)†	.558
1967—	Richmond	.574
	Toledo (3rd)†	.525
1968—	Toledo	.565
	Jacksonville (4th)†	.514
1969—	Tidewater	.563
	Syracuse (3rd)†	.536
1970—	Syracuse‡	.600
1971—	Rochester‡	.614
1972—	Louisville	.563
	Tidewater (3rd)†	.545
1973—	Charleston	.586
	Pawtucket y†	.534
1974—	Memphis	.613
	Rochester x‡	.611
1975—	Tidewater‡	.610
1976—	Rochester	.638
	Syracuse (2nd)†	.590
1977—	Pawtucket	.571
	Charleston (2nd)‡	.557
1978—	Charleston	.607
	Richmond (4th)†	.511
1979—	Columbus‡	.612
1980—	Columbus‡	.593
1981—	Columbus‡	.633
1982—	Richmond	.590
	Tidewater (3rd)†	.540
1983—	Columbus‡	.593
	Tidewater (4th)†	.511
1984—	Columbus	.590
	Pawtucket (4th)†	.536
1985—	Syracuse	.564
	Tidewater (4th)†	.540
1986—	Richmond‡	.571
1987—	Tidewater	.579
	Columbus†	.550
1988—	Rochester z	.546
	Tidewater	.546
1989—	Syracuse	.572
	Richmond z	.555
1990—	Rochester z	.614
	Columbus	.596
1991—	Columbus z	.590
	Pawtucket	.552
1992—	Columbus z	.660
	Scranton W.B.	.592
1993—	Charlotte z	.610
	Rochester	.525

*Won split-season playoff. †Won four-team playoff. ‡Won championship and four-team playoff. §Defeated Havana in game to decide fourth place, then won four-team playoff. xLeague was divided into Northern, Southern divisions. yLeague divided into American, National divisions. zLeague divided into Eastern, Western divisions; won playoffs. (NOTE—Known as Eastern League in 1884, New York State League in 1885, International League in 1886-87, International Association in 1888, International League in 1889-90, Eastern Association in 1891 and Eastern League from 1892 until 1912.)

MEXICAN LEAGUE

FINAL STANDINGS

FIRST HALF

NORTHERN ZONE

Team	W	L	T	Pct.	GB
Monterrey Sultans	39	26	2	.600	......
Nuevo Laredo	36	29	2	.554	3
Monclova	36	31	0	.537	4
Torreon	34	32	1	.515	5½
Jalisco	33	33	1	.500	6½
Monterrey Industrials	30	35	2	.462	9
Aguascalientes	28	39	0	.418	12
Saltillo	27	40	0	.403	13

SOUTHERN ZONE

Team	W	L	T	Pct.	GB
Mexico City Red Devils	43	23	1	.652	......
Mexico City Tigers	42	23	1	.646	½
Tabasco	34	29	4	.540	7½
Aguila	32	34	1	.485	11
Minatitlan	31	33	3	.484	11
Yucatan	29	34	3	.460	12½
Campeche	25	39	1	.391	17
Puebla	23	42	0	.354	19½

SECOND HALF

NORTHERN ZONE

Team	W	L	T	Pct.	GB
Nuevo Laredo	40	24	1	.625	......
Aguascalientes	39	25	0	.609	1
Monclova	37	26	0	.587	2½
Monterrey Sultans	36	29	0	.554	4½
Monterrey Industrials	31	32	2	.492	8½
Jalisco	28	32	1	.467	10
Torreon	27	38	0	.415	13½
Saltillo	24	40	0	.375	16

SOUTHERN ZONE

Team	W	L	T	Pct.	GB
Mexico City Red Devils	38	24	0	.613	......
Tabasco	32	30	1	.516	6
Mexico City Tigers	32	31	1	.508	6½
Aguila	33	32	0	.508	6½
Puebla	29	32	1	.475	8½
Minatitlan	29	33	0	.468	9
Campeche	24	35	1	.407	12½
Yucatan	22	38	0	.367	15

COMPOSITE

NORTHERN ZONE

Team	M.R.	M.T.	Tab.	Agu.	Min.	Yuc.	Pue.	Cam.	N.L.	M.S.	Mva.	Ags.	Jal.	M.I.	Tor.	Sal.	W	L	T	Pct.	GB
Nuevo Laredo	2	1	2	2	2	3	3	3	....	4	9	8	12	6	9	10	76	53	3	.589	......
Monterrey Sultans	1	3	2	2	1	2	3	1	10	....	8	6	10	7	11	8	75	55	2	.577	1½
Monclova	2	1	1	3	2	4	4	1	7	6	....	6	9	10	6	11	73	57	0	.562	3½
Aguascalientes	2	3	3	2	2	0	2	4	8	8	8	....	5	9	7	6	67	64	0	.511	10
Jalisco	1	3	2	2	2	2	1	2	2	3	5	11	....	9	8	8	61	65	2	.484	13½
Monterrey Indus.	1	2	2	3	3	3	1	3	6	4	5	4	7	....	7	9	61	67	4	.477	14½
Torreon	2	1	3	3	1	3	1	3	4	3	8	7	6	7	....	9	61	70	1	.466	16
Saltillo	1	0	2	2	0	1	4	2	4	6	3	8	6	5	7	....	51	80	0	.389	26

SOUTHERN ZONE

Team	M.R.	M.T.	Tab.	Agu.	Min.	Yuc.	Pue.	Cam.	N.L.	M.S.	Mva.	Ags.	Jal.	M.I.	Tor.	Sal.	W	L	T	Pct.	GB
M.C. Red Devils	....	7	9	11	7	6	11	8	3	2	3	2	3	3	2	3	81	47	1	.633	......
Mexico City Tigers	8	....	8	6	8	9	7	10	3	1	3	1	1	2	3	4	74	54	2	.578	7
Tabasco	3	6	....	9	10	6	11	8	2	2	3	1	1	1	1	2	66	59	5	.528	13½
Aguila	3	7	5	....	8	10	9	9	2	2	1	2	2	1	2	1	65	66	1	.496	17½
Minatitlan	7	6	5	6	....	4	8	7	2	3	2	1	1	3	4	1	60	66	3	.476	20
Yucatan	5	4	7	4	9	....	3	7	1	1	0	4	2	1	1	2	51	72	3	.415	27½
Puebla	3	7	2	7	6	10	....	6	1	1	0	2	1	3	3	2	52	74	1	.413	28
Campeche	6	3	6	5	5	7	6	....	1	3	1	0	2	1	1	2	49	74	2	.398	29½

Playoffs—Monterrey Sultans defeated Monclova, four games to one; Nuevo Laredo defeated Aguascalientes, four games to one; Mexico City Red Devils defeated Aguila, four games to none; Tabasco defeated Mexico City Tigers, four games to three. Nuevo Laredo defeated Monterrey Sultans, four games to one, in Northern Zone finals; Tabasco defeated Mexico City Red Devils, four games to one, in Southern Zone finals. Tabasco defeated Nuevo Laredo, four games to one, in final series to capture league championship.

(Compiled by Ana Luisa Perea Talarico, League Statistician, Mexico, D.F.)

BATTING

TEAM

Team	Avg.	G	AB	R	OR	H	TB	2B	3B	HR	RBI	SH	SF	HP	BB	Int. BB	SO	SB	CS	LOB
M.C. Red Devils	.320	129	4301	765	570	1378	2000	228	26	114	706	29	50	43	445	38	480	73	49	923
Monclova	.306	130	4252	664	611	1299	1844	213	31	90	616	74	48	39	434	43	580	74	71	910
Mexico City Tigers	.302	130	4165	744	682	1258	1889	211	15	130	696	68	46	31	509	40	605	101	47	910
Torreon	.296	132	4491	675	687	1330	1898	219	29	97	604	43	32	39	394	41	607	59	33	962
Jalisco	.295	128	4123	595	646	1218	1717	185	22	90	553	65	35	42	425	34	533	40	30	932
Monterrey Sultans	.295	132	4299	723	590	1269	1814	199	26	98	659	45	35	55	523	39	680	120	59	940
Nuevo Laredo	.286	132	4375	693	555	1253	1859	183	15	131	646	48	25	46	507	35	634	59	47	983
Saltillo	.286	131	4203	572	753	1203	1635	158	29	72	535	76	41	34	478	29	662	39	41	971
Monterrey Ind.	.285	132	4181	587	642	1193	1694	184	22	91	530	92	31	43	489	42	492	74	62	966
Yucatan	.283	126	3981	582	659	1127	1606	194	9	89	527	53	26	32	485	30	599	86	50	898
Aguascalientes	.278	131	4132	629	639	1148	1650	162	35	90	566	94	36	44	470	42	520	78	69	898
Tabasco	.275	130	4072	577	515	1119	1576	165	23	82	515	76	31	24	558	52	647	116	65	976
Minatitlan	.268	129	4009	545	556	1073	1507	185	18	71	505	57	35	40	475	32	597	53	35	917
Aguila	.262	132	4115	518	542	1078	1481	166	15	69	468	90	31	28	536	25	565	52	55	981
Puebla	.259	127	4034	516	628	1044	1513	147	26	90	468	69	28	42	426	32	664	68	28	875
Campeche	.246	125	3876	448	558	953	1378	143	9	88	412	81	27	26	462	28	535	44	63	858

INDIVIDUAL

(Leading qualifiers for batting championship—362 or more plate appearances)

Player, Team	Avg.	G	AB	R	H	TB	2B	3B	HR	RBI	SH	SF	HP	BB	Int. BB	SO	SB	CS
Simmons, Nelson, Jalisco	.382	109	369	81	141	270	27	0	34	95	0	4	1	71	11	45	1	3
Mangham, Eric, Mexico City Tigers	.373	99	351	87	131	199	29	3	11	56	8	3	8	41	4	46	33	12
Garcia, Cornelio, Yucatan	.362	116	406	98	147	201	27	3	7	41	3	2	3	86	0	76	45	18
Stark, Matt, Mexico City Red Devils	.361	122	413	101	149	266	24	0	31	114	0	5	5	99	11	41	2	2
Monell, Johnny, M.C. Red Devils	.356	120	432	94	154	238	19	4	19	101	0	14	7	52	9	28	6	5
Perez Tovar, Raul, Minatitlan	.349	123	453	68	158	213	36	2	5	52	2	6	4	42	9	42	6	6
Gonzalez, Jose, Monterrey Sultans	.349	105	398	76	139	201	21	10	7	48	0	0	5	46	2	65	22	13
Garbey, Barbaro, Mexico City Tigers	.348	129	463	71	161	251	27	0	21	102	0	4	1	61	14	43	5	2
Sanchez, Armando, M.C. Red Devils	.347	116	452	79	157	202	26	2	5	55	10	4	3	34	2	28	3	3
Carrillo, Matias, Mexico City Tigers	.345	115	414	113	143	293	36	0	38	125	0	5	7	59	13	61	28	11

Departmental leaders: G—Six players tied at 132; AB—Fentanes, 526; R—Carrillo, 113; H—Avila, 169; TB—Carrillo, 293; 2B—Azocar, 37; 3B—Jo. Gonzalez, D. Fernandez, 10; HR—Carrillo, 38; RBI—Carrillo, 125; SH—H. Garcia, 19; SF—Monell, 14; HP—Escalera, 14; BB—E. Castro, 125; IBB—Stockstill, 19; SO—Tillman, 113; SB—Co. Garcia, 45; CS—Co. Garcia, 18.

(All players—listed alphabetically)

Player, Team	Avg.	G	AB	R	H	TB	2B	3B	HR	RBI	SH	SF	HP	BB	Int. BB	SO	SB	CS
Abrego, Jesus, Monclova	.332	99	286	44	95	127	15	4	3	29	7	3	4	35	1	41	1	7
Abril, Ramon, Jalisco	.281	102	292	41	82	94	10	1	0	33	15	2	6	25	0	24	0	3
Aganza, Ruben, Monclova	.324	113	401	65	130	213	21	1	20	69	3	5	5	31	1	47	2	3
Agramon, Antonio, Monterrey Ind.	.225	25	40	4	9	10	1	0	0	2	0	0	3	5	0	7	0	1
Aguilar, Enrique, Aguascalientes	.292	130	459	79	134	209	14	2	19	74	9	8	7	30	3	36	6	1
Aguilera, Antonio, Monterrey Sultans	.278	110	309	59	86	109	15	1	2	36	10	2	2	48	4	51	18	6
Alexander, Gary, Saltillo	.273	20	55	5	15	28	2	1	3	15	1	1	0	17	0	16	0	0
Alfaro, Jesus, Yucatan	.281	124	398	65	112	216	29	0	25	97	3	4	4	79	5	66	3	1
Almeida, Shammar, Saltillo	.216	59	88	8	19	25	4	1	0	8	1	1	1	17	1	25	1	2
Almodobar, Ricardo, Monterrey Ind.	.211	81	142	23	30	35	3	1	0	7	12	0	3	6	0	16	1	2
Alvarado, Ivan, Campeche	.125	6	8	0	1	1	0	0	0	0	0	0	0	0	0	0	0	0
Alvarez, Chris, Monterrey Industrials	.301	51	163	12	49	62	8	1	1	23	0	3	3	38	4	9	1	4
Alvarez Ortiz, Hector Javier, Torreon	.262	121	423	43	111	147	25	1	3	51	2	3	4	20	2	47	7	6
Arauz, Ignacio, Monclova	.284	43	95	10	27	30	3	0	0	10	1	1	0	4	0	26	0	0
Arias, Everardo, Mexico City Tigers	.219	65	105	19	23	26	3	0	0	9	2	0	0	5	0	24	3	2
Arredondo, Hernando, Puebla	.077	11	13	2	1	1	0	0	0	0	2	0	0	0	0	4	0	0
Arredondo, J. Alfredo, Aguascalientes	.326	94	215	43	70	82	5	2	1	20	12	0	2	36	1	28	9	10
Arredondo, Luis, Jalisco	.3..	124	479	80	165	231	24	3	12	52	0	3	2	49	8	52	20	7
Arvizu, Javier, Campeche	.260	33	77	9	20	30	7	0	1	15	0	0	0	11	1	17	1	0
Arzate, Martin, Monterrey Industrials	.205	105	307	27	63	79	10	0	2	19	10	2	1	36	1	27	6	1
Avila Torres, Ruben, Torreon	.337	132	501	93	169	272	25	0	26	112	0	9	5	43	1	62	5	0
Ayala, Mario, Monclova	.000	5	3	0	0	0	0	0	0	0	0	0	0	0	0	3	0	0
Aylward, Jim, Tabasco	.000	2	7	0	0	0	0	0	0	1	0	0	1	0	1	0	0	0
Azocar, Oscar, Yucatan	.333	126	489	84	163	232	37	1	10	81	5	7	3	24	5	20	7	4
Baca, Manuel, Campeche	.189	42	127	7	24	36	6	0	2	17	3	2	1	5	0	27	0	0
Balderas, Abelardo, Minatitlan	.167	21	48	7	8	9	1	0	0	3	1	0	0	5	0	11	0	2
Barrera, Jesus Antonio, Aguila	.233	97	159	16	37	48	5	3	0	7	3	0	1	22	0	17	1	4
Barrera, Nelson, Campeche	.298	114	389	53	116	213	19	0	26	75	2	0	7	44	2	46	3	5
Bellazetin, Jose Juan, Mex. City Tigers	.347	83	251	51	87	111	13	1	3	46	3	7	0	52	0	25	0	0
Beltran, Gerardo, Aguila	.255	99	294	38	75	111	13	1	7	38	8	2	8	33	8	51	2	6
Beristain, Gregorio, Jalisco	.233	80	219	20	51	61	7	0	1	19	8	2	2	16	0	31	0	1
Blocker, Terry, Minatitlan	.309	110	408	70	126	188	26	6	8	59	1	5	0	50	6	49	14	1
Bocardo, Manuel, Tabasco	.000	4	5	0	0	0	0	0	0	0	0	0	0	0	0	0	0	0
Brown, Chris, Monterrey Sultans	.250	7	24	4	6	7	1	0	0	1	0	1	0	1	0	0	0	0
Brown, Todd, Tabasco	.343	121	431	67	148	251	35	1	22	95	2	6	2	50	4	56	11	10
Brown, Tony, Torreon	.250	13	56	6	14	20	3	0	1	9	1	0	0	3	0	13	0	0
Burke, Norberto, Monterrey Sultans	.293	19	41	4	12	12	0	0	0	3	1	0	1	6	0	9	1	0
Camacho, Adulfo, Mexico City Tigers	.265	112	358	68	95	118	20	0	1	34	13	3	1	62	0	52	6	4
Camarero, Genaro, Minatitlan	.118	13	17	0	2	2	0	0	0	1	0	0	0	1	0	7	0	0
Campos, Francisco, Campeche	.148	48	61	4	9	10	1	0	0	5	0	1	0	4	0	14	0	0
Canizales, Juan Carlos, Mont. Sultans	.287	112	352	58	101	161	13	4	13	54	3	3	1	28	4	76	5	1
Carmona, Rafael, Monterrey Ind.	.286	10	14	2	4	7	1	1	0	2	1	0	0	4	0	4	0	1
Carrasco, Ernesto, Nuevo Laredo	.180	43	50	8	9	10	1	0	0	6	1	0	0	1	0	9	1	0
Carrillo, Matias, Mexico City Tigers	.345	115	414	113	143	293	36	0	38	125	0	5	7	59	13	61	28	11
Castaneda, Nick, Monterrey Sultans	.342	57	202	32	69	115	18	2	8	44	0	3	2	37	2	30	0	0
Castaneda, Rafael, Mexico City Tigers	.268	122	365	54	98	125	12	3	3	36	11	2	2	45	0	41	5	2
Castelan, Miguel Angel, Tabasco	.284	82	197	21	56	67	4	2	1	16	6	1	1	10	1	38	3	4
Castro, Arnoldo, Minatitlan	.230	110	408	46	94	120	15	1	3	29	10	2	2	19	0	36	2	3
Castro, Eddie, Minatitlan	.323	128	390	88	126	209	29	0	18	92	0	4	7	125	10	74	8	6
Cazarin, Manuel, Minatitlan	.288	104	375	32	108	141	18	0	5	54	5	2	4	25	3	39	2	3
Cervera, Francisco, Puebla	.234	122	380	54	89	166	14	3	19	46	7	1	11	60	1	81	6	3
Chan, Armando, Monclova	.050	15	20	2	1	1	0	0	0	0	1	0	0	2	0	10	0	0
Chavez, Jorge, Minatitlan	.000	3	1	0	0	0	0	0	0	0	0	0	0	0	0	0	0	0
Chavez Barajas, J. Heriberto, Tabasco	.000	8	1	0	0	0	0	0	0	0	0	0	0	0	0	1	0	1
Chisum, Luis David, Mex. City Tigers	.361	37	97	16	35	47	4	1	2	12	0	2	0	7	2	15	3	0
Coachman, Pete, Jalisco	.349	76	249	50	87	120	18	0	5	42	3	2	5	43	2	28	7	1
Cobos, Rogelio, Mexico City Red Devils	.250	5	8	1	2	5	0	0	1	2	0	0	1	0	0	2	0	0
Cole, Mike, Campeche	.283	16	60	9	17	23	1	1	1	5	2	0	0	10	0	6	4	1
Contreras, Cuitlahuac, Torreon	.234	74	141	17	33	46	5	1	2	19	2	1	1	6	0	36	0	0
Contreras, Silvano, Tabasco	.241	72	137	19	33	52	4	0	5	23	1	1	0	22	0	43	6	3
Cornejo, Edgar, Saltillo	.198	52	111	15	22	34	6	0	2	6	4	0	1	10	0	18	0	0
Corrales, Virgilio, Torreon	.000	6	10	0	0	0	0	0	0	0	0	0	0	0	0	2	0	0
Cruz, Fernando, Mexico City Tigers	.201	59	164	13	33	44	5	0	2	21	2	1	0	9	0	28	0	1
Cruz, Luis Alfonso, Yucatan	.300	117	424	67	127	198	18	1	17	74	1	1	1	40	8	48	8	5
Cruz, Marco Antonio, Nuevo Laredo	.257	100	315	33	81	98	8	0	3	38	5	2	9	35	0	66	0	0
Cueto, Raul, Tabasco	.224	26	49	6	11	16	2	0	1	5	2	0	0	5	0	13	0	1
Davis, Mark, Minatitlan	.328	58	180	42	59	109	10	2	12	52	0	4	5	45	1	39	11	3
Dean, Kevin, Minatitlan	.240	15	50	5	12	17	3	1	0	9	0	0	0	6	0	17	0	3
DeLeon, Aguilar Ramiro, Jalisco	.265	67	113	5	30	36	6	0	0	17	2	3	1	5	1	15	1	0
Delima, Rafael, Tabasco	.327	55	150	36	49	98	9	2	12	36	0	1	1	31	1	35	6	1
Diaz, Luis Fernando, Nuevo Laredo	.311	127	457	80	142	218	31	0	15	71	1	3	3	64	5	105	0	4
Diaz, Remigio, Monterrey Sultans	.286	117	434	86	124	150	16	2	2	42	10	0	1	42	0	47	31	7
Dominguez, David, Aguila	.298	120	426	57	127	195	23	0	15	74	4	1	0	63	4	79	1	1

Player, Team	Avg.	G	AB	R	H	TB	2B	3B	HR	RBI	SH	SF	HP	BB	Int. BB	SO	SB	CS
Dominguez, Fausto, Jalisco	.234	73	154	16	36	47	6	1	1	14	4	1	1	5	0	32	0	1
Duarte, Felix Jose, Minatitlan	.000	1	2	0	0	0	0	0	0	0	0	0	0	1	0	1	0	0
Duarte, Rene Jacobo, Minatitlan	.236	86	212	21	50	63	10	0	1	12	4	3	1	18	0	36	1	1
Durazo, Raul, Monterrey Industrials	.167	5	6	0	1	1	0	0	0	0	0	0	0	0	0	0	0	0
Escalera, Ruben, Aguascalientes	.273	109	373	73	102	148	15	5	7	51	5	3	14	66	5	57	11	8
Espinoza, Antonio, Puebla	.200	11	30	3	6	6	0	0	0	1	0	0	0	3	0	8	0	0
Espinoza, Javier, Monterrey Ind.	.285	124	417	61	119	155	14	5	4	49	17	6	1	59	6	53	9	5
Esquer, Navarro Ramon, Torreon	.289	121	470	97	136	200	24	5	10	47	6	1	1	54	6	70	18	4
Estrada, Francisco, Minatitlan	.181	50	127	14	23	31	5	0	1	9	4	1	2	18	0	5	0	0
Estrada, Hector, Puebla	.279	118	419	44	117	177	16	1	14	70	7	4	3	16	4	38	1	1
Estrada, Roberto, Puebla	.280	118	404	43	113	142	13	2	4	49	13	9	5	32	5	49	3	6
Estrada, Ruben, Nuevo Laredo	.248	69	157	19	39	48	5	2	0	14	1	0	1	25	4	17	1	4
Felice, Jason, Campeche	.270	11	37	5	10	14	1	0	1	5	0	0	0	4	0	8	1	1
Felix, Arturo, Yucatan	.223	98	188	21	42	51	4	1	1	9	7	1	0	30	0	31	4	4
Fentanes, P. Oscar, Torreon	.312	129	526	65	164	222	31	6	5	80	5	6	10	23	0	64	2	1
Fernandez, Daniel, M.C. Red Devils	.339	111	445	106	151	214	28	10	5	54	4	2	2	49	1	33	29	9
Fernandez, Joey, Saltillo	.309	39	136	29	42	63	6	0	5	28	0	2	1	27	5	16	2	0
Firova, Dan, Nuevo Laredo	.000	1	4	0	0	0	0	0	0	0	0	0	0	0	0	0	0	0
Flores, Francisco J., Minatitlan	.333	2	3	0	1	1	0	0	0	0	0	0	0	0	0	0	0	0
Ford, Curt, Mexico City Red Devils	.367	41	169	39	62	87	11	1	4	28	0	1	2	20	0	16	7	5
Franco, Manuel, Monterrey Ind.	.239	74	180	18	43	55	8	2	0	21	1	2	4	4	0	30	3	4
Garbey, Barbaro, Mexico City Tigers	.348	129	463	71	161	251	27	0	21	102	0	4	1	61	14	43	5	2
Garcia, Carlos Miguel, Aguila	.276	84	210	37	58	67	7	1	0	12	6	2	2	47	0	32	6	10
Garcia, Cornelio, Yucatan	.362	116	406	98	147	201	27	3	7	41	3	2	3	86	0	76	45	18
Garcia, Heriberto, Aguila	.258	123	399	59	103	114	9	1	0	31	19	1	3	63	0	38	9	7
Garcia, Jose Antonio, Minatitlan	.000	3	3	1	0	0	0	0	0	0	0	0	0	0	0	0	0	0
Garcia, Jose Luis, Monterrey Sultans	.255	66	145	25	37	58	9	0	4	22	1	1	7	32	2	25	0	1
Garcia, Juan Manuel, Campeche	.083	12	12	0	1	1	0	0	0	1	0	0	0	0	0	4	0	0
Garcia, Martin, Monclova	.238	65	164	12	39	56	6	1	3	22	3	2	1	15	1	27	3	4
Garcia, Ramiro, Mexico City Red Devils	.333	3	9	1	3	3	0	0	0	0	0	0	0	0	0	1	0	0
Garcia, Zenon, Mexico City Tigers	.000	1	0	1	0	0	0	0	0	0	0	0	0	0	0	0	0	0
Garibay, Luis Alberto, Mex. City Tigers	.273	17	44	4	12	14	0	1	0	8	0	0	0	3	0	11	0	0
Garza Garza, Gerardo, Mex. City Tigers	.276	104	315	34	87	102	12	0	1	32	7	5	3	22	1	27	0	2
Garzon, Eliseo, Tabasco	.251	119	375	50	94	154	14	2	14	47	9	3	2	59	3	82	7	2
Gastelum, Carlos, Aguila	.181	95	265	18	48	63	6	0	3	26	15	2	1	9	0	37	0	1
Gavia, Jesus, Aguila	.207	90	217	21	45	53	5	0	1	18	2	1	1	19	0	33	0	1
Gil, Geronimo, Mexico City Red Devils	.000	1	1	0	0	0	0	0	0	0	0	0	0	0	0	0	1	0
Gomez, Alejandro, Jalisco	.244	46	86	12	21	22	1	0	0	3	4	0	0	7	0	10	1	0
Gonzalez, Alfonso, Aguila	.200	17	25	1	5	6	1	0	0	5	0	0	0	1	0	5	0	0
Gonzalez, Denio, Jalisco	.200	29	90	12	18	37	1	0	6	12	1	1	3	19	1	25	0	0
Gonzalez, Jesus, Aguila	.208	101	322	28	67	84	14	0	1	22	10	2	0	33	0	17	0	1
Gonzalez, Jose, Monterrey Sultans	.349	105	398	76	139	201	21	10	7	48	0	0	5	46	2	65	22	13
Gonzalez, Mario A., Yucatan	.244	45	135	13	33	56	5	0	6	21	2	1	2	11	0	26	1	1
Gonzalez, Pedro, Yucatan	.221	45	68	3	15	19	4	0	0	5	0	0	2	15	1	27	1	1
Guerrero, Francisco, Mex. City Tigers	.267	118	360	57	96	141	12	0	11	46	8	4	4	67	2	79	11	6
Guerrero, Jaime, Aguascalientes	.225	72	178	28	40	57	2	3	3	17	6	0	3	16	0	38	4	3
Guerrero, Javier, Aguascalientes	.203	41	69	8	14	19	3	1	0	6	0	0	0	4	0	24	0	0
Guerrero, Pedro, Jalisco	.293	31	99	14	29	40	5	0	2	19	0	3	1	12	1	17	0	0
Guizar, Hector, Campeche	.216	89	218	18	47	52	5	0	0	17	12	5	0	26	0	27	2	6
Gutierrez, Andres, Minatitlan	.245	68	159	28	39	49	6	2	0	12	8	0	3	23	0	40	3	2
Gutierrez, Arnoldo Ivan, Jalisco	.214	12	14	2	3	3	0	0	0	1	1	0	0	1	0	5	0	0
Gutierrez, Felipe, Monclova	.285	92	291	33	83	107	15	0	3	31	11	2	2	11	1	28	1	8
Gutierrez, Jose Luis, Campeche	.500	3	4	0	2	2	0	0	0	1	0	0	0	1	0	0	0	0
Guzman, Marco Antonio, Agua.	.271	115	343	44	93	149	18	1	12	57	10	4	1	55	3	53	1	0
Hernandez, Miguel, Jalisco	.226	90	221	20	50	58	6	1	0	17	14	0	2	22	1	12	0	0
Hernandez A., Martin, Campeche	.229	40	48	8	11	15	2	1	0	6	2	0	2	5	0	14	1	0
Hernandez B., Juan Carlos, Puebla	.167	39	30	10	5	6	1	0	0	6	4	1	0	2	0	4	0	0
Herrera, Isidro, Campeche	.308	119	402	66	124	162	22	2	4	48	7	3	0	74	7	36	10	17
Herrera, Ricardo, Jalisco	.236	50	174	24	41	49	3	1	1	11	3	0	0	17	1	21	4	3
Hill, Orsino, Monterrey Sultans	.281	47	167	20	47	70	11	0	4	23	1	2	3	12	1	37	1	2
Hinshaw, George, Aguascalientes	.148	7	27	3	4	5	1	0	0	0	0	0	0	4	2	6	0	0
Ibarra, Jose Alberto, Aguila	.245	62	163	17	40	60	9	1	3	22	1	2	0	15	1	40	1	0
Infante, Alexis, Tabasco	.291	123	461	77	134	156	14	4	0	49	14	3	7	45	2	38	13	5
Iturbe, Pedro, Puebla	.268	102	295	33	79	94	7	4	0	16	4	1	2	28	2	53	4	1
Jacas, David, Torreon	.278	25	90	20	25	44	2	1	5	11	0	1	1	16	2	11	2	0
Jackson, Kenny, Saltillo	.281	115	413	82	116	219	26	4	23	69	5	6	8	49	3	102	3	3
Jimenez, Alfonso, Campeche	.228	92	324	43	74	99	11	1	4	19	9	3	1	34	3	41	5	5
Jimenez, Eduardo, Monterrey Sultans	.331	129	447	75	148	231	22	2	19	90	0	7	3	88	6	67	4	0
Jimenez, Javier, Campeche	.160	13	25	3	4	7	0	0	1	4	0	0	0	0	0	9	0	0
Jimenez, Jose Luis, Saltillo	.274	29	73	7	20	25	2	0	1	4	0	1	1	4	0	27	1	0
Johnson, Roy, Puebla	.309	121	376	58	116	182	13	1	17	64	1	4	2	85	16	38	1	1
Jones, Barry, Aguascalientes	.291	58	206	27	60	89	5	3	6	29	0	2	1	21	4	21	3	4
Lagunes, Antonio, Campeche	.077	9	13	2	1	4	0	1	0	1	0	0	0	1	0	5	0	0
Leal, Guadalupe, Monclova	.328	106	338	53	111	160	17	1	10	51	5	2	2	20	7	46	4	3
Lee, Terry, Campeche	.314	26	86	10	27	41	2	0	4	11	0	0	1	8	1	8	0	1
Lennon, Patrick, Torreon	.351	27	97	18	34	54	5	0	5	15	0	1	0	11	0	31	0	0
Leyva, German, Monclova	.331	114	441	85	146	199	20	9	5	44	5	3	1	62	9	37	12	7
Loaiza, Sabino, Campeche	.000	1	0	0	0	0	0	0	0	0	0	0	0	0	0	0	0	0
Lopez, Alfredo, Jalisco	.287	101	164	26	47	61	11	0	1	16	3	2	3	8	1	31	0	3
Lopez, Gonzalo, Monclova	.290	107	397	52	115	153	18	4	4	49	11	2	2	29	1	48	0	6
Lopez, Jesus Manuel, Jalisco	.000	5	0	0	0	0	0	0	0	0	0	0	0	0	0	0	0	0
Lopez, Jose Juan, Minatitlan	.000	2	1	0	0	0	0	0	0	0	0	0	0	0	0	5	0	0
Lopez, Jose Miguel, Yucatan	.250	3	4	1	1	1	0	0	0	0	0	0	0	2	0	0	0	0
Lopez, Salvador, Aguascalientes	.267	95	300	38	80	110	11	2	5	39	10	2	1	17	0	24	8	10
Lopez, Victor M., Jalisco	.182	6	11	3	2	5	0	0	1	2	0	0	0	0	0	6	0	0
Loredo, Jorge Luis, Campeche	.190	74	153	17	29	44	4	1	3	8	5	0	4	14	0	34	1	5
Luna, Jose Luis, Saltillo	.228	55	136	6	31	33	2	0	0	13	4	2	0	8	0	14	0	1
Machiria, Pablo, Aguila	.333	128	495	76	165	245	25	8	13	76	3	6	4	23	2	46	2	3
Machorro, Roberto, Monterrey Sultans	.400	7	5	2	2	4	0	1	0	2	0	0	0	0	0	1	0	0
Magana, Gabriel, Yucatan	.230	78	152	23	35	39	4	0	0	13	6	0	3	26	0	41	3	3
Mangham, Eric, Mexico City Tigers	.373	99	351	87	131	199	29	3	11	56	8	3	8	41	4	46	33	12
Marquez, Edwin, Mexico City Tigers	.000	2	0	0	0	0	0	0	0	0	0	0	0	0	0	0	0	0
Marquez, Victor, Torreon	.227	46	88	10	20	29	2	2	1	9	4	0	0	5	0	18	1	0
Marrujo, Hector, Tabasco	.216	77	125	12	27	28	1	0	0	4	4	0	0	7	0	27	5	1

Player, Team	Avg.	G	AB	R	H	TB	2B	3B	HR	RBI	SH	SF	HP	BB	Int. BB	SO	SB	CS
Martinez, Grimaldo, Monclova	.241	124	398	48	96	118	11	4	1	51	13	8	3	38	1	46	13	8
Martinez, Luis Carlos, Saltillo	.207	11	29	5	6	8	2	0	0	2	1	0	0	0	0	8	0	0
Martinez, Raul, Torreon	.285	103	365	43	104	140	9	0	9	46	3	0	5	20	1	29	1	0
McCray, Rodney, Monterrey Sultans	.050	16	40	13	2	3	1	0	0	3	3	2	1	17	0	11	8	2
McDonough, Gilberto, Minatitlan	.171	38	41	7	7	7	0	0	0	0	0	0	2	3	0	12	1	1
Melendez, Francisco, Aguila	.291	96	316	43	92	131	12	0	9	49	2	3	1	63	6	28	0	4
Mendez, Ramon, Aguascalientes	.340	27	47	10	16	17	1	0	0	6	1	0	0	0	0	9	0	2
Mendez, Roberto, M.C. Red Devils	.278	84	216	33	60	86	9	1	5	30	2	2	4	11	0	42	9	4
Mere, Pedro, Nuevo Laredo	.328	132	461	87	151	233	22	3	18	84	8	1	7	63	2	57	8	5
Meza, Alfredo, Monterrey Sultans	.242	73	198	20	48	56	5	0	1	25	3	3	6	20	2	32	0	1
Mojica, Hector, Jalisco	.250	7	4	0	1	2	1	0	0	1	0	0	1	0	0	0	0	0
Monell, Johnny, M.C. Red Devils	.356	120	432	94	154	238	19	4	19	101	0	14	7	52	9	28	6	5
Monroy, Francisco, Monterrey Sultans	.333	12	24	6	8	10	2	0	0	2	0	0	0	3	0	5	0	0
Monroy, Victor Hugo, Mex. City Tigers	.246	77	228	29	56	91	9	1	8	36	3	2	1	10	0	18	0	0
Montalvo, Ivan, Mexico City Tigers	.375	13	8	3	3	5	2	0	0	2	1	0	0	2	0	3	0	0
Moore, Bobby, Nuevo Laredo	.340	108	435	82	148	199	24	3	7	43	8	2	4	46	1	27	23	7
Mora, Andres, Nuevo Laredo	.244	123	410	43	100	169	9	0	20	64	1	2	5	50	8	71	0	1
Morales, Alejandro, Torreon	.200	7	5	2	1	1	0	0	0	0	0	0	0	0	0	2	0	0
Morales, Florentino, Mex. City Tigers	.297	79	165	23	49	53	4	0	0	17	1	0	1	16	0	22	1	2
Moreno, Roberto, Minatitlan	.199	53	136	8	27	28	1	0	0	14	1	2	1	1	0	31	0	0
Morones, Martin, Jalisco	.325	112	366	63	119	179	17	8	9	64	0	2	3	57	2	29	5	4
Munoz, Noe, Mexico City Red Devils	.290	118	369	47	107	127	12	1	2	47	3	1	7	44	1	43	4	4
Narvaez, Arquimides, Monclova	.000	4	6	0	0	0	0	0	0	0	0	0	0	0	0	1	0	0
Navarro, Ruben, Mexico City Tigers	.222	27	63	5	14	20	4	1	0	2	0	1	0	7	2	20	0	0
Naveda, Edgar, Monterrey Industrials	.330	132	467	98	154	244	34	1	18	70	4	6	1	73	1	58	6	7
Nelson, Gerome, Minatitlan	.321	39	134	28	43	53	4	3	0	7	1	0	1	31	1	15	6	4
Nelson, Rob, Saltillo	.250	84	260	37	65	119	12	0	14	52	1	3	0	72	6	83	0	1
Noris, Rogelio, Aguila	.257	113	334	32	86	110	10	1	4	26	13	2	0	25	1	42	6	8
Ochoa, Edgar, Nuevo Laredo	.000	3	3	0	0	0	0	0	0	0	0	0	0	0	0	0	0	0
Orantes, Ramon, Monterrey Sultans	.250	3	4	2	1	4	0	0	1	2	0	0	0	0	0	0	0	0
Ortega, Roberto, Jalisco	.219	72	73	11	16	19	1	1	0	12	0	1	0	7	1	12	0	1
Ortiz, Alejandro, Nuevo Laredo	.297	130	461	93	137	252	25	0	30	102	0	7	5	78	8	76	1	1
Osuna, Hector Manuel, Saltillo	.288	33	59	7	17	20	1	1	0	5	3	0	1	0	0	12	0	0
Pacho, Carlos, Yucatan	.333	3	3	0	1	1	0	0	0	0	0	0	0	0	0	1	0	0
Pacho, Juan Jose, Yucatan	.243	117	374	45	91	110	16	0	1	23	13	0	2	32	0	43	6	2
Pardo, Alberto Judas, Yucatan	.250	10	24	1	6	9	1	1	0	3	0	0	0	6	1	2	0	0
Pardo, Victor Manuel, Puebla	.264	123	413	51	109	132	12	1	3	35	8	2	5	40	0	47	3	3
Pena, Carlos, Monterrey Sultans	.083	5	12	0	1	2	1	0	0	0	0	0	0	1	0	5	0	0
Pena, Luis Alberto, Mont. Industrials	.225	90	182	16	41	67	9	1	5	26	2	0	1	32	5	44	0	1
Peralta, Amado, Minatitlan	.282	110	309	42	87	144	11	2	14	64	4	3	7	78	9	77	1	4
Perez, Alfredo, Mexico City Tigers	.000	3	2	0	0	0	0	0	0	0	0	0	0	0	0	1	0	0
Perez, Francisco, Minatitlan	.268	106	313	41	84	112	14	1	4	26	4	1	1	10	1	77	3	4
Perez Solis, Fausto Enrique, Torreon	.000	2	3	1	0	0	0	0	0	0	0	0	0	0	0	2	0	0
Perez Tovar, Raul, Minatitlan	.349	123	453	68	158	213	36	2	5	52	2	6	4	42	9	42	6	6
Pina, Joseph M., Torreon	.200	5	20	3	4	4	0	0	0	2	0	0	1	1	0	6	0	0
Ponce, Hector, Campeche	.243	62	148	19	36	39	3	0	0	5	4	0	0	11	0	16	5	7
Porras, Leonardo, Tabasco	.000	3	4	0	0	0	0	0	0	0	0	0	0	1	0	0	0	0
Pulido, Jesus, Mexico City Tigers	.244	23	41	5	10	14	1	0	1	4	1	0	2	3	0	9	0	0
Quintero, Guillermo, Mont. Sultans	.111	25	9	8	1	1	0	0	0	0	0	0	0	1	0	1	0	0
Quiroz, Jose Julian, Puebla	.179	64	162	10	29	37	5	0	1	13	1	1	0	12	1	22	0	0
Ramirez, Efren, Puebla	.223	89	247	27	55	79	12	0	4	24	2	1	7	32	2	49	2	1
Ramirez, Enrique, Nuevo Laredo	.262	130	489	59	128	148	17	0	1	40	16	1	1	23	0	29	14	7
Ramirez, Roberto, M.C. Red Devils	.500	4	2	1	1	2	1	0	0	0	0	0	0	0	0	1	0	0
Ramos, Enrique, Monterrey Sultans	.350	18	20	6	7	7	0	0	0	4	0	0	0	6	0	6	2	0
Reyes, Juan, Mexico City Red Devils	.274	71	241	23	66	95	11	0	6	38	0	0	1	23	3	49	0	2
Reyes, Ramon, Mexico City Red Devils	.333	17	12	3	4	4	0	0	0	0	0	0	0	0	0	2	0	1
Reyna, Luis, Campeche	.195	33	113	10	22	31	4	1	1	10	2	0	1	11	1	13	4	2
Reza, Silva Hector, Torreon	.158	16	19	4	3	3	0	0	0	0	0	0	1	0	0	4	0	0
Ritchie, Greg, Monterrey Industrials	.356	56	174	29	62	68	3	0	1	15	6	0	1	38	2	37	8	6
Rivera, Alberto, Jalisco	.269	108	301	34	81	96	13	1	0	24	10	2	5	37	0	43	4	2
Rivera, Eleazar, Yucatan	.233	48	90	11	21	30	1	1	2	13	3	0	1	11	2	18	1	0
Rivera, German, Aguila	.261	131	440	67	115	181	21	0	15	63	7	4	4	68	3	66	6	4
Rivera, Paul, Aguascalientes	.000	1	0	0	0	0	0	0	0	0	0	0	0	0	0	0	0	0
Robles, Humberto, Mont. Industrials	.000	2	1	0	0	0	0	0	0	0	0	0	0	1	0	0	0	0
Robles, Juan Jose, Mont. Industrials	.318	15	22	4	7	10	0	0	1	3	0	0	4	0	5	0	0	0
Robles Acuna, Javier, Torreon	.278	114	353	54	98	136	14	6	4	36	12	1	2	26	0	57	8	6
Rodriguez, Cecilio, Saltillo	.276	49	134	22	37	40	3	0	0	10	4	1	0	18	1	8	1	2
Rodriguez, Fernando, Torreon	.303	20	33	2	10	14	1	0	1	4	0	1	2	1	0	5	0	0
Rodriguez, Genaro, Monclova	.285	72	207	25	59	74	12	0	1	34	5	1	2	12	2	27	0	3
Rodriguez, Guillermo, Campeche	.235	72	230	17	54	75	10	1	3	16	7	0	0	11	0	37	0	1
Rodriguez, Hector, Puebla	.240	124	437	54	105	169	16	3	14	54	7	2	2	32	2	106	4	7
Rodriguez, Jose Luis, Saltillo	.357	91	230	24	82	99	9	1	2	37	6	1	2	28	1	36	3	2
Rodriguez, Juan Francisco, Agua.	.277	127	455	59	126	159	18	3	3	52	17	2	2	60	0	24	9	8
Rojas, Francisco J., Mont. Industrials	.226	43	53	9	12	15	3	0	0	5	1	0	3	3	0	11	0	0
Rojas, Homar, Monterrey Industrials	.278	109	356	35	99	123	11	2	3	50	3	3	3	36	4	48	3	1
Romero, Marco Antonio, Nuevo Laredo	.298	110	400	72	119	183	11	1	17	78	2	4	6	46	2	55	7	4
Romero, Oscar, Aguila	.305	112	410	58	125	177	23	1	9	52	4	4	3	31	2	62	5	3
Rosell, Omar, Minatitlan	.000	1	1	0	0	0	0	0	0	0	0	0	0	0	0	1	0	0
Rubio, Marco Antonio, Saltillo	.307	114	349	38	107	130	12	1	3	45	6	5	3	33	2	32	4	4
Rubio, Sergio, Yucatan	.111	15	27	1	3	5	0	1	0	3	0	0	0	0	0	6	0	1
Ruiz, Demetrio, Campeche	.236	108	305	22	72	83	8	0	1	16	10	2	0	25	0	25	0	2
Ruiz, Juan De Dios, Torreon	.296	124	466	59	138	207	32	2	11	65	1	3	3	25	2	65	7	10
Ruiz, Vicente, Torreon	.313	16	32	6	10	15	3	1	0	5	0	0	0	0	0	7	0	0
Saenz, Ricardo, Mexico City Tigers	.280	118	410	63	115	212	20	1	25	91	3	5	1	39	2	83	1	2
Saiz Aguilar, Herminio, Tabasco	.263	104	304	29	80	91	11	0	0	23	9	0	7	22	0	40	0	0
Salazar, Carlos, Puebla	.198	41	86	11	17	34	2	0	5	21	0	0	1	17	0	34	1	0
Salgado, Eduardo, Nuevo Laredo	.125	47	32	6	4	6	0	1	0	2	0	0	1	5	0	15	0	2
Salinas, Rogelio, Puebla	.252	96	294	26	74	100	12	1	4	20	3	0	5	17	0	41	2	0
Samaniego, Manuel, Monclova	.330	36	112	21	37	42	3	1	0	14	1	1	2	13	1	6	0	1
Sambo, Ramon, Torreon	.237	34	114	19	27	32	3	1	0	9	3	0	0	26	0	16	5	1
Sanchez, Alejandro, Monclova	.291	130	485	93	141	239	22	2	24	79	0	7	9	43	4	87	21	11
Sanchez, Andres, Puebla	.197	37	76	9	15	20	5	0	0	12	0	0	0	14	0	20	0	0
Sanchez, Armando, M.C. Red Devils	.347	116	452	79	157	202	26	2	5	55	10	4	3	34	2	28	3	3
Sanchez, Gerardo, Nuevo Laredo	.290	132	507	89	147	236	29	3	18	88	3	2	4	55	4	56	1	10

Player, Team	Avg.	G	AB	R	H	TB	2B	3B	HR	RBI	SH	SF	HP	BB	Int. BB	SO	SB	CS
Sanchez, Orlando, Aguascalientes	.278	119	421	59	117	174	22	1	11	59	3	2	1	44	11	51	1	3
Sanchez, Raul, Mexico City Tigers	.200	11	10	3	2	4	0	1	0	1	1	0	0	0	0	3	0	0
Sanchez, Roque, Campeche	.194	51	103	5	20	23	3	0	0	3	3	1	1	6	0	11	2	1
Sandoval, Jose Luis, M.C. Red Devils	.274	33	113	19	31	46	4	1	3	16	0	1	2	12	1	15	2	1
Santos, Julio, Jalisco	.429	10	7	2	3	3	0	0	0	0	0	0	0	0	0	1	0	0
See, Larry, Aguascalientes	.300	57	200	35	60	98	15	1	7	39	1	3	3	36	9	22	1	4
Shamburg, Ken, Yucatan	.222	13	45	5	10	12	2	0	0	4	0	0	0	5	1	9	0	0
Shepherd, Ron, Yucatan	.251	54	171	23	43	76	6	0	9	23	1	0	0	14	4	51	1	0
Sievers, Carlos, Yucatan	.229	57	109	11	25	31	1	1	1	10	0	0	0	9	0	25	0	1
Simmons, Nelson, Jalisco	.382	109	369	81	141	270	27	0	34	95	0	4	1	71	11	45	1	3
Smith, Gregory, Saltillo	.238	21	80	9	19	28	3	0	2	9	0	1	0	7	3	13	0	0
Smith, Mike, Mexico City Tigers	.000	4	0	3	0	0	0	0	0	0	0	0	0	0	0	0	0	0
Sommers, Jesus, Jalisco	.281	120	406	35	114	158	20	0	8	45	0	1	4	35	4	72	0	1
Stark, Matt, Mexico City Red Devils	.361	122	413	101	149	266	24	0	31	114	0	5	5	99	11	41	2	2
Steels, James, Monterrey Industrials	.334	130	473	96	158	278	27	3	29	100	1	3	4	61	8	50	18	11
Stephenson, Phil, Aguila	.323	119	381	64	123	198	26	5	13	71	2	9	5	77	7	49	3	0
Stockstill, David, Torreon	.335	132	472	71	158	212	20	2	10	61	4	5	2	83	19	36	0	1
Tatis, Bernardo, Puebla	.315	116	397	87	125	199	18	7	14	59	4	4	1	81	9	70	40	6
Taylor, Dwight, Aguascalientes	.281	93	345	52	97	120	8	3	3	25	5	1	0	23	4	39	31	10
Tejada, Wilfredo, Mexico City Tigers	.000	1	1	1	0	0	0	0	0	0	0	0	1	0	0	0	0	0
Tejeda, Arturo, Nuevo Laredo	.158	15	19	0	3	7	0	2	0	0	0	0	0	1	0	6	0	0
Tejeda, Juan, Campeche	.000	1	2	1	0	0	0	0	0	0	0	0	0	1	0	0	0	0
Tellez, Alonso, Monterrey Industrials	.311	132	488	55	152	222	22	6	12	88	5	6	2	28	4	42	5	6
Tillman, Rusty, Tabasco	.268	122	410	62	110	195	20	1	21	77	0	3	2	63	13	113	29	8
Tiquet, Lazaro, Puebla	.258	103	353	48	91	120	14	3	3	32	9	1	6	36	0	47	4	0
Tirado, Federico, Puebla	.000	3	4	0	0	0	0	0	0	0	0	0	0	0	0	2	0	0
Tirado, Victor, Puebla	.225	49	102	5	23	27	4	0	0	9	3	0	0	3	0	21	0	1
Torres, Eduardo, Saltillo	.255	126	404	61	103	146	14	4	7	54	2	4	2	82	3	71	12	13
Torres, Eleuterio, Campeche	.000	1	1	0	0	0	0	0	0	0	0	0	0	0	0	0	0	0
Torres, Raymundo, Campeche	.221	123	385	59	85	172	15	0	24	66	5	5	6	75	4	84	3	0
Tovar, Jose De Jesus, Saltillo	.143	14	35	7	5	5	0	0	0	2	1	0	0	5	0	14	0	0
Trafton, Todd, Mexico City Red Devils	.342	70	240	50	82	144	13	2	15	59	1	3	4	29	5	19	3	3
Trapaga, More Julio, Nuevo Laredo	.148	43	54	11	8	8	0	0	0	4	1	1	0	2	0	18	1	1
Traver, Jim, Monterrey Sultans	.316	126	487	73	154	225	20	0	17	118	0	8	3	36	8	46	3	5
Trevino, Alejandro, Monterrey Sultans	.288	84	212	32	61	88	10	1	5	35	4	1	7	42	4	35	2	4
Uzcanga, Ali, Aguascalientes	.200	6	5	1	1	1	0	0	0	1	0	0	0	0	0	3	0	0
Valdez, Baltazar, Aguascalientes	.299	105	341	40	102	163	16	3	13	66	6	3	2	33	3	52	1	2
Valdez, Francisco J., Mont. Industrials	.296	88	240	26	71	88	9	1	2	30	3	2	8	18	1	25	2	3
Valdez, Luis Alberto, Tabasco	.286	58	161	12	46	56	6	2	0	15	4	1	0	13	1	21	0	2
Valdez Castro, Edgar, Tabasco	.000	3	1	1	0	0	0	0	0	0	0	0	0	0	0	0	0	0
Valdez R., Jesus, Aguascalientes	.325	55	126	22	41	53	4	4	0	19	0	0	0	7	0	14	1	3
Valencia, Carlos, Aguascalientes	.287	120	407	57	117	170	27	1	8	61	5	7	8	33	1	42	5	8
Valenzuela, Armando, Saltillo	.277	113	415	51	115	129	5	3	1	27	15	3	6	28	1	34	8	8
Valenzuela, Eduardo, Saltillo	.330	81	191	23	63	75	9	0	1	20	5	1	3	7	0	19	0	0
Valenzuela, Horacio, Tabasco	.217	116	350	39	76	114	5	0	11	62	0	8	4	69	14	55	1	1
Valenzuela, Jose Luis, Torreon	.237	62	93	21	22	28	0	3	0	4	2	0	0	16	0	19	3	3
Valenzuela, Leonardo, Tabasco	.298	114	363	58	108	144	17	2	5	47	5	2	0	63	7	40	1	7
Valle, Jose Luis, Minatitlan	.272	126	404	51	110	156	25	0	7	50	12	1	4	27	0	38	2	2
Valverde, Raul, Jalisco	.311	99	341	53	106	150	12	4	8	62	2	6	3	10	1	36	1	3
Vargas, Trinidad, Monterrey Sultans	.251	107	275	47	69	83	12	1	0	21	8	0	3	26	1	55	13	7
Vazquez, Felipe, M.C. Red Devils	.170	31	53	3	9	11	2	0	0	1	0	0	0	4	0	10	0	3
Vazquez, Jose, Mexico City Red Devils	.500	3	2	1	1	1	0	0	0	0	0	0	0	0	0	1	0	0
Vega, Edgar, Nuevo Laredo	.303	51	122	12	37	44	1	0	2	12	1	0	0	6	0	25	2	1
Velazquez, Armando, Aguila	.253	93	146	16	37	46	4	1	1	8	4	2	0	9	0	28	3	5
Veliz, Martin, Jalisco	.111	6	9	1	1	1	0	0	0	0	0	0	0	0	0	2	0	0
Verdugo, Ricardo, Yucatan	.214	12	14	3	3	4	1	0	0	2	0	0	0	0	0	3	0	0
Verdugo, Vicente, M.C. Red Devils	.299	127	442	69	132	166	26	1	2	48	5	7	2	13	0	33	2	2
Villaescusa, Fernando, Yucatan	.317	91	284	41	90	101	8	0	1	31	4	3	2	21	0	9	3	2
Villagomez, David, Tabasco	.000	6	6	0	0	0	0	0	0	0	0	0	0	0	0	2	0	0
Villegas, Fernando, Saltillo	.338	35	74	9	25	27	2	0	0	3	2	0	1	5	0	17	1	1
Villela, Carlos, Saltillo	.299	96	338	43	101	122	6	6	1	40	11	4	0	35	1	50	0	2
Vizcarra, Marco Antonio, Mont. Ind.	.236	79	203	34	48	57	9	0	0	16	16	0	4	17	0	10	4	4
Vizcarra, Roberto, Mont. Industrials	.299	129	501	84	150	228	28	1	16	56	14	4	7	49	5	43	15	12
Williams, Eddie, Monterrey Sultans	.352	59	210	40	74	127	17	0	12	34	1	1	4	21	4	29	0	2
Willson, James George, Yucatan	.329	47	155	22	51	73	10	0	4	34	1	5	1	19	0	31	0	2
Wong, Julian, Tabasco	.257	97	269	42	69	89	8	3	2	25	9	2	2	42	2	21	5	3
Yepiz, Gerardo, Aguascalientes	.234	43	47	11	11	11	0	0	0	4	1	0	0	11	0	5	1	1
Yuriar, Jesus, Monclova	.324	108	358	50	116	152	18	3	4	59	11	8	0	26	3	47	10	7
Zamudio, Rafael, Monterrey Sultans	.306	66	124	22	38	51	4	0	3	20	0	0	1	13	1	25	5	1
Zazueta, Mauricio, M.C. Red Devils	.287	89	310	39	89	123	24	2	2	48	2	5	3	15	2	52	2	2
Zulueta, Felix, Yucatan	.270	71	126	11	34	38	4	0	0	11	2	1	2	17	1	20	2	1
Zuniga, Armando, Mont. Industrials	.273	22	33	4	9	10	1	0	0	0	2	0	0	6	0	8	0	0

The following pitchers, listed alphabetically by club, with games in parentheses, had no plate appearances, primarily through use of designated hitters:

AGUASCALIENTES—Cardenas, Benito (26); Cervantes, Lauro (25); Cervantes, Rafael (7); Enriquez, Martin (19); Jimenez, German (20); Lopez, Jonas (39); Medvin, Scott (17); Molina, Jose Joaquin (9); Normand, Guy (20); Palacios, Vicente (38); Parnet, Mike (3); Vargas, Ignacio (19); Velazquez, Ildefonso (16); Villanueva, Luis (41); Villegas, Jose Angel (38); Zamudio, Pablo (4).

AGUILA—Arias, Daniel (6); Baez, Sixto (38); Cabrales, Gabriel (43); Cazares, Juan (42); Contreras, Benjamin (20); Diaz, Cesar (7); Gutierrez, Jose Arturo (2); Hernandez, Manuel (24); Lopez, Rodrigo (2); Luevano, Juan (26); Macias, Abraham (12); Martinez, Uriel (4); Meza, Leobardo (17); Munoz, Miguel (28); Pulido, Alfonso (28); Sanchez, Hector (29); Sandoval, Carlos (9); Solis, Jesus (30); Soto, Ramon (15).

CAMPECHE—Araujo, Andy (20); Browning, Mike (50); Dominguez, Herminio (13); Fuentes, David (4); Lara, Hugo (24); Lopez, Juan (8); Lopez Sanchez, Juan (1); Manzano, Fernando (8); May, Scott (19); Oren, Victor (6); Ortega, Harvey (1); Ortiz, Gregorio (3); Rojo, Oscar (32); Sanchez, Efrain (2); Sangeado, Juan Carlos (6); Sierra, Abel (26); Sulu, Mario (3); Taylor, Terry (3); Tinoco, Ruben (31); Toledo, Mario (32); Valencia, Jose (15); Velazquez, Pedro (26); Zamorano, Gabriel (2).

JALISCO—Castaneda, Aurelio (46); Castellanos, Humberto (33); Castillo, Felipe (31); Cazares, Rosario (18); Chavez, Jose Guadalupe (34); Flores, Ignacio (2); Hernandez, Encarnacion (31); Iniguez, Dario (28); Jaime Granillo, Ismael (12); Lizarraga, Hugo (30); Lugo, Urbano (29); Munoz, Ricardo (14); Sanchez, Jose Luis (7); Sombra, Francisco (27); Zavaleta, Marcelino (2).

MEXICO CITY RED DEVILS—Barojas, Salome (13); Carrasco, Alejandro (3); Cecena, Jose Isabel (20); Cordoba, Francisco (43); Cruz, Javier (19); Del Toro, Miguel Alfonso (5); Dessens, Elmer (14); Garcia, Francisco (5); Herrera, Jose Luis (2); Jimenez, Saul (18); Kraemer, Joe (3); Loaiza, Esteban (4); Martinez, Filiberto (28); Mendez, Luis Fernando (26); Mendoza, Marco Antonio (8); Moreno, Leobardo (28); McMurtry, Joe Graig (17); Pavlas, Dave (11); Pina, Rafael (9); Reyes, Dennis (7); Reyes, Oscar (2); Rivera, Hector (1); Vazquez, Adrian (15).

MEXICO CITY TIGERS—Candia, Rodolfo (5); DeLaCruz, Carlos (10); Galvez, Balbino (13); Garibay, Daniel (26); Hernandez, Jose Manuel (46); Marquez, Isidro (14); Martin, Daniel (5); Mora, Eleazar (33); Moreno, Angel (12); Onofre, Artemio (1); Parra, Julio Cesar (2); Rios, Jesus (25); Robles, Felix (10); Rodriguez, Mario Alberto (39); Salas, Ernesto (30); Valdez, Ismael (26).

MINATITLAN—Acosta, Francisco (7); Aguilar, Miguel (29); Camacho, Adrian (17); Camarena, Martin (19); DeLeon, Luis (10); Diaz, Octavio (2); Garcia, Miguel (14); Gomez Rios, Martin (15); Hernandez, Julio (9); Herrera, Roberto (12); Martinez, Martin (2); Pulido, Antonio (6); Reyes, Flavio (15); Sauveur, Richie (7); Sinohui, David (36); Soto, Fernando (31); Velazquez, Israel (27); Weber, Weston (7).

MONCLOVA—Antunez, Martin (48); Castillo, Luis Trinidad (26); Eave, Gary (3); Espinoza, Carlos (5); Garcia, David (3); Garza, Armando (25); Gomez, Jesus (2); Hansen, Mike (5); Herrera, Calixto (46); Leal, Gerardo (3); Montano, Francisco (23); Murillo, Felipe (29); Rodriguez, Ignacio (45); Smith, Daryl (24); Solano, Julio (47); Valdez, Rodolfo (26); Valenzuela, Ramon Loreto (24).

MONTERREY INDUSTRIALS—Acosta, Gerardo (1); Boyd, Oil Can (15); Garibay, Roberto (25); Hernandez, Martin (27); Huerta, Luis Enrique (28); Lara, Jorge (40); Lopez, Raul (19); Montalvo, Rafael (24); Ochoa, Porfirio (25); Ontiveros, Juan (33); Peraza, Oswald Jose (9); Purata, Julio (26); Rodriguez, Mario (22); Stowell, Steve (5); Valdez Soto, Armando (30); Veliz Arballo, Francisco (50).

MONTERREY SULTANS—Acosta, Aaron (30); Barrera, Enrique (1); Benitez, Francisco (1); Cano, Ezequiel (21); DeAnda, Alfredo (1); Diaz, Marcos (1); Edwards, Wayne (18); Elvira, Narciso (7); Gonzalez, Arturo (26); Granillo, Carlos (48); Heredia, Hector (52); Munoz, Leonardo (2); Orozco, Jaime (25); Pelcastregui, Leonardo (5); Perez, Leonardo (1); Quinones, Enrique (26); Raygoza, Martin (26); Solis, Ricardo (23); Villarreal, Antonio (42).

NUEVO LAREDO—Alvarez, Juan Jesus (28); Baller, Jay (61); Barraza, Ernesto (28); Barrera, Sigfrido (1); Couoh, Enrique (43); Cruz, Miguel (30); Lind, Orlando (23); Loynd, Mike (9); Mena, Evaristo (1); Moreno, Ricardo (15); Quiroz, Aaron (6); Rodriguez, Rene (26); Valdez, Jose Luis (9); Valenzuela, Mario (3); Vega Velarde, Obed (21); Watson, Preston (15).

PUEBLA—Acosta, Carlos (4); August, Don (11); Bennett, Chris (27); Carman, Don (22); Garcia, Jorge Luis (11); Harrison, Phil (7); Morales, Isidro (19); Noriega, Eduardo (29); Ramos, Jorge Luis (6); Roesler, Mike (19); Saenz, Alfredo (9); Saldana, Gerardo (24); Sosa, Mario (10); Soto Cruz, Antonio (8); Valdez, Efrain (16); Valenzuela, Saul (29); Villegas, Ramon (22); Zamudio, Aurelio (28).

SALTILLO—Barron, Avelino (17); Berenguer, Juan (20); Cosio, Mario Alberto (23); DeAvila, Lizandro (13); Escamilla, Sergio (7); Ibarra, Jose Antonio (8); Lara, Eddie (8); Leyva, Filiberto (29); Moreno, Jesus (30); Navarro, Adolfo (14); Navarro, Luis (6); Olivas, Anselmo (2); Olmos, Arturo (8); Puig, Benny (15); Rodriguez, Raul (23); Romero Cobos, Hector Manuel (24); Sanchez, Martin (30); Sandoval, Guillermo (21); Straker, Les (4); Valencia, Jorge (44).

TABASCO—Acosta, Martin (7); Alvarez, Martin (46); Chevez Cruz, Humberto (9); Colorado, Salvador (16); Diaz, Alejandro (2); Felix, Antonio (26); Garcia-Luna, Jose Antonio (11); Herrera, Enrique (45); Lopez, Emigdio (29); Morales, Celestino (3); Moreno, Francisco (3); Osuna, Ricardo (20); Perez, Joaquin (7); Retes, Lorenzo (29); Rodriguez, Ulises (43); Romero, Juan Jose (30); Ruiz, Cecilio (29); Saldana, Edgardo (39); Serna, Ramon (14); Tejeda Sanchez, Felix (1).

TORREON—Alicea, Miguel (11); Cervantes, Roberto (4); Cruz Canto, Andres (27); Garcia, Salvador (16); Grajales, Norberto (45); Mead, Timber (22); Miranda, Julio Cesar (47); McClellan, Paul (3); Ochoa, Gerardo (3); Palafox, Juan Manuel (28); Palomo, Ricardo (3); Perry, Jeff (50); Pimentel, Roberto (44); Quintero, Victor Hugo (20); Renteria, Hilario (22); Rincon, Ricardo (57); Rodriguez, Rosario (13); Velazquez, Ernesto (29).

YUCATAN—Carranza, Javier (23); Castro, Rodrigo (42); Chavarin, Jose Angel (7); Esquer, Mercedes (23); Gamboa, Ezequiel (6); Garcia, Juan (26); Jimenez, Isaac (24); Ledon, Juan Carlos (41); Merodio, Ramon (15); Neri, Braulio (27); Osuna, Roberto (24); Perea, Juan Alberto (4); Rodriguez, Eric (8); Rodriguez, Salvador (4); Uribe, Juan Carlos (29); Velez, Arturo (8).

GRAND SLAMS—Avila, 3; S. Contrer∵ Mere, V.H. Monroy, Reyes, M. Romero, Steels, Tillman, R. Torres, 2 each; Alexander, Alfaro, H. Alvarez, Bellazetin, Todd Brown, Canizales, Carrillo, E. Castro, Cervera, C. Contreras, DeLima, L.F. Diaz, D. Dominguez, Garzon, Je. Gonzalez, Machiria, Melendez, Mora, E. Rivera, H. Rodriguez, J.F. Rodriguez, J. Ruiz, Salazar, Al. Sanchez, Ar. Sanchez, G. Sanchez, See, Sommers, F. Valdez, L. Valenzuela, Valverde, 1 each.

AWARDED FIRST BASE ON CATCHER'S INTERFERENCE—DeLima (Gavia); Mora (Narvaez); Al. Sanchez (F. Dominguez); Ar. Sanchez (Ef. Ramirez); B. Valdez (M. Cruz); L. Valenzuela (R. Duarte); Valverde (Luna); Zamudio (V. Lopez).

PITCHING

TEAM

Team	ERA	G	CG	ShO	Sv.	IP	H	R	ER	HR	HB	BB	Int. BB	SO	WP	Bk.
Nuevo Laredo	3.78	132	21	4	38	1124.2	1112	555	472	78	36	512	33	861	65	1
Tabasco	3.96	130	30	13	23	1071.2	1135	515	471	84	42	402	28	536	37	2
Aguila	3.98	132	32	8	29	1103.0	1092	540	488	109	29	439	25	551	32	4
Monterrey Sultans	4.00	132	27	6	28	1103.2	1230	590	491	61	38	415	26	555	39	4
Monclova	4.03	130	24	5	29	1099.2	1165	611	493	87	37	484	35	620	68	2
Minatitlan	4.09	129	27	6	33	1053.0	1109	556	478	89	27	485	26	560	33	1
Mexico City Red Devils	4.20	129	26	5	31	1075.0	1093	570	502	99	43	471	19	708	43	4
Campeche	4.25	125	19	7	27	1042.2	1018	558	492	78	34	548	68	502	43	4
Monterrey Industrials	4.50	132	25	3	32	1091.1	1248	642	546	89	51	483	46	553	45	3
Puebla	4.59	127	45	8	16	1057.2	1195	630	539	72	32	476	32	543	46	2
Aguascalientes	4.70	131	26	4	31	1084.2	1232	639	567	96	48	457	51	504	61	3
Torreon	4.72	132	10	1	27	1114.1	1304	687	585	128	41	460	30	650	55	2
Jalisco	4.98	128	18	5	24	1051.0	1230	646	582	86	23	444	41	599	72	2
Mexico City Tigers	5.18	130	34	6	23	1069.1	1262	682	616	119	36	477	36	601	51	1
Yucatan	5.19	126	32	4	20	1021.1	1186	659	589	123	41	512	28	527	62	1
Saltillo	5.69	131	28	1	20	1080.2	1332	753	683	94	50	551	58	530	47	5

INDIVIDUAL

(Leading qualifiers for earned-run average leadership—107 or more innings)

Pitcher, Team	W	L	Pct.	ERA	G	GS	CG	GF	ShO	Sv.	IP	H	R	ER	HR	HB	BB	Int. BB	SO	WP
Man. Hernandez, Aguila	13	9	.591	2.20	24	24	14	0	4	0	180.1	139	47	44	10	2	67	2	126	7
Araujo, Campeche	9	9	.500	2.63	20	20	8	0	2	0	133.1	113	47	39	11	5	33	7	31	4
Ri. Osuna, Tabasco	8	3	.727	2.84	20	16	4	1	1	0	107.2	107	36	34	7	5	36	1	57	3
Lugo, Jalisco	17	5	.773	2.88	29	28	10	1	1	0	206.0	182	74	66	15	4	75	5	164	15
Lind, Nuevo Laredo	13	7	.650	2.95	23	23	4	0	1	0	158.2	142	66	52	6	3	64	2	121	7
Carman, Puebla	8	9	.471	2.98	22	20	8	2	4	1	142.0	129	57	47	8	2	59	2	85	4
J. J. Alvarez, Nuevo Laredo	13	11	.542	3.07	28	28	4	0	1	0	193.2	175	80	66	9	8	68	3	163	4
G. Jimenez, Aguascalientes	10	4	.714	3.09	20	20	3	0	0	0	139.2	134	52	48	6	4	46	5	55	7
Bennett, Puebla	13	11	.542	3.19	27	26	16	1	2	0	197.2	185	91	70	9	5	46	2	135	7
Luevano, Aguila	9	11	.450	3.23	26	26	1	0	0	0	170.0	148	71	61	7	3	78	3	83	4

Departmental leaders: G—Baller, 61; W—Lugo, J. Moreno, 17; L—A. Cruz, Ro. Osuna, Sierra, F. Soto, 14; Pct.—Cordoba, .818; GS—F. Soto, 30; CG—Bennett, 16; GF—Baller, 61; ShO—E. Lopez, 6; Sv.—Baller, 30; IP—Lugo, 206.0; H—F. Soto, 229; R—Palafox, 116; ER—Palafox, 103; HR—Rios, 24; HB—Palafox, 17; BB—M. Smith, 110; IBB—Sierra, 23; SO—Lugo, 164; WP—Castaneda, 20.

(All pitchers—listed alphabetically)

Pitcher, Team	W	L	Pct.	ERA	G	GS	CG	GF	ShO	Sv.	IP	H	R	ER	HR	HB	BB	Int. BB	SO	WP
A. Acosta, Monterrey Sultans	2	2	.500	4.95	30	5	1	25	0	2	63.2	83	38	35	5	3	28	1	37	3
C. Acosta, Puebla	0	0	.000	60.75	4	0	0	4	0	0	1.1	6	10	9	0	1	5	0	2	0

Pitcher, Team	W	L	Pct.	ERA	G	GS	CG	GF	ShO	Sv.	IP	H	R	ER	HR	HB	BB	Int. BB	SO	WP
C.E. Acosta, Mont. Industrials	0	0	.000	54.00	1	0	0	1	0	0	0.1	2	2	2	0	0	2	0	0	0
F. Acosta, Minatitlan	0	1	.000	6.75	7	1	0	6	0	0	10.2	16	8	8	1	0	5	0	3	0
M. Acosta, Tabasco	0	0	.000	4.38	7	0	0	7	0	0	12.1	8	6	6	0	1	7	0	4	0
Aguilar, Minatitlan	9	3	.750	3.79	29	18	2	11	0	0	133.0	120	60	56	9	2	64	2	82	5
Alicea, Torreon	2	1	.667	3.72	11	0	0	11	0	1	9.2	10	5	4	0	0	8	1	5	1
J.J. Alvarez, Nuevo Laredo	13	11	.542	3.07	28	28	4	0	1	0	193.2	175	80	66	9	8	68	3	163	8
M. Alvarez, Tabasco	2	2	.500	5.48	46	0	0	46	0	2	47.2	51	33	29	4	3	21	1	21	6
Antunez, Monclova	4	7	.364	3.52	48	5	0	43	0	1	64.0	65	29	25	4	1	27	3	30	3
Araujo, Campeche	9	9	.500	2.63	20	20	8	0	4	0	133.1	113	47	39	11	5	33	7	31	4
Arias, Aguila	0	0	.000	9.00	6	0	0	6	0	0	7.0	12	7	7	1	0	6	1	3	0
August, Puebla	4	6	.400	3.21	11	11	4	0	0	0	73.0	90	31	26	2	1	17	2	31	3
Azocar, Yucatan	0	0	.000	18.00	1	0	0	1	0	0	1.0	3	2	2	0	0	1	0	0	0
Baez, Aguila	5	3	.625	1.75	38	0	0	38	0	12	56.2	33	15	11	1	6	33	5	34	5
Baller, Nuevo Laredo	7	3	.700	2.09	61	0	0	61	0	30	81.2	64	24	19	6	1	25	4	85	4
Barojas, Mexico City Red Devils	0	0	.000	2.25	13	0	0	13	0	2	16.0	17	7	4	0	1	5	0	6	0
Barraza, Nuevo Laredo	15	8	.652	3.40	28	27	7	1	1	0	177.1	185	84	67	9	4	86	0	115	11
E. Barrera, Monterrey Sultans	0	0	.000	0.00	1	0	0	1	0	0	1.0	1	1	0	0	0	0	0	1	0
S. Barrera, Nuevo Laredo	0	0	.000	54.00	1	0	0	1	0	0	0.1	2	2	2	0	0	2	0	0	0
Barron, Saltillo	0	4	.000	11.05	17	4	0	13	0	0	29.1	50	38	36	4	3	20	5	20	2
Benitez, Monterrey Sultans	0	0	.000	0.00	1	0	0	1	0	0	1.0	1	0	0	0	0	1	0	0	1
Bennett, Puebla	13	11	.542	3.19	27	26	16	1	2	0	197.2	185	91	70	9	5	46	2	135	7
Berenguer, Saltillo	1	5	.167	6.14	20	1	1	19	0	11	29.1	35	26	20	1	2	16	2	32	0
Boyd, Monterrey Industrials	0	3	.000	4.91	15	1	0	14	0	11	25.2	24	14	14	1	1	16	2	20	1
Browning, Campeche	5	6	.455	2.96	50	2	1	49	0	22	82.0	80	28	27	7	0	23	9	35	2
Cabrales, Aguila	3	5	.375	5.29	43	3	0	40	0	11	63.0	74	42	37	9	1	32	4	34	2
Camacho, Minatitlan	1	0	1.000	3.72	17	0	0	17	0	0	19.1	22	10	8	1	0	14	0	7	1
Camarena, Minatitlan	1	3	.250	5.40	19	4	0	15	0	0	41.2	57	27	25	4	0	22	2	14	0
Candia, Mexico City Tigers	0	0	.000	13.50	5	0	0	5	0	1	5.1	9	8	8	1	0	4	0	1	0
Cano, Monterrey Sultans	5	6	.455	5.56	21	18	1	3	0	0	98.2	124	68	61	7	6	44	1	42	5
Cardenas, Aguascalientes	5	4	.556	4.88	26	13	2	13	0	0	96.0	104	58	52	8	6	32	3	29	3
Carman, Puebla	8	9	.471	2.98	22	20	8	2	4	1	142.0	129	57	47	8	2	59	2	85	4
Carranza, Yucatan	7	12	.368	5.81	23	22	4	1	0	0	136.1	170	99	88	16	3	70	4	77	4
Carrasco, Mexico City Red Devils	0	0	.000	0.00	3	0	0	3	0	0	4.2	5	1	0	0	0	0	0	4	0
Castaneda, Jalisco	7	12	.368	4.85	46	6	1	40	0	14	105.2	126	62	57	7	1	38	8	78	20
Castellanos, Jalisco	4	8	.333	5.42	33	7	0	27	0	1	84.2	108	56	51	5	5	26	3	39	2
F. Castillo, Jalisco	3	4	.429	4.82	31	4	0	28	0	8	65.1	77	45	35	2	3	34	6	25	7
L.T. Castillo, Monclova	10	10	.500	3.67	26	26	3	0	2	0	149.2	171	78	61	16	3	35	1	85	2
Castro, Yucatan	1	1	.500	6.50	42	0	0	42	0	2	18.0	26	14	13	2	2	11	3	11	1
J. Cazares, Aguila	1	3	.250	2.67	42	1	0	41	0	5	30.1	20	13	9	3	2	22	0	19	2
R. Cazares, Jalisco	3	5	.375	3.69	18	8	2	10	1	0	63.1	68	33	26	5	1	29	1	33	4
Cecena, Mexico City Red Devils	6	0	1.000	1.69	20	0	0	20	0	8	32.0	23	6	6	2	1	18	1	32	2
L. Cervantes, Aguascalientes	11	6	.647	4.64	25	25	2	0	1	0	137.2	182	80	71	16	2	42	5	44	5
Ra. Cervantes, Aguascalientes	0	0	.000	11.57	7	0	0	7	0	0	7.0	12	9	9	3	1	2	0	1	2
Ro. Cervantes, Torreon	0	0	.000	7.04	4	0	0	4	0	0	7.2	9	6	6	1	3	2	1	3	0
Chavarin, Yucatan	0	0	.000	6.14	7	0	0	7	0	0	7.1	9	5	5	0	0	5	0	8	2
Chavez, Jalisco	1	2	.333	3.81	34	1	0	33	0	0	56.2	63	28	24	4	2	23	3	28	1
Chevez, Tabasco	0	0	.000	13.50	9	0	0	9	0	0	6.0	9	9	9	3	0	6	0	3	0
Colorado, Tabasco	8	1	.889	3.11	16	11	2	5	2	1	72.1	79	27	25	5	2	5	0	22	0
B. Contreras, Aguila	0	1	.000	6.94	20	0	0	20	0	0	35.0	47	30	27	7	2	27	0	17	0
C. Contreras, Torreon	0	0	.000	0.00	2	0	0	2	0	0	2.0	1	0	0	0	0	0	0	2	0
Cordoba, Mexico City Red Devils	9	2	.818	3.23	43	4	1	39	0	4	106.0	96	44	38	8	2	47	4	71	3
Cosio, Saltillo	3	10	.231	8.07	23	20	2	3	0	0	90.1	139	83	81	11	8	45	6	23	1
Couoh, Nuevo Laredo	7	2	.778	2.24	43	3	0	40	0	5	88.1	67	24	22	6	1	28	5	95	8
A. Cruz, Torreon	7	14	.333	4.89	27	27	2	0	1	0	154.2	193	101	84	13	0	65	2	86	9
J. Cruz, Mexico City Red Devils	1	3	.250	4.21	19	0	0	19	0	0	36.1	30	19	17	3	4	17	2	17	2
M. Cruz, Nuevo Laredo	3	3	.500	3.12	30	0	0	30	0	1	57.2	58	27	20	5	2	25	5	37	1
DeAnda, Monterrey Sultans	0	0	.000	9.00	1	0	0	1	0	0	1.0	1	1	1	0	0	3	0	2	0
DeAvila, Saltillo	3	3	.500	7.15	13	5	1	8	0	0	34.0	39	28	27	1	4	25	3	24	6
DeLaCruz, Mexico City Tigers	1	0	1.000	4.50	10	0	0	10	0	5	10.0	10	5	5	1	1	5	0	9	1
L. DeLeon, Minatitlan	1	1	.500	1.91	10	3	0	7	0	6	28.1	23	8	6	1	0	7	2	13	0
R. DeLeon, Jalisco	1	0	1.000	8.74	9	0	0	9	0	0	11.1	15	12	11	1	1	6	0	8	2
Del Toro, Mexico City Red Devils	0	0	.000	7.94	5	0	0	5	0	0	5.2	7	7	5	1	2	5	0	2	3
Dessens, Mexico City Red Devils	3	1	.750	2.35	14	0	0	14	0	2	30.2	31	8	8	2	0	5	1	16	1
A. Diaz, Tabasco	0	0	.000	27.00	2	0	0	2	0	0	1.2	5	5	5	3	0	2	0	1	0
C. Diaz, Aguila	1	1	.500	7.27	7	0	0	7	0	0	8.2	10	8	7	3	1	6	1	4	0
M. Diaz, Monterrey Sultans	0	0	.000	0.00	1	0	0	1	0	0	1.0	1	0	0	0	0	0	0	0	0
O. Diaz, Minatitlan	0	0	.000	21.60	2	0	0	2	0	0	1.2	4	4	4	1	0	2	0	1	0
Dominguez, Campeche	3	7	.300	4.59	13	13	0	0	0	0	68.2	79	44	35	6	2	38	5	28	3
Eave, Monclova	0	3	.000	11.12	3	3	0	0	0	0	11.1	22	16	14	3	4	7	1	6	2
Edwards, Monterrey Sultans	6	5	.545	2.14	18	10	5	8	1	1	84.0	67	26	20	1	2	44	1	66	3
Elvira, Monterrey Sultans	0	1	.000	0.00	7	0	0	7	0	0	4.1	5	1	0	0	0	5	0	5	0
Enriquez, Aguascalientes	9	6	.600	3.49	19	18	7	1	2	0	116.0	109	55	45	4	3	45	2	67	5
Escamilla, Saltillo	0	0	.000	7.71	7	0	0	7	0	0	4.2	7	4	4	1	0	3	0	1	0
Espinoza, Monclova	1	0	1.000	3.72	5	0	0	5	0	0	9.2	11	4	4	0	0	4	0	8	1
Esquer, Yucatan	10	9	.526	4.74	23	22	9	1	1	0	148.0	166	78	78	21	3	49	2	114	11
An. Felix, Tabasco	4	10	.286	5.08	26	15	1	11	0	1	88.2	80	58	50	7	5	91	5	67	7
Ar. Felix, Yucatan	0	0	.000	5.40	1	0	0	1	0	0	1.2	2	1	1	1	0	3	0	2	1
Flores, Jalisco	0	0	.000	8.64	2	0	0	2	0	0	8.1	11	8	8	1	1	4	1	4	1
Fuentes, Campeche	0	0	.000	2.25	4	0	0	4	0	0	4.0	3	1	1	0	0	3	0	3	2
Galvez, Mexico City Tigers	8	3	.727	5.10	13	13	3	0	0	0	84.2	104	53	48	11	1	36	2	45	3
Gamboa, Yucatan	0	0	.000	13.50	6	0	0	6	0	0	6.2	13	12	10	2	0	6	0	1	0
D. Garcia, Monclova	0	0	.000	3.38	3	1	0	2	0	0	5.1	8	4	2	0	1	2	0	4	0
F. Garcia, Mexico City Red Devils	1	0	1.000	8.59	5	1	0	4	0	1	7.1	10	9	7	3	0	6	0	4	2
Jorge Garcia, Puebla	0	1	.000	19.50	11	2	0	9	0	1	12.0	30	27	26	2	0	9	4	5	2
Jose Garcia, Minatitlan	5	1	.833	2.30	42	3	1	39	0	2	74.1	71	25	19	3	4	41	0	40	1
Juan Garcia, Yucatan	3	4	.429	6.88	26	6	0	20	0	2	52.1	79	49	40	8	0	24	4	30	4
Ma. Garcia, Monclova	0	0	.000	0.00	1	0	0	1	0	0	1.0	0	0	0	0	0	0	0	0	0
Mi. Garcia, Minatitlan	0	1	.000	4.19	14	0	0	14	0	1	19.1	22	12	9	3	0	7	0	8	1
Z. Garcia, Mexico City Tigers	1	0	1.000	8.37	16	1	0	15	0	0	23.2	47	24	22	5	1	11	3	6	4
Garcia-Luna, Tabasco	1	0	1.000	5.60	11	1	0	10	0	0	17.2	24	13	11	2	0	15	0	2	3
D. Garibay, Mexico City Tigers	8	6	.571	5.15	26	26	2	0	0	0	146.2	157	89	84	10	2	80	3	57	8
R. Garibay, Monterrey Industrials	5	10	.333	5.57	25	21	2	4	0	0	137.1	153	98	85	17	10	80	3	47	4
S. Garibay, Torreon	0	0	.000	8.87	16	0	0	16	0	1	22.1	38	25	22	5	0	19	1	15	1
Garza, Monclova	0	2	.000	6.02	25	0	0	25	0	0	52.1	61	39	35	2	1	31	2	35	6

Pitcher, Team	W	L	Pct.	ERA	G	GS	CG	GF	ShO	Sv.	IP	H	R	ER	HR	HB	BB	Int. BB	SO	WP
J. Gomez, Monclova	0	0	.000	5.40	2	0	0	2	0	0	3.1	4	2	2	2	0	0	0	2	0
M. Gomez, Minatitlan	0	2	.000	3.46	15	4	0	11	0	0	26.0	23	13	10	2	1	19	3	13	2
Gonzalez, Monterrey Sultans	13	8	.619	4.12	26	26	3	0	0	0	146.1	160	82	67	7	2	56	3	75	2
Grajales, Torreon	4	1	.800	3.86	45	0	0	45	0	1	60.2	76	36	26	5	1	23	3	29	0
Granillo, Monterrey Sultans	3	0	1.000	3.46	48	0	0	49	0	4	26.0	34	13	10	3	2	5	1	12	2
Gutierrez, Aguila	0	0	.000	0.00	2	0	0	2	0	0	2.1	2	0	0	0	0	1	0	0	0
Hansen, Monclova	0	0	.000	6.43	5	5	0	0	0	0	21.0	33	21	15	3	0	12	0	13	1
Harrison, Puebla	2	3	.400	5.77	7	6	2	1	0	0	34.1	42	25	22	2	1	28	1	17	0
Heredia, Monterrey Sultans	6	3	.667	3.33	52	0	0	52	0	14	51.1	58	21	19	2	0	21	6	39	2
E. Hernandez, Jalisco	3	3	.500	9.67	31	2	0	29	0	4	49.1	87	55	53	12	1	21	1	29	4
Jo. Hernandez, Mex. City Tigers	1	3	.250	5.87	46	2	0	44	0	2	46.0	60	31	30	5	2	25	1	27	2
Ju. Hernandez, Minatitlan	3	4	.429	6.06	9	7	2	2	0	0	35.2	43	27	24	3	3	19	0	22	1
Man. Hernandez, Aguila	13	9	.591	2.20	24	24	14	0	4	0	180.1	139	47	44	10	2	67	2	126	7
Mar. Hernandez, Mont. Ind.	8	11	.421	5.34	27	26	4	1	0	0	141.2	184	98	84	12	8	58	3	81	7
C. Herrera, Monclova	6	4	.600	4.32	46	1	0	45	0	3	66.2	75	51	32	7	6	47	6	31	11
E. Herrera, Tabasco	4	10	.286	5.67	45	2	0	43	0	4	60.1	78	41	38	4	2	28	4	32	3
J. Herrera, M.C. Red Devils	0	0	.000	0.00	2	0	0	2	0	0	2.0	1	0	0	0	0	1	0	0	1
R. Herrera, Minatitlan	1	1	.500	4.09	12	0	0	12	0	1	22.0	25	16	10	2	1	11	1	11	4
Huerta, Monterrey Industrials	12	11	.522	4.36	28	27	3	1	0	0	163.0	188	96	79	16	11	61	3	77	3
Ibarra, Saltillo	1	0	1.000	7.27	8	0	0	8	0	0	8.2	10	9	7	1	0	8	0	3	2
Iniguez, Jalisco	8	6	.571	4.55	28	21	2	7	0	2	124.2	146	70	63	10	0	42	4	68	2
Jaime Granillo, Jalisco	0	0	.000	6.75	12	1	0	11	0	0	21.1	28	20	16	2	2	10	2	11	1
G. Jimenez, Aguascalientes	10	4	.714	3.09	20	20	3	0	0	0	139.2	134	52	48	6	4	46	5	55	7
I. Jimenez, Yucatan	11	7	.611	3.24	24	24	8	0	2	0	158.1	157	67	57	5	13	60	4	90	8
S. Jimenez, M.C. Red Devils	3	1	.750	6.35	18	0	0	18	0	3	34.0	35	25	24	5	1	15	2	17	4
Kraemer, Mexico City Red Devils	0	0	.000	0.00	3	0	0	3	0	1	6.2	1	0	0	0	0	3	0	2	0
E. Lara, Saltillo	1	0	1.000	10.67	8	0	0	8	0	1	14.1	21	17	17	2	2	15	1	2	0
H. Lara, Campeche	3	2	.600	2.47	24	1	0	23	0	1	47.1	33	14	13	2	3	17	4	22	0
J. Lara, Monterrey Industrials	8	4	.667	3.50	40	0	0	40	0	1	74.2	57	30	29	8	7	43	5	38	0
Ge. Leal, Monclova	0	0	.000	21.60	3	0	0	3	0	0	1.2	5	8	4	0	1	3	0	0	0
Gu. Leal, Monclova	0	0	.000	0.00	1	0	0	1	0	0	1.0	0	0	0	0	0	0	0	0	0
Ledon, Yucatan	5	5	.500	4.03	41	4	2	37	0	4	60.1	52	32	27	4	4	29	6	22	6
Leyva, Saltillo	3	4	.429	6.79	29	3	0	26	0	2	53.0	73	41	40	4	6	32	5	19	1
Lind, Nuevo Laredo	13	7	.650	2.95	23	23	4	0	1	0	158.2	142	66	52	6	3	64	2	121	9
Lizarraga, Jalisco	7	6	.538	6.14	30	12	2	18	0	0	85.0	109	60	58	15	0	35	5	28	2
E. Loaiza, Mexico City Red Devils	1	1	.500	5.18	4	3	0	1	0	0	24.1	32	18	14	3	0	4	1	15	0
S. Loaiza, Campeche	1	5	.167	5.57	19	10	0	9	0	0	63.0	67	47	39	5	3	51	3	27	1
E. Lopez, Tabasco	13	10	.565	3.41	29	27	12	2	6	0	187.1	195	76	71	12	10	38	4	85	4
Jonas Lopez, Aguascalientes	3	6	.333	4.59	39	4	1	35	0	2	82.1	86	50	42	9	0	34	4	29	4
Jose Lopez, Minatitlan	8	13	.381	4.69	29	16	3	13	0	2	124.2	156	80	65	19	4	57	5	69	0
Juan Lopez, Aguila	0	0	.000	4.91	8	0	0	8	0	0	14.2	11	8	8	0	0	10	0	5	3
Ra. Lopez, Monterrey Industrials	1	2	.333	6.92	19	2	0	17	0	0	39.0	57	32	30	7	0	13	2	21	1
Ro. Lopez, Aguila	0	0	.000	36.00	2	0	0	2	0	0	1.0	3	4	4	0	0	3	0	0	0
S. Lopez, Campeche	0	0	.000	0.00	1	0	0	1	0	0	1.2	2	0	0	0	0	1	0	0	0
Loynd, Nuevo Laredo	6	1	.857	3.15	9	9	0	0	0	0	60.0	53	23	21	2	3	21	0	68	1
Luevano, Aguila	9	11	.450	3.23	26	26	1	0	0	0	170.0	148	71	61	7	3	78	3	83	4
Lugo, Jalisco	17	5	.773	2.88	29	28	10	1	1	0	206.0	182	74	66	15	4	75	5	164	15
Macias, Aguila	0	0	.000	5.69	12	0	0	12	0	1	12.2	14	9	8	0	1	13	0	14	1
Manzano, Campeche	0	0	.000	1.35	8	0	0	8	0	0	6.2	5	1	1	1	1	9	0	6	1
Marquez, Mexico City Tigers	3	1	.750	1.90	14	0	0	14	0	5	23.2	21	5	5	0	0	11	4	12	3
Martin, Mexico City Tigers	0	0	.000	15.30	5	2	0	3	0	0	10.0	14	17	17	4	1	9	1	3	1
F. Martinez, M.C. Red Devils	11	7	.611	4.42	28	23	7	5	0	0	142.2	150	86	70	15	4	59	1	104	4
M. Martinez, Minatitlan	0	0	.000	18.00	1	0	0	0	0	0	1.0	2	2	2	0	1	0	0	0	0
U. Martinez, Aguila	0	0	.000	13.50	4	0	0	4	0	0	2.2	4	4	4	0	0	3	0	0	0
May, Campeche	9	7	.563	4.35	19	19	2	0	1	0	118.0	113	65	57	11	1	63	5	87	3
McClellan, Torreon	0	3	.000	13.97	3	3	0	0	0	0	9.2	16	15	15	5	0	8	0	7	0
McMurtry, M.C. Red Devils	1	2	.333	5.08	17	0	0	17	0	6	28.1	30	17	16	2	0	13	2	25	0
Mead, Torreon	10	10	.500	4.75	22	21	7	1	0	0	132.2	179	81	70	17	3	42	5	70	4
Medvin, Aguascalientes	4	5	.444	4.33	17	8	2	9	1	3	60.1	67	35	29	4	11	31	5	34	6
Mena, Nuevo Laredo	0	0	.000	27.00	1	0	0	1	0	0	0.2	3	2	2	1	0	1	0	1	0
Mendez, Mexico City Red Devils	10	9	.526	3.73	26	22	3	4	0	0	135.0	136	60	56	13	5	46	2	78	3
Mendoza, Mexico City Red Devils	0	1	.000	11.25	8	0	0	8	0	0	8.0	13	11	10	1	1	7	0	9	0
Merodio, Yucatan	4	7	.364	6.32	15	14	1	1	0	0	72.2	92	64	51	15	4	49	1	30	3
Meza, Aguila	3	2	.600	5.19	17	7	1	10	1	1	52.0	42	30	30	2	0	29	1	31	2
Miranda, Torreon	3	7	.300	6.04	47	0	0	47	0	2	56.2	77	44	38	10	1	32	5	54	3
Mojica, Jalisco	0	0	.000	7.36	2	0	0	2	0	0	3.2	6	3	3	0	0	0	0	3	0
Molina, Aguascalientes	0	5	.000	3.55	9	0	0	9	0	0	12.2	8	11	5	2	3	9	0	5	3
Montalvo, Monterrey Industrials	0	5	.000	6.32	24	1	0	23	0	9	37.0	56	26	26	2	1	17	7	26	1
Montano, Monclova	9	6	.600	3.43	23	23	7	0	2	0	152.1	139	64	58	13	2	56	6	81	7
Mora, Mexico City Tigers	1	3	.250	10.69	33	2	0	31	0	0	33.2	63	44	40	5	0	18	1	23	1
C. Morales, Tabasco	0	0	.000	0.00	3	0	0	3	0	0	0.1	0	0	0	0	0	2	0	1	1
I. Morales, Puebla	0	0	.000	5.40	19	0	0	20	0	1	13.1	14	8	8	3	2	10	0	9	1
A. Moreno, Mexico City Tigers	0	4	.000	5.96	12	7	0	5	0	1	45.1	58	37	30	5	0	20	2	23	3
F. Moreno, Tabasco	1	0	1.000	6.35	3	0	0	3	0	0	5.2	7	4	4	0	0	2	0	3	1
J. Moreno, Saltillo	17	10	.630	4.94	30	28	11	2	0	0	184.0	206	104	101	16	8	83	8	114	1
L. Moreno, M.C. Red Devils	10	7	.588	5.37	28	25	5	3	1	0	134.0	143	89	80	16	6	68	0	101	7
R. Moreno, Nuevo Laredo	0	2	.000	6.57	15	4	0	11	0	0	24.2	30	21	18	2	1	11	0	16	5
L. Munoz, Monterrey Sultans	0	0	.000	2.20	4	0	0	4	0	0	3.0	3	1	0	0	0	3	0	0	1
M. Munoz, Aguila	14	11	.560	3.82	28	27	9	1	3	0	174.1	178	80	74	20	3	33	3	66	0
R. Munoz, Jalisco	0	1	.000	4.57	14	7	0	7	0	0	43.1	52	26	22	1	0	24	2	17	2
Murillo, Monclova	5	3	.625	4.48	29	10	0	19	0	6	94.1	114	56	47	6	4	37	4	37	3
A. Navarro, Saltillo	2	6	.250	6.57	16	10	0	6	0	0	63.0	76	51	46	8	2	38	0	38	4
L. Navarro, Saltillo	0	0	.000	9.00	6	0	0	6	0	0	11.0	20	11	11	2	0	6	0	3	2
Neri, Yucatan	4	11	.267	5.61	27	22	4	5	0	0	126.2	138	85	79	15	8	78	3	62	8
Noriega, Puebla	1	4	.200	6.10	29	6	1	23	0	1	48.2	65	38	33	4	4	33	2	21	2
Normand, Aguascalientes	5	9	.357	4.26	20	19	4	1	2	1	120.1	134	69	57	10	3	68	3	49	9
G. Ochoa, Torreon	0	0	.000	3.38	2	1	0	1	0	0	5.1	4	2	2	0	0	3	0	1	0
P. Ochoa, Monterrey Industrials	3	0	1.000	4.27	25	2	0	23	0	1	46.1	57	26	22	3	0	17	3	12	0
Olivas, Saltillo	0	0	.000	23.63	2	0	0	2	0	0	2.2	5	7	7	0	0	4	0	1	1
Olmos, Saltillo	2	3	.400	3.61	8	8	2	0	1	0	42.1	41	23	17	2	1	23	2	27	0
Onofre, Mexico City Tigers	0	0	.000	0.00	1	0	0	1	0	0	1.1	1	0	0	0	0	0	0	1	0
Ontiveros, Monterrey Industrials	1	2	.333	5.44	33	1	0	32	0	5	46.1	62	30	28	5	0	11	0	20	1
Oren, Campeche	0	0	.000	0.00	6	0	0	6	0	0	2.0	3	0	0	0	0	1	0	1	0
Orozco, Monterrey Sultans	6	10	.375	3.89	25	23	6	2	2	0	145.2	172	80	63	10	6	33	3	61	3

— 368 —

Pitcher, Team	W	L	Pct.	ERA	G	GS	CG	GF	ShO	Sv.	IP	H	R	ER	HR	HB	BB	Int. BB	SO	WP
H. Ortega, Campeche	0	0	.000	....	1	0	0	1	0	0	0.0	2	3	3	0	0	1	0	0	0
R. Ortega, Jalisco	0	0	.000	12.00	4	0	0	4	0	0	6.0	7	8	8	1	0	5	0	1	0
Ortiz, Campeche	0	0	.000	23.63	3	1	0	2	0	0	2.2	6	7	7	1	0	11	0	0	1
Ri. Osuna, Tabasco	8	3	.727	2.84	20	16	3	4	1	0	107.2	107	36	34	7	5	36	1	57	3
Ro. Osuna, Yucatan	8	14	.364	4.67	24	24	10	0	1	0	165.2	200	93	86	15	1	71	2	87	5
Palacios, Aguascalientes	4	4	.500	3.94	38	2	0	36	0	20	59.1	47	27	26	4	0	40	3	57	11
Palafox, Torreon	8	8	.500	4.94	28	27	4	1	0	0	187.2	225	116	103	23	17	60	4	87	10
Palomo, Torreon	0	0	.000	31.50	3	0	0	3	0	0	2.0	4	7	7	0	0	4	0	2	0
Parnet, Aguascalientes	1	1	.500	15.43	3	0	0	3	0	0	2.1	8	4	4	0	0	3	1	3	0
Parra, Mexico City Tigers	0	0	.000	4.50	2	0	0	2	0	0	2.0	3	1	1	0	0	0	1	0	0
Pavlas, Mexico City Red Devils	5	3	.625	3.49	11	11	1	0	0	0	56.2	59	24	22	0	3	19	0	32	3
Pelcastregui, Monterrey Sultans	0	0	.000	2.08	5	0	0	5	0	0	4.1	8	1	1	0	0	7	0	3	2
Peraza, Monterrey Industrials	2	0	1.000	3.95	9	0	0	9	0	4	13.2	16	10	6	0	0	11	1	10	5
Perea, Yucatan	0	0	.000	13.50	4	0	0	4	0	0	4.2	10	7	7	1	0	4	0	1	1
J. Perez, Tabasco	0	1	.000	7.94	7	2	0	5	0	1	11.1	14	11	10	0	1	14	1	6	2
L. Perez, Monterrey Sultans	0	0	.000	7.20	1	1	0	0	0	0	5.0	6	4	4	0	0	2	1	3	0
Perry, Torreon	10	7	.588	3.11	50	4	1	46	0	14	98.1	99	41	34	7	4	34	3	61	5
Pimentel, Torreon	2	3	.400	4.02	44	0	0	40	0	1	69.1	81	37	31	3	5	23	0	46	1
Pina, Mexico City Red Devils	1	1	.500	7.36	9	1	0	8	0	0	14.2	21	12	12	0	0	15	0	13	0
Puig, Saltillo	4	6	.400	4.13	15	12	4	3	0	1	85.0	87	51	39	6	2	46	4	26	1
Al. Pulido, Aguila	9	10	.474	4.10	28	25	3	3	0	0	140.1	162	70	64	19	1	25	0	48	1
An. Pulido, Minatitlan	0	0	.000	4.00	6	0	0	6	0	0	9.0	8	4	4	0	0	2	0	3	0
Purata, Monterrey Industrials	7	11	.389	4.13	26	25	5	1	1	0	154.2	157	80	71	10	5	75	3	84	2
Quinones, Monterrey Sultans	7	4	.636	2.96	26	8	0	18	0	1	76.0	66	35	25	4	3	18	2	20	2
Quintero, Torreon	2	5	.286	6.37	20	9	0	11	0	1	59.1	74	45	42	13	0	25	0	27	4
A. Quiroz, Nuevo Laredo	1	2	.333	6.45	6	5	0	1	0	0	22.1	32	16	16	4	0	13	2	21	0
J. Quiroz, Puebla	0	0	.000	3.45	14	0	0	14	0	1	15.2	13	10	6	3	0	5	1	14	0
Ramirez, Mexico City Red Devils	14	5	.737	3.40	25	24	8	1	4	0	156.1	136	65	59	8	9	65	2	100	2
Ramos, Puebla	0	0	.000	4.91	6	0	0	6	0	0	11.0	12	6	6	1	0	8	0	4	0
Raygoza, Monterrey Sultans	15	7	.682	3.28	26	26	8	0	2	0	186.1	198	79	68	6	6	44	1	81	1
Renteria, Torreon	8	7	.533	4.86	22	22	0	0	0	0	113.0	129	72	61	17	2	34	2	52	3
Retes, Tabasco	8	7	.533	4.30	29	24	5	5	1	0	127.2	129	71	61	12	4	63	1	42	5
D. Reyes, Mexico City Red Devils	0	1	.000	5.06	7	1	0	6	0	0	5.1	4	4	3	1	0	9	0	5	0
F. Reyes, Minatitlan	0	1	.000	4.61	15	0	0	15	0	0	13.2	15	8	7	1	0	9	2	6	0
O. Reyes, Mexico City Red Devils	0	0	.000	6.00	2	0	0	2	0	0	3.0	4	2	2	1	0	2	0	1	0
Rincon, Torreon	7	3	.700	3.17	57	4	0	53	0	8	82.1	80	33	29	8	0	36	3	81	5
Rios, Mexico City Tigers	13	11	.542	4.82	25	25	10	0	3	0	162.1	176	97	87	24	6	50	6	123	7
Ritchie, Monterrey Industrials	0	0	.000	9.00	2	0	0	2	0	0	5.0	6	5	5	0	0	2	0	6	1
Rivera, Mexico City Red Devils	0	0	.000	0.00	1	1	0	0	0	0	3.0	2	0	0	0	0	0	0	1	0
Robles, Mexico City Tigers	0	1	.000	5.27	10	0	0	10	0	0	13.2	18	8	8	2	1	10	0	5	0
E. Rodriguez, Yucatan	0	0	.000	2.25	8	0	0	8	0	0	12.0	9	4	3	0	0	6	0	6	1
I. Rodriguez, Monclova	3	2	.400	5.12	45	1	0	44	0	0	38.2	38	30	22	2	2	26	2	32	5
M. Rodriguez, Monterrey Ind.	3	4	.429	4.83	22	10	0	12	0	0	63.1	82	40	34	7	0	35	1	23	4
M.A. Rodriguez, Mex. City Tigers	6	3	.667	5.34	39	0	0	39	0	0	60.2	79	41	36	3	4	24	6	24	2
Ra. Rodriguez, Saltillo	7	11	.389	5.07	23	21	4	2	0	0	129.2	163	79	73	12	3	31	2	76	6
Re. Rodriguez, Nuevo Laredo	1	3	.250	6.80	26	1	0	26	0	1	43.2	46	36	33	7	3	31	5	13	5
Ro. Rodriguez, Torreon	0	0	.000	3.24	13	0	0	13	0	0	8.1	7	5	3	0	1	11	0	7	2
S. Rodriguez, Yucatan	0	1	.000	11.25	4	2	0	2	0	0	8.0	10	11	10	1	1	9	0	2	0
U. Rodriguez, Tabasco	2	1	.667	3.92	43	0	0	43	0	2	39.0	43	19	17	3	1	25	4	17	3
Roesler, Puebla	6	4	.600	3.24	19	4	3	15	1	5	50.0	51	24	18	1	0	25	2	43	4
Rojo, Campeche	3	8	.273	4.44	32	8	2	24	0	0	79.0	79	50	39	7	0	42	7	40	4
H.M. Romero, Saltillo	0	0	.000	5.36	24	0	0	24	0	0	42.0	54	30	25	7	3	25	0	18	5
J. Romero, Tabasco	6	3	.667	3.38	30	0	0	30	0	1	53.1	53	26	20	3	4	30	3	31	1
Ruiz, Puebla	9	9	.500	3.47	29	27	7	2	3	0	181.1	204	75	70	14	1	32	2	120	1
Saenz, Puebla	1	1	.500	2.84	9	2	1	7	1	1	25.1	27	8	8	0	0	19	2	7	2
Salas, Mexico City Tigers	2	1	.667	4.28	30	0	0	30	0	2	48.1	58	25	23	4	2	17	1	26	2
E. Saldana, Tabasco	2	9	.182	4.32	39	10	1	29	0	12	89.2	100	46	43	7	5	40	4	43	5
G. Saldana, Puebla	0	2	.000	4.46	24	3	0	21	0	1	38.1	43	22	19	3	4	27	2	15	2
E. Sanchez, Campeche	0	0	.000	32.40	2	0	0	2	0	0	1.2	6	6	6	0	0	0	0	2	0
H. Sanchez, Aguila	6	8	.429	3.14	29	13	4	16	0	1	100.1	106	40	35	13	0	20	3	39	1
J.J. Sanchez, Jalisco	0	0	.000	3.86	7	0	0	7	0	0	9.1	9	4	4	0	0	10	0	2	3
M. Sanchez, Saltillo	1	3	.250	4.94	30	1	0	29	0	3	54.2	64	35	30	3	1	30	7	28	5
C. Sandoval, Aguila	0	0	.000	18.78	9	0	0	9	0	0	7.2	24	16	16	3	0	5	0	4	2
G. Sandoval, Saltillo	2	6	.250	6.97	21	12	0	9	0	1	62.0	83	54	48	4	3	55	3	21	2
Sangeado, Campeche	0	0	.000	5.68	6	0	0	6	0	0	6.1	7	4	4	0	1	9	0	7	2
Sauveur, Minatitlan	3	3	.500	3.27	7	7	1	0	0	0	44.0	40	19	16	1	0	23	1	31	0
Serna, Tabasco	1	0	1.000	2.83	14	7	0	7	0	0	41.1	35	13	13	3	3	12	0	30	0
Sierra, Campeche	7	14	.333	3.83	26	26	5	0	1	0	152.2	147	68	65	7	3	73	13	82	2
Sinohui, Minatitlan	7	4	.636	2.79	36	0	0	36	0	19	58.0	45	18	18	9	1	22	2	38	2
D. Smith, Monclova	8	5	.615	3.97	24	17	4	7	0	3	111.0	99	59	49	3	2	74	1	91	18
M. Smith, Mexico City Tigers	14	10	.583	5.08	27	26	7	1	2	0	172.0	189	109	97	18	8	110	3	103	9
Solano, Monclova	7	5	.583	2.39	47	0	0	47	0	24	60.1	54	23	16	5	1	20	6	45	2
J. Solis, Aguila	2	2	.500	6.71	30	1	0	29	0	0	52.1	65	45	39	8	3	37	5	15	7
R. Solis, Monterrey Sultans	7	11	.389	4.43	23	23	6	0	1	0	144.1	180	81	71	7	4	39	5	67	2
Sombra, Jalisco	2	4	.333	3.98	29	9	1	18	1	1	63.1	75	32	28	3	1	21	0	31	6
Sosa, Puebla	0	2	.000	11.88	10	0	0	10	0	1	8.1	10	11	11	1	0	7	1	2	0
A. Soto, Puebla	0	1	.000	5.14	8	0	0	8	0	0	14.0	11	9	8	0	0	14	0	5	2
F. Soto, Minatitlan	13	14	.481	4.20	31	30	11	1	2	1	197.1	229	101	92	20	4	55	6	91	4
R. Soto, Aguila	0	0	.000	6.54	15	1	0	14	0	0	31.2	38	24	23	5	4	12	0	10	1
Stowell, Monterrey Industrials	1	0	1.000	3.60	6	1	0	5	0	1	5.0	6	2	2	0	0	8	1	4	3
Straker, Saltillo	1	1	.500	3.52	4	4	0	0	0	0	15.1	16	6	6	2	0	11	0	7	1
Sulu, Campeche	1	1	.500	1.35	3	1	0	2	0	0	6.2	4	4	1	1	1	2	0	4	2
Taylor, Campeche	1	1	.500	3.57	3	3	0	0	0	0	17.2	16	7	7	0	1	14	0	12	2
A. Tejeda, Nuevo Laredo	0	0	.000	9.00	1	0	0	1	0	0	1.0	2	1	1	0	0	0	0	0	0
F. Tejeda, Tabasco	0	0	.000	....	1	0	0	1	0	0	0.0	1	2	2	0	0	1	0	0	0
J. Tejeda, Campeche	3	5	.375	5.24	20	1	0	10	1	0	55.0	62	36	32	6	3	21	3	25	3
Tinoco, Campeche	4	2	.333	5.16	31	8	0	23	0	1	66.1	65	41	38	2	2	37	4	24	2
Toledo, Campeche	0	2	.000	3.71	32	2	0	30	0	0	60.2	59	29	25	2	3	36	5	29	1
Torres, Campeche	0	0	.000	0.00	4	0	0	4	0	0	4.1	4	0	0	0	0	2	0	2	0
Uribe, Yucatan	2	2	.500	4.54	27	0	0	27	0	1	37.2	42	21	19	4	5	26	2	20	2
A. Valdez, Monterrey Industrials	7	12	.368	5.20	30	24	6	6	0	1	150.2	170	102	87	13	9	59	6	65	8
E. Valdez, Puebla	4	12	.250	4.50	16	16	5	0	0	0	102.0	118	63	51	11	5	39	2	43	4
I. Valdez, Mexico City Tigers	16	7	.696	3.94	26	25	11	1	1	0	173.2	192	87	76	16	8	55	3	113	7
J. Valdez, Nuevo Laredo	0	0	.000	15.00	9	0	0	9	0	1	9.0	21	16	15	0	1	10	1	5	1

Pitcher, Team	W	L	Pct.	ERA	G	GS	CG	GF	ShO	Sv.	IP	H	R	ER	HR	HB	BB	Int. BB	SO	WP
R. Valdez, Monclova	15	5	.750	3.48	26	26	9	0	1	0	176.0	171	83	68	14	5	53	1	86	5
Jorge Valencia, Saltillo	5	3	.625	4.54	44	0	0	44	0	4	81.1	86	46	41	6	4	48	10	27	4
Jose Valencia, Campeche	1	3	.250	10.80	15	1	0	14	0	1	25.0	40	33	30	4	2	29	2	15	5
M. Valenzuela, Nuevo Laredo	0	0	.000	7.20	3	0	0	3	0	0	5.0	7	6	4	0	1	3	1	2	1
R. Valenzuela, Monclova	2	2	.500	4.07	24	2	1	22	0	1	59.2	73	28	27	5	2	17	2	20	1
S. Valenzuela, Puebla	5	10	.333	7.76	29	15	1	14	0	1	87.0	120	82	75	9	5	40	4	33	7
Vargas, Aguascalientes	2	2	.500	4.28	19	0	0	19	0	0	48.1	62	27	23	1	1	21	3	20	2
Vazquez, Mexico City Red Devils	4	2	.667	5.00	15	13	1	2	0	0	63.0	85	42	35	13	2	27	0	36	2
Vega Velarde, Nuevo Laredo	4	6	.400	5.06	21	17	2	4	0	0	94.1	114	62	53	9	3	60	2	52	6
E. Velazquez, Torreon	5	8	.385	4.74	29	19	1	10	0	0	106.1	113	69	56	17	3	60	2	63	7
Il. Velazquez, Aguascalientes	5	7	.417	4.66	16	12	1	4	0	0	67.2	71	39	35	4	3	19	0	23	2
Is. Velazquez, Minatitlan	6	8	.429	4.26	27	22	5	5	4	1	107.2	105	63	51	5	1	60	0	64	9
P. Velazquez, Campeche	2	0	1.000	5.70	26	0	0	26	0	1	30.0	20	20	19	4	3	31	1	22	4
Velez, Yucatan	0	0	.000	6.43	8	0	0	8	0	0	7.0	8	5	5	0	1	5	1	1	0
Veliz Arballo, Monterrey Ind.	4	4	.500	3.54	50	5	1	45	0	4	76.1	84	38	30	8	2	38	7	44	5
Villanueva, Aguascalientes	0	2	.000	6.46	41	0	0	41	0	3	23.2	34	17	17	1	2	13	1	19	4
Villarreal, Monterrey Sultans	5	2	.714	3.18	42	1	0	42	0	3	73.2	67	34	26	5	2	36	2	50	3
J.A. Villegas, Aguascalientes	5	3	.625	5.72	38	5	0	33	0	3	83.1	107	59	53	8	4	35	7	27	4
R. Villegas, Puebla	6	7	.455	4.23	22	17	4	5	0	0	106.1	122	56	50	10	1	48	1	38	2
Vizcarra, Monterrey Industrials	0	1	.000	42.43	4	1	0	3	0	0	2.1	11	15	11	2	0	3	1	2	0
Watson, Nuevo Laredo	6	4	.600	4.67	15	15	4	0	1	0	96.1	96	51	50	10	5	50	1	64	3
Weber, Minatitlan	0	2	.000	4.63	7	3	0	2	0	0	11.2	11	6	6	1	0	10	1	6	2
Zamorano, Campeche	0	0	.000	19.64	2	0	0	2	0	0	3.2	10	8	8	1	0	1	0	1	0
A. Zamudio, Puebla	1	2	.333	6.26	28	0	0	28	0	1	50.1	67	42	35	5	1	31	2	28	2
P. Zamudio, Aguascalientes	0	0	.000	16.20	4	0	0	4	0	0	5.0	10	12	9	1	2	6	0	6	0
Zavaleta, Jalisco	0	1	.000	40.50	2	0	0	2	0	0	0.2	3	3	3	1	0	0	0	1	1
Zuniga, Monterrey Industrials	0	0	.000	0.00	1	0	0	1	0	0	0.2	0	0	0	0	0	0	1	0	0

BALKS—DeAvila, Man. Hernandez, Luevano, Ramirez, Rojo, E. Velazquez, 2 each; A. Acosta, Carranza, Castellanos, R. Cervantes, Cosio, Edwards, Enriquez, Garza, Gonzalez, Huerta, I. Jimenez, H. Lara, Jonas Lopez, F. Martinez, Mendez, Mora, Neri, Noriega, Retes, I. Rodriguez, R. Rodriguez, J.J. Romero, H.M. Romero, F. Soto, E. Valdez, J.L. Valdez, Valdez Soto, R. Valenzuela, P. Velazquez, 1 each.

COMBINATION SHUTOUTS—Cardenas-Villanueva-Palacios, L. Cervantes-Cardenas-Villanueva-Medvin, L. Cervantes-Palacios, L. Cervantes-Sanchez, Jimenez-Miranda, Medvin-Villanueva, Velazquez-Villegas, Aguascalientes; Pulido-Baez 2, Hernandez-Cazares-Cabrales, Luevano-Cabrales, Luevano-Cazares-Cabrales, Pulido-Cabrales, Sanchez-Baez, Aguila; Araujo-Browning, May-Browning, Sierra-Browning, Sierra-Toledo-Tinoco, Toledo-Sulu-Fuentes-Manzano-Lara, Campeche; Iniguez-Castaneda, Lizarraga-Castellanos, Lugo-Castaneda, Jalisco; Mendez-Garcia, Moreno-Cecena, Mexico City Red Devils; Salas-Marquez, Valdez-Moreno-Marquez, Mexico City Tigers; Acosta-J. Garcia-Camacho-Aguilar-DeLeon, Sauveur-Lopez, Soto-DeLeon, Velazquez-Camacho-J. Garcia-Jaime Granillo-Aguilar-DeLeon, Minatitlan; Castillo-Antunez, Montano-Solano, Valdez-Herrera, Monclova; Hernandez-Boyd, Hernandez-Lara-Boyd, Hernandez-Lara-Ochoa, Huerta-Boyd, Jimenez-Peraza, Monterrey Industrials; Edwards-Villarreal, Gonzalez-Granillo-Heredia, Monterrey Sultans; Barraza-Baller 2, Couoh-Moreno, Lind-Rodriguez, Loynd-Baller, Loynd-Couoh, Vega Velarde-Baller, Vega Velarde-Couoh, Vega Velarde-Moreno, Nuevo Laredo; Villegas-Roesler 2, Puebla; Moreno-Berenguer, Saltillo; Colorado-Rodriguez, Ruiz-Alvarez-Saldana, Tabasco; Rincon-Perry 2, Mead-Perry, Palafox-Rincon, Palafox-Rincon-Alicea, Quintero-Grajales-Rincon, Renteria-Rincon, Torreon; S. Rodriguez-Esquer, Yucatan.

NO-HIT GAMES—Olmos, Saltillo, defeated Aguascalientes, 2-0, March 21; Meza, Aguila, defeated Nuevo Laredo, 3-0, June 13; Velazquez, Minatitlan, defeated Campeche, 2-0, June 19.

FIELDING

TEAM

Team	Pct.	G	PO	A	E	DP	PB		Team	Pct.	G	PO	A	E	DP	PB
Yucatan	.978	126	3064	1324	101	113	15		Torreon	.975	132	3343	1458	124	159	14
Saltillo	.978	131	3242	1465	107	142	9		Minatitlan	.974	129	3159	1345	121	118	17
Aguascalientes	.978	131	3254	1568	107	154	7		Jalisco	.974	128	3153	1391	121	145	8
Mexico City Red Devils	.977	129	3225	1394	111	118	9		Nuevo Laredo	.972	132	3374	1448	140	141	24
Mexico City Tigers	.977	130	3208	1379	109	129	8		Puebla	.969	127	3173	1361	144	124	10
Tabasco	.976	130	3215	1388	112	138	14		Monterrey Sultans	.969	132	3311	1506	154	121	12
Campeche	.976	125	3128	1327	108	129	11		Monterrey Industrials	.969	130	3274	1515	152	152	15
Aguila	.976	132	3309	1432	115	131	9		Monclova	.968	130	3299	1421	157	147	25

Triple plays—Jalisco, Mexico City Red Devils, Monterrey Sultans, Nuevo Laredo, Tabasco, Torreon.

INDIVIDUAL

FIRST BASEMEN

Player, Team	Pct.	G	PO	A	E	DP		Player, Team	Pct.	G	PO	A	E	DP
Ortega, Jalisco	1.000	47	158	5	0	19		Salinas, Puebla	.990	71	572	32	6	55
See, Aguascalientes	1.000	44	417	32	0	52		Simmons, Jalisco	.990	45	375	18	4	38
Estrada, Nuevo Laredo	1.000	19	126	5	0	13		Willson, Yucatan	.990	12	92	5	1	12
Almeida, Saltillo	1.000	17	92	5	0	9		Quiroz, Puebla	.990	40	358	22	4	40
Javier Guerrero, Agua.	1.000	16	85	11	0	14		Zamudio, Monterrey Sultans	.990	18	90	5	1	7
Tatis, Puebla	1.000	11	65	4	0	6		Aganza, Monclova	.989	59	491	38	6	52
H. Valenzuela, Tabasco	.997	80	665	31	2	71		B. Valdez, Aguascalientes	.989	29	246	15	3	26
Peralta, Minatitlan	.996	34	274	10	1	36		Ortiz, Nuevo Laredo	.988	12	81	3	1	7
Carrillo, Mexico City Tigers	.996	31	225	12	1	17		Blocker, Minatitlan	.986	34	259	19	4	29
Azocar, Yucatan	.995	114	1009	70	5	95		Salazar, Puebla	.985	19	114	18	2	12
Avila, Torreon	.995	126	1115	83	6	131		Traver, Monterrey Sultans	.985	124	1131	52	18	100
Stephenson, Aguila	.995	36	332	32	2	34		Sommers, Jalisco	.985	62	439	20	7	61
Melendez, Aguila	.994	92	847	49	5	80		Fernandez, Saltillo	.982	21	163	2	3	23
Tillman, Tabasco	.994	71	617	33	4	62		Guerrero, Jalisco	.982	12	100	8	2	9
Castro, Monclova	.993	85	718	46	5	79		Contreras, Tabasco	.979	42	225	13	5	16
Rodriguez, Campeche	.993	67	563	36	4	59		Hernandez A., Campeche	.977	13	40	2	1	4
Nelson, Saltillo	.993	59	512	44	4	47								
Stark, Mexico City Red Devils	.993	116	1003	57	8	87		**(Fewer Than Ten Games)**						
H. Rojas, Monterrey Industrials	.993	41	379	18	3	40		Williams, Monterrey Sultans	1.000	7	28	2	0	1
Steels, Monterrey Industrials	.992	65	559	49	5	65		Rodriguez, Torreon	1.000	6	25	4	0	3
Barrera, Campeche	.992	53	444	29	4	49		Trafton, Mexico City Red Devils	1.000	4	13	0	0	0
Garbey, Mexico City Tigers	.991	107	851	69	8	97		Barrera, Aguila	1.000	4	27	1	0	1
Romero, Nuevo Laredo	.991	110	940	91	9	104		Sanchez, Monclova	1.000	4	29	0	0	3
Sanchez, Aguascalientes	.991	107	951	45	9	112		Pulido, Mexico City Tigers	1.000	3	6	0	0	0
Alvarez, Monterrey Industrials	.991	12	99	10	1	11		Contreras, Torreon	1.000	3	9	0	0	1
								J. Valdez R., Aguascalientes	1.000	3	15	0	0	2

Player, Team	Pct.	G	PO	A	E	DP
Escalera, Aguascalientes	1.000	3	12	1	0	1
Monroy, Mexico City Tigers	1.000	2	2	0	0	0
Aylward, Tabasco	1.000	2	23	1	0	2
Ramirez, Yucatan	1.000	2	3	2	0	1
P. Gonzalez, Yucatan	1.000	2	4	0	0	0
Villaescusa, Yucatan	1.000	2	6	0	0	0
Pardo, Puebla	1.000	2	14	0	0	0
Diaz, Nuevo Laredo	1.000	2	12	0	0	2
Jones, Aguascalientes	1.000	2	2	0	0	0
Guzman, Aguascalientes	1.000	2	18	1	0	1
Ramirez, Mexico City Red Devils	1.000	1	1	0	0	0
Castaneda, Mexico City Tigers	1.000	1	3	0	0	0
Arzate, Monterrey Industrials	1.000	1	3	0	0	1
Beltran, Aguila	1.000	1	4	1	0	0
Aguilar, Tabasco	1.000	1	2	0	0	0
Alfaro, Yucatan	1.000	1	3	0	0	0
Zulueta, Yucatan	1.000	1	2	0	0	0
Bennett, Puebla	1.000	1	1	2	0	0
Tejeda, Nuevo Laredo	1.000	1	3	0	0	1
Osuna, Saltillo	1.000	1	0	1	0	0
C. Rodriguez, Saltillo	1.000	1	2	0	0	0
Cornejo, Saltillo	1.000	1	2	0	0	0
J. Gonzalez, Monterrey Sultans	1.000	1	2	0	0	0
V. Ruiz, Torreon	1.000	1	3	0	0	2
Gu. Leal, Monclova	1.000	1	5	1	0	1
Rivera, Yucatan	1.000	1	1	0	0	0
Beristain, Jalisco	1.000	1	2	0	0	1
Pena, Monterrey Industrials	.982	9	51	5	1	8
Sanchez, Puebla	.981	7	48	3	1	6
Camarero, Minatitlan	.977	6	43	0	1	3
Arvizu, Campeche	.967	3	27	2	1	2
Ibarra, Aguila	.958	5	21	2	1	1
J. Reyes, Mexico City Red Devils	.942	8	59	6	4	10
G. Rodriguez, Monclova	.941	3	12	4	1	2
Chan, Monclova	.939	6	28	3	2	3
Abrego, Monclova	.909	1	9	1	1	0
Firova, Nuevo Laredo	.900	1	9	0	1	1
Gavia, Aguila	.889	1	7	1	1	1
Reyna, Campeche	.857	2	11	1	2	2
Espinoza, Monterrey Industrials	.800	1	4	0	1	0
Valverde,	.750	1	2	1	1	0

Triple plays—Avila, Estrada, Tillman.

SECOND BASEMEN

Player, Team	Pct.	G	PO	A	E	DP
Arias, Mexico City Tigers	1.000	14	20	27	0	8
R. Sanchez, Campeche	1.000	12	21	18	0	4
Valdez, Tabasco	.996	51	101	129	1	31
Rodriguez, Aguascalientes	.992	125	296	365	5	93
Beristain, Jalisco	.992	30	53	72	1	21
Barrera, Aguila	.990	71	84	113	2	28
J. Gonzalez, Aguila	.989	79	148	222	4	57
Villaescusa, Yucatan	.989	28	42	44	1	8
Balderas, Minatitlan	.988	18	37	43	1	17
C. Rodriguez, Saltillo	.988	30	72	87	2	22
Vilela, Saltillo	.985	85	239	223	7	60
Sanchez, Mexico City Red Devils	.985	38	99	92	3	22
Contreras, Torreon	.983	14	25	34	1	11
Castro, Minatitlan	.982	110	302	306	11	73
Magana, Yucatan	.982	71	138	137	5	38
Morales, Mexico City Tigers	.982	35	46	61	2	14
Abril, Jalisco	.980	94	211	240	9	67
Verdugo, Mexico City Red Devils	.979	24	41	51	2	17
Rob. Vizcarra, Mont. Industrials	.978	129	318	408	16	107
Camacho, Mexico City Tigers	.978	105	243	286	12	63
Vargas, Monterrey Sultans	.977	48	93	121	5	24
Rivera, Jalisco	.976	27	60	64	3	26
Gutierrez, Monclova	.976	12	21	20	1	6
Guizar, Campeche	.976	38	81	79	4	19
Sanchez, Puebla	.976	11	16	24	1	3
Mere, Nuevo Laredo	.975	124	268	356	16	92
Navarro, Torreon	.974	120	292	350	17	88
Wong, Tabasco	.974	87	184	228	11	55
Felix, Yucatan	.971	70	117	119	7	28
Pardo, Puebla	.971	119	263	334	18	86
Zazueta, Mexico City Red Devils	.969	73	181	190	12	49
Loredo, Campeche	.969	50	105	111	7	31
Canizales, Monterrey Sultans	.967	100	217	229	15	52
C. Garcia, Aguila	.967	64	119	145	9	35
M. Garcia, Monclova	.964	23	31	49	3	14
Martinez, Monclova	.963	121	275	304	22	86
Trapaga, Nuevo Laredo	.937	17	24	35	4	9
Tovar, Saltillo	.936	11	22	22	3	8

(Fewer Than Ten Games)

Player, Team	Pct.	G	PO	A	E	DP
Quintero, Monterrey Sultans	1.000	9	6	8	0	4
Jimenez, Saltillo	1.000	8	15	12	0	2
Alvarado, Campeche	1.000	6	10	6	0	3
V. Ruiz, Torreon	1.000	6	12	19	0	6
Hernandez, Puebla	1.000	5	4	4	0	0
M.A. Vizcarra, Mont. Industrials	1.000	4	11	8	0	1
Perez, Mexico City Tigers	1.000	3	1	1	0	0

Player, Team	Pct.	G	PO	A	E	DP
Herrera, Jalisco	1.000	3	8	9	0	1
Leyva, Monclova	1.000	3	4	8	0	2
Santos, Jalisco	1.000	3	2	3	0	0
Veliz, Jalisco	1.000	3	6	4	0	3
Franco, Monterrey Sultans	1.000	2	2	1	0	0
Fentanes, Torreon	1.000	2	2	6	0	1
Peralta, Minatitlan	1.000	1	4	2	0	0
Arzate, Monterrey Industrials	1.000	1	0	1	0	0
Cazarin, Minatitlan	1.000	1	0	3	0	0
Aguilar, Tabasco	1.000	1	2	0	0	0
V. Tirado, Puebla	1.000	1	4	4	0	1
Estrada, Nuevo Laredo	1.000	1	2	2	0	0
Martinez, Saltillo	1.000	1	0	2	0	0
Burke, Monterrey Sultans	1.000	1	2	3	0	0
Zuniga, Monterrey Industrials	1.000	1	2	0	0	1
Rodriguez, Torreon	1.000	1	1	1	0	0
Silva, Torreon	1.000	1	2	2	0	1
Acuna, Torreon	1.000	1	0	3	0	0
Aguilar, Aguascalientes	1.000	1	4	3	0	1
Yepiz, Aguascalientes	.971	9	12	21	1	2
Romero, Aguascalientes	.969	7	17	14	1	7
Marrujo, Tabasco	.958	4	8	15	1	5
A. Valenzuela, Saltillo	.938	4	9	6	1	3
Arredondo, Puebla	.929	7	8	5	1	2
Moreno, Minatitlan	.929	4	7	6	1	1
Chisum, Mexico City Tigers	.909	6	9	11	2	3
Arredondo, Aguascalientes	.857	2	3	3	1	2
Lopez, Yucatan	.833	2	2	3	1	2
Durazo, Monterrey Industrials	.833	2	4	1	1	0
Jaime Guerrero, Agua.	.800	1	1	3	1	1
Valle, Minatitlan	.750	2	2	4	2	0

Triple plays—Contreras, Herrera.

THIRD BASEMEN

Player, Team	Pct.	G	PO	A	E	DP
Camacho, Mexico City Tigers	1.000	19	5	16	0	1
Loredo, Campeche	1.000	13	7	10	0	1
R. Sanchez, Campeche	.977	35	30	54	2	10
Cornejo, Saltillo	.975	11	12	27	1	3
Jimenez, Saltillo	.967	14	9	20	1	2
Alfaro, Yucatan	.966	123	104	296	14	30
Mere, Nuevo Laredo	.966	14	7	21	1	1
Infante, Tabasco	.962	30	26	49	3	7
Aguilar, Aguascalientes	.960	126	76	263	14	21
Rivera, Jalisco	.960	31	19	53	3	7
Castaneda, Mexico City Tigers	.955	122	128	232	17	30
Leyva, Monclova	.953	108	102	246	17	24
Aguilar, Tabasco	.951	100	75	197	14	26
Rubio, Saltillo	.949	113	91	261	19	24
Cazarin, Minatitlan	.947	39	39	86	7	12
Barrera, Campeche	.946	56	52	89	8	18
Aganza, Monclova	.946	22	33	55	5	5
Sanchez, Mexico City Red Devils	.945	45	32	72	6	8
Gonzalez, Jalisco	.942	25	22	43	4	7
Peralta, Minatitlan	.939	66	48	122	11	12
J. Ruiz, Torreon	.937	122	100	256	24	27
Vargas, Monterrey Sultans	.936	30	22	51	5	4
Gutierrez, Monclova	.935	37	29	58	6	6
Franco, Monterrey Sultans	.934	66	52	131	13	14
C. Rodriguez, Saltillo	.933	10	4	10	1	1
Rodriguez, Puebla	.929	125	99	241	26	31
Moreno, Minatitlan	.926	35	24	64	7	4
Coachman, Jalisco	.923	75	48	120	14	13
Romero, Aguila	.920	102	61	205	23	19
Rivera, Aguila	.918	102	74	218	26	23
Burke, Monterrey Sultans	.914	18	5	27	3	2
Ortiz, Nuevo Laredo	.908	121	76	189	27	22
Naveda, Monterrey Industrials	.891	125	89	247	41	23
Aguilera, Monterrey Sultans	.891	37	18	72	11	5
Carrasco, Nuevo Laredo	.765	11	7	6	4	2

(Fewer Than Ten Games)

Player, Team	Pct.	G	PO	A	E	DP
Verdugo, Mexico City Red Devils	1.000	9	8	19	0	3
Guizar, Campeche	1.000	9	7	12	0	1
M.A. Vizcarra, Mont. Industrials	1.000	9	5	20	0	3
Marrujo, Tabasco	1.000	5	2	7	0	0
Beristain, Jalisco	1.000	5	6	10	0	3
Yepiz, Aguascalientes	1.000	4	0	8	0	0
Barrera, Aguila	1.000	2	0	2	0	0
Zulueta, Yucatan	1.000	2	1	1	0	0
Estrada, Nuevo Laredo	1.000	2	1	2	0	0
R. Garcia, M.C. Red Devils	1.000	1	1	1	0	0
Valle, Minatitlan	1.000	1	1	1	0	1
Gutierrez, Minatitlan	1.000	1	2	2	0	0
Chavez, Minatitlan	1.000	1	0	1	0	0
Valdez, Campeche	1.000	1	2	2	0	1
Garcia, Campeche	1.000	1	0	2	0	0
Sanchez, Puebla	1.000	1	0	1	0	0
R. Diaz, Monterrey Sultans	1.000	1	0	1	0	0
Canizales, Monterrey Sultans	1.000	1	1	1	0	1
Hernandez, Monterrey Ind.	1.000	1	1	0	0	0
Zuniga, Monterrey Industrials	1.000	1	0	2	0	0

Player, Team	Pct.	G	PO	A	E	DP
F. Rojas, Monterrey Industrials...	1.000	1	0	1	0	0
Fentanes P., Torreon	1.000	1	0	3	0	0
M. Garcia, Monclova	1.000	1	1	1	0	0
Rodriguez, Aguascalientes	1.000	1	0	1	0	0
Arredondo, Aguascalientes	1.000	1	0	2	0	1
Felix, Yucatan	.955	7	8	13	1	1
Contreras, Torreon	.944	5	4	13	1	2
Williams, Monterrey Sultans	.941	8	5	11	1	1
Garbey, Mexico City Tigers	.917	5	1	10	1	1
Brown, Monterrey Sultans	.913	7	5	16	2	1
Wong, Tabasco	.909	5	0	10	1	0
Tillman, Tabasco	.900	1	9	0	1	2
Monell, Mexico City Red Devils	.833	7	0	15	3	0
Salazar, Puebla	.833	2	0	5	1	0
Valencia, Aguascalientes	.833	2	0	5	1	1
Samaniego, Monclova	.800	1	1	3	1	1
J. Vazquez, M.C. Red Devils	.750	2	0	3	1	0
J. Gonzalez, Monterrey Sultans	.500	1	0	1	1	0
Trevino, Monterrey Sultans	.333	1	0	1	2	0
Orantes, Monterrey Sultans	.000	2	0	0	1	0
C. Garcia, Aguila	.000	1	0	0	1	0

Triple plays—Saiz, Williams.

SHORTSTOPS

Player, Team	Pct.	G	PO	A	E	DP
A. Valenzuela, Saltillo	.985	110	184	338	8	73
Gutierrez, Monclova	.976	39	65	96	4	26
Sandoval, M.C. Red Devils	.974	33	61	123	5	23
A. Jimenez, Campeche	.973	90	175	257	12	54
Moreno, Minatitlan	.973	10	17	19	1	8
J.J. Pacho, Yucatan	.972	116	179	341	15	58
Verdugo, Mexico City Red Devils	.970	95	146	304	14	57
Vargas, Monterrey Sultans	.969	27	44	80	4	31
Cornejo, Saltillo	.968	25	31	61	3	16
Contreras, Torreon	.968	27	37	53	3	13
Jaime Guerrero, Agua.	.967	66	125	224	12	49
Arredondo, Aguascalientes	.966	80	137	256	14	56
Gomez, Jalisco	.965	41	50	89	5	23
Rivera, Jalisco	.963	45	69	139	8	32
R. Diaz, Monterrey Sultans	.963	112	182	357	21	54
Guerrero, Mexico City Tigers	.961	117	169	330	20	60
Barrera, Jalisco	.959	15	31	40	3	11
Ramirez, Nuevo Laredo	.958	130	209	390	26	87
Valle, Minatitlan	.956	122	203	361	26	66
Guizar, Campeche	.956	40	77	117	9	25
M.A. Vizcarra, Mont. Industrials	.955	65	109	191	14	47
Marrujo, Tabasco	.954	59	52	94	7	16
Acuna, Torreon	.954	112	214	322	26	75
M. Garcia, Monclova	.953	30	44	58	5	15
H. Garcia, Aguila	.952	121	202	358	28	68
Infante, Tabasco	.951	97	170	299	24	66
Cervera, Puebla	.950	120	214	361	30	74
Beristain, Jalisco	.947	47	79	136	12	22
Almodobar, Monterrey Ind.	.939	73	109	170	18	34
Lopez, Monclova	.937	79	123	246	25	44
Felix, Yucatan	.937	19	20	39	4	11
Arias, Mexico City Tigers	.921	29	34	48	7	12
Hernandez B., Puebla	.919	13	9	25	3	5
Herrera, Jalisco	.917	28	40	59	9	17
Trapaga, Nuevo Laredo	.900	16	17	19	4	3
J. Rojas, Monterrey Industrials	.867	35	27	38	10	12

(Fewer Than Ten Games)

Player, Team	Pct.	G	PO	A	E	DP
Martinez, Saltillo	1.000	8	10	16	0	2
Chavez, Tabasco	1.000	6	1	3	0	0
C. Rodriguez, Saltillo	1.000	6	2	11	0	1
Uzcanga, Aguascalientes	1.000	6	4	9	0	3
Zazueta, Mexico City Red Devils	1.000	3	1	1	0	1
Camacho, Mexico City Tigers	1.000	3	1	7	0	1
Santos, Jalisco	1.000	3	1	5	0	1
C. Garcia, Aguila	1.000	3	1	3	0	0
Loredo, Campeche	1.000	2	0	4	0	0
Magana, Yucatan	1.000	2	1	1	0	0
Quintero, Monterrey Sultans	1.000	2	1	3	0	2
Munoz, Mexico City Red Devils	1.000	1	5	0	0	0
J. Vazquez, M.C. Red Devils	1.000	1	0	1	0	0
Flores, Minatitlan	1.000	1	3	3	0	0
Velazquez, Aguila	1.000	1	0	1	0	0
Barrera, Campeche	1.000	1	2	5	0	0
R. Sanchez, Campeche	1.000	1	0	1	0	0
Sanchez, Puebla	1.000	1	2	1	0	0
Arredondo, Puebla	1.000	1	0	1	0	0
Ortiz, Nuevo Laredo	1.000	1	1	4	0	0
Cruz, Mexico City Tigers	1.000	1	3	1	0	0
Rubio, Saltillo	1.000	1	1	2	0	0
Naveda, Monterrey Industrials	1.000	1	2	1	0	0
Carmona, Monterrey Industrials	1.000	1	0	2	0	0
Fentanes P., Torreon	1.000	1	1	0	0	0
Perez Solis, Torreon	1.000	1	3	1	0	0
J. Ruiz, Torreon	1.000	1	1	1	0	0
I. Rodriguez, Monclova	1.000	1	2	5	0	0
Javier Guerrero, Agua.	1.000	1	1	0	0	0

Player, Team	Pct.	G	PO	A	E	DP
Yepiz, Aguascalientes	.964	8	9	18	1	2
Zuniga, Monterrey Industrials	.960	9	10	14	1	7
Silva, Torreon	.871	7	8	19	4	2
V. Ruiz, Torreon	.750	3	0	3	1	0
Ayala, Monclova	.750	3	1	2	1	0
Jimenez, Saltillo	.750	3	2	1	1	0
Azocar, Yucatan	.667	1	2	0	1	0
Agramon, Monterrey Industrials	.000	1	0	0	1	0

Triple plays—Sandoval, Trapaga.

OUTFIELDERS

Player, Team	Pct.	G	PO	A	E	DP
Mangham, Mexico City Tigers	1.000	88	132	12	0	0
Velazquez, Aguascalientes	1.000	73	85	7	0	1
Perez, Minatitlan	1.000	66	94	2	0	0
Brown, Tabasco	1.000	61	115	2	0	0
Nelson, Minatitlan	1.000	37	69	1	0	0
Zulueta, Yucatan	1.000	27	49	0	0	0
Jacas, Torreon	1.000	25	41	1	0	1
McDonough, Minatitlan	1.000	22	21	1	0	0
Stockstill, Torreon	1.000	20	38	3	0	0
Williams, Monterrey Sultans	1.000	20	38	1	0	0
Bellazetin, Mexico City Tigers	1.000	19	15	0	0	0
Reyna, Campeche	1.000	17	17	0	0	0
Cole, Campeche	1.000	16	31	4	0	0
Ramos, Monterrey Sultans	1.000	16	11	0	0	0
Agramon, Monterrey Industrials	1.000	16	15	0	0	0
Lennon, Torreon	1.000	16	27	1	0	0
Simmons, Jalisco	1.000	16	28	0	0	0
Dean, Minatitlan	1.000	13	15	1	0	0
Zazueta, Mexico City Red Devils	1.000	12	16	0	0	0
Azocar, Yucatan	1.000	12	18	0	0	0
Zamudio, Monterrey Sultans	1.000	12	15	0	0	0
Carrasco, Nuevo Laredo	1.000	11	3	0	0	0
Arvizu, Campeche	1.000	10	16	1	0	0
Rubio, Yucatan	1.000	10	17	0	0	0
Yuriar, Monclova	.995	108	204	9	1	0
Valverde, Jalisco	.993	86	135	3	1	0
Monell, Mexico City Red Devils	.991	112	208	10	2	3
Aguilera, Monterrey Sultans	.990	67	93	6	1	1
Arredondo, Jalisco	.990	119	289	5	3	1
R. Mendez, M.C. Red Devils	.989	55	89	1	1	1
Stephenson, Aguila	.989	44	83	3	1	1
Alvarez, Torreon	.988	119	247	10	3	3
R. Torres, Campeche	.987	97	222	10	3	2
Gutierrez, Minatitlan	.987	38	71	3	1	0
Moore, Nuevo Laredo	.986	108	197	11	3	0
Carrillo, Mexico City Tigers	.986	88	193	11	3	1
R. Estrada, Puebla	.985	80	129	3	2	0
Sambo, Torreon	.985	34	60	4	1	1
Valencia, Aguascalientes	.984	106	177	13	3	4
Tovar, Minatitlan	.983	115	226	10	4	1
DeLima, Tabasco	.983	123	280	10	5	3
Fernandez, M.C. Red Devils	.982	110	214	7	4	0
Torres, Saltillo	.982	124	320	11	6	1
Ponce, Campeche	.982	53	100	7	2	2
Johnson, Puebla	.981	24	50	1	1	0
Espinoza, Monterrey Industrials	.980	120	286	12	6	2
Diaz, Nuevo Laredo	.980	126	189	8	4	2
Iturbe, Puebla	.979	98	187	3	4	0
J. Valdez R., Aguascalientes	.979	33	46	1	1	0
Cruz, Yucatan	.978	117	256	14	6	0
Tellez, Monterrey Industrials	.977	132	203	14	5	6
Arzate, Monterrey Industrials	.977	99	167	6	4	1
Noris, Aguascalientes	.977	105	239	11	6	1
Dominguez, Aguascalientes	.977	120	201	7	5	2
Herrera, Campeche	.976	113	189	11	5	0
Alvarez, Monterrey Industrials	.976	23	39	1	1	0
Tiquet, Puebla	.975	99	148	6	4	1
C. Garcia, Yucatan	.974	116	184	6	5	0
Baca, Campeche	.972	40	69	0	2	0
Gu. Leal, Monclova	.970	78	119	12	4	3
Morones, Jalisco	.970	101	160	3	5	0
Tatis, Puebla	.970	103	209	17	7	2
Tillman, Tabasco	.969	48	88	7	3	2
Castelan, Yucatan	.969	56	94	0	3	0
Taylor, Aguascalientes	.968	89	208	6	7	0
Trafton, Mexico City Red Devils	.968	66	87	4	3	0
Machiria, Minatitlan	.968	121	195	14	7	1
S. Lopez, Aguascalientes	.967	76	113	6	4	0
McCray, Monterrey Sultans	.967	16	28	1	1	0
Beltran, Aguascalientes	.966	88	169	4	6	2
Garcia, Monterrey Industrials	.966	32	55	2	2	1
Steels, Monterrey Industrials	.966	69	137	5	5	1
Blocker, Minatitlan	.966	68	140	2	5	1
J. Gonzalez, Monterrey Sultans	.966	102	214	12	8	1
Davis, Minatitlan	.966	58	112	1	4	0
Sanchez, Monclova	.966	121	245	9	9	2
Hill, Monterrey Sultans	.965	34	50	5	2	3
Shepherd, Yucatan	.964	41	78	3	3	0
Valenciana, Yucatan	.964	33	53	1	2	0
Estrada, Nuevo Laredo	.964	19	26	1	1	0
Ritchie, Monterrey Industrials	.963	36	51	1	2	0
Jimenez, Monterrey Sultans	.963	107	212	19	9	1

Player, Team	Pct.	G	PO	A	E	DP
Saenz, Mexico City Tigers	.962	95	168	11	7	1
Jones, Aguascalientes	.962	54	99	3	4	1
Lee, Campeche	.962	19	25	0	1	0
Sanchez, Nuevo Laredo	.960	132	202	16	9	3
Ford, Mexico City Red Devils	.958	41	66	3	3	1
Escalera, Aguascalientes	.957	107	211	12	10	2
L. Valenzuela, Tabasco	.955	99	158	13	8	3
See, Aguascalientes	.950	13	17	2	1	1
A. Lopez, Jalisco	.948	72	91	1	5	0
Jackson, Saltillo	.948	115	178	23	11	3
Villegas, Saltillo	.944	26	33	1	2	1
Aguilar, Jalisco	.944	18	16	1	1	1
Sievers, Yucatan	.942	30	46	3	3	1
Lopez, Monclova	.942	24	45	4	3	0
Fentanes P., Torreon	.941	125	181	11	12	2
Salgado, Nuevo Laredo	.941	22	14	2	1	0
Castro, Monclova	.940	26	44	3	3	0
Quiroz, Puebla	.938	16	13	2	1	0
Navarro, Mexico City Tigers	.938	14	15	0	1	0
Chisum, Mexico City Tigers	.922	28	44	3	4	0
P. Gonzalez, Yucatan	.917	17	21	1	2	0
J.L. Rodriguez, Saltillo	.912	27	30	1	3	0
Ibarra, Aguila	.906	23	27	2	3	0
Brown, Torreon	.900	13	17	1	2	0
G. Rodriguez, Monclova	.895	19	17	0	2	0

Player, Team	Pct.	G	PO	A	E	DP	PB
Cruz, Mexico City Tigers	.988	51	224	18	3	0	5
Garzon, Tabasco	.987	117	477	66	7	10	7
Ramirez, Yucatan	.987	82	333	42	5	3	6
Ma. Cruz, Nuevo Laredo	.985	98	647	68	11	13	14
Samaniego, Monclova	.984	35	159	23	3	1	9
H. Estrada, Puebla	.982	105	455	36	9	3	7
Campos, Campeche	.982	46	95	12	2	2	1
M. Gonzalez, Yucatan	.981	37	146	11	3	0	6
Pulido, Mexico City Tigers	.981	16	45	6	1	1	0
V. Tirado, Puebla	.980	43	140	9	3	1	2
Trevino, Monterrey Sultans	.980	80	303	40	7	6	5
F. Vazquez, M.C. Red Devils	.980	28	87	11	2	1	0
Arauz, Monclova	.979	32	118	21	3	3	6
Dominguez, Jalisco	.978	73	246	22	6	2	4
Meza, Monterrey Sultans	.976	67	286	46	8	4	7
Abrego, Monclova	.975	83	376	52	11	8	9
E. Valenzuela, Saltillo	.974	73	265	37	8	5	5
Estrada, Minatitlan	.974	49	203	22	6	0	5
Vega, Nuevo Laredo	.972	48	220	26	7	4	9
Luna, Saltillo	.969	51	187	30	7	7	2
Cueto, Tabasco	.964	20	75	5	3	0	5
J. Jimenez, Campeche	.962	11	23	2	1	0	3
Duarte, Minatitlan	.961	56	194	30	9	2	8
H. Rojas, Mont. Industrials	.947	11	34	2	2	1	1

(Fewer Than Ten Games)

Player, Team	Pct.	G	PO	A	E	DP
Sanchez, Mexico City Tigers	1.000	9	6	1	0	0
Espinoza, Puebla	1.000	9	15	0	0	0
Abrego, Monclova	1.000	9	12	0	0	0
L.A. Garibay, Mexico City Tigers	1.000	8	6	1	0	0
A. Gonzalez, Aguila	1.000	8	8	0	0	0
Monroy, Monterrey Sultans	1.000	8	6	0	0	0
Gutierrez, Jalisco	1.000	8	7	0	0	0
Canizales, Monterrey Sultans	1.000	7	12	1	0	0
R. Reyes, Mexico City Red Devils	1.000	6	4	0	0	0
Montalvo, Mexico City Tigers	1.000	6	7	0	0	0
Sanchez, Puebla	1.000	6	6	0	0	0
Tejeda, Nuevo Laredo	1.000	6	6	0	0	0
Munoz, Mexico City Red Devils	1.000	5	4	0	0	0
M. Gonzalez, Yucatan	1.000	5	5	0	0	0
Shamburg, Yucatan	1.000	5	7	0	0	0
Pina, Torreon	1.000	5	5	1	0	0
Lagunes, Campeche	1.000	4	4	0	0	0
Contreras, Torreon	1.000	4	2	0	0	0
Martinez, Monclova	1.000	4	4	0	0	0
Hinshaw, Aguascalientes	1.000	4	9	0	0	0
Guerrero, Jalisco	1.000	4	11	0	0	0
C. Garcia, Aguila	1.000	3	7	0	0	0
Gutierrez, Campeche	1.000	3	3	0	0	0
Garza, Mexico City Tigers	1.000	3	5	1	0	1
Rodriguez, Torreon	1.000	3	7	0	0	0
Garcia, Campeche	1.000	2	3	0	0	0
Pardo, Puebla	1.000	2	2	0	0	0
F. Valdez, Monterrey Industrials	1.000	2	1	0	0	0
Zuniga, Monterrey Industrials	1.000	2	1	0	0	0
Ramirez, Mexico City Red Devils	1.000	1	1	0	0	0
Durate, Minatitlan	1.000	1	2	0	0	0
Aguilar, Tabasco	1.000	1	1	2	0	0
Rodriguez, Campeche	1.000	1	2	0	0	0
C. Pacho, Yucatan	1.000	1	1	1	0	0
V. Tirado, Puebla	1.000	1	1	0	0	0
Cervera, Puebla	1.000	1	1	0	0	0
Mere, Nuevo Laredo	1.000	1	1	3	0	0
Trapaga, Nuevo Laredo	1.000	1	1	1	0	0
Naveda, Monterrey Industrials	1.000	1	2	0	0	0
Morales, Torreon	1.000	1	1	0	0	0
Nelson, Saltillo	.917	7	11	0	1	0
Felice, Campeche	.917	5	10	1	1	0
Carmona, Monterrey Industrials	.900	9	8	1	1	0
Almeida, Saltillo	.875	5	7	0	1	0
Pena, Monterrey Industrials	.857	3	6	0	1	0
Loredo, Campeche	.800	4	4	0	1	0

Triple plays—Monell, Salgado.

(Fewer Than Ten Games)

Player, Team	Pct.	G	PO	A	E	DP	PB
Pena, Monterrey Sultans	1.000	5	13	3	0	0	0
J. Lopez, Jalisco	1.000	5	5	0	0	0	0
Machorro, Monterrey Sultans	1.000	4	5	1	0	0	0
J.A. Garcia, Minatitlan	1.000	3	5	0	0	0	0
Bocardo, Tabasco	1.000	3	11	0	0	0	1
Porras, Tabasco	1.000	3	4	0	0	0	1
Verdugo, Yucatan	1.000	3	7	0	0	0	0
Ochoa, Nuevo Laredo	1.000	3	3	0	0	0	0
Corrales, Torreon	1.000	3	11	1	0	0	0
F. Tirado, Puebla	1.000	2	4	2	0	0	1
Contreras, Torreon	1.000	2	2	1	0	0	2
R. Mendez, M.C. Red Devils	1.000	1	3	1	0	0	0
Tejada, Mexico City Tigers	1.000	1	3	0	0	0	0
Salazar, Puebla	1.000	1	1	0	0	0	0
Morales, Torreon	1.000	1	3	0	0	0	0
Valenzuela, Torreon	1.000	1	2	0	0	0	0
Pardo, Torreon	.979	8	43	4	1	0	2
J.J. Robles, Mont. Industrials	.944	7	16	1	1	0	3
Stark, Mexico City Red Devils	.917	3	10	1	1	0	0
Torres, Torreon	.905	5	16	3	2	0	0
M. Garcia, Monclova	.900	1	4	5	1	2	0
V. Lopez, Jalisco	.895	6	12	5	2	1	0
Cobos, Mexico City Red Devils	.889	7	8	0	1	0	0
Narvaez, Monclova	.889	3	6	2	1	0	0

Triple play—Munoz.

CATCHERS

Player, Team	Pct.	G	PO	A	E	DP	PB
Mendez, Aguascalientes	1.000	24	58	3	0	0	1
Gavia, Aguila	.996	68	216	30	1	3	3
Marquez, Torreon	.994	46	155	20	1	3	2
Gastelum, Aguila	.993	95	369	45	3	4	6
Cazarin, Minatitlan	.992	48	221	30	2	4	4
Rivera, Yucatan	.992	39	108	16	1	2	3
Martinez, Torreon	.991	102	502	71	5	11	9
Monroy, Mexico City Tigers	.991	49	206	21	2	7	3
M. Hernandez, Jalisco	.991	89	368	61	4	6	3
Ruiz, Campeche	.990	108	439	57	5	9	7
Guzman, Aguascalientes	.990	107	411	81	5	18	4
Osuna, Saltillo	.989	29	87	6	1	0	1
Garza, Mexico City Tigers	.989	101	499	52	6	11	5
F. Valdez, Mont. Industrials	.989	81	305	52	4	5	7
Munoz, M.C. Red Devils	.988	113	631	56	8	8	9

PITCHERS

Player, Team	Pct.	G	PO	A	E	DP
Baller, Nuevo Laredo	1.000	61	1	7	0	0
Rincon, Torreon	1.000	57	2	6	0	1
Heredia, Monterrey Sultans	1.000	52	3	7	0	2
Antunez, Monclova	1.000	48	3	9	0	0
Granillo, Monterrey Sultans	1.000	47	1	5	0	1
Miranda, Torreon	1.000	47	4	10	0	2
Alvarez, Tabasco	1.000	46	2	6	0	0
Hernandez, Mexico City Tigers	1.000	45	2	15	0	2
Herrera, Tabasco	1.000	45	2	14	0	2
Valencia, Saltillo	1.000	44	2	14	0	1
Rodriguez, Tabasco	1.000	43	2	8	0	0
Villarreal, Monterrey Sultans	1.000	43	5	18	0	1
Cazares, Aguila	1.000	42	1	8	0	1
Castro, Yucatan	1.000	42	1	6	0	0
Villanueva, Aguascalientes	1.000	41	1	7	0	0
Lara, Monterrey Industrials	1.000	40	6	12	0	1
Saldana, Tabasco	1.000	39	4	11	0	0
J. Lopez, Aguascalientes	1.000	39	3	16	0	1
Baez, Aguila	1.000	38	5	13	0	1
Chavez, Jalisco	1.000	34	2	6	0	0
Mora, Mexico City Tigers	1.000	33	3	3	0	0
Ontiveros, Monterrey Industrials	1.000	32	0	6	0	0
Soto, Minatitlan	1.000	31	8	22	0	0
Salas, Mexico City Tigers	1.000	30	4	4	0	1
Solis, Aguila	1.000	30	2	4	0	1
Acosta, Monterrey Sultans	1.000	30	4	7	0	1
Castillo, Jalisco	1.000	30	4	22	0	2
Leyva, Saltillo	1.000	29	1	10	0	1
Aguilar, Minatitlan	1.000	29	1	16	0	1
Mi. Cruz, Nuevo Laredo	1.000	29	3	8	0	2
Munoz, Aguila	1.000	28	10	40	0	4
Pulido, Saltillo	1.000	28	8	26	0	3
Ruiz, Tabasco	1.000	28	1	24	0	2
Velazquez, Torreon	1.000	28	11	10	0	1
Uribe, Yucatan	1.000	27	1	10	0	0
Sombra, Jalisco	1.000	27	1	20	0	0
Cardenas, Aguascalientes	1.000	26	6	24	0	2
Sierra, Campeche	1.000	26	3	22	0	3

Player, Team	Pct.	G	PO	A	E	DP
Valdez, Monclova	1.000	26	8	20	0	0
Ramirez, Mexico City Red Devils	1.000	25	7	45	0	0
J. Garcia, Yucatan	1.000	25	2	8	0	0
Ochoa, Monterrey Industrials	1.000	25	2	9	0	2
Romero Cobos, Saltillo	1.000	24	2	1	0	0
Velazquez, Campeche	1.000	24	3	3	0	0
Osuna, Yucatan	1.000	24	6	26	0	0
Valenzuela, Monclova	1.000	24	5	2	0	0
Montalvo, Monterrey Industrials	1.000	24	3	12	0	0
Esquer, Yucatan	1.000	23	3	20	0	1
Solis, Monterrey Sultans	1.000	23	3	25	0	5
Rodriguez, G., Monterrey Ind.	1.000	22	5	9	0	1
Renteria, Torreon	1.000	22	4	14	0	2
Sandoval, Saltillo	1.000	21	5	15	0	2
Cecena, Mexico City Red Devils	1.000	20	4	11	0	0
Contreras, Aguila	1.000	20	6	6	0	1
Osuna, Tabasco	1.000	20	3	18	0	1
Berenguer, Saltillo	1.000	20	1	5	0	1
Lopez, Monterrey Industrials	1.000	19	3	2	0	0
Jimenez, Mexico City Red Devils	1.000	18	1	3	0	0
Camarena, Minatitlan	1.000	18	2	4	0	0
McMurtry, M.C. Red Devils	1.000	17	1	6	0	0
Camacho, Minatitlan	1.000	17	0	3	0	0
Meza, Aguila	1.000	17	0	6	0	0
Barron, Saltillo	1.000	17	1	5	0	0
Garcia, Mexico City Tigers	1.000	16	1	3	0	0
A. Navarro, Saltillo	1.000	16	2	2	0	1
Valdez, Puebla	1.000	16	4	17	0	0
Garibay, Torreon	1.000	16	0	5	0	0
Rios, Minatitlan	1.000	15	2	3	0	0
Reyes, Minatitlan	1.000	15	0	2	0	0
Soto, Aguila	1.000	15	1	1	0	0
Merodio, Yucatan	1.000	15	5	9	0	0
Watson, Nuevo Laredo	1.000	15	5	13	0	1
Valencia, Campeche	1.000	15	0	3	0	0
Boyd, Monterrey Industrials	1.000	15	0	5	0	1
Dessens, Mexico City Red Devils	1.000	14	1	3	0	0
I. Marquez, Mexico City Tigers	1.000	14	2	7	0	0
M. Garcia, Minatitlan	1.000	14	1	3	0	0
Quiroz, Puebla	1.000	14	0	6	0	1
Moreno, Nuevo Laredo	1.000	14	3	4	0	1
Barojas, Mexico City Red Devils	1.000	13	0	4	0	0
Rodriguez, Torreon	1.000	13	1	1	0	0
Herrera, Minatitlan	1.000	12	0	8	0	1
Jaime Granillo, Jalisco	1.000	12	1	2	0	0
Macias, Aguila	1.000	11	2	1	0	0
Pavlas, Mexico City Red Devils	1.000	11	1	6	0	1
Garcia-Luna, Tabasco	1.000	11	1	7	0	2
Robles, Mexico City Tigers	1.000	10	1	2	0	0
DeLaCruz, Mexico City Tigers	1.000	10	0	4	0	1
DeLeon, Minatitlan	1.000	10	3	4	0	0
Garcia, Puebla	1.000	10	2	1	0	0
Sosa, Puebla	1.000	10	0	1	0	0
Lopez, Tabasco	.982	29	12	43	1	5
Lugo, Jalisco	.982	28	14	40	1	3
Moreno, Saltillo	.980	30	9	40	1	1
Valdez, Mexico City Tigers	.976	26	8	32	1	2
L.F. Mendez, M.C. Red Devils	.972	26	8	27	1	2
Palafox, Torreon	.971	28	6	28	1	1
Luevano, Aguila	.971	26	12	21	1	0
Villegas, Puebla	.971	22	8	25	1	1
Retes, Tabasco	.970	29	10	22	1	2
Browning, Campeche	.968	50	6	24	1	1
D. Garibay, Mexico City Tigers	.967	25	10	19	1	0
L. Cervantes, Aguascalientes	.966	25	7	21	1	3
Purata, Monterrey Industrials	.964	26	8	46	2	2
Orozco, Monterrey Sultans	.964	24	5	22	1	2
Barraza, Nuevo Laredo	.964	28	12	41	2	5
R. Rodriguez, Saltillo	.963	23	4	22	1	2
Cordoba, Mexico City Red Devils	.962	44	10	15	1	0
Valenzuela, Puebla	.960	28	6	18	1	0
Iniguez, Jalisco	.958	27	6	17	1	1
Lind, Nuevo Laredo	.957	23	16	29	2	2
Lizarraga, Jalisco	.957	30	3	19	1	5
Rios, Mexico City Tigers	.957	25	5	17	1	2
Villegas, Aguascalientes	.955	37	4	17	1	2
Velazquez, Minatitlan	.952	27	7	13	1	1
Cruz Canto, Torreon	.952	27	12	28	2	5
Rodriguez, Nuevo Laredo	.952	26	5	15	1	1
A. Gonzalez, Monterrey Sultans	.952	26	5	35	2	4
Galvez, Mexico City Tigers	.952	13	3	17	1	1
A. Valdez Soto, Mont. Industrials	.950	27	11	27	2	6
Dominguez, Campeche	.950	13	4	15	1	1
Moreno, Mexico City Red Devils	.947	28	6	30	2	1
Murillo, Monclova	.944	29	2	15	1	2
Zamudio, Puebla	.941	28	2	14	1	1
Huerta, Monterrey Industrials	.941	28	6	26	2	0
Quinones, Monterrey Sultans	.941	26	5	11	1	1
Edwards, Monterrey Sultans	.941	18	2	14	1	0
Cazares, Jalisco	.941	18	4	12	1	0
Colorado, Tabasco	.941	16	4	12	1	1
Couoh, Nuevo Laredo	.938	43	7	8	1	0
Tinoco, Campeche	.938	31	1	14	1	1
Alvarez, Nuevo Laredo	.938	28	13	32	3	2
Lara, Campeche	.938	24	2	13	1	3

Player, Team	Pct.	G	PO	A	E	DP
August, Puebla	.938	12	9	21	2	2
Mead, Torreon	.935	22	12	17	2	2
J.L. Garcia, Minatitlan	.933	42	2	12	1	2
Castellanos, Jalisco	.933	33	1	13	1	0
Raygoza, Monterrey Sultans	.933	26	9	33	3	3
Cano, Monterrey Sultans	.933	21	3	11	1	1
Carman, Puebla	.931	23	9	18	2	0
Castaneda, Jalisco	.929	44	1	12	1	0
Cabrales, Aguila	.929	43	3	10	1	3
Sinohui, Minatitlan	.929	35	4	9	1	1
Jimenez, Yucatan	.929	24	6	46	4	7
Hernandez, Aguila	.927	24	16	35	4	3
Sanchez, Aguila	.926	29	6	19	2	3
Veliz Arballo, Mont. Industrials	.923	50	2	10	1	2
Pimentel, Torreon	.923	43	4	8	1	0
Hernandez, Mont. Industrials	.923	27	3	21	2	2
Castillo, Monclova	.923	26	8	16	2	1
Cosio, Saltillo	.923	23	2	11	1	1
Jimenez, Aguascalientes	.923	20	4	20	2	2
Quintero, Torreon	.923	18	7	5	1	1
Velazquez, Aguascalientes	.923	15	7	5	1	0
A. Vazquez, M.C. Red Devils	.923	14	0	12	1	1
May, Campeche	.920	19	6	17	2	1
Loaiza, Campeche	.917	19	2	9	1	1
Garibay, Monterrey Industrials	.914	24	7	25	3	1
Sanchez, Saltillo	.909	30	2	8	1	1
Roesler, Puebla	.909	19	1	9	1	0
Enriquez, Aguascalientes	.905	19	4	15	2	0
Martinez, Mexico City Red Devils	.903	28	3	25	3	2
Carranza, Yucatan	.903	22	3	25	3	3
Smith, Mexico City Tigers	.900	27	9	27	4	5
Neri, Yucatan	.900	27	6	21	3	2
Smith, Monclova	.900	24	7	11	2	0
Tejeda, Campeche	.900	20	5	13	2	1
DeAvila, Saltillo	.900	13	5	4	1	2
Rojo, Campeche	.895	32	5	12	2	1
Puig, Saltillo	.895	15	3	14	2	2
Palacios, Aguascalientes	.889	38	4	4	1	0
Garza, Monclova	.889	23	3	13	2	0
Cruz, Mexico City Red Devils	.889	19	2	6	1	1
Ledon, Yucatan	.882	41	1	14	2	0
Normand, Aguascalientes	.880	20	5	17	3	1
Vega Velarde, Nuevo Laredo	.880	20	8	14	3	1
Rodriguez, Mexico City Tigers	.875	39	1	6	1	0
E. Hernandez, Jalisco	.875	31	0	7	1	1
Montano, Monclova	.875	23	4	17	3	1
Herrera, Monclova	.867	46	3	10	2	4
Araujo, Campeche	.867	20	8	18	4	1
Serna, Tabasco	.857	14	0	6	1	0
Munoz, Jalisco	.857	14	2	10	2	0
Moreno, Mexico City Tigers	.857	12	2	4	1	0
Lopez, Minatitlan	.852	29	2	21	4	0
Bennett, Puebla	.848	24	6	12	27	7	2
Grajales, Torreon	.833	45	5	10	3	3
Medvin, Aguascalientes	.824	17	5	9	3	1
Solano, Monclova	.800	47	0	12	3	1
Vargas, Aguascalientes	.800	19	0	4	1	0
Perry, Torreon	.773	50	5	12	5	0
I. Rodriguez, Monclova	.750	45	2	10	4	1
Romero, Tabasco	.750	30	3	3	2	0
Toledo, Campeche	.733	32	0	11	4	0
Saldana, Puebla	.727	24	2	6	3	2
Noriega, Puebla	.714	30	2	3	2	1
Morales, Puebla	.667	19	0	2	1	0
Felix, Tabasco	.600	26	0	3	2	0

(Fewer Than Ten Games)

Player, Team	Pct.	G	PO	A	E	DP
Pina, Mexico City Red Devils	1.000	9	0	4	0	0
Sandoval, Aguila	1.000	9	0	1	0	0
Saenz, Puebla	1.000	9	0	4	0	0
Valdez, Nuevo Laredo	1.000	9	0	5	0	1
Loynd, Nuevo Laredo	1.000	9	3	8	0	0
Molina, Aguascalientes	1.000	9	1	1	0	0
Velez, Yucatan	1.000	8	0	1	0	0
Soto, Puebla	1.000	8	1	5	0	0
Olmos, Jalisco	1.000	8	3	7	0	0
Lara, Saltillo	1.000	8	0	2	0	0
D. Reyes, Mexico City Red Devils	1.000	7	1	1	0	1
Acosta, Minatitlan	1.000	7	1	1	0	1
Diaz, Aguila	1.000	7	0	2	0	0
Perez, Tabasco	1.000	7	1	1	0	0
Acosta C., Tabasco	1.000	7	1	0	0	0
Chavarin, Yucatan	1.000	7	0	1	0	0
Harrison, Puebla	1.000	7	3	11	0	1
Escamilla, Saltillo	1.000	7	0	1	0	0
R. Cervantes, Aguascalientes	1.000	7	0	1	0	0
Weber, Minatitlan	1.000	7	0	3	0	0
Sanchez, Jalisco	1.000	7	0	1	0	0
Quiroz, Nuevo Laredo	1.000	6	1	2	0	0
L. Navarro, Saltillo	1.000	6	0	2	0	0
Candia, Mexico City Tigers	1.000	5	1	3	0	0
Pelcastregui, Monterrey Sultans	1.000	5	0	2	0	1
Hansen, Monclova	1.000	5	4	4	0	0

Player, Team	Pct.	G	PO	A	E	DP
Loaiza, Mexico City Red Devils ...	1.000	4	2	2	0	0
F. Garcia, M.C. Red Devils	1.000	4	0	3	0	0
Rodriguez, Yucatan	1.000	4	0	1	0	0
Ramos, Puebla	1.000	4	0	1	0	0
Straker, Saltillo	1.000	4	1	1	0	0
Rod. Vizcarra, Mont. Industrials	1.000	4	0	1	0	0
Cervantes, Torreon	1.000	4	0	2	0	0
Kraemer, Mexico City Red Devils	1.000	3	2	0	0	0
Carrasco, M.C. Red Devils	1.000	3	0	1	0	1
Morales, Tabasco	1.000	3	0	1	0	0
Sulu, Campeche	1.000	3	1	2	0	1
F. Valdez, Monterrey Industrials	1.000	3	1	3	0	0
Parnet, Aguascalientes	1.000	3	0	2	0	0
Herrera, Mexico City Red Devils	1.000	2	1	0	0	0
Diaz, Tabasco	1.000	2	1	0	0	0
E. Sanchez, Campeche	1.000	2	0	1	0	0
Ritchie, Monterrey Industrials	1.000	2	1	0	0	0
Ochoa, Torreon	1.000	2	0	2	0	0
Flores, Jalisco	1.000	2	0	5	0	0
Mojica, Jalisco	1.000	2	0	1	0	0
F. Vazquez, M.C. Red Devils	1.000	1	0	1	0	0
Onofre, Mexico City Tigers	1.000	1	1	0	0	0
J.L. Sanchez, Campeche	1.000	1	0	1	0	0
Perez, Monterrey Sultans	1.000	1	0	4	0	0
D. Garcia, Monclova	1.000	1	0	1	0	0
Hernandez, Minatitlan	.889	9	1	7	1	0
Sauveur, Minatitlan	.875	7	0	7	1	1
Taylor, Campeche	.800	3	3	1	1	0
Jose Peraza, Mont. Industrials	.500	9	0	1	1	0
Ge. Leal, Monclova	.500	3	0	1	1	0
Zavaleta, Jalisco	.500	2	0	1	1	0

LEAGUE CHAMPIONS

Year	Team	Pct.
1955—	Mexico City Tigers*	.539
1956—	Mexico City Reds	.692
1957—	Yucatan	.567
	Mex. C. Reds (2nd)†	.550
1958—	Nuevo Laredo	.625
1959—	Poza Rica	.575
	Mex. C. Reds (3rd)†	.507
1960—	Mexico City Tigers	.538
1961—	Veracruz	.575
1962—	Monterrey	.592
1963—	Puebla	.606
1964—	Mexico City Reds	.586
1965—	Mexico City Reds	.590
1966—	Mexico City Tigers‡	.614
	Mexico City Reds	.571
1967—	Jalisco	.607
1968—	Mexico City Reds	.586
1969—	Reynosa	.591
1970—	Aguila§	.580
	Mexico City Reds	.607
1971—	Jalisco§	.558
	Saltillo	.593
1972—	Saltillo	.636
	Cordoba§	.541
1973—	Saltillo	.656
	Mexico City Reds x	.590
1974—	Jalisco	.627
	Mexico City Reds x	.551
1975—	Tampico x	.541
	Cordoba	.649
1976—	Mexico City Reds x	.543
	Union Laguna	.547
1977—	Mexico City Reds	.623
	Nuevo Laredo x	.507
1978—	Aguascalientes x	.589
	Union Laguna	.523
1979—	Saltillo	.704
	Puebla x	.628
1980—	No champion y	
1981—	Mexico City Reds	.615
	Reynosa	.492
1982—	Ciudad Juarez x	.570
	Mexico City Tigers	.508
1983—	Campeche z	.614
	Ciudad Juarez	.535
1984—	Yucatan z	.560
	Ciudad Juarez	.509
1985—	Mexico City Reds z	.606
	Nuevo Laredo	.5275
1986—	Puebla z	.682
	Monclova	.598
1987—	Mexico City Reds z	.605
	Monterrey	.536
1988—	Mexico City Reds z	.646
	Nuevo Laredo	.602
1989—	Nuevo Laredo z	.621
	Yucatan	.539
1990—	Nuevo Laredo	.618
	Leon z	.565
1991—	Monterrey z	.683
	Mexico City Reds	.627
1992—	Mexico City Tigers z	.594
	Nuevo Laredo	.538
1993—	Nuevo Laredo	.589
	Tabasco z	.528

*Defeated Nuevo Laredo, two games to none, in playoff for pennant. †Won four-team playoff. ‡Won split-season playoff. §League divided into Northern, Southern divisions; won two-team playoff. xLeague divided into Northern, Southern zones; sub-divided into Eastern, Western divisions, won eight-team playoff. yA players strike on July 1 forced the cancellation of the regular season and playoff schedule. zLeague divided into Northern, Southern zones; four clubs from each zone qualified for postseason play. Won final series for league championship.

PACIFIC COAST LEAGUE

FINAL STANDINGS

FIRST HALF

NORTHERN DIVISION

Team	W	L	T	Pct.	GB
Portland (Twins)	42	29	0	.592	......
Edmonton (Marlins)	39	32	0	.549	3
Vancouver (Angels)	34	36	0	.486	7½
Calgary (Mariners)	34	36	0	.486	7½
Tacoma (Athletics)	32	39	0	.451	10

SOUTHERN DIVISION

Team	W	L	T	Pct.	GB
Tucson (Astros)	38	33	0	.535	......
Colorado Springs (Rockies)	35	34	0	.507	2
Phoenix (Giants)	34	37	0	.479	4
Albuquerque (Dodgers)	34	38	0	.472	4½
Las Vegas (Padres)	32	40	0	.444	6½

SECOND HALF

NORTHERN DIVISION

Team	W	L	T	Pct.	GB
Portland (Twins)	45	27	0	.625	......
Vancouver (Angels)	38	32	0	.543	6
Tacoma (Athletics)	37	35	0	.514	8
Calgary (Mariners)	34	36	0	.486	10
Edmonton (Marlins)	33	37	0	.471	11

SOUTHERN DIVISION

Team	W	L	T	Pct.	GB
Tucson (Astros)	45	27	0	.625	......
Albuquerque (Dodgers)	37	34	0	.521	7½
Colorado Springs (Rockies)	31	41	0	.431	14
Phoenix (Giants)	30	42	0	.417	15
Las Vegas (Padres)	26	45	0	.366	18½

COMPOSITE

Team	Port.	Tuc.	Van.	Edm.	Alb.	Cal.	Tac.	C.S.	Phoe.	L.V.	W	L	T	Pct.	GB
Portland (Twins)	....	6	11	11	10	8	8	10	12	11	87	56	0	.608	......
Tucson (Astros)	10	....	8	7	9	10	12	9	9	9	83	60	0	.580	4
Vancouver (Angels)	5	8	....	9	10	7	9	7	9	8	72	68	0	.514	13½
Edmonton (Marlins)	5	8	6	....	10	7	7	10	9	10	72	69	0	.511	14
Albuquerque (Dodgers)	6	7	6	6	....	8	11	8	10	9	71	72	0	.497	16
Calgary (Mariners)	8	6	7	9	7	....	7	5	8	11	68	72	0	.486	17½
Tacoma (Athletics)	7	4	7	9	5	9	....	10	7	11	69	74	0	.483	18
Colorado Springs (Rockies)	6	7	8	6	8	10	6	....	6	9	66	75	0	.468	20
Phoenix (Giants)	4	7	7	7	6	8	9	9	....	7	64	79	0	.448	23
Las Vegas (Padres)	5	7	8	5	7	5	5	7	9	....	58	85	0	.406	29

Major league affiliations in parentheses.

Playoffs—Tucson defeated Portland, four games to two, to win league championship.

Regular-season attendance—Albuquerque, 390,652; Calgary, 278,140; Colorado Springs, 189,293; Edmonton, 261,361; Las Vegas, 386,310; Phoenix, 246,414; Portland, 186,010; Tacoma, 316,475; Tucson, 307,791; Vancouver, 349,726. Total, 2,912,172. Playoffs (6 games)—21,433. Class AAA All-Star Game at Albuquerque—10,541.

Managers—Albuquerque, Bill Russell; Calgary, Keith Bodie; Colorado Springs, Brad Mills; Edmonton, Sal Rende; Las Vegas, Russ Nixon; Phoenix, Carlos Alfonso; Portland, Scott Ullger; Tacoma, Bob Boone; Tucson, Rick Sweet; Vancouver, Max Olivares.

All-Star team: 1B—J.R. Phillips, Phoenix; 2B—James Mouton, Tucson; 3B—Eddie Perez, Vancouver; SS—Kurt Abbott, Tacoma; OF—Billy Ashley, Albuquerque; Rikkert Faneyte, Phoenix; Nigel Wilson, Edmonton; C—Brian Johnson, Las Vegas; DH—Bernardo Brito, Portland; RHP—Dave Weathers, Edmonton; LHP—Carlos Pulido, Portland; Relief Pitcher—Todd Williams, Albuquerque; Most Valuable Player—James Mouton, Tucson; Manager of the Year—Scott Ullger, Portland.

BATTING

TEAM

Team	Avg.	G	AB	R	OR	H	TB	2B	3B	HR	RBI	SH	SF	HP	BB	Int. BB	SO	SB	CS	LOB
Calgary	.298	140	4848	810	790	1446	2239	304	54	127	752	39	62	37	492	17	849	141	79	1047
Portland	.298	143	4778	831	708	1425	2151	289	58	107	765	45	65	40	524	26	745	110	56	1026
Tucson	.297	143	4995	850	762	1486	2183	311	76	78	782	50	50	42	558	36	821	80	69	1069
Colorado Springs	.295	141	4730	795	800	1397	2184	280	63	127	737	49	43	52	461	28	905	134	88	963
Albuquerque	.293	143	4995	806	837	1463	2242	291	55	126	749	55	53	44	398	35	802	79	61	967
Edmonton	.292	141	4824	729	728	1408	2079	281	51	96	676	49	38	38	451	28	837	89	63	1015
Las Vegas	.288	143	4929	739	855	1419	2132	271	53	112	677	72	36	43	506	23	867	114	48	1110
Vancouver	.286	140	4636	746	731	1326	1862	250	41	68	670	63	54	40	512	29	858	183	73	974
Phoenix	.281	143	4940	726	792	1389	2085	260	53	110	668	57	45	39	496	33	933	145	80	1057
Tacoma	.281	143	4850	744	772	1362	2023	263	52	98	676	45	47	29	531	29	1007	130	76	1060

INDIVIDUAL

(Leading qualifiers for batting championship—389 or more plate appearances)

*Bats lefthanded.   †Switch-hitter.

Player, Team	Avg.	G	AB	R	H	TB	2B	3B	HR	RBI	SH	SF	HP	BB	Int. BB	SO	SB	CS
Lindeman, Jim, Tucson	.362	101	390	72	141	219	28	7	12	88	0	7	5	41	4	68	5	0
Brumley, Mike, Tucson†	.353	93	346	65	122	163	25	8	0	47	0	6	0	44	6	71	24	10
McGriff, Terry, Edmonton	.345	105	339	62	117	171	29	2	7	55	0	3	1	49	2	29	2	1
Brooks, Jerry, Albuquerque	.344	116	421	67	145	214	28	4	11	71	3	7	2	21	2	44	3	4
Johnson, Brian, Las Vegas	.339	115	416	58	141	218	35	6	10	71	0	5	5	41	2	53	0	0

Player, Team	Avg.	G	AB	R	H	TB	2B	3B	HR	RBI	SH	SF	HP	BB	Int. BB	SO	SB	CS
Traxler, Brian, Albuquerque*	.333	127	441	81	147	237	36	3	16	83	0	3	2	46	14	38	0	2
Pye, Eddie, Albuquerque	.329	101	365	53	120	176	21	7	7	66	4	3	7	32	0	43	5	9
Carter, Jeff, Portland†	.325	101	381	73	124	159	21	7	0	48	1	3	3	63	1	53	17	12
Turang, Brian, Calgary	.324	110	423	83	137	203	20	11	8	54	5	4	3	40	2	48	24	8
Bruett, J.T., Portland*	.322	90	320	70	103	138	17	6	2	40	10	3	3	55	3	38	12	11

Departmental leaders: G—Garrison, 138; AB—Mouton, 546; R—Mouton, 126; H—Mouton, 172; TB—Mouton, 286; 2B—Mouton, 42; 3B—Tinsley, 18; HR—Phillips, 27; RBI—Ashley, 100; SH—Lopez, Schunk, 13; SF—Pirkl, 10; HP—Bates, N. Wilson, 10; BB—R. Williams, 88; IBB—Traxler, 14; SO—Ashley, 143; SB—R. Williams, 50; CS—Hubbard, Mouton, 18.

(All players—listed alphabetically)

Player, Team	Avg.	G	AB	R	H	TB	2B	3B	HR	RBI	SH	SF	HP	BB	Int. BB	SO	SB	CS
Abbott, Kurt, Tacoma	.319	133	480	75	153	247	36	11	12	79	4	3	2	33	4	123	19	9
Adamson, Joel, Edmonton*	.333	5	3	1	1	1	0	0	0	0	0	0	0	0	0	0	0	0
Agosto, Juan, 19 L.V.-32 Tuc.*	.000	51	1	0	0	0	0	0	0	0	0	0	0	0	0	0	0	0
Aldrete, Mike, Tacoma*	.320	37	122	20	39	75	11	2	7	21	1	0	0	26	5	22	2	2
Alicea, Ed, Colorado Springs†	.337	67	205	44	69	88	8	4	1	23	3	1	0	20	3	30	3	5
Allanson, Andy, Phoenix	.354	50	161	31	57	94	15	2	6	23	1	2	1	10	1	18	7	4
Allen, Steve, 2 Albu.-35 C.S.	.000	37	8	0	0	0	0	0	0	0	1	0	0	0	0	5	0	0
Allison, Dana, Tacoma	.000	23	1	0	0	0	0	0	0	0	0	0	0	0	0	0	0	0
Anderson, Garret, Vancouver*	.293	124	467	57	137	191	34	4	4	71	1	5	0	31	8	95	3	4
Anderson, Scott, Edmonton	.000	44	6	0	0	0	0	0	0	0	1	0	0	0	0	3	0	0
Ansley, Willie, Tucson	.262	125	382	71	100	149	20	7	5	61	5	3	3	79	0	93	22	9
Armas, Marcos, Tacoma	.290	117	434	69	126	214	27	8	15	89	1	6	3	35	1	113	4	0
Arnsberg, Brad, Tacoma	.000	22	1	0	0	0	0	0	0	0	0	0	0	0	0	0	0	0
Ashby, Andy, Colorado Springs	.000	7	4	0	0	0	0	0	0	0	1	0	0	0	0	2	0	0
Ashby, Billy, Albuquerque	.297	125	482	88	143	260	31	4	26	100	0	5	2	35	1	143	6	4
Ausmus, Brad, Colorado Springs	.270	76	241	31	65	89	10	4	2	33	2	3	1	27	1	41	10	6
Ayrault, Bob, 3 Cal.-11 Albu.	.000	14	1	0	0	0	0	0	0	0	0	0	0	0	0	1	0	0
Barberie, Bret, Edmonton†	.421	4	19	3	8	13	2	0	1	8	0	0	1	0	0	2	0	1
Barrett, Tom, Tucson†	.279	69	204	31	57	73	3	5	1	19	4	0	1	24	0	14	5	2
Barron, Tony, Albuquerque	.290	107	259	42	75	123	22	1	8	36	2	2	2	27	1	59	6	5
Basso, Mike, Las Vegas	.253	34	91	12	23	41	6	0	4	17	3	0	0	9	0	25	1	0
Bates, Jason, Colorado Springs†	.267	122	449	76	120	184	21	2	13	62	3	3	10	45	4	99	9	8
Batista, Tony, Tacoma	.167	4	12	1	2	3	1	0	0	1	0	0	1	1	0	4	0	0
Bean, Billy, Las Vegas*	.353	53	167	31	59	95	11	2	7	40	0	4	2	32	3	14	3	1
Beard, Garrett, Tacoma	.143	19	49	3	7	11	4	0	0	2	2	0	0	4	0	8	1	1
Bell, Eric, Tucson*	.083	22	12	1	1	1	0	0	0	1	5	0	0	1	0	5	0	0
Bellinger, Clay, Phoenix	.256	122	407	50	104	148	20	3	6	49	7	5	4	38	4	81	7	7
Benavides, Freddie, Colorado Springs	.438	5	16	3	7	8	1	0	0	2	0	0	0	1	0	0	0	0
Berroa, Geronimo, Edmonton	.327	90	327	64	107	196	33	4	16	68	0	3	4	36	3	71	1	2
Bethea, Steve, Las Vegas†	.180	39	61	7	11	13	2	0	0	2	1	0	0	14	1	22	0	1
Bochtler, Doug, 12 C.S.-7 L.V.	.111	19	18	0	2	3	1	0	0	2	2	0	0	1	0	6	0	0
Boone, Bret, Calgary	.332	71	274	48	91	139	18	3	8	56	0	6	1	28	0	58	3	8
Borrelli, Dean, Tacoma	.243	76	210	29	51	65	7	2	1	19	3	2	2	18	0	37	1	0
Boucher, Denis, Las Vegas	.200	24	10	0	2	2	0	0	0	2	1	0	0	0	0	3	0	0
Bournigal, Rafael, Albuquerque	.277	134	465	75	129	166	25	0	4	55	8	5	3	29	1	18	3	5
Brantley, Mickey, Phoenix	.364	65	247	45	90	149	23	6	8	49	0	4	1	22	1	22	2	1
Brito, Bernardo, Portland	.339	85	319	64	108	192	18	3	20	72	0	6	4	26	5	65	0	2
Brocail, Doug, Las Vegas*	.267	10	15	2	4	5	1	0	0	0	1	0	0	0	0	2	0	0
Brooks, Jerry, Albuquerque	.344	116	421	67	145	214	28	4	11	71	3	7	2	21	2	44	3	4
Brosius, Scott, Tacoma	.297	56	209	38	62	103	13	2	8	41	2	3	4	21	0	50	8	5
Bross, Terry, Phoenix	.333	54	3	0	1	1	0	0	0	0	0	0	0	0	0	1	0	0
Brown, Jarvis, Las Vegas	.308	100	402	74	124	178	27	9	3	47	5	2	5	41	1	55	22	5
Brown, Jeff, Las Vegas*	.000	1	2	0	0	0	0	0	0	0	0	0	0	0	0	2	0	0
Brown, Kevin, Phoenix*	.077	26	13	1	1	2	1	0	0	0	0	5	0	2	0	6	0	0
Browne, Jerry, Tacoma†	.240	6	25	3	6	6	0	0	0	2	0	0	0	0	0	4	1	0
Bruett, J.T., Portland*	.322	90	320	70	103	138	17	6	2	40	10	3	3	55	3	38	12	11
Brumley, Mike, Tucson†	.353	93	346	65	122	163	25	8	0	47	0	6	0	44	6	71	24	10
Brummett, Greg, Phoenix	.143	18	14	1	2	2	0	0	0	0	0	2	0	2	0	5	0	0
Brundage, Dave, Calgary*	.000	5	1	0	0	0	0	0	0	0	0	0	0	0	0	1	0	0
Bruske, Jim, Tucson	.462	13	13	2	6	14	2	0	2	4	3	0	0	0	0	2	0	0
Buccheri, Jim, Tacoma	.276	90	293	45	81	102	9	3	2	40	10	1	2	39	1	46	12	9
Buckley, Travis, Colorado Springs	.000	6	1	0	0	0	0	0	0	0	0	0	0	0	0	1	0	0
Burke, John, Colorado Springs†	.400	8	10	2	4	5	1	0	0	1	0	1	0	1	0	0	0	0
Busch, Mike, Albuquerque	.283	122	431	87	122	228	32	4	22	70	0	5	8	53	4	89	1	2
Bustillos, Albert, Albuquerque	.000	20	2	0	0	0	0	0	0	0	0	0	0	0	0	0	0	0
Calcagno, Danny, Phoenix	.206	16	34	4	7	8	1	0	0	2	0	1	1	8	1	8	1	0
Campbell, Kevin, Tacoma	.000	40	1	0	0	0	0	0	0	0	0	0	0	0	0	1	0	0
Canale, George, Colorado Springs*	.287	39	115	15	33	59	9	1	5	15	0	1	1	10	2	20	2	1
Candaele, Casey, Tucson†	.296	6	27	4	8	9	1	0	0	4	0	0	0	3	1	2	1	2
Capel, Mike, Tucson	.000	25	2	0	0	0	0	0	0	0	0	0	0	0	0	1	0	0
Capra, Nick, Edmonton	.278	106	389	71	108	156	19	4	7	44	4	4	2	58	0	42	20	13
Carlson, Dan, Phoenix	.067	13	15	0	1	1	0	0	0	0	0	0	0	1	0	6	0	0
Carter, Jeff, Portland†	.325	101	381	73	124	159	21	7	0	48	1	3	3	63	1	53	17	12
Carter, Larry, Phoenix	.143	8	7	3	1	1	0	0	0	0	1	0	0	0	0	3	0	0
Carter, Steve, Tucson*	.247	40	146	26	36	46	7	0	1	17	0	0	2	11	2	13	6	2
Case, Mike, Colorado Springs	.333	3	3	0	1	1	0	0	0	0	0	0	0	0	0	0	0	0
Castellano, Pedro, Colorado Springs	.313	90	304	61	95	156	21	2	12	60	1	8	6	36	0	63	3	5
Castillo, Braulio, 39 C.S.-17 Tuc.	.363	56	212	40	77	111	20	4	2	37	0	4	4	22	2	54	9	3
Cedeno, Roger, Albuquerque†	.222	6	18	1	4	7	1	1	0	4	0	0	0	3	0	3	0	1
Chimelis, Joel, Phoenix	.309	80	262	40	81	140	14	3	13	46	1	2	3	22	1	41	4	3
Colbert, Craig, Phoenix	.222	13	45	5	10	17	2	1	1	7	0	1	1	0	0	11	0	0
Cole, Stu, Colorado Springs	.281	104	324	54	91	134	22	3	5	35	2	2	1	36	1	36	10	6
Compres, Fidel, Las Vegas	.000	24	1	0	0	0	0	0	0	0	0	0	0	0	0	1	0	0
Correia, Rod, Vancouver	.271	60	207	43	56	86	10	4	4	28	3	5	1	15	1	25	11	4
Costello, Fred, Tucson	.143	14	14	0	2	2	0	0	0	1	2	0	0	1	0	8	0	0
Cruz, Fausto, Tacoma	.243	21	74	13	18	22	2	1	0	6	2	0	0	5	0	16	3	3
Cummings, John, Calgary*	.333	11	3	0	1	1	0	0	0	0	0	0	0	0	0	2	0	0
Daal, Omar, Albuquerque*	.000	6	1	0	0	0	0	0	0	0	0	0	0	0	0	0	0	0
Dalesandro, Mark, Vancouver	.299	26	107	16	32	48	8	1	2	15	0	1	1	8	1	13	1	0
Darwin, Jeff, Edmonton	.000	25	2	0	0	0	0	0	0	0	0	0	0	0	0	0	0	0
Dattola, Kevin, Tacoma†	.193	25	57	6	11	12	1	0	0	2	0	0	0	4	0	12	1	1

Player, Team	Avg.	G	AB	R	H	TB	2B	3B	HR	RBI	SH	SF	HP	BB	Int. BB	SO	SB	CS
Daugherty, Jack, Tucson†	.390	42	141	23	55	74	9	2	2	29	0	2	3	26	2	12	1	0
Davenport, Adell, Phoenix	.300	14	40	5	12	19	1	0	2	8	0	0	0	3	0	10	0	1
Davis, Kevin, Vancouver†	.271	62	210	24	57	77	8	3	2	25	3	3	1	7	0	41	3	4
Davis, Rick, Las Vegas	.000	34	5	0	0	0	0	0	0	0	0	0	0	0	0	2	0	0
Dayley, Ken, Albuquerque*	.000	9	1	0	0	0	0	0	0	0	0	0	0	0	0	0	0	0
Deak, Brian, Calgary	.247	80	235	43	58	103	12	0	11	41	4	2	5	41	0	65	5	1
De Los Santos, Luis, Edmonton	.311	125	425	49	132	167	25	2	2	66	0	8	2	25	1	56	0	3
Dixon, Eddie, Tucson	.000	50	7	0	0	0	0	0	0	0	1	0	0	0	0	4	0	0
Dodge, Thomas, Vancouver†	.235	7	17	3	4	5	1	0	0	4	0	3	0	1	0	2	3	0
Dozier, D.J., Las Vegas	.270	43	122	25	33	55	10	3	2	13	0	2	0	25	1	34	6	4
Drees, Tom, Portland†	.000	31	2	0	0	0	0	0	0	1	0	0	0	0	0	1	0	0
Duncan, Andres, Tucson†	.500	5	4	1	2	2	0	0	0	0	0	0	0	1	0	0	0	0
Edmonds, Jim, Vancouver*	.315	95	356	59	112	175	28	4	9	74	2	4	0	41	4	81	6	8
Elliott, Donnie, Las Vegas	.000	8	6	0	0	0	0	0	0	0	0	0	0	0	0	4	0	0
Eusebio, Tony, Tucson	.324	78	281	39	91	116	20	1	1	43	1	0	1	22	0	40	1	1
Everett, Carl, Edmonton†	.309	35	136	28	42	81	13	4	6	16	1	0	2	19	0	45	12	1
Fabregas, Jorge, Vancouver*	.231	4	13	1	3	4	1	0	0	1	0	0	0	1	0	3	0	0
Faneyte, Rikkert, Phoenix	.312	115	426	71	133	193	23	2	11	71	2	3	8	40	1	72	15	9
Faries, Paul, Phoenix	.303	78	327	56	99	129	14	5	2	32	3	1	1	22	1	30	18	11
Fariss, Monty, Edmonton	.256	74	254	32	65	102	11	4	6	37	1	2	2	43	0	74	1	5
Felix, Junior, Edmonton†	.355	7	31	7	11	13	2	0	0	5	0	0	0	4	0	8	0	0
Fernandez, Danny, Phoenix	.263	42	118	17	31	36	3	1	0	7	2	2	1	17	0	24	1	2
Fisher, Brian, Phoenix	.000	14	6	0	0	0	0	0	0	0	3	0	0	0	0	5	0	0
Flora, Kevin, Vancouver	.330	30	94	17	31	36	2	0	1	12	2	1	1	10	0	20	6	2
Forbes, P.J., Vancouver	.250	5	16	1	4	6	2	0	0	3	1	0	0	0	0	3	0	0
Fox, Eric, Tacoma†	.312	92	317	49	99	156	14	5	11	52	7	3	1	41	3	48	18	8
Fredrickson, Scott, Colorado Springs	.000	23	2	1	0	0	0	0	0	0	1	0	0	0	0	2	0	0
Furtado, Tim, Calgary	.188	6	16	1	3	4	1	0	0	1	1	0	0	2	0	3	0	0
Gainer, Jay, Colorado Springs*	.294	86	293	51	86	133	11	3	10	74	1	4	1	22	2	70	4	2
Garrelts, Scott, Las Vegas	.000	1	1	0	0	0	0	0	0	0	0	0	0	0	0	1	0	0
Garrison, Webster, Tacoma	.303	138	544	91	165	225	29	5	7	73	2	5	2	58	2	64	17	9
Gates, Brent, Tacoma†	.341	12	44	7	15	25	7	0	1	4	0	0	1	4	1	6	2	0
Girardi, Joe, Colorado Springs	.484	8	31	6	15	21	1	1	1	6	0	0	0	3	0	3	1	0
Gleaton, Jerry Don, Edmonton*	.000	46	6	0	0	0	0	0	0	0	1	0	0	0	0	4	0	0
Gomez, Fabio, Tacoma	.282	67	252	28	71	89	10	1	2	29	0	5	3	20	1	47	5	9
Gonzales, Larry, Vancouver	.261	81	264	30	69	84	9	0	2	27	5	3	2	26	2	28	5	1
Gonzalez, Paul, Las Vegas*	.240	75	267	36	64	104	11	4	7	34	1	2	1	21	1	64	3	2
Goodwin, Tom, Albuquerque*	.260	85	289	48	75	93	5	5	1	28	5	4	2	30	2	51	21	6
Grant, Mark, 4 Tuc.-1 Van.	.333	5	3	0	1	1	0	0	0	0	0	0	0	0	0	1	0	0
Grifol, Pedro, Portland	.330	28	94	14	31	45	4	2	2	17	2	2	0	4	0	14	0	0
Gross, Kip, Albuquerque	.214	59	14	1	3	3	0	0	0	0	0	0	0	2	0	4	0	0
Grotewold, Jeff, Portland*	.252	52	151	27	38	68	6	3	6	30	1	1	2	27	0	41	2	1
Gruber, Kelly, Vancouver	.458	8	24	4	11	15	1	0	1	5	0	1	0	2	0	4	0	0
Gutierrez, Ricky, Las Vegas	.417	5	24	4	10	14	4	0	0	4	0	0	0	0	0	4	4	0
Hale, Chip, Portland*	.280	55	211	37	59	83	15	3	1	24	3	1	0	21	1	13	2	1
Hamilton, Joey, Las Vegas	.000	8	5	0	0	0	0	0	0	0	0	0	0	0	0	3	0	0
Hansell, Greg, Albuquerque	.083	26	12	1	1	1	0	0	0	1	3	0	0	2	0	6	0	0
Hanselman, Carl, Phoenix*	.188	21	16	2	3	3	0	0	0	0	2	0	0	0	0	7	0	0
Harris, Reggie, Calgary	.000	17	3	0	0	0	0	0	0	1	0	0	0	0	0	1	0	0
Hartgraves, Dean, Tucson	.100	23	10	0	1	1	0	0	0	0	0	0	0	0	0	3	0	0
Hartsock, Jeff, Phoenix	.167	12	6	0	1	1	0	0	0	0	4	0	0	1	0	3	0	0
Hawblitzel, Ryan, Colorado Springs	.077	30	26	0	2	2	0	0	0	0	1	0	0	0	0	7	0	0
Hecht, Steve, Phoenix*	.314	48	169	27	53	69	8	1	2	20	1	2	0	20	0	23	9	1
Heffernan, Bert, Phoenix*	.286	16	49	7	14	17	1	1	0	6	1	0	0	9	1	11	2	2
Henderson, Dave, Tacoma	.182	3	11	1	2	3	1	0	0	2	0	1	0	0	0	2	0	0
Higgins, Kevin, Las Vegas*	.359	40	142	22	51	62	8	0	1	22	1	1	0	18	1	8	1	1
Hill, Orsino, Vancouver*	.222	9	36	4	8	16	3	1	1	4	0	0	0	0	0	11	0	0
Holley, Bobby, Calgary	.263	12	38	8	10	22	2	2	2	9	2	2	0	2	0	8	1	0
Holmes, Darren, Colorado Springs	.000	3	1	0	0	0	0	0	0	0	0	0	0	0	0	0	0	0
Hosey, Dwayne, Las Vegas†	.264	32	110	21	29	50	4	4	3	12	0	0	4	11	1	17	7	4
Hosey, Steve, Phoenix	.292	129	455	70	133	229	40	4	16	85	0	5	3	66	5	129	16	10
Howard, Chris, Calgary	.320	94	331	40	106	147	23	0	6	55	5	2	5	23	1	62	1	5
Howard, Matt, Albuquerque	.154	18	26	3	4	6	0	1	0	4	1	1	0	3	0	2	1	1
Howell, Pat, Portland†	.209	114	369	57	77	100	11	3	2	29	6	3	1	12	0	77	36	10
Howitt, Dann, Calgary*	.279	95	333	57	93	178	20	1	21	77	1	7	1	39	2	67	7	5
Hubbard, Trent, Colorado Springs	.314	117	439	83	138	199	24	8	7	56	5	1	6	47	3	57	33	18
Hudek, John, Tucson†	.000	13	2	0	0	0	0	0	0	0	0	0	0	0	0	2	0	0
Huisman, Rick, 14 Phoe.-2 Tuc.	.067	16	15	0	1	1	0	0	0	2	0	0	0	0	0	11	0	0
Hurst, Bruce, 1 L.V.-3 C.S.*	.000	4	5	0	0	0	0	0	0	0	1	0	0	1	0	4	0	0
Hurst, Jonathan, Albuquerque	.267	18	15	4	4	4	0	0	0	2	1	0	0	1	0	4	0	0
Jackson, Chuck, Edmonton	.279	36	129	23	36	61	4	3	5	11	0	0	9	2	0	30	0	1
Jackson, John, Vancouver*	.289	55	201	28	58	81	9	4	2	20	6	3	2	17	0	29	12	4
Jeffcoat, Mike, Edmonton*	.000	33	2	0	0	0	0	0	0	0	0	0	0	0	0	1	0	0
Jelic, Chris, Las Vegas	.208	46	130	16	27	41	4	2	2	14	2	1	1	18	0	22	2	0
Jeter, Shawn, Calgary*	.156	11	32	3	5	7	2	0	0	3	0	2	0	4	1	10	3	0
Johnson, Brian, Las Vegas	.339	115	416	58	141	218	35	6	10	71	0	5	5	41	2	53	0	0
Johnson, Erik, Phoenix	.248	101	363	33	90	108	8	5	0	33	2	3	1	29	2	51	3	9
Johnson, Juan, Phoenix†	.000	1	4	0	0	0	0	0	0	0	0	0	0	0	0	1	0	0
Johnstone, John, Edmonton	.087	30	23	0	2	2	0	0	0	1	1	0	0	1	0	9	0	0
Jones, Chris, Colorado Springs	.280	46	168	41	47	98	5	5	12	40	0	4	2	19	2	47	8	2
Jones, Todd, Tucson*	.000	41	2	0	0	0	0	0	0	1	0	0	0	0	0	1	0	0
Jorgensen, Terry, Portland	.307	61	238	37	73	107	18	2	4	44	1	1	1	19	2	28	1	0
Juden, Jeff, Tucson	.050	27	40	2	2	2	0	0	0	3	5	0	1	1	0	24	0	0
Katzaroff, Rob, Phoenix	.154	9	26	2	4	4	0	0	0	3	0	1	0	3	0	4	0	1
Killeen, Tim, Tacoma*	.444	3	9	4	4	4	0	0	0	0	0	0	0	1	0	0	0	0
Kipila, Jeff, Vancouver	.313	32	99	18	31	53	7	0	5	21	1	1	0	15	0	20	2	1
Knudson, Mark, Colorado Springs	.000	5	4	1	0	0	0	0	0	0	3	0	0	0	0	1	0	0
Kramer, Randy, Edmonton	.000	46	6	0	0	0	0	0	0	0	1	0	0	0	0	1	0	0
Kutzler, Jerry, Albuquerque*	.350	37	20	5	7	15	2	0	2	3	2	0	0	1	0	6	0	0
Landrum, Ced, Portland*	.000	4	4	0	0	0	0	0	0	0	0	0	0	0	0	1	0	0
Layana, Tim, Phoenix	.000	55	1	0	0	0	0	0	0	0	0	0	0	0	0	1	0	0
Lee, Derek, Portland*	.315	106	381	79	120	194	30	7	10	80	4	4	4	60	2	51	16	5
Lemon, Don, Edmonton	.059	21	17	1	1	1	0	0	0	2	2	0	0	1	0	5	0	0
Leskanic, Curt, Colorado Springs	.273	9	11	0	3	3	0	0	0	1	3	0	0	0	0	3	0	0

Player, Team	Avg.	G	AB	R	H	TB	2B	3B	HR	RBI	SH	SF	HP	BB	Int. BB	SO	SB	CS
Lindeman, Jim, Tucson	.362	101	390	72	141	219	28	7	12	88	0	7	5	41	4	68	5	0
Linskey, Mike, Las Vegas*	.000	30	17	0	0	0	0	0	0	0	2	0	0	2	0	11	0	1
Liriano, Nelson, Colorado Springs†	.358	79	293	48	105	158	23	6	6	46	2	3	1	32	1	34	9	13
List, Paul, Colorado Springs	.300	18	50	9	15	24	7	1	0	5	0	0	0	3	0	8	0	0
Litton, Greg, Calgary	.318	49	170	35	54	94	16	3	6	27	0	2	1	25	0	36	3	1
Lopez, Luis, Las Vegas†	.305	131	491	52	150	216	36	6	6	58	13	3	5	27	3	62	8	0
Lyden, Mitch, Edmonton	.306	50	160	34	49	90	15	1	8	31	0	2	0	5	0	34	1	1
Lydy, Scott, Tacoma	.293	95	341	70	100	161	22	6	9	41	2	3	1	50	3	87	12	4
Mack, Quinn, Calgary*	.308	84	325	48	100	145	25	1	6	39	1	2	0	17	2	41	9	6
Mahomes, Pat, Portland	.000	17	1	0	0	0	0	0	0	0	0	0	0	0	0	1	0	0
Maksudian, Mike, Portland*	.314	76	264	57	83	143	16	7	10	49	0	4	0	45	3	51	5	1
Manahan, Anthony, Calgary	.302	117	451	70	136	184	31	4	3	62	3	3	2	38	0	48	19	4
Marquez, Isidrio, Albuquerque	.000	9	1	0	0	0	0	0	0	0	0	0	0	0	0	1	0	0
Marshall, Randy, Colorado Springs*	.400	11	5	1	2	2	0	0	0	1	0	0	0	0	0	0	0	0
Martinez, Carmelo, Calgary	.255	42	149	21	38	55	5	0	4	18	1	0	1	22	0	25	4	0
Martinez, Dave, Phoenix*	.467	3	15	4	7	7	0	0	0	2	0	0	0	1	0	1	1	0
Martinez, Fili, Albuquerque*	.000	4	3	0	0	0	0	0	0	0	0	0	0	0	0	0	0	0
Martinez, Jose, 13 Edm.- 14 L.V.	.136	27	22	2	3	4	1	0	0	0	0	1	0	0	0	9	0	0
Martinez, Manuel, Tacoma	.305	20	59	9	18	23	2	0	1	6	1	0	0	4	0	12	2	3
Martinez, Pablo, Las Vegas†	.231	76	251	24	58	70	4	1	2	20	10	2	3	18	3	46	8	2
Martinez, Pedro A., Las Vegas*	.083	15	12	0	1	1	0	0	0	0	1	0	0	0	0	6	0	0
Martinez, Ray, Vancouver	.252	114	357	54	90	127	24	2	3	35	4	4	7	35	0	64	5	6
Massarelli, John, Tucson	.281	114	423	66	119	161	28	4	2	42	5	2	2	46	4	61	37	14
Masteller, Dan, Portland*	.322	61	211	35	68	110	13	4	7	47	1	7	1	24	3	25	3	4
Mathews, Terry, Tucson*	.250	16	4	1	1	1	0	0	0	0	0	0	0	0	0	0	0	0
Maurer, Ron, Albuquerque	.293	58	116	19	34	50	7	0	3	14	4	0	0	11	1	17	1	1
Maynard, Tow, Calgary	.143	9	21	7	3	3	0	0	0	0	0	0	0	5	0	7	4	1
McCarty, Dave, Portland	.385	40	143	42	55	90	11	0	8	31	0	3	1	27	2	25	5	2
McGehee, Kevin, Phoenix	.000	4	5	1	0	0	0	0	0	0	0	0	0	1	0	2	0	0
McGriff, Terry, Edmonton	.345	105	339	62	117	171	29	2	7	55	0	3	1	49	2	29	2	1
McNamara, Jim, Phoenix*	.196	50	158	10	31	39	5	0	1	23	1	2	0	12	1	29	1	0
Meares, Pat, Portland	.296	18	54	6	16	21	5	0	0	3	2	0	1	3	0	11	0	0
Mejia, Roberto, Colorado Springs	.299	77	291	51	87	148	15	2	14	48	0	3	1	18	0	56	12	5
Mercedes, Henry, Tacoma	.238	85	256	37	61	88	13	1	4	32	3	7	1	31	2	53	1	2
Mercedes, Luis, Phoenix	.291	70	244	28	71	82	5	3	0	15	1	1	4	36	0	30	14	6
Metzinger, Bill, Colorado Springs	.500	12	2	0	1	1	0	0	0	1	0	0	0	0	0	1	0	0
Mikulik, Joe, Tucson	.301	94	296	48	89	129	24	2	4	45	1	1	1	14	2	39	9	6
Miller, Kurt, Edmonton	.143	9	7	0	1	1	0	0	0	0	1	0	0	0	0	1	0	0
Miller, Orlando, Tucson	.304	122	471	86	143	252	29	16	16	89	1	4	7	20	0	95	2	4
Mimbs, Mark, Albuquerque*	.000	19	3	0	0	0	0	0	0	0	0	0	0	0	0	1	0	0
Minutelli, Gino, Phoenix*	.000	49	2	0	0	0	0	0	0	0	0	0	0	0	2	2	0	0
Mondesi, Raul, Albuquerque	.280	110	425	65	119	191	22	7	12	65	0	5	2	18	4	85	13	10
Montgomery, Ray, Tucson	.340	15	50	9	17	28	3	1	2	6	1	0	1	5	0	7	1	2
Moore, Marcus, Colorado Springs†	.000	32	1	0	0	0	0	0	0	0	1	0	0	0	0	0	0	0
Morales, Willie, Tacoma	.000	2	3	0	0	0	0	0	0	0	0	0	1	0	1	0	0	0
Mota, Andy, 3 Tuc.-29 Px. -70 C.S.	.301	102	345	46	104	162	29	4	7	61	4	4	6	21	4	57	8	5
Mouton, James, Tucson	.315	134	546	126	172	286	42	12	16	92	7	9	8	72	0	82	40	18
Munoz, Jose, Albuquerque†	.288	127	438	66	126	160	21	5	1	54	8	3	1	29	3	46	6	3
Munoz, Mike, Colorado Springs*	.000	40	1	0	0	0	0	0	0	0	0	0	0	0	0	1	0	0
Murray, Calvin, Phoenix	.316	5	19	4	6	9	1	1	0	0	0	0	0	2	0	5	1	1
Myers, Jimmy, Phoenix	.143	31	7	0	1	1	0	0	0	0	0	0	0	0	0	4	0	0
Myers, Mike, Edmonton*	.200	28	35	2	7	10	1	1	0	2	1	0	0	2	0	9	0	0
Natal, Bob, Edmonton	.318	17	66	16	21	38	6	1	3	16	0	0	1	8	0	10	0	0
Neel, Troy, Tacoma*	.360	13	50	11	18	25	4	0	1	9	0	0	0	6	2	9	2	1
Nevin, Phil, Tucson	.286	123	448	67	128	185	21	3	10	93	0	7	3	52	1	99	8	1
Nichols, Rod, Albuquerque	.185	22	27	0	5	5	0	0	0	4	1	1	2	1	0	4	0	1
Nied, David, Colorado Springs	.500	3	2	0	1	1	1	0	0	0	0	0	0	0	0	0	0	0
Nieves, Melvin, Las Vegas†	.308	43	159	31	49	82	10	1	7	24	0	0	2	18	0	42	2	2
Nolte, Eric, 10 Cal.-23 Albu. *	.143	33	7	0	1	1	0	0	0	0	0	0	0	0	0	4	0	0
Olander, Jim, Colorado Springs	.300	57	200	43	60	100	16	3	6	25	1	1	2	31	1	40	4	1
Ortiz, Hector, Albuquerque	.182	18	44	0	8	11	1	1	0	3	2	0	1	0	0	6	0	0
Ortiz, Ray, Portland*	.283	111	357	42	101	138	18	2	5	53	0	6	1	14	2	58	2	1
Osuna, Al, Tucson	.000	13	7	0	0	0	0	0	0	0	0	0	0	0	0	6	0	0
Owens, J., Colorado Springs	.310	55	174	24	54	89	11	3	6	43	0	3	5	21	0	56	5	3
Painter, Lance, Colorado Springs*	.148	26	27	1	4	4	0	0	0	2	2	0	0	1	0	7	0	1
Paquette, Craig, Tacoma	.268	50	183	29	49	81	8	0	8	29	0	2	1	14	0	54	3	3
Parker, Rick, Tucson	.308	29	120	28	37	58	9	3	2	12	0	0	0	14	1	20	6	2
Parks, Derek, Portland	.311	107	363	63	113	189	23	1	17	71	0	6	4	48	1	57	0	0
Parrish, Lance, Albuquerque	.273	11	33	4	9	11	2	0	0	1	0	0	3	5	0	4	0	0
Pedrique, Al, Edmonton	.305	121	403	54	123	145	14	1	2	42	8	4	7	44	4	43	5	6
Peek, Tim, Tacoma	.000	60	1	0	0	0	0	0	0	0	0	0	0	0	0	0	0	0
Pegues, Steve, Las Vegas	.352	68	270	52	95	152	20	5	9	50	0	3	1	7	0	43	12	5
Perez, Eddie, Vancouver	.306	96	363	66	111	182	23	6	12	70	1	3	3	28	5	83	21	7
Perschke, Greg, Albuquerque	.167	33	12	1	2	2	0	0	0	1	2	0	0	1	0	8	0	0
Peters, Reed, Phoenix	.300	96	240	43	72	111	16	4	5	31	3	2	1	41	0	18	8	3
Pettis, Gary, Tacoma†	.237	26	76	16	18	22	4	0	0	6	2	0	0	22	0	24	5	2
Phillips, J.R., Phoenix*	.263	134	506	80	133	253	35	2	27	94	0	6	6	53	9	127	7	5
Pirkl, Greg, Calgary	.308	115	445	67	137	226	24	1	21	94	1	10	6	13	1	50	3	3
Polidor, Gus, Edmonton	.285	72	249	26	71	100	16	2	3	40	5	1	2	17	3	17	1	1
Pose, Scott, Edmonton*	.284	109	398	61	113	133	8	6	0	27	5	1	1	42	3	36	19	9
Pye, Eddie, Albuquerque	.329	101	365	53	120	176	21	7	7	66	4	3	7	32	0	43	5	3
Quinones, Luis, 64 Tuc.- 12 Cal.†	.257	76	175	21	45	73	13	3	3	25	5	3	0	34	5	33	0	3
Rambo, Dan, Phoenix	.500	18	4	1	2	2	1	0	0	0	0	0	0	0	0	0	0	0
Rapp, Pat, Edmonton	.250	17	24	3	6	7	1	0	0	2	3	0	0	2	0	6	0	0
Reed, Steve, Colorado Springs	.000	11	0	0	0	0	0	0	0	0	0	0	0	0	0	0	0	0
Renteria, Ed, Edmonton	.265	24	68	6	18	21	0	0	1	8	1	1	1	7	1	12	0	1
Reyes, Gilberto, Colorado Springs	.236	73	174	22	41	78	6	2	9	29	5	1	2	22	1	36	1	1
Reynolds, Shane, Tucson	.222	25	27	3	6	8	2	0	0	7	2	0	0	2	0	5	0	0
Reynoso, Armando, Colorado Springs	.333	4	3	0	1	2	1	0	0	0	0	0	0	2	0	1	0	0
Ricker, Troy, Colorado Springs	.045	9	22	0	1	1	0	0	0	1	0	0	0	0	1	9	0	0
Ridenour, Dana, Colorado Springs	.286	39	21	4	6	8	0	1	0	3	0	0	0	3	0	2	0	0
Robbins, Doug, Tacoma	.226	57	164	23	37	57	9	1	3	18	1	2	2	20	0	37	1	0
Rodriguez, Henry, Albuquerque*	.296	46	179	26	53	88	13	5	4	30	0	3	2	14	0	37	1	2
Ross, Sean, Colorado Springs*	.303	34	119	15	36	58	13	3	1	14	0	1	0	5	1	20	3	3

Player, Team	Avg.	G	AB	R	H	TB	2B	3B	HR	RBI	SH	SF	HP	BB	Int. BB	SO	SB	CS
Russo, Paul, Portland	.281	83	288	43	81	139	24	2	10	47	0	6	0	29	0	69	0	1
Sager, A.J., Las Vegas	.167	21	12	1	2	2	0	0	0	0	2	0	1	0	0	5	0	0
Sanders, Scott, Las Vegas	.212	26	33	2	7	9	2	0	0	1	4	0	0	0	0	10	0	0
Sanford, Mo, Colorado Springs	.150	20	20	1	3	4	1	0	0	2	3	0	0	0	0	7	0	0
Santana, Andres, Edmonton†	.228	61	171	20	39	44	3	1	0	11	3	3	0	12	0	15	5	3
Scarsone, Steve, Phoenix	.257	19	70	13	18	32	1	2	3	9	0	0	2	8	1	21	2	0
Scheid, Rich, Edmonton*	.167	38	12	0	2	3	1	0	0	2	2	0	0	1	0	7	0	0
Schunk, Jerry, Portland	.270	118	397	53	107	143	28	1	2	47	13	4	5	18	1	23	5	3
Scott, Gary, Portland	.291	54	189	26	55	74	8	4	1	28	1	6	7	27	0	33	3	1
Seminara, Frank, Las Vegas	.053	22	19	1	1	1	0	0	0	1	4	0	0	2	0	5	0	1
Shepherd, Keith, Colorado Springs	.111	38	9	0	1	2	1	0	0	0	0	0	0	0	0	4	0	0
Sherman, Darrell, Las Vegas*	.265	82	272	52	72	84	8	2	0	11	7	1	2	38	0	27	20	10
Shockey, Scott, Tacoma*	.254	21	71	2	18	26	5	0	1	12	0	0	1	8	0	17	1	0
Simms, Mike, Las Vegas	.268	129	414	74	111	212	25	2	24	80	0	4	6	67	4	114	1	1
Sims, Mark, Portland†	.000	50	3	0	0	0	0	0	0	0	0	0	0	0	0	1	0	0
Small, Jeff, Edmonton	.271	92	328	29	89	126	19	6	2	39	2	1	2	10	1	56	3	3
Smiley, Reuben, Phoenix*	.300	99	313	58	94	145	16	7	7	37	0	1	0	15	3	67	24	3
Smith, Jack, Calgary	.286	128	458	61	131	191	30	3	8	57	8	7	1	37	1	73	5	9
Snow, J.T., Vancouver†	.340	23	94	19	32	58	9	1	5	24	1	0	1	10	0	13	0	0
Snyder, Randy, Edmonton†	.266	38	94	12	25	34	6	0	1	10	0	0	0	7	1	28	0	1
Soriano, Fred, Tacoma	.167	2	6	3	1	2	1	0	0	3	0	0	0	2	0	3	0	0
Spearman, Vernon, Albuquerque*	.254	62	185	31	47	63	6	5	0	15	4	0	0	17	0	28	11	4
Springer, Dennis, Albuquerque	.158	35	19	0	3	3	0	0	0	0	3	0	0	0	0	3	0	0
Staton, Dave, Las Vegas	.270	11	37	8	10	31	0	0	7	11	0	1	0	3	0	9	0	0
Stevens, Matt, Portland	1.000	54	1	0	1	1	0	0	0	0	0	0	0	0	0	0	0	0
Strawberry, Darryl, Albuquerque*	.316	5	19	3	6	11	2	0	1	2	0	0	0	0	0	5	1	0
Strittmatter, Mark, Colorado Springs	.200	5	10	1	2	3	1	0	0	2	0	0	1	0	0	2	0	0
Strong, Joe, Las Vegas†	.000	21	1	0	0	0	0	0	0	0	1	0	0	0	0	0	0	0
Sveum, Dale, 12 Tac. -33 Cal.†	.313	45	163	41	51	89	12	1	8	32	0	1	1	30	1	39	2	2
Tatum, Jim, Colorado Springs	.222	13	45	5	10	18	2	0	2	7	0	0	1	2	0	9	0	1
Taylor, Rob, Phoenix	.211	49	19	1	4	5	1	0	0	1	3	0	0	2	0	10	0	0
Tejero, Fausto, Vancouver	.153	20	59	2	9	9	0	0	0	2	1	1	1	4	1	12	1	1
Thompson, Mark, Colorado Springs	.125	4	8	1	1	1	0	0	0	0	0	0	0	1	0	4	0	0
Tinsley, Lee, Calgary†	.302	111	450	95	136	227	25	18	10	63	3	4	2	50	1	98	34	11
Torres, Salomon, Phoenix	.200	14	25	3	5	5	0	0	0	3	3	0	0	1	0	15	0	0
Trafton, Todd, Tucson	.250	8	20	3	5	8	1	1	0	2	0	0	1	2	0	4	0	1
Traxler, Brian, Albuquerque*	.333	127	441	81	147	237	36	3	16	83	0	3	2	46	14	38	0	2
Treadwell, Jody, Albuquerque	.316	40	19	4	6	12	1	1	1	3	2	0	1	0	0	2	0	0
Tucker, Scooter, Tucson	.274	98	318	54	87	114	20	2	1	37	2	2	2	47	8	37	1	5
Turang, Brian, Calgary	.324	110	423	83	137	203	20	11	8	54	5	4	3	40	2	48	24	8
Turner, Chris, Vancouver	.276	90	283	50	78	104	12	1	4	57	0	8	5	49	1	44	6	1
Turner, Matt, Edmonton	.000	12	2	0	0	0	0	0	0	0	1	0	0	0	0	2	0	0
Turner, Shane, Calgary*	.303	86	323	46	98	122	22	1	0	38	2	5	7	32	1	57	6	5
Van Burkleo, Ty, Vancouver*	.274	105	361	47	99	140	19	2	6	56	1	4	2	51	3	89	7	3
Van Ryn, Ben, Albuquerque*	.125	6	8	1	1	2	1	0	0	0	0	0	0	0	0	4	0	0
Vatcher, Jim, Las Vegas	.317	103	293	36	93	135	17	2	7	45	5	2	4	35	0	46	3	4
Velasquez, Guillermo, Las Vegas*	.333	30	129	23	43	66	6	1	5	24	0	2	1	10	1	19	0	0
Veres, Dave, Tucson	.211	44	19	2	4	9	2	0	1	4	0	1	0	1	0	9	0	0
Vierra, Joey, Albuquerque*	.000	29	0	0	0	0	0	0	0	1	0	0	0	0	0	0	0	0
Wade, Scott, Portland	.324	11	37	6	12	17	3	1	0	4	0	2	2	10	0	10	1	1
Waggoner, Aubrey, Calgary*	.263	13	38	9	10	20	2	1	2	4	0	0	0	15	0	17	3	0
Wakamatsu, Don, Albuquerque	.337	54	181	30	61	95	11	1	7	31	0	4	4	15	2	31	0	1
Walewander, Jim, Vancouver†	.305	102	351	77	107	124	12	1	1	43	5	3	9	60	1	57	36	6
Walker, Mike, Calgary	.333	28	3	1	1	2	1	0	0	1	0	0	0	0	0	1	0	0
Wall, Donnie, Tucson	.125	25	24	1	3	4	1	0	0	1	1	0	0	0	0	9	0	0
Walter, Gene, Edmonton*	1.000	6	1	0	1	1	0	0	0	0	0	0	0	0	0	0	0	0
Walters, Dan, Las Vegas	.287	66	223	26	64	93	14	0	5	39	0	1	1	14	0	26	1	2
Walton, Jerome, Vancouver	.313	54	176	34	55	74	11	1	2	20	8	1	1	16	0	24	5	4
Ward, Kevin, Colorado Springs	.233	23	73	12	17	32	2	2	3	13	2	1	2	9	0	16	1	1
Wassenaar, Rob, 13 C.S. -21 Phoe.	.400	34	5	0	2	2	0	0	0	0	0	0	0	2	0	0	0	0
Weathers, Dave, Edmonton	.156	22	32	4	5	7	2	0	0	2	2	0	0	2	0	13	0	0
Wedge, Eric, Colorado Springs	.267	38	90	17	24	39	6	0	3	13	0	0	2	16	1	22	0	0
Wells, Terry, Colorado Springs*	1.000	16	1	0	1	2	1	0	0	0	0	0	0	0	0	0	0	0
Whitmore, Darrell, Edmonton	.355	73	273	52	97	152	24	2	9	62	0	3	0	22	0	53	11	8
Williams, Reggie, Vancouver†	.274	130	481	92	132	167	17	6	2	53	9	6	5	88	2	99	50	17
Williams, Todd, Albuquerque	.000	65	1	0	0	0	0	0	0	0	0	0	0	0	0	1	0	0
Wilson, Jim, Calgary	.254	18	63	10	16	22	3	0	1	9	1	2	2	6	0	13	0	0
Wilson, Nigel, Edmonton*	.292	96	370	66	108	199	26	7	17	68	1	2	10	25	7	108	8	3
Wilson, Steve, Albuquerque*	.273	13	11	0	3	4	1	0	0	2	0	0	1	0	0	6	0	0
Windes, Rodney, Tucson*	.000	13	1	0	0	0	0	0	0	0	0	0	0	0	0	0	0	0
Witkowski, Mat, Las Vegas	.283	91	286	49	81	96	6	3	1	35	4	0	3	33	1	42	10	2
Witmeyer, Ron, Tacoma*	.254	132	452	52	115	154	22	4	3	52	2	4	1	57	3	96	7	3
Worrell, Tim, Las Vegas	.176	15	17	0	3	3	0	0	0	0	2	0	0	0	0	11	0	0
Worrell, Todd, Albuquerque	.000	7	1	0	0	0	0	0	0	0	0	0	0	1	0	1	0	0
Yaughn, Kip, Edmonton	.000	1	1	0	0	0	0	0	0	0	1	0	0	0	0	0	0	0
Young, Gerald, Calgary†	.298	26	104	19	31	46	8	2	1	10	1	0	2	20	0	16	7	9
Young, Ray, Las Vegas	.000	14	1	0	0	0	0	0	0	0	0	0	0	0	0	1	0	0

The following pitchers, listed alphabetically by club, with games in parentheses, had no plate appearances, primarily through use of designated hitters:

ALBUQUERQUE—Allen, Steve (2); James, Mike (16); Martinez, Pedro J. (1).

CALGARY—Ayrault, Bob (3); Barton, Shawn (51); Carman, Don (6); Converse, Jim (23); Czarkowski, Mark (9); DeLucia, Rich (8); Grater, Mark (9); Gunderson, Eric (5); Holman, Brad (21); Kent, Troy (9); McCullers, Lance (33); Nelson, Jeff (5); Nolte, Eric (10); Parkins, Bob (3); Picota, Len (22); Powell, Dennis (12); Remlinger, Mike (19); St. Claire, Randy (27); Shinall, Zak (33); Swan, Russ (9); Wainhouse, Dave (14); Wapnick, Steve (32).

COLORADO SPRINGS—Seanez, Rudy (3); Zavaras, Clint (6).

EDMONTON—McGraw, Tom (5); Newlin, Jim (4).

LAS VEGAS—Agosto, Juan (19); Campbell, Mike (21); Ettles, Mark (47); Pena, Jim (39); Seanez, Rudy (14).

PHOENIX—Peltzer, Kurt (12); Van Landingham, Bill (1).

PORTLAND—Casian, Larry (7); Chapin, Darrin (48); Garces, Rich (36); Henry, Jon (26); LaPoint, Dave (13); Merriman, Brett (39); Munoz, Oscar (5); Neidlinger, Jim (29); Ontiveros, Steve (20); Pulido, Carlos (33); Tsamis, George (3); Willis, Carl (2).

TACOMA—Briscoe, John (9); Chitren, Steve (14); Guzman, Dionini (21); Hillegas, Shawn (9); Horsman, Vince (26); Jiminez, Miguel (8); Osteen, Gavin (16); Patrick, Bronswell (35); Phoenix, Steve (11); Raczka, Mike (55); Shikles, Larry (38); Slusarski, Joe (24); Smith, Tim (6); Smithberg, Roger (28); Van Poppel, Todd (16); Young, Curt (10).

TUCSON—Edens, Tom (5); Huisman, Rick (2); Hurta, Bob (8); Robinson, Jeff (13); Walton, Bruce (13); Williams, Brian (2).

VANCOUVER—Anderson, Brian (2); Bennett, Erik (18); Burcham, Tim (13); Butcher, Mike (14); Charland, Colin (6); Edenfield, Ken (2); Egloff, Bruce (12); Farrell, John (12); Fritz, John (8); Gamez, Bob (9); Grant, Mark (1); Green, Otis (26); Hathaway, Hilly (12); Holzemer, Mark (24); Leftwich, Phil (20); Lewis, Scott (24); Nielsen, Jerry (33); Peck, Steve (31); Percival, Troy (18); Pico, Jeff (18); Scott, Darryl (46); Springer, Russ (11); Swingle, Paul (37); Zappelli, Mark (17).

GRAND SLAMS—S. Hosey, R. Ortiz, Pye, 2 each; Bellinger, Brito, Brosius, Castellano, Edmonds, Faneyte, Fox, Hubbard, Lee, Lyden, Masteller, McCarty, O. Miller, Nevin, Pegues, Pirkl, C. Turner, Vatcher, Ward, 1 each.

AWARDED FIRST BASE ON CATCHER'S INTERFERENCE—Brooks (Snyder); Castillo (Maksudian); Hubbard (C. Turner); C. Jones (Borrelli); J. Munoz (C. Howard); Pedrique (C. Howard); Peters (Brooks); Van Burkleo (Calcagno); Velasquez (Calcagno); Witmeyer (Maksudian).

PITCHING

TEAM

Team	ERA	G	CG	ShO	Sv.	IP	H	R	ER	HR	HB	BB	Int. BB	SO	WP	Bk.
Tucson	4.42	143	6	6	37	1267.2	1418	762	623	79	48	461	26	946	79	7
Portland	4.58	143	12	4	37	1212.0	1322	708	617	110	29	498	16	800	62	20
Vancouver	4.68	140	9	7	36	1198.2	1293	731	623	85	46	503	23	899	59	15
Edmonton	4.73	141	14	5	35	1216.0	1382	729	639	121	33	417	16	869	52	15
Tacoma	4.85	143	4	6	35	1235.1	1414	772	666	104	42	498	37	765	42	9
Phoenix	4.91	143	5	3	30	1257.2	1475	792	686	99	39	498	34	920	91	26
Colorado Springs	5.04	141	12	10	34	1192.0	1413	800	667	80	40	545	22	895	85	15
Calgary	5.21	140	9	3	30	1201.0	1397	790	695	109	46	534	28	765	90	6
Las Vegas	5.39	143	11	1	31	1236.0	1519	855	740	141	45	470	34	950	84	16
Albuquerque	5.39	143	3	2	45	1257.1	1488	837	753	121	36	505	48	870	94	18

INDIVIDUAL

(Leading qualifiers for earned-run average leadership— 115 or more innings)

*Throws lefthanded.

Pitcher, Team	W	L	Pct.	ERA	G	GS	CG	GF	ShO	Sv.	IP	H	R	ER	HR	HB	BB	Int. BB	SO	WP
Mahomes, Portland	11	4	.733	3.03	17	16	3	1	1	0	115.2	89	47	39	11	1	54	1	94	4
Reynolds, Tucson	10	6	.625	3.62	25	20	2	1	0	1	139.1	147	74	56	4	3	21	0	106	4
Wall, Tucson	6	4	.600	3.83	25	22	0	2	0	0	131.2	147	73	56	11	2	35	3	89	4
Weathers, Edmonton	11	4	.733	3.83	22	22	3	0	1	0	141.0	150	77	60	12	2	47	2	117	4
Walker, Calgary	13	8	.619	4.03	28	27	3	0	1	0	169.2	197	91	76	11	5	47	2	131	10
Gross, Albuquerque	13	7	.650	4.05	59	7	0	25	0	13	124.1	115	58	56	7	2	41	6	96	9
Pulido, Portland*	10	6	.625	4.19	33	22	1	5	0	0	146.0	169	74	68	8	2	45	1	79	8
Taylor, Phoenix	10	8	.556	4.24	49	12	0	11	0	2	144.1	166	85	68	15	4	49	4	110	7
Nichols, Albuquerque	8	5	.615	4.30	21	21	3	0	1	0	127.2	132	68	61	16	3	50	3	79	9
Painter, Colorado Springs*	9	7	.563	4.30	23	22	4	0	1	0	138.0	165	90	66	10	5	44	2	91	6

Departmental leaders: G—T. Williams, 65; W—Drees, 15; L—Johnstone, 15; Pct.—Mahomes, Weathers, .733; GS—Hawblitzel, 28; CG—Five pitchers tied with 4; GF—T. Williams, 50; ShO—Drees, 2; Sv.—T. Williams, 21; IP—Walker, 169.2; H—Hawblitzel, 221; R—Hawblitzel, 129; ER—Hawblitzel, 113; HR—Drees, 23; HB—Myers, 10; BB—Juden, 76; IBB—Dixon, Rambo, Treadwell, 7; SO—Sanders, 161; WP—Ridenour, 16.

(All pitchers—listed alphabetically)

Pitcher, Team	W	L	Pct.	ERA	G	GS	CG	GF	ShO	Sv.	IP	H	R	ER	HR	HB	BB	Int. BB	SO	WP
Adamson, Edmonton*	1	2	.333	6.92	5	5	0	0	0	0	26.0	39	21	20	5	0	13	0	7	0
Agosto, 19 L.V.-32 Tuc.*	7	3	.700	5.29	51	0	0	18	0	3	51.0	66	32	30	4	3	29	5	33	6
Allen, 2 Albu.-35 C.S.	6	4	.600	4.10	37	0	0	16	0	2	63.2	73	34	29	5	0	28	4	32	1
Allison, Tacoma*	3	3	.500	4.48	23	5	0	5	0	0	62.1	75	35	31	7	0	19	1	30	0
Anderson, Vancouver*	0	1	.000	12.38	2	2	0	0	0	0	8.0	13	12	11	3	1	6	0	2	1
Anderson, Edmonton	5	4	.556	3.53	44	1	0	14	0	4	66.1	74	30	26	6	2	15	2	52	1
Arnsberg, Tacoma	3	2	.600	7.48	21	0	0	8	0	1	27.2	31	25	23	2	7	21	2	12	1
Ashby, Colorado Springs	4	2	.667	4.10	7	6	1	0	0	0	41.2	45	25	19	2	3	12	0	35	3
Ayrault, 3 Cal.-11 Albu.	2	2	.500	7.11	14	0	0	3	0	1	19.0	29	15	15	2	2	9	3	16	0
Barrett, Tucson	1	0	1.000	0.00	3	0	0	3	0	0	4.0	3	0	0	0	0	1	0	1	0
Barton, Calgary*	3	1	.750	3.56	51	0	0	18	0	4	60.2	64	29	24	5	2	27	6	29	3
Bell, Tucson*	4	6	.400	4.05	22	16	3	1	1	0	106.2	131	59	48	8	1	39	0	53	5
Bennett, Vancouver	6	6	.500	6.05	18	12	0	1	0	1	80.1	101	57	54	10	4	21	0	51	3
Bochtler, 12 C.S.-7 L.V.	1	9	.100	6.18	19	18	1	0	0	0	90.1	123	67	62	5	1	37	2	68	3
Borrelli, Tacoma	0	0	.000	0.00	1	0	0	0	0	0	1.0	1	1	0	0	0	1	0	0	0
Boucher, Las Vegas*	4	7	.364	6.43	24	7	1	2	0	1	70.0	101	59	50	12	6	27	3	46	4
Briscoe, Tacoma	1	1	.500	2.92	9	0	0	8	0	6	12.1	13	5	4	1	0	9	3	16	1
Brocail, Las Vegas	4	2	.667	3.68	10	8	0	1	0	1	51.1	51	26	21	4	1	14	0	32	2
Bross, Phoenix	4	4	.500	3.97	54	0	0	28	0	5	79.1	76	39	35	5	1	37	1	69	4
Brown, Las Vegas*	0	0	.000	9.00	1	0	0	1	0	0	5.0	9	5	5	1	0	0	0	4	0
Brown, Phoenix*	6	10	.375	4.94	23	20	0	0	0	0	120.1	134	74	66	12	2	60	2	75	5
Brummett, Phoenix	7	7	.500	3.62	18	18	1	0	0	0	107.0	114	56	43	3	2	27	3	84	3
Brundage, Calgary*	0	1	.000	2.25	4	1	0	2	0	0	8.0	8	4	2	0	1	4	0	4	1
Bruske, Tucson	4	2	.667	3.78	12	9	0	1	0	1	66.2	77	36	28	4	0	18	2	42	3
Buckley, Colorado Springs	1	2	.333	6.00	6	1	0	1	0	0	9.0	12	13	6	0	3	7	0	5	2
Burcham, Vancouver	0	2	.000	11.30	13	0	0	7	0	1	14.1	29	19	18	2	0	8	2	11	0
Burke, Colorado Springs	3	2	.600	3.14	8	8	0	0	0	0	48.2	44	22	17	0	2	23	0	38	1
Bustillos, Albuquerque	2	1	.667	4.45	20	0	0	4	0	2	30.1	37	15	15	4	0	13	4	17	2
Butcher, Vancouver	2	3	.400	4.44	14	1	0	5	0	3	24.1	21	16	12	3	1	12	0	12	3
Campbell, Tacoma	3	5	.375	2.75	40	0	0	28	0	12	55.2	42	19	17	5	2	19	6	46	4
Campbell, Las Vegas	2	1	.667	5.40	21	0	0	9	0	1	31.2	39	20	19	9	0	9	2	24	6
Capel, Tucson	0	4	.000	7.16	25	1	0	13	0	3	32.2	46	30	26	3	3	11	1	33	5
Carlson, Phoenix	5	6	.455	6.56	13	12	0	0	0	0	70.0	79	54	51	12	5	32	1	48	4
Carman, Calgary*	1	0	1.000	3.55	6	0	0	1	0	0	12.2	12	6	5	1	1	2	1	6	0
Carter, Phoenix	3	1	.750	2.88	7	7	0	0	0	0	34.1	28	14	11	2	2	15	0	31	1
Casian, Portland*	1	0	1.000	0.00	7	0	0	5	0	2	7.2	9	0	0	0	0	2	1	2	0
Chapin, Portland	5	2	.714	4.31	47	0	0	35	0	14	56.1	58	28	27	5	1	24	2	43	6

Pitcher, Team	W	L	Pct.	ERA	G	GS	CG	GF	ShO	Sv.	IP	H	R	ER	HR	HB	BB	Int. BB	SO	WP
Charland, Vancouver*	3	2	.600	3.86	6	6	0	0	0	0	32.2	37	22	14	0	0	17	0	27	0
Chitren, Tacoma	1	0	1.000	3.00	14	0	0	6	0	1	24.0	21	9	8	0	1	14	2	27	2
Cole, Colorado Springs	0	0	.000	18.00	1	0	0	1	0	0	1.0	2	2	2	0	0	2	0	0	0
Compres, Las Vegas	1	1	.500	5.54	24	0	0	9	0	4	26.0	33	16	16	1	2	10	1	7	2
Converse, Calgary	7	8	.467	5.40	23	22	4	0	0	0	121.2	144	86	73	6	3	64	1	78	8
Costello, Tucson	6	2	.750	3.69	14	14	0	0	0	0	83.0	92	42	34	6	6	33	1	36	1
Cummings, Calgary*	3	4	.429	4.13	11	10	0	0	0	0	65.1	69	40	30	6	2	21	2	42	7
Czarkowski, Calgary*	1	4	.200	7.61	9	8	0	0	0	0	36.2	62	33	31	4	2	11	0	11	1
Daal, Albuquerque*	1	1	.500	3.38	6	0	0	4	0	2	5.1	5	2	2	1	0	3	1	2	0
Darwin, Edmonton	2	2	.500	8.51	25	0	0	14	0	2	30.2	50	34	29	5	0	10	2	22	1
Dattola, Tacoma	0	0	.000	9.00	1	0	0	1	0	0	1.0	2	2	1	0	0	1	0	0	0
Davis, Las Vegas	1	8	.111	7.14	34	4	0	12	0	3	51.2	94	54	41	5	2	20	3	27	3
Dayley, Albuquerque*	0	0	.000	12.19	9	1	0	0	0	0	10.1	14	15	14	1	0	12	1	9	5
DeLucia, Calgary	1	5	.167	5.73	8	7	0	1	0	1	44.0	45	30	28	6	0	20	1	38	4
Dixon, Tucson	4	3	.571	4.15	50	0	0	18	0	0	80.1	92	54	37	6	1	22	7	41	7
Drees, Portland*	15	10	.600	6.22	31	24	3	0	0	0	153.1	183	112	106	23	7	62	1	83	6
Edenfield, Vancouver	0	0	.000	0.00	2	0	0	2	0	0	3.2	1	0	0	0	1	1	0	5	0
Edens, Tucson	1	0	1.000	6.14	5	0	0	1	0	0	7.1	9	5	5	0	1	3	0	6	0
Egloff, Vancouver	0	0	.000	3.50	12	0	0	7	0	1	18.0	20	10	7	0	1	3	0	9	0
Elliott, Las Vegas	2	5	.286	6.37	8	7	0	0	0	0	41.0	48	32	29	6	1	24	0	44	3
Ettles, Las Vegas	3	6	.333	4.71	47	0	0	41	0	15	49.2	58	28	26	2	2	22	6	29	13
Farrell, Vancouver	4	5	.444	3.99	12	12	2	0	0	0	85.2	83	44	38	7	8	28	1	71	4
Fisher, Phoenix	3	4	.429	8.08	14	9	0	1	0	0	49.0	75	52	44	6	1	15	1	25	4
Fredrickson, Colorado Springs	1	3	.250	5.47	23	0	0	18	0	7	26.1	25	16	16	3	0	19	3	20	2
Fritz, Vancouver	3	1	.750	4.07	8	7	0	0	0	0	42.0	52	22	19	3	0	18	1	29	2
Gamez, Vancouver*	1	0	1.000	4.73	9	0	0	3	0	0	13.1	11	9	7	0	0	9	0	15	2
Garces, Portland	1	3	.250	8.33	35	7	0	5	0	0	54.0	70	55	50	4	0	64	0	48	3
Garrelts, Las Vegas	0	0	.000	21.00	1	1	0	0	0	0	3.0	10	7	7	0	0	2	0	1	3
Gleaton, Edmonton*	3	1	.750	3.99	46	0	0	25	0	7	65.1	73	30	29	7	1	26	2	46	2
Gonzales, Vancouver	0	0	.000	0.00	1	0	0	1	0	0	1.0	1	0	0	0	0	1	0	1	0
Grahe, Vancouver	1	1	.500	4.50	4	2	0	0	0	0	6.0	4	3	3	1	0	2	0	5	1
Grant, 4 Tuc.-1 Van.	1	0	1.000	0.87	5	0	0	2	0	0	10.1	5	1	1	0	0	6	0	11	0
Grater, Calgary	0	1	.000	7.71	9	0	0	7	0	0	11.2	19	10	10	1	2	6	0	4	2
Green, Vancouver*	2	8	.200	5.61	25	18	1	3	0	0	109.0	109	71	68	8	9	53	0	97	10
Gross, Albuquerque	13	7	.650	4.05	59	7	0	25	0	13	124.1	115	58	56	7	2	41	6	96	9
Gunderson, Calgary*	0	1	.000	18.90	5	0	0	1	0	0	6.2	14	15	14	1	2	8	0	3	1
Guzman, Tacoma*	2	7	.222	7.32	20	16	0	1	0	0	87.1	130	87	71	7	4	44	1	50	8
Hamilton, Las Vegas	3	2	.600	4.40	8	8	0	0	0	0	47.0	49	25	23	0	4	22	1	33	6
Hansell, Albuquerque	5	10	.333	6.93	26	20	0	3	0	0	101.1	131	86	78	9	3	60	1	60	10
Hanselman, Phoenix	2	6	.250	5.98	21	13	0	5	0	0	87.1	115	66	58	8	2	35	3	45	7
Harris, Calgary	8	6	.571	5.20	17	15	1	0	0	0	88.1	74	55	51	7	8	61	1	75	10
Hartgraves, Tucson*	1	6	.143	6.37	23	10	0	2	0	0	77.2	90	65	55	7	4	40	0	42	5
Hartsock, Phoenix	2	5	.286	5.53	12	7	0	2	0	0	55.1	83	36	34	3	1	20	1	35	4
Hathaway, Vancouver*	7	0	1.000	4.09	12	12	0	0	0	0	70.1	60	38	32	5	2	27	0	44	4
Hawblitzel, Colorado Springs	8	13	.381	6.15	29	28	2	0	0	0	165.1	221	129	113	16	4	49	0	90	3
Henry, Portland	6	5	.545	5.70	26	13	0	4	0	1	94.2	122	68	60	13	5	30	0	62	2
Hillegas, Tacoma	2	3	.400	5.48	9	9	0	0	0	0	47.2	62	31	29	4	1	13	0	29	0
Holman, Calgary	8	4	.667	4.74	21	13	1	2	0	0	98.2	109	59	52	5	3	42	0	54	7
Holmes, Colorado Springs	1	0	1.000	0.00	3	2	0	0	0	0	8.2	1	1	0	0	0	1	0	9	0
Holzemer, Vancouver*	9	6	.600	4.82	24	23	2	0	0	0	145.2	158	94	78	4	4	70	2	80	5
Horsman, Tacoma*	1	2	.333	4.28	26	0	0	10	0	3	33.2	37	25	16	11	0	9	2	23	1
Howard, Calgary	0	0	.000	0.00	1	0	0	1	0	0	1.0	3	0	0	0	0	0	0	0	0
Howard, Albuquerque	0	0	.000	0.00	1	0	0	1	0	0	1.2	0	0	0	0	0	0	0	2	0
Hudek, Tucson	3	1	.750	3.79	13	1	0	3	0	0	19.0	17	11	8	1	2	11	1	18	1
Huisman, 14 Phoe.-2 Tuc.	4	4	.500	6.04	16	14	0	0	0	0	76.0	84	59	51	5	1	46	0	63	13
Hurst, 1 L.V.-3 C.S.*	1	2	.333	7.78	4	4	0	0	0	0	19.2	30	19	17	1	0	4	1	15	0
Hurst, Albuquerque	7	2	.778	4.15	18	15	0	0	0	0	86.2	101	47	40	12	4	29	0	62	2
Hurta, Tucson*	2	1	.667	6.00	8	0	0	4	0	1	12.0	11	8	8	0	3	13	0	10	1
James, Albuquerque	1	0	1.000	7.47	16	0	0	5	0	2	31.1	38	28	26	5	4	19	3	32	2
Jeffcoat, Edmonton*	4	3	.571	4.14	33	0	0	14	0	3	54.1	58	25	25	2	1	6	1	32	1
Jimenez, Tacoma	2	3	.400	4.78	8	8	0	0	0	0	37.2	32	23	20	4	0	24	0	34	3
Johnstone, Edmonton	4	15	.211	5.18	30	21	1	6	0	4	144.1	167	95	83	16	6	59	2	126	9
Jones, Tucson	4	2	.667	4.44	41	0	0	28	0	12	48.2	49	26	24	5	0	31	2	45	5
Juden, Tucson	11	6	.647	4.63	27	27	0	0	0	0	169.0	174	102	87	8	9	76	0	156	15
Kent, Calgary	0	1	.000	11.45	9	0	0	0	0	0	11.0	21	16	14	0	1	8	2	10	2
Kipila, Vancouver	0	0	.000	0.00	1	0	0	1	0	0	1.0	1	0	0	0	0	0	0	1	0
Knudson, Colorado Springs	3	1	.750	2.25	5	5	1	0	1	0	28.0	30	12	7	0	0	8	0	15	1
Kramer, Edmonton	5	4	.556	5.52	46	0	0	20	0	5	62.0	76	45	38	3	1	24	2	44	8
Kutzler, Albuquerque	5	6	.455	5.58	35	11	0	5	0	1	100.0	124	70	62	10	2	31	1	50	4
Layana, Phoenix	3	2	.600	4.81	55	0	0	38	0	9	67.1	80	42	36	5	5	24	4	55	8
LaPoint, Portland*	6	4	.600	6.09	13	13	0	0	0	0	75.1	99	60	51	7	0	29	0	40	4
Leftwich, Vancouver	7	7	.500	4.64	20	20	1	0	0	0	126.0	138	74	65	8	2	45	1	102	4
Lemon, Edmonton	3	3	.500	5.21	21	11	0	1	0	0	74.1	89	48	43	10	1	20	1	52	2
Leskanic, Colorado Springs	4	3	.571	4.47	9	7	1	1	1	0	44.1	39	24	22	3	2	26	0	38	1
Lewis, Tucson	3	1	.750	1.37	24	0	0	18	0	9	39.1	31	7	6	1	2	9	2	38	1
Linskey, Las Vegas*	4	5	.444	4.68	30	13	0	6	0	1	107.2	130	68	56	7	1	46	3	77	3
Mahomes, Portland	11	4	.733	3.03	17	16	3	1	1	0	115.2	89	47	39	11	1	54	1	94	4
Marquez, Albuquerque	1	0	1.000	1.50	9	0	0	3	0	2	12.0	7	2	2	0	0	3	0	10	2
Marshall, Colorado Springs*	1	0	1.000	3.86	11	1	0	5	0	1	21.0	35	20	9	2	0	6	0	12	2
F. Martinez, Albuquerque*	0	2	.000	4.32	4	1	0	0	0	0	8.1	11	8	4	1	0	1	0	2	1
J. Martinez, 13 Edm.-14 L.V.	8	7	.533	6.01	27	18	3	2	0	0	115.1	148	88	77	18	2	39	0	45	5
P.A. Martinez, Las Vegas*	3	5	.375	4.72	15	14	1	0	0	0	87.2	94	49	46	8	1	40	4	65	3
P.J. Martinez, Albuquerque	0	0	.000	3.00	1	1	0	0	0	0	3.0	1	1	1	0	1	0	0	4	0
Mathews, Tucson	5	0	1.000	3.55	16	4	0	4	0	2	33.0	40	14	13	1	3	11	1	34	1
McCullers, Tucson	4	5	.444	5.67	33	10	0	15	0	1	87.1	106	62	55	17	2	40	2	42	6
McGehee, Phoenix	0	3	.000	4.91	4	4	0	0	0	0	22.0	28	16	12	1	5	8	1	16	1
McGraw, Edmonton*	2	0	1.000	5.59	5	2	0	1	0	0	9.2	12	7	6	1	6	4	0	6	0
Merriman, Portland	5	0	1.000	3.00	39	0	0	33	0	15	48.0	46	19	16	0	3	18	0	29	2
Metzinger, Colorado Springs	1	0	1.000	10.07	12	0	0	5	0	0	19.2	25	24	22	4	0	19	0	21	6
Miller, Edmonton	3	3	.500	4.50	9	9	0	0	0	0	48.0	42	24	24	2	0	34	0	19	5
Mimbs, Albuquerque*	0	1	.000	10.13	19	1	0	3	0	1	18.2	20	21	21	0	0	16	1	12	2
Minutelli, Phoenix*	2	2	.500	4.02	49	0	0	34	0	11	53.2	55	28	24	1	0	26	0	57	6
Moore, Colorado Springs	1	5	.167	4.47	30	0	0	14	0	4	44.1	54	26	22	3	1	29	0	38	4
Munoz, Colorado Springs*	1	2	.333	1.67	40	0	0	13	0	3	37.2	46	10	7	0	0	9	0	30	2

Pitcher, Team	W	L	Pct.	ERA	G	GS	CG	GF	ShO	Sv.	IP	H	R	ER	HR	HB	BB	Int. BB	SO	WP
Munoz, Portland	2	2	.500	4.31	5	5	0	0	0	0	31.1	29	18	15	2	0	17	1	29	6
Myers, Phoenix	2	5	.286	3.68	31	3	0	5	0	0	58.2	69	35	24	2	3	22	2	20	5
Myers, Edmonton*	7	14	.333	5.18	27	27	3	0	0	0	161.2	195	109	93	20	10	52	1	112	7
Neidlinger, Portland	9	8	.529	5.19	29	24	3	1	0	0	157.2	175	106	91	22	5	54	3	112	4
Nelson, Calgary	1	0	1.000	1.17	5	0	0	4	0	1	7.2	6	1	1	0	1	2	0	6	2
Newlin, Edmonton	0	0	.000	13.50	4	0	0	1	0	0	6.0	11	9	9	1	2	4	0	3	1
Nichols, Albuquerque	8	5	.615	4.30	21	21	3	0	1	0	127.2	132	68	61	16	3	50	3	79	9
Nied, Colorado Springs	0	2	.000	9.00	3	3	0	0	0	0	15.0	24	17	15	3	2	6	0	11	0
Nielsen, Vancouver*	2	5	.286	4.20	33	5	0	10	0	0	55.2	70	32	26	4	0	20	3	45	2
Nolte, 10 Cal.-23 Albu.*	3	5	.375	6.34	33	7	0	3	0	1	71.0	101	60	50	9	0	30	1	63	8
Ontiveros, Portland	7	6	.538	2.87	20	16	2	2	0	0	103.1	90	40	33	5	4	20	0	73	2
Ortiz, Portland*	0	0	.000	18.00	1	0	0	0	0	0	2.0	6	4	4	0	0	2	0	2	2
Osteen, Tacoma*	7	7	.500	5.08	16	15	0	0	0	0	83.1	89	51	47	4	1	31	1	46	0
Osuna, Tucson*	3	1	.750	4.50	13	4	0	3	0	1	30.0	26	16	15	1	5	17	0	38	4
Painter, Colorado Springs*	9	7	.563	4.30	23	22	4	0	1	0	138.0	165	90	66	10	5	44	2	91	6
Parkins, Calgary	0	0	.000	10.13	3	0	0	3	0	0	2.2	6	3	3	1	0	0	0	3	1
Patrick, Tacoma	3	8	.273	7.05	35	13	1	12	0	1	104.2	156	87	82	12	4	42	3	56	3
Peck, Vancouver	5	3	.625	4.85	31	7	0	5	0	0	72.1	91	47	39	4	4	29	2	47	3
Peek, Tacoma	9	6	.600	3.95	60	0	0	25	0	5	86.2	103	46	38	8	5	28	5	63	0
Peltzer, Phoenix*	2	0	1.000	6.75	12	0	0	8	0	2	16.0	16	13	12	0	1	7	3	16	0
Pena, Las Vegas*	1	2	.333	6.10	39	0	0	16	0	1	51.2	69	41	35	12	3	16	2	31	4
Percival, Vancouver	0	1	.000	6.27	18	0	0	11	0	4	18.2	24	14	13	0	2	13	1	19	2
Perschke, Albuquerque	7	4	.636	6.36	33	13	0	5	0	0	104.2	146	76	74	12	2	24	3	63	6
Peters, Phoenix	0	0	.000	18.00	1	0	0	0	0	0	2.0	4	4	4	0	0	2	0	2	1
Phoenix, Tacoma	0	2	.000	6.97	11	5	0	1	0	0	31.0	42	27	24	4	0	27	2	21	2
Pico, Vancouver	3	1	.750	4.21	18	0	0	4	0	0	25.2	29	18	12	2	1	20	3	16	1
Picota, Calgary	1	2	.333	6.14	22	0	0	17	0	5	29.1	32	22	20	1	0	16	0	10	5
Powell, Calgary	3	2	.600	3.60	12	4	0	2	0	1	40.0	37	16	16	3	1	19	1	30	0
Pulido, Portland*	10	6	.625	4.19	33	22	1	5	0	0	146.0	169	74	68	8	2	45	1	79	8
Raczka, Tacoma*	2	1	.667	5.37	55	0	0	11	0	0	60.1	65	39	36	6	3	30	2	40	3
Rambo, Phoenix	1	3	.250	7.14	18	5	0	2	0	0	51.2	77	44	41	6	0	33	7	31	10
Rapp, Edmonton	8	3	.727	3.43	17	17	4	0	1	0	107.2	89	45	41	4	1	34	0	93	2
Reed, Colorado Springs	0	0	.000	0.00	11	0	0	10	0	7	12.1	8	1	0	0	1	3	1	10	1
Remlinger, Calgary*	4	3	.571	5.53	19	18	0	0	0	0	84.2	100	57	52	8	2	52	0	51	5
Reyes, Colorado Springs	0	0	.000	9.00	1	0	0	1	0	0	1.0	2	1	1	0	0	1	0	0	0
Reynolds, Tucson	10	6	.625	3.62	25	20	2	1	0	1	139.1	147	74	56	4	3	21	0	106	4
Reynoso, Colorado Springs	2	1	.667	3.22	4	4	0	0	0	0	22.1	19	10	8	1	1	8	0	22	2
Ridenour, Colorado Springs	8	8	.500	5.21	39	16	1	6	0	0	121.0	156	83	70	9	6	58	5	105	16
Robinson, Tucson	1	0	1.000	5.06	13	0	0	6	0	1	21.1	22	12	12	2	0	9	3	15	2
Sager, Las Vegas	6	5	.545	3.70	21	11	2	3	1	1	90.0	91	49	37	7	5	18	1	58	5
St. Claire, Calgary	4	6	.400	6.79	27	0	0	13	0	3	51.2	70	40	39	4	2	13	2	45	4
Sanders, Las Vegas	5	10	.333	4.96	24	24	4	0	0	0	152.1	170	101	84	19	6	62	2	161	4
Sanford, Colorado Springs	3	6	.333	5.23	20	17	0	1	0	0	105.0	103	64	61	8	4	57	2	104	7
Scheid, Edmonton*	5	7	.417	5.07	38	12	0	15	0	0	110.0	130	68	62	8	4	38	1	84	4
Schunk, Portland	0	0	.000	0.00	1	0	0	0	0	0	1.0	0	0	0	0	0	0	0	0	0
Scott, Vancouver	7	1	.875	2.09	46	0	0	33	0	15	51.2	35	12	12	4	1	19	2	57	3
Seanez, 3 C.S.-14 L.V.	0	1	.000	6.75	17	0	0	11	0	0	22.2	27	18	17	3	0	12	0	19	7
Seminara, Las Vegas	8	5	.615	5.43	21	19	0	1	0	0	114.1	136	79	69	15	4	52	1	99	2
Shepherd, Colorado Springs	3	6	.333	6.78	37	1	0	20	0	8	67.2	90	61	51	2	4	44	2	57	15
Shikles, Tacoma	7	7	.500	4.49	38	21	1	10	1	2	148.1	179	85	74	13	6	34	4	68	5
Shinall, Calgary	2	1	.667	5.01	33	0	0	19	0	5	46.2	55	29	26	6	4	18	3	25	4
Simms, Las Vegas	0	0	.000	0.00	1	0	0	1	0	0	1.0	2	1	0	0	0	0	0	2	0
Sims, Portland*	3	1	.750	3.41	50	0	0	22	0	3	66.0	69	33	25	6	0	36	3	32	4
Slusarski, Tacoma	7	5	.583	4.76	24	21	1	0	1	0	113.1	133	67	60	6	1	40	1	61	2
Smith, Calgary	0	0	.000	0.00	1	0	0	1	0	0	1.0	1	0	0	0	0	0	0	0	0
Smith, Tacoma	3	0	1.000	7.15	6	4	0	0	0	0	22.2	31	18	18	2	0	11	1	16	2
Smithberg, Tacoma	3	3	.500	1.78	28	0	0	12	0	4	50.2	50	14	10	1	2	11	1	25	2
Snyder, Edmonton	0	0	.000	22.50	2	0	0	2	0	0	2.0	7	5	5	2	1	1	0	2	0
Springer, Albuquerque	3	8	.273	5.99	35	18	0	5	0	0	130.2	173	104	87	18	2	39	1	69	7
Springer, Vancouver	5	4	.556	4.27	11	9	0	0	0	0	59.0	58	37	28	5	0	33	1	40	4
Stevens, Portland	5	3	.625	1.98	53	0	0	16	0	2	81.2	75	27	18	2	1	35	3	60	6
Strong, Las Vegas	1	3	.250	5.67	21	0	0	5	0	0	27.0	37	23	17	4	2	10	1	18	0
Swan, Calgary*	2	1	.667	8.44	9	0	0	3	0	0	10.2	14	11	10	1	0	8	0	7	0
Swingle, Vancouver	2	9	.182	6.92	37	4	0	11	0	1	67.2	85	61	52	4	1	32	1	61	3
Taylor, Phoenix	10	8	.556	4.24	49	12	0	11	0	2	144.1	166	85	68	15	4	49	4	110	7
Thompson, Colorado Springs	3	0	1.000	2.70	4	4	2	0	0	0	33.1	31	13	10	1	1	11	0	22	3
Torres, Phoenix	7	4	.636	3.50	14	14	4	0	1	0	105.1	105	43	41	5	2	27	0	99	7
Traxler, Albuquerque*	1	0	1.000	11.57	2	0	0	2	0	0	2.1	3	3	3	0	2	2	0	1	2
Treadwell, Albuquerque	5	4	.556	4.70	39	10	0	6	0	0	105.1	119	58	55	7	7	52	7	102	11
Tsamis, Portland*	1	2	.333	8.36	3	3	0	0	0	0	14.0	27	15	13	2	0	5	0	10	0
Turner, Edmonton	0	0	.000	0.66	12	0	0	12	0	10	13.2	9	1	1	0	0	2	0	15	0
Van Landingham, Phoenix	0	1	.000	6.43	1	1	0	0	0	0	7.0	8	6	5	0	0	2	0	2	0
Van Poppel, Tacoma	4	8	.333	5.83	16	16	0	0	0	0	78.2	67	53	51	5	4	54	0	71	2
Van Ryn, Albuquerque*	1	4	.200	10.73	6	6	0	0	0	0	24.1	35	30	29	1	0	17	0	9	0
Vatcher, Las Vegas	0	0	.000	9.00	2	0	0	2	0	0	3.0	7	3	3	0	0	0	0	0	3
Veres, Tucson	6	10	.375	4.90	43	15	1	18	0	5	130.1	156	88	71	7	2	32	1	122	5
Vierra, Albuquerque	0	4	.000	4.91	29	0	0	15	0	1	33.0	38	22	18	3	2	18	6	24	4
Wainhouse, Calgary	0	1	.000	4.02	13	0	0	10	0	5	15.2	10	7	7	2	1	7	1	7	2
Walker, Calgary	13	8	.619	4.03	28	27	3	0	1	0	169.2	197	91	76	11	5	47	2	131	10
Wall, Tucson	6	4	.600	3.83	25	22	0	2	0	0	131.2	147	73	56	11	2	35	3	89	4
Walter, Edmonton*	2	0	1.000	7.88	6	0	0	2	0	0	8.0	13	7	7	1	0	3	0	4	2
Walton, Tucson	2	0	1.000	1.80	13	0	0	12	0	7	15.0	12	4	3	0	0	3	1	14	1
Wapnick, Calgary	1	5	.167	4.96	32	2	0	7	0	2	61.2	74	39	34	8	1	24	3	26	0
Wassenaar, 13 C.S.-21 Phe.	2	4	.333	6.56	34	4	0	9	0	2	70.0	117	54	51	9	2	24	2	50	7
Weathers, Edmonton	11	4	.733	3.83	22	22	3	0	1	0	141.0	150	77	60	12	6	47	2	117	4
Wells, Colorado Springs*	2	3	.400	6.67	16	2	0	7	0	1	27.0	33	23	20	3	0	25	0	22	4
Williams, Tucson	1	0	1.000	0.00	2	0	0	0	0	0	3.0	1	0	0	0	0	0	0	6	0
Williams, Albuquerque	5	5	.500	4.99	65	0	0	50	0	21	70.1	87	44	39	2	1	31	6	56	6
Willis, Portland	0	0	.000	2.25	2	0	0	1	0	0	4.0	6	2	1	0	0	1	0	2	0
Wilson, Albuquerque*	0	3	.000	4.38	13	12	0	0	0	0	51.1	57	29	25	5	2	14	0	44	4
Windes, Tucson*	1	3	.250	9.00	13	0	0	3	0	0	12.0	20	13	12	3	1	6	0	10	0
Worrell, Las Vegas	5	6	.455	5.48	15	14	2	0	0	0	87.0	102	61	53	13	2	26	1	89	0
Worrell, Albuquerque	1	0	1.000	1.04	7	2	0	1	0	0	8.2	7	2	1	1	0	2	0	13	0
Yaughn, Edmonton	1	0	1.000	0.00	1	0	0	0	0	0	5.0	6	0	0	0	1	0	0	2	0

Pitcher, Team	W	L	Pct.	ERA	G	GS	CG	GF	ShO	Sv.	IP	H	R	ER	HR	HB	BB	Int. BB	SO	WP
Young, Tacoma*	6	1	.857	1.93	10	10	1	0	0	0	65.1	53	23	14	2	1	16	0	31	1
Young, Las Vegas	1	2	.333	6.10	14	0	0	8	0	2	20.2	29	15	14	1	0	8	0	20	3
Zappelli, Vancouver	0	1	.000	3.91	17	0	0	7	0	1	25.1	31	12	11	2	2	5	1	13	2
Zavaras, Colorado Springs	0	0	.000	2.25	6	0	0	1	0	0	8.0	5	3	2	0	0	11	0	9	0

BALKS—Linskey, 6; Holzemer, Sims, 5 each; Huisman, 4; Brummett, Drees, Fisher, Garces, Gross, Hartsock, LaPoint, Metzinger, Nichols, Nolte, Veres, Wall, 3 each; Ashby, Bross, K. Brown, Butcher, Green, Guzman, Henry, Jeffcoat, Johnstone, Kramer, Layana, Leskanic, Ontiveros, Painter, Peck, Perschke, Remlinger, Sager, Scheid, Seminara, Taylor, Torres, Treadwell, Wilson, C. Young, 2 each; Adamson, Allen, B. Anderson, Arnsberg, Boucher, Carman, Czarkowski, Daal, Davis, Dayley, Hanselman, Hathaway, Holman, Horsman, Marshall, J. Martinez, P. Martinez, Miller, Mimbs, Minutelli, M. Myers, Newlin, Nielsen, Osteen, Peek, Pulido, Rapp, Reed, Ridenour, Sanders, Sanford, Seanez, Shikles, Stevens, Strong, Swingle, Vierra, Wassenaar, Weathers, Wells, Windes, 1 each.

COMBINATION SHUTOUTS—Hurst-Kutzler-Treadwell-Gross-Williams, Albuquerque; Harris-Wainhouse, Powell-McCullers, Calgary; Bochtler-Moore-Munoz, Burke-Munoz-Allen, Hawblitzel-Munoz-Reed, Hawblitzel-Wassenaar, Leskanic-Munoz-Allen, Reynoso-Shepherd, Wells-Allen-Munoz-Shepherd-Fredrickson, Colorado Springs; Scheid-Gleaton-Darwin, Weathers-Johnstone, Yaughn-Kramer-Jeffcoat, Edmonton; Brown-Minutelli, Carter-Minutelli, Phoenix; Mahomes-Merriman, Portland; Smith-Smithberg-Raczka-Campbell, Van Poppel-Campbell, Van Poppel-Peek-Raczka-Campbell, Young-Peek, Tacoma; Juden-Capel, Mathews-Williams-Dixon, Veres-Edens-Jones, Veres-Jones, Wall-Bruske, Tucson; Charland-Swingle, Farrell-Butcher, Green-Peck-Pico-Lewis, Holzemer-Scott, Nielsen-Green, Springer-Scott, Vancouver.

NO-HIT GAMES—None.

FIELDING

TEAM

Team	Pct.	G	PO	A	E	DP	PB	Team	Pct.	G	PO	A	E	DP	PB
Albuquerque	.972	143	3772	1702	155	144	21	Las Vegas	.969	143	3708	1526	169	125	22
Portland	.972	143	3636	1503	146	117	11	Tacoma	.969	143	3706	1566	171	136	21
Vancouver	.972	140	3596	1469	147	123	26	Colorado Springs	.967	141	3576	1558	175	135	15
Edmonton	.971	141	3648	1532	152	132	14	Phoenix	.967	143	3773	1625	184	158	11
Calgary	.971	140	3603	1611	156	168	13	Tucson	.962	143	3803	1653	217	137	21

Triple plays—Calgary, Edmonton, Portland, Tucson.

INDIVIDUAL

FIRST BASEMEN

*Throws lefthanded.

Player, Team	Pct.	G	PO	A	E	DP
Aldrete, Tacoma*	.970	4	30	2	1	5
Allanson, Phoenix	.968	3	26	4	1	5
G. Anderson, Vancouver*	1.000	5	37	3	0	4
Armas, Tacoma	.983	67	537	32	10	53
Bean, Las Vegas*	1.000	13	103	13	0	12
Beard, Tacoma	1.000	3	14	1	0	3
Bellinger, Phoenix	1.000	1	8	1	0	2
Berroa, Edmonton	.947	13	84	6	5	8
Borrelli, Tacoma	1.000	1	6	1	0	1
Brosius, Tacoma	.966*	4	25	3	1	3
Brumley, Tucson	1.000	7	51	2	0	4
Busch, Albuquerque	.977	17	112	13	3	11
Canale, Colorado Springs	.995	29	203	15	1	15
Castellano, Colorado Springs	.981	35	281	30	6	29
Chimelis, Phoenix	1.000	6	32	2	0	6
Colbert, Phoenix	1.000	2	20	1	0	6
Cole, Colorado Springs	1.000	1	4	0	0	1
Daugherty, Tucson*	.988	38	310	19	4	24
Davenport, Phoenix	1.000	1	12	0	0	3
Deak, Calgary	1.000	1	9	0	0	0
De Los Santos, Edmonton	.986	112	850	63	13	81
Fariss, Edmonton	.990	24	190	18	2	23
Furtado, Calgary	.833	1	5	0	1	0
Gainer, Colorado Springs*	.989	65	504	49	6	54
Gonzales, Vancouver	1.000	10	67	7	0	6
Grotewold, Portland	.889	2	7	1	1	2
Higgins, Las Vegas	1.000	1	2	0	0	0
Holley, Calgary	.952	2	16	4	1	0
Hosey, Phoenix	1.000	9	62	4	0	7
Jelic, Las Vegas	.950	5	19	0	1	0
Jorgensen, Portland	1.000	13	101	10	0	6
Kipila, Vancouver	1.000	1	3	1	0	0
Lindeman, Tucson	.987	84	715	45	10	64
Lyden, Edmonton	.982	7	52	4	1	4
Maksudian, Portland	.996	32	246	23	1	21
Martinez, Calgary	1.000	13	96	12	0	9
Masteller, Portland*	.988	39	303	28	4	28
McCarty, Portland*	.994	21	143	20	1	8
Mota, Colorado Springs	.900	3	9	0	1	0
Ortiz, Portland*	.968	22	166	13	6	20
Owens, Colorado Springs	1.000	1	6	0	0	1
Parker, Tucson	1.000	1	13	0	0	1
Perez, Vancouver	.972	10	62	8	2	3
Phillips, Phoenix*	.978	129	1135	93	28	117
Pirkl, Calgary	.986	108	918	71	14	121
Quinones, 11 Tuc.-5 Cal.	.992	16	122	8	1	11
Reyes, Colorado Springs	.971	12	94	6	3	14
Robbins, Tacoma	.976	5	39	1	1	2
Rodriguez, Albuquerque*	.982	28	254	17	5	28
Russo, Portland	.976	23	187	17	5	20
Scarsone, Phoenix	1.000	1	7	0	0	1
Schunk, Portland	1.000	1	1	0	0	0
Shockey, Tacoma*	.994	19	146	9	1	16

Player, Team	Pct.	G	PO	A	E	DP
Simms, Las Vegas	.987	92	762	45	11	57
Smith, Calgary	1.000	1	2	0	0	1
Snow, Vancouver*	.991	23	200	13	2	27
Snyder, Edmonton	1.000	3	5	0	0	2
Staton, Las Vegas	.969	10	88	5	3	13
Sveum, 1 Tac.-6 Cal.	.984	7	58	4	1	7
Tatum, Colorado Springs	1.000	1	1	0	0	0
Trafton, Tucson	1.000	3	30	1	0	4
TRAXLER, Albuquerque*	.995	115	969	89	5	98
Tucker, Tucson	.993	17	121	12	1	12
Turner, Vancouver	.983	8	55	4	1	5
Turner, Calgary	1.000	1	5	2	0	0
Van Burkleo, Vancouver*	.984	96	765	51	13	68
Velasquez, Las Vegas	.990	30	278	28	3	29
Ward, Colorado Springs	1.000	1	12	0	0	0
Wedge, Colorado Springs	.977	12	74	10	2	8
Wilson, Calgary	.991	11	106	2	1	15
Witkowski, Las Vegas	1.000	2	4	0	0	0
Witmeyer, Tacoma*	.991	62	404	30	4	35

Triple plays—Fariss, Lindeman, McCarty, Pirkl.

SECOND BASEMEN

Player, Team	Pct.	G	PO	A	E	DP
Barberie, Edmonton	.952	4	8	12	1	0
Barrett, Tucson	.979	24	30	62	2	7
Bates, Colorado Springs	1.000	7	13	26	0	8
Bethea, Las Vegas	1.000	19	19	25	0	3
Boone, Calgary	.976	64	146	180	8	51
Brosius, Tacoma	.923	8	31	17	4	4
Browne, Vancouver	.778	1	3	4	2	2
Buccheri, Tacoma	1.000	3	1	0	0	0
Candaele, Tucson	.727	1	3	5	3	3
Carter, Portland	.970	91	207	208	13	46
Chimelis, Phoenix	.978	29	59	72	3	28
Cole, Colorado Springs	1.000	11	22	23	0	5
Correia, Vancouver	.963	17	38	39	3	8
Cruz, Tacoma	.818	2	6	3	2	1
Davis, Vancouver	.992	26	58	68	1	23
Faries, Phoenix	1.000	21	50	66	0	21
Flora, Vancouver	.950	11	16	22	2	5
Forbes, Vancouver	1.000	5	15	13	0	2
GARRISON, Tacoma	.972	112	225	333	16	64
Gates, Tacoma	.984	12	27	36	1	9
Gutierrez, Las Vegas	.900	5	9	9	2	4
Hale, Portland	.946	35	69	89	9	18
Hecht, Phoenix	.976	41	83	123	5	31
Higgins, Las Vegas	1.000	3	4	6	0	2
Howard, Albuquerque	.969	12	9	22	1	5
Hubbard, Colorado Springs	.909	8	12	8	2	3
Jackson, Edmonton	.895	5	8	9	2	4
E. Johnson, Phoenix	.984	45	82	100	3	28
Liriano, Colorado Springs	.975	50	103	173	7	38
Litton, Calgary	1.000	9	31	25	0	13
Lopez, Las Vegas	.982	60	141	189	6	50

— 384 —

Player, Team	Pct.	G	PO	A	E	DP
Manahan, Calgary	.983	41	95	132	4	28
P. Martinez, Las Vegas	.857	2	6	6	2	0
Martinez, Vancouver	.986	14	40	28	1	9
Maurer, Albuquerque	1.000	2	1	0	0	0
Mejia, Colorado Springs	.979	72	166	204	8	49
Mota, 21 Phoe.-2 C.S.	.943	23	30	36	4	4
Mouton, Tucson	.936	126	277	354	43	75
Munoz, Albuquerque	.982	68	126	207	6	48
Paquette, Tacoma	1.000	1	1	1	0	1
Pedrique, Edmonton	.946	16	34	36	4	12
Polidor, Edmonton	1.000	11	32	30	0	6
Pye, Albuquerque	.973	82	181	245	12	53
Quinones, 1 Tuc.-5 Cal.	.967	6	15	14	1	4
Renteria, Edmonton	.948	14	31	42	4	12
Santana, Edmonton	.939	36	89	96	12	20
Scarsone, Phoenix	.966	12	22	34	2	5
Schunk, Portland	1.000	11	20	20	0	5
Scott, Portland	1.000	12	21	36	0	8
Small, Edmonton	.974	64	121	180	8	43
Smith, Calgary	1.000	4	7	17	0	4
Sveum, Tacoma	1.000	11	23	19	0	5
Turang, Calgary	.978	17	33	58	2	15
Turner, Calgary	.912	5	13	18	3	7
Walewander, Vancouver	.980	73	155	193	7	47
Witkowski, Las Vegas	.974	76	122	179	8	35

Triple plays—Hale, Mouton.

THIRD BASEMEN

Player, Team	Pct.	G	PO	A	E	DP
Alicea, Colorado Springs	1.000	6	0	4	0	0
Allanson, Phoenix	.667	1	1	1	1	0
Armas, Tacoma	1.000	4	0	10	0	0
Barrett, Tucson	.940	39	24	55	5	5
Beard, Tacoma	.900	9	3	15	2	1
Bellinger, Phoenix	.910	78	43	128	17	18
Bethea, Las Vegas	1.000	4	1	0	0	0
Brosius, Tacoma	.935	30	15	85	7	7
Browne, Tacoma	1.000	3	0	8	0	0
Brumley, Tucson	.941	6	4	12	1	0
Busch, Albuquerque	.881	108	57	218	37	17
Calcagno, Phoenix	.000	1	0	0	1	0
Capra, Edmonton	.944	70	58	144	12	7
Castellano, Colorado Springs	.954	52	31	115	7	10
Chimelis, Phoenix	.940	46	16	94	7	10
Colbert, Phoenix	.833	2	2	3	1	0
Cole, Colorado Springs	.892	66	38	111	18	11
Cruz, Tacoma	.976	12	18	22	1	5
Dalesandro, Vancouver	.918	26	19	59	7	8
Davenport, Phoenix	.788	9	10	16	7	1
Davis, Vancouver	.884	14	7	31	5	4
De Los Santos, Edmonton	1.000	4	1	5	0	2
Faries, Phoenix	1.000	4	0	14	0	4
Gomez, Tacoma	.872	32	26	49	11	3
Gonzales, Vancouver	.889	9	3	13	2	0
Gonzalez, Las Vegas	.933	70	31	137	12	16
Grotewold, Portland	1.000	1	1	0	0	0
Gruber, Vancouver	1.000	2	0	4	0	0
Hale, Portland	.951	16	5	34	2	3
Hecht, Phoenix	1.000	2	0	1	0	0
Higgins, Las Vegas	.944	30	20	48	4	7
Holley, Calgary	.905	6	8	11	2	0
Hubbard, Colorado Springs	1.000	5	2	10	0	1
Jackson, Edmonton	.923	26	25	59	7	11
Jelic, Las Vegas	.887	30	11	52	8	2
Johnson, Las Vegas	.956	19	15	28	2	2
E. Johnson, Phoenix	.885	9	4	19	3	0
Jorgensen, Portland	.966	43	34	79	4	4
Liriano, Colorado Springs	.913	13	7	14	2	1
Litton, Calgary	.988	24	21	59	1	6
Maksudian, Portland	.857	10	5	13	3	0
Manahan, Calgary	.899	43	12	77	10	9
Martinez, Vancouver	.936	14	6	38	3	5
Maurer, Albuquerque	.957	14	7	15	1	3
Mercedes, Phoenix	.813	13	2	24	6	6
Mota, 1 Tuc.- 1 Phoe.	.500	2	0	3	3	0
Mota, Colorado Springs	1.000	1	0	1	0	0
Munoz, Albuquerque	.908	40	18	61	8	1
NEVIN, Tucson	.891	96	50	186	29	11
Paquette, Tacoma	.911	50	31	113	14	9
Parker, Tucson	1.000	2	0	1	0	0
Parks, Portland	1.000	2	0	2	0	0
Pedrique, Edmonton	1.000	23	14	46	0	5
Perez, Vancouver	.905	77	35	166	21	11
Peters, Phoenix	.875	14	4	24	4	3
Pirkl, Calgary	1.000	1	2	1	0	1
Polidor, Edmonton	1.000	2	1	1	0	0
Pye, Albuquerque	1.000	2	0	4	0	0
Quinones, 33 Tuc. -3 Cal.	.947	36	22	50	4	3
Renteria, Edmonton	.824	5	2	12	3	1
Russo, Portland	.939	54	24	115	9	4
Scarsone, Phoenix	.923	4	5	7	1	1
Schunk, Portland	1.000	2	2	5	0	0
Scott, Portland	.928	23	18	46	5	4

Player, Team	Pct.	G	PO	A	E	DP
Simms, Las Vegas	1.000	2	1	0	0	0
Small, Edmonton	.964	25	18	62	3	8
Smith, Calgary	1.000	4	1	7	0	0
Sveum, Calgary	.944	11	9	25	2	2
Tatum, Colorado Springs	.903	11	7	21	3	3
Tucker, Tucson	1.000	2	0	2	0	0
Turang, Calgary	.786	7	3	8	3	1
Turner, Calgary	.951	59	23	112	7	13
Walewander, Vancouver	.941	7	1	15	1	1
Witkowski, Las Vegas	1.000	6	2	7	0	1

Triple plays—Nevin, Russo, Turner.

SHORTSTOPS

Player, Team	Pct.	G	PO	A	E	DP
Abbott, Tacoma	.951	129	210	367	30	76
Alicea, Colorado Springs	.946	8	8	27	2	7
Barrett, Tucson	.917	3	2	9	1	0
Bates, Colorado Springs	.940	112	161	293	29	66
Batista, Tacoma	1.000	4	6	9	0	2
Bellinger, Phoenix	.951	53	72	143	11	34
Benavides, Colorado Springs	1.000	5	4	12	0	1
Bethea, Las Vegas	.867	6	5	8	2	0
BOURNIGAL, Albuquerque	.980	133	196	427	13	97
Brosius, Tacoma	1.000	2	3	4	0	1
Brumley, Tucson	.914	22	26	59	8	8
Candaele, Tucson	1.000	2	6	5	0	2
Cole, Colorado Springs	.880	7	9	13	3	3
Correia, Vancouver	.944	43	67	120	11	20
Cruz, Tacoma	1.000	6	9	18	0	4
Davis, Vancouver	.881	13	12	25	5	7
Duncan, Phoenix	.500	4	1	0	1	0
Faries, Phoenix	.987	53	62	164	3	32
Garrison, Tacoma	1.000	5	4	10	0	1
Gutierrez, Las Vegas	1.000	1	2	5	0	2
Hale, Portland	1.000	4	5	11	0	1
Hubbard, Colorado Springs	1.000	1	1	2	0	0
E. Johnson, Phoenix	.965	52	77	144	8	31
J. Johnson, Phoenix	.900	1	2	7	1	2
Jorgensen, Portland	.944	5	7	10	1	4
Liriano, Colorado Springs	.929	17	33	45	6	14
Litton, Calgary	.909	2	6	4	1	0
Lopez, Las Vegas	.924	69	89	191	23	33
Manahan, Calgary	.930	28	53	93	11	23
P. Martinez, Las Vegas	.941	74	91	259	22	38
Martinez, Vancouver	.943	85	120	241	22	40
Maurer, Albuquerque	.931	25	18	63	6	9
Meares, Portland	.938	18	28	48	5	9
Miller, Tucson	.945	118	180	389	33	74
Paquette, Tacoma	.667	1	0	2	1	0
Pedrique, Edmonton	.931	85	118	233	26	44
Polidor, Edmonton	.969	60	75	179	8	35
Pye, Albuquerque	1.000	4	1	5	0	0
Quinones, Tucson	1.000	14	10	27	0	6
Santana, Edmonton	1.000	2	1	3	0	1
Scarsone, Phoenix	1.000	2	2	7	0	1
Schunk, Portland	.959	105	160	309	20	54
Scott, Portland	.927	18	33	56	7	16
Small, Edmonton	1.000	2	0	1	0	0
Smith, Calgary	.948	113	156	351	28	90
Soriano, Portland	1.000	2	3	5	0	0
Sveum, Tacoma	1.000	1	1	2	0	0
Turang, Calgary	.750	1	0	3	1	0
Turner, Calgary	1.000	1	1	6	0	0
Walewander, Vancouver	1.000	7	8	15	0	4

Triple plays—Manahan, Polidor.

OUTFIELDERS

Player, Team	Pct.	G	PO	A	E	DP
Aldrete, Tacoma*	1.000	23	45	3	0	2
Alicea, Colorado Springs	.891	47	51	6	7	1
Allanson, Phoenix	.667	2	3	1	2	0
G. Anderson, Vancouver*	.988	106	161	10	2	1
Ansley, Tucson	.958	116	174	9	8	2
Armas, Tacoma	1.000	2	1	0	0	0
Ashley, Albuquerque	.952	116	211	7	11	0
Ausmus, Colorado Springs	1.000	3	2	0	0	0
Barrett, Tucson	1.000	3	1	0	0	0
Barron, Albuquerque	.967	77	82	5	3	2
Bean, Las Vegas*	.981	36	46	7	1	0
Berroa, Edmonton	.985	53	126	4	2	2
Brantley, Phoenix	1.000	44	72	1	0	0
Brito, Portland	.951	36	37	2	2	0
Brooks, Albuquerque	1.000	20	19	2	0	1
Brosius, Tacoma	.964	16	27	0	1	0
Ja. Brown, Las Vegas	.963	97	217	16	9	1
Browne, Tacoma	1.000	1	4	0	0	0
Bruett, Portland*	.991	87	213	11	2	2
Brumley, Tucson	.943	51	80	3	5	1
Buccheri, Tacoma	.989	85	181	7	2	2
Canale, Colorado Springs	1.000	9	17	2	0	1
Candaele, Tucson	1.000	4	3	0	0	0

Player, Team	Pct.	G	PO	A	E	DP
Capra, Edmonton	.985	36	62	3	1	0
Carter, Portland	1.000	3	4	0	0	0
Carter, Tucson	.923	35	56	4	5	1
Castillo, 38 C.S. - 12 Tuc.	.970	50	91	5	3	1
Cedeno, Albuquerque	.923	5	12	0	1	0
Chimelis, Phoenix	.500	2	1	0	1	0
Cole, Colorado Springs	.800	6	4	0	1	0
Cruz, Tacoma	1.000	1	1	0	0	0
Dattola, Tacoma	.909	19	28	2	3	1
Daugherty, Tucson*	1.000	2	3	0	0	0
Davis, Vancouver	1.000	4	2	1	0	0
Deak, Calgary	1.000	2	2	0	0	0
Dozier, Las Vegas	.897	31	24	2	3	1
Edmonds, Vancouver*	.983	76	167	4	3	0
Everett, Edmonton	.976	34	69	12	2	0
Faneyte, Phoenix	.987	104	223	11	3	2
Faries, Phoenix	1.000	5	9	0	0	0
Fariss, Edmonton	.990	56	95	2	1	1
Felix, Edmonton	1.000	7	18	1	0	0
Flora, Vancouver	1.000	2	5	0	0	0
Fox, Tacoma*	.981	77	198	6	4	2
Furtado, Calgary	.833	3	5	0	1	0
Garrison, Tacoma	.973	21	34	2	1	1
Gomez, Tacoma	.974	30	71	3	2	0
Goodwin, Albuquerque	.986	77	145	1	2	0
Hecht, Phoenix	1.000	6	8	0	0	0
Henderson, Tacoma	1.000	3	7	0	0	0
Hill, Vancouver	1.000	6	5	1	0	0
Hosey, Las Vegas	.957	27	43	1	2	0
Hosey, Phoenix	.961	107	166	5	7	0
HOWELL, Portland	.993	110	270	14	2	1
Howitt, Calgary	.984	88	174	5	3	3
Hubbard, Colorado Springs	.981	95	193	9	4	1
Jackson, Edmonton	.667	3	1	1	1	0
Jackson, Vancouver*	.989	46	90	3	1	0
Jeter, Calgary	1.000	9	15	0	0	0
Jones, Colorado Springs	.974	46	107	5	3	0
Katzaroff, Phoenix	1.000	8	16	1	0	1
Kipila, Vancouver	1.000	6	10	0	0	0
Landrum, Portland	1.000	2	1	0	0	0
Lee, Portland	.971	102	188	10	6	4
Lindeman, Tucson	.938	26	28	2	2	0
List, Colorado Springs	.944	16	16	1	1	0
Litton, Calgary	1.000	5	7	0	0	0
Lydy, Tacoma	.970	88	182	9	6	3
Mack, Calgary*	.983	63	113	3	2	0
Manahan, Calgary	1.000	1	2	0	0	0
Martinez, Calgary	1.000	13	18	2	0	0
Martinez, Phoenix*	1.000	3	5	1	0	0
Martinez, Tacoma	1.000	19	33	6	0	1
Massarelli, Tucson	.932	94	129	8	10	3
Masteller, Portland*	.975	19	38	1	1	0
Maynard, Calgary	1.000	8	13	0	0	0
McCarty, Portland*	.977	22	42	1	1	0
Mercedes, Tacoma	1.000	1	2	0	0	0
Mercedes, Phoenix	.924	58	104	6	9	1
Mikulik, Tucson	.970	79	156	5	5	1
Mondesi, Albuquerque	.957	105	211	10	10	2
Montgomery, Tucson	1.000	14	33	1	0	0
Mota, 6 Phoe.-68 C.S.	.971	74	128	6	4	1
Munoz, Albuquerque	1.000	5	3	0	0	0
Murray, Phoenix	.867	5	13	0	2	0
Nevin, Tucson	1.000	23	18	1	0	0
Nieves, Las Vegas	.988	41	79	4	1	1
Olander, Colorado Springs	.988	47	81	1	1	0
Ortiz, Portland*	.946	74	114	8	7	0
Owens, Colorado Springs	.917	10	10	1	1	0
Parker, Tucson	.957	28	64	2	3	0
Pegues, Las Vegas	.982	64	103	5	2	2
Perez, Vancouver	1.000	1	1	0	0	0
Peters, Phoenix	.982	72	107	4	2	1
Pettis, Tacoma	.963	25	76	3	3	0
Phillips, Phoenix*	.750	1	3	0	1	0
Pose, Edmonton	.970	99	192	4	6	1
Renteria, Edmonton	1.000	2	5	0	0	0
Ricker, Colorado Springs	.500	8	3	0	3	0
Rodriguez, Albuquerque*	1.000	24	23	1	0	0
Ross, Colorado Springs*	.942	31	64	1	4	0
Sherman, Las Vegas	.981	73	152	6	3	1
Simms, Las Vegas	.857	10	11	1	2	0
Smiley, Phoenix*	.918	67	88	1	8	0
Spearman, Albuquerque*	.985	56	130	5	2	1
Strawberry, Albuquerque*	1.000	5	7	0	0	0
Tinsley, Calgary	.988	108	241	4	3	0
Turang, Calgary	.965	88	185	6	7	1
Turner, Calgary	1.000	19	30	2	0	0
Van Burkleo, Vancouver*	1.000	12	16	0	0	0
Vatcher, Las Vegas	.968	79	139	11	5	3
Wade, Portland	1.000	6	6	1	0	0
Waggoner, Calgary	1.000	9	7	0	0	0
Walewander, Vancouver	1.000	4	1	1	0	0
Walton, Vancouver	1.000	47	82	3	0	0
Ward, Colorado Springs	1.000	20	32	2	0	0
Whitmore, Edmonton	.978	72	171	7	4	3
Williams, Vancouver	.987	127	293	6	4	4

Player, Team	Pct.	G	PO	A	E	DP
Wilson, Edmonton*	.985	85	121	13	2	1
Witmeyer, Tacoma*	.968	64	89	2	3	0
Young, Calgary	.937	26	58	1	4	0

Triple play—Howell.

CATCHERS

Player, Team	Pct.	G	PO	A	E	DP	PB
Allanson, Phoenix	.983	39	213	20	4	1	2
Ausmus, Colorado Springs	.987	63	391	57	6	4	4
Barron, Albuquerque	1.000	5	6	2	0	0	2
Basso, Las Vegas	.981	33	200	12	4	2	6
Beard, Tacoma	.955	6	21	0	1	0	0
Borrelli, Tacoma	.980	71	359	37	8	3	8
Brooks, Albuquerque	.976	75	414	42	11	3	13
Calcagno, Phoenix	.970	15	84	14	3	0	1
Colbert, Phoenix	.982	9	51	5	1	0	1
Deak, Calgary	.972	53	266	47	9	4	3
Dodge, Vancouver	1.000	7	31	3	0	0	1
Eusebio, Tucson	.994	73	450	46	3	6	9
Fabregas, Vancouver	1.000	3	30	3	0	0	0
Fernandez, Phoenix	.978	41	230	35	6	0	2
Girardi, Colorado Springs	.977	8	40	3	1	0	0
Gonzales, Vancouver	1.000	52	289	31	0	1	5
Grifol, Portland	.978	28	171	10	4	2	5
Grotewold, Portland	.941	31	149	11	10	1	4
Heffernan, Phoenix	.992	16	112	8	1	2	2
Higgins, Las Vegas	1.000	9	48	4	0	1	2
Howard, Calgary	.988	89	506	65	7	8	10
Johnson, Las Vegas	.987	78	498	39	7	2	12
Lyden, Edmonton	.993	22	129	12	1	1	3
Maksudian, Portland	.981	28	146	12	3	2	3
Massarelli, Tucson	1.000	5	35	5	0	0	0
McGRIFF, Edmonton	.996	83	505	38	2	1	8
McNamara, Phoenix	.976	44	251	30	7	3	3
Mercedes, Tacoma	.969	72	328	50	12	10	10
Morales, Tacoma	1.000	1	4	1	0	0	0
Natal, Edmonton	.986	17	119	19	2	0	0
Ortiz, Albuquerque	.978	18	78	11	2	0	0
Owens, Colorado Springs	.959	35	191	17	9	2	7
Parks, Portland	.993	69	376	47	3	5	2
Parrish, Albuquerque	1.000	11	67	7	0	0	2
Peters, Phoenix	1.000	1	2	0	0	0	0
Reyes, Colorado Springs	.972	46	217	27	7	2	2
Robbins, Tacoma	1.000	22	87	8	0	1	3
Snyder, Edmonton	.957	27	144	10	7	4	3
Strittmatter, Colorado Springs	1.000	4	15	1	0	0	0
Tejero, Vancouver	.991	14	96	13	1	0	3
Tucker, Tacoma	.993	78	500	55	4	9	12
Turner, Vancouver	.990	74	469	52	5	4	17
Wakamatsu, Albuquerque	.989	53	329	35	4	0	4
Walters, Las Vegas	.992	41	245	14	2	3	2
Wedge, Colorado Springs	.986	12	60	12	1	0	2

Triple play—Maksudian.

PITCHERS

Player, Team	Pct.	G	PO	A	E	DP
Adamson, Edmonton*	1.000	5	0	5	0	0
Agosto, 19 L.V.-32 Tuc.*	.875	51	4	10	2	1
Allen, 2 Albu.-35 C.S.	.857	37	6	6	2	2
Allison, Tacoma*	1.000	23	2	12	0	0
B. Anderson, Vancouver*	1.000	2	1	0	0	0
Anderson, Edmonton	1.000	44	4	7	0	1
Arnsberg, Tacoma	1.000	21	1	5	0	1
Ashby, Colorado Springs	1.000	7	4	8	0	0
Ayrault, 3 Cal.-11 Albu.	1.000	14	0	1	0	0
Barrett, Tucson	1.000	3	1	1	0	0
Barton, Calgary*	.864	51	9	10	3	0
Bell, Tucson*	.923	22	6	18	2	0
Bennett, Vancouver	.944	18	7	10	1	0
Bochtler, 12 C.S.-7 L.V.	1.000	19	5	11	0	0
Boucher, Las Vegas*	.950	24	5	14	1	0
Briscoe, Tacoma	1.000	9	0	3	0	0
Brocail, Las Vegas	1.000	10	3	9	0	0
Bross, Phoenix	.895	54	2	15	2	1
Brown, Phoenix*	.946	23	8	27	2	3
Brummett, Phoenix	.800	18	0	8	2	1
Brundage, Calgary*	1.000	4	1	3	0	0
Bruske, Tucson	.944	12	4	13	1	1
Buckley, Colorado Springs	1.000	6	0	1	0	0
Burcham, Vancouver	1.000	13	0	1	0	0
Burke, Colorado Springs	1.000	8	2	12	0	2
Bustillos, Albuquerque	1.000	20	1	8	0	0
Butcher, Vancouver	.667	14	0	4	2	1
Campbell, Tacoma	1.000	40	6	7	0	0
Capel, Tucson	.889	25	2	6	1	0
Carlson, Phoenix	1.000	13	6	5	0	0
Carman, Calgary*	1.000	6	0	4	0	0
Carter, Phoenix	.857	7	3	3	1	0
Casian, Portland*	1.000	7	1	1	0	0
Chapin, Portland	.857	47	2	10	2	1
Charland, Vancouver*	1.000	6	0	1	0	0

Player, Team	Pct.	G	PO	A	E	DP
Chitren, Tacoma	1.000	14	2	3	0	1
Compres, Las Vegas	1.000	24	0	4	0	0
Converse, Calgary	.929	23	8	18	2	4
Costello, Tucson	1.000	14	4	10	0	1
Cummings, Calgary*	.867	11	5	8	2	1
Czarkowski, Calgary*	1.000	9	3	7	0	0
Daal, Albuquerque*	1.000	6	0	2	0	0
Darwin, Edmonton	1.000	25	0	3	0	1
Davis, Las Vegas	.857	34	5	7	2	1
Dayley, Albuquerque*	1.000	9	0	1	0	0
DeLucia, Calgary	1.000	8	1	4	0	0
Dixon, Tucson	.833	50	5	20	5	1
Drees, Portland*	.974	31	14	23	1	2
Edens, Tucson	1.000	5	1	1	0	1
Egloff, Vancouver	1.000	12	0	2	0	0
Elliott, Las Vegas	1.000	8	4	4	0	0
Ettles, Las Vegas	.889	47	3	5	1	0
Farrell, Vancouver	.929	12	3	10	1	1
Fisher, Phoenix	1.000	14	6	8	0	0
Fredrickson, Colorado Springs	1.000	23	1	1	0	0
Fritz, Vancouver	1.000	8	4	8	0	0
Gamez, Vancouver*	1.000	9	0	1	0	0
Garces, Portland	1.000	35	6	13	0	1
Gleaton, Edmonton*	1.000	46	3	7	0	0
Grahe, Vancouver	1.000	4	3	1	0	0
Grant, 4 Tuc.-1 Van.	1.000	5	0	2	0	0
Grater, Calgary	1.000	9	0	3	0	0
Green, Vancouver*	.920	25	5	18	2	2
GROSS, Albuquerque	1.000	59	13	25	0	0
Gunderson, Calgary*	1.000	5	1	0	0	0
Guzman, Tacoma*	.958	20	5	18	1	1
Hamilton, Las Vegas	1.000	8	6	6	0	0
Hansell, Albuquerque	.917	26	8	14	2	1
Hanselman, Phoenix	.917	21	5	6	1	1
Harris, Las Vegas	.895	17	5	12	2	0
Hartsock, Phoenix	1.000	12	3	6	0	1
Hartgraves, Tucson*	.944	23	6	11	1	1
Hathaway, Vancouver*	.900	12	2	7	1	0
Hawblitzel, Colorado Springs	.940	29	22	25	3	6
Henry, Portland	.941	26	7	9	1	0
Hillegas, Tacoma	.857	9	1	5	1	0
Holman, Calgary	.909	21	5	15	2	1
Holmes, Colorado Springs	1.000	3	0	1	0	0
Holzemer, Vancouver*	.906	24	3	26	3	2
Horsman, Tacoma*	1.000	26	2	4	0	0
Hudek, Tucson	.857	13	2	4	1	0
Huisman, 14 Phoe.-2 Tuc.	1.000	16	5	3	0	0
Hurst, 1 L.V.-3 C.S.*	.750	4	1	5	2	0
Hurst, Albuquerque	1.000	18	5	9	0	1
Hurta, Tucson*	1.000	8	1	0	0	1
James, Albuquerque	1.000	16	0	3	0	0
Jeffcoat, Edmonton*	1.000	33	3	8	0	0
Jiminez, Tacoma	.909	8	3	7	1	2
Johnstone, Edmonton	.895	30	4	13	2	0
Jones, Tucson	1.000	41	1	10	0	0
Juden, Tucson	.900	27	10	17	3	2
Kent, Calgary	1.000	9	1	1	0	0
Knudson, Colorado Springs	.900	5	4	5	1	0
Kramer, Edmonton	1.000	46	8	7	0	0
Kutzler, Albuquerque	.939	35	13	18	2	0
LaPoint, Portland*	.933	13	2	12	1	0
Layana, Phoenix	.958	55	6	17	1	0
Leftwich, Vancouver	.885	20	9	14	3	0
Lemon, Edmonton	.923	21	5	7	1	0
Leskanic, Colorado Springs	1.000	9	2	5	0	1
Lewis, Vancouver	1.000	24	2	4	0	0
Linskey, Las Vegas*	.960	30	3	21	1	0
Mahomes, Portland	1.000	17	15	19	0	2
Marquez, Albuquerque	1.000	9	0	3	0	0
Marshall, Colorado Springs*	1.000	11	1	3	0	1
F. Martinez, Albuquerque*	1.000	4	0	4	0	0
Martinez, 13 Edm.-14 L.V.	.952	27	6	14	1	0
P.A. Martinez, Las Vegas*	.944	15	3	14	1	0
P.J. Martinez, Albuquerque	1.000	1	1	0	0	0
Mathews, Tucson	.667	16	4	0	2	0
McCullers, Calgary	.947	33	7	11	1	1
McGehee, Phoenix	1.000	4	1	5	0	1
McGraw, Edmonton*	1.000	5	2	1	0	0
Merriman, Portland	1.000	39	1	7	0	0
Metzinger, Colorado Springs	1.000	12	4	1	0	0
Miller, Edmonton	1.000	9	7	16	0	2
Mimbs, Albuquerque*	1.000	19	0	4	0	0
Minutelli, Phoenix*	.889	49	2	6	1	0
Moore, Colorado Springs	1.000	30	3	5	0	0
Munoz, Portland	1.000	5	2	6	0	0
Munoz, Colorado Springs*	.913	40	6	15	2	0
Myers, Phoenix	1.000	31	5	16	0	1
Myers, Edmonton*	.930	27	10	30	3	2
Neidlinger, Portland	1.000	29	9	10	0	1
Nelson, Calgary	1.000	5	0	4	0	1
Newlin, Edmonton	1.000	4	0	1	0	0
Nichols, Albuquerque	.955	21	8	13	1	2
Nielsen, Vancouver*	.818	33	1	8	2	1
Nolte, 10 Cal.-23 Albu.*	.900	33	1	8	1	0
Ontiveros, Portland	.966	20	14	14	1	1
Osteen, Tacoma*	1.000	16	7	16	0	2
Osuna, Tucson*	1.000	13	0	5	0	0
Painter, Colorado Springs*	.977	23	14	29	1	3
Parkins, Calgary	1.000	3	1	0	0	0
Patrick, Tacoma	.969	35	7	24	1	1
Peck, Vancouver	1.000	31	6	10	0	2
Peek, Tucson	1.000	60	5	15	0	0
Peltzer, Phoenix*	1.000	12	1	3	0	0
Pena, Las Vegas*	1.000	39	3	6	0	1
Percival, Vancouver	1.000	18	1	2	0	0
Perschke, Albuquerque	1.000	33	11	10	0	1
Phoenix, Tacoma	1.000	11	1	4	0	0
Pico, Vancouver	.625	18	0	5	3	0
Picota, Calgary	1.000	22	0	5	0	0
Powell, Calgary*	.909	12	2	8	1	0
Pulido, Portland*	1.000	33	6	23	0	3
Raczka, Tacoma*	1.000	55	6	10	0	0
Rambo, Phoenix	1.000	18	3	8	0	0
Rapp, Edmonton	.960	17	7	17	1	1
Reed, Colorado Springs	1.000	11	0	1	0	0
Remlinger, Calgary*	.875	19	6	15	3	2
Reynolds, Tucson	.886	25	6	25	4	1
Reynoso, Colorado Springs	1.000	4	2	8	0	0
Ridenour, Colorado Springs	.926	39	7	18	2	1
Robinson, Tucson	1.000	13	2	3	0	0
Sager, Las Vegas	.958	21	5	18	1	3
St. Claire, Calgary	.941	27	5	11	1	0
Sanders, Las Vegas	.941	24	14	18	2	1
Sanford, Colorado Springs	.933	20	7	7	1	3
Scheid, Edmonton*	1.000	38	5	16	0	2
Scott, Vancouver	.933	46	5	9	1	1
Seminara, Las Vegas	.870	21	11	9	3	0
Shepherd, Colorado Springs	.941	37	5	11	1	0
Shikles, Tacoma	.929	38	11	15	2	0
Shinall, Calgary	1.000	33	5	8	0	0
Sims, Portland*	.960	50	3	21	1	1
Slusarski, Tacoma	.950	24	4	15	1	2
Smith, Calgary	1.000	1	0	1	0	1
Smith, Tacoma	1.000	6	2	3	0	0
Smithberg, Tacoma	.941	28	3	13	1	2
Springer, Albuquerque	.912	35	7	24	3	0
Springer, Vancouver	.909	11	4	6	1	2
Stevens, Portland	.947	53	6	12	1	2
Strong, Las Vegas	.857	21	1	5	1	1
Swan, Calgary*	1.000	9	0	2	0	0
Swingle, Vancouver	.857	37	2	4	1	0
Taylor, Phoenix	1.000	49	8	18	0	1
Thompson, Colorado Springs	1.000	4	1	8	0	1
Torres, Phoenix	.923	14	8	16	2	0
Treadwell, Albuquerque	1.000	39	2	13	0	2
Tsamis, Portland*	1.000	3	0	1	0	0
Turner, Edmonton	1.000	12	1	1	0	0
Van Landingham, Phoenix	1.000	1	2	1	0	0
Van Poppel, Tacoma	.800	14	3	5	2	0
Van Ryn, Albuquerque*	1.000	6	2	2	0	0
Vatcher, Las Vegas	1.000	2	1	0	0	0
Veres, Tucson	.943	43	10	23	2	2
Vierra, Albuquerque*	.778	22	3	5	2	0
Wainhouse, Calgary	1.000	14	1	3	0	2
Walker, Calgary	1.000	28	8	16	0	2
Wall, Calgary	.974	25	7	30	1	3
Walter, Edmonton*	1.000	6	1	1	0	0
Walton, Tucson	1.000	13	0	1	0	0
Wapnick, Calgary	1.000	32	6	5	0	2
Wassenaar, 13 C.S.-21 Phoe.	.941	34	7	9	1	0
Weathers, Edmonton	.875	22	9	12	3	0
Wells, Colorado Springs*	1.000	16	1	4	0	0
Williams, Albuquerque	.920	65	8	15	2	4
Willis, Portland	.500	2	0	1	1	0
Wilson, Tacoma*	1.000	13	4	9	0	0
Windes, Tucson*	.833	13	3	2	1	0
Worrell, Las Vegas	.786	15	3	8	3	0
Yaughn, Edmonton	1.000	1	0	2	0	1
Young, Tacoma*	1.000	10	3	8	0	1
Young, Las Vegas	1.000	14	1	5	0	0
Zappelli, Vancouver	.909	17	1	9	1	1
Zavaras, Colorado Springs	1.000	6	1	0	0	0

The following players did not have any fielding statistics at the positions indicated or appeared only as a designated hitter, pinch-hitter or pinch-runner: Borrelli, p; Je. Brown, p; Brundage, of; M. Campbell, p; Capra, 2b; Case, ph; Cole, p; Dattola, p; Edenfield, p; Garrelts, p; Garrison, 3b; Gonzales, p; Higgins, of; Holley, of; C. Howard, of, p; M. Howard, p; B. Johnson, of; Killeen, dh; Kipila, p; Moore, of; Neel, dh, ph; Nied, p; R. Ortiz, p; Peters, 1b, 2b, ss, p; Reyes, p; Schunk, p; Seanez, p; Simms, p; Snyder, p; Trafton, of; Traxler, p; B. Williams, p; Witkowski, p; Todd Worrell, p.

Year	Team	Pct.
1903—	Los Angeles	.630
1904—	Tacoma	.589
	Tacoma§	.571
	Los Angeles§	.571
1905—	Tacoma	.583
	Los Angeles*	.604
1906—	Portland	.657
1907—	Los Angeles	.608
1908—	Los Angeles	.585
1909—	San Francisco	.623
1910—	Portland	.567
1911—	Portland	.589
1912—	Oakland	.591
1913—	Portland	.559
1914—	Portland	.574
1915—	San Francisco	.570
1916—	Los Angeles	.601
1917—	San Francisco	.561
1918—	Vernon	.569
	Los Angeles (2nd)x	.548
1919—	Vernon	.613
1920—	Vernon	.556
1921—	Los Angeles	.574
1922—	San Francisco	.638
1923—	San Francisco	.617
1924—	Seattle	.545
1925—	San Francisco	.643
1926—	Los Angeles	.599
1927—	Oakland	.615
1928—	San Francisco*	.630
	Sacramento§§	.626
	San Francisco§§	.626
1929—	Mission	.643
	Hollywood*	.592
1930—	Los Angeles	.576
	Hollywood*	.650
1931—	Hollywood	.626
	San Francisco*	.608
1932—	Portland	.587
1933—	Los Angeles	.610
1934—	Los Angeles z	.786
	Los Angeles z	.689
1935—	Los Angeles	.648
	San Francisco*	.608
1936—	Portland‡	.549
1937—	Sacramento	.573
	San Diego (3rd)†	.545

Year	Team	Pct.
1938—	Los Angeles	.590
	Sacramento (3rd)†	.537
1939—	Seattle	.589
	Sacramento (4th)†	.500
1940—	Seattle‡	.629
1941—	Seattle‡	.598
1942—	Sacramento	.590
	Seattle (3rd)†	.539
1943—	Los Angeles	.710
	S. Francisco (2nd)†	.574
1944—	Los Angeles	.586
	S. Francisco (3rd)†	.509
1945—	Portland	.622
	S. Francisco (4th)†	.525
1946—	San Francisco‡	.628
1947—	Los Angeles††	.567
1948—	Oakland‡	.606
1949—	Hollywood‡	.583
1950—	Oakland	.590
1951—	Seattle‡	.593
1952—	Hollywood	.606
1953—	Hollywood	.589
1954—	San Diego y	.604
1955—	Seattle	.552
1956—	Los Angeles	.637
1957—	San Francisco	.601
1958—	Phoenix	.578
1959—	Salt Lake City	.552
1960—	Spokane	.601
1961—	Tacoma	.630
1962—	San Diego	.604
1963—	Spokane	.620
	Oklahoma City a	.632
1964—	Arkansas	.609
	San Diego a	.576
1965—	Oklahoma City a	.628
	Portland	.547
1966—	Seattle a	.561
	Tulsa	.578
1967—	San Diego a	.574
	Spokane	.541
1968—	Tulsa a	.642
	Spokane	.586
1969—	Tacoma a	.589
	Eugene	.603
1970—	Spokane a	.644
	Hawaii	.671

Year	Team	Pct.
1971—	Salt Lake City	.534
	Tacoma	.545
1972—	Albuquerque	.622
	Eugene	.534
1973—	Tucson	.583
	Spokane a	.563
1974—	Spokane a	.549
	Albuquerque	.535
1975—	Salt Lake City	.556
	Hawaii a	.611
1976—	Salt Lake City	.625
	Hawaii a	.531
1977—	Phoenix a	.579
	Hawaii	.541
1978—	Tacoma b	.584
	Albuquerque b	.557
1979—	Albuquerque	.581
	Salt Lake City c	.541
1980—	Albuquerque	.578
	Hawaii	.539
1981—	Albuquerque*	.712
	Tacoma	.561
1982—	Albuquerque*	.594
	Spokane	.545
1983—	Albuquerque	.594
	Portland*	.528
1984—	Hawaii	.621
	Edmonton*	.486
1985—	Vancouver*	.522
	Phoenix	.563
1986—	Vancouver	.616
	Las Vegas*	.563
1987—	Calgary	.596
	Albuquerque*	.542
1988—	Vancouver	.599
	Las Vegas*	.529
1989—	Albuquerque	.563
	Vancouver*	.514
1990—	Albuquerque*	.641
	Edmonton	.553
1991—	Albuquerque	.580
	Tucson*	.564
1992—	Colorado Springs*	.596
	Portland	.576
1993—	Portland	.608
	Tucson*	.580

*Won split-season playoff. †Won four-team playoff. ‡Won pennant and four-team playoff. §Tied for second-half title with Tacoma winning playoff. §§Tied for second-half title, with Sacramento winning playoff. ††Ended regular season in tie with San Francisco and won one-game playoff for pennant, then won four-club playoff. xWon playoff from first-place Vernon and awarded championship. yDefeated Hollywood in one-game play-off for pennant. zWon both halves, no playoff. aLeague was divided into Northern, Southern divisions in 1963, 1969-70-71, and Eastern, Western divisions in 1964 through 1968 and 1972 through 1977, won two-team playoff. bLeague divided into Eastern and Western divisions, Tacoma and Albuquerque declared co-champions following cancellation of four-team playoff due to continuing rain and wet grounds. cWon second-half title and defeated Hawaii in four-team playoff.

EASTERN LEAGUE

FINAL STANDINGS

Team	Har.	C.A.	Bow.	Alb.	Bing.	Lon.	Read.	N.B.	W	L	T	Pct.	GB
Harrisburg (Expos)	....	13	12	9	13	15	15	17	94	44	0	.681	......
Canton-Akron (Indians)	7	....	12	13	10	8	13	12	75	63	0	.543	19
Bowie (Orioles)	8	8	....	10	12	11	11	12	72	68	0	.514	23
Albany (Yankees)	9	7	10	....	11	12	11	10	70	68	0	.507	24
Binghamton (Mets)	7	10	8	9	....	13	7	14	68	72	0	.486	27
London (Tigers)	5	10	9	8	7	....	13	11	63	75	0	.457	31
Reading (Phillies)	5	7	9	9	13	7	....	12	62	78	0	.443	33
New Britain (Red Sox)	3	8	8	10	6	9	8	....	52	88	0	.371	43

London club represented London, Ontario, Can.

Major league affiliations in parentheses.

Playoffs—Harrisburg defeated Albany, three games to one; Canton-Akron defeated Bowie, three games to two; Harrisburg defeated Canton-Akron, three games to two, to win league championship.

Regular-season attendance—Albany, 137,541; Binghamton, 225,467; Bowie, 254,861; Canton-Akron, 273,639; Harrisburg, 250,476; London, 103,840; New Britain, 140,915; Reading, 313,083. Total—1,699,822. Playoffs (14 games)—19,486. Class AA All-Star Game at Memphis—6,335.

Managers—Albany, Mike Hart (through June 27) and Bill Evers (from June 28); Binghamton, Steve Swisher; Bowie, Don Buford; Canton-Akron, Brian Graham; Harrisburg, Jim Tracy; London, Tom Runnells; New Britain, Jim Pankovits; Reading, Don McCormack. Managerial record of team with more than one manager: Albany, Hart (36-35), Evers (34-33).

All-Star team: 1B—Cliff Floyd, Harrisburg; 2B—Quilvio Veras, Binghamton; 3B—Butch Huskey, Binghamton; SS—Robert Eenhorn, Albany; OF—Manny Ramirez, Canton-Akron; Omar Ramirez, Canton-Akron; Rondell White, Harrisburg; C—Gregg Zaun, Bowie; DH—T.R. Lewis, Bowie; Alan Zinter, Binghamton; P—Albie Lopez, Canton-Akron; Felipe Lira, London; Gabe White, Harrisburg; Most Valuable Player—Cliff Floyd, Harrisburg; Pitcher of the Year—Joey Eischen, Harrisburg; Manager of the Year—Jim Tracy, Harrisburg.

BATTING

TEAM

Team	Avg.	G	AB	R	OR	H	TB	2B	3B	HR	RBI	SH	SF	HP	BB	Int. BB	SO	SB	CS	LOB
Harrisburg	.278	138	4672	802	569	1301	2125	230	42	170	738	44	32	47	507	23	1006	187	73	945
Canton-Akron	.273	138	4667	713	639	1276	1861	234	36	93	624	39	47	52	511	24	738	131	59	1014
Bowie	.264	140	4609	600	594	1219	1784	213	44	88	545	32	52	42	463	24	832	156	83	953
Albany	.261	138	4556	661	636	1189	1789	240	42	92	591	34	25	46	444	17	936	143	83	904
London	.259	138	4626	570	684	1197	1658	217	26	64	505	28	35	48	473	17	854	183	84	965
Binghamton	.253	140	4573	634	630	1159	1758	206	45	101	582	50	45	42	541	23	914	120	62	1007
Reading	.253	140	4569	551	651	1157	1657	186	37	80	506	40	31	44	417	15	881	113	53	951
New Britain	.234	140	4569	502	630	1069	1499	200	25	60	454	53	34	57	455	23	967	60	68	918

INDIVIDUAL

(Leading qualifiers for batting championship—378 or more plate appearances)

*Bats lefthanded.   †Switch-hitter.

Player, Team	Avg.	G	AB	R	H	TB	2B	3B	HR	RBI	SH	SF	HP	BB	Int. BB	SO	SB	CS
Ramirez, Manny, Canton-Akron	.340	89	344	67	117	200	32	0	17	79	0	5	2	45	10	68	2	2
Floyd, Cliff, Harrisburg*	.329	101	380	82	125	228	17	4	26	101	0	2	5	54	12	71	31	10
White, Rondell, Harrisburg	.328	90	372	72	122	194	16	10	12	52	0	3	5	22	1	72	21	6
Giles, Brian, Canton-Akron*	.327	123	425	64	139	192	17	6	8	64	7	4	4	57	4	43	18	12
Ramirez, Omar, Canton-Akron	.314	125	516	116	162	219	24	6	7	53	4	1	5	53	2	49	24	6
Veras, Quilvio, Binghamton†	.306	128	444	87	136	175	19	7	2	51	4	5	9	91	0	62	52	19
Lewis, T.R., Bowie	.304	127	480	73	146	191	26	2	5	64	0	7	3	36	4	80	22	8
Barnwell, Richard, Albany	.298	131	463	98	138	209	24	7	11	50	3	2	13	77	3	101	33	13
Wawruck, Jim, Bowie*	.297	128	475	59	141	184	21	5	4	44	5	2	1	43	3	66	28	12
Martin, Chris, Harrisburg	.294	116	395	68	116	162	23	1	7	54	7	3	6	40	2	48	16	7

Departmental leaders: G—Huskey, 139; AB—Huskey, 526; R—O. Ramirez, 116; H—O. Ramirez, 162; TB—Jordan, 234; 2B—Jordan, 33; 3B—Tyler, 17; HR—Floyd, Murray, 26; RBI—Floyd, 101; SH—Kimberlin, 11; SF—Alfonzo, 11; HP—Perry, 15; BB—Veras, 91; IBB—Floyd, 12; SO—Robertson, 126; SB—Penn, 53; CS—Veras, 19.

(All players—listed alphabetically)

Player, Team	Avg.	G	AB	R	H	TB	2B	3B	HR	RBI	SH	SF	HP	BB	Int. BB	SO	SB	CS
Alder, Jimmy, London	.193	42	119	8	23	32	7	1	0	7	0	0	0	11	0	42	2	1
Alfonzo, Ed, Bowie	.264	130	459	45	121	164	22	3	5	49	5	11	4	37	1	49	14	4
Allen, Ron, Reading	.182	15	11	1	2	4	0	1	0	3	0	0	0	1	0	4	0	0
Allison, Tom, Binghamton†	.200	63	130	16	26	37	7	2	0	5	3	0	1	20	0	34	5	0
Alstead, Jason, Bowie*	.298	53	124	25	37	53	4	3	2	13	3	1	2	11	1	18	12	5
Andrews, Shane, Harrisburg	.260	124	442	77	115	202	29	2	18	70	1	4	1	64	2	118	10	6
Ausanio, Joe, Harrisburg	.000	19	1	0	0	0	0	0	0	0	0	0	0	0	0	0	0	0
Baines, Harold, Bowie*	.000	2	6	0	0	0	0	0	0	0	0	0	0	1	0	1	0	0
Barker, Tim, Harrisburg	.308	49	185	40	57	87	10	1	4	16	6	2	2	30	0	32	7	4
Barnwell, Richard, Albany	.298	131	463	98	138	209	24	7	11	50	3	2	13	77	3	101	33	13
Batista, Miguel, Harrisburg	.250	26	20	2	5	6	1	0	0	3	1	0	0	2	0	9	0	0
Bautista, Danny, London	.285	117	424	55	121	162	21	1	6	48	4	6	2	32	1	69	28	12
Beams, Mike, New Britain	.236	84	263	26	62	95	16	1	5	36	4	0	2	28	1	74	3	4
Bell, David, Canton-Akron*	.292	129	483	69	141	192	20	2	9	60	2	6	3	43	0	54	3	4
Bethea, Scott, New Britain*	.228	117	395	47	90	105	13	1	0	30	8	4	2	32	4	48	3	4
Bieser, Steve, Reading†	.312	53	170	21	53	68	6	3	1	19	1	0	2	15	1	24	9	5
Bradbury, Miah, Harrisburg	.313	9	32	4	10	18	5	0	1	6	1	0	0	1	0	1	0	0

Player, Team	Avg.	G	AB	R	H	TB	2B	3B	HR	RBI	SH	SF	HP	BB	Int. BB	SO	SB	CS
Brady, Pat, Reading*	.236	46	140	23	33	56	8	0	5	14	2	1	2	30	1	28	1	3
Brito, Mario, Harrisburg	.000	36	2	0	0	0	0	0	0	0	0	0	0	0	0	1	0	0
Brown, Bryan, New Britain	.230	34	113	13	26	42	5	1	3	17	0	3	3	11	0	20	0	0
Brown, Greg, Reading	.167	18	6	0	1	1	0	0	0	0	0	0	0	1	0	3	0	0
Bryant, Shawn, Canton-Akron	.000	27	0	0	0	0	0	0	0	0	0	0	1	0	0	0	0	0
Butterfield, Chris, Binghamton†	.211	77	237	32	50	97	10	5	9	37	2	4	1	24	1	72	0	4
Cameron, Stanton, Bowie	.276	118	384	65	106	198	27	1	21	64	0	6	6	84	2	103	6	7
Carpenter, Bubba, Albany*	.321	14	53	8	17	27	4	0	2	14	0	1	0	7	0	4	2	2
Carroll, Kevin, New Britain	.149	56	168	9	25	31	6	0	0	6	4	0	1	6	0	58	1	1
Carter, Andy, Reading*	.000	4	2	0	0	0	0	0	0	0	3	0	0	0	0	0	0	0
Castillo, Juan, Binghamton	.067	26	15	0	1	1	0	0	0	0	0	0	0	0	0	8	0	0
Chick, Bruce, New Britain	.259	55	193	20	50	69	8	1	3	14	2	2	1	8	0	39	2	3
Colombino, Carlo, Reading	.228	86	325	31	74	90	8	1	2	22	2	1	3	19	0	48	4	5
Corbin, Archie, Harrisburg	.000	42	3	0	0	0	0	0	0	0	0	0	0	0	0	1	0	0
Cornelius, Brian, London*	.262	64	229	21	60	83	11	0	4	24	2	0	3	23	4	36	1	4
Cornelius, Reid, Harrisburg	.154	27	13	2	2	2	0	0	0	0	1	0	0	0	0	6	0	0
Crowley, Jim, New Britain	.241	109	369	49	89	143	19	1	11	51	4	2	4	59	0	95	3	7
Daniel, Mike, Harrisburg	.333	3	6	1	2	4	1	0	1	0	0	0	0	0	0	1	0	0
Davis, Glenn, Bowie	.333	2	6	2	2	6	1	0	1	1	0	0	0	1	0	1	0	0
Davis, Jay, Binghamton*	.279	119	409	52	114	140	15	4	1	35	2	3	1	21	2	71	5	7
Decillis, Dean, London	.293	54	208	28	61	89	13	0	5	26	0	1	0	25	1	22	1	0
Dedrick, Jim, Bowie†	.000	39	2	0	0	0	0	0	0	0	1	0	0	0	0	0	0	0
Delgado, Alex, New Britain	.184	33	87	10	16	21	2	0	1	9	4	2	4	4	0	11	2	1
Dellicarri, Joe, Binghamton	.250	85	252	37	63	83	15	1	1	19	6	2	3	30	2	49	2	2
Devarez, Cesar, Bowie	.224	57	174	14	39	48	7	1	0	17	2	2	2	5	0	21	5	1
Devereaux, Mike, Bowie	.286	2	7	1	2	3	1	0	0	2	0	0	0	0	0	2	0	0
DeBerry, Joe, Albany*	.256	125	446	58	114	183	19	7	12	63	2	5	3	24	1	111	3	7
DeHart, Rick, Harrisburg	.000	12	3	0	0	0	0	0	0	0	0	0	0	1	0	3	0	0
Diaz, Rafael, Harrisburg	.000	32	3	0	0	0	0	0	0	0	1	0	1	0	1	2	2	0
Dixon, Colin, New Britain	.210	66	214	11	45	64	10	0	3	22	2	1	5	9	0	47	1	2
Doolan, Blake, Reading	.000	27	5	0	0	0	0	0	0	0	0	0	0	0	0	2	0	0
Dorn, Chris, Binghamton	.000	23	1	0	0	0	0	0	0	0	0	0	0	0	0	0	0	0
Douma, Todd, Binghamton*	.000	15	3	0	0	0	0	0	0	0	0	0	0	0	0	1	0	0
Dziadkowiec, Andy, Binghamton*	.210	67	176	19	37	54	12	1	1	18	3	2	0	18	1	38	0	1
Eenhoorn, Robert, Albany*	.280	82	314	48	88	136	24	3	6	46	3	3	1	21	1	39	3	5
Eischen, Joey, Harrisburg*	.188	20	16	2	3	5	2	0	0	1	1	0	0	0	0	6	0	0
Erickson, Greg, Albany†	.100	3	10	2	1	1	0	0	0	0	0	0	0	2	0	1	0	0
Escobar, John, Reading	.193	65	202	15	39	52	4	0	3	17	3	1	0	16	1	42	0	1
Farmer, Mike, Reading†	.182	23	11	0	2	2	0	0	0	0	1	0	0	1	0	3	1	1
Fernandez, Jose, Reading*	.248	38	129	8	32	46	5	0	3	18	2	1	0	12	0	37	0	0
Fernandez, Sid, Binghamton*	.000	2	1	0	0	0	0	0	0	0	1	0	0	0	0	0	0	0
Ferretti, Sam, Bowie	.238	60	164	24	39	57	6	0	4	18	3	3	0	18	0	30	2	2
Figga, Mike, Albany	.227	6	22	3	5	5	0	0	0	1	0	0	0	2	0	9	1	0
Fitzpatrick, Rob, Harrisburg	.226	99	341	44	77	122	10	1	11	46	2	2	5	36	0	82	6	8
Flannelly, Tim, Albany*	.272	53	184	21	50	69	9	2	2	18	1	1	1	10	0	30	5	1
Flores, Miguel, Canton-Akron	.292	116	435	73	127	166	20	5	3	54	4	3	3	59	0	39	36	9
Floyd, Cliff, Harrisburg*	.329	101	380	82	125	228	17	4	26	101	0	2	5	54	12	71	31	10
Fox, Andy, Albany*	.275	65	236	44	65	92	16	1	3	24	2	0	2	32	1	54	12	6
Friedman, Jason, New Britain*	.248	81	294	22	73	93	15	1	1	24	1	4	3	20	4	50	2	0
Fulton, Greg, Harrisburg†	.000	1	4	0	0	0	0	0	0	0	0	0	0	0	0	3	0	0
Gaddy, Bob, Reading	.000	22	3	0	0	0	0	0	0	0	1	0	0	0	0	2	0	0
Geisler, Phil, Reading	.270	48	178	25	48	73	14	1	3	14	1	0	3	17	2	50	4	2
Giles, Brian, Canton-Akron*	.327	123	425	64	139	192	17	6	8	64	7	4	4	57	4	43	18	12
Givens, Jim, London†	.263	82	262	24	69	92	8	3	3	28	5	4	2	16	2	45	17	3
Goedhart, Darrell, Reading	.333	27	12	2	4	4	0	0	0	1	0	0	0	1	0	2	0	0
Goergen, Todd, Reading†	.000	3	4	2	0	0	0	0	0	0	0	0	0	1	0	2	0	0
Gonzalez, Javier, Binghamton	.230	94	257	30	59	96	7	0	10	36	0	3	5	24	0	65	0	0
Gonzalez, Pete, London	.156	25	64	5	10	13	3	0	0	6	0	1	2	14	0	12	0	0
Grable, Rob, Reading	.233	37	120	10	28	37	4	1	1	10	0	1	1	18	1	27	2	1
Griffin, Mark, Harrisburg*	.151	24	53	5	8	10	2	0	0	6	1	1	1	1	0	9	5	1
Hammonds, Jeffrey, Bowie	.283	24	92	13	26	38	3	0	3	10	1	1	2	9	0	18	4	3
Hankins, Mike, Albany†	.223	63	175	16	39	41	2	0	0	12	5	1	0	29	0	27	2	2
Hardge, Mike, Harrisburg	.244	99	386	70	94	147	15	10	6	35	3	1	3	37	0	97	27	8
Harriger, Denny, Binghamton	.125	35	16	1	2	2	0	0	0	0	1	0	1	1	0	5	0	0
Harvey, Raymond, Canton-Akron*	.244	14	41	5	10	11	1	0	0	4	3	1	1	7	0	5	0	1
Hatteberg, Scott, New Britain*	.278	68	227	35	63	98	10	2	7	28	1	0	1	42	3	38	1	3
Haynes, Heath, Harrisburg	.250	57	4	0	1	1	0	0	0	0	0	0	0	0	0	1	0	0
Henderson, Rod, Harrisburg	.333	5	3	0	1	2	1	0	0	1	0	0	0	0	0	2	0	0
Hernandez, Jose, Canton-Akron	.200	45	150	19	30	42	6	0	2	17	1	0	0	10	0	39	9	2
Higginson, Bob, London*	.308	63	224	25	69	104	15	4	4	35	0	3	0	19	0	37	4	3
Hill, Eric, Reading	.000	21	3	0	0	0	0	0	0	1	0	0	0	0	0	2	0	0
Holland, Tim, Bowie	.249	130	449	49	112	166	17	5	9	53	2	2	3	25	1	123	9	8
Holman, Craig, Reading†	.455	24	11	2	5	8	0	0	1	1	1	0	0	0	0	2	0	3
Horne, Tyrone, Harrisburg*	.359	35	128	22	46	68	8	1	4	22	1	0	1	22	0	37	3	2
Howard, Tim, Harrisburg*	.300	28	100	13	30	44	6	1	2	15	0	3	0	23	1	8	2	0
Hunter, Bert, Binghamton	.224	92	308	38	69	100	10	3	5	30	6	2	3	24	0	85	9	7
Huskey, Butch, Binghamton	.251	139	526	72	132	232	23	1	25	98	0	2	8	48	3	102	11	2
Hyde, Mickey, Reading	.285	94	277	32	79	104	6	2	5	30	2	2	1	14	0	43	3	4
Jackson, Jeff, Reading	.238	113	374	45	89	136	14	3	9	51	1	1	2	30	1	117	20	8
Jacobs, Frank, Binghamton*	.269	109	346	50	93	143	17	3	9	46	0	0	4	42	3	72	2	3
Jacome, Jason, Binghamton*	.091	14	11	3	1	1	0	0	0	0	1	0	0	2	0	1	0	0
Jordan, Kevin, Albany	.283	135	513	87	145	234	33	4	16	87	0	4	9	41	2	53	8	4
Kimberlin, Keith, Reading†	.264	137	504	56	133	158	13	3	2	29	11	3	5	57	1	70	19	7
Krause, Ron, Harrisburg*	.288	17	59	12	17	27	5	1	1	8	0	1	1	4	0	14	2	0
Leach, Jalal, Albany*	.282	125	457	64	129	208	19	9	14	79	0	4	1	47	3	113	15	12
Ledesma, Aaron, Binghamton	.267	66	206	23	55	82	12	0	5	22	4	1	2	14	0	43	2	1
Lennon, Pat, Canton-Akron	.257	45	152	24	39	60	7	1	4	23	0	2	1	30	1	45	4	2
Leshnock, Donnie, Albany*	.000	1	3	0	0	0	0	0	0	0	0	0	0	0	0	0	0	0
Lewis, Mica, Reading	.189	74	243	29	46	62	12	2	0	16	1	1	1	32	0	47	13	2
Lewis, T.R., Bowie	.304	127	480	73	146	191	26	2	5	64	0	7	3	36	4	80	22	8
Livesey, Jeff, Albany	.154	32	104	6	16	20	4	0	0	6	4	0	0	7	0	22	0	0
Lockett, Ron, Reading†	.242	105	368	53	89	150	18	5	11	53	2	3	2	27	3	79	12	2
Long, Steve, Binghamton	.333	38	12	1	4	4	0	0	0	0	2	1	0	1	0	3	0	0
Looney, Brian, Harrisburg*	.000	8	3	0	0	0	0	0	0	0	0	0	0	0	0	3	0	0

Player, Team	Avg.	G	AB	R	H	TB	2B	3B	HR	RBI	SH	SF	HP	BB	Int. BB	SO	SB	CS
Lopez, Luis, Canton-Akron	.277	60	231	30	64	86	16	0	2	41	2	3	5	13	0	16	0	3
Lowery, David, Binghamton†	.050	12	20	0	1	3	0	1	0	0	0	1	0	0	0	5	0	0
Mahay, Ron, New Britain*	.120	8	25	2	3	6	0	0	1	2	0	0	0	1	0	6	1	0
Marchok, Chris, Reading*	1.000	40	1	0	1	1	0	0	0	0	0	0	0	0	0	0	0	0
Marrero, Oreste, Harrisburg*	.333	85	255	39	85	135	18	1	10	49	3	4	0	22	2	46	3	3
Marshall, Randy, Binghamton*	.000	7	1	0	0	0	0	0	0	0	2	0	0	0	0	0	0	0
Martin, Chris, Harrisburg	.294	116	395	68	116	162	23	1	7	54	7	3	6	40	2	48	16	7
Martindale, Ryan, Canton-Akron	.219	105	310	44	68	119	19	1	10	39	4	3	9	23	0	71	1	3
Martinez, Chito, Bowie*	.077	5	13	5	1	1	0	0	0	0	0	0	0	2	0	2	0	0
Mendenhall, Kirk, London	.204	97	275	41	56	66	5	1	1	18	4	3	5	30	0	45	21	4
Millares, Jose, Bowie	.280	30	50	6	14	19	1	2	0	5	2	0	7	1	0	9	1	1
Miller, Brent, Bowie*	.257	113	404	35	104	150	13	0	11	66	0	4	2	19	5	41	6	1
Milne, Darren, London*	.050	5	20	2	1	1	0	0	0	0	0	0	0	2	0	7	0	0
Mitchell, John, New Britain	.000	8	2	0	0	0	0	0	0	0	0	0	0	0	0	1	0	0
Moler, Jason, Reading	.283	38	138	15	39	56	11	0	2	19	0	1	2	12	0	31	1	1
Moore, Boo, New Britain	.209	96	301	35	63	106	8	1	11	32	0	2	4	32	3	102	1	7
Morrison, Jim, New Britain	.221	77	249	30	55	79	10	1	4	25	4	1	3	29	0	81	11	8
Mota, Carlos, Canton-Akron	.286	35	84	12	24	25	1	0	0	10	2	0	0	4	0	12	2	2
Mouton, Lyle, Albany	.255	135	491	74	125	201	22	3	16	76	2	1	7	50	2	125	18	14
Murray, Glenn, Harrisburg	.253	127	475	82	120	227	21	4	26	96	0	2	8	56	1	111	16	7
Norris, Bill, New Britain*	.259	119	398	43	103	137	17	4	3	36	8	2	1	21	1	69	4	6
Nuneviller, Thomas, Reading	.230	71	226	24	52	69	11	0	2	32	0	1	3	16	0	23	3	0
Obando, Sherman, Bowie	.241	19	58	8	14	25	2	0	3	12	0	3	1	9	0	11	1	0
Odor, Rouglas, Canton-Akron	.209	86	263	39	55	77	9	2	3	18	3	3	1	22	0	65	10	3
Ortiz, Bo, Bowie	.200	8	30	1	6	8	0	1	0	3	2	0	1	1	0	5	0	0
Oster, Paul, Albany†	.208	39	106	11	22	31	7	1	0	8	2	0	1	6	0	27	1	0
Otero, Ricky, Binghamton*	.264	124	503	63	133	180	21	10	2	54	7	4	7	38	2	57	29	15
Peguero, Julio, Canton-Akron†	.226	65	177	19	40	56	6	5	0	14	4	1	1	17	1	32	5	1
Pemberton, Rudy, London	.276	124	471	70	130	205	22	4	15	67	0	3	12	24	1	80	14	12
Penn, Shannon, London†	.260	128	493	78	128	153	13	6	0	36	7	4	8	54	1	95	53	17
Perez, Yorkis, Harrisburg*	.000	34	1	0	0	0	0	0	0	0	0	0	0	0	0	1	0	0
Perona, Joe, London	.269	102	349	34	94	130	17	2	5	29	3	2	4	28	1	56	2	5
Perry, Herbert, Canton-Akron	.269	89	327	52	88	138	21	1	9	55	0	6	15	37	2	47	7	4
Pineda, Jose, Albany	.150	38	107	12	16	24	2	0	2	12	1	1	2	11	0	40	0	0
Posada, Jorge, Albany	.280	7	25	3	7	7	0	0	0	0	0	0	0	2	0	7	0	0
Pratte, Evan, London†	.238	121	408	44	97	134	24	2	3	46	1	3	3	45	2	77	5	2
Pride, Curtis, Harrisburg*	.356	50	180	51	64	121	6	3	15	39	2	2	4	12	0	36	21	5
Ramirez, Danny, Bowie	.065	15	31	3	2	2	0	0	0	0	0	0	1	1	0	6	0	0
Ramirez, Manny, Canton-Akron	.340	89	344	67	117	200	32	0	17	79	0	5	2	45	10	68	2	2
Ramirez, Omar, Canton-Akron	.314	125	516	116	162	219	24	6	7	53	4	1	5	53	2	49	24	6
Rappoli, Paul, New Britain*	.213	115	356	49	76	111	16	5	3	26	6	2	6	64	4	77	6	9
Reich, Andy, Binghamton	1.000	24	1	0	1	1	0	0	0	1	0	0	0	0	0	0	0	0
Rendina, Mike, London*	.282	135	475	59	134	196	30	1	10	77	0	3	0	55	1	96	8	4
Rice, Lance, Harrisburg†	.235	46	136	12	32	45	10	0	1	20	2	2	0	16	0	22	0	1
Roa, Joe, Binghamton	.000	32	4	0	0	0	0	0	0	0	0	0	0	0	0	1	0	0
Robertson, Jason, Albany*	.228	130	483	65	110	166	30	4	6	41	3	2	4	43	3	126	35	12
Rodriguez, Carlos, Albany†	.368	38	152	16	56	72	14	1	0	30	5	0	2	12	1	9	2	4
Rodriguez, Tony, New Britain	.228	99	355	37	81	105	16	4	0	31	4	5	4	16	0	52	8	7
Rosado, Ed, Reading†	.171	31	76	6	13	16	3	0	0	9	0	0	1	4	1	12	0	1
Roso, Jimmy, Bowie†	.231	52	117	12	27	32	5	0	0	9	1	1	4	10	0	35	2	1
Rueter, Kirk, Harrisburg*	.250	9	8	1	2	2	0	0	0	0	1	0	0	0	0	0	0	0
Rundels, Matt, Harrisburg	.342	34	117	27	40	63	5	0	6	17	0	0	2	14	0	31	8	2
Rusk, Troy, Reading*	.243	41	144	14	35	61	6	1	6	26	0	2	0	11	0	45	0	0
Saltzgaber, Brian, London	.212	87	241	28	51	68	9	1	2	17	1	2	5	41	1	59	13	3
Sanchez, Gordon, Albany	.215	65	195	23	42	56	11	0	1	21	1	0	2	19	0	34	3	1
Sanders, Tracy, Canton-Akron*	.213	42	136	20	29	54	6	2	5	20	0	1	1	31	1	30	4	1
Sandy, Tim, Binghamton*	.242	70	157	29	38	65	8	2	5	26	3	1	1	30	1	26	0	1
Sarbaugh, Mike, Canton-Akron	.249	85	277	29	69	110	13	5	6	31	0	4	0	20	1	44	3	3
Schall, Gene, Reading	.326	82	285	51	93	158	12	4	15	60	0	3	10	24	0	56	2	1
Sellers, Rick, London	.264	72	239	31	63	92	11	0	6	31	0	0	0	45	2	55	5	3
Silcox, Rusty, Binghamton	.000	3	1	0	0	0	0	0	0	0	0	0	0	0	0	0	0	0
Simons, Mitch, Harrisburg	.234	29	77	5	18	21	1	1	0	5	2	1	0	7	0	14	2	0
Skinner, Joel, Canton-Akron	.239	15	46	6	11	20	3	0	2	5	1	0	0	6	0	16	0	0
Sparks, Greg, Canton-Akron*	.231	35	117	11	27	48	9	0	4	23	1	3	0	18	2	33	0	1
Sued, Nick, Canton-Akron	.254	24	63	5	16	21	2	0	1	6	1	0	0	4	0	8	0	0
Tatum, Willie, New Britain†	.276	43	152	25	42	52	7	0	1	21	0	0	8	20	0	38	4	5
Taylor, Sam, Reading*	.277	49	173	31	48	75	12	0	5	27	1	4	1	30	0	24	9	3
Thomas, Mike, Harrisburg*	.250	25	4	1	1	2	1	0	0	1	0	0	0	1	0	3	0	0
Thoutsis, Paul, New Britain*	.291	64	213	17	62	78	12	2	0	21	1	2	0	27	1	24	0	2
Tokheim, David, Reading*	.292	65	257	30	75	104	11	6	2	25	3	0	0	12	0	36	9	6
Tovar, Edgar, Harrisburg	.262	12	42	5	11	11	0	0	0	3	1	0	1	0	0	4	0	1
Tyler, Brad, Bowie*	.236	129	437	85	103	191	24	17	10	44	1	3	1	84	2	89	24	11
Urbina, Ugueth, Harrisburg	.000	11	10	0	0	0	0	0	0	0	3	0	0	0	0	7	0	0
Vargas, Hector, Canton-Akron	.222	29	90	9	20	25	2	0	1	8	0	0	2	12	0	22	3	0
Velarde, Randy, Albany	.235	5	17	2	4	7	0	0	1	2	0	0	0	2	0	2	0	0
Veras, Quilvio, Binghamton†	.306	128	444	87	136	175	19	7	2	51	4	5	9	91	0	62	52	19
Walker, Pete, Binghamton	.250	45	4	0	1	1	0	0	0	1	2	1	0	0	0	1	0	0
Waller, Casey, Reading†	.260	53	169	25	44	66	8	4	2	18	1	4	5	15	3	20	1	0
Wallin, Les, New Britain*	.231	69	195	22	45	64	10	0	3	23	0	2	4	26	2	37	1	3
Washington, Kyle, Bowie	.252	120	389	50	98	150	23	4	7	33	4	5	2	39	3	96	16	12
Wawruck, Jim, Bowie*	.297	128	475	59	141	184	21	5	4	44	5	2	1	43	3	66	28	12
White, Derrick, Harrisburg	.228	21	79	14	18	25	1	0	2	12	0	1	2	5	0	17	2	0
White, Gabe, Harrisburg*	.125	16	8	1	1	2	1	0	0	0	0	0	0	0	0	4	0	0
White, Rondell, Harrisburg	.328	90	372	72	122	194	16	10	12	52	0	3	5	22	1	72	21	6
Wiegandt, Scott, Reading*	.000	56	2	0	0	0	0	0	0	0	1	0	0	0	0	0	0	0
Williams, Ted, London	.240	32	125	17	30	38	8	0	0	4	1	0	2	12	2	21	10	5
Wilstead, Randy, Harrisburg*	.259	45	108	10	28	47	7	0	4	15	0	1	0	12	2	21	1	1
Winston, Darrin, Harrisburg	.000	24	0	0	0	0	0	0	0	0	0	0	0	1	0	0	0	0
Woods, Tyrone, Harrisburg	.252	106	318	51	80	145	15	1	16	59	2	1	2	35	0	77	4	1
Zaun, Gregg, Bowie†	.306	79	258	25	79	98	15	0	3	38	0	1	1	27	4	26	4	7
Zinter, Alan, Binghamton†	.262	134	432	68	113	217	24	4	24	87	0	5	1	90	7	105	1	0

The following pitchers, listed alphabetically by club, with games in parentheses, had no plate appearances, primarily through use of designated hitters:

ALBANY—Batchelor, Rich (36); Carper, Mark (25); Dunbar, Matt (15); Faw, Brian (45); Frazier, Ron (12); Garagozzo, Keith (17); Gogolewski, Doug (13); Haller, Jim (41); Hines, Rich (14); Hodges, Darren (30); Jean, Domingo (11); Karp, Ryan (3); Ojala, Kirt (1); Pettitte, Andy (1); Polak, Rich (21); Popplewell, Tom (34); Prybylinski, Bruce (2); Quirico, Rafael (36); Taylor, Brien (27); Witt, Mike (1).

BINGHAMTON—Gunderson, Eric (20); Guzik, Bob (15); Knackert, Brent (15); McCready, Jim (14); Miller, Pat (2); Rogers, Bryan (62).

BOWIE—Borowski, Joe (9); Chaves, Rafael (45); DuBois, Brian (13); Farrar, Terry (24); Forney, Rick (1); Krivda, Rick (22); Mercedes, Jose (26); Mussina, Mike (2); Paveloff, Dave (32); Ricci, Chuck (34); Ryan, Kevin (16); Satre, Jason (13); Schullstrom, Erik (24); Smith, Daryl (3); Smith, Mark (5); Taylor, Tom (40); Valenzuela, Fernando (1); Wood, Brian (8).

CANTON-AKRON—Abbott, Paul (13); Alexander, Jerry (6); Allen, Chad (18); Byrd, Paul (2); Charland, Colin (5); Dyer, Mike (17); Embree, Alan (1); Garcia, Apolinar (42); Gardella, Mike (21); Hernandez, Fernando (2); Jones, Calvin (43); Lopez, Albie (16); McCarthy, Greg (33); Mlicki, Dave (6); Nagy, Charles (2); Power, Ted (7); Rivera, Roberto (8); Robinson, Napoleon (9); Romanoli, Paul (30); Shuey, Paul (27); Soper, Mike (8); Stone, Eric (13); Trice, Walt (19); Turek, Joe (3); Valdez, Rafael (5); Veres, Randolf (13); Wilkins, Mike (11).

HARRISBURG—Johnson, Chris (1); Puig, Benito (14).

LONDON—Blomdahl, Ben (17); Braley, Jeff (9); Carlyle, Ken (12); Edmondson, Brian (5); Garcia, Mike (6); Gomez, Henrique (29); Greene, Rich (23); Guilfoyle, Mike (49); Henry, Jim (33); Kelley, Rich (7); Lima, Jose (27); Lira, Felipe (22); Lumley, Mike (27); Pfaff, Jason (23); Schwarber, Tom (48); Stidham, Phil (33); Thompson, Justin (14); Undorf, Bob (19); Warren, Brian (22); Wolf, Steve (14).

NEW BRITAIN—Carter, Glenn (12); Ciccarella, Joe (30); Dzafic, Bernhard (45); Fischer, Tom (16); Hansen, Brent (15); Hoy, Pete (51); Mintz, Steve (43); Mosley, Tony (15); Painter, Gary (14); Riley, Ed (14); Rodriguez, Francisco (28); Shea, John (48); Smith, Tim (28); Uhrhan, Kevin (9); Vanegmond, Tim (29).

READING—Borland, Toby (44); Bottalico, Ricky (49); Hassinger, Brad (1); Sullivan, Mike (31).

GRAND SLAMS—Barnwell, Crowley, 2 each; Bautista, Carpenter, Eenhoorn, Fitzpatrick, Giles, Huskey, Jackson, Jordan, Lockett, Murray, Pemberton, Rendina, Sanders, 1 each.

AWARDED FIRST BASE ON CATCHER'S INTERFERENCE—Jackson 4 (Carroll, Hatteberg, Pineda, Posada); Hardge 2 (Hatteberg, Livesey); Hankins 2 (J. Gonzalez 2); Carroll (Mota); Griffin (Moler); Jacobs (Carroll); Lopez (Hatteberg); Tyler (P. Gonzalez); Wawruck (Martindale).

PITCHING

TEAM

Team	ERA	G	CG	ShO	Sv.	IP	H	R	ER	HR	HB	BB	Int. BB	SO	WP	Bk.
Harrisburg	3.48	138	8	10	36	1212.0	1086	569	469	75	48	538	19	1056	66	18
Bowie	3.67	140	12	9	35	1215.1	1179	594	495	86	30	453	13	887	57	13
New Britain	3.94	140	12	7	26	1235.1	1228	630	541	68	55	454	34	863	65	25
Albany	3.95	138	7	6	37	1181.2	1124	636	519	82	39	509	20	902	79	18
Binghamton	4.08	140	12	12	34	1201.2	1295	630	545	98	53	387	6	717	52	11
Canton-Akron	4.27	138	4	6	43	1202.2	1176	639	571	101	57	536	26	966	80	17
Reading	4.31	140	8	12	37	1191.0	1224	651	571	106	40	429	24	823	61	17
London	4.32	138	12	5	30	1218.2	1255	684	585	112	56	505	24	914	68	35

INDIVIDUAL

(Leading qualifiers for earned-run average leadership—112 or more innings)

*Throws lefthanded.

Pitcher, Team	W	L	Pct.	ERA	G	GS	CG	GF	ShO	Sv.	IP	H	R	ER	HR	HB	BB	Int. BB	SO	WP
Harriger, Binghamton	13	10	.565	2.95	35	24	4	4	3	1	170.2	174	69	56	8	7	40	0	89	9
Krivda, Bowie*	7	5	.583	3.08	22	22	0	0	0	0	125.2	114	46	43	10	2	50	0	108	1
Lira, London	10	4	.714	3.38	22	22	2	0	0	0	152.0	157	63	57	16	6	39	2	122	10
Taylor, Albany*	13	7	.650	3.48	27	27	1	0	0	0	163.0	127	83	63	7	8	102	0	150	12
Farrar, Bowie*	7	7	.500	3.49	24	21	2	0	0	0	116.0	114	51	45	10	4	40	0	85	5
Eischen, Harrisburg*	14	4	.778	3.62	20	20	0	0	0	0	119.1	122	62	48	11	4	60	0	110	9
Blomdahl, London	6	6	.500	3.71	17	17	3	0	0	0	119.0	108	58	49	7	7	42	1	72	4
Bryant, Canton-Akron*	10	5	.667	3.72	27	27	0	0	0	0	172.0	179	80	71	11	7	61	3	111	11
Rodriguez, New Britain	7	11	.389	3.74	28	26	4	1	1	0	170.2	147	79	71	17	4	78	4	151	7
Smith, New Britain	7	13	.350	3.79	28	28	3	0	1	0	180.1	192	91	76	9	11	44	5	81	5

Departmental leaders: G—Rogers, 62; W—Eischen, 14; L—Holman, Lima, T. Smith, 13; Pct.—Eischen, .778; GS—Vanegmond, 29; CG—Harriger, Holman, Long, Rodriguez, 4; GF—Schwarber, 42; ShO—Harriger, 3; Sv.—Jones, 22; IP—Vanegmond, 190.1; H—T. Smith, 192; R—Vanegmond, 99; ER—Goedhart, 88; HR—Castillo, 27; HB—Vanegmond, 14; BB—B. Taylor, 102; IBB—Weigandt, 7; SO—Vanegmond, 163; WP—Carper, 17.

(All pitchers—listed alphabetically)

Pitcher, Team	W	L	Pct.	ERA	G	GS	CG	GF	ShO	Sv.	IP	H	R	ER	HR	HB	BB	Int. BB	SO	WP
Abbott, Canton-Akron	4	5	.444	4.06	13	12	1	0	0	0	75.1	72	34	34	4	1	28	2	86	7
Alexander, Canton-Akron	1	0	1.000	6.00	6	0	0	2	0	1	9.0	8	7	6	1	1	7	0	6	1
Allen, Canton-Akron	0	1	.000	5.16	18	0	0	4	0	1	22.2	34	20	13	1	2	12	0	10	0
Allen, Reading	4	5	.444	4.45	15	15	0	0	0	0	85.0	82	45	42	8	1	35	0	63	6
Ausanio, Harrisburg	2	0	1.000	1.21	19	0	0	15	0	6	22.1	16	3	3	1	0	4	1	30	0
Barnwell, Albany	0	0	.000	0.00	1	0	0	1	0	0	2.0	2	0	0	0	0	0	0	2	0
Batchelor, Albany	1	3	.250	0.89	36	0	0	32	0	19	40.1	27	9	4	1	1	12	0	40	3
Batista, Harrisburg	13	5	.722	4.34	26	26	0	0	0	0	141.0	139	79	68	11	4	86	0	91	10
Bethea, New Britain	0	0	.000	0.00	1	0	0	1	0	0	1.0	1	0	0	0	0	1	0	0	0
Bieser, Reading	0	0	.000	0.00	1	0	0	1	0	0	1.0	0	0	0	0	0	1	0	1	0
Blomdahl, London	6	6	.500	3.71	17	17	3	0	0	0	119.0	108	58	49	7	7	42	1	72	4
Borland, Reading	2	2	.500	2.52	44	0	0	37	0	13	53.2	38	17	15	2	0	20	1	74	1
Borowski, Bowie	3	0	1.000	0.00	9	0	0	5	0	0	17.2	11	0	0	0	0	11	3	17	0
Bottalico, Reading	3	3	.500	2.25	49	0	0	37	0	20	72.0	63	22	18	4	2	26	3	65	3
Braley, London	1	2	.333	4.73	9	0	0	5	0	2	13.1	19	10	7	2	1	6	2	6	1
Brito, Harrisburg	4	3	.571	2.68	36	0	0	22	0	10	50.1	41	17	15	5	3	11	3	51	0
Brown, Reading	5	6	.455	5.72	18	17	1	0	0	0	94.1	119	72	60	10	5	29	1	42	4
Bryant, Canton-Akron*	10	5	.667	3.72	27	27	0	0	0	0	172.0	179	80	71	11	7	61	3	111	11
Byrd, Canton-Akron	0	0	.000	3.60	2	1	0	1	0	0	10.0	7	4	4	2	0	3	0	8	1
Carlyle, London	4	6	.400	3.69	12	12	1	0	0	0	78.0	72	40	32	8	5	35	1	50	0
Carper, Albany	7	10	.412	4.52	25	25	0	0	0	0	155.1	148	96	78	9	4	70	3	98	17
Carter, Reading*	1	1	.500	2.82	4	4	0	0	0	0	22.1	15	8	7	1	1	12	0	16	0
Carter, New Britain	5	4	.556	3.14	12	12	2	0	1	0	80.1	67	31	28	6	1	35	0	55	6
Castillo, Binghamton	7	11	.389	4.56	26	26	2	0	0	0	165.2	167	93	84	27	13	55	1	118	7
Charland, Canton-Akron*	2	2	.500	7.43	5	5	0	0	0	0	23.0	33	20	19	6	0	8	0	18	1

Pitcher, Team	W	L	Pct.	ERA	G	GS	CG	GF	ShO	Sv.	IP	H	R	ER	HR	HB	BB	Int. BB	SO	WP
Chaves, Bowie	2	5	.286	3.94	45	0	0	40	0	20	48.0	56	23	21	4	1	16	2	39	4
Ciccarella, New Britain*	0	4	.000	4.22	30	0	0	30	0	15	32.0	31	19	15	1	1	23	4	34	5
Corbin, Harrisburg	5	3	.625	3.68	42	2	0	21	0	4	73.1	43	31	30	0	2	59	1	91	6
Cornelius, Harrisburg	10	7	.588	4.17	27	27	1	0	0	0	157.2	146	95	73	10	13	82	1	119	8
Dedrick, Bowie	8	3	.727	2.54	38	6	1	14	1	3	106.1	84	36	30	4	3	32	1	78	1
DeHart, Harrisburg*	2	4	.333	7.68	12	7	0	1	0	0	34.0	45	31	29	5	2	19	0	18	2
Diaz, Harrisburg	5	4	.556	3.56	31	8	0	7	0	0	91.0	86	46	36	4	5	31	1	62	8
Doolan, Reading	7	8	.467	5.09	27	15	1	3	0	0	109.2	135	70	62	13	5	36	0	61	3
Dorn, Binghamton	2	1	.667	5.44	23	1	0	6	0	0	41.1	48	27	25	8	0	17	0	22	1
Douma, Binghamton*	0	3	.000	6.90	15	4	0	6	0	0	30.0	46	26	23	4	1	16	0	23	4
DuBois, Bowie*	6	1	.857	2.52	13	13	0	0	0	0	75.0	71	36	21	2	1	29	0	37	5
Dunbar, Albany*	1	0	1.000	2.66	15	0	0	6	0	0	23.2	23	8	7	0	0	6	0	18	0
Dyer, Canton-Akron	7	4	.636	5.55	17	17	0	0	0	0	94.0	90	64	58	8	4	55	0	75	12
Dzafic, New Britain	2	7	.222	4.04	45	0	0	24	0	2	64.2	86	38	29	3	5	17	3	31	1
Edmondson, London	0	4	.000	6.26	5	5	1	0	0	0	23.0	30	23	16	2	0	13	0	17	1
Eischen, Harrisburg*	14	4	.778	3.62	20	20	0	0	0	0	119.1	122	62	48	11	4	60	0	110	9
Embree, Canton-Akron*	0	0	.000	3.38	1	1	0	0	0	0	5.1	3	2	2	0	0	3	0	4	0
Farmer, Reading*	5	10	.333	5.03	22	18	0	1	0	0	102.0	125	62	57	18	1	34	2	64	8
Farrar, Bowie*	7	7	.500	3.49	24	21	2	0	0	0	116.0	114	51	45	10	4	40	0	85	5
Faw, Albany	9	5	.643	5.23	45	5	1	17	0	4	86.0	95	61	50	5	6	36	2	52	4
Fernandez, Binghamton*	0	1	.000	1.80	2	2	0	0	0	0	10.0	6	2	2	0	0	3	0	11	0
Fischer, New Britain*	0	2	.000	12.46	16	0	0	7	0	0	17.1	36	25	24	4	1	15	0	12	4
Forney, Bowie	0	0	.000	1.29	1	1	0	0	0	0	7.0	1	1	1	1	1	1	0	4	0
Frazier, Albany	4	3	.571	3.84	12	12	0	0	0	0	79.2	93	43	34	5	1	16	0	65	3
Gaddy, Reading*	6	4	.600	2.51	22	8	1	2	1	0	75.1	64	22	21	3	3	29	0	55	3
Garagozzo, Albany*	4	6	.400	4.48	17	14	1	1	0	0	86.1	88	49	43	7	1	24	1	71	1
Garcia, Canton-Akron	8	4	.667	3.89	42	7	0	9	0	3	111.0	103	53	48	12	7	37	2	110	5
Garcia, London	1	0	1.000	5.56	6	0	0	2	0	0	11.1	12	8	7	0	0	6	0	12	1
Gardella, Canton-Akron*	2	1	.667	4.37	21	0	0	7	0	4	22.2	26	14	11	2	1	22	2	14	0
Goedhart, Reading	9	12	.429	5.20	27	26	1	0	0	0	152.1	160	94	88	17	2	54	0	110	10
Goergen, Reading	2	1	.667	3.06	3	3	0	0	0	0	17.2	14	7	6	2	2	4	0	10	0
Gogolewski, Albany	4	1	.800	2.21	13	0	0	8	0	1	20.1	20	7	5	2	0	4	0	10	0
Gomez, London	4	3	.571	3.53	29	6	0	6	0	1	71.1	56	30	28	5	6	27	2	67	5
Greene, London	2	2	.500	6.52	23	0	0	11	0	0	29.0	31	22	21	1	1	20	3	19	3
Guilfoyle, London*	1	2	.333	3.73	49	0	0	18	0	3	41.0	43	19	17	2	2	16	0	35	0
Gunderson, Binghamton*	2	1	.667	5.24	20	1	0	7	0	1	22.1	20	14	13	1	2	14	0	26	1
Guzik, Binghamton	1	1	.500	8.06	15	0	0	6	0	0	22.1	36	20	20	5	0	7	0	12	0
Haller, Albany*	2	2	.500	3.99	41	0	0	17	0	0	67.2	66	37	30	5	4	29	2	53	8
Hansen, New Britain	2	11	.154	4.92	15	15	1	0	0	0	93.1	99	55	51	9	4	30	2	56	2
Harriger, Binghamton	13	10	.565	2.95	35	24	4	4	3	1	170.2	174	69	56	8	7	40	0	89	9
Hassinger, Reading	0	0	.000	9.00	1	0	0	1	0	0	2.0	4	2	2	0	0	0	0	0	1
Haynes, Harrisburg	8	0	1.000	2.59	57	0	0	22	0	5	66.0	46	27	19	2	2	19	4	78	4
Henderson, Harrisburg	5	0	1.000	1.82	5	5	0	0	0	0	29.2	20	10	6	0	0	15	0	25	2
Henry, London*	1	3	.250	5.28	33	0	0	9	0	0	30.2	33	20	18	1	1	28	0	25	4
Hernandez, Canton-Akron	0	1	.000	11.74	2	2	0	0	0	0	7.2	14	11	10	1	1	5	0	8	0
Hill, Reading	2	3	.400	4.59	21	7	0	3	0	0	68.2	72	44	35	10	1	30	2	37	6
Hines, Albany*	0	1	.000	2.08	14	0	0	3	0	0	26.0	17	9	6	1	0	11	2	27	0
Hodges, Albany	10	10	.500	4.72	30	24	2	1	0	0	152.2	161	89	80	18	2	61	2	96	6
Holland, Bowie	0	0	.000	0.00	1	0	0	1	0	0	1.0	1	0	0	0	0	0	0	2	0
Holman, Reading	8	13	.381	4.14	24	24	4	0	1	0	139.0	134	73	64	5	12	43	1	86	6
Hoy, New Britain	9	4	.692	3.84	51	0	0	21	0	0	79.2	86	38	34	3	5	41	6	37	5
Jacome, Binghamton*	8	4	.667	3.21	14	14	0	0	0	0	87.0	85	36	31	6	4	38	1	56	3
Jean, Albany	5	3	.625	2.51	11	11	1	0	0	0	61.0	42	24	17	1	5	33	0	41	4
Johnson, Harrisburg	0	0	.000	13.50	1	0	0	0	0	0	1.1	1	2	2	0	0	2	0	1	0
Jones, Canton-Akron	5	5	.500	3.30	43	0	0	36	0	22	62.2	40	25	23	1	1	26	2	73	12
Karp, Albany*	0	0	.000	4.15	3	0	0	0	0	0	13.0	13	7	6	1	0	9	0	10	2
Kelley, London*	0	0	.000	9.00	7	0	0	0	0	0	5.0	7	5	5	1	0	5	0	3	3
Knackert, Binghamton	1	3	.250	5.56	15	6	0	2	0	0	43.2	59	30	27	2	4	13	0	27	1
Krivda, Bowie*	7	5	.583	3.08	22	22	0	0	0	0	125.2	114	46	43	10	2	50	0	108	1
Lima, London	8	13	.381	4.07	27	27	2	0	0	0	177.0	160	96	80	19	5	59	4	138	8
Lira, London	10	4	.714	3.38	22	22	2	0	2	0	152.0	157	63	57	16	6	39	2	122	10
Long, Binghamton	12	8	.600	3.96	38	19	4	4	0	1	156.2	165	87	69	9	7	58	0	70	6
Looney, Harrisburg*	3	2	.600	2.38	8	8	1	0	1	0	56.2	36	15	15	2	1	17	1	76	0
Lopez, Canton-Akron	9	4	.692	3.11	16	16	2	0	0	0	110.0	79	44	38	10	5	47	0	80	6
Lumley, London	4	2	.667	4.57	26	1	0	5	0	0	41.1	32	22	21	3	6	20	1	26	5
Marchok, Reading*	2	5	.286	5.59	40	3	0	17	0	0	77.1	82	52	48	8	3	19	4	50	0
Marshall, Binghamton*	0	3	.000	8.49	7	7	0	0	0	0	35.0	61	39	33	3	0	8	0	21	1
McCarthy, Canton-Akron*	2	3	.400	4.72	33	0	0	19	0	6	34.1	28	18	18	1	2	37	2	39	6
McCready, Binghamton	1	1	.500	3.44	14	0	0	4	0	0	18.1	18	7	7	0	0	4	1	12	0
Mercedes, Bowie	6	8	.429	4.78	26	23	0	0	0	0	147.0	170	86	78	13	2	65	0	75	10
Millares, Bowie	0	0	.000	81.00	1	0	0	0	0	0	0.2	3	6	6	1	0	3	0	0	0
Miller, Binghamton	0	0	.000	9.00	2	0	0	2	0	0	2.0	3	2	2	1	0	1	0	2	0
Mintz, New Britain	2	4	.333	2.08	43	1	0	20	0	5	69.1	52	22	16	3	2	30	5	51	6
Mitchell, New Britain	1	1	.500	1.04	8	1	0	4	0	1	17.1	15	2	2	0	2	8	0	8	2
Milicki, Canton-Akron	2	1	.667	0.39	6	6	0	0	0	0	23.0	15	2	1	0	2	8	0	21	2
Mosley, New Britain*	0	0	.000	6.17	15	0	0	5	0	0	11.2	12	9	8	1	0	9	0	11	0
Mussina, Bowie	1	0	1.000	2.25	2	2	0	0	0	0	8.0	5	2	2	1	0	0	0	10	0
Nagy, Canton-Akron	0	0	.000	1.13	2	2	0	0	0	0	8.0	8	1	1	0	0	2	0	4	0
Ojala, Albany*	1	0	1.000	0.00	1	1	0	0	0	0	6.1	5	0	0	0	0	2	0	6	2
Painter, New Britain	3	6	.333	4.06	14	14	0	0	0	0	77.2	76	44	35	4	3	29	1	57	5
Paveloff, Bowie	4	5	.556	1.73	32	0	0	21	0	1	57.1	50	21	11	1	1	19	3	31	2
Perez, Harrisburg*	4	2	.667	3.45	34	0	0	15	0	3	44.1	49	26	17	3	0	20	1	58	6
Pettitte, Albany*	1	0	1.000	3.60	1	1	0	0	0	0	5.0	5	4	2	0	0	2	0	6	0
Pfaff, Albany	9	4	.400	5.73	23	23	1	0	0	0	132.0	176	90	84	9	4	45	1	62	9
Polak, Albany	3	4	.429	4.55	21	0	0	16	0	5	27.2	34	18	14	1	1	10	1	16	0
Popplewell, Albany	1	3	.250	5.88	34	4	1	12	0	1	64.1	60	45	42	3	5	48	2	59	11
Power, Canton-Akron	0	0	.000	4.67	7	3	0	0	0	0	17.1	22	10	9	2	1	8	0	16	0
Prybylinski, Albany	0	0	.000	1.93	2	0	0	1	0	0	4.2	4	1	1	0	1	1	0	1	0
Puig, Harrisburg*	0	1	.000	2.45	14	0	0	3	0	1	18.1	16	5	5	1	2	7	0	10	0
Quirico, Albany*	4	10	.286	3.52	36	11	0	15	0	7	94.2	92	46	37	15	1	33	2	79	6
Ramirez, Albany	0	0	.000	0.00	1	0	0	1	0	0	1.0	1	0	0	0	0	0	0	1	0
Reich, Binghamton	0	4	.000	3.34	24	0	0	14	0	4	35.0	38	15	13	4	0	9	0	16	4
Ricci, Bowie	7	4	.636	3.20	34	1	0	16	0	5	81.2	72	35	29	7	3	20	0	83	8
Riley, New Britain*	4	6	.400	3.55	14	14	1	0	0	0	83.2	85	39	33	5	0	29	0	50	1

Pitcher, Team	W	L	Pct.	ERA	G	GS	CG	GF	ShO	Sv.	IP	H	R	ER	HR	HB	BB	Int. BB	SO	WP
Rivera, Canton-Akron*	0	1	.000	5.02	8	0	0	4	0	0	14.1	22	8	8	0	2	3	0	6	0
Roa, Binghamton	12	7	.632	3.87	32	23	2	0	1	0	167.1	190	80	72	9	10	24	0	73	3
Robinson, Canton-Akron	3	2	.600	4.56	9	7	0	0	0	0	47.1	49	28	24	6	4	18	1	26	2
Rodriguez, New Britain	7	11	.389	3.74	28	26	4	1	0	0	170.2	147	79	71	17	4	78	4	151	7
Rogers, Binghamton	5	4	.556	2.34	62	0	0	40	0	8	84.2	80	29	22	4	0	25	2	42	6
Romanoli, Canton-Akron*	1	2	.333	4.54	30	0	0	15	0	0	39.2	37	22	20	5	4	21	3	38	2
Rueter, Harrisburg*	5	0	1.000	1.36	9	8	1	1	1	0	59.2	47	10	9	4	0	7	0	36	1
Ryan, Bowie	3	10	.231	5.30	16	15	2	1	0	0	88.1	106	67	52	8	1	34	0	40	5
Sarbaugh, Canton-Akron	0	0	.000	0.00	3	0	0	3	0	0	3.0	2	0	0	0	0	2	0	0	0
Satre, Bowie	7	3	.700	3.11	13	13	2	0	0	0	84.0	68	35	29	7	4	20	0	65	2
Schullstrom, Bowie	5	10	.333	4.27	24	14	2	4	0	1	109.2	119	63	52	6	3	45	0	97	7
Schwarber, London	5	2	.714	5.03	48	0	0	42	0	16	53.2	54	34	30	7	1	28	3	58	3
Shea, New Britain*	4	2	.667	3.65	48	0	0	12	0	1	56.2	48	27	23	2	2	22	3	62	5
Shuey, Canton-Akron	4	8	.333	7.30	27	7	0	10	0	0	61.2	76	50	50	13	3	36	3	41	5
Silcox, Binghamton	0	1	.000	6.97	3	3	0	0	0	0	10.1	10	9	8	1	0	9	0	8	1
D. Smith, Bowie	0	0	.000	2.45	3	3	0	0	0	0	22.0	14	7	6	1	1	11	0	23	0
M. Smith, Bowie	0	1	.000	8.22	5	1	0	3	0	0	7.2	11	7	7	1	0	1	0	4	2
Smith, New Britain	7	13	.350	3.79	28	28	3	0	1	0	180.1	192	91	76	9	11	44	5	81	5
Soper, Canton-Akron	1	3	.250	5.63	8	0	0	4	0	0	8.0	8	5	5	1	0	4	1	11	0
Sparks, Canton-Akron*	0	0	.000	20.25	1	0	0	0	0	0	1.1	4	3	3	1	0	0	0	0	0
Stidham, London	2	2	.500	2.38	33	0	0	8	0	2	34.0	40	18	9	3	2	19	3	39	2
Stone, Canton-Akron	3	0	1.000	3.05	13	0	0	4	0	0	20.2	17	8	7	1	0	17	3	15	0
Sullivan, Reading	0	3	.000	3.38	31	0	0	12	0	4	45.1	42	20	17	2	2	13	3	29	5
Tavarez, Canton-Akron	2	1	.667	0.95	3	2	1	0	1	0	19.0	14	2	2	0	2	1	0	11	0
Taylor, Albany*	13	7	.650	3.48	27	1	0	0	0	0	163.0	127	83	63	7	8	102	0	150	12
Taylor, Bowie	4	7	.364	5.62	40	4	0	19	0	4	89.2	90	65	56	9	2	47	1	69	5
Thomas, Harrisburg*	2	2	.500	4.73	25	0	0	14	0	0	32.1	34	18	17	3	1	19	2	40	1
Thompson, London*	3	6	.333	4.09	14	14	1	0	0	0	83.2	96	51	38	9	2	37	0	72	4
Trice, Canton-Akron*	3	2	.600	5.61	19	3	0	6	0	1	51.1	65	36	32	6	3	24	0	30	3
Turek, Canton-Akron	1	0	1.000	2.25	3	3	0	0	0	0	16.0	11	4	4	1	0	7	0	7	0
Uhrhan, New Britain	0	1	.000	11.57	9	0	0	3	0	0	9.1	14	12	12	4	0	6	0	3	0
Undorf, London	0	1	.000	3.58	19	0	0	5	0	1	32.2	37	17	13	2	5	6	0	15	1
Urbina, Harrisburg	4	5	.444	3.99	11	11	3	0	1	0	70.0	66	32	31	5	5	32	1	45	1
Valdez, Canton-Akron	1	0	1.000	0.00	5	0	0	3	0	1	11.1	7	1	0	0	0	2	0	12	1
Valenzuela, Bowie*	0	0	.000	1.50	1	1	0	0	0	0	6.0	4	1	1	0	1	0	0	4	0
Vanegmond, New Britain	6	12	.333	3.97	29	29	1	0	1	0	190.1	182	99	84	18	14	44	1	163	11
Veres, Canton-Akron	1	5	.167	4.89	13	12	0	0	0	0	57.0	59	33	31	3	3	19	1	49	3
Walker, Binghamton	4	9	.308	3.44	45	10	0	33	0	19	99.1	89	45	38	6	5	46	1	89	5
Warren, London	3	3	.500	5.83	22	1	0	13	0	5	29.1	36	19	19	6	0	9	0	21	1
White, Harrisburg*	7	2	.778	2.16	16	16	2	0	1	0	100.0	80	30	24	4	2	28	0	80	5
Wiegandt, Reading*	6	2	.750	3.56	56	0	0	16	0	0	73.1	75	41	29	3	0	44	7	60	5
Wilkins, Canton-Akron	3	3	.500	3.89	11	5	0	1	0	0	44.0	44	30	19	3	1	13	1	37	0
Winston, Harrisburg*	1	0	1.000	4.63	24	0	0	9	0	1	44.2	53	30	23	4	2	19	2	36	3
Witt, Albany	0	0	.000	0.00	1	0	0	1	0	0	2.0	2	0	0	0	0	0	0	2	0
Wolf, London	2	5	.286	4.99	14	10	1	2	0	0	61.1	56	39	34	9	2	45	1	55	3
Wood, Bowie	1	0	1.000	3.38	8	0	0	3	0	1	13.1	13	6	5	1	0	8	3	15	0
Zaun, Bowie	0	0	.000	0.00	1	0	0	0	0	0	2.1	1	0	0	0	0	0	0	0	0

BALKS—Lima, 13; B. Taylor, 8; Bryant, 7; Carper, Farmer, A. Garcia, Henry, T. Smith, 4 each; Blomdahl, Hill, Knackert, Mitchell, Painter, Perez, Riley, Rodriguez, Thomas, Vanegmond, 3 each; Carlyle, G. Carter, Doolan, Douma, Farrar, Gomez, Greene, Haynes, Henderson, Hodges, Krivda, Paveloff, Puig, Rivera, Roa, Ryan, White, Wolf, 2 each; R. Allen, Bethea, Borowski, Brown, Castillo, Corbin, Diaz, Dubois, Eischen, Frazier, Gaddy, Goedhart, Gogolewski, Guilfoyle, Hansen, Harriger, Holman, Hoy, Jacome, Jones, Kelley, Lira, Long, Lopez, Marchok, Mercedes, Pfaff, Polak, Quirico, Satre, Schwarber, Shea, Sullivan, Tavarez, T. Taylor, Thompson, Turek, Undorf, Urbina, Wiegandt, 1 each.

COMBINATION SHUTOUTS—Garagozzo-Batchelor, Hodges-Quirico-Batchelor, Ojala-Gogolewski, Quirico-Batchelor-Haller, Taylor-Faw, Taylor-Faw-Batchelor, Albany; Roa-Walker 2, Harriger-Long-Rogers, Jacome-McCready-Walker, Jacome-Rogers, Jacome-Walker, Long-McCready-Walker, Roa-McCready-Walker, Binghamton; Krivda-Paveloff 2, Dubois-Ricci, Farrar-Dedrick, Farrar-Smith, Mercedes-Chaves, Satre-Ricci-Taylor, Schullstrom-Chaves, Bowie; Abbott-Shuey-Gardella-McCarthy, Bryant-Power-McCarthy, Dyer-Romanoli-Jones, Tavarez-Romanoli, Turek-Allen-Trice, Canton-Akron; Batista-Haynes-Ausanio, Corbin-Haynes-Diaz-Thomas, Cornelius-Corbin, Cornelius-Haynes, White-Corbin, White-Perez-Brito, Harrisburg; Carlyle-Undorf, Blomdahl-Henry-Warren, Blomdahl-Lumley, Lima-Greene, Lira-Stidham-Schwarber, London; Carter-Mintz-Dzafic, Painter-Ciccarella, Smith-Mintz, New Britain; Allen-Wiegandt-Borland, Brown-Marchok-Bottalico, Carter-Hill-Sullivan, Doolan-Bottalico, Farmer-Bottalico, Gaddy-Borland, Gaddy-Marchok, Goedhart-Sullivan, Hill-Borland, Holman-Brown-Borland-Bottalico, Reading.

NO-HIT GAMES—Holman-Brown-Borland-Bottalico, Reading, defeated New Britain, 2-0 (first game), September 4.

FIELDING

TEAM

Team	Pct.	G	PO	A	E	DP	PB	Team	Pct.	G	PO	A	E	DP	PB
Reading	.975	140	3573	1511	133	112	20	Binghamton	.968	140	3605	1575	170	140	11
Canton-Akron	.973	138	3608	1469	143	127	25	Bowie	.968	140	3646	1484	170	117	16
Harrisburg	.971	138	3636	1310	147	108	22	New Britain	.966	140	3706	1502	182	127	14
London	.969	138	3656	1453	161	102	23	Albany	.965	138	3545	1416	181	130	34

Triple plays—Reading 2.

INDIVIDUAL

FIRST BASEMEN

*Throws lefthanded.

Player, Team	Pct.	G	PO	A	E	DP
Brady, Reading	.981	5	49	3	1	3
Cameron, Bowie	1.000	3	14	3	0	3
Cornelius, London	1.000	1	5	0	0	1
Daniel, Harrisburg	1.000	1	1	1	0	0
Davis, Bowie	1.000	2	10	2	0	0
DeBerry, Albany*	.983	125	1042	87	19	97
Dixon, New Britain	.983	21	164	10	3	17

Player, Team	Pct.	G	PO	A	E	DP
Flannelly, Albany	1.000	1	4	0	0	0
Floyd, Harrisburg*	.969	61	483	23	16	38
Friedman, New Britain*	.986	67	510	70	8	40
Hankins, Albany	1.000	3	29	0	0	4
Harvey, Canton-Akron*	.972	11	94	10	3	11
Jacobs, Binghamton	.982	72	651	55	13	68
Lennon, Canton-Akron	1.000	1	2	0	0	0
Lewis, Bowie	.988	53	454	34	6	35
Lockett, Reading*	.987	98	897	72	13	75
L. Lopez, Canton-Akron	.990	35	277	22	3	29
Marrero, Harrisburg*	.993	44	273	25	2	24

FIRST BASEMEN (continued)

Player, Team	Pct.	G	PO	A	E	DP
Millares, Bowie	1.000	1	1	0	0	0
Miller, Bowie	.989	87	720	73	9	64
Moler, Reading	1.000	2	21	1	0	0
Mota, Canton-Akron	1.000	1	10	2	0	2
Obando, Bowie	1.000	3	11	0	0	1
Oster, Albany*	.980	14	92	5	2	10
Perona, London	1.000	11	77	2	0	6
Perry, Canton-Akron	.990	46	354	42	4	39
RENDINA, London*	.992	132	1071	107	9	82
Roso, Bowie	1.000	1	3	1	0	0
Rusk, Reading	1.000	2	13	2	0	1
Saltzgaber, London	1.000	4	22	1	0	0
Sanchez, Albany	1.000	1	1	0	0	0
Sarbaugh, Canton-Akron	.988	22	160	7	2	14
Schall, Reading	.997	35	281	25	1	21
Sparks, Canton-Akron*	.989	34	260	19	3	24
Tatum, New Britain	.988	34	304	25	4	27
Thoutsis, New Britain	1.000	1	7	0	0	1
Wallin, New Britain*	.977	27	202	15	5	27
D. White, Harrisburg	.989	21	171	11	2	17
Wilstead, Harrisburg*	.981	17	99	5	2	10
Woods, Harrisburg	.989	13	82	9	1	7
Zinter, Binghamton	.990	72	656	43	7	63
Sarbaugh, Canton-Akron	1.000	17	7	17	0	2
Simons, Harrisburg	.808	7	7	14	5	0
Sued, Canton-Akron	1.000	1	0	1	0	0
Tyler, Bowie	.963	12	6	20	1	1
Woods, Harrisburg	1.000	1	0	1	0	0

Triple play—Lockett.

SECOND BASEMEN

Player, Team	Pct.	G	PO	A	E	DP
Alfonzo, Bowie	.952	20	27	52	4	9
Allison, Binghamton	.979	23	37	56	2	20
Barnwell, Albany	.667	1	1	1	1	0
Bell, Canton-Akron	.974	17	39	35	2	5
Bethea, New Britain	.941	40	62	97	10	21
Crowley, New Britain	.942	102	176	262	27	58
Escobar, Reading	.953	35	70	93	8	24
Ferretti, Bowie	1.000	11	11	16	0	5
FLORES, Canton-Akron	.974	109	221	295	14	80
Hankins, Albany	1.000	5	5	12	0	2
Hardge, Harrisburg	.972	98	194	221	12	50
Jordan, Albany	.967	133	261	359	21	93
Krause, Harrisburg	.984	13	30	33	1	7
Lewis, Reading	.958	59	90	137	10	21
Lowery, Binghamton	1.000	3	5	7	0	0
Martin, Harrisburg	.963	26	48	56	4	11
Mendenhall, London	.900	4	1	8	1	0
Millares, Bowie	.860	16	22	27	8	7
Odor, Canton-Akron	1.000	8	11	25	0	4
Penn, London	.958	110	197	311	22	50
Pratte, London	.955	34	50	97	7	18
Ramirez, Bowie	.974	11	16	22	1	3
Rundels, Harrisburg	.857	2	3	3	1	1
Sarbaugh, Canton-Akron	1.000	10	15	31	0	5
Simons, Harrisburg	1.000	5	4	15	0	1
Tyler, Bowie	.963	112	209	286	19	56
Vargas, Canton-Akron	1.000	5	9	12	0	2
Veras, Binghamton	.966	127	274	372	23	81
Waller, Reading	.975	53	90	148	6	28
Zaun, Bowie	1.000	1	2	0	0	0

Triple play—Waller.

SHORTSTOPS

Player, Team	Pct.	G	PO	A	E	DP
Allison, Binghamton	.954	25	29	54	4	17
Barker, Harrisburg	.944	47	65	119	11	21
Bell, Canton-Akron	.956	11	9	34	2	8
Bethea, New Britain	.936	59	101	146	17	25
Butterfield, Binghamton	.899	22	28	52	9	7
Dellicarri, Binghamton	.936	84	124	243	25	57
Eenhoorn, Albany	.922	82	143	221	31	47
Escobar, Reading	1.000	9	9	19	0	2
Ferretti, Bowie	1.000	4	7	10	0	2
Flores, Canton-Akron	.950	79	107	195	16	36
Givens, London	.989	25	32	55	1	16
Hankins, Albany	1.000	5	5	12	0	1
J. Hernandez, Canton-Akron	.968	45	75	134	7	25
Holland, Bowie	.931	128	202	337	40	69
KIMBERLIN, Reading	.963	134	183	424	23	68
Krause, Harrisburg	.900	3	3	6	1	1
Ledesma, Binghamton	.910	20	36	65	10	15
Lowery, Binghamton	1.000	1	2	0	0	0
Martin, Harrisburg	.970	74	97	194	9	41
Mendenhall, London	.960	62	102	162	11	23
Odor, Canton-Akron	.962	73	87	164	10	39
Pratte, London	.894	12	19	23	5	6
Ramirez, Bowie	1.000	1	2	1	0	1
Rodriguez, Albany	.942	38	48	97	9	21
T. Rodriguez, New Britain	.950	96	179	276	24	59
Rundels, Harrisburg	1.000	5	7	15	0	4
Sarbaugh, Canton-Akron	1.000	4	1	5	0	0
Simons, Harrisburg	1.000	2	1	1	0	0
Tovar, Harrisburg	.897	12	12	23	4	5
Vargas, Canton-Akron	.980	16	15	34	1	4
Velarde, Albany	.944	3	5	12	1	2

Triple play—Kimberlin.

THIRD BASEMEN

Player, Team	Pct.	G	PO	A	E	DP
Alder, London	.816	31	24	38	14	4
ALFONZO, Bowie	.967	108	75	187	9	14
Andrews, Harrisburg	.927	123	74	217	23	17
Bell, Canton-Akron	.943	103	69	214	17	32
Bethea, New Britain	.500	2	0	2	2	0
Brady, Reading	1.000	1	0	1	0	0
Butterfield, Binghamton	1.000	2	1	6	0	1
Colombino, Reading	.948	85	64	156	12	14
Crowley, New Britain	.800	3	3	1	1	0
Decillis, London	.889	25	16	24	5	2
Dixon, New Britain	.955	32	30	55	4	7
Erickson, Albany	.875	3	2	5	1	0
Escobar, Reading	.935	20	16	42	4	2
Ferretti, Bowie	.960	22	8	64	3	1
Flannelly, Albany	.925	47	31	80	9	5
Flores, Canton-Akron	.750	2	2	1	1	0
Fox, Albany	.917	64	59	150	19	15
Grable, Reading	.981	37	28	77	2	6
Hankins, Albany	.917	27	12	54	6	5
J. Hernandez, Canton-Akron	1.000	1	0	1	0	0
Holland, Bowie	1.000	1	0	1	0	0
Huskey, Binghamton	.921	138	101	297	34	26
Lowery, Binghamton	1.000	2	1	0	0	0
Mendenhall, London	.978	27	15	30	1	3
Millares, Bowie	1.000	4	5	4	0	0
Miller, Bowie	.800	5	5	3	2	1
Norris, New Britain	.951	116	79	194	14	20
Perry, Canton-Akron	.917	25	22	44	6	3
Pratte, London	.938	74	53	128	12	11
Rundels, Harrisburg	.931	9	7	20	2	2
Saltzgaber, London	.667	1	0	2	1	0

OUTFIELDERS

Player, Team	Pct.	G	PO	A	E	DP
Alder, London	.750	8	5	1	2	0
Alstead, Bowie	.972	43	69	1	2	0
Barnwell, Albany	.986	44	65	4	1	1
Bautista, London	.989	107	256	13	3	2
Beams, New Britain	.961	69	139	9	6	1
Bieser, Reading	1.000	14	23	1	0	0
Brady, Reading	1.000	38	93	4	0	0
Brown, New Britain	1.000	27	54	1	0	0
Butterfield, Binghamton	.986	53	66	3	1	0
Cameron, Bowie	.972	115	194	11	6	3
Carpenter, Albany*	.941	9	15	1	1	0
Chick, Reading	.981	54	99	6	2	2
Cornelius, London	.982	58	101	6	2	1
Davis, Binghamton*	.964	93	150	11	6	1
Devereaux, Bowie	1.000	2	5	0	0	0
Ferretti, Bowie	1.000	1	5	1	0	0
Flores, Canton-Akron	1.000	1	1	1	0	0
Floyd, Harrisburg*	.966	43	81	4	3	0
Geisler, Reading*	1.000	48	96	6	0	1
Giles, Canton-Akron*	.974	100	186	2	5	0
Griffin, Harrisburg	1.000	18	24	0	0	0
Hammonds, Bowie	1.000	21	48	2	0	0
Hankins, Albany	1.000	1	1	0	0	0
Higginson, London	.982	58	100	11	2	2
Horne, Harrisburg	.982	35	54	2	1	0
Howard, Binghamton	.979	28	42	4	1	0
Hunter, Binghamton	.990	89	175	16	2	4
Hyde, Reading	.991	69	109	4	1	0
Jackson, Bowie	.938	96	163	4	11	0
Leach, Albany*	.961	111	210	9	9	2
Lennon, Canton-Akron	.920	32	43	3	4	0
Lewis, Reading	.960	8	23	1	1	0
L. Lopez, Canton-Akron	1.000	1	1	1	0	0
Mahay, New Britain*	.889	7	15	1	2	0
Martin, Harrisburg	1.000	7	7	0	0	0
Martinez, Bowie*	1.000	2	5	0	0	0
Mendenhall, London	1.000	3	3	1	0	0
Millares, Bowie	1.000	3	0	1	0	0
Moore, New Britain	.976	63	115	6	3	1
Morrison, New Britain	.988	73	154	8	2	1
Mouton, Albany	.975	114	189	6	5	1
Murray, Harrisburg	.975	123	270	6	7	1
Nuneviller, Reading	1.000	38	61	1	0	0
Obando, Bowie	.955	16	21	0	1	0
Ortiz, Bowie	.941	8	16	0	1	0
Oster, Albany*	.938	11	14	1	1	0
Otero, Binghamton	.976	124	238	9	6	
Peguero, Canton-Akron	.949	48	74	1	4	
Pemberton, London	.966	115	215	11	8	

Player, Team	Pct.	G	PO	A	E	DP
Penn, London	.000	1	0	0	1	0
Perry, Canton-Akron	1.000	2	2	0	0	0
Pride, Harrisburg	.972	39	69	0	2	0
M. Ramirez, Canton-Akron	.967	84	142	4	5	0
O. Ramirez, Canton-Akron	.980	120	278	9	6	1
Rappoli, New Britain	.949	110	193	13	11	2
Rice, Harrisburg	1.000	2	1	0	0	0
Robertson, Albany*	.986	129	274	5	4	0
Rundels, Harrisburg	1.000	20	37	0	0	0
Saltzgaber, London	.986	70	142	2	2	0
Sanders, Canton-Akron	.944	30	64	3	4	0
Sandy, Binghamton	.987	49	74	2	1	1
Sarbaugh, Canton-Akron	.941	15	16	0	1	0
Schall, Reading	1.000	12	17	0	0	0
Simons, Harrisburg	1.000	4	8	0	0	0
Taylor, Reading*	.971	47	96	4	3	2
Thoutsis, New Britain	.990	50	97	1	1	1
Tokheim, Reading*	.963	64	151	6	6	0
Tyler, Bowie	.968	16	25	5	1	2
Velarde, Albany	.500	1	1	0	1	0
Washington, Bowie	.950	106	201	9	11	2
WAWRUCK, Bowie*	.991	121	210	4	2	0
R. White, Harrisburg	.995	85	179	4	1	0
Williams, London	.933	17	27	1	2	0
Woods, Harrisburg	.973	73	106	3	3	1
Zinter, Binghamton	.900	13	16	2	2	0

Triple play—Tokheim.

CATCHERS

Player, Team	Pct.	G	PO	A	E	DP	PB
Bieser, Reading	.980	31	176	25	4	3	6
Bradbury, Harrisburg	1.000	5	35	9	0	1	1
Carroll, New Britain	.976	55	302	29	8	3	4
Daniel, Harrisburg	1.000	1	8	0	0	0	0
Delgado, New Britain	.987	30	200	24	3	2	2
Devarez, Bowie	.986	55	316	36	5	3	6
Dziadkowiec, Binghamton	.991	65	296	25	3	1	6
Fernandez, Reading	.979	38	216	18	5	1	4
Figga, Albany	.971	6	31	2	1	0	2
Fitzpatrick, Harrisburg	.978	94	713	78	18	11	15
Fulton, Harrisburg	1.000	1	13	1	0	0	1
GONZALEZ, Binghamton	.9917	93	429	54	4	4	5
Gonzalez, London	.971	25	148	20	5	1	2
Hatteberg, New Britain	.978	67	410	45	10	4	8
Leshnock, Albany	1.000	1	8	1	0	0	2
Livesey, Albany	.979	32	204	25	5	2	6
L. Lopez, Canton-Akron	1.000	2	3	0	0	0	0
Martindale, Canton-Akron	.9915	101	625	77	6	3	17
Moler, Reading	.988	33	211	28	3	2	5
Mota, Canton-Akron	.969	29	168	19	6	0	5
Perona, London	.990	70	480	36	5	2	8
Pineda, Albany	.977	38	225	32	6	4	7
Posada, Albany	.958	7	39	7	2	0	2
Rice, Harrisburg	.997	41	305	26	1	0	5
Rosado, Reading	.984	30	156	29	3	3	2
Roso, Bowie	.986	38	193	14	3	2	6
Rusk, Reading	.978	16	82	8	2	0	3
Saltzgaber, London	1.000	2	7	1	0	0	1
Sanchez, Albany	.989	63	427	37	5	5	15
Sellers, London	.981	50	323	37	7	4	12
Skinner, Canton-Akron	.985	10	62	4	1	1	1
Sued, Canton-Akron	.985	23	124	10	2	0	2
Zaun, Bowie	.979	61	421	51	10	1	4
Zinter, Binghamton	.953	7	37	4	2	0	0

PITCHERS

Player, Team	Pct.	G	PO	A	E	DP
Abbott, Canton-Akron	1.000	13	4	10	0	0
Alexander, Canton-Akron	.000	6	0	0	1	0
Allen, Canton-Akron	.778	18	3	4	2	1
Allen, Reading	.944	15	5	12	1	1
Ausanio, Harrisburg	1.000	19	3	3	0	0
Batchelor, Albany	1.000	36	1	5	0	1
Batista, Harrisburg	.929	26	6	20	2	0
Bethea, New Britain	1.000	1	1	0	0	0
Blomdahl, London	.875	17	8	13	3	1
Borland, Reading	.882	44	4	11	2	1
Borowski, Bowie	1.000	9	0	2	0	0
Bottalico, Reading	.929	49	3	10	1	0
Braley, London	1.000	9	4	4	0	0
Brito, Harrisburg	1.000	36	8	10	0	0
Brown, Harrisburg	1.000	18	4	16	0	0
Bryant, Canton-Akron*	.927	27	12	39	4	1
Byrd, Canton-Akron	1.000	2	1	0	0	0
Carlyle, London	.889	12	9	15	3	1
Carper, Albany	.900	25	14	22	4	2
Carter, Reading*	1.000	4	0	2	0	2
Carter, New Britain	.903	12	10	18	3	0
Castillo, Binghamton	.947	26	15	21	2	2
Charland, Canton-Akron*	1.000	5	0	2	0	0
Chaves, Bowie	.833	45	3	7	2	2
Ciccarella, New Britain*	1.000	30	0	3	0	0
Corbin, Harrisburg	1.000	42	3	9	0	0

Player, Team	Pct.	G	PO	A	E	DP
Cornelius, Harrisburg	.912	27	11	20	3	0
Dedrick, Bowie	1.000	38	8	19	0	3
DeHart, Harrisburg	.800	12	2	2	1	0
Diaz, Harrisburg	.880	31	7	15	3	3
Doolan, Reading	.971	27	12	21	1	1
Dorn, Binghamton	1.000	23	1	6	0	1
Douma, Binghamton*	1.000	15	0	6	0	0
DuBois, Bowie	.810	13	3	14	4	0
Dunbar, Albany*	1.000	15	1	4	0	0
Dyer, Canton-Akron	.844	17	8	19	5	2
Dzafic, New Britain	1.000	45	7	12	0	2
Edmondson, London	.889	5	2	6	1	0
Eischen, Harrisburg*	.789	20	3	12	4	0
Farmer, Reading*	.870	22	6	14	3	0
Farrar, Bowie*	.853	24	11	18	5	0
Faw, Albany	.909	45	6	14	2	0
Fernandez, Binghamton*	1.000	2	1	2	0	0
Fischer, New Britain*	1.000	16	2	3	0	0
Forney, Bowie	1.000	1	1	0	0	0
Frazier, Albany	.833	12	3	7	2	0
Gaddy, Reading*	.958	22	7	16	1	0
Garagozzo, Albany*	.857	17	2	10	2	0
Garcia, Canton-Akron*	1.000	42	7	23	0	1
Garcia, London	1.000	6	0	3	0	0
Gardella, Canton-Akron*	.750	21	1	2	1	0
Goedhart, Reading	.962	27	10	15	1	1
Goergen, Reading	1.000	3	1	2	0	1
Gogolewski, Albany	1.000	13	2	0	0	0
Gomez, London	1.000	29	4	12	0	0
Greene, London	1.000	23	2	4	0	2
Guilfoyle, London*	1.000	49	3	5	0	0
Gunderson, Binghamton*	1.000	20	2	7	0	0
Guzik, Binghamton	1.000	15	4	1	0	0
Haller, Albany*	1.000	41	3	8	0	1
Hansen, New Britain	1.000	15	13	11	0	1
HARRIGER, Binghamton	1.000	35	26	26	0	1
Hassinger, Reading	1.000	1	0	2	0	0
Haynes, Harrisburg	1.000	57	2	7	0	0
Henderson, Harrisburg	1.000	5	1	8	0	0
Henry, London*	.875	33	1	6	1	0
F. Hernandez, Canton-Akron	1.000	2	1	1	0	0
Hill, Reading	.917	21	4	7	1	0
Hines, Albany*	.875	14	3	4	1	0
Hodges, Albany	.944	30	19	15	2	0
Holman, Reading	.971	24	15	19	1	3
Hoy, New Britain	.957	51	9	13	1	2
Jacome, Binghamton*	1.000	14	7	15	0	3
Jean, Albany	.952	11	11	9	1	2
Jones, Canton-Akron	1.000	43	6	7	0	0
Karp, Albany*	1.000	3	0	2	0	0
Kelley, London*	1.000	7	1	1	0	0
Knackert, Binghamton	.929	15	5	8	1	1
Krivda, Bowie*	.917	22	2	20	2	2
Lima, London	.925	27	14	23	3	0
Lira, London	.919	22	12	22	3	0
Long, Binghamton	.900	38	27	27	6	5
Looney, Harrisburg*	1.000	8	1	6	0	0
A. Lopez, Canton-Akron	.941	16	6	10	1	0
Lumley, London	1.000	26	1	8	0	0
Marchok, Reading*	.909	40	11	9	2	0
Marshall, Binghamton*	.917	7	3	8	1	0
McCarthy, Canton-Akron*	1.000	33	2	3	0	1
McCready, Binghamton	1.000	14	0	2	0	0
Mercedes, Bowie	1.000	26	9	25	0	0
Miller, Binghamton	1.000	2	0	1	0	0
Mintz, New Britain	.952	43	4	16	1	0
Mitchell, New Britain	1.000	8	2	2	0	0
Mlicki, Canton-Akron	1.000	6	1	2	0	0
Mosley, New Britain*	.750	15	1	2	1	1
Mussina, Bowie	1.000	2	1	2	0	0
Nagy, Canton-Akron	1.000	2	2	0	0	0
Painter, New Britain	.947	14	4	14	1	1
Paveloff, Binghamton	1.000	32	9	12	0	0
Perez, Harrisburg*	.833	34	1	4	1	0
Pettitte, Albany*	1.000	1	0	1	0	0
Pfaff, London	1.000	23	11	17	0	1
Polak, Albany	1.000	21	3	3	0	0
Popplewell, Albany	1.000	34	1	3	0	0
Power, Canton-Akron	1.000	7	0	3	0	0
Puig, Harrisburg*	.750	14	1	2	1	1
Quirico, Albany*	1.000	36	2	18	0	0
Reich, Binghamton	.909	24	5	5	1	0
Ricci, Bowie	.938	34	6	9	1	0
Riley, New Britain*	.933	14	2	12	1	0
Rivera, Canton-Akron*	1.000	8	3	2	0	0
Roa, Binghamton	.982	32	24	30	1	1
Robinson, Canton-Akron	.846	9	3	8	2	0
F. Rodriguez, New Britain	.957	28	16	28	2	1
Rogers, Binghamton	1.000	62	10	9	0	2
Romanoli, Canton-Akron*	.900	30	2	7	1	0
Rueter, Harrisburg*	1.000	9	3	19	0	2
Ryan, Bowie	.955	16	7	14	1	1
Satre, Bowie	.944	13	11	6	1	0
Schullstrom, Bowie	.941	24	10	6	1	1
Schwarber, London	1.000	48	5	9	0	1

Player, Team	Pct.	G	PO	A	E	DP
Shea, New Britain*	1.000	48	1	8	0	0
Shuey, Canton-Akron	1.000	27	2	8	0	2
Silcox, Binghamton	.667	3	2	0	1	0
D. Smith, Bowie	.750	3	1	2	1	0
M. Smith, Bowie	1.000	5	1	1	0	0
Smith, New Britain	.961	28	19	30	2	0
Soper, Canton-Akron	1.000	8	0	1	0	0
Sparks, Canton-Akron*	.000	1	0	0	1	0
Stidham, London	.800	33	3	5	2	0
Stone, Canton-Akron	1.000	13	0	2	0	1
Sullivan, Reading	1.000	31	3	6	0	1
Tavarez, Canton-Akron	1.000	3	1	3	0	1
Taylor, Albany*	.800	27	4	20	6	1
Taylor, Bowie	.909	40	4	6	1	0
Thomas, Harrisburg*	1.000	25	0	4	0	0
Thompson, London*	.938	14	3	12	1	1

Player, Team	Pct.	G	PO	A	E	DP
Trice, Canton-Akron*	.778	19	2	5	2	0
Turek, Canton-Akron	1.000	3	0	3	0	0
Uhrhan, New Britain	1.000	9	1	1	0	0
Undorf, London	.923	19	4	8	1	2
Urbina, Harrisburg	1.000	11	7	5	0	1
Valenzuela, Bowie*	1.000	1	0	2	0	0
Vanegmond, New Britain	.945	29	19	33	3	2
Veres, Canton-Akron	1.000	13	6	3	0	0
Walker, Binghamton	.929	45	5	21	2	1
Warren, London	1.000	22	1	6	0	0
G. White, Harrisburg*	1.000	16	3	10	0	0
Wiegandt, Reading*	1.000	56	4	10	0	2
Wilkins, Canton-Akron	.714	11	2	8	4	1
Winston, Harrisburg*	1.000	24	3	9	0	2
Wolf, London	1.000	14	6	3	0	1
Wood, Bowie	.875	8	3	4	1	0

The following players did not have any fielding statistics at the positions indicated or appeared only as a designated hitter, pinch-hitter or pinch-runner: Allison, of; Andrews, ss; Baines, dh; Barnwell, p; Bethea, of; Bieser, p; Dedrick, of; Delgado, 1b; Embree, p; Givens, of; Holland, p; Huskey, ss; Johnson, p; Martin, 3b; Millares, ss, p; Mota, of; Ojala, of; Perona, 3b; Prybylinski, p; D. Ramirez, p; Sarbaugh, p; Tyler, 1b; Valdez, p; Vargas, of; Wilstead, of; Witt, p; Zaun, 3b, p; Zinter, 3b.

LEAGUE CHAMPIONS

Year	Team	Pct.	Year	Team	Pct.	Year	Team	Pct.
1923—	Williamsport	.661	1950—	Wilkes-Barre‡	.652	1974—	Thetford Miners (2nd)c	.536
1924—	Williamsport	.654	1951—	Wilkes-Barre‡	.612		Pittsfield (2nd)	.496
1925—	York§	.583		Scranton (2nd)†	.562	1975—	Reading	.613
	Williamsport§	.583	1952—	Albany	.603		Bristol*	.587
1926—	Scranton	.627		Binghamton (2nd)‡	.562	1976—	Three Rivers	.601
1927—	Harrisburg	.630	1953—	Reading	.682		West Haven d	.576
1928—	Harrisburg	.603		Binghamton (2nd)‡	.636	1977—	West Haven e	.623
1929—	Binghamton	.597	1954—	Wilkes-Barre	.576		Three Rivers	.551
1930—	Wilkes-Barre	.572		Albany (3rd)‡	.540	1978—	Reading	.642
1931—	Harrisburg	.597	1955—	Reading	.613		Bristol*	.580
1932—	Wilkes-Barre	.561		Allentown (2nd)‡	.565	1979—	West Haven f	.597
1933—	Binghamton	.690	1956—	Schenectady†	.609	1980—	Holyoke*	.561
1934—	Binghamton	.694	1957—	Binghamton	.607		Waterbury	.540
	Williamsport*	.603		Reading (3rd)‡	.529	1981—	Glens Falls	.615
1935—	Scranton	.657	1958—	Lancaster x	.568		Bristol*	.577
	Binghamton*	.580		Binghamton (6th)‡	.493	1982—	West Haven*	.614
1936—	Scranton*	.609	1959—	Springfield†	.607		Lynn	.590
	Elmira	.629	1960—	Williamsport y	.551	1983—	Lynn	.554
1937—	Elmira†	.622		Springfield (3rd)y	.496		New Britain‡	.518
1938—	Binghamton	.622	1961—	Springfield	.612	1984—	Waterbury	.543
	Elmira (3rd)‡	.522	1962—	Williamsport	.593		Vermont‡	.536
1939—	Scranton†	.571		Elmira (2nd)‡	.514	1985—	Albany	.540
1940—	Scranton	.568	1963—	Charleston	.593		Vermont‡	.514
	Binghamton (2nd)‡	.554	1964—	Elmira	.586	1986—	Reading	.566
1941—	Wilkes-Barre	.630	1965—	Pittsfield	.607		Vermont‡	.554
	Elmira (3rd)‡	.514	1966—	Elmira	.633	1987—	Pittsfield	.630
1942—	Albany	.600	1967—	Binghamton z	.586		Harrisburg‡	.550
	Scranton (2nd)‡	.593		Elmira	.532	1988—	Glens Falls	.584
1943—	Scranton	.630	1968—	Pittsfield	.604		Albany‡	.522
	Elmira (2nd)‡	.568		Reading (2nd)‡	.579	1989—	Albany‡	.657
1944—	Hartford	.723	1969—	York	.640		Harrisburg	.522
	Binghamton (4th)‡	.474	1970—	Waterbury a	.560	1990—	Albany	.568
1945—	Utica	.615		Reading a	.553		London‡	.547
	Albany (3rd)‡	.564	1971—	Three Rivers	.569	1991—	Harrisburg	.621
1946—	Scranton†	.691		Elmira b	.561		Albany‡	.543
1947—	Utica†	.652	1972—	West Haven b	.600	1992—	Canton-Akron	.580
1948—	Scranton†	.636		Three Rivers	.559		Binghamton‡	.572
1949—	Albany	.664	1973—	Reading b	.551	1993—	Harrisburg‡	.681
	Binghamton (4th)‡	.500		Pittsfield	.551		Canton-Akron	.543

*Won split-season playoff. †Won championship and four-team playoff. ‡Won four-team playoff. §Tied for pennant, York winning playoff. xLeague was divided into Northern, Southern divisions and played a split season; Lancaster over-all season leader. yPlayoff finals canceled after one game because of rain with Williamsport and Springfield declared playoff co-champions. zLeague was divided into Eastern, Western divisions; Binghamton won playoff. aTied for pennant, Waterbury winning playoff. bLeague was divided into American, National divisions; won playoff. cLeague was divided into American and National divisions; won four-team playoff. dLeague was divided into Northern, Southern divisions, won playoff. eLeague was divided into New England and Canadian-American divisions; won playoff. fWon both halves of split season (no playoffs). (NOTE—Known as New York-Pennsylvania League prior to 1938.)

SOUTHERN LEAGUE

FINAL STANDINGS

FIRST HALF

EAST DIVISION

Team	W	L	T	Pct.	GB
Greenville (Braves)	39	32	0	.549	.....
Orlando (Cubs)	38	33	0	.535	1
Carolina (Pirates)	37	33	0	.529	1½
Knoxville (Blue Jays)	33	38	0	.465	6
Jacksonville (Mariners)	32	39	0	.451	7

WEST DIVISION

Team	W	L	T	Pct.	GB
Nashville (Twins)	40	31	0	.563	.....
Birmingham (White Sox)	35	36	0	.493	5
Huntsville (Athletics)	34	37	0	.479	6
Chattanooga (Reds)	34	38	0	.472	6½
Memphis (Royals)	33	38	0	.465	7

SECOND HALF

EAST DIVISION

Team	W	L	T	Pct.	GB
Knoxville (Blue Jays)	38	33	0	.535	.....
Carolina (Pirates)	37	34	0	.521	1
Greenville (Braves)	36	35	0	.507	2
Orlando (Cubs)	33	37	1	.471	4½
Jacksonville (Mariners)	27	42	1	.391	10

WEST DIVISION

Team	W	L	T	Pct.	GB
Birmingham (White Sox)	43	28	0	.606	.....
Chattanooga (Reds)	38	31	0	.551	4
Huntsville (Athletics)	37	33	0	.529	5½
Nashville (Twins)	32	39	0	.451	11
Memphis (Royals)	30	39	0	.435	12

COMPOSITE

Team	Birm.	Grn.	Caro.	Chat.	Nash.	Orl.	Hunt.	Knox.	Mem.	Jack.	W	L	T	Pct.	GB
Birmingham (White Sox)	....	4	5	11	9	6	12	6	11	10	78	64	0	.549	.....
Greenville (Braves)	10	....	14	7	5	6	4	9	10	10	75	67	0	.528	3
Carolina (Pirates)	5	10	....	7	11	10	6	6	10	9	74	67	0	.525	3½
Chattanooga (Reds)	5	7	7	....	9	8	10	12	7	7	72	69	0	.511	5½
Nashville (Twins)	7	9	3	7	....	8	8	8	13	9	72	70	0	.507	6
Orlando (Cubs)	8	10	6	6	6	....	7	9	7	12	71	70	1	.504	6½
Huntsville (Athletics)	12	10	8	8	7	7	....	7	6	7	71	70	0	.504	6½
Knoxville (Blue Jays)	8	7	10	10	6	7	7	....	6	10	71	71	0	.500	7
Memphis (Royals)	5	4	4	8	11	7	9	8	....	7	63	77	0	.450	14
Jacksonville (Mariners)	4	6	6	5	7	5	11	4	7	....	59	81	1	.421	18

Carolina's home games played in Zebulon, N.C.

Major league affiliations in parentheses.

Playoffs—Birmingham defeated Nashville, three games to none; Knoxville defeated Greenville, three games to two; Birmingham defeated Knoxville, three games to one, to win league championship.

Regular-season attendance—Birmingham, 277,096; Carolina, 328,207; Chattanooga, 270,671; Greenville, 232,369; Huntsville, 282,731; Jacksonville, 250,002; Knoxville, 140,868; Memphis, 230,181; Nashville, 178,737; Orlando, 217,716. Total, 2,408,578. Playoffs (12 games)—12,630. Class AA All-Star Game at Memphis—6,335.

Managers—Birmingham, Terry Francona; Carolina, Spin Williams (April 8 through May 20 and August 11 through end of season), John Wockenfuss (May 21 through August 10); Chattanooga, Pat Kelly; Greenville, Bruce Kimm; Huntsville, Casey Parsons; Jacksonville, Marc Hill; Knoxville, Garth Iorg; Memphis, Tom Poquette; Nashville, Phil Roof; Orlando, Tommy Jones. Managerial records of team with more than one manager: Carolina, Williams (29-38), Wockenfuss (45-29).

All-Star team: 1B—Jim Bowie, Huntsville; 2B—Ruben Santana, Jacksonville; 3B—Joe Randa, Memphis; SS—Alex Gonzalez, Knoxville; OF—Jerry Wolak, Birmingham; Les Norman, Memphis; Rich Becker, Nashville; Marc Newfield, Jacksonville; C—(tie) Carlos Delgado, Knoxville, and George Williams, Huntsville; DH—Jamie Dismuke, Chattanooga; RHP—Scott Ruffcorn, Birmingham; LHP—Huck Flener, Knoxville; Relief Pitcher—Chris Bushing, Chattanooga; Most Valuable Player—Carlos Delgado, Knoxville; Outstanding Pitcher—Oscar Munoz, Nashville; Manager of the Year—Terry Francona, Birmingham.

BATTING

TEAM

Team	Avg.	G	AB	R	OR	H	TB	2B	3B	HR	RBI	SH	SF	HP	BB	Int. BB	SO	SB	CS	LOB
Knoxville	.273	142	4663	630	653	1273	1789	224	29	78	574	41	27	57	439	39	930	160	86	969
Orlando	.266	142	4737	686	673	1262	1938	256	27	122	629	79	42	39	516	29	928	96	83	1002
Memphis	.265	140	4701	627	656	1245	1841	232	35	98	589	44	47	60	447	19	846	79	66	999
Huntsville	.264	141	4620	678	676	1221	1795	230	22	100	624	43	54	64	502	22	972	111	60	985
Jacksonville	.264	141	4735	624	679	1248	1894	235	18	125	579	58	37	69	471	23	850	130	82	1020
Birmingham	.260	142	4598	630	564	1196	1745	211	40	86	541	32	43	53	453	18	926	159	83	904
Chattanooga	.259	142	4663	628	583	1207	1817	216	35	108	577	38	37	45	415	22	1122	144	87	892
Nashville	.257	142	4717	672	651	1213	1832	224	31	111	613	48	40	61	584	23	925	164	53	1046
Carolina	.256	141	4733	615	626	1213	1755	202	38	88	548	76	38	67	427	31	842	109	67	992
Greenville	.254	142	4665	602	631	1184	1760	233	38	89	540	43	36	52	476	20	852	97	79	935

BATTING

INDIVIDUAL

(Leading qualifiers for batting championship—383 or more plate appearances)

*Bats lefthanded.   †Switch-hitter.

Player, Team	Avg.	G	AB	R	H	TB	2B	3B	HR	RBI	SH	SF	HP	BB	Int. BB	SO	SB	CS
Bowie, Jim, Huntsville*	.333	138	501	77	167	244	33	1	14	101	1	8	0	56	8	52	8	3
Hyers, Tim, Knoxville*	.306	140	487	72	149	190	26	3	3	61	5	2	2	53	5	51	12	3
Dismuke, Jamie, Chattanooga*	.306	136	497	69	152	236	22	1	20	91	0	4	14	48	6	60	4	2
Wolak, Jerry, Birmingham	.305	137	525	78	160	230	35	4	9	64	2	4	8	26	2	95	16	12

— 398 —

Player, Team	Avg.	G	AB	R	H	TB	2B	3B	HR	RBI	SH	SF	HP	BB	Int. BB	SO	SB	CS
Casillas, Adam, Memphis*	.304	126	450	53	137	194	33	6	4	50	2	5	4	59	3	18	3	3
Delgado, Carlos, Knoxville*	.303	140	468	91	142	245	28	0	25	102	0	5	6	102	18	98	10	3
Santana, Ruben, Jacksonville	.301	128	499	79	150	238	21	2	21	84	3	5	9	38	7	101	13	8
Merchant, Mark, Chattanooga†	.301	109	336	56	101	168	16	0	17	61	0	3	3	50	2	79	3	5
Randa, Joe, Memphis	.295	131	505	74	149	223	31	5	11	72	0	10	3	39	2	64	8	7
Williams, George, Huntsville†	.295	124	434	80	128	200	26	2	14	77	1	6	14	67	0	66	6	3

Departmental leaders: G—Gonzalez, 142; AB—Bowers, 577; R—Becker, Gonzalez, 93; H—Bowie, 167; TB—Gonzalez, 253; 2B—Wolak, 35; 3B—Durham, 10; HR—C. Delgado, 25; RBI—C. Delgado, 102; SH—Ratliff, 14; SF—Randa, 10; HP—Lis, 16; BB—C. Delgado, 102; IBB—C. Delgado, 18; SO—Cordova, 153; SB—Wilson, 43; CS—Durham, 25.

(All players—listed alphabetically)

Player, Team	Avg.	G	AB	R	H	TB	2B	3B	HR	RBI	SH	SF	HP	BB	Int. BB	SO	SB	CS
Adams, Tommy, Jacksonville	.276	61	232	19	64	92	12	2	4	20	2	3	0	14	2	34	4	0
Adriana, Sharnol, Knoxville	.215	64	177	19	38	43	3	1	0	18	2	2	2	24	2	59	9	8
Alicea, Ed, Greenville†	.065	14	31	5	2	2	0	0	0	2	0	0	0	5	0	9	1	0
Alvarez, Clemente, Birmingham	.225	35	111	8	25	32	4	0	1	8	1	1	1	11	0	28	0	4
Arias, Amador, Chattanooga†	.215	18	65	6	14	17	1	1	0	2	1	0	0	4	0	23	1	1
Aude, Rich, Carolina	.289	120	422	66	122	207	25	3	18	73	1	6	12	50	7	79	8	4
Backlund, Brett, Carolina	.400	21	15	2	6	9	0	0	1	7	2	0	0	2	0	3	0	0
Banister, Jeff, Carolina	.333	8	15	2	5	6	1	0	0	4	0	0	1	1	0	0	0	0
Battle, Howard, Knoxville	.278	141	521	66	145	197	21	5	7	70	1	3	7	45	3	94	12	9
Beard, Garrett, Huntsville	.262	18	61	8	16	21	3	1	0	6	0	1	1	6	0	13	1	1
Beasley, Tony, Carolina	.202	82	252	39	51	76	7	3	4	13	3	1	0	23	2	52	11	6
Beatty, Blaine, Carolina*	.091	18	11	1	1	1	0	0	0	1	1	1	0	0	0	2	0	0
Beauchamp, Kash, Chattanooga	.400	18	60	16	24	47	6	1	5	15	1	0	2	10	0	9	1	1
Becker, Rich, Nashville*	.287	138	516	93	148	232	25	7	15	66	2	3	3	94	5	117	29	7
Beeler, Pete, Jacksonville	.207	18	58	6	12	18	3	0	1	6	1	0	1	6	0	13	0	0
Belcher, Kevin, Birmingham	.222	111	360	38	80	136	13	2	13	50	0	5	4	45	2	81	11	6
Boltz, Brian, Greenville*	.250	9	4	0	1	1	0	0	0	0	0	0	0	0	0	1	0	0
Bowers, Brent, Knoxville	.248	141	577	63	143	189	23	4	5	43	13	0	3	21	1	121	36	19
Bowie, Jim, Huntsville*	.333	138	501	77	167	244	33	1	14	101	1	8	0	56	8	52	8	3
Bradley, Scott, Greenville*	.333	26	57	6	19	24	2	0	1	11	0	0	1	5	1	8	0	0
Bragg, Darren, Jacksonville*	.264	131	451	74	119	184	26	3	11	46	4	3	7	81	3	82	19	11
Brito, Jorge, Huntsville	.278	18	36	6	10	25	3	0	4	11	0	1	2	10	1	10	0	0
Brown, Adam, Orlando*	.500	2	6	0	3	4	1	0	0	1	0	0	0	0	0	0	0	0
Brown, Brant, Orlando*	.315	28	111	17	35	64	11	3	4	23	0	1	4	6	1	19	2	1
Buckley, Travis, 2 Chat. - 10 Jack.	.000	12	1	0	0	0	0	0	0	0	0	0	0	0	0	1	0	0
Buckley, Troy, Chattanooga	.256	14	43	4	11	15	1	0	1	4	1	0	0	1	0	5	0	0
Burgos, John, Chattanooga*	.000	31	1	0	0	0	0	0	0	0	0	0	0	1	0	0	0	0
Burlingame, Dennis, Greenville	.333	15	6	1	2	2	0	0	0	1	2	0	0	1	0	1	0	0
Busby, Wayne, Orlando	.203	27	74	8	15	20	5	0	0	4	1	1	1	10	1	16	1	1
Bushing, Chris, Chattanooga	.000	61	2	0	0	0	0	0	0	0	0	0	0	0	0	2	0	0
Butler, Rich, Knoxville*	.095	6	21	3	2	4	0	0	1	0	0	0	0	0	0	4	0	0
Cairo, Sergio, Birmingham	.228	68	189	20	43	51	2	0	2	13	0	1	1	28	0	28	6	3
Campanis, Jim, Jacksonville	.245	70	212	16	52	68	7	0	3	22	4	0	7	23	0	43	0	2
Canate, Willie, Knoxville	.270	9	37	8	10	15	2	0	1	4	0	0	0	5	0	2	2	1
Casillas, Adam, Memphis*	.304	126	450	53	137	194	33	6	4	50	2	5	4	59	3	18	3	3
Cecena, Jose, Carolina	.000	14	1	0	0	0	0	0	0	0	0	0	0	0	0	0	0	0
Cepicky, Scott, Birmingham*	.242	66	236	30	57	92	12	1	7	35	2	2	1	34	3	67	4	0
Clayton, Craig, Jacksonville	.298	59	215	23	64	79	8	2	1	23	5	1	2	17	0	29	10	5
Coffman, Kevin, Jacksonville	.000	11	2	0	0	0	0	0	0	0	0	0	0	0	0	0	0	0
Cole, Butch, Memphis	.257	80	292	33	75	97	16	0	2	36	1	3	5	13	0	39	5	3
Cole, Victor, Carolina†	.000	27	1	0	0	0	0	0	0	0	0	0	0	0	0	0	0	0
Coleman, Ken, Birmingham	.233	50	129	11	30	33	3	0	0	14	3	2	1	13	0	25	2	1
Colvard, Benny, Memphis	.236	56	182	20	43	65	10	4	0	25	1	1	1	8	0	39	0	1
Coomer, Ron, Birmingham	.324	69	262	44	85	142	18	0	13	50	0	2	0	15	3	43	1	1
Corbett, Sherm, Orlando*	.500	5	4	1	2	2	0	0	0	0	0	0	0	0	0	2	0	0
Corbin, Ted, Nashville†	.333	5	15	2	5	6	1	0	0	1	0	0	0	2	0	1	0	0
Cordova, Marty, Nashville	.250	138	508	83	127	224	30	5	19	77	0	3	13	64	3	153	10	5
Cornelius, Brian, Jacksonville*	.286	48	168	28	48	68	11	0	3	17	4	0	2	8	1	28	5	5
Courtright, John, Chattanooga*	.000	27	16	0	0	0	0	0	0	0	0	0	0	0	0	8	0	0
Cox, Darron, Chattanooga	.217	89	300	35	65	93	9	5	3	26	7	1	3	38	2	63	7	4
Crockett, Russ, Orlando	.204	33	98	15	20	24	4	0	0	3	2	0	3	7	0	14	1	1
Cruz, Fausto, Huntsville	.335	63	251	45	84	112	15	2	3	31	4	2	1	20	0	42	2	0
Culberson, Calvain, Chattanooga	.333	39	3	0	1	1	0	0	0	0	0	0	0	0	0	0	0	0
Cummings, Midre, Carolina*	.295	63	237	33	70	109	17	2	6	26	2	0	1	14	1	23	5	3
Czarkowski, Mark, Jacksonville*	.000	25	2	0	0	0	0	0	0	0	0	0	0	0	0	1	0	0
Dattola, Kevin, Huntsville†	.253	91	296	43	75	124	17	1	10	32	4	3	4	32	5	70	12	6
Dauphin, Phil, Orlando*	.264	81	299	53	79	132	16	2	11	35	3	3	3	30	0	40	7	10
Davisson, Sean, Orlando	.000	2	1	0	0	0	0	0	0	0	0	0	0	0	0	0	0	0
De Los Santos, Alberto, Carolina	.223	47	148	17	33	44	5	3	0	10	2	0	2	5	1	18	4	3
Delanuez, Rex, Nashville	.236	115	352	71	83	133	20	3	8	43	4	6	13	93	4	80	23	4
Delgado, Carlos, Knoxville*	.303	140	468	91	142	245	28	0	25	102	0	5	6	102	18	98	10	3
Delgado, Tim, Orlando	.167	9	6	0	1	1	0	0	0	0	0	0	0	1	0	2	0	0
De Los Santos, Mariano, Carolina*	.000	8	4	0	0	0	0	0	0	0	0	0	0	0	1	0	0	0
Dempsey, John, Memphis*	.250	1	4	0	1	1	0	0	0	0	0	0	0	0	0	1	0	0
Diaz, Carlos, Memphis	.215	54	163	13	35	47	3	0	3	25	0	3	1	3	0	33	1	0
Diaz, Eddy, Jacksonville	.251	77	259	36	65	99	16	0	6	26	7	4	2	17	1	31	6	3
Diaz, Kiki, Memphis	.282	21	78	12	22	24	2	0	0	5	0	0	13	2	1	7	1	1
Dickson, Lance, Orlando	.250	9	4	0	1	1	0	0	0	0	0	0	0	1	0	1	0	0
DiSarcina, Glenn, Birmingham*	.400	3	5	1	2	2	0	0	0	1	0	0	0	2	0	2	0	0
Dismuke, Jamie, Chattanooga*	.306	136	497	69	152	236	22	1	20	91	0	4	14	48	6	60	4	2
Dunn, Steve, Nashville*	.262	97	366	48	96	162	20	2	14	60	0	1	4	35	3	88	1	2
Durant, Mike, Nashville	.243	123	437	58	106	155	23	1	8	57	4	3	6	44	1	68	17	3
Durham, Ray, Birmingham†	.271	137	528	83	143	194	22	10	3	37	5	5	14	42	2	100	39	25
Ebright, Chris, Orlando*	.283	113	318	49	90	143	21	1	10	56	2	6	1	50	3	61	2	0
Edge, Tim, Carolina	.219	46	160	12	35	52	6	0	3	16	2	0	1	11	0	41	1	2
Erdman, Brad, Orlando	.181	69	171	12	31	39	5	0	1	17	3	1	6	18	5	42	2	2
Ferry, Mike, Chattanooga*	.087	28	23	0	2	2	0	0	0	0	3	0	0	0	0	10	0	0
Franco, Matt, Orlando*	.316	68	237	31	75	118	20	1	7	37	1	2	2	29	2	30	3	6
Fuller, Jon, Chattanooga	.270	46	148	22	40	59	8	1	3	17	1	4	2	12	0	41	3	1

Player, Team	Avg.	G	AB	R	H	TB	2B	3B	HR	RBI	SH	SF	HP	BB	Int. BB	SO	SB	CS
Galvez, Balvino, Orlando	.000	3	2	0	0	0	0	0	0	0	0	0	0	0	0	0	0	0
Garber, Jeff, Memphis	.281	81	253	40	71	120	13	0	12	32	2	0	5	26	2	61	1	3
Gardner, John, 7 Orl. - 19 Birm.	1.000	26	1	0	1	1	0	0	0	0	0	0	0	0	0	0	0	0
Garner, Kevin, Chattanooga*	.151	19	53	6	8	15	1	0	2	5	0	0	0	9	1	26	2	1
Garza, Alejandro, Carolina	.000	35	4	0	0	0	0	0	0	0	1	0	0	0	0	2	0	0
Gates, Brent, Huntsville†	.333	12	45	7	15	22	4	0	1	11	1	0	0	7	0	9	0	0
Gibralter, Steve, Chattanooga	.237	132	477	65	113	177	25	3	11	47	3	4	7	20	2	108	7	12
Gill, Chris, Chattanooga	.000	1	2	0	0	0	0	0	0	0	0	0	0	0	0	0	0	0
Gillis, Tim, Greenville	.251	135	451	58	113	183	22	3	14	62	2	3	7	51	3	103	1	6
Gillum, K.C., Chattanooga*	.245	66	216	31	53	82	9	1	6	24	1	1	1	19	3	61	3	6
Giovanola, Ed, Greenville*	.281	120	384	70	108	154	21	5	5	43	4	6	2	84	3	49	6	7
Glanville, Doug, Orlando	.264	73	296	42	78	127	14	4	9	40	6	5	2	12	0	41	15	7
Gomez, Fabio, Huntsville	.259	60	220	26	57	90	10	1	7	33	3	1	2	17	0	43	5	3
Gomez, Rudy, Orlando	.329	56	140	26	46	57	8	0	1	17	8	2	3	25	0	31	5	3
Gonzalez, Alex, Knoxville	.289	142	561	93	162	253	29	7	16	69	0	6	6	39	2	110	38	13
Gordon, Keith, Chattanooga	.291	116	419	69	122	196	26	3	14	59	0	2	4	19	0	132	13	18
Grace, Mike, Orlando	.271	120	425	65	115	189	29	3	13	76	4	6	2	35	4	56	2	3
Grayum, Richie, Orlando*	.295	92	234	45	69	114	13	1	10	33	3	1	3	45	1	66	1	10
Green, Shawn, Knoxville*	.283	99	360	40	102	132	14	2	4	34	6	1	5	26	2	72	4	9
Green, Tom, Carolina	.238	98	311	42	74	111	14	4	5	48	2	4	8	32	1	66	4	7
Grifol, Pedro, Nashville	.203	58	197	22	40	68	13	0	5	29	5	3	2	11	0	38	0	1
Guerrero, Mike, Memphis	.265	24	68	7	18	24	6	0	0	4	4	0	0	4	0	7	0	2
Halter, Shane, Memphis	.258	81	306	50	79	98	7	0	4	20	10	3	2	30	1	74	4	7
Hammond, Greg, Chattanooga	.281	9	32	3	9	12	3	0	0	5	1	0	0	2	1	6	0	1
Hancock, Lee, Carolina*	.500	25	10	3	5	6	1	0	0	3	1	0	0	0	0	2	0	0
Harrah, Doug, Carolina	.000	6	2	0	0	0	0	0	0	0	0	0	0	0	0	1	0	0
Hart, Chris, Huntsville	.256	103	301	39	77	108	7	3	6	42	5	1	11	10	0	82	12	5
Hartsock, Jeff, Orlando	.000	8	2	0	0	0	0	0	0	0	0	0	0	0	0	0	0	0
Hassinger, Brad, Greenville	1.000	12	1	1	1	1	0	0	0	0	0	0	0	0	0	0	0	0
Heath, Lee, Greenville†	.243	112	432	47	105	150	15	6	6	36	1	2	7	23	0	108	16	18
Helfand, Eric, Huntsville*	.228	100	302	38	69	118	15	2	10	48	3	7	8	43	2	78	1	1
Henderson, Derek, Knoxville	.241	13	29	4	7	7	0	0	0	1	1	0	2	3	0	7	1	1
Hernandez, Jose, Orlando	.304	71	263	42	80	118	8	3	8	33	5	1	0	20	1	60	8	4
Hocking, Denny, Nashville†	.267	107	409	54	109	150	9	4	8	50	3	2	4	34	0	66	15	5
Hodge, Tim, Knoxville*	.242	102	289	21	70	91	18	0	1	31	2	1	5	34	3	79	5	1
Holley, Bobby, Jacksonville	.247	108	388	59	96	159	22	1	13	66	2	2	6	43	5	50	7	5
Hood, Randy, Birmingham	.250	11	20	6	5	10	3	1	0	2	0	0	2	3	0	6	0	0
Hook, Chris, Chattanooga†	.000	28	17	0	0	0	0	0	0	0	2	0	0	0	0	8	0	0
Hope, John, Carolina	.000	21	11	1	0	0	0	0	0	0	3	0	0	1	0	6	0	0
Hostetler, Mike, Greenville	.077	19	13	0	1	1	0	0	0	0	2	0	0	1	0	6	0	0
Houk, Tom, 48 Nash. -43 Chat.	.237	91	278	36	66	86	6	4	2	29	4	0	1	48	0	57	6	4
Houston, Tyler, Greenville*	.279	84	262	27	73	104	14	1	5	33	3	4	2	13	4	50	5	3
Hughes, Troy, Greenville	.266	109	383	49	102	172	20	4	14	59	0	3	5	44	1	67	7	3
Hunter, Bobby, Carolina†	.000	46	2	0	0	0	0	0	0	0	0	0	0	0	0	0	0	0
Hyers, Tim, Knoxville*	.306	140	487	72	149	190	26	3	3	61	5	2	2	53	5	51	12	3
Jackson, Kenny, Jacksonville	.000	4	10	1	0	0	0	0	0	1	0	0	0	1	0	4	0	0
Jarvis, Kevin, Chattanooga*	.400	7	5	1	2	2	0	0	0	1	0	0	0	1	0	0	0	0
Jaster, Scott, Memphis	.251	55	183	24	46	77	11	1	6	24	0	2	1	19	1	41	6	1
Jenkins, Bernie, Chattanooga	.252	102	290	31	73	93	9	1	3	26	1	2	2	21	1	71	18	7
Jennings, Lance, Memphis	.205	98	327	27	67	90	11	0	4	33	1	2	6	21	0	83	0	1
Jensen, John, Orlando*	.266	62	192	27	51	83	10	2	6	34	0	2	2	18	2	45	4	3
Johns, Doug, Huntsville	.200	44	5	0	1	1	0	0	0	1	0	0	0	1	0	1	0	0
Johnson, Chris, Orlando	1.000	15	1	0	1	1	0	0	0	0	0	0	0	0	0	0	0	0
Johnson, Earnie, Orlando*	.250	54	4	1	1	1	0	0	0	0	0	0	0	2	0	0	0	0
Johnson, Herman, Huntsville	.333	2	3	0	1	1	0	0	0	0	0	0	0	0	0	2	1	0
Johnson, Jack, Orlando	.232	33	82	9	19	25	6	0	0	5	3	1	1	12	0	22	0	1
Johnson, Mark D., Memphis*	.197	61	213	24	42	67	4	3	5	22	3	2	1	14	1	24	6	2
Johnson, Mark P., Carolina*	.233	125	399	48	93	161	18	4	14	52	2	3	3	66	7	93	6	2
Jones, Dan, Carolina	.250	11	8	0	2	2	0	0	0	0	0	0	0	0	0	4	0	0
Jones, Motorboat, Chattanooga	.225	26	89	10	20	27	4	0	1	10	2	1	0	9	0	17	3	2
Kapano, Corey, Orlando	.255	89	263	44	67	105	12	1	8	35	3	2	1	20	0	58	17	4
Kelly, Pat, Greenville	.255	72	212	23	54	66	10	1	0	17	5	1	1	14	1	30	2	5
Kennedy, Bo, Chattanooga	.000	2	1	0	0	0	0	0	0	0	0	0	1	0	1	0	0	0
Kessinger, Keith, Chattanooga†	.311	56	161	24	50	68	9	0	3	28	5	0	0	24	2	18	0	3
Kieschnick, Brooks, Orlando	.341	25	91	12	31	45	8	0	2	10	0	0	7	1	9	19	1	2
Kizziah, Daren, Knoxville	1.000	27	1	0	1	1	0	0	0	0	0	0	0	0	0	0	0	0
Klonoski, Jason, Nashville*	.000	57	1	0	0	0	0	0	0	0	0	0	0	0	0	0	0	0
Koelling, Brian, Chattanooga	.277	110	430	64	119	160	17	6	4	47	4	3	2	32	1	105	34	13
Kounas, Tony, Jacksonville	.278	49	158	22	44	70	14	0	4	22	1	1	2	14	0	24	2	1
Kowitz, Brian, Greenville*	.278	122	450	63	125	170	20	5	5	48	1	1	2	60	0	56	13	10
Krevokuch, Jim, Carolina	.253	125	395	58	100	133	15	3	4	30	3	2	15	53	1	38	4	3
Kuehl, John, Huntsville†	.240	111	379	49	91	156	28	2	11	67	4	8	7	36	4	107	3	0
Lane, Brian, Chattanooga	.264	114	425	60	112	179	29	4	10	57	0	3	2	41	0	134	1	1
Leiper, Dave, Carolina*	.000	8	3	0	0	0	0	0	0	0	0	0	0	0	0	0	0	0
Leiper, Tim, Carolina*	.258	44	132	11	34	41	4	0	1	11	1	0	2	10	0	6	0	1
Lewis, Mica, Orlando	.244	42	86	14	21	27	3	0	1	10	2	0	0	14	0	19	3	1
Lieber, Jon, 4 Mem. -6 Caro.*	.000	10	3	0	0	0	0	0	0	0	0	0	0	0	0	2	0	0
Lis, Joe, Knoxville	.290	129	448	66	130	189	29	3	8	64	2	5	16	42	1	58	6	9
Loaiza, Steve, Carolina	.000	7	7	0	0	0	0	0	0	0	0	0	0	0	0	1	0	0
Lofton, Rod, Chattanooga	.111	10	27	1	3	3	0	0	0	2	1	0	0	7	0	11	2	0
Lomon, Kevin, Greenville	.200	13	10	0	2	2	0	0	0	0	2	0	0	0	0	4	0	0
Long, Kevin, Memphis*	.272	79	301	47	82	111	14	6	1	20	2	2	5	37	2	56	7	11
Lonigro, Greg, Orlando	.273	62	216	20	59	83	12	0	4	22	1	2	0	5	0	33	4	5
Magallanes, Willie, Orlando	.176	7	17	1	3	3	0	0	0	0	0	0	0	2	1	3	1	0
Mann, Kelly, Orlando	.244	28	82	11	20	28	3	1	1	7	2	0	2	11	1	11	0	0
Manning, Henry, Birmingham	.179	30	106	7	19	30	3	1	2	9	0	0	3	3	0	25	0	1
Marquez, Jesus, Jacksonville*	.313	11	32	7	10	16	0	0	2	5	1	1	2	9	1	9	3	2
Martinez, Edgar, Jacksonville	.357	4	14	2	5	8	0	0	1	3	0	0	0	2	0	1	0	0
Mashore, Damon, Huntsville†	.233	70	253	35	59	79	7	2	3	20	1	2	4	25	0	64	18	4
Masteller, Dan, Nashville*	.273	36	121	19	33	45	3	0	3	16	2	0	1	11	0	19	2	1
Matos, Francisco, Huntsville	.275	123	461	69	127	148	12	3	1	32	4	3	4	22	1	54	16	6
May, Lee, Memphis†	.205	14	39	3	8	8	0	0	0	0	0	0	0	0	0	16	2	0
Maynard, Tow, Jacksonville	.215	60	195	21	42	55	5	1	2	8	0	1	1	15	0	50	17	7
McCreary, Bob, Nashville†	.000	38	2	0	0	0	0	0	0	0	0	0	0	0	0	0	0	0

Player, Team	Avg.	G	AB	R	H	TB	2B	3B	HR	RBI	SH	SF	HP	BB	Int. BB	SO	SB	CS
McCurry, Jeff, Carolina	.000	23	1	0	0	0	0	0	0	0	0	0	0	0	0	1	0	0
McDonald, Mike, Nashville*	.257	82	268	28	69	104	12	1	7	31	2	4	0	30	2	63	1	3
McDonnell, Shawn, Orlando†	.213	18	47	2	10	12	2	0	0	8	0	1	4	1	0	14	0	0
Melvin, Bill, Orlando	.667	36	3	1	2	2	0	0	0	3	1	0	0	0	0	0	0	0
Merchant, Mark, Chattanooga†	.301	109	336	56	101	168	16	0	17	61	0	3	3	50	2	79	3	5
Miller, Damian, Nashville	.231	4	13	0	3	3	0	0	0	0	0	0	0	0	0	4	0	0
Miller, Paul, Carolina	.111	6	9	1	1	1	0	0	0	0	1	0	0	1	0	5	0	0
Miranda, Geovany, Birmingham	.094	12	32	2	3	3	0	0	0	0	1	0	0	1	0	6	0	0
Morales, Jorge, Jacksonville	.282	55	170	15	48	66	9	0	3	25	3	1	1	9	0	39	9	5
Morland, Michael, Knoxville	.232	45	112	7	26	32	4	1	0	15	3	0	0	10	0	31	1	1
Morones, Geno, Orlando	.000	4	4	0	0	0	0	0	0	0	0	0	0	0	0	1	0	0
Mota, Domingo, Memphis	.214	56	196	22	42	58	7	3	1	16	3	3	1	11	0	48	10	9
Mota, Willie, Nashville†	.234	64	201	16	47	67	10	2	2	26	2	3	1	9	1	33	1	1
Nava, Lipso, Jacksonville	.254	114	397	52	101	142	20	0	7	41	12	3	13	31	1	43	5	6
Neff, Marty, Carolina	.222	20	63	2	14	17	3	0	0	5	0	0	0	0	0	18	0	1
Neill, Mike, Huntsville*	.246	54	179	30	44	55	8	0	1	15	0	1	1	34	0	45	3	4
Newfield, Marc, Jacksonville	.307	91	336	48	103	178	18	0	19	51	0	3	5	33	1	35	1	1
Norman, Les, Memphis	.291	133	484	78	141	234	32	5	17	81	7	2	14	50	3	88	11	9
Nunez, Rogelio, Birmingham†	.214	83	257	22	55	71	10	3	0	21	6	2	1	5	0	53	2	4
O'Connor, Kevin, Greenville*	.189	122	355	63	67	107	15	2	7	30	4	0	7	62	1	63	18	10
Olmeda, Jose, Greenville†	.279	122	451	61	126	190	33	2	9	51	5	9	0	29	2	63	15	7
Ortiz, Javier, Carolina	.339	33	109	17	37	64	10	1	5	24	0	3	2	15	3	18	1	1
Osik, Keith, Carolina	.280	103	371	47	104	159	21	2	10	47	4	1	9	30	1	46	0	2
Perez, Eddie, Greenville	.333	28	84	15	28	52	6	0	6	17	0	2	0	2	0	8	1	0
Picota, Len, Jacksonville	.500	11	2	0	1	1	0	0	0	0	0	0	0	0	0	0	0	0
Pierce, Jeff, 33 Birm. - 13 Chat.	.000	46	1	0	0	0	0	0	0	0	0	0	0	0	0	0	0	0
Pledger, Kinnis, Birmingham*	.242	125	393	70	95	159	10	6	14	56	5	4	3	74	0	120	19	6
Polcovich, Kevin, Carolina	.273	4	11	1	3	3	0	0	0	1	2	0	0	1	0	1	0	0
Polley, Dale, Greenville	.333	42	3	1	1	1	0	0	0	0	0	0	0	0	0	1	0	0
Potts, Mike, Greenville*	.071	25	14	2	1	1	0	0	0	0	1	0	0	3	0	7	0	0
Purdy, Alan, Carolina	.268	18	56	9	15	20	3	1	0	9	2	0	2	3	1	11	0	0
Raabe, Brian, Nashville	.286	134	524	80	150	195	23	2	6	52	10	4	10	56	1	28	18	8
Raasch, Glen, Orlando	.214	5	14	0	3	3	0	0	0	1	1	0	0	0	0	4	0	0
Randa, Joe, Memphis	.295	131	505	74	149	223	31	5	11	72	0	10	3	39	2	64	8	7
Ratliff, Daryl, Carolina	.284	121	454	59	129	152	15	4	0	47	14	5	2	35	0	58	29	13
Ray, Johnny, Chattanooga	.000	30	2	0	0	0	0	0	0	0	0	0	0	0	0	2	0	0
Reams, Ron, Knoxville	.227	96	299	39	68	102	14	1	6	33	4	2	2	11	2	69	16	3
Reese, Pokey, Chattanooga	.212	102	345	35	73	107	17	4	3	37	3	7	1	23	1	77	8	5
Relaford, Desi, Jacksonville†	.244	133	472	49	115	163	16	4	8	47	6	4	7	50	1	103	16	12
Reyes, Carlos, Greenville*	.000	33	2	0	0	0	0	0	0	0	0	0	0	0	0	1	0	0
Ripplemeyer, Brad, Greenville	.191	95	277	25	53	79	14	0	4	27	3	3	6	31	4	74	0	2
Ritter, Darren, Greenville	.333	35	3	0	1	1	0	0	0	0	0	0	0	0	0	1	0	0
Rivera, David, Nashville	.237	105	325	41	77	97	7	2	3	33	8	1	5	17	1	42	35	9
Roa, Hector, Greenville	.246	123	447	50	110	164	28	4	6	58	2	2	8	24	0	72	6	7
Robertson, Mike, Birmingham*	.270	138	511	73	138	208	31	3	11	73	0	8	3	59	4	97	10	5
Robinson, Jim, Orlando	.231	20	52	3	12	14	2	0	0	1	1	0	0	6	0	14	1	0
Robinson, Scott, Chattanooga	.231	21	13	1	3	9	1	1	1	1	0	0	0	0	0	6	0	0
Rodriguez, Roman, Carolina	.182	4	11	0	2	2	0	0	0	0	0	0	0	0	0	3	0	0
Rosario, Gabriel, Knoxville	.500	1	4	0	2	2	0	0	0	0	0	0	0	0	0	1	0	1
Saenz, Olmedo, Birmingham	.347	49	173	30	60	99	17	2	6	29	0	1	5	20	2	21	2	1
Salles, John, Orlando	.071	33	14	1	1	1	0	0	0	2	0	0	0	0	0	9	0	0
Sanchez, Ozzie, Greenville*	.220	33	100	8	22	37	3	0	4	13	0	0	3	12	0	28	2	0
Sandberg, Ryne, Orlando	.222	4	9	0	2	2	0	0	0	1	0	0	0	3	1	1	0	1
Santana, Ruben, Jacksonville	.301	128	499	79	150	238	21	2	21	84	3	5	9	38	7	101	13	8
Schreiber, Bruce, Carolina	.260	94	296	42	77	100	11	3	2	28	9	3	2	20	1	50	1	2
Schutz, Carl, Greenville*	.000	22	1	0	0	0	0	0	0	0	0	0	0	0	0	0	0	0
Scruggs, Tony, Jacksonville	.241	61	224	26	54	88	11	1	7	38	2	1	2	13	0	53	5	4
Sheppard, Don, Knoxville	.281	72	249	32	70	89	11	1	2	27	2	2	1	14	0	70	5	5
Simmons, Enoch, Huntsville	.229	43	140	24	32	48	7	0	3	20	0	4	1	17	0	39	5	2
Smith, Bubba, Nashville	.219	37	137	12	30	56	8	0	6	21	0	1	2	7	0	52	0	2
Sondrini, Joe, Carolina	.222	60	185	21	41	49	8	0	0	13	8	0	2	13	3	33	2	3
Spann, Tookie, Chattanooga	.071	8	14	0	1	1	0	0	0	0	0	0	0	0	0	6	0	0
Sparma, Blase, Greenville	.143	28	21	1	3	5	0	1	0	2	0	0	1	0	0	6	0	0
Stahoviak, Scott, Nashville*	.272	93	331	40	90	153	25	1	12	56	1	4	1	56	2	95	10	2
Steenstra, Kennie, Orlando	.083	15	12	0	1	1	0	0	0	1	0	0	0	1	0	7	0	0
Stevens, Dave, Orlando	.083	11	12	0	1	1	0	0	0	1	0	0	0	0	0	3	0	0
Stewart, Carl, Chattanooga	.000	10	1	0	0	0	0	0	0	0	0	0	0	1	0	1	0	0
Strange, Keith, Birmingham	.235	6	17	1	4	4	0	0	0	3	0	0	0	0	0	5	0	0
Strauss, Julio, Orlando	.000	15	1	0	0	0	0	0	0	0	0	0	0	0	0	1	0	0
Swann, Pedro, Greenville*	.306	44	157	19	48	70	9	2	3	21	1	0	1	9	0	23	2	2
Swartzbaugh, Dave, Orlando	.000	10	10	0	0	0	0	0	0	0	2	0	0	2	0	5	0	0
Tafoya, Dennis, Carolina	.250	49	8	0	2	4	0	1	0	1	1	0	0	0	0	4	0	0
Tatar, Kevin, Chattanooga	.000	4	1	0	0	0	0	0	0	0	0	0	0	0	0	0	0	0
Tedder, Scott, Birmingham*	.254	39	118	20	30	38	5	0	1	12	2	1	0	19	0	15	1	4
Thomas, Keith, Carolina	.238	94	336	40	80	138	9	2	15	52	1	4	2	22	0	110	12	6
Timmons, Ozzie, Orlando	.284	107	359	65	102	182	22	2	18	58	2	1	2	62	3	80	5	11
Tomlin, Randy, Carolina*	.000	2	2	0	0	0	0	0	0	0	0	0	0	0	0	0	0	0
Torres, Paul, Orlando	.255	19	55	10	14	27	4	0	3	10	0	0	0	0	0	18	3	0
Tucker, Mike, Memphis*	.279	72	244	38	68	110	7	4	9	35	0	3	4	42	0	51	12	5
Upshaw, Lee, Greenville*	.375	35	16	1	6	7	1	0	0	4	2	0	0	0	0	2	0	0
Van Slyke, Andy, Carolina*	.000	2	4	0	0	0	0	0	0	1	0	0	0	1	0	3	0	0
Vasquez, Marcos, Greenville	.143	43	7	0	1	1	0	0	0	1	0	0	0	0	0	3	0	0
Vice, Darryl, Orlando†	.273	62	220	36	60	78	5	2	3	24	7	1	0	28	0	31	6	5
Viera, Jose, Orlando	.091	3	11	0	1	1	0	0	0	1	0	0	0	1	0	1	0	0
Vitiello, Joe, Memphis	.288	117	413	62	119	193	25	2	15	66	0	5	5	57	2	95	2	0
Wade, Terrell, Greenville*	.000	8	1	0	0	0	0	0	0	0	0	0	0	0	0	0	0	0
Waggoner, Aubrey, Jacksonville*	.245	34	102	29	25	46	8	2	3	7	0	1	0	40	0	34	7	3
Waggoner, Jim, Huntsville*	.140	57	129	12	18	24	3	0	1	8	0	1	0	29	0	38	2	2
Wakefield, Tim, Carolina	.143	9	7	0	1	1	0	0	0	2	0	0	0	0	0	3	0	0
Walker, Dennis, Birmingham	.214	46	126	10	27	41	4	2	2	16	1	1	3	1	0	32	2	0
Walker, Mike, Orlando	.000	16	1	0	0	0	0	0	0	0	0	0	0	0	0	1	0	0
Wallace, Derek, Orlando	.267	15	15	4	4	4	0	0	0	0	5	0	0	0	0	3	0	0
Ward, Turner, Knoxville†	.261	7	23	6	6	8	0	0	0	0	0	0	0	7	0	3	2	0
Warner, Mike, Greenville*	.350	5	20	4	7	11	0	2	0	3	0	0	0	2	0	4	2	1

Player, Team	Avg.	G	AB	R	H	TB	2B	3B	HR	RBI	SH	SF	HP	BB	Int. BB	SO	SB	CS
White, Billy, Orlando	.242	40	120	14	29	48	11	1	2	14	2	2	0	15	1	28	1	2
White, Rick, Carolina	.111	12	9	0	1	1	0	0	0	1	1	0	0	0	0	1	0	0
Williams, Dave, Greenville	.000	45	1	0	0	0	0	0	0	0	0	0	0	0	0	0	0	0
Williams, George, Huntsville†	.295	124	434	80	128	200	26	2	14	77	1	6	14	67	0	66	6	3
Williams, Jimmy, Orlando*	.083	15	12	0	1	1	0	0	0	0	1	0	0	0	0	6	0	0
Willis, Travis, Orlando	.000	61	3	0	0	0	0	0	0	0	0	0	0	0	0	2	0	0
Wilson, Brandon, Birmingham	.270	137	500	76	135	170	19	5	2	48	4	3	3	52	0	77	43	10
Wolak, Jerry, Birmingham	.305	137	525	78	160	230	35	4	9	64	2	4	8	26	2	95	16	12
Wolfe, Joel, Huntsville	.299	36	134	20	40	55	6	0	3	18	1	0	0	13	1	24	6	3
Womack, Tony, Carolina*	.304	60	247	41	75	86	7	2	0	23	4	4	1	17	2	34	21	6
Wood, Jason, Huntsville	.230	103	370	44	85	119	21	2	3	36	9	3	2	33	0	97	2	4
Woodall, Brad, Greenville†	.222	8	9	2	2	2	0	0	0	1	2	0	0	0	0	2	0	0
Young, Ernie, Huntsville	.208	45	120	26	25	45	5	0	5	15	2	2	2	24	0	36	8	5
Zambrano, Roberto, Orlando	.135	13	37	4	5	6	1	0	0	1	0	0	6	0	3	0	0
Zimmerman, Mike, Carolina	.000	33	1	0	0	0	0	0	0	0	1	0	0	0	0	0	0	0

The following pitchers, listed alphabetically by club, with games in parentheses, had no plate appearances, primarily through use of designated hitters:

BIRMINGHAM—Adkins, Steve (26); Andujar, Luis (6); Baldwin, Jim (17); Barfield, John (13); Boehringer, Brian (7); Campos, Frank (9); Carter, Jeff (13); Ellis, Bob (12); Gajkowski, Steve (1); Gardner, John (19); Gordon, Tony (37); Johnson, Barry (13); Keyser, Brian (2); Leach, Terry (4); Locklear, Dean (9); Manon, Ramon (2); Merigliano, Frank (2); Mongiello, Mike (7); Olsen, Steve (25); Perigny, Don (48); Pierce, Jeff (33); Ruffcorn, Scott (20); Ruffin, Johnny (11); Schrenk, Steve (8); Thomas, Larry (1).

CAROLINA—Christiansen, Jason (2); Miceli, Dan (13); Parkinson, Eric (2); Piatt, Doug (3); Smith, Zane (4); Toliver, Fred (33).

CHATTANOOGA—Anderson, Mike (2); Garcia, Vic (15); Holcomb, Scott (6); Kilgo, Ray (53); Lynch, Dave (3); Shaw, Kevin (25).

GREENVILLE—Lovelace, Vance (11); Strange, Don (27).

HUNTSVILLE—Acre, Mark (19); Allison, Dana (19); Baker, Scott (25); Briscoe, John (30); Chitren, Steve (33); Connolly, Craig (20); Garland, Chaon (24); Jimenez, Miguel (20); Karsay, Steve (2); Latter, Dave (6); Osteen, Gavin (12); Phoenix, Steve (11); Shaw, Curt (28); Smith, Tim (9); Smithberg, Roger (27); Strebeck, Rich (23); Sturtze, Tanyon (28); Wojciechowski, Steve (13).

JACKSONVILLE—Bicknell, Greg (24); Buckley, Travis (10); Cummings, John (7); Darwin, Jeff (27); Fleming, Dave (4); Foster, Kevin (12); Glinatsis, George (9); Hampton, Mike (15); Harris, Reggie (9); Kent, Troy (14); King, Kevin (16); Knackert, Brent (4); Newlin, Jim (8); Parris, Steve (7); Perkins, Paul (36); Phillips, Tony (27); Plantenberg, Erik (34); Remlinger, Mike (7); Russell, Lee (17); Salkeld, Roger (14); Schanz, Scott (49); Villone, Ron (11); Weber, Weston (18).

KNOXVILLE—Baptist, Travis (7); Brow, Scott (3); Brown, Daren (46); Crabtree, Tim (27); Cromwell, Nate (6); Duey, Kyle (37); Flener, Greg (38); Ganote, Joe (33); Grove, Scott (10); Heble, Kurt (6); Jordan, Ricardo (25); Karsay, Steve (19); Montoya, Al (5); Newlin, Jim (13); Ohlms, Mark (7); Phillips, Randy (5); Renko, Steve (12); Rogers, Jim (19); Small, Aaron (48); Spoljaric, Paul (7); Ward, Tony (11).

MEMPHIS—Ahern, Brian (18); Bevil, Brian (6); Bittiger, Jeff (2); Campbell, Jim (11); Chrisman, Jim (8); Fyhrie, Mike (22); Givens, Brian (14); Harris, Doug (22); Karchner, Matt (6); Landress, Roger (26); Lieber, Jon (4); Limbach, Chris (42); Mason, Mike (1); Miceli, Dan (6); Morton, Kevin (20); Myers, Rodney (12); Perez, Vladimir (18); Peters, Doug (6); Piatt, Doug (11); Pierce, Ed (37); Richards, Dave (7); Roesler, Mike (3); Sanchez, Alex (15); Ventura, Jose (20); Wagner, Hector (10).

NASHVILLE—Barcelo, Marc (2); Best, Jayson (3); Gavaghan, Sean (20); Guardado, Ed (10); Henry, Jon (6); Johnson, Greg (31); Konieczki, Dominic (42); Mansur, Jeff (33); Misuraca, Mike (25); Munoz, Oscar (20); Newman, Alan (14); Radke, Brad (13); Ritchie, Todd (12); Robinson, Bob (35); Schullstrom, Erik (4); Watkins, Scott (13); Wissler, Bill (29).

ORLANDO—Czajkowski, Jim (10); Harkey, Mike (1); Taylor, Aaron (28); Trinidad, Hector (4).

GRAND SLAMS—Thomas, 3; Hart, Kuehl, Pledger, Stahoviak, G. Williams, 2 each; Colvard, C. Delgado, Ebright, Glanville, K. Gordon, Helfand, Hocking, Jaster, Mark Johnson (Carolina), Kessinger, Kapano, Merchant, Scruggs, C. Smith, 1 each.

AWARDED FIRST BASE ON CATCHER'S INTERFERENCE—Houston 4 (Campanis, Durant, Manning, Nunez); Hocking 3 (Jennings, Kounas, G. Williams); Adams (J. Robinson); Cordova (G. Williams); Dauphin (G. Williams); Gibralter (Campanis); Matos (Edge); Olmeda (C. Delgado).

PITCHING

TEAM

Team	ERA	G	CG	ShO	Sv.	IP	H	R	ER	HR	HB	BB	Int. BB	SO	WP	Bk.
Birmingham	3.36	142	17	12	39	1222.2	1104	564	456	84	57	446	10	1022	70	9
Chattanooga	3.56	141	10	4	43	1228.0	1185	583	486	92	57	422	36	857	60	8
Carolina	3.75	141	8	6	48	1249.1	1211	626	521	93	61	431	38	951	73	11
Greenville	3.84	142	7	6	36	1248.1	1203	631	533	86	61	572	34	967	83	10
Nashville	4.01	142	15	8	26	1246.1	1303	651	556	117	46	396	13	943	77	7
Knoxville	4.11	142	7	11	37	1214.2	1277	653	555	95	45	461	10	885	90	23
Jacksonville	4.15	141	5	5	21	1226.2	1189	679	565	117	47	500	26	912	75	20
Huntsville	4.15	141	8	14	30	1207.1	1198	676	557	98	55	588	32	949	83	14
Orlando	4.22	142	10	6	31	1243.1	1317	673	583	110	76	440	37	869	77	20
Memphis	4.32	140	9	10	24	1213.2	1275	656	583	113	62	474	10	838	54	12

INDIVIDUAL

(Leading qualifiers for earned-run average leadership— 114 or more innings)

*Throws lefthanded.

Pitcher, Team	W	L	Pct.	ERA	G	GS	CG	GF	ShO	Sv.	IP	H	R	ER	HR	HB	BB	Int. BB	SO	WP
Baldwin, Birmingham	8	5	.615	2.25	17	17	4	0	0	0	120.0	94	48	30	6	6	43	0	107	7
Hostetler, Greenville	8	5	.615	2.72	19	19	2	0	0	0	135.2	122	48	41	9	7	36	3	105	6
Ruffcorn, Birmingham	9	4	.692	2.73	20	20	3	0	3	0	135.0	108	47	41	6	4	52	0	141	7
Munoz, Nashville	11	4	.733	3.08	20	20	1	0	0	0	131.2	123	56	45	10	4	51	0	139	12
Upshaw, Greenville*	9	9	.500	3.29	34	14	0	8	0	2	120.1	109	49	44	5	4	56	4	99	11
Flener, Knoxville*	13	6	.684	3.30	38	16	2	10	2	4	136.1	130	56	50	9	3	39	1	114	9
Ferry, Chattanooga	13	8	.619	3.42	28	28	4	0	1	0	186.2	176	85	71	17	5	30	1	111	9
Courtright, Chattanooga*	5	11	.313	3.50	27	27	1	0	0	0	175.0	179	81	68	5	8	70	6	96	5
Fyhrie, Memphis	11	4	.733	3.54	22	22	3	0	0	0	131.1	143	59	52	11	9	59	0	59	7
Karsay, 19 Knox.-2 Hunt.	8	4	.667	3.58	21	20	1	0	0	0	118.0	111	50	47	11	7	35	1	122	5

Departmental leaders: G—Bushing, Willis, 61; W—Ferry, Flener, 13; L—C. Shaw, 16; Pct.—Fyhrie, Munoz, .733; GS—Ferry, Hook, C. Shaw, Sturtze, 28; CG—Baldwin, Ferry, Mansur, 4; GF—Willis, 57; ShO—Ruffcorn, 3; Sv.—Bushing, 29; IP—Ferry, 186.2; H—Salles, 203; R—Salles, 103; ER—Sturtze, 88; HR—Wissler, 23; HB—C. Shaw, 14; BB—C. Shaw, 89; IBB—Hunter, E. Johnson, 8; SO—Ruffcorn, 141; WP—Coffman, C. Shaw, 19.

(All pitchers—listed alphabetically)

Pitcher, Team	W	L	Pct.	ERA	G	GS	CG	GF	ShO	Sv.	IP	H	R	ER	HR	HB	BB	Int. BB	SO	WP
Acre, Huntsville	1	1	.500	2.42	19	0	0	19	0	10	22.1	22	10	6	2	0	3	1	21	2
Adkins, Birmingham*	1	4	.200	4.14	26	3	0	8	0	2	50.0	46	25	23	2	1	20	2	40	2
Adriana, Knoxville	0	0	.000	13.50	1	0	0	1	0	0	2.0	5	3	3	1	0	1	0	0	0
Ahern, Memphis	4	9	.308	5.34	18	18	0	0	0	0	97.2	113	69	58	11	10	46	0	63	10
Allison, Huntsville*	2	3	.400	1.80	19	0	0	6	0	0	40.0	40	9	8	5	0	4	2	18	1
Anderson, Chattanooga	1	1	.500	1.20	2	2	1	0	0	0	15.0	10	3	2	0	0	1	0	14	0
Andujar, Birmingham	5	0	1.000	1.82	6	6	0	0	0	0	39.2	31	9	8	3	5	18	0	48	1
Backlund, Carolina	7	5	.583	4.58	20	20	0	0	0	0	106.0	115	66	54	22	5	28	3	94	7
Baker, Huntsville*	10	4	.714	4.14	25	25	1	0	1	0	130.1	141	73	60	7	4	84	0	97	8
Baldwin, Birmingham	8	5	.615	2.25	17	4	0	0	0	0	120.0	94	48	30	6	6	43	0	107	7
Baptist, Knoxville*	1	3	.250	4.09	7	7	0	0	0	0	33.0	37	17	15	2	2	7	0	24	3
Barcelo, Nashville	1	0	1.000	3.86	2	2	0	0	0	0	9.1	9	5	4	2	1	5	0	5	1
Barfield, Birmingham*	5	2	.714	3.86	13	5	1	5	1	1	42.0	57	24	18	1	1	5	0	18	0.
Beatty, Carolina*	7	3	.700	2.85	18	13	2	2	0	0	94.2	68	42	30	8	2	35	0	67	4
Best, Nashville	1	0	1.000	11.81	3	0	0	2	0	1	5.1	11	7	7	3	0	4	0	7	1
Bevil, Memphis	3	3	.500	4.36	6	6	0	0	0	0	33.0	36	17	16	4	0	14	0	26	3
Bicknell, Jacksonville	6	6	.500	4.31	24	12	2	4	1	1	94.0	96	59	45	14	5	28	0	45	5
Bittiger, Memphis	1	0	1.000	1.59	2	2	0	0	0	0	11.1	6	2	2	1	1	3	0	11	0
Boehringer, Birmingham	2	1	.667	3.54	7	7	1	0	0	0	40.2	41	20	16	3	2	14	0	29	1
Boltz, Greenville*	1	2	.333	3.23	9	8	0	0	1	0	39.0	33	15	14	2	2	17	0	22	1
Bowie, Huntsville*	0	0	.000	4.00	8	0	0	7	0	0	9.0	9	5	4	2	0	4	0	4	1
Bradley, Greenville	0	0	.000	0.00	1	0	1	0	0	0	1.0	0	0	0	0	0	0	0	0	0
Bragg, Jacksonville	0	0	.000	9.00	1	0	0	1	0	0	1.0	3	1	1	0	0	0	0	0	0
Briscoe, Huntsville	4	0	1.000	3.03	30	0	0	28	0	16	38.2	28	14	13	3	1	16	1	62	0
Brow, Knoxville	1	2	.333	3.32	3	3	1	0	0	0	19.0	13	8	7	0	0	9	0	12	2
Brown, Knoxville	4	5	.444	5.00	46	2	0	25	0	10	72.0	72	44	40	4	3	32	1	67	8
Buckley, 2 Chat. - 10 Jack.	2	4	.333	5.75	12	11	0	0	0	0	56.1	64	41	36	8	4	22	0	44	3
Burgos, Chattanooga*	2	2	.500	3.56	31	1	0	14	0	1	48.0	33	21	19	2	2	14	4	35	4
Burlingame, Greenville	4	4	.500	5.00	15	12	0	2	0	0	66.2	76	52	37	6	3	37	1	35	10
Bushing, Chattanooga*	6	1	.857	2.31	61	0	0	50	0	29	70.0	50	20	18	7	2	23	3	84	2
Campbell, Memphis*	1	1	.500	5.82	11	0	0	4	0	1	21.2	23	14	14	0	0	10	0	11	1
Campos, Birmingham	2	4	.333	3.25	9	9	0	0	0	0	55.1	49	29	20	4	3	26	0	41	7
Carter, Birmingham	2	1	.667	1.02	13	0	0	12	0	8	17.2	9	2	2	1	0	6	0	21	0
Casillas, Memphis*	0	1	.000	9.00	3	0	0	2	0	0	3.0	7	3	3	1	0	0	0	1	1
Cecena, Carolina	3	3	.500	2.20	14	0	0	5	0	0	16.1	10	4	4	1	0	6	1	21	1
Chitren, Huntsville	2	1	.667	5.17	32	0	0	13	0	1	55.2	53	38	32	7	10	35	3	39	8
Chrisman, Memphis	0	0	.000	4.66	8	0	0	0	0	0	19.1	20	11	10	4	1	5	0	15	0
Christiansen, Carolina*	0	0	.000	0.00	2	0	0	1	0	0	2.2	3	0	0	0	0	1	0	2	0
Clayton, Jacksonville	0	0	.000	0.00	3	0	0	3	0	0	4.0	3	0	0	0	1	1	0	1	0
Coffman, Jacksonville	1	7	.125	5.40	10	10	0	0	0	0	50.0	33	33	30	0	2	47	0	45	19
Cole, Memphis	0	0	.000	81.00	1	0	0	1	0	0	0.2	6	6	6	1	0	4	0	1	1
Cole, Carolina	0	4	.000	5.93	27	0	0	13	0	8	41.0	39	30	27	5	2	31	2	35	6
Connolly, Huntsville	1	1	.500	5.59	20	0	0	5	0	1	37.0	37	23	23	3	4	12	1	29	2
Corbett, Orlando*	2	1	.667	3.16	5	4	0	0	0	0	25.2	32	11	9	0	0	9	0	16	1
Courtright, Chattanooga*	5	11	.313	3.50	27	27	1	0	0	0	175.0	179	81	68	5	8	70	6	96	5
Crabtree, Knoxville	9	14	.391	4.08	27	27	4	0	2	0	158.2	178	93	72	11	10	59	0	67	7
Cromwell, Knoxville*	0	1	.000	11.00	6	1	0	3	0	0	9.0	15	13	11	2	1	10	0	11	1
Culberson, Chattanooga	6	6	.500	2.99	37	0	0	15	0	1	105.1	82	38	35	11	6	36	0	86	3
Cummings, Jacksonville*	2	2	.500	3.15	7	7	1	0	0	0	45.2	50	24	16	1	1	9	0	35	1
Czajkowski, Orlando	1	2	.333	2.84	10	0	0	4	0	1	19.0	15	7	6	0	1	3	1	16	0
Czarkowski, Jacksonville*	0	3	.000	4.19	25	4	0	5	0	1	58.0	68	36	27	5	0	16	2	26	0
Darwin, Jacksonville	3	5	.375	2.97	27	0	0	22	0	7	36.1	29	17	12	1	3	17	3	39	0
Dattola, Huntsville	0	0	.000	0.00	2	0	0	2	0	0	2.0	0	0	0	0	0	0	0	1	0
Delanuez, Nashville	0	0	.000	9.00	3	0	0	2	0	0	3.0	7	3	3	1	0	0	0	3	0
Delgado, Orlando	1	3	.250	5.90	9	6	0	2	0	0	39.2	53	28	26	7	2	15	0	23	2
M. De Los Santos, Carolina	1	2	.333	4.73	8	8	0	0	0	0	40.0	49	24	21	1	4	15	1	34	2
Dickson, Orlando*	2	3	.400	3.83	9	9	0	0	0	0	49.1	37	22	21	7	0	17	1	46	5
Duey, Knoxville	2	3	.400	6.88	37	1	0	15	0	0	68.0	92	57	52	7	0	27	0	40	6
Ebright, Orlando*	0	0	.000	0.00	3	0	0	3	0	0	4.0	4	0	0	0	0	0	0	2	0
Ellis, Birmingham	6	3	.667	3.10	12	12	2	0	1	0	81.1	68	33	28	2	4	21	0	77	6
Ferry, Chattanooga	13	8	.619	3.42	28	28	4	0	1	0	186.2	176	85	71	17	5	30	1	111	9
Fleming, Jacksonville*	0	2	.000	4.41	4	4	0	0	0	0	16.1	16	9	8	2	1	7	0	10	0
Flener, Knoxville*	13	6	.684	3.30	38	16	2	10	2	4	136.1	130	56	50	9	3	39	1	114	9
Foster, Jacksonville	4	4	.500	3.97	12	12	1	0	1	0	65.2	53	32	29	2	4	29	0	72	5
Fyhrie, Memphis	11	4	.733	3.56	22	22	3	0	0	0	131.1	143	59	52	11	9	59	0	59	7
Gajkowski, Birmingham	0	0	.000	0.00	1	0	0	0	0	0	2.1	0	0	0	0	0	0	0	2	0
Galvez, Orlando	1	0	1.000	8.44	3	1	0	0	0	0	10.2	16	14	10	1	1	3	0	9	1
Ganote, Knoxville	8	6	.571	4.15	33	19	1	6	0	0	138.2	149	70	64	11	5	52	0	87	13
Garcia, Chattanooga	0	2	.000	5.85	15	0	0	3	0	0	20.0	24	15	13	5	1	11	2	14	3
Gardner, 7 Orl. - 19 Birm.	2	5	.286	5.50	26	8	0	10	0	1	75.1	70	52	46	5	10	43	0	46	3
Garland, Huntsville	3	3	.500	7.26	23	3	0	0	0	0	48.1	58	40	39	7	0	35	6	37	6
Garza, Carolina	4	3	.571	3.69	35	4	0	5	0	1	68.1	63	34	28	2	5	24	2	45	4
Gavaghan, Nashville	4	0	1.000	0.49	20	1	0	5	0	0	36.2	21	3	2	0	4	12	1	30	3
Givens, Memphis*	1	3	.250	4.58	14	4	0	7	0	2	35.1	37	22	18	4	1	11	0	29	3
Glinatsis, Jacksonville	5	2	.714	6.75	9	5	0	0	0	0	34.2	39	26	26	4	0	15	0	25	1
Gordon, Birmingham*	3	2	.600	2.58	37	0	0	9	0	1	45.1	32	17	13	0	1	35	2	49	5
Grove, Knoxville	0	2	.000	7.16	10	0	0	6	0	0	16.1	18	13	13	3	1	9	0	10	1
Guardado, Nashville*	4	0	1.000	1.24	10	10	2	0	2	0	65.1	53	10	9	1	2	10	0	57	2
Hampton, Jacksonville*	6	4	.600	3.71	15	14	1	1	0	0	87.1	71	43	36	3	4	33	1	84	2
Hancock, Carolina*	7	3	.700	2.53	25	11	0	3	0	0	99.2	87	42	28	3	4	32	2	85	5
Harkey, Orlando	0	0	.000	1.69	1	1	0	0	0	0	5.1	4	1	1	0	0	2	0	5	0
Harrah, Carolina	1	4	.200	9.47	6	6	1	0	0	0	25.2	40	28	27	3	3	9	0	17	0
Harris, Memphis	3	6	.333	4.67	22	12	1	4	0	0	86.2	99	52	45	6	3	13	0	38	3
Harris, Jacksonville	1	4	.200	4.78	9	8	0	1	0	0	37.2	33	24	20	4	3	22	0	30	3
Hartsock, Orlando	3	4	.429	3.47	45	4	0	8	1	0	49.1	43	24	19	2	2	17	0	24	2
Hassinger, Greenville	3	1	.750	1.57	12	0	0	3	0	0	23.0	19	4	4	1	0	8	3	11	2
Heble, Knoxville	0	1	.000	3.72	6	0	0	2	0	0	9.2	12	5	4	1	1	4	0	13	1
Henry, Nashville	4	2	.667	2.74	6	6	1	0	1	0	42.2	41	14	13	5	3	7	0	20	1
Holcomb, Chattanooga*	0	2	.000	13.50	6	0	0	2	0	0	4.0	5	6	6	1	1	5	2	3	1
Hook, Chattanooga	12	8	.600	3.62	28	28	1	0	0	0	166.2	163	85	67	7	12	66	2	122	9
Hope, Carolina	9	4	.692	4.37	21	20	0	0	0	0	111.1	123	69	54	7	8	29	4	66	10
Hostetler, Greenville	8	5	.615	2.72	19	19	2	0	0	0	135.2	122	48	41	9	7	36	3	105	6

Pitcher, Team	W	L	Pct.	ERA	G	GS	CG	GF	ShO	Sv.	IP	H	R	ER	HR	HB	BB	Int. BB	SO	WP
Houk, Chattanooga	0	0	.000	0.00	1	0	0	0	0	0	1.0	0	0	0	0	0	0	0	1	0
Hunter, Carolina	5	3	.625	1.01	46	0	0	21	0	7	71.0	54	11	8	1	3	35	8	53	1
Jarvis, Chattanooga	3	1	.750	1.69	7	3	2	0	0	0	37.1	26	7	7	0	1	11	0	18	1
Jimenez, Huntsville	10	6	.625	2.94	20	19	0	0	0	0	107.0	92	49	35	10	4	64	0	105	6
Johns, Huntsville*	7	5	.583	2.97	40	6	0	11	0	1	91.0	82	41	30	3	2	31	4	56	2
Johnson, Birmingham	2	0	1.000	3.32	13	1	0	8	0	1	21.2	27	11	8	2	0	6	0	16	2
C. Johnson, Orlando	0	1	.000	2.96	15	1	0	3	0	1	27.1	31	12	9	1	4	15	2	14	3
E. Johnson, Orlando*	6	5	.545	5.94	53	0	0	18	0	2	66.2	84	47	44	4	4	31	8	58	5
Johnson, Nashville	3	1	.750	2.80	31	0	0	27	0	13	35.1	30	12	11	3	1	10	1	54	2
Jones, Carolina	0	5	.000	4.82	11	9	0	1	0	1	52.1	63	30	28	4	4	21	0	34	7
Jordan, Knoxville*	1	4	.200	2.45	25	0	0	8	0	2	36.2	33	17	10	2	0	18	1	35	0
Karchner, Memphis	3	2	.600	4.20	6	5	0	1	0	0	30.0	34	16	14	2	4	4	0	14	1
Karsay, 19 Knox.-2 Hunt.	8	4	.667	3.58	21	20	1	0	0	0	118.0	111	50	47	11	7	35	1	122	5
Kennedy, Chattanooga	1	1	.500	6.75	2	2	0	0	0	0	9.1	12	7	7	0	0	5	0	10	0
Kent, Jacksonville	0	0	.000	5.21	14	0	0	5	0	1	19.0	26	14	11	3	1	5	1	17	1
Keyser, Birmingham	0	2	.000	5.73	2	2	1	0	0	0	11.0	15	9	7	0	0	6	0	5	0
Kilgo, Chattanooga*	11	7	.611	2.80	53	1	0	20	0	6	80.1	92	30	25	2	5	31	6	61	4
King, Jacksonville*	2	0	1.000	3.14	16	0	0	8	0	1	28.2	25	10	10	3	1	7	2	13	3
Kizziah, Knoxville	3	0	1.000	2.83	27	1	0	10	0	0	54.0	47	25	17	5	4	18	0	33	2
Klonoski, Nashville*	4	6	.400	3.16	56	0	0	24	0	3	77.0	69	33	27	3	3	34	3	56	1
Knackert, Jacksonville	0	1	.000	2.57	4	2	0	1	0	1	14.0	6	4	4	1	3	4	0	10	0
Konieczki, Nashville*	2	6	.250	6.66	42	0	0	23	0	4	48.2	65	47	36	4	1	16	1	39	5
Landress, Memphis	3	4	.429	3.14	26	0	0	14	0	2	51.2	55	21	18	4	2	15	3	25	1
Latter, Huntsville	0	0	.000	15.00	6	0	0	4	0	0	9.0	19	15	15	1	1	7	2	5	0
Leach, Birmingham	0	0	.000	4.15	4	0	0	1	0	1	4.1	4	2	2	0	0	2	1	5	0
Leiper, Carolina	2	1	.667	1.48	8	4	2	0	1	0	30.1	26	6	5	1	1	5	0	16	0
Lieber, 4 Mem.-6 Caro.	6	3	.667	5.07	10	10	0	0	0	0	55.0	71	31	31	7	1	16	0	45	3
Limbach, Memphis*	3	4	.429	2.73	42	5	0	24	0	6	92.1	85	34	28	5	0	22	0	82	2
Loaiza, Carolina	2	1	.667	3.77	7	7	1	0	0	0	43.0	39	18	18	5	0	12	1	40	3
Locklear, Birmingham*	2	0	1.000	6.14	9	2	0	4	0	0	22.0	29	17	15	1	1	11	0	20	1
Lomon, Greenville	3	4	.429	3.86	13	13	1	0	1	0	79.1	76	41	34	4	4	31	2	68	4
Long, Memphis*	0	0	.000	0.00	1	0	0	1	0	0	0.2	2	0	0	0	0	0	0	0	0
Lovelace, Greenville*	2	0	1.000	1.65	11	0	0	3	0	1	16.1	10	4	3	0	1	12	1	21	1
Lynch, Chattanooga*	0	0	.000	0.00	3	0	0	2	0	1	2.1	0	0	0	0	0	0	0	3	0
Manon, Birmingham	10	7	.588	3.63	25	22	2	2	1	0	131.1	134	63	53	10	6	65	0	88	10
Mansur, Nashville*	10	8	.556	4.25	33	19	4	4	0	0	158.2	180	82	75	22	0	38	3	89	5
Mason, Memphis*	1	0	1.000	0.00	1	0	0	1	0	0	2.0	0	0	0	0	0	1	0	0	0
McCreary, Nashville	3	8	.273	5.31	38	5	1	12	0	1	78.0	111	55	46	12	3	20	0	42	6
McCurry, Carolina	2	1	.667	2.79	23	0	0	15	0	0	29.0	24	11	9	1	0	14	2	14	2
Melvin, Orlando	0	1	.000	3.88	36	1	0	13	0	1	65.0	57	34	28	11	3	40	2	60	12
Merigliano, Birmingham	0	1	.000	27.00	2	0	0	1	0	0	1.2	4	5	5	1	0	2	0	3	1
Miceli, 40 Mem.-13 Caro.	6	6	.500	4.69	53	0	0	41	0	17	71.0	65	38	37	9	4	43	4	87	4
Miller, Carolina	2	2	.500	2.82	6	6	0	0	0	0	38.1	31	15	12	3	0	12	1	33	4
Misuraca, Nashville	6	6	.500	3.82	25	17	2	2	1	0	113.0	103	57	48	9	5	40	0	80	7
Mongiello, Birmingham	0	1	.000	1.54	7	1	0	4	0	1	11.2	5	6	2	0	2	4	0	9	3
Montoya, Knoxville*	1	0	1.000	5.14	5	0	0	2	0	0	7.0	8	4	4	1	1	3	0	9	3
Morones, Orlando	2	2	.500	4.88	4	4	1	0	0	0	24.0	29	14	13	2	2	9	0	14	1
Morton, Memphis*	3	6	.333	4.81	20	9	1	4	0	1	73.0	88	48	39	12	1	29	1	59	3
Munoz, Nashville	11	4	.733	3.08	20	20	1	0	0	0	131.2	123	56	45	10	4	51	0	139	12
Myers, Memphis	3	6	.333	5.62	12	12	1	0	1	0	65.2	73	46	41	8	10	32	0	42	3
Newlin, 8 Jack.-13 Knox.	1	3	.250	7.21	21	1	2	2	0	0	43.2	63	40	35	5	1	16	1	30	3
Newman, Nashville*	1	6	.143	6.03	14	11	1	1	0	0	65.2	75	52	44	4	1	40	0	35	5
Ohlms, Knoxville	1	0	1.000	2.70	7	0	0	6	0	1	6.2	6	2	2	0	0	3	0	4	1
Olsen, Birmingham	10	9	.526	4.75	25	25	1	0	1	0	142.0	156	87	75	22	7	52	2	92	4
Osteen, Huntsville*	7	3	.700	2.30	11	11	2	0	0	0	70.1	56	21	18	1	2	25	1	46	2
Parkinson, Carolina	0	0	.000	2.08	2	0	0	0	0	0	4.1	4	2	1	0	0	1	0	2	0
Parris, Jacksonville	0	1	.000	5.93	7	1	0	0	0	0	13.2	15	9	9	3	2	6	0	5	0
Perez, Memphis	1	0	1.000	3.00	18	1	1	9	1	3	42.0	37	15	14	2	1	11	0	35	2
Perigny, Birmingham	3	4	.429	4.22	48	0	0	25	0	3	70.1	69	38	33	9	5	15	1	57	7
Perkins, Jacksonville	2	4	.333	5.40	36	1	0	14	0	1	60.0	69	40	36	10	0	23	2	34	3
Peters, Memphis	1	2	.333	5.87	6	6	0	0	0	0	23.0	32	16	15	4	0	10	0	14	1
Phillips, Knoxville	2	2	.500	6.12	5	5	0	0	0	0	25.0	32	20	17	3	2	12	0	12	3
Phillips, Jacksonville	1	3	.250	1.72	27	0	0	22	0	5	31.1	34	6	6	1	0	5	1	26	1
Phoenix, Huntsville	2	2	.500	1.40	11	0	0	7	0	1	19.1	13	5	3	0	0	2	2	15	0
Piatt, 11 Mem.-3 Caro.	0	1	.000	10.06	14	0	0	3	0	0	17.0	29	19	19	2	2	7	0	11	1
Picota, Jacksonville	0	4	.000	4.87	11	0	0	4	0	0	20.1	26	20	11	3	1	12	2	7	4
Pierce, Memphis*	6	5	.545	3.74	37	2	0	18	0	1	67.1	65	35	28	5	3	34	3	53	3
Pierce, 33 Birm.-13 Chat.	3	4	.429	2.60	46	0	0	34	0	22	69.1	51	22	20	4	3	16	1	67	3
Plantenberg, Jacksonville*	2	1	.667	2.01	34	0	0	13	0	1	44.2	38	11	10	0	0	14	1	49	1
Polley, Greenville*	8	1	.889	4.12	42	0	0	18	0	2	59.0	44	28	27	8	3	21	2	66	2
Potts, Greenville*	7	6	.538	3.88	25	25	1	0	0	0	141.2	131	79	61	7	1	86	2	116	5
Raabe, Nashville	0	0	.000	54.00	1	0	0	1	0	0	1.0	8	6	6	1	0	0	0	0	0
Radke, Nashville	2	6	.250	4.62	13	13	1	0	0	0	76.0	81	42	39	6	6	16	0	76	0
Ray, Nashville	3	7	.300	6.82	30	8	0	5	0	0	62.0	79	55	47	10	2	28	6	46	3
Remlinger, Jacksonville*	1	3	.250	6.58	7	7	0	0	0	0	39.2	40	30	29	7	0	19	0	23	2
Renko, Knoxville	1	3	.250	3.63	12	5	0	1	0	0	34.2	38	21	14	1	1	8	0	30	7
Reyes, Greenville	8	1	.889	2.06	33	2	0	10	0	2	70.0	64	22	16	5	3	24	1	57	3
Richards, Memphis*	0	1	.000	3.68	7	3	0	2	0	1	22.0	12	9	9	2	1	12	0	24	0
Ritchie, Nashville	3	2	.600	3.66	12	10	0	0	0	0	46.2	46	21	19	2	0	15	0	41	6
Ritter, Greenville	4	6	.400	6.06	35	3	0	15	0	3	65.1	81	48	44	7	4	26	1	49	4
Rivera, Nashville	0	0	.000	18.00	1	0	0	0	0	0	2.0	2	2	2	0	0	2	0	2	0
Robinson, Nashville	2	4	.333	5.16	35	0	0	20	0	3	45.1	64	34	26	3	5	15	2	26	5
Robinson, Chattanooga	6	5	.545	3.54	20	18	0	0	0	0	112.0	114	60	44	12	5	40	1	58	5
Roesler, Memphis	5	1	.667	2.38	3	3	2	0	1	0	22.2	11	7	6	0	1	4	0	16	1
Rogers, Knoxville	7	7	.500	4.04	19	19	0	0	0	0	100.1	107	54	45	9	2	33	1	80	5
Ruffcorn, Birmingham	9	4	.692	2.73	20	20	3	0	3	0	135.0	108	47	41	6	4	52	0	141	7
Ruffin, Birmingham	0	0	.000	2.82	11	0	0	10	0	2	22.1	16	9	7	2	0	9	1	23	0
Russell, Jacksonville	4	9	.308	5.52	17	17	0	0	0	0	89.2	115	67	55	14	2	32	1	52	5
Salkeld, Jacksonville	4	3	.571	3.27	14	14	0	0	0	0	77.0	71	39	28	8	5	29	1	56	2
Salles, Orlando	11	9	.550	4.38	33	26	1	6	0	1	176.2	203	103	86	19	11	50	2	115	7
Sanchez, Memphis	1	4	.200	4.37	15	10	0	4	0	0	70.0	64	36	34	5	1	35	0	47	2
Sanchez, Greenville*	0	0	.000	18.00	1	0	0	1	0	0	1.0	2	2	2	0	1	2	0	1	0
Schanz, Jacksonville	7	4	.636	2.56	49	3	0	21	0	1	102.0	77	38	29	11	2	51	5	81	5
Schrenk, Birmingham	5	1	.833	1.17	8	8	2	0	1	0	61.2	31	11	8	2	1	7	0	51	3

Pitcher, Team	W	L	Pct.	ERA	G	GS	CG	GF	ShO	Sv.	IP	H	R	ER	HR	HB	BB	Int. BB	SO	WP
Schullstrom, Nashville	1	0	1.000	4.85	4	3	0	0	0	0	13.0	16	7	7	1	0	6	0	11	1
Schutz, Greenville*	2	1	.667	5.06	22	0	0	16	0	3	21.1	17	17	12	3	1	22	1	19	2
Shaw, Huntsville*	6	16	.273	4.93	28	28	2	0	1	0	151.2	141	98	83	8	14	89	2	132	19
Shaw, Chattanooga	0	1	.000	3.82	25	0	0	7	0	1	37.2	50	19	16	4	0	9	2	14	3
Small, Knoxville	4	4	.500	3.39	48	9	0	32	0	16	93.0	99	44	35	5	2	40	4	44	8
Smith, Huntsville	1	3	.250	3.35	9	6	1	1	1	0	43.0	46	22	16	5	1	18	0	31	4
Smith, Carolina*	1	2	.333	3.05	4	4	0	0	0	0	20.2	20	10	7	1	1	5	0	13	1
Smithberg, Huntsville	4	2	.667	2.21	27	0	0	13	0	0	36.2	34	15	9	3	2	16	1	36	2
Sparma, Greenville	5	12	.294	4.85	28	27	1	1	0	0	150.1	170	95	81	12	13	68	0	97	15
Spoljaric, Knoxville*	4	1	.800	2.28	7	7	0	0	0	0	43.1	30	12	11	3	1	22	0	51	2
Steenstra, Orlando	8	3	.727	3.59	14	14	2	0	2	0	100.1	103	47	40	4	9	25	0	60	5
Stevens, Orlando	6	1	.857	4.22	11	11	1	0	1	0	70.1	69	36	33	7	2	35	0	49	1
Stewart, Chattanooga	3	4	.429	5.03	10	10	1	0	0	0	53.2	57	35	30	6	4	24	0	47	4
Strange, Greenville	1	1	.500	3.65	27	0	0	24	0	18	24.2	27	11	10	3	0	9	1	27	2
Strauss, Orlando	0	2	.000	3.54	15	0	0	4	0	0	28.0	22	12	11	4	0	15	5	21	0
Strebeck, Huntsville	2	2	.500	5.18	23	0	0	7	0	0	48.2	54	38	28	7	1	22	3	29	4
Sturtze, Huntsville	5	12	.294	4.78	28	28	1	0	1	0	165.2	169	102	88	16	6	85	2	112	11
Swartzbaugh, Orlando	1	3	.250	4.23	10	9	1	0	0	0	66.0	52	33	31	5	3	18	0	59	2
Tafoya, Carolina	5	4	.556	3.09	49	0	0	17	0	0	81.2	87	35	28	3	5	21	4	55	1
Tatar, Chattanooga	0	1	.000	1.93	4	4	0	0	0	0	14.0	9	4	3	1	2	5	0	7	0
Taylor, Orlando	5	4	.556	4.85	28	3	0	16	0	0	55.2	73	37	30	6	5	15	2	37	3
Thomas, Birmingham*	0	1	.000	5.14	1	1	0	0	0	0	7.0	9	5	4	1	1	1	1	5	0
Toliver, Carolina	2	2	.500	3.15	33	0	0	24	0	12	40.0	32	16	14	3	3	24	4	48	3
Tomlin, Carolina*	1	0	1.000	0.75	2	2	0	0	0	0	12.0	7	1	1	1	0	1	0	9	0
Trinidad, Orlando	1	3	.250	6.57	4	4	1	0	0	0	24.2	34	19	18	5	1	7	0	13	2
Upshaw, Greenville*	9	9	.500	3.29	34	14	0	8	0	2	120.1	109	49	44	5	4	56	4	99	11
Vasquez, Greenville	4	5	.444	4.61	43	4	0	16	0	3	82.0	96	47	42	1	2	37	7	61	3
Ventura, Memphis	2	5	.286	3.94	20	12	0	2	0	0	82.1	88	40	36	6	5	45	0	61	1
Villone, Jacksonville*	3	4	.429	4.38	11	11	0	0	0	0	63.2	49	34	31	6	1	41	3	66	9
Wade, Greenville*	2	1	.667	3.21	8	8	1	0	1	0	42.0	32	16	15	6	1	29	0	40	2
Wagner, Memphis	2	4	.333	4.50	10	4	0	2	0	0	36.0	38	19	18	4	1	4	0	19	0
Wakefield, Carolina	3	5	.375	6.99	9	9	1	0	0	0	56.2	68	48	44	5	5	22	0	36	3
Walker, Orlando	2	3	.400	7.31	16	2	0	6	0	1	28.1	42	26	23	4	6	9	4	21	5
Wallace, Orlando	5	7	.417	5.03	15	15	2	0	0	0	96.2	105	59	54	12	10	28	3	69	9
Ward, Knoxville*	1	1	.500	1.71	11	0	0	6	0	3	21.0	17	5	4	1	0	10	0	23	0
Watkins, Nashville	0	1	.000	5.94	13	0	0	3	0	0	16.2	19	15	11	2	1	7	0	17	2
Weber, Jacksonville	2	1	.667	1.69	17	0	0	8	0	1	26.2	25	6	5	1	1	7	1	12	2
White, Carolina	4	3	.571	3.50	12	12	1	0	0	0	69.1	59	29	27	5	4	12	0	52	4
Williams, Greenville	2	4	.333	4.15	45	0	0	16	0	3	56.1	51	29	26	5	9	27	5	35	3
Williams, Orlando*	5	5	.500	2.48	15	14	0	0	0	0	90.2	84	29	25	4	2	38	1	65	2
Willis, Orlando	8	6	.571	2.84	61	1	0	57	0	24	82.1	91	37	26	2	2	22	6	56	8
Wissler, Nashville	10	10	.500	3.95	29	25	2	1	0	0	175.1	169	88	77	23	6	48	2	115	7
Wojciechowski, Huntsville*	4	6	.400	5.32	13	13	1	0	1	0	67.2	91	50	40	6	2	30	1	52	5
Woodall, Greenville	2	4	.333	3.38	8	7	1	1	0	0	53.1	43	24	20	1	2	24	0	38	6
Zimmerman, Carolina	2	3	.400	3.60	33	0	0	23	0	9	45.0	40	26	18	2	4	21	2	30	2

BALKS—Flener, 8; Newlin, 5; Baker, Hampton, C. Shaw, Wallace, 4 each; Crabtree, Czarkowski, E. Johnson, Limbach, Myers, 3 each; Backlund, Baldwin, Courtright, Cummings, Garcia, Gavaghan, R. Harris, Hope, Jimenez, Karsay, Perkins, R. Phillips, Salles, Steenstra, Toliver, Vasquez, J. Williams, 2 each; Ahern, Barcelo, Barfield, Boehringer, Boltz, Buckley, Burlingame, Bushing, Campbell, Campos, Czajkowski, Ferry, Foster, Fyhrie, Gardner, Glinatsis, Grove, Hartsock, Hook, Johns, B. Johnson, Jones, Kilgo, Kizziah, Knackert, Lieber, Locklear, Mansur, Melvin, Miceli, Miller, Misuraca, Perigny, A. Phillips, J. Pierce, Polley, Potts, Richards, Ritchie, Salkeld, A. Sanchez, Sparma, Spoljaric, Strauss, Strebeck, Sturtze, Taylor, Upshaw, Walker, Ward, Watkins, White, D. Williams, Wojciechowski, Woodall, Zimmerman, 1 each.

COMBINATION SHUTOUTS—Adkins-Carter, Andujar-Adkins, Olsen-Perigny, Ruffcorn-Gordon-Pierce, Birmingham; Backlund-Garza-Hunter, Backlund-Toliver, Harrah-Hancock-Toliver, Loaiza-Hunter, Smith-Zimmerman, Carolina; Courtright-Ray, Ray-Bushing-Garcia, Tatar-Jarvis-Pierce, Chattanooga; Boltz-Reyes, Hostetler-Schutz, Sparma-Polley-Strange, Upshaw-Strange, Greenville; Baker-Smithberg, Jimenez-Allison-Briscoe, Jimenez-Briscoe, Jimenez-Chitren-Allison, Jimenez-Johns, Osteen-Smithberg, Osteen-Smithberg-Briscoe, Sturtze-Briscoe, Huntsville; Hampton-Darwin, Hampton-Schanz-Darwin, Knackert-Perkins, Jacksonville; Flener-Duey-Brown, Flener-Small, Flener-Small-Brown, Rogers-Brown, Rogers-Ganote-Newlin, Rogers-Renko-Jordan-Small, Spoljaric-Duey, Knoxville; Bevil-Limbach-Miceli, Fyhrie-Miceli, Morton-Miceli, Myers-Richards, Sanchez-Limbach, Ventura-Pierce, Ventura-Piatt-Pierce, Memphis; Guardado-Konieczki, McCreary-Konieczki-Johnson, Misuraca-Mansur, Ritchie-Misuraca-Klonoski, Nashville; Stevens-Melvin-Willis, Williams-Willis, Orlando.

NO-HIT GAMES—Sturtze, Huntsville, defeated Chattanooga, 5-0, June 13; Myers, Memphis, defeated Knoxville, 3-0 (first game), August 8.

FIELDING

TEAM

Team	Pct.	G	PO	A	E	DP	PB
Orlando	.973	142	3730	1609	148	139	15
Knoxville	.972	142	3644	1603	151	125	23
Greenville	.971	142	3745	1665	163	152	18
Chattanooga	.970	141	3684	1488	160	115	10
Memphis	.970	140	3641	1505	160	120	14
Carolina	.969	141	3748	1555	167	140	19
Nashville	.969	142	3739	1547	167	112	9
Birmingham	.966	142	3668	1405	179	108	33
Jacksonville	.966	141	3680	1465	183	102	16
Huntsville	.964	141	3622	1451	190	126	26

Triple plays—Greenville, Huntsville.

INDIVIDUAL

FIRST BASEMEN

*Throws lefthanded.

Player, Team	Pct.	G	PO	A	E	DP
Adriana, Knoxville	.983	5	57	2	1	0
Aude, Carolina	.985	90	790	49	12	74
Banister, Carolina	1.000	1	4	1	0	0
Beard, Huntsville	1.000	1	0	1	0	0
Bowie, Huntsville*	.988	136	1078	96	14	99
Bradley, Greenville	1.000	9	44	3	0	3
B. Brown, Orlando*	.989	28	237	27	3	31
Troy Buckley, Chattanooga	1.000	1	4	2	0	0
Campanis, Jacksonville	.966	6	23	5	1	0
Casillas, Memphis*	.997	40	352	26	1	24
Cepicky, Birmingham	.962	3	24	1	1	0
Coleman, Birmingham	1.000	4	29	3	0	1
Coomer, Birmingham	.857	1	6	0	1	0
Cornelius, Jacksonville	1.000	6	53	2	0	4
Diaz, Jacksonville	1.000	1	2	0	0	1
Dismuke, Chattanooga	.986	135	1104	94	15	98
Dunn, Nashville*	.987	81	700	73	10	50
Ebright, Orlando*	.986	72	574	52	9	57
Erdman, Orlando	1.000	2	7	0	0	0
Franco, Orlando	.994	51	441	39	3	34
Fuller, Chattanooga	1.000	1	4	0	0	1
Gillis, Greenville	.989	108	819	92	10	88
Grifol, Nashville	1.000	1	1	0	0	1

— 405 —

Player, Team	Pct.	G	PO	A	E	DP
Holley, Jacksonville	.991	49	414	32	50	31
Houk, Nashville	.980	8	45	5	51	5
HYERS, Knoxville*	.996	140	1209	116	30	105
Johns, Huntsville*	1.000	2	1	0	1	0
Johnson, Carolina*	.993	54	492	39	35	45
Kessinger, Chattanooga	1.000	1	3	0	3	0
Kounas, Jacksonville	1.000	8	60	10	70	4
Kuehl, Huntsville	.957	14	59	7	69	6
Lane, Chattanooga	.944	2	16	1	18	1
Lonigro, Orlando	1.000	2	3	0	3	0
Masteller, Nashville*	.993	15	136	3	40	10
McDonald, Nashville	1.000	1	1	0	1	1
Merchant, Chattanooga	.978	6	41	4	46	2
Morales, Jacksonville	1.000	5	42	5	47	1
Mota, Nashville	.982	42	351	37	95	28
Newfield, Jacksonville	.995	44	407	19	28	28
Norman, Memphis	.882	4	15	0	17	1
O'Connor, Greenville	.992	32	223	21	46	25
Perez, Greenville	.979	16	122	15	40	16
Robertson, Birmingham*	.990	137	1063	108	83	93
Sanchez, Greenville	1.000	5	49	5	54	2
Scruggs, Jacksonville	1.000	1	1	0	1	0
Simmons, Huntsville	.909	3	10	0	11	1
Smith, Jacksonville	.983	33	273	24	02	22
Stahoviak, Nashville	1.000	5	33	1	34	3
Torres, Orlando	1.000	1	3	0	3	0
Vitiello, Memphis	.981	100	830	53	00	79

Triple play—Gillis.

SECOND BASEMEN

Player, Team	Pct.	G	PO	A	E	DP
Adriana, Knoxville	.963	35	62	95	63	28
Alicea, Greenville	.950	4	8	11	20	4
Arias, Chattanooga	.951	16	32	46	82	10
Beasley, Carolina	.968	69	145	189	45	48
Busby, Orlando	1.000	3	3	7	10	1
Clayton, Jacksonville	1.000	1	1	0	1	0
Coleman, Birmingham	.957	25	36	52	92	14
Crockett, Orlando	.967	18	39	48	90	12
Diaz, Jacksonville	.959	26	24	47	74	4
Durham, Birmingham	.945	120	227	284	41	59
Garber, Memphis	.990	25	33	66	00	8
Gates, Huntsville	1.000	12	32	28	60	10
Giovanola, Greenville	.967	20	34	54	91	9
Gomez, Huntsville	.958	7	13	10	24	5
Gomez, Orlando	.958	33	43	71	19	8
Grace, Orlando	1.000	2	0	1	1	0
Hood, Birmingham	1.000	1	2	1	3	0
Houk, 7 Nash.-11 Chat.	.963	18	40	39	82	12
Kelly, Greenville	.962	38	60	91	57	15
Kessinger, Chattanooga	1.000	11	17	28	45	4
Koelling, Chattanooga	.968	105	222	289	28	58
Krevokuch, Carolina	1.000	2	2	1	3	0
T. Leiper, Carolina	.900	4	4	5	10	1
Lewis, Orlando	.000	2	0	0	1	0
Lis, Knoxville	.976	111	197	281	90	56
Lofton, Chattanooga	1.000	3	7	3	10	0
Lonigro, Orlando	.973	26	49	60	12	15
Matos, Huntsville	.970	113	161	257	31	51
Miranda, Birmingham	.846	6	5	6	13	1
Mota, Memphis	.955	53	119	113	43	30
Nava, Jacksonville	.986	17	28	44	73	12
O'Connor, Greenville	1.000	1	1	2	1	0
OLMEDA, Greenville	.977	98	230	288	30	88
Polcovich, Carolina	1.000	3	4	13	17	3
Purdy, Carolina	.967	16	23	36	61	9
Raabe, Nashville	.995	50	72	114	87	29
Reams, Knoxville	.667	1	0	2	3	0
Relaford, Jacksonville	.957	8	20	24	46	1
Rivera, Nashville	.933	98	182	224	35	37
Rodriguez, Carolina	1.000	2	1	4	5	0
Rosario, Knoxville	1.000	1	6	3	9	0
Sandberg, Orlando	1.000	2	3	8	11	2
Santana, Jacksonville	.968	101	164	259	37	49
Schreiber, Carolina	.923	4	7	5	13	0
Sondrini, Carolina	.969	58	116	166	91	32
Tucker, Memphis	.962	72	153	176	42	39
Vice, Orlando	.963	46	96	141	46	31
Waggoner, Huntsville	.989	27	41	47	89	11
White, Orlando	.975	32	67	87	58	19
Wilson, Birmingham	1.000	1	3	7	10	1
Zambrano, Orlando	.000	1	0	0	1	0

Triple plays—Kelly, Matos.

THIRD BASEMEN

Player, Team	Pct.	G	PO	A	E	DP
Battle, Knoxville	.933	141	88	319	36	17
Beard, Huntsville	.837	16	13	23	43	4
Beasley, Carolina	1.000	5	2	3	5	0

Player, Team	Pct.	G	PO	A	E	DP
Busby, Orlando	.952	12	12	28	42	3
Clayton, Jacksonville	.908	43	20	79	09	2
Coleman, Birmingham	.889	9	5	11	18	1
Coomer, Birmingham	.935	54	37	106	53	8
Cruz, Huntsville	.930	26	19	34	57	7
Diaz, Jacksonville	.667	3	0	2	3	0
Franco, Orlando	.800	3	3	1	5	0
Fuller, Chattanooga	1.000	2	2	3	5	0
Garber, Memphis	.875	18	13	36	56	3
Gillis, Greenville	.945	41	17	69	91	5
GIOVANOLA, Greenville	.963	107	60	227	98	23
Gomez, Huntsville	.871	52	29	86	32	9
Gomez, Orlando	.867	9	4	9	15	1
Grace, Orlando	.952	112	61	216	91	25
Grayum, Orlando	1.000	1	0	2	2	0
Henderson, Knoxville	.889	3	3	5	9	1
Holley, Jacksonville	.894	34	21	63	94	2
Houk, 14 Nash.-26 Chat.	.939	40	36	72	15	12
Kapano, Orlando	.833	8	2	8	12	1
Kelly, Greenville	.975	16	9	30	40	2
Kessinger, Chattanooga	.962	9	8	17	26	2
Krevokuch, Carolina	.928	123	88	245	59	17
Kuehl, Huntsville	.838	37	16	46	74	5
Lane, Chattanooga	.924	104	83	186	91	16
T. Leiper, Carolina	.927	20	9	29	41	2
Lofton, Chattanooga	1.000	3	6	4	10	0
Lonigro, Orlando	1.000	1	0	7	7	0
Matos, Huntsville	1.000	2	1	2	3	0
McDonald, Nashville	.778	5	2	12	18	0
Mota, Nashville	.941	10	4	12	17	2
Nava, Jacksonville	.942	71	47	133	91	7
Raabe, Nashville	.926	48	23	90	22	4
Randa, Memphis	.942	125	97	309	31	23
Relaford, Jacksonville	.667	1	1	1	3	1
Saenz, Birmingham	.899	47	38	87	39	10
Santana, Jacksonville	.875	3	2	5	8	0
Schreiber, Carolina	.958	9	5	18	24	0
Stahoviak, Nashville	.893	80	55	146	25	7
Vice, Orlando	.737	8	3	11	19	2
Viera, Orlando	.786	3	1	10	14	0
Waggoner, Huntsville	.932	17	6	35	44	3
Walker, Birmingham	.831	40	19	40	71	1
Williams, Huntsville	1.000	2	3	0	3	0
Zambrano, Orlando	.917	8	3	8	12	1

Triple play—Giovanola.

SHORTSTOPS

Player, Team	Pct.	G	PO	A	E	DP
Adriana, Knoxville	1.000	3	3	2	5	1
Arias, Chattanooga	1.000	2	5	5	10	3
Beasley, Carolina	1.000	6	8	12	20	1
Busby, Orlando	.949	13	18	38	59	9
Coleman, Birmingham	.935	9	8	21	31	5
Corbin, Nashville	1.000	4	5	11	16	1
Crockett, Orlando	.972	14	24	46	72	6
Cruz, Huntsville	.960	39	81	109	98	27
E. Diaz, Memphis	.952	21	33	66	04	10
DiSarcina, Birmingham	.889	3	4	4	9	1
Garber, Memphis	.947	20	29	42	75	9
Gill, Chattanooga	1.000	1	1	4	5	0
Gomez, Orlando	1.000	14	16	36	52	8
GONZALEZ, Knoxville	.956	142	224	428	82	92
Grace, Orlando	.933	8	18	24	45	0
Guerrero, Memphis	.947	21	23	49	76	6
Halter, Memphis	.959	81	142	229	87	47
Hernandez, Orlando	.961	71	136	205	55	43
Hocking, Nashville	.937	100	144	300	74	46
Holley, Jacksonville	.974	7	13	24	38	1
Houk, 12 Nash.-1 Chat.	.902	13	15	31	51	5
Kelly, Greenville	.955	17	20	44	67	8
Kessinger, Chattanooga	.918	32	57	77	46	9
Koelling, Chattanooga	.900	5	9	9	20	1
Lane, Chattanooga	1.000	2	1	1	2	0
Lofton, Chattanooga	1.000	4	5	8	13	4
Lonigro, Orlando	.974	38	47	103	54	22
Matos, Huntsville	.871	10	9	18	31	5
Miranda, Birmingham	.933	4	3	11	15	2
Nava, Jacksonville	.915	16	20	34	59	9
Olmeda, Greenville	.914	21	21	53	81	11
Polcovich, Carolina	1.000	1	0	2	2	0
Purdy, Carolina	1.000	2	4	5	9	1
Raabe, Nashville	.961	33	44	104	54	18
Reese, Chattanooga	.951	102	181	300	06	62
Relaford, Jacksonville	.934	124	136	361	32	59
Roa, Greenville	.940	112	179	338	50	80
Rodriguez, Carolina	1.000	2	0	5	5	2
Santana, Jacksonville	1.000	1	0	1	1	0
Schreiber, Carolina	.930	76	101	206	30	49
Stahoviak, Nashville	1.000	3	0	3	3	0
Wilson, Birmingham	.937	133	214	308	57	61
Womack, Carolina	.961	60	102	169	82	38
Wood, Huntsville	.932	99	161	277	70	45

OUTFIELDERS

Player, Team	Pct.	G	PO	A	E	DP
Adams, Jacksonville	.968	55	109	11	24	2
Adriana, Knoxville	1.000	3	2	0	2	0
Alicea, Greenville	1.000	3	5	1	6	1
Beauchamp, Chattanooga	1.000	17	23	1	24	0
Becker, Nashville*	.981	131	303	5	14	1
Belcher, Birmingham	.973	84	142	4	50	1
Bowers, Knoxville	.983	141	285	8	98	1
Bragg, Jacksonville	.970	129	306	14	30	5
Butler, Knoxville	1.000	5	11	0	11	0
Cairo, Birmingham	.979	63	85	9	96	2
Canate, Knoxville	1.000	9	17	1	18	0
Casillas, Memphis*	.965	49	78	4	85	0
Cepicky, Birmingham	.938	9	13	2	16	0
Clayton, Jacksonville	1.000	6	12	0	12	0
Cole, Memphis	.969	78	150	5	60	0
Colvard, Greenville	.846	14	11	0	13	0
CORDOVA, Nashville	.991	130	209	7	18	0
Cornelius, Jacksonville	.972	36	69	1	72	0
Crockett, Orlando	1.000	1	3	0	3	0
Cummings, Carolina	.964	58	99	7	10	1
Dattola, Huntsville	.949	82	160	9	78	1
Dauphin, Orlando*	.988	77	165	3	70	1
Delanuez, Nashville	.976	95	194	11	10	2
A. De Los Santos, Carolina	.857	35	48	0	56	0
Diaz, Jacksonville	.987	46	70	7	78	1
Durant, Orlando	1.000	1	1	0	1	0
Ebright, Orlando*	.667	5	2	0	3	0
Garber, Memphis	1.000	16	22	3	25	0
Gibralter, Chattanooga	.976	131	319	7	34	2
Gillum, Chattanooga	.962	58	93	7	04	2
Glanville, Orlando	.972	70	168	8	81	3
Gordon, Chattanooga	.981	110	196	13	13	3
Grayum, Orlando	.988	57	77	2	80	0
Green, Knoxville*	.956	99	172	3	83	1
Green, Carolina	.969	90	183	6	95	3
Hart, Huntsville	.967	94	134	11	50	3
Heath, Huntsville	.975	103	150	8	62	2
Helfand, Huntsville	1.000	1	1	0	1	0
Hodge, Knoxville	.981	31	51	1	53	0
Holley, Jacksonville	.947	10	17	1	19	0
Hood, Birmingham	1.000	9	9	2	11	1
Houk, Nashville	.800	3	4	0	5	0
Hughes, Greenville	.969	98	172	14	92	2
Jackson, Jacksonville	1.000	3	4	0	4	0
Jaster, Memphis	.976	44	77	6	85	0
Jenkins, Chattanooga	.981	84	151	2	56	0
Jensen, Orlando	.969	42	60	3	65	1
Johns, Huntsville*	1.000	2	3	2	5	1
Johnson, Memphis	.986	32	62	8	71	1
Johnson, Carolina*	1.000	24	28	1	29	0
Jones, Chattanooga	1.000	22	37	1	38	0
Kapano, Orlando	.980	56	91	6	99	1
Kelly, Greenville	1.000	3	5	1	6	1
Kieschnick, Orlando	.885	23	22	1	26	0
Kowitz, Greenville*	.989	117	257	6	66	1
Kuehl, Huntsville	1.000	1	4	0	4	0
T. Leiper, Carolina	.960	16	22	2	25	1
Lewis, Orlando	.946	27	35	0	37	0
Long, Memphis*	.985	77	190	8	01	1
Magallanes, Orlando	1.000	4	7	0	7	0
Marquez, Jacksonville*	.833	11	10	0	12	0
Mashore, Huntsville	.983	68	167	9	79	4
Masteller, Nashville*	.952	13	19	1	21	0
May, Memphis	1.000	12	17	0	17	0
Maynard, Jacksonville	.952	50	98	2	05	1
McDonald, Nashville	1.000	60	106	9	15	0
Merchant, Chattanooga	.976	25	37	3	41	0
Morales, Jacksonville	1.000	3	3	0	3	0
Neff, Carolina	1.000	16	17	2	19	0
Neill, Huntsville*	.973	48	70	2	74	1
Newfield, Jacksonville	.968	24	28	2	31	0
Norman, Memphis	.972	121	258	17	83	3
O'Connor, Greenville	.983	84	110	4	16	0
Olmeda, Greenville	1.000	2	2	0	2	0
Ortiz, Carolina	.980	25	45	4	50	0
Pledger, Birmingham	.980	113	192	5	01	2
Ratliff, Carolina	.986	113	303	11	17	3
Reams, Knoxville	.969	84	145	12	62	2
Relaford, Jacksonville	.000	1	0	0	1	0
Rivera, Nashville	.833	6	5	0	6	0
Robertson, Birmingham*	.667	1	2	0	3	0
Sanchez, Greenville*	.952	16	19	1	21	0
Santana, Jacksonville	.933	10	12	2	15	0
Scruggs, Jacksonville	.956	45	83	3	90	1
Sheppard, Knoxville	.923	64	101	7	17	0
Simmons, Huntsville	.961	40	71	3	77	0
Spann, Chattanooga	1.000	1	1	0	1	0
Stahoviak, Nashville	1.000	2	1	0	1	0
Swann, Greenville	.932	26	38	3	44	0
Tedder, Birmingham*	1.000	33	56	3	59	0
Thomas, Carolina	.953	78	136	5	48	0
Timmons, Orlando	.968	97	169	14	89	3
Torres, Orlando	1.000	14	16	1	17	0
Waggoner, Jacksonville	1.000	22	56	0	56	0
Waggoner, Huntsville	.889	5	8	0	9	0
T. Ward, Knoxville	1.000	7	20	0	20	0
Warner, Greenville*	.933	5	14	0	15	0
Williams, Huntsville	.975	50	72	7	81	1
Wolak, Birmingham	.972	136	300	9	18	2
Wolfe, Huntsville	1.000	34	63	3	66	0
Young, Orlando	.963	41	97	8	09	4
Zambrano, Orlando	1.000	2	2	0	2	0

Triple plays—Hart, Kowitz.

CATCHERS

Player, Team	Pct.	G	PO	A	E	DP	PB
Alvarez, Birmingham	.993	34	277	27	06	1	5
Banister, Carolina	.882	2	15	0	17	0	0
Beeler, Jacksonville	.982	17	103	6	11	1	4
Bradley, Greenville	.982	13	51	3	55	0	1
Brito, Huntsville	1.000	1	1	0	1	0	0
A. Brown, Orlando	1.000	1	9	0	9	0	0
Troy Buckley, Chattanooga	.967	10	52	7	61	1	1
Campanis, Jacksonville	.983	50	374	38	19	4	6
Cox, Chattanooga	.987	88	519	87	14	3	7
Delgado, Knoxville	.983	107	683	103	00	8	16
Dempsey, Memphis	1.000	1	5	0	5	0	0
C. Diaz, Memphis	.994	53	275	35	12	4	10
DURANT, Nashville	.9923	95	590	61	56	7	5
Edge, Carolina	.975	45	309	40	58	2	1
Erdman, Orlando	.995	66	368	33	03	5	7
Fuller, Chattanooga	.974	44	274	29	11	2	1
Grifol, Nashville	.995	49	336	48	86	3	3
Hammond, Chattanooga	1.000	9	51	12	63	2	1
Helfand, Huntsville	.985	93	602	63	75	12	12
Houston, Greenville	.980	63	410	34	53	4	8
Jennings, Memphis	.984	98	596	68	75	8	4
J. Johnson, Orlando	.969	33	174	16	96	1	0
Kounas, Jacksonville	.988	40	224	25	52	1	3
Mann, Orlando	.993	27	131	20	52	2	3
Manning, Birmingham	.985	29	173	30	06	3	3
McDonnell, Orlando	.978	18	79	10	91	1	2
Miller, Nashville	1.000	3	26	3	29	0	1
Morales, Jacksonville	.952	46	242	14	69	3	3
Morland, Knoxville	.988	44	210	31	44	3	7
Mota, Nashville	1.000	1	1	0	1	0	0
Nunez, Birmingham	.986	80	550	66	25	5	22
Osik, Carolina	.9918	100	662	69	37	11	18
Perez, Greenville	1.000	6	24	4	28	0	0
Raasch, Orlando	1.000	5	29	1	30	0	2
Ripplemeyer, Greenville	.987	78	497	55	59	4	9
Robinson, Orlando	.984	19	110	11	23	3	1
Strange, Birmingham	.977	6	41	2	44	0	3
Williams, Huntsville	.979	61	355	56	20	5	14

PITCHERS

Player, Team	Pct.	G	PO	A	E	DP
Acre, Huntsville	1.000	19	1	4	5	0
Adkins, Birmingham*	.923	26	4	8	13	1
Adriana, Knoxville	1.000	1	1	0	1	1
Ahern, Memphis	.867	18	6	20	30	2
Allison, Huntsville*	1.000	19	0	9	9	1
Anderson, Chattanooga	1.000	2	3	1	4	0
Andujar, Birmingham	1.000	6	1	8	9	0
Backlund, Carolina	1.000	20	6	16	22	0
Baker, Huntsville*	.857	25	4	32	42	2
Baldwin, Birmingham	.929	17	15	24	42	2
Baptist, Knoxville*	1.000	7	0	6	6	0
Barcelo, Nashville	1.000	2	1	2	3	0
Barfield, Birmingham*	1.000	13	6	10	16	0
Beatty, Carolina*	1.000	18	6	11	17	1
Bevil, Memphis	1.000	6	1	6	7	1
Bicknell, Jacksonville	.864	24	6	13	22	0
Bittiger, Nashville	1.000	2	0	1	1	0
Boehringer, Birmingham	.933	7	3	11	15	1
Boltz, Greenville*	1.000	9	1	3	4	0
Bradley, Greenville	1.000	1	1	0	1	0
Briscoe, Huntsville	.750	30	0	3	4	0
Brow, Knoxville	1.000	3	2	4	6	0
Brown, Knoxville	.947	46	5	13	19	2
Travis Buckley, 2 Cht.-10 Jax.	.909	12	6	4	11	0
Burgos, Chattanooga*	1.000	31	0	6	6	0
Burlingame, Greenville	1.000	15	5	7	12	1
Bushing, Chattanooga	.800	61	3	5	10	1
Campbell, Memphis*	1.000	11	1	4	5	0
Campos, Birmingham	1.000	9	5	14	19	2
Carter, Birmingham	1.000	13	1	2	3	0
Cecena, Carolina	.667	14	0	2	3	0
Chitren, Huntsville	1.000	32	1	4	5	0
Chrisman, Birmingham	1.000	8	2	1	3	0
Clayton, Jacksonville	1.000	3	1	0	1	0
Coffman, Jacksonville	1.000	10	1	3	4	1
Cole, Carolina	1.000	27	2	3	5	0
Connolly, Huntsville	1.000	20	4	7	11	0

Player, Team	Pct.	G	PO	A	E	DP
Corbett, Orlando*	1.000	5	2	5	7	0
Courtright, Chattanooga*	.978	27	12	33	46	1
Crabtree, Knoxville	.906	27	18	30	53	4
Cromwell, Knoxville*	.000	6	0	0	1	0
Culberson, Chattanooga	.950	37	7	12	20	1
Cummings, Jacksonville*	.875	7	1	6	8	0
Czajkowski, Orlando	1.000	10	2	3	5	0
Czarkowski, Jacksonville*	.947	25	6	12	19	1
Darwin, Jacksonville	1.000	27	1	1	2	0
Delanuez, Nashville	1.000	3	1	0	1	0
Delgado, Orlando	1.000	9	0	4	4	0
M. De Los Santos, Carolina	.778	8	1	6	9	0
Dickson, Orlando*	1.000	9	2	8	10	0
Duey, Knoxville	.941	37	4	12	17	1
Ellis, Birmingham	.875	12	6	15	24	0
Ferry, Chattanooga	.923	28	8	16	26	0
Fleming, Jacksonville*	1.000	4	3	6	9	0
Flener, Knoxville*	.974	38	12	25	38	1
Foster, Jacksonville	.900	12	5	4	10	1
Fyhrie, Memphis	1.000	22	5	19	24	2
Galvez, Orlando	.667	3	1	1	3	0
Ganote, Knoxville	.935	33	10	19	31	2
Garcia, Chattanooga	.667	15	0	2	3	0
Gardner, 7 Orl.- 19 Birm.	.800	26	2	10	15	2
Garland, Huntsville	.909	23	3	7	11	2
Garza, Carolina	1.000	35	1	15	16	0
Gavaghan, Nashville	.900	20	3	6	10	0
Givens, Memphis*	1.000	14	5	9	14	0
Glinatsis, Jacksonville	.600	9	2	1	5	0
Gordon, Birmingham*	1.000	37	3	2	5	0
Grove, Knoxville	1.000	10	3	4	7	1
Guardado, Nashville*	.933	10	2	12	15	3
Hampton, Jacksonville*	.917	15	6	16	24	0
Hancock, Carolina*	.926	25	4	21	27	2
Harkey, Orlando	1.000	1	0	1	1	0
Harrah, Carolina	1.000	6	1	4	5	0
Harris, Memphis	.867	22	3	10	15	0
Harris, Jacksonville	1.000	9	3	5	8	0
Hartsock, Orlando	1.000	8	4	6	10	1
Hassinger, Greenville	1.000	12	2	5	7	0
Henry, Nashville	.900	6	3	6	10	0
Holcomb, Chattanooga*	1.000	6	1	2	3	0
Hook, Chattanooga	.892	28	11	22	37	1
Hope, Carolina	.971	21	9	25	35	1
Hostetler, Greenville	.867	19	14	12	30	1
Hunter, Carolina	1.000	46	4	17	21	2
Jarvis, Chattanooga	1.000	7	1	5	6	1
Jimenez, Huntsville	.958	20	8	15	24	0
Johns, Huntsville*	.955	40	19	23	44	2
Johnson, Birmingham	1.000	13	0	3	3	0
C. Johnson, Orlando	.889	15	5	3	9	0
E. Johnson, Orlando*	.875	53	6	8	16	2
Johnson, Nashville	1.000	31	2	3	5	0
Jones, Carolina	.933	11	6	8	15	1
Jordan, Knoxville*	.846	25	2	9	13	0
Karchner, Memphis	1.000	6	6	3	9	1
Karsay, 19 Knox.-2 Hunt.	.783	21	11	7	23	1
Kennedy, Chattanooga	1.000	2	0	4	4	0
Kent, Jacksonville	.500	14	1	0	2	0
Keyser, Birmingham	1.000	2	0	8	8	0
Kilgo, Chattanooga*	1.000	53	6	16	22	0
King, Jacksonville*	1.000	16	2	4	6	0
Kizziah, Knoxville	.938	27	3	12	16	1
Klonoski, Nashville*	1.000	56	12	15	27	1
Knackert, Jacksonville	1.000	4	0	1	1	0
Konieczki, Nashville*	.800	42	1	7	10	1
Landress, Memphis	.846	26	1	10	13	0
Latter, Huntsville	1.000	6	0	1	1	0
D. Leiper, Carolina*	1.000	8	0	4	4	0
Lieber, 4 Mem.-6 Caro.	.909	10	3	7	11	1
Limbach, Memphis*	.857	42	1	11	14	1
Loaiza, Carolina	1.000	7	2	5	7	0
Locklear, Birmingham*	1.000	9	2	6	8	0
Lomon, Greenville	.800	13	3	9	15	0
Lovelace, Greenville*	.800	11	3	1	5	0
Manon, Birmingham	.935	25	12	17	31	1
MANSUR, Nashville*	1.000	33	14	33	47	3
Mason, Memphis*	1.000	1	0	1	1	0
McCreary, Nashville	1.000	38	10	16	26	1
McCurry, Carolina	.500	23	0	1	2	0
Melvin, Orlando	1.000	36	9	3	12	1
Miceli, 40 Mem.- 13 Caro.	1.000	53	5	8	13	1
Miller, Carolina	1.000	6	6	6	12	1
Misuraca, Nashville	1.000	25	13	14	27	2
Mongiello, Birmingham	1.000	7	0	5	5	1
Morones, Orlando	1.000	4	0	1	1	0
Morton, Memphis*	1.000	20	1	17	18	1
Munoz, Nashville	.929	20	11	15	28	0
Myers, Memphis	.882	12	2	13	17	1
Newlin, 8 Jack.- 13 Knox.	.900	21	9	9	20	0
Newman, Nashville*	.833	14	1	9	12	0
Ohlms, Knoxville	1.000	7	0	2	2	0
Olsen, Birmingham	.917	25	4	7	12	1
Osteen, Huntsville*	.933	11	2	12	15	0
Parris, Jacksonville	1.000	7	0	4	4	0
Perez, Memphis	.889	18	5	3	9	1
Perigny, Birmingham	.909	48	5	5	11	0
Perkins, Nashville	1.000	36	2	4	6	0
Peters, Memphis	1.000	6	1	3	4	1
Phillips, Jacksonville	.833	27	1	4	6	0
Phillips, Knoxville	.750	5	1	2	4	0
Phoenix, Huntsville	1.000	11	2	2	4	0
Piatt, 11 Mem.-3 Caro.	1.000	14	1	3	4	0
Picota, Jacksonville	1.000	11	3	3	6	0
Pierce, Memphis*	.944	37	1	16	18	0
Pierce, 33 Birm.- 13 Chat.	1.000	46	6	8	14	1
Plantenberg, Jacksonville*	1.000	34	3	7	10	0
Polley, Greenville	.889	42	3	13	18	1
Potts, Greenville*	.841	25	7	30	44	2
Radke, Nashville	.952	13	8	12	21	0
Ray, Chattanooga	1.000	30	1	5	6	1
Remlinger, Jacksonville*	.900	7	5	4	10	0
Renko, Knoxville	.833	12	2	3	6	0
Reyes, Greenville	.909	33	5	15	22	1
Richards, Memphis*	1.000	7	1	3	4	0
Ritchie, Nashville	.889	12	4	12	18	1
Ritter, Greenville	.941	35	7	9	17	0
Robinson, Nashville	.889	35	2	6	9	1
Robinson, Chattanooga	.972	20	10	25	36	2
Roesler, Memphis	1.000	3	0	2	2	0
Rogers, Knoxville	1.000	9	8	8	16	0
Ruffcorn, Birmingham	.977	20	19	24	44	1
Ruffin, Birmingham	1.000	11	3	2	5	0
Russell, Jacksonville	.933	17	9	19	30	2
Salkeld, Jacksonville	1.000	14	4	12	16	0
Salles, Orlando	.935	33	15	28	46	1
Sanchez, Memphis	1.000	15	5	8	13	0
Schanz, Jacksonville	1.000	49	8	13	21	0
Schrenk, Birmingham	1.000	8	9	15	24	0
Schullstrom, Nashville	1.000	4	0	2	2	0
Schutz, Greenville*	1.000	22	1	2	3	0
Shaw, Chattanooga	1.000	25	1	3	4	0
Shaw, Huntsville*	.974	28	7	31	39	2
Small, Knoxville	1.000	48	10	10	20	3
Smith, Huntsville	1.000	9	5	4	9	0
Smith, Carolina*	1.000	4	2	2	4	1
Smithberg, Huntsville	1.000	27	3	7	10	0
Sparma, Greenville	.870	28	19	21	46	1
Spoljaric, Knoxville*	.923	7	3	9	13	1
Steenstra, Orlando	.972	14	17	18	36	3
Stevens, Orlando	.947	11	6	12	19	1
Stewart, Chattanooga	1.000	10	6	7	13	0
Strange, Greenville	1.000	27	4	1	5	1
Strauss, Greenville	.857	15	3	3	7	1
Strebeck, Huntsville	.900	23	3	6	10	0
Sturtze, Huntsville	.944	28	11	23	36	3
Swartzbaugh, Orlando	1.000	10	4	8	12	2
Tafoya, Carolina	.933	49	8	20	30	3
Tatar, Chattanooga	1.000	4	2	3	5	0
Taylor, Orlando	1.000	28	4	6	10	1
Toliver, Orlando	1.000	33	0	8	8	1
Tomlin, Carolina*	1.000	4	0	1	1	0
Trinidad, Orlando	1.000	4	4	7	11	4
Upshaw, Greenville*	.962	34	4	21	26	0
Vasquez, Greenville	.944	43	5	12	18	4
Ventura, Memphis	.933	20	5	9	15	1
Villone, Jacksonville*	.933	11	4	10	15	0
Wade, Greenville*	1.000	8	2	4	6	0
Wagner, Memphis	.833	10	1	4	6	0
Wakefield, Carolina	.769	9	4	6	13	0
Walker, Orlando	.846	16	4	7	13	2
Wallace, Orlando	1.000	15	7	12	19	0
A. Ward, Knoxville*	1.000	11	0	6	6	0
Watkins, Nashville	1.000	13	0	3	3	0
Weber, Nashville	.889	17	2	6	9	1
White, Carolina	.947	12	7	11	19	3
Williams, Greenville	.923	45	5	7	13	0
Williams, Orlando*	.966	15	3	25	29	0
Willis, Orlando	.933	61	1	13	15	1
Wissler, Nashville	.972	29	16	19	36	0
Wojciechowski, Huntsville*	.810	13	6	11	21	0
Woodall, Greenville	1.000	8	4	17	21	1
Zimmerman, Carolina	.929	33	3	10	14	1

The following players did not have any fielding statistics at the positions indicated or appeared only as a designated hitter, pinch-hitter or pinch-runner: Alicea, 3b, ss; Beasley, of; Best, p; Bowie, p; Bragg, p; Casillas, p; Christiansen, p; G. Cole, p; Dattola, p; Davisson, 2b; Ebright, p; Gajkowski, p; Garner, dh, ph; Heble, p; Holley, 2b; Houk, p; Houston, of; Kounas, of; Jensen, 3b; H. Johnson, dh, ph; Leach, p; Long, p; Lynch, p; Martinez, dh; Merigliano, p; Montoya, p; Osik, 3b; Osteen, 1b; Parkinson, p; Raabe, p; Rivera, p; O. Sanchez, p; L. Thomas, p; Van Slyke, of; D. Walker, of.

Year	Team	Pct.
1904—	Macon	.598
1905—	Macon	.625
1906—	Savannah	.637
1907—	Charleston	.620
1908—	Jacksonville	.694
1909—	Chattanooga*	.738
	Augusta	.702
1910—	Columbus	.588
1911—	Columbus*	.681
	Columbia	.710
1912—	Jacksonville*	.679
	Columbus	.632
1913—	Savannah	.754
	Savannah	.593
1914—	Savannah*	.667
	Albany	.650
1915—	Macon	.588
	Columbus*	.686
1916—	Augusta*	.617
	Columbia	.631
1917—	Charleston	.741
	Columbia*	.667
1918—	Did not operate.	
1919—	Columbia	.585
1920—	Columbia	.633
1921—	Columbia	.642
1922—	Charleston	.625
1923—	Charlotte*	.653
	Macon	.580
1924—	Augusta	.612
1925—	Spartanburg	.620
1926—	Greenville	.662
1927—	Greenville	.622
1928—	Asheville	.664
1929—	Asheville	.605
	Knoxville*	.634
1930—	Greenville*	.620
	Macon	.643
1931-35—	Did not operate.	
1936—	Jacksonville	.652
	Columbus*	.650
1937—	Columbus	.572
	Savannah (3rd)†	.565
1938—	Savannah	.574
	Macon (2nd)†	.570
1939—	Columbus	.601
	Augusta (2nd)†	.597
1940—	Savannah	.627
	Columbus (2nd)†	.583
1941—	Macon	.643
	Columbia (2nd)†	.636
1942—	Charleston	.620
	Macon (2nd)†	.585
1943-45—	Did not operate.	
1946—	Columbus	.568
	Augusta (4th)†	.547
1947—	Columbus	.575
	Savannah (2nd)†	.563
1948—	Charleston	.572
	Greenville (3rd)†	.549
1949—	Macon‡	.623
1950—	Macon‡	.588
1951—	Montgomery	.607
1952—	Columbia	.649
	Montgomery (3rd)†	.558
1953—	Jacksonville	.679
	Savannah (2nd)†	.571
1954—	Jacksonville	.593
	Savannah (2nd)†	.571
1955—	Columbia	.636
	Augusta (3rd)†	.543
1956—	Jacksonville‡	.621
1957—	Augusta	.636
	Charlotte (2nd)†	.562
1958—	Augusta	.550
	Macon (3rd)†	.500
1959—	Knoxville	.557
	Gastonia (4th)†	.504
1960—	Columbia	.597
	Savannah (3rd)†	.561
1961—	Asheville	.635
1962—	Savannah	.662
	Macon (3rd)†	.576
1963—	Augusta*	.661
	Lynchburg	.662
1964—	Lynchburg	.579
1965—	Columbus	.572
1966—	Mobile	.629
1967—	Birmingham	.604
1968—	Asheville	.614
1969—	Charlotte	.579
1970—	Columbus	.569
1971—	Did not operate as league—clubs were members of Dixie Association.	
1972—	Asheville	.583
	Montgomery§	.561
1973—	Montgomery§	.580
	Jacksonville	.559
1974—	Jacksonville	.565
	Knoxville§	.533
1975—	Orlando	.587
	Montgomery§	.545
1976—	Montgomery x	.591
	Orlando	.540
1977—	Montgomery x	.628
	Jacksonville	.522
1978—	Knoxville x	.611
	Savannah	.500
1979—	Columbus	.587
	Nashville x	.576
1980—	Memphis	.576
	Charlotte x	.500
1981—	Nashville	.566
	Orlando x	.556
1982—	Jacksonville	.576
	Nashville x	.535
1983—	Birmingham x	.628
	Jacksonville	.531
1984—	Charlotte x	.510
	Knoxville	.483
1985—	Charlotte	.545
	Huntsville x	.542
1986—	Huntsville	.553
	Columbus x	.500
1987—	Charlotte	.586
	Birmingham x	.476
1988—	Greenville	.604
	Chattanooga x	.566
1989—	Birmingham x	.615
	Greenville	.504
1990—	Orlando	.590
	Memphis x	.507
1991—	Greenville	.611
	Orlando x	.535
1992—	Greenville x	.699
	Chattanooga	.629
1993—	Birmingham x	.549
	Knoxville	.500

*Won split season playoff. †Won four-club playoff. ‡Won championship and four-club playoff. §League was divided into Eastern and Western divisions; won playoff. xLeague was divided into Eastern and Western divisions and played split season; won playoff.

TEXAS LEAGUE

FINAL STANDINGS

FIRST HALF

EAST DIVISION

Team	W	L	T	Pct.	GB
Jackson (Astros)	41	27	0	.603	....
Arkansas (Cardinals)	37	31	0	.544	4
Tulsa (Rangers)	31	37	0	.456	10
Shreveport (Giants)	29	39	0	.426	12

WEST DIVISION

Team	W	L	T	Pct.	GB
El Paso (Brewers)	36	31	0	.537	....
San Antonio (Dodgers)	33	34	0	.493	3
Midland (Angels)	33	35	0	.485	3½
Wichita (Padres)	31	37	0	.456	5½

SECOND HALF

EAST DIVISION

Team	W	L	T	Pct.	GB
Shreveport (Giants)	37	31	0	.544	....
Tulsa (Rangers)	35	32	0	.522	1½
Jackson (Astros)	32	35	0	.478	4½
Arkansas (Cardinals)	30	38	0	.441	7

WEST DIVISION

Team	W	L	T	Pct.	GB
El Paso (Brewers)	40	28	0	.588	....
Wichita (Padres)	37	31	0	.544	3
Midland (Angels)	34	33	1	.507	5½
San Antonio (Dodgers)	25	42	1	.373	14½

COMPOSITE

Team	E.P.	Jack.	Wich.	Mid.	Ark.	Tul.	Shrv.	S.A.	W	L	T	Pct.	GB
El Paso (Brewers)	....	7	20	18	3	4	3	21	76	59	0	.563	....
Jackson (Astros)	3	....	5	5	16	20	19	5	73	62	0	.541	3
Wichita (Padres)	12	5	....	18	5	6	6	16	68	68	0	.500	8½
Midland (Angels)	14	5	14	....	4	5	6	19	67	68	1	.496	9
Arkansas (Cardinals)	7	16	5	6	....	11	15	7	67	69	0	.493	9½
Tulsa (Rangers)	6	11	4	5	21	....	15	4	66	69	0	.489	10
Shreveport (Giants)	7	13	4	4	17	17	....	4	66	70	0	.485	10½
San Antonio (Dodgers)	10	5	16	12	3	6	6	....	58	76	1	.433	17½

Arkansas club represented Little Rock, Ark.

Major league affiliations in parentheses.

Playoffs—Jackson defeated Shreveport, three games to one; El Paso defeated Wichita, three games to one; Jackson defeated El Paso, three games to none, to win league championship.

Regular-season attendance—Arkansas, 285,757; El Paso, 306,948; Jackson, 148,230; Midland, 196,464; San Antonio, 189,251; Shreveport, 203,479; Tulsa, 325,135; Wichita, 236,378. Total—1,891,642. Playoffs (11 games)—20,440. Class AA All-Star Game at Memphis—6,335. Texas League All-Star Game at Wichita—5,164.

Managers—Arkansas, Joe Pettini; El Paso, Tim Ireland; Jackson, Sal Butera; Midland, Don Long; San Antonio, Glenn Hoffman; Shreveport, Ron Wotus; Tulsa, Stan Cliburn; Wichita, Dave Tremblay.

All-Star team: 1B—Roberto Petagine, Jackson; 2B—P.J. Forbes, Midland; 3B—Cris Colon, Tulsa; SS—Wes Weger, El Paso; OF—Brian Hunter, Jackson; Dwayne Hosey, Wichita; John Mabry, Arkansas; C—Jorge Fabregas, Midland; DH—Trey McCoy, Tulsa; LHP—Ben VanRyn, San Antonio; Scott Karl, El Paso; RHP—James Dougherty, Jackson; Rick Helling, Tulsa; Rick Gorecki, San Antonio; Bryce Florie, Wichita; Player of the Year—Roberto Petagine, Jackson; Pitcher of the Year—Ben VanRyn, San Antonio; Manager of the Year—Sal Butera, Jackson.

BATTING

TEAM

Team	Avg.	G	AB	R	OR	H	TB	2B	3B	HR	RBI	SH	SF	HP	BB	Int. BB	SO	SB	CS	LOB
Midland	.285	136	4639	729	729	1322	1881	229	39	84	656	70	54	64	471	22	799	68	59	988
El Paso	.275	135	4610	703	635	1266	1833	245	59	68	629	41	36	58	448	28	824	144	91	913
Jackson	.267	135	4387	615	570	1171	1780	224	23	113	556	31	36	52	409	40	975	115	80	883
Wichita	.267	136	4502	631	640	1200	1763	198	37	97	559	37	37	52	435	23	980	196	119	900
Tulsa	.260	136	4360	547	602	1135	1758	196	26	125	506	22	28	72	365	15	908	91	77	875
San Antonio	.247	135	4504	533	570	1114	1696	204	39	100	488	55	31	37	385	33	918	74	70	852
Arkansas	.247	136	4330	550	531	1069	1668	239	30	100	495	44	33	46	415	46	824	83	67	924
Shreveport	.247	136	4420	497	528	1090	1548	222	22	64	440	51	30	46	374	45	824	83	67	924

INDIVIDUAL

(Leading qualifiers for batting championship—367 or more plate appearances)

*Bats lefthanded. †Switch-hitter.

Player, Team	Avg.	G	AB	R	H	TB	2B	3B	HR	RBI	SH	SF	HP	BB	Int. BB	SO	SB	CS
Petagine, Roberto, Jackson*	.334	128	437	73	146	231	36	2	15	90	0	5	4	84	14	89	6	5
Forbes, P.J., Midland	.319	126	498	90	159	231	23	2	15	64	14	2	4	26	1	50	6	8
Dodson, Bo, El Paso*	.312	101	330	58	103	165	27	4	9	59	0	2	6	42	4	69	1	6
Pritchett, Chris, Midland*	.308	127	464	61	143	191	30	6	2	66	6	7	2	61	2	72	3	7
Palmeiro, Orlando, Midland*	.305	131	535	85	163	192	19	5	0	64	18	3	2	42	1	35	18	14
Kellner, Frank, Jackson†	.301	121	355	51	107	150	27	2	4	36	2	6	2	38	5	51	11	12
Katzaroff, Robbie, Shreveport	.300	104	406	52	122	152	22	4	0	30	5	4	8	35	3	33	15	13
Colon, Cris, Tulsa†	.300	124	490	63	147	213	27	3	11	47	4	5	5	13	0	76	6	3
Hunter, Brian, Jackson	.294	133	523	84	154	216	22	5	10	52	5	2	1	34	4	85	35	18
Thompson, Fletcher, Jackson*	.294	98	316	54	93	124	15	2	4	29	7	1	1	55	2	83	23	12
Grebeck, Brian, Midland	.294	118	405	65	119	162	20	4	5	54	6	7	8	64	1	81	6	1
Smith, Ed, El Paso	.294	118	419	64	123	182	23	6	8	69	0	2	3	38	4	97	15	5

Departmental leaders: G—Mabry, 136; AB—Palmeiro, 535; R—Forbes, 90; H—Palmeiro, 163; TB—McCoy, 243; 2B—Petagine, 36; 3B—Battle, 12; HR—McCoy, 29; RBI—McCoy, 95; SH—Palmeiro, 18; SF—Holbert, 9; HP—McCoy, 19; BB—Petagine, 84; IBB—Petagine, 14; SO—Madsen, 136; SB—Hunter, 35; CS—Cedeno, 20.

Player, Team	Avg.	G	AB	R	H	TB	2B	3B	HR	RBI	SH	SF	HP	BB	Int. BB	SO	SB	CS
Abbe, Chris, San Antonio	.205	82	254	32	52	100	7	1	13	36	0	4	6	35	5	61	0	3
Abercrombie, John, Wichita	.254	71	181	21	46	74	7	0	7	31	1	1	7	8	0	44	6	5
Alvarez, Jorge, San Antonio	.271	93	251	26	68	104	24	0	4	34	1	3	1	20	3	34	9	8
Anderson, Paul, Arkansas	.273	18	11	1	3	4	1	0	0	0	1	0	0	1	0	3	0	0
Anderson, Tom, Jackson	.250	8	8	1	2	2	0	0	0	1	0	0	0	1	0	0	0	0
Ard, Johnny, Shreveport	.000	3	1	0	0	0	0	0	0	0	0	0	0	0	0	0	0	0
Aversa, Joe, Arkansas†	.181	95	199	23	36	44	4	2	0	5	2	1	1	17	0	34	3	1
Barber, Brian, Arkansas	.286	25	28	4	8	10	0	1	0	2	1	0	1	4	0	6	0	0
Basse, Mike, El Paso*	.267	108	386	65	103	130	14	5	1	36	4	2	4	51	2	72	26	13
Battle, Allen, Arkansas	.274	108	390	71	107	164	24	12	3	40	2	3	6	45	0	75	20	12
Bellomo, Kevin, Shreveport	.083	10	12	0	1	1	0	0	0	1	0	0	0	2	0	7	0	0
Beltran, Rigo, Arkansas*	.143	19	14	1	2	3	1	0	0	0	0	2	0	0	0	5	0	0
Bene, Bill, San Antonio	.000	46	3	0	0	0	0	0	0	0	0	0	0	0	0	1	0	0
Berumen, Andres, Wichita	.000	7	3	0	0	0	0	0	0	0	0	0	0	0	0	2	0	0
Bethea, Steve, Wichita†	.265	15	49	2	13	13	0	0	0	1	0	0	0	4	0	16	0	1
Bish, Brent, Wichita	.266	24	64	12	17	21	2	1	0	6	0	1	1	6	0	19	2	2
Blanco, Henry, San Antonio	.195	117	374	33	73	124	19	1	10	42	2	1	4	29	0	80	3	3
Boykin, Tyrone, Midland	.280	35	132	29	37	52	3	3	2	17	0	2	2	17	0	17	1	0
Brakebill, Mark, Midland	.230	62	222	21	51	77	9	1	5	32	2	5	9	4	0	60	0	6
Brosnan, Jason, San Antonio*	.000	3	1	0	0	0	0	0	0	0	1	0	0	0	0	1	0	0
Brumley, Duff, 12 Ark.-6 Tul.	.000	18	13	0	0	0	0	0	0	0	1	0	0	0	0	9	0	0
Bruno, Julio, Wichita	.285	70	246	34	70	98	17	1	3	24	1	1	2	11	3	46	3	5
Bruske, Jim, Jackson	.308	16	26	3	8	15	1	0	2	4	0	0	0	1	0	3	0	0
Bryand, Renay, Wichita*	.000	52	3	0	0	0	0	0	0	0	0	0	0	0	0	1	0	0
Calcagno, Dan, Shreveport	.500	3	4	1	2	2	0	0	0	0	0	0	0	1	0	1	0	0
Campillo, Rob, El Paso	.000	4	11	0	0	0	0	0	0	0	0	0	0	0	0	4	0	0
Carlson, Dan, Shreveport	.111	15	18	0	2	2	0	0	0	0	0	0	0	0	0	3	0	0
Carter, Mike, El Paso	.370	17	73	16	27	39	4	1	2	16	0	0	0	3	0	7	6	4
Castellanos, Miguel, Tulsa	.169	49	142	10	24	33	4	1	1	13	0	2	0	12	0	29	1	1
Castillo, Ben, Tulsa	.228	86	272	34	62	91	12	1	5	14	2	1	8	20	0	53	6	3
Castleberry, Kevin, El Paso*	.300	98	327	46	98	123	9	5	2	49	0	3	2	26	3	38	13	3
Castro, Juan, San Antonio	.276	118	424	55	117	177	23	8	7	41	17	3	2	30	3	40	12	11
Castro, Nelson, San Antonio	.200	5	5	1	1	1	0	0	0	0	0	0	0	0	0	2	0	0
Cavanagh, Mike, Shreveport	.571	4	7	3	4	8	1	0	1	3	0	0	0	1	0	2	0	0
Cedeno, Roger, San Antonio†	.288	122	465	70	134	174	12	8	4	30	4	1	1	45	2	90	28	20
Chimelis, Joel, Shreveport	.202	36	114	10	23	46	5	0	6	18	0	2	2	8	0	14	3	0
Cholowsky, Dan, Arkansas	.217	68	212	31	46	69	10	2	3	16	1	1	2	38	3	54	10	2
Christopherson, Eric, Shreveport	.152	15	46	5	7	9	2	0	0	2	0	0	0	9	0	10	1	1
Cimorelli, Frank, Arkansas	.000	37	2	0	0	0	0	0	0	0	1	0	0	0	0	1	0	0
Cirillo, Jeff, El Paso	.341	67	249	53	85	132	16	2	9	41	0	3	5	26	1	37	2	3
Clark, Terry, Wichita	.000	19	1	0	0	0	0	0	0	0	0	0	0	0	0	0	0	0
Claus, Todd, Midland†	.188	18	32	7	6	9	1	1	0	3	1	0	0	10	0	10	1	0
Clinton, Jim, Tulsa	.083	6	12	0	1	1	0	0	0	0	0	0	0	1	0	4	0	0
Cohick, Emmitt, Midland*	.270	105	356	59	96	157	18	5	11	53	9	2	5	35	2	91	6	2
Cole, Mark, El Paso†	.313	5	16	3	5	6	1	0	0	1	0	0	1	2	0	5	1	0
Coleman, Paul, Arkansas	.244	123	401	44	98	149	24	3	7	30	3	3	8	32	3	97	8	6
Collier, Anthony, San Antonio*	.207	83	193	21	40	60	8	0	4	15	1	1	2	10	3	43	2	4
Colon, Cris, Tulsa†	.300	124	490	63	147	213	27	3	11	47	4	5	5	13	0	76	6	3
Correa, Edwin, San Antonio	.000	2	1	0	0	0	0	0	0	0	0	0	0	0	0	0	0	0
Costello, Fred, Jackson	.000	12	16	0	0	0	0	0	0	0	0	0	0	0	0	9	0	0
Couture, Mike, El Paso	.000	4	4	0	0	0	0	0	0	0	0	0	0	0	0	3	0	0
Creek, Doug, Arkansas*	.074	25	27	3	2	2	0	0	0	0	1	0	0	4	0	10	0	0
Cromwell, Nate, Wichita*	.300	21	10	2	3	6	0	0	1	1	1	0	0	1	0	2	0	0
Dalesandro, Mark, Midland	.294	57	235	33	69	84	9	0	2	36	0	5	4	8	2	30	1	1
Daspit, Jimmy, San Antonio	.000	15	6	0	0	0	0	0	0	0	2	0	0	0	0	3	0	0
Davenport, Adell, Shreveport	.262	103	370	43	97	163	21	0	15	62	0	4	5	29	6	73	4	2
Davis, Kevin, Midland†	.276	47	156	29	43	71	5	1	7	28	1	2	1	18	1	31	6	3
Davis, Matt, Shreveport†	.270	131	423	44	114	151	25	0	4	42	2	2	1	52	7	64	3	5
Deak, Darrel, Arkansas†	.242	121	414	63	100	181	22	1	19	73	1	5	10	58	6	103	4	8
Delahoya, Javier, San Antonio	.077	21	13	1	1	1	0	0	0	0	1	0	0	1	0	10	0	0
Decillis, Dean, Shreveport	.200	2	5	0	1	1	0	0	0	1	0	0	0	0	0	0	0	0
Diggs, Tony, El Paso†	.143	18	63	5	9	13	1	0	1	3	3	0	1	1	0	14	3	0
Dodson, Bo, El Paso*	.312	101	330	58	103	165	27	4	9	59	0	2	6	42	4	69	1	6
Doffek, Scott, San Antonio*	.259	26	85	5	22	29	7	0	0	8	0	0	1	2	0	6	1	1
Doran, Bill, El Paso†	.364	5	11	3	4	5	1	0	0	0	0	0	0	3	0	2	0	0
Dougherty, James, Jackson	.333	52	3	0	1	2	1	0	0	0	0	0	0	0	0	1	0	0
Duncan, Andres, Shreveport†	.147	35	75	4	11	18	2	1	1	5	1	1	1	5	1	25	2	0
Ellis, Paul, Arkansas*	.333	24	78	5	26	32	3	0	1	11	0	0	3	16	0	2	0	2
Elster, Kevin, San Antonio	.282	10	39	5	11	15	2	1	0	7	0	0	0	4	0	4	0	0
Epley, Daren, Tulsa*	.151	20	53	4	8	11	0	0	1	2	0	0	0	5	0	9	1	0
Eversgerd, Bryan, Arkansas	.000	62	0	0	0	0	0	0	0	0	0	0	0	0	0	0	0	0
Fabregas, Jorge, Midland*	.289	113	409	63	118	168	26	3	6	56	0	3	1	31	6	60	1	1
Faccio, Luis, Arkansas	.167	8	6	1	1	1	0	0	0	0	0	0	0	0	0	4	0	0
Fanning, Steve, Arkansas	.213	97	249	28	53	76	14	0	3	20	1	1	2	26	1	71	5	3
Faulkner, Craig, Arkansas	.237	104	299	34	71	134	18	0	15	55	1	1	3	26	0	78	0	0
Felix, Nick, 27 Wich.-15 E.P.*	.200	42	5	0	1	2	1	0	0	1	0	0	0	0	0	1	0	0
Fernandez, Dan, Shreveport	.188	48	128	12	24	34	5	1	1	13	4	1	0	14	2	32	1	2
Florez, Tim, Shreveport	.255	106	318	33	81	105	17	2	1	26	3	2	2	16	4	43	3	5
Florie, Bryce, Wichita	.095	27	21	0	2	3	1	0	0	1	2	0	0	3	0	11	0	0
Forbes, P.J., Midland	.319	126	498	90	159	231	23	2	15	64	14	2	4	26	1	50	6	6
Gallaher, Kevin, Jackson	.000	4	5	0	0	0	0	0	0	0	0	0	0	1	0	1	0	0
Garrett, Clifton, Midland*	.359	11	39	3	14	16	2	0	0	5	2	1	1	4	0	4	2	0
Gash, Darius, Wichita†	.269	91	271	34	73	105	9	4	5	37	2	3	3	20	1	58	15	6
Gies, Chris, Tulsa	.000	26	1	0	0	0	0	0	0	0	0	0	0	0	0	0	0	0
Gieseke, Mark, Wichita†	.244	15	41	5	10	13	3	0	0	4	0	0	0	4	0	9	0	0
Gil, Benji, Tulsa	.275	101	342	45	94	156	9	1	17	59	0	3	7	35	2	89	20	12
Gill, Steve, 39 Wich.-70 E.P.*	.246	109	329	50	81	122	18	4	5	43	1	0	9	28	2	67	14	12
Gilmore, Tony, Jackson	.172	47	145	14	25	35	4	0	2	7	0	0	4	7	1	29	1	0
Gonzales, Ben, Jackson	.500	41	4	1	2	2	0	0	0	0	0	0	0	0	0	2	0	0
Gonzalez, Paul, Wichita*	.270	59	215	36	58	92	7	3	7	33	0	2	3	25	2	55	5	5
Gorecki, Rick, San Antonio	.182	26	22	1	4	4	0	0	0	2	1	0	0	1	0	9	0	0
Grebeck, Brian, Midland	.294	118	405	65	119	162	20	4	5	54	6	7	8	64	1	81	6	1

Player, Team	Avg.	G	AB	R	H	TB	2B	3B	HR	RBI	SH	SF	HP	BB	Int. BB	SO	SB	CS
Greer, Rusty, Tulsa*	.291	129	474	76	138	220	25	6	15	59	1	3	4	53	4	79	10	5
Griffiths, Brian, Shreveport	.222	24	27	0	6	6	0	0	0	3	0	0	0	2	0	11	0	1
Groppuso, Mike, Jackson	.241	114	370	41	89	137	18	0	10	49	0	1	5	35	4	121	3	3
Hajek, Dave, Jackson	.292	110	332	50	97	136	20	2	5	27	1	3	2	17	2	14	6	5
Hall, Billy, Wichita†	.270	124	486	80	131	184	27	7	4	46	4	4	4	36	1	88	29	19
Hamilton, Joey, Wichita	.125	15	16	0	2	2	0	0	0	1	1	0	1	0	0	10	0	0
Hancock, Brian, El Paso*	.000	11	1	0	0	0	0	0	0	0	0	0	0	0	0	1	0	0
Hancock, Chris, Shreveport*	.087	23	23	1	2	5	0	0	1	2	3	0	0	0	0	16	0	0
Hanselman, Carl, Shreveport*	.182	15	11	1	2	2	0	0	0	0	0	0	0	0	0	5	0	0
Harris, Vince, Wichita†	.274	112	350	55	96	113	13	2	0	36	3	1	4	45	0	45	27	16
Hatcher, Chris, Jackson	.259	101	367	45	95	161	15	3	15	64	0	3	11	11	0	104	5	8
Hecht, Steve, Shreveport*	.298	49	168	25	50	79	8	6	3	11	1	0	1	11	1	25	5	3
Heffernan, Bert, Shreveport*	.235	33	98	8	23	25	2	0	0	7	0	1	3	10	1	14	1	1
Heinkel, Don, Wichita*	.200	33	5	1	1	1	0	0	0	0	0	0	0	0	0	2	0	0
Henderson, Lee, Wichita	.176	31	74	7	13	13	0	0	0	3	0	0	2	7	0	18	1	2
Hill, Chris, Jackson*	.250	58	8	1	2	2	0	0	0	1	1	0	0	1	0	6	0	0
Holbert, Ray, Wichita	.260	112	388	56	101	139	13	5	5	48	3	9	2	54	0	87	30	17
Hollandsworth, Todd, San Antonio*	.251	126	474	57	119	212	24	9	17	63	2	5	5	29	2	101	24	12
Hosey, Dwayne, Wichita†	.291	86	326	52	95	172	19	2	18	61	0	4	2	25	4	44	13	4
Howard, Matt, San Antonio	.287	41	122	12	35	42	5	1	0	5	2	0	3	16	1	14	4	5
Huckaby, Ken, San Antonio	.220	28	82	4	18	19	1	0	0	5	0	1	2	2	1	7	0	0
Hunter, Brian, Jackson	.294	133	523	84	154	216	22	5	10	52	5	2	1	34	4	85	35	18
Hurta, Bob, Jackson*	.000	36	9	1	0	0	0	0	0	0	0	1	0	1	0	6	0	0
Hyde, Rich, Shreveport	.000	6	5	0	0	0	0	0	0	0	0	0	0	0	0	4	0	0
Hyzdu, Adam, Shreveport	.202	86	302	30	61	96	17	0	6	25	1	1	1	20	2	82	0	5
Ingram, Garey, San Antonio	.269	84	305	43	82	124	14	5	6	33	2	2	5	31	0	50	19	6
Jackson, John, Midland*	.325	70	243	43	79	110	18	2	3	34	6	4	10	40	1	43	12	8
Johnson, Steve, Arkansas	.167	11	6	0	1	1	0	0	0	2	0	0	0	0	0	4	0	0
Jones, Dax, Shreveport	.284	118	436	59	124	165	19	5	4	36	3	2	4	26	6	53	13	8
Jones, Kiki, San Antonio	.000	3	1	0	0	0	0	0	0	0	1	0	0	0	0	1	0	0
Jones, Stacy, Shreveport	.000	24	1	0	0	0	0	0	0	0	0	0	0	0	0	1	0	0
Kappesser, Bob, El Paso	.249	67	173	25	43	60	9	1	2	23	3	2	2	20	0	29	7	3
Kasper, Kevin, Shreveport	.215	65	121	13	26	31	5	0	0	11	0	0	0	14	0	23	4	2
Katzaroff, Robbie, Shreveport	.300	104	406	52	122	152	22	4	0	30	5	4	8	35	3	33	15	13
Kellner, Frank, Jackson†	.301	121	355	51	107	150	27	2	4	36	2	6	2	38	5	51	11	12
Kellogg, Geoff, Wichita	.231	22	13	0	3	3	0	0	0	0	1	0	0	2	0	1	0	0
Kelly, John, Arkansas	.000	51	1	0	0	0	0	0	0	0	0	0	0	0	0	1	0	0
Ketchen, Doug, Jackson	.114	27	35	2	4	4	0	0	0	2	0	0	2	0	0	14	0	0
Kipila, Jeff, Midland	.232	59	203	32	47	92	7	1	12	47	0	4	3	32	1	67	0	0
Kirkpatrick, Jay, San Antonio*	.320	27	97	17	31	57	6	1	6	17	0	0	0	14	4	15	0	1
Kliafas, Stephen, San Antonio	.143	6	14	2	2	2	0	0	0	0	0	0	1	2	0	6	0	0
Knox, Kerry, Arkansas*	.067	22	15	2	1	1	0	0	0	0	5	0	0	0	0	3	0	0
Leskanic, Curt, Wichita	.000	7	5	0	0	0	0	0	0	1	0	0	0	0	0	3	0	0
Lewis, Al, El Paso*	.258	113	380	53	98	142	22	5	4	48	1	3	2	57	2	58	4	3
Lewis, Anthony, Arkansas*	.264	112	326	48	86	157	28	2	13	50	1	3	0	25	3	98	3	4
Lifgren, Kelly, Wichita*	.143	37	7	0	1	1	0	0	0	0	0	0	0	0	0	4	0	0
List, Paul, Tulsa	.200	40	125	8	25	30	3	1	0	6	0	3	3	10	0	30	2	6
Lofton, Rodney, El Paso	.265	67	200	39	53	77	8	5	2	21	5	1	5	13	0	40	16	1
Lopez, Pedro, Wichita	.204	50	142	12	29	48	7	0	4	14	1	0	1	22	2	24	3	0
Lott, Billy, San Antonio	.254	114	418	49	106	172	17	2	15	49	1	2	1	23	3	111	5	11
Lowery, Terrell, Tulsa	.240	66	258	29	62	78	5	1	3	14	1	1	1	28	1	50	10	12
Luce, Roger, Tulsa	.193	101	321	35	62	104	14	2	8	29	0	1	4	17	0	107	2	1
Lukachyk, Rob, El Paso*	.265	113	362	58	96	161	24	7	9	63	2	5	7	52	3	75	8	10
Mabry, John, Arkansas*	.290	136	528	68	153	237	32	2	16	72	3	5	4	27	2	68	7	15
Madsen, Lance, Jackson	.221	116	353	58	78	168	19	1	23	65	2	4	4	43	3	136	2	6
Magallanes, Ever, Tulsa*	.326	55	184	20	60	79	12	2	1	14	1	1	1	16	1	22	0	4
Magnusson, Brett, San Antonio	.111	13	9	1	1	2	1	0	0	0	1	0	0	4	0	3	0	0
Makarewicz, Scott, Jackson	.246	92	285	31	70	107	14	1	7	35	1	3	8	17	2	51	1	1
Martinez, Francisco, Arkansas	.000	2	4	0	0	0	0	0	0	0	0	0	0	0	0	2	0	0
Martinez, Pablo, Wichita†	.277	45	130	19	36	49	5	1	2	14	1	1	1	11	1	24	8	5
Masters, Dave, Shreveport	.333	14	3	1	1	2	1	0	0	0	0	0	0	0	0	1	0	0
Matheny, Mike, El Paso†	.254	107	339	39	86	117	21	2	2	28	1	1	2	17	2	73	1	4
Mathews, Terry, Jackson*	.182	17	22	2	4	7	0	0	1	2	1	0	0	1	0	8	0	0
Maurer, Ron, San Antonio	.189	11	37	6	7	11	1	0	1	4	1	0	0	7	0	12	0	1
McCoy, Trey, Tulsa	.293	125	420	72	123	243	27	3	29	95	0	2	19	65	4	79	3	2
McDavid, Ray, Wichita*	.270	126	441	65	119	180	18	5	11	55	0	8	6	70	6	104	33	17
McDowell, Oddibe, Tulsa*	.342	34	114	26	39	72	7	1	8	31	3	1	1	20	2	24	3	3
McFarlin, Jason, Shreveport*	.186	21	59	12	11	15	2	1	0	1	1	0	2	4	0	12	4	1
McFarlin, Terry, San Antonio†	.000	52	3	0	0	0	0	0	0	0	0	0	0	0	0	0	0	0
Melendez, Dan, San Antonio*	.241	47	158	25	38	70	11	0	7	30	0	5	1	11	0	29	0	0
Miller, Barry, Shreveport*	.288	129	452	59	130	203	30	2	13	82	1	8	5	49	7	91	5	4
Miller, Roger, Shreveport	.247	61	194	19	48	64	10	0	2	12	3	0	3	14	1	24	0	2
Mimbs, Mark, San Antonio*	.000	49	3	0	0	0	0	0	0	0	2	0	0	0	0	1	0	0
Montgomery, Ray, Jackson	.281	100	338	50	95	147	16	3	10	59	1	6	6	36	1	54	12	6
Montgomery, Steve, Arkansas	.333	6	6	2	2	3	1	0	0	0	0	0	0	1	0	0	0	0
Morman, Alvin, Jackson*	.208	19	24	2	5	7	2	0	0	3	0	0	0	0	0	9	0	0
Morrow, Timmie, Tulsa	.246	108	390	46	96	152	25	2	9	45	3	2	8	19	1	98	11	14
Mota, Gary, Jackson	.144	27	90	7	13	24	2	0	3	8	2	1	0	2	0	25	1	1
Munoz, Orlando, Midland†	.263	36	118	24	31	41	8	1	0	10	2	0	1	20	0	23	0	4
Murray, Calvin, Shreveport	.188	37	138	15	26	32	6	0	0	3	1	2	1	14	0	29	12	6
Myers, Jim, Shreveport	.000	29	3	0	0	0	0	0	0	0	3	0	0	0	0	1	0	0
Nevers, Tom, Jackson	.272	55	184	21	50	65	8	2	1	10	1	1	2	16	2	36	7	2
Nilsson, Dave, El Paso*	.471	5	17	5	8	12	1	0	1	7	0	0	0	2	0	4	1	1
Ortiz, Hector, San Antonio	.214	49	131	6	28	36	5	0	1	16	3	1	1	9	2	17	0	2
Palmeiro, Orlando, Midland*	.305	131	535	85	163	192	19	5	0	64	18	3	0	42	1	35	18	14
Parra, Jose, San Antonio	.083	17	12	0	1	1	0	0	0	0	1	0	0	0	0	6	0	0
Paskievitch, Tom, Wichita	.000	7	1	0	0	0	0	0	0	0	0	0	0	1	0	0	0	0
Peltzer, Kurt, Shreveport	.333	30	3	1	1	1	0	0	0	0	0	0	0	0	0	1	0	0
Petagine, Roberto, Jackson*	.334	128	437	73	146	231	36	2	15	90	0	5	4	84	14	89	6	5
Pimentel, Wander, Arkansas	.204	27	49	3	10	10	0	0	0	5	1	0	1	0	0	9	0	0
Piotrowicz, Brian, San Antonio	.000	6	4	0	0	0	0	0	0	0	1	0	0	0	0	0	0	0
Pote, Lou, Shreveport	.074	19	27	1	2	2	0	0	0	0	1	0	0	0	0	15	0	0
Prager, Howard, Arkansas*	.316	59	158	31	50	81	8	1	7	21	2	2	2	28	5	34	4	2
Pritchett, Chris, Midland*	.308	127	464	61	143	191	30	6	2	66	6	7	2	61	2	72	3	7

Player, Team	Avg.	G	AB	R	H	TB	2B	3B	HR	RBI	SH	SF	HP	BB	Int. BB	SO	SB	CS
Proctor, Murph, San Antonio†	.252	91	294	38	74	99	10	0	5	42	1	3	1	45	4	45	1	4
Pugh, Scott, Wichita*	.316	26	79	15	25	38	1	0	4	11	0	0	2	4	0	17	0	1
Rambo, Dan, Shreveport	.375	15	8	1	3	3	0	0	0	3	3	0	0	2	0	1	0	0
Raven, Luis, Midland	.257	43	167	21	43	63	12	1	2	30	1	0	1	5	1	45	4	2
Riesgo, Nikco, El Paso	.280	30	93	15	26	55	6	1	7	21	0	1	5	9	1	23	2	0
Rolls, David, Tulsa	.240	72	221	23	53	77	9	0	5	23	2	2	6	22	0	51	1	2
Ronan, Marc, Arkansas*	.214	96	281	33	60	99	16	1	7	34	3	3	2	26	2	47	1	3
Rosselli, Joe, Shreveport	.167	4	6	1	1	1	0	0	0	0	0	0	0	0	0	2	0	0
Rumsey, Dan, Midland*	.059	19	51	3	3	4	1	0	0	1	1	0	1	4	0	15	0	0
Sager, A.J., Wichita	.167	11	12	0	2	2	0	0	0	0	1	0	0	0	0	5	0	1
Sanders, Tracy, Wichita*	.323	77	266	44	86	146	13	4	13	47	0	1	2	34	1	67	6	5
Santos, Gerald, Arkansas	.000	58	2	0	0	0	0	0	0	0	0	0	0	2	0	1	0	0
Savinon, Odalis, Arkansas	.200	15	20	3	4	5	1	0	0	1	0	0	1	1	0	3	0	1
Scott, Kevin, Jackson	.284	50	109	11	31	38	4	0	1	13	0	0	2	3	0	26	2	1
Shackle, Rick, Arkansas	.400	10	5	1	2	2	0	0	0	0	0	0	0	0	0	2	0	0
Shireman, Jeff, Arkansas†	.285	107	333	32	95	121	20	0	2	32	5	4	1	25	3	43	3	7
Simmons, Scott, Arkansas	.045	13	22	0	1	1	0	0	0	0	2	0	0	0	0	5	0	0
Simon, Rich, Shreveport	.000	52	0	0	0	0	0	0	0	0	1	0	0	0	0	0	0	0
Simonson, Bob, Tulsa	.237	34	118	11	28	44	4	0	4	14	0	0	3	6	0	27	3	1
Singleton, Duane, El Paso*	.230	125	456	52	105	144	21	6	2	61	2	5	3	34	0	90	23	19
Small, Mark, Jackson	.000	52	3	2	0	0	0	0	0	0	2	0	0	1	0	3	0	0
Smith, Ed, El Paso	.294	118	419	64	123	182	23	6	8	69	0	2	3	38	4*	97	13	5
Smith, Ira, Wichita	.231	13	39	7	9	11	0	1	0	4	1	0	0	4	0	9	0	2
Smith, Shad, Wichita	.154	24	13	1	2	2	0	0	0	0	3	0	0	0	0	7	0	0
Snedeker, Sean, San Antonio	.154	12	13	0	2	3	1	0	0	1	0	0	0	0	0	2	0	1
Spann, Tookie, Wichita	.274	79	281	30	77	120	17	1	8	42	2	1	3	15	1	64	6	1
Spearman, Vernon, San Antonio*	.259	56	162	22	42	50	4	2	0	13	5	0	1	11	0	21	13	4
Staton, Dave, Wichita	.417	5	12	2	5	8	3	0	0	2	0	0	0	2	0	3	0	0
Strong, Joe, Wichita†	.000	4	1	0	0	0	0	0	0	1	1	0	0	0	0	1	0	0
Sweeney, Mark, Midland*	.356	51	188	41	67	111	13	2	9	32	0	4	6	27	3	22	1	1
Tahan, Kevin, Arkansas	.154	35	65	5	10	16	1	1	1	5	0	0	4	0	0	16	1	0
Tejero, Fausto, Midland	.130	26	69	3	9	15	1	1	1	7	1	1	2	8	0	17	0	0
Thomas, Royal, San Antonio	.000	47	5	0	0	0	0	0	0	1	1	0	0	0	0	4	0	0
Thompson, Fletcher, Jackson*	.294	98	316	64	93	124	15	2	4	29	7	1	1	55	2	83	23	12
Thurston, Jerry, Wichita	.244	78	197	22	48	64	10	0	2	22	3	0	6	14	0	62	2	0
Torres, Salomon, Shreveport	.227	12	22	1	5	5	0	0	0	2	2	0	0	1	0	5	0	0
Turco, Frank, Tulsa	.267	118	423	45	113	154	13	2	8	39	5	2	1	27	0	86	13	8
Van Ryn, Ben, San Antonio*	.182	21	22	1	4	6	2	0	0	5	0	0	0	3	0	13	0	0
Vierra, Joey, San Antonio*	.500	9	2	0	1	1	0	0	0	0	0	0	0	0	0	1	0	0
Ward, Ricky, Shreveport	.256	33	90	8	23	31	8	0	0	5	1	0	1	7	0	8	0	1
Wasinger, Mark, Midland	.214	39	117	17	25	35	4	0	2	17	0	1	1	15	1	26	0	1
Weber, Pete, Shreveport*	.194	105	278	33	54	86	14	0	6	27	1	1	5	26	4	84	7	5
Weger, Wes, El Paso	.291	123	471	69	137	186	24	5	5	53	7	2	4	31	4	44	9	9
Wengert, Bill, Wichita	.150	28	20	3	3	3	0	0	0	1	6	0	0	1	0	9	1	0
Whitaker, Steve, Shreveport*	.000	4	1	0	0	0	0	0	0	0	1	0	0	0	0	0	0	0
White, Chris, Jackson	.000	16	7	0	0	0	0	0	0	0	0	0	0	0	0	5	0	0
Whitehurst, Wally, Wichita	1.000	4	1	0	1	1	0	0	0	0	0	0	0	0	0	0	0	0
Windes, Rodney, Jackson*	.000	42	13	0	0	0	0	0	0	0	0	0	0	1	0	5	0	0
Yockey, Mark, Shreveport*	.000	48	4	0	0	0	0	0	0	0	0	0	1	0	0	2	0	0
Young, Dmitri, Arkansas†	.247	45	166	13	41	65	11	2	3	21	0	2	9	1	29	4	4

The following pitchers, listed alphabetically by club, with games in parentheses, had no plate appearances, primarily through use of designated hitters:

ARKANSAS—Davis, Clint (28); Perez, Mike (4).

EL PASO—Archer, Kurt (54); Boze, Marshall (13); Carter, Glenn (18); Correa, Ramser (5); Dell, Tim (48); Farmer, Howard (4); Felix, Nick (15); Gamez, Francisco (15); Hunter, Jim (14); Johnson, Dane (15); Karl, Scott (27); Kiefer, Mark (11); Kloek, Kevin (23); Pitcher, Scott (14); Richards, Dave (35); Rogers, Tom (48); Taylor, Scott (17).

JACKSON—Kent, Troy (2).

MIDLAND—Anderson, Brian (2); Bennett, Erik (11); Charland, Colin (10); Chavez, Tony (5); Edenfield, Ken (48); Fritz, John (20); Gamez, Bob (44); Gledhill, Chance (28); Heredia, Julian (46); Holdridge, Dave (27); Lewis, Scott (1); Musset, Jose (59); Perez, Beban (3); Purdy, Shawn (5); Ratekin, Mark (7); Stroud, Derek (13); Watson, Ron (36); Williams, Shad (27).

SAN ANTONIO—Henderson, Ryan (23); Kutzler, Jerry (2); Marquez, Isidro (30); Valdez, Ismael (3).

SHREVEPORT—Gardella, Mike (5); Vanderweele, Doug (1).

TULSA—Alberro, Jose (17); Arner, Mike (27); Brumley, Duff (6); Dreyer, Steve (5); Goetz, Barry (38); Helling, Ricky (26); Hurst, Jim (11); Miller, Kurt (18); Moody, Ritchie (47); Oliver, Darren (46); Perez, Dave (33); Reed, Bob (14); Romero, Brian (21); Rowley, Steve (20); Sadecki, Steve (9).

WICHITA—Freitas, Mike (8); Hoeme, Steve (44); Huber, Jeff (15); Pena, Jim (10).

GRAND SLAMS—Faulkner, 2; Coleman, Collier, K. Davis, Luce, McCoy, McDowell, Morrow, Petagine, Proctor, Ronan, E. Smith, Sweeney, 1 each.

AWARDED FIRST BASE ON CATCHER'S INTERFERENCE—B. Miller 4 (Ellis, Luce, Makarewicz, Rolls); Doffek (Lopez); Faulkner (Rolls); P. Martinez (Matheny); Rolls (Tahan).

PITCHING

TEAM

Team	ERA	G	CG	ShO	Sv.	IP	H	R	ER	HR	HB	BB	Int. BB	SO	WP	Bk.
San Antonio	3.45	135	5	9	35	1199.0	1165	570	460	74	48	417	30	957	52	13
Shreveport	3.46	136	6	7	38	1166.0	1137	528	448	68	48	412	18	828	61	4
Arkansas	3.49	136	8	13	32	1154.0	1098	531	448	103	35	369	52	921	69	15
Jackson	3.77	135	4	10	43	1143.0	1118	570	479	95	45	389	26	915	63	11
El Paso	3.88	135	9	11	40	1201.0	1268	635	518	85	64	427	36	753	51	18
Tulsa	4.01	135	5	12	33	1138.1	1088	602	507	103	57	412	26	945	60	17
Wichita	4.12	136	8	7	34	1176.2	1171	640	539	99	53	457	29	901	90	13
Midland	4.78	136	10	3	29	1197.2	1322	729	636	124	77	419	18	851	85	10

*Throws lefthanded.

(Leading qualifiers for earned-run average leadership— 109 or more innings)

Pitcher, Team	W	L	Pct.	ERA	G	GS	CG	GF	ShO	Sv.	IP	H	R	ER	HR	HB	BB	Int. BB	SO	WP
Van Ryn, San Antonio*	14	4	.778	2.21	21	21	1	0	0	0	134.1	118	43	33	5	4	37	1	144	2
Karl, El Paso*	13	8	.619	2.45	27	27	4	0	2	0	180.0	172	67	49	9	6	35	0	95	6
Brumley, 12 Ark.-6 Tul.	7	7	.500	2.93	18	18	2	0	1	0	110.2	87	43	36	13	3	35	6	121	4
Parra, San Antonio	1	8	.111	3.15	17	17	0	0	0	0	111.1	103	46	39	10	6	12	2	87	1
Gorecki, San Antonio	6	9	.400	3.35	26	26	1	0	0	0	156.0	136	76	58	6	5	62	2	118	5
Helling, Tulsa	12	8	.600	3.60	26	26	2	0	2	0	177.1	150	76	71	14	10	46	1	188	3
Fritz, Midland	9	5	.643	3.61	20	20	2	0	1	0	129.2	125	61	52	12	8	42	0	85	12
Delahoya, San Antonio	8	10	.444	3.66	21	21	1	0	0	0	125.1	122	61	51	14	8	42	0	107	2
Thomas, San Antonio	4	6	.400	3.94	47	6	0	16	0	2	109.2	116	58	48	11	3	44	5	52	4
Florie, Wichita	11	8	.579	3.96	27	27	0	0	0	0	154.2	128	80	68	8	10	100	2	133	25

Departmental leaders: G—Eversgerd, 62; W—Van Ryn, 14; L—Ketchen, 12; Pct.—Morman, .800; GS—Five pitchers tied with 27; CG—P. Anderson, Karl, 4; GF—Dougherty, Simon, 50; ShO—P. Anderson, Helling, Karl, 2; Sv.—Dougherty, 36; IP—Karl, 180.0; H—Holdridge, 202; R—Holdridge, 117; ER—Holdridge, 102; HR—Barber, 19; HB—Gledhill, 12; BB—Florie, 100; IBB—Santos, 11; SO—Helling, 188; WP—Florie, 25.

(All pitchers—listed alphabetically)

Pitcher, Team	W	L	Pct.	ERA	G	GS	CG	GF	ShO	Sv.	IP	H	R	ER	HR	HB	BB	Int. BB	SO	WP
Alberro, Tulsa	0	0	.000	0.95	17	0	0	16	0	5	19.0	11	2	2	0	0	8	1	24	2
Anderson, Midland*	0	1	.000	3.38	2	0	0	2	0	0	10.2	16	5	4	2	0	0	0	9	0
Anderson, Arkansas	6	9	.400	3.76	17	17	4	0	2	0	107.2	102	52	45	9	2	24	4	81	5
Anderson, Jackson	2	5	.286	6.05	8	8	0	0	0	0	38.2	47	30	26	5	2	20	1	27	4
Archer, El Paso	9	8	.529	4.90	54	0	0	28	0	11	104.2	129	63	57	10	8	38	8	50	6
Ard, Shreveport	0	0	.000	0.00	3	0	0	2	0	0	5.0	1	0	0	0	0	4	0	0	0
Arner, Tulsa	1	0	1.000	4.53	27	0	0	12	0	0	57.2	58	33	29	8	2	14	0	37	1
Barber, Arkansas	9	8	.529	4.02	24	24	1	0	0	0	143.1	154	70	64	19	4	56	2	126	10
Bellomo, Shreveport*	0	0	.000	0.00	1	0	0	1	0	0	0.2	1	0	0	0	0	0	0	0	0
Beltran, Arkansas*	5	5	.500	3.25	18	16	0	1	0	0	88.2	74	39	32	8	6	38	1	82	11
Bene, San Antonio	5	6	.455	4.84	46	0	0	12	0	1	70.2	50	43	38	3	4	53	1	82	15
Bennett, Midland	5	4	.556	6.49	11	11	0	0	0	0	69.1	87	57	50	12	6	17	1	33	1
Berumen, Wichita	3	1	.750	5.74	7	7	0	0	0	0	26.2	35	17	17	2	1	11	2	17	3
Boze, El Paso	10	3	.769	2.71	13	13	1	0	0	0	86.1	78	36	26	5	4	32	2	48	6
Brosnan, San Antonio*	0	2	.000	4.43	3	3	0	0	0	0	20.1	21	11	10	1	0	7	0	10	1
Brumley, 12 Ark.-6 Tul.	7	7	.500	2.93	18	18	2	0	1	0	110.2	87	43	36	13	3	35	6	121	4
Bruske, Jackson	9	5	.643	2.31	15	15	1	0	0	0	97.1	86	34	25	6	2	22	1	83	2
Bryand, Wichita*	3	5	.375	2.41	52	0	0	15	0	2	71.0	67	29	19	4	0	32	2	63	5
Carlson, Shreveport	7	4	.636	2.24	15	15	2	0	1	0	100.1	86	30	25	9	0	26	3	81	5
Carter, El Paso	3	5	.375	5.12	18	9	0	4	0	0	63.1	65	44	36	10	2	22	1	47	2
Castro, San Antonio	2	1	.667	4.94	5	5	0	0	0	0	27.1	35	16	15	2	1	4	0	15	0
Charland, Midland*	6	2	.750	5.01	10	10	0	0	0	0	59.1	66	37	33	9	0	17	0	54	3
Chavez, Midland	0	0	.000	4.15	5	0	0	3	0	1	8.2	11	5	4	1	0	4	1	9	2
Cimorelli, Arkansas	1	1	.500	2.54	37	0	0	9	0	1	56.2	44	20	16	3	3	23	5	36	2
Clark, Wichita	3	0	1.000	2.43	19	0	0	3	0	0	29.2	27	10	8	2	1	7	0	30	2
Correa, San Antonio	0	2	.000	8.00	2	2	0	0	0	0	9.0	17	8	8	2	0	8	0	8	1
Correa, El Paso	1	0	1.000	5.06	5	1	0	2	0	0	10.2	15	15	6	2	0	7	1	5	2
Costello, Jackson	8	3	.727	2.82	12	12	0	0	0	0	60.2	57	24	19	2	3	13	0	45	1
Couture, El Paso	0	0	.000	13.50	1	0	0	0	0	0	1.1	2	3	2	0	0	5	0	2	1
Creek, Arkansas*	11	10	.524	4.02	25	25	1	0	1	0	147.2	142	75	66	15	3	48	1	128	10
Cromwell, Wichita*	3	5	.375	4.13	21	11	1	2	1	0	89.1	90	49	41	9	4	38	4	86	8
Daspit, San Antonio	3	8	.273	4.43	15	15	0	0	0	0	81.1	92	48	40	5	8	33	0	58	5
Davis, Arkansas	2	0	1.000	1.95	28	0	0	10	0	1	37.0	22	10	8	1	3	10	3	37	0
Davis, Shreveport	0	0	.000	0.00	1	0	0	1	0	0	0.1	0	0	0	0	0	0	0	0	0
Delahoya, San Antonio	8	10	.444	3.66	21	21	1	0	0	0	125.1	122	61	51	14	8	42	0	107	2
Dell, El Paso	4	2	.667	5.13	48	3	0	17	0	1	105.1	151	71	60	5	8	32	4	56	7
Dougherty, Jackson	2	2	.500	1.87	52	0	0	50	0	36	53.0	39	15	11	3	1	21	0	55	0
Dreyer, Tulsa	2	2	.500	3.73	5	5	1	0	1	0	31.1	26	13	13	4	0	8	1	27	0
Edenfield, Midland	5	8	.385	4.61	48	3	1	19	0	4	93.2	93	56	48	10	8	35	5	84	14
Eversgerd, Arkansas*	4	4	.500	2.18	62	0	0	32	0	0	66.0	60	24	16	3	1	19	4	68	7
Faccio, Arkansas	0	3	.000	8.37	8	0	0	1	0	0	23.2	33	23	22	3	2	7	1	20	0
Fanning, Arkansas	1	0	1.000	1.80	3	0	0	3	0	0	5.0	4	1	1	0	1	0	0	4	0
Farmer, El Paso	2	1	.667	3.33	4	1	0	0	0	0	24.1	14	9	9	2	2	10	0	16	0
Felix, 27 Wich.-15 E.P.*	2	1	.667	4.32	42	0	0	13	0	4	66.2	61	36	32	6	9	32	4	69	1
Florie, Wichita	11	8	.579	3.96	27	27	0	0	0	0	154.2	128	80	68	8	10	100	2	133	25
Freitas, Wichita	0	2	.000	10.57	8	0	0	7	0	0	7.2	13	14	9	1	0	2	0	4	2
Fritz, Midland	9	5	.643	3.61	20	20	2	0	1	0	129.2	125	61	52	12	8	42	0	85	12
Gallaher, Jackson	2	2	.500	2.63	4	4	0	0	0	0	24.0	14	7	7	3	2	10	0	30	6
Gamez, Midland*	5	2	.714	3.26	44	0	0	13	0	0	60.2	68	27	22	7	2	18	0	50	5
Gamez, El Paso	2	8	.200	5.40	15	14	1	0	0	0	68.1	92	45	41	3	8	25	1	26	0
Gardella, Shreveport*	0	0	.000	1.04	5	0	0	3	0	1	8.2	4	1	1	0	0	3	0	11	0
Gies, Tulsa	1	5	.167	5.02	26	8	0	9	0	1	66.1	67	42	37	8	4	24	1	28	0
Gieseke, Wichita*	0	0	.000	5.40	1	0	0	0	0	0	1.2	2	1	1	0	0	1	0	1	0
Gill, 1 Wich.-3 E.P.*	0	0	.000	0.00	4	0	0	4	0	0	5.0	1	0	0	0	0	4	0	2	0
Gledhill, Midland	6	11	.353	5.41	28	23	1	1	0	0	141.1	169	102	85	14	12	41	3	66	5
Goetz, Tulsa	2	3	.400	6.55	38	0	0	13	0	0	56.1	70	51	41	12	2	44	2	57	7
Gonzales, Jackson	2	2	.500	5.12	41	0	0	17	0	0	65.0	90	43	37	7	2	15	1	36	5
Gorecki, San Antonio	6	9	.400	3.35	26	26	1	0	0	0	156.0	136	76	58	6	5	62	2	118	5
Griffiths, Shreveport	5	11	.313	4.85	24	23	1	0	0	0	133.2	152	85	72	8	7	68	1	83	18
Hajek, Jackson	0	0	.000	27.00	2	0	0	2	0	0	2.0	4	6	6	0	0	1	0	2	1
Hamilton, Wichita	4	9	.308	3.97	15	15	0	0	0	0	90.2	101	56	40	3	5	36	2	50	2
Hancock, El Paso*	1	0	1.000	7.04	10	6	0	1	0	0	30.2	40	26	24	5	1	30	1	15	3
Hancock, Shreveport*	8	8	.500	4.06	23	23	0	0	0	0	124.0	126	71	56	13	7	52	2	93	8
Hanselman, Shreveport	1	5	.167	2.91	15	6	0	3	0	2	55.2	54	23	18	4	6	13	0	36	2
Heinkel, Wichita	2	5	.286	5.47	33	0	0	21	0	5	49.1	59	33	30	8	3	6	1	41	2
Helling, Tulsa	12	8	.600	3.60	26	26	2	0	2	0	177.1	150	76	71	14	10	46	1	188	3
Henderson, San Antonio	0	0	.000	2.52	23	0	0	20	0	5	25.0	19	10	7	0	0	16	2	22	1
Heredia, Midland	5	3	.625	3.12	46	1	0	19	0	0	89.1	77	42	31	10	8	19	6	99	3
Hill, Jackson*	6	4	.600	3.86	58	3	0	37	0	2	105.0	90	52	45	9	7	53	6	93	8
Hoeme, Wichita	2	3	.400	2.42	44	0	0	37	0	19	48.1	41	17	13	2	1	16	3	47	3
Holdridge, Midland	8	10	.444	6.08	27	27	1	0	1	0	151.0	202	117	102	13	11	55	0	123	13
Huber, Wichita*	3	1	.750	3.26	15	0	0	8	0	3	19.1	16	9	7	2	3	9	0	18	1
Hunter, El Paso	3	1	.750	2.45	14	0	0	2	0	1	22.0	20	8	6	1	0	6	1	10	0

— 414 —

Pitcher, Team	W	L	Pct.	ERA	G	GS	CG	GF	ShO	Sv.	IP	H	R	ER	HR	HB	BB	Int. BB	SO	WP
Hurst, Tulsa*	2	3	.400	3.26	11	7	0	2	0	1	49.2	41	21	18	6	0	12	0	44	0
Hurta, Jackson*	7	9	.438	4.42	36	12	0	10	0	2	93.2	101	55	46	8	3	38	1	72	5
Hyde, Shreveport	1	1	.500	7.78	6	3	0	1	0	0	19.2	33	17	17	1	2	2	1	14	1
Johnson, El Paso	2	2	.500	3.91	15	1	0	10	0	1	25.1	23	12	11	2	0	10	1	26	1
Johnson, Arkansas	2	2	.500	4.33	11	3	0	5	0	0	27.0	30	18	13	3	0	7	0	18	0
Jones, San Antonio	0	1	.000	4.50	3	3	0	0	0	0	14.0	14	9	7	1	1	8	0	7	0
Jones, Shreveport	4	1	.800	3.58	24	2	0	9	0	1	50.1	53	21	20	2	1	19	1	28	0
Kappesser, El Paso	0	0	.000	0.00	2	0	0	2	0	0	3.0	2	0	0	0	0	1	0	1	0
Karl, El Paso*	13	8	.619	2.45	27	27	4	0	2	0	180.0	172	67	49	9	6	35	0	95	6
Kasper, Shreveport	0	0	.000	30.86	1	0	0	0	0	0	2.1	9	8	8	0	0	3	0	0	0
Kellogg, Wichita	7	11	.389	5.37	22	21	2	0	0	0	124.0	137	83	74	16	4	45	1	71	7
Kelly, Arkansas	2	4	.333	3.55	51	0	0	45	0	27	58.1	53	28	23	4	1	12	5	40	1
Kent, Jackson	1	0	1.000	2.45	2	0	0	0	0	0	3.2	2	1	1	1	0	1	0	1	0
Ketchen, Jackson	7	12	.368	4.11	27	27	3	0	1	0	159.2	160	91	73	12	6	50	2	104	10
Kiefer, El Paso	3	4	.429	4.01	11	11	0	0	0	0	51.2	48	29	23	5	2	19	0	44	6
Kloek, El Paso	9	6	.600	4.11	23	23	1	0	1	0	135.2	148	75	62	11	7	53	4	97	5
Knox, Arkansas*	4	4	.500	2.78	22	11	0	2	0	0	81.0	78	30	25	9	3	14	3	61	1
Kutzler, San Antonio	1	0	1.000	1.59	2	0	0	0	0	0	5.2	3	1	1	0	0	0	0	3	1
Leskanic, Wichita	3	2	.600	3.45	7	7	0	0	0	0	44.1	37	20	17	3	3	17	0	42	4
Lewis, El Paso	0	0	.000	1.59	2	0	0	1	0	0	5.2	3	1	1	0	0	0	0	2	0
Lewis, Midland	1	0	1.000	1.50	1	1	0	0	0	0	6.0	6	1	1	0	0	0	0	2	0
Lifgren, Wichita	5	3	.625	5.35	37	4	0	13	0	2	74.0	88	47	44	9	1	28	3	45	3
Marquez, San Antonio	1	4	.200	2.84	30	0	0	29	0	12	31.2	34	13	10	1	1	8	3	25	1
Martinez, Arkansas	0	1	.000	6.43	2	2	0	0	0	0	7.0	9	5	5	0	1	1	0	3	0
Masters, Shreveport	0	2	.000	1.07	14	0	0	5	0	2	25.1	21	8	3	0	2	15	0	25	4
Mathews, Jackson	6	5	.545	3.67	17	17	0	0	0	0	103.0	116	55	42	11	3	29	2	74	1
McFarlin, San Antonio	4	7	.364	2.83	52	0	0	24	0	4	95.1	87	37	30	2	3	37	4	77	7
Miller, Tulsa	6	8	.429	5.06	18	18	0	0	0	0	96.0	102	69	54	8	5	45	2	68	8
Mimbs, San Antonio*	3	3	.500	1.60	49	0	0	23	0	10	67.2	49	21	12	0	2	18	7	77	2
Montgomery, Arkansas	3	3	.500	3.94	6	6	0	0	0	0	32.0	34	17	14	2	0	12	2	19	2
Moody, Tulsa*	3	2	.600	2.15	47	0	0	39	0	16	67.0	58	27	16	1	2	34	2	61	10
Morman, Jackson*	8	2	.800	2.96	19	19	0	0	0	0	97.1	77	35	32	7	5	28	0	101	5
Musset, Midland	2	6	.250	5.49	59	0	0	49	0	21	62.1	59	38	38	9	5	32	2	59	4
Myers, Shreveport	2	2	.500	2.01	29	0	0	14	0	1	49.1	50	14	11	1	2	19	3	23	4
Oliver, Tulsa*	7	5	.583	1.96	46	0	0	25	0	6	73.1	51	18	16	1	9	41	5	77	9
Parra, San Antonio	1	8	.111	3.15	17	17	0	0	0	0	111.1	103	46	39	10	6	12	2	87	1
Paskievitch, Wichita	1	2	.333	7.00	7	0	0	5	0	0	9.0	11	8	7	1	1	8	2	5	0
Peltzer, Shreveport*	4	3	.571	3.19	30	0	0	15	0	1	42.1	33	16	15	2	3	9	0	28	0
Pena, Wichita*	2	0	1.000	1.69	10	1	0	4	0	0	16.0	10	5	3	0	0	2	0	12	2
Perez, Midland*	0	1	.000	19.64	3	0	0	0	0	0	3.2	8	8	8	0	1	2	0	1	1
Perez, Tulsa	9	10	.474	4.02	33	14	1	6	0	2	125.1	119	64	56	11	7	34	7	111	3
Perez, Arkansas	0	0	.000	7.36	4	0	0	0	0	0	3.2	7	3	3	0	1	0	0	4	0
Piotrowicz, San Antonio	0	0	.000	4.66	6	2	0	2	0	0	19.1	31	18	10	4	0	7	0	12	1
Pitcher, El Paso	2	0	1.000	8.24	13	0	0	7	0	1	19.2	32	24	18	3	0	10	0	12	1
Pote, Shreveport	8	7	.533	4.07	19	19	0	0	0	0	108.1	111	53	49	10	0	45	1	81	3
Purdy, Midland	2	2	.500	5.06	5	5	1	0	0	0	32.0	38	19	18	2	1	9	0	18	2
Rambo, Shreveport	7	5	.583	3.18	15	15	1	0	0	0	102.0	98	46	36	1	4	27	1	61	2
Ratekin, Midland	3	1	.750	4.67	7	6	2	0	0	0	44.1	50	25	23	5	4	11	0	24	2
Reed, Tulsa	5	7	.417	4.32	14	14	0	0	0	0	75.0	88	45	36	5	5	22	0	34	3
Richards, El Paso*	2	2	.500	3.80	35	0	0	10	0	0	64.0	66	31	27	4	1	26	4	54	4
Rogers, El Paso*	4	3	.571	1.74	48	2	0	35	0	23	72.1	50	17	14	2	2	23	6	55	1
Romero, Tulsa*	5	6	.455	3.91	21	18	1	1	0	0	94.1	98	47	41	4	4	34	2	72	1
Rosselli, Shreveport*	0	1	.000	3.13	4	4	0	0	0	0	23.0	22	9	8	1	0	7	0	19	1
Rowley, Tulsa	8	7	.533	6.04	20	19	0	0	0	0	92.1	103	71	62	13	5	33	1	63	11
Sadecki, Tulsa	0	1	.000	3.94	9	0	0	7	0	0	16.0	16	10	7	2	0	4	0	12	0
Sager, Wichita	5	3	.625	3.19	11	11	2	0	1	0	73.1	69	30	26	5	1	16	0	49	1
Santos, Arkansas	3	6	.333	2.63	57	0	0	19	0	4	82.0	80	36	24	8	3	41	11	65	12
Shackle, Arkansas	4	1	.800	4.57	10	6	0	1	0	0	41.1	48	24	21	5	1	12	2	19	2
Simmons, Arkansas*	6	3	.667	2.70	13	10	0	0	0	0	76.2	68	26	23	1	0	18	3	35	4
Simon, Shreveport	2	7	.222	4.33	52	0	0	50	0	26	54.0	56	32	26	7	4	24	4	38	5
Small, Jackson	7	2	.778	3.19	51	0	0	18	0	6	95.2	84	71	34	30	8	41	6	64	8
Smith, Shreveport	6	3	.667	3.76	24	13	0	3	0	0	95.2	95	43	40	6	4	37	1	65	3
Snedeker, San Antonio	4	5	.444	4.35	12	12	2	0	1	0	70.1	92	42	34	6	1	17	2	36	0
Strong, Wichita	1	0	1.000	6.75	4	3	0	1	0	0	14.2	13	13	11	2	0	11	0	13	0
Stroud, Midland*	1	1	.500	4.61	13	0	0	4	0	0	13.2	16	7	7	0	2	9	3	13	0
Taylor, El Paso	6	6	.500	3.80	17	16	1	1	0	0	104.1	105	53	44	4	11	31	2	76	0
Thomas, San Antonio	4	6	.400	3.94	47	6	0	16	0	2	109.2	116	58	48	11	3	44	5	52	4
Torres, Shreveport	7	4	.636	2.70	12	12	0	0	2	0	83.1	67	27	25	6	3	12	0	67	3
Valdez, San Antonio	1	0	1.000	1.38	3	2	0	0	0	0	13.0	12	2	2	0	0	4	0	11	0
Vanderweele, Shreveport	0	0	.000	0.00	1	0	0	0	0	0	2.0	0	0	0	0	0	0	0	3	0
Van Ryn, San Antonio*	14	4	.778	2.21	21	21	0	0	0	0	134.1	118	43	33	5	4	37	1	144	1
Vierra, San Antonio*	1	0	1.000	5.40	9	0	0	4	0	1	11.2	14	7	7	1	4	1	6	1	1
Watson, Midland	2	1	.667	3.88	36	0	0	18	0	1	46.1	39	22	20	2	6	43	2	41	8
Wengert, Wichita	7	7	.500	4.10	28	25	3	1	1	0	162.1	167	86	74	16	8	43	3	106	15
Whitaker, Shreveport*	1	0	1.000	1.08	4	1	0	2	0	0	8.1	5	1	1	0	0	7	0	12	0
White, Jackson	3	5	.375	7.35	16	11	0	1	0	0	60.0	80	54	49	3	3	25	2	44	5
Whitehurst, Wichita	1	0	1.000	1.27	4	4	0	0	0	0	21.1	11	4	3	1	0	5	0	14	4
Williams, Midland	7	10	.412	4.71	27	27	2	0	0	0	175.2	192	100	92	16	3	65	1	91	9
Windes, Jackson*	5	4	.556	2.93	41	7	0	6	0	2	95.1	84	34	31	7	3	22	4	84	5
Yockey, Shreveport*	3	6	.333	2.13	48	0	0	19	0	6	71.2	60	23	17	2	3	20	0	60	2

BALKS—Karl, Romero, 7 each; Beltran, Van Ryn, 4 each; Castro, Cromwell, Helling, Kiefer, 3 each; P. Anderson, Barber, Bene, Edenfield, Farmer, Florie, Goetz, Heredia, Hurta, D. Johnson, Knox, Moody, Richards, Santos, Small, Wengert, White, Windes, 2 each; Alberro, T. Anderson, Brumley, Carter, Charland, Costello, Creek, Delahoya, Dell, Eversgerd, Gledhill, Gorecki, Griffiths, Hamilton, Heinkel, Henderson, Holdridge, Huber, Kutzler, Morman, Paskievitch, B. Perez, D. Perez, Pote, Rambo, Rowley, Strong, Stroud, Whitehurst, Williams, Yockey, 1 each.

COMBINATION SHUTOUTS—Barber-Kelly, Beltran-Davis-Kelly, Beltran-Perez-Eversgerd, Brumley-Eversgerd, Knox-Kelly, Montgomery-Santos, Simmons-Davis-Eversgerd, Simmons-Davis-Kelly, Simmons-Kelly, Arkansas; Archer-Hunter-Felix, Farmer-Hunter-Correa, Gamez-Rogers, Karl-Rogers, Karl-Rogers-Hunter, Kiefer-Archer, Kloek-Archer, Kloek-Rogers-Archer, El Paso; Bruske-Dougherty, Bruske-Small-Hurst, Costello-Gonzales-Dougherty, Costello-Hill-Hurta-Dougherty, Costello-Small-Dougherty, Gallaher-Windes-Small, Morman-Hurta, Morman-Small-Hill-Dougherty, Windes-Hill-Dougherty, Jackson; Fritz-Musset, Midland; Castro-Mimbs, Daspit-McFarlin-Henderson-Mimbs, Delahoya-McFarlin, Delahoya-Mimbs-Henderson, Gorecki-Mimbs, Parra-Bene, Parra-Mimbs, Van Ryn-Marquez, San Antonio; Pote-Ard, Pote-Smith-Peltzer, Pote-Yockey, Rambo-Jones, Whitaker-Gardella, Shreveport; Romero-Perez 2, Brumley-Romero-Moody, Helling-Goetz-Romero, Helling-Oliver, Hurst-Alberro, Perez-Goetz, Reed-Moody, Rowley-Arner, Tulsa; Florie-Bryand-Hoeme, Leskanic-Heinkel, Lifgren-Bryand, Whitehurst-Felix, Wichita.

NO-HIT GAMES—None.

FIELDING

TEAM

Team	Pct.	G	PO	A	E	DP	PB	Team	Pct.	G	PO	A	E	DP	PB
Shreveport	.972	136	3498	1404	143	164	13	Wichita	.966	136	3530	1490	174	110	26
Arkansas	.971	136	3462	1363	143	89	13	San Antonio	.966	135	3597	1487	181	97	8
Midland	.968	136	3593	1421	167	126	25	Tulsa	.965	135	3415	1310	172	103	7
El Paso	.967	135	3603	1601	177	160	15	Jackson	.962	135	3429	1486	192	135	8

INDIVIDUAL

FIRST BASEMEN

*Throws lefthanded.

Player, Team	Pct.	G	PO	A	E	DP
Abbe, San Antonio	1.000	1	1	0	0	0
Abercrombie, Wichita	.976	44	336	23	9	33
Bish, Wichita	1.000	2	7	2	0	1
Blanco, San Antonio	.984	7	58	5	1	2
Brakebill, Midland	.960	3	21	3	1	1
Castellanos, Tulsa	.962	4	24	1	1	1
Dalesandro, Midland	1.000	2	15	2	0	2
Davenport, Shreveport	.976	14	81	2	2	9
Dodson, El Paso*	.990	88	756	54	8	73
Epley, Tulsa*	1.000	1	11	1	0	1
Fanning, Arkansas	.960	8	21	3	1	0
Faulkner, Arkansas	.973	41	325	35	10	21
Forbes, Midland	1.000	1	9	0	0	1
Gieseke, Wichita*	1.000	13	80	9	0	8
Gill, El Paso*	1.000	8	27	0	0	3
Greer, Tulsa*	.993	129	1055	93	8	86
Heffernan, Shreveport	1.000	2	15	2	0	2
Kasper, Shreveport	1.000	1	1	0	0	0
Kipila, Midland	1.000	5	46	1	0	7
Kirkpatrick, San Antonio	.992	26	225	22	2	20
Lewis, El Paso	1.000	4	5	0	0	0
Madsen, Jackson	1.000	7	56	8	0	4
Makarewicz, Jackson	1.000	2	0	3	0	0
Melendez, San Antonio*	.997	42	328	45	1	26
MILLER, Shreveport*	.996	126	1040	92	5	121
Petagine, Jackson*	.988	127	1033	110	14	114
Prager, Arkansas*	.980	56	399	32	9	32
Pritchett, Midland	.984	126	1075	88	19	96
Proctor, San Antonio*	.993	66	518	64	4	30
Pugh, Wichita*	.995	26	172	12	1	10
Raven, Midland	1.000	2	18	2	1	3
Riesgo, El Paso	1.000	3	17	1	0	5
Rolls, Tulsa	1.000	3	19	1	0	3
Scott, Jackson	.940	8	44	3	3	3
Smith, El Paso	.979	55	479	42	11	54
Spann, Wichita	.990	75	622	61	7	39
Tahan, Arkansas	.957	3	20	2	1	0
Weber, Shreveport*	1.000	2	4	0	0	1
Young, Arkansas	.982	44	348	27	7	18

SECOND BASEMEN

Player, Team	Pct.	G	PO	A	E	DP
Alvarez, San Antonio	.954	34	53	72	6	9
Aversa, Arkansas	1.000	15	13	14	0	3
Bethea, Wichita	.952	4	5	15	1	2
Bish, Wichita	1.000	10	20	31	0	6
Castellanos, Tulsa	1.000	2	0	4	0	0
Castleberry, El Paso	.981	64	129	181	6	54
J. Castro, San Antonio	.923	5	9	15	2	3
Chimelis, Shreveport	1.000	20	36	56	0	15
Cirillo, El Paso	.973	40	66	113	5	28
Cole, El Paso	.893	3	15	10	3	4
Colon, Tulsa	.952	6	9	11	1	2
Davis, Midland	1.000	2	2	9	0	4
Deak, Arkansas	.967	119	219	273	17	52
Doffek, San Antonio	.935	20	37	49	6	9
Doran, El Paso	1.000	5	4	12	0	3
Fanning, Arkansas	.957	15	18	27	2	3
Florez, Shreveport	.965	94	167	269	16	70
FORBES, Midland	.970	122	251	372	19	74
Grebeck, Midland	.967	6	13	16	1	5
Hajek, Jackson	.978	66	112	158	6	35
Hall, Wichita	.964	117	209	373	22	72
Harris, Wichita	1.000	2	4	5	0	0
Hecht, Shreveport	.955	29	41	65	5	20
Howard, San Antonio	.985	32	51	77	2	13
Ingram, San Antonio	.912	66	98	183	27	21
Kasper, Shreveport	1.000	4	6	8	0	5
Kellner, Jackson	.962	9	12	13	1	4
Lofton, El Paso	.956	38	73	124	9	25
Magallanes, Tulsa	.969	55	97	150	8	28
Martinez, Wichita	.952	6	7	13	1	1
Munoz, Midland	1.000	3	9	6	0	0
Pimentel, Arkansas	1.000	7	7	9	0	2
Pritchett, Midland	1.000	1	1	4	0	0
Shireman, Arkansas	1.000	1	0	3	0	0
Thompson, Jackson	.932	86	160	211	27	46
Turco, Tulsa	.930	75	115	150	20	29
Ward, Shreveport	.947	8	10	8	1	1
Wasinger, Midland	1.000	3	0	8	0	2

THIRD BASEMEN

Player, Team	Pct.	G	PO	A	E	DP
Alvarez, San Antonio	.864	26	14	24	6	2
Aversa, Arkansas	.953	57	17	105	6	2
Bethea, Wichita	.600	6	1	5	4	1
Bish, Wichita	1.000	3	0	4	0	0
BLANCO, San Antonio	.944	111	92	163	15	18
Brakebill, Midland	.886	58	26	91	15	2
Bruno, Wichita	.917	69	51	115	15	13
Castellanos, Tulsa	.933	31	17	53	5	2
Castleberry, El Paso	.900	9	3	6	1	1
Chimelis, Shreveport	.881	65	41	115	21	5
Cirillo, El Paso	.920	21	17	29	4	1
Claus, Midland	.850	9	4	13	3	0
Clinton, Tulsa	1.000	3	2	4	0	0
Cole, El Paso	.667	1	0	2	1	0
Colon, Tulsa	.916	96	51	145	18	14
Dalesandro, Midland	.867	31	28	44	11	5
Davenport, Shreveport	.900	83	58	122	20	25
Davis, Midland	1.000	5	2	7	0	1
Davis, Midland	1.000	20	9	41	0	4
Doffek, San Antonio	.900	4	3	6	1	0
Fanning, Arkansas	.920	37	17	52	6	7
Gonzalez, Wichita	.931	59	31	104	10	8
Grebeck, Midland	.966	10	9	19	1	3
Groppuso, Jackson	.873	111	62	165	33	21
Hajek, Jackson	.965	22	14	41	2	2
Hecht, Shreveport	.857	8	4	8	2	1
Howard, San Antonio	1.000	1	1	1	0	0
Kasper, Shreveport	.914	28	17	36	5	3
Kellner, Jackson	.917	10	6	16	2	2
Lewis, El Paso	.907	83	52	163	22	16
Lofton, El Paso	1.000	2	1	1	0	0
Lott, San Antonio	1.000	2	1	1	0	0
Madsen, Jackson	.885	10	3	20	3	0
Martinez, Wichita	1.000	4	3	4	0	0
Maurer, San Antonio	.808	8	6	15	5	1
Munoz, Midland	.961	25	21	52	3	5
Ortiz, San Antonio	1.000	1	0	1	0	0
Pimentel, Arkansas	1.000	1	0	1	0	0
Rolls, Tulsa	.917	10	12	21	3	2
Smith, El Paso	.926	13	5	20	2	4
Turco, Tulsa	.909	34	2	8	1	0
Ward, Shreveport	.964	14	9	18	1	1
Wasinger, Midland	.933	9	6	22	2	0
Young, Arkansas	1.000	1	0	2	0	0

SHORTSTOPS

Player, Team	Pct.	G	PO	A	E	DP
Alvarez, San Antonio	.920	18	17	29	4	4
Aversa, Arkansas	1.000	11	4	11	0	1
Bethea, Wichita	.875	4	3	11	2	2
Bish, Wichita	.947	5	4	14	1	2
Blanco, San Antonio	1.000	2	0	1	0	0
Castleberry, El Paso	.957	20	31	57	4	18
J. Castro, San Antonio	.946	110	160	299	26	51
Chimelis, Shreveport	.875	7	3	11	2	1
Cholowsky, Arkansas	1.000	1	0	2	0	0
Claus, Midland	1.000	2	1	4	0	0
Clinton, Tulsa	1.000	3	4	3	0	0
Colon, Tulsa	.859	23	29	50	13	8
Davis, Midland	.934	31	49	65	8	15
Davis, Shreveport	.960	113	192	291	20	78
Decillis, Shreveport	.500	1	0	1	1	0
Duncan, Shreveport	.940	30	37	73	7	14
Elster, San Antonio	.918	10	14	31	4	3
Fanning, Arkansas	.974	37	42	70	3	15
Florez, Shreveport	.857	3	2	4	1	1
Gil, Tulsa	.959	101	159	285	19	56
Grebeck, Midland	.948	97	163	254	23	59
Hajek, Jackson	.969	5	10	21	1	5

Player, Team	Pct.	G	PO	A	E	DP
Holbert, Wichita	.934	102	155	267	30	49
Howard, San Antonio	1.000	1	2	2	0	0
Kasper, Shreveport	.833	9	6	9	3	2
Kellner, Jackson	.967	94	121	256	13	56
Kliafas, San Antonio	1.000	6	6	7	0	2
Martinez, Wichita	.964	28	42	91	5	10
Maurer, San Antonio	1.000	3	6	11	0	3
Munoz, Midland	.929	8	10	16	2	5
Nevers, Jackson	.900	52	69	128	22	29
Pimentel, Jackson	.918	15	11	34	4	3
SHIREMAN, Arkansas	.971	99	142	229	11	37
Turco, Tulsa	.918	15	19	26	4	7
Weger, El Paso	.936	122	205	349	38	77

OUTFIELDERS

Player, Team	Pct.	G	PO	A	E	DP
Abercrombie, Wichita	1.000	1	1	0	0	0
Alvarez, San Antonio	.929	8	12	1	1	0
Basse, El Paso*	.964	95	155	5	6	0
Battle, Arkansas	.980	105	241	5	5	2
Bellomo, Shreveport*	1.000	7	5	0	0	0
Boykin, Midland	.970	18	32	0	1	0
M. Carter, El Paso	1.000	13	25	0	0	0
Castellanos, Tulsa	1.000	12	19	3	0	1
Castillo, Tulsa	.924	83	130	3	11	0
Cedeno, San Antonio	.961	113	213	6	9	2
Cohick, Midland*	.981	92	198	7	4	1
Coleman, Arkansas	.958	117	197	10	9	0
Collier, San Antonio*	1.000	39	58	2	0	0
Couture, El Paso	1.000	3	2	0	0	0
Dalesandro, Midland	1.000	1	2	0	0	0
Diggs, El Paso	.930	17	35	5	3	1
Epley, Tulsa*	1.000	11	19	1	0	0
Fanning, Arkansas	1.000	4	4	0	0	0
Garrett, Midland*	.957	11	22	0	1	0
Gash, Wichita	.964	72	125	7	5	3
Gieseke, Wichita*	1.000	2	1	0	0	0
Gill, 32 Wich.-63 E.P.*	.9892	95	169	15	2	5
Hajek, Jackson	1.000	7	7	1	0	0
Harris, Wichita	.982	87	156	11	3	2
Hatcher, Jackson	.941	60	78	2	5	0
Hecht, Shreveport	1.000	9	12	1	0	0
Hollandsworth, San Antonio*	.956	120	246	13	12	2
Hosey, Wichita	.924	56	85	0	7	0
Hunter, Jackson	.953	131	276	9	14	3
Hyzdu, Shreveport	.973	80	136	8	4	4
Ingram, San Antonio	1.000	1	3	1	0	0
Jackson, Midland*	.976	63	122	1	3	0
D. Jones, Shreveport	.973	105	236	13	7	1
Kappesser, El Paso	1.000	9	0	1	0	0
Kasper, Shreveport	1.000	3	2	0	0	0
Katzaroff, Shreveport	.981	103	236	18	5	3
Kellner, Jackson	.833	4	4	1	1	0
Kipila, Midland	1.000	17	28	1	0	0
Lewis, Arkansas*	.978	68	85	6	2	0
List, Tulsa	.928	38	64	0	5	0
Lott, San Antonio	.978	109	166	13	4	4
Lowery, Wichita	.988	66	152	6	2	0
Lukachyk, El Paso	.978	100	172	10	4	0
MABRY, Arkansas	.9893	136	262	15	3	6
Madsen, Jackson	.971	90	126	9	4	1
McCoy, Tulsa	1.000	10	16	1	0	0
McDavid, Wichita	.964	122	259	8	10	4
McDowell, Tulsa*	1.000	32	64	3	0	2
McFarlin, Shreveport*	1.000	19	33	1	0	0
Montgomery, Jackson	.964	99	151	9	6	1
Morrow, Tulsa	.954	108	203	5	10	1
Mota, Jackson	1.000	23	27	2	0	0
Murray, Shreveport	.976	37	79	2	2	2
Palmeiro, Midland	.973	130	307	12	9	3
Raven, Midland	.976	23	38	3	1	0
Riesgo, El Paso	1.000	2	3	0	0	0
Rumsey, Midland	1.000	14	20	0	0	0
Sanders, Wichita	.926	60	82	5	7	0
Savinon, Arkansas	1.000	9	9	1	0	0
Scott, Jackson	1.000	13	13	1	0	1
Simonson, Tulsa	.909	32	40	0	4	0
Singleton, El Paso	.975	123	288	20	8	5
Smith, El Paso	.957	23	21	1	1	0
Smith, Wichita	.882	9	15	0	2	0
Spearman, San Antonio*	.989	39	85	6	1	1
Sweeney, Midland*	.989	49	85	3	1	1
Tahan, Arkansas	1.000	2	4	0	0	0
Turco, Tulsa	.933	27	41	1	3	0
Weber, Shreveport*	.991	77	103	5	1	1

CATCHERS

Player, Team	Pct.	G	PO	A	E	DP	PB
Abbe, San Antonio	.987	74	524	65	8	10	7
Abercrombie, Wichita	1.000	8	17	5	0	0	0
Calcagno, Shreveport	1.000	2	7	2	0	0	1
Campillo, El Paso	1.000	4	20	3	0	0	0
Cavanagh, Shreveport	1.000	4	5	1	0	1	1
Christopherson, Shreveport	.981	15	98	8	2	2	2

Player, Team	Pct.	G	PO	A	E	DP	PB
Dalesandro, Midland	.991	17	92	14	1	2	4
Ellis, Arkansas	.994	23	151	21	1	2	1
Fabregas, Midland	.985	106	620	99	11	7	17
Faulkner, Arkansas	.979	28	167	18	4	0	2
Fernandez, Shreveport	.989	47	244	34	3	9	4
Gilmore, Jackson	.984	46	278	34	5	4	4
Heffernan, Shreveport	.984	25	169	10	3	4	0
Henderson, Wichita	.980	31	179	18	4	0	2
Huckaby, San Antonio	.978	26	149	29	4	4	0
Kappesser, El Paso	.968	43	238	33	9	6	6
Lopez, Wichita	.986	50	312	46	5	2	11
Luce, Tulsa	.989	97	642	69	8	8	4
Lukachyk, El Paso	1.000	1	2	0	0	0	1
Magnusson, San Antonio	1.000	3	6	1	0	0	0
Makarewicz, Jackson	.989	85	577	58	7	7	4
Matheny, El Paso	.986	102	524	100	9	18	8
R. Miller, Shreveport	.987	58	330	46	5	5	5
Nilsson, El Paso	1.000	5	31	9	0	1	0
Ortiz, San Antonio	.978	48	311	42	8	3	1
Rolls, Tulsa	.969	47	324	23•	11	1	3
RONAN, Arkansas	.994	93	564	65	4	6	9
Scott, Jackson	.980	18	93	7	2	1	0
Tahan, Arkansas	.984	19	58	3	1	0	1
Tejero, Midland	.973	26	147	31	5	3	3
Thurston, Wichita	.980	78	397	46	9	4	13

PITCHERS

Player, Team	Pct.	G	PO	A	E	DP
Alberro, Tulsa	1.000	17	2	3	0	0
Anderson, Midland*	1.000	2	1	2	0	0
Anderson, Arkansas	.964	17	8	19	1	2
Anderson, Jackson	1.000	8	3	8	0	2
Archer, El Paso	.833	54	5	5	2	2
Ard, Shreveport	1.000	3	0	1	0	0
Arner, Tulsa	.923	27	4	8	1	1
Barber, Arkansas	.917	24	11	11	2	0
Beltran, Arkansas*	1.000	18	6	21	0	0
Bene, San Antonio	1.000	46	5	5	0	1
Bennett, Midland	1.000	11	11	6	0	0
Berumen, Wichita	1.000	7	1	8	0	0
Boze, El Paso	.913	13	8	13	2	3
Brosnan, San Antonio*	1.000	3	0	4	0	0
Brumley, 12 Arkansas.-6 Tulsa	.833	18	7	8	3	0
BRUSKE, Jackson	1.000	15	13	18	0	1
Bryand, Wichita*	1.000	52	3	12	0	0
Carlson, Shreveport	.850	15	11	6	3	0
G. Carter, Tulsa	1.000	18	7	10	0	2
N. Castro, San Antonio	.857	5	3	3	1	0
Charland, Midland*	.846	10	4	7	2	2
Chavez, Midland	.500	5	0	1	1	0
Cimorelli, Arkansas	.955	37	6	15	1	2
Clark, Wichita	.800	19	0	4	1	0
Correa, San Antonio	1.000	2	0	1	0	0
Correa, San Antonio	1.000	5	0	3	0	1
Costello, Jackson	1.000	12	4	10	0	1
Creek, Arkansas*	.848	25	6	22	5	2
Cromwell, Wichita*	1.000	21	3	11	0	0
Daspit, San Antonio	.955	15	10	11	1	1
Davis, Arkansas	1.000	28	4	3	0	0
Delahoya, San Antonio	.950	21	16	22	2	0
Dell, El Paso	1.000	48	6	19	0	1
Dougherty, Jackson	.944	52	4	13	1	5
Dreyer, Tulsa	1.000	5	3	6	0	0
Edenfield, Midland	.952	48	2	18	1	1
Eversgerd, Arkansas*	.889	62	6	10	2	2
Faccio, Arkansas	1.000	8	2	2	0	0
Farmer, El Paso	.833	4	1	4	1	1
Felix, 27 Wich.-15 E.P.*	.895	42	1	16	2	0
Florie, Wichita	.930	27	16	24	3	3
Freitas, Wichita	1.000	8	3	1	0	0
Fritz, Midland	1.000	20	7	17	0	0
Gallaher, Jackson	1.000	4	2	2	0	0
Gamez, El Paso	.857	15	5	7	2	1
Gamez, Midland*	.933	44	6	8	1	0
Gies, Tulsa	1.000	26	6	14	0	1
Gill, 1 Wich.-3 E.P.*	1.000	4	0	1	0	0
Gledhill, Midland	.971	28	15	18	1	0
Goetz, Tulsa	1.000	38	3	5	0	2
Gonzales, Jackson	.958	41	9	14	1	2
Gorecki, San Antonio	.892	26	18	15	4	2
Griffiths, Shreveport	.889	24	6	10	2	2
Hajek, Jackson	1.000	2	1	0	0	0
Hamilton, Wichita	1.000	15	11	9	0	1
Hancock, Shreveport*	.852	23	2	21	4	5
Hancock, El Paso*	.857	10	2	4	1	0
Hanselman, Shreveport	1.000	15	8	6	0	0
Heinkel, Wichita	1.000	33	8	13	0	0
Helling, Tulsa	.925	26	10	27	3	1
Henderson, San Antonio	1.000	23	2	7	0	0
Heredia, Midland	.905	46	5	14	2	1
Hill, Jackson*	.810	58	5	12	4	2
Hoeme, Wichita	1.000	44	5	1	0	0
Holdridge, Midland	.795	27	15	16	8	6
Huber, Wichita*	.857	15	1	5	1	0

— 417 —

Player, Team	Pct.	G	PO	A	E	DP
Hunter, El Paso	.714	14	2	3	2	0
Hurst, Tulsa*	.933	11	3	11	1	1
Hurta, Jackson*	.844	36	9	18	5	1
Hyde, Shreveport	1.000	6	1	6	0	1
Johnson, El Paso	1.000	15	1	5	0	0
Johnson, Arkansas	1.000	11	1	2	0	0
S. Jones, Shreveport	.833	24	1	4	1	0
Jones, San Antonio	1.000	3	0	2	0	0
Karl, El Paso*	.968	27	13	47	2	2
Kellogg, Wichita	1.000	22	13	17	0	1
Kelly, Arkansas	.909	51	5	5	1	0
Ketchen, Jackson	.972	27	11	24	1	2
Kiefer, El Paso	1.000	11	3	7	0	1
Kloek, El Paso	1.000	23	6	12	0	0
Knox, Arkansas*	1.000	22	2	14	0	0
Kutzler, San Antonio	1.000	2	1	0	0	0
Leskanic, Wichita	.846	7	7	4	2	0
Lewis, Midland	.500	1	1	0	1	0
Lifgren, Wichita	.933	37	3	11	1	0
Marquez, San Antonio	.867	30	2	11	2	0
Martinez, Arkansas	1.000	2	2	2	0	0
Masters, Shreveport	1.000	14	0	5	0	0
Mathews, Jackson	.970	17	17	15	1	1
McFarlin, San Antonio	.878	52	13	23	5	0
Miller, Tulsa	.870	18	6	14	3	0
Mimbs, San Antonio*	.941	49	6	10	1	0
Montgomery, Arkansas	1.000	6	0	3	0	0
Moody, Tulsa*	1.000	47	4	14	0	0
Morman, Jackson*	.895	19	3	14	2	0
Musset, Midland	1.000	59	7	8	0	0
Myers, Shreveport	.889	29	3	5	1	2
Oliver, Tulsa*	.955	46	6	15	1	0
Parra, San Antonio	.912	17	15	16	3	0
Paskievitch, Wichita	1.000	7	0	2	0	0
Peltzer, Shreveport*	.944	30	5	12	1	1
Pena, Wichita*	1.000	10	3	7	0	0
Perez, Midland*	1.000	3	0	1	0	0
Perez, Tulsa	.947	33	15	21	2	0
Perez, Arkansas	1.000	4	0	2	0	0
Piotrowicz, San Antonio	.667	6	1	1	1	0
Pitcher, El Paso	1.000	13	0	1	0	0
Pote, Shreveport	1.000	19	8	10	0	1
Purdy, Midland	.818	5	3	6	2	1
Rambo, Shreveport	.889	15	5	11	2	0
Ratekin, Midland	.900	7	5	4	1	1
Reed, Tulsa	.952	14	3	17	1	1
Richards, El Paso*	1.000	35	1	3	0	0
Rogers, El Paso*	.737	48	1	13	5	0
Romero, Tulsa*	.909	21	2	18	2	1
Rosselli, Shreveport*	1.000	4	0	4	0	0
Rowley, Tulsa	.905	20	7	12	2	0
Sadecki, Tulsa	.500	9	0	1	1	0
Sager, Wichita	1.000	11	3	12	0	1
Santos, Arkansas	.962	57	6	19	1	1
Shackle, Arkansas	1.000	10	3	4	0	0
Simmons, Arkansas*	1.000	13	3	15	0	1
Simon, Shreveport	1.000	52	3	5	0	0
Small, Jackson	.952	51	8	12	1	1
Smith, Shreveport	1.000	24	3	3	0	0
Snedeker, San Antonio	1.000	12	11	17	0	1
Strong, Wichita	1.000	4	0	4	0	0
Stroud, Midland*	1.000	13	1	1	0	0
Taylor, El Paso	.880	17	8	14	3	2
Thomas, San Antonio	.968	47	14	16	1	1
Torres, Shreveport	.889	12	1	7	1	1
Valdez, San Antonio	1.000	3	1	1	0	0
Vanderweele, Shreveport	1.000	1	1	0	0	0
Van Ryn, San Antonio*	.947	21	4	14	1	2
Vierra, San Antonio*	1.000	9	2	6	0	0
Watson, Midland	1.000	36	2	6	0	1
Wengert, Wichita	.972	28	14	21	1	0
White, Jackson	.895	16	3	14	2	2
Whitehurst, Wichita	.333	4	1	0	2	0
Williams, Midland	.972	27	16	19	1	1
Windes, Jackson*	.912	41	5	26	3	1
Yockey, Shreveport*	.917	48	4	7	1	2

The following players did not have any fielding statistics at the positions indicated or appeared only as a designated hitter, pinch-hitter or pinch-runner: Bellomo, p; Castleberry, of; Claus, 2b; Couture, p; M. Davis, p; Doffek, of; Fanning, p; Gardella, p; Gieseke, p; Groppuso, ss; Kappesser, 2b; Kasper, p; Kent, p; A. Lewis, 2b; Lofton, ss, of; Lukachyk, 1b, 3b; Staton, p; Ward, of; Wasinger, 1b; Whitaker, p.

LEAGUE CHAMPIONS

Year	Team	Pct.	Year	Team	Pct.	Year	Team	Pct.
1888—	Dallas	.671	1922—	Fort Worth	.694	1952—	Dallas	.571
1889—	Houston	.551		Fort Worth	.711		Shreveport (3rd)§	.522
1890—	Galveston	.705	1923—	Fort Worth	.632	1953—	Dallas‡	.571
1892—	Houston	.741	1924—	Fort Worth	.689	1954—	Shreveport	.559
	Houston	.613		Fort Worth	.763		Houston (2nd)§	.553
1895—	Dallas	.754	1925—	Fort Worth	.711	1955—	Dallas	.581
	Fort Worth*	.750		Fort Worth y	.653		Shreveport (3rd)§	.540
1896—	Fort Worth	.757	1926—	Dallas	.574	1956—	Houston‡	.623
	Houston*	.679	1927—	Wichita Falls	.654	1957—	Dallas	.662
	Galveston	.548	1928—	Houston*	.679		Houston (2nd)§	.630
1897—	San Antonio†	.657		Wichita Falls	.731	1958—	Fort Worth	.582
	Galveston†	.717	1929—	Dallas*	.588		Cor. Christi (3rd)§	.507
1898—	League disbanded.			Wichita Falls	.620	1959—	Victoria	.589
1899—	Galveston	.632	1930—	Wichita Falls	.697		Austin (2nd)§	.548
	Galveston	.762		Fort Worth*	.632	1960—	Rio Grande Valley	.590
1900-01—	Did not operate.		1931—	Houston a	.625		Tulsa (3rd)	.528
1902—	Corsicana	.866		Houston	.734	1961—	Amarillo	.643
	Corsicana	.682	1932—	Beaumont*	.640		San Antonio (3rd)§	.532
1903—	Paris-Waco	.615		Dallas	.727	1962—	El Paso	.571
	Dallas*	.648	1933—	Houston	.623		Tulsa (2nd)§	.550
1904—	Corsicana*	.615		San Antonio (4th)§	.523	1963—	San Antonio	.564
	Fort Worth	.800	1934—	Galveston‡	.579		Tulsa (3rd)§	.529
1905—	Fort Worth	.545	1935—	Oklahoma City‡	.590	1964—	San Antonio†	.607
1906—	Fort Worth	.677	1936—	Dallas	.604	1965—	Tulsa	.574
	Cleburne x	.609		Tulsa (3rd)§	.519		Albuquerque b	.550
1907—	Austin	.629	1937—	Oklahoma City	.635	1966—	Arkansas	.579
1908—	San Antonio	.664		Fort Worth (3rd)§	.535	1967—	Albuquerque	.557
1909—	Houston	.601	1938—	Beaumont	.635	1968—	Arkansas	.586
1910—	Dallas†	.586	1939—	Houston	.606		El Paso b	.562
	Houston†	.586		Fort Worth (4th)§	.540	1969—	Amarillo	.593
1911—	Austin	.575	1940—	Houston‡	.652		Memphis b	.504
1912—	Houston	.626	1941—	Houston	.673	1970—	Albuquerque a	.615
1913—	Houston	.620		Dallas (4th)§	.519		Memphis	.507
1914—	Houston†	.671	1942—	Beaumont	.605	1971—	Did not operate as league—clubs	
	Waco†	.671		Shreveport (2nd)§	.576		were members of Dixie Association.	
1915—	Waco	.592	1943-44-45—	Did not operate.		1972—	Alexandria	.600
1916—	Waco	.587	1946—	Fort Worth	.656		El Paso b	.557
1917—	Dallas	.600		Dallas (2nd)§	.591	1973—	San Antonio	.590
1918—	Dallas	.584	1947—	Houston‡	.623		Memphis b	.558
1919—	Shreveport*	.677	1948—	Fort Worth‡	.601	1974—	Victoria b	.581
	Fort Worth	.651	1949—	Fort Worth	.649		El Paso	.555
1920—	Fort Worth	.703		Tulsa (2nd)§	.584	1975—	Lafayette c	.558
	Fort Worth	.750	1950—	Beaumont	.595		Midland c	.604
1921—	Fort Worth	.691		San Antonio (4th)§	.513	1976—	Amarillo b	.600
	Fort Worth	.662	1951—	Houston‡	.619		Shreveport	.515

Year	Team	Pct.	Year	Team	Pct.	Year	Team	Pct.
1977—	El Paso	.600	1983—	Jackson	.507	1989—	Arkansas d	.585
	Arkansas d	.485		Beaumont d	.500		Wichita	.537
1978—	El Paso d	.593	1984—	Beaumont	.654	1990—	San Antonio	.582
	Jackson	.567		Jackson d	.610		Shreveport d	.489
1979—	Arkansas d	.571	1985—	El Paso	.632	1991—	Shreveport d	.632
	Midland	.563		Jackson d	.537		El Paso	.596
1980—	Arkansas d	.596	1986—	El Paso d	.630	1992—	Shreveport	.566
	San Antonio	.544		Jackson	.533		Wichita d	.515
1981—	San Antonio	.571	1987—	Wichita d	.515	1993—	El Paso	.563
	Jackson d	.507		Jackson	.515		Jackson d	.541
1982—	El Paso	.559	1988—	El Paso	.552			
	Tulsa d	.515		Tulsa d	.522			

*Won split-season playoff. †Won playoff for title. ‡Finished first and won four-club playoff. §Won four-club playoff. xTitle to Cleburne by default. yTied with Dallas in second half and won playoff for championship. zFort Worth disbanded. aTied with Beaumont at end of first half and won title in best-of-five series played as part of second-half schedule. bLeague divided into Eastern, Western divisions; won two-team playoff. cLeague divided into Eastern, Western divisions; declared co-champions when playoffs were not completed. dLeague divided into Eastern and Western divisions and played split-season; won playoffs. NOTE—Championship awarded to winner of four-team playoff, 1933-51; first-place team and playoff winner co-champions, 1952-64.

CALIFORNIA LEAGUE

FIRST HALF

NORTHERN DIVISION

Team	W	L	T	Pct.	GB
Modesto (Athletics)	42	26	0	.618	......
San Jose (Giants)	41	27	0	.603	1
Stockton (Brewers)	37	31	0	.544	5
Central Valley (Rockies)	26	42	0	.382	16
Bakersfield (Dodgers)	18	50	0	.265	24

SOUTHERN DIVISION

Team	W	L	T	Pct.	GB
High Desert (Marlins)	44	24	0	.647	......
Riverside (Mariners)	36	32	0	.529	8
Rancho Cucamonga (Padres)	35	33	0	.515	9
San Bernardino (Independent)	31	37	0	.456	13
Palm Springs (Angels)	30	38	0	.441	14

SECOND HALF

NORTHERN DIVISION

Team	W	L	T	Pct.	GB
Stockton (Brewers)	42	26	0	.618	......
San Jose (Giants)	38	30	0	.559	4
Central Valley (Rockies)	35	33	0	.515	7
Modesto (Athletics)	30	38	0	.441	12
Bakersfield (Dodgers)	24	44	0	.353	18

SOUTHERN DIVISION

Team	W	L	T	Pct.	GB
*High Desert (Marlins)	41	28	0	.594	......
*Riverside (Mariners)	40	29	0	.580	1
San Bernardino (Independent)	31	37	0	.456	9 ½
Palm Springs (Angels)	31	37	0	.456	9 ½
Rancho Cucamonga (Padres)	29	39	0	.426	11 ½

*High Desert defeated Riverside in one-game playoff to decide second-half championship.

COMPOSITE

Team	H.D.	Sto.	S.J.	Riv.	Mod.	R.C.	S.B.	P.S.	C.V.	Bak.	W	L	T	Pct.	GB
High Desert (Marlins)	....	3	5	13	9	13	15	11	6	10	85	52	0	.620	......
Stockton (Brewers)	9	....	12	5	9	10	5	5	14	10	79	57	0	.581	5 ½
San Jose (Giants)	7	7	....	7	13	7	6	7	14	11	79	57	0	.581	5 ½
Riverside (Mariners)	7	7	5	....	5	13	13	14	6	6	76	61	0	.555	9
Modesto (Athletics)	3	11	6	7	....	6	9	9	9	12	72	64	0	.529	12 ½
Rancho Cucamonga (Padres)	6	2	5	5	6	....	13	11	6	10	64	72	0	.471	20 ½
San Bernardino (Independent)	5	7	6	6	3	6	....	10	8	11	62	74	0	.456	22 ½
Palm Springs (Angels)	7	7	5	6	3	9	8	....	7	9	61	75	0	.449	23 ½
Central Valley (Rockies)	6	5	4	6	10	6	4	5	....	15	61	75	0	.449	23 ½
Bakersfield (Dodgers)	2	8	9	6	6	2	1	3	5	....	42	94	0	.309	42 ½

Major league affiliations in parentheses.

Playoffs—High Desert defeated Riverside, three games to one; Modesto defeated Stockton, three games to one; High Desert defeated Modesto, three games to two, to win league championship.

Regular-season attendance—Bakersfield, 149,095; Central Valley, 77,547; High Desert, 191,697; Modesto, 100,016; Palm Springs, 105,039; Rancho Cucamonga, 331,005; Riverside, 68,821; San Bernardino, 88,468; San Jose, 133,138; Stockton, 108,629. Total, 1,353,455. Playoffs (13 games)—30,893. All-Star Game—3,413.

Managers—Bakersfield, Rick Dempsey; Central Valley, Paul Zuvella; High Desert, Fredi Gonzalez; Modesto, Ted Kubiak; Palm Springs, Mario Mendoza; Rancho Cucamonga, Keith Champion; Riverside, Dave Myers; San Bernardino, Greg Mahlberg; San Jose, Dick Dietz; Stockton, Lamar Johnson.

All-Star team: 1B—John Toale, High Desert; 2B—Arquimedez Pozo, Riverside; 3B—Bryn Kosco, High Desert; SS—Kurt Ehmann, San Jose; OF—Tim Clark, High Desert; Ira Smith, Rancho Cucamonga; Ernie Young, Modesto; C—Izzy Molina, Modesto; DH—Kevin Riggs, Stockton; P—Sid Roberson, Stockton; John Pricher, Palm Springs; Russ Brock, Modesto; John Burke, Central Valley; Most Valuable Player—Tim Clark, High Desert; Pitcher of the Year—Sid Roberson, Stockton; Rookie of the Year—Arquimedez Pozo, Riverside; Manager of the Year—Fredi Gonzalez, High Desert.

BATTING

TEAM

Team	Avg.	G	AB	R	OR	H	TB	2B	3B	HR	RBI	SH	SF	HP	BB	Int. BB	SO	SB	CS	LOB
High Desert	.289	137	4683	939	769	1355	2067	238	60	118	841	22	67	61	721	20	909	230	90	1068
Rancho Cucamonga	.287	136	4766	775	821	1369	2056	283	43	106	712	22	47	48	538	17	867	128	85	1050
Stockton	.285	136	4634	776	659	1320	1933	225	35	106	703	52	54	55	617	25	792	211	103	1065
Riverside	.278	136	4716	760	711	1310	1889	259	34	84	681	35	53	48	566	18	852	109	70	1059
Central Valley	.269	136	4640	666	719	1250	1742	187	25	85	592	49	42	46	607	17	873	161	80	1083
Modesto	.269	136	4479	750	666	1204	1771	222	27	97	662	57	54	53	740	11	856	108	87	1098
San Bernardino	.267	136	4679	732	797	1248	1963	232	21	147	662	43	43	56	544	23	1030	115	77	997
Palm Springs	.263	136	4611	656	717	1211	1624	201	40	44	598	38	43	39	585	13	814	208	117	1008
San Jose	.260	136	4569	696	683	1189	1696	219	27	78	615	40	49	64	580	18	795	216	81	1046
Bakersfield	.251	136	4664	558	766	1170	1699	195	26	94	504	31	32	63	405	14	1065	100	75	976

INDIVIDUAL

(Leading qualifiers for batting championship—367 or more plate appearances)

*Bats lefthanded.   †Switch-hitter.

Player, Team	Avg.	G	AB	R	H	TB	2B	3B	HR	RBI	SH	SF	HP	BB	Int. BB	SO	SB	CS
Clark, Tim, High Desert*	.363	128	510	109	185	298	42	10	17	126	0	13	4	56	3	65	2	5
Riggs, Kevin, Stockton*	.347	108	377	84	131	164	18	3	3	45	1	4	1	101	3	46	12	15
Smith, Ira, Rancho Cucamonga	.346	92	347	71	120	183	30	6	7	47	2	3	5	55	1	41	32	16
Pozo, Arquimedez, Riverside	.342	127	515	98	176	271	44	6	13	83	1	5	2	56	4	56	10	10
Turner, Brian, San Bernardino*	.325	109	406	69	132	224	23	3	21	68	2	3	2	49	4	75	4	2
Martinez, Manny, San Bernardino	.322	109	459	84	148	213	26	3	11	52	6	4	5	41	2	60	28	21
Stefanski, Michael, Stockton	.322	97	345	58	111	167	22	2	10	57	1	2	5	49	2	45	6	1
Hardtke, Jason, Rancho Cucamonga†	.319	130	523	98	167	252	38	7	11	85	2	6	2	61	2	54	7	8
McFarlin, Jason, San Jose*	.311	97	395	71	123	172	20	4	7	53	7	4	3	29	0	67	49	10
Shockey, Greg, Riverside*	.311	95	354	61	110	138	10	0	6	63	1	4	4	50	5	50	2	2

Departmental leaders: G—Toale, 134; AB—Hardtke, 523; R—K. Moore, 120; H—Clark, 185; TB—Clark, 298; 2B—A. Pozo, 44; 3B—Clark, 10; HR—Toale, 28; RBI—Clark, 126; SH—McCracken, 12; SF—Clark, 13; HP—J. Martin, 13; BB—K. Moore, 114; IBB—Giambi, 7; SO—J. Martin, 131; SB—K. Moore, 71; CS—Riley, 25.

(All players—listed alphabetically)

Player, Team	Avg.	G	AB	R	H	TB	2B	3B	HR	RBI	SH	SF	HP	BB	Int. BB	SO	SB	CS
Albrecht, Andrew, San Jose*	.259	76	239	33	62	89	13	4	2	32	3	1	6	29	3	42	6	7
Alicea, Edwin, Central Valley*	.306	12	49	5	15	20	2	0	1	5	1	0	2	5	0	5	0	2
Anderson, Chris, Palm Springs	.238	103	353	51	84	121	19	6	2	45	2	4	9	30	0	50	3	5
Anderson, Cliff, Bakersfield*	.139	12	36	4	5	8	3	0	0	3	3	0	1	0	13	0	1
Anderson, Steve, San Bernardino*	.274	113	405	61	111	180	21	0	16	76	0	1	5	33	4	74	3	4
Baber, Larue, Rancho Cucamonga	.333	3	3	1	1	1	0	0	0	1	0	0	0	1	0	1	1	0
Barns, Jeff, Modesto†	.308	53	143	17	44	52	8	0	0	14	8	2	0	24	0	9	1	1
Bates, Tommy, San Bernardino	.159	15	44	8	7	11	1	0	1	5	0	2	1	10	0	10	2	0
Beard, Garrett, Modesto	.268	83	284	46	76	115	17	2	6	33	3	3	3	63	0	55	3	2
Bellomo, Kevin, San Jose	.235	33	102	7	24	33	2	2	1	15	0	1	1	12	0	22	1	1
Benjamin, Mike, San Jose	.000	2	8	1	0	0	0	0	0	0	0	0	1	1	0	0	0	0
Bish, Brent, Rancho Cucamonga	.210	52	143	22	30	42	8	2	0	13	0	0	4	11	0	21	4	4
Bonnici, James, Riverside	.307	104	375	49	115	165	21	1	9	58	3	1	9	58	2	72	0	0
Boykin, Tyrone, Palm Springs	.325	77	286	48	93	117	13	1	3	40	2	3	0	51	0	52	22	8
Bream, Scott, Rancho Cucamonga†	.281	113	405	70	114	153	15	6	4	52	4	3	2	74	3	85	30	14
Bruno, Julio, Rancho Cucamonga	.308	54	201	37	62	86	11	2	3	16	1	2	1	19	2	56	15	6
Bryant, Craig, Riverside	.258	61	236	38	61	93	15	4	3	28	1	2	2	36	0	39	8	4
Bucchieri, Jim, Modesto	.286	2	7	3	2	2	0	0	0	1	0	0	1	2	0	2	0	0
Buchanan, Shawn, San Bernardino	.258	53	182	39	47	68	11	2	2	29	3	4	5	50	1	38	11	7
Burnett, Roger, San Bernardino	.286	72	245	34	70	103	15	0	6	33	4	1	2	25	1	39	3	2
Calcagno, Dan, San Jose.	.250	25	64	10	16	17	1	0	0	6	0	3	0	11	0	8	1	1
Carmona, Greg, Stockton†	.170	20	47	9	8	9	1	0	0	7	1	0	0	18	0	11	5	5
Case, Mike, Central Valley	.276	124	449	54	124	181	20	2	11	80	6	7	7	53	2	120	21	6
Casper, Tim, San Jose†	.143	13	21	3	3	5	0	1	0	1	0	1	0	5	0	10	0	3
Cervantes, Manny, Riverside*	.333	2	3	0	1	1	0	0	0	0	0	0	0	0	0	1	0	0
Cervantes, Ray, San Bernardino	.209	82	244	37	51	68	5	0	4	19	7	0	2	43	0	52	3	5
Clark, Tim, High Desert*	.363	128	510	109	185	298	42	10	17	126	0	13	4	56	3	65	2	5
Claus, Todd, Palm Springs†	.190	42	105	17	20	29	4	1	1	8	2	1	0	13	0	24	1	0
Clayton, Craig, Riverside	.328	60	235	37	77	97	13	2	1	32	0	5	2	30	2	30	4	4
Clemens, Troy, San Jose*	.291	96	306	36	89	106	15	1	0	31	2	4	3	35	4	34	1	1
Cole, Mark, Stockton†	.240	79	242	30	58	77	8	1	3	34	3	3	2	17	1	40	7	3
Cookson, Brent, San Jose	.256	67	234	43	60	123	10	1	17	50	2	5	3	43	1	73	14	6
Cooper, Tim, San Bernardino	.281	60	217	32	61	108	13	2	10	44	2	5	5	40	1	49	4	4
Counsell, Craig, Central Valley*	.280	131	471	79	132	179	26	3	5	59	5	4	3	95	1	68	14	8
Couture, Mike, Stockton	.241	32	87	22	21	33	6	0	2	9	1	1	1	17	0	28	14	2
Cruz, Fausto, Modesto	.236	43	165	21	39	45	3	0	1	20	5	4	0	25	0	34	6	4
Dalesandro, Mark, Palm Springs	.244	46	176	22	43	57	5	3	1	25	0	7	0	15	1	20	3	2
DeHart, Rick, San Bernardino*	.000	9	1	0	0	0	0	0	0	0	0	0	0	0	0	0	0	0
DelaCruz, Marcelino, Central Valley	.176	11	34	6	6	8	2	0	0	2	0	0	1	6	0	6	0	0
Demerson, Tim, San Bernardino	.261	115	426	73	111	159	21	3	7	46	9	3	11	39	1	89	24	4
Diggs, Tony, Stockton†	.295	81	285	48	84	107	14	3	1	31	1	3	3	43	2	34	31	11
Dobrolsky, Bill, Stockton	.211	67	190	18	40	45	2	0	1	21	2	1	5	16	0	43	2	1
Dodge, Tom, Palm Springs†	.270	97	366	47	99	115	9	2	1	44	2	4	7	35	1	38	13	10
Doran, Bill, Stockton†	.500	1	2	0	1	1	0	0	0	0	0	0	0	1	0	1	0	1
Dotolo, C.L., San Jose	.197	58	157	17	31	40	9	0	0	22	4	3	3	23	0	36	1	3
Drinkwater, Sean, Rancho Cucamonga	.270	121	486	69	131	192	29	1	10	84	1	12	2	35	1	78	2	3
Duncan, Andres, San Jose†	.225	36	111	17	25	33	1	2	1	12	2	2	2	12	0	28	14	3
Dunn, Nathan, Bakersfield	.214	4	14	1	3	3	0	0	0	1	0	0	3	0	2	0	0
Ebel, Dino, Bakersfield	.280	19	50	7	14	19	5	0	0	4	2	2	0	4	0	7	0	1
Echevarria, Angel, Central Valley	.271	104	358	45	97	135	16	2	6	52	5	3	5	44	0	74	6	5
Edmondson, Gavin, Bakersfield	.185	45	119	14	22	25	3	0	0	8	1	0	3	7	0	31	2	1
Ehmann, Kurt, San Jose	.262	123	439	81	115	152	20	1	5	57	3	4	11	75	2	69	12	9
Encarnacion, Anito, R. Cucamonga	.194	22	62	5	12	19	4	0	1	6	0	0	2	5	1	10	0	0
Everett, Carl, High Desert†	.289	59	253	48	73	127	12	6	10	52	0	1	6	22	0	73	24	9
Fairman, Andy, Stockton*	.265	122	456	59	121	190	20	2	15	70	6	7	1	39	5	51	4	8
Felix, Lauro, Modesto	.205	102	302	55	62	78	6	2	2	35	8	2	1	69	0	70	7	4
Ferguson, Jim, 12 P.S.-23 S.B.	1.000	35	1	0	1	1	0	0	0	0	0	0	0	0	0	0	0	0
Figga, Michael, San Bernardino	.266	83	308	48	82	176	17	1	25	71	2	3	2	17	0	84	2	3
Filson, Matt, Bakersfield*	.233	98	283	33	66	114	16	4	8	37	0	4	9	36	2	84	1	3
Frazier, Terance, Modesto	.276	96	340	48	94	107	9	2	0	29	6	2	7	25	1	57	22	8
Freeburg, Ryan, San Bernardino*	.241	120	432	57	104	156	19	3	9	57	1	6	5	47	2	121	5	7
Freehling, Rick, San Bernardino†	.091	3	11	3	1	1	0	0	0	0	0	0	3	0	3	0	0
Furtado, Tim, Riverside	.161	43	112	7	18	23	2	0	1	10	2	1	1	8	1	22	1	1
Garcia, Karim, Bakersfield*	.241	123	460	61	111	206	20	9	19	54	0	2	2	37	4	109	5	4
Gennaro, Brad, Rancho Cucamonga*	.285	127	481	77	137	213	23	7	13	70	4	3	5	30	0	88	3	9
Giambi, Jason, Modesto*	.291	89	313	72	91	147	16	2	12	60	1	3	10	73	7	47	2	3
Gieseke, Mark, Rancho Cucamonga†	.353	5	17	4	6	8	2	0	0	3	0	0	1	5	1	0	0	0
Gilliam, Bo, San Bernardino	.280	39	157	19	44	69	8	1	5	28	1	1	3	8	2	34	3	2
Glenn, Leon, Stockton*	.276	114	431	77	119	197	27	3	15	76	1	6	4	49	4	110	35	15
Gonzalez, Mauricio, Central Valley*	.281	83	263	30	74	95	8	2	3	27	2	1	2	19	3	37	1	5
Gousha, Sean, High Desert	.183	45	126	22	23	25	2	0	0	11	3	3	5	26	0	47	0	1
Griffey, Craig, Riverside	.241	58	191	30	46	67	4	4	3	25	3	7	2	17	3	25	10	2
Gruber, Kelly, Palm Springs	.222	5	9	0	2	2	0	0	0	1	0	0	1	0	2	0	0
Hagy, Gary, Palm Springs	.179	104	340	35	61	71	8	1	0	24	7	2	2	42	0	61	6	6
Hardtke, Jason, Rancho Cucamonga†..	.319	130	523	98	167	252	38	7	11	85	2	6	2	61	2	54	7	8
Hardwick, Bill, Stockton*	.000	61	1	0	0	0	0	0	0	0	0	0	0	0	0	0	0	0
Harris, Mike, Stockton*	.309	104	363	64	112	162	17	3	9	65	8	4	6	63	4	56	19	7
Henderson, Lee, Rancho Cucamonga	.266	56	177	28	47	61	11	0	1	23	2	1	1	16	0	36	0	1
Hirsch, Chris, Palm Springs	.276	44	145	19	40	70	10	1	6	22	1	1	3	23	0	35	1	2
Hostetler, Brian, Stockton*	.423	11	26	5	11	13	2	0	0	4	0	0	0	7	0	2	1	0
Huyler, Mike, Stockton	.281	92	338	66	95	129	19	3	3	34	11	2	2	43	1	48	16	5
Hyzdu, Adam, San Jose	.291	44	165	35	48	104	11	3	13	38	1	2	0	29	0	53	1	1
Jaime, Angel, Bakersfield	.230	46	152	21	35	40	5	0	0	8	4	0	4	18	0	34	14	6
Jenkins, Brett, San Jose	.233	52	189	25	44	76	11	0	7	25	0	2	1	16	1	25	1	0
Johnson, Herman, Modesto	.000	5	6	1	0	0	0	0	0	1	0	0	0	1	0	0	0	0
Jones, Terry, Central Valley	.288	21	73	16	21	22	1	0	0	7	1	0	1	10	0	15	5	0
King, Clay, San Jose	.303	51	188	27	57	81	9	0	5	33	0	3	3	20	1	34	0	1
Kirkpatrick, Jay, Bakersfield*	.288	103	375	42	108	153	21	0	8	63	1	3	4	35	2	78	1	4

Player, Team	Avg.	G	AB	R	H	TB	2B	3B	HR	RBI	SH	SF	HP	BB	Int. BB	SO	SB	CS
Kliafas, Stephen, Bakersfield	.235	88	328	40	77	93	13	0	1	24	5	2	2	13	1	37	4	1
Koehler, Jim, Riverside*	.190	12	42	7	8	17	1	1	2	12	0	0	0	5	0	11	1	1
Kosco, Bryn, High Desert	.307	121	450	96	138	250	25	3	27	121	0	8	5	62	3	97	1	6
Krenke, Keith, Central Valley	.125	15	40	3	5	7	2	0	0	4	0	2	1	4	0	9	0	0
Latham, Chris, Bakersfield†	.185	6	27	1	5	6	1	0	0	3	0	0	0	4	0	5	2	2
Lee, Derrek, Rancho Cucamonga	.274	20	73	13	20	30	5	1	1	10	0	1	0	10	0	20	0	2
Lewis, Tyrone, Bakersfield	.232	83	332	31	77	91	8	3	0	23	5	0	4	16	1	67	4	6
Liriano, Nelson, Central Valley†	.364	6	22	3	8	12	0	2	0	4	0	0	0	6	0	0	0	2
List, Paul, Central Valley	.292	33	120	21	35	69	6	2	8	27	0	1	2	17	0	19	0	3
Livesey, Steve, San Bernardino	.308	4	13	2	4	5	1	0	0	3	0	0	1	0	0	5	0	0
Lohry, Adin, San Bernardino*	.250	28	84	13	21	24	3	0	0	7	2	1	3	13	0	17	2	1
Lopez, Pedro, Rancho Cucamonga	.252	37	103	25	26	39	10	0	1	9	0	0	2	24	1	19	0	1
Loretta, Mark, Stockton	.363	53	201	36	73	91	4	1	4	31	2	2	2	22	0	17	8	2
Lund, Ed, Bakersfield	.261	66	203	20	53	63	4	0	2	21	0	1	6	21	0	25	2	1
Luzinski, Ryan, Bakersfield	.279	48	147	18	41	62	10	1	3	9	0	0	5	13	0	24	2	2
Malinoski, Chris, High Desert	.304	111	368	62	112	151	24	3	3	72	1	6	12	81	2	54	7	7
Manahan, Austin, R. Cucamonga†	.290	43	145	17	42	64	8	1	4	22	1	2	1	11	0	38	7	2
Marquez, Jesus, Riverside*	.308	12	39	3	12	14	2	0	0	6	1	0	0	6	0	9	2	2
Martin, Darryl, Central Valley	.212	10	33	6	7	9	2	0	0	1	1	0	0	1	0	5	1	1
Martin, Jim, Bakersfield	.259	118	441	60	114	173	17	3	12	50	0	4	13	45	2	131	27	12
Martinez, Manny, San Bernardino	.322	109	459	88	148	213	26	3	11	52	6	4	5	41	2	60	28	21
Martinez, Ramon, High Desert†	.265	118	412	73	109	137	10	6	2	46	6	3	2	49	2	79	46	11
Maxwell, Trent, Riverside	.500	4	2	0	1	1	0	0	0	1	0	0	0	0	0	1	0	0
Maynard, Tow, Riverside	.228	36	136	19	31	45	10	2	0	19	1	0	1	16	0	28	16	2
McCaffery, Dennis, Palm Springs	.251	75	239	25	60	70	6	2	0	25	3	1	2	26	0	59	10	6
McCracken, Quinton, Central Valley†	.292	127	483	94	141	178	17	7	2	58	12	4	2	78	4	90	60	19
McFarlin, Jason, San Jose*	.311	97	395	71	123	172	20	4	7	53	7	4	3	29	0	67	49	10
McKamie, Sean, Bakersfield	.328	21	67	15	22	32	4	0	2	12	1	0	2	7	0	6	4	3
McNair, Fred, Riverside	.270	112	400	70	108	173	21	4	14	65	1	4	5	41	2	91	6	7
Mirabelli, Doug, San Jose	.270	113	371	58	100	126	19	2	1	48	2	4	4	72	1	55	0	4
Molina, Izzy, Modesto	.261	125	444	61	116	170	26	5	6	69	4	11	3	44	0	85	2	8
Montgomery, Don, San Jose	.167	34	96	8	16	21	2	0	1	9	0	0	0	9	0	18	0	0
Moore, Kerwin, High Desert†	.269	132	510	120	137	193	20	9	6	52	3	5	6	114	3	95	71	16
Moore, Mike, Bakersfield	.288	100	403	61	116	182	25	1	13	58	0	4	3	29	0	103	23	10
Moore, Vince, Rancho Cucamonga*	.258	39	159	33	41	67	8	0	6	23	0	1	3	15	0	52	9	7
Motuzas, Jeff, San Bernardino	.156	52	154	16	24	37	7	0	2	13	1	3	2	13	1	45	2	3
Mowry, David, Rancho Cucamonga*	.243	22	74	9	18	39	0	0	7	23	0	1	2	6	0	24	0	0
Mulligan, Sean, Rancho Cucamonga	.280	79	268	29	75	109	10	3	6	36	0	4	3	34	0	33	1	3
Munoz, Orlando, Palm Springs†	.270	64	237	38	64	78	8	3	0	24	3	5	2	47	0	25	23	14
Murray, Calvin, San Jose	.281	85	345	61	97	150	24	1	9	42	2	0	4	40	0	63	42	10
Neill, Mike, Modesto*	.194	17	62	4	12	15	3	0	0	4	0	0	0	12	0	12	0	1
North, Tim, High Desert†	.000	9	4	4	0	0	0	0	0	0	0	0	1	1	0	0	1	1
Norton, Rick, Modesto*	.200	44	120	14	24	37	0	0	0	9	1	2	0	20	0	37	1	2
O'Neill, Tom, San Jose	.000	2	5	0	0	0	0	0	0	0	0	0	0	0	0	2	0	0
Oakland, Mike, Central Valley	.235	62	221	20	52	68	10	0	2	27	1	2	1	22	0	35	0	3
Ortman, Ben, Central Valley	.130	7	23	3	3	3	0	0	0	0	0	0	0	3	0	7	1	0
Orton, John, Palm Springs	.000	2	7	0	0	0	0	0	0	0	0	0	0	1	0	1	0	0
Ostermeyer, Bill, San Bernardino	.194	16	36	3	7	8	1	0	0	0	0	0	0	6	0	10	0	1
Otanez, Willis, San Bernardino	.262	95	325	34	85	130	11	2	10	39	4	2	2	29	1	63	1	4
Patterson, John, San Jose†	.235	16	68	8	16	26	7	0	1	14	0	0	2	7	1	12	6	0
Pearce, Jeff, Rancho Cucamonga*	.281	101	324	51	91	129	17	0	7	55	0	5	2	30	1	52	12	9
Perez, Danny, Stockton	.292	10	24	4	7	12	3	1	0	0	0	0	2	0	0	2	1	1
Pezzoni, Ron, San Jose	.256	100	340	51	87	120	18	0	5	53	1	2	0	50	3	42	11	5
Phillips, Steve, San Bernardino*	.274	57	208	29	57	97	11	1	9	38	0	1	1	37	1	71	3	4
Pineiro, Mike, Central Valley	.308	34	117	19	36	48	3	0	3	14	0	1	0	17	0	22	0	0
Powell, Ken, Rancho Cucamonga	.268	22	41	10	11	17	1	1	1	7	2	0	0	4	0	12	0	0
Pozo, Arquimedez, Riverside	.342	127	515	98	176	271	44	6	13	83	1	5	2	56	4	56	10	10
Pozo, Yohel, Central Valley	.333	1	3	1	1	1	0	0	0	0	0	0	0	0	0	1	0	0
Prater, Andy, High Desert	.125	2	8	1	1	1	0	0	0	0	0	0	0	0	0	0	0	0
Pugh, Scott, Rancho Cucamonga*	.294	96	327	39	96	134	19	2	5	43	4	2	5	26	2	52	3	2
Ramirez, Roberto, Modesto	.257	41	140	17	36	53	8	0	3	14	0	2	1	17	0	36	2	5
Raven, Luis, Palm Springs	.277	85	343	38	95	140	20	2	7	52	1	2	3	22	0	84	15	11
Reed, Jeff, San Jose*	.500	4	10	2	5	6	1	0	0	2	0	0	0	1	0	0	0	0
Reid, Derek, San Jose	.188	29	80	9	15	18	1	1	0	8	0	0	1	6	0	16	5	2
Renteria, Edinson, High Desert	.314	56	207	43	65	83	12	0	2	27	0	3	2	22	1	33	1	4
Ricker, Troy, Central Valley	.222	27	90	11	20	25	2	0	1	9	0	0	5	11	0	31	2	2
Riggs, Kevin, Stockton*	.347	108	377	84	131	164	18	3	3	45	1	4	1	101	3	46	12	15
Riley, Marquis, Palm Springs	.264	130	508	93	134	151	10	2	1	42	5	2	0	90	1	117	69	25
Rios, Eddie, Bakersfield	.283	29	113	19	32	57	4	0	7	17	2	0	2	8	0	17	2	3
Robbs, Bill, Rancho Cucamonga	.258	47	120	19	31	43	4	1	2	16	0	1	2	18	1	29	0	3
Robertson, Tommy, Riverside*	.251	96	339	50	85	122	9	5	6	51	1	6	6	43	2	53	10	2
Rodarte, Raul, Riverside	.289	106	402	79	116	152	19	1	5	48	6	2	0	51	0	66	13	14
Rogers, Lamarr, Central Valley	.264	112	406	68	107	131	14	2	2	33	7	4	4	68	1	54	29	15
Romero, Wilfredo, Bakersfield	.351	20	77	8	27	35	5	0	1	12	0	0	0	5	0	16	4	2
Ross, Sean, Central Valley*	.314	9	35	5	11	19	0	1	2	11	0	1	0	5	0	5	2	0
Salvador, Felix, Modesto	.125	11	16	2	2	3	1	0	0	0	0	0	0	0	0	5	0	0
Samples, Todd, Stockton	.264	122	401	63	106	151	21	3	6	48	4	10	28	1	63	36	12
Samuels, Scott, High Desert*	.297	76	219	43	65	101	10	4	6	40	0	1	1	45	0	55	12	4
Scalzitti, Will, Central Valley	.242	75	248	25	60	76	10	0	2	17	3	1	1	17	1	40	0	1
Schmidt, Tom, Central Valley	.245	126	478	61	117	191	15	1	19	62	1	5	4	40	2	107	5	3
Schwenke, Matthew, Bakersfield†	.220	13	41	2	9	9	0	0	0	4	0	0	0	3	0	12	0	0
Scott, Tim, San Bernardino	.219	98	356	46	78	124	11	1	11	35	1	1	2	24	1	64	3	5
Sheets, Andy, Riverside	.193	52	176	23	34	48	9	1	1	12	6	4	0	17	1	51	2	2
Shockey, Greg, Riverside*	.311	95	354	61	110	138	10	0	6	63	1	4	4	50	6	50	2	1
Shockey, Scott, Modesto*	.303	97	350	62	106	188	20	1	20	87	2	3	6	64	3	70	1	1
Simmons, Enoch, Modesto	.209	26	86	12	18	26	2	0	2	14	0	1	1	7	0	16	2	2
Simmons, Nelson, Palm Springs†	.329	20	76	13	25	48	8	0	5	23	0	1	0	10	0	7	1	1
Simpson, Jay, Palm Springs†	.260	77	246	31	64	99	12	1	7	29	4	0	4	12	1	54	14	8
Skeels, Andy, Rancho Cucamonga*	.318	32	66	11	21	30	9	0	0	10	1	0	1	15	0	14	1	0
Skeels, Mark, High Desert†	.277	91	300	48	83	125	16	4	6	56	1	2	8	69	2	62	3	1
Smith, Bubba, Riverside	.421	5	19	5	8	11	3	0	0	3	0	0	0	0	0	6	0	0
Smith, Chris, Palm Springs	.279	40	154	27	43	60	7	2	2	21	0	0	1	16	0	20	3	4
Smith, Frank, Bakersfield	.258	102	299	36	77	109	11	3	5	30	0	3	2	32	0	91	1	7
Smith, Ira, Rancho Cucamonga	.346	92	347	71	120	183	30	6	7	47	2	3	5	55	1	41	32	16

Player, Team	Avg.	G	AB	R	H	TB	2B	3B	HR	RBI	SH	SF	HP	BB	Int. BB	SO	SB	CS
Smith, Joel, Palm Springs	.234	86	295	37	69	107	16	2	6	47	3	5	2	24	1	61	2	2
Smith, Tim, San Bernardino	.000	17	1	0	0	0	0	0	0	0	0	0	0	0	0	0	0	0
Snyder, Randy, High Desert†	.294	20	68	13	20	36	5	1	3	17	0	3	1	9	0	11	0	0
Sobolewski, Mark, Modesto	.229	130	507	66	116	160	23	3	5	60	9	9	8	42	0	100	0	4
Soriano, Fred, Modesto	.250	11	40	6	10	14	2	1	0	5	1	0	1	1	0	12	1	0
Spiezio, Scott, Modesto†	.255	32	110	12	28	42	9	1	1	13	1	0	1	23	0	19	1	5
Staton, Dave, Rancho Cucamonga	.317	58	221	37	70	145	21	0	18	58	0	1	1	30	1	52	0	0
Stefanski, Michael, Stockton	.322	97	345	58	111	167	22	2	10	57	1	2	5	49	2	45	6	1
Stela, Jose, Palm Springs	.261	10	23	4	6	7	1	0	0	4	0	0	1	7	1	4	2	0
Strittmatter, Mark, Central Valley	.263	59	179	21	47	61	8	0	2	15	2	3	2	31	0	29	3	0
Swanson, John, Palm Springs*	.293	29	92	17	27	40	8	1	1	13	0	0	0	19	0	17	3	1
Sweeney, Mark, Palm Springs*	.355	66	245	41	87	120	18	3	3	47	0	3	2	42	6	29	9	6
Tavarez, Jesus, High Desert†	.293	109	444	104	130	188	21	8	7	71	3	5	4	57	0	66	47	14
Tejcek, John, Riverside	.286	64	241	42	69	97	12	2	4	36	4	2	4	28	0	46	4	4
Tejero, Fausto, Palm Springs	.300	7	20	2	6	8	2	0	0	1	1	0	0	2	0	1	0	1
Toale, John, High Desert*	.286	134	517	108	148	268	30	3	28	125	0	11	2	84	4	101	1	3
Torres, Tony, High Desert	.230	89	287	45	66	84	9	3	1	25	5	3	2	24	0	69	14	8
Triessl, Mike, Riverside	.333	3	3	1	1	1	0	0	0	0	0	0	0	0	0	0	0	0
Turner, Brian, San Bernardino*	.325	109	406	69	132	224	23	3	21	68	2	3	2	49	4	75	4	2
Turner, Ryan, Central Valley	.294	112	422	64	124	188	23	1	13	67	2	3	5	62	2	88	11	5
Twitty, Sean, San Bernardino	.301	78	289	54	87	131	18	1	8	38	2	4	0	45	2	90	13	2
Unroe, Tim, Stockton	.251	108	382	57	96	165	21	6	12	63	3	4	7	36	0	96	9	10
Urso, Joe, Palm Springs	.257	96	346	51	89	114	17	1	2	41	2	2	1	57	1	53	9	5
Wachter, Derek, Riverside	.293	115	420	75	123	217	20	4	22	108	3	11	6	64	2	93	3	3
Waldenberger, Dave, Riverside†	.247	96	336	40	83	123	20	1	6	52	1	3	4	43	2	87	4	3
Walker, Dane, Modesto*	.296	122	443	94	131	182	22	1	9	67	7	1	0	94	0	55	16	16
Ward, Ricky, San Jose	.182	41	143	17	26	30	4	0	0	12	3	3	2	13	0	14	2	2
Watts, Craig, Bakersfield	.144	34	118	5	17	20	0	0	1	5	0	1	0	7	1	38	0	0
Wedge, Eric, Central Valley	.304	6	23	6	7	16	0	0	3	11	0	0	0	2	1	6	0	0
Whitford, Eric, Stockton	.188	8	16	1	3	3	0	0	0	0	0	0	0	2	0	3	1	1
Widger, Chris, Riverside	.264	97	360	44	95	154	28	2	9	58	3	4	3	19	0	64	5	4
Wilder, Willie, Riverside	.275	63	200	37	55	76	16	1	1	19	0	4	3	35	1	47	11	6
Williams, Leroy, Bakersfield	.240	62	192	18	46	57	8	0	1	17	2	4	0	25	0	43	0	1
Wimmer, Chris, San Jose	.264	123	493	76	130	168	21	4	3	53	7	6	8	42	1	72	49	12
Wittig, Paul, Bakersfield	.129	23	62	7	8	12	1	0	1	2	1	0	0	7	0	27	1	1
Wolfe, Joel, Modesto	.350	87	300	54	105	154	29	1	6	56	0	6	6	51	0	42	18	14
Young, Ernie, Modesto	.306	85	301	83	92	191	18	6	23	71	0	3	4	72	0	92	23	7

The following pitchers, listed alphabetically by club, with games in parentheses, had no plate appearances, primarily through use of designated hitters:

BAKERSFIELD—Brosnan, Jason (9); Castro, Nelson (20); Colson, Brent (39); Costello, Chris (16); Garcia, Jose (27); Herges, Matt (51); Hubbs, Dan (19); Iglesias, Mike (6); Jacobsen, Joe (6); Kenady, Jason (8); Martinez, Jesus (30); Miran, Sal (33); Osuna, Tony (14); Pincavitch, Kevin (6); Salcedo, Jose (16); Sinacori, Chris (31); Snedeker, Sean (13); Thomas, Carlos (39); Veras, Dario (7); Watts, Burgess (10); Weaver, Eric (38); White, Brandon (1); Worrell, Todd (2); Zerbe, Chad (14).

CENTRAL VALLEY—Acevedo, Juan (27); Alston, Garvin (26); Bailey, Roger (22); Bochtler, Doug (8); Burke, John (20); Duke, Kyle (28); Eiffert, Mike (13); Ericson, Mike (38); Grimes, Mike (26); Hovey, Jim (23); Hutchins, Jason (20); Johnson, Jason (7); Kotarski, Mike (52); Metzinger, Bill (14); Mineer, Dave (8); Moore, Marcus (8); Nied, David (1); Peever, Lloyd (17); Schneider, Phil (19); Seanez, Rudy (5); Thompson, Mark (11); Voisard, Mark (21).

HIGH DESERT—Adamson, Joel (22); Berumen, Andres (14); Corsi, Jim (3); Darensbourg, Vic (1); Juelsgaard, Jarod (17); Kendrena, Ken (40); Kerfut, George (28); Lemon, Don (5); Magill, Jim (14); McGraw, Tom (6); Newlin, Jim (17); Parisotto, Barry (32); Patterson, Jim (33); Person, Robert (28); Spencer, Stan (13); Stafford, Jerry (27); Whitman, Ryan (12); Whitten, Mike (43); Wiley, Warren (11); Yaughn, Kip (6).

MODESTO—Brock, Russ (27); Chouinard, Bob (24); Connolly, Craig (22); Dressendorfer, Kirk (5); Fermin, Ramon (31); Grigsby, Ben (39); Haught, Gary (12); Ingram, Todd (32); Mejia, Delfino (12); Myers, Tom (44); Pierce, Bob (36); Plaster, Allen (21); Rossiter, Mike (20); Smock, Greg (7); Strebeck, Rich (11); Sudbury, Craig (42); Wasdin, John (3); Wengert, Don (12); Wojciechowski, Steve (14).

PALM SPRINGS—Burcham, Tim (21); Butler, Mike (27); Ferguson, Jim (12); Janicki, Pete (1); Johnson, Dominick (45); Keling, Korey (31); Marcon, Dave (8); Montoyo, Norm (28); Morrison, Keith (27); Perez, Beban (33); Pricher, John (49); Purdy, Shawn (5); Ratekin, Mark (21); Rinehart, Dallas (7); Silverio, Vic (19); Szczepanski, Joe (26); Trujillo, Jose (36); Wernig, Pat (13).

RANCHO CUCAMONGA—Baker, Jared (9); Barnes, Jonathan (14); Beckett, Bob (37); Brown, Jeff (38); Cairncross, Cameron (29); Campbell, Mike (2); Clark, Terry (8); Compton, Clint (39); Dale, Ron (8); Davis, Rich (8); Dishman, Glenn (2); Garrelts, Scott (9); Grzelaczyk, Ken (33); Hamilton, Joey (2); Hernandez, Fernando (17); Hoeme, Steve (8); Huber, Jeff (42); Hurst, Bruce (1); Kerr, Jason (6); Loiselle, Rich (14); Martin, Tom (47); Paskievitch, Tom (31); Strong, Joe (7); Waldron, Joe (30); White, Darell (2).

RIVERSIDE—Adam, Dave (27); Borski, Jeff (47); Davis, Tim (18); Evans, Dave (8); Glinatsis, George (14); Gutierrez, Jim (27); King, Kevin (25); Lowe, Derek (27); Mecir, Jim (26); Perkins, Paul (11); Phillips, Tony (25); Rees, Sean (18); Rosenberg, Steve (6); Sullivan, Dan (34); Villone, Ron (16); Wiley, Chuck (31); Youngblood, Todd (26).

SAN BERNARDINO—Conte, Mike (7); Edwards, Todd (7); Grimes, Mike (4); Hovey, Jim (22); Malone, Todd (39); Pedraza, Rodney (24); Perez, Carlos (20); Rose, Scott (28); Shoemaker, Steve (25); Sutch, Ray (52); Sutherland, John (43); Suzuki, Makoto (49); Tajima, Toshio (37); Wilkins, Dean (20).

SAN JOSE—Alvarez, Ivan (10); Black, Harry (1); Crowe, Ron (8); Dour, Brian (18); Heckman, Andy (30); Hicks, Charles (36); Huisman, Rick (4); Hyde, Rich (23); McLeod, Brian (12); Myers, Jeff (5); Peltzer, Kurt (17); Peterson, Mark (37); Richey, Jeff (21); Stonecipher, Eric (26); Vanderweele, Doug (25); Van Landingham, Bill (27); Wanke, Chuck (27); Whitaker, Steve (22); Wilson, Trevor (2).

STOCKTON—Allen, Chad (26); Blair, Don (4); Boze, Marshall (14); Browne, Byron (27); Correa, Ramser (21); Criminger, John (29); Dorn, Chris (22); Duda, Steve (2); Fetty, Pat (32); Gerstein, Ron (36); Hampton, Mark (19); Hancock, Brian (13); Hill, Tyrone (19); McKeon, Brian (27); Murphy, Matt (2); Pruitt, Don (16); Roberson, Sid (24); Steinmetz, Earl (28); Thibault, Ryan (1).

GRAND SLAMS—Clark, Cole, McNair, Molina, Wachter, Wedge, 2 each; Cookson, Hyzdu, Kosco, J. Martin, McKamie, V. Moore, Murray, Pearce, S. Phillips, Samuels, Schmidt, Scott, N. Simmons, M. Skeels, Chris Smith, J. Smith, Snyder, Tavarez, B. Turner, Young, 1 each.

AWARDED FIRST BASE ON CATCHER'S INTERFERENCE—I. Smith 2 (Dodge, Gousha); Wolfe 2 (Freeburg, Hostetler); S. Anderson (Scalzitti); Bream (Snyder); Burnett (Widger); Fairman (Lohry); Furtado (Dodge); Stefanski (Figga); R. Turner (Henderson); Williams (Molina).

PITCHING

TEAM

Team	ERA	G	CG	ShO	Sv.	IP	H	R	ER	HR	HB	BB	Int. BB	SO	WP	Bk.
Stockton	3.98	136	7	10	38	1202.0	1239	659	531	77	77	592	16	781	69	11
Riverside	4.25	137	8	5	42	1207.1	1286	711	570	68	61	491	12	831	68	22
San Jose	4.35	136	7	8	35	1195.1	1212	683	578	85	44	631	12	868	72	13
Modesto	4.47	136	5	7	43	1184.1	1207	666	588	115	43	562	25	897	76	9
Palm Springs	4.53	136	14	5	27	1211.0	1319	717	610	77	51	513	40	803	70	14

Team	ERA	G	CG	ShO	Sv.	IP	H	R	ER	HR	HB	BB	Int. BB	SO	WP	Bk.
Central Valley	4.57	136	6	7	28	1204.0	1200	719	612	94	62	653	7	1063	108	17
Bakersfield	4.60	136	1	5	19	1194.1	1235	766	610	105	43	722	26	912	86	31
High Desert	4.61	137	14	7	28	1198.1	1318	769	614	130	44	469	9	814	65	18
San Bernardino	4.76	136	9	6	31	1208.2	1274	797	639	117	41	629	21	917	92	14
Rancho Cucamonga	5.10	136	4	3	28	1196.0	1336	821	678	91	67	641	16	967	97	25

INDIVIDUAL

(Leading qualifiers for earned-run average leadership— 109 or more innings)

*Throws lefthanded.

Pitcher, Team	W	L	Pct.	ERA	G	GS	CG	GF	ShO	Sv.	IP	H	R	ER	HR	HB	BB	Int. BB	SO	WP
Roberson, Stockton*	12	8	.600	2.60	24	23	6	0	1	0	166.0	157	68	48	8	12	34	0	87	6
Pedraza, San Bernardino	9	7	.563	3.18	24	23	2	0	1	0	141.2	145	74	50	7	3	33	1	95	9
Burke, Central Valley	7	8	.467	3.18	20	20	2	0	0	0	119.0	104	62	42	5	3	64	0	114	8
Keling, Palm Springs	8	8	.500	3.29	31	21	2	1	0	0	158.2	152	69	58	9	3	62	1	131	7
Perez, San Bernardino*	8	7	.533	3.44	20	18	3	0	0	0	131.0	120	57	50	0	0	44	0	98	9
Gutierrez, Riverside	12	9	.571	3.78	27	27	2	0	0	0	171.1	182	95	72	15	4	53	2	84	5
Brock, Modesto	12	4	.750	3.81	27	26	1	0	0	0	139.1	137	69	59	12	5	44	0	121	4
Whitaker, San Jose*	8	10	.444	3.82	22	21	1	1	0	0	127.1	106	70	54	9	5	114	0	94	7
Ratekin, Palm Springs	7	7	.500	3.89	21	21	6	0	1	0	143.1	151	78	62	5	6	46	0	66	5
Vanderweele, San Jose	10	6	.625	3.89	25	24	3	1	0	0	171.0	188	78	74	17	3	55	3	106	8

Departmental leaders: G—Hardwick, 61; W—Morrison, Van Landingham, 14; L—Martinez, 13; Pct.—Berumen, .818; GS—Several pitchers tied with 27; CG—Adamson, Ratekin, Roberson, 6; GF—Pricher, 45; ShO—Adamson, 3; Sv.—Pricher, 26; IP—Butler, 179.1; H—Morrison, 200; R—Person, 115; ER—Van Landingham, 93; HR—Vanderweele, 17; HB—Mecir, 15; BB—Weaver, 118; IBB—D. Johnson, 7; SO—Van Landingham, 171; WP—Beckett, 25.

(All pitchers—listed alphabetically)

Pitcher, Team	W	L	Pct.	ERA	G	GS	CG	GF	ShO	Sv.	IP	H	R	ER	HR	HB	BB	Int. BB	SO	WP
Acevedo, Central Valley	9	8	.529	4.40	27	20	1	3	0	0	118.2	119	68	58	8	9	58	0	107	12
Adam, Riverside	12	8	.600	4.05	27	27	1	0	0	0	169.0	180	91	76	11	10	51	0	98	8
Adamson, High Desert*	5	5	.500	4.58	22	20	6	1	3	0	129.2	160	83	66	13	4	30	0	72	5
Allen, Stockton	1	3	.250	1.78	26	0	0	21	0	8	30.1	39	10	6	0	1	10	0	17	1
Alston, Central Valley	5	9	.357	5.46	25	24	1	0	0	0	117.0	124	81	71	11	8	70	0	90	10
Alvarez, San Jose*	3	4	.429	5.32	10	9	0	0	0	0	44.0	34	28	26	4	1	42	1	32	3
Anderson, Palm Springs	0	0	.000	0.00	1	0	0	1	0	0	1.0	1	1	0	0	1	1	0	1	0
Bailey, Central Valley	4	7	.364	4.84	22	22	1	0	1	0	111.2	139	78	60	9	6	56	1	84	7
Baker, Rancho Cucamonga	1	5	.167	7.29	9	9	0	0	0	0	42.0	57	44	34	2	5	30	0	21	2
Barnes, Rancho Cucamonga	5	5	.500	5.67	14	13	0	0	0	0	79.1	88	60	50	10	3	54	0	59	9
Barns, Modesto	0	0	.000	0.00	1	0	0	0	0	0	1.0	1	0	0	0	0	0	0	0	0
Beckett, Rancho Cucamonga*	2	4	.333	6.02	37	10	0	14	0	4	83.2	75	62	56	7	2	93	1	88	25
Berumen, High Desert	9	2	.818	3.62	14	13	1	0	0	0	92.0	85	45	37	8	7	36	1	74	6
Black, San Jose*	0	0	.000	9.00	1	1	0	0	0	0	1.0	2	1	1	0	1	0	0	2	0
Blair, Stockton	2	2	.500	3.95	4	2	0	0	0	0	13.2	19	8	6	2	0	3	0	4	0
Bochtler, Central Valley	3	1	.750	3.40	8	8	0	0	0	0	47.2	40	23	18	2	1	28	0	43	2
Borski, Riverside	3	4	.429	2.58	47	0	0	28	0	8	76.2	71	39	22	4	3	37	0	46	5
Boze, Stockton	7	2	.778	2.65	14	14	0	0	0	0	88.1	82	36	26	4	7	41	2	54	6
Brock, Modesto	12	4	.750	3.81	27	26	1	0	0	0	139.1	137	69	59	12	5	44	0	121	4
Brosnan, Bakersfield*	4	1	.800	3.47	9	6	0	1	0	0	36.1	36	20	14	2	2	15	0	34	4
Brown, Rancho Cucamonga*	6	6	.500	5.68	38	8	1	10	0	0	95.0	137	75	60	7	7	28	3	63	5
Browne, Stockton	10	5	.667	4.07	27	27	0	0	0	0	143.2	117	73	65	9	11	117	1	110	13
Burcham, Palm Springs	6	5	.545	3.43	21	12	0	3	0	0	94.1	95	43	36	2	1	34	4	68	3
Burke, Central Valley	7	8	.467	3.18	20	20	2	0	0	0	119.0	104	62	42	5	3	64	0	114	8
Burnett, San Bernardino	0	0	.000	36.00	1	0	0	1	0	0	1.0	6	4	4	1	0	0	0	2	0
Butler, Palm Springs*	8	10	.444	4.62	27	27	4	0	1	0	179.1	197	112	92	11	4	61	1	123	5
Cairncross, R. Cucamonga*	10	11	.476	5.12	29	26	0	0	0	0	154.2	182	112	88	10	13	81	1	122	8
Campbell, Rancho Cucamonga	1	0	1.000	1.93	2	0	0	1	0	0	4.2	1	1	1	0	0	4	0	4	0
Case, Central Valley	0	0	.000	0.00	2	0	0	2	0	0	1.1	2	1	0	0	0	1	0	0	0
Castro, Bakersfield	4	7	.364	4.27	20	20	0	0	0	0	86.1	100	47	41	5	4	37	0	54	2
Cervantes, San Bernardino	0	0	.000	0.00	2	0	0	2	0	0	2.2	3	0	0	0	0	2	0	2	0
Chouinard, Modesto	8	10	.444	4.26	24	24	1	0	0	0	145.2	154	75	69	15	4	56	1	82	4
Clark, Rancho Cucamonga	0	2	.000	4.66	8	0	0	2	0	0	9.2	7	5	5	1	0	4	2	7	0
Claus, Palm Springs	0	0	.000	0.00	1	0	0	0	0	0	1.0	1	0	0	0	0	1	0	0	0
Clemens, San Jose	0	0	.000	4.50	2	0	0	2	0	0	2.0	3	1	1	0	1	2	0	2	1
Colson, Bakersfield*	2	4	.333	5.60	39	1	0	12	0	1	54.2	64	37	34	6	2	39	6	37	5
Compton, Rancho Cucamonga	3	3	.500	4.62	39	1	0	8	0	0	74.0	82	50	38	5	6	50	0	59	6
Connolly, Modesto	5	0	1.000	3.60	22	1	0	5	0	0	55.0	45	22	22	3	3	22	1	45	5
Conte, San Bernardino	0	1	.000	12.27	6	0	0	2	0	0	7.1	10	15	10	0	3	12	1	2	0
Correa, Stockton	4	3	.571	4.52	21	10	0	6	0	3	67.2	78	38	34	2	1	30	1	32	2
Corsi, High Desert	0	1	.000	3.00	3	3	0	0	0	0	9.0	11	3	3	1	0	2	0	6	0
Costello, Bakersfield	3	3	.500	6.89	16	7	0	2	0	0	49.2	54	44	38	11	3	35	0	34	6
Criminger, Stockton	5	5	.500	4.47	29	0	0	6	0	0	58.1	61	35	29	3	7	30	2	50	8
Crowe, San Jose	2	0	1.000	1.84	8	0	0	4	0	0	14.2	11	5	3	0	0	5	1	8	0
Dale, Rancho Cucamonga	0	0	.000	10.13	8	0	0	1	0	0	13.1	20	19	15	0	0	13	1	8	3
Darensbourg, High Desert*	0	0	.000	0.00	1	0	0	1	0	0	1.0	1	0	0	0	0	0	0	1	0
Davis, Rancho Cucamonga	0	2	.000	8.00	8	0	0	2	0	1	9.0	13	9	8	2	1	4	0	10	0
Davis, Riverside*	3	0	1.000	1.76	18	0	0	17	0	7	30.2	14	6	6	1	1	9	0	56	1
DeHart, San Bernardino	4	3	.571	3.04	9	9	0	0	0	0	53.1	56	28	18	4	0	25	0	44	0
Dishman, Rancho Cucamonga*	0	1	.000	7.15	2	2	0	0	0	0	11.1	14	9	9	0	1	5	0	6	1
Dobrolsky, Stockton	1	0	1.000	0.00	3	0	0	3	0	0	3.0	2	0	0	0	0	1	0	0	1
Dodge, Palm Springs	0	0	.000	13.50	2	0	0	1	0	0	2.0	3	3	3	1	0	1	0	1	0
Dorn, Stockton	3	2	.600	4.06	22	0	0	9	0	4	37.2	43	21	17	2	1	16	1	31	0
Dour, San Jose	4	1	.800	1.52	18	0	0	15	0	10	29.2	21	5	5	2	0	16	0	16	0
Dressendorfer, Modesto	0	0	.000	3.97	5	5	0	0	0	0	11.1	14	5	5	2	0	15	0	15	0
Duda, Stockton	1	0	1.000	4.50	2	0	0	1	0	0	10.0	10	6	5	1	2	4	0	7	0
Duke, Central Valley*	3	3	.500	3.07	28	0	0	24	0	9	41.0	42	14	14	1	2	12	0	40	4
Edwards, San Bernardino*	0	1	.000	16.20	7	0	0	1	0	0	6.2	13	16	12	2	2	10	0	6	1
Eiffert, Central Valley*	1	4	.200	7.65	13	1	0	5	0	0	20.0	19	20	17	1	3	28	0	12	15
Ericson, Central Valley	0	5	.000	5.78	38	1	0	11	0	0	67.0	90	46	43	6	0	27	2	51	6
Evans, Riverside	3	2	.600	4.54	8	8	1	0	1	0	41.2	41	22	21	5	5	23	0	42	2
Ferguson, 11 P.S.-23 S.B.	3	4	.429	5.23	34	1	0	14	0	2	43.0	39	31	25	0	3	37	2	30	5
Fermin, Modesto	4	6	.400	6.15	31	5	0	8	0	1	67.1	78	56	46	7	5	37	5	47	10
Fetty, Stockton	4	7	.364	4.40	32	0	0	17	0	1	43.0	41	29	21	3	2	26	3	27	2
Garcia, Bakersfield	0	3	.000	6.83	27	0	0	22	0	4	29.0	47	23	22	6	0	12	1	25	3

Pitcher, Team	W	L	Pct.	ERA	G	GS	CG	GF	ShO	Sv.	IP	H	R	ER	HR	HB	BB	Int. BB	SO	WP
Garrelts, Rancho Cucamonga	0	5	.000	5.16	9	8	0	1	0	1	29.2	39	23	17	0	0	17	0	32	3
Gerstein, Stockton*	8	4	.667	5.32	36	7	1	9	0	0	86.1	103	59	51	2	2	63	3	49	7
Glinatsis, Riverside	1	0	1.000	4.54	14	3	0	6	0	2	35.2	40	24	18	1	1	9	0	30	2
Grigsby, Modesto	5	6	.455	4.78	39	0	0	10	0	6	90.1	90	49	48	12	3	42	2	72	9
Grimes, 26 C.V. -4 S.B.	1	3	.250	5.55	30	0	0	9	0	1	58.1	64	40	36	9	5	25	1	56	1
Grzelaczyk, Rancho Cucamonga	12	7	.632	4.30	33	24	1	2	0	1	165.1	180	93	79	13	4	51	1	100	8
Gutierrez, Riverside	12	9	.571	3.78	27	27	2	0	0	0	171.1	182	95	72	15	4	53	2	84	5
Hamilton, Rancho Cucamonga	1	0	1.000	4.09	2	2	0	0	0	0	11.0	11	5	5	0	1	2	0	6	0
Hampton, Stockton	2	1	.667	5.51	19	3	0	2	0	1	47.1	55	36	29	4	2	25	0	21	3
Hancock, Stockton*	2	4	.333	4.69	13	9	0	1	0	0	55.2	57	39	29	10	7	31	0	42	1
Hardwick, Stockton*	6	2	.750	2.90	61	0	0	41	0	14	83.2	95	32	27	4	5	30	0	59	5
Haught, Modesto	0	1	.000	5.09	12	0	0	4	0	0	23.0	25	14	13	3	1	17	2	15	0
Heckman, San Jose*	5	1	.833	2.44	30	0	0	19	0	7	59.0	45	20	16	3	2	23	0	40	2
Herges, Bakersfield	2	6	.250	3.69	51	0	0	17	0	2	90.1	70	49	37	6	10	56	6	84	4
Hernandez, Rancho Cucamonga	7	5	.583	4.15	17	17	1	0	0	0	99.2	90	54	46	8	2	67	0	121	4
Hicks, San Jose	5	4	.556	5.27	36	0	0	20	0	7	68.1	63	48	40	5	5	42	0	48	5
Hill, Stockton*	1	3	.250	4.50	19	17	0	1	0	1	66.0	43	45	33	5	6	60	0	65	7
Hoeme, Rancho Cucamonga	1	0	1.000	6.48	8	0	0	4	0	0	8.1	8	9	6	1	1	5	0	4	0
Hostetler, Stockton	0	0	.000	0.00	1	0	0	1	0	0	1.0	0	0	0	0	0	2	0	2	0
Hovey, 23 C.V.-22 S.B.*	2	7	.222	9.09	45	1	0	14	0	1	69.1	124	92	70	7	6	53	1	44	9
Hubbs, Bakersfield	2	1	.667	1.81	19	1	0	8	0	1	44.2	36	12	9	4	0	15	1	44	3
Huber, Rancho Cucamonga*	4	1	.800	3.14	42	0	0	41	0	18	48.2	43	22	17	4	0	18	0	43	4
Huisman, San Jose	2	1	.667	2.31	4	4	1	0	0	0	23.1	19	6	6	0	2	12	0	15	1
Hurst, Rancho Cucamonga*	0	0	.000	8.31	1	1	0	0	0	0	4.1	4	5	4	0	0	1	0	6	0
Hutchins, Central Valley	1	3	.250	9.15	20	0	0	9	0	1	20.2	14	21	21	4	5	37	0	27	7
Hyde, San Jose	2	0	1.000	4.79	23	1	0	11	0	2	47.0	59	31	25	4	1	14	2	34	3
Iglesias, Bakersfield	1	2	.333	5.59	6	3	0	0	0	0	19.1	26	16	12	2	1	12	0	10	3
Ingram, Modesto	5	7	.417	5.48	32	0	0	24	0	9	42.2	49	30	26	4	2	18	3	39	11
Jacobsen, Bakersfield	1	0	1.000	4.58	6	0	0	3	0	2	19.2	22	16	10	1	0	8	0	23	3
Janicki, Palm Springs	0	0	.000	10.80	1	1	0	0	0	0	1.2	3	2	2	0	0	2	0	2	0
Johnson, Palm Springs	2	4	.333	5.72	45	0	0	12	0	0	50.1	51	34	32	6	3	39	7	47	19
Johnson, Central Valley	3	1	.750	2.45	7	6	0	1	0	0	40.1	31	12	11	4	0	13	0	33	1
Juelsgaard, High Desert	6	5	.545	5.56	17	16	0	1	0	0	79.1	81	57	49	8	1	58	0	58	4
Keling, Palm Springs	8	8	.500	3.29	31	21	2	1	0	0	158.2	152	69	58	9	3	62	1	131	7
Kenady, Bakersfield*	0	4	.000	6.15	8	6	0	1	0	0	26.1	26	27	18	3	1	29	0	17	4
Kendrena, High Desert	6	0	1.000	6.62	40	0	0	25	0	4	66.2	78	50	49	16	4	26	1	63	7
Kerfut, High Desert	3	0	1.000	5.85	28	0	0	5	0	4	67.2	86	60	44	11	3	23	0	35	3
Kerr, Rancho Cucamonga*	0	1	.000	11.57	6	0	0	4	0	0	11.2	17	15	15	4	1	8	0	7	0
King, Riverside*	3	2	.600	1.57	25	0	0	14	0	5	46.0	37	10	8	0	1	20	1	28	1
Kotarski, Central Valley*	6	2	.750	3.87	52	0	0	32	0	11	88.1	87	44	38	9	3	37	3	81	3
Lemon, High Desert	0	1	.000	3.70	5	5	0	0	0	0	24.1	35	17	10	2	0	2	0	17	4
Loiselle, Rancho Cucamonga	5	8	.385	5.77	14	14	1	0	0	0	82.2	109	64	53	5	5	34	1	53	1
Lowe, Riverside	12	9	.571	5.26	27	26	3	1	2	0	154.0	189	104	90	9	2	60	0	80	12
Malone, San Bernardino*	3	9	.250	7.03	38	11	0	8	0	2	88.1	91	76	69	13	2	89	0	75	17
Marcon, Palm Springs*	0	1	.000	5.06	8	0	0	5	0	0	10.2	15	7	6	0	0	4	0	6	0
Martin, Rancho Cucamonga*	1	4	.200	5.61	47	1	0	16	0	0	59.1	72	41	37	4	7	39	2	53	9
Martinez, Bakersfield*	4	13	.235	4.14	30	21	0	2	0	0	145.2	144	95	67	12	5	75	0	108	6
Magill, High Desert	1	0	1.000	6.65	14	0	0	8	0	0	23.0	26	21	17	3	0	23	0	18	2
McCaffery, Palm Springs	0	0	.000	9.00	1	0	0	1	0	0	1.0	1	1	1	0	0	1	0	0	0
McGraw, High Desert*	2	3	.400	3.55	6	6	1	0	0	0	38.0	38	17	15	3	1	7	0	31	1
McKeon, Stockton	4	2	.667	4.80	27	5	0	9	0	2	60.0	69	37	32	8	3	23	1	32	2
McLeod, San Jose	0	2	.000	7.23	12	0	0	3	0	0	18.2	12	16	15	1	6	27	2	14	5
Mecir, Riverside	9	11	.450	4.33	26	26	1	0	0	0	145.1	160	89	70	3	15	58	2	85	4
Mejia, San Jose	1	1	.500	6.35	12	0	0	3	0	0	22.2	30	18	16	4	0	10	0	18	2
Metzinger, Central Valley	0	1	.000	7.24	14	0	0	3	0	0	27.1	31	25	22	5	4	25	0	28	7
Mineer, Central Valley	0	0	.000	6.97	8	0	0	3	0	0	10.1	12	8	8	0	2	13	0	8	4
Miran, Bakersfield*	2	5	.286	3.45	32	7	0	12	0	0	75.2	83	40	29	9	3	27	5	48	3
Montoya, Palm Springs*	1	3	.250	4.81	28	4	0	8	0	0	63.2	83	38	34	0	3	21	5	35	6
Moore, Central Valley	1	0	1.000	0.75	8	0	0	8	0	2	12.0	7	3	1	0	0	9	0	15	1
Morrison, Palm Springs	14	6	.700	4.14	27	27	2	0	1	0	176.0	200	108	81	16	10	55	0	107	7
Motuzas, San Bernardino	0	0	.000	0.00	2	0	0	1	0	0	2.0	4	0	0	0	0	0	0	1	0
Murphy, Stockton*	0	0	.000	1.50	2	2	0	0	0	0	12.0	11	3	2	1	0	2	0	11	0
Myers, San Jose*	3	2	.600	5.17	5	5	0	0	0	0	31.1	38	21	18	4	0	19	0	16	0
Myers, Modesto*	5	1	.833	3.72	44	0	0	18	0	3	58.0	55	30	24	2	3	40	2	43	4
Newlin, High Desert	3	0	1.000	2.86	17	0	0	9	0	3	28.1	30	15	9	3	2	9	1	23	0
Nied, Central Valley	0	1	.000	3.00	1	1	0	0	0	0	3.0	1	1	1	0	0	3	0	3	0
Osuna, Bakersfield	0	2	.000	4.91	14	2	0	11	0	2	18.1	19	10	10	2	0	5	0	20	0
Parisotto, High Desert	6	5	.545	4.03	32	14	1	11	0	3	118.1	137	71	53	10	5	34	1	92	4
Paskievitch, Rancho Cucamonga	3	0	1.000	1.19	31	0	0	10	0	1	45.1	26	9	6	1	4	18	4	45	5
Patterson, High Desert	7	6	.538	5.10	33	1	0	12	0	1	67.0	71	49	38	9	3	44	1	51	3
Pedraza, San Bernardino	9	7	.563	3.18	24	23	2	0	1	0	141.2	145	74	50	7	3	33	1	95	9
Peever, Central Valley	2	4	.333	4.19	16	7	1	6	1	4	66.2	65	31	31	6	1	17	0	69	5
Peltzer, Central Valley	2	3	.400	2.93	17	0	0	9	0	3	27.2	28	16	9	3	0	8	0	20	3
Perez, Palm Springs*	3	3	.500	5.11	33	0	0	7	0	0	49.1	52	36	28	8	4	30	3	27	5
Perez, San Bernardino*	8	7	.533	3.44	20	18	3	0	0	0	131.0	120	57	50	12	0	44	0	98	9
Perkins, Riverside	1	0	1.000	4.80	11	0	0	8	0	0	15.0	18	11	8	1	3	7	1	10	2
Person, High Desert	12	10	.545	4.69	28	26	4	1	1	0	169.0	184	115	88	13	4	48	0	107	9
Peterson, San Jose*	4	1	.800	3.43	37	7	1	19	1	0	81.1	95	36	31	5	2	15	0	45	3
Phillips, Riverside	3	1	.750	1.80	25	0	0	23	0	15	30.0	22	8	6	1	2	4	1	19	0
Pierce, Modesto	1	1	.500	1.87	36	0	0	27	0	14	53.0	41	11	11	2	2	28	1	44	1
Pincavitch, Bakersfield	1	2	.333	1.99	6	5	0	0	0	0	31.2	27	11	7	2	1	25	2	32	6
Pineiro, Central Valley	0	0	.000	0.00	1	0	0	1	0	0	1.0	0	0	0	0	0	0	0	1	0
Plaster, Modesto	4	4	.500	4.70	21	18	0	0	0	0	95.2	89	55	50	11	3	61	1	89	3
Pricher, Palm Springs	3	5	.375	3.17	49	0	0	45	0	26	54.0	41	20	19	3	3	25	4	61	0
Pruitt, Stockton	2	3	.400	5.99	16	12	0	0	0	0	67.2	84	48	45	7	5	21	2	40	5
Purdy, Palm Springs	1	1	.500	3.67	5	3	0	2	0	1	27.0	30	12	11	2	3	5	2	17	1
Ratekin, Palm Springs	7	7	.500	3.89	21	21	6	1	0	0	143.1	151	78	62	5	6	46	0	66	5
Rees, Riverside*	0	1	.000	6.19	18	1	0	3	0	1	32.0	52	27	22	0	1	11	0	27	2
Richey, San Jose	3	1	.750	3.43	21	0	0	16	0	4	29.0	34	13	11	2	1	11	1	30	1
Rinehart, Palm Springs	1	4	.200	11.92	7	6	0	0	0	0	25.2	37	34	34	3	1	16	1	14	5
Roberson, Stockton*	12	8	.600	2.60	24	23	6	0	1	0	166.0	157	68	48	8	12	34	0	87	6
Rose, San Bernardino	9	10	.474	4.26	28	25	1	0	1	0	173.1	184	110	82	16	10	63	6	73	10
Rosenberg, Riverside*	0	0	.000	1.17	6	0	0	1	0	0	7.2	5	1	1	0	0	1	0	13	1
Rossiter, Modesto	8	6	.571	4.34	20	17	2	0	0	0	112.0	120	62	54	14	1	45	0	96	5

Pitcher, Team	W	L	Pct.	ERA	G	GS	CG	GF	ShO	Sv.	IP	H	R	ER	HR	HB	BB	Int. BB	SO	WP
Salcedo, Bakersfield	1	0	1.000	7.27	16	0	0	10	0	0	26.0	35	26	21	4	0	19	0	23	0
Schneider, Central Valley*	8	1	.889	3.11	19	0	0	4	0	0	37.2	30	16	13	3	1	25	0	42	1
Seanez, Central Valley	0	2	.000	9.72	5	1	0	1	0	0	8.1	9	9	9	0	1	11	0	7	1
Shoemaker, San Bernardino	9	6	.600	5.40	24	23	0	1	0	0	126.2	146	92	76	16	3	56	1	116	3
Silverio, Palm Springs	1	6	.143	6.08	19	12	0	1	0	0	66.2	88	50	45	5	3	45	3	28	1
Simpson, Palm Springs	0	0	.000	13.50	2	0	0	2	0	0	2.0	3	3	3	1	0	1	0	2	0
Sinacori, Bakersfield	2	6	.250	5.54	31	3	0	20	0	6	39.0	42	29	24	1	3	37	1	39	2
Skeels, Rancho Cucamonga	0	0	.000	10.80	1	0	0	1	0	0	1.2	3	2	2	0	2	1	0	0	0
Smith, San Bernardino	6	4	.600	4.38	16	15	0	1	0	0	88.1	84	47	43	13	2	45	3	72	2
Smock, Modesto*	0	0	.000	5.11	7	0	0	0	0	0	12.1	7	10	7	2	0	7	1	14	3
Snedeker, Bakersfield	1	5	.167	5.58	13	5	0	2	0	0	40.1	51	31	25	4	0	16	0	20	1
Spencer, High Desert	4	4	.500	4.09	13	13	0	0	0	0	61.2	67	33	28	4	3	18	0	38	1
Stafford, High Desert*	7	4	.636	4.93	27	7	1	8	0	2	80.1	85	55	44	14	2	42	1	45	8
Steinmetz, Stockton	4	1	.800	3.92	28	3	0	2	0	0	59.2	73	36	26	2	3	22	0	41	1
Stonecipher, San Jose	5	7	.417	5.91	26	15	0	5	0	0	115.2	146	94	76	8	5	71	0	69	11
Strebeck, Modesto	1	0	1.000	3.86	11	0	0	10	0	0	14.0	11	6	6	2	0	11	0	12	1
Strong, Rancho Cucamonga	1	0	1.000	2.70	7	0	0	6	0	1	10.0	10	3	3	0	0	2	0	13	2
Sudbury, Modesto	2	6	.250	8.27	42	1	0	21	0	4	69.2	105	74	64	9	8	50	6	39	9
Sullivan, Riverside	2	3	.400	6.99	34	0	0	11	0	1	55.1	72	49	43	3	3	31	2	27	8
Sutch, San Bernardino	1	5	.167	4.64	51	6	0	19	0	6	114.1	123	72	59	10	5	64	2	88	12
Sutherland, San Bernardino	3	7	.300	4.99	43	1	0	24	0	1	70.1	73	46	39	7	0	37	2	59	5
Suzuki, San Bernardino	4	4	.500	3.68	48	1	0	35	0	12	80.2	59	37	33	5	2	56	4	87	12
Szczepanski, Palm Springs*	2	3	.400	4.86	26	0	0	6	0	0	33.1	48	19	18	0	1	14	3	13	3
Tajima, San Bernardino	1	3	.250	5.46	13	3	0	3	0	0	29.2	28	24	18	2	1	17	0	22	1
Thibault, Stockton*	0	0	.000	0.00	1	0	0	1	0	0	1.0	0	0	0	0	0	1	0	0	0
Thomas, Bakersfield	5	9	.357	4.33	38	8	0	7	0	1	97.2	89	51	47	8	4	75	0	82	12
Thompson, Central Valley	3	2	.600	2.20	11	11	0	0	0	0	69.2	46	19	17	3	5	18	0	72	3
Trujillo, Palm Springs	3	6	.333	4.72	36	0	0	16	0	0	34.1	32	19	18	5	3	13	3	30	1
Turner, San Bernardino*	0	0	.000	0.00	1	0	0	1	0	0	1.0	0	0	0	0	0	3	0	0	0
Urso, Palm Springs	0	0	.000	3.00	2	0	0	2	0	0	3.0	2	1	1	0	1	2	0	2	0
Vanderweele, San Jose	10	6	.625	3.89	25	24	3	1	0	0	171.0	188	78	74	17	3	55	3	106	8
Van Landingham, San Jose	14	8	.636	5.12	27	27	1	0	0	0	163.1	167	103	93	7	1	87	0	171	15
Veras, Bakersfield	1	0	1.000	7.43	7	0	0	1	0	0	13.1	13	11	11	1	0	8	2	11	0
Villone, Riverside*	7	4	.636	4.21	16	16	0	0	0	0	83.1	74	47	39	5	4	62	0	82	7
Voisard, Central Valley	3	6	.333	6.12	21	14	0	1	0	0	82.1	72	58	56	6	1	53	0	61	6
Waldron, Rancho Cucamonga*	1	2	.333	5.91	30	0	0	8	0	0	35.0	43	28	23	6	1	11	0	31	0
Wanke, San Jose*	6	7	.462	5.08	27	20	0	4	0	2	131.0	137	91	74	9	9	75	2	98	4
Wasdin, Modesto	0	3	.000	3.86	3	3	0	0	0	0	16.1	17	9	7	0	0	4	0	11	0
Watts, Bakersfield	0	0	.000	6.35	10	0	0	3	0	0	22.2	30	19	16	4	0	9	0	9	1
Weaver, Bakersfield	6	11	.353	4.28	28	27	0	0	0	0	157.2	135	89	75	10	2	118	2	110	16
Wengert, Modesto	3	6	.333	4.73	12	12	0	0	0	0	70.1	75	42	37	8	3	29	0	43	4
Wernig, Palm Springs*	1	1	.500	6.75	13	1	0	4	0	0	21.1	24	17	16	0	1	18	1	15	1
Whitaker, San Jose*	8	10	.444	3.82	22	21	1	0	0	0	127.1	106	70	54	9	5	114	0	94	7
White, Bakersfield	0	0	.000	27.00	1	0	0	0	0	0	1.0	2	3	3	0	0	3	0	2	0
White, Rancho Cucamonga	0	0	.000	1.35	2	0	0	1	0	1	6.2	5	2	1	0	1	1	0	6	2
Whitman, High Desert	8	2	.800	3.73	12	5	0	2	0	0	50.2	49	26	21	3	0	21	0	31	2
Whitten, High Desert*	5	2	.714	2.22	43	0	0	33	0	13	52.2	44	20	13	0	3	30	3	26	3
Wiley, Riverside	3	2	.600	4.61	31	0	0	10	0	2	54.2	65	44	28	5	2	25	3	49	4
Wiley, High Desert	1	2	.333	7.23	11	0	0	7	0	0	18.2	25	15	15	6	2	3	0	13	0
Wilkins, San Bernardino	1	2	.333	7.50	20	0	0	14	0	4	24.0	25	24	20	4	5	23	0	26	1
Wilson, San Jose*	1	0	1.000	0.00	2	2	0	0	0	0	10.0	4	0	0	0	0	3	0	8	0
Wojciechowski, Modesto*	8	2	.800	2.55	14	14	1	0	1	0	84.2	64	29	24	3	0	36	0	52	1
Worrell, Bakersfield	0	0	.000	0.00	2	2	0	0	0	0	2.0	1	0	0	0	0	0	0	5	0
Yaughn, High Desert	0	0	.000	6.86	6	6	0	0	0	0	21.0	25	17	16	3	3	13	0	13	3
Youngblood, Riverside	2	5	.286	6.10	26	3	0	7	0	0	59.0	64	44	40	4	4	30	0	55	4
Zerbe, Bakersfield*	0	10	.000	5.91	14	12	1	1	0	0	67.0	83	60	44	2	2	47	0	41	2

BALKS—Cairncross, Lowe, 9 each; Grzelaczyk, 8; Adamson, 7; Castro, Miran, C. Perez, 6 each; Martinez, 5; Acevedo, Roberson, Silverio, Van Landingham, 4 each; Beckett, Herges, Patterson, Rees, Stonecipher, Villone, C. Wiley, 3 each; Alston, Criminger, Ericson, Garcia, Keling, Kenady, Malone, Metzinger, Pricher, Strebeck, Sutch, Suzuki, Thompson, Vanderweele, Waldron, Wanke, W. Wiley, Zerbe, 2 each; Adam, Alvarez, Bailey, Berumen, Blair, Brock, Burke, Chouinard, Compton, Correa, Dishman, Ferguson, Grigsby, Grimes, Gutierrez, Hampton, Hancock, Hernandez, Hubbs, Hyde, Iglesias, Ingram, Janicki, Juelsgaard, Kotarski, Magill, McCaffery, Mineer, T. Myers, Osuna, Parisotto, B. Perez, Person, Phillips, Pruitt, Ratekin, Smith, Snedeker, Tajima, Trujillo, Watts, Wengert, Whitten, Wojciechowski, Youngblood, 1 each.

COMBINATION SHUTOUTS—Brosnan-Hubbs-Sinacori, Castro-Hubbs-Sinacori, Martinez-Hubbs, Weaver-Costello, Weaver-Hubbs-Jacobson, Bakersfield; Alston-Ericson-Metzinger-Duke, Bailey-Seanez, Johnson-Kotarski, Thompson-Kotarski, Voisard-Kotarski, Central Valley; Berumen-Whitten, Corsi-Person, Parisotto-Kerfut, Whittman-Kerfut, High Desert; Brock-Grigsby, Brock-Pierce, Dressendorfer-Rossiter-Ingram, Grigsby-Plaster-Fermin, Rossiter-Pierce, Wojciechowski-Ingram, Modesto; Keling-Pricher 3, Burcham-Johnson-Keling, Burcham-Trujillo, Palm Springs; Barnes-Strong, Cairncross-Brown-Huber, Grzelaczyk-Huber, Rancho Cucamonga; Adam-Borski-Davis, Gutierrez-Borski, Riverside; De-Hart-Suzuki, Smith-Sutherland, San Bernardino; Alvarez-Heckman, Vanderweele-Peltzer-Dour, Vanderweele-Richey-Peterson, Van Landingham-Heckman, Wanke-Dour, Whitaker-Hyde, Wilson-Crowe, San Jose; Roberson-Hardwick 2, Brown-Gerstein, Correa-Steinmetz-Dorn, Hill-Allen, Hill-McKeon-Hardwick, Hill-Steinmetz-Dorn, McKeon-Hardwick-Steinmetz, Pruitt-Fetty, Stockton.

NO-HIT GAMES—None.

FIELDING

TEAM

Team	Pct.	G	PO	A	E	DP	PB
San Jose	.972	136	3586	1537	146	128	16
Modesto	.967	136	3553	1480	174	138	29
Stockton	.966	136	3606	1616	183	132	14
Palm Springs	.964	136	3633	1595	196	152	19
Central Valley	.963	136	3612	1460	197	100	17
Riverside	.961	137	3622	1551	210	138	27
High Desert	.960	137	3595	1588	215	147	34
Bakersfield	.959	136	3583	1559	220	129	30
Rancho Cucamonga	.958	136	3588	1499	225	143	22
San Bernardino	.956	136	3626	1582	240	122	26

INDIVIDUAL

FIRST BASEMEN

*Throws lefthanded.

Player, Team	Pct.	G	PO	A	TC	DP
Albrecht, San Jose	1.000	2	1	1	2	0
Anderson, Palm Springs	1.000	5	35	3	38	1
Barns, Modesto	.983	23	160	13	176	17
Beard, Modesto	.983	71	599	53	663	59
Bish, Rancho Cucamonga	1.000	10	48	10	58	6
Bonnici, Riverside	.992	27	245	12	259	24
Case, Central Valley	.983	86	665	50	727	44
Clark, High Desert*	.974	15	137	14	155	17
Clemens, San Jose	.989	88	734	53	796	65

Player, Team	Pct.	G	PO	A	E	DP
Dalesandro, Palm Springs	1.000	4	42	5	47	4
Dodge, Palm Springs	.974	27	249	15	271	26
Dotolo, San Jose	.952	4	19	1	21	2
Encarnacion, R. Cucamonga	.948	12	86	6	97	4
Fairman, Stockton*	.984	90	816	44	874	83
Freeburg, San Bernardino	.974	32	273	26	307	28
Furtado, Riverside	.988	11	79	6	86	7
Gieseke, Rancho Cucamonga*	.976	5	40	1	42	3
Gilliam, San Bernardino	.917	1	11	0	12	1
Glenn, Stockton	.981	55	490	25	525	38
Gousha, High Desert	.750	1	3	0	4	1
Hardtke, Rancho Cucamonga	1.000	2	13	1	14	2
Harris, Stockton*	1.000	1	1	0	1	0
King, San Jose	.992	29	229	18	249	27
KIRKPATRICK, Bakersfield	.993	102	882	78	967	84
Kosco, High Desert	.982	23	199	16	219	11
Lee, Rancho Cucamonga	.960	14	115	6	126	19
Lopez, Rancho Cucamonga	1.000	2	9	1	10	1
Lund, Bakersfield	1.000	13	75	5	80	6
Malinoski, High Desert	.900	2	9	0	10	1
McNair, Riverside	.986	104	942	75	031	89
Montgomery, San Jose	.988	32	229	19	251	19
Mowry, Rancho Cucamonga*	.973	9	67	5	74	6
Norton, Modesto	1.000	6	47	2	49	5
Oakland, Central Valley	.975	62	508	44	566	38
Ostermeyer, San Bernardino	1.000	4	6	2	8	1
Pearce, Rancho Cucamonga*	1.000	1	3	0	3	0
Pugh, Rancho Cucamonga*	.986	93	752	44	807	73
Raven, Palm Springs	.982	56	527	34	571	52
Rodarte, Riverside	.500	1	1	0	2	0
Scott, San Bernardino	.984	7	57	3	61	4
Shockey, Modesto*	.986	36	258	19	281	26
Simmons, Palm Springs	.977	14	117	11	131	12
Skeels, High Desert	1.000	1	2	0	2	1
Smith, Riverside	1.000	4	45	1	46	6
Smith, Bakersfield	1.000	1	2	0	2	0
J. Smith, Palm Springs	.974	20	181	9	195	16
Spiezio, Modesto	1.000	3	21	0	21	4
Staton, Rancho Cucamonga	.958	8	63	6	72	11
Stefanski, Stockton	1.000	2	9	1	10	0
Swanson, Palm Springs*	1.000	14	111	18	129	21
Sweeney, Palm Springs*	.952	4	20	0	21	3
Toale, High Desert	.989	101	940	55	006	102
Turner, San Bernardino*	.987	101	895	72	980	72
C. Watts, Bakersfield	.984	26	229	16	249	19
Williams, Bakersfield	.864	5	18	1	22	2
Wolfe, Modesto	1.000	7	53	4	57	9

SECOND BASEMEN

Player, Team	Pct.	G	PO	A	E	DP
Alicea, Central Valley	1.000	1	2	3	5	1
Anderson, Palm Springs	.935	6	13	16	31	4
Anderson, Bakersfield	.960	8	6	18	25	1
Anderson, San Bernardino	.955	107	223	329	578	62
Bates, San Bernardino	1.000	4	10	13	23	2
Benjamin, San Jose	1.000	1	0	2	2	1
Bish, Rancho Cucamonga	.952	11	24	35	62	9
Carmona, Stockton	1.000	3	2	4	6	0
Casper, San Jose	1.000	9	15	30	45	6
Cervantes, San Bernardino	.961	35	67	104	178	24
Claus, Palm Springs	1.000	3	4	6	10	1
Cole, Stockton	.983	52	90	144	238	29
DelaCruz, Central Valley	1.000	1	2	1	3	0
Doran, Stockton	1.000	1	2	0	2	0
Dotolo, San Jose	1.000	2	3	10	13	1
Duncan, San Jose	.800	2	1	3	5	1
Ebel, Bakersfield	.956	14	32	33	68	10
Felix, Modesto	.958	9	26	20	48	4
Freeburg, San Bernardino	.750	2	2	1	4	0
Gonzalez, Central Valley	.932	13	23	32	59	5
Hardtke, Rancho Cucamonga	.967	112	226	309	553	88
Huyler, Stockton	.971	15	29	39	70	6
Kliafas, Bakersfield	1.000	3	9	4	13	0
Lewis, Bakersfield	.960	81	175	236	428	63
Liriano, Central Valley	1.000	1	1	3	4	1
Malinoski, High Desert	.966	60	119	161	290	46
Manahan, Rancho Cucamonga	.952	16	33	47	84	9
Martinez, High Desert	.950	8	17	21	40	4
McCracken, Central Valley	.951	28	52	64	122	12
McKamie, Bakersfield	.929	7	11	15	28	4
Munoz, Palm Springs	.982	48	123	155	283	39
O'Neill, San Jose	1.000	1	1	2	3	1
Otanez, Bakersfield	.500	1	1	1	4	0
Patterson, San Jose	1.000	1	2	2	4	3
Pozo, Riverside	.963	123	249	367	640	89
Renteria, High Desert	1.000	1	1	2	3	1
Riggs, Stockton	.964	87	180	226	421	57
Rios, Bakersfield	.953	29	54	89	150	13
Rodarte, Riverside	.960	19	43	53	100	13
Rogers, Central Valley	.978	97	168	278	456	44
Salvador, Modesto	1.000	2	0	1	1	0
Scott, San Bernardino	1.000	3	4	6	10	1
Smith, San Bernardino	1.000	1	1	0	1	0
Sobolewski, Modesto	.965	128	293	341	657	82

Player, Team	Pct.	G	PO	A	E	DP
Soriano, Modesto	1.000	1	1	3	4	2
Torres, High Desert	.940	80	154	225	403	49
Urso, Palm Springs	.977	84	165	260	435	59
Ward, San Jose	1.000	9	16	19	35	3
Whitford, Stockton	1.000	4	4	7	11	1
WIMMER, San Jose	.992	119	254	343	602	83

THIRD BASEMEN

Player, Team	Pct.	G	PO	A	E	DP
Alicea, Central Valley	1.000	3	0	3	3	0
Anderson, Palm Springs	.920	72	44	140	200	7
Anderson, Bakersfield	1.000	1	0	7	7	0
Anderson, San Bernardino	1.000	1	0	1	1	0
Barns, Modesto	.900	15	12	24	40	3
Bates, San Bernardino	.333	1	0	1	3	0
Beard, Modesto	.750	2	2	1	4	0
Bish, Rancho Cucamonga	.914	22	14	39	58	6
Bonnici, Riverside	.818	3	5	4	11	1
Bruno, Rancho Cucamonga	.874	54	39	107	167	10
Case, Central Valley	1.000	1	1	1	2	1
Cervantes, San Bernardino	.909	20	8	32	44	2
Claus, Palm Springs	.901	28	18	55	81	2
Clayton, Riverside	.922	57	39	127	180	8
Cole, Stockton	.836	17	14	37	61	1
Cooper, San Bernardino	.877	22	15	49	73	3
DelaCruz, Central Valley	1.000	1	3	2	5	0
Diggs, Stockton	1.000	1	2	1	3	0
Dodge, Palm Springs	.500	1	1	0	2	1
Dotolo, San Jose	.936	49	40	92	141	2
Drinkwater, Rancho Cucamonga	.921	33	17	65	89	4
Duncan, San Jose	.931	14	6	21	29	2
Dunn, Bakersfield	.933	4	4	10	15	0
Ebel, Bakersfield	.889	3	1	7	9	1
Ehmann, San Jose	.925	11	12	25	40	1
Felix, Modesto	1.000	5	7	11	18	1
Freeburg, San Bernardino	.853	16	5	24	34	0
Giambi, Modesto	.911	88	49	145	213	10
Gonzalez, Central Valley	.889	11	2	22	27	1
Gruber, Palm Springs	.500	4	0	1	2	0
Hardtke, Rancho Cucamonga	.878	14	9	27	41	2
Huyler, Stockton	.909	11	4	16	22	2
Jenkins, San Jose	.817	20	21	37	71	5
King, San Jose	.919	26	15	42	62	3
Kosco, High Desert	.879	87	53	180	265	16
Lewis, Bakersfield	1.000	1	0	3	3	0
Liriano, Central Valley	1.000	2	3	2	5	1
Livesey, San Bernardino	.600	1	0	3	5	1
Loretta, Stockton	1.000	1	1	1	2	0
Malinoski, High Desert	.916	38	24	85	119	6
Manahan, Rancho Cucamonga	.932	25	18	50	73	12
McKamie, Bakersfield	.826	5	5	14	23	1
Munoz, Palm Springs	1.000	1	0	6	6	0
Norton, Modesto	.857	2	0	6	7	0
O'Neill, San Jose	1.000	1	1	0	1	0
Otanez, Bakersfield	.918	87	54	192	268	20
Renteria, High Desert	.938	20	4	56	64	3
Rodarte, Riverside	.905	15	9	29	42	0
Salvador, Modesto	1.000	5	2	3	5	1
Schmidt, Central Valley	.895	122	73	217	324	12
Scott, San Bernardino	.889	89	48	177	253	16
C. Smith, Palm Springs	.933	40	23	75	105	12
Spiezio, Modesto	.935	27	21	51	77	6
Stefanski, Stockton	.900	15	10	26	40	1
Tejcek, Riverside	.773	4	3	14	22	0
UNROE, Stockton	.936	104	78	244	344	16
Waldenberger, Riverside	.915	63	50	134	201	13
Ward, San Jose	.918	28	14	53	73	5
Williams, Bakersfield	.854	39	24	52	89	5

SHORTSTOPS

Player, Team	Pct.	G	PO	A	E	DP
Albrecht, San Jose	1.000	1	1	0	1	0
Alicea, Central Valley	1.000	2	2	1	3	0
Anderson, Palm Springs	.908	23	41	68	120	24
Anderson, Bakersfield	1.000	2	1	8	9	2
Barns, Modesto	.960	7	3	21	25	4
Bates, San Bernardino	.851	10	13	27	47	7
Benjamin, San Jose	1.000	1	1	3	4	2
Bish, Rancho Cucamonga	1.000	1	2	1	3	1
Bream, Rancho Cucamonga	.928	52	63	130	208	32
Bryant, Riverside	.924	55	79	175	275	32
Burnett, San Bernardino	.936	72	92	186	297	38
Carmona, Stockton	.926	16	21	42	68	9
Cervantes, San Bernardino	.903	32	43	96	154	11
Claus, Palm Springs	1.000	1	2	1	3	0
Cole, Stockton	1.000	8	7	9	16	2
Cooper, San Bernardino	.875	32	49	84	152	21
Counsell, Central Valley	.9436	124	233	353	621	60
Cruz, Modesto	.945	43	90	117	219	21
DelaCruz, Central Valley	1.000	2	2	2	4	0
Dotolo, San Jose	1.000	4	2	2	4	1
Drinkwater, Rancho Cucamonga	.935	93	136	270	434	54
Duncan, San Jose	.917	20	22	55	84	11

Player, Team	Pct.	G	PO	A	E	DP
Ebel, Bakersfield	1.000	1	1	1	2	0
EHMANN, San Jose	.9442	112	176	315	520	62
Felix, Modesto	.948	83	135	249	405	67
Gonzalez, Central Valley	.789	12	10	20	38	3
Hagy, Palm Springs	.938	104	159	322	513	69
Huyler, Stockton	.946	75	104	231	354	45
Jaime, Bakersfield	.865	39	66	114	208	31
Kliafas, Bakersfield	.974	85	135	272	418	49
Liriano, Central Valley	1.000	2	1	4	5	1
Loretta, Stockton	.943	52	74	172	261	32
Malinoski, High Desert	1.000	6	5	11	16	3
Manahan, Rancho Cucamonga	1.000	1	1	0	1	0
Martinez, High Desert	.930	107	195	367	604	85
McKamie, Bakersfield	.963	5	11	15	27	3
Munoz, Palm Springs	.939	17	21	41	66	10
North, High Desert	1.000	2	1	2	3	2
Otanez, Bakersfield	.967	8	11	18	30	2
Renteria, High Desert	.950	30	43	91	141	18
Rodarte, Riverside	.938	28	36	85	129	14
Salvador, Modesto	.750	2	1	2	4	1
Sheets, Riverside	.934	52	80	159	256	42
Soriano, Modesto	.980	9	12	38	51	6
Waldenberger, Riverside	.833	6	8	17	30	3
Whitford, Stockton	.818	3	3	6	11	2
Wimmer, San Jose	1.000	6	6	16	22	1

OUTFIELDERS

Player, Team	Pct.	G	PO	A	E	DP
Albrecht, San Jose	.982	29	54	2	57	0
Alicea, Central Valley	1.000	6	8	0	8	0
Barns, Modesto	1.000	5	3	0	3	0
Bellomo, San Jose*	.982	31	52	2	55	0
Bish, Rancho Cucamonga	1.000	6	5	0	5	0
Boykin, Palm Springs	.979	76	132	6	141	2
Bream, Rancho Cucamonga	1.000	67	139	7	146	2
Buccheri, Modesto	1.000	2	5	0	5	0
Buchanan, San Bernardino	.941	52	87	9	102	1
Case, Central Valley	.966	40	80	5	88	0
Cervantes, San Bernardino	1.000	3	2	0	2	0
Clark, High Desert*	.974	78	141	9	154	2
Claus, Palm Springs	1.000	3	6	0	6	0
Cookson, San Jose	.969	57	90	4	97	0
Cooper, San Bernardino	1.000	6	9	0	9	0
Couture, Stockton	1.000	27	35	4	39	2
Demerson, San Bernardino	.961	107	190	5	203	1
Diggs, Stockton	.959	80	178	9	195	0
Echevarria, Central Valley	.961	90	141	8	155	2
Everett, High Desert	.985	54	124	6	132	2
Filson, Bakersfield	.868	23	31	2	38	1
Frazier, Modesto	.981	75	153	6	162	0
Freeburg, San Bernardino	1.000	8	6	1	7	0
Garcia, Bakersfield*	.940	110	193	12	218	1
Gennaro, Rancho Cucamonga*	.956	127	201	18	229	1
Gilliam, San Bernardino	.951	30	38	1	41	0
Glenn, Stockton	.913	30	39	3	46	0
Gonzalez, Central Valley	1.000	5	3	0	3	0
Griffey, Riverside	.971	55	96	6	105	0
Harris, Stockton*	.977	100	162	7	173	1
Hyzdu, San Jose	.963	39	72	5	80	0
Jones, Central Valley	.974	19	36	2	39	0
Koehler, Riverside*	.923	7	10	2	13	0
Krenke, Central Valley	.944	10	16	1	18	1
Latham, Bakersfield	.923	6	12	0	13	0
List, Central Valley	.935	31	58	0	62	0
Marquez, Riverside*	.958	11	22	1	24	1
Martin, Central Valley	1.000	9	15	0	15	0
Martin, Bakersfield*	.976	98	157	3	164	0
Martinez, San Bernardino	.983	101	222	15	241	1
Maynard, Riverside	.949	32	73	1	78	0
McCaffery, Palm Springs	.966	63	105	8	117	2
McCracken, Central Valley	.941	82	101	11	119	1
McFarlin, San Jose*	.976	96	191	13	209	4
McNair, Riverside	.714	4	5	0	7	0
Moore, High Desert	.973	128	251	4	262	2
Moore, High Desert	.972	96	203	9	218	2
Moore, Rancho Cucamonga*	.933	39	95	3	105	0
Murray, San Jose	.991	85	203	9	214	2
Neill, Modesto*	1.000	16	28	0	28	0
Ortman, Central Valley	1.000	6	11	2	13	1
Pearce, Rancho Cucamonga*	.948	73	119	8	134	1
Perez, Stockton	1.000	10	11	0	11	0
Pezzoni, San Jose	.977	79	123	4	130	0
Phillips, San Bernardino*	.989	44	84	5	90	0
Powell, Rancho Cucamonga	.846	13	11	0	13	0
Ramirez, Modesto	.887	32	53	2	62	0
Raven, Palm Springs	.917	26	30	3	36	0
Reid, San Jose	.909	6	10	0	11	0
Renteria, High Desert	1.000	1	2	0	2	0
Ricker, Central Valley	.960	25	47	1	50	1
Riggs, Stockton	1.000	10	12	1	13	0
RILEY, Palm Springs	.984	129	297	12	314	3
Robbs, Rancho Cucamonga	.944	36	46	5	54	2
Robertson, Riverside	.948	92	139	7	154	2

Player, Team	Pct.	G	PO	A	E	DP
Rodarte, Riverside	1.000	12	22	2	24	1
Romero, Bakersfield	.972	20	33	2	36	0
Ross, Central Valley*	.929	8	13	0	14	0
Salvador, Modesto	1.000	1	1	0	1	0
Samples, Stockton	.980	122	233	9	247	0
Samuels, High Desert	.988	48	75	4	80	1
Scalzitti, Central Valley	1.000	4	0	1	1	0
Shockey, Riverside*	.963	90	171	11	189	1
Simmons, Modesto	1.000	15	32	2	34	0
Simmons, Palm Springs	1.000	1	2	0	2	0
Simpson, Palm Springs	.982	63	104	6	112	1
Smith, Bakersfield	.951	74	131	6	144	0
Smith, Rancho Cucamonga	.970	91	153	6	164	1
Swanson, Palm Springs*	.905	10	17	2	21	1
Sweeney, Palm Springs*	.955	59	125	2	133	0
Tavarez, High Desert	.958	108	194	10	213	0
Tejcek, Riverside	.992	59	120	3	124	1
Turner, Central Valley	.967	98	170	7	183	1
Twitty, San Bernardino	.964	71	129	3	137	1
Unroe, Stockton	.750	6	3	0	4	0
Wachter, Stockton	.978	65	130	6	139	0
Waldenberger, Riverside	1.000	10	15	1	16	0
Walker, Modesto	.960	107	160	6	173	1
Widger, Riverside	1.000	1	2	0	2	0
Wilder, Riverside	.961	57	97	2	103	1
Wolfe, Modesto	.982	78	155	6	164	0
Young, Modesto	.984	84	178	8	189	1

CATCHERS

Player, Team	Pct.	G	PO	A	E	DP	PB
Bonnici, Riverside	.986	55	328	22	355	1	14
Calcagno, San Jose	.987	25	131	25	158	1	7
Cervantes, San Bernardino	1.000	1	1	0	1	0	0
Clemens, San Jose	1.000	6	17	4	21	1	0
Couture, Stockton	1.000	2	1	1	2	1	0
Dalesandro, Palm Springs	.974	40	229	37	273	6	5
Dobrolsky, Stockton	.967	65	303	48	363	4	5
Dodge, Palm Springs	.975	49	280	37	325	2	9
Edmondson, Bakersfield	.974	39	194	29	229	5	6
Figga, San Bernardino	.979	77	491	70	573	8	10
Freeburg, San Bernardino	.952	13	54	5	62	0	5
Furtado, Riverside	.959	15	41	6	49	1	3
Gousha, High Desert	.985	43	239	31	274	3	14
Henderson, R. Cucamonga	.970	55	355	39	406	7	12
Hirsch, Palm Springs	.967	33	213	21	242	4	3
Hostetler, Stockton	.952	10	49	10	62	2	1
Johnson, Modesto	1.000	3	16	1	17	0	0
Lohry, San Bernardino	.990	25	180	13	195	3	3
Lopez, Rancho Cucamonga	.966	35	231	28	268	1	7
Lund, Bakersfield	.981	42	280	27	313	5	8
Luzinski, Bakersfield	.990	41	269	41	313	3	12
Maxwell, Riverside	1.000	2	2	0	2	0	0
Mirabelli, San Jose	.989	113	737	99	845	9	8
Molina, Modesto	.983	118	740	119	874	11	20
Montgomery, San Jose	1.000	1	2	0	2	0	1
Motuzas, San Bernardino	.976	38	218	27	251	1	8
Mulligan, Rancho Cucamonga	.965	44	251	23	284	3	3
Norton, Modesto	.983	25	156	21	180	3	9
Orton, Palm Springs	1.000	2	11	1	12	0	0
Pineiro, Central Valley	.995	23	189	17	207	5	2
Pozo, Central Valley	1.000	1	7	2	9	1	0
Prater, High Desert	1.000	2	20	4	24	1	0
Reed, San Jose	1.000	4	19	2	21	0	0
Scalzitti, Central Valley	.975	66	450	67	530	8	10
Schwenke, Bakersfield	.982	9	49	6	56	0	0
Skeels, Rancho Cucamonga	.987	24	137	13	152	2	0
SKEELS, High Desert	.992	80	449	42	495	3	17
J. Smith, Palm Springs	1.000	5	26	4	30	1	0
Snyder, High Desert	.958	19	121	17	144	0	3
Stefanski, Stockton	.981	80	452	65	527	5	9
Stela, San Bernardino	.949	9	49	7	59	0	0
Strittmatter, Central Valley	.996	57	405	61	468	6	5
Tejero, Palm Springs	.974	7	31	7	39	0	2
Wedge, Central Valley	1.000	4	30	0	30	0	0
Widger, Riverside	.974	80	470	63	547	6	10
Wittig, Bakersfield	.975	22	138	21	163	0	4

PITCHERS

Player, Team	Pct.	G	PO	A	E	DP
Acevedo, Central Valley	.962	27	3	22	26	1
Adam, Riverside	.929	27	14	25	42	2
Adamson, High Desert*	.895	22	10	24	38	2
Allen, Stockton	.909	26	2	8	11	2
Alston, Central Valley	.938	25	8	7	16	0
Alvarez, San Jose*	.875	10	1	6	8	1
Bailey, Central Valley	.960	22	6	18	25	0
Baker, Rancho Cucamonga	.857	9	3	3	7	1
Barnes, Rancho Cucamonga	.643	14	6	3	14	0
Beckett, Rancho Cucamonga*	.929	37	3	10	14	0
Berumen, High Desert	.905	14	7	12	21	1
Blair, Stockton	1.000	4	0	1	1	0
Bochtler, Central Valley	.917	8	2	9	12	0
Borski, Riverside	.882	47	3	12	17	0

Player, Team	Pct.	G	PO	A	E	DP
Boze, Stockton	1.000	14	8	13	21	2
Brock, Modesto	1.000	27	13	22	35	3
Brosnan, Bakersfield*	.900	9	0	9	10	0
Brown, Rancho Cucamonga*	1.000	38	4	14	18	0
Browne, Stockton	.913	27	5	16	23	3
Burcham, Palm Springs	.947	21	3	15	19	2
Burke, Central Valley	.875	20	13	22	40	2
Butler, Palm Springs*	.914	27	6	26	35	1
Cairncross, R. Cucamonga*	.911	29	6	45	56	2
Campbell, Rancho Cucamonga	1.000	2	0	1	1	0
Case, Central Valley	.500	2	1	0	2	0
Castro, Bakersfield	.900	20	6	12	20	0
Chouinard, Modesto	.971	24	8	25	34	0
Clark, Rancho Cucamonga	1.000	8	1	4	5	0
Colson, Bakersfield	1.000	39	3	20	23	0
Compton, Rancho Cucamonga	.900	39	2	7	10	0
Connolly, Modesto	1.000	22	3	8	11	0
Conte, San Bernardino	.667	6	2	0	3	0
Correa, Stockton	.917	21	2	9	12	1
Corsi, High Desert	1.000	3	0	2	2	1
Costello, Bakersfield	.700	16	3	4	10	1
Criminger, Stockton	.923	29	3	9	13	1
Crowe, San Jose	1.000	8	0	4	4	0
Dale, Rancho Cucamonga	1.000	8	1	2	3	1
Davis, Rancho Cucamonga	1.000	8	1	3	4	0
Davis, Riverside*	1.000	18	4	4	8	0
DeHart, San Bernardino	.889	9	2	6	9	0
Dishman, Rancho Cucamonga*	1.000	2	1	2	3	1
Dorn, Stockton	1.000	22	3	6	9	0
Dour, San Jose	1.000	18	2	5	7	0
Dressendorfer, Modesto	.667	5	1	1	3	0
Duda, Stockton	1.000	2	0	1	1	0
Duke, Central Valley*	1.000	28	0	11	11	2
Eiffert, Central Valley*	.833	13	0	5	6	1
Ericson, Central Valley	.933	38	8	6	15	0
Evans, Riverside	1.000	8	4	3	7	0
Ferguson, 12 P.S.-23 S.B.	1.000	35	0	8	8	1
Fermin, Modesto	.750	31	3	6	12	0
Fetty, Stockton	1.000	32	2	4	6	0
Garcia, Bakersfield	.900	27	4	5	10	0
Garrelts, Rancho Cucamonga	.500	9	0	1	2	0
Gerstein, Stockton*	.958	36	7	16	24	2
Glinatsis, Riverside	1.000	14	5	0	5	0
Grigsby, Modesto	.957	39	9	13	23	2
Grimes, 26 C.V.-4 S.B.	1.000	30	4	4	8	0
Grzelaczyk, Rancho Cucamonga	.938	33	7	23	32	4
Gutierrez, Riverside	1.000	27	11	16	27	1
Hamilton, Rancho Cucamonga	1.000	2	0	7	7	0
Hampton, Stockton	1.000	19	0	6	6	1
Hancock, Stockton*	1.000	13	1	11	12	2
Hardwick, Stockton*	.917	61	1	10	12	0
Haught, Modesto	.833	12	2	3	6	0
Heckman, San Jose*	1.000	30	2	5	7	2
Herges, Bakersfield	.917	51	4	7	12	2
Hernandez, Rancho Cucamonga	.950	17	7	12	20	1
Hicks, San Jose	.882	36	6	9	17	0
Hill, Stockton*	.875	19	2	5	8	0
Hoeme, Rancho Cucamonga	1.000	8	0	2	2	0
Hovey, 23 C.V.-22 S.B.*	.941	45	5	11	17	0
Hubbs, Bakersfield	.800	19	3	5	10	0
Huber, Rancho Cucamonga*	.882	42	4	11	17	0
Huisman, San Jose	1.000	4	0	3	3	0
Hurst, Rancho Cucamonga	1.000	1	0	1	1	0
Hutchins, Central Valley	.500	20	1	0	2	0
Hyde, San Jose	.923	23	3	9	13	0
Iglesias, Bakersfield	1.000	6	3	1	4	0
Ingram, Modesto	1.000	32	2	6	8	0
Jacobsen, Bakersfield	1.000	6	0	2	2	0
Johnson, Palm Springs	1.000	45	4	8	12	1
Johnson, Central Valley	1.000	7	2	6	8	3
Juelsgaard, High Desert	.889	17	5	11	18	0
Keling, Palm Springs	.957	31	10	35	47	4
Kenady, Bakersfield*	.500	8	0	1	2	0
Kendrena, High Desert	1.000	40	4	7	11	0
Kerfut, High Desert	1.000	28	4	9	13	0
Kerr, Rancho Cucamonga*	1.000	6	4	1	5	0
King, Riverside*	1.000	25	3	13	16	0
Kotarski, Central Valley*	.864	52	4	15	22	1
Lemon, High Desert	1.000	5	2	6	8	2
Loiselle, Rancho Cucamonga	1.000	14	6	8	14	2
Lowe, Riverside	.941	27	17	31	51	2
Magill, High Desert	1.000	14	0	3	3	0
Malone, San Bernardino*	1.000	38	5	5	10	1
Marcon, Palm Springs*	1.000	8	1	1	2	0
Martin, Rancho Cucamonga*	1.000	47	7	8	15	0
Martinez, Bakersfield*	.844	30	7	20	32	0
McGraw, High Desert	.929	6	0	13	14	1
McKeon, Stockton	1.000	27	7	17	24	2
McLeod, San Jose	.750	12	3	0	4	0
Mecir, Riverside	.939	26	12	19	33	0
Mejia, Modesto	1.000	12	1	3	4	0
Metzinger, Central Valley	1.000	14	1	2	3	0
Miran, Bakersfield*	.960	32	7	17	25	2
Montoya, Palm Springs	1.000	28	5	11	16	3
Moore, Central Valley	.667	8	1	1	3	0
Morrison, Palm Springs	.939	27	17	29	49	0
Murphy, Stockton	1.000	2	1	2	3	0
Myers, San Jose	1.000	5	1	6	7	0
Myers, Modesto*	.760	44	6	13	25	1
Newlin, High Desert	.625	17	0	5	8	1
Osuna, Bakersfield	.889	14	2	6	9	0
Parisotto, High Desert	.882	32	7	8	17	0
Paskievitch, R. Cucamonga	.941	31	1	15	17	1
Patterson, High Desert	.750	33	4	5	12	0
Pedraza, San Bernardino	.917	24	16	28	48	2
Peever, Central Valley	.929	16	7	6	14	0
Peltzer, San Jose*	.909	17	2	8	11	2
Perez, Palm Springs*	.864	33	8	11	22	1
Perez, San Bernardino*	.935	20	4	25	31	1
Perkins, Riverside	.500	11	0	1	2	0
Person, High Desert	.854	28	13	28	48	1
Peterson, San Jose*	1.000	37	4	18	22	2
Phillips, Riverside	1.000	25	5	4	9	1
Pierce, Modesto	.769	36	1	9	13	0
Pincavitch, Bakersfield	.667	6	1	5	9	0
Pineiro, Central Valley	1.000	1	0	1	1	0
Plaster, Modesto	.789	21	6	9	19	0
Pricher, Palm Springs	1.000	49	0	10	10	0
Pruitt, Stockton	1.000	16	3	10	13	1
Purdy, Palm Springs	.900	5	3	6	10	1
Ratekin, Palm Springs	.917	21	10	23	36	1
Rees, Riverside*	.800	18	0	4	5	0
Richey, San Jose	.833	21	1	4	6	1
Rinehart, Palm Springs	1.000	7	2	5	7	0
Roberson, Stockton*	1.000	24	9	28	37	2
ROSE, San Bernardino	1.000	28	23	27	50	3
Rosenberg, Riverside*	1.000	6	1	0	1	0
Rossiter, Modesto	1.000	20	5	11	16	2
Salcedo, Bakersfield	.750	16	0	3	4	1
Schneider, Central Valley*	.900	19	1	8	10	0
Seanez, Central Valley	1.000	5	0	2	2	0
Shoemaker, San Bernardino	.851	25	12	28	47	2
Silverio, Palm Springs	.833	19	6	9	18	0
Sinacori, Bakersfield	.667	31	2	2	6	0
Smith, San Bernardino	.964	16	8	19	28	0
Smock, Modesto*	1.000	7	0	2	2	0
Snedeker, Bakersfield	.941	13	6	10	17	0
Spencer, High Desert	1.000	13	4	9	13	1
Stafford, High Desert*	.867	27	2	11	15	1
Steinmetz, Stockton	.875	28	1	6	8	0
Stonecipher, San Jose	.914	26	7	25	35	3
Strebeck, Modesto	1.000	11	3	1	4	0
Strong, Rancho Cucamonga	1.000	7	0	3	3	0
Sudbury, Modesto	.889	42	8	16	27	4
Sullivan, Riverside	1.000	34	3	10	13	1
Sutch, San Bernardino	.853	51	9	20	34	1
Sutherland, San Bernardino	1.000	43	5	9	14	3
Suzuki, San Bernardino	.833	48	4	6	12	3
Szczepanski, Palm Springs*	.889	26	2	6	9	0
Tajima, San Bernardino	1.000	13	1	4	5	1
Thomas, Bakersfield	.871	38	12	15	31	2
Thompson, Central Valley	.818	11	8	10	22	2
Trujillo, Palm Springs	.833	36	3	2	6	0
Vanderweele, San Jose	.974	25	13	24	38	3
Van Landingham, San Jose	.912	27	11	20	34	1
Veras, Bakersfield	1.000	7	1	0	1	0
Villone, Riverside*	.789	16	5	10	19	1
Voisard, Central Valley	.952	21	9	11	21	1
Waldron, Rancho Cucamonga*	1.000	30	3	1	4	0
Wanke, San Jose*	.878	27	5	31	41	2
Wasdin, Modesto	1.000	3	0	4	4	0
B. Watts, Bakersfield	.938	28	16	29	48	1
Weaver, Bakersfield	1.000	12	7	11	18	2
Wengert, Modesto	1.000	13	0	3	3	0
Wernig, Palm Springs*	1.000	13	0	3	3	0
Whitaker, San Jose*	.933	22	2	26	30	0
White, Rancho Cucamonga	1.000	2	0	2	2	0
Whitman, High Desert	1.000	12	4	11	15	0
Whitten, High Desert*	1.000	43	5	9	14	0
Wiley, Riverside	.813	31	4	9	16	0
Wiley, High Desert	1.000	11	2	1	3	0
Wilkins, San Bernardino	1.000	20	0	3	3	0
Wilson, San Jose*	1.000	2	1	1	2	0
Wojciechowski, Modesto*	.962	14	3	22	26	0
Yaughn, High Desert	1.000	6	0	1	1	0
Youngblood, Riverside	1.000	26	5	5	10	2
Zerbe, Bakersfield*	.875	14	2	19	24	3

The following players did not have any fielding statistics at the positions indicated or appeared only as a designated hitter, pinch-hitter or pinch-runner: Ch. Anderson, p; S. Anderson, ss; Baber, of; Barns, p; Beard, c; Black, p; Bream, 2b; Burnett, p; Casper, 3b; M. Cervantes, dh, ph; R. Cervantes, p; Claus, p; Clemens, p; Darensbourg, p; DelaCruz, of; Dobrolsky, p; Dodge, of; Dotolo, of; Edwards, p; Freehling, dh; Hostetler, p; Jaime, 2b; Janicki, p; Kliafas, 3b; Malone, of; McCaffery, p; Mineer, p; Molina, of; Motuzas, of, p; Munoz, c; Nied, p; Simpson, p; A. Skeels, of, p; Suzuki, of; Thibault, p; Torres, 3b; Triessl, c; B. Turner, of, p; Urso, p; B. White, p; Worrell, p.

LEAGUE CHAMPIONS

Year	Team	Pct.	Year	Team	Pct.	Year	Team	Pct.
1914—	Fresno	.571	1962—	San Jose§	.686	1978—	Visalia§	.698
1915—	Modesto	.857		Reno	.587		Lodi	.607
1916-40—	Did not operate.		1963—	Modesto	.589	1979—	San Jose§	.636
1941—	Fresno	.643		Stockton§	.687		Reno	.525
	S. Barbara (2nd)*	.597	1964—	Fresno	.638	1980—	Stockton§	.638
1942—	Santa Barbara†	.642		Fresno	.600		Visalia	.507
1943-44-45—	Did not operate.		1965—	San Jose	.586	1981—	Visalia	.621
1946—	Stockton‡	.600		Stockton§	.614		Lodi§	.521
1947—	Stockton‡	.679	1966—	Modesto	.577	1982—	Modesto§	.671
1948—	Fresno	.607		Modesto	.671		Visalia	.586
	S. Barbara (3rd)*	.529	1967—	San Jose§	.676	1983—	Visalia	.621
1949—	Bakersfield	.612		Modesto	.586		Redwood§	.529
	San Jose (4th)*	.543	1968—	San Jose	.629	1984—	Modesto§	.597
1950—	Ventura	.607		Fresno§	.623		Bakersfield	.486
	Modesto (2nd)*	.586	1969—	Stockton§	.600	1985—	Fresno§	.575
1951—	Santa Barbara‡	.599		Visalia	.614		Stockton	.566
1952—	Fresno†	.629	1970—	Bakersfield	.667	1986—	Palm Springs	.613
1953—	San Jose‡	.664		Bakersfield	.671		Stockton§	.585
1954—	Modesto†	.623	1971—	Visalia§	.583	1987—	Fresno§	.559
1955—	Stockton	.733		Fresno	.500		Reno	.535
	Fresno§	.718	1972—	Modesto§	.547	1988—	Stockton	.657
1956—	Fresno§	.650		Bakersfield	.629		Riverside§	.599
1957—	Visalia x	.622	1973—	Lodi§	.657	1989—	Stockton	.627
	Salinas (4th)*	.504		Bakersfield	.571		Bakersfield§	.577
1958—	Fresno*	.639	1974—	Fresno§	.607	1990—	Visalia	.638
	Bakersfield	.672		San Jose	.579		Stockton§	.582
1959—	Bakersfield	.592	1975—	Reno	.614	1991—	San Jose	.676
	Modesto§	.643		Reno	.614		High Desert§	.537
1960—	Reno	.614	1976—	Salinas	.650	1992—	Stockton§	.610
	Reno	.657		Reno§	.547		Visalia	.551
1961—	Reno	.743	1977—	Salinas	.564	1993—	High Desert§	.620
	Reno	.643		Lodi§	.579		Modesto	.529

*Won four-club playoff. †League disbanded June 28. ‡Won championship and four-club playoff. §Won split-season playoff. xWon both halves of split season.

CAROLINA LEAGUE

FINAL STANDINGS

FIRST HALF

NORTHERN DIVISION

Team	W	L	T	Pct.	GB
Wilmington (Royals)	44	25	0	.638	......
Frederick (Orioles)	35	35	0	.500	9½
Lynchburg (Red Sox)	32	37	0	.464	12
Prince William (Yankees)	30	40	0	.429	14½

SOUTHERN DIVISION

Team	W	L	T	Pct.	GB
Kinston (Indians)	38	31	0	.551	......
Durham (Braves)	35	34	0	.507	3
Winston-Salem (Reds)	33	37	0	.471	5½
Salem (Pirates)	31	39	0	.443	7½

SECOND HALF

NORTHERN DIVISION

Team	W	L	T	Pct.	GB
Frederick (Orioles)	43	27	0	.614	......
Prince William (Yankees)	37	33	0	.529	6
Lynchburg (Red Sox)	33	37	0	.471	10
Wilmington (Royals)	30	40	0	.429	13

SOUTHERN DIVISION

Team	W	L	T	Pct.	GB
Winston-Salem (Reds)	39	31	0	.557	......
Durham (Braves)	34	35	0	.493	4½
Kinston (Indians)	33	36	0	.478	5½
Salem (Pirates)	30	40	0	.429	9

COMPOSITE

Team	Fre.	Wil.	Kin.	W.S.	Dur.	P.W.	Lyn.	Sal.	W	L	T	Pct.	GB
Frederick (Orioles)	....	12	11	10	8	12	13	12	78	62	0	.557	......
Wilmington (Royals)	8	....	12	12	7	12	9	14	74	65	0	.532	3½
Kinston (Indians)	9	7	....	9	11	13	12	10	71	67	0	.514	6
Winston-Salem (Reds)	10	8	11	....	12	11	11	9	72	68	0	.514	6
Durham (Braves)	12	13	8	8	....	8	11	9	69	69	0	.500	8
Prince William (Yankees)	8	8	7	9	12	....	10	13	67	73	0	.479	11
Lynchburg (Red Sox)	7	11	8	9	8	10	....	12	65	74	0	.468	12½
Salem (Pirates)	8	6	10	11	11	7	8	....	61	79	0	.436	17

Major league affiliations in parentheses.

Playoffs—Wilmington defeated Frederick, two games to none; Winston-Salem defeated Kinston, two games to one; Winston-Salem defeated Wilmington, three games to one, to win league championship.

Regular-season attendance—Durham, 305,692; Frederick, 351,146; Kinston, 134,506; Lynchburg, 100,113; Prince William, 209,273; Salem, 145,657; Wilmington, 332,132; Winston-Salem, 164,509. Total, 1,743,028. Playoffs (9 games)—20,099. All-Star Game—3,581.

Managers—Durham, Leon Roberts; Frederick, Pete Mackanin; Kinston, Dave Keller; Lynchburg, Mark Meleski; Prince William, Trey Hillman; Salem, Scott Little; Wilmington, Ron Johnson; Winston-Salem, Mark Berry.

All-Star team: 1B—Tate Seefried, Prince William; 2B—Tony Graffanino, Durham; 3B—Scott McClain, Frederick; SS—Eric Owens, Winston-Salem; OF—Curtis Goodwin, Frederick; Chad Mottola, Winston-Salem; Alex Ochoa, Frederick; C—Jorge Posada, Prince William; DH—Bubba Smith, Winston-Salem; Starting Pitcher—Julian Tavarez, Kinston; Relief Pitcher—Ian Doyle, Kinston; Most Valuable Player—Bubba Smith, Winston-Salem; Manager of the Year—(tie) Dave Keller, Kinston, and Pete Mackanin, Frederick.

BATTING

TEAM

Team	Avg.	G	AB	R	OR	H	TB	2B	3B	HR	RBI	SH	SF	HP	BB	Int. BB	SO	SB	CS	LOB
Winston-Salem	.273	140	4863	734	700	1329	2074	211	27	160	665	25	36	50	425	11	956	131	68	988
Durham	.265	140	4591	671	628	1218	1836	234	33	106	574	62	29	46	444	21	1060	151	108	860
Wilmington	.258	139	4673	623	558	1207	1754	211	39	86	550	56	46	47	444	15	964	110	79	980
Kinston	.256	138	4574	586	589	1172	1698	209	28	87	503	53	38	47	419	18	949	96	84	915
Lynchburg	.255	139	4684	635	665	1195	1821	246	28	108	567	53	46	52	480	9	1051	46	47	1034
Frederick	.251	140	4545	605	552	1143	1653	211	37	75	527	56	33	64	491	5	854	159	72	956
Prince William	.251	140	4639	633	656	1166	1726	222	37	88	555	36	34	50	478	19	1060	113	81	953
Salem	.251	140	4672	619	758	1171	1832	197	25	138	539	42	32	45	417	12	1028	151	94	862

INDIVIDUAL

(Leading qualifiers for batting championship—378 or more plate appearances)

*Bats lefthanded.   †Switch-hitter.

Player, Team	Avg.	G	AB	R	H	TB	2B	3B	HR	RBI	SH	SF	HP	BB	Int. BB	SO	SB	CS
Colon, Felix, Lynchburg	.320	98	319	52	102	172	22	0	16	58	2	7	1	45	0	65	0	1
Belk, Tim, Winston-Salem	.306	134	509	89	156	227	23	3	14	65	2	2	6	48	3	76	9	7
Smith, Bubba, Winston-Salem	.301	92	342	55	103	200	16	0	27	81	0	4	7	35	1	109	1	0
Marini, Marc, Kinston*	.300	124	440	65	132	189	34	4	5	53	6	9	3	63	4	70	7	6
Therrien, Dominic, Durham*	.300	117	387	53	116	166	26	3	6	55	1	4	0	34	3	49	10	7
Wollenburg, Doug, Durham	.299	113	361	49	108	152	21	4	5	42	13	4	6	27	2	61	6	7
Fleming, Carlton, Prince William†	.299	120	442	72	132	150	14	2	0	25	6	1	0	80	2	23	21	10
Juday, Robert, Lynchburg†	.297	114	354	67	105	134	15	1	4	32	8	3	2	83	2	58	5	5
Maxwell, Pat, Kinston*	.293	103	400	46	117	152	17	3	4	35	3	2	3	22	3	32	6	4
Ladell, Cleveland, Winston-Salem	.284	132	531	90	151	240	15	7	20	66	4	5	3	16	0	95	24	7

Departmental leaders: G—Goodwin, Perna, 138; AB—Goodwin, 555; R—Goodwin, 98; H—Belk, Goodwin, 156; TB—Ladell, 240; 2B—Marini, 34; 3B—Goodwin, 10; HR—C. Smith, 27; RBI—Mottola, 91; SH—Burton, Wollenburg, 13; SF—Marini, Seitzer, Strickland, 9; HP—Hill, 18; BB—Juday, 83; IBB—Seven players tied with 4; SO—Seefried, 150; SB—Goodwin, 61; CS—Cotton, 24.

Player, Team	Avg.	G	AB	R	H	TB	2B	3B	HR	RBI	SH	SF	HP	BB	Int. BB	SO	SB	CS
Alstead, Jason, Frederick*	.228	21	57	6	13	14	1	0	0	1	4	0	0	12	0	8	2	1
Andujar, Juan, Kinston	.253	111	407	42	103	134	12	5	3	31	8	1	2	17	0	92	15	9
Arias, Amador, Winston-Salem†	.263	58	179	25	47	50	3	0	0	12	4	1	0	7	0	28	5	6
Arntzen, Brian, Kinston	.220	20	50	1	11	16	2	0	1	6	1	0	0	4	0	17	3	1
Ashton, Jeff, Winston-Salem	.500	4	2	2	1	1	0	0	0	0	0	0	0	2	0	0	0	0
Ayrault, Joe, Durham	.254	119	390	45	99	138	21	0	6	52	8	3	7	23	0	103	1	4
Azuaje, Jesus, Kinston	.455	3	11	1	5	7	2	0	0	0	0	0	0	2	0	1	0	2
Baez, Diogenes, Lynchburg*	.231	13	26	2	6	7	1	0	0	1	1	0	0	3	0	1	1	1
Bakkum, Scott, Lynchburg	.000	26	2	0	0	0	0	0	0	0	0	0	0	0	0	1	0	0
Belk, Tim, Winston-Salem	.306	134	509	89	156	227	23	3	14	65	2	2	6	48	3	76	9	7
Bess, John, Winston-Salem†	.242	11	33	4	8	14	0	0	2	7	0	0	1	7	0	7	2	1
Bonifay, Ken, Salem*	.277	100	361	59	100	175	19	1	18	60	0	6	4	42	1	63	12	2
Brown, Michael, Salem*	.271	126	436	71	118	212	25	3	21	70	0	7	2	61	4	109	6	4
Brown, Randy, Lynchburg	.236	128	483	57	114	159	25	7	2	45	2	4	13	25	0	127	10	8
Buckley, Troy, Winston-Salem	.265	64	215	19	57	81	10	1	4	29	1	3	0	15	0	31	0	3
Burnett, Roger, Prince William	.189	18	53	3	10	17	1	0	2	7	1	0	1	6	0	7	1	0
Burton, Darren, Wilmington†	.277	134	549	82	152	215	23	5	10	45	13	4	1	48	1	111	30	10
Calder, Joe, Salem	.231	13	39	4	9	14	2	0	1	6	0	1	0	3	1	15	1	0
Caraballo, Gary, Wilmington	.303	39	145	20	44	64	8	3	2	26	0	0	5	20	1	25	3	0
Carey, Tim, Lynchburg*	.220	49	141	9	31	38	7	0	0	11	0	0	0	17	0	45	1	0
Carvajal, Jovino, Prince William†	.265	120	445	52	118	159	20	9	1	42	8	3	1	21	1	69	17	13
Castaldo, Gregg, Frederick	.216	75	208	23	45	53	8	0	0	13	8	2	5	27	0	61	2	3
Charbonnet, Mark, Kinston*	.245	96	319	35	78	122	13	5	7	34	3	1	3	11	0	89	8	8
Coates, Tom, Durham	.267	93	221	31	59	96	10	3	7	24	2	1	1	28	1	63	8	4
Colon, Felix, Lynchburg	.320	98	319	52	102	172	22	0	16	58	2	7	1	45	0	65	0	1
Conger, Jeff, Salem*	.230	110	391	40	90	116	12	1	4	31	7	1	1	31	2	125	24	10
Cooper, Tim, Prince William	.301	58	193	33	58	83	9	2	4	29	2	4	5	30	0	49	2	5
Cotton, John, Kinston*	.264	127	454	81	120	181	16	3	13	51	5	2	11	59	1	130	28	24
Crosby, Mike, Kinston*	.217	72	203	20	44	62	9	0	3	17	4	2	3	7	0	45	1	2
Dando, Pat, Wilmington	.237	82	253	25	60	91	11	1	6	29	1	2	1	13	0	74	1	1
Davis, Glenn, Frederick	.273	3	11	1	3	4	1	0	0	2	0	0	0	1	0	3	0	0
Deller, Bob, Prince William*	.265	53	166	30	44	65	8	2	3	22	1	0	1	19	0	45	6	1
Dempsey, John, Wilmington*	.176	18	34	3	6	8	2	0	0	4	0	0	0	2	0	5	0	0
Devarez, Cesar, Frederick	.290	38	124	15	36	50	8	0	2	16	1	0	1	12	1	18	1	4
Dunbar, Matt, Prince William*	.000	49	1	0	0	0	0	0	0	0	0	0	0	0	0	1	0	0
Eierman, John, Lynchburg*	.273	119	399	56	109	178	20	2	15	62	3	7	1	62	0	97	2	2
Encarnacion, Angelo, Salem	.256	70	238	20	61	84	12	1	3	24	0	1	0	13	1	27	1	4
Epps, Scott, Prince William	.196	34	92	12	18	25	4	0	1	17	0	1	1	9	0	24	0	0
Erickson, Greg, Prince William†	.274	80	288	44	79	96	11	3	0	21	3	0	0	25	0	54	10	5
Espinosa, Ramon, Salem	.269	54	208	30	56	92	8	2	8	25	2	0	1	6	0	36	11	6
Farrell, Jon, Salem	.238	105	386	58	92	163	9	1	20	51	1	0	8	40	0	103	5	4
Flannelly, Tim, Prince William*	.281	73	274	45	77	122	18	3	7	40	1	1	3	42	3	39	7	3
Fleming, Carlton, Prince William†	.299	120	442	72	132	150	14	2	0	25	6	1	0	80	2	23	21	10
Franklin, Micah, Winston-Salem†	.232	20	69	10	16	28	1	1	3	6	1	0	2	10	1	19	0	1
Garvey, Don, Salem	.204	54	152	19	31	46	6	0	3	12	2	0	1	10	0	22	4	6
George, Curtis, Kinston	.214	31	70	11	15	20	5	0	0	2	3	0	1	6	0	17	1	1
Gill, Chris, Winston-Salem	.161	42	93	10	15	21	3	0	1	6	1	0	7	10	0	21	0	4
Gilliam, Bo, Prince William	.250	86	340	37	85	134	13	3	10	55	0	5	2	11	2	84	4	3
Gonzalez, Raul, Wilmington	.269	127	461	59	124	193	30	3	11	55	1	4	4	54	1	58	13	5
Gonzalez, Ricky, Winston-Salem	.276	10	29	5	8	8	0	0	0	0	0	0	0	4	0	7	1	0
Goodwin, Curtis, Frederick*	.281	138	555	98	156	197	15	10	2	42	7	1	1	52	0	90	61	15
Graffanino, Tony, Durham	.275	123	459	78	126	211	30	5	15	69	2	4	4	45	1	78	24	11
Graham, Tim, Lynchburg*	.130	8	23	6	3	4	1	0	0	3	1	0	0	13	0	8	0	2
Gresham, Kris, Frederick	.218	66	188	22	41	68	13	1	4	17	3	0	7	13	0	41	1	0
Guerrero, Mike, Wilmington	.273	44	150	24	41	47	4	1	0	7	7	0	0	32	0	20	4	12
Halter, Shane, Wilmington	.299	54	211	44	63	96	8	5	5	32	12	4	2	27	2	55	5	4
Hammond, Greg, Winston-Salem	.190	46	137	11	26	37	5	0	2	11	2	0	4	9	0	47	1	0
Hanel, Marcus, Salem	.185	69	195	18	36	52	6	2	2	16	9	2	4	18	2	65	5	3
Harrison, Mike, Winston-Salem	.252	72	238	20	60	82	10	0	4	23	0	1	1	15	0	46	2	1
Harvey, Ray, Kinston*	.284	88	335	36	95	127	19	2	3	39	3	1	3	28	1	43	3	6
Hecker, Doug, Lynchburg	.237	127	490	57	116	208	23	3	21	73	0	2	6	36	0	149	0	0
Hill, Lew, Prince William†	.250	116	460	66	115	182	22	3	13	57	3	4	18	29	0	124	12	7
Hinton, Steve, Wilmington*	.247	104	344	43	85	122	11	1	8	42	1	4	1	46	1	79	4	5
Hodge, Roy, Frederick	.205	67	166	17	34	45	9	1	0	12	3	0	1	18	0	29	4	1
Hubbard, Mark, Prince William*	.218	114	376	41	82	109	17	2	2	26	5	1	3	37	3	101	5	11
Jimenez, Manny, Durham	.225	127	427	55	96	138	16	4	6	29	10	1	7	21	0	93	7	9
Johnson, J.J., Lynchburg	.255	25	94	10	24	39	3	0	4	17	2	2	7	0	0	20	1	2
Jones, Motorboat, Durham	.300	90	330	58	99	185	21	4	19	69	0	3	4	30	0	47	8	4
Juday, Rick, Salem	.133	9	30	1	4	6	2	0	0	3	1	0	0	0	0	8	0	1
Juday, Robert, Lynchburg†	.297	114	354	67	105	134	15	1	4	32	8	3	2	83	2	58	5	5
Kelly, Pat, Durham	.281	35	128	27	36	45	6	0	1	12	2	0	2	13	1	19	5	4
Knowles, Eric, Durham	.193	105	353	33	68	96	16	0	4	37	2	2	4	30	0	96	2	5
Ladell, Cleveland, Winston-Salem	.284	132	531	90	151	240	15	7	20	66	4	5	3	16	0	95	24	0
Link, Bryan, Frederick*	.333	6	24	3	8	14	3	0	1	2	0	0	0	3	0	5	0	0
Lohry, Adin, Prince William*	.000	1	2	0	0	0	0	0	0	0	0	0	0	1	0	2	0	0
Mahay, Ron, Lynchburg*	.213	73	254	28	54	79	8	1	5	23	4	1	5	11	1	63	2	5
Malave, Jose, Lynchburg	.301	82	312	42	94	147	27	1	8	54	0	5	3	36	3	54	2	3
Marini, Marc, Kinston*	.300	124	440	65	132	189	34	4	5	53	6	9	3	63	4	70	7	6
Marks, Lance, Durham	.213	113	385	55	82	137	21	2	10	56	5	4	3	40	0	111	6	5
Marshall, Jason, Wilmington	.240	92	279	34	67	87	13	2	1	27	2	2	3	18	0	49	0	2
Martin, Jeff, Lynchburg	.182	62	192	25	35	64	7	2	6	22	4	0	3	23	0	78	0	0
Martinez, Ramon, Wilmington	.253	24	75	8	19	23	4	0	0	9	1	1	1	11	0	9	1	4
Marx, Tim, Salem	.233	13	43	2	10	10	0	0	0	5	1	1	0	7	0	9	1	1
Maxwell, Pat, Kinston*	.293	103	400	46	117	152	17	3	4	35	3	2	3	22	3	32	6	4
McCall, Rod, Kinston*	.208	71	245	32	51	91	13	0	9	33	0	4	3	32	2	85	3	1
McClain, Scott, Frederick	.260	133	427	65	111	164	22	2	9	54	3	2	6	70	0	88	10	6
McConathy, Doug, Frederick*	.217	100	322	25	70	108	13	2	7	41	1	3	3	30	3	37	1	0
McKeel, Walt, Lynchburg	.239	80	247	28	59	95	17	2	5	32	6	3	3	26	0	40	0	1
Meade, Paul, Kinston†	.240	117	404	47	97	143	17	1	9	45	5	3	3	23	2	80	5	5
Mendoza, Francisco, Wilmington	.236	42	123	12	29	43	9	1	1	15	1	0	1	12	0	31	0	1
Mercedes, Feliciano, Frederick†	.228	123	400	45	91	126	17	6	2	35	10	1	0	44	0	91	17	7

Player, Team	Avg.	G	AB	R	H	TB	2B	3B	HR	RBI	SH	SF	HP	BB	Int. BB	SO	SB	CS
Millares, Jose, Frederick	.251	85	299	38	75	113	11	0	9	36	2	2	12	23	0	44	4	4
Mitchell, Tony, Kinston†	.245	96	318	43	78	122	16	2	8	44	2	5	3	33	2	88	5	4
Moore, Vince, Durham*	.292	87	319	53	93	151	14	1	14	64	1	2	6	29	2	93	21	8
Mota, Domingo, Wilmington	.194	14	36	1	7	10	1	1	0	6	2	1	1	2	0	6	0	1
Mottola, Chad, Winston-Salem	.280	137	493	76	138	232	25	3	21	91	0	3	2	62	2	109	13	7
Motuzas, Jeff, Prince William	.208	16	53	5	11	17	4	1	0	3	0	1	0	1	0	20	0	1
Munda, Steve, Prince William	.000	37	1	0	0	0	0	0	0	0	0	0	0	0	0	1	0	0
Neff, Marty, Salem	.227	89	344	39	78	146	12	1	18	50	2	2	2	14	0	87	5	7
Ochoa, Alex, Frederick	.276	137	532	84	147	225	29	5	13	90	1	6	9	46	0	67	34	13
Ortiz, Basilio, Frederick	.282	104	351	72	99	161	18	7	10	60	6	1	7	44	0	65	12	11
Owens, Billy, Frederick†	.350	17	60	8	21	25	4	0	0	8	0	1	0	3	0	8	0	0
Owens, Eric, Winston-Salem	.271	122	487	74	132	195	25	4	10	63	4	7	4	53	0	69	21	12
Ozuna, Mateo, Winston-Salem	.306	93	304	54	93	126	17	2	4	29	1	3	3	26	1	36	32	7
Patrizi, Mike, Kinston	.133	7	15	1	2	3	1	0	0	0	0	0	0	2	0	4	0	1
Perna, Bobby, Winston-Salem†	.265	138	525	89	139	220	27	0	18	70	3	4	3	64	1	116	6	1
Pineda, Jose, Prince William	.143	6	21	5	3	3	0	0	0	3	0	0	0	4	0	9	0	0
Polcovich, Kevin, Salem	.255	94	282	44	72	91	10	3	1	25	6	3	12	49	0	42	13	6
Ponder, Marcus, Salem	.230	39	126	17	29	39	4	0	2	12	1	0	1	8	0	24	10	3
Posada, Jorge, Prince William†	.259	118	410	71	106	188	27	2	17	61	1	6	6	67	4	90	17	5
Pough, Clyde, Kinston	.270	120	418	66	113	172	18	1	13	57	1	4	5	59	2	95	8	3
Pueschner, Craig, Winston-Salem	.182	33	99	14	18	23	0	1	1	6	2	0	2	2	0	34	5	1
Purdy, Alan, Salem	.234	15	47	9	11	15	4	0	0	0	1	0	2	4	0	12	0	0
Ragland, Trace, Salem*	.237	91	278	35	66	106	13	0	9	32	3	2	1	32	1	77	1	3
Ramey, Arthur, Winston-Salem	.071	6	14	0	1	1	0	0	0	0	0	0	0	1	0	7	0	1
Ramirez, Alex, Kinston	.167	3	12	0	2	2	0	0	0	0	1	0	0	0	0	5	0	1
Ramirez, Dan, Frederick	.215	41	130	11	28	32	4	0	0	9	2	2	3	7	0	26	3	3
Robinson, Don, Durham*	.228	117	390	52	89	136	11	3	10	47	5	3	3	45	1	112	15	9
Rodriguez, Steve, Lynchburg	.274	120	493	78	135	176	26	3	3	42	8	3	4	31	0	69	20	13
Ronca, Joe, Salem	.286	92	290	41	83	136	13	2	12	51	0	3	1	26	0	60	5	7
Rose, Pete, Kinston*	.218	74	284	33	62	95	10	1	7	30	6	1	2	25	0	34	1	3
Salcedo, Edwin, Prince William	.163	23	80	8	13	23	4	0	2	6	0	0	2	3	0	22	0	2
Sanchez, Ozzie, Durham*	.243	14	37	8	9	17	2	0	2	5	0	0	2	11	3	8	0	0
Sanford, Chance, Salem*	.255	115	428	54	109	170	21	5	10	37	3	2	1	33	0	80	11	10
Schmidt, David, Lynchburg†	.158	6	19	2	3	9	0	0	2	4	0	0	0	0	0	7	0	0
Scott, George, Lynchburg	.230	80	196	26	45	58	6	2	1	21	5	2	2	18	0	32	1	3
Seefried, Tate, Prince William*	.265	125	464	63	123	219	25	4	21	89	3	6	2	50	4	150	8	3
Seitzer, Brad, Frederick	.253	130	439	44	111	171	24	3	10	68	3	9	5	58	1	95	3	3
Selby, Bill, Lynchburg*	.251	113	394	57	99	144	22	1	7	38	2	7	3	24	2	66	1	2
Smith, Bubba, Winston-Salem	.301	92	342	55	103	200	16	0	27	81	0	4	7	35	1	109	1	0
Smith, Dave, Lynchburg	.308	4	13	1	4	6	0	1	0	2	0	0	0	0	0	1	0	0
Smith, Tom, Wilmington†	.213	92	296	33	63	93	11	2	5	32	0	1	2	27	1	92	5	5
Stewart, Andy, Kinston	.277	110	361	54	100	150	20	3	8	42	0	1	8	26	0	88	7	1
Stewart, Brady, Wilmington	.217	87	258	22	56	62	6	0	0	21	5	1	3	14	0	61	7	3
Strickland, Chad, Wilmington	.249	122	409	51	102	136	16	6	2	46	7	3	3	23	0	46	4	3
Sued, Nick, Kinston	.249	62	189	26	47	60	5	1	2	25	3	3	2	26	1	22	2	3
Sutko, Glenn, Winston-Salem	.000	31	1	0	0	0	0	0	0	0	0	0	0	0	0	0	0	0
Swail, Steve, Durham*	.263	48	133	16	35	44	6	0	1	12	2	0	1	12	0	39	1	3
Swann, Pedro, Durham*	.346	61	182	27	63	93	8	2	6	27	0	1	1	19	0	38	6	12
Tallman, Troy, Frederick	.189	55	143	16	27	43	7	0	3	12	2	2	2	19	0	48	3	0
Therrien, Dominic, Durham*	.300	117	387	53	116	166	26	3	6	55	1	4	0	34	3	49	10	7
Thomas, Keith, Salem	.266	25	94	17	25	45	8	0	4	11	1	0	2	7	0	30	8	1
Tucker, Mike, Wilmington*	.305	61	239	42	73	109	14	2	6	44	0	4	2	34	4	49	12	2
Twitty, Sean, Prince William	.192	36	125	13	24	38	9	1	1	15	0	1	1	13	0	50	1	2
Vasquez, Chris, Winston-Salem*	.262	67	233	29	61	103	10	1	10	31	0	1	1	11	1	52	1	1
Waldrop, Tom, Durham*	.441	11	34	9	15	23	5	0	1	3	1	0	0	4	0	8	0	1
Walker, Hugh, Wilmington*	.258	126	450	66	116	205	20	3	21	71	1	7	10	35	4	106	14	14
Warner, Mike, Durham*	.319	77	263	55	84	125	18	4	5	32	3	3	2	50	3	45	29	12
Waszgis, B.J., Frederick	.248	31	109	12	27	40	4	0	3	9	0	1	2	9	0	30	1	1
Williams, Juan, Durham*	.231	124	403	49	93	146	16	2	11	44	6	1	1	36	4	120	11	12
Wollenburg, Doug, Durham	.299	113	361	49	108	152	21	4	5	42	13	3	6	27	2	61	6	7
Womack, Tony, Salem*	.299	72	304	41	91	114	11	3	2	18	2	1	2	13	0	34	28	14
Zambrano, Jose, Lynchburg	.245	72	233	32	57	104	16	2	9	27	5	0	4	20	1	70	0	2
Zimmerman, Phil, Durham	.208	39	72	9	15	18	3	0	0	1	0	0	7	0	20	1	0	

The following pitchers, listed alphabetically by club, with games in parentheses, had no plate appearances, primarily through use of designated hitters:

DURHAM—Blair, Dirk (44); Boltz, Brian (15); Brock, Chris (12); Burgess, Kurt (48); Chiles, Barry (14); Clontz, Brad (51); Hassinger, Brad (14); Koller, Jerry (27); Leahy, Tom (28); Lomon, Kevin (14); May, Darrell (9); Place, Mike (5); Ramirez, Leo (8); Ryder, Scott (10); Schmidt, Jason (22); Seelbach, Chris (25); Steinmetz, Earl (6); Wade, Terrell (5); Wilder, John (35); Woodall, Brad (6).

FREDERICK—Benavides, Alvaro (25); Benitez, Armando (12); Borowski, Joe (42); Cusey, Lee (16); DuBois, Brian (10); Eshelman, Vaughn (24); Forney, Rick (27); Haynes, Jimmy (27); Klingenbeck, Scott (23); Lemp, Chris (52); Pavelof, Dave (24); Polasek, John (55); Ryan, Kevin (15); Sackinsky, Brian (18); Smith, Mark (31).

KINSTON—Brown, Clarence (31); Crawford, Carlos (28); Doyle, Ian (47); Fleet, Joe (41); Fronio, Jason (32); Hernandez, Fernando (8); Logsdon, Kevin (31); McCarthy, Greg (9); Morgan, Scott (28); Perez, Cesar (10); Ramos, Cesar (2); Rivera, Roberto (19); Ruyak, Todd (18); Shuey, Paul (15); Tavarez, Julian (18); Thobe, John (4); Welch, Dave (46); Williams, Greg (2); Williams, Matt (27).

LYNCHBURG—Bennett, Joel (29); Donovan, Bret (15); Faino, Jeff (40); Gakeler, Dan (30); Glaze, Gettys (27); Henkel, Bob (18); Hudson, Joe (49); Johnston, Dan (20); Maloney, Ryan (18); Miller, Todd (25); Niles, Tom (32); Painter, Gary (15).

PRINCE WILLIAM—Brown, Chuck (2); Carter, Tom (26); Croghan, Andy (39); Frazier, Ron (15); Garagozzo, Keith (11); Gully, Scott (59); Jean, Domingo (1); Karp, Ryan (8); Pettitte, Andy (26); Prybylinski, Bruce (11); Ralph, Curt (32); Seiler, Keith (31); Short, Ben (11); Sullivan, Grant (34); Wiley, Jim (36).

SALEM—Christiansen, Jason (57); DeLosSantos, Mariano (18); Doorneweerd, Dave (15); Evans, Sean (45); Harrah, Doug (24); Jones, Dan (11); Konuszewski, Dennis (39); LaPlante, Michel (11); Lawrence, Sean (4); Loaiza, Esteban (17); Martin, Jim (17); McCurry, Jeff (41); Mesewicz, Mark (48); Mooney, Troy (15); Parkinson, Eric (17); Pisciotta, Marc (20); Ruebel, Matt (19); Rychel, Kevin (53); Teich, Mike (12); Wilson, Gary (15).

WILMINGTON—Baez, Francisco (28); Bevil, Brian (12); Bladow, Dave (30); Bunch, Mel (10); Chrisman, Jim (24); Eddy, Chris (55); Fyhrie, Mike (5); Gross, John (28); Harrison, Brian (26); Hodges, Kevin (3); Huffman, Jason (4); Landress, Roger (20); Lieber, Jonathan (17); Perez, Dario (33); Rea, Shayne (14); Smith, Jeff (51); Toth, Bob (25); Wagner, Hector (13).

WINSTON-SALEM—Angel, Jason (10); Cullop, Glen (39); Dodd, Scott (1); Duff, Scott (7); Garcia, Vic (26); Hrusovsky, John (52); Jarvis, Kevin (21); Kummerfeldt, Jason (5); Loftin, Bill (24); McCann, Joe (32); McClain, Chuck (10); Nix, Jim (11); O'Laughlin, Chuck (3); Quinones, Rene (50); Ruyak, Todd (7); Shaw, Kevin (25); Steph, Rodney (28); Stewart, Carl (14); Tuttle, Dave (15).

GRAND SLAMS—Belk, J. Williams, 2 each; Cotton, Halter, Millares, Mottola, Perna, Posada, Robinson, Rose, C. Smith, Wollenburg, 1 each.

AWARDED FIRST BASE ON CATCHER'S INTERFERENCE—Graffanino 2 (Gresham, McKeel); Charbonnet (Strickland); Hecker (Salcedo); Kelly (Gresham); Ladell (Je. Martin); Marini (McKeel); Salcedo (Buckley); Wollenburg (Posada).

PITCHING

TEAM

Team	ERA	G	CG	ShO	Sv.	IP	H	R	ER	HR	HB	BB	Int. BB	SO	WP	Bk.
Frederick	3.20	140	8	12	45	1218.0	1127	552	433	92	51	448	16	1161	100	16
Wilmington	3.32	139	8	9	43	1225.2	1158	558	452	84	39	353	12	896	72	13
Kinston	3.62	138	11	7	35	1210.0	1080	589	487	91	64	526	0	1097	81	28
Prince William	3.84	140	7	7	34	1213.2	1201	656	518	83	33	427	2	910	85	7
Durham	4.03	138	4	4	36	1220.1	1182	628	546	114	60	465	23	1026	64	15
Lynchburg	4.11	139	18	9	25	1209.2	1297	665	552	109	44	402	29	949	99	11
Winston-Salem	4.18	140	11	7	39	1228.1	1251	700	571	140	45	482	15	906	84	16
Salem	4.43	140	6	2	41	1232.1	1305	758	606	135	65	495	13	977	137	17

INDIVIDUAL

(Leading qualifiers for earned-run average leadership—112 or more innings)

*Throws lefthanded.

Pitcher, Team	W	L	Pct.	ERA	G	GS	CG	GF	ShO	Sv.	IP	H	R	ER	HR	HB	BB	Int. BB	SO	WP
Fronio, Kinston	7	9	.438	2.41	32	20	2	3	0	0	138.1	95	46	37	6	15	66	0	147	11
Tavarez, Kinston	11	5	.688	2.42	18	18	2	0	0	0	119.0	102	48	32	6	7	28	0	107	3
Lieber, Wilmington	9	3	.750	2.67	17	16	2	0	0	0	114.2	125	47	34	4	2	9	1	89	3
Forney, Frederick	14	8	.636	2.78	27	27	2	0	0	0	165.0	156	64	51	11	7	64	0	175	12
Toth, Wilmington	8	7	.533	2.91	25	24	0	1	0	0	151.2	129	57	49	13	3	40	1	129	7
Klingenbeck, Frederick	13	4	.765	2.98	23	23	0	0	0	0	139.0	151	62	46	7	2	35	1	146	5
Haynes, Frederick	12	8	.600	3.03	27	27	0	0	1	0	172.1	139	73	58	13	1	61	1	174	20
Pettitte, Prince William*	11	9	.550	3.04	26	26	2	0	1	0	159.2	146	68	54	7	5	47	0	129	8
Williams, Kinston*	12	12	.500	3.17	27	27	2	0	1	0	153.1	125	65	54	6	8	100	0	134	12
Sackinsky, Frederick	6	8	.429	3.20	18	18	1	0	0	0	123.0	117	55	43	13	2	37	2	112	17

Departmental leaders: G—Gully, 59; W—Forney, 14; L—Bennett, Glaze, M. Williams, 12; Pct.—Klingenbeck, .765; GS—Bennett, 29; CG—Henkel, 7; GF—Hrusovsky, 40; ShO—Bakkum, 4; Sv.—Hrusovsky, 25; IP—Bennett, 181.0; H—Bakkum, 201; R—Steph, 101; ER—Logsdon, 85; HR—Bakkum, McCann, 23; HB—Fronio, 15; BB—M. Williams, 100; IBB—Bennett, Faino, 6; SO—Bennett, 221; WP—Rychel, 27.

(All pitchers—listed alphabetically)

Pitcher, Team	W	L	Pct.	ERA	G	GS	CG	GF	ShO	Sv.	IP	H	R	ER	HR	HB	BB	Int. BB	SO	WP
Angel, Winston-Salem	3	5	.375	6.75	10	10	0	0	0	0	42.2	53	37	32	8	3	25	0	14	5
Baez, Wilmington*	1	2	.333	5.05	28	0	0	11	0	1	35.2	38	22	20	2	0	12	1	29	4
Bakkum, Lynchburg	12	11	.522	3.77	26	26	6	0	4	0	169.2	201	87	71	23	2	31	0	98	7
Benavides, Frederick	1	2	.333	5.17	25	0	0	9	0	0	38.1	42	27	22	4	9	21	3	31	4
Benitez, Frederick	3	0	1.000	0.66	12	0	0	10	0	4	13.2	7	1	1	0	0	4	0	29	1
Bennett, Lynchburg	7	12	.368	3.83	29	29	3	0	1	0	181.0	151	93	77	17	4	67	6	221	18
Bevil, Wilmington	7	1	.875	2.30	12	12	2	0	0	0	74.1	46	21	19	2	4	23	0	61	4
Bladow, Wilmington	3	2	.600	4.83	30	0	0	14	0	1	50.1	45	29	27	3	2	24	1	33	3
Blair, Durham	4	5	.444	3.21	44	0	0	23	0	12	81.1	78	32	29	7	3	17	1	69	3
Boltz, Durham*	3	0	1.000	3.67	15	5	0	5	0	1	41.2	35	21	17	3	0	11	1	27	0
Borowski, Frederick	1	1	.500	3.61	42	2	0	27	0	11	62.1	61	30	25	5	3	37	0	70	8
Brock, Durham	5	2	.714	2.51	12	12	1	0	0	0	79.0	63	28	22	7	5	35	0	67	6
Brown, Prince William	0	0	.000	5.40	2	1	0	0	0	0	6.2	4	4	4	1	2	6	0	4	2
Brown, Prince William	4	3	.571	3.29	31	8	0	7	0	2	82.0	77	40	30	6	7	42	0	62	5
Buckley, Winston-Salem	0	0	.000	0.00	1	0	0	1	0	0	1.0	0	0	0	0	0	1	0	1	0
Bunch, Wilmington	5	3	.625	2.33	10	10	1	0	0	0	65.2	52	22	17	3	1	14	0	54	2
Burgess, Durham*	6	5	.545	4.40	48	0	0	25	0	4	75.2	84	40	37	4	2	20	3	61	5
Carter, Prince William*	8	10	.444	4.39	26	26	1	0	0	0	145.2	160	87	71	11	0	53	0	105	11
Castaldo, Frederick	0	1	.000	3.38	2	0	0	1	0	0	2.2	2	1	1	0	0	2	0	2	0
Chiles, Durham	1	0	1.000	5.03	14	2	0	1	0	0	34.0	31	21	19	5	0	10	1	17	1
Chrisman, Wilmington	3	0	1.000	2.16	24	1	0	7	0	0	41.2	35	11	10	3	2	17	0	33	1
Christiansen, Salem*	1	1	.500	3.15	57	0	0	22	0	4	71.1	48	30	25	5	4	24	2	70	2
Clontz, Durham	1	7	.125	2.75	51	0	0	38	0	10	75.1	69	32	23	5	4	26	1	79	6
Conger, Salem*	0	0	.000	0.00	1	0	0	0	0	0	0.0	0	1	0	0	1	0	0	0	0
Crawford, Kinston	7	9	.438	3.65	28	28	4	0	1	0	165.0	158	87	67	11	10	46	0	124	8
Croghan, Prince William	5	11	.313	4.80	39	14	1	19	0	11	105.0	117	66	56	9	3	27	0	80	6
Cullop, Winston-Salem	6	0	1.000	1.52	39	0	0	11	0	2	65.0	37	12	11	2	3	21	3	48	5
Cusey, Frederick	1	1	.500	3.58	16	1	0	3	0	1	27.2	23	11	11	2	1	9	0	16	1
DeLosSantos, Salem	9	5	.643	3.36	18	18	2	0	1	0	99.0	90	46	37	8	5	41	0	80	8
Dodd, Winston-Salem*	0	0	.000	18.00	1	0	0	1	0	0	1.0	3	2	2	0	0	1	0	1	0
Donovan, Lynchburg	3	10	.231	5.72	31	16	0	7	0	0	107.0	136	82	68	18	6	33	2	63	7
Doorneweerd, Salem	2	8	.200	5.48	15	15	1	0	0	0	70.2	70	54	43	12	3	44	0	47	12
Doyle, Kinston	5	1	.833	3.08	47	0	0	38	0	23	52.2	44	20	18	9	1	29	0	51	6
Dubois, Frederick*	6	2	.750	1.55	10	8	1	0	2	0	58.0	50	19	10	2	0	13	1	55	4
Duff, Winston-Salem*	2	0	1.000	10.57	7	0	0	2	0	0	7.2	20	13	9	1	0	6	0	10	3
Dunbar, Prince William*	6	2	.750	1.73	49	0	0	20	0	4	73.0	50	21	14	0	3	30	1	66	6
Eddy, Wilmington*	2	2	.500	2.83	55	0	0	38	0	14	54.0	39	23	17	4	3	37	1	67	8
Eshelman, Frederick*	7	10	.412	3.89	24	24	0	1	0	0	143.1	128	70	62	10	7	59	0	122	7
Evans, Salem	1	4	.200	5.56	45	3	0	10	0	0	66.1	67	50	41	8	6	33	0	70	11
Faino, Lynchburg*	6	3	.667	3.16	40	8	0	12	0	1	105.1	93	45	37	6	4	47	6	79	4
Fleet, Kinston	2	2	.500	4.34	40	1	0	8	0	0	66.1	61	37	32	7	1	36	0	54	12
Forney, Frederick	14	8	.636	2.78	27	27	2	0	0	0	165.0	156	64	51	11	7	64	0	175	12

— 434 —

Pitcher, Team	W	L	Pct.	ERA	G	GS	CG	GF	ShO	Sv.	IP	H	R	ER	HR	HB	BB	Int. BB	SO	WP
Frazier, Prince William	8	3	.727	2.14	15	15	1	0	0	0	101.0	79	34	24	5	1	23	0	108	4
Fronio, Kinston	7	9	.438	2.41	32	0	2	3	0	0	138.1	95	46	37	6	15	66	0	147	11
Fyhrie, Wilmington	3	2	.600	3.68	5	5	0	0	0	0	29.1	32	15	12	3	0	8	0	19	1
Gakeler, Lynchburg	3	3	.500	1.49	30	0	0	19	0	9	42.1	31	13	7	3	2	11	0	28	2
Garagozzo, Prince William*	5	4	.556	2.59	11	11	0	0	0	0	66.0	44	23	19	3	4	21	0	52	4
García, Winston-Salem	1	0	1.000	3.53	26	0	0	12	0	1	43.1	33	20	17	6	2	19	2	43	1
Garvey, Salem	0	0	.000	0.00	1	0	0	1	0	0	1.0	2	0	0	0	0	0	0	0	0
Glaze, Lynchburg	5	12	.294	3.97	27	25	2	2	0	1	163.1	191	90	72	8	8	49	3	137	12
Gresham, Frederick	0	0	.000	9.00	1	0	0	1	0	0	1.0	2	1	1	0	0	1	0	0	0
Gross, Wilmington	11	10	.524	3.60	28	28	2	0	1	0	175.0	180	91	70	14	9	55	1	100	13
Gully, Prince William	5	6	.455	4.52	59	0	0	20	0	1	87.2	76	56	44	7	2	50	1	72	13
Harrah, Salem	8	5	.615	4.23	24	19	0	1	0	0	115.0	125	61	54	14	6	26	0	85	4
Harrison, Wilmington	13	6	.684	3.28	26	26	1	0	1	0	173.0	168	76	63	16	2	38	0	98	6
Hassinger, Durham	4	1	.800	2.08	14	0	0	4	0	0	30.1	20	12	7	2	4	4	0	25	0
Haynes, Frederick	12	8	.600	3.03	27	27	2	0	1	0	172.1	139	73	58	13	1	61	1	174	20
Henkel, Lynchburg	8	7	.533	4.29	18	18	7	0	2	0	113.1	120	60	54	10	8	27	2	96	15
Hernandez, Kinston	2	3	.400	1.76	8	8	0	0	0	0	51.0	34	15	10	1	2	18	0	53	1
Hodges, Wilmington	1	0	1.000	0.00	3	0	0	1	0	0	4.2	2	0	0	0	1	3	0	1	0
Hrusovsky, Winston-Salem	2	4	.333	3.86	52	0	0	40	0	25	58.1	53	27	25	4	4	27	2	61	6
Hudson, Lynchburg	8	6	.571	4.06	49	1	0	30	0	6	84.1	97	46	38	1	2	38	2	62	10
Huffman, Wilmington	0	0	.000	3.38	4	0	0	0	0	0	5.1	7	6	2	0	0	0	0	1	0
Jarvis, Winston-Salem	8	7	.533	3.41	21	20	2	0	1	0	145.0	133	68	55	13	0	48	2	101	6
Jean, Prince William	0	0	.000	0.00	1	0	0	0	0	0	1.2	1	0	0	0	0	0	0	1	0
Johnston, Lynchburg	0	1	.000	6.33	20	0	0	15	0	3	27.0	37	23	19	2	1	13	3	21	5
Jones, Salem	5	3	.625	3.96	11	11	0	0	0	0	61.1	61	36	27	11	2	21	0	50	8
Jones, Frederick	0	2	.000	9.95	4	2	0	0	0	0	12.2	24	17	14	4	0	1	0	7	0
Karp, Prince William*	3	2	.600	2.20	8	8	1	0	1	0	49.0	35	17	12	4	2	12	0	34	5
Klingenbeck, Frederick	13	4	.765	2.98	23	23	0	0	0	0	139.0	151	62	46	7	2	35	1	146	5
Koller, Durham	8	10	.444	4.57	27	26	1	0	0	0	157.2	168	91	80	20	8	47	1	102	7
Konuszewski, Salem	4	10	.286	4.63	39	13	0	7	0	1	103.0	121	66	53	14	5	43	3	81	6
Kummerfeldt, Winston-Salem	1	1	.500	5.32	5	4	0	0	0	0	23.2	31	16	14	3	2	9	0	21	4
Landress, Wilmington	2	2	.500	3.86	20	0	0	5	0	2	28.0	23	16	12	1	1	11	4	18	1
LaPlante, Salem*	3	2	.600	3.44	11	11	0	0	0	0	65.1	71	35	25	6	0	19	0	44	10
Lawrence, Salem*	1	3	.250	10.20	4	4	0	0	0	0	15.0	25	19	17	1	9	0	14	2
Leahy, Durham	1	7	.125	5.28	28	0	0	16	0	4	44.1	40	30	26	4	6	24	2	36	7
Lemp, Frederick	4	1	.800	3.56	52	0	0	33	0	8	60.2	51	32	24	5	4	35	1	51	5
Lieber, Wilmington	9	3	.750	2.67	17	16	2	0	0	0	114.2	125	47	34	4	2	9	1	89	3
Loaiza, Salem	6	7	.462	3.39	17	17	3	0	0	0	109.0	113	53	41	7	4	30	0	61	8
Loftin, Winston-Salem	3	2	.600	3.41	24	0	0	18	0	3	34.1	30	17	13	2	2	22	2	23	2
Logsdon, Kinston*	6	7	.462	6.14	31	20	1	10	0	3	124.2	146	94	85	11	5	57	0	105	6
Lomon, Durham	4	2	.667	3.71	14	14	1	0	0	0	85.0	80	36	35	6	2	30	1	68	5
Maloney, Lynchburg*	0	0	.000	7.07	18	0	0	12	0	0	28.0	41	25	22	4	1	18	2	13	2
Martin, Salem*	2	0	1.000	6.95	17	0	0	5	0	0	22.0	25	19	17	4	5	12	0	18	0
May, Durham*	5	2	.714	2.09	9	9	0	0	0	0	51.2	44	18	12	4	1	16	0	47	2
McCann, Winston-Salem	11	8	.579	4.67	32	23	0	3	0	1	160.0	185	92	83	23	3	47	1	84	4
McCarthy, Kinston*	0	0	.000	1.69	9	0	0	6	0	2	10.2	8	4	2	0	0	13	0	14	2
McClain, Winston-Salem	2	6	.250	6.38	10	7	0	1	0	0	42.1	46	40	30	6	2	31	0	30	3
McCurry, Salem	1	4	.200	3.89	41	0	0	36	0	22	44.0	41	21	19	3	0	15	3	32	5
Mesewicz, Salem*	4	4	.500	2.76	48	0	0	12	0	1	65.1	57	24	20	7	3	15	0	75	4
Miller, Lynchburg	4	0	1.000	3.38	25	0	0	8	0	0	50.2	54	22	19	1	1	17	1	23	4
Mooney, Salem	0	2	.000	6.29	15	2	0	3	0	1	34.1	47	30	24	6	3	19	0	13	6
Morgan, Kinston	2	3	.400	4.10	28	0	0	14	0	3	41.2	28	19	19	5	2	15	0	54	4
Munda, Prince William	1	1	.500	3.68	37	0	0	15	0	0	66.0	69	36	27	7	3	33	0	48	8
Niles, Lynchburg	7	7	.500	5.07	32	15	0	6	0	0	108.1	121	68	61	15	4	53	1	82	12
Nix, Winston-Salem	3	3	.500	3.57	11	4	0	3	0	0	35.1	37	24	14	8	0	15	0	33	2
O'Laughlin, Winston-Salem*	0	1	.000	6.75	3	1	0	0	0	0	9.1	17	9	7	1	1	5	0	8	2
Painter, Lynchburg	2	2	.500	2.15	15	1	0	10	0	5	29.1	24	8	7	1	1	8	1	26	1
Parkinson, Salem	2	8	.200	5.85	17	9	0	2	0	0	67.2	96	52	44	4	3	25	0	43	9
Paveloff, Frederick	2	1	.667	0.73	24	0	0	22	0	15	24.2	16	4	2	2	2	8	1	28	1
Perez, Kinston	0	0	.000	2.70	10	0	0	3	0	0	13.1	7	4	4	0	0	7	0	20	0
Perez, Wilmington	3	9	.250	4.06	33	3	0	13	0	1	68.2	77	41	31	8	4	14	0	56	4
Pettitte, Prince William*	11	9	.550	3.04	26	26	2	0	1	0	159.2	146	68	54	7	5	47	0	129	8
Pisciotta, Salem	0	0	.000	2.95	20	0	0	18	0	12	18.1	23	13	6	0	0	13	0	13	2
Place, Durham	1	2	.333	3.13	5	5	0	0	0	0	31.2	30	15	11	3	0	9	3	26	1
Polasek, Frederick*	3	4	.429	3.36	55	0	0	14	0	5	59.0	39	24	22	3	5	31	2	56	7
Prybylinski, Prince William	4	3	.571	4.71	11	11	0	0	0	0	65.0	74	42	34	6	0	13	0	40	0
Quinones, Winston-Salem*	3	1	.750	3.95	50	0	0	10	0	1	70.2	76	41	31	6	3	21	2	65	2
Ralph, Prince William	3	3	.500	5.11	32	0	0	30	0	15	37.0	39	23	21	2	1	11	0	41	2
Ramirez, Durham	0	1	.000	6.75	8	0	0	1	0	0	10.2	13	10	8	0	2	10	2	10	1
Ramos, Kinston	0	0	.000	27.00	2	0	0	0	0	0	2.0	6	7	6	2	0	2	0	1	1
Rea, Wilmington	0	2	.000	6.64	11	1	0	2	0	0	20.1	23	18	15	0	0	13	0	11	5
Rivera, Kinston*	2	3	.400	6.17	19	1	0	9	0	0	35.0	44	26	24	4	1	4	0	32	0
Ronca, Salem	0	0	.000	9.00	1	0	0	1	0	0	1.0	1	1	1	0	2	2	0	0	0
Ruebel, Salem*	1	4	.200	5.94	19	1	0	4	0	0	33.1	34	31	22	6	3	32	3	29	8
Ruyak, 7 W.S.-18 Kin.*	1	1	.500	4.65	25	0	0	15	0	5	31.0	30	17	16	4	3	11	0	20	0
Ryan, Frederick	0	3	.000	2.43	15	2	0	4	0	1	33.1	28	11	9	3	2	9	0	23	3
Rychel, Salem	5	4	.556	3.95	53	2	0	11	0	0	73.0	68	41	32	3	10	44	2	86	27
Ryder, Salem	0	0	.000	5.48	10	0	0	3	0	1	23.0	23	14	14	3	2	15	0	26	0
Sackinsky, Frederick	6	8	.429	3.20	18	18	1	0	0	0	121.0	117	55	43	13	2	37	2	112	17
Schmidt, Lynchburg	7	11	.389	4.94	22	22	0	0	0	0	116.2	128	69	64	12	8	47	3	110	4
Seelbach, Durham	9	9	.500	4.93	25	25	0	0	0	0	131.1	133	85	72	15	7	74	1	112	10
Seiler, Prince William*	3	3	.500	3.92	31	0	0	16	0	1	43.2	47	26	19	2	1	9	0	21	2
Shaw, Winston-Salem	2	3	.400	4.30	25	0	0	11	0	3	46.0	46	24	22	6	2	18	1	34	4
Short, Prince William	0	0	.000	3.79	11	0	0	2	0	0	19.0	23	10	8	2	1	9	0	20	0
Shuey, Kinston	1	0	1.000	4.84	15	0	0	7	0	0	22.1	29	12	12	1	1	8	0	27	4
Smith, Wilmington	2	7	.222	3.94	51	0	0	39	0	24	64.0	66	33	28	4	4	25	2	60	6
Smith, Frederick	5	6	.455	3.84	31	6	0	6	0	0	82.0	87	48	35	8	5	21	4	64	5
Steinmetz, Durham	0	0	.000	12.27	6	0	0	3	0	0	11.0	21	15	15	4	1	10	0	12	0
Steph, Winston-Salem	7	11	.389	3.92	28	28	4	0	2	0	167.2	166	101	73	21	8	57	0	130	14
Stewart, Winston-Salem	5	2	.714	3.24	14	14	1	0	0	0	80.2	65	38	29	9	5	35	0	69	5
Sued, Kinston	0	0	.000	0.00	1	0	0	1	0	0	1.0	1	0	0	0	0	1	0	1	0
Sullivan, Prince William*	3	8	.273	5.89	34	15	0	4	0	1	96.1	122	74	63	8	3	44	0	35	9
Sutko, Winston-Salem	5	7	.417	4.30	28	14	2	7	0	0	98.1	112	54	47	11	3	33	0	68	10
Tallman, Frederick	0	0	.000	0.00	2	0	0	2	0	0	1.1	0	0	0	0	0	2	0	0	0

Pitcher, Team	W	L	Pct.	ERA	G	GS	CG	GF	ShO	Sv.	IP	H	R	ER	HR	HB	BB	Int. BB	SO	WP
Tavarez, Kinston	11	5	.688	2.42	18	18	2	0	0	0	119.0	102	48	32	6	7	28	0	107	3
Teich, Salem*	1	0	1.000	3.50	12	0	0	1	0	0	18.0	18	17	7	0	0	3	0	12	0
Thobe, Kinston	1	2	.333	3.13	4	0	0	0	0	0	23.0	26	11	8	1	1	9	0	11	1
Toth, Wilmington	8	7	.533	2.91	25	24	0	1	0	0	151.2	129	57	49	13	3	40	1	129	7
Tuttle, Winston-Salem	7	7	.500	5.53	15	15	2	0	1	0	86.1	98	61	53	8	1	39	0	58	6
Vasquez, Winston-Salem	0	0	.000	0.00	2	0	0	2	0	0	1.1	1	0	0	0	0	1	0	0	0
Wade, Durham*	2	1	.667	3.27	5	5	0	0	0	0	33.0	26	13	12	3	1	18	0	47	0
Wagner, Wilmington	1	7	.125	3.38	13	13	0	0	0	0	69.1	71	30	26	4	1	10	0	37	4
Welch, Kinston*	9	6	.600	3.47	46	2	0	13	0	0	83.0	62	38	32	12	1	34	0	83	4
Wilder, Durham	5	3	.625	3.86	35	8	0	15	0	3	77.0	75	36	33	5	2	36	2	58	2
Wiley, Prince William	2	8	.200	4.73	36	12	0	7	0	1	91.1	114	69	48	9	2	39	0	54	5
Williams, Kinston*	0	1	.000	9.00	2	1	0	0	0	0	3.0	6	3	3	1	0	1	0	2	1
Williams, Kinston*	12	12	.500	3.17	27	27	2	0	1	0	153.1	125	65	54	6	8	100	0	134	12
Wilson, Salem	5	5	.500	5.74	15	15	0	0	0	0	78.1	102	58	50	15	2	25	0	54	3
Woodall, Durham	3	1	.750	3.00	6	5	1	0	1	0	30.0	21	10	10	2	2	6	1	27	4

BALKS—M. Williams, 6; DeLosSantos, 5; Bladow, Crawford, Haynes, Konuszewski, Morgan, Ruyak, 4 each; Harrah, Kummerfeldt, Lomon, Sutko, Welch, Wilder, 3 each; Baez, Bakkum, Duff, Forney, Fronio, Hudson, Jarvis, Klingenbeck, Koller, Lemp, Loftin, Logsdon, Niles, Ruebel, 2 each; Blair, Burgess, Carter, Castaldo, Chiles, Cullop, Donovan, Doorneweerd, Eddy, Eshelman, Faino, Fleet, Frazier, Gakeler, Garagozzo, Glaze, Gross, Harrison, Johnston, S. Jones, Karp, LaPlante, Leiber, May, McClain, Parkinson, C. Perez, D. Perez, Pettitte, Place, Polasek, Quinones, Sackinsky, Schmidt, Short, Shuey, J. Smith, M. Smith, Tavarez, Toth, Wade, Wiley, 1 each.

COMBINATION SHUTOUTS—Seelbach-Blair, Seelbach-Blair-Burgess-Clontz, Wilder-Ryder-Leahy, Durham; Forney-Polasek 2, Forney-Benitez, Forney-Lemp-Polasek, Forney-Polasek-Borowski, Haynes-Paveloff, Haynes-Ryan-Borowski, Klingenbeck-Polasek, Smith-Polasek, Frederick; Bennett-Gakeler, Fronio-Logsdon, Hernandez-Doyle, Tavarez-Morgan-Perez, Williams-Doyle, Williams-Welch-Doyle, Kinston; Glaze-Gakeler, Lynchburg; Carter-Dunbar-Ralph, Frazier-Dunbar-Ralph, Frazier-Seiler, Garagozzo-Gully, Wiley-Gully-Croghan, Prince William; Jones-Rychel-Mesewicz-Konuszewski-Pisciotta, Salem; Bevil-Perez, Bunch-Smith, Harrison-Eddy, Harrison-Eddy-Smith, Lieber-Landress-Baez-Eddy, Perez-Landress-Eddy, Wagner-Perez, Wilmington; Steph-Nix-Hrusovsky, Sutko-Cullop, Sutko-Quinones, Winston-Salem.

NO-HIT GAMES—None.

FIELDING

TEAM

Team	Pct.	G	PO	A	E	DP	PB
Lynchburg	.970	139	3629	1478	160	155	19
Durham	.969	138	3661	1398	164	101	22
Kinston	.965	138	3630	1513	188	124	21
Frederick	.962	140	3654	1349	195	90	35
Wilmington	.961	139	3677	1471	207	129	19
Winston-Salem	.959	140	3685	1491	220	108	34
Prince William	.957	140	3641	1633	235	107	46
Salem	.957	140	3697	1576	238	107	10

Triple plays—Durham, Salem.

INDIVIDUAL

FIRST BASEMEN

*Throws lefthanded.

Player, Team	Pct.	G	PO	A	E	DP
Belk, Winston-Salem	.986	122	1052	117	17	83
Bess, Winston-Salem	1.000	1	1	0	0	0
Bonifay, Salem	1.000	19	176	17	0	6
BROWN, Salem*	.989	115	1082	73	13	78
Buckley, Winston-Salem	1.000	5	34	7	0	3
Calder, Salem	.958	5	45	1	2	2
Carey, Lynchburg	1.000	5	23	0	0	3
Charbonnet, Kinston*	1.000	1	6	0	0	0
Colon, Lynchburg	.992	29	227	16	2	23
Dando, Wilmington*	.980	19	139	9	3	19
Davis, Frederick	1.000	2	13	2	0	1
Deller, Prince William	1.000	1	3	0	0	2
Epps, Prince William	.941	3	27	5	2	1
Erickson, Prince William	.750	1	3	0	1	0
Garvey, Salem	.968	4	30	0	1	2
Gresham, Frederick	1.000	5	16	3	0	3
Harrison, Winston-Salem	.941	3	16	0	1	0
Harvey, Kinston*	.980	21	186	10	4	19
Hecker, Lynchburg	.987	110	919	70	13	112
Hinton, Wilmington*	.975	81	651	54	18	49
Hubbard, Prince William*	.964	19	176	9	7	14
Marks, Durham	.982	98	784	50	15	56
McCall, Kinston*	.988	50	396	30	5	43
McClain, Frederick	.800	1	3	1	1	0
McConathy, Frederick	.978	32	257	12	6	16
Mendoza, Wilmington	1.000	1	4	0	0	0
Millares, Frederick	1.000	3	16	4	0	1
Owens, Frederick	1.000	12	103	4	0	5
Pough, Kinston	.993	72	614	71	5	47
Ramey, Winston-Salem	1.000	1	2	0	0	0
Robinson, Durham	1.000	4	31	5	0	3
Ronca, Salem	1.000	1	9	0	0	0
Sanchez, Durham*	.970	4	31	1	1	1
Seefried, Prince William	.987	119	1127	91	16	85
Seitzer, Frederick	.981	99	762	62	16	54
Selby, Lynchburg	1.000	2	9	1	0	1
Smith, Winston-Salem	.980	17	136	9	3	13
A. Stewart, Wilmington	.987	49	435	21	6	38
Swail, Durham	1.000	3	6	1	0	1
Swann, Durham	.931	5	23	4	2	1
Wollenburg, Durham	.973	39	276	14	8	24

Triple plays—Brown, Marks.

SECOND BASEMEN

Player, Team	Pct.	G	PO	A	E	DP
Arias, Winston-Salem	.946	50	57	134	11	24
Ashton, Winston-Salem	1.000	2	2	2	0	0
Azuaje, Kinston	1.000	3	5	8	0	0
Castaldo, Frederick	.946	56	95	116	12	22
Colon, Lynchburg	1.000	2	0	2	0	1
Cotton, Kinston	1.000	4	7	5	0	3
Erickson, Prince William	.957	26	56	56	5	19
Fleming, Prince William	.962	116	231	299	21	55
Garvey, Salem	.984	14	25	38	1	11
Gill, Winston-Salem	.932	28	31	51	6	8
Gonzalez, Winston-Salem	1.000	4	3	4	0	0
GRAFFANINO, Durham	.968	103	186	263	15	43
Juday, Winston-Salem	.958	19	33	36	3	12
Kelly, Durham	.969	10	10	21	1	1
Marshall, Wilmington	.938	10	14	16	2	5
Martinez, Wilmington	.976	24	52	70	3	19
Maxwell, Kinston	.962	102	208	270	19	60
Meade, Kinston	.978	36	84	93	4	26
Millares, Frederick	.965	73	130	171	11	38
Mota, Wilmington	.930	12	22	31	4	7
Ozuna, Winston-Salem	.924	81	108	183	24	18
Polcovich, Salem	.975	15	34	44	2	7
Purdy, Salem	.955	6	12	9	1	0
Ramirez, Frederick	.944	19	27	40	4	2
Rodriguez, Lynchburg	.964	119	236	348	22	86
Sanford, Lynchburg	.931	108	172	284	34	48
Schmidt, Lynchburg	1.000	2	0	7	0	1
Scott, Lynchburg	1.000	1	1	0	0	0
Smith, Lynchburg	.944	4	9	8	1	4
B. Stewart, Wilmington	.945	44	64	107	10	19
Tucker, Wilmington	.965	61	120	157	10	33
Wollenburg, Durham	.959	35	47	70	5	19
Zimmerman, Durham	.952	5	7	13	1	3

Triple play—Graffanino.

THIRD BASEMEN

Player, Team	Pct.	G	PO	A	E	DP
Bonifay, Salem	.930	67	49	138	14	17
Buckley, Winston-Salem	.875	6	5	9	2	0
Burnett, Prince William	.867	5	2	11	2	1
Caraballo, Wilmington	.882	38	36	61	13	9
Castaldo, Frederick	1.000	1	1	0	0	0
Colon, Lynchburg	1.000	3	2	4	0	0
Cooper, Prince William	.883	50	32	127	21	11
Dempsey, Wilmington	.800	6	3	9	3	3
Epps, Prince William	.936	17	10	34	3	3
Erickson, Prince William	.907	14	11	28	4	3
Flannelly, Prince William	.903	59	47	148	21	12
Garvey, Salem	.839	24	17	35	10	1
George, Kinston	.833	17	8	42	10	7
Juday, Salem	.909	8	8	12	2	1
Juday, Lynchburg	.929	68	41	117	12	17
Kelly, Durham	.958	24	19	27	2	2
Marshall, Wilmington	.938	60	52	99	10	14
Maxwell, Kinston	1.000	2	0	2	0	0
McClain, Frederick	.938	132	113	235	23	12
Meade, Kinston	.953	53	36	106	7	11
Mendoza, Wilmington	.899	39	30	68	11	6
Millares, Frederick	.818	3	4	5	2	0
Neff, Salem	.821	19	7	25	7	1
Perna, Winston-Salem	.904	134	111	239	37	23
Polcovich, Salem	.903	8	4	24	3	1
Posada, Prince William	.727	1	1	7	3	0
Purdy, Salem	1.000	7	2	11	0	0
Ramey, Winston-Salem	1.000	1	1	2	0	0
Ramirez, Frederick	.500	3	0	1	1	0
Ronca, Salem	.879	24	15	43	8	4
Rose, Kinston	.892	74	49	140	23	13
Schmidt, Lynchburg	.818	3	5	4	2	1
Seitzer, Frederick	.933	8	7	7	1	0
Selby, Durham	.951	73	57	98	8	13
A. Stewart, Wilmington	.905	6	8	11	2	2
B. Stewart, Wilmington	1.000	7	2	5	0	0
THERRIEN, Durham	.957	98	80	166	11	15
Wollenburg, Durham	.882	23	18	27	6	3
Zimmerman, Durham	.903	21	12	16	3	4

SHORTSTOPS

Player, Team	Pct.	G	PO	A	E	DP
Andujar, Kinston	.914	111	135	330	44	62
Arias, Winston-Salem	.857	5	2	4	1	0
Brown, Lynchburg	.945	126	205	363	33	85
Burnett, Prince William	.966	7	7	21	1	3
Castaldo, Frederick	.938	10	9	21	2	5
Cooper, Prince William	1.000	2	0	4	0	1
Erickson, Prince William	.944	38	52	101	9	19
Garvey, Salem	.909	3	2	8	1	2
George, Kinston	.848	9	12	16	5	3
Gill, Winston-Salem	.944	10	12	22	2	5
Gonzalez, Winston-Salem	.947	6	8	10	1	0
Guerrero, Wilmington	.954	43	77	131	10	27
Halter, Wilmington	.939	53	84	146	15	27
JIMENEZ, Durham	.950	126	213	317	28	61
Juday, Lynchburg	.952	20	32	47	4	17
Kelly, Durham	1.000	4	2	6	0	2
Knowles, Prince William	.903	103	152	305	49	40
Marshall, Wilmington	.916	21	27	60	8	7
Martinez, Wilmington	.400	1	0	2	3	0
McClain, Frederick	1.000	2	0	1	0	0
Meade, Kinston	.970	23	38	58	3	14
Mercedes, Frederick	.900	120	127	303	48	43
Owens, Winston-Salem	.943	121	215	347	34	57
Perna, Winston-Salem	1.000	3	2	5	0	2
Polcovich, Salem	.944	67	73	213	17	29
Purdy, Salem	1.000	3	8	7	0	4
Ramírez, Frederick	.926	18	21	42	5	6
Rodriguez, Lynchburg	1.000	1	0	2	0	0
B. Stewart, Wilmington	.931	28	34	60	7	13
Wollenburg, Durham	.872	15	14	20	5	2
Womack, Salem	.927	72	130	223	28	38
Zimmerman, Durham	.875	10	7	21	4	4

Triple plays—Jimenez, Polcovich.

OUTFIELDERS

Player, Team	Pct.	G	PO	A	E	DP
Alstead, Frederick	1.000	15	23	3	0	0
Baez, Lynchburg	.952	10	20	0	1	0
Belk, Winston-Salem	.875	7	6	1	1	1
Bonifay, Salem	1.000	6	10	0	0	0
Burton, Wilmington	.972	128	303	14	9	6
Carvajal, Prince William	.969	118	202	16	7	3
Charbonnet, Kinston*	.982	75	108	0	2	0
Coates, Durham	.960	62	68	4	3	0
Conger, Salem*	.942	106	166	13	11	3
Cotton, Kinston	.974	125	214	9	6	1
Deller, Prince William	.966	35	55	2	2	0

THIRD BASEMEN (continued)

Player, Team	Pct.	G	PO	A	E	DP
Eierman, Lynchburg	.977	114	199	12	5	6
Encarnacion, Salem	1.000	1	1	0	0	0
Erickson, Prince William	1.000	2	5	0	0	0
Espinosa, Salem	.956	52	129	1	6	0
Farrell, Salem	.964	71	151	9	6	1
Franklin, Winston-Salem	.974	19	36	1	1	0
Garvey, Salem	1.000	11	12	0	0	0
Gilliam, Prince William	.946	61	84	3	5	0
Gonzalez, Wilmington	.969	125	227	19	8	4
Goodwin, Frederick*	.976	136	271	9	7	3
Graham, Lynchburg	1.000	8	18	1	0	0
Hanel, Salem	1.000	1	1	0	0	0
Harvey, Kinston*	.967	24	29	0	1	0
Hill, Prince William	.955	106	202	9	10	0
Hinton, Wilmington*	1.000	13	18	1	0	1
Hodge, Frederick	.935	43	55	3	4	1
Hubbard, Prince William*	.973	91	167	13	5	4
Johnson, Lynchburg	.952	25	38	2	2	0
Jones, Winston-Salem	.981	77	140	12	3	2
Juday, Lynchburg	1.000	5	8	3	0	0
Ladell, Winston-Salem	.964	124	310	12	12	4
Link, Frederick*	.857	6	6	0	1	0
Mahay, Lynchburg*	.973	71	173	6	5	3
Malave, Lynchburg	.933	77	129	10	10	3
Marini, Kinston*	.972	117	169	6	5	1
Millares, Frederick	.800	3	4	0	1	0
Mitchell, Kinston	.940	85	134	7	9	0
Moore, Durham*	.968	86	207	6	7	1
Mottola, Winston-Salem	.940	137	214	20	15	4
Neff, Salem	.882	54	60	7	9	0
Ochoa, Frederick	.943	133	169	13	11	2
ORTIZ, Frederick	.989	98	171	11	2	1
Ponder, Salem	.930	27	38	2	3	0
Pueschner, Winston-Salem	1.000	32	41	0	0	0
Ragland, Durham	.938	52	67	9	5	1
Ramey, Winston-Salem	1.000	3	4	0	0	0
Ramirez, Kinston	.750	3	3	0	1	0
Robinson, Durham	.933	105	162	6	12	1
Ronca, Salem	.941	39	44	4	3	0
Scott, Lynchburg	.993	65	132	5	1	1
Seitzer, Frederick	1.000	2	1	0	0	0
T. Smith, Wilmington	.989	59	88	3	1	0
Swann, Durham	1.000	16	17	2	0	0
Thomas, Salem	1.000	24	36	1	0	0
Twitty, Prince William	.903	18	24	4	3	0
Vasquez, Winston-Salem	.910	41	58	3	6	0
Waldrop, Durham*	.923	9	12	0	1	0
Walker, Wilmington	.965	105	184	7	7	1
Warner, Durham*	.970	74	152	9	5	2
Williams, Durham	.978	112	169	11	4	1
Zambrano, Lynchburg	.976	67	118	6	3	0

CATCHERS

Player, Team	Pct.	G	PO	A	E	DP	PB
Arntzen, Kinston	1.000	19	119	16	0	2	3
AYRAULT, Durham	.992	108	739	98	7	5	14
Bess, Winston-Salem	.975	10	66	13	2	1	5
Buckley, Winston-Salem	.991	33	191	18	2	2	3
Carey, Lynchburg	.985	25	176	20	3	1	3
Crosby, Kinston	.983	71	520	68	10	8	8
Dempsey, Wilmington	.964	10	25	2	1	0	2
Devarez, Frederick	.996	37	238	38	1	1	5
Encarnacion, Salem	.962	67	449	82	21	3	5
Epps, Prince William	1.000	14	55	11	0	0	2
Gresham, Frederick	.978	47	359	34	9	3	11
Hammond, Winston-Salem	.963	46	243	45	11	3	11
Hanel, Salem	.983	66	449	57	9	2	4
Harrison, Winston-Salem	.990	68	448	40	5	2	15
Lohry, Prince William	1.000	1	4	0	0	0	1
Mahay, Lynchburg*	1.000	1	1	1	0	0	0
Martin, Lynchburg	.979	58	358	62	9	4	8
Marx, Salem	.965	13	98	11	4	2	1
McKeel, Lynchburg	.982	70	390	59	8	3	8
Motuzas, Prince William	.978	15	78	13	2	0	2
Patrizi, Kinston	1.000	7	37	3	0	0	0
Pineda, Prince William	1.000	6	47	4	0	0	0
Posada, Prince William	.985	107	676	91	12	1	38
Salemcedo, Prince William	.953	7	36	5	2	0	3
A. Stewart, Wilmington	.984	33	164	25	3	6	5
Strickland, Wilmington	.977	110	733	126	20	11	10
Sued, Kinston	.994	59	429	38	3	0	10
Swail, Durham	.991	42	295	25	3	4	8
Tallman, Frederick	.987	51	415	31	6	1	11
Walker, Wilmington	1.000	1	2	0	0	0	2
Waszgis, Frederick	.989	23	159	23	2	0	8

PITCHERS

Player, Team	Pct.	G	PO	A	E	DP
Angel, Winston-Salem	.950	10	9	10	1	1
Baez, Wilmington*	1.000	28	1	4	0	0
Bakkum, Lynchburg	.971	26	11	22	1	6
Benavides, Frederick	.941	25	6	10	1	3

Player, Team	Pct.	G	PO	A	E	DP
Benitez, Frederick	1.000	12	0	1	0	0
Bennett, Lynchburg	.913	29	7	14	2	0
Bevil, Wilmington	1.000	12	3	6	0	2
Bladow, Wilmington	1.000	30	4	10	0	1
Blair, Durham	.882	44	7	8	2	1
Boltz, Durham*	.857	15	1	5	1	0
Borowski, Frederick	.857	42	3	9	2	0
Brock, Durham	.968	12	8	22	1	1
Brown, Kinston	.957	31	9	13	1	0
Buckley, Winston-Salem	1.000	1	0	1	0	0
Bunch, Wilmington	.875	10	3	11	2	1
Burgess, Durham*	1.000	48	3	13	0	0
Carter, Prince William*	.903	26	3	25	3	0
Chiles, Durham	.875	14	3	4	1	1
Chrisman, Wilmington	.833	24	7	3	2	2
Christiansen, Salem*	1.000	57	3	7	0	0
Clontz, Durham	.889	51	3	21	3	0
Crawford, Kinston	.889	28	17	39	7	6
Croghan, Prince William	.958	39	8	15	1	0
Cullop, Winston-Salem	.950	39	3	16	1	1
Cusey, Frederick	1.000	16	1	0	0	0
DeLosSantos, Salem	.960	18	7	17	1	1
Donovan, Lynchburg*	1.000	31	2	15	0	1
Doorneweerd, Salem	.889	15	2	6	1	0
Doyle, Kinston	1.000	47	7	7	0	0
Dubois, Frederick*	.960	10	5	19	1	1
Duff, Winston-Salem*	.750	7	0	3	1	0
Dunbar, Prince William*	.962	49	4	21	1	2
Eddy, Wilmington*	.800	55	2	10	3	0
Eshelman, Frederick*	.935	24	8	21	2	1
Evans, Salem	.950	45	5	14	1	1
Faino, Lynchburg*	.852	40	8	15	4	1
Fleet, Kinston	.867	40	3	10	2	0
Forney, Frederick	.923	27	5	19	2	2
Frazier, Prince William	.739	15	9	8	6	0
Fronio, Kinston	1.000	32	4	8	0	3
Fyhrie, Wilmington	1.000	5	3	2	0	0
Gakeler, Lynchburg	1.000	30	7	6	0	0
Garagozzo, Prince William*	.875	11	1	13	2	0
Garcia, Winston-Salem	.889	26	3	5	1	1
Glaze, Lynchburg	.957	27	15	30	2	2
Gresham, Frederick	1.000	1	1	0	0	0
Gross, Wilmington	.879	28	12	17	4	1
Gully, Prince William	.958	59	11	12	1	0
Harrah, Salem	1.000	24	10	13	0	0
Harrison, Wilmington	.973	26	9	27	1	2
Hassinger, Durham	1.000	14	4	4	0	0
Haynes, Frederick	.938	27	10	20	2	1
Henkel, Lynchburg	.917	18	1	10	1	0
Hernandez, Kinston	.714	8	2	3	2	0
Hodges, Wilmington	1.000	3	0	1	0	0
Hrusovsky, Winston-Salem	1.000	52	3	2	0	0
Hudson, Lynchburg	1.000	49	3	16	0	2
Huffman, Wilmington	1.000	4	0	1	0	0
Jarvis, Winston-Salem	.881	21	20	17	5	3
Johnston, Lynchburg	1.000	20	2	8	0	0
Jones, Salem	1.000	11	3	4	0	0
Jones, Frederick	.667	4	2	0	1	0
Karp, Prince William*	.923	8	3	9	1	0
Klingenbeck, Frederick	.880	23	12	10	3	1
Koller, Durham	1.000	27	7	19	0	0
Konuszewski, Salem	.958	39	4	19	1	0
Kummerfeldt, Winston-Salem	.857	5	3	3	1	1
Landress, Wilmington	.833	20	2	3	1	0
LaPlante, Salem	1.000	11	7	14	0	0
Lawrence, Salem*	.667	4	0	2	1	0
Leahy, Durham	1.000	28	1	7	0	0
Lemp, Frederick	.875	52	3	4	1	0
Lieber, Wilmington	.943	17	11	22	2	0
Loaiza, Salem	.971	17	13	20	1	1
Loftin, Winston-Salem	.750	24	1	2	1	0
Logsdon, Kinston*	.923	31	7	29	3	2
Lomon, Durham	.920	14	8	15	2	0
Maloney, Lynchburg*	1.000	18	4	8	0	1
Martin, Salem*	1.000	17	0	4	0	1
May, Durham*	.923	9	3	9	1	1
McCANN, Winston-Salem	1.000	32	17	33	0	5
McCarthy, Kinston*	.800	9	1	3	1	0
McClain, Winston-Salem	.857	10	6	12	3	0
McCurry, Salem	1.000	41	3	1	0	0
Mesewicz, Salem*	.700	48	2	5	3	2
Miller, Lynchburg	.923	25	1	11	1	1
Mooney, Salem	1.000	15	4	3	0	0
Morgan, Kinston	1.000	28	1	2	0	0
Munda, Prince William	.882	37	5	10	2	0
Niles, Lynchburg	.882	32	7	8	2	1
Nix, Winston-Salem	1.000	11	2	4	0	1
O'Laughlin, Winston-Salem*	.667	3	0	2	1	0
Painter, Lynchburg	1.000	15	2	5	0	1
Parkinson, Salem	.850	17	6	11	3	1
Paveloff, Frederick	1.000	24	4	4	0	0
Perez, Wilmington	.900	33	8	10	2	0
Pettitte, Prince William*	.953	26	5	36	2	0
Pisciotta, Salem	1.000	20	0	3	0	0
Place, Durham	1.000	5	3	8	0	0
Polasek, Frederick*	.882	55	7	8	2	0
Prybylinski, Prince William	.947	11	2	16	1	1
Quinones, Winston-Salem*	.933	50	6	8	1	1
Ralph, Prince William	1.000	32	3	6	0	0
Ramirez, Durham	1.000	8	1	3	0	0
Rea, Wilmington	1.000	11	0	2	0	0
Rivera, Kinston*	1.000	19	6	3	0	1
Ruebel, Salem*	.857	19	2	4	1	0
Ruyak, 7 W.S.- 18 Kin.*	1.000	25	2	5	0	0
Ryan, Frederick	1.000	15	0	2	0	0
Rychel, Salem	.950	53	6	13	1	1
Ryder, Durham	1.000	10	0	6	0	0
Sackinsky, Frederick	.944	18	7	10	1	0
Schmidt, Durham	1.000	22	8	16	0	2
Seelbach, Durham	.840	25	6	15	4	0
Seiler, Prince William*	.900	31	3	6	1	0
Shaw, Winston-Salem	1.000	25	1	8	0	1
Short, Prince William	1.000	11	0	4	0	0
Shuey, Kinston	.800	15	3	1	1	1
J. Smith, Wilmington	.818	51	2	7	2	0
Smith, Frederick	.957	31	7	15	1	0
Steinmetz, Durham	1.000	6	0	1	0	0
Steph, Winston-Salem	.891	28	19	30	6	2
Stewart, Winston-Salem	1.000	14	17	6	0	0
Sullivan, Prince William*	.955	34	3	18	1	2
Sutko, Winston-Salem	1.000	28	9	10	0	0
Tavarez, Kinston	.939	18	12	19	2	2
Teich, Salem*	.400	12	0	2	3	0
Thobe, Kinston	.800	4	4	4	2	1
Toth, Wilmington	1.000	25	7	11	0	1
Tuttle, Winston-Salem	.947	15	10	8	1	2
Wade, Durham*	1.000	5	0	1	0	0
Wagner, Wilmington	.938	13	5	10	1	0
Welch, Kinston*	1.000	46	4	9	0	0
Wilder, Durham	1.000	35	7	13	0	0
Wiley, Prince William	1.000	36	9	17	0	0
M. Williams, Kinston*	.971	27	3	31	1	0
Wilson, Salem	1.000	15	9	13	0	0
Woodall, Durham*	1.000	6	1	5	0	0

The following players did not have any fielding statistics at the positions indicated or appeared only as a designated hitter, pinch-hitter or pinch-runner: Andujar, 2b; Ch. Brown, p; Castaldo, p; Conger, p; Crosby, 1b; Dodd, p; Garvey, p; Gill, of; Ri. Gonzales, 3b; Graffanino, ss; Guerrero, 2b; M. Harrison, 3b; Jean, p; Ladell, c; Marini, 1b; Marks, 3b; Meade, of; Mota, 3b; C. Perez, p; Polcovich, of; Pough, of; Ramos, p; Ronca, p; B. Stewart, of; Strickland, 1b; Sued, p; Tallman, p; Vasquez, p; Waldrop, 1b; G. Williams, p; Wollenburg, of.

LEAGUE CHAMPIONS

Year	Team	Pct.	Year	Team	Pct.	Year	Team	Pct.
1945—	Danville	.681	1955—	HP-Thomasville	.580		Greensboro§	.590
1946—	Greensboro	.599		Danville (2nd)†	.533		Wilson (2nd)†	.535
	Raleigh (2nd)†	.563	1956—	HP-Thomasville	.591	1964—	Kinston§	.572
1947—	Burlington	.613		Fayetteville (4th)§	.523		Winston-Salem§†	.590
	Raleigh (3rd)†	.574	1957—	Durham	.632	1965—	Peninsula§	.597
1948—	Raleigh	.592		HP-Thomasville	.622		Durham§	.580
	Martinsville (2nd)†	.570	1958—	Danville	.576		Tidewater†	.528
1949—	Danville	.601		Burlington (4th)†	.511	1966—	Kinston§	.547
	Burlington (4th)†	.500	1959—	Raleigh	.600		Winston-Salem§	.586
1950—	Winston-Salem*	.693		Wilson (2nd)†	.550		Rocky Mount†	.533
1951—	Durham	.600	1960—	Greensboro‡	.636	1967—	Durham x (West.)	.536
	Wins-Salem (2nd)†	.583		Burlington	.586		Raleigh (East.)	.542
1952—	Raleigh	.581	1961—	Wilson	.594	1968—	Salem (West.)	.607
	Reidsville (4th)†	.536	1962—	Durham	.636		Ral-Dur (East.)	.597
1953—	Raleigh	.593		Wilson	.600		HP-Thom. y (W.)	.493
	Danville (2nd)†	.572		Kinston (2nd)†	.593	1969—	Rocky M (East.)	.569
1954—	Fayetteville*	.628	1963—	Kinston§	.538		Salem (West.)	.542

Year	Team	Pct.	Year	Team	Pct.	Year	Team	Pct.
	Ral-Dur z (East.)	.560	1978—	Peninsula	.696	1987—	Salem‡	.576
1970—	Winston-Salem‡	.586		Lynchburg‡	.614		Kinston	.536
	Burlington	.597	1979—	Winston-Salem a	.607	1988—	Kinston§	.629
1971—	Peninsula‡	.647	1980—	Peninsula‡	.714		Lynchburg	.486
	Kinston	.623		Durham	.600	1989—	Durham	.609
1972—	Salem‡	.657	1981—	Peninsula	.522		Prince William‡	.522
	Burlington	.632		Hagerstown‡	.507	1990—	Kinston	.652
1973—	Lynchburg	.588	1982—	Alexandria‡	.597		Frederick‡	.544
	Winston-Salem‡	.557		Durham	.588	1991—	Kinston‡	.645
1974—	Salem	.671	1983—	Lynchburg‡	.691		Lynchburg	.482
	Salem	.582		Winston-Salem	.529	1992—	Lynchburg	.570
1975—	Rocky Mount	.667	1984—	Lynchburg‡	.645		Peninsula‡	.536
	Rocky Mount	.614		Durham	.486	1993—	Wilmington	.532
1976—	Winston-Salem	.618	1985—	Lynchburg	.679		Winston-Salem‡	.514
	Winston-Salem	.551		Winston-Salem‡	.417			
1977—	Lynchburg	.591	1986—	Hagerstown	.655			
	Peninsula‡	.556		Winston-Salem‡	.594			

*Won championship and four-club playoff. †Won four-club playoff. ‡Won split-season playoff. §League was divided into Eastern, Western divisions. xWon eight-club, two-division playoff. yWon eight-club, two-division playoff against Raleigh-Durham. zWon eight-club, two-division playoff against Burlington. aWon both halves of split season (no playoffs).

FLORIDA STATE LEAGUE

FINAL STANDINGS

FIRST HALF

EAST DIVISION

Team	W	L	T	Pct.	GB
Lakeland (Tigers)	38	30	1	.559	......
West Palm Beach (Expos)	37	30	0	.552	½
St. Lucie (Mets)	37	30	0	.552	½
Osceola (Astros)	28	38	0	.424	9
Daytona (Cubs)	28	39	0	.418	9 ½
Vero Beach (Dodgers)	24	41	0	.369	12 ½
Fort Lauderdale (Red Sox)	22	43	0	.338	14 ½

WEST DIVISION

Team	W	L	T	Pct.	GB
Clearwater (Phillies)	44	24	0	.647	......
Charlotte (Rangers)	40	27	1	.597	3 ½
Sarasota (White Sox)	37	29	0	.561	6
St. Petersburg (Cardinals)	37	30	0	.552	6 ½
Dunedin (Blue Jays)	34	33	0	.507	9 ½
Fort Myers (Twins)	27	39	0	.409	16

SECOND HALF

EAST DIVISION

Team	W	L	T	Pct.	GB
St. Lucie (Mets)	41	22	0	.651	......
Vero Beach (Dodgers)	32	36	0	.471	11 ½
West Palm Beach (Expos)	32	37	0	.464	12
Lakeland (Tigers)	27	33	0	.450	12 ½
Daytona (Cubs)	29	37	0	.439	13 ½
Osceola (Astros)	28	36	0	.438	13 ½
Fort Lauderdale (Red Sox)	24	42	0	.364	18 ½

WEST DIVISION

Team	W	L	T	Pct.	GB
Charlotte (Rangers)	44	22	0	.667	......
Sarasota (White Sox)	40	28	0	.588	5
St. Petersburg (Cardinals)	38	28	0	.576	6
Dunedin (Blue Jays)	34	31	0	.523	9 ½
Clearwater (Phillies)	31	36	0	.463	13 ½
Fort Myers (Twins)	28	40	0	.412	17

COMPOSITE

Team	Char.	StL	Sar.	St.P.	Clw.	Dun.	Lak.	WPB	Osc.	Day.	V.B.	Ft.M.	Ft.L.	W	L	T	Pct.	GB
Charlotte (Rangers)	...	5	9	5	5	6	10	6	9	7	6	6	10	84	49	1	.632	......
St. Lucie (Mets)	7	...	6	6	5	7	4	4	7	8	8	8	8	78	52	0	.600	4 ½
Sarasota (White Sox)	2	6	...	4	6	8	9	6	5	7	7	8	9	77	57	0	.575	7 ½
St. Petersburg (Cardinals)	6	4	7	...	7	6	4	8	6	7	5	6	9	75	58	0	.564	9
Clearwater (Phillies)	6	7	4	4	...	6	5	8	8	6	5	6	10	75	60	0	.556	10
Dunedin (Blue Jays)	3	4	3	5	5	...	6	7	4	8	6	10	7	68	64	0	.515	15 ½
Lakeland (Tigers)	0	5	3	5	7	6	...	6	6	8	11	5	3	65	63	1	.508	16 ½
West Palm Beach (Expos)	6	8	4	4	4	3	6	...	7	7	7	9	4	69	67	0	.507	16 ½
Osceola (Astros)	3	3	5	6	4	8	3	4	...	3	7	4	6	56	74	0	.431	26 ½
Daytona (Cubs)	5	3	5	3	3	4	5	5	8	...	5	6	7	57	76	0	.429	27
Vero Beach (Dodgers)	4	3	4	7	7	6	1	5	3	5	...	7	4	56	77	0	.421	28
Fort Myers (Twins)	5	2	4	6	5	1	5	3	6	6	4	...	8	55	79	0	.410	29 ½
Fort Lauderdale (Red Sox)	2	2	3	3	2	3	7	5	5	4	6	4	...	46	85	0	.351	37

Charlotte played home games in Port Charlotte, Fla.

Osceola played home games in Kissimmee, Fla.

Major league affiliations in parentheses.

Playoffs—Clearwater defeated Charlotte, two games to one; St. Lucie defeated Lakeland, two games to one; Clearwater defeated St. Lucie, three games to one, to win league championship.

Regular-season attendance—Charlotte, 90,792; Clearwater, 86,508; Daytona, 95,089; Dunedin, 77,382; Fort Lauderdale, 28,240; Fort Myers, 95,054; Lakeland, 25,248; Osceola, 51,527; St. Lucie, 69,078; St. Petersburg, 123,275; Sarasota, 91,883; Vero Beach, 72,861; West Palm Beach, 69,289. Total, 976,226. Playoffs (10 games), 4,061. All-Star Game, 3,114.

Managers—Charlotte, Tommy Thompson; Clearwater, Bill Dancy; Daytona, Bill Hayes; Dunedin, Dennis Holmberg; Fort Lauderdale, Demarlo Hale; Fort Myers, Steve Liddle; Lakeland, Gerry Groninger; Osceola, Tim Tolman; St. Lucie, John Tamargo; St. Petersburg, Terry Kennedy; Sarasota, Dave Huppert; Vero Beach, Joe Vavra; West Palm Beach, Rob Leary.

All-Star team: 1B—Chris Weinke, Dunedin; 2B—Chris Demetral, Vero Beach; 3B—Eduardo Lantigua, Vero Beach; SS—Edgardo Alfonzo, St. Lucie; LF—Rich Butler, Dunedin; CF—Randy Curtis, St. Lucie; RF—Rick Holifield, Dunedin; C—Jason Moler, Clearwater, and Ken Huckaby, Vero Beach; DH—Doug Radziewicz, St. Petersburg; RHP—Rodney Henderson, West Palm Beach; John Dettmer, Charlotte; LHP—Chris Roberts, St. Lucie; B.J. Wallace, West Palm Beach; Relievers—Clint Davis, St. Petersburg; Jim McCready, St. Lucie; Most Valuable Player—Randy Curtis, St. Lucie; Manager of the Year—John Tamargo, St. Lucie.

BATTING

TEAM

Team	Avg.	G	AB	R	OR	H	TB	2B	3B	HR	RBI	SH	SF	HP	BB	Int. BB	SO	SB	CS	LOB
Clearwater	.276	135	4525	659	566	1249	1769	243	35	69	584	44	42	48	479	25	704	111	96	944
Dunedin	.272	132	4402	650	571	1199	1777	198	52	92	567	57	28	59	484	35	789	179	102	934
St. Petersburg	.272	133	4486	562	502	1221	1605	216	30	36	494	62	42	41	450	38	724	155	86	986
St. Lucie	.272	134	4266	593	467	1159	1562	174	47	45	535	29	50	36	453	20	607	172	101	896
Vero Beach	.269	133	4439	582	672	1194	1608	184	22	62	517	56	40	69	395	15	815	117	86	906
Charlotte	.269	134	4460	595	459	1199	1591	192	34	44	534	50	33	48	525	24	799	117	91	998
Lakeland	.261	129	4253	558	527	1112	1535	175	49	50	492	47	46	34	505	31	803	133	80	943
Daytona	.259	133	4407	577	608	1141	1592	181	36	66	508	60	41	51	451	10	796	114	88	919
West Palm Beach	.254	136	4469	549	544	1133	1574	220	31	53	482	51	33	41	435	27	807	139	82	920
Osceola	.251	130	4261	503	621	1071	1418	142	62	27	447	24	42	38	367	10	753	139	105	835
Sarasota	.251	134	4436	579	518	1114	1585	204	42	61	504	26	44	47	447	26	812	98	50	929
Fort Lauderdale	.245	131	4393	494	682	1075	1418	157	30	42	422	66	33	36	417	22	827	94	63	905
Fort Myers	.241	134	4434	500	664	1067	1457	210	27	42	438	44	36	40	454	24	815	142	65	930

(Leading qualifiers for batting championship—367 or more plate appearances)
*Bats lefthanded.   †Switch-hitter.

Player, Team	Avg.	G	AB	R	H	TB	2B	3B	HR	RBI	SH	SF	HP	BB	Int. BB	SO	SB	CS
Radziewicz, Doug, St. Petersburg*	.342	123	439	66	150	202	36	2	4	72	1	5	5	73	11	58	6	8
Demetral, Chris, Vero Beach*	.325	122	437	63	142	185	22	3	5	48	6	3	2	69	2	47	6	6
Garcia, Omar, St. Lucie	.322	129	485	73	156	196	17	7	3	76	2	5	2	57	2	47	25	8
Curtis, Randy, St. Lucie*	.319	126	467	91	149	209	30	12	2	38	4	4	5	93	2	72	52	17
Colon, Dennis, Osceola*	.316	118	469	51	148	186	20	6	2	59	0	3	0	17	1	41	10	4
Cairo, Miguel, Vero Beach	.315	90	346	50	109	124	10	1	1	23	10	0	7	28	0	22	23	16
Grable, Rob, Clearwater	.313	98	351	60	110	162	27	5	5	55	0	5	7	49	3	72	16	9
Dubose, Brian, Lakeland*	.313	122	448	74	140	213	27	11	8	68	0	4	4	49	5	97	18	18
Auralia, Richard, Charlotte	.309	122	440	80	136	177	16	5	5	56	9	7	3	75	4	57	15	18
Coughlin, Kevin, Sarasota*	.308	112	415	53	128	157	19	2	2	32	4	2	0	42	5	51	4	4
Zuber, Jon, Clearwater*	.308	129	494	70	152	214	37	5	5	69	3	4	0	49	5	47	6	6

Departmental leaders: G—Guggiana, 134; AB—Guggiana, 514; R—Curtis, 91; H—Garcia, Wilson, 156; TB—Holifield, Zuber, 214; 2B—Zuber, 37; 3B—Abreu, 17; HR—Holifield, 20; RBI—Weinke, 98; SH—Petersen, 17; SF—Fisher, 10; HP—Holifield, 16; BB—Curtis, 93; IBB—Radziewicz, 11; SO—Holifield, 129; SB—Curtis, 52; CS—Holbert, 22.

(All players—listed alphabetically)

Player, Team	Avg.	G	AB	R	H	TB	2B	3B	HR	RBI	SH	SF	HP	BB	Int. BB	SO	SB	CS
Abreu, Bob, Osceola*	.283	129	474	62	134	204	21	17	5	55	1	3	1	51	1	90	10	14
Adams, Bill, Vero Beach*	.133	18	45	8	6	10	1	0	1	7	0	0	0	7	0	16	3	3
Alder, Jimmy, Lakeland	.200	41	135	13	27	47	6	1	4	16	1	0	0	14	1	39	2	2
Alfonzo, Edgardo, St. Lucie	.294	128	494	75	145	202	18	3	11	86	4	9	5	57	3	51	26	16
Allen, Matt, West Palm Beach	.211	57	152	10	32	42	10	0	0	8	5	0	8	13	0	41	4	0
Anthony, Mark, Dunedin	.250	2	4	1	1	1	0	0	0	1	0	0	0	1	0	0	0	0
Auralia, Richard, Charlotte	.309	122	440	80	136	177	16	5	5	56	9	7	3	75	4	57	15	18
Austin, James, West Palm Beach	.236	33	89	2	21	26	3	1	0	9	1	1	1	6	0	20	2	2
Ayala, Moises, Lakeland	.500	3	2	1	1	4	0	0	1	4	0	0	0	1	0	0	0	0
Badorek, Mike, St. Petersburg	.000	29	1	0	0	0	0	0	0	0	0	0	0	0	0	0	0	0
Barry, Jeff, St. Lucie†	.257	114	420	68	108	147	17	5	4	50	2	6	5	49	4	37	17	14
Beals, Greg, St. Lucie	.233	22	60	6	14	21	2	1	1	8	0	2	0	9	0	11	0	0
Beasley, Andy, St. Petersburg*	.143	13	35	1	5	5	0	0	0	3	1	0	1	7	0	10	0	0
Bennett, Gary, Clearwater	.327	17	55	5	18	21	0	0	1	6	2	0	1	3	0	10	0	1
Berblinger, Jeff, St. Petersburg	.186	19	70	7	13	14	1	0	0	5	2	0	1	5	0	10	3	1
Berry, Perry, Osceola	.259	84	239	25	62	88	8	6	2	31	2	6	2	24	1	55	8	5
Bethke, Jamie, Charlotte†	.000	1	1	0	0	0	0	0	0	0	0	0	0	0	0	0	0	0
Blackburn, Tyres, Dunedin	.000	1	2	0	0	0	0	0	0	0	0	0	0	0	0	0	0	0
Blazier, Ron, Clearwater	.000	28	2	0	0	0	0	0	0	0	1	0	0	0	0	1	0	0
Bradish, Mike, Sarasota	.226	32	106	6	24	30	3	0	1	17	0	0	1	15	0	23	0	0
Bradshaw, Terry, St. Petersburg*	.291	125	461	84	134	186	25	6	5	51	7	5	7	82	1	60	43	17
Brady, Doug, Sarasota†	.252	115	449	75	113	156	16	6	5	44	4	5	6	55	2	54	26	9
Brede, Brent, Fort Myers*	.330	53	182	27	60	72	10	1	0	27	2	0	1	32	3	19	8	4
Bright, Brian, Fort Lauderdale	.301	75	259	25	78	104	11	0	5	35	2	4	5	10	0	47	1	2
Brito, Tilson, Dunedin	.269	126	465	80	125	170	21	3	6	44	10	3	10	59	0	60	27	16
Brooks, Eric, Dunedin	.197	43	142	18	28	35	4	0	1	10	2	1	3	17	2	21	1	2
Brown, Adam, Daytona*	.284	36	109	17	31	51	8	0	4	23	0	3	0	15	1	21	0	1
Brown, Brant, Daytona*	.342	75	266	26	91	122	8	7	3	33	4	0	1	11	0	38	8	7
Brown, Bryan, Fort Lauderdale	.312	55	205	24	64	92	9	2	5	29	3	3	1	19	1	37	0	1
Brown, Matt, Fort Myers	.164	60	201	8	33	35	2	0	0	17	5	4	0	11	0	41	1	2
Brown, Mike, Vero Beach	.174	39	86	9	15	15	0	0	0	9	1	2	3	8	0	14	0	0
Buchanan, Shawn, Sarasota	.274	30	106	18	29	38	5	2	0	11	1	1	3	23	1	23	1	3
Burguillos, Carlos, Lakeland	.286	15	28	6	8	9	1	0	0	5	2	2	0	7	1	2	1	1
Burke, Alan, Clearwater	.111	8	27	2	3	6	0	0	1	3	0	0	0	2	0	7	0	0
Burns, Michael, Osceola	.183	123	438	43	80	120	17	1	7	56	0	3	4	35	2	110	10	12
Burrough, Butch, Fort Myers	.210	77	248	28	52	94	12	3	8	30	2	2	3	35	2	75	8	4
Busby, Wayne, Daytona	.231	9	26	5	6	9	1	1	0	3	0	0	0	5	0	9	1	0
Butler, Rich, Dunedin*	.306	110	444	68	136	204	19	8	11	65	1	4	3	48	10	64	11	13
Cabrera, Carlos, Dunedin†	.200	4	15	1	3	3	0	0	0	1	0	0	0	2	0	2	0	1
Cairo, Miguel, Vero Beach	.315	90	346	50	109	124	10	1	1	23	10	0	7	28	0	22	23	16
Cairo, Sergio, Charlotte	.369	34	122	15	45	66	4	1	5	25	2	0	2	15	0	11	3	4
Cantu, Mike, St. Petersburg	.289	127	463	54	134	194	28	1	10	75	1	7	7	40	6	81	2	6
Cappuccio, Carmine, Sarasota*	.189	24	90	9	17	26	2	2	1	12	0	0	4	11	0	10	3	0
Carey, Todd, Fort Lauderdale*	.245	118	444	41	109	142	14	5	3	31	5	3	0	24	1	44	2	6
Castillo, Alberto, St. Lucie	.258	105	333	37	86	122	21	0	5	42	2	7	3	28	1	46	0	2
Cerio, Steve, St. Petersburg	.301	52	176	20	53	78	14	1	3	29	0	3	0	12	1	33	1	2
Chavez, Raul, Osceola	.228	58	197	13	45	52	5	1	0	16	1	1	1	8	0	19	1	1
Chick, Bruce, Fort Lauderdale	.289	39	159	13	46	58	9	0	1	14	2	0	0	4	2	34	1	2
Cholowsky, Dan, St. Petersburg	.288	54	208	30	60	78	12	0	2	22	0	0	2	20	2	54	6	8
Civit, Xavier, West Palm Beach	.100	11	30	1	3	3	0	0	0	0	1	0	0	0	0	11	0	0
Clark, Tony, Lakeland†	.265	36	117	14	31	40	4	1	1	22	2	2	0	18	2	32	0	1
Clinton, Jim, Charlotte	.175	86	285	26	50	62	9	0	1	23	7	2	4	18	1	72	4	3
Colbrunn, Greg, West Palm Beach	.387	8	31	6	12	19	2	1	1	5	0	0	0	4	0	1	0	0
Coleman, Ken, Sarasota†	.188	11	32	4	6	6	0	0	0	2	0	1	0	6	0	4	1	1
Colmenares, Carlos, Dunedin	.000	4	2	1	0	0	0	0	0	0	0	0	0	0	0	0	0	0
Colon, Dennis, Osceola*	.316	118	469	51	148	186	20	6	2	59	0	3	0	17	1	41	10	4
Coquillette, Trace, West Palm Beach	.278	6	18	2	5	8	3	0	0	3	1	0	0	2	0	5	0	0
Corbin, Ted, Fort Myers†	.236	91	339	46	80	95	11	2	0	22	5	3	8	36	0	47	22	8
Coughlin, Kevin, Sarasota*	.308	112	415	53	128	157	19	2	2	32	4	2	0	42	5	51	4	4
Crespo, Felipe, Dunedin†	.299	96	345	51	103	153	16	8	6	39	5	2	4	47	3	40	18	5
Crespo, Mike, Charlotte†	.131	30	99	5	13	17	4	0	0	6	4	0	0	5	0	35	0	1
Cruz, Ruben, Osceola	.251	79	243	20	61	72	6	1	1	28	1	4	2	12	0	15	2	2
Curtis, Randy, St. Lucie*	.319	126	467	91	149	209	30	12	2	38	4	4	5	93	2	72	52	17
Daniel, Chuck, Daytona	.000	15	0	0	0	0	0	0	0	0	1	0	0	1	0	0	0	0
Daniel, Mike, West Palm Beach	.245	106	359	39	88	132	27	1	5	48	0	5	3	43	3	71	2	1
Davis, Tim, Fort Lauderdale	.071	4	14	0	1	1	0	0	0	1	0	0	0	1	0	2	0	0
Davisson, Sean, Daytona	.184	33	76	9	14	16	2	0	0	6	1	0	6	7	0	21	6	2
Delgado, Alex, Fort Lauderdale	.253	63	225	26	57	72	5	0	2	25	7	1	5	9	1	21	2	2
Delgado, Tim, Daytona	.000	17	1	0	0	0	0	0	0	0	0	0	0	0	0	0	0	0
Demetral, Chris, Vero Beach*	.325	122	437	63	142	185	22	3	5	48	6	3	2	69	2	47	6	6

Player, Team	Avg.	G	AB	R	H	TB	2B	3B	HR	RBI	SH	SF	HP	BB	Int. BB	SO	SB	CS
DeArmas, Rollie, Clearwater	.000	3	3	0	0	0	0	0	0	0	0	0	0	0	0	1	0	0
DeSantis, Dom, Clearwater	.000	49	1	0	0	0	0	0	0	0	0	0	0	0	0	1	0	0
DiFelice, Mike, St. Petersburg	.227	30	97	5	22	24	2	0	0	8	2	2	1	11	1	13	1	0
Dimare, Gino, Fort Lauderdale*	.230	81	278	36	64	67	3	0	0	23	6	3	2	41	1	41	12	8
DiSarcina, Glenn, Sarasota*	.283	120	477	73	135	186	29	5	4	47	0	6	2	33	4	77	11	5
Dorante, Luis, Fort Lauderdale	.074	14	27	1	2	3	1	0	0	1	2	1	0	7	0	8	0	0
Doster, David, Clearwater	.357	9	28	4	10	15	3	1	0	2	0	0	0	2	0	2	0	0
Dotel, Angel, Vero Beach*	.221	88	263	33	58	83	9	2	4	15	2	0	0	35	4	56	2	5
Dubose, Brian, Lakeland*	.313	122	448	74	140	213	27	11	8	68	0	4	4	49	5	97	18	18
Duncan, Andres, Fort Myers†	.364	5	22	3	8	11	0	0	1	1	0	0	0	3	0	6	4	2
Durkin, Marty, Fort Lauderdale†	.259	97	332	43	86	123	16	3	5	32	4	0	1	21	3	73	15	5
Edwards, Jay, Clearwater	.253	124	430	57	109	140	23	4	0	53	6	5	1	48	1	64	21	11
Edwards, Mike, Charlotte	.279	130	458	73	128	194	26	2	12	79	1	3	4	82	2	70	11	6
Estalella, Robert, Clearwater	.229	11	35	4	8	8	0	0	0	4	0	0	0	2	0	3	0	0
Evangelista, George, Charlotte	.231	98	321	39	74	91	12	1	1	18	6	2	10	41	0	62	6	6
Evans, Stan, Clearwater*	.271	39	133	13	36	43	5	1	0	12	1	1	0	14	0	12	4	3
Facione, Chris, Lakeland	.333	3	6	1	2	4	0	1	0	1	0	0	0	0	0	2	0	0
Faircloth, Eugene, Sarasota	.222	5	9	1	2	3	1	0	0	1	0	1	1	1	0	2	1	0
Fermin, Carlos, Lakeland	.252	86	278	25	70	83	11	1	0	19	3	0	1	25	2	38	3	2
Fernandez, Mike, Fort Myers	.267	107	375	47	100	138	29	3	1	37	6	7	3	45	5	73	14	2
Ferreira, Tony, Fort Lauderdale†	.185	42	124	10	23	27	2	1	0	6	4	0	1	25	0	30	2	3
Fisher, David, Clearwater	.240	126	430	54	103	150	25	2	6	54	8	10	8	52	1	42	11	17
Flores, Jose, Osceola†	.243	124	452	47	110	123	11	1	0	39	6	4	1	39	0	64	12	11
Fryman, Troy, Sarasota*	.239	78	285	42	68	105	16	3	5	46	0	1	3	31	3	55	0	0
Fully, Ed, St. Lucie	.239	117	393	49	94	122	12	5	2	29	6	3	2	17	1	66	15	9
Garcia, Omar, St. Lucie	.322	129	485	73	156	196	17	7	3	76	2	5	2	57	2	47	25	8
Garrow, David, Fort Myers	.208	109	351	33	73	94	15	0	2	25	3	2	0	25	0	62	11	4
Geisler, Phil, Clearwater*	.305	87	344	72	105	181	23	4	15	62	2	1	6	29	3	70	4	5
Gerald, Ed, St. Petersburg†	.199	52	176	17	35	55	12	4	0	17	1	2	0	17	0	58	2	1
Glanville, Doug, Daytona	.293	61	239	47	70	88	10	1	2	21	4	0	3	28	0	24	18	15
Gomez, Mike, Clearwater	.286	124	496	63	142	170	21	2	1	44	6	2	4	26	2	23	7	11
Gomez, Rudy, Daytona	.265	40	147	20	39	45	4	1	0	12	3	3	0	19	0	24	3	5
Gonzalez, Pedro, Lakeland	.250	63	200	20	50	62	4	1	2	25	2	3	2	31	4	28	7	2
Grable, Rob, Clearwater	.313	98	351	60	110	162	27	5	5	55	0	5	7	49	3	72	16	9
Graham, Greg, St. Lucie†	.196	26	56	10	11	12	1	0	0	4	0	0	1	13	0	10	1	2
Graham, John, Fort Lauderdale*	.237	55	177	23	42	60	6	3	2	14	4	0	4	18	0	53	2	2
Graham, Tim, Fort Lauderdale*	.259	53	162	34	42	61	5	7	0	11	3	2	0	32	4	31	8	3
Gray, Dan, Vero Beach	.200	1	5	1	1	1	0	0	0	1	0	0	0	0	0	1	0	1
Green, Steve, Vero Beach	.188	15	48	5	9	10	1	0	0	3	0	0	3	11	0	11	0	1
Griffin, Marc, West Palm Beach*	.319	69	226	34	72	88	6	2	2	18	4	0	2	29	1	34	23	8
Grimm, John, Lakeland	.000	16	0	0	0	0	0	0	0	0	0	0	0	2	0	0	0	0
Grissom, Antonio, West Palm Beach	.225	40	138	16	31	42	3	1	2	7	2	0	1	19	0	20	9	7
Grudzielanek, Mark, West Palm Beach	.267	86	300	41	80	106	11	6	1	34	0	0	7	14	0	42	17	10
Guggiana, Todd, Charlotte*	.286	134	514	53	147	193	34	0	4	79	2	5	4	41	7	62	7	4
Hardge, Mike, West Palm Beach	.228	27	92	14	21	28	2	1	1	12	4	3	0	14	0	16	5	6
Harley, Al, Osceola†	.228	121	391	42	89	120	12	8	1	51	2	6	8	36	2	67	20	13
Hartung, Andy, Daytona	.295	44	173	24	51	75	10	1	4	32	0	0	2	23	0	33	1	1
Hayden, David, Clearwater	.310	97	290	42	90	103	13	0	0	27	1	2	6	39	1	38	8	9
Hazlett, Steve, Fort Myers	.339	29	115	19	39	48	5	2	0	6	2	0	1	15	1	21	12	5
Heisler, Laurence, Clearwater	.000	19	2	0	0	0	0	0	0	0	0	0	0	0	0	0	0	0
Helsel, Ron, Dunedin	.333	9	30	4	10	12	2	0	0	0	0	0	3	1	0	4	1	0
Henry, Harold, Sarasota	.203	37	123	16	25	37	9	0	1	7	0	0	5	12	1	34	7	5
Higginson, Bob, Lakeland*	.300	61	223	42	67	101	11	7	3	25	2	2	1	40	1	31	8	3
Hines, Keith, Dunedin	.230	45	152	21	35	57	6	2	4	28	5	1	1	14	0	28	8	0
Holbert, Aaron, St. Petersburg	.265	121	457	60	121	151	18	3	2	31	15	1	4	28	2	61	45	22
Holifield, Rick, Dunedin*	.275	127	407	84	112	214	18	12	20	68	6	4	16	56	6	129	30	13
Hood, Randy, Sarasota	.182	47	143	14	26	34	6	1	0	9	1	1	6	12	1	36	3	2
Hopp, Dean, Clearwater†	.098	26	51	5	5	9	1	0	1	4	5	0	3	4	0	16	0	1
Horincewich, Tom, Fort Myers*	.217	45	161	19	35	46	9	1	0	12	2	1	0	19	3	19	1	1
Horne, Tyrone, West Palm Beach*	.295	82	288	43	85	138	19	2	10	44	1	3	0	40	1	72	11	10
Hubbard, Mike, Daytona	.294	68	245	25	72	91	10	3	1	20	2	5	5	18	0	41	10	6
Huckaby, Ken, Vero Beach	.267	79	281	22	75	103	14	1	4	41	3	2	2	11	1	35	2	1
Hymel, Gary, West Palm Beach	.259	37	112	15	29	49	9	1	3	10	1	1	2	7	0	31	2	2
Johnson, Jack, Daytona	.111	3	9	0	1	1	0	0	0	0	0	0	0	0	0	3	0	0
Johnson, Keith, Vero Beach	.238	111	404	37	96	130	22	0	4	48	6	5	4	18	0	71	13	13
Johnson, Matthew, Dunedin	.209	54	148	19	31	45	5	0	3	18	5	0	3	18	0	31	3	2
Johnson, Reggie, Vero Beach	.263	84	270	27	71	95	16	1	2	29	5	3	2	17	0	73	5	6
Jones, Keith, St. Petersburg*	.244	102	324	40	79	99	12	4	0	25	5	0	0	14	2	40	21	9
Kapano, Corey, Daytona	.200	7	25	2	5	6	1	0	0	3	0	0	0	0	0	8	3	1
Keister, Tripp, St. Lucie*	.500	3	4	0	2	2	0	0	0	0	0	0	0	1	0	1	0	1
Kennedy, Darryl, Charlotte	.280	106	347	47	97	123	23	0	1	30	5	2	1	47	0	38	5	7
Kieschnick, Brooks, Daytona*	.182	6	22	1	4	6	2	0	0	2	0	0	1	0	0	4	0	1
Killen, Brent, Lakeland*	.243	45	136	17	33	46	10	0	1	18	1	1	3	36	0	22	2	3
King, Jason, St. Lucie†	.294	12	34	11	10	11	1	0	0	5	0	1	0	7	0	4	0	2
Koeyers, Ramsey, West Palm Beach	.167	4	12	0	2	2	0	0	0	3	0	1	0	0	0	5	8	0
Kontorinis, Andrew, Fort Myers*	.255	114	408	44	104	143	24	3	3	59	3	4	6	40	5	42	4	5
Lamar, Johnny, Lakeland*	.269	102	346	43	93	133	16	6	4	37	0	2	0	35	3	67	10	2
Landrum, Tito, Vero Beach	.232	116	396	50	92	136	13	2	9	42	5	4	9	41	1	95	8	6
Landry, Lonny, Lakeland	.500	2	4	0	2	4	2	0	0	1	0	0	0	0	0	1	0	0
Lane, Dan, West Palm Beach	.228	66	193	25	44	59	9	0	2	24	4	1	2	26	3	31	2	2
Lantigua, Ed, Vero Beach	.271	119	439	70	119	173	16	4	10	79	1	7	10	31	1	107	10	2
Larkin, James, Fort Lauderdale*	.203	47	158	11	32	39	7	0	0	17	2	0	0	7	0	34	1	0
Larregui, Ed, Daytona	.237	95	329	26	78	104	10	5	2	34	5	2	2	15	0	24	1	11
Larson, Danny, Clearwater*	.248	47	129	14	32	39	5	1	0	16	3	3	0	8	0	38	8	2
LaValliere, Mike, Sarasota*	.306	32	108	6	33	35	2	0	0	14	0	3	1	19	1	5	2	0
LeVangie, Dana, Fort Lauderdale	.188	80	250	17	47	52	5	0	0	11	2	0	6	26	0	46	0	2
Loeb, Marc, Dunedin	.238	75	248	20	59	75	10	0	2	27	2	1	1	29	0	57	4	4
Lowery, Terrell, Charlotte	.300	65	257	46	77	111	7	9	3	36	1	1	2	46	2	47	14	15
LoDuca, Paul, Vero Beach	.313	39	134	17	42	48	6	0	0	13	0	1	2	13	0	22	0	0
Lutz, Brent, Dunedin	.264	84	246	38	65	95	12	3	4	33	3	2	5	31	1	60	16	8
Manahan, Austin, West Palm Beach†	.237	77	274	34	65	95	14	2	4	29	1	2	0	26	0	78	7	3
Maness, Dwight, Vero Beach	.259	118	409	57	106	153	21	4	6	42	8	7	15	32	0	105	22	13
Manning, Henry, Sarasota	.228	27	79	8	18	21	3	0	0	4	0	0	2	1	0	12	0	0
Marrero, Kenny, Lakeland	.250	9	8	0	2	2	0	0	0	0	0	0	0	2	0	2	0	0

Player, Team	Avg.	G	AB	R	H	TB	2B	3B	HR	RBI	SH	SF	HP	BB	Int. BB	SO	SB	CS
Mashore, Justin, Lakeland	.256	118	442	64	113	141	11	4	3	30	16	5	6	37	4	92	26	13
Matos, Domingo, West Palm Beach	.251	46	171	23	43	64	10	1	3	20	1	2	1	6	0	34	4	0
McClinton, Tim, St. Lucie	.211	49	161	22	34	49	7	1	2	17	0	0	0	9	0	37	6	1
McConnell, Chad, Clearwater	.240	90	300	43	72	113	17	3	6	37	0	2	4	51	2	98	9	5
McConnell, Tim, Lakeland	.273	81	253	34	69	100	16	3	3	43	5	6	0	41	2	48	9	3
McDonnell, Shawn, Daytona†	.277	42	141	18	39	47	2	0	2	14	1	0	1	20	1	18	2	2
McGuire, Ryan, Fort Lauderdale*	.324	58	213	23	69	97	12	2	4	38	1	3	2	27	3	34	2	4
McNabb, Buck, Osceola*	.285	125	487	69	139	171	15	7	1	35	4	1	6	52	2	66	28	15
Mediavilla, Ricky, St. Petersburg	.205	30	83	5	17	18	1	0	0	8	5	2	3	7	0	13	7	0
Merloni, Louis, Fort Lauderdale	.244	44	156	14	38	47	1	1	2	21	0	4	1	13	1	26	1	1
Meza, Larry, St. Petersburg*	.272	86	257	31	70	83	11	1	0	22	1	2	0	37	4	41	3	6
Millan, Bernie, St. Lucie†	.270	122	459	33	124	136	12	0	0	54	6	5	1	22	2	28	2	9
Miller, Damian, Fort Myers	.212	87	325	31	69	86	12	1	1	26	1	0	0	31	0	44	6	3
Milne, Darren, Lakeland	.196	71	204	19	40	63	6	1	5	18	2	2	0	23	0	33	6	5
Miranda, Geovany, Sarasota	.175	19	63	7	11	13	0	1	0	2	1	0	1	1	0	8	3	0
Moler, Jason, Clearwater	.289	97	350	59	101	167	17	2	15	64	0	4	3	46	3	40	5	7
Molina, Jose, Daytona	.143	3	7	0	1	1	0	0	0	1	0	0	0	2	0	0	0	1
Montero, Danny, Daytona	1.000	1	1	1	1	1	0	0	0	0	0	0	0	0	0	0	0	0
Moore, Tim, Fort Myers†	.252	69	222	32	56	95	15	3	6	32	1	4	0	28	0	52	17	3
Morel, Plinio, St. Petersburg	.000	3	3	1	0	0	0	0	0	0	0	0	0	0	0	0	0	0
Moreno, Jorge, Lakeland†	.000	2	1	0	0	0	0	0	0	0	0	1	0	0	0	1	0	0
Morgan, Kevin, Lakeland	.237	112	417	45	99	121	12	2	2	34	3	4	2	32	2	84	9	7
Morris, Rod, Charlotte*	.206	33	107	11	22	26	0	2	0	6	2	0	0	7	0	24	2	3
Morrow, Chris, Vero Beach*	.310	88	316	47	98	161	18	3	13	66	0	3	1	21	6	40	7	3
Mota, Willie, Fort Myers†	.235	39	149	13	35	47	6	0	2	5	2	0	0	8	0	21	1	1
Munoz, J.J., Clearwater*	.000	56	2	1	0	0	0	0	0	0	0	0	0	0	0	0	0	0
Murphy, James, Fort Lauderdale*	.296	54	186	28	55	63	4	2	0	21	1	2	1	24	0	23	9	9
Norman, Kenny, Fort Myers*	.207	84	237	27	49	61	9	0	1	8	0	0	4	11	0	67	12	7
Northrup, Kevin, West Palm Beach	.296	131	459	65	136	183	29	0	6	63	4	5	3	70	7	76	10	7
Nunez, Bernie, Daytona	.231	124	458	51	106	173	18	2	15	73	3	6	3	37	3	119	5	3
O'Brien, John, St. Petersburg	.320	9	25	2	8	12	1	0	1	5	0	1	1	2	0	3	0	0
O'Neal, Kelley, Lakeland*	.275	117	436	66	120	149	14	3	3	36	4	3	7	48	1	73	28	10
Ogden, Jamie, Fort Myers*	.242	118	396	37	96	150	22	4	8	46	4	1	6	34	1	89	7	1
Ortiz, Nick, Fort Lauderdale	.205	36	112	9	23	37	9	1	1	14	4	0	0	9	0	39	2	1
Ozoria, Claudio, West Palm Beach	.199	81	226	28	45	62	5	3	2	18	5	1	1	9	2	57	8	3
Perozo, Ed, Fort Lauderdale†	.219	49	160	18	35	51	5	1	3	18	1	0	2	11	2	35	0	0
Petersen, Chris, Daytona	.214	130	473	66	101	111	10	0	0	28	17	1	9	58	0	105	19	11
Pettiford, Cecil, Lakeland	.000	33	2	0	0	0	0	0	0	0	0	0	0	0	0	1	0	0
Phillips, Chris, Fort Myers	.264	54	197	32	52	63	9	1	0	15	2	2	2	26	0	34	9	9
Pimentel, Wander, St. Petersburg	.190	23	58	3	11	11	0	0	0	4	1	0	0	3	0	8	0	0
Pinkney, Alton, Vero Beach*	.239	14	46	8	11	11	0	0	0	1	0	0	1	9	0	7	4	2
Poe, Charles, Sarasota	.249	95	313	45	78	139	16	6	11	47	2	0	4	33	0	91	5	8
Powell, Ken, Charlotte	.302	31	116	15	35	39	1	0	1	20	1	1	1	13	1	32	3	2
Prybylinski, Don, St. Petersburg	.191	67	209	27	40	51	11	0	0	18	6	1	3	16	0	39	2	0
Puchales, Javier, Vero Beach*	.337	77	279	46	94	100	6	0	0	27	6	1	3	17	0	44	4	5
Radziewicz, Doug, St. Petersburg*	.342	123	439	66	150	202	36	2	4	72	1	5	5	73	11	58	6	8
Randall, Mark, Clearwater	.000	52	1	0	0	0	0	0	0	0	0	0	0	0	0	1	0	0
Rea, Clarke, Lakeland*	.141	24	71	4	10	12	2	0	0	8	1	2	0	10	0	21	1	0
Reyes, Jimmy, Sarasota†	.256	17	43	2	11	13	0	1	0	3	0	0	0	6	0	8	2	0
Reyes, Roberto, West Palm Beach	.140	16	43	4	6	6	0	0	0	3	1	0	1	6	0	8	1	0
Robledo, Nilson, Sarasota	.259	74	259	35	67	108	18	1	7	34	3	5	2	13	2	63	0	1
Rodriguez, Adam, Lakeland	.167	3	6	4	1	4	0	0	1	3	0	0	0	2	0	0	0	0
Ronan, Marc, St. Petersburg*	.310	25	87	13	27	32	5	0	0	6	3	2	0	6	0	10	0	0
Roper, Chad, Fort Myers	.248	125	454	46	112	162	17	3	9	65	4	5	6	43	2	96	1	2
Rosado, Edwin, Clearwater†	.204	39	137	22	28	45	7	2	2	12	2	2	1	29	1	30	4	1
Rosario, Gabriel, Dunedin	.224	72	219	19	49	58	3	3	0	18	6	0	4	7	0	24	12	6
Ross, Tony, Osceola	.160	9	25	3	4	4	0	0	0	1	0	0	1	1	0	9	0	0
Rudolph, Mason, St. Lucie	.188	22	64	7	12	16	2	1	0	5	1	0	0	2	0	19	0	0
Ruff, Dan, Lakeland*	.284	101	349	47	99	155	17	6	9	65	2	8	5	36	2	65	1	5
Rundels, Matt, West Palm Beach	.115	8	26	2	3	5	0	1	0	2	0	1	0	3	1	4	3	1
Rusk, Troy, Clearwater*	.296	61	199	30	59	99	8	1	10	40	1	0	0	23	0	55	0	3
Saenz, Olmedo, Sarasota	.256	33	121	13	31	48	9	4	0	27	1	1	2	9	0	18	3	1
Saffer, Jon, West Palm Beach*	.208	7	24	3	5	5	0	0	0	2	1	0	1	2	0	5	1	3
Sandberg, Ryne, Daytona	.200	2	5	2	1	4	0	0	1	2	0	0	0	1	0	0	0	0
Sandy, Tim, St. Lucie*	.067	4	15	0	1	2	1	0	0	1	0	0	0	1	0	3	0	0
Santana, Raul, West Palm Beach	.230	74	256	23	59	89	11	2	5	27	2	2	1	14	1	47	1	3
Saunders, Chris, St. Lucie	.252	123	456	45	115	149	14	4	4	64	1	4	1	40	4	89	6	7
Schofield, Dick, Dunedin	.200	11	30	4	6	8	2	0	0	4	2	0	0	3	0	7	0	1
Schulte, Rich, Osceola*	.227	19	44	4	10	10	0	0	0	3	1	1	0	3	0	7	2	3
Scott, Kevin, Osceola	.253	30	75	11	19	26	5	1	0	9	0	4	0	4	0	17	2	1
Sheppard, Don, Dunedin	.310	39	116	12	36	44	5	4	0	10	2	0	0	17	1	26	6	4
Shockey, Greg, Fort Myers*	.259	16	54	8	14	17	3	0	0	5	0	1	0	12	2	7	4	2
Simons, Mitch, West Palm Beach	.256	45	156	24	40	49	4	1	1	13	1	2	3	19	0	9	14	3
Sirak, Ken, Clearwater*	.196	25	51	8	10	16	3	0	1	5	2	0	1	6	0	16	1	0
Smith, Dan, Daytona	.249	102	334	50	83	126	11	4	8	36	6	5	3	25	0	65	15	5
Smith, Dave, Fort Lauderdale	.225	36	120	22	27	31	2	1	0	8	1	2	1	17	1	31	7	1
Smith, Dwight, Daytona*	.313	5	16	3	5	9	4	0	0	2	0	0	1	3	0	4	0	1
Smith, John, St. Lucie	.268	110	365	66	98	166	19	8	11	56	1	4	11	48	1	86	22	13
Smith, Mike, Charlotte	.235	86	327	33	77	110	16	4	3	43	3	3	3	37	0	55	3	6
Snopek, Chris, Sarasota	.245	107	371	61	91	150	21	4	10	50	3	6	1	65	2	67	3	2
Soto, Emison, Fort Lauderdale	.151	45	139	13	21	38	5	0	4	12	4	1	2	6	0	36	1	1
Steverson, Todd, Dunedin	.271	106	413	68	112	185	32	4	11	54	3	1	1	44	2	118	15	12
Stutheit, Tim, Daytona	.167	5	12	1	2	2	0	0	0	1	0	0	0	5	0	7	1	0
Stynes, Chris, Dunedin	.304	123	496	72	151	210	28	5	7	48	4	4	3	25	2	40	19	9
Teel, Garrett, Vero Beach	.000	5	9	0	0	0	0	0	0	0	0	0	0	2	0	0	0	0
Terilli, Joey, Daytona*	.213	70	216	29	46	62	10	3	0	19	2	1	2	40	1	27	4	2
Texidor, Jose, Charlotte	.319	19	72	14	23	27	4	0	0	4	0	0	0	5	1	11	2	0
Thomas, Brian, Charlotte*	.289	34	135	25	39	52	3	2	2	11	3	0	0	18	1	29	4	1
Thomas, Tim, Lakeland	.167	15	48	5	8	11	1	1	0	2	1	0	2	8	0	13	1	1
Tokheim, David, Clearwater*	.329	41	155	27	51	63	8	2	0	11	1	1	2	14	4	17	7	5
Torres, Paul, Daytona	.278	100	353	63	98	164	17	5	13	43	1	3	8	52	0	94	5	4
Tosar, Mike, West Palm Beach*	.267	33	101	9	27	30	3	0	0	11	1	0	0	7	0	17	4	0
Tovar, Edgar, West Palm Beach	.229	116	467	52	107	138	21	2	2	32	11	2	3	16	2	33	4	5
Townley, Jason, Dunedin	.500	2	4	1	2	2	0	0	0	1	0	0	0	1	0	0	0	0

Player, Team	Avg.	G	AB	R	H	TB	2B	3B	HR	RBI	SH	SF	HP	BB	Int. BB	SO	SB	CS
Tranberg, Mark, Clearwater	.000	15	1	0	0	0	0	0	0	0	0	0	0	0	0	1	0	0
Tredaway, Chad, Daytona†	.256	66	242	32	62	74	12	0	0	21	3	4	0	27	2	25	4	3
Tremie, Chris, Sarasota	.162	14	37	2	6	7	1	0	0	5	0	0	3	2	0	4	0	0
Truby, Chris, Osceola	.000	3	13	0	0	0	0	0	0	0	0	0	0	0	0	2	0	0
Turvey, Joe, St. Petersburg*	.259	18	27	1	7	8	1	0	0	3	1	0	0	2	1	15	0	0
Valdez, Pedro, Daytona*	.287	60	230	27	66	108	16	1	8	49	0	5	2	9	1	30	3	4
Valrie, Kerry, Sarasota	.212	115	386	47	82	136	14	2	12	52	2	7	4	17	1	81	19	7
Vazquez, Jose, St. Petersburg	.254	29	71	10	18	20	2	0	0	3	0	0	0	6	1	18	5	0
Velez, Jose, St. Petersburg†	.236	81	178	12	42	49	3	2	0	15	3	0	0	6	1	32	0	1
Ventress, Leroy, Daytona†	.183	17	60	8	11	12	1	0	0	4	0	0	0	10	1	17	2	1
Vilet, Tom, Clearwater	.185	18	27	4	5	5	0	0	0	4	0	0	1	3	0	11	0	0
Vinas, Julio, Sarasota	.246	18	65	5	16	23	2	1	1	7	0	0	0	5	0	13	0	0
Vinyard, Derek, Fort Lauderdale†	.210	85	281	34	59	64	3	1	0	19	6	1	5	33	0	65	26	8
Vogel, Mike, Sarasota†	.239	71	247	21	59	66	7	0	0	21	2	3	0	29	1	48	2	0
Vorbeck, Eric, Vero Beach	.194	51	129	17	25	29	4	0	0	12	1	2	2	16	0	27	5	2
Walker, Dennis, Sarasota	.355	30	107	16	38	48	5	1	1	13	0	1	0	7	1	25	2	2
Wallin, Les, Fort Lauderdale*	.297	47	155	23	46	74	16	0	4	25	1	1	0	27	2	13	0	1
Warner, Ron, St. Petersburg	.289	103	311	42	90	116	8	3	4	37	7	4	5	31	2	39	5	1
Webb, Lonnie, Vero Beach	.258	31	97	15	25	38	5	1	2	8	0	3	0	6	0	23	2	2
Weinke, Chris, Dunedin*	.284	128	476	68	135	206	16	2	17	98	1	4	2	66	8	78	8	6
Welch, Mike, Charlotte*	.231	50	173	15	40	49	7	1	0	10	2	1	1	13	1	45	4	2
Wells, Robert, Clearwater	.000	12	1	0	0	0	0	0	0	0	0	0	0	0	0	1	0	0
White, Billy, Daytona	.336	38	125	19	42	64	9	2	3	22	4	1	5	16	0	23	2	0
White, Derrick, West Palm Beach	.200	6	25	1	5	5	0	0	0	1	0	0	1	0	0	2	2	0
White, Jimmy, Osceola*	.275	125	447	80	123	177	9	12	7	37	0	3	5	54	1	120	24	17
Williams, Lanny, Charlotte	.229	58	175	15	40	54	5	0	3	18	2	1	6	12	0	59	5	2
Wilson, Desi, Charlotte*	.305	131	511	83	156	200	21	7	3	70	0	2	7	50	4	90	29	11
Wilstead, Randy, West Palm Beach*	.333	60	201	33	67	101	19	3	3	35	0	2	1	39	6	39	3	1
Winston, Todd, Osceola	.156	72	212	28	33	47	9	1	1	21	6	2	7	26	0	57	10	6
Withem, Shannon, Lakeland	.000	16	3	0	0	0	0	0	0	0	0	0	0	0	0	1	0	0
Wolff, Jim, Daytona	.224	24	67	5	15	20	5	0	0	5	0	1	1	3	0	12	1	1
Wyngarden, Brett, Osceola	.255	22	55	5	14	18	4	0	0	6	0	1	0	5	0	14	0	1
Yelton, Rob, Lakeland	.300	24	90	14	27	31	4	0	0	13	0	0	1	8	0	9	0	2
Young, Dmitri, St. Petersburg†	.315	69	270	31	85	119	13	3	5	43	0	5	2	24	3	28	3	4
Zambrano, Jose, Fort Lauderdale	.158	23	57	6	9	15	3	0	1	5	0	0	0	6	0	24	0	1
Zuber, Jon, Clearwater*	.308	129	494	70	152	214	37	5	5	69	3	4	0	49	5	47	6	6

The following pitchers, listed alphabetically by club, with games in parentheses, had no plate appearances, primarily through use of designated hitters:

CHARLOTTE—Brownholtz, Joe (24); Curtis, Chris (27); Dettmer, John (27); Fajardo, Hector (2); Gandolph, Dave (34); Geeve, Dave (24); Giberti, Dave (31); Henderson, Daryl (16); Heredia, Wilson (34); Lacy, Kerry (4); Magee, Dan (30); Manuel, Barry (3); Newcomb, Chris (21); Patterson, Dan (47); Reed, Bob (1); Sadecki, Steve (24); Schuermann, Lance (46); Smith, Dan S. (1); Washington, Tyrone (23).

CLEARWATER—Boldt, Sean (2); Bottalico, Ricky (13); Brown, Greg (11); Corry, Steve (1); DeJesus, Jose (11); Gilmore, Joel (7); Gomes, Wayne (9); Holman, Craig (7); Humphry, Trevor (9); Juhl, Mike (21); Kirkland, Kris (2); Mitchell, Larry (9); Rama, Shelby (7); Sepeda, Jamie (26); Trisler, John (27).

DAYTONA—Adams, Terry (13); Bradford, Troy (11); Broome, John (1); Burlingame, Ben (8); Corbett, Sherman (5); Dickson, Lance (3); Dreyer, Darren (4); Franklin, Jay (39); Howze, Ben (20); James, Todd (5); Kirk, Charles (20); Meyer, Jay (33); Morones, Eugenio (13); Ratliff, Jon (8); Rodriguez, Cristobal (29); Schramm, Carl (34); Steenstra, Ken (13); Strauss, Julio (14); Taylor, Aaron (15); Tidwell, Mike (39); Wallace, Derek (14); White, Fred (7); Whitfill, Mike (1).

DUNEDIN—Arias, Alfredo (3); Carrara, Giovanni (27); Daniels, Lee (2); Darley, Ned (5); Gray, Dennis (26); Grove, Scott (30); Heble, Kurt (41); Hotchkiss, Tom (43); Jordan, Ricardo (15); Kotes, Chris (10); Lindsay, Tim (22); Montoya, Al (50); Phillips, Randy (17); Singer, Tom (26); Spoljaric, Paul (4); Steed, Ricky (22); Timlin, Mike (4); Weber, Ben (55); Williams, Woody (2).

FORT LAUDERDALE—Allen, Ron (26); Amos, Chad (42); Bennett, Shayne (23); Blais, Mike (3); Brooks, Wes (19); Davis, Chris (8); Gonzalez, Mel (21); Hansen, Brent (14); Hayward, Steve (13); Hoy, Pete (4); Johnson, Jeff (14); Kennedy, Greg (12); Klvac, Dave (21); Lawrence, Randy (5); Martinez, Cesar (18); Mosley, Tony (17); Nies, Joel (20); Osterkamp, Ken (39); Perez, Hilario (6); Santamaria, Silverio (41).

FORT MYERS—Barcelo, Marc (7); Bigham, Dave (5); Dixon, Roger (25); Garcia, Luis (55); Gavaghan, Sean (19); Johnson, Greg (2); Kohl, Jim (17); Konieczki, Dominic (12); Legault, Kevin (18); Naulty, Dan (7); Radke, Brad (14); Roberts, Brett (28); Robinson, Bob (15); Saccavino, Paul (23); Sweeney, Mark (26); Swope, Mark (26); Thelen, Jeff (10); Watkins, Scott (10).

LAKELAND—Ahearne, Pat (25); Berlin, Mike (9); Coppeta, Greg (36); Edmondson, Brian (19); Greene, Rich (26); Guilfoyle, Mike (9); Gullickson, Bill (5); Henry, Jim (4); Kelley, Rich (26); Kosenski, John (35); Kostich, Bill (11); Mendenhall, Casey (15); Mysel, Dave (12); Raffo, Greg (35); Stidham, Phil (25); Thompson, Justin (11); Walsh, Dennis (7).

OSCEOLA—Anderson, Tom (16); Brown, Duane (2); Edens, Tom (3); Gallaher, Kevin (21); Guerry, Kyle (56); Hennis, Randy (14); Holliday, Brian (6); Kent, Troy (24); Lane, Kevin (58); Lewis, Jim (4); Mercado, Hector (2); Micki, Doug (26); Nieto, Roy (42); Padron, Oscar (2); Powers, Steve (36); Sewell, Joe (38); Waring, Ken (4); Wheeler, Ken (26); White, Chris (13).

ST. LUCIE—Beckerman, Andy (20); Carpenter, Bob (23); Crawford, Joe (34); Fernandez, Sid (1); Fiegel, Todd (25); Fuller, Mark (40); Guzik, Bob (19); Jacomb, Jason (14); Kindell, Scott (1); McCready, Jim (40); Miller, Pat (21); Petcka, Joe (3); Pulsipher, Bill (13); Roberts, Chris (25); Schorr, Brad (27); Smith, Ottis (22); Vitko, Joe (2).

ST. PETERSBURG—Arrandale, Matt (2); Bailey, Roy (31); Botkin, Alan (49); Brumley, Duff (8); Corona, John (59); Corrigan, Cory (4); Davis, Clint (29); Hisey, Jason (17); Johnson, Steve (22); Jolley, Mike (11); Lowe, Sean (25); Martinez, Francisco (13); Matranga, Jeff (5); McGarity, Jeremy (34); Miller, Eric (26); Montgomery, Steve (14); Romanoli, Paul (17); Simmons, Scott (13); Slininger, Dennis (17); Wiseman, Dennis (2).

SARASOTA—Andujar, Luis (18); Boehringer, Brian (18); Christman, Scott (2); Dunne, Mike (7); Ellis, Bob (15); Fordham, Tom (2); Gajkowski, Steve (43); Gordon, Tony (2); Heathcott, Mike (26); Johnson, Barry (18); Johnston, Sean (12); Keating, Dave (22); Levine, Alan (27); Locklear, Dean (18); Merigliano, Frank (18); Stieb, Dave (2); Tagle, Henry (17); Thomas, Larry (8); Tolar, Kevin (23).

VERO BEACH—Brosnan, Jason (23); Correa, Ed (10); Daspit, Jim (1); Duran, Roberto (8); Gutierrez, Rafael (15); Hamilton, Ken (32); Henderson, Ryan (30); James, Mike (30); Jones, Keith (15); Lavigne, Martin (22); Licursi, Rich (25); Linares, Rich (45); Nichting, Chris (4); Pincavitch, Kevin (6); Prado, Jose (12); Pyc, Dave (23); Rodriguez, Felix (32); Salcedo, Jose (8); Sinacori, Chris (16); Veras, Dario (24); Walden, Ronnie (3); Watts, Brandon (8); White, Brandon (8); Zerbe, Chad (10).

WEST PALM BEACH—Arteaga, Ivan (4); Aucoin, Derek (38); Baxter, Bob (33); Connolly, Matt (6); DeHart, Rick (7); Gentile, Scott (25); Henderson, Rodney (22); Larosa, Mark (54); Looney, Brian (18); McDonald, Kevin (15); Norris, Joe (26); Powers, Terry (24); Rushworth, Jim (24); Schmidt, Curt (44); Thomas, Mike (25); Wallace, Billy (25); Wetteland, John (2); Winston, Darrin (8); Woodring, Jason (4).

GRAND SLAMS—Ruff, 2; Alder, Alfonzo, Ayala, Bright, Burns, Burrough, Butler, Castillo, Horne, Huckaby, Lantigua, C. McConnell, McDonnell, Miller, O'Neal, Perozo, M. Smith, Valdez, Zuber, 1 each.

AWARDED FIRST BASE ON CATCHER'S INTERFERENCE—Durkin 5 (Castillo, Prybylinski, Rea, Turvey, Wolff); Burns 3 (Brooks, Loeb, LaValliere); Cantu 2 (Brooks, Hubbard); Radziewicz 2 (Winston 2); Demetral (T. McConnell); M. Edwards (Ma. Brown); Hayden (Gray); Lamar (Prybylinski); Lantigua (Rodriguez); McGuire (Gonzalez); Stynes (Ma. Brown); B. Thomas (Wolff); Velez (Santana); Young (Brooks).

TEAM

Team	ERA	G	CG	ShO	Sv.	IP	H	R	ER	HR	HB	BB	Int. BB	SO	WP	Bk.
Charlotte	2.97	134	9	15	47	1192.1	1080	459	394	36	36	415	13	789	54	18
St. Lucie	3.08	130	13	9	43	1125.1	1115	467	385	43	48	324	19	718	36	16
St. Petersburg	3.09	133	8	16	41	1185.1	1074	502	407	54	33	455	21	794	50	12
Sarasota	3.14	134	29	11	29	1171.0	1057	518	409	40	36	419	25	793	58	13
West Palm Beach	3.42	136	3	10	42	1192.0	1082	544	453	31	55	473	12	963	55	24
Clearwater	3.55	135	10	5	34	1189.2	1253	566	469	47	39	389	29	738	70	12
Lakeland	3.59	129	8	8	28	1129.1	1121	527	450	47	53	406	9	697	54	14
Dunedin	3.60	132	3	9	27	1147.1	1079	571	459	69	46	524	27	829	88	18
Daytona	3.80	133	9	10	26	1164.0	1154	608	491	59	68	410	17	673	59	22
Osceola	3.85	130	6	9	32	1124.2	1207	621	481	65	37	439	42	697	78	12
Vero Beach	4.20	133	3	4	33	1164.1	1138	672	543	80	51	593	45	849	79	30
Fort Myers	4.31	134	10	2	30	1180.0	1317	664	565	47	51	479	33	792	70	9
Fort Lauderdale	4.45	131	18	7	20	1162.1	1257	682	575	71	35	536	15	719	75	24

INDIVIDUAL

(Leading qualifiers for earned-run average leadership— 109 or more innings)

*Throws lefthanded.

Pitcher, Team	W	L	Pct.	ERA	G	GS	CG	GF	ShO	Sv.	IP	H	R	ER	HR	HB	BB	Int. BB	SO	WP
Linares, Vero Beach	4	4	.500	1.81	45	7	0	29	0	13	109.1	97	36	22	4	2	28	5	80	1
Dettmer, Charlotte	16	3	.842	2.15	27	27	5	0	2	0	163.0	132	44	39	6	7	33	0	128	2
Pyc, Vero Beach*	7	8	.467	2.38	23	15	1	2	0	0	113.1	97	41	30	1	1	47	2	78	5
Roberts, St. Lucie*	13	5	.722	2.75	25	25	3	0	2	0	173.1	162	64	53	3	7	36	0	111	2
Boehringer, Sarasota	10	4	.714	2.80	18	17	3	0	0	0	119.0	103	47	37	2	1	51	2	92	2
Geeve, Charlotte	11	8	.579	2.85	24	23	1	1	1	0	132.2	141	52	42	7	3	19	0	80	8
Henderson, West Palm Beach	12	7	.632	2.90	22	22	1	1	0	1	143.0	110	50	46	3	6	44	0	127	8
Edmondson, Lakeland	8	5	.615	2.99	19	19	1	0	0	0	114.1	115	44	38	6	3	43	0	64	7
Wallace, West Palm Beach*	11	8	.579	3.28	25	24	0	0	0	0	137.1	112	61	50	2	11	65	0	126	5
Fiegel, St. Lucie*	10	7	.588	3.39	25	16	0	5	0	0	116.2	122	60	44	7	3	42	0	71	4

Departmental leaders: G—Corona, 59; W—Dettmer, 16; L—B. Roberts, 16; Pct.—Dettmer, .842; GS—Badorek, B. Roberts, 28; CG—Ellis, 8; GF—Larosa, 43; ShO—Brooks, 3; Sv.—Cl. Davis, Larosa, 19; IP—Schorr, 181.2; H—Wheeler, 196; R—Wheeler, 101; ER—B. Roberts, 84; HR—Mlicki, 16; HB—B. Wallace, 11; BB—Gray, 97; IBB—D. Brown, 10; SO—Levine, 129; WP—Singer, 17.

(All pitchers—listed alphabetically)

Pitcher, Team	W	L	Pct.	ERA	G	GS	CG	GF	ShO	Sv.	IP	H	R	ER	HR	HB	BB	Int. BB	SO	WP
Adams, Daytona	3	5	.375	4.97	13	13	0	0	0	0	70.2	78	47	39	2	1	43	0	35	9
Ahearne, Lakeland	6	15	.286	4.46	25	24	2	0	0	0	147.1	160	87	73	8	6	48	0	51	3
Allen, West Palm Beach	0	0	.000	0.00	1	0	0	1	0	0	1.0	1	1	0	0	1	1	0	0	0
Allen, Fort Lauderdale*	6	5	.545	5.03	26	10	1	5	0	0	78.2	80	48	44	4	6	56	1	45	4
Amos, Fort Lauderdale	3	2	.600	6.97	42	0	0	21	0	4	50.1	53	43	39	7	5	30	1	40	6
Anderson, Osceola	2	8	.200	3.01	16	16	1	0	1	0	98.2	109	50	33	2	8	28	1	72	8
Andujar, Sarasota	6	6	.500	1.99	18	11	2	4	0	1	86.0	67	26	19	2	3	28	0	76	1
Arias, Dunedin	0	0	.000	8.10	3	0	0	2	0	0	3.1	6	3	3	0	0	2	0	2	1
Arrandale, St. Petersburg	1	0	1.000	1.29	2	0	0	2	0	0	14.0	8	2	2	1	0	3	0	11	1
Arteaga, West Palm Beach	0	3	.000	8.04	4	4	0	0	0	0	15.2	23	14	14	1	1	9	0	10	0
Aucoin, West Palm Beach	4	4	.500	4.23	38	6	0	6	0	1	87.1	89	48	41	5	0	44	3	62	8
Badorek, St. Petersburg	15	7	.682	3.44	29	28	2	1	0	0	170.0	170	76	65	6	4	53	1	60	3
Bailey, St. Petersburg	2	3	.400	3.89	31	0	0	8	0	1	44.0	34	22	19	4	1	17	1	29	0
Barcelo, Fort Myers	1	1	.500	2.74	7	3	0	3	0	0	23.0	18	10	7	1	1	4	0	24	1
Baxter, West Palm Beach*	2	2	.500	2.28	33	0	0	18	0	6	59.1	55	20	15	1	0	5	1	29	2
Beckerman, St. Lucie	2	0	1.000	0.38	20	0	0	19	0	14	26.2	16	3	1	0	1	2	0	28	1
Bennett, Fort Lauderdale	1	2	.333	1.72	23	0	0	18	0	6	31.1	26	8	6	1	0	11	1	23	2
Berlin, Lakeland	1	5	.167	9.69	9	8	1	1	1	0	39.0	62	45	42	3	3	23	1	18	4
Bigham, Fort Myers*	8	3	.727	3.40	53	0	0	18	0	5	84.2	87	37	32	3	6	22	2	60	2
Blais, Fort Lauderdale	1	1	.500	1.50	3	0	0	3	0	0	6.0	4	1	1	0	0	3	1	7	0
Blazier, Clearwater	9	8	.529	3.94	27	23	1	1	0	0	155.1	171	80	68	8	6	40	1	86	1
Boehringer, Sarasota	10	4	.714	2.80	18	17	3	0	0	0	119.0	103	47	37	2	1	51	2	92	2
Boldt, Clearwater	0	0	.000	9.00	2	0	0	1	0	0	3.0	7	5	3	0	1	0	2	1	0
Botkin, St. Petersburg*	3	3	.500	3.17	49	0	0	10	0	0	48.1	45	21	17	1	3	25	6	24	6
Bottalico, Clearwater*	1	0	1.000	2.75	13	0	0	9	0	4	19.2	19	6	6	0	0	5	0	19	0
Bradford, Daytona	3	5	.375	5.53	11	10	0	0	0	0	53.2	58	35	33	7	3	27	1	39	3
Brooks, Fort Lauderdale	8	5	.615	3.89	19	18	4	0	3	0	127.1	124	62	55	7	2	42	0	85	4
Broome, Daytona	0	1	.000	4.50	1	1	0	0	0	0	6.0	6	3	3	0	0	0	0	1	0
Brosnan, Vero Beach*	0	2	.000	4.56	23	0	0	9	0	1	25.2	30	22	13	1	1	19	2	32	4
Brown, Osceola	2	1	.667	5.02	35	0	0	15	0	0	52.0	65	32	29	4	2	31	10	27	9
Brown, Clearwater	8	3	.727	2.94	11	11	0	0	1	0	67.1	76	29	22	1	3	11	0	21	4
Brownholtz, Charlotte*	4	0	1.000	1.56	24	5	0	6	0	2	69.1	62	15	12	1	2	19	0	48	3
Brumley, St. Petersburg	5	1	.833	0.64	8	8	0	0	0	0	56.0	26	5	4	2	2	13	0	67	1
Burlingame, Daytona	0	1	.000	7.79	8	1	0	2	0	0	17.1	27	16	15	4	2	9	0	10	0
Carpentier, St. Lucie	2	1	.667	3.50	23	1	0	5	0	0	36.0	39	19	14	3	5	12	1	10	3
Carrara, Dunedin	6	11	.353	3.45	27	24	1	1	0	0	140.2	136	69	54	14	4	59	0	108	10
Christman, Sarasota*	0	1	.000	0.87	2	2	0	0	0	0	10.1	5	4	1	0	1	5	0	6	0
Civit, West Palm Beach	0	0	.000	4.50	2	0	0	2	0	0	2.0	1	1	1	0	0	4	0	1	0
Connolly, West Palm Beach	1	1	.500	4.91	6	0	0	0	0	0	14.2	14	9	8	0	1	9	0	8	0
Coppeta, Lakeland*	3	4	.429	2.41	36	3	0	13	0	1	67.1	63	20	18	2	4	21	0	37	3
Corbett, Daytona*	0	3	.000	3.04	5	4	0	0	0	0	26.2	26	15	9	1	1	11	0	20	1
Corona, St. Petersburg*	3	4	.429	2.82	59	0	0	35	0	16	60.2	52	26	19	3	1	22	4	51	1
Correa, Vero Beach	3	4	.429	4.45	10	10	0	0	0	0	54.2	61	34	27	6	3	22	0	56	8
Corrigan, St. Petersburg	0	1	.000	9.00	4	0	0	2	0	0	5.0	9	5	5	1	0	2	0	5	0
Corry, Clearwater	0	0	.000	1.50	1	1	0	0	0	0	6.0	8	5	1	0	1	2	0	2	0
Crawford, St. Lucie*	3	3	.500	3.65	34	0	0	19	0	5	37.0	38	15	15	0	2	14	5	24	0
Curtis, Charlotte	8	8	.500	3.99	27	26	1	0	0	0	151.0	159	76	67	6	8	51	0	55	4
Daniel, Daytona	2	2	.500	3.00	15	0	0	12	0	2	24.0	17	10	8	4	2	7	1	9	1
Daniels, Dunedin	0	1	.000	6.23	2	1	0	1	0	0	4.1	6	4	3	0	0	2	0	5	1

Pitcher, Team	W	L	Pct.	ERA	G	GS	CG	GF	ShO	Sv.	IP	H	R	ER	HR	HB	BB	Int. BB	SO	WP
Darley, Dunedin	2	0	1.000	2.59	5	4	0	1	0	0	24.1	18	8	7	4	0	12	0	12	0
Daspit, Vero Beach	0	0	.000	0.00	1	1	0	0	0	0	3.0	4	0	0	0	0	2	0	2	0
Davis, Fort Lauderdale	2	6	.250	6.96	8	8	0	0	0	0	42.2	69	42	33	2	0	8	1	10	4
Davis, St. Petersburg	1	0	1.000	1.93	29	0	0	26	0	19	28.0	26	8	6	0	0	10	0	44	0
Delgado, Daytona	6	7	.462	1.70	17	13	1	1	1	0	84.2	78	31	16	1	5	28	1	44	3
Dettmer, Charlotte	16	3	.842	2.15	27	27	5	0	2	0	163.0	132	44	39	6	7	33	0	128	2
DeArmas, Clearwater	0	0	.000	18.00	2	0	0	2	0	0	2.0	7	4	4	1	0	1	0	0	1
DeHart, West Palm Beach	1	3	.250	3.00	7	7	1	0	1	0	42.0	42	14	14	0	1	17	0	33	2
DeJesus, Clearwater	3	6	.333	4.07	11	10	1	0	0	0	55.1	65	32	25	5	0	19	0	33	2
DeSantis, Clearwater	1	3	.250	3.45	49	1	0	14	0	3	88.2	92	43	34	3	4	27	8	42	10
Dickson, Daytona*	1	2	.333	3.18	3	3	0	0	0	0	17.0	17	7	6	0	0	3	0	18	3
Dixon, Fort Myers*	4	12	.250	4.21	25	25	1	0	0	0	151.2	168	87	71	6	6	82	2	109	16
Dotel, Vero Beach*	0	0	.000	0.00	1	0	0	1	0	0	1.0	1	0	0	0	0	0	0	2	0
Dreyer, Daytona	2	2	.500	1.80	4	4	1	0	1	0	30.0	22	8	6	1	1	3	0	17	1
Dunne, Sarasota	1	1	.500	5.47	7	1	0	1	0	0	24.2	30	17	15	4	0	8	0	11	1
Duran, Vero Beach*	1	1	.500	3.72	8	0	0	2	0	0	9.2	10	4	4	0	0	8	1	9	0
Edens, Osceola	1	0	1.000	0.00	3	1	0	0	0	0	4.0	5	0	0	0	1	1	0	4	0
Edmondson, Lakeland	8	5	.615	2.99	19	19	1	0	0	0	114.1	115	44	38	6	3	43	0	64	7
Ellis, Sarasota	7	8	.467	2.51	15	15	8	0	2	0	104.0	81	37	29	3	3	31	1	79	6
Fajardo, Charlotte	0	0	.000	1.80	2	1	0	0	0	0	5.0	5	1	1	0	0	1	0	3	0
Fernandez, St. Lucie*	0	0	.000	4.50	1	1	0	0	0	0	4.0	3	2	2	1	0	1	0	7	0
Ferreira, Fort Lauderdale	0	0	.000	0.00	1	0	0	1	0	0	1.0	1	1	0	0	0	1	0	0	0
Fiegel, St. Lucie*	10	7	.588	3.39	25	16	0	5	0	0	116.2	122	60	44	7	3	42	0	71	4
Fordham, Sarasota*	0	0	.000	0.00	2	0	0	1	0	0	5.0	3	1	0	0	0	3	2	5	1
Franklin, Daytona	3	11	.214	4.49	39	15	4	16	1	3	132.1	146	80	66	8	8	39	2	64	3
Fuller, St. Lucie	4	3	.571	1.90	40	0	0	18	0	2	47.1	53	13	10	0	3	12	2	31	0
Gajkowski, Sarasota	3	3	.500	2.07	43	0	0	38	0	15	69.2	52	21	16	1	4	17	5	46	5
Gallaher, Osceola	7	7	.500	3.80	21	21	1	0	1	0	135.0	132	68	57	7	4	57	1	93	8
Gandolph, Charlotte*	4	2	.667	3.92	34	0	0	9	0	2	43.2	49	23	19	0	2	29	0	24	1
Garcia, Fort Myers	4	1	.800	4.04	55	2	0	28	0	10	89.0	105	53	40	4	1	31	7	54	5
Gavaghan, Fort Myers	1	3	.250	2.61	19	0	0	13	0	4	31.0	37	10	9	1	0	8	1	24	2
Geeve, Charlotte	11	8	.579	2.85	24	23	1	1	1	0	132.2	141	52	42	7	3	19	0	80	8
Gentile, West Palm Beach	8	9	.471	4.03	25	25	0	0	0	0	138.1	132	72	62	8	7	54	0	108	6
Giberti, Charlotte*	11	4	.733	3.70	31	20	2	2	1	1	141.0	132	63	58	7	3	52	0	85	8
Gilmore, Clearwater	5	0	1.000	3.30	7	7	0	0	0	0	43.2	45	18	16	3	1	7	0	22	4
Gomes, Clearwater	0	0	.000	1.17	9	0	0	8	0	4	7.2	4	1	1	0	0	9	0	13	2
Gonzalez, Fort Lauderdale	0	4	.000	4.84	21	2	0	5	0	2	48.1	52	31	26	2	0	34	1	37	0
Gordon, Sarasota*	0	0	.000	1.50	2	0	0	2	0	0	6.0	4	1	1	0	1	4	0	6	1
Gray, Dunedin*	8	10	.444	3.57	26	26	0	0	0	0	141.1	115	71	56	7	7	97	1	108	6
Greene, Lakeland	2	3	.400	6.20	26	0	0	11	0	2	40.2	57	28	28	1	1	16	1	32	5
Grimm, Lakeland	2	1	.667	2.45	16	0	0	15	0	3	18.1	12	7	5	2	0	11	0	17	0
Grove, Dunedin	3	2	.600	2.40	30	0	0	15	0	4	45.0	34	20	12	1	1	23	3	32	2
Guerry, Osceola*	1	2	.333	3.35	56	0	0	12	0	1	48.1	46	27	18	1	2	34	4	26	5
Guilfoyle, Lakeland*	0	0	.000	0.96	9	0	0	9	0	5	9.1	5	1	1	0	0	3	0	10	0
Gullickson, Lakeland	1	0	1.000	6.87	5	5	0	0	0	0	18.1	24	14	14	2	1	4	0	9	1
Gutierrez, Vero Beach	1	4	.200	7.20	15	6	0	7	0	0	40.0	42	38	32	4	6	33	2	22	8
Guzik, St. Lucie	0	3	.000	3.70	19	5	1	12	0	6	48.2	52	26	20	4	5	7	0	26	1
Hamilton, Vero Beach	6	6	.500	4.54	32	12	0	5	0	1	105.0	113	55	53	10	1	45	3	70	5
Hansen, Fort Lauderdale	4	6	.400	2.63	14	14	4	0	2	0	102.2	94	37	30	6	4	37	2	59	1
Hayward, Fort Lauderdale	1	4	.200	5.18	13	5	0	5	0	0	40.0	43	25	23	1	0	32	2	37	8
Heathcott, Sarasota	11	10	.524	3.61	26	26	6	0	1	0	179.1	174	90	72	5	4	62	7	83	16
Heble, Dunedin	6	1	.857	2.49	41	0	0	21	0	4	50.2	35	16	14	1	3	34	1	66	4
Heisler, Clearwater	1	3	.250	3.26	19	2	0	7	0	0	49.2	49	18	18	3	2	19	3	27	5
Henderson, Charlotte*	7	2	.778	2.64	16	16	0	0	0	0	92.0	71	32	27	2	1	33	0	81	3
Henderson, West Palm Beach	12	7	.632	2.90	22	22	1	0	1	0	143.0	110	50	46	3	6	44	0	127	8
Henderson, Vero Beach	0	3	.000	3.97	30	0	0	25	0	10	34.0	29	24	15	2	0	28	4	34	4
Hennis, Osceola	0	3	.000	3.31	14	14	0	0	0	0	35.1	21	13	13	3	2	15	0	26	2
Henry, Lakeland*	1	1	.500	5.12	4	3	0	0	0	0	19.1	24	13	11	1	2	5	0	14	4
Heredia, Charlotte	1	5	.167	3.72	34	0	0	29	0	15	38.2	30	17	16	0	1	20	1	26	4
Hisey, St. Petersburg	6	6	.500	3.54	17	17	0	0	0	0	96.2	75	50	38	5	1	38	0	70	6
Holliday, Osceola	0	0	.000	2.35	6	3	0	1	0	1	7.2	6	2	2	0	0	2	0	4	1
Holman, Clearwater	0	0	.000	2.50	7	1	0	2	0	0	18.0	17	7	5	1	0	1	0	7	1
Hotchkiss, Dunedin	0	3	.000	5.40	43	0	0	18	0	0	66.2	76	48	40	4	6	28	3	52	10
Howze, Daytona	2	7	.222	4.55	20	13	1	4	0	1	85.0	95	53	43	12	4	46	1	29	6
Hoy, Fort Lauderdale	0	0	.000	0.00	4	0	0	4	0	1	4.1	2	0	0	0	0	0	0	4	0
Humphry, Clearwater	0	1	.000	6.75	9	0	0	2	0	0	13.1	18	11	10	0	1	13	1	7	2
Jacome, St. Lucie*	6	3	.667	3.08	14	14	2	0	2	0	99.1	106	37	34	2	0	23	1	66	2
James, Vero Beach	2	3	.400	4.92	30	1	0	15	0	5	60.1	54	37	33	2	5	33	5	60	5
James, Daytona*	0	1	.000	8.44	5	0	0	0	0	0	5.1	10	6	5	0	3	2	0	1	3
Johnson, Sarasota	5	0	1.000	0.66	18	1	0	7	0	1	54.1	33	5	4	1	2	8	0	35	1
Johnson, Fort Myers	0	0	.000	0.00	2	0	0	2	0	1	2.0	1	0	0	0	0	1	0	4	1
Johnson, Fort Lauderdale	0	2	.000	6.61	14	0	0	4	0	1	16.1	17	19	12	2	4	15	1	10	2
Johnson, Dunedin	0	0	.000	0.00	1	0	0	1	0	0	1.0	1	0	0	0	0	0	0	0	0
Johnson, St. Petersburg	6	2	.750	2.80	21	3	0	6	0	0	54.2	56	18	17	2	2	22	4	40	1
Johnston, Sarasota*	6	5	.545	4.50	12	12	1	0	0	0	72.0	74	43	36	7	0	30	0	29	0
Jolley, St. Petersburg	2	0	1.000	0.35	11	2	0	4	0	1	26.0	14	3	1	0	0	5	0	12	2
Jones, Vero Beach	4	7	.364	5.32	15	15	0	0	0	0	69.1	63	46	41	4	7	45	1	44	2
Jordan, Dunedin*	2	0	1.000	4.38	15	0	0	3	0	1	24.2	20	13	12	0	1	15	1	24	3
Juhl, Clearwater*	2	1	.667	0.96	21	0	0	13	0	4	28.0	23	6	3	0	0	3	0	24	1
Keating, Sarasota*	2	0	1.000	3.55	22	0	0	14	0	3	33.0	37	16	13	0	0	16	2	28	2
Kelley, Lakeland*	4	5	.444	3.05	26	9	0	10	0	2	85.2	78	31	29	2	4	31	1	45	5
Kennedy, Fort Lauderdale*	3	6	.333	3.66	12	12	1	0	0	0	78.2	79	41	32	0	1	43	0	44	3
Kent, Osceola	0	0	.000	1.93	24	0	0	20	0	15	23.1	21	10	5	0	0	11	4	21	2
Kindell, St. Lucie*	0	1	.000	0.00	1	0	0	0	0	0	1.0	2	1	0	0	0	0	0	0	0
Kirk, Daytona	1	2	.333	6.08	20	0	0	10	0	4	26.2	38	23	18	1	1	6	1	20	0
Kirkland, Clearwater	0	1	.000	15.00	2	0	0	2	0	0	3.0	7	5	5	0	0	3	2	0	1
Klvac, Fort Lauderdale*	4	9	.308	4.46	21	19	3	1	0	0	127.0	138	76	63	13	3	59	0	72	8
Kohl, Fort Myers	1	1	.500	5.13	17	0	0	7	0	0	26.1	35	20	15	0	2	11	5	10	1
Konieczki, Fort Myers*	0	2	.000	3.78	12	0	0	9	0	2	16.2	18	7	7	0	1	16	0	15	1
Kontorinis, Fort Myers	0	0	.000	9.00	1	0	0	1	0	0	1.0	2	1	1	0	1	1	0	1	0
Kosenski, Lakeland	3	3	.500	2.74	35	2	0	8	0	3	65.2	45	24	20	3	2	43	2	42	7
Kostich, Lakeland*	0	1	.000	2.57	11	0	0	2	0	0	21.0	29	14	6	0	3	6	1	18	0
Kotes, Dunedin	2	2	.500	2.57	10	8	0	0	0	0	42.0	37	17	12	1	0	12	0	41	1
Lacy, Charlotte	0	0	.000	1.93	4	0	0	3	0	2	4.2	2	2	1	0	1	3	0	3	1

Pitcher, Team	W	L	Pct.	ERA	G	GS	CG	GF	ShO	Sv.	IP	H	R	ER	HR	HB	BB	Int. BB	SO	WP
Lane, Osceola	3	10	.231	2.69	58	0	0	34	0	11	60.1	54	31	18	0	3	31	3	31	4
Larkin, Fort Lauderdale	0	0	.000	27.00	1	0	0	1	0	0	1.1	3	5	4	1	0	3	0	0	0
Larson, Clearwater*	0	0	.000	9.00	1	0	0	0	0	0	1.0	2	1	1	0	0	1	0	0	0
Lavigne, Vero Beach*	7	8	.467	5.56	22	19	0	3	0	0	90.2	104	65	56	11	9	45	1	76	5
Lawrence, Fort Lauderdale	0	0	.000	22.50	5	0	0	2	0	0	8.0	27	22	20	0	0	4	0	5	1
LaRosa, West Palm Beach*	3	3	.500	2.57	54	0	0	43	0	19	70.0	59	28	20	2	5	21	2	79	5
Levine, Sarasota	11	8	.579	3.68	27	26	5	0	1	0	161.1	169	87	66	6	7	50	3	129	11
Lewis, Osceola	0	0	.000	2.35	4	0	0	0	0	0	7.2	8	4	2	1	0	2	0	3	0
LeGault, Fort Myers	3	9	.250	5.71	18	18	3	0	0	0	110.1	142	80	70	4	4	33	1	60	4
Licursi, Vero Beach	3	0	1.000	5.09	25	0	0	4	0	0	46.0	38	30	26	7	1	31	3	36	5
Linares, Vero Beach	4	4	.500	1.81	45	7	0	29	0	13	109.1	97	36	22	4	2	28	5	80	1
Lindsay, Dunedin	1	1	.500	2.55	22	1	0	6	0	0	42.1	52	16	12	2	0	14	0	17	5
Locklear, Sarasota*	7	0	1.000	3.69	18	2	1	6	1	0	53.2	55	25	22	2	2	16	0	37	1
Looney, West Palm Beach*	4	6	.400	3.14	18	16	0	1	0	0	106.0	108	48	37	2	5	29	0	109	2
Lowe, St. Petersburg	6	11	.353	4.27	25	25	0	0	0	0	132.2	152	80	63	6	6	62	1	87	4
Magee, Charlotte*	6	3	.667	4.15	30	14	0	4	0	0	89.0	76	44	41	3	0	51	0	64	6
Manuel, Charlotte	0	0	.000	0.00	3	0	0	1	0	0	4.2	6	0	0	0	0	2	0	4	0
Martinez, Fort Lauderdale*	3	11	.214	5.47	18	16	2	1	0	0	97.0	124	65	59	6	2	44	0	45	4
Martinez, St. Petersburg	3	2	.600	1.37	13	1	1	2	1	0	65.2	55	13	10	2	0	22	0	38	0
Matranga, St. Petersburg	2	0	1.000	2.22	5	3	0	1	0	0	28.1	23	10	7	1	0	6	0	21	3
McCready, St. Lucie	6	4	.600	1.76	40	0	0	30	0	16	61.1	51	18	12	0	2	22	6	40	2
McDonald, West Palm Beach	2	3	.400	5.65	15	0	0	4	0	1	28.2	34	19	18	0	2	22	1	18	3
McGarity, St. Petersburg	9	7	.563	3.88	34	7	0	7	0	0	92.2	102	48	40	7	2	47	0	48	4
Mendenhall, Lakeland	9	5	.643	3.59	15	15	0	1	0	1	77.2	88	38	31	2	5	20	0	49	5
Mercado, Osceola*	1	1	.500	5.19	2	2	0	0	0	0	8.2	9	7	5	0	0	6	1	5	0
Merigliano, Sarasota	0	1	.000	2.10	18	0	0	14	0	8	25.2	12	6	6	0	0	12	1	21	1
Meyer, Daytona*	3	2	.600	3.47	33	1	0	11	0	2	49.1	48	23	19	1	1	23	2	29	0
Meza, St. Petersburg	0	0	.000	0.00	2	0	0	1	0	0	1.2	0	0	0	0	0	0	0	0	0
Miller, St. Petersburg	1	1	.500	1.15	26	0	0	6	0	1	31.1	19	6	4	0	3	18	1	35	2
Miller, St. Lucie	4	1	.800	3.15	21	4	0	7	0	0	45.2	54	17	16	4	2	9	1	30	3
Mitchell, Clearwater	4	4	.500	3.00	9	4	1	1	0	0	57.0	50	23	19	0	0	21	1	45	4
Milcki, Osceola	11	10	.524	3.91	26	23	0	0	0	0	158.2	158	81	69	16	2	65	1	111	9
Montgomery, St. Petersburg	2	1	.667	2.66	14	5	0	7	0	3	40.2	33	14	12	2	0	9	0	34	1
Montoya, Dunedin*	7	4	.636	3.59	50	1	0	22	0	5	80.1	78	37	32	2	2	26	5	35	5
Morones, Daytona	5	1	.833	1.76	13	6	1	1	1	0	51.0	44	10	10	0	3	16	2	27	3
Mosley, Fort Lauderdale*	2	1	.667	4.78	17	0	0	9	0	0	26.1	36	18	14	0	0	10	0	19	0
Munoz, Clearwater*	5	2	.714	2.45	56	0	0	33	0	9	77.0	59	22	21	2	2	26	4	81	11
Mysel, Lakeland	4	5	.444	3.60	12	12	1	0	0	0	70.0	59	36	28	2	6	28	0	46	2
Naulty, Fort Myers	0	3	.000	5.70	7	6	0	0	0	0	30.0	41	22	19	4	6	14	1	20	3
Newcomb, Charlotte	4	0	1.000	2.00	21	0	0	8	0	1	36.0	35	11	8	0	1	10	1	26	2
Nichting, Vero Beach	0	1	.000	4.15	4	4	0	0	0	0	17.1	18	9	8	2	0	6	0	18	1
Nies, Fort Lauderdale	5	9	.357	3.55	20	19	3	0	2	0	126.2	123	60	50	11	3	31	0	85	6
Nieto, Osceola	3	3	.500	4.50	42	0	0	18	0	2	66.0	76	45	33	2	4	36	7	39	8
Norris, West Palm Beach	7	4	.636	2.67	26	13	0	4	0	0	81.0	62	27	24	3	9	29	0	63	6
Osterkamp, Fort Lauderdale*	1	1	.500	1.81	39	0	0	13	0	3	49.2	51	12	10	3	3	20	2	19	4
Padron, Osceola	0	0	.000	18.00	2	0	0	1	0	0	2.0	7	4	4	0	0	1	0	0	0
Patterson, Charlotte	5	6	.455	2.51	47	0	0	24	0	7	68.0	55	22	19	2	1	28	4	41	5
Perez, Fort Lauderdale	0	4	.000	7.90	6	6	0	0	0	0	27.1	50	29	24	1	1	18	0	12	3
Petcka, St. Lucie	0	1	.000	7.82	3	2	0	0	0	0	12.2	18	12	11	3	0	4	0	7	0
Pettiford, Lakeland	2	1	.667	2.32	32	2	0	12	0	1	73.2	58	25	19	3	2	32	1	71	2
Phillips, Dunedin	7	6	.538	3.83	17	17	0	0	0	0	110.1	99	51	47	12	5	30	3	87	5
Pincavitch, Vero Beach	0	0	.000	4.66	6	0	0	0	0	0	9.2	11	10	5	0	0	10	1	3	1
Powers, Osceola*	4	8	.333	4.32	36	11	0	4	0	0	93.2	105	62	45	0	0	41	4	66	7
Powers, West Palm Beach	6	3	.667	4.25	24	13	0	1	0	0	91.0	89	52	43	1	3	45	0	57	1
Prado, Vero Beach	3	4	.429	4.37	12	9	0	0	0	0	55.2	45	31	27	2	1	29	3	31	1
Pulsipher, St. Lucie*	7	3	.700	2.24	13	13	3	0	1	0	96.1	63	27	24	2	0	39	0	102	3
Pyc, Vero Beach*	7	8	.467	2.38	23	15	1	2	0	0	113.1	97	41	30	1	1	47	2	78	5
Radke, Fort Myers	3	5	.375	3.82	14	14	0	0	0	0	92.0	85	42	39	3	4	21	1	69	3
Radziewicz, St. Petersburg*	0	0	.000	0.00	1	0	0	1	0	0	1.0	0	0	0	0	0	2	0	1	0
Raffo, Lakeland	3	2	.600	1.73	35	0	0	16	0	2	52.0	36	13	10	1	1	19	1	39	0
Rama, Clearwater	3	2	.600	4.26	7	6	2	0	0	0	38.0	35	19	18	0	1	18	0	12	0
Randall, Clearwater	6	8	.429	5.11	52	2	0	23	0	0	75.2	99	47	43	4	4	26	1	41	5
Ratliff, Daytona	2	4	.333	3.95	8	8	0	0	0	0	41.0	50	29	18	0	5	23	0	15	3
Reed, Charlotte	1	0	1.000	0.00	1	1	0	0	0	0	6.0	2	0	0	0	0	1	0	4	1
Roberts, Fort Myers	9	16	.360	4.35	28	28	3	0	0	0	173.2	184	93	84	6	4	86	5	108	10
Roberts, St. Lucie*	13	5	.722	2.75	25	25	3	0	2	0	173.1	162	64	53	3	7	36	0	111	2
Robinson, Fort Myers	0	1	.000	3.26	15	0	0	11	0	4	19.1	28	9	7	2	0	3	1	15	4
Rodriguez, Daytona	1	1	.500	3.18	29	0	0	18	0	4	39.2	30	15	14	2	2	16	1	31	2
Rodriguez, Vero Beach	8	8	.500	3.75	32	20	2	7	1	0	132.0	109	71	55	15	6	71	1	80	9
Romanoli, St. Petersburg*	4	4	.500	4.29	17	0	0	7	0	0	21.0	21	14	10	2	2	21	2	17	1
Rushworth, West Palm Beach	1	1	.500	3.91	24	0	0	8	0	0	46.0	43	24	20	0	1	19	0	23	3
Saccavino, Fort Myers	5	8	.385	4.70	23	19	2	4	0	0	105.1	122	63	55	2	6	49	3	55	6
Sadecki, Charlotte	3	2	.600	2.01	24	0	0	5	0	1	40.1	40	9	9	0	2	11	0	37	0
Salcedo, Vero Beach	0	0	.000	3.65	8	0	0	5	0	0	12.1	9	6	5	1	1	6	0	10	0
Santa Maria, Fort Lauderdale	2	7	.222	3.91	41	2	0	20	0	5	71.1	61	37	31	2	1	35	0	61	15
Schmidt, West Palm Beach	4	6	.400	3.17	44	2	0	22	0	5	65.1	63	32	23	3	0	25	3	51	1
Schorr, St. Lucie	11	10	.524	3.72	27	26	4	1	0	0	181.2	192	87	75	8	10	52	1	75	7
Schramm, Daytona	8	4	.667	3.50	34	13	0	9	0	2	121.0	119	58	47	4	6	29	0	89	9
Schuermann, Charlotte*	1	4	.200	2.07	46	0	0	24	0	16	65.1	40	20	15	1	1	28	2	59	2
Schulte, Osceola	0	0	.000	0.00	1	0	0	1	0	0	1.0	1	0	0	0	0	1	0	0	0
Sepeda, Clearwater	9	9	.500	3.60	26	26	2	0	2	0	160.0	165	81	64	8	5	63	3	97	7
Sewell, Osceola	4	3	.571	5.18	38	0	0	16	0	2	57.1	84	42	33	7	2	14	3	32	7
Simmons, St. Petersburg*	4	5	.444	3.43	13	13	1	1	0	0	78.2	70	38	30	1	0	31	0	54	6
Sinacori, Vero Beach	3	5	.375	4.15	16	5	0	5	0	1	47.2	63	27	22	5	0	16	3	29	3
Singer, Dunedin*	9	11	.450	4.01	26	26	0	0	0	0	137.0	139	75	61	6	5	71	4	90	17
Slininger, St. Petersburg	3	3	.500	4.42	12	12	0	0	0	0	71.1	75	40	35	8	4	25	1	40	8
Smith, Charlotte*	1	0	1.000	0.00	1	1	0	0	0	0	7.0	3	0	0	0	0	0	0	5	1
Smith, St. Lucie*	10	7	.588	3.57	22	21	0	1	0	0	133.2	140	65	53	6	8	48	2	83	8
Spoljaric, Dunedin*	3	0	1.000	1.38	4	4	0	0	0	0	26.0	16	5	4	0	2	12	0	29	2
Steed, Dunedin	4	9	.308	5.03	22	20	2	0	1	0	111.0	120	81	62	10	3	62	1	66	9
Steenstra, Daytona	5	3	.625	2.55	13	13	1	0	1	0	81.1	64	26	23	2	8	12	1	57	2
Stidham, Lakeland	2	1	.667	1.52	25	0	0	23	0	9	29.2	22	6	5	2	2	15	1	24	0
Stieb, Sarasota	1	1	.500	5.84	2	2	0	0	0	0	12.1	18	10	8	2	1	5	2	14	1
Strauss, Daytona	0	1	.000	3.79	14	0	0	11	0	3	19.0	12	9	8	1	3	5	0	19	1

Pitcher, Team	W	L	Pct.	ERA	G	GS	CG	GF	ShO	Sv.	IP	H	R	ER	HR	HB	BB	Int. BB	SO	WP
Sweeney, Fort Myers*	8	7	.533	3.92	39	13	1	7	0	0	114.2	110	56	50	5	5	55	1	77	6
Swope, Fort Myers	3	4	.429	4.99	26	4	0	10	0	1	57.2	74	42	32	4	4	23	2	32	3
Tagle, Sarasota*	1	1	.500	2.87	17	0	0	10	0	1	15.2	13	8	5	1	1	10	1	9	0
Taylor, Daytona	1	0	1.000	4.56	15	1	0	8	0	2	23.2	21	13	12	1	3	8	0	17	0
Thelen, Fort Myers	3	1	.750	6.75	10	2	0	1	0	0	24.0	33	18	18	2	0	7	1	14	0
Thomas, Sarasota*	4	2	.667	2.48	8	8	3	0	2	0	61.2	52	19	17	3	0	15	0	27	1
Thomas, West Palm Beach*	1	3	.250	3.29	25	0	0	19	0	9	27.1	19	13	10	0	2	23	2	28	1
Thompson, Lakeland*	4	4	.500	3.56	11	11	0	0	0	0	55.2	65	25	22	1	1	16	0	46	3
Tidwell, Daytona*	4	2	.667	3.07	39	0	0	19	0	2	58.2	40	25	20	0	2	19	2	41	1
Timlin, Dunedin	0	0	.000	1.00	4	0	0	2	0	1	9.0	4	1	1	0	0	0	0	8	0
Tolar, Sarasota*	2	6	.250	5.35	23	11	0	8	0	1	77.1	75	55	46	1	6	51	1	60	8
Tranberg, Clearwater	7	3	.700	2.50	14	13	2	0	0	0	75.2	78	26	21	1	3	18	0	59	2
Trisler, Clearwater	10	6	.625	4.69	27	22	0	1	0	0	117.0	138	74	61	6	4	49	0	71	6
Veras, Vero Beach	2	2	.500	2.80	24	0	0	8	0	2	54.2	59	23	17	2	1	14	5	31	3
Vitko, St. Lucie	0	0	.000	1.29	2	2	0	0	0	0	7.0	4	1	1	0	1	0	1	5	0
Vorbeck, Vero Beach	0	0	.000	18.00	1	0	0	1	0	0	1.0	3	2	2	0	0	1	0	1	0
Walden, Vero Beach*	1	1	.500	4.00	3	3	0	0	0	0	9.0	9	5	4	0	1	7	0	2	1
Wallace, West Palm Beach*	11	8	.579	3.28	25	24	0	0	1	0	137.1	112	61	50	2	11	65	0	126	5
Wallace, Daytona	5	6	.455	4.20	14	12	0	1	0	1	79.1	85	50	37	6	2	23	2	34	5
Walsh, Lakeland*	0	0	.000	5.56	7	0	0	1	0	0	11.1	11	9	7	1	2	4	0	3	0
Waring, Osceola	1	1	.500	2.60	4	0	0	0	0	0	17.1	16	5	5	0	0	6	0	16	1
Washington, Charlotte	1	2	.333	5.14	23	0	0	9	0	0	35.0	40	28	20	1	3	24	5	16	3
Watkins, Fort Myers*	2	2	.500	2.93	20	0	0	10	0	3	27.2	27	14	9	0	0	12	0	41	2
Watts, Vero Beach*	0	1	.000	4.08	8	0	0	1	0	0	17.2	14	11	8	4	0	16	0	12	2
Weber, Dunedin	8	3	.727	2.92	55	0	0	36	0	12	83.1	87	36	27	4	7	25	5	45	7
Wells, Clearwater	1	0	1.000	0.98	12	1	0	7	0	2	27.2	23	5	3	0	2	6	1	24	0
Wetteland, West Palm Beach	0	0	.000	0.00	2	2	0	0	0	0	3.0	0	0	0	0	0	1	0	5	0
Wheeler, Osceola	10	14	.417	4.35	26	23	3	2	1	0	159.1	196	101	77	14	5	38	2	70	6
White, Vero Beach	0	5	.000	8.45	8	6	0	0	0	0	33.0	43	35	31	1	2	18	3	20	3
White, Osceola	6	3	.667	3.36	13	12	1	0	0	0	88.1	88	37	33	8	2	19	1	51	1
F. White, Daytona	0	3	.000	8.15	7	2	0	1	0	0	17.2	22	16	16	1	2	11	0	5	1
W. White, Daytona	0	0	.000	0.00	1	0	0	0	0	0	2.0	1	0	0	0	0	1	0	0	0
Whitfill, Daytona	0	0	.000	0.00	1	0	0	0	0	0	1.0	0	0	0	0	0	0	0	1	0
Williams, Dunedin	0	0	.000	0.00	2	0	0	0	0	0	4.0	0	0	0	0	0	2	0	2	0
Winston, West Palm Beach*	2	0	1.000	1.46	8	2	1	3	0	0	24.2	18	6	4	0	0	3	0	21	0
Wiseman, St. Petersburg	1	1	.500	1.59	2	2	0	0	0	0	17.0	10	3	3	0	1	5	0	6	0
Withem, Lakeland	10	2	.833	3.42	16	16	2	0	1	0	113.0	108	47	43	5	5	24	0	62	3
Woodring, West Palm Beach	0	1	.000	4.32	4	0	0	2	0	0	8.1	9	5	4	0	0	5	0	4	3
Zerbe, Vero Beach*	1	0	1.000	6.57	10	0	0	1	0	0	12.1	12	10	9	0	2	13	1	11	3

BALKS—D. Wallace, 11; Ro. Henderson, Nies, Phillips, F. Rodriguez, B. Wallace, 6 each; Curtis, Dettmer, Lowe, Sepeda, Singer, 5 each; Hayward, Jacome, Kelley, Lavigne, Magee, Prado, Pyc, Schorr, 4 each; Gallaher, Hisey, Kennedy, Levine, Linares, O. Smith, 3 each; Adams, Amos, Aucoin, Bennett, Berlin, Bigham, Boehringer, Delgado, Fiegel, Greene, D. Henderson, S. Johnson, Klvac, Larosa, McDonald, Montoyo, Nieto, T. Powers, B. Roberts, Sweeney, Trisler, C. White, 2 each; Ahearne, Anderson, Bailey, Baxter, Blazier, Brooks, G. Brown, Christman, DeJesus, Ellis, Fordham, Fuller, Gajkowski, Geeve, Guerry, Gutierrez, Hamilton, Hansen, Heathcott, Heble, Ry. Henderson, Hennis, Henry, Hotchkiss, Howze, M. James, B. Johnson, G. Johnson, J. Johnson, Johnston, Jones, Kent, Kotes, Licursi, Looney, Mendenhall, Meyer, Mitchell, Mysel, Newcomb, Perez, Pincavitch, S. Powers, Pulsipher, Rama, Ratliff, C. Roberts, C. Rodriguez, Rushworth, Saccavino, Santamaria, Schmidt, Schramm, Simmons, Steed, Steenstra, Strauss, L. Thomas, Thompson, Walsh, Watkins, Weber, B. White, Zerbe, 1 each.

COMBINATION SHUTOUTS—Curtis-Sadecki, Dettmer-Brownholtz, Dettmer-Fajardo-Newcomb-Magee-Gandolph-Lacy, Geeve-Gandolph-Patterson, Geeve-Sadecki-Schuermann-Brownholtz, Henderson-Brownholtz, Henderson-Heredia, Magee-Newcomb, Magee-Sadecki-Brownholtz-Heredia, Magee-Sadecki-Newcomb, Smith-Schuermann, Charlotte; Tranberg-Heisler-DeSantis-Randall-Gomes, Tranberg-Wells, Clearwater; Delgado-Rodriguez, Dickson-Kirk-Tidwell-Franklin, Morones-Tidwell-Strauss, Steenstra-Kirk, Steenstra-Schramm-Daniel, Daytona; Carrara-Grove-Montoya, Gray-Kotes-Heble, Gray-Lindsay-Weber, Kotes-Lindsay-Montoya-Hotchkiss, Phillips-Heble-Grove, Singer-Grove, Singer-Heble-Hotchkiss-Weber, Spoljaric-Montoya-Lindsay, Dunedin; Fort Lauderdale; Roberts-Gavaghan, Sweeney-Watkins, Fort Myers; Edmondson-Coppeta-Stidham, Kelley-Kosenski-Coppeta-Guilfoyle, Mysel-Pettiford, Thompson-Walsh-Stidham, Withem-Stidham, Lakeland; Anderson-Powers-Lane, Gallaher-Edens-Holliday-Sewell, Hennis-Powers-Lane-Guerry, Holliday-Wheeler, Mlicki-Brown-Guerry, Wheeler-Guerry-Brown-Powers, Osceola; Roberts-Fuller, Smith-Beckerman, Smith-Fiegel, Vitko-Schorr, St. Lucie; Hisey-Davis 2, Badorek-Johnson-Davis, Badorek-Simmons, Brumley-Bailey, Brumley-Corona-Davis, Brumley-Corona-McGarity-Romanoli-Davis, Brumley-McGarity-Romanoli-Davis, Hisey-Botkin-Bailey-Corona, Jolley-Bailey-Meza-Miller-Corona, Lowe-Martinez, Lowe-McGarity-Romanoli-Davis, Martinez-Jolley-Botkin-Miller-Corona, Montgomery-Miller-Corona, Simmons-Bailey-Romanoli, St. Petersburg; Andujar-Gajkowski, Andujar-Merigliano, Andujar-Tagle, Locklear-Gajkowski, Sarasota; Correa-James, Pyc-Linares, Rodriguez-Linares, Vero Beach; Henderson-Aucoin, Henderson-Thomas, Norris-Baxter-Larosa, Norris-Connolly-Schmidt, Powers-Winston-Larosa, Wallace-Norris, Wallace-Rushworth, Wetteland-Wallace-Thomas, West Palm Beach.

NO-HIT GAMES—Rodriguez, Vero Beach, defeated Sarasota, 11-0, August 28.

FIELDING

TEAM

Team	Pct.	G	PO	A	E	DP	PB	Team	Pct.	G	PO	A	E	DP	PB
Charlotte	.975	134	3577	1640	135	127	14	St. Petersburg	.967	133	3556	1500	173	129	15
St. Lucie	.972	130	3376	1552	142	152	14	Fort Myers	.963	134	3540	1538	193	127	23
Clearwater	.972	135	3569	1623	151	128	23	Dunedin	.963	132	3442	1536	191	121	29
West Palm Beach	.971	136	3576	1520	151	85	30	Daytona	.962	133	3492	1583	198	151	15
Sarasota	.970	134	3513	1653	160	101	27	Vero Beach	.961	133	3493	1435	201	131	21
Lakeland	.969	129	3388	1596	157	124	20	Osceola	.959	130	3374	1528	211	153	29
Fort Lauderdale	.968	131	3487	1577	170	121	18								

INDIVIDUAL

FIRST BASEMEN

*Throws lefthanded.

Player, Team	Pct.	G	PO	A	E	DP
Bradish, Sarasota	1.000	27	260	14	0	14
A. Brown, Daytona	1.000	2	6	1	0	0
B. Brown, Daytona*	.993	75	643	55	5	63
Burns, Osceola	.981	45	384	28	8	38
Busby, Daytona	1.000	1	2	0	0	0
Cantu, St. Petersburg	.987	19	135	18	2	15

Player, Team	Pct.	G	PO	A	E	DP
Carey, Fort Lauderdale	1.000	4	27	1	0	1
Cerio, St. Petersburg	1.000	4	10	0	0	2
Colbrunn, West Palm Beach	.988	8	74	5	1	2
Colon, Osceola	.994	34	295	17	2	28
Coughlin, Sarasota*	.989	26	243	18	3	16
Cruz, Osceola*	.979	41	354	27	8	45
Daniel, West Palm Beach	.993	55	488	44	4	27
DeArmas, Clearwater	1.000	1	5	0	0	0
Dorante, Fort Lauderdale	1.000	1	10	1	0	3
Dotel, Vero Beach*	.986	70	517	48	8	57

Player, Team	Pct.	G	PO	A	E	DP
Dubose, Lakeland	.994	122	1166	101	8	100
Durkin, Fort Lauderdale	1.000	2	9	1	0	1
Edwards, Charlotte	.993	49	431	26	3	36
Fernandez, Fort Myers	.976	15	112	9	3	9
Fryman, Sarasota	.992	75	744	78	7	52
Garcia, St. Lucie	.992	129	1222	90	10	130
Garrow, Fort Myers	.875	2	7	0	1	2
Geisler, Clearwater*	1.000	1	10	1	0	1
Graham, St. Lucie	1.000	1	7	0	0	2
Guggiana, Charlotte	1.000	12	118	15	0	14
Hartung, Daytona	.991	9	98	9	1	6
Hymel, West Palm Beach	.958	6	43	3	2	6
R. Johnson, Vero Beach	.978	58	417	22	10	43
Kapano, Daytona	1.000	6	48	6	0	5
Killen, Lakeland	1.000	1	9	1	0	1
Kontorinis, Fort Myers	.987	102	910	66	13	85
Lantigua, Vero Beach	.971	9	65	3	2	5
Larkin, Fort Lauderdale	.889	1	8	0	1	0
LeVangie, Fort Lauderdale	1.000	2	6	0	0	2
Loeb, Dunedin	1.000	1	5	0	0	0
Lutz, Dunedin	.935	5	40	3	3	5
Manahan, West Palm Beach	1.000	1	2	0	0	0
Matos, West Palm Beach	.980	37	323	27	7	22
McGuire, Fort Lauderdale*	.991	56	513	61	5	46
Meza, St. Petersburg	1.000	1	2	0	0	0
Millan, St. Lucie	.958	4	22	1	1	4
Moler, Clearwater*	.969	12	85	8	3	7
Morrow, Vero Beach*	.976	18	108	13	3	12
Mota, Fort Myers	.991	22	213	17	2	22
O'Brien, St. Petersburg	1.000	7	60	3	0	4
Perozo, Fort Lauderdale	.985	33	246	24	4	20
Radziewicz, St. Petersburg*	.991	99	775	76	8	67
Rosado, Clearwater	.981	6	48	4	1	3
Ruff, Lakeland	.990	11	101	3	1	8
Rusk, Clearwater	.971	8	58	8	2	6
Scott, Osceola	.991	27	187	23	2	24
Terilli, Daytona*	1.000	3	30	1	0	3
Torres, Daytona	.989	37	318	27	4	44
Valdez, Daytona*	.984	13	120	6	2	15
Vogel, Sarasota	.988	8	81	4	1	6
Walker, Sarasota	.947	4	31	5	2	3
Wallin, Fort Lauderdale*	.993	45	391	23	3	29
Weinke, Dunedin*	.984	128	1142	101	20	99
White, West Palm Beach	1.000	4	38	4	0	2
Wilson, Charlotte*	.986	77	769	48	12	63
Wilstead, West Palm Beach*	.994	33	268	40	2	18
Wolff, Daytona	1.000	1	2	0	0	0
Young, St. Petersburg	1.000	24	234	13	0	26
ZUBER, Clearwater*	.996	117	1050	88	5	91

SECOND BASEMEN

Player, Team	Pct.	G	PO	A	E	DP
Berblinger, St. Petersburg	.990	18	35	65	1	14
Berry, Osceola	.969	16	28	35	2	9
Brady, Sarasota	.962	110	200	363	22	57
Brito, Dunedin	1.000	3	2	13	0	2
Cabrera, Dunedin	1.000	4	8	6	0	2
Cairo, Vero Beach	.963	48	110	151	10	40
Cholowsky, St. Petersburg	.965	39	63	102	6	21
Clinton, Charlotte	1.000	20	37	44	0	16
Coleman, Sarasota	1.000	3	9	7	0	2
Colmenares, Dunedin	.500	2	1	0	1	0
Coquillette, West Palm Beach	.960	6	8	16	1	0
Corbin, Fort Myers	.964	39	72	117	7	22
Crespo, Dunedin	.949	88	198	269	25	58
T. Davis, Fort Lauderdale	.941	4	5	11	1	3
Davisson, Daytona	.917	7	15	18	3	3
Demetral, Vero Beach	.961	83	158	236	16	49
Doster, Clearwater	.972	6	14	21	1	4
Durkin, Fort Lauderdale	.946	17	41	47	5	9
Evangelista, Charlotte	.971	35	49	83	4	19
Fermin, Lakeland	.949	16	30	45	4	9
Ferreira, Fort Lauderdale	.980	39	84	108	4	19
Fisher, Clearwater	.949	8	14	23	2	6
Gomez, Clearwater	.960	118	265	364	26	78
Gomez, Daytona	.938	19	41	65	7	14
Graham, St. Lucie	.959	9	21	26	2	9
Grudzielanek, West Palm Beach	.977	30	50	75	3	13
Hardge, West Palm Beach	.983	26	48	66	2	10
Harley, Osceola	.946	118	231	364	34	80
Hayden, Clearwater	1.000	8	14	31	0	4
Horincewich, Fort Myers	.972	44	94	148	7	31
Hubbard, Daytona	1.000	1	1	4	0	0
Johnson, Dunedin	.975	21	28	50	2	9
King, St. Lucie	.975	9	17	22	1	3
Lane, West Palm Beach	.989	21	31	59	1	6
Mediavilla, St. Petersburg	1.000	1	0	1	0	1
Meza, St. Petersburg	.967	40	61	117	6	22
MILLAN, St. Lucie	.969	117	272	386	21	105
Miranda, Sarasota	1.000	13	20	41	0	8
Murphy, Fort Lauderdale	.980	42	84	108	4	24
O'Neal, Lakeland	.963	114	250	375	24	71
Ortiz, Fort Lauderdale	.932	9	23	32	4	6
Phillips, Fort Myers	.959	54	99	179	12	28

Player, Team	Pct.	G	PO	A	E	DP
Pimentel, St. Petersburg	.984	16	27	33	1	4
Reyes, Sarasota	.959	11	21	26	2	4
Reyes, West Palm Beach	.714	4	3	7	4	0
Rosario, Dunedin	.947	26	32	58	5	10
Rundels, West Palm Beach	.944	7	12	22	2	7
Sandberg, Daytona	1.000	2	3	4	0	2
Simons, West Palm Beach	.968	24	35	57	3	4
Sirak, Clearwater	1.000	2	1	6	0	1
Da. Smith, Daytona	1.000	6	16	16	0	4
Smith, Fort Lauderdale	.939	22	48	60	7	17
M. Smith, Charlotte	.977	86	157	272	10	54
Stutheit, Daytona	.893	5	10	15	3	3
Thomas, Lakeland	1.000	4	4	5	0	1
Tosar, West Palm Beach	.952	32	50	110	8	14
Tredaway, Daytona	.968	65	129	202	11	50
Warner, St. Petersburg	.944	39	66	104	10	18
Webb, Vero Beach	1.000	3	9	3	0	0
W. White, Daytona	.950	36	63	126	10	29

THIRD BASEMEN

Player, Team	Pct.	G	PO	A	E	DP
Alder, Lakeland	.867	34	25	60	13	4
Allen, West Palm Beach	1.000	2	1	1	0	0
Beals, St. Lucie	1.000	1	0	2	0	0
Berry, Osceola	.912	31	26	67	9	10
Bradish, Sarasota	.714	2	3	2	2	0
Brito, Dunedin	.923	3	3	9	1	0
Burns, Osceola	.920	34	33	59	8	10
Busby, Daytona	.889	4	4	4	1	2
Cairo, Vero Beach	.964	13	12	15	1	2
Carey, Fort Lauderdale	.875	2	0	7	1	0
Cholowsky, St. Petersburg	.926	16	12	38	4	4
Clinton, Charlotte	1.000	1	1	5	0	0
Coleman, Sarasota	.824	5	2	12	3	0
Colon, Osceola	.910	67	48	155	20	9
Demetral, Vero Beach	1.000	3	1	4	0	0
Doster, Clearwater	.909	3	2	8	1	2
Durkin, Fort Lauderdale	.897	34	28	76	12	5
Edwards, Charlotte	.909	79	52	148	20	10
Evangelista, Charlotte	.966	62	49	123	6	9
Fermin, Lakeland	.890	52	36	110	18	5
Fernandez, Fort Myers	.833	7	6	9	3	1
Garrow, Fort Myers	.857	4	2	4	1	0
Gomez, Daytona	.898	18	11	33	5	8
Grable, Clearwater	.928	95	83	225	24	18
Graham, St. Lucie	1.000	6	7	10	0	1
Grudzielanek, West Palm Beach	.900	7	3	6	1	0
Guggiana, Charlotte	.800	1	1	3	1	0
Hartung, Daytona	.793	9	7	16	6	3
Hayden, Clearwater	.938	34	28	63	6	5
Johnson, Dunedin	.800	3	2	10	3	1
R. Johnson, Vero Beach	.839	19	13	34	9	5
Killen, Lakeland	.960	41	27	94	5	6
Kontorinis, Fort Myers	.500	1	0	1	1	0
Lane, West Palm Beach	.948	44	21	89	6	7
Lantigua, Vero Beach	.887	104	83	167	32	20
Larkin, Fort Lauderdale	.844	41	36	72	20	10
Lutz, Dunedin	1.000	1	1	0	0	0
Manahan, West Palm Beach	.908	75	54	134	19	8
Merloni, Fort Lauderdale	.941	20	13	55	4	2
Meza, St. Petersburg	.897	39	34	53	10	7
Millan, St. Lucie	1.000	1	2	1	0	0
Moler, Clearwater	1.000	1	0	1	0	0
Mota, Fort Myers	.750	1	1	2	1	0
Murphy, Fort Lauderdale	1.000	2	0	1	0	0
Ortiz, Fort Lauderdale	.981	16	20	31	1	4
Pimentel, St. Petersburg	.667	2	1	1	1	0
Reyes, Sarasota	.800	4	0	4	1	0
Reyes, West Palm Beach	.920	6	7	16	2	1
Roper, Fort Myers	.904	125	96	243	36	22
Rosado, Clearwater	1.000	2	2	0	0	0
Rosario, Dunedin	.938	14	10	20	2	3
Rundels, West Palm Beach	.833	2	2	3	1	0
Saenz, Sarasota	.933	31	15	55	5	6
Saunders, St. Lucie	.915	123	65	259	30	22
Simons, West Palm Beach	1.000	7	4	9	0	0
Sirak, Clearwater	.714	4	0	5	2	0
Da. Smith, Daytona	.902	95	72	166	26	14
Snopek, Sarasota	.919	88	69	180	22	18
Soto, Fort Lauderdale	.912	28	26	57	8	5
STYNES, Dunedin	.938	116	83	234	21	22
Thomas, Lakeland	.946	10	8	27	2	4
Torres, Daytona	.886	10	13	18	4	1
Truby, Osceola	.857	3	3	9	2	0
Walker, Sarasota	.955	10	4	17	1	0
Warner, St. Petersburg	.991	46	40	70	1	7
W. White, Daytona	1.000	1	1	0	0	0
Young, St. Petersburg	.912	48	26	77	10	6
Zuber, Clearwater*	1.000	1	0	1	0	0

SHORTSTOPS

Player, Team	Pct.	G	PO	A	E	DP
Alfonzo, St. Lucie	.954	124	183	425	29	90
Auralia, Charlotte	.964	122	200	445	24	82

Player, Team	Pct.	G	PO	A	E	DP	PB
Berry, Osceola	.895	10	12	22	4	5	
Brady, Sarasota	.882	3	8	7	2	2	
Brito, Dunedin	.938	117	195	365	37	65	
Busby, Daytona	.857	2	3	3	1	0	
Cairo, Vero Beach	.948	26	50	78	7	16	
CAREY, Fort Lauderdale	.970	107	190	351	17	67	
Clinton, Charlotte	.963	16	29	49	3	8	
Coleman, Sarasota	1.000	2	1	6	0	1	
Colmenares, Dunedin	.833	2	3	2	1	2	
Corbin, Fort Myers	.947	54	94	155	14	32	
DiSarcina, Sarasota	.954	114	179	383	27	51	
Duncan, Fort Myers	.962	5	9	16	1	4	
Evangelista, Charlotte	.667	1	0	2	1	0	
Fermin, Lakeland	.952	24	33	86	6	10	
Fisher, Clearwater	.953	113	198	350	27	69	
Flores, Osceola	.943	124	200	414	37	91	
Garrow, Fort Myers	.922	81	146	246	33	48	
Gomez, Daytona	.923	4	2	10	1	0	
Graham, St. Lucie	.875	7	6	15	3	4	
Grudzielanek, West Palm Beach	.905	21	32	54	9	7	
Harley, Osceola	.667	1	1	1	1	0	
Hayden, Clearwater	.957	24	40	72	5	12	
Holbert, St. Petersburg	.947	119	220	351	32	77	
K. Johnson, Vero Beach	.952	111	181	315	25	62	
Johnson, Dunedin	1.000	3	0	1	0	0	
King, St. Lucie	1.000	3	3	6	0	2	
Merloni, Fort Lauderdale	.957	18	27	63	4	10	
Miranda, Sarasota	.882	4	6	9	2	1	
Morgan, Lakeland	.950	110	184	365	29	79	
Ortiz, Fort Lauderdale	.881	12	13	39	7	3	
Petersen, Daytona	.967	130	253	450	24	105	
Pimentel, St. Petersburg	.909	5	4	6	1	1	
Reyes, Sarasota	1.000	2	3	5	0	0	
Rosario, Dunedin	.907	14	18	31	5	8	
Schofield, Dunedin	.964	11	14	13	1	1	
Simons, West Palm Beach	1.000	2	2	4	0	0	
Sirak, Clearwater	1.000	2	0	3	0	0	
Snopek, Sarasota	.977	15	25	60	2	10	
Thomas, Lakeland	.750	1	1	2	1	0	
Tovar, West Palm Beach	.951	116	169	333	26	49	
Warner, St. Petersburg	.909	19	31	39	7	6	

OUTFIELDERS

Player, Team	Pct.	G	PO	A	E	DP	
Abreu, Osceola	.961	121	179	18	8	4	
Adams, Vero Beach*	1.000	15	23	1	0	0	
Allen, West Palm Beach	1.000	3	1	0	0	0	
Anthony, Dunedin	1.000	1	0	1	0	0	
Austin, West Palm Beach*	1.000	4	5	0	0	0	
Barry, St. Lucie	.994	98	167	12	1	5	
BRADSHAW, St. Petersburg	.997	125	293	10	1	2	
Brede, Fort Myers*	.968	48	83	7	3	0	
Bright, Fort Lauderdale	.989	57	83	5	1	1	
Brown, Fort Lauderdale	1.000	23	41	3	0	0	
Buchanan, Sarasota	.957	29	43	1	2	0	
Burguillos, Lakeland	1.000	13	14	2	0	0	
Burke, Clearwater	1.000	6	12	0	0	0	
Burrough, Fort Myers	.960	44	69	3	3	1	
Butler, Dunedin	.988	103	157	7	2	0	
Cairo, Charlotte	.989	34	87	2	1	0	
Cappuccio, Sarasota	1.000	22	34	1	0	1	
Cerio, St. Petersburg	.980	38	48	2	1	0	
Chick, Fort Lauderdale	.976	38	75	7	2	2	
Civit, West Palm Beach	.800	10	8	0	2	0	
Clark, Lakeland	.944	20	34	0	2	0	
Clinton, Charlotte	.979	55	87	6	2	2	
Coughlin, Sarasota*	.988	87	162	3	2	1	
Cruz, Osceola*	1.000	6	12	2	0	0	
Curtis, St. Lucie*	.989	123	259	16	3	4	
Davisson, Daytona	.900	13	8	1	1	1	
Demetral, Vero Beach	1.000	1	1	0	0	0	
Dimare, Fort Lauderdale*	.980	50	95	3	2	0	
Dotel, Vero Beach*	.958	19	22	1	1	0	
Durkin, Fort Lauderdale	.920	36	43	3	4	0	
Edwards, Clearwater	.987	119	280	13	4	5	
Evans, Clearwater	1.000	38	66	4	0	0	
Facione, Lakeland	.750	3	3	0	1	0	
Fernandez, Fort Myers	.986	33	60	8	1	1	
Fully, St. Lucie	.969	112	207	11	7	4	
Garrow, Fort Myers	.902	24	45	1	5	0	
Geisler, Clearwater*	.995	85	186	7	1	1	
Gerald, St. Petersburg	.967	44	82	5	3	2	
Glanville, Daytona	.950	60	123	11	7	4	
J. Graham, Fort Lauderdale*	.970	48	97	0	3	0	
T. Graham, Fort Lauderdale	.980	48	95	3	2	1	
Green, Vero Beach	1.000	12	18	0	0	0	
Griffin, West Palm Beach	.970	66	124	5	4	0	
Grissom, West Palm Beach	.975	39	79	0	2	0	
Grudzielanek, West Palm Beach	1.000	20	20	0	0	0	
Hazlett, Fort Myers	.972	29	68	2	2	0	
Heisel, Fort Lauderdale	1.000	6	11	2	0	0	
Henry, Sarasota	1.000	28	39	2	0	1	
Higginson, Lakeland	.979	56	88	7	2	0	
Hines, Dunedin	.913	45	74	10	8	0	

Player, Team	Pct.	G	PO	A	E	DP	PB
Holifield, Dunedin*	.957	122	255	9	12	2	
Hood, Sarasota	.967	42	56	3	2	0	
Horne, West Palm Beach	.965	69	105	5	4	1	
Johnson, Dunedin	1.000	2	1	0	0	0	
Jones, St. Petersburg*	.973	92	173	7	5	1	
Kieschnick, Daytona	1.000	4	9	1	0	0	
Lamar, Lakeland	.958	74	90	1	4	0	
Landrum, Vero Beach	.957	115	212	12	10	3	
Landry, Lakeland	.500	1	1	0	1	0	
Larregui, Daytona	.962	84	167	9	7	2	
Larson, Clearwater*	.978	29	42	3	1	0	
Lowery, Charlotte	.976	65	156	5	4	0	
Lutz, Dunedin	.967	18	26	3	1	1	
Maness, Vero Beach	.960	118	271	17	12	6	
Mashore, Lakeland	.980	118	281	14	6	1	
McClinton, St. Lucie	.963	18	26	0	1	0	
McConnell, Clearwater	.941	87	103	8	7	0	
McNabb, Osceola	.976	115	223	18	6	5	
Mediavilla, St. Petersburg	1.000	16	22	1	0	0	
Meza, St. Petersburg	1.000	1	2	1	0	1	
Milne, Lakeland	.973	61	99	9	3	2	
Montero, Daytona	1.000	1	1	0	0	0	
Moore, Fort Myers*	.986	66	126	11	2	3	
Morris, Charlotte*	.985	28	62	2	1	0	
Morrow, Vero Beach*	.969	36	60	2	2	0	
Norman, Fort Myers	.972	79	133	8	4	2	
Northrup, West Palm Beach	.983	128	210	19	4	0	
Nunez, Daytona	.952	118	228	10	12	4	
Ogden, Fort Myers*	.971	106	217	16	7	0	
Ozoria, West Palm Beach	.962	72	123	5	5	0	
Perozo, Fort Lauderdale	1.000	9	10	0	0	0	
Pettiford, Lakeland	1.000	1	2	0	0	0	
Pinkney, Vero Beach	.600	2	3	0	2	0	
Poe, Sarasota	.975	90	145	10	4	1	
Powell, Charlotte	.974	28	35	3	1	0	
Puchales, Vero Beach*	.950	62	127	6	7	1	
Radziewicz, St. Petersburg*	.952	36	56	3	3	0	
Reyes, West Palm Beach	1.000	6	9	2	0	0	
Rosario, Dunedin	.923	12	8	4	1	0	
Ross, Osceola	.923	6	12	0	1	0	
Ruff, Lakeland	.980	67	93	5	2	1	
Saffer, West Palm Beach	1.000	7	14	1	0	0	
Sandy, St. Lucie	1.000	1	3	0	0	0	
Schulte, Osceola	1.000	12	25	1	0	1	
Sheppard, Dunedin	.938	29	44	1	3	0	
Shockey, Fort Myers*	1.000	12	12	2	0	1	
Simons, West Palm Beach	1.000	13	22	1	0	0	
Dw. Smith, Daytona	1.000	3	3	0	0	0	
J. Smith, St. Lucie	.986	45	69	2	1	0	
Soto, Fort Lauderdale	.955	14	17	4	1	3	
Steverson, Dunedin	.994	68	149	5	1	0	
Terilli, Daytona*	.980	53	90	6	2	0	
Texidor, Charlotte	1.000	19	31	0	0	0	
Thomas, Charlotte	.990	34	96	1	1	0	
Tokheim, Charlotte*	1.000	41	78	4	0	1	
Torres, Daytona	.964	53	80	1	3	0	
Valdez, Daytona*	.983	27	56	1	1	0	
Valrie, Sarasota	.961	114	188	11	8	1	
Vazquez, St. Petersburg	.969	26	31	0	1	0	
Velez, St. Petersburg*	.937	75	94	10	7	3	
Ventress, Daytona	1.000	8	12	1	0	0	
Vilet, Clearwater	1.000	12	15	0	0	0	
Vinyard, Fort Lauderdale	.985	79	191	6	3	2	
Vorbeck, Vero Beach	.973	44	66	5	2	1	
Warner, St. Petersburg	1.000	3	1	0	0	0	
Welch, Charlotte*	.978	49	87	1	2	1	
J. White, Osceola	.960	123	270	16	12	4	
Williams, Charlotte	.973	52	61	11	2	2	
Wilson, Charlotte*	.971	55	90	9	3	0	
Winston, Osceola	.966	17	27	1	1	0	
Zambrano, Fort Lauderdale	.977	18	38	5	1	3	
Zuber, Clearwater*	.969	18	30	1	1	0	

CATCHERS

Player, Team	Pct.	G	PO	A	E	DP	PB
Allen, West Palm Beach	.975	53	328	29	9	1	16
Ayala, Lakeland	1.000	2	2	0	0	0	0
Beals, St. Lucie	.985	15	62	5	1	2	1
Beasley, St. Petersburg	.989	11	77	9	1	0	1
Bennett, Clearwater	1.000	10	70	12	0	0	1
Bethke, Charlotte	1.000	1	2	0	0	0	0
Brooks, Dunedin	.988	43	287	43	4	6	8
A. Brown, Daytona	.950	8	50	7	3	1	1
Brown, Fort Myers	.990	60	339	46	4	0	11
Brown, Vero Beach	.989	38	174	13	2	0	1
Burns, Osceola	.980	38	217	31	5	1	9
Castillo, St. Lucie	.983	105	604	80	12	9	11
Cerio, St. Petersburg	1.000	1	1	0	0	0	0
Chavez, Osceola	.986	57	303	62	5	6	11
Crespo, Charlotte	.983	30	211	25	4	3	4
Daniel, West Palm Beach	.997	39	272	21	1	0	7
DeArmas, Clearwater	1.000	1	4	0	0	0	0
Delgado, Fort Lauderdale	.978	59	337	63	9	7	6

Player, Team	Pct.	G	PO	A	E	DP	PB
DiFelice, St. Petersburg	.964	30	165	23	7	2	1
Dorante, Fort Lauderdale	.951	10	36	3	2	0	0
Durkin, Fort Lauderdale	1.000	1	3	0	0	0	0
Estalella, Clearwater	1.000	9	47	8	0	2	0
Faircloth, Sarasota	1.000	5	19	5	0	0	3
Gonzalez, Lakeland	.987	60	321	54	5	5	9
Gray, Vero Beach	.938	1	14	1	1	0	0
Hopp, Clearwater	.991	23	100	13	1	0	2
Hubbard, Daytona	.979	67	353	62	9	5	10
Huckaby, Vero Beach	.980	79	481	99	12	14	13
Hymel, West Palm Beach	1.000	19	89	13	0	0	3
Johnson, Daytona	.923	3	10	2	1	0	0
R. Johnson, Vero Beach	1.000	5	7	1	0	0	0
Kapano, Daytona	1.000	2	3	0	0	0	0
KENNEDY, Charlotte	.986	105	591	97	10	6	10
Koeyers, West Palm Beach	1.000	4	32	2	0	0	1
LaValliere, Sarasota	.987	21	141	14	2	0	3
LeVangie, Fort Lauderdale	.982	73	378	65	8	5	12
Loduca, Vero Beach	.992	29	209	26	2	1	6
Loeb, Dunedin	.984	48	262	39	5	5	10
Lutz, Dunedin	.991	50	290	42	3	4	10
Manning, Sarasota	.992	27	110	17	1	1	1
Marrero, Sarasota	1.000	8	18	1	0	0	0
McConnell, Lakeland	.977	50	257	35	7	2	7
McDonnell, Daytona	.986	37	185	25	3	3	1
Meza, St. Petersburg	.500	1	0	1	1	0	0
Miller, Fort Myers	.985	78	465	62	8	4	12
Moler, Clearwater	.981	73	345	76	8	4	15
Molina, Daytona	1.000	3	13	2	0	0	0
Morel, St. Petersburg	1.000	3	13	0	0	0	0
Prybylinski, St. Petersburg	.961	66	355	62	17	4	9
Rea, Lakeland	.987	14	63	15	1	3	3
Robledo, Sarasota	.974	59	381	36	11	1	14
Rodriguez, Lakeland	.929	3	12	1	1	0	0
Ronan, St. Petersburg	.989	24	155	30	2	4	3
Rosado, Clearwater	.988	23	143	18	2	2	4
Rudolph, St. Lucie	.990	22	92	9	1	0	2
Rusk, Clearwater	.957	11	36	9	2	2	1
Santana, West Palm Beach	.994	42	279	31	2	2	3
Scott, Osceola	1.000	3	13	1	0	0	0
Soto, Fort Lauderdale	.917	3	13	9	2	0	0
Teel, Vero Beach	.933	5	14	0	1	0	1
Townley, Dunedin	.889	2	6	2	1	1	1
Tremie, Sarasota	1.000	14	71	13	0	2	1
Turvey, St. Petersburg	.942	17	57	8	4	0	1
Vinas, Sarasota	.982	16	93	14	2	2	1
Vogel, Daytona	.938	4	15	0	1	0	2
Williams, Charlotte	1.000	3	8	2	0	0	0
Winston, Osceola	.968	36	190	22	7	4	7
Wolff, Daytona	.966	24	99	13	4	1	3
Wyngarden, Osceola	.950	7	18	1	1	1	2
Yelton, Lakeland	1.000	8	56	5	0	0	1

PITCHERS

Player, Team	Pct.	G	PO	A	E	DP
Adams, Daytona	.895	13	9	8	2	2
Ahearne, Lakeland	.930	25	17	23	3	1
Allen, Fort Lauderdale*	.958	26	7	16	1	2
Allen, West Palm Beach	1.000	1	0	1	0	0
Amos, Fort Lauderdale	1.000	42	5	4	0	0
Anderson, Osceola	.800	16	6	14	5	0
Andujar, Sarasota	.870	18	9	11	3	1
Arias, Dunedin	1.000	3	1	0	0	0
Arrandale, St. Petersburg	1.000	2	0	1	0	0
Arteaga, West Palm Beach	.800	4	0	4	1	1
Aucoin, West Palm Beach	.889	38	5	19	3	0
Badorek, St. Petersburg	.968	29	18	12	1	0
Bailey, St. Petersburg	1.000	31	4	2	0	0
Barcelo, Fort Myers	.800	7	2	2	1	0
Baxter, West Palm Beach*	1.000	33	7	11	0	3
Beckerman, St. Lucie	1.000	20	2	2	0	0
Bennett, Fort Lauderdale	.875	23	4	3	1	1
Berlin, Lakeland	1.000	9	3	2	0	0
Bigham, Fort Myers*	.947	53	4	14	1	1
Blais, Fort Lauderdale	1.000	3	0	1	0	0
Blazier, Clearwater	.933	27	12	16	2	1
Boehringer, Sarasota	.941	18	5	27	2	2
Boldt, Clearwater	1.000	2	1	1	0	0
Botkin, St. Petersburg*	.947	49	4	14	1	1
Bottalico, Clearwater	1.000	13	1	2	0	1
Bradford, Daytona	.933	11	5	9	1	0
Brooks, Fort Lauderdale	.946	19	12	23	2	2
Broome, Daytona	1.000	1	1	2	0	0
Brosnan, Vero Beach*	1.000	23	4	3	0	0
Brown, Osceola	1.000	35	1	6	0	0
Brown, Clearwater	.917	11	10	12	2	0
Brownholtz, Charlotte*	1.000	24	4	15	0	1
Brumley, St. Petersburg	.889	8	3	5	1	0
Burlingame, Daytona	1.000	8	2	3	0	0
Carpenter, St. Lucie	.900	23	2	7	1	0
Carrara, Dunedin	.970	27	13	19	1	2
Christman, Sarasota*	1.000	2	0	4	0	0
Connolly, West Palm Beach	1.000	6	1	1	0	0
Coppeta, Lakeland*	1.000	36	2	16	0	1

Player, Team	Pct.	G	PO	A	E	DP
Corbett, Daytona*	.800	5	1	3	1	0
Corona, St. Petersburg*	.938	59	3	12	1	1
Correa, Vero Beach	.850	10	3	14	3	4
Corrigan, St. Petersburg	1.000	4	0	1	0	0
Corry, Clearwater	1.000	1	1	0	0	0
Crawford, St. Lucie*	1.000	34	3	7	0	0
Curtis, Charlotte	.944	27	15	36	3	3
Daniel, Daytona	.800	15	2	6	2	0
Daniels, Dunedin	1.000	2	1	0	0	0
Darley, Dunedin	.833	5	3	2	1	0
Daspit, Vero Beach	1.000	1	1	0	0	0
C. Davis, Fort Lauderdale	.818	8	4	5	2	0
Davis, St. Petersburg	1.000	29	2	2	0	1
DeHart, West Palm Beach	1.000	7	2	9	0	0
DeJesus, Clearwater	1.000	11	6	1	0	0
Delgado, Daytona	.955	17	7	14	1	0
DeSantis, Clearwater	.929	49	8	18	2	0
Dettmer, Charlotte	.944	27	11	23	2	0
Dickson, Daytona*	.667	3	0	2	1	0
Dixon, Fort Myers*	.837	25	7	29	7	2
Dreyer, Daytona	1.000	4	0	8	0	0
Dunne, Sarasota	1.000	7	6	2	0	0
Duran, Vero Beach*	.667	8	1	1	1	0
Edens, Osceola	1.000	3	1	0	0	0
Edmondson, Lakeland	1.000	19	5	13	0	0
Ellis, Sarasota	1.000	15	10	23	0	1
Fajardo, Charlotte	1.000	2	0	1	0	0
Fiegel, St. Lucie*	.778	25	8	13	6	0
Fordham, Sarasota	1.000	2	0	2	0	0
Franklin, Daytona	.846	39	7	15	4	0
Fuller, St. Lucie	1.000	40	2	12	0	0
Gajkowski, Sarasota	1.000	43	6	17	0	3
Gallaher, Osceola	.857	21	12	12	4	0
Gandolph, Charlotte*	1.000	34	2	11	0	2
Garcia, Fort Myers	1.000	55	5	9	0	2
Gavaghan, Fort Myers	1.000	19	2	4	0	1
Geeve, Charlotte	.971	24	13	20	1	1
Gentile, West Palm Beach	.972	25	11	24	1	4
Giberti, Charlotte*	.850	31	6	28	6	0
Gilmore, Clearwater	1.000	7	3	4	0	0
Gomes, Clearwater	.000	9	0	0	1	0
Gonzalez, Fort Lauderdale	.857	21	6	6	2	0
Gray, Dunedin*	.860	26	7	36	7	3
Greene, Lakeland	1.000	26	2	10	0	1
Grimm, Lakeland	1.000	16	1	0	0	0
Grove, Dunedin	1.000	30	3	6	0	0
Guerry, Osceola*	1.000	56	2	7	0	1
Guilfoyle, Lakeland*	1.000	9	0	3	0	0
Gullickson, Lakeland	1.000	5	3	2	0	0
Gutierrez, Vero Beach	.545	15	2	4	5	0
Guzik, St. Lucie	.875	19	2	5	1	0
Hamilton, Vero Beach	1.000	32	10	9	0	1
Hansen, Fort Lauderdale	.941	14	7	9	1	0
Hayward, Fort Lauderdale	1.000	13	5	5	0	0
Heathcott, Sarasota	.945	26	12	40	3	1
Heble, Dunedin	1.000	41	1	2	0	0
Heisler, Clearwater	1.000	19	3	11	0	3
Henderson, Charlotte*	.969	16	8	23	1	0
Henderson, West Palm Beach	1.000	22	18	14	0	0
Henderson, Vero Beach	1.000	30	3	3	0	0
Hennis, Osceola	1.000	14	6	7	0	0
Henry, Lakeland*	1.000	4	2	5	0	1
Heredia, Charlotte	1.000	34	1	5	0	1
Hisey, St. Petersburg	.960	17	8	16	1	1
Holliday, Osceola	1.000	6	1	0	0	0
Holman, Clearwater	.800	7	1	3	1	0
Hotchkiss, Dunedin	.857	43	5	1	1	0
Howze, Daytona	1.000	20	5	12	0	0
Hoy, Fort Lauderdale	1.000	4	0	1	0	0
Humphry, Clearwater	1.000	9	1	2	0	0
Jacome, St. Lucie*	.929	14	8	18	2	2
James, Vero Beach	1.000	30	3	13	0	0
James, Daytona*	1.000	5	1	2	0	0
Johnson, Sarasota	.778	18	1	6	2	0
Johnson, Fort Lauderdale	.000	14	0	0	1	0
Johnson, St. Petersburg	1.000	21	3	3	0	0
Johnston, Sarasota*	.929	12	7	6	1	0
Jolley, St. Petersburg	.833	11	2	3	1	0
Jones, Vero Beach	.867	15	4	9	2	2
Jordan, Dunedin*	1.000	15	4	7	0	0
Juhl, Clearwater*	.909	21	3	7	1	1
Keating, Sarasota*	.909	22	2	8	1	1
Kelley, Lakeland*	.952	26	3	17	1	0
Kennedy, Fort Lauderdale*	.967	12	11	18	1	4
Kent, Osceola	1.000	24	2	5	0	0
Kirk, Daytona	1.000	20	2	5	0	3
Kirkland, Clearwater	1.000	2	0	2	0	0
Klvac, Fort Lauderdale*	.897	21	2	24	3	1
Kohl, Fort Myers	1.000	17	2	10	0	0
Konieczki, Fort Myers*	1.000	12	0	3	0	1
Kosenski, Lakeland	1.000	35	4	10	0	2
Kostich, Lakeland*	.667	11	1	1	1	0
Kotes, Dunedin	.750	10	2	4	2	0
Lane, Osceola	.789	58	2	13	4	0
LaRosa, West Palm Beach*	.818	54	3	6	2	0

Player, Team	Pct.	G	PO	A	E	DP
Lavigne, Vero Beach*	.960	22	4	20	1	0
Lawrence, Fort Lauderdale	1.000	5	1	1	0	0
Legault, Fort Myers	.957	18	6	16	1	1
Levine, Sarasota	.887	27	16	31	6	1
Lewis, Osceola	1.000	4	1	1	0	0
Licursi, Vero Beach	1.000	25	1	6	0	0
Linares, Vero Beach	.909	45	3	17	2	1
Lindsay, Dunedin	1.000	22	7	8	0	2
Locklear, Sarasota*	.938	18	0	15	1	0
Looney, West Palm Beach*	.958	18	8	15	1	0
Lowe, St. Petersburg	.872	25	11	23	5	0
Magee, Charlotte*	.950	30	3	16	1	0
Manuel, Charlotte	1.000	3	0	1	0	0
Martinez, Fort Lauderdale*	.957	18	7	15	1	0
Martinez, St. Petersburg	.952	13	9	11	1	2
Matranga, St. Petersburg	1.000	5	4	1	0	0
McCready, St. Lucie	.889	40	2	6	1	0
McDonald, West Palm Beach	.909	15	3	7	1	0
McGarity, St. Petersburg	.714	34	6	9	6	0
Mendenhall, Lakeland	.947	15	7	11	1	1
Mercado, Osceola*	.750	2	0	3	1	0
Merigliano, Sarasota	1.000	18	3	3	0	1
Meyer, Daytona*	.923	33	5	7	1	0
Miller, St. Petersburg	1.000	26	1	5	0	2
Miller, St. Lucie	1.000	21	1	8	0	1
Mitchell, Clearwater	.800	9	4	4	2	0
Mlicki, Osceola	.920	26	5	18	2	1
Montgomery, St. Petersburg	1.000	14	2	3	0	0
Montoya, Dunedin*	.966	50	9	19	1	3
Morones, Daytona	.917	13	5	6	1	0
Mosley, Fort Lauderdale*	1.000	17	0	4	0	0
Munoz, Clearwater*	.941	56	4	12	1	1
Mysel, Lakeland	.867	12	4	9	2	1
Naulty, Fort Myers	1.000	7	2	5	0	0
Newcomb, Charlotte	.500	21	0	4	4	0
Nichting, Vero Beach	.600	4	0	3	2	0
Nies, Fort Lauderdale	.933	20	4	10	1	1
Nieto, Osceola	.786	42	2	9	3	0
Norris, West Palm Beach	.933	26	3	11	1	1
Osterkamp, Fort Lauderdale*	1.000	39	4	11	0	1
Padron, Osceola	1.000	2	1	0	0	0
Patterson, Charlotte	.875	47	4	10	2	0
Perez, Fort Lauderdale	1.000	6	1	7	0	0
Petcka, St. Lucie	.000	3	0	0	1	0
Pettiford, Lakeland	1.000	32	4	14	0	0
Phillips, Dunedin	1.000	17	6	16	0	0
Pincavitch, Vero Beach	.667	6	0	4	2	0
Powers, Osceola*	.722	36	7	6	5	0
Powers, West Palm Beach	1.000	24	9	19	0	1
Prado, Vero Beach	1.000	12	2	5	0	0
Pulsipher, St. Lucie*	.929	13	2	11	1	0
Pyc, Vero Beach*	1.000	23	5	18	0	0
Radke, Fort Myers	1.000	14	5	3	0	0
Raffo, Lakeland	.875	35	4	3	1	0
Rama, Clearwater	.889	7	4	4	1	1
Randall, Clearwater	.955	52	8	13	1	0
Ratliff, Daytona	.818	8	2	7	2	1
Reed, Charlotte	1.000	1	1	0	0	0
Roberts, Fort Myers	.914	28	10	22	3	3
Roberts, St. Lucie*	1.000	25	13	19	0	2
Robinson, Fort Myers	1.000	15	1	3	0	1

Player, Team	Pct.	G	PO	A	E	DP
Rodriguez, Daytona	.818	29	2	7	2	1
Rodriguez, Vero Beach	.917	32	5	6	1	0
Romanoli, St. Petersburg*	1.000	17	1	2	0	0
Rushworth, West Palm Beach	1.000	24	6	13	0	0
Saccavino, Fort Myers	.895	23	8	9	2	1
Sadecki, Charlotte	1.000	24	3	9	0	0
Salcedo, Vero Beach	1.000	8	0	1	0	0
Santamaria, Fort Lauderdale	.895	41	7	10	2	0
Schmidt, West Palm Beach	.947	44	4	14	1	0
Schorr, St. Lucie	.894	27	9	33	5	3
Schramm, Daytona	.963	34	13	13	1	0
Schuermann, Charlotte*	1.000	46	2	7	0	1
Sepeda, Clearwater	.925	26	11	26	3	0
Sewell, Osceola	1.000	38	8	5	0	1
Simmons, St. Petersburg*	.957	13	3	19	1	0
Sinacori, Vero Beach	.889	16	5	11	2	1
Singer, Dunedin*	.892	26	9	24	4	0
Slininger, St. Petersburg	.957	12	10	12	1	1
SMITH, St. Lucie*	1.000	22	6	31	0	2
Spoljaric, Dunedin*	1.000	4	2	8	0	0
Steed, Dunedin	.783	22	6	12	5	0
Steenstra, Daytona	.905	13	1	18	2	2
Stidham, Lakeland	1.000	25	1	5	0	1
Stieb, Sarasota	1.000	2	0	2	0	0
Strauss, Daytona	1.000	14	1	2	0	0
Sweeney, Fort Myers*	.824	39	2	12	3	2
Swope, Fort Myers	.933	26	5	9	1	2
Tagle, Sarasota*	.800	17	1	3	1	0
Taylor, Daytona	.833	15	2	3	1	0
Thelen, Fort Myers	1.000	10	0	9	0	0
Thomas, Sarasota*	1.000	8	10	14	0	1
Thomas, West Palm Beach*	.917	25	1	10	1	0
Thompson, Lakeland*	.929	11	2	11	1	0
Tidwell, Daytona*	.875	39	5	9	2	0
Timlin, Dunedin	1.000	4	1	2	0	0
Tolar, Sarasota*	.944	23	4	13	1	3
Tranberg, Clearwater	.933	14	5	9	1	1
Trisler, Clearwater	1.000	27	9	15	0	1
Veras, Vero Beach	.867	24	6	7	2	1
Vitko, St. Lucie	1.000	2	0	2	0	0
Walden, Vero Beach*	1.000	3	0	4	0	0
Wallace, West Palm Beach*	.920	25	4	19	2	0
Wallace, Daytona	.808	14	12	9	5	0
Walsh, Lakeland*	1.000	7	1	4	0	1
Waring, Osceola	1.000	4	1	3	0	0
Washington, Charlotte	1.000	23	7	4	0	2
Watkins, Fort Myers*	1.000	20	1	1	0	0
Watts, Vero Beach*	1.000	8	1	1	0	0
Weber, Dunedin	.958	55	7	16	1	1
Wells, Clearwater	.750	12	0	3	1	0
Wheeler, Osceola	.939	26	14	17	2	2
White, Osceola	.800	8	2	2	1	0
C. White, Osceola	.905	13	11	8	2	2
F. White, Daytona	.750	7	1	5	2	0
Whitfill, Daytona	1.000	1	0	1	0	0
Williams, Dunedin	1.000	2	0	1	0	0
Winston, West Palm Beach*	1.000	8	1	3	0	0
Wiseman, St. Petersburg	1.000	2	1	5	0	1
Withem, Lakeland	.966	16	14	14	1	0
Woodring, West Palm Beach	1.000	4	2	2	0	0
Zerbe, Vero Beach*	1.000	10	2	1	0	0

The following players did not have any fielding statistics at the positions indicated or appeared only as a designated hitter, pinch-hitter or pinch-runner: Alder, of; Beasley, 1b; Blackburn, of; Brede, 1b; Brant Brown, of; Civit, p; Coleman, 1b; M. Daniel, 3b; DeArmas, p; Dotal, p; S. Fernandez, p; Ferreira, p; Gordon, p; Green, 1b; Holbert, 2b; Hood, ss; G. Johnson, p; M. Johnson, p; R. Johnson, of; Keister, pr, dh; D. Kennedy, of; Kindell, p; Kontorinis, p; Lacy, p; Larkin, p; Larson, p; Meza, ss, p; Miranda, 3b; Moreno, dh, ph, pr; Ozorio, 2b; Prybylinski, of; Radziewicz, p; Randall, of; Ronan, of; Schulte, p; Dan Smith (Charlotte), p; Dave Smith, ss; Steverson, 2b; Tosar, ss; Vorbeck, p; Walker, of; Wetteland, p; W. White, p.

LEAGUE CHAMPIONS

Year	Team	Pct.
1919—	Sanford*	.605
	Orlando*	.703
1920—	Tampa	.654
	Tampa	.722
1921—	Orlando	.635
1922—	St. Petersburg	.503
	St. Petersburg	.618
1923—	Orlando	.667
	Orlando	.678
1924—	Lakeland	.695
	Lakeland	.683
1925—	St. Petersburg	.667
	Tampa†	.696
1926—	Sanford	.647
	Sanford	.623
1927—	Orlando†	.600
	Miami	.661
1928-35—	Did not operate.	
1936—	Gainesville	.542
	St. Augustine (4th)†	.492
1937—	Gainesville§	.616

Year	Team	Pct.
1938—	Leesburg	.626
	Gainesville (2nd)‡	.615
1939—	Sanford§	.787
1940—	Daytona Beach	.619
	Orlando (4th)‡	.507
1941—	St. Augustine	.659
	Leesburg (4th)‡	.488
1942-45—	Did not operate.	
1946—	Orlando§	.681
1947—	St. Augustine	.625
	Gainesville (2nd)‡	.584
1948—	Orlando	.643
	Daytona Beach (2nd)‡	.616
1949—	Gainesville	.635
	St. Augustine (3rd)‡	.556
1950—	Orlando	.629
	DeLand (3rd)‡	.590
1951—	DeLand§	.643
1952—	DeLand x	.704
	Palatka (3rd)‡	.569
1953—	Daytona Beach†	.657

Year	Team	Pct.
	DeLand	.703
1954—	Jacksonville Beach	.629
	Lakeland†	.594
1955—	Orlando	.671
	Orlando	.643
1956—	Cocoa	.614
	Cocoa	.671
1957—	Palatka	.629
	Tampa†	.681
1958—	St. Petersburg	.732
	St. Petersburg	.681
1959—	Tampa	.591
	St. Petersburg†	.612
1960—	Lakeland	.731
	Palatka†	.614
1961—	Tampa†	.710
	Sarasota	.696
1962—	Sarasota	.689
	Fort Lauderdale†	.623
1963—	Sarasota	.645
	Sarasota	.667

Year	Team	Pct.	Year	Team	Pct.	Year	Team	Pct.
1964—	Fort Lauderdale†	.629	1974—	West Palm Beach d	.598	1984—	Tampa	.532
	St. Petersburg	.594		Fort Lauderdale	.626		Fort Lauderdale f	.521
1965—	Fort Lauderdale	.627	1975—	St. Petersburg d	.652	1985—	Fort Myers g	.590
	Fort Lauderdale	.634		Miami	.581		Fort Lauderdale	.550
1966—	Leesburg†	.781	1976—	Tampa	.559	1986—	St. Petersburg g	.647
	St. Petersburg	.700		Lakeland d	.536		West Palm Beach	.593
1967—	St. Petersburg y	.691	1977—	Lakeland d	.616	1987—	Fort Lauderdale g	.616
	Orlando	.638		West Palm Beach	.583		Osceola	.576
1968—	Miami	.613	1978—	Lakeland	.565	1988—	Osceola	.606
	Orlando z	.579		Miami§	.539		St. Lucie h	.532
1969—	Miami a	.606	1979—	Fort Lauderdale	.643	1989—	Port Charlotte h	.540
	Orlando	.606		Winter Haven e	.577		St. Petersburg	.540
1970—	Miami b	.662	1980—	Daytona Beach	.628	1990—	West Palm Beach	.697
	St. Petersburg	.600		Fort Lauderdale d	.606		Vero Beach h	.585
1971—	Miami b	.667	1981—	Fort Myers	.554	1991—	Clearwater	.623
	Daytona Beach	.586		Daytona Beach f	.504		West Palm Beach h	.550
1972—	Miami c	.562	1982—	Fort Lauderdale f	.621	1992—	Sarasota	.639
	Daytona Beach	.606		Tampa	.546		Lakeland i	.530
1973—	St. Petersburg d	.575	1983—	Daytona Beach	.634	1993—	St. Lucie	.600
	West Palm Beach	.580		Vero Beach f	.515		Clearwater f	.556

*Split-season playoff abandoned after each team won three games. †Won split-season playoff. ‡Won four-club playoff. §Won championship and four-club playoff. xWon both halves of split season. yLeague divided into Eastern and Western divisions with split season. St. Petersburg and Orlando won both halves of split season; St. Petersburg won playoff. zLeague divided into Eastern and Western divisions. Miami won regular-season pennant on basis of highest won-lost percentage. Orlando won four-club playoff involving first two teams in each division. aLeague divided into Southern and Central divisions. Miami won playoff between division leaders. (NOTE—Pennant awarded to playoff winner in 1936.) bLeague divided into Eastern and Western divisions. Miami won regular-season pennant on basis of highest won-loss percentage, and also won four-club playoff involving first two teams in each division. cLeague divided into Eastern and Western divisions. Won four-club playoff involving first two teams in each division. dLeague divided into Northern and Southern divisions. Won four-club playoff involving first two teams in each division. eLeague divided into Northern and Southern divisions. Same two clubs won both halves; won playoffs. fWon split-season playoff. gLeague divided into Western, Central and Southern divisions. Won four-club playoff. hLeague divided into Eastern, Western and Central divisions; played split-season. Won six-club playoff. iLeague divided into Eastern, Western and Central divisions; played split-season. Won eight-club playoff.

MIDWEST LEAGUE

FINAL STANDINGS

FIRST HALF

NORTHERN DIVISION

Team	W	L	T	Pct.	GB
Rockford (Royals)	43	22	0	.662	....
Madison (Athletics)	39	28	0	.582	5
Kane County (Marlins)	39	29	0	.574	5½
South Bend (White Sox)	34	32	0	.515	9½
Appleton (Mariners)	34	32	0	.515	9½
Fort Wayne (Twins)	33	33	0	.500	10½
Beloit (Brewers)	29	36	0	.446	14

SOUTHERN DIVISION

Team	W	L	T	Pct.	GB
Springfield (Cardinals)	41	26	0	.612	....
Clinton (Giants)	36	29	0	.554	4
Burlington (Expos)	35	31	0	.530	5½
Peoria (Cubs)	29	40	0	.420	13
Quad City (Astros)	25	40	0	.385	15
Cedar Rapids (Angels)	24	40	0	.375	15½
Waterloo (Padres)	22	45	0	.328	19

SECOND HALF

NORTHERN DIVISION

Team	W	L	T	Pct.	GB
South Bend (White Sox)	43	27	0	.614	....
Madison (Athletics)	38	30	0	.559	4
Rockford (Royals)	35	32	0	.522	6½
Kane County (Marlins)	36	33	0	.522	6½
Fort Wayne (Twins)	35	34	0	.507	7½
Beloit (Brewers)	31	38	0	.449	11½
Appleton (Mariners)	28	41	0	.406	14½

SOUTHERN DIVISION

Team	W	L	T	Pct.	GB
Clinton (Giants)	44	25	0	.638	....
Springfield (Cardinals)	37	32	0	.536	7
Waterloo (Padres)	32	34	0	.485	10½
Quad City (Astros)	31	34	0	.477	11
Peoria (Cubs)	30	39	0	.435	14
Cedar Rapids (Angels)	30	40	0	.429	14½
Burlington (Expos)	29	40	0	.420	15

COMPOSITE

Team	Cln.	Rock.	Spr.	Mad.	S.B.	K.C.	F.W.	Burl.	App.	Bel.	Q.C.	Peo.	Wat.	C.R.	W	L	T	Pct.	GB
Clinton (Giants)	....	2	2	5	5	4	6	5	3	9	10	8	8	8	80	54	0	.597	....
Rockford (Royals)	6	....	3	5	6	8	11	4	7	7	5	5	7	4	78	54	0	.591	1
Springfield (Cardinals)	4	3	....	6	5	2	4	10	2	5	9	8	9	11	78	58	0	.574	3
Madison (Athletics)	3	8	2	....	5	9	6	3	11	10	5	6	3	6	77	58	0	.570	3½
South Bend (White Sox)	3	8	3	8	....	9	4	5	9	9	2	5	5	7	77	59	0	.566	4
Kane County (Marlins)	4	6	5	5	5	....	8	4	10	4	4	5	5	6	75	62	0	.547	6½
Fort Wayne (Twins)	2	3	4	8	10	5	....	4	9	6	4	4	5	4	68	67	0	.504	12½
Burlington (Expos)	7	4	4	5	3	4	4	....	3	3	8	5	8	6	64	71	0	.474	16½
Appleton (Mariners)	3	6	6	3	4	4	5	5	....	8	5	7	3	3	62	73	0	.459	18½
Beloit (Brewers)	5	5	3	4	5	6	7	3	6	....	5	4	4	3	60	74	0	.448	20
Quad City (Astros)	4	1	4	3	4	3	4	5	2	3	....	10	6	7	56	74	0	.431	22
Peoria (Cubs)	4	3	6	2	3	3	4	9	1	3	4	....	10	7	59	74	0	.428	23
Waterloo (Padres)	5	1	5	2	3	2	3	6	3	4	7	4	....	9	54	79	0	.406	25½
Cedar Rapids (Angels)	4	4	3	2	1	3	1	8	5	5	7	6	5	....	54	80	0	.403	26

Kane County's home games played in Geneva, Ill.

Quad City's home games played in Davenport, Ia.

Major league affiliations in parentheses.

Playoffs—South Bend defeated Rockford, two games to none; Clinton defeated Springfield, two games to none; South Bend defeated Clinton, three games to one, to win league championship.

Regular-season attendance—Appleton, 56,036; Beloit, 65,728; Burlington, 77,492; Cedar Rapids, 114,105; Clinton, 62,873; Fort Wayne, 318,506; Kane County, 354,327; Madison, 101,219; Peoria, 100,811; Quad City, 103,797; Rockford, 68,206; South Bend, 229,883; Springfield, 110,189; Waterloo, 51,329. Total, 1,814,501. Playoffs (8 games), 14,565. All-Star Game—6,061.

Managers—Appleton, Carlos Lezcano; Beloit, Wayne Krenchicki; Burlington, Lorenzo Bundy; Cedar Rapids, Mitch Seoane; Clinton, Jack Mull; Fort Wayne, Jim Dwyer; Kane County, Carlos Tosca; Madison, Gary Jones; Peoria, Steve Roadcap; Quad City, Steve Dillard; Rockford, Mike Jirschele; South Bend, Tony Franklin; Springfield, Mike Ramsey; Waterloo, Ed Romero.

All-Star team: 1B—Ken Tirpack, Fort Wayne; 2B—Joe Biasucci, Springfield; 3B—Mike Gulan, Springfield; SS—Chad Fonville, Clinton; OF—Anthony Byrd, Fort Wayne; Johnny Damon, Rockford; Carmine Cappuccio, South Bend; C—Charles Johnson, Kane County; DH—Scott Talanoa, Beloit; LHP—Ugueth Urbina, Burlington; RHP—Tim Davis, Appleton; LH Reliever—Vic Darensbourg, Kane County; RH Reliever—Kirk Bullinger, Springfield; Most Valuable Player—Joe Biasucci, Springfield; Manager of the Year—Jack Mull, Clinton.

BATTING

TEAM

Team	Avg.	G	AB	R	OR	H	TB	2B	3B	HR	RBI	SH	SF	HP	BB	Int. BB	SO	SB	CS	LOB
South Bend	.269	136	4539	659	583	1222	1721	216	44	65	579	38	43	66	455	21	952	155	72	976
Rockford	.269	132	4272	630	537	1148	1639	234	43	57	552	41	43	71	480	22	851	239	96	937
Clinton	.258	134	4251	679	559	1096	1577	179	34	78	576	60	40	64	502	13	975	214	81	903
Kane County	.255	137	4473	602	560	1139	1574	219	33	50	527	46	50	39	528	29	892	127	85	993
Appleton	.253	135	4330	604	669	1095	1639	227	43	77	531	37	36	73	467	30	1039	131	102	893
Springfield	.253	136	4317	662	548	1091	1721	206	26	124	589	32	31	52	517	15	1131	144	83	927
Peoria	.252	138	4379	578	644	1103	1522	218	21	53	509	110	37	69	469	19	914	81	68	945
Quad City	.252	130	4179	570	530	1052	1496	180	30	68	496	42	38	72	403	19	957	169	98	865
Madison	.252	135	4340	636	521	1092	1638	214	34	88	567	72	48	62	488	12	1086	105	75	950
Beloit	.250	134	4279	641	712	1068	1627	191	37	98	547	46	37	41	514	13	1004	182	94	847
Fort Wayne	.249	135	4485	578	585	1117	1616	203	37	74	506	21	36	69	505	19	946	136	70	1010
Burlington	.248	135	4400	616	595	1093	1691	224	31	104	562	51	37	52	473	24	1079	125	61	971
Waterloo	.248	134	4060	525	685	1008	1475	172	29	79	453	51	29	63	360	8	987	158	65	802
Cedar Rapids	.231	134	4220	580	732	976	1432	167	26	79	492	64	35	54	565	11	1017	132	69	919

(Leading qualifiers for batting championship—378 or more plate appearances)

*Bats lefthanded. †Switch-hitter.

Player, Team	Avg.	G	AB	R	H	TB	2B	3B	HR	RBI	SH	SF	HP	BB	Int. BB	SO	SB	CS
Bush, Homer, Waterloo	.322	130	472	63	152	192	19	3	5	51	1	1	1	19	0	87	39	14
Jennings, Robin, Peoria*	.308	132	474	64	146	194	29	5	3	65	5	3	4	46	2	73	11	11
Fonville, Chad, Clinton†	.306	120	447	80	137	176	16	10	1	44	5	2	9	40	2	48	52	16
Cappuccio, Carmine, South Bend*	.305	101	383	59	117	165	26	5	4	52	0	1	6	42	6	56	2	6
Benard, Marvin, Clinton*	.301	112	349	84	105	138	14	2	5	50	2	0	4	56	1	66	42	10
Perez, Dan, Beloit	.300	106	377	70	113	172	17	6	10	59	1	2	5	56	0	64	23	8
Tirpack, Ken, Fort Wayne*	.294	127	473	71	139	206	34	3	9	70	0	6	6	68	4	103	1	4
Ball, Jeff, Quad City	.293	112	389	69	114	188	28	2	14	76	1	5	7	58	3	62	40	19
Byrd, Anthony, Fort Wayne	.292	123	479	84	140	227	19	10	16	79	0	3	3	58	4	79	24	11
Murphy, Steve, Rockford*	.292	110	349	56	102	135	17	5	2	49	13	1	7	48	0	69	29	14

Departmental leaders: G—C. Johnson, Stovall, 135; AB—Mathews, 518; R—Burton, 95; H—Bush, 152; TB—C. Johnson, 230; 2B—Pridy, 38; 3B—Damon, 13; HR—Biasucci, 26; RBI—C. Johnson, 94; SH—Ri. Perez, 29; SF—Gubanich, 12; HP—Gipson, 27; BB—Sutton, 95; IBB—Hmielewski, 10; SO—Wallace, 145; SB—Burton, 74; CS—Burton, 24.

(All players—listed alphabetically)

Player, Team	Avg.	G	AB	R	H	TB	2B	3B	HR	RBI	SH	SF	HP	BB	Int. BB	SO	SB	CS
Alcantara, Israel, Burlington	.245	126	470	65	115	201	26	3	18	73	1	5	7	20	2	125	6	7
Alimena, Charles, Clinton*	.249	110	309	36	77	110	12	0	7	44	3	6	6	38	0	77	2	5
Antoon, Jeff, Rockford	.278	60	205	27	57	78	13	1	2	35	0	2	2	12	0	41	3	0
Aracena, Luinis, Madison	.270	42	89	7	24	27	3	0	0	6	1	1	0	5	0	20	2	3
Arias, Georgie, Cedar Rapids	.217	74	253	31	55	101	13	3	9	41	1	2	3	31	1	65	6	1
Atencio, Enrique, Appleton	.232	101	358	45	83	119	9	6	5	49	2	3	4	9	0	77	6	3
Baber, Larue, Waterloo	.272	90	254	31	69	90	15	0	2	19	3	2	1	19	0	71	13	8
Ball, Jeff, Quad City	.293	112	389	69	114	188	28	2	14	76	1	5	7	58	3	62	40	19
Ballara, Juan, Springfield	.246	60	195	24	48	73	8	1	5	29	1	2	2	12	0	42	1	1
Banks, Brian, Beloit†	.245	38	147	21	36	55	5	1	4	19	0	0	1	7	0	34	1	2
Bell, George, South Bend	.125	2	8	1	1	1	0	0	0	0	0	0	0	1	0	1	0	0
Bellomo, Kevin, Clinton	.254	24	67	10	17	20	3	0	0	5	3	0	5	10	0	6	3	0
Benard, Marvin, Clinton*	.301	112	349	84	105	138	14	2	5	50	2	0	4	56	1	66	42	10
Benitez, Yamil, Burlington	.273	111	411	70	112	188	21	5	15	61	6	3	3	29	1	99	18	7
Berry, Mike, Burlington	.239	31	92	15	22	27	2	0	1	6	3	0	0	20	0	22	0	1
Biasucci, Joe, Springfield	.289	119	398	76	115	229	30	3	26	86	4	5	7	62	3	110	15	6
Biermann, Steve, Springfield†	.091	3	11	0	1	1	0	0	0	0	0	0	0	0	0	6	0	1
Bonds, Bobby, Waterloo	.248	102	359	44	89	119	12	3	4	35	4	3	4	30	1	124	30	11
Bowrosen, Ricky, South Bend	.159	32	88	9	14	25	5	0	2	9	0	0	8	11	0	37	0	1
Boyzuick, Mike, Beloit	.266	108	346	50	92	135	18	2	7	43	0	4	3	57	2	70	2	4
Bradish, Mike, South Bend	.285	47	172	21	49	69	11	0	3	26	0	2	2	9	1	46	0	1
Bradley, Byron, Peoria	.301	49	176	28	53	69	13	0	1	22	0	1	1	15	0	33	4	3
Bridges, Kary, Quad City*	.281	65	263	37	74	92	9	0	3	24	1	3	2	31	1	18	15	10
Briggs, Stoney, Waterloo	.257	125	421	57	108	160	15	5	9	55	4	5	12	30	1	103	21	8
Brooks, Ramy, Rockford	.255	120	415	74	106	189	34	2	15	65	1	3	7	60	1	91	14	5
Brown, Armann, Fort Wayne	.194	41	124	11	24	27	3	0	0	10	0	0	5	18	0	27	13	1
Bruce, Andy, Springfield	.255	105	364	61	93	171	13	1	21	70	0	3	6	44	3	136	1	2
Bryant, Craig, Appleton	.300	51	170	33	51	83	11	3	5	29	4	1	3	18	2	32	12	2
Burton, Essex, South Bend†	.255	134	501	95	128	153	6	8	1	36	8	2	4	85	0	94	74	24
Bush, Homer, Waterloo	.322	130	472	63	152	192	19	3	5	51	1	1	1	19	0	87	39	14
Byrd, Anthony, Fort Wayne	.292	123	479	84	140	227	19	10	16	79	0	3	3	58	4	79	24	11
Cabrera, Jolbert, Burlington	.254	128	507	62	129	157	24	2	0	38	11	4	7	39	0	93	31	11
Cacini, Ron, Quad City	.182	7	22	3	4	7	0	0	1	1	0	0	1	3	0	6	1	0
Cameron, Mike, South Bend	.238	122	411	52	98	122	14	5	0	30	2	5	6	27	0	101	19	10
Cappuccio, Carmine, South Bend*	.305	101	383	59	117	165	26	5	4	52	0	1	6	42	6	56	2	6
Carrion, German, Waterloo†	.218	48	110	11	24	27	3	0	0	7	5	0	4	4	0	18	1	2
Casanova, Raul, Waterloo	.256	76	227	32	58	88	12	0	6	30	5	0	1	21	2	46	0	1
Castro, Antonio, Cedar Rapids	.087	34	46	8	4	6	2	0	0	3	4	0	0	8	0	22	2	0
Cavanagh, Mike, Clinton	.241	39	87	13	21	38	5	0	4	16	4	2	0	15	0	30	0	1
Centeno, Henri, Quad City	.251	102	295	42	74	88	5	3	1	24	4	3	8	30	0	50	23	9
Christian, Eddie, Kane County†	.268	112	366	49	98	138	21	5	3	46	3	10	0	58	6	77	9	11
Clapinski, Chris, Kane County†	.210	82	214	22	45	59	12	1	0	27	8	4	1	31	0	55	3	8
Claus, Marc, Fort Wayne	.206	81	248	29	51	60	7	1	0	9	6	1	4	24	1	60	7	4
Connell, Lino, Cedar Rapids†	.179	75	240	20	43	44	1	0	0	24	12	5	2	31	0	70	6	6
Cora, Manny, Waterloo†	.329	22	73	8	24	31	4	0	1	11	0	0	0	5	0	6	1	1
Costic, Tim, Fort Wayne*	.238	85	273	28	65	97	14	3	4	29	2	1	1	26	1	75	5	7
Cromer, D.T., Madison*	.262	98	321	37	84	124	20	4	4	41	7	2	1	22	0	72	8	6
Crowe, Ron, Clinton	.000	34	0	0	0	0	0	0	0	0	0	0	0	1	0	0	0	0
Cunningham, Earl, Peoria	.194	43	139	15	27	50	6	1	5	15	0	0	4	10	0	38	2	1
Damon, Johnny, Rockford*	.290	127	511	82	148	214	25	13	5	50	3	3	6	52	1	83	59	18
Daniels, Morisse, Cedar Rapids	.242	110	368	53	89	121	7	2	7	36	3	0	2	54	1	113	25	8
Dawson, Dwayne, Quad City	.000	32	2	0	0	0	0	0	0	0	0	0	0	0	0	2	0	0
Delaney, Sean, Rockford	.178	20	45	7	8	8	0	0	0	2	0	0	2	0	0	15	1	0
Deutsch, John, Peoria*	.246	43	130	18	32	57	10	0	5	13	2	0	1	22	1	32	0	5
Devers, Edgar, South Bend*	.197	33	66	9	13	16	3	0	0	10	2	0	1	6	0	21	0	0
DeLeon, Roberto, Waterloo	.266	114	391	51	104	167	20	5	11	59	9	4	3	19	0	67	6	2
Diaz, Eddy, Appleton	.333	46	189	28	63	90	14	2	3	33	0	0	0	15	2	13	13	9
DiFelice, Mike, Springfield	.350	8	20	5	7	7	1	0	0	3	0	0	1	2	0	3	0	1
Dorencz, Mark, Quad City	.182	50	165	18	30	48	3	3	3	15	4	4	3	13	0	40	2	2
Doyle, Tom, Burlington*	.079	13	38	3	3	5	2	0	0	4	0	0	1	0	0	13	0	0
Dumas, Mike, Beloit	.230	76	174	48	40	43	9	0	2	19	0	2	0	27	0	30	13	11
Dunckel, Bill, Cedar Rapids	.125	12	32	2	4	6	2	0	0	2	0	0	0	4	0	5	0	0
Duran, Iggy, Waterloo	.196	88	240	21	47	67	7	2	3	18	5	1	2	17	0	62	1	1
Durkin, Chris, Quad City*	.273	25	77	14	21	32	6	1	1	6	0	0	0	15	3	13	6	4
Ealy, Tracey, Clinton†	.253	122	396	60	100	147	13	5	8	65	5	2	3	36	2	93	24	12
Eicher, Mike, Springfield	.172	38	87	10	15	21	3	0	1	11	1	3	1	16	0	28	1	0
Eidle, Scott, Quad City*	.258	56	194	34	50	75	12	2	3	24	0	0	1	33	4	60	4	0
Eldridge, Brian, Madison	.245	85	253	37	62	79	12	1	1	22	8	1	4	27	0	48	5	4

Player, Team	Avg.	G	AB	R	H	TB	2B	3B	HR	RBI	SH	SF	HP	BB	Int. BB	SO	SB	CS
Ellstrom, Rich, Waterloo	.224	44	116	19	26	38	10	1	0	5	3	1	3	21	0	38	5	0
Ellsworth, Ben, Springfield†	.189	29	74	6	14	17	3	0	0	8	0	0	1	5	0	13	0	2
Encarnacion, Anito, Waterloo	.091	20	44	1	4	5	1	0	0	5	0	1	0	2	1	9	0	0
Erdman, Brad, Peoria	.246	20	57	7	14	18	1	0	1	10	3	1	2	6	0	12	2	0
Evans, Tim, Quad City*	.277	124	440	62	122	174	24	5	6	53	3	3	6	36	2	76	11	7
Faircloth, Eugene, South Bend	.250	2	4	0	1	1	0	0	0	0	0	0	0	0	0	3	0	0
Fantauzzi, John, Waterloo*	.226	119	367	57	83	137	10	1	14	41	2	3	6	48	0	115	0	0
Felder, Ken, Beloit	.182	32	99	12	18	35	4	2	3	8	0	0	2	10	0	40	1	1
Fonville, Chad, Clinton†	.306	120	447	80	137	176	16	10	1	44	5	2	9	40	2	48	52	16
Francisco, David, Madison	.277	129	484	87	134	180	24	8	2	50	9	4	12	50	1	108	27	16
Francisco, Vincente, Madison†	.249	116	325	36	81	99	10	4	0	29	15	1	2	21	0	61	4	4
Fraraccio, Dan, South Bend	.274	49	135	23	37	47	10	0	0	21	1	1	3	6	0	29	0	1
Frazier, Bradley, Kane County*	.000	39	1	0	0	0	0	0	0	0	0	0	0	0	0	0	0	0
Fryman, Troy, South Bend*	.318	51	173	34	55	95	7	6	7	41	0	4	3	33	1	45	2	0
Gamble, Freddie, Kane County*	.242	58	99	17	24	33	3	3	0	10	0	0	0	6	0	9	5	3
Garrett, Clifton, Cedar Rapids*	.323	36	127	26	41	49	4	2	0	11	3	0	0	30	0	22	14	6
Gay, Brad, Beloit	.194	36	98	12	19	30	5	0	2	15	0	1	0	13	0	31	1	0
Gerteisen, Aaron, Springfield†	.333	4	6	1	2	2	0	0	0	1	0	0	1	3	0	2	1	0
Gipson, Charles, Appleton	.256	109	348	63	89	104	13	1	0	20	9	1	27	61	0	76	21	16
Gonzalez, Jim, Quad City	.227	47	154	20	35	46	9	1	0	15	1	1	4	14	1	36	2	2
Good, Thomas, Rockford*	.188	9	32	3	6	6	0	0	0	2	0	0	0	3	0	7	3	1
Gorman, Paul, Beloit	.237	22	59	13	14	21	4	0	1	3	2	0	1	14	0	6	0	3
Greene, Charlie, Waterloo	.178	84	213	19	38	52	8	0	2	20	6	3	3	13	0	33	0	0
Griffey, Craig, Appleton	.255	37	102	14	26	39	7	0	2	20	1	3	1	12	0	18	9	3
Grissom, Antonio, Burlington	.251	73	271	40	68	106	13	5	5	27	4	1	3	35	2	60	22	11
Gubanich, Creighton, Madison	.268	119	373	65	100	180	19	2	19	78	2	12	11	63	2	105	3	3
Guillen, Jose, Madison†	.268	104	332	44	89	114	17	4	0	25	9	1	2	52	0	69	16	11
Gulan, Mike, Springfield	.259	132	455	81	118	223	28	4	23	76	3	3	9	34	0	135	8	4
Guzik, Brian, Cedar Rapids	.252	36	115	20	29	43	5	0	3	10	1	1	3	15	0	29	0	1
Haar, Richard, Burlington	.211	24	71	9	15	18	3	0	0	8	0	2	1	10	0	16	2	2
Hamlin, Jonas, Beloit	.217	121	428	57	93	167	19	2	17	62	2	2	3	40	2	119	3	2
Hardwick, Joe, Cedar Rapids	.227	62	194	44	44	58	5	3	1	14	3	1	14	34	0	57	22	7
Harkrider, Timothy, Cedar Rapids†	.253	54	190	29	48	59	11	0	0	14	8	0	1	22	0	28	7	4
Hauswirth, Trenton, Rockford	.171	37	105	6	18	21	3	0	0	14	1	3	3	15	0	42	0	0
Henry, Antoine, Springfield	.273	18	66	12	18	25	4	0	1	11	1	0	0	11	0	13	5	1
Herrera, Edgar, Fort Wayne	.195	37	113	8	22	29	4	0	1	13	1	0	0	12	0	28	1	0
Herrera, Jose, Madison*	.214	4	14	1	3	3	0	0	0	0	1	0	0	0	0	6	1	1
Hickey, Mike, Appleton*	.286	69	255	35	73	99	14	3	2	41	1	3	1	38	1	49	14	7
Hightower, Vee, Peoria†	.200	2	10	0	2	2	0	0	0	0	0	0	0	0	0	1	1	0
Hill, Orsino, Cedar Rapids*	.271	54	199	36	54	92	17	0	7	30	0	4	6	19	1	51	0	0
Hirsch, Chris, Cedar Rapids	.194	13	36	4	7	11	1	0	1	6	0	0	0	10	0	15	0	0
Hmielewski, Chris, Burlington*	.274	125	412	69	113	184	25	2	14	70	3	5	3	74	10	99	4	2
Hood, Randy, South Bend	.235	6	17	5	4	6	2	0	0	1	0	0	3	6	0	3	1	1
Horn, Jeff, Fort Wayne	.195	66	200	19	39	61	7	0	5	23	1	4	4	18	0	51	1	2
Hostetler, Brian, Beloit*	.197	73	218	20	43	64	7	1	4	17	1	1	1	34	3	44	2	1
Hughes, Bobby, Beloit	.277	98	321	42	89	157	11	3	17	56	5	0	6	23	0	76	1	3
Hurst, Jimmy, South Bend	.244	123	464	79	113	199	26	0	20	79	0	5	8	37	3	141	15	2
Hust, Gary, Madison	.223	118	364	52	81	147	20	2	14	54	4	1	0	51	1	141	7	4
Hymel, Gary, Burlington	.275	50	182	28	50	99	14	1	11	41	0	4	5	3	0	60	1	0
Ibanez, Raul, Appleton*	.274	52	157	26	43	67	9	0	5	21	1	2	1	24	2	31	0	2
Imperial, Jason, Beloit	.120	15	50	4	6	8	2	0	0	2	0	1	1	1	0	19	0	0
Jennings, Robin, Peoria*	.308	132	474	64	146	194	29	5	3	65	5	3	4	46	2	73	11	11
Jensen, Marcus, Clinton†	.262	104	324	53	85	146	24	2	11	56	0	4	4	66	5	98	1	2
Johns, Keith, Springfield	.259	132	467	74	121	153	24	1	2	40	9	5	4	70	0	68	40	20
Johnson, Charles, Kane County	.275	135	488	74	134	230	29	5	19	94	0	4	2	62	9	111	9	1
Johnson, Jack, Peoria	.188	39	96	10	18	25	7	0	0	10	4	2	1	23	0	33	3	0
Jordan, Tim, Springfield*	.100	3	10	2	1	1	0	0	0	1	0	0	1	0	0	5	0	0
Kerns, Mickey, Cedar Rapids	.193	91	300	30	58	102	15	1	9	34	3	6	1	19	1	85	8	7
Kessler, David, Cedar Rapids	.265	13	34	5	9	9	0	0	0	5	0	1	0	11	0	9	1	0
Killeen, Tim, Madison*	.202	76	243	33	49	94	15	0	10	36	0	1	3	39	1	70	0	0
King, Clay, Clinton	.214	39	126	14	27	35	5	0	1	16	1	2	0	7	0	19	0	0
Kingston, Mark, Peoria†	.254	64	224	25	57	85	14	1	4	24	3	3	5	28	0	44	3	0
Knauss, Tom, Fort Wayne	.188	55	186	26	35	57	3	2	5	22	0	1	8	21	2	44	5	3
Koehler, Jim, Appleton*	.242	115	372	52	90	179	28	5	17	60	2	5	6	55	4	95	4	6
Landinez, Carlos, Springfield	.214	47	126	18	27	34	7	0	0	3	2	0	2	6	0	19	5	4
Landry, Todd, Beloit	.302	38	149	26	45	63	6	0	4	24	0	2	0	4	0	36	4	4
Lawson, David, Appleton*	.252	113	333	59	84	149	26	3	11	38	2	1	5	65	6	129	6	14
Lawton, Matt, Fort Wayne*	.285	111	340	50	97	151	21	3	9	38	0	2	8	65	3	42	23	15
LaChance, Vince, Burlington*	.164	19	61	6	10	20	1	0	3	12	0	0	1	5	0	18	0	0
Leary, Rob, Madison*	.143	8	28	2	4	4	0	0	0	0	0	0	2	0	0	10	0	0
Lee, Charles, Burlington	.219	68	228	33	50	76	12	1	4	21	5	1	2	32	0	65	16	5
LeGree, Keith, Fort Wayne*	.242	49	178	28	43	62	6	2	3	14	0	0	3	21	2	51	1	2
Lesher, Brian, Madison	.274	119	394	63	108	146	13	5	5	47	6	6	9	46	0	102	20	9
Linares, Mario, Quad City	.256	57	199	18	51	70	10	0	3	22	2	0	4	10	0	22	1	0
Listach, Pat, Beloit†	.250	4	12	2	3	3	0	0	0	1	0	0	1	1	0	2	2	0
Llanos, Aurelio, Appleton†	.252	81	246	35	62	103	15	4	6	30	1	3	2	15	2	67	6	6
Long, Ryan, Rockford	.290	107	396	46	115	178	27	6	8	68	2	5	18	16	3	76	16	6
Lopez, Rene, Fort Wayne	.250	92	340	26	85	108	12	1	3	44	1	5	2	45	0	57	0	1
Lucca, Louis, Kane County	.277	127	419	52	116	163	25	2	6	53	2	7	9	60	0	58	4	10
Machado, Robert, South Bend	.306	75	281	34	86	112	14	3	2	33	2	4	4	19	0	59	1	2
Mader, Chris, South Bend	.262	18	61	6	16	21	2	0	1	8	0	0	0	11	0	8	2	0
Madsen, Dan, Peoria†	.211	80	265	39	56	80	16	4	0	32	7	2	10	37	2	60	9	8
Marabella, Tony, Burlington	.286	17	42	7	12	24	6	0	2	11	0	1	0	6	1	6	0	0
Markiewicz, Brandon, Cedar Rapids	.264	120	425	56	112	167	18	5	9	55	4	2	6	37	3	68	6	8
Marquez, Jesus, Appleton*	.273	61	216	23	59	80	7	1	4	27	1	2	2	13	2	47	5	4
Martin, Steve, Cedar Rapids	.265	56	181	33	48	74	7	2	5	15	3	3	5	27	1	56	11	1
Martinez, Eduard, Appleton	.152	10	33	3	5	7	0	1	0	0	0	0	0	0	0	8	0	0
Martinez, Gabriel, Beloit	.242	94	285	40	69	93	14	5	0	24	15	4	1	14	0	52	22	10
Martinez, Javier, Cedar Rapids†	.155	33	97	15	15	18	3	0	0	7	2	2	0	13	0	17	1	2
Mathews, Byron, South Bend*	.245	131	518	75	127	157	10	7	2	58	11	5	2	48	1	110	30	13
Mayes, Craig, Clinton*	.296	75	226	25	67	90	12	1	3	37	3	3	0	10	0	52	1	0
McCubbin, Shane, Burlington	.149	40	121	12	18	28	4	0	2	13	6	1	0	11	0	45	1	0
McGinnis, Shane, Peoria	.184	38	103	5	19	21	2	0	0	11	2	2	2	10	0	31	2	3
McGlone, Brian, Quad City*	.204	97	250	28	51	55	4	0	0	15	16	2	0	31	0	80	5	8

Player, Team	Avg.	G	AB	R	H	TB	2B	3B	HR	RBI	SH	SF	HP	BB	Int. BB	SO	SB	CS
Medina, Ricardo, Peoria	.254	88	283	30	72	95	14	0	3	29	2	2	1	40	1	37	0	5
Mendez, Emilio, Peoria	.190	14	21	3	4	4	0	0	0	1	1	0	0	0	0	8	0	0
Mendoza, Francisco, Beloit†	.061	27	49	3	3	6	0	0	1	5	3	1	1	3	0	18	2	0
Miller, Joey, Fort Wayne	.243	67	169	30	41	58	8	3	1	9	0	1	3	25	0	60	20	7
Miller, Roger, Clinton	.192	10	26	1	5	8	0	0	1	4	1	1	0	2	0	3	0	0
Minchk, Kevin, Waterloo*	.205	33	73	7	15	17	2	0	0	6	1	0	2	10	0	21	0	0
Montilla, Julio, Rockford†	.273	84	289	34	79	104	13	3	2	27	3	3	2	17	0	38	6	10
Moore, Mark, Madison	.158	12	19	0	3	4	1	0	0	5	0	1	1	2	0	4	0	0
Morales, Francisco, Peoria	.204	19	49	9	10	22	1	1	3	11	4	0	0	9	0	16	0	0
Morales, Jorge, Appleton	.194	38	103	8	20	26	6	0	0	9	0	1	2	6	0	26	1	1
Morel, Plinio, Springfield	.227	26	75	3	17	19	2	0	0	3	0	0	1	4	0	17	0	0
Morillo, Cesar, Rockford†	.260	101	327	47	85	113	13	3	3	36	5	2	3	30	3	65	4	1
Morones, Geno, Peoria	.000	13	1	0	0	0	0	0	0	0	0	0	0	0	0	1	0	0
Mowry, Dave, Waterloo*	.239	46	142	16	34	61	4	1	7	25	0	1	1	28	3	41	1	0
Mumma, Bob, South Bend	.160	9	25	5	4	4	0	0	0	0	0	0	0	3	0	9	0	1
Murphy, Steve, Rockford*	.292	110	349	56	102	135	17	5	2	49	13	1	7	48	0	69	29	14
Myers, Rod, Rockford*	.259	129	474	69	123	184	24	5	9	68	6	4	5	58	6	117	49	16
Nava, Marlo, Fort Wayne	.259	115	455	48	118	153	25	2	2	47	4	4	4	23	0	61	9	3
Newhouse, Andre, Rockford	.240	94	271	42	65	89	18	0	2	28	2	4	6	26	†	68	24	8
O'Neill, Doug, Burlington	.212	67	203	26	43	64	6	3	3	20	2	1	2	33	1	69	3	1
O'Neill, Tom, Clinton	.247	88	215	41	53	84	13	3	4	34	10	6	5	40	0	46	6	3
Orie, Kevin, Peoria	.269	65	238	28	64	104	17	1	7	45	2	2	10	21	1	51	3	5
Pages, Javier, Burlington	.261	96	295	35	77	118	20	0	7	47	7	4	3	44	0	74	2	2
Pearson, Eddie, South Bend†	.326	48	190	23	62	81	16	0	1	26	0	3	1	13	2	29	0	1
Penix, Troy, Madison*	.254	66	236	35	60	106	10	3	10	45	1	2	1	20	4	39	1	1
Perez, Dan, Beloit	.300	106	377	70	113	172	17	6	10	59	1	2	5	56	0	64	23	8
Perez, Ralph, Waterloo*	.125	4	8	0	1	1	0	0	0	0	0	0	0	0	0	2	0	0
Perez, Richard, Peoria	.243	109	370	60	90	104	12	1	0	34	29	5	8	31	0	64	5	8
Petering, Todd, Clinton*	.146	27	48	9	7	7	0	0	0	2	4	1	0	8	0	17	1	1
Pico, Brandon, Peoria*	.156	8	32	5	5	8	1	1	0	3	0	0	0	1	0	6	0	0
Pike, Dave, Beloit	.000	35	1	0	0	0	0	0	0	0	0	0	0	0	0	0	0	0
Polidor, Wil, South Bend†	.283	42	120	14	34	44	2	4	0	9	2	0	0	1	0	15	0	1
Powell, Corey, Burlington	.279	115	433	55	121	188	18	5	13	62	1	3	3	29	3	97	2	1
Powell, Gordon, Beloit	.273	47	172	27	47	77	16	1	4	19	0	1	0	6	0	51	8	3
Pridy, Todd, Kane County*	.272	132	475	63	129	216	38	5	13	75	0	5	4	55	8	129	5	2
Probst, Alan, Quad City	.273	49	176	18	48	70	9	2	3	28	0	3	3	16	1	48	2	0
Puchkov, Yevgeny, Cedar Rapids*	.116	19	43	2	5	5	0	0	0	1	3	0	0	7	0	11	0	0
Raasch, Glen, Peoria	.274	53	197	17	54	76	13	0	3	18	1	1	2	7	0	47	1	2
Radmanovich, Ryan, Fort Wayne*	.289	62	204	36	59	100	7	5	8	38	2	2	7	30	2	60	8	2
Ramirez, Roberto, Madison	.309	14	55	9	17	24	4	0	1	7	0	1	1	3	0	10	2	2
Ramos, Eddie, Quad City	.258	125	446	52	115	166	18	0	11	63	2	6	5	26	2	117	7	5
Ramos, Papo, Clinton	.308	3	13	2	4	4	0	0	0	0	0	0	0	0	0	3	0	1
Redmond, Mike, Kane County	.200	43	100	10	20	22	2	0	0	10	2	0	4	6	0	17	2	0
Reid, Derek, Clinton	.298	15	57	5	17	19	2	0	0	7	1	0	0	1	0	6	3	2
Renteria, Edgar, Kane County	.203	116	384	40	78	89	8	0	1	35	6	3	0	35	0	94	7	8
Rhein, Jeff, Quad City	.208	53	159	15	33	48	5	2	2	16	2	1	2	14	0	49	14	7
Rich, Ted, South Bend	.228	26	79	5	18	27	1	1	2	11	1	1	2	6	0	23	1	1
Richardson, Scott, Beloit	.276	125	475	76	131	180	26	7	3	64	6	5	1	42	0	85	50	12
Riesgo, Nikco, Beloit	.194	9	31	7	6	12	0	0	2	6	0	0	0	9	0	8	1	2
Roach, Petie, Clinton*	.174	28	92	8	16	22	3	0	1	7	2	2	0	13	0	26	0	1
Robbs, Bill, Waterloo	.273	6	22	1	6	10	2	1	0	2	0	0	1	0	0	6	0	0
Roberts, John, Waterloo	.249	126	390	65	97	157	20	5	10	46	3	3	14	65	0	90	33	10
Robertson, Robbie, Appleton*	.285	105	340	49	97	139	16	7	4	46	0	2	3	42	3	63	7	7
Robinson, Dan, Kane County*	.242	105	363	60	88	121	23	2	2	34	1	0	1	50	3	90	5	7
Rodgers, John, Peoria	.220	37	91	16	20	23	3	0	0	5	3	0	4	25	0	24	2	1
Rodriques, Cecil, Beloit	.238	104	349	50	83	136	21	4	8	49	3	3	2	43	1	94	18	12
Roman, Vince, Quad City†	.282	81	291	52	82	108	10	2	4	29	3	1	2	28	1	75	29	15
Rosario, Mel, Waterloo†	.210	32	105	15	22	47	6	2	5	15	0	0	2	7	1	37	5	2
Ross, Jackie, Beloit†	.243	122	415	64	101	122	7	4	2	41	4	8	3	63	0	101	23	14
Rudolph, Greg, Springfield	.242	90	277	35	67	88	11	2	2	24	4	1	5	36	0	63	9	5
Rumsey, Dan, Cedar Rapids*	.178	16	45	3	8	13	2	0	1	5	0	0	0	5	0	20	1	0
Rundels, Matt, Burlington	.271	64	203	36	55	82	7	4	4	17	3	1	5	38	1	36	14	7
Saenz, Olmedo, South Bend	.360	13	50	3	18	24	4	1	0	7	0	0	0	7	0	7	1	1
Santini, Aaron, Fort Wayne	.194	46	139	17	27	35	3	1	1	7	1	0	2	17	0	31	7	1
Saugstad, Mark, Clinton	.111	5	9	0	1	1	0	0	0	0	0	0	0	0	0	4	0	0
Sbrocco, Jon, Clinton*	.268	56	179	28	48	58	6	2	0	17	5	0	4	29	0	31	8	6
Schmidt, Keith, Beloit	.085	15	47	3	4	6	2	0	0	2	0	0	1	3	0	18	0	0
Schulte, Rich, Quad City*	.229	50	188	26	43	76	8	5	5	20	3	2	1	12	0	48	6	5
Serrano, Nestor, Appleton	.085	19	47	4	4	6	0	1	0	2	0	0	1	3	0	10	0	2
Shabazz, Basil, Springfield	.297	64	239	44	71	99	12	2	4	18	2	0	2	29	2	66	29	16
Sheets, Andy, Appleton	.263	69	259	32	68	89	10	4	1	25	4	2	3	20	1	59	7	7
Sheff, Chris, Kane County	.272	129	456	79	124	171	22	5	5	50	3	5	2	58	2	100	33	10
Sheldon, Scott, Madison	.213	131	428	67	91	139	22	1	8	67	3	8	8	49	3	121	8	7
Simmons, Josh, Peoria†	.290	30	69	20	20	26	4	1	0	4	1	0	1	29	2	23	1	2
Simmons, Mark, Cedar Rapids	.192	58	203	25	39	45	6	0	0	23	7	0	2	33	0	57	8	4
Simonton, Benji, Clinton	.255	100	310	52	79	141	18	4	12	49	0	2	6	40	2	112	8	7
Sisco, Steve, Rockford	.287	124	460	62	132	168	22	4	2	57	4	5	2	42	2	65	25	10
Smith, Chris, Cedar Rapids	.260	70	246	29	64	94	11	2	5	39	1	1	3	28	2	35	1	2
Smith, Coleman, Peoria	.056	6	18	4	1	1	0	0	0	1	1	0	0	3	0	6	0	0
Smith, Craig, Beloit	.218	53	147	16	32	48	11	1	1	15	4	0	3	13	1	38	3	1
Smith, Dan, Peoria	.276	8	29	2	8	12	1	0	1	3	1	0	0	1	0	7	1	0
Snopek, Chris, South Bend	.389	22	72	20	28	53	8	1	5	18	0	2	3	15	0	13	1	1
Soto, Rafael, Peoria†	.236	114	330	39	78	85	3	2	0	25	17	3	2	18	0	43	8	6
Stasio, Chris, Clinton	.188	31	69	8	13	16	0	0	1	5	1	0	1	2	0	31	0	2
Stela, Jose, Cedar Rapids	.231	53	173	12	40	55	9	0	2	15	0	0	3	15	0	22	3	2
Stewart, Reggie, Waterloo	.212	28	33	7	7	9	2	0	0	3	0	1	4	1	0	11	2	5
Stovall, Darond, Springfield*	.257	135	460	73	118	205	19	4	20	81	2	1	0	53	2	143	18	12
Stricklin, Scott, Fort Wayne*	.065	9	31	1	2	2	0	0	0	0	0	0	0	4	0	7	0	0
Stutheit, Tim, Peoria	.119	19	42	4	5	10	2	0	1	4	2	1	2	8	0	11	1	0
Sutherland, Alex, Appleton	.240	103	325	40	78	116	20	0	6	31	2	2	1	20	2	62	5	4
Sutton, Larry, Rockford*	.269	113	361	67	97	144	24	1	7	50	0	8	8	95	5	65	3	5
Sylvestri, Tony, Kane County†	.259	106	360	40	95	114	13	3	0	31	11	7	3	36	0	37	9	9
Talanoa, Scott, Beloit	.287	87	258	55	74	161	12	0	25	66	0	4	8	71	6	86	5	3
Taylor, Gary, Springfield*	.274	100	307	42	84	108	15	3	1	37	0	4	4	54	1	89	0	1

Player, Team	Avg.	G	AB	R	H	TB	2B	3B	HR	RBI	SH	SF	HP	BB	Int. BB	SO	SB	CS
Terilli, Joe, Peoria*	.246	21	65	11	16	22	3	0	1	10	3	0	0	21	1	12	2	0
Thielen, D.J., Clinton	.231	124	446	72	103	172	18	3	15	68	1	4	6	29	0	125	21	6
Thomas, Gene, Clinton†	.203	28	59	12	12	13	1	0	0	1	2	0	1	9	0	13	10	2
Tirpack, Ken, Fort Wayne*	.294	127	473	71	139	206	34	3	9	70	0	6	6	68	4	103	1	4
Tomberlin, Justin, Fort Wayne	.258	45	151	20	39	54	10	1	1	16	1	2	5	7	0	21	0	0
Torino, Damian, Quad City	.138	26	65	2	9	13	1	0	1	6	0	0	0	5	0	33	0	0
Tosone, Joe, Burlington	.151	28	73	6	11	12	1	0	0	4	0	0	0	13	0	28	0	2
Triessl, Mike, Appleton	.185	34	81	9	15	23	5	0	1	8	3	1	2	14	0	32	0	0
Tucker, Robert, Cedar Rapids	.226	81	266	34	60	81	10	1	3	29	1	1	1	38	0	56	2	2
Valdez, Pedro, Peoria*	.316	65	234	33	74	108	11	1	7	36	5	4	0	10	4	40	2	2
Valette, Ramon, Fort Wayne	.238	112	382	46	91	129	20	0	6	38	2	4	4	23	0	89	12	7
Vaske, Terry, Peoria*	.213	21	47	10	10	17	4	0	1	7	2	0	0	11	1	13	0	0
Vazquez, Jose, Springfield	.257	37	70	13	18	19	1	0	0	6	1	0	0	18	0	18	5	4
Vidro, Jose, Burlington*	.240	76	287	39	69	94	19	0	2	34	4	2	5	28	3	54	3	2
Vinas, Julio, South Bend	.319	55	188	24	60	104	15	1	9	37	2	1	1	12	1	29	1	1
Vogel, Mike, South Bend†	.269	24	78	7	21	31	7	0	1	8	0	0	1	8	0	24	1	0
Walker, Steve, Peoria†	.249	128	466	60	116	168	27	2	7	58	8	5	7	21	4	123	15	6
Wallace, Brian, Appleton	.215	117	396	46	85	121	17	2	5	42	4	4	9	37	3	145	15	9
Walls, Eric, Rockford*	.219	15	32	8	7	8	1	0	0	1	1	0	2	4	0	9	3	2
White, Jason, Madison	.267	119	382	61	102	168	24	0	14	55	6	6	7	36	0	100	1	4
Williams, Ed, Springfield†	.236	53	182	25	43	58	6	3	1	19	0	2	2	18	2	36	2	1
Wilson, Craig, South Bend	.259	132	455	56	118	164	27	2	5	59	7	6	8	49	2	50	4	4
Wilson, Pookie, Kane County*	.249	129	469	74	117	129	18	2	0	27	10	2	9	52	0	55	34	15
Winslow, Bryant, Quad City	.238	114	404	59	96	140	19	2	7	59	0	4	23	28	1	122	1	5
Wolff, Mike, Cedar Rapids	.246	120	407	63	100	179	18	5	17	72	5	5	2	74	1	104	8	8
Wong, Kevin, Clinton	.156	30	77	10	12	18	4	1	0	5	0	1	1	9	0	14	2	0
Woods, Kenny, Clinton	.281	108	320	56	90	114	10	1	4	44	7	2	4	41	1	55	30	5
Wulf, Eric, Kane County*	.261	82	272	22	71	89	15	0	1	35	0	3	4	19	1	60	2	1
Zarate, Vince, Peoria	.260	61	123	16	32	36	4	0	0	13	4	0	1	14	0	25	3	0

The following pitchers, listed alphabetically by club, with games in parentheses, had no plate appearances, primarily through use of designated hitters:

APPLETON—Aschoff, Jerry (9); Bruce, Tim (12); Cody, Ron (26); Cope, Robin (3); Davis, Tim (16); Deal, Jamon (11); Estes, Shawn (19); Evans, Dave (5); Graham, Rich (43); Harikkala, Tim (15); Kostich, Bill (20); Kovach, Ty (3); Lisiecki, Dave (20); Nickell, Julian (24); O'Donnell, Erik (6); Rivera, Oscar (13); Sanchez, Jose (26); Urso, Salvatore (36); Witte, Larry (28); Worley, Bob (45).

BELOIT—Aronetz, Cameron (30); Blair, Don (21); Boddicker, Mike (1); Demyan, Kirk (50); Droll, Jeff (4); Duda, Steve (6); Fetty, Pat (2); Froning, Tom (4); Hampton, Mark (11); Jones, Bob (25); Kyslinger, Dan (36); Meek, Darryl (24); O'Laughlin, Chuck (2); Paul, Andy (8); Sadler, Alden (20); Schenbeck, Tommy (38); Thibault, Ryan (40); Torrez, Rafael (10); Wunsch, Kelly (12).

BURLINGTON—Arteaga, Ivan (20); Clelland, Rich (30); DaSilva, Fernando (11); Eggert, Dave (51); Falteisek, Steve (14); Hostetler, Jeff (32); Kermode, Alfred (19); Maloney, Ryan (11); Martinez, Williams (2); Pacheco, Alex (13); Paxton, Darrin (41); Perez, Carlos (12); Phelps, Tom (8); Pisciotta, Scott (24); Reyes, Alberto (53); Rushworth, Jim (24); Stull, Everett (15); Urbina, Ugueth (16).

CEDAR RAPIDS—Chavez, Tony (41); Fermin, Miguel (9); Hingle, Larry (28); Marcon, Dave (30); Mejia, Juan (13); Rinehart, Dallas (16); Schmidt, Jeff (26); Sebach, Kyle (26); Simas, Bill (35); Snyder, John (21); Valencia, Max (14); Van Dyke, Roderick (7); White, Steve (41); Williard, Brian (23).

CLINTON—Baine, Dave (3); Brewington, Jamie (26); Castillo, Mariano (40); Fultz, Aaron (26); Gambs, Chris (21); Grande, Mark (2); Heckman, Andy (11); Henrikson, Dan (12); Locklear, Jeff (28); McLain, Mike (36); Myers, Jason (1); Myers, Jeff (18); Richey, Jeff (40); Rosenbohm, Jim (23); Valdez, Carlos (35).

FORT WAYNE—Caridad, Ron (27); Correa, Jose (41); Fultz, Aaron (1); Gandarillas, Gus (52); Gavaghan, Sean (11); Hawkins, Latroy (26); Legault, Kevin (12); Linebarger, Keith (35); Miller, Shawn (8); Moten, Scott (30); Naulty, Dan (18); Ohme, Kevin (15); Sartain, Dave (5); Serafini, Dan (27); Tatar, Jason (2); Taylor, Todd (25); Watkins, Scott (15).

KANE COUNTY—Carrasco, Hector (28); Darensbourg, Vic (46); Donahue, Matt (31); Juelsgaard, Jarod (11); Leahy, Pat (25); Lynch, John (2); Mendoza, Reynol (26); Petersen, Matt (30); Pettit, Doug (52); Saunders, Tony (23); Tidwell, Jason (25); Vlcek, Jim (33); Whisenant, Matt (15); Wiley, Warren (7).

MADISON—Acre, Mark (28); Adams, Bill (5); Banks, Jim (44); Belliard, Carlos (26); Bennett, Bob (26); Bojan, Tim (43); Foster, Clifton (26); Gienger, Craig (15); Haught, Gary (17); Hollins, Stacy (26); Lemke, Steve (16); Martinez, Julio (10); Mejia, Delfino (5); Moncion, Manuel (3); Sawyer, Zachary (25); Smock, Greg (40); Urbina, Bill (10); Wasdin, John (9); Wengert, Don (13).

PEORIA—Bliss, Bill (12); Broome, John (6); Burlingame, Ben (20); Daniel, Chuck (19); Gardner, Scott (39); Gavlick, Daryle (51); Guerra, Esmili (27); Hassel, Jay (12); Hutcheson, Dave (15); Kenny, Brian (6); Kerley, Collin (31); Lee, Tony (41); Lopez, Orlando (4); Rodriguez, Cristobal (17); Sanchez, Adrian (16); Schulhofer, Adam (5); Telemaco, Amaury (23); Trinidad, Hector (22).

QUAD CITY—Bjornson, Craig (39); Evans, Jim (27); Gutierrez, Tony (11); Holt, Chris (26); Krislock, Zak (7); Loughlin, Mark (19); Murphy, Pat (42); Ponte, Ed (39); Rees, Ricky (2); Rees, Sean (12); Rose, Heath (7); Smith, Chuck (23); Walker, Jim (26); Westbrook, Destry (27).

ROCKFORD—Bovee, Mike (20); Bunch, Mel (19); Burley, Rich (9); Clinkscales, Sherard (20); Connolly, Chris (34); Dickens, John (32); Dorlarque, Aaron (28); Downs, John (5); Evans, Bart (27); Haas, Jeff (24); Myers, Rodney (12); Page, Duane (16); Peters, Doug (11); Pittsley, Jim (15); Rawitzer, Kevin (5); Rusch, Glendon (2); Sheehan, Chris (31); Weglarz, John (23).

SOUTH BEND—Bertotti, Mike (17); Call, Mike (26); Cary, Chuck (8); Culberson, Don (9); Dixon, Jim (10); Fritz, Greg (11); Gay, Chris (12); Jenkins, Jon (16); Johnston, Sean (15); Keating, Dave (6); Lindemann, Wayne (12); McCaskill, Kirk (1); McDermott, Jim (6); Moore, Tim (26); Pierson, Jason (26); Sirotka, Mike (7); Tagle, Henry (11); Watkins, Jason (37); Winiarski, Ron (34); Woodfin, Chris (11); Woods, Brian (2); Worrell, Steve (36).

SPRINGFIELD—Bailey, Roy (9); Blake, Todd (24); Bullinger, Kirk (50); Carrillo, Joe (15); DeGrasse, Tim (49); Frascatore, John (27); Hammond, Allan (1); Johnson, Steve (5); Jolley, Mike (5); Knowles, Greg (54); Lucchetti, Larry (20); Mathews, Tim (25); Miller, Eric (24); Oehrlein, Dave (13); Ruiz, Diego (1); Slininger, Dennis (13); Smith, Chad (13); Smith, Mike (14); Spiller, Derron (31).

WATERLOO—Anthony, Greg (7); Arroyo, Luis (17); Baker, Jared (18); Barnes, Jon (10); Burns, Jerry (19); D'Amato, Brian (21); Doyle, Tom (4); Dunckel, Keith (30); Erdos, Todd (11); Hanson, Craig (28); Hermanson, Mike (18); Hollinger, Adrian (44); Kindler, Tom (20); Loiselle, Rich (10); Long, Joey (33); Sandt, Tom (17); Schmitt, Todd (51); Waldron, Joe (16).

GRAND SLAMS—Chris Smith, Talanoa, 2 each; Arias, Atencio, Biasucci, Byrd, Cora, Cromer, Ealy, Gubanich, Hughes, Hust, Knauss, Lawson, Lopez, Thielen, Vidro, Walker, Wolff, 1 each.

AWARDED FIRST BASE ON CATCHER'S INTERFERENCE—Johns 4 (Greene, Horn, Pages, Tucker); DeLeon 3 (Pages 2, Tucker); Triessl 3 (Brooks, Rodgers, Stela); Griffey 2 (Hostetler 2); Sheff 2 (Machado, F. Morales); Vidro 2 (Gubanich, C. Johnson); Alcantara (J. Morales); Ballara (Pages); Clapinski (Horn); Cromer (Machado); Cunningham (Tucker); Gipson (Pages); Gulan (F. Morales); Hickey (Casanova); Hurst (Jensen); Markiewicz (Vinas); Mayes (Rodgers); Medina (Cavanagh); Penix (Gonzalez); Pridy (Cavanagh); Roberts (Pages); Roman (Killeen); Santini (Sutherland); Sheldon (Cavanagh); Tirpack (Vinas); Woods (Gubanich).

PITCHING

TEAM

Team	ERA	G	CG	ShO	Sv.	IP	H	R	ER	HR	HB	BB	Int. BB	SO	WP	Bk.
Madison	3.39	135	7	7	37	1146.1	985	521	432	74	35	494	47	965	65	22
Fort Wayne	3.49	135	9	16	41	1178.1	1089	585	457	53	49	511	11	1136	86	32
Springfield	3.53	136	10	8	41	1137.0	1058	548	446	73	36	336	7	995	59	14
Kane County	3.56	137	9	7	45	1184.2	1079	560	468	72	85	491	34	1074	80	31
Burlington	3.59	135	8	6	26	1138.0	1029	595	454	81	62	534	19	1107	95	20
Rockford	3.61	132	13	11	38	1127.0	1063	537	452	43	51	466	2	1001	98	17
Clinton	3.61	134	6	16	52	1126.2	989	559	452	87	60	546	15	1021	80	15
South Bend	3.79	136	18	14	40	1177.2	1126	583	496	83	60	395	13	870	74	13
Peoria	4.08	138	15	16	25	1174.1	1148	644	532	75	79	429	15	986	84	27
Quad City	4.10	130	16	11	23	1067.1	1088	630	495	93	55	441	12	967	66	24
Appleton	4.27	135	8	7	35	1145.2	1151	669	544	84	68	495	14	967	123	39
Cedar Rapids	4.48	134	11	3	26	1133.2	1214	732	564	100	69	479	13	947	76	23
Beloit	4.49	134	14	4	32	1139.0	1208	712	568	75	83	514	22	958	85	24
Waterloo	4.75	133	6	5	33	1066.1	1073	685	563	101	55	595	31	836	110	26

INDIVIDUAL

(Leading qualifiers for earned-run average leadership — 112 or more innings)

*Throws lefthanded.

Pitcher, Team	W	L	Pct.	ERA	G	GS	CG	GF	ShO	Sv.	IP	H	R	ER	HR	HB	BB	Int. BB	SO	WP
Hawkins, Fort Wayne	15	5	.750	2.06	26	23	4	1	3	0	157.1	110	53	36	5	4	41	0	179	9
Holt, Quad City	11	10	.524	2.27	26	26	10	0	3	0	186.1	162	70	47	10	3	54	1	176	9
Trinidad, Peoria	7	6	.538	2.47	22	22	4	0	0	0	153.0	142	56	42	6	4	29	1	118	7
Mathews, Springfield	12	9	.571	2.71	25	25	5	0	2	0	159.1	121	59	48	7	6	29	0	144	1
Sheehan, Rockford	9	5	.643	2.83	31	12	2	15	0	6	117.2	97	40	37	8	3	22	1	101	10
Arteaga, Burlington	6	5	.545	2.83	20	20	2	0	0	0	127.0	114	57	40	7	7	47	1	111	10
Mendoza, Kane County	12	5	.706	2.86	26	23	3	3	0	2	163.2	129	59	52	5	9	45	3	153	14
Sebach, Cedar Rapids	6	9	.400	3.04	26	26	4	0	0	0	154.0	138	73	52	7	14	70	1	138	8
Nickell, Appleton	7	7	.500	3.06	24	23	2	1	0	0	150.0	135	54	51	8	7	41	0	151	7
Foster, Madison	10	8	.556	3.14	26	26	1	0	0	0	140.1	106	62	49	6	4	92	3	146	8

Departmental leaders: G—Knowles, 54; W—Call, Hawkins, 15; L—Hanson, Schmidt, 14; Pct.—U. Urbina, .909; GS—Carrasco, 28; CG—Holt, 10; GF—Gandarillas, 48; ShO—Hawkins, Holt, 3; Sv.—Bullinger, 33; IP—Holt, 186.1; H—Call, 187; R—Schmidt, 105; ER—Hollins, 86; HR—Hollins, Moore, 21; HB—Leahy, 23; BB—Foster, 92; IBB—Banks, Lee, 8; SO—Hawkins, 179; WP—J. Sanchez, 27.

(All pitchers — listed alphabetically)

Pitcher, Team	W	L	Pct.	ERA	G	GS	CG	GF	ShO	Sv.	IP	H	R	ER	HR	HB	BB	Int. BB	SO	WP
Acre, Madison	0	0	.000	0.29	28	0	0	27	0	20	31.1	9	1	1	1	0	13	0	41	4
Adams, Madison	0	2	.000	3.38	5	5	0	0	0	0	18.2	21	10	7	2	0	8	0	22	1
Anthony, Waterloo	1	2	.333	6.66	7	7	0	0	0	0	25.2	29	21	19	8	0	10	1	11	2
Aracena, Madison	1	0	1.000	0.00	5	0	0	5	0	1	4.1	1	0	0	0	0	3	1	3	0
Aronetz, Beloit*	1	1	.500	3.29	30	0	0	12	0	5	38.1	39	19	14	2	2	16	1	38	0
Arroyo, Waterloo*	5	7	.417	4.52	17	16	1	1	0	0	95.2	99	59	48	11	6	46	1	59	5
Arteaga, Burlington	6	5	.545	2.83	20	20	2	0	0	0	127.0	114	57	40	7	7	47	1	111	10
Aschoff, Appleton*	3	4	.429	6.10	9	6	0	0	0	0	38.1	45	28	26	3	1	29	0	26	4
Baber, Waterloo	0	0	.000	0.00	1	0	0	1	0	0	1.0	1	2	0	0	0	3	0	1	0
Bailey, Springfield	1	2	.333	5.25	9	0	0	4	0	1	12.0	19	7	7	1	2	7	1	7	1
Baine, Clinton*	0	1	.000	10.97	3	3	0	0	0	0	10.2	16	13	13	1	1	9	0	6	0
Baker, Waterloo	6	7	.462	5.64	15	15	2	0	0	0	81.1	82	60	51	13	3	54	2	62	6
Banks, Madison	4	1	.800	2.62	44	0	0	23	0	4	55.0	39	24	16	1	1	46	8	66	6
Barnes, Waterloo	5	3	.625	2.86	10	10	0	0	0	0	56.2	51	27	18	1	1	23	0	46	5
Belliard, Madison*	5	3	.625	3.63	26	11	0	1	0	0	86.2	81	44	35	3	2	54	2	64	8
Bennett, Madison	7	8	.467	3.28	26	17	0	3	0	1	107.0	103	45	39	7	1	23	3	102	4
Bertotti, South Bend*	5	7	.417	3.49	17	16	2	0	2	0	111.0	93	51	43	5	6	44	2	108	7
Bjornson, Quad City*	0	6	.000	5.08	39	0	0	17	0	3	51.1	63	34	29	4	2	18	1	37	5
Blair, Beloit	9	6	.600	3.40	21	21	6	0	1	0	135.0	130	60	51	10	2	11	0	126	3
Blake, Springfield*	9	6	.600	4.31	24	18	1	2	0	0	117.0	125	61	56	11	3	25	0	98	7
Bliss, Peoria	3	4	.429	5.56	12	12	0	0	0	0	66.1	67	49	41	8	5	41	0	38	8
Boddicker, Beloit	0	0	.000	2.25	1	1	0	0	0	0	4.0	3	1	1	0	0	1	0	4	1
Bojan, Madison	8	5	.615	3.70	43	5	0	14	0	2	92.1	78	45	38	5	5	43	3	78	5
Bovee, Rockford	5	9	.357	4.21	20	20	2	0	0	0	109.0	118	58	51	1	6	30	0	111	15
Brewington, Clinton	13	5	.722	4.78	26	25	1	0	0	0	133.2	126	78	71	20	5	61	1	111	19
Broome, Peoria	0	1	.000	7.88	6	0	0	4	0	0	8.0	12	8	7	1	1	4	0	3	0
Bruce, Appleton	2	1	.667	1.29	12	0	0	9	0	3	21.0	12	8	3	1	1	5	0	25	2
Bullinger, Springfield	1	3	.250	2.28	50	0	0	46	0	33	51.1	26	19	13	5	2	21	1	72	6
Bunch, Rockford	6	4	.600	2.12	19	11	1	8	0	4	85.0	79	24	20	4	2	18	0	71	6
Burley, Rockford*	4	2	.667	5.26	9	6	0	1	0	0	37.2	43	26	22	3	1	26	0	15	3
Burlingame, Peoria	9	7	.563	3.56	20	20	4	0	1	0	126.1	122	59	50	9	15	32	0	102	9
Burns, Waterloo	5	4	.556	5.09	19	7	0	3	0	1	63.2	68	44	36	8	3	33	1	37	6
Cacini, Quad City	0	0	.000	0.00	1	0	0	1	0	0	0.1	0	0	0	0	0	0	0	0	0
Call, South Bend	15	7	.682	3.78	26	26	4	0	0	0	176.1	187	87	74	14	5	31	1	109	2
Caridad, Fort Wayne	6	8	.429	3.51	27	27	0	0	0	0	143.2	138	68	56	7	11	91	2	124	20
Carrasco, Kane County	6	12	.333	4.11	28	28	0	0	0	0	149.0	153	90	68	11	11	76	6	127	13
Carrillo, Springfield*	0	1	.000	5.04	15	1	0	1	0	1	30.1	34	19	17	4	0	14	0	21	5
Cary, South Bend	1	1	.500	2.00	8	3	0	4	0	1	18.0	13	4	4	0	2	1	0	28	4
Castillo, Clinton	4	2	.667	3.39	40	0	0	19	0	6	69.0	64	31	26	3	1	19	1	59	1
Castro, Cedar Rapids	2	1	.667	7.27	13	2	0	7	0	0	26.0	25	22	21	1	2	23	0	22	3
Cavanagh, Clinton	0	0	.000	18.00	1	0	0	0	0	0	2.0	4	4	4	2	0	3	0	0	1
Chavez, Cedar Rapids	4	5	.444	1.52	41	0	0	35	0	16	59.1	44	17	10	1	2	24	2	87	3
Claus, Fort Wayne	0	0	.000	0.00	1	0	0	0	0	0	1.2	2	0	0	0	0	1	0	0	0
Clelland, Burlington	5	7	.417	3.71	30	12	0	5	0	1	97.0	94	57	40	9	4	61	0	86	15
Clinkscales, Rockford	5	3	.625	6.75	20	13	0	4	0	0	61.1	57	58	46	0	7	83	0	46	13

Pitcher, Team	W	L	Pct.	ERA	G	GS	CG	GF	ShO	Sv.	IP	H	R	ER	HR	HB	BB	Int. BB	SO	WP
Cody, Appleton	5	7	.417	5.56	26	10	0	7	0	0	90.2	98	67	56	18	3	26	0	52	7
Connell, Cedar Rapids	0	0	.000	0.00	1	0	0	1	0	0	1.0	1	0	0	0	0	1	0	0	0
Connolly, Rockford*	6	3	.667	3.98	34	0	0	16	0	3	74.2	83	37	33	1	2	31	1	50	5
Cope, Appleton	0	0	.000	6.19	3	2	0	0	0	0	16.0	17	12	11	0	2	11	0	5	3
Correa, Fort Wayne	4	5	.444	2.63	41	0	0	18	0	9	96.0	81	33	28	7	1	36	1	107	5
Crowe, Clinton	4	3	.571	3.13	33	1	0	18	0	8	60.1	56	34	21	2	3	17	2	52	8
Culberson, South Bend	0	1	.000	9.60	9	1	0	5	0	8	15.0	24	18	16	1	1	14	1	7	6
D'Amato, Waterloo	1	0	1.000	5.11	21	0	0	11	0	0	24.2	31	19	14	4	1	7	0	17	2
Daniel, Peoria	1	1	.500	1.86	19	0	0	18	0	10	19.1	14	4	4	0	0	5	1	19	1
Darensbourg, Kane County*	9	1	.900	2.14	46	0	0	31	0	16	71.1	58	17	17	3	4	28	3	89	2
Davis, Appleton*	10	2	.833	1.85	16	10	3	4	2	0	77.2	54	20	16	5	2	33	0	89	4
Dawson, Quad City	0	5	.000	5.44	31	0	0	17	0	0	41.1	48	30	25	6	2	31	1	29	4
DaSilva, Burlington	0	4	.000	4.75	11	10	0	0	0	0	60.2	66	38	32	10	3	18	2	50	1
Deal, Appleton	0	1	.000	12.32	11	1	0	3	0	0	19.0	31	38	26	3	0	25	0	15	6
Delaney, Rockford	0	0	.000	0.00	1	0	0	1	0	0	1.0	0	0	0	0	0	1	0	0	0
Demyan, Beloit	8	7	.533	3.38	50	0	0	28	0	4	90.2	94	49	34	3	6	44	4	70	11
DeGrasse, Springfield	4	3	.571	2.20	49	0	0	17	0	1	77.2	56	28	19	2	2	32	1	90	9
DeLeon, Waterloo	0	0	.000	1.80	3	0	0	3	0	0	5.0	4	1	1	0	0	4	0	4	2
Dickens, Rockford*	2	0	1.000	3.94	32	0	0	13	0	2	61.2	57	28	27	3	3	34	0	60	5
Dixon, South Bend	0	0	.000	4.85	10	0	0	5	0	0	13.0	17	8	7	1	1	5	0	10	2
Donahue, Kane County	3	2	.600	4.70	31	0	0	14	0	2	67.0	66	39	35	7	6	31	3	70	2
Dorlarque, Rockford	2	3	.400	1.46	28	0	0	26	0	16	49.1	37	12	8	3	3	12	0	51	4
Downs, Rockford	1	3	.250	5.46	5	5	0	0	0	0	28.0	36	22	17	3	3	11	0	21	2
Doyle, Waterloo	0	0	.000	6.75	4	0	0	1	0	0	6.2	7	6	5	2	2	6	0	7	2
Droll, Beloit	0	3	.000	7.64	4	4	0	0	0	0	17.2	32	20	15	2	2	8	0	5	2
Duda, Beloit	2	1	.667	4.46	6	6	0	0	0	0	36.1	45	18	18	2	2	11	1	30	2
Dumas, Beloit	0	0	.000	18.00	1	0	0	1	0	0	1.0	1	6	2	1	1	3	0	1	1
Dunckel, Waterloo	1	2	.333	6.96	30	3	0	10	0	0	53.0	74	56	41	8	2	41	3	32	15
Duran, Waterloo	1	0	1.000	1.42	5	0	0	5	0	0	6.1	2	1	1	0	0	4	0	7	0
Eggert, Burlington*	5	4	.556	2.83	51	0	0	31	0	8	60.1	59	22	19	3	1	24	4	83	1
Eldridge, Madison	0	0	.000	12.00	3	0	0	3	0	0	3.0	6	4	4	0	0	1	0	0	0
Ellsworth, Springfield	0	0	.000	0.00	1	0	0	1	0	0	1.0	0	0	0	0	0	0	0	0	0
Erdos, Waterloo	1	9	.100	8.31	11	11	0	0	0	0	47.2	64	51	44	9	4	31	2	27	8
Estes, Appleton*	5	9	.357	7.24	19	18	0	0	0	0	83.1	108	85	67	3	7	52	1	65	19
Evans, Rockford	10	4	.714	4.36	27	16	0	4	0	0	99.0	95	52	48	5	4	60	0	120	10
Evans, Appleton	2	1	.667	2.28	5	5	0	0	0	0	27.2	21	9	7	0	2	15	0	23	5
Evans, Quad City	7	11	.389	4.17	26	26	1	0	0	0	159.2	165	96	74	12	6	65	1	126	4
Falteisek, Burlington	3	5	.375	5.90	14	14	0	0	0	0	76.1	86	59	50	4	2	35	0	63	4
Fermin, Cedar Rapids	2	1	.667	3.33	9	2	0	3	0	0	24.1	23	10	9	1	1	4	1	27	0
Fetty, Beloit	0	0	.000	9.00	2	0	0	2	0	0	3.0	5	4	3	0	1	1	0	1	0
Foster, Madison	10	8	.556	3.14	26	26	1	0	0	0	140.1	106	62	49	6	4	92	3	146	8
Frascatore, Springfield	7	12	.368	3.78	27	26	2	1	1	0	157.1	157	84	66	6	3	33	0	126	2
Frazier, Kane County*	5	0	1.000	5.93	39	0	0	11	0	1	30.1	35	24	20	3	1	26	4	23	2
Fritz, South Bend*	2	7	.222	5.18	11	10	3	1	0	0	66.0	88	44	38	3	3	35	1	20	7
Froning, Beloit*	0	1	.000	10.29	4	1	0	1	0	0	7.0	15	12	8	0	1	7	0	4	0
Fultz, 26 Clin. - 1 F.W.*	14	8	.636	3.55	27	26	2	0	1	0	152.0	142	67	60	8	11	64	2	147	10
Gambs, Clinton	9	5	.643	4.02	21	21	0	0	0	0	112.0	100	56	50	12	2	76	2	82	8
Gandarillas, Fort Wayne	5	5	.500	3.26	52	0	0	48	0	25	66.1	66	37	24	8	1	22	2	59	5
Gardner, Peoria	5	6	.455	5.40	39	9	1	12	0	3	88.1	81	60	53	7	7	36	1	99	7
Gavaghan, Fort Wayne	3	1	.750	1.23	11	0	0	5	0	1	22.0	14	5	3	0	0	7	0	25	2
Gavlick, Peoria*	6	7	.462	1.30	51	0	0	36	0	9	55.1	43	17	8	1	0	18	3	49	2
Gay, South Bend*	0	0	.000	5.16	12	0	0	2	0	1	22.2	25	16	13	2	0	9	0	14	1
Gienger, Madison	0	1	.000	2.54	15	0	0	6	0	0	28.1	28	10	8	3	2	10	2	20	2
Graham, Appleton	2	3	.400	4.46	43	0	0	14	0	2	76.2	75	48	38	7	9	31	2	59	9
Grande, Clinton	0	0	.000	7.71	2	0	0	1	0	0	2.1	3	4	2	0	1	3	0	1	1
Guerra, Peoria*	1	4	.200	5.79	27	0	0	7	0	0	37.1	37	28	24	1	2	14	0	25	3
Gutierrez, Quad City*	1	0	1.000	4.35	11	1	0	1	0	0	20.2	24	18	10	3	1	14	0	17	2
Haas, Rockford*	4	2	.667	3.90	24	4	1	8	1	2	67.0	67	37	29	4	4	21	0	37	5
Hammond, Springfield	0	0	.000	27.00	1	0	0	1	0	0	1.0	2	3	3	0	1	2	0	1	1
Hampton, Beloit	1	4	.200	6.43	11	7	0	0	0	0	42.0	53	36	30	7	2	24	0	19	2
Hanson, Waterloo	7	14	.333	4.90	28	16	1	3	0	0	112.0	120	78	61	10	6	62	2	90	9
Harikkala, Appleton	3	3	.500	6.52	15	4	0	5	0	0	38.2	50	30	28	3	2	12	2	33	4
Hassel, Peoria	3	5	.375	5.82	12	11	0	0	0	0	55.2	75	41	36	6	1	20	0	37	4
Haught, Madison	7	1	.875	2.58	17	12	2	1	0	0	83.2	62	27	24	8	2	29	2	75	1
Hawkins, Fort Wayne	15	5	.750	2.06	26	23	4	1	3	0	157.1	110	53	36	4	4	41	0	179	9
Heckman, Clinton*	2	1	.667	1.74	11	1	0	5	0	0	20.2	18	6	4	2	2	4	0	24	0
Henrikson, Clinton*	3	2	.600	2.65	12	4	0	4	0	0	34.0	27	14	10	4	2	17	1	27	1
Hermanson, Waterloo	3	6	.333	4.74	18	18	0	0	0	0	81.2	79	51	43	9	4	52	2	57	6
Hingle, Cedar Rapids*	9	13	.409	4.91	28	24	1	3	0	1	146.2	166	103	80	15	4	64	0	115	21
Hmielewski, Burlington*	0	0	.000	3.86	5	0	0	5	0	0	4.2	7	8	2	0	3	3	0	5	0
Hollinger, Waterloo	8	3	.727	2.54	44	0	0	18	0	5	60.1	44	23	17	3	3	40	4	67	4
Hollins, Madison	10	11	.476	5.14	26	26	2	0	1	0	150.2	145	100	86	21	8	52	6	105	4
Holt, Quad City	11	10	.524	2.27	26	26	10	0	3	0	186.1	162	70	47	10	3	54	1	176	9
Hostetler, Burlington*	1	6	.143	6.56	32	0	0	8	0	1	59.0	59	49	43	5	4	51	4	56	6
Hust, Madison	0	0	.000	0.00	1	0	0	0	0	0	0.0	0	0	0	0	1	0	0	0	0
Hutcheson, Peoria	4	3	.571	2.33	15	12	1	1	1	0	89.0	71	26	23	2	5	29	0	82	3
Jenkins, South Bend	2	1	.667	1.93	16	0	0	6	0	1	23.1	10	9	5	0	1	26	0	31	10
Johnson, Springfield	1	3	.250	5.91	5	5	0	0	0	0	21.1	26	17	14	1	1	7	0	16	0
Johnston, South Bend*	8	3	.727	2.20	15	15	2	0	2	0	98.0	83	30	24	3	4	28	0	59	4
Jolley, Springfield	2	1	.667	3.52	5	5	0	0	0	0	30.2	27	13	12	4	1	9	0	26	0
Jones, Beloit*	10	10	.500	4.11	25	25	4	0	0	0	144.2	159	82	66	8	9	65	1	115	5
Juelsgaard, Kane County	3	0	1.000	3.81	11	2	1	3	0	0	26.0	21	11	11	0	1	7	0	18	2
Keating, South Bend*	1	0	1.000	3.12	6	0	0	2	0	1	8.2	5	3	3	0	0	2	0	6	0
Kenny, Peoria	0	0	.000	3.68	5	0	0	3	0	0	7.1	3	3	3	0	1	1	0	9	0
Kerley, Peoria	6	9	.400	4.41	31	17	1	4	0	0	134.2	148	75	66	11	6	44	0	129	9
Kermode, Burlington	0	1	.000	3.67	19	0	0	10	0	3	27.0	29	11	11	2	1	9	1	32	2
Kindler, Waterloo	0	7	.000	6.75	20	11	0	3	0	0	69.1	80	64	52	2	6	48	0	46	4
Knowles, Springfield	11	4	.733	2.58	54	0	0	27	0	3	73.1	62	25	21	2	1	22	3	59	3
Kostich, Appleton*	0	2	.000	0.91	20	0	0	11	0	3	29.2	28	7	3	0	1	8	1	33	1
Kovach, Appleton	1	0	1.000	7.27	3	1	0	0	0	0	8.2	10	7	7	1	0	5	0	5	0
Krislock, Quad City	2	0	1.000	7.94	7	0	0	3	0	0	11.1	15	14	10	4	3	8	0	17	4
Kyslinger, Beloit	4	5	.444	3.60	35	0	0	25	0	15	40.0	24	19	16	1	4	21	2	52	1
Lawson, Appleton*	0	0	.000	0.00	1	0	0	1	0	0	0.2	2	0	0	0	4	2	1	0	1
Leahy, Kane County	8	11	.421	3.22	25	25	2	0	0	0	139.2	124	68	50	6	23	43	2	106	12

Pitcher, Team	W	L	Pct.	ERA	G	GS	CG	GF	ShO	Sv.	IP	H	R	ER	HR	HB	BB	Int. BB	SO	WP
Lee, Peoria	1	4	.200	5.19	41	3	0	11	0	1	76.1	72	56	44	7	7	46	8	53	7
Legault, Fort Wayne	1	1	.500	3.38	12	0	0	3	0	2	26.2	28	13	10	1	2	12	1	28	4
Lemke, Madison	7	0	1.000	3.50	16	0	0	9	0	0	36.0	41	17	14	1	4	6	1	22	1
Lesher, Madison*	0	0	.000	6.00	2	0	0	2	0	0	3.0	3	2	2	0	0	3	0	2	0
Lindemann, South Bend*	3	2	.600	4.26	12	11	1	0	0	0	69.2	76	37	33	4	4	21	0	48	1
Linebarger, Fort Wayne	5	7	.417	4.25	35	11	1	12	1	0	97.1	113	60	46	3	5	43	2	76	6
Lisiecki, Appleton	2	3	.400	3.22	20	0	0	6	0	1	36.1	22	15	13	1	1	20	1	58	1
Llanos, Appleton	0	0	.000	20.25	2	0	0	2	0	0	4.0	7	9	9	2	1	5	0	2	0
Locklear, Clinton*	7	2	.778	3.07	28	10	0	8	0	0	108.1	103	51	37	9	2	44	0	90	5
Loiselle, Waterloo	1	5	.167	3.94	10	10	1	0	1	0	59.1	55	28	26	3	4	29	1	47	6
Long, Waterloo*	4	3	.571	4.86	33	7	0	7	0	0	96.1	96	56	52	7	3	36	2	90	9
Lopez, Peoria*	1	1	.500	5.11	4	4	1	0	1	0	24.2	22	16	14	3	2	7	0	16	0
Loughlin, Quad City*	4	6	.400	3.57	19	12	1	1	0	0	70.2	66	37	28	6	8	26	0	60	4
Lucchetti, Springfield	10	5	.667	3.16	20	20	1	0	0	0	111.0	98	50	39	6	4	51	1	88	7
Lynch, Kane County	1	0	1.000	3.00	2	0	0	0	0	0	9.0	4	4	3	1	0	12	0	3	0
Maloney, Burlington*	0	1	.000	3.00	11	0	0	3	0	0	15.0	16	11	5	0	0	6	0	8	2
Marcon, Cedar Rapids*	10	5	.667	2.96	30	5	1	10	0	1	82.0	87	34	27	4	4	17	1	60	2
Martinez, Madison	1	0	1.000	4.58	10	1	0	3	0	1	19.2	18	11	10	1	0	15	0	13	1
Martinez, Burlington	0	0	.000	0.00	2	0	0	1	0	0	2.2	3	1	0	0	0	1	0	1	0
Mathews, Springfield	12	9	.571	2.71	25	25	5	0	2	0	159.1	121	59	48	7	6	29	0	144	1
McCaskill, South Bend	1	0	1.000	1.50	1	1	0	0	0	0	6.0	3	2	1	0	0	3	0	5	0
McDermott, South Bend	1	0	1.000	5.56	6	0	0	4	0	1	11.1	11	7	7	3	0	1	0	5	0
McLain, Clinton	4	3	.571	2.93	36	1	0	20	0	7	73.2	66	36	24	5	9	23	4	78	1
Meek, Beloit	5	10	.333	5.19	24	17	1	1	0	0	109.1	108	81	63	7	17	52	3	64	11
Mejia, Madison	2	1	.667	2.79	5	0	0	4	0	1	9.2	9	4	3	0	0	2	2	8	1
Mejia, Cedar Rapids*	0	2	.000	4.76	13	1	0	6	0	0	28.1	38	17	15	1	1	13	2	30	1
Mendoza, Kane County	12	5	.706	2.86	26	23	3	3	0	2	163.2	129	59	52	5	9	45	3	153	14
Miller, Springfield	2	1	.667	0.91	24	0	0	12	0	2	29.2	22	4	3	1	1	9	0	32	2
Miller, Fort Wayne	0	0	.000	5.81	8	2	0	2	0	0	26.1	32	28	17	2	2	14	1	18	2
Moncion, Madison	0	0	.000	0.00	3	0	0	1	0	0	6.0	1	0	0	0	0	2	1	8	0
Moore, South Bend	11	9	.550	4.52	26	26	4	0	0	0	165.1	156	89	83	21	12	52	0	108	8
Morones, Peoria	0	2	.000	2.45	13	0	0	8	0	0	18.1	12	8	5	0	3	7	1	21	1
Moten, Fort Wayne	7	11	.389	5.05	30	22	0	4	0	1	140.2	152	99	79	8	11	63	2	141	7
Murphy, Quad City	4	5	.444	4.81	42	0	0	17	0	1	63.2	59	38	34	2	7	32	2	52	6
Ja. Myers, Clinton*	0	0	.000	0.00	1	0	0	0	0	0	3.0	0	0	0	0	0	2	0	5	0
Je. Myers, Clinton*	8	6	.571	2.71	18	18	2	0	1	0	99.2	83	41	30	3	5	57	0	91	8
Myers, Rockford	7	3	.700	1.79	12	12	5	0	2	0	85.1	65	22	17	3	1	18	0	65	3
Naulty, Fort Wayne	6	8	.429	3.26	18	18	3	0	2	0	116.0	101	45	42	5	2	48	0	96	7
Nickell, Appleton	7	7	.500	3.06	24	23	2	1	0	0	150.0	135	54	51	8	7	41	0	151	7
O'Donnell, Appleton	0	1	.000	4.00	6	2	0	1	0	0	18.0	18	11	8	2	1	4	0	11	1
O'Laughlin, Beloit*	0	0	.000	0.00	2	0	0	1	0	0	3.1	4	1	0	1	0	1	0	1	1
Oehrlein, Springfield*	3	4	.429	4.92	13	13	0	0	0	0	60.1	70	38	33	6	0	21	0	52	1
Ohme, Fort Wayne*	3	2	.600	2.53	15	4	0	6	0	0	46.1	38	19	13	1	1	15	1	45	5
Pacheco, Burlington	3	5	.375	4.19	13	7	0	2	0	1	43.0	47	31	20	3	3	12	0	24	3
Page, Rockford	2	0	1.000	5.87	16	0	0	9	0	2	23.0	27	18	15	0	2	13	0	16	6
Paul, Beloit	1	3	.250	2.96	8	8	1	0	0	0	54.2	53	22	18	1	1	30	0	52	5
Paxton, Beloit*	6	1	.857	2.88	41	3	0	8	0	1	75.0	57	28	24	5	8	34	1	110	4
Perez, Burlington*	1	0	1.000	3.24	12	1	0	5	0	0	16.2	13	6	6	0	0	9	0	21	0
Peters, Rockford	2	2	.500	3.11	11	7	0	1	0	0	46.1	46	25	16	0	2	13	0	34	2
Petersen, Kane County	9	11	.450	4.89	30	22	1	3	1	3	141.2	139	85	77	15	10	46	2	118	9
Pettit, Kane County	5	10	.333	2.45	52	0	0	38	0	17	77.0	67	26	21	7	2	16	5	63	1
Phelps, Burlington*	2	4	.333	3.73	8	8	0	0	0	0	41.0	36	18	17	4	1	13	0	33	2
Pierson, South Bend*	13	9	.591	4.70	26	25	2	0	0	0	147.1	160	92	77	16	5	43	1	107	8
Pike, Beloit	2	3	.400	4.84	35	0	0	12	0	3	57.2	57	42	31	4	9	41	4	72	5
Pisciotta, Burlington	9	12	.429	4.06	24	24	1	0	0	0	135.1	129	85	61	7	8	79	1	112	16
Pittsley, Rockford	5	5	.500	4.26	15	15	2	0	1	0	80.1	76	43	38	3	5	32	0	87	5
Ponte, Quad City	3	6	.333	4.01	39	0	0	34	0	17	51.2	48	27	23	5	5	18	4	67	1
Rawitzer, Rockford*	3	0	1.000	1.50	5	5	0	0	0	0	30.0	23	7	5	0	1	11	0	34	0
R. Rees, Quad City	7	3	.700	3.56	17	13	0	1	0	0	81.0	82	44	32	4	2	27	0	62	2
S. Rees, Quad City*	3	3	.500	5.19	12	9	0	0	0	0	52.0	60	34	30	4	1	17	0	45	4
Reyes, Burlington	7	6	.538	2.68	53	0	0	41	0	11	74.0	52	33	22	7	6	26	3	80	5
Richey, Clinton	2	1	.667	1.03	40	0	0	39	0	28	52.1	19	7	6	2	1	17	0	75	2
Rinehart, Cedar Rapids	1	2	.333	5.29	16	4	0	5	0	0	47.2	59	37	28	4	2	17	0	40	6
Rivera, Appleton	2	2	.500	3.53	13	13	0	0	0	0	71.1	70	33	28	5	5	22	0	33	5
Rodriguez, Peoria	3	2	.600	2.67	17	1	0	10	0	2	30.1	26	13	9	1	5	14	0	28	3
Rose, Quad City*	1	2	.333	5.30	7	2	1	2	0	0	18.2	18	12	11	0	3	8	0	14	1
Rosenbohm, Clinton	6	8	.429	4.89	23	23	1	0	1	0	106.2	98	74	58	8	13	86	1	91	7
Ruiz, Springfield*	1	0	1.000	0.00	1	1	0	0	0	0	6.1	2	1	0	0	1	1	0	2	0
Rusch, Rockford*	0	1	.000	3.38	2	2	0	0	0	0	8.0	10	6	3	0	0	7	0	8	1
Rushworth, Burlington	2	0	1.000	0.83	24	0	0	8	0	0	32.2	16	7	3	0	2	11	1	40	5
Sadler, Beloit	6	6	.500	4.11	20	20	1	0	0	0	116.0	126	67	53	9	9	47	1	87	10
Sanchez, Peoria	1	2	.333	12.13	16	0	0	7	0	0	23.0	44	35	31	2	3	16	0	12	5
Sanchez, Appleton*	8	11	.421	4.56	26	25	2	1	1	0	130.1	132	80	66	11	11	79	1	133	27
Sandt, Waterloo	1	0	1.000	3.68	17	1	0	9	0	1	29.1	27	12	12	2	0	14	3	23	3
Sartain, Fort Wayne*	1	1	.500	2.57	5	0	0	3	0	1	7.0	3	2	2	1	0	2	0	7	0
Saunders, Kane County*	6	1	.857	2.27	23	10	2	1	0	1	83.1	72	23	21	3	2	32	3	87	2
Sawyer, Madison	3	6	.333	3.83	25	2	0	6	0	0	49.1	50	28	21	4	3	20	6	25	5
Schenbeck, Beloit	6	4	.600	6.13	38	10	1	21	0	3	94.0	117	72	64	7	7	39	2	78	8
Schmidt, Cedar Rapids	3	14	.176	4.90	26	25	3	0	0	0	152.1	166	105	83	16	16	58	3	107	11
Schmitt, Waterloo	1	4	.200	1.99	51	0	0	47	0	25	58.2	41	15	13	0	6	33	5	76	5
Schulhofer, Peoria	0	4	.000	10.34	4	4	0	0	0	0	15.2	19	18	18	1	2	12	0	12	7
Sebach, Cedar Rapids	6	9	.400	3.04	26	26	4	0	0	0	140.2	138	73	52	7	14	70	1	138	4
Serafini, Fort Wayne*	10	8	.556	3.65	27	27	1	0	1	0	140.2	117	72	57	5	6	83	0	147	12
Sheehan, Rockford	9	5	.643	2.83	31	12	2	15	0	6	117.2	97	40	37	8	3	22	1	101	10
Simas, Cedar Rapids	5	8	.385	4.95	35	6	0	19	0	6	80.0	93	60	44	8	3	36	1	62	4
Sirotka, South Bend*	0	1	.000	6.10	7	1	0	3	0	0	10.1	12	8	7	3	0	6	0	12	0
Slininger, Springfield	8	1	.889	2.96	13	13	1	0	0	0	76.0	69	34	25	6	4	21	0	57	4
C. Smith, Springfield	1	3	.250	7.20	13	5	0	3	0	0	35.0	48	36	28	3	5	9	0	33	2
Smith, Quad City	7	5	.583	4.64	22	17	2	3	0	0	110.2	109	73	57	16	6	52	0	103	8
M. Smith, Springfield	4	0	1.000	6.80	14	4	0	4	0	0	42.1	50	36	32	5	1	18	0	32	5
Smock, Madison	2	0	1.000	2.45	40	0	0	18	0	7	47.2	32	15	13	2	1	22	4	47	6
Snyder, Cedar Rapids	5	6	.455	5.91	21	16	0	1	0	0	99.0	125	88	65	13	8	39	1	79	6
Spiller, Springfield*	1	0	1.000	2.25	31	0	0	8	0	0	44.0	44	14	11	3	0	10	0	39	3
Stull, Burlington	4	9	.308	3.83	15	15	1	0	0	0	82.1	68	44	35	8	3	59	0	85	13

Pitcher, Team	W	L	Pct.	ERA	G	GS	CG	GF	ShO	Sv.	IP	H	R	ER	HR	HB	BB	Int. BB	SO	WP
Sylvestri, Kane County	0	0	.000	0.00	1	0	0	1	0	0	1.0	0	0	0	0	0	0	0	2	0
Tagle, South Bend*	0	1	.000	2.51	11	0	0	9	0	1	14.1	12	7	4	0	3	3	1	10	2
Tatar, Fort Wayne	0	0	.000	2.57	2	0	0	1	0	0	7.0	4	2	2	0	0	2	0	7	0
Taylor, Fort Wayne*	0	5	.000	5.14	25	0	0	15	0	0	49.0	54	32	28	0	2	23	1	40	2
Telemaco, Peoria	8	11	.421	3.45	23	23	3	0	0	0	143.2	129	69	55	9	5	54	0	133	8
Thibault, Beloit*	4	5	.444	4.59	40	2	0	12	0	2	64.2	64	44	33	4	4	44	2	65	8
Tidwell, Kane County	3	1	.750	3.22	25	7	0	0	0	0	81.0	68	34	29	4	8	38	1	78	5
Torrez, Beloit	0	0	.000	7.71	10	0	0	3	0	0	16.1	21	18	14	2	2	10	0	13	3
Trinidad, Peoria	7	6	.538	2.47	22	22	4	0	0	0	153.0	142	56	42	6	4	29	1	118	7
Urbina, Burlington	10	1	.909	1.99	16	16	4	0	1	0	108.1	78	30	24	7	7	36	1	107	6
Urbina, Madison	2	3	.400	4.50	10	8	0	1	0	0	46.0	41	31	23	0	0	22	2	30	2
Urso, Appleton*	4	4	.500	3.35	36	1	0	18	0	3	53.2	57	24	20	2	1	24	1	50	7
Valdez, Clinton	4	7	.364	3.99	35	2	0	14	0	0	90.1	74	47	40	6	2	44	1	85	8
Valencia, Cedar Rapids	0	2	.000	5.75	14	0	0	6	0	0	20.1	21	17	13	3	2	15	0	14	1
Van Dyke, Cedar Rapids	0	0	.000	10.03	7	0	0	5	0	0	11.2	14	18	13	2	3	10	0	14	0
Vaske, Peoria	0	0	.000	16.20	2	0	0	2	0	0	1.2	4	3	3	0	0	0	0	1	0
Vlcek, Kane County	3	1	.750	3.65	33	0	0	11	0	1	61.2	64	33	25	2	4	35	2	54	4
Waldron, Waterloo*	3	3	.500	2.53	16	1	0	5	0	1	32.0	19	11	9	1	1	19	2	30	3
Walker, Quad City*	3	11	.214	5.13	25	24	1	1	1	0	131.2	140	92	75	12	6	48	1	121	12
Wasdin, Madison	2	3	.400	1.86	9	9	0	0	0	0	48.1	32	11	10	1	1	9	1	40	2
Watkins, South Bend	6	3	.667	1.57	37	0	0	27	0	16	63.0	37	13	11	2	6	24	3	57	1
Watkins, Fort Wayne*	2	0	1.000	3.26	15	0	0	8	0	1	30.1	26	13	11	0	1	9	0	31	0
Weglarz, Rockford	5	5	.500	2.87	23	4	0	13	0	3	62.2	47	22	20	2	2	23	0	72	3
Wengert, Madison	6	5	.545	3.32	13	13	2	0	0	0	78.2	79	30	29	5	1	18	0	46	6
Westbrook, Quad City*	3	1	.750	2.48	27	0	0	14	0	2	36.1	29	11	10	3	0	21	0	20	3
Whisenant, Kane County*	2	6	.250	4.69	15	15	0	0	0	0	71.0	68	45	37	3	3	56	0	74	8
White, Cedar Rapids	2	4	.333	4.60	41	0	0	23	0	2	76.1	84	52	39	5	4	31	0	41	6
Wiley, Kane County	0	1	.000	1.50	7	0	0	3	0	0	12.0	11	2	2	2	1	0	0	9	0
Williard, Cedar Rapids	5	8	.385	4.76	23	23	1	0	0	0	124.2	130	79	66	17	3	57	1	111	4
Winiarski, South Bend	4	4	.500	4.85	34	0	0	18	0	3	55.2	59	38	30	4	4	18	0	31	7
Witte, Appleton	3	9	.250	4.28	28	14	1	3	0	0	101.0	111	57	48	8	9	22	0	62	3
Woodfin, South Bend	0	0	.000	1.62	11	0	0	7	0	4	16.2	10	3	3	1	3	0	0	4	0
Woods, South Bend	1	0	1.000	3.86	2	1	0	1	0	0	7.0	7	5	3	0	2	3	0	4	2
Worley, Appleton	3	3	.500	2.21	45	0	0	41	0	22	53.0	48	23	13	1	2	23	4	37	4
Worrell, South Bend*	2	2	.667	1.68	36	0	0	24	0	10	59.0	37	12	11	0	2	23	1	57	2
Wunsch, Beloit*	1	5	.167	4.83	12	12	0	0	0	0	63.1	58	39	34	5	1	39	1	61	5

BALKS—Nickell, 12; Clinkscales, 8; Leahy, 7; Taylor, 6; Caridad, Donahue, Hassel, Kindler, Meek, Mendoza, Naulty, J. Sanchez, U. Urbina, 5 each; Arteaga, Dunckel, J. Evans, Guerra, Jones, Rosenbohm, Schmidt, Charles Smith, Snyder, Stull, Thibault, 4 each; Arroyo, Baker, Belliard, Blair, Burlingame, Frascatore, Harikkala, Holt, Johnston, Kerley, Legault, Long, Mathews, J. Mejia, Petersen, Pittsley, Rivera, A. Sanchez, Wasdin, Whisenant, White, 3 each; Bjornson, Brewington, Davis, Dawson, Eggert, Estes, D. Evans, Foster, Fultz, Graham, Haught, Hawkins, Juelsgaard, Knowles, Kyslinger, Lee, Lindemann, Linebarger, Locklear, Marcon, McDermott, E. Miller, Moten, Je. Myers, Pierson, Pisciotta, Ponte, R. Rees, S. Rees, Sawyer, Schmitt, Serafini, W. Urbina, Valencia, Vlcek, Wunsch, 2 each; Adams, Baber, Banks, Barnes, Bennett, Bertotti, Blake, Bliss, Bojan, Bruce, Buehl, Carrasco, Carrillo, Chavez, Cody, Connolly, Cope, Correa, Deal, Demyan, Downs, Duda, Erdos, B. Evans, Falteisek, Gambs, Gardner, Gavaghan, Gavlick, Haas, Hansen, Henrikson, Hermanson, Hingle, Hollinger, Hollis, Hutcheson, Kostich, Kovach, Lesher, Lisiecki, Lucchetti, McLain, D. Mejia, Moore, Morones, Murphy, R. Myers, Ohme, Paxton, Perez, Pettit, Rose, Sartain, Saunders, Schenbeck, Schulhofer, Sebach, Simas, Sirotka, Slininger, Smock, Tidwell, Torrez, Trinidad, Urso, Walker, J. Watkins, S. Watkins, 1 each.

COMBINATION SHUTOUTS—Cody-Graham-Kostich-Worley, Nickell-Witte-Worley, Rivera-Worley, Witte-Worley, Appleton; Duda-Kyslinger, Jones-Kyslinger-Thibault, Wunsch-Thibault, Beloit; Paxton-Kermode, Phelps-Hostetler-Rushworth, Pisciotta-Clelland-Martinez, Pisciotta-Perez-Rushworth, Urbina-Reyes, Burlington; Schmidt-White-Simas, Williard-Snyder-Hingle, Cedar Rapids; Fultz-Castillo 2, Fultz-Richey 2, Gambs-Castillo-Richey 2, Brewington-Jason Myers-Locklear, Brewington-Richey, Gambs-McLain, Locklear-Crowe, Jeff Myers-Crowe-McLain, Jeff Myers-McLain-Crowe, Rosenbohm-Richey, Clinton; Caridad-Correa, Caridad-Correa-Sartain, Caridad-Gavaghan-Gandarillas, Hawkins-Moten-Gandarillas, Moten-Correa-Gandarillas, Moten-Gandarillas, Naulty-Gandarillas, Naulty-Watkins, Serafini-Correa-Gandarillas-Legault, Fort Wayne; Carrasco-Mendoza, Carrasco-Pettit, Leahy-Darensbourg, Leahy-Petersen-Darensbourg, Saunders-Pettit, Saunders-Tidwell, Kane County; Belliard-Haught-Acre, Bojan-Banks-Acre, Foster-Lemke-Smock, Foster-Smock-Acre, Sawyer-Moncion-Bojan-Lemke, Wasdin-Bojan, Madison; Bliss-Gavlick, Bliss-Kenny, Burlingame-Gavlick, Gardner-Morones-Kerley, Hassel-Gardner-Morones, Hutcheson-Lee-Gavlick, Kerley-Gardner, Kerley-Gavlick, Telemaco-Lee, Telemaco-Lee-Daniel, Trinidad-Gavlick, Trinidad-Kenny, Trinidad-Rodriguez, Peoria; R. Rees-Murphy 2, Evans-Westbrook, Holt-Ponte, R. Rees-Dawson-Bjornson-Ponte, R. Rees-Loughlin-Ponte, Smith-Murphy, Quad City; Bovee-Connolly, Bovee-Weglarz, Bunch-Sheehan, Clinkscales-Weglarz, Evans-Connolly-Dorlarque, Pittsley-Dickens-Sheehan, Rawitzer-Haas, Rockford; Bertotti-Watkins, Bertotti-Watkins-Keating-Woodfin-Worrell, Call-Worrell, Cary-Watkins, Johnston-Culberson, Johnston-Jenkins, Johnston-Jenkins-Worrell, Lindemann-Winiarski, Pierson-Cary, Pierson-Winiarski-Worrell, South Bend; Blake-Bullinger, Jolley-Bailey-Blake, Lucchetti-Bullinger, Mathews-Bullinger, Slininger-Spiller-Knowles, Springfield; Arroyo-Schmitt 2, Baker-Bullinger-Schmitt, Hermanson-Long-Hollinger-Schmitt, Waterloo.

NO-HIT GAMES—Gardner-Lee, Peoria, defeated Springfield, 2-1, April 28; Hollins, Madison, defeated Springfield, 3-0, July 7; Mathews, Springfield, defeated Burlington, 4-0, August 13.

FIELDING

TEAM

Team	Pct.	G	PO	A	E	DP	PB	Team	Pct.	G	PO	A	E	DP	PB
Madison	.969	135	3439	1400	156	82	33	Quad City	.961	130	3262	1338	185	109	22
Rockford	.968	132	3381	1451	161	131	24	Beloit	.960	134	3417	1307	195	97	39
Peoria	.966	138	3523	1423	174	106	25	Fort Wayne	.960	135	3535	1341	204	116	22
Kane County	.966	137	3554	1470	178	111	16	Appleton	.958	135	3437	1498	215	112	29
Clinton	.964	134	3380	1348	175	107	14	Waterloo	.957	133	3199	1324	204	114	34
South Bend	.964	136	3533	1451	186	112	16	Burlington	.955	135	3414	1297	222	97	29
Springfield	.964	136	3411	1457	184	93	30	Cedar Rapids	.953	134	3401	1401	237	100	25

Triple plays—Fort Wayne, Kane County.

INDIVIDUAL

FIRST BASEMEN

*Throws lefthanded.

Player, Team	Pct.	G	PO	A	E	DP	Player, Team	Pct.	G	PO	A	E	DP
Alimena, Clinton*	.988	100	711	34	9	64	Bowrosen, South Bend	1.000	1	3	0	0	0
Antoon, Rockford	.984	7	56	4	1	4	Boyzuick, Beloit	1.000	3	8	1	0	0
Ball, Quad City	.989	19	176	6	2	20	Bradish, South Bend	.977	26	201	8	5	15
Banks, Beloit	1.000	2	9	0	0	0	Brooks, Rockford	.988	11	73	9	1	11
							Bruce, Springfield	.980	70	664	32	14	37
							Claus, Fort Wayne	1.000	2	13	1	0	0
							Costic, Fort Wayne*	.978	11	83	6	2	7

Player, Team	Pct.	G	PO	A	E	DP
Cromer, Madison*	.983	20	165	4	3	13
Deutsch, Peoria*	.978	35	244	25	6	13
Doyle, Burlington	.972	5	31	4	1	1
Dumas, Beloit	1.000	1	7	0	0	0
Dunckel, Cedar Rapids	.923	8	44	4	4	2
Eicher, Springfield	.947	2	17	1	1	2
Encarnacion, Waterloo	1.000	1	1	0	0	0
Fantauzzi, Waterloo*	.986	106	860	68	13	76
Fryman, South Bend	.994	51	467	29	3	43
Greene, Waterloo	1.000	5	32	3	0	2
Gubanich, Madison	.889	3	8	0	1	0
Guzik, Cedar Rapids	.973	28	241	14	7	16
Hamlin, Springfield	.981	67	585	34	12	45
Hmielewski, Burlington*	.981	115	859	85	18	62
Hughes, Beloit	.980	10	44	6	1	5
Hymel, Burlington	1.000	1	3	0	0	0
Ibanez, Appleton	.976	11	79	2	2	4
Imperial, Beloit	.973	6	34	2	1	4
Jennings, Peoria*	1.000	8	56	11	0	6
Johnson, Peoria	1.000	2	23	1	0	0
King, Clinton	.979	21	134	9	3	12
Kingston, Peoria	.988	62	522	42	7	47
Koehler, Appleton*	.981	101	806	61	17	72
Landry, Beloit*	.993	38	275	30	2	19
Leary, Madison*	.963	8	49	3	2	4
Linares, Quad City	1.000	1	5	1	0	0
Llanos, Appleton	.980	26	186	11	4	14
Mader, South Bend	1.000	2	1	0	0	0
Markiewicz, Cedar Rapids	.989	86	719	64	9	58
Mayes, Clinton	.900	2	8	1	1	0
Medina, Peoria	.989	34	255	22	3	17
Mendoza, Beloit	.962	6	22	3	1	2
Minchk, Waterloo*	.980	10	46	2	1	5
Morales, Appleton	1.000	1	2	0	0	0
Morillo, Rockford	.987	10	71	4	1	8
Mowry, Waterloo*	.994	22	146	13	1	10
Pages, Burlington	1.000	1	1	0	0	0
Pearson, South Bend	.982	42	347	35	7	25
Polidor, South Bend	.800	2	4	0	1	0
Powell, Burlington	.958	16	105	9	5	8
Powell, Beloit	1.000	3	20	3	0	1
Pridy, Kane County*	.984	107	870	58	15	77
Probst, Quad City	1.000	1	9	1	0	1
Raasch, Peoria	1.000	4	29	1	0	0
Ramos, Quad City	.988	19	164	7	2	12
Rich, South Bend	.990	22	181	17	2	14
Richardson, Beloit	.980	8	45	4	1	1
Riesgo, Beloit	1.000	2	17	4	0	0
Roach, Clinton*	.984	14	114	9	2	15
Robertson, Appleton*	.989	11	78	9	1	5
Robinson, Kane County	.990	38	275	21	3	17
Rundels, Burlington	.974	6	36	2	1	6
Stasio, Clinton	.980	27	137	7	3	8
Stutheit, Peoria	1.000	2	13	1	0	2
Sutton, Rockford*	.989	107	911	76	11	92
Talanoa, Beloit	.975	73	550	32	15	51
TIRPACK, Fort Wayne	.9924	125	984	74	8	89
Valdez, Peoria*	1.000	2	13	1	0	0
Vaske, Peoria	1.000	3	11	1	0	2
Wallace, Appleton	1.000	3	29	2	0	6
White, Madison*	.9921	116	909	102	8	50
Winslow, Quad City	.993	91	764	58	6	58
Wolff, Cedar Rapids	.974	16	144	7	4	8
Wulf, Kane County	.944	3	16	1	1	3

Triple play—Costic.

SECOND BASEMEN

Player, Team	Pct.	G	PO	A	E	DP
Atencio, Appleton	.974	27	45	69	3	11
Ball, Quad City	1.000	10	13	16	0	5
Berry, Burlington	.937	22	30	44	5	13
Biasucci, Springfield	.956	108	164	270	20	47
Bridges, Quad City	.978	32	49	85	3	16
Bryant, Appleton	1.000	2	1	1	0	1
Burton, South Bend	.963	132	283	308	23	69
Bush, Waterloo	.930	127	215	289	38	61
Cacini, Quad City	.750	4	6	9	5	1
Carrion, Waterloo	1.000	6	7	17	0	1
Castro, Cedar Rapids	1.000	2	2	2	0	2
CENTENO, Quad City	.982	96	170	214	7	57
Clapinski, Kane County	.944	66	121	149	16	31
Claus, Fort Wayne	.956	58	104	137	11	31
Connell, Cedar Rapids	.945	36	66	89	9	17
DeLeon, Waterloo	1.000	3	3	3	0	1
Diaz, Appleton	.972	41	73	101	5	27
Dumas, Beloit	.946	32	64	58	7	10
Eldridge, Madison	.972	64	103	141	7	25
Ellsworth, Springfield	.938	20	32	44	5	10
Fonville, Clinton	1.000	2	0	2	0	0
Fraraccio, South Bend	1.000	5	3	10	0	1
Gamble, Kane County	.986	32	57	86	2	16
Gipson, Appleton	.953	48	83	138	11	24
Guillen, Madison	.964	81	136	182	12	28

Player, Team	Pct.	G	PO	A	E	DP
Haar, Burlington	.963	22	29	48	3	9
Hickey, Appleton	.893	22	36	56	11	14
Landinez, Springfield	.923	15	22	26	4	4
Marabella, Burlington	.889	11	16	8	3	3
Martinez, Cedar Rapids	.968	32	48	74	4	15
McGinnis, Peoria	1.000	1	2	1	0	0
Mendoza, Beloit	1.000	2	3	7	0	1
Montilla, Rockford	.952	5	10	10	1	5
Morillo, Rockford	1.000	6	9	17	0	3
Nava, Fort Wayne	.959	64	110	146	11	29
O'Neill, Clinton	.979	75	125	154	6	39
Perez, Peoria	.968	92	140	218	12	44
Polidor, South Bend	1.000	6	11	10	0	3
Powell, Beloit	1.000	4	6	4	0	3
Puchkov, Cedar Rapids	.961	15	15	34	2	6
Richardson, Beloit	.947	94	193	222	23	45
Rudolph, Springfield	1.000	2	1	4	0	0
Rundels, Burlington	.957	12	18	27	2	3
Santini, Fort Wayne	.956	29	49	60	5	15
Sbrocco, Clinton	.956	55	90	106	9	23
Sheets, Appleton	.941	4	5	11	1	2
Simmons, Peoria	.894	16	12	30	5	4
Simmons, Cedar Rapids	.953	57	97	146	12	22
Sisco, Rockford	.967	124	254	332	20	87
Smith, Beloit	.953	22	29	52	4	7
D. Smith, Peoria	1.000	1	1	3	0	1
Soto, Peoria	.967	38	61	84	5	20
Stutheit, Peoria	.931	6	12	15	2	3
Sylvestri, Kane County	.968	57	112	131	8	25
Vidro, Burlington	.974	74	107	153	7	33
Wong, Clinton	.943	22	40	43	5	10
Zarate, Peoria	.833	4	5	5	2	0

Triple play—Sylvestri.

THIRD BASEMEN

Player, Team	Pct.	G	PO	A	E	DP
Alcantara, Burlington	.846	125	98	216	57	19
Antoon, Rockford	.800	4	1	3	1	0
Arias, Cedar Rapids	.905	72	59	159	23	14
Baber, Waterloo	1.000	1	1	1	0	1
Ball, Quad City	.895	18	7	27	4	2
Berry, Burlington	1.000	3	0	6	0	0
Biermann, Springfield	1.000	2	0	2	0	1
Bowrosen, South Bend	.873	23	14	48	9	5
Boyzuick, Beloit	.916	95	79	172	23	14
Bradish, South Bend	.886	15	7	24	4	1
Bradley, Peoria	.920	46	33	93	11	5
Bridges, Quad City	.910	19	14	47	6	6
Bryant, Appleton	1.000	1	2	0	0	0
Carrion, Waterloo	.778	7	4	3	2	1
Castro, Cedar Rapids	.783	10	5	13	5	3
Clapinski, Kane County	1.000	3	0	3	0	0
Claus, Fort Wayne	.500	3	0	1	1	0
Connell, Cedar Rapids	.898	23	13	40	6	3
DeLeon, Waterloo	.900	14	8	28	4	2
Diaz, Appleton	1.000	1	1	3	0	0
Dumas, Beloit	1.000	1	1	0	0	0
Duran, Waterloo	.914	82	60	163	21	18
Eldridge, Madison	.828	13	0	24	5	0
Ellstrom, Waterloo	.969	43	24	71	3	3
Ellsworth, Springfield	.923	6	3	9	1	1
Encarnacion, Waterloo	1.000	2	1	1	0	1
Fonville, Clinton	.750	2	3	3	2	1
Fraraccio, South Bend	.895	35	28	57	10	3
Gorman, Beloit	.902	22	12	34	5	3
Gubanich, Madison	.935	22	16	42	4	1
Gulan, Springfield	.922	129	78	255	28	15
Hauswirth, Rockford	.800	6	4	4	2	0
Hickey, Appleton	.935	13	5	24	2	2
Imperial, Beloit	.943	10	9	24	2	1
King, Clinton	.935	11	8	21	2	1
Kingston, Peoria	1.000	1	1	0	0	0
Knauss, Fort Wayne	.832	55	41	83	25	7
Landinez, Springfield	1.000	3	3	2	0	1
Linares, Quad City	.667	1	1	1	1	0
Long, Rockford	.880	99	59	184	33	16
LUCCA, Kane County	.932	122	82	235	23	24
Mader, South Bend	.951	16	10	29	2	2
Marabella, Burlington	1.000	1	0	2	0	0
Markiewicz, Cedar Rapids	.893	32	20	55	9	4
Martinez, Appleton	.808	8	4	17	5	2
McGinnis, Peoria	.917	36	24	53	7	5
McGlone, Quad City	.885	15	6	17	3	2
Medina, Peoria	.974	44	26	88	3	15
Morillo, Rockford	.895	28	19	58	9	3
Nava, Fort Wayne	.917	52	34	77	10	8
O'Neill, Clinton	.813	9	3	10	3	0
Perez, Peoria	.893	19	5	20	3	1
Petering, Clinton	1.000	1	0	2	0	0
Polidor, South Bend	.895	27	15	53	8	6
Puchkov, Cedar Rapids	1.000	3	4	3	0	0
Raasch, Peoria	1.000	1	0	2	0	0
Ramos, Quad City	.818	90	54	157	47	13

Player, Team	Pct.	G	PO	A	E	DP
Rudolph, Springfield	1.000	3	2	4	0	0
Rundels, Burlington	.870	8	6	14	3	1
Saenz, South Bend	.913	13	11	31	4	2
Saugstad, Clinton	.750	4	2	4	2	1
Serrano, Appleton	.833	7	3	12	3	2
Sheldon, Madison	.921	119	60	221	24	18
Simmons, Peoria	1.000	3	2	3	0	0
Smith, Beloit	.923	22	6	18	2	2
D. Smith, Peoria	.870	8	4	16	3	2
Snopek, South Bend	.959	21	19	51	3	3
Sylvestri, Kane County	.961	29	10	39	2	4
Thielen, Clinton	.899	116	85	246	37	24
Tomberlin, Fort Wayne	.784	34	22	36	16	5
Wallace, Appleton	.929	115	79	224	23	15
Wong, Clinton	1.000	2	1	4	0	0
Woods, Clinton	1.000	1	2	0	0	0

Triple play—Lucca.

SHORTSTOPS

Player, Team	Pct.	G	PO	A	E	DP
Biermann, Springfield	.909	2	3	7	1	1
Bryant, Appleton	.939	47	81	134	14	24
Cabrera, Burlington	.929	126	173	300	36	51
Cacini, Quad City	.769	3	1	9	3	2
Carrion, Waterloo	.914	21	24	29	5	4
Castro, Cedar Rapids	.800	9	6	10	4	3
Centeno, Quad City	.875	3	1	6	1	1
Claus, Fort Wayne	.966	14	17	39	2	6
Connell, Cedar Rapids	.929	16	32	47	6	9
Cora, Waterloo	.940	22	26	53	5	9
DeLeon, Waterloo	.935	101	137	220	25	44
Diaz, Appleton	.938	4	7	8	1	1
Dorencz, Quad City	.932	49	55	136	14	22
Dumas, Beloit	.972	29	52	53	3	12
Duran, Waterloo	1.000	3	1	0	0	0
Ellstrom, Waterloo	1.000	1	1	0	0	1
Fonville, Clinton	.934	119	164	314	34	43
V. Francisco, Madison	.941	114	134	262	25	33
Fraraccio, South Bend	.600	2	1	2	2	1
Gipson, Appleton	.884	26	38	61	13	14
Guillen, Madison	.911	25	13	38	5	4
Haar, Burlington	1.000	1	1	3	0	0
Harkrider, Cedar Rapids	.935	54	64	124	13	22
Johns, Springfield	.943	132	151	415	34	52
Landinez, Springfield	.955	11	4	17	1	1
Listach, Beloit	1.000	3	3	7	0	1
Long, Rockford	.929	4	5	8	1	3
Martinez, Beloit	.939	92	109	242	23	35
McGlone, Quad City	.927	81	118	198	25	44
Mendez, Peoria	.935	14	14	29	3	7
Mendoza, Beloit	.980	18	22	28	1	5
Montilla, Rockford	.944	79	105	231	20	51
Morillo, Rockford	.949	45	69	155	12	32
Orie, Peoria	.949	56	74	149	12	26
Perez, Peoria	1.000	6	8	13	0	3
Petering, Clinton	.800	2	2	2	1	0
Polidor, South Bend	.875	9	7	14	3	4
Renteria, Kane County	.934	114	173	306	34	56
Rundels, Burlington	.861	10	9	22	5	3
Santini, Fort Wayne	.917	18	17	38	5	4
Sheets, Appleton	.965	65	93	183	10	33
Sheldon, Madison	.977	20	30	54	2	9
Smith, Cedar Rapids	.900	66	81	180	29	25
Smith, Beloit	.918	16	21	24	4	3
Soto, Peoria	.924	80	106	174	23	24
Sylvestri, Kane County	.949	30	38	74	6	14
Valette, Fort Wayne	.939	111	156	289	29	50
Wallace, Appleton	1.000	1	1	2	0	0
WILSON, South Bend	.963	132	166	388	21	60
Wong, Clinton	1.000	2	4	4	0	2
Woods, Clinton	.920	30	28	53	7	14

Triple play—Valette.

OUTFIELDERS

Player, Team	Pct.	G	PO	A	E	DP
Aracena, Madison	.938	20	29	1	2	0
Atencio, Appleton	.957	75	102	8	5	0
Baber, Waterloo	.947	74	101	6	6	4
Ball, Quad City	.913	33	42	0	4	0
Banks, Beloit	.980	35	47	2	1	0
Bellomo, Clinton*	1.000	23	42	3	0	1
Benard, Clinton*	.974	111	179	10	5	2
Benitez, Burlington	.945	104	167	4	10	0
Berry, Burlington	1.000	2	5	2	0	1
Bonds, Waterloo	.941	93	184	9	12	3
Bridges, Quad City	.846	12	9	2	2	0
Briggs, Waterloo	.967	122	190	16	7	4
Brown, Fort Wayne	.933	34	40	2	3	0
Byrd, Fort Wayne	.965	117	236	9	9	3
Cacini, Quad City	1.000	1	1	0	0	0
Cameron, South Bend	.985	112	248	13	4	4
Cappuccio, South Bend	.955	85	133	17	7	3
Centeno, Quad City	1.000	1	2	0	0	0
CHRISTIAN, Kane County*	1.000	104	177	5	0	0
Claus, Fort Wayne	1.000	6	12	5	0	1
Costic, Fort Wayne*	.976	54	80	3	2	1
Cromer, Madison*	.947	52	68	4	4	0
Cunningham, Peoria	.963	18	26	0	1	0
Damon, Rockford*	.977	127	240	14	6	5
Daniels, Cedar Rapids	.933	106	161	5	12	0
Devers, South Bend	.960	21	22	2	1	1
Diaz, Appleton	1.000	2	3	0	0	0
Dumas, Beloit	.500	5	2	0	2	0
Dunckel, Cedar Rapids	1.000	4	7	0	0	0
Durkin, Quad City*	.926	18	25	0	2	0
Ealy, Clinton	.973	99	136	7	4	1
Eicher, Springfield	.958	32	41	5	2	0
Eidle, Quad City	.964	47	77	3	3	0
T. Evans, Quad City*	.973	120	212	7	6	2
Felder, Beloit	.907	30	38	1	4	0
D. Francisco, Madison	.976	129	266	13	7	3
Gamble, Kane County	1.000	4	3	0	0	0
Garrett, Cedar Rapids*	1.000	22	32	0	0	0
Gerteisen, Springfield	1.000	3	5	0	0	0
Gipson, Appleton	.948	37	71	2	4	0
Good, Rockford*	1.000	9	17	0	0	0
Griffey, Springfield	.933	37	53	3	4	0
Grissom, Burlington	.958	64	109	5	5	3
Hardwick, Cedar Rapids	.965	61	136	3	5	3
Henry, Springfield	.929	18	12	1	1	0
Herrera, Fort Wayne	.929	35	52	0	4	0
Herrera, Madison*	1.000	4	6	1	0	0
Hickey, Appleton	.958	32	65	4	3	1
Hill, Cedar Rapids	1.000	1	3	0	0	0
Hood, South Bend	.857	6	5	1	1	0
Hostetler, Beloit	1.000	3	5	0	0	0
Hurst, South Bend	.898	70	98	8	12	1
Hust, Madison	.961	108	144	4	6	1
Ibanez, Appleton	1.000	4	2	0	0	0
Jennings, Peoria*	.963	120	163	20	7	4
Jordan, Springfield	1.000	3	3	0	0	0
Kerns, Cedar Rapids	.941	61	89	6	6	2
Koehler, Appleton*	1.000	13	18	0	0	0
LaChance, Burlington	.973	17	31	5	1	2
Landinez, Springfield	.889	13	8	0	1	0
Landry, Beloit*	.667	1	2	0	1	0
Lawson, Appleton*	.955	104	158	13	8	0
Lawton, Fort Wayne	.959	47	65	6	3	1
Lee, Burlington	.974	64	107	4	3	2
LeGree, Fort Wayne	.987	44	69	5	1	1
Lesher, Madison*	.976	114	193	9	5	2
Llanos, Appleton	.933	21	27	1	2	0
Madsen, Peoria*	.971	79	129	3	4	1
Marquez, Appleton*	.924	60	88	3	8	2
Martin, Cedar Rapids	.941	54	93	3	6	0
Mathews, South Bend	.975	127	267	7	7	2
Medina, Peoria	1.000	4	1	0	0	0
Mendoza, Beloit	.800	1	4	0	1	0
J. Miller, Fort Wayne	.885	38	45	1	6	1
Murphy, Rockford	.993	103	124	12	1	1
Roderick Myers, Rockford*	.969	123	208	10	7	2
Newhouse, Rockford	.963	32	48	4	2	0
O'Neill, Burlington	.945	59	116	4	7	2
Orie, Peoria	1.000	3	3	0	0	0
Perez, Beloit	.990	96	180	9	2	4
Perez, Waterloo	1.000	4	4	0	0	0
Petering, Clinton	.963	20	24	2	1	0
Pico, Peoria*	1.000	8	18	0	0	0
Powell, Burlington	.961	56	93	6	4	2
Radmanovich, Fort Wayne	.968	51	84	6	3	1
Ramirez, Madison	.929	9	11	2	1	0
Ramos, Clinton	1.000	2	3	0	0	0
Reid, Clinton	1.000	7	8	2	0	0
Rhein, Quad City*	.986	49	69	2	1	0
Richardson, Beloit	.974	20	36	1	1	0
Riesgo, Clinton	1.000	6	14	1	0	0
Roach, Clinton*	.923	14	21	3	2	1
Robbs, Waterloo	1.000	2	5	1	0	0
Roberts, Waterloo	.957	114	170	9	8	3
Robertson, Appleton*	.909	52	75	5	8	0
Robinson, Kane County	.960	71	94	3	4	0
Rodriques, Beloit	.951	102	165	9	9	1
Roman, Quad City	.942	77	110	4	7	1
Ross, Beloit	.982	114	211	10	4	2
Rudolph, Springfield	.943	81	99	1	6	0
Rumsey, Cedar Rapids	.889	14	16	0	2	0
Rundels, Burlington	.976	30	40	1	1	0
Schmidt, Beloit	1.000	13	17	0	0	0
Schulte, Quad City	.986	50	71	1	1	0
Serrano, Appleton	.800	9	7	1	2	1
Shabazz, Springfield	.941	64	107	5	7	0
Sheff, Kane County	.975	125	190	4	5	1
Simonton, Clinton	.948	81	89	3	5	0
C. Smith, Peoria	1.000	6	13	0	0	0
Stasio, Clinton	1.000	1	1	0	0	0
Stewart, Waterloo	.867	19	13	0	2	0

Player, Team	Pct.	G	PO	A	E	DP
Stovall, Springfield*	.958	134	247	6	11	1
Stutheit, Peoria	1.000	1	1	0	0	0
Taylor, Springfield	.967	65	82	6	3	1
Terilli, Peoria*	1.000	20	24	4	0	1
Thomas, Clinton	.964	23	26	1	1	0
Tosone, Burlington*	.974	27	35	2	1	0
Triessi, Appleton	1.000	3	3	0	0	0
Valdez, Peoria*	.975	24	38	1	1	1
Vazquez, Springfield	.957	34	40	4	2	2
Walker, Peoria	.969	126	264	15	9	3
Walls, Rockford*	.955	11	20	1	1	0
Wilson, Kane County*	.981	126	205	5	4	0
Wolff, Cedar Rapids	.978	96	165	15	4	3
Woods, Clinton	.976	87	111	10	3	2
Zarate, Peoria	.958	33	46	0	2	0

CATCHERS

Player, Team	Pct.	G	PO	A	E	DP	PB
Ballara, Springfield	.987	56	406	47	6	6	12
Brooks, Rockford	.987	100	718	94	11	6	13
Casanova, Waterloo	.976	59	361	50	10	8	15
Cavanagh, Clinton	.980	34	205	38	5	1	3
Delaney, Rockford	1.000	18	102	13	0	1	2
DiFelice, Springfield	1.000	8	52	9	0	1	3
Eldridge, Madison	.941	2	15	1	1	0	0
Encarnacion, Waterloo	.920	5	21	2	2	0	3
Erdman, Peoria	.982	20	152	13	3	1	4
Faircloth, South Bend	1.000	1	7	1	0	0	0
Gay, Beloit	.989	29	154	20	2	0	7
Gonzalez, Quad City	.978	42	283	35	7	4	5
Greene, Waterloo	.970	77	428	93	16	11	15
Gubanich, Madison	.9901	86	523	78	6	6	25
Hauswirth, Rockford	1.000	29	179	23	0	1	9
Hirsch, Cedar Rapids	1.000	6	32	5	0	0	1
Horn, Fort Wayne	.988	63	504	62	7	10	5
Hostetler, Beloit	.980	48	318	33	7	3	19
Hughes, Beloit	.972	76	519	61	17	7	13
Hymel, Burlington	.974	22	166	23	5	2	3
Ibanez, Appleton	1.000	4	17	0	0	0	0
JENSEN, Clinton	.9902	90	641	73	7	5	7
Johnson, Kane County	.988	118	852	140	12	9	15
Johnson, Peoria	.988	35	220	30	3	5	5
Kessler, Cedar Rapids	.961	10	64	10	3	2	4
Killeen, Madison	.979	58	410	50	10	4	6
Linares, Quad City	.990	38	271	39	3	5	4
Lopez, Fort Wayne	.994	69	580	73	4	11	15
Machado, South Bend	.979	73	490	66	12	6	9
Mayes, Clinton	1.000	18	115	7	0	1	3
McCubbin, Burlington	.962	28	222	29	10	5	10
Miller, Clinton	1.000	10	69	12	0	1	1
Moore, Madison	.983	12	54	4	1	0	2
Morales, Peoria	.970	17	115	14	4	1	0
Morales, Appleton	.969	33	200	22	7	3	10
Morel, Springfield	.986	26	184	22	3	1	4
Mumma, South Bend	1.000	9	68	4	0	2	0
Pages, Burlington	.984	89	725	81	13	6	15
Powell, Burlington	1.000	2	1	2	0	0	1
Probst, Quad City	.995	45	334	28	2	1	9
Raasch, Peoria	1.000	39	277	23	0	3	5
Redmond, Kane County	.996	34	213	26	1	1	1
Rodgers, Peoria	.978	37	240	28	6	3	4
Rosario, Waterloo	.986	9	62	11	1	0	1
Stela, Cedar Rapids	.987	51	334	47	5	6	5
Stricklin, Fort Wayne	.986	8	69	4	1	0	2
Sutherland, Appleton	.989	97	616	89	8	3	14
Torino, Quad City	.979	15	85	7	2	1	4
Triessi, Appleton	.978	24	123	12	3	0	5
Tucker, Cedar Rapids	.974	73	537	58	16	5	15
Vinas, South Bend	.968	55	333	30	12	7	7
Vogel, South Bend	1.000	2	11	2	0	0	0
Williams, Springfield	.985	53	333	54	6	1	11
Wulf, Kane County	1.000	3	4	0	0	0	0

PITCHERS

Player, Team	Pct.	G	PO	A	E	DP
Acre, Madison	1.000	28	3	2	0	0
Adams, Madison	.667	5	1	1	1	0
Anthony, Waterloo	1.000	7	1	4	0	0
Aracena, Madison	1.000	5	0	1	0	1
Aronetz, Beloit*	.909	30	5	5	1	1
Arroyo, Waterloo*	.906	17	7	22	3	1
Arteaga, Burlington	.913	20	9	12	2	1
Aschoff, Appleton*	.900	9	1	8	1	0
Bailey, Springfield	.667	9	0	2	1	0
Baine, Clinton*	1.000	3	1	1	0	0
Baker, Waterloo	.870	15	6	14	3	2
Banks, Madison	1.000	44	3	5	0	0
Barnes, Waterloo	.929	10	4	9	1	3
Belliard, Madison*	.889	26	3	13	2	0
Bennett, Madison	1.000	26	14	17	0	1
Bertotti, South Bend*	.852	17	2	21	4	0

Player, Team	Pct.	G	PO	A	E	DP
Bjornson, Quad City*	.938	39	3	12	1	0
Blair, Beloit	.895	21	9	8	2	1
Blake, Springfield*	1.000	24	6	17	0	1
Bliss, Peoria	.846	12	5	6	2	0
Bojan, Madison	1.000	43	8	9	0	1
Bovee, Rockford	1.000	20	6	16	0	0
Brewington, Clinton	.931	26	5	22	2	0
Bruce, Appleton	1.000	12	0	1	0	0
Bullinger, Springfield	1.000	50	2	10	0	1
Bunch, Rockford	.889	19	6	10	2	3
Burley, Rockford*	.917	9	0	11	1	0
Burlingame, Peoria	.970	20	8	24	1	1
Burns, Waterloo	1.000	19	2	7	0	0
Cacini, Quad City	1.000	1	0	1	0	0
Call, South Bend	.960	26	18	30	2	1
Caridad, Fort Wayne	.824	27	16	26	9	0
Carrasco, Kane County	.737	28	8	20	10	0
Carrillo, Springfield*	1.000	15	1	7	0	0
Cary, South Bend*	1.000	8	0	3	0	0
Castillo, Clinton	.917	40	4	7	1	0
Castro, Cedar Rapids	1.000	13	2	3	0	1
Chavez, Cedar Rapids	1.000	41	5	8	0	1
Clelland, Burlington	1.000	30	10	13	0	2
Clinkscales, Rockford	.905	20	4	15	2	3
Cody, Appleton	1.000	26	2	15	0	2
Connell, Cedar Rapids	1.000	1	1	0	0	0
Connolly, Rockford*	.952	34	5	15	1	1
Cope, Appleton	1.000	3	0	2	0	0
Correa, Fort Wayne	.933	41	6	8	1	0
Crowe, Clinton	1.000	33	7	10	0	0
Culberson, South Bend	1.000	9	1	4	0	1
D'Amato, Waterloo	1.000	21	0	2	0	0
Daniel, Peoria	1.000	19	1	1	0	0
Darensbourg, Kane County*	.882	46	2	13	2	1
DaSilva, Burlington	1.000	11	5	10	0	0
Davis, Appleton*	.952	16	5	15	1	0
Dawson, Quad City	.857	31	1	5	1	0
Deal, Appleton	.667	11	0	2	1	0
DeGrasse, Springfield	.875	49	2	5	1	0
DeLeon, Waterloo	1.000	3	1	2	0	0
Demyan, Beloit	.813	50	5	8	3	1
Dickens, Rockford*	1.000	32	1	10	0	0
Dixon, South Bend	1.000	10	2	2	0	0
Donahue, Kane County	1.000	31	2	9	0	1
Dorlarque, Rockford	.923	28	6	6	1	0
Downs, Rockford	.500	5	1	0	1	0
Doyle, Waterloo*	1.000	4	0	1	0	0
Droll, Beloit	1.000	4	0	4	0	0
Duda, Beloit	1.000	6	4	4	0	0
Dumas, Beloit	1.000	1	0	2	0	0
Dunckel, Waterloo	.833	30	8	12	4	1
Duran, Waterloo	1.000	5	0	1	0	0
Eggert, Burlington*	.857	51	3	9	2	1
Eldridge, Madison	1.000	3	1	0	0	0
Ellsworth, Springfield	1.000	1	1	0	0	0
Erdos, Waterloo	1.000	11	4	9	0	0
Estes, Appleton*	.846	19	4	18	4	1
Evans, Rockford	.714	27	4	6	4	0
Evans, Appleton	1.000	5	1	4	0	0
J. Evans, Quad City	.977	26	6	37	1	1
Falteisek, Burlington	.933	14	10	18	2	0
Fermin, Cedar Rapids	1.000	9	2	2	0	0
Fetty, Beloit	1.000	2	1	0	0	0
Foster, Madison	.872	26	13	21	5	0
Frascatore, Springfield	.939	27	14	32	3	1
Frazier, Kane County*	1.000	39	1	8	0	1
Fritz, South Bend*	.882	11	4	11	2	2
Froning, Beloit*	1.000	4	0	1	0	0
Fultz, 26 Clin.- 1 F.W.*	.926	27	2	23	2	0
Gambs, Clinton	.941	21	8	8	1	0
Gandarillas, Fort Wayne	.917	52	5	6	1	0
Gardner, Madison	.920	39	9	14	2	1
Gavaghan, Fort Wayne	.900	11	1	8	1	0
Gavlick, Peoria*	.714	51	1	9	4	2
Gay, South Bend*	.500	12	0	1	1	0
Gienger, Madison	.875	15	2	5	1	1
Graham, Appleton	.952	43	9	11	1	0
Guerra, Peoria*	.875	27	4	3	1	0
Gutierrez, Quad City*	.857	11	1	5	1	0
Haas, Rockford*	1.000	24	6	20	0	2
Hampton, Beloit	.875	11	3	4	1	0
Hanson, Waterloo	.955	28	7	14	1	0
Harikkala, Appleton	.750	15	3	6	3	0
Hassel, Peoria	1.000	12	3	4	0	0
Haught, Madison	.944	17	7	10	1	0
Hawkins, Fort Wayne	.882	26	12	18	4	1
Heckman, Clinton	1.000	11	1	4	0	0
Henrikson, Clinton*	.800	12	0	4	1	0
Hermanson, Waterloo	.944	18	4	13	1	2
Hingle, Cedar Rapids*	.974	28	9	28	1	2
Hmielewski, Burlington*	1.000	5	0	1	0	0
Hollinger, Waterloo	1.000	44	3	7	0	0
Hollins, Madison	.923	26	11	13	2	1
Holt, Quad City	1.000	26	14	35	0	1
Hostetler, Burlington*	.846	32	2	9	2	0

Player, Team	Pct.	G	PO	A	E	DP
Hutcheson, Peoria	.867	15	4	9	2	0
Jenkins, South Bend	.600	16	2	1	2	0
Johnson, Springfield	1.000	5	2	2	0	0
Johnston, South Bend*	.920	15	7	16	2	2
Jolley, Springfield	1.000	5	3	1	0	0
Jones, Beloit*	.952	25	6	14	1	1
Juelsgaard, Kane County	.900	11	2	7	1	1
Keating, South Bend*	1.000	6	1	2	0	0
Kenny, Peoria	1.000	5	0	1	0	0
Kerley, Peoria	.871	31	12	15	4	1
Kermode, Burlington	1.000	19	2	6	0	1
Kindler, Waterloo	.778	20	3	11	4	0
Knowles, Burlington	1.000	54	4	6	0	0
Kostich, Appleton*	.778	20	3	4	2	0
Krislock, Quad City	.000	7	0	0	2	0
Kyslinger, Beloit	1.000	35	2	9	0	0
Leahy, Kane County	.857	25	10	20	5	1
Lee, Peoria	1.000	41	4	13	0	0
Legault, Fort Wayne	1.000	12	1	2	0	0
Lemke, Madison	1.000	16	8	10	0	1
Lindemann, South Bend*	.885	12	6	17	3	3
Linebarger, Fort Wayne	.852	35	7	16	4	0
Lisiecki, Appleton	1.000	20	1	2	0	0
Locklear, Clinton*	1.000	28	4	12	0	0
Loiselle, Waterloo	.889	10	1	7	1	0
Long, Waterloo*	.968	33	7	23	1	2
Lopez, Peoria*	.889	4	1	7	1	0
Loughlin, Quad City*	.947	19	6	12	1	1
Lucchetti, Springfield	.944	20	3	14	1	3
Lynch, Kane County	.667	2	0	2	1	0
Maloney, Burlington*	.667	11	1	1	1	1
Marcon, Cedar Rapids	.818	30	0	9	2	0
Martinez, Madison	1.000	10	0	3	0	0
Mathews, Madison	.917	25	11	33	4	1
McCaskill, South Bend	1.000	1	0	1	0	0
McDermott, South Bend	1.000	6	1	3	0	0
McLain, Clinton	.800	36	1	11	3	0
Meek, Beloit	.882	24	6	24	4	3
Mejia, Madison	1.000	5	1	1	0	0
Mejia, Cedar Rapids*	.778	13	2	5	2	0
Mendoza, Kane County	.898	26	9	35	5	2
Miller, Springfield	1.000	24	0	1	0	0
S. Miller, Fort Wayne	1.000	8	2	2	0	0
Moore, South Bend	.893	26	8	17	3	1
Morones, Peoria	.833	13	4	1	1	0
Moten, Fort Wayne	.914	30	7	25	3	1
Murphy, Quad City	1.000	42	5	17	0	1
Ja. Myers, Clinton*	1.000	1	0	1	0	0
Je. Myers, Clinton*	.938	18	3	12	1	0
Rodney Myers, Rockford	.930	12	13	27	3	1
Naulty, Fort Wayne	.750	18	1	8	3	0
Nickell, Appleton	.875	24	10	18	4	2
O'Donnell, Appleton	1.000	6	0	3	0	0
O'Laughlin, Beloit*	1.000	2	1	0	0	0
Oehrlein, Springfield*	.818	13	2	7	2	0
Ohme, Fort Wayne*	1.000	15	1	9	0	0
Pacheco, Burlington	.750	13	3	3	2	0
Page, Rockford	1.000	16	1	1	0	0
Paul, Beloit	.857	8	6	6	2	0
Paxton, Burlington*	.917	41	4	18	2	2
Perez, Burlington*	1.000	12	0	5	0	1
Peters, Rockford	.933	11	5	9	1	1
Petersen, Kane County	.857	30	6	18	4	0
Pettit, Kane County	.750	52	2	7	3	0
Phelps, Burlington	1.000	8	1	7	0	0
Pierson, South Bend*	.943	26	6	27	2	0
Pike, Beloit	.833	35	1	4	1	0
Pisciotta, Burlington	.919	24	9	25	3	1
Pittsley, Rockford	.889	15	5	11	2	1
Ponte, Quad City	.950	39	4	15	1	2

Player, Team	Pct.	G	PO	A	E	DP
Rawitzer, Rockford*	.833	5	2	3	1	0
R. Rees, Quad City	1.000	17	4	11	0	1
S. Rees, Quad City*	1.000	12	2	7	0	2
Reyes, Burlington	1.000	53	4	10	0	0
Richey, Clinton	1.000	40	2	11	0	2
Rinehart, Cedar Rapids	1.000	16	3	11	0	0
Rivera, Appleton	.905	13	6	13	2	0
Rodriguez, Peoria	.909	17	5	5	1	0
Rose, Quad City*	.857	7	1	5	1	0
Rosenbohm, Clinton	.900	23	5	13	2	2
Ruiz, Springfield*	.500	1	1	0	1	0
Rusch, Rockford*	1.000	2	0	1	0	0
Rushworth, Burlington	1.000	24	1	11	0	0
Sadler, Beloit	.885	20	8	15	3	0
Sanchez, Peoria	.750	36	3	4	2	0
Sanchez, Appleton	.962	26	7	18	1	1
Sandt, Waterloo	1.000	17	1	4	0	0
Sartain, Fort Wayne*	1.000	5	1	1	0	0
Saunders, Kane County*	.714	23	2	8	4	1
Sawyer, Madison	1.000	25	7	7	0	1
Schenbeck, Beloit	.941	38	4	12	1	0
Schmidt, Cedar Rapids	.842	26	8	24	6	1
Schmitt, Waterloo	.833	51	3	7	2	0
Schulhofer, Peoria	.857	4	6	0	1	0
SEBACH, Cedar Rapids	1.000	26	19	32	0	2
Serafini, Fort Wayne*	.806	27	6	23	7	0
Sheehan, Rockford	1.000	31	13	17	0	1
Simas, Cedar Rapids	.783	35	5	13	5	0
Sirotka, South Bend*	.000	7	0	0	1	0
Slininger, Springfield	.963	13	4	22	1	2
C. Smith, Springfield	1.000	13	1	6	0	1
Smith, Quad City	.821	22	4	19	5	0
M. Smith, Springfield	.889	14	4	4	1	0
Smock, Madison*	.714	40	0	5	2	0
Snyder, Cedar Rapids	.741	21	5	15	7	0
Spiller, Springfield*	1.000	31	2	6	0	1
Stull, Burlington	1.000	15	4	15	0	1
Tagle, South Bend*	1.000	11	0	3	0	0
Tatar, Fort Wayne	1.000	2	1	0	0	0
Taylor, Fort Wayne*	.947	25	0	18	1	0
Telemaco, Peoria	.875	23	15	20	5	0
Thibault, Beloit*	.700	40	2	5	3	0
Tidwell, Kane County	1.000	25	6	8	0	0
Torrez, Beloit	1.000	10	1	1	0	0
Trinidad, Peoria	1.000	22	13	35	0	1
Urbina, Burlington	1.000	16	7	13	0	1
Urbina, Madison	.889	10	2	6	1	0
Urso, Appleton*	.938	36	7	23	2	0
Valdez, Clinton	.800	35	6	10	4	0
Valencia, Cedar Rapids	1.000	14	1	4	0	0
Vlcek, Kane County	.824	33	3	11	3	0
Waldron, Waterloo*	.857	16	1	5	1	1
Walker, Quad City*	.946	25	5	30	2	0
Wasdin, Madison	1.000	9	5	10	0	0
Watkins, South Bend	1.000	37	6	7	0	0
Watkins, Fort Wayne*	.909	15	2	8	1	0
Weglarz, Rockford	.889	23	1	7	1	0
Wengert, Madison	1.000	13	8	21	0	1
Westbrook, Quad City	1.000	27	2	4	0	0
Whisenant, Kane County*	.867	15	9	17	4	1
White, Cedar Rapids	.800	41	2	14	4	0
Wiley, Kane County	1.000	7	0	1	0	1
Williard, Cedar Rapids	.828	23	8	16	5	0
Winiarski, South Bend	1.000	34	2	5	0	1
Witte, Appleton	.892	28	10	23	4	4
Woodfin, South Bend	1.000	11	1	3	0	0
Woods, South Bend	1.000	2	0	3	0	0
Worley, Appleton	.944	45	3	14	1	3
Worrell, South Bend*	.933	36	5	9	1	0
Wunsch, Beloit*	.556	12	1	4	4	0

The following players did not have any fielding statistics at the positions indicated or appeared only as a designated hitter, pinch-hitter or pinch-runner: Arias, ss; Baber, p; Bell, dh; Boddicker, p; Broome, p; Carrion, of; Casanova, 3b; Cavanagh, p; Claus, p; Dawson, of; Delaney, p; DeLeon, of; Ellstrom, 2b; Grande, p; Greene, 3b, ss; Hammond, p; Harkrider, 3b; Hightower, of; Hughes, 3b, of; Hurst, 1b; Hust, p; Kovach, p; Kyslinger, of; Lawson, p; Lesher, p; Llanos, p; R. Long, 2b; Marabella, 1b; W. Martinez, p; Moncion, p; J. Morales, 3b; Penix, dh, ph; Sheets, of; Stewart, 1b; Sylvestri, of, p; Van Dyke, p; Vaske, p; Winslow, of.

LEAGUE CHAMPIONS

Year	Team	Pct.	Year	Team	Pct.	Year	Team	Pct.
1947 —	Belleville	.667	1956 —	Paris y	.656	1963 —	Clinton	.710
	Belleville	.672		Dubuque	.603		Clinton	.629
1948 —	West Frankfort*	.708	1957 —	Decatur y	.683	1964 —	Clinton	.667
1949 —	Centralia	.627		Clinton	.623		Fox Cities z	.667
	Paducah (4th)†	.454	1958 —	Michigan City	.623	1965 —	Burlington	.667
1950 —	Centralia‡	.675		Waterloo z	.613		Burlington	.677
1951 —	Paris§	.700	1959 —	Waterloo	.613	1966 —	Fox Cities z	.689
	Danville (4th)†	.432		Waterloo	.613		Cedar Rapids	.762
1952 —	Danville x	.685	1960 —	Waterloo	.629	1967 —	Wisconsin Rapids	.685
	Decatur (3rd)†	.584		Waterloo	.677		Appleton z	.587
1953 —	Decatur*	.576	1961 —	Waterloo	.613	1968 —	Decatur	.656
1954 —	Decatur	.587		Quincy	.594		Quad Cities z	.648
	Danville (2nd)‡	.528	1962 —	Dubuque z	.667	1969 —	Appleton	.648
1955 —	Dubuque*	.587		Waterloo	.625		Appleton	.690

Year	Team	Pct.	Year	Team	Pct.	Year	Team	Pct.
1970—	Quincy z	.691	1978—	Appleton a	.708	1986—	Springfield	.621
	Quad Cities	.581		Burlington	.500		Waterloo b	.557
1971—	Appleton	.642	1979—	Waterloo	.600	1987—	Springfield	.671
	Quad Cities a	.548		Quad Cities a	.579		Kenosha b	.586
1972—	Appleton	.598	1980—	Waterloo a	.610	1988—	Cedar Rapids a	.621
	Danville a	.584		Quad Cities	.532		Kenosha	.579
1973—	Wisconsin Rapids a	.562	1981—	Wausau a	.636	1989—	South Bend a	.644
	Danville	.537		Quad Cities	.570		Springfield	.541
1974—	Appleton	.593	1982—	Madison	.626	1990—	Cedar Rapids	.657
	Danville a	.517		Appleton b	.579		Quad City a	.579
1975—	Waterloo a	.727	1983—	Appleton c	.635	1991—	Clinton a	.583
	Quad Cities	.624		Springfield	.576		Madison	.558
1976—	Waterloo a	.600	1984—	Appleton c	.640	1992—	Quad City	.664
	Cedar Rapids	.595		Springfield	.504		Cedar Rapids a	.594
1977—	Waterloo	.580	1985—	Kenosha b	.568	1993—	Clinton	.597
	Burlington a	.511		Peoria	.536		South Bend a	.566

*Won championship and four-club playoff. †Won four-club playoff. ‡Playoff finals canceled because of bad weather. §Won both halves of split season. xWon first half of split season and tied Paris for second-half title. yWon first-half title and four-team playoff. zWon split season playoff. aLeague divided into Northern and Southern divisions and played split season. Playoff winner. bLeague divided into Northern, Central and Southern divisions. Playoff winner. cLeague divided into Northern, Central and Southern divisions; regular-season and playoff winner. (NOTE— Known as Illinois State League in 1947-48 and Mississippi-Ohio Valley League from 1949 through 1955.)

NEW YORK - PENN LEAGUE

FINAL STANDINGS

McNAMARA DIVISION

Team	W	L	T	Pct.	GB
Pittsfield (Mets)	40	35	0	.533	....
Utica (Red Sox)	38	38	0	.500	2½
Glens Falls (Cardinals)	37	40	0	.481	4
Oneonta (Yankees)	36	40	0	.474	4½

PINCKNEY DIVISION

Team	W	L	T	Pct.	GB
Watertown (Indians)	46	32	0	.590	....
Geneva (Cubs)	43	34	0	.558	2½
Elmira (Marlins)	31	44	0	.413	13½
Auburn (Astros)	30	46	0	.395	15

STEDLER DIVISION

Team	W	L	T	Pct.	GB
St. Catharines (Blue Jays)	49	29	0	.628	....
Niagara Falls (Tigers)	47	31	0	.603	2
Batavia (Phillies)	38	39	0	.494	10½
Erie (Rangers)	36	41	0	.468	12½
Welland (Pirates)	35	42	0	.455	13½
Jamestown (Expos)	31	46	0	.403	17½

COMPOSITE

Team	St.C.	N.F.	Wat.	Gen.	Pit.	Utl.	Bat.	G.F.	One.	Erie	Wel.	Elm.	Jam.	Aub.	W	L	T	Pct.	GB
St. Catharines (Blue Jays)	....	3	3	2	3	2	5	2	3	5	10	2	6	3	49	29	0	.628	....
Niagara Falls (Tigers)	5	....	2	2	1	2	9	4	1	4	5	3	6	3	47	31	0	.603	2
Watertown (Indians)	1	2	....	6	3	1	4	2	3	2	3	10	2	8	46	32	0	.590	3
Geneva (Cubs)	2	2	6	....	2	2	2	2	2	2	2	8	3	8	43	34	0	.558	5½
Pittsfield (Mets)	1	3	1	2	....	5	3	9	7	2	1	2	1	3	40	35	0	.533	7½
Utica (Red Sox)	2	2	3	2	6	....	2	7	5	3	3	1	2	0	38	38	0	.500	10
Batavia (Phillies)	3	5	0	2	1	2	....	0	3	5	6	3	6	2	38	39	0	.494	10½
Glens Falls (Cardinals)	2	0	2	1	5	5	4	....	6	1	2	4	1	4	37	40	0	.481	11½
Oneonta (Yankees)	1	3	1	2	4	9	1	6	....	3	1	1	1	3	36	40	0	.474	12
Erie (Rangers)	3	4	2	2	2	1	3	1	1	....	4	2	7	2	36	41	0	.468	12½
Welland (Pirates)	4	3	2	2	2	1	2	2	3	4	....	3	5	2	35	42	0	.455	13½
Elmira (Marlins)	2	1	2	6	2	2	1	0	2	2	1	....	3	7	31	44	0	.413	16½
Jamestown (Expos)	2	2	1	3	2	2	2	3	6	3	1	....	1	31	46	0	.403	17½	
Auburn (Astros)	1	1	6	4	1	1	0	1	7	2	2	4	3	....	30	46	0	.395	18

Major league affiliations in parentheses.

Playoffs—Niagara Falls defeated St. Catharines, one game to none; Pittsfield defeated Watertown, one game to none; Niagara Falls defeated Pittsfield, two games to none, to win league championship.

Regular-season attendance—Auburn, 30,325; Batavia, 41,539; Elmira, 65,106; Erie, 65,316; Geneva, 34,634; Glens Falls, 78,925; Jamestown, 40,588; Niagara Falls, 50,190; Oneonta, 55,144; Pittsfield, 46,682; St. Catharines, 46,535; Utica, 77,645; Watertown, 40,082; Welland, 35,664. Total—708,175. Playoffs (4 games)—3,875.

Managers—Auburn, Manny Acta; Batavia, Al LeBoeuf; Elmira, Lynn Jones; Erie, Doug Sisson; Geneva, Jerry Weinstein; Glens Falls, Steve Turco; Jamestown, Tim Torricelli; Niagara Falls, Larry Parrish; Oneonta, Mark Newman; Pittsfield, Howard Freiling; St. Catharines, J.J. Cannon; Utica, Dave Holt; Watertown, Mike Young; Welland, Larry Smith.

All-Star team: 1B—Greg Thomas, Watertown; 2B—T.J. O'Donnell, Utica; 3B—Adam Melhuse, St. Catharines; SS—Mike Neal, Watertown; OF—Ruben Rivera, Oneonta; Noel Rodriguez, Auburn; Jermaine Allensworth, Welland; Ron Brown, Elmira; C—Wes Shook, Erie, and Ramsey Koeyers, Jamestown; DH—Wes Shook, Erie; RHP—Joshua Neese, Niagara Falls; Adam Meinershagen, St. Catharines; LHP—Casey Whitten, Watertown; Silvio Censale, Batavia; Most Valuable Player—Ruben Rivera, Oneonta; Manager of the Year—J.J. Cannon, St. Catharines.

BATTING

TEAM

Team	Avg.	G	AB	R	OR	H	TB	2B	3B	HR	RBI	SH	SF	HP	BB	Int. BB	SO	SB	CS	LOB
St. Catharines	.258	78	2588	357	279	668	957	96	20	51	296	28	20	22	247	10	560	89	67	534
Watertown	.258	78	2567	442	372	662	921	120	23	31	369	17	26	46	342	9	605	97	31	585
Niagara Falls	.253	78	2620	393	304	662	914	129	21	27	301	13	25	25	230	4	570	195	83	463
Utica	.252	76	2503	383	365	631	942	148	20	41	328	27	28	59	255	8	601	69	41	539
Auburn	.252	76	2555	351	423	643	889	111	21	31	300	13	21	31	257	5	542	62	31	547
Pittsfield	.251	75	2434	322	316	610	804	98	18	20	271	27	19	26	236	9	570	89	58	511
Welland	.250	77	2565	349	381	640	902	112	21	36	303	14	15	50	200	2	562	63	39	513
Erie	.247	77	2670	379	379	660	975	105	18	58	325	9	23	48	260	8	505	86	52	566
Geneva	.246	77	2519	397	383	620	874	116	12	38	320	37	18	55	259	7	567	130	76	496
Oneonta	.244	76	2510	361	364	612	907	89	43	40	302	21	22	33	285	8	554	61	44	536
Elmira	.243	75	2489	351	372	606	863	112	8	43	299	26	22	40	310	10	514	50	33	582
Glens Falls	.242	77	2562	312	387	621	821	117	13	19	266	42	18	26	266	4	518	84	52	562
Batavia	.239	77	2566	296	319	614	849	122	28	19	235	27	19	41	229	9	541	82	43	555
Jamestown	.237	77	2510	337	386	596	941	114	36	53	286	11	18	19	269	11	657	52	33	501

INDIVIDUAL

(Leading qualifiers for batting championship—211 or more plate appearances)

*Bats lefthanded.   †Switch-hitter.

Player, Team	Avg.	G	AB	R	H	TB	2B	3B	HR	RBI	SH	SF	HP	BB	Int. BB	SO	SB	CS
Danapilis, Eric, Niagara Falls	.341	65	208	35	71	91	9	1	3	28	0	1	6	33	0	36	8	4
O'Donnell, T.J., Utica	.329	68	255	47	84	120	22	1	4	33	3	1	9	18	1	24	5	5
Shook, Wes, Erie	.321	68	268	48	86	153	12	2	17	52	0	2	8	18	1	43	1	2
Wiseley, Mike, Niagara Falls*	.321	73	287	46	92	113	19	1	0	28	4	6	3	8	3	35	27	8
Allensworth, Jermaine, Welland	.308	67	263	44	81	108	16	4	1	32	2	1	12	24	0	38	18	3
Thomas, Greg, Watertown*	.307	73	277	48	85	142	20	5	9	63	0	1	2	27	3	47	3	4
McMillon, Bill, Elmira*	.305	57	226	38	69	105	14	2	6	35	0	0	4	31	4	43	5	4

Player, Team	Avg.	G	AB	R	H	TB	2B	3B	HR	RBI	SH	SF	HP	BB	Int. BB	SO	SB	CS
Collier, Louis, Welland	.303	50	201	35	61	74	6	2	1	19	1	1	5	12	0	31	8	7
Rodriguez, Noel, Auburn	.300	69	273	41	82	120	12	4	6	54	0	7	3	12	0	52	0	2
Sefcik, Kevin, Batavia	.299	74	281	49	84	122	24	4	2	28	7	5	3	27	2	22	20	6

Departmental leaders: G—Raleigh, 77; AB—Stewart, 301; R—Prieto, Stewart, 53; H—Wiseley, 92; TB—Shook, 153; 2B—Dowler, 26; 3B—Forkner, 9; HR—Shook, 17; RBI—Thomas, 63; SH—Garcia, 10; SF—Rodriguez, 7; HP—Kendall, 16; BB—Neal, 55; IBB—Several players tied with 4; SO—Raleigh, 99; SB—Barker, 37; CS—Biernat, 15.

(All players—listed alphabetically)

Player, Team	Avg.	G	AB	R	H	TB	2B	3B	HR	RBI	SH	SF	HP	BB	Int. BB	SO	SB	CS
Agbayni, Benny, Pittsfield	.251	51	167	26	42	60	6	3	2	22	0	0	0	20	0	43	7	2
Aguado, Victor, Utica	.208	9	24	3	5	7	2	0	0	1	1	0	0	1	0	5	0	2
Aldridge, Steve, Oneonta*	.313	34	112	21	35	42	5	1	0	12	0	1	2	12	0	18	2	2
Allensworth, Jermaine, Welland	.308	67	263	44	81	108	16	4	1	32	2	1	12	24	0	38	18	3
Almond, Greg, Glens Falls	.255	68	239	33	61	86	17	1	2	30	1	1	2	31	1	47	4	5
Alongi, Douglas, Geneva*	.275	60	182	29	50	63	6	2	1	22	2	0	1	33	1	32	17	9
Angeli, Douglas, Utica*	.218	75	252	20	55	68	7	3	0	15	7	1	1	18	0	33	5	6
Baez, Diogenes, Utica*	.272	50	151	30	41	58	9	1	2	20	1	0	1	13	2	20	5	4
Bando, Sal, Glens Falls*	.188	27	69	4	13	18	5	0	0	7	0	1	3	7	0	24	0	0
Barker, Glen, Niagara Falls	.217	72	253	49	55	89	11	4	5	23	2	3	4	24	0	71	37	12
Basey, Marsalis, Auburn	.232	39	142	20	33	42	6	0	1	8	2	2	1	10	0	15	6	4
Batista, Juan, Jamestown	.239	75	280	45	67	110	10	3	9	32	0	2	6	21	0	97	4	6
Bell, Brent, Batavia	.240	41	154	14	37	49	6	3	0	15	0	0	2	13	2	37	3	0
Berblinger, Jeff, Glens Falls	.312	38	138	26	43	58	9	0	2	21	1	3	3	11	0	14	9	4
Berg, Dave, Elmira	.263	75	281	37	74	101	13	1	4	28	4	3	8	34	1	37	7	4
Bierek, Kurt, Oneonta*	.234	70	274	36	64	97	6	6	5	37	1	1	3	19	2	49	4	4
Biernat, Joe, Geneva*	.287	69	247	44	71	95	8	2	4	26	7	1	2	28	0	40	23	15
Bonifazio, Anthony, Utica	.207	22	82	10	17	20	0	0	1	10	0	1	2	2	0	24	1	2
Bonneau, Britton, Geneva†	.208	9	24	5	5	7	2	0	0	5	1	2	1	2	0	7	2	1
Booker, Kevin, Geneva	.255	52	157	28	40	59	8	1	3	17	2	0	4	10	1	52	11	4
Borrero, Richie, Utica	.158	44	120	10	19	27	2	0	2	14	1	3	1	11	0	39	3	1
Borzello, Mike, Glens Falls	.111	13	18	1	2	2	0	0	0	0	0	0	1	3	0	7	0	0
Brainard, Matthew, Batavia	.212	63	226	23	48	70	13	3	1	16	2	1	2	22	0	51	7	5
Broome, Corey, Niagara Falls*	.219	47	137	17	30	42	4	1	2	20	0	2	0	6	0	36	6	3
Brown, Ron, Elmira	.284	75	285	52	81	132	22	1	9	54	1	3	2	37	2	60	4	2
Brown, Shawn, Niagara Falls	.291	71	247	37	72	86	6	4	0	21	0	3	1	16	0	40	29	6
Cabreja, Alexis, Erie	.226	46	159	23	36	52	9	2	1	27	0	1	1	9	0	36	5	2
Cabrera, Alex, Geneva	.246	53	167	29	41	61	5	0	5	27	0	1	5	9	0	49	4	5
Callan, Brett, Auburn	.264	42	129	16	34	45	6	1	1	15	0	0	1	25	0	35	8	0
Campos, Jesus, Jamestown	.242	70	285	43	69	90	6	6	1	22	0	2	2	18	0	39	9	9
Cannaday, Aaron, Welland	.221	47	163	23	36	62	8	0	6	33	0	0	2	24	0	66	2	1
Cawhorn, Gerad, Watertown	.254	66	232	28	59	75	9	2	1	29	0	4	6	26	0	51	3	4
Cedeno, Eddie, Auburn	.287	39	150	27	43	62	8	1	3	16	0	0	2	4	0	36	2	2
Chapman, Eric, Watertown	.233	64	215	28	50	72	4	3	4	24	2	0	1	21	0	62	14	4
Childers, Terry, Pittsfield	.121	21	66	4	8	10	2	0	0	2	1	1	0	4	0	24	0	0
Clark, Brian, Erie*	.249	65	233	33	58	88	11	2	5	26	2	3	5	24	0	47	11	4
Collier, Daniel, Utica	.217	67	226	39	49	107	11	1	15	48	0	2	7	29	1	95	4	0
Collier, Louis, Welland	.303	50	201	35	61	74	6	2	1	19	1	1	5	12	0	31	8	7
Collum, Gary, Pittsfield	.275	54	211	32	58	67	9	0	0	17	2	1	0	9	2	33	15	4
Conant, Scott, Niagara Falls	.000	3	5	0	0	0	0	0	0	0	0	0	0	0	0	2	0	1
Cossins, Tim, Erie	.400	4	10	1	4	5	1	0	0	3	0	0	0	2	0	0	0	1
Crispin, Carlos, Auburn†	.188	32	85	10	16	17	1	0	0	8	0	0	0	10	0	21	1	2
Cromer, Brandon, St. Catharines*	.230	75	278	29	64	92	9	2	5	20	3	1	1	21	2	64	2	4
Cumberbatch, Abdiel, Oneonta†	.289	45	142	30	41	56	3	6	0	18	2	3	0	33	0	28	20	5
Danapilis, Eric, Niagara Falls	.341	65	208	35	71	91	9	1	3	28	0	1	6	33	0	36	8	4
Dean, Mark, Glens Falls†	.231	52	156	21	36	41	3	1	0	10	7	3	3	16	0	31	7	6
Deares, Greg, Glens Falls*	.248	69	250	28	62	80	12	0	2	31	5	1	1	25	0	42	6	4
Debrand, Juan, Utica	.500	4	2	1	1	1	0	0	0	1	1	0	0	0	0	0	0	0
Debrand, Rafael, St. Catharines*	.218	66	229	43	50	57	7	0	0	19	8	3	1	35	0	41	9	12
de la Cruz, Lorenzo, St. Catharines	.000	6	16	2	0	0	0	0	0	0	1	0	1	0	0	5	0	0
DeJesus, Malvin, Niagara Falls	.254	54	142	26	36	49	7	3	0	15	1	1	1	19	0	29	20	10
DePastino, Joe, Utica	.253	62	221	28	56	73	9	1	2	32	1	5	4	16	0	51	3	2
DeSimone, Raymond, Erie*	.241	65	249	35	60	81	6	6	1	19	0	2	0	23	3	41	18	6
Diaz, Cesar, Pittsfield	.188	14	48	6	9	10	1	0	0	8	0	0	2	3	0	11	4	0
Dickerson, Robert, Niagara Falls*	.228	56	171	29	39	62	8	3	3	23	0	0	0	15	0	44	14	4
Dixon, Tyrone, Niagara Falls	.272	50	147	24	40	48	4	2	0	13	2	0	2	18	0	25	16	8
Dominow, Eric, Erie*	.216	62	204	23	44	58	6	1	2	17	1	1	2	18	0	34	4	1
Dowler, Demetrius, Geneva	.271	75	291	49	79	104	26	2	5	38	2	2	8	24	0	54	21	11
Duross, Gabe, Geneva*	.276	62	225	35	62	99	15	2	6	41	2	0	3	14	9	14	9	5
Durso, Joe, St. Catharines	.324	43	145	20	47	79	6	1	8	30	0	2	3	14	1	21	1	1
Estrada, Osmani, Erie	.267	60	225	24	60	83	11	0	4	22	1	2	6	17	1	26	1	7
Ford, Eric, Utica	.194	33	103	14	20	34	9	1	1	11	0	0	2	6	0	28	1	1
Forkner, Timothy, Auburn*	.285	72	267	32	76	108	14	9	0	39	1	1	3	38	0	29	3	3
Foster, Jeff, Jamestown*	.231	28	91	15	21	32	1	2	2	13	0	1	0	10	1	30	1	1
Froschauer, Trevor, Auburn	.190	45	137	22	26	61	3	1	10	20	0	1	4	27	0	54	0	0
Fuller, Aaron, Utica†	.250	53	176	31	44	50	3	0	1	17	5	3	4	20	0	26	24	4
Galvez, Ricardo, Geneva	.333	2	3	1	1	1	0	0	0	0	0	0	0	0	0	2	0	0
Garcia, Osmel, Glens Falls	.214	57	168	27	36	42	6	0	0	13	10	0	1	7	0	38	7	4
Garrett, Bryan, Watertown†	.221	69	217	40	48	58	4	3	0	24	5	1	2	24	0	62	17	4
George, Curtis, Watertown	.200	2	5	1	1	1	0	0	0	0	0	0	0	0	0	2	1	0
Gibson, Michael, Geneva	.177	30	62	11	11	12	1	0	0	3	2	0	0	14	0	16	3	2
Gipner, Marcus, Oneonta†	.000	3	3	0	0	0	0	0	0	0	0	0	0	0	0	2	0	0
Goldberg, Lonnie, Erie	.254	72	283	39	72	88	11	1	1	37	3	3	1	32	0	40	22	10
Gosselin, Patrick, Welland	.284	33	109	21	31	40	7	1	0	10	1	1	3	12	0	19	1	2
Grapenthien, Dan, Auburn	.237	47	173	16	41	48	7	0	0	20	0	4	4	16	0	54	0	2
Gross, William, Elmira	.231	4	13	1	3	3	0	0	0	0	1	0	1	0	0	5	0	0
Grubb, Chris, Jamestown†	.220	53	132	14	29	40	4	2	1	14	1	1	0	24	0	22	6	0
Guerrero, Rafael, Pittsfield	.269	8	26	8	7	8	1	0	0	1	0	0	0	2	0	5	1	1
Gyselman, Jeffrey, Batavia	.192	36	120	7	23	32	5	2	0	8	3	1	2	8	0	33	1	1
Haag, Jeffrey, Watertown*	.200	5	10	1	2	2	0	0	0	1	0	0	1	2	0	1	0	0
Haar, Rich, Jamestown	.351	21	57	10	20	29	5	2	0	6	1	1	1	10	1	13	3	0
Haggas, Josh, Pittsfield	.182	45	143	11	26	33	5	1	0	20	1	1	2	11	0	33	0	1

Player, Team	Avg.	G	AB	R	H	TB	2B	3B	HR	RBI	SH	SF	HP	BB	Int. BB	SO	SB	CS
Hansen, Elston, Oneonta	.272	67	239	45	65	108	16	3	7	32	0	3	5	35	1	46	2	3
Harrell, Matt, Jamestown	.200	25	55	9	11	14	3	0	0	6	0	0	0	7	0	13	0	0
Harris, Eric, Pittsfield	.222	52	185	18	41	69	7	0	7	35	1	1	0	16	0	68	2	3
Harris, G.G., Welland	.295	31	112	16	33	49	6	2	2	21	0	2	2	8	0	21	2	0
Hayes, Emanuel, St. Catharines	.136	27	66	5	9	10	1	0	0	2	1	0	1	13	0	30	4	2
Hayward, Joe, Utica*	.243	36	74	7	18	23	5	0	0	2	0	0	1	21	0	18	1	0
Hearn, Sean, St. Catharines*	.299	44	174	33	52	85	7	1	8	45	1	1	2	7	0	45	13	2
Held, Daniel, Batavia	.205	45	151	18	31	50	8	1	3	16	1	2	6	16	0	40	2	3
Henley, Robert, Jamestown	.257	60	206	25	53	92	10	4	7	29	1	1	1	20	1	60	0	1
Henry, Antoine, Glens Falls	.296	51	186	38	55	72	15	1	0	7	2	0	1	29	1	31	18	5
Henson, Joe, Glens Falls*	.191	18	47	4	9	10	1	0	0	2	1	0	0	8	0	8	2	0
Hernandez, Rafael, Pittsfield	.220	49	159	17	35	43	8	0	0	11	5	2	4	7	1	39	4	1
Hernandez, Ramon, Batavia	.229	10	35	3	8	9	1	0	0	4	0	0	0	0	0	7	1	0
Hill, Michael, Erie*	.251	63	203	30	51	75	10	1	4	28	0	3	3	31	3	49	3	2
Hodson, Blair, Watertown*	.288	60	191	34	55	74	13	0	2	27	1	1	6	19	0	33	4	1
Holland, Rod, Watertown*	.051	13	39	3	2	2	0	0	0	1	0	0	1	0	0	12	0	0
House, Mitch, Welland	.247	62	227	39	56	100	13	2	9	41	0	1	6	27	1	48	2	2
Hunt, Riegal, Welland*	.154	8	26	3	4	7	0	0	1	2	0	0	1	2	0	12	0	0
Jackson, Kuron, Geneva	.263	50	133	25	35	52	6	1	3	17	4	3	3	11	0	22	7	6
Johnson, J.J., Utica	.288	43	170	33	49	80	17	4	2	27	2	3	7	9	1	34	5	3
Johnston, Tom, Welland	.156	10	32	0	5	5	0	0	0	1	0	0	0	1	0	10	0	0
Jones, Donny, Utica	.200	21	65	6	13	18	2	0	1	4	2	1	2	1	0	18	0	2
Jones, Kenneth, Geneva	.240	13	25	4	6	8	2	0	0	1	0	0	0	2	0	11	0	1
Josepher, Rick, Oneonta	.000	4	1	0	0	0	0	0	0	0	0	0	0	2	0	0	0	0
Jumonville, Joe, Glens Falls	.219	60	224	19	49	70	12	0	3	22	1	2	0	4	0	28	1	1
Kelley, Erskine, Geneva	.264	42	159	21	42	68	7	2	5	20	0	1	2	7	0	41	3	2
Kendall, Jeremy, Batavia	.280	73	275	48	77	105	17	4	1	23	3	2	16	27	1	60	31	13
Kester, Timothy, Auburn	.000	15	2	0	0	0	0	0	0	0	0	0	0	0	0	2	0	0
Kingston, Mark, Geneva†	.222	3	9	0	2	2	0	0	0	1	0	0	0	0	0	3	0	0
Kinnon, Duane, Niagara Falls*	.253	66	229	20	58	85	14	2	3	32	0	4	2	12	0	40	2	10
Klaas, Klint, Auburn	.204	35	113	12	23	36	4	0	3	18	2	2	0	19	0	41	1	2
Koeyers, Ramsey, Jamestown	.223	65	233	25	52	77	9	2	4	29	0	2	2	10	0	69	1	1
Kulle, Robert, Watertown	.211	45	128	18	27	47	6	1	4	19	0	3	2	12	0	48	2	1
Kulpa, Steven, Geneva	.230	56	165	18	38	51	10	0	1	17	1	2	0	18	4	45	4	3
LaChance, Vince, Jamestown*	.288	39	139	16	40	68	9	2	5	18	2	0	0	10	2	32	4	3
Ledee, Ricky, Oneonta	.255	52	192	32	49	92	7	6	8	20	1	1	2	25	0	46	7	5
Lefebvre, Ryan, Watertown*	.150	6	20	1	3	3	0	0	0	2	1	0	1	0	0	2	0	1
Lewis, Brian, Oneonta*	.208	30	72	11	15	22	2	1	1	4	0	0	1	11	0	17	1	2
Lewis, Kevin, Pittsfield	.203	54	187	22	38	61	8	0	5	22	0	2	0	21	1	50	1	1
Lewis, Robert, Watertown	.268	59	198	30	53	69	10	0	2	29	2	4	2	30	0	38	4	1
Llanos, Victor, Glens Falls	.258	46	132	18	34	48	8	3	0	19	1	0	1	9	1	31	1	3
Lombardi, John, St. Catharines	.333	4	12	1	4	7	0	0	1	4	0	0	1	0	0	3	0	0
Lugo, Arquimedes, Auburn	.000	22	1	0	0	0	0	0	0	0	0	0	0	0	0	1	0	0
Luna, Richard, Welland	.220	33	91	9	20	25	1	2	0	6	1	1	1	12	0	16	5	3
Lyman, Jason, Watertown	.213	31	80	14	17	24	3	2	0	7	0	0	4	14	0	25	2	1
Madden, Joseph, Batavia	.235	62	230	24	54	72	6	3	2	27	1	3	0	17	0	55	3	2
Maize, Dave, Pittsfield†	.400	16	25	2	10	10	0	0	0	2	0	0	1	3	0	3	2	1
Marabella, Tony, Jamestown	.243	52	185	25	45	78	13	1	6	24	0	1	1	16	3	32	1	0
Marine, Del, Niagara Falls	.264	55	182	29	48	81	12	0	7	32	0	1	3	20	0	48	5	5
Marrero, Kenny, Niagara Falls	.221	31	77	9	17	27	7	0	1	11	0	1	1	0	0	17	0	0
Marte, Pedro, Watertown†	.263	43	133	41	35	36	1	0	0	11	2	3	0	34	0	38	23	5
Martinez, Dalvis, Niagara Falls	.220	31	100	8	22	26	4	0	0	12	0	0	0	9	1	28	1	1
Martinez, Matt, Elmira	.225	64	218	43	49	57	5	0	1	19	2	3	6	27	0	29	14	4
Matvey, Michael, Glens Falls	.289	70	239	37	69	99	11	5	3	42	6	1	4	29	1	43	7	4
Mayfield, Chris, Batavia	.095	8	21	3	2	2	0	0	0	1	0	0	1	5	0	7	1	1
Mazion, Rodney, Pittsfield	.266	46	184	25	49	58	5	2	0	18	7	1	1	10	0	39	16	6
McCabe, Brett, Geneva	.271	38	107	20	29	36	4	0	1	15	0	0	2	10	0	25	3	0
McDonald, Dan, Batavia	.238	35	122	16	29	38	6	0	1	5	0	2	2	17	0	22	1	3
McGinn, Shaun, Batavia	.000	3	6	0	0	0	0	0	0	0	0	0	0	1	0	1	0	0
McGinnis, Shane, Geneva	.318	13	44	9	14	15	1	0	0	3	0	0	0	7	0	12	0	0
McLamb, Brian, Oneonta†	.227	54	194	20	44	55	7	2	0	18	0	1	3	19	0	61	4	3
McMillon, Bill, Elmira*	.305	57	226	38	69	105	14	2	6	35	0	4	3	31	4	43	5	4
McMullen, Jon, Batavia*	.293	65	249	31	73	108	13	2	6	37	0	0	1	21	3	58	2	1
Melendez, Jorge, Erie	.128	14	47	6	6	9	0	0	1	5	0	1	0	8	0	11	0	0
Melhuse, Adam, St. Catharines†	.256	73	266	40	68	101	14	2	5	32	2	3	0	45	4	61	4	0
Mendez, Emilio, Geneva	.144	51	139	18	20	22	2	0	0	11	4	1	7	11	0	46	5	4
Mendez, Sergio, Welland	.248	32	121	12	30	36	4	1	0	10	0	0	4	0	0	28	0	1
Milligan, Ricky, Geneva	.228	53	123	18	28	47	7	3	2	12	0	1	2	20	0	47	4	4
Mitchell, John, Welland	.219	50	178	24	39	53	7	2	1	19	0	2	2	14	0	21	1	2
Moen, Rob, Elmira	.286	49	182	16	52	68	10	0	2	16	6	3	3	15	0	28	2	4
Montero, Danny, Geneva	.063	9	16	1	1	2	1	0	0	2	0	0	0	2	0	7	0	1
Moore, Andy, Utica	.130	7	23	2	3	6	1	1	0	2	0	0	0	2	0	10	0	0
Moore, Charlton, Batavia	.122	16	49	9	6	9	1	1	0	2	2	0	0	5	0	20	0	0
Morales, Francisco, Geneva	.195	45	123	12	24	34	4	0	2	20	0	2	1	15	0	41	1	0
Moreno, Jorge, Niagara Falls†	.188	55	101	16	19	23	4	0	0	7	0	0	1	14	0	36	4	6
Mota, Santo, Glens Falls†	.289	10	38	6	11	13	2	0	0	7	1	0	0	6	0	6	9	2
Moultrie, Patrick, St. Catharines*	.269	73	264	29	71	86	6	3	1	19	7	0	4	16	0	46	18	13
Mummau, Robert, St. Catharines	.241	75	257	35	62	86	9	3	3	21	2	0	5	23	1	44	7	12
Murphy, Neal, Batavia	.167	39	150	11	25	33	5	0	1	10	0	0	0	5	0	26	1	0
Navas, Silverio, Oneonta†	.270	55	189	21	51	60	3	0	2	15	7	2	2	14	0	30	1	3
Neal, Michael, Watertown	.291	67	234	47	68	101	15	3	4	43	2	3	6	55	4	45	7	1
O'Donnell, T.J., Utica	.329	68	255	47	84	120	22	1	4	33	3	1	9	18	1	24	5	5
Oram, Jon, Watertown	.189	29	74	11	14	19	2	0	1	5	0	1	1	5	0	21	0	1
Ordway, Kirk, Niagara Falls	.181	40	116	17	21	33	9	0	1	11	1	1	1	7	0	35	3	2
Ortiz, Nick, Utica	.269	63	197	31	53	75	10	1	2	26	1	2	6	19	0	56	4	1
Paez, Raul, Welland†	.236	39	148	10	35	44	3	0	2	14	0	1	2	10	0	25	1	0
Pagano, Scott, Niagara Falls†	.167	5	6	1	1	4	0	0	1	1	0	0	0	0	0	4	0	0
Patton, Gregory, Utica	.225	54	169	22	38	57	8	1	3	24	1	1	4	23	1	45	0	2
Pearson, Cory, Erie	.209	69	230	27	48	71	9	4	2	24	0	3	15	14	0	74	13	8
Peterson, Nate, Auburn*	.260	69	277	35	72	97	17	1	2	29	1	0	5	17	0	34	5	2
Petillo, Bruce, Batavia	.228	19	57	12	13	21	5	0	1	5	0	0	1	12	1	15	0	0
Petrulis, Paul, Pittsfield	.283	69	237	33	67	83	7	2	1	30	0	5	3	40	1	52	6	9
Pico, Brandon, Geneva*	.269	45	167	22	45	68	7	2	4	24	3	1	1	8	0	29	7	4
Prater, Andrew, Elmira	.199	45	156	11	31	47	7	0	3	15	3	0	3	17	0	30	1	4

Player, Team	Avg.	G	AB	R	H	TB	2B	3B	HR	RBI	SH	SF	HP	BB	Int. BB	SO	SB	CS
Prieto, Richard, Watertown†	.292	68	219	53	64	99	15	4	4	40	1	1	8	39	2	61	11	1
Purdy, Alan, Welland	.167	7	24	2	4	4	0	0	0	0	0	0	1	2	0	2	0	0
Pyle, John, Erie	.125	13	32	5	4	7	0	0	1	4	0	0	2	5	0	7	0	0
Quade, Scott, Jamestown	.140	47	121	6	17	25	0	4	0	4	3	1	0	20	0	31	1	1
Querecuto, Juan, St. Catharines	.274	57	223	29	61	99	8	3	8	39	0	2	2	10	1	47	0	4
Raleigh, Matt, Jamestown	.236	77	263	51	62	124	17	0	15	42	0	4	1	39	0	99	5	2
Ramirez, Angel, St. Catharines	.273	6	22	2	6	7	1	0	0	2	0	0	0	0	0	7	0	2
Reed, Patrick, Welland	.253	46	158	22	40	58	10	1	2	24	3	1	2	12	0	48	10	6
Renteria, David, Oneonta	.233	43	129	19	30	37	7	0	0	16	3	1	0	14	0	25	1	3
Ritz, Trey, Glens Falls*	.209	31	86	7	18	23	1	2	0	7	1	1	0	5	0	15	3	4
Rivera, Maximo, Welland†	.243	32	115	17	28	35	5	1	0	11	3	0	0	4	0	27	4	8
Rivera, Ruben, Oneonta	.276	55	199	45	55	113	7	6	13	47	1	3	5	32	1	66	12	5
Rodriguez, Noel, Auburn	.300	69	273	41	82	120	12	4	6	54	0	7	3	12	0	52	0	2
Roggendorf, Kristian, St. Catharines*	.296	58	179	19	53	83	8	2	6	21	0	3	1	20	0	46	2	1
Saffer, Jonathan, Jamestown*	.258	61	225	31	58	85	17	5	0	18	3	1	2	31	1	46	11	5
Sagmoen, Marc, Erie*	.304	6	23	6	7	10	1	1	0	2	0	1	1	3	0	7	0	0
Sanchez, Sergio, Elmira	.133	17	45	3	6	6	0	0	0	3	0	0	1	0	0	13	0	0
Santucci, Steven, Glens Falls	.254	68	209	21	53	75	5	1	5	23	2	0	2	27	0	58	9	7
Schmitz, Mike, Oneonta	.180	69	245	22	44	63	7	3	2	32	2	4	1	17	1	65	0	3
Schulz, Pat, Watertown	.198	24	86	14	17	23	6	0	0	9	0	1	2	13	0	16	4	2
Sefcik, Kevin, Batavia	.299	74	281	49	84	122	24	4	2	28	7	5	3	27	2	22	20	6
Seminoff, Rich, Elmira*	.211	67	218	34	46	87	8	0	11	40	0	1	5	35	1	72	3	0
Senkowitz, Mark, Utica	.285	42	137	25	39	59	8	3	2	23	0	1	5	14	1	28	2	3
Shook, Wes, Erie	.321	68	268	48	86	153	12	2	17	52	0	2	8	18	1	43	1	2
Sigler, Brad, Geneva*	.154	6	13	3	2	2	0	0	0	1	0	0	0	6	0	5	0	1
Sims, Mike, Elmira	.176	24	85	6	15	18	3	0	0	7	0	0	0	7	0	18	0	0
Sims, Wesley, Erie†	.239	74	284	38	68	97	8	0	7	22	0	0	1	31	0	49	2	5
Small, Andru, Elmira	.216	56	176	25	38	51	8	1	1	16	2	2	3	34	0	72	2	1
Smith, Sloan, Oneonta†	.198	34	116	14	23	33	5	1	1	10	3	1	6	15	0	33	3	2
Smith, Tad, Pittsfield*	.278	37	115	12	32	40	6	1	0	7	0	0	2	8	1	28	2	2
Snyder, Jared, Geneva	.209	51	148	15	31	44	7	0	2	22	5	1	10	16	0	29	5	1
Soliz, Steven, Watertown	.297	56	209	30	62	74	12	0	0	35	2	3	1	15	0	41	2	0
Sollecito, Gabriel, Niagara Falls†	.000	23	0	0	0	0	0	0	0	0	0	0	0	1	0	0	0	0
Southard, Scott, Elmira	.238	74	281	34	67	81	11	0	1	20	6	4	1	24	0	41	3	4
Stewart, Shannon, St. Catharines	.279	75	301	53	84	112	15	2	3	29	3	2	3	33	1	43	25	11
Stratton, John, Utica*	.249	53	173	22	43	65	14	1	2	19	2	3	3	17	1	44	2	2
Strickland, Erick, Elmira*	.259	59	212	30	55	84	11	3	4	34	1	2	1	35	2	32	8	4
Stutz, John, Glens Falls	.203	54	182	7	37	45	6	1	0	14	2	2	3	13	0	51	1	3
Sullivan, Charlie, Pittsfield*	.269	55	156	20	42	61	11	4	0	17	2	1	3	22	3	26	3	1
Taylor, Mike, Glens Falls*	.233	35	86	5	20	25	3	1	0	6	1	0	0	13	0	7	0	1
Terrell, Matt, Pittsfield	.270	65	226	37	61	80	9	2	2	25	3	1	4	37	0	59	17	3
Thomas, Greg, Watertown*	.307	73	277	48	85	142	20	5	9	63	0	1	2	27	3	47	3	4
Thompson, Angelo, Jamestown	.223	66	215	20	48	68	10	2	2	28	0	2	3	28	2	70	5	3
Thompson, Mike, Batavia	.239	30	92	11	22	31	4	1	1	11	3	0	2	11	0	36	1	1
Torres, Jaime, Oneonta	.260	28	104	13	27	36	6	0	1	8	0	0	1	9	0	9	2	0
Tosone, Joe, Jamestown	.174	10	23	2	4	9	0	1	1	0	0	0	1	5	0	4	1	1
Trimble, Robin, Oneonta*	.219	43	160	13	35	40	3	1	0	12	1	1	1	9	2	36	0	2
Triplett, Al, Erie	.215	37	93	16	20	28	2	0	2	14	1	1	3	14	0	12	5	3
Turnbull, Tony, Elmira	.103	9	29	3	3	3	0	0	0	2	0	0	0	2	0	10	0	0
Unrat, Christopher, Erie*	.290	36	124	25	36	70	5	1	8	22	0	0	0	11	0	27	1	1
Vaught, Craig, St. Catharines	.237	47	156	17	37	53	5	1	3	13	0	1	0	7	0	57	4	3
Velandia, Jorge, Niagara Falls	.193	72	212	30	41	55	11	0	1	22	3	2	0	19	0	48	22	4
Verduzco, Steven, Auburn	.222	64	239	30	53	65	7	1	1	19	5	0	3	19	1	48	8	1
Vindivich, John, Auburn*	.255	66	220	36	56	74	12	0	2	19	0	3	2	22	2	58	13	3
Walker, John, Utica*	.298	37	94	14	28	35	5	1	0	12	2	2	1	15	0	13	6	4
Walker, Shon, Welland*	.195	35	118	15	23	34	3	1	2	9	0	0	0	14	0	52	4	0
Warner, Randy, Pittsfield	.215	19	65	10	14	25	3	1	2	8	1	0	0	4	0	21	1	1
White, Chad, Auburn†	.291	66	247	47	72	94	12	2	2	29	2	1	1	34	2	33	15	8
Wieczorek, Theod, Auburn	.160	34	100	7	16	20	2	1	0	6	3	0	0	3	0	29	0	0
Wiegandt, Bryan, Batavia	.281	27	96	6	27	30	1	1	0	10	0	2	2	7	0	18	2	1
Williams, Mark, Glens Falls	.137	38	95	10	13	14	1	0	0	5	0	3	1	23	0	37	0	0
Williamson, Joel, Welland	.207	23	82	9	17	23	3	0	1	9	0	1	2	3	0	16	1	0
Wilson, Preston, Pittsfield	.552	8	29	6	16	26	5	1	1	12	0	1	1	7	0	7	1	1
Wiltz, Stan, Welland	.255	51	184	24	47	64	11	0	2	14	3	2	4	5	1	25	1	1
Wiseley, Mike, Niagara Falls*	.321	73	287	46	92	113	19	1	0	28	4	6	3	35	2	35	27	8
Woodall, Kevin, Erie	.000	3	3	0	0	0	0	0	0	1	0	0	0	2	0	0	0	0
Wuerch, Jason, Oneonta*	.103	13	39	4	4	4	0	0	0	2	0	1	0	7	0	10	1	2
Yaroshuk, Ernie, Oneonta*	.300	29	100	15	30	49	3	5	2	18	0	1	1	12	1	13	1	0
Young, James, Geneva†	.181	43	72	19	13	17	1	0	1	9	0	2	4	17	0	26	8	3
Yselonia, John, Welland*	.148	16	54	3	8	13	2	0	1	8	0	0	2	8	0	16	0	1
Zuniga, David, Pittsfield	.268	61	205	33	55	60	3	1	0	14	4	0	6	17	0	29	7	2

The following pitchers, listed alphabetically by club, with games in parentheses, had no plate appearances, primarily through use of designated hitters:

AUBURN—Czanstkowski, Tom (10); Dault, Don (20); Diorio, Mike (15); Grzanich, Mike (16); Hartnett, Bill (12); Humphrey, Rich (29); Rhine, Kendall (16); Schulte, Troy (8); Smith, Kevin (13); Spring, Joshua (26); Wagner, Bill (7).

BATAVIA—Agostinelli, Pete (24); Barstad, Scott (8); Censale, Silvio (9); Costa, Tim (10); Eggleston, Scott (15); Fiore, Tony (16); Franek, Tom (15); Genke, Mike (18); Gomes, Wayne (5); Irwin, Tom (26); Kirkland, Kris (11); Metheney, Nelson (7); Pugh, Tim (22); Swan, Tyrone (15); Wood, Mike (22).

ELMIRA—Bowen, Mitch (18); Chergey, Dan (15); Dominguez, Johnny (6); Filbeck, Ryan (13); Gomez, Phil (12); Larkin, Andy (14); Minyard, Sam (3); Mix, Greg (17); Nunez, Clemente (14); Thornton, Paul (16); Valdes, Marc (3); VanZandt, Jon (17); Walania, Alan (22); Ward, Bryan (14).

ERIE—Davis, Jeff (27); Franklin, Jim (17); Gerhart, Bert (15); Hartmann, Pete (15); Kell, Bob (18); Kunz, Devin (5); Lesch, Paul (19); Moody, Eric (17); Morvay, Joe (17); O'Brien, Mark (20); Seip, Rodney (16); Smith, Chris (3); Tipton, Shawn (10); Wozney, Kevin (7).

GENEVA—Ball, Tom (15); Bobbitt, Greg (6); Donnelly, Brendan (21); Dreyer, Darren (3); Farrow, Jim (15); Hill, Shawn (34); Hillman, Greg (14); Hogan, Sean (17); Jenkins, Mike (20); Kendrick, Scott (1); Locey, Tony (29); Ratliff, Jon (3); Twiggs, Greg (14); Walker, Wade (13); Woodall, Brent (23).

GLENS FALLS—Alexander, Eric (15); Arrandale, Matt (12); Benes, Alan (7); Britt, Ken (35); Cain, Sheldon (24); Croushore, Rich (31); Grasser, Craig (36); Jolley, Mike (2); Kehrli, Ed (16); Larson, Joe (18); Magnelli, Tony (29); Ottmers, Marc (9); Pontes, Dan (20); Redovian, Dan (8); Windham, Mike (11).

JAMESTOWN—Alfonseca, Tony (15); Brown, Nathan (2); Bullock, Joshua (23); DaSilva, Fernando (15); Harrison, Bob (24); Knieper, Aaron (15); Leon, Mike (20); Pacheco, Alex (6); Phelps, Tom (16); Respondek, Mark (18); Schneider, Tom (14); Stutts, Dennis (26); Weber, Neil (16).

NIAGARA FALLS—Arguto, Sam (7); Gaillard, Ed (3); Goldsmith, Gary (21); Hunt, Bill (14); Jackson, Rod (15); Magrini, Paul (2); McFarland, Toby (25); Moehler, Brian (12); Neese, Joshua (21); Nowak, Steve (2); Reincke, Corey (20); Richardson, Mike (24); Rodriguez, Dave (25); Rosengren, John (15); Salazar, Mike (15); Santos, Henry (7); Smith, Cameron (2).

ONEONTA—Alazaus, Shawn (28); Cumberland, Chris (16); Drumheller, Albert (16); Gordon, Mike (3); Heberling, Keith (4); Jerzembeck, Mike (14); Kozeniewski, Blaise (24); Lankford, Frank (16); Leshnock, Donnie (11); Musselwhite, Jim (5); Rathbun, Jason (7); Resz, Greg (24); Shelby, Tony (3); Standish, Scott (20); Thomforde, Jim (15); Wharton, Joe (13); Whitworth, Clint (10).

PITTSFIELD—Bellman, Bill (4); Cosman, Jeff (14); Engle, Tom (15); Grennan, Steve (21); Isringhausen, Jason (15); Jones, Scott (12); Kenny, Sean (7); Ludwick, Eric (10); McDill, Allen (21); Newell, Brandon (16); Shaffer, Travis (7); Swanson, Dave (15); Tam, Jeff (21); Welch, Mike (17).

ST. CATHARINES—Adkins, Tim (16); Beltran, Alonso (15); Brown, Chad (18); Cheek, Jeff (18); Hurtado, Ed (15); Maldonado, Jason (13); Meiners, Doug (15); Meinershagen, Adam (13); Muir, Harry (21); Pearlman, Dave (18); Steinert, Bob (8); Torres, Dilson (17).

UTICA—Berryman, Bob (21); Bogott, Kurt (13); Bush, Craig (16); Cormier, Eric (18); Johnson, Jeff (19); Johnston, Dan (4); Lawrence, Randy (14); McKinley, Leif (21); Orellano, Rafael (12); Perez, Hilario (16); Peterson, Dean (16); Renfroe, Chad (16); Senior, Shawn (13); Telgheder, Jim (2); Tyrrell, Jim (28).

WATERTOWN—Augustine, Bob (19); Delamaza, Roland (15); Dempsey, Wes (20); Diaz, German (11); Driskill, Travis (21); Garza, Roberto (11); Hanson, Kris (9); Key, Denny (3); Kirkreit, Daron (7); Kline, Steve (13); Neilson, Mike (10); Plumlee, Chris (23); Runion, Tony (4); Sexton, Jeff (17); Sides, Craig (3); Sinner, Greg (1); Smith, Fred (2); Whitten, Chuck (14); Williams, Greg (1).

WELLAND—Abramavicius, Jason (14); Beck, Brian (22); Chamberlain, Matt (8); Fairfax, Ken (11); Garcia, Ramon (2); Isom, Jeff (22); Johnson, Jason (6); Lutt, Jeff (26); Mattson, Craig (18); Morel, Ramon (16); Nuttle, Jamie (21); Pelka, Brian (15); Perez, Gil (14); Peters, Chris (16); Phillips, Jason (14); Pickich, Jeff (21); Ryan, Matt (16).

GRAND SLAMS—Collier, 2; Allensworth, Blair, Hearn, J.J. Johnson, Klaas, Lachance, Marrero, Reed, Rivera, Seminoff, Shook, 1 each.

AWARDED FIRST BASE ON CATCHER'S INTERFERENCE—M. Martinez 2 (Froschauer, Trimble); Baez (Trimble); Batista (Melendez); Bell (Shook); Bierek (Diaz); Cabrera (M. Sims); Garrett (Snyder); Goldberg (Stratton); Petrulis (Stratton); Raleigh (Borrero); Snyder (Prater).

PITCHING

TEAM

Team	ERA	G	CG	ShO	Sv.	IP	H	R	ER	HR	HB	BB	Int. BB	SO	WP	Bk.
St. Catharines	2.87	78	7	13	21	680.0	525	279	217	40	22	235	0	609	30	7
Niagara Falls	3.05	78	6	7	25	695.1	574	304	236	23	46	342	17	626	66	12
Batavia	3.24	77	4	6	18	674.2	624	319	243	23	27	256	4	528	60	12
Pittsfield	3.36	75	9	5	21	638.0	548	316	238	26	31	247	3	562	53	11
Watertown	3.71	78	6	4	26	667.1	662	372	275	46	30	230	10	560	59	10
Erie	3.74	77	5	2	17	686.2	619	379	285	56	45	220	8	613	31	13
Geneva	3.78	77	3	3	20	671.0	636	383	282	43	37	318	10	570	85	25
Oneonta	3.83	77	2	5	21	658.1	658	364	280	28	30	276	7	558	49	11
Welland	3.98	77	2	3	21	658.0	624	381	291	35	36	269	2	564	80	21
Utica	3.99	76	2	5	20	649.0	644	365	288	35	31	268	6	530	56	11
Elmira	4.00	75	6	2	15	645.1	685	372	287	36	60	216	7	545	60	14
Jamestown	4.02	77	5	3	17	656.2	684	386	293	36	39	231	5	481	45	7
Glens Falls	4.15	77	1	10	21	676.1	722	387	312	44	34	246	10	547	52	8
Auburn	4.25	76	11	3	10	650.2	640	423	307	36	53	291	15	573	77	10

INDIVIDUAL

(Leading qualifiers for earned-run average leadership—62 or more innings)

*Throws lefthanded.

Pitcher, Team	W	L	Pct.	ERA	G	GS	CG	GF	ShO	Sv.	IP	H	R	ER	HR	HB	BB	Int. BB	SO	WP
Meinershagen, St. Catharines	8	1	.889	1.88	13	13	1	0	1	0	86.0	53	19	18	2	3	26	0	87	1
Kester, Auburn	4	6	.400	2.06	15	13	4	1	1	0	96.1	78	40	22	2	10	19	1	83	5
Thornton, Elmira	3	5	.375	2.26	16	7	1	7	0	2	63.2	51	29	16	2	1	27	0	59	1
Beltran, St. Catharines	11	2	.846	2.36	15	15	1	0	1	0	99.0	63	36	26	4	6	28	0	101	2
Rosengren, Niagara Falls*	7	3	.700	2.41	15	15	0	0	0	0	82.0	52	32	22	3	6	38	0	91	6
Whitten, Watertown*	6	3	.667	2.42	14	14	0	0	0	0	81.2	75	28	22	8	3	18	0	81	5
Hurtado, St. Catharines	10	2	.833	2.50	15	15	3	0	1	0	101.0	69	34	28	6	4	34	0	87	3
DeLaMaza, Watertown	10	3	.769	2.52	15	15	1	0	0	0	100.0	90	39	28	8	3	14	0	81	0
Neese, Niagara Falls	12	3	.800	2.54	21	8	0	2	0	0	71.0	44	24	20	2	3	34	1	73	2
Jerzembeck, Oneonta	8	4	.667	2.68	14	14	0	0	0	0	77.1	70	25	23	1	3	26	0	76	2

Departmental leaders: G—Grasser, 36; W—Neese, 12; L—Five pitchers tied with 8; Pct.—Meinershagen, .889; GS—Fiore, Morel, Seip, Weber, 16; CG—Grzanich, Kester, Larkin, 4; GF—Grasser, 36; ShO—Several pitchers tied with 1; Sv.—Grasser, 19; IP—Cormier, 104.2; H—Cumberland, 109; R—Grzanich, 63; ER—Rhine, 52; HR—Grzanich, 11; HB—Larkin, 12; BB—Rhine, 48; IBB—Richardson, 7; SO—Isringhausen, 104; WP—Rhine, 21.

(All pitchers—listed alphabetically)

Pitcher, Team	W	L	Pct.	ERA	G	GS	CG	GF	ShO	Sv.	IP	H	R	ER	HR	HB	BB	Int. BB	SO	WP
Abramavicius, Welland*	2	4	.333	3.12	14	7	1	6	1	1	52.0	44	22	18	4	2	10	0	43	2
Adkins, St. Catharines*	5	6	.455	3.54	16	15	1	0	1	0	96.2	80	43	38	5	2	45	0	91	5
Agostinelli, Batavia*	3	2	.600	2.59	24	1	1	13	1	4	41.2	31	12	12	1	1	13	0	36	2
Alazaus, Oneonta*	2	1	.667	0.98	28	0	0	18	0	6	36.2	23	5	4	1	0	21	1	37	2
Alexander, Glens Falls*	5	5	.500	3.21	15	15	1	0	1	0	87.0	86	35	31	4	6	32	0	55	5
Alfonseca, Jamestown	2	2	.500	6.15	15	4	0	3	0	1	33.2	31	26	23	3	3	22	1	29	4
Arguto, Niagara Falls	0	0	.000	0.00	7	0	0	7	0	6	8.0	1	0	0	0	0	4	0	14	1
Arrandale, Glens Falls	3	4	.429	4.59	12	12	0	0	0	0	68.2	77	42	35	6	2	14	0	53	4
Augustine, Watertown	0	1	.000	6.43	19	0	0	5	0	1	28.0	26	25	20	2	1	29	1	29	12
Ball, Geneva*	5	2	.714	4.55	15	11	0	0	0	0	61.1	85	48	31	7	5	23	0	43	13
Barstad, Batavia	0	2	.000	5.02	8	0	0	3	0	0	14.1	14	8	8	1	1	15	0	9	2
Beck, Welland*	3	1	.750	4.08	22	0	0	7	0	1	35.1	34	21	16	1	2	25	0	25	9
Bellman, Pittsfield	0	1	.000	1.93	4	0	0	3	0	0	9.1	8	6	2	0	0	4	0	3	1
Beltran, St. Catharines	11	2	.846	2.36	15	15	1	0	1	0	99.0	63	36	26	4	6	28	0	101	2
Benes, Glens Falls	0	4	.000	3.65	7	7	0	0	0	0	37.0	39	20	15	2	2	14	0	29	2
Berryman, Utica	2	3	.400	3.65	21	0	0	14	0	5	24.2	23	14	10	0	1	15	4	30	3
Bobbitt, Geneva*	2	0	1.000	3.42	6	4	0	1	0	0	23.2	27	11	9	1	0	8	0	16	2
Bogott, Utica*	1	7	.125	4.45	13	10	0	0	0	0	56.2	64	37	28	4	3	23	0	53	8
Borzello, Glens Falls	0	0	.000	14.40	2	0	0	2	0	0	5.0	15	8	8	2	1	1	0	3	1
Bowen, Elmira	1	2	.333	4.70	18	0	0	11	0	2	46.0	55	37	24	0	7	14	0	45	10

Pitcher, Team	W	L	Pct.	ERA	G	GS	CG	GF	ShO	Sv.	IP	H	R	ER	HR	HB	BB	Int. BB	SO	WP
Britt, Glens Falls	2	4	.333	5.62	35	0	0	13	0	1	41.2	49	30	26	2	5	10	1	32	2
Brown, St. Catharines*	2	0	1.000	1.74	18	0	0	18	0	10	20.2	7	4	4	2	0	5	0	23	0
Brown, Jamestown*	0	1	.000	3.00	2	2	0	0	0	0	3.0	1	1	1	0	0	6	0	6	0
Bullock, Jamestown	5	3	.625	2.97	23	0	0	19	0	6	36.1	25	14	12	2	1	14	1	35	3
Bush, Utica	3	3	.500	5.35	16	12	0	1	0	0	65.2	67	44	39	6	1	28	0	51	7
Cain, Glens Falls	5	2	.714	2.45	24	4	0	6	0	0	51.1	48	19	14	2	4	15	1	55	4
Censale, Batavia*	5	2	.714	2.08	9	9	1	0	0	0	52.0	39	20	12	1	0	19	0	54	3
Chamberlain, Welland	2	3	.400	3.86	8	7	0	1	0	0	37.1	41	19	16	0	0	9	0	28	2
Cheek, St. Catharines	2	3	.400	5.04	18	0	0	11	0	2	30.1	34	20	17	2	0	8	0	25	4
Chergey, Elmira	3	5	.375	3.50	15	10	1	1	0	0	79.2	85	34	31	5	8	14	0	53	3
Cormier, Utica	7	5	.583	3.10	18	15	1	1	0	0	104.2	95	39	36	4	2	39	1	93	7
Cosman, Pittsfield	2	7	.222	4.19	14	14	1	0	0	0	81.2	84	49	38	3	7	31	0	46	4
Costa, Batavia	3	4	.429	4.94	10	9	0	0	0	0	51.0	56	32	28	1	2	19	0	37	5
Croushore, Glens Falls	4	1	.800	3.05	31	0	0	11	0	1	41.1	38	16	14	1	2	22	4	36	6
Cumberland, Oneonta*	4	4	.500	3.34	15	15	0	0	0	0	89.0	109	43	33	2	0	28	0	62	6
Czanstkowski, Auburn	5	1	.833	2.50	10	8	2	1	0	0	57.2	56	30	16	3	3	19	0	29	7
Danapilis, Niagara Falls	1	0	1.000	0.00	1	0	0	1	0	0	3.2	4	0	0	0	0	3	0	5	1
Dault, Auburn	0	3	.000	4.00	20	0	0	5	0	0	36.0	38	32	16	2	4	21	3	51	4
Davis, Erie	0	5	.000	3.65	27	0	0	24	0	13	37.0	32	18	15	3	4	10	2	41	2
DaSilva, Jamestown	3	8	.273	4.19	15	14	0	1	0	0	92.1	107	58	43	6	1	25	0	59	2
Dempsey, Watertown*	2	4	.333	4.50	20	0	0	8	0	2	24.0	26	16	12	0	0	14	1	27	3
DeLaMaza, Watertown	10	3	.769	2.52	15	15	1	0	0	0	100.0	90	39	28	8	3	14	0	81	0
Diaz, Watertown	0	0	.000	2.91	11	0	0	3	0	1	21.2	22	10	7	1	0	12	0	20	7
Diorio, Auburn	3	7	.300	5.13	15	15	0	0	0	0	79.0	98	57	45	6	3	27	0	57	6
Dominguez, Elmira*	0	2	.000	10.00	6	0	0	3	0	0	9.0	7	12	10	1	2	11	0	8	0
Donnelly, Geneva	4	0	1.000	6.28	21	3	0	7	0	1	43.0	39	34	30	4	6	29	0	29	7
Dreyer, Geneva	2	1	.667	3.66	3	3	0	0	0	0	19.2	22	9	8	1	1	4	1	10	0
Driskill, Watertown	5	4	.556	4.14	21	8	0	7	0	3	63.0	62	38	29	4	5	21	0	53	6
Drumheller, Oneonta*	3	1	.750	5.04	16	0	0	7	0	0	30.1	28	18	17	2	2	11	0	28	2
Eggleston, Batavia	5	1	.833	2.03	15	3	0	5	0	1	44.1	42	21	10	2	1	23	1	37	3
Engle, Pittsfield	7	7	.500	3.21	15	14	3	0	1	0	84.0	57	35	30	5	8	35	1	100	4
Fairfax, Welland	1	3	.250	5.85	11	4	0	0	0	0	32.1	33	30	21	5	3	21	0	22	11
Farrow, Geneva	3	6	.333	4.65	15	12	0	1	0	1	71.2	76	48	37	4	3	23	0	52	10
Filbeck, Elmira	4	3	.571	4.71	13	13	0	0	0	0	57.1	70	35	30	1	5	24	0	42	13
Fiore, Batavia	2	8	.200	3.05	16	16	1	0	0	0	97.1	82	51	33	1	4	40	0	55	15
Franek, Batavia	3	5	.375	3.34	15	15	0	0	0	0	86.1	86	39	32	3	5	21	0	40	2
Franklin, Erie	1	4	.200	6.16	17	2	0	5	0	1	30.2	38	29	21	2	0	12	1	34	2
Gaillard, Niagara Falls	1	2	.333	3.68	3	3	0	0	0	0	14.2	15	6	6	0	0	4	0	12	0
Garcia, Welland	0	2	.000	12.60	2	2	0	0	0	0	5.0	10	11	7	0	0	5	0	1	0
Garza, Watertown	1	2	.333	6.05	11	0	0	5	0	0	19.1	29	22	13	1	3	5	1	12	1
Genke, Batavia	2	3	.400	6.03	18	2	0	6	0	1	37.1	51	26	25	3	4	7	0	22	5
Gerhart, Erie	6	4	.600	2.88	15	15	2	0	0	0	97.0	82	42	31	10	4	13	0	68	1
Goldsmith, Niagara Falls	4	2	.667	2.30	21	5	0	12	0	6	54.2	43	21	14	3	4	20	3	64	4
Gomes, Batavia	1	0	1.000	1.23	5	0	0	3	0	0	7.1	1	1	1	0	0	6	0	11	0
Gomez, Elmira	2	2	.500	4.35	12	0	0	2	0	1	41.1	45	29	20	4	6	14	0	17	2
Gordon, Oneonta	0	3	.000	6.91	3	3	1	0	0	0	14.1	13	12	11	0	2	11	0	15	3
Grasser, Glens Falls	2	1	.667	2.06	36	0	0	36	0	19	39.1	30	13	9	1	2	14	1	39	3
Grennan, Pittsfield*	3	0	1.000	1.85	21	0	0	13	0	6	39.0	17	8	8	1	4	20	1	44	2
Grzanich, Auburn	5	8	.385	4.82	16	14	4	1	1	0	93.1	106	63	50	11	3	27	0	71	7
Hanson, Watertown	4	2	.667	3.43	9	9	0	0	0	0	44.2	44	23	17	3	2	13	0	31	1
Harrison, Jamestown	1	4	.200	3.38	24	0	0	19	0	6	26.2	27	16	10	0	5	9	0	25	3
Hartman, Erie*	6	7	.462	4.18	15	15	1	0	0	0	88.1	74	51	41	5	3	43	0	98	6
Hartnett, Auburn	5	2	.286	4.30	12	1	1	1	0	0	60.2	49	34	29	2	7	31	0	69	6
Heberling, Oneonta*	2	1	.667	0.99	4	3	0	0	0	0	27.1	20	4	3	0	0	8	0	27	0
Hill, Geneva	5	4	.556	2.25	34	0	0	32	0	12	40.0	26	12	10	2	2	18	2	55	1
Hillman, Geneva*	3	5	.375	3.30	14	14	0	0	0	0	76.1	76	51	28	8	3	42	0	85	7
Hogan, Geneva*	1	1	.500	7.25	17	0	0	5	0	0	22.1	27	25	18	4	3	21	0	23	11
Humphrey, Auburn	4	3	.571	2.50	29	0	0	26	0	9	39.2	34	18	11	2	3	10	2	49	2
Hunt, Niagara Falls*	2	1	.667	2.20	14	0	0	3	0	0	16.1	11	6	4	1	3	8	2	16	2
Hurtado, St. Catharines	10	2	.833	2.50	15	15	3	0	1	0	101.0	69	34	28	6	4	34	0	87	3
Irwin, Batavia	1	3	.250	2.72	26	0	0	18	0	8	43.0	40	16	13	0	4	11	1	43	8
Isom, Welland*	1	1	.500	5.83	22	0	0	11	0	2	29.1	35	23	19	2	2	9	0	28	4
Isringhausen, Pittsfield	7	4	.636	3.29	15	15	2	0	0	0	90.1	68	45	33	7	3	28	0	104	8
Jackson, Niagara Falls	1	3	.250	3.91	15	8	0	4	0	1	53.0	51	26	23	3	1	36	0	34	13
Jenkins, Geneva	3	3	.500	4.25	20	0	0	6	0	1	36.0	30	21	17	2	1	14	0	30	2
Jerzembeck, Oneonta	8	4	.667	2.68	14	14	0	0	0	0	77.1	70	25	23	1	3	26	0	76	2
Johnson, Welland	1	5	.167	4.63	6	6	1	0	0	0	35.0	33	24	18	0	2	9	0	19	1
Johnson, Utica	0	2	.000	5.40	19	0	0	10	0	3	28.1	20	22	17	1	2	19	0	23	4
Johnston, Utica	0	0	.000	2.35	4	0	0	2	0	0	7.2	3	2	2	0	2	5	0	10	1
Jolley, Glens Falls	0	0	.000	0.00	2	0	0	2	0	0	5.0	4	2	0	0	0	3	0	4	0
Jones, Pittsfield	0	1	.000	7.71	14	0	0	8	0	2	21.0	17	23	18	1	5	31	0	15	7
Kehrli, Glens Falls	0	2	.000	11.52	16	0	0	7	0	0	27.1	45	37	35	6	3	16	0	18	5
Kell, Erie*	2	0	1.000	1.87	18	1	0	10	0	1	33.2	16	8	7	2	3	18	0	44	1
Kendrick, Geneva	0	0	.000	18.00	1	0	0	1	0	0	1.0	1	2	2	1	0	2	0	1	0
Kenny, Pittsfield	0	0	.000	1.50	7	0	0	4	0	0	12.0	11	2	2	0	1	2	0	4	0
Kester, Auburn	4	6	.400	2.06	15	13	4	1	1	0	96.1	78	40	22	2	10	19	1	83	6
Key, Watertown	2	1	.667	6.14	3	2	0	0	0	0	14.2	18	11	10	4	1	4	0	5	1
Kirkland, Batavia	2	0	1.000	0.64	11	0	0	10	0	2	14.0	9	2	1	0	3	1	0	17	1
Kirkreit, Watertown	4	1	.800	2.23	7	7	1	0	0	0	36.1	33	14	9	1	0	11	0	44	1
Kline, Watertown*	5	4	.556	3.19	13	13	2	1	0	0	79.0	77	36	28	3	4	12	0	45	5
Knieper, Jamestown	4	5	.444	4.42	15	11	0	2	0	1	79.1	83	47	39	7	7	27	1	40	5
Kozeniewski, Oneonta	2	1	.667	4.86	24	0	0	11	0	1	37.0	45	29	20	3	4	17	0	21	4
Kunz, Erie*	0	2	.000	7.43	5	4	0	0	0	0	13.1	23	19	11	2	6	5	0	9	2
Lankford, Oneonta	4	5	.444	3.34	16	7	0	1	0	0	64.2	60	41	24	3	1	22	0	61	5
Larkin, Elmira	5	7	.417	2.97	14	14	4	0	1	0	88.0	74	43	29	1	12	23	0	89	3
Larson, Glens Falls*	3	4	.429	5.65	18	11	0	1	0	0	63.2	77	51	40	9	1	17	1	41	3
Lawrence, Utica	1	1	.500	5.56	14	0	0	4	0	0	22.2	28	20	14	1	1	15	0	13	2
Leon, Jamestown*	0	2	.000	3.23	20	0	0	11	0	0	30.2	34	14	11	0	3	10	0	33	0
Lesch, Erie	1	2	.333	5.33	19	0	0	6	0	0	25.1	31	21	15	3	1	10	2	19	1
Leshnock, Oneonta	0	5	.000	5.21	11	0	0	5	0	0	19.0	23	15	11	0	2	8	0	12	4
Lewis, Oneonta	0	1	.000	9.00	1	0	0	0	0	0	1.0	1	1	1	0	0	1	0	1	0
Locey, Geneva	2	2	.500	3.34	29	0	0	13	0	4	62.0	52	29	23	3	4	32	2	61	4
Ludwick, Pittsfield	4	4	.500	3.18	10	10	1	0	0	0	51.0	51	27	18	0	0	18	0	40	4

— 473 —

Pitcher, Team	W	L	Pct.	ERA	G	GS	CG	GF	ShO	Sv.	IP	H	R	ER	HR	HB	BB	Int. BB	SO	WP
Lugo, Auburn	1	2	.333	3.64	22	0	0	7	0	0	47.0	38	20	19	0	4	21	3	39	4
Luft, Welland	0	2	.000	5.86	26	0	0	11	0	2	27.2	24	21	18	3	0	16	0	16	2
Magnelli, Glens Falls	3	2	.600	5.72	27	1	0	2	0	0	39.1	53	34	25	3	1	15	0	34	5
Magrini, Niagara Falls	0	0	.000	3.38	2	0	0	0	0	0	2.2	3	1	1	0	0	2	0	0	0
Maize, Pittsfield	0	0	.000	0.00	2	0	0	2	0	0	1.2	0	0	0	0	0	2	0	1	0
Maldonado, St. Catharines	1	1	.500	0.99	13	0	0	4	0	1	36.1	16	7	4	2	1	15	0	38	2
Mattson, Welland	2	1	.667	2.12	18	0	0	6	0	1	29.2	25	13	7	2	0	5	0	32	5
McDill, Pittsfield*	2	3	.400	5.40	5	5	0	0	0	0	28.1	31	22	17	0	1	15	0	24	3
McFarland, Niagara Falls*	2	0	1.000	1.16	25	1	0	6	0	2	38.2	28	11	5	0	4	19	1	22	3
McKinley, Utica	2	1	.667	4.23	21	3	0	10	0	3	44.2	58	26	21	1	2	7	0	28	4
Meiners, St. Catharines	5	6	.455	3.96	15	15	1	0	0	0	91.0	89	52	40	8	1	32	0	56	3
Meinershagen, St. Catharines	8	1	.889	1.88	13	13	1	0	1	0	86.0	53	19	18	2	3	26	0	87	1
Metheney, Batavia	3	0	1.000	2.96	7	7	0	0	0	0	27.1	24	10	9	2	0	7	0	16	0
Minyard, Elmira*	0	0	.000	2.35	3	0	0	2	0	0	7.2	6	3	2	1	1	4	1	7	3
Mix, Elmira	3	3	.500	4.17	17	1	0	8	0	2	45.1	51	26	21	4	4	17	0	38	4
Moehler, Niagara Falls	6	5	.545	3.22	12	11	0	0	0	0	58.2	51	33	21	3	4	27	0	38	8
Moody, Erie	3	3	.500	3.83	17	7	0	4	0	0	54.0	54	30	23	3	2	13	1	33	3
Morales, Geneva	0	0	.000	9.00	1	0	0	1	0	0	2.0	3	2	2	0	0	2	0	0	1
Morel, Welland	7	8	.467	4.21	16	16	0	0	0	0	77.0	90	45	36	7	5	21	0	51	6
Morvay, Erie	2	3	.400	2.82	18	2	0	8	0	2	38.1	32	18	12	0	2	14	1	42	1
Muir, St. Catharines	4	1	.800	2.30	21	2	0	11	0	2	47.0	44	26	12	2	2	14	0	29	4
Musselwhite, Oneonta	1	1	.500	2.25	5	4	0	0	0	0	20.0	15	7	5	0	0	8	0	18	1
Neese, Niagara Falls	12	3	.800	2.54	21	21	0	0	2	0	71.0	44	24	20	2	3	34	1	73	2
Neilson, Watertown*	0	0	.000	4.61	10	0	0	6	0	1	13.2	10	13	7	0	1	14	3	15	0
Newell, Pittsfield	2	0	1.000	3.54	16	0	2	4	0	2	48.1	54	25	19	2	1	13	0	32	5
Nowak, Niagara Falls	0	0	.000	8.44	2	0	0	2	0	0	5.1	10	5	5	0	0	4	1	8	0
Nunez, Elmira	4	3	.571	3.98	14	9	0	3	0	0	63.1	66	31	28	4	5	17	0	34	7
Nuttle, Welland	0	0	.000	0.65	21	0	0	18	0	10	27.2	13	2	2	0	1	10	0	43	2
O'Brien, Erie*	2	3	.400	2.86	20	6	1	3	1	0	66.0	57	32	21	8	2	21	1	63	2
Oram, Watertown	0	0	.000	14.73	3	0	0	3	0	0	3.2	7	6	6	0	2	1	0	2	0
Orellano, Utica*	1	2	.333	5.79	11	0	0	7	0	2	18.2	22	15	12	4	1	7	0	13	1
Ottmers, Glens Falls	4	3	.571	2.30	9	9	0	0	0	0	47.0	35	17	12	3	0	30	0	48	3
Pacheco, Jamestown	0	1	.000	3.21	6	1	0	1	0	0	14.0	11	7	5	0	0	4	0	15	4
Pearlman, St. Catharines	0	1	.000	5.52	18	0	0	11	0	1	31.0	39	20	19	2	3	14	0	25	2
Pelka, Welland	8	4	.667	3.59	15	15	0	0	0	0	85.1	87	40	34	3	4	24	0	71	7
Perez, Welland	1	0	1.000	3.86	14	0	0	2	0	0	18.2	14	11	8	1	2	16	0	14	0
Perez, Utica	3	2	.600	3.03	16	3	0	1	0	0	29.2	39	20	10	1	1	11	1	15	2
Peters, Welland*	1	0	1.000	4.55	16	0	0	4	0	0	27.2	33	16	14	0	2	20	1	25	5
Peterson, Utica	1	4	.200	5.36	16	5	0	7	0	2	42.0	45	28	25	5	1	7	0	26	1
Phelps, Jamestown*	3	8	.273	4.58	16	15	1	0	0	0	92.1	102	62	47	4	5	37	1	74	7
Phillips, Welland	4	6	.400	3.53	14	14	0	0	0	0	71.1	60	44	28	2	9	36	0	66	15
Pickich, Welland	2	1	.667	4.37	21	2	0	2	0	0	47.1	35	27	23	5	1	19	0	54	4
Plumlee, Watertown	1	2	.333	5.21	23	0	0	21	0	15	19.0	18	13	11	2	0	16	0	15	4
Pontes, Glens Falls	2	3	.400	3.83	20	6	0	2	0	0	44.2	49	26	19	0	1	18	2	40	3
Pugh, Batavia*	1	2	.333	4.36	22	0	0	6	0	1	33.0	41	21	16	4	1	16	0	25	3
Rathbun, Oneonta	2	0	1.000	2.67	7	6	1	0	0	0	30.1	27	9	9	1	3	15	0	26	0
Ratliff, Geneva	1	1	.500	3.21	3	3	0	0	0	0	14.0	12	8	5	0	2	8	0	7	0
Redovian, Glens Falls	0	0	.000	4.05	8	1	0	0	0	0	13.1	13	6	6	1	2	6	0	9	1
Reincke, Niagara Falls	1	1	.500	7.02	20	1	0	5	0	1	33.1	35	29	26	3	5	23	0	26	7
Renfroe, Utica	7	4	.636	2.78	16	15	0	0	0	0	90.2	69	40	28	6	8	39	0	73	5
Respondek, Jamestown*	1	1	.500	6.19	18	0	0	5	0	1	32.0	48	28	22	2	1	11	0	26	3
Resz, Oneonta	3	0	1.000	3.76	24	0	0	18	0	9	26.1	18	14	11	2	4	16	1	16	4
Rhine, Auburn	0	2	.000	9.82	16	10	0	2	0	0	47.2	61	62	52	2	10	48	1	36	21
Richardson, Niagara Falls	3	4	.429	4.58	24	2	0	7	0	0	53.0	56	29	27	1	5	29	7	37	4
Ritz, Glens Falls	0	0	.000	7.71	3	0	0	1	0	0	7.0	9	7	6	0	1	3	0	6	1
Rodriguez, Niagara Falls	0	1	.000	2.25	25	0	0	8	0	1	44.0	31	15	11	0	5	36	1	45	6
Rosengren, Niagara Falls*	7	3	.700	2.41	15	15	0	0	0	0	82.0	52	32	22	3	6	38	0	91	6
Runion, Watertown	0	1	.000	6.75	4	1	0	0	0	0	8.0	7	9	6	0	0	9	0	8	4
Ryan, Welland	0	1	.000	2.08	16	0	0	12	0	5	17.1	11	10	4	0	1	12	1	25	5
Salazar, Niagara Falls*	3	4	.429	3.17	15	15	0	0	0	0	82.1	80	36	29	1	1	24	0	68	4
Santos, Niagara Falls*	2	1	.667	2.34	7	7	0	0	0	0	42.1	29	15	11	3	2	17	0	50	0
Schneider, Jamestown*	6	5	.545	3.93	14	14	2	0	0	0	87.0	102	50	38	5	7	23	1	44	9
Schulte, Auburn	2	1	.667	5.00	8	0	0	6	0	1	9.0	9	5	5	2	0	4	2	11	1
Seip, Erie	8	2	.800	3.17	16	16	1	0	0	0	93.2	76	41	33	9	4	19	0	82	2
Senior, Utica*	7	2	.778	3.89	13	13	1	0	0	0	76.1	84	40	33	2	3	34	0	77	8
Sexton, Watertown	1	1	.500	2.67	17	1	1	9	1	2	33.2	35	15	10	1	1	10	3	30	3
Shaffer, Pittsfield	1	1	.500	2.89	7	0	0	4	0	1	18.2	17	10	6	1	0	7	0	21	3
Shelby, Oneonta*	0	0	.000	17.47	3	0	0	0	0	0	5.2	14	12	11	0	0	6	0	0	0
Sides, Watertown	0	0	.000	8.74	3	3	0	0	0	0	11.1	16	15	11	0	1	7	0	8	4
Sinner, Watertown	0	0	.000	9.00	1	1	0	0	0	0	1.0	2	2	1	0	0	1	0	1	0
Smith, Niagara Falls	0	0	.000	18.00	2	2	0	0	0	0	5.0	12	11	10	0	0	6	0	0	2
Smith, Watertown	0	0	.000	6.75	2	0	0	0	0	0	2.2	1	2	2	0	0	6	0	1	0
Smith, Auburn*	0	1	.000	7.63	10	0	0	5	0	0	15.1	14	16	13	1	3	14	0	12	0
Smith, Erie	1	1	.500	8.10	3	1	0	0	0	0	6.2	9	6	6	0	0	4	0	2	2
Sollecito, Niagara Falls	2	1	.667	0.34	23	0	0	21	0	14	26.2	18	4	1	0	3	10	1	23	3
Spring, Auburn	3	4	.429	3.57	26	0	0	10	0	0	40.1	34	27	16	1	2	25	3	35	6
Standish, Oneonta	2	3	.400	4.35	20	3	0	5	0	1	49.2	58	33	24	2	2	22	2	45	1
Steinert, St. Catharines	0	2	.000	1.50	8	3	0	4	0	2	18.0	10	5	3	2	0	8	0	24	2
Stutts, Jamestown	0	1	.000	3.34	26	0	0	11	0	2	35.0	29	17	13	1	2	7	0	31	1
Swan, Batavia	5	4	.556	3.19	15	15	1	0	1	0	87.1	83	43	31	2	1	34	0	86	8
Swanson, Pittsfield*	6	3	.667	2.99	15	13	2	2	0	0	81.1	60	34	27	5	0	28	0	63	8
Tam, Pittsfield	3	3	.500	3.35	21	1	0	13	0	0	40.1	50	21	15	0	1	7	0	31	1
Telgheder, Utica	0	0	.000	0.00	2	0	0	1	0	0	2.0	0	1	0	0	1	1	0	0	0
Thomforde, Oneonta	2	7	.222	5.14	15	15	0	0	0	0	75.1	73	52	43	5	7	34	0	64	11
Thompson, Batavia*	0	0	.000	0.00	1	0	0	0	0	0	1.0	1	0	0	0	1	0	1	0	0
Thornton, Elmira	3	5	.375	2.26	16	7	1	7	0	2	63.2	51	29	16	2	1	27	0	59	1
Tipton, Erie*	3	1	.750	1.88	10	0	6	6	0	4	14.1	16	6	3	1	1	7	0	15	2
Torres, St. Catharines	1	4	.200	3.13	17	0	0	12	0	3	23.0	21	13	8	3	0	6	0	23	2
Twiggs, Geneva*	5	6	.455	3.16	14	14	2	0	1	0	79.2	65	39	28	4	1	37	2	67	6
Tyrrell, Utica*	3	2	.600	3.38	28	0	0	14	0	3	34.2	27	17	13	0	2	18	0	25	3
Valdes, Elmira	0	2	.000	5.59	3	3	0	0	0	0	9.2	8	9	6	0	3	7	0	15	0
Van Zandt, Elmira	1	2	.333	6.52	17	0	0	13	0	4	29.0	42	22	21	3	2	15	0	28	3
Wagner, Auburn*	1	3	.250	4.08	7	7	0	0	0	0	28.2	25	19	13	2	1	25	0	31	8
Walania, Elmira	3	3	.500	3.07	22	0	0	19	0	4	44.0	43	21	15	4	2	13	4	47	0

Player, Team			Avg.	G	AB	R	H	TB	2B	3B	HR	RBI	SH	SF	HP	BB	Int. BB	SO	SB	CS
Walker, Geneva	5	2	.714	3.12	13	13	1	0	0	0	0	83.2	76	38	29	2	4	36	1	47	15
Ward, Elmira*	2	5	.286	4.99	14	11	0	2	0	0	1	61.1	82	41	34	6	4	26	2	63	5
Weber, Jamestown*	6	5	.545	2.77	16	16	2	0	1	0	0	94.1	84	46	29	3	4	36	0	80	3
Welch, Pittsfield	3	1	.750	1.45	17	0	0	14	0	9		31.0	23	9	5	0	0	6	1	34	3
Wharton, Oneonta	0	1	.000	1.45	13	0	0	8	0	4		18.2	13	8	3	1	0	5	1	30	1
Whitten, Watertown*	6	3	.667	2.42	14	14	0	0	0	0	0	81.2	75	28	22	8	3	18	0	81	5
Whitworth, Oneonta	1	2	.333	7.07	10	6	0	0	0	0	0	35.2	48	36	28	3	3	17	0	20	2
G. Williams, Watertown*	0	1	.000	0.00	1	0	0	0	1	0	0	0.0	1	1	0	0	2	1	0	0	
J. Williams, Watertown*	5	2	.714	3.77	19	5	1	4	1	1		62.0	63	34	26	7	3	11	0	52	2
Willming, Erie	1	4	.200	4.18	18	8	0	3	0	0	5	75.1	64	47	35	7	9	22	0	55	1
Wiltz, Welland	0	0	.000	9.00	1	0	0	1	0	0	2	2.0	2	2	2	0	0	2	0	1	0
Windham, Glens Falls	4	5	.444	2.65	11	11	0	0	0	0	0	57.2	55	24	17	2	1	16	0	44	5
Wood, Batavia	2	3	.400	3.38	22	0	0	8	0	1		37.1	24	17	14	1	3	19	1	39	3
Woodall, Geneva*	2	1	.667	1.30	23	0	0	7	0	1		34.2	19	6	5	0	2	20	2	44	4
Woodall, Erie	0	0	.000	20.25	2	0	0	0	0	0	0	1.1	0	3	3	0	0	2	0	0	0
Wozney, Erie	0	0	.000	6.17	7	0	0	2	0	1		11.2	15	8	8	1	1	7	0	8	0

BALKS—Locey, Pelka, Ward, 5 each; Ball, Phillips, Thornton, 4 each; Bogott, Bush, Donnelly, Eggleston, Farrow, Hillman, Hurtado, O'Brien, Pickich, Salazar, Seip, Tam, Weber, 3 each; Arrandale, Augustine, Chamberlain, Cumberland, DaSilva, Engle, Fairfax, Franek, Garza, Grennan, Hartnett, Irwin, Jerzembeck, Kester, Kunz, Lawrence, Ludwick, Moehler, Muir, Neese, Pontes, Rathbun, Senior, Swan, Walker, Whitworth, J. Williams, 2 each; Abramavicius, Adkins, Alfonseca, Arguto, Beck, Benes, Bobbitt, Bowen, Britt, Chergey, Cosman, Dault, DeLaMaza, Dominguez, Dreyer, Drumheller, Franklin, Garcia, Gomes, Grzanich, Hartmann, Hogan, Humphrey, Hunt, Isom, Jackson, Jenkins, Kehrli, Kirkreit, Larkin, Lugo, Maldonado, McKinley, Metheney, Moody, Nunez, Peters, Phelps, Rosengren, Runion, Shelby, Sides, Sollecito, Spring, Thomforde, Wagner, Welch, Willming, Windham, Wood, B. Woodall, Wozney, 1 each.

COMBINATION SHUTOUTS—Censale-Barstad, Costa-Agostinelli, Fiore-Wood, Swan-Irwin, Batavia; Nunez-Chergey-Walania, Elmira; Willming-Morvay, Erie; Ball-Locey, Ratliff-Farrow, Geneva; Arrandale-Britt, Cain-Grasser, Ottmers-Cain-Croushore, Ottmers-Croushore-Cain, Ottmers-Jolley-Grasser, Pontes-Britt-Grasser, Windham-Britt-Magnelli, Windham-Magnelli-Cain-Grasser, Windham-Pontes-Cain-Croushore-Grasser, Glens Falls; Alfonseca-Stutts-Harrison, DaSilva-Bullock, Jamestown; Gaillard-Arguto, Jackson-Goldsmith, Moehler-Hunt, Neese-Rodriguez-Hunt-Jackson-Sollecito, Rosengren-Goldsmith, Rosengren-Goldsmith-Arguto, Salazar-Richardson-Sollecito, Niagara Falls; Engle-Grennan, Heberling-Kozeniewski-Resz, Jerzembeck-Alazaus-Resz, Jerzembeck-Resz, Jerzembeck-Standish-Alazaus, Rathbun-Kozeniewski-Drumheller-Alazaus, Oneonta; Cosman-Grennan, Engle-Grennan, Engle-Welch, Pittsfield; Adkins-Torres, Beltran-Torres-Brown, Hurtado-Steinert, Meiners-Cheek, Meinershagen-Brown, Meinershagen-Torres, Muir-Brown, Steinert-Muir, St. Catharines; Cormier-Lawrence-Orellano, Cormier-McKinley, Cormier-Tyrrell-Perez, Peterson-Perez-Telgheder-McKinley-Tyrrell, Renfroe-Tyrrell-Johnson, Utica; Hanson-Plumlee, Watertown; Pelka-Ryan, Phillips-Mattson-Beck-Nuttle, Welland.

NO-HIT GAMES—Twiggs, Geneva, defeated Auburn, 5-0 (second game), June 30; Larkin, Elmira, defeated Welland, 6-0, July 25; Agostinelli, Batavia, defeated Welland, 4-0 (second game), September 1.

FIELDING

TEAM

Team	Pct.	G	PO	A	E	DP	PB	Team	Pct.	G	PO	A	E	DP	PB
St. Catharines	.968	78	2040	770	93	54	17	Watertown	.953	78	2002	770	137	59	10
Glens Falls	.960	77	2029	806	119	50	11	Jamestown	.950	77	1970	845	148	53	19
Oneonta	.956	76	1975	790	126	68	19	Utica	.950	77	1947	800	145	53	38
Pittsfield	.955	75	1914	700	122	37	15	Niagara Falls	.950	78	2086	811	154	67	15
Batavia	.954	77	2024	855	138	68	19	Erie	.949	77	2060	833	154	64	14
Geneva	.954	77	2013	805	136	62	23	Welland	.943	77	1974	793	166	49	34
Elmira	.954	75	1936	895	137	69	23	Auburn	.942	76	1952	808	169	59	43

Triple play—Pittsfield.

INDIVIDUAL

FIRST BASEMEN

*Throws lefthanded.

Player, Team	Pct.	G	PO	A	E	DP
Bando, Glens Falls	.985	7	60	4	1	5
Bierek, Oneonta	.982	17	146	16	3	18
Cabrera, Geneva	.935	17	119	11	9	10
Cawhorn, Watertown	1.000	6	45	0	0	2
Clark, Erie*	1.000	1	5	0	0	0
Danapilis, Niagara Falls	.983	8	50	9	1	4
Debrand, St. Catharines*	1.000	1	2	0	0	1
DePastino, Erie	.985	24	186	7	3	12
Dominow, Erie*	.987	59	500	32	7	38
Duross, Geneva*	.987	51	418	38	6	33
Durso, St. Catharines	1.000	1	1	0	0	1
Ford, Utica	.957	18	145	10	7	10
Froschauer, Auburn	.935	6	28	1	2	4
Grapenthien, Auburn	.975	44	369	16	10	30
Harrell, Jamestown	1.000	2	17	1	0	1
Harris, Pittsfield	.972	51	435	22	13	22
Harris, Welland	.981	27	243	21	5	20
Held, Batavia	.987	41	356	22	5	27
Henson, Glens Falls*	.982	13	101	8	2	5
Hernandez, Pittsfield	1.000	1	4	0	0	0
Hill, Erie*	.983	28	204	21	4	19
Hodson, Watertown	.971	12	92	10	3	13
House, Welland	.972	4	35	0	1	2
Josepher, Oneonta	1.000	3	4	0	0	0
Kingston, Geneva	1.000	1	1	1	0	0
Kinnon, Niagara Falls*	.971	59	449	21	14	43
Llanos, Glens Falls	.985	21	123	8	2	10
Marine, Niagara Falls	.957	6	39	6	2	1
McCabe, Geneva	.985	16	118	10	2	14
McMullen, Batavia	.981	16	146	11	3	13
Moore, Utica	1.000	7	77	3	0	5
Moreno, Niagara Falls	.978	29	130	5	3	9
Murphy, Batavia	.985	21	180	11	3	12

Player, Team	Pct.	G	PO	A	E	DP
O'Donnell, Utica	.953	9	58	3	3	7
Ortiz, Utica	.969	4	29	2	1	1
Paez, Welland*	.987	35	282	15	4	16
Petersen, Auburn	.900	1	9	0	1	0
Querecuto, St. Catharines	.976	6	35	6	1	1
RALEIGH, Jamestown	.993	76	692	49	5	42
Roggendorf, St. Catharines*	.985	53	414	37	7	30
Sanchez, Elmira	1.000	3	1	0	0	1
Santucci, Glens Falls	1.000	1	2	0	0	0
Schmitz, Oneonta	.989	54	433	28	5	32
Seminoff, Elmira*	.977	62	605	40	15	52
Senkowitz, Utica	.970	8	62	2	2	1
Small, Elmira	.988	17	161	9	2	15
Smith, Pittsfield	.981	26	195	9	4	8
Stratton, Utica	.986	17	119	19	2	9
Stutz, Glens Falls	.988	37	307	17	4	16
Taylor, Glens Falls*	.989	13	86	3	1	6
Thomas, Watertown*	.982	61	503	42	10	37
Thompson, Batavia*	1.000	1	11	0	0	1
Vaught, St. Catharines	.981	25	189	16	4	16
Wieczorek, Auburn	.973	31	239	12	7	14
Wuerch, Oneonta	.977	6	39	3	1	4
Yselonia, Welland	.976	12	108	12	3	8

Triple play—E. Harris.

SECOND BASEMEN

Player, Team	Pct.	G	PO	A	E	DP
Aguado, Utica	1.000	1	3	2	0	1
Basey, Auburn	.943	37	84	97	11	20
Berblinger, Glens Falls	.979	34	58	82	3	13
Berg, Elmira	.983	10	24	35	1	9
Biernat, Geneva	.926	44	76	86	13	19
Bonneau, Geneva	1.000	8	12	24	0	7
Brown, Niagara Falls	.954	59	111	139	12	32

— 475 —

Player, Team	Pct.	G	PO	A	E	DP
Cedeno, Auburn	.924	33	78	92	14	20
Crispin, Auburn	1.000	9	9	23	0	4
Dean, Glens Falls	.783	4	9	9	5	2
DeJesus, Niagara Falls	.962	20	38	38	3	9
DeSimone, Erie	.625	4	1	4	3	1
Dowler, Geneva	.952	24	39	41	4	6
Estrada, Erie	.955	16	34	50	4	8
Goldberg, Erie	.954	38	59	108	8	15
Gosselin, Welland	.945	31	63	74	8	22
Grubb, Jamestown	.957	28	63	70	6	11
Haar, Jamestown	1.000	2	2	2	0	0
Hansen, Oneonta	.940	32	61	80	9	13
Hayes, St. Catharines	.929	4	8	5	1	2
Hernandez, Pittsfield	.946	12	22	31	3	5
Hernandez, Batavia	1.000	2	4	6	0	2
Jackson, Geneva	.969	16	24	38	2	10
Johnston, Welland	.967	7	8	21	1	1
Luna, Welland	.954	28	50	75	6	10
Lyman, Watertown	.944	9	17	17	2	3
Marabella, Jamestown	.950	51	116	151	14	23
Marte, Watertown	.600	2	1	2	2	0
Martinez, Niagara Falls	.917	2	6	5	1	3
Martinez, Elmira	.947	50	84	129	12	29
Matvey, Glens Falls	.971	24	40	61	3	12
Moen, Elmira	.938	6	6	9	1	2
MUMMAU, St. Catharines	.965	75	142	190	12	40
Navas, Oneonta	.985	44	88	105	3	29
O'Donnell, Utica	.960	57	94	147	10	24
Oram, Watertown	.978	12	19	25	1	6
Ordway, Niagara Falls	.963	7	12	14	1	5
Prieto, Watertown	.943	64	127	155	17	33
Purdy, Welland	.933	4	5	9	1	0
Quade, Jamestown	1.000	2	4	6	0	1
Renteria, Oneonta	1.000	3	6	11	0	1
Ritz, Glens Falls	.936	22	44	59	7	8
Rivera, Welland	.843	9	20	23	8	4
Sanchez, Elmira	.951	14	25	52	4	9
Sefcik, Batavia	.964	72	134	212	13	33
Sims, Erie	.962	24	39	62	4	13
Sullivan, Pittsfield	.921	43	59	92	13	11
Vaught, St. Catharines	1.000	1	0	1	0	0
Walker, Utica	.963	27	45	59	4	9
Wiegandt, Batavia	1.000	3	6	6	0	1
Zuniga, Pittsfield	.957	25	36	54	4	7

THIRD BASEMEN

Player, Team	Pct.	G	PO	A	E	DP
Aldridge, Oneonta	.917	4	2	9	1	1
Basey, Auburn	1.000	1	0	2	0	0
Batista, Jamestown	.857	74	59	157	36	9
Berg, Elmira	.909	62	31	158	19	11
Bierek, Oneonta	.845	43	26	72	18	5
Biernat, Geneva	.914	23	17	36	5	3
Brainard, Batavia	.816	49	33	82	26	4
Broome, Niagara Falls	.714	3	1	4	2	0
Brown, Niagara Falls	.800	13	5	27	8	1
Cawhorn, Watertown	.884	56	41	111	20	9
Conant, Niagara Falls	.800	1	2	2	1	0
Crispin, Auburn	.800	8	1	11	3	2
DeJesus, Niagara Falls	.912	22	2	29	3	2
DePastino, Utica	.912	41	31	72	10	5
DeSimone, Erie	.839	19	14	33	9	5
Dixon, Niagara Falls	.765	12	7	19	8	2
Estrada, Erie	1.000	1	2	2	0	0
Forkner, Auburn	.891	69	47	133	22	12
Fuller, Utica	1.000	2	1	1	0	0
Goldberg, Erie	.890	35	15	66	10	7
Grubb, Jamestown	.800	4	1	7	2	0
Haggas, Pittsfield	.928	40	25	65	7	6
Hansen, Oneonta	.825	27	21	59	17	6
Hayes, St. Catharines	.500	1	1	0	1	0
Hernandez, Pittsfield	.892	33	20	63	10	4
Hernandez, Batavia	.778	1	4	3	2	0
House, Welland	.870	31	24	63	13	6
Jumonville, Glens Falls	.929	56	46	110	12	6
KULPA, Geneva	.932	54	39	97	10	8
Lewis, Watertown	.837	16	11	30	8	3
Llanos, Glens Falls	.914	12	22	10	3	0
Lyman, Watertown	1.000	1	3	0	0	0
Marine, Niagara Falls	1.000	4	0	3	0	0
Martinez, Niagara Falls	.937	27	18	56	5	6
Matvey, Glens Falls	1.000	3	1	5	0	1
McGinn, Batavia	.750	2	1	2	1	0
McGinnis, Oneonta	.926	9	4	21	2	1
Melhuse, St. Catharines	.927	73	37	140	14	12
Moreno, Niagara Falls	.800	2	5	3	2	0
O'Donnell, Utica	.667	1	1	1	1	0
Oram, Watertown	.750	9	2	16	6	1
Ordway, Niagara Falls	.810	17	7	27	8	1
Ortiz, Utica	.892	40	28	55	10	2
Quade, Jamestown	1.000	1	0	5	0	0
Querecuto, St. Catharines	1.000	3	4	6	0	0
Raleigh, Jamestown	1.000	2	0	1	0	0
Renteria, Oneonta	.923	3	2	10	1	0

Player, Team	Pct.	G	PO	A	E	DP
Sefcik, Batavia	.667	2	2	4	3	0
Sigler, Geneva	.875	4	2	5	1	0
Sims, Erie	.925	12	11	26	3	3
Small, Elmira	.881	13	6	31	5	2
Stutz, Glens Falls	.909	11	10	20	3	1
Triplett, Erie	.767	17	10	23	10	2
Vaught, St. Catharines	.857	2	1	5	1	1
Wiegandt, Batavia	.929	24	23	42	5	3
Wilson, Pittsfield	.700	8	5	9	6	0
Wiltz, Welland	.873	47	40	105	21	6

SHORTSTOPS

Player, Team	Pct.	G	PO	A	E	DP
Aguado, Utica	.953	8	12	29	2	2
Angeli, Batavia	.923	75	128	230	30	47
Biernat, Geneva	.929	7	6	7	1	4
Cedeno, Auburn	.900	3	1	8	1	0
Collier, Welland	.887	49	74	138	27	21
Crispin, Auburn	.854	12	9	32	7	3
Cromer, St. Catharines	.923	75	82	204	24	32
Dean, Glens Falls	.938	39	55	96	10	17
DeJesus, Niagara Falls	.887	19	22	41	8	9
Estrada, Erie	.907	41	40	106	15	20
Foster, Jamestown	.880	26	25	56	11	7
George, Watertown	.875	2	3	4	1	1
Haar, Jamestown	.970	19	24	41	2	10
Hayes, St. Catharines	.667	4	2	6	4	1
Hernandez, Pittsfield	.667	2	1	1	1	0
Hernandez, Batavia	.923	5	4	8	1	2
Jackson, Geneva	.962	35	39	88	5	11
Johnston, Welland	.889	2	1	7	1	1
Luna, Welland	.923	3	3	9	1	0
Lyman, Watertown	.947	13	13	23	2	8
Martinez, Niagara Falls	.000	1	0	1	1	0
Matvey, Glens Falls	.922	32	41	89	11	9
McLamb, Oneonta	.932	49	67	125	14	22
Mendez, Geneva	.894	51	51	126	21	22
Mota, Glens Falls	.894	10	11	31	5	5
Neal, Watertown	.891	64	91	154	30	30
Oram, Watertown	.778	5	3	4	2	0
Ortiz, Utica	.907	19	28	40	7	11
Patton, Utica	.895	54	85	153	28	24
Petrulis, Pittsfield	.945	39	47	74	7	6
Purdy, Welland	.625	3	1	4	3	2
Quade, Jamestown	.931	42	63	85	11	12
Renteria, Oneonta	.947	30	42	83	7	21
Ritz, Glens Falls	1.000	2	2	4	0	1
Rivera, Welland	.859	22	28	39	11	7
Sanchez, Elmira	1.000	1	1	2	0	1
Sims, Erie	.904	37	47	104	16	17
SOUTHARD, Elmira	.927	74	82	234	25	42
Triplett, Erie	.800	1	0	4	1	0
Velandia, Niagara Falls	.918	72	82	186	24	33
Verduzco, Auburn	.884	64	76	167	32	28
Zuniga, Pittsfield	.927	37	57	95	12	11

Triple play—Zuniga.

OUTFIELDERS

Player, Team	Pct.	G	PO	A	E	DP
Agbayni, Pittsfield	.969	42	62	1	2	0
Aldridge, Oneonta	.750	1	3	0	1	0
Allensworth, Welland	.979	67	140	2	3	0
Alongi, Geneva*	.985	59	127	3	2	2
Baez, Utica	.983	45	59	0	1	0
BARKER, Niagara Falls	.993	72	148	3	1	2
Bell, Batavia	.959	41	65	5	3	0
Bonifazio, Elmira	.926	18	24	1	2	0
Booker, Geneva	.912	36	51	1	5	0
Brown, Elmira	.930	73	113	7	9	2
Cabreja, Erie	.941	29	47	1	3	0
Cabrera, Geneva	1.000	21	39	2	0	0
Callan, Auburn	1.000	1	2	0	0	0
Campos, Jamestown	.958	70	151	10	7	1
Chapman, Watertown	.960	62	119	1	5	0
Clark, Erie*	.947	61	103	5	6	1
Collier, Utica	.875	47	54	2	8	1
Collum, Pittsfield*	.976	54	74	9	2	0
Cumberbatch, Oneonta	.940	40	76	3	5	1
Danapilis, Niagara Falls	.924	38	70	3	6	1
Dean, Glens Falls	1.000	6	7	0	0	0
Deares, Glens Falls	.974	64	109	4	3	1
Debrand, St. Catharines*	.967	62	111	7	4	2
de la Cruz, St. Catharines	1.000	6	6	0	0	0
DeSimone, Erie	.953	39	35	6	2	1
Dickerson, Niagara Falls*	.875	34	47	2	7	1
Dixon, Niagara Falls	.971	35	33	1	1	0
Dowler, Geneva	.941	54	87	8	6	2
Ford, Utica	1.000	9	8	0	0	0
Fuller, Utica	.981	50	99	3	2	2
Garcia, Glens Falls	.953	51	98	3	5	1
Garrett, Watertown	.978	69	127	5	3	0
Gibson, Watertown	1.000	21	25	0	0	0
Grubb, Jamestown	.963	17	25	1	1	0

Player, Team	Pct.	G	PO	A	E	DP
Guerrero, Pittsfield	1.000	8	12	2	0	0
Harris, Welland	1.000	1	1	0	0	0
Hayes, St. Catharines	1.000	10	16	1	0	0
Hayward, Utica	.500	4	1	0	1	0
Hearn, St. Catharines*	.968	43	86	6	3	1
Henry, Glens Falls	.955	50	101	4	5	0
Hernandez, Pittsfield	1.000	2	5	0	0	0
Hernandez, Batavia	1.000	1	1	0	0	0
Hill, Erie*	.944	27	32	2	2	1
Holland, Watertown	1.000	12	7	0	0	0
Hunt, Welland	.667	7	4	2	3	0
Jer. Johnson, Utica	.957	43	87	3	4	1
Jones, Utica	.960	17	23	1	1	0
Jones, Geneva	.750	2	3	0	1	0
Kelley, Welland	.974	40	72	4	2	1
Kendall, Batavia	.969	73	149	9	5	3
Klaas, Jamestown	.800	9	7	1	2	1
Kulle, Watertown	.987	44	75	2	1	2
LaChance, Jamestown	.946	35	50	3	3	1
Ledee, Oneonta*	.970	51	91	6	3	2
Lefebvre, Watertown*	1.000	6	9	1	0	0
Lewis, Oneonta	.938	26	29	1	2	0
Madden, Batavia	.950	58	109	4	6	1
Marte, Watertown	.948	38	51	4	3	0
Martinez, Elmira	1.000	2	1	0	0	0
Matvey, Glens Falls	.750	9	9	0	3	0
Mayfield, Batavia	.909	6	10	0	1	0
Mazion, Pittsfield	.941	45	108	3	7	1
McDonald, Batavia	1.000	25	35	0	0	0
McMillon, Elmira*	.931	55	66	1	5	0
Milligan, Utica	.952	43	54	5	3	0
Mitchell, Welland	.918	47	51	5	5	2
Moen, Elmira	.944	30	31	3	2	2
Moore, Batavia	1.000	16	13	1	0	0
Moreno, Niagara Falls	1.000	20	18	1	0	1
Moultrie, St. Catharines*	.963	69	100	3	4	0
Navas, Oneonta	1.000	1	1	0	0	0
Pearson, Erie	.953	69	134	7	7	1
Petersen, Auburn	.895	41	67	1	8	0
Pico, Geneva*	.914	42	72	2	7	0
Quade, Jamestown	1.000	2	1	0	0	0
Querecuto, St. Catharines	.950	10	19	0	1	0
Ramirez, St. Catharines	.917	6	11	0	1	0
Reed, Welland	.921	45	80	2	7	0
Renteria, Oneonta	1.000	1	0	1	0	0
Rivera, Oneonta	.976	55	111	9	3	3
Rodriguez, Auburn	.952	59	97	3	5	1
Saffer, Jamestown	.896	47	57	3	7	0
Sagmoen, Erie*	1.000	6	15	1	0	0
Santucci, Glens Falls	.955	62	97	9	5	1
Schulz, Watertown	.971	24	34	0	1	0
Small, Elmira	1.000	4	2	0	0	0
Smith, Oneonta	.949	34	71	4	4	1
Stewart, St. Catharines	1.000	32	81	0	0	0
Strickland, Elmira	.968	48	90	2	3	1
Taylor, Glens Falls*	1.000	6	6	1	0	0
Terrell, Pittsfield	.963	64	122	8	5	2
Thompson, Jamestown	.879	64	96	6	14	0
Thompson, Batavia*	.786	19	20	2	6	0
Tosone, Jamestown*	.917	9	11	0	1	0
Triplett, Erie	.962	16	25	0	1	0
Vindivich, Auburn	.958	60	83	9	4	1
Walker, Welland*	.941	28	47	1	3	0
Warner, Pittsfield	1.000	19	26	2	0	0
White, Auburn	.949	64	140	8	8	2
Wiseley, Niagara Falls	.991	71	108	5	1	1
Woodall, Erie	.833	1	4	1	1	0
Wuerch, Oneonta	.929	8	13	0	1	0
Yaroshuk, Oneonta	.960	27	24	0	1	0
Young, Geneva	.973	32	33	3	1	1

CATCHERS

Player, Team	Pct.	G	PO	A	E	DP	PB
Aldridge, Oneonta	1.000	24	164	12	0	1	8
Almond, Glens Falls	.993	41	247	38	2	1	3
Borrero, Utica	.955	41	200	32	11	1	20
Borzello, Glens Falls	.979	11	39	7	1	0	1
Brainard, Batavia	.990	13	93	9	1	2	1
Broome, Niagara Falls	.979	39	251	25	6	3	4
Callan, Auburn	.978	39	286	29	7	6	18
Cannaday, Welland	.966	23	148	24	6	2	8
Childers, Pittsfield	.983	21	161	13	3	1	4
Cossins, Erie	1.000	3	27	3	0	0	0
Diaz, Pittsfield	.982	12	101	9	2	0	0
DURSO, St. Catharines	.997	40	314	23	1	1	4
Froschauer, Auburn	.978	38	267	39	7	2	23
Gipner, Oneonta	1.000	1	4	2	0	0	1
Gross, Elmira	1.000	1	7	0	0	0	0
Gyselman, Batavia	.993	35	240	46	2	5	10
Haag, Watertown	1.000	1	7	0	0	0	0
Harrell, Jamestown	.964	12	46	8	2	0	3
Henley, Jamestown	.978	26	143	36	4	3	2
Koeyers, Jamestown	.983	48	291	46	6	3	14

Player, Team	Pct.	G	PO	A	E	DP	PB
Lewis, Pittsfield	.988	46	298	36	4	2	11
Lewis, Watertown	.996	30	191	34	1	2	6
Lombardi, St. Catharines	1.000	2	22	1	0	0	1
Maize, Pittsfield	1.000	2	5	2	0	0	0
Marine, Niagara Falls	.994	38	288	27	2	1	8
Marrero, Niagara Falls	.964	17	99	9	4	1	3
Melendez, Erie	.967	13	110	8	4	0	4
Mendez, Welland	.981	32	232	32	5	1	15
Montero, Geneva	1.000	9	50	4	0	0	6
Morales, Geneva	.990	32	187	19	2	0	8
Murphy, Batavia	.988	12	78	6	1	2	3
Petersen, Auburn	.938	3	15	0	1	0	2
Petillo, Batavia	.994	19	138	24	1	1	5
Prater, Elmira	.987	44	324	42	5	2	9
Pyle, Erie	.963	12	71	6	3	0	2
Querecuto, St. Catharines	.991	39	297	35	3	1	12
Senkowitz, Utica	.980	19	132	13	3	0	6
Shook, Erie	.991	30	206	20	2	1	5
Sims, Elmira	.995	24	182	22	1	0	9
Snyder, Geneva	.987	51	336	35	5	3	9
Soliz, Watertown	.976	52	367	34	10	3	4
Stratton, Utica	.975	32	184	46	6	3	12
Torres, Oneonta	1.000	22	158	24	0	1	1
Trimble, Oneonta	.983	33	247	42	5	8	9
Turnbull, Elmira	.918	7	38	7	4	0	5
Unrat, Erie	.965	25	209	13	8	0	3
Williams, Glens Falls	.977	38	269	31	7	2	7
Williamson, Welland	.980	23	169	26	4	1	11

PITCHERS

Player, Team	Pct.	G	PO	A	E	DP
Abramavicius, Welland*	1.000	14	2	6	0	0
Adkins, St. Catharines*	.947	16	10	8	1	0
Agostinelli, Batavia*	1.000	24	2	14	0	1
Alazaus, Oneonta*	.929	28	3	10	1	0
Alexander, Glens Falls	.963	15	10	16	1	1
Alfonseca, Jamestown	1.000	15	3	6	0	1
Arguto, Niagara Falls	1.000	7	0	1	0	0
Arrandale, Glens Falls	.905	12	5	14	2	1
Augustine, Watertown	1.000	19	5	4	0	2
Ball, Geneva*	.667	8	6	6	5	0
Barstad, Batavia	1.000	8	0	1	0	0
Beck, Welland*	.857	22	3	3	1	0
Bellman, Pittsfield	.750	4	2	1	1	0
Beltran, St. Catharines	1.000	15	10	7	0	0
Benes, Glens Falls	1.000	7	0	2	0	0
Bobbitt, Geneva*	1.000	6	1	4	0	0
Bogott, Utica*	1.000	13	3	9	0	0
Borzello, Glens Falls	.500	2	0	1	1	0
Bowen, Elmira	.813	18	3	10	3	1
Britt, Glens Falls	1.000	35	0	3	0	0
Brown, St. Catharines*	1.000	18	4	4	0	1
Bullock, Jamestown*	1.000	23	1	13	0	2
Bush, Utica	.889	16	1	7	1	2
Cain, Glens Falls	.714	24	0	5	2	0
Censale, Batavia*	1.000	5	1	3	0	0
Chamberlain, Welland	.833	8	3	7	2	0
Cheek, St. Catharines	.875	18	2	5	1	0
Chergey, Elmira	.905	15	3	16	2	1
Cormier, Utica	1.000	18	5	13	0	0
Cosman, Pittsfield	.833	14	8	12	4	0
Costa, Batavia	.933	10	4	10	1	0
Croushore, Glens Falls	.875	31	1	6	1	0
Cumberland, Oneonta*	.842	15	5	11	3	1
Czanstkowski, Auburn	1.000	10	4	13	0	0
Danapilis, Niagara Falls	1.000	1	2	0	0	0
DaSilva, Jamestown	.769	15	3	7	3	0
Dault, Auburn	.857	20	1	5	1	0
Davis, Batavia	.846	27	3	8	2	0
Delamaza, Watertown	.938	15	9	21	2	2
Dempsey, Watertown*	.800	20	0	4	1	0
Diaz, Watertown	1.000	11	1	1	0	0
Diorio, Auburn	.944	15	5	12	1	0
Dominguez, Elmira*	.667	6	3	1	2	0
Donnelly, Geneva	.571	21	3	1	3	0
Dreyer, Geneva	1.000	3	0	3	0	0
Driskill, Watertown	1.000	21	6	3	0	1
Drumheller, Oneonta*	1.000	16	3	6	0	0
Eggleston, Batavia	1.000	15	1	5	0	0
Engle, Pittsfield	.882	15	4	11	2	0
Fairfax, Welland	1.000	11	2	7	0	0
Farrow, Geneva	.792	15	6	13	5	1
Filbeck, Elmira	1.000	13	7	9	0	0
Fiore, Batavia	.868	16	11	22	5	2
Franek, Batavia	.875	15	4	17	3	2
Franklin, Erie	.800	17	2	6	2	1
Gaillard, Niagara Falls	1.000	3	0	1	0	0
Garcia, Welland	.000	2	0	0	1	0
Garza, Watertown	1.000	11	1	2	0	0
Genevabe, Batavia	.857	15	1	5	1	0
Gerhart, Erie	.947	15	7	11	1	3
Goldsmith, Niagara Falls	1.000	21	8	7	0	1
Gomes, Batavia	1.000	5	2	0	0	0
Gomez, Elmira	.900	12	4	5	1	0

Player, Team	Pct.	G	PO	A	E	DP
Gordon, Oneonta	1.000	3	2	3	0	0
Grasser, Glens Falls	1.000	36	1	3	0	0
Grennan, Pittsfield*	1.000	21	1	13	0	0
Grzanich, Auburn	.913	16	7	14	2	0
Hanson, Watertown	1.000	9	1	5	0	0
Harrison, Jamestown	.833	24	3	2	1	0
Hartmann, Erie*	.889	15	6	10	2	0
Hartnett, Auburn	.909	12	3	7	1	0
Heberling, Oneonta*	1.000	4	0	3	0	2
Hill, Geneva	1.000	34	1	4	0	0
Hillman, Geneva*	.789	14	3	12	4	0
Hogan, Geneva*	1.000	17	1	2	0	0
Humphrey, Auburn	1.000	29	3	9	0	0
Hunt, Niagara Falls*	1.000	14	1	0	0	0
Hurtado, St. Catharines	1.000	15	13	11	0	1
Irwin, Batavia	1.000	26	2	7	0	0
Isom, Welland*	1.000	22	2	4	0	0
Isringhausen, Pittsfield	.792	15	5	14	5	2
Jackson, Niagara Falls	.826	15	5	14	4	0
Jenkins, Geneva	.875	20	1	6	1	0
Jerzembeck, Oneonta	1.000	14	6	9	0	0
Johnson, Welland	.700	6	1	6	3	0
Jeff Johnson, Utica	.800	19	0	4	1	0
Johnston, Utica	1.000	4	1	3	0	0
Jolley, Glens Falls	1.000	2	0	3	0	0
Jones, Pittsfield	1.000	12	3	4	0	0
Kehrli, Glens Falls	1.000	16	1	6	0	0
Kell, Erie*	.600	18	0	3	2	0
Kenny, Pittsfield	1.000	7	0	4	0	0
Kester, Auburn	.875	15	5	23	4	2
Kirkland, Batavia	1.000	11	0	4	0	0
Kirkreit, Watertown	.600	7	2	1	2	0
KLINE, Watertown*	1.000	13	7	19	0	0
Knieper, Jamestown	.833	15	3	7	2	2
Kozeniewski, Oneonta	.700	24	3	4	3	0
Kunz, Erie*	.667	5	1	5	3	0
Lankford, Oneonta	.833	16	8	2	2	1
Larkin, Elmira	.864	14	4	15	3	0
Larson, Glens Falls*	1.000	18	1	12	0	1
Lawrence, Utica	1.000	14	4	2	0	0
Leon, Jamestown*	1.000	20	2	5	0	0
Lesch, Erie	1.000	19	3	3	0	0
Leshnock, Oneonta	.833	11	1	4	1	1
Locey, Geneva	1.000	29	2	6	0	0
Ludwick, Pittsfield	.929	10	2	11	1	0
Lugo, Auburn	1.000	22	3	12	0	1
Lutt, Welland	1.000	26	0	8	0	0
Magnelli, Glens Falls	.800	27	5	3	2	1
Maldonado, St. Catharines	.833	13	1	4	1	0
Mattson, Welland	.833	18	1	4	1	0
McDill, Pittsfield*	.833	5	0	5	1	0
McFarland, Niagara Falls*	1.000	25	2	7	0	0
McKinley, Utica	.714	21	2	8	4	0
Meiners, St. Catharines	.952	15	7	13	1	1
Meinershagen, St. Catharines	1.000	13	1	8	0	0
Metheney, Batavia	.750	7	1	2	1	0
Minyard, Elmira*	.750	3	1	2	1	0
Mix, Elmira	.769	17	3	7	3	0
Moehler, Niagara Falls	.900	12	8	10	2	1
Moody, Erie	.944	17	8	9	1	1
Morel, Welland	.909	16	6	4	1	1
Morvay, Erie	.857	18	5	7	2	3
Muir, St. Catharines	.857	21	6	6	2	1
Musselwhite, Oneonta	1.000	5	2	1	0	0
Neese, Niagara Falls	.769	21	3	7	3	0
Neilson, Watertown*	1.000	10	0	2	0	0
Newell, Pittsfield	.867	16	4	9	2	1
Nowak, Niagara Falls	1.000	2	0	1	0	0
Nunez, Elmira	.933	14	3	11	1	1
Nuttle, Welland	1.000	21	4	0	0	0
O'Brien, Erie*	.900	20	4	14	2	1
Orellano, Utica*	.800	12	0	4	1	0
Ottmers, Glens Falls	.429	9	1	2	4	0
Pacheco, Jamestown	.857	6	2	4	1	0
Pearlman, St. Catharines	1.000	18	2	6	0	0
Pelka, Welland	.857	15	5	7	2	0
Perez, Welland	1.000	14	3	7	0	0
Perez, Utica	.857	16	4	8	2	0
Peters, Welland*	1.000	16	1	2	0	1
Peterson, Utica	.909	16	4	6	1	0
Phelps, Jamestown*	.962	16	6	19	1	1
Phillips, Welland	.875	14	8	6	2	0
Pickich, Welland	.909	21	3	7	1	1
Plumlee, Watertown	1.000	23	0	2	0	1
Pontes, Glens Falls	.900	20	1	8	1	0
Pugh, Batavia*	.750	22	1	5	2	0
Rathbun, Oneonta	1.000	7	3	4	0	2
Redovian, Glens Falls	.667	8	1	1	1	0
Reincke, Niagara Falls	.833	20	3	2	1	0
Renfroe, Utica	.952	16	11	9	1	0
Respondek, Jamestown*	.750	18	0	6	2	0
Resz, Oneonta	.750	24	2	1	1	0
Rhine, Auburn	.889	16	2	14	2	0
Richardson, Niagara Falls	1.000	24	1	5	0	0
Rodriguez, Niagara Falls	.750	25	0	6	2	0
Rosengren, Niagara Falls*	.733	15	2	9	4	0
Runion, Watertown	1.000	4	0	3	0	0
Ryan, Welland	1.000	16	1	2	0	0
Salazar, Niagara Falls*	.923	15	1	23	2	0
Santos, Niagara Falls*	1.000	7	2	1	0	0
Schneider, Jamestown*	.714	14	1	14	6	2
Schulte, Auburn	1.000	8	1	1	0	1
Seip, Erie	.971	16	16	17	1	0
Senior, Utica*	.944	13	2	15	1	3
Sexton, Watertown	.857	17	1	5	1	1
Shaffer, Pittsfield	1.000	7	0	2	0	0
Shelby, Oneonta*	1.000	1	0	1	0	0
Sides, Watertown	.333	3	1	0	2	0
Smith, Niagara Falls	.500	2	0	1	1	0
Smith, Erie	.750	3	2	1	1	0
Smith, Watertown	.667	2	0	2	1	0
Smith, Auburn*	.600	13	1	2	2	0
Sollecito, Niagara Falls	1.000	23	0	6	0	1
Spring, Auburn	.800	26	2	6	2	0
Standish, Oneonta	.769	20	3	7	3	1
Steinert, St. Catharines	1.000	8	1	2	0	0
Stutts, Jamestown	1.000	26	2	6	0	0
Swan, Batavia	.750	15	6	12	6	0
Swanson, Pittsfield*	1.000	15	2	8	0	0
Tam, Pittsfield	.857	21	2	4	1	1
Telgheder, Utica	1.000	2	1	0	0	0
Thomforde, Oneonta	.714	15	3	7	4	0
Thornton, Elmira	.826	16	8	11	4	3
Tipton, Erie*	.833	10	1	4	1	0
Torres, St. Catharines	.857	17	2	4	1	0
Twiggs, Geneva*	.810	14	3	14	4	0
Tyrrell, Utica*	.667	28	4	2	3	0
Valdes, Elmira	.800	3	2	2	1	0
VanZandt, Elmira	1.000	17	3	3	0	1
Wagner, Auburn*	.778	7	1	6	2	0
Walania, Elmira	.944	22	6	11	1	0
Walker, Geneva	.900	13	10	17	3	3
Ward, Elmira*	.900	14	3	6	1	0
Weber, Jamestown*	1.000	16	7	12	0	2
Welch, Pittsfield	1.000	17	1	2	0	0
Wharton, Oneonta	.667	13	1	3	2	0
Whitten, Watertown*	1.000	14	5	11	0	1
Whitworth, Oneonta	.818	10	9	0	2	1
J. Williams, Watertown*	1.000	19	5	4	0	0
Willming, Erie	.958	18	3	20	1	1
Windham, Glens Falls	.909	11	2	8	1	0
Wood, Batavia	.875	22	2	5	1	1
Woodall, Geneva*	.900	23	3	6	1	0
Wozney, Erie	1.000	7	0	1	0	0

The following players did not have any fielding statistics at the positions indicated or appeared only as a designated hitter, pinch-hitter or pinch-runner: Bando, of; Berg, of; Berryman, p; N. Brown, p; Conant, 2b; J. DeBrand, 2b, ss; Galvez, ph, dh; Hodson, of; Kendrick, p; Key, p; B. Lewis, p; Magrini, p; Maize, 3b, p; Morales, p; Oram, p; Prieto, 3b; Ratliff, p; Ritz, p; Sanchez, 3b; W. Sims, of; Sinner, p; T. Smith, 3b; Sullivan, ss; M. Thompson, p; G. Williams, p; Wiltz, p; K. Woodall, p; Zuniga, 3b.

LEAGUE CHAMPIONS

Year	Team	Pct.	Year	Team	Pct.	Year	Team	Pct.
1939 —	Olean*	.631	1948 —	Lockport*	.603	1958 —	Erie (2nd)†	.598
1940 —	Olean*	.625	1949 —	Bradford*	.635		Wellsville	.556
1941 —	Jamestown	.618	1950 —	Hornell	.653		Geneva (2nd)†	.548
	Bradford (2nd)†	.549		Olean (2nd)†	.568	1959 —	Wellsville†	.635
1942 —	Jamestown*	.672	1951 —	Olean	.622	1960 —	Erie	.643
1943 —	Lockport	.591		Hornell (3rd)†	.568		Wellsville (2nd)†	.535
	Wellsville (3rd)†	.532	1952 —	Hamilton	.659	1961 —	Geneva	.616
1944 —	Lockport	.608		Jamestown (2nd)†	.643		Olean (4th)†	.512
	Jamestown (2nd)†	.565	1953 —	Jamestown*	.704	1962 —	Jamestown	.580
1945 —	Batavia	.677	1954 —	Corning*	.621		Auburn (3rd)†	.521
1946 —	Jamestown‡	.672	1955 —	Hamilton*	.656	1963 —	Auburn	.585
	Batavia‡	.672	1956 —	Wellsville*	.617		Batavia (3rd)†	.485
1947 —	Jamestown*	.690	1957 —	Wellsville	.632	1964 —	Auburn§	.622

Year	Team	Pct.	Year	Team	Pct.	Year	Team	Pct.
1965—	Binghamton	.677	1977—	Oneonta y	.671		Auburn	.603
	Binghamton	.607		Batavia	.600	1986—	Oneonta	.766
1966—	Auburn x	.620	1978—	Oneonta	.729		St. Catharines z	.632
	Binghamton	.646		Geneva z	.718	1987—	Geneva y	.632
1967—	Auburn	.667	1979—	Geneva	.725		Watertown	.579
1968—	Auburn	.645		Oneonta z	.618	1988—	Oneonta y	.632
	Oneonta (2nd) *	.558	1980—	Oneonta y	.662		Jamestown	.618
1969—	Oneonta	.662		Geneva	.649	1989—	Pittsfield	.697
1970—	Auburn	.623	1981—	Oneonta y	.658		Jamestown y	.579
1971—	Oneonta	.662		Jamestown	.649	1990—	Oneonta a	.667
1972—	Niagara Falls	.686	1982—	Oneonta	.566		Geneva	.662
1973—	Auburn	.667		Niagara Falls y	.553	1991—	Pittsfield	.662
1974—	Oneonta	.768	1983—	Utica y	.649		Jamestown a	.654
1975—	Newark	.688		Newark	.649	1992—	Hamilton	.737
	Newark	.714	1984—	Newark	.622		Geneva b	.547
1976—	Elmira	.727		Little Falls y	.587	1993—	Niagara Falls b	.603
	Elmira	.703	1985—	Oneonta*	.705		Pittsfield	.533

*Won championship and four-club playoff. †Won four-club playoff. ‡Jamestown and Batavia declared co-champions; Batavia defeated Jamestown in final of four-club playoff. §Won championship and two-club playoff. xWon split-season playoff. yLeague divided into Eastern and Western Divisions; won playoff. zLeague divided into Wrigley and Yawkey Divisions; won playoff. aLeague divided into Eastern, Western and Stedler divisions; won playoff. bLeague divided into McNamara, Pinckney and Stedler divisions; won playoff. (NOTE—Known as Pennsylvania-Ontario-New York League from 1939 through 1956.)

NORTHWEST LEAGUE

NORTH DIVISION

Team	W	L	T	Pct.	GB
Bellingham (Mariners)	44	32	0	.579	
Everett (Giants)	42	34	0	.553	2
Spokane (Padres)	35	41	0	.461	9
Yakima (Dodgers)	30	46	0	.395	14

SOUTH DIVISION

Team	W	L	T	Pct.	GB
Boise (Angels)	41	35	0	.539	
Eugene (Royals)	40	36	0	.526	1
Southern Oregon (Athletics)	37	39	0	.487	4
Bend (Rockies)	35	41	0	.461	6

COMPOSITE

Team	Bell.	Ever.	Boi.	Eug.	S.O.	Spo.	Bend	Yak.	W	L	T	Pct.	GB
Bellingham (Mariners)	....	8	2	3	5	12	3	11	44	32	0	.579	....
Everett (Giants)	8	....	4	3	3	10	3	11	42	34	0	.553	2
Boise (Angels)	5	3	....	7	10	3	11	2	41	35	0	.539	3
Eugene (Royals)	4	4	9	....	7	2	10	4	40	36	0	.526	4
Southern Oregon (Athletics)	2	4	6	9	....	4	8	4	37	39	0	.487	7
Spokane (Padres)	4	6	4	5	3	....	3	10	35	41	0	.461	9
Bend (Rockies)	4	5	5	6	8	4	....	4	35	41	0	.461	9
Yakima (Dodgers)	5	5	5	3	3	6	3	....	30	46	0	.395	14

Southern Oregon played home games in Medford and Cline Falls.

Major league affiliations in parentheses.

Playoffs—Boise defeated Bellingham, two games to none, to win league championship.

Regular-season attendance—Bellingham, 74,900; Bend, 60,612; Boise, 151,080; Eugene, 121,283; Everett, 87,874; Southern Oregon, 78,202; Spokane, 126,028; Yakima, 86,822. Total—786,801. Playoffs (2 games)—4,759.

Managers—Bellingham, Mike Goff; Bend, Howie Bedell; Boise, Tom Kotchman; Eugene, John Mizerock; Everett, Norm Sherry; Southern Oregon, Dick Scott; Spokane, Tim Flannery; Yakima, John Shoemaker.

All-Star team: 1B—Jason Thompson, Spokane; 2B—Mark Simmons, Boise; 3B—Doug Newstrom, Yakima; SS—Brett King, Everett; OF—Todd Greene, Boise; Aaron Iatarola, Boise; Keith Williams, Everett; C—Mike Sweeney, Eugene; DH—Sal Fasano, Eugene; RHP—Bob Wolcott, Bellingham; LHP—Glenn Dishman, Spokane; RH Reliever—Matt Mantei, Bellingham; LH Reliever—Steve Day, Everett; Most Valuable Player—Todd Greene, Boise; Manager of the Year—Dick Scott, Southern Oregon.

BATTING

TEAM

Team	Avg.	G	AB	R	OR	H	TB	2B	3B	HR	RBI	SH	SF	HP	BB	Int. BB	SO	SB	CS	LOB
Boise	.258	76	2527	432	360	651	962	113	21	52	378	27	25	48	409	23	510	59	38	624
Southern Oregon	.255	76	2521	407	440	643	919	133	16	37	341	15	28	35	395	21	572	101	41	592
Everett	.252	76	2615	403	399	659	972	118	18	53	331	36	13	35	415	20	622	113	54	669
Spokane	.249	76	2550	401	440	636	881	123	19	28	333	15	25	36	322	19	563	82	40	592
Yakima	.247	76	2563	376	440	632	894	106	21	38	323	17	20	33	357	15	563	82	40	592
Eugene	.240	76	2467	333	306	593	870	102	17	47	284	16	27	44	283	13	603	148	42	516
Bend	.239	76	2519	360	385	602	925	95	21	62	304	29	14	39	308	18	616	115	59	537
Bellingham	.239	76	2535	385	327	605	849	105	14	37	327	21	22	51	367	21	548	81	56	582

INDIVIDUAL

(Leading qualifiers for batting championship—205 or more plate appearances)

*Bats lefthanded.   †Switch-hitter.

Player, Team	Avg.	G	AB	R	H	TB	2B	3B	HR	RBI	SH	SF	HP	BB	Int. BB	SO	SB	CS
Simmons, Mark, Boise	.304	58	230	46	70	87	9	1	2	24	2	2	0	39	0	57	18	5
Williams, Keith, Everett	.302	75	288	57	87	154	21	5	12	49	2	0	3	48	4	73	21	7
Burke, Jamie, Boise	.301	66	226	32	68	84	11	1	1	30	2	2	5	39	3	28	2	3
Thompson, Jason, Spokane*	.300	66	240	36	72	120	25	1	7	38	0	5	1	37	6	47	3	2
Mueller, Bill, Everett†	.300	58	200	31	60	75	8	2	1	24	6	2	3	42	1	17	13	6
Hickman, Braxton, Eugene*	.299	67	234	30	70	103	16	1	5	30	1	1	2	27	6	48	1	3
Newstrom, Doug, Yakima*	.297	75	279	51	83	110	17	2	2	36	1	3	1	53	4	44	11	1
Zaletel, Brian, Everett	.293	54	184	29	54	84	11	2	5	27	2	3	3	23	1	48	5	2
Prieto, Chris, Spokane*	.289	73	280	64	81	111	17	5	1	28	0	3	5	47	0	30	36	3
Iatarola, Aaron, Boise*	.289	57	218	36	63	100	12	2	7	39	2	2	2	28	2	46	4	1

Departmental leaders: G—Greene, Roach, 76; AB—Greene, 305; R—Prieto, 64; H—K. Williams, 87; TB—K. Williams, 154; 2B—Thompson, 25; 3B—Latham, 6; HR—Greene, 15; RBI—Greene, 71; SH—B. King, 9; SF—Subero, 6; HP—Boyd, 15; BB—Kennedy, 65; IBB—Kennedy, 7; SO—Haley, 83; SB—Prieto, 36; CS—Perez, 14.

(All players—listed alphabetically)

Player, Team	Avg.	G	AB	R	H	TB	2B	3B	HR	RBI	SH	SF	HP	BB	Int. BB	SO	SB	CS
Anderson, Cliff, Yakima*	.222	23	81	7	18	25	4	0	1	7	0	1	2	7	2	19	1	0
Anderson, Jamie, Bend	.063	7	16	1	1	1	0	0	0	2	1	1	0	2	0	2	0	1
Aracena, Luinis, Southern Oregon	.213	28	80	6	17	18	1	0	0	4	0	0	1	9	0	22	2	1
Augustine, Andy, Bellingham	.200	7	20	5	4	7	0	0	1	5	0	0	0	6	0	8	0	0
Banks, Tony, Southern Oregon*	.250	49	172	29	43	68	11	1	4	22	0	1	32	3	25	9	4
Barger, Michael, Bellingham	.261	68	203	30	53	66	7	3	0	23	1	1	5	26	1	26	15	6
Barrett, Scott, Everett	.259	35	108	14	28	42	6	1	2	21	1	0	2	10	1	20	0	0
Barwick, Lyall, Boise	.286	59	210	31	60	87	13	4	2	31	2	3	8	12	0	27	2	6
Bengoechea, Brandy, Southern Oregon	.292	31	72	11	21	24	1	1	0	11	2	1	3	8	0	16	2	1
Bernhardt, Steven, Bend	.191	54	162	16	31	41	7	0	1	9	3	2	2	19	1	24	5	3
Berube, Joe, Bellingham*	.252	44	139	17	35	49	6	1	2	28	1	3	5	23	2	38	4	1
Bostock, Jim, Spokane*	.237	57	169	28	40	47	5	1	0	16	3	3	2	16	0	36	7	1

— 480 —

Player, Team	Avg.	G	AB	R	H	TB	2B	3B	HR	RBI	SH	SF	HP	BB	Int. BB	SO	SB	CS
Boyd, Greg, Bend*	.223	70	224	39	50	88	6	1	10	33	0	1	15	40	3	61	3	2
Buckley, Mat, Boise	.214	19	56	9	12	12	0	0	0	6	2	0	2	10	1	7	2	0
Burke, Jamie, Boise	.301	66	226	32	68	84	11	1	1	30	2	2	5	39	3	28	2	3
Byington, Jimmie, Eugene	.259	53	170	23	44	73	5	0	8	32	1	1	3	14	0	45	9	1
Cabrera, Antonio, Bellingham	.220	48	123	22	27	39	3	0	3	15	1	2	3	14	0	42	4	2
Cardenas, Johnny, Bellingham	.204	47	157	17	32	45	5	1	2	24	2	1	7	17	0	34	1	0
Carr, Jeremy, Eugene	.228	42	136	33	31	43	2	5	0	12	2	2	6	20	1	18	30	3
Cavalli, Brian, Boise	.235	14	34	4	8	13	2	1	0	4	1	1	2	3	0	12	0	1
Cepeda, Malcolm, Eugene	.091	4	11	1	1	1	0	0	0	2	0	1	0	2	0	4	0	0
Clifford, Jim, Bellingham*	.269	62	193	39	52	93	14	0	9	40	0	1	6	36	1	63	8	6
Compton, Scott, Yakima†	.148	19	27	4	4	5	1	0	0	2	0	0	1	6	0	8	1	0
Corps, Erick, Spokane†	.000	4	7	1	0	0	0	0	0	1	0	0	0	0	0	3	0	0
Cox, Steve, Southern Oregon*	.316	15	57	10	18	30	4	1	2	16	0	2	0	5	0	15	0	0
Cristopher, Carlos, Bend*	.293	22	41	13	12	18	1	1	1	5	3	0	0	7	0	8	5	2
Cuevas, Eduardo, Spokane	.250	2	8	0	2	2	0	0	0	1	0	0	0	0	0	0	0	1
D'Amico, Jeff, Southern Oregon	.263	33	114	12	30	48	9	0	3	15	2	1	1	9	1	25	2	1
Dandridge, Brad, Spokane	.238	64	248	26	59	83	8	2	4	41	1	4	5	16	1	38	2	0
Davis, Melvin, Everett	.146	26	96	12	14	21	1	0	2	9	1	1	1	12	1	29	9	3
Dermendziev, Tony, Bend*	.217	19	60	8	13	13	0	0	0	5	0	0	0	6	0	19	8	1
Diaz, Freddie, Boise†	.293	26	75	13	22	34	4	1	2	14	3	0	0	9	0	11	1	3
Diaz, Lino, Eugene	.251	53	183	19	46	58	7	1	1	23	2	4	3	13	0	25	6	2
Dilone, Juan, Southern Oregon†	.211	54	152	19	32	43	6	1	1	19	4	2	1	22	1	52	7	5
Donati, John, Boise	.193	52	109	15	21	33	3	0	3	16	1	5	1	19	0	37	2	4
Doty, Derrin, Boise	.261	64	211	50	55	81	13	2	3	33	2	1	6	46	0	45	11	3
Duke, Darrick, Eugene	.286	49	147	26	42	56	6	1	2	25	2	0	3	21	0	29	5	2
Dunavan, Chad, Bellingham	.223	48	130	18	29	45	11	1	1	12	1	0	1	11	1	48	3	2
Dunn, Billy, Eugene	.187	40	123	13	23	28	2	0	1	6	0	0	2	22	0	21	8	4
Dunn, Nathan, Yakima	.308	4	13	1	4	5	1	0	0	1	0	0	0	2	0	1	0	0
Evans, Mike, Eugene*	.207	56	193	25	40	69	6	1	7	25	1	1	1	19	2	55	4	3
Fasano, Sal, Eugene	.267	49	176	25	47	90	11	1	10	36	0	2	6	19	2	49	4	3
Galligani, Marcel, Southern Oregon	.287	63	223	44	64	95	11	1	6	32	2	4	4	40	1	65	12	5
Gerald, Dwayne, Eugene	.206	55	170	16	35	46	1	2	2	13	0	0	9	57	10	57	10	2
Gillis, Troy, Spokane	.118	7	17	0	2	2	0	0	0	1	0	0	0	1	0	8	0	0
Giudice, John, Bend	.234	57	184	28	43	66	8	0	5	17	2	0	6	36	0	57	5	2
Good, Thomathan, Eugene*	.244	44	123	22	30	36	4	1	0	13	3	2	3	15	0	26	19	5
Greene, Todd, Boise	.269	76	305	55	82	148	15	3	15	71	0	3	9	34	6	44	4	3
Grunewald, Keith, Bend†	.275	56	182	29	50	67	4	2	3	22	1	1	0	30	1	43	7	2
Guevara, Giomar, Bellingham	.227	62	211	31	48	65	8	3	1	23	4	0	2	34	2	46	4	7
Guiel, Aaron, Boise*	.298	35	104	24	31	51	6	4	2	12	2	0	4	26	1	21	3	0
Gulseth, Mark, Everett*	.240	60	196	29	47	78	10	0	7	35	1	2	2	36	0	50	0	1
Gump, Christopher, Everett	.253	21	75	4	19	22	3	0	0	4	1	0	2	4	0	18	0	4
Haley, Rick, Yakima*	.264	63	220	28	58	96	14	0	8	50	0	1	3	28	1	83	2	1
Harkrider, Timothy, Boise†	.400	3	10	4	4	6	2	0	0	1	0	0	0	5	0	0	0	0
Harris, Eric, Southern Oregon	.245	50	155	27	38	68	9	0	7	26	1	1	8	23	2	55	5	4
Harris, John, Yakima	.135	47	89	12	12	15	0	0	1	5	0	0	3	22	0	44	7	7
Hartwell, Eddie, Everett*	.226	32	93	17	21	37	5	1	3	14	0	1	1	26	1	18	2	1
Hawkins, Richard, Yakima	.266	55	207	30	55	74	8	1	3	24	0	0	2	24	2	41	5	3
Heath, Jason, Bellingham	.146	22	41	4	6	6	0	0	0	1	0	0	1	4	0	12	3	0
Hickman, Braxton, Eugene*	.299	67	234	30	70	103	16	1	5	30	1	1	2	27	6	48	1	3
Higgins, Mike, Bend	.269	51	167	23	45	78	10	1	7	19	0	1	1	20	1	47	3	4
Holdren, Nathan, Bend	.227	62	203	30	46	96	10	2	12	43	0	1	4	24	5	78	8	0
Iatarola, Aaron, Boise*	.289	57	218	36	63	100	12	2	7	39	2	2	2	28	2	46	4	1
Ibanez, Raul, Bellingham*	.284	43	134	16	38	47	5	2	0	15	0	1	0	21	1	23	0	3
Jackson, Vince, Yakima†	.237	22	59	11	14	19	2	0	1	6	1	0	0	7	0	13	1	2
Jaime, Angel, Spokane	.262	50	168	29	44	64	8	3	2	25	2	2	1	18	0	27	9	4
Jimenez, Oscar, Eugene	.266	62	184	34	49	83	15	2	5	18	1	1	8	40	0	65	16	4
Johnson, Earl, Spokane	.246	63	199	33	49	54	3	1	0	14	5	1	1	16	0	49	19	3
Johnson, Herman, Southern Oregon	.500	1	2	0	1	1	0	0	0	0	0	0	0	0	0	0	0	0
Jones, Terry, Bend	.290	33	138	21	40	53	5	4	0	18	2	0	0	12	1	19	16	6
Jorgensen, Randy, Bellingham*	.263	67	228	42	60	88	13	0	5	32	2	2	4	37	2	33	7	4
Keel, David, Southern Oregon*	.267	61	195	38	52	64	9	0	1	18	0	0	3	47	5	31	12	1
Kennedy, David, Boise	.238	74	248	53	59	107	14	2	10	49	0	2	0	65	7	63	2	0
Kessler, David, Boise	.269	9	26	4	7	7	0	0	0	4	0	0	1	6	1	6	0	0
Kim, Bobby, Boise	.167	8	18	0	3	3	0	0	0	0	0	0	0	1	0	5	1	0
King, Brett, Everett	.226	69	243	43	55	71	10	0	2	24	9	0	5	40	2	63	26	11
King, Hank, Boise	.165	54	139	14	23	26	1	1	0	11	8	1	5	22	0	31	3	4
Latham, Chris, Yakima†	.260	54	192	46	50	76	2	6	4	17	0	1	1	39	0	53	25	9
Loomis, Geoff, Southern Oregon	.247	70	255	33	63	89	15	1	3	50	0	5	2	26	1	37	5	4
Lootens, Brian, Everett*	.216	40	125	17	27	35	5	0	1	11	1	0	0	11	0	35	4	3
Luzinski, Ryan, Yakima	.257	69	237	32	61	89	10	3	4	46	3	4	4	41	4	44	6	1
Martinez, Eduard, Bellingham	.193	45	119	14	23	36	7	0	2	9	0	0	1	10	2	35	2	0
Martinez, Javier, Boise†	.083	7	24	3	2	2	0	0	0	0	0	0	0	2	0	5	0	0
Mason, Andy, Everett	.143	7	7	3	1	1	0	0	0	0	0	0	2	0	0	1	0	0
McDonald, Jason, Southern Oregon†	.295	35	112	26	33	42	5	2	0	8	2	0	0	31	2	17	22	4
McKinnis, Roy, Spokane	.241	58	191	35	46	63	8	0	3	27	1	2	10	25	0	45	2	3
Miller, Roy, Bellingham	.224	55	165	26	37	46	3	0	2	15	2	2	5	28	2	42	4	7
Moore, Mark, Southern Oregon	.242	48	153	24	37	59	12	2	2	24	0	2	6	31	3	36	2	3
Morales, Willie, Southern Oregon	.269	60	208	34	56	75	16	0	1	27	1	4	4	19	2	36	0	3
Mueller, Bill, Everett†	.300	58	200	31	60	75	8	2	1	24	6	2	3	42	1	17	13	6
Munoz, Mario, Bend	.235	58	187	28	44	65	10	3	1	11	0	0	0	17	1	49	5	2
Myrow, John, Bend	.200	70	260	27	52	76	12	0	4	24	8	3	4	16	0	62	12	5
Newstrom, Doug, Yakima*	.297	75	279	51	83	110	17	2	2	36	1	3	1	53	4	44	11	1
Oglesby, Luke, Eugene*	.204	45	147	19	30	37	5	1	0	10	2	3	6	22	0	42	26	5
Ortman, Ben, Bend	.288	63	226	38	65	92	5	5	4	27	4	0	0	34	2	44	18	12
Patel, Manny, Bellingham*	.233	66	227	41	53	70	8	0	3	38	2	4	7	54	3	43	12	9
Perez, Neifi, Bend†	.260	75	296	35	77	105	11	4	3	32	4	3	2	19	2	43	19	14
Phillips, Gary, Everett	.239	54	180	24	43	72	8	0	7	31	0	0	2	25	1	45	4	4
Pineiro, Mike, Bend	.077	5	13	1	1	2	1	0	0	0	0	0	0	0	0	1	0	1
Pitts, Kevin, Yakima	.235	60	226	23	53	88	13	2	6	32	1	1	3	13	0	69	2	4
Porter, Jason, Bend	.000	6	8	1	0	0	0	0	0	0	1	0	1	1	0	2	0	0
Post, David, Yakima	.252	60	210	34	53	66	8	1	1	22	3	1	4	35	1	27	7	4
Powell, Kenny, Spokane	.000	5	14	1	0	0	0	0	0	0	0	0	1	2	0	7	0	0
Prieto, Chris, Spokane*	.289	73	280	64	81	111	17	5	1	28	0	3	5	47	0	30	36	3

Player, Team	Avg.	G	AB	R	H	TB	2B	3B	HR	RBI	SH	SF	HP	BB	Int. BB	SO	SB	CS
Rackley, Keifer, Bellingham*	.246	33	114	21	28	38	4	0	2	15	1	2	0	12	1	16	3	1
Ravitz, David, Yakima	.185	28	92	12	17	24	4	0	1	4	2	0	1	6	0	8	1	1
Reese, Mat, Southern Oregon*	.244	47	123	25	30	43	5	1	2	23	0	3	1	27	0	36	6	2
Reynolds, Chance, Everett†	.231	12	26	3	6	6	0	0	0	1	0	0	2	2	0	10	0	0
Rhone, O.J., Eugene	.272	48	125	12	34	43	9	0	0	8	1	2	0	4	0	29	7	3
Richardson, Jeff, Southern Oregon	.227	37	110	11	25	29	2	1	0	10	0	0	1	15	0	31	9	2
Rivera, Alex, Spokane	.000	1	1	0	0	0	0	0	0	0	0	0	0	0	0	0	0	0
Rivera, Santiago, Spokane†	.210	49	119	13	25	32	7	0	0	14	1	1	0	22	2	33	3	1
Roach, Petie, Everett*	.264	76	284	37	75	95	10	2	2	32	2	2	2	54	4	76	3	2
Romero, Wilfredo, Yakima	.255	13	51	8	13	13	0	0	0	1	0	1	2	1	0	12	3	0
Rosario, Melvin, Spokane†	.229	41	140	17	32	49	5	0	4	19	0	0	0	8	2	36	2	1
Salvador, Felix, Southern Oregon	.172	30	87	16	15	16	1	0	0	5	0	1	0	18	0	16	4	0
Sanders, Pat, Southern Oregon*	.214	45	126	10	27	43	6	2	2	12	1	1	0	15	0	39	2	0
Sbrocco, Jon, Everett*	.333	2	3	0	1	1	0	0	0	0	0	0	1	0	0	0	0	0
Scheibe, Britton, Spokane†	.182	46	99	11	18	20	2	0	0	11	2	2	2	13	0	39	0	2
Serrano, Nestor, Bellingham	.204	29	93	8	19	22	3	0	0	12	0	1	3	12	2	11	3	3
Simmons, Mark, Boise	.304	58	230	46	70	87	9	1	2	24	2	2	0	39	0	57	18	5
Singleton, Chris, Everett*	.265	58	219	39	58	89	14	4	3	18	5	1	1	18	0	46	14	3
Smith, Jason, Bend	.211	46	152	22	32	64	5	0	9	36	0	0	4	24	1	59	1	2
Smith, Toby, Eugene	.111	28	45	3	5	11	3	0	1	4	0	0	0	9	0	24	0	0
Speakman, Willie, Boise†	.233	70	227	31	53	69	7	0	3	28	0	3	2	32	3	46	2	4
Spiezio, Scott, Southern Oregon†	.328	31	125	32	41	64	10	2	3	19	0	0	0	16	0	18	0	1
Stadler, Mike, Spokane	.000	1	1	0	0	0	0	0	0	0	0	0	0	0	0	1	0	0
Stafford, Mitch, Everett*	.176	16	34	6	6	6	0	0	0	3	0	1	0	4	0	12	1	0
Stasio, Chris, Everett	.000	1	3	0	0	0	0	0	0	0	0	0	0	0	0	1	0	0
Sturdivant, Marcus, Bellingham*	.256	64	238	34	61	87	8	3	4	32	2	0	2	22	1	28	8	5
Subero, Carlos, Eugene†	.243	68	251	26	61	69	5	0	1	21	2	6	1	18	1	50	6	3
Sweeney, Mike, Eugene	.240	53	175	32	42	74	10	2	6	29	0	1	3	30	0	41	1	0
Tessicini, David, Everett*	.292	27	65	13	19	25	3	0	1	7	1	0	2	1	1	13	3	3
Thomas, Gene, Everett†	.170	17	53	6	9	12	0	0	1	3	1	0	1	10	0	16	6	4
Thompson, Jason, Spokane*	.300	66	240	36	72	120	25	1	7	38	0	5	1	37	6	47	3	2
Uribe, Dilone, Yakima*	.188	16	32	2	6	9	0	0	1	3	0	0	1	3	0	7	0	0
Vizcaino, Julian, Boise	.140	23	57	8	8	12	1	0	1	5	0	0	0	16	0	19	2	1
West, Chris, Spokane*	.265	68	226	37	60	88	14	1	4	37	0	1	2	26	5	57	1	2
Williams, Keith, Everett	.302	75	288	57	87	154	21	5	12	49	2	0	3	48	4	73	21	7
Williams, Leroy, Yakima	.241	39	141	17	34	50	5	1	3	23	1	2	3	16	0	33	1	1
Wojtkowski, Steve, Eugene†	.238	6	21	1	5	6	1	0	0	2	0	0	0	4	0	4	1	1
Woodridge, Dickie, Spokane*	.264	70	250	42	66	92	13	5	1	34	2	2	4	49	1	21	16	5
Yard, Bruce, Yakima	.225	44	129	18	29	36	5	1	0	12	2	0	0	22	1	12	0	1
Zahner, Kevin, Yakima	.218	33	110	11	24	30	4	1	0	4	1	3	1	14	0	18	0	2
Zaletel, Brian, Everett	.293	54	184	29	54	84	11	2	5	27	2	2	3	23	1	48	5	2
Zanolla, Dan, Spokane	.216	57	194	31	42	62	10	2	2	21	1	1	0	23	2	16	3	2

The following pitchers, listed alphabetically by club, with games in parentheses, had no plate appearances, primarily through use of designated hitters:

BELLINGHAM—Apana, Matt (14); Bruce, Tim (8); Carmona, Rafael (24); Collett, John (1); Crow, Dean (25); Doughty, Brian (14); Franklin, Ryan (15); Harikkala, Tim (4); Krueger, Bob (13); Mantei, Matt (26); Montane, Ivan (15); Santana, Marino (15); Sosa, Brian (18); Theron, Greg (23); Thompson, John (17); Wolcott, Bob (15).

BEND—Calvin, Derrick (13); Conley, Curt (20); Dewett, Martin (14); Eiffert, Mike (7); Goodrich, Jon (17); Henderson, Chris (27); Holland, Jay (21); Johnson, Jason (8); Lasbury, Bob (13); McClinton, Pat (18); Moore, Joel (15); Neier, Chris (15); Rekar, Bryan (13); Schneider, Philip (4); Sobkoviak, Jeff (15); Wehn, Kevin (13); Zolecki, Mike (14).

BOISE—Blanchette, Bill (20); Brown, Willard (15); Drysdale, Brooks (18); Edsell, Geoff (13); Fontes, Brian (14); Grenert, Geoff (26); Hancock, Ryan (3); Harris, Bryan (16); Kane, Mike (12); Knox, Jeff (3); Lloyd, John (13); Lorraine, Andy (6); Mejia, Juan (3); Myers, Matt (11); Nedeau, John (24); Puffer, Aaron (19); Purdy, Shawn (1); Razhigaev, Rudolf (9); Runzi, Andy (5); Slade, Shawn (24).

EUGENE—Aminoff, Matt (17); Atkinson, Neil (23); Bacon, Rich (16); Brassington, Phil (11); Brewer, Nevin (10); Burley, Rich (22); Flury, Pat (27); Granger, Jeff (8); Grundy, Phillip (15); Hogue, Jay (21); Kosman, Cody (16); Lopez, Andres (9); Ralston, Kris (15); Rawitzer, Kevin (6); Santos, Juan (9); Towns, Ryan (15).

EVERETT—Altman, Heath (15); Anderson, Clark (17); Baine, Dave (1); Baumann, Matt (14); Bourgeois, Steve (15); Day, Steve (30); Drumm, Doug (20); Franko, Kris (13); Grande, Marc (21); Hanneman, Blair (19); Martin, Jeff (25); Saugstad, Mark (12); Smith, Brent (9); Smith, Brook (17); Soult, Dave (12).

SOUTHERN OREGON—Baldwin, Scott (15); Conte, Mike (18); Gienger, Craig (4); King, Rich (22); Kubinski, Tim (12); Lemke, Steve (8); Lowe, Jason (22); MacCauley, John (25); Manning, Derek (15); Michalak, Chris (16); Rajotte, Jason (9); Urbina, Bill (13); Walsh, Matt (3); Whitaker, Ryan (27); Zongor, Steve (27).

SPOKANE—Clark, Byron (13); Dishman, Glenn (12); Doyle, Tom (6); Drewien, Dan (23); Erdos, Todd (16); Fargas, Hector (21); Kaufman, Brad (25); Keagle, Greg (15); Matos, Alberto (5); McLain, Brian (14); Mix, Derek (24); Schlutt, Jason (35); White, Kyle (23); Winchester, Martin (17); Wolff, Bryan (25).

YAKIMA—Baxter, Herbert (25); Binkley, Brett (14); Bland, Nathan (16); Botts, Jacob (13); Cook, Kenny (24); Duran, Roberto (20); Garcia, Jose (36); Groot, Fransiscus (12); Iglesias, Mike (10); Jacobsen, Joe (25); Lagarde, Joe (15); Perez, Jayson (17); Pincavitch, Kevin (9); Spykstra, Dave (13); Watts, Brandon (2); Winslett, Dax (18).

GRAND SLAMS—Holdren, 3; Iatarola, 2; Byington, Greene, Gulseth, E. Harris, Hickman, B. King, Luzinski, J. Smith, Speakman, Sturdivant, West, 1 each.

AWARDED FIRST BASE ON CATCHER'S INTERFERENCE—Singleton 5 (Luzinski 2, Heath, McKinnis, Speakman); B. Dunn 2 (Heath, Moore); Spiezio 2 (Higgins 2); Bernhardt (Cavalli); L. Diaz (Speakman); Giudice (Zahner); Greene (Rosario); Gulseth (Sweeney); Hawkins (Rosario); B. King (Speakman); Ravitz (Cardenas); Roach (Heath); Zaletel (Dandridge).

PITCHING

TEAM

Team	ERA	G	CG	ShO	Sv.	IP	H	R	ER	HR	HB	BB	Int. BB	SO	WP	Bk.
Bellingham	3.38	76	4	8	20	681.1	571	327	256	41	25	338	10	559	77	13
Eugene	3.43	76	1	6	22	669.0	569	306	255	30	40	336	29	622	47	6
Boise	4.05	76	5	6	18	663.2	608	360	299	48	44	301	27	603	61	15
Bend	4.06	76	3	2	15	667.0	671	385	301	45	30	319	9	534	71	12
Everett	4.24	76	1	2	18	687.2	614	399	324	44	53	404	14	610	53	15
Southern Oregon	4.54	76	3	6	18	666.0	691	440	336	50	40	303	22	495	39	19
Yakima	4.59	76	0	2	13	665.0	653	440	339	40	40	439	25	537	80	15
Spokane	4.80	76	4	4	10	658.0	644	440	351	56	49	416	14	569	66	18

INDIVIDUAL

(Leading qualifiers for earned-run average leadership—61 or more innings)

*Throws lefthanded.

Pitcher, Team	W	L	Pct.	ERA	G	GS	CG	GF	ShO	Sv.	IP	H	R	ER	HR	HB	BB	Int. BB	SO	WP
Franko, Everett*	5	0	1.000	1.47	13	12	0	0	0	0	79.1	59	15	13	0	1	25	0	72	2
Harris, Boise*	8	3	.727	1.89	16	16	1	0	0	0	105.0	80	29	22	4	8	29	1	96	5
Dishman, Spokane*	6	3	.667	2.20	12	12	2	0	2	0	77.2	59	25	19	3	1	13	0	79	3
Doughty, Bellingham	5	4	.556	2.49	14	14	1	0	0	0	76.0	65	30	21	4	0	42	1	39	9
Wolcott, Bellingham	8	4	.667	2.64	15	15	1	0	0	0	95.1	70	31	28	7	6	26	1	79	6
Ralston, Eugene	7	3	.700	2.74	15	15	1	0	0	0	82.0	52	29	25	5	3	36	3	75	1
Kubinski, Southern Oregon*	5	5	.500	2.83	12	12	1	0	0	0	70.0	67	36	22	4	6	18	0	51	2
Bland, Yakima*	4	6	.400	2.84	16	13	0	1	0	0	63.1	54	34	20	2	0	29	1	43	3
Michalak, Southern Oregon*	7	3	.700	2.85	16	15	0	0	0	0	79.0	77	41	25	2	6	36	0	57	4
Franklin, Bellingham	5	3	.625	2.92	15	14	1	0	1	0	74.0	72	38	24	2	3	27	0	55	7

Departmental leaders: G—Garcia, 36; W—Day, 9; L—Wolff, 9; Pct.—Day, .818; GS—Br. Smith, 17; CG—Lorraine, 3; GF—Garcia, 30; ShO—Dishman, Manning, 2; Sv.—Mantei, 12; IP—Harris, 105.0; H—Neier, Sobkoviak, 90; R—Altman, 62; ER—Conte, 52; HR—Erdos, 13; HB—Br. Smith, 10; BB—Altman, Erdos, 53; IBB—Atkinson, Baxter, Cook, 7; SO—Harris, 96; WP—Baxter, Mix, Wolff, 12.

(All pitchers—listed alphabetically)

Pitcher, Team	W	L	Pct.	ERA	G	GS	CG	GF	ShO	Sv.	IP	H	R	ER	HR	HB	BB	Int. BB	SO	WP
Altman, Everett	2	5	.286	5.42	15	15	0	0	0	0	73.0	69	62	44	5	8	53	0	64	7
Aminoff, Eugene	0	1	.000	3.60	17	0	0	6	0	2	40.0	41	19	16	1	1	17	1	42	6
Anderson, Everett	2	1	.667	5.27	17	1	0	4	0	2	41.0	49	30	24	4	2	7	0	24	1
Apana, Bellingham	5	3	.625	4.43	14	14	0	0	0	0	61.0	50	38	30	7	4	43	0	59	7
Aracena, Southern Oregon	0	0	.000	4.91	3	0	0	2	0	0	3.2	2	2	2	1	0	2	0	0	0
Atkinson, Eugene*	2	3	.400	4.34	23	4	0	7	0	3	47.2	50	28	23	2	3	26	7	43	5
Bacon, Eugene	2	3	.400	7.28	16	0	0	2	0	0	29.2	33	27	24	0	2	26	0	29	7
Baine, Everett*	0	0	.000	0.00	1	1	0	0	0	0	4.1	2	0	0	0	0	3	0	7	0
Baldwin, Southern Oregon*	3	3	.500	6.11	15	10	0	0	0	0	56.0	70	47	38	7	3	26	1	40	6
Baumann, Everett	2	2	.500	6.04	14	0	0	4	0	0	22.1	13	19	15	1	3	27	0	20	3
Baxter, Yakima*	4	1	.800	3.44	25	0	0	6	0	0	49.2	41	35	19	7	1	38	7	54	12
Bengoechea, Southern Oregon	0	0	.000	9.00	1	0	0	1	0	0	2.0	3	2	2	1	0	1	0	0	0
Binkley, Yakima*	1	1	.500	5.93	14	0	0	8	0	2	13.2	15	10	9	1	0	7	0	14	1
Blanchette, Boise*	2	0	1.000	1.64	20	0	0	5	0	0	22.0	20	5	4	0	1	6	1	14	4
Bland, Yakima*	4	6	.400	2.84	16	13	0	1	0	0	63.1	54	34	20	2	0	29	1	43	3
Botts, Yakima	1	6	.143	6.80	13	9	0	0	0	0	47.2	56	48	36	4	4	45	0	40	5
Bourgeois, Everett	5	3	.625	4.21	15	15	0	0	0	0	77.0	62	44	36	7	7	44	0	77	4
Brassington, Eugene	1	3	.250	2.42	11	8	0	2	0	1	48.1	35	14	13	2	7	19	1	32	3
Brewer, Eugene	3	0	1.000	0.97	10	8	0	0	0	0	37.0	26	7	4	0	0	17	0	31	3
Brown, Boise	5	4	.556	3.87	15	15	0	0	0	0	83.2	64	41	36	4	7	42	1	68	6
Bruce, Bellingham	3	0	1.000	4.97	6	0	0	1	0	0	12.2	10	8	7	0	0	9	1	14	0
Burley, Eugene*	3	3	.500	3.00	22	2	0	6	0	2	45.0	30	18	15	4	3	24	6	42	2
Calvin, Bend	0	2	.000	3.91	13	0	0	3	0	0	23.0	22	10	10	2	0	12	0	11	4
Carmona, Bellingham	2	3	.400	3.79	23	0	0	9	0	0	35.2	33	19	15	1	1	14	1	30	4
Clark, Spokane*	0	0	.000	14.66	13	0	0	4	0	0	11.2	20	22	19	2	3	12	1	9	3
Collett, Bellingham	0	0	.000	0.00	1	0	0	0	0	0	1.0	1	0	0	0	0	0	0	0	5
Conley, Bend*	2	1	.667	3.57	20	0	0	15	0	2	35.1	30	18	14	0	2	16	1	27	2
Conte, Southern Oregon	2	4	.333	8.41	18	7	0	4	0	0	55.2	71	55	52	5	8	31	0	31	4
Cook, Yakima	3	1	.750	6.28	24	0	0	5	0	0	43.0	39	38	30	1	1	44	7	33	6
Crow, Bellingham	5	3	.625	1.89	25	0	0	12	0	4	47.2	31	14	10	1	0	21	1	38	0
Day, Everett*	9	2	.818	1.79	30	0	0	23	0	7	45.1	35	14	9	2	6	21	4	47	5
DeWett, Bend*	1	2	.333	2.92	14	0	0	5	0	0	37.0	30	14	12	0	0	30	0	36	1
Dilone, Southern Oregon	0	0	.000	20.25	2	0	0	1	0	0	2.2	8	6	6	1	1	0	0	1	1
Dishman, Spokane*	6	3	.667	2.20	12	12	2	0	2	0	77.2	59	25	19	3	1	13	0	79	3
Doughty, Bellingham	5	4	.556	2.49	14	14	1	0	0	0	76.0	65	30	21	4	0	42	1	39	9
Doyle, Everett*	0	0	.000	13.50	6	0	0	2	0	0	6.0	12	9	9	0	3	6	0	5	2
Drewien, Spokane	1	0	1.000	5.28	23	0	0	3	0	0	29.0	28	21	17	2	4	21	0	31	3
Drumm, Everett	1	0	1.000	8.22	20	4	0	5	0	0	38.1	48	44	35	4	1	36	3	39	0
Drysdale, Boise*	2	2	.500	2.73	18	0	0	14	0	11	26.1	22	8	8	1	1	9	0	32	0
Duran, Yakima*	2	2	.500	6.98	20	3	0	6	0	0	40.0	37	34	31	3	6	42	0	50	10
Edsell, Boise	4	3	.571	6.89	13	13	0	0	0	0	64.0	64	52	49	10	3	40	0	63	6
Eiffert, Bend*	0	1	.000	10.80	7	3	0	1	0	0	8.1	15	21	10	0	4	17	0	4	7
Erdos, Spokane	5	6	.455	3.19	16	15	0	0	0	0	90.1	73	39	32	13	3	53	2	64	1
Fargas, Spokane	2	2	.500	5.93	21	0	0	2	0	0	41.0	49	34	27	4	4	24	0	28	2
Flury, Eugene	2	2	.500	3.27	27	0	0	19	0	7	33.0	25	15	12	0	1	22	1	34	4
Fontes, Boise	2	5	.286	6.10	14	9	0	0	0	0	51.2	63	45	35	10	6	29	2	41	9
Franklin, Bellingham	5	3	.625	2.92	15	14	1	0	1	0	74.0	72	38	24	2	3	27	0	55	7
Franko, Everett*	5	0	1.000	1.47	13	12	0	0	0	0	79.1	59	15	13	0	1	25	0	72	2
Galligan, Southern Oregon	0	0	.000	9.00	2	0	0	2	0	0	2.0	1	4	2	0	1	5	0	2	0
Garcia, Yakima	2	2	.500	2.42	36	0	0	30	0	5	44.2	40	14	12	1	3	19	2	19	2
Gienger, Southern Oregon	3	0	1.000	2.19	4	4	0	0	0	0	24.2	20	9	6	1	1	6	0	11	0
Goodrich, Bend	1	2	.333	4.91	17	0	0	5	0	0	22.0	30	18	12	1	1	9	0	13	3
Grande, Everett	3	3	.500	3.88	21	1	0	6	0	0	48.2	43	27	21	3	2	38	1	59	7
Granger, Eugene*	3	3	.500	3.00	8	7	0	0	0	0	36.0	28	17	12	2	1	10	1	56	1
Grenert, Boise	3	4	.429	4.30	26	1	0	11	0	1	46.0	51	24	22	1	3	20	5	44	4
Groot, Yakima	2	6	.250	7.56	12	7	0	1	0	0	41.2	48	42	35	6	5	37	1	27	3
Grundy, Eugene	3	5	.375	3.26	15	13	0	0	0	0	69.0	68	31	25	7	5	37	1	61	6
Hancock, Boise	1	0	1.000	3.31	3	3	0	0	0	0	16.1	14	9	6	1	0	8	1	18	0
Hanneman, Everett	0	2	.000	6.57	19	1	0	9	0	1	24.2	22	20	18	0	3	33	0	21	4
Harikkala, Bellingham	1	0	1.000	1.13	4	0	0	0	0	0	8.0	3	1	1	0	1	2	0	12	0
Harris, Boise*	8	3	.727	1.89	16	16	1	0	0	0	105.0	80	29	22	4	8	29	1	96	5
Henderson, Bend	4	3	.571	2.36	27	0	0	20	0	8	42.0	34	14	11	2	1	16	1	38	7
Hogue, Bend*	3	2	.600	5.83	21	0	0	12	0	1	29.1	35	22	19	2	2	10	1	27	0
Holland, Bend	0	0	.000	10.80	2	0	0	1	0	0	1.2	1	3	2	0	1	4	0	1	0
Iglesias, Yakima	0	3	.000	7.63	10	5	0	0	0	0	30.2	42	29	26	1	2	21	1	24	4
Jacobsen, Yakima	1	0	1.000	2.39	25	0	0	7	0	3	37.2	27	16	10	0	1	28	2	55	1
Johnson, Bend	4	1	.800	0.79	8	4	0	4	0	3	34.0	30	10	3	2	2	10	0	27	4
Kane, Boise	0	1	.000	9.95	12	0	0	3	0	0	12.2	11	18	14	1	2	18	1	14	6
Kaufman, Spokane	5	4	.556	6.88	25	8	1	11	0	4	53.2	56	56	41	8	3	41	2	48	4
Keagle, Spokane	3	3	.500	3.25	15	15	1	0	0	0	83.0	80	37	30	2	7	40	2	77	4
King, Southern Oregon	1	2	.333	3.40	22	0	0	7	0	3	55.2	63	32	21	5	6	14	1	49	0

Pitcher, Team	W	L	Pct.	ERA	G	GS	CG	GF	ShO	Sv.	IP	H	R	ER	HR	HB	Int. BB	BB	SO	WP
Knox, Boise	0	0	.000	0.00	3	0	0	0	0	0	2.1	1	0	0	0	0	2	1	3	0
Kosman, Eugene	3	2	.600	3.00	16	0	0	8	0	2	30.0	27	11	10	1	2	22	6	29	2
Krueger, Bellingham*	2	0	1.000	3.58	13	3	0	0	0	0	27.2	25	13	11	2	2	11	0	17	3
Kubinski, Southern Oregon*	5	5	.500	2.83	12	12	1	0	0	0	70.0	67	36	22	4	6	18	0	51	2
Lagarde, Yakima	5	4	.556	3.31	15	12	0	2	0	2	70.2	69	28	26	4	0	28	0	45	7
Lasbury, Bend	1	0	1.000	6.29	13	1	0	5	0	1	24.1	31	22	17	3	0	19	0	16	1
Lemke, Southern Oregon	1	0	1.000	4.40	8	0	0	4	0	1	14.1	13	11	7	2	0	6	0	11	1
Lloyd, Boise	0	3	.000	5.09	13	8	0	0	0	0	53.0	60	41	30	6	0	27	2	54	6
Lopez, Eugene*	2	0	1.000	2.41	9	0	0	2	0	0	18.2	15	6	5	0	0	8	0	15	0
Lorraine, Boise*	4	1	.800	1.29	6	6	3	0	1	0	42.0	33	6	6	3	2	6	0	39	0
Lowe, Southern Oregon	0	4	.000	6.98	22	1	0	8	0	0	29.2	31	32	23	1	1	42	4	29	5
MacCauley, Southern Oregon	2	1	.667	4.21	25	3	0	11	0	4	51.1	54	29	24	5	0	20	5	32	3
Manning, Southern Oregon*	5	4	.556	3.63	15	13	2	0	2	0	79.1	71	35	32	5	3	21	2	63	4
Mantei, Bellingham	1	1	.500	5.96	26	0	0	21	0	12	25.2	26	19	17	2	1	15	0	34	4
Martin, Everett	5	5	.500	3.00	25	0	0	13	0	4	54.0	38	22	18	4	4	20	2	44	3
Matos, Spokane	0	0	.000	7.11	5	0	0	0	0	0	6.1	9	7	5	2	0	10	0	6	1
McClinton, Bend*	3	2	.600	4.98	18	1	0	6	0	0	34.1	34	23	19	3	0	22	0	30	3
McLain, Spokane	1	6	.143	5.87	14	9	0	2	0	0	38.1	37	28	25	4	2	23	0	30	3
Mejia, Boise*	1	2	.333	2.40	3	3	0	0	0	0	15.0	14	8	4	2	1	4	0	13	2
Michalak, Southern Oregon*	7	3	.700	2.85	16	15	0	0	0	0	79.0	77	41	25	2	6	36	0	57	4
Mix, Spokane	2	1	.667	7.13	24	1	0	6	0	0	41.2	42	38	33	4	5	46	0	41	12
Montane, Bellingham	5	4	.556	3.93	15	15	1	0	0	0	73.1	55	36	32	7	3	37	0	53	9
Moore, Bend	4	7	.364	3.21	15	15	0	0	0	0	89.2	75	35	32	2	2	31	1	79	6
Myers, Boise	0	0	.000	4.09	11	0	0	5	0	0	11.0	10	5	5	0	2	1	2	10	2
Nedeau, Boise	2	3	.400	3.26	24	0	0	6	0	0	38.2	33	15	14	2	3	9	1	26	0
Neier, Bend	3	5	.375	4.79	15	15	0	0	0	0	77.0	90	55	41	6	3	32	2	58	5
Perez, Yakima	0	0	.000	4.13	17	0	0	7	0	0	28.1	26	16	13	0	2	19	1	14	4
Pincavitch, Yakima	3	4	.429	1.89	9	9	0	0	0	0	57.0	40	22	12	2	5	29	1	43	7
Puffer, Boise	4	2	.667	5.40	19	0	0	6	0	1	28.1	29	21	17	1	0	14	3	28	4
Purdy, Boise	1	0	1.000	0.00	1	1	0	0	0	0	6.0	2	2	0	0	0	5	2	1	0
Rajotte, Southern Oregon*	1	0	.000	6.28	9	0	0	1	0	0	14.1	15	15	10	2	1	9	2	14	2
Ralston, Eugene	7	3	.700	2.74	15	15	1	0	0	0	82.0	52	29	25	5	3	36	3	75	1
Rawitzer, Eugene*	1	0	1.000	0.50	6	4	0	0	0	0	18.0	13	1	1	0	1	5	0	20	0
Razhigaev, Boise*	0	0	.000	6.35	9	0	0	1	0	0	5.2	13	4	4	0	0	6	0	3	2
Rekar, Bend	3	5	.375	4.08	13	13	1	0	0	0	75.0	81	36	34	8	1	18	2	59	8
Runzi, Boise	0	0	.000	9.00	5	1	0	2	0	0	7.0	10	7	7	1	1	5	0	10	1
Santana, Bellingham	0	1	.000	5.82	15	0	0	8	0	0	21.2	27	19	14	3	0	22	1	24	4
Santos, Eugene*	0	2	.000	11.66	9	0	0	3	0	0	14.2	18	20	19	1	4	14	1	12	2
Saugstad, Everett	1	1	.500	5.86	12	0	0	2	0	0	27.2	30	18	18	1	4	19	1	17	1
Schlutt, Spokane*	5	4	.556	3.38	35	0	0	28	0	5	48.0	45	25	18	2	1	23	2	40	3
Schneider, Bend*	1	0	1.000	0.00	4	0	0	4	0	0	7.0	1	1	0	0	0	0	0	9	0
Slade, Boise	2	2	.500	5.33	24	0	0	18	0	5	27.0	34	20	16	1	4	15	4	26	4
Brent Smith, Everett	1	7	.125	6.55	9	9	0	0	0	0	34.1	41	26	25	5	2	24	1	19	1
Brook Smith, Everett*	5	3	.625	4.40	17	17	0	0	0	0	92.0	83	51	45	7	10	47	0	79	11
Smith, Eugene	1	1	.500	2.35	14	0	0	8	0	4	23.0	14	8	6	1	1	7	0	31	0
Sobkoviak, Bend	4	6	.400	4.44	15	15	1	0	0	0	77.0	90	50	38	4	6	38	1	34	7
Sosa, Bellingham	1	3	.250	2.83	18	0	0	8	0	0	35.0	26	13	11	1	1	17	2	30	8
Soult, Everett	1	0	1.000	1.05	12	0	0	9	0	4	25.2	20	7	3	0	2	21	2	21	2
Spykstra, Yakima	2	6	.250	5.20	13	12	0	0	0	0	55.1	65	43	32	3	4	36	2	39	11
Theron, Bellingham	1	1	.500	3.25	23	0	0	5	0	0	52.2	46	25	19	1	2	19	0	47	5
Thompson, Bellingham	0	2	.000	4.24	17	1	0	7	0	0	34.0	31	23	16	3	1	33	2	28	11
Towns, Eugene	4	3	.571	3.46	15	15	0	0	0	0	67.2	59	33	26	2	4	36	0	43	5
Urbina, Southern Oregon	3	5	.375	5.36	13	9	0	0	0	0	48.2	58	41	29	3	1	22	2	28	2
Walsh, Southern Oregon	1	0	1.000	2.08	3	0	0	0	0	0	4.1	4	1	1	0	0	3	0	1	0
Watts, Yakima*	0	2	.000	8.00	2	2	0	0	0	0	9.0	8	8	8	3	0	7	0	12	1
Wehn, Bend	1	0	1.000	7.03	13	1	0	2	0	0	24.1	30	20	19	3	5	15	0	14	4
Whitaker, Southern Oregon	2	3	.400	4.40	27	0	0	15	0	0	45.0	39	25	22	6	0	21	2	42	3
White, Spokane	1	0	1.000	3.35	23	0	0	4	0	0	40.1	43	17	15	1	4	23	3	33	4
Winchester, Spokane*	1	3	.250	7.41	17	4	0	3	0	0	34.0	39	32	28	4	2	37	2	31	7
Winslett, Yakima	0	2	.000	5.51	8	4	0	0	0	0	32.2	46	23	20	2	6	10	0	25	3
Wolcott, Bellingham	8	4	.667	2.64	15	15	1	0	0	0	95.1	70	31	28	7	6	26	1	79	6
Wolff, Spokane	3	9	.250	5.53	25	8	0	7	0	1	57.0	52	50	35	4	5	44	0	48	12
Zolecki, Bend	4	3	.571	4.42	14	8	1	3	0	1	55.0	47	35	27	7	2	30	1	78	5
Zongor, Southern Oregon*	2	4	.333	3.90	27	0	0	17	0	3	27.2	24	17	12	0	2	19	3	33	2

BALKS—Altman, 5; Baldwin, Johnson, Keagle, Manning, 4 each; Drumm, Edsell, Franklin, Harris, Lopez, Michalak, Montane, Pincavitch, Whitaker, Winslett, Wolff, 3 each; Apana, Botts, Groot, Kaufman, Krueger, Kubinski, Lloyd, McClinton, Mix, Nedeau, Rekar, Santana, 2 each; Anderson, Baxter, Bland, Bourgeois, Brown, Dishman, Drewien, Erdos, Fargas, Fontes, Franco, Grande, Grenert, Grundy, Hanneman, Iglesias, King, Lagarde, Lowe, Matos, Neier, Puffer, Ralston, Razhigaev, Saugstad, Schlutt, T. Smith, Sobkoviak, Soult, Spykstra, Wehn, White, Wolcott, Zolecki, Zongor, 1 each.

COMBINATION SHUTOUTS—Apana-Theron-Mantei, Doughty-Crow, Franklin-Bruce-Santana, Montane-Crow-Mantei, Montane-Theron-Bruce-Mantei, Wolcott-Crow, Wolcott-Mantei, Bellingham; Brown-Grenert, Johnson-Zolecki, Rekar-Goodrich-Johnson, Bend; Brown-Myers-Razhigaev-Puffer, Harris-Knox-Grenert, Harris-Nedeau-Blanchette-Slade, Lorraine-Nedeau, Boise; Brassington-Flury, Brewer-Smith-Brassington-Atkinson, Granger-Aminoff, Ralston-Bacon-Flury, Ralston-Burley-Flury, Towns-Bacon-Santos-Kosman, Eugene; Smith-Martin, Smith-Martin-Drumm, Everett; Baldwin-MacCauley, Kubinski-Lowe-Zongor-Whitaker, Michalak-MacCauley, Michalak-Whitaker, Southern Oregon; Erdos-Kaufman-Schlutt, Erdos-Mix-Schlutt, Spokane; Bland-Jacobsen, Bland-Lagarde, Yakima.

NO-HIT GAMES—Apana-Theron-Mantei, Bellingham, defeated Spokane, 4-0, June 23; Dishman, Spokane, defeated Yakima, 1-0, July 17.

FIELDING

TEAM

Team	Pct.	G	PO	A	E	DP	PB	Team	Pct.	G	PO	A	E	DP	PB
Eugene	.966	76	2007	832	101	76	17	Spokane	.955	76	1974	742	127	58	17
Everett	.963	76	2063	873	113	61	30	Bend	.955	76	2001	916	138	67	19
Boise	.963	76	1991	774	107	60	14	Yakima	.947	76	1995	850	160	65	15
Bellingham	.962	76	2044	840	113	59	36	Southern Oregon	.946	76	1998	831	163	61	15

FIRST BASEMEN

*Throws lefthanded.

Player, Team	Pct.	G	PO	A	E	DP
Bostock, Spokane	1.000	7	37	4	0	5
Boyd, Bend	.966	39	339	30	13	30
Cepeda, Eugene	1.000	3	27	3	0	5
Clifford, Bellingham*	.989	37	324	31	4	23
Cox, Southern Oregon*	.983	14	104	11	2	7
DONATI, Boise	.993	51	289	13	2	28
Galligani, Southern Oregon	.973	31	236	20	7	20
Gerald, Eugene	.976	12	76	5	2	2
Gulseth, Everett	.979	29	213	19	5	13
Haley, Yakima*	.968	54	438	39	16	36
Hickman, Eugene*	.980	63	491	44	11	57
Holdren, Bend	.984	42	396	28	7	30
Jorgensen, Bellingham*	.988	45	386	26	5	33
Kennedy, Boise	.973	46	372	23	11	27
Kim, Boise	1.000	1	1	0	0	0
Loomis, Southern Oregon	.972	4	34	1	1	4
Lootens, Everett	1.000	1	1	0	0	0
Martinez, Bellingham	1.000	1	2	1	0	0
McKinnis, Spokane	.985	9	60	7	1	9
Moore, Southern Oregon	.800	4	4	0	1	1
Morales, Southern Oregon	1.000	1	1	0	0	0
Newstrom, Yakima	1.000	2	5	1	0	0
Pitts, Yakima*	1.000	1	4	0	0	1
Roach, Everett*	.980	51	451	32	10	41
Sanders, Southern Oregon*	.991	30	212	13	2	17
Smith, Eugene	.956	4	42	1	2	5
Spiezio, Southern Oregon	1.000	6	59	4	0	4
Stasio, Everett	1.000	1	5	1	0	1
Thompson, Spokane*	.978	66	507	37	12	39
Williams, Yakima	.963	27	209	22	9	21

SECOND BASEMEN

Player, Team	Pct.	G	PO	A	E	DP
Anderson, Bend	.895	5	7	10	2	4
Bengoechea, Southern Oregon	1.000	2	1	0	0	0
Bernhardt, Bend	.950	8	7	12	1	3
Bostock, Spokane	.889	10	8	16	3	0
Cabrera, Bellingham	1.000	3	0	2	0	0
Carr, Eugene	.954	39	69	96	8	21
Cristopher, Bend	.979	14	27	20	1	2
Cuevas, Spokane	1.000	2	7	5	0	3
Diaz, Eugene	.923	8	11	13	2	5
Dilone, Southern Oregon	.913	23	38	46	8	9
Dunn, Yakima	.889	2	5	3	1	1
Dunn, Eugene	.966	37	55	89	5	18
Gillis, Spokane	1.000	1	1	1	0	0
Grunewald, Bend	.965	36	56	111	6	19
Guiel, Boise	.854	21	22	48	12	6
Gump, Everett	.945	21	48	55	6	11
King, Boise	.947	13	15	21	2	6
Loomis, Southern Oregon	.947	26	66	59	7	12
Martinez, Boise	.889	7	8	8	2	1
McDonald, Southern Oregon	.955	33	70	77	7	16
Miller, Bellingham	.984	12	24	36	1	7
Mueller, Everett	.966	50	86	143	8	25
Newstrom, Yakima	1.000	1	3	5	0	2
Patel, Bellingham	.953	66	93	194	14	34
Perez, Bend	.934	24	49	64	8	9
Post, Yakima	.937	53	96	158	17	27
Ravitz, Yakima	.963	21	45	58	4	11
Salvador, Southern Oregon	1.000	2	0	4	0	0
Sbrocco, Everett	1.000	1	1	4	0	1
Simmons, Boise	.939	35	43	80	8	16
Stafford, Everett	.935	11	19	24	3	7
Tessicini, Everett	1.000	3	1	4	0	0
Vizcaino, Boise	.971	18	26	41	2	9
WOODRIDGE, Spokane	.962	70	110	191	12	37
Yard, Yakima	.885	6	9	14	3	3

THIRD BASEMEN

Player, Team	Pct.	G	PO	A	E	DP
Bengoechea, Southern Oregon	.810	15	17	17	8	1
Bernhardt, Bend	.924	30	22	51	6	3
Bostock, Spokane	.923	8	6	6	1	0
Burke, Boise	.873	57	34	90	18	9
Cabrera, Bellingham	.880	41	16	72	12	2
D'Amico, Southern Oregon	.778	5	7	7	4	2
Diaz, Eugene	.942	47	29	84	7	6
Dilone, Southern Oregon	.938	14	7	38	3	1
Gerald, Eugene	.920	35	20	49	6	1
Greene, Bellingham	1.000	1	0	1	0	0
Heath, Bellingham	.600	2	2	1	2	0
Loomis, Southern Oregon	.859	27	25	54	13	6
Martinez, Bellingham	.851	23	11	29	7	2
Miller, Bellingham	.923	25	15	33	4	4
MUÑOZ, Bend	.889	54	31	113	18	9
Newstrom, Yakima	.842	71	59	96	29	12
Phillips, Everett	.958	35	29	62	4	4
Post, Yakima	1.000	2	0	3	0	0
Serrano, Bellingham	.714	5	4	6	4	1
Simmons, Boise	.871	21	15	39	8	4
Spiezio, Southern Oregon	.859	23	17	38	9	2
Vizcaino, Boise	1.000	5	4	7	0	0
West, Spokane	.794	32	19	35	14	1
Williams, Yakima	1.000	2	1	4	0	1
Wojtkowski, Eugene	.893	6	9	16	3	0
Yard, Yakima	.833	7	0	5	1	0
Zaletel, Everett	.879	45	28	74	14	5
Zanolla, Spokane	.898	48	32	83	13	11

SHORTSTOPS

Player, Team	Pct.	G	PO	A	E	DP
Anderson, Yakima	.926	20	36	64	8	16
Anderson, Bend	1.000	2	1	6	0	1
Bengoechea, Southern Oregon	.889	11	13	19	4	2
Bernhardt, Bend	1.000	8	3	22	0	1
Bostock, Spokane	.914	30	38	68	10	15
Buckley, Boise	.892	17	24	34	7	8
Cabrera, Bellingham	1.000	1	0	1	0	0
Corps, Spokane	1.000	4	4	5	0	2
D'Amico, Southern Oregon	.906	25	36	60	10	11
Diaz, Boise	.929	24	36	55	7	11
Dunn, Yakima	1.000	1	0	5	0	0
Galligani, Southern Oregon	.903	19	35	49	9	8
Gerald, Eugene	.880	15	18	26	6	6
Grunewald, Bend	.929	18	23	55	6	7
Guevara, Bellingham	.941	62	83	172	16	35
Harkrider, Boise	.909	3	6	4	1	0
Jaime, Yakima	.882	38	58	84	19	16
King, Everett	.921	67	120	193	27	35
King, Boise	.954	40	52	94	7	16
Miller, Bellingham	.917	20	30	47	7	10
Mueller, Everett	.913	4	11	10	2	3
Perez, Bend	.938	56	78	180	17	33
Phillips, Everett	1.000	1	2	1	0	0
S. Rivera, Spokane	.869	46	53	80	20	22
Salvador, Southern Oregon	.942	28	50	80	8	18
SUBERO, Eugene	.945	68	127	185	18	40
Tessicini, Everett	.962	15	19	32	2	8
Yard, Yakima	.954	23	41	63	5	13
Zanolla, Spokane	.953	14	17	24	2	2

OUTFIELDERS

Player, Team	Pct.	G	PO	A	E	DP
Aracena, Southern Oregon	.963	25	49	3	2	0
Banks, Southern Oregon*	.979	39	89	3	2	0
Barger, Bellingham	.992	64	126	2	1	0
Barwick, Boise	.977	50	77	7	2	0
Bernhardt, Bend	.857	6	6	0	1	0
Berube, Bellingham	.976	25	40	1	1	0
Byington, Eugene	.969	51	87	6	3	1
Compton, Yakima	.900	15	8	1	1	0
Cristopher, Bend	1.000	4	3	1	0	0
Dandridge, Spokane	.988	41	73	6	1	1
Davis, Everett	.958	22	44	2	2	0
Dermendziev, Bend	.960	19	22	2	1	0
Dilone, Southern Oregon	.900	14	17	1	2	0
DOTY, Boise	1.000	53	83	3	0	1
Duke, Spokane	.935	34	51	7	4	0
Dunavan, Bellingham	.923	40	46	2	4	1
Evans, Eugene	.971	27	33	1	1	0
Galligani, Southern Oregon	.857	15	24	0	4	0
Giudice, Bend	.920	53	71	10	7	2
Good, Eugene*	1.000	30	27	0	0	0
Greene, Boise	.979	76	136	4	3	0
Guiel, Boise	1.000	9	12	1	0	0
Harris, Southern Oregon	.934	41	67	4	5	1
Harris, Yakima	.971	43	68	0	2	0
Hartwell, Everett	.971	25	31	2	1	0
Hawkins, Yakima	.957	52	82	6	4	0
Heath, Bellingham	1.000	3	3	0	0	0
Iatarola, Boise*	.988	42	82	3	1	1
Jackson, Yakima*	1.000	16	20	0	0	0
Jaime, Yakima	1.000	4	3	1	0	0
Jimenez, Eugene	.947	61	66	5	4	1
Johnson, Spokane	.967	59	139	8	5	1
Jones, Bend	.985	31	57	7	1	0
Jorgensen, Bellingham*	1.000	13	19	2	0	0
Keel, Southern Oregon	.957	57	84	5	4	1
Kim, Boise	1.000	2	3	0	0	0
King, Boise	1.000	1	1	0	0	0
Latham, Yakima	.936	51	83	5	6	0
Lootens, Everett	.986	37	63	8	1	2
Mason, Everett	1.000	2	2	0	0	0
Myrow, Bend	.954	69	136	9	7	2
Oglesby, Eugene	1.000	39	77	2	0	1

NORTHWEST LEAGUE · CLASS A · NORTHWEST LEAGUE

Player, Team	Pct.	G	PO	A	E	DP
Ortman, Bend	.976	55	76	5	2	0
Pitts, Yakima*	.900	59	88	2	10	0
Powell, Spokane	1.000	5	1	0	0	0
Prieto, Spokane*	.962	73	119	9	5	0
Rackley, Bellingham	.941	32	46	2	3	0
Ravitz, Yakima	1.000	2	3	0	0	0
Reese, Southern Oregon*	.945	38	47	5	3	1
Rhone, Eugene	.964	39	51	2	2	0
Richardson, Southern Oregon	.983	35	57	1	1	1
A. Rivera, Spokane	1.000	1	1	0	0	0
Roach, Everett*	.944	27	33	1	2	0
Romero, Yakima	.962	13	24	1	1	0
Scheibe, Spokane	.978	39	40	4	1	0
Serrano, Bellingham	.972	22	35	0	1	0
Simmons, Boise	1.000	8	14	1	0	0
Singleton, Everett*	.974	55	106	6	3	0
Sturdivant, Bellingham*	.956	62	121	8	6	2
Thompson, Spokane*	1.000	1	1	0	0	0
Williams, Everett	.973	73	106	3	3	0
Yard, Yakima	1.000	6	13	1	0	0

CATCHERS

Player, Team	Pct.	G	PO	A	E	DP	PB
Augustine, Bellingham	.974	7	35	2	1	0	2
Barrett, Everett	.989	34	233	33	3	2	17
Berube, Bellingham	.933	4	27	1	2	1	4
Cardenas, Bellingham	.987	46	346	34	5	1	15
Cavalli, Boise	.989	12	77	9	1	0	3
CECERE, Everett	.994	46	317	39	2	4	11
Dandridge, Spokane	.984	24	172	17	3	0	6
Evans, Eugene	1.000	5	8	1	0	0	0
Fasano, Eugene	.997	34	276	38	1	7	5
Heath, Bellingham	.857	6	17	1	3	0	4
Higgins, Bend	.970	44	290	31	10	4	9
Ibanez, Bellingham	.993	20	137	15	1	0	11
Johnson, Southern Oregon	.933	1	12	2	1	0	1
Kessler, Boise	1.000	9	44	10	0	0	1
Kim, Boise	1.000	2	2	1	0	0	1
Luzinski, Yakima	.985	43	289	44	5	2	5
McKinnis, Spokane	.985	39	291	29	5	3	6
Moore, Southern Oregon	.965	32	199	23	8	1	7
Morales, Southern Oregon	.982	48	281	53	6	3	8
Pineiro, Bend	.972	5	32	3	1	0	1
Porter, Bend	.950	4	16	3	1	0	2
Reynolds, Everett	1.000	8	54	7	0	0	5
Rosario, Spokane	.967	16	132	16	5	0	5
Smith, Bend	.977	31	214	40	6	3	4
Speakman, Boise	.989	66	472	51	6	0	9
Stadler, Spokane	1.000	1	6	0	0	0	0
Sweeney, Eugene	.983	43	364	46	7	0	12
Uribe, Yakima	.988	13	67	12	1	0	4
West, Spokane	1.000	2	10	0	0	0	5
Zahner, Yakima	.977	29	184	32	5	1	6

PITCHERS

Player, Team	Pct.	G	PO	A	E	DP
Altman, Everett	.897	15	5	21	3	1
Aminoff, Eugene	1.000	17	2	5	0	0
Anderson, Everett	.917	17	4	7	1	0
Apana, Bellingham	.929	14	6	7	1	0
Atkinson, Eugene*	1.000	23	1	12	0	1
Bacon, Eugene	.857	16	1	5	1	3
Baine, Everett*	1.000	1	1	2	0	0
Baldwin, Southern Oregon*	.882	15	2	13	2	2
Baumann, Everett	.500	14	1	1	2	0
Baxter, Yakima*	1.000	25	2	8	0	0
Bengoechea, Southern Oregon	1.000	1	1	0	0	0
Binkley, Yakima*	.667	14	0	2	1	0
Blanchette, Boise*	1.000	20	1	8	0	0
Bland, Yakima*	.889	16	1	7	1	0
Botts, Boise	.923	13	6	6	1	0
Bourgeois, Everett	.917	15	4	7	1	0
Brassington, Eugene	1.000	11	5	17	0	2
Brewer, Eugene	.875	10	1	6	1	0
Brown, Boise	.933	15	3	11	1	2
Bruce, Bellingham	1.000	8	0	3	0	1
Burley, Eugene*	.941	22	1	15	1	0
Calvin, Bend	1.000	13	1	8	0	0
Carmona, Bellingham	1.000	23	2	8	0	0
Clark, Spokane*	1.000	13	0	2	0	0
Collett, Bellingham	1.000	1	1	1	0	0
Conley, Bend*	1.000	20	0	6	0	1
Conte, Southern Oregon	.833	18	4	16	4	2
Cook, Yakima	1.000	24	6	5	0	2
Crow, Bellingham	1.000	25	1	6	0	1
Day, Everett*	1.000	30	0	11	0	0
DeWett, Bend*	1.000	14	0	7	0	0
Dilone, Southern Oregon	1.000	2	0	1	0	0
Dishman, Spokane*	.947	12	5	13	1	0
Doughty, Bellingham	1.000	14	5	12	0	2
Doyle, Spokane*	1.000	6	0	1	0	0

Player, Team	Pct.	G	PO	A	E	DP
Drewien, Spokane	.857	23	3	3	1	0
Drumm, Everett	.833	20	1	4	1	2
Drysdale, Boise	1.000	18	1	4	0	0
Duran, Yakima*	.889	20	2	6	1	0
Edsell, Boise	1.000	13	5	14	0	2
Eiffert, Bend*	.000	7	0	0	1	0
Erdos, Spokane	.900	16	3	6	1	0
Fargas, Spokane	1.000	21	1	2	0	0
Flury, Eugene	.900	27	5	4	1	0
Fontes, Boise	.917	14	5	6	1	0
Franklin, Bellingham	.929	15	6	20	2	0
Franko, Everett*	.952	13	4	16	1	2
Garcia, Yakima	.941	36	1	15	1	2
Gienger, Southern Oregon	1.000	4	3	0	0	0
Goodrich, Bend	.600	17	2	1	2	1
Grande, Everett	1.000	21	3	6	0	1
Granger, Eugene*	.667	8	2	2	0	0
Grenert, Boise	.909	26	1	9	1	1
Groot, Yakima	1.000	12	2	7	0	0
Grundy, Eugene	.700	15	4	3	3	0
Hancock, Boise	1.000	3	1	5	0	1
Hanneman, Everett	1.000	19	3	2	0	1
Harikkala, Bellingham	1.000	4	0	1	0	0
Harris, Boise*	.960	16	4	20	1	3
Henderson, Bend	.778		3	4	2	1
Hogue, Eugene*	1.000	21	3	0	0	0
Iglesias, Yakima	.800	10	3	5	2	0
Jacobsen, Yakima	1.000	25	2	6	0	0
Johnson, Bend	1.000	8	3	4	0	1
Kane, Boise	1.000	12	0	3	0	0
Kaufman, Spokane	.923	25	2	10	1	0
Keagle, Eugene	.957	15	10	12	1	1
King, Southern Oregon	.750	22	0	3	1	1
Kosman, Eugene	1.000	16	1	13	0	2
Krueger, Bellingham*	1.000	13	0	6	0	0
Kubinski, Southern Oregon*	.833	12	3	12	3	0
LAGARDE, Yakima	1.000	15	7	21	0	2
Lasbury, Bend	.833	13	0	5	1	1
Lemke, Southern Oregon	.000	8	0	1	1	0
Lloyd, Boise	.818	13	5	4	2	1
Lopez, Eugene*	1.000	9	5	0	0	0
Lorraine, Boise*	1.000	6	3	6	0	1
Lowe, Southern Oregon	.857	22	3	3	1	1
MacCauley, Southern Oregon	.867	25	2	11	2	1
Manning, Southern Oregon*	.889	15	4	20	3	1
Mantei, Bellingham	1.000	26	4	7	0	0
Martin, Everett	.833	25	1	9	2	0
McClinton, Bend*	1.000	18	2	9	0	0
McLain, Spokane	1.000	14	3	5	0	0
Mejia, Boise*	1.000	3	2	8	0	2
Michalak, Southern Oregon*	.973	16	9	27	1	2
Mix, Spokane	.750	24	2	4	2	0
Montane, Bellingham	.950	15	8	11	1	0
Moore, Bend	.844	15	10	17	5	1
Myers, Boise	1.000	11	0	2	0	0
Nedeau, Boise	1.000	24	9	13	0	0
Neier, Bend	1.000	15	5	8	0	1
Perez, Yakima	1.000	17	3	5	0	0
Pincavitch, Yakima	.815	9	4	18	5	1
Puffer, Boise	.667	19	0	2	1	0
Purdy, Boise	1.000	1	0	3	0	1
Rajotte, Southern Oregon*	.600	9	0	3	2	0
Ralston, Eugene	.957	15	9	13	1	1
Rawltzer, Eugene*	.667	6	1	1	1	0
Rekar, Bend	.909	13	5	15	2	1
Santana, Bellingham	1.000	15	1	4	0	0
Santos, Eugene*	1.000	9	2	2	0	0
Saugstad, Everett	1.000	12	3	4	0	0
Schlutt, Spokane*	.933	35	2	12	1	0
Schneider, Bend*	.500	4	0	1	1	0
Slade, Boise	1.000	24	1	7	0	0
Brent Smith, Everett	.857	9	3	3	1	0
Brook Smith, Everett*	.893	17	3	22	3	0
Smith, Spokane	.857	14	3	3	1	1
Sobkoviak, Bend	.938	15	5	10	1	1
Sosa, Bellingham	.818	18	4	5	2	1
Soult, Everett	1.000	12	4	3	0	0
Spykstra, Yakima	1.000	13	9	4	0	0
Theron, Bellingham	.938	23	3	12	1	0
Thompson, Bellingham	1.000	17	6	2	0	0
Towns, Eugene	.941	15	5	11	1	1
Urbina, Southern Oregon	.938	13	4	11	1	1
Watts, Yakima*	.857	2	2	4	1	0
Wehn, Bend	1.000	13	1	3	0	0
Whitaker, Southern Oregon	1.000	27	2	7	0	1
White, Spokane	1.000	23	4	1	0	0
Winchester, Spokane*	.667	17	0	2	1	0
Winslett, Yakima	1.000	8	4	2	0	0
Wolcott, Bellingham	.920	15	9	14	2	2
Wolff, Spokane	.938	25	4	11	1	1
Zolecki, Bend	.900	14	2	7	1	0
Zongor, Southern Oregon*	.875	27	3	4	1	0

The following players did not have any fielding statistics at the positions indicated or appeared only as a designated hitter, pinch-hitter or pinch-runner: Aracena, p; Cabrera, 1b; Carr, 3b; Cecere, 3b, ss; Dilone, ss; N. Dunn, 3b; Galligani, p; Gillis, ss, of; Holland, p; Knox, p; Matos, p; Munoz, 2b; Razhigaev, p; Runzi, p; Sanders, of; Thomas, of; Walsh, p.

LEAGUE CHAMPIONS

Year	Team	Pct.	Year	Team	Pct.	Year	Team	Pct.
1901—	Portland	.675	1950—	Yakima	.613	1974—	Bellingham	.619
1902—	Butte	.608	1951—	Spokane	.655		Eugene c	.571
1903—	Butte	.578	1952—	Victoria	.631	1975—	Portland	.545
1904—	Boise	.625	1953—	Salem	.635		Eugene d	.684
1905—	Vancouver	.586		Spokane*	.590	1976—	Portland	.556
	Everett*	.667	1954—	Vancouver*	.636		Walla Walla d	.639
1906—	Tacoma	.600		Lewiston	.629	1977—	Bellingham e	.618
1907—	Aberdeen	.625	1955—	Salem	.646		Portland	.667
1908—	Vancouver	.578		Eugene*	.639	1978—	Grays Harbor f	.671
1909—	Seattle	.653	1956—	Yakima	.691		Eugene	.514
1910—	Spokane	.596		Yakima	.619	1979—	Central Oregon d	.606
1911—	Vancouver	.628	1957—	Eugene	.576		Walla Walla	.571
1912—	Seattle	.600		Wenatchee*	.647	1980—	Bellingham g	.643
1913—	Vancouver	.600	1958—	Lewiston	.621		Eugene g	.529
1914—	Vancouver	.632		Yakima*	.594	1981—	Medford d	.600
1915—	Seattle	.564	1959—	Salem	.623		Bellingham	.557
1916—	Spokane	.622		Yakima*	.563	1982—	Medford	.757
1917—	Great Falls	.592	1960—	Yakima	.638		Salem d	.486
1918—	Seattle	.588		Yakima	.562	1983—	Medford h	.735
1919—	Seattle	.590	1961—	Lewiston*	.621		Bellingham	.588
1920—	Victoria	.600		Yakima	.600	1984—	Tri-Cities h	.622
1921—	Yakima	.710	1962—	Wenatchee*	.574		Medford	.608
	Yakima	.660		Tri-City	.580	1985—	Everett h	.541
1922—	Calgary†	.600	1963—	Lewiston	.594		Eugene	.541
1923-36—	Did not operate.			Yakima*	.613	1986—	Bellingham h	.608
1937—	Wenatchee	.603	1964—	Eugene*	.636		Eugene	.608
	Tacoma*	.627		Yakima*	.611	1987—	Spokane c	.711
1938—	Yakima	.583	1965—	Lewiston	.667		Everett	.653
	Bellingham (2nd)†	.511		Tri-City*	.681	1988—	Southern Oregon	.605
1939—	Wenatchee	.601	1966—	Tri-City	.679		Spokane d	.553
	Tacoma (2nd)†	.533	1967—	Medford	.607	1989—	Southern Oregon	.600
1940—	Spokane	.587	1968—	Tri-City	.600		Spokane d	.547
	Tacoma (4th)†	.500	1969—	Rogue Valley	.633	1990—	Boise	.697
1941—	Spokane	.669	1970—	Lewiston a	.538		Spokane d	.645
1942—	Vancouver	.594		Coos Bay-No. Bend	.563	1991—	Boise d	.658
1943-45—	Did not operate.		1971—	Tri-City a	.625		Yakima	.579
1946—	Wenatchee	.622		Bend	.538	1992—	Bellingham d	.566
1947—	Vancouver	.566	1972—	Lewiston a	.675		Bend	.566
1948—	Spokane	.614		Walla Walla	.513	1993—	Bellingham	.579
1949—	Yakima	.660	1973—	Walla Walla b	.638		Boise d	.539
	Vancouver (2nd)†	.615		Portland	.563			

*Won split-season playoff. †Won four-club playoff. §League disbanded June 18. aLeague divided into Northern and Southern divisions, declared champion under league rules. bLeague divided into Eastern and Western divisions, declared champion under league rules. cLeague divided into Eastern and Western divisions; won two-team playoff. dLeague divided into Northern and Southern divisions; won two-team playoff. eLeague divided into Affiliate and Independent divisions; won two-team playoff. fDeclared league champion after winning one-game playoff. Balance of playoff canceled due to rain and wet grounds. gDeclared co-champion after winning one game. Balance of playoff canceled due to rain and wet grounds. hLeague divided into Washington and Oregon divisions; won two-team playoff. (NOTE—Known as Pacific Northwest League 1901-02, Pacific National League 1903-04, Northwestern League 1905-18, Pacific Coast International League 1919-22 and Western International League 1937-54.)

SOUTH ATLANTIC LEAGUE

FINAL STANDINGS

FIRST HALF

NORTHERN DIVISION

Team	W	L	T	Pct.	GB
Greensboro (Yankees)	45	25	0	.643	....
Charleston (W.Va.) (Reds)	38	32	0	.543	7
Hagerstown (Blue Jays)	34	36	0	.486	11
Fayetteville (Tigers)	31	38	0	.449	13½
Spartanburg (Phillies)	28	42	0	.400	17
Hickory (White Sox)	26	43	0	.377	18½
Asheville (Astros)	26	43	0	.377	18½

SOUTHERN DIVISION

Team	W	L	T	Pct.	GB
Savannah (Cardinals)	47	23	0	.671	....
Macon (Braves)	41	29	0	.586	6
Columbus (Indians)	40	30	0	.571	7
Albany (Orioles)	39	31	0	.557	8
Charleston (SC) (Rangers)	34	36	0	.486	13
Augusta (Pirates)	31	39	0	.443	16
Capital City (Mets)	28	41	0	.406	18½

SECOND HALF

NORTHERN DIVISION

Team	W	L	T	Pct.	GB
Fayetteville (Tigers)	44	28	0	.611	....
Greensboro (Yankees)	40	31	0	.563	3½
Hagerstown (Blue Jays)	40	32	0	.556	4
Charleston (W.Va.) (Reds)	38	32	0	.543	5
Spartanburg (Phillies)	34	38	0	.472	10
Hickory (White Sox)	26	45	0	.366	17½
Asheville (Astros)	25	45	0	.357	18

SOUTHERN DIVISION

Team	W	L	T	Pct.	GB
Savannah (Cardinals)	47	25	0	.653	....
Columbus (Indians)	46	26	0	.639	1
Capital City (Mets)	36	36	0	.500	11
Macon (Braves)	33	38	0	.465	13½
Albany (Orioles)	32	40	0	.444	15
Charleston (SC) (Rangers)	31	41	0	.431	16
Augusta (Pirates)	28	43	0	.394	18½

COMPOSITE

Team	Sav.	C'us	Gbr.	CWV	Fay.	Mac.	Hag.	Alb.	CSC	C.C.	Spt.	Aug.	Hick.	Ash.	W	L	T	Pct.	GB
Savannah (Cardinals)	...	11	6	2	6	9	4	9	11	7	5	12	5	7	94	48	0	.662	....
Columbus (Indians)	6	...	4	7	5	8	3	13	9	6	4	9	6	6	86	56	0	.606	8
Greensboro (Yankees)	2	4	...	7	8	4	10	6	7	6	7	4	11	9	85	56	0	.603	8½
Charleston (W.Va.) (Reds)	5	1	5	...	4	3	10	4	5	4	10	6	10	9	76	64	0	.543	17
Fayetteville (Tigers)	2	3	8	12	...	4	3	3	7	10	4	8	6	6	75	66	0	.532	18½
Macon (Braves)	7	4	4	5	3	...	5	6	8	6	4	10	6	6	74	67	0	.525	19½
Hagerstown (Blue Jays)	4	5	4	6	12	3	...	4	3	5	7	4	8	9	74	68	0	.521	20
Albany (Orioles)	3	3	2	4	5	8	4	...	9	12	4	8	4	5	71	71	0	.500	23
Charleston (SC) (Rangers)	5	5	1	3	5	3	5	3	...	8	6	7	6	3	65	77	0	.458	29
Capital City (Mets)	7	6	2	4	1	6	3	4	6	...	9	6	5	5	64	77	0	.454	29½
Spartanburg (Phillies)	5	4	5	4	4	4	2	5	...	8	5	9	62	80	0	.437	32
Augusta (Pirates)	0	7	3	2	4	6	4	7	6	0	...	6	6	59	82	0	.418	34½
Hickory (White Sox)	3	2	5	4	3	1	8	4	2	3	7	2	...	8	52	88	0	.371	41
Asheville (Astros)	1	1	7	4	6	2	3	3	5	2	7	2	8	...	51	88	0	.367	41½

Capital City played home games in Columbia, S.C.

Playoffs—Greensboro defeated Fayetteville, two games to one; Savannah defeated Greensboro, three games to two, to win league championship.

Regular-season attendance—Albany, 140,140; Asheville, 121,573; Augusta, 115,051; Capital City, 144,054; Charleston (S.C.), 98,670; Charleston (W.Va.), 110,118; Columbus, 122,137; Fayetteville, 100,321; Greensboro, 201,222; Hagerstown, 95,702; Hickory, 283,727; Macon, 96,450; Savannah, 106,287; Spartanburg, 53,975. Total—1,789,427. Playoffs (8 games)—13,869. All-Star Game—4,648.

Managers—Albany, Mike O'Berry; Asheville, Bobby Ramos; Augusta, Trent Jewett; Capital City, Ron Washington; Charleston (S.C.), Walt Williams; Charleston (W.Va.), Tom Nieto; Columbus, Mike Brown; Fayetteville, Mark Wagner; Greensboro, Bill Evers; Hagerstown, Jim Nettles; Hickory, Fred Kendall; Macon, Randy Ingle; Savannah, Chris Maloney; Spartanburg, Roy Majtyka.

All-Star team: 1B—D.J. Boston, Hagerstown; 2B—Donovan Mitchell, Asheville; 3B—Eric Chavez, Albany; SS—Derek Jeter, Greensboro; OF—Jose Herrera, Hagerstown; Matt Luke, Greensboro; Derek Hacopian, Columbus; DH—Nick Delvecchio, Greensboro; C—Jason Kendall, Augusta; RHP—J.J. Thobe, Columbus; LHP—Ryan Karp, Greensboro; Most Valuable Player—D.J. Boston, Hagerstown; Most Outstanding Pitcher—Ryan Karp, Greensboro; Manager of the Year—Chris Maloney, Savannah.

BATTING

TEAM

Team	Avg.	G	AB	R	OR	H	TB	2B	3B	HR	RBI	SH	SF	HP	BB	Int. BB	SO	SB	CS	LOB
Greensboro	.266	141	4699	763	633	1249	1857	248	39	94	665	27	42	82	644	16	994	190	78	1096
Spartanburg	.261	142	4717	630	649	1231	1653	219	31	47	547	69	47	68	442	13	849	124	82	1000
Augusta	.259	141	4694	627	711	1218	1664	219	34	53	545	31	43	55	412	13	948	149	80	914
Hagerstown	.258	142	4733	681	621	1221	1860	258	42	99	614	32	34	53	474	19	1049	189	89	961
Columbus	.255	142	4777	700	552	1218	1835	224	30	111	614	28	46	91	414	16	1015	176	73	971
Asheville	.252	139	4577	595	801	1155	1678	243	26	76	518	30	37	49	422	5	1053	176	112	886
Macon	.252	141	4630	611	529	1168	1685	210	44	73	534	56	44	59	443	26	994	167	105	931
Albany	.247	142	4663	631	636	1152	1664	234	28	74	552	25	36	65	507	17	959	127	63	1083
Savannah	.247	142	4662	670	472	1151	1618	209	33	64	579	40	50	66	640	11	1021	134	59	1018
Charleston (S.C.)	.242	142	4714	582	690	1142	1645	223	41	66	491	38	34	38	493	11	1021	162	100	962
Fayetteville	.242	141	4685	600	627	1134	1630	210	41	68	600	23	34	56	718	15	1142	127	75	1092
Charleston (W.Va.)	.242	140	4576	660	678	1106	1647	220	42	79	576	27	52	69	596	14	1101	140	77	1003
Capital City	.241	141	4570	624	713	1101	1494	206	35	39	541	48	41	50	590	16	1085	178	76	993
Hickory	.224	140	4586	540	692	1028	1410	166	36	48	443	42	33	56	493	7	1051	153	80	939

(Leading qualifiers for batting championship—383 or more plate appearances)

*Bats lefthanded.   †Switch-hitter.

Player, Team	Avg.	G	AB	R	H	TB	2B	3B	HR	RBI	SH	SF	HP	BB	Int. BB	SO	SB	CS
Rupp, Brian, Savannah	.320	122	472	80	151	208	31	7	4	81	1	5	3	48	2	70	3	2
Herrera, Jose, Hagerstown*	.317	95	388	60	123	170	22	5	5	42	5	4	7	26	1	63	36	20
Hacopian, Derek, Columbus	.315	131	454	81	143	244	29	0	24	82	1	7	13	60	6	69	4	2
Boston, D.J., Hagerstown*	.315	127	464	77	146	228	35	4	13	93	0	3	4	54	6	77	31	11
Brito, Luis, Spartanburg†	.313	127	467	56	146	170	16	4	0	33	8	3	1	11	0	47	9	12
Pecorilli, Aldo, Savannah	.305	141	515	75	157	243	30	7	14	93	0	8	6	81	7	86	16	11
White, Don, Capital City	.304	114	441	86	134	173	18	6	3	41	9	1	5	54	0	75	43	14
Thomas, Tim, Fayetteville	.303	104	380	80	115	164	31	3	4	48	2	3	3	82	0	85	5	1
Owens, Billy, Albany†	.297	120	458	64	136	196	23	2	11	66	1	5	2	49	6	70	3	5
Grijak, Kevin, Macon*	.296	120	389	50	115	172	26	5	7	58	2	12	6	37	4	37	9	5

Departmental leaders: G—Pecorilli, 141; AB—Luke, 549; R—McEwing, 94; H—Luke, Pecorilli, 157; TB—Luke, 267; 2B—Chavez, 38; 3B—Henry, 12; HR—Hacopian, 24; RBI—Burke, 96; SH—McEwing, 15; SF—Burke, 14; HP—Delvecchio, 23; BB—Keister, Wilson, 91; IBB—Delvecchio, 9; SO—Kimsey, 168; SB—Hawkins, 67; CS—Hinds, 22.

(All players—listed alphabetically)

Player, Team	Avg.	G	AB	R	H	TB	2B	3B	HR	RBI	SH	SF	HP	BB	Int. BB	SO	SB	CS
Adams, Jason, Capital City†	.175	31	80	18	14	16	2	0	0	5	0	0	0	13	0	33	3	1
Albaladejo, Randy, Asheville	.231	66	225	20	52	76	22	1	0	20	1	2	2	9	0	49	2	2
Anderson, Charlie, Savannah	.247	46	146	17	36	59	7	2	4	20	1	2	0	10	1	37	3	1
Anthony, Mark, Hagerstown	.176	11	34	6	6	12	0	0	2	5	0	0	2	7	0	13	0	0
Aquino, Geronimo, Hickory	.000	4	10	0	0	0	0	0	0	0	0	0	0	0	0	8	0	0
Arntzen, Brian, Columbus	.188	35	112	10	21	29	5	0	1	10	2	0	11	0	24	0	1
Ashby, Chris, Greensboro	.750	1	4	2	3	3	0	0	0	0	0	0	0	1	0	0	0	0
Ashton, Jeff, Charleston (W.Va.)	.167	5	6	1	1	1	0	0	0	2	0	2	1	3	0	3	0	0
Austin, Jake, Augusta†	.294	123	449	71	132	185	24	4	7	54	6	1	9	32	4	85	14	7
Barnden, Myles, Albany*	.362	12	47	6	17	26	3	0	2	11	0	0	0	6	0	5	0	1
Bautista, Juan, Albany	.237	98	295	24	70	91	17	2	0	28	3	4	7	14	0	72	11	3
Beamon, Trey, Augusta*	.271	104	373	64	101	131	18	6	0	45	0	4	6	48	2	60	19	6
Bell, Curt, Fayetteville	.143	4	14	0	2	2	0	0	0	1	0	0	1	0	0	5	0	0
Benbow, Lou, Hagerstown	.166	71	193	22	32	44	5	2	1	12	2	2	2	13	0	47	2	1
Bennett, Gary, Spartanburg	.254	42	126	18	32	38	4	1	0	15	2	1	1	12	0	22	0	2
Berrios, Harry, Albany	.207	46	145	16	30	46	5	1	3	16	0	2	5	18	1	20	2	0
Bess, John, Charleston (W.Va.)†	.229	106	358	35	82	127	16	7	5	67	2	2	6	47	2	107	10	5
Bethke, Jamie, Charleston (S.C.)†	.247	103	352	31	87	109	19	0	1	31	4	4	0	32	2	54	3	10
Bigler, Jeff, Spartanburg*	.260	66	231	26	60	88	23	1	1	35	0	2	3	23	3	43	0	0
Billingsley, Marvin, Asheville*	1.000	28	1	0	1	1	0	0	0	0	0	0	0	0	0	0	0	0
Black, Keith, Savannah	.238	125	442	68	105	133	11	1	5	59	5	7	13	76	1	80	22	11
Blanton, Garrett, Savannah	.178	84	241	34	43	67	10	4	2	22	0	0	8	37	0	64	3	2
Boston, D.J., Hagerstown*	.315	127	464	77	146	228	35	4	13	93	0	3	4	54	6	77	31	11
Boulware, Benjamin, Hickory	.193	18	57	6	11	13	2	0	0	3	0	1	0	8	0	10	2	1
Brito, Luis, Spartanburg†	.313	127	467	56	146	170	16	4	0	33	8	3	1	11	0	47	9	12
Brock, Tarrik, Fayetteville*	.215	116	427	60	92	117	8	4	3	47	5	4	5	54	2	108	25	16
Brophy, E.J., Spartanburg	.185	51	162	12	30	40	4	0	2	14	3	0	4	12	0	27	0	1
Bryant, Pat, Columbus	.263	121	483	82	127	205	26	2	16	61	0	2	13	43	1	117	43	11
Buckley, Terrell, Macon	.196	42	107	10	21	26	3	1	0	9	3	1	2	14	0	30	9	6
Burguillos, Carlos, Fayetteville	.292	68	240	45	70	102	11	6	3	40	3	3	0	30	0	26	13	6
Burke, Alan, Spartanburg	.281	129	481	62	135	215	29	0	17	96	0	14	5	49	0	92	1	1
Burr, Chris, Charleston (S.C.)	.235	118	409	36	96	150	18	3	10	65	1	4	8	48	2	95	0	4
Burton, Steve, Charleston (S.C.)*	.237	118	354	39	84	127	16	0	9	44	4	1	0	47	2	101	1	4
Byrne, Clayton, Albany	.276	122	457	64	126	176	26	3	6	55	6	3	4	42	0	69	23	11
Calder, Joe, Augusta	.205	12	39	6	8	9	1	0	0	3	1	0	1	0	0	18	0	0
Campusano, Genaro, Char. (S.C.)	.174	29	69	3	12	23	2	0	3	11	0	1	0	6	0	40	0	0
Cardenas, Epi, Columbus	.242	119	472	53	114	161	25	5	4	68	0	4	7	26	1	72	1	3
Carmona, William, Spartanburg	.200	4	10	2	2	2	0	0	0	3	0	0	0	2	0	1	0	0
Carpenter, Brian, Savannah	.000	28	1	0	0	0	0	0	0	0	0	0	0	0	0	1	0	0
Cedeno, Eddie, Asheville	.097	9	31	3	3	4	1	0	0	1	0	0	1	0	0	10	0	1
Chambers, Mark, Macon	.205	15	39	6	8	8	0	0	0	4	0	0	0	3	0	11	4	1
Chavez, Eric, Albany	.250	139	476	74	119	215	38	2	18	74	0	4	5	79	6	124	3	3
Childers, Terry, Capital City	.250	3	8	2	2	3	1	0	0	0	0	0	0	0	0	3	0	0
Clark, Howie, Albany*	.235	7	17	2	4	4	0	0	0	1	0	0	0	0	0	3	1	0
Claudio, Patricio, Columbus	.256	98	312	48	80	100	8	6	0	26	1	0	2	23	0	67	40	12
Clyburn, Danny, Augusta	.265	127	457	55	121	177	21	4	9	66	0	5	5	37	1	97	5	5
Colon, Hector, Savannah	.231	100	295	39	68	75	5	1	0	18	3	3	4	30	0	33	13	5
Coolbaugh, Mike, Hagerstown	.244	112	389	58	95	168	23	1	16	62	4	4	3	32	5	94	4	3
Correa, Miguel, Macon†	.265	131	495	58	131	203	26	8	10	61	2	5	4	30	5	84	18	17
Cossins, Tim, Charleston (S.C.)	.146	27	89	8	13	15	2	0	0	10	0	1	3	7	0	21	0	1
Cradle, Cobi, Charleston (W.Va.)*	.352	44	159	34	56	68	9	0	1	12	1	0	2	35	0	19	16	6
Cradle, Rickey, Hagerstown	.254	129	441	72	112	185	26	4	13	62	1	4	11	68	2	125	19	14
Cranford, Jay, Augusta	.267	128	469	55	125	174	31	0	6	72	3	9	6	32	0	101	17	2
Curtis, Kevin, Albany	.200	59	180	26	36	64	7	0	7	27	1	1	3	38	0	36	4	3
Daubach, Brian, Capital City*	.280	102	379	50	106	152	19	3	7	72	1	7	5	52	5	84	6	1
Delgado, Geno, Albany	.209	78	206	33	43	58	9	3	0	14	3	1	3	28	0	35	14	5
DeLosSantos, Reynaldo, Spartanburg*	.231	37	104	12	24	33	2	2	1	11	4	0	0	9	1	31	1	1
Delvecchio, Nick, Greensboro*	.270	137	485	90	131	230	30	3	21	80	0	2	23	80	9	156	4	3
DeJesus, Malvin, Fayetteville	.119	17	59	8	7	7	0	0	0	2	0	0	0	7	0	14	2	1
Diaz, Einar, Columbus	.000	1	3	0	0	0	0	0	0	0	0	0	0	0	0	1	0	0
Dietz, Steve, Fayetteville†	.181	36	105	14	19	24	3	1	0	13	0	1	0	18	0	17	2	4
Doster, David, Spartanburg	.274	60	223	34	61	85	15	0	3	20	6	1	3	25	1	36	1	0
Dotel, Mariano, Hagerstown†	.207	99	270	31	56	74	10	4	0	16	10	3	1	20	0	91	6	5
Doucette, Darren, Savannah*	.249	91	225	22	56	86	12	3	4	21	0	2	3	53	3	87	0	1
Dudek, Steve, Savannah*	.174	23	46	1	8	9	1	0	0	2	1	0	0	3	0	11	0	0
Duplessis, Dave, Columbus*	.289	52	187	26	54	89	7	2	8	32	0	2	15	12	0	60	0	1
Duran, Felipe, Columbus	.185	48	119	15	22	33	2	0	3	15	2	1	4	6	0	22	4	2
Durso, Joe, Hagerstown	.171	15	41	3	7	9	2	0	0	5	0	0	0	4	0	9	0	0
Eaddy, Keith, Albany	.262	86	229	40	60	86	13	2	3	18	1	0	1	41	0	69	12	9
Eggleston, Wayne, Charleston (S.C.)	.227	91	216	34	49	73	13	4	1	10	3	1	2	23	1	54	7	5
Elliott, Greg, Asheville*	.269	120	424	50	114	174	25	1	11	55	0	4	3	42	2	95	17	10

Player, Team	Avg.	G	AB	R	H	TB	2B	3B	HR	RBI	SH	SF	HP	BB	Int. BB	SO	SB	CS
Espinosa, Ramon, Augusta	.297	70	266	32	79	100	9	3	2	27	1	3	2	12	2	51	17	5
Evans, Jason, Hickory†	.212	82	274	26	58	69	6	1	1	29	3	2	2	31	2	56	11	4
Evans, Matt, Fayetteville*	.266	138	515	76	137	216	28	0	17	94	0	6	2	88	5	125	5	3
Evans, Stan, Spartanburg*	.273	83	275	52	75	95	13	2	1	24	4	3	4	46	2	48	17	12
Evans, Tom, Hagerstown	.257	119	389	47	100	148	25	1	7	54	0	4	3	53	2	61	9	2
Faircloth, Eugene, Hickory	.173	25	81	4	14	16	2	0	0	4	1	0	2	3	0	25	0	1
Farmer, Randy, Capital City	.230	16	61	5	14	16	2	0	0	1	2	1	2	1	0	9	1	1
Feeley, Peter, Fayetteville	.251	98	323	33	81	111	18	3	2	36	1	2	3	49	0	76	6	5
Flores, Joe, Capital City	.167	34	96	12	16	24	2	0	2	9	1	0	0	18	0	28	3	1
Franklin, Micah, Charleston (W.Va.)†..	.262	102	343	56	90	163	14	4	17	68	3	6	18	47	4	109	6	1
Fraraccio, Dan, Hickory	.211	41	147	13	31	45	9	1	1	15	0	1	3	6	0	21	2	2
French, Ronnie, Savannah	.197	70	152	30	30	46	4	0	4	12	0	0	4	22	0	44	4	1
Frias, Hanley, Charleston (S.C.)	.230	132	473	61	109	149	20	4	4	37	4	4	3	40	0	108	27	14
Frye, Dan, Charleston (W.Va.)	.267	134	472	64	126	202	35	7	9	70	1	8	2	76	0	122	13	15
Garcia, Adrian, Macon	.267	47	105	13	28	39	4	2	1	11	4	0	0	6	0	44	2	3
Garcia, Guillermo, Capital City	.289	119	429	64	124	165	28	2	3	72	1	3	10	49	1	60	10	8
Garr, Ralph, Macon	.224	57	143	19	32	49	10	2	1	23	1	1	1	21	0	54	5	1
Garvey, Don, Augusta	.169	43	124	12	21	30	3	0	2	6	2	2	3	10	0	18	2	2
Gholston, Rico, Augusta	.231	120	415	52	96	149	20	3	9	46	1	4	4	26	1	130	2	1
Gill, Chris, Charleston (W.Va.)	.000	1	2	1	0	0	0	0	0	0	0	0	0	1	0	0	0	0
Gonzalez, Jimmy, Asheville	.221	43	149	16	33	50	5	0	4	15	2	1	0	7	0	37	3	1
Gonzalez, Ricky, Charleston (W.Va.)	.115	34	52	6	6	7	1	0	0	5	1	1	0	9	0	8	2	1
Grapenthien, Dan, Asheville	.204	28	98	7	20	28	6	1	0	6	0	0	1	8	0	31	1	3
Grijak, Kevin, Macon*	.296	120	389	50	115	172	26	5	7	58	2	12	6	37	4	37	9	5
Hacopian, Derek, Columbus	.315	131	454	81	143	244	29	0	24	82	1	7	13	60	6	69	4	2
Hammell, Al, Capital City	.174	11	23	4	4	5	1	0	0	3	0	0	3	0	0	6	0	0
Hansen, Elston, Greensboro	.239	48	155	29	37	66	4	2	7	30	3	1	2	19	1	43	0	1
Harmes, Kris, Hagerstown*	.276	130	482	68	133	206	29	1	14	73	2	2	4	69	0	86	3	4
Harris, G.G., Augusta	.288	15	52	7	15	21	4	1	0	3	0	0	0	5	0	10	0	1
Harris, Marc, Hickory	.188	79	250	24	47	60	10	0	1	14	2	1	2	21	0	74	15	8
Hawkins, Kraig, Greensboro†	.254	131	418	66	106	121	13	1	0	45	9	3	1	67	1	112	67	18
Haws, Scott, Spartanburg*	.244	73	234	23	57	67	7	0	1	21	1	1	0	37	0	44	2	3
Hearn, Sean, Hagerstown*	.279	24	86	12	24	36	3	0	3	9	0	0	1	6	1	22	2	0
Hence, Sam, Columbus	.269	88	268	36	80	118	16	2	6	33	0	4	14	10	0	57	5	7
Henry, Santiago, Hagerstown	.275	115	404	64	111	189	30	12	8	54	3	1	2	20	0	110	13	4
Hernandez, Ramon, Spartanburg	.176	7	17	0	3	4	1	0	0	1	0	1	0	0	0	5	0	0
Herrera, Jose, Hagerstown*	.317	95	388	60	123	170	22	5	5	42	5	4	7	26	1	63	36	20
Herrmann, Gary, Spartanburg	.000	15	6	0	0	0	0	0	0	0	0	0	0	0	0	2	0	0
Hidalgo, Richard, Asheville	.270	111	403	49	109	168	23	3	10	55	2	5	4	30	0	76	21	13
Hieb, Dave, Charleston (S.C.)	.231	5	13	1	3	5	2	0	0	1	0	0	0	1	0	2	0	0
Hinds, Robert, Greensboro	.227	126	503	80	114	134	14	3	0	50	1	2	13	72	0	101	50	22
Hines, Keith, Hagerstown	.222	59	189	26	42	61	7	3	2	17	2	1	2	12	1	37	7	4
Hobson, Todd, Asheville	.214	76	234	44	50	81	12	5	3	17	1	0	3	29	0	95	15	6
Hodge, Roy, Albany	.258	29	97	25	25	32	3	2	0	11	0	0	0	13	0	21	1	0
Hollrah, Scot, Hickory*	.236	59	148	23	35	39	4	0	0	8	2	3	3	18	1	34	10	6
Jackson, Damian, Columbus	.269	108	350	70	94	137	19	3	6	45	5	1	5	41	0	61	26	7
Jenkins, Dee, Charleston (W.Va.)*	.292	133	480	93	140	204	32	4	8	58	4	4	3	73	2	104	27	9
Jesperson, Bob, Charleston (W.Va.)	.209	53	91	7	19	28	4	1	1	4	0	1	2	7	0	30	3	2
Jeter, Derek, Greensboro	.295	128	515	85	152	203	14	11	5	71	2	4	11	58	1	95	18	9
Keeline, Jason, Macon	.215	121	353	35	76	80	4	0	0	28	5	1	5	30	0	70	6	5
Keenan, Bradley, Charleston (W.Va.) ...	.198	29	96	13	19	26	5	1	0	6	0	0	1	11	1	24	0	0
Keister, Tripp, Capital City*	.274	101	314	60	86	104	11	2	1	39	8	4	3	91	0	60	33	17
Kendall, Jason, Augusta	.276	102	366	43	101	129	17	4	1	40	0	5	7	22	1	30	8	5
Killen, Brent, Fayetteville*	.269	68	223	42	60	97	15	2	6	41	0	2	2	48	0	45	1	4
Kimsey, Keith, Fayetteville	.245	120	469	79	115	203	19	6	19	85	0	3	2	50	2	168	2	0
King, Jason, Capital City†	.207	94	304	34	63	81	12	3	0	37	3	3	1	54	1	49	7	4
Kiraly, Jeff, Capital City*	.214	132	491	60	105	156	20	2	9	58	0	6	1	44	1	131	3	2
Knott, John, Macon	.262	113	309	66	81	145	16	3	14	49	2	4	17	71	1	96	9	12
Kopriva, Dan, Charleston (W.Va.)	.244	121	402	69	98	143	22	7	3	70	2	9	10	75	2	57	6	6
Kratz, Ron, Spartanburg*	.184	28	87	4	16	19	0	0	1	8	2	1	2	3	0	29	0	0
Kupsey, John, Spartanburg	.271	35	118	18	32	53	10	1	3	20	0	3	8	0	23	4	0	
Ladd, Jeff, Hagerstown	.211	22	57	8	12	25	4	0	3	11	0	1	0	12	0	25	2	1
Larson, Danny, Spartanburg*	.250	34	112	16	28	39	4	2	1	10	2	3	7	19	2	29	1	3
Lawler, Brian, Spartanburg	.185	18	54	5	10	13	3	0	0	2	0	0	1	3	0	19	0	0
Levias, Andres, Hickory†	.165	25	85	8	14	19	2	0	1	7	1	0	3	6	0	17	6	2
Lidle, Kevin, Fayetteville	.213	58	197	29	42	73	14	1	5	25	0	1	1	34	0	42	2	0
Livsey, Shawn, Asheville†	.263	124	453	50	119	153	26	1	2	60	1	6	9	62	0	92	26	15
Lombardi, John, Hagerstown	.238	8	21	2	5	5	0	0	0	1	1	0	1	1	0	4	0	0
Long, R.D., Greensboro†	.241	58	170	21	41	62	4	4	3	20	4	1	0	33	0	45	6	4
Luke, Matt, Greensboro*	.286	135	549	83	157	267	37	5	21	91	0	6	7	47	4	79	11	3
Mader, Chris, Hickory	.270	120	396	54	107	155	25	1	7	49	0	4	6	81	1	90	2	0
Magdaleno, Ricky, Char. (W.Va.)	.239	131	447	49	107	139	15	4	3	25	6	1	1	37	0	103	8	3
Malloy, Marty, Macon*	.293	109	376	55	110	141	19	3	2	36	3	3	2	39	3	70	24	8
Malone, Scott, Charleston (S.C.)*	.288	130	458	70	132	210	34	4	12	71	4	5	2	59	3	75	20	9
Manrique, Marco, Albany	.216	100	319	26	69	95	14	0	4	48	3	3	2	20	2	44	3	2
Manship, Jeff, Charleston (W.Va.)	.244	84	287	45	70	105	12	1	7	36	0	6	3	32	0	80	8	3
Marine, Del, Fayetteville	.280	25	75	4	21	28	7	0	0	4	0	0	0	16	0	25	1	0
Marshall, Jason, Columbus	.130	15	46	3	6	10	1	0	1	5	1	2	2	1	0	13	1	0
Martin, Andy, Savannah*	.235	54	149	17	35	45	5	1	1	16	0	3	0	23	2	42	1	0
Martin, Jerry, Charleston (S.C.)	.500	28	2	0	1	1	0	0	0	0	0	0	0	0	0	0	1	0
Martin, Matt, Charleston (W.Va.)†	.223	58	121	19	27	36	6	0	1	10	0	0	2	18	0	23	1	2
Martinez, Angel, Hagerstown*	.263	94	338	41	89	134	16	1	9	46	0	1	6	19	0	71	1	1
Martinez, Jacen, Capital City†	.221	35	104	15	23	25	2	0	0	6	7	0	3	12	0	34	4	3
Marx, Tim, Augusta	.278	53	162	28	45	62	8	0	3	21	2	2	2	34	0	18	3	4
Matos, Malvin, Charleston (S.C.)	.223	105	359	47	80	128	17	2	9	32	1	0	3	24	0	114	6	9
McCloughan, Scot, Hagerstown*	.231	12	26	4	6	6	0	0	0	5	0	0	0	3	0	10	0	0
McCraw, Johnny, Asheville	.283	26	60	8	17	27	4	0	2	14	2	0	0	12	0	24	1	2
McEwing, Joe, Savannah	.249	138	511	94	127	164	35	4	0	43	15	4	4	89	0	73	22	9
McKinnon, Sandy, Hickory	.251	64	263	29	66	82	10	3	0	21	1	2	1	21	0	47	17	12
Meggers, Mike, Charleston (W.Va.)	.206	116	388	43	80	134	14	2	12	49	2	5	3	33	1	118	3	5
Mejia, Miguel, Albany	.165	23	79	11	13	19	0	3	0	3	2	0	2	4	0	22	7	2
Meluskey, Mitch, Columbus†	.246	101	342	36	84	117	18	3	3	47	4	7	4	35	4	69	1	1
Menechino, Frank, Hickory	.281	50	178	35	50	74	6	3	4	19	1	1	4	33	0	28	11	2
Mercado, Rafael, Columbus	.152	36	99	14	15	26	2	0	3	13	2	1	5	5	1	27	0	1

— 490 —

Player, Team	Avg.	G	AB	R	H	TB	2B	3B	HR	RBI	SH	SF	HP	BB	Int. BB	SO	SB	CS
Mercedes, Guillermo, Char. (S.C.)	.239	127	457	55	109	125	12	2	0	30	8	3	2	47	0	60	41	17
Metcalf, Scott, Albany	.256	115	375	48	96	128	16	2	4	45	1	2	5	35	1	69	6	0
Michael, Jeff, Albany	.270	49	163	20	44	50	6	0	0	14	5	1	3	14	0	21	5	1
Milne, Blaine, Savannah	.219	11	32	0	7	8	1	0	0	1	0	1	0	1	0	4	1	0
Miranda, Geovany, Hickory	.234	33	107	13	25	28	3	0	0	6	4	2	0	5	1	8	4	2
Mitchell, Donovan, Asheville*	.291	113	453	67	132	167	20	3	3	45	2	1	1	33	1	52	28	18
Mompres, Danilo, Capital City	.133	5	15	2	2	2	0	0	0	1	0	0	0	0	0	4	0	0
Mora, Melvin, Asheville	.285	108	365	66	104	136	22	2	2	31	5	8	9	36	0	46	20	13
Moreno, Jorge, Fayetteville†	.227	17	66	7	15	18	0	0	1	8	0	0	2	3	0	18	1	2
Moreno, Juan, Capital City	.159	31	107	10	17	24	1	3	0	9	2	2	0	10	0	36	6	2
Morris, Rod, Charleston (S.C.)*	.235	17	51	8	12	16	0	2	0	3	0	0	0	4	0	13	3	0
Mota, Santo, Savannah†	.248	62	202	32	50	63	3	2	2	25	5	1	0	29	0	41	14	10
Mumma, Bob, Hickory	.213	23	61	8	13	21	3	1	1	5	1	0	0	10	0	16	0	1
Murphy, Jeff, Savannah†	.226	98	345	40	78	122	21	1	7	47	3	4	5	49	1	105	2	1
Murphy, Mike, Spartanburg	.289	133	509	70	147	197	29	6	3	60	9	2	9	35	1	91	33	14
Nagy, Jeff, Charleston (W.Va.)	.160	29	100	19	16	20	1	0	1	8	1	0	4	20	0	31	10	4
Noel, Jason, Macon	.228	118	373	48	85	122	15	2	6	44	5	3	5	33	3	109	23	19
Norton, Greg, Hickory†	.244	71	254	36	62	90	12	2	4	36	1	4	1	41	1	44	0	2
Nunez, Ramon, Macon	.286	115	377	57	108	157	18	5	7	40	6	2	4	37	2	73	6	5
Nunnally, Jon, Columbus*	.251	125	438	81	110	174	15	2	15	56	4	6	3	63	0	108	17	11
O'Brien, John, Savannah	.249	68	265	31	66	119	11	0	14	66	0	6	2	13	2	62	0	0
Ollison, Ron, Spartanburg	.267	100	322	43	86	107	8	2	3	35	5	2	6	30	1	51	10	7
Ordonez, Magglio, Hickory	.216	84	273	32	59	90	14	4	3	20	2	0	0	26	0	66	5	5
Osentowski, Jared, Capital City	.203	86	300	38	61	76	13	1	0	25	3	3	7	24	0	99	18	3
Owens, Billy, Albany†	.297	120	458	64	136	196	23	2	11	66	1	5	2	49	6	70	3	5
Parker, Corey, Fayetteville*	.225	110	377	48	85	121	20	2	4	52	0	2	5	66	3	70	3	6
Parra, Franklin, Charleston (S.C.)†	.213	125	446	52	95	135	13	6	5	25	3	3	3	37	0	99	18	13
Patrizi, Mike, Capital City	.200	2	5	1	1	3	0	1	0	0	0	0	1	0	0	1	0	1
Patton, Scott, Hickory	.181	38	116	13	21	24	3	0	0	11	2	0	2	22	0	50	5	3
Paulino, Nelson, Macon†	.231	99	325	45	75	96	10	1	3	24	5	5	0	19	0	49	24	5
Pearson, Eddie, Hickory†	.242	87	343	37	83	116	15	3	4	40	5	1	1	20	0	59	5	1
Pecorilli, Aldo, Savannah	.305	141	515	75	157	243	30	7	14	93	0	8	6	81	7	86	16	11
Petillo, Bruce, Spartanburg	.250	2	8	3	2	3	1	0	0	0	0	0	0	0	0	2	0	0
Pineda, Jose, Greensboro	.000	4	6	0	0	0	0	0	0	0	0	0	0	0	0	2	0	0
Polcovich, Kevin, Augusta	.271	14	48	9	13	15	2	0	0	4	2	1	0	7	0	8	2	1
Polidor, Wil, Hickory†	.233	15	43	4	10	10	0	0	0	3	1	0	1	2	0	7	1	1
Ponder, Marcus, Augusta	.225	47	138	18	31	42	1	2	2	5	0	0	0	12	0	36	4	5
Probst, Alan, Asheville	.258	40	124	14	32	51	4	0	5	21	0	1	0	12	0	34	0	2
Pueschner, Craig, Charleston (W.Va.)	.182	26	99	24	18	28	2	1	2	5	2	0	3	12	0	22	10	6
Purdy, Alan, Augusta	.107	12	28	3	3	5	2	0	0	1	0	0	1	0	0	4	0	0
Randle, Mike, Hickory	.000	3	6	1	0	0	0	0	0	0	0	0	0	0	0	0	0	0
Rea, Clarke, Fayetteville*	.168	27	95	9	16	21	2	0	1	8	0	0	1	14	1	18	1	0
Rennhack, Mike, Asheville†	.272	118	441	57	120	186	30	3	10	52	2	3	3	37	0	90	16	10
Reyes, Jimmy, Hickory†	.218	77	262	38	57	72	1	7	0	23	8	4	3	42	0	64	9	3
Rich, Ted, Hickory	.164	16	55	5	9	16	1	0	2	9	1	0	0	1	0	21	0	0
Richardson, Eric, Hickory	.231	119	412	40	95	112	9	1	2	30	5	2	4	19	0	75	42	15
Riemer, Matt, Albany	.130	11	23	1	3	3	0	0	0	2	0	1	0	2	0	5	1	1
Rivera, Maximo, Augusta†	.273	5	11	1	3	3	0	0	0	0	0	0	0	0	0	3	1	0
Roberts, Lonell, Hagerstown†	.240	131	501	78	120	158	21	4	3	46	2	3	4	53	1	103	54	15
Robinson, Dwight, Capital City*	.292	116	407	59	119	171	34	3	4	51	3	3	6	53	2	74	5	4
Rodriguez, Nerio, Hickory	.206	82	262	31	54	79	9	2	4	32	0	2	3	27	0	70	4	0
Rodriguez, Noel, Spartanburg	.263	38	133	23	35	46	8	0	1	12	1	0	2	9	0	31	3	0
Rojas, Roberto, Fayetteville*	.254	120	492	68	125	157	17	6	1	29	5	1	2	41	1	118	30	16
Roman, Mark, Fayetteville	.125	14	24	4	3	3	0	0	0	2	0	0	0	8	0	11	1	0
Romano, Scott, Greensboro	.282	121	418	75	118	180	33	4	7	62	2	3	9	63	0	69	14	7
Romero, Phil, Spartanburg	.213	45	141	17	30	38	6	1	0	14	9	4	4	15	0	10	5	4
Rumfield, Toby, Charleston (W.Va.)	.225	97	333	36	75	112	20	1	5	50	0	4	3	26	1	74	6	4
Rupp, Brian, Savannah	.320	122	472	80	151	208	31	7	4	81	1	5	3	48	2	70	3	2
Ruth, Pat, Spartanburg	.286	4	14	1	4	5	1	0	0	1	2	0	0	0	0	4	3	0
Sagmoen, Marc, Charleston (S.C.)*	.295	63	234	44	69	108	13	4	6	34	3	3	3	23	0	39	16	4
Sallee, Andy, Spartanburg*	.239	93	305	37	73	106	10	4	5	38	1	4	1	18	2	58	5	2
Sanchez, Yuri, Fayetteville*	.203	111	340	53	69	88	7	6	0	30	7	3	2	73	0	125	20	9
Santana, Jose, Asheville†	.238	133	429	50	102	130	13	3	3	30	9	2	9	28	0	69	9	9
Schmidt, Keith, Albany*	.152	18	46	3	7	8	1	0	0	1	0	0	0	3	1	14	1	0
Sealy, Scot, Charleston (S.C.)	.143	2	7	0	1	1	0	0	0	0	0	0	0	0	0	4	0	0
Secrist, Reed, Augusta*	.267	90	266	38	71	111	16	3	6	47	2	4	1	27	1	43	4	1
Seesz, Brian, Charleston (S.C.)*	.200	20	55	6	11	12	1	0	0	5	1	0	0	9	0	8	0	1
Serra, Jose, Albany	.213	111	390	62	83	103	15	1	1	23	1	1	5	35	0	51	26	6
Shelton, Derek, Greensboro	.291	23	55	7	16	23	4	0	1	6	1	1	0	6	0	4	0	0
Shirley, Al, Capital City	.146	72	240	32	35	64	9	4	4	22	0	2	2	50	1	121	12	5
Silvia, Brian, Charleston (W.Va.)	.264	23	53	7	14	18	2	1	0	4	0	1	0	4	0	12	0	0
Simonson, Bob, Charleston (S.C.)	.250	11	32	4	8	16	3	1	1	6	0	0	0	0	0	8	2	1
Sly, Kian, Macon*	.179	21	56	2	10	18	2	0	2	7	2	0	0	4	2	25	2	1
Smith, Bobby, Macon	.245	108	384	53	94	136	16	7	4	38	8	0	5	23	1	81	12	8
Smith, Demond, Capital City†	.000	1	2	0	0	0	0	0	0	0	0	0	0	0	0	0	0	0
Smith, Eric, Spartanburg	.000	35	2	0	0	0	0	0	0	0	0	0	0	0	0	0	0	0
Solomon, Steve, Spartanburg*	.288	81	306	59	88	115	16	4	1	33	7	1	8	39	0	49	14	5
Soto, Miguel, Macon	.221	40	104	10	23	29	3	0	1	10	1	0	0	7	1	18	1	0
Spencer, Shane, Greensboro	.269	122	431	89	116	191	35	2	12	80	0	8	3	52	0	62	14	2
Stahlhoefer, Larry, Augusta	.245	77	220	22	54	66	9	0	1	25	2	1	1	15	0	35	4	6
Stanczak, Jack, Charleston (S.C.)	.256	79	281	34	72	105	14	5	3	30	0	2	4	41	1	50	9	5
Starks, Fred, Hickory*	.150	20	20	2	3	3	0	0	0	0	0	0	0	3	0	9	0	0
Sumner, Chad, Savannah	.212	89	297	37	63	83	10	2	2	22	1	1	2	18	0	56	2	1
Suplee, Ray, Greensboro	.280	90	353	54	99	148	30	2	5	46	1	2	6	30	0	72	1	3
Swinton, Jermaine, Asheville	.188	89	272	39	51	102	8	2	13	44	0	4	1	45	1	137	5	3
Taylor, Jamie, Columbus*	.226	111	402	46	91	136	21	0	8	46	2	4	0	36	2	115	4	2
Tena, Dario, Augusta†	.263	87	308	45	81	92	9	1	0	19	3	1	2	31	0	56	39	16
Thomas, Duane, Albany	.077	8	13	2	1	3	0	1	0	0	0	0	1	1	0	11	0	1
Thomas, Juan, Hickory	.229	90	328	51	75	137	14	6	12	46	1	3	7	35	1	124	2	4
Thomas, Tim, Fayetteville	.303	104	380	80	115	164	31	3	4	48	2	3	3	82	0	85	5	1
Thompson, Billy, Fayetteville	.275	42	142	14	39	50	6	1	1	19	0	2	2	20	1	28	2	2
Tijerina, Tony, Capital City†	.309	53	175	15	54	69	9	3	0	21	2	3	0	14	0	25	3	0
Tobin, Shawn, Albany	.229	20	35	3	8	8	0	0	0	4	1	1	1	3	0	1	1	0

Player, Team	Avg.	G	AB	R	H	TB	2B	3B	HR	RBI	SH	SF	HP	BB	Int. BB	SO	SB	CS
Tooch, Chuck, 17 Aug.-42 C.C.	.219	59	160	19	35	48	10	0	1	14	0	1	1	14	0	60	2	0
Torres, Jaime, Greensboro	.283	25	92	9	26	34	5	0	1	12	1	1	2	7	0	7	1	0
Toth, David, Macon	.246	104	353	38	87	121	22	0	4	40	5	3	7	28	1	53	6	5
Townsend, Charles, Columbus*	.236	104	314	43	74	125	15	3	10	40	1	3	2	23	1	84	1	0
Tremie, Chris, Hickory	.187	49	155	7	29	40	6	1	1	17	1	0	4	9	0	26	0	0
Ugueto, Jesus, Savannah	.228	47	127	17	29	38	6	0	1	12	2	2	2	13	0	25	1	0
Velandia, Jorge, Fayetteville	.160	37	106	15	17	21	4	0	0	11	0	2	3	13	0	21	5	0
Vlasis, Chris, Savannah*	.211	71	199	36	42	50	6	1	0	19	4	0	9	45	0	39	21	8
Waldrop, Tom, Macon*	.246	107	342	46	84	143	16	5	11	52	2	4	1	36	3	90	7	4
Walker, Shon, Augusta*	.208	64	226	26	47	67	11	0	3	26	0	2	2	19	1	85	2	5
Waszgis, B.J., Albany	.307	86	300	45	92	147	25	3	8	52	0	5	6	27	0	55	4	0
Webb, Kevin, Asheville	.225	76	267	32	60	97	14	1	7	39	1	0	2	11	1	78	9	4
Welch, Mike, Charleston (S.C.)*	.303	67	238	33	72	101	20	3	1	37	0	1	1	41	0	43	6	2
Wells, Beck, Charleston (S.C.)	.216	22	74	9	16	23	4	0	1	7	1	1	3	4	0	21	0	2
White, Andre, Columbus*	.278	115	367	55	102	130	15	2	3	35	3	0	2	19	0	48	29	12
White, Don, Capital City	.304	114	441	86	134	173	18	6	3	41	9	1	5	54	0	75	43	14
White, Eric, Columbus	.143	2	7	1	1	1	0	0	0	0	0	0	0	0	0	1	0	0
Wilkerson, Wayne, Char. (W.Va.)*	.216	102	287	39	62	86	10	1	4	27	2	2	5	30	1	55	11	3
Williams, Clifford, Asheville	.067	11	15	0	1	1	0	0	0	0	0	0	0	1	0	7	0	0
Wills, Shawn, Spartanburg	.223	116	403	60	90	121	17	1	4	53	4	4	6	44	1	86	21	17
Wilson, Tom, Greensboro	.249	120	394	55	98	150	20	1	10	63	3	8	4	91	0	112	2	5
Wipf, Mark, Capital City+	.210	127	471	51	99	133	15	2	5	58	6	4	5	36	5	107	17	7
Woodall, Kevin, Charleston (S.C.)	.244	24	45	7	11	13	0	1	0	2	1	0	0	2	0	12	3	0
Wooten, William, Fayetteville	.250	5	16	2	4	7	0	0	1	5	0	0	0	3	0	3	0	0
Wuerch, Jason, Greensboro*	.232	51	151	18	35	45	5	1	1	9	0	0	0	19	0	35	2	1
Yeske, Kyle, Albany	.224	109	313	36	70	106	13	1	7	40	1	1	10	35	0	92	6	6
Zapata, Ramon, Augusta	.247	81	235	31	58	80	10	3	2	32	3	3	2	37	0	47	6	7
Zosky, Eddie, Hagerstown	.100	5	20	2	2	2	0	0	0	1	0	1	0	2	0	1	0	0

The following pitchers, listed alphabetically by club, with games in parentheses, had no plate appearances, primarily through use of designated hitters:

ALBANY—Benitez, Armando (40); Brewer, Brian (6); Chatterton, Craig (25); Chavez, Carlos (20); Conner, Scott (37); Cusey, Lee (11); Devereux, Chuck (27); Emerson, Scott (27); Fregoso, Dan (6); Griffin, Ryan (2); Jarvis, Matt (29); Lane, Aaron (29); Lombardi, John T. (4); Porter, Mike (10); Powell, Jim (6); Sackinsky, Brian (9); Shenk, Larry (54); Stephenson, Garrett (30); Walker, Jim (10).

ASHEVILLE—Bottoms, Derrick (3); Centeno, Jose (43); Czanstkowski, Tom (10); Fesh, Sean (65); Henriquez, Oscar (27); Krislock, Zak (48); Lewis, Ed (12); Madrigal, Vic (31); McCutchen, Jim (16); Narcisse, Tyrone (29); Tenbarge, Jeff (36); Valdez, Vic (30); Young, Dan (32).

AUGUSTA—Bonilla, Miguel (15); Chamberlain, Matt (6); Doorneweerd, Dave (13); Fairfax, Ken (5); Ford, John (31); Garcia-Luna, Francisco (7); Klamm, Ed (26); LaPlante, Michel (14); Lawrence, Sean (22); Martin, Jim (5); Mesewicz, Mark (12); Nuttle, Jamie (12); Pisciotta, Marc (34); Pontbriant, Matt (3); Ruebel, Matt (23); Salamon, John (47); Santana, Manuel (38); Sosa, Jose (33); Townsend, Rich (53); Wilkins, Marc (48); Wilson, Gary (20).

CAPITAL CITY—Beckerman, Andy (25); Bellman, Bill (11); Bullock, Craig (30); Cotner, Andy (27); Engle, Tom (15); Hiljus, Erik (27); Hokanson, Mark (44); Kohl, Jim (20); Kroon, Marc (29); Lyons, Steve (27); Petcka, Joe (25); Pulsipher, Bill (6); Ramirez, Hector (14); Reichenbach, Eric (56); Shanahan, Chris (13); Stark, Greg (41).

CHARLESTON (S.C.)—Anderson, Mike (30); Brandenburg, Mark (44); Eyre, Scott (26); Kimel, Jack (36); Lacy, Kerry (58); Manning, Dave (37); Martinez, Ramiro (27); Perez, Paulino (37); Reynoso, Querbin (15); Runion, Jeff (15); Vaughn, Heath (32); Wheeler, Earl (11); Wiley, Chad (40).

CHARLESTON (W.Va.)—Angel, Jason (19); Brothers, John (46); Brunson, Bill (37); Etheridge, Roger (13); Fox, Chad (27); Garcia, Fermin (35); Kummerfeldt, Jason (23); Langford, Rich (4); Lister, Martin (51); Loftin, Bill (9); Maberry, Lou (57); Nix, Jim (26); O'Laughlin, Chuck (2); Pickett, Cecil (44); Reed, Chris (21); Ruyak, Todd (14); Stewart, Carl (2); Tuttle, Dave (13).

COLUMBIA—Beauchamp, Jim (27); Cabrera, Jose (26); Campbell, Alfred (2); Carter, John (29); Diaz, German (5); Gibbs, Paul (23); Harris, Hernando (26); Koller, Rodney (47); Neilson, Mike (5); Perez, Cesar (45); Resendez, Oscar (32); Ruyak, Todd (9); Sharts, Scott (43); Smith, Fred (18); Thobe, John (19); Williams, Jeff (6); York, Chuck (26).

FAYETTEVILLE—Adams, Art (3); Arguto, Sam (23); Bauer, Matt (40); Berlin, Mike (18); Bussa, Todd (39); Cedeno, Blas (28); Crombie, Kevin (28); Gaillard, Ed (11); Grimm, John (23); Maxcy, Brian (39); Miller, Trever (28); Mysel, Dave (12); Navarro, Rich (41); Santos, Henry (8); Sodowsky, Clint (27); Whiteside, Sean (24).

GREENSBORO—Antolick, Jeff (13); Buddie, Mike (27); Cindrich, Jeff (35); Coleman, Bill (59); DeJean, Michel (20); Heberling, Keith (11); Inman, Bert (26); Karp, Ryan (19); Long, Joe (36); Mendoza, Ramiro (2); Musselwhite, Jim (11); Pool, Bruce (55); Prybylinski, Bruce (8); Rivera, Mariano (10); Santiago, Sandi (29); Short, Ben (6); Underwood, Bill (22); Wallace, Kent (13); Wharton, Joe (16).

HAGERSTOWN—Brandow, Derek (40); Cornett, Brad (31); Daniels, Lee (33); Darley, Ned (24); Dolson, Andy (29); Doman, Roger (26); Jersild, Aaron (44); Largusa, Levon (6); Lindsay, Tim (16); Lutz, Brent (1); Maldonado, Jason (8); Mallory, Trevor (26); Meinershagen, Adam (5); Renko, Steve (23); Robinson, Ken (40); Silva, Jose (24).

HICKORY—Bennett, Shedrick (41); Bertotti, Mike (9); Brincks, Mark (30); Culberson, Don (29); Elsbernd, Dave (19); Fitzpatrick, Dave (6); Fordham, Tom (8); Gay, Chris (13); Lehman, Toby (39); Lindemann, Wayne (15); Malaver, Johnny (9); McCormack, Andy (14); McGraw, Doug (5); McKinion, Mickey (17); Ogden, Jason (9); Pratt, Rich (13); Proctor, Bill (21); Quirk, John (10); Soto, Juan (3); Theodile, Bob (8); Woods, Brian (10).

MACON—Arnold, Jim (27); Bock, Jeff (3); Brock, Chris (14); Burlingame, Dennis (6); Butler, Jason (31); Cromer, Burke (17); D'Andrea, Mike (26); Giard, Ken (40); May, Darrell (17); Murray, Matt (15); Place, Mike (31); Ramirez, Leo (36); Rusciano, Chris (19); Simmons, John (36); Thobe, Tom (43); Turnier, Aaron (12); Wade, Terrell (14).

SAVANNAH—Alkire, Jeff (28); Busby, Mike (23); Carrillo, Joe (6); Cochran, Jamie (58); Davis, Ray (26); Goodman, Doug (60); Jones, Steve (56); Lucchetti, Larry (9); Martinez, Francisco (14); Matranga, Jeff (15); Matulevich, Jeff (34); Ottmers, Marc (4); Smith, Chad (20); Stanley, Karl (22); Tranbarger, Mark (56); Witasick, Jerry (1).

SPARTANBURG—Agostinelli, Pete (6); Alger, Kevin (38); Anderson, Chad (29); Boldt, Sean (17); Brown, Dan (39); Corry, Steve (15); Doolan, Blake (8); Edwards, Sam (15); Humphry, Trevor (10); Irwin, Tom (20); Lundberg, Bryan (2); Martinez, Ben (1); Mitchell, Larry (19); Mitchell, Bob (32); Nutt, Steve (46); Rama, Shelby (10); Tranberg, Mark (11).

GRAND SLAMS—Harmes, 2; Bigler, Black, Bryant, Burke, Burton, Cardenas, T. Evans, Franklin, Hansen, Henry, Hidalgo, Kimsey, Knott, Paulino, Sallee, Spencer, Swinton, Wilkerson, Wipf, 1 each.

AWARDED FIRST BASE ON CATCHER'S INTERFERENCE—Claudio 2 (Albaladejo, Soto); M. Evans 2 (Silvia 2); Hawkins 2 (Albaladejo, A. Martinez); C. Cradle (A. Martinez); Doucette (G. Garcia); Lawler (Harmes); O'Brien (Waszgis); Romero (A. Garcia); Rumfield (Albaladejo); Sallee (Probst); Santana (A. Martinez); B. Smith (Tremie); Townsend (Silvia); Waszgis (Nerio Rodriguez); Wilkerson (Manrique); Wills (Manrique).

PITCHING

TEAM

Team	ERA	G	CG	ShO	Sv.	IP	H	R	ER	HR	HB	BB	Int. BB	SO	WP	Bk.
Savannah	2.72	142	7	19	53	1257.1	1086	472	380	67	48	409	9	1150	49	6
Macon	3.03	141	10	16	35	1231.2	1054	529	414	58	46	476	11	1138	92	13

Team	ERA	G	CG	ShO	Sv.	IP	H	R	ER	HR	HB	BB	Int. BB	SO	WP	Bk.
Columbus	3.21	142	6	10	56	1246.1	1067	552	444	62	42	517	15	994	82	12
Albany	3.51	142	13	12	29	1215.2	1155	636	474	60	47	525	11	1010	87	23
Greensboro	3.66	141	3	14	42	1228.2	1108	633	499	81	46	518	19	1097	100	15
Hagerstown	3.67	142	10	5	36	1231.1	1164	621	502	76	59	482	8	1049	82	7
Fayetteville	3.69	141	7	13	44	1245.2	1205	627	511	67	67	479	12	1027	84	10
Charleston (W.Va.)	3.83	140	2	5	44	1227.2	1103	678	523	52	85	623	21	1016	91	20
Augusta	3.84	141	6	8	22	1214.1	1202	711	518	70	82	437	17	1051	73	12
Spartanburg	3.99	142	20	5	20	1229.0	1208	649	545	72	60	506	8	955	89	6
Charleston (S.C.)	4.06	142	4	11	44	1248.2	1191	690	563	80	72	586	38	1022	88	22
Capital City	4.14	141	9	7	30	1221.2	1251	713	562	74	71	559	3	894	96	15
Hickory	4.17	140	11	5	22	1228.1	1186	692	569	84	52	566	8	937	71	27
Asheville	4.96	139	10	2	28	1194.1	1294	801	658	88	59	605	27	830	128	22

INDIVIDUAL

(Leading qualifiers for earned-run average leadership— 114 or more innings)

*Throws lefthanded.

Pitcher, Team	W	L	Pct.	ERA	G	GS	CG	GF	ShO	Sv.	IP	H	R	ER	HR	HB	BB	Int. BB	SO	WP
Thobe, Columbus	11	2	.846	1.91	19	19	2	0	1	0	132.0	105	36	28	6	1	25	0	106	3
Cornett, Hagerstown	10	8	.556	2.40	31	21	3	7	1	3	172.1	164	77	46	6	5	31	2	161	6
Busby, Savannah	12	2	.857	2.44	23	21	1	0	1	0	143.2	116	49	39	8	10	31	0	125	5
Alkire, Savannah*	15	6	.714	2.46	28	28	0	0	0	0	171.2	143	56	47	10	11	68	0	175	8
Silva, Hagerstown	12	5	.706	2.52	24	24	0	0	0	0	142.2	103	50	40	6	4	62	0	161	9
Cabrera, Columbus	11	6	.647	2.67	26	26	1	0	0	0	155.1	122	54	46	8	1	53	2	105	8
York, Columbus*	10	7	.588	2.79	26	26	1	0	0	0	158.0	127	59	49	8	2	78	0	182	15
Carter, Columbus	17	7	.708	2.79	29	29	1	0	0	0	180.1	147	72	56	7	7	48	0	134	8
Stephenson, Albany	16	7	.696	2.84	30	24	3	3	2	1	171.1	142	65	54	6	5	44	0	147	3
Carpenter, Savannah	10	8	.556	2.86	28	28	0	0	0	0	154.1	145	55	49	8	2	41	0	147	2

Departmental leaders: G—Fesh, 65; W—Carter, 17; L—Lyons, 16; Pct.—Karp, .929; GS—C. Anderson, Carter, Jarvis, Narcisse, 29; CG—Jarvis, 8; GF—Fesh, 58; ShO—R. Martinez, Matranga, L. Mitchell, Stephenson, 2; Sv.—Cochran, 46; IP—C. Anderson, 191.1; H—C. Anderson, 216; R—Young, 114; ER—Young, 97; HR—Buddie, 19; HB—Petcka, 18; BB—Hiljus, 111; IBB—Fesh, 8; SO—York, 182; WP—Krislock, 25.

(All pitchers—listed alphabetically)

Pitcher, Team	W	L	Pct.	ERA	G	GS	CG	GF	ShO	Sv.	IP	H	R	ER	HR	HB	BB	Int. BB	SO	WP
Adams, Fayetteville	0	1	.000	3.52	3	0	0	1	0	0	7.2	8	3	3	1	0	4	0	6	0
Agostinelli, Spartanburg*	0	0	.000	5.79	6	0	0	3	0	0	9.1	13	9	6	1	1	3	0	8	1
Alger, Spartanburg*	1	3	.250	3.55	38	1	0	16	0	1	63.1	48	34	25	5	2	42	0	86	7
Alkire, Savannah*	15	6	.714	2.46	28	28	0	0	0	0	171.2	143	56	47	10	11	68	0	175	8
Anderson, Spartanburg	7	14	.333	4.42	29	29	5	0	0	0	191.1	216	111	94	12	10	65	0	129	7
Anderson, Charleston (S.C.)	3	1	.750	3.42	30	0	0	13	0	0	50.0	44	24	19	4	1	30	1	26	6
Angel, Charleston (W.Va.)	3	2	.600	5.13	19	7	0	4	0	0	59.2	62	39	34	2	5	33	2	28	5
Antolick, Greensboro	6	2	.750	2.96	13	13	1	0	0	0	73.0	63	32	24	1	3	24	1	57	5
Arguto, Fayetteville	2	3	.400	2.92	23	0	0	21	0	6	24.2	19	8	8	1	2	15	0	22	6
Arnold, Macon	8	9	.471	3.12	27	27	1	0	0	0	164.1	142	67	57	5	16	56	0	124	13
Bauer, Fayetteville*	6	5	.545	2.90	40	0	0	16	0	5	62.0	57	30	20	2	3	23	1	81	4
Beauchamp, Columbus	5	6	.455	4.43	27	22	0	2	0	0	130.0	148	85	64	5	7	76	0	78	13
Beckerman, Capital City	5	1	.833	0.90	25	0	0	22	0	10	30.0	19	5	3	0	1	10	0	41	2
Bellman, Capital City	1	1	.500	9.56	11	0	0	3	0	0	16.0	30	20	17	2	1	13	0	8	4
Benitez, Albany	5	1	.833	1.52	40	0	0	34	0	14	53.1	31	10	9	2	2	19	0	83	4
Bennett, Hickory	8	7	.533	3.29	41	4	0	28	0	6	112.0	112	50	41	10	3	23	1	98	3
Berlin, Fayetteville	4	2	.667	3.24	18	5	1	6	0	2	58.1	50	29	21	1	2	28	1	44	6
Bertotti, Hickory*	3	3	.500	2.11	9	9	2	0	0	0	59.2	42	19	14	2	1	29	1	77	2
Billingsley, Asheville*	8	12	.400	4.15	28	28	0	0	0	0	169.0	169	99	78	9	5	75	0	110	24
Blanton, Savannah	0	0	.000	9.00	1	0	0	0	0	0	1.0	2	1	1	0	0	0	0	2	1
Bock, Macon	2	1	.667	2.16	3	3	1	0	0	0	16.2	12	9	4	0	0	8	0	11	2
Boldt, Spartanburg	0	0	.000	5.84	17	0	0	8	0	4	24.2	34	17	16	7	0	12	2	24	2
Bonilla, Augusta	1	0	1.000	7.16	15	0	0	6	0	0	27.2	43	30	22	3	2	10	0	23	3
Bottoms, Asheville*	0	0	.000	19.80	3	0	0	1	0	0	5.0	12	12	11	1	0	7	1	3	1
Brandenburg, Charleston (S.C.)	6	3	.667	1.46	44	0	0	18	0	4	80.0	62	23	13	2	3	22	6	67	0
Brandow, Hagerstown	4	5	.444	3.66	40	1	0	27	0	6	76.1	76	38	31	5	4	34	1	62	6
Brewer, Albany*	0	3	.000	2.57	6	3	0	0	0	0	21.0	19	14	6	1	1	21	0	19	3
Brincks, Hickory	2	4	.333	3.84	30	0	0	15	0	0	68.0	64	32	29	6	0	26	0	60	3
Brock, Macon	7	5	.583	2.70	14	14	1	0	0	0	80.0	61	37	24	3	2	33	0	92	8
Brothers, Charleston (W.Va.)	5	3	.625	4.43	46	4	0	15	0	1	89.1	94	58	44	5	5	40	3	70	11
Brown, Spartanburg	6	6	.500	2.95	39	0	0	27	0	3	61.0	53	25	20	2	1	14	3	43	3
Brunson, Charleston (W.Va.)*	5	6	.455	3.93	37	15	0	4	0	0	123.2	119	68	54	10	11	50	1	103	7
Buddie, Greensboro	13	10	.565	4.87	27	26	0	0	0	0	155.1	138	104	84	19	8	89	0	143	22
Bullock, Capital City	7	6	.538	4.13	30	21	2	3	1	1	143.2	158	78	66	11	4	45	0	57	8
Burlingame, Macon	4	1	.800	2.03	6	6	1	0	1	0	40.0	34	13	9	0	1	19	0	30	9
Busby, Savannah	12	2	.857	2.44	23	21	1	0	1	0	143.2	116	49	39	8	10	31	0	125	5
Bussa, Fayetteville	4	3	.571	3.65	39	0	0	17	0	7	79.0	70	33	32	2	3	36	1	92	6
Butler, Macon*	2	6	.250	4.54	31	9	2	11	1	1	83.1	74	54	42	11	0	49	0	61	7
Cabrera, Columbus	11	6	.647	2.67	26	26	1	0	0	0	155.1	122	54	46	8	1	53	2	105	8
Campbell, Columbus	0	0	.000	27.00	2	0	0	1	0	0	1.2	4	5	5	0	0	1	0	1	1
Carpenter, Savannah	10	8	.556	2.86	28	28	0	0	0	0	154.1	145	55	49	8	2	41	0	147	2
Carrillo, Savannah*	0	0	.000	5.23	6	0	0	3	0	0	10.1	9	6	6	1	3	10	0	11	1
Carter, Columbus	17	7	.708	2.79	29	29	1	0	0	0	180.1	147	72	56	7	7	48	0	134	8
Cedeno, Fayetteville	6	6	.500	3.15	28	22	1	3	1	0	148.2	145	64	52	11	11	55	0	103	6
Centeno, Asheville*	1	2	.333	4.19	43	0	0	16	0	1	66.2	79	41	31	5	2	20	2	29	3
Chamberlain, Augusta	2	4	.333	2.25	6	6	2	0	0	0	36.0	35	16	9	0	3	7	0	29	0
Chatterton, Albany	3	2	.600	5.00	25	1	0	12	0	1	45.0	53	35	25	3	6	24	1	47	5
Chavez, Albany	1	3	.250	5.29	20	0	0	13	0	3	34.0	33	20	20	3	3	18	0	28	6
Childers, Capital City	0	0	.000	0.00	1	0	0	1	0	0	1.0	1	0	0	0	0	1	0	0	1
Cindrich, Greensboro	6	7	.462	3.82	35	5	0	5	0	0	110.2	97	64	47	4	8	62	2	88	7
Cochran, Savannah	4	1	.800	1.55	58	0	0	54	0	46	64.0	51	14	11	1	2	22	3	62	4
Coleman, Greensboro	5	3	.625	2.57	59	0	0	41	0	14	70.0	54	24	20	5	3	23	4	82	5
Conner, Albany	6	6	.500	5.14	37	13	0	8	0	0	115.2	133	92	66	8	2	71	2	90	12
Cornett, Hagerstown	10	8	.556	2.40	31	21	3	7	1	3	172.1	164	77	46	6	5	31	2	161	6

Pitcher, Team	W	L	Pct.	ERA	G	GS	CG	GF	ShO	Sv.	IP	H	R	ER	HR	HB	BB	Int. BB	SO	WP
Corry, Spartanburg	0	2	.000	6.75	15	4	0	9	0	0	29.1	28	23	22	3	0	21	0	22	4
Cotner, Capital City*	3	2	.600	4.71	27	0	0	11	0	1	28.2	24	15	15	4	2	18	0	32	2
Crombie, Fayetteville	2	1	.667	4.57	28	0	0	13	0	0	41.1	46	23	21	3	2	14	1	25	5
Cromer, Macon	0	0	.000	3.19	17	0	0	10	0	3	31.0	33	18	11	1	3	22	4	16	3
Culberson, Hickory	2	1	.667	4.56	29	0	0	19	0	5	53.1	49	33	27	2	2	32	2	43	5
Cusey, Albany	2	0	1.000	2.22	11	0	0	5	0	0	24.1	23	8	6	0	0	5	0	20	0
Czanstkowski, Asheville	1	1	.500	4.70	10	0	0	3	0	0	23.0	32	18	12	1	2	7	1	17	7
D'Andrea, Macon	8	7	.533	4.03	26	23	0	1	0	0	136.1	129	68	61	11	5	55	1	156	3
Daniels, Hagerstown	2	4	.333	3.43	33	0	0	28	0	12	39.1	31	20	15	2	2	26	1	38	5
Darley, Hagerstown	5	3	.625	5.01	24	6	0	6	0	0	55.2	48	38	31	4	9	39	0	40	0
Davis, Savannah	9	7	.563	3.63	26	26	1	0	1	0	131.1	141	73	53	10	3	53	0	120	7
Delgado, Albany	0	0	.000	0.00	1	0	0	1	0	0	1.0	0	0	0	0	0	1	0	1	0
Devereux, Albany	3	2	.600	4.33	27	1	0	9	0	1	62.1	69	38	30	6	1	15	0	48	1
DeJean, Greensboro	2	3	.400	5.00	20	0	0	18	0	9	18.0	22	12	10	1	0	8	2	16	1
Diaz, Columbus	0	2	.000	5.91	5	0	0	0	0	0	10.2	10	9	7	0	2	12	0	11	1
Dolson, Hagerstown*	10	11	.476	3.64	29	25	4	1	1	0	163.0	148	74	66	10	10	58	0	143	12
Doman, Hagerstown	8	6	.571	4.11	26	26	0	0	0	0	146.2	153	78	67	11	6	73	0	102	15
Doolan, Spartanburg	2	2	.500	1.70	8	8	1	0	0	0	58.1	50	16	11	2	0	9	1	34	2
Doorneweerd, Augusta	1	5	.167	1.98	13	13	0	0	0	0	77.1	60	30	17	3	4	30	0	70	2
Edwards, Spartanburg	3	6	.333	4.38	15	15	3	0	1	0	98.2	105	49	48	8	5	25	1	63	5
Elsbernd, Hickory	2	9	.182	4.37	19	19	2	0	0	0	105.0	107	74	51	6	2	41	1	71	5
Emerson, Albany*	10	9	.526	3.54	27	27	1	0	0	0	147.1	143	72	58	6	7	62	1	115	10
Engle, Capital City	0	2	.000	5.40	15	1	0	4	0	1	30.0	30	19	18	2	1	20	1	38	3
Etheridge, Charleston (W.Va.) * ..	3	3	.500	7.21	13	8	0	0	0	0	43.2	43	41	35	2	4	35	0	28	1
Evans, Fayetteville*	0	0	.000	0.00	1	0	0	0	0	0	1.0	0	0	0	0	0	0	0	1	0
Eyre, Charleston (S.C.) *	11	7	.611	3.45	26	26	0	0	0	0	143.2	115	74	55	6	6	59	1	154	2
Fairfax, Augusta	3	2	.600	4.32	5	5	0	0	0	0	25.0	29	14	12	1	4	9	0	17	3
Fesh, Asheville*	10	6	.625	3.61	65	0	0	58	0	20	82.1	75	39	33	4	5	37	8	49	4
Fitzpatrick, Hickory	0	1	.000	7.50	6	0	0	2	0	1	12.0	17	11	10	2	2	3	0	13	0
Ford, Augusta *	1	1	.500	2.49	31	0	0	8	0	2	43.1	42	17	12	1	0	11	1	40	2
Fordham, Hickory*	4	3	.571	3.88	8	8	1	0	0	0	48.2	36	21	21	3	0	21	0	27	3
Fox, Charleston (W.Va.)	9	12	.429	5.37	27	26	0	0	0	0	135.2	138	100	81	7	13	97	0	81	15
Fregoso, Albany	3	1	.750	1.93	6	6	0	0	0	0	28.0	17	7	6	0	1	17	0	23	4
Gaillard, Fayetteville	5	2	.714	4.09	11	11	0	0	0	0	61.2	64	30	28	8	4	20	0	41	1
Garcia, Charleston (W.Va.)	6	7	.462	4.33	35	12	0	0	0	0	116.1	127	74	56	11	2	51	5	79	1
Garcia-Luna, Augusta	3	1	.750	4.26	7	7	0	0	0	0	31.2	34	15	15	2	0	3	0	29	0
Garvey, Augusta	0	0	.000	9.00	1	0	0	1	0	0	2.0	4	3	2	0	0	1	0	1	0
Gay, Hickory*	3	2	.600	3.06	13	8	2	4	0	0	70.2	67	30	24	3	2	19	0	43	1
Giard, Macon	1	7	.125	3.84	41	1	0	16	0	2	68.0	59	37	29	2	1	27	0	58	5
Gibbs, Columbus	1	1	.500	1.63	23	0	0	7	0	3	55.1	32	15	10	0	8	27	0	68	2
Goodman, Savannah	5	3	.625	3.26	60	0	0	16	0	0	77.1	66	33	28	2	2	29	1	45	4
Griffin, Albany	0	0	.000	0.00	2	0	0	0	0	0	2.1	1	0	0	0	0	0	0	2	0
Grijak, Macon	0	0	.000	4.50	2	0	0	2	0	0	2.0	3	1	1	0	0	0	0	2	0
Grimm, Fayetteville	0	2	.000	1.45	23	0	0	15	0	10	37.1	18	7	6	1	1	14	2	58	4
Harris, Columbus	7	8	.467	4.24	26	17	0	4	0	0	119.0	113	67	56	7	4	44	0	82	6
Heberling, Greensboro*	8	1	.889	2.07	11	11	0	0	0	0	69.2	47	18	16	3	3	18	0	74	3
Henriquez, Asheville	9	10	.474	4.44	27	26	2	0	1	0	150.0	154	95	74	12	10	70	2	117	7
Herrmann, Spartanburg*	7	3	.700	3.13	13	13	0	0	0	0	83.1	74	40	29	6	3	31	0	76	6
Hiljus, Capital City	7	10	.412	4.32	27	27	1	0	0	0	145.2	114	76	70	8	4	111	1	157	17
Hokanson, Capital City	4	3	.571	6.15	44	0	0	16	0	0	67.1	86	55	46	6	7	33	0	41	10
Humphry, Spartanburg	1	7	.125	11.78	10	9	0	0	0	0	36.2	57	54	48	3	5	29	0	29	6
Inman, Greensboro	7	10	.412	5.20	26	23	0	1	0	0	126.1	147	99	73	11	3	61	2	90	16
Irwin, Spartanburg	2	3	.400	5.75	20	0	0	8	0	1	36.0	44	30	23	3	1	15	0	20	1
Jarvis, Albany*	11	13	.458	3.06	29	29	8	0	1	0	185.1	173	82	63	7	5	82	4	118	10
Jersild, Hagerstown*	3	2	.600	3.68	44	0	0	18	0	3	71.0	74	39	29	4	4	25	2	59	4
Jesperson, Charleston (W.Va.)	3	1	.750	1.37	20	0	0	8	0	0	26.1	13	10	4	1	3	15	2	19	6
Jones, Savannah	6	5	.545	2.51	56	0	0	21	0	4	68.0	61	30	19	4	4	26	0	69	6
Karp, Greensboro*	13	1	.929	1.81	17	17	0	0	0	0	109.1	73	26	22	2	2	40	0	132	6
Killen, Fayetteville	0	0	.000	18.00	1	0	0	1	0	0	1.0	5	4	2	0	0	1	0	0	0
Kimel, Charleston (S.C.) *	9	7	.563	3.97	36	11	1	6	0	0	118.0	121	70	52	8	3	34	2	98	4
King, Capital City	0	0	.000	9.00	1	0	0	1	0	0	2.0	2	1	1	0	0	1	0	1	0
Klamm, Augusta*	10	10	.500	3.94	26	25	3	0	0	0	132.1	122	71	58	9	4	53	0	113	7
Kohl, Capital City	1	2	.333	5.79	20	0	0	7	0	2	28.0	42	26	18	1	2	7	0	17	0
Koller, Columbus	9	5	.643	2.24	47	0	0	23	0	6	68.1	51	21	17	4	1	19	1	37	1
Krislock, Asheville	4	6	.400	4.09	48	4	0	17	0	5	99.0	91	55	45	6	5	56	4	90	25
Kroon, Capital City	2	11	.154	3.47	29	19	0	8	0	2	124.1	123	65	48	6	5	70	0	122	10
Kummerfeldt, Char. (W.Va.)	5	6	.455	3.89	23	13	1	6	0	0	83.1	102	54	36	3	3	32	3	67	6
Lacy, Charleston (S.C.)	0	6	.000	3.15	58	0	0	57	0	36	60.0	49	25	21	1	5	32	5	54	6
Lane, Albany*	2	10	.167	4.97	29	11	0	8	0	0	76.0	92	62	42	6	6	42	2	48	6
Langford, Charleston (W.Va.)	0	1	.000	1.33	4	4	0	0	0	0	20.1	12	5	3	1	1	10	0	34	3
Largusa, Hagerstown*	3	1	.750	2.17	6	6	0	0	0	0	29.0	16	10	7	2	2	16	0	33	2
Lawrence, Augusta*	6	8	.429	3.12	22	22	0	0	0	0	121.0	108	59	42	9	4	50	1	96	6
LaPlante, Augusta	5	5	.500	3.46	14	14	0	0	0	0	83.1	89	37	32	5	3	10	1	80	4
Lehman, Hickory	4	3	.571	3.51	39	7	1	25	0	7	102.2	84	49	40	6	12	57	1	91	9
Lewis, Asheville	0	2	.000	7.91	12	0	0	3	0	1	19.1	24	18	17	2	1	15	0	15	2
Lindemann, Hickory*	6	8	.429	3.62	15	15	2	0	1	0	99.1	95	51	40	11	1	32	0	58	3
Lindsay, Hagerstown	1	1	.500	6.43	16	1	0	7	0	0	35.0	49	27	25	1	0	10	0	23	1
Lister, Charleston (W.Va.)*	1	2	.333	2.08	51	0	0	46	0	32	52.0	38	16	12	0	2	31	0	57	6
Loftin, Charleston (W.Va.)	4	1	.800	1.94	9	9	0	0	0	0	51.0	47	24	11	0	4	22	0	19	2
Lombardi, Albany	0	2	.000	5.40	4	4	0	0	0	0	20.0	25	14	12	1	0	18	0	9	1
Long, Greensboro	6	4	.600	3.95	36	7	0	10	0	4	100.1	96	56	44	8	5	33	2	63	6
Lucchetti, Savannah	2	1	.667	2.86	9	1	0	3	0	0	22.0	16	8	7	0	0	6	0	29	0
Lundberg, Spartanburg	1	0	1.000	1.15	2	2	0	0	0	0	15.2	13	2	2	0	1	6	0	13	1
Lyons, Capital City	8	16	.333	3.69	27	25	4	0	1	0	163.1	165	97	67	5	11	75	0	91	12
Maberry, Charleston (W.Va.)	8	4	.667	1.62	57	0	0	18	0	4	94.2	55	23	17	3	2	28	0	103	3
Madrigal, Asheville	1	5	.167	3.92	31	9	0	7	0	0	87.1	73	47	38	9	4	37	4	85	5
Malaver, Hickory	1	1	.500	10.38	9	0	0	4	0	0	13.0	20	19	15	2	0	14	0	6	3
Maldonado, Hagerstown	1	0	1.000	3.00	8	0	0	2	0	0	12.0	11	4	4	0	1	6	0	9	1
Mallory, Hagerstown	7	10	.412	4.06	26	26	3	0	1	0	148.2	145	81	67	14	5	49	0	92	8
Manning, Charleston (S.C.)	6	7	.462	3.03	37	10	0	8	0	2	116.0	112	54	39	3	7	39	4	83	11
Martin, Savannah	0	0	.000	18.00	1	0	0	1	0	0	1.0	2	2	2	0	0	2	0	0	0
Martin, Charleston (S.C.)	8	10	.444	4.18	28	28	1	0	1	0	161.2	157	83	75	18	4	61	2	109	7
Martin, Augusta*	0	0	.000	5.87	5	0	0	1	0	0	7.2	6	6	5	0	2	3	1	5	3
Martin, Charleston (W.Va.)	0	0	.000	0.00	1	0	0	1	0	0	0.2	0	0	0	0	1	0	0	0	0

Pitcher, Team	W	L	Pct.	ERA	G	GS	CG	GF	ShO	Sv.	IP	H	R	ER	HR	HB	BB	Int. BB	SO	WP
Martinez, Savannah	7	3	.700	1.89	14	14	2	0	0	0	95.1	70	28	20	4	1	23	1	79	2
Martinez, Charleston (S.C.) *	6	10	.375	5.85	27	27	2	0	2	0	124.2	129	91	81	10	10	90	4	129	11
Matranga, Savannah	11	3	.786	1.49	15	15	3	0	2	0	103.0	74	24	17	8	4	13	0	90	4
Matulevich, Savannah	4	4	.500	4.80	34	1	0	13	0	0	50.2	61	31	27	4	1	14	1	42	0
Maxcy, Fayetteville	12	4	.750	2.93	39	12	1	20	1	9	113.2	111	51	37	2	13	42	3	101	5
May, Macon*	10	4	.714	2.24	17	17	0	0	0	0	104.1	81	29	26	6	1	22	1	111	3
McCormack, Hickory*	4	7	.364	4.64	14	14	0	0	0	0	83.1	89	47	43	5	3	26	0	67	3
McCutchen, Asheville	1	2	.333	7.30	16	0	0	4	0	1	24.2	24	22	20	3	2	23	0	23	5
McGraw, Hickory	1	0	1.000	1.38	5	0	0	2	0	0	13.0	13	4	2	0	0	7	0	14	1
McKinion, Hickory	2	8	.200	5.04	17	15	0	0	0	0	85.2	83	57	48	12	9	48	0	54	6
Meinershagen, Hagerstown	0	3	.000	7.36	5	5	0	0	0	0	25.2	37	22	21	3	0	11	0	16	3
Mendoza, Greensboro	0	1	.000	2.45	2	0	0	1	0	0	3.2	3	1	1	0	0	5	0	3	0
Mesewicz, Augusta*	0	2	.000	4.11	12	0	0	8	0	0	15.1	14	9	7	2	0	3	0	17	3
Metcalf, Albany	0	0	.000	9.00	1	0	0	1	0	0	1.0	2	1	1	1	0	0	0	1	0
Miller, Fayetteville*	8	13	.381	4.19	28	28	2	0	0	0	161.0	151	99	75	7	5	67	0	116	10
L. Mitchell, Spartanburg	6	6	.500	4.10	19	19	4	0	2	0	116.1	113	55	53	3	3	54	0	114	14
R. Mitchell, Spartanburg	6	9	.400	4.53	32	20	1	6	0	0	129.0	134	83	65	6	13	62	0	83	13
Mora, Asheville	0	0	.000	0.00	1	0	0	1	0	0	0.2	1	0	0	0	0	0	0	0	0
Murray, Macon	7	3	.700	1.83	15	15	3	0	0	0	83.2	70	24	17	3	3	27	0	77	0
Musselwhite, Greensboro	5	3	.625	2.79	11	10	0	1	0	0	67.2	60	29	21	4	2	24	0	60	4
Mysel, Fayetteville	5	2	.714	2.61	12	12	1	0	1	0	72.1	69	25	21	2	6	16	0	46	0
Narcisse, Asheville	6	12	.333	4.38	29	29	2	0	0	0	160.1	173	95	78	11	12	66	0	114	9
Navarro, Fayetteville*	1	5	.167	2.85	41	0	0	17	0	5	75.2	59	27	24	4	3	23	3	96	3
Neilson, Columbus*	0	0	.000	6.00	5	0	0	2	0	0	9.0	6	6	6	2	1	6	0	2	2
Nix, Charleston (W.Va.)	7	2	.778	2.23	26	5	1	18	0	5	60.2	28	19	15	1	5	24	3	75	5
Nutt, Spartanburg*	6	5	.545	3.12	46	0	0	20	0	3	69.1	59	30	24	1	7	31	0	44	5
Nuttle, Augusta	1	2	.333	6.35	12	0	0	9	0	4	11.1	6	11	8	1	0	11	0	17	1
Ogden, Hickory	0	1	.000	3.24	9	0	0	5	0	0	16.2	19	8	6	2	0	8	0	18	1
O'Laughlin, Charleston (W.Va.)*	0	0	.000	0.00	2	0	0	0	0	0	1.1	2	0	0	0	0	0	0	0	0
Ottmers, Savannah	2	2	.500	4.29	4	4	0	0	0	0	21.0	20	12	10	1	0	12	0	13	1
Perez, Columbus	0	0	.000	0.59	45	0	0	45	0	35	46.0	21	4	3	1	0	19	0	50	3
Perez, Charleston (S.C.)	4	4	.500	4.29	37	2	0	13	0	0	77.2	78	40	37	6	7	34	4	60	6
Petcka, Capital City	12	6	.667	3.77	25	25	1	0	1	0	155.0	141	81	65	13	18	58	0	101	10
Pickett, Charleston (W.Va.)*	1	2	.333	6.75	44	1	0	5	0	0	44.0	42	40	33	1	5	48	0	65	6
Pisciotta, Augusta	5	2	.714	2.68	34	0	0	28	0	12	43.2	31	18	13	0	5	17	1	49	5
Place, Macon	6	5	.545	2.35	31	9	1	11	0	2	99.2	91	44	26	3	0	23	0	74	3
Pontbriant, Augusta*	0	2	.000	3.27	3	3	0	0	0	0	11.0	13	13	4	0	2	6	0	12	1
Pool, Greensboro*	2	6	.250	4.79	55	0	0	23	0	3	67.2	68	39	36	4	2	33	3	73	7
Porter, Albany	0	0	.000	4.80	10	0	0	6	0	0	15.0	14	19	8	0	0	25	0	11	7
Powell, Albany	0	2	.000	4.55	6	6	0	0	0	0	27.2	29	19	14	0	0	13	0	29	4
Pratt, Hickory*	1	4	.200	3.68	13	4	0	6	0	2	44.0	36	23	18	3	7	24	1	29	1
Proctor, Hickory	3	4	.429	6.75	21	0	0	15	0	1	29.1	29	23	22	0	1	18	0	19	2
Prybylinski, Greensboro	3	0	1.000	2.01	6	2	0	2	0	1	22.1	17	5	5	1	0	2	0	20	0
Pulsipher, Capital City*	2	3	.400	2.08	6	6	1	0	0	0	43.1	34	17	10	1	1	12	0	29	1
Quirk, Hickory*	3	4	.429	4.97	10	10	0	0	0	0	50.2	55	34	28	3	1	31	1	30	3
Rama, Spartanburg	4	6	.400	3.21	10	10	1	0	0	0	70.0	62	28	25	4	2	36	0	32	2
Ramirez, Capital City	4	6	.400	5.34	14	14	0	0	0	0	64.0	86	51	38	2	2	23	0	42	7
Ramirez, Macon	4	4	.500	3.10	36	0	0	35	0	17	40.2	34	18	14	1	2	13	1	43	1
Reed, Charleston (W.Va.)	7	9	.438	4.09	21	21	0	0	0	0	112.1	99	63	51	1	10	58	0	84	6
Reichenbach, Capital City	6	4	.600	3.96	56	0	0	41	0	12	77.1	77	39	34	6	6	30	1	58	2
Renko, Hagerstown	4	2	.667	3.40	23	1	0	12	0	5	42.1	35	20	16	2	1	11	1	45	5
Resendez, Columbus	7	3	.700	4.75	32	2	1	9	0	2	66.1	61	43	35	5	2	45	3	49	8
Reynoso, Charleston (S.C.)	1	9	.100	5.38	15	15	0	0	0	0	75.1	102	56	45	8	8	23	2	37	2
Rivera, Greensboro	1	0	1.000	2.06	10	10	0	0	0	0	39.1	31	12	9	0	0	15	0	32	2
Robinson, Hagerstown	4	7	.364	4.65	40	0	0	24	0	7	71.2	74	43	37	6	6	31	1	65	5
Ruebel, Augusta*	5	5	.500	2.42	23	7	1	6	1	0	63.1	51	28	17	2	5	34	4	50	1
Runion, Charleston (S.C.)	2	7	.222	8.40	15	15	0	0	0	0	60.0	73	60	56	2	3	49	2	32	8
Rusciano, Macon	0	2	.000	5.86	19	1	0	10	0	1	35.1	34	26	23	4	4	24	1	33	5
Ruyak, 14 Chr. (W.V) -9 Col.*	4	0	1.000	2.47	23	1	0	5	0	2	43.2	31	13	12	2	4	14	1	41	0
Sackinsky, Albany	3	4	.429	3.20	9	8	0	0	0	0	50.2	50	29	18	2	0	16	0	41	5
Salamon, Augusta	1	2	.333	3.54	47	0	0	14	0	1	61.0	43	37	24	1	9	42	2	59	5
Santana, Augusta	3	6	.333	3.35	38	13	0	4	0	0	110.0	113	65	41	7	4	35	1	85	2
Santiago, Greensboro	1	1	.500	6.42	29	0	0	12	0	0	47.2	54	44	34	10	2	26	1	36	6
Santos, Fayetteville*	3	2	.600	4.70	8	8	0	0	0	0	44.0	43	25	23	3	3	30	0	29	6
Secrist, Augusta	0	0	.000	9.00	2	0	0	2	0	0	2.0	3	2	2	0	0	0	0	0	0
Shanahan, Capital City*	1	1	.500	2.93	13	0	0	4	0	0	15.1	17	5	5	2	1	4	0	16	2
Sharts, Columbus	3	3	.500	3.99	43	0	0	25	0	6	65.1	66	39	29	7	4	39	6	45	4
Shenk, Albany	5	2	.714	2.10	53	0	0	29	0	9	85.2	57	25	20	4	4	11	0	101	3
Short, Greensboro	0	0	.000	2.53	6	0	0	2	0	0	10.2	11	3	3	1	0	5	1	17	1
Silva, Hagerstown	12	5	.706	2.52	24	24	0	0	0	0	142.2	103	50	40	6	4	62	0	161	9
Simmons, Macon*	0	5	.000	2.66	35	0	0	10	0	1	67.2	49	25	20	8	3	25	2	59	2
Smith, Savannah	1	0	1.000	2.27	20	2	0	4	0	1	43.2	33	15	11	2	1	14	1	47	1
Smith, Spartanburg	2	7	.222	2.62	35	1	0	25	0	8	55.0	51	19	16	1	5	30	1	52	7
Smith, Columbus	1	6	.143	7.17	18	0	0	14	0	1	21.1	24	21	17	1	1	18	3	20	5
Sodowsky, Fayetteville	14	10	.583	5.09	27	27	1	0	0	0	155.2	177	101	88	11	6	51	0	80	4
Sosa, Augusta	3	9	.250	5.92	33	15	0	3	0	0	106.1	125	88	70	8	9	32	0	62	10
Soto, Hickory	0	2	.000	3.60	3	3	0	0	0	0	15.0	13	7	6	0	1	8	0	9	0
Soto, Macon	0	0	.000	0.00	1	0	0	1	0	0	1.0	0	0	0	0	0	1	0	1	0
Spencer, Greensboro	0	0	.000	4.50	2	0	0	2	0	0	4.0	5	2	2	0	0	2	0	5	0
Stahlhoefer, Augusta	0	0	.000	0.00	1	0	0	0	0	0	1.0	0	0	0	0	0	0	0	1	0
Stanley, Savannah	0	1	.000	2.33	22	0	0	9	0	1	27.0	13	7	7	1	1	14	2	36	1
Stark, Capital City	1	3	.250	4.15	41	1	0	11	0	1	86.2	99	60	40	4	5	27	0	41	6
Starks, Hickory	1	7	.125	7.43	14	5	0	5	0	0	40.0	44	40	33	2	1	47	0	34	10
Stephenson, Hagerstown	16	7	.696	2.84	30	24	3	3	2	1	171.1	142	65	54	6	5	44	0	147	3
Stewart, Charleston (W.Va.)	0	0	.000	0.84	2	2	0	0	0	0	10.2	4	2	1	0	3	4	0	9	2
Tenbarge, Asheville	5	10	.333	6.58	36	12	1	9	0	0	104.0	135	89	76	7	4	64	4	54	14
Theodile, Hickory	0	4	.000	6.75	8	8	0	0	0	0	45.1	63	40	34	1	1	21	0	23	5
Thobe, Columbus	11	2	.846	1.91	19	19	2	0	0	0	132.0	105	36	28	6	1	25	0	106	3
Thobe, Macon*	7	5	.583	2.93	69	43	0	22	0	5	70.1	70	25	21	0	2	16	1	55	8
Tooch, 1 Aug. - 1 C.C.	0	0	.000	12.00	2	0	0	1	0	0	3.0	4	4	4	1	0	3	0	4	0
Townsend, Augusta*	3	2	.250	5.30	53	0	0	23	0	2	69.2	79	53	41	8	5	23	4	79	2
Tranbarger, Savannah*	5	2	.714	3.14	56	1	0	11	0	1	66.0	56	25	23	3	3	29	0	50	2
Tranberg, Spartanburg	8	1	.889	1.98	11	11	4	0	1	0	81.2	54	24	18	5	1	21	0	83	3
Turnier, Macon*	0	1	.000	4.88	12	0	2	0	0	1	24.0	21	18	13	1	2	20	0	14	9

Pitcher, Team	W	L	Pct.	ERA	G	GS	CG	GF	ShO	Sv.	IP	H	R	ER	HR	HB	BB	Int. BB	SO	WP
Tuttle, Charleston (W.Va.)	8	3	.727	3.54	13	13	0	0	0	0	81.1	66	37	32	3	3	36	1	74	6
Underwood, Greensboro	3	1	.750	3.83	22	3	0	4	0	3	47.0	45	25	20	4	2	27	0	36	3
Valdez, Asheville	0	6	.000	6.15	30	7	0	10	0	0	60.0	72	49	41	5	0	30	0	23	5
Vaughn, Charleston (S.C.)	3	1	.750	3.81	32	0	0	4	0	0	52.0	40	28	22	3	4	38	2	79	11
Wade, Macon*	8	2	.800	1.73	14	14	0	0	0	0	83.1	57	16	16	1	1	36	0	121	11
Walker, Albany	1	4	.200	2.96	10	9	1	0	1	0	48.2	49	24	16	4	3	21	1	29	3
Wallace, Greensboro	4	2	.667	3.00	13	10	2	2	1	2	66.0	63	31	22	2	2	12	0	49	3
Welch, Charleston (S.C.)*	0	0	.000	0.00	1	0	0	1	0	0	0.2	1	0	0	0	0	2	0	2	0
Wharton, Greensboro	1	1	.500	3.15	16	0	0	14	0	6	20.0	14	7	7	1	1	9	1	21	3
Wheeler, Charleston (S.C.)	3	3	.500	2.06	11	6	0	3	0	0	48.0	46	14	11	4	3	14	1	19	1
Whiteside, Fayetteville*	3	5	.375	4.65	24	16	0	4	0	0	100.2	113	68	52	8	3	41	0	85	18
Wiley, Charleston (S.C.)	3	2	.600	3.84	40	2	0	14	0	2	79.2	60	42	34	5	8	54	2	72	13
Wilkins, Augusta	5	6	.455	4.21	48	5	0	14	0	1	77.0	83	52	36	4	13	31	1	73	10
Williams, Asheville	0	0	.000	189.00	1	0	0	0	0	0	0.1	6	8	7	0	0	3	0	1	0
Williams, Columbus*	1	0	1.000	15.43	6	0	0	1	0	0	4.2	11	8	8	0	0	2	0	4	2
Wilson, Augusta	3	7	.300	5.47	20	6	0	4	0	0	51.0	66	35	31	4	3	11	0	42	3
Witasick, Savannah	1	0	1.000	4.50	1	1	0	0	0	0	6.0	7	3	3	0	0	2	0	8	0
Woodall, Charleston (S.C.)	0	0	.000	20.25	2	0	0	1	0	0	1.1	2	6	3	0	0	5	0	1	0
Woods, Hickory	2	5	.286	2.51	10	10	0	0	0	0	61.0	49	20	17	3	3	31	0	53	2
York, Columbus*	10	7	.588	2.79	26	26	1	0	0	0	158.0	127	59	49	8	2	78	0	182	15
Young, Asheville*	5	14	.263	6.12	32	24	2	0	1	0	142.2	174	114	97	13	7	95	1	101	16
Zapata, Augusta	0	0	.000	0.00	3	0	0	3	0	0	2.1	2	1	0	0	0	2	0	0	0

BALKS—Je. Martin, 7; Klamm, 6; Lane, Narcisse, Sodowsky, Stephenson, 5 each; Cabrera, Hiljus, McCormack, 4 each; Bertotti, Billingsley, Cromer, Elsbernd, Henriquez, Madrigal, Manning, Pickett, Place, Reed, Reynoso, York, Young, 3 each; Arnold, Bennett, Brunson, Buddie, Busby, Carter, Chavez, Devereax, Doman, Emerson, Fordham, Gay, Hokanson, Kroon, Lacy, Lehman, Lewis, Musselwhite, Pool, Ruyak, Salamon, Stark, Starks, Townsend, Walker, Wallace, Wharton, Wiley, 2 each; Agostinelli, Angel, Antolick, Arguto, Beauchamp, Beckerman, Bock, Brincks, Brock, Brothers, Burlingame, Butler, Carpenter, Conner, Cornett, Cotner, Davis, Edwards, Etheridge, Eyre, Fesh, Fitzpatrick, Fox, Fregoso, Gaillard, Garcia, Goodman, Herrmann, Jarvis, Jersild, Jones, Karp, Kimel, Krislock, Kummerfeldt, Langford, Lindemann, Maberry, Malaver, Mallory, R. Mitchell, Murray, Mysel, Navarro, Nix, Nutt, Ogden, Petcka, Poitbriant, Powell, Pratt, Pulsipher, Rama, Robinson, Runion, Santiago, Santos, Shanahan, Short, Silva, F. Smith, J. Thobe, Tuttle, Underwood, Valdez, Vaughn, Wheeler, Wilson, Woods, 1 each.

COMBINATION SHUTOUTS—Conner-Walker-Benitez, Emerson-Benitez, Emerson-Shenk, Lombardi-Devereux-Shenk, Stephenson-Benitez, Stephenson-Shenk, Walker-Conner-Benitez, Walker-Conner-Shenk, Albany; Doorneweerd-Townsend-Wilkins-Ruebel-Pisciotta, Garcia-Luna-Mesewicz-Pisciotta, Klamm-Ford-Wilkins, Klamm-Pisciotta, Lawrence-Ford, Santana-Salamon-Townsend, Sosa-Townsend-Pisciotta, Augusta; Bullock-Cotner-Reichenbach, Hiljus-Bullock, Lyons-Stark-Reichenbach, Ramirez-Kroon, Capital City; Eyre-Brandenburg-Lacy, Eyre-Wiley, Eyre-Wiley-Kimel-Lacy, Manning-Wiley-Perez-Brandenburg, Martin-Brandenburg-Lacy, Martin-Lacy, Reynoso-Manning-Lacy, Wheeler-Brandenburg-Lacy, Charleston (S.C.); Brunson-Brothers, Fox-Ruyak, Reed-Brothers-Nix, Reed-Pickett-Maberry, Tuttle-Lister, Charleston (W.Va.); Cabrera-Perez, Cabrera-Resendez, Cabrera-Sharts, Carter-Koller-Perez, Carter-Perez, Thobe-Gibbs-Perez, Thobe-Koller, Thobe-Perez, Thobe-Resendez-Sharts, York-Sharts-Perez, Columbus; Sodowsky-Grimm 2, Berlin-Grimm, Gaillard-Bussa, Maxcy-Whiteside, Miller-Cedeno, Mysel-Bauer, Mysel-Bussa, Mysel-Grimm-Navarro-Bussa, Sodowsky-Cedeno-Navarro-Arguto, Fayetteville; Karp-Santiago 2, Antolick-Cindrich-DeJean, Cindrich-Long-DeJean, Heberling-Underwood, Inman-Pool, Inman-Underwood, Karp-Long, Long-Wharton, Prybylinski-Cindrich-Coleman, Rivera-Santiago-Pool-Coleman, Wallace-Coleman-DeJean, Wallace-Pool-DeJean, Greensboro; Darley-Brandow, Mallory-Renko-Brandow, Hagerstown; Bertotti-Lehman, Lindemann-Culberson, McKinion-Fitzpatrick, Pratt-Lehman, Hickory; Wade-Butler-Ramirez 2, Arnold-Butler, Arnold-Giard-Ramirez, Arnold-Simmons, Brock-Simmons-Ramirez, Butler-Giard, D'Andrea-Place, May-Cromer-Ramirez, May-Place-Ramirez, May-Simmons, Murray-Thobe, Wade-Butler-Giard-Simmons, Wade-Ramirez, Macon; Busby-Cochran 2, Alkire-Stanley-Cochran, Alkire-Stanley-Goodman-Cochran, Busby-Jones, Busby-Jones-Cochran, Busby-Stanley, Carpenter-Cochran, Carpenter-Lucchetti-Stanley, Carpenter-Matulevich-Jones-Smith, Davis-Jones-Cochran, Davis-Tranbarger-Jones-Smith, Martinez-Tranbarger-Stanley, Matranga-Cochran, Matranga-Jones, Savannah.

NO-HIT GAMES—Lindemann, Hickory, defeated Albany, 1-0, May 15; Stephenson, Albany, defeated Macon, 1-0, June 9; Martinez, Charleston (S.C.), defeated Macon, 1-0 (five innings), July 16; Sadowsky-Cedeno-Navarro-Arguto, Fayetteville, defeated Greensboro, 8-0, August 3.

FIELDING

TEAM

Team	Pct.	G	PO	A	E	DP	PB
Savannah	.968	142	3772	1479	172	110	25
Macon	.966	141	3695	1464	181	104	24
Columbus	.965	142	3739	1516	191	133	25
Fayetteville	.964	142	3737	1623	201	112	30
Spartanburg	.963	142	3687	1615	203	125	25
Charleston (S.C.)	.961	142	3746	1411	209	125	29
Capital City	.961	141	3665	1590	213	131	47
Greensboro	.961	141	3686	1463	210	106	33
Hagerstown	.960	141	3694	1446	213	114	20
Hickory	.957	140	3685	1459	230	85	21
Albany	.953	142	3647	1445	251	108	28
Asheville	.952	139	3583	1654	263	137	38
Charleston (W.Va.)	.952	140	3683	1367	255	102	35
Augusta	.945	141	3643	1416	297	109	23

INDIVIDUAL

FIRST BASEMEN

*Throws lefthanded.

Player, Team	Pct.	G	PO	A	E	DP
Bess, Charleston (W.Va.)	.974	10	69	7	2	8
Bigler, Spartanburg*	.990	63	551	41	6	57
Boston, Hagerstown*	.989	123	1039	79	12	87
Burke, Spartanburg	.983	73	652	35	12	42
Burr, Charleston (S.C.)	.990	55	373	28	4	39
Burton, Charleston (S.C.)	.990	99	775	55	8	71
Calder, Augusta	1.000	5	30	1	0	4
Carmona, Spartanburg	.938	3	24	6	2	2
E. Chavez, Albany	.977	5	35	8	1	8
Coolbaugh, Hagerstown	.992	15	115	4	1	7
Curtis, Augusta	.875	2	14	0	2	2
Daubach, Capital City	.989	46	392	43	5	42
DeLosSantos, Spartanburg	1.000	1	3	0	0	0
Delvecchio, Greensboro	.987	127	1033	113	15	90
Doucette, Charleston (W.Va.)*	.983	55	331	22	6	26
Dudek, Savannah*	1.000	1	5	0	0	0
Duplessis, Columbus*	.986	34	275	15	4	29
Evans, Fayetteville*	.976	58	527	46	14	33
Evans, Hagerstown	1.000	1	4	2	0	0
Frye, Charleston (W.Va.)	.977	71	564	43	14	36
Gholston, Augusta	.978	116	942	72	23	78
Grapenthien, Asheville	.970	26	250	12	8	21
Grijak, Macon	.992	84	617	34	5	47
Hacopian, Columbus	.969	7	59	3	2	5
Harmes, Hagerstown	.970	11	62	3	2	6
Harris, Augusta	.968	10	83	7	3	5
Keenan, Charleston (W.Va.)	.983	28	212	15	4	19
Killen, Fayetteville	1.000	4	25	4	0	1
Kiraly, Capital City*	.982	97	849	65	17	74
Knott, Macon	.979	47	303	20	7	22
Kopriva, Charleston (W.Va.)	.983	24	153	16	3	15
Kupsey, Spartanburg	1.000	1	3	0	0	0
Lawler, Spartanburg	.960	2	22	2	1	0
Mader, Hickory	.964	8	78	2	3	3
Malone, Charleston (S.C.)	1.000	8	28	1	0	3
Manrique, Albany	1.000	2	6	0	0	1
Manship, Charleston (W.Va.)	1.000	6	33	1	0	2
Martin, Savannah	1.000	40	273	15	0	22
Martin, Charleston (W.Va.)	1.000	1	3	1	0	0
McCraw, Asheville	.970	12	95	3	3	9
Mercado, Columbus	1.000	25	157	9	0	15
Metcalf, Albany	.985	20	124	9	2	9
Mumma, Hickory	.985	9	56	8	1	4

Player, Team	Pct.	G	PO	A	E	DP
Murphy, Savannah	1.000	3	27	1	0	1
Nunez, Macon	.983	36	270	19	5	19
O'Brien, Savannah	.998	68	589	48	1	42
Owens, Albany	.991	113	942	73	9	70
Parker, Fayetteville*	.984	81	744	61	13	60
Pearson, Hickory	.980	64	547	41	12	37
Rich, Hickory	.993	16	125	13	1	8
Robinson, Capital City	1.000	1	1	0	0	1
Rumfield, Charleston (W.Va.)	.976	14	112	8	3	7
Sallee, Spartanburg	.985	12	56	10	1	8
Secrist, Augusta	.985	9	63	4	1	0
Shelton, Greensboro	1.000	3	23	2	0	1
Silvia, Charleston (W.Va.)	1.000	2	8	2	0	1
Stahlhoefer, Augusta	.968	16	82	8	3	4
Sumner, Savannah	.941	2	14	2	1	0
Swinton, Asheville	.975	55	440	37	12	36
Taylor, Columbus	1.000	3	3	0	0	0
Thomas, Hickory	.985	45	367	34	6	27
Tobin, Albany	.981	11	49	2	1	5
TOWNSEND, Columbus*	.993	101	792	42	6	64
Waldrop, Macon*	1.000	2	1	0	0	0
Webb, Asheville	.991	57	536	37	5	51
Welch, Charleston (S.C.)*	1.000	1	1	0	0	0
Wooten, Fayetteville	1.000	1	12	1	0	0
Wuerch, Greensboro	1.000	17	111	5	0	11

SECOND BASEMEN

Player, Team	Pct.	G	PO	A	E	DP
Anderson, Savannah	.973	19	26	46	2	13
Ashton, Charleston (W.Va.)	1.000	3	8	10	0	2
Benbow, Hagerstown	1.000	2	1	1	0	0
Black, Savannah	.955	123	209	320	25	58
Boulware, Hickory	.960	18	32	40	3	8
Burke, Spartanburg	.870	4	12	8	3	2
Cardenas, Columbus	.969	73	133	178	10	44
Cedeno, Asheville	.973	7	11	25	1	10
Clark, Albany	.833	5	6	4	2	2
Colon, Savannah	1.000	1	0	1	0	0
Coolbaugh, Hagerstown	.945	40	60	95	9	18
DeJesus, Fayetteville	.926	17	31	57	7	8
Delgado, Albany	.954	48	86	101	9	20
Dietz, Fayetteville	.961	20	28	45	3	7
Doster, Spartanburg	.960	60	111	205	13	43
Eggleston, Charleston (S.C.)	.922	41	63	79	12	25
Evans, Hickory	.873	23	40	49	13	7
Farmer, Capital City	.919	6	16	18	3	1
Frias, Charleston (S.C.)	.955	106	169	235	19	57
Garcia, Capital City	.850	5	4	13	3	2
Garvey, Augusta	.943	34	50	98	9	22
Gonzalez, Charleston (W.Va.)	.958	15	12	11	1	2
Hansen, Greensboro	.947	6	9	9	1	0
Harmes, Hagerstown	.857	2	3	3	1	1
Henry, Hagerstown	.961	108	194	277	19	59
Hernandez, Spartanburg	.917	3	5	6	1	0
Hinds, Greensboro	.957	124	209	347	25	68
Hollrah, Hickory	.938	28	43	47	6	9
Jenkins, Charleston (W.Va.)	.958	129	234	337	25	55
Knott, Macon	1.000	1	1	1	0	1
R. Long, Greensboro	.931	16	27	40	5	5
Malloy, Macon	.959	99	187	263	19	37
Martin, Charleston (W.Va.)	1.000	10	13	14	0	3
Martinez, Spartanburg	1.000	1	0	2	0	0
Martinez, Capital City	.970	34	65	98	5	21
Menechino, Hickory	.977	49	102	148	6	21
Michael, Albany	1.000	4	10	4	0	0
Mitchell, Asheville	.950	99	204	309	27	69
Mora, Asheville	.943	35	69	96	10	18
Nunez, Macon	1.000	7	5	12	0	3
Nunnally, Columbus	.936	75	138	197	23	44
Ollison, Spartanburg	.952	39	67	111	9	24
Osentowski, Capital City	.947	83	144	228	21	47
Parra, Charleston (S.C.)	.943	12	19	31	3	5
Paulino, Macon	.955	48	87	103	9	17
Polcovich, Augusta	1.000	1	2	1	0	0
Purdy, Augusta	.944	5	10	7	1	1
Randle, Hickory	.667	2	4	0	2	0
Reyes, Hickory	.961	26	51	47	4	10
Rivera, Albany	.846	5	3	8	2	0
Romero, Spartanburg	.943	40	74	126	12	19
Serra, Albany	.950	106	181	237	22	54
Stahlhoefer, Augusta	.965	25	36	47	3	9
THOMAS, Fayetteville	.983	104	209	306	9	57
Tooch, 10 Aug.-24 C.C.	.932	34	54	70	9	15
Ugueto, Savannah	.968	7	12	18	1	4
Velandia, Fayetteville	.906	7	11	18	3	2
Wells, Charleston (S.C.)	1.000	1	2	1	0	0
Zapata, Augusta	.943	77	136	178	19	30

THIRD BASEMEN

Player, Team	Pct.	G	PO	A	E	DP
Anderson, Savannah	.854	21	8	27	6	4
Ashton, Charleston (W.Va.)	1.000	1	0	2	0	0
Austin, Augusta	.904	117	74	228	32	13
Barnden, Albany	1.000	1	0	2	0	0
Benbow, Hagerstown	1.000	4	2	6	0	0
Cardenas, Columbus	.910	38	18	73	9	7
E. Chavez, Albany	.894	131	79	243	38	23
Coolbaugh, Hagerstown	.931	35	22	72	7	4
Delgado, Albany	.818	4	4	5	2	1
Dietz, Fayetteville	1.000	2	1	2	0	0
Duran, Columbus	.800	2	1	3	1	0
Eggleston, Charleston (S.C.)	.909	6	3	7	1	1
Elliott, Asheville	.898	110	73	261	38	24
Evans, Hagerstown	.908	104	87	179	27	16
Farmer, Capital City	.800	3	3	5	2	1
Feeley, Fayetteville	.876	74	49	128	25	15
Flores, Capital City	.750	2	3	3	2	1
Fraraccio, Hickory	1.000	2	2	9	0	0
Frias, Charleston (S.C.)	1.000	1	0	3	0	0
Frye, Charleston (W.Va.)	.884	59	40	90	17	12
Garcia, Capital City	.960	13	14	10	1	0
Garvey, Augusta	1.000	1	1	0	0	0
Gill, Charleston (W.Va.)	1.000	1	0	1	0	0
Gonzalez, Charleston (W.Va.)	.667	6	2	2	2	0
Hansen, Greensboro	.873	19	14	41	8	4
Harmes, Hagerstown	.875	7	3	11	2	0
Hernandez, Spartanburg	.857	4	3	3	1	0
Hollrah, Hickory	.914	13	5	27	3	0
Killen, Fayetteville	.956	61	33	142	8	10
Knott, Macon	.890	41	27	62	11	4
Kopriva, Charleston (W.Va.)	.891	77	69	136	25	10
Kratz, Spartanburg	.880	22	25	41	9	4
Kupsey, Spartanburg	.952	23	12	28	2	4
Lawler, Spartanburg	.833	2	1	4	1	0
R. Long, Greensboro	.955	11	5	16	1	1
Mader, Hickory	.894	71	40	155	23	11
Marine, Fayetteville	.882	6	5	10	2	0
Martin, Charleston (W.Va.)	.857	9	9	15	4	1
Michael, Albany	.960	10	9	15	1	0
Mitchell, Asheville	.906	10	6	23	3	4
Mora, Asheville	.810	7	9	8	4	2
Norton, Hickory	.914	59	42	127	16	11
Nunez, Macon	.882	17	5	25	4	1
Ollison, Spartanburg	.929	42	24	81	8	3
Osentowski, Capital City	.700	5	2	5	3	1
Parra, Charleston (S.C.)	.890	62	59	95	19	7
Paulino, Macon	.833	2	0	5	1	0
Probst, Asheville	.667	2	1	3	2	0
Purdy, Augusta	1.000	1	0	2	0	0
Reyes, Hickory	.667	4	2	0	1	0
ROBINSON, Capital City	.961	113	79	265	14	21
Romano, Greensboro	.889	111	98	191	36	17
Rupp, Savannah	.912	48	41	73	11	2
Sallee, Spartanburg	.867	63	40	116	24	6
Secrist, Augusta	.767	27	14	42	17	3
Smith, Macon	.885	92	65	167	30	17
Stanczak, Charleston (S.C.)	.888	77	53	160	27	19
Sumner, Savannah	.938	86	52	145	13	9
Taylor, Columbus	.947	102	76	225	17	19
Tooch, 3 Aug.-12 C.C.	.852	15	7	16	4	1
Ugueto, Savannah	.750	4	1	2	1	0
Velandia, Fayetteville	1.000	7	2	8	0	1
Webb, Asheville	.800	21	10	30	10	2
E. White, Columbus	.800	2	2	2	1	2
Woodall, Charleston (S.C.)	.600	1	2	1	2	0
Wooten, Fayetteville	1.000	1	1	1	0	0
Wuerch, Greensboro	1.000	7	6	13	0	0

SHORTSTOPS

Player, Team	Pct.	G	PO	A	E	DP
Bautista, Albany	.892	98	124	249	45	39
Benbow, Hagerstown	.918	67	77	169	22	32
Brito, Spartanburg	.941	127	198	376	36	76
Cardenas, Columbus	.895	4	6	11	2	2
Cedeno, Asheville	1.000	2	2	12	0	2
Cranford, Augusta	.870	118	168	286	68	55
Delgado, Albany	.896	21	16	27	5	5
Dietz, Fayetteville	.908	14	21	38	6	6
Dotel, Hagerstown	.922	91	126	216	29	32
Duran, Columbus	.976	40	49	113	4	19
Elliott, Asheville	.957	5	7	15	1	1
Evans, Hagerstown	1.000	1	1	0	0	0
Farmer, Capital City	.926	7	5	20	2	4
Flores, Capital City	.905	32	48	85	14	13
Fraraccio, Hickory	.917	39	70	118	17	16
Frias, Charleston (S.C.)	.875	8	11	10	3	4
Frye, Charleston (W.Va.)	1.000	3	2	0	0	0
Garvey, Augusta	.941	7	5	11	1	3
Gonzalez, Charleston (W.Va.)	1.000	8	6	14	0	1
Hinds, Greensboro	1.000	2	2	6	0	0
Jackson, Columbus	.908	106	191	324	52	68
Jeter, Greensboro	.889	126	158	292	56	57
Keeline, Greensboro	.958	120	157	323	21	50
King, Capital City	.940	94	166	305	30	54
Kratz, Spartanburg	1.000	1	1	0	0	0
R. Long, Greensboro	.902	19	26	48	8	7

Player, Team	Pct.	G	PO	A	E	DP
Magdaleno, Charleston (W.Va.)	.913	131	201	310	49	54
Malloy, Macon	1.000	2	0	1	0	1
Martin, Charleston (W.Va.)	.933	21	18	24	3	8
MERCEDES, Charleston (S.C.)	.962	127	214	337	22	63
Michael, Albany	.878	35	40	82	17	16
Miranda, Hickory	.950	33	49	83	7	11
Mompres, Capital City	.857	5	5	13	3	4
Mora, Asheville	.833	3	1	4	1	0
Mota, Savannah	.927	61	78	149	18	26
Norton, Hickory	.980	13	15	34	1	7
Ollison, Spartanburg	.900	14	19	35	6	6
Parra, Charleston (S.C.)	.907	11	14	25	4	7
Paulino, Macon	.953	39	43	80	6	13
Polcovich, Augusta	.872	14	9	32	6	5
Polidor, Hickory	.922	14	23	36	5	4
Purdy, Augusta	.846	5	2	9	2	4
Reyes, Hickory	.905	47	75	126	21	16
Riemer, Albany	.980	9	10	40	1	3
Robinson, Capital City	.833	1	1	4	1	1
Rupp, Savannah	.914	66	102	174	26	32
Sallee, Spartanburg	.900	5	6	12	2	2
Sanchez, Fayetteville	.927	110	161	311	37	46
Santana, Asheville	.931	133	210	413	46	79
Tooch, 4 Aug.-8 C.C.	.932	12	16	25	3	7
Ugueto, Savannah	.978	26	22	66	2	17
Velandia, Fayetteville	.944	22	34	68	6	14
Woodall, Charleston (S.C.)	1.000	2	2	1	0	1
Zapata, Augusta	.813	4	2	11	3	1
Zosky, Hagerstown	1.000	5	10	15	0	6

OUTFIELDERS

Player, Team	Pct.	G	PO	A	E	DP
Adams, Capital City	.953	26	35	6	2	0
Anthony, Hagerstown	.846	5	11	0	2	0
Aquino, Hickory	1.000	3	3	0	0	0
Beamon, Augusta	.969	81	181	5	6	5
Berrios, Albany	.971	40	62	5	2	2
Blanton, Savannah	.951	80	124	11	7	1
Brock, Fayetteville*	.950	114	178	12	10	3
Bryant, Columbus	.961	113	185	11	8	3
Buckley, Macon	1.000	35	53	1	0	0
Burguillos, Fayetteville	.929	54	72	7	6	0
Burke, Spartanburg	.946	35	51	2	3	1
Burton, Charleston (S.C.)	1.000	4	9	0	0	0
Byrne, Albany	.956	121	250	13	12	1
Campusano, Charleston (S.C.)	.800	7	4	0	1	0
Chambers, Macon	.929	15	12	1	1	0
Claudio, Columbus	.984	88	182	7	3	2
Clyburn, Augusta	.959	101	156	9	7	2
Colon, Savannah	.948	94	141	4	8	0
Coolbaugh, Hagerstown	1.000	10	16	2	0	0
Correa, Macon	.976	127	231	8	6	2
Cradle, Charleston (W.Va.) *	.991	44	110	1	1	0
Cradle, Hagerstown	.949	124	185	18	11	3
Curtis, Albany	.954	47	79	4	4	1
Daubach, Capital City	1.000	1	1	0	0	0
DeLosSantos, Spartanburg	.840	13	20	1	4	0
Dotel, Hagerstown	1.000	6	11	1	0	0
Dudek, Savannah*	1.000	14	9	0	0	0
Eaddy, Albany	.883	56	80	3	11	0
Eggleston, Charleston (S.C.)	.800	6	3	1	1	0
Espinosa, Augusta	.922	65	114	4	10	1
Evans, Hickory	.945	38	63	6	4	0
Evans, Spartanburg	.967	77	103	13	4	1
Feeley, Fayetteville	.944	18	17	0	1	0
Franklin, Charleston (W.Va.)	.952	76	134	5	7	2
French, Savannah	.978	49	42	3	1	0
Frias, Charleston (S.C.)	.914	23	31	1	3	0
Garr, Macon	.963	54	71	8	3	1
Garvey, Augusta	1.000	2	1	0	0	0
Gonzalez, Charleston (W.Va.)	1.000	3	0	1	0	0
Grijak, Macon	.963	14	24	2	1	0
Hacopian, Columbus	.976	32	39	1	1	0
Harris, Hickory	.943	75	137	11	9	1
Hawkins, Greensboro	.977	126	274	19	7	1
Hearn, Hagerstown*	.981	22	48	3	1	0
Hence, Columbus	.943	74	94	6	6	1
Henry, Hagerstown	1.000	6	6	1	0	0
Herrera, Hagerstown*	.945	88	150	6	9	0
Hidalgo, Asheville	.974	108	197	30	6	6
Hines, Hagerstown	.937	47	69	5	5	1
Hobson, Asheville	.963	44	72	5	3	2
Hodge, Albany	.950	27	53	4	3	2
Jesperson, Charleston (W.Va.)	.910	32	55	6	6	1
Keister, Capital City*	.982	90	155	8	3	3
Kimsey, Fayetteville	.962	108	171	8	7	2
Larson, Spartanburg*	.909	31	48	2	5	2
Levias, Hickory	.969	25	61	2	2	0
Livsey, Asheville	.974	113	216	11	6	0
LUKE, Greensboro*	.9871	134	218	11	3	2
Malone, Charleston (S.C.)	.964	127	196	16	8	3
Manship, Charleston (W.Va.)	.974	56	110	2	3	1
Martin, Charleston (W.Va.)	1.000	3	2	0	0	0

Player, Team	Pct.	G	PO	A	E	DP
Matos, Charleston (S.C.)	.955	102	225	10	11	3
McCloughan, Hagerstown	1.000	1	2	0	0	0
McEwing, Savannah	.982	138	262	13	5	4
McKinnon, Hickory	.967	63	169	5	6	0
Meggers, Charleston (W.Va.)	.968	111	177	7	6	1
Mejia, Albany	.927	22	37	1	3	0
Metcalf, Albany	.975	29	36	3	1	0
Mora, Asheville	.969	34	56	6	2	2
Moreno, Fayetteville	.955	16	20	1	1	1
Moreno, Capital City	1.000	13	24	1	0	1
Morris, Charleston (S.C.) *	1.000	15	30	0	0	0
Murphy, Spartanburg	.968	124	201	8	7	1
Nagy, Charleston (W.Va.)	.966	29	54	2	2	1
Noel, Macon	.978	118	170	8	4	1
Nunnally, Columbus	.979	46	88	5	2	2
Ordonez, Hickory	.959	72	131	10	6	2
Parker, Fayetteville*	.875	5	7	0	1	0
Parra, Charleston (S.C.)	.944	34	81	4	5	1
Patton, Hickory	.984	37	58	4	1	0
Pecorilli, Savannah	.962	33	47	3	2	0
Ponder, Augusta	.972	39	65	4	2	1
Pueschner, Charleston (W.Va.)	.942	24	47	2	3	0
Rennhack, Asheville	.981	101	141	12	3	1
Richardson, Hickory	.972	118	238	7	7	1
Riemer, Albany	1.000	2	3	0	0	0
Roberts, Hagerstown	.957	128	254	10	12	2
Robinson, Capital City	1.000	2	3	0	0	0
Rodriguez, Asheville	.921	26	34	1	3	0
Rojas, Fayetteville*	.964	119	234	5	9	2
Ruth, Spartanburg	.833	2	5	0	1	0
Sagmoen, Charleston (S.C.) *	.992	63	118	4	1	3
Sallee, Spartanburg	.833	5	9	1	2	0
Schmidt, Albany	.885	12	19	4	3	0
Secrist, Augusta	1.000	12	13	1	0	0
Shirley, Capital City	.911	71	127	6	13	2
Simonson, Charleston (S.C.)	1.000	10	10	3	0	1
Sly, Macon	1.000	18	36	1	0	1
Smith, Capital City	.000	1	0	0	1	0
Solomon, Spartanburg*	.990	51	91	4	1	0
Spencer, Greensboro	.967	81	138	10	5	2
Suplee, Greensboro	.950	76	111	3	6	1
Swinton, Asheville	.857	5	5	1	1	0
Tena, Augusta	.966	80	132	10	5	4
Thomas, Albany	1.000	3	2	0	0	0
Ugueto, Savannah	1.000	1	2	0	0	0
Vlasis, Savannah	.973	69	103	5	3	1
Waldrop, Macon*	.954	95	137	7	7	0
Walker, Augusta*	.941	59	87	8	6	1
Welch, Charleston (S.C.) *	.965	64	103	8	4	1
Wells, Charleston (S.C.)	1.000	3	6	0	0	0
A. White, Columbus*	.970	108	186	8	6	3
White, Capital City	.956	113	223	15	11	1
Wilkerson, Charleston (W.Va.)*	.951	87	129	8	7	1
Wills, Spartanburg	.9868	105	215	10	3	1
Wipf, Capital City	.980	120	221	21	5	5
Woodall, Charleston (S.C.)	1.000	17	18	3	0	1
Wuerch, Greensboro	1.000	14	23	1	0	0
Yeske, Albany	.983	103	164	8	3	0

CATCHERS

Player, Team	Pct.	G	PO	A	E	DP	PB
Albaladejo, Asheville	.960	65	415	60	20	2	19
Arntzen, Columbus	.997	35	275	30	1	2	4
Ashby, Greensboro	1.000	1	4	2	0	0	2
Bell, Fayetteville	1.000	4	32	3	0	0	0
Bennett, Spartanburg	.992	36	199	35	2	2	4
Bess, Charleston (W.Va.)	.976	79	585	77	16	4	23
Bethke, Charleston (S.C.)	.986	97	726	51	11	5	16
Brophy, Spartanburg	.991	44	297	50	3	3	8
Cossins, Charleston (S.C.)	.988	24	148	18	2	3	4
E. Diaz, Columbus	1.000	1	3	1	0	0	1
Durso, Hagerstown	.989	14	78	11	1	0	4
Faircloth, Hickory	.961	23	130	19	6	1	2
Garcia, Macon	.988	26	147	13	2	1	4
Garcia, Capital City	.980	96	632	92	15	8	36
Gonzalez, Asheville	.964	40	214	29	9	1	12
Hammell, Capital City	1.000	11	50	4	0	1	2
Harmes, Hagerstown	.980	52	348	38	8	2	5
Haws, Spartanburg	.988	69	438	68	6	7	12
Hieb, Charleston (S.C.)	.962	5	23	2	1	0	2
Kendall, Augusta	.964	62	472	65	20	2	8
Ladd, Hagerstown	.992	13	110	10	1	1	2
Lawler, Spartanburg	.889	1	7	1	1	0	0
Lidle, Fayetteville	.982	57	392	47	8	3	14
Lombardi, Hagerstown	1.000	5	25	1	0	0	1
Lutz, Hagerstown	1.000	1	2	0	0	0	0
Manrique, Albany	.967	88	616	66	23	3	12
Marine, Fayetteville	.964	14	94	14	4	0	7
Marshall, Columbus	1.000	15	88	9	0	0	0
Martinez, Hagerstown	.976	69	493	68	14	1	8
Marx, Augusta	.978	49	356	41	9	5	2
Meluskey, Columbus	.990	99	639	87	7	9	20
Metcalf, Albany	.967	9	47	12	2	0	4

Player, Team	Pct.	G	PO	A	E	DP	PB
Milne, Savannah	.984	9	54	8	1	1	0
Mumma, Hickory	1.000	10	36	6	0	0	4
MURPHY, Savannah	.993	89	757	81	6	7	15
Patrizi, Capital City	.941	2	15	1	1	0	1
Pecorilli, Savannah	.981	52	360	43	8	4	10
Petilo, Spartanburg	1.000	2	11	2	0	0	1
Pineda, Greensboro	1.000	3	10	2	0	0	0
Probst, Asheville	.979	37	196	32	5	5	6
Rea, Fayetteville	.996	27	228	23	1	3	7
Rodriguez, Hickory	.976	72	476	45	13	1	12
Roman, Fayetteville	1.000	6	22	2	0	0	0
Rumfield, Charleston (W.Va.)	.970	55	384	41	13	1	8
Sealy, Charleston (S.C.)	1.000	2	15	3	0	0	1
Secrist, Augusta	.974	10	37	1	1	0	3
Seesz, Charleston (S.C.)	.991	16	97	15	1	1	6
Shelton, Greensboro	1.000	13	85	7	0	1	1
Silvia, Charleston (W.Va.)	.915	15	59	6	6	1	4
Soto, Macon	.996	28	185	38	1	2	5
Stahlhoefer, Augusta	.983	30	215	23	4	3	10
Thompson, Fayetteville	.984	40	274	38	5	2	2
Tijerina, Capital City	.986	43	241	39	4	4	8
Tobin, Albany	1.000	4	10	0	0	0	1
Torres, Greensboro	.993	17	127	18	1	0	1
Toth, Macon	.985	101	786	107	14	8	15
Tremie, Hickory	.990	49	343	44	4	3	3
Waszgis, Albany	.981	51	369	49	8	5	12
Wells, Charleston (S.C.)	1.000	6	46	0	0	0	0
Williams, Asheville	1.000	10	31	5	0	1	1
Wilson, Greensboro	.986	113	850	92	13	2	29

PITCHERS

Player, Team	Pct.	G	PO	A	E	DP
Agostinelli, Spartanburg*	1.000	6	1	3	0	0
Alger, Spartanburg*	.882	38	2	13	2	0
Alkire, Savannah*	.976	28	9	31	1	4
Anderson, Spartanburg	.975	29	14	25	1	1
Anderson, Charleston (S.C.)	.867	30	7	6	2	0
Angel, Charleston (W.Va.)	.769	19	6	4	3	0
Antolick, Greensboro	.853	13	12	17	5	1
Arguto, Fayetteville	1.000	23	1	0	0	0
Arnold, Macon	.821	27	9	14	5	0
Bauer, Fayetteville*	1.000	40	2	12	0	0
Beauchamp, Columbus	.957	27	5	17	1	1
Beckerman, Capital City	.875	25	2	5	1	0
Bellman, Capital City	1.000	11	2	3	0	0
Benitez, Albany	.500	40	0	1	1	0
Bennett, Hickory	.957	41	3	19	1	0
Berlin, Fayetteville	.929	18	6	7	1	1
Bertotti, Hickory*	.875	9	3	11	2	1
Billingsley, Asheville*	.804	28	9	28	9	1
Bock, Macon	1.000	3	1	1	0	0
Boldt, Spartanburg	.875	17	2	5	1	0
Bonilla, Augusta	1.000	15	1	6	0	1
Brandenburg, Charleston (S.C.)	.941	44	4	12	1	1
Brandow, Hagerstown	.923	40	3	9	1	0
Brewer, Albany*	1.000	6	3	7	0	1
Brincks, Hickory	1.000	30	3	9	0	0
Brock, Macon	.950	14	9	10	1	1
Brothers, Charleston (W.Va.)	.850	46	2	15	3	1
Brown, Spartanburg	.950	39	7	12	1	2
Brunson, Charleston (W.Va.)*	.909	37	6	14	2	1
Buddie, Greensboro	.974	27	16	21	1	1
Bullock, Capital City	.909	30	17	23	4	4
Burlingame, Macon	1.000	6	1	4	0	0
Busby, Savannah	.970	23	16	16	1	1
Bussa, Fayetteville	.947	39	6	12	1	3
Butler, Macon*	.786	31	3	8	3	1
Cabrera, Columbus	.840	26	6	15	4	1
Carpenter, Savannah	.821	28	6	17	5	1
Carrillo, Savannah*	1.000	6	1	2	0	1
Carter, Columbus	.814	29	11	24	8	2
Cedeno, Fayetteville	.956	28	20	23	2	1
Centeno, Capital City*	.917	43	4	7	1	0
Chamberlain, Augusta	.933	6	5	9	1	0
Chatterton, Albany	1.000	25	4	5	0	0
C. Chavez, Albany	1.000	20	0	6	0	0
Cindrich, Greensboro	.800	35	8	8	4	1
Cochran, Savannah	.933	58	5	9	1	1
Coleman, Greensboro	.923	59	6	6	1	0
Conner, Spartanburg	.929	37	11	15	2	2
Cornett, Hagerstown	.917	31	7	15	2	1
Corry, Spartanburg	1.000	15	1	5	0	0
Cotner, Capital City*	1.000	27	3	4	0	0
Crombie, Fayetteville	1.000	28	3	7	0	1
Cromer, Macon	1.000	17	0	5	0	0
Culberson, Hickory	.818	29	5	4	2	0
Cusey, Albany	1.000	11	0	1	0	0
Czanstkowski, Asheville	.667	10	0	2	1	0
D'ANDREA, Macon	1.000	26	12	13	0	4
Daniels, Hagerstown	.750	33	2	4	2	0
Darley, Hagerstown	1.000	24	3	12	0	0
Davis, Savannah	.774	26	4	20	7	2
DeJean, Greensboro	1.000	20	1	4	0	0
Devereux, Albany	.900	27	6	3	1	0
Dolson, Hagerstown*	.935	29	14	15	2	0
Doman, Hagerstown	.868	26	12	21	5	1
Doolan, Spartanburg	.938	8	5	10	1	0
Doorneweerd, Augusta	.917	13	3	8	1	0
Edwards, Spartanburg	.941	15	7	9	1	2
Elsbernd, Hickory	.870	19	7	13	3	0
Emerson, Albany*	.957	27	9	35	2	2
Engle, Capital City	.500	15	1	0	1	0
Etheridge, Charleston (W.Va.)*.	.923	13	2	10	1	1
Eyre, Charleston (S.C.)*	.900	26	7	20	3	1
Fairfax, Augusta	1.000	5	1	2	0	0
Fesh, Asheville*	.913	65	5	16	2	2
Fitzpatrick, Hickory	1.000	6	0	1	0	0
Ford, Augusta*	.889	31	1	7	1	1
Fordham, Hickory*	1.000	8	0	3	0	1
Fox, Charleston (W.Va.)	.738	27	15	16	11	1
Fregoso, Albany	1.000	6	9	2	0	0
Gaillard, Fayetteville	.857	11	4	8	2	0
Garcia-Luna, Augusta	1.000	7	1	2	0	0
Garcia, Charleston (W.Va.)	1.000	35	9	11	0	0
Gay, Hickory*	.846	13	3	8	2	0
Giard, Macon	1.000	40	7	4	0	0
Gibbs, Columbus	1.000	23	6	7	0	0
Goodman, Savannah	1.000	60	4	12	0	0
Grimm, Fayetteville	1.000	23	1	3	0	0
Harris, Columbus	.875	26	8	20	4	1
Heberling, Greensboro*	1.000	11	4	14	0	0
Henriquez, Asheville	.939	27	13	18	2	0
Herrmann, Spartanburg*	.727	13	0	8	3	2
Hiljus, Capital City	.947	27	12	6	1	4
Hokanson, Capital City	.905	44	4	15	2	2
Humphry, Spartanburg	1.000	10	3	1	0	0
Inman, Greensboro	.935	26	15	28	3	3
Irwin, Spartanburg	.900	20	1	8	1	0
Jarvis, Albany*	.939	29	8	23	2	2
Jersild, Hagerstown*	.833	44	6	9	3	0
Jesperson, Charleston (W.Va.)..	.875	20	1	6	1	0
Jones, Savannah	1.000	56	6	15	0	0
Karp, Greensboro*	1.000	17	8	15	0	1
Kimel, Charleston (S.C.)*	.850	36	2	32	6	1
Klamm, Augusta*	.917	26	10	12	2	0
Kohl, Capital City	1.000	20	2	6	0	1
Koller, Columbus	1.000	47	5	12	0	1
Krislock, Asheville	.824	48	4	10	3	1
Kroon, Capital City	.824	29	5	9	3	0
Kummerfeldt, Char. (W.Va.)	1.000	23	8	8	0	1
Lacy, Charleston (S.C.)	.941	58	6	10	1	0
Lane, Albany*	.919	29	5	29	3	0
Langford, Charleston (W.Va.)	.833	4	1	4	1	0
LaPlante, Augusta	.800	14	3	13	4	0
Largusa, Hagerstown*	1.000	6	0	3	0	0
Lawrence, Augusta*	.815	22	6	16	5	1
Lehman, Hickory	.842	39	9	7	3	0
Lewis, Asheville	.857	12	2	4	1	1
Lindemann, Hickory*	.952	15	7	13	1	2
Lindsay, Hagerstown	1.000	16	3	4	0	0
Lister, Charleston (W.Va.)*	.833	51	0	5	1	0
Loftin, Charleston (W.Va.)	.909	9	4	6	1	0
Lombardi, Albany	1.000	4	1	3	0	0
J. Long, Greensboro	.926	36	12	13	2	1
Lucchetti, Savannah	1.000	9	3	1	0	0
Lundberg, Spartanburg	1.000	2	1	1	0	0
Lyons, Capital City	.892	27	17	16	4	2
Maberry, Charleston (W.Va.)	.909	57	1	9	1	0
Madrigal, Asheville	1.000	31	8	13	0	1
Malaver, Hickory	1.000	9	1	3	0	0
Maldonado, Hagerstown	1.000	8	1	0	0	0
Mallory, Hagerstown	.962	26	10	15	1	0
Manning, Charleston (S.C.)	.929	37	6	20	2	0
Martin, Savannah	1.000	1	1	0	0	0
Martin, Augusta*	1.000	5	1	0	0	0
Martin, Charleston (S.C.)	.912	28	8	23	3	3
Martinez, Savannah	.969	14	7	24	1	2
Martinez, Charleston (S.C.)*	.786	27	3	8	3	1
Matranga, Savannah	1.000	15	4	17	0	0
Matulevich, Savannah	1.000	34	2	10	0	0
Maxcy, Fayetteville	.974	39	9	29	1	1
May, Macon*	1.000	17	6	13	0	2
McCormack, Hickory*	.963	14	5	21	1	0
McCutchen, Asheville	.667	16	1	5	3	0
McGraw, Hickory	.500	5	0	1	1	0
McKinion, Hickory	.929	17	7	6	1	0
Meinershagen, Hagerstown	1.000	5	0	3	0	0
Mendoza, Greensboro.	1.000	2	0	1	0	0
Mesewicz, Augusta*	.800	12	0	4	1	0
Miller, Fayetteville	.909	28	17	33	5	2
L. Mitchell, Spartanburg	1.000	19	10	9	0	1
R. Mitchell, Spartanburg	1.000	32	9	11	0	0
Murray, Macon	.778	15	5	9	4	0
Musselwhite, Greensboro	1.000	11	16	7	0	0
Mysel, Fayetteville	1.000	12	7	13	0	1
Narcisse, Asheville	.923	29	15	33	4	0
Navarro, Fayetteville*	1.000	41	6	14	0	0
Neilson, Columbus*	1.000	5	0	2	0	0
Nix, Charleston (W.Va.)	.800	26	0	4	1	0

Player, Team	Pct.	G	PO	A	E	DP
Nutt, Spartanburg*	1.000	46	4	16	0	1
O'Laughlin, Char. (W.Va.)*	1.000	2	0	1	0	1
Ogden, Hickory	1.000	9	0	1	0	0
Ottmers, Savannah	.857	4	2	4	1	0
Perez, Columbus	1.000	45	1	2	0	0
Perez, Charleston (S.C.)	.950	37	7	12	1	1
Petcka, Capital City	.840	25	9	12	4	0
Pickett, Charleston (W.Va.)*	.667	44	0	2	1	0
Pisciotta, Augusta	1.000	34	0	9	0	0
Place, Macon	.931	31	7	20	2	1
Pontbriant, Augusta*	1.000	3	0	1	0	0
Pool, Greensboro*	.938	55	4	11	1	2
Porter, Albany	.333	10	0	1	2	0
Powell, Albany	1.000	6	0	6	0	1
Pratt, Hickory*	1.000	13	5	4	0	0
Proctor, Hickory	1.000	21	2	4	0	1
Prybylinski, Greensboro	1.000	6	2	7	0	0
Pulsipher, Capital City*	.857	6	3	9	2	0
Quirk, Hickory*	.833	10	0	5	1	0
Rama, Spartanburg	.933	10	7	7	1	0
Ramirez, Capital City	1.000	14	1	7	0	0
Ramirez, Macon	.846	36	5	6	2	1
Reed, Charleston (W.Va.)	.800	21	5	15	5	0
Reichenbach, Capital City	.952	56	5	15	1	1
Renko, Hagerstown	.800	23	4	4	2	0
Resendez, Columbus	.923	32	2	10	1	0
Reynoso, Charleston (S.C.)	.955	15	6	15	1	1
Rivera, Greensboro	1.000	10	2	6	0	0
Robinson, Hagerstown	1.000	40	8	10	0	1
Ruebel, Augusta*	.889	23	3	13	2	0
Runion, Charleston (S.C.)	.867	15	4	9	2	1
Rusciano, Macon	.857	19	1	5	1	1
Ruyak, 14 Char.(W.Va.)-9 Col.*	.929	23	3	10	1	0
Sackinsky, Albany	1.000	9	7	1	0	0
Salamon, Augusta	.769	47	7	3	3	0
Santana, Augusta	.944	38	8	9	1	0
Santiago, Greensboro	.786	29	6	5	3	0
Santos, Fayetteville*	1.000	8	3	3	0	0
Shanahan, Capital City*	1.000	13	0	1	0	0
Sharts, Columbus	.800	43	3	5	2	0
Shenk, Albany	1.000	54	6	8	0	0
Short, Greensboro	1.000	6	3	2	0	0
Silva, Hagerstown	1.000	24	7	16	0	0
Simmons, Macon*	.778	36	3	11	4	1
Smith, Savannah	1.000	20	7	7	0	0
Smith, Spartanburg	1.000	35	3	8	0	2
Smith, Columbus	1.000	18	2	2	0	0
Sodowsky, Fayetteville	.975	27	12	27	1	3
Sosa, Augusta	.947	33	4	14	1	0
Soto, Hickory	1.000	3	0	5	0	0
Stanley, Savannah	1.000	22	1	2	0	0
Stark, Capital City	.933	41	5	9	1	0
Starks, Hickory	.882	14	7	8	2	2
Stephenson, Albany	.833	30	15	15	6	0
Tenbarge, Asheville	.818	36	7	11	4	2
Theodile, Hickory	.857	8	1	5	1	0
Thobe, Columbus	.893	19	5	20	3	1
Thobe, Macon*	.926	43	4	21	2	0
Townsend, Augusta*	1.000	53	6	12	0	1
Tranbarger, Savannah*	.929	56	1	12	1	1
TRANBERG, Spartanburg	1.000	11	6	19	0	0
Turnier, Macon*	1.000	12	1	5	0	0
Tuttle, Charleston (W.Va.)	1.000	13	7	15	0	2
Underwood, Greensboro	1.000	22	2	5	0	0
Valdez, Asheville	.938	30	6	9	1	0
Vaughn, Charleston (S.C.)	.800	32	1	7	2	0
Wade, Macon*	1.000	14	1	6	0	1
Walker, Albany	1.000	10	1	11	0	0
Wallace, Greensboro	1.000	13	4	3	0	0
Wharton, Greensboro	1.000	16	4	2	0	0
Wheeler, Charleston (S.C.)	.875	11	5	9	2	0
Whiteside, Fayetteville*	.939	24	5	26	2	0
Wiley, Charleston (S.C.)	.767	40	3	20	7	0
Wilkins, Augusta	.840	48	8	13	4	1
Wilson, Augusta	1.000	20	9	5	0	0
Woods, Hickory	1.000	10	4	5	0	1
York, Columbus*	.870	26	5	15	3	0
Young, Asheville*	.897	32	8	18	3	1
Zapata, Augusta	1.000	3	1	0	0	0

The following players did not have any fielding statistics at the positions indicated or appeared only as a designated hitter, pinch-hitter or pinch-runner: A. Adams, p; Charles Anderson, ss; Austin, of; Blanton, p; Bottoms, p; Burton, 3b; Campbell, p; Childers, p; Delgado, p; G. Diaz, p; Dietz, of; M. Evans, p; A. Garcia, of; Garvey, p; Griffin, p; Grijak, p; Haws, of; Hollrah, ss; Killen, p; King, p; Malloy, of; Marine, 1b; A. Martin, of; M. Martin, p; Marx, of; McCraw, 2b, of; Metcalf, p; Mora, p; Nuttle, p; Ollison, of; Parra, 1b; Polidor, 2b; Randle, 3b; Roman, of; Secrist, 2b, p; Serra, 1b; Solomon, 2b; M. Soto, 1b, p; Spencer, p; Stahlhoefer, p; Stewart, p; Tena, 2b; J. Thomas, of; Tooch, p; Welch, p; C. Williams, 3b, p; J. Williams, p; Wills, 2b; Witasick, p; Woodall, 2b, p.

LEAGUE CHAMPIONS

Year	Team	Pct.	Year	Team	Pct.	Year	Team	Pct.
1948—	Lincolnton*	.627	1968—	Spartanburg	.597	1981—	Greensboro‡	.695
1949—	Newton-Conover	.667		Greenwood‡	.597		Greenwood	.549
	Ruth'ford Co. (2nd)†	.627	1969—	Greenwood‡	.587	1982—	Greensboro‡	.681
1950—	Newton-Conover	.627		Shelby	.565		Florence	.546
	Lenoir (2nd)†	.626	1970—	Greenville	.576	1983—	Columbia	.620
1951—	Morganton	.645		Greenville	.619		Gastonia‡	.587
	Shelby (2nd)†	.604	1971—	Greenwood	.631	1984—	Charleston	.549
1952—	Lincolnton	.649		Greenwood	.759		Asheville‡	.510
	Shelby (2nd)†	.645	1972—	Spartanburg‡	.788	1985—	Florence‡	.599
1953-59—	League inactive.			Greenville	.652		Greensboro	.540
1960—	Lexington	.707	1973—	Spartanburg‡	.646	1986—	Columbia‡	.682
	Salisbury (2nd)†	.650		Gastonia	.619		Asheville	.643
1961—	Salisbury	.627	1974—	Gastonia	.606	1987—	Asheville	.655
	Shelby (4th)†	.481		Gastonia	.672		Myrtle Beach‡	.597
1962—	Statesville	.563	1975—	Spartanburg	.543	1988—	Charleston (S.C.)	.616
	Statesville	.700		Spartanburg	.614		Spartanburg	.500
1963—	Greenville†	.576	1976—	Asheville	.544	1989—	Gastonia	.657
	Salisbury	.631		Greenwood‡	.600		Augusta‡	.535
1964—	Rock Hill	.672	1977—	Greenwood	.557	1990—	Columbia	.580
	Salisbury‡	.631		Gastonia‡	.590		Charleston (W.Va.)‡	.538
1965—	Salisbury	.641	1978—	Greenwood	.614	1991—	Charleston (W.Va.)	.648
	Rock Hill‡	.603		Greenwood	.565		Columbia‡	.614
1966—	Spartanburg	.682	1979—	Greenwood‡	.565	1992—	Columbia	.572
	Spartanburg	.767		Spartanburg	.525		Myrtle Beach‡	.522
1967—	Spartanburg	.730	1980—	Greensboro	.590	1993—	Savannah‡	.662
	Spartanburg	.567		Charleston	.561		Greensboro	.603

*Won championship and four-club playoff. †Won four-club playoff. ‡Won split-season playoff. (NOTE—Known as Western Carolina League from 1948 through 1962 and known as Western Carolinas League through 1979.)

APPALACHIAN LEAGUE

NORTH DIVISION

Team	W	L	T	Pct.	GB
Burlington (Indians)	44	24	0	.647	......
Bluefield (Orioles)	44	24	0	.647	......
Danville (Braves)	38	30	0	.559	6
Princton (Reds)	26	42	0	.382	18
Martinsville (Phillies)	22	46	0	.324	22

SOUTH DIVISION

Team	W	L	T	Pct.	GB
Elizabethton (Twins)	37	30	0	.552	......
Johnson City (Cardinals)	37	31	0	.544	½
Huntington (Cubs)	33	35	0	.485	4½
Kingsport (Mets)	30	38	0	.441	7½
Bristol (Tigers)	28	39	0	.418	9

Team	Burl.	Blue.	Dan.	Eliz.	J.C.	Hun.	Kng.	Brs.	Pri.	Mar.	W	L	T	Pct.	GB
Burlington (Indians)	....	7	6	3	1	3	4	7	8	5	44	24	0	.647	......
Bluefield (Orioles)	3	....	6	3	7	3	3	3	9	7	44	24	0	.647	......
Danville (Braves)	4	4	....	3	3	6	3	3	4	8	38	30	0	.559	6
Elizabethton (Twins)	2	1	2	....	6	5	6	7	2	5	37	30	0	.552	6½
Johnson City (Cardinals)	3	3	2	4	....	6	8	4	3	4	37	31	0	.544	7
Huntington (Cubs)	2	1	4	5	4	....	6	5	2	4	33	35	0	.485	11
Kingsport (Mets)	0	2	1	4	2	4	....	8	4	5	30	38	0	.441	14
Bristol (Tigers)	3	2	1	3	6	5	2	....	2	4	28	39	0	.418	15½
Princeton (Reds)	2	1	6	3	2	2	1	2	....	7	26	42	0	.382	18
Martinsville (Phillies)	5	3	2	2	0	1	5	1	3	....	22	46	0	.324	22

Major league affiliations in parentheses.

Playoffs—Burlington defeated Elizabethton, two games to none, to win league championship.

Regular-season attendance—Bluefield, 47,281; Bristol, 29,868; Burlington, 61,088; Danville, 80,539; Elizabethton, 18,422; Huntington, 51,365; Johnson City, 37,751; Kingsport, 25,467; Martinsville, 58,368; Princeton, 32,606. Total—442,755. Playoffs (2 games)—1,164.

Managers—Bluefield, Andy Etchebarren; Bristol, Ruben Amaro; Burlington, Jim Gabella; Danville, Bruce Benedict; Elizabethton, Ray Smith; Huntington, Steve Kolinsky; Johnson City, Joe Cunningham; Kingsport, Ron Gideon; Martinsville, Ramon Henderson; Princeton, Tommy Dunbar.

All-Star team: 1B—Bryan Link, Bluefield; 2B—Jesus Azuaje, Burlington; 3B—Myles Barnden, Bluefield; SS—Enrique Wilson, Elizabethton; OF—Andre King, Danville; Randy Warner, Kingsport; Damon Hollins, Danville; C—Cesar Diaz, Kingsport; DH—Shawn Wooten, Bristol; RHP—Calvin Maduro, Bluefield; LHP—Javier DeJesus, Elizabethton; Relief Pitcher—Cesar Ramos, Burlington; Most Valuable Player—Bryan Link, Bluefield; Manager of the Year—Joe Cunningham, Johnson City.

BATTING

TEAM

Team	Avg.	G	AB	R	OR	H	TB	2B	3B	HR	RBI	SH	SF	HP	BB	Int. BB	SO	SB	CS	LOB
Bluefield	.273	68	2336	475	341	638	956	113	14	59	408	21	31	32	382	7	510	114	47	552
Elizabethton	.267	67	2269	415	301	605	934	119	18	58	341	9	22	34	234	7	408	71	28	457
Burlington	.265	68	2291	402	287	608	898	113	15	49	348	17	25	32	270	9	445	106	54	481
Kingsport	.261	68	2254	337	396	589	908	112	9	63	281	19	10	26	265	4	503	44	36	503
Danville	.257	68	2272	327	311	584	811	108	25	23	262	19	26	30	225	8	501	75	36	482
Johnson City	.251	68	2218	344	352	556	811	89	20	42	290	19	23	38	317	8	474	90	42	516
Huntington	.249	68	2187	381	361	545	829	89	15	55	329	23	25	38	297	10	468	59	43	475
Bristol	.245	67	2201	314	414	539	855	106	24	54	274	14	13	19	235	6	558	74	42	439
Princeton	.244	68	2234	315	390	545	751	90	28	20	263	32	28	33	222	8	445	80	44	449
Martinsville	.238	68	2269	319	476	541	798	94	11	47	276	11	7	44	244	10	575	74	39	469

INDIVIDUAL

(Leading qualifiers for batting championship—184 or more plate appearances)

*Bats lefthanded. †Switch-hitter.

Player, Team	Avg.	G	AB	R	H	TB	2B	3B	HR	RBI	SH	SF	HP	BB	Int. BB	SO	SB	CS
Wooten, Shawn, Bristol	.350	52	177	26	62	102	12	2	8	39	0	2	3	24	2	20	1	2
Link, Bryan, Bluefield*	.338	68	266	64	90	151	17	1	14	60	0	5	1	42	1	38	9	9
Diaz, Cesar, Kingsport	.327	55	211	36	69	116	12	1	11	37	0	1	6	15	2	41	0	1
Foster, Jim, Bluefield	.326	61	218	59	71	124	21	1	10	45	0	3	4	42	1	34	3	1
White, Eric, Burlington	.321	68	249	41	80	104	19	1	1	45	0	5	4	27	0	37	14	9
Hollins, Damon, Danville	.321	62	240	37	77	117	15	2	7	51	0	3	1	19	0	30	10	2
Venezia, Danny, Elizabethton	.310	62	258	47	80	97	9	1	2	36	0	3	2	18	0	34	21	8
King, Andre, Danville	.309	60	223	41	69	91	10	6	0	18	0	1	5	36	2	40	15	5
Catalanotto, Frank, Bristol*	.307	55	199	37	61	89	9	5	3	22	3	0	3	15	1	19	3	6
Warner, Randy, Kingsport	.305	58	223	37	68	125	12	0	15	37	0	1	1	13	0	55	1	0

Departmental leaders: G—Dalton, Link, McKinnon, E. White, 68; AB—Herrera, Link, 266; R—Link, 64; H—Link, 90; TB—Link, 151; 2B—J. Foster, 21; 3B—Wieser, 8; HR—P. Wilson, 16; RBI—Link, 60; SH—Carvajal, 8; SF—Ramey, 7; HP—Wallace, 10; BB—Barnden, 58; IBB—McKinnon, 4; SO—Rupp, 79; SB—Bartee, 27; CS—Carvajal, 11.

(All players—listed alphabetically)

Player, Team	Avg.	G	AB	R	H	TB	2B	3B	HR	RBI	SH	SF	HP	BB	Int. BB	SO	SB	CS
Acevedo, Jesus, Elizabethton	.105	5	19	1	2	2	0	0	0	1	0	1	0	0	0	5	0	0
Adams, Jason, Kingsport†	.216	14	51	6	11	13	2	0	0	0	1	0	0	11	0	15	2	2
Allen, Dell, Martinsville†	.192	12	26	3	5	6	1	0	0	2	1	0	0	6	0	11	0	0
Amador, Hiram, Martinsville†	.235	61	234	38	55	91	7	1	9	35	1	1	1	26	0	49	5	1
Arano, Eloy, Bristol†	.217	31	83	11	18	25	5	1	0	9	1	2	1	0	0	22	1	0
Asermely, Bill, Bluefield	.244	30	90	10	22	30	1	2	1	10	0	0	0	17	1	26	1	1
Ayala, Moises, Bristol	.000	8	22	0	0	0	0	0	0	0	1	0	0	0	0	9	0	0
Azuaje, Jesus, Burlington	.280	62	254	46	71	104	10	1	7	41	1	3	0	22	0	53	19	2
Baker, Jason, Elizabethton*	.298	60	248	45	74	110	19	4	3	26	1	2	2	20	1	27	16	2
Barnden, Myles, Bluefield*	.288	65	212	52	61	96	13	2	6	53	0	2	2	58	1	46	5	5
Bartee, Kimera, Bluefield	.246	66	264	59	65	96	15	2	4	37	3	2	3	44	0	66	27	6

Player, Team	Avg.	G	AB	R	H	TB	2B	3B	HR	RBI	SH	SF	HP	BB	Int. BB	SO	SB	CS
Bass, Jason, Bristol*	.210	35	119	21	25	47	6	2	4	13	0	0	2	14	0	42	2	2
Batiste, Darnell, Burlington*	.286	13	14	4	4	4	0	0	0	6	0	1	0	7	0	4	0	0
Baucom, Chad, Elizabethton	.204	21	49	9	10	15	2	0	1	5	0	0	3	13	0	14	0	0
Bautista, Juan, Johnson City	.156	29	77	10	12	15	1	1	0	4	0	0	1	5	0	16	4	0
Benitez, Fernando, Danville†	.286	20	49	8	14	17	3	0	0	2	1	1	1	6	0	14	1	0
Betts, Todd, Burlington*	.232	56	168	40	39	69	9	0	7	27	0	1	3	32	2	26	6	1
Biermann, Steve, Johnson City†	.284	33	116	10	33	38	5	0	0	17	1	0	0	6	0	16	2	3
Blanco, Pedro, Elizabethton†	.202	38	129	14	26	34	3	1	1	12	0	0	1	8	1	22	8	1
Bonneau, Britton, Huntington†	.255	51	153	25	39	62	7	2	4	26	5	1	4	22	1	34	4	4
Brennan, Shawn, Danville	.107	29	56	6	6	7	1	0	0	4	1	1	1	4	0	16	0	0
Bridgers, Brandon, Bluefield	.249	63	205	39	51	61	6	2	0	26	6	1	4	31	0	36	22	8
Broach, Donald, Princeton	.232	55	181	29	42	52	5	1	1	19	2	1	4	15	0	31	8	3
Brown, Armann, Elizabethton	.269	50	182	31	49	70	8	2	3	21	0	1	2	19	0	41	7	3
Campbell, Camp, Burlington	.000	23	1	0	0	0	0	0	0	0	0	0	0	0	0	0	0	0
Carvajal, Jhonny, Princeton	.292	67	253	41	74	94	10	5	0	16	8	0	4	29	1	31	7	11
Castaneda, Hector, Bluefield*	.179	22	56	8	10	14	4	0	0	8	1	1	0	9	0	12	0	0
Catalanotto, Frank, Bristol*	.307	55	199	37	61	89	9	5	3	22	3	0	3	15	1	19	3	6
Chambers, Brad, Huntington*	.100	3	10	1	1	1	0	0	0	2	0	0	0	0	0	1	0	0
Chambers, Mack, Burlington	.132	28	53	9	7	7	0	0	0	3	0	0	1	7	0	18	2	0
Christmon, Drew, Bristol*	.208	33	101	12	21	38	4	2	3	13	0	0	1	15	0	32	5	0
Christopher, Chris, Johnson City†	.299	55	204	34	61	81	5	3	3	28	1	3	2	35	1	21	18	5
Clark, Howie, Bluefield*	.294	58	180	29	53	74	10	1	3	30	1	4	4	26	2	34	5	2
Cline, Pat, Huntington	.188	33	96	17	18	30	6	0	2	13	1	3	1	17	0	28	0	0
Coleman, Ronnie, Burlington†	.189	42	74	25	14	21	2	1	1	3	1	0	3	37	0	30	12	8
Columna, Jose, Danville	.289	43	149	26	43	62	9	2	2	13	0	0	3	18	0	36	1	3
Concepcion, Yamil, Princeton	.153	32	85	6	13	19	3	0	1	8	0	0	1	2	0	24	1	2
Cordero, Edward, Bristol	.000	1	1	0	0	0	0	0	0	0	0	0	0	0	0	0	0	0
Corey, Bryan, Bristol	.105	39	95	14	10	13	3	0	0	3	0	1	0	2	0	35	2	3
Cornish, Tim, Martinsville	.194	19	62	10	12	20	3	1	1	4	0	0	0	7	0	19	4	2
Costello, Brian, Martinsville	.254	60	209	28	53	78	8	1	5	19	0	0	3	37	1	52	6	3
Cox, Chris, Danville	.242	19	66	12	16	27	5	0	2	8	0	0	0	8	0	26	1	0
Cradle, Cobi, Princeton*	.238	27	105	21	25	40	4	4	1	11	3	1	1	14	1	15	7	2
Crafton, David, Bristol*	.000	1	2	1	0	1	0	0	0	0	0	0	0	1	0	2	0	0
Dailey, Jason, Danville	.185	12	27	3	5	7	2	0	0	0	0	0	1	0	0	9	0	0
Dalton, Dee, Johnson City	.271	68	240	36	65	115	13	2	11	46	3	2	5	30	0	56	5	4
Daly, Rob, Kingsport	.303	62	238	47	72	110	16	2	6	32	4	1	2	24	1	23	1	2
DeBruhl, Randy, Princeton	.272	58	184	37	50	81	12	2	5	36	0	4	4	32	1	67	0	3
Diaz, Cesar, Kingsport	.327	55	211	36	69	116	12	1	11	37	0	1	6	15	2	41	0	1
Diaz, Einar, Burlington	.299	60	231	40	69	105	15	3	5	33	2	4	4	8	0	7	7	3
Diaz, Linardo, Martinsville	.221	35	68	12	15	25	1	0	3	12	0	1	2	12	1	28	3	1
Dicken, Rongie, Johnson City	.203	31	74	12	15	20	1	2	0	3	1	0	0	8	0	23	10	1
Dishington, Nathan, Johnson City*	.157	36	121	13	19	29	5	1	1	7	0	2	2	16	0	52	3	1
Dold, Jon, Princeton	.244	44	127	12	31	42	6	1	1	21	0	3	2	13	0	18	5	1
Domino, Rob, Princeton	.244	34	86	8	21	31	4	0	2	7	1	0	3	7	0	14	1	1
Donohue, Pat, Johnson City*	.198	36	101	15	20	32	1	1	3	12	2	1	0	19	0	23	1	1
Dorsey, James, Kingsport	.256	43	129	14	33	54	9	0	4	19	2	3	0	13	0	21	0	2
Duke, Mitch, Princeton*	.156	26	64	7	10	12	2	0	0	3	0	1	1	11	0	12	0	0
Dye, Jermaine, Danville	.277	25	94	6	26	40	6	1	2	12	0	2	0	8	1	10	4	1
Ellis, Kevin, Huntington	.267	59	225	44	60	114	11	2	13	48	0	2	0	25	3	43	6	5
Epperson, Chad, Kingsport†	.342	38	117	15	40	65	7	0	6	26	1	0	1	18	0	24	3	1
Estalella, Robert, Martinsville	.295	35	122	14	36	56	11	0	3	19	0	0	2	14	2	24	0	1
Eusebio, Ralph, Huntington	.216	47	116	25	25	33	2	0	2	12	2	1	6	25	2	25	4	4
Facione, Chris, Bristol	.289	48	173	27	50	70	10	2	2	16	1	0	0	16	0	26	15	2
Farrell, Mike, Kingsport	.205	44	112	18	23	30	5	1	0	10	0	0	3	21	0	31	2	1
Ferrante, Steve, Elizabethton	.217	18	46	9	10	17	4	0	1	8	0	0	1	7	0	16	0	0
Fitzgerald, Barry, Martinsville*	.192	26	78	8	15	27	3	0	3	7	0	0	0	5	0	29	0	0
Foster, Jim, Bluefield	.326	61	218	59	71	124	21	1	10	45	0	3	3	42	1	34	3	1
Fric, Sean, Huntington	.268	53	190	36	51	85	8	1	8	37	0	2	4	29	1	41	5	1
Garcia, Luis, Bristol	.211	24	57	7	12	16	1	0	1	7	1	0	0	3	0	11	3	1
Garcia, Luis A., Danville	.240	30	104	14	25	29	4	0	0	8	7	1	0	6	0	13	2	0
Gerteisen, Aaron, Johnson City†	.252	63	222	49	56	72	8	1	2	28	5	2	3	55	0	35	19	9
Guerrero, Rafael, Kingsport	.234	51	188	25	44	59	10	1	1	18	0	1	1	15	0	23	4	4
Guzman, Ismael, Bristol	.303	33	109	15	33	51	6	0	4	21	0	1	1	4	0	16	2	3
Hall, Darran, Princeton†	.197	49	142	17	28	31	3	0	0	5	3	0	1	14	0	40	17	5
Hamilton, Jason, Bristol*	.249	56	173	30	43	72	11	0	6	29	0	2	2	31	0	44	5	3
Hawkins, Wes, Bluefield	.246	49	179	29	44	62	10	1	2	37	2	4	4	26	0	39	10	1
Herde, Kevin, Johnson City	.264	22	53	5	14	19	5	0	0	7	1	0	3	7	0	11	0	3
Herrera, Edgar, Elizabethton	.286	67	266	48	76	117	15	1	8	48	0	3	1	22	2	52	1	2
Hobbie, Matt, Burlington*	.282	25	85	15	24	31	1	0	2	14	1	0	1	15	0	16	6	4
Hobbs, Shane, Martinsville	.193	44	135	14	26	35	7	1	0	14	0	0	3	13	0	23	0	1
Hollins, Damon, Danville	.321	62	240	37	77	117	15	2	7	51	0	0	3	19	0	30	10	5
Johnson, Artis, Huntington	.294	33	102	17	30	36	6	0	0	10	1	1	2	20	2	20	2	3
Johnson, Michael, Kingsport	.255	19	51	6	13	15	2	0	0	3	0	0	0	3	0	19	0	0
Johnson, Todd, Burlington	.299	52	184	33	55	72	11	0	2	27	1	4	2	20	2	27	7	2
Jones, Ben, Elizabethton	.273	40	139	26	38	50	12	0	0	19	1	0	2	8	0	15	7	4
Jones, Bobby, Bristol	.278	47	144	27	40	72	10	2	6	24	0	4	0	22	1	38	4	4
Jones, Paul, Bluefield*	.286	9	35	9	10	21	2	0	3	5	0	0	0	0	0	6	0	0
Keenan, Chris, Bristol	.141	28	78	10	11	21	3	2	1	4	1	0	0	6	0	46	2	0
Key, Jeffrey, Martinsville*	.251	61	219	37	55	95	8	1	10	35	1	0	4	26	2	69	8	5
Khoury, Tony, Huntington	.293	30	41	8	12	17	0	1	1	11	0	3	0	4	0	8	1	0
King, Andre, Danville	.309	60	223	41	69	91	10	6	0	18	0	1	5	36	2	40	15	5
King, Anthony, Huntington*	.189	28	74	8	14	19	2	0	1	6	0	0	2	8	1	23	2	2
King, Thomas, Huntington†	.266	44	124	16	33	45	6	0	2	21	3	1	1	13	0	35	7	2
Knauss, Tom, Elizabethton	.243	54	206	36	50	86	15	3	5	34	0	4	3	20	0	37	2	1
Lackey, Steve, Kingsport	.146	53	171	14	25	29	4	0	0	9	3	0	0	14	0	30	3	4
Landry, Lonny, Bristol	.232	41	142	20	33	52	6	3	1	7	1	0	0	16	0	52	14	9
LaBarca, Argenis, Princeton	.224	31	98	11	22	32	5	1	1	13	3	1	3	12	0	14	0	1
Lemons, Rich, Burlington*	.329	51	155	31	51	74	9	1	4	24	1	3	0	21	1	41	8	5
Lewandowski, John, Burlington	.000	1	2	0	0	0	0	0	0	0	0	0	0	0	0	0	0	0
Link, Bryan, Bluefield*	.338	68	266	64	90	151	17	1	14	60	0	5	1	42	1	38	9	9
Lofton, James, Princeton†	.224	50	174	26	39	50	4	2	1	13	6	3	0	19	0	41	11	5
Lopez, Richard, Johnson City	.276	54	210	39	58	75	7	2	2	17	0	2	6	35	1	41	12	7
Magee, James, Danville	.243	10	37	4	9	10	1	0	0	1	0	0	1	0	0	10	3	0

Player, Team	Avg.	G	AB	R	H	TB	2B	3B	HR	RBI	SH	SF	HP	BB	Int. BB	SO	SB	CS
Marrero, Elieser, Johnson City	.361	18	61	10	22	36	8	0	2	14	0	1	1	12	0	9	2	2
Martin, Ariel, Huntington†	.232	45	151	18	35	45	5	1	1	13	1	3	1	14	1	35	2	1
Martin, Lincoln, Bluefield†	.273	64	245	50	67	100	15	0	6	34	1	4	5	44	1	52	26	7
Martinez, Dalvis, Bristol	.229	9	35	3	8	14	4	1	0	4	0	0	0	3	1	6	0	1
Maxwell, Jason, Huntington	.291	61	179	50	52	84	7	2	7	38	2	1	4	35	0	39	6	4
McCroskey, Jackie, Princeton*	.253	29	95	21	24	48	10	1	4	12	0	1	2	15	2	26	0	3
McGlawn, Tom, Martinsville	.159	23	63	7	10	11	1	0	0	1	1	0	0	8	0	12	4	1
McKinnon, Tom, Johnson City*	.301	68	256	42	77	132	13	6	10	53	2	4	4	25	4	51	4	2
Mercedes, Juan, Huntington	.157	39	102	11	16	16	0	0	0	5	2	0	2	8	0	24	3	3
Minton, Rusty, Johnson City	.000	3	3	0	0	0	0	0	0	0	0	0	0	0	0	1	0	0
Montero, Danny, Huntington	.292	33	89	20	26	36	3	2	1	9	2	1	2	12	0	16	4	3
Moon, Ray, Princeton	.224	26	67	8	15	19	1	0	1	10	2	1	3	10	1	9	4	3
Morris, Bob, Huntington*	.288	50	170	29	49	66	8	3	1	24	3	1	2	24	0	29	6	8
Motte, James, Elizabethton	.288	45	153	32	44	83	7	1	10	27	3	1	1	15	0	29	3	2
Moyle, Mike, Burlington	.250	4	8	1	2	2	0	0	0	0	0	0	1	0	1	1	0	0
Ordaz, Luis, Princeton	.300	57	217	28	65	94	9	7	2	39	0	5	2	7	2	32	3	1
Palmer, Travis, Kingsport	.067	8	15	0	1	1	0	0	0	0	1	0	0	2	0	10	0	0
Paragin, Bill, Danville	.135	16	37	6	5	7	2	0	0	0	1	0	0	5	0	10	0	0
Pellot, Victor, Johnson City	.143	14	28	2	4	5	1	0	0	1	0	0	0	1	0	7	0	1
Pichardo, Sandy, Kingsport*	.302	51	192	25	58	71	6	2	1	15	4	0	3	22	1	25	12	10
Pierre-Louis, Danton, Martinsville*	.261	35	115	14	30	46	5	1	3	17	3	0	2	8	0	35	5	3
Ramey, Jeff, Princeton	.271	63	240	31	65	81	10	3	0	43	3	7	0	23	0	36	17	3
Ramirez, Alex, Burlington	.270	64	252	44	68	129	14	4	13	58	0	3	4	13	1	52	12	9
Ramirez, Richard, Burlington	.227	64	203	30	46	63	9	1	2	23	4	0	4	21	0	35	3	5
Ramos, Cesar, Burlington	.000	29	1	0	0	0	0	0	0	0	0	0	0	0	0	1	0	0
Reece, John, Danville*	.160	29	81	11	13	15	0	1	0	4	0	0	4	8	0	25	1	0
Reed, Ken, Bluefield	.217	21	46	9	10	20	1	0	3	15	1	1	2	3	0	20	1	0
Riemer, Matt, Bluefield	.241	61	224	38	54	80	6	1	6	35	5	3	3	18	0	65	8	6
Robinson, Darek, Johnson City†	.192	47	146	18	28	33	5	0	0	6	3	0	0	13	0	29	4	0
Rodriguez, Adam, Bristol	.221	42	131	19	29	52	4	2	5	19	1	1	1	13	1	36	5	1
Rodriguez, Nate, Martinsville	.245	57	208	22	51	52	1	0	0	16	4	1	7	10	0	15	4	6
Rojas, Freddy, Kingsport	.297	41	128	22	38	57	8	1	3	14	1	0	1	28	0	50	4	2
Rolen, Scott, Martinsville	.313	25	80	8	25	30	5	0	0	12	0	1	7	10	0	15	3	4
Rupp, Chad, Elizabethton	.246	67	228	54	56	102	14	1	10	36	0	5	9	44	2	79	0	1
Sanders, Rod, Princeton	.183	40	82	8	15	17	2	0	0	5	1	0	1	5	0	25	0	1
Sanjurjo, Jose, Bristol	.308	26	91	8	28	37	3	0	2	18	1	1	0	3	0	23	2	2
Saturnino, Sherton, Danville†	.254	45	142	25	36	50	5	0	1	15	0	1	7	7	0	39	9	4
Selmo, Feliberto, Danville	.236	16	55	5	13	15	2	0	0	7	0	0	1	7	0	15	3	2
Serrato, Jacob, Huntington	.071	12	14	0	1	2	1	0	0	1	0	0	0	1	0	3	0	1
Sexson, Richie, Burlington	.186	40	97	11	18	24	3	0	1	5	2	1	1	18	2	21	1	1
Shankle, Ron, Bluefield	.275	29	80	14	22	30	5	0	1	8	1	0	1	10	0	25	0	1
Shelley, Jason, Danville	.111	14	18	4	2	3	1	0	0	1	0	0	0	0	0	9	3	1
Shipman, Mike, Martinsville	.238	45	160	20	38	52	8	0	2	11	0	1	1	9	0	49	1	1
Shirley, Al, Kingsport	.180	43	133	22	24	31	5	1	0	11	2	1	4	42	1	57	6	5
Sigler, Brad, Huntington*	.250	9	20	4	5	6	1	0	0	2	0	0	2	7	0	4	1	0
Silvia, Brian, Princeton	.176	5	17	1	3	3	0	0	0	1	0	0	0	2	0	1	1	1
Simon, Randall, Danville*	.254	61	232	28	59	87	17	1	3	31	0	2	2	10	2	34	1	2
Smith, Ronald, Huntington*	.205	49	156	22	32	57	4	0	7	26	1	1	3	19	1	28	3	0
Smith, Sean, Danville*	.287	49	157	17	45	58	5	1	2	23	1	2	1	21	2	21	1	3
Stingley, Derek, Martinsville	.254	34	126	32	32	55	9	4	2	20	0	0	6	17	0	31	18	5
Strehlow, Rob, Johnson City	.250	8	4	1	1	1	0	0	0	1	0	0	0	0	0	1	0	0
Stricklin, Scott, Elizabethton*	.224	38	125	18	28	33	2	0	1	15	4	1	0	16	0	17	1	0
Strus, George, Johnson City†	.278	15	36	3	10	14	1	0	1	6	0	0	2	1	0	13	0	0
Stutts, Angelo, Danville	.244	29	78	10	19	22	3	0	0	8	0	1	2	3	0	21	2	2
Surratt, Jamie, Johnson City	.111	34	9	0	1	1	0	0	0	0	0	0	0	1	0	2	0	0
Tatrow, Dan, Johnson City	.000	7	3	0	0	0	0	0	0	0	0	0	0	1	0	6	0	0
Thompson, Leroy, Burlington*	.243	54	169	23	41	68	9	3	4	32	1	0	2	17	0	54	3	3
Tinsley, Charles, Martinsville	.100	22	50	9	5	9	1	0	1	4	0	0	1	9	0	29	2	1
Tupper, Craig, Bristol	.176	27	85	7	15	24	3	0	2	7	0	0	1	10	0	24	3	1
Ugueto, Hector, Johnson City	.250	36	100	14	25	30	5	0	0	8	1	0	3	12	0	19	3	1
Valdez, Ken, Bristol	.211	24	71	8	15	24	1	1	2	7	1	0	0	6	0	31	2	1
Valentin, Jose, Elizabethton†	.208	9	24	3	5	6	1	0	0	3	0	0	0	4	0	2	0	0
Venezia, Danny, Elizabethton	.310	62	258	47	80	97	9	1	2	36	0	3	2	18	0	34	21	8
Wallace, Joe, Johnson City	.227	51	154	31	35	65	9	0	7	32	0	2	10	36	0	40	2	2
Warner, Ken, Danville	.235	60	221	37	52	61	5	2	0	35	3	6	2	28	0	47	16	7
Warner, Randy, Kingsport	.305	58	223	37	68	125	12	0	15	37	0	1	1	13	0	55	1	0
Watts, Josh, Martinsville*	.245	58	216	31	53	76	9	1	4	38	0	1	3	20	1	56	10	3
Whatley, Gabe, Huntington*	.263	51	175	30	46	75	12	1	5	25	1	1	5	26	0	32	3	3
White, Eric, Burlington	.321	68	249	41	80	104	19	1	1	45	0	5	4	27	0	37	14	9
White, Jarvis, Bluefield	.222	16	36	6	8	9	1	0	0	5	0	0	1	10	0	9	0	0
White, Maximo, Princeton	.176	12	17	3	3	5	0	1	0	0	0	0	1	2	0	9	1	0
Wiegandt, Bryan, Martinsville	.255	29	98	12	25	34	6	0	1	10	1	1	2	12	2	29	1	0
Wieser, Mike, Danville	.243	58	206	27	50	86	11	8	3	21	5	1	2	23	1	76	2	4
Williams, Norman, Burlington	.209	37	91	9	19	21	2	0	0	7	3	0	3	4	1	22	6	2
Wilson, Enrique, Elizabethton†	.289	58	197	42	57	112	8	4	13	50	0	2	6	14	1	18	5	4
Wilson, Preston, Kingsport	.232	66	259	44	60	118	10	0	16	48	0	2	3	24	0	75	6	2
Winterlee, Scott, Kingsport	.278	12	36	6	10	14	4	0	0	2	0	0	0	0	0	6	0	0
Wooten, Shawn, Bristol	.350	52	177	26	62	102	12	2	8	39	0	3	2	24	2	20	1	2
Wyrick, Chris, Bristol	.221	33	113	11	25	36	5	0	2	12	1	1	6	0	25	5	1

The following pitchers, listed alphabetically by club, with games in parentheses, had no plate appearances, primarily through use of designated hitters:

BLUEFIELD—Barrett, Rich (2); Brewer, Brian (6); Brown, Cory (9); Chavez, Carlos (14); Dawley, Joe (20); Fregosi, Dan (6); Griffin, Ryan (15); Kitchen, Ron (16); Knott, Shawn (4); Maduro, Calvin (14); Percibal, Bill (13); Porter, Mike (9); Rinderknecht, Bob (11); Saneaux, Francisco (6); Trimarco, Mike (19); Ziegler, Shane (14).

BRISTOL—Brazoban, Candy (15); Brown, Alvin (15); Fuduric, Anton (13); Furusato, Yasutara (11); Granger, Greg (13); Hunt, Bill (12); Meredith, Ryan (19); Nakagawa, Shinya (24); Norman, Steve (16); Nowak, Steve (16); Roberts, Willis (10); Severino, Jose (4); Skrmetta, Matt (8); Smith, Cameron (9); Timko, John (13); Weber, Eric (16); Wilson, Mike (7).

BURLINGTON—Brabant, Dan (12); DeLaRosa, Maximo (14); Dinnen, Kevin (30); Done, Jose (1); Hritz, Derrick (9); Kline, Steve (2); Leyva, Damian (17); Mackey, Jason (22); Martinez, Johnny (11); Palmer, Brett (10); Runion, Tony (3); Williams, Greg (11); Wisler, Brian (4); Zubiri, Jon (5).

DANVILLE—Betti, Rich (11); Bock, Jeff (5); Bradshaw, Craig (22); Brown, Darold (11); Byrd, Matt (25); Christmas, Maurice (14); Cromer, Burke (3); Danley, Mike (13); Havens, Bill (13); Hostetler, Marcus (20); Howard, Jim (9); Jacobs, Ryan (10); Paige, Carey (13); Schutz, Carl

(12); Shafer, Bill (23); Yan, Esteban (14).

ELIZABETHTON—Bowers, Shane (7); Carrasco, Troy (14); Cobb, Trevor (13); DeJesus, Javier (12); Dowhower, Deron (20); Lehoisky, Russ (23); Miller, Shawn (13); O'Brien, Brian (14); Oiler, David (19); Perkins, Dan (10); Sampson, Ben (11); Schooler, Aaron (17).

HUNTINGTON—Bobbitt, Greg (10); Bryant, Chris (12); Childress, Bill (16); Garcia, Alfredo (3); Gonzalez, Geremis (12); Hennessy, Sean (11); Kurtz, Rodd (11); Lavenia, Mark (21); Lopez, Orlando (9); Lynch, Mike (14); Ortiz, Dan (17); Weber, Dave (14).

JOHNSON CITY—Almanza, Armando (3); Battles, Jeff (13); Bledsoe, Randy (5); Carroll, Dave (6); Charles, Domingo (9); Corrigan, Cory (11); Marchesi, Jim (20); Marquardt, Scott (4); Sailors, Jim (14); Scott, Ron (21); Stanton, Duane (24); Stewart, Chris (29); Stoppello, Jason (4); Wagner, Dale (16); Witasick, Gerald (12).

KINGSPORT—Baker, Derek (14); Carr, Bob (19); Collier, Ervin (16); Cotner, Andy (6); Gontkosky, Bob (14); Kenny, Sean (13); Krablin, Justin (4); Mast, Brian (13); McDill, Allen (9); Moreno, Juan (20); Roque, Rafael (14); Sutton, Derek (11); Tatis, Ramon (13); Wolff, Tom (3).

MARTINSVILLE—Barstad, Scott (9); Dabalack, Darin (19); Foster, Mark (13); Genke, Mike (2); Hamilton, Paul (7); Humphry, Trevor (18); Hunter, Rich (13); Lundberg, Bryan (13); McClurg, Clint (11); Mejias, Fernando (8); O'Connor, Brian (8); Olson, Chris (11); Phipps, Chris (14); Rife, Jackie (13); Sanders, Lance (12); Szarko, Andy (25).

PRINCETON—Chandler, Jason (14); Etheridge, Roger (9); Fernandez, Luis (15); Franklin, Joel (16); Fuccillo, Joe (13); Hagan, Danny (17); Keenan, Brad (14); Meier, Pat (14); Morales, Armando (1); Mullins, Chris (14); Murphy, Jeff (16); Robbins, Jason (17); Rutledge, Murry (12); Sullivan, Bill (27).

GRAND SLAMS—Thompson, 3; Amador, Herrera, 2 each; Brown, Clark, Dalton, Ellis, Fric, Gerteisen, Guzman, Venezia, P. Wilson, 1 each.

AWARDED FIRST BASE ON CATCHER'S INTERFERENCE—Brown (A. Rodriguez); Coleman (Shipman); Hawkins (E. Diaz); Rupp (C. Diaz); Shirley (E. Diaz); E. Wilson (E. Diaz).

PITCHING

TEAM

Team	ERA	G	CG	ShO	Sv.	IP	H	R	ER	HR	HB	BB	Int. BB	SO	WP	Bk.
Danville	3.38	68	1	3	23	591.2	511	311	222	29	35	252	5	514	46	8
Burlington	3.57	68	4	6	19	594.2	523	287	236	32	33	301	22	508	46	16
Elizabethton	3.58	67	2	1	15	570.2	484	301	227	42	31	282	15	511	61	8
Bluefield	4.04	68	6	1	15	599.1	584	341	269	57	30	216	11	507	52	11
Johnson City	4.21	68	1	2	21	588.0	565	352	275	55	22	240	3	558	38	8
Huntington	4.42	68	3	2	15	572.2	594	361	281	41	33	232	3	465	59	12
Princeton	4.51	68	4	5	10	586.1	587	390	294	36	23	321	10	484	83	22
Kingsport	4.71	68	5	4	17	573.0	616	396	300	52	37	218	3	430	54	11
Bristol	5.37	67	2	3	16	573.1	593	414	342	59	42	348	4	469	72	24
Martinsville	5.49	68	2	2	7	582.1	693	476	355	67	40	281	1	441	61	19

INDIVIDUAL

(Leading qualifiers for earned-run average leadership—54 or more innings)

*Throws lefthanded.

Pitcher, Team	W	L	Pct.	ERA	G	GS	CG	GF	ShO	Sv.	IP	H	R	ER	HR	HB	BB	Int. BB	SO	WP
Etheridge, Princeton*	3	2	.600	1.49	9	9	1	0	0	0	54.1	40	14	9	2	2	28	1	60	3
Mackey, Burlington*	6	0	1.000	2.15	22	5	0	7	0	1	54.1	28	14	13	3	3	36	1	53	4
Martinez, Burlington	6	1	.857	2.22	11	10	1	0	0	0	73.0	63	21	18	3	1	25	2	54	3
Miller, Elizabethton	5	0	1.000	2.63	13	11	1	2	0	0	68.1	60	26	20	4	5	23	2	35	5
Lundberg, Martinsville	3	4	.429	2.78	13	12	1	0	0	0	71.1	71	30	22	4	3	21	0	60	5
DeJesus, Elizabethton*	9	0	1.000	2.99	12	12	0	0	0	0	78.1	55	27	26	9	3	36	0	79	6
Yan, Danville	4	7	.364	3.03	14	14	0	0	0	0	71.1	73	46	24	4	5	24	1	50	3
Hagan, Princeton*	2	1	.667	3.17	17	6	0	3	0	1	59.2	44	23	21	2	1	35	1	63	10
Bryant, Huntington*	5	4	.556	3.18	12	12	0	0	0	0	65.0	57	28	23	0	1	37	0	56	11
Battles, Johnson City	5	4	.556	3.20	13	13	0	0	0	0	81.2	82	38	29	4	2	15	0	69	2
Carrasco, Elizabethton*	2	4	.333	3.20	14	10	0	3	0	2	70.1	46	32	25	2	3	39	3	75	6

Departmental leaders: G—Dinnen, 30; W—DeJesus, Maduro, 9; L—Foster, Gonzalez, 9; Pct.—DeJesus, 1.000; GS—Several pitchers tied with 14; CG—Maduro, 3; GF—Ramos, 27; ShO—Several pitchers tied with 1; Sv.—Ramos, 14; IP—Maduro, 91.0; H—Norman, 100; R—Phipps, 63; ER—Hunter, 52; HR—Chavez, 15; HB—Rife, Roque, 7; BB—Fuduric, 52; IBB—Several pitchers tied with 3; SO—Maduro, 83; WP—A. Brown, Chavez, 14.

(All pitchers—listed alphabetically)

Pitcher, Team	W	L	Pct.	ERA	G	GS	CG	GF	ShO	Sv.	IP	H	R	ER	HR	HB	BB	Int. BB	SO	WP
Almanza, Johnson City*	1	1	.500	4.15	3	0	0	0	0	0	4.1	6	2	2	1	0	3	0	4	0
Baker, Kingsport	5	6	.455	4.19	14	14	2	0	0	0	81.2	92	47	38	7	4	31	0	45	5
Barrett, Bluefield*	0	0	.000	15.00	2	0	0	0	0	0	3.0	6	5	5	0	0	4	1	1	1
Barstad, Martinsville	1	1	.500	9.37	9	0	0	2	0	0	16.1	18	17	17	3	0	10	0	15	2
Battles, Johnson City	5	4	.556	3.20	13	13	0	0	0	0	81.2	82	38	29	4	2	15	0	69	2
Betti, Danville*	2	1	.667	2.10	11	5	0	1	0	0	34.1	20	13	8	0	2	19	0	28	1
Bledsoe, Johnson City	1	1	.500	5.81	5	5	0	0	0	0	26.1	34	20	17	4	3	8	0	17	1
Bobbitt, Huntington*	3	2	.600	3.56	10	10	0	0	0	0	60.2	54	27	24	3	4	9	0	30	6
Bock, Danville	0	0	.000	7.11	5	0	0	1	0	0	6.1	6	5	5	0	0	3	0	2	1
Bowers, Elizabethton	2	0	1.000	4.76	7	1	0	4	0	0	11.1	13	7	6	0	0	1	0	13	3
Brabant, Burlington	5	3	.625	4.82	12	12	1	0	1	0	65.1	64	38	35	5	2	34	3	48	4
Bradshaw, Danville*	3	1	.750	2.63	22	0	0	8	0	1	37.2	33	15	11	2	1	10	1	33	2
Brazoban, Bristol	0	2	.000	9.43	15	0	0	8	0	0	21.0	33	28	22	3	1	20	0	16	4
Brewer, Bluefield*	3	0	1.000	1.38	6	3	1	2	0	0	26.0	18	8	4	1	2	10	0	18	2
Brown, Bristol	2	2	.500	6.23	15	6	0	4	0	1	39.0	27	30	27	1	4	47	0	30	14
Brown, Bluefield*	2	5	.286	5.79	9	9	0	0	0	0	46.2	56	31	30	2	5	17	0	37	5
Brown, Danville*	1	0	1.000	1.42	11	1	0	3	0	0	19.0	12	8	3	0	1	19	0	19	2
Bryant, Huntington*	5	4	.556	3.18	12	12	0	0	0	0	65.0	57	28	23	0	1	37	0	56	11
Byrd, Danville	5	2	.714	1.96	25	0	0	15	0	7	41.1	23	10	9	2	2	17	2	57	5
Campbell, Burlington	4	5	.444	3.57	23	6	0	4	0	0	63.0	60	33	25	4	4	29	2	50	3
Carr, Kingsport*	1	2	.333	4.45	19	0	0	18	0	4	28.1	26	14	14	3	1	4	0	23	4
Carrasco, Elizabethton*	2	4	.333	3.20	14	10	0	3	0	2	70.1	46	32	25	2	3	39	3	75	6
Carroll, Johnson City*	4	1	.800	1.83	6	6	1	0	0	0	34.1	27	8	7	3	1	10	0	22	1
Chandler, Princeton	2	6	.250	4.04	14	14	1	0	0	0	75.2	77	47	34	5	1	23	0	53	6
Charles, Johnson City	1	4	.200	7.20	9	8	0	1	0	0	35.0	52	33	28	2	0	10	0	17	3
Chavez, Bluefield*	6	3	.667	3.73	14	13	0	0	0	0	82.0	80	43	34	15	3	37	1	71	14
Childress, Huntington*	4	1	.800	2.49	16	0	0	14	0	6	43.1	37	19	12	3	4	16	0	57	7

Pitcher, Team	W	L	Pct.	ERA	G	GS	CG	GF	ShO	Sv.	IP	H	R	ER	HR	HB	BB	Int. BB	SO	WP
Christmas, Danville	7	5	.583	4.32	14	14	1	0	0	0	81.1	94	50	39	8	5	15	0	60	3
Cobb, Elizabethton*	5	4	.556	3.92	13	13	1	0	0	0	82.2	71	48	36	7	5	40	0	53	7
Collier, Kingsport	1	4	.200	6.39	16	3	0	6	0	2	43.2	51	40	31	7	6	19	0	27	5
Concepcion, Princeton	0	0	.000	18.00	2	0	0	2	0	0	3.0	5	7	6	2	0	3	0	1	1
Corrigan, Johnson City	3	0	1.000	1.86	11	6	0	3	0	1	48.1	26	15	10	2	1	8	0	46	1
Cotner, Kingsport*	4	0	1.000	1.26	6	0	0	2	0	0	14.1	10	6	2	0	1	7	0	18	2
Cromer, Danville	0	1	.000	3.86	3	0	0	3	0	0	2.1	4	2	1	0	2	1	1	1	1
Dabalack, Martinsville	2	1	.667	5.13	19	0	0	5	0	0	40.1	45	29	23	4	0	16	0	25	1
Danley, Danville*	2	1	.667	8.69	13	1	0	3	0	0	19.2	21	25	19	1	3	25	0	17	4
Dawley, Bluefield	3	1	.750	3.52	20	0	0	15	0	3	30.2	34	20	12	1	1	14	3	30	3
Delarosa, Burlington	7	2	.778	3.77	14	14	0	0	1	0	76.1	53	38	32	3	5	37	2	69	3
DeJesus, Elizabethton*	9	0	1.000	2.99	12	12	0	0	0	0	78.1	55	27	26	9	3	36	0	79	6
Dinnen, Burlington	3	2	.600	3.00	30	0	0	5	0	1	45.0	45	19	15	2	1	20	2	38	2
Done, Burlington	0	0	.000	6.00	1	1	0	0	0	0	3.0	2	2	2	0	0	3	0	1	0
Dowhower, Elizabethton	0	2	.000	3.69	20	0	0	11	0	1	31.2	11	17	13	1	3	30	1	40	12
Etheridge, Princeton*	3	2	.600	1.49	9	9	1	0	0	0	54.1	40	14	9	2	2	28	1	60	3
Fernandez, Princeton*	0	1	.000	5.74	15	0	0	5	0	1	26.2	28	18	17	2	1	20	1	13	3
Foster, Martinsville*	1	9	.100	4.93	13	13	0	0	0	0	69.1	77	55	38	3	6	42	1	50	6
Franklin, Princeton	3	1	.750	3.42	16	0	0	9	0	1	23.2	20	16	9	3	0	13	0	30	4
Fregoso, Bluefield	3	2	.600	4.33	6	5	0	1	0	0	27.0	22	15	13	2	0	13	0	22	2
Fuccillo, Princeton*	1	2	.333	9.45	13	0	0	7	0	1	13.1	10	22	14	0	1	19	0	14	9
Fuduric, Bristol	1	6	.143	7.38	13	13	0	0	0	0	53.2	52	54	44	7	3	52	1	40	7
Furusato, Bristol	1	1	.500	8.36	11	0	0	4	0	0	14.0	16	15	13	2	2	9	0	16	3
Garcia, Huntington	1	2	.333	4.95	3	3	0	0	0	0	20.0	23	11	11	2	2	1	0	11	0
Genke, Martinsville	0	1	.000	9.00	2	2	0	0	0	0	8.0	14	10	8	4	0	2	0	4	0
Gontkosky, Kingsport*	7	3	.700	3.54	14	11	2	0	0	0	76.1	82	42	30	7	5	18	0	56	5
Gonzalez, Huntington	3	9	.250	6.25	12	12	1	0	0	0	67.2	82	59	47	6	5	38	0	42	5
Granger, Bristol	3	3	.500	4.28	13	13	0	0	0	0	73.2	74	40	35	12	4	27	0	62	2
Griffin, Bluefield	3	2	.600	2.91	15	4	0	10	0	5	46.1	42	22	15	6	3	13	0	29	3
Hagan, Princeton*	2	1	.667	3.17	17	6	0	3	0	1	59.2	44	23	21	2	1	35	1	63	10
Hamilton, Martinsville	1	1	.500	14.18	7	1	0	3	0	0	13.1	29	22	21	4	1	13	0	2	2
Havens, Danville	1	1	.500	3.82	13	2	0	3	0	0	35.1	38	20	15	3	0	14	0	22	2
Hennessy, Huntington*	0	1	.000	8.83	11	0	0	7	0	0	17.1	36	20	17	2	1	4	0	17	0
Hostetler, Danville	0	1	.000	2.05	20	0	0	12	0	5	30.2	18	8	7	0	3	5	0	36	1
Howard, Danville	2	2	.500	3.89	9	8	0	0	0	0	39.1	31	29	17	0	4	26	0	31	5
Hritz, Burlington*	2	2	.500	4.50	9	8	0	0	0	0	44.0	44	25	22	0	4	30	1	39	3
Humphry, Martinsville	3	1	.750	1.64	18	0	0	14	0	3	33.0	25	8	6	1	4	13	0	40	8
Hunt, Bristol*	0	1	.000	2.03	12	0	0	10	0	8	13.1	7	4	3	0	1	8	1	14	2
Hunter, Martinsville	0	6	.000	9.55	13	9	0	1	0	0	49.0	82	61	52	9	4	27	0	36	4
Jacobs, Danville*	4	3	.571	4.01	10	10	0	0	0	0	42.2	35	24	19	5	1	25	0	32	5
Keenan, Princeton	1	1	.500	6.05	14	0	0	6	0	2	19.1	16	16	13	0	3	20	0	21	7
Kenny, Kingsport	1	2	.333	1.77	13	0	0	11	0	4	20.1	9	4	4	1	1	6	2	16	1
Khoury, Huntington	0	1	.000	3.63	12	0	0	8	0	1	22.1	17	9	9	1	2	11	1	22	3
Kitchen, Bluefield	1	2	.333	5.18	16	0	0	6	0	0	40.0	49	33	23	3	1	7	1	24	2
Kline, Burlington*	1	1	.500	4.91	2	1	0	0	0	0	7.1	11	4	4	0	0	2	1	4	0
Knott, Bluefield	1	0	1.000	3.00	4	0	0	2	0	0	6.0	5	2	2	0	3	1	0	6	0
Krablin, Kingsport	1	0	1.000	4.76	4	1	0	0	0	0	11.1	13	9	6	0	0	4	0	9	2
Kurtz, Huntington*	4	3	.571	4.75	11	11	0	0	0	0	60.2	71	42	32	8	2	18	0	42	4
Lavenia, Huntington*	2	3	.400	4.24	21	0	0	16	0	5	34.0	27	19	16	3	2	14	0	35	6
Lehoisky, Elizabethton	2	8	.200	5.79	23	0	0	19	0	4	46.2	48	37	30	5	1	23	2	55	5
Leyva, Burlington*	0	1	.000	4.91	17	0	0	10	0	1	25.2	32	18	14	1	1	17	0	22	3
Lopez, Huntington*	7	1	.875	3.19	9	8	2	0	1	0	53.2	55	28	19	1	4	17	0	46	4
Lundberg, Martinsville	3	4	.429	2.78	13	12	0	1	0	0	71.1	71	30	22	4	3	21	0	60	5
Lynch, Huntington	2	1	.667	5.70	14	3	0	6	0	2	36.1	29	26	23	5	1	25	1	40	9
Mackey, Burlington*	6	0	1.000	2.15	22	5	0	7	0	1	54.1	28	14	13	3	3	36	1	53	4
Maduro, Bluefield	9	4	.692	3.96	14	14	3	0	0	0	91.0	90	46	40	4	3	17	0	83	4
Marchesi, Johnson City	3	2	.600	5.24	20	3	0	6	0	1	34.1	40	28	20	6	2	17	1	27	2
Marquardt, Johnson City	0	0	.000	3.60	4	2	0	1	0	0	10.0	11	4	4	1	0	4	0	11	3
Martinez, Burlington	6	1	.857	2.22	11	10	1	0	0	0	73.0	63	21	18	3	1	25	2	54	3
Mast, Kingsport	2	4	.333	4.83	13	9	0	2	0	1	59.2	63	39	32	3	3	24	0	60	5
McClurg, Martinsville	1	1	.500	4.71	11	0	0	5	0	0	21.0	17	19	11	1	2	14	0	18	3
McDill, Kingsport*	5	2	.714	2.19	9	9	0	0	0	0	53.1	52	19	13	1	0	14	0	42	0
Meier, Princeton	1	3	.250	8.24	14	0	0	7	0	0	19.2	26	20	18	4	1	18	2	18	4
Mejias, Martinsville	1	0	1.000	6.32	8	0	0	6	0	0	15.2	22	11	11	2	0	3	0	11	3
Meredith, Bristol	4	0	1.000	4.85	19	0	0	11	0	2	29.2	27	17	16	7	1	16	0	38	3
Miller, Elizabethton	5	1	1.000	2.63	13	11	1	2	0	0	68.1	60	26	20	4	5	23	2	35	5
Morales, Princeton	0	0	.000	36.00	1	0	0	0	0	0	1.0	4	4	4	0	0	0	0	2	0
Moreno, Kingsport	1	4	.200	3.86	20	0	0	14	0	5	42.0	37	23	18	4	0	10	1	37	6
Mullins, Princeton	3	7	.300	4.60	14	14	0	0	0	0	74.1	87	58	38	2	2	49	0	51	12
Murphy, Princeton	4	4	.500	3.84	16	10	0	3	0	0	70.1	79	36	30	4	6	20	1	52	2
Nakagawa, Bristol*	2	2	.500	3.34	24	0	0	13	0	4	29.2	35	13	11	1	1	7	1	40	3
Norman, Bristol	3	6	.333	5.26	13	13	1	0	0	0	77.0	100	54	45	7	6	18	0	43	9
Nowak, Bristol	2	1	.667	5.03	16	0	0	5	0	0	34.0	39	20	19	3	2	16	0	28	3
O'Brien, Elizabethton*	1	5	.167	3.64	14	0	0	7	0	1	29.2	36	21	12	2	4	17	3	39	2
O'Connor, Martinsville	3	2	.600	4.28	8	7	0	1	0	0	40.0	48	23	19	4	2	11	0	34	3
Oiler, Elizabethton*	2	2	.500	3.47	19	1	0	9	0	4	36.1	37	24	14	5	0	16	1	32	4
Olson, Martinsville	2	3	.400	5.26	11	9	1	1	0	0	53.0	64	33	31	5	3	23	0	27	5
Ortiz, Huntington*	1	2	.333	4.79	17	0	0	11	0	1	35.2	33	25	19	4	2	24	0	42	2
Paige, Danville	2	4	.333	4.21	13	13	0	0	0	0	66.1	59	37	31	3	3	32	0	58	6
Palmer, Burlington*	0	1	.000	7.04	10	0	0	8	0	0	15.1	18	17	12	3	3	13	3	13	5
Percibal, Bluefield	6	0	1.000	3.81	13	13	2	0	0	0	82.2	71	48	35	7	1	33	0	81	8
Perkins, Elizabethton	3	3	.500	5.00	10	10	0	0	0	0	45.0	46	33	25	3	5	25	0	30	5
Phipps, Martinsville	0	6	.000	8.84	14	6	0	5	0	2	38.2	63	63	38	12	0	26	0	28	5
Porter, Bluefield	0	0	.000	5.56	9	0	0	8	0	3	11.1	11	7	7	2	0	13	0	12	2
Ramos, Burlington	3	3	.500	1.88	29	0	0	27	0	14	38.1	32	8	8	2	2	10	3	38	2
Rife, Martinsville	0	2	.000	5.87	13	2	0	2	0	0	30.2	26	24	20	1	7	20	1	19	4
Rinderknecht, Bluefield*	0	0	.000	5.14	11	0	0	3	0	0	14.0	17	9	8	2	1	3	1	11	0
Robbins, Princeton	1	5	.167	6.55	17	5	0	4	0	1	44.0	50	41	32	0	2	20	1	34	3
Roberts, Bristol	2	3	.400	1.38	10	2	0	2	0	0	26.0	24	16	4	0	1	11	0	23	2
Roque, Kingsport*	1	3	.250	6.15	14	7	0	4	0	0	45.1	58	44	31	9	7	26	0	36	8
Runion, Burlington	0	0	.000	3.00	3	2	0	0	0	0	12.0	10	4	4	1	0	6	0	6	2
Rutledge, Princeton	4	5	.444	3.80	12	10	2	2	1	0	64.0	63	43	27	4	0	25	1	42	7
Sailors, Johnson City*	0	6	.000	4.42	14	13	0	1	0	0	77.1	72	44	38	10	2	31	0	81	3
Sampson, Elizabethton*	4	1	.800	1.91	11	6	0	2	0	1	42.1	33	12	9	1	1	15	1	34	5

Pitcher, Team	W	L	Pct.	ERA	G	GS	CG	GF	ShO	Sv.	IP	H	R	ER	HR	HB	BB	Int. BB	SO	WP
Sanders, Martinsville	2	3	.400	4.50	12	7	1	2	0	0	50.0	55	43	25	8	3	18	0	40	3
Saneaux, Bluefield	2	1	.667	3.62	6	6	0	0	0	0	32.1	30	14	13	3	4	14	0	28	4
Schooler, Elizabethton	2	1	.667	3.86	17	1	0	8	0	2	28.0	28	17	12	3	1	17	2	26	1
Schutz, Danville*	1	0	1.000	0.66	12	0	0	9	0	4	13.2	6	1	1	0	0	6	0	25	1
Scott, Johnson City*	2	1	.667	3.70	21	0	0	15	0	9	24.1	18	11	10	2	5	17	0	22	4
Severino, Bristol	0	0	.000	35.10	4	0	0	2	0	0	3.1	12	13	13	3	0	6	0	2	0
Shafer, Danville	4	1	.800	2.32	23	0	0	9	0	6	50.1	38	18	13	1	3	11	0	43	4
Skrmetta, Bristol	2	3	.400	4.89	8	5	0	1	0	0	35.0	30	23	19	1	3	22	1	29	6
Smith, Bristol	3	1	.750	3.58	9	7	1	0	0	0	37.2	25	22	15	5	6	22	0	33	2
Stanton, Johnson City	5	2	.714	3.90	24	0	0	14	0	2	32.1	25	19	14	1	0	20	1	36	3
Stewart, Johnson City	2	1	.667	2.93	29	0	0	10	0	7	43.0	21	18	14	2	1	25	0	49	7
Stoppello, Johnson City*	0	0	.000	11.81	4	0	0	1	0	0	5.1	9	7	7	0	1	6	0	5	0
Strehlow, Johnson City	0	0	.000	5.40	2	0	0	1	0	0	1.2	1	1	1	0	0	5	0	1	0
Sullivan, Princeton	1	4	.200	5.30	27	0	0	16	0	3	37.1	38	25	22	3	3	28	2	30	12
Surratt, Martinsville	5	2	.714	4.29	29	0	0	8	0	1	35.2	41	28	17	4	2	17	1	43	1
Sutton, Kingsport*	0	4	.000	7.99	11	8	1	1	0	0	41.2	51	45	37	7	1	19	0	31	3
Szarko, Martinsville	2	5	.286	3.58	25	0	0	18	0	2	32.2	37	28	13	2	5	22	0	32	2
Tatis, Kingsport*	0	2	.000	6.12	13	3	0	5	0	1	42.2	51	42	29	1	5	23	0	25	4
Tatrow, Johnson City	0	0	.000	7.71	3	0	0	1	0	0	2.1	5	2	2	1	0	2	0	3	0
Timko, Bristol	0	1	.000	7.13	13	0	0	6	0	0	24.0	27	19	19	0	3	24	0	16	4
Trimarco, Bluefield	3	3	.500	4.21	19	0	0	9	0	2	36.1	35	26	17	6	1	11	3	24	2
Wagner, Johnson City	1	3	.250	9.00	16	0	0	5	0	0	24.0	30	32	24	4	3	24	0	30	2
Weber, Huntington	1	5	.167	4.66	14	9	0	0	0	0	56.0	73	48	29	3	3	18	1	25	3
Weber, Bristol	2	4	.333	4.87	16	5	0	2	0	0	44.1	43	33	24	6	3	33	0	24	6
Williams, Burlington*	3	1	.750	4.39	11	4	0	2	0	2	41.0	31	30	20	2	3	29	2	48	2
Wilson, Bristol	1	3	.250	6.50	7	3	0	1	0	0	18.0	22	13	13	1	1	10	0	15	2
Wisler, Burlington	1	1	.500	3.60	4	0	0	1	0	0	5.0	7	4	2	1	0	2	0	10	1
Witasick, Johnson City	4	3	.571	4.12	12	12	0	0	0	0	67.2	65	42	31	8	0	19	0	74	5
Wolff, Kingsport	1	2	.333	10.95	3	3	0	0	0	0	12.1	21	22	15	2	3	13	0	5	2
Yan, Danville	4	7	.364	3.03	14	14	0	0	0	0	71.1	73	46	24	4	5	24	1	50	3
Ziegler, Bluefield	2	1	.667	4.13	14	1	0	6	0	2	24.0	18	12	11	3	2	9	1	30	2
Zubiri, Burlington	3	1	.750	3.81	5	5	0	0	0	0	26.0	23	12	11	2	4	8	0	15	3

BALKS—Chandler, 6; Kurtz, Norman, 5 each; Foster, Martinez, Rutledge, 4 each; Charles, Fuccillo, Mackey, O'Connor, Sanders, Skrmetta, Smith, 3 each; Baker, D. Brown, Carrasco, Dabalack, Danley, Delarosa, Etheridge, Furusato, Gonzalez, Kitchen, Lehoisky, Leyva, McDill, Phipps, Robbins, Sutton, E. Weber, Williams, Wilson, 2 each; Brazoban, C. Brown, Bryant, Campbell, Carr, Chavez, Cobb, Corrigan, Cromer, Dawley, Dowhower, Fuduric, Gontkosky, Griffin, Havens, Hennessy, Hostetler, Howard, Hritz, Hunt, Hunter, Keenan, Lopez, Maduro, Marquardt, McClurg, Meier, Mejias, Meredith, Miller, Moreno, Mullins, Murphy, Nowak, Ortiz, Percibal, Perkins, Porter, Ramos, Rife, Roque, Sailors, Scott, Severino, Sullivan, Szarko, Timko, Trimarco, D. Weber, Witasick, Wolff, Ziegler, 1 each.

COMBINATION SHUTOUTS—Brown-Trimarco, Bluefield; Granger-Nakagawa, Roberts-Brown-Hunt, Wilson-Nakagawa, Bristol; Campbell-Dinnen-Leyva, Delarosa-Mackey, Martinez-Ramos, Zubiri-Mackey, Burlington; Christmas-Bradshaw-Byrd, Christmas-Shafer, Paige-Havens-Byrd, Danville; Perkins-Dowhower, Elizabethton; Kurtz-Weber-Ortiz, Huntington; Corrigan-Marchesi, Carroll-Stewart, Johnson City; Baker-Mast, Gontkosky-Kenny, Gontkosky-Mast, McDill-Carr, Kingsport; O'Connor-Humphry, O'Connor-Olson-Humphry, Martinsville; Etheridge-Fuccillo-Fernandez, Hagan-Meier-Franklin, Hagan-Robbins, Rutledge-Keenan, Princeton.

NO-HIT GAMES—Paige-Havens-Byrd, Danville, defeated Bristol, 4-0, July 21.

FIELDING

TEAM

Team	Pct.	G	PO	A	E	DP	PB	Player, Team	Pct.	G	PO	A	E	DP	PB
Burlington	.963	68	1784	822	101	68	12	Kingsport	.948	68	1719	685	133	59	23
Bluefield	.952	68	1798	721	127	48	19	Danville	.947	68	1775	652	136	41	20
Elizabethton	.951	67	1712	712	124	50	17	Huntington	.946	68	1718	739	140	52	33
Johnson City	.951	68	1764	704	128	51	30	Princeton	.945	68	1759	730	146	64	19
Bristol	.948	67	1720	715	133	52	20	Martinsville	.932	68	1747	780	183	67	17

Triple play—Kingsport.

INDIVIDUAL

FIRST BASEMEN

*Throws lefthanded.

Player, Team	Pct.	G	PO	A	E	DP
Batiste, Burlington	.900	2	8	1	1	2
Baucom, Elizabethton	1.000	2	1	1	0	0
Brennan, Danville	1.000	3	12	0	0	1
Clark, Bluefield	.917	1	11	0	1	1
Concepcion, Princeton	1.000	1	6	48	2	0
DALY, Kingsport	.986	48	395	42	6	34
DeBruhl, Princeton	.971	7	64	3	2	8
Dold, Princeton	.974	5	34	4	1	5
Donohue, Johnson City	1.000	2	13	1	0	0
Ellis, Huntington	.857	1	3	3	1	0
Facione, Bristol	.875	2	5	2	1	1
Fitzgerald, Martinsville	.955	13	118	9	6	15
Hamilton, Bristol*	.976	52	419	23	11	32
Hobbs, Martinsville	.976	40	351	18	9	24
Jones, Bluefield*	.986	8	66	7	1	4
Lewandowski, Burlington	.917	1	11	0	1	1
Link, Bluefield*	.982	52	452	36	9	33
Martin, Huntington*	.981	31	243	15	5	18
McKinnon, Johnson City	.963	68	539	32	22	45
Palmer, Kingsport	1.000	1	2	0	0	0
Pierre-Louis, Martinsville*	.954	22	202	7	10	21
Ramey, Princeton	.972	53	465	26	14	44
Reed, Bluefield	1.000	9	61	4	0	4
Rojas, Kingsport	.980	20	183	16	4	20
Rupp, Elizabethton	.980	67	533	55	12	47
Sexson, Burlington	.988	40	309	15	4	32

Player, Team	Pct.	G	PO	A	E	DP
Sigler, Huntington	1.000	1	12	0	0	1
Simon, Danville*	.980	58	463	37	10	26
Smith, Huntington	.987	42	353	28	5	28
Tatrow, Johnson City	1.000	1	3	0	0	0
Ugueto, Johnson City	1.000	1	8	0	0	0
Wieser, Danville	.973	14	105	3	3	6
White, Burlington	.986	42	333	18	5	24
Wooten, Bristol	.981	24	151	6	3	10

Triple play—Daly.

SECOND BASEMEN

Player, Team	Pct.	G	PO	A	E	DP
AZUAJE, Burlington	.986	57	122	162	4	40
Biermann, Johnson City	.891	10	15	26	5	5
Blanco, Elizabethton	.946	9	17	18	2	1
Bonneau, Huntington	.915	30	38	69	10	14
Carvajal, Princeton	.962	59	101	174	11	37
Catalanotto, Bristol	.957	55	96	128	10	21
Chambers, Burlington	.957	23	23	43	3	10
Clark, Bluefield	.910	14	28	43	7	10
Columna, Danville	.891	12	11	30	5	4
Corey, Bristol	1.000	7	12	7	0	1
Dicken, Johnson City	.962	22	45	56	4	9
Farrell, Kingsport	.941	14	21	27	3	4
Garcia, Bristol	.980	13	15	34	1	5
Johnson, Kingsport	.914	17	29	24	5	6
LaBarca, Princeton	1.000	1	0	3	0	0

— 506 —

Player, Team	Pct.	G	PO	A	E	DP
Martin, Bluefield	.939	55	87	129	14	25
Martinez, Bristol	1.000	4	11	13	0	5
McGlawn, Martinsville	.856	22	31	46	13	7
Morris, Huntington	.912	50	84	123	20	26
Ordaz, Princeton	.963	11	22	30	2	8
Pichardo, Kingsport	.938	47	84	112	13	31
Robinson, Johnson City	.975	43	74	82	4	19
Rodriguez, Martinsville	.924	46	95	124	18	27
Shankle, Bluefield	1.000	5	13	8	0	3
Venezia, Elizabethton	.963	60	144	166	12	39
Warner, Danville	.939	58	92	122	14	19
White, Burlington	.857	4	3	3	1	0
White, Princeton	.900	3	5	4	1	3
Wiegandt, Martinsville	.946	6	13	22	2	2

THIRD BASEMEN

Player, Team	Pct.	G	PO	A	E	DP
Amador, Martinsville	1.000	1	2	0	0	0
Arano, Bristol	.818	28	19	35	12	3
Azuaje, Burlington	1.000	4	1	2	0	0
Barnden, Bluefield	.899	63	36	115	17	7
BETTS, Burlington	.912	47	21	93	11	9
Biermann, Johnson City	.955	18	16	26	2	4
Blanco, Princeton	.897	11	6	20	3	1
Carvajal, Princeton	1.000	1	2	3	0	1
Chambers, Burlington	.600	2	0	3	2	0
Columna, Danville	.000	1	0	0	1	0
Concepcion, Princeton	.871	14	7	20	4	0
Cornish, Martinsville	.814	16	11	37	11	2
Cox, Danville	.909	18	12	48	6	1
Dalton, Johnson City	.840	7	1	20	4	0
Diaz, Burlington	.750	2	2	1	1	2
Donohue, Johnson City	.920	29	12	57	6	3
Ellis, Huntington	.910	38	23	58	8	5
Farrell, Kingsport	1.000	5	2	7	0	0
Garcia, Bristol	1.000	2	3	1	0	1
Garcia, Danville	.958	8	6	17	1	1
Knauss, Elizabethton	.862	54	33	104	22	12
LaBarca, Princeton	.864	26	15	36	8	4
Martinez, Bristol	.833	6	3	7	2	1
Motte, Elizabethton	1.000	4	4	4	0	0
Ordaz, Princeton	.914	30	23	51	7	7
Ramey, Princeton	.800	3	3	5	2	0
Reed, Bluefield	.667	4	1	3	2	0
Rodriguez, Martinsville	.957	7	5	17	1	1
Rodriguez, Bristol	1.000	2	3	2	0	0
Rolen, Martinsville	.889	25	23	57	10	5
Shankle, Bluefield	.889	12	5	11	2	0
Ugueto, Johnson City	.792	22	15	27	11	2
Valdez, Bristol	.735	19	15	21	13	1
Wallace, Johnson City	.833	6	2	13	3	0
Watts, Martinsville	.850	4	5	12	3	1
Wieser, Danville	.924	43	35	99	11	8
Whatley, Huntington	.856	30	24	53	13	5
White, Burlington	.894	24	24	77	12	7
White, Princeton	.200	3	0	1	4	0
Wiegandt, Martinsville	.926	20	13	37	4	5
Wilson, Elizabethton	1.000	1	0	1	0	0
Wilson, Kingsport	.873	65	45	127	25	10
Wooten, Bristol	.894	22	22	37	7	6
Wyrick, Bristol	.909	4	3	7	1	1

SHORTSTOPS

Player, Team	Pct.	G	PO	A	E	DP
Amador, Martinsville	.891	60	98	205	37	35
Arano, Bristol	.833	4	2	8	2	0
Azuaje, Burlington	.895	9	5	12	2	1
Betts, Burlington	1.000	4	5	2	0	1
Biermann, Johnson City	.952	7	5	15	1	1
Carvajal, Princeton	.919	8	15	19	3	4
Columna, Danville	.795	20	18	40	15	4
Corey, Bristol	.919	31	41	73	10	13
Dalton, Johnson City	.929	61	101	186	22	37
Farrell, Kingsport	.913	21	24	49	7	9
Garcia, Bristol	.897	11	15	20	4	2
Garcia, Danville	.914	22	37	48	8	10
LaBarca, Princeton	1.000	1	0	3	0	0
Lackey, Kingsport	.903	53	74	141	23	30
Lofton, Princeton	.900	49	63	143	23	28
Magee, Danville	.903	10	12	16	3	7
Maxwell, Huntington	.957	44	60	140	9	23
Mercedes, Huntington	.884	35	38	92	17	10
Motte, Elizabethton	.939	20	28	49	5	11
Ordaz, Princeton	.925	13	13	36	4	6
RAMIREZ, Burlington	.955	64	102	195	14	37
Riemer, Bluefield	.918	61	90	179	24	25
Rodriguez, Martinsville	.958	8	4	19	1	2
Selmo, Danville	.869	15	21	32	8	3
Shankle, Bluefield	.836	12	20	31	10	4
Surratt, Johnson City	1.000	1	0	1	0	0
Wieser, Danville	1.000	5	8	15	0	2
White, Princeton	.800	4	1	7	2	0

Player, Team	Pct.	G	PO	A	E	DP
Wiegandt, Martinsville	1.000	3	4	6	0	3
Wilson, Elizabethton	.908	49	50	138	19	18
Wyrick, Bristol	.935	29	44	99	10	17

Triple play—Lackey.

OUTFIELDERS

Player, Team	Pct.	G	PO	A	E	DP
Adams, Kingsport	.972	14	34	1	1	0
Asermely, Bluefield	1.000	5	5	0	0	0
Baker, Elizabethton*	.959	57	113	4	5	1
Bartee, Bluefield	.970	66	124	5	4	1
Bass, Bristol*	.854	25	34	1	6	0
Bautista, Johnson City	.900	20	25	2	3	1
Blanco, Elizabethton	1.000	8	10	0	0	0
Bonneau, Huntington	.912	22	30	1	3	0
Brennan, Danville	.935	25	28	1	2	0
Bridgers, Bluefield	.979	63	134	4	3	1
Broach, Princeton	.955	51	100	7	5	2
Brown, Elizabethton	.908	40	66	3	7	1
Chambers, Huntington	1.000	1	1	0	0	0
Christmon, Bristol	1.000	22	17	4	0	1
Christopher, Johnson City	.968	47	87	3	3	1
Clark, Bluefield	.800	6	8	0	2	0
Coleman, Burlington	.977	41	43	0	1	0
Cornish, Martinsville	1.000	2	2	0	0	0
Costello, Martinsville	.895	57	91	3	11	1
Cradle, Princeton*	.970	27	59	5	2	0
Dailey, Danville	1.000	3	3	1	0	0
Diaz, Martinsville	.868	24	33	0	5	0
Dishington, Johnson City	.932	35	53	2	4	0
Dold, Princeton	.906	26	26	3	3	0
Dorsey, Kingsport	.973	42	72	1	2	0
Dye, Danville	.963	24	51	1	2	0
Ellis, Huntington	1.000	3	5	0	0	0
Eusebio, Huntington	.953	45	78	3	4	1
Facione, Bristol	.989	45	89	4	1	0
Farrell, Kingsport	1.000	1	1	0	0	0
Fric, Huntington	.946	57	104	1	6	0
Gerteisen, Johnson City	.961	53	93	5	4	1
Guerrero, Kingsport	.914	51	93	3	9	1
Guzman, Bristol	.978	27	42	2	1	1
Hall, Princeton*	.944	43	65	2	4	0
Hawkins, Bluefield	.947	49	69	2	4	1
Herrera, Elizabethton	.935	65	109	7	8	1
Hobbie, Burlington*	.971	24	33	1	1	1
Hollins, Danville*	.946	62	95	11	6	1
Johnson, Huntington	.906	28	28	1	3	0
Jones, Elizabethton	.933	32	24	4	2	0
Jones, Bristol	.923	41	67	5	6	0
Keenan, Bristol	.882	14	15	0	2	0
Key, Martinsville	.912	47	60	1	6	0
King, Danville	.957	60	133	1	6	0
A. King, Huntington*	.857	26	18	0	3	0
T. King, Huntington	.947	44	65	6	4	1
Landry, Bristol	.934	32	51	6	4	1
Lemons, Burlington	.938	51	59	2	4	0
Link, Bluefield*	1.000	15	27	2	0	1
Lopez, Johnson City	.982	31	52	3	1	0
McCroskey, Princeton*	.882	18	30	0	4	0
Moon, Princeton	.815	18	21	1	5	0
Palmer, Kingsport	.875	6	7	0	1	0
Pellot, Johnson City	.909	12	7	3	1	0
Ramey, Princeton	.857	4	6	0	1	0
A. Ramirez, Burlington	.930	64	85	8	7	3
Reece, Danville*	1.000	13	13	0	0	0
Rojas, Kingsport	.875	3	6	1	1	0
Sanders, Princeton	.907	36	33	6	3	4
Sanjurjo, Bristol	1.000	18	25	5	0	0
Saturnino, Danville	.854	23	35	0	6	0
Shelley, Danville	.923	9	23	0	2	0
Shirley, Kingsport	.922	43	82	1	7	0
Stingley, Martinsville	.879	31	53	5	8	0
Strehlow, Johnson City	1.000	2	2	0	0	0
Stutts, Johnson City	1.000	9	8	0	0	0
Surratt, Johnson City	1.000	3	3	0	0	0
Thompson, Burlington*	.960	28	21	3	1	0
Tinsley, Martinsville	.786	14	11	0	3	0
Ugueto, Johnson City	.933	12	13	1	1	1
WARNER, Kingsport	1.000	58	78	5	0	0
Watts, Martinsville	1.000	46	65	5	0	2
Whatley, Huntington	.941	15	15	1	1	0
White, Bluefield	.941	14	16	0	1	0
N. Williams, Burlington	.949	35	35	2	2	0

CATCHERS

Player, Team	Pct.	G	PO	A	E	DP	PB
Acevedo, Elizabethton	1.000	4	26	1	0	0	3
Ayala, Bristol	.980	8	45	4	1	0	3
Baucom, Elizabethton	.989	13	83	8	1	0	8
Benitez, Danville	.977	19	113	14	3	1	8
Castaneda, Bluefield	.985	21	114	17	2	0	3
Cline, Huntington	.974	30	174	10	5	1	17

Player, Team	Pct.	G	PO	A	E	DP	PB
DeBruhl, Princeton	.978	32	198	21	5	3	10
Diaz, Kingsport	.979	43	291	30	7	2	11
Diaz, Burlington	.976	42	313	54	9	3	7
Domino, Princeton	.968	31	192	22	7	3	5
Duke, Princeton	.961	14	68	5	3	0	5
Epperson, Kingsport	.976	16	111	10	3	0	5
Estalella, Martinsville	.975	27	210	25	6	1	9
Ferrante, Elizabethton	.971	10	62	4	2	0	4
Fitzgerald, Martinsville	.950	6	17	2	1	0	2
Foster, Bluefield	.9839	55	378	52	7	2	16
Herde, Johnson City	.986	20	117	20	2	0	6
Hobbs, Martinsville	1.000	4	23	1	0	0	0
Johnson, Burlington	.983	28	197	29	4	2	5
Khoury, Huntington	1.000	16	67	7	0	0	6
Marrero, Johnson City	.994	15	154	18	1	1	10
Montero, Huntington	.964	32	185	28	8	2	10
Moyle, Burlington	1.000	1	3	0	0	0	0
Paragin, Danville	.972	16	99	4	3	0	2
Ramey, Princeton	.889	2	8	0	1	0	1
Reed, Bluefield	.900	3	8	1	1	0	0
RODRIGUEZ, Bristol	.9841	40	259	52	5	3	7
Serrato, Huntington	1.000	11	33	1	0	0	6
Shipman, Martinsville	.965	37	182	37	8	4	6
Silvia, Princeton	.967	3	28	1	1	0	3
Smith, Danville	.980	47	315	28	7	3	10
Stricklin, Elizabethton	.9840	38	276	32	5	1	5
Strus, Johnson City	1.000	3	6	0	0	0	0
Tupper, Bristol	.990	27	168	32	2	3	10
Valentin, Elizabethton	.977	9	81	3	2	1	2
Wallace, Johnson City	.978	40	277	39	7	1	14
Winterlee, Kingsport	.957	12	40	4	2	0	7

Player, Team	Pct.	G	PO	A	E	DP
Havens, Danville	1.000	13	4	6	0	1
Hennessy, Huntington*	.500	11	0	2	2	0
Hostetler, Danville	1.000	20	2	7	0	0
Howard, Bluefield	.750	9	5	4	3	0
Hritz, Burlington*	.800	9	0	8	2	0
Humphry, Martinsville	1.000	18	2	4	0	0
Hunt, Bristol	1.000	12	3	1	0	0
Hunter, Martinsville	1.000	13	1	6	0	1
Jacobs, Danville*	1.000	10	2	4	0	0
Keenan, Princeton	1.000	14	1	3	0	0
Kenny, Kingsport	.900	13	4	5	1	0
Khoury, Huntington	1.000	12	3	2	0	0
Kitchen, Bluefield	.909	16	3	7	1	2
Kline, Burlington*	1.000	2	0	2	0	0
Knott, Bluefield	1.000	4	0	1	0	0
Krablin, Kingsport	1.000	4	3	0	0	0
Kurtz, Huntington*	.947	11	8	10	1	1
Lavenia, Huntington*	1.000	21	3	1	0	0
Lehoisky, Elizabethton	.700	23	3	4	3	1
Leyva, Burlington*	.889	11	7	1	1	0
Lopez, Huntington*	.800	9	2	14	4	0
LUNDBERG, Martinsville	1.000	13	2	17	0	2
Lynch, Huntington	.857	14	1	5	1	0
Mackey, Burlington*	1.000	22	3	12	0	2
Maduro, Bluefield	.913	14	12	9	2	2
Marchesi, Johnson City	.727	20	4	4	3	3
Marquardt, Johnson City	1.000	4	0	2	0	0
Martinez, Burlington	1.000	11	3	12	0	0
Mast, Kingsport	1.000	13	5	5	0	0
McClurg, Martinsville	1.000	11	2	6	0	0
McDill, Kingsport*	1.000	9	4	5	0	0
Meier, Princeton	1.000	14	1	1	0	0
Mejias, Martinsville	1.000	8	1	3	0	1
Meredith, Bristol	1.000	19	3	2	0	0
Miller, Elizabethton	.952	13	6	14	1	0
Moreno, Kingsport	.667	20	1	1	1	0
Mullins, Princeton	.875	14	8	13	3	1
Murphy, Princeton	.867	16	8	5	2	0
Nakagawa, Bristol*	.857	24	1	5	1	0
Norman, Bristol	.900	13	3	15	2	0
Nowak, Bristol	1.000	16	1	3	0	0
O'Brien, Elizabethton*	1.000	14	5	3	0	0
O'Connor, Martinsville	.800	8	3	5	2	1
Oiler, Elizabethton*	.889	19	5	3	1	1
Olson, Martinsville	.909	11	1	9	1	1
Ortiz, Huntington*	1.000	17	4	5	0	0
Paige, Danville	.857	13	5	13	3	2
Palmer, Burlington*	.000	10	0	0	1	0
Percibal, Bluefield	.917	13	1	10	1	0
Perkins, Elizabethton	.818	10	5	4	2	0
Phipps, Martinsville	.857	14	4	2	1	0
Porter, Bluefield	1.000	9	1	2	0	0
Ramos, Burlington	.800	29	2	6	2	2
Rife, Martinsville	1.000	13	1	3	0	0
Rinderknecht, Bluefield*	.800	11	1	3	1	0
Robbins, Princeton	1.000	17	1	4	0	1
Roberts, Bristol	.900	10	3	6	1	0
Roque, Kingsport*	.867	14	3	10	2	0
Rutledge, Princeton	.778	12	4	10	4	0
Sailors, Johnson City*	.579	14	1	10	8	0
Sampson, Elizabethton	1.000	11	3	8	0	0
Sanders, Martinsville	.909	12	5	5	1	1
Saneaux, Bluefield	.667	6	1	1	1	0
Schooler, Elizabethton	.857	17	2	4	1	0
Schutz, Danville*	1.000	12	0	1	0	0
Scott, Johnson City*	1.000	21	2	3	0	1
Severino, Bristol	1.000	4	0	2	0	0
Shafer, Danville	.923	23	3	9	1	0
Skrmetta, Bristol	1.000	8	1	2	0	0
Smith, Bristol	.857	9	3	3	1	0
Stanton, Johnson City	1.000	24	3	5	0	0
Stewart, Johnson City	.667	29	2	2	2	1
Strehlow, Johnson City	1.000	2	0	1	0	0
Sullivan, Johnson City	1.000	27	1	11	0	0
Surratt, Johnson City	.800	29	0	4	1	0
Sutton, Kingsport*	1.000	11	1	6	0	0
Szarko, Martinsville	.875	25	0	7	1	2
Tatis, Kingsport*	1.000	13	4	9	0	0
Timko, Bristol	.600	13	1	2	2	0
Trimarco, Bluefield	.818	19	2	7	2	1
Wagner, Johnson City	1.000	16	0	1	0	0
Weber, Huntington	.929	14	5	8	1	0
Weber, Bristol	1.000	16	1	6	0	1
G. Williams, Burlington*	.923	11	2	10	1	1
Wilson, Bristol	.800	7	2	2	1	0
Witasick, Johnson City	1.000	12	3	6	0	0
Wolff, Kingsport	.600	3	1	2	2	0
Yan, Danville	.875	14	8	6	2	0
Ziegler, Bluefield	.500	14	0	1	1	0
Zubiri, Burlington	1.000	5	0	4	0	0

PITCHERS

Player, Team	Pct.	G	PO	A	E	DP
Baker, Kingsport	.889	14	7	9	2	2
Barstad, Martinsville	.600	9	0	3	2	0
Battles, Johnson City	.900	13	5	13	2	0
Betti, Danville*	.900	11	2	7	1	0
Bledsoe, Johnson City	1.000	5	0	1	0	0
Bobbitt, Huntington*	.923	10	2	22	2	2
Bowers, Elizabethton	1.000	7	1	3	0	0
Brabant, Burlington	1.000	12	4	7	0	0
Bradshaw, Danville*	1.000	22	1	6	0	0
Brazoban, Bristol	.833	15	1	4	1	0
Brewer, Bluefield*	1.000	6	5	5	0	0
Brown, Bristol	.692	15	1	8	4	0
Brown, Bluefield	1.000	9	3	3	0	0
Brown, Danville*	1.000	11	0	3	0	0
Bryant, Huntington*	.933	12	4	10	1	0
Byrd, Danville	1.000	25	3	9	0	1
Campbell, Burlington	1.000	23	3	7	0	0
Carr, Kingsport*	.833	19	1	4	1	0
Carrasco, Elizabethton*	.824	14	3	11	3	0
Carroll, Johnson City*	1.000	6	2	6	0	0
Chandler, Princeton	.933	14	4	10	1	0
Charles, Johnson City	1.000	9	3	2	0	0
Chavez, Bluefield	.824	14	4	10	3	0
Childress, Huntington*	1.000	16	1	3	0	0
Christmas, Danville	.889	14	2	6	1	0
Cobb, Elizabethton*	.853	13	9	20	5	2
Collier, Kingsport	.800	16	3	9	3	0
Concepcion, Princeton	1.000	2	1	1	0	0
Corrigan, Johnson City	.889	11	2	6	1	1
Cotner, Kingsport*	.500	6	0	1	1	0
Cromer, Danville	1.000	3	1	1	0	0
Dabalack, Martinsville	1.000	19	1	2	0	0
Danley, Danville*	.600	13	0	3	2	0
Dawley, Bluefield	.889	20	4	4	1	0
DeJesus, Elizabethton*	1.000	12	4	12	0	1
Delarosa, Burlington	.789	14	5	10	4	0
Dinnen, Burlington	1.000	30	3	10	0	0
Done, Burlington	1.000	1	1	0	0	0
Dowhower, Elizabethton	.800	20	0	4	1	0
Etheridge, Princeton*	1.000	9	1	12	0	0
Fernandez, Princeton*	1.000	15	1	1	0	0
Foster, Martinsville*	.909	13	1	9	1	1
Franklin, Princeton	1.000	16	2	3	0	0
Fregoso, Bluefield	.750	6	2	1	1	1
Fuccillo, Princeton*	.500	13	0	2	2	0
Fuduric, Bristol	.714	13	2	3	2	0
Furusato, Bristol	.500	11	0	1	1	0
Garcia, Huntington	1.000	3	1	2	0	0
Genke, Princeton	.667	2	0	2	1	0
Gontkosky, Kingsport*	.963	14	8	18	1	2
Gonzalez, Huntington	.850	12	3	14	3	1
Granger, Bristol	.882	13	3	12	2	0
Griffin, Bluefield	.875	15	6	8	2	0
Hagan, Princeton*	.957	17	8	14	1	2
Hamilton, Martinsville	1.000	7	1	1	0	0

The following players did not have any fielding statistics at the positions indicated or appeared only as a designated hitter, pinch-hitter or pinch-runner: Allen, dh, ph; Almanza, p; Barrett, p; Bock, p; Campbell, of; Cordero, ss; Crafton, dh; M. Johnson, ss; Maxwell, 1b, 3b; McGlawn, of; Minton, of; Morales, p; Morris, 3b; Runion, p; Sigler, 3b; Stoppello, p; Tatrow, p; Valdez, of; Wallace, 1b; E. White, of; Wisler, p; Wooten, of.

Year	Team	Pct.
1921—	Greenville	.608
	Johnson City*	.627
1922—	Bristol	.557
1923—	Knoxville	.635
1924—	Knoxville*	.642
	Bristol	.607
1925—	Greenville	.667
1926-36—	Did not operate.	
1937—	Elizabethton	.559
	Pennington Gap*	.580
1938—	Elizabethton	.664
	Greenville (3rd)†	.571
1939—	Elizabethton‡	.597
1940—	Johnson City§	.726
	Elizabethton	.750
1941—	Johnson City	.614
	Elizabethton*	.661
1942—	Bristol	.667
	Bristol x	.660
1943—	Bristol	.755
	Bristol y	.617
1944—	Kingsport‡	.575
1945—	Kingsport‡	.670
1946—	New River‡	.675
1947—	Pulaski	.648
	New River (3rd)†	.516
1948—	Pulaski‡	.680
1949—	Bluefield‡	.721
1950—	Bluefield	.600
	Bluefield z	.745

Year	Team	Pct.
1951—	Kingsport‡	.659
1952—	Johnson City	.595
	Welch (3rd)†	.509
1953—	Welch*	.705
	Johnson City	.672
1954—	Bluefield‡	.619
1955—	Salem**	.689
1956—	Did not operate.	
1957—	Bluefield	.701
1958—	Johnson City	.662
1959—	Morristown	.603
1960—	Wytheville	.614
1961—	Middlesboro	.591
1962—	Bluefield	.671
1963—	Bluefield	.652
1964—	Johnson City	.662
1965—	Salem	.614
1966—	Marion	.623
1967—	Bluefield	.627
1968—	Marion	.583
1969—	Pulaski a	.576
	Johnson City	.544
1970—	Bluefield	.638
1971—	Bluefield a	.609
	Kingsport	.559
1972—	Bristol a	.588
	Covington	.586
1973—	Kingsport	.757
1974—	Bristol a	.754
	Bluefield	.536

Year	Team	Pct.
1975—	Marion	.515
	Johnson City a	.603
1976—	Johnson City a	.714
	Bluefield	.600
1977—	Kingsport	.623
1978—	Elizabethton	.594
1979—	Paintsville	.800
1980—	Paintsville	.657
1981—	Paintsville	.657
1982—	Bluefield a	.681
	Johnson City	.478
1983—	Paintsville	.653
1984—	Elizabethton b	.580
	Pulaski	.536
1985—	Bristol c	.638
1986—	Johnson City	.667
	Pulaski b	.621
1987—	Burlington b	.729
	Johnson City	.609
1988—	Kingsport b	.644
	Burlington	.529
1989—	Elizabethton b	.691
	Pulaski	.618
1990—	Elizabethton	.761
1991—	Pulaski b	.662
	Burlington	.597
1992—	Elizabethton b	.742
	Bluefield b	.597
1993—	Burlington b	.647
	Elizabethton	.552

*Won split-season playoff. †Won four-team playoff. ‡Won championship and four-team playoff. §Johnson City, first-half winner, won playoff involving six clubs. xWon both halves and defeated second-place Elizabethton in playoff. yWon both halves, but Erwin won four-team playoff. zWon both halves, but Bristol won two-club playoff. **Salem and Johnson City declared playoff co-champions when weather forced cancellation of final series. aLeague was divided into Northern, Southern divisions; declared league champion, based on highest won-lost percentage. bLeague was divided into Northern and Southern divisions; won playoff. cBristol declared league champion based on regular-season record.

ARIZONA LEAGUE

FINAL STANDINGS

Team	Ath.	Car.	Gia.	Ang.	Brw.	Pad.	Rck.	Mar.	W	L	T	Pct.	GB
Athletics	....	4	5	4	5	5	6	6	35	20	0	.636	......
Cardinals	4	....	4	5	5	4	3	6	31	22	0	.585	3
Giants	3	4	....	5	5	4	5	5	31	24	0	.564	4
Angels	4	3	3	....	4	4	6	5	29	26	1	.527	6
Brewers	3	3	3	4	....	6	4	6	29	27	0	.518	6½
Padres	2	4	4	4	2	....	3	5	24	31	0	.436	11
Rockies	2	2	3	2	4	5	....	3	21	32	1	.396	13
Mariners	2	2	2	2	2	3	5	....	18	36	0	.333	16½

Games played in Mesa, Peoria, Scottsdale and Tempe.

Club names are major league affiliations.

Playoffs—No playoffs scheduled.

Regular-season attendance—No total official attendance figures reported.

Managers—Angels, Bill Lachemann; Athletics, Bruce Hines; Brewers, Ralph Dickenson; Cardinals, Roy Silver; Giants, Alan Bannister; Mariners, Marty Martinez; Padres, Ken Berry; Rockies, P.J. Carey.

All-Star team: 1B—Harold Herdocia, Angels; 2B—Franklin Garcia, Brewers; 3B—Dave Madsen, Cardinals; SS—Juan Henderson, Angels; OF—Tony Dermendziev, Rockies; Jason Herrick, Angels; Alex Rivera, Padres; Jose Soriano, Athletics; C—Joel Galarza, Giants; DH—John Jones, Athletics; LHP—Jason Myers, Giants; RHP—Gustavo Gil, Athletics; LH Reliever—Bret Morfin, Giants; RH Reliever—Jose Carrasco, Angels; Most Valuable Player—Jason Myers, Giants; Manager of the Year—Roy Silver, Cardinals.

BATTING

TEAM

Team	Avg.	G	AB	R	OR	H	TB	2B	3B	HR	RBI	SH	SF	HP	BB	Int. BB	SO	SB	CS	LOB
Athletics	.266	55	1862	353	289	495	713	83	27	27	277	6	17	20	237	7	417	76	31	372
Brewers	.266	56	1912	326	322	508	648	58	26	10	252	11	31	46	204	6	438	148	37	407
Giants	.264	55	1907	321	288	503	693	86	31	14	265	10	19	31	230	6	439	85	33	433
Mariners	.246	54	1801	277	338	443	598	65	27	12	215	13	20	25	217	1	433	79	23	399
Cardinals	.246	53	1740	271	234	428	560	58	28	6	216	17	19	25	216	4	376	77	35	370
Angels	.246	56	1779	261	239	437	583	69	25	9	200	30	22	40	248	8	334	38	30	415
Padres	.230	55	1812	243	292	417	549	69	18	9	179	13	16	18	206	3	508	94	42	380
Rockies	.221	54	1729	241	291	382	527	70	18	13	187	8	17	27	212	4	443	111	31	359

INDIVIDUAL

(Leading qualifiers for batting championship—151 or more plate appearances)

*Bats lefthanded.   †Switch-hitter.

Player, Team	Avg.	G	AB	R	H	TB	2B	3B	HR	RBI	SH	SF	HP	BB	Int. BB	SO	SB	CS
Jones, John, Athletics	.341	50	170	38	58	88	9	3	5	39	0	2	3	28	2	33	1	3
Galarza, Joel, Giants	.326	42	132	26	43	70	12	3	3	26	0	1	1	17	0	26	4	4
Henderson, Juan, Angels†	.323	54	192	37	62	82	11	3	1	16	2	0	7	29	1	29	10	6
Cook, Jason, Mariners	.319	45	160	31	51	75	10	4	2	24	2	3	3	16	0	20	9	1
Garcia, Franklin, Brewers	.314	56	236	43	74	88	5	3	1	32	0	3	1	25	0	31	36	10
DeLeon, Santo, Mariners	.309	43	152	31	47	63	5	4	1	15	2	0	2	16	0	32	19	2
Sanchez, Cecilio, Brewers*	.302	44	149	22	45	55	6	2	0	23	1	1	0	7	0	29	6	2
Espinal, Juan, Padres	.301	37	136	23	41	60	11	1	2	19	0	1	1	15	1	40	3	3
Herrick, Jason, Angels*	.301	56	196	34	59	85	9	4	3	36	1	2	2	41	2	51	5	4
Garcia, Vincente, Rockies	.299	38	137	13	41	51	10	0	0	13	0	1	0	27	12	2		

Departmental leaders: G—Franklin Garcia, Herrick, 56; AB—Franklin Garcia, 236; R—Vargas, 46; H—Franklin Garcia, 74; TB—Franklin Garcia, Jones, 88; 2B—Hamburg, H. Ramirez, 14; 3B—Canizaro, Vargas, 6; HR—Hamburg, Jones, F. Soriano, 5; RBI—Canizaro, 41; SH—O. Rodriguez, 7; SF—Four players tied with 5; HP—Cantrell, 15; BB—Herrick, 41; IBB—Herdocia, Klassen, H. Ramirez, 3; SO—F. Cruz, 58; SB—Franklin Garcia, 36; CS—Franklin Garcia, 10.

(All players—listed alphabetically)

Player, Team	Avg.	G	AB	R	H	TB	2B	3B	HR	RBI	SH	SF	HP	BB	Int. BB	SO	SB	CS
Acosta, Eduardo, Brewers†	.320	8	25	6	8	9	1	0	0	4	0	0	0	6	0	7	3	0
Alguacil, Jose, Giants*	.241	42	145	28	35	46	6	1	1	13	3	1	1	6	0	23	8	1
Aquino, Pedro, Mariners	.292	34	120	18	35	47	9	0	1	23	0	3	1	9	0	8	1	0
Augustine, Andy, Mariners†	.125	3	8	0	1	2	1	0	0	1	0	0	0	1	0	5	0	0
Batista, Dario, Mariners†	.265	30	102	22	27	31	4	0	0	7	3	0	0	14	0	18	8	1
Batista, Tony, Athletics	.327	24	104	21	34	50	6	2	2	17	0	2	0	6	1	14	6	2
Benner, Brian, Giants	.245	32	110	11	27	40	3	2	2	14	0	1	3	18	0	36	2	1
Bogatyrev, Ilya, Angels	.274	25	62	12	17	18	1	0	0	6	0	0	0	11	0	16	1	2
Bowden, Joe, Padres	.143	20	56	10	8	12	2	1	0	2	0	1	0	7	0	21	6	2
Bowen, Glenn, Cardinals	.190	32	79	12	15	18	1	1	0	11	3	1	1	14	0	27	2	0
Brady, Michael, Mariners	.169	26	83	15	14	18	1	0	1	5	0	1	1	11	0	29	1	2
Brannon, Paul, Mariners	.368	5	19	2	7	11	2	1	0	2	0	0	0	1	0	6	0	0
Canizaro, Jason, Giants	.261	49	180	34	47	78	10	6	3	41	0	0	3	22	1	40	12	3
Cantrell, Derrick, Brewers	.247	49	154	31	38	44	4	1	0	21	1	5	15	16	0	35	30	5
Cardona, Alex, Cardinals	.339	19	56	9	19	25	2	0	0	10	0	0	2	4	0	7	0	0
Carr, Jeffrey, Athletics	.139	26	36	4	5	7	2	0	0	4	0	0	0	7	0	4	1	0
Cartaya, Luis, Padres	.222	22	81	5	18	20	2	0	0	5	0	0	2	5	0	12	4	0
Cedeno, Jose, Rockies	.205	46	156	21	32	52	7	2	3	14	1	0	4	17	0	49	8	3
Chambers, Shawn, Athletics†	.000	13	1	0	0	0	0	0	0	0	0	0	0	0	0	1	0	0
Christopherson, Eric, Giants	.409	8	22	7	9	12	1	1	0	4	0	0	0	9	0	1	0	0

Player, Team	Avg.	G	AB	R	H	TB	2B	3B	HR	RBI	SH	SF	HP	BB	Int. BB	SO	SB	CS
Colon, Marlon, Cardinals	.111	19	45	5	5	6	1	0	0	4	0	1	1	4	0	7	0	0
Cook, Jason, Mariners	.319	45	160	31	51	75	10	4	2	24	2	3	3	16	0	20	9	1
Cordero, Pablo, Giants	.290	29	107	10	31	39	2	3	0	14	1	0	1	2	0	18	4	0
Corps, Erick, Padres†	.281	43	153	28	43	59	8	4	0	18	1	0	1	33	0	23	4	6
Cruz, Devei, Giants	.341	29	82	8	28	31	3	0	0	15	3	1	0	4	0	5	3	0
Cruz, Francisco, Padres	.161	37	112	16	18	26	2	3	0	7	2	1	1	12	1	58	6	1
Cuevas, Eduardo, Padres	.295	35	139	17	41	49	6	1	0	13	1	0	1	4	0	12	9	3
Cullen, Geoff, Angels*	.118	15	34	2	4	6	2	0	0	3	0	1	1	4	0	1	0	0
Current, Jeremy, Cardinals	.178	25	73	6	13	14	1	0	0	3	1	1	2	5	0	24	4	1
Darwin, Brian, Athletics	.235	29	68	12	16	18	2	0	0	7	0	0	2	10	0	25	7	2
Davis, Melvin, Giants	.259	23	85	12	22	29	1	3	0	8	0	0	1	5	0	14	6	0
Davis, Stacey, Mariners*	.172	36	122	18	21	32	2	3	1	12	1	1	1	13	0	47	2	1
Delacruz, Marcelino, Rockies	.203	23	74	10	15	19	4	0	0	5	1	0	0	10	0	16	6	3
DeLeon, Jose, Mariners	.238	25	84	8	20	21	1	0	0	9	0	1	2	5	0	22	5	1
DeLeon, Santo, Mariners	.309	43	152	31	47	63	5	4	1	15	2	0	2	16	0	32	19	2
Denbow, Don, Giants	.200	39	130	27	26	41	7	1	2	17	0	2	4	24	1	57	4	0
Denny, Shawn, Mariners	.167	2	6	1	1	1	0	0	0	2	1	0	0	2	0	1	0	0
Dermendziev, Tony, Rockies*	.318	30	110	24	35	46	2	3	1	18	0	1	2	14	0	23	17	0
Derotal, Francisco, Padres	.239	45	163	21	39	63	8	2	4	24	0	2	1	10	0	47	6	1
Diaz, Javier, Rockies	.215	39	135	17	29	47	8	2	2	16	0	2	0	16	1	29	6	1
Domenico, Brian, Athletics	.000	16	1	0	0	0	0	0	0	0	0	0	0	0	0	1	0	0
Domingo, Tyrone, Mariners	.200	13	35	4	7	8	1	0	0	2	0	0	0	5	0	6	1	2
Dumas, Chris, Mariners	.245	32	106	15	26	38	3	3	1	11	1	1	2	9	0	29	4	2
Edwards, Randy, Rockies	.132	24	68	10	9	15	2	2	0	8	0	1	3	11	0	22	7	0
Espinal, Juan, Padres	.301	37	136	23	41	60	11	1	2	19	0	1	1	15	1	40	3	3
Feliz-Nova, Jose, Brewers	.267	44	120	20	32	46	4	5	0	15	0	5	0	12	1	36	2	1
Fernandez, Randy, Cardinals*	.256	31	90	17	23	32	2	2	1	10	1	0	0	8	0	22	9	0
Figueroa, Danny, Rockies	.273	28	88	22	24	30	4	1	0	6	0	1	1	11	0	19	8	1
Figueroa, Walter, Brewers*	.240	35	104	17	25	37	6	3	0	10	0	1	1	2	0	28	3	0
French, Anton, Cardinals†	.274	34	106	19	29	39	3	2	1	17	1	1	0	10	0	22	15	5
Fryman, Jarod, Brewers	.103	31	58	8	6	9	0	0	1	2	3	1	4	15	0	23	0	0
Fuertes, Pedro, Brewers	.203	33	69	9	14	15	1	0	0	4	0	0	3	8	0	18	2	1
Galarza, Joel, Padres	.326	42	132	26	43	70	12	3	3	26	0	1	1	17	0	26	4	4
Gambill, Chad, Rockies	.214	46	159	23	34	54	8	0	4	24	0	1	4	21	1	39	1	2
Garcia, Francisco, Brewers	.171	19	35	2	6	7	1	0	0	1	0	0	0	1	0	9	1	0
Garcia, Franklin, Brewers	.314	56	236	43	74	88	5	3	1	32	0	3	1	25	0	31	36	10
Garcia, Vincente, Rockies	.299	38	137	13	41	51	10	0	0	13	0	0	1	18	0	27	12	2
German, Juan, Athletics	.227	36	97	13	22	30	3	1	1	13	0	0	2	12	0	25	2	1
Gibson, Derrick, Rockies	.151	34	119	13	18	24	2	2	0	10	0	1	3	5	0	55	3	0
Gillis, Troy, Padres	.283	26	92	14	26	28	2	0	0	7	0	2	2	12	0	29	8	1
Goebel, Matt, Angels	.273	9	11	1	3	4	1	0	0	0	0	0	0	1	0	4	1	0
Gonzalez, Jesus, Giants	.053	7	19	2	1	1	0	0	0	0	0	0	1	1	0	5	1	0
Green, Bert, Cardinals	.221	33	95	16	21	26	3	1	0	11	1	0	3	7	0	17	3	2
Griffin, Chad, Athletics*	.155	26	58	7	9	16	2	1	1	3	1	0	2	5	0	18	2	0
Ham, Kevin, Angels	.220	49	150	18	33	47	8	0	2	14	0	1	5	17	1	36	1	2
Hamburg, Leon, Athletics	.279	48	165	38	46	77	14	1	5	27	0	3	3	35	1	42	9	3
Harpe, Daniel, Padres.	.000	6	1	0	0	0	0	0	0	0	0	0	0	0	0	0	0	0
Harper, Otis, Cardinals†	.220	29	91	14	20	29	1	4	0	11	0	0	1	10	0	29	4	2
Hartwell, Eddie, Angels*	.382	19	68	17	26	34	4	2	0	4	0	0	5	16	0	10	2	5
Hatfield, Rick, Rockies*	.167	36	108	9	18	24	6	0	0	12	1	1	3	5	0	12	1	1
Hause, Brendan, Athletics*	.667	1	3	0	2	2	0	0	0	0	2	0	0	1	0	1	0	0
Heffernan, Bert, Giants*	.320	7	25	3	8	8	0	0	0	4	0	0	0	6	1	2	2	1
Henderson, Juan, Angels†	.323	54	192	37	62	82	11	3	1	16	2	0	7	29	1	29	10	6
Herdocia, Harold, Brewers	.280	52	186	18	52	63	5	0	2	27	1	3	0	25	3	38	0	1
Herrick, Jason, Angels*	.301	56	196	34	59	85	9	4	3	36	1	2	2	41	2	51	5	4
Hodge, Jim, Brewers	.233	46	133	18	31	48	6	1	3	20	0	2	2	11	2	37	1	0
Hoover, Will, Rockies	.100	18	40	6	4	5	1	0	0	3	0	1	0	9	1	23	1	0
Houser, Kyle, Rockies	.176	37	119	14	21	23	2	0	1	11	2	2	1	14	0	16	1	1
Iverson, Eric, Cardinals*	.176	10	17	0	3	4	1	0	0	0	0	0	0	1	0	4	0	0
Jimenez, Ruben, Cardinals†	.237	43	135	21	32	38	2	2	0	7	0	0	3	25	1	30	9	8
Johnson, Juan, Giants†	.241	43	158	36	38	48	8	1	0	18	0	3	3	26	0	34	22	6
Jones, John, Athletics	.341	50	170	38	58	88	9	3	5	39	0	2	3	28	2	33	1	3
Klassen, Danny, Brewers	.222	38	117	26	26	37	5	0	2	20	1	4	8	24	3	28	14	3
Lee, Derrek, Padres	.327	15	52	11	17	26	1	1	2	5	0	0	0	6	1	7	4	0
Leger, Gus, Angels	.125	14	32	4	4	9	1	2	0	2	1	1	1	5	0	12	1	0
Leibee, Skye, Athletics*	.000	14	0	0	0	0	0	0	0	0	0	0	0	1	0	0	0	0
Lopez, Carlos, Mariners†	.245	36	110	13	27	31	2	1	0	10	0	0	2	12	0	43	1	3
Lopez, Richard, Cardinals	.429	4	14	1	6	6	0	0	0	0	0	0	0	0	0	2	0	0
Luckett, Zaven, Padres	.227	33	97	15	22	27	3	1	0	11	0	1	1	18	0	41	7	5
Lugo, Jesus, Cardinals	.292	38	137	18	40	49	7	1	0	23	0	3	3	22	0	10	2	1
Machado, Mike, Rockies	.130	13	46	4	6	7	1	0	0	1	0	0	1	4	0	15	3	2
Madsen, Dave, Cardinals	.287	53	181	32	52	84	12	4	4	38	0	5	0	37	1	38	4	2
Malekovic, Brett, Padres	.153	19	59	3	9	11	0	1	0	2	0	0	0	8	0	21	2	0
Martinez, Gabby, Padres	.224	29	76	11	17	22	5	0	0	10	0	1	0	2	0	30	3	2
Martinez, Greg, Brewers†	.632	5	19	6	12	12	0	0	0	3	0	0	1	4	0	5	7	1
Martinez, Pablo, Giants	.286	13	35	4	10	10	0	0	0	4	0	0	0	5	0	5	2	1
Martinez, Victor, Mariners	.212	16	52	8	11	16	0	1	1	6	0	0	2	1	0	8	3	1
Marval, Raul, Giants	.234	19	47	8	11	13	2	0	0	3	0	1	0	3	0	4	3	1
Mathis, Joe, Mariners*	.250	36	84	14	21	27	4	1	0	9	0	1	0	5	0	26	7	1
Maxwell, Trent, Mariners	.159	19	44	6	7	7	0	0	0	5	1	1	0	4	0	16	1	0
Mazara, Hommy, Angels*	.217	54	207	29	45	62	7	5	0	21	3	2	4	18	0	38	3	5
McLeod, Michael, Athletics*	.257	51	175	34	45	59	7	2	1	26	0	1	2	24	0	24	10	3
McMillan, Thomas, Cardinals	.267	25	60	16	16	21	5	0	0	5	1	3	1	17	0	15	4	3
Mealing, Al, Brewers*	.256	48	133	23	31	34	1	1	0	12	2	0	2	12	0	31	12	5
Medina, Alger, Rockies	.291	29	79	19	23	32	3	3	0	5	0	1	3	26	1	21	26	6
Melendez, Enrique, Rockies†	.188	15	32	3	6	7	1	0	0	3	1	0	0	7	0	14	1	2
Meyer, Alan, Padres	.000	8	1	0	0	0	0	0	0	0	0	0	0	1	0	0	0	0
Millan, Jorge, Cardinals	.247	29	93	15	23	30	5	1	0	10	2	0	0	16	0	16	3	2
Milsitz, John, Brewers	.212	21	33	3	7	9	2	0	0	7	0	1	0	9	0	13	1	0
Mojica, Francis, Athletics	.000	24	1	0	0	0	0	0	0	0	0	0	0	0	0	1	0	0
Molina, Ben, Angels	.263	27	80	9	21	31	6	2	0	10	0	1	1	10	0	4	0	2
Molina, Luis, Mariners	.214	39	112	19	24	29	3	1	0	6	1	3	2	30	0	13	7	4
Monday, Mike, Angels	.175	24	63	13	11	13	2	0	0	7	2	3	2	10	0	18	1	1
Montgomery, Trent, Athletics	1.000	15	1	0	1	1	0	0	0	0	0	0	0	0	0	0	0	0

Player, Team	Avg.	G	AB	R	H	TB	2B	3B	HR	RBI	SH	SF	HP	BB	Int. BB	SO	SB	CS
Moschetti, Mike, Athletics	.263	30	99	26	26	38	4	1	2	19	0	0	1	11	0	16	4	2
Newman, Damon, Athletics	.000	10	1	0	0	0	0	0	0	0	0	0	0	0	0	1	0	0
Norton, Chris, Cardinals	.229	27	83	10	19	30	5	3	0	11	0	1	1	11	1	23	0	0
Nunez, Francisco, Brewers	.252	52	163	21	41	53	2	5	0	24	1	4	2	23	0	32	2	1
Nunez, Isaias, Cardinals*	.234	51	184	27	43	50	3	2	0	22	0	3	2	18	0	33	2	1
Ortega, Randy, Athletics	.250	36	88	14	22	30	5	0	1	12	0	2	2	20	1	13	2	2
Peguero, Juan, Giants	.289	30	90	11	26	33	3	2	0	13	0	0	3	1	0	31	0	4
Perez, Sergio, Giants†	.100	12	20	3	2	4	0	1	0	2	0	0	1	5	0	7	0	0
Perozo, Jose, Angels	.235	55	221	31	52	66	6	4	0	14	4	2	4	20	1	24	5	3
Pomierski, Joe, Mariners*	.225	48	173	19	39	61	8	4	2	29	1	3	2	19	0	39	4	1
Pooschke, Mark, Giants	.212	38	113	23	24	37	5	4	0	15	0	2	3	20	0	44	6	3
Pozo, Yohel, Rockies	.284	21	74	5	21	28	4	0	1	17	0	3	0	4	0	13	1	1
Pridgen, Matt, Rockies†	.263	19	38	8	10	13	1	1	0	1	0	1	0	4	0	15	2	1
Quintana, Eddy, Athletics	.224	47	170	18	38	47	7	1	0	19	0	1	2	16	0	44	3	0
Ramirez, Hiram, Giants	.294	54	201	31	59	84	14	1	3	34	2	1	1	26	3	40	3	2
Randolph, Edward, Mariners†	.269	19	52	6	14	21	4	0	1	12	0	1	3	6	0	13	2	1
Reynolds, Paul, Giants†	.200	7	20	1	4	6	2	0	0	4	0	0	0	5	0	2	0	0
Rivera, Alex, Padres	.297	46	165	22	49	59	8	1	0	14	4	1	2	13	0	28	10	5
Robles, Rafael, Cardinals†	.270	42	126	19	34	42	4	2	0	18	3	0	5	21	1	34	5	6
Rodriguez, Miguel, Brewers	.308	27	65	8	20	23	1	1	0	9	0	0	1	2	0	12	1	1
Rodriguez, Nelson, Padres	.188	30	101	10	19	23	4	0	0	6	3	2	1	9	0	20	4	2
Rodriguez, Orlando, Angels*	.202	41	124	18	25	34	5	2	0	18	7	2	5	22	0	22	0	0
Roques, Aaron, Padres	.165	32	103	10	17	22	3	1	0	14	0	1	2	12	0	40	7	4
Salvador, Felix, Athletics	.387	9	31	5	12	12	0	0	0	4	1	1	0	4	0	4	1	1
Sanchez, Cecilio, Brewers*	.302	44	149	22	45	55	6	2	0	23	1	1	0	7	0	29	6	2
Sanchez, Marcos, Padres†	.195	36	118	17	23	25	2	0	0	15	1	3	2	16	0	30	5	6
Sanders, Mike, Padres	.188	4	16	1	3	3	0	0	0	0	0	0	0	0	0	6	1	0
Simmons, Enoch, Athletics	.538	4	13	4	7	11	1	0	1	3	0	0	0	3	0	2	1	0
Singleton, Scott, Padres	.000	15	0	0	0	0	0	0	0	0	0	0	0	0	0	0	0	0
Soriano, Fred, Athletics	.260	41	131	34	34	62	5	4	5	19	2	1	1	21	0	41	7	2
Soriano, Jose, Athletics	.265	48	181	30	48	74	7	5	3	31	1	2	0	12	1	51	8	3
Soto, Wilson, Brewers	.301	41	123	31	37	50	6	2	1	19	1	1	3	12	0	30	20	5
Stadler, Mike, Padres	.107	21	56	6	6	11	2	0	1	5	1	0	0	11	0	20	3	1
Sterling, Henry, Giants	.094	23	32	3	3	3	0	0	0	2	0	1	2	3	0	11	0	0
Talbott, Ricky, Padres	.029	17	35	3	1	3	0	1	0	2	0	0	0	12	0	22	2	0
Taylor, Sam, Angels	.245	52	159	27	39	52	4	3	1	21	2	5	8	26	0	29	9	4
Tiffany, Ted, Angels*	.161	24	56	7	9	10	1	0	0	3	4	0	0	8	0	11	1	0
Tinoco, Luis, Mariners	.259	39	112	20	29	40	4	2	1	20	1	1	1	31	1	41	4	1
Torres, Derrick, Brewers	.253	38	99	19	25	36	3	1	2	11	1	2	3	7	0	30	1	2
Urena, Santiago, Giants	.222	10	18	3	4	4	0	0	0	1	0	0	5	0	0	5	0	1
Valentino, Rob, Mariners	.211	23	71	8	15	20	1	2	0	7	0	1	0	9	0	12	2	0
Vargas, Julio, Athletics	.287	50	195	46	56	74	6	6	0	25	1	2	0	15	1	37	12	6
Vega, Ramon, Giants	.279	22	68	13	19	22	3	0	0	8	1	1	5	0	0	19	1	1
Velazquez, Edgard, Rockies	.245	39	147	20	36	50	4	2	2	20	2	2	0	16	0	35	7	5
Ventura, Leonardo, Athletics	.192	35	73	9	14	17	3	0	0	7	0	0	0	6	0	19	0	1
Williams, Curtis, Cardinals*	.200	34	75	14	15	17	0	1	0	4	2	1	0	14	0	18	9	2
Zwisler, Josh, Brewers	.337	35	89	13	30	36	4	1	0	15	0	1	0	10	0	10	6	0

The following pitchers, listed alphabetically by club, with games in parentheses, had no plate appearances, primarily through use of designated hitters:

ANGELS—Aguirre, Jose (11); Andujar, Guillermo (5); Bawlson, Jeff (15); Blyleven, Todd (11); Carrasco, Jose (18); Cintron, Jose (12); Egloff, Bruce (4); Knox, Jeff (13); Mayer, Aaron (17); Perisho, Matt (11); Purdy, Shawn (2); Thurmond, Travis (12); Vega, Orlando (6); Warren, Deshawn (9).

ATHLETICS—Gil, Gus (14); Huber, Aaron (12); Kubinski, Tim (1); Luft, Tom (17); Moncion, Manuel (1); Perez, Juan (12); Smith, Andy (8); Walsh, Matt (9); Wasdin, John (1).

BREWERS—Benny, Pete (14); Calderon, Jose (12); Gaskill, Derek (13); Gold, Steve (19); Hillis, Jon (16); Jaen, Juan (13); Krause, Kevin (12); Mercado, Gabriel (17); Paul, Andy (5); Perkins, Scott (7); Prempas, Lyle (10); Preston, George (9); Sheldon, Shane (11); Snure, Jeremy (16); Tijerina, Tano (10).

CARDINALS—Alexis, Julio (14); Almanza, Armando (20); Barrick, Troy (24); Bledsoe, Randy (4); Conway, Keith (28); Cruise, Mark (23); Curran, Tighe (27); Lair, Scott (6); Manon, Julio (15); Martin, Mike (11); Parker, Freddie (8); Ramirez, Rafael (9); Welch, Travis (10).

GIANTS—Abreu, Jose (22); Abreu, Juan (12); Brown, Kevin (1); Carrasco, Joel (12); Grundt, Ken (4); McMullen, Mike (14); Mercedes, Bob (10); Mitchell, Kendrick (14); Morfin, Bret (21); Murray, Jim (15); Myers, Jason (13); Pinder, Chris (22); Vasquez, Jorge (26).

MARINERS—Bieniasz, Derek (6); Coffman, Kevin (4); Cope, Robin (2); Craig, Casey (9); Daniels, John (13); Dessellier, Chris (12); Golden, Chuck (14); Green, Chris (24); Hinchliffe, Brett (10); Mitchell, Kelvin (3); Newton, Geronimo (21); Updike, Jon (21); Vallejo, Julio (2); Vanhof, John (5); Williams, Brian (16).

PADRES—Baron, Jim (13); Burgos, Ali (1); Clark, Byron (5); Duncan, Devohn (13); Estrella, Alejandro (3); Garrett, Harold (14); Johnson, Byron (3); Jones, Jeff (12); Lachappa, Matt (12); Matos, Alberto (12); Paniagua, Feliz (16); Sandt, Tom (1); White, Darell (19); Willis, Marcus (17).

ROCKIES—Barnes, Keith (11); Barry, Dan (12); Burdick, Morgan (16); Dewett, Martin (3); Fernandez, Fernando (16); Garrett, Neil (11); Hutchins, Jason (1); Matos, Jose (18); McAdams, Dennis (22); Mineer, Dave (10); Mora, Jaihe (14); Tafoya, Greg (9); Thomson, John (11); Viano, Jacob (22); Walls, Doug (10); Wright, Jamey (11).

GRAND SLAMS—Herrick, Klassen, 1 each.

AWARDED FIRST BASE ON CATCHER'S INTERFERENCE—Galarza 4 (Bowen, Stadler, Talbott, Zwisler); Dumas (O. Rodriguez); Fernandez (Monday); Hatfield (O. Rodriguez); Jones (Galarza); Leger (Hatfield); Moschetti (O. Rodriguez).

PITCHING

TEAM

Team	ERA	G	CG	ShO	Sv.	IP	H	R	ER	HR	HB	BB	Int. BB	SO	WP	Bk.
Angels	3.34	56	10	6	8	483.0	405	239	179	10	21	188	2	455	45	9
Cardinals	3.47	53	0	5	14	463.2	456	234	179	12	15	159	3	463	51	11
Padres	3.72	55	2	1	9	476.1	421	292	197	10	44	251	7	439	56	14
Rockies	3.92	54	2	1	8	457.0	468	291	199	10	29	176	2	350	76	11
Athletics	3.97	55	0	1	15	478.0	479	289	211	24	34	186	6	391	57	17
Giants	4.09	55	0	1	12	489.0	453	288	222	9	23	295	8	446	49	6
Brewers	4.68	56	3	4	9	492.1	473	322	256	11	30	287	8	439	75	18
Mariners	4.78	54	0	1	9	459.0	458	338	244	14	36	228	3	405	67	10

INDIVIDUAL

(Leading qualifiers for earned-run average leadership—45 or more innings)

*Throws lefthanded.

Pitcher, Team	W	L	Pct.	ERA	G	GS	CG	GF	ShO	Sv.	IP	H	R	ER	HR	HB	BB	Int. BB	SO	WP
Myers, Giants*	8	1	.889	1.69	13	13	0	0	0	0	74.2	50	19	14	0	2	16	0	105	3
Duncan, Padres	3	3	.500	1.96	13	7	1	5	0	3	46.0	37	18	10	0	5	28	1	39	5
Welch, Cardinals	7	1	.875	2.04	10	10	0	0	0	0	57.1	44	14	13	0	1	12	0	67	3
Ramirez, Cardinals*	2	2	.500	2.34	9	9	0	0	0	0	50.0	49	18	13	2	1	16	0	41	4
Barnes, Rockies	5	4	.556	2.67	11	11	1	0	0	0	60.2	60	30	18	0	1	14	0	38	8
Aguirre, Angels	5	5	.500	2.75	11	11	5	0	1	0	72.0	51	29	22	0	4	18	0	62	6
Garrett, Rockies	1	1	.500	2.91	11	10	1	0	1	0	55.2	50	27	18	2	2	10	0	42	2
Tijerina, Brewers	6	1	.857	2.94	10	10	1	0	0	0	64.1	51	34	21	0	3	24	0	55	7
Montgomery, Athletics	4	3	.571	3.12	15	7	0	2	0	0	57.2	51	30	20	0	3	19	2	41	4
Domenico, Athletics	4	1	.800	3.17	15	11	0	1	0	1	59.2	47	27	21	2	4	39	1	59	14

Departmental leaders: G—Conway, 28; W—Myers, 8; L—Walls, 7; Pct.—Ju. Abreu, 1.000; GS—H. Garrett, McMullen, 14; CG—Aguirre, 5; GF—Barrick, 23; ShO—Paul, 2; Sv.—Barrick, 12; IP—Gil, 75.2; H—Krause, 72; R—McMullen, 60; ER—McMullen, 45; HR—Gil, 6; HB—Golden, 9; BB—McMullen, 53; IBB—Vasquez, 4; SO—Myers, 105; WP—Five pitchers tied with 14.

(All pitchers—listed alphabetically)

Pitcher, Team	W	L	Pct.	ERA	G	GS	CG	GF	ShO	Sv.	IP	H	R	ER	HR	HB	BB	Int. BB	SO	WP
Jose Abreu, Giants	1	1	.500	4.58	22	0	0	9	0	0	35.1	39	24	18	2	1	27	0	20	4
Juan Abreu, Giants*	7	0	1.000	4.11	12	12	0	0	0	0	61.1	54	30	28	1	4	46	0	46	4
Aguirre, Angels	5	5	.500	2.75	11	11	5	0	1	0	72.0	51	29	22	0	4	18	0	62	6
Alexis, Cardinals	1	2	.333	6.50	14	7	0	1	0	0	45.2	63	46	33	2	2	13	0	30	1
Almanza, Cardinals*	4	1	.800	3.21	20	4	0	6	0	0	42.0	38	19	15	2	3	14	0	56	14
Andujar, Angels	0	0	.000	4.00	5	0	0	1	0	0	9.0	8	5	4	0	1	2	0	8	0
Barnes, Rockies*	5	4	.556	2.67	11	11	1	0	0	0	60.2	60	30	18	0	1	14	0	38	8
Baron, Padres*	1	3	.250	4.44	13	8	1	2	0	1	48.2	38	33	24	0	6	38	0	36	5
Barrick, Cardinals	3	0	1.000	1.01	24	0	0	23	0	12	26.2	18	3	3	0	0	4	0	23	3
Barry, Rockies*	1	1	.500	3.66	12	0	0	2	0	0	19.2	26	15	8	1	1	6	0	15	1
Bawlson, Angels*	4	2	.667	3.51	15	6	2	1	0	0	59.0	55	32	23	0	1	21	1	54	12
Benny, Brewers	1	3	.250	7.21	14	8	0	1	0	0	43.2	56	44	35	2	2	37	0	29	10
Bieniasz, Mariners	0	0	.000	4.85	6	0	0	1	0	0	13.0	11	8	7	0	1	4	0	15	2
Bledsoe, Cardinals	4	0	1.000	0.72	4	4	0	0	0	0	25.0	11	3	2	0	3	8	0	26	0
Blyleven, Angels	4	4	.500	3.60	11	11	1	0	0	0	70.0	69	35	28	3	5	17	0	49	5
Brown, Giants	1	0	1.000	0.00	1	0	0	1	0	1	3.0	0	0	0	0	0	0	0	6	0
Burdick, Rockies	1	0	1.000	4.94	16	2	0	2	0	0	27.1	39	19	15	0	2	12	0	14	4
Burgos, Padres	0	0	.000	0.00	1	0	0	0	0	0	2.0	1	1	0	0	0	2	0	2	0
Calderon, Brewers	0	0	.000	2.77	12	0	0	0	0	0	13.0	15	9	4	0	0	14	0	13	2
Carr, Athletics	0	0	.000	0.00	1	0	0	1	0	0	1.0	0	0	0	0	0	0	0	0	0
Carrasco, Giants	0	0	.000	11.66	12	0	0	2	0	0	14.2	23	25	19	2	4	14	0	12	6
Carrasco, Angels	3	3	.500	1.54	18	1	0	11	0	4	35.0	28	10	6	0	1	14	1	43	0
Chambers, Athletics*	1	1	.500	4.09	13	8	0	1	0	1	44.0	43	23	20	4	2	14	0	36	1
Cintron, Angels	0	3	.000	2.81	12	2	0	2	0	0	32.0	27	14	10	2	0	10	0	17	1
Clark, Padres*	1	2	.333	6.00	5	5	0	0	0	0	24.0	26	20	16	0	1	10	1	26	2
Coffman, Mariners	0	1	.000	1.29	4	0	0	0	0	0	7.0	3	4	1	0	0	5	0	6	1
Conway, Cardinals*	1	1	.500	2.97	28	0	0	4	0	0	39.1	31	13	13	1	2	21	0	47	5
Cope, Mariners	3	4	.429	5.08	11	11	0	0	0	0	62.0	66	42	35	3	1	20	0	62	4
Craig, Mariners	0	1	.000	8.03	9	1	0	2	0	1	12.1	15	13	11	0	1	9	0	5	0
Cruise, Cardinals	3	2	.600	1.60	23	1	0	9	0	2	33.2	25	10	6	0	1	7	2	28	2
Curran, Cardinals*	2	1	.667	3.69	27	0	0	8	0	0	31.2	37	17	13	0	0	9	1	38	6
Daniels, Mariners	3	4	.429	3.40	13	8	0	0	0	0	53.0	46	30	20	0	5	13	0	50	8
Dessellier, Mariners	1	5	.167	6.56	12	10	0	0	0	0	48.0	62	50	35	0	4	36	0	32	8
DeWett, Rockies*	0	0	.000	0.00	3	0	0	3	0	1	4.0	3	0	0	0	0	0	0	3	0
Domenico, Athletics	4	1	.800	3.17	15	11	0	1	0	1	59.2	47	27	21	2	4	39	1	59	14
Duncan, Padres	3	3	.500	1.96	13	7	1	5	0	3	46.0	37	18	10	0	5	28	1	39	5
Egloff, Angels	1	0	1.000	0.00	4	0	0	4	0	0	6.0	6	0	0	0	0	0	0	6	1
Estrella, Padres	0	0	.000	9.00	3	0	0	1	0	0	4.0	6	5	4	0	0	2	0	4	1
Fernandez, Rockies	1	4	.200	1.00	16	0	0	5	0	1	27.0	19	14	3	0	2	9	0	14	3
Garrett, Padres	6	5	.545	3.24	14	14	0	0	0	0	72.1	64	40	26	3	5	31	2	83	6
Garrett, Rockies	1	1	.500	2.91	11	10	1	0	1	0	55.2	50	27	18	2	2	10	0	42	2
Gaskill, Brewers	2	0	1.000	3.12	13	1	0	8	0	1	26.0	22	10	9	0	1	14	0	19	2
Gil, Athletics	7	1	.875	4.52	14	13	0	0	0	0	75.2	63	43	38	6	3	31	0	63	8
Gold, Brewers	2	1	.667	5.29	19	0	0	7	0	0	34.0	36	24	20	0	3	15	1	29	3
Golden, Mariners	2	1	.667	6.12	14	6	0	1	0	0	50.0	52	50	34	1	9	37	0	46	14
Green, Mariners	2	5	.286	3.72	24	0	0	21	0	6	36.1	29	21	15	2	4	16	1	31	1
Griffin, Athletics	0	0	.000	9.00	1	0	0	1	0	0	1.0	3	1	1	0	0	1	0	0	1
Grundt, Giants*	0	0	.000	2.25	4	0	0	0	0	0	4.0	5	1	1	0	0	0	0	2	1
Harpe, Padres	1	0	1.000	2.61	6	0	0	2	0	0	10.1	5	3	3	0	3	5	0	5	0
Hillis, Brewers	2	3	.400	4.03	16	0	0	9	0	1	22.1	23	13	10	0	3	12	1	24	8
Hinchliffe, Mariners	0	4	.000	5.08	10	8	0	0	0	0	44.1	55	32	25	4	3	5	0	29	4
Huber, Athletics	1	2	.333	5.81	12	2	0	3	0	1	31.0	45	29	20	3	6	12	0	21	4
Hutchins, Rockies	1	0	1.000	0.00	1	0	0	0	0	0	0.0	0	6	6	0	2	4	0	0	0
Jaen, Brewers	0	1	.000	9.35	13	1	0	4	0	0	17.1	23	21	18	1	0	14	0	8	2
Johnson, Padres*	0	0	.000	0.00	3	0	0	2	0	0	5.0	1	0	0	0	0	2	0	5	1
Jones, Padres	3	5	.375	3.80	12	9	0	0	0	0	47.1	39	27	20	0	1	24	1	35	14
Knox, Angels	2	1	.667	3.51	13	3	0	7	0	1	33.1	28	16	13	2	2	9	0	32	4
Krause, Brewers	4	4	.500	4.50	12	12	0	0	0	0	64.0	72	38	32	1	1	34	0	36	6
Kubinski, Athletics*	0	1	.000	6.00	1	1	0	0	0	0	3.0	5	2	2	1	0	0	0	3	0
Lair, Cardinals	1	3	.250	5.92	6	6	0	0	0	0	24.1	26	22	16	0	2	16	0	23	3
LaChappa, Padres*	2	4	.333	4.18	12	10	0	1	0	0	56.0	59	37	26	2	6	25	0	73	9
Leibee, Athletics*	4	4	.500	0.99	14	2	0	8	0	3	27.1	27	10	3	0	1	10	0	20	3
Luft, Athletics	1	1	.500	6.32	17	0	0	11	0	3	31.1	35	36	22	1	1	21	3	26	10
Manon, Cardinals	2	3	.400	5.13	15	4	0	1	0	0	33.1	44	21	19	2	0	12	0	22	5
Martin, Cardinals	1	5	.167	5.54	11	9	0	1	0	0	39.0	53	30	24	1	1	11	0	44	2
Matos, Padres	0	2	.000	6.28	11	0	0	8	0	0	14.1	14	15	10	1	4	13	1	13	3
Matos, Rockies	0	2	.000	4.97	18	1	0	5	0	0	25.1	32	19	14	1	1	12	0	15	4
Mayer, Angels	0	1	.000	4.82	17	0	0	12	0	3	18.2	10	11	10	1	2	17	0	19	4
McAdams, Rockies	3	1	.750	4.08	22	0	0	16	0	3	28.2	34	14	13	0	0	12	2	35	3
McMullen, Giants	1	6	.143	6.33	14	14	0	0	0	0	64.0	70	60	45	1	5	53	0	44	12
Mercado, Brewers	1	4	.200	4.93	17	1	0	10	0	3	34.2	34	24	19	0	2	18	1	36	4

Pitcher, Team	W	L	Pct.	ERA	G	GS	CG	GF	ShO	Sv.	IP	H	R	ER	HR	HB	BB	Int. BB	SO	WP
Mercedes, Giants*	1	0	1.000	5.40	10	0	0	3	0	0	13.1	10	9	8	0	0	14	0	9	1
Meyer, Padres	0	0	.000	8.10	8	0	0	1	0	0	10.0	11	17	9	0	1	14	0	8	3
Mineer, Rockies*	1	0	1.000	2.19	10	0	0	2	0	0	12.1	11	6	3	0	0	5	0	10	2
Mitchell, Mariners*	0	0	.000	2.70	3	0	0	0	0	0	3.1	4	1	1	0	0	2	0	2	0
Mitchell, Giants*	0	2	.000	1.77	14	0	0	3	0	0	20.1	15	7	4	1	3	12	0	25	3
Mojica, Athletics	6	2	.750	4.15	24	0	0	19	0	5	30.1	31	19	14	1	3	8	0	33	0
Moncion, Athletics	0	0	.000	10.80	1	1	0	0	0	0	3.1	7	5	4	2	0	1	0	0	0
Montgomery, Athletics	4	3	.571	3.12	15	7	0	2	0	0	57.2	51	30	20	0	3	19	2	41	4
Mora, Rockies	0	1	.000	11.05	14	0	0	8	0	0	14.2	21	22	18	2	5	16	0	6	10
Morfin, Giants*	4	3	.571	3.40	21	3	0	8	0	3	42.1	41	19	16	1	0	24	2	37	3
Murray, Giants*	5	4	.556	3.30	15	12	0	1	0	0	71.0	58	36	26	0	0	23	1	72	4
Myers, Giants*	8	1	.889	1.69	13	13	0	0	0	0	74.2	50	19	14	0	2	16	0	105	3
Newman, Athletics	0	0	.000	4.08	9	2	0	0	0	0	17.2	17	12	8	0	1	8	0	10	3
Newton, Mariners*	1	4	.200	2.23	21	1	0	12	0	1	40.1	31	27	10	0	1	23	2	39	7
Paniagua, Padres*	2	2	.333	4.50	16	2	0	2	0	0	36.0	40	25	18	2	1	12	1	19	2
Parker, Cardinals	0	1	.000	5.17	8	0	0	0	0	0	15.2	17	18	9	0	0	16	0	18	3
Paul, Brewers	4	1	.800	1.25	5	5	2	0	2	0	36.0	18	7	5	0	1	9	0	55	3
Perez, Athletics*	4	1	.800	2.31	12	0	0	1	0	0	35.0	34	12	9	2	1	9	0	31	4
Perisho, Angels*	7	3	.700	3.66	11	11	0	0	1	0	64.0	58	32	26	1	2	23	0	65	2
Perkins, Brewers	0	0	.000	20.25	7	0	0	3	0	0	4.0	5	10	9	0	0	9	0	4	3
Pinder, Giants	1	1	.500	5.72	22	0	0	9	0	0	39.1	41	33	25	1	3	39	1	30	5
Prempas, Brewers*	2	3	.400	5.35	10	9	0	0	0	0	38.2	37	28	23	2	5	31	1	52	8
Preston, Brewers	2	5	.286	3.66	9	9	0	0	0	0	46.2	33	23	19	2	1	28	0	48	5
Purdy, Angels	1	0	1.000	2.08	2	2	0	0	0	0	13.0	7	3	3	0	1	1	0	11	0
Ramirez, Cardinals	2	2	.500	2.34	9	9	0	0	0	0	50.0	49	18	13	2	1	16	0	41	4
Sandt, Padres	0	0	.000	0.00	1	0	0	1	0	0	2.0	2	1	0	0	1	0	0	0	0
Sheldon, Brewers	0	0	.000	12.54	11	0	0	6	0	0	9.1	12	16	13	1	3	15	1	9	9
Singleton, Padres	0	1	.000	1.88	15	0	0	9	0	2	28.2	24	9	6	0	3	8	0	28	0
Smith, Athletics	1	2	.333	9.00	8	2	0	1	0	0	19.0	32	24	19	2	2	6	0	7	0
Snure, Brewers*	3	1	.750	4.70	16	0	0	5	0	2	38.1	36	21	20	2	5	13	2	22	3
Tafoya, Rockies*	0	0	.000	3.07	9	0	0	1	0	0	14.2	20	5	5	0	0	4	0	14	1
Talbott, Padres	1	0	1.000	0.00	3	0	0	0	0	0	5.0	2	0	0	0	0	1	0	0	0
Thomson, Rockies	3	5	.375	4.62	11	11	0	0	0	0	50.2	43	40	26	0	3	31	0	36	14
Thurmond, Angels	0	0	.000	4.26	12	0	0	5	0	0	19.0	20	14	9	0	0	8	0	19	2
Tijerina, Brewers	6	1	.857	2.94	10	10	1	0	0	0	64.1	51	34	21	0	3	24	0	55	7
Updike, Mariners	1	3	.250	5.97	21	0	0	9	0	0	34.2	36	27	23	3	2	22	0	32	5
Vallejo, Mariners*	0	1	.000	121.50	2	1	0	0	0	0	0.2	4	10	9	0	1	8	0	0	0
Vanhof, Mariners*	0	0	.000	1.64	5	2	0	1	0	0	11.0	7	2	2	0	1	4	0	12	2
Vargas, Athletics	0	1	.000	5.79	5	0	0	5	0	1	4.2	7	6	3	0	1	1	0	4	1
Vasquez, Giants	3	6	.333	3.55	26	1	0	22	0	8	45.2	47	25	18	0	1	27	4	38	4
Vega, Angels	0	0	.000	6.97	6	0	0	3	0	0	10.1	11	12	8	1	1	13	0	7	2
Viano, Rockies	2	2	.500	3.27	22	1	0	8	0	1	33.0	24	15	12	1	3	6	0	32	6
Walls, Rockies	2	7	.222	4.56	10	10	0	0	0	0	47.1	51	40	24	2	2	26	0	50	11
Walsh, Athletics	2	0	1.000	1.62	9	5	0	1	0	0	33.1	29	9	6	0	5	6	0	33	3
Warren, Angels*	2	4	.333	4.10	9	9	1	0	1	0	41.2	27	26	19	0	1	34	0	63	6
Wasdin, Athletics	0	0	.000	3.00	1	1	0	0	0	0	3.0	3	1	1	0	0	1	0	0	0
Welch, Cardinals	7	1	.875	2.04	10	10	0	0	0	0	57.1	44	14	13	0	1	12	0	67	3
White, Padres	2	2	.500	3.63	19	0	0	8	0	2	39.2	28	20	16	1	5	22	0	33	4
Williams, Mariners	2	3	.400	3.35	16	5	0	7	0	1	43.0	37	21	16	1	2	24	0	44	11
Willis, Padres	3	2	.600	3.24	17	0	0	11	0	5	25.0	24	19	9	0	2	14	0	27	1
Wright, Rockies	1	3	.250	4.00	8	0	0	0	0	0	36.0	35	19	16	1	5	20	0	26	7

BALKS—Jaen, 5; Joel Carrasco, Manon, 4; Burdick, Hillis, Meyer, Mora, Smith, 3 each; Alexis, Blyleven, Daniels, Domenico, Gaskill, Gil, Lachappa, Luft, Mercado, Mojica, Perisho, Prempas, Sandt, Tijerina, Vega, Walls, Walsh, 2 each; Juan Abreu, Aguirre, Almanza, Baron, Benny, Bieniasz, Chambers, Cintron, Conway, Craig, Duncan, Fernandez, Golden, Green, Hinchliffe, Jones, Lair, Leibee, A. Matos, McAdams, Paniagua, Parker, Perez, Ramirez, Singleton, Snure, Thomson, Updike, Vallejo, Vargas, Vasquez, White, Williams, 1 each.

COMBINATION SHUTOUTS—Perisho-Egloff, Warren-Carrasco, Warren-Cintron-Bawlson-Knox, Angels; Gil-Leibee, Athletics; Gaskill-Gold, Preston-Gold, Brewers; Alexis-Conway-Barrick, Lair-Curran-Barrick, Welch-Almanza-Manon, Welch-Curran, Welch-Curran-Barrick, Cardinals; Myers-Vasquez, Giants; Williams-Newton-Green, Mariners; Baron-Paniagua-Jones-Matos, Padres.

NO-HIT GAMES—None.

FIELDING

TEAM

Team	Pct.	G	PO	A	E	DP	PB	Team	Pct.	G	PO	A	E	DP	PB
Cardinals	.958	53	1391	552	85	39	19	Mariners	.945	54	1377	593	114	40	20
Angels	.954	56	1449	561	98	46	9	Athletics	.942	55	1434	572	123	43	17
Giants	.951	55	1467	644	109	62	17	Padres	.940	55	1429	532	125	36	27
Brewers	.951	56	1477	663	111	45	28	Rockies	.937	54	1371	595	133	43	32

INDIVIDUAL

FIRST BASEMEN

*Throws lefthanded.

Player, Team	Pct.	G	PO	A	E	DP
Alguacil, Giants	.974	11	68	6	2	3
Aquino, Mariners	.967	31	282	13	10	22
Carr, Athletics	1.000	2	2	0	0	0
Cedeno, Rockies	.971	44	390	11	12	31
Colon, Cardinals	1.000	9	40	4	0	5
Cruz, Giants	1.000	1	5	0	0	1
Davis, Mariners	.973	26	209	8	6	15
Delacruz, Rockies	1.000	3	28	1	0	3
Derotal, Padres	.971	21	158	7	5	17
Diaz, Rockies	.889	1	8	0	1	0
Feliz-Nova, Brewers	1.000	2	5	0	0	0
Figueroa, Brewers*	1.000	1	1	1	0	0
Fryman, Brewers	.971	8	28	5	1	0
Hatfield, Rockies	1.000	7	63	3	0	5
Hause, Athletics*	1.000	1	2	1	0	0
Herdocia, Angels	.983	52	434	25	8	35
Jones, Athletics	.988	10	82	3	1	4
Lee, Padres	.985	15	115	14	2	6
Madsen, Cardinals	1.000	1	10	2	0	1
Malekovic, Padres	.935	14	84	2	6	4
Martinez, Padres	.971	12	92	7	3	4
Martinez, Giants	1.000	1	1	0	0	0
McLeod, Athletics	1.000	1	18	0	0	0
Monday, Angels	1.000	2	7	1	0	1
Nunez, Brewers	.987	51	403	43	6	36
NUNEZ, Cardinals*	.991	50	431	15	4	27
Pomierski, Mariners	1.000	2	10	0	0	1
Quintana, Athletics	.984	46	408	21	7	34
Ramirez, Giants	.981	49	425	30	9	54

Player, Team	Pct.	G	PO	A	E	DP
Sanchez, Brewers*	.962	9	47	3	2	5
Tiffany, Angels*	.949	5	36	1	2	3
Valentino, Mariners	1.000	1	6	0	0	0

Triple play—F. Nunez.

SECOND BASEMEN

Player, Team	Pct.	G	PO	A	E	DP
Alguacil, Giants	.909	2	6	4	1	2
Batista, Athletics	1.000	6	11	12	0	2
Bogatyrev, Angels	1.000	7	5	9	0	1
Canizaro, Giants	.954	48	102	106	10	33
Cartaya, Padres	.944	15	32	35	4	8
Colon, Cardinals	1.000	1	2	0	0	0
Cook, Mariners	1.000	1	0	1	0	1
Corps, Padres	.944	7	8	9	1	2
Cuevas, Padres	.889	15	20	36	7	6
Darwin, Athletics	1.000	1	3	1	0	0
Delacruz, Rockies	1.000	2	4	4	0	1
S. DeLeon, Mariners	.962	10	25	26	2	7
Denny, Angels	1.000	1	2	1	0	0
Domingo, Mariners	.875	11	14	21	5	5
Figueroa, Rockies	.795	8	19	16	9	3
Franklin Garcia, Brewers	.966	56	155	153	11	31
GARCIA, Rockies	.973	38	86	92	5	23
Gillis, Padres	.952	19	45	34	4	6
Griffin, Athletics	.940	22	20	27	3	3
Jimenez, Cardinals	.926	42	65	86	12	15
Lopez, Mariners	.938	34	42	80	8	18
Martinez, Giants	.842	8	8	8	3	1
Melendez, Rockies	.912	12	10	21	3	3
Millan, Cardinals	.986	17	30	41	1	12
Molina, Mariners	.944	6	5	12	1	1
Moschetti, Athletics	.932	13	19	22	3	3
Perez, Giants	.950	8	12	7	1	2
Perozo, Angels	.954	51	88	120	10	32
Robles, Cardinals	1.000	3	3	4	0	0
F. Soriano, Athletics	.937	13	28	31	4	11
Soto, Brewers	.800	6	1	3	1	0
Vargas, Athletics	.971	15	31	37	2	7

Triple play—Franklin Garcia.

THIRD BASEMEN

Player, Team	Pct.	G	PO	A	E	DP
Alguacil, Giants	.924	33	27	94	10	14
Batista, Athletics	.952	16	20	39	3	8
Cartaya, Padres	.700	3	1	6	3	2
Cedeno, Rockies	1.000	1	2	2	0	1
Cook, Mariners	.886	14	11	28	5	2
Corps, Padres	1.000	3	0	8	0	0
Cruz, Giants	.964	24	9	45	2	2
Cuevas, Padres	.769	8	3	17	6	0
Delacruz, Rockies	.945	16	17	35	3	1
Diaz, Rockies	.819	38	25	70	21	3
Espinal, Padres	.872	35	33	69	15	4
Feliz-Nova, Brewers	.900	34	17	73	10	5
Figueroa, Rockies	1.000	3	0	4	0	0
Fryman, Brewers	.863	22	9	35	7	3
Fuertes, Brewers	.811	21	8	22	7	1
Gonzalez, Giants	.889	7	4	12	2	2
Hamburg, Athletics	1.000	1	1	0	0	0
Jones, Athletics	.743	25	12	40	18	4
Lopez, Mariners	1.000	1	0	1	0	0
MADSEN, Cardinals	.966	52	30	110	5	10
Mazara, Angels	.858	54	35	122	26	9
Millan, Cardinals	.500	3	0	1	1	0
Nunez, Brewers	1.000	1	2	1	0	0
Perozo, Angels	.800	2	0	4	1	0
Pomierski, Mariners	.805	43	29	78	26	8
Robles, Cardinals	.857	2	0	6	1	1
Rodriguez, Padres	1.000	1	2	0	0	0
Sanchez, Padres	.813	6	6	7	3	1
Soto, Brewers	.667	1	0	2	1	0
Vargas, Athletics	.787	17	13	35	13	1

SHORTSTOPS

Player, Team	Pct.	G	PO	A	E	DP
Acosta, Brewers	.967	8	9	20	1	4
Batista, Athletics	1.000	2	3	3	0	0
Bogatyrev, Angels	.909	5	3	7	1	0
Cartaya, Padres	1.000	3	1	6	0	2
Cedeno, Rockies	.667	1	0	4	2	1
Cook, Mariners	.950	27	29	84	6	7
Corps, Padres	.924	28	37	96	11	14
Cruz, Giants	1.000	4	3	7	0	2
Delacruz, Rockies	.882	2	3	12	2	3
Domingo, Mariners	.333	1	1	0	2	0
Figueroa, Rockies	.829	17	18	40	12	7
Fryman, Brewers	1.000	1	1	2	0	0
Green, Cardinals	.897	31	35	87	14	9
HENDERSON, Angels	.927	53	59	145	16	23
Houser, Rockies	.890	37	43	127	21	20
Johnson, Giants	.889	43	60	116	22	22
Klassen, Brewers	.922	31	45	97	12	18
Martinez, Giants	.500	1	0	1	1	0
Marval, Giants	.877	15	17	40	8	11
Molina, Mariners	.955	33	34	92	6	19
Moschetti, Athletics	.900	3	2	7	1	1
Quintana, Athletics	1.000	1	2	4	0	0
Robles, Cardinals	.929	32	44	74	9	13
Rodriguez, Padres	.923	26	38	58	8	8
Salvador, Athletics	.828	8	6	18	5	5
F. Soriano, Athletics	.907	27	26	71	10	11
Soto, Brewers	.870	21	33	54	13	7
Urena, Giants	.800	5	2	2	1	0
Vargas, Athletics	.864	23	20	56	12	4

OUTFIELDERS

Player, Team	Pct.	G	PO	A	E	DP
Alguacil, Giants	1.000	1	3	0	0	0
Batista, Mariners	1.000	29	50	1	0	1
Benner, Giants	.875	32	23	5	4	1
Bowden, Padres	.955	16	21	0	1	0
Brady, Mariners	.897	22	33	2	4	0
Cantrell, Brewers	.976	46	73	9	2	3
Cordero, Giants	.930	25	50	3	4	0
Cruz, Padres	.948	33	71	2	4	0
Cuevas, Padres	1.000	4	1	0	0	0
Current, Cardinals	.872	21	32	2	5	0
Darwin, Athletics	.935	20	27	2	2	0
Davis, Mariners	1.000	5	3	0	0	0
J. DeLeon, Mariners	.927	19	34	4	3	0
S. DeLeon, Mariners	.953	27	40	1	2	0
DENBOW, Giants	.983	37	54	5	1	0
Dermendziev, Rockies	1.000	21	33	2	0	1
Derotal, Padres	1.000	20	30	2	0	1
Dumas, Mariners	.966	26	26	2	1	0
Edwards, Rockies	.967	20	24	5	1	0
Feliz-Nova, Brewers	1.000	2	1	0	0	0
Fernandez, Cardinals*	.962	28	48	3	2	0
Figueroa, Brewers*	.955	18	19	2	1	0
French, Cardinals	.919	26	32	2	3	1
Gambill, Rockies	.962	44	70	6	3	0
German, Athletics	.961	27	43	6	2	1
Gibson, Rockies	.821	18	22	1	5	0
Ham, Angels	.916	49	74	2	7	2
Hamburg, Athletics	.944	45	79	6	5	1
Harper, Cardinals	.975	25	39	0	1	0
Hartwell, Angels	.938	8	15	0	1	0
Herrick, Angels*	.957	53	83	5	4	2
Hodge, Brewers	.950	31	38	0	2	0
Jones, Athletics	1.000	2	5	0	0	0
Leger, Angels	.960	14	24	0	1	0
Lopez, Cardinals	1.000	4	8	0	0	0
Luckett, Padres	.980	29	49	1	1	0
Lugo, Cardinals	.903	31	26	2	3	0
Machado, Rockies	1.000	4	7	0	0	0
Martinez, Brewers	.909	5	9	1	1	0
Mathis, Mariners	.938	26	30	0	2	0
Matos, Padres	1.000	1	1	0	0	0
McLeod, Athletics	.966	37	51	5	2	0
McMillan, Cardinals	.970	21	30	2	1	0
Mealing, Brewers	.927	37	50	1	4	1
Medina, Rockies	.886	20	29	2	4	0
Peguero, Padres	.967	21	27	2	1	0
Pooschke, Giants	.887	35	51	4	7	0
Pridgen, Rockies	.929	15	13	0	1	0
Ramirez, Giants	1.000	2	2	0	0	0
Rivera, Padres	.933	44	81	3	6	1
Roques, Padres	.949	27	33	4	2	1
Sanchez, Brewers*	.959	33	42	5	2	1
Sanders, Padres	.857	4	6	0	1	0
Simmons, Athletics	1.000	2	4	0	0	0
F. Soriano, Athletics	1.000	3	1	0	0	0
J. Soriano, Athletics	.976	43	77	4	2	2
Taylor, Angels	.979	47	92	3	2	1
Tiffany, Angels*	.962	18	22	3	1	1
Tinoco, Mariners	.947	30	34	2	2	0
Torres, Brewers	.909	33	26	4	3	0
Vega, Giants	.979	22	42	4	1	1
Velazquez, Rockies	.924	37	70	3	6	0
Williams, Cardinals*	.844	27	23	4	5	2

Triple play—Mealing.

CATCHERS

Player, Team	Pct.	G	PO	A	E	DP	PB
Aquino, Mariners	1.000	1	4	1	0	1	0
Augustine, Mariners	1.000	3	22	5	0	0	1
Bowen, Cardinals	.984	32	217	34	4	1	12
Cardona, Athletics	.981	18	140	13	3	3	4
Carr, Athletics	.935	24	81	5	6	0	5
Christopherson, Giants	1.000	7	40	4	0	0	1
Colon, Cardinals	1.000	2	8	2	0	0	1
Cullen, Angels	1.000	4	13	0	0	0	1
Galarza, Giants	.981	31	216	42	5	4	9

Player, Team	Pct.	G	PO	A	E	DP	PB
Francisco Garcia, Brewers	.980	19	82	16	2	1	2
Goebel, Angels	1.000	4	9	0	0	0	0
Hatfield, Rockies	.961	28	168	31	8	2	12
Heffernan, Giants	.983	5	49	8	1	0	1
Hoover, Rockies	.977	17	78	8	2	1	19
Martinez, Padres	.963	16	73	4	3	0	4
Martinez, Mariners	.969	15	113	11	4	0	4
Maxwell, Mariners	.990	17	85	12	1	0	2
Millan, Cardinals	.000	1	0	0	0	0	1
Milisitz, Brewers	.951	18	87	11	5	0	5
Molina, Angels	1.000	8	47	2	0	0	0
Monday, Angels	.979	19	130	13	3	0	3
Norton, Cardinals	.989	12	85	8	1	1	1
ORTEGA, Athletics	.990	33	182	14	2	1	5
Pozo, Rockies	1.000	20	116	14	0	1	1
Ramirez, Giants	.923	6	17	7	2	0	1
Randolph, Mariners	.979	9	39	7	1	0	9
Reynolds, Giants	1.000	7	42	5	0	0	2
Robles, Cardinals	1.000	1	1	0	0	0	0
Rodriguez, Brewers	.983	23	101	13	2	0	11
Rodriguez, Angels	.980	36	265	29	6	3	5
Sanchez, Padres	.985	25	174	21	3	0	12
Stadler, Padres	.940	21	141	17	10	0	8
Sterling, Giants	.988	23	73	6	1	0	3
Talbott, Padres	.982	9	52	3	1	0	3
Valentino, Mariners	.982	21	139	23	3	1	4
Ventura, Athletics	.958	33	131	30	7	1	7
Zwisler, Brewers	.958	30	153	29	8	0	10

PITCHERS

Player, Team	Pct.	G	PO	A	E	DP
Jose Abreu, Giants	1.000	22	1	4	0	0
Juan Abreu, Giants*	.833	12	1	4	1	0
Aguirre, Angels*	1.000	11	1	13	0	1
Alexis, Cardinals	.833	14	1	4	1	0
Almanza, Cardinals*	.900	20	2	7	1	0
Andujar, Angels	1.000	5	0	2	0	0
Barnes, Rockies*	.808	11	5	16	5	1
Baron, Padres*	.917	13	1	10	1	1
Barrick, Cardinals	.750	24	1	2	1	0
Barry, Rockies*	1.000	12	1	5	0	0
Bawlson, Angels*	1.000	15	3	5	0	0
Benny, Brewers	1.000	14	2	6	0	0
Bieniasz, Mariners	1.000	6	0	1	0	0
Bledsoe, Cardinals	1.000	4	0	2	0	0
Blyleven, Angels	.765	11	2	11	4	2
Burdick, Rockies	.875	16	1	6	1	0
Calderon, Brewers	1.000	12	0	1	0	0
Carrasco, Giants	1.000	12	1	0	0	0
Carrasco, Angels	1.000	18	0	4	0	0
Chanibers, Athletics*	.900	13	4	5	1	0
Cintron, Angels	1.000	12	2	1	0	0
Clark, Padres*	1.000	5	1	1	0	0
Coffman, Mariners	1.000	4	1	1	0	0
Conway, Cardinals*	1.000	28	0	2	0	0
COPE, Mariners	1.000	11	4	13	0	1
Craig, Mariners	.857	9	1	5	1	0
Cruise, Cardinals	.900	23	3	6	1	1
Curran, Cardinals*	.833	27	1	4	1	0
Daniels, Mariners	.846	13	3	8	2	0
Dessellier, Mariners	.875	12	3	4	1	0
DeWett, Rockies*	1.000	3	0	1	0	0
Domenico, Athletics	.786	15	4	7	3	0
Duncan, Padres	.857	13	4	8	2	0
Egloff, Angels	1.000	4	0	2	0	0
Fernandez, Rockies	.900	16	1	8	1	0
Garrett, Padres	.733	14	5	6	4	0
Garrett, Rockies	.941	11	3	13	1	1
Gaskill, Brewers	1.000	13	1	5	0	0
Gil, Athletics	.786	14	4	7	3	0
Gold, Brewers	1.000	19	1	2	0	0
Golden, Mariners	.875	14	3	4	1	0

Player, Team	Pct.	G	PO	A	E	DP
Green, Mariners	1.000	24	4	6	0	1
Grundt, Giants*	1.000	4	0	1	0	0
Harpe, Padres	1.000	6	0	1	0	0
Hillis, Brewers	.750	16	5	1	2	0
Hinchliffe, Mariners	.875	10	2	5	1	0
Huber, Athletics	1.000	12	0	2	0	0
Jaen, Brewers	1.000	13	1	0	0	1
Johnson, Padres*	1.000	3	1	1	0	1
Jones, Padres	.833	12	2	3	1	0
Knox, Angels	1.000	13	3	2	0	0
Krause, Brewers	.875	12	6	15	3	0
Kubinski, Athletics*	1.000	1	0	1	0	0
LaChappa, Padres*	1.000	12	0	10	0	0
Lair, Cardinals	.333	6	0	1	2	0
Leibee, Athletics*	.667	14	0	4	2	0
Luft, Athletics	.667	17	1	3	2	0
Manon, Cardinals	.800	15	1	7	2	0
Martin, Cardinals	1.000	4	0	4	0	0
Matos, Cardinals	1.000	11	1	0	0	0
Matos, Rockies	.500	18	0	1	1	0
Mayer, Angels	1.000	17	1	5	0	0
McAdams, Rockies	1.000	22	1	3	0	0
McMullen, Giants	.833	14	1	19	4	2
Mercado, Brewers	1.000	17	3	7	0	0
Mercedes, Giants*	1.000	10	0	1	0	0
Meyer, Padres	.000	8	0	0	3	0
Mineer, Rockies	1.000	10	0	2	0	0
Mitchell, Mariners*	1.000	3	0	1	0	0
Mitchell, Giants*	1.000	14	1	3	0	1
Mojica, Athletics	1.000	24	1	4	0	0
Moncion, Athletics	1.000	1	2	1	0	0
Montgomery, Athletics	1.000	15	3	11	0	1
Mora, Rockies	.750	14	0	3	1	0
Morfin, Giants*	1.000	21	3	8	0	1
Murray, Giants*	.769	15	1	9	3	1
Myers, Giants*	1.000	13	1	8	0	0
Newman, Athletics	1.000	9	1	4	0	0
Newton, Mariners*	.929	21	3	10	1	1
Paniagua, Padres*	1.000	16	0	8	0	2
Parker, Cardinals	1.000	8	0	2	0	0
Paul, Brewers	1.000	5	2	3	0	0
Perez, Athletics*	1.000	12	2	12	0	0
Perisho, Angels*	.750	11	2	10	4	0
Pinder, Giants	.929	22	2	11	1	0
Prempas, Brewers*	1.000	10	3	3	0	0
Preston, Brewers	1.000	9	3	6	0	0
Purdy, Angels	1.000	2	1	3	0	0
Ramirez, Cardinals	.833	9	1	4	1	0
Sandt, Cardinals	.000	2	0	0	1	0
Singleton, Padres	.750	15	1	2	1	0
Smith, Athletics	.750	8	1	2	1	0
Snure, Brewers*	.833	16	2	3	1	0
Tafoya, Rockies*	1.000	9	0	3	0	0
Talbott, Padres	1.000	5	1	1	0	0
Thomson, Rockies	.947	11	7	11	1	1
Thurmond, Angels	1.000	12	1	2	0	0
Tijerina, Brewers	.900	10	3	6	1	0
Updike, Mariners	.857	21	0	6	1	0
Vallejo, Mariners*	1.000	2	0	1	0	0
Vanhof, Mariners*	.750	5	0	3	1	0
Vargas, Athletics	1.000	5	1	1	0	0
Vasquez, Giants	1.000	26	2	3	0	0
Vega, Angels	1.000	6	0	2	0	0
Viano, Rockies	1.000	22	2	6	0	1
Walls, Rockies	.833	10	3	2	1	0
Walsh, Athletics	.875	9	0	7	1	0
Warren, Angels*	.833	9	5	5	2	0
Wasdin, Athletics	1.000	1	0	1	0	0
Welch, Cardinals	1.000	10	2	5	0	0
White, Padres	.875	19	4	10	2	0
Williams, Mariners	.737	16	4	10	5	0
Willis, Padres	1.000	17	1	2	0	0
Wright, Rockies	1.000	8	1	1	0	0

The following players did not have any fielding statistics at the positions indicated or appeared only as a designated hitter, pinch-hitter or pinch-runner: D. Batista, 3b; Bogatyrev, 3b; Brannon, dh, ph; Brown, p; Burgos, p; Canizaro, ss; Carr, p; S. DeLeon, 3b; Estrella, p; Griffin, ss, of, p; Hause, of; Hutchins, p; Iverson, of; C. Lopez, of; Millan, c; L. Molina, of; Ortega, of; Perkins, p; Randolph, ss; N. Rodriguez, 2b; Sheldon, p; Simmons, 2b; Vargas, 1b, of, c.

LEAGUE CHAMPIONS

Year	Team	Pct.	Year	Team	Pct.	Year	Team	Pct.
1988—	Peoria Brewers	.690	1990—	Peoria Brewers	.679	1992—	Scottsdale A's	.607
1989—	Peoria Brewers	.732	1991—	Scottsdale A's	.650	1993—	Scottsdale A's	.636

DOMINICAN SUMMER LEAGUE

FINAL STANDINGS

SANTO DOMINGO WEST DIVISION

Team	W	L	T	Pct.	GB
Oakland	49	23	2	.681	......
New York Mets	48	24	2	.667	1
Pittsburgh	39	29	1	.574	8
Yankees/San Diego	33	36	0	.478	14½
Detroit/St. Louis	34	38	0	.472	15
Toronto West	26	44	0	.371	22
Chicago/Texas	17	52	1	.246	30½

SAN PEDRO DE MACORIS DIVISION

Team	W	L	T	Pct.	GB
Toyo Carp	52	18	0	.743	......
California	42	28	0	.600	10
Baltimore/White Sox	36	34	0	.514	16
Houston	35	35	0	.500	17
Atlanta	28	42	0	.400	24
San Fran./Phila./Houston	17	53	0	.243	35

SANTO DOMINGO EAST DIVISION

Team	W	L	T	Pct.	GB
Toronto East	50	17	0	.746	......
Los Angeles I	39	31	0	.557	12½
Seattle	34	34	1	.500	16½
Montreal	29	38	1	.433	21
Milwaukee	27	40	1	.403	23
Florida	25	44	1	.362	26

CIBAO DIVISION

Team	W	L	T	Pct.	GB
Angels/Dodgers	42	28	0	.600	......
Cleveland	39	31	0	.557	3
Kansas City/Rockies	24	46	0	.343	18

Club names are major league affiliations.

Playoffs—Angels/Dodgers defeated Toyo Carp, two games to none; Toronto East defeated Oakland, two games to none; Angels/Dodgers defeated Toronto East, three games to one, to win league championship.

Managers—Angels/Dodgers, Antonio Bautista; Atlanta, Jose Salado; Baltimore/White Sox, Juan R. Benhardt; California, Daniel de Leon; Cleveland, Alejandro Taveras; Detroit/St. Louis, Felix Nivar; Florida, Edmundo Borrome; Toyo Carp, Manuel Castillo; Houston, Juan Mercedes; Kansas City/Rockies, Julio Alcala; Los Angeles I, Teodoro Martinez; Milwaukee, Cesar Prebox; Montreal, Hilario Soriano; New York Mets, Roberto Marte; Oakland, Luis Martinez; Pittsburgh, Hall Dyer; San Francisco/Philadelphia/Houston, Elvio Jimenez; Seattle, Ramon de los Santos; Toronto East, Ramon Webster; Toronto West, Julio Cesar Paula; Yankees/San Diego, Victor Mata.

BATTING

TEAM

Team	Avg.	G	AB	R	OR	H	TB	2B	3B	HR	RBI	SH	SF	HP	BB	Int. BB	SO	SB	CS	LOB
Toronto East	.299	67	2204	472	273	658	957	92	27	51	383	11	27	39	346	12	308	155	63	473
Baltimore/White Sox	.289	70	2494	529	525	720	1013	116	6	55	419	16	34	30	376	9	357	92	17	408
Los Angeles I	.286	69	2263	449	345	648	853	79	33	20	368	61	32	65	407	12	400	80	56	608
Houston	.284	70	2386	490	427	678	937	115	24	32	384	26	25	29	378	14	354	51	94	546
Toyo Carp	.284	70	2463	544	234	700	1012	107	44	39	427	12	36	52	343	16	338	130	42	411
Montreal	.274	68	2225	391	414	609	860	74	6	55	337	20	20	44	345	11	382	94	60	544
New York Mets	.274	74	2325	445	333	638	916	90	13	54	364	27	26	41	356	11	387	107	63	539
California	.273	70	2333	456	401	636	858	128	17	20	358	27	19	41	437	13	394	111	71	576
Cleveland	.273	70	2378	399	347	650	867	118	31	17	313	13	20	30	293	14	404	92	67	507
Oakland	.271	74	2391	426	328	649	891	96	19	36	332	25	24	29	388	14	412	103	60	593
Atlanta	.266	70	2365	347	511	628	825	122	12	17	280	28	24	32	272	5	365	90	43	536
Milwaukee	.266	68	2170	325	441	578	739	72	16	19	260	47	20	38	292	7	281	72	48	539
Angels/Dodgers	.263	70	2218	402	335	583	774	84	46	5	318	36	22	36	388	5	314	133	52	544
Pittsburgh	.258	69	2266	422	340	585	829	93	17	39	323	33	23	67	348	15	379	179	69	366
Detroit/St. Louis	.256	72	2214	363	427	567	816	93	24	36	292	24	24	44	279	7	420	146	74	477
Florida	.256	69	2190	316	404	560	738	66	14	28	254	30	23	55	246	8	434	77	52	499
Toronto West	.254	70	2167	337	406	550	746	86	19	24	273	33	27	32	342	7	402	144	88	503
Yankees/San Diego	.253	67	2201	340	335	556	734	80	19	20	265	20	29	47	325	17	379	110	61	533
Seattle	.250	69	2161	369	445	540	779	85	5	48	318	20	20	50	328	5	451	84	54	502
K.C./Rockies	.242	70	2211	330	457	534	688	85	18	11	255	26	18	34	347	15	347	105	67	493
Chicago/Texas	.209	70	2121	253	417	443	551	55	10	11	197	22	19	37	319	3	446	119	54	492
S.F./Phil./Houston	.203	70	2310	272	532	469	623	82	9	18	204	14	14	33	283	4	434	51	21	507

INDIVIDUAL

(Leading qualifiers for batting championship—170 or more plate appearances)

Player, Team	Avg.	G	AB	R	H	TB	2B	3B	HR	RBI	SH	SF	HP	BB	Int. BB	SO	SB	CS
Abreu, Junior, Milwaukee	.403	65	243	45	98	131	12	3	5	39	1	3	0	42	3	13	17	8
Zerpa, Mauro, Baltimore/White Sox	.377	44	159	34	60	85	10	0	5	32	2	3	2	23	1	10	5	0
Garcia, Miguel, Cleveland	.376	51	173	41	65	89	14	5	0	29	0	1	2	41	3	17	8	4
Pena, Charlies, Toyo Carp	.372	70	282	74	105	171	22	7	10	69	0	4	3	44	3	31	13	4
Mendoza, Jesus, Baltimore/White Sox	.371	61	248	62	92	135	17	1	8	52	3	5	2	27	0	15	11	3
Cesar, Angel, Los Angeles I	.367	65	240	54	88	120	14	6	2	46	4	3	6	40	2	17	9	4
Villalona, Kadil, Toronto East	.361	65	249	52	90	125	8	6	5	45	0	2	4	30	2	19	17	7
Vilonar, Henry, New York Mets	.355	72	242	47	86	123	13	3	6	38	2	1	6	33	2	43	12	6
Salomon, Domingo, Atlanta	.353	56	215	32	76	103	23	2	0	26	2	6	2	14	1	19	8	3
Mota, Alfonzo, California	.348	62	224	56	78	107	17	3	2	46	1	0	6	57	7	22	13	7

Departmental leaders: G—D. Ramirez, 73; AB—C. Brito, 291; R—Soto, 80; H—C. Pena, 105; TB—C. Pena, 171; 2B—Salomon, 23; 3B—M. Gonzalez, 10; HR—Adolfo, 15; RBI—C. Brito, C. Pena, 69; SH—Pimentel, J. Sosa, 14; SF—C. Brito, Salvador, 7; HP—Agnoly, 18; BB—F. Castro, 89; IBB—A. Mota, S. Nunez, 7; SO—R. Fernandez, 79; SB—Alcantara, F. Castro, 46; CS—Di. Brito, 17.

Player, Team	Avg.	G	AB	R	H	TB	2B	3B	HR	RBI	SH	SF	HP	BB	Int. BB	SO	SB	CS
Abad, Irvin, Toronto West	.281	70	217	40	61	74	7	3	0	23	1	5	2	44	1	33	11	15
Abreu, Junior, Milwaukee	.403	65	243	45	98	131	12	3	5	39	1	3	0	42	3	13	17	8
Acosta, Roberto, Toronto East	.000	1	1	0	0	0	0	0	0	0	0	0	0	0	0	0	0	0
Adino, Robert, Milwaukee	.300	59	237	26	71	96	11	1	4	36	0	3	3	10	0	26	3	4
Adolfo, Carlos, Montreal	.305	63	220	55	67	124	10	1	15	66	1	3	1	54	4	52	6	3
Agnoly, Earl, Florida	.321	69	246	49	79	96	9	4	0	28	3	0	18	24	1	21	20	8
Agromonte, Freddy, Los Angeles I	.000	2	0	0	0	0	0	0	0	0	0	0	0	0	0	0	0	0
Agustin, Filiberto, S.F./Phil./Hou.	.278	68	263	43	73	102	10	2	5	31	2	1	3	19	0	47	15	5
Albino, Eliazer, Yankees/San Diego	.286	8	14	1	4	4	0	0	0	1	0	0	0	1	0	4	3	0
Alcantara, Jose, Toyo Carp	.332	69	283	74	94	127	11	8	2	41	1	5	2	41	1	18	46	11
Alejo, Nigel, Florida	.188	66	218	14	41	57	7	0	3	28	2	4	5	33	0	51	2	7
Almanzar, Richard, Detroit/St. Louis	.311	62	222	46	69	83	9	1	1	30	1	2	2	32	0	12	32	14
Almonte, Hector, Florida	.000	2	2	0	0	0	0	0	0	0	2	0	0	0	0	1	0	0
Almonte, Waddy, Baltimore/White Sox	.342	53	222	53	76	116	19	0	7	41	3	2	1	22	1	16	4	2
Alvarado, Basilio, Montreal	.308	45	182	21	56	74	9	0	3	31	0	0	4	6	1	26	0	4
Alvaro, Luis, Toyo Carp	.285	53	214	50	61	91	13	1	5	37	0	0	2	29	1	33	11	2
Alzualde, Daniel, California	.207	47	121	19	25	33	5	0	1	11	1	1	0	21	0	9	2	1
Andujar, Eliezer, California	.306	49	134	37	41	53	10	1	0	17	2	1	6	44	0	28	19	6
Aquino, Julio, Los Angeles I	.100	3	10	0	1	2	1	0	0	1	0	0	0	2	0	1	0	0
Araiz, Jhonattan, Montreal	.237	24	59	7	14	15	1	0	0	5	1	1	0	19	0	15	3	3
Arias, Alberto, Oakland	.224	33	76	12	17	22	2	0	1	8	0	1	0	15	1	10	1	0
Arias, David, Seattle	.264	61	201	37	53	93	17	1	7	31	0	5	4	34	1	44	1	1
Arias, Jose, New York Mets	.273	55	161	25	44	56	6	0	2	17	0	2	3	25	1	32	3	4
Arias, Rogelio, Kansas City/Rockies	.172	45	134	13	23	29	4	1	0	17	4	0	0	13	1	9	3	2
Arrendel, Eduard, Houston	.365	33	85	14	31	35	4	0	0	14	2	3	1	13	0	7	5	0
Arvelo, Luis, Milwaukee	.000	1	0	0	0	0	0	0	0	0	0	0	0	0	0	0	0	0
Asencio, Alexander, Angels/Dodgers	.248	62	218	38	54	73	7	6	0	37	1	6	4	38	1	28	10	3
Asencio, Jose, Toronto West	.235	61	179	18	42	59	9	1	2	23	2	0	2	36	1	36	4	7
Avila, Edwin, California	.000	1	1	0	0	0	0	0	0	0	0	0	0	0	0	1	0	0
Ayala, Fernando, Los Angeles I	.000	1	3	0	0	0	0	0	0	0	0	0	0	0	0	0	0	0
Aybar, Jose Soriano, New York Mets	.000	1	1	0	0	0	0	0	0	0	0	0	0	0	0	1	0	0
Aybar, Ramon, Detroit/St. Louis	.237	25	76	13	18	20	2	0	0	4	0	0	1	11	0	24	17	6
Baez, Victor, Angels/Dodgers	.292	34	106	7	31	38	7	0	0	18	4	1	2	10	0	13	2	2
Balcazar, Carlos, California	.326	45	89	14	29	40	11	0	0	13	1	0	1	27	1	24	1	0
Barazarte, Wilfred, Los Angeles I	.268	42	164	24	44	64	5	6	1	26	2	2	3	20	0	25	2	2
Bautista, Perfecto, Detroit/St. Louis	.143	13	35	6	5	5	0	0	0	3	0	0	1	6	0	9	2	1
Beras, Iluminado, California	.247	36	77	12	19	24	5	0	0	15	1	1	1	3	0	7	1	0
Berroa, Gabriel, Seattle	.250	46	124	26	31	44	7	0	2	10	0	1	1	19	0	23	5	4
Betancourt, Damaso, Los Angeles I	.000	2	4	0	0	0	0	0	0	0	0	0	0	0	0	2	0	0
Bido, Jorge, Houston	.213	60	211	39	45	61	7	0	3	31	1	3	1	30	0	30	6	2
Blanco, Ender, Montreal	.161	23	56	9	9	11	2	0	0	4	3	0	0	15	0	27	0	0
Blanco, Tirso, Houston	.320	52	172	47	55	82	9	0	6	36	2	0	2	38	3	33	13	1
Bonilla, Ramon, Oakland	.324	58	182	33	59	73	12	1	0	26	0	6	0	23	1	24	5	0
Borges, Andry, Kansas City/Rockies	.304	66	237	32	72	88	7	3	1	26	6	1	6	22	3	31	7	11
Brazoban, Delfin, Toronto West	.000	1	0	0	0	0	0	0	0	0	0	0	0	1	0	0	0	0
Brea, Juan, New York Mets	.235	22	51	8	12	20	2	0	2	11	0	2	1	4	1	4	0	1
Brea, Rafael, Toronto West	.265	70	234	59	62	84	9	5	1	28	3	1	7	54	0	51	30	11
Brito, Cirilo, Toyo Carp	.313	70	291	68	91	152	16	9	9	69	0	7	6	21	4	35	9	5
Brito, Diolis, Chicago/Texas	.314	63	229	42	72	91	9	2	2	22	1	3	4	30	0	29	36	17
Brito, Domingo, San Fran./Phil./Hou.	.223	49	179	26	40	50	4	0	2	11	2	0	0	27	0	30	6	1
Brito, Edgar, Toronto West	.259	67	232	22	60	87	16	1	3	25	5	3	3	20	2	21	11	13
Brito, Hernan, Milwaukee	.214	39	84	8	18	29	6	1	1	7	0	0	1	25	0	21	0	2
Brito, Jose, California	.000	1	1	0	0	0	0	0	0	0	0	0	0	1	0	0	0	0
Brito, Jose, Milwaukee	.500	1	2	1	1	1	0	0	0	0	0	0	0	0	0	0	0	0
Brito, Silvano, Seattle	.197	44	127	24	25	27	2	0	0	8	2	1	0	3	0	28	18	10
Brito, Vicente, Toronto West	.268	66	209	40	56	69	4	0	3	31	5	3	0	30	0	19	10	4
Brown, Alfonso, Los Angeles I	.339	59	227	45	77	102	9	5	2	56	0	2	3	43	2	30	14	10
Bryan, Leonaldo, California	.251	60	199	36	50	77	10	1	5	37	2	1	2	28	0	48	8	8
Caballero, Javier, Balt./White Sox	.237	26	97	16	23	37	2	0	4	14	1	1	0	6	0	21	0	0
Cabarcas, Carlos, K.C./Rockies	.147	37	75	11	11	14	3	0	0	9	3	1	0	18	0	19	3	0
Cabrera, Jairo, Toyo Carp	.295	58	193	34	57	65	4	2	0	29	1	3	2	22	1	12	0	2
Cabrera, Orlando, Montreal	.344	38	122	24	42	53	6	1	1	17	1	4	2	18	1	11	14	5
Cadet, Javier, Chicago/Texas	.153	24	59	6	9	9	0	0	0	4	0	0	1	9	0	22	0	1
Campos, Jesus, Montreal	.280	11	50	12	14	16	2	0	0	8	0	0	0	3	0	1	6	0
Campusano, Carlos, Milwaukee	.209	54	148	32	31	38	1	3	0	15	10	0	4	19	0	25	5	8
Caraballo, Deivis, Toronto West	.244	50	135	11	33	40	3	2	0	20	5	1	3	28	0	35	6	2
Cardenas, Nelson, Cleveland	.289	13	38	8	11	11	0	0	0	3	0	0	3	5	3	12	3	2
Carrasco, Ruddy, Toronto West	.238	58	193	29	46	68	7	0	5	20	1	5	5	23	1	31	16	4
Castillo, Amaury, Houston	.318	54	211	26	67	90	11	0	4	38	2	1	2	13	4	41	2	2
Castillo, Edwin, Toyo Carp	.267	25	75	12	20	21	1	0	0	10	1	0	0	1	0	5	0	0
Castillo, Juan, Milwaukee	.306	56	196	42	60	67	5	1	0	21	4	1	3	40	1	13	20	5
Castillo, Luis, Florida	.282	69	266	48	75	96	7	1	4	31	2	3	2	36	1	22	21	13
Castillo, Victor, Toronto West	.000	1	1	0	0	0	0	0	0	0	0	0	0	0	0	0	0	0
Castro, Cesar, California	.197	34	61	13	12	15	0	0	1	9	2	0	2	17	0	16	6	2
Castro, Francisco, Angels/Dodgers	.312	69	221	58	69	86	11	3	0	30	2	1	7	89	1	14	46	13
Castro, Jose, Oakland	.307	57	192	52	59	76	7	2	2	26	4	1	1	59	1	30	25	15
Castro, Jose Luis, Seattle	.270	64	215	37	58	82	10	1	4	48	0	5	0	32	0	16	6	5
Cedeno, Ruddy, Houston	.242	61	219	47	53	69	9	2	1	24	5	0	4	57	1	32	15	5
Cesar, Angel, Los Angeles I	.367	65	240	54	88	120	14	6	2	46	4	3	6	40	2	17	9	4
Collado, Hugo, Oakland	.000	1	0	0	0	0	0	0	0	0	0	0	0	0	0	0	0	0
Contreras, Franklin, Houston	.132	22	53	9	7	10	0	0	1	5	0	0	1	11	0	10	0	1
Cordero, Edward, Detroit/St. Louis	.227	33	97	15	22	40	8	2	2	11	1	0	4	12	0	25	3	3
Croes, Estefano, Montreal	.273	25	77	16	21	22	1	0	0	6	2	0	0	13	0	6	3	3
Cruz, Jose, Baltimore/White Sox	.243	38	107	10	26	28	2	0	0	11	0	2	2	4	0	19	10	1
Cuevas, Francisco, Florida	.000	1	1	0	0	0	0	0	0	0	0	0	0	0	0	1	0	0
Cuevas, Javier, San Fran./Phil./Hou.	.211	38	123	22	26	32	6	0	0	12	0	1	0	21	0	28	3	3
Davalillo, David, California	.302	47	179	37	54	74	10	2	2	25	2	2	0	22	0	15	3	5
DeLaCruz, Henry, Atlanta	.167	2	6	0	1	2	0	0	0	0	0	0	0	0	0	3	0	0
DeLaCruz, Jesus, California	.258	43	132	22	34	45	11	0	0	15	1	1	10	22	0	18	2	5
DeLaCruz, Jocelin, K.C./Rockies	.188	30	69	8	13	16	3	0	0	4	3	0	2	9	0	10	0	2
DeLaCruz, Rafael, Chicago/Texas	.179	65	207	25	37	42	5	0	0	18	0	1	5	22	0	58	9	8
DeLaCruz, Wilfredo, Yankees/S.D.	.242	19	62	9	15	17	2	0	0	4	0	0	1	4	0	11	10	1

Player, Team	Avg.	G	AB	R	H	TB	2B	3B	HR	RBI	SH	SF	HP	BB	Int. BB	SO	SB	CS
DeLaRosa, Elvis, Detroit/St. Louis	.258	71	217	43	56	80	9	0	5	37	2	6	3	41	2	56	5	2
DeLaRosa, Luis, Pittsburgh	.265	52	151	23	40	57	8	0	3	21	3	2	3	23	0	34	6	2
DeLeon, Felix, Yankees/San Diego	.299	67	251	48	75	108	14	5	3	36	2	3	1	23	0	15	16	8
DeLeon, Javier, Toronto West	1.000	1	1	1	1	2	1	0	0	0	0	0	0	0	0	0	0	1
DeLeon, Ruben, Chicago/Texas	.120	32	100	5	12	13	1	0	0	4	0	0	1	14	0	21	0	1
Delgado, Pedro, Kansas City/Rockies	.284	64	208	31	59	67	6	1	0	20	2	4	4	13	1	27	10	4
Delgado, Wilson, Seattle	.292	60	171	19	50	58	8	0	0	26	7	0	1	34	0	25	5	9
DeLosSantos, Alex, Florida	.239	65	226	30	54	75	7	1	4	30	3	2	1	24	1	60	7	6
DeLosSantos, Jose, Atlanta	.239	54	184	25	44	62	10	1	2	23	2	3	6	23	0	50	8	4
Devers, Jose M., Seattle	.237	25	59	8	14	17	3	0	0	6	0	0	1	5	0	20	1	1
Diaz, Emenegildo, Toyo Carp	.199	48	141	27	28	41	6	2	1	19	2	2	9	20	0	32	4	0
Diaz, Jacobo, California	.227	52	128	28	29	35	4	1	0	13	3	1	0	20	0	10	7	5
Diaz, Richard, Florida	.234	62	209	28	49	58	6	0	1	18	6	4	3	17	0	44	2	3
Dijol, Julio M., Chicago/Texas	.133	57	166	14	22	27	3	1	0	9	5	1	3	40	0	57	3	1
Domero, Richard, Pittsburgh	.162	20	37	5	6	10	1	0	1	4	2	0	1	9	0	16	0	0
Dominguez, Ramon, Yankees/S.D.	.154	12	26	6	4	4	0	0	0	5	0	2	2	5	0	12	0	0
Duncan, Juan, Seattle	.247	48	162	26	40	47	3	2	0	17	2	0	2	14	1	33	9	5
Encarnacion, Juan, Detroit/St. Louis	.251	72	251	36	63	123	13	4	13	49	1	3	6	15	0	65	6	7
Encarnacion, Pedro, Balt./White Sox	.273	52	154	31	42	58	5	1	3	24	3	1	3	27	1	9	3	0
Escalante, Carlos, Chicago/Texas	.228	42	136	14	31	36	2	0	1	11	2	1	2	16	0	26	2	0
Escoto, Marlon, Milwaukee	.174	10	23	1	4	4	0	0	0	2	2	0	0	1	0	7	1	1
Espinosa, Jose, New York Mets	.220	43	118	21	26	39	1	0	4	9	2	0	3	15	1	39	0	2
Estrada, Horacio, Milwaukee	.000	1	2	1	0	0	0	0	0	0	0	0	1	0	0	0	0	0
Evangelista, German, Cleveland	.244	67	217	41	53	80	7	7	2	39	1	2	6	40	3	48	13	8
Fana, Alberto, San Fran./Phil./Hou.	.223	46	166	10	37	48	6	1	1	18	0	3	1	9	0	20	1	3
Faneyte, Reynaldo, Toronto East	.341	50	182	30	62	96	10	3	6	35	1	3	5	16	0	38	5	9
Felix, Juan, Milwaukee	.262	51	183	31	48	66	10	1	2	24	7	4	2	24	2	15	3	2
Feliz, Claudio, Chicago/Texas	.125	17	32	1	4	5	1	0	0	0	0	0	2	6	0	13	0	1
Fermin, Jose, Florida	.295	61	190	32	56	60	4	0	0	16	2	1	7	22	2	21	8	2
Fernandez, Jose M., Montreal	.319	65	251	40	80	120	8	1	10	49	0	1	5	32	1	23	2	5
Fernandez, Juan, Atlanta	.267	39	146	22	39	47	2	0	2	17	2	1	0	10	0	27	3	1
Fernandez, Pedro, Atlanta	.330	33	112	19	37	61	12	3	2	22	4	2	2	8	0	22	7	5
Fernandez, Robert, Cleveland	.197	59	188	33	37	60	11	0	4	30	0	3	3	30	0	79	2	5
Figuereo, Roberto, Atlanta	.259	50	193	26	50	55	3	1	0	15	6	1	2	18	1	15	11	5
Fisher, Carlos, California	.239	20	67	12	16	18	0	1	0	9	2	1	0	12	0	12	1	4
Flobil, Reyes, Kansas City/Rockies	.154	12	39	0	6	6	0	0	0	2	0	0	1	1	0	6	0	0
Francois, Aldo, Toronto East	.103	24	29	6	3	3	0	0	0	2	0	0	1	5	0	10	2	1
Freire, Alex, Houston	.315	65	232	43	73	101	13	3	3	39	0	1	5	29	2	24	6	1
Galan, Manolo, Baltimore/White Sox	.294	50	180	33	53	76	5	0	6	35	0	3	4	22	2	18	0	0
Garcia, Amaury, Florida	.283	64	237	35	67	90	5	3	4	29	4	0	5	31	0	41	9	6
Garcia, Apostol, Detroit/St. Louis	.193	65	150	24	29	31	2	0	0	6	8	0	6	15	0	32	14	4
Garcia, Eusebio, Florida	.333	4	3	1	1	3	0	0	1	0	1	0	0	0	0	2	0	0
Garcia, Jose, Baltimore/White Sox	.287	26	108	11	31	43	6	0	2	27	1	1	2	1	0	11	0	0
Garcia, Julio, Yankees/San Diego	.289	14	45	3	13	15	2	0	0	3	0	0	1	1	0	3	0	0
Garcia, Miguel, Cleveland	.376	51	173	41	65	89	14	5	0	29	0	1	2	41	3	17	8	4
Garcia, Miguel, Los Angeles I	.275	44	167	41	46	50	1	0	1	18	6	2	5	39	1	31	12	7
Garcia, Roberto, Chicago/Texas	.196	38	112	12	22	28	3	0	1	15	0	1	2	25	0	45	2	2
Garcia, Wandel, Kansas City/Rockies	.272	55	184	25	50	66	10	0	2	29	0	2	1	23	0	34	5	5
German, Julian, Detroit/St. Louis	.178	44	90	13	16	20	0	2	0	8	2	0	1	10	0	18	6	2
German, Rigoberto, Detroit/St. Louis	.333	44	132	20	44	52	8	0	0	16	0	1	5	14	0	19	10	3
Giron, Roberto, Toronto West	.000	1	1	0	0	0	0	0	0	0	0	0	0	0	0	0	0	0
Gomez, Bernis, Chicago/Texas	.261	69	226	32	59	76	8	3	1	32	1	5	2	34	2	28	17	4
Gomez, Ramon, Baltimore/White Sox	.232	43	112	26	26	32	3	0	1	13	0	0	2	20	0	25	6	0
Gonzalez, Ever, Yankees/San Diego	.242	40	95	18	23	24	1	0	0	7	1	1	7	16	0	25	10	2
Gonzalez, Freddy, Montreal	.227	35	75	12	17	30	1	0	4	11	0	0	4	14	0	18	6	4
Gonzalez, Juan, Milwaukee	.500	1	2	1	1	1	0	0	0	0	0	0	0	0	0	0	0	0
Gonzalez, Julio, Toyo Carp	.257	51	179	25	46	77	7	3	6	31	0	1	8	23	3	27	8	2
Gonzalez, Luis, Milwaukee	.224	46	107	11	24	26	2	0	0	10	3	0	4	15	0	17	2	5
Gonzalez, Manuel, Angels/Dodgers	.262	66	237	42	62	86	4	10	0	39	5	1	3	41	0	43	17	8
Gonzalez, Singerton, Angels/Dodgers	.192	45	130	20	25	34	7	1	0	15	3	2	0	24	0	13	2	2
Gonzalez, Victor, Oakland	.227	43	75	13	17	18	1	0	0	7	2	0	2	20	0	13	4	4
Gonzalez, Wikleman, Pittsburgh	.299	69	244	47	73	110	10	3	7	47	0	3	9	40	3	15	24	8
Griffin, Juan, Houston	.277	32	94	21	26	37	4	2	1	16	1	1	2	13	1	24	7	1
Gross, Rafael, Angels/Dodgers	.314	67	242	47	76	97	9	3	2	29	5	1	3	41	1	24	14	6
Grullon, Bernardo, Angels/Dodgers	.000	8	0	1	0	0	0	0	0	0	0	0	0	0	0	0	0	0
Guerra, Robert, California	.154	31	91	12	14	18	4	0	0	11	1	2	1	16	0	23	1	3
Guerrero, Diogenes, Oakland	.258	64	209	38	54	92	8	3	8	33	1	1	2	28	3	58	6	4
Guerrero, Hamlet, New York Mets	.221	36	77	14	17	24	1	0	2	13	2	0	6	7	0	10	2	1
Guerrero, Ramon, California	.261	64	226	46	59	85	7	2	5	47	0	5	2	30	1	43	4	5
Guerrero, Vladimir, Montreal	.333	34	105	19	35	42	4	0	1	14	1	2	2	8	0	13	4	2
Guerrero, Wilton, Angels/Dodgers	.355	8	31	6	11	13	0	1	0	4	2	0	0	4	0	3	2	0
Guillen, Carlos, Houston	.250	18	56	12	14	22	4	2	0	8	1	1	1	8	0	12	0	0
Guillen, Franklin, Florida	.000	1	2	0	0	0	0	0	0	0	0	0	0	0	0	1	0	0
Guillen, Jose, Pittsburgh	.226	63	234	39	53	97	3	4	11	41	0	2	5	21	1	55	10	7
Guillermo, Henry, Chicago/Texas	.188	57	186	16	35	41	4	1	0	13	1	3	6	14	0	21	5	1
Henriquez, Fabio, Milwaukee	.257	32	101	17	26	31	5	0	0	6	0	1	0	30	0	18	1	0
Henriquez, Ramon, Detroit/St. Louis	.317	59	205	30	65	106	10	2	9	50	0	4	1	16	1	28	3	4
Hernandez, Carlos, Houston	.306	67	245	52	75	99	13	4	1	36	3	6	5	27	3	29	36	9
Hernandez, Darwin, Pittsburgh	.199	52	146	24	29	35	3	0	1	17	3	2	5	30	2	24	8	3
Hernandez, Jose, Oakland	.245	36	102	15	25	31	2	2	0	15	2	2	0	4	1	12	4	0
Hernandez, Raul, Pittsburgh	.317	58	202	38	64	89	11	1	4	28	3	3	9	25	0	29	15	6
Hernandez, Renny, Atlanta	.240	60	225	26	54	62	5	0	1	24	3	1	13	0	24	6	4	
Herrera, Alvaro, California	.292	40	137	17	40	59	12	2	1	27	1	1	2	1	30	3	37	2
Hidalgo, Bernardino, Detroit/St. Louis	.195	29	77	10	15	19	2	1	0	4	1	1	6	11	0	16	4	3
Hiraldo, Manolo, Pittsburgh	.167	31	66	12	11	16	3	1	0	8	4	0	4	8	0	26	1	0
Jacobo, Ramon, Yankees/San Diego	.214	39	84	9	18	29	2	0	3	14	0	0	0	16	0	19	2	5
James, John, Toronto West	1.000	1	1	1	1	1	0	0	0	0	0	0	0	0	0	0	0	0
Jasco, Eliton, Chicago/Texas	.188	48	160	28	30	41	6	1	1	15	3	0	2	25	0	35	23	5
Jasson, Tomas, California	.205	31	88	15	18	28	5	1	1	11	3	1	1	12	0	28	3	2
Jimenez, Daniel, New York Mets	.252	56	147	21	37	50	5	1	2	21	3	1	2	6	0	49	7	2
Jimenez, Elvis, Kansas City/Rockies	.211	69	223	29	47	67	7	5	1	20	0	2	1	24	0	43	9	1
Jimenez, Ivan, Los Angeles I	.264	33	87	15	23	34	4	0	1	17	1	1	7	18	0	23	1	2
Jimenez, Jose, Cleveland	.229	32	105	11	24	36	5	2	1	9	0	0	3	14	0	22	1	1
Jose, Heriberto, Kansas City/Rockies	.159	55	138	21	22	27	2	0	1	10	4	0	3	25	0	16	6	5

Player, Team	Avg.	G	AB	R	H	TB	2B	3B	HR	RBI	SH	SF	HP	BB	Int. BB	SO	SB	CS
Lantigua, Miguel A., New York Mets	.211	32	71	7	15	21	0	0	2	7	0	2	0	14	1	22	3	4
Lantigua, Nixon, Pittsburgh	.205	27	44	9	9	11	2	0	0	5	1	0	0	6	0	7	3	3
Lara, Edward, Oakland	.343	56	198	24	68	86	7	4	1	34	1	4	2	17	0	22	5	9
Ledesma, Felipe, Angels/Dodgers	.279	57	201	42	56	74	11	2	1	33	3	1	2	25	1	28	6	6
Liriano, Ramon, Milwaukee	.000	1	1	0	0	0	0	0	0	0	0	0	0	0	0	1	0	0
Lopez, Jose L., San Fran./Phil./Hou.	.187	38	241	28	45	63	9	0	3	17	2	2	3	33	0	67	5	0
Lopez, Mendy, Kansas City/Rockies	.276	28	98	15	27	36	5	2	0	20	1	3	0	11	0	5	2	3
Lugo, Urbino, Cleveland	.308	54	182	31	56	71	10	1	1	24	0	0	1	10	0	10	11	5
Luna, Roberto, Cleveland	.095	17	21	3	2	3	1	0	0	1	0	0	0	5	0	6	1	1
Macias, Jose, Montreal	.313	64	211	60	66	92	12	1	4	26	5	0	9	59	0	26	38	16
Madera, Darlen, Oakland	.204	55	137	24	28	33	5	0	0	6	3	0	2	18	0	16	6	2
Maldonado, Franklin, Chicago/Texas	.131	45	122	12	16	20	4	0	0	10	2	3	1	21	1	36	6	5
Marquez, Alexander, Yankees/S.D.	.257	55	187	32	48	61	8	1	1	20	1	1	0	30	0	43	6	4
Marquez, Felix, Seattle	.086	16	35	1	3	4	1	0	0	1	0	1	0	4	0	13	0	0
Martinez, Aristide, Atlanta	.313	59	211	33	66	95	16	2	3	27	1	1	3	37	3	25	8	2
Martinez, Claudio, Los Angeles I	.201	64	179	32	36	41	2	0	1	19	4	3	11	27	1	45	12	7
Martinez, Cristian, K.C./Rockies	.266	33	79	14	21	35	5	0	3	12	0	0	1	20	1	18	3	2
Martinez, David, Toronto West	.118	27	51	9	6	7	1	0	0	2	0	0	0	13	0	12	4	1
Martinez, Federico, Atlanta	.205	42	117	20	24	25	1	0	0	10	0	0	2	25	0	20	4	0
Martinez, Jose Luis, Cleveland	.277	38	101	14	28	40	7	1	1	13	0	0	3	13	1	20	1	1
Martinez, Jose R., Seattle	.209	45	129	15	27	37	1	0	3	17	0	2	5	22	0	34	1	3
Martinez, Juan J., Toronto East	.304	67	273	41	83	131	15	3	9	63	0	4	4	17	2	45	7	6
Martinez, Leo, Yankees/San Diego	.286	6	21	2	6	6	0	0	0	2	1	0	0	2	0	3	1	1
Martinez, Rafael, Los Angeles I	.292	56	185	33	54	73	7	3	2	30	3	5	2	36	2	27	5	6
Mateo, Francisco, Milwaukee	1.000	1	1	0	1	1	0	0	0	0	0	0	0	0	0	0	0	0
Mateo, Victor, Toyo Carp	.316	11	38	4	12	14	2	0	0	6	0	0	0	4	0	7	4	1
Matos, Jose Luis, Cleveland	.174	8	23	1	4	6	0	1	0	1	0	1	0	0	0	6	1	2
Matos, Miguel, San Fran./Phil./Hou.	.212	69	259	26	55	67	6	0	2	32	0	4	2	27	0	54	2	0
Matos, Wellinton, Toyo Carp	.214	22	56	10	12	15	1	1	0	7	1	0	2	4	1	18	0	1
Mega, Pedro, Los Angeles I	.233	31	90	26	21	25	2	1	0	9	4	1	3	27	1	23	3	1
Melendez, Pastor, Pittsburgh	.280	67	243	44	68	82	8	3	0	27	2	3	3	39	4	29	42	14
Melo, Juan, Yankees/San Diego	.252	52	147	25	37	48	3	1	2	15	5	2	4	27	2	20	3	5
Mendez, Carlos, Yankees/San Diego	.256	42	125	16	32	34	2	0	0	12	0	2	0	11	1	19	2	2
Mendez, Rodolfo, Toyo Carp	.275	27	102	25	28	51	4	2	5	21	0	1	4	13	0	20	3	2
Mendoza, Carlos, New York Mets	.240	36	96	25	23	27	1	0	1	14	1	1	1	23	1	10	7	5
Mendoza, Jesus, Baltimore/White Sox	.371	61	248	62	92	135	17	1	8	52	3	5	2	27	0	15	11	3
Mercedes, Matias, Detroit/St. Louis	.221	60	204	31	45	71	13	2	3	23	4	3	3	17	0	35	11	7
Meza, German, Seattle	.197	33	71	10	14	22	2	0	2	13	4	1	8	6	0	9	4	3
Miranda, Walter, Florida	.250	4	8	1	2	2	0	0	0	1	0	0	0	1	0	1	0	0
Montero, Joselyn, Florida	.301	68	256	32	77	111	10	0	8	47	0	5	5	18	0	58	1	3
Mora, Raymond, Cleveland	.319	25	69	17	22	32	4	3	0	12	0	1	0	8	0	9	1	1
Morales, Jose, Atlanta	.185	42	135	18	25	30	3	1	0	11	1	1	2	21	0	41	3	5
Moreno, Juan, New York Mets	.205	43	117	15	24	38	8	0	2	18	0	1	1	11	0	20	2	0
Mota, Alfonzo, California	.348	62	224	56	78	107	17	3	2	46	1	0	6	57	7	22	13	7
Mota, Cristian, Cleveland	.255	49	165	21	42	50	6	1	0	11	0	3	2	7	0	22	5	2
Mota, Gleydel, New York Mets	.291	60	189	49	55	78	10	2	3	27	1	2	1	47	2	34	17	9
Munoz, Juan, Pittsburgh	.222	57	153	25	34	41	5	1	0	13	7	1	5	21	2	11	9	5
Navas, Jose, Oakland	.237	40	135	17	32	37	5	0	0	24	2	3	1	19	0	21	2	0
Nieves, Miguel, Milwaukee	.201	54	144	21	29	45	4	3	2	14	5	2	6	22	0	25	6	3
Noriega, Kelvin, Yankees/San Diego	.266	67	237	35	63	85	9	2	3	40	1	5	3	46	5	24	6	4
Nova, Pascual, Yankees/San Diego	.243	62	181	29	44	65	9	0	4	30	0	6	9	34	1	65	14	8
Novas, Teodoro, Seattle	.257	53	167	25	43	56	7	0	2	25	1	1	2	21	1	22	8	4
Nunez, Euripides, Balt./White Sox	.195	54	123	38	24	28	1	0	1	14	0	2	6	32	0	29	13	3
Nunez, Julio C., Toronto East	.000	1	0	0	0	0	0	0	0	0	0	0	0	0	0	0	0	0
Nunez, Maximo, Toronto East	.263	67	262	49	69	116	17	3	8	48	0	3	1	22	0	38	6	5
Nunez, Primitivo, Pittsburgh	.235	64	200	46	47	59	5	2	1	20	4	1	10	33	0	37	21	7
Nunez, Sergio, Kansas City/Rockies	.341	70	249	63	85	113	18	2	2	35	0	1	3	50	7	17	32	16
Oliva, Osvaldo, Atlanta	.240	60	225	29	54	82	13	0	5	30	2	0	4	26	0	71	6	1
Oliveros, Ricardo, Montreal	.226	22	62	8	14	17	1	1	0	5	1	0	0	11	0	10	1	0
Olmedo, Juan, Milwaukee	.200	15	35	5	7	7	0	0	0	1	0	0	0	4	1	8	1	0
Ossers, Edwin, Toyo Carp	.232	36	82	18	19	27	2	3	0	10	0	3	0	12	0	21	2	3
Ovalles, Homy, Montreal	.172	20	58	5	10	16	3	0	1	5	0	0	3	0	0	21	0	0
Ozoria, Douglas, Yankees/San Diego	.217	52	161	22	35	43	8	0	0	13	1	1	2	26	2	32	7	0
Ozuna, Rafael, Angels/Dodgers	.245	61	212	36	52	62	4	3	0	29	5	3	4	34	0	18	8	5
Padilla, Rafael, Baltimore/White Sox	.280	48	150	26	42	65	6	1	5	19	0	2	2	15	1	29	0	1
Patrone, Carlos, Atlanta	.319	43	166	21	53	73	14	0	2	24	1	3	2	5	0	8	1	0
Paulino, Arturo, Oakland	.285	48	137	25	39	60	7	1	4	17	0	2	3	18	2	26	7	4
Paulino, Esteban, New York Mets	.241	20	29	7	7	10	0	0	1	3	1	0	0	5	0	4	1	0
Paulino, John, San Fran./Phil./Hou.	.196	45	143	12	28	37	6	0	1	13	1	2	2	26	1	24	3	1
Pedra, Juan, Los Angeles I	.296	50	152	27	45	54	7	1	0	20	5	2	3	32	0	20	1	5
Pemberton, Juan, Montreal	.212	43	146	21	31	35	1	0	1	14	0	1	4	16	1	26	3	1
Pena, Alejandro, Cleveland	.283	63	233	45	66	98	17	0	5	31	4	2	5	21	1	21	21	7
Pena, Angel, Angels/Dodgers	.280	50	168	27	47	57	3	2	1	24	4	1	1	10	0	41	6	0
Pena, Charlies, Toyo Carp	.372	70	282	74	105	171	22	7	10	69	0	4	3	44	3	31	13	4
Pena, Jose Aridio, Cleveland	.308	11	26	5	8	8	0	0	0	2	1	0	1	0	0	3	1	0
Pena, Ramon, Toronto East	.308	49	143	19	44	60	4	0	4	21	2	0	5	30	0	18	6	4
Peralta, Alexander, Yankees/S.D.	.200	60	190	27	38	53	5	5	0	15	4	1	8	23	1	33	9	5
Perdomo, Felix, Toyo Carp	.280	59	225	60	63	74	7	2	0	35	2	4	5	48	1	28	20	2
Perez, Cesar, Chicago/Texas	.222	24	72	10	16	20	1	0	1	5	3	0	0	11	0	13	5	1
Perez, Cesar, Los Angeles I	.250	2	4	0	1	1	0	0	0	1	0	0	0	0	0	0	0	0
Perez, Eduis, Los Angeles I	.000	2	3	0	0	0	0	0	0	1	0	0	0	0	0	1	0	0
Perez, Edwin, Cleveland	.285	45	137	26	39	45	4	1	0	17	2	2	1	17	1	17	3	5
Perez, Juan, Oakland	.000	1	0	0	0	0	0	0	0	0	0	0	0	0	0	0	0	0
Perez, Marcos, Houston	.279	44	147	24	41	50	6	0	1	19	1	2	2	7	0	17	2	3
Perez, Nelson, San Fran./Phil./Hou.	.281	59	224	22	63	81	10	1	2	31	2	1	2	13	2	37	1	2
Perez, Santiago, Detroit/St. Louis	.263	58	171	28	45	55	6	2	0	17	3	2	2	20	0	22	17	8
Perez, Wilman, Florida	.187	54	166	27	31	53	5	4	3	14	1	0	2	24	2	66	4	1
Pierret, Juan, Los Angeles I	.500	2	2	0	1	1	0	0	0	0	0	0	0	0	0	0	0	0
Pimentel, Jose, Los Angeles I	.324	61	216	45	70	95	6	2	5	35	14	5	4	34	1	34	9	6
Pineda, Andres L., Florida	.000	2	1	0	0	0	0	0	0	0	1	0	0	1	0	0	0	0
Pineda, Hector, San Fran./Phil./Hou.	.150	35	113	7	17	23	4	1	0	7	0	0	2	18	0	33	2	1
Piters, Moises, California	.359	36	76	16	30	43	7	0	2	11	0	0	2	13	0	11	7	4
Polanco, Enohel, New York Mets	.311	53	148	33	46	79	9	3	6	31	1	1	4	38	0	25	6	6
Polanco, Juan, Oakland	.262	61	195	36	51	71	5	0	5	31	1	1	2	34	3	36	6	4

Player, Team	Avg.	G	AB	R	H	TB	2B	3B	HR	RBI	SH	SF	HP	BB	Int. BB	SO	SB	CS
Polo, Reynaldo, Atlanta	.182	20	66	11	12	12	0	0	0	4	0	0	2	12	0	15	9	2
Portes, Miguel, Yankees/San Diego	.322	61	214	35	69	86	8	0	3	28	1	3	5	23	4	15	14	9
Prensi, Dagoberto, Toronto West	.290	68	241	33	70	114	15	1	9	44	0	4	8	22	1	49	23	9
Puente, Roberto, Seattle	.268	60	190	35	51	96	6	0	13	46	0	3	4	37	2	70	2	0
Quezada, Adalberto, S.F./Phil./Hou.	.189	48	164	23	31	38	2	1	1	10	0	0	10	26	0	32	8	4
Ramirez, Daniel, New York Mets	.321	73	271	48	87	116	14	3	3	50	4	4	5	27	1	28	23	12
Ramirez, Jorge, Angels/Dodgers	.170	37	112	16	19	33	4	5	0	12	0	1	5	11	0	32	1	1
Ramirez, Jose Luis, Pittsburgh	.280	55	186	34	52	78	13	2	3	32	4	1	6	39	2	33	10	1
Ramirez, Jose, Milwaukee	.000	1	2	0	0	0	0	0	0	0	0	0	0	0	0	1	0	0
Ramirez, Juan, Milwaukee	.143	14	35	4	5	5	0	0	0	1	0	0	2	6	0	6	0	0
Ramos, Ambiorix, Florida	.000	2	1	0	0	0	0	0	0	0	0	0	0	1	0	1	0	0
Ramos, Jose, Houston	.234	60	201	44	47	63	9	2	1	25	5	1	0	59	0	33	13	6
Rayo, Francisco, Angels/Dodgers	.297	33	37	6	11	19	1	2	1	5	1	0	2	3	0	8	1	0
Rendon, Juan, Chicago/Texas	.281	59	224	34	63	80	4	2	3	34	3	5	6	17	0	23	5	3
Reyes, Francis, Toyo Carp	.207	29	82	10	17	18	1	0	0	7	1	0	0	11	1	12	2	3
Reyes, Jose, Detroit/St. Louis	.231	32	78	5	18	22	1	0	1	7	0	1	1	10	0	21	1	1
Reyes, Jose, Pittsburgh	.341	35	88	21	30	54	9	0	5	30	2	2	3	21	1	14	7	1
Reyes, Luis, Florida	.667	2	3	0	2	2	0	0	0	0	0	0	0	1	0	0	0	0
Reyes, Pablo, Cleveland	.276	54	192	29	53	68	7	4	0	20	0	2	2	18	0	19	6	6
Reyes, Renee, Toyo Carp	.190	47	147	30	28	46	7	4	1	25	1	4	4	33	0	28	3	3
Reyes, Winston, San Fran./Phil./Hou.	.245	70	249	38	61	83	13	3	1	23	2	1	2	44	1	30	1	0
Rincones, Wanner, Balt./White Sox	.314	54	169	40	53	86	12	0	7	48	0	4	1	50	0	16	2	1
Rivera, Juan, Chicago/Texas	.207	41	116	14	24	29	3	1	0	5	2	0	2	25	0	30	4	4
Roa, Frank, Kansas City/Rockies	.262	59	191	40	50	64	5	3	1	23	0	1	4	18	0	30	19	14
Roche, Marlon, Houston	.338	59	204	46	69	91	13	3	1	37	2	2	2	32	0	22	7	0
Rodriguez, Alberto, Oakland	.236	42	110	20	26	41	7	1	2	9	3	3	0	12	0	33	4	3
Rodriguez, Eddy, Los Angeles I	.400	9	30	5	12	13	1	0	0	8	0	1	1	6	0	4	0	0
Rodriguez, Jose, Atlanta	.263	63	236	46	62	83	17	2	0	29	2	3	0	35	0	33	6	5
Rodriguez, Luis, Los Angeles I	.236	55	195	40	46	69	4	5	3	30	3	2	9	27	2	44	4	4
Rodriguez, Oakland	.319	57	160	51	51	76	7	3	4	26	1	0	2	56	0	25	18	8
Rojas, Jose, Montreal	.189	50	143	16	27	29	2	0	0	13	4	1	3	24	0	24	4	7
Rojas, Roberto, Pittsburgh	.259	28	81	12	21	24	3	0	0	8	0	2	0	10	0	20	3	4
Romero, Jovanny, Milwaukee	.267	7	15	3	4	4	0	0	0	2	0	0	0	4	0	3	0	2
Rondon, Alexander, Oakland	.271	59	166	27	45	59	9	1	1	21	2	0	6	28	0	13	3	3
Roque, Francisco, Milwaukee	.204	61	181	13	37	43	4	1	0	20	6	0	2	17	0	18	7	4
Rosario, Felix, Toronto East	.308	66	237	67	73	117	10	5	8	63	1	4	1	50	3	33	32	6
Rosario, Nelson, Toronto East	.000	1	0	1	0	0	0	0	0	0	0	0	0	0	0	0	0	0
Rosario, Sotero, Milwaukee	.288	42	111	20	32	45	7	0	2	16	4	0	2	4	0	24	1	1
Ruan, Rafael, Montreal	.276	63	232	42	64	108	6	1	12	48	0	5	6	21	2	34	4	2
Ruiz, Cesar, Detroit/St. Louis	.273	67	209	43	57	89	10	8	2	27	1	1	3	49	4	38	15	9
Ruiz, Justo, Baltimore/White Sox	.222	32	99	15	22	33	3	1	2	17	0	0	1	11	0	24	5	0
Ruiz, Wilmer, Los Angeles I	.500	1	2	1	1	2	1	0	0	1	0	0	0	0	0	0	0	0
Salazar, Charlie, Yankees/San Diego	.164	21	61	8	10	17	4	0	1	6	1	0	0	12	0	13	0	0
Salazar, Tomas, Baltimore/White Sox	.195	36	87	8	17	19	2	0	0	9	0	1	1	19	0	24	0	0
Salcedo, Elias, Kansas City/Rockies	.129	9	31	0	4	4	0	0	0	0	0	0	2	1	0	8	0	0
Salomon, Domingo, Atlanta	.353	56	215	32	76	103	23	2	0	26	2	6	2	14	1	19	8	3
Salvador, Freddy, Balt./White Sox	.273	58	165	41	45	54	6	0	1	26	0	7	2	51	2	23	8	2
Sanavia, Enrique, Los Angeles I	.262	22	61	10	16	26	4	0	2	12	0	0	4	11	0	17	0	0
Sanchez, Jose, Yankees/San Diego	.189	20	53	3	10	11	1	0	0	4	0	0	3	10	0	17	3	7
Sanchez, Nelson, Toronto East	.218	58	147	25	32	49	7	2	2	23	1	2	7	21	1	24	7	1
Sanchez, Omar, Toronto East	.333	66	225	66	75	91	8	4	0	30	4	2	2	69	1	24	40	12
Santa, Milciades, Toronto West	.311	68	228	37	71	90	10	3	1	35	4	5	0	39	0	39	17	15
Santana, Francisco, Oakland	.222	49	90	15	20	28	3	1	1	13	3	0	4	11	0	33	3	0
Santana, Franklin, S.F./Phil./Hou.	.210	31	105	6	22	24	2	0	0	4	1	0	0	8	0	10	0	1
Santana, Luis, Angels/Dodgers	.172	19	58	7	10	16	2	2	0	7	0	2	1	13	0	12	0	1
Santana, Miguel, Pittsburgh	.280	52	132	36	37	53	7	0	3	20	2	1	3	17	0	25	19	8
Santana, Ramon, Houston	.293	68	256	56	75	127	13	6	9	60	1	4	1	41	0	40	11	3
Santander, Vicente, Florida	.170	50	153	19	26	35	6	0	1	11	3	3	7	13	1	44	3	3
Santelise, Osvaldo, Balt./White Sox	.147	13	34	5	5	7	2	0	0	1	0	0	0	5	0	17	3	0
Santos, Rafael, Pittsburgh	.000	1	1	0	0	0	0	0	0	0	0	0	0	0	0	1	0	0
Schecker, Luis, Oakland	.262	57	172	19	45	70	7	0	6	31	0	0	2	20	0	26	3	3
Sepulveda, Elvin, Seattle	.132	20	53	3	7	7	0	0	0	3	0	0	3	8	0	19	0	2
Serafin, Ricardo, San Fran./Phil./Hou.	.198	28	81	9	16	20	4	0	0	2	2	0	2	12	0	22	4	0
Sierra, Santo, Montreal	.252	38	131	22	33	47	5	0	3	12	1	1	4	25	1	36	0	5
Solano, Fausto, Toronto East	.318	67	264	79	84	115	8	1	7	26	1	3	2	49	3	35	25	9
Soriano, Carlos, New York Mets	.312	63	202	49	63	102	9	0	10	48	0	4	5	43	0	27	6	5
Soriano, Juan C., New York Mets	.285	65	172	33	49	63	5	0	3	25	5	2	2	31	0	21	4	6
Sosa, Gamalier, California	.274	57	168	35	46	56	6	2	0	22	0	1	2	38	1	22	8	1
Sosa, Juan, Los Angeles I	.278	63	237	51	66	81	7	4	0	39	14	3	4	45	0	52	8	2
Sosa, Ramon, Cleveland	.311	57	219	28	68	93	16	0	3	37	0	2	0	15	2	35	5	4
Soto, Manuel, Baltimore/White Sox	.296	66	280	80	83	111	15	2	3	36	3	1	0	40	0	51	28	4
Sterling, Jose, Atlanta	.242	41	128	19	31	33	2	0	0	17	2	1	4	24	0	13	10	6
Suarez, Ramon, Kansas City/Rockies	.156	32	90	9	14	18	4	0	0	9	1	0	0	17	0	21	1	2
Suero, Miguel, Milwaukee	.182	21	22	1	4	4	0	0	0	1	0	0	1	1	0	3	0	0
Tatis, Fernando, Chicago/Texas	.273	59	198	22	54	73	5	1	4	34	2	1	4	27	0	12	7	3
Tatis, Milton, Yankees/San Diego	.255	23	47	12	12	24	2	2	2	10	2	1	1	12	1	8	1	1
Taveras, Franklin, Cleveland	.250	27	92	15	23	28	3	1	0	7	2	1	0	7	0	23	2	4
Tejada, Jose, Florida	.000	1	2	0	0	0	0	0	0	0	0	0	0	0	0	0	0	0
Tremols, Johanny, Pittsburgh	.190	25	58	7	11	13	2	0	0	2	0	1	0	6	0	3	1	0
Ulloa, Cristian, Toronto West	.174	48	149	16	26	32	2	2	0	12	2	0	1	20	1	45	2	1
Urena, Fausto, Angels/Dodgers	.245	70	245	49	60	86	14	6	0	36	1	2	4	45	1	37	18	5
Urvina, Dan, Los Angeles I	.000	1	2	0	0	0	0	0	0	1	0	0	0	1	0	0	0	0
Valdespino, Jose, Toronto East	.224	64	192	37	43	54	5	0	2	27	1	4	7	37	0	24	8	3
Valdez, Socrates, Seattle	.290	51	155	38	45	68	6	1	5	26	3	0	9	26	0	24	11	3
Valera, Johanny, New York Mets	.247	35	89	15	22	37	3	0	4	18	1	2	1	12	0	17	2	0
Valera, Willy, Cleveland	.250	42	136	21	34	46	6	3	0	18	2	0	0	13	0	25	4	4
Vargas, Cesar, Toronto West	.158	40	95	21	15	19	2	1	0	10	5	0	1	12	0	31	10	6
Vargas, Franklin, California	.313	45	134	29	42	48	4	1	0	22	4	0	0	26	0	19	16	10
Vasquez, Carlos, Los Angeles I	.000	2	3	0	0	0	0	0	0	0	0	0	0	0	0	1	0	0
Ventura, Wilfredo, Oakland	.236	23	55	5	13	18	2	0	1	5	0	0	0	6	0	14	2	1
Veras, Gabriel, Seattle	.196	40	102	14	20	22	2	0	0	5	1	0	1	21	0	25	4	1
Veras, Quivilo, Milwaukee	.200	30	70	6	14	15	1	0	0	8	2	1	1	13	0	14	0	0
Villalobos, Carlos, Seattle	.295	60	200	51	59	99	10	0	10	36	0	1	6	30	0	46	9	2
Villalona, Kadil, Toronto East	.361	65	249	52	90	125	8	6	5	45	0	2	4	30	2	19	17	7

Player, Team	Avg.	G	AB	R	H	TB	2B	3B	HR	RBI	SH	SF	HP	BB	Int. BB	SO	SB	CS
Vilonar, Henry, New York Mets	.355	72	242	47	86	123	13	3	6	38	2	1	6	33	2	43	12	6
Wilson, Jaime, Kansas City/Rockies	.181	56	166	19	30	38	6	1	0	17	0	0	8	32	2	47	5	0
Zapata, Luis, Montreal	.200	19	45	2	9	9	0	0	0	3	0	1	0	4	0	13	0	0
Zerpa, Mauro, Baltimore/White Sox	.377	44	159	34	60	85	10	0	5	32	2	3	2	23	1	10	5	0
Zorrilla, Delio, Toyo Carp	.260	32	73	23	19	22	3	0	0	11	2	0	4	17	0	11	5	1
Zorrilla, Julio, New York Mets	.174	48	144	28	25	33	3	1	1	14	4	1	0	15	0	17	12	0

PITCHING

TEAM

Team	ERA	G	CG	ShO	Sv.	IP	H	R	ER	HR	HB	BB	Int. BB	SO	WP	Bk.
Toyo Carp	2.52	70	15	5	18	622.2	526	234	174	21	13	238	0	390	28	4
Cleveland	3.19	70	6	2	11	595.1	531	347	220	9	36	321	11	387	33	12
Toronto East	3.22	67	6	3	24	575.1	578	273	206	18	32	251	12	399	41	6
Angels/Dodgers	3.45	70	9	3	11	589.2	564	335	226	11	32	289	20	363	31	9
Oakland	3.53	74	18	2	13	627.0	541	328	245	20	52	305	10	412	43	5
Pittsburgh	3.63	69	3	1	13	598.2	544	340	241	28	22	379	5	493	59	10
Los Angeles I	3.80	70	4	5	18	596.1	561	345	252	36	38	306	1	416	54	6
New York Mets	3.81	74	6	4	16	611.0	563	333	260	53	42	295	16	446	54	9
Yankees/San Diego	3.94	69	5	4	14	580.2	559	335	254	26	44	290	6	402	57	13
California	4.04	70	2	4	25	616.2	619	401	277	35	26	309	19	392	51	13
Chicago/Texas	4.05	70	7	1	7	570.2	614	417	258	32	34	298	4	295	49	6
Houston	4.51	70	7	2	11	607.0	607	427	304	19	61	320	2	364	83	14
Toronto West	4.53	70	6	4	13	582.2	563	406	293	26	45	392	20	365	79	11
Florida	4.58	70	7	3	12	567.0	616	404	290	29	52	334	15	369	75	8
Montreal	4.85	68	9	1	10	567.2	621	414	306	45	70	332	2	309	64	3
Detroit/St. Louis	4.96	72	3	5	15	582.2	604	427	322	35	57	398	13	412	58	8
K.C./Rockies	5.23	70	2	2	13	579.2	674	457	337	14	32	355	1	298	50	11
Atlanta	5.40	70	4	1	10	608.0	695	511	365	25	47	441	16	318	80	13
S.F./Phil./Houston	5.48	70	10	0	6	599.2	741	532	364	23	34	312	7	333	64	26
Milwaukee	5.52	68	16	2	8	561.1	644	441	344	37	48	329	10	390	68	17
Baltimore/White Sox	5.76	70	4	2	11	609.1	684	525	390	57	31	420	7	446	104	17
Seattle	12.33	69	9	0	14	567.0	573	445	365	56	51	412	15	373	73	14

INDIVIDUAL

(Leading qualifiers for earned-run average leadership—80 or more innings)

Pitcher, Team	W	L	Pct.	ERA	G	GS	CG	GF	ShO	Sv.	IP	H	R	ER	HR	HB	BB	Int. BB	SO	WP
Avila, Edwin, California	4	2	.667	1.09	18	8	0	10	2	4	82.2	54	27	10	0	4	28	2	78	6
Silva, Hernan, Oakland	7	2	.778	1.40	14	12	2	1	2	0	90.0	57	23	14	2	8	27	0	62	3
Aracena, Ramon, Toyo Carp	7	2	.778	1.59	13	12	3	1	0	0	85.0	66	22	15	4	2	25	0	54	3
Martinez, Gustavo, Ang./Dod.	8	4	.667	1.83	14	13	5	0	1	0	88.2	72	47	18	1	6	21	4	44	0
Ramirez, Felix, Toyo Carp	9	4	.692	1.95	18	14	5	4	2	1	110.2	87	39	24	2	3	44	0	96	3
Lois, Newman, Houston	3	2	.600	2.21	15	13	1	0	1	0	89.2	65	39	22	0	6	41	0	60	11
Colome, Jesus, Chicago/Texas	5	5	.500	2.31	16	13	3	3	0	0	97.1	81	42	25	5	1	46	2	58	7
Sanchez, Jesus, New York Mets	7	3	.700	2.40	16	13	2	1	2	0	82.1	63	30	22	6	2	36	0	94	5
Diese, Jose, Toyo Carp	10	3	.769	2.66	18	13	4	4	1	1	91.1	80	38	27	1	1	37	0	52	4
Liquet, Wilton, Angels/Dodgers	7	3	.700	2.79	13	13	2	0	0	0	84.0	75	30	26	1	3	22	2	71	7

Departmental leaders: G—Edward Perez, 33; W—Diese, 10; L—Connors, 12; Pct.—Delgado, 1.000; GS—Agramonte, 18; CG—Carmona, F. Ramirez, 5; GF—Edward Perez, 31; ShO—E. Avila, F. Ramirez, J. Sanchez, Silva, 2; Sv.—Romero, 13; IP—L. Figueroa, 117.1; H—V. Rodriguez, 125; R—Connors, 85; ER—Connors, 68; HR—Carmona, 12; HB—L. Figueroa, 15; BB—Albino, 63; IBB—Paulino, 7; SO—Montoya, 97; WP—Ja. DeLeon, Vicentino, 16.

(All pitchers—listed alphabetically)

Pitcher, Team	W	L	Pct.	ERA	G	GS	CG	GF	ShO	Sv.	IP	H	R	ER	HR	HB	BB	Int. BB	SO	WP
Abreu, Jose Mi., S.F./Phil./Hou.	0	2	.000	6.17	5	1	0	4	0	0	11.2	15	16	8	0	4	15	0	5	3
Abreu, Kennedy, California	3	5	.375	6.00	17	8	0	4	0	1	51.0	72	46	34	2	4	19	1	26	3
Abreu, Pedro, Pittsburgh	5	3	.625	3.78	14	13	2	1	0	1	78.2	87	46	33	4	1	27	0	54	3
Acosta, Roberto, Toronto East	7	4	.636	2.25	19	6	3	11	1	4	76.0	74	31	19	2	1	19	1	42	2
Agramonte, Freddy, L.A. I	8	3	.727	3.22	18	18	1	0	0	0	86.2	63	42	31	7	12	50	0	54	3
Aguasvivas, Jose, Pittsburgh	0	3	.000	4.79	17	0	0	11	0	0	20.2	25	14	11	1	0	7	0	13	1
Aguilar, Carlos, Yankees/S.D.	3	1	.750	4.13	11	11	0	0	0	0	61.0	57	35	28	2	4	36	0	36	6
Albino, Rogers, Chicago/Texas	2	7	.222	5.31	16	14	1	2	0	0	76.1	85	63	45	6	4	63	1	32	9
Alcantara, Miguel, K.C./Rockies	4	4	.500	6.10	27	0	0	8	0	0	62.0	82	53	42	1	2	28	0	24	4
Almanzar, Carlos, Toronto East	5	2	.714	3.38	16	9	0	5	0	2	69.1	60	35	26	5	3	32	2	59	3
Almonte, Hector, Florida	1	6	.143	4.79	13	7	1	4	0	1	56.1	59	39	30	2	10	29	2	20	6
Alvarez, Juan, Montreal	2	4	.333	3.67	13	6	1	6	0	1	41.2	50	27	17	5	6	21	0	20	3
Alvarez, Marcos, Detroit/St. L.	4	4	.429	4.08	15	5	1	5	0	1	53.0	51	39	24	2	4	26	2	33	5
Alvarez, Melvin, Montreal	1	0	1.000	2.57	4	0	0	3	0	1	7.0	7	2	2	0	1	2	0	6	0
Aquino, Julio, Los Angeles I	3	6	.333	3.04	18	1	0	14	0	5	50.1	50	27	17	2	1	11	0	31	5
Aracena, Ramon, Toyo Carp	7	2	.778	1.59	13	12	3	1	0	0	85.0	66	22	15	4	2	25	0	54	3
Arias, Cesarin, Chicago/Texas	2	5	.286	1.70	13	5	0	2	0	0	42.1	34	22	8	0	2	18	0	19	1
Arias, Juan, Detroit/St. Louis	1	2	.333	11.32	11	1	0	2	0	0	20.2	27	27	26	1	5	34	2	8	2
Arias, Julio A., Toyo Carp	6	3	.667	3.19	17	12	3	3	1	2	98.2	86	45	35	4	2	27	0	44	5
Arias, Miguel, Angels/Dodgers	1	2	.333	9.82	10	6	0	2	0	0	25.2	36	35	28	1	1	24	0	22	1
Arvelo, Luis, Milwaukee	0	1	.000	81.82	1	0	0	0	0	0	0.1	3	4	3	0	0	1	0	0	0
Avila, Edwin, California	4	2	.667	1.09	18	8	0	10	2	4	82.2	54	27	10	0	4	28	2	78	6
Avila, Jose, Pittsburgh	0	1	.000	1.42	3	1	0	1	0	0	6.1	3	3	1	0	0	9	0	5	2
Ayala, Fernando, Los Angeles I	8	3	.727	3.07	17	15	1	1	0	0	91.0	72	48	31	5	3	43	0	81	11
Aybar, Jose V., New York Mets	1	3	.750	2.00	12	0	0	10	0	4	18.0	15	6	4	0	0	13	1	14	1
Aybar, Manuel, Detroit/St. Louis	4	4	.500	3.15	13	11	1	1	0	0	71.1	54	33	25	1	3	33	0	66	4
Baez, Homer, Pittsburgh	4	1	.800	1.86	9	9	0	0	0	0	48.1	29	14	10	4	0	36	0	41	1
Balbuena, Roberto, Chi./Texas	3	6	.333	2.20	25	1	0	21	0	6	65.0	64	33	18	1	8	28	0	54	1
Barrios, Manuel, Houston	6	1	.857	4.63	13	12	2	0	0	0	77.2	77	57	40	1	5	23	0	59	11

Pitcher, Team	W	L	Pct.	ERA	G	GS	CG	GF	ShO	Sv.	IP	H	R	ER	HR	HB	BB	Int. BB	SO	WP
Batista, Mario, Pittsburgh	4	2	.667	4.30	16	6	0	4	0	0	52.1	34	29	25	4	5	53	0	54	12
Bautista, Juan, Atlanta	0	0	.000	11.37	4	0	0	1	0	0	6.1	8	9	8	0	1	4	0	4	3
Bautista, Perfecto, Detroit/St. L.	0	0	.000	81.81	1	0	0	0	0	0	0.1	1	3	3	0	1	1	0	0	1
Bautista, Sudequi, Yankees/S.D.	0	1	.000	10.31	7	5	0	1	0	0	18.1	20	25	21	0	5	31	0	17	5
Bele, Roble, Chicago/Texas	0	1	.000	1.17	3	0	0	3	0	0	7.2	6	4	1	0	0	4	1	4	1
Belioso, Chester, Yankees/S.D.	3	1	.750	2.45	10	6	1	3	0	2	47.2	32	14	13	2	8	21	0	51	4
Berroa, Gabriel, Seattle	0	0	.000	0.00	1	0	0	1	0	0	1.0	0	0	0	0	1	0	1	0	0
Betancourt, Damaso, L.A. I	3	4	.429	2.57	24	4	1	18	1	8	73.2	55	29	21	3	4	29	0	75	6
Blanco, Ender, Montreal	0	1	.000	15.00	1	0	0	0	0	0	3.0	3	6	5	3	0	5	0	3	1
Blanco, Roger, Seattle	0	5	.000	8.75	11	7	0	1	0	0	23.2	33	31	23	2	8	21	0	12	1
Blanco, Romer, Chicago/Texas	0	1	.000	4.40	3	3	0	0	0	0	14.1	10	10	7	0	2	9	0	10	3
Bonilla, Danny, Seattle	7	2	.778	2.87	28	0	0	11	0	3	84.2	75	36	27	6	1	28	5	80	7
Brazoban, Delfin, Toronto West	2	3	.400	6.75	19	3	0	14	0	0	52.0	57	48	39	6	7	45	3	33	6
Brito, Jose, California	1	1	.500	6.34	11	5	0	4	0	0	6.0	13	5	4	2	0	3	0	2	0
Brito, Jose, Milwaukee	2	1	.667	1.19	3	3	2	0	0	0	22.2	21	10	3	1	1	12	0	18	0
Brito, Silvano, Seattle	0	0	.000	10.78	1	0	0	1	0	0	1.2	2	2	2	0	1	0	0	0	0
Burgos, Alix, Yankees/San Diego	0	1	.000	2.51	8	0	0	7	0	2	14.1	16	5	4	2	0	2	0	5	0
Burgos, Danny, Yankees/S.D.	0	1	.000	1.13	3	0	0	2	0	0	8.0	3	2	1	0	1	2	0	2	0
Cabarcas, Carlos, K.C./Rockies	0	0	.000	....	1	0	0	1	0	0	0.0	2	0	0	0	0	0	0	0	0
Cabrera, Carlos, Oakland	2	1	.667	4.02	11	6	0	1	0	0	31.1	25	18	14	0	8	28	2	24	1
Campusano, Carlos, Seattle	2	1	.667	6.05	15	1	0	6	0	0	38.2	37	31	26	5	4	30	0	22	3
Cana, Nelson, Florida	5	5	.500	3.61	14	13	1	0	0	0	77.1	79	53	31	4	3	48	1	69	13
Carderon, Jorge, Atlanta	3	4	.429	5.17	13	12	1	0	0	0	62.2	80	50	36	2	2	54	1	25	8
Carmona, Roberto, Seattle	8	7	.533	4.56	17	16	5	0	0	0	100.2	90	59	51	12	7	52	1	94	6
Carrion, Jorge, Milwaukee	3	3	.500	6.96	14	4	0	3	0	0	42.2	55	37	33	5	4	29	0	23	5
Carrion, Jose, Montreal	0	4	.000	10.97	10	5	0	3	0	0	21.1	30	37	26	3	11	34	0	12	7
Cartaya, Anibal, Balt./White Sox	0	3	.000	9.25	17	0	0	7	0	1	24.1	27	29	25	4	1	31	0	22	4
Carvajal, Tomas, California	1	1	.500	7.00	3	2	0	0	0	0	9.0	14	11	7	0	1	2	1	8	0
Castillo, Luis, Florida	0	0	.000	0.00	1	0	0	1	0	0	1.0	1	0	0	0	1	0	0	0	0
Castillo, Miguel, Balt./White Sox.	3	2	.600	6.50	17	2	0	8	1	1	45.2	31	44	33	2	3	55	0	62	15
Castillo, Sandy, Atlanta	3	3	.500	3.34	14	9	2	2	0	0	67.1	65	39	25	3	5	31	0	41	4
Castillo, Victor, Toronto West	2	3	.400	4.35	20	7	0	10	0	3	62.0	66	46	30	1	2	49	4	55	13
Cera, Aquiles, Angels/Dodgers	2	2	.500	3.83	21	0	0	5	0	1	49.1	54	33	21	2	0	24	0	24	5
Collado, Hugo, Oakland	2	5	.286	5.21	13	9	0	2	0	1	46.2	48	39	27	3	5	38	0	14	8
Colome, Jesus, Chicago/Texas	5	5	.500	2.31	16	13	3	3	0	0	97.1	81	42	25	5	1	46	2	58	7
Colon, Bartolo, Cleveland	6	1	.857	2.59	11	10	2	1	1	1	66.0	44	24	19	0	0	33	0	48	2
Connors, Wilson, S.F./Phil./Hou.	2	12	.143	8.02	17	15	2	2	0	0	76.1	107	85	68	1	2	51	0	44	14
Cordova, Luis, Yankees/S.D.	2	3	.400	7.50	13	0	0	6	0	0	18.0	14	21	15	1	2	25	0	16	4
Cornielle, Marcelo, Houston	2	3	.400	6.75	20	0	0	10	0	2	30.2	35	29	23	1	6	22	0	14	7
Coronado, Osvaldo, N.Y. Mets	1	1	.500	3.94	3	3	0	0	0	0	16.0	17	11	7	2	1	9	0	8	2
Croes, Estefano, Montreal	0	0	.000	1.86	5	1	0	3	0	1	9.2	9	3	2	0	0	6	0	6	1
Cruz, Raymol, S.F./Phil./Hou.	0	5	.000	4.71	17	6	1	9	0	0	57.1	78	49	30	2	3	33	1	27	7
Cruz, Victor, Milwaukee	1	4	.200	6.46	16	7	1	4	0	0	54.1	63	55	39	7	4	41	0	31	7
Cuevas, Francisco, Florida	0	3	.000	3.33	15	3	0	7	0	1	27.0	22	19	10	0	2	27	0	16	6
Curillan, Darwin, Yankees/S.D.	0	2	.000	9.45	4	2	0	1	0	0	6.2	8	9	7	0	1	14	0	3	3
DeLaCruz, Francisco, Toyo Carp	4	1	.800	2.91	10	7	0	1	0	1	46.1	40	16	15	1	2	24	0	32	5
DeLaCruz, Fernando, K.C./R.	2	5	.286	4.64	14	8	0	2	0	0	54.1	59	38	28	0	2	39	0	29	5
DeLaCruz, Henry, Atlanta	1	2	.333	4.41	17	3	0	7	0	1	51.0	56	41	25	0	4	37	3	26	2
DeLaCruz, Jesus, New York Mets	1	0	1.000	6.25	5	0	0	4	0	0	8.2	11	7	6	1	1	5	0	2	1
DeLaCruz, Juan, Pittsburgh	3	2	.600	3.50	14	3	0	4	0	0	46.1	44	25	18	4	1	20	1	37	8
DeLaRosa, L., Detroit/St. Louis	0	0	.000	0.00	1	0	0	0	0	0	0.0	0	0	0	0	0	0	0	0	0
DeLaRosa, Raul, Balt./White Sox	4	1	.800	3.97	13	12	0	0	0	0	65.2	60	39	29	3	5	47	0	37	5
DeLosSantos, Cornelio, Florida	0	0	.000	18.00	1	0	0	0	0	0	2.0	3	4	4	0	0	4	0	1	0
DeLosSantos, Jose, Milwaukee	4	3	.571	3.84	20	4	2	9	1	1	61.0	59	29	26	5	6	23	2	22	2
DeLosSantos, Valerio, Milwaukee	1	7	.125	6.50	19	8	1	4	0	0	63.2	91	57	46	2	4	37	0	39	9
Decena, Sotero, Milwaukee	0	0	.000	4.90	4	0	0	3	0	0	3.2	6	5	2	0	4	0	0	4	2
DelaCruz, Juan, Houston	6	6	.500	4.81	17	15	3	1	1	0	95.1	118	72	51	4	6	41	0	32	6
DeLeon, Felix, Yankees/S.D.	0	0	.000	0.00	1	0	0	0	0	0	0.2	0	0	0	0	0	0	0	0	0
DeLeon, Javier, Toronto West	1	7	.125	8.27	18	3	0	5	0	0	41.1	53	44	38	3	4	39	2	19	16
DeLeon, Julio Cesar, Yan./S.D.	1	1	.500	4.86	6	1	0	2	0	0	16.2	16	11	9	1	2	10	0	6	2
DeLeon, Nicanor, Atlanta	0	0	.000	14.88	17	1	0	5	0	0	26.0	36	61	43	1	9	55	0	17	14
Delgado, Manuel, Toronto East	8	0	1.000	4.08	14	11	1	2	0	1	70.2	82	38	32	2	6	16	0	47	4
DeLosSantos, Americo, KC/R	1	2	.333	7.41	18	2	0	4	0	0	37.2	49	37	31	4	2	26	0	22	4
DeLosSantos, S., California	6	3	.667	3.64	17	12	0	2	1	0	71.2	67	37	29	2	3	40	1	58	11
Diaz, Richard, Florida	0	0	.000	0.00	1	0	0	1	0	0	1.1	2	1	0	0	0	2	0	2	0
Diese, Jose, Toyo Carp	10	3	.769	2.66	18	10	4	4	1	1	91.1	80	38	27	1	1	37	0	52	4
Dijol, Julio Cesar, Chi./Tex.	0	0	.000	6.74	1	0	0	0	0	0	2.2	2	3	2	0	1	1	0	1	1
Done, Johnny, Toronto West	4	5	.444	2.39	14	13	1	0	0	0	75.1	64	33	20	2	8	23	1	47	6
Dotel, Octavio, New York Mets	6	2	.750	4.10	15	11	0	1	0	0	59.1	46	30	27	1	6	38	1	48	6
Doval, Eliezer, Atlanta	1	0	1.000	4.24	14	0	0	7	0	1	34.0	47	29	16	2	1	15	1	14	3
Duncan, Juan, Seattle	0	0	.000	18.00	1	0	0	1	0	0	2.0	6	5	4	0	0	1	0	0	0
Duran, Juan, Toyo Carp	5	1	.833	1.55	18	4	0	13	0	6	58.0	45	14	10	1	0	15	0	34	1
Dykhoff, Radhames, Balt./W.S.	1	0	1.000	1.93	6	0	0	5	0	1	9.1	8	3	2	1	1	4	0	4	2
Encarnacion, Alex, Montreal	0	4	.000	5.46	7	5	0	1	0	0	29.2	26	27	18	5	5	22	0	21	5
Encarnacion, Eliel, Ang./Dod.	4	1	.800	4.30	17	4	0	7	0	1	46.0	45	28	22	2	4	37	0	24	5
Escobar, Kelvin, Toronto East	2	1	.667	4.13	8	7	0	0	0	0	32.2	34	17	15	2	1	25	0	31	4
Espriella, Alex, Seattle	2	3	.400	5.55	15	4	0	2	0	0	47.0	43	35	29	1	5	38	0	31	7
Estrado, Horacio, Milwaukee	1	2	.333	4.41	22	3	0	2	0	0	51.0	39	33	25	5	5	37	1	60	10
Falcon, Dehan, Montreal	4	2	.667	5.11	10	10	1	0	0	0	44.0	51	29	25	1	5	20	0	26	6
Faulkner, Jose, Balt./White Sox.	0	4	.000	9.41	16	0	0	7	0	2	36.1	60	50	38	10	2	23	1	13	7
Feblex, Narciso, Toronto West	5	6	.455	5.06	25	2	0	19	0	6	48.0	54	39	27	1	0	39	3	45	5
Felix, Antonio, Cleveland	2	3	.400	4.07	26	1	0	12	0	3	42.0	38	34	19	0	5	37	3	17	5
Felix, Claudio, Chicago/Texas	0	0	.000	6.77	1	0	0	1	0	0	1.1	3	1	1	0	0	0	0	1	0
Ferreira, Marcos, Balt./W.S.	3	2	.600	4.47	17	5	0	7	1	1	52.1	69	32	26	5	3	26	0	36	4
Figuereo, Leonardo, Montreal	7	6	.538	3.30	22	12	3	6	0	1	117.1	103	67	43	6	15	44	0	62	6
Figueroa, Julio, Montreal	3	5	.375	3.62	25	0	2	13	0	5	87.0	102	49	35	7	6	30	2	57	5
Franco, Wander, Balt./White Sox	7	3	.700	3.98	15	11	0	2	0	1	74.2	77	48	33	3	2	37	0	55	3
Fuente, Joel, Yankees/San Diego	6	2	.750	2.43	10	10	1	0	0	0	55.2	47	26	15	3	3	22	0	56	6
Garcia, Andres, Cleveland	0	2	.000	5.94	14	6	0	2	0	0	33.1	29	30	22	0	0	41	0	15	3
Garcia, Emerson, Yankees/S.D.	1	6	.143	3.48	12	11	0	0	0	0	64.2	69	34	25	2	5	19	0	38	8
Garcia, Eusebio, Florida	2	3	.400	4.50	11	10	0	0	0	0	52.0	54	39	26	5	2	37	0	27	10
Garcia, Jose, Atlanta	1	5	.167	4.55	13	11	0	0	0	0	61.1	62	41	31	3	4	41	1	32	2
Garcia, Roberto, Chicago/Texas	0	1	.000	26.87	1	0	0	0	0	0	0.2	5	5	2	0	2	1	0	0	0
Gautier, Julio, Montreal	1	0	1.000	3.86	3	0	0	1	0	0	9.1	7	5	4	1	3	11	0	2	2

Pitcher, Team	W	L	Pct.	ERA	G	GS	CG	GF	ShO	Sv.	IP	H	R	ER	HR	HB	BB	Int. BB	SO	WP
German, Julian, Detroit/St. Louis	0	0	.000	0.00	3	0	0	3	0	0	4.1	2	0	0	0	0	2	0	4	0
Geronimo, Julio C., Pittsburgh	2	1	.667	3.48	16	3	0	4	0	1	41.1	35	23	16	1	3	19	0	38	7
Giron, Juan, Toronto West	4	5	.444	3.76	17	11	2	2	0	0	79.0	64	47	33	1	9	50	2	31	5
Giron, Roberto, Toronto West	4	4	.500	3.56	12	11	2	1	1	1	65.2	59	38	26	4	3	30	1	42	10
Gomez, Alex, California	4	2	.667	5.44	14	7	1	2	0	1	27.1	42	25	16	0	2	13	1	16	2
Gomez, Bernis, Chicago/Texas	0	0	.000	5.41	2	0	0	2	0	0	3.1	4	3	2	1	0	3	0	1	2
Gomez, Manuel, Detroit/St. Louis	1	0	1.000	1.59	14	0	0	7	0	4	22.2	13	6	4	0	1	16	1	18	0
Gomez, Miguel, Toronto East	4	0	1.000	3.77	11	11	1	0	0	0	57.1	53	34	24	0	0	36	0	35	5
Gonzalez, Cristian, Cleveland	0	0	.000	4.90	5	0	0	2	0	0	3.2	6	4	2	0	1	4	1	3	0
Gonzalez, Generoso, Det./St. L.	0	2	.000	6.16	7	5	0	1	0	0	19.0	16	25	13	1	5	32	0	13	9
Gonzalez, Jesus, Cleveland	1	2	.333	3.20	14	2	0	7	0	2	25.1	27	15	9	0	2	12	0	10	1
Gonzalez, Juan, Milwaukee	6	8	.429	4.57	18	17	4	0	0	0	106.1	116	73	54	2	13	54	3	69	15
Gonzalez, Lariel, K.C./Rockies	0	4	.000	9.38	14	7	0	3	0	1	24.0	32	34	25	0	3	46	1	17	2
Gonzalez, Maximo, Oakland	1	0	1.000	7.10	4	1	0	1	0	0	12.2	11	11	10	0	4	3	0	6	0
Gonzalez, Singuerton, Ang./Dod.	0	0	.000	4.50	1	0	0	1	0	0	2.0	4	1	1	0	0	1	0	1	0
Gonzalez, Teodoro, Yankees/S.D.	2	1	.667	1.00	6	0	0	6	0	0	9.0	4	2	1	0	0	5	1	7	0
Graterol, Belker, Toronto West	2	5	.286	3.95	13	13	1	0	0	0	70.2	59	39	31	5	4	29	0	40	1
Grullon, Bernardo, Ang./Dod.	0	1	.000	5.63	5	1	0	1	0	0	8.0	5	7	5	0	4	12	0	9	0
Guerrero, Vladimir, Montreal	0	0	.000	2.25	3	0	0	0	0	0	8.0	10	3	2	0	1	4	0	6	1
Guillen, Angel, S.F./Phil./Hou.	1	6	.143	4.91	17	4	0	6	0	1	51.1	71	54	28	1	4	25	1	23	3
Guillen, Franklin, Florida	3	2	.600	4.09	19	2	1	11	0	3	55.0	53	30	25	0	7	23	3	25	8
Guillen, Ramon, Toronto East	2	0	1.000	2.53	18	2	0	6	0	3	46.1	49	21	13	0	4	22	3	26	2
Gutierrez, Javier, Seattle	3	3	.500	5.68	17	9	2	5	0	1	52.1	54	40	33	6	7	34	3	24	12
Hacen, Abraham, Balt./W.S.	4	1	.800	5.66	14	11	1	2	0	4	55.2	54	45	35	4	1	43	0	31	10
Hernandez, Etanislao., California	0	0	.000	5.41	2	0	0	1	0	0	51.1	50	46	31	3	1	41	3	34	2
Hernandez, Julio, California	0	0	.000	12.00	1	0	0	0	0	0	3.0	3	4	4	0	0	4	0	1	1
Hinetrosa, Wilfredo, Pittsburgh	0	1	.000	3.17	6	1	0	3	0	0	5.2	7	5	2	0	0	8	0	1	1
Israel, Charles, K.C./Rockies	2	8	.200	4.92	15	13	0	0	0	0	71.1	78	54	39	2	3	34	0	44	8
James, John, Toronto West	0	2	.000	5.85	13	1	0	5	0	0	32.1	25	32	21	1	4	51	1	18	11
Jimenez, Jose, Detroit/St. Louis	3	5	.375	3.52	12	12	0	0	0	0	56.1	61	47	22	3	6	35	0	30	1
Jimenez, Jose, K.C./Rockies	0	0	.000	2.25	4	0	0	2	0	0	4.0	1	1	1	0	0	8	0	3	3
Lantigua, Enemencio, Florida	0	1	.000	3.86	3	2	0	0	0	0	14.0	12	8	6	1	2	6	0	3	1
Lara, Crespo, Oakland	6	2	.750	3.81	13	6	1	5	0	1	52.0	55	28	22	6	3	10	0	22	1
Lara, Yovanny, Montreal	2	2	.500	7.40	20	4	0	9	0	0	62.0	88	60	51	7	1	54	0	24	11
Leon, Luis, Montreal	2	3	.400	9.78	17	0	0	8	0	1	23.0	29	30	25	3	5	32	0	14	9
Liberato, Ambiorix, Yan./S.D.	0	2	.000	2.40	5	4	0	0	0	0	15.0	11	5	4	0	0	3	0	11	0
Linares, Juan, New York Mets	2	1	.667	2.39	25	0	0	21	0	10	37.2	28	18	10	2	2	23	2	36	3
Linares, Mario, Toyo Carp	7	0	1.000	2.18	21	7	0	12	1	3	70.1	60	23	17	2	1	42	0	34	3
Linares, Roman, New York Mets	2	4	.333	3.93	11	6	1	5	0	1	50.1	50	23	22	7	2	10	3	28	0
Liquet, Wilton, Angels/Dodgers	7	3	.700	2.79	13	13	2	0	0	0	84.0	75	30	26	1	3	22	2	71	7
Liriano, Eddy, Detroit/St. Louis	0	3	.000	10.21	9	3	0	4	0	0	24.2	34	32	28	4	4	30	1	12	8
Lois, Newman, Houston	3	2	.600	2.21	15	13	1	0	1	0	89.2	65	39	22	0	6	41	0	60	11
Lopez, Johan, Houston	5	4	.556	4.07	15	15	1	0	0	0	86.1	83	56	39	5	10	37	0	74	10
Lopez, Juan, S.F./Phil./Hou.	2	3	.400	4.36	24	0	0	19	0	4	33.0	40	28	16	1	0	12	3	11	4
Lopez, Luis A., Detroit/St. Louis	2	2	.500	5.15	8	7	0	0	0	0	36.2	45	23	21	3	4	13	0	28	3
Lorenzo, Cristian, Pittsburgh	3	3	.500	6.46	20	1	0	11	0	4	30.2	38	30	22	2	0	15	1	34	1
Luis, Cristian, Houston	2	2	.500	4.55	17	3	0	8	0	2	31.2	31	24	16	0	3	25	0	24	5
Macey, Fausto, S.F./Phil./Hou.	7	4	.636	3.81	15	13	5	1	0	0	101.2	114	63	43	6	1	38	0	42	7
Macias, Jose, Montreal	1	0	1.000	6.00	3	0	0	3	0	0	6.0	5	6	4	0	0	3	0	2	2
Maldonado, Rosendo, Houston	2	2	.500	5.35	9	7	0	0	0	0	35.1	38	25	21	1	1	11	0	19	3
Malena, Juancito, Cleveland	6	4	.600	3.24	20	8	0	3	0	1	75.0	72	38	27	0	3	32	0	45	0
Mante, Carlos, Oakland	1	4	.200	5.14	14	10	1	2	0	1	49.0	46	36	28	0	5	38	0	41	8
Marte, Barneris, S.F./Phil./Hou.	1	1	.500	7.57	22	0	0	12	0	1	52.1	77	62	44	3	2	28	1	18	1
Marte, Damaso, Seattle	2	5	.286	6.55	17	15	2	0	0	0	56.1	62	48	41	5	7	50	0	29	4
Martin, Daniel, Angels/Dodgers	0	0	.000	1.38	8	0	0	7	0	1	13.0	13	4	2	0	0	3	0	5	0
Martinez, Fausto., Seattle	5	2	.714	3.61	26	0	0	21	0	10	47.1	50	22	19	3	1	24	3	26	1
Martinez, Gustavo, Ang./Dod.	8	4	.667	1.83	14	13	5	0	1	0	88.2	72	47	18	1	6	21	4	44	0
Martinez, Juan R., Chi./Tex.	0	4	.000	4.08	7	7	0	0	0	0	35.1	37	28	16	0	1	16	0	19	0
Martinez, Osvaldo, Detroit/St. L.	4	7	.364	3.51	13	12	0	1	0	0	66.2	69	32	26	4	4	26	1	53	6
Martinez, Starling, Pittsburgh	0	0	.000	4.50	7	1	0	1	0	0	8.0	14	6	4	0	1	7	0	4	2
Mateo, Francisco, Milwaukee	0	0	.000	4.50	1	0	0	1	0	0	2.0	2	1	1	0	0	0	0	2	0
Matos, Santos, Seattle	0	1	.000	25.20	6	3	0	2	0	0	5.0	5	16	14	1	1	19	0	2	5
Medina, David, Yankees/S.D.	3	2	.600	2.88	13	3	1	7	0	3	40.2	43	24	13	1	2	12	0	21	4
Medina, Tomas, Houston	1	6	.143	4.28	19	1	0	10	0	2	33.2	28	24	16	0	9	26	0	16	11
Mejia, Robert, Yankees/S.D.	2	2	.500	2.10	12	0	0	8	0	3	30.0	36	10	7	1	0	8	5	10	1
Melian, Jonathan, Seattle	0	1	.000	20.79	4	3	0	0	0	0	4.1	5	10	10	0	0	11	0	1	1
Mena, Eddy, Detroit/St. Louis	2	1	.667	5.74	17	2	0	7	0	1	42.1	47	32	27	0	4	38	0	30	6
Mendoza, Juan C., Atlanta	0	0	.000	19.91	6	0	0	3	0	0	6.1	10	22	14	0	3	22	0	2	10
Mendoza, Marcos, Ang./Dod.	4	2	.667	2.98	12	9	1	1	1	0	54.1	50	30	18	1	2	26	1	48	3
Mercedes, Carlos, Balt./W.S.	1	3	.250	15.43	14	0	0	6	0	0	18.2	29	42	32	5	3	25	2	10	10
Mercedes, Matias, Detroit/St. L.	0	0	.000	2.25	3	0	0	2	0	0	4.0	2	1	1	0	0	4	0	1	0
Mesa, Rafael, Cleveland	7	2	.778	2.63	16	8	1	2	0	1	72.0	65	34	21	4	6	18	0	51	1
Miranda, Walter, Florida	5	5	.500	4.66	14	12	1	1	0	0	56.0	47	42	29	3	9	45	1	61	3
Montano, Lenny, Seattle	0	1	.000	10.27	10	0	0	2	0	0	23.2	35	32	27	6	2	26	3	7	6
Montero, Olmedo, K.C./R.	0	0	.000	8.21	4	0	0	2	0	0	7.2	12	10	7	1	2	4	0	1	1
Montoya, Wilmer, Cleveland	6	4	.600	2.82	19	11	2	6	1	1	83.0	65	47	26	0	4	49	3	97	12
Morel, Jose, Pittsburgh	3	4	.429	2.79	11	9	1	1	0	1	58.0	47	25	18	2	1	34	0	49	8
Moreno, Juan, Oakland	3	1	.750	3.33	13	3	0	3	0	1	48.2	42	23	18	2	2	35	1	36	5
Moreno, Julio, Balt./W.S.	1	2	.333	12.54	16	2	0	7	0	0	28.0	45	42	39	7	3	28	1	11	14
Mota, Marcos, New York Mets	4	4	.500	3.88	12	12	0	0	0	0	58.0	61	36	25	3	6	19	2	21	6
Mozquea, Alberto, SF/Phil/Hou	1	9	.100	5.08	15	14	1	1	0	0	72.2	73	57	41	4	8	49	0	67	11
Nin, Sandy, Toyo Carp	4	4	.500	4.48	25	4	0	17	0	4	62.1	62	37	31	6	2	24	0	44	4
Nixon, Luis, Angels/Dodgers	5	3	.625	3.84	14	11	1	1	1	0	65.2	75	37	28	2	1	28	2	40	4
Nova, Wilson, Yankees/S.D.	1	2	.333	8.10	15	1	0	5	0	0	30.0	45	38	27	4	0	21	0	16	2
Nunez, Julio, Toronto East	6	5	.545	3.02	27	0	0	10	0	1	59.2	64	27	20	1	7	28	1	42	2
Ojeda, Erick, New York Mets	6	1	.857	2.55	13	9	3	1	0	0	74.0	47	24	21	5	6	34	3	84	14
Olivier, Richard, Yankees/S.D.	4	5	.444	3.70	14	14	2	0	0	0	87.2	85	45	36	5	7	25	0	60	8
Olmedo, Juan, Milwaukee	1	0	1.000	1.62	3	3	1	0	0	0	16.2	11	4	3	0	0	3	0	17	0
Paredes, Roberto, Cleveland	3	2	.600	2.75	25	0	0	18	0	10	36.0	23	15	11	0	3	16	0	21	0
Parra, Nelson, Yankees/S.D.	4	0	1.000	1.95	10	0	0	4	0	1	27.2	20	6	6	1	3	16	0	28	2
Pascual, Carlos, K.C./Rockies	1	1	.500	1.64	20	0	0	10	0	0	38.1	23	14	7	0	5	24	0	17	4
Pascual, Felipe, California	0	0	.000	6.00	3	0	0	2	1	0	32.2	35	35	23	5	0	34	0	18	2
Pascual, Osvaldo, Chi./Tex.	3	6	.333	7.23	25	2	0	20	0	1	61.0	80	62	49	5	5	36	0	31	7
Patino, Leonaldo, California	6	5	.545	4.36	15	10	0	2	0	0	64.0	65	42	31	6	3	28	1	42	7

Pitcher, Team	W	L	Pct.	ERA	G	GS	CG	GF	ShO	Sv.	IP	H	R	ER	HR	HB	BB	Int. BB	SO	WP
Paulino, Mario, Angels/Dodgers..	5	3	.625	1.31	28	0	0	27	0	7	41.1	31	9	6	0	1	17	7	24	2
Paz, Ivan, New York Mets............	3	1	.750	6.45	11	1	0	0	0	0	22.1	15	17	16	4	0	21	1	17	4
Pena, Elvio, Cleveland.................	0	0	.000	4.50	1	0	0	0	0	0	2.0	3	2	1	1	0	1	0	0	0
Pena, Jesus, Pittsburgh...............	6	3	.667	2.37	18	10	0	7	0	2	68.1	48	27	18	1	2	51	1	79	5
Pena, Moises, New York Mets......	0	1	.000	9.00	2	2	0	0	0	0	3.0	4	7	3	0	0	8	0	3	2
Pena, Nelson A., Pittsburgh.........	2	1	.667	3.31	19	0	0	9	0	2	32.2	31	19	12	1	3	24	0	26	4
Peralta, Alexander, Yan./S.D.	0	0	.000	13.50	3	0	0	3	0	0	4.0	9	6	6	0	0	2	0	1	0
Peralta, Jose, Detroit/St. Louis ...	7	3	.700	4.76	29	0	0	28	0	6	51.0	45	35	27	4	4	17	6	35	0
Perez, Angel, California...............	3	4	.429	2.00	21	2	1	17	0	8	63.0	49	23	14	0	0	12	4	35	1
Perez, Cesar, Chicago/Texas......	0	1	.000	3.86	3	2	0	0	0	0	16.1	15	9	7	1	0	6	0	9	1
Perez, Cesar, Los Angeles I..........	4	2	.667	4.16	24	5	0	5	0	1	71.1	74	43	33	5	2	36	0	46	4
Perez, Eduis, Los Angeles I..........	3	1	.750	3.13	22	3	0	11	0	3	54.2	51	28	19	5	3	20	0	25	1
Perez, Edward, K.C./Rockies.......	3	2	.600	2.08	33	0	0	31	0	12	47.2	47	21	11	0	1	10	0	23	1
Perez, J. Cesar, Cleveland............	4	6	.400	2.99	17	13	0	2	0	1	75.1	54	47	25	1	8	44	1	47	4
Perez, Juan, Oakland..................	7	0	1.000	2.48	11	4	1	6	0	0	36.1	37	17	10	0	2	18	2	38	4
Perez, Luis, California..................	4	0	1.000	4.11	21	1	0	15	0	9	57.0	62	37	26	9	2	19	0	29	3
Peroso, Alberto, Atlanta...............	2	5	.286	6.23	17	8	0	7	0	0	52.0	70	47	36	3	6	40	2	23	10
Pierrot, Juan, Los Angeles I.........	1	3	.250	4.71	11	8	0	2	0	1	36.1	35	23	19	1	3	24	0	14	2
Pinales, Demetrio, Atlanta...........	4	6	.400	5.47	19	4	0	4	0	0	54.1	54	49	33	3	4	33	2	33	5
Pineda, Juan, K.C./Rockies.........	2	2	.500	2.64	8	7	1	1	0	0	44.1	48	21	13	0	2	7	0	18	2
Pineda, Leonel, Florida................	4	7	.364	3.64	14	14	2	0	0	0	89.0	115	56	36	5	7	18	3	51	2
Placencia, Leonardo, Cleveland...	0	1	.000	2.67	16	2	0	8	0	1	27.0	26	19	8	1	2	17	0	9	1
Polanco, Carlos, California..........	2	2	.500	4.69	12	2	0	5	0	2	40.1	40	25	21	2	1	31	5	13	5
Polanco, Jose, K.C./Rockies........	2	9	.182	5.96	16	14	0	1	0	0	71.0	99	59	47	3	4	28	0	33	7
Puesan, Antonio, K.C./Rockies....	2	3	.400	5.50	13	12	1	0	0	0	54.0	54	39	33	1	3	54	0	19	7
Quezada, Edward, Montreal.........	4	3	.571	3.47	10	10	1	0	0	0	57.0	59	32	22	0	9	22	0	24	2
Quintana, Urbano, SF/Ph./Ho.	0	5	.000	7.15	17	7	0	5	0	0	56.2	72	64	45	1	6	20	0	43	8
Quiroz, Diego, Oakland................	6	1	.857	2.08	17	1	1	14	0	4	34.2	24	11	8	0	6	18	2	33	0
Ramirez, Felix, Toyo Carp...........	9	4	.692	1.95	18	14	5	4	2	1	110.2	87	39	24	2	3	44	0	96	3
Ramirez, Jose, Milwaukee...........	3	5	.375	8.36	19	10	3	3	1	1	61.1	92	71	57	6	2	42	1	51	8
Ramirez, Juan, Milwaukee...........	4	2	.667	3.68	22	0	0	22	0	6	36.2	36	20	15	0	3	11	3	31	2
Ramirez, Raul, New York Mets.....	3	2	.600	4.54	9	9	0	0	0	0	35.2	31	25	18	2	3	16	0	21	1
Ramos, Ambiorix, Florida............	2	3	.400	3.27	18	0	0	16	0	2	33.0	36	15	12	2	1	11	0	33	6
Randolph, Robert, Toronto West..	2	4	.333	4.47	16	6	0	8	0	3	56.1	62	40	28	2	4	37	3	35	6
Rayo, Francisco, Ang./Dod.	6	1	.857	2.79	24	0	0	9	0	1	61.1	59	27	19	1	1	23	4	29	1
Reyes, Luis, Florida.....................	2	3	.400	3.79	16	0	0	14	0	4	40.1	43	24	17	1	1	20	3	28	4
Reynoso, Edison, Houston...........	2	1	.667	5.47	18	0	0	8	0	0	26.1	31	21	16	2	3	24	0	15	3
Reynoso, Gabriel, Toronto East ...	4	1	.800	4.46	9	9	0	0	0	0	42.1	44	25	21	1	5	29	0	32	11
Rijo, Jose, Houston......................	2	1	.667	5.46	19	0	0	6	0	2	29.2	29	22	18	2	3	18	0	14	3
Rijo, Julio, California..................	5	1	.833	4.14	14	7	0	4	0	0	54.1	51	36	25	4	3	33	0	32	7
Rivera, Juan C., Chicago/Texas..	0	2	.000	6.10	4	2	0	2	0	0	10.1	15	13	7	1	1	6	0	4	1
Rivera, Santos, Yankees/S.D.......	1	2	.333	3.52	9	0	0	6	0	3	15.1	16	6	6	0	1	6	0	13	1
Rodriguez, Alan, Houston............	1	4	.200	4.09	21	1	0	10	0	1	33.0	29	21	15	0	6	21	1	16	4
Rodriguez, Dauryn, Florida..........	0	1	.000	14.63	7	0	0	1	0	1	8.0	12	18	13	1	3	16	0	6	3
Rodriguez, Luis, Los Angeles I.....	0	0	.000	3.00	1	0	0	1	0	0	3.0	3	2	1	0	1	4	0	2	0
Rodriguez, Santos, Pittsburgh.....	0	0	.000	0.00	1	0	0	1	0	0	0.1	0	0	0	0	0	1	0	0	0
Rodriguez, Tomas, Det./St. L......	2	2	.500	10.67	11	5	1	2	0	0	27.0	25	38	32	4	7	49	0	15	9
Rodriguez, Vicente, Chi./Tex.	2	10	.167	3.99	16	15	2	0	0	0	94.2	125	81	42	5	7	28	0	34	5
Romero, Ramon, Toronto East.....	5	3	.625	1.67	29	0	0	27	0	13	43.0	35	10	8	1	3	19	4	44	0
Rosado, Jose, Atlanta..................	7	7	.500	2.92	23	5	1	16	1	3	86.1	86	38	28	3	5	30	3	43	5
Rosario, Juan, Florida..................	0	1	.000	13.50	5	3	0	0	0	0	9.1	20	17	14	1	3	10	0	7	5
Rosario, Michael, Cleveland.........	4	3	.571	2.66	11	8	1	1	1	0	50.2	52	18	15	1	1	5	0	19	1
Rosario, Nelson, Toronto East.....	7	1	.875	3.23	13	12	1	0	0	0	78.0	83	35	28	4	2	25	1	41	8
Rosario, Ruben, Detroit/St. Louis	3	1	.750	3.66	10	5	0	3	0	1	39.1	36	20	16	5	0	18	0	34	0
Rosiles, Jose, California..............	3	2	.600	5.27	8	6	0	0	0	0	3.1	2	2	2	0	2	2	0	0	1
Ruiz, Mauricio, Balt./White Sox ..	1	6	.143	3.57	13	13	2	0	0	0	75.2	87	42	30	6	0	22	0	60	2
Ruiz, Wilmer, Los Angeles I.........	3	1	.750	5.19	18	1	0	9	0	0	34.2	40	24	20	1	2	32	0	26	5
Sabino, Miguel, Chicago/Texas...	0	0	.000	0.86	6	0	0	5	0	0	13.1	11	7	1	2	1	2	0	3	2
Salcedo, Mateo, Pittsburgh..........	4	2	.667	3.91	15	12	0	0	0	0	66.2	70	42	29	3	3	27	0	37	0
Saldana, Roberto, Cleveland........	0	1	.000	13.50	3	1	0	0	0	0	4.0	9	7	6	0	0	2	1	1	0
Samboy, Javier, New York Mets ..	2	0	1.000	5.65	6	2	0	3	0	0	14.1	25	11	9	3	0	3	0	7	0
Sanchez, Jesus, New York Mets ..	7	3	.700	2.40	16	13	2	1	2	0	82.1	63	30	22	6	2	36	0	94	5
Sanchez, Richard, N.Y. Mets........	0	0	.000	5.00	15	1	0	6	0	0	27.0	24	19	15	2	5	20	2	15	5
Saneaux, Francisco, Balt./W.S. ..	4	3	.571	3.12	8	8	0	0	0	0	43.1	31	25	15	3	1	25	0	52	13
Santana, Kelvin, Seattle...............	1	0	1.000	6.26	14	0	0	5	0	0	23.0	26	33	16	3	2	22	0	9	3
Santive, Antonio, Oakland...........	1	1	.500	5.08	12	2	1	6	0	0	28.1	32	18	16	1	1	17	1	16	1
Santos, Juan C., Balt./White Sox	3	2	.600	7.76	18	0	0	12	0	0	26.2	45	33	23	2	3	18	2	13	7
Santos, Rafael, Pittsburgh...........	3	2	.600	5.77	18	0	0	8	0	2	34.1	34	32	22	1	2	41	2	21	4
Segura, Armando, Oakland..........	4	1	.800	3.86	16	0	0	10	0	3	39.2	27	22	17	1	1	31	1	16	4
Selmo, Alexandre, Atlanta...........	4	6	.400	6.79	14	13	0	0	0	0	59.2	75	54	45	4	3	54	1	25	9
Sena, Samuel, Detroit/St. Louis...	1	2	.333	4.60	6	4	0	0	0	0	29.1	39	22	15	1	3	10	0	18	3
Serrano, Domingo, Yankees/S.D.	0	0	.000	9.31	5	1	0	2	0	0	9.2	8	11	10	1	0	10	0	5	1
Severino, Ramon, New York Mets	1	0	1.000	5.29	19	0	0	9	0	1	32.1	39	25	19	5	2	23	1	10	3
Silva, Hernan, Oakland................	7	2	.778	1.40	14	12	2	1	2	0	90.0	57	23	14	2	8	27	0	62	3
Sojo, Luis, Houston.....................	3	3	.500	6.45	20	3	0	10	0	2	37.2	43	37	27	3	3	31	1	21	9
Sosa, Helpy, Oakland..................	5	3	.625	3.93	14	12	6	1	0	1	84.2	85	49	37	2	4	21	0	48	3
Suriel, Rosendo, New York Mets ..	7	3	.700	4.50	21	5	0	7	0	0	72.0	87	44	36	10	6	17	0	38	1
Tapia, Benito H., Balt./White Sox	4	2	.667	5.09	16	6	0	3	0	0	53.0	61	51	30	2	3	36	1	40	8
Tejada, Jose, Florida...................	1	3	.250	7.35	14	3	1	6	0	0	45.1	58	39	37	4	1	38	2	20	8
Toribio, Herminio, Los Angeles I ..	0	3	.000	9.95	8	1	0	3	0	0	19.0	35	30	21	4	3	11	0	14	4
Torres, Yason, Angels/Dodgers ..	0	6	.000	5.77	13	13	0	0	0	0	48.1	42	46	31	0	9	49	0	21	3
Uceta, Victor, Oakland................	1	1	.500	4.11	11	3	1	4	0	1	35.0	25	20	16	1	2	19	1	35	2
Umanzor, Kenny, Atlanta.............	2	4	.333	5.53	22	4	0	14	0	5	40.2	46	31	25	1	0	25	2	33	5
Urena, Fausto, Angels/Dodgers ..	0	0	.000	4.50	1	0	0	0	0	0	2.0	3	1	1	0	0	2	0	1	0
Urvina, Dan, Los Angeles I...........	4	3	.571	4.41	12	11	1	0	0	0	65.1	74	40	32	1	2	34	1	45	12
Valdez, Angel, Montreal..............	2	4	.333	5.40	11	5	1	3	0	0	41.2	42	29	25	4	2	22	0	24	3
Valdez, Eugenio, Oakland............	3	1	.750	1.84	5	5	4	0	0	0	38.0	27	13	8	2	1	2	0	21	3
Valdez, Orlando, S.F./Phil./Hou. .	3	6	.333	4.26	16	11	1	2	0	0	86.2	94	54	41	4	4	41	1	53	6
Vasquez, Carlos, Los Angeles I....	1	2	.333	6.10	6	2	0	1	0	0	10.1	9	9	7	2	2	12	0	3	1
Vasquez, Lioner, K.C./Rockies....	2	5	.286	5.06	14	5	0	2	0	0	37.1	42	31	21	1	0	25	0	31	2
Ventura, Isidro, Detroit/St. Louis	0	0	.000	10.11	1	0	0	0	0	0	2.2	4	3	3	1	1	5	0	4	0
Ventura, Jose, Detroit/St. Louis ..	1	0	1.000	7.15	6	0	0	3	0	2	11.1	13	9	9	1	1	8	0	10	1
Veras, Gabriel, Seattle.................	0	0	.000	0.00	1	0	0	0	0	0	3.2	1	0	0	0	0	0	0	2	0
Vicentino, Andy, Seattle..............	4	3	.571	7.44	15	11	0	2	0	0	52.0	49	45	43	6	5	55	0	33	16

Pitcher, Team	W	L	Pct.	ERA	G	GS	CG	GF	ShO	Sv.	IP	H	R	ER	HR	HB	BB	Int. BB	SO	WP
Villareal, Modesto, K.C./Rockies .	3	1	.750	11.51	14	2	0	0	0	0	22.2	43	41	29	1	1	20	0	14	0
Wilson, Jaime, K.C./Rockies........	0	0	.000	8.11	2	0	0	1	0	0	3.1	3	4	3	0	2	2	0	3	0
Zambrano, Oliver, Chi./Tex.	0	4	.000	7.85	9	6	0	2	0	0	28.2	37	31	25	3	1	31	0	14	8
Zapata, Juan, Milwaukee.............	1	4	.200	8.54	12	9	2	1	0	0	39.0	50	42	37	2	6	35	0	23	8

FIELDING

TEAM

Team	Pct.	G	PO	A	E	DP	PB	Team	Pct.	G	PO	A	E	DP	PB
Toyo Carp	.961	70	1866	771	108	67	5	Florida	.938	70	1701	743	161	68	14
Toronto East	.952	67	1726	773	126	57	16	Yankees/San Diego	.938	69	1742	771	167	52	12
New York Mets	.950	74	1833	720	134	57	9	Baltimore/White Sox	.935	70	1864	772	184	75	4
Seattle	.947	69	1701	717	135	59	9	California	.934	70	1866	830	191	61	9
Milwaukee	.945	68	1684	703	138	53	25	Detroit/St. Louis	.933	72	1748	776	180	69	10
Montreal	.945	68	1703	833	147	72	7	Cleveland..................	.932	70	1773	803	187	55	25
Oakland	.941	74	1881	867	173	63	18	Atlanta	.930	70	1810	899	205	77	12
Toronto West	.941	70	1748	791	160	61	21	Houston	.929	70	1755	747	192	44	14
Angels/Dodgers	.940	70	1769	842	167	62	18	K.C./Rockies	.929	70	1738	794	194	78	17
Los Angeles I	.940	70	1789	779	163	53	15	Chicago/Texas	.919	70	1712	793	224	54	22
Pittsburgh	.940	69	1796	781	164	47	18	S.F./Phil./Hou.	.910	70	1743	820	250	49	7

INDIVIDUAL

Player, Team	Pos.	Pct.	PO	A	E	DP	PB	Player, Team	Pos.	Pct.	PO	A	E	DP	PB
Abad, Tor. West	INF	.965	170	164	12	6	0	Bautista, Yan./S.D.	P	.500	1	0	1	0	0
Abreu, California........	P	.900	2	7	1	0	0	Belioso, Yankees/S.D. ..	P	1.000	1	12	0	0	0
Abreu, Milwaukee	INF	.930	115	125	18	8	0	Beras, California	C	.966	117	25	5	0	3
Abreu, Pittsburgh	P	.952	1	19	1	0	0	Berroa, Seattle	INF	.879	69	62	18	8	0
Abreu, SF/Ph./Hou.	P	1.000	3	1	0	0	0	Betancourt, L.A. I........	P	1.000	4	13	0	2	0
Acosta, Toronto East..	P	.960	4	20	1	2	0	Bido, Houston............	OF	.955	97	9	5	0	0
Adino, Milwaukee	OF/INF	.973	315	13	9	3	0	Blanco, Houston	OF	.918	72	6	7	0	0
Adolfo, Montreal	OF	.930	100	6	8	1	0	Blanco, Montreal	INF	.968	145	8	5	0	0
Agnoly, Florida	INF/OF	.986	483	25	7	6	0	Blanco, Seattle	P	.875	2	5	1	0	0
Agromonte, L.A. I	P	.862	6	19	4	0	0	Bonilla, Oakland..........	C/OF	.947	111	15	7	0	6
Aguasvivas, Pitts.	P	1.000	1	5	0	1	0	Bonilla, Seattle	P	.895	2	15	2	0	0
Aguilar, Yankees/S.D. ..	P	.955	5	16	1	0	0	Borges, K.C./Rockies .	OF	.902	99	12	12	3	0
Agustin, SF/Ph./Hou. ...	OF	.892	137	12	18	2	0	Brazoban, Tor. West...	P	.875	2	5	1	1	0
Albino, Chi./Texas......	P	.760	3	16	6	0	0	Brea, New York Mets ...	C/DH	.957	80	8	4	1	1
Albino, Yankees/S.D. .	INF	.833	3	2	1	1	0	Brea, Toronto West.....	INF/DH	.903	59	71	14	5	0
Alcantara, K.C./Rock.	P	.545	1	5	5	0	0	Brito, Chicago/Texas .	OF	.936	93	9	7	0	0
Alcantara, Toyo Carp .	INF	.969	193	149	11	15	0	H. Brito, Milwaukee.....	C/OF	.952	164	16	9	3	1
Alejo, Florida	INF	.913	65	155	21	11	0	J. Brito, Milwaukee	P	1.000	3	1	0	1	0
Almanzar, Det./St. L...	INF	.902	102	118	24	14	0	Brito, Seattle	OF	.957	60	7	3	0	0
Almanzar, Tor. East....	P	.950	7	12	1	2	0	Brito, S.F./Phil./Hou..	INF	.922	98	114	18	7	0
Almonte, Balt./W.S.....	OF	.961	92	7	4	1	0	Brito, Toyo Carp	OF/INF	.988	233	8	3	0	0
Almonte, Florida	P	.824	3	11	3	1	0	E. Brito, Toronto West	OF/INF	.973	489	24	14	6	0
Alvarado, Montreal	C/INF	.949	223	59	15	2	2	V. Brito, Toronto West	INF	.929	79	144	17	19	0
Alvarez, Detroit/St. L.	P	.800	1	3	1	0	0	Brown, Los Angeles I..	OF	.829	62	6	14	1	0
Alvarez, Montreal	P	.900	6	3	1	2	0	Bryan, California.........	OF	.958	82	10	4	1	0
Alvaro, Toyo Carp......	P	.986	69	4	1	1	0	A. Burgos, Yan./S.D...	P	1.000	0	9	0	0	0
Alzualde, California	C/INF	.973	171	44	8	2	0	D. Burgos, Yan./S.D...	P	1.000	0	3	0	0	0
Andujar, California	OF	.897	67	3	8	1	0	Caballero, Balt./W.S...	OF	.938	14	1	1	0	0
Aquino, Los Angeles I.	OF/P	.833	7	13	4	1	0	Cabarcas, K.C./Rock..	C	.957	50	16	3	1	3
Aracena, Toyo Carp....	P	1.000	1	7	0	0	0	Cabrera, Montreal	INF	.982	86	76	3	12	0
Arias, Ang./Dod.........	P	.900	1	8	1	0	0	Cabrera, Oakland........	P	.692	3	6	4	0	0
Arias, Chicago/Texas	P	1.000	2	10	0	0	0	Cabrera, Toyo Carp	P	.979	308	68	8	1	4
Arias, Detroit/St. L....	P	.800	1	3	1	1	0	Cadet, Chicago/Texas	C	.912	89	14	10	0	8
Arias, K.C./Rockies	C	.976	175	29	5	3	5	Calderon, Atlanta........	P	.893	8	17	3	0	0
Arias, New York Mets .	C/INF	.981	275	30	6	1	5	Campos, Montreal	OF	.933	25	3	2	0	0
Arias, Oakland	C/I/O	.956	122	8	6	0	2	Campusano, Milw.......	INF	.912	69	107	17	11	0
Arias, Toyo Carp........	P	1.000	3	19	0	0	0	Campusano, Seattle....	P	.800	1	7	2	0	0
Arraiz, Montreal.........	INF	.972	60	46	3	7	0	Cana, Florida	P	.879	5	24	4	1	0
Arrendel, Houston	C	.959	125	16	6	0	5	Caraballo, Tor. West...	OF	.914	80	5	8	2	0
Asencio, Ang./Dod.....	OF	.956	93	16	5	6	0	Cardenas, Cleveland...	INF	1.000	12	21	0	0	0
Asencio, Tor. West	C/INF	.972	277	33	9	3	8	Carmona, Seattle........	P	.950	1	18	1	0	0
Avila, California	P	.862	9	16	4	2	0	Carrasco, Tor. West....	OF	.927	94	8	8	2	0
Avila, Pittsburgh........	P	.500	1	0	1	0	0	Carrion, Milwaukee.....	P	.917	1	10	1	1	0
Ayala, Los Angeles I ..	P	.900	3	15	2	0	0	Carrion, Montreal	P	.625	5	3	0	0	0
M. Aybar, Det./St. L. ..	P	.917	2	20	2	2	0	Cartaya, Balt./W.S......	P	.727	3	5	3	0	0
R. Aybar, Det./St. L. ..	OF/INF	.972	14	21	1	3	0	Carvajal, California......	P	1.000	1	0	0	0	0
Aybar, New York Mets	P	1.000	1	4	0	0	0	Castillo, Atlanta..........	P	.917	5	17	2	2	0
Baez, Angels/Dodgers	C	.981	167	43	4	1	6	Castillo, Balt./W.S.......	P	.900	5	4	1	1	0
Baez, Pittsburgh	P	.917	2	9	1	1	0	Castillo, Florida..........	INF	.943	151	180	20	20	0
Balbuena, Chi./Texas..	P	.889	2	6	1	0	0	Castillo, Houston	INF	.875	59	67	18	2	0
Balcazar, California	C/INF	.967	161	15	6	1	1	Castillo, Milwaukee.....	OF	.979	132	9	3	0	0
Barazarte, L.A. I........	C/INF	.921	137	49	16	7	0	Castillo, Toyo Carp.....	C	.983	108	10	2	0	5
Barrios, Houston........	P	.864	8	11	3	0	0	Castillo, Toronto West	P	.789	1	14	4	2	0
Batista, Detroit/St. L..	OF/INF	.929	12	1	1	1	0	Castro, Ang./Dod.......	OF	.920	105	10	10	1	0
Batista, Pittsburgh	P	1.000	5	3	0	0	0	Castro, California........	C/INF	.967	70	17	3	1	5
Bautista, Atlanta	P	1.000	0	2	0	0	0	Castro, Oakland	OF/INF	.893	78	98	21	5	0

Player, Team	Pos.	Pct.	PO	A	E	DP	PB
Castro, Seattle	OF/INF	.963	173	7	7	0	0
Cedeno, Houston	INF	.852	79	186	46	9	0
Cera, Angels/Dodgers	P	.900	0	9	1	0	0
Cesar, Los Angeles I	INF	.968	150	156	10	5	0
Collado, Oakland	P	.813	2	11	3	1	0
Colome, Chi./Texas	P	1.000	4	15	0	1	0
Colon, Cleveland	P	.913	7	14	2	0	0
Connors, SF/Phil/Hou	P	.923	7	5	1	0	0
Contreras, Houston	C	.982	95	13	2	0	5
Cordero, Det./St. L	INF	.888	36	67	13	1	0
Cordova, Yan./S.D.	P	.857	3	3	1	0	0
Cornielle, Houston	P	.889	3	5	1	1	0
Coronado, N.Y. Mets	P	1.000	2	3	0	0	0
Croes, Montreal	INF	.882	14	31	6	6	0
Cruz, Balt./White Sox	INF	.878	39	4	6	0	0
Cruz, Milwaukee	P	.889	2	6	1	0	0
Cruz, S.F./Phil./Hou.	P	.938	9	6	1	0	0
Cuevas, Florida	P	1.000	0	5	0	0	0
Cuevas, SF/Phil/Hou	INF	.883	78	66	19	2	0
Curillon, Yan./S.D.	P	.667	2	2	2	1	0
Davalillo, California	INF	.932	66	113	13	12	0
DeLaCruz, Atlanta	C/P	.917	5	6	1	0	0
DeLaCruz, California	INF	.952	61	97	8	13	0
DeLaCruz, Chi./Texas	OF	.965	131	7	5	1	0
DeLaCruz, Houston	P	.800	11	5	4	2	0
F. DeLaCruz, KC/R	P	.850	3	14	3	1	0
J. DeLaCruz, KC/R	OF	.976	38	3	1	2	0
DeLaCruz, N.Y. Mets	P	1.000	0	1	0	0	0
DeLaCruz, Pittsburgh	P	.857	0	6	1	0	0
DeLaCruz, Toyo Carp.	P	1.000	3	4	0	0	0
DeLaRosa, Balt./W.S.	P	.867	8	5	2	1	0
DeLaRosa, Det./St.L.	C/INF	.982	443	92	10	3	8
DeLaRosa, Pittsburgh	P	.965	53	2	2	0	0
DeLosSantos, Atlanta	OF	.913	90	5	9	0	0
DeLosSantos, Calif.	P	.846	1	10	2	0	0
DeLosSantos, Florida	P	.918	100	12	10	6	0
DeLosSantos, KC/R	P	.833	3	7	2	0	0
J. DeLosSantos, Mil.	P	.714	3	2	2	1	0
V. DeLosSantos, Mil.	P	.833	0	5	1	0	0
DeLeon, Atlanta	P	.700	2	5	3	0	0
DeLeon, Chi./Tex.	C	.954	148	37	9	0	5
DeLeon, Toronto West	P	.818	2	7	2	0	0
F. DeLeon, Yan./S.D.	INF/OF	.943	181	99	17	6	0
J.C. DeLeon, Yan/SD.	P	.833	2	3	1	0	0
Delgado, KC/Rockies.	INF	.955	306	14	15	0	0
Delgado, Seattle	INF	.938	96	148	16	12	0
Delgado, Toronto East	P	.778	4	10	4	0	0
Devers, Seattle	INF	.761	19	35	17	2	0
Diaz, California	OF	.877	65	6	10	1	0
Diaz, Florida	OF	.951	108	9	6	3	0
Diaz, Toyo Carp	INF	.977	365	12	9	2	0
Diese, Toyo Carp	P	.895	1	16	2	1	0
Dijol, Chicago/Texas	INF	.886	114	73	24	7	0
Domero, Pittsburgh	C/OF	.944	55	13	4	0	2
Dominguez, Yan./S.D.	C	.982	47	9	1	0	4
Done, Toronto West	P	1.000	2	17	0	0	0
Dotel, New York Mets.	P	.846	1	10	2	1	0
Doval, Atlanta	P	1.000	4	5	0	0	0
Duncan, Seattle	INF/OF	.948	101	81	10	9	0
Duran, Toyo Carp	P	1.000	2	14	0	0	0
Dykhoff, Balt./WS	P	.800	4	0	1	0	0
Encarnacion, An/Do...	P	.571	0	4	3	0	0
Encarnacion, B/WS...	OF	.923	80	4	7	0	0
Encarnacion, D/StL	OF	.879	110	13	17	3	0
Encarnacion, Mont....	P	.900	2	7	1	0	0
Escalante, Ch/Tx	INF	.970	272	15	9	0	0
Escobar, Toronto East	P	.889	1	7	1	0	0
Escoto, Milwaukee....	DH/INF	.914	30	2	3	0	0
Espinosa, N.Y.M.	INF	.954	130	35	8	5	0
Espirella, Seattle	P	.929	2	11	1	0	0
Estrada, Milwaukee	OF/P	1.000	2	5	0	0	0
Evangelista, Cle.	OF	.905	79	7	9	2	0
Falcon, Montreal	P	1.000	2	11	0	0	0
Fana, SF/Phil/Hou	C	.930	166	48	16	1	3
Faneyte, Tor E	INF	.883	39	97	18	3	0
Farra, Yan./S.D.	P	.750	0	3	1	0	0
Faulkner, Balt./WS....	P	.750	2	1	1	0	0
Febles, Toronto West..	P	.727	1	7	3	0	0
Felix, Chicago/Texas.	INF	.877	25	39	9	3	0
Felix, Cleveland	P	.929	2	11	1	0	0
Felix, Milwaukee	INF	.957	83	137	10	8	0
Fermin, Florida	INF/OF	.956	98	11	5	1	0
J. Fernandez, Atlanta	C	.952	171	29	10	1	9
P. Fernandez, Atlanta.	OF	.897	47	5	6	0	0
Fernandez, Cleveland	OF	.906	78	9	9	0	0
Fernandez, Montreal...	INF	.929	103	223	25	9	0
Ferreira, Balt./W.S.	P	.800	7	9	4	0	0
Figuereo, Atlanta	INF	.925	130	155	23	17	0
Figuereo, Montreal....	P	.906	7	22	3	1	0
Figueroa, Montreal	P	.909	3	17	2	0	0
Fisher, California	INF	.833	21	84	21	7	0
Flobil, K.C./Rockies	INF	.852	13	10	4	0	0
Franco, Balt./W.S.	P	.941	10	6	1	0	0
Francois, Tor. East	INF	.862	6	19	4	2	0
Freire, Houston	INF	.986	540	32	8	2	0
Fuentes, Yan./S.D.	P	1.000	5	13	0	1	0
Galan, Balt./W.S.	C/INF	.988	302	26	4	0	0
Garcia, Atlanta	P	.875	2	5	1	0	0
Garcia, Balt./W.S.	INF	.937	123	10	9	1	0
Garcia, Chi./Texas	OF/INF	.922	44	3	4	0	0
A. Garcia, Cleveland	P	.857	1	11	2	2	0
M. Garcia, Cleveland	INF	.974	242	17	7	2	0
Garcia, Det./St. L	OF/INF	.880	84	107	26	13	0
A. Garcia, Florida	INF	.927	129	112	19	11	0
E. Garcia, Florida	P	.917	1	10	1	0	0
Garcia, K.C./Rockies..	INF	.959	271	55	14	5	0
Garcia, Los Angeles I.	OF	.960	90	7	4	1	0
E. Garcia, Yan./S.D.	P	.950	1	18	1	1	0
J. Garcia, Yan./S.D.	INF	.922	16	31	4	1	0
Gautier, Montreal	P	1.000	0	2	0	0	0
J. German, Det./St. L.	OF/INF	.846	19	14	6	3	0
R. German, Det./St. L.	OF/INF	.956	62	3	3	1	0
Geronimo, Pittsburgh .	P	.909	1	9	1	0	0
J. Giron, Tor. West	P	.923	4	8	1	0	0
R. Giron, Tor. West	P	.929	1	12	1	0	0
Gomez, Balt./W.S.	OF	.875	37	5	6	0	0
Gomez, California	P	.875	0	7	1	0	0
Gomez, Chi/Tex	C/I/0	.895	111	144	30	10	2
Gomez, Det./St. L.	P	1.000	1	2	0	0	0
Gomez, Toronto East	P	.773	4	13	5	0	0
M. Gonzalez, An/Do....	OF	.909	98	12	11	2	0
S. Gonzalez, An/Do....	OF	.733	18	4	8	1	0
Gonzalez, Cleveland....	P	1.000	0	4	0	0	0
Gonzalez, Det/StL	P	1.000	0	3	0	0	0
Gonzalez, KC/Rockies	P	.889	4	4	1	0	0
J. Gonzalez, Milw.	P	.895	3	14	2	1	0
L. Gonzalez, Milw.	OF/INF	.986	70	3	1	0	0
Gonzalez, Montreal	OF	1.000	32	6	0	1	0
M. Gonzalez, Oakland .	P	1.000	2	2	0	0	0
V. Gonzalez, Oakland ..	OF	.978	43	1	1	0	0
Gonzalez, Pittsburgh ..	C/INF	.986	506	48	8	0	5
Gonzalez, Toyo Carp ...	OF	.962	24	1	1	0	0
E. Gonzalez, Yan./SD..	INF	.917	43	45	8	1	0
T. Gonzalez, Yan./S.D.	P	1.000	0	1	0	0	0
Graterol, Tor West	P	.842	0	16	3	0	0
Griffin, Houston	C	.966	131	38	6	0	4
Gross, Ang/Dod	INF	.916	70	170	22	10	0
Guerra, California	INF	.846	43	78	22	6	0
Guerrero, Ang/Dod	INF	.971	15	18	1	2	0
Guerrero, California	OF	.926	70	5	6	0	0
Guerrero, Montreal	O/I/P	.940	75	7	5	2	0
Guerrero, NY Mets	OF/DH	.950	34	4	2	0	0
Guerrero, Oakland	OF/INF	.967	79	9	3	3	0
Guillen, Florida	P	.882	5	10	2	1	0
Guillen, Houston	INF	.902	18	37	6	2	0
Guillen, Pittsburgh	OF	.947	112	12	7	4	0
Guillen, SF/Ph/Hou	P	.875	10	11	3	0	0
Guillen, Toronto East..	P	1.000	3	7	0	1	0
Guillermo, Chi./Texas	C/INF	.946	234	28	15	1	7
Gutierrez, Seattle	P	.909	1	9	1	1	0
Hacen, Balt./W.S.	P	.846	6	5	2	0	0
Henriquez, Det./St. L..	OF/INF	.993	385	14	3	3	0
Henriquez, Milwaukee	OF/INF	1.000	36	6	0	0	0
Hernandez, Atlanta	INF	.895	75	129	24	10	0
E. Hernandez, Calif.	P	.818	1	8	2	0	0
J.C. Hernandez, Calif.	P	1.000	0	1	0	0	0
Hernandez, Houston	INF	.938	181	134	21	9	0
Hernandez, Oakland ...	OF/INF	.964	49	5	2	1	0
D. Hernandez, Pitts.	INF	.910	83	129	21	11	0
R. Hernandez, Pitts. ...	OF/INF	.874	27	63	13	8	0
Herrera, California	INF	.989	352	20	4	2	0
Hidalgo, Det./St. L.	OF	.913	38	4	4	0	0
Hinetrosa, Pittsburgh .	P	.667	0	2	1	0	0
Hiraldo, Pittsburgh	OF	.815	21	1	5	0	0

Player, Team	Pos.	Pct.	PO	A	E	DP	PB
Israel, K.C./Rockies....	P	.905	3	16	2	0	0
Jacobo, Yankees/S.D.	OF/INF	.945	205	18	13	3	0
James, Toronto West..	P	1.000	0	5	0	0	0
Jasco, Chi./Texas	INF	.943	91	124	13	6	0
Jasson, California.......	INF	.826	32	82	24	3	0
Jimenez, Cleveland	C	.951	114	22	7	0	6
Jimenez, Det./St. L.	P	.909	2	18	2	0	0
E. Jimenez, KC/Rock..	OF	.918	135	11	13	2	0
J. Jimenez, KC/Rock..	P	.667	2	0	1	0	0
Jimenez, L.A. I...........	C/INF	.968	160	23	6	1	6
Jimenez, N.Y. Mets....	INF	.981	274	34	6	3	0
Jose, KC/Rock	INF	.873	68	104	25	11	0
Lantigua, Florida	P	1.000	2	4	0	0	0
Lantigua, NYM	C/IF	.958	141	19	7	0	1
Lantigua, Pittsburgh ..	C/OF	.917	39	5	4	0	1
Lara, Montreal	P	.667	2	4	3	0	0
C. Lara, Oakland	P	1.000	1	16	0	0	0
E. Lara, Oakland	INF	.945	74	148	13	13	0
Ledesma, An/Do........	INF	.928	68	86	12	7	0
Leon, Montreal	P	.750	0	3	1	0	0
Liberato, Yan/SD	P	1.000	1	3	0	1	0
J. Linares, NYM	P	.727	0	8	3	0	0
R. Linares, NYM	P	.875	1	6	1	1	0
Linares, Toyo Carp	P	.818	3	6	2	0	0
Liquet, An/Do	P	.900	5	13	2	1	0
Lois, Houston	P	.912	14	17	3	3	0
Lopez, Det/StL	P	1.000	2	3	0	0	0
Lopez, Houston	P	.895	10	7	2	2	0
Lopez, KC/Rockies	INF	.894	52	75	15	6	0
Jo. Lopez, SF/Ph/Ho...	OF	.875	111	8	17	1	0
Ju. Lopez, SF/Ph/Ho..	P	.778	4	3	2	0	0
Lorenzo, Pittsburgh	P	.833	1	4	1	1	0
Lugo, Cleveland	INF	.950	139	88	12	5	0
Luis, Houston	P	.667	2	2	2	0	0
Luna, Cleveland	C	.942	41	8	3	0	9
Macey, SF/Ph/Ho	P	.853	13	16	5	0	0
Macias, Montreal	INF	.954	100	44	7	6	0
Madera, Oakland	OF	.970	58	7	2	0	0
Maldonado, Chi/Tex....	OF	.938	70	6	5	0	0
Maldonado, Houston...	P	1.000	1	3	0	0	0
Malena, Cleveland	P	1.000	1	14	0	1	0
Mante, Oakland	P	.714	0	5	2	0	0
Mante, Seattle............	P	.950	3	16	1	0	0
Marquez, Seattle	C	.959	40	7	2	1	0
Marquez, Yan./S.D.	OF/INF	.945	118	3	7	1	0
Marte, SF/Phi/Hou......	P	.938	9	6	1	0	0
Martin, Ang/Dod	P	.500	0	1	1	0	0
Martinez, Ang/Dod	P	.895	5	12	2	0	0
A. Martinez, Atlanta	INF	.989	430	37	5	4	0
F. Martinez, Atlanta	OF	.939	82	10	6	1	0
Martinez, Chi/Tex.......	P	1.000	0	4	0	0	0
Martinez, Cleveland	INF	.950	221	9	12	1	0
Martinez, Det/St.L......	P	.929	2	11	1	0	0
Martinez, KC/Rockies	OF	.956	37	6	2	3	0
C. Martinez, L.A. I	OF	.962	90	11	4	4	0
R. Martinez, L.A. I	INF/OF	.979	519	29	12	2	0
Martinez, Pittsburgh....	P	.500	0	1	1	0	0
F. Martinez, Seattle....	P	1.000	1	8	0	0	0
J.R. Martinez, Seattle..	OF	.962	48	3	2	0	0
Martinez, Tor East	INF/C	.985	560	48	9	2	1
Martinez, Tor West	INF	.808	10	32	10	1	0
Martinez, Y/SD	INF	.941	16	16	2	2	0
Mateo, Toyo Carp	INF	.857	6	24	5	4	0
Matos, Cleveland	INF	.794	11	16	7	1	0
Matos, Seattle............	P	.500	1	1	2	0	0
Matos, SF/Ph/Ho	INF	.964	460	43	19	2	0
Matos, Toyo Carp	INF	.994	149	7	1	1	0
Medina, Houston	P	.889	3	5	1	1	0
Medina, Yankees/SD..	P	.833	1	9	2	0	0
Medrano, Seattle........	C	.983	290	65	6	3	3
Mega, Los Angeles I...	INF/DH	.975	16	23	1	0	0
Mejia, Yankees/SD	P	1.000	1	6	0	1	0
Melendes, Pittsburgh..	INF	.929	125	162	22	11	0
Melo, Yan/SD...........	INF/DH	.917	58	107	15	6	0
Mena, Dt/StL	P	.778	2	5	2	0	0
Mendez, Toyo Carp	OF	.935	39	4	3	1	0
Mendoza, An/Do........	P	.938	4	11	1	0	0
Mendoza, Balt./WS	INF	.945	151	124	16	10	0
Mendoza, NYM	OF	.952	17	3	1	1	0
Mercedes, Balt/WS	P	.800	3	1	1	0	0
Mercedes, Dt/StL	OF/INF	.942	111	52	10	8	0
Mesa, Cleveland.........	P	.875	4	17	3	3	0
Meza, Seattle	OF	.952	36	4	2	0	0
Miranda, Florida	P	.929	2	11	1	0	0
Montano, Seattle.........	P	.857	2	4	1	0	0
Montero, Florida	C/OF	.952	368	66	22	1	11
Montero, KC/Rock......	P	1.000	1	0	1	0	0
Montoya, Cleveland	P	.952	6	14	1	0	0
Mora, Cleveland..........	OF	.848	26	2	5	0	0
Morales, Atlanta	OF	.897	48	4	6	0	0
Morel, Oakland	P	1.000	0	2	0	0	0
Morel, Pittsburgh	P	.909	3	7	1	1	0
Moreno, Balt/WS........	P	.667	2	2	2	0	0
Moreno, NYM	OF	.929	24	2	2	0	0
Moreno, Oakland	P	.938	3	12	1	0	0
Mota, California	INF	.900	111	96	23	7	0
Mota, Cleveland..........	INF	.873	38	65	15	3	0
G. Mota, NYM	OF	.984	117	6	2	2	0
M. Mota, NYM	P	1.000	3	10	0	0	0
Mozquea, SF/Ph/Ho....	P	.870	13	7	3	0	0
Munoz, Pittsburgh	INF	.955	214	42	12	1	0
Navas, Cleveland	INF	.885	49	82	17	5	0
Nieves, Milwaukee......	INF/DH	.864	43	78	19	8	0
Nin, Toyo Carp	P	1.000	3	5	0	2	0
Nixon, Ang/Dod..........	P	.870	3	17	3	2	0
Noriega, Yan/SD.........	OF/INF	.970	213	15	7	2	0
P. Nova, Yan/SD.........	OF/INF	.961	91	8	4	0	0
W. Nova, Yan/SD........	P	.833	1	4	1	0	0
Nunez, Balt/WS	INF	.912	76	89	16	10	0
Nunez, KC/Rockies	INF	.960	171	214	16	24	0
Nunez, Pittsburgh	INF	.909	101	149	25	3	0
J.C. Nunez, Tor East ...	P	1.000	0	2	0	0	0
M. Nunez, Tor East	OF	.966	99	13	4	4	0
Ojeda, New York Mets.	P	.833	2	8	2	0	0
Oliva, Atlanta	INF	.977	241	14	6	0	0
Oliver, Yan/S.D.	P	.774	7	17	7	1	0
Oliveros, Montreal	C/INF	.974	135	17	4	1	2
Olmedo, Milwaukee	OF/P	.889	6	2	1	0	0
Ortiz, Seattle	INF	.984	462	16	8	3	0
Ossers, Toyo Carp	INF	.886	23	47	9	6	0
Ovalles, Montreal	INF	.864	19	38	9	2	0
Ozorio, Yan/S.D.	INF	.868	64	101	25	9	0
Ozuna, Ang/Dod	INF	.901	107	201	34	13	0
Padilla, Balt/WS	OF	.932	52	3	4	1	0
Paredes, Cleveland	P	.929	2	11	1	0	0
Pascual, California	P	1.000	4	4	0	0	0
Pascual, Chi./Tex.......	P	.750	1	8	3	0	0
Pascual, KC/Rockies ...	P	.857	3	9	2	1	0
Patino, California	P	.818	1	17	4	0	0
Patrone, Atlanta	C	.985	161	34	3	0	3
Paulino, Ang/Dod	P	.913	4	17	2	1	0
Paulino, NY Mets	INF	.829	10	19	6	1	0
Paulino, Oakland........	INF	.959	69	71	6	6	0
Paulino, SF/Phil/Hou..	INF	.883	69	59	17	5	0
Paz, New York Mets ...	P	.667	0	2	1	0	0
Pedra, Los Angeles I...	C	.980	291	10	6	0	8
Pemberton, Montreal ..	INF	.979	355	15	8	0	0
Pena, Ang/Dod	C	.944	197	57	15	2	12
A. Pena, Cleveland	OF	.936	124	8	9	1	0
J. Pena, Cleveland	P	.943	26	7	2	0	3
Pena, New York Mets..	P	.000	0	0	2	0	0
J. Pena, Pittsburgh	P	1.000	2	10	0	0	0
N.A. Pena, Pittsburgh..	P	.500	0	1	1	0	0
Pena, Toyo Carp	OF	.982	155	5	3	0	0
Pena, Toronto East	C/DH	.895	15	2	2	0	2
Peralta, Det/St.L	P	.889	3	13	2	1	0
Peralta, Yan/SD..........	INF	.927	92	111	16	11	0
Perdomo, Toyo Carp ...	INF	.934	85	197	20	23	0
A. Perez, California	P	.929	2	11	1	2	0
L. Perez, California	P	1.000	1	8	0	0	0
Perez, Chi/Tex...........	I/O/P	.942	123	7	8	3	0
E. Perez, Cleveland	INF	.923	112	105	18	7	0
J.C. Perez, Cleveland ..	P	.848	6	22	5	0	0
Perez, Det/St.L...........	INF/OF	.869	59	47	16	4	0
Perez, Florida	INF/OF	.850	79	57	160	5	0
Perez, Houston	OF	.857	30	12	7	0	0
Perez, KC/Rockies	P	.824	5	9	3	0	0
C. Perez, Los Angeles I	P	.818	2	16	4	0	0
E. Perez, Los Angeles I	P	.889	1	7	1	0	0
Perez, Oakland	P	1.000	1	10	0	1	0
Perez, SF/Phil/Hou	INF	.874	57	144	29	12	0
Perozo, Atlanta	P	.800	2	10	3	0	0
Pierrot, Los Angeles I..	P	.600	0	6	4	0	0
Pimentel, LA I	OF/INF	.921	88	5	8	0	0

Player, Team	Pos.	Pct.	PO	A	E	DP	PB
Pinales, Atlanta	P	.909	2	18	2	0	0
Pineda, Florida	P	.808	5	16	5	1	0
Pineda, KC/Rockies	P	1.000	1	7	0	0	0
Pineda, SF/Phi/Hou	INF	.874	51	46	14	6	0
Piters, California	C	1.000	76	11	0	0	0
Placencia, Cleveland	P	.875	1	6	1	0	0
Polanco, California	P	1.000	4	7	0	0	0
Polanco, KC/Rockies	P	.950	5	14	1	0	0
Polanco, NY Mets	INF	.902	71	122	21	13	0
Polanco, Oakland	INF	.873	85	121	30	15	0
Polo, Atlanta	INF	.775	19	60	23	8	0
Portes, Yan/SD	C/INF	.954	171	36	10	0	2
Prensi, Toronto West	OF	.952	110	10	6	2	0
Puente, Seattle	OF	.956	82	4	4	2	0
Puesan, KC/Rockies	P	.762	2	14	5	0	0
Quezada, Montreal	P	.929	2	11	1	0	0
Quezada, SF/Phi/Hou	OF	.837	75	2	15	0	0
Quintana, SF/Phi/Ho	P	.857	10	8	3	1	0
Quiroz, Oakland	P	1.000	1	1	0	0	0
Ramirez, Ang/Dod	INF	.912	45	38	8	2	0
Jo. Ramirez, Milw	P	.706	0	12	5	0	0
Ju. Ramirez, Milw	INF/P	.946	18	35	3	2	0
D. Ramirez, NY Mets	OF/INF	.968	170	9	6	1	0
R. Ramirez, NY Mets	P	1.000	4	3	0	0	0
Ramirez, Pittsburgh	OF/INF	.944	95	7	6	2	0
Ramos, Florida	P	.917	0	11	1	3	0
Ramos, Houston	INF	.909	81	108	19	8	0
Randolph, Tor West	P	.895	1	16	2	0	0
Rayo, Ang/Dod	P	.813	4	9	3	0	0
Rendon, Milwaukee	OF/INF	.928	83	7	7	0	0
Reyes, Cleveland	INF	.907	62	74	14	12	0
Reyes, Det/St.L	C/INF	.955	134	15	7	1	2
Reyes, Florida	P	.857	2	4	1	0	0
Reyes, Pittsburgh	C/OF	.949	164	40	11	0	7
Reyes, SF/Phi/Hou	INF	.919	189	162	31	9	0
F. Reyes, Toyo Carp	INF	.824	14	47	13	3	0
R. Reyes, Toyo Carp	INF	.914	33	105	13	4	0
Reynoso, Houston	P	.889	3	5	1	0	0
Reynoso, Tor East	P	.692	3	6	4	0	0
Rijo, California	P	.714	2	8	4	0	0
Rijo, Houston	P	.818	3	6	2	1	0
Rincones, Balt/WS	INF	.908	59	89	15	10	0
Rivera, Chi/Tex	INF/P	.906	25	4	3	0	0
Rivera, Yan/SD	P	.667	0	6	3	0	0
Roa, KC/Rockies	INF	.883	72	87	21	11	0
Roche, Houston	INF	.914	70	4	7	0	0
Rodriguez, Atlanta	OF	.958	87	5	4	1	0
Rodriguez, Chi/Tex	P	.767	4	19	7	0	0
Rodriguez, Det/St.L	P	.833	1	4	1	0	0
Rodriguez, Florida	P	1.000	1	2	0	0	0
Rodriguez, Houston	P	1.000	3	2	0	0	0
E. Rodriguez, LA I	OF/DH	.933	13	1	1	0	0
L. Rodriguez, LA I	INF/P	.882	60	134	26	9	0
Rodriguez, Oakland	INF	.932	104	87	14	9	0
Rojas, Montreal	P	.881	8	133	19	18	0
Rojas, Pittsburgh	OF/INF	1.000	17	2	0	0	0
Romero, Milwaukee	OF	1.000	8	0	0	0	0
Romero, Tor East	P	1.000	0	1	0	0	0
Rondon, Oakland	C/INF	.957	220	45	12	0	7
Roque, Milwaukee	C/INF	.977	281	53	8	2	12
Rosado, Atlanta	P	.897	2	24	3	1	0
Rosario, Cleveland	P	.846	1	10	2	0	0
Rosario, Det/St.L	P	1.000	1	2	0	0	0
Rosario, Florida	P	.800	1	3	1	0	0
Rosario, Milwaukee	INF	.930	79	28	8	3	0
F. Rosario, Tor East	OF	.940	85	9	6	2	0
N. Rosario, Tor East	P	.852	3	20	4	2	0
Ruan, Montreal	OF	.941	60	4	4	1	0
J. Ruiz, Balt/WS	INF	.816	20	42	14	5	0
M. Ruiz, Balt/WS	P	.909	11	9	2	2	0
Ruiz, Det/St.L	INF	.912	121	118	23	8	0
Ruiz, Los Angeles I	P	.846	3	8	2	0	0
Salazar, Balt/WS	C	.963	105	24	5	2	0
Salazar, Yan/SD	C/INF	.966	127	16	5	1	5
Salcedo, Pittsburgh	P	1.000	4	5	0	2	0
Saldana, Cleveland	P	1.000	0	3	0	0	0
Salomon, Atlanta	INF	.889	115	189	38	17	0
Salvador, Balt/WS	INF/C	.977	347	39	9	0	4
Samboy, NY Mets	P	1.000	0	2	0	0	0
J. Sanchez, NY Mets	P	.857	6	6	2	0	0
R. Sanchez, NY Mets	P	1.000	0	4	0	0	0
N. Sanchez, Tor East	INF	.919	93	55	13	3	0
O. Sanchez, Tor East	INF/OF	.944	165	140	18	8	0
Sanchez, Yan/SD	OF/INF	.870	20	0	3	0	0
Saneaux, Balt/WS	P	1.000	5	4	0	1	0
Santa, Tor West	INF	.877	67	147	30	11	0
Santana, Ang/Dod	INF	.978	39	49	2	5	0
Santana, Houston	OF/INF	.903	109	12	13	1	0
Santana, Oakland	INF	.978	297	13	7	2	0
Santana, Pittsburgh	OF	.904	56	10	7	1	0
Santana, Seattle	P	.857	1	5	1	0	0
Santana, SF/Phi/Hou	C	.964	124	37	6	1	4
Santander, Florida	C/INF	.942	92	5	6	0	3
Santelise, Balt/WS	INF	.933	14	0	1	0	0
Santive, Oakland	P	.857	3	3	1	0	0
Santos, Pittsburgh	P	.875	2	5	1	0	0
Santos Perez, B/WS	P	1.000	4	2	0	0	0
Saravia, LA I	C	1.000	11	1	0	1	1
Scheker, Oakland	INF	.968	345	16	12	0	0
Segura, Oakland	P	.700	4	3	3	0	0
Selmo, Atlanta	P	.913	2	19	2	1	0
Sena, Det/St.L	P	.600	0	3	2	0	0
Sepulveda, Seattle	C	.966	66	19	3	0	6
Serafin, SF/Phi/Hou	OF	.800	41	3	11	0	0
Severino, NY Mets	P	1.000	2	1	0	0	0
Sierra, Montreal	OF	.944	62	5	4	1	0
Silva, Oakland	P	.933	5	23	2	2	0
Sojo, Houston	P	.857	7	5	2	1	0
Solano, Tor East	INF	.944	117	223	20	23	0
Soriano, Chi/Tex	INF	.857	39	63	17	11	0
C. Soriano, NY Mets	OF/INF	.914	50	141	18	8	0
J.C. Soriano, NY Mets	INF	.960	110	105	9	12	0
Sosa, California	OF/INF	.981	197	15	4	0	0
Sosa, Cleveland	C	.972	326	62	11	2	7
Sosa, LA I	INF	.910	74	209	28	16	0
Sosa, Oakland	P	.941	1	15	1	0	0
Soto, Balt/WS	INF	.902	123	217	37	27	0
Sterling, Atlanta	INF	.883	78	88	22	14	0
Suarez, KC/Rockies	C	.957	132	25	7	1	8
Suero, Milwaukee	OF/INF	.941	15	1	1	0	0
Suriel, NY Mets	P	.826	4	15	4	2	0
Tapia, Balt/WS	P	.923	7	5	1	1	0
Tatis, Chi/Tex	INF	.857	86	135	37	11	0
Tatis, Yan/SD	C/INF	.992	107	19	1	1	1
Taveras, Cleveland	INF	.848	34	55	16	6	0
Tejada, Florida	P	.818	0	9	2	0	0
Toribio, LA I	P	.600	1	2	2	0	0
Torres, Ang/Dod	P	.875	2	12	2	1	0
Tremols, Pittsburgh	C/INF	.950	105	10	6	0	3
Uceta, Oakland	P	.923	4	8	1	0	0
Ulloa, Tor West	C	.962	237	45	11	1	13
Umanzor, Atlanta	P	1.000	2	7	0	0	0
Urena, Ang/Dod	INF	.982	719	25	14	5	0
Urvina, LA I	P	.810	1	16	4	0	0
Valdespino, Tor East	C	.982	380	61	8	1	13
Valdez, Montreal	P	.909	2	8	1	0	0
Valdez, Oakland	P	1.000	0	11	0	0	0
Valdez, Seattle	INF	.940	70	71	9	8	0
Valdez, SF/Phi/Hou	P	.957	9	13	1	0	0
Valera, Cleveland	INF	.919	57	91	13	7	0
Valera, NY Mets	C	.966	141	27	6	0	0
Vargas, California	P	.933	65	5	5	0	0
Vargas, Tor West	OF/INF	.941	62	2	4	0	0
Vasquez, KC/Rockies	P	.857	4	14	3	1	0
Ventura, Oakland	C/OF	.976	68	13	2	0	3
Veras, Milwaukee	C	.941	123	21	9	1	12
Veras, Seattle	INF	.898	43	71	13	10	0
Vicentino, Seattle	P	1.000	1	13	0	0	0
Villalobos, Seattle	OF/INF	.943	28	5	2	0	0
Villalona, Tor East	OF	.973	138	8	4	2	0
Villareal, KC/Rockies	P	1.000	1	4	0	0	0
Vilomar, NY Mets	OF/INF	.952	77	3	4	0	0
Viloria, Yan/SD	OF/INF	.967	112	7	4	1	0
Wilson, KC/Rockies	OF/C	.881	81	15	13	2	1
Zambrano, Chi/Tex	P	.800	1	7	2	0	0
Zapata, Milwaukee	P	1.000	0	5	0	0	0
Zapata, Montreal	P	.959	75	19	4	0	3
Zerpa, Balt/WS	INF/OF	.953	153	30	9	1	0
Zorrilla, NY Mets	INF	.945	86	70	9	5	0
Zorrilla, Toyo Carp	OF	.979	46	1	1	0	0

GULF COAST LEAGUE

EASTERN DIVISION

Team	W	L	T	Pct.	GB
Mets	39	20	0	.661	....
Braves	32	26	0	.552	6½
Expos	27	31	0	.466	11½
Cubs	19	40	0	.322	20

NORTHERN DIVISION

Team	W	L	T	Pct.	GB
Astros	35	24	0	.593	....
Marlins	32	28	0	.533	3½
Yankees	30	29	0	.508	5
Blue Jays	22	38	0	.367	13½

WESTERN DIVISION

Team	W	L	T	Pct.	GB
Rangers	40	20	0	.667	....
White Sox	32	27	0	.542	7½
Red Sox	32	28	0	.533	8
Orioles	30	28	0	.517	9
Royals	29	30	0	.492	10½
Twins	23	36	0	.390	16½
Pirates	21	38	0	.356	18½

COMPOSITE

Team	Rng.	Mets	Ast.	Brv.	W.S.	R.S.	Mrl.	Ori.	Yan.	Ryl.	Exp.	Twi.	B.J.	Pir.	Cubs	W	L	T	Pct.	GB
Rangers	....	0	0	0	5	9	0	6	0	6	0	7	0	7	0	40	20	0	.667	....
Mets	0	....	0	10	0	0	0	0	0	13	0	0	0	16	39	20	0	.661	½
Astros	0	0	....	0	0	0	10	0	10	0	0	15	0	0	0	35	24	0	.593	4½
Braves	0	9	0	....	0	0	0	0	0	0	8	0	0	0	15	32	26	0	.552	7
White Sox	5	0	0	0	....	4	0	4	0	3	0	6	0	8	0	32	27	0	.542	7½
Red Sox	1	0	0	0	6	....	0	4	0	6	0	9	0	6	0	32	28	0	.533	8
Marlins	0	0	10	0	0	0	....	0	9	0	0	13	0	0	0	32	28	0	.533	8
Orioles	4	0	0	0	4	0	6	....	0	3	0	6	0	7	0	30	28	0	.517	9
Yankees	0	0	9	0	0	0	0	11	....	0	0	10	0	0	0	30	29	0	.508	9½
Royals	4	0	0	0	7	4	0	6	0	....	0	4	0	4	0	29	30	0	.492	10½
Expos	0	7	0	11	0	0	0	0	0	0	....	0	0	9	0	27	31	0	.466	12
Twins	3	0	0	0	4	1	0	3	0	6	0	....	0	6	0	23	36	0	.390	16½
Blue Jays	0	0	5	0	0	0	7	0	10	0	0	0	....	0	0	22	38	0	.367	18
Pirates	3	0	0	0	1	4	0	3	0	6	0	4	0	....	0	21	38	0	.356	18½
Cubs	0	4	0	5	0	0	0	0	0	0	10	0	0	0	....	19	40	0	.322	20½

Games played in Bradenton and Sarasota, Fla.

Club names are major league affiliations.

Playoffs—Astros defeated Mets, one game to none; Rangers defeated Astros, two games to none, to win league championship.

Regular-season attendance—No official attendance figures reported.

Managers—Astros, Julio Linares; Blue Jays, Hector Torres; Braves, Jim Saul; Cubs, Butch Hughes; Expos, Nelson Norman; Marlins, Jim Hendry; Mets, Junior Roman; Orioles, Oneri Fleita; Pirates, Woody Huyke; Rangers, Chino Cadahia; Red Sox, Felix Maldonado; Royals, Bob Herold; Twins, Jose Marzan; White Sox, Mike Rojas; Yankees, Glenn Sherlock.

All-Star team: 1B—David Catlett, Braves; 2B—Carlos Cabrera, Blue Jays; 3B—Mike Bell, Rangers; SS—Gavin Jackson, Red Sox; OF—Charles Peterson, Pirates; Juan Ramirez, Mets; Romulo Vizcaino, Twins; C—Larry Ephan, Rangers; Starting Pitcher—John Lombardi, Orioles; Relief Pitcher—Julio Santana, Rangers; Manager of the Year—Chino Cadahia, Rangers.

BATTING

TEAM

Team	Avg.	G	AB	R	OR	H	TB	2B	3B	HR	RBI	SH	SF	HP	BB	Int. BB	SO	SB	CS	LOB
Astros	.261	59	1990	286	252	520	684	95	24	7	230	11	12	31	187	0	367	76	22	437
Marlins	.261	60	2028	318	239	529	682	85	16	12	277	8	24	30	213	1	389	60	26	433
Rangers	.255	59	1924	313	234	491	660	75	29	12	249	6	22	42	258	5	350	133	50	425
Mets	.250	59	1962	314	239	491	651	85	21	11	232	19	19	35	259	2	361	100	32	443
Expos	.247	58	1959	249	239	484	640	72	15	18	203	18	20	27	208	2	413	40	18	423
Braves	.246	58	1921	275	262	472	620	74	19	12	213	12	15	48	178	0	348	66	23	398
Red Sox	.244	60	1988	241	212	485	633	89	13	11	198	26	20	44	217	9	355	53	27	479
White Sox	.242	59	1910	281	202	463	637	87	24	13	229	32	21	33	293	2	389	115	64	450
Royals	.242	59	1945	235	244	471	628	77	22	12	196	14	18	29	155	3	392	78	31	395
Cubs	.238	59	1848	243	341	440	546	54	14	8	175	51	14	46	222	1	364	92	57	382
Pirates	.237	59	1929	218	288	458	610	72	22	12	187	8	16	26	187	2	378	65	34	423
Blue Jays	.237	60	1976	235	336	469	622	87	21	8	195	13	13	22	178	0	438	76	32	408
Yankees	.226	59	1930	237	249	436	593	71	22	14	195	11	21	34	231	3	507	79	27	455
Twins	.216	59	1885	248	305	408	537	65	14	12	196	7	16	37	218	0	403	66	25	404
Orioles	.207	58	1852	200	251	383	466	42	16	3	148	24	15	28	189	2	438	122	40	390

INDIVIDUAL

(Leading qualifiers for batting championship—162 or more plate appearances)

*Bats lefthanded. †Switch-hitter.

Player, Team	Avg.	G	AB	R	H	TB	2B	3B	HR	RBI	SH	SF	HP	BB	Int. BB	SO	SB	CS
Ephan, Larry, Rangers	.350	56	180	42	63	86	16	2	1	38	0	0	6	41	3	30	0	1
Lobaton, Jose, Yankees	.345	44	165	30	57	80	8	6	1	16	1	2	19	0	28	24	2
Rodriguez, Maximo, Marlins	.326	48	187	30	61	79	8	5	0	29	0	2	1	10	1	26	3	2

Player, Team	Avg.	G	AB	R	H	TB	2B	3B	HR	RBI	SH	SF	HP	BB	Int. BB	SO	SB	CS
Jackson, Gavin, Red Sox	.318	41	157	29	50	61	7	2	0	11	2	0	10	14	0	18	11	5
Bell, Mike, Rangers	.317	60	230	48	73	107	13	6	3	34	1	2	4	27	0	23	9	2
Mendez, Carlos, Royals	.313	50	163	18	51	73	10	0	4	27	0	2	4			15	6	1
Catlett, David, White Sox	.311	54	193	33	60	90	11	2	5	33	2	3	5	31	0	19	11	5
Aranzamendi, Alex, Marlins	.309	42	149	13	46	60	8	0	2	31	0	2	0	13	0	17	1	1
Diaz, Ed, Rangers	.305	43	154	27	47	70	10	5	1	23	0	2	4	19	1	21	12	5
Ramirez, Juan, Mets	.304	52	204	37	62	78	4	3	2	31	2	4	3	15	0	45	10	3

Departmental leaders: G—Bell, 60; AB—Abad, Bell, 230; R—Arvelo, 50; H—Bell, 73; TB—Bell, 107; 2B—Ephan, 16; 3B—Macon, 7; HR—Niethammer, 6; RBI—Ephan, 38; SH—Scopio, 9; SF—T. Nelson, 8; HP—Macon, 13; BB—Ephan, 41; IBB—Ephan, 3; SO—McClure, 66; SB—Ozario, 39; CS—Ozario, 11.

(All players—listed alphabetically)

Player, Team	Avg.	G	AB	R	H	TB	2B	3B	HR	RBI	SH	SF	HP	BB	Int. BB	SO	SB	CS
Abad, Andy, Red Sox*	.248	59	230	24	57	73	9	2	1	28	2	4	2	25	0	27	2	2
Abreu, Guillermo, Twins	.200	25	60	9	12	14	2	0	0	9	1	0	1	4	0	10	1	0
Alfonzo, Robert, Mets†	.261	40	134	13	35	37	2	0	0	19	1	1	1	12	0	11	9	3
Alonso, Marcelino, Orioles	.256	36	78	9	20	24	2	1	0	6	2	1	0	8	0	15	4	0
Alvarez, Clemente, White Sox	.000	2	5	0	0	0	0	0	0	0	0	0	0	1	0	2	0	1
Amezcua, Adan, Astros	.297	48	145	14	43	62	13	3	0	24	0	1	1	12	0	19	1	0
Aquino, Geronimo, White Sox	.103	13	29	1	3	4	1	0	0	2	0	0	0	1	0	12	0	1
Aranzamendi, Alex, Marlins	.309	42	149	13	46	60	8	0	2	31	0	2	0	13	0	17	1	1
Arias, Ramon, Red Sox†	.200	14	20	3	4	5	1	0	0	2	0	0	0	8	0	6	0	0
Arrollado, Courtney, Red Sox	.161	17	56	6	9	9	0	0	0	1	1	0	1	7	1	16	2	2
Arvelo, Tomas, Mets	.227	56	207	50	47	56	6	0	1	17	3	0	3	40	0	49	25	3
Ashby, Chris, Yankees	.211	49	175	24	37	49	12	0	0	23	0	2	6	32	0	45	5	3
Avalos, Gilbert, Cubs	.297	33	111	22	33	44	6	1	1	8	1	1	2	14	0	17	14	2
Babin, Brady, Marlins	.237	54	186	29	44	48	2	1	0	21	0	6	3	18	0	25	3	3
Baker, Keivi, Orioles	.172	29	64	9	11	13	2	0	0	5	1	0	1	13	0	16	2	0
Barberie, Bret, Marlins†	.250	2	8	0	2	2	0	0	0	1	0	0	0	1	0	1	0	0
Baucom, Chad, Twins	.057	11	35	1	2	3	1	0	0	1	0	0	2	1	0	9	0	0
Beaumont, Hamil, Yankees	.208	39	125	14	26	36	5	1	1	11	2	0	0	18	0	56	2	3
Becker, David, Blue Jays	.209	38	110	14	23	32	7	1	0	8	1	0	5	20	0	37	8	1
Bell, Mike, Rangers	.317	60	230	48	73	107	13	6	3	34	1	2	4	27	0	23	9	2
Beyna, Terry, Astros	.275	41	120	24	33	43	6	2	0	23	0	4	3	16	0	13	2	1
Blackburn, Tyres, White Sox	.256	31	78	9	20	23	1	1	0	5	2	0	2	6	0	22	6	1
Borges, Mariano, Pirates	.225	29	102	8	23	33	6	2	0	7	0	1	1	1	0	20	1	3
Boulware, Benjamin, White Sox	.208	33	106	19	22	31	3	0	2	11	1	4		20	0	11	13	1
Bourne, Charles, Blue Jays	.244	44	160	26	39	45	6	0	0	11	1	1	1	17	0	57	10	2
Bowers, Ray, Astros	.274	55	208	24	57	73	13	0	1	21	0	1	6	4	0	43	10	2
Bowles, John, Red Sox*	.191	48	152	14	29	36	4	0	1	13	4	1	5	18	0	20	0	1
Bowman, Delshon, Orioles	.127	31	79	8	10	11	1	0	0	5	1	2	2	11	0	36	8	4
Bowman, Paul, Mets	.000	10	0	0	0	0	0	0	0	0	0	0	0	0	0	0	0	0
Bradley, Ken, Mets	.269	36	130	16	35	49	9	1	1	15	0	0	0	1	0	26	4	4
Brandon, Jelani, Royals	.238	53	151	18	36	54	5	5	1	18	2	1	0	23	0	36	4	2
Brea, Juan, Mets	.383	19	60	12	23	37	3	4	1	10	0	2	6	10	0	10	0	1
Brea, Vincente, Orioles	.324	12	34	5	11	12	1	0	0	2	0	0	0	4	0	11	0	0
Brewer, Doug, Braves	.282	41	142	17	40	48	4	2	0	16	0	1	6	2	0	17	5	1
Brinkley, Joshua, Royals	.270	16	63	6	17	19	2	0	0	4	0	1	2	2	0	8	2	1
Brown, Roosevelt, Braves*	.113	26	80	4	9	14	1	2	0	5	1	0	1	2	0	9	2	0
Brown, Vick, Yankees	.245	52	212	31	52	61	7	1	0	15	1	3	7	19	1	44	18	2
Burgos, Carlos, Royals	.333	3	3	0	1	1	0	0	0	2	0	0	0	0	0	0	0	0
Cabrera, Carlos, Blue Jays†	.303	52	201	35	61	89	14	4	2	23	2	2	0	14	0	23	12	6
Campos, Jesus, Expos	.125	2	8	1	1	1	0	0	0	1	0	0	0	2	0	1	0	0
Carone, Richard, White Sox	.239	27	88	12	21	33	4	1	1	14	2	1	1	8	0	19	2	0
Carr, Chuck, Marlins†	.417	3	12	4	5	9	1	0	1	3	0	0	0	0	0	2	3	0
Carter, Rickey, Braves	.138	25	87	8	12	16	1	0	1	9	0	1	4	4	0	20	2	1
Casique, Willie, Twins	.241	10	29	4	7	8	1	0	0	2	0	1	0	0	4	0	1	
Castle, Ryan, Cubs	.275	25	80	15	22	31	3	0	2	10	2	2	1	9	0	11	6	1
Castro, Ruben, Twins	.267	40	135	19	36	48	8	2	0	12	1	0	3	21	0	18	3	2
Catlett, David, White Sox	.311	54	193	33	60	90	11	2	5	33	2	3	5	31	0	19	11	5
Cepeda, Malcolm, Royals	.265	48	155	15	41	55	4	2	2	20	0	1	0	11	1	37	4	1
Chambers, Bradley, Cubs*	.297	24	74	9	22	31	6	0	1	10	2	1	2	9	0	7	0	2
Chancey, Bob, Orioles	.143	29	84	7	12	15	3	0	0	3	0	0	1	4	0	39	3	0
Cicero, Frank, Cubs	.241	29	83	13	20	24	2	1	0	9	2	1	5	7	0	14	2	1
Civit, Xavier, Expos	.304	33	102	16	31	37	4	1	0	15	1	1	6	22	0	0		
Clark, Kevin, Red Sox	.204	40	137	14	28	40	9	0	1	19	0	4	3	16	1	24	1	1
Coquillette, Trace, Expos	.252	44	159	27	40	56	4	3	2	11	1	3	7	37	0	28	16	3
Cormenares, Carlos, Blue Jays	.233	9	30	3	7	8	1	1	0	1	1	0	0	1	0	8	0	1
Crick, Jeffrey, Twins	.127	24	71	7	9	10	1	0	0	5	1	0	1	7	0	29	0	0
Cruz, Brian, Braves	.211	22	57	11	12	17	5	0	0	5	0	0	3	11	0	6	0	0
Cruz, Hiram, Twins	.215	39	107	21	23	33	4	0	2	11	0	0	0	18	0	38	8	2
Culp, Randy, Expos	.271	55	210	31	57	88	14	1	5	23	0	2	3	18	0	56	0	0
Cunningham, Jamil, Cubs	.179	40	106	16	19	25	1	1	1	12	5	0	7	6	0	25	9	6
Cunningham, Paul, Pirates	.167	25	78	5	13	16	3	0	0	7	0	1	0	8	0	12	0	0
Davila, Vic, Blue Jays*	.302	50	182	23	55	77	10	3	2	20	2	2	2	13	0	42	4	3
Delgado, Jose, Pirates†	.254	33	118	15	30	40	6	2	0	9	1	0	0	17	1	16	10	2
Deno, Ariel, Rangers	.200	14	25	4	5	5	0	0	0	4	0	0	1	0	0	7	0	1
DeJesus, Jose, Cubs	.150	33	80	13	12	14	2	0	0	4	3	0	4	10	0	20	1	0
Diaz, Ed, Rangers	.305	43	154	27	47	70	10	5	1	23	0	2	4	19	1	21	12	5
Doezie, David, Twins	.126	31	87	11	11	13	2	0	0	8	0	1	0	9	0	25	1	0
Dolney, Dan, Astros*	.316	26	57	12	18	30	7	1	1	8	0	0	1	15	0	9	1	0
Domingo, Tyrone, Braves	.067	4	15	3	1	1	0	0	0	0	0	0	0	0	0	6	1	0
Dondero, Daron, Royals	.127	35	71	4	9	13	2	1	0	7	0	0	0	11	0	34	0	0
Dunwoody, Todd, Marlins*	.193	31	109	13	21	27	2	2	0	7	1	1	2	7	0	28	5	0
Dye, Jermaine, Braves*	.347	31	124	17	43	57	14	0	0	27	0	1	5	5	0	13	5	0
Ephan, Larry, Rangers	.350	56	180	42	63	86	16	2	1	38	0	6	4	41	3	30	0	1
Estrada, Josue, Expos	.243	55	214	24	52	66	5	3	1	32	0	4	2	20	1	48	2	1
Faggett, Ethan, Red Sox*	.172	23	58	4	10	14	2	0	0	2	0	1	0	10	0	15	5	1
Fantauzzi, Hiram, Marlins	.264	37	121	22	32	49	9	1	2	15	0	3	1	12	0	39	5	2
Farner, Matt, Blue Jays*	.181	27	94	12	17	19	2	0	0	6	1	0	0	19	0	22	6	3

Player, Team	Avg.	G	AB	R	H	TB	2B	3B	HR	RBI	SH	SF	HP	BB	Int. BB	SO	SB	CS
Fellhauer, David, Mets*	.288	30	104	19	30	44	7	2	1	15	0	1	6	11	1	16	2	0
Ferrier, Ross, Mets	.277	43	155	23	43	61	10	1	2	21	0	1	7	20	0	27	1	2
Ford, Eric, Red Sox	.273	8	33	5	9	12	1	1	0	3	0	1	0	5	0	8	0	0
Fortin, Troy, Twins	.257	30	101	6	26	35	3	0	2	15	0	1	1	8	0	11	3	0
Foster, Jeff, Expos*	.179	8	28	4	5	6	1	0	0	1	1	1	0	5	0	7	0	0
Franklin, James, Braves	.236	41	148	18	35	47	4	1	2	22	0	0	1	15	0	48	4	1
Frazier, Jason, Marlins†	.111	12	18	3	2	2	0	0	0	2	0	0	0	2	0	2	0	0
Frazier, Tyrone, Royals	.200	39	90	11	18	19	1	0	0	4	0	0	3	13	0	27	7	2
Freeberger, George, Orioles	.133	26	60	5	8	9	1	0	0	4	3	1	1	9	0	20	1	1
Friedrich, Steven, White Sox	.262	28	84	10	22	24	2	0	0	11	1	1	3	6	0	12	7	5
Fuller, Aaron, Red Sox†	.545	6	11	5	6	8	0	1	0	2	0	0	0	3	0	3	0	0
Gabriel, Denio, Orioles†	.221	44	154	19	34	52	4	4	2	8	1	1	2	7	0	40	11	5
Galarza, Eduardo, Pirates†	.256	38	121	9	31	36	5	0	0	15	0	3	1	6	0	12	0	0
Garcia, Carlos, Twins	.240	16	50	7	12	17	3	1	0	6	0	1	1	4	0	14	3	2
Garcia, Eduard, Cubs	.211	45	133	13	28	37	4	1	1	13	3	0	1	8	0	29	2	1
Garcia, Jesus, Orioles	.237	48	156	20	37	41	4	0	0	16	8	3	1	21	1	32	14	6
Garcia, Luis, Rangers†	.182	41	99	9	18	19	1	0	0	5	2	0	2	8	0	25	10	7
Gargiulo, Michael, Orioles*	.162	26	74	8	12	13	1	0	0	6	0	0	2	8	0	16	1	3
Genden, Eric, Marlins	.232	40	112	21	26	35	3	0	2	21	0	2	3	17	0	41	0	0
Gibralter, David, Red Sox	.267	49	180	23	48	71	14	0	3	27	1	2	7	11	1	34	1	1
Gil, Dan, Cubs	.272	48	151	13	41	44	3	0	0	19	3	2	1	20	0	25	4	8
Gipner, Marcus, Yankees†	.207	47	174	17	36	38	2	0	0	19	0	2	0	20	1	39	3	0
Goligoski, Jason, White Sox*	.258	54	163	30	42	64	12	2	2	27	3	3	1	34	0	18	16	9
Gomez, Paul, Mets	.150	10	20	2	3	5	0	1	0	3	0	0	1	9	0	3	2	0
Gonzalez, Carlos, Expos	.272	22	81	6	22	28	4	1	0	8	0	0	0	3	0	21	0	0
Gonzalez, Mario, Rangers†	.284	53	183	33	52	62	10	0	0	15	1	3	2	32	0	19	21	3
Gordon, Adrian, Twins	.241	37	112	11	27	31	2	1	0	8	0	0	3	17	0	29	5	3
Gosch, Grant, Astros*	.154	12	26	3	4	4	0	0	0	3	0	0	2	0	0	8	0	0
Graham, John, Red Sox*	.385	9	39	7	15	24	4	1	1	6	1	0	4	0	5	3	2
Gross, William, Marlins	.220	23	59	4	13	18	3	1	0	9	0	1	1	6	0	11	0	0
Hagen, Sean, Pirates†	.189	32	106	11	20	26	4	1	0	8	2	0	3	10	0	26	1	0
Hairston, Jeff, Pirates	.202	29	99	5	20	32	2	2	2	12	0	0	3	3	0	29	2	6
Halbruner, Rich, Blue Jays*	.230	41	126	20	29	51	9	2	3	19	2	0	0	17	0	32	0	2
Hall, Ronnie, Expos	.226	49	177	21	40	49	6	0	1	13	1	0	5	19	0	32	4	3
Hall, Todd, White Sox	.241	34	83	15	20	30	8	1	0	11	1	1	2	16	0	7	4	2
Hamilton, Joe, Red Sox*	.170	15	47	3	8	11	0	0	1	2	0	0	0	8	0	13	0	0
Hammer, Ben, Astros*	.250	44	108	19	27	31	4	0	0	12	2	0	3	18	0	19	4	1
Hayward, Joe, Red Sox*	.333	8	24	7	8	15	1	0	2	6	0	1	1	7	0	2	0	0
Helsel, Ron, Blue Jays	.286	5	14	2	4	6	2	0	0	1	0	0	1	3	0	2	0	0
Hidalgo, Jose, Orioles	.205	38	122	12	25	33	4	2	0	15	1	2	6	9	0	16	5	2
Hightower, Aaron, Blue Jays	.257	54	202	25	52	76	9	6	1	37	0	7	3	11	0	40	13	3
Hiraldo, Jerry, Mets	.221	32	104	15	23	33	6	2	0	12	3	2	0	17	0	20	2	1
Hobert, Billy Joe, White Sox	.256	15	39	3	10	12	2	0	0	4	1	0	0	6	0	5	1	1
Hofer, Raymond, Braves	.240	27	96	12	23	26	1	1	0	8	0	1	1	3	0	16	1	2
Hubley, Greg, Marlins	.296	48	142	27	42	51	5	2	0	21	2	0	4	19	0	28	11	3
Hunter, Burt, Cubs*	.226	9	31	2	7	8	1	0	0	2	0	0	0	2	0	8	2	0
Hunter, Toril, Twins†	.190	28	100	6	19	22	3	0	0	8	1	0	9	4	0	23	4	2
Izquierdo, Nelson, White Sox	.318	11	22	5	7	8	1	0	0	3	1	0	0	3	0	2	0	0
Jackson, Gavin, Red Sox	.318	41	157	29	50	61	7	2	0	11	2	0	10	14	0	18	11	5
Jefferson, David, Marlins	.263	15	38	4	10	14	1	0	1	6	0	0	0	2	0	3	0	0
Johnson, Damon, Marlins	.276	39	127	12	35	39	4	0	0	7	0	0	1	5	0	34	4	0
Johnson, Mike, Twins	.379	7	29	4	11	15	2	1	0	6	0	0	1	4	0	4	0	0
Keefe, Jamie, Pirates	.500	5	14	3	7	7	0	0	0	2	1	0	0	2	0	2	3	1
Kern, Mike, Royals	.169	39	89	7	15	24	4	1	1	6	0	0	0	5	0	24	1	1
Kieschnick, Brooks, Cubs*	.222	3	9	2	2	3	1	0	0	0	0	0	0	0	0	1	0	0
King, Kevin, Blue Jays	.115	17	52	5	6	6	0	0	0	2	0	0	2	4	0	21	3	0
Kingman, Brendan, Marlins	.251	57	203	34	51	73	14	1	2	37	0	4	2	25	0	36	0	0
Knighten, Dwon, Cubs	.250	34	88	12	22	25	1	0	0	14	4	0	2	10	0	14	6	3
Lamb, David, Orioles†	.179	16	56	4	10	11	1	0	0	6	0	0	0	10	0	8	2	0
Landaker, David, Astros	.500	10	32	12	16	21	5	0	0	4	0	0	3	6	0	6	2	1
Lane, Ryan, Twins	.145	43	138	15	20	27	3	2	0	5	3	1	2	15	0	38	3	1
Larkin, Jim, Red Sox	.276	8	29	6	8	9	1	0	0	3	0	0	3	2	0	5	1	1
Larson, Kirk, Astros	.200	3	5	0	1	1	0	0	0	0	0	0	0	2	0	0	0	0
Lebron, Ruben, Red Sox†	.294	14	34	4	10	11	1	0	0	2	0	0	1	0	0	7	0	1
Lee, Angelo, Astros	.248	46	145	21	36	56	7	2	3	25	1	2	1	11	0	36	8	5
Lee, Jason, Braves	.206	27	97	8	20	21	1	0	0	6	4	2	0	4	0	12	1	1
Leger, Tim, Pirates	.190	31	105	12	20	23	3	0	0	10	1	0	0	17	0	19	4	1
Levias, Andres, White Sox	.209	39	86	18	18	26	2	3	0	5	6	2	3	14	1	15	9	4
Lewis, Andreaus, Rangers	.261	56	203	44	53	72	3	5	2	15	0	1	5	35	0	50	25	9
Lewis, Greg, Rangers	.000	3	9	1	0	0	0	0	0	0	0	0	0	1	0	2	1	0
Lewis, Jeffrey, Marlins	.231	40	78	14	18	18	0	0	0	8	0	0	3	9	0	29	7	5
Linares, Ruben, Orioles	.157	38	127	7	20	20	0	0	0	5	0	1	1	6	0	29	3	3
Lobaton, Jose, Yankees	.345	44	165	30	57	80	8	6	1	16	1	2	2	19	0	28	24	3
Lopez, Miguel, Royals	.200	47	145	15	29	34	5	0	0	12	2	3	2	10	0	23	0	2
Lopez, Orangel, Yankees	.224	32	116	13	26	37	4	0	1	12	1	0	2	13	0	15	2	3
Lopez, Yamil, Astros	.143	23	42	5	6	6	0	0	0	2	0	0	2	3	0	13	0	1
Lorenzo, Wilson, Red Sox	.169	24	65	2	11	14	3	0	0	7	3	0	2	3	0	12	0	0
Lyde, Alfredo, Pirates	.154	20	52	4	8	10	0	1	0	2	0	0	1	6	0	22	1	0
Mackert, Jamie, Pirates	.353	5	17	4	6	10	1	0	1	4	0	0	1	0	0	4	0	0
Macon, Leland, Rangers	.264	56	193	35	51	72	1	7	2	27	1	1	13	14	0	25	29	5
Magee, James, Braves	.283	16	60	14	17	26	4	1	1	8	0	0	8	5	0	12	4	0
Maize, Dave, Mets†	.100	3	10	0	1	1	0	0	0	0	0	0	0	0	0	2	0	0
Martinez, Felix, Royals	.255	37	165	23	42	49	5	1	0	12	1	0	3	17	0	26	22	5
Martinez, Humberto, Red Sox	.197	26	66	7	13	16	1	1	0	5	0	0	9	0	20	0	0
Martinez, Luis, Expos	.230	19	61	8	14	16	2	0	0	3	2	2	1	7	0	13	0	0
Martinez, Ramon, Royals	.237	37	97	16	23	28	5	0	0	9	2	2	2	8	0	6	3	0
Mathews, Delmer, Braves*	.147	34	34	4	5	5	0	0	0	3	0	1	1	2	0	8	1	0
Matos, Pasqual, Braves	.227	36	119	12	27	34	3	1	0	15	1	1	2	8	0	32	3	1
McClure, Craig, White Sox	.245	58	200	36	49	69	8	3	2	25	3	1	3	40	0	66	17	5
McCoy, Justin, Royals	.148	39	81	3	12	16	2	1	0	7	0	1	2	3	0	22	0	1
McKinnon, Sandy, White Sox	.182	6	11	2	2	2	0	0	0	1	0	0	0	2	0	4	0	0
Medrano, Anthony, Blue Jays	.266	39	158	20	42	51	9	0	0	9	1	0	2	10	0	13	6	2
Mejia, Miguel, Orioles	.246	35	130	21	32	41	3	3	0	12	0	0	2	13	1	23	18	5
Melendez, Osmin, Orioles†	.193	48	140	13	27	31	2	1	0	6	2	2	1	19	0	18	9	1

— 532 —

Player, Team	Avg.	G	AB	R	H	TB	2B	3B	HR	RBI	SH	SF	HP	BB	Int. BB	SO	SB	CS
Mendez, Carlos, Royals	.313	50	163	18	51	73	10	0	4	27	0	4	2	4	1	15	6	1
Mendoza, Francisco, Royals	.545	11	44	12	24	36	7	1	1	11	0	1	1	3	0	7	0	0
Menechino, Frank, White Sox	.244	17	45	10	11	20	4	1	1	9	0	0	4	12	0	4	3	1
Meran, Jorge, Expos	.153	17	59	6	9	10	1	0	0	2	2	0	1	7	0	19	1	0
Merloni, Louis, Red Sox	.357	4	14	4	5	6	1	0	0	1	0	0	1	1	0	1	1	1
Milliard, Ralph, Marlins	.234	53	192	35	45	60	15	0	0	25	0	1	6	30	0	17	11	5
Molina, Jose, Cubs	.218	33	78	5	17	19	2	0	0	4	4	0	0	12	0	12	3	2
Montilla, Miguel, Cubs	.216	40	125	15	27	30	1	1	0	7	2	1	1	23	1	35	3	4
Moore, David, White Sox	.239	47	134	16	32	40	3	1	1	16	2	0	0	21	0	47	4	4
Morales, Hery, Mets†	.215	40	130	26	28	37	7	1	0	14	4	1	1	30	0	25	1	0
Morales, Jesus, Mets	.167	35	114	10	19	23	4	0	0	7	1	0	2	19	0	21	2	3
Mosquera, Julio, Blue Jays	.259	35	108	9	28	35	3	2	0	15	2	1	1	8	0	16	3	3
Mota, Guillermo, Mets	.249	43	169	23	42	56	7	2	1	22	1	1	3	7	0	37	1	0
Mucker, Kelcey, Twins*	.138	9	29	6	4	4	0	0	0	2	0	0	0	4	0	10	2	0
Murphy, Pat, Red Sox*	.273	5	22	4	6	6	0	0	0	1	0	0	0	2	1	1	1	1
Navarro, Tito, Mets†	.286	4	14	2	4	7	1	1	0	5	0	0	2	3	0	1	1	0
Nelson, Andre, Cubs	.200	4	15	3	3	3	0	0	0	0	0	0	1	2	0	7	2	0
Nelson, Travion, Yankees	.179	57	195	24	35	59	10	1	4	22	0	8	1	21	0	54	3	3
Niethammer, Marc, Expos*	.197	49	157	21	31	53	4	0	6	18	0	1	5	26	1	55	0	1
Nolte, Bruce, Marlins	.271	36	70	11	19	27	3	1	1	12	0	1	0	10	0	10	0	1
Norman, Tyrone, Red Sox	.185	22	65	8	12	14	2	0	0	2	2	0	0	7	1	7	5	1
Norton, Gregory, White Sox†	.222	3	9	1	2	2	0	0	0	2	0	0	0	1	0	1	0	1
Ojeda, Miguel, Pirates	.278	27	97	9	27	41	3	1	3	11	1	0	2	10	0	18	2	0
Ortiz, Javier, Pirates	.304	8	23	5	7	10	3	0	0	6	0	1	0	8	0	7	0	0
Osentowski, Jared, Mets	.118	4	17	0	2	2	0	0	0	0	0	0	0	2	0	1	0	0
Ouimet, Steve, Rangers	.227	34	97	9	22	32	3	2	1	16	0	2	0	15	0	15	0	1
Ozario, Yudith, Mets	.230	55	213	38	49	60	7	2	0	13	3	1	5	33	0	35	39	11
Pachot, John, Expos	.306	35	121	13	37	43	4	1	0	16	4	2	0	2	0	7	0	1
Pagan, Angel, Orioles†	.278	34	115	12	32	46	5	3	1	30	3	1	1	17	0	33	7	1
Palmer, James, Yankees	.217	50	175	22	38	56	6	3	2	23	3	1	3	17	0	48	7	7
Palmer, Travis, Pirates	.222	6	18	2	4	4	0	0	0	1	0	0	0	1	0	5	1	1
Patterson, Jacob, Twins*	.207	44	140	14	29	43	6	1	2	16	0	2	5	13	0	34	1	0
Patterson, Jarrod, Mets*	.241	46	166	27	40	57	9	1	2	25	1	4	0	24	1	28	1	3
Patton, Greg, Red Sox	.563	4	16	6	9	11	2	0	0	5	0	0	0	2	0	2	0	2
Patton, Scott, White Sox	.189	50	159	19	30	42	8	2	0	16	2	1	1	31	1	46	10	7
Payano, Adolfo, Royals	.325	40	114	23	37	46	7	1	0	8	1	1	4	8	0	16	15	5
Pearson, Kevin, Twins	.142	42	120	13	17	21	1	0	1	6	0	0	1	20	0	21	5	2
Perez, Luis, Twins	.250	43	144	31	36	41	5	0	0	14	0	1	2	22	0	28	12	2
Perez, Pablo, Yankees	.227	19	44	7	10	19	1	4	0	4	0	0	0	9	0	8	2	2
Perez, Tomas, Expos†	.243	52	189	27	46	57	3	1	2	21	4	2	0	23	0	25	8	3
Peterson, Charles, Pirates	.303	49	188	28	57	77	11	3	1	23	0	1	0	22	0	22	8	6
Pico, Brandon, Cubs*	.385	10	39	3	15	20	3	1	0	9	0	0	0	2	0	2	3	3
Poe, Charles, White Sox	.308	3	13	2	4	10	3	0	1	2	0	0	0	1	0	3	0	1
Polanco, Felipe, Pirates	.293	38	133	16	39	47	4	2	0	13	1	0	6	8	0	20	13	7
Prieto, Alejandro, Royals	.246	43	114	14	28	31	3	0	0	6	4	0	0	9	1	13	4	2
Ramirez, Juan, Mets	.304	52	204	37	62	78	4	3	2	31	2	4	3	15	0	45	10	3
Ramos, Juan, Astros	.221	50	140	14	31	42	3	4	0	17	2	1	4	9	0	33	4	4
Reeves, Glenn, Marlins	.282	48	177	36	50	60	6	2	0	19	3	1	2	22	0	29	6	3
Rennspies, Dustin, Braves	.286	15	28	7	8	8	1	0	0	5	0	0	0	7	0	3	1	0
Reyes, Roberto, Expos	.304	30	112	17	34	49	6	3	1	15	2	1	0	9	0	18	9	3
Reynolds, Paul, Cubs	.261	48	142	16	37	45	8	0	0	13	3	2	10	28	0	33	4	7
Rice, Charles, Pirates†	.206	41	126	17	26	41	2	2	3	14	0	1	8	26	1	46	0	1
Ridenour, Jim, White Sox	.308	7	13	3	4	4	0	0	0	2	0	0	2	2	0	2	0	0
Rivera, Wilfredo, Red Sox	.268	53	183	17	49	66	15	1	0	21	1	5	4	19	1	29	2	2
Rivers, Jon, Blue Jays	.191	51	178	13	34	43	5	2	0	19	1	0	1	16	0	31	7	2
Roberson, Gerald, Braves	.281	42	153	34	43	56	7	3	0	8	0	0	3	21	0	17	14	3
Rodriguez, Maximo, Marlins	.326	48	187	30	61	79	7	8	5	29	0	2	1	10	1	26	3	2
Root, Derek, Astros*	.282	41	131	12	37	45	8	0	0	16	0	0	2	12	0	21	1	2
Roskos, John, Marlins	.175	11	40	6	7	11	1	0	1	3	0	0	1	5	0	11	1	1
Ross, Tony, Astros	.316	37	133	29	42	53	4	2	1	9	0	0	2	8	0	19	11	1
Rounsifer, Aaron, Red Sox	.267	23	60	3	16	20	4	0	0	6	1	0	1	2	1	17	2	0
Salazar, Marlon, Cubs	.000	2	1	0	0	0	0	0	0	0	0	0	0	0	0	0	0	0
Samuel, Quvia, Yankees†	.252	57	202	22	51	69	9	0	3	21	2	2	6	28	1	65	4	5
Sanchez, Dan, White Sox†	.179	26	28	0	5	8	1	1	0	7	0	2	0	3	0	5	1	1
Sanchez, Juan, Cubs	.232	27	69	9	16	17	1	0	0	6	2	0	0	9	0	10	2	2
Santiago, Carlos, Blue Jays	.277	38	119	12	33	35	2	0	0	9	0	0	1	10	0	21	3	1
Sasser, Robert, Braves	.239	33	113	19	27	31	4	0	0	7	0	2	4	6	0	25	2	1
Sauer, John, Cubs	.169	29	65	12	11	12	1	0	0	1	1	0	0	10	0	17	5	1
Saylor, Jamie, Astros*	.235	51	162	39	38	47	5	2	0	14	1	0	0	23	0	28	5	3
Schwab, Christopher, Expos*	.220	56	218	21	48	62	12	1	0	20	0	0	0	22	0	53	0	3
Scopio, Joe, Cubs†	.156	43	90	18	14	15	1	0	0	2	9	0	4	15	0	21	14	5
Seguignol, Fernando, Yankees†	.217	45	161	16	35	50	3	3	2	20	0	0	5	9	0	37	2	0
Selmo, Feliberto, Braves	.263	33	118	16	31	43	5	2	1	12	3	2	1	18	0	15	1	6
Shanklin, Whitney, Rangers	.197	29	71	8	14	18	1	0	1	7	0	0	1	16	0	26	4	5
Sheffield, Tony, Red Sox*	.177	43	130	11	23	33	3	2	1	17	1	1	1	17	1	47	6	2
Shows, Travis, Rangers	.063	11	16	1	1	1	0	0	0	1	0	0	1	2	0	8	0	0
Shumpert, Derek, Yankees†	.153	43	131	9	20	21	1	0	0	5	1	0	2	16	0	57	7	2
Simmons, Edwon, Orioles	.208	27	77	10	16	17	1	0	0	5	0	1	0	6	0	20	2	1
Smith, Akili, Pirates	.200	29	95	13	19	29	3	2	1	9	0	0	1	10	0	18	1	1
Smith, David, Red Sox	.300	3	10	3	3	3	0	0	0	1	0	1	0	2	0	2	0	0
Smith, Larry, Royals	.169	31	71	7	12	14	2	0	0	4	2	1	1	5	0	23	3	0
Spry, Shane, White Sox*	.239	43	117	19	28	34	6	0	0	10	4	2	1	15	0	24	6	3
Starks, Fred, White Sox	.294	9	17	2	5	9	0	2	0	6	0	2	1	3	0	1	0	0
Staton, Tarrence, Pirates*	.357	32	115	23	41	57	9	2	1	18	0	0	1	8	0	14	10	3
Stone, Craig, Blue Jays	.160	30	94	5	15	18	3	0	0	3	0	0	2	7	0	36	0	1
Swafford, Derek, Pirates*	.190	32	121	10	23	28	1	2	0	5	1	0	1	4	0	15	5	1
Tebbs, Nathan, Red Sox†	.260	43	146	21	38	44	4	1	0	4	4	7	0	15	1	16	7	1
Thomas, Juan, White Sox	.305	19	59	12	18	28	3	2	1	9	0	0	1	12	0	12	5	5
Thomas, Nathan, Cubs*	.200	7	5	0	1	1	0	0	0	1	0	0	0	0	0	2	1	0
Thomas, Rob, Braves	.500	2	2	0	1	1	0	0	0	0	0	0	0	0	0	0	0	0
Tillman, Bennie, Braves*	.259	33	116	18	30	45	1	4	2	14	0	1	4	13	0	31	3	0
Tolbert, Andrew, Braves	.189	29	90	10	17	18	1	0	0	7	0	1	1	14	0	17	4	1
Torres, Denny, Yankees	.236	20	55	8	13	18	3	1	0	4	0	1	0	10	0	11	0	3
Torres, Matt, Pirates	.174	18	46	5	8	10	2	0	0	5	0	2	1	6	0	8	0	0

Player, Team	Avg.	G	AB	R	H	TB	2B	3B	HR	RBI	SH	SF	HP	BB	Int. BB	SO	SB	CS
Trammell, Gary, Astros*	.288	59	215	25	62	77	5	5	0	19	1	2	3	14	0	38	11	3
Tremie, Chris, White Sox†	.000	2	4	0	0	0	0	0	0	0	0	0	0	0	0	0	0	0
Truby, Chris, Astros	.228	57	215	30	49	66	10	2	1	24	2	1	1	22	0	30	16	1
Turlais, John, Pirates*	.227	25	75	10	17	21	4	0	0	4	0	2	1	2	0	15	1	0
Ulises, Pedro, Orioles†	.220	40	132	13	29	34	5	0	0	8	0	0	7	13	0	38	10	2
Unrat, Christopher, Rangers*	.258	12	31	3	8	10	2	0	0	5	0	2	1	4	1	4	1	0
Valdez, Trovin, Orioles†	.212	39	151	16	32	38	2	2	0	6	2	0	0	9	0	23	21	5
Valentin, Jose, Twins†	.262	32	103	18	27	38	6	1	1	19	4	1	14	0	19	0	2
Vaninetti, Gene, Blue Jays	.162	43	148	11	24	31	5	1	0	12	0	0	1	8	0	41	1	0
Vaske, Terry, Cubs*	.261	31	88	16	23	36	3	2	2	10	3	1	1	12	0	17	2	5
Vazquez, Jorge, Braves	.239	16	46	10	11	15	4	0	0	4	0	0	2	8	0	22	2	0
Vessel, Andrew, Rangers	.219	51	192	23	42	59	10	2	1	31	0	6	1	8	0	28	6	2
Vielleux, Billy, Cubs	.283	36	99	11	28	34	2	2	0	10	2	1	1	10	0	18	6	4
Vindivich, Paul, Royals	.291	52	175	24	51	77	9	4	3	26	0	2	6	4	0	33	1	1
Vizcaino, Romulo, Twins†	.279	47	179	26	50	73	9	4	2	27	0	2	11	0	14	14	3
Vollmer, Scott, White Sox	.273	43	132	19	36	45	9	0	0	11	1	2	2	17	0	11	3	4
Walker, John, Red Sox*	.250	1	4	1	1	1	0	0	0	0	0	0	1	0	0	1	0	0
Walker, Roderic, Rangers	.152	27	79	7	12	13	1	0	0	8	0	0	1	9	0	23	6	2
Walls, Eric, Royals*	.282	24	71	10	20	32	2	5	0	9	0	2	0	5	0	12	5	4
Weathersby, Len, Royals	.158	33	76	6	12	13	1	0	0	7	0	0	2	3	0	26	0	1
White, Jarvis, Orioles	.263	5	19	2	5	5	0	0	0	0	0	0	0	2	0	5	1	0
Williams, Harold, White Sox*	.280	52	186	18	52	69	6	4	1	21	1	2	2	17	0	40	4	5
Williams, Ray, Rangers	.185	57	162	19	30	34	4	0	0	20	1	3	1	26	0	44	8	6
Williams, Richard, Braves†	.000	2	3	0	0	0	0	0	0	0	0	0	0	0	0	0	0	0
Winterlee, Scott, Mets	.455	4	11	1	5	8	3	0	0	2	0	1	0	1	0	3	0	0
Witt, Joe, Astros*	.189	39	106	13	20	27	5	1	0	9	2	0	1	13	0	30	0	2
Wojtkowski, Steve, Royals*	.143	26	70	9	10	13	3	0	0	1	0	1	0	13	0	12	3	1
Wolf, Brian, Pirates*	.150	26	80	4	12	12	0	0	0	2	0	1	0	11	0	28	2	1
Wolff, James, Cubs	.212	11	33	4	7	13	2	2	0	5	0	2	0	1	0	8	2	0
Zorrilla, Miguel, Twins†	.259	41	116	19	30	41	3	1	2	16	0	2	1	19	0	25	1	3
Zuleta, Julio, Cubs	.245	17	53	3	13	15	0	1	0	6	0	0	3	3	0	12	0	0

The following pitchers, listed alphabetically by club, with games in parentheses, had no plate appearances, primarily through use of designated hitters:

ASTROS—Baptist, Brett (19); Blanco, Alberto (9); Creek, Ryan (12); Crossley, Chad (17); Linehan, Andy (12); Mercado, Hector (11); Padron, Oscar (15); Phillips, Jon (3); Ramos, Edgar (14); Runyan, Sean (12); Steinke, Brock (15); Tucker, Julien (11); Walter, Mike (17).

BRAVES—Barrera, Davy (12); Betti, Rich (9); Bryant, Shane (14); Cain, Travis (9); Danley, Mike (3); Faile, Bill (11); Gann, Charlie (17); Green, Jason (12); Hostetler, Marcus (3); Leroy, John (10); Lollie, Adrian (3); Miller, Jerrod (13); Millwood, Kevin (12); Olszewski, Eric (13); Rigney, Justin (11); Warner, Mike (1).

BLUE JAYS—Arias, Alfredo (22); Ashley, Billy (12); Coe, Brent (1); Corral, Ruben (20); Geraldo, Tony (16); Hartshorn, Tyson (9); Johnson, Mike (16); Lee, Jeremy (9); Pett, Jose (4); Sinnes, Dave (6); Smith, Keilan (1); Stefanoff, Mike (11); Stone, Matt (15); Volkert, Oreste (14); Young, Reggie (14).

CUBS—Beashore, Gary (3); Blanco, Rosmel (6); Broome, John (11); Castro, Gamalier (14); Garcia, Alfredo (10); Kendrick, Scott (9); Liriano, Orlando (12); Love, Farley (5); Pacheco, Jose (4); Pimentel, Bob (4); Porzio, Mike (10); Rain, Steve (10); Rose, Tim (10); Sabino, Miguel (3); Tomberlin, Lance (14); Urbina, Jose (4); Whitfill, Mike (13).

EXPOS—Ausanio, Joe (5); Baker, Jason (7); Brown, Nathan (1); Detwiler, Brian (17); Durocher, Jayson (7); Foster, Kris (17); Handy, Russ (11); Hylton, Jim (11); Kermode, Alfred (4); Mainville, Martin (6); Markham, Andy (11); Paniagua, Jose (4); Schmidt, Curt (1); Taveras, Roberto (17); Vializ, Arce (15); Woodring, Jason (14).

MARLINS—Bavousett, Brian (11); Carl, Todd (10); Cunnane, Bill (16); Delgado, Ernesto (11); Ehler, Dan (10); Foshie, Joshua (1); Harms, Mike (18); Heredia, Felix (12); Howard, Tom (8); Ireland, Rich (8); Johnson, Scott (19); Matthews, Fred (17); Mays, Marcus (12); Touchett, Sean (13).

METS—Adair, Scott (11); Atwater, Joe (11); Coronado, Osvaldo (12); Grennan, Steve (1); Kindell, Scott (14); Krablin, Justin (10); McEntire, Ethan (10); McGinn, Mark (9); Pack, Steve (12); Pena, Moises (18); Quillin, Ty (17); Ramirez, Hector (1); Spang, Bob (4); Vitko, Joe (1); Wolff, Tom (10); Young, Tyson (17).

ORIOLES—Anderson, Matt (3); Barrett, Rich (6); Cafaro, Rocco (14); Dykhoff, Radhames (14); Galvez, Reynaldo (15); Gulledge, Derek (18); Hale, Deshane (3); Holter, Brian (9); Karns, Tim (11); Kitchen, Ron (2); Lane, Mike (11); Lombardi, John T. (10); Pena, Alex (19); Price, Tobias (13); Romano, Manuel (7); Singleton, Kendrick (5); Smith, Byrond (3); Trimarco, Mike (1).

PIRATES—Bullard, Jason (4); Davis, Kane (11); Duer, Doug (4); Ford, John (6); Garcia, Ramon (14); Goldman, Ben (12); Johnson, Jason (9); Keener, Kevin (7); Leiper, Dave (7); Mooney, Troy (5); Pickford, Kevin (9); Reid, Rayon (13); Ryan, Matt (9); Serna, Joe (7); Sharer, Tony (7); Skjerpen, Trevor (14); Temple, Jason (11); Ward, Kerry (11); Whitehead, Steve (6).

RANGERS—Cather, Mike (25); Delzine, Domingo (20); Evans, Brent (2); Fajardo, Hector (6); Falmier, Ryan (14); Farmer, Jason (2); Howell, Ken (5); Jackson, Mike (15); Knighton, Toure (8); O'Flynn, Gardner (18); Ocasio, Mark (12); Oropeza, Igor (12); Perez, Leopardo (19); Reynoso, Querbin (6); Rosenkranz, Terry (8); Runion, Jeff (3); Santana, Julio (26); Smith, Dan (12).

RED SOX—Amos, Chad (11); Asher, Ray (6); Becker, Kevin (14); Bennett, Shayne (2); Blais, Mike (22); Bogott, Kurtiss (3); Bonilla, Welnis (5); Cook, Jacob (8); Dewalt, Mark (6); Fernandes, Jim (6); Hayward, Steve (2); Hobson, Daren (1); Kennedy, Greg (3); Kivac, Dave (7); Martinez, Cesar (1); Mejia, Carlos (12); Padilla, Roy (13); Peterson, Dean (3); Phillip, Craig (3); Pinango, Simon (13); Senior, Shawn (3); Suppan, Jeff (10); Telgheder, Jim (7).

ROYALS—Acevedo, Milt (15); Anderson, Eric L. (12); Bennett, Matt (11); Brixey, Dustin (14); Campusano, Anibal (15); Downs, John (3); Fitzpatrick, Ken (12); Givens, Brian (4); Hodges, Kevin (12); Huffman, Jason (13); Lopez, Andres (7); Page, Duane (2); Ray, Ken (13); Rea, Shayne (9); Rusch, Glendon (11); Smith, Jarrod (12).

TWINS—Alvarado, Luis (13); Anderson, Eric T. (12); Belcher, Jim (1); Debrino, Bob (26); Fidge, Darren (12); Gourdin, Tom (24); Herrera, Raul (11); Johnson, Greg (1); Pina, Pedro (17); Sartain, Dave (5); Sosa, Alex (3); Stadelhofer, Mike (5); Tatar, Jason (12); Wilson, Ricardo (15); Woodman, Harold (13).

WHITE SOX—Baldwin, Bill (11); Bales, Joe (4); Broome, Curt (15); Christman, Scott (4); Dixon, Jim (3); Dunne, Mike (3); Fitzpatrick, Dave (3); Forbes, Adam (7); Fordham, Tom (3); Garcia, Ariel (12); Gomez, Augustine (13); Hassen, Ted (14); Leiber, Zane (15); Lundquist, Dave (11); Matznick, Dan (9); McCormack, Andy (1); McKinion, Mickey (9); Merigliano, Frank (3); Ogden, Jason (4); Pratt, Rich (3); Proctor, Bill (2); Quirk, John (4); Sirotka, Mike (3); Theodile, Bob (10); Woodfin, Chris (4); Woods, Brian (2).

YANKEES—Berry, Jason (15); Brown, Chuck (16); Estrella, Alejandro (1); Ferguson, Howard (10); Gordon, Mike (11); Janzen, Martin (5); Leshnock, Donnie (3); Medina, Rafael (5); Mendoza, Ramiro (15); Mittauer, Casey (21); Rios, Dan (24); Rivera, Mariano (2); Rush, Tony (8); Santaella, Alexis (17); Santiago, Sandi (1); Shelby, Tony (10); Short, Ben (2).

GRAND SLAMS—Aranzamendi, Catlett, O. Lopez, Menechino, Nolte, 1 each.

AWARDED FIRST BASE ON CATCHER'S INTERFERENCE—Bell 2 (Valentin 2); Rodriguez 2 (Abezcua 2); Ephan (Valentin); Fellhauer (Matos); L. Garcia (V. Brea); R. Hall (H. Morales); A. Lewis (Fortin); Mathews (H. Morales); Ross (Mosquera).

PITCHING

TEAM

Team	ERA	G	CG	ShO	Sv.	IP	H	R	ER	HR	HB	BB	Int. BB	SO	WP	Bk.
White Sox	2.59	59	2	5	15	521.2	421	202	150	7	29	197	15	406	31	15
Red Sox	2.65	60	4	5	12	526.2	426	212	155	13	45	203	1	479	45	6
Royals	2.72	59	2	4	16	508.2	446	244	154	4	22	202	1	343	51	2
Yankees	2.95	59	2	2	13	512.1	451	249	168	10	28	168	1	449	40	13
Expos	2.99	58	6	7	12	518.1	437	239	172	4	39	224	2	338	45	15
Rangers	3.06	60	3	6	16	515.0	474	234	175	18	43	178	1	368	24	6
Braves	3.19	58	0	3	14	504.2	421	262	179	13	38	248	3	455	56	16
Astros	3.22	59	4	3	15	508.2	472	252	182	9	28	205	2	430	51	12
Mets	3.27	59	0	5	20	520.2	476	239	189	16	28	189	0	372	53	10
Marlins	3.29	60	1	2	13	519.1	506	239	190	7	23	196	1	422	50	8
Orioles	3.39	58	2	5	16	504.2	440	251	190	13	30	227	1	337	47	7
Pirates	3.46	59	0	2	12	505.1	464	288	194	9	38	238	2	398	38	14
Twins	3.88	59	4	0	14	497.0	488	305	214	11	32	272	2	374	49	7
Cubs	4.42	59	0	1	7	508.2	553	341	250	16	51	206	0	321	73	28
Blue Jays	4.68	60	2	2	13	512.0	525	336	266	15	38	240	0	400	41	22

INDIVIDUAL

(Leading qualifiers for earned-run average leadership—48 or more innings)

*Throws lefthanded.

Pitcher, Team	W	L	Pct.	ERA	G	GS	CG	GF	ShO	Sv.	IP	H	R	ER	HR	HB	BB	Int. BB	SO	WP
Lombardi, Orioles	7	1	.875	0.92	10	10	0	0	0	0	59.0	32	10	6	0	2	27	0	45	2
Atwater, Mets*	7	1	.875	0.93	11	10	0	0	0	0	58.0	44	9	6	0	2	6	0	44	2
Miller, Braves	5	2	.714	1.07	13	7	0	1	0	0	50.2	31	12	6	2	3	16	0	43	6
Taveras, Expos	2	4	.333	1.48	17	5	0	12	0	3	54.2	52	21	9	0	4	18	0	37	2
Rusch, Royals*	4	2	.667	1.60	11	10	0	0	0	0	62.0	43	14	11	0	1	11	0	48	2
Gordon, Yankees	4	2	.667	1.67	11	9	0	1	0	0	64.2	43	23	12	0	0	27	0	61	6
Pinango, Red Sox*	0	4	.000	1.73	13	7	0	1	0	1	52.0	36	17	10	1	2	17	0	57	3
Reid, Pirates	4	3	.571	1.74	13	8	0	1	0	1	62.0	50	16	12	1	2	15	0	39	3
Cafaro, Orioles	2	2	.500	1.79	14	8	1	2	0	1	80.2	58	21	16	1	3	12	0	57	2
Hodges, Royals	7	2	.778	2.03	12	10	0	2	0	0	71.0	52	25	16	0	7	25	0	40	3

Departmental leaders: G—Santana, 26; W—Atwater, Creek, Hodges, Lombardi, 7; L—Eric T. Anderson, Fidge, 8; Pct.—Atwater, Lombardi, .875; GS—Several pitchers tied with 12; CG—Durocher, 3; GF—Debrino, 19; ShO—Durocher, 2; Sv.—Debrino, 11; IP—Cafaro, 80.2; H—Geraldo, 81; R—Lane, 49; ER—Lane, 37; HR—Adair, J. Broome, 5; HB—Several pitchers tied with 8; BB—Price, Vializ, 43; IBB—Leiber, 5; SO—Tatar, 73; WP—Several pitchers tied with 11.

(All pitchers—listed alphabetically)

Pitcher, Team	W	L	Pct.	ERA	G	GS	CG	GF	ShO	Sv.	IP	H	R	ER	HR	HB	BB	Int. BB	SO	WP
Acevedo, Royals*	4	6	.400	2.90	15	3	0	7	0	0	40.1	34	20	13	1	1	16	1	22	5
Adair, Mets	3	2	.600	4.59	11	9	0	1	0	0	51.0	66	30	26	5	3	13	0	29	1
Alvarado, Twins	3	5	.375	3.39	13	10	1	0	0	0	58.1	65	34	22	0	3	21	0	40	7
Amos, Red Sox	3	0	1.000	1.50	11	0	0	9	0	2	18.0	13	3	3	1	1	4	1	21	1
Anderson, Royals	1	4	.200	4.03	12	7	1	2	0	0	44.2	47	34	20	1	2	19	0	18	10
Anderson, Twins*	2	8	.200	5.36	12	9	1	0	0	0	45.1	49	44	27	2	2	36	0	35	3
Anderson, Orioles*	0	0	.000	0.00	3	3	0	0	0	0	4.0	3	0	0	0	2	5	0	5	0
Aquino, White Sox	1	1	.500	4.15	2	0	0	1	0	0	4.1	4	2	2	0	0	0	0	1	0
Arias, Blue Jays	2	3	.400	2.92	22	4	0	16	0	6	49.1	46	23	16	1	3	16	0	44	4
Asher, Red Sox	2	1	.667	1.60	6	6	1	0	0	0	33.2	21	13	6	0	2	14	0	28	4
Ashley, Blue Jays	0	2	.000	6.86	12	0	0	2	0	0	19.2	19	19	15	1	6	19	0	15	3
Atwater, Mets*	7	1	.875	0.93	11	10	0	0	0	0	58.0	44	9	6	0	2	6	0	44	2
Ausanio, Expos	0	0	.000	0.00	5	0	0	4	0	0	5.0	3	1	0	0	0	1	0	6	0
Baker, Expos	1	1	.500	2.25	7	7	0	0	0	0	32.0	26	14	8	0	1	11	0	24	4
Baldwin, White Sox	0	2	.000	6.75	11	0	0	5	0	0	13.1	11	11	10	0	1	17	0	12	4
Bales, White Sox	0	0	.000	6.19	4	4	0	0	0	0	16.0	19	11	11	1	2	10	0	11	0
Baptist, Astros	2	0	1.000	5.02	19	0	0	7	0	1	37.2	49	32	21	0	3	22	0	22	5
Barrera, Braves	0	3	.000	2.94	12	4	0	4	0	0	33.2	28	20	11	0	5	21	0	22	2
Barrett, Orioles*	0	1	.000	0.98	6	0	0	3	0	2	18.1	13	2	2	1	1	3	0	11	0
Bavousett, Marlins	4	0	1.000	2.33	11	0	0	6	0	0	27.0	24	8	7	0	3	5	0	10	2
Beashore, Cubs	0	1	.000	6.75	3	1	0	2	0	1	8.0	10	7	6	1	1	1	0	6	2
Becker, Red Sox	4	3	.571	4.75	14	5	0	7	0	2	53.0	58	35	28	1	5	28	0	45	4
Belcher, Twins	1	0	1.000	0.00	1	1	0	0	0	0	1.0	1	0	0	0	0	0	0	1	0
Bennett, Royals	2	2	.500	4.76	11	3	0	4	0	1	34.0	35	29	18	0	0	27	0	25	8
Bennett, Red Sox	0	0	.000	1.29	2	1	0	1	0	1	7.0	2	1	1	0	1	1	0	4	1
Berry, Yankees	1	2	.333	0.85	15	0	0	2	0	0	31.2	20	10	3	0	3	12	0	20	1
Betti, Braves*	1	0	1.000	0.89	9	2	0	5	0	2	20.1	10	5	2	1	1	8	0	27	1
Blais, Red Sox*	3	1	.750	1.38	22	0	0	17	0	4	26.0	15	6	4	0	2	8	0	22	2
Blanco, Astros*	0	1	.000	2.00	9	1	0	1	0	1	18.0	15	4	4	0	1	11	0	32	2
Blanco, Cubs	0	5	.000	11.44	6	6	0	0	0	0	19.2	22	33	25	0	7	30	0	5	11
Bogott, Red Sox*	0	1	.000	1.80	3	2	0	0	0	0	15.0	10	3	3	1	2	4	0	20	3
Bonilla, Red Sox	0	1	.000	13.50	5	0	0	1	0	0	5.1	12	8	8	0	1	1	0	1	1
Bowman, Mets	2	3	.400	5.02	10	2	0	5	0	4	28.2	28	19	16	2	2	18	0	18	5
Brixey, Royals	2	1	.667	4.65	14	1	0	6	0	2	31.0	30	22	16	0	3	17	0	11	4
Broome, White Sox	5	3	.625	2.57	15	4	1	3	0	0	63.0	56	24	18	0	0	25	4	32	2
Broome, Cubs	3	6	.333	5.66	11	11	0	0	0	0	55.2	79	42	35	5	5	14	0	25	3
Brown, Yankees	3	3	.500	3.59	16	6	0	5	0	1	52.2	51	28	21	2	1	13	0	54	2
Brown, Expos*	0	0	.000	0.00	1	1	0	0	0	0	1.0	0	0	0	0	0	0	0	1	0
Bryant, Braves	4	4	.500	2.97	14	0	0	4	0	3	63.2	66	30	21	1	2	13	0	40	6
Bullard, Pirates	0	1	.000	3.86	4	0	0	1	0	0	7.0	11	3	3	0	1	2	0	8	1
Cafaro, Orioles	2	2	.500	1.79	14	8	1	2	0	1	80.2	58	21	16	1	3	12	0	57	2
Cain, Braves	1	2	.333	4.50	9	4	0	2	0	0	30.0	24	24	15	0	3	20	0	33	8
Campusano, Royals	1	0	1.000	4.67	15	0	0	9	0	2	27.0	35	21	14	1	0	13	0	10	5

Pitcher, Team	W	L	Pct.	ERA	G	GS	CG	GF	ShO	Sv.	IP	H	R	ER	HR	HB	BB	Int. BB	SO	WP
Carl, Marlins	1	2	.333	6.00	10	0	0	4	0	1	18.0	23	12	12	0	0	17	0	20	6
Castro, Cubs*	2	3	.400	2.88	13	0	0	7	0	1	40.2	35	21	13	3	2	19	0	31	11
Cather, Rangers	1	1	.500	1.76	25	0	0	17	0	4	30.2	20	7	6	0	3	9	0	30	2
Chambers, Cubs	0	1	.000	6.75	1	0	0	1	0	0	1.1	2	1	1	0	0	1	0	1	0
Christman, White Sox*	0	0	.000	0.00	4	2	0	1	0	1	11.1	3	1	0	0	0	4	0	15	0
Civit, Expos	0	0	.000	6.75	5	0	0	4	0	1	8.0	7	6	6	0	1	5	0	7	0
Coe, Blue Jays*	0	0	.000	13.50	1	0	0	0	0	0	1.1	1	2	2	0	0	3	0	2	1
Cook, Red Sox	1	1	.500	2.03	8	1	0	4	0	0	13.1	8	3	3	0	1	13	0	10	2
Cormenares, Blue Jays	0	0	.000	8.10	2	0	0	2	0	0	3.1	5	3	3	0	1	0	0	4	1
Coronado, Mets	3	3	.500	5.36	12	6	0	6	0	1	43.2	54	26	26	1	1	20	0	19	1
Corral, Blue Jays	3	5	.375	5.92	20	3	0	7	0	0	48.2	53	40	32	2	1	26	0	32	6
Creek, Astros	7	3	.700	2.34	12	11	2	1	1	1	69.1	53	22	18	0	4	30	0	62	6
Crossley, Astros	2	1	.667	5.22	17	0	0	8	0	2	29.1	27	19	17	2	2	10	0	21	4
Cunnane, Marlins	3	3	.500	2.70	16	9	0	4	0	2	66.2	75	32	20	1	0	8	0	64	4
Danley, Braves*	0	0	.000	7.20	3	0	0	3	0	0	5.0	6	6	4	0	5	3	0	4	0
Davis, Pirates	0	0	.000	7.07	11	4	0	5	0	0	28.0	34	30	22	0	0	19	1	24	3
Delgado, Marlins	4	3	.571	3.08	11	11	0	0	0	0	61.1	61	27	21	0	4	19	0	46	5
Delzine, Rangers	5	0	1.000	1.82	20	1	0	6	0	1	39.2	39	10	8	0	1	5	0	17	1
Detwiler, Expos	1	2	.333	4.97	17	0	0	9	0	3	41.2	48	25	23	1	1	21	2	26	4
DeBrino, Twins	1	4	.200	3.48	25	0	0	19	0	11	41.1	34	19	16	0	2	27	0	47	7
DeWalt, Red Sox	1	1	.500	3.54	6	2	0	2	0	1	20.1	16	11	8	0	5	6	0	12	6
Dixon, White Sox	0	1	.000	0.90	3	0	0	1	0	0	10.0	8	2	1	0	0	1	0	7	0
Downs, Royals	0	0	.000	1.50	3	3	0	0	0	0	12.0	12	3	2	0	1	2	0	11	0
Duer, Pirates	0	1	.000	11.25	4	0	0	2	0	0	4.0	6	5	5	0	0	6	0	3	1
Dunne, White Sox	0	0	.000	0.00	3	2	0	0	0	0	5.2	3	1	0	0	1	9	0	9	0
Durocher, Expos	2	3	.400	3.46	7	7	3	0	2	0	39.0	32	23	15	0	3	13	0	21	3
Dykhoff, Orioles*	1	2	.333	3.40	14	3	0	1	0	1	45.0	37	22	17	2	2	11	0	29	3
Ehler, Marlins	2	3	.400	4.73	10	7	0	1	0	0	40.0	45	25	21	2	3	15	0	38	2
Estrella, Yankees	0	1	.000	30.38	1	1	0	0	0	0	2.2	12	9	9	1	0	0	0	4	0
Evans, Rangers*	0	0	.000	36.00	1	0	0	0	0	0	1.0	4	5	4	0	2	0	0	1	0
Faile, Braves	3	0	1.000	1.73	11	0	0	4	0	2	26.0	15	9	5	1	1	18	0	9	6
Fajardo, Rangers	3	1	.750	1.80	6	6	0	0	0	0	30.0	21	8	6	0	0	5	0	27	0
Falmier, Rangers	1	0	1.000	3.90	14	0	0	2	0	1	27.2	18	12	12	3	4	10	0	17	0
Farmer, Rangers	0	1	.000	18.00	2	0	0	0	0	0	2.0	3	5	4	1	0	3	0	2	0
Ferguson, Yankees	0	6	.000	4.57	10	7	0	2	0	1	43.1	49	40	22	1	2	18	0	32	2
Fernandes, Red Sox	2	0	1.000	0.86	6	2	0	2	0	0	21.0	14	3	2	0	3	8	0	17	2
Fidge, Twins	1	8	.111	4.19	12	12	1	0	0	0	66.2	72	48	31	1	8	27	0	31	6
Fitzpatrick, White Sox	1	0	1.000	0.00	3	0	0	2	0	0	6.0	3	2	0	0	0	1	0	10	0
Fitzpatrick, Royals	4	3	.571	2.57	12	10	1	1	0	1	56.0	58	25	16	0	4	20	0	35	2
Forbes, White Sox*	0	1	.000	2.31	7	0	0	4	0	1	11.2	4	5	3	0	0	4	1	16	0
Ford, Pirates*	0	0	.000	0.00	6	0	0	5	0	1	7.0	2	0	0	0	0	3	0	9	0
Fordham, White Sox*	1	0	1.000	1.80	3	0	0	2	0	0	10.0	9	2	2	0	0	3	0	12	1
Foshie, Marlins	0	0	.000	0.00	1	0	0	0	0	0	2.0	2	0	0	0	0	3	0	2	0
Foster, Expos	1	6	.143	3.43	17	3	0	8	0	1	44.2	44	26	17	0	6	16	0	30	6
Galarza, Pirates	0	1	.000	2.38	7	0	0	7	0	0	11.1	11	6	3	0	1	4	1	3	1
Galvez, Orioles	1	1	.500	6.60	15	0	0	8	0	1	30.0	32	28	22	1	6	15	0	13	2
Gann, Braves	1	0	1.000	5.55	17	0	0	14	0	4	24.1	31	17	15	0	0	9	0	14	2
Garcia, Cubs	2	6	.250	3.40	10	8	0	2	0	0	55.2	54	29	21	0	4	7	0	38	3
Garcia, White Sox	5	2	.714	3.15	12	11	0	0	0	0	68.2	71	34	24	4	8	12	0	36	3
Garcia, Pirates	2	0	1.000	3.93	14	4	0	9	0	3	36.2	38	19	16	0	1	9	0	26	1
Geraldo, Blue Jays	2	5	.286	4.17	16	11	0	1	0	0	73.1	81	47	34	2	5	34	0	46	5
Givens, Royals*	0	1	.000	3.38	4	4	0	0	0	0	8.0	7	3	3	0	0	1	0	11	0
Goldman, Pirates	1	1	.500	5.91	12	0	0	5	0	0	21.1	22	19	14	1	7	25	0	11	9
Gomez, White Sox	1	0	1.000	2.08	13	0	0	11	0	6	17.1	10	4	4	0	2	9	2	28	1
Gordon, Yankees	4	2	.667	1.67	11	9	0	1	0	0	64.2	43	23	12	0	0	27	0	61	6
Gourdin, Twins	1	2	.333	4.59	24	4	0	8	0	3	51.0	53	34	26	1	3	17	0	33	5
Green, Braves	3	2	.600	2.91	12	10	0	0	0	0	43.1	27	21	14	0	0	36	0	63	6
Grennan, Mets*	0	0	.000	0.00	1	1	0	0	0	0	4.0	1	1	0	0	1	0	0	3	0
Gulledge, Orioles*	4	1	.800	3.62	18	0	0	17	0	4	32.1	41	14	13	1	0	5	0	19	2
Hale, Orioles*	0	0	.000	0.00	3	0	0	0	0	0	4.0	2	0	0	0	0	0	0	2	0
Handy, Expos	1	2	.333	3.42	11	10	0	0	0	0	47.1	33	25	18	1	4	39	0	23	11
Harms, Marlins	2	3	.400	3.66	18	0	0	11	0	3	39.1	41	20	16	0	2	10	0	22	3
Hartshorn, Blue Jays	0	4	.000	6.08	9	4	0	4	0	1	26.2	36	26	18	0	0	18	0	18	0
Hassen, White Sox	3	3	.500	2.74	14	0	0	7	0	1	23.0	17	12	7	0	0	18	2	19	2
Hayward, Red Sox	1	1	.500	1.17	5	2	0	2	0	0	7.2	7	3	1	0	1	1	0	3	0
Helsel, Blue Jays	0	0	.000	0.00	1	0	0	0	0	0	0.1	1	0	0	0	0	0	0	1	0
Heredia, Marlins*	5	1	.833	2.47	12	12	0	0	0	0	62.0	50	18	17	0	2	11	0	53	1
Herrera, Twins	5	4	.556	2.81	11	11	0	0	0	0	64.0	59	28	20	1	4	21	0	41	5
Hobson, Red Sox	0	0	.000	0.00	1	0	0	0	0	0	1.0	1	0	0	0	0	2	0	2	1
Hodges, Royals	7	2	.778	2.03	12	10	0	2	0	0	71.0	52	25	16	0	7	25	0	40	3
Holter, Orioles	1	0	1.000	1.93	9	0	0	6	0	2	14.0	7	5	3	0	1	9	0	8	2
Hostetler, Braves	2	0	1.000	1.00	3	0	0	3	0	0	9.0	2	1	1	0	1	2	1	12	0
Howard, Marlins*	2	4	.333	3.18	8	6	1	0	0	0	34.0	35	16	12	0	0	20	0	31	5
Howell, Rangers	1	0	1.000	2.08	6	4	0	1	0	0	13.0	8	3	3	1	0	5	0	17	0
Huffman, Royals	2	0	1.000	0.79	13	0	0	10	0	5	22.2	14	8	2	0	0	13	0	21	0
Hylton, Expos	3	3	.500	3.23	11	3	0	4	0	0	30.2	32	18	11	0	2	17	0	16	0
Ireland, Marlins*	1	2	.333	3.12	8	4	0	2	0	0	26.0	12	11	9	0	0	23	0	19	10
Jackson, Rangers	1	4	.200	5.88	15	5	0	4	0	0	26.0	33	25	17	1	1	9	0	12	2
Janzen, Yankees	0	1	.000	1.21	5	5	0	0	0	0	22.1	20	5	3	0	1	3	0	19	0
Johnson, Twins	0	0	.000	0.00	1	0	0	0	0	0	1.0	0	0	0	0	0	2	0	2	0
Johnson, Pirates	1	4	.200	2.33	9	9	0	0	0	0	54.0	48	22	14	0	1	14	0	39	0
Johnson, Blue Jays	0	2	.000	4.87	16	1	0	7	0	1	44.1	51	40	24	4	2	22	0	31	4
Johnson, Marlins	2	2	.500	2.82	19	0	0	12	0	2	38.1	41	16	12	3	1	12	0	30	1
Karns, Orioles	5	4	.556	4.09	11	11	0	0	0	0	55.0	47	32	25	0	4	39	0	28	8
Keener, Pirates*	1	0	1.000	6.08	7	0	0	0	0	0	13.1	17	11	9	0	3	15	0	12	0
Kendrick, Cubs	1	2	.333	7.32	9	7	0	1	0	0	35.2	44	37	29	2	1	15	0	17	9
Kennedy, Red Sox*	0	0	.000	2.77	3	2	0	0	0	0	13.0	12	4	4	0	2	3	0	14	1
Kermode, Expos	0	0	.000	3.00	4	0	0	1	0	0	6.0	5	2	2	0	0	1	0	5	0
Kindell, Mets	1	0	1.000	1.48	14	0	0	3	0	1	24.1	16	6	4	0	1	6	0	21	2
Kitchen, Orioles	0	0	.000	0.00	2	0	0	1	0	0	2.0	3	0	0	0	0	1	0	2	0
Klvac, Red Sox	0	3	.000	2.92	5	1	1	0	0	0	37.0	27	15	12	0	4	15	0	26	3
Knighton, Rangers	3	1	.750	2.31	8	7	0	0	0	0	35.0	33	12	9	0	5	12	0	25	1
Krablin, Mets	3	0	1.000	3.76	10	5	0	3	0	1	38.1	40	23	16	2	1	4	0	36	1
Lane, Orioles	3	7	.300	7.09	11	10	0	0	0	0	47.0	56	49	37	3	6	34	0	36	11

Pitcher, Team	W	L	Pct.	ERA	G	GS	CG	GF	ShO	Sv.	IP	H	R	ER	HR	HB	BB	Int. BB	SO	WP
Lee, Blue Jays	1	4	.200	4.71	9	7	0	0	0	0	28.2	29	15	15	0	5	8	0	22	2
Leiber, White Sox	0	2	.000	2.66	15	0	0	7	0	3	20.1	12	10	6	0	2	21	5	11	2
Leiper, Pirates*	0	0	.000	1.69	7	4	0	0	0	0	21.1	17	4	4	0	2	0	0	24	0
Leroy, Braves	2	2	.500	2.05	10	2	0	4	0	1	26.1	21	9	6	1	0	8	1	32	2
Leshnock, Yankees	0	0	.000	1.35	3	0	0	1	0	0	6.2	4	1	1	0	1	2	0	7	2
Linehan, Astros*	2	1	.667	5.12	12	0	0	6	0	0	19.1	26	12	11	1	0	6	0	13	1
Liriano, Cubs	1	1	.500	3.89	12	3	0	6	0	1	34.2	40	18	15	0	4	10	0	24	9
Lollie, Braves	0	0	.000	0.00	3	0	0	2	0	0	4.0	2	1	0	0	0	3	0	3	0
Lombardi, Orioles	7	1	.875	0.92	10	10	0	0	0	0	59.0	32	10	6	0	2	27	0	45	2
Lopez, Royals*	2	1	.667	1.76	7	0	0	4	0	2	15.1	9	4	3	0	0	2	0	18	1
Love, Cubs	1	0	1.000	3.00	5	0	0	0	0	0	9.0	12	8	3	0	0	6	0	7	0
Lundquist, White Sox	5	3	.625	3.14	11	10	0	0	0	0	63.0	70	26	22	0	4	15	0	40	2
Mainville, Expos	1	2	.333	5.25	6	5	0	0	0	0	24.0	26	15	14	0	2	4	0	12	0
Markham, Expos	5	4	.556	3.13	11	10	2	0	1	0	72.0	59	31	25	1	6	21	0	45	5
Martinez, Red Sox*	0	0	.000	0.00	1	1	0	0	0	0	3.0	1	0	0	0	0	2	0	3	0
Mathews, Braves	2	4	.333	4.50	14	12	0	0	0	0	62.0	65	42	31	4	8	26	0	59	4
Matthews, Marlins	0	0	.000	3.46	17	0	0	8	0	2	26.0	17	13	10	0	5	23	0	15	2
Matznick, White Sox	0	2	.000	2.13	9	9	0	0	0	0	25.1	17	11	6	0	1	12	0	35	1
Mays, Marlins*	4	5	.444	3.79	12	11	0	1	0	0	61.2	66	34	26	1	2	19	1	47	6
McCormack, White Sox*	0	0	.000	0.00	1	1	0	0	0	0	6.0	1	0	0	0	0	0	0	7	0
McEntire, Mets*	4	1	.800	2.53	10	7	0	0	0	0	42.2	36	12	12	0	2	14	0	41	7
McGinn, Mets	1	1	.500	5.06	9	1	0	0	0	0	16.0	10	11	9	0	3	16	0	9	5
McKinion, White Sox	1	1	.500	3.06	6	2	0	3	0	2	17.2	13	6	6	0	1	5	0	10	5
Medina, Yankees	2	0	1.000	0.66	5	5	0	0	0	0	27.1	16	6	2	0	1	12	0	21	1
Mejia, Red Sox*	5	4	.556	3.20	12	9	0	2	0	0	56.1	43	25	20	3	8	31	0	59	2
Mendoza, Yankees	4	5	.444	2.79	15	9	0	3	0	1	67.2	59	26	21	3	4	7	0	61	3
Mercado, Astros*	5	4	.556	2.42	11	11	1	0	1	0	67.0	49	26	18	1	1	29	0	59	10
Merigliano, White Sox	1	1	.500	2.25	3	0	0	3	0	0	4.0	2	1	1	0	0	1	0	8	0
Miller, Braves	5	2	.714	1.07	13	7	0	1	0	0	50.2	31	12	6	2	3	16	0	43	4
Millwood, Braves	3	3	.500	3.06	12	9	0	1	0	0	50.0	36	27	17	3	4	28	0	49	5
Mittauer, Yankees	6	1	.857	2.68	21	0	0	16	0	3	40.1	34	17	12	0	4	4	0	34	2
Mooney, Pirates	2	2	.500	1.75	5	5	0	0	0	0	25.2	20	13	5	0	0	13	0	16	4
Ocasio, Rangers	3	1	.750	3.88	12	9	0	2	0	1	46.1	46	24	20	3	4	32	0	28	1
O'Flynn, Rangers*	4	3	.571	0.67	18	0	0	5	0	0	27.0	23	7	2	2	3	5	1	15	1
Ogden, White Sox	1	0	1.000	1.50	4	0	0	0	0	0	6.0	4	2	1	0	0	1	0	3	1
Olszewski, Braves	3	3	.500	5.58	13	0	0	3	0	0	30.2	33	25	19	0	3	20	0	26	3
Oropeza, Rangers	6	0	1.000	2.73	12	10	1	0	0	0	56.0	48	23	17	2	6	22	0	43	2
Pacheco, Cubs	0	0	.000	4.50	4	2	0	2	0	2	18.0	18	10	9	0	3	3	0	11	3
Pack, Mets	5	3	.625	4.19	12	11	0	0	0	0	58.0	52	34	27	1	3	18	0	41	3
Padilla, Red Sox*	0	1	.000	2.35	13	1	0	3	0	0	30.2	25	10	8	0	2	17	0	18	5
Padron, Astros	3	2	.600	3.09	15	0	0	9	0	2	23.1	24	9	8	0	0	7	1	22	2
Page, Royals	0	0	.000	0.00	2	0	0	0	0	0	4.0	2	0	0	0	0	3	0	2	0
Paniagua, Expos	3	0	1.000	0.67	4	4	1	0	0	0	27.0	13	2	2	0	2	5	0	25	1
Pena, Orioles	3	1	.750	2.68	19	0	0	11	0	1	37.0	38	18	11	2	1	8	0	28	4
Pena, Mets	1	2	.333	2.83	18	0	0	11	0	2	41.1	32	22	13	1	1	16	0	40	8
Perez, Rangers	1	4	.200	3.99	19	0	0	6	0	2	29.1	37	23	13	1	2	13	0	23	3
Peterson, Red Sox	1	0	1.000	3.60	3	2	0	0	0	0	15.0	14	8	6	1	0	4	0	10	0
Pett, Blue Jays	1	1	.500	3.60	4	4	0	0	0	0	10.0	10	4	4	0	0	3	0	7	0
Phillip, Red Sox	1	1	.500	4.50	3	2	0	0	0	0	8.0	13	6	4	0	0	2	0	9	0
Phillips, Astros*	0	1	.000	3.38	3	0	0	2	0	0	2.2	1	5	1	0	0	3	0	6	0
Pickford, Pirates*	0	4	.000	3.41	9	7	0	0	0	0	34.1	24	19	13	1	3	20	0	28	0
Pimentel, Cubs	0	1	.000	2.25	4	0	0	3	0	0	8.0	8	7	2	1	2	6	0	9	1
Pina, Twins	3	1	.750	3.72	17	0	0	6	0	0	36.1	41	21	15	3	3	24	1	23	2
Pinango, Red Sox*	0	4	.000	1.73	13	7	0	1	0	1	52.0	36	17	10	1	2	17	0	57	3
Porzio, Cubs*	1	3	.250	3.83	10	8	0	2	0	0	42.1	42	26	18	1	3	30	0	30	1
Pratt, White Sox*	1	0	1.000	2.70	3	0	0	0	0	0	10.0	10	3	3	0	0	2	0	10	0
Price, Orioles*	2	5	.286	5.54	13	6	1	2	0	1	37.1	36	27	23	0	1	43	0	28	7
Proctor, White Sox	0	0	.000	0.00	2	0	0	0	0	0	4.0	4	1	0	0	0	2	0	1	0
Quillin, Mets	3	1	.750	2.70	17	0	0	17	0	6	26.2	18	8	8	2	0	15	0	27	1
Quirk, White Sox*	2	0	1.000	0.86	4	0	0	0	0	0	21.0	16	2	2	0	1	2	0	10	3
Rain, Cubs	1	3	.250	3.89	10	6	0	3	0	0	37.0	37	20	16	0	2	17	0	29	5
Ramirez, Mets	1	0	1.000	0.00	1	1	0	0	0	0	7.0	5	1	0	0	0	1	0	6	0
Ramos, Astros	5	2	.714	2.16	14	12	0	0	0	0	75.0	59	23	18	0	3	13	0	70	4
Ray, Royals	2	3	.400	2.28	13	7	0	3	0	0	47.1	44	21	12	1	0	17	0	45	6
Rea, Royals	0	0	.000	0.00	6	0	0	6	0	3	11.0	5	2	0	0	0	4	0	10	1
Reid, Pirates	4	3	.571	1.74	13	8	0	1	0	1	62.0	50	16	12	1	2	15	0	39	3
Rennspies, Braves	0	0	.000	13.50	1	0	0	1	0	0	1.1	2	2	2	0	0	2	0	0	0
Reyes, Expos	1	0	1.000	0.00	1	0	0	1	0	0	1.0	0	0	0	0	0	0	0	1	0
Reynoso, Rangers	3	1	.750	1.97	6	5	1	0	0	0	32.0	29	15	7	0	4	5	0	15	3
Rigney, Braves*	2	1	.667	3.47	11	0	0	7	0	2	23.1	22	10	9	0	1	14	1	18	2
Rios, Yankees	2	1	.667	3.52	24	0	0	17	0	6	38.1	34	18	15	0	5	16	0	29	9
Rivera, Yankees	0	1	.000	2.25	2	2	0	0	0	0	4.0	3	1	1	0	0	1	0	3	0
Romano, Orioles	0	2	.000	3.55	7	6	0	1	0	1	25.1	22	14	10	1	1	12	0	15	4
Rose, Cubs	2	2	.500	3.04	10	1	0	5	0	0	23.2	25	9	8	0	0	6	0	22	3
Rosenkranz, Rangers*	0	0	.000	9.58	8	0	0	1	0	0	10.1	16	12	11	2	0	4	0	6	4
Ruiz, Cubs*	0	0	.000	1.86	4	1	0	2	0	1	9.2	7	2	2	0	0	2	0	6	2
Runion, Rangers	1	0	1.000	7.02	6	3	0	1	0	0	16.2	15	15	13	1	6	22	0	13	4
Runyan, Astros*	4	3	.571	2.98	12	12	0	0	0	0	66.1	66	35	22	2	2	24	0	52	4
Rusch, Royals*	4	2	.667	1.60	11	10	0	0	0	0	62.0	43	14	11	0	1	11	0	48	2
Rush, Yankees*	0	0	.000	12.60	8	0	0	2	0	0	10.0	21	16	14	1	0	10	0	7	2
Ryan, Pirates	1	1	.500	2.33	9	0	0	5	0	2	19.1	17	8	5	0	1	9	0	20	0
Sabino, Cubs	0	0	.000	5.59	3	0	0	2	0	0	9.2	13	10	6	1	8	0	0	4	0
Santaella, Yankees	3	5	.375	3.24	17	4	1	8	0	1	41.2	35	22	15	2	2	21	1	42	7
Santana, Rangers	4	1	.800	1.38	26	0	0	12	0	7	39.0	31	9	6	0	1	7	0	50	1
Santiago, Yankees	0	0	.000	4.50	1	0	0	1	0	0	2.0	3	2	1	0	0	0	0	1	0
Sartain, Twins*	1	0	1.000	6.43	5	0	0	1	0	0	7.0	9	6	5	0	0	7	0	6	0
Schmidt, Expos	1	0	1.000	0.00	1	1	0	0	0	0	5.0	1	0	0	0	0	0	0	7	0
Senior, Red Sox*	3	0	1.000	1.93	8	1	0	1	0	0	14.0	10	7	3	0	1	6	0	17	0
Serna, Pirates	0	0	.000	0.00	7	0	0	6	0	3	9.0	2	0	0	0	1	7	0	15	1
Sharer, Pirates	0	1	.000	7.71	7	0	0	2	0	0	9.1	15	10	8	1	1	6	0	5	3
Shelby, Yankees*	4	1	.800	2.67	10	10	1	0	0	0	54.0	46	25	16	0	3	22	0	48	3
Short, Yankees	1	0	1.000	0.00	2	1	0	0	0	0	3.0	2	0	0	0	1	0	0	3	0
Singleton, Orioles	1	1	.500	5.19	5	0	0	0	0	0	8.2	10	8	5	1	2	5	0	6	0
Sinnes, Blue Jays	1	0	1.000	0.00	6	0	0	6	0	2	9.2	3	0	0	0	0	1	0	11	0

Pitcher, Team	W	L	Pct.	ERA	G	GS	CG	GF	ShO	Sv.	IP	H	R	ER	HR	HB	BB	Int. BB	SO	WP
Sirotka, White Sox*	0	0	.000	0.00	3	0	0	1	0	0	5.0	4	1	0	0	0	2	0	8	0
Skjerpen, Pirates	4	0	1.000	1.77	14	0	0	6	0	2	35.2	23	16	7	2	5	13	0	31	2
Smith, Rangers	3	2	.600	2.87	12	10	1	0	0	0	53.1	50	19	17	1	3	8	0	27	3
Smith, Orioles	0	0	.000	0.00	3	0	0	2	0	0	4.0	0	0	0	0	0	1	0	5	0
Smith, Royals	0	5	.000	3.22	12	1	0	2	0	0	22.1	19	13	8	0	3	16	0	16	4
Smith, Blue Jays	0	0	.000	2.45	1	0	0	0	0	0	3.2	4	1	1	0	0	1	0	4	0
Sosa, Twins	0	0	.000	18.00	3	0	0	2	0	0	3.0	6	7	6	0	2	6	0	1	0
Spang, Mets	1	0	1.000	2.70	4	2	0	1	0	1	10.0	9	3	3	1	1	1	0	2	2
Stadelhofer, Twins	0	1	.000	5.40	5	2	0	0	0	0	10.0	9	7	6	2	0	8	0	13	1
Stefanoff, Blue Jays	1	2	.333	16.69	11	1	0	2	0	0	18.1	21	34	34	0	7	36	0	12	11
Steinke, Astros	3	2	.600	4.73	15	2	0	3	0	0	26.2	33	19	14	1	0	16	1	22	5
Stone, Blue Jays*	5	2	.714	3.22	15	10	0	2	0	1	64.1	52	28	23	3	4	27	0	56	0
Suppan, Red Sox	4	3	.571	2.18	10	9	2	1	1	0	57.2	52	20	14	0	3	16	0	64	2
Tatar, Twins	5	1	.833	2.57	12	11	1	1	0	0	66.2	52	26	19	1	2	29	0	73	2
Taveras, Expos	2	4	.333	1.48	17	5	0	12	0	3	54.2	52	21	9	4	4	18	0	37	2
Telgheder, Red Sox	1	2	.333	3.38	7	1	0	3	0	1	18.2	16	11	7	2	1	2	0	17	2
Temple, Pirates	4	5	.444	5.08	11	7	0	0	0	0	39.0	35	35	22	3	3	32	0	36	8
Theodile, White Sox	5	2	.714	2.59	10	8	1	1	1	1	66.0	45	24	19	2	6	23	0	42	2
Thomas, Cubs*	0	0	.000	8.31	5	2	0	1	0	0	13.0	15	15	12	0	2	14	0	10	4
Tomberlin, Cubs	2	2	.500	4.02	14	2	0	7	0	0	47.0	49	29	21	1	5	19	0	18	2
Touchett, Marlins	2	0	1.000	3.71	13	0	0	10	0	3	17.0	14	7	7	0	1	11	0	25	1
Tucker, Astros	2	3	.400	3.95	11	10	1	0	0	0	54.2	55	36	24	2	8	22	0	33	5
Trimarco, Orioles	0	0	.000	9.00	1	0	0	1	0	0	1.0	3	1	1	0	0	0	0	0	0
Turlais, Pirates	0	0	.000	18.00	1	0	0	0	0	0	2.0	7	5	4	0	1	0	0	0	0
Vaske, Astros	1	1	.500	1.29	4	0	0	4	0	1	7.0	8	1	1	1	2	1	0	4	0
Vializ, Expos	3	3	.500	3.92	15	2	0	4	0	0	43.2	37	25	19	1	6	43	0	32	4
Vitko, Mets	0	0	.000	0.00	1	1	0	0	0	0	3.0	1	0	0	0	0	1	0	2	1
Volkert, Blue Jays	2	3	.400	3.38	14	3	0	1	0	2	48.0	54	24	18	0	0	6	0	34	3
Walter, Astros	0	1	.000	2.79	17	0	0	16	0	8	19.1	15	10	6	0	4	12	0	16	3
Ward, Pirates	1	7	.125	4.26	11	9	0	0	0	0	50.2	53	36	24	1	4	20	0	35	1
Warner, Braves	0	0	.000	9.00	1	0	0	1	0	0	1.0	0	1	1	0	1	1	0	1	0
Whitehead, Pirates	0	3	.000	2.51	6	2	0	3	0	0	14.1	12	11	4	0	1	6	0	14	0
Whitfill, Cubs	2	2	.500	1.91	13	1	0	9	0	1	33.0	33	16	7	0	0	5	0	24	4
Wilson, Twins	0	1	.000	8.05	15	0	0	11	0	0	19.0	24	24	17	0	3	24	1	9	8
Wolff, Mets	2	2	.500	2.73	10	3	0	2	0	1	33.0	26	16	10	1	4	13	0	29	3
Woodfin, White Sox	1	0	1.000	0.00	4	0	0	2	0	0	5.0	1	1	0	0	0	0	0	7	0
Woodman, Twins	0	1	.000	1.37	13	0	0	8	0	0	26.1	14	7	4	0	0	23	0	19	3
Woodring, Expos	2	1	.667	0.76	14	0	0	9	0	3	35.2	19	5	3	0	1	9	0	20	3
Woods, White Sox	0	0	.000	2.25	2	2	0	0	0	0	8.0	4	3	2	0	1	6	0	6	2
Young, Blue Jays	4	5	.444	3.90	14	12	1	0	0	0	62.1	59	30	27	2	4	31	0	61	1
Young, Mets	2	1	.667	3.34	17	0	0	14	0	0	35.0	38	18	13	4	6	10	0	18	7

BALKS—R. Young, 11; Castro, 8; Al. Garcia, 5; Baptist, Barrera, Hostetler, Kendrick, 4 each; C. Broome, Corral, Foster, Leiber, Mays, M. Pena, Rios, Rose, Shelby, Skjerpen, Taveras, Tucker, 3 each; Eric T. Anderson, R. Blanco, Bryant, Cafaro, Delgado, R. Garcia, Geraldo, M. Johnson, Keener, Lundquist, Mathews, Mercado, Mercado, A. Pena, Pickford, Pina, Porzio, Ramos, Theodile, Vializ, 2 each; Arias, Barrett, Becker, Berry, C. Brown, Carl, Cather, Christman, Civit, Cormenares, Coronado, Crossley, Cunnane, Danley, Detwiler, Durocher, Faile, Farmer, Fernandes, Fidge, Galarza, Goldman, Gomez, Gordon, Gourdin, Hartshorn, Hassen, Hayward, Heredia, Huffman, Hylton, Jackson, J. Johnson, Knighton, Krablin, Lane, Leshnock, Markham, McGinn, Medina, Millwood, Mittauer, Ocasio, Ogden, Olszewski, Paniagua, Phillip, Pimentel, Pinango, Quillin, Quirk, Rain, Reid, Rusch, Sabino, Serna, Short, Singleton, D. Smith, Stefanoff, Tatar, Telgheder, Urbina, Wolff, Woodring, 1 each.

COMBINATION SHUTOUTS—Ramos-Blanco-Walter, Astros; Green-Miller-Leroy-Betti, Green-Faile-Gann, Green-Millwood-Gann, Braves; Volkert-Hartshorn, Young-Lee-Sinnes, Blue Jays; Whitfill-Garcia, Cubs; Hylton-Woodring, Mainville-Taveras, Paniagua-Kermode, Vializ-Detwiler, Expos; Cunnane-Foshie-Bavouset, Heredia-Bavouset, Marlins; Adair-Spang, Atwater-Kindell-Quillin, Atwater-McGinn-Krablin-Wolff, Atwater-Pena-Quillin, McEntire-Young-Kindell, Mets; Anderson-Dykhoff-Price-Gulledge, Anderson-Smith-Karns, Hale-Pena-Gulledge, Lombardi-Barrett, Lombardi-Cafaro-Galvez, Orioles; Leiper-Skjerpen, Reid-Ryan, Pirates; Delzine-O'Flynn-Cather, Fajardo-Howell-Santana, Fajardo-Ocasio, Knighton-Delzine-Perez-Santana, Ocasio-Santana-Cather, Oropeza-Perez-Delzine-Santana, Rangers; Asher-Pinango-Blais-Amos, Mejia-Blais, Suppan-Padilla-Blais, Suppan-Padilla-Blais-Amos, Red Sox; Fitzpatrick-Smith-Brixey, Hodges-Campusano-Huffman, Hodges-Huffman-Rea, Rusch-Fitzpatrick, Royals; Garcia-Gomez, Matznick-Dunne-Fitzpatrick-Leiber, Quirk-Broome-Leiber, Quirk-Gomez-Leiber, White Sox; Brown-Mittauer, Mendoza-Rios, Yankees.

NO-HIT GAMES—Green-Faile-Gann, Braves, defeated Expos, 3-0, August 4.

FIELDING

TEAM

Team	Pct.	G	PO	A	E	DP	PB	Team	Pct.	G	PO	A	E	DP	PB
Marlins	.961	60	1558	670	90	57	16	Blue Jays	.949	60	1536	700	119	48	12
Expos	.960	58	1555	750	95	53	18	Royals	.949	59	1526	672	118	37	24
Rangers	.959	60	1545	693	95	50	14	Braves	.946	58	1514	596	121	42	10
White Sox	.959	60	1565	637	94	45	6	Astros	.944	59	1526	660	130	48	12
Mets	.957	59	1562	637	99	54	11	Twins	.943	59	1491	574	125	31	10
Red Sox	.956	58	1580	662	102	46	15	Cubs	.939	59	1526	602	138	48	14
Orioles	.955	59	1514	651	101	49	13	Pirates	.938	59	1516	631	142	37	15
Yankees	.950	59	1537	642	115	30	16								

INDIVIDUAL

FIRST BASEMEN

*Throws lefthanded.

Player, Team	Pct.	G	PO	A	E	DP	Player, Team	Pct.	G	PO	A	E	DP
Abad, Red Sox*	1.000	11	84	7	0	7	Chambers, Cubs	.985	9	57	10	1	6
Baucom, Twins	.943	3	33	0	2	4	Civit, Expos	1.000	2	20	1	0	0
Becker, Blue Jays	1.000	1	4	0	0	0	Crick, Twins	.952	13	92	7	5	3
Beyna, Astros	1.000	1	4	0	0	0	Culp, Rangers	1.000	2	5	0	0	0
Bowles, Red Sox	.966	31	261	23	10	22	Delgado, Pirates	1.000	1	3	0	0	0
Catlett, Braves	.984	53	457	40	8	37	Dondero, Royals	1.000	1	5	0	0	0
Cepeda, Royals	.987	46	363	11	5	17	Ephan, Rangers	.970	6	29	3	1	0
							Fantauzzi, Marlins	.985	18	121	11	2	12
							Fellhauer, Mets*	.968	23	197	13	7	23
							Ford, Red Sox	.968	4	29	1	1	2

— 538 —

Player, Team	Pct.	G	PO	A	E	DP
Galarza, Pirates	.979	6	44	2	1	3
Gonzalez, Expos	1.000	18	174	13	0	19
Halbruner, Blue Jays*	.994	33	303	13	2	27
Hall, White Sox	1.000	1	1	2	0	0
Hidalgo, Orioles	.977	35	282	19	7	27
Izquierdo, White Sox	1.000	1	1	2	0	0
D. Johnson, Marlins	1.000	1	4	1	0	0
Kern, Royals	1.000	2	11	0	0	0
Kingman, Marlins	.991	47	429	27	4	40
Linares, Orioles	.981	28	242	11	5	17
M. Lopez, Royals	1.000	1	2	0	0	0
Mathews, Braves*	1.000	6	44	2	0	0
Mendez, Royals	1.000	3	16	1	0	0
Mendoza, Royals	1.000	7	53	5	0	3
Niethammer, Expos	.989	40	411	23	5	35
Ouimet, Rangers	.987	26	205	17	3	12
Palmer, Pirates	1.000	4	35	2	0	5
Patterson, Twins*	.970	35	274	16	9	16
Patterson, Mets	.994	38	328	26	2	25
Pearson, Twins	.978	13	78	10	2	4
Reynolds, Cubs	.961	28	212	12	9	13
Rice, Pirates	.963	30	250	11	10	12
Root, Astros*	.965	36	284	17	11	26
Rounsifer, Red Sox	.982	23	157	10	3	9
Samuel, Yankees	.972	52	470	19	14	24
Sauer, Cubs	1.000	3	29	0	0	0
Seguignol, Yankees	.950	3	17	2	1	0
Spry, White Sox*	.974	19	139	13	4	7
C. Stone, Blue Jays	.982	29	246	21	5	17
Thomas, White Sox	.969	12	119	6	4	10
Thomas, Cubs*	1.000	2	10	0	0	0
Torres, Yankees	.984	8	58	5	1	5
Vaske, Cubs	.991	27	195	19	2	23
Vindivich, Royals	.983	18	111	7	2	11
Williams, White Sox*	.975	34	287	19	8	21
WILLIAMS, Rangers	.992	41	332	24	3	30
Witt, Astros	.980	35	229	18	5	18
Wolf, Pirates*	.985	23	191	9	3	11

SECOND BASEMEN

Player, Team	Pct.	G	PO	A	E	DP
Abreu, Twins	1.000	1	2	0	0	0
Alfonzo, Mets	.962	39	87	91	7	25
Avalos, Cubs	.944	11	21	13	2	5
Barberie, Marlins	1.000	2	3	4	0	1
Bell, Rangers	1.000	1	1	1	0	0
Boulware, White Sox	.951	33	63	73	7	9
Brea, Mets	1.000	1	1	0	0	0
Brinkley, Expos	.973	6	15	21	1	3
V. Brown, Yankees	.987	21	36	41	1	7
Cabrera, Blue Jays	.949	45	106	118	12	23
Castle, Cubs	.900	19	39	33	8	12
Castro, Twins	.984	18	36	24	1	2
Coquillette, Expos	.944	42	80	123	12	19
Cormenares, Blue Jays	1.000	1	0	1	0	0
Cruz, Twins	.948	33	72	56	7	6
Cunningham, Cubs	.904	30	56	48	11	11
Davila, Blue Jays	.919	18	32	47	7	13
Diaz, Rangers	.967	40	78	100	6	17
Domingo, Braves	1.000	1	5	2	0	0
Dondero, Royals	1.000	1	3	1	0	0
Frazier, Marlins	1.000	4	3	4	0	2
Friedrich, White Sox	.978	22	38	51	2	9
Gabriel, Orioles	.800	4	5	7	3	2
Garcia, Twins	.913	14	29	34	6	8
Garcia, Orioles	.950	23	37	78	6	16
Gonzalez, Rangers	.972	20	46	57	3	13
Hunter, Cubs	.972	7	14	21	1	5
Keefe, Pirates	1.000	5	5	13	0	2
Knighten, Cubs	1.000	2	0	2	0	0
Larson, Astros	1.000	2	2	4	0	1
Lebron, Red Sox	.963	6	14	12	1	0
Lee, Braves	.922	23	45	61	9	15
Lobaton, Yankees	.964	20	45	63	4	11
M. Lopez, Royals	.857	4	5	7	2	0
Lopez, Yankees	.929	16	33	32	5	5
Lopez, Astros	.938	23	27	33	4	5
F. Martinez, Royals	.948	21	45	46	5	8
R. Martinez, Royals	.973	35	71	108	5	19
Melendez, Orioles	.987	35	65	90	2	15
Menechino, White Sox	.979	13	22	25	1	6
MILLIARD, Marlins	.984	52	111	142	4	29
J. Morales, Mets	.967	20	36	52	3	11
Murphy, Red Sox	.960	5	13	11	1	3
Nolte, Marlins	.968	12	14	16	1	4
Norman, Red Sox	.918	16	27	29	5	4
Osentowski, Mets	1.000	2	5	4	0	1
Polanco, Pirates	.939	29	65	73	9	13
Prieto, Royals	.951	12	15	24	2	3
J. Ramos, Astros	1.000	1	0	1	0	0
Reyes, Expos	.964	10	19	34	2	7
Roberson, Braves	.938	33	63	89	10	16
Sanchez, White Sox	1.000	3	4	6	0	0

Player, Team	Pct.	G	PO	A	E	DP
Selmo, Braves	.917	3	6	5	1	0
Smith, Red Sox	1.000	2	4	8	0	0
Swafford, Pirates	.921	30	60	68	11	9
Tebbs, Red Sox	.950	38	49	64	6	14
Torres, Yankees	.880	6	10	12	3	1
Trammell, Astros	.964	55	102	112	8	33
Walker, Red Sox	1.000	1	2	0	0	0
Williams, Rangers	1.000	4	2	7	0	0

THIRD BASEMEN

Player, Team	Pct.	G	PO	A	E	DP
Alfonzo, Mets	.667	1	0	2	1	0
Aranzamendi, Marlins	.958	32	18	96	5	7
Arvelo, Mets	1.000	3	2	7	0	0
Avalos, Cubs	.750	2	2	1	1	0
Bell, Rangers	.937	58	35	144	12	8
Beyna, Astros	.815	11	4	18	5	1
Bowles, Red Sox	.750	4	1	5	2	2
Brea, Mets	1.000	2	2	6	0	0
Brinkley, Expos	1.000	3	1	3	0	0
Carter, Braves	1.000	1	2	0	0	0
Casique, Twins	.400	1	0	2	3	0
Castro, Twins	.903	16	11	17	3	0
Chambers, Cubs	.833	4	0	10	2	0
Crick, Twins	.903	12	12	16	3	1
Culp, Expos	.867	44	25	79	16	6
Cunningham, Pirates	.820	24	15	35	11	1
Davila, Blue Jays	.928	23	14	63	6	6
DeJesus, Cubs	.958	31	31	61	4	4
Domingo, Braves	1.000	1	1	1	0	0
Dondero, Royals	.900	14	3	15	2	0
Dye, Braves	.900	3	2	7	1	2
Friedrich, White Sox	1.000	2	0	1	0	0
Fuller, Red Sox	1.000	1	0	1	0	0
Gabriel, Orioles	.924	27	28	57	7	3
Galarza, Pirates	.944	28	18	49	4	4
Gibralter, Red Sox	.865	48	40	95	21	5
Gonzalez, Rangers	1.000	1	1	4	0	0
Hall, White Sox	.893	14	10	15	3	1
Hamilton, Red Sox	1.000	2	1	6	0	1
Hofer, Braves	.844	21	16	38	10	8
Hunter, Cubs	.769	3	3	7	3	0
Izquierdo, White Sox	.733	9	5	6	4	0
D. Johnson, Marlins	.806	13	10	19	7	1
Kingman, Marlins	.826	8	6	13	4	1
Larkin, Red Sox	.800	8	2	10	3	1
Lee, Braves	.667	1	0	2	1	0
Leger, Pirates	.667	2	0	4	2	0
Linares, Orioles	.875	4	0	7	1	0
M. Lopez, Royals	.894	29	21	55	9	2
Lopez, Yankees	.880	6	4	18	3	0
Mackert, Pirates	1.000	5	0	9	0	0
Melendez, Orioles	.886	10	12	19	4	1
Mendoza, Royals	.941	7	3	13	1	0
Milliard, Marlins	.857	2	3	3	1	0
Moore, White Sox	.934	45	34	80	8	11
J. Morales, Mets	.800	10	6	14	5	3
MOTA, Mets	.943	41	40	93	8	11
Nolte, Marlins	.818	15	6	30	8	1
Norton, White Sox	1.000	3	1	7	0	1
Osentowski, Mets	.813	3	2	10	3	2
Pagan, Orioles	1.000	1	3	4	0	1
Palmer, Yankees	.915	48	32	108	13	3
Perez, Yankees	1.000	3	0	5	0	0
Polanco, Pirates	1.000	7	3	14	0	0
Reyes, Expos	.885	15	10	36	6	3
Sanchez, White Sox	.800	3	2	2	1	0
Sasser, Braves	.884	33	15	61	10	2
Scopio, Cubs	.800	3	1	7	2	0
Simmons, Orioles	.859	24	16	39	9	3
Tebbs, Red Sox	.750	2	0	3	1	0
Torres, Yankees	.941	7	6	10	1	0
Trammell, Astros	1.000	3	1	6	0	0
Truby, Astros	.889	50	30	139	21	10
Valentin, Twins	1.000	1	0	1	0	0
Vaninetti, Blue Jays	.888	39	26	93	15	6
Vielleux, Cubs	.847	27	16	56	13	6
Williams, Rangers	1.000	7	2	8	0	0
Wojtkowski, Royals	.929	22	14	38	4	1
Zorrilla, Twins	.856	37	23	78	17	7

SHORTSTOPS

Player, Team	Pct.	G	PO	A	E	DP
Abreu, Twins	.934	22	29	56	6	6
Aranzamendi, Marlins	.778	6	9	12	6	6
Arrollado, Red Sox	.885	10	12	34	6	5
Arvelo, Mets	.905	52	80	158	25	29
Avalos, Cubs	.872	20	28	40	10	8
Babin, Marlins	.917	54	67	165	21	30
Brinkley, Expos	.692	2	4	5	4	2
V. Brown, Yankees	.892	31	40	92	16	13

Player, Team	Pct.	G	PO	A	E	DP
Cabrera, Blue Jays	.882	7	11	19	4	2
Casique, Twins	.885	7	5	18	3	3
Civit, Expos	1.000	1	1	1	0	0
Cormenares, Blue Jays	.824	8	10	18	6	4
Cruz, Twins	.667	2	2	0	1	0
Cunningham, Cubs	.800	3	2	2	1	2
Davila, Blue Jays	.900	7	10	17	3	1
Delgado, Pirates	.847	31	38	73	20	11
Domingo, Braves	1.000	2	0	5	0	1
Dondero, Royals	.882	16	11	34	6	3
J. Foster, Expos	1.000	2	4	5	0	1
Frazier, Marlins	1.000	3	0	2	0	0
Friedrich, White Sox	1.000	1	1	0	0	0
Gabriel, Orioles	1.000	3	0	7	0	0
Garcia, Orioles	.911	19	24	58	8	6
Goligoski, White Sox	.938	54	81	159	16	23
Gonzalez, Rangers	.953	31	50	92	7	18
Hagen, Pirates	.863	30	41	98	22	12
Hall, White Sox	.931	8	9	18	2	2
Hofer, Braves	.750	3	3	3	2	1
Izquierdo, White Sox	.500	1	0	1	1	0
Jackson, Red Sox	.957	40	61	118	8	14
Lamb, Orioles	.927	10	16	22	3	4
Landaker, Astros	.857	5	2	16	3	0
Lane, Twins	.929	40	50	94	11	8
Lobaton, Yankees	.897	23	32	81	13	7
M. Lopez, Royals	.500	1	2	0	2	0
Lopez, Yankees	.944	6	3	14	1	1
Lopez, Astros	1.000	1	1	2	0	0
Magee, Braves	.900	16	24	39	7	4
F. Martinez, Royals	.832	33	34	90	25	18
Medrano, Blue Jays	.948	39	58	142	11	20
Melendez, Orioles	1.000	1	2	0	0	1
Merloni, Red Sox	.952	4	7	13	1	3
Montilla, Cubs	.900	39	74	97	19	19
J. Morales, Mets	.833	4	3	7	2	0
Mosquera, Blue Jays	1.000	1	1	0	0	0
Mota, Mets	1.000	1	2	2	0	0
Navarro, Mets	.909	3	5	5	1	3
Nolte, Marlins	1.000	4	1	6	0	1
Pagan, Orioles	.933	30	52	87	10	24
Patton, Red Sox	1.000	4	7	9	0	1
PEREZ, Expos	.964	52	121	205	12	39
Prieto, Royals	.861	31	27	72	16	6
Reyes, Expos	.938	4	3	12	1	0
Roberson, Braves	.960	8	9	15	1	3
Sanchez, White Sox	.789	10	4	11	4	2
Saylor, Astros	.890	49	61	149	26	24
Selmo, Braves	.925	30	39	84	10	13
Smith, Red Sox	1.000	1	2	2	0	1
Tebbs, Red Sox	.905	4	6	13	2	3
Trammell, Astros	.714	4	4	6	4	1
Truby, Astros	.861	6	12	19	5	5
Vaninetti, Blue Jays	1.000	2	0	2	0	0
Vielleux, Cubs	.909	4	4	6	1	1
Walker, Rangers	.830	26	26	47	15	8
Williams, Rangers	.878	12	12	24	5	3

OUTFIELDERS

Player, Team	Pct.	G	PO	A	E	DP
Abad, Red Sox*	.991	51	109	6	1	3
Alonso, Orioles	.982	34	49	6	1	0
Aquino, White Sox	.818	11	8	1	2	0
Beaumont, Yankees	.878	39	38	5	6	0
Becker, Blue Jays	1.000	1	1	0	0	0
Blackburn, White Sox	.974	29	34	3	1	2
Borges, Pirates	.952	26	54	5	3	0
Bourne, Blue Jays	.889	24	30	2	4	0
Bowers, Astros	.963	47	73	4	3	0
Bowman, Orioles	.917	27	41	3	4	0
Bradley, Mets	.895	24	49	2	6	0
Brandon, Royals	.972	50	99	5	3	0
Brewer, Braves	.984	34	61	1	1	1
Brinkley, Expos	1.000	1	3	1	0	1
Brown, Braves	.846	12	18	4	4	0
Campos, Expos	1.000	1	1	0	0	0
Carr, Marlins	.900	3	9	0	1	0
Carter, Braves	1.000	2	2	1	0	0
Chancey, Orioles	.850	23	31	3	6	1
Civit, Expos	1.000	11	16	2	0	0
DeJesus, Cubs	1.000	1	1	0	0	0
Dunwoody, Marlins*	.979	30	45	1	1	0
Dye, Braves	.958	27	44	2	2	1
ESTRADA, Expos	1.000	54	95	4	0	0
Faggett, Red Sox*	.950	13	19	0	1	0
Fantauzzi, Marlins	.960	17	22	2	1	0
Farner, Blue Jays*	.958	25	46	0	2	0
Ferrier, Mets	.985	34	59	6	1	0
Ford, Red Sox	1.000	3	2	0	0	0
Fortin, Twins	1.000	1	2	0	0	0
Franklin, Cubs	.962	37	50	0	2	0
Frazier, Royals	.942	34	46	3	3	1
Gabriel, Orioles	1.000	1	1	0	0	0

Player, Team	Pct.	G	PO	A	E	DP
E. Garcia, Cubs	.974	41	72	3	2	0
Garcia, Rangers	.982	38	52	2	1	0
Genden, Marlins	1.000	27	26	1	0	0
Gil, Cubs	.979	43	84	8	2	3
Gordon, Twins	.952	36	58	2	3	0
Gosch, Astros*	1.000	11	7	0	0	0
Graham, Red Sox*	1.000	9	21	1	0	1
Hairston, Pirates	.846	26	31	2	6	1
Hall, Expos	.938	47	58	2	4	0
Hammer, Astros	.975	33	36	3	1	0
J. Hayward, Red Sox	1.000	3	5	1	0	0
Helsel, Blue Jays	1.000	3	7	0	0	0
Hightower, Blue Jays	.976	48	79	1	2	0
Hiraldo, Mets	.944	14	16	1	1	0
Hobert, Marlins	1.000	12	13	1	0	0
Hubley, Marlins	.966	39	54	3	2	1
Hunter, Twins	.895	27	50	1	6	0
Jefferson, Marlins	.905	14	19	0	2	0
D. Johnson, Marlins	1.000	4	4	0	0	0
M. Johnson, Twins	.909	7	10	0	1	0
Kern, Royals	.958	32	46	0	2	0
Kieschnick, Cubs	1.000	2	3	1	0	0
King, Blue Jays	.913	16	20	1	2	0
Knighten, Cubs	.978	27	43	1	1	0
Lee, Astros	.886	34	39	0	5	0
Leger, Astros	.967	27	56	2	2	0
Levias, White Sox	.986	35	67	1	1	0
A. Lewis, Rangers	.989	47	86	1	1	1
Lewis, Marlins	.972	31	30	5	1	0
Lyde, Pirates	1.000	9	10	3	0	1
Macon, Rangers	.963	55	70	7	3	0
H. Martinez, Red Sox	1.000	23	34	0	0	0
R. Martinez, Royals	.500	1	1	0	1	0
McClure, White Sox	.978	52	89	2	2	0
McKinnon, White Sox	1.000	4	10	1	0	1
Mejia, Cubs	.976	33	80	3	2	0
Meran, Expos	1.000	11	22	1	0	0
Mucker, Twins	1.000	1	1	0	0	0
Nelson, Cubs	1.000	4	9	1	0	0
Nelson, Yankees	.980	57	97	1	2	0
Nolte, Marlins	1.000	4	4	1	0	0
Ortiz, Pirates	1.000	3	4	1	0	1
OZARIO, Mets	1.000	55	110	3	0	0
Patton, White Sox	.982	50	50	4	1	0
Payano, Royals	.984	37	57	3	1	0
Pearson, Twins	.973	28	34	2	1	0
Perez, Twins	.960	40	86	10	4	3
Peterson, Pirates	.943	39	75	7	5	0
Pico, Cubs*	1.000	8	11	0	0	0
Poe, White Sox	1.000	2	4	0	0	0
Polanco, Pirates	1.000	1	2	0	0	0
J. Ramirez, Mets	.981	52	103	3	2	0
J. Ramos, Astros	.974	48	76	0	2	0
Reeves, Marlins	.989	45	84	3	1	0
Rivera, Red Sox	.953	51	76	5	4	2
Rivers, Blue Jays	.971	50	61	5	2	0
Ross, Astros	.987	37	70	5	1	1
Sanchez, Cubs	.955	26	40	2	2	1
Santiago, Blue Jays	.923	29	33	3	3	1
Sauer, Cubs	.903	22	27	1	3	0
Schwab, Expos	.949	53	71	3	4	0
Scopio, Cubs	.973	32	70	2	2	0
Seguignol, Yankees	.987	43	69	6	1	0
Shanklin, Rangers	.857	9	6	0	1	0
Sheffield, Red Sox*	.919	43	50	7	5	0
Shumpert, Yankees	.924	43	72	1	6	0
Smith, Pirates	.892	27	31	2	4	0
R. Smith, Royals	.929	21	12	1	1	0
Spry, White Sox*	1.000	10	11	0	0	0
Starks, White Sox	1.000	4	6	0	0	0
Staton, Pirates*	.906	29	44	4	5	3
Tillman, Braves	.966	29	55	1	2	0
Tolbert, Royals	1.000	24	34	2	0	0
Ulises, Orioles	.975	35	71	6	2	3
Valdez, Orioles	.988	38	76	3	1	1
Vazquez, Braves	.963	13	25	1	1	0
VESSEL, Rangers	1.000	49	81	12	0	4
Vindivich, Royals	1.000	11	8	1	0	0
Vizcaino, Twins	.947	47	85	4	5	0
Walls, Royals*	.964	22	26	1	1	0
Weathersby, Royals	.949	29	35	2	2	0
White, Orioles	1.000	3	2	1	0	0
Williams, Braves	1.000	1	1	0	0	0

CATCHERS

Player, Team	Pct.	G	PO	A	E	DP	PB
Abezcua, Astros	.971	46	276	23	9	1	6
Alvarez, White Sox	1.000	1	4	0	0	0	0
Arias, Red Sox	.976	11	35	5	1	1	2
Ashby, Yankees	.966	27	212	18	8	1	8
Baker, Orioles	.983	23	107	9	2	0	6
Baucom, Twins	.929	6	34	5	3	1	1
Becker, Blue Jays	.977	32	222	29	6	1	3

Player, Team	Pct.	G	PO	A	E	DP	PB
Beyna, Astros	.986	16	62	8	1	1	3
Bradley, Mets	1.000	1	1	0	0	0	0
Brea, Mets	.987	13	63	12	1	0	1
Brea, Orioles	.965	12	71	12	3	0	2
Burgos, Royals	1.000	3	2	0	0	0	0
Carone, White Sox	.989	25	149	23	2	0	2
Cicero, Cubs	.964	20	99	8	4	2	4
CLARK, Red Sox	.983	36	246	40	5	1	8
Cruz, Braves	.972	22	122	15	4	1	2
Culp, Expos	.921	6	29	6	3	0	4
Davila, Blue Jays	1.000	1	8	0	0	0	0
Deno, Rangers	.905	10	19	0	2	0	1
Doezie, Twins	.974	22	101	13	3	0	4
Dolney, Astros	.990	21	93	10	1	0	3
Ephan, Rangers	.982	46	281	41	6	5	9
Fortin, Twins	.980	20	129	18	3	1	2
Frazier, Marlins	1.000	2	5	0	0	0	0
Freeberger, Orioles	.969	26	110	13	4	1	4
Gargiulo, Orioles	1.000	12	60	10	0	0	1
Gipner, Yankees	.984	23	173	17	3	0	4
Gomez, Mets	.974	7	36	2	1	0	1
Gross, Marlins	1.000	21	111	12	0	1	1
Lorenzo, Red Sox	.990	24	170	25	2	1	5
Maize, Mets	1.000	3	19	1	0	0	0
Martinez, Expos	.979	19	108	29	3	1	6
Matos, Braves	.968	36	259	39	10	3	5
McCoy, Royals	.958	39	140	19	7	1	15
Mendez, Royals	.981	39	182	28	4	2	7
Molina, Cubs	.960	31	143	27	7	1	5
H. Morales, Mets	.971	40	258	43	9	1	8
Mosquera, Blue Jays	.965	32	179	39	8	3	9
Niethammer, Expos	1.000	2	9	3	0	0	2
Ojeda, Pirates	.983	23	151	22	3	3	8
Ouimet, Rangers	1.000	1	2	0	0	0	0
Pachot, Expos	.974	35	214	48	7	4	6
Perez, Yankees	.964	15	71	10	3	0	2
Rennspies, Braves	.928	13	71	6	6	0	3
Reynolds, Cubs	.966	12	54	2	2	0	4
Ridenour, White Sox	1.000	5	23	4	0	2	1
Rodriguez, Marlins	.975	43	284	29	8	2	14
Roskos, Marlins	.909	3	18	2	2	1	1
Shows, Rangers	.979	11	44	2	1	1	4
Torres, Pirates	.964	18	109	23	5	1	3
Tremie, White Sox	1.000	2	11	0	0	0	0
Turlais, Pirates	.994	24	150	20	1	2	4
Unrat, Rangers	.962	9	45	5	2	0	0
Valentin, Twins	.966	19	120	22	5	0	3
Vindivich, Royals	.946	9	33	2	2	0	2
Vollmer, White Sox	.977	36	228	27	6	3	3
Winterlee, Mets	1.000	2	14	2	0	0	0
Wolff, Cubs	1.000	6	19	7	0	0	1
Zuleta, Cubs	.880	6	20	2	3	0	0

PITCHERS

Player, Team	Pct.	G	PO	A	E	DP
Acevedo, Royals*	1.000	15	3	9	0	0
Adair, Mets	.917	11	4	7	1	0
Alvarado, Twins	.813	13	3	10	3	1
Amos, Red Sox	1.000	11	1	1	0	0
Anderson, Royals	1.000	12	2	6	0	0
Anderson, Twins*	.750	12	1	8	3	0
Anderson, Orioles*	1.000	3	0	1	0	0
Aquino, White Sox	1.000	2	0	1	0	0
Arias, Blue Jays	.800	22	4	4	2	1
Asher, Red Sox	.917	6	5	6	1	1
Ashley, Blue Jays	.500	12	1	1	2	0
Atwater, Mets*	1.000	11	8	8	0	0
Ausanio, Expos	1.000	5	0	1	0	0
Baker, Expos	.875	7	1	6	1	0
Baldwin, White Sox	.333	11	1	0	2	0
Bales, White Sox	1.000	4	0	4	0	0
Baptist, Astros	.900	19	2	7	1	1
Barrera, Braves	1.000	12	1	6	0	0
Barrett, Orioles*	1.000	6	0	5	0	1
Bavousett, Marlins	1.000	11	1	2	0	0
Beashore, Cubs	1.000	3	2	1	0	0
Becker, Red Sox	.846	14	3	8	2	2
Bennett, Royals	.750	11	1	2	1	0
Bennett, Red Sox	1.000	2	1	0	0	0
Berry, Yankees	.667	15	1	1	1	0
Betti, Braves*	.857	9	4	2	1	0
Blais, Red Sox	.833	22	5	5	2	2
Blanco, Astros*	1.000	9	1	1	0	0
Blanco, Cubs	.750	6	2	1	1	0
Bogott, Red Sox*	1.000	3	1	3	0	1
Bowman, Mets	.917	10	3	8	1	0
Brixey, Royals	1.000	14	3	6	0	1
Broome, White Sox	.933	15	6	8	1	0
Broome, Cubs	1.000	11	4	8	0	0
C. Brown, Yankees	1.000	16	1	7	0	1
Bryant, Braves	.810	14	6	11	4	0
Bullard, Pirates	1.000	4	0	2	0	0
Cafaro, Orioles	.905	14	4	15	2	1

Player, Team	Pct.	G	PO	A	E	DP
Cain, Braves	.818	9	5	4	2	0
Campusano, Royals	1.000	15	1	3	0	0
Carl, Marlins	1.000	10	4	1	0	0
Castro, Cubs*	.545	13	1	5	5	1
Cather, Rangers	1.000	25	0	3	0	0
Chambers, Cubs	1.000	1	1	1	0	0
Christman, White Sox*	1.000	4	1	1	0	0
Civit, Expos	1.000	5	0	1	0	0
Cook, Red Sox	1.000	8	0	1	0	0
Cormenares, Blue Jays	1.000	2	1	1	0	0
Coronado, Mets	.929	12	5	8	1	1
Corral, Blue Jays	.714	20	3	7	4	1
Creek, Astros	.917	12	3	8	1	1
Crossley, Astros	.833	17	4	1	1	0
Cunnane, Marlins	.778	16	6	8	4	0
Danley, Braves*	1.000	3	1	1	0	0
Davis, Pirates	.833	11	2	3	1	0
DeBrino, Twins	1.000	26	1	5	0	1
Delgado, Marlins	.909	11	4	6	1	0
Delzine, Rangers	1.000	20	6	8	0	1
Detwiler, Expos	1.000	17	3	6	0	0
DeWalt, Red Sox	1.000	6	2	3	0	0
Dixon, White Sox	1.000	3	0	1	0	0
Downs, Royals	1.000	3	0	2	0	0
Dunne, White Sox	1.000	3	0	1	0	0
Durocher, Astros	1.000	7	2	6	0	1
Dykhoff, Orioles*	.929	14	5	8	1	0
Ehler, Marlins	1.000	10	1	4	0	0
Evans, Rangers*	.000	2	0	1	0	0
Faile, Braves	1.000	11	1	6	0	0
Fajardo, Marlins	1.000	6	3	9	0	1
Falmier, Rangers	.875	14	5	2	1	1
Farmer, Rangers	1.000	2	0	1	0	0
Ferguson, Yankees	1.000	10	2	10	0	0
Fernandes, Red Sox	.900	6	3	6	1	2
Fidge, Twins	1.000	12	4	6	0	0
Fitzpatrick, White Sox	1.000	3	0	1	0	0
Fitzpatrick, Royals	.800	12	3	5	2	0
Forbes, White Sox*	.000	7	0	1	0	0
Ford, Pirates*	1.000	6	0	2	0	0
Fordham, White Sox*	1.000	3	0	2	0	0
K. Foster, Expos	.833	17	6	9	3	0
Galarza, Pirates	1.000	7	4	9	0	0
Gann, Braves	1.000	17	2	2	0	0
A. Garcia, Cubs	1.000	10	1	11	0	0
Garcia, White Sox	.950	12	7	12	1	1
Garcia, White Sox	.818	14	4	5	2	1
Geraldo, Blue Jays	.944	16	5	12	1	1
Givens, Royals*	1.000	4	1	2	0	0
Goldman, Pirates	1.000	12	1	5	0	0
Gomez, White Sox	1.000	13	0	2	0	0
Gordon, Yankees	.842	11	1	15	3	1
Gourdin, Twins	.917	24	4	7	1	0
Green, Braves	1.000	12	4	1	0	0
Gulledge, Orioles	1.000	18	2	7	0	0
Handy, Expos	.727	11	3	5	3	0
Harms, Marlins	1.000	18	3	3	0	0
Hartshorn, Blue Jays	1.000	9	1	3	0	0
Hassen, White Sox	.667	14	2	2	2	0
S. Hayward, Red Sox	1.000	2	1	2	0	1
Heredia, Marlins*	1.000	12	6	4	0	0
Herrera, Twins	1.000	11	15	13	0	1
HODGES, Royals	1.000	12	8	22	0	0
Holter, Orioles	1.000	9	5	2	0	0
Hostetler, Braves	.500	3	0	1	1	0
Howard, Marlins*	1.000	8	1	2	0	0
Howell, Rangers	1.000	6	0	1	0	0
Huffman, Royals	1.000	13	0	3	0	0
Hylton, Expos	.778	11	2	5	2	0
Ireland, Marlins*	.714	8	1	4	2	0
Jackson, Rangers	.867	15	3	10	2	0
Janzen, Yankees	1.000	5	1	4	0	0
Johnson, Pirates	.923	9	2	10	1	0
Johnson, Blue Jays	.750	16	3	9	4	0
S. Johnson, Marlins	1.000	19	4	6	0	1
Karns, Orioles	.917	11	3	8	1	0
Keener, Pirates*	1.000	7	0	1	0	0
Kendrick, Cubs	.833	9	3	7	2	0
Kennedy, Red Sox*	1.000	3	0	3	0	0
Kermode, Expos	1.000	4	1	0	0	0
Kindell, Mets*	.800	14	0	4	1	0
Kitchen, Orioles	1.000	2	0	1	0	0
Klvac, Red Sox*	.923	7	0	12	1	0
Knighton, Rangers	.769	22	2	8	3	0
Krablin, Mets	.500	10	0	2	2	0
Lane, Orioles	1.000	11	2	7	0	0
Lee, Blue Jays	1.000	9	0	3	0	0
Leiber, White Sox	.875	15	3	4	1	0
Leiper, Pirates*	.667	7	1	1	1	0
Leroy, Braves	.500	10	0	1	1	0
Leshnock, Yankees	.000	3	0	0	1	0
Linehan, Astros*	1.000	12	3	3	0	0
Liriano, Cubs	.800	12	4	4	2	0
Lollie, Braves	1.000	3	0	1	0	0
Lombardi, Orioles	.929	10	6	7	1	1

COAST LE!

Player, Team	Pct.	G	PO	A	E	DP
A. Lopez, Royals*	1.000	7	0	5	0	0
Love, Cubs	1.000	5	0	2	0	0
Lundquist, White Sox	.833	11	4	6	2	1
Mainville, Expos	.909	6	1	9	1	0
Markham, Expos	.882	11	4	11	2	1
Mathews, Braves*	.864	14	3	16	3	0
Matthews, Marlins	1.000	17	4	7	0	0
Matznick, White Sox	1.000	9	3	2	0	0
Mays, Marlins*	.933	12	3	11	1	0
McCormack, White Sox*	1.000	1	0	1	0	0
McEntire, Mets*	.786	10	5	6	3	2
McGinn, Mets	.750	9	1	2	1	0
McKinion, White Sox	1.000	6	2	4	0	0
Medina, Yankees	1.000	5	2	3	0	0
Mejia, Red Sox*	1.000	12	3	9	0	0
Mendoza, Yankees	1.000	15	2	11	0	0
Mercado, Astros*	.909	11	3	17	2	0
Merigliano, White Sox	1.000	3	0	1	0	0
Miller, Braves	.818	13	4	5	2	0
Millwood, Braves	.750	12	3	3	2	0
Mittauer, Yankees	1.000	21	1	2	0	0
Mooney, Pirates	.929	5	2	11	1	0
O'Flynn, Rangers*	.727	18	4	4	3	0
Ocasio, Rangers	.789	12	3	12	4	0
Ogden, White Sox	1.000	4	0	2	0	0
Olszewski, Braves	.786	13	5	6	3	0
Oropeza, Rangers	.875	12	3	11	2	1
Pacheco, Cubs	1.000	4	1	5	0	0
Pack, Mets	.900	12	5	13	2	0
Padilla, Red Sox*	.857	13	1	11	2	0
Padron, Astros	1.000	15	4	3	0	0
Paniagua, Expos	1.000	4	0	5	0	0
Pena, Orioles	.900	19	2	7	1	0
Pena, Mets	.600	18	1	2	2	0
Perez, Rangers	.500	19	2	3	5	0
Peterson, Red Sox	1.000	3	1	1	0	0
Pett, Blue Jays	1.000	4	0	1	0	0
Phillip, Red Sox	.500	3	0	2	2	0
Pickford, Pirates*	1.000	9	4	3	0	0
Pimentel, Cubs	.750	4	0	6	2	0
Pina, Twins	.600	17	0	3	2	0
Pinango, Red Sox*	.875	13	1	6	1	1
Porzio, Cubs*	.909	10	2	8	1	1
Pratt, White Sox*	.750	3	2	1	1	0
Price, Orioles*	.429	13	0	3	4	0
Proctor, White Sox	1.000	2	0	1	0	0
Quillin, Mets	1.000	17	3	1	0	0
Quirk, White Sox*	1.000	4	0	6	0	0
Rain, Cubs	1.000	10	2	10	0	0
H. Ramirez, Mets	1.000	1	0	1	0	0
E. Ramos, Astros	.875	14	6	8	2	0
Ray, Royals	.818	13	1	8	2	1
Rea, Royals	1.000	6	1	4	0	0
Reid, Pirates	1.000	13	0	6	0	0
Reyes, Expos	1.000	1	0	1	0	0
Reynoso, Rangers	1.000	6	1	6	1	0

Player, Team	Pct.	G	PO	A	E	DP
Rigney, Braves*	1.000	11	2	3	0	0
Rios, Yankees	.889	24	3	5	1	0
Rivera, Yankees	1.000	2	0	1	0	0
Romano, Orioles	1.000	7	1	5	0	0
Rose, Cubs	1.000	10	2	2	0	0
Rosenkranz, Rangers*	.667	8	1	1	1	0
Runion, Rangers	1.000	6	0	3	0	0
Runyan, Astros*	.909	12	2	8	1	0
Rusch, Royals*	1.000	11	0	3	0	0
Rush, Royals*	.500	8	0	1	1	0
Ryan, Pirates	.800	9	1	3	1	0
Santaella, Yankees	.857	17	2	4	1	0
Santana, Rangers	1.000	26	3	2	0	0
Santiago, Yankees	1.000	1	0	2	0	0
Sartain, Twins*	1.000	5	0	1	0	0
Schmidt, Expos	1.000	1	0	1	0	0
Senior, Red Sox*	1.000	3	0	1	0	0
Serna, Pirates	.500	7	0	1	1	0
Sharer, Pirates	.000	7	0	0	1	0
Shelby, Yankees*	.905	10	3	16	2	0
Singleton, Orioles	.667	5	1	1	1	0
Sinnes, Blue Jays	1.000	6	0	1	0	0
Sirotka, White Sox*	1.000	3	0	1	0	0
Skjerpen, Pirates	1.000	14	1	6	0	0
Smith, Rangers	.929	12	4	9	1	1
Spang, Mets	1.000	4	0	1	0	0
Stefanoff, Blue Jays	.800	11	2	2	1	0
Steinke, Astros	.800	15	1	3	1	0
M. Stone, Blue Jays*	.813	15	4	9	3	2
Suppan, Red Sox	1.000	10	4	16	0	1
Tatar, Twins	1.000	12	2	10	0	0
Taveras, Expos	.905	17	10	9	2	1
Telgheder, Red Sox	1.000	7	2	2	0	0
Temple, Pirates	.700	11	3	4	3	0
Theodile, White Sox	.857	10	4	8	2	1
Thomas, Cubs*	.556	5	2	3	4	1
Tomberlin, Cubs	.857	14	3	9	2	2
Touchett, Marlins	1.000	13	0	2	0	0
Tucker, Astros	.688	11	3	8	5	0
Turlais, Pirates	1.000	1	0	1	0	0
Urbina, Cubs*	1.000	4	4	1	0	0
Vaske, Cubs	.500	4	0	1	1	1
Vializ, Expos	.933	15	3	11	1	2
Volkert, Blue Jays	.875	14	1	6	1	1
Walter, Astros	.000	17	0	0	1	0
Ward, Pirates	.875	11	5	9	2	0
Warner, Braves	1.000	1	0	1	0	0
Whitehead, Pirates	.833	6	1	4	1	0
Whitfill, Cubs	1.000	13	3	8	0	0
Wilson, Twins	.600	15	3	0	2	0
Wolff, Mets	1.000	10	1	3	0	0
Woodman, Twins	.750	13	0	3	1	0
Woodring, Expos	1.000	14	0	2	0	0
Woods, White Sox	.750	2	2	1	1	0
Young, Mets	1.000	17	1	6	0	0
Young, Blue Jays	.917	14	4	7	1	1

The following players did not have any fielding statistics at the positions indicated or appeared only as a designated hitter, pinch-hitter or pinch-runner: D. Becker, 3b; Belcher, p; Bonilla, p; N. Brown, p; Castle, ss; R. Castro, ss; Coe, p; H. Cruz, of; J. Cunningham, of; R. Cunningham, ss; DeJesus, 2b, ss; Dondero, of; Duer, p; Estrella, p; Foshie, p; J. Frazier, 3b, of; T. Frazier, 1b; Friedrich, 1b; Fuller, 2b; Galvez, p; E. Garcia, 2b, ss; J. Garcia, 3b; P. Gomez, 3b; Grennan, p; Hale, p; Helsel, p; Hobson, p; L. Hunter, ss; G. Johnson, ss; Larson, 3b; Lebron, 1b; Ja. Lee, ss; G. Lewis, dh, pr; M. Lopez, of; C. Martinez, p; F. Martinez, 3b; Molina, 1b; Norman, 3b; Page, p; J. Palmer, 2b; Phillips, p; Rennspies, p; Reynolds, of; Sabino, p; Salazar, 3b; of; Scopio, ss; Short, p; B. Smith, p; J. Smith, p; K. Smith, p; L. Smith, 1b, 2b; Sosa, p; Stadelhofer, p; R. Thomas, of; Trimarco, p; Valentin, of; Vitko, p; Vollmer, 2b; Witt, of; Woodfin, p; Zuleta, of.

LEAGUE CHAMPIONS

Year	Team	Pct.
1964—	Sarasota Braves	.610
1965—	Bradenton Astros	.632
1966—	New York AL	.667
1967—	Kansas City	.614
1968—	Oakland	.650
1969—	Montreal	.585
1970—	Chicago AL	.600
1971—	Kansas City	.755
1972—	Chicago NL a	.651
	Kansas City a	.651
1973—	Texas	.732
1974—	Chicago NL	.702
1975—	Texas	.774
1976—	Texas	.704

Year	Team	Pct.
1977—	Chicago AL	.731
1978—	Texas	.600
1979—	Houston	.635
1980—	Kansas City-Blue	.635
1981—	Kansas City-Gold	.688
1982—	New York AL	.667
1983—	Texas	.645
	Los Angeles b	.617
1984—	White Sox	.651
	Rangers b	.571
1985—	Yankees d	.705
	Rangers	.532
1986—	Reds	.548
	Dodgers b	.541

Year	Team	Pct.
1987—	Dodgers b	.683
	Royals	.635
1988—	Yankees b	.714
	Royals	.619
1989—	Yankees c	.651
	Dodgers	.635
1990—	Expos	.635
	Dodgers c	.603
1991—	Orioles	.593
	Expos e	.533
1992—	Royals f	.695
	Expos	.593
1993—	Rangers g	.667
	Astros	.593

(Note—Known as Sarasota Rookie League in 1964 and Florida Rookie League in 1965.) aDeclared co-champions; no playoff. bLeague divided into Northern and Southern divisions; won one-game playoff for league championship. cLeague divided into Northern and Southern divisions; won best-of-three playoff for league championship. dYankees declared champion based on winning percentage when one-game playoff against Rangers was rained out. eLeague divided into Northern, Southern and Central divisions; won best-of-three playoff for league championship. fLeague divided into Eastern, Central and Western divisions; won three-team playoff. gLeague divided into Eastern, Northern and Western divisions; won three-team playoff.

PIONEER LEAGUE

NORTHERN DIVISION

Team	W	L	T	Pct.	GB
Billings (Reds)	49	26	0	.653	....
Medicine Hat (Blue Jays)	39	34	0	.534	9
Great Falls (Dodgers)	37	35	0	.514	10 ½
Lethbridge (Independent)	29	44	0	.397	19

SOUTHERN DIVISION

Team	W	L	T	Pct.	GB
Helena (Brewers)	43	30	0	.589	....
Pocatello (Independent)	37	38	0	.493	7
Idaho Falls (Braves)	36	40	0	.474	8 ½
Butte (Independent)	26	49	0	.347	18

COMPOSITE

Team	Bil.	Hel.	M.H.	G.F.	Poc.	I.F.	Leth.	But.	W	L	T	Pct.	GB
Billings (Reds)	....	4	8	12	3	4	11	7	49	26	0	.653	....
Helena (Brewers)	2	....	3	2	10	11	6	9	43	30	0	.589	5
Medicine Hat (Blue Jays)	8	2	....	9	2	5	7	6	39	34	0	.534	9
Great Falls (Dodgers)	4	5	7	....	3	4	10	4	37	35	0	.514	10 ½
Pocatello (Independent)	4	6	5	3	....	6	3	10	37	38	0	.493	12
Idaho Falls (Braves)	3	5	2	3	10	....	4	9	36	40	0	.474	13 ½
Lethbridge (Independent)	5	1	8	4	4	3	....	4	29	44	0	.397	19
Butte (Independent)	0	7	1	2	6	7	3	....	26	49	0	.347	23

Major league affiliations in parentheses.

Playoffs—Billings defeated Helena, two games to one, to win league championship.

Regular-season attendance—Billings, 101,490; Butte, 19,750; Great Falls, 59,924; Helena, 39,210; Idaho Falls, 37,385; Lethbridge, 28,053; Medicine Hat, 25,102; Pocatello, 45,638. Total, 335,366. Playoffs (3 games), 7,669.

Managers—Billings, Donnie Scott; Butte, John Shelby; Great Falls, Jon Debus; Helena, Mike Epstein (June 17 through June 27), Harry Dunlop (June 28 through end of season); Idaho Falls, Paul Runge; Lethbridge, Phillip Wellman; Medicine Hat, Omar Malave; Pocatello, Ernie Rodriguez (June 17 through August 31), John Stein (September 1 through end of season). Managerial records of teams with more than one manager: Helena, Epstein (4-7), Dunlop (39-23); Pocatello, Rodriguez (34-34), Stein (3-4).

All-Star team: 1B—Will Fitzpatrick, Pocatello; 2B—Michael Eaglin, Idaho Falls; 3B—Adam Burton, Idaho Falls; SS—Jeff Patzke, Medicine Hat; OF—Willie Brown, Lethbridge; Derek Vaughn, Pocatello; Marty Watson, Butte; C—Paul Bako, Billings; DH—Todd Takayoshi, Pocatello; Pitchers—Daniel Camacho, Great Falls; Todd Etler, Billings; Fabian Salmon, Helena; Manager of the Year—Harry Dunlop, Helena.

TEAM

Team	Avg.	G	AB	R	OR	H	TB	2B	3B	HR	RBI	SH	SF	HP	BB	Int. BB	SO	SB	CS	LOB
Pocatello	.289	75	2499	451	487	721	998	107	19	44	372	34	40	57	360	10	502	100	53	630
Idaho Falls	.286	76	2573	472	460	735	1068	132	30	47	399	15	35	30	308	11	524	128	66	523
Butte	.280	75	2414	398	543	677	987	112	27	48	356	8	12	22	307	4	536	84	38	541
Billings	.279	75	2466	447	299	687	1006	120	20	53	387	17	40	34	287	6	427	121	51	517
Helena	.268	75	2427	448	358	650	967	113	21	54	381	34	21	52	379	6	592	123	48	592
Medicine Hat	.265	73	2377	387	308	629	920	95	20	52	328	28	20	38	239	4	537	45	47	489
Great Falls	.258	72	2400	339	399	618	842	108	19	26	287	22	19	33	241	8	544	69	45	501
Lethbridge	.246	73	2334	328	416	575	838	94	20	43	280	23	15	40	244	9	543	101	52	465

INDIVIDUAL

(Leading qualifiers for batting championship—205 or more plate appearances)

*Bats lefthanded.   †Switch-hitter.

Player, Team	Avg.	G	AB	R	H	TB	2B	3B	HR	RBI	SH	SF	HP	BB	Int. BB	SO	SB	CS
Takayoshi, Todd, Pocatello*	.358	69	243	38	87	113	9	1	5	40	0	3	2	50	0	25	3	1
Ramirez, Angel, Medicine Hat	.352	62	227	40	80	110	8	5	4	30	1	1	4	8	0	43	15	9
Bingham, David, Pocatello	.348	55	178	42	62	91	8	3	5	30	1	3	10	28	0	45	8	2
Sexton, Chris, Billings	.333	72	273	63	91	125	14	4	4	46	0	8	1	35	1	27	13	4
Fitzpatrick, Will, Pocatello*	.330	57	194	33	64	105	14	0	9	58	1	6	6	38	0	52	0	2
Eaglin, Michael, Idaho Falls	.326	66	236	50	77	96	5	4	2	35	2	2	1	29	0	48	28	11
Bako, Paul, Billings*	.314	57	194	34	61	84	11	0	4	30	1	3	1	22	0	37	5	1
McInnes, Chris, Helena†	.312	64	218	49	68	95	14	5	1	37	2	2	4	45	1	42	29	4
Vaughn, Derek, Pocatello	.311	72	299	60	93	128	14	3	5	43	2	4	3	52	4	52	40	13
Segura, Juan, Lethbridge	.306	66	242	33	74	87	13	0	0	25	2	2	9	13	0	53	4	2

Departmental leaders: G—Mahalik, 74; AB—Vaughn, 299; R—Sexton, 63; H—Vaughn, 93; TB—Vaughn, 128; 2B—Bugg, Oyas, 17; 3B—A. Brown, 9; HR—W. Brown, 16; RBI—Fitzpatrick, 58; SH—Cephas, 8; SF—Gann, 9; HP—Bingham, Newman, 10; BB—Takayoshi, 50; IBB—Yselonia, 4; SO—W. Brown, 86; SB—Vaughn, 40; CS—Vaughn, 13.

(All players—listed alphabetically)

Player, Team	Avg.	G	AB	R	H	TB	2B	3B	HR	RBI	SH	SF	HP	BB	Int. BB	SO	SB	CS
Acosta, Ed, Helena†	.209	30	43	10	9	9	0	0	0	2	4	0	0	1	0	13	0	1
Akers, Chad, Billings†	.267	65	247	54	66	92	14	3	2	35	1	3	8	24	0	26	14	7
Allen, John, Lethbridge	.050	8	20	0	1	1	0	0	0	1	1	0	0	1	0	11	0	1
Anderson, Cliff, Great Falls*	.298	37	141	19	42	58	9	2	1	22	3	1	1	5	1	27	1	3
Ashton, Jeff, Billings	.235	58	183	28	43	75	10	2	6	29	2	4	3	33	0	42	13	1
Baker, Jason, Billings	.308	34	91	18	28	33	3	1	0	9	2	1	0	8	0	16	1	3
Bako, Paul, Billings*	.314	57	194	34	61	84	11	0	4	30	1	3	1	22	0	37	5	1
Banks, Brian, Helena†	.396	12	48	8	19	28	1	1	2	8	0	1	0	11	0	8	1	2
Baugh, Gavin, Billings	.245	70	249	40	61	91	12	3	4	29	2	1	1	24	1	60	11	1
Benitez, Fernando, Idaho Falls†	.400	3	10	3	4	6	2	0	0	2	0	1	0	1	0	2	0	0
Biltimier, Mike, Great Falls*	.240	69	250	35	60	81	12	0	3	29	0	2	4	35	2	62	1	4
Bingham, David, Pocatello	.348	55	178	42	62	91	8	3	5	30	1	3	10	28	0	45	8	2
Bishop, Stephen, Idaho Falls	.382	20	68	13	26	38	6	0	2	10	0	0	9	1	1	11	1	2

Player, Team	Avg.	G	AB	R	H	TB	2B	3B	HR	RBI	SH	SF	HP	BB	Int. BB	SO	SB	CS
Bobb, Jason, Butte	.000	15	1	0	0	0	0	0	0	0	0	0	0	0	0	1	0	0
Bock, Jeff, Idaho Falls	.000	15	1	0	0	0	0	0	0	0	0	0	0	0	0	0	0	0
Boka, Ben, Lethbridge	.165	35	109	7	18	24	3	0	1	7	1	0	1	10	0	40	2	1
Bonifazio, Anthony, Lethbridge	.169	25	77	6	13	22	3	0	2	10	0	0	5	8	0	24	0	2
Bostic, Dwaine, Great Falls	.143	4	14	0	2	2	0	0	0	0	0	0	0	1	1	2	0	1
Boyle, Jeff, Pocatello	.208	60	159	24	33	41	6	1	0	15	3	2	1	13	1	43	5	4
Breuer, Jim, Great Falls	.178	40	118	16	21	25	4	0	0	8	1	1	6	6	0	49	3	0
Browder, Cam, Idaho Falls*	.273	54	128	28	35	59	12	0	4	17	0	1	2	32	3	23	2	4
Brown, Adrian, Lethbridge	.266	69	282	47	75	114	12	9	3	27	3	0	5	17	1	34	22	7
Brown, Willie, Lethbridge*	.244	65	213	43	52	110	6	2	16	44	0	1	4	40	1	86	11	6
Bugg, Jason, Idaho Falls*	.245	56	200	37	49	79	17	2	3	29	0	2	2	21	1	45	8	2
Burrill, Casey, Idaho Falls	.296	44	152	16	45	69	9	0	5	25	0	1	1	6	0	12	1	1
Burton, Adam, Idaho Falls	.262	64	202	46	53	104	16	4	9	48	1	7	3	43	0	75	19	5
Campillo, Rob, Helena	.250	33	92	13	23	32	3	0	2	19	0	0	3	17	0	22	3	3
Candelaria, Ben, Medicine Hat*	.264	62	208	24	55	79	7	1	5	34	5	4	3	27	1	49	3	3
Carew, Jeff, Butte	.000	14	1	0	0	0	0	0	0	0	0	0	0	0	0	1	0	0
Carranza, Pedro, Pocatello	.273	64	227	44	62	106	12	4	8	48	1	4	4	43	1	42	3	6
Carter, Chris, Helena	.234	32	94	13	22	32	7	0	1	14	3	0	1	15	0	28	2	2
Caruso, Gene, Pocatello†	.250	27	8	4	2	3	1	0	0	1	0	0	0	0	0	3	1	0
Cephas, Ruben, Helena†	.230	60	191	33	44	49	3	1	0	19	8	1	5	25	0	38	26	6
Clark, Brian, Great Falls*	.182	9	11	0	2	3	1	0	0	4	0	0	1	5	0	10	0	0
Colmenares, Carlos, Medicine Hat	.154	10	26	8	4	6	2	0	0	3	1	0	1	5	0	10	0	0
Cook, Steve, Butte	.254	37	138	19	35	45	4	0	2	15	0	1	1	19	0	20	4	2
Cordova, Luis, Lethbridge*	.279	68	251	28	70	92	10	3	2	38	1	2	0	29	0	33	9	4
Daunic, Willie, Medicine Hat*	.252	46	143	20	36	43	4	0	1	17	2	1	2	29	0	20	0	3
Davis, Eddie, Great Falls	.224	60	205	32	46	80	8	1	8	44	0	1	5	28	1	54	11	10
de la Cruz, Lorenzo, Medicine Hat	.298	62	208	44	62	118	11	6	11	43	3	2	7	23	0	59	5	1
Denman, Ralph, Idaho Falls*	.217	37	115	18	25	35	5	1	1	9	1	0	0	22	5	2	2	2
DeRosa, Jeff, Butte	.251	46	175	31	44	50	6	0	0	20	1	0	2	12	1	32	2	3
Diieso, Tony, Idaho Falls	.264	32	72	18	19	27	5	0	1	8	1	0	1	5	0	24	2	2
Dunn, Nathan, Great Falls	.313	22	83	11	26	40	5	0	3	12	2	2	1	7	1	8	1	1
Dunn, Todd, Helena	.307	43	150	33	46	91	11	2	10	42	1	2	6	22	1	52	5	2
Durrwachter, Doug, Billings	.256	18	43	12	11	15	1	0	1	4	1	0	2	12	0	6	6	1
Eaglin, Michael, Idaho Falls	.326	66	236	50	77	96	5	4	2	35	2	2	1	29	0	48	28	11
Eddie, Steve, Billings	.286	67	231	31	66	85	8	1	3	38	3	0	2	23	0	33	5	9
Fitzpatrick, Will, Pocatello*	.330	57	194	33	64	105	14	0	9	58	1	6	8	38	0	52	0	2
Gann, Stephen, Billings	.301	71	266	46	80	113	14	2	5	51	1	9	8	22	3	33	14	6
Garcia, Freddy, Medicine Hat	.239	72	264	47	63	108	8	2	11	42	1	4	2	31	1	71	4	5
Garcia, Luis, Idaho Falls	.215	27	107	17	23	29	4	1	0	13	3	3	1	4	0	15	3	1
Garcia, Orlando, Pocatello	.233	50	150	13	35	38	3	0	0	16	5	0	2	4	0	25	2	8
Gatti, Dominic, Butte	.289	64	239	44	69	102	7	1	4	35	1	0	3	40	0	34	17	9
Gay, Brad, Helena	.272	29	92	15	25	47	5	1	5	23	2	1	1	10	0	28	2	1
Greenlee, Darren, Pocatello	.143	6	21	1	3	3	0	0	0	2	0	1	0	3	1	5	0	0
Guerrero, Wilton, Great Falls	.297	66	256	44	76	83	5	1	0	21	5	0	3	24	1	33	20	8
Haddock, Doug, Lethbridge	.214	26	42	5	9	10	1	0	0	1	0	0	3	0	0	13	3	0
Hardy, Hayland, Helena	.277	66	235	43	65	115	9	1	13	52	3	2	8	39	0	85	3	2
Harris, D.J., Pocatello	.271	59	155	30	42	69	8	2	5	28	2	4	5	23	1	39	9	5
Hendricks, Kacy, Butte*	.000	17	1	0	0	0	0	0	0	0	0	0	0	0	0	1	0	0
Hernaiz, Juan, Great Falls	.349	52	186	24	65	85	7	2	3	19	1	0	3	42	4	5	8	5
Hill, Clayton, Helena	.234	53	158	23	37	61	10	1	4	27	1	1	2	28	0	46	3	1
Holland, Rod, Butte*	.326	36	129	26	42	57	10	1	1	18	1	2	0	22	0	29	11	1
Huff, Matt, Butte	.276	63	232	40	64	111	11	6	8	46	0	2	2	26	1	52	7	2
Hughes, Danan, Helena	.233	10	30	8	7	13	1	1	1	4	0	0	2	8	1	11	0	1
Hunt, Chris, Pocatello*	.282	66	195	26	55	64	7	1	0	18	2	0	3	36	2	24	1	1
Ignash, Reggie, Butte	.242	52	157	34	38	52	3	1	3	25	1	1	2	23	1	50	16	5
Jeffery, Scott, Medicine Hat*	1.000	16	1	0	1	1	0	0	0	0	0	0	0	0	0	0	0	0
Jones, Matt, Lethbridge*	.247	28	97	16	24	35	5	0	2	11	0	1	4	5	0	15	1	2
Jones, Ryan, Medicine Hat	.246	47	171	20	42	56	5	0	3	27	0	1	3	12	0	46	1	1
Keefe, Jamie, Lethbridge	.204	46	137	27	28	32	2	1	0	9	4	2	1	26	1	27	11	5
King, Tiger, Butte	.259	71	232	34	60	88	10	3	4	25	1	2	3	21	1	58	2	3
Kinney, Mike, Great Falls	.232	50	164	23	38	50	6	3	0	16	1	1	3	13	0	44	10	3
Klassen, Danny, Helena	.200	18	45	8	9	10	1	0	0	3	1	0	2	7	0	11	2	1
Landry, Todd, Helena	.315	29	124	27	39	66	10	1	5	24	0	1	2	8	1	20	4	1
Lea, Corey, Lethbridge	.272	39	114	15	31	38	5	1	0	7	1	0	1	10	0	34	11	8
Lidle, Cory, Pocatello	.000	21	4	0	0	0	0	0	0	0	2	0	0	0	0	2	0	0
Loretta, Mark, Helena	.321	6	28	5	9	13	1	0	1	8	0	0	1	4	0	4	0	0
Lussier, Pat, Lethbridge	.293	51	167	16	49	74	10	0	5	26	1	1	5	11	0	33	1	6
Lutz, Richard, Medicine Hat	.000	1	4	0	0	0	0	0	0	0	0	0	0	0	0	1	0	0
Lymberopoulos, Nick, Pocatello	.000	6	2	0	0	0	0	0	0	0	0	0	0	0	0	0	0	0
Mackie, Ed, Helena	.190	36	105	8	20	29	1	1	2	12	0	1	9	9	0	45	0	2
Mahalik, John, Butte	.271	74	258	25	70	88	15	0	1	27	1	1	0	21	0	52	10	0
Marshall, Jason, Lethbridge	.222	8	18	4	4	7	0	0	1	4	0	0	2	0	0	2	1	0
Martinez, Greg, Helena†	.290	52	183	45	53	61	4	2	0	19	3	5	6	30	0	26	29	6
Martinez, Hector, Medicine Hat	.307	26	101	15	31	48	11	0	2	15	1	1	0	5	1	14	0	0
McBride, Gator, Idaho Falls	.289	49	142	25	41	61	6	4	2	20	0	1	3	13	0	27	8	3
McCubbin, Shane, Medicine Hat	.340	15	47	10	16	28	1	1	3	9	0	0	1	4	0	14	1	1
McInnes, Chris, Helena†	.312	64	218	49	68	95	14	5	1	37	2	2	4	45	1	42	29	4
Mendoza, Alonso, Pocatello†	.276	55	170	32	47	64	9	1	2	24	4	4	7	18	0	18	9	4
Mills, Tony, Lethbridge	.193	38	88	13	17	17	0	0	0	6	4	0	0	13	0	18	11	3
Minear, Clint, Butte	.000	16	1	0	0	0	0	0	0	0	0	0	0	0	0	1	0	0
Monds, Wonder, Idaho Falls	.299	60	214	47	64	105	13	8	4	35	2	0	2	25	1	43	17	5
Moon, Ray, Billings	.214	16	42	6	9	10	1	0	0	3	0	0	3	0	0	5	1	1
Moreno, Erik, Idaho Falls	.283	49	138	21	39	52	4	0	3	20	0	1	0	31	1	24	0	1
Morgan, David, Medicine Hat	.238	62	210	35	50	74	9	0	5	34	2	2	5	36	0	57	2	1
Morrill, Craig, Butte	.000	16	1	0	0	0	0	0	0	0	0	0	0	0	0	0	0	0
Newman, Bruce, Idaho Falls*	.295	45	122	17	36	52	5	1	3	22	2	2	10	12	0	29	6	4
Olexa, Mike, Helena	.252	59	214	35	54	85	14	1	5	34	0	2	3	12	2	42	4	7
Oyas, Dan, Billings	.271	68	255	35	69	108	17	2	6	49	1	6	1	29	0	44	15	4
Patzke, Jeff, Medicine Hat†	.293	71	273	45	80	98	11	2	1	22	3	1	2	34	1	31	5	7
Perez, Eddie, Idaho Falls	.308	43	117	20	36	49	4	0	3	16	0	1	0	15	0	25	6	3
Pitts, Jon, Butte	.349	41	149	19	52	69	9	1	2	26	0	2	3	5	0	19	0	0
Polis, Peter, Medicine Hat	.118	11	34	0	4	5	1	0	0	3	0	0	0	2	0	13	0	0
Pollock, Jason, Pocatello	.248	59	129	27	32	37	3	1	0	7	4	0	4	16	0	47	8	1
Postiff, J.P., Pocatello	.277	62	191	34	53	62	6	0	1	21	5	2	2	33	1	42	6	2

Player, Team	Avg.	G	AB	R	H	TB	2B	3B	HR	RBI	SH	SF	HP	BB	Int. BB	SO	SB	CS
Powers, Robert, Helena	.274	41	106	30	29	34	3	1	0	8	1	0	0	36	0	29	4	2
Ramirez, Angel, Medicine Hat	.352	62	227	40	80	110	8	5	4	30	1	1	4	8	0	43	15	9
Rash, Joshua, Great Falls	.277	54	177	38	49	63	6	4	0	20	2	2	1	24	0	49	6	3
Reiber, Lee, Lethbridge	.183	42	109	10	20	28	5	0	1	12	3	1	3	18	1	37	1	2
Richardson, Brian, Great Falls	.225	54	178	16	40	51	11	0	0	13	1	2	3	14	1	47	1	2
Rios, Eduardo, Great Falls	.271	26	107	18	29	45	4	3	2	13	0	2	1	9	0	11	2	4
Robinson, Eli, Billings	.128	13	39	7	5	8	0	0	1	5	0	0	1	4	0	17	4	0
Rodriguez, Jose, Idaho Falls	.272	54	195	30	53	74	10	1	3	35	0	7	0	20	3	41	1	2
Romero, Wilfredo, Great Falls	.276	15	58	12	16	21	5	0	0	9	0	0	0	2	0	9	2	1
Ruff, Tony, Idaho Falls	.295	40	132	21	39	48	4	1	1	18	0	2	2	7	0	21	9	7
Salazar, Julian, Pocatello	.293	52	174	42	51	74	7	2	4	21	2	3	7	31	0	37	5	4
Salzano, Jerry, Helena	.260	66	227	30	59	78	12	2	1	18	4	2	3	25	0	39	6	3
Sanders, Tony, Medicine Hat	.262	63	225	44	59	86	9	3	4	33	3	1	2	20	0	49	6	5
Schwenke, Matt, Great Falls†	.228	29	79	6	18	22	4	0	0	4	2	0	0	10	0	21	0	0
Segura, Juan, Lethbridge	.306	66	242	33	74	87	13	0	0	25	2	2	9	13	0	53	4	2
Sexton, Chris, Billings	.333	72	273	63	91	125	14	4	4	46	0	8	1	35	1	27	13	4
Sievers, Jason, Butte	.310	36	113	21	35	42	7	0	0	21	1	0	1	26	0	30	1	1
Smith, Craig, Helena	.321	7	28	6	9	14	2	0	1	4	0	0	2	1	1	2	0	1
Steed, Dave, Great Falls	.200	42	120	13	24	32	4	2	0	16	4	3	3	27	0	28	1	0
Takayoshi, Todd, Pocatello*	.358	69	243	38	87	113	9	1	5	40	0	3	2	50	0	25	3	1
Thomas, Chris, Helena	.250	8	16	6	4	5	1	0	0	4	1	0	0	9	0	1	0	0
Thomas, Rod, Billings	.257	65	230	38	59	98	11	2	8	35	3	4	4	23	1	60	11	6
Tomasello, John, Butte*	.240	49	179	27	43	84	12	1	9	31	0	2	2	15	0	60	1	1
Toney, Mike, Medicine Hat	.000	11	1	0	0	0	0	0	0	0	0	0	0	0	0	0	0	0
Towle, Justin, Billings	.263	47	137	29	36	63	6	0	7	23	1	1	1	27	1	37	4	4
Valdez, Miguel, Idaho Falls*	.358	39	134	29	48	60	5	2	1	28	0	2	0	15	1	24	7	9
Vasquez, Eddy, Medicine Hat	.221	71	281	45	62	88	9	1	5	27	6	2	7	7	0	74	4	12
Vaughn, Derek, Pocatello	.311	72	299	60	93	128	14	3	5	43	2	8	4	24	3	52	40	13
Vazquetelles, Darren, Idaho Falls	.253	37	87	16	22	24	0	1	0	15	2	4	0	14	0	13	5	2
Watkins, William, Billings	.268	66	235	46	63	97	10	3	6	30	1	1	2	22	0	44	15	4
Watson, Marty, Butte	.303	62	218	46	66	121	12	5	11	41	0	4	3	34	0	62	10	7
Watts, Craig, Great Falls	.325	26	83	15	27	46	4	0	5	15	0	1	1	7	0	19	0	0
Wells, David, Idaho Falls	1.000	18	1	0	1	1	0	0	0	0	0	0	0	0	0	0	0	0
Williams, Juan, Butte	.000	20	1	0	0	0	0	0	0	0	0	0	0	0	0	0	0	0
Wingate, Ervan, Great Falls	.198	38	126	13	25	39	12	1	0	18	0	0	1	15	0	21	0	0
Winget, Jeremy, Butte*	.303	44	142	22	43	50	5	1	0	18	1	1	0	29	0	20	2	3
Wittig, Paul, Great Falls	.273	15	44	4	12	16	1	0	1	5	0	0	0	6	0	17	1	0
Yselonia, John, Lethbridge*	.244	36	119	18	29	56	7	1	6	23	0	4	1	14	4	23	2	2

The following pitchers, listed alphabetically by club, with games in parentheses, had no plate appearances, primarily through use of designated hitters:

BILLINGS—Connors, Chad (19); Etler, Todd (15); Fussell, Denny (18); Harvell, Albert (17); Hebel, Jon (12); Lyons, Curt (15); Magre, Pete (14); McKenzie, Scott (14); Moses, Mike (18); Sullivan, Scott (18); Tweedlie, Brad (11); Wilkerson, Steve (15); Witzel, Dave (22).

BUTTE—Beard, Richie (20); Harris, John (14); Kelley, Chris (23); LaPoint, Jason (12); Seaton, Billy (6); Starr, Chris (8); Week, Ben (9).

GREAT FALLS—Ashworth, Kym (11); Camacho, Dan (28); Carpenter, Brian (14); Costello, Craig (13); Hubbs, Dan (3); Kenady, Jason (17); Markham, Dan (18); Perez, George (22); Rolocut, Brian (18); Rosario, Juan (2); Sarmiento, Dan (6); Scheffler, Craig (15); Sikes, Ken (16); Troutman, Keith (27); Vukson, John (16).

HELENA—Arias, Wagner (17); Cole, Jim (18); Droll, Jeff (4); Duda, Steve (5); England, Dave (2); Kopitzke, Chad (18); Maloney, Sean (17); Mercado, Gabriel (3); Murphy, Matt (5); Rhoda, Gary (14); Rodriguez, Francisco (18); Salmon, Fabian (13); Schmitt, Chris (13); Wagner, Joe (8); Werner, Rich (14); Wilstead, Judd (11).

IDAHO FALLS—Blaine, Jim (14); Evangelista, Alberto (15); Gagnon, Clint (13); Martineau, Yves (16); Nelson, Earl (16); Randall, Jim (13); Rusciano, Chris (1); Simmons, Jason (21); Stoecklin, Tony (27); Thomas, Jason (26); Turnier, Aaron (9); Tyner, Marcus (21).

LETHBRIDGE—Ballance, Dale (20); Bonilla, Miguel (16); Davidson, Rodney (17); DeLeon, Elcilio (19); Dillinger, John (15); Hyman, Terry (3); Kath, Merlin (17); Musso, Sam (15); Ohman, Shawn (16); Roman, Dan (15); Solomon, Ray (23); Terminie, Chad (9).

MEDICINE HAT—Adkins, Bob (14); Grant, Brian (14); Kennedy, Scott (19); Leystra, Jeff (28); Patterson, Bob (26); Romano, Mike (9); Sievert, Mark (15); Sinclair, Steve (15); Sinnes, Dave (19); Smith, Keilan (15); Vogelgesang, Joe (12); Young, Reggie (2).

POCATELLO—Atwood, Jason (12); Birdt, Lou (18); Dempsey, Steve (4); Diaz, Rafael (15); Evenhus, Jason (14); Graham, Mark (4); Ishii, Galen (19); Matthews, Ron (2); May, Steve (14); Orta, Edgar (6); Ploeger, Tim (14); Post, Jeff (6); Pruitt, Don (5); Woods, Barry (17); Wright, Scott (9).

GRAND SLAMS—Ashton, Davis, Eaglin, Fitzpatrick, Harris, Oyas, Towle, Vasquez, 1 each.

AWARDED FIRST BASE ON CATCHER'S INTERFERENCE—G. Martinez 3 (Boka, Rodriguez, Towle); Baugh (Morgan); Diieso (Carter); R. Jones (Reiber); McInnes (Rodriguez); Reiber (Morgan).

PITCHING

TEAM

Team	ERA	G	CG	ShO	Sv.	IP	H	R	ER	HR	HB	BB	Int. BB	SO	WP	Bk.
Medicine Hat	3.24	73	0	3	20	613.2	554	308	221	33	34	246	4	467	50	9
Billings	3.30	75	10	6	17	637.2	574	299	234	31	35	287	8	546	78	15
Helena	3.90	73	4	5	22	633.0	653	358	274	49	46	260	8	562	53	13
Lethbridge	4.57	73	11	3	19	614.2	623	416	312	41	32	304	11	486	62	15
Great Falls	4.60	72	1	2	23	626.0	576	399	320	34	46	366	4	575	107	15
Idaho Falls	5.20	76	3	4	16	652.1	749	460	377	52	26	285	14	554	71	18
Pocatello	5.49	75	15	2	7	634.1	752	487	387	56	39	319	7	603	94	30
Butte	6.78	75	7	1	17	596.1	811	543	449	71	48	298	2	412	90	13

INDIVIDUAL

(Leading qualifiers for earned-run average leadership—61 or more innings)

*Throws lefthanded.

Pitcher, Team	W	L	Pct.	ERA	G	GS	CG	GF	ShO	Sv.	IP	H	R	ER	HR	HB	BB	Int. BB	SO	WP
Camacho, Great Falls	5	2	.714	1.38	28	0	0	13	0	5	65.1	38	14	10	6	6	18	1	79	9
Salmon, Helena	8	3	.727	2.64	13	13	1	0	1	0	81.2	84	37	24	13	12	25	0	62	5
Etler, Billings	8	1	.889	2.71	15	15	1	0	1	0	89.2	75	33	27	4	7	30	0	55	4
Grant, Medicine Hat*	5	4	.556	2.84	14	13	0	0	0	0	73.0	61	33	23	4	2	34	0	49	4
Bonilla, Lethbridge	4	8	.333	2.87	16	15	5	0	1	0	106.2	105	46	34	8	8	24	1	59	7

— 545 —

Pitcher, Team	W	L	Pct.	ERA	G	GS	CG	GF	ShO	Sv.	IP	H	R	ER	HR	HB	BB	Int. BB	SO	WP
Lyons, Billings	7	3	.700	3.00	15	12	2	0	0	0	84.0	89	35	28	3	3	20	0	64	10
Caruso, Pocatello*	7	5	.583	3.17	16	14	7	0	2	0	110.2	83	52	39	8	12	58	1	163	12
Costello, Great Falls	4	2	.667	3.21	12	12	0	0	0	0	70.0	61	30	25	0	4	26	0	59	10
Sinclair, Medicine Hat*	5	2	.714	3.33	15	12	0	0	0	0	78.1	87	41	29	5	1	16	0	45	5
Hebel, Billings	6	2	.750	3.45	12	11	2	1	0	0	62.2	61	32	24	4	1	24	2	65	8

Departmental leaders: G—Camacho, Leystra, 28; W—Etler, Lidle, Salmon, 8; L—Dillinger, 10; Pct.—Etler, .889; GS—Lidle, 16; CG—Caruso, 7; GF—Leystra, 26; ShO—Caruso, Nelson, Sullivan, 2; Sv.—Troutman, 16; IP—Caruso, 110.2; H—Bonilla, 105; R—Roman, 67; ER—Minear, 56; HR—Salmon, 13; HB—Caruso, Salmon, 12; BB—Roman, 62; IBB—Five pitchers tied with 3; SO—Caruso, 163; WP—Ploeger, 18.

(All pitchers—listed alphabetically)

Pitcher, Team	W	L	Pct.	ERA	G	GS	CG	GF	ShO	Sv.	IP	H	R	ER	HR	HB	BB	Int. BB	SO	WP
Adkins, Medicine Hat	3	3	.500	4.74	14	11	0	1	0	0	49.1	51	39	26	4	4	37	1	25	3
Arias, Helena	4	3	.571	5.89	17	6	0	5	0	1	47.1	46	32	31	6	2	28	1	36	5
Ashworth, Great Falls*	3	3	.500	2.44	11	11	0	0	0	0	59.0	43	25	16	4	1	14	0	52	9
Atwood, Pocatello	1	5	.167	8.31	12	7	0	0	0	0	43.1	61	42	40	6	2	29	1	20	3
Ballance, Lethbridge*	4	2	.667	3.88	20	3	0	3	0	2	51.0	44	29	22	2	0	25	1	32	5
Beard, Butte	2	4	.333	6.32	20	4	0	16	0	3	31.1	40	25	22	3	5	14	0	28	5
Birdt, Pocatello	1	2	.333	9.69	8	0	0	3	0	0	13.0	25	18	14	2	1	4	1	11	3
Blaine, Idaho Falls	0	0	.000	7.50	14	0	0	3	0	1	24.0	31	27	20	1	4	11	1	19	4
Bobb, Butte	2	9	.182	8.65	15	10	0	2	0	1	52.0	87	58	50	9	6	32	0	38	12
Bock, Idaho Falls	3	2	.600	2.84	15	1	0	8	0	1	31.2	15	16	10	2	0	12	1	21	1
Bonilla, Lethbridge	4	8	.333	2.87	16	15	5	0	1	0	106.2	105	46	34	8	8	24	1	59	7
Browder, Idaho Falls*	0	0	.000	0.00	3	0	0	2	0	0	2.0	1	0	0	0	0	2	0	2	0
Camacho, Great Falls	5	2	.714	1.38	28	0	0	13	0	5	65.1	38	14	10	6	6	18	1	79	5
Carew, Butte	2	6	.250	7.45	13	11	1	2	0	0	54.1	83	55	45	12	5	19	0	35	3
Carpenter, Great Falls	4	2	.667	4.99	14	1	0	7	0	0	30.2	28	18	17	1	3	22	1	38	6
Caruso, Pocatello*	7	5	.583	3.17	16	14	7	0	2	0	110.2	83	52	39	8	12	58	0	163	12
Cole, Helena	1	0	1.000	2.82	18	1	0	11	0	8	54.1	57	24	17	3	0	20	0	53	4
Colmenares, Medicine Hat	0	0	.000	0.00	1	0	0	0	0	0	1.0	0	0	0	0	0	0	0	0	0
Connors, Billings	2	2	.500	2.12	19	0	0	8	0	5	29.2	20	9	7	0	3	20	0	32	6
Costello, Great Falls	4	2	.667	3.21	12	12	0	0	0	0	70.0	61	30	25	0	4	26	0	59	10
Davidson, Lethbridge*	1	5	.167	11.44	17	4	0	4	0	0	28.1	45	46	36	3	0	20	0	25	9
Dempsey, Pocatello	0	0	.000	9.00	4	0	0	2	0	0	8.0	15	9	8	3	0	1	0	6	0
DeLeon, Lethbridge	2	4	.333	4.07	19	2	1	7	0	1	42.0	38	24	19	1	4	29	3	49	4
Diaz, Pocatello*	2	3	.400	4.38	15	8	0	2	0	0	49.1	56	34	24	1	2	30	0	31	6
Dillinger, Lethbridge	3	10	.231	3.92	15	15	3	0	0	0	80.1	65	51	35	2	5	60	1	94	9
Droll, Helena	0	2	.000	2.16	4	2	0	2	0	0	8.1	9	5	2	0	0	2	0	11	1
Duda, Helena	3	1	.750	5.18	5	4	0	0	0	0	24.1	24	15	14	1	3	8	0	21	2
England, Helena	0	2	.000	10.80	2	2	0	0	0	0	5.0	7	6	6	1	2	1	0	8	0
Etler, Billings	8	1	.889	2.71	15	15	1	0	1	0	89.2	75	33	27	4	7	30	0	55	4
Evangelista, Idaho Falls	4	2	.667	6.15	15	11	0	0	0	0	60.0	68	46	41	5	1	35	1	41	12
Evenhus, Pocatello	6	2	.750	4.85	14	6	1	4	0	0	59.1	69	40	32	4	1	22	3	44	2
Fussell, Billings*	1	0	1.000	8.22	18	0	0	7	0	0	23.0	39	22	21	4	0	13	1	15	7
Gagnon, Idaho Falls	3	3	.500	8.10	13	8	0	0	0	0	46.2	69	49	42	10	2	21	0	42	4
Graham, Pocatello*	0	0	.000	9.45	4	0	0	2	0	0	6.2	10	7	7	3	0	4	0	7	2
Grant, Medicine Hat*	5	4	.556	2.84	14	13	0	0	0	0	73.0	61	33	23	4	2	34	0	49	4
Haddock, Lethbridge	1	2	.333	5.75	13	0	0	7	0	2	20.1	21	17	13	2	3	13	0	13	2
Harris, Pocatello	0	0	.000	6.43	5	0	0	4	0	1	7.0	14	10	5	0	0	3	0	10	7
Harris, Butte	1	3	.250	6.85	14	4	0	2	0	0	47.1	50	43	36	3	2	39	0	43	8
Harvell, Billings*	5	3	.625	4.62	17	9	2	1	1	1	60.1	61	45	31	4	1	40	0	45	5
Hebel, Billings	6	2	.750	3.45	12	11	2	1	0	0	62.2	61	32	24	4	1	24	2	65	8
Hendricks, Butte*	1	1	.500	6.15	17	1	0	4	0	1	52.2	67	43	36	4	3	30	0	30	6
Hubbs, Great Falls	1	1	.500	1.17	3	1	0	0	0	0	7.2	3	1	1	0	2	2	0	12	0
Hyman, Lethbridge	0	0	.000	18.00	3	0	0	0	0	0	2.0	1	4	4	0	1	6	0	1	2
Ishii, Pocatello*	3	2	.600	6.37	19	0	0	6	0	0	29.2	32	25	21	3	2	17	0	40	6
Jeffery, Medicine Hat*	1	4	.200	4.18	16	0	0	11	0	2	28.0	29	14	13	3	2	3	1	21	0
Kath, Lethbridge	1	1	.500	5.08	17	0	0	8	0	1	33.2	43	25	19	4	1	11	2	15	4
Kelley, Butte	3	2	.600	5.69	23	6	0	15	0	6	61.2	88	50	39	5	6	21	1	47	17
Kenady, Great Falls*	5	5	.500	3.79	17	10	0	4	0	0	59.1	52	29	25	4	7	30	0	52	4
Kennedy, Medicine Hat	3	2	.600	3.09	19	0	0	6	0	0	32.0	20	13	11	2	4	21	0	31	7
Kopitzke, Helena	4	1	.800	4.30	18	1	0	8	0	1	29.1	31	20	14	5	4	8	1	21	2
Landry, Butte	0	0	.000	3.38	2	0	0	2	0	0	2.2	4	1	1	0	0	0	0	3	0
LaPoint, Butte*	5	3	.625	4.81	12	10	2	1	0	0	67.1	93	52	36	6	2	19	0	37	5
Leystra, Medicine Hat	3	2	.600	2.51	28	0	0	26	0	11	46.2	37	17	13	3	3	15	0	56	3
Lidle, Pocatello	8	4	.667	4.13	17	16	3	0	1	0	106.2	104	59	49	6	5	54	0	91	14
Lymberopoulos, Pocatello	0	1	.000	16.50	5	2	0	2	0	0	6.0	14	18	11	1	0	8	0	5	1
Lyons, Billings	7	3	.700	3.00	15	12	2	0	0	0	84.0	89	35	28	3	3	20	0	64	10
Magre, Billings	2	5	.286	4.56	14	8	0	6	0	0	49.1	49	32	25	3	3	22	0	34	7
Maloney, Helena	2	2	.500	4.34	17	3	1	10	0	0	47.2	55	31	23	2	2	11	1	35	3
Markham, Great Falls*	1	5	.167	6.26	18	6	0	1	0	0	41.2	50	44	29	1	3	36	1	29	8
Martineau, Idaho Falls	3	8	.273	5.01	16	15	1	1	1	0	82.2	91	53	46	4	5	29	1	75	9
Matthews, Pocatello	0	0	.000	12.00	2	1	0	0	0	0	3.0	5	7	4	0	0	6	0	4	1
May, Pocatello	1	1	.500	2.57	14	0	0	11	0	3	21.0	27	8	6	0	2	3	0	20	1
McKenzie, Billings	1	2	.333	3.60	14	1	0	5	0	0	30.0	27	16	12	2	1	14	0	37	6
Mercado, Helena	1	0	1.000	8.31	3	1	0	1	0	0	8.2	9	8	8	1	0	3	0	5	1
Minear, Pocatello*	3	5	.375	6.43	16	14	2	1	1	0	78.1	94	59	56	11	8	24	0	53	7
Morrill, Butte	2	3	.400	10.43	15	4	0	6	0	1	33.2	53	49	39	2	3	35	0	20	13
Moses, Billings*	3	0	1.000	1.63	18	1	1	6	0	0	38.2	30	13	7	1	1	15	0	27	8
Murphy, Helena*	4	0	1.000	1.41	5	5	0	0	0	0	32.0	21	5	5	1	0	9	0	33	0
Musso, Lethbridge	1	0	1.000	5.40	15	0	0	13	0	10	16.2	16	10	10	1	2	8	0	12	1
Nelson, Idaho Falls*	5	7	.417	4.38	16	15	2	1	2	0	76.0	82	50	37	2	5	48	2	72	6
Ohman, Lethbridge	3	4	.429	4.46	16	13	1	2	0	0	78.2	91	56	39	5	2	29	0	68	4
Orta, Pocatello	0	0	.000	13.89	6	2	0	1	0	0	11.2	25	20	18	4	0	10	0	9	0
Patterson, Medicine Hat*	3	4	.429	2.35	26	0	0	9	0	1	53.2	51	29	14	2	4	18	0	38	2
Perez, Great Falls*	1	0	1.000	7.17	22	0	0	10	0	0	37.2	42	35	30	2	2	30	0	29	7
Ploeger, Pocatello	4	7	.364	5.63	14	12	4	2	0	0	78.1	101	63	49	8	3	29	2	82	18
Post, Pocatello	0	1	.000	8.68	6	0	0	3	0	0	9.1	23	14	9	0	0	9	0	9	0
Postiff, Pocatello	0	0	.000	7.71	2	0	0	1	0	0	2.1	5	2	2	0	0	1	0	1	0
Pruitt, Pocatello	1	4	.200	9.58	5	5	0	0	0	0	20.2	35	25	22	2	1	10	0	14	1
Randall, Idaho Falls*	1	1	.500	5.85	19	4	0	2	0	0	47.2	51	34	31	5	0	22	1	36	10
Rhoda, Helena*	6	3	.667	4.20	14	14	2	0	0	0	79.1	79	40	37	7	5	32	0	82	4
Rodriguez, Helena	2	1	.667	2.41	18	1	0	9	0	5	41.0	31	19	11	0	1	17	3	63	8

Pitcher, Team	W	L	Pct.	ERA	G	GS	CG	GF	ShO	Sv.	IP	H	R	ER	HR	HB	BB	Int. BB	SO	WP
Rolocut, Great Falls	4	2	.667	5.03	17	8	0	2	0	0	48.1	45	34	27	1	2	44	0	40	17
Roman, Lethbridge*	3	5	.375	5.80	15	15	0	0	0	0	76.0	74	67	49	7	3	62	0	65	8
Romano, Medicine Hat	4	1	.800	2.63	9	8	0	0	0	0	41.0	34	20	12	1	7	11	0	28	3
Rosario, Great Falls	0	1	.000	21.94	2	2	0	0	0	0	5.1	11	13	13	3	5	6	0	4	0
Rusciano, Idaho Falls	1	0	1.000	0.00	1	1	0	0	0	0	6.0	4	0	0	0	2	1	0	6	0
Salmon, Helena	8	3	.727	2.64	13	13	1	0	1	0	81.2	84	37	24	13	12	25	0	62	5
Sarmiento, Great Falls*	2	3	.400	6.35	6	4	0	1	0	0	22.2	20	18	16	1	0	14	0	15	2
Scheffler, Great Falls*	5	3	.625	5.75	15	10	1	2	0	1	61.0	68	46	39	5	2	27	0	56	7
Schmitt, Helena*	3	3	.500	1.62	23	2	0	20	0	7	44.1	32	12	8	1	7	26	2	48	5
Seaton, Butte	2	4	.333	8.65	6	6	0	0	0	0	26.0	39	25	25	7	3	9	0	7	4
Sievert, Medicine Hat	6	3	.667	5.00	15	15	0	0	0	0	63.0	63	40	35	2	3	30	0	52	12
Sikes, Great Falls	1	1	.500	7.01	16	4	0	2	0	1	43.2	52	40	34	4	4	39	0	37	16
Simmons, Idaho Falls	2	4	.333	3.95	21	0	0	8	0	2	43.1	53	28	19	6	0	15	3	21	6
Sinclair, Medicine Hat*	5	2	.714	3.33	15	12	0	0	0	0	78.1	87	41	29	5	1	16	0	45	5
Sinnes, Medicine Hat	3	4	.429	2.20	19	4	0	5	0	2	45.0	37	20	11	3	1	25	1	45	3
Smith, Medicine Hat	1	1	.500	2.84	15	4	0	5	0	1	38.0	28	14	12	3	1	11	0	37	2
Solomon, Lethbridge	2	2	.500	3.60	23	0	0	18	0	3	30.0	31	15	12	3	0	8	3	23	5
Starr, Butte	3	5	.375	6.53	8	7	2	1	0	0	40.0	53	35	29	4	3	10	0	29	1
Stoecklin, Idaho Falls*	3	2	.600	2.42	27	0	0	24	0	8	44.2	36	14	12	1	3	14	1	51	3
Sullivan, Billings	5	0	1.000	1.67	18	7	2	9	2	3	54.0	33	13	10	1	6	25	0	79	2
Terminie, Lethbridge	4	1	.800	3.67	9	6	1	0	1	0	49.0	49	26	20	3	3	9	0	30	2
Thomas, Idaho Falls*	3	1	.750	4.19	26	0	0	11	0	3	43.0	48	23	20	2	0	17	0	36	4
Tomasello, Butte*	0	0	.000	6.75	1	0	0	0	0	0	1.1	1	1	1	0	0	3	0	0	0
Toney, Medicine Hat	0	2	.000	0.38	11	0	0	6	0	2	23.2	13	4	1	0	0	13	1	12	2
Troutman, Great Falls	1	1	.500	1.71	27	0	0	23	0	16	42.0	26	12	8	2	2	12	1	48	2
Turnier, Idaho Falls*	4	0	1.000	4.50	9	3	0	3	0	0	30.0	27	15	15	3	0	9	0	24	2
Tweedlie, Billings	3	3	.500	4.30	11	8	0	1	0	1	44.0	28	22	21	2	3	31	1	31	8
Tyner, Idaho Falls	2	3	.400	6.06	21	4	0	8	0	1	52.0	61	43	35	3	2	22	1	64	4
Vazquetelles, Idaho Falls	0	0	.000	148.50	1	0	0	0	0	0	0.2	6	11	11	1	1	5	0	0	0
Vogelgesang, Medicine Hat	2	1	.667	5.46	12	4	0	4	0	3	29.2	37	21	18	1	2	6	0	19	4
Vukson, Great Falls	0	4	.000	9.10	16	4	0	4	0	0	29.2	37	42	30	0	3	45	0	24	10
Wagner, Helena	3	2	.600	2.61	8	7	0	0	0	0	41.1	39	17	12	1	3	20	0	30	2
Week, Butte	0	2	.000	7.98	9	0	7	0	3	1	14.2	22	13	13	3	1	13	1	18	3
Wells, Idaho Falls	2	7	.222	5.52	18	9	0	2	0	0	62.0	90	51	38	7	1	22	2	44	6
Werner, Helena	1	2	.333	5.19	14	1	0	1	0	0	43.1	70	40	25	2	2	14	0	31	5
Wilkerson, Billings	2	2	.500	3.00	15	3	0	8	0	2	30.0	28	15	10	1	4	18	2	26	3
Williams, Butte*	0	2	.000	6.00	19	1	0	9	0	2	33.0	38	34	22	2	1	30	0	26	6
Wilstead, Helena	1	5	.167	8.50	11	10	0	0	0	0	42.1	55	46	40	5	3	36	0	17	6
Wingate, Great Falls	0	0	.000	0.00	1	0	0	1	0	0	2.0	0	0	0	0	1	0	0	1	0
Winget, Butte*	0	0	.000	3.38	2	0	0	2	0	0	2.2	3	1	1	0	0	0	1	0	0
Witzel, Billings	4	3	.571	2.34	22	0	0	13	0	2	42.1	34	12	11	2	2	15	2	36	4
Woods, Pocatello	3	1	.750	4.66	17	2	0	12	0	2	36.2	37	25	19	4	5	16	0	31	7
Wright, Pocatello	0	0	.000	6.94	9	0	0	4	0	1	11.2	11	9	9	1	3	14	0	5	7
Young, Medicine Hat	0	1	.000	2.38	2	2	0	0	0	0	11.1	6	3	3	0	0	6	0	7	0

BALKS—Caruso, Martineau, Sullivan, Woods, 5 each; Diaz, Grant, McKenzie, Wilstead, 4 each; Ashworth, Atwood, Ballance, Dillinger, Musso, Post, Sikes, Stoecklin, 3 each; Arias, Cole, Evangelista, Evenhus, Kelley, LaPoint, May, Nelson, Starr, Thomas, Toney, Tweedlie, Vukson, Week, Williams, 2 each; Beard, Birdt, Blaine, Bonilla, Carew, Carpenter, Costello, Davidson, DeLeon, Dempsey, Fussell, Hebel, Hubbs, Kenady, Lidle, Magre, Markham, Minear, Murphy, Orta, Patterson, Ploeger, Rodriguez, Rolocut, Roman, Scheffler, Schmitt, Sinclair, Solomon, Terminie, Turnier, Vazquetelles, Vogelgesang, Wagner, Wells, Werner, Witzel, Wright, 1 each.

COMBINATION SHUTOUTS—Harvell-Tweedlie-Witzel-Sullivan, Sullivan-Magre, Billings; Costello-Camacho, Rolocut-Troutman, Great Falls; Murphy-Rodriguez, Murphy-Schmitt, Rhoda-Schmitt, Helena; Martineau-Bock, Idaho Falls; Bonilla-Ohman-Solomon, Lethbridge; Grant-Kennedy-Leystra, Grant-Smith-Vogelgesang, Sievert-Patterson-Leystra, Medicine Hat.

NO-HIT GAMES—Costello-Camacho, Great Falls, defeated Lethbridge, 8-0, July 11; Romano-Kennedy-Leystra, Medicine Hat, defeated Lethbridge, 4-1, September 4.

FIELDING

TEAM

Team	Pct.	G	PO	A	E	DP	PB	Team	Pct.	G	PO	A	E	DP	PB
Billings	.961	75	1913	806	111	67	14	Butte	.952	75	1789	792	131	65	14
Pocatello	.958	75	1903	807	118	67	15	Idaho Falls	.950	76	1957	822	147	70	11
Helena	.957	73	1899	802	120	57	5	Lethbridge	.947	73	1844	785	148	60	28
Great Falls	.957	72	1878	743	118	51	16	Medicine Hat	.946	73	1841	789	149	67	20

Triple plays—Billings, Idaho Falls.

INDIVIDUAL

FIRST BASEMEN

*Throws lefthanded.

Player, Team	Pct.	G	PO	A	E	DP
Bako, Billings	.958	5	42	4	2	3
BILTIMIER, Great Falls*	.989	61	487	32	6	38
Bishop, Idaho Falls	.987	10	73	5	1	5
Browder, Idaho Falls*	.991	48	312	20	3	32
Bugg, Idaho Falls	.966	6	56	0	2	6
Burrill, Idaho Falls	.983	17	101	14	2	9
Carter, Helena	1.000	8	42	3	0	3
Caruso, Pocatello*	1.000	1	5	0	0	0
Daunic, Medicine Hat*	.968	24	200	13	7	21
Dunn, Helena	1.000	1	1	0	0	1
Eddie, Billings	.984	64	529	39	9	47
Fitzpatrick, Pocatello	.987	53	431	22	6	31
Greenlee, Pocatello	1.000	1	9	0	0	0
Haddock, Lethbridge	1.000	2	13	1	0	2
Hardy, Helena	1.000	2	9	0	0	2
Harris, Pocatello	.933	3	11	3	1	0
Hunt, Pocatello	1.000	4	9	0	0	2

Player, Team	Pct.	G	PO	A	E	DP
Jones, Lethbridge*	.975	27	220	13	6	20
Jones, Medicine Hat	.983	44	385	17	7	33
Landry, Helena*	.969	20	163	24	6	12
Lussier, Lethbridge	.987	9	72	4	1	11
Morgan, Medicine Hat	.980	6	41	7	1	3
Morrill, Butte	1.000	1	1	0	0	0
Olexa, Helena	1.000	4	26	2	0	0
Postiff, Pocatello	.988	15	77	8	1	12
Richardson, Great Falls	1.000	1	1	0	0	0
Robinson, Billings	.956	10	60	5	3	5
Rodriguez, Idaho Falls	.969	15	116	10	4	8
Salzano, Helena	.988	43	321	22	4	24
Takayoshi, Pocatello	1.000	12	87	6	0	7
Thomas, Helena	.953	6	38	3	2	3
Tomasello, Butte*	.975	45	359	28	10	33
Watts, Great Falls	.983	14	107	6	2	8
Winget, Butte*	.996	32	233	19	1	25
Yselonia, Lethbridge	.991	36	306	26	3	24

Triple plays—Burrill, Eddie.

SECOND BASEMEN

Player, Team	Pct.	G	PO	A	E	DP
Acosta, Helena	1.000	1	1	0	0	0
Akers, Billings	.985	29	53	75	2	12
Allen, Lethbridge	.929	8	13	13	2	5
Anderson, Great Falls	.991	29	59	50	1	14
Ashton, Billings	.990	39	88	103	2	26
Bingham, Pocatello	.943	11	15	18	2	4
Boyle, Butte	.936	14	21	23	3	5
Burton, Idaho Falls	.962	9	24	27	2	8
Colmenares, Medicine Hat	.917	3	6	5	1	2
Cook, Butte	.936	34	70	91	11	23
DeRosa, Butte	.904	35	75	66	15	15
Dunn, Great Falls	.958	11	21	25	2	3
Durrwachter, Billings	1.000	1	0	2	0	1
EAGLIN, Idaho Falls	.955	66	129	191	15	41
Gann, Billings	.885	5	10	13	3	1
Garcia, Pocatello	1.000	1	1	0	0	0
Harris, Pocatello	.950	14	29	28	3	10
Keefe, Lethbridge	.940	45	109	110	14	28
King, Butte	.951	7	17	22	2	4
McBride, Idaho Falls	.786	6	6	5	3	2
McInnes, Helena	.947	58	115	117	13	24
Mills, Lethbridge	.903	25	44	49	10	11
Powers, Helena	.970	17	29	35	2	10
Rios, Great Falls	.985	26	56	77	2	14
Salazar, Pocatello	.957	50	86	116	9	22
Segura, Lethbridge	1.000	1	4	0	0	0
Sexton, Billings	.875	5	7	7	2	2
Smith, Helena	.966	5	8	20	1	4
Vasquez, Medicine Hat	.920	70	122	144	23	36
Vazquetelles, Idaho Falls	1.000	3	4	2	0	0
Wingate, Great Falls	.953	9	24	17	2	2

Triple play — Eaglin.

THIRD BASEMEN

Player, Team	Pct.	G	PO	A	E	DP
Ashton, Billings	.872	14	11	23	5	3
Baugh, Lethbridge	.877	63	61	146	29	18
Bishop, Idaho Falls	.944	7	5	12	1	0
Boyle, Pocatello	.864	10	6	13	3	1
Bugg, Idaho Falls	.841	25	14	44	11	4
Burton, Idaho Falls	.786	23	10	34	12	3
Carranza, Pocatello	.9386	63	51	163	14	16
Colmenares, Medicine Hat	1.000	2	1	4	0	1
Cook, Butte	1.000	2	3	3	0	0
Dunn, Great Falls	.923	6	2	10	1	0
Gann, Billings	.926	58	34	103	11	9
Garcia, Medicine Hat	.891	72	63	175	29	18
Haddock, Lethbridge	.917	8	8	14	2	1
Harris, Pocatello	.714	4	3	2	2	0
Hunt, Pocatello	.500	1	0	1	1	0
Lussier, Lethbridge	1.000	4	1	3	0	0
Mackie, Helena	.936	33	13	60	5	4
MAHALIK, Butte	.9389	73	61	154	14	16
McBride, Idaho Falls	.862	19	12	44	9	3
Mills, Lethbridge	.571	1	0	4	3	0
Olexa, Helena	.900	8	3	6	1	1
Postiff, Pocatello	.800	3	2	2	1	0
Powers, Helena	.848	23	13	43	10	2
Richardson, Great Falls	.839	50	28	107	26	7
Romero, Great Falls	1.000	1	0	1	0	0
Salzano, Helena	.938	22	16	44	4	3
Sexton, Billings	.917	5	11	11	2	1
Vazquetelles, Idaho Falls	.714	5	0	5	2	0
Wingate, Great Falls	.814	20	11	37	11	3

Triple play — Gann.

SHORTSTOPS

Player, Team	Pct.	G	PO	A	E	DP
Acosta, Helena	.794	11	5	22	7	3
Akers, Billings	.857	4	7	5	2	0
Anderson, Great Falls	.892	8	10	23	4	2
Baugh, Lethbridge	.833	6	7	8	3	0
Bostic, Great Falls	.778	2	2	5	2	1
Boyle, Pocatello	.962	38	43	82	5	12
Burton, Idaho Falls	.942	30	44	69	7	13
Colmenares, Medicine Hat	.875	3	5	9	2	3
DeRosa, Butte	.804	11	13	24	9	5
Durrwachter, Billings	.878	15	17	26	6	7
Eddie, Billings	.923	4	9	15	2	3
Garcia, Idaho Falls	.933	27	47	78	9	23
Garcia, Pocatello	.899	44	49	102	17	18
Guerrero, Great Falls	.925	64	76	184	21	30
Harris, Pocatello	.882	10	10	20	4	1
KING, Butte	.929	64	106	194	23	33
Klassen, Helena	.905	18	25	42	7	8
Loretta, Butte	1.000	6	11	18	0	2
Mahalik, Butte	.750	1	0	3	1	0
McInnes, Helena	1.000	1	0	2	0	0
Mills, Lethbridge	1.000	4	3	9	0	0
Olexa, Helena	.920	43	81	125	18	23

OUTFIELDERS

Player, Team	Pct.	G	PO	A	E	DP
Patzke, Medicine Hat	.927	71	119	223	27	37
Powers, Helena	.000	1	0	0	1	0
Salazar, Pocatello	1.000	2	0	1	0	0
Segura, Lethbridge	.891	65	66	205	33	29
Sexton, Billings	.924	59	74	156	19	33
Smith, Helena	.909	3	3	7	1	0
Vazquetelles, Idaho Falls	.937	24	34	70	7	15

Triple play — Vazquetelles.

OUTFIELDERS

Player, Team	Pct.	G	PO	A	E	DP
Acosta, Helena	.889	7	6	2	1	0
Akers, Billings	1.000	3	4	0	0	0
Baker, Billings	.975	25	39	0	1	0
Banks, Helena	.962	12	25	0	1	0
Bingham, Pocatello	.962	41	44	7	2	1
Bonifazio, Lethbridge	.900	18	27	0	3	0
Breuer, Great Falls	.941	28	45	3	3	0
Browder, Idaho Falls*	1.000	5	8	1	0	0
A. BROWN, Lethbridge	.992	61	119	4	1	0
W. Brown, Lethbridge	.973	59	101	9	3	0
Bugg, Idaho Falls	.909	10	9	1	1	0
Candelaria, Medicine Hat	.958	36	43	3	2	2
Cephas, Helena*	.951	56	89	9	5	0
Cordova, Lethbridge*	.981	50	96	6	2	2
Daunic, Medicine Hat*	1.000	9	16	0	0	0
Davis, Great Falls	.944	46	61	6	4	1
de la Cruz, Medicine Hat	.937	58	89	15	7	4
Denman, Idaho Falls	.944	23	33	1	2	0
Diieso, Idaho Falls	.941	11	16	0	1	0
Dunn, Helena	.959	42	93	1	4	0
Gatti, Butte	.986	54	65	5	1	0
Harris, Pocatello	1.000	15	18	2	0	1
Hernaiz, Great Falls	.941	49	107	4	7	0
Hill, Helena	.898	45	44	0	5	0
Holland, Butte	.931	31	51	3	4	0
Huff, Butte	.961	50	93	6	4	2
Hughes, Helena	1.000	9	17	2	0	0
Hunt, Pocatello	.920	14	20	3	2	0
Ignash, Butte	.944	36	64	3	4	1
Kinney, Great Falls	.957	40	65	2	3	1
Landry, Helena*	1.000	10	11	0	0	0
Lea, Lethbridge	.921	20	32	3	3	2
Lidle, Pocatello	1.000	2	1	0	0	0
Lussier, Lethbridge	.944	15	15	2	1	1
Martinez, Helena	.989	52	85	7	1	1
McBride, Idaho Falls	1.000	14	19	3	0	1
Mendoza, Pocatello	.885	52	64	5	9	0
Mills, Lethbridge	1.000	2	6	0	0	0
Monds, Idaho Falls	.920	57	73	8	7	2
Moon, Billings	1.000	12	10	1	0	0
Newman, Idaho Falls	.967	37	58	1	2	1
Oyas, Idaho Falls	.966	68	100	14	4	5
Perez, Idaho Falls	.948	39	54	1	3	1
Pollock, Great Falls	.862	49	45	5	8	0
Postiff, Pocatello	1.000	16	12	1	0	0
Ramirez, Medicine Hat	.959	60	131	8	6	1
Rash, Great Falls	.988	48	81	1	1	0
Richardson, Great Falls	1.000	1	1	0	0	0
Romero, Great Falls	1.000	13	22	0	0	0
Ruff, Idaho Falls	.857	33	34	2	6	0
Salzano, Helena	1.000	2	1	0	0	0
Sanders, Medicine Hat	.980	57	88	8	2	2
Sexton, Billings	1.000	1	2	0	0	0
Thomas, Billings	.919	63	86	5	8	2
Valdez, Idaho Falls*	.955	34	61	2	3	0
Vaughn, Pocatello	.933	72	120	6	9	1
Vazquetelles, Idaho Falls	.333	2	0	1	2	0
Watkins, Billings	.985	66	123	5	2	0
Watson, Butte	.969	58	114	9	4	1

Triple play — Browder.

CATCHERS

Player, Team	Pct.	G	PO	A	E	DP	PB
Bako, Billings	.988	40	281	41	4	5	7
Benitez, Idaho Falls	1.000	3	24	4	0	0	1
Bingham, Pocatello	1.000	3	10	2	0	1	2
Boka, Lethbridge	.977	34	233	19	6	0	10
Burrill, Idaho Falls	.987	12	67	8	1	0	2
Campillo, Helena	.991	32	189	35	2	2	1
Carter, Helena	.990	24	170	21	2	1	1
Gay, Helena	.983	29	191	39	4	1	3
Hunt, Pocatello	.986	33	265	19	4	3	4
Marshall, Lethbridge	1.000	6	26	3	0	0	2
Martinez, Medicine Hat	.993	21	129	20	1	1	3
McCubbin, Butte	.964	9	49	5	2	0	4
Moreno, Idaho Falls	.9939	46	295	32	2	1	3
Morgan, Medicine Hat	.969	45	314	28	11	6	14
Pitts, Butte	.958	36	221	32	11	0	7
Polis, Medicine Hat	.957	9	58	8	3	0	3
Postiff, Pocatello	.994	23	148	22	1	3	1
Reiber, Lethbridge	.975	40	234	41	7	2	16

Player, Team	Pct.	G	PO	A	E	DP	PB
Rodriguez, Idaho Falls	.959	29	175	14	8	2	5
Schwenke, Great Falls	.995	27	177	16	1	1	6
Sievers, Butte	.975	32	154	40	5	3	3
STEED, Great Falls	.9940	39	295	35	2	2	7
Takayoshi, Pocatello	.985	26	179	24	3	3	8
Thomas, Helena	1.000	1	10	2	0	0	0
Towle, Billings	.976	40	272	48	8	4	7
Wittig, Great Falls	.992	15	108	13	1	1	3

Triple play—Towle.

PITCHERS

Player, Team	Pct.	G	PO	A	E	DP
Adkins, Medicine Hat	.308	14	1	3	9	1
Arias, Helena	1.000	17	1	4	0	0
Ashworth, Great Falls*	.813	11	0	13	3	0
Atwood, Pocatello	.900	12	3	6	1	1
Ballance, Lethbridge*	.900	20	1	8	1	0
Beard, Butte	.800	20	0	4	1	1
Birdt, Pocatello	1.000	8	0	5	0	1
Blaine, Idaho Falls	.750	14	2	1	1	0
Bobb, Butte	1.000	15	2	7	0	1
Bock, Idaho Falls	1.000	15	6	6	0	1
Bonilla, Lethbridge	.960	16	6	18	1	0
Browder, Idaho Falls*	1.000	3	0	1	0	0
Camacho, Great Falls	.833	28	3	7	2	0
Carew, Butte	.875	13	2	5	1	0
Carpenter, Great Falls	.846	14	1	10	2	0
CARUSO, Pocatello*	1.000	16	3	14	0	1
Cole, Helena	1.000	18	4	4	0	0
Connors, Billings	.923	19	5	7	1	0
Costello, Great Falls	.938	12	5	10	1	3
Davidson, Lethbridge*	1.000	17	0	5	0	0
DeLeon, Lethbridge	1.000	19	3	4	0	0
Dempsey, Pocatello	1.000	4	3	1	0	0
Diaz, Pocatello*	.909	15	2	8	1	0
Dillinger, Lethbridge	.857	15	6	12	3	1
Droll, Helena	1.000	4	1	1	0	0
Duda, Helena	1.000	5	1	5	0	0
England, Helena	1.000	2	0	2	0	0
Etler, Billings	.962	15	7	18	1	1
Evangelista, Idaho Falls	.714	15	3	12	6	2
Evenhus, Pocatello	.941	14	4	12	1	2
Fussell, Billings*	.857	18	1	5	1	0
Gagnon, Idaho Falls	.600	13	2	1	2	0
Grant, Medicine Hat*	.900	14	3	15	2	2
Haddock, Lethbridge	.857	13	1	5	1	0
Harris, Pocatello	1.000	5	1	1	0	0
Harris, Butte	.938	14	4	11	1	0
Harvell, Billings*	.923	17	0	12	1	0
Hebel, Billings	.846	12	4	7	2	0
Hendricks, Butte*	1.000	17	3	4	0	1
Hubbs, Great Falls	1.000	3	0	1	0	0
Hyman, Lethbridge	1.000	3	0	1	0	0
Ishii, Pocatello*	1.000	19	1	5	0	0
Jeffery, Medicine Hat*	1.000	16	2	4	0	0
Kath, Lethbridge	.765	17	5	8	4	2
Kelley, Butte	.941	23	5	11	1	1
Kenady, Great Falls*	1.000	17	1	6	0	0
Kennedy, Medicine Hat	1.000	19	1	5	0	0
Kopitzke, Helena	1.000	18	2	5	0	0
Landry, Helena*	1.000	2	1	0	0	0
LaPoint, Butte*	.846	12	2	9	2	1
Leystra, Medicine Hat	.800	28	3	5	2	0
Lidle, Pocatello	.903	17	6	22	3	0

Player, Team	Pct.	G	PO	A	E	DP
Lymberopoulos, Pocatello	1.000	5	0	2	0	1
Lyons, Billings	1.000	15	5	9	0	2
Magre, Billings	.833	14	4	11	3	1
Maloney, Helena	.833	17	5	10	3	0
Markham, Great Falls*	.667	18	2	6	4	0
Martineau, Idaho Falls	.882	16	2	13	2	1
Matthews, Pocatello	1.000	2	0	1	0	0
May, Pocatello	.750	14	1	2	1	0
McKenzie, Billings	.778	14	1	6	2	0
Minear, Butte*	.889	16	1	7	1	1
Morrill, Butte	.875	15	5	2	1	0
Moses, Billings*	1.000	18	1	7	0	0
Murphy, Helena*	.917	5	4	7	1	1
Musso, Lethbridge	1.000	15	2	5	0	0
Nelson, Idaho Falls*	.963	16	5	21	1	3
Ohman, Lethbridge*	.875	16	2	5	1	0
Patterson, Medicine Hat*	.818	26	1	8	2	1
Perez, Great Falls*	.889	22	2	6	1	0
Ploeger, Pocatello	.867	14	3	10	2	1
Post, Pocatello	1.000	6	0	1	0	0
Pruitt, Pocatello	1.000	5	1	5	0	1
Randall, Idaho Falls*	.600	13	1	2	2	0
Rhoda, Helena*	.846	14	4	7	2	0
Rodriguez, Helena	1.000	18	0	6	0	0
Rolocut, Great Falls	1.000	17	2	7	0	1
Roman, Lethbridge*	.750	15	0	3	1	0
Romano, Medicine Hat	.923	9	4	8	1	1
Rusciano, Idaho Falls	1.000	1	0	1	0	0
Salmon, Helena	.895	13	10	7	2	0
Sarmiento, Great Falls*	1.000	6	5	6	0	1
Scheffler, Great Falls*	.909	15	1	9	1	1
Schmitt, Helena*	.875	23	2	12	2	0
Seaton, Butte	1.000	6	5	5	0	0
Sievert, Medicine Hat	1.000	15	2	14	0	0
Sikes, Great Falls	.714	16	2	3	2	1
Simmons, Idaho Falls	1.000	21	2	10	0	0
Sinclair, Medicine Hat*	.950	15	4	15	1	1
Sinnes, Medicine Hat	.875	19	4	10	2	2
Smith, Medicine Hat	1.000	15	2	5	0	0
Solomon, Lethbridge	.667	23	1	5	3	0
Starr, Butte	1.000	8	6	9	0	1
STOECKLIN, Idaho Falls*	1.000	27	4	13	0	0
Sullivan, Billings	.800	18	4	4	2	0
Terminie, Lethbridge	.933	9	4	10	1	1
Thomas, Idaho Falls*	.938	26	3	12	1	0
Tomasello, Butte*	1.000	1	1	0	0	0
Toney, Medicine Hat	1.000	11	3	5	0	0
Troutman, Great Falls	1.000	27	5	2	0	0
Turnier, Idaho Falls*	1.000	9	2	7	0	0
Tweedlie, Billings	.917	11	3	8	1	0
Tyner, Idaho Falls	.818	21	4	5	2	0
Vogelgesang, Medicine Hat	.857	12	1	5	1	0
Vukson, Great Falls	1.000	16	3	3	0	0
Wagner, Helena	.923	8	4	8	1	1
Week, Butte	1.000	9	0	3	0	0
Wells, Idaho Falls	.889	18	8	8	2	1
Werner, Helena	1.000	14	2	8	0	0
Wilkerson, Billings	1.000	15	4	7	0	0
Williams, Butte*	.846	19	4	7	2	0
Wilstead, Helena	.778	11	4	3	2	1
Winget, Butte*	1.000	2	0	1	0	0
Witzel, Billings	1.000	22	5	5	0	0
Woods, Pocatello	1.000	17	2	2	0	0
Wright, Pocatello	.857	9	2	4	1	1

Triple play—Tweedlie.

The following players did not have any fielding statistics at the positions indicated or appeared only as a designated hitter, pinch-hitter or pinch-runner: Bishop, of; Carranza, ss; Clark, dh, ph; Colmenares, of, p; L. Garcia (Pocatello), 3b; Graham, p; Greenlee, of; Lutz, dh; McInnes, 3b, of; Mercado, p; Olexa, 2b, of; Orta, p; Postiff, p; Rosario, p; C. Smith, 3b; Steed, 3b; Takayoshi, of; Vazquetelles, p; Watts, 3b; Williams, of; Wingate, of, p; Young, p.

LEAGUE CHAMPIONS

Year	Team	Pct.
1939—	Twin Falls*	.581
1940—	Salt Lake City	.608
	Ogden (4th)*	.492
1941—	Boise	.623
	Ogden (2nd)*	.598
1942—	Pocatello†	.690
	Boise	.683
1943-44-45—	Did not operate.	
1946—	Twin Falls‡	.585
	Salt Lake City†	.585
1947—	Salt Lake City	.618
	Twin Falls†	.600
1948—	Pocatello	.611
	Twin Falls (2nd)*	.595
1949—	Twin Falls	.624
	Pocatello (3rd)*	.595
1950—	Pocatello	.635
	Billings (3rd)*	.571
1951—	Salt Lake City	.618

Year	Team	Pct.
	Great Falls (3rd)*	.559
1952—	Pocatello	.595
	Idaho Falls (2nd)*	.573
1953—	Ogden	.679
	Salt Lake City (4th)*	.527
1954—	Salt Lake City	.595
	Great Falls (4th)*	.530
1955—	Boise	.588
	Magic Valley (4th)*	.489
1956—	Boise	.561
1957—	Salt Lake City	.650
	Billings†	.582
1958—	Great Falls	.582
	Boise†	.615
1959—	Boise	.633
	Billings (2nd)*	.523
1960—	Boise†	.686
	Idaho Falls	.650
1961—	Boise	.638

Year	Team	Pct.
1962—	Boise§	.565
	Billings†	.706
1963—	Idaho Falls	.702
	Magic Valley†	.643
1964—	Treasure Valley	.615
1965—	Treasure Valley	.530
1966—	Ogden	.591
1967—	Ogden	.621
1968—	Ogden	.609
1969—	Ogden	.620
1970—	Idaho Falls	.629
1971—	Great Falls	.643
1972—	Billings	.694
1973—	Billings	.629
1974—	Idaho Falls	.569
1975—	Great Falls	.577
1976—	Great Falls	.577
1977—	Lethbridge	.629

Year	Team	Pct.	Year	Team	Pct.	Year	Team	Pct.
1978—	Billings x	.735	1984—	Billings	.691	1989—	Great Falls z	.791
1979—	Helena	.623		Helena y	.647		Butte	.621
	Lethbridge y	.559	1985—	Great Falls	.771	1990—	Great Falls z	.706
1980—	Lethbridge y	.743		Salt Lake City y	.657		Salt Lake	.618
	Billings	.629	1986—	Salt Lake City z	.643	1991—	Salt Lake City z	.700
1981—	Calgary	.657		Great Falls	.571		Great Falls	.657
	Butte y	.557	1987—	Salt Lake City z	.700	1992—	Salt Lake	.697
1982—	Medicine Hat y	.629		Helena	.657		Billings z	.697
	Idaho Falls	.600	1988—	Great Falls z	.754	1993—	Billings z	.653
1983—	Billings y	.614		Butte	.629		Helena	.589
	Calgary	.600						

*Won four-club playoff. †Won split-season playoff. ‡Ended first half in tie with Salt Lake City and won one-game playoff. §Ended first half in tie with Billings and Great Falls and won playoff. xBillings (first place) defeated Idaho Falls (second place) in First Place-Second Place playoff. yLeague divided into Northern and Southern divisions; won two-club playoff. zWon two-club playoff.

MINOR LEAGUE INDEX

OTHER BOOKS AVAILABLE
FROM THE SPORTING NEWS LIBRARY